2004

ALMANAC *Plus*

108TH CONGRESS
2ND SESSION

VOLUME LX

Congressional Quarterly Inc.

1255 22nd Street N.W.
Washington, D.C. 20037

President & Publisher Robert W. Merry
Editor, Sr. V.P. David Rapp

Executive Editors
Susan Benkelman, Anne Q. Hoy, Mike Mills

Design Director
Jamie Baylis

Managing Editors
David Hawkings, Mark Stencel, Randy Wynn

Senior Editors
Jan Austin, Adriel Bettelheim, John Cranford,
Mike Christensen, Caitlin Hendel

Politics Editor
Bob Benenson

Department Editors
John Bicknell, Jonathan Broder, Paul Hendrie,
Katherine Rizzo, Jodi Schneider

Deputy Editors
Maureen Conners, Pat Joy, Maureen Lorenzetti,
Marileen Maher, Greg McDonald, Frank Oliveri,
Michael Remez, Joe Warminksy

Reporters
Jonathan Allen, Susan Crabtree,
Michael R. Crittenden, John M. Donnelly, Ben Evans,
Susan Ferrechio, Liriel Higa, Martin Kady II,
Stephen J. Norton, Keith Perine, Anne Plummer,
Isaiah J. Poole, Daphne Retter, Joseph J. Schatz,
Kate Schuler, Amol Sharma, Tim Starks, Seth Stern,
Bill Swindell, Joelle Tessler, Alex Wayne,
Kathryn A. Wolfe

CQ
2004
ALMANAC *Plus*

Editor
Jan Austin

Production Editor
Melinda W. Nahmias

Copy Editors
Chris Kapler, Melinda W. Nahmias,
Jessica Scheuer, Kathleen Silvassy, Charles Southwell,
Lisa Weintraub, Chris Wright

Art Directors
Marilyn Gates-Davis, Jamey Fry

Staff Photographer
Scott J. Ferrell

Graphics
Yolie Dawson, Jacob Freedman, Brian Taylor

News Research
Nell Benton (Supervisor),
Alecia Marzullo Burke (Senior Researcher),
Seth Goldman, Rachel Kapochunas, Emi Kolawole,
Daniel Link

Indexer
Susan Nedrow

BUSINESS OPERATIONS
General Manager, Sr. V.P. Keith White

Advertising Sales, V.P. Beth Bronder

Circulation Sales
Vice President Jim Gale
National Sales Manager Sean F. Doyle
Senior Sales Representatives Joanna Matthews,
David Stevens

Marketing, V.P. Lance Matthiesen

Chief Financial Officer Diane Atwell

Chief Information Officer Larry Tunks

Customer Relations
Customer Service Manager Lorri Porter
Managing Deputy LaWanda D. Council

Strategy & Development
Strategy & Development Neil Maslansky

CQ Press
General Manager, Sr. V.P. John A. Jenkins

Published by
CONGRESSIONAL QUARTERLY INC.

Chairman Paul C. Tash
Vice Chairman Andrew P. Corty
Founder Nelson Poynter
(1903-1978)

Congressional Quarterly Inc.

Congressional Quarterly Inc. is a publishing and information services company and the recognized national leader in political journalism. For more than half a century, CQ has served clients in the fields of business, government, news and education with complete, timely and nonpartisan information on Congress, politics and national issues.

The flagship publication is the CQ Weekly, a news magazine on government, commerce and politics. It covers all the forces that shape public policy, from Capitol Hill to K Street to the White House.

CQ Today is a legislative news-daily providing a morning news report on Congress and the scheduled hearings and markups of congressional committees. It provides a comprehensive breaking news report of everything that just happened or is about to happen on Capitol Hill.

CQ also offers the most comprehensive, detailed and up-to-the-minute legislative tracking information on the World Wide Web. CQ.com provides immediate access to exclusive CQ coverage of bill action, votes, schedules and member profiles, with direct links to relevant texts of bills, committee reports, testimony and verbatim transcripts.

CQ Press, a division of Congressional Quarterly Inc., serves the academic and education markets with a variety of reference works and political science text books, both in print and online, plus reference books on the federal government, national elections and politics.

The CQ Press catalogue includes the signature CQ reference work, "Politics in America 2006," with original profiles of every member of the 109th Congress, written and edited by the CQ staff.

CQ Press also publishes a unique weekly publication — The CQ Researcher — with each weekly issue focused exclusively on a single topic of current interest. And CQ Press offers a line of print and Web-based directories, such as the Congressional Staff Directory.

The "Congressional Quarterly Almanac®," published annually, provides a legislative history for each session of Congress. "Congress and the Nation," published every four years, provides a record of government for a presidential term.

The 2004 CQ Almanac

This book marks the 60th edition of the CQ Almanac. Beginning with the first session of the 79th Congress in 1945, Congressional Quarterly has produced and published an annual account of the major legislative action in each session of Congress.

The 2004 edition covers the second session of the 108th Congress. It begins with an overview of the year, followed by 17 chapters filled with narrative accounts of major legislation. A special chapter on Politics & Elections analyzes the presidential and congressional races that culminated in the Nov. 2 elections.

Each chapter was written especially for the book, based on reporting and analysis done throughout the year by Congressional Quarterly's news staff. We added "Plus" to our title in 2001 to highlight the original nature of the material.

The 2004 Almanac provides a detailed look at all the major bills considered during the year — whether or not they became law. It examines how the bills changed as they moved from committee markup to floor votes and conference negotiations. The stories also identify and explain the main provisions of the bills and look at the roles played by individual members of Congress.

Perhaps the biggest piece of legislation in 2004 was a bill reorganizing the nation's intelligence community in an effort to correct the kind of intelligence errors that preceded the Sept. 11, 2001, terrorist attacks.

Meanwhile, Republicans succeeded in holding the line on discretionary spending, allowing a less-than-inflation increase for domestic programs.

Although lawmakers did not finish all the appropriations bills by the start of the new fiscal year, they did complete the appropriations process before adjournment. It was the first time in three years that the spending bills did not spill over into the following session.

To finish work on the intelligence overhaul and the nine-bill omnibus appropriations package, Congress returned after the elections for a lame-duck session, the 12th since World War II.

Other major legislation cleared during the year included a 10-year, $137 billion corporate tax bill and a $146 billion, 10-year extension of middle-class tax cuts. An attempt to rewrite the nation's energy policy failed, as did a six-year highway reauthorization.

The Politics & Elections chapter chronicles all the main events of the presidential election campaign, beginning with the primaries, and includes maps and official results. The state and district races that will determine the shape of the 109th Congress are also detailed.

In addition, the Almanac contains a series of data-filled reference appendixes:

● **Congress and its members.** An 11-page glossary of terms that arise in discussing Congress and legislation, and a list of members of the House and Senate in the second session of the 108th Congress.

● **Vote studies.** CQ's popular annual analysis of voting patterns in Congress. Here, the story was one of intense partisanship. CQ's study of party unity showed that Republicans and Democrats retreated only slightly from the record level of polarization reflected in their votes in 2003, the most partisan year in the five decades CQ has done these annual analyses.

Other studies analyze the level of presidential support and member participation during the year, providing aggregate scores for each chamber along with individual ratings for each member.

● **Key votes.** An account of the votes chosen by CQ editors as most critical in determining the outcome of congressional action on major issues during the year.

● **Texts.** The president's State of the Union address and the Democratic response, excerpts from the Sept. 11 commission's report, and key election speeches.

● **Public laws.** A detailed list of all the bills enacted into law during the year.

● **Roll call votes.** A complete set of roll call vote charts for both chambers, describing every vote and showing every member's position on each vote.

CQ produces the Almanac for public policy specialists, scholars, journalists, and all interested citizens and students of the U.S. legislative system.

We believe our 60th edition remains true to the mandate laid out more than 50 years ago by CQ founders Nelson and Henrietta Poynter: "Congressional Quarterly presents the facts in as complete, concise and unbiased form as we know how. The editorial comment on the acts and votes of Congress, we leave to our subscribers."

Jan Austin
Editor, CQ Almanac

CQ *"By providing a link between the local newspaper and Capitol Hill we hope Congressional Quarterly can help to make public opinion the only effective pressure group in the country. Since many citizens other than editors are also interested in Congress, we hope that they too will find Congressional Quarterly an aid to a better understanding of their government."*

Foreword, Congressional Quarterly, Vol. I, 1945
Henrietta Poynter, 1901-1968
Nelson Poynter, 1903-1978

SUMMARY TABLE OF CONTENTS

Table of Contents

Chapter 1 – Inside Congress

Chapter 2 – Appropriations

Chapter 3 – Banking & Financial Services

Chapter 4 – Budget

Chapter 5 – Congressional Affairs

Chapter 6 – Defense & Homeland Security

Chapter 7 – Education

Chapter 8 – Employment & Labor

Chapter 9 – Energy & Environment

Chapter 10 – Health

Chapter 11 – Intelligence & Foreign Policy

Chapter 12 – Legal Affairs

Chapter 13 — Taxes

Chapter 14 — Technology & Communications

Chapter 15 – Trade

Chapter 16 — Transportation & Infrastructure

Chapter 17 — NASA, Postal Service, Welfare

Chapter 18 — Politics & Elections

Appendixes

Congress and Its Members

Vote Studies

Key Votes

Texts

Public Laws

Roll Call Votes

General Index

Chapter 1

INSIDE CONGRESS

Campaigning Trumps Legislating

Election-year politics and relentless partisanship dominated the second session of the 108th Congress. Republican leaders, who controlled both chambers, intentionally front-loaded their agenda so that their highest priorities — including a new round of tax cuts and the creation of a Medicare prescription drug benefit — came up in 2003, knowing that the second session would be so tied up by election-year posturing that little would be accomplished.

With the exception of a groundbreaking overhaul of the intelligence community — a late addition to the agenda — no major legislative themes dominated Congress' work in 2004. Instead, the year was mostly about positioning for the Nov. 2 elections. Hanging over the entire session was President Bush's campaign for re-election and Massachusetts Democratic Sen. John Kerry's attempt to unseat him. The race was so tight for so much of the year that lawmakers from both parties became active participants.

Legislating was also limited by an abbreviated congressional calendar that was tailored to accommodate members' needs to campaign. In addition to short work weeks, Congress broke early for its summer recess to allow for the Democratic convention in Boston the last week of July. Lawmakers also had an unexpected break in early June when Washington effectively shut down for a week of tributes to President Ronald Reagan, following his death June 5.

By September, appropriators were resigned to moving nine of the 13 annual spending bills in a single, omnibus package; five were never even debated on the Senate floor. The other main agenda item, the intelligence overhaul, had become a top priority in late July after a blue-ribbon commission released recommendations for correcting intelligence failures that preceded the Sept. 11, 2001, terrorist attacks.

At that point, lawmakers had little choice but to return for a post-election lame-duck session, which ran from Nov. 16 to Dec. 8, to complete the appropriations and intelligence legislation.

In the work done column, Republicans could point to the intelligence overhaul, the largest reorganization of the intelligence community since World War II, and to their success in holding total regular discretionary spending to below $821.9 billion, as Bush demanded, a 4.6 percent increase over fiscal 2004. Non-emergency discretionary spending not related to defense or homeland security was held to a below-inflation 1 percent increase.

Congress cleared two tax cut bills. The first was a $137 billion 10-year corporate tax cut that also carried a $10 billion buyout of tobacco farmers. The second was a $146 billion bill that extended several popular tax breaks for families and individuals that had been enacted in 2001 and 2003 but were due to expire.

While only one fiscal 2005 appropriations measure — the defense bill — made it into law by the start of the fiscal year, the other 12 were enacted before Congress adjourned. In 2002 and 2003, Congress was unable finish the omnibus until the following session. Lawmakers also continued to fund the military presence in Iraq and Afghanistan, approving $25 billion in emergency supplemental appropriations as part of the fiscal 2005 defense spending bill.

A bill reauthorizing federal aid for special education programs cleared, as did a bill that allowed companies to reduce their pension contributions while Congress tried to agree on a plan to overhaul the pension system. In a victory for social conservatives, lawmakers cleared a bill that made it a separate offense to harm a fetus while committing a federal crime against a pregnant woman.

But the legislative landscape was also strewn with casualties, many of them the result not of partisan conflict but of intraparty disputes among Republicans. Thanks to a disagreement between GOP moderates and conservatives over tax cuts, Congress failed to approve an annual budget resolution for only the third time since the modern budget law was written in 1974.

Republicans were unable to revive a bill sought by Bush to overhaul the nation's energy policies because of regional disputes over the clean fuel additive called methyl tertiary butyl ether (MTBE) that had been shown to pollute groundwater. A six-year reauthorization of federal highway and transit programs died when House-Senate conferees could not agree on how to distribute the money.

Partisan disagreements were largely to blame for the death of several bills that were part of the GOP campaign for revamping the rules of civil litigation, including bills to limit class action lawsuits, cap damages in medical malpractice cases and create a no-fault fund to pay victims of asbestos exposure.

The 1996 welfare overhaul law, which had expired two years earlier, was left on autopilot because lawmakers could not agree on how to reauthorize and update it. The reauthorization of Head Start, the early childhood development program, failed when Democrats blocked it from reaching the Senate floor, convinced Republicans would rewrite it themselves once the bill got to a House-Senate conference.

A 10-year-old ban on certain kinds of assault weapons was allowed to expire, a consequence of Republican opposi-

Session Highlights

CONGRESS DID:

- Overhaul the nation's intelligence community in response to recommendations of the independent Sept. 11 commission.
- Hold the increase in regular, non-security discretionary spending to a below-inflationary 1 percent.
- Appropriate $25 billion for the military occupations of Iraq and Afghanistan.
- Increase the statutory limit on federal borrowing by $800 billion, or 11 percent, to $8.18 trillion.
- Cut business taxes $137 billion over a decade, the biggest changes to the corporate tax code in 18 years.
- Extend a collection of tax breaks, mainly for middle-income families, at a 10-year cost of $146 billion.
- Reauthorize federal programs for educating disabled students.
- Reduce corporate pension contributions through 2005.
- Ease federal inmates' access to genetic testing that could exonerate them.
- Guarantee some rights of crime victims under federal law.
- Extend a ban on new Internet-access taxes through 2007.
- End subsidies for growing tobacco after making a final $10 billion payment to farmers.
- Recognize the fetus under federal law as an entity distinct from the pregnant woman.

CONGRESS DID NOT:

- Adopt an annual budget resolution, the third such failure since the current budget law was enacted in 1974.
- Complete any of the nine domestic appropriations bills before the start of fiscal 2005.
- Finish a long-term rewrite of highway and mass transit law.
- Clear a comprehensive overhaul of federal energy policy.
- Reauthorize federal welfare programs.
- Reauthorize vocational and technical education programs.
- Reauthorize the Head Start program for low-income children.
- Extend a program of federal unemployment compensation.
- Create a compensation pool for victims of asbestos exposure.
- Rewrite federal bankruptcy law.
- Tighten regulations of Fannie Mae and Freddie Mac.
- Extend a 10-year ban on semiautomatic assault weapons.
- Limit the reach of class action lawsuits.
- Advance a constitutional amendment to ban gay marriage.
- Complete a plan for quickly reconstituting the House after a catastrophic attack.
- Cap non-economic damages in medical malpractice suits.
- Shield the firearms industry from liability for gun violence.
- Consider legislation to permit imports of prescription drugs.
- Stiffen penalties for broadcasting indecent material.
- Block rules mandating corporate expensing of stock options.
- Curtail new Labor Department overtime regulations.
- Revamp the governance of the U.S. Postal Service.

tion so strong that the GOP sank one of its own bills — the Senate's gun liability bill — when it was amended to include a renewal of the assault weapons ban.

Other casualties included measures that were put on the agenda to rally political support. A proposed constitutional amendment to ban gay marriage failed in both chambers, for example, but Republicans were able to use the issue to draw social conservatives to the polls. In a pattern repeated annually since 2001, House Republicans passed a permanent extension of the estate tax, but the bill had no chance in the Senate.

Sharpening Party Differences

The partisan acrimony that characterized the year reflected the heated presidential campaign, but it also was part of a trend in which lawmakers increasingly played to their core constituencies rather than seeking cooperation across the aisle to get legislation through. Congressional Quarterly's annual study of party-unity votes — those in which a majority of one party voted against a majority of the other — showed 2004 to be the second-most partisan year in the five decades the votes studies had been done. The most partisan was 2003. *(Party unity, p. B-8)*

The election campaign permeated Congress, with stump speeches for the candidates common on the floor. Off Capitol Hill, lawmakers were active in the campaigns, often acting as surrogates. Republicans held press conferences and conference calls to attack Kerry and his running mate, Sen. John Edwards of North Carolina, both of whom were noticeably absent from the Senate for most of the year. Kerry deployed three Democratic lawmakers — Sen. Richard J. Durbin of Illinois, Rep. Stephanie Tubbs Jones of Ohio, and Rep. Ed Pastor of Arizona — to spread his political message and coordinate it with congressional Democrats.

Perhaps the most surprising development was the decision by Senate Majority Leader Bill Frist, R-Tenn., to campaign actively against Minority Leader Tom Daschle, who was in a tough re-election race in South Dakota against former Rep. John Thune. Frist's actions violated no formal rules, but they ended a decades-old unwritten agreement that no Senate leader would campaign against the other. It was not clear that Frist's involvement made the difference, but Daschle lost in November.

The impact of the election went beyond campaigning. Lawmakers from both parties used the machinery of Congress and their votes to polish their images with voters and separate themselves from the competition. Party leaders worked to sharpen their distinctions and to rally their troops to vote in ways that highlighted those distinctions. They also sought votes that they believed would put members of the other party in a bad light.

A Halting Start for Bush and the GOP

For Republicans, the year did not get off to a promising start. The growing federal budget deficit, which the Congressional Budget Office projected would reach a record $521 billion for fiscal 2004, was a cloud over the party that had come to power in 1995 promising to balance the budget. (The final deficit was $412.1 billion — still the largest nominal deficit in the country's history.) Members were also unnerved by White House projections in January that showed the new Medicare prescription drug benefit, enacted two months earlier, would cost $139 billion more than they had been led to believe.

Bush's Jan. 20 State of the Union address was less a bold outline for a second term than a defense against an onslaught of criticism by Democrats contending for their party's nomination. His fiscal 2005 budget, released Feb. 2, called for a 7 percent jump in defense spending, stringent limits on most domestic programs and $1.3 trillion in tax cuts over the next decade. Bush said he would halve the deficit projected for fiscal 2004 by fiscal 2007. Conservative Republicans, especially in the House, vowed to cut deeper. (*Bush text, p. D-3; budget, p. 4-3*)

The escalating insurgent attacks in Iraq tested GOP support for the war. And Bush's insistence that the economy was recovering — a position supported by most economic indicators — came across as tone-deaf to some Republicans from manufacturing states such as Ohio and Michigan, where unemployment was getting worse.

Bush would regain the support of most Hill Republicans later in the year as he hit his campaign stride — particularly at the Republican National Convention in New York, where he laid out an ambitious agenda for a second term, mounted a stronger defense of his actions in Iraq and convinced the GOP base that Kerry would be far worse.

For much of the year, though, the Republican agenda had a bumpy ride in Congress.

Budget Woes

Both chambers wrote budget plans that largely followed Bush's proposal, though they sought to reduce the deficit more quickly and did not not come close to the $1.3 trillion in tax cuts he proposed. But a small group of GOP moderates joined with Democrats to add language to the Senate budget resolution that would have restored so-called pay-as-you-go rules, requiring Congress to offset any new tax cuts or entitlement spending with revenue increases or spending cuts.

After weeks of negotiations in which the moderates refused to back down, House and Senate Republican budget writers gave up and produced a conference report without their support. That ensured there would be no final budget resolution, since it left Republicans without enough votes to adopt it in the Senate. The House adopted the conference report in May, but the Senate did not even bother to take it up. (*Budget resolution, p. 4-9*)

In the end, the inability to finalize a budget resolution slowed work on the spending bills but had little other practical impact. The appropriators held to the $821.9 billion cap on discretionary spending that was contained in the abandoned budget. The budget resolution would have allowed tax cuts to move through Congress under the protective umbrella of a budget reconciliation bill that could not be filibustered in the Senate. But the two tax bills that Republicans planned to move — the middle-class tax cuts and the corporate tax bill — had enough support to clear without the cover of reconciliation.

It was the difficulty imposed by tight spending limits — combined with the shortened legislative calendar and the constant partisan bickering on Capitol Hill — that ensured that most of the spending bills would, once again, be bundled in a huge year-end omnibus measure.

Putting nine of the 13 annual spending bills into a single package, which cleared Nov. 20 (PL 108-447), allowed the White House and GOP leaders to dictate their terms. The take-it-or-leave-it approach, together with a strategy of deferring most painful spending decisions until after the elections, ultimately allowed Congress to hold overall discretionary spending to a 4.6 percent increase over fiscal 2004.

Bush and Congress did make room for significant increases in defense and homeland security spending. The defense appropriations bill gave the Pentagon a 7 percent increase over fiscal 2004, while the Department of Homeland Security got an increase of more than 9 percent. Foreign operations also got a boost, getting 13 percent more than in the previous year's bill, excluding supplemental spending.

Because of heavy lobbying by House Majority Leader Tom DeLay, R-Texas, Bush also got most of the increase he had requested for NASA to begin work on his proposal to send humans to the moon and Mars. (*Appropriations, p. 2-3*)

Republican Tax Bills

The corporate tax law (PL 108-357), enacted Oct. 22, was built around a change in the tax code that was critical to ending European Union (EU) sanctions that were costing U.S. companies $4 billion a year. (*Corporate taxes, p. 13-3*)

The EU sanctions were in response to a subsidy for U.S. corporations that the World Trade Organization had ruled was illegal. The bill to repeal the subsidy became must-pass legislation, and both chambers loaded it up with tax breaks for assorted industries and constituencies. The final bill also contained a buyout of tobacco farmers and a new deduction for state sales taxes, both added by Bill Thomas, R-Calif., chairman of the House Ways and Means Committee.

There was strong Senate support for combining a tobacco buyout with new regulation of tobacco products, but that was a non-starter in the House and it was dropped. To maintain support in the Senate, negotiators loaded the final bill with still more add-ons, including tax breaks for ethanol, timber and shipping. The bill became such a special-interest grab bag that even Thomas called it "Miss Piggy." Bush skipped the usual White House ceremony and quietly signed the measure while on the campaign trail.

The other major tax law (PL 108-311) extended three middle-class tax cuts — benefits for married couples, a $1,000-per-child tax credit and an expanded 10 percent bracket — that were part of Bush's 2001 and 2003 tax cuts (PL 107-16, PL 108-27) and were due to expire at the end of 2004. The bill was broadly popular, particularly in an election year: The House backed the final bill, 339-65, and the Senate cleared it, 92-3. It was enacted Oct. 4. (*Middle-class tax cut, p. 13-8*)

Congress also cleared a four-year moratorium on Internet access taxes (PL 108-435) while lawmakers continued to de-

108th Congress, 2nd Session: By the Numbers

The second session of the 108th Congress began, as the Constitution and federal law require, Jan. 20, 2004, at noon. Under the terms of the annual adjournment resolution (H Con Res 531), the House adjourned sine die Dec. 7 at 8:38 p.m.; the Senate adjourned sine die Dec. 8 at 10:54 p.m. The following are some statistical comparisons of the two chambers over the past decade:

		2004	2003	2002	2001	2000	1999	1998	1997	1996	1995
Days in Session	Senate	133	167	149	173	141	162	143	153	132	211
	House	110	133	123	142	135	137	119	132	122	168
Time in Session	Senate	1,032	1,454	1,043	1,236	1,018	1,184	1,095	1,093	1,037	1,839
(hours)	House	879	1,015	772	922	1,054	1,125	999	1,004	919	1,525
Avg. Length Daily	Senate	7.8	8.7	7	7.1	7.2	7.3	7.7	7.1	7.9	8.7
Session (hours)	House	8	7.6	6.3	6.5	7.8	8.2	8.4	7.6	7.5	9.1
Public Laws Enacted		300	198	241	136	410	170	241	153	245	88
Bills/Resolutions	Senate	1,317	2,398	1,558	2,212	1,546	2,352	1,321	1,840	860	1,801
Introduced	House	2,338	4,616	2,711	4,318	2,701	4,241	2,254	3,728	1,899	3,430
	TOTAL	3,655	7,014	4,269	6,530	4,247	6,593	3,575	5,568	2,759	5,231
Recorded Votes	Senate	216	459	253	380	298	374	314	298	306	613
	House[1]	544	677	484	512	603	611	547	640	455	885
	TOTAL	760	1,136	739	892	901	985	861	938	761	1,498
Vetoes		0	0	0	0	7[2]	5	5	3[3]	6	11

SOURCE: Congressional Record

[1] Includes quorum calls
[2] Includes pocket vetoes
[3] Does not include line-item vetoes

bate whether to make the ban permanent. (*Internet taxes*, p. 13-11)

Energy, Highway Bills Postponed

For the third year in a row, Republicans were unable to complete a comprehensive energy bill. The House adopted the conference report on a $31.1 billion measure (HR 6) in late 2003, but the Senate was deadlocked over a liability waiver for producers of MTBE. The dispute was regional and pitted senators from Gulf Coast states where MTBE producers were located against those from states that worried about getting saddled with the bill for MTBE cleanups. (*Energy policy*, p. 9-4)

The House passed a new version of the same bill in June. But when Republican Sen. Pete V. Domenici of New Mexico tried drafting a Senate bill without the MTBE provision, supporters and critics of other provisions began to waiver and the effort collapsed. Some of the tax incentives in the energy bill were cleared as part of the corporate tax package.

Efforts to write a six-year reauthorization bill for surface transportation programs (HR 3550), a job that was delayed in the first session, collapsed in the face of multiple problems. Bush threatened to veto both the House and Senate versions because they exceeded the $256 billion authorization level he proposed — the House bill called for $283.2 billion, the Senate $318.9 billion. The White House also rejected a so-called reopener clause in the House bill that would have stopped most highway funding at the end of fiscal 2005 unless the authorization level was

increased. (*Surface transportation*, p. 16-3)

By the end of the session, Republican negotiators had come up with a $299 billion total for the bill that the White House seemed willing to consider, but the conferees could not agree on a formula for distributing highway money to the states. The differences were regional rather than partisan, between states that paid more in highway taxes than they got in highway construction and those that paid less. Every proposal had winners and losers, and no member of Congress wanted to be a loser, especially in an election year.

Fetal Protection, 'Tort Reform'

Social conservatives scored a victory with enactment in April of a law (PL 108-212) that for the first time gave federal legal status to a fetus. The measure made it a separate offense to harm a fetus during the commission of a federal crime against a pregnant woman. It included exceptions for abortions performed with the woman's consent, and for cases in which the fetus was harmed by medical treatment of the pregnant woman or an act of the woman herself. Sen. Dianne Feinstein, D-Calif., narrowly lost a bid to substitute language that would have made harm to the fetus a separate crime, but without establishing a separate legal status for the fetus. Abortion-rights supporters worried that by creating such an identity, the bill would lay the groundwork for a challenge to *Roe v. Wade*, the 1973 Supreme Court ruling that guaranteed a woman's right to an abortion. (*Fetal protection*, p. 12-3)

Republicans were unable to send any of the trio of bills aimed at what they called "tort reform" to the White

House. The fate of legislation to limit class action lawsuits (S 2062, HR 1115) was a reminder of the election-year mood in Congress. The bill had more than 60 supporters in the Senate, but Frist pulled it from the floor to prevent Democrats from offering amendments to extend federal unemployment insurance and increase the minimum wage. Both parties hoped to use the outcome on the campaign trail — Republicans to demonstrate Democrats' ties to trial lawyers, Democrats to paint Republicans as anti-labor. (*Class action lawsuits, p. 12-7*)

A bill to limit damages in medical malpractice suits passed the House in 2003, but a similar measure had little chance in the Senate, where Democrats rejected the damage caps as unfair to injured plaintiffs. Frist held two cloture votes on versions of the bill in 2004; although Republicans did not come close to the 60 votes needed to cut off debate, they did get another campaign issue against the Democrats. (*Medical malpractice, p. 12-12*)

The third main tort bill (S 2290) would have created a no-fault fund to compensate victims of asbestos exposure, financed by businesses and their insurers in exchange for ending their civil liability. It failed because the main players, which included organized labor, could not agree on such basic issues as the size of the fund and the criteria for establishing eligibility for beneficiaries. (*Asbestos, p. 12-6*)

Congress started, but did not finish, a spate of telecommunications bills including measures on spyware and online pirating. A bill to crack down on identity theft by imposing tougher penalties and making it easier for prosecutors to go after the perpetrators was enacted in July (PL 108-275).

Education, Welfare

In an exception to the partisan wrangling, lawmakers managed to cut through their differences and clear a rewrite of the law governing special education. The law (PL 108-446) reauthorized the Individuals with Disabilities Education Act (IDEA), through 2011 with provisions to increase federal funding, establish stronger certification standards for special education teachers and allow more flexibility in an effort to reduce paperwork. The compromise did not make IDEA funding mandatory, as some Senate Democrats wanted, and it did not include a House provision that would have eliminated a student's disability as a factor in determining appropriate discipline for breaking school rules. (*Special education, p. 7-3*)

Several other education bills stalled, including a reauthorization of Head Start, the early childhood development program for low-income children, and a bill to rewrite the nation's main job-training programs. In both cases, Democrats blocked a conference to prevent Republicans from excluding them and writing the final bills to suit themselves.

An attempt to reauthorize the 1996 welfare overhaul law was another casualty of the year's partisanship. The House had passed a bill in 2003, and the Senate took up its version in March, agreeing to add an extra $6 billion for child care over five years as proposed by GOP moderate Olympia J. Snowe of Maine. Instead of backing the bill, Senate Democrats tried to attach an increase in the minimum wage. An attempt to limit debate on the bill failed, 51-47, nine votes short of the 60 required. Instead, Congress cleared a short-

term extension to keep the program going until the end of March 2005. (*Welfare, p. 17-5*)

Battle Over Judicial Nominations

The standoff over Bush's judicial nominees that roiled the Senate in 2003 continued throughout the second session. The fight was over the Democratic minority's use of the filibuster to erect a 60-vote hurdle to the confirmation of judicial nominees they opposed. The issue was of great importance to both sides because it was widely assumed that there would be at least one Supreme Court vacancy during the next administration. With the disclosure in October that Chief Justice William H. Rehnquist was being treated for thyroid cancer, a high court vacancy appeared increasingly likely.

Senate Democrats held up all of Bush's judicial nominees until May, angered because the president used recess appointments to seat two nominees who had been blocked in the first session. They eventually let 25 nominees go through after Bush promised not to make any more recess appointments for the rest of the year, but they continued to fight others, mostly because of their ideological views.

All told, Democrats blocked 10 of Bush's appellate court nominees on procedural votes in the 108th Congress and threatened to block several others. By the end of the year Bush had filled 203 lifetime seats on federal district and appellate courts, or 24 percent of the total. (*Judges, p. 12-17*)

The White House and Senate GOP leaders argued that Congress had a constitutional duty to give each of the president's nominees an up-or-down vote. The Democrats argued that use of the filibuster to block such a vote was a time-honored means of protecting the rights of the minority.

On Dec. 23, the White House announced that Bush intended to resubmit the names of 20 judicial nominees who failed to win confirmation during his first term, including seven of the appeals court nominees whom Democrats had blocked by filibusters. Frist signaled that he might proceed in 2005 with a plan known on Capitol Hill as the "nuclear option" to effectively eliminate the filibuster as an means for thwarting presidential nominees. Frist had moved such a proposal (S Res 138), through the Rules Committee in 2003 but did not act on it in 2004. Democrats threatened to shut down the Senate if the majority deprived them of the filibuster.

War in Iraq

The war in Iraq was never far from lawmakers' minds. The United States handed over limited sovereignty to a provisional Iraqi government June 28, an event that Bush hailed as a major step in his ambitious plan to transform that nation into a bastion of democracy in the Middle East. "Let freedom reign," he scrawled across a note from his national security adviser, Condoleezza Rice, informing him that the transfer had taken place.

But for congressional overseers, the handover, which officially concluded the U.S.-led occupation 15 months after Bush launched the invasion of Iraq, was more of a legal milestone than a major turning point. The reality was that the United States planned to keep at least 140,000 Army soldiers and Marines in Iraq for the foreseeable future to battle insurgents and bolster the nascent government. Efforts to rebuild Iraq's infrastructure and shattered economy were only just beginning.

Congressional Leaders: 108th Congress, 2nd Session

House

Speaker of the House — J. Dennis Hastert, R-Ill.

REPUBLICANS
Majority Leader — Tom DeLay, Texas
Majority Whip — Roy Blunt, Mo.
Conference Chairwoman — Deborah Pryce, Ohio
Conference Vice Chairman — Jack Kingston, Ga.
Conference Secretary — John T. Doolittle, Calif.
Policy Committee Chairman — Christopher Cox, Calif.
Chairman, National Republican Congressional Committee — Thomas M. Reynolds, N.Y.
Chief Deputy Majority Whip — Eric Cantor, Va.

DEMOCRATS
Minority Leader — Nancy Pelosi, Calif.
Minority Whip — Steny H. Hoyer, Md.
Caucus Chairman — Robert Menendez, N.J.
Caucus Vice Chairman — James E. Clyburn, S.C.
Assistant to the Minority Leader — John M. Spratt Jr., S.C.
Chairman, Democratic Congressional Campaign Committee — Robert T. Matsui, Calif.
Senior Chief Deputy Minority Whip — John Lewis, Ga.

Senate

President Pro Tempore — Ted Stevens, R-Alaska

REPUBLICANS
Majority Leader — Bill Frist, Tenn.
Majority Whip — Mitch McConnell, Ky.
Conference Chairman — Rick Santorum, Pa.
Conference Vice Chairwoman — Kay Bailey Hutchison, Texas
Policy Committee Chairman — Jon Kyl, Ariz.
Chairman, National Republican Senatorial Committee — George Allen, Va.
Chief Deputy Majority Whip — Robert F. Bennett, Utah

DEMOCRATS
Minority Leader — Tom Daschle, S.D.
Minority Whip — Harry Reid, Nev.
Conference Chairman — Tom Daschle, S.D.
Conference Secretary — Barbara A. Mikulski, Md.
Policy Committee Chairman — Byron L. Dorgan, N.D.
Steering & Coordination Committee Chairwoman — Hillary Rodham Clinton, N.Y.
Chairman, Democratic Senatorial Campaign Committee — Jon Corzine, N.J.
Chief Deputy Minority Whip — John B. Breaux, La.

The bills for the military operation, which was costing more than $5 billion a month, continued to roll in. There was mounting frustration on Capitol Hill over the administration's refusal to provide long-term estimates of the war's costs. Bush declined to seek full funding for war operations for fiscal 2005 and requested an incremental $25 billion war fund in May only after being pressed by GOP appropriators. As evidence of their frustration, while lawmakers agreed to provide the supplemental funds as part of the defense spending bill (PL 108-375), they rejected an administration request for near-total discretion over the money, instead allocating all but $1.5 billion to specific uses.

The $25 billion brought to more than $200 billion the amount appropriated for military operations in Iraq and Afghanistan and related expenses, since Sept. 11, 2001.

Abu Ghraib Prison Torture

Congress had more to worry about than just funding the war, however. In late April lawmakers were stunned by published photographs showing sadistic abuse of Iraqi prisoners by U.S military personnel at the Abu Ghraib prison near Baghdad. The graphic pictures, splashed across news pages and television screens, showed naked prisoners piled into pyramids, covered with hoods, and threatened by dogs and electrodes. Defense Secretary Donald H. Rumsfeld and other top Pentagon officials were summoned to back-to-back hearings by the House and Senate Armed Services committees, and the Defense secretary publicly apologized to the Iraqi prisoners. "Our country had an obligation to treat them right," he said. "We didn't, and that was wrong."

Democrats called for Rumsfeld's ouster, but Bush voiced full confidence in his Defense secretary.

John W. Warner, R-Va., chairman of the Senate Armed Services Committee promised to "go where the evidence leads us, no matter how embarrassing or incriminating it may be." But Duncan Hunter, R-Calif., his House counterpart, joined with other House Republicans to urge Warner to let the military conduct its own investigations.

Ultimately, Congress backed away from its demands for detailed information on the treatment of prisoners in Iraq, Afghanistan and Guantánamo Bay, Cuba. Instead, it was the Pentagon that took the lead. In August, a panel appointed by Rumsfeld and chaired by former Defense Secretary James R. Schlesinger issued a report that blamed the abuses on failures of military leadership, but found no evidence that they were an intentional policy by top officials to squeeze information out of the detainees.

The one legislative response came in the fiscal 2005 defense authorization law, which ordered the Defense secretary to draft a new policy, based on minimum standards set by Congress, to guarantee that prisoners would be treated humanely. It also required the secretary to certify that those who interrogated detainees were properly trained, and called for regular reports to Congress on how the new policy was being implemented. (*Defense authorization, p. 6-3*)

Intelligence Overhaul

The reorganization of the intelligence community, Congress' last major act of the year, came at the prodding of the independent, bipartisan National Commission on Terrorist

Attacks Upon the United States — also know as the 9-11 commission — and the emotional lobbying by some of the victims' families. (*Intelligence overhaul, p. 11-3*)

The commission's report, which was released July 22, called for a restructuring of the intelligence community with a new national intelligence director to coordinate the 15 intelligence agencies.

Both chambers wrote overhaul legislation, parting ways over two main issues: the extent of the new intelligence director's powers and a House plan to include new immigration restrictions. The Senate voted to give the intelligence director near-total control over intelligence budgets and personnel, including the Pentagon spy agencies that accounted for 80 percent of intelligence spending. The House leaned more to the Pentagon position, which was to to restrict the director's authority and allow the Defense Department to continue managing its own intelligence budget and personnel.

House Republicans, led by Judiciary Chairman F. James Sensenbrenner Jr., R-Wis., also wanted to include stronger immigration enforcement to make it harder for potential terrorists to get into the country. Sensenbrenner's plan, which included letting the government deport illegal immigrants more rapidly, were strongly opposed by most senators.

Under tremendous political pressure from the Sept. 11 commission and the victims' families, House and Senate negotiators managed to reach a deal during the lame-duck session. They wrote a draft conference report that gave the intelligence director the power to set the budget for all of the intelligence agencies but not to make operational decisions. The conferees left out most of the immigration provisions.

The deal almost collapsed in the face of opposition from Sensenbrenner and Hunter. Hunter argued that the plan would compromise real-time intelligence to U.S. troops but was ultimately satisfied by the insertion of language stating the arrangement would not "abrogate" the military chain of command. Sensenbrenner was promised a vote on his immigration provisions early in the 109th Congress. The intelligence bill was signed into law Dec. 17 (PL 108-458).

Looking Ahead to the 109th

The Nov. 2 election returned Bush to the White House with 51 percent of the popular vote, increased Republican control of both chambers of Congress, and sent Democrats into a new round of soul-searching. Senate Republicans picked up four seats, expanding their majority for the next Congress to 55, including several hard-right freshmen who strengthened the conservative ranks within the caucus. House Republicans ended up with their largest elected majority since 1995: 232 seats, a net gain of three. (*Politics, pp. 18-3, 18-14, 18-17*)

Both parties began organizing for a new Congress during the November lame-duck session.

Senate Republicans agreed in their party caucus to dilute one element of their "seniority rules" tradition. The caucus voted, 27-26, by secret ballot to adopt a proposal by Trent Lott, R-Miss., that allowed Frist to appoint half of all open seats on the most coveted panels, known as "A" committees. Other seats on those committees would continue to be filled based on seniority. Lott praised the vote an attempt to fix "a hide-bound, muscle-bound, dysfunctional institution" by

---

Lame-Duck Sessions Since World War II

The 2004 lame-duck session was the 12th since World War II. Such post-election sessions were happening with increasing frequency: They had occurred every two years since 1998.

2004 Nov. 16-Dec. 8 (10 days)
Appropriations; overhaul of intelligence community

2002 Nov. 7-22 (10 days)
Appropriations; creation of Homeland Security Department; defense authorization

2000 Nov. 13-Dec. 15 (11 days)
Appropriations

1998 Dec. 17-19 (three days)
Impeachment of President Bill Clinton

1994 Nov. 29-Dec. 1 (three days)
Creation of the World Trade Organization under the General Agreement on Tariffs and Trade

1982 Nov. 29-Dec. 23 (21 days)
Appropriations; gas tax increase to fund highway repairs

1980 Nov. 12 - Dec. 16 (23 days)
Appropriations; budget resolution; tax reconciliation; creation of superfund

1974 Nov. 18-Dec. 20 (22 days)
Appropriations; approval of Nelson A. Rockefeller as vice president; mass transit; benefits for Korean and Vietnam War veterans

1970 Nov. 16-Jan. 2, 1971 (31 days)
Appropriations; aid to Cambodia; repeal Gulf of Tonkin resolution

1954 Nov. 8-Dec. 2 (13 days)
Condemnation of Sen. Joseph R. McCarthy, R-Wis.

1950 Nov. 27-Jan. 2, 1951 (22 days)
Supplemental defense spending; excess profits tax; extension of federal rent controls; aid to Yugoslavia

1948 Dec. 31 (one day)
Congressional housekeeping

---

giving Frist more weapons to prevent Republican senators from going their own way.

But the change left defenders of the seniority system — moderates, senators from swing states and senior members — sputtering in anger over the jab at their independence. "I think it's a punitive measure, by any interpretation," said Snowe.

On the other side of the aisle, Daschle's defeat set off a scramble to reorganize the Senate Democratic leadership, producing an almost entirely new slate of leaders for the 109th Congress. Minority Whip Harry Reid of Nevada, who had just won his own re-election easily to a fourth Senate term, was elected the new minority leader without any contest. Richard J. Durbin of Illinois took Reid's place as the new

minority whip, warding off a challenge from Byron L. Dorgan of North Dakota, who stayed in his position as Senate Democratic Policy Committee chairman at Reid's request.

Meanwhile, Barbara A. Mikulski of Maryland stepped down as secretary of the Democratic caucus, the No. 3 elected position in the Democratic leadership. She was replaced by Debbie Stabenow of Michigan, who had been in the Senate just four years.

DeLay's Ethics Troubles

On the House side, both parties retained their leadership for the new Congress.

In their Nov. 17 organizing meeting, Republicans focused on protecting DeLay, their majority leader. DeLay — a combative party leader and lightning rod for Democratic attacks — was the engineer of a 2003 redistricting plan in Texas that forced some Democrats out of their seats. Three of De-Lay's political associates had been indicted by an Austin grand jury in September in a scheme to funnel corporate campaign contributions to GOP state legislative candidates in 2002. The case was tied to DeLay's bid to create enough GOP legislative power in Austin to redraw the state's congressional district lines.

For most of the year, DeLay also had been the subject of an investigation by the House ethics committee, triggered by a complaint from Chris Bell, D-Texas, one of the lawmakers who lost his seat because of the redistricting. *(2003 Almanac, p. 14-7)*

In October, the ethics committee admonished DeLay for two of three issues raised by Bell: drawing the federal government into the hunt for Texas Democratic legislators who left the state in 2003 to stall DeLay's redistricting effort, and for raising "an appearance of impropriety" by appearing at a private fundraiser for energy company officials while a major energy bill was being negotiated in 2002. De-Lay was also admonished separately for offering in 2003 to endorse the congressional candidacy of Brad Smith if his father, Rep. Nick Smith, R-Mich., voted for the Medicare overhaul bill. *(Ethics, p. 5-4)*

In none of the cases was a written ethics or House rule violated. The ethics panel also scolded Bell, saying he had exaggerated his charges. DeLay cited those facts as evidence that he had been cleared of any wrongdoing. He called Bell a "partisan stalker" and a sore loser and blamed Democrats for engaging in "the politics of personal destruction."

The committee postponed action on the third of Bell's complaints related to the grand jury investigation.

Meeting on Nov. 17, the House Republican Conference

agreed to alter their caucus rules in a way that would allow DeLay to keep his leadership job even if he were indicted. Previously, House Republican caucus rules required that a party leader or committee chairman indicted on a felony charge had to step aside until the case was resolved. Although the rule had never been invoked, DeLay contended that it made Republican leaders vulnerable to politically motivated criminal investigations.

The new rule let the caucus decide if one of their leaders should step down if indicted. It gave the Republican Steering Committee, an arm of the leadership, 30 days to review a case and make a recommendation on which the full conference would vote. A leader who was convicted of a felony had to be removed immediately.

GOP leaders also drafted a series of proposed changes to the rules of the House aimed at blunting the powers of the ethics committee. The changes still had to be submitted for approval to the Republican caucus in January before being put to the full House for a formal vote. One of the proposed changes was to prohibit admonishments except when the behavior at issue violated a specific law or House rule. If that had been in the rules in 2004, the ethics committee would have had a more difficult time finding grounds for rebuking DeLay.

A second proposed change would effectively kill an ethics complaint unless the panel chairman and ranking member found within 45 days that it had merit. Under the existing House rules, if the 45 days passed without action, the case automatically passed to an investigative subcommittee. A third proposal would give targeted members a right to respond to the ethics panel's conclusions before a decision was made final or made public.

It also became clear that Speaker J. Dennis Hastert, R-Ill., would replace ethics Chairman Joel Hefley, R-Colo., who had served for three terms and who was widely criticized by his GOP colleagues for the admonishments of DeLay.

Under pressure from the rank-and-file Republicans, who were getting complaints from their constituents, GOP leaders decided in January to drop the rule change that would have let DeLay keep his post if indicted, and it abandoned the attempt to strip out the House rule that let the ethics committee punish actions that bring discredit on the House even if there was no rule specifically addressing that behavior. "It's never a good idea to tie your shoelaces together right out of the gate," said Rep. J.D. Hayworth, R-Ariz.

The other changes in House rules planned by the leadership were made at the start of the 109th, and Hefley was replaced. ◆

Chapter 2

APPROPRIATIONS

Omnibus Bill Wraps Up 2004

Displaying fiscal restraint not seen since the heady days of the Republican takeover of Congress a decade earlier, Congress held discretionary spending for fiscal 2005 to $821.9 billion — a cap the White House and GOP leaders had agreed on at the start of the year. That was a 4.6 percent increase over fiscal 2004, but a less-than-inflation increase for domestic spending other than for homeland security. Yet Republicans had to wait until after Election Day to achieve that goal.

After finishing just four fiscal 2005 spending bills before the election, appropriators bundled the remaining nine bills into an omnibus package during their lame-duck session. Congress cleared it Nov. 20, and President Bush signed it into law Dec. 8 (HR 4818 — PL 108-447).

In the interim, three stopgap "continuing resolutions" were enacted to fund agencies governed by the nine bills.

From the start of the year, it was an open secret that election-year considerations and a tight squeeze on domestic spending would mean that most of the annual spending bills would end up rolled into one, a process that allowed congressional leaders and the president to take the legislative shortcuts necessary to assure that spending and policies were shaped on their terms.

The House managed to pass 12 of the 13 regular spending bills before the election; the exception was the VA-HUD measure. Senate leaders declined to call up seven of their bills for floor debate and amendment.

The omnibus contained $388.4 billion in discretionary spending, an increase of just 1 percent over comparable fiscal 2004 levels. Combined with the four previously enacted fiscal 2005 bills — for defense (PL 108-287), the Department of Homeland Security (PL 108-334), military construction (PL 108-324) and the District of Columbia (PL 108-335) — non-emergency discretionary spending totaled $821.9 billion. That overall figure covered increases of 7 percent for defense and 9 percent for the Department of Homeland Security, which meant significant cuts or flat funding for many domestic programs.

Republican leaders also succeeded in spiking every policy rider that had drawn a presidential veto threat, including provisions to block new overtime pay rules, lift the ban on travel by U.S. citizens to Cuba and curb the administration's ability to privatize federal jobs. A bid to add language permitting the importation of prescription drugs also died.

Unlike previous years, veteran appropriators were generally unable to use gimmicks to evade the spending limits. However, money was so tight in some domestic bills — especially those for the departments of Labor, Health and Human Services, and Education, and for the departments of Veterans Affairs and Housing and Urban Development — that appropriators negotiated with the White House for add-ons totaling about $5 billion.

Bush got $300 million more than Congress had planned for his Millennium Challenge Account, which provided aid to countries that worked toward human rights and democracy. Bush and House Majority Leader Tom DeLay, R-Texas,

insisted on $300 million more for NASA. Another $1.2 billion went to politically popular veterans' health programs. The energy and water bill got an extra $800 million.

Much of the additional spending was financed by a 0.8 percent across-the-board discretionary cut in every non-defense, non-homeland-security bill, which produced about $3.1 billion in savings. Appropriators also used $1 billion generated by adopting a calendar-year budget for public housing authorities, $300 million in unused defense money and $283 million in unexpected receipts from a crime fund.

Of the add-ons, only $300 million for the Low-Income Home Energy Assistance Program and $93 million in humanitarian aid for war-torn Sudan were designated as emergency spending outside the $821.9 billion cap.

Congress and the White House also had a safety valve in the form of supplemental emergency spending bills that did not count under the discretionary cap. A $25 billion supplemental for war and reconstruction in Iraq and Afghanistan was enacted as part of the defense bill. Another $16.5 billion was appropriated in two bills to aid stricken farmers in the Midwest and victims of a series of hurricanes that devastated Florida (PL 108-303, PL 108-324).

Lame-Duck Bargaining

Negotiations on the omnibus, which was attached to the foreign operations bill, began after Bush's re-election, and the gain of extra GOP seats in Congress guaranteed that his budget limits would be enforced. Senate appropriators had squeezed $8 billion more into their bills than had their House counterparts, mostly using accounting maneuvers. About $6 billion worth of Senate increases were dropped.

Democrats derided the process and accused Republican leaders of using the must-pass omnibus to ram through threadbare spending measures that might not have passed on their own. But the package contained thousands of hometown projects requested by lawmakers, ensuring that many Democrats voted for the bill despite their criticism.

Although the package contained little in the way of controversial policy changes, it did carry provisions to renew a law governing the satellite television industry, improve rural air service and settle water rights claims on the Snake River. More contentious ideas, such as weakening country-of-origin food labeling rules, were left out to avoid trouble.

One clumsily drafted House provision delayed enactment, however. It would have permitted leaders of the Appropriations committees and their aides to look at individual tax returns as part of their oversight of the IRS but without criminal and civil penalties for releasing tax information. Senate GOP leaders quickly won adoption of a resolution (H Con Res 528) striking the provision; the House cleared the fix Dec. 6.

The fiscal 2005 omnibus was the second such multiple-bill spending package considered during the year. In January, the Senate cleared a fiscal 2004 omnibus (PL 108-199) containing seven appropriations bills that had not been enacted before Congress adjourned in December 2003. ◆

Appropriations Mileposts
108th Congress — Second Session

Bill	House Action	Senate Action	House Final*	Senate Final*	President Signed	Story
FY 2005 Agriculture (HR 4766, S 2803, incorporated in HR 4818 — PL 108-447)	Passed 7/13/04	Panel approved 9/14/04	11/20/04	11/20/04	12/8/04	2-5
FY 2005 Commerce-Justice-State (HR 4754, S 2809, incorporated in HR 4818 — PL 108-447)	Passed 7/8/04	Panel approved 9/15/04	11/20/04	11/20/04	12/8/04	2-8
FY 2005 Defense (HR 4613 — PL 108-287)	Passed 6/22/04	Passed 6/24/04	7/22/04	7/22/04	8/5/04	2-12
FY 2005 District of Columbia (HR 4850 — PL 108-335)	Passed 7/20/04	Passed 9/22/04	10/6/04	10/6/04	10/18/04	2-16
FY 2005 Energy-Water Development (HR 4614, incorporated in 4818 — PL 108-447)	Passed 6/25/04	——	11/20/04	11/20/04	12/8/04	2-19
FY 2005 Foreign Operations (HR 4818 — PL 108-447)	Passed 7/15/04	Passed 9/23/04	11/20/04	11/20/04	12/8/04	2-22
FY 2005 Homeland Security (HR 4567 — 108-334)	Passed 6/18/04	Passed 9/14/04	10/9/04	10/11/04	10/18/04	2-26
FY 2005 Interior (HR 4568, S 2804, incorporated in HR 4818 — PL 108-447)	Passed 6/17/04	Panel approved 9/14/04	11/20/04	11/20/04	12/8/04	2-30
FY 2005 Labor-HHS-Education (HR 5006, S 2810, incorporated in HR 4818 — PL 108-447)	Passed 9/9/04	Panel approved 9/15/04	11/20/04	11/20/04	12/8/04	2-33
FY 2005 Legislative Branch (HR 4755, incorporated in HR 4818 — PL 108-447)	Passed 7/12/04	Passed 9/21/04	11/20/04	11/20/04	12/8/04	2-37
FY 2005 Military Construction (HR 4837 — PL 108-324)	Passed 7/22/04	Passed 9/20/04	10/9/04	10/11/04	10/13/04	2-40
FY 2005 Transportation-Treasury (HR 5025, S 2806, incorporated in HR 4818 — PL 108-447)	Passed 9/22/04	Panel approved 9/14/04	11/20/04	11/20/04	12/8/04	2-43
FY 2005 VA-HUD (HR 5041, S 2825, incorporated in HR 4818 — PL 108-447)	Panel approved 7/22/04	Panel approved 9/21/04	11/20/04	11/20/04	12/8/04	2-47
FY 2005 War Supplemental (HR 4613 — PL 108-287)	Passed 6/22/04	Passed 6/24/04	7/22/04	7/22/04	8/5/04	2-51
FY 2004 Disaster Supplementals (HR 5005 — PL 108-303) (HR 4837 — 108-324)	—— ——	—— 9/20/04	9/7/04 10/9/04	9/7/04 10/11/04	9/8/04 10/13/04	2-53

* Adoption of conference report

Some Fallow Times for Agriculture

Congress cleared an $86.2 billion fiscal 2005 agriculture appropriations bill as part of the year-end omnibus spending package. President Bush signed the measure into law Dec. 8 (HR 4818 — PL 108-447).

The bill funded Agriculture Department programs, including food and nutrition programs such as food stamps, crop insurance and other farm programs, rural conservation, and foreign food aid. It also covered food safety programs, including those of the Food and Drug Administration (FDA).

The total, which does not include a 0.8 percent across-the-board cut in all non-security discretionary spending, was just slightly less than provided in the fiscal 2004 law.

Eighty percent of the spending in the bill was guaranteed by formulas, mainly in the 2002 farm law (PL 107-171), for crop subsidies, nutrition and some conservation programs. The remaining $17 billion was discretionary spending, which the appropriators could allocate. The discretionary total was 2 percent more than the president requested but about 1 percent less than under the fiscal 2004 Agriculture spending law (PL 108-199). (*2002 Almanac, p. 4-3; 2003 Almanac, p. 2-35*)

The squeeze on discretionary spending meant cuts in some of the smaller programs that were authorized under the farm act. Rural development, conservation and renewable energy suffered some of the biggest cuts. The biggest increases in the bill were for food safety and domestic nutrition programs.

The House passed an $83.7 billion version of the bill in July. Senate appropriators approved an $84.1 billion version in September, but that bill did not reach the floor. Instead, appropriators returning after the November elections incorporated the measure into the nine-bill omnibus. With Republican leaders setting the terms of the omnibus, conferees dropped several provisions opposed by the White House, including House language that would have made it easier for Americans to import prescription drugs from Canada and Senate provisions to ease the sale of medical supplies and farm goods to Cuba.

Highlights

The fiscal 2005 agriculture bill included the following components:

● **Agriculture programs.** $27.1 billion, a 18 percent cut from fiscal 2004, for accounts ranging from crop supports to soil conservation and environmental programs. More than

BoxScore 2005
Agriculture
Fiscal Year

Bill:
HR 4818 — PL 108-447
Legislative Action:
House passed HR 4766 (H Rept 108-584), 389-31, on July 13.
Senate Appropriations Committee approved S 2803 (S Rept 108-340) by voice vote Sept. 14.
House adopted the conference report on HR 4818 (H Rept 108-792), 344-51, on Nov. 20.
Senate cleared the bill, 65-30, on Nov. 20.
President signed Dec. 8.

half the total, $16.5 billion went to the Commodity Credit Corporation (CCC), the main source of funding for crop price supports, export promotion, disposition of surplus commodities and some rural development and conservation programs. The total was 28 percent less than the CCC got in fiscal 2004, reflecting the fact that market prices for many commodities had increased and fewer farmers had losses that qualified for reimbursement. The bill also included $4.1 billion for the Federal Crop Insurance Corporation, a 9 percent increase over fiscal 2004.

● **Food and nutrition programs.** $52.5 billion for food stamps and other domestic nutrition programs — an increase of 11 percent or $5.3 billion from fiscal 2004. The biggest single program, food stamps, accounted for $35.2 billion of the total, an increase of 14 percent or $4.2 billion over fiscal 2004. The bill also included a $3 billion food stamp contingency fund. WIC, the supplemental nutrition program for women, infants and children, received $5.3 billion in discretionary funds, a 14 percent increase.

● **Conservation.** $999.9 million in discretionary spending for conservation programs, 3 percent less than provided in fiscal 2004. The bill also reduced spending on some mandatory programs from the amounts authorized under the 2002 farm law. The Environmental Quality Incentives Program, an entitlement program providing assistance to livestock producers and farmers for water quality improvements, got $1 billion, compared with an authorization of $1.2 billion. The Wetlands Reserve Program, which offered landowners incentives to protect and restore wetlands, was limited to 154,500 acres, rather than the 250,000 acres allowed in the farm law.

● **Rural development.** $2.4 billion, virtually the same as the previous year, for rural development programs that provided assistance for housing, community facilities and infrastructure, and business development in low-income areas. The Rural Business Investment Program, designed to create jobs in sparsely populated areas, was cut to $10 million, 77 percent below its authorized level.

● **Trade and international food aid.** $1.5 billion, virtually the same as in fiscal 2004, to provide food aid abroad and promote U.S. agricultural exports. Most of the total, $1.3 billion, was for the Food for Peace program, also known as PL 480, to provide commodities to developing countries and emerging democracies.

● **Food safety.** $1.5 billion for the Food and Drug Administration, a 5 percent increase from fiscal 2004 but 2 percent

Where the Money Goes

Agriculture Spending

(figures are in thousands of dollars of new budget authority)

	Fiscal 2004 Appropriation	Fiscal 2005 Bush Request	House Passed	Senate Panel Approved	Conference Report *
GRAND TOTAL	$86,761,836	$83,586,539	$83,670,594	$84,053,760	$86,190,567
Total adjusted for scorekeeping**	$86,585,013	$82,938,539	$83,221,594	$83,141,760	$85,275,959
MAIN COMPONENTS					
Domestic food programs	$47,262,481	$50,422,047	$50,236,739	$50,512,886	$52,533,133
Agricultural programs	32,848,079	26,934,522	26,927,128	26,986,917	27,093,737
Rural development programs	2,447,943	2,209,733	2,398,507	2,441,042	2,433,235
Foreign food and export assistance	1,503,398	1,520,914	1,508,711	1,549,540	1,533,201
Conservation programs	1,026,969	909,479	1,034,165	993,881	999,901
FDA, other agencies	1,475,639	1,589,844	1,555,844	1,560,594	1,556,119

* Totals do not reflect a 0.8 percent across-the-board cut in discretionary spending.

** Adjustments based on Congressional Budget Office criteria for determining discretionary spending; the adjusted total is used to assess compliance with 302(b) allocations.

TABLE: House, Senate Appropriations committees

less than requested, for the agency charged with regulating food, cosmetics, drugs and medical devices. The spending boost followed the December 2003 discovery in Washington state of a cow infected with bovine spongiform encephalopathy, or mad cow disease. The total also included $215 million for counterterrorism food safety programs. As in previous years, Congress rejected an administration proposal to charge a new user fee for inspecting meat and poultry.

The Animal and Plant Health Inspection Service (APHIS) also benefited from the concern over food safety, getting $820 million, a 14 percent increase. The Food Safety and Inspection Service received $824 million, a 6 percent increase.

Legislative Action

House Subcommittee Action

The House Agriculture Appropriations Subcommittee approved a draft of the bill by voice vote June 14, after adding language to make it easier for Americans to import prescription drugs from foreign countries. The measure included $16.8 billion in discretionary spending, the amount the subcommittee had been allocated.

The drug import amendment by ranking Democrat Marcy Kaptur of Ohio, was adopted 8-6 over the objections of several members, including Chairman Henry Bonilla, R-Texas, who said he was "blindsided" by the proposal.

It would have barred the FDA from using funds in the bill to enforce the ban on prescription drug imports by people other than wholesalers or pharmacists. A similar provision was added to the fiscal 2004 agriculture spending bill in full committee over Bonilla's objections, but it was later stripped in conference.

Under the 2003 Medicare overhaul law (PL 108-173), prescription drugs could be imported only from Canada, and only if the Health and Human Services (HHS) secretary certified the drugs were safe and would reduce consumers'

costs. HHS Secretary Tommy G. Thompson said he could not make such a certification. (*2003 Almanac, p. 11-3*)

Bonilla made a variety of small cuts to avoid large reductions in some farm programs. Food safety was one of the few areas slated to get more money; conservation programs were among the hardest hit. The subcommittee draft included:

• $1.5 billion for the FDA, 5 percent above the fiscal 2004 level.

• $825 million for the Food Safety and Inspection Service, a 6 percent increase.

• $814 million for APHIS, a 13 percent increase over fiscal 2004.

• $4.9 billion for WIC, a 6 percent increase.

• $994 million for discretionary conservation programs, a 3 percent decrease.

• $2.4 billion for rural development programs, a 2 percent drop from fiscal 2004.

House Appropriations Committee

The full Appropriations Committee approved the $83.7 billion bill (HR 4766 — H Rept 108-584) by voice vote June 23. The bill was virtually unchanged from the subcommittee draft. Committee members did not challenge the drug importation provision.

Democrats blamed GOP leaders who set the overall discretionary allocations — not Republican appropriators — for the spending reductions.

House Floor Action

The House passed the bill, 389-31, on July 13 after adding another controversial provision, this one to bar spending on a proposed taxpayer-funded buyout of tobacco farmers. It was widely expected that this and other amendments would be dropped later in conference. (*House vote 370, p. H-122*)

The White House issued a statement the day of the vote reiterating its opposition to the drug import language, which House GOP leaders also opposed.

During floor debate, the House:

• Agreed by voice vote to the tobacco provision, offered by Jeff Flake, R-Ariz., and other members who opposed a $9.6 billion tobacco buyout that Senate leaders were in the midst of adding to corporate tax legislation (PL 108-357). House Appropriations panel spokesman John Scofield said the language could undercut the buyout and imperil the tax bill, and would be "dropped like a bad habit." (*Tobacco, p. 13-5*)

• Adopted by voice vote, an amendment by Carolyn B. Maloney, D-N.Y., and Henry A. Waxman, D-Calif., aimed at allowing over-the-counter sales of the "morning after" contraceptive Plan B. The FDA announced in May that it would not allow sale of Plan B without a prescription. The amendment proposed to bar the FDA from spending funds to "restrict to prescription use a contraceptive that is determined to be safe and effective" without a doctor's supervision. Republicans accepted the amendment with little debate, saying the language mirrored existing law, and it was later retained in the conference report.

• Adopted by voice vote an amendment by Bonilla that made several small changes to the bill, including increasing discretionary funds for conservation programs to $1 billion.

• Adopted by voice vote a proposal by Anthony Weiner, D-N.Y., to increase funding for APHIS to $837 million.

Senate Subcommittee Action

The Senate Agriculture Appropriations Subcommittee approved a draft of the spending bill by voice vote Sept. 8, after renewing their fight with the Bush administration over restrictions on trade with Cuba. Like the House version, the bill included $16.8 billion in discretionary spending.

The committee adopted by voice vote an amendment by Byron L. Dorgan, D-N.D., to make it easier for farmers and medical suppliers to travel to Cuba to promote exports. The proposal, cosponsored by Larry E. Craig, R-Idaho, was popular with Midwest farmers eager to build sales to Cuba, but anathema to anti-Castro Cuban-Americans who opposed any weakening of the 42-year trade embargo. Both Florida, where Cuban-Americans were politically potent, and the Farm Belt were were considered key battlegrounds in the coming presidential election.

The Senate had added similar language to the fiscal 2004 agriculture bill, but it was abandoned at White House insistence.

The Senate draft included:

• $1.5 billion for the FDA, roughly the same as in the House bill.

• $824 million for the Food Safety and Inspection Service, close to the House amount.

• $792 million for APHIS, $45 million less than in the House bill.

• $5.2 billion for WIC, $125 million of which was classified as emergency funding.

• $994 million for conservation programs, $40 million less than the House-passed bill

• $2.4 billion for rural development programs, $43 million more than in the House bill.

Senate Appropriations Committee

The Senate Appropriations Committee approved the $84.1 billion bill (S 2803 — S Rept 108-340) by voice vote Sept. 14, after rejecting an attempt to move up the start date for mandatory country-of-origin labels on meat, fruit, vegetables and other food products.

The committee rejected, on a 14-14 tie, an amendment by Dorgan that would have moved the program's start date to Jan. 1, 2005, from Sept. 30, 2006. The program, authorized in the 2002 farm law, was originally scheduled to begin Sept. 30, 2004, but Congress had delayed the onset as part of the fiscal 2004 agriculture spending law.

The new labeling regimen was backed by Midwestern farmers, who feared competition from Canadian beef producers; they said putting the country of origin on food labels would help consumers avoid foods from areas where diseases such as mad cow disease had been identified.

Meatpackers and food producers, as well as ranchers in the Southwest where Mexican and U.S. meat often was mixed in packing houses, argued that the mandate would drive up their costs and, consequently, consumer prices.

Appropriations Chairman Ted Stevens, R-Alaska, said he supported the labeling program but opposed the amendment because he doubted House appropriators would relent. Bonilla had led the effort in 2003 to delay implementation of the law.

Stevens and another longtime supporter of the labeling amendment, Conrad Burns, R-Mont., also argued that it would be difficult for the Agriculture Department to be ready to implement the program on such short notice.

While the committee rejected Dorgan's labeling amendment, it left intact his amendment on Cuba despite bitter opposition by the Bush administration.

Conference/Final Action

The differences between the two versions were resolved with relative ease, and the measure cleared as part of the nine-bill omnibus. The House adopted the conference report (HR 4818 — H Rept 108-792), 344-51, on Nov. 20 and the Senate cleared the omnibus, 65-30, later the same day. (*House vote 542, p. H-174; Senate vote 215, p. S-46*)

Faced with stiff White House opposition, conferees dropped the Senate provision aimed at easing travel to Cuba to promote and sell agricultural and medical goods. They also struck the House language that would have prohibited the FDA from enforcing existing laws barring the importation of prescription drugs.

Among other decisions, the conferees:

• Provided $5.3 billion for WIC, more than either chamber had recommended with none of the money classified as emergency spending.

• Agreed to $820 million for APHIS, roughly splitting the difference between the two bills.

• Leaned toward the Senate on discretionary conservation programs, agreeing to $999 million, about $6 million more than in the Senate bill but $35 million less than the House wanted. ◆

C-J-S Escapes Contentious Riders

The spending bill for the departments of Commerce, Justice and State (C-J-S) and related agencies was relatively free of the high-profile policy riders and polarizing debates that had weighed it down in recent years. Still, like virtually all the other fiscal 2005 domestic spending bills, it was wrapped into an end-of-year omnibus package that did not clear until Nov. 20. President Bush signed the measure into law Dec. 8 (HR 4818 — PL 108-447)

The final bill provided $43.7 billion for the three departments along with the federal judiciary and a number of independent agencies, including the Federal Communications Commission, Federal Trade Commission, Small Business Administration (SBA) and the Securities and Exchange Commission.

The total was more than either chamber had recommended and 3 percent more than was appropriated for fiscal 2004. Most of the spending — $40 billion — was discretionary, which meant it was under the annual control of the appropriators. Totals do not include a 0.8 percent general cut in non-security discretionary spending, and a 0.54 percent across-the-board cut in the C-J-S bill.

The House passed a $43.5 billion C-J-S bill in July. The Senate Appropriations Committee approved a companion bill with virtually the same bottom line in September.

Among the winners in the final bill were the National Oceanic and Atmospheric Administration (NOAA), the FBI and the Patent and Trademark Office, all of which got significantly more than in fiscal 2004. Funding was sharply reduced for the SBA, due largely to an administration plan to make the SBA's popular 7(a) loan guarantee program self-sustaining.

The final bill did not include House language that would have temporarily blocked new Bush administration rules limiting Cuban-Americans' ability to send supplies to family members in Cuba.

Highlights

The following are major components of the fiscal 2005 Commerce, Justice, State appropriations law:

● **Commerce Department.** $6.7 billion, a 13 percent increase over fiscal 2004. More than half the spending, $3.9 billion, was for NOAA, which got 17 percent more than Bush requested and 6.5 percent more than in fiscal 2004. NOAA monitors the environment, manages fisheries and coastlines, and makes weather forecasts. The Patent and Trademark Office got $1.54 billion, 26 percent more than in

---

BoxScore 2005 Fiscal Year

Commerce-Justice-State

Bill:
HR 4818 — PL 108-447

Legislative Action:

House passed HR 4754 (H Rept 108-576), 397-18, on July 8.

Senate Appropriations Committee approved S 2809 (S Rept 108-344), 29-0, on Sept. 15.

House adopted the conference report on HR 4818 (H Rept 108-792), 344-51, on Nov. 20.

Senate cleared the bill, 65-30, on Nov. 20.

President signed Dec. 8.

---

fiscal 2004, in part through an increase in fees.

● **Justice Department.** $20.9 billion, a 5 percent increase over fiscal 2004 and 4 percent more than requested. The funds included $5.2 billion for the FBI — 14 percent more than in fiscal 2004 and 2 percent above the request — mainly for staff, training and information technology.

Local law enforcement assistance grants, perennially popular with lawmakers, received $3 billion, 43 percent more than the president requested but 3 percent less than in 2004.

As requested by the administration, the bill combined funds distributed under the popular Byrne Grant Program's state formula and the Local Law Enforcement Block Grant Program. But it retained $170 million of discretionary grants under the Byrne program, named for Edward Byrne, a slain New York City police officer, to be directed to hundreds of local and state law enforcement agencies.

Funding for the hiring grants under the Community Oriented Policing Services' (COPS) — the centerpiece of the Clinton-era initiative aimed at improving local community policing — was reduced to $10 million, compared with $119 million in fiscal 2004. Bush had requested no funding for COPS hiring.

● **State Department.** $8.3 billion for the State Department plus $600 million for the Broadcasting Board of Governors, which is responsible for all U.S. government-sponsored international broadcasting services. The total was 6 percent below fiscal 2004 funding and 3 percent less than Bush requested.

● **The judiciary.** $5.5 billion for the federal judiciary, a 6.5 percent increase but nearly 4 percent less than the judicial branch sought. By law, Bush was required to pass along the budget requested by the federal courts without making changes.

Legislative Action

House Subcommittee Action

The House C-J-S Appropriations Subcommittee approved a $43.5 billion draft of the bill by voice vote June 15 with no amendments. Discretionary spending accounted for $39.8 billion.

The measure included:

● $5.8 billion for Commerce, more than half of it, $3.2 billion, for NOAA. House appropriators kept funding for the agency low — $543 million below the fiscal 2004 level — to position themselves for negotiations with the Senate, which

Where the Money Goes

Commerce-Justice-State Spending

(figures are in thousands of dollars of new budget authority)

	Fiscal 2004 Appropriation	Fiscal 2005 Bush Request	House Passed	Senate Panel Approved	Conference Report *
GRAND TOTAL	**$42,242,023**	**$43,216,594**	**$43,483,066**	**$43,467,214**	**$43,681,207**
Total adjusted for scorekeeping**	**$38,272,362**	**$40,277,848**	**$40,517,815**	**$40,494,815**	**$40,729,055**
MAIN COMPONENTS					
Justice Department	$19,850,274	$20,059,739	$20,786,195	$20,389,055	$20,863,618
FBI	4,590,748	5,115,270	5,215,270	5,111,547	5,215,270
Community Oriented Policing Services	748,324	43,618	686,702	755,969	606,446
Commerce Department	5,942,779	6,057,989	5,756,925	6,919,139	6,703,158
National Oceanic and Atmospheric Administration	3,701,011	3,373,498	3,158,000	4,141,793	3,940,000
U.S. Patent and Trademark Office	1,222,460	1,523,407	1,523,407	1,544,754	1,544,754
State Department	8,837,162	8,551,541	8,420,709	7,981,308	8,283,227
Federal Judiciary	5,157,436	5,704,626	5,545,865	5,361,623	5,495,172
Federal Communications Commission	273,947	292,958	279,851	282,346	281,098
Federal Trade Commission	185,505	205,430	203,430	282,346	205,430
Small Business Administration	711,281	678,400	742,781	761,917	579,516

* Totals do not include a 0.8 percent across-the-board cut in discretionary spending.

** Adjustments based on Congressional Budget Office criteria for determining discretionary spending; the adjusted total is used to assess compliance with 302(b) allocations.

TABLE: House, Senate Appropriations committees

---

typically pushed for much higher NOAA funding.

• $20.8 billion for the Department of Justice, more than $900 million above Bush's request. Most of the increase was for the COPS program; the House bill recommended $687 million for the program, including $113 million in hiring grants. The COPS funding was part of $3 billion included for Office of Justice programs. The appropriators recommended $5.2 billion for the FBI.

House appropriators endorsed the administration proposal to consolidate the Byrne formula grants and Local Law Enforcement Block Grant programs in order to provide more flexibility and ease administrative burdens on the states and localities that received the funding. They recommended $634 million for the combined program, $125 million more than requested, but they also included $110 million for the Byrne discretionary grant program, an item that was not in Bush's budget.

• $8.4 billion for the State Department and $610 million for the Broadcasting Board of Governors.

• $5.5 billion for the judiciary.

House Committee Action

The full Appropriations Committee approved the bill (HR 4754 — H Rept 108-576) by voice vote June 23. There was little debate over the funding levels, but appropriators agreed to add a controversial restriction on the release of gun ownership information

During the markup, the committee:

• Adopted, 42-19, a provision by Todd Tiahrt, R-Kan., to block disclosure of most crime gun trace information collected by the Bureau of Alcohol, Tobacco, Firearms and Explosives and stored in a federal database. The data revealed the seller or dealer of guns used in crimes. Under the amendment, the information could be disclosed only to "a federal, state or local law enforcement agency or a prosecutor . . . for use in a bona fide criminal investigation."

The provision, which built on similar language in the fiscal 2004 C-J-S law (PL 108-199), was a response to a June 8 ruling by a federal district judge that New York City could access gun trace information as part of a case against firearms manufacturer Beretta USA Corp. Tiahrt argued that releasing the information even on a limited basis could put informants and undercover police officers in jeopardy

Gun control advocates Patrick J. Kennedy, D-R.I., and James P. Moran, D-Va., argued that the real aim of the amendment was to block the information from being introduced as evidence in civil lawsuits. A number of municipalities had filed lawsuits against gunmakers in a bid to make them liable for the costs of gun violence. Tiahrt and others said the suits were meant to drive gunmakers out of business.

• Adopted by voice vote an amendment by ranking Democrat David R. Obey of Wisconsin to bar the use of funds in the bill to justify the use of torture.

• Adopted by voice vote a proposal by Maurice D. Hinchey, D-N.Y., to require the Justice Department inspector general to provide a report to Congress on the contents of administration memos that made recommendations about the treatment of suspected terrorists and enemy combatants.

House Floor Action

The House passed the $43.5 billion bill on July 8 by a vote of 397-18 after an often-heated debate that covered issues ranging from the war on terrorism to Cuba policy and small-business loans. *(House vote 346, p. H-114)*

Both parties saw the debate as a chance to score important points in an election year, even though it was widely assumed the bill would end up as part of an omnibus package written in a conference where GOP leaders could jettison

any provisions they opposed.

During the debate, the House:

● **Patriot Act.** Rejected, on a 210-210 tie, a proposal by Bernard Sanders, I-Vt., to bar the Justice Department from using funds in the bill to seek the records of library and bookstore patrons, as allowed by the 2001 anti-terrorism law (PL 107-56) known as the Patriot Act. At one point, the tally stood at 219-200 in favor of the amendment. Despite vociferous objections from Democrats, GOP leaders held the balloting open for more than 30 minutes until they were able to prevail. The White House had warned that any language weakening the Patriot Act would draw a veto. (*House vote 339, p. H-112*)

● **Cuba.** Adopted, 221-194, an amendment by Jeff Flake, R-Ariz., to temporarily block new Bush administration regulations that limited the ability of Cuban-Americans to send supplies to family members in Cuba, and also restricted personal baggage carried by travelers to the island nation. Parcels bound for Cuba, for example, could not include seeds, clothing, fishing equipment or veterinary medicines. (*House vote 329, p. H-110*)

"It is unreasonable for our government to prevent Americans from sending clothes, personal hygiene items, seeds, etc., to people in Cuba who are struggling under the dictatorship of Fidel Castro," Flake argued. House Majority Leader Tom DeLay, R-Texas, responded that Flake "does not intend to help Fidel Castro's brutal regime grind its boot heel of tyranny deeper into the necks of Cuban people, but that is exactly what this amendment will do."

● **Small business.** Adopted, 281-137, a proposal by Small Business Chairman Donald Manzullo, R-Ill., to add $79 million for the SBA's 7(a) loan program, thereby maintaining funding at the fiscal 2004 level. The amendment received the support of 87 Republicans. (*House vote 328, p. H-110*)

In other action, the House:

● Adopted, 306-113, a proposal by Todd Akin, R-Mo., to prohibit use of funds in the bill for HIV/AIDS programs that did not explicitly oppose legalizing sex trafficking and prostitution. (*House vote 340, p. H-112*)

● Rejected by voice vote an amendment by Brad Sherman, D-Calif., that would have barred the use of funds in the bill to hold enemy combatants apprehended without charge on U.S. soil for more than 30 days. The Supreme Court had ruled June 28 that Yaser Esam Hamdi, a U.S. citizen detained in Afghanistan and held in South Carolina as an enemy combatant, had the right to challenge his detention before a "neutral decision maker."

● Rejected, 148-268, an amendment by Sam Farr, D-Calif., to bar the Justice Department from spending fiscal 2005 funds to prevent 10 states from implementing laws allowing the medical use of marijuana. (*House vote 334, p. H-112*)

Senate Committee Action

The Senate Appropriations Committee approved a $43.5 billion version of the bill (S 2809 — S Rept 108-344), 29-0, on Sept. 15, steering clear of contentious policy questions. Like the House bill, the measure included $39.8 billion in discretionary spending.

As had been the case in recent years, the biggest funding difference between the two bills concerned spending for the Commerce Department. Senate appropriators recommended

$6.9 billion, $1.2 billion more than in the House bill. Most of the increase was for NOAA, which was slated to get $4.1 billion. Senate appropriators had long favored the agency, in part because of the strong support of Ernest F. Hollings, D-S.C., who helped shape it 34 years before. Other Senate appropriators, particularly those from coastal regions, viewed the NOAA account as a way to target marine and fishery research funding to their states. (*1970 Almanac, p. 462*)

Senate appropriators also recommended:

● $20.4 billion for the Justice Department, splitting the difference between the $20 billion requested by Bush and the $20.8 billion in the House bill. Senate appropriators recommended $2.6 billion for Office of Justice programs, and $756 million for the COPS program, including $180 million for hiring grants. They included $5.1 billion for the FBI.

As in previous years, Senate appropriators resisted the administration plan to consolidate the popular Byrne Grant Program and the Local Law Enforcement Block Grants. The bill included a total of $768 million for the two separate programs and the Byrne discretionary grants.

● $8 billion for the State Department and $561 million for the Broadcasting Board of Governors, $489 million less than in the House bill.

● $5.4 billion for the federal judiciary, $184 million below the House figure.

Conference/Final Action

The final bill was completed as part of the conference on the omnibus spending package (HR 4818 — H Rept 108-792). The House adopted the conference report, 344-51, on Nov. 20; the Senate cleared the omnibus, 65-30, later the same day. (*House vote 542, p. H-174; Senate vote 215, p. S-46*)

While the C-J-S bill had few controversial policy provisions, negotiators were still called upon to resolve several significant disagreements.

● **Commerce.** The Senate prevailed on Commerce Department spending, although it did not get all it wanted. The final total, $6.7 billion, was $216 million less than in the Senate bill but $946 million above the House figure. The extra money beyond what the House recommended went to NOAA.

● **COPS.** The final bill provided $606 million for the overall program, less than recommended by either chamber. Just $10 million of that was for hiring, a 92 percent cut from fiscal 2004, and half of that was directed for school resource officers. The president had requested no funding for hiring. Conferees also provided more than Bush requested to fund crime labs, particularly for reducing backlogs of biological evidence.

● **Cuba.** Negotiators abandoned the House language that would have temporarily blocked administration restrictions on the amount of supplies that family members could send to Cuba. The White House had warned that the House provision could provoke a veto.

● **Gun checks.** Conferees retained Tiahrt's provision to block disclosure of information collected by the Bureau of Alcohol, Tobacco, Firearms and Explosives tracing the history of firearms used in crimes.

● **Justice Department.** The House prevailed here: The final figure of $20.9 billion for the department was just $77 million above the House total but $475 million more

than the Senate wanted to spend.

● **Law enforcement grants.** The final bill followed the House version in providing $634 million for a new Edward Byrne Memorial Justice Assistance Grant program that combined funds distributed under the Byrne Grant Program's state formula and Local Law Enforcement Block Grants. It also provided $170 million for Byrne discretionary grants.

● **FBI.** Like the House version, the final bill provided $5.2 billion for the FBI, about $100 million more then either Bush or the Senate wanted. Most of the new money was to fund staff, training and information technology to improve the agency's intelligence and counterterrorism capabilities. The bill also provided for retention and relocation bonuses for FBI personnel and enabled the FBI director to waive the mandatory retirement age of 57 and allow employees to work until they are 65.

● **SBA.** The bill provided $580 million for the SBA, 18.5 percent less than it got for fiscal 2004. The total was also less than the president requested or either chamber recommended. Conferees eliminated the subsidy for the 7(a) loan program, embracing the administration's plan to make the program self-sustaining. That was accomplished by making permanent an increase in fees paid by borrowers and lenders in the program for loans that went into effect Oct. 1.

The bill also increased the total loan level for the 7(a) program to $16 million, raised the federal guarantee level for a loan from $1 million to $1.5 million, and increased the maximum loan amount from $250,000 to $350,000 for low-paperwork SBA Express loans.

● **Patent and Trademark Office.** Conferees agreed to appropriate $1.54 billion for the Patent and Trademark Office. The money came from patent and trademark registration fees : $1.3 billion from existing fees and $209 million resulting from a fee increase requested by the administration and enacted as part of the omnibus. The administration said the change would help the office reduce a two-year backlog in patent processing. ◆

Quick Action on Pentagon Funding

With lawmakers from both parties anxious to demonstrate support for U.S. troops in Iraq and Afghanistan, Congress cleared a $417.5 billion defense appropriations bill July 22 with near-unanimous bipartisan support. The bill was the only fiscal 2005 spending measure to clear before Congress left for a six-week summer recess, and the only one to be enacted before the new fiscal year began on Oct. 1. President Bush signed it into law Aug. 5 (HR 4613 — PL 108-287).

The final bill closely tracked the fiscal 2005 defense authorization measure, which was still in conference, and provided all but $1.6 billion sought by the administration for Bush's robust defense agenda. The total included a record $391.2 billion for the Pentagon's core budget — a 7 percent increase over fiscal 2004 funding, excluding supplemental spending — and an emergency $25 billion war appropriation to pay for operations in Iraq and Afghanistan.

The $25 billion was available upon enactment, enabling the Pentagon to tap it to cover shortfalls in the final months of fiscal 2004. That provision proved prescient: just hours after the conference report was filed July 21, the Government Accountability Office (GAO) estimated that the Pentagon would face a $12.3 billion shortfall before Sept. 30. Defense officials said they would need only about $2.8 billion more before the end of the fiscal year and could reprogram the money from other accounts. Appropriators had insisted all along that the shortfall would be higher.

Inclusion of the $25 billion war fund gave a special urgency to the bill in Congress. Quick action was also aided by the fact that lawmakers had debated most of the contentious defense issues as part of the defense authorization bill (PL 108-375). *(Defense authorization, p. 6-3)*

While the administration got much of what it wanted, it did not get everything. Appropriators refused to give the president the nearly unlimited authority he had sought to spend the $25 billion war fund, instead restricting all but $2 billion of the money to specific accounts.

"Transformation" programs to remake the military into a leaner, more technologically savvy force — a top priority for Defense Secretary Donald H. Rumsfeld — did not fare well. Lawmakers reduced Bush's request for the Future Combat System, the centerpiece of the Army's modernization effort, and slashed spending for the space-based radar, an Air Force program to develop near-continuous global radar imagery and tracking of moving targets. They also cut back his request for the Air Force's transformation communications satellites, a program aimed at providing U.S. war fighters

---

BoxScore **2005** Fiscal Year

Defense

Bill:
HR 4613 — PL 108-287

Legislative Action:

House passed HR 4613 (H Rept 108-553), 403-17, on June 22.

Senate passed HR 4613, amended (S Rept 108-284), 98-0, on June 24.

Senate voted, 96-0, on July 22 to deem the bill cleared pending House adoption.

House adopted the conference report (H Rept 108-662), 410-12, on July 22.

President signed Aug. 5.

---

with global access to secure, high-bandwidth links.

The cuts to transformation programs reflected concerns in Congress about a looming procurement shortfall. Lawmakers warned that there were simply more big-ticket weapons programs in the development pipeline than the Pentagon would be able to afford. Still, in an election year, appropriators kept their knives sheathed much of the time. The only major weapons systems to have its funding terminated was the RAH-66 Comanche attack helicopter, which the Army had decided earlier in the year to cancel.

Lawmakers added $1.5 billion to Bush's request to replace equipment and munitions used in Iraq and Afghanistan and to deploy more armored vehicles. They also agreed to fully fund Bush's plan to deploy the first elements of a national missile defense system later in the year.

The bill also included $1.4 billion for non-defense emergency needs, such as the new U.S. diplomatic mission in Iraq, suppression of wildfires in the western United States and extra security at the national party conventions.

Highlights

The following are major spending components and selected individual items in the bill:

● **Operations and maintenance.** $121.1 billion, a 4 percent increase over fiscal 2004 but about $800 million less than requested. *(2003 Almanac, p. 2-42)*

● **Procurement.** $77.7 billion, a 6 percent increase over fiscal 2004 and 4 percent more than requested.

● **Military personnel.** $103.7 billion, a 5 percent increase over fiscal 2004 but 1 percent less than requested. The funds included enough to cover a 3.5 percent pay increase, as requested. The emergency war fund included an additional $1.3 billion that could be used later, if needed, to cover a permanent increase in troop levels.

● **R&D.** $69.9 billion for research, development and testing, a 7 percent increase over fiscal 2004 and 3 percent more than Bush sought.

● **Missile defense.** $10 billion, 2 percent less than Bush requested but 10 percent above fiscal 2004 spending. The total included $4.6 billion, as Bush requested, for the ground-based midcourse missile defense, the centerpiece of the president's plan to deploy a limited missile defense system in 2004.

● **Future Combat System.** $2.9 billion, 8 percent less than the $3.2 billion requested for the futuristic Army program linking vehicles, weapons and sensors. The conference re-

Where the Money Goes

Defense Spending

(figures are in thousands of dollars of new budget authority)

	Fiscal 2004 Appropriation	Fiscal 2005 Bush Request	House Passed	Senate Passed	Conference Report
GRAND TOTAL	**$430,462,007**	**$417,807,305**	**$416,933,400**	**$416,298,400**	**$417,509,612**
Total adjusted for scorekeeping*	**$365,772,453**	**$392,824,305**	**$391,170,100**	**$384,012,400****	**$391,170,312**
MAIN COMPONENTS					
Procurement	$73,516,939	$74,662,317	$77,354,791	$76,466,514	$77,679,803
Research & Development	65,217,884	67,772,288	68,946,512	68,768,845	69,932,182
Military personnel	98,453,681	104,811,558	104,191,558	103,869,413	103,731,158
Operations & Maintenance	115,914,877	121,874,589	120,568,274	121,410,132	121,062,969
Emergency war spending	64,706,554	25,000,000	25,000,000	25,000,000	25,000,000
Defense health program	15,730,013	17,640,411	17,959,186	18,064,811	18,171,436

* Adjustments based on Congressional Budget Office criteria for determining discretionary spending; adjusted total is used to assess compliance with 302(b) allocations.

**Does not include $7,158,000 in emergency spending, which brought the total to $391,170,400.

Table: House and Senate Appropriations committees

port expressed concerns about the initiative, assigned the money to specific accounts and required a report on the program's future. The cut coincided with the Army's July 21 announcement that it was restructuring the program, adding $25 billion to the $92 billion price tag and delaying completion by two years, to 2014, to provide more time to develop and field high-risk technologies.

● **F/A-22 Raptor fighter.** $4.1 billion, all but $30 million of the amount requested to procure 24 F/A-22 Raptor fighter jets, the Air Force's next-generation, premier fighter. However, conferees ordered an independent cost assessment of the program. Critics said the program, originally envisioned for air-to-air combat with Soviet fighters, was a Cold War relic. Jerry Lewis, R-Calif., had tried unsuccessfully to cut funding for the aircraft when he became chairman of the House Defense Appropriations Subcommittee in 1999. *(1999 Almanac, p. 2-40)*

● **Shipbuilding.** $10.4 billion, nearly 5 percent more than Bush sought but 4 percent less than existing spending. The total included money to build one *Virginia*-class submarine and three DDG-51 destroyers. The bill dropped House language that would have delayed procurement of the first DD(X) next-generation destroyer and added funds to build a second ship.

● **Joint Strike Fighter.** $4.4 billion to continue development of the fighter, 4 percent less than requested and about the same as fiscal 2004 funding. The conference report ordered the Pentagon to review the management of the program, which had been delayed because the aircraft was overweight, and report to Congress by Dec. 15.

● **Refueling tankers.** $100 million for the Air Force to initiate a program to replace its aging fleet of refueling tankers. Conferees dropped House language specifying that the Pentagon should sign a deal with Boeing Co.

● **Space-based radar.** $75 million, less than a quarter of the $328 million sought by Bush. Senators agreed to House language directing the Pentagon to revamp the program.

● **Defense health program.** $18.2 billion, a 15.5 percent increase over fiscal 2004 and 3 percent above Bush's request. An additional $683 million was included in the $25 billion emergency fund for additional health costs, including those of reserves.

● **Non-defense funds.** $1.4 billion in emergency funds, including: $665 million for the State Department's new diplomatic mission in Iraq, $500 million to fight wildfires in the West, $95 million in relief for victims of ethnic cleansing in Sudan's Darfur region, and $50 million to bolster security at the Democratic and Republican national conventions.

Legislative Action

House Committee Action

The House Appropriations Committee approved a $416.9 billion version of the bill (HR 4613 — H Rept 108-553) by voice vote June 16. The Defense Appropriations Subcommittee had approved a draft by voice vote in a closed session June 2. The main change made by the full committee was the addition of $780 million in emergency non-defense funds.

The bill called for $391.2 billion in core Pentagon funding. Major components were $120.6 billion for operations and maintenance, $104.2 billion for military personnel, $77.4 billion for procurement and $68.9 billion for research and development.

An additional $25 billion in emergency money would be available upon enactment for Iraq and Afghanistan. Committee Chairman C.W. Bill Young, R-Fla., and other appropriators wanted to give the Pentagon quick access to the money to cover any shortfalls in Iraq and Afghanistan. Young said the military was burning through the $65.1 billion war supplemental Congress provided in late 2003 (PL 108-106) and that it might need as much as $10 billion to make it through fiscal 2004. John P. Murtha of Pennsylvania, the senior Democrat on the Defense Subcommittee, predicted that the Army would run out of war money three

months early if it did not have access to the $25 billion fund. (*2003 Almanac, p. 2-83*)

In a sign of increasing assertiveness on how war funds should be spent, the appropriators assigned all but $2 billion of the fund to 22 specific accounts. The Pentagon "would have preferred $25 billion in a pool that was a pretty fluid pool," said Lewis, who was serving his sixth and final year as chairman of the Defense Subcommittee. "We have distributed that $25 billion package in a way that we think reflects the needs out there."

Major items in the basic Pentagon budget included:

• $9.7 billion for ballistic missile defense — full funding for initial deployment of the antimissile interceptors, but $500 million less than the $10.2 billion that Bush requested for the program.

• A $100 million fund to begin buying 100 midair refueling tankers. Appropriators concurred with language in the House defense authorization bill directing the Pentagon to sign a contract for the tankers with Boeing by March 2005. The Boeing deal had been delayed for more than two years by concerns about the need for the planes, the best way to acquire them and alleged ethics lapses among the program's proponents. (*Tankers, p. 6-7*)

• $4.1 billion for 24 F/A-22 fighters.

• $10.2 billion for shipbuilding, including full funding for one *Virginia*-class submarine. The committee included $1.2 billion, 17 percent less than Bush requested, for the Navy's new DD(X) destroyer. It dropped the funding requested to start construction, warning that an overly ambitious development schedule presented a "potential 'rush to failure,'" and recommended more time for development.

• $2.9 billion for the Army's Future Combat System.

• $4.4 billion for Joint Strike Fighter development.

• $75 million, 77 percent less than requested, for the Air Force's space-based radar. The report lambasted the program, saying the system was "neither affordable nor likely to produce the results claimed by its advocate," that it would consume a disproportionate share of resources and was a less-pressing priority than many Pentagon needs.

• $2.2 billion in unrequested procurement funds to replenish armored combat vehicles, helicopters, trucks and ammunition used in Iraq and Afghanistan.

During the markup, the full committee:

• Adopted by voice vote an amendment by Lewis that added $685 million in emergency spending for the U.S. diplomatic mission in Iraq and $95 million in emergency humanitarian aid for refugees in Sudan and Chad.

• Adopted by voice vote an amendment by Steny H. Hoyer, D-Md., the House minority whip, reaffirming U.S. policy against the use of torture. Members had been outraged by revelations that U.S. military personnel had brutalized and humiliated detainees at Iraq's Abu Ghraib prison. (*Abu Ghraib, p. 6-5*)

• Adopted by voice vote an amendment by ranking full committee Democrat David R. Obey of Wisconsin to require a presidential report by Oct. 1 estimating the costs of war and reconstruction in Iraq and Afghanistan for fiscal 2006 through 2011. A Pentagon spokeswoman said the department did "not have credible information to accurately project the costs of war or reconstruction in fiscal 2005, much less beyond fiscal 2006."

House Floor Action

The House easily passed the $416.9 billion bill June 22 on a bipartisan vote of 403-17. Virtually all the "no" votes came from the most liberal House Democrats, who viewed the military budget as excessive. (*House vote 284, p. H-96*)

The only contentious change to the bill was made as part of the rule for floor debate. The rule automatically added language to make it possible for both chambers to avoid a separate vote on increasing the limit on the national debt. The language stated that the government "shall take all steps necessary to guarantee the full faith and credit of the government." That was enough to put a debt limit increase within the scope of the conference on the defense bill, potentially saving Republicans from having to cast a separate, potentially embarrassing vote on the debt in an election year. The rule was adopted, 221-197. (*House vote 280, p. H-94; debt limit, p. 4-13*)

The House rejected, 202-218, an amendment by Jay Inslee, D-Wash, to bar the Pentagon from suspending the collective bargaining or due process rights of its civilian employees. Congress had allowed the Pentagon, as part of the fiscal 2004 defense authorization bill (PL 108-136), to revise personnel rules for its civilian workforce. Inslee, Norm Dicks, D-Wash., and others said an initial draft of the new rules released in February would eliminate traditional worker protections. Murtha opposed the amendment, saying he feared it would cause the White House to veto the bill. (*House vote 283, p. H-96*)

In a statement of policy released the day of the House debate, the White House Office of Management and Budget generally supported the bill but criticized the lack of flexibility it would give the president in using the $25 billion war fund.

Senate Committee Action

Senate appropriators rushed to complete their version of the bill before the July Fourth recess, holding subcommittee and full committee markups just hours apart June 22. Both panels approved the $416.3 billion Senate measure (S 2559 — S Rept 108-284) by voice vote. No amendments were proposed in either markup.

The appropriators included the $25 billion in emergency funds for Iraq and Afghanistan, giving the administration more flexibility than the House wanted but less than Bush requested. Any transfers would require five days' advance notice to Congress, and the administration would have to provide quarterly reports on the use of the money. The report accompanying the bill said that the committee approach "provides necessary financial flexibility and ensures proper congressional oversight."

Like the House bill, the Senate version recommended $391.2 billion in core Pentagon funding, though $7.2 billion of it was considered emergency spending to stay within Senate spending caps. The bill included $121.4 billion for operations and maintenance, $103.9 billion for personnel, $76.5 billion for procurement and $68.8 billion for research and development.

Major items included:

• $10.2 billion, the full amount requested, for missile defense programs.

• $3 billion for the Army's Future Combat System.

• $4.1 billion for 24 F/A-22 fighters.

- $4.6 billion for the Joint Strike Fighter.
- $10.2 billion for shipbuilding. The bill recommended $1.4 billion, Bush's full request, for the DD(X) destroyer program, including construction of the first ship, plus $99 million for advance procurement of a second DD(X).
- $228 million for space-based radar, $100 million less than requested.
- $110 million for the tanker replacement fund, though the bill did not direct the Pentagon to sign the Boeing contract. Appropriations Chairman Ted Stevens, R-Alaska, opposed including that language in an appropriations bill.

Senate Floor Action

Stevens whisked the measure through the Senate on a 98-0 vote June 24, after disposing of 43 amendments in a little over four hours. (*Senate vote 149, p. S-32*)

Most of the amendments were earmarks that had been agreed to in advance and were adopted by voice vote. Stevens was moving so fast he provided only dollar amounts for some amendments without saying what the money was for. By contrast, it had taken the Senate more than a month to complete its version of the fiscal 2005 defense authorization bill (S 2400), which had finally passed June 23.

Angry Democrats initially threatened to delay action on the spending bill because of the GOP ploy to use it as a vehicle to pass a debt limit increase. Stevens strongly defended the debt limit plan at first, but when it became clear that the controversy would slow down his timetable, he promised Democrats he would abandon it.

During the debate, the Senate:

- Adopted, 89-9, an amendment by Robert C. Byrd of West Virginia, the ranking Democrat on the Appropriations Committee, to express the sense of the Senate that future requests for military funding, including for war operations, should be included in the president's regular budget. The administration preferred to pay for war costs through incremental emergency supplemental spending requests, and had irritated lawmakers by refusing to provide estimates of future war costs. Byrd complained that the administration ignored similar language in the fiscal 2004 law (PL 108-87). (*Senate vote 147, p. S-32*)
- Adopted by voice vote an amendment by Mike DeWine, R-Ohio, to add $95 million in emergency funds for the Darfur region of Sudan and Chad. However, the Republican majority defeated a Democratic attempt to increase the amount. A proposal by Joseph R. Biden Jr. of Delaware to increase the amount by another $118 million was tabled (killed), 53-45. (*Senate vote 148, p. S-32*)

Conference/Final Action

House and Senate appropriators wrapped up their negotiations July 13 and approved the conference report in a 10-minute meeting the following evening. The Senate, anxious to get the job finished, adopted the conference report by a vote of 96-0 on July 22, pending adoption by the other chamber. That came a little more than an hour later on a 410-12 vote. (*Senate vote 163, p. S-35; House vote 418, p. H-136*)

The differences between the two chambers' bills were relatively minor. And with 140,000 U.S. soldiers in Iraq and the United States under continuing threat of another major terrorist attack, there was little doubt that the bill would be finished with relative ease.

The following were among the issues resolved:

- **DD(X).** Conferees largely adopted the Senate position. The agreement provided $1.4 billion for the next-generation Navy destroyer, including $221 million for advance procurement of the first ship at the Ingalls shipyard in Mississippi, home state of Thad Cochran, the No. 2 Republican on the Senate Appropriations Committee. House conferees also agreed to include $84 million for advance procurement to build a second DD(X) at the Bath Iron Works in Maine, Ingalls' only rival in the destroyer trade. Maine Republicans Olympia J. Snowe and Susan Collins pressed for the extra funding.
- **Space-based radar.** The conferees adopted the tougher House position and provided only $75 million.
- **Army recapitalization.** Conferees added $1.5 billion to Bush's request to help the Army and Marine Corps replace vehicles, helicopters and ammunition used in Iraq and Afghanistan, $700 million less than the amount added in the House version of the bill. The funding included $625 million to purchase and field one additional brigade of Stryker armored vehicles, reflecting the concerns of defense overseers in Congress that some U.S. soldiers in Iraq, particularly reservists, were not being adequately protected.
- **Troop strength.** The conference report sidestepped the question of whether to endorse a permanent increase in force strength, a matter that was being debated as part of the fiscal 2005 defense authorization bill. But it included $1.3 billion in the $25 billion war fund to pay for war-related personnel expenses and to cover a permanent troop level increase if the final version of the defense authorization bill required one — which it did.
- **Debt limit.** The final bill did not address the debt limit.
- **Senate discretionary spending.** The conference report included language setting an overall fiscal 2005 discretionary spending limit of $821.4 billion for the Senate. That was the cap provided in the conference report on the fiscal 2005 budget resolution (S Con Res 95 — H Rept 108-498). The House had adopted the conference report, but the measure had stalled in the Senate, making it difficult for that chamber to bring up spending bills. (*Budget resolution, p. 4-9*) ◆

D.C. Gets Vote of Confidence

The Senate cleared a $560 million fiscal 2005 spending bill for the District of Columbia on Oct. 6 — the earliest the annual measure had been completed since 1996. President Bush signed the legislation into law Oct. 18 (HR 4850 — PL 108-335).

The $560 million was mainly a payment in lieu of local taxes, from which the federal government is exempt. The amount was a 3 percent increase over fiscal 2004 and essentially equal to Bush's request. The total was subject to a further 0.8 percent cut in discretionary spending enacted as part of the year-end omnibus spending bill (PL 108-447).

In addition to the federal payment, the bill put the federal government's legally required seal of approval on the city's $8.3 billion budget — a prerequisite for D.C. officials to reorder their own programs. The timely enactment, just five days after the start of the fiscal year, was particularly important to the municipal government for that reason.

In contrast to previous years, the D.C. spending measure sped through committee and floor consideration in both chambers with little controversy. The House passed its version of the bill by a lopsided vote in July, and the Senate passed its by voice vote in September. It was the first time in several years that the conference report on the D.C. bill was not part of a year-end omnibus agreement.

While the measure retained several social policy riders added by GOP conservatives in previous years, Rodney Frelinghuysen, R-N.J., chairman of the House District of Columbia Appropriations Subcommittee, and his Senate counterpart, Mike DeWine, R-Ohio, succeeded in keeping the measure free of any new dictates on local affairs.

The bill also gave a vote of confidence to the District, which had balanced its budget for seven straight years. Its bonds were considered a grade-A investment by all three major rating agencies. The measure allowed the District to reduce its emergency reserve fund from 7 percent to 2 percent and its contingency reserve fund from 6 percent to 4 percent.

Highlights

Following are highlights of the fiscal 2005 D.C. bill:
● **Education.** The law provided $40 million for District school improvements, as requested, which was virtually the same as in the previous year. The total included $14 million, an 8 percent increase over fiscal 2004, for a voucher program created under the fiscal 2004 spending law (PL 108-199) that helped low-income parents send their children to private schools. Tuition subsidies for District

BoxScore 2005
Fiscal Year
District of Columbia

Bill:
HR 4850 — PL 108-335
Legislative Action:
House passed HR 4850
(H Rept 108-610), 371-54,
on July 20.
Senate passed HR 4850,
amended with text of S 2826
(S Rept 108-354), by voice
vote Sept. 22.
House adopted the conference
report (H Rept 108-734),
377-36, on Oct. 6.
Senate cleared the bill by
voice vote Oct. 6.
President signed Oct. 18.

high school graduates attending out-of-state universities and colleges were increased 52 percent, to $25.6 million. The bill also provided $13 million to improve D.C. public schools, and an equal amount for charter schools.
● **D.C. courts.** $409 million, nearly three-fourths of the federal payment, to fund courts and court-related services, a 12 percent increase over fiscal 2004, but 11 percent less than Bush requested.
● **Capital projects.** $14 million for capital projects, including $4.8 million for the D.C. water and sewer authority, $3 million for the Anacostia Waterfront Initiative and $6 million for the Unified Communications Center. The bill also provided $8 million in unrequested funds for a new bioterrorism and forensics laboratory.
● **Social spending.** Unrequested funds including $5 million for improvements to the city's foster care system, $6 million to improve the city's public school libraries, and $1 million for family literacy.
● **Homeland security.** $15 million for emergency planning and security costs to the District, the amount Bush requested and 37 percent above the fiscal 2004 total.
● **Chief financial officer.** $32.5 million in unrequested funds to the District's chief financial officer for education, public safety, health, economic development and infrastructure initiatives.
● **Legislative riders.** The bill renewed existing prohibitions on the use of both federal and local funds for the distribution of sterile hypodermic needles aimed at reducing the spread of AIDS; for abortions except to save the life of the woman or in cases of rape or incest; to lobby for statehood; or to enforce a D.C. ruling that the Boy Scouts reinstate and compensate two homosexual scout leaders.

It prohibited the use of federal, but not local, funds to implement the District's policy of granting health insurance benefits to domestic partners.

It also retained language that prevented a city initiative on medical marijuana from taking effect. And it limited fees for attorneys who brought special-education lawsuits against the city to $4,000 for each action filed.

Legislative Action

House Subcommittee, Committee Action

The House District of Columbia Appropriations Subcommittee approved the bill by voice vote July 7, and the full committee followed suit on July 14 (HR 4850 — H Rept 108-610).

Where the Money Goes

District of Columbia Spending

(figures are in thousands of dollars of new budget authority)

	Fiscal 2004 Appropriation	Fiscal 2005 Bush Request	House Passed	Senate Passed	Conference Report *
TOTAL FEDERAL FUNDS	**$541,783**	**$560,359**	**$560,000**	**$560,000**	**$560,000**
Total D.C. Budget	**$7,460,858**	**$8,243,789**	**$8,253,500**	**$8,286,608**	**$8,265,417**
FEDERAL FUNDS: MAIN COMPONENTS					
Court System	$166,775	$228,069	$202,110	$195,010	$190,800
New bioterrorism and forensics lab	—	—	—	8,000	8,000
Resident tuition subsidies	16,900	17,000	25,600	21,200	25,600
Emergency planning and security	10,935	15,000	15,000	15,000	15,000
Chief financial officer	32,159	—	19,000	32,500	32,500
School improvement	39,764	40,000	40,000	40,000	40,000
Foster care improvements	13,917	—	5,000	5,000	5,000

* Totals do not include a 0.8 percent across-the-board cut in discretionary spending.

TABLE: House Appropriations Committee

Frelinghuysen dissuaded conservatives from trying to add any new policy riders that might hold up the bill.

The bill called for a $560 million federal payment to the city, virtually the same as Bush's request, and gave the required congressional blessing to an $8.25 billion budget for fiscal 2005.

City officials said they were glad no new policy riders had been attached so far. But the office of Mayor Anthony A. Williams complained that the bill effectively froze payments to the city for emergency planning and security in a year that would include the presidential inauguration. The bill included $15 million in such payments for fiscal 2005, a 37 percent boost over the $11 million provided the previous year. However, the city actually spent $15 million in fiscal 2004, using $4.1 million left over from an earlier appropriation.

Funding for schools remained almost flat at $40 million, including $14 million for the new voucher program and $13 million each for public and charter school improvements. Frelinghuysen said the voucher funding would provide scholarships of $7,500 to 1,250 low-income students in the 2004-05 school year

However, appropriators also included $25.6 million — about 50 percent more than Bush requested — for a five-year-old program that subsidized tuition for city residents at state colleges and universities nationwide. Williams pushed hard for the increase, saying it was needed to cover rising tuition costs and rapid growth of the program.

Items added to the bill that Bush did not request included $6 million to improve school libraries, $1 million for family literacy programs and $5 million for foster-care programs.

To make room for the increased tuition aid and other additions, appropriators trimmed Bush's requested funding level for the city's court and related services by about 7 percent to $427 million. The administration's courts request was intended to go toward renovating a building in the city's Judiciary Square area, a cost that would now be phased in over two years. The White House issued a statement of adminis-

tration policy saying the president "strongly opposes" any plan to allow the city to enter into a contract for the renovations without funding for the whole project.

Appropriators said the panel lacked the resources to provide more than $10 million — about a third of what was provided the previous year — to upgrade the District's sewer system. The project was expected to cost $1.3 billion and take between 15 and 40 years to complete.

House Floor Action

The spending bill made it through the House unscathed on a 371-54 vote July 20, after appropriators successfully fended off the addition of any controversial riders. Del. Eleanor Holmes Norton, D-D.C., hailed the quick passage as "nothing short of a new day," although she said she still took "strong exception" to some provisions added in prior years that remained in the bill. (*House vote 399, p. H-132*)

An amendment to cut all discretionary spending by 1 percent was defeated, 113-309. Sponsor Joel Hefley, R-Colo., said he planned to offer the same amendment to other appropriations bills considered by the House. (*House vote 398, p. H-130*)

Senate Committee, Floor Action

The Senate Appropriations Committee made quick work of its D.C. spending bill (S 2826 — S Rept 108-354), approving the chairman's draft 28-1 on Sept 21 with no major changes or controversial riders. The Senate passed HR 4850 by voice vote and without debate Sept. 22 after substituting the text of its own bill.

The measure included $560 million in federal funds and approved an overall city budget of $8.29 billion, slightly more than under the House version.

Larry E. Craig, R-Idaho, decided not to offer an amendment to repeal District gun control laws after a Sept. 20 meeting with D.C. subcommittee Chairman DeWine, who opposed such a provision. Spokesman Dan Whiting said Craig decided to wait for a House debate on a stand-

Authorization Bill For D.C. Clears

Congress cleared a stand-alone District of Columbia authorization bill that covered a range of changes to federal and local laws governing the city. President Bush signed the measure into law Oct. 30 (HR 3797 — PL 108-386)

House Government Reform Committee Chairman Thomas M. Davis III, R-Va., the bill's sponsor, said members of Congress had not been doing their job as authorizers. "Up to this point, the District has had no choice but to go through the appropriations process for assistance on authorization-related matters," Davis said.

Davis said the bill would start a process that would allow Congress to work with the District to consider annual changes to federal laws regarding the city, without slowing the D.C. appropriations bill.

Davis' committee approved the bill (H Rept 108-551) by voice vote Feb. 26. The House passed the measure by voice vote June 21.

The bill:

• Required the District's school board to submit a plan for allocating school funds to the City Council no later than March 1 each year, including a breakdown of how much money would go to each school. The plan also had to specify the amount of funds allocated to each school that would be controlled by the school itself, and a breakdown of other funds that would benefit that school, including money for personnel, equipment and supplies.

• Gave city courts the authority to enter into multi-year contracting and leasing agreements.

• Changed the public school system's fiscal year from Oct. 1-Sept. 30 to July 1-June 30, starting in fiscal 2007.

• Gave the city council 56 days to review the mayor's proposed budget, six days longer than under prior law.

• Allowed the city to offer its employees "flex-time" under the same guidelines that applied to federal workers.

• Transferred oversight of District-chartered banks from the Office of the Comptroller, which regulated federally chartered banks, to the Federal Deposit Insurance Corporation, which regulated state-chartered banks.

alone bill (HR 3193) to repeal those laws. The House passed that bill Sept. 29, but the Senate never took it up. *(Guns, p. 12-13)*

A catchall amendment, adopted by voice vote, cut in half a proposed $8.7 million increase for the out-of-state tuition aid. The bill provided $21.2 million, rather than the $25.6 million in the House version. Richard J. Durbin, D-

Ill., championed the change after discovering that the city had yet to spend $9 million in fiscal 2004 funding. Norton said the city held onto the funds to ensure that the money lasted through the fall and winter semesters.

Like the House bill, the measure included $14 million for vouchers, $13 million for public schools, an equal amount for charter schools and $6 million for school library improvements.

Senate appropriators added a somewhat different list of unrequested items than their House counterparts, including $5 million for transportation assistance and $32.5 million for the chief financial officer — $13.5 million more than in the House bill. The bill also included $8 million to design and plan a bioterrorism and forensic lab. DeWine, a former prosecutor, added the lab — which was not part of Bush's budget request — in order to allow law enforcement in the District to process evidence without seeking help from an already busy FBI crime lab.

To make up for the extras, the committee cut even more than the House did from the courts and judicial services request, reducing the funds to $412 million.

Conference/Final Action

Thanks to the agreement among Republican and Democratic appropriators not to fight over social issues, Congress quickly finished the D.C. spending bill. Conferees reached unanimous agreement without amendments or debate. The House adopted the conference report (H Rept 108-734), 377-36, on Oct. 6, and the Senate cleared the bill by voice vote later the same day. *(House vote 498, p. H-160)*

Differences resolved in pre-conference negotiations included:

• $25.6 million for out-of-state tuition, as the House recommended. Durbin relented in his effort to cut the funding level in favor of taking up the issue in the Senate Governmental Affairs Committee the next year. The conference committee did limit administrative costs to $1.2 million, and Durbin said he would request a review of the program by the Government Accountability Office.

• $6 million for the Unified Communications Center, $1 million less than in Bush's budget or in either bill.

• $6 million for school libraries and $1 million for family-literacy programs, as recommended by the House.

• $2.5 million for transportation assistance. The Senate sought $5 million; the House bill contained no funding.

• $32.5 million for the District's chief financial officer, as recommended by the Senate.

• $8 million for a bioterrorism and forensics lab, as recommended by the Senate.

• $409.3 million for the courts and court services, less than either chamber recommended, to make room for the combined House-Senate add-ons.

• $4.8 million for the D.C. water and sewer authority, less than half the amount in either chamber's bill or in Bush's request. The funds were for a long-term plan to eliminate sewer overflow into the Anacostia and Potomac rivers during storms, and they had to be matched by the local water authority. ◆

Dispute Centers on Nuclear Waste

A dispute over funding for the Yucca Mountain nuclear waste dump in Nevada nearly derailed the fiscal 2005 energy and water spending bill. The popular measure cleared at the last moment as part of the year-end omnibus after top appropriators managed to find extra money for the project. President Bush signed the measure into law Dec. 8 (HR 4818 — PL 108-447).

The bill appropriated $29 billion to fund energy research, nuclear weapons programs and civilian water projects. The total was 2 percent more than Bush requested and 5 percent more than what was appropriated for fiscal 2004. The total does not count a 0.8 percent across-the-board cut in discretionary spending that was part of the omnibus.

The bulk of the funding — $23 billion — was for the Energy Department, including $6.5 billion for nuclear weapons programs. In a blow for the Bush administration, no money was provided for research into a nuclear "bunker buster," a weapon to penetrate underground enemy strongholds.

The measure also funded civil works projects carried out by the Army Corps of Engineers, including flood control and the construction of dams and waterways that make the bill a perennial favorite with members hoping to steer federal spending to their home districts.

But the dispute over Yucca Mountain nearly caused appropriators to give up on the bill. Congress in 2002 endorsed Bush's decision to make Yucca Mountain the nation's permanent repository for high-level nuclear waste (PL 107-200). But funding the project had become an annual battle between nuclear energy proponents, who supported it, and lawmakers from Nevada, who vigorously opposed it. Waste storage was a major impediment to the future of the nuclear power industry. *(2002 Almanac, p. 8-8)*

This time, the debate was complicated by a White House proposal to tap an off-budget trust fund financed by nuclear utilities to pay part of the cost. Senate Democratic Whip Harry Reid of Nevada, a fierce opponent of the project, thwarted legislation that would have authorized the use of the fund. That left energy and water appropriators with a shortage of money for Yucca Mountain.

The House passed a bill that provided only a fraction of the $880 million requested by the White House. The Senate Energy and Water Appropriations Subcommittee never produced a bill because it was unable to solve the Yucca problem. Reid and other opponents vowed to block extensive use of the trust fund. Pete V. Domenici, R-N.M., who chaired the subcommittee, floated a proposal to pay for the project in fiscal 2005 with a surcharge on nuclear utilities. Conservatives and utilities companies opposed that idea, calling it a tax that

would be passed on to consumers.

Top appropriators were able to resolve the problem only when the energy and water bill was wrapped into the multibill omnibus. They then could take money from other spending bills to fund Yucca Mountain.

Highlights

The energy and water bill included the following major components:

● **Energy Department.** $23 billion, about 80 percent of the funding in the bill, with nearly 40 percent of that going to the National Nuclear Security Administration, the agency responsible for maintaining U.S. nuclear weapons and reducing the threat from weapons of mass destruction.

● **Nuclear weapons.** Of the nuclear security funds, $6.2 billion was for nuclear weapons programs, slightly less than Bush wanted and 5 percent more than the fiscal 2004 level. An additional $300 million transferred from defense spending brought the total to $6.5 billion. Congress rejected a White House request for funds to research a low-yield nuclear weapon known as the Robust Nuclear Earth Penetrator designed to destroy underground bunkers. The Bush administration sought $28 million and stressed it was only funding a study — not building a weapon — but Office of Management and Budget projections showing a cost of $485 million through 2009 raised lawmakers' suspicions that the United States was trying to build a new round of nuclear weapons.

● **Nuclear waste disposal.** $577 million for Yucca Mountain, roughly the same as in fiscal 2004, but only two-thirds of what Bush requested. The funding came from accounts for commercial and defense nuclear waste disposal.

● **Basic energy research.** $3.6 billion, nearly 6 percent more than fiscal 2004 spending or Bush's request, for research on nuclear physics, biological and environmental sciences, fusion and related fields.

● **Energy supply.** $946 million for energy supply programs, including renewable energy resources and nuclear power. The amount was 13 percent more than requested and 29 percent more than in the fiscal 2004 law.

● **Army Corps of Engineers.** $4.7 billion for popular river dredging, sewer, erosion and other water projects — 14 percent above Bush's request and 3 percent more than the fiscal 2004 level. Although lawmakers did not fund any new projects, they rejected Bush's request to cut many of the 41 existing water projects with annual costs over $100 million.

● **Interior Department.** $972 million for water and dam projects in Western states operated by the Bureau of Reclamation, 5 percent more than requested and 3 percent more than in fiscal 2004.

BoxScore 2005
Fiscal Year

Energy-Water

Bill:
HR 4818 — PL 108-447

Legislative Action:

House passed HR 4614 (H Rept 108-554), 370-16, on June 25.

House adopted the conference report on HR 4818 (H Rept 108-792), 344-51, on Nov. 20.

Senate cleared the bill, 65-30, on Nov. 20.

President signed Dec. 8.

Where the Money Goes

Energy-Water Spending

(figures are in thousands of dollars of new budget authority)

	Fiscal 2004 Appropriation	Fiscal 2005 Bush Request	House Passed	Senate Bill	Conference Report *
GRAND TOTAL	$27,756,375	$28,470,382	$28,525,000	N/A	$29,020,000
Total adjusted for scorekeeping **	$27,253,463	$27,938,382	$27,993,000	N/A	$28,488,000
MAIN COMPONENTS					
Energy Department	$21,967,429	$23,147,833	$22,478,342	N/A	$23,002,804
Nuclear weapons activities	6,235,502	6,568,453	6,514,424	N/A	6,526,471
Nuclear waste disposal (Yucca Mountain)	576,578	880,000	131,000	N/A	577,000
Defense nuclear non-proliferation	1,319,779	1,348,647	1,348,647	N/A	1,420,397
Science	3,431,335	3,431,718	3,599,964	N/A	3,628,902
Army Corps of Engineers	4,580,380	4,120,000	4,832,280	N/A	4,705,190
Interior Department	980,641	970,333	1,021,162	N/A	1,020,338
Independent agencies	227,925	232,216	193,216	N/A	291,668
Nuclear Regulatory Commission	80,065	129,175	129,175	N/A	129,175

* Conference totals do not include a 0.8 percent across-the-board cut in discretionary accounts.

** Adjustments based on Congressional Budget Office criteria for determining discretionary spending; the adjusted total is used to assess compliance with 302(b) allocations.

TABLE: House Appropriations Committee

Legislative Action

House Committee Action

The House Appropriations Committee approved a $28.5 billion version of the bill (HR 4614 — H Rept 108-554) by voice vote June 16. The committee made virtually no changes to a draft that the Energy and Water Development Subcommittee approved by voice vote June 9.

The bill included $22.5 billion for the Energy Department, 3 percent less than Bush requested.

● **Yucca Mountain.** Although House appropriators routinely backed funding for Yucca Mountain, the bill provided only $131 million, about a quarter of the $880 million Bush requested. The administration assumed that $749 million of the total would come from the Nuclear Waste Fund, which contained about $15 billion in utility industry contributions intended to pay for waste disposal. But Subcommittee Chairman David L. Hobson, R-Ohio, said it would be too difficult to get Congress to authorize the use of those funds. "I don't like going forward with so little money for Yucca Mountain, but we are playing the hand that we were dealt," he said. The administration said the project needed an average annual budget of about $1.3 billion to stay on track for a 2010 opening.

Historically, the House had been the chamber to boost funds for Yucca while the Senate tried to cut them. The House version of the fiscal 2004 energy and water bill included $765 million for the project, nearly 30 percent more than Bush requested; the two chambers finally settled on $580 million (PL 108-137). (*2003 Almanac, p. 2-49*)

● **Corps.** The draft included $4.8 billion for Corps projects, a 5 percent increase over fiscal 2004. Bush had targeted the Corps for a 10 percent cut, to $4.1 billion. The panel did not add new projects, but it did not cut existing projects with annual costs over $100 million. "Members won't receive as

many water earmarks as they might like, but we did take care of their top priorities," Hobson said.

● **Renewable energy.** The subcommittee proposed $343 million, 8 percent less than Bush requested, for renewable-energy programs. The draft included $64 million, or two-thirds of what Bush sought, to develop hydrogen fuel cell technology. Hobson criticized the Energy Department for favoring its own laboratories in awarding $150 million in hydrogen research grants and said it had not secured adequate funding from the private sector.

● **Nuclear weapons.** The panel included $6.5 billion for nuclear weapons, a cut of less than 1 percent from Bush's budget. They left out the $28 million requested for research on a low-yield nuclear weapon designed to destroy underground bunkers. The bill also left out funding for a facility to make plutonium pits — the triggers in modern nuclear weapons — following a Defense Department report outlining major cutbacks to the U.S. stockpile over the next several years.

House Floor Action

The House passed the $28.5 billion bill by a vote of 370-16 on June 25. (*House vote 325, p. H-108*)

Much of the debate concerned an amendment by West Coast Democrats aimed at compensating victims of price gouging in the California power crisis of 2000 and 2001.

During the debate, the House:

● Adopted by voice vote an amendment by Anna G. Eshoo, D-Calif., to prohibit use of funds in the bill to deny public access to documents related to market manipulation by Enron Corp. and others. The amendment was agreed to after Republicans refused to support a proposal by Eshoo to require the Federal Energy Regulatory Commission to step up its reimbursement of consumers who had to pay artificially inflated electricity prices when power wholesalers, such as Enron, manipulated the energy supply.

• Rejected, 151-235, an amendment by Democrats Martin T. Meehan of Massachusetts and Adam B. Schiff of California to add $30 million to a program that cleaned up highly enriched uranium at reactor sites in Russia and elsewhere. *(House vote 323, p. H-108)*

• Rejected, 163-224, an amendment by Heather A. Wilson, R-N.M., that would have provided $5 million in additional funding for two non-proliferation programs. *(House vote 322, p. H-108)*

Conference/Final Action

Appropriators managed to solve the Yucca Mountain funding puzzle just in time to clear the energy and water measure as part of the nine-bill omnibus spending package. The House adopted the conference report (HR 4818 — H Rept 108-792), 344-51, Nov. 20. The Senate cleared the omnibus, 65-30, later the same day. *(House vote 542, p. H-174; Senate vote 215, p. S-46)*

Hobson and Domenici had largely resolved differences between the House-passed energy and water bill and a Senate draft, but the Yucca Mountain problem appeared intractable. With time running out, staff discussions had shifted to whether a short-term or long-term extension of fiscal 2004 energy and water funding would be better.

But the two Appropriations chairmen — Sen. Ted Stevens, R-Alaska, and Rep. C.W. Bill Young, R-Fla. — were loath to let Yucca hold up funding, particularly for the popular water projects. After marathon negotiations, the two freed up $800 million, mostly through cuts to other domestic appropriations bills. With White House blessing, they used the money to fund Yucca Mountain at the previous year's level of $577 million and increase spending for nuclear and defense projects favored by Domenici and Hobson. Although Domenici lost on funding for the bunker buster, he won additional funding for the Sandia and Los Alamos National Laboratories in New Mexico.

Hobson won funding for nuclear non-proliferation efforts in Russia, and for an Energy Department program that helped scientists maintain the nation's nuclear weapons stockpile without conducting explosive tests. ◆

Foreign Aid Bill Rewards Allies

Congress boosted funding for foreign aid and export assistance, continuing a trend evident since Sept. 11, 2001, though at a slower pace than the president sought. The fiscal 2005 foreign operations bill provided $19.8 billion, 13 percent more than was available for fiscal 2004 excluding supplemental funds, but 7 percent less than President Bush requested. The measure, which also served as the vehicle for the omnibus appropriations package, was signed into law Dec. 8 (HR 4818 — PL 108-447).

The bill's total does not reflect a 0.8 percent across-the-board reduction in discretionary spending enacted as part of the omnibus.

The fiscal 2005 bill did not include funding for the war in Iraq. Bush was expected to request supplemental spending for that purpose in 2005. Congress had provided $87.5 billion in supplemental funds in fiscal 2004 for military operations and reconstruction in Iraq and Afghanistan and related expenses (PL 108-106). (*2003 Almanac, p. 2-83*)

The foreign operations bill funded most U.S. foreign assistance, including bilateral aid administered by the U.S. Agency for International Development (USAID), as well as U.S. military assistance and contributions to the World Bank and other international financial institutions.

The fiscal 2005 bill rewarded U.S. allies in the war on terror, including Israel, Egypt, Jordan, Afghanistan and Pakistan. Lawmakers also fully funded a major Bush initiative to fight HIV/AIDS in the developing world. But they scaled back another big-ticket White House initiative — the Millennium Challenge Account (MCA) — which got about 60 percent of the funding Bush requested. The MCA was created to assist developing nations that made progress in human rights, democratization and economic policies.

A central issue during consideration of the bill was aid for Darfur, a region in western Sudan where as many as 10,000 black Africans were dying each month because of an ethnic cleansing campaign by government-backed Muslim mercenaries.

Bill Highlights

The following are major components of the final bill:

● **Bilateral economic aid.** $13.3 billion in the category of bilateral economic aid, which included the costs of running USAID. The total included $2.5 billion for the Economic Support Fund — $360 million of it for Israel and $535 million for Egypt. The appropriation was 16 percent more than

BoxScore **2005** *Fiscal Year*

Foreign Operations

Bill:
HR 4818 — PL 108-447

Legislative Action:

House passed HR 4818 (H Rept 108-599), 365-41, on July 15.

Senate passed HR 4818, amended to reflect S 2812 (S Rept 108-346), by voice vote Sept. 23.

House adopted the conference report (H Rept 108-792), 344-51, on Nov. 20.

Senate cleared the bill, 65-30, on Nov. 20.

President signed Dec. 8.

under the fiscal 2004 law, although supplemental spending added another $20.9 billion in fiscal 2004 spending.

● **Military assistance.** $5 billion, 12 percent above fiscal 2004 not counting emergency spending. Israel, traditionally the lead recipient of U.S. aid, got $2.2 billion in military assistance, a 3 percent increase and equal to the president's request. Egypt received $1.3 billion, a very slight increase, as requested, although the bill reduced the Egyptian government's control over the money. Afghanistan got $400 million to train and equip a new national army — about eight times fiscal 2004 spending. Pakistan received $300 million under a new program aimed at capturing al Qaeda forces on its border with Afghanistan. Poland, a U.S. ally in the Iraq war, received $66 million in military assistance, a 230 percent increase. The legislation also granted Bush the authority to lead an international effort to forgive Iraq's debt.

● **HIV/AIDS.** $2.3 billion to combat global HIV/AIDS, tuberculosis and malaria, about 4 percent more than Bush requested. The total, which was spread across several accounts, included $1.4 billion for Bush's Global AIDS Initiative and $336 million for the Global Fund to Fight AIDS, Tuberculosis and Malaria. An additional $600 million in the Labor-Health and Human Services portion of the omnibus, plus a few million elsewhere in the budget brought total U.S. international AIDS funding for fiscal 2005 to $2.9 billion.

● **Millennium Challenge Account.** $1.5 billion for the MCA. That was $1 billion less than Bush had requested, the largest such cut in the foreign operations bill. Appropriators maintained — as they had the previous year — that the fledgling program could not absorb the sums requested. But, they insisted they were still on track to meet the president's original goal of $9.3 billion by fiscal 2006.

● **Sudan.** $404 million for relief efforts in the Darfur region of Sudan where government-sponsored mercenaries had waged a campaign of ethnic cleansing against black African Muslims. Of the total, $93 million was designated as "emergency" funds that did not count against the allocation for the bill. Another $95 million in emergency aid was provided in the fiscal 2005 defense spending bill (PL 108-287).

Legislative Action

House Subcommittee Action

The House Foreign Operations Appropriations Subcommittee approved a $19.4 billion draft of the bill by voice

Where the Money Goes

Foreign Operations Spending

(figures are in thousands of dollars of new budget authority)

	Fiscal 2004 Appropriation	Fiscal 2005 Bush Request	House Passed	Senate Passed	Conference Report *
GRAND TOTAL	**$17,504,418****	**$21,360,830**	**$19,428,145**	**$19,653,500**	**$19,839,960**
MAIN COMPONENTS					
U.S. Agency for International Development	$4,445,129	$3,971,000	$4,248,800	$4,208,000	$4,191,500
Peace Corps	308,171	401,000	330,000	310,000	320,000
Millennium Challenge Corporation	994,100	2,500,000	1,250,000	1,120,000	1,500,000
Global HIV/AIDS Initiative	488,103	1,450,000	1,260,000	1,450,000	1,385,000
Andean Counterdrug Initiative	726,687	731,000	731,000	731,000	731,000
Military aid for Israel	2,147,256	2,220,000	2,220,000	2,220,000	2,220,000
Military aid for Egypt	1,292,330	1,300,000	1,300,000	1,300,000	1,300,000
World Bank	1,047,347	1,181,988	957,500	940,678	957,500
Other international financial institutions	335,694	310,743	310,743	193,222	271,531

* Totals do not reflect a 0.8 percent across-the-board cut in discretionary spending.

** Does not include $21,212,600 in supplemental spending (PL 108-106).

TABLE: House, Senate Appropriations committees

vote June 23 that generally endorsed Bush's priorities.

The draft included:

- **HIV/AIDS.** $2.2 billion for HIV/AIDS programs, the full amount requested by Bush but 47 percent above fiscal 2004 funding. The total included $400 million for the Global Fund, $300 million more than requested.
- **MCA.** $1.25 billion for the MCA, half the amount Bush requested. Subcommittee Chairman Jim Kolbe, R-Ariz., said the reduction reflected the committee's tight spending allocation, not displeasure with the program. But lawmakers in both chambers also expressed concern that the fledgling aid program could not absorb that much money in the coming year — the first in which the program, created in 2004 (PL 108-199), would actually hand out grants.
- **Family planning.** $432 million for family planning programs, including $25 million for the United Nations Population Fund (UNFPA), with the caveat that the administration could withhold the U.N. money if required by U.S. laws barring aid for abortion. The Bush administration had decided not to release $34 million appropriated for UNFPA in fiscal 2004 on the grounds that it would violate the Kemp-Kasten amendment. The Kemp-Kasten language, added to the foreign aid bill in 1985 and repeated annually, prohibited aid to any organization that "supports or participates in the management" of a program of coercive abortion or involuntary sterilization. (*2002 Almanac, p. 2-18; 1985 Almanac, p. 367*)
- **Iraq debt.** Authority to transfer money from Iraq reconstruction funds in the fiscal 2004 supplemental to pay for canceling Iraq's debt to the United States.

House Committee Action

The House Appropriations Committee approved the bill by voice vote July 9 (HR 4818 — H Rept 108-599), after Republicans turned back an attempt to ensure that family planning money in the bill would be distributed. The debate centered on UNFPA funding.

During the markup, the committee:

- Rejected, 26-32, an amendment by Nita M. Lowey of New York, ranking Democrat on the Foreign Operations Subcommittee, that would have released funds to UNFPA for use in six specific nations, even if the administration blocked general funding for the U.N. agency. Lowey said all six nations — Afghanistan, Iraq, Jordan, Kenya, Pakistan and Tanzania — prohibited or strongly restricted abortion. Kolbe opposed the amendment, arguing that the language would turn the bill into a lightning rod for anti-abortion groups and jeopardize its passage.
- Rejected by voice vote an amendment by Sam Farr, D-Calif., to increase the limit on U.S. military personnel in Colombia from 400 to 500.

House Floor Action

The House passed the $19.4 billion measure July 15 by a vote of 365-41. Much of the debate focused on two longtime Middle Eastern allies that many lawmakers considered to have been less than steadfast — Egypt and Saudi Arabia. While the administration salvaged aid to Egypt, it was not able to beat back a largely symbolic amendment barring aid to the Saudi government. (*House vote 390, p. H-128*)

During the floor debate, the House:

- Rejected, 131-287, an effort by Tom Lantos of California, top Democrat on the International Relations Committee, to convert $570 million of the bill's $1.3 billion in military aid for Egypt into economic assistance. (*House vote 381, p. H-126*)

Lantos led a bipartisan group of lawmakers who argued that Egypt faced no major military threat and that the money would be better spent on desperately needed economic and social programs. The proposal also tapped an undercurrent of anger among lawmakers who contended that Egypt had not assisted U.S. military operations in Iraq and Af-

ghanistan, or done enough to combat the spread of radical Islam and anti-Americanism. "When the United States needed Egypt's support, the powerful Egyptian military on the whole has been AWOL," Lantos said.

But the Bush administration mounted a lobbying blitz against the amendment. In a letter to Congress, Secretary of State Colin L. Powell argued that reducing military aid to Egypt would seriously damage U.S. objectives in the Middle East. Powell said the aid was a cornerstone of the 1979 Camp David peace accords between Egypt and Israel and a vital part of the administration's efforts to combat terrorism. He also cautioned that a reduction in military aid could cause Egypt's government to cancel $2.2 billion worth of military purchases from U.S. contractors.

• Adopted, 217-191, an amendment by Anthony Weiner, D-N.Y., to eliminate funds for Saudi Arabia, a nation many lawmakers believed had shielded Islamic terrorists. Weiner said the language would remove $25,000 in funding for Saudi military education and training and make Saudi Arabia ineligible to receive discounts to purchase such training. The amendment was seen as largely symbolic, but the administration strongly opposed it. (*House vote 389, p. H-128*)

• Adopted, 270-132, an amendment by Bernard Sanders, I-Vt., to prohibit the Export-Import Bank from approving direct loans or loan guarantees to companies incorporated offshore in the Caribbean. The provision was dropped in conference. (*House vote 386, p. H-128*)

• Adopted, 241-166, an amendment by George Nethercutt, R-Wash., to bar economic aid to any country that was party to the International Criminal Court and did not pledge that it would not surrender U.S. nationals to the court. (*House vote 387, p. H-128*)

• Rejected, 111-312, a proposal by Brad Sherman, D-Calif., to reduce World Bank funding and increase the amount for child survival. (*House vote 380, p. H-126*)

• Rejected, 133-288, a proposal by Mark Kennedy, R-Minn., to reduce funding for the World Bank and increase funds for the MCA and the HIV/AIDS initiative. (*House vote 382, p. H-126*)

Senate Committee Action

The Senate Appropriations Committee approved a $19.6 billion version of the bill by a vote of 29-0 on Sept. 15 (S 2812 — S Rept 108-346). The Foreign Operations Subcommittee had forwarded the draft to the full committee without a formal vote.

The central issue in the markup was the deteriorating situation in Darfur. A few hours before the meeting, Senate leaders agreed to a proposal by Patrick J. Leahy, D-Vt., to allow Bush to redirect up to $150 million in unspent funds for use in Darfur relief efforts. The funds were part of the $18.4 billion in supplemental spending enacted in late 2003 (PL 108-106) for reconstruction in Iraq; only $1 billion had been spent.

The bill also included an extra $75 million for refugee, disaster and famine assistance, with the understanding the money could be used for Darfur relief.

During the markup, the committee:

• Adopted by voice vote an amendment by Sam Brownback, R-Kan., to eliminate Egypt's veto over how U.S. aid to promote democracy in that country could be spent. Brown-

back said Egypt was the only nation with such a veto.

• Adopted by voice vote a proposal by Richard J. Durbin, D-Ill., to add $150 million in emergency spending to the bill for the Global Fund to Fight AIDS, Tuberculosis and Malaria.

The bill approved at the end of the markup included:

• **HIV/AIDS.** $2.4 billion to combat AIDS. Like their House counterparts, Senate appropriators provided $400 million for the Global Fund, including the $150 million in emergency spending added by Durbin.

• **MCA.** $1.1 billion for the MCA, less than half of the $2.5 billion requested by Bush. White House spokesman Scott McClellan described the MCA as a "groundbreaking initiative," and said Bush would press lawmakers to find more money for it in conference.

• **Family planning.** $450 million for family planning programs, including $34 million for UNFPA. The bill attempted to soften the Kemp-Kasten provision by specifying only that a recipient organization could not directly support coercive abortions or involuntary sterilization. And in a provision that drew a White House veto threat, the appropriators sought to revise the so-called Mexico City policy, which barred U.S. funds for any organization that was involved in abortions, even if it did so with its own money. The Senate bill would have allowed the funds if the organization's activities did not violate local or U.S. law.

• **Sudan.** $615 million for assistance to the Darfur region — including $150 million to be transferred from funds appropriated for reconstruction projects in Iraq and Afghanistan subject to congressional approval.

• **Iraq debt.** Authority for the administration to transfer $360 million from Iraqi reconstruction funds to eliminate Iraq's debt to the United States. The debt relief was part of a broader plan proposed by the administration Sept. 14 to reshuffle $3.5 billion in Iraq reconstruction funds, shifting money away from big-ticket infrastructure projects to pay for increased security. Attacks by Iraqi insurgents had slowed or halted reconstruction projects.

Senate Floor Action

The Senate passed what had become a $19.7 billion bill by voice vote Sept. 23, after inserting the text of S 2812. The situation in Darfur continued to occupy center state.

The Senate adopted by voice vote an amendment by Jon Corzine, D-N.J., and Mike DeWine, R-Ohio, to add $75 million in emergency funding for logistical support of an African Union peacekeeping force that might be deployed in the Darfur region. The funds would be available upon a request from the White House.

Barbara Boxer, D-Calif, won voice vote approval for an amendment to earmark $10 million to reduce the threat that man-portable air defense systems could be acquired by terrorists or by state sponsors of terrorism.

Conference/Final Action

The foreign aid bill not only became part of the year-end appropriations package, as expected, but it served as the vehicle for the eight other unfinished fiscal 2005 bills. The House adopted the conference report (H Rept 108-792) by a vote of 344-51 on Nov. 20, and the Senate cleared the omnibus, 65-30, later the same day. (*House vote 542, p. H-174;*

Senate vote 215, p. S-46)

The following were among the issues resolved by conferees on the foreign operations section of the omnibus:

● **MCA.** Appropriators had planned to provide no more than half what Bush had requested for the program, but Joshua B. Bolten, the White House budget director, made it clear after the election that the president expected them to "reallocate funds more in line with the president's request for this important program." In the end, they tapped some of the $3.1 billion that was saved through the across-the-board discretionary spending cut in the omnibus to bring MCA funding up to $1.5 billion. The 0.8 percent cut applied to all fiscal 2005 spending bills — except those related to defense and homeland security — including other provisions in the foreign operations bill.

● **Sudan.** The final bill provided $403 million for relief and peacekeeping efforts in the Darfur region — $311 million in regular funding, as proposed by the House, plus $75 million in emergency funds to support African Union peacekeeping efforts in Sudan, as backed by the Senate, and $18 million for humanitarian aid. Conferees dropped the Senate provision that would have allowed the transfer of $150 million from unspent Iraq reconstruction funds.

On Dec. 7, the Senate cleared a separate bill authorizing $300 million in U.S. aid to Sudan. Bush signed the measure Dec. 23 (PL 108-497).

● **HIV/AIDS.** Conferees agreed to $2.3 billion for international HIV/AIDS programs, about $80 million more than passed by the House and $137 less than in the Senate bill. Although both versions had directed $400 million of the total to the Global Fund, the final bill provided only $248 million. It also authorized use of $88 million appropriated but not used in fiscal 2004 because the organization could not find matching donations from other countries. The fund had agreed to match U.S. contributions on a two-to-one basis. That brought the amount available for the Global Fund in fiscal 2005 to $336 million.

● **Family planning.** The final bill included $441 million for family planning programs, $34 million of it for UNFPA. Conferees dropped Senate provisions that would have loosened the Kemp-Kasten restrictions and revised the Mexico City policy.

● **Iraq debt.** Authorization to use Iraq reconstruction money to cancel Iraq's debt to the United States was enacted Sept. 30 as part of the first fiscal 2005 short-term continuing resolution (PL 108-309). That law allowed the transfer of $360 million, as proposed by the Senate.

● **Saudi Arabia.** The final bill prohibited aid to Saudi Arabia, but added a provision allowing the president to waive the ban if he certified that the Saudis were cooperating with efforts to combat international terrorism and that the funds would assist that effort. ◆

Homeland Bill Sheds Some Baggage

The fiscal 2005 Department of Homeland Security spending bill was a top priority in Congress, but it nearly sank under the weight of controversial add-ons before the November election. At the last moment, the bill shook free of its baggage and cleared just as members were about to leave town to campaign. The bill provided $33.1 billion for the Department of Homeland Security, which was in its second year of operations. President Bush signed the measure into law Oct. 18 (HR 4567 — PL 108-334), making it one of four fiscal 2005 appropriations bills enacted before the election.

The bill got off to an easy start, with both chambers recommending $33.1 billion for the department. The House passed its version in June; the Senate followed suit in September, and it was widely assumed the measure would be enacted before Oct. 1, the start of the new fiscal year. But the bill's must-pass nature spelled trouble, making it an irresistible target for members trying to rush other legislation into law. The Senate attached $3 billion in emergency drought aid for farmers, appropriators planned to add several billion dollars in hurricane assistance in conference, and for a time there was a dispute over attaching an extension of milk subsidies.

Negotiators were able to reach agreement only after the bill had become so bogged down that leaders gave up using it to carry the emergency disaster aid.

Like the initial House and Senate versions, the final bill provided $32 billion in discretionary spending, 9 percent more than the fiscal 2004 law (PL 108-90), and 3 percent more than Bush requested. The total included $2.5 billion in previously appropriated funds for Bush's Project Bioshield, aimed at stockpiling vaccines and chemicals for a biological or chemical attack. (*2003 Almanac, p. 2-56*)

In the absence of an authorization bill for the new department and firm new guidelines on congressional oversight, appropriators included a number of spending restrictions. Hundreds of millions of dollars for high-profile initiatives such as the entry-exit program known as US VISIT and the airline passenger screening program called Secure Flight could not be spent until appropriators approved a departmental spending plan for the programs. The conference report required the department to submit more than 40 studies, plans and reports on topics ranging from hiring practices to data-mining strategy. The appropriators also blocked several of the department's plans to shift components and create new programs, including rail security initiatives and an office to manage geospatial mapping.

BoxScore 2005
Homeland Security — Fiscal Year

Bill:
HR 4567 — PL 108-334

Legislative Action:
House passed HR 4567 (H Rept 108-541), 400-5, on June 18.

Senate passed HR 4567, 93-0, on Sept. 14, after substituting the text of S 2537 (S Rept 108-280).

House adopted the conference report (H Rept 108-774), 368-0, on Oct. 9.

Senate cleared the bill by voice vote Oct. 11.

President signed Oct. 18.

Highlights

The following are major elements of the fiscal 2005 law:

● **Border protection.** The Bureau of Customs and Border Protection got an appropriation of $5.3 billion; when combined with about $1.1 billion expected from various immigration and inspection user fees, that translated to $6.3 billion — 7 percent more than fiscal 2004 funding but 2 percent less than requested.

The bureau — formed by combining inspectors and other personnel from the old U.S. Customs Service, the Immigration and Naturalization Service (INS), the Animal and Plant Health Inspection Service, and the U.S. Border Patrol — was responsible for securing U.S. borders and examining incoming visitors and trade to the United States.

● **Immigration and customs enforcement.** The Bureau of Immigration and Customs Enforcement received $3.2 billion; together with $200 million in expected immigration user fees and other funds, that brought the total to $3.4 billion — 8 percent less than in fiscal 2004 and 5 percent less than requested. The cut was due largely to a decision by appropriators to move funding for air and marine interdiction activities to the Bureau of Customs and Border Protection.

The Bureau of Immigration and Customs Enforcement combined the investigative, intelligence, and interdiction elements of the old Customs Service and the INS, along with the protective functions of the FBI, and was responsible for enforcing immigration and customs laws in the United States, as well as for investigating fraud, forced labor, trade agreement non-compliance, money laundering, smuggling and cargo theft.

● **TSA.** The Transportation Security Administration (TSA), charged with protecting the nation's airports, airlines and other means of transport, received $5.2 billion, a 12.5 percent increase over fiscal 2004 funding and 2 percent more than requested. Most of the extra money was for passenger and baggage screening and other aviation security activities, including $118 million for 100 additional air cargo inspectors and research into related technologies. The bill required that the TSA triple the percentage of air cargo inspected on passenger planes. The bill assumed that $1.9 billion of the total would be offset by passenger and other user fees. An existing cap of 45,000 full-time screeners was renewed. The measure prohibited the department from implementing the controversial Computer Assisted Passenger Prescreening System (CAPPS) II until a number of conditions were met.

Where the Money Goes

Homeland Security Spending

(figures are in thousands of dollars of new budget authority)

	Fiscal 2004 Appropriation	Fiscal 2005 Bush Request	House Passed	Senate Passed	Conference Report
GRAND TOTAL	$37,048,446*	$32,189,925	$33,085,401	$36,128,460**	$33,085,460
Total adjusted for scorekeeping*	$30,262,263	$32,189,925	$33,085,401	$33,082,460	$33,085,460
MAIN COMPONENTS					
Customs and Border Protection	$5,943,107	$6,201,122	$6,254,619	$6,087,591	$6,349,275
Immigration and Customs Enforcement	3,679,614	3,532,500	3,588,600	3,660,032	3,367,178
Transportation Security Administration	4,578,045	5,042,016	5,115,416	5,226,935	5,150,375
State and local first-responder grants	3,267,608	3,061,255	3,423,900	2,845,081	3,086,300
Firefighter grants	745,575	500,000	650,000	700,000	715,000
U.S. VISIT Program	328,053	340,000	340,000	340,000	340,000
Coast Guard	6,764,313	7,335,230	7,306,630	7,469,130	7,373,280
Secret Service	1,134,128	1,162,758	1,182,758	1,162,758	1,175,008
Information Analysis/Infrastructure Protection	834,347	864,576	854,576	875,576	893,708

* Includes $4.7 billion in "advance appropriations" for future years for Project Bioshield and $2 billion in disaster aid (PL 108-303).

** Includes $3 billion in emergency disaster relief for Midwestern farmers that was removed and attached to the military construction bill (HR 4837).

*** Adjustments based on Congressional Budget Office criteria for determining discretionary spending; adjusted total is used to assess compliance with 302(b) allocations.

TABLE: House, Senate Appropriations committees

● **Coast Guard.** The bill provided $7.4 billion for the Coast Guard, a 9 percent increase over fiscal 2004 and virtually the same as the president's request. The total included $724 million for the next phase of the Coast Guard's "Deepwater" program aimed at replacing aging vessels and aircraft that operated more than 50 miles from shore.

● **First-responders.** Conferees agreed to $4 billion for the Office for State and Local Government Coordination and Preparedness, intended as a "one-stop shop" for state and local first-responders seeking federal funds.

The funding included $715 million for firefighters; $1.5 billion for basic formula grants, 40 percent of which were divided evenly among the states; $1.2 billion for a grant program that favored high-threat, high-density urban areas; and $180 million for state and local law enforcement terrorism prevention grants. The mix reflected demands for more help from lawmakers representing New York and other vulnerable urban areas. The fiscal 2004 law had allotted $1.7 billion for basic grants and $725 million for high-threat areas.

● **Project Bioshield.** The bill included an advance appropriation of $2.5 billion for Project Bioshield, a program to encourage private drug companies to develop vaccines and treatments for chemical and biological weapons. The program included expedited review procedures and funding to buy the products for the strategic national stockpile once they were developed and approved.

The $2.5 billion could be obligated through fiscal 2008 and was in addition to an $890 million advance appropriation in the fiscal 2004 Homeland Security law.

● **Information Analysis and Infrastructure Protection.** The section of the department responsible for analyzing information on terrorist threats, identifying and mitigating U.S. vulnerabilities to terrorism, and issuing public alerts received $894 million — 7 percent above fiscal 2004 fund-

ing and 3 percent more than requested.,

● **Science and technology.** The bill appropriated $1.1 billion for the bureau charged with promoting the development and deployment of cutting-edge technologies and new capabilities, including countermeasures to terrorist threats involving weapons of mass destruction. The funding was 22 percent above the fiscal 2004 level and 7 percent more than Bush requested.

● **Citizenship and immigration.** The department's Bureau of Citizenship and Immigration Services was funded primarily through immigration user fees, which were expected to bring in $1.6 billion in fiscal 2005. The bill appropriated an additional $160 million for the agency, bringing the total to $1.7 billion. The total was about the same as requested and 4 percent below what the bureau got in fiscal 2004.

Legislative Action

House Subcommittee Action

The House Homeland Security Appropriations Subcommittee gave voice vote approval June 3 to a $31.9 billion draft of the bill, $30.8 billion of which was discretionary spending. Subcommittee Chairman Harold Rogers, R-Ky., noted that the bill had not yet been adjusted for $1.2 billion for the Coast Guard, which was being transferred from the defense appropriations bill.

Rogers barred members from adding earmarks for special projects, warning that there was "an insatiable appetite" for security funding and that not every spending request could be met. But David R. Obey of Wisconsin, the Appropriations Committee's top Democrat, complained that the bill left a wide range of programs underfunded. "We're nibbling around the edges," he said, "and we're going to pay for it big time."

- **First-responders.** The draft called for $4.1 billion for first-responders, 14 percent more than Bush requested. The total included $1.25 billion for basic formula grants and $1 billion for grants that favored high-threat urban areas, including $100 million for rail security. The White House had requested $1.5 billion for urban grants. The draft also included $125 million for port security and $600 million for firefighters. Rogers said billions of dollars in already appropriated grant money had yet to reach the local level and that until it did, he saw no need to "put billions more in the pipeline."
- **TSA.** $5.1 billion, $1.9 billion of which was from expected fees. The total included $118 million for air cargo security, including funds to hire 100 additional inspectors, double the percentage of inspected air cargo in passenger planes, and research new cargo-screening technologies.

The draft prohibited spending funds on the CAPPS II system until a number of problems were solved. It also continued the 45,000 cap on TSA screeners.

House Committee Action

The full Appropriations Committee approved the bill (HR 4567 — H Rept 108-541) by voice vote June 9. The total had grown to $33.1 billion with the inclusion of $1.2 billion for the Coast Guard.

Before approving the measure, the committee adopted, 35-17, a controversial amendment by Rosa DeLauro, D-Conn., to block any contract between the department and companies that had offshore headquarters to avoid U.S. taxes. DeLauro's target was Accenture Ltd., which was incorporated in Bermuda and had won a $10 billion contract to build the US VISIT computer system to track foreign visitors to the United States. Accenture had beaten out Lockheed Martin Corp. and Computer Sciences Corp.

Rogers postponed a brewing dispute over the distribution of first-responder grants by persuading John E. Sweeney, R-N.Y., to hold off on an amendment requiring that more fire and police grants go to areas at high risk for terrorism.

On other amendments, the committee:
- Rejected, 26-28, a proposal by Obey to establish a $3 billion emergency reserve — including more funds for emergency preparedness and first-responder programs, transportation security, Customs and border protection and bioterrorism preparedness — which would be available if the president submitted a supplemental request.
- Rejected, 27-30, an amendment by Martin Olav Sabo, D-Minn., to require that 60 percent of air cargo on commercial airplanes be inspected.

House Floor Action

The House passed the $33.1 billion bill, 400-5, on June 18. Democrats' efforts to add funds for firefighters, air cargo inspections and other purposes were rebuffed at almost every turn. *(House vote 275, p. H-94)*
- **First-responders.** The debate over the distribution of first-responder grants that had been sidestepped in committee produced a full-blown fight on the floor. In a nearly three-hour debate that extended past midnight, New Yorkers from both parties, backed by metropolitan-area lawmakers from Illinois, California and Florida, clashed with members from both parties representing districts in Iowa, Kentucky and Tennessee that stood to lose money if the formu-

las were changed. The White House issued a statement of administration policy on June 17 that called for focusing more of the first-responder money on high-threat areas.

The House:
- Rejected, 171-237, Sweeney's proposal to shift $450 million from formula grants to the program for high-density urban areas. Under the bill, the formula grants already were getting about $440 million less than in fiscal 2004. *(House vote 266, p. H-90)*
- Rejected, 113-292, an attempt by Carolyn B. Maloney, D-N.Y., to limit the number of urban security grants to 80. Maloney said that would help to ensure that the money was concentrated on New York and other spots at high risk for a terrorist attack. *(House vote 271, p. H-92)*
- **Offshore contracts.** DeLauro's proposal to block all contracts with expatriate companies was dropped on a point of order, and an attempt to restore the language failed, 182-221. However, the portion of the amendment preventing the department from signing such contracts in the future remained. *(House vote 268, p. H-92)*
- **Privatization.** The House adopted, 242-163, an amendment by Lucille Roybal-Allard, D-Calif., to prevent the department from carrying out plans to have private businesses bid on work that was being performed by some 1,100 federal workers at the Bureau of Citizenship and Immigration Services. *(House vote 269, p. H-92)*
- **TSA.** An attempt by Peter A. DeFazio, D-Ore., to lift the 45,000 limit on aviation screeners was rejected, 180-228. *(House vote 265, p. H-90)*
- **Air cargo.** The House rejected, 191-211, an amendment by Edward J. Markey, D-Mass., to bar the use of funds in the bill for any cargo security plan that allowed unscreened cargo on passenger planes. *(House vote 273, p. H-92)*

Senate Committee Action

The Senate Appropriations Committee approved a $33.1 billion Homeland Security spending bill (S 2537 — S Rept 108-280) by a vote of 29-0 on June 17. The Homeland Security Subcommittee had approved the measure by voice vote the previous day.

Spending levels included:
- $3.8 billion for first-responder grants, $365 million below the House figure. The Senate total included $2.8 billion for state and local programs ($1.4 billion for formula grants and $1.2 billion for high-threat urban areas), and $700 million for firefighter grants.
- $5.2 billion for the TSA, including $1.9 billion in expected fees. Like the House version, the Senate bill included $118 million to add 100 additional air cargo inspectors and research new technologies.

Subcommittee Chairman Thad Cochran, R-Miss., said he received more than 1,000 requests from other senators for earmarks, but none were added to the bill.

The panel agreed by voice vote to an amendment by Robert C. Byrd, D-W.Va., to require the Government Accountability Office to carry out a privacy study of the CAPPS II airline passenger screening system.

Senate Floor Action

The Senate passed HR 4567 by a vote of 93-0 in the waning hours of Sept. 14, after substituting the text of its own

bill. (*Senate vote 184, p. S-39*)

During five days of debate, Cochran defeated more than a dozen Democratic amendments that would have added billions of dollars for programs ranging from port and rail security to urban area anti-terrorism grants. "All these activities were popular, and anybody who was offering amendments for firefighters, those were difficult," Cochran said afterward. "But we didn't lose on a single recorded vote."

However, the Senate made several significant additions to the bill, all backed by bipartisan majorities. The Senate:

● **Drought aid.** Attached $3 billion in emergency disaster aid for for farmers suffering crop losses from drought in 2003 and 2004. Midwestern lawmakers from both parties had been clamoring for the assistance for months, and they redoubled their efforts after Congress, in less than a day, assembled a $2 billion measure (PL 108-303) to aid victims of Hurricane Charley. The amendment was approved by voice vote Sept. 14. (*Disaster supplementals, p. 2-53*)

● **Homeland funding increases.** Added $784 million for various Homeland Security Department programs, including $200 million for Canadian border security, $40 million for radiation detection devices and $81 million for rail and transit security. Bipartisan agreement was reached once offsetting revenue in the form of a Customs fee extension was identified. The funds were added in a series of amendments.

● **Privatization.** Agreed to a proposal by Patrick J. Leahy, D-Vt., to prevent the department from contracting work carried out by the Bureau of Citizenship and Immigration Services. The amendment was adopted by voice vote Sept. 8. The White House issued a policy statement the same day warning that such a provision could trigger a veto of the bill.

● **Offshore contracts.** Agreed by voice vote Sept. 13 to an amendment by Carl Levin, D-Mich., to block the department from giving contracts to companies that incorporated offshore to avoid U.S. taxes.

Conference/Final Action

House and Senate conferees had a working agreement on most of the funding issues by early October, but unrelated riders nearly hijacked plans to clear the bill before Congress adjourned for the elections. They missed the Oct. 8 targeted adjournment date, but managed to file the conference report (H Rept 108-774) on Oct. 9. The House adopted the report an hour and a half later, 368-0, and the Senate cleared the bill by voice vote Oct. 11. (*House vote 530, p. H-170*)

Democrats tried with little effect to add more money for priorities such as explosives detection systems at airports, improved communications for first-responders, and additional border patrol and immigration staff. "It's fair to say this hardly reflects the rhetoric we hear about homeland security being a priority," said Sabo. Rogers stuck to his position. "Spending more money than we need, just for the sake of saying we spent more, does not make us safe," he said.

In March, the department had revealed that a projected $1.2 billion budget shortfall would force a hiring freeze at three of its agencies that protected the borders and enforced immigration laws: Customs and Border Protection, Immigration and Customs Enforcement, and Citizenship and Immigration Services. But Rogers said the department, not Congress, had to fix that problem. "More money is not what they need," he said. "They need some organizational push."

Sen. Barbara A. Mikulski, D-Md., failed to persuade conferees to shift more of the first-responder funding formula toward high-risk areas.

An objection from House Ways and Means Chairman Bill Thomas, R-Calif., forced the conferees to drop the Senate's plan to add $784 million for various security programs paid for by extending Customs user fees. Thomas, who intended to use the fees to offset part of the corporate tax cut bill (HR 4520), said the Senate provision violated the House's prerogative to initiate revenue measures.

Meanwhile, the Senate's decision to add $3 billion in emergency drought aid drew demands from House conservatives that the money be offset with cuts elsewhere in the measure, a proposal that did not sit well with the appropriators.

Appropriators also were waiting to use the conference report to carry emergency funds for hurricane-ravaged Florida. Bush had requested a total of $12.9 billion for such aid — in addition to $2 billion enacted in early September (PL 108-303). The leadership hoped to clear the funds before the planned adjournment and did not want to risk a stand-alone emergency aid bill that would be a magnet for amendments in the Senate.

Sen. Herb Kohl, D-Wis., added yet another twist in conference by proposing to attach a two-year extension of the Milk Income Loss Contract program. The program, which was due to expire at the end of fiscal 2005, provided financial assistance to dairy producers when domestic milk prices fell below a specified level. When Senate conferees voted to include the milk provision, Rogers and several other GOP conferees balked, and the conference recessed.

The bill also faced a White House veto threat over the proposal to bar the department from privatizing immigration services jobs.

Lawmakers had all but given up on clearing the bill before the election, when the problems began to melt away.

The bill's fate had become so complicated that by the night of Oct. 8, Appropriations Chairman C.W. Bill Young, R-Fla., gave up hopes of using it as a vehicle for either the emergency hurricane aid or the drought assistance, moving those provisions to the conference report on the fiscal 2005 military construction bill. (*Military construction, p. 2-40*)

The dairy language was dropped when Arlen Specter of Pennsylvania, the lone Senate GOP holdout for the provisions, was persuaded to back down and sign the conference report.

Conferees kept the language barring the use of federal funds to privatize immigration officers' jobs. However, a spokesman said Homeland Security Secretary Tom Ridge had informed lawmakers that he would put off the competitive-sourcing initiative, rendering the veto threat moot. ◆

River Dispute Slows Interior Bill

The fiscal 2005 Interior Department spending bill cleared in the lame-duck session as part of a nine-bill omnibus appropriations package that was signed Dec. 8 (HR 4818 — PL 108-447).

The House passed its version of the Interior bill in June, and Senate appropriators approved a similar measure in September, but further action in the regular session was blocked in part by a dispute over the Missouri River.

The $20 billion bill funded Interior Department agencies, including the Bureau of Land Management, U.S. Fish and Wildlife Service, National Park Service, U.S. Geological Survey, and Bureau of Indian Affairs. It also paid for the Agriculture Department's Forest Service, some Energy programs, the Indian Health Service, and arts and cultural agencies.

The total, which does not include a 0.8 percent across-the-board cut in all non-defense discretionary spending, was nearly 2 percent above President Bush's request, but it was still about 2 percent below the fiscal 2004 law (PL 108-108). (*2003 Almanac, p. 2-60*)

Given the tight spending limits, appropriators held off on a number of White House initiatives in conservation, clean energy and the arts in order to fund core accounts in the bill, such as those for American Indians and for fighting wildfires on national lands. Lawmakers deferred to future years about $257 million requested for clean-coal technology, and they pared administration initiatives in the arts and humanities by a total of $38 million, including a program championed by first lady Laura Bush.

The House originally passed the bill at $20 billion; the Senate committee version called for $20.3 billion. The Missouri River dispute that held up the Senate bill pitted senators from the northern Plains, who wanted to keep more of the water upstream in their drought-plagued states, against those from states downriver who wanted the water for commercial navigation and for other uses.

Highlights

The final bill included the following main components:
- **Wildfires.** $3 billion for fighting wildfires, 14 percent more than Bush requested. Of the total, $1.7 billion went to the Forest Service and $743 million was for the Bureau of Land Management. The total included $500 million in unrequested emergency firefighting funds that could be tapped if necessary. Another $500 million in fiscal 2004 funds was enacted as part of the fiscal 2005 defense appropriations law (PL 108-287).

BoxScore 2005
Interior — Fiscal Year

Bill:
HR 4818 — PL 108-447
Legislative Action:
House passed HR 4568 (H Rept 108-542), 334-86, on June 17.
Senate Appropriations Committee approved S 2804 (S Rept 108-341), 29-0, on Sept. 14.
House adopted the conference report on HR 4818 (H Rept 108-792), 344-51, on Nov. 20.
Senate cleared the bill, 65-30, on Nov. 20.
President signed Dec. 8.

- **Land acquisition.** $167 million for land acquisition, scattered across several accounts. That was 24 percent less than the $220 million that Bush sought and 2 percent more than the $177 million appropriated for fiscal 2004.
- **BLM.** $1.8 billion for the Bureau of Land Management, virtually the same as Bush's request and 7 percent less than the fiscal 2004 level. The total included $849 million to manage some 260 million acres of public land and $743 million for wildland fire management.
- **National Park Service.** $2.3 billion, just slightly less than requested and 4 percent above fiscal 2004 spending, with nearly three-quarters of the funds, or $1.7 billion, going to park service operations.
- **Fish and Wildlife Service.** $1.3 billion, virtually the same as fiscal 2004 spending. The service was responsible for migratory birds, threatened and endangered species, and some marine mammals.
- **Forest Service.** $4.3 billion, 13 percent less than fiscal 2004 spending but 1 percent above Bush's request, to manage more than 190 million acres of public land with uses ranging from timber and mineral production to recreation. The total included $1.7 billion of the firefighting funds.
- **Energy-related programs.** $1.3 billion, a drop of 23 percent from fiscal 2004, for Energy Department programs devoted to energy conservation, fossil fuel research and the Strategic Petroleum Reserve. Most Energy Department programs were funded in the energy and water portion of the omnibus. (*Energy and water, p. 2-19*)
- **Indian affairs.** $5.5 billion for Indian programs, about 2 percent more than requested. The total included $2.3 billion for the Bureau of Indian Affairs and $3 billion for the Indian Health Service.
- **Arts programs.** $123 million for the National Endowment for the Arts (NEA), an increase of 2 percent over the previous year. The National Endowment for the Humanities (NEH) received $140 million, a 3.4 percent increase, and the Smithsonian Institution got $624 million, a 4.6 percent increase. Taken together, the programs got about 4.5 percent less than Bush sought.

Legislative Action

House Subcommittee Action

The House Interior Appropriations Subcommittee approved a $20.2 billion draft of the bill by voice vote June 3.

The total was equal to Bush's request, but the appropria-

Where the Money Goes

Interior Spending

(figures are in thousands of dollars of new budget authority)

	Fiscal 2004 Appropriation	Fiscal 2005 Bush Request	House Passed	Senate Panel Approved	Conference Report *
GRAND TOTAL	**$20,514,187**	**$19,686,285**	**$20,030,125**	**$20,256,914**	**$20,044,977**
Total adjusted for scorekeeping**	**$20,093,841**	**$19,743,285**	**$20,091,125**	**$19,777,914**	**$20,090,977**
MAIN COMPONENTS					
Interior Department	**$9,847,964**	**$9,971,299**	**$9,744,451**	**$9,875,304**	**$9,888,199**
Bureau of Land Management	1,893,233	1,759,355	1,746,817	1,776,432	1,756,205
U.S. Fish and Wildlife Service	1,308,405	1,326,053	1,263,204	1,309,479	1,310,941
Bureau of Indian Affairs	2,300,814	2,253,795	2,334,851	2,276,116	2,329,865
National Park Service	2,258,581	2,360,544	2,267,809	2,360,242	2,348,841
U.S. Forest Service	**4,939,899**	**4,238,103**	**4,246,398**	**4,271,185**	**4,298,384**
Department of Energy programs	**1,713,772**	**1,335,632**	**1,373,046**	**1,490,928**	**1,324,103**
National Endowment for the Arts	**120,972**	**139,400**	**130,972**	**120,972**	**122,972**
National Endowment for the Humanities	**135,310**	**162,000**	**141,999**	**135,310**	**139,999**
Smithsonian Institution	**596,279**	**628,025**	**619,825**	**627,025**	**623,825**

* Totals do not include a 0.8 percent across-the-board cut in discretionary spending.

**Adjustments based on Congressional Budget Office criteria for determining discretionary spending; adjusted total is used to assess compliance with 302(b) allocations.

TABLE: House, Senate Appropriations committees

---

tors rearranged the funding, putting more money into areas such as firefighting and American Indian health care, at the expense of the president's call for funding increases for the arts and energy and land conservation programs.

David R. Obey of Wisconsin, the top Democrat on the full Appropriations Committee, said a "woefully inadequate" budget allocation put the GOP "at war with itself" over the priorities in the bill.

The bill included:

• $121 million for the NEA and $138 million for the NEH. The funding did not include an $18 million increase urged by Laura Bush for an NEA program designed to bring 300 years of American dance, musical and literary heritage to the 50 states.

• $49 million for land acquisition, $121 million less than was spent in fiscal 2004, with a proviso that the money be spent only on administrative costs for managing already acquired lands. Chairman Charles H. Taylor, R-N.C., took a hard line on acquisition, saying the government should better manage its existing holdings before acquiring more land for forest, conservation and park programs.

• $1.4 billion for energy programs, but appropriators postponed for a year a $237 million request for an initiative called FutureGen aimed at developing clean-burning power plants.

• $3 billion for fighting wildfires, including $500 million in emergency funds.

• $2.3 billion for the National Park Service, including $1.7 billion for operations. The subcommittee included a stern rebuke to agency managers whom the panel viewed as spending too much on their own travel and doing a poor job on construction supervision and personnel decisions.

• $1.7 billion for the Bureau of Land Management.

• $5.5 billion for Indian health, education and construction programs and Bureau of Indian Affairs operations.

The total included a 4 percent increase for the Indian Health Service.

House Committee Action

The full Appropriations Committee approved the bill (HR 4568 — H Rept 108-542) by voice vote June 9.

In the only significant change to the subcommittee draft, the committee shifted $227 million for a low-income energy assistance program, reflecting a decision to transfer jurisdiction over the program to the spending bill for the departments of Labor, Health and Human Services, and Education. That reduced the bill's total to $20 billion.

The committee rejected by voice vote an attempt by Obey to add $229 million requested by Bush but dropped by the committee for land acquisition and water conservation funds.

House Floor Action

After adding a bit more money for the arts, and sparring over forest conservation and national park policies, the House passed the $20 billion bill by a vote of 334-86 on June 17. (*House vote 264, p. H-90*)

The two-day debate turned into a tug of war that illustrated deep regional and philosophical differences over federal land stewardship.

During the debate, the House:

• Rejected, 198-224, an attempt by Rush D. Holt, D-N.J., to retain a Clinton administration plan to ban the use of snowmobiles in Yellowstone and Grand Teton National parks. Bush wanted to reverse the Clinton ban and allow a new generation of snowmobiles that manufacturers said were cleaner and quieter. Holt argued that the vehicles shattered the pristine experience for visitors that was intended when the parks were established. (*House vote 263, p. H-90*)

• Adopted, 222-205, an amendment by Steve Chabot,

R-Ohio, to bar roadbuilding in the Tongass National Forest in Alaska. Don Young, R-Alaska, angrily denounced the proposal, saying 96 percent of the forest was off-limits to logging and that the fraction open to harvesting was vital to the economy. "But this is an easy, cheap vote for somebody from Ohio, somebody who does not know squat about the people of Alaska," Young fumed. (*House vote 253, p. H-86*)

• Rejected, 202-215, a proposal by Maurice D. Hinchey, D-N.Y., and Charles Bass, R-N.H., for a one-year moratorium on a program that destroyed bison with the aim of eradicating a bacterial disease from the herd. Hinchey urged other ways of combating the illness. Denny Rehberg, R-Mont., argued that the bacteria could threaten the livelihood of Western cattle ranchers. (*House vote 261, p. H-88*)

• Adopted, 241-185, an amendment by Louise M. Slaughter, D-N.Y., to add $10 million for the NEA and $3.5 million for the NEH, bringing the totals for the agencies to $131 million and $142 million, respectively. The increases were for a program championed by the first lady. (*House vote 248, p. H-84*)

Senate Committee Action

The Senate Appropriations Committee approved its version of the bill (S 2804 — S Rept 108-341) on Sept. 14 by a vote of 29-0. The Interior Appropriations Subcommittee had approved a draft informally in June. The bill totaled $20.3 billion — only $268 million more than the $20 billion House version.

Like their House counterparts, the appropriators focused on funding core programs and recommended cuts in some Bush initiatives to make room for these priorities.

The committee-approved bill included:

• $3 billion for wildland fire activities including, if needed, $500 million in emergency supplemental funds.

• $217 million for land acquisition — less than requested but more than the $49 million in the House bill. House appropriators argued that the government should better manage its current holdings before acquiring more land for forest, conservation and park programs.

• $2.4 billion, $92 million more than in the House bill, for the National Park Service, including $1.7 billion for operations.

• $1.8 billion, $29 million more than in the House bill, for the Bureau of Land Management.

• $5.5 billion for Indian programs, virtually the same as in the House version, including $3 billion for the Indian Health Service.

• $1.5 billion, $118 million above the House figure, for energy programs. The Senate bill included $18 million for FutureGen.

• $121 million for the NEA and $135 million for the NEH. The totals were equal to fiscal 2004 funding, but they were $10 million and $7 million, respectively, below the levels in the House-passed bill.

The committee markup was dominated by policy issues, including management of the Missouri River and cleanup of abandoned coal mines. The panel:

• Rejected, 9-14, an attempt by Missouri Republican Christopher S. Bond to strike bill language that would allow the Army Corp of Engineers to adjust the flow of the Missouri River so that more water could be kept in drought-plagued states upstream. The provision was included in the bill by Interior Subcommittee Chairman Conrad Burns, R-Mont., and the panel's top Democrat, Byron L. Dorgan of North Dakota. States downstream argued that holding more water would hurt barge traffic and cause other problems.

• Adopted by voice vote an amendment by Robert C. Byrd, D-W.Va., to extend the Abandoned Mine Land Reclamation Fund for nine months while the authorizing committees worked out modifications to the program. The fund, which was due to expire Sept. 30, was administered by the government but financed by industry. It paid for environmental cleanup of abandoned mines and subsidized the medical insurance of some former miners.

Conference/Final Acton

House and Senate conferees completed the Interior bill with relative ease as part of the omnibus spending package assembled after the November election. The House adopted the conference report on the omnibus (H Rept 108-792) by a vote of 344-51 on Nov. 20, and the Senate cleared the bill, 65-30, later the same day. (*House vote 542, p. H-174; Senate vote 215, p. S-46*)

The following are some of the differences resolved by the negotiators:

• **Land acquisition.** The $167 million for land in the final bill was much closer to the Senate's $217 million than the $49 million in the House bill.

• **FutureGen.** Following the Senate lead, the bill included $18 million for the project.

• **Wildfires.** The $3 billion, including $500 million in emergency funds, conformed to both bills; Bush did not request the emergency money.

• **Weatherization.** Like the Senate bill, the omnibus provided $230 million for low-income weatherization grants, but like the House, it did not count the money as part of the Interior bill.

• **Tongass.** As expected, Senate Appropriations Chairman Ted Stevens, R-Alaska, prevailed in removing the House provision that would have halted roadbuilding in the Tongass National Forest.

• **Missouri River.** Bond won on the Missouri River, persuading conferees to drop the Senate amendment that would have required the corps to keep more of the water upstream when needed to respond to drought.

• **Abandoned mines.** Conferees retained Byrd's amendment reauthorizing the Abandoned Mine Land Reclamation Fund through June 30, 2005. ◆

Overtime Rules Draw Veto Threat

The fiscal 2005 bill for the departments of Labor, Health and Human Services, and Education — the largest of the domestic spending bills — cleared Nov. 20 as part of the year-end omnibus appropriations package. President Bush signed the omnibus into law Dec. 8 (HR 4818 — PL 108-447).

The Labor-HHS measure, which provided a total of $497.6 billion, broke with a recent tradition of providing substantial increases for major education and medical research programs. Less than a third of the bill — $143.3 billion — was discretionary funds that the appropriators could allocate as they chose. That was about 1 percent more than Bush had requested and 3 percent more than fiscal 2004 spending, which meant it barely kept up with inflation. The remainder of the bill was mandatory spending for programs such as Medicaid, Medicare and unemployment insurance. *(2003 Almanac, p. 2-64)*

The numbers do not include a 0.8 percent across-the-board cut in discretionary accounts enacted in the omnibus.

From the outset, appropriators struggled to squeeze the many programs covered by the bill within tight spending caps. The House in September passed a $496.7 billion version of the bill with $142.5 billion in discretionary spending. Mirroring Bush's request, it proposed increases of $1 billion each for Title I programs for low-income schools and state grants for educating disabled students, as well an additional $726 million for the National Institutes of Health (NIH).

A week later, the Senate Appropriations Committee approved a more generous $499.5 billion measure that included $2.8 billion more than the House bill, mainly for Title I, NIH and other health and education programs. Sen. Arlen Specter, R-Pa., chairman of the Labor-HHS Appropriations Subcommittee, was able to include the extra money without busting his discretionary spending cap by using a series of accounting maneuvers that were not acceptable to the White House.

The biggest differences facing conferees in reconciling the two bills was the Senate's extra money and language in both versions to block new Labor Department overtime pay rules, which drew a veto threat. The sheer size of the bill also made the negotiations slow-going.

In the end, conferees dropped the Senate's accounting gimmicks and funded major education and health programs at levels below what either Bush or the appropriators had sought. GOP leaders dropped the overtime pay language, as they had the previous year. The final bill included a provision that allowed doctors, hospitals and insurers to refuse to provide abortions on moral grounds without losing federal funds.

BoxScore 2005 Fiscal Year
Labor-HHS-Education

Bill:
HR 4818 — PL 108-447
Legislative Action:
House passed HR 5006 (H Rept 108-636), 388-13, Sept. 9.
Senate Appropriations Committee approved S 2810 (S Rept 108-345), 29-0, Sept. 15.
House adopted the conference report on HR 4818 (H Rept 108-792), 344-51, Nov. 20.
Senate cleared the bill, 65-30, Nov. 20.
President signed Dec. 8.

Highlights

The fiscal 2005 Labor-HHS-Education law included $96.6 billion in advance fiscal 2006 appropriations, $400 million in advance fiscal 2007 appropriations and $12.5 billion from trust funds. The measure traditionally included advance appropriations for the first quarter of the succeeding fiscal year for certain education and health programs. The following are the law's major funding components:

● **Education.** $59.7 billion, including $15 billion in advance funds for fiscal 2006. The total was $1.4 billion or 2 percent more than the fiscal 2004 appropriation, but $306 million less than Bush requested. It included:

● $12.8 billion for Title I grants to low-income school districts, a 4 percent increase over fiscal 2004 but less than requested by Bush or included in the House or Senate bill.

● $10.7 billion for state grants for special education, a 6 percent increase over fiscal 2004 but less than Bush or either chamber sought.

● $12.4 billion for Pell grants, a 4 percent increase but less than Bush or either chamber sought. The bill maintained the maximum Pell grant award at its previous level of $4,050.

● **Health and Human Services.** $375.3 billion, including $304.5 billion in fiscal 2005 appropriations, $68.1 billion in advance fiscal 2006 appropriations and $2.8 billion from trust funds.

About a fifth of the total, $64.2 billion, was discretionary spending, a 3 percent increase over fiscal 2004. It included $28.6 billion for NIH, $4.5 billion for the Centers for Disease Control and Prevention (CDC), and $6.9 billion for Head Start, the early childhood program for low-income children.

The rest of the money was for mandatory programs, including $177.5 billion for grants to states under Medicaid, the federal-state health program for the poor, and $119.8 billion for Medicare.

● **Labor.** $15.4 billion for the Labor Department — $11.5 billion in appropriations and $3.9 billion from trust funds — virtually the same as fiscal 2004 funding.

Legislative Action

House Subcommittee Action

The House Labor-HHS Subcommittee approved a $496.6 billion draft of the bill, 18-0, on July 8. The bill's $142.5 billion in discretionary funding was about $200 mil-

Where the Money Goes

Labor-HHS-Education Spending

(figures are in thousands of dollars of new budget authority)

	Fiscal 2004 Appropriation	Fiscal 2005 Bush Request	House Passed	Senate Panel Approved	Conference Report *
GRAND TOTAL	$479,817,978	$496,434,577	$496,665,511	$499,489,511	$497,552,511
Total adjusted for scorekeeping**	$471,035,821	$492,213,162	$492,407,596	$489,014,096	$493,254,096
MAIN COMPONENTS					
Department of Labor	$15,283,808	$15,179,349	$14,904,358	$15,432,189	$15,399,053
Training and employment Services	5,145,464	5,326,292	5,112,728	5,377,662	5,361,957
Department of Health and Human Services	360,327,552	374,327,562	374,298,336	375,556,107	375,307,532
Centers for Disease Control and Prevention	4,367,165	4,213,554	4,228,778	4,538,592	4,533,911
National Institutes of Health	27,800,048	28,526,871	28,526,871	28,900,300	28,600,048
Low-Income Home Energy Assistance grants	2,115,956	2,291,700	2,249,000	2,000,500	2,200,000
Department of Education	58,246,623	59,974,897	60,317,016	61,484,313	59,668,693
Title I Grants to school districts	12,342,309	13,342,309	13,342,309	13,457,607	12,842,309
Special education grants to states	10,068,106	11,068,106	11,068,106	11,228,981	10,675,147

* Totals do not reflect a 0.8 percent across-the-board cut in discretionary spending.

** Adjustments based on Congressional Budget Office criteria for determining discretionary spending; the adjusted total is used to assess compliance with 302(b) allocations.

TABLE: House, Senate Appropriations committees

lion more than Bush requested, but it was slightly less than what the government said would be needed to keep all programs running at existing levels in fiscal 2005.

David R. Obey of Wisconsin, the top Democrat on both the subcommittee and the full committee, said the discretionary total was insufficient to meet critical medical research and education needs. Obey maintained, as he had at other appropriations markups, that GOP leaders were insisting on a draconian domestic budget to limit the deficit created because of tax cuts for the wealthy.

House appropriators embraced many of Bush's requests, including:

• $13.3 billion for Title I aid, a $1 billion increase over fiscal 2004 spending. Democrats argued that the funding was insufficient compared with the $20.5 billion authorized under the 2002 "No Child Left Behind" education law (PL 107-110). They said the money was critical to prepare low-income children to meet the law's requirement that all students be proficient in math and reading by 2014. Republicans said the proposed boost was adequate, even generous, given that many states still had large amounts of unspent funds. *(2001 Almanac, p. 8-3)*

• $11.1 billion for special-education grants, a $1 billion increase over fiscal 2004.

• $12.8 billion for Pell grants, an $823 million increase.

• $28.5 billion for NIH, a $726 million increase.

To compensate for some of the bigger increases, the subcommittee cut funds for other programs or kept their increases below the rate of inflation. It proposed to end a $297 million state block grant for innovative education efforts, and cut the budget for the CDC by 3 percent to $4.2 billion. It left out or reduced funding for administration priorities such as job-training programs administered by community colleges and a program to help prisoners make the transition back to society.

During the markup, the subcommittee rejected, on a party-line 7-11 vote, a proposal by Obey to add $7.4 billion for discretionary programs, offset by rolling back tax cuts enacted in 2001 and 2003 (PL 107-16, PL 108-27) for those with annual incomes above $1 million. *(2003 Almanac, p. 17-3)*

House Committee Action

The full House Appropriations Committee approved the $496.6 billion bill (HR 5006 — H Rept 108-636) by voice vote July 14, after narrowly defeating an attempt to block major portions of the new Labor Department overtime rule.

Most of the debate focused on the Democratic amendment to block the rule and a GOP amendment to further tighten restrictions on federal funding for abortions.

During the markup, the committee:

• Rejected, on a 29-31 party-line vote, an amendment by Obey to block the Labor Department from enforcing any rule that would take away any worker's overtime pay eligibility.

Democrats had tried for two years to block Labor Department plans to implement new rules revising the eligibility standards for overtime pay. Democrats contended that as many as 6 million workers would lose their eligibility for overtime pay as their jobs were reclassified. The Bush administration disputed that number and said the new rules would allow 1.3 million low-income workers to qualify for overtime for the first time. A veto threat in 2003 had led the leadership to strip a similar amendment from the fiscal 2004 Labor-HHS bill once it was wrapped into an omnibus spending package (PL 108-199). *(Overtime, p. 8-5; 2003 Almanac, p. 12-6)*

• Adopted by voice vote an amendment by Dave Weldon, R-Fla., to deny funding in the bill to government agencies that discriminated against health providers or insurance companies because they refused to provide, cover or refer abortion services. Weldon said some jurisdictions were pre-

venting hospitals that banned abortion services, particularly Catholic hospital chains, from acquiring medical clinics that provided such services.

• Adopted by voice vote an amendment by Randy "Duke" Cunningham, R-Calif., to bar any new policies on the consolidation of federally backed student loans until Congress reauthorized the Higher Education Act.

• Rejected, 20-36, a proposal by Virgil H. Goode Jr., R-Va., to bar funding for a proposed agreement with Mexico under which Mexican workers in the United States would pay Social Security payroll taxes and then receive equivalent benefits from the Mexican pension system when they retired in Mexico. The deal also would extend a comparable arrangement to Americans working in Mexico.

• Rejected, 25-31, an Obey amendment to increase overall funding in the bill by $7.4 billion, of which $5.6 billion would go to the Education Department, offset by reducing tax cuts for people with annual incomes of over $1 million.

House Floor Action

After two days of debate, the House passed what was calculated as a $496.7 billion Labor-HHS bill by a lopsided vote that reflected political expediency on both sides of the aisle. The vote, taken Sept. 9, was 388-13. All 192 Democrats present voted in favor of the bill; the dissenters were all Republicans, generally from the party's most fiscally conservative wing. (House vote 440, p. H-142)

Democrats wanted to avoid a repeat of the previous year, when Subcommittee Chairman Ralph Regula, R-Ohio, dropped all the Democratic earmarks in the bill after the caucus voted en bloc against the measure. That did not stop Democrats from complaining that the bill would again shortchange important education and health care programs. (2003 Almanac, p. 2-64)

• **Overtime rules.** Before passage, GOP leaders gave minority Democrats a chance for a rare victory by allowing Obey to offer his amendment on overtime pay rules. The amendment was adopted, 223-193, with 22 mostly moderate Republicans crossing party lines to show their pro-labor sympathies. (House vote 434, p. H-140)

Although Republican leaders expected to drop the language in conference, they still fought to defeat it, delaying the vote the night of Sept. 8 to gain more time to lobby.

• **Other amendments.** During the floor debate, the House:

• Rejected, 178-225, an attempt by J.D. Hayworth, R-Ariz., to prevent the Social Security Administration from implementing the reciprocal pension agreement with Mexico. Hayworth said the agreement could pose a financial threat to Social Security. Sixty-one Republicans voted against the amendment. (House vote 439, p. H-142)

• Adopted, 413-3, an amendment by Dale E. Kildee, D-Mich., to eliminate certain types of student college loans that guaranteed lenders a higher-return rate than other federally subsidized loans. Kildee said that a loophole in the Higher Education Act (PL 105-244) allowed some lenders, at an annual cost to taxpayers of $1 billion, to receive a 9.5 percent return on certain federally backed loans rather than the current rate of 3.5 percent for most loans. (House vote 436, p. H-142)

• Adopted, 268-148, an amendment by George Miller, D-Calif., to require the Pension Benefit Guaranty Corpora-

tion (PBGC) to make public the financial status of company pension plans that carried negative balances. The amendment was later dropped in conference. (House vote 429, p. H-140)

Senate Committee Action

The Senate Appropriations Committee approved a $499.5 billion version of the bill (S 2810 — S Rept 108-345) by a vote of 29-0 on Sept. 15. The Labor-HHS Subcommittee had forwarded its draft of the measure to the full committee without a formal vote.

Subcommittee Chairman Specter managed to add $3.6 billion above House levels for education and health programs through a series of accounting maneuvers. Specter gained $3.2 billion by proposing to shift certain mandatory Supplemental Security Income payments by a few days so they would fall in fiscal 2006. He got another $100 million by extending employer fees for H-1B visas and $200 million by recouping unspent money from the new Medicare prescription drug program. Officially, the bill still met its $142.3 billion discretionary spending cap.

The bill included:

• $28.9 billion for NIH, $380 million more than in Bush's request or the House bill.

• $13.5 billion for Title I programs, $118 million more than the House bill and Bush's budget request.

• $11.2 billion for special-education grants to states, $161 million more than the House bill and the Bush request. The maximum annual amount for a Pell grant would remain at $4,050, the same amount contained in the House bill and in Bush's budget.

The committee adopted, 16-13, an amendment by Tom Harkin of Iowa, ranking Democrat on the subcommittee, to prevent the Labor Department from taking away overtime pay rights from any worker who was previously eligible, while maintaining the new rights for low-income workers who earned up to $23,660 a year.

The bill was never expected to go to the full Senate.

Conference/Final Action

With Republican leaders and the White House insisting on tight domestic discretionary spending limits, conferees meeting in the post-election lame-duck session dropped the Senate's accounting maneuvers and allocated less to Title I grants for low-income schools and programs for disabled students than the president had called for.

The House adopted the conference report on the omnibus (HR 4818 — H Rept 108-792), 344-51, on Nov. 20. The Senate cleared the bill, 65-30, later the same day. (House vote 542, p. H-174; Senate vote 215, p. S-46)

Specter, a champion of expanded education and health spending, said there were "many, many, many disappointments" in the bill. Senate Democrats echoed his complaints, noting that important medical research and education programs would receive the smallest percentage increase in years once across-the-board cuts in the omnibus were applied.

• **Title I grants.** $12.8 billion, a $500 million increase over fiscal 2004, compared with increases of $1 billion and $1.1 billion recommended in the House and Senate bills, respectively.

"We all understand, the committee on appropriations plays the cards that they are dealt. In this instance, they

have been dealt a set of cards with a great big deficit and not much room to work," said George Miller of California, the ranking Democrat on the House Education and the Workforce Committee. "I must say, however, that I am deeply disappointed in the figures for education."

Conferees dropped Senate language — which had been in the fiscal 2004 law — prohibiting the Education Department from using a new formula to calculate student aid eligibility.

Critics such as Sen. Jon Corzine, D-N.J., said failure to renew the provision banning use of the formula would result in nearly 90,000 students losing their eligibility for Pell grants.

The department had changed its policy for distributing Title I funds for low-income schools, using child poverty estimates calculated by the Census Bureau on an annual, rather than biennial, basis in order to more closely track the migration of poor students. Under the new formula, 10 states — Kansas, Maine, Massachusetts, Michigan, Minnesota, Missouri, New Hampshire, New Jersey, North Dakota and Pennsylvania — stood to lose as much as 10 percent of their Title I funding, according to the Center on Education Policy, a nonpartisan think tank.

● **Special education.** $10.7 billion for state special-education grants, $393 million less than in the House bill or Bush's budget and $554 million less than Senate appropriators sought. A five-year reauthorization of the Individuals with Disabilities Education Act (PL 108-446), signed Dec. 3, called for $12.4 billion for state grants in fiscal 2005. (*Special education, p. 7-3*)

● **Pell grants.** $12.5 billion, $365 million less than Bush or either chamber sought.

● **NIH.** $28.6 billion for NIH, $73 million more than in the House version but $300 million less than in the Senate bill. Appropriators had been scaling back the size of NIH in-

creases since completing a doubling of the NIH budget over five years in fiscal 2003. (*2002 Almanac, p. 2-24*)

● **CDC.** $4.5 billion, $321 million more than the House recommended but $9 million less than in the Senate bill.

● **HIV/AIDS.** $607 million, drawn from a number of accounts, for international AIDS, tuberculosis and malaria programs.

● **Community health centers.** $1.7 billion, $88 million less than Bush or the House recommended and $119 million less than in the Senate bill.

● **Head Start.** $6.9 billion, equal to the House amount but $45 million less than in the Senate bill. The total included an advance appropriation of $1.4 billion for fiscal 2006.

● **LIHEAP.** $2.2 billion for the Low-Income Home Energy Assistance Program (LIHEAP). A last-minute lobbying campaign by lawmakers from the Northeast and Midwest persuaded conferees to add $300 million in emergency funding in response to rising natural gas and heating oil costs. The House had recommended $2.25 billion, the Senate bill $2 billion.

Some of the bitterest debate was on social policy riders.

● **Abortion.** At the urging of House conservatives, appropriators included the House language permitting health care providers to refuse to provide or fund abortions if they objected on moral or religious grounds — without jeopardizing their federal funding. Democrats complained that the language was a "radical change" in policy that would chip away at abortion rights.

● **Overtime rules.** Under a veto threat, conferees dropped language that would have blocked portions of the new Labor Department overtime rules.

● **Student loans.** Conferees also dropped Kildee's language that would have barred use of funds for loans that guaranteed lenders a higher than normal rate of return. ◆

Smooth Sailing for Capitol Funding

The fiscal 2005 spending bill for the legislative branch was the first of the year's domestic appropriations bills to pass both chambers, but Republican leaders held off finishing it to avoid the appearance of putting Congress' interests ahead of the nation's. Instead, the $3.6 billion bill became part of the omnibus appropriations package that cleared Nov. 20. President Bush signed the omnibus into law Dec. 8 (HR 4818 — PL 108-447).

The bill provided a less-than-inflation 1 percent increase over what the legislative branch got in both regular and supplemental legislation for fiscal 2004. That was a point of pride for Jack Kingston, R-Ga., the chairman of the House Legislative Branch Appropriations Subcommittee. "We held the line," Kingston said. "I think Congress has to lead the way." The final bill was subject to a further 0.8 percent across-the-board cut in discretionary spending enacted as part of the omnibus.

The bill covered the operations of Congress and its affiliated agencies, including the Library of Congress, the Government Accountability Office (GAO), the Government Printing Office (GPO) and the Congressional Budget Office (CBO). It also paid for House and Senate overhead, including staff salaries, office expenses and mail, and it included funds for maintenance and security for the Capitol complex and grounds.

The main winners in the fiscal 2005 bill were the Capitol Police, who got a 6 percent increase over fiscal 2004, and the Library of Congress, which got a 5 percent boost. The House got a 4 percent increase for its operations. To make room for these and other modest increases, appropriators cut funding for the Architect of the Capitol by 12.5 percent and reduced the GPO budget by 10 percent.

Highlights

The following are the main components of the bill:
- **House and Senate.** $1 billion for staff salaries and expenses of House leaders, members and committees, a 4 percent increase over fiscal 2004 spending, and $726 million for comparable expenses in the Senate, a 2 percent boost. The totals allowed for modest salary increases for Capitol Hill staff, at the discretion of individual lawmakers. The totals did not include $113 million in mandatory spending for salaries and benefits of the members themselves, which is permanently appropriated.
- **Architect of the Capitol.** $353 million, $50 million less than in fiscal 2004, rather than the 45 percent increase re-

BoxScore 2005 Fiscal Year
Legislative Branch

Bill:
HR 4818 — PL 108-447
Legislative Action:
House passed HR 4755 (H Rept 108-577), 327-43, on July 12.
Senate passed HR 4755, amended to reflect S 2666 (S Rept 108-307), 94-2, on Sept. 21.
House adopted the conference report on HR 4818 (H Rept 108-792), 344-51, on Nov. 20.
Senate cleared the bill, 65-30, on Nov. 20.
President signed Dec. 8.

quested by Architect Alan M. Hantman. Conferees authorized the architect to transfer $10.6 million of the $29 million provided for his Capitol Building account to the underground Capitol Visitor Center, but they expressed their displeasure with what they said was "the architect's ongoing inability to provide the committees with accurate cost estimates and delivery schedules on this very important and high-profile project." The appropriators also forced the resignation of Richard McSeveney, the man who had been brought in to improve management in the architect's office. McSeveney's $171,000 salary and benefits package was zeroed out in the conference report. He resigned Nov. 22, the first business day after the report language was made public.

- **Capitol Police.** Although appropriators gave Capitol Police Chief Terrance W. Gainer a $13 million increase over fiscal 2004, bringing his total to $232 million, they criticized him in the conference report for exceeding his budget authority and declaring emergencies to justify excess spending. They went on to direct the GAO to audit police spending back to fiscal 2002 and report by Jan. 31. The bill did not include funding for increased staffing levels requested by Gainer.

Legislative Action

House Subcommittee Action

The House Legislative Branch Appropriations Subcommittee agreed by voice vote June 16 to a draft of the bill that allotted $2.75 billion for House operations and for the various agencies that support Congress. By custom, the House measure did not include Senate expenses, leaving it to that chamber to fill in its own numbers. The total was about $3 million below the fiscal 2004 level (PL 108-83) and $395 million below what was requested by the various House offices and ancillary agencies. (*2003 Almanac, p. 2-69*)

The draft called for a 20 percent cut in funding for the Architect of the Capitol, leaving a total of $272 million. It included no additional funding for construction or startup of the Capitol Visitor Center; $15 million was requested. Total spending on the underground complex on the East Front had already reached $351 million, almost 60 percent more than originally agreed to but sufficient to complete the complex by the summer of 2006.

The bill also directed the Architect to contract with a private company to manage and operate the Capitol Power Plant before fiscal 2006. In the meantime, the budget for the

Where the Money Goes

Legislative Branch Spending

(figures are in thousands of dollars of new budget authority)

	Fiscal 2004 Appropriation	Fiscal 2005 Bush Request	House Passed*	Senate Passed	Conference Report **
GRAND TOTAL	**$3,527,460**	**$3,969,283**	**$2,749,522**	**$3,574,000**	**$3,571,000**
MAIN COMPONENTS					
House of Representatives	$1,008,479	$1,066,344	$1,044,281	$1,044,281	$1,048,581
Senate	712,488	759,708	N/A	725,067	726,067
Capitol Police	219,795	291,641	232,328	226,925	232,328
Architect of the Capitol	402,976	584,944	271,666	372,677	352,724
Government Printing Office	134,767	151,058	121,324	120,735	120,753
Library of Congress	523,001	562,631	543,488	544,092	549,760
Congressional Budget Office	33,620	35,455	34,790	34,790	34,919
Government Accountability Office	457,606	480,535	473,500	470,000	470,973

*By custom, the House bill is silent on accounts that are the exclusive purview of the Senate.
** Totals do not include a 0.8 across-the-board cut in discretionary spending.

TABLE: House Appropriations Committee

plant was cut by 31 percent, from $81 million in fiscal 2004 to $56 million in fiscal 2005.

Appropriators also proposed to trim the GPO by 10 percent, bringing it to $121 million.

The cuts made room for small increases for most other congressional agencies, including:

• $1 billion for House operations, a 4 percent increase over fiscal 2004 that members hoped would help stem the tide of House aides seeking higher-paying jobs elsewhere.

• $232 million for the Capitol Police — an increase of nearly 6 percent over fiscal 2004 spending, but $60 million less than Gainer had requested. Gainer was hoping to expand the force for the fourth time in as many years, but the appropriators' report cautioned that "at this point these large increases in personnel are too much for any agency to absorb in such a short period of time."

• $543 million for the Library of Congress, a 4 percent increase above fiscal 2004.

• $474 million for the GAO, also a 4 percent increase.

During the markup, the subcommittee:

• Adopted by voice vote an amendment by Mark Steven Kirk, R-Ill., to eliminate the Capitol Police's mounted patrol unit, which had been authorized in the fiscal 2004 law, for an estimated savings of $1.8 million over a decade. The report urged Gainer to start clearing his "public pronouncements" with congressional leaders in advance. Gainer had been making TV appearances to promote the horse patrols.

• Rejected, 5-5, an amendment by Ray LaHood, R-Ill., to bar lame-duck lawmakers from filing ethics complaints against sitting members. The proposal would have nullified a complaint against Majority Leader Tom DeLay, R-Texas, filed by Rep. Chris Bell, D-Texas. *(Ethics, p. 5-4)*

House Committee Action

The full House Appropriations Committee approved the bill (HR 4755 — H Rept 108-577) by voice vote June 23.

Kingston said House appropriators demonstrated fiscal restraint and set a good example for the rest of Congress. "We have taken a sleepy, quiet bill and turned it into a vivid example of how to limit government spending," he declared afterwards. James P. Moran of Virginia, the subcommittee's ranking Democrat, gave grudging support to the bill, saying flat funding for the legislative branch, although "a little too restrictive," was justified in a year of soaring deficits. But he cautioned against using the bill as a precedent for future cuts, saying it would "impose real harm to this institution and its ability to operate."

During the markup, the committee:

• Adopted by voice vote a manager's amendment by Kingston that called on congressional leaders to evaluate laws governing compensation for the heads of various agencies controlled by Congress, such as the Architect of the Capitol and CBO. It also directed the GAO to determine whether there was any unnecessary overlap between four offices that review economic policies and outlook: CBO, the Congressional Research Service, the Joint Economic Committee and the Joint Committee on Taxation.

• Adopted by voice vote proposals by Moran and John T. Doolittle, R-Calif., to explore opportunities to provide dental and vision insurance for staff and members.

• Adopted by voice vote an amendment by Sam Farr, D-Calif., to prohibit the building of a perimeter fence around the Capitol Building.

• Rejected by voice vote an attempt by Kingston to cut funding for the Joint Economic Committee by 50 percent, to $2 million. The joint committee, created nearly six decades earlier, advised lawmakers from both parties on the economy.

House Floor Action

The House passed the bill by an overwhelming vote of 327-43 on July 12. *(House vote 362, p. H-120)*

During the debate, the House:

• Rejected, 115-252, a proposal by physicist Rush D. Holt, D-N.J., to revive the work, if not the bureaucracy, of

the Office of Technology Assessment. The agency had advised Congress on scientific and technology issues for nearly a quarter-century. Republicans labeled it wasteful and closed it after taking power in 1995. *(House vote 359, p. H-118)*

• Rejected, 87-278, an amendment by Joel Hefley, R-Colo., to cut legislative branch spending by 1 percent across the board. *(House vote 360, p. H-118)*

Senate Committee Action

With minimal debate, the Senate Appropriations Committee approved its version of the bill (S 2666 — S Rept 108-307) by a vote of 29-0 on July 15. The Legislative Branch Subcommittee had waived its right to consider the bill, forwarding the draft to the full committee. In a rare exception to the partisan squabbling that prevailed elsewhere in Congress, ranking subcommittee Democrat Richard J. Durbin of Illinois described the measure as "comprehensive, thorough and fair, especially in light of the tight funding constraints under which we are operating."

The bill recommended $2.5 billion for the Senate and the legislative branch operations it shared with the House, just 0.3 percent more than the comparable amount appropriated for fiscal 2004. When combined with the House bill, the measure brought total legislative branch spending to $3.5 billion — about the same as the fiscal 2004 level.

Subcommittee Chairman Ben Nighthorse Campbell, R-Colo., said he agreed with the overall call for flat funding, but called some House provisions "penny-wise but pound-foolish." Campbell, a former police officer, was a particular champion of the mounted police unit.

The Senate bill called for:

• $725 million for Senate operations, a 2 percent boost.

• $227 million for the Capitol Police, a 3 percent increase compared with the 6 percent boost in the House bill. The Senate bill did not call for abolishing the mounted patrols. The funding level and fate of the horse unit were the most significant differences between the two bills. "It should be easy, except for the damned horses," said Moran, looking ahead to conference.

• $308 million for Architect of the Capitol, a 10 percent cut from fiscal 2004.

• $121 million for the GPO, a 10 percent cut.

• $544 million for the Library of Congress, virtually the same as the House.

• $470 million for the GAO.

Senate Floor Action

The Senate passed HR 4755 by a vote of 94-2 on Sept. 21 after adding the text of its own bill. The combined bill totaled $3.6 billion. As passed by the Senate, the measure called for $373 million for the architect. *(Senate vote 186, p. S-40)*

Conference/Final Action

The conference, as expected, was relatively easy. House and Senate conferees agreed to a $3.6 billion bill, which was folded into the conference report on the fiscal 2005 omnibus (HR 4818 — H Rept 108-792). The House adopted the conference report, 344-51, on Nov. 20, and the Senate cleared the omnibus, 65-30, later the same day. *(House vote 542, p. H-174; Senate vote 215, p. S-46)*

On the biggest issue in conference — the Capitol Police — the Senate came around to the 6 percent increase advocated by the House. The Senate prevailed in the dispute over continuing the new mounted police unit, although the conference report asked for a GAO report on the unit. House appropriators expected to do away with the program after Campbell, its champion, retired at the end of the 108th Congress.

The conference agreement included House language prohibiting construction of a fence around the Capitol. It also required a GAO study on the feasibility of contracting with a private company to manage the Capitol power plant and included provisions to move forward with such a contract if the GAO recommended it. ◆

Green Light for Military Housing

With U.S. forces fighting in Iraq and elsewhere, Congress easily agreed on a $10 billion spending bill for military construction projects in the United States and overseas, family housing, and the costs of base realignment and closing. The measure, one of four fiscal 2005 appropriations bills to clear before lawmakers adjourned for the elections, also carried $14.5 billion in emergency hurricane and drought relief aid. President Bush signed the bill into law Oct. 13 (HR 4837 — PL 108-324). (*Disaster aid, p. 2-53*)

The total for military construction was not in dispute. Both chambers called for $10 billion — $450 million, or 5 percent, more than Bush requested. The extra funds covered home-state projects that members added to the president's request. The chance to bring home military construction dollars in an election year also helped speed the bill along.

The funding amounted to $687 million, or 7 percent, more than Congress provided in the fiscal 2004 law (PL 108-132). When the military construction funds in the 2003 Iraq war supplemental (PL 108-106) were counted, the increase over fiscal 2004 shrank to $162 million, or 2 percent — less than the rate of inflation. (*2003 Almanac, p. 2-83*)

The main issue confronting members was how to increase a statutory limit of $850 million for a program that encouraged private construction of military family housing. The Pentagon expected to hit the cap in November, which would have left at least 50,000 families in several states waiting for better homes. House appropriators tried to increase the cap, but Budget Committee Chairman Jim Nussle, R-Iowa, was able to knock the provision out during floor debate because it would have pushed the bill over its spending allocation.

Senate appropriators also wanted to lift the cap, as did the Bush administration, but the Senate bill was silent on the issue because of the spending problem.

The problem was resolved when conferees on the fiscal 2005 defense authorization bill (PL 108-375) — which included military construction accounts — agreed to eliminate any restriction on spending for the housing program. Negotiators on the military construction bill then quickly completed their work and got the bill cleared just as lawmakers were preparing to leave for the campaign trail. (*Defense authorization, p. 6-3*)

Highlights

The following are the main components of the fiscal 2005 military construction law:
• **Military construction.** $4.5 billion for military construc-

BoxScore 2005
Military Construction — Fiscal Year

Bill:
HR 4837 — PL 108-324
Legislative Action:
House passed HR 4837 (H Rept 108-607), 420-1, on July 22.
Senate passed HR 4837, amended with the text of S 2674 (S Rept 108-309), 91-0, on Sept. 20.
House adopted the conference report (H Rept 108-773), 374-0, on Oct. 9.
Senate cleared the bill by voice vote Oct. 11.
President signed Oct. 13.

tion for the active forces in the Army, Navy and Air Force and for the Defense agencies — a 7 percent increase over Bush's request but a cut of 1.5 percent from fiscal 2004. The bill also appropriated $945 million in construction funds for the National Guard and reserve forces, up nearly 30 percent from the previous year and 52 percent more than requested.
• **Family and military housing.** $4.1 billion for family and military personnel housing, 6 percent above fiscal 2004 spending, but 3 percent less than requested.
• **Base closings.** $246 million, as requested, for costs associated with base closings and realignments, 34 percent less than was appropriated in fiscal 2004. The next round of base closings was scheduled for 2005.
• **NATO.** $161 million for the U.S. contribution to NATO infrastructure improvements, about the same as in fiscal 2004 and 3 percent less than requested.

Legislative Action

House Committee Action

The House Appropriations Committee approved its version of the $10 billion bill (HR 4837 — H Rept 108-607) by voice vote July 9. The Military Construction Subcommittee had approved a draft of the bill by voice vote July 6.

The full committee agreed by voice vote to an amendment by Subcommittee Chairman Joe Knollenberg, R-Mich., that would have increased the cap on spending for private military housing by $500 million, bringing the total to $1.35 billion. The amendment also exempted the funds from being counted against the panel's spending allocation.

The Military Housing Privatization Initiative, instituted under the fiscal 1996 defense authorization law (PL 104-106), allowed private developers and property managers to build or renovate and manage many of the homes needed by service members and their families. The Defense Department provided loans, loan guarantees and other help to the developer; military families used their housing allowances and got other DoD assistance to pay the rent. As a result, the Pentagon was able to get more houses built faster because it did not have to pay as much up front. When Congress began the program, it limited the federal contribution to $850 million. (*1996 Almanac, p. 8-12*)

There was bipartisan support for increasing the cap, but the Congressional Budget Office (CBO) had ruled in 2003 that the long-term cost of any increase had to be scored in

Where the Money Goes

Military Construction Spending

(figures are in thousands of dollars of new budget authority)

	Fiscal 2004 Appropriation*	Fiscal 2005 Bush Request	House Passed	Senate Passed	Conference Report
GRAND TOTAL	$9,840,861	$9,553,375	$10,003,000	$10,003,000	$10,003,000**
MAIN COMPONENTS					
Military construction	$5,314,219	$4,824,977	$5,294,432	$5,345,384	$5,461,295
NATO infrastructure	161,300	165,800	165,800	165,800	160,800
Family housing	3,820,100	4,171,596	4,151,766	4,163,814	4,052,903
Base realignment and closure	370,427	246,116	246,116	246,116	246,116
General provisions	55,000	63,000	63,000	—	—

*Fiscal 2004 figures include supplemental spending (PL 108-106) and rescissions.

**Total does not include $14.5 billion in emergency disaster aid that was attached to the bill.

TABLE: House, Senate Appropriations committees

the first budget year. That meant CBO would treat the committee's $500 million increase as adding $1.2 billion to the bill — money that appropriators could get only by making cuts elsewhere.

"It would be outrageous and a morale-buster to put a freeze on the most important military housing program in our nation's history, especially during a war," said Chet Edwards of Texas, the top Democrat on the Military Construction Subcommittee. Appropriations Chairman C.W. Bill Young, R-Fla., called it "one of the best programs we've ever done."

In its report accompanying the bill, the committee said CBO's approach was "unmerited and exaggerates the financial risk to the federal government." The committee counted only the additional $500 million in fiscal 2005, and the administration supported the appropriators' approach. But CBO scored the long-term cost anyway.

House Floor Action

The House passed the bill, 420-1, on July 22, but the $500 million increase in the housing cap fell in the face of a challenge by Budget Chairman Nussle. He raised a point of order that the provision violated a House rule against legislating on an appropriations bill. (*House vote 417, p. H-136*)

The rule for floor debate could have protected the provision, but it did not. Edwards called the House's action a "slap in the face" to military families. Many members agreed with him, but not quite enough: The rule was adopted July 21, by a 212-211 vote. (*House vote 401, p. H-132*)

GOP leaders backed Nussle, but did so away from the microphones, leaving him as the lone target for critics. Nussle introduced a stand-alone bill (HR 4879) to eliminate the cap, and it quickly passed, 423-0, though his critics derided it as an inadequate "fig leaf." (*House vote 406, p. H-132*)

Senate Committee Action

The Senate Appropriations Committee approved its version of the bill (S 2674 — S Rept 108-309) by a vote of 29-0 on July 15. The measure was considered so uncomplicated that the Military Construction Subcommittee sent it directly to the full committee without holding a markup. Like the House version, the bill recommended $10 billion, including $5.3 billion for military construction and $4.2 billion for family housing.

The Senate bill was silent on the housing spending cap. Kay Bailey Hutchison, R-Texas, chairwoman of the Military Construction Subcommittee, said appropriators deferred to the Armed Services Committee, which planned to address the issue in conference on the defense authorization bill. "If the authorizing bill doesn't support raising the cap, I have the support of my committee to go along with the House on the appropriations bill," Hutchison said. However, the fact that she made that statement before the House dropped its provision created some uncertainty.

Senate Floor Action

The Senate passed the bill, 91-0, on Sept. 20, after inserting the text of its own measure. (*Senate vote 185, p. S-40*)

Before passage, the Senate adopted two amendments sponsored jointly by Hutchison and Dianne Feinstein, D-Calif., both by voice vote. The first required the Pentagon to assess the impact on military families if Congress should fail to lift the spending cap on the housing program. The White House's Office of Management and Budget had issued a statement the same day advocating lifting or eliminating the cap. The amendment ensured that the conference committee on the final bill could revisit the issue.

The second amendment provided $1.5 million for the Independent Overseas Basing Commission, created under the fiscal 2004 military construction law to assess overseas infrastructure needs. Feinstein said appropriators had dropped several proposals for overseas construction because they needed more information on the administration's plans, announced earlier in the year, to bring 60,000 to 70,000 troops home in the next decade. She expressed hope that the commission would provide details on the planned restructuring of U.S. forces in Europe and Korea.

Conference/Final Action

House and Senate conferees wrapped up their work on the military construction bill Oct. 8 as Congress was rushing headlong toward the election break. The House adopted the conference report (H Rept 108-773), 374-0, on Oct. 9, and

the Senate cleared the bill by voice vote Oct. 11. (*House vote 529, p. H-170*)

The conferees thought their biggest obstacle was removed Oct. 8, when negotiators on the defense authorization bill filed their conference report, including language eliminating the restriction on privatized housing. Differences in the military construction spending provisions already had been ironed out.

But the bill faced one more hurdle. Because the measure was ready to clear, Young decided to make it the vehicle for a package of disaster relief that lawmakers were determined to send to the White House before leaving town. The $14.5 billion relief package led to more wrangling on the bill.

The relief included $11.6 billion in emergency funds to help Florida and other states hit by a series of unusually deadly hurricanes. The other $2.8 billion was for farmers and ranchers who had suffered from drought and other natural disasters. But that money was taken from an agricultural conservation program championed by Tom Harkin, D-Iowa, prompting Harkin to delay final action on the military construction bill until Oct. 11. Harkin backed off when the Senate adopted by voice vote, a non-binding motion (S Res 465) urging conferees on one of the unfinished appropriations bills to restore the cuts. ◆

Bush Prevails on Cuba, Privatization

After several starts and stops, the fiscal 2005 Transportation-Treasury bill cleared Nov. 20 as part of the omnibus spending package negotiated in the lame-duck session. President Bush signed the omnibus into law Dec. 8 (HR 4818 — PL 108-447).

The bill provided $90.5 billion for the Transportation and Treasury departments, as well as the White House, Office of Personal Management (OPM), General Services Administration and several smaller agencies. The total, which does not count a 0.8 percent across-the-board cut in the omnibus, was virtually even with fiscal 2004 spending and about 2 percent more than Bush requested.

However, discretionary spending, the funds over which the appropriators had control, dropped to $25.9 billion, a 9 percent cut from fiscal 2004.

House appropriators initially approved an $89.8 billion bill, with $25.3 billion in discretionary funds. The House bill was dismantled on the floor as a result of turf wars between authorizers and appropriators, though at the time lawmakers knew the full committee version would be considered in conference. The Senate Appropriations Committee approved a version of the bill in September that totaled $90.8 billion, with $25.4 billion in discretionary funds. That measure did not make it to the Senate floor.

Instead, the bill was completed as part of the nine-bill omnibus. Republican leaders dumped bill provisions opposed by the White House, including a Senate proposal to halt enforcement of the ban on travel to Cuba and language from both versions of the bill that would have limited the administration's ability to privatize federal jobs. The White House failed, however, to strike a House ban on Canadian and Mexican trucks that do not comply with U.S. safety laws.

Highlights

The following are major components of the fiscal 2005 Transportation-Treasury law:

● **Highways.** Release of a record $34.7 billion from the Highway Trust Fund to pay for construction and repairs on the Interstate Highway system and other roads. The previous record was set by the fiscal 2004 law, which released $33.6 billion. The president requested 3 percent less. (*2003 Almanac, p. 2-74*)

● **Transit.** $7.7 billion for public mass transit programs, including $1.5 billion for new projects. The total was about 6 percent below both fiscal 2004 funding and Bush's request.

BoxScore 2005
Fiscal Year
Transportation-Treasury

Bill:
HR 4818 — PL 108-447

Legislative Action:

House passed HR 5025 (H Rept 108-671), 397-12, on Sept. 22.

Senate Appropriations Committee approved S 2806 (S Rept 108-342), 29-0, on Sept. 14.

House adopted the conference report on HR 4818 (H Rept 108-792), 344-51, on Nov. 20.

Senate cleared the bill, 65-30, on Nov. 20.

President signed Dec. 8.

● **FAA.** $13.6 billion for the Federal Aviation Administration (FAA), about 2 percent below the previous year's spending and Bush's request. The total included $3.5 billion for grants to airports and $7.8 billion for FAA operations.

● **Amtrak.** A $1.2 billion subsidy for Amtrak, about the same as in fiscal 2004 but 35 percent more than requested. Amtrak had requested $1.8 billion, but said it could "muddle through" on what it got. The bill also required the national passenger railroad to start repaying a $100 million federal loan within five years. (*Amtrak, p. 16-7*)

● **Treasury.** $11.2 billion, 1 percent above fiscal 2004 spending but 3 percent less than Bush sought. More than 90 percent of the funds — $10.3 billion — was for the IRS.

● **OPM.** $18.2 billion for the government's human resources agency, virtually all of it mandatory spending for federal employee retirement plans.

● **Executive Office of the President.** $770 million, slightly less than requested. For the fourth year, appropriators turned down Bush's request to consolidate White House funding into a single account.

Legislative Action

House Subcommittee Action

The House Appropriations Subcommittee on Transportation, Treasury and Independent Agencies approved a draft of the bill by voice vote July 15, after adding controversial language to restrict outsourcing of government jobs.

The draft called for $89.9 billion, about $1 billion more than Bush requested. Discretionary spending was cut 11 percent, to $25.4 billion. The overall total, however, remained essentially the same as in fiscal 2004 due to projected increases in mandatory spending — mainly on federal employee benefits — and larger withdrawals from the highway trust fund.

Major elements of the draft included:

● $34.6 billion in highway spending, nearly $1 billion more than Bush requested.

● $900 million for Amtrak, equal to Bush's request but half the amount that David L. Gunn, the passenger railroad's president and CEO, said Amtrak needed to continue safe operations. The draft required that the passenger rail service pay off a $100 million federal loan that had been deferred in the past and spend $500 million on Northeast Corridor and other capital expenses.

Where the Money Goes

Transportation-Treasury Spending

(figures are in thousands of dollars of new budget authority)

	Fiscal 2004 Appropriation	Fiscal 2005 Bush Request	House Passed*	Senate Panel Approved	Conference Report **
GRAND TOTAL*	$46,141,907	$43,748,430	$43,540,159	$44,052,003	$43,980,159
Total adjusted for scorekeeping**	$45,883,353	$43,969,721	$43,581,450	$43,700,450	$44,199,493
Limits on obligations and exempt obligations	($44,429,981)	($44,934,835)	($46,272,912)	($46,750,608)	($46,527,289)
MAIN COMPONENTS					
Federal Aviation Administration***	$10,500,046	$10,466,000	$10,293,000	$10,363,427	$10,395,927
Federal Highway Administration***	177,447	—	—	100,000	855,000
Federal Railroad Administration	1,446,664	1,088,421	1,082,027	1,437,074	1,443,444
Federal Transit Administration***	1,453,716	1,314,123	1,201,947	993,024	963,500
Department of the Treasury	11,100,446	11,610,415	11,247,519	11,184,146	11,248,086
Executive Office of the President	781,992	774,476	727,167	754,206	770,016
General Services Administration	645,219	242,775	1,825,057	97,432	96,732
Office of Personnel Management	17,511,730	18,519,841	18,221,508	18,219,150	18,214,050

* Includes items struck on the floor.

** Totals do not include a 0.8 percent across-the-board cut in discretionary spending.

*** Does not include money from trust funds, which are budgeted as limits on obligations.

**** Adjustments based on Congressional Budget Office criteria for determining discretionary spending; adjusted total is used to assess compliance with 302(b) allocations.

TABLE: House, Senate Appropriations committees

• $14 billion for the FAA, a 4 percent cut from fiscal 2004, including $3.5 billion for airport-improvement grants. The total also included $102 million for the Essential Air Service program, which provides subsidies to keep airlines flying into small airports; Bush requested $50 million.

• $7.2 billion for transit programs, about the same as the president's request. But New Starts, the Transportation Department mechanism for funding heavy and light rail and commuter buses, was slashed by 22 percent from fiscal 2004 to $1 billion.

• An extension of war risk insurance through 2005.

• Extension of an existing provision that effectively barred banks from getting into the real estate business.

During the markup, the committee:

• **Outsourcing.** Adopted by voice vote an amendment by Steny H. Hoyer, D-Md., to impose a governmentwide ban on contracting out certain government jobs unless the private contractor could demonstrate that it could perform the work at a savings of 10 percent or $10 million, whichever was less. Similar language in the fiscal 2004 bill triggered a White House veto threat and pushed the bill into the year-end omnibus, where the restriction was limited to jobs at the Interior and Defense departments. Subcommittee Chairman Ernest Istook, R-Okla., conceded that he did not have the votes to delete Hoyer's language and said he would wait until the bill reached the floor.

• **Mexican identification cards.** Adopted, 9-7, an amendment by John Culberson, R-Texas, to prohibit banks from accepting Mexican identification documents known as "matricula cards" as a valid form of identification. The cards, which Mexican consular offices issued by the thousands, included the holder's name, date and place of birth, U.S. address and photograph. They were widely used by immigrants, including those in the country illegal-

ly, to set up bank accounts, obtain mortgages and get other services.

House Committee Action

The House Appropriations Committee approved the bill (HR 5025 — H Rept 108-671) by voice vote July 22.

During the markup, the committee:

• Narrowly rejected, 25-26, an attempt by Ed Pastor, D-Ariz., to strike the ban on allowing banks to accept the Mexican identity cards.

• Approved, 42-16, a Hoyer amendment to give civilian government workers the same 3.5 percent cost-of-living raise their military counterparts were expected to get. Bush had proposed a 1.5 percent increase for civilian employees.

• Adopted by voice vote an amendment to prohibit the imposition of a 10 percent local match proposed by Bush for some airports in the Essential Air Service program.

• Rejected, 26-29, an amendment by Rosa DeLauro, D-Conn., to bar federal agencies from contracting with expatriate corporations.

House Floor Action

The House voted, 397-12, on Sept. 22 to pass a shell of the bill following a chaotic battle in which transportation authorizers and appropriators took turns killing whole sections of the measure. (*House vote 465, p. H-152*)

The meltdown occurred Sept. 14, after GOP leaders declined to choose sides in a long-running turf battle between Don Young, R-Alaska, who chaired the Transportation and Infrastructure Committee, and C.W. Bill Young, R-Fla., outgoing chairman of the Appropriations Committee. Instead, the leadership allowed a rule for floor debate that, unlike most such rules, left unauthorized appropriations in the bill open to challenge.

The spending was vulnerable because the 1998 surface transportation law (PL 105-178) had expired at the end of fiscal 2003. Unable to agree on a new highway bill, Congress had passed a series of short-term extensions of the 1998 law which did not provide for new spending or programs. (*Surface transportation, p. 16-3*)

In all, the House cut about $47 billion from accounts for federal highways, highway safety, mass transit, Amtrak and the Airport Improvement Program. Istook assured members that the funds would be restored in conference.

The authorizers vs. appropriators dispute went back at least to the 1998 law, known as TEA-21, which was pushed through Congress by Bud Shuster, R-Pa. (1973-2001), then-chairman of the Transportation and Infrastructure Committee. The law tied highway spending to gas tax revenues and put much of the annual spending on highway projects off-limits to the appropriators. Two years later, the 2000 FAA reauthorization (PL 106-181), known as AIR-21, created similar limits on aviation funding. (*1998 Almanac, p. 24-3; 2000 Almanac, p. 21-3*)

Before passing what remained of the bill, the House adopted a number of politically loaded amendments, though it was widely assumed that most of them would be dropped in conference.

● **Cuba.** The House added several provisions aimed at weakening sanctions against Cuba, despite a blunt White House warning that Bush would veto a bill that contained such language. However, Cuban-American lawmakers were pleased that Jeff Flake, R-Ariz., did not offer what had become an annual proposal to lift the broad U.S. ban on travel to Cuba. Flake said the fact that Florida, home to a powerful anti-Castro constituency, was a swing state in the upcoming presidential election made the topic too hot to handle. He vowed to resume his effort when "the electoral smoke clears."

During the debate on Cuba, the House:

● Adopted, 225-174, an amendment by Jim Davis, D-Fla., to prohibit use of funds in the bill to implement new Bush administration travel restrictions that allowed individuals to visit immediate relatives in Cuba only once every three years for a maximum of two consecutive weeks. (*House vote 460, p. H-150*)

● Adopted by voice vote a proposal by Barbara Lee, D-Calif., to lift a recently issued rule that sharply restricted educational travel to Cuba.

● Adopted by voice vote an amendment by Maxine Waters, D-Calif., to bar use of funds in the bill to implement any restrictions on private commercial sales of agricultural commodities, medicine or medical supplies to Cuba.

● Rejected, 188-225, an attempt by Charles B. Rangel, D-N.Y., to prohibit the use of funds to enforce the U.S. economic embargo on Cuba. (*House vote 461, p. H-150*)

● **Outsourcing.** The House adopted, 210-187, an amendment by Chris Van Hollen, D-Md., to prohibit the Office of Management and Budget (OMB) from enforcing a 2003 regulation allowing thousands of federal jobs to be contracted out to the private sector. This provision, too, drew a White House veto threat. (*House vote 457, p. H-150*)

● **Foreign trucks.** Also prompting a veto threat was an amendment by John W. Olver, D-Mass., adopted, 339-70, to bar the Transportation Department from implementing an administration plan to give Mexican and Canadian trucks operating in the United States a two-year exemption from meeting federal safety standards. (*House vote 462, p. H-150*)

● **Mexican identification cards.** Michael G. Oxley, R-Ohio, succeeded in striking the committee language aimed at preventing financial institutions from accepting Mexican matricula cards. The White House strongly opposed the provision, saying it would make it harder to enforce regulations of the 2002 anti-terrorism law known as the Patriot Act (PL 107-56) which required banks to do a better job of identifying customers. Oxley prevailed, 222-177. (*House vote 452, p. H-148*)

● **Other amendments.** On other issues, the House:

● Adopted, 404-8, an amendment by Charles W. Stenholm, D-Texas, to prevent the Treasury Department from dipping into various retirement trust funds to circumvent the statutory limit on the federal debt when Congress had not yet passed an increase. (*House vote 463, p. H-150*)

● Rejected, 189-211, another attempt by DeLauro to bar the use of the funds in the bill to enter into contracts with companies located in Bermuda, Barbados, the Cayman Islands, Antigua or Panama, parts of the Caribbean commonly used as tax havens. (*House vote 453, p. H-148*)

Senate Subcommittee, Committee Action

The Senate Appropriations Committee approved a $90.8 billion version of the bill (S 2806 — S Rept 108-342), 29-0, on Sept. 14. The Subcommittee on Transportation, Treasury and General Government had approved it by voice vote Sept. 9, after adding provisions to limit government outsourcing of jobs and restrict enforcement of the ban on travel to Cuba.

Major elements of the bill included:

● $1.2 billion for Amtrak — equal to its fiscal 2004 funding and $317 million more than the White House sought or than House appropriators recommended.

● $34.9 billion in highway spending, $259 million above the House committee bill and $1.3 billion more than requested.

● $7.8 billion for transit programs, including $1.5 billion in grants for New Starts.

● $13.9 billion for the FAA, including $3.5 billion for the Airport Improvement Program and $102 million for Essential Air Services.

● A 3.5 percent pay raise for federal civilian workers.

During the subcommittee markup, the appropriators:

● Adopted, 9-6, an amendment by Barbara A. Mikulski, D-Md., designed to block the administration from enforcing the 2003 rule on privatizing federal jobs.

● Agreed by voice vote to an amendment by Byron L. Dorgan, D-N.D., to prohibit the Treasury Department's Office of Foreign Assets Control from using funds in the bill to enforce the Cuba travel ban. Dorgan said the office was devoting most of its resources to enforcing the ban. "We ought to be tracking terrorists," he said.

Subcommittee Chairman Richard C. Shelby, R-Ala., accepted the language in the interest of moving the bill along, but warned that was likely to attract a "strenuous" veto threat from the president.

Conference/Final Action

When lawmakers returned to Washington in November to assemble the multi-bill omnibus, the Transportation-

Treasury bill was one of those seen as posing problems. But Bush's electoral victory and the larger GOP majorities being sent to both chambers in the 109th Congress gave Republican leaders the clout to remove most hurdles with relative ease. The House adopted the conference report on the omnibus (HR 4818 — H Rept 108-792), 344-51, on Nov. 20, and the Senate cleared the package, 65-30, later the same day. (*House vote 542, p. H-174; Senate vote 215, p. S-46*)

The final bill:

● **Cuba.** Dropped provisions from the House and Senate bills that would have weakened sanctions on Cuba.

● **Outsourcing.** Dropped language from the both bills that would have prevented the White House from enforcing its 2003 rule on privatizing federal jobs.

● **Amtrak.** Provided $1.2 billion for Amtrak, following the Senate's lead, and specified that at least $500 million go to capital grants as proposed by the House. The conference report required the passenger railroad to repay its $100 million loan in five equal installments over five years. It also required Amtrak to develop an operating and capital plan for fiscal 2005 before it could receive the funds in the bill.

● **Transit.** Leaned toward the Senate in providing $7.7 billion for mass transit, with $1.5 billion for New Starts.

● **Highways.** Stuck closer to the House in releasing $34.7 billion for federal-aid highways, $1.1 billion more than Bush's request. The Senate would have gone higher, providing $1.3 billion more than requested.

● **FAA.** Provided $14 billion for the FAA, $335 million less than requested. The House wanted $391 million more than Bush requested; the Senate proposed $418 million less than Bush wanted. Conferees included $3.5 billion for airport improvement grants, paid for in part with rescissions, and $102 million for the Essential Air Services, including $50 million in fees. They ruled out requiring matching funds.

● **Post Office.** Provided $507 million for biohazard detection efforts by the U.S. Post office as the Senate sought, but dropped a Senate plan to make the funds emergency spending not subject to regular budget rules.

● **Pay increase.** Included the 3.5 percent cost-of-living pay increase for civilian employees.

● **War risk insurance.** Extended war risk insurance through 2005, as recommended by both chambers.

● **Real estate.** Renewed an existing provision that effectively barred banks from getting into the real estate business, a provision that was in both bills.

● **Tax inspection.** Added a provision in conference that would have given the chairmen or designated staff of the House and Senate Appropriations committees access to information in tax returns. Under existing law, members and designated staff of the House Ways and Means, Senate Finance and Joint Taxation committees had such access. However, they were subject to criminal and civil penalties for improperly disclosing information — penalties that were not included in the omnibus. An outcry over the provision held up the omnibus temporarily. The delay ended when GOP leaders agreed to delete the provision in an enrolling resolution (H Con Res 528). The Senate adopted the resolution Nov. 20, and the House did so on Dec. 6. ◆

NASA Gets Help From Bush, DeLay

Stiff competition over funds among supporters of veterans' and space programs held up the fiscal 2005 spending bill for the departments of Veterans Affairs (VA) and Housing and Urban Development (HUD) until the end of the lame-duck session in November. Appropriators were able to finish the measure only by dipping into the funding for other bills as part of a year-end omnibus spending package. The VA-HUD bill cleared as part of the omnibus, which President Bush signed into law Dec. 8 (HR 4818 — PL 108-447).

"We were helped dramatically in the omnibus," said James T. Walsh, R-N.Y., chairman of the House VA-HUD Appropriations Subcommittee. "It would have been a very difficult bill to pass stand-alone."

The $133.2 billion fiscal 2005 bill funded its namesake departments, as well as NASA, the EPA, the National Science Foundation (NSF), the Corporation for National and Community Service, and scores of smaller offices. Discretionary spending — the portion that was under the control of the appropriators — amounted to $93.9 billion. That was 3 percent above fiscal 2004 spending and 2 percent more than Bush requested. The totals do not include a 0.8 percent across-the-board discretionary spending cut enacted as part of the omnibus.

The VA-HUD bill was an annual exercise in controversy, because it required members to balance veterans' health care, the most politically attractive issue, against programs such as space flight, rent vouchers and basic scientific research that often came without built-in constituencies.

In this case, Bush and House Majority Leader Tom DeLay, R-Texas, fought vigorously for a large increase in NASA's budget. The president wanted to re-orient the agency away from the space shuttle and the International Space Station, and toward travel to the moon and Mars. DeLay's suburban Houston district was home to many employees of the nearby Lyndon B. Johnson Space Center.

Faced with a tight discretionary spending allocation, House appropriators in July decided to cut back on NASA's budget to make room for other spending. Because of the NASA cuts, DeLay refused to bring the bill to the House floor. Senate appropriators tried to solve the problem in September by adding money but classifying some of it as "emergency" funds that did not count against the allocation. The White House rejected that idea, too.

The stalemate continued until Congress reconvened in November. After winning re-election by more than 3 million votes, Bush was in a position to demand — and receive

BoxScore 2005
VA-HUD — Fiscal Year

Bill:
HR 4818 — PL 108-447

Legislative Action:

House Appropriations Committee approved HR 5041 (H Rept 108-674) by voice vote July 22.

Senate Appropriations Committee approved S 2825 (S Rept 108-353), 29-0, on Sept. 21.

House adopted the conference report on HR 4818 (H Rept 108-792), 344-51, on Nov. 20.

Senate cleared the bill, 65-30, on Nov. 20.

President signed Dec. 8.

— special treatment for his priorities. The final bill provided $16.2 billion for NASA, just $44 million shy of what the president had requested. The increase was at the expense of most other agencies in the VA-HUD bill, except for the Veterans Health Administration, which got part of its funds from the across-the-board cut in all non-security discretionary spending.

Highlights

Following are major components of the fiscal 2005 VA-HUD spending bill:

● **Veterans.** $66 billion, a 7 percent increase over fiscal 2004 funding and 2 percent more than Bush sought. About $35.1 billion of the VA funding was mandatory spending, mainly for veterans' compensation and pensions.

The bill included $28.3 billion — 5.5 percent more than was spent in fiscal 2004 and 4 percent more than Bush sought — for the Veterans Health Administration, which provided health care through veterans' hospitals, outpatient clinics and other facilities. An additional $2 billion in fees expected in fiscal 2005 brought total veterans' health care funding to $30.3 billion.

● **HUD.** $32 billion, a 3 percent increase over fiscal 2004 funding, although all of the increase and more went to the Section 8 rent-subsidy program. Most other HUD programs received cutbacks. As it had in the past, Congress ignored Bush's requests to turn Section 8 subsidies into a block grant or eliminate the HOPE VI program for revitalizing public housing. A one-time savings of nearly $1 billion was achieved by requiring all public housing communities to start their fiscal year on Jan. 1.

● **NASA.** $16.2 billion, a 5 percent increase over fiscal 2004 and virtually the same as Bush requested.

● **EPA.** $8.1 billion, 4 percent more than Bush requested but still 3 percent below fiscal 2004 spending.

● **NSF.** $5.5 billion, 1 percent below fiscal 2004 spending and 4 percent less than Bush requested.

● **Corporation for National and Community Service.** $578 million, including $290 million for AmeriCorps. The total was about the same as fiscal 2004 funding but 10 percent less than Bush wanted.

Legislative Action

House Subcommittee, Committee Action

The House Appropriations Committee approved a $132.2 billion VA-HUD bill (HR 4818 — H Rept 108-674),

Where the Money Goes

VA-HUD Spending

(figures are in thousands of dollars of new budget authority)

	Fiscal 2004 Appropriation	Fiscal 2005 Bush Request	House Panel Approved	Senate Panel Approved	Conference Report *
GRAND TOTAL	**$127,683,430**	**$131,436,824**	**$132,238,084**	**$134,238,029**	**$133,169,084**
Total adjusted for scorekeeping**	**$123,480,430**	**$127,235,824**	**$128,037,084**	**$128,037,029**	**$128,968,084**
MAIN COMPONENTS					
Department of Veterans Affairs	$61,845,163	$64,761,609	$65,961,609	$66,057,412	$65,961,589
Veterans Health Administration	26,844,296	27,133,370	28,333,370	28,354,193	28,328,370
Department of Housing and Urban Development	31,202,259	31,519,359	32,579,049	32,217,763	32,040,080
Public and Indian Housing	30,537,857	29,571,400	30,993,800	31,020,045	30,261,000
Environmental Protection Agency	8,365,817	7,789,245	7,753,069	8,500,408	8,088,189
Hazardous Substance Superfund	1,257,537	1,381,416	1,257,537	1,381,416	1,257,537
State and Tribal Assistance Grants	2,705,543	1,979,500	2,197,400	2,724,000	2,458,425
NASA	15,378,032	16,244,000	15,149,369	16,379,200	16,200,000
National Science Foundation	5,577,845	5,744,690	5,466,960	5,747,000	5,516,960
Corporation for National and Community Service	581,027	642,232	572,000	590,061	577,844

* Totals do not reflect a 0.8 percent across-the-board cut in discretionary spending.

** Adjustments based on Congressional Budget Office criteria for determining discretionary spending; the adjusted total is used to assess compliance with 302(b) allocations.

TABLE: House, Senate Appropriations committees

including $92.9 billion in discretionary spending, by voice vote July 22. The committee proposed increases for veterans' health care and housing while cutting space, science and environmental programs. The VA-HUD subcommittee had approved the measure without amendment two days earlier, also by voice vote.

The only substantive amendment added a package of about 1,230 earmarks for member projects. "We dealt with the president's priorities in the bill; now we'll deal with yours," Subcommittee Chairman Walsh told appropriators as he introduced his amendment. The earmarks did not add money; they only told agencies how to spend what otherwise would have been undirected funds.

The attempt to cut NASA funding brought a swift response from DeLay, who said he would not bring the bill to the House floor unless it provided significantly more for the space agency. A letter from White House Budget Director Joshua B. Bolten to Appropriations Chairman C.W. Bill Young, R-Fla., warned of a veto unless NASA and other presidential priorities got more money.

As approved by the committee, the bill included:

● **NASA.** $15.1 billion, a 1.5 percent reduction from fiscal 2004 and $1.1 billion, or 7 percent, less than Bush requested. The cuts were mainly in programs related to the president's 30-year plan to put humans on the moon and Mars. The appropriators were apologetic in their committee report, saying that if more money became available, they could increase NASA funding. NASA said the proposed cut would jeopardize not only the president's proposed missions to the moon and Mars but also the space shuttle's return to flight following the February 2003 *Columbia* disaster.

● **Veterans.** $66 billion for Veterans Affairs, including $28.3 billion for veterans' health care. The appropriators rejected a proposal by Bush to increase co-payments for pre-

scription drugs and other services and institute an annual enrollment fee for some veterans.

The committee rejected, 28-35, an attempt by Democrats to increase funds for veterans' health care by $1.5 billion, offset by repealing certain tax cuts for people making more than $1 million a year. Walsh said the amendment would fall to a budget point of order on the House floor if it was retained.

● **HUD.** $32.6 billion, $1.1 billion more than Bush requested. The increase was for Section 8 rent vouchers; the committee recommended $20 billion, compared with $18.5 billion in Bush's budget, and rejected the administration proposal to turn the program into block grants administered by local governments. Advocates for low-income housing and congressional allies from both parties warned that cuts in Section 8 could leave thousands of families homeless. To allow for the Section 8 increase, Walsh said, the committee cut remaining HUD programs by an average of about 4 percent.

● **EPA.** $7.8 billion, 7 percent below fiscal 2004 funding and $36 million less than Bush proposed. As Bush asked, the cuts were mainly to an account that made grants and loans to states and Indian tribes for water pollution control projects. The EPA's Clean Water State Revolving Fund was cut from $1.4 billion in 2004 to $850 million under the bill.

● **NSF.** $5.5 billion in 2005, a 2 percent cut from fiscal 2004 spending. Many science interest groups and some appropriators said research efforts crucial to the U.S. economy would be hurt.

Senate Committee Action

The Senate Appropriations Committee approved a $134.2 billion version of the bill (S 2825 — S Rept 108-353) by a vote of 29-0 on Sept. 21. The panel's VA-HUD Subcommittee had forwarded a draft without a formal vote Sept. 9.

Like their House counterparts, the appropriators had a $92.9 billion limit on discretionary funds, but they added an extra $2 billion to the bill by designating it as "emergency spending" not subject to the limits. That allowed them to increase funding for veterans' health and housing, as well as for other accounts including NASA and the EPA.

Senate appropriators further complicated the bill's prospects by adding a rider to extend a subsidy for milk production that was due to expire in 2005. The amendment, by Herb Kohl, D-Wis., was adopted 18-5. It proposed to extend the deadline for the Milk Income Loss Contract program by two years and adjust the subsidy so that it would take effect when milk prices dropped below $17.10 per hundredweight, up from $16.94 under existing law. Some Western senators complained that the proposal would limit milk production so that large dairies — more common in the West — that exceeded the cap would not get subsidies for all of their milk. Dianne Feinstein, D-Calif., cited Congressional Budget Office estimates showing the amendment would cost $2.4 billion.

These were the main components of the Senate bill:
- **Veterans.** $66.1 billion for the VA, of which $28.4 billion was for the Veterans Health Administration. The totals were about the same as in the House bill, except that $1.2 billion in the Senate version was labeled as emergency spending. Christopher S. Bond, R-Mo., chairman of the VA-HUD Subcommittee, said use of emergency funds for veterans' health care was justified by "unprecedented and unanticipated demand by veterans seeking medical services" and the surge of returning veterans from conflicts in Iraq and Afghanistan
- **HUD.** $32.2 billion, about $360 million less than in the House bill. The total included $20.8 billion for Section 8 vouchers, about $2.3 billion more than requested. Like the House, Senate appropriators rejected Bush's block grant proposal. The committee freed up about $1 billion by directing public housing authorities to begin their fiscal years on Jan. 1, which meant the fiscal 2005 bill would have to fund housing authorities only through December 2005.
- **NASA.** $16.4 billion for the space agency, $1 billion above the fiscal 2004 level and $1.2 billion more than in the House bill. The total included $800 million in emergency spending proposed by Barbara A. Mikulski, D-Md., and Kay Bailey Hutchison, R-Texas, and adopted by voice vote. The two senators said the additional money was needed to return the space shuttle to flight and repair the Hubble telescope, which NASA said was likely to fail after 2008 without a servicing mission.
- **EPA.** $8.5 billion, $711 million more than Bush requested and $747 million more than the House recommended. The extra funds allowed Senate appropriators to bring grants for states and Indian tribes to $2.7 billion, a 38 percent increase over Bush's budget.
- **NSF.** $5.7 billion, $280 million more than in the House bill.

Conference/Final Action

Despite pressure to clear out all of the fiscal 2005 spending bills after the Nov. 2 elections, appropriators remained stalemated over the funding levels for NASA and veterans. The impasse was broken only after Senate Appropriations Chairman Ted Stevens, R-Alaska, won White House approval to increase total discretionary spending, and Republican leaders agreed on a series of cuts and accounting maneuvers in the overall omnibus package to pay for the increases.

The House adopted the conference report on the omnibus (HR 4818 — H Rept 108-792) by a vote of 344-51 on Nov. 20; the Senate cleared the bill, 65-30, later the same day. (*House vote 542, p. H-174; Senate vote 215, p. S-46*)

Walsh credited DeLay for getting the extra NASA funds and for boosting the discretionary spending total for VA-HUD from the $92.9 billion cap that had been set in the spring to $93.9 billion in the final bill.
- **NASA.** Conferees initially agreed to $15.9 billion for NASA, 3 percent above the fiscal 2004 amount but still $344 million short of Bush's request. DeLay intervened at the last minute, instructing them in no uncertain terms to add another $300 million. That brought the total to $16.2 billion, just $44 million less than requested. The increased funding restored some of the cuts that appropriators had made to programs related to Bush's goals for travel to the moon and Mars.

The conferees also gave NASA "unrestrained" authority to transfer money within its accounts — a rare exception for any agency. The conference report said NASA needed such flexibility to move to a new accounting method.
- **Veterans.** Despite the increase for NASA, the negotiators managed to include $28.3 billion for veterans' health care — $1.2 billion more than the president had requested — without the emergency designation used by the Senate. The extra costs for both NASA and veterans' health were offset by reductions for other agencies in the VA-HUD bill, and by using part of the cushion created in the omnibus through the 0.8 percent across-the-board cut and other maneuvers.
- **HUD.** Although the department as a whole did relatively well — getting $32 billion, an increase of $838 million or 2 percent over fiscal 2004 — most individual agencies were cut. The one big winner was the Section 8 rental subsidy program, which received $20.2 billion, an increase of $969 million or 5 percent over fiscal 2004.

Funding was cut by about 4 percent for a number of accounts, including those for public housing construction, community development, and housing programs serving groups such as the elderly and people with disabilities. The HOME investment partnership program was cut by 5 percent. Smaller programs were also cut, including block grants for American Indian housing, down 4 percent; housing opportunities for people with AIDS, down 3 percent and programs for the homeless, down 1 percent.

Conferees provided $144 million for the HOPE VI program, created to rebuild run-down public housing. Bush recommended eliminating the program, but it was popular with local officials.
- **EPA.** Conferees roughly split the difference between the two chambers, providing $8.1 billion for the EPA, still 3 percent below fiscal 2004 spending. State and tribal assistance grants received $3.6 billion, more than Bush requested but 7 percent less than in the previous year. Walsh said the cutback "won't make a dramatic difference if we do it just once," because a revolving loan program constitutes the largest part of the account. "But at some point," he added,

"the rubber meets the road, and people won't be able to do projects around the country."

● **NSF.** The $5.5 billion in the final bill was closer to the House version than to either Bush's budget or the Senate version, both of which called for a 3 percent increase in the agency's funding to $5.7 billion.

● **Corporation for National and Community Service.** The final bill provided $578 million, about $6 million more than in the House bill and $12 million less than the Senate recommended. Although the White House had warned that Bush might veto a stand-alone VA-HUD bill that did not include more money for AmeriCorps, the dominant program under the service agency, it was not an issue once the entire omnibus was at stake. Funding in the final bill was enough to support 70,000 volunteers, 5,000 fewer than Bush wanted. ◆

$25 Billion for Iraq, Afghanistan Wars

Congress approved $25 billion in emergency spending for operations in Iraq and Afghanistan as part of the fiscal 2005 defense appropriations bill signed into law Aug. 5 (PL 108-287). The supplemental funds were available upon enactment. (*Defense, p. 2-12*)

The Bush administration requested the funds May 12, after insisting for months that no additional money would be needed until after the November election. The wars in Iraq and Afghanistan had been funded entirely through supplemental appropriations, rather than through the annual Defense Department spending bill. The last infusion of money had come from a huge, $87.5 billion bill (PL 108-106) cleared Nov. 6, 2003. (*2003 Almanac, p. 2-83*)

Despite repeated assurances from the Pentagon, lawmakers were not convinced that those funds would be enough to last until 2005. Democrats complained that President Bush was trying to hide the war's hefty cost from voters. Defense-minded Republicans expressed concern that Bush's timetable would force the Pentagon to take money from other defense accounts to pay for the war.

Then in May, with stepped up fighting in Iraq, the White House shifted its position. Bush announced May 5 that he would seek a $25 billion "contingency reserve fund" for fiscal 2005, to be followed by a full fiscal 2005 request "when we can better estimate precise costs."

Bush's request consisted of $20 billion for operations and maintenance for the various military branches and $5 billion for unspecified activities, with virtually unlimited authority for Defense Secretary Donald H. Rumsfeld to "transfer the funds provided herein to any appropriation or fund" within the Pentagon budget.

The debate in Congress centered on the questions of how much to provide, whether the funds would be needed before the end of fiscal 2004, and the degree of flexibility to give the president in spending the money.

At first, House appropriators and authorizers were more inclined than their Senate counterparts to restrict the president's latitude in spending the money, but senators ultimately agreed to keep a tight rein on the funds. Despite Pentagon protests that the funds would not be needed before October, Congress made the money available upon enactment of the bill in August. Between then and Oct. 1, the Defense Department ended up obligating about $2 billion from the $25 billion total.

Congress included authorization for the funds in the fiscal 2005 defense authorization bill, enacted Oct. 28 (PL 108-375). (*Defense authorization, p. 6-3*)

The $25 billion brought to more than $200 billion the amount Congress had appropriated since Sept. 11, 2001, for the wars in Iraq and Afghanistan and enhanced security at military facilities.

Highlights

The following are highlights of the emergency supplemental:
- $1.25 billion for additional military personnel costs stemming from the international war on terrorism.
- $683 million for the Defense Health Program, including costs associated with improving medical readiness for Ready Reserve members and their families.
- $20.2 billion for operations and maintenance.
- $1.38 billion for procurement, including equipment for Guard and Reserve units and kits to upgrade the armor on equipment being used in Iraq.
- Authority to transfer up to $1.5 billion among accounts, following approval by the congressional defense committees.
- An increase of $700 million in the amount of fiscal year 2004 funds that could be transferred, for a total of $2.8 billion.

Legislative Action

House Action

The House Appropriations Committee included the $25 billion in its version of the defense bill approved by voice vote June 16. The House passed the bill, 403-17, on June 22. (*House vote 284, p. H-96*)

The bill divided the supplemental money into 22 specific accounts, allowing the president to transfer only $1 billion among accounts with the prior approval of the House and Senate Defense Appropriations subcommittees. "They would have preferred $25 billion in a pool that was a pretty fluid pool," said Jerry Lewis, R-Calif., who was serving his final year as chairman of the Defense Subcommittee. "We have distributed that $25 billion package in a way that we think reflects the needs out there."

The measure allowed for the Defense Department to tap into the money as soon as the bill was signed. While Defense Department officials continued to insist they could wait until Oct. 1, House Appropriations Chairman C.W. Bill Young, R-Fla., and other appropriators were worried the money could be needed before that. Young said the military was burning through the last war supplemental so fast that it might need as much as $10 billion more to make it through fiscal 2004.

An expected showdown over the size of the war fund was averted in the committee after top Democrat David R. Obey of Wisconsin decided not to offer an amendment he had drawn up that would have added another $50 billion. Democrats argued that the fund should reflect the true costs of war operations in fiscal 2005. "The public gets the facts on the installment plan," Obey complained.

But Obey was forced to back down in the face of strong opposition from Republicans and some Democrats, including John P. Murtha of Pennsylvania, the ranking member on the Defense Appropriations Subcommittee, who backed Bush's plan to wait until early 2005 to seek additional war funding.

Obey instead offered an amendment to require the administration to submit a report to Congress by Oct. 1 esti-

mating the costs of war and reconstruction in Iraq and Afghanistan for the next six budget cycles, from fiscal 2006 through fiscal 2011. The president could waive the requirement if he certified in writing that the estimates could not be provided because of national security concerns. The amendment was adopted by voice vote after Lewis said he did not oppose it.

A Pentagon spokeswoman said that the Defense secretary "has repeatedly emphasized that we do not have credible information to accurately project the costs of war or reconstruction in fiscal 2005, much less beyond fiscal 2006."

Senate Action

A sense of urgency over the war funds enabled Senate Appropriations Chairman Ted Stevens, R-Alaska, to whisk the defense bill through committee and floor action in a matter of three days. The Senate passed the measure, 98-0 on June 24. (*Senate vote 149, p. S-32*)

Like the House version, it made the supplemental funds available upon enactment. However, the Senate bill would have put the funds in the Iraq Freedom Fund, created in 2003 (PL 108-11), and required a separate presidential emergency request to spend the money as well as a five-day prior notification to transfer the funds from the Freedom Fund.

The Senate voted, 89-9, June 24 to add language by Robert C. Byrd, D-W.Va., expressing the sense of the Senate that Bush should include future requests for war funding in his regular defense budget. (*Senate vote 147, p. S-32*)

Final Action

Eager to depart for the August recess, the Senate adopted the conference report on the defense appropriations bill by a vote of 96-0 on July 22, pending adoption by the other chamber. That came a little more than an hour later on a 410-12 vote. (*Senate vote 163, p. S-35; House vote 418, p. H-136*) ◆

Mother Nature Exacts Heavy Toll

Responding to a string of devastating hurricanes in Florida, Congress cleared two emergency supplemental spending bills before the November elections. The second of the measures also included drought relief for farmers and ranchers.

After Hurricane Charley swept through Florida in late August, Congress quickly cleared a $2 billion stand-alone bill that was signed into law Sept. 8 (HR 5005 — PL 108-103).

Less than five weeks later — with Florida reeling from three more hurricanes and farm-state lawmakers pressing for drought aid in advance of the election — Congress agreed to a $14.5 billion emergency aid package. The supplemental funds cleared as part of the fiscal 2005 military construction appropriations bill, which was signed into law Oct. 13 (HR 4837 — PL 108-324).

Round One: Hurricane Charley

Hurricane Charley, the first of four such storms to pound Florida, struck on Aug. 13. On Sept. 6, President Bush sent Congress a formal request for $2 billion to replenish the coffers of the Federal Emergency Management Agency (FEMA). The next day, as lawmakers returned to the Capitol from their summer recess, House Appropriations Chairman C.W. Bill Young, a Florida Republican, introduced the bill (HR 5005).

With FEMA expected to run out of money the next day, the measure aiding a swing state in the fall presidential race was on its way to the White House by nightfall. The House passed the bill by voice vote Sept. 7. The Senate had earlier "deemed" the bill passed, also by voice vote, so once the Senate received it from the House, it was automatically cleared for the president.

Round Two: More Hurricanes, Drought

As hurricanes Frances, Ivan and Jeanne bore down on Florida and disaster costs continued to spiral, the White House requested an additional $3.1 billion on Sept. 14 and $7.1 billion more Sept. 27.

While lawmakers did not begrudge Florida the emergency funding, a must-pass supplemental spending bill so close to the election was an irresistible target for members trying to get other pre-election spending priorities into law.

GOP leaders planned to attach the hurricane aid to the fiscal 2005 Homeland Security spending bill (HR 4567), but before they could act, farm-state senators added $3 billion in aid for drought-stricken farmers and ranchers to the measure. Senate Minority Leader Tom Daschle, who was in a tight re-election battle in South Dakota against Republican former

BoxScore 2004
Disaster Supplementals — Fiscal Year

Bills:
HR 5005 — PL 108-303;
HR 4837 — PL 108-324

Legislative Action:
House passed HR 5005 by voice vote, Sept. 7.
Senate cleared HR 5005 by voice vote, Sept. 7.
President signed Sept. 8.

Senate passed HR 4567, 93-0, on Sept. 14.
House adopted the conference report on HR 4837 (H Rept 108-773), 374-0, on Oct. 9.
Senate cleared the bill by voice vote Oct. 11.
President signed Oct. 13.

Rep. John Thune (1997-2003), led the group of farm-state Democrats who argued farmers and ranchers in Western states deserved help just as much as did storm-battered Floridians. (*Homeland Security, p. 2-26*)

The White House issued a plea for Congress to keep the supplemental focused on hurricane relief. But Majority Leader Bill Frist, R-Tenn., concluded that supporters of the drought aid, including Midwest Republicans, would be able to muster the 60 votes needed to waive a point of order, so he allowed the amendment to go through by voice vote Sept. 14.

Once the Homeland Security bill reached conference, it was bogged down with other add-ons. With GOP leaders anxious to unravel the mess and send lawmakers home and onto the campaign trail, Young decided instead to attach both the disaster assistance and the drought aid to the military construction bill, which was completed but was still in conference. (*Military construction, p. 2-40*)

By Oct. 8, Young had persuaded the White House to request another $1.6 billion in hurricane relief for his home state. The final disaster aid package included $11.6 billion in emergency funds for hurricane victims and $2.8 billion for farmers and ranchers who had suffered crop losses in 2003 or 2004 from drought, plus agricultural producers, primarily in Florida and surrounding areas, hurt by the hurricanes. The emergency hurricane funding did not count against the fiscal 2005 budget cap. To satisfy House conservatives who insisted that the drought package be offset by cuts to other programs, GOP appropriators included reductions to the Conservation Security Program created in the 2002 farm bill (PL 107-171) at the behest of Sen. Tom Harkin, D-Iowa.

The House adopted the conference report (H Rept 108-773) on the military construction bill, including the supplemental funding, 374-0, on Oct. 9. But Harkin was incensed at the cuts in the conservation program, and he delayed final Senate action until Oct. 11. (*House vote 529, p. H-170*)

Harkin relented after the Senate adopted by voice vote a non-binding motion (S Res 465) to instruct conferees on either the agriculture spending bill (HR 4766) or the year-end omnibus to restore the cuts. At his request, the Senate adopted by voice vote a second resolution (S Con Res 144) directing that the cuts in the disaster aid conference report be stricken and the drought money be treated as emergency funding, The vote was symbolic; the House did not take up the resolution. The Senate cleared the military construction bill by voice vote. Oct. 11, and Bush signed it into law. ◆

Chapter 3

BANKING & FINANCIAL SERVICES

Fannie, Freddie Overhaul Dies

Legislation to overhaul the regulation of Fannie Mae and Freddie Mac died at the end of the session, the victim of partisan tensions, lobbying clout and questions about how to effectively regulate the two mortgage finance giants. The Senate Banking, Housing and Urban Affairs Committee approved a bill in April, but the House took no action. White House objections led to the canceling of a House markup in October 2003.

The drive to strengthen regulation of Fannie Mae and Freddie Mac was set in motion by an accounting scandal at Freddie Mac in 2003 that required a $5 billion earnings restatement and led to the ouster of top executives. The scandal and the rapid growth of both institutions raised new concerns about their stability and the potential impact on both the housing industry and the financial markets if either of them should fail.

Between them, the two companies owned or guaranteed almost half the nation's $8.3 trillion in existing residential mortgages. Although they had long been public corporations, both were originally set up by Congress as government-sponsored enterprises (GSEs). That status allowed them to borrow in financial markets at rates almost as low as those available to the U.S. Treasury. Each also benefited from an unused $2.25 billion line of credit with the U.S. Treasury.

Fannie and Freddie bought mortgages from banks and other lenders, freeing up cash for new home loans at lower rates than might otherwise be available. They bundled the mortgages together and sold the pooled loans, called mortgage-backed securities, to investors. To hedge against potential losses, Fannie and Freddie also bought and sold complex, unregulated financial instruments called derivatives.

Given the history and size of the institutions, investors almost universally expected that the federal government would step in if either were about to fail, a possibility that no one in Congress wanted to entertain.

The existing regulator — the Office of Federal Housing Enterprise Oversight (OFHEO) located in the Department of Housing and Urban Development (HUD) — was a tiny agency that was not equipped to rein in the two financial behemoths. Just days before the 2003 accounting scandal broke, for example, the OFHEO issued a rosy report about corporate governance at both companies.

In testimony before the Senate Banking Committee on Feb. 24, Federal Reserve Board Chairman Alan Greenspan said Fannie and Freddie had grown so large that the safety of the entire housing finance system depended upon their risk managers doing "everything just right." He said Congress should create a new regulator "with a free hand to set appropriate capital standards," and that the legislation should also rein in the size and composition of the companies' investment portfolios. Greenspan said the GSEs should focus on mortgage-backed securities, not complex, high-risk financial instruments.

BoxScore

Bill:

S 1508

Legislative Action:

Senate Banking Committee approved S 1508, 12-9, April 1.

cial instruments.

There was, however, no agreement on what sort of structure should replace the OFHEO or where it should be housed. Any new regulator had to be able to effectively monitor the companies' complicated financial dealings, while also knowing something about housing.

Any attempt to tighten regulation also ran up against the vigorous opposition of Fannie and Freddie, backed by a legendary lobbying operation. The companies said that stricter regulation would harm their ability to expand home ownership. Based on 2003 registration forms filed with the Senate, the two companies employed more than 100 lobbyists between them and spent almost $25 million on lobbying in 2003. Their lobbying operation was filled with former lawmakers, congressional relatives and former administration officials. They also regularly sponsored events in the home districts of legislators.

"We're swimming in a river with some of the most powerful lobbyists that Washington has ever seen," said Richard C. Shelby, R-Ala., who chaired the Senate Banking Committee.

Michael G. Oxley, R-Ohio, chairman of the House Financial Services Committee, had negotiated a bill in 2003 that proposed to divide oversight of Fannie and Freddie between HUD and a new Treasury Department agency. The White House derailed the bill just hours before a scheduled markup in October 2003, saying the measure would create a regulator with too little power to do its job. (*2003 Almanac, p. 4-8*)

Legislative Action

Senate Committee Action

The Senate Banking Committee approved Shelby's bill (S 1508) in a 12-9 vote on April 1. The measure proposed a new safety and soundness regulator that could raise minimum capital requirements for the two enterprises above the 2.5 percent limit dictated by existing law. The only Democrat to vote in favor of the bill was Sen. Zell Miller of Georgia, who often broke ranks with his party.

The bill proposed to:

• Abolish the OFHEO and replace it with a new regulator, the Federal Housing Enterprise Supervisory Agency. The new agency would oversee Fannie and Freddie as well as the 12 federal home loan banks that were overseen by the Federal Housing Finance Board, created in the wake of the savings and loan scandal of the late 1980s.

• Establish an executive director who would sit on a board that would include the heads of HUD, the Treasury Department, and the Securities and Exchange Commission.

The structure was modeled after agencies such as the Pension Benefit Guaranty Corporation.

• Give the agency flexibility to adjust risk-based capital standards, designed to take into account the amount of risk inherent in the practices of Fannie and Freddie, when determining how much cash the two should set aside as protection against unforeseen shocks.

• Empower the agency to appoint a receiver to liquidate assets in the unlikely event that either Fannie or Freddie became unable to make payments on their debts. The OFHEO had only more limited conservatorship powers.

The establishment of a receiver was seen as a remote possibility because Fannie Mae and Freddie Mac's senior debt was rated safer than almost any other in the market. But the receivership provision was the most controversial element in Shelby's bill. Critics said it would undermine the long-held market perception that the federal government would bail out the two GSEs if they were unable to meet their financial obligations.

Greenspan supported a receivership for the same reasons. He said it would make it easier for other companies to compete in the secondary mortgage market.

Moody's Investors Service had said receivership powers would not cause it to lower its ratings on Fannie Mae or Freddie Mac's debt. But Democrats worried that receivership could wind up leading to higher mortgage rates as investors demanded, in essence, an insurance policy against the possibility that other creditors could take precedence over bondholders.

During the markup, the committee:

• Adopted by voice vote a compromise amendment by Robert F. Bennett, R-Utah, to give Congress the right to reject the appointment of a receiver. That change led Bennett and other Republicans to vote for the bill.

• Rejected, 9-12, an amendment by Paul S. Sarbanes, D-Md., that included a provision to create a five-person commission to regulate Fannie Mae and Freddie Mac. The proposal was intended partly to protect against the chance that the executive director would simply be the agent of any president who placed more emphasis on finance than on housing. The amendment also included language to ensure that minimum capital requirements were raised only in the face of concern about unsafe or unsound practices. Democrats opposed giving the new regulator what they said was too much power to increase capital requirements without adequately considering the effect on housing markets.

• Adopted by voice vote a Democratic amendment to require Fannie and Freddie to invest more in affordable housing. The companies would be required to deposit about $450 million into a fund to be used for grants and subsidies aimed at providing rental housing to low-income families. They would have to stop buying mortgages that included language that forced customers to take complaints to arbitration. Fannie Mae already had adopted such a policy.

For many Democrats, the problem with Fannie and Freddie was not that they posed big risks to the nation's financial system but that they did not do enough to help homebuyers who made less than the national median income.

Postscript

The 2003 scandal at Freddie Mac resulted in an investigation into accounting practices at the sister company, Fannie Mae. On Sept. 22, 2004, the OFHEO released an interim report stating that Fannie Mae willfully misapplied certain accounting rules and used a "cookie jar" reserve to help guarantee stable earnings growth. The report also alleged that the firm deferred certain expenses in 1998 so the company's earnings results would trigger executives' bonus targets.

On Dec. 15, the Securities and Exchange Commission released a statement by its chief accountant that said Fannie Mae's accounting practices from 2001 to mid-2004 "did not comply in material respects" with generally accepted accounting practices. The statement advised Fannie to restate its financial results for those four years, a change the company had said could cause it to record as much as $9 billion in unreported losses. The accounting missteps related to derivatives and certain loan transactions.

A week later, on Dec. 21, Fannie Mae's board announced the departure of two top executives, Chairman and CEO Franklin D. Raines and Vice Chairman and CFO J. Timothy Howard.

Shelby applauded the executive shapeup, as did Richard H. Baker, R-La., a longtime critic of Fannie and Freddie and chairman of a House Financial Services subcommittee. But both lawmakers said the executives' departures did not change the need for comprehensive regulations, which they vowed to pursue in the 109th Congress. ◆

Stock Option Accountability

In a rebuff to regulators, the House voted by a wide margin to block plans for a new accounting rule that would require companies to count employee stock options as expenses. The Senate Banking, Housing and Urban Affairs Committee refused to act on a companion bill, and the legislation died at the end of the session.

The Financial Accounting Standards Board (FASB) rule required companies to value employee stock options and deduct the expense from company earnings. That had the potential of forcing many companies to report losses rather than profits on their income statements. The rule took effect at the end of 2004, but the FASB voted in October to delay implementation until June 15, 2005.

Stock options permit the owner to purchase stock in the future at a price determined when the options are granted. If stock prices rise, the options holder can reap big gains by pocketing the difference between the price on the date of the options grant and the price on the date the options are exercised. Companies receive tax breaks when workers exercise such options.

The House bill would have stopped the rule and required companies to count as expenses only those options granted to the five most highly compensated executives, using a technique that regulators said would diminish the value of those options.

The House GOP leadership made the legislation a priority, making sure that it reached the floor before the August recess. The House vote was as far as the legislation got, however. Richard C. Shelby, R-Ala., chairman of the Senate Banking Committee, refused to hold a vote on a companion Senate bill (S 1890), saying that Congress should not interfere with regulators. "Obviously, there's some sentiment to override FASB," he said in June. "I'm certainly against that. I think we set up FASB to do its job."

Shelby had the support of the ranking Democrat on his committee, Paul S. Sarbanes of Maryland.

The attempt to block the new accounting rule came just two years after Congress signed off on the toughest corporate fraud law since the Great Depression. That law (PL 107-204) was known as Sarbanes-Oxley after its sponsors, Sarbanes and Michael G. Oxley, R-Ohio. Enacted following scandals at Enron Corp. and WorldCom Inc., it boosted the FASB's stature by enhancing its power to raise money and emphasizing its independence from Congress. (*2002 Almanac, p. 11-3*)

But with the FASB stock options rule close to taking hold and memories of the financial scandals fading, times had changed at least in the House. Oxley, who chaired the Financial Services Committee, had declined to call up the stock options bill for a vote in 2003. He said he changed his mind because "this decision is going to affect the entire economy, particularly start-ups." Start-up companies said they depended on stock options to attract workers because the chances of big rewards later could make up for lower pay in the beginning.

Intel Corp., Cisco Systems Inc., Genentech Inc. and other technology companies that relied heavily on stock options to compensate executives and other workers led the lobbying campaign against the FASB rule.

Legislative Action

House Committee Action

The House Financial Services Committee approved the bill, 45-13, on June 15 (HR 3574 — H Rept 108-609, Part 1). The Subcommittee on Capital Markets, Insurance and Government-Sponsored Enterprises had approved it by voice vote May 12.

The bill included provisions to:

• Require that companies count as expenses the stock options of their five most highly compensated individuals. Small businesses would be exempt.

• Require companies to estimate the value of those options assuming "zero volatility," meaning that the underlying stock would neither rise nor fall in price.

BoxScore

Bills:
HR 3574, S 1890

Legislative Action:

House passed HR 3574 (H Rept 108-609, Part 1), 312-111, on July 20.

• Prohibit the Securities and Exchange Commission (SEC) from recognizing the FASB accounting rule until an economic analysis was completed by the departments of Commerce and Labor.

"Hundreds of thousands of employees annually are given an ability to invest in their own company with their own intellect and hard work, and if it pays off and the company value is enhanced, you share in that growth without the corporation having to expense the cost of that action at the time of the grant," said Republican Richard H. Baker of Louisiana, the bill's sponsor. "That structure is a good thing."

Brad Sherman, D-Calif., offered an amendment to strip the "zero volatility" language; it failed, 14-43. A separate Sherman amendment, adopted by voice vote, required a joint study by the Commerce and Labor departments on the effect of expensing stock options, to be completed within one year.

Although Baker made changes to the bill that he said would keep it out of the hands of other committees, a turf battle with the Energy and Commerce Committee delayed floor action for weeks. The Energy and Commerce Committee ultimately was discharged.

House Floor Action

The House passed the bill by a broad bipartisan vote of 312-111 on July 20 amid heavy lobbying by the technology companies. (*House vote 397, p. H-130*)

Democrats and Republicans from technology-rich districts backed the bill. "Implementation of these new accounting rules would have a disastrous impact on American companies and, most importantly, American workers," said Anna G. Eshoo, D-Calif. "If companies are forced to expense stock options, most likely they will drop broad-based stock option plans."

The vote was a disappointment to a minority of lawmakers of both parties, including six Republicans on the Financial Services Committee who voted against the bill. "The real issue we are debating today is whether or not we in the House want to set a dangerous precedent and politicize the process of setting accounting standards," said Paul E. Gillmor, R-Ohio, who voted against it. "The Financial Accounting Standards rule does not in any way, despite the implication of some other statements, prevent the issuance of stock options. It just says you have to honestly tell the shareholders what their real cost is."

During the floor debate the House:

• Rejected, 126-296, an amendment by Sherman to strip the "zero volatility" language. (*House vote 394, p. H-130*)

• Rejected, 114-308, a proposal by Carolyn B. Maloney, D-N.Y., to add language stating that nothing in the bill limited the authority of the SEC to establish accounting standards or principles. (*House vote 395, p. H-130*)

• Rejected, 127-293, an amendment by Paul E. Kanjorski, D-Pa., to require that the SEC oversee the process of setting accounting standards for stock options and express the

sense of Congress that preserving the independence of the FASB was crucial. *(House vote 396, p. H-130)*

Senate Committee

Companion legislation in the Senate (S 1890) sponsored by Michael B. Enzi, R-Wyo., enjoyed wide support — it had 30 cosponsors, including 10 Democrats. But the bill was bottled up in committee by Shelby, who argued that politics should not interfere with the FASB's independence and rule-making authority. Four senators, including John McCain, R-Ariz., and

Richard J. Durbin, D-Ill., also strongly opposed the legislation as undermining the integrity and independence of the FASB. A bipartisan group of senators including Republican Peter G. Fitzgerald of Illinois and Democrat Carl Levin of Michigan introduced a resolution urging their colleagues not to interfere with the FASB's efforts to strengthen accounting standards.

There was talk of trying to add stock options provisions to the omnibus appropriations package in the lame-duck session, but the leadership ordered that the must-pass spending bill be kept clean to ensure swift enactment. ◆

Terrorism Insurance Extension Dies

Despite a major push by the insurance industry, legislation to extend a federal terrorism insurance program beyond its Dec. 31, 2005, expiration date died at the end of the Congress. The House Financial Services Committee approved a reauthorization bill, but the Senate Banking Housing and Urban Affairs committee did not consider a companion measure.

The Terrorism Risk Insurance Act (PL 107-297) was enacted in November 2002 to help stabilize the commercial property and casualty insurance markets in the wake of the Sept. 11, 2001, terrorist attacks. It required insurers to provide coverage against terrorism but made the federal government responsible for 90 percent of claims above a certain threshold, set at $15 billion in 2005. The government's responsibility topped out at $100 billion. *(2002 Almanac, p. 11-10)*

The law authorized a three-year program to give the private insurance market a transition period in which to develop pricing and risk models so it could offer terrorism coverage without the federal government backstop. To date, however, the industry had not developed alternatives.

Insurance and real estate companies pressed for an extension in 2004, saying they already were negotiating insurance policies that went beyond the 2005 expiration date.

Critics said the program amounted to a federal subsidy for insurers and maintained that the industry would have to find ways to insure against terrorism if Congress did not extend the 2001 act.

Both the House bill and a companion Senate measure (S 2764) introduced by Christopher J. Dodd, D-Conn., would have extended the expiration date to Dec. 31, 2007. One of the key disputes was over whether to include a so-called soft landing clause that would allow policies written before the expiration date to keep the federal backstop until they expired. The Senate bill included such a clause, and it had support from House Democrats.

The House committee approved its bill in September, but the Senate Banking Committee put off action until the 109th Congress. With the Senate bill stuck, Richard

BoxScore

Bill:
HR 4634
Legislative Action:
House Financial Services Committee approved HR 4634 (H Rept 108-780) by voice vote Sept. 29.

H. Baker, R-La., tried to add the language to the House intelligence overhaul bill (HR 10) just before the end of the regular session, but he was rebuffed by the Rules Committee.

Legislative Action

House Committee Action

The House Financial Services Committee approved its bill (HR 4634 — H Rept 108-780) by voice vote Sept. 29. Bipartisan approval of the legislation followed negotiations between committee Chairman Michael G. Oxley, R-Ohio, and ranking Democrat Barney Frank of Massachusetts that resulted in the inclusion of group life insurance coverage — a Democratic priority — in the bill.

The compromise ended a period of rare partisan tension in the committee over the summer, sparked by a GOP leadership decision in June to halt work on a bipartisan bill and and instead back a measure (HR 4634) by Pete Sessions, R-Texas. Sessions was not a member of the committee but was in a tight re-election race against a Democrat and stood to gain insurance industry contributions as a result. Angry committee Democrats responded by introducing their own two-year extension (HR 4772).

During the markup, the committee adopted by voice vote an amendment by Oxley and other panel members adding the group life coverage.

Two other amendments were withdrawn to ensure bipartisan support for the base bill. One, offered by Brad Sherman, D-Calif., and Ginny Brown-Waite, R-Fla., requested that the Treasury Department compile an annual report for Congress on the cost and availability of homeowners' insurance for losses resulting from hurricanes, earthquakes and other disasters.

The second was a version of the soft-landing clause. Instead of the Dec. 31, 2007, expiration date, the amendment would have allowed policies written before that date to remain under the federal backstop until they expired. It was offered by Democrats Michael E. Capuano of Massachusetts and Steve Israel of New York.

Senate Committee

In the Senate, Banking Chairman Richard C. Shelby, R-Ala., put off consideration of Dodd's bill until 2005 in order to hold hearings on the issue.

Shelby resisted pressure from both sides of the aisle to take up Dodd's bill, saying he wanted to hold hearings in 2005 and get the results of a Treasury Department study due in June on the effects of 2001 act. ◆

Chapter 4

BUDGET

CQ

Bush Proposes Tight Budget

On Feb. 2, President Bush sent Congress a $2.36 trillion fiscal 2005 budget that called for a 7 percent jump in defense spending, stringent limits on most domestic programs and $1.3 trillion in tax cuts over the next decade.

The White House said that if Bush's budget were fully implemented, the $521 billion deficit projected for fiscal 2004 would be cut in half by 2007. However, the budget left out several big-ticket items that seemed sure to add to the deficit — particularly the ongoing military and reconstruction operations in Iraq and Afghanistan, and an expected change in the alternative minimum tax (AMT), without which upper-middle-income taxpayers would lose many of the benefits of Bush's 2001 and 2003 tax cuts.

The Congressional Budget Office issued its own calculation of the president's budget in March. Both Congress and the White House subsequently used the CBO numbers, which are used in the following account as well.

CBO said that Bush's budget would produce deficits of $478 billion in fiscal 2004 and $358 billion in 2005.

Bush called for capping fiscal 2005 discretionary spending — the approximately one-third of the budget controlled by the congressional appropriations process — at $822.9 billion, a 4.2 percent increase over fiscal 2004, excluding supplemental spending. Virtually all of the additional spending was requested for defense and homeland security programs, leaving non-defense discretionary spending to grow by 0.5 percent.

The conventional wisdom was that if Bush won a second term, he would spend some of his political capital in 2005 on domestic issues with substantial budgetary consequences, such as overhauling Medicare and Social Security in anticipation of the looming retirement of the baby boom generation. "They don't want any attention paid to this budget because the real budget is the 2006 budget," said Urban Institute President Robert D. Reischauer, a former CBO director. "That's when the administration really wants to come forward and debate these questions."

2004. However, the total included $2.5 billion previously appropriated for Bush's Project Bioshield initiative to stockpile vaccines and medications for use in responding to a bioterror attack. (*Bioshield, p. 10-3*)

● **Non-defense spending.** Bush's request for a 0.5 percent increase in nondefense discretionary spending amounted to a cut for most programs when inflation was factored in. CBO projected inflation of 1.7 percent in fiscal 2005. Substantial increases requested for several accounts left even bigger cuts for many other programs. Bush asked for $21.3 billion in discretionary spending for foreign operations, a whopping 22 percent increase over fiscal 2004 spending. The foreign aid request included $2.8 billion, a 17 percent increase, for programs to combat HIV/AIDS overseas and $2.5 billion, a 152 percent boost, for the Millennium Challenge Account, Bush's new program to deliver foreign aid to countries that adopted democratic reforms.

Bush also requested increases of $2.1 billion, or 8 percent, for grants for special-education programs and for low-income school districts.

Seven of the 15 Cabinet-level agencies faced outright cuts under Bush's budget: Agriculture (8 percent), Commerce (1 percent), Health and Human Services (2 percent), Justice (3 percent), Treasury (4 percent), Transportation (4 percent) and the EPA (13 percent). Some of the cuts were aimed at hardy perennials that had survived earlier assaults. These included a proposal to eliminate funds for congressional earmarks in programs under the departments of Education, and Housing and Urban Development. Bush also proposed a 13 percent cut for the Army Corps of Engineers, whose water projects were dear to lawmakers, especially in an election year.

● **Taxes.** Bush called for a total of $1.3 trillion in new tax cuts in fiscal 2005-2014. The bulk of the reductions, $1.1 trillion, came from proposals to remove the expiration dates from nearly all of the 2001 and 2003 tax cuts. Those cuts were scheduled to begin expiring at the end of 2004 and

Bush's Budget Priorities

● **Defense.** Bush requested $420.8 billion for defense, a 7 percent increase over fiscal 2004, excluding supplemental funds. The total included $401.7 billion for the Pentagon, as well as funds for Energy Department nuclear activities. It did not count costs in fiscal 2005 for operations in Iraq and Afghanistan. The administration subsequently requested — and Congress agreed to — $25 billion in supplemental appropriations for fiscal 2005. (*War supplemental, p. 2-51; 2003 Almanac, p. 2-83*)

● **Homeland security.** CBO said Bush proposed about $31 billion in discretionary spending for homeland security, an increase of 15 percent over fiscal

Totals From Fiscal 2005 Budget Proposal

The president's fiscal 2005 budget proposed $2.36 trillion in new spending, or budget authority. Actual outlays, which include spending approved in prior years, were estimated at $2.4 trillion. The administration forecast that outlays would exceed revenues in each year, with budget deficits totaling $1.87 trillion.

(fiscal years, in billions of dollars)

	Estimated			Proposed		
	2004	**2005**	**2006**	**2007**	**2008**	**2009**
Budget authority	$2,345	$2,355	$2,487	$2,624	$2,761	$2,902
Outlays	2,319	2,400	2,473	2,592	2,724	2,853
Revenue	1,798	2,036	2,206	2,351	2,485	2,616
Deficit	−521	−364	−268	−241	−239	−237

SOURCE: Office of Management and Budget

Bush Proposals by Appropriations Panel

The White House offered the following breakdown to show how discretionary budget authority would be allocated among the Appropriations subcommittees under the president's budget:

(in billions of dollars)	2004 Enacted	2005 Proposed	2004-05 Percentage Change
Agriculture	$17.7	$16.4	−6.8%
Commerce, Justice, State	38.7	39.4	1.8
Defense	366.1	392.5	7.2
District of Columbia	0.5	0.6	2.8
Energy and water development	27.3	27.0	−1.1
Foreign operations	17.5	21.3	21.7
Homeland Security	27.1	28.3	4.8
Interior	20.0	20.0	−0.5
Labor, HHS, Education	140.9	141.8	0.6
Legislative branch	3.5	4.0	11.4
Military construction	9.3	9.5	2.2
Transportation, Treasury	28.7	26.0	−9.4
VA, HUD, NASA and EPA	90.1	92.0	2.1
Allowances	—	− 0.4	—
TOTALS*	**$787.3**	**$818.4**	**4.0%**

* Excludes $87.3 billion in supplemental budget authority for fiscal 2004 appropriated for military and reconstruction operations in Iraq and Afghanistan.

NOTE: Figures may not add due to rounding

SOURCE: Office of Management and Budget

to sunset at the end of 2010. The expiration dates were necessary to get the tax cuts through the Senate under budget reconciliation rules that would protect them from filibusters. Bush's proposal included:

- Permanently extending the reduction in income tax rates, treatment of taxes for married couples, the $1,000-per-year child tax credit and the estate tax repeal, among other provisions, resulting in $904 billion in tax cuts over 10 years.
- Making permanent the 15 percent maximum tax rate on capital gains and dividend income, resulting in $157 billion in tax cuts.
- Making permanent an increase from $25,000 to $100,000 in the amount of investment that small businesses could deduct immediately from their taxable income, for a total of $34 billion in tax reductions.
- Making the research and experimentation tax credit permanent, yielding $58 billion in cuts.
- Extending — for 2004 and 2005 only — exemptions and credits that saved many upper-middle-income taxpayers from being drawn into the AMT, a parallel tax system designed to prevent the use of tax benefits to avoid all taxes. The change would yield an additional $23 billion in tax cuts.
- Enacting new health insurance tax breaks at a cost of $59 billion in tax cuts and $54 billion in additional outlays.
- **Deficit.** CBO calculated that under Bush's budget, the deficit would reach $358 billion in fiscal 2005, gradually falling to $258 billion in 2009 for a cumulative $1.38 trillion

deficit in fiscal 2005 through 2009. The White House's Office of Management and Budget (OMB), which prepared the president's budget, said the deficit would go from $364 billion in fiscal 2005 to $237 billion in 2009; the cumulative total was $1.35 trillion for that period.

None of the calculations included expected supplemental spending for the war. Also, Bush's budget assumed that after fiscal 2005, outlays for all non-defense discretionary spending — a category that included the Homeland Security Department — would shrink. OMB said that even programs that Bush wanted to increase in fiscal 2005 — including Title I grants to subsidize schools in low income areas, the Women, Infants and Children food program, and the National Institutes of Health — would be targeted for cuts in subsequent years if Bush won a second term.

Bush's spending goals also assumed that some programs would be funded partially through proposed user fees that Congress had previously rejected, including a new annual enrollment fee for relatively better-off veterans seeking Department of Veterans Affairs medical care and higher prescription drug co-payments for veterans. Without the fee increases, Congress would have to make even deeper cuts to programs than Bush proposed in order to live within the president's overall spending limit.

As it had the previous year, the White House submitted a budget covering five years, arguing that longer-term projections could not be trusted. Critics said the decision to look out only five years allowed the White House to hide a bleak deficit picture and the impact of making the 2001 and 2003 tax cuts permanent.

- **Budget enforcement.** Bush called for reviving budget rules to require that increases in entitlement programs such as Medicare be offset with savings in other mandatory programs. Unlike earlier so-called PAYGO rules, tax cuts would not have to be offset with other revenue increases under Bush's plan, and tax increases could not be used to finance spending increases.

The president also proposed reinstating the statutory caps on appropriations that were in place — though often violated — from fiscal 1991 through fiscal 2002. The caps would apply to both budget authority and outlays, the actual money disbursed by Treasury in any given year.

Appropriators Feel the Squeeze

The outlook for domestic spending was so tight that appropriators said Bush's initiatives would have to compete with what House Appropriations Chairman C.W. "Bill" Young, R-Fla., called "proven programs and traditional congressional priorities." The almost $4 billion boost proposed

(Continued on p. 4-8)

Bush's Fiscal 2005 Proposal by Agency

New budget authority and expected outlays by fiscal year. For year-to-year comparisons, the administration adjusted the fiscal 2003 figures for several agencies and departments to account for creation of the Department of Homeland Security.

(figures in millions of dollars)

	BUDGET AUTHORITY			OUTLAYS		
	2003 Actual	2004 Estimate	2005 Proposed	2003 Actual	2004 Estimate	2005 Proposed
Legislative Branch	3,861	3,919	4,376	3,427	4,269	4,373
The Judiciary	5,164	5,452	6,043	5,123	5,306	5,903
Agriculture	78,386	78,434	83,283	72,390	77,739	81,778
Commerce	5,811	5,894	5,837	5,676	6,194	6,147
Defense – Military	439,523	442,692	402,633	388,870	435,674	429,746
Education	63,256	63,258	66,434	57,400	62,815	64,342
Energy	20,558	20,992	22,098	19,385	20,623	22,496
Health and Human Services	515,887	556,401	571,589	505,345	547,898	579,889
Homeland Security	30,841	28,845	31,414	31,967	30,663	31,119
Housing and Urban Development	34,435	34,707	34,042	37,474	46,177	38,943
Interior	10,432	10,415	10,591	9,210	9,965	9,784
Justice	23,683	24,936	21,776	21,539	23,488	23,680
Labor	69,104	60,031	57,321	69,593	59,949	56,995
State	10,271	10,572	10,893	9,261	11,301	11,109
Transportation	54,441	58,557	58,376	50,807	58,010	58,959
Treasury	367,871	369,587	396,511	366,987	368,981	395,200
Veterans Affairs	58,934	60,296	65,285	56,887	60,318	67,314
Corps of Engineers	4,840	4,588	3,989	4,751	4,308	4,189
Other Defense—Civil Programs	39,950	41,612	42,039	39,883	41,881	42,038
Environmental Protection Agency	7,945	8,381	7,636	8,061	8,129	8,277
Executive Office of the President	2,569	18,779	342	387	6,612	9,880
General Services Administration	1,332	442	230	573	778	581
International Assistance Programs	18,471	13,376	18,257	13,462	17,365	16,597
NASA	15,391	15,379	16,245	14,552	14,604	16,386
National Science Foundation	5,430	5,617	5,770	4,736	5,346	5,586
Office of Personnel Management	57,317	60,571	63,688	54,136	57,568	60,880
Small Business Administration	1,625	4,097	681	1,558	3,978	683
Social Security Administration						
(On-budget)	46,157	48,494	53,698	46,333	48,620	54,406
(Off-budget)	463,280	483,524	501,333	461,401	481,875	499,865
Other Independent Agencies						
(On-budget)	14,459	16,213	17,337	12,158	16,351	17,656
(Off-budget)	5,386	2,200	−253	−5,245	−4,956	−250
Allowances	—	—	−798	—	—	−767
Undistributed offsetting receipts	−210,450	−212,995	−223,941	−210,450	−212,995	−223,941
(On-budget)	(−117,303)	(−116,055)	(−120,065)	(−117,303)	(−116,055)	(−120,065)
(Off-budget)	(−93,147)	(−96,940)	(−103,876)	(−93,147)	(−96,940)	(−103,876)
TOTALS	$2,266,160	$2,345,266	$2,354,755	$2,157,637	$2,318,834	$2,399,843

Figures may not add due to rounding.

SOURCE: Office of Management and Budget

Bush's Fiscal 2005 Proposal by Function

A breakdown, in millions of dollars per fiscal year, of governmental spending by function rather than agency

	BUDGET AUTHORITY			OUTLAYS		
	2003 Actual	2004 Estimate	2005 Proposed	2003 Actual	2004 Estimate	2005 Proposed
NATIONAL DEFENSE						
Department of Defense — military	$437,863	$441,709	$402,633	$387,319	$434,777	$429,554
Atomic energy defense activities	16,365	16,753	17,220	16,029	16,631	17,759
Defense-related activities	1,957	2,085	3,245	1,572	2,276	3,273
Total, National defense	**$456,185**	**$460,547**	**$423,098**	**$404,920**	**$453,684**	**$450,586**
INTERNATIONAL AFFAIRS						
International development and humanitarian assistance	15,116	30,058	13,117	10,332	17,880	21,021
International security assistance	10,058	7,888	7,899	8,619	9,545	8,192
Conduct of foreign affairs	7,210	7,656	7,992	6,683	7,953	7,842
Foreign information and exchange activities	1,013	996	1,037	959	1,009	1,074
International financial programs	−1,691	−5,271	−476	−5,385	−2,151	−291
Total, International affairs	**$31,706**	**$41,327**	**$29,569**	**$21,208**	**$34,236**	**$37,838**
GENERAL SCIENCE, SPACE AND TECHNOLOGY						
General science and basic research	8,668	9,033	9,134	7,993	8,713	8,970
Space flight, research and supporting activities	14,386	14,344	15,325	12,880	13,578	15,383
Total, General science, space and technology	**$23,054**	**$23,377**	**$24,459**	**$20,873**	**$22,291**	**$24,353**
ENERGY						
Energy supply	−758	−126	466	−2,101	−363	375
Energy conservation	881	878	876	897	882	877
Emergency energy preparedness	180	176	177	182	176	177
Energy information, policy, and regulation	245	279	364	247	262	345
Total, Energy	**$548**	**$1,207**	**$1,883**	**−$775**	**$957**	**$1,774**
NATURAL RESOURCES AND ENVIRONMENT						
Water resources	5,653	5,666	4,645	5,492	5,655	5,003
Conservation and land management	10,638	10,126	10,179	9,739	10,360	9,982
Recreational resources	2,931	2,995	3,086	2,872	2,982	3,172
Pollution control and abatement	8,079	8,546	7,793	8,208	8,299	8,431
Other natural resources	4,505	4,867	4,583	3,392	4,369	4,311
Total, Natural resources and environment	**$31,806**	**$32,200**	**$30,286**	**$29,703**	**$31,665**	**$30,899**
AGRICULTURE						
Farm income stabilization	20,054	15,296	18,280	18,409	15,741	18,064
Agricultural research and services	4,607	4,160	4,073	4,191	4,380	4,258
Total, Agriculture	**$24,661**	**$19,456**	**$22,353**	**$22,600**	**$20,121**	**$22,322**
COMMERCE AND HOUSING CREDIT						
Mortgage credit	−286	104	−361	−4,591	2,213	−4,900
Postal Service	5,462	2,260	−216	−5,169	−4,896	−213
(On-budget)	(76)	(60)	(37)	(76)	(60)	(37)
(Off-budget)	(5,386)	(2,200)	(−253)	(−5,245)	(−4,956)	(−250)
Deposit insurance	1	1	1	−1,369	−1,451	−1,521
Other advancement of commerce	9,737	11,674	8,668	9,522	11,857	9,348
Total, Commerce and housing credit	**$14,914**	**$14,039**	**$8,092**	**−$1,607**	**$7,723**	**$2,714**
(On-budget)	(9,528)	(11,839)	(8,345)	(3,638)	(12,679)	(2,964)
(Off-budget)	(5,386)	(2,200)	(−253)	(−5,245)	(−4,956)	(−250)
TRANSPORTATION						
Ground transportation	40,316	43,675	43,606	37,491	42,789	43,818
Air transportation	21,478	17,499	18,099	23,343	18,598	18,530
Water transportation	6,624	7,101	7,298	5,907	6,426	7,045
Other transportation	295	294	491	328	331	506
Total, Transportation	**$68,713**	**$68,569**	**$69,494**	**$67,069**	**$68,144**	**$69,899**
COMMUNITY AND REGIONAL DEVELOPMENT						
Community development	5,718	5,486	4,707	6,346	6,914	6,619
Area and regional development	2,956	2,902	2,129	2,397	2,617	2,930
Disaster relief and insurance	8,025	7,924	6,113	10,107	9,226	7,468
Total, Community and regional development	**$16,699**	**$16,312**	**$12,949**	**$18,850**	**$18,757**	**$17,017**
EDUCATION, TRAINING, EMPLOYMENT, AND SOCIAL SERVICES						
Elementary, secondary and vocational education	36,396	38,275	39,379	31,473	37,554	37,830
Higher education	23,573	21,660	23,703	22,697	21,572	23,158
Research and general education aids	2,939	3,064	3,080	2,973	3,236	3,059
Training and employment	7,378	7,114	7,237	8,372	7,345	6,880
Other labor services	1,594	1,610	1,596	1,480	1,610	1,621
Social services	15,749	16,204	16,822	15,573	15,894	16,472
Total, Educ., training, employment and social services	**$87,629**	**$87,927**	**$91,817**	**$82,568**	**$87,211**	**$89,020**

	BUDGET AUTHORITY			OUTLAYS		
	2003 Actual	2004 Estimate	2005 Proposed	2003 Actual	2004 Estimate	2005 Proposed
HEALTH						
Health care services	$200,842	$219,339	$216,289	$192,608	$213,557	$220,618
Health research and training	28,052	28,985	29,461	24,044	27,037	28,985
Consumer and occupational health and safety	2,793	2,966	3,030	2,924	2,907	2,994
Total, Health	**$231,687**	**$251,290**	**$248,780**	**$219,576**	**$243,501**	**$252,597**
MEDICARE						
Total, Medicare	**$249,947**	**$271,030**	**$293,574**	**$249,433**	**$270,451**	**$294,249**
INCOME SECURITY						
General retirement and disability insurance	6,449	6,266	6,605	7,047	6,907	6,919
Federal employee retirement and disability	86,830	91,217	94,569	85,154	89,295	92,832
Unemployment compensation	57,464	48,827	43,205	57,054	48,287	43,191
Housing assistance	28,796	29,231	29,739	35,325	37,328	37,533
Food and nutrition assistance	43,349	48,591	51,119	42,526	46,614	48,509
Other income security	106,602	112,063	117,087	107,326	111,064	119,165
Total, Income security	**$329,490**	**$336,195**	**$342,324**	**$334,432**	**$339,495**	**$348,149**
SOCIAL SECURITY						
Total, Social Security	**$476,571**	**$497,823**	**$516,457**	**$474,680**	**$496,174**	**$514,989**
(On-budget)	(13,291)	(14,299)	(15,124)	(13,279)	(14,299)	(15,124)
(Off-budget)	(463,280)	(483,524)	(501,333)	(461,401)	(481,875)	(499,865)
VETERANS' BENEFITS AND SERVICES						
Income security for veterans	30,893	31,775	34,356	29,885	32,441	37,152
Veterans' education, training and rehabilitation	2,205	2,468	2,522	2,265	2,621	2,806
Hospital and medical care for veterans	24,668	27,364	27,823	24,019	26,599	26,797
Veterans' housing	543	−1,916	−28	524	−1,921	−22
Other veterans' benefits and services	782	743	771	325	714	740
Total, Veterans' benefits and services	**$59,071**	**$60,434**	**$65,444**	**$ 57,018**	**$60,454**	**$67,473**
ADMINISTRATION OF JUSTICE						
Federal law enforcement activities	18,193	19,180	20,717	15,813	18,843	21,672
Federal litigative and judicial activities	9,164	9,421	10,488	9,085	9,365	10,340
Federal correctional activities	5,256	5,561	5,645	5,384	5,290	5,889
Criminal justice assistance	7,076	8,557	3,931	5,126	8,105	4,881
Total, Administration of justice	**$39,689**	**$42,719**	**$40,781**	**$35,408**	**$41,603**	**$42,782**
GENERAL GOVERNMENT						
Legislative functions	3,144	3,158	3,557	2,840	3,459	3,559
Executive direction and management	537	582	602	706	578	605
Central fiscal operations	11,693	10,126	11,355	11,472	9,940	10,550
General property and records management	914	745	509	201	1,084	873
Central personnel management	213	207	526	204	207	526
General purpose fiscal assistance	7,591	7,537	2,577	7,379	7,693	2,570
Other general government	2,821	3,114	1,785	2,079	3,982	1,984
Deductions for offsetting receipts	−1,894	−1,519	−1,519	−1,894	−1,519	−1,519
Total, General government	**$25,019**	**$23,950**	**$19,392**	**$22,987**	**$25,424**	**$19,148**
NET INTEREST						
Interest on Treasury debt securities (gross)	318,141	319,157	349,805	318,141	319,157	349,805
Interest received by on-budget trust funds	−72,523	−67,388	−68,915	−72,523	−67,388	−68,915
Interest received by off-budget trust funds	−83,545	−86,286	−91,918	−83,545	−86,286	−91,918
Other interest	−6,461	−7,431	−9,990	−6,538	−7,352	−9,990
Other investment income	−2,459	−1,867	−1,073	−2,459	−1,867	−1,073
Total, Net interest	**$153,153**	**$156,185**	**$177,909**	**$153,076**	**$156,264**	**$177,909**
(On-budget)	(236,698)	(242,471)	(269,827)	(236,621)	(242,550)	(269,827)
(Off-budget)	(−83,545)	(−86,286)	(−91,918)	(−83,545)	(−86,286)	(−91,918)
ALLOWANCES AND OFFSETTING RECEIPTS						
Total, Allowances	—	—	−$798	—	—	−$767
Total, Undistributed offsetting receipts	**−$54,382**	**−$59,321**	**−$63,108**	**−$54,382**	**−$59,321**	**−$63,108**
(On-budget)	(−44,780)	(−48,667)	(−51,150)	(−44,780)	(−48,667)	(−51,150)
(Off-budget)	(−9,602)	(−10,654)	(−11,958)	(−9,602)	(−10,654)	(−11,958)
TOTALS	**$2,266,160**	**$2,345,266**	**$2,354,755**	**$2,157,637**	**$2,318,834**	**$2,399,843**
(On-budget)	(1,890,641)	(1,956,482)	(1,957,551)	(1,794,628)	(1,938,855)	(2,004,104)
(Off-budget)	(375,519)	(388,784)	(397,204)	(363,009)	(379,979)	(395,739)

Figures may not add due to rounding.

SOURCE: Office of Management and Budget

(Continued from p. 4-4)

for foreign aid, in particular, seemed dead on arrival. "With pressing domestic needs and the 1 percent discretionary increase ceiling, the administration . . . will have a difficult task of convincing our colleagues of the need for this increase," said Jim Kolbe, R-Ariz., who chaired the House Foreign Operations Appropriations Subcommittee.

Many budget insiders predicted that Congress would not accept Bush's demands on appropriations, and that gridlock was a probable outcome.

Meanwhile, GOP conservatives were ready to take a tougher line on spending. Conservative voters, the GOP political base, were unhappy with the earmark-laden fiscal 2004 omnibus spending law (PL 108-199) enacted in January, and many conservatives were outraged to learn of administration estimates that the 2003 Medicare prescription drug law (PL 108-173) would cost 35 percent more in the next decade than CBO had estimated. *(2003 Almanac, p. 11-3)*

Economic Assumptions

The economic assumptions behind Bush's budget included a 4.4 percent economic growth rate in calendar 2004 as measured by real gross domestic product (GDP). That was a relatively conservative estimate compared with growth forecasts of 4.8 percent by CBO and 4.6 percent by the Blue Chip consensus, an average of 50 top private-sector forecasters. Still, it was a significant increase over OMB's previous forecast. In the fiscal 2004 budget, when the recovery was still anemic and there were fears of a double-dip recession, OMB predicted 3.6 percent growth for 2004. *(2003 Almanac, p. 5-3)*

"The economic outlook appears brighter now than at any time in recent years," the White House said, crediting "expansionary fiscal" policies and "improvements in the tax system," in part, for the rebound.

Some analysts said the administration could be setting itself up to unveil some good news about the deficit later in the year. Overall, however, economists of all stripes praised officials for refraining from proffering the kinds of rosy economic scenarios that would help them understate deficit projections.

The White House also projected that the jobless rate, always a major issue in an election year, would be a bit higher than it had hoped a year earlier. The budget assumed 5.6 percent unemployment in 2004, compared with its previous prediction of 5.5 percent. Both CBO and the Blue Chip consensus projected 5.8 percent unemployment for the remainder of 2004, down slightly from the estimated 6 percent unemployment rate for 2003.

OMB, CBO and private-sector projections agreed that interest rates and inflation would remain low through the next

Economic Forecasts Compared

	2004	2005	2006	2007	2008	2009
Real GDP growth *(chain-weighted)*						
OMB	4.4%	3.6%	3.4%	3.3%	3.2%	3.1%
OMB 2003	3.6	3.5	3.3	3.2	3.1	3.1
CBO	4.8	4.2	3.2	2.7	2.8	2.8
Blue Chip	4.6	3.7	3.3	3.1	3.2	3.2
Inflation *(CPI)*						
OMB	1.4	1.5	1.8	2.1	2.4	2.5
OMB 2003	2.1	2.1	2.2	2.2	2.3	2.3
CBO	1.6	1.7	2.0	2.2	2.2	2.2
Blue Chip	1.7	2.1	2.3	2.4	2.4	2.4
Unemployment						
OMB	5.6	5.4	5.2	5.1	5.1	5.1
OMB 2003	5.5	5.2	5.1	5.1	5.1	5.1
CBO	5.8	5.3	5.0	5.1	5.2	5.2
Blue Chip	5.8	5.5	5.4	5.3	5.3	5.2
91-day Treasury bills						
OMB	1.3	2.4	3.3	4.0	4.3	4.4
OMB 2003	3.6	4.3	4.4	4.4	4.5	4.5
CBO	1.3	3.0	4.0	4.6	4.6	4.6
Blue Chip	1.3	2.6	3.7	3.9	4.1	4.1
10-year Treasury notes						
OMB	4.6	5.0	5.4	5.6	5.8	5.8
OMB 2003	5.0	5.3	5.4	5.5	5.6	5.6
CBO	4.6	5.4	5.5	5.5	5.5	5.5
Blue Chip	4.7	5.4	5.5	5.6	5.6	5.6

This comparison of the forecasts of the White House's Office of Management and Budget (OMB), the Congressional Budget Office (CBO) and the Blue Chip consensus of private economists uses annual percentage changes in inflation-adjusted gross domestic product (GDP) and the consumer price index (CPI). The unemployment rate and the Treasury bill and note interest rates are annual averages. The OMB forecast (and the OMB forecast from a year before) assumes enactment of the president's budget and therefore is not strictly comparable with those of CBO and the Blue Chip.

SOURCE: Office of Management and Budget, Congressional Budget Office

five years, but the administration predicted much lower interest rates than others did for calendar year 2005, allowing the White House to assume lower costs for servicing the national debt. CBO and private-sector forecasters predicted an average yield of 5.4 percent for 10-year Treasury notes in 2005, while the White House projected a 5.0 percent yield.

While economic assumptions provide the crucial underpinning to budget calculations, they frequently turn out to be incorrect. Small changes in economic assumptions can affect out-year deficits by hundreds of billions of dollars, often far more than the spending and tax cut proposals that are hotly debated in Congress. OMB acknowledged, for example, that if its GDP figure was wrong by 1 percentage point every year, the deficit would grow by an additional $511.1 billion over five years.

Inaccuracies of that magnitude in economic forecasting were common, according to an October 2003 study by CBO. The study found that CBO, the White House and the Blue Chip consensus all were at least a percentage point off in their forecasts for real GDP growth for the previous six consecutive years. ◆

Budget Plans Fall by the Wayside

For the third time since 1974 — the second since President Bush took office — Congress was unable to agree on a budget resolution to guide tax and spending decisions for the year.

Republicans in both chambers agreed with relative ease to separate budget plans for fiscal 2005 that largely tracked Bush's austere non-defense spending proposals — though neither could come close to the $1.3 trillion in tax cuts over 10 years outlined in his budget.

The central goal in both the House and Senate was to trim the deficit a bit more quickly than Bush, whose budget projected a $358 billion shortfall for fiscal 2005, and ease the way for a modest dose of additional tax cuts. The House agreed to a conference report that reflected those aims, but a fierce split among Republicans over whether to pay for the tax cuts doomed final action in the Senate.

The conference agreement was essentially a stopgap plan to put the budget on autopilot through an election year. It allowed for $821.4 billion in discretionary spending for the 13 fiscal 2005 appropriations bills, about $1.5 billion less than Bush requested. It included instructions for a reconciliation bill, protected from filibuster in the Senate, that would cut taxes by $27.5 billion. That was enough for a one-year extension of three popular tax cuts slated to shrink at the end of the year.

When the House and Senate debated their respective versions of the budget, Republican appropriators generally supported the plans, although they complained that the spending caps were so tight that the appropriations bills could stall in both chambers. There was speculation, which turned out to be prescient, that leaders would have to assemble yet another major omnibus spending package after the November elections to finish the process.

The stumbling block between the chambers was a dispute over whether to revive pay-as-you-go budget rules requiring that all tax cuts and new entitlement spending be offset with spending cuts or revenue increases. The so-called PAY-GO rules, first enacted in 1993, had expired at the end of fiscal 2002.

On the one side was a small group of GOP moderates who joined with Democrats to insert language in the Senate version of the budget resolution to restore pay-as-you-go. On the other side were House Republican leaders, backed by the White House, who adamantly opposed anything that would make tax cuts more difficult. "I'd rather not have a budget resolution than have pay-as-you-go for taxes," said House Majority Whip Roy Blunt of Missouri.

Despite months of effort, Senate Majority Leader Bill

BoxScore

Bill:
S Con Res 95
Legislative Action:
Senate adopted S Con Res 95, 51-45, on March 12.
House adopted H Con Res 393 (H Rept 108-441), 215-212, on March 25, and later inserted the text into S Con Res 95.
House adopted the conference report on S Con Res 95 (H Rept 108-498), 216-213, on May 19.

Frist, R-Tenn., was unable to bridge the differences. In the end, the conference report reflected mainly the views of House Republicans, and it never came to the Senate floor.

For the House, the main drawback to operating without a budget resolution was the resulting need to vote on a separate bill to raise the federal debt limit. Under what was known as the Gephardt rule, passage of a House debt limit bill was automatic if both chambers adopted a conference report on the budget resolution. (*Debt limit, p. 4-13*)

In the Senate, the lack of a budget resolution meant there was no procedural protection for tax cut legislation. The budget resolution would have put the tax cuts into a reconciliation bill that would have come to the Senate floor under special rules that barred filibusters and limited amendments. It took only 51 votes in the Senate to pass a reconciliation bill, as opposed to the 60 needed to shut down a filibuster. Republicans were less concerned about this than in previous years, however, because their tax cut agenda was much less ambitious than in 2001 and 2003.

GOP conservative Sen. Judd Gregg of New Hampshire said the budget debate was less intense "because the tax issue is basically muted . . . there is not significant tax policy in this bill," he said. "There's a lot of posturing because it's a presidential year — a lot of political votes are being cast — but the intensity of the fight over taxes isn't there."

The other main consequence for the Senate was that without a budget resolution to set spending limits, it took only a simple majority to add money to the appropriations bills on the floor. With a budget resolution in place, amendments that added spending could have been knocked down with points of order that could only be waived with 60 votes. That significantly slowed the appropriations process in the Senate.

Both chambers found ways around the inconvenience of not having a budget resolution, however.

Highlights

Following are major elements of the conference report on the fiscal 2005 budget resolution as adopted by the House:
● **Discretionary spending.** A cap of $821.4 billion on discretionary spending — the approximately one-third of the budget controlled by the congressional appropriations process. Bush later agreed to an additional $500 million to fight wildfires, bringing the total available to appropriators to $821.9 billion. The budget recommended: $420.8 billion for defense, a 7 percent increase over the fiscal 2004 level excluding supplemental spending; $31.2 billion for homeland security, an increase of about 15 percent; and

$369.4 billion for all other discretionary programs, a freeze at fiscal 2004 levels.

● **Supplemental war spending.** An additional $50 billion in discretionary funds in fiscal 2005 for military activities in Iraq and Afghanistan, which did not count against the discretionary cap. Bush did not include the war costs in his fiscal 2005 budget, but the administration advised Congress that it would be requesting as much as $50 billion in supplemental funds, probably in January 2005. The administration shifted its stance May 5, asking Congress for $25 billion, which was considered a down payment. (*War supplemental, p. 2-51*)

● **Tax cuts.** Instructions for a $27.5 billion reconciliation bill to extend three expiring tax breaks: the $1,000 child tax credit, an expanded 10 percent income tax bracket, and tax relief for married couples. All three were enacted as part of the 2001 tax law (PL 107-16) and accelerated in 2003 (PL 108-27). Without additional legislation, they would revert to the 2001 schedule at the end of 2004 and expire at the end of 2010. The projected cost of a one-year extension was comprised of $22.9 billion in lost revenue and $4.6 billion in anticipated outlays, mainly for refundable tax credits.

The resolution also allowed for another $27.7 billion in tax cuts that would not be part of a reconciliation bill.

● **Budget enforcement.** A rule that was good only until April 15, 2005, that made tax cuts or increases in entitlement spending subject to a 60-vote point of order in the Senate unless they were fully offset. The rule did not apply to the $27.5 billion tax-reconciliation bill.

● **Deficit.** An expected deficit of $367.4 billion in fiscal 2005, declining to $174.2 in fiscal 2009.

● **Mandatory spending.** Conferees dropped a House plan to require cuts in existing mandatory programs.

Legislative Action

Senate Committee Action

The Senate Budget Committee got started first, approving a budget resolution (S Con Res 95) March 4 that recommended tighter spending constraints and quicker deficit reduction than the president had requested. The committee approved the five-year budget on a 12-10 party-line vote following a two-day markup.

Drafted by Chairman Don Nickles, R-Okla., the Senate resolution recommended:

● **Discretionary spending.** An $814 billion cap on fiscal 2005 discretionary budget authority, about $7 billion less than Bush requested. The budget recommended $414 billion for defense, nearly $7 billion less than Bush requested, $31 billion for homeland security, and $369 billion for all other accounts.

Senate Appropriations Chairman Ted Stevens, R-Alaska, and Armed Services Chairman John W. Warner, R-Va., vowed to restore the defense funding, and Nickles assured them that would happen on the floor or later in the appropriations process.

Nickles needed to stick to the $814 billion limit because that was the limit for fiscal 2005 set by the fiscal 2004 budget resolution (H Con Res 95). A budget resolution that exceeded that amount would have been subject to a 60-vote point of order when it came to the Senate floor. (*2003 Almanac, p. 5-8*)

● **War spending.** An additional $30 billion in discretionary funds for military operations in Iraq and Afghanistan, pending a request by the president. The money would not count against the discretionary cap.

● **Taxes.** Tax cuts of $138.6 billion over the period 2005 through 2009, of which $80.6 billion would be protected from filibuster as part of a tax-reconciliation bill. Conceding they could not meet the White House goal of permanently extending the tax cuts of 2001 and 2003, Senate GOP leaders settled for a five-year extension of the three tax breaks set to expire after 2004, and moved the repeal of estate taxes up to 2009 from 2010. "We don't do much on taxes," Nickles said.

● **Mandatory spending.** A second reconciliation bill that would cut $11 billion from Medicaid over five years and $3 billion from the earned-income tax credit for the working poor, as well as increasing revenue by $7.6 billion by extending expiring Customs user fees. Of the total, $18.2 billion would be used to offset outlays anticipated as a result of the refundable portions of the child tax credit and marriage penalty relief. The remaining $3.4 billion would go to reduce the deficit.

● **Debt limit.** A third reconciliation bill to increase the $7.4 trillion limit on the national debt by $664 billion.

● **Pay-as-you-go.** The committee defeated, 10-12, an attempt by Russell D. Feingold, D-Wis., to renew pay-as-you-go rules to 2009 with no exception for the tax cuts approved in the budget resolution.

Senate Floor Action

The Senate adopted the budget resolution, 51-45, in the early morning of March 12, after four days of debate and votes on dozens of amendments. (*Senate vote 58, p. S-14*)

In a blow to Bush's tax cut agenda, the Senate adopted the Feingold amendment to reinstate pay-as-you-go rules for both taxes and entitlement spending. "This is a major step toward restoring the discipline and beginning the long hard road of balancing the budget," Feingold said.

But that victory for deficit hawks was sandwiched between two votes that rejected the committee's proposed cuts in defense and mandatory spending. The Senate also adopted amendments allowing for more than $12 billion in additional spending on veterans' medical care, education, medical research and other programs — most of it to be paid for from an "allowances" category often used to assume unidentified savings.

The Senate increased the discretionary spending cap to $819.7 billion, and floor amendments added various mechanisms that could increase the total further. Also, the Senate agreed to exempt $2.5 billion in previously appropriated money for Project Bioshield from the discretionary cap, creating room for $2.5 billion more in new spending. The amendment, by Robert C. Byrd, D-W.Va., was adopted by voice vote. Bioshield was a Bush initiative to stockpile vaccines and medications to combat a bioterror attack.

As adopted by the Senate, the resolution assumed a fiscal 2005 deficit of $341.1 billion, about $20 billion less than predicted under Bush's budget, falling to $227 billion in 2007 and $200.3 billion in 2009.

● **Pay-as-you-go.** Feingold succeeded in adding language to

require that any tax cut or new entitlement spending proposed in the five-year window of the budget resolution be offset or face a 60-vote point of order in the Senate. The vote was 51-48. (*Senate vote 38, p. S-11*)

Nickles and other GOP leaders opposed the move, arguing that the budget resolution already required offsets for spending increases, and that tax cuts should not be subject to deficit-reduction rules requiring offsets. Feingold responded that reinstating the rules would not bar tax cuts. "It just makes it a little harder," he said.

Four Republicans — Olympia J. Snowe and Susan Collins of Maine, Lincoln Chafee of Rhode Island and John McCain of Arizona — defied their leadership and voted for the amendment. The outcome momentarily stunned GOP leaders. But Feingold, himself, said he would vote to override the pay-as-you-go rules to allow an extension of the three expiring tax cuts covered by the reconciliation instructions, and that sentiment was echoed by many other lawmakers.

- **Defense.** Warner won a 95-4 vote to increase the recommended level of defense spending by $6.9 billion, erasing the cuts made by the committee. That brought the total for defense to $420.8 billion. (*Senate vote 37, p. S-11*)

- **Mandatory cuts.** Eight Republicans joined all but one Democrat in a 53-43 vote to eliminate the instructions to the Finance Committee to cut $11 billion from Medicaid and $3 billion from the earned-income tax credit. The proposed cuts were strongly opposed by the National Governors Association. "This is not the time to cut Medicaid," said Max Baucus, D-Mont., who sponsored the amendment. (*Senate vote 39, p. S-12*)

- **Taxes.** An amendment, adopted by voice vote, to prevent tax increases for families receiving the child credit brought the tax-reconciliation package to $82.6 billion. Byrd failed on a 47-52 vote to eliminate the requirement for a tax reconciliation bill. (*Senate vote 36, p. S-11*)

House Committee Action

The House Budget Committee approved its version of the budget resolution (H Con Res 393 — H Rept 108-441) by a vote of 24-19, on March 17.

Under pressure from defense hawks, Chairman Jim Nussle, R-Iowa, dropped initial plans to shave about $2 billion from Bush's defense request. A group of almost three dozen Republicans, led by Armed Services Chairman Duncan Hunter of California, threatened to vote against the budget resolution if it contained such cuts. GOP leaders had pledged to put "everything on the table," including defense.

The House budget projected a fiscal 2005 deficit of $376.8 billion, falling to $239.8 in 2007 and $233.9 in 2009.

Highlights of the House budget included:

- **Discretionary spending.** A limit of $821.3 billion in discretionary spending. The total allowed $420.6 billion for defense (although some of the funding was in a separate homeland security category that did not exist in the Senate bill). Domestic spending unrelated to homeland security was frozen at fiscal 2003 levels. The $2.5 billion for Project Bioshield was included under the discretionary cap.

- **War spending.** An additional $50 billion in fiscal 2005 for operations in Iraq and Afghanistan, exempt from the discretionary limit.

- **Taxes.** Tax cuts of $145.8 billion over five years, of which

$137.6 billion could be protected under a reconciliation bill. The resolution recommended including extensions of the 10 percent tax bracket, the marriage penalty relief and the $1,000 child tax credit.

- **Mandatory spending.** Instructions to five House committees to produce a reconciliation bill that would achieve a combined $13.2 billion in savings from mandatory programs in fiscal 2005 through 2009.

- **Debt limit.** An increase of $690 million in the federal debt limit bringing the total to $8.1 trillion. Under a version of the so-called Gephardt rule, adopted at the start of the 108th Congress, the House would be deemed to have passed a bill increasing the debt limit by that amount once both chambers had adopted the budget resolution conference report.

Republicans handily defeated more than two dozen Democratic amendments aimed at reshaping budget priorities.

The bigger challenge for House leaders was a brief rebellion by GOP moderates who tried to revive strict budget enforcement rules. After delaying the completion of the resolution for a week, the moderates were mollified by a vote on a separate bill that called for caps on annual appropriations and a pay-as-you-go requirement for new entitlement spending. At the insistence of Speaker J. Dennis Hastert of Illinois and other GOP leaders, the tax cuts would not be affected. The committee approved the enforcement bill (HR 3973 — H Rept 108-442) by voice vote March 17, but it went no further.

House Floor Action

House Republicans pushed the resolution to adoption on a 215-212 vote March 25. Ten Republicans voted against the plan; no Democrats backed it. (*House vote 92, p. H-34*)

Before the final vote, the House rejected four alternative budgets — three offered by Democrats and one by GOP conservatives. The alternatives were:

- A Democratic leadership proposal, defeated 194-232, to allow discretionary spending to keep pace with inflation, with a balanced budget projected by 2012. The plan included extensions of the $1,000 child tax credit, marriage penalty relief, and the expanded 10 percent tax bracket, along with some other tax relief. Beyond that, however, it would have set up pay-as-you-go rules for both tax cuts and increases in entitlement programs. It also called for repeal of some of the 2001 and 2003 tax cuts for those who made more than $500,000 a year. (*House vote 91, p. H-34*)

- A proposal by the Congressional Black Caucus, rejected 119-302, that called for $43.3 billion more in fiscal 2005 discretionary spending than the GOP budget, including more for homeland security, education and law enforcement. It would have repealed recent tax breaks for individuals with incomes above $200,000. (*House vote 88, p. H-32*)

- A plan by the group of fiscally conservative Democrats known as the "Blue Dogs," which was rejected 183-243. The substitute, which won the support of 12 Republicans, included a one-year extension of the three expiring tax cuts, but it would have renewed pay-as-you-go rules for other tax cuts or mandatory spending increases. The amendment called for $822.9 billion in fiscal 2005 discretionary spending and promised a balanced budget by 2012. (*House vote 89, p. H-34*)

- A proposal by the Republican Study Committee, a

Budget Amendment Dies

The House Judiciary Committee began marking up a proposed constitutional amendment to balance the budget (H J Res 22) on Sept. 22, but recessed without a final vote, after Democrats blasted the measure as hypocritical.

The House last adopted a balanced-budget amendment in 1995, as part of the GOP majority's "Contract With America." Nearly 10 years later, a few GOP conservatives and leaders sought to resurrect the issue in advance of the 2004 election as a way to force a controversial vote for Democrats. (*1995 Almanac, p. 2-34*)

The proposed amendment would have required a three-fifths majority vote of both chambers to enact legislation that would result in a deficit, though it included an exception for times of military conflict. The changes to the Constitution would have taken effect during the fiscal 2010 budget cycle at the earliest, or later if it took the states longer to ratify the amendment. A constitutional amendment must be ratified by three-fourths of the states.

The attempt to embarrass Democrats backfired. When the Judiciary Committee began marking up the resolution, Chairman F. James Sensenbrenner Jr., R-Wis., ran into a torrent of criticism from Democrats. "The gall and hypocrisy of this amendment is breathtaking," said Jerrold Nadler of New York, noting the huge tax cuts and record deficits that were incurred under a Republican administration. Republicans defeated a Democratic amendment to remove Social Security receipts and outlays from the total figure used to determine whether the budget was balanced. Sensenbrenner then recessed the markup and did not reconvene it.

group of the most conservative House Republicans, which was defeated 116-309. It called for a 1 percent cut from fiscal 2004 levels for non-security-related discretionary spending, and a 1 percent reduction in the growth of non-Social Security entitlement spending each year. The amendment would have provided reconciliation protection for $182.6 billion in tax cuts. (*House vote 90, p. H-34*)

House GOP leaders worked to keep rebellion among a few party members from spreading to the rank and file. Veterans' Affairs Committee Chairman Christopher H. Smith, R-N.J., argued that the Budget Committee's recommended funding level for veterans' programs was $1.2 billion below the level in the Senate's budget resolution. Smith ultimately voted against the resolution, but leaders persuaded other wary Veterans' Committee members that the Senate's apparently higher veterans' funding level would actually be offset by unspecified spending cuts elsewhere. Veterans Affairs Secretary Anthony J. Principi stepped in to help by endorsing Nussle's plan.

Conference

Republican leaders and budget writers spent nearly two months trying to strike a deal on tax cuts that both Senate

moderates and the rest of the party would accept. But House GOP leaders flatly rejected any proposal that could limit their ability to cut taxes or extend existing tax cuts, and the Senate moderates refused to accept any proposal that exempted tax cuts from pay-as-you-go rules. With patience running out and other options exhausted, Republican negotiators decided on a long-shot strategy. They completed a conference report on the budget and essentially dared the Senate moderates to block it. "We have exhausted all negotiations," Frist said. "This is the best we can do."

On May 19, budget leaders filed a conference report (H Rept 108-498) on a stripped down version of the resolution that covered only fiscal 2005. The agreement included restoring pay-as-you-go rules, but only through April 15, 2005, with an exemption for any tax cuts that were part of a 2004 reconciliation bill. The House adopted the report later May 19 by a 216-213 vote. (*House vote 198, p. H-68*)

But in the Senate, where Republicans had just 51 seats plus Georgia Democrat Zell Miller who routinely voted with them, GOP leaders could afford to lose only two votes from within their own ranks and remain assured of adopting the budget. Rather than risk defeat, Frist held off. The Senate never took up the resolution.

Postscript

House Republicans had prepared for the possibility that the Senate would not act: The rule for floor debate on the conference report included language that deemed the budget resolution to be in force in the House as if it had been adopted by both chambers. That gave the Appropriations Committee a discretionary spending total of $821.4 billion to use in drafting the 13 fiscal 2005 spending bills. The rule was adopted 220-204. (*House vote 192, p. H-66*)

Meanwhile, David R. Obey of Wisconsin, the ranking Democrat on the House Appropriations Committee, agreed to work with the majority party to help move along the 13 appropriations bills. In return, Republican leaders agreed to hold a floor vote on a Democratic proposal to boost fiscal 2005 discretionary spending in the budget conference report by $14.2 billion. The proposed increase included more funds for homeland security, veterans' health care, education and deficit reduction.

Obey was under no illusion that he would prevail, but he relished the chance for a vote on Democratic priorities. "The country needs to know who stands where," he told reporters. The resolution (H Res 685) was defeated 184-230, on June 24. The Rules Committee had refused to let Obey offer a similar proposal when the budget resolution was originally on the House floor. (*House vote 301, p. H-100*)

The lack of a budget resolution was a bigger headache for Senate appropriators. It meant that Stevens did not have an official spending allocation to divide among his 13 subcommittees. More important, it left GOP leaders procedurally defenseless against Democratic attempts to add money to the spending bills on the floor.

Senate leaders finally got the budget enforcement tool they needed with a provision added to the conference report on the only fiscal 2005 spending bill cleared before the August recess — the defense appropriations bill. Signed into law Aug. 5 (PL 108-287), the measure set a fiscal 2005 discretionary spending limit in the Senate of $821.4 billion. ◆

Debt Limit Dilemmas

The House cleared legislation Nov. 18 that raised the nation's debt limit by 11 percent to $8.18 trillion. President Bush signed the bill into law the next day (S 2986 — PL 108-145).

The bill, introduced by Senate Majority Leader Bill Frist, R-Tenn., increased the nation's borrowing authority from the previous statutory level of $7.38 trillion, which had been enacted in May 2003 (PL 108-24). If Congress had failed to clear the increase, the government would have been unable to pay interest on existing notes and bonds, redeem maturing securities or borrow additional funds. *(2003 Almanac, p. 5-12)*

The Treasury Department had asked GOP leaders to act on the issue before Congress recessed in October, but Republicans delayed a vote until after the November election to prevent Democrats from using the issue to embarrass them during the campaign.

The House cleared the bill on the date the Treasury Department cited as the deadline for raising the debt limit. Treasury had used a number of accounting maneuvers to avoid breaching the debt ceiling up to that point, but the department said it had exhausted all of its options. Treasury Secretary John W. Snow told Congress in a Nov. 16 letter that the department would suspend new investments to be credited to the Civil Service Retirement and Disability Fund. Snow also postponed until Nov. 19 an announcement of $84 billion in sales of four-week bills, three- and six-month bills and two-year notes.

The debt ceiling applies to the sum of the public debt — including Treasury securities, savings bonds and other government notes — and the government's obligations to federal trust funds, primarily Social Security and Medicare.

Failing to raise the ceiling is never an option: The alternative of a government default is unthinkable. But Democrats used the occasion to blame President Bush's tax cuts for restoring the deficit and adding to the accumulated red ink.

Legislative Action

House Republicans had given themselves a way to avoid voting on a stand-alone bill. As part of the rules set at the start of the 108th Congress, the GOP majority revived the so-called Gephardt rule — named for former House Democratic leader Richard A. Gephardt of Missouri (1977-2003) — which allowed the chamber to escape an up-or-down vote on the debt limit. Instead, the House was considered to have passed a debt limit increase and sent it to the Senate when both chambers adopted the conference report on the annual budget resolution.

The problem was that House and Senate Republicans were unable in 2004 to agree on a budget resolution, and the Senate never voted on the conference report (S Con Res 95

BoxScore

Bill:
S 2986 — PL 108-145
Legislative Action:
Senate passed S 2986, 52-44, on Nov. 17.
House cleared the bill, 208-204, on Nov. 18.
President signed Nov. 19.

— H Rept 108-498). That made the Gephardt rule mute.

House Republicans tried a second ploy in June, seeking to include the debt limit increase in the must-pass defense appropriations bill. They added language to the House version of the defense bill (HR 4613) declaring that the government, "shall take all steps necessary to guarantee the full faith and credit of the government." That minimal reference made the debt limit a germane subject once the bill got to conference, without requiring either chamber to vote on it. Republicans hoped that would prevent Senate Democrats from offering amendments on the topic, or even debating it at length.

House Democrats were unable to block the strategy. But two days later the defense bill moved to the Senate, where the minority party has more leverage. Democrats made it plain the issue would delay passage of the bill — and the onset of senators' July Fourth recess. Senate Appropriations Chairman Ted Stevens, R-Alaska — who initially supported the plan — relented, announcing on the floor June 24 that the conference report would not include a debt limit increase.

When Congress eventually took up the debt limit in the lame-duck session, Democrats used the debate to fire a broadside at GOP fiscal policies. No Republicans spoke in favor of the measure before the Senate passed it Nov. 17 by a vote of 52-44. The House cleared the bill, 208-204, the next day, with 10 Republicans joining Democrats in voting against it. *(Senate vote 213, p. S-45; House vote 536, p. H-172)* ◆

Deficit Record

The federal government set a new deficit record in fiscal 2004, although the Bush administration emphasized, as it had the previous year, that the red ink was actually relatively modest when measured against the size of the economy.

Fiscal 2004 ended Sept. 30 with a federal deficit of $412.1 billion. That was $34.6 billion or 9 percent above the previous record of $377.6 billion, which was set in fiscal 2003. As a percent of the gross domestic product (GDP), however, the shortfall looked somewhat less alarming. The fiscal 2005 deficit represented 3.6 percent of GDP — the highest ratio since 1993, but nothing like the 6 percent mark hit in 1983.

The final deficit was less than the $445 billion projected in July, when the White House and the Office of Management and Budget issued its mid-session review of the budget.

Chapter 5

CONGRESSIONAL AFFAIRS

Continuity of Congress Bills Stall

The House passed legislation to ensure rapid elections to fill House vacancies in the event of a catastrophe — a possibility Congress had been contemplating with renewed focus since the Sept. 11, 2001, terrorist attacks. However, the House rejected a proposal to amend the constitution so that some House vacancies could be filled by appointment. A Senate subcommittee approved a separate proposal for a constitutional amendment, but the Senate took no further action on either plan.

Though there was no clear proof, it was widely assumed that hijackers aboard United Airlines Flight 93, which crashed in a field in Pennsylvania on Sept. 11, were headed for either the U.S. Capitol or the White House. An attack on the nation's capital could leave tens or even hundreds of lawmakers dead, making it impossible for Congress to function effectively and undercutting the legitimacy of any actions it might attempt to take.

At the end of 2003, House Republican leaders coalesced behind a bill (HR 2844) that would require states to hold special elections within 45 days if the Speaker declared that more than 100 House seats were vacant. The House passed that measure overwhelmingly in April 2004.

Proponents said the six-week delay was an appropriate price to pay for retaining the direct election of members, a hallmark of the House. But many Democrats argued that the 45-day time limit was not long enough to put together special elections. Some members said that to keep Congress functioning, governors should be allowed to appoint House members until elections could be held. That, however, required amending the Constitution.

House GOP leaders opposed any method other than elections to fill vacant seats, but they allowed a vote on a proposed constitutional amendment (H J Res 83) in exchange for securing Democratic support for the special-election bill. H J Res 83 was soundly defeated in June.

The Senate, unlike the House, had a process for replacing members who died, resigned or were removed from office: Under the 17th Amendment, states could fill senatorial vacancies, a power most states gave to the governor. But that did not deal with the possibility of incapacitated senators or a large-scale attack. In May, a Senate Judiciary subcommittee approved a proposed constitutional amendment (S J Res 23) that would allow the House and Senate to set terms for replacing their members in a catastrophe. Even if the Senate had endorsed that proposal, it would have been doomed in the House. "Traditionally, the House has not been interested in Senate efforts to pass a constitutional amendment to appoint House members,"

BoxScore

Bills:
HR 2844, H J Res 83, S J Res 23

Legislative Action:
House passed HR 2844 (H Rept 108-404, Parts 1, 2), 306-97, on April 22.
House rejected H J Res 83 (H Rept 108-503), 63-353, on June 2.
Senate subcommittee approved S J Res 23 by voice vote May 13.

said House Judiciary Committee spokesman Jeff Lungren.

Legislative Action

House Special Election Bill

● **Committee action.** Brushing aside the concerns of Democrats, the House Judiciary Committee approved the special-election bill (HR 2844 — H Rept 108-404, Part 2) by a vote of 18-10 on Jan. 21. The measure had the support of Speaker J. Dennis Hastert, R-Ill. The House Administration Committee approved it in November 2003. (*2003 Almanac, p. 6-4*)

Under the bill:

● States would be required to hold special elections within 45 days of the Speaker announcing that more than 100 vacancies existed in the House of Representatives.

● States did not need to hold the special election if a regularly scheduled general election to fill the seat was to occur within 75 days of the Speaker's announcement.

● Parties would be required to nominate their candidates within 10 days of the Speaker's announcement.

● Any challenge to the Speaker's announcement would have to be filed within two days in the federal district court with jurisdiction over that congressional district, and heard by a three-judge panel that would have three days from the filing to issue a final decision. The governor could intervene to support or oppose the challenge. The decision of the three-judge panel would not be subject to further judicial review.

Judiciary Chairman F. James Sensenbrenner Jr., R-Wis., said the bill "will protect the people's right to chosen representation." He and Rules Chairman David Dreier, R-Calif., were the bill's main sponsors.

Democrats, who cast all of the "no" votes in the Judiciary Committee, reiterated concerns that a 45-day period for electing new members was too short. "Perhaps for smaller states that might be adequate," said Linda T. Sánchez, D-Calif., "but in California it would be a logistical feat."

"There needs to be ability in the worst-case scenario for the House to be reconstituted on a temporary basis," said Zoe Lofgren, D-Calif.

Existing law allowed states to decide when to hold special elections to fill vacancies in their House delegations. In the previous 15 years or so it had taken an average of four months to fill a House vacancy.

● **Floor action.** The House passed the bill April 22 by a lopsided, bipartisan vote of 306-97. The outcome belied the level of dissatisfaction, especially among House Democrats. (*House vote 130, p. H-48*)

Many Democrats said they preferred to amend the Constitution to permit the appointment of replacement House members after disasters, at least until the states could hold special elections. "The bill before us today does not give us a viable plan," said Martin Frost, D-Texas. "We would find ourselves without a functioning Congress perhaps for months under this bill."

The sponsors replied that any procedure allowing for an appointed House member would undo one of the central tenets of the founders: that one chamber of the national legislature should be "the people's house," its members unalterably subject to a popular vote.

Democrats also complained that they had essentially been left out of deliberations on the bill sent to the floor — a slight all the more offensive on a matter of institutional, not political, importance.

Wary of passing such a bill by a razor-thin partisan margin, Republican leaders promised a floor debate on a constitutional amendment later in the year. And they allowed for the consideration of several Democratic amendments to the bill, two of which they accepted on voice votes. One required that any special elections adhere to federal election laws. The other sought to guarantee that members of the military overseas would have enough time to vote in any of the quick special elections.

House Constitutional Amendment

● **Committee action.** The House Judiciary Committee voted 17-12 on May 5 to send the proposed constitutional amendment (H J Res 83 — H Rept 108-503) to the floor with an unfavorable recommendation. The vote fell along party lines, with Democrats complaining that the measure, offered by Brian Baird, D-Wash., had not been given a fair and sufficient hearing.

Sensenbrenner said the founding fathers explicitly rejected the idea of appointing lawmakers to the House.

Under the proposed constitutional amendment:

● If a majority of House lawmakers were killed or incapacitated in a catastrophe, governors would appoint replacements to fill each vacant seat in their state delegation, choosing from a list of at least two names provided by the representative before taking office.

● The same process would occur if the House adopted a resolution declaring that extraordinary circumstances

threatened its ability to represent the interests of the people.

● The governor would have to make the appointment within seven days after the member's death or incapacity had been certified. The individual appointed would serve until the member regained capacity or until another member was elected to fill the vacancy. The state would hold an election to fill the vacancy at such time and in accordance with procedures provided for under state law, and the individual appointed to fill the vacancy in the meantime could be a candidate. The measure would not apply to members of the House who died or were incapacitated prior to the catastrophic event that required the appointment of members under this measure.

● Congress would be allowed to establish criteria for determining whether a member of the House or Senate was dead or incapacitated and would have the power to enforce this provision through appropriate legislation.

● The resolution provided seven years for ratification by three-fourths (38) of the states.

The committee rejected two motions by Lofgren to delay the committee markup for at least two weeks so lawmakers could hold additional hearings on the matter.

● **Floor action.** The House overwhelmingly rejected the proposal June 2. The votes was 63-353. (*House vote 219, p. H-74*)

Many lawmakers, particularly Republicans, said they opposed appointing members under any circumstances; others balked at the idea of amending the Constitution.

Baird tried, but failed, to get the Rules Committee to allow an open floor debate so that other similar measures could be considered. The House rejected, 194-221, an attempt by Lofgren to send the bill back to committee for further discussion and hearings on the topic. (*House vote 218, p. H-74*)

Senate Constitutional Amendment

The Senate Judiciary Subcommittee on the Constitution, Civil Rights and Property Rights gave voice vote approval May 13 to a proposed constitutional amendment (S J Res 23) that would allow each chamber to set the terms for replacing its members through legislation. The action would be required if one-fourth of either chamber was killed or incapacitated. The bill's sponsor, panel Chairman John Cornyn, R-Texas, said the intent was to allow the two chambers to manage continuity issues separately. ◆

Ethics Panel Admonishes DeLay

The House ethics committee was busier than at any time since 1997, when the House revamped the procedures for policing its members' behavior, and party leaders tacitly blessed an informal truce under which members refrained from alleging ethical lapses by other members.

Two highly publicized investigations dominated the committee's attention in 2004, and the panel resolved each by admonishing Majority Leader Tom DeLay, R-Texas.

The Senate Ethics Committee announced one new investigation during the year, into whether Richard C. Shelby

of Alabama leaked classified information to reporters in 2002, while he was the top Republican on the Select Intelligence Committee.

DeLay Admonished

On June 15, Rep. Chris Bell, D-Texas, filed a complaint with the ethics panel, formally the Committee on Standards of Official Conduct, maintaining that DeLay, the Republican floor leader, had broken House rules, federal law or Texas law in three instances. Bell alleged that DeLay had:

• Solicited campaign donations from Westar Energy Inc., the largest electricity provider in Kansas, in return for favorable consideration of the company's views in writing the energy overhaul bill (HR 6). (*2003 Almanac, p. 9-3*)

• Pressured Federal Aviation Administration (FAA) officials to help find Texas Democratic legislators who had left the state in 2003 in a bid to block the congressional redistricting plan then being pushed by DeLay. (*2003 Almanac, p. 14-6*)

• Participated in a scheme to subvert state law by funneling corporate contributions to Texas state House candidates in 2002.

On Oct. 6, the ethics panel — with bipartisan unanimity — admonished DeLay for going "beyond the bounds of acceptable conduct" by sponsoring a golf fundraiser for energy company executives, including Westar officials, just before the start of conference negotiations on the energy bill and by soliciting FAA help to locate the Texas legislators. The committee also warned DeLay that it had identified a clear pattern of misbehavior and would be on the lookout for additional instances when he pushed the bounds of acceptable conduct in pursuing his legislative and political goals.

"In view of the number of instances to date in which the committee has found it necessary to comment on conduct in which you have engaged, it is clearly necessary for you to temper your future actions to assure that you are in full compliance at all times with the applicable House rules and standards of conduct," the panel wrote.

Six days earlier, the committee had admonished DeLay for improperly offering to endorse the congressional candidacy of Brad Smith as long as his father, Rep. Nick Smith, R-Mich., reversed his position and voted to clear the Medicare prescription drug law (PL 108-173) in November 2003. (*2003 Almanac, p. 11-3*)

The ethics committee postponed action on the third part of Bell's complaint, which was based on facts also being investigated by the district attorney in Austin, Ronnie Earle. The panel by custom defers to prosecutors in such cases. On Sept. 21, a grand jury in Austin indicted three of DeLay's political advisers. They were charged with using the Texans for a Republican Majority Political Action Committee, which DeLay chaired, to illegally funnel corporate political donations to Texas state legislative candidates. Election of a GOP majority in the state House in 2002 was essential to DeLay's campaign to rewrite the state's congressional district lines to favor Republicans the following year.

Although DeLay was neither identified as a target of Earle's inquiry nor subpoenaed in the case, House Republicans voted in a Nov. 17 closed session to allow the majority leader to continue in this post even if he were indicted. They changed an 11-year-old caucus rule that had required party leaders or committee chairmen to relinquish those jobs if charged with a felony. (The caucus reversed the decision in January 2005 after Republicans complained of being tarred in local newspapers and on talk radio for condoning the rules change.)

Three other lawmakers connected to the DeLay cases also were upbraided. The ethics panel faulted Smith, who was retiring, for initially making false allegations in the Medicare matter, including that he had been offered a bribe.

It said Rep. Candice S. Miller, R-Mich., had wrongly suggested a threat of political retaliation against Smith if he did not change his vote. The committee also faulted Bell, who lost his bid for renomination to a second term, for including innuendo, speculation and unwarranted conclusions in his complaint against DeLay.

The 2004 events were not DeLay's first run-in with the ethics committee. In 1999, he received a warning from the panel for threatening to retaliate against a trade association unless it hired a Republican as its president. DeLay was then the GOP whip. (*1999 Almanac, p. 8-17*)

Other House Ethics Cases

In other action, the House ethics committee:

• Admonished Karen McCarthy, D-Mo., for not reimbursing her campaign committee for thousands of dollars she spent on a trip to the Grammy Awards ceremony in New York early in 2003.

• Opened an examination of whether John Conyers Jr., D-Mich., violated House rules by using his Detroit district office to conduct campaign activity.

• Began an investigation into whether Curt Weldon, R-Pa., used his office to help his daughter's lobbying firm.

• Was asked to consider whether Jim McDermott, D-Wash., violated House rules in 1996.

In October, U.S. District Judge Thomas F. Hogan ordered McDermott to pay $60,000 in damages and eight years' worth of attorneys' fees to Rep. John A. Boehner, R-Ohio, for leaking a transcript of an illegally recorded cellular phone conversation among the House leadership in 1996. When McDermott appealed the award, David L. Hobson, R-Ohio, filed the ethics complaint against McDermott. (*1997 Almanac, p. 1-35*)

Shelby Investigated

The Senate Ethics Committee in August announced it was investigating whether Shelby leaked classified information to reporters in 2002, while he was the top Republican on the Select Intelligence Committee. The panel said it had gotten matter on referral from the Justice Department.

The FBI had been investigating whether Shelby illegally, or at least inappropriately, disclosed the content of National Security Agency (NSA) intercepts that were discussed during closed-door testimony before the House and Senate Intelligence committees in June 2002 during an investigation into intelligence activities prior to the Sept. 11 terrorist attacks. (*2002 Almanac, p. 7-18*)

Shelby's office released a statement Aug. 6 denying any wrongdoing by the senator.

The Justice Department investigation focused on Shelby after news reports in June 2002 disclosed that the NSA had intercepted two messages Sept. 10, 2001, saying that an event was planned, but had not translated them until Sept. 12. A report aired by CNN said that the messages were, "Tomorrow is zero hour" and "the match begins tomorrow."

That information apparently came from closed-door testimony by Lt. Gen. Michael Hayden, the NSA director, that was delivered to the Intelligence Committee the same day as the CNN report. Vice President Dick Cheney complained about the leak, and Intelligence Committee leaders called on the Justice Department to find the source. ◆

Senate Restructures Committees

After grueling negotiations and opposition from chairmen trying to protect their turf, the Senate agreed in October to make changes to its standing rules to enhance the power of committees responsible for intelligence and homeland security programs. The changes came at the urging of the independent Sept. 11 commission, but they fell well short of the bipartisan panel's recommendations.

The Senate adopted the new committee plan in October, although it was not set to take effect until the start of the 109th Congress. The House planned to deal with its own reorganization issues at that time. House leaders did not say whether their reorganization would mirror that of the Senate.

The Commission on Terrorist Attacks Upon the United States was created by Congress (PL 107-306) to review the events leading up to the Sept. 11, 2001, terrorist attacks. Much of its highly publicized report, issued July 22, dealt with shortcomings in the intelligence community. It led to the enactment in December of a bill overhauling the intelligence agencies (PL 108-458). *(Intelligence overhaul, p. 11-3)*

But the panel also called on Congress to consolidate its oversight of homeland security in one committee and grant the panel new authority over intelligence appropriations.

John Lehman, a Republican member of the commission, told the House Government Reform Committee Aug. 3: "The most important thing to do is to fix the congressional issues. . . . Fix that first if there has to be a priority, because the rest of the system that we're recommending will not function properly without Congress fixing its own committee structure and jurisdiction."

Highlights

The final resolution adopted by the Senate made only part of the recommended changes.

● **Intelligence Committee.** The Senate raised the status of the Intelligence Committee to category "A," to give its members more time to focus on intelligence issues. Under Senate rules, senators could serve on no more than two "A" panels.

The resolution also ended the eight-year term limit for Intelligence members; gave the majority and minority leaders power to appoint all panel members, including the chair and vice chair; and reduced the size of the committee from 17 to 15 members.

Rejecting one of the main directives of the Sept. 11 commission, however, the Senate did not give the Intelligence Committee budget authority, leaving that power instead with the Appropriations Committee. The Intelligence Committee was also denied on-demand sequential referral, which would have given it automatic jurisdiction of all legislation that included intelligence-related material.

● **Appropriations.** The resolution created a new Senate Appropriations subcommittee to handle the intelligence budget,

---

BoxScore

Bill:
S Res 445

Legislative Action:
Senate adopted S Res 445, 79-6, on Oct. 9.

---

but left it to the appropriators to decide what adjustments to make to avoid exceeding the panel's limit of 13 subcommittees. It said the reorganization should occur "as soon as possible after the convening of the 109th Congress."

● **Homeland Security.** The Governmental Affairs Committee was given formal jurisdiction over some functions of the Department of Homeland Security and renamed the Homeland Security and Governmental Affairs Committee. But the panel did not gain jurisdiction over two of the department's largest agencies: the Transportation Security Administration (TSA) and the Coast Guard.

Background

In its 567-page report, the 10-member Sept. 11 commission recommended changes to the congressional committee structure aimed at giving the Intelligence Committee more clout and creating a Homeland Security panel that would keep tabs on the fledgling Homeland Security Department.

At the time, at least 17 committees in the two chambers had some responsibility for intelligence matters. "Congressional oversight for intelligence — and counterterrorism — is now dysfunctional," the commission wrote. "Congress should address this problem." The commission recommended establishing a joint House-Senate Intelligence committee.

The problem was that such changes ran counter to the interests of powerful chairmen and ranking members. As Sen. Pat Roberts, R-Kan., chairman of the Intelligence Committee, explained. "The No. 1 issue for any chairman of any committee is that you don't give up your turf under any circumstances — not a spadeful."

The two chambers had created committees specifically to oversee intelligence matters in the mid-1970s after evidence of wrongdoing by the CIA. The Senate experienced a protracted turf war in 1976 when members tried to create a single Intelligence panel by taking jurisdiction from existing committees, especially Armed Services and Judiciary. At the time, eight committees had access to CIA documents and information. *(1976 Almanac, p. 294)*

Ultimately, the Senate's Select Intelligence Committee was established without spending power. After equally intense partisan wrangling, the House followed suit a year later. *(1976 Almanac, p. 294; 1977 Almanac, p. 376)*

Efforts to consolidate intelligence oversight had been going on for at least two decades before that. In 1956, for example, the Senate, in a 27-59 vote, crushed a proposal by Mike Mansfield, D-Mont. (1953-77), to establish a joint intelligence panel. *(1956 Almanac, p. 509)*

In 1987, the Tower Commission investigating the Iran-contra scandal suggested a joint committee on intelligence to cut down on leaks of classified information. The idea was championed by Republicans, then in the minority, but it

eventually fizzled out. *(1987 Almanac, p. 61)*

The Senate Governmental Affairs Committee, the panel tapped to oversee homeland security, had not generally been considered a premier assignment. Its jurisdiction included the civil service and Postal Service, the census, archives and the general oversight of the executive branch.

When Congress was debating the law (PL 107-296) that created the Homeland Security Department, Senate leaders put Governmental Affairs in charge of its work, and the panel had been dealing with domestic security issues since. *(2002 Almanac, p. 7-3)*

In 2004, the committee — led by Chairwoman Susan Collins, R-Maine, and ranking Democrat Joseph I. Lieberman of Connecticut — gained new stature for successfully guiding the intelligence overhaul bill through to enactment. But the panel still lacked the clout to keep key pieces of homeland security oversight from other powerful committees.

Legislative Action

Senate Floor Action

The Senate adopted its reorganization plan (S Res 445) by a vote of 79-6 on Oct. 9 during the chamber's first weekend session in 11 months. *(Senate vote 208, p. S-44)*

The resolution was put together by a 22-member leadership group and shepherded through the balky chamber by Republican Whip Mitch McConnell of Kentucky and Democratic Whip Harry Reid of Nevada. Once the measure was on the floor, senators from panels such as Appropriations, Finance, Judiciary and Commerce who felt slighted teamed up to help one another chip away at the reorganization plan.

The resolution broadened the jurisdiction of the Governmental Affairs Committee and gave it a new name. But the chairmen of other Senate committees reclaimed jurisdiction over so many parts of the Homeland Security Department during the bill's drafting and floor debate that Collins and Lieberman ended up voting against the resolution.

As drafted, the plan left jurisdiction over the TSA and Coast Guard in the hands of the Commerce, Science and Transportation Committee. Additional pieces of the department were claimed by other committees

During the floor debate, the Senate:

• Adopted by voice vote an amendment by Saxby Chambliss, R-Ga., to keep immigration issues under Judiciary Committee purview. Chambliss chaired the Judiciary subcommittee that handled immigration.

• Adopted by voice vote an amendment by Max Baucus of Montana, the ranking Democrat on the Finance Committee, to allow Finance to retain oversight of part of the Bureau of Customs and Border Protection.

• Defeated, 33-63, an attempt by John McCain, R-Ariz., Collins and Lieberman to reclaim the TSA for the Governmental Affairs panel. *(Senate vote 201, p. S-43)*

• Adopted, 54-41, a proposal by Judiciary Chairman Orrin G. Hatch, R-Utah, to reclaim jurisdiction over the Secret Service. Judiciary had had jurisdiction over the agency for 56 years. "If you've got something that's not broken, why fix it?" asked ranking Judiciary Democrat Patrick J. Leahy of Vermont. *(Senate vote 202, p. S-43)*

Collins said at one point that the resolution, as amended, would leave a Homeland Security Committee with jurisdiction over less than 38 percent of the Department of Homeland Security's budget and just 8 percent of its personnel. She became so disgusted by the turn of events that she voted to kill the resolution by delay Oct. 8. Only two other senators did so, however, and cloture was invoked, 88-3. *(Senate vote 204, p. S-44)*

The Senate also:

• Adopted, 50-35, a proposal by Budget Chairman Don Nickles, R-Okla., to give the Budget Committee sole jurisdiction over the congressional budget process. At the time, Governmental Affairs and Budget shared jurisdiction. *(Senate vote 206, p. S-44)*

• Defeated, 23-74, a proposal by McCain that would have given the Intelligence Committee power over intelligence spending as well as policy. *(Senate vote 200, p. S-43)*

• Adopted, 44-41, along party lines, a proposal to strike language that would have merged the Military Construction Appropriations subcommittee into the Defense subcommittee to allow for a new intelligence panel. The amendment was offered by Kay Bailey Hutchison, R-Texas, who chaired the Military Construction Subcommittee and stood to lose her chairmanship. The amendment left it up to the Appropriations Committee to decide how to make room for the intelligence subcommittee. *(Senate vote 207, p. S-44)* ◆

Chapter 6

DEFENSE & HOMELAND SECURITY

Lengthy Debate on Defense Bill

For the third year in a row, the annual defense authorization bill was enacted after appropriators had completed the companion spending bill, reducing the influence of the House and Senate Armed Services committees on military funding. But the authorizers retained their say on matters of policy, weighing in on the future of a troubled refueling plane program, base closures, troop levels, military pay and benefits, and hundreds of other issues.

The fiscal 2005 defense bill authorized $445.6 billion for the Department of Defense and for Energy Department nuclear programs. President Bush signed the bill into law Oct. 28 (HR 4200 — PL 108-375).

The defense authorization debate was lengthy, in part because it was the arena where the big fights on defense were played out — a factor that allowed the appropriators to move more quickly.

The Senate alone took 16 legislative days to wade through hundreds of amendments until lawmakers passed their version of the authorization bill in late June — more than a month after the House had passed its bill. It took weeks more for a conference to convene, as recesses, national party conventions, the Abu Ghraib prison scandal and a proposed reorganization of the intelligence community diverted members' attention. But once they sat down for negotiations, conferees managed to resolve the disputes that had divided the House and the Senate.

Conferees rejected a House attempt to delay the 2005 round of military base closings, authorized the largest increase in troop levels in decades and authorized the Air Force to sign a new contract to purchase, but not lease, up to 100 refueling tanker planes. They also dropped House "Buy American" provisions, increased military pay and benefits, and eliminated a statutory cap on spending for a military family housing privatization program.

Overall, the measure authorized $144.5 billion for operations and maintenance, $106.5 billion for personnel, $74.2 billion for weapons procurement, $66.5 billion for research and development and $17.5 billion for weapons-related and environmental cleanup activities of the Energy Department. It also authorized $17.7 billion for defense health costs and $10 billion for military construction and family housing.

Highlights

The following are highlights of the 2004 bill:

● **Iraq supplemental.** The measure authorized $25 billion in emergency funds for ongoing operations in Iraq and Afghanistan, as requested by the president, and made the mon-

BoxScore

Bill:
HR 4200 — PL 108-375

Legislative Action:

House passed HR 4200 (H Rept 108-491, Parts 1-2), 391-34, on May 20.

Senate passed S 2400 (S Rept 108-260), 97-0, on June 23, then inserted the text into HR 4200.

House adopted the conference report (H Rept 108-767), 359-14, on Oct. 9.

Senate cleared the bill by voice vote Oct. 9.

President signed Oct. 28.

ey available upon enactment. However, Congress rejected a Pentagon request for full discretion in using the funds. The money was actually appropriated in the fiscal 2005 defense spending bill (PL 108-287) signed Aug. 5. (*Appropriations, p. 2-12*)

● **Airborne refueling tankers.** The bill authorized the Air Force to start a new 10-year program to purchase — not lease — up to 100 refueling tanker planes in a new full-and-open competition. The provision replaced language in the fiscal 2004 authorization law (PL 108-136) that authorized the Air Force to lease 20 KC-767A aerial tankers from Boeing Co. and buy 80 more. That deal had been on hold amid criminal charges against a former Defense Department and Boeing employee, and questions about the cost effectiveness of the entire program. (*2003 Almanac, p. 7-3*)

● **Troop strength.** Congress authorized the largest increase in troop strength in decades, requiring the Army to add 20,000 active-duty personnel in fiscal 2005 for a total of 502,400, and the Marine Corps to add 3,000 for a total of 178,000. Initial funding was provided as part of the Iraq supplemental. The totals were established as statutory minimums. In addition, the bill authorized, but did not require, the Army to grow by 10,000 troops and the Marine Corps to grow by 6,000 by 2009.

● **Weapons systems.** The final bill authorized:

● $9.9 billion for missile defense, including interceptors being installed in Alaska and California as part of the first national anti-missile shield. The total was 11 percent above fiscal 2004 spending but about 2 percent less than requested.

● $3.5 billion to continue development of the Joint Strike Fighter, a next-generation fighter with versions to be used by the Air Force, the Navy and the Marine Corps.

● $4.2 billion for 24 F/A-22 Raptor fighters, as requested. The Air Force's controversial, next-generation fighter, intended to replace the F-15 and F-16, had been plagued by cost overruns and technical problems. It already had become the most expensive jet fighter ever built.

● $2.9 billion, $270 million less than requested, for the Army's Future Combat System. Of the total, $700 million was contingent on the program meeting a number of goals.

● $1.5 billion for the DD(X) destroyer, including a requested $221 million for detail design and advanced construction of the first ship, plus $84 million for design of a second ship.

● **Base closures.** Conferees rejected a House provision to delay until 2007 a round of base closures scheduled for 2005, defying the House majority and almost half the Senate, and

backing the administration, which said it could save billions of dollars by closing unneeded bases.

● **Military housing.** The conference agreement repealed a statutory cap on funding for a popular military housing privatization program. The cap had limited total federal contributions for the program to $850 million, a point the government expected to reach before the end of the year. Without legislative relief, an estimated 60,000 military families would have been unable to get new or renovated homes. Appropriators waited until this provision was finalized before completing the fiscal 2005 military construction spending bill (PL 108-324). (*Appropriations, p. 2-40*)

● **Benefits.** The bill authorized a 3.5 percent pay raise as requested, expanded benefits for survivors of deceased military personnel, concurrent receipt of full pensions and full disability payments for military retirees considered 100 percent disabled, and expanded access for reservists to the military's TRICARE health system.

● **"Buy American."** Conferees jettisoned a House provision that would have banned defense trade with countries that required "offsets" in the form of local investment by the U.S. defense firms that wanted to sell them U.S.-made weapons.

Legislative Action

House Committee Action

The House Armed Services Committee approved a $447.1 billion defense authorization bill (HR 4200 — H Rept 108-491, Parts 1-2) late May 12 after a marathon markup that lasted nearly 14 hours. The measure, approved 60-0, included $25 billion in emergency spending for Iraq. The committee's six subcommittees had approved portions of the bill May 5-6. While the bill closely followed Bush's funding request, it parted ways with the administration on several key points, including provisions to increase the size of the military, delay the next round of base closures by two years and give the president only minimum flexibility in deciding how to spend the $25 billion war fund.

● **Troop strength.** In a reflection of growing concern over the increased strain on the armed forces and reserves due to the war in Iraq, the committee called for the addition of 10,000 Army troops per year and 3,000 Marines per year in in fiscal 2005 through 2007. The totals would be a statutory minimum. The increase was to be funded initially under the $25 billion emergency war fund.

Secretary of Defense Donald H. Rumsfeld had asked lawmakers to give the Pentagon flexibility to adjust troop levels. Rumsfeld was concerned that the cost of the added soldiers would divert funds needed to modernize weapons. He also said the answer was retraining people who were already in the Army, not adding more. But with volunteer soldiers being required to stay longer in Iraq than they originally signed on for and troops being diverted from Korea to bolster the force in Iraq, senators were not receptive to Rumsfeld's pitch.

● **Base closings.** The bill included an amendment by Joel Hefley, R-Colo., to delay the next round of military base closures scheduled for 2005 until 2007. The amendment was adopted by voice vote. Hefley and others said it was premature to start closing bases until Congress had more answers about the needs of the U.S. military and about plans for ex-

isting facilities in Europe and Asia. The delay — which the committee adopted in place of a proposal by Gene Taylor, D-Miss., to kill the Base Realignment and Closure program — was similar to a provision approved by the Readiness Subcommittee, which Hefley chaired.

● **Nuclear weapons.** The bill included $27.6 million, as requested, to continue studying the feasibility of developing a nuclear bomb, known as the Robust Nuclear Earth Penetrator, that could burrow deep into the earth to destroy underground enemy bunkers. Supporters stressed that the program was only a study. Critics argued that any research on a new nuclear weapon would deal a blow to U.S. counterproliferation efforts and encourage other countries to follow suit. They said the $485 million the Energy Department planned to spend on the program in fiscal 2005-09 suggested that the administration was conducting more than a simple study.

The committee rejected separate attempts by Ellen O. Tauscher, D-Calif., and Martin T. Meehan, D-Mass., to cut $36.6 million from the nuclear "bunker buster" and shift the money to other programs.

● **Missile defense.** The committee endorsed $10 billion of the president's $10.2 billion request for anti-missile programs. Democrats focused much of their criticism on the Pentagon's plan to start deploying the system in September, arguing that it had not been adequately tested. However, they were unable, as they had been in the Strategic Forces Subcommittee, to reduce the funding.

The committee rejected, 26-31, an attempt by John M. Spratt Jr. of South Carolina, the second-ranking Democrat on the committee, to redirect $150 million to shorter range anti-missile systems. The panel also rejected, 26-34, an amendment by Loretta Sanchez, D-Calif., to prevent use of money authorized in the bill to fund space-based interceptor components of the ballistic missile defense system.

● **Iraq war.** The full committee added language authorizing the $25 billion war fund that Bush had requested to pay for operations in Iraq and Afghanistan during the first months of fiscal 2005. In place of the unlimited flexibility Bush wanted, however, the committee specified how the money should be spent, allowing the Pentagon to transfer only $2.5 billion between accounts without asking for prior congressional approval. The committee recommended that $1.2 billion from the fund go toward costs associated with the proposed increases in Army and Marine troop strength.

● **Aerial tanker.** To get the tanker program back on track, Chairman Duncan Hunter, R-Calif., called for a "fresh start" in which the Air Force would sign a new multi-year contract to lease 20 Boeing KC-767s and buy 80 more. The bill authorized $98.5 million for the program and provided for an independent commission to review the contract. In its report accompanying the bill, the committee said it was "deeply concerned" that the ongoing investigations into alleged wrongdoing, "while necessary and proper, are needlessly delaying the pressing requirement to proceed with the acquisition of a replacement aircraft for our aging fleet of KC-135 tankers."

● **Military family housing.** The committee gave voice vote approval to an amendment by Jeff Miller, R-Fla., to eliminate the spending cap on the program to privatize construction of military housing, using some extra discretionary budget authority that committee staff produced by finding a

Hill Steps Aside on Abu Ghraib Abuses

Lawmakers expressed outrage and disgust in early May when photos surfaced showing abuse of detainees by U.S. military personnel at the Abu Ghraib prison near Baghdad. Defense Secretary Donald H. Rumsfeld and other top Pentagon officials were summoned for back-to-back hearings by the House and Senate Armed Services committees. Democrats called for Rumsfeld's ouster. Both chambers adopted resolutions condemning the abuses and calling for investigations.

In the end, however, Congress left the investigations to the Pentagon and backed away from demands for detailed information about detainee operations and policies in Iraq, Afghanistan and Guantánamo Bay, Cuba.

On May 6, soon after the world saw the startling photos of Iraqi prisoners stripped naked, posed in humiliating positions with U.S. soldiers leering over them, some covered with hoods and threatened with electrocution, the House adopted a non-binding resolution (H Res 627) condemning the abuse and urging an investigation. The resolution was adopted, 365-50, on May 6. (*House vote 150, p. H-54*)

Four days later, the Senate voted 92-0 to adopt a similar measure (S Res 356). (*Senate vote 86, p. S-21*)

In the months that followed, three House committees — Armed Services, International Relations and Judiciary — shot down resolutions of inquiry requesting that the Bush administration provide Congress with documents about its policies affecting the treatment of detainees in Iraq and elsewhere. Senate Judiciary Committee Democrats sought unsuccessfully in June to get their GOP colleagues to subpoena the Justice Department for detainee-related documents.

Senate Armed Services was more aggressive in its pursuit of reports of prisoner abuses than its House counterpart, which showed little appetite for such inquiries. Duncan Hunter, R-Calif., chairman of the House panel, criticized his Senate counterpart, John W. Warner, R-Va., for holding hearings on the issue. But Warner stressed the limitations of those hearings, calling them an "inquiry" rather than an investigation, and saying the job of investigating the abuses should be left to the Defense Department.

In the end, it was the Pentagon, not Congress, that investigated the incidents and issued reports on how they happened. An independent panel, appointed by Rumsfeld and chaired by former Defense Secretary James R. Schlesinger, released a report Aug. 24 that blamed prisoner abuses on military leadership failures at all levels of command, but found no evidence that the Abu Ghraib abuses were part of a high-level policy to gain intelligence from prisoners.

An Army report, also released in September, concluded that the prison abuses at Abu Ghraib were the result of individual misconduct, a lack of discipline and a failure of leadership.

The only binding legislation on the abuses was buried deep within the fiscal 2005 defense authorization law (PL 108-375) enacted Oct. 28. In addition to sense-of-Congress language expressing outrage and a desire to see a thorough investigation, the law set minimum criteria for a new policy to be drafted by the Defense secretary to ensure humane treatment of detainees. It also required the secretary to certify the proper training of those who handled or interrogated detainees, including training on the Geneva Conventions. (*Defense authorization, p. 6-3*)

The law also required regular reports to Congress on the development and implementation of the new policies, any criminal investigations arising from detentions, and "aggregate data" on foreign national detainees in U.S. custody. A Senate provision that would have required the Pentagon to turn over details on the number of detainees at specific locations was dropped in conference.

By the end of the year, three soldiers had been sentenced for the abuses and a fourth arraigned. The first, Spc. Jeremy Sivits, got one year in jail in May after agreeing to testify against six other accused Americans. Spc. Armin J. Cruz, the first military intelligence soldier to stand trial, was sentenced to eight months in September. U.S. army reservist Staff Sgt. Ivan (Chip) Frederick, the highest-ranking U.S. soldier charged in the scandal, was sentenced to eight years in prison. Pfc. Lynndie England was arraigned; her trial was announced for 2005.

new way to score the tanker provisions. But the committee rejected, on a 20-30 party-line vote, a proposal by Susan A. Davis, D-Calif., to shift $414 million from missile defense programs to build military housing in several states.

- **Civilian workers.** The panel adopted, by voice vote, an amendment by Jim Langevin, D-R.I., to specify that any job performed by 10 or more Defense Department civilians could not be outsourced to a private contractor unless a competition was held that compared the competing parties' costs, ability to meet quality and reliability standards and other criteria.
- **Weapons systems.** The authorization included:
  - $4.6 billion, as requested, to continue development of

the F-35 Joint Strike Fighter.
  - $4.1 billion for 24 F/A-22 Raptor fighters.
  - $3 billion for the Army's Future Combat System (FCS), as recommended by the Tactical Air and Land Forces Subcommittee. The total was $245 million less than requested, and the committee directed that $750 million of the remaining money be held until the Army reported to the Congress on the program's progress. In its report, the committee said it was "greatly concerned about the Army's ability to deliver these capabilities within cost and schedule estimates. The Army has never managed any program of the size and complexity of FCS."
  - $1.2 billion for the DD(X) destroyer. The committee

eliminated $221 million requested to begin constructing the first ship, saying it should be delayed to allow more testing.

• **"Buy American."** Hunter, who was an avid supporter of a strong domestic defense industry, included language to bar U.S. defense contractors from investing in a foreign country's economy as a condition of selling weapons to that nation. Hunter and many Democrats argued that the practice was siphoning U.S. defense industry jobs abroad. The Pentagon and defense industry trade groups strongly opposed the so-called Buy American provision, saying it threatened the nation's 6-to-1 defense trade surplus with Europe.

Hunter had clashed sharply with his Senate counterpart, Armed Services Chairman John W. Warner, R-Va., the previous year in an effort to include domestic-content requirements for U.S.-made weapons in the fiscal 2004 defense authorization bill.

• **Colombia.** The committee adopted, 32-24, an amendment by Taylor to cap the number of U.S. troops in Colombia at 500. An aide said the existing cap of 400 for contractors would not be affected.

House Floor Action

The House passed the $447.2 billion bill, 391-34, on May 20. An en bloc amendment by Hunter, adopted by voice vote, made a number of small changes, including strengthening the tanker provisions to instruct the Air Force to enter into an agreement to buy the 80 tankers by March 1, 2005. The amendment also specified that the $25 billion in war funds would be available upon enactment of the bill. (*House vote 206, p. H-70*)

• **Base closings.** Lawmakers soundly rejected, 162-259, an attempt by Mark Kennedy, R-Minn., to scratch the base closing delay language. Among those voting in support of the delay — even after the language drew an explicit veto threat from the White House — were 103 Republicans, or 45 percent of the caucus, a rare instance of parochial political considerations triumphing over House GOP loyalty to the president. (*House vote 200, p. H-68*)

• **Prisoner abuse.** The House adopted, 416-4, an amendment by Hunter condemning the abuse of prisoners at Abu Ghraib prison in Iraq. Henry A. Waxman, D-Calif., later offered a motion to recommit the bill so non-binding language calling for a congressional investigation could be added. The motion failed, 202-224. (*House votes 199, 205, pp. H-68, H-70; Abu Ghraib, p. 6-5*)

The House also voted, 308-114, to urge the Pentagon to raze the Abu Ghraib prison. Opponents said the Iraqi people, not the Pentagon, should decide the prison's fate. (*House vote 201, p. H-68*)

• **Nuclear weapons.** Tauscher tried again to cut $36.6 million from research on a nuclear bunker buster and spend the money instead on a conventional version. Republicans argued the government needed to pursue all weapons programs if it was to maintain a credible deterrence of its enemies. The amendment was rejected, 204-214. (*House vote 203, p. H-68*)

• **Other amendments.** The House also:

• Adopted, 231-191, an amendment by Virgil H. Goode Jr., R-Va., to allow members of the armed services to assist the Homeland Security Department with border protection. Democrats opposed the amendment, arguing it would un-

necessarily strain the military. It was subsequently dropped in conference. (*House vote 196, p. H-66*)

• Adopted, 290-132, an amendment to authorize a Pentagon training program for the Taiwanese military, which also was dropped in conference. (*House vote 204, p. H-70*)

• Adopted, 410-0, a proposal by Ike Skelton, D-Mo., to direct the Defense Department to develop a comprehensive policy to prevent and respond to sexual assault involving members of the armed forces. (*House vote 202, p. H-68*)

• Rejected, 202-221, an amendment by Davis that would have allowed female service members stationed overseas to obtain abortions at military hospitals as long as they paid for them. (*House vote 197, p. H-66*)

Senate Committee Action

The Senate Armed Services Committee approved a $422.2 billion version of the bill (S 2400 — S Rept 108-260) by a vote of 25-0 on May 6. The bottom line was the same as for the House bill, minus the $25 billion emergency war fund.

Ordinarily the bill would have been the committee's top priority, but at that point the panel was focused on just-released photos of U.S. military personnel abusing prisoners at Abu Ghraib prison. The panel concluded the markup just in time to convene a high-profile hearing the next day to take testimony from Rumsfeld on the incidents.

The bill, which largely mirrored the president's request, omitted some of the more controversial House provisions, such as the delay in base closings and the Buy American language. The bill also contained no authorization to proceed on the tanker deal with Boeing.

The authorizations included:

• Authority, but not a requirement for the Army to add 30,000 soldiers over four years.

• $10.2 billion for missile defense as requested, including funds to buy 36 more Patriot PAC-3 interceptors.

• $3.4 billion, as requested, to continue development of the Joint Strike Fighter.

• $3.4 billion for 22 F/A-22 Raptor fighters, rather than the 24 that Bush proposed, for a savings of $280 million. The committee cited backups in the delivery schedule.

• $3.2 billion, as requested, for the Army's Future Combat System .

• $1.5 billion for the DD(X), including the requested $221 million for detail design and advanced construction of the first ship and $99 million for detail design of a second ship.

Senate Floor Action

The Senate passed the bill, 97-0, just before midnight June 23. The vote came after 16 days of debate that began May 17. The addition of the $25 billion war fund during floor debate brought the bill's total to $447.2 billion. (*Senate vote 146, p. S-32*)

With more than 100 amendments pending on the authorization, Majority Leader Bill Frist, R-Tenn., filed a motion June 16 to invoke cloture and move toward a final vote but backed off after determining he lacked the 60 votes needed. Under pressure from appropriators who were eager to get the $25 billion for Iraq to the president's desk, the Senate finally completed its work.

• **Iraq war fund.** An amendment by Warner, adopted

Aerial Tanker Lease Under Scrutiny

The saga of the aerial tankers began with the fiscal 2002 defense appropriations act (PL 107-117), which authorized the Air Force to negotiate with Boeing Co. to lease 100 of its 767 passenger jets, modified to become KC-767 tankers. Ted Stevens of Alaska — then ranking Republican on the Senate Appropriations Committee and its Defense Subcommittee — said he wrote the leasing provision out of concern for the military's increasing refueling requirements in the war on terrorism. Aides said he was supported by Democratic senators, including Daniel K. Inouye of Hawaii, then the Defense Subcommittee chairman, and Patty Murray of Washington, where Boeing was then based and where it still built 767s. (*2001 Almanac, p. 2-13*)

The original idea was apparently Boeing's. The company had pitched it to the Air Force in February 2001. Before that, the Air Force had not requested replacements for its fleet of more than 500 KC-135 tankers, many of which were built during the Eisenhower administration. The Air Force had said those planes would not need to be replaced for years.

After the provision became law, the Air Force became an advocate for the lease proposal, discussing for the first time what was termed a serious corrosion problem in the tankers and urging their rapid replacement. The Air Force, Boeing and their congressional allies all said that by leasing the planes, rather than buying them, the Air Force could obtain more planes sooner because fewer dollars would be required up front.

Plan Comes Under Attack

Almost immediately, Sen. John McCain, R-Ariz., began to criticize the deal as "corporate welfare." McCain said the Defense Department did not conduct its own formal evaluation of alternatives to the Boeing deal and that the Pentagon document that established the need for the planes was written to fit the Boeing KC-767. An early version of the document even had the plane's name in the title, he said. McCain's voice was amplified by taxpayer groups and a host of government agencies.

Over the following three years, criticisms were leveled by the Congressional Budget Office, the Congressional Research Service, the Pentagon's Program Analysis and Evaluation Office, the Office of Management and Budget, the Pentagon's inspector general, the Defense Science Board and the Government Accountability Office. They said the planes were not needed as quickly as the Air Force maintained because the corrosion problem had been overstated, and/or that leasing them would cost billions more than buying them.

Proponents of the deal continued to argue that the planes would be needed sooner rather than later and that leasing them was the only way to get them quickly.

Although the Senate Armed Services Committee, resisted, the fiscal 2004 defense authorization law (PL 108-136) allowed the Air Force to lease up to 20 tankers and purchase no fewer than 80. (*2003 Almanac, p. 7-3*)

On Nov. 24, 2003, the day President Bush signed that bill, Boeing revealed it had fired two of its top executives, Chief Financial Officer Mike Sears and a missile-defense executive, Darleen Druyun. Druyun, a former principal deputy assistant secretary for Air Force acquisition and management, had secretly negotiated her post-government work with Boeing while overseeing the tanker program and other Boeing initiatives, the company said. A month later, Boeing's chief executive, Phil Condit, stepped down. Almost immediately, Defense Secretary Donald H. Rumsfeld suspended the tanker program.

The drumbeat of criticism continued into 2004, including a Pentagon advisory board statement that the KC-135 corrosion problem was not as bad as the Air Force had argued and a Pentagon inspector general report that said the proposal did not satisfy the military requirement for refueling planes, did not protect taxpayers with complete auditing standards and used "questionable" pricing assumptions.

In May, Rumsfeld deferred action on the program until November, pending further studies of the refueling requirements and the best way to meet them.

On Oct. 1, Druyun was sentenced to nine months in jail after admitting that while serving as a senior Air Force official, she accepted a higher than justified price for the tankers, part of more than $4 billion in favors she did for Boeing to repay the company for deciding to hire her and two of her relatives.

The House tried to "restart" the lease/buy plan as part of the fiscal 2005 defense authorization law, but Senate conferees refused. The final bill (PL 108-375) barred the Air Force from leasing the planes and authorized it to start over, negotiating a contract to purchasing 100 aerial refueling planes. (*Defense authorization, p. 6-3*)

Even then, however, the argument continued. On Oct. 8, Norm Dicks, D-Wash., suggested in a House floor colloquy with Armed Services Chairman Duncan Hunter, R-Calif., that they had won in conference. "The most important point," Dicks said, "is we don't have to go back and have yet another procurement, because if we did that, it would take years and years before we would start getting tankers."

The next day, John W. Warner, R-Va., Senate Armed Services chairman, inserted in the Congressional Record a written exchange with McCain. In direct contrast to Dicks' contention, McCain said the bill specified "the Air Force cannot acquire, by lease or purchase, Boeing 767s without full and open competition."

Boeing Chief Executive Officer Harry C. Stonecipher asserted that the law did not require a new competition. But the parent company of Boeing's archrival, French-based Airbus, said the law was "ambiguous" and made it clear it stood ready to bid for the contract.

95-0, added the $25 billion emergency war fund to the bill. Most of the money would be allocated; the Pentagon would be able to transfer up to $2.5 billion among accounts with congressional approval. (*Senate vote 106, p. S-25*)

● **Base closing.** An attempt by Trent Lott, R-Miss., to effectively postpone the 2005 base closing round failed, 47-49. Lott's amendment would have confined the 2005 closures to overseas bases and revised the method of selecting domestic basis for closure in 2007. But the 2005 round had strong support from Warner, as well as from Carl Levin of Michigan, ranking Democrat on the Armed Services Committee, and the committee's No. 2 Republican, John McCain of Arizona. (*Senate vote 98, p. S-23*)

● **Troop strength.** Over administration objections, the Senate voted overwhelmingly to add 20,000 soldiers to the Army in fiscal 2005, bringing the total to 502,400, but without establishing that as the new statutory minimum. The amendment, by Jack Reed, D-R.I., was adopted 93-4. (*Senate vote 129, p. S-29*)

"We didn't have enough people on the ground" in Iraq, said McCain. "And now we are paying a very, very heavy price for that incredible mistake on the part of the civilian leadership in the Pentagon of the United States. And why were they so reluctant to send additional troops? The dirty little secret is . . . they didn't have them."

While the added troops would not be of immediate assistance in Iraq, many senators believed the United States was in the global war on terrorism for the long haul and would need a bigger military to wage it.

Senators ultimately agreed to a compromise by Warner to tap emergency spending funds — either the pending $25 billion request or a future one — to pay for the estimated $1.7 billion cost of adding the troops.

● **"Buy American."** Going the opposite way from the House, the Senate adopted, 54-46, a McCain amendment to allow the Defense secretary to waive existing Buy American laws for a handful of close U.S. allies. (*Senate vote 135, p. S-30*)

● **Tankers.** A McCain amendment adopted by voice vote without debate required that any tanker contract be reviewed by the Pentagon inspector general and the Government Accountability Office, and that it meet Office of Management and Budget scoring rules for leases. A Senate Republican aide said the provision could mean the Air Force would have to pay up front for leased planes, negating the reason for leasing them in the first place. McCain was a strong opponent of the leasing proposal.

● **Military benefits.** Senators agreed to significantly expand benefits for service members and their families. The Senate:

● Adopted, 82-0, a proposal to authorize medical and dental care for Reserve Officer Training Corps participants who became injured or ill in the line of duty. The amendment, by Kay Bailey Hutchison, R-Texas, also proposed to extend disability coverage to service academy cadets and midshipmen. (*Senate vote 95, p. S-23*)

● Adopted, 70-25, a proposal to give members of the National Guard and the reserve access to the military's TRICARE health system regardless of whether they were deployed. Under existing law, reservists were covered only while on active duty and for a limited time period afterward. The amendment, by Minority Leader Tom Daschle, D-S.D.,

and Lindsey Graham, R-S.C., required that reservists pay 28 percent of the cost. (*Senate vote 105, p. S-25*)

The vote defied the Pentagon and Warner, who argued that the cost — estimated at $14.2 billion over 10 years — was too high and that the new benefit would remove an incentive for soldiers to join the regular forces. "We're talking about a very, very significant, permanent entitlement for the reserves, which is extremely costly," Warner said. But Daschle and Graham said recruiting and retaining reservists might be increasingly difficult without improved benefits.

Warner beat back Democratic attempts to expand the benefits even further. The Senate:

● Rejected an amendment by Jon Corzine of New Jersey to reduce the retirement age for reservists from 60 to 55. The vote was 49-49, short of the 60 votes required to overcome a budgetary point of order. (*Senate vote 136, p. S-30*)

● Rejected, 49-48, on a similar point of order a Daschle proposal for mandatory veterans' health benefits to cover inflation and population increases. (*Senate vote 145, p. S-31*)

● **Nuclear weapons.** The Senate defeated, 42-55, a proposal by Edward M. Kennedy, D-Mass., and Dianne Feinstein, D-Calif., to eliminate the $36.6 million for a study of the nuclear bunker buster. (*Senate vote 113, p. S-27*)

● **Missile defense.** Democrats lost four separate party-line votes aimed mainly at requiring more stringent testing of missile defense components. The Senate:

● Rejected, 42-57, on June 17 a proposal by Barbara Boxer, D-Calif., to require the Pentagon's testing director to oversee tests of the system and certify that it was ready before deployment. Warner said adopting the amendment would "put a halt on this system." (*Senate vote 124, p. S-28*)

● Rejected a similar proposal by Reed that called for the independent testing office to run the exercises, but would not have made deployment contingent on such testing. Warner altered Reed's amendment to require the Defense secretary to set criteria for operationally realistic testing of prototypes after consulting with the Pentagon's testing director. Warner's second-degree amendment was adopted, 55-44, on June 17. The modified Reed amendment was then adopted by voice vote. (*Senate vote 125, p. S-29*)

● Rejected, 44-56, a proposal by Levin to shift $515.5 million for ground-based midcourse interceptors to nuclear nonproliferation and other anti-terrorism activities. (*Senate vote 133, p. S-30*)

● Rejected, 45-53, an attempt by Reed to tie the $550.5 million to certification by the independent testing office that the system was effective and suitable for combat. (*Senate vote 139, p. S-31*)

● **Other amendments.** The Senate also:

● Voted, 54-43, to table (kill) a proposal by Christopher J. Dodd, D-Conn., to prohibit the use of private contractors to conduct prisoner interrogations at U.S. military facilities. Warner and other Republicans said the amendment would not give the Defense Department sufficient time to hire and train enough U.S. military personnel to perform the interrogations. (*Senate vote 118, p. S-27*)

● Rejected, 46-52, a proposal by Patrick J. Leahy, D-Vt., to create a new criminal penalty for "war profiteering" by contractors abroad. An alternative by Warner, adopted 97-0, proposed to extend the jurisdiction of U.S. courts over such alleged crimes overseas, but without creating a new

criminal statute. *(Senate votes 119, 120, p. S-28)*

• Adopted by voice vote an amendment by Ron Wyden, D-Ore., to prohibit contracting out work that is "closely associated with inherently governmental work" unless no government employees could do it. The amendment also would bar such outsourcing if giving the work to the contractor would create the appearance of a conflict of interest.

• Rejected, 49-50, an amendment to revise a 1977 law (PL 95-223) that prohibited U.S. firms from doing business with states that sponsored terrorism. The language, by Frank R. Lautenberg, D-N.J., was designed to block companies from maneuvering around the law by using foreign subsidiaries to conduct business with countries such as Iran. *(Senate vote 101, p. S-24)*

• Rejected, on a 48-48 tie, a proposal by Maria Cantwell, D-Wash., to delete bill language permitting on-site burial of nuclear waste held in holding tanks at the Savannah River Site in South Carolina, rather than requiring shipment to a planned nuclear waste repository at Yucca Mountain, Nev. *(Senate vote 107, p. S-25)*

• Rejected, 40-58, a proposal by Robert C. Byrd, D-W. Va., to limit the number of U.S. military troops and civilian contractors in Colombia to 500 each. *(Senate vote 140, p. S-31)*

• **Hate crimes, indecency.** The Senate also adopted the following amendments unrelated to the bill; they were dropped in conference:

• An amendment by Gordon H. Smith, R-Ore., to broaden categories covered by federal hate crimes to include crimes motivated by the victim's gender, sexual orientation or disability, adopted, 65-33. *(Senate vote 114, p. S-27)*

• A proposal by Sam Brownback, R-Kan., to add language tripling fines for broadcast indecency, adopted, 99-1. However, Byron L. Dorgan, D-N.D., succeeded in adding provisions to Brownback's amendment to block the Federal Communications Commission from rolling back media ownership restrictions. The same proposal had stalled earlier anti-indecency legislation. *(Senate vote 134, p. S-30; indecency, p. 14-3)*

Conference/Final Action

The House-Senate conference on the bill did not officially convene until Sept. 29, but aides and members had been negotiating informally since mid-July. The conference report on what ended up as a $445.6 billion bill (H Rept 108-767) was filed after midnight on Oct. 8 as Congress raced to complete its work before heading home to campaign. The House adopted the conference report, 359-14, in the early morning hours of Oct. 9, and the Senate cleared the bill by voice vote later the same day. *(House vote 528, p. H-170)*

The lengthy talks covered hundreds of issues, though only a relative handful were particularly troublesome. The following are among the decisions made by the conferees:

• **Iraq funds.** Both chambers agreed that Congress should allocate the $25 billion for Iraq to specific accounts, rather than leaving the decision up to the Pentagon. The bill specified that $16.4 billion be used for operations and maintenance, $1.3 billion to pay for increased Army and Marine troop levels, $1.5 billion for increased fuel costs and $1.2 billion for additional procurement. The bill mandated

large increases over administration requests to protect U.S. forces in Iraq, including $572 million more for additional "up armor" Humvees, $250 million more for ballistic armor for other Humvees and trucks and $435 million more for body armor. The Pentagon could transfer $1.5 billion of the total among accounts after consulting with Congress.

• **Tankers.** The tanker issue was the last to be resolved. Conferees rejected the House requirement that the Air Force sign a new contract with Boeing to lease 20 planes and buy 80. They barred the Air Force from leasing the planes and authorized a new, multi-year contract to buy 100 planes. Even after the conference report had been cleared, conferees continued to argue about whether the compromise would require Boeing to compete with other companies to build the tankers.

• **Base closings.** The conferees agreed to allow the next round to proceed in 2005, but set new criteria for closing bases and required seven of the nine members of the base-closing commission to approve each closure.

• **Prisoner abuse.** The conference agreement required the Defense secretary to establish procedural policies for U.S. military and contract personnel to prevent the abuse of prisoners held as part of the global war on terrorism. The policies were to be issued within 150 days of enactment and given to Congress immediately; the Defense secretary was required to report to Congress on their implementation one year later.

• **National Guard and reserves.** The bill expanded access to the military's TRICARE health care system for the National Guard and reservists. Reservists on active duty who re-enlisted in the reserves were made eligible for one year of TRICARE while not on active duty for each 90 days of active duty service. Under previous law, reservists were allowed access to the health care network only for brief periods while not serving on active duty. The bill also permanently gave reservists and their families access to TRICARE benefits 90 days before they were activated.

The law continued a provision of the fiscal 2004 authorization that extended TRICARE to the Guard and reservists who lacked health insurance and did not have access to employer health plans.

• **Veterans' benefits.** The bill increased benefits for surviving dependents of deceased military personnel from 35 percent of retired pay to 55 percent by fiscal 2008. It also allowed military retirees who were 100 percent disabled to receive both their full pensions and disability benefits in 2005, earlier than under the fiscal 2004 law.

• **Active duty benefits.** The bill permanently increased the family separation allowance from $100 per month to $250, and increased imminent danger pay from $150 per month to $225.

• **Nuclear waste storage.** The conference report retained a Senate provision that reclassified high-level nuclear waste remaining from Cold War bomb manufacturing as incidental waste, enabling South Carolina to bury waste from the military's Savannah River site on location rather than requiring shipment to a planned permanent repository at Yucca Mountain in Nevada.

• **Civilian workers.** The final bill limited the ability of the Pentagon to contract out work being done by civilian employees unless it would save 10 percent or $10 million.

• **Colombia.** Conferees dropped the House cap of 500 U.S.

military personnel, agreeing instead to limits of 800 for military personnel and 600 for U.S. contractors, as requested.

● **Sexual assault.** The final bill required the Pentagon to develop a uniform policy for all services for preventing and responding to sexual assault. It also expanded the mission of a task force established under the 2004 defense authoriza-

tion law, by having it examine sexual assaults throughout the military and report to Congress within 12 months of its initial meeting. The conference report said conferees expected the renamed Defense Task Force on Sexual Assault in the Military Services to provide an independent assessment of policies implemented by the services. ◆

Coast Guard Enters New Phase

Congress cleared a bill to help modernize and expand the Coast Guard, which had taken on significant new duties in guarding the U.S. coast since the Sept. 11, 2001, terrorist attacks. The bill authorized $8.2 billion in appropriations for the Coast Guard in fiscal 2005, about 12 percent more than President Bush requested. The president signed the bill into law Aug. 9 (HR 2443 — PL 108-293).

The bill authorized a personnel level of 45,500, and included $1.1 billion — $422 million more than requested — for the Coast Guard's 20-year program to replace its deteriorating ships and aircraft, known as Deepwater. It also extended training bonuses and housing-related privileges to the Coast Guard as a way to encourage enlistment and bring the service in line with benefits given to other military branches.

The House passed a version of the reauthorization bill in 2003 (HR 2443 — H Rept 108-233) that would have authorized $7.1 billion for fiscal 2004 but did not cover fiscal 2005. The bill stalled over a House provision that would have required the Coast Guard to approve security plans for foreign vessels entering U.S. ports. The Bush administration opposed it because of the extra money it would require. The Senate passed a version of the bill in 2004 that did not include the proposal, and conferees ultimately agreed to drop it, paving the way for quick enactment.

The Coast Guard was under the new Department of Homeland Security, which began operating in 2003. The fiscal 2004 Homeland Security spending law included $6.8 billion for the Coast Guard. Despite the new authorization, the service got $7.4 billion in fiscal 2005 (PL 108-334), virtually the same as Bush requested. (*Appropriations, p. 2-26*)

Legislative Action

Senate Floor Action

The Senate passed its two-year version of the Coast Guard reauthorization bill (HR 2443) by voice vote March 30. The measure was an update of a bill (S 733) that the Senate Commerce, Science and Transportation Com-

BoxScore

Bill:
HR 2443 — PL 108-293
Legislative Action:
Senate passed HR 2443, amended, by voice vote March 30.
House adopted the conference report (H Rept 108-617), 425-1, on July 21
Senate cleared the bill by voice vote July 22.
President signed Aug. 9.

mittee had approved in July 2003.

The new version authorized $7.1 billion in appropriations for fiscal 2004 and $7.8 billion for 2005. It required foreign vessels bound for U.S. ports to have security plans that conformed to international maritime treaties, but it did not require the Coast Guard to approve the plans. For the Deepwater program, the Senate proposed authorizing $702 million in fiscal 2004 and $708 million in fiscal 2005.

House Committee Action

On April 21, the House Transportation and Infrastructure Committee approved a new bill (HR 3879 — H Rept 108-482) that proposed to authorize almost $8 billion for fiscal 2005. Like the earlier House bill it proposed to tighten security procedures, requiring each foreign vessel entering a U.S. port to submit a security plan to the Coast Guard for approval. It also required that the Coast Guard develop a procedure to certify "classification societies" — private or quasi-governmental entities that served as vessel safety inspection bodies for foreign governments that lacked the resources to do the job themselves.

The bill authorized $1.1 billion for the Deepwater program. The panel's Coast Guard and Maritime Transportation Subcommittee had increased the amount from $858 million when it approved the bill March 10. The decision to add more money was made despite a Government Accountability Office report issued March 9 that cited management problems in the program.

The Transportation Committee also gave voice vote approval May 12 to a bill (HR 4251 — H Rept 108-775) endorsing policy proposals that had been requested by the Coast Guard, including language expressly authorizing Coast Guard personnel to carry handguns and make arrests.

Conference/Final Action

After more than two months of negotiations, House and Senate conferees reached agreement and filed the conference report (H Rept 108-617) on July 20. The House adopted the conference report July 21 by a vote of 425-1, and the Senate cleared the bill by voice vote the following day. (*House vote 404, p. H-134*)

The following are some of the main decisions made by the conferees:

• With fiscal 2004 three-quarters over, conferees agreed to confine the bill to a one-year, $8.2 billion authorization for fiscal 2005, an amount that would allow the Coast Guard to raise its payroll to an authorized level of 45,500 people.

• Conferees settled their biggest disagreement — over security of foreign commercial vessels — by leaving existing law in place. In general, that meant the security plans for arriving ships were checked by their country of origin or by classification societies. The Coast Guard evaluated foreign ships based on their history, where they were registered and the reliability of the classification society. If the evaluation revealed a potential threat, the Coast Guard intercepted the vessel.

The House strongly supported its plan to require the Coast Guard to do the certification. Members voted 395-19 on May 6 to instruct conferees to retain the House language. But the administration and House GOP leaders preferred the Senate version because it promised to cost much less. The Coast Guard said it did not have enough money or personnel to evaluate security plans of an estimated 10,000 foreign-registered vessels. *(House vote 148, p. H-54)*

• Conferees kept the House's $1.1 billion spending level for the Deepwater program. However, the conference report included a provision requiring the Coast Guard to report to Congress on the performance of the project's contractors.

• House provisions allowing Coast Guard personnel to carry handguns and make arrests also were retained. ◆

Chapter 7

EDUCATION

IDEA Reauthorization Clears

After two years of legislative wrangling, Congress cleared a rewrite of the law governing special education for the nation's 6.7 million disabled students. The bill reauthorized the Individuals with Disabilities Education Act (IDEA), through 2011, with provisions to increase federal funding, raise teacher standards and give parents more flexibility in dealing with program rules. President Bush signed the bill into law Dec. 3 (HR 1350 — PL 108-446).

IDEA — which was first enacted in 1975 (PL 94-142) and last rewritten in 1997 (PL 105-17) — authorized federal assistance to help support special education and related programs. To qualify for the money, states and school districts were required to provide a free, "appropriate" public education to each eligible child with a disability in the "least restrictive environment."

The main controversies in 2004 centered on disciplinary standards for special-needs students and whether to make program funding mandatory, rather than allowing congressional appropriators to decide how much would actually be spent on a year-to-year basis.

The House passed an IDEA reauthorization bill in April 2003 with mainly Republican support. The measure, sponsored by Michael N. Castle, R-Del., focused on reducing paperwork requirements for special education programs, limiting parents' ability to take legal action against school districts and making discipline for children with disabilities similar to that for other students. *(2003 Almanac, p. 8-5)*

The Senate Health, Education, Labor and Pensions (HELP) Committee took a less confrontational approach. Chairman Judd Gregg, R-N.H., worked with ranking Democrat Edward M. Kennedy of Massachusetts to co-author a bipartisan bill that was substantially different from the House version, particularly in the areas of student discipline, teacher qualifications, legal fees stemming from lawsuits by parents and paperwork reduction for school officials.

The Senate passed the Gregg-Kennedy bill in May 2004, but Senate Democrats delayed sending it to conference until they were assured that they would have a meaningful role in shaping the conference agreement.

Conferees agreed on a final bill just before the end of the November lame-duck session. The compromise maintained the existing requirement that administrators consider disabilities when disciplining special education students. It also established stronger certification standards for special education teachers, and denied funding to states if their local school districts did not comply with bill provisions. Funding remained discretionary.

BoxScore

Bill:
HR 1350 — PL 108-446
Legislative Action:
Senate passed HR 1350, 95-3, on May 13, after inserting the text of S 1248 (S Rept 108-185).
House adopted the conference report on HR 1350 (H Rept 108-779), 397-3, on Nov. 19.
Senate cleared the bill by voice vote Nov. 19.
President signed Dec. 3.

The bill authorized $12.4 billion in fiscal 2005; the amount actually appropriated was $10.7 billion.

Highlights

The 2004 IDEA reauthorization law included these components:

● **State grants.** The $12.4 billion was for grants to help states pay for special education programs in fiscal 2005. The authorization increased annually until it reached $26.1 billion in fiscal 2011. If Congress appropriated the full amounts, by fiscal 2011 the federal government would be paying states an amount equal to 40 percent of the extra cost of educating children with disabilities. The 40 percent benchmark was set in the 1975 law, but had never been met.

● **Discipline.** As under previous law, school authorities could remove a child with disabilities from the classroom for up to 10 days for breaking school behavior codes.

Following the Senate lead, the bill left in place a requirement that school officials establish whether the disciplinary infraction was directly related to the child's disability. (In a change from previous law, the child could be removed from the school while the determination was being made.)

If the infraction was not a result of the disability, the child would be subject to the same discipline as other students. If it was linked to the disability, a behavioral intervention plan would be developed and the child would return to the classroom. Under prior law, if the infraction involved weapons or drugs, the student could be removed from the school for up to 45 days, with further extensions possible. The new law added "committing serious bodily injury" to the list and clarified that the removal was for 45 school days.

As before, disabled students who were removed from school for disciplinary reasons had to continue to receive educational services in an alternative setting.

● **Paperwork.** The law established a 15-state demonstration program that would give parents the choice of having their child's individualized education program (IEP) reviewed every three years, instead of every year, significantly reducing paperwork requirements. The IEP spelled out the specific special education and related services that were to be provided to meet the child's needs. A second pilot program allowed the Education Department to waive certain IDEA provisions for as many as 15 states to reduce paperwork requirements.

● **Identifying disabled children.** School districts were allowed to use up to 15 percent of their IDEA funds for so-called pre-referral services to help children before they were

Head Start Bill Blocked

Legislation to reauthorize Head Start, the early childhood development program, fell victim to the partisanship that dominated the Senate all year. Democrats blocked the bill from reaching the Senate floor, fearing it would be altered in a Republicans-only conference.

House GOP leaders eked out a one-vote margin of victory in July 2003 (HR 2210) for a bill that would have allowed eight states to experiment with integrating their own early childhood programs with Head Start, which is federally funded but operated locally by groups, such as churches and nonprofit organizations.

President Bush wanted to go further, proposing that states assume significant control over Head Start, but House Republicans anticipated strong resistance and settled for the pilot program.

In October 2003, the Senate Health, Education, Labor and Pensions Committee unanimously approved a bipartisan Head Start bill (S 1940) written by Chairman Judd Gregg, R-N.H., and ranking Democrat Edward M. Kennedy of Massachusetts. Gregg dropped the pilot program, which was opposed by key committee Republicans, as well as a House plan to allow faith-based hiring at Head Start centers run by church groups. (*2003 Almanac, p. 8-3*)

Senate Democrats prevented the Gregg-Kennedy bill from going to the floor in 2004. They were concerned that if it were allowed to pass, Republicans in charge of the Senate-House conference committee would include the pilot project in the final bill, leaving Democrats helpless to stop it.

identified as being disabled and in need of special education. The aim was to reduce what the measure called the "inappropriate overidentification" of children, especially minority and children with limited proficiency in English, as having a disability. Also, the bill prohibited the use of a discrepancy between a child's achievement and intellectual ability as a basis to determine whether the child had a specific learning disability.

● **Teacher certification.** The new law required that special education teachers be "highly qualified" by the end of the 2005-06 school year, the same deadline required for general classroom teachers under the 2002 No Child Left Behind Act (PL 107-110). To meet the requirement, all special education teachers, whether or not they taught core subjects, had to hold a bachelors' degree and be fully certified in special education, or have passed a state special education license exam. Those teaching core subjects would need additional certification.

● **State oversight.** States were required to file a plan showing how they would ensure that all disabled children were receiving a free, "appropriate" education. The Education Department could withhold federal funding for states that failed to comply.

Legislative Action

Senate Floor Action

After two days of generally harmonious debate, the Senate passed its version of the bill May 13 by a vote of 95-3. (*Senate vote 94, p. S-22*)

The bipartisan tone was in part due to the collaboration between Gregg and Kennedy, who sought a sober and respectful debate as a mark of respect for parents and teachers of special-needs children, some of whom watched the debate from the visitors' gallery. Kennedy's advocacy for the disabled dated to before IDEA's initial enactment in 1975.

● **Mandatory funding.** Tom Harkin, D-Iowa, and Chuck Hagel, R-Neb., tried but failed to insert language in the bill requiring mandatory increases in IDEA funding, rather than leaving it to the annual discretion of the appropriators. They proposed mandatory increases of $2.2 billion per year over six years to reach the 40 percent threshold. "Recent history leaves no doubt that discretionary increases will not get us to full funding," Harkin said. The Senate had approved a similar amendment by voice vote during the debate over the 2001 education law, but the language was dropped in conference. (*2001 Almanac, p. 8-3*)

Because the Harkin-Hagel amendment did not propose offsetting cuts to compensate for the mandatory funding, it was subject to a budget point of order that required 60 votes to overcome. The vote to waive the budget rule was 56-41, four short of the number needed. (*Senate vote 93, p. S-22*)

● **State grants.** Instead of making the funding mandatory, the Senate adopted, 96-1, an amendment by Gregg to authorize discretionary funding levels that would reach the 40 percent mark by 2011. The House bill had a similar provision aimed at reaching 40 percent by 2010. The Gregg amendment authorized $12.4 billion for IDEA grants in fiscal 2005, rising to $26.1 billion by 2011. The underlying Senate bill had simply indicated "such sums as may be necessary." (*Senate vote 92, p. S-22*)

● **Discipline.** In one of the main departures from the House bill, the Senate measure did not seek to change existing law requiring that school officials consider whether a disciplinary infraction was the result of a child's disability.

Under the House bill, disabled students would have been subject to the same disciplinary procedures as non-disabled students for any violation of school policy. School officials would not have been required to determine whether the violation was due to a disability.

School administrators, represented by groups such as the National School Boards Association, supported the House version, saying it would allow local districts to evaluate discipline on a case-by-case basis and eliminate a two-tiered disciplinary system. Disability rights groups adamantly opposed such a change. The Consortium for Citizens With Disabilities said the House provision "would potentially increase school dropout rates and delinquency" and "lead to an explosion of litigation."

● **Complaint procedures.** The Senate approved by voice vote a Gregg amendment to allow school districts to recover attorneys' fees when a parent filed a frivolous lawsuit alleging that their disabled child had received inadequate schooling. The amendment clarified that the parents would

not be responsible for the cost. The bill retained an existing requirement that the attorney fees be set by the court. The House bill proposed that governors set the attorneys' fees in IDEA cases in which the parents prevailed.

The Senate bill allowed a two-year limit for parents to file complaints after an incident in which a school allegedly failed to uphold the law. The House bill provided a one-year deadline. The Senate bill did not include a House provision that offered the alternative of voluntary binding arbitration if both the parents and the school agreed to the procedure.

● **Paperwork.** Like the House bill, the Senate measure sought to ease the burden of paperwork for teachers. The Senate gave voice vote approval to an amendment by Rick Santorum, R-Pa., to permit as many as 15 states to obtain waivers from the Education Department for demonstration projects to reduce paperwork required under IDEA. States would not be able to waive civil rights protections in their quest to reduce record-keeping. The conservative senator attracted support for his amendment from a group normally among his adversaries, the National Education Association, the nation's largest teachers' union.

The House bill allowed for a 10-state demonstration project. It included a second demonstration project that would give parents the option of having a multi-year IEP for their child. The Senate legislation allowed that option only for students between the ages of 18 and 21.

Conference/Final Action

House and Senate conferees did not formally convene until the lame-duck session, although aides had worked for weeks on a final bill. The conferees reached a bipartisan agreement Nov. 17. The House adopted the conference report (H Rept 108-779) by a vote of 397-3 on Nov. 19, and the Senate cleared the measure by voice vote later that night. *(House vote 537, p. H-174)*

Senate Democrats had agreed to go to conference only after Gregg and Kennedy reached an agreement in late September on how negotiations would be conducted. Senate conferees were finally appointed Oct. 11. ◆

Vocational Education Bill Stalls

Committees in both chambers approved bills to rewrite the nation's main vocational and technical education program, but the legislation went no further because of the campaign-shortened legislative year. Lawmakers working on the bills stressed the importance of ensuring that vocational education gave students both the academic and technical skills needed to succeed in the high-tech workplace of the 21st century.

Congress worked in a mostly bipartisan manner to reauthorize and update the 1998 Carl D. Perkins Vocational and Technical Education Act (PL 105-332), which was the main source of federal grants to the states for career and technical education. The Perkins grants supported training and programs for many low-income students, from high-schoolers to adults changing careers.

Both bills proposed new standards and levels of accountability to strengthen the academic content of vocational education programs. The House bill also proposed to merge the Perkins state grants and the smaller Tech-Prep program, which provided specialized courses in math, science and technology to make it easier for students to transfer to a vocational school or community college. The Senate bill kept the funding streams separate.

President Bush, in April, called for overhauling the Perkins program by transferring the money to a new high school and vocational college program. Under the proposal, participating schools would offer four years of English, three years of math, three years of science and three-and-a-half

BoxScore

Bills:
HR 4496, S 2686

Legislative Action:

House Education and the Workforce Committee approved HR 4496 (H Rept 108-659) by voice vote July 21.

Senate Health, Education, Labor and Pensions Committee approved S 2686 (S Rept 108-384) by voice vote Sept. 22.

years of social studies as part of their curriculum for vocational students. Congress did not consider the Bush plan.

For fiscal 2005, Congress appropriated $1.2 billion for Perkins grants and $107 million for Tech-Prep. Bush had requested $1 billion for Perkins grants and nothing for Tech-Prep.

House Committee Action

The House Education and the Workforce Committee approved its version of the bill (HR 4496 — H Rept 108-659) by voice vote July 21, despite Democratic complaints that the measure should focus more on retraining workers who lost their jobs because of outsourcing to foreign countries. The Education Reform Subcommittee approved the measure July 14.

The bill, sponsored by Michael N. Castle, R-Del., authorized $1.3 billion in fiscal 2005 and "such sums as may be necessary" for fiscal 2006 through 2010. States would be required to ensure that vocational education courses led to a degree and that schools offered challenging academic work in a coordinated curriculum.

The bill proposed to merge funding for the Perkins and Tech-Prep programs, a step Castle said would give the states greater flexibility. In subcommittee, Castle added a "hold harmless" provision, specifying that states would get at least as much as they received in combined Tech-Prep and Perkins grant funds in fiscal 2004, and that they would have to spend at least what they did in 2004 on tech-prep activi-

Job Training Bill Dies

Legislation to renew the nation's main job training program — the 1998 Workforce Investment Act (PL 105-220) — died at the end of the 108th Congress. Both chambers passed versions of the bill (HR 1261) in 2003. The House appointed conferees in June 2004, but Senate Democrats blocked efforts to go to conference, fearing they would be excluded from the final GOP-controlled negotiations.

The 1998 job training act consolidated more than 60 programs into block grants allocated to the states. It also allowed adults to use vouchers for training and education, and established one-stop career centers where recipients could learn about job leads, apply for aid and receive counseling.

The House version of the reauthorization bill — which passed 220-204 on May 8, 2003 — would have allowed faith-based groups receiving aid to discriminate in hiring based on religion. The 1998 law banned such discrimination. The bill also would have consolidated funding for adults, dislocated workers and employment services into a single state block grant. Most Democrats opposed both provisions.

The Senate version — which passed by voice vote Nov. 14, 2003 — included neither the faith-based provision, nor the consolidation proposed by the House.

ties. But some Democrats argued that money for the Tech-Prep program would erode without its own dedicated financial stream.

The bill emphasized student achievement in core academic subjects, as defined by the 2002 No Child Left Behind education law (PL 107-110), and stressed math and science education that incorporated the use of technology. States could impose sanctions on local recipients that received technical assistance but failed to show improvements. States also could get incentive grants for accomplishments, such as developing links between secondary and postsecondary education, integrating rigorous academic and technical coursework and achieving successful outcomes for special populations.

During the markup, the committee:

• Rejected, 21-23, an amendment by John F. Tierney, D-Mass., to keep the Perkins and Tech-Prep programs separate,

• Rejected, 20-24, a proposal by Rush D. Holt, D-N.J., for a new $250 million annual job-training program for high-tech manufacturing that could be utilized by workers who lost their jobs to outsourcing to foreign countries. "If we are going to keep the jobs in the United States that everyone is so concerned about with outsourcing, we can do it only if our workforce has the necessary skills," Holt said. But Chairman John A. Boehner, R-Ohio, said appropriators would never fund such a costly program.

• Adopted, 46-0, an alternative proposed by Boehner that added "advanced manufacturing" as a career field to be covered under the bill.

Senate Committee Action

The Senate Health, Education, Labor and Pensions Committee approved a similar bill (S 2686 — S Rept 108-384) by voice vote Sept. 22. The measure, sponsored by Michael B. Enzi, R-Wyo., had bipartisan support and was cosponsored by ranking panel Democrat Edward M. Kennedy of Massachusetts. Unlike the House measure, the bill did not seek to merge the Perkins and Tech-Prep programs. The measure was expected to authorize about $1.4 billion for fiscal 2005 and $10.1 billion through 2011, although amounts were not specified in the bill. ◆

Chapter 8

EMPLOYMENT & LABOR

Corporations Get Pension Relief

With thousands of companies lobbying for relief, Congress temporarily reduced the amount many employers were required to contribute to their employee pension plans. The White House threatened more than once to veto the bill, but President Bush won enough changes to enable him to sign it into law April 10 (HR 3108 — PL 108-218).

The bill temporarily changed the benchmark used by employers to calculate the value of the assets in their pension plans. Instead of the low, 30-year Treasury bond rate, they could use an index based on higher-paying corporate bonds. The new formula was available for companies with defined-benefit plans — plans that paid employees a set amount after retirement. It immediately increased the assumed value of the companies' pension assets and reduced the amount of cash they had to add to their plans in a given year to cover expected liabilities.

Enactment came just in time to help about 30,000 companies whose first-quarter pension contributions were due April 15. The change was expected to reduce the companies' pension contributions by $80 billion over two years. Airlines and steelmakers with chronically underfunded pensions plans won an additional layer of relief.

Although some prominent Democrats such as Sen. Edward M. Kennedy of Massachusetts were deeply disappointed at the minimal aid given to multi-employer plans, which were common in unionized industries such as trucking and construction, most Democrats ultimately decided they had to support the final bill.

Many companies threatened to freeze or terminate their defined-benefit plans if Congress failed to approve the new funding rules. For the previous two years, they had been allowed under a 2002 law (PL 107-147) to adjust the benchmark for valuing their assets to 120 percent of the four-year interest rate on 30-year Treasury bonds. But when the law expired Dec. 31, 2003, the rate had reverted to 105 percent of the bond rate.

Work on the bill began in the first session of the 108th Congress. The House version of HR 3108, passed in October 2003, was limited to a temporary change in the benchmark rate for single-employer plans. In November, the House passed a tax extension bill (HR 3521) that included the single-employer provisions plus special relief for airlines with chronically underfunded pensions. The airline provisions were expected to be of particular benefit to Northwest Airlines and UAL Corp.'s United Airlines, which said its emergence from bankruptcy protection hinged partly on reducing its pension obligations. *(2003 Almanac, p. 12-3)*

The Senate passed an amended version of HR 3108 in

BoxScore

Bill:
HR 3108 — PL 108-218
Legislative Action:
Senate passed HR 3108, amended, 86-9, on Jan. 28.
House adopted the conference report (H Rept 108-457), 336-69, on April 2.
Senate cleared the bill, 78-19, on April 8.
President signed April 10.

January 2004 that added help for steelmakers with chronically underfunded pensions, as well as relief for a range of multi-employer plans.

The Bush administration, which had supported the House bill, warned Congress against passing legislation that would excuse troubled companies from fully funding their pensions. It said those companies could pose a risk to the financial health of the Pension Benefit Guaranty Corporation (PBGC), the government agency responsible for insuring the pensions of 44 million Americans. With more than $800 million a year from fees charged to corporate pension sponsors, and more than $30 billion in assets, the PBGC was in no immediate danger of running out of money. Still, the administration and many lawmakers worried that if too many troubled plans collapsed, the PBGC would have to turn to taxpayers to bail it out.

In January, Bush Cabinet officials who sat on the board of the PBGC warned of a possible veto if the final bill included special help for chronically underfunded plans, such as those of the airlines, or relief for multi-employer plans. As the legislation went through Congress with strong bipartisan support, the administration dropped its objections to the airline and steel provisions. It narrowed its focus to multi-employer plans and to a Senate provision that would have opened the door for a range of companies to delay reducing their pension shortfalls. The final bill eliminated the broad relief and offered help to only about 4 percent of the nation's 1,600 multi-employer plans. The deal was enough to win the support of the White House.

Highlights

The following are the main components of the new law:
● **Single-employer plans.** The law temporarily allowed companies with defined-benefit pension plans to use a blend of corporate bond index rates created by the Treasury Department as the benchmark for determining their funding liability. The provision was good through Dec. 31, 2005.
● **Airlines and steel.** Under existing law, employers whose pension funding fell below 90 percent of liabilities for two out of three years were required to make additional payments, known as "deficit reduction contributions." The bill allowed airlines and steel companies to pay just 20 percent of their catch-up payments in 2004 and 2005, saving them an additional $1.6 billion.
● **Multi-employer plans.** The bill gave about 4 percent of multi-employer plans a two-year deferral for up to 80 percent of the catch-up payments required of chronically underfunded plans. To be eligible, a plan had to have a net investment loss

of 10 percent or larger for 2002, and the plan's actuary had to certify that the plan was expected to have a funding deficiency in 2004, 2005 or 2006. Qualifying plans could not increase their pension benefits during the deferral period, unless the increase was already negotiated under an existing collective bargaining agreement or if contributions to the plan exceeded the annual charges attributable to the benefit change.

● **Greyhound Lines Inc.** Greyhound Line was allowed to skip catch-up payments for two years. Also, in calculating its pension contributions, it was allowed to use an alternate mortality table that more closely reflected the ages of the beneficiaries in its plan. Greyhound had closed its plan to new entrants in 1983, and its average pension recipient was 70.

Legislative Action

Senate Floor Action

Brushing aside White House objections, the Senate pressed ahead with its expanded pension bill, passing it Jan. 28 by a bipartisan vote of 86-9. The temporary relief for single-employer plans was similar to the provisions in the House bill, but the Senate measure also included special aid for financially struggling airlines and steelmakers, as well as for multi-employer plans. (*Senate vote 5, p. S-5*)

Before passage, the Senate rejected an attempt by Jon Kyl, R-Ariz., to limit the liability of the PBGC for underfunded pension plans if the plans' sponsors were allowed to make less than full catch-up payments. The Senate voted 67-25 to table (kill) the amendment. (*Senate vote 4, p. S-5*)

The Senate bill proposed to:

● Allow the steel and airline companies with chronically underfunded pensions to reduce their catch-up contributions by 80 percent in 2004 and 60 percent in 2005.

● Allow any company with a chronic funding shortfall to apply to the Treasury Department to defer catch-up contributions.

● Allow Greyhound Lines Inc. to escape the extra payments for two years and to use alternate mortality tables.

● Permit multi-employer plans that had losses between mid-2002 and mid-2006 to delay accounting for their pension shortfall for up to three years.

● Require multi-employer plans to provide increased disclosure to participants, including information about the value of assets and benefit payments.

Under existing law, underfunded multi-employer plans could spread out their catch-up payments over 15 years. But when each year brought additional losses, the required annual contributions piled up. Also, pension contributions often were part of multi-year union contracts, which made it difficult to renegotiate pension benefits to avoid underfunding. By postponing the date to begin amortizing the extra contributions, companies could escape hefty excise taxes levied on underfunded plans, and have time to negotiate new pension contributions.

The added provisions sparked strong opposition from the Bush administration. On Jan. 22, three Cabinet members — Treasury Secretary John W. Snow, Labor Secretary Elaine L. Chao and then-Commerce Secretary Donald L. Evans — warned Majority Leader Bill Frist, R-Tenn., that they would recommend a veto if the bill singled out financially struggling companies for special pension funding relief.

But lawmakers in both chambers said the industries deserved help as they attempted to rebound. Airlines had been able to fully fund their pensions as recently as 2000, but the decline in air travel following the Sept. 11, 2001, terrorist attacks, a rise in oil prices and a boost in airline competition had left many airlines struggling. Steelmakers also were having problems with their pension plans at a time of increased global competition and falling prices.

"They didn't cause 9/11," Trent Lott, R-Miss., said of the nation's airlines. "They have not been responsible for the increasing and up-and-down prices of fuel. A number of factors that have played into their economic situation, they can't be blamed for."

"This relief is needed to help protect the pensions and jobs of workers in these industries," said Kennedy. "They are industries that can come back and must come back to help drive our economic recovery."

Conference/Final Action

With the April 15 deadline approaching, Republican conferees filed a conference report on the bill (H Rept 108-457) on April 1. The House adopted the report, 336-69, on April 2, sending it to the Senate just as House members were about to leave for a two-week recess. The Senate, which stayed in town, cleared the bill April 8 by a vote of 78-19. (*House vote 117, p. H-42; Senate vote 68, p. S-17*)

John A. Boehner, R-Ohio, chairman of the House Education and the Workforce Committee, presided over the conference. He acknowledged that the legislation lacked the level of multi-employer relief many members wanted. But he told the House, "We need to get this bill finished, and we need to get it finished today."

Disagreement over multi-employer relief nearly sank the bill. The Senate, led by Kennedy, insisted that any pension funding bill include relief for multi-employer plans. The Bush administration wanted the relief dropped. Boehner ended the talks March 26 after four straight days of closed-door meetings failed to produce an agreement. "These talks are in serious danger, this bill is in serious jeopardy," he said.

On April 1, Boehner made a last attempt at a compromise, offering relief for the most severely underfunded multi-employer plans. When Democrats demanded more, Republicans moved on and approved the conference report. The vote was 9-5, with all Democrats opposed.

Kennedy took to the Senate floor to rail against White House intervention, calling the multi-employer provisions "punitive, unfair and discriminatory." But pressure to clear the measure was enormous. Republicans and Democrats were hearing from companies back home that they desperately needed Congress to act fast. Kennedy ultimately voted for the conference report, as did the other Senate Democratic conferee, Max Baucus of Montana. "A lot of people need this bill passed," said Baucus. Even stalwart liberal Democrats such as Barbara Boxer of California and Hillary Rodham Clinton of New York voted to clear the measure.

The nine "nay" votes were from Republicans. "I fear that Congress is encouraging irresponsible underfunding of corporate pensions, and it will ultimately come back to haunt us," said Peter G. Fitzgerald of Illinois, one of the nine. ◆

Democrats Fail to Halt New Overtime Rules

Attempts to block new Labor Department rules on overtime pay won majority support in both chambers, but a determined White House used veto threats to force lawmakers to back down. None of the provisions became law.

The Labor Department rule, which took effect Aug. 23, revised the types of jobs eligible for overtime pay under the Fair Labor Standards Act. The administration argued that the previous rules, which had not been updated since 1949, excluded many workers and were so outdated that workers often had to take their employers to court to find out if they were eligible for overtime.

The department said the new rules would make many low-income workers eligible for overtime pay for the first time. Opponents, including organized labor, contended that as many as 6 million other white-collar workers could lose their eligibility because the new rules reclassified their jobs as professional or team leadership positions that were exempt.

Democrats had been trying to stop the Labor Department from implementing the rules for two years. An amendment included in the fiscal 2004 omnibus appropriations bill (PL 108-199) was stripped because of a persistent veto threat. (*2003 Almanac, p. 2-33*)

In response to the criticism, the Labor Department revised its proposal in April 2004 to guarantee overtime pay for police, firefighters, nurses and paramedics. The annual income ceiling for workers automatically eligible for overtime was set at $23,660, nearly triple the $8,060 threshold under the 1949 law. The department said the changes guaranteed overtime pay to 1.3 million additional workers, and that only about 107,000 highly paid workers would lose their eligibility. Labor unions said as many as 6 million would still lose their eligibility.

On May 4, the Senate adopted an amendment by Tom Harkin, D-Iowa, to exempt from the rule any employee who would lose existing overtime status; it let stand the part of the rule that allowed more workers to qualify for the extra pay. The Senate agreed, 52-47, to append the language to its version of the corporate tax bill (S 1637). (*Senate vote 79, p. S-20; corporate taxes, p. 13-3*)

On Sept. 9, the House adopted a similar amendment to the fiscal 2005 Labor, Health and Human Services (HHS), and Education bill (HR 5006). The proposal, by David R. Obey of Wisconsin, ranking Democrat on the Appropriations Committee, was adopted, 223-193. (*House vote 434, p. H-140; appropriations, p. 2-33*)

Harkin also added the overtime language to the Senate version of the Labor-HHS bill (S 2810) when the Appropriations Committee marked it up Sept. 15. It was clear at that point, however, that the bill would be included in the omnibus and would not go separately to the Senate floor.

All of the amendments were dropped in conference at White House insistence. ◆

Minimum Wage A Non-Starter

Republicans successfully blocked Democrats from getting a floor vote in either chamber on a proposal to raise the minimum wage.

Democrats wanted to increase the minimum wage to $7 an hour over two years. They argued that because the wage had not kept up with inflation — it had been $5.15 an hour since 1997 — millions of Americans had joined the ranks of the "working poor." Democrats used the dispute as one of several issues in the 2004 elections to paint Republicans as unfriendly to workers.

Republicans countered that an increase would result in more unemployment, because businesses forced to raise salaries would reduce their workforce. They also maintained that few workers actually earned the minimum wage for very long; the proportion of hourly workers at or below the minimum wage had fallen from 13.4 percent in 1979 to 2.9 percent in 2003, according to the Bureau of Labor Statistics. The influential U.S. Chamber of Congress lobbied all year against a wage increase.

Sen. Edward M. Kennedy of Massachusetts and other Democrats tried to attach a minimum wage increase to two separate measures: a welfare reauthorization bill (HR 4) and a class action lawsuit overhaul (S 2062). Republican leaders attempted to limit debate and block the amendments by invoking cloture; when they failed to get the 60 votes needed, they withdrew the underlying legislation rather than allow a vote on the minimum wage. Senate GOP leaders did not allow a stand-alone minimum wage bill (S 2370) to come to the Senate floor. (*Welfare, p. 17-5; class action, p. 12-7*)

House Republican leaders used their majority status in committees and their control of the Rules Committee to prevent any proposed minimum wage increase from reaching the floor.

Republicans discussed raising the minimum wage to a lesser amount — Democratic aides put the figure at $6.25 — but the plan was never offered as stand-alone legislation or as an amendment. ◆

Chapter 9

ENERGY & ENVIRONMENT

Aiding California's Water Supply

Congress agreed to provide new federal funds for the huge California Federal Bay-Delta (CalFed) project, authorizing $389 million for the project over the next six fiscal years, plus $6 million for other water projects. President Bush signed the bill into law Oct. 25 (HR 2828 — PL 108-361).

Members of California's congressional delegation had been pushing for nearly five years to get more federal funding for CalFed. The state-federal program was first authorized in 1996 (PL 104-208) to improve water quality and storage in the San Francisco Bay and the Sacramento-San Joaquin River Delta region, which supplies water to the fertile farmland of the state's Central Valley.

The federal portion of the program expired in 2000, and appropriators were unwilling to continue funding it without an authorization. But conflicts among farmers, environmental groups and others within and outside the state kept compromise elusive until election-year momentum brought the parties together.

"Without CalFed there is not going to be enough water to meet California's needs," said Senate sponsor Dianne Feinstein, D-Calif. "The last time California increased its water infrastructure was the 1960s." The state's population had about doubled since then.

The bill authorized funding mainly to increase water storage, but it also authorized money to improve water supplies, stabilize aging levees and restore ecosystems statewide.

The bill's price tag had fallen significantly over time. In the 107th Congress, Feinstein sought $2.4 billion for the program. The bill she introduced in 2004 called for $880 million; the final bill was less than half that.

The House and Senate passed similar versions of the legislation, but lawmakers differed over a controversial House provision that would have automatically authorized future water projects in the program unless Congress specifically rejected them. Pete V. Domenici, R-N.M., Senate Energy and Natural Resources chairman and other Senate authorizers opposed the House language, and it was ultimately dropped.

Legislative Action

Senate Committee Action

The Senate Energy and Natural Resources Committee gave voice vote approval April 28 to a version of Feinstein's bill (S 1097 — S Rept 108-268) that called for $389 million over six years for CalFed. The reduced cost, less than half the $880 million Feinstein initially sought, helped win the support of Western senators on the panel who were con-

BoxScore

Bill:
HR 2828 — PL 108-361

Legislative Action:

House passed HR 2828 (H Rept 108-573, Part 1) by voice vote July 9.

Senate passed HR 2828, amended, by voice vote Sept. 15.

House cleared the bill by voice vote Oct. 6.

President signed Oct. 25.

cerned that the California project would use up federal funds that otherwise would be available to their states.

The revised bill also clarified that funding would come from a variety of agencies, including the EPA, the Army Corps of Engineers and the Fish and Wildlife Service, not just the Bureau of Reclamation. Western states looked to the bureau to fund water projects, and Western senators did not want all the money devoted to California.

House Committee Action

The House Resources Committee approved a similar bill (HR 2828 — H Rept 108-573, Part 1) by voice vote May 5. However, the House bill included a provision to limit congressional authority to review some future projects.

During the markup, the committee:

• Adopted by voice vote a substitute amendment by bill sponsor Ken Calvert, R-Calif., that cut the cost from $1.2 billion for several projects to $389 million over the next four years for the CalFed Bay-Delta Program. To speed up the approval of water projects, the substitute provided for the Interior secretary to determine which projects were feasible and notify Congress. The projects would be authorized automatically unless both chambers disapproved within 120 days.

• Rejected, 11-28, an attempt by George Miller, D-Calif., to substitute the text of the Senate committee-approved bill, which did not contain the automatic authorization provision. Republicans, including committee Chairman Richard W. Pombo of California, said the language was necessary to expedite projects and the money would still be subject to appropriations.

House, Senate, Final Action

The House passed the bill by voice vote July 9, although some California Democrats said the proposed latitude for the Interior Department would set a dangerous precedent.

The Senate passed HR 2828 by voice vote Sept. 15, after substituting a revised version of Feinstein's measure. The Senate bill required Congress to approve individual projects through the normal legislative process. But to bridge differences with the House, Feinstein added language to require Interior Department "involvement" in any projects that were held up for significant periods.

The Senate bill also added $6 million to the $389 million reported out of committee. Feinstein said the money would finance a feasibility study on water storage and a temperature control system at Folsom Dam northeast of Sacramento.

After negotiations involving California's Republican Gov. Arnold Schwarzenegger, House members accepted the Senate compromise and cleared the bill by voice vote Oct. 6. ◆

Water Projects Bill Dries Up

A politically popular but controversial water projects bill died at the end of the session because of a dispute over whether to overhaul the way the Army Corps of Engineers planned and evaluated water projects. The legislation would have reauthorized the Water Resources Development Act, under which the Corps conducted dozens of navigation, flood control, dredging and other water projects. A new water resources bill had not been enacted since 2000 (PL 106-541).

The Corps had been sharply criticized in recent years in newspaper exposes and reports from the Army inspector general and the Government Accountability Office, which said the agency exaggerated the benefits and underestimated the negative effects of water projects. But lawmakers disagreed over what kind of action, if any, to take. Port authorities and other government entities hoping to expedite Corps projects feared that extra scrutiny would unnecessarily slow down projects and drive up costs. Environmentalists and fiscal watchdog organizations, on the other hand, wanted any reauthorization to be part of a broad overhaul of the way the Corps did business.

The same disagreement torpedoed a similar reauthorization in the 107th Congress.

The House tried to address the problem in 2003, passing a reauthorization bill (HR 2557) that required independent peer reviews of projects that were deemed controversial or that cost more than $50 million — roughly 30 percent of those covered by the bill. (*2003 Almanac, p. 9-14*)

Spurred by environmental groups, the Senate Environment and Public Works Committee approved a bill by voice vote June 23, that proposed to subject a broader range of projects to the peer review process.

The Senate bill — later introduced as S 2773 (S Rept 108-314) — also included a provision to create a 23-member Corps of Engineers River Stewardship Commission with seats for representatives of environmental groups, the hydroelectric power industry, recreational user groups, state and Indian tribal governments and "other affected interests." The commission would investigate Corps management and environmental practices and submit a report to Congress.

The committee adopted, 10-9, an amendment to require the Corps to restore, in equal measure, wetlands and fish or wildlife habitats that it disrupted in the course of its projects. Barbara Boxer, D-Calif., said the same requirement was imposed on private sector building projects, but Christopher S. Bond, R-Mo., chairman of the Environment and Public Works Transportation and Infrastructure Subcommittee, said some projects would not go forward because of "excessive mitigation requirements."

The Senate bill included $3.2 billion to improve navigation in the upper Mississippi River and Illinois River waterway area. The project had been the subject of several critical reports, but waterways interests said existing locks dated to the 1930s and needed to be replaced. An October review of the Corps' justification for the upper Mississippi River project by the National Academy of Sciences concluded that the project was unnecessary. "Implementing some nonstructural measures for managing waterway congestion would decrease congestion, reduce shipping costs and use the existing waterway more efficiently," the report said.

A last-minute effort to revive the bill at the end of the session died; authorizers said they were close but ran out of time. ◆

No Agreement on Energy Bill

For a third straight year, Congress was unable to pass a comprehensive energy bill. The conference report on a massive, $31.1 billion bill (HR 6) that won House passage in 2003 but was halted in the Senate got no further in 2004. Energy interests claimed a modest victory when some of the bill's tax incentives were enacted as part of a separate corporate tax package (PL 108-357).

Lawmakers could not overcome regional differences over the gasoline additive methyl tertiary butyl ether (MTBE), a clean-fuel additive that had been shown to pollute groundwater.

House Majority Leader Tom DeLay, R-Texas, insisted that the bill include a liability waiver for makers of the chemical, many of which were located in Texas and other Gulf Coast states. Senate Democrats and some Republican moderates rejected the waiver, fearing taxpayers could be saddled with the bill for cleaning up MTBE without the

ability to seek damages from the manufacturers. They had enough votes to keep the conference report from coming up in the Senate.

In a largely symbolic vote, the House passed a bill (HR 4503) on June 15 that contained essentially the same provisions as the stranded measure. The bill passed, 244-178, with support from almost nine out of 10 Republicans and opposition from about three out of four Democrats. (*House vote 241, p. H-82*)

In the Senate, Pete V. Domenici, R-N.M., the chairman of the Energy and Natural Resources Committee, drafted a $14 billion bill (S 2095) that dropped the MTBE liability waiver and some other contentious provisions. But without the waiver, other deals that held the measure together began to pull apart, and the bill never mustered enough support to break a threatened Democratic filibuster.

A range of energy-related tax incentives did find their

way into the corporate tax bill (PL 108-357). The most significant was a decision to make oil and gas drilling eligible for a provision that cut the top tax rate for manufacturing to 32 percent from 35 percent. Other provisions included accelerated depreciation for the Alaska gas pipeline, expanded tax credits for renewable energy technologies, deductions for the cost of pollution control equipment, tax credits for biodiesel fuel blends and tax-free bonds for the construction of certain environmentally friendly buildings. (*Corporate tax bill, p. 13-3*) ◆

Chapter 10

HEALTH

Project Bioshield Authorized

More than a year after Congress rallied around a Bush administration initiative to bolster the nation's bioterror defenses, lawmakers agreed on a mechanism to fund the effort. A plan by Senate negotiators to give appropriators discretion over how to parcel out money to expand the country's store of vaccines dislodged the Project Bioshield authorization, which had been held up since mid-2003.

The House, which passed a nearly identical bill in 2003, cleared the measure July 14. President Bush, who proposed the initiative in his 2003 State of the Union address, signed the bill into law July 21 (S 15 — PL 108-276).

The legislation authorized funding for purchase of vaccines and other countermeasures against biological terror agents such as smallpox, anthrax and botulism toxin, as well as other pathogens such as Ebola and plague. The bill guaranteed $5.6 billion for the program over 10 years but gave appropriators ultimate discretion over how the initiative would be funded year by year.

The legislation also allowed the government to simplify the process for awarding research and development grants for biomedical countermeasures, and it gave the government authority to distribute critically needed medicines and vaccines in an emergency, even if they had not yet been approved by the Food and Drug Administration (FDA).

"Bioshield is without question the most important step we can take to improve our nation's biodefense capabilities," Health and Human Services (HHS) Secretary Tommy G. Thompson said. Thompson said the legislation would allow the government to immediately purchase up to 75 million doses of an anthrax vaccine under development that was expected to be available in 2005 and would ensure that enough smallpox vaccine was stockpiled for every American.

Highlights

The following are the main components of the new law:
- **Strategic stockpile.** The measure authorized $5.6 billion in fiscal 2004 through 2013 to purchase bioterrorism countermeasures for the Strategic National Stockpile. The stockpile, authorized in 2002 (PL 107-188), was a national repository of antibiotics, chemical antidotes and other items that would be disbursed to state and local authorities in an emergency. Of the total, $890 million could be obligated in fiscal 2004, and $3.4 billion could be used in the first five years.
- **Research and development.** HHS was allowed to use expedited procedures for approving grants for research and development of countermeasures for use against biological, chemical, nuclear and radiological agents. The authority also could be used to respond to emergency health threats. HHS could bypass the usual peer review process for award-

BoxScore

Bill:
S 15 — PL 108-276
Legislative Action:
Senate passed S 15, 99-0, on May 19.
House cleared the bill, 414-2, on July 14.
President signed July 21.

ing grants of less than $1.5 million. The department also could waive competitive bidding rules when only a few companies provided goods and services needed for research and development. The law gave the National Institutes of Health flexibility to hire up to 30 people to respond to urgent research and development needs.
- **Emergency use.** HHS was given the authority to distribute drugs and treatments not yet approved by the FDA in the case of a national emergency involving an actual or potential attack with biological, chemical, radiological or nuclear agents. HHS could use the authority only if the Homeland Security or Defense departments determined there was a national emergency, or the potential for one.

Background

In a proposal highlighted in his 2003 State of the Union speech, Bush called for a new Project Bioshield to provide incentives to pharmaceutical companies and others to develop new vaccines and antidotes for use in case of a bioterrorist attack. The proposal included expedited procedures to finance high-priority research and development; unlimited, permanent mandatory funding to purchase items for the Strategic Stockpile; and authority for the government during an emergency to allow promising, but unapproved, drugs and treatments for bioterrorism attacks.

The Senate Health, Education, Labor and Pensions Committee approved an authorization bill that reflected Bush's request in March 2003, and prospects for quick passage appeared good, especially because deliberations were taking place at a time when the nation's terror alert system was raised in the opening days of the conflict in Iraq.

But before floor debate could begin in the Senate, Robert C. Byrd of West Virginia, the ranking Democrat on the Appropriations Committee, put a hold on the bill, objecting that the permanent mandatory funding would take control over funding out of the hands of the appropriators.

The administration and bill supporters said that a guaranteed funding stream was crucial to assure companies that the government would purchase the vaccines and antidotes they developed. Otherwise, they said, drugmakers and biotechnology companies could not justify the investment in costly and time-consuming research and development for products that would have no other uses.

In July 2003, the House overwhelmingly passed a bioshield bill (HR 2122 — H Rept 108-147) that contained a compromise funding mechanism. The $5.6 billion would be discretionary spending, giving appropriators authority over the funds. The appropriators would provide the entire amount as an advance 10-year appropriation — thereby en-

suring a continuous flow of funds over that period. *(2003 Almanac, p. 11-15)*

Eager to get the initiative going, Congress included in the fiscal 2004 Homeland Security appropriations law (PL 108-90) an advance appropriation of $5.6 billion over 10 years, $890 million of it in fiscal 2004. The rest of the funds still had to be authorized. *(2003 Almanac, p. 2-56)*

Legislative Action

Byrd said he would back the hybrid funding plan in the House-passed bill, but in early 2004 Senate Budget Chairman Don Nickles, R-Okla., tried to revive the guaranteed funding language as part of the Senate's version of the fiscal 2005 budget resolution (S Con Res 95). Byrd and other appropriators prevailed on the floor with an amendment stripping Nickles' language from the resolution. Byrd and Nickles later reached an agreement that satisfied Byrd's concerns but acknowledged the need for continuous funding. That agreement cleared the way for Senate passage. *(Budget resolution, p. 4-9)*

The Senate passed the bioshield authorization, 99-0, on May 19, after approving the compromise by voice vote. The House cleared the bill July 14 by a 414-2 vote. *(Senate vote 99, p. S-23; House vote 376, p. H-124)* ◆

Stalemate on Drug Importation

Splits among Republicans and resistance from the White House sidetracked attempts to allow Americans to import drugs from Canada and other countries, where they often cost less. The House passed a bill (HR 2427) in 2003 to allow drug imports from Canada and 24 other industrialized countries. Several bills were introduced in the Senate but none saw committee or floor action. GOP leaders were not eager to force a vote and send the president a popular bill he might have to veto in the midst of an election campaign.

The idea of allowing Americans to import cheaper prescription drugs was popular, especially among seniors, and lawmakers expected it to have strong appeal in the November elections. Democrats and GOP moderates generally supported liberalizing imports, as did some conservatives who saw it as a free-trade issue.

But the Bush administration and GOP leaders in Congress opposed it, saying it could open the U.S. market to a flood of unsafe or counterfeit medicines. Opponents also likened the practice to imposing foreign price controls on the U.S. drug market. Drug prices in countries such as Canada were typically lower than in the United States because of price controls in government-run medical systems.

The bill that passed the House in July 2003 would have allowed the importation of medicines from 25 industrialized countries. The issue was ultimately addressed in the 2003 Medicare prescription drug law (PL 108-173), which reaffirmed existing law by allowing the import of drugs from Canada but only if the Health and Human Services (HHS) secretary certified that the practice was safe and would save consumers money. HHS Secretary Tommy G. Thompson said he could not do that given his existing resources. *(2003 Almanac, pp. 11-14, 11-3)*

Thompson and Mark McClellan, head of the Centers for Medicare and Medicaid Services, both testified in 2004 that they would be willing to work with Congress on plans to give the Food and Drug Administration (FDA) the resources and direction needed to make such a certification possible. FDA officials warned, however, that the added responsibilities would cost hundreds of millions of dollars and that the cost ultimately could be passed on to consumers.

Senate Bills

Several bills were introduced in the Senate in 2004 by central players in the debate. All three of the following bills proposed to allow individuals to import personal supplies of prescription drugs from Canada upon enactment. The bills applied only to FDA-approved drugs from FDA-approved plants.

• The lead bill (S 2493) was introduced by Judd Gregg, R-N.H., chairman of the Health, Education, Labor and Pensions (HELP) Committee. Under Gregg's bill, commercial imports of prescription drugs could be imported from Canada within a year and from the European Union (EU) within three years. Registration fees and annual user fees would help pay for the program. Gregg's bill included stricter inspection and certification requirements on manufacturers and importers and a higher user fee than a separate bipartisan proposal.

Gregg was forced to call off a HELP Committee markup of his bill in July because he did not have a solid majority of Republicans behind it; panel Democrats said the bill was too restrictive.

• A bipartisan group of senators led by Democrat Byron L. Dorgan of North Dakota and Republican moderate Olympia J. Snowe of Maine offered an alternative bill (S 2328) that would have required the FDA to set up a system to allow pharmacists and wholesalers to import drugs from Canada within 90 days of enactment, and from the EU and a list of other developed countries after one year. Commercial importers would need to register with the FDA and pay a 1 percent fee to cover the costs of regulating the practice.

The bill included penalties for manufacturers that interfered with importation by limiting supply or increasing prices.

Other Democrats behind the measure included Edward M. Kennedy of Massachusetts, his party's senior member on the HELP Committee, and Minority Leader Tom Daschle of South Dakota. Commerce Chairman John McCain of Arizona was among the GOP sponsors. The measure also was endorsed by the influential seniors' lobby AARP.

Backers hoped to circumvent Gregg's committee and

bring their bill directly to the floor, but Senate Majority Leader Bill Frist, R-Tenn., was unwilling to cooperate.

• Charles E. Grassley, R-Iowa, chairman of the Finance Committee, introduced a bill (S 2307) to require the FDA to set up a system for commercial imports from Canada within 90 days. After two years, the system for individuals and commercial buyers could be extended to the EU and certain other developed countries. User fees would pay for the added FDA costs. To appease drugmakers, Grassley included a 20 percent increase in the research and development tax credit, but he also included penalties for drug companies that tried to interfere with the imports. ◆

Chapter 11

INTELLIGENCE & FOREIGN POLICY

Intelligence Overhaul Enacted

Hoping to rectify the intelligence failures that preceded the Sept. 11, 2001, terrorist attacks, Congress cleared the most extensive overhaul of the U.S. intelligence community since World War II. President Bush signed the measure into law Dec. 17 (S 2845 — PL 108-458).

Congressional action was sparked by the recommendations of the National Commission on Terrorist Attacks Upon the United States, an independent bipartisan commission formed to investigate the circumstances surrounding the events of Sept. 11. When the commission came out with its report on July 22, it was an immediate best seller. On Capitol Hill, House and Senate committees quickly embraced the commission's work. (*Sept. 11 commission, p. 11-8*)

While there was broad support in both chambers and both parties for a major intelligence overhaul, Congress did not embrace all of the commission's recommendations. Proposals to make the total for the annual intelligence budget public and to give the new director of national intelligence near unilateral power over the military intelligence budget, for example, were left on the cutting-room floor.

The law focused on creating a new management structure to oversee the 15 sprawling and sometimes-competing intelligence agencies. It established a new director of national intelligence to set the strategic direction for much of the intelligence community, advise the president on foreign intelligence and coordinate U.S. intelligence operations around the globe. The director was given authority to develop budgets throughout the intelligence community, but he had limited influence over military intelligence spending, an area the Pentagon fought aggressively to protect while the bill was being written.

The Senate version of the bill (S 2845), which passed overwhelmingly in early October, called for a powerful new intelligence director with near unilateral authority over the intelligence community. The measure was guided through committee and floor debate with rare bipartisan cooperation by its sponsors, Maine Republican Susan Collins and Connecticut Democrat Joseph I. Lieberman.

The House bill (HR 10), passed two days later, also proposed a new national intelligence director, but with less power to set budgets and move money and personnel among agencies. The House bill also incorporated a series of immigration provisions not recommended by the commission, including controversial proposals to make it easier to deport illegal residents without judicial review and to bar states from issuing driver's licenses to people in the country illegally.

There was little progress in reconciling the two measures

BoxScore

Bill:
S 2845 — PL 108-458

Legislative Action:

Senate passed S 2845, 96-2, on Oct. 6.

House passed HR 10 (H Rept 108-724, Parts 1-5), 282-134, on Oct. 8, subsequently inserting the text into S 2845.

House adopted the conference report (H Rept 108-796), 336-75, on Dec. 7.

Senate cleared the bill, 89-2, on Dec. 8.

President signed Dec. 17.

before the Nov. 2 elections. Although House and Senate conferees agreed on the need to create a director of national intelligence, the discussions broke down when they tried to define the director's specific budgetary powers. Pentagon advocates, led by members of the House and Senate Armed Services committees, pushed hard to limit the director's powers to civilian agencies such as the CIA, which controlled only about 20 percent of the estimated $40 billion intelligence budget. The Defense Department controlled the other 80 percent, including money for "combat support" agencies such as the National Security Agency (NSA) and the Defense Intelligence Agency (DIA).

But Senate negotiators, who had already given up one of their key proposals — to declassify the overall intelligence funding figure — said they had conceded as much as they could.

After weeks with no progress in conference, it took a weekend session shortly before Thanksgiving to break the logjam. House Armed Services Chairman Duncan Hunter, R-Calif., who had been the primary holdout on the bill, agreed to language promising that the director of national intelligence would not "abrogate" the military chain of command. The conference agreement also left out some of the most controversial immigration proposals.

The final agreement also included provisions on foreign policy, aid to Afghanistan, border security initiatives, biometrics programs, immigration rules and new standards for airport screening.

Highlights

Following are the main components of the new law:

● **Director of National Intelligence.** The law created a Director of National Intelligence (DNI) to be appointed by the president and confirmed by the Senate. The DNI was authorized to set government-wide priorities for collecting and analyzing intelligence, and to serve as principal intelligence adviser to the president. By fiscal 2009, the director had to move out of offices at CIA headquarters.

● **Budget authority.** The DNI was given the authority to "develop and determine" the annual budgets for national intelligence programs, including the CIA, parts of the NSA, the National Reconnaissance Office (NRO) and the National Geospatial-Intelligence Agency. However, the DNI's authority did not extend to joint military intelligence programs or tactical battlefield intelligence.

Military intelligence agencies would maintain control of day-to-day implementation of their budget and of all tactical

battlefield intelligence operations. While the DNI would write the budget, the money for all of the Defense intelligence agencies would actually flow through the Pentagon.

In setting up the budgets, the DNI could not "abrogate" the chain of command in the military. Total spending on intelligence would remain secret. The DNI could transfer up to $150 million or 5 percent of an agency's budget to other intelligence agencies, but the transfers could not terminate any procurement programs.

● **Personnel.** The law authorized 500 new personnel billets for the DNI, and allowed him to transfer up to 150 personnel from other agencies to his office for up to two years.

● **Intelligence centers.** The law created a National Intelligence Council to be composed of senior analysts within the government and from the private sector. The council would be in charge of writing the National Intelligence Estimates, assessments that reflect the collective judgement of the intelligence community on critical issues.

The law created a National Counterterrorism Center to be the primary organization for analyzing and integrating U.S. intelligence on global terrorism. The office would conduct strategic operational planning but would not direct the execution of counterterrorism operations. A separate National Counterproliferation Center was established to collect and analyze intelligence related to nuclear weapons and other weapons of mass destruction. The DNI was also directed to create special groups to focus on competitive, or alternative analysis, known as "red-teaming" to poke holes in conventional wisdom within the intelligence community.

● **Civil liberties.** The law created a Civil Liberties Protection Officer, as well as a Privacy and Civil Liberties Board, but conferees weakened the board's powers by removing subpoena powers.

● **CIA.** Several top-level CIA positions were abolished, including assistant directors of central intelligence for collection, analysis and production and administration. The law also reiterated that the CIA could not conduct any policing powers within the United States.

● **FBI.** The FBI was required to establish a national intelligence workforce to create a career track for FBI agents interested in intelligence. The law also created a reserve corps of retired FBI employees to serve during a national emergency.

● **Transportation security.** The Homeland Security secretary was required to develop a "national strategy for transportation security" that set priorities for guarding transportation systems. The law also directed the Transportation Security Administration (TSA), the agency responsible for securing the nation's airports and all other modes of transportation, to integrate names on the various terrorist watch lists, screen airport employees and develop a plan to screen all carry-on bags for explosives; the law authorized $250 million for research and development for such screening.

The Homeland Security Department was required to deploy biometric screening at airports.

● **Border security and immigration.** The law provided a wide range of new rules for border security, including the addition of 2,000 full-time border agents per year for five years, and 40,000 new beds for detention of illegal immigrants. The law also prohibited judicial review of visa revocations, taking away an appeals process.

● **Security clearances.** The president was given 180 days to designate a single agency to conduct security clearances for government employees and contractors with access to classified information.

● **Drivers license standards.** The Homeland Security and Transportation departments were required to develop national standards for the documents states could accept as the basis for issuing drivers' licenses, since licenses were used to board airplanes. The new standards could not infringe on a state's power to decide who was eligible for licenses.

● **Wire-tapping.** The law allowed the FBI to conduct surveillance of alleged "lone wolf" terrorists who were not connected to any foreign power but could be acting alone in planning terrorist activities. Prior law allowed such surveillance only if the individual was thought to be connected to a foreign power or organization.

● **Foreign policy provisions.** This law contained provisions intended to improve diplomatic outreach to the Muslim world. It authorized "such sums as may be necessary" for Afghanistan, and called for the United States to improve diplomatic relations with Saudi Arabia and Pakistan. It also created educational grants for American schools in Muslim countries.

Legislative Action

Committees in both chambers used the usually quiet August recess to hold hearings and study the recommendations of the Sept. 11 commission. Members of the commission, along with family members of Sept. 11 victims, also kept up pressure for a bill during the recess and throughout the fall, holding news conferences and meeting with members to argue passionately for changes in intelligence, border, and aviation security, and other areas they said were critical in preventing another attack.

Senate Committee Action

After a 10-hour markup that spanned two days, the Senate Governmental Affairs Committee approved its bill (S 2840 — S Rept 108-359) by a vote of 14-0 on Sept. 22. Collins and Lieberman worked to strike a middle path between panel members who wanted to give the new intelligence director more power and Pentagon officials who wanted to give him considerably less.

Central elements of the Senate bill included:

● A national intelligence director with the authority to determine funding levels for nearly the entire intelligence community, including spy agencies that fell under the Defense Department. The director would be able to transfer unlimited funds among the agencies and would have wide personnel powers.

● Public disclosure of the total budget for intelligence, though not the details.

● A National Counterterrorism Center with the authority to engage in operational planning — although not to tell Pentagon spy agencies how to carry out their duties.

Carl Levin of Michigan, the ranking Democrat on the Armed Services Committee, dominated the markup with 14 amendments, most of them aimed at curbing the new director's authority over military intelligence personnel, budgets and operations. The committee either rejected Levin's amendments outright or modified them so they did not

erode the director's proposed budgetary or personnel power.

Levin argued unsuccessfully that the national intelligence director should not be able to transfer military intelligence personnel or reprogram money within the Pentagon's intelligence agencies. The panel did adopt some of Levin's amendments that clarified the lines of authority between the intelligence director and the military agencies that would fall under his mandate.

One of those proposals, adopted by voice vote, made it clear that the National Counterterrorism Center could not assign duties to specific elements of the armed forces. Another specified that certain joint operations of military and intelligence agencies that were solely military in nature would not fall under the director's budget authority.

Levin failed on several other amendments, including an attempt to deny the national intelligence director the power to transfer any military personnel.

The committee also turned back a proposal backed by a coalition of senators who were pushing for a much more powerful director who would have day-to-day operational control of both civilian and military intelligence agencies.

Arlen Specter, R-Pa., a former Senate Intelligence chairman, proposed giving the new director power not only to control the budgets of all the intelligence agencies but also to direct day-to-day operations, potentially taking significant power out of the hands of Pentagon intelligence chiefs. The committee rejected the amendment, 5-12.

The committee also adopted by voice vote an amendment by George V. Voinovich, R-Ohio, calling on the president to name a single agency to process all government security clearances — an idea aimed at clearing a massive backlog of clearance requests.

Senate Floor Action

Collins and Lieberman kept the measure — which was introduced as a clean bill (S 2845) — largely intact on the floor, turning back virtually every amendment, including proposals offered by some of the most senior members of the Senate. The debate fell more along committee than party lines, but despite predictions of fierce turf battles and close votes it rarely became partisan or heated. The Senate passed the bill, 96-2, on Oct. 6. (*Senate vote 199, p. S-42*)

When the debate began Sept. 27, the chamber faced as many as 300 amendments. But Collins and Lieberman negotiated behind the scenes while the bill was on the Senate floor, convincing members of their respective parties to withdraw most amendments. Other amendments were ruled out of order, or tabled. Many were adopted by voice vote, but only after being rewritten to Collins and Lieberman's liking.

The two senators first agreed with Levin to limit the director's authority to transfer individual military personnel, while allowing the money and the billet slots for those individuals' jobs to be moved among intelligence agencies. The Senate adopted Levin's rewritten amendment by voice vote. Levin originally sought to deny the intelligence director authority to transfer active military personnel within the national intelligence system. Under the compromise, "the slots can be moved, but the national intelligence director can't go in and say, 'I want Col. Murkowski,' " Lieberman explained.

Collins and Lieberman also negotiated middle ground with Armed Services Chairman John W. Warner, R-Va.,

over which military intelligence programs would fall under the "national intelligence program" to be run by the intelligence director. The Senate adopted by voice vote a Warner amendment that was reworked to give both the national intelligence director and the Pentagon a say in joint military intelligence programs.

During the floor debate, the Senate also:

• Tabled (killed) an amendment by Specter to set a 10-year fixed term for the DNI, thereby increasing his independence from the president. The vote to table was 93-4. (*Senate vote 191, p. S-41*)

• Tabled, 78-19, a Specter amendment to give the national intelligence director much more power over day-to-day operations of all the intelligence agencies, including those at the Pentagon. (*Senate vote 192, p. S-41*)

• Tabled, 62-29, an amendment by Robert C. Byrd of West Virginia, ranking Democrat on the Appropriations Committee, to sharply curtail the director's budget authority and impose strict conditions on his power to transfer personnel or funds among the 15 intelligence agencies. (*Senate vote 195, p. S-42*)

Byrd, along with Appropriations Chairman Ted Stevens, R-Alaska, and other top appropriators tried throughout the fall to put the brakes on the intelligence overhaul. Byrd earlier warned the Senate to "think twice before we attempt to reorganize crucial intelligence activities with one eye on the clock and one eye on the polls." That sentiment had the backing of a coalition of national security luminaries led by Henry Kissinger, who argued that a major intelligence shake-up could cause years of "turmoil" at the agencies.

But Lieberman argued, "We've received warning after warning that if you're going to do this right, you've got to give this national director real power." Collins agreed. "If we impose these kinds of restrictions," she said, "we really are not improving the current system in any significant way."

• Tabled, 55-37, an amendment by Stevens to strike the language requiring public disclosure of the overall intelligence budget. (*Senate vote 196, p. S-42*)

By the time the final roll call came in the Senate, leaders from both sides of the aisle were using the terms "bipartisan" and "historic" to describe the final version of the legislation. "We stuck together on every single issue," Collins said of her relationship with Lieberman. "We are going to conference with a very strong bill."

House Committee Action

House Republican leaders, who initially were cool to the idea of a major intelligence overhaul, kept a firm hand on their legislation. In September, Speaker J. Dennis Hastert, R-Ill., introduced an overhaul bill (HR 10) written by the leadership, then divided responsibility for marking up portions of the legislation among at least 10 House committees. Five approved sections of the measure.

Central elements of the House bill included:

• A national intelligence director who would "manage and oversee" implementation of the budget for the non-military intelligence agencies. Funding for Pentagon agencies would be funneled through the department's comptroller, preserving the Pentagon's budget control. On the controversial issue of reprogramming, the bill proposed to cap the

House vs. Senate Overhaul Plans

PROVISION	HOUSE-PASSED BILL	SENATE-PASSED BILL
National intelligence program	Redefine the "national foreign intelligence program" as the "national intelligence program," to include the CIA but explicitly exclude joint military intelligence programs and tactical intelligence programs.	Has largely same definition as House, but would require a study to see if certain joint military and tactical intelligence programs also should fall under rubric of "national intelligence program."
National intelligence director	Director would be appointed by the president and confirmed by the Senate. If the Senate did not vote within 30 legislative days, appointment would take effect. The CIA director at the time of enactment (in this case Porter J. Goss) would automatically become national intelligence director without Senate confirmation.	Director would be appointed by the president and confirmed by the Senate. The bill has no provision about promoting the current CIA director to national intelligence director.
Budget authority	Intelligence director would "manage and oversee" intelligence program and help implement agency budgets, but would not have power to execute the budget or parcel out money to intelligence agencies. Military intelligence funding would be funneled through the Pentagon.	Intelligence director would get separate appropriations account from Treasury, and set and execute budgets, with input from Defense officials on military intelligence agencies.
Personnel powers	Intelligence director would have power to hire and fire intelligence employees, but not those in the military. Director's "concurrence" would be required for appointment of directors of National Security Agency (NSA), National Reconnaissance Office (NRO) and National Geospatial-Intelligence Agency (NGA).	Intelligence director would have power to hire and fire employees and transfer them among agencies. In cases involving active duty military, only the job and title could be transferred, not the individual. Director's concurrence would be necessary for appointment of NSA, NRO, NGA and Defense Intelligence Agency directors.
National Counterterrorism Center	A new National Counterterrorism Center would act as a central repository for terrorism intelligence, but could do only strategic operational planning. Center would not be empowered to tell field operatives how to execute their missions.	Similar to House language, but would give the center power to assign missions and tasks to intelligence agencies. The bill would not allow center to tell agents how to carry out their missions.
Immigration	Bill would allow expedited deportation of illegal immigrants charged with a crime if they had not been in the United States for up to five years. Existing law allowed extra appeals and judicial reviews if immigrants had been in country for two years.	No similar provisions. The Senate rejected amendments that sought to add immigration language.
Civil liberties	Bill would create a civil liberties officer. Language to create a Privacy and Civil Liberties Oversight Board added by Intelligence Committee was deleted by the Rules Committee before the bill went to the floor.	Bill would create a Privacy and Civil Liberties Oversight Board with power to investigate civil liberties violations in the intelligence community. An ombudsman would deal with disputes and act as internal watchdog.
Intelligence budget classification	Intelligence funding would remain classified.	Bill would declassify "top line," grand total for intelligence spending, estimated at $40 billion.

amount of money the director could transfer among agencies to $100 million per year.

• A National Counterterrorism Center that would have authority to conduct broad strategic planning but no operational powers.

• Continued classification of the intelligence budget.

• Criminal and immigration provisions intended to strengthen the 2001 law known as the USA Patriot Act (PL 107-56) by, for example, making it easier to search and monitor so-called lone wolf terrorists, and by deporting aliens without judicial review. It proposed a federal standard for state driver's licenses, identification cards and birth certificates; a new formula for distributing first-responder aid to the states; and more border security and immigration agents. (*2001 Almanac, p. 14-3*)

During the Sept. 29 markups, GOP leaders turned back almost every Democratic amendment that would have substantially changed the measure to bring it in line with the Collins-Lieberman bill.

• **Intelligence.** An exception was the Intelligence Committee, which approved provisions creating the DNI by a vote of 17-2 (H Rept 108-724, Part 1). The panel's new

PROVISION	HOUSE-PASSED BILL	SENATE-PASSED BILL
Aviation security	Bill would mandate biometric technology standards for air travelers; turn over "no fly list" authority to the Transportation Security Administration; require explosives screening for carry-on baggage; and protect anonymity of federal air marshals so they would not have to publicly identify themselves at airport security checks.	Bill would mandate consolidation of "no fly list"; create pilot projects for blast-resistant cargo holds; require explosives detection systems for carry-on baggage.
National ID standards	Bill would require federal standards for state-issued driver's licenses, identification cards and birth certificates.	Similar to House provisions.
Homeland security grant formula	Money for local police and fire first-responder grants would be distributed based on threat of terrorism. Each state would receive at least .25 percent of annual grant funding; states with international or water borders would receive a minimum of .45 percent.	First 10 percent of total funding for first-responder grants would go to high threat urban areas. The remaining 90 percent would be distributed based on threat of terrorism, with each state guaranteed 0.75 percent of total.
Security clearances	Bill would create a multi-agency database to handle all security clearances. Applications would have to be cleared within 120 days.	President would be required to designate a single agency to handle all security clearances and set uniform standards for processing applications.
Money laundering	Bill would increase funding for Treasury Department's Financial Crimes Enforcement Network by $36 million to improve technology; equate the possession of counterfeiting technology with the act of counterfeiting; promote greater coordination of international efforts to combat money laundering and terrorist financing.	No similar provision.
Other intelligence centers	The national intelligence director would be authorized to create other intelligence centers, but bill did not offer specifics.	Bill would create a National Counterproliferation Center, and allow creation of other intelligence centers.
FBI intelligence duties	FBI director would be required to establish an intelligence directorate with authority to manage all FBI intelligence operations. The FBI mandatory retirement age would increase from 60 to 65. The bill would create a "reserve service" of former FBI employees who could be called on in times of emergency.	No comparable FBI provision, but would allow the FBI to increase salaries and benefits for agents and create an "Intelligence Career Service."
Inspector general	CIA's inspector general would have jurisdiction over office of national intelligence director, which would not have a separate inspector general.	National intelligence director's office would include an inspector general, as well as an ombudsman.
Information sharing	National intelligence director would have authority to set information sharing policies; FBI would get authority to create a program for sharing information with federal, state and foreign governments and the private sector.	Bill would authorize creation of a massive database for sharing information at every level of government, with layers of security built in to limit access based on rank and security clearance.

chairman, Peter Hoekstra, R-Mich., joined with ranking Democrat Jane Harman of California to find agreement on several provisions aimed at bringing the bill modestly closer to the Senate version, including one to create a civil liberties board and another to remove the $100 million cap on the new director's ability to transfer money among agencies.

But Republicans united to quash on 8-11 party line votes other Democratic attempts to give the DNI greater budget execution authority and more power over hiring and firing. They also rejected a Democratic amendment to remove a provision allowing the president to appoint the CIA direc-

tor — the freshly sworn-in Porter J. Goss, R-Fla., the committee's former chairman — to the position of national intelligence director without Senate confirmation.

Harman and six other Democrats supported the measure but with caveats. Harman said, "Collins-Lieberman remains the best bill."

● **Armed Services.** The committee endorsed Hastert's proposal to limit the authority of the national intelligence director, particularly where it would affect Defense intelligence agencies. The panel approved its portion of the bill by a vote of 59-0 (H Rept 108-274, Part 2).

The 9-11 Commission

The National Commission on Terrorist Attacks Upon the United States — also know as the 9-11 commission — was an independent, bipartisan panel created by Congress in 2002 as part of the fiscal 2003 intelligence authorization act (PL 107-306).

The law, signed Nov. 27, 2002, instructed the commission to provide a "full and complete accounting of the circumstances surrounding the [Sept. 11, 2001] attacks, and the extent of the United States' preparedness for, and immediate response to, the attacks." It was also directed to report its findings to Congress and the president, along with "recommendations for corrective measures that can be taken to prevent acts of terrorism."

The panel consisted of 10 members, divided evenly between Democrats and Republicans. It was authorized to conduct investigations, hold hearings and issue subpoenas. The commission's final report came out July 22, 2004. The initial deadline was in May, but Congress agreed to extend it by two months (PL 108-207). The commission closed Aug. 21.

The 10 members of the commission were:

- Thomas H. Kean, former Republican governor of New Jersey, chairman.
- Lee H. Hamilton, D-Ind., who served in the House from 1965 to 1999, vice chairman.
- Fred Fielding, who served as White House counsel in the Reagan administration.
- Former Sen. Slade Gorton, R-Wash. (1981-87; 1989-2001).
- John F. Lehman, former secretary of the Navy under President Ronald Reagan.
- James R. Thompson, a former Republican governor of Illinois (1977-91).
- Richard Ben-Veniste, former federal Watergate prosecutor and chief Democratic counsel of the Senate Whitewater Committee.
- Jamie S. Gorelick, a Democrat and former deputy attorney general (1994-97).
- Former Sen. Bob Kerrey, D-Neb. (1989-2001).
- Former Rep. Tim Roemer, D-Ind. (1991-2003).

The committee rejected, 26-33, an amendment by Jim Cooper, D-Tenn., to substitute a modified version of the Collins-Lieberman bill. Hunter said the proposal was tantamount to risking the lives of U.S. military personnel. He said those who voted for the Hastert bill instead would be thanked by "the soldiers, sailors, airmen and Marines whose lives depend on the very strong lifeline" of intelligence data on the battlefield.

The committee rejected, 26-32, a proposal to authorize the director to recommend candidates to head Pentagon intelligence agencies. Hastert's bill required the director and Defense secretary to agree on nominees. An amendment to give the director unlimited authority to transfer funds was defeated, 25-33. The committee also rejected an amend-

ment to make the total for intelligence spending public.

- **Government Reform.** The committee gave voice vote approval to provisions (H Rept 108-274, Part 4) that dealt with drivers license standards and administrative rules.

In its closest vote, the committee rejected, 18-18, an amendment to put a single agency in charge of conducting security clearance investigations for federal employees and contractors.

- **Judiciary.** The committee approved portions of the bill covering immigration, border security and driver's license rules by a vote of 19-12 (H Rept 108-274, Part 5). Chairman F. James Sensenbrenner Jr. of Wisconsin led his GOP colleagues in defeating more than a dozen Democratic amendments, many of them designed to bring the legislation in line with the Senate bill. Republicans also turned back Democrats' attempts to strip out a handful of provisions that critics argued would erode civil liberties and unfairly restrict the rights of non-citizens.

The panel rejected by voice vote an attempt to strike a provision that would make it more difficult for people to win asylum. Under existing law, asylum-seekers had to show that they faced persecution based in part on race, religion, nationality or membership in a certain social group. The bill required that one of the criteria be the "central motive" behind the persecution, and allowed judges to require asylum seekers to corroborate their claims of persecution.

The committee added language dovetailing with a recommendation of the Sept. 11 commission that there be a new privacy and civil liberties oversight board, but only after agreeing, 19-15, to a proposal by Sensenbrenner that eliminated the board's subpoena power.

- **Financial Services.** The committee, which handled provisions targeting money laundering and other sources of terrorist financing, approved its portion of the bill by voice vote Sept. 29 (H Rept 108-274, Part 3).

House Floor Action

The House voted 282-134 on Oct. 8 to pass a somewhat revised version of HR 10 that was assembled by the Rules Committee from the five committee-reported proposals. The bill proposed significantly less power for the DNI than the Senate version, and less authority than the Sept. 11 commission had recommended. *(House vote 523, p. H-168)*

House GOP leaders succeeded in turning back Democratic amendments aimed at strengthening the powers of the DNI and weakening the restrictions on driver's licenses.

Most of the debate centered on an amendment by Robert Menendez, D-N.J., that would have substituted the Senate bill. The amendment failed 203-213, making it clear that a large majority of House Republicans would rally behind their leadership's legislation. *(House vote 510, p. H-164)*

The GOP leadership-controlled Rules Committee did not allow a vote on a bipartisan substitute (HR 5150), sponsored by Republican Christopher Shays of Connecticut and Democrat Carolyn B. Maloney of New York. Their amendment also included the text of another Senate bill (S 2774) to implement the recommendations of the Sept. 11 panel on homeland security, diplomacy and foreign aid.

In a highly unusual maneuver, the House first backed a proposal by Christopher H. Smith, R-N.J., to drop language that would make it easier to deport illegal immigrants back to

countries that had been known to torture criminal suspects. The vote was 212-203. But Sensenbrenner called for another roll call on the amendment and persuaded enough Republicans to switch that they managed to defeat Smith's proposal, 203-210. *(House votes 517, 521, pp. H-166, H-168)*

The House also adopted, 283-132, an amendment by Mark Green, R-Wis., to make attending a terrorist training camp a deportable offense. The House adopted, 333-84, an amendment by Robert W. Goodlatte, R-Va., to allow pre-trial detention without bail for suspected terrorists. *(House votes 516, 515, p. H-166)*

The House adopted by voice vote a leadership-approved amendment by John Hostettler, R-Ind., to modify the provisions on aliens from countries that used torture. The foreign terrorism suspects and their supporters would be detained in the United States instead, under the authority of the Department of Homeland Security.

Conference/Final Action

In the last roll call votes of the session, the House embraced the conference report on the bill (H Rept 108-796) on Dec. 7 by a lopsided and bipartisan vote of 336-75, and the Senate cleared the bill 89-2 the next day. *(House vote 544, p. H-176; Senate vote 216, p. S-47)*

Because both versions of the bill originally passed in early October, Republicans in Congress and the White House had hoped that the sweeping intelligence overhaul could make it to the president's desk in time for the Nov. 2 election. But conferees remained far apart as the election approached, pushing final action into the lame-duck session.

Once the elections were over, the political pressure to strike a deal faded and prospects for the bill looked slim. Among the chief sticking points were whether to declassify the total spent on intelligence and what to do about the House's immigration provisions. The biggest dispute, however, was still over exactly how much budget authority to give the DNI.

The Sept. 11 commission, some family members of Sept. 11 victims and a bipartisan coalition of House members and senators backed the Senate plan to create a powerful national intelligence director, wresting budgetary control of the intelligence apparatus away from the Defense Department. The Pentagon camp, led by Hunter, flatly opposed giving the intelligence director day-to-day authority over the Pentagon's intelligence agencies and their budgets.

The White House backed the Senate plan. But in a rare departure from the administration on national security, Gen. Richard B. Myers, chairman of the Joint Chiefs of Staff, said in a letter to Hunter that he backed the weaker House version.

On Nov. 20, Hunter derailed a tentative conference agreement on the bill that included a DNI with the power to set budget levels for the intelligence agencies, although much of the money would flow through the Pentagon. In an emotional caucus meeting, Hunter convinced a majority of House Republicans that the provisions would disrupt the military chain of command and interfere with the real-time flow of intelligence between commanders and troops on the battlefield, including his own son who had fought in Iraq.

Hastert, who had scheduled floor action for Nov. 20, pulled the bill; although there were enough Democratic "aye" votes to ensure adoption of the conference report, Hastert was unwilling to fracture his caucus or allow Democrats to provide the deciding votes.

Hunter was joined by Sensenbrenner, who was angry that Senate negotiators had rejected his provision barring states from issuing driver's licenses to illegal immigrants. "The 19 9/11 hijackers had 63 validly issued U.S. driver's licenses," he said in a statement.

In the end, Collins and Lieberman agreed to language that slightly softened the budgetary powers of the DNI. What sealed the deal was one word — abrogate. Collins and Lieberman agreed Dec. 5 to insert language saying essentially that the DNI's budgetary powers would not abrogate the military chain of command. That was enough to win over Hunter.

Hastert, meanwhile, promised Sensenbrenner a chance to take up the driver's license legislation and other dropped immigration provisions in a new bill soon after the 109th Congress convened in January. ◆

Details of the Intelligence Overhaul Law

The final act of the 109th Congress was to send President Bush a wide-ranging bill overhauling the nation's intelligence community. The initiative was spawned by the report of the National Commission on Terrorist Attacks Upon the United States, which studied intelligence failures prior to Sept. 11, 2001. The House adopted the conference report Dec. 7; the Senate cleared the bill Dec. 8; and the president signed the legislation (PL 108-458) Dec. 17. Following are the major provisions of the new intelligence law:

Director of National Intelligence

The law began by creating the position of director of national intelligence (DNI) to serve as head of the U.S. intelligence community. The DNI was to act as principal adviser to the president, the National Security Council and the Homeland Security Council on intelligence matters.

● **Role of the director.** The director, who had to be appointed by the president and confirmed by the Senate, was charged with ensuring that all federal departments and agencies, the Joint Chiefs, and relevant committees of Congress had access to the intelligence they need to carry out their missions. The DNI was given access to all national intelligence acquired by any federal department or agency, unless the president or existing law provided otherwise.

Other responsibilities included monitoring the implementation of intelligence operations — though the DNI was not directly in charge of the CIA's clandestine operations — and creating governmentwide priorities and standards for collecting and analyzing intelligence. The director also was charged with overseeing the coordination of relations with the intelligence or security services of foreign governments and international organizations.

The DNI could not serve simultaneously as CIA director.

• **Budget authority.** The director was given the power to "develop and determine" the annual budgets for the National Intelligence Program, including the CIA and parts of the National Security Agency, National Reconnaissance Office and National Geospatial Intelligence Agency. It did not include joint military intelligence programs or tactical intelligence and related activities, both of which were purely military intelligence functions. The DNI could participate in creation of those budgets.

However, the director could not "abrogate" the military chain of command, meaning the intelligence chief could not use his budgetary powers to override decisions by military leaders.

The DNI could tell the intelligence agency comptrollers how to allocate money but lacked day-to-day power over budgetary operations at the agencies.

The director was authorized to "reprogram," or transfer, funds within the intelligence community up to a limit of $150 million or 5 percent of an agency budget per year, whichever was less. Such transfers required approval from the director of the Office of Management and Budget, and they could not terminate any program.

• **Personnel.** The law authorized 500 new personnel billets to staff the new DNI office. The director was allowed to detail up to 150 personnel within the intelligence community to the office for up to two years, and could transfer personnel among intelligence agencies for up to two years.

• **Office of the Director of National Intelligence.** The law established the office and specified that it include a principal deputy director of national intelligence, a general counsel, a civil liberties protection officer, a director of science and technology, a national counterintelligence executive and up to four deputy directors appointed by the DNI. Only one of the deputy directors could be an active military officer.

Information Sharing

The law required the DNI to establish a far-reaching system within the intelligence community to share information from agency to agency.

• **Governmentwide standards.** The director was given responsibility for establishing uniform procedures, technology standards and policies for information sharing, and for purchasing whatever equipment and technology was needed to build the appropriate technological architecture.

• **Protecting sources.** The director was expected to create across-the-board standards for keeping secret the sources and methods being used by spies to collect sensitive information.

Improving Analysis and Coordination

• **National Intelligence Council.** The council, appointed by the DNI, was to be composed of senior analysts within the intelligence community and experts from the private sector. It would be responsible for creating the National Intelligence Estimates similar to the report used to justify the invasion of Iraq. The DNI was allowed to hire private sector contractors to provide help in crafting these intelligence estimates.

• **National Counterterrorism Center.** The center, created in the Office of the DNI, was to be the primary government organization for analyzing and integrating intelligence on international terrorism and counterterrorism. It was authorized to conduct strategic planning for big-picture intelligence goals, but was not allowed to assign responsibilities or direct intelligence operations for individual intelligence agencies.

The center was to absorb the current Terrorist Threat Integration Center, which was created by executive order. The center's director would work for the DNI, after being appointed by the president and confirmed by the Senate.

• **National Counterproliferation Center.** The center, to be created by the president, would serve as the primary organization within the government for analyzing and integrating all intelligence related to the proliferation of weapons of mass destruction.

The president could waive any portion of this section if he believed it was in the interest of national security. This section also authorized creation of specialized intelligence centers to focus on specific threats, such as bioterrorism, or geographic areas, such as North Korea.

• **"Red teaming."** The DNI was directed to set up a group responsible for producing an alternative, or competitive, analysis of intelligence. This so-called red team analysis is a common tool used to poke holes in intelligence assumptions and test conclusions of the regular analysts. It was put into the law in the wake of the faulty intelligence used to declare that Iraq had weapons of mass destruction. The DNI was required to appoint a special officer who would conduct investigations into whether intelligence analyses lacked objectivity or had been compromised by politics.

Differences in analytic judgment of intelligence were supposed to be fully considered and brought to policy makers' attention.

Civil Liberties

• **Civil Liberties Protection Office.** An office to protect civil liberties was to be created within the Office of the DNI and charged with ensuring that the civil liberties and privacy of U.S. citizens were protected when intelligence activities and policies were being carried out.

• **Oversight board.** A new Privacy and Civil Liberties Oversight Board was created within the Executive Office of the President to review executive-branch policies and regulations on terrorism to ensure protection of privacy and civil liberties. The board was weakened in conference, leaving it without subpoena powers. Also, the law allowed the DNI to withhold information from the oversight board if it was in the interest of national security.

• **CIA.** The law reiterated that the CIA lacked the power to conduct any police, subpoena or law enforcement operations inside the United States.

Other Intelligence Changes

• **Education and training.** The DNI was supposed to develop new education and linguistic training requirements for the intelligence community in an effort to improve the spy agencies' abilities to penetrate terrorist cells and interpret intercepted communications. A new intelligence-community scholarship program was created to offer scholarships to college students interested in going into the intelligence field.

• **"Open source" intelligence.** The law required the DNI to ensure that the intelligence community was making adequate use of "open source" intelligence — meaning publicly available, unclassified information that might contain clues or insights into national security threats. It recommended that a special center be created for this purpose.

• **Reserve Corps.** The DNI was also authorized to establish a National Intelligence Reserve Corps of former or retired intelligence employees who could be called on to work at intelligence agencies during a national emergency.

• **CIA changes.** The CIA director was given 180 days from enactment to submit to the DNI and congressional intelligence committees a strategy for improving intelligence analysis and human intelligence.

The CIA was directed to develop a more effective foreign language program and to hire people with "diverse" backgrounds, a move aimed at getting more agents with Arab or Middle-Eastern backgrounds into the clandestine services.

The law abolished several top-level CIA positions, including assis-

tant directors of central intelligence for collection, analysis and production, and administration.

- **Defense-CIA coordination.** The CIA and Department of Defense, often depicted as competitive and turf-conscious on intelligence matters, were required to develop new procedures to improve coordination between military and civilian intelligence operations. The procedures were to include language guaranteeing that top officials at the CIA and Defense knew exactly what intelligence activities the other was pursuing.

The law also required creation of an "information-sharing environment" — a virtual, multi-agency information-sharing system designed to share intelligence data, not only within the federal government but also with state and local law enforcement authorities. To create the system, the law authorized $20 million in fiscal 2005 and 2006.

- **FBI changes.** The FBI, which shouldered much of the blame for pre-Sept. 11 intelligence failures, was required to create a new "national intelligence workforce" intended to establish a career track within the agency for domestic intelligence work. The provision addresses concerns that career success at the FBI had hinged more on being a top criminal agent than on being a collector or analyst of intelligence. The FBI's Office of Intelligence was elevated to a "Directorate of Intelligence" as part of this effort.

The law also created a Reserve Service of former or retired FBI employees who could be called on to help the FBI during a national emergency, as determined by the FBI director. The mandatory FBI retirement age was raised to 65 from 60.

- **Security clearances.** In an attempt to break up the backlog in processing security clearances, the law required the president to select a single department or agency to be responsible for oversight of all such clearances. Agencies also were required to accept security clearances from other agencies to reduce repetitive processing. The law set a goal of processing 90 percent of security clearance applications within 60 days. Existing waits often were more than a year.

The law also called on the president-elect, shortly after a presidential election, to submit to the agency in charge of clearances all the names of candidates being considered for national security positions so the clearances could be processed quickly.

Transportation Security

The secretary of Homeland Security was told to develop a national strategy for transportation security that set threat priorities and laid out a damage-recovery plan in case of another attack. The Transportation Security Administration (TSA) had been criticized for focusing to too great an extent on "fighting the last war," meaning concentrating on airplane security alone.

- **Biometric technology.** The law required the Homeland Security Department to begin deploying a biometric screening system at airports. Such systems obtain biological information through methods such as retinal or iris scanning, fingerprints, or face recognition to identify individual travelers. Within two years, the TSA was to integrate that system with the biometric identification systems used by the Justice and State departments. The TSA was required to establish national technology requirements for this system by March 31, 2005, along with a list of products and vendors that met the standards. The law authorized $20 million for the TSA to research and develop advanced biometric technologies for use in aviation security.

- **Advanced passenger screening.** The law directed the TSA to test a new airline passenger screening system that ran names through "no fly" lists and an integrated terrorist watch list, and to establish a procedure that allowed passengers to dispute their inclusion on the list. This was in response to the problem of mistaken identities in which people were blocked from flying because their names were similar to that of someone on the no-fly list.

- **Employee screening.** Employees who worked for the airport, airlines or security services would also have to undergo screening, filling what critics said had been a hole in airport security.

- **Baggage screening.** Within 90 days of enactment, the TSA was required to submit a plan to Congress for screening all passengers and their carry-on bags for explosives. The law authorized $250 million for research and development of devices to detect biological, radiological and nuclear materials at airport checkpoints and another $150 million to test experimental weapons-detection technologies at five airports in fiscal 2005 and 2006.

In addition, the law authorized $400 million a year — up from $250 million — for airport security improvement projects.

- **Air marshals.** The law directed the TSA to come up with rules to make it easier for armed air marshals to protect their anonymity. Air marshals complained that because of a strict business dress code, their cover was easily blown on airplanes. The law also required the Homeland Security Department to train air marshals in foreign countries so they could travel on foreign airliners bound for U.S. airspace.

- **Other aviation security measures.** The TSA was directed to revise the list of prohibited items on airplanes to include butane lighters, a reaction to the "shoe bomber" incident in 2001.

The Federal Aviation Administration was told to come up with improved pilot licensing standards to reduce the chance of fraud.

The law also urged the president to pursue diplomatic discussions with foreign governments to limit the easy availability of shoulder-fired missiles that could threaten airplanes on takeoff and landing.

The law authorized $900 million in fiscal 2005 through 2007 to improve cargo security on airplanes. It also authorized $2 million for a test program to evaluate blast-resistant cargo containers for airplanes.

- **Maritime security.** The law required the secretary of Homeland Security to implement a program for screening passengers and crew members on cruise ships against terrorist databases. Such a rule would lead to creation of the maritime equivalent of no-fly lists. However, the secretary could waive the requirements if they were deemed impractical.

Border Security and Immigration

This section of the law addressed the concerns of the Sept. 11 commission that immigration rules and border security were partially to blame for allowing terrorists to enter and move around the country freely even though some were here on expired visas

- **Border agents and Customs.** The Homeland Security Department was authorized to add 2,000 full-time border patrol agents every year between fiscal 2006 and 2010. It was allowed to hire 800 new immigration investigators and provide 40,000 new beds for detention facilities that housed illegal aliens during that time. To patrol the northern border, the law authorized the use of unmanned airplanes and other technologies such as video sensors. The law also expanded the presence of U.S. immigration officers in foreign airports, increasing the number of foreign "pre-inspection" stations from 25 to 50.

- **Visa requirements.** The law required that all visa applicants be interviewed in person by a U.S. consular official. It created a new visa and passport security program to investigate how terrorists used fraudulent documents and which countries facilitated such actions. The State Department was required to report to Congress by May 31, 2005, on the feasibility of giving border agents access to real-time, constantly updated information on stolen passports. The measure also required creation of a Visa and Passport Security Program at the State Department.

- **Illegal immigrant treatment.** The law created a Human Smuggling and Trafficking Center aimed at halting terrorist entries into the United States and cracking down on human smuggling. Anyone who had received military-style training from a terrorist orga-

nization could be deported. The law also barred entry into the United States by any foreign national who had committed torture or other atrocities abroad. If such individuals were already in the country, they can be deported. The law also prohibited judicial review of visa revocations, taking away an appeals process for people whose visas had been revoked.

- **Consular officers.** The secretary of State was authorized to add 150 new consular officers per year between fiscal 2006 and 2009 for consulates around the world. Most aliens applying for non-immigrant visas had to be interviewed in person by a consular official, not a foreign national. Consular officers would get training to help them better detect fraudulent documents.

- **Fraudulent travel documents.** The law called on the president to lead efforts to draw up international agreements to better track terrorist travel and crack down on use of stolen or falsified passports and visas, and to help establish an international system for "real time" verification of visas and passports.

- **Immigration security.** The secretary of Homeland Security was put in charge of the "immigration security initiative," which placed U.S. immigration officers at foreign airports. The measure authorized $105 million over three years to carry out the program.

- **Driver's license standards.** The Homeland Security and Transportation departments were required to develop federal standards for the types of documents that states could accept in issuing driver's licenses. In what some critics called a "loophole," the law stated that such federal regulations could not infringe on a state's power to decide who was eligible for a driver's license.

- **Birth certificates.** The Health and Human Services Department was directed to establish federal standards for state-issued birth certificates, although the department was not allowed to require that all states adhere to a specific design.

- **Social Security numbers.** The law required the Social Security Administration to create minimum standards for verifying documents used by people seeking an original or replacement Social Security card. The law limited people to three replacement cards in a year or 10 for their entire life. The law created an interagency task force composed of Social Security and Homeland Security officials to be responsible for combating Social Security card fraud. States were prohibited from displaying Social Security numbers on driver's licenses, a standard practice for years in many states.

- **Terrorist travel information.** The Homeland Security Department was required to set up a program to oversee dissemination of terrorist travel intelligence to all federal authorities involved in transportation security.

- **Identification standards.** States were required to certify to the Transportation Department that they were meeting minimum federal standards for issuing driver's licenses, birth certificates and other identification documents. The departments of Transportation and Homeland Security were instructed to write such standards within 18 months of enactment. The measure was aimed at getting a national standard for IDs used to board airplanes.

Terrorism Prevention

- **"Lone wolf" terrorist.** The law amended the Foreign Intelligence Surveillance Act (PL 95-511) to allow the FBI to conduct surveillance on a single terrorist who might not be connected to any foreign power or agent of a foreign power. Prior law allowed surveillance on U.S. soil of people suspected of spying for a foreign power, but critics said that prevented monitoring of a potential terrorist who was working as a "lone wolf." This provision also required amending the 2001 Patriot Act (PL 107-56).

- **Pre-trial imprisonment.** Terrorist suspects had to be denied bail and held in jail until trial, unless they could prove they were not flight risks or dangers to society.

- **Material support to terrorists.** The law made it a crime to pro-

vide material support — meaning money, lodging, advice, training or any other aid — to help carry out an act of terrorism. The provisions expires at the end of 2006.

- **Terrorist hoaxes.** The law also made it a crime for anyone to convey false or misleading information about a terrorist attack or possible terrorist attack. If convicted, the suspect could receive five years in prison. If the hoax caused bodily harm or death to anyone, the suspect could be sentenced to 20 years to life in prison.

- **Weapons of mass destruction.** The law specified that it was a crime to use the mail or any postal-like service to carry out an attack with a weapon of mass destruction.

- **Biological and radiological weapons.** Criminal penalties were expanded for production, possession and use of radiological explosive devices, or "dirty bombs," and the variola virus, which is the carrier of smallpox.

- **Grand jury information.** Existing law permitted sharing of grand jury information with state and local governments to help enforce federal laws. The new law expanded that authority to allow the sharing of grand jury information with foreign governments to help U.S. law enforcement. Foreign intelligence could be shared with foreign governments, but only after the Justice Department and the DNI submitted guidelines.

- **Criminal background checks.** Private employers were allowed to ask the Justice Department to conduct criminal background checks on private security officers, but the employer would have to have written consent from the employee to do the investigation.

Financial Provisions

- **Financial Crimes Network.** The law authorized $35.5 million in fiscal 2005 to boost the Treasury Department's Financial Crimes Enforcement Network, with most of the money going to a program designed to securely receive and analyze data from financial institutions. The law also extended provisions in the Money Laundering and Financial Crimes Strategy Act (PL 105-310) and required the Treasury Department to submit to Congress a national strategy for combating money laundering. This section also made terrorist-financing provisions in the Patriot Act permanent. All the provisions were geared toward better tracking of terrorist financial networks.

- **Currency engraving.** The Bureau of Engraving and Printing was authorized to print currency and other sensitive documents for foreign governments. This was designed to allow the bureau to test anti-counterfeiting measures that could be used in future upgrades of U.S. currency, while also helping U.S. allies in the developing world to upgrade their currency systems. The printing of money for foreign countries had to be consistent with U.S. foreign policy.

- **Financial market emergencies.** The law expanded the authority of the Securities and Exchange Commission to take emergency actions to halt trading and close financial markets in case of a national emergency. The SEC was allowed to extend emergency orders for up to 30 business days, up from 10 days in prior law.

- **Bank examiner rules.** Senior federal bank examiners were barred from accepting employment at a bank they had investigated for at least one year after leaving the Federal Deposit Insurance Corporation.

- **Reports to Congress.** Within 270 days of enactment, the Treasury Department was required to submit a report on the effectiveness of U.S. efforts to stop terrorist financing. The agreement also required the department to work more closely with the International Monetary Fund to battle global terrorist financing.

Foreign Policy Provisions

The Sept. 11 commission recommended significant outreach efforts to improve U.S. diplomatic relations throughout the world, and the law included several provisions aimed at accomplishing this goal.

- **Terrorist sanctuaries.** A "sense of Congress" provision stated that the United States should be aggressive in identifying terrorist sanctuaries and countries that sheltered terrorists. It recommended that the United States help countries that unknowingly harbored terrorists to come up with strategies for eliminating the conditions that created the terrorist sanctuaries.

- **Export Administration Act.** The law amended the Export Administration Act of 1979 (PL 96-72) to ensure that regulations relating to state sponsors of terrorism also applied to all terrorist sanctuaries.

- **Pakistan.** The law declared that a stable Pakistan was critical to the stability of the region and the United States should help Pakistan fully control its territorial borders. The law waived existing restrictions on foreign assistance to Pakistan through fiscal 2006.

- **Afghanistan.** The law reiterated U.S. support for democracy in Afghanistan, backed efforts to slow down the narcotics trade and called for the president to create a long-term strategy for Afghanistan. It authorized "such sums as may be necessary" for assistance to Afghanistan in fiscal 2005 and 2006. The law created the position of a "coordinator for assistance" to Afghanistan and called for the Afghan government, with U.S. assistance, to disarm Afghan warlords.

- **Saudi diplomacy.** The law expressed a sense of Congress that Saudi Arabia should remain a key ally, but that the Saudi government had not done a good job preventing financial support from flowing to terrorists in Saudi Arabia. The president was required to submit to Congress within 180 days of enactment a new strategy for collaborating with Saudi Arabia, including intelligence cooperation. The president had to submit a similar report outlining a long-term strategy for dealing with Pakistan within 180 days.

- **"Moral leadership."** In a section dealing with efforts to combat Islamic terrorism, the law acknowledged the U.S. reputation in the Islamic world had suffered and stated that the United States should offer an example of "moral leadership" to the world by treating people humanely and respecting Muslim traditions.

- **Using media in diplomacy.** The law called on the State Department to promote a free press in the Muslim world. The measure authorized the secretary of State to make grants to the National Endowment for Democracy to fund a private sector group to manage a "media network" of individuals and government officials that would help develop free and independent media in the Islamic world. No specific amount of money was authorized.

- **Muslim outreach.** A pilot program was created to provide scholarship grants to American-sponsored schools in Muslim countries. The State Department was directed to establish an "International Youth Opportunity Fund" to improve public education in predominantly Muslim countries, but no specific amount of money was authorized. The law authorized continued funding — with no specific dollar figure — for the Middle East Partnership Initiative, a program designed to promote the rule of law in the Middle East.

- **Human rights.** The law reiterated U.S. support of the U.N. Human Rights Commission and called on the president and State Department to establish training courses in multilateral diplomacy for Foreign Service officers.

- **Free trade.** The measure declared that the United States would work toward creating a "Middle East Free Trade Area" by 2013 and use economic policies and free trade to combat the conditions that lead to terrorism.

Homeland Security

This section began with a sense-of-Congress statement that the Department of Homeland Security needed to develop a unified "incident command system" so there was a national communications and response plan in case of another major terrorist attack.

- **Capital region aid.** The law authorized mutual aid between local governments and regional authorities in the Washington area. The aid could be used by regional or local authorities to share emergency services or resources in responding to a terrorist attack.

- **Emergency communications.** The law had several provisions aimed at improving emergency-communications systems. It called on Congress to pass a law to set aside certain radio spectrum and analog television spectrum for emergency responders. It also required the Department of Homeland Security to work with the Commerce Department to establish a program to enhance public safety communications and authorized $118 million over five years for the program.

- **First-responder funding.** The law did not change the formula for distributing first-responder grants, although both the House and Senate versions called for a greater emphasis on high-threat areas while guaranteeing a minimum to all states. Congress recommended that the 109th Congress should overhaul the formula, with no specific recommendation for how to do so.

- **Alert system.** The law authorized a pilot study to see whether the Homeland Security Department could develop a homeland security warning system similar to the AMBER Alert system commonly used to disseminate information about missing children.

- **Counternarcotics office.** The duties of the counternarcotics office were expanded to allow the director to serve on the Joint Terrorism Task Force to facilitate the investigations of connections between terrorism and narcotic trafficking.

- **Geospatial Management.** The law created an Office of Geospatial Management in the Department of Homeland Security to coordinate mapping, satellite analysis and other geographic technologies in an effort to improve terrorism intelligence.

- **Civil liberties.** The law required the department's inspector general to designate a senior staff member to handle civil rights and civil liberties cases for the department. The official would review complaints and initiate investigations when there were allegations of violations of civil rights or civil liberties. However, this section did not contain any new civil liberties protections and did not give any subpoena powers to the civil liberties offices in Homeland Security or the DNI.

Miscellaneous Provisions

- **Financial disclosure forms.** The Office of Government Ethics was required to submit a report to Congress on conflict of interest rules regarding financial disclosure reporting for government officials.

- **Plane tickets on bankrupt airlines.** The law extended for an additional year — through Nov. 19, 2005 — a provision in existing law that required airlines to honor tickets on other airlines that have suspended service or gone out of business.

- **FBI computers.** The law required the FBI to maintain state-of-the-art information-technology systems and to report annually to the House and Senate Judiciary committees on the progress of those systems. ◆

Intelligence Sharing Emphasized

The annual bill to authorize the nation's intelligence agencies was held prisoner for weeks while lawmakers struggled to complete a reorganization of the intelligence community. Within hours of final action on the larger overhaul, Congress on Dec. 8 cleared the authorization bill. President Bush signed the measure into law Dec. 23 (HR 4548 — PL 108-487).

The bill set budget levels and policy for fiscal 2005 at the nation's 15 spy agencies. The intelligence budget is classified — a classified annex showing dollar amounts and personnel ceilings for each intelligence program is available to members only — but intelligence experts estimated that it amounted to about $40 billion. Pentagon agencies accounted for about 80 percent of the total, with the rest going to the CIA and smaller agencies in the departments of Justice, State and Energy.

Most of the bill was classified, but the portion made public required the director of national intelligence, a position created under the overhaul bill (PL 108-458), to conduct an intelligence assessment to identify countries or regions that were sanctuaries for terrorists. (*Overhaul, p. 11-3*)

It also authorized more funding for language studies, required that senior intelligence officers demonstrate high proficiency in a foreign language and authorized partnerships with educational institutions to encourage the study of foreign languages. This emphasis followed criticism that the intelligence community did not have enough translators of Middle Eastern languages before the Sept. 11, 2001, attacks.

The bill created a chief information officer to manage large-scale information-sharing projects for agencies within the intelligence community and direct research and development initiatives. The conference report said terrorism-related intelligence needed to be shared among far more individuals and agencies than traditional foreign intelligence, which usually relates to the internal plans and intentions of a sovereign nation.

Other provisions allowed the use of intelligence funds to support combined operations against drug traffickers and terrorist organizations in Colombia, and allowed the CIA director to authorize increases of up to 2 percent in civilian personnel ceilings with approval from the Office of Management and Budget.

The House passed its version of the bill in June, and the Senate followed in October. The differences appeared to have been settled, but House GOP leaders refused to name conferees because the process would have given Democrats an opening on the floor to express dissatisfaction with the

BoxScore

Bill:
HR 4548 — PL 108-487

Legislative Action:

House passed HR 4548 (H Rept 108-558), 360-61, on June 23.

Senate passed HR 4548 by voice vote Oct. 11, after incorporating the text of S 2386 (S Rept 108-258, S Rept 108-300).

House adopted the conference report (H Rept 108-798) by voice vote Dec. 7.

Senate cleared the bill Dec. 8 by voice vote.

President signed Dec. 23.

overhaul bill, which was stuck in conference. As prospects for a formal conference dwindled late in the session, it looked increasingly likely that Congress would adjourn without clearing the authorization bill. The measure was not must-pass legislation, because the intelligence programs were automatically authorized and funded in "black" sections of the annual defense appropriations bill.

Although Congress cleared the authorization measure shortly before adjourning, the defense spending bill had been law for more than four months (PL 108-287). "When we don't pass our authorization bills," said Peter Hoekstra, R-Mich., chairman of the House Select Committee on Intelligence, "we cede some of our influence to appropriators."

Senate Committee Action

The Senate Select Intelligence Committee approved its version of the bill May 4 (S 2386 — S Rept 108-258), including a provision to abolish the traditional eight-year term limit for committee members.

Both Democrats and Republicans said term limits — imposed to prevent members from being co-opted by the intelligence community — discouraged expertise in intelligence issues, which took years to develop.

In a statement released after the session, the committee said the bill would improve security and reduce administrative duties for spies with non-official cover. A committee staffer said it "would basically let operatives with non-official cover live their lives more easily without leaving a trail." He declined to give more details.

The Senate bill also proposed to amend the 1978 Foreign Intelligence Surveillance Act (PL 95-511) to allow surveillance of a suspected foreign terrorist, even if the person could not be linked to a foreign power or terrorist group. The so-called lone wolf provision was later enacted as part of the intelligence overhaul law. (*1978 Almanac, p. 186*)

The Senate Armed Services committee approved classified portions of the bill July 8 (S Rept 108-300).

House Committee Action

The usually bipartisan House Intelligence Committee fractured along party lines, approving its version of the bill (HR 4548 — H Rept 108-558) by a vote of 11-8 on June 16. Democrats voted against the bill after five of their amendments were rejected. They then took the unusual step of holding a news conference to air their complaints, arguing that the bill was not adequate to fund the war on terrorism.

Goss Replaces Tenet at CIA

Porter J. Goss, R-Fla., became the 19th director of central intelligence on Sept. 24, after being confirmed by the Senate two days earlier. Goss succeeded George J. Tenet, whose resignation was announced June 3.

Goss, a CIA case officer in the 1960s, was the head of the House Select Committee on Intelligence from 1997 until he resigned to head the CIA. Goss had announced his plans to retire from Congress at the end of the session, and there was widespread speculation that he might become the next CIA director.

Democrats reacted skeptically when President Bush announced his choice of Goss for the job Aug. 10, warning that the Florida Republican had to demonstrate that he was not too partisan to head the spy agency. Bush called Goss the "right man to lead this important agency at this critical moment."

The Senate Select Intelligence Committee approved Goss' nomination, 12-4, in a closed-door session Sept. 21. In hearings prior to the vote, Democrats questioned the nominee closely, but Goss was largely unflappable. Asked about his willingness to overhaul the CIA, he told Ron Wyden, D-Ore., "I don't think there's any question about my commitment to reform. Otherwise I wouldn't be here."

All nine Republicans on the panel and three Democrats voted in favor of the nomination. The four Democrats who voted "no" said Goss' record indicated he would be too close to the Bush White House to serve as an independent director and embrace the major intelligence shake-up that was needed.

The Senate confirmed Goss' nomination by a vote of 77-17 on Sept. 22, and he was sworn in two days later. (*Senate vote 187, p. S-40*)

Tenet's resignation was effective July 11, the seventh anniversary of his appointment to the job in 1997 by President Bill Clinton. Before becoming director, he had served as deputy to then-Director John M. Deutch.

Tenet had come under sharp criticism for intelligence failures that preceded the Sept. 11 terrorist attacks, and for faulty intelligence that Saddam Hussein was stockpiling weapons of mass destruction. He resigned as two potentially critical intelligence reports were being prepared.

On July 9, the Senate Intelligence panel released a detailed report on the intelligence used by Bush to justify the war in Iraq, which painted a damning picture of the CIA. The committee charged that the agency not only relied on flawed and outdated intelligence, but also failed to correct those flaws or even inform policy makers just how shaky their key judgments were.

On July 22, the bipartisan, independent Sept. 11 commission published a bestseller that examined U.S. intelligence failings surrounding Sept. 11 and called for a complete restructuring of the intelligence community. By the end of the year, that report led to enactment of an intelligence overhaul law (PL 108-458) that created a new director of national intelligence and narrowed the job of the CIA director to managing the agency, rather than also serving as the overall director of national intelligence. (*Overhaul, p. 11-3*)

Committee Chairman Porter J. Goss, R-Fla., and ranking Democrat Jane Harman of California did agree to exclude two of the more controversial Senate provisions — the lone-wolf provision and the section exempting DIA personnel from the 1974 Privacy Act.

But Democrats complained that the panel's GOP majority rejected amendments to open the markup of non-sensitive matters to the public, provide more funding for counterterrorism efforts, and increase oversight and investigate prisoner abuse at the Abu Ghraib prison in Iraq. Other Democratic amendments would have restructured intelligence gathering and investigated U.S. dealings with former Iraqi exile leader Ahmed Chalabi. The FBI was investigating administration accusations that Chalabi informed Iran that U.S. intelligence had broken Tehran's spy code. (*Abu Ghraib, p. 6-5*)

A Republican aide called the Democrats' complaints a political ploy, noting that they had not tried to work out their amendments in advance, as was typically done on the committee.

The GOP-written committee report on the bill contained some pointed criticism of the CIA, particularly its human intelligence operation. "For too long, the CIA has been ignoring its core mission activities," the report said. "There is a dysfunctional denial of any need for corrective action."

The committee said the human intelligence program was at least five years from being "viable" and "continues down a road leading over a proverbial cliff." It cited "misallocation and redirection of resources, poor prioritization of objectives, micromanagement of field operations and a continued political aversion to operational risk."

The comments drew a strong and blunt response from retiring CIA Director George J. Tenet.

In a June 23 letter to Goss that the CIA made public, Tenet said some of the report's conclusions were "ill-informed" or "frankly absurd." He said the CIA was in the midst of a years-long effort to "recruit, train and deploy experienced case officers."

"The damage done by inattention to the clandestine service during the first half of the 1990s," he wrote, "cannot be repaired in the blink of an eye."

House Floor Action

The partisanship continued on the House floor June 23, when members passed the bill, 360-61, after rejecting, 197-224, a Democratic motion to send the measure back to the Intelligence Committee. That was a marked change from the previous year when only nine House members voted against the authorization bill. (*House votes 300, 299, p. H-100*)

Democrats said the GOP-written bill would authorize less than one-third the money needed for counterterrorism in fiscal 2005 and complained that they were not allowed to offer an amendment to increase the funding. Republicans said that Democrats were resorting to election-year grandstanding.

Goss said the bill would authorize a record amount of intelligence spending, 16 percent more than Bush had requested. He said it would exceed Bush's request for human intelligence activities by 22 percent. It would also create a chief information officer to improve coordination among intelligence agencies. Goss said the House bill mostly tracked the Senate version.

Senate Floor Action

The bill languished through the summer and into the fall as lawmakers debated possible changes to the intelligence community. The real push for an overhaul did not come until after the independent Sept. 11 commission released its recommendations in late July. On Oct. 11, less than a week after passing their version of the intelligence overhaul bill, senators passed the authorization by voice vote.

During the floor debate the Senate:

• Agreed by voice vote to delete the provision abolishing term limits for Intelligence Committee members. The Senate had voted to end the term limits as part of a separate committee reorganization resolution (S Res 445) adopted Oct. 9. (*Committee reorganization, p. 5-6*)

• Agreed by voice vote to strike a provision that would have allowed Defense Intelligence Agency (DIA) personnel to conceal their identities when gathering intelligence on U.S. citizens. Under a 30-year-old law (PL 93-579), federal agents were required to identify themselves when collecting information stateside. The CIA was prohibited from domestic spying in all circumstances. Other intelligence agencies, including the DIA, could gather information inside the United States but only if their agents disclosed who they were to their sources. (*1974 Almanac, p. 292*)

Final Action

The Senate appointed conferees Oct. 16, but House leaders waited until Dec. 7 after final agreement was reached on the intelligence overhaul bill. Within minutes of voting on the overhaul, conferees filed their report on the authorization bill (H Rept 108-798) and the House adopted it by voice vote. The Senate cleared the bill by voice vote the next day. ◆

Foreign Affairs Bill Stranded

A bill to authorize funds for the State Department, foreign aid, U.N. dues and the Peace Corps died at the end of the Congress, leaving the appropriators free rein to write spending bills for foreign operations and the State Department. (*Appropriations, pp. 2-8, 2-22*)

A fiscal 2004 State Department authorization bill (S 925) reached the Senate floor in July 2003, but Majority Leader Bill Frist, R-Tenn., pulled it after Democrats tried to tack on unrelated amendments to raise the minimum wage. (*2003 Almanac, p. 10-3*)

The House passed its own bill (HR 1950) in 2003 that would have authorized $45.3 billion through fiscal 2007, mainly for the State Department, public diplomacy and non-military foreign aid. It also included $9.3 billion for the Millennium Challenge Account (MCA) for fiscal 2004 through 2006. A Bush administration priority, the MCA was created to aid poor countries that met benchmarks in human rights, democracy and economic policy. Without Senate action, the bill went no further.

In March 2004, the Senate Foreign Relations Committee tried again, approving a combined fiscal 2005 State Department and foreign aid authorization bill (S 2144). The impetus came from Chairman Richard G. Lugar, R-Ind., who argued that Congress had an important role to play as the government tried to define its role in places like Iraq, Haiti and

BoxScore

Bill:
S 2144
Legislative Action:
Senate Foreign Relations Committee approved S 2144 (S Rept 108-248), 19-0, on March 4.

other war-ravaged countries.

But the measure never reached the Senate floor. GOP aides said Frist did not schedule floor time because he expected a replay of the 2003 minimum wage fight.

Background

Congress had not passed a comprehensive foreign aid authorization bill since 1985, the last time Lugar chaired the Foreign Relations Committee. Separate legislation to authorize State Department operations had an only slightly better track record. In the previous three Congresses, the State Department authorization bills had been signed into law after the provisions already had been enacted as part of the appropriations process or included in an omnibus measure to shield them from a veto (*1999 Almanac, p. 14-3; 1998 Almanac, p. 2-45; 1996 Almanac, p. 9-3*)

The absence of such legislation meant reduced influence for the Foreign Relations Committee and the companion House International Relations Committee, chaired by Henry J. Hyde, R-Ill. On the other hand, the Foreign Operations Appropriations subcommittees had increased clout because they made the decisions about foreign aid.

The House and Senate Armed Services committees found themselves legislating on how troops should act in nation-building programs.

Foreign policy authorizers said it was difficult to pinpoint exactly when they started to be marginalized. Several members pointed to the tenure from 1995-2001 of Jesse Helms, R-N.C. (1973-2003), as Senate Foreign Relations chairman. Helms was adroit at blocking proposals he did not like, but he was not widely known for his zeal in passing foreign policy legislation. However, Helms did make an effort to pass foreign aid legislation in 2000, opting to divide the proposals into a series of smaller bills rather than trying to pass one mammoth piece. (*2000 Almanac, p. 11-3*)

Others said the situation was more endemic and could not be blamed on one chairman. Foreign policy can change rapidly, and the Constitution was written to give the president great power to react to those changes without congressional approval.

Also, foreign policy issues generally ranked low among the priorities of U.S. voters, giving such measures little momentum through Congress. That meant legislators were prone to abandon legislation at the first hint of trouble or if opponents managed to attach unpalatable provisions to the bill.

After the Sept. 11, 2001, terrorist attacks, the administration and Congress were forced to put international affairs back on their plates. But most of the response was military, a trend that intensified with the war in Iraq.

Lugar and other foreign policy experts said relying on the military to achieve foreign policy objectives had some serious ripple effects. Perhaps the biggest, was that the United States did not have enough troops to handle the needs for both fighting wars and the postwar occupations such interventions required. Lugar said the United States had to find new and innovative ways to fulfill its global responsibilities while maintaining an adequate force to pro-

tect itself. "We still have a daunting set of prospects here," Lugar said at a March 3 hearing. "Somebody's going to have to fill in the blanks."

Legislative Action

Senate Committee Action

The Senate Foreign Relations Committee approved the authorization bill (S 2144 — S Rept 108-248), 19-0, on March 4. The totals matched President Bush's overall fiscal 2005 budget request — $10.9 billion for the State Department and $18.3 billion in foreign aid — but the panel made several adjustments.

For example, the bill called for $2 billion for the MCA, $500 million less than Bush requested. Lugar argued that the new program, in existence for just a few weeks, was not ready for the pressure of doling out so much money so soon. The bill included $351 million for the Peace Corps, $50 million less than requested.

During the same markup, Lugar hedged his bets with a separate, more focused bill aimed at giving the State Department greater control over nation-building programs. The committee approved the measure (S 2127 — S Rept 108-247), 19-0. The bill proposed guidelines for the State Department to administer assistance to war-torn nations in coordination with the White House. A new office of International Stabilization and Reconstruction would be created within the State Department and given an emergency fund and a contingent of volunteers from fields such as medicine and law enforcement, who could be sent abroad quickly to take over nation-building programs.

The separate bill went no further. ◆

Chapter 12

LEGAL AFFAIRS

Abortion Services 'Conscience Clause'

Congress agreed to deny federal aid to states and localities that compel health care providers, facilities or insurance companies to provide, fund or refer abortion services. The language — enacted as part of the fiscal 2005 omnibus appropriations bill — significantly expanded the "conscience clause" under federal law that shields doctors and other health care providers from discrimination lawsuits when they refuse to perform abortions and cite their personal opposition to the procedure. The bill was signed into law Dec. 8 (HR 4818 — PL 108-447).

The House Appropriations Committee added the language, by Dave Weldon, R-Fla., to its version of the Labor-Health and Human Services-Education spending bill (HR 5006). Many lawmakers expected the provision to be stripped out during conference negotiations with the Senate, where a majority of members generally supported abortion rights. But the language survived at the insistence of House conservatives, whose leverage was strengthened by Election Day polls suggesting social conservatives played a pivotal role in the outcome of races nationwide.

Weldon said expanding the conscience clause would prevent situations in which cities or states denied licenses to hospitals, such as those run by the Roman Catholic Church, that refused to perform abortions. Opponents said the language marked a significant policy shift that could make it more difficult for many women to obtain abortions or other forms of reproductive health care.

Senate Democrats, led by Barbara Boxer of California, contemplated delaying action on the omnibus to protest the provision. They backed off after Republican leaders promised a vote on legislation to repeal the provision in early 2005. The vote was symbolic, since House GOP leaders were almost certain to shelve such legislation. (*Appropriations, p. 2-33*)

Lawmakers who supported the bill said it was a matter of simple justice to recognize fetuses as distinct victims under the law. Sam Brownback, R-Kan., displayed large photographs of dead fetuses to underscore that point.

The crucial vote came on a substitute by Dianne Feinstein, D-Calif., that would have enabled prosecutors to charge defendants in such criminal cases with a separate offense for interrupting or terminating a pregnancy, but would not have established a separate legal status for a fetus. The amendment was defeated, 49-50. (*Senate vote 61, p. S-15*)

"The only difference," Feinstein said, "is our substitute does not include a new, unprecedented definition of when life begins."

Mike DeWine, R-Ohio, said Feinstein's amendment would create "a legal fiction" in that it would not explicitly recognize that a crime against a pregnant woman could result in two victims. "If you believe there is a second victim, you cannot vote for the Feinstein amendment," DeWine said. The Bush administration also weighed in, releasing a statement of administration policy the day of the Senate debate opposing Feinstein's language.

Feinstein lost by a single vote after she unsuccessfully sought unanimous consent to change her amendment to clarify the language on additional criminal penalties.

John Kerry of Massachusetts, the presumed Democratic presidential nominee, interrupted his campaign and made his second appearance of the year in the Senate to vote for Feinstein's amendment and against the underlying bill.

Republicans also blocked an amendment by Patty Murray, D-Wash., to combat domestic violence. Murray proposed expanding the Family and Medical Leave Act (PL 103-3) to allow workers to take emergency leave to deal with incidents of domestic or sexual violence. The amendment also would have extended unemployment benefits to people who lost their jobs because of domestic violence or sexual assault, and allowed states to extend Medicaid benefits to cover services related to domestic violence.

Business groups, such as the U.S. Chamber of Commerce and the National Federation of Independent Business, opposed the amendment, saying it would dramatically expand workplace law and unduly burden small businesses.

Murray failed, 46-53, to overcome a procedural challenge to the amendment; she was 14 votes shy of the 60 needed to prevail. (*Senate vote 62, p. S-15*) ◆

Attempt to Ban Gay Marriage Fails

A proposed constitutional amendment to ban gay marriage, a top priority for social conservatives, failed in both the House and Senate. As a backup, the House passed a bill to bar federal courts from hearing challenges to portions of a 1996 law known as the Defense of Marriage Act, but the Senate did not take up the bill.

The proposed constitutional amendment was drafted in response to a Massachusetts Supreme Judicial Court ruling in November 2003 that same-sex couples had a right to wed under the Massachusetts Constitution. In a separate case in

June 2003, the Supreme Court had ruled in *Lawrence v. Texas* that homosexuals had a constitutional right to engage in consensual relations.

Social conservatives pointed to the rulings as evidence that the institution of marriage was under threat from an activist judiciary. They warned that the Massachusetts decision would lead to similar rulings in state and federal courts that would effectively legalize gay marriage in all 50 states. They also said they were convinced that sooner or later, the Supreme Court would rule the 1996 Defense of Marriage Act

Chapter 12

LEGAL AFFAIRS

Penalties for Harming a Fetus

In a victory for social conservatives, Congress cleared legislation that for the first time gave federal legal status to a fetus. The bill made it a separate offense to harm a fetus during the commission of a federal crime against a pregnant woman. President Bush strongly supported the bill and signed it into law April 1 (HR 1997—PL 108-212).

Under the new statute, federal prosecutors could file at least two charges against a criminal defendant, one for injury to the pregnant woman and another for harm to the embryo or fetus. The prosecutor would not have to show that the defendant knew the victim was pregnant or intended to harm the fetus. The measure created exceptions for abortions performed with consent, medical treatment of a pregnant woman and the actions of a pregnant woman regarding her own fetus.

Twenty-nine states had fetal homicide laws that applied to "unborn children" in different stages of prenatal development, but prior to enactment, there was no provision under federal law for separate criminal charges or added punishment for federal crimes that affect pregnancies.

Most lawmakers agreed that a crime against a woman affecting her pregnancy should carry extra punishment. What made the bill controversial was a provision that defined an "unborn child" as "a member of the species homo sapiens, at any stage of development, who is carried in the womb."

Abortion rights advocates argued that the bill could lay the foundation for a legal challenge to the 1973 Supreme Court ruling in *Roe v. Wade* on the grounds that a fetus has rights equal to those of the pregnant woman. *Roe* established a constitutional right to an abortion.

Social conservatives said the sole purpose of the legislation, sponsored by Melissa A. Hart, R-Pa., was to affirm the value of human life.

"This bill . . . treats an unborn victim of violence as something more than just a torn spleen or a bruised appendix," said Steve Chabot, R-Ohio. "We in Congress should reserve for unborn victims of violence a distinct place and a protective shield under criminal law."

The House passed similar bills in 1999 and 2001, but the Senate never considered them. (*1999 Almanac, p. 18-33; 2001 Almanac, p. 14-16*)

The legislation gained fresh momentum in the 108th Congress with the discoveries in April 2003 of the bodies of Laci Peterson, a Modesto, Calif., woman, and her unborn son, whom the family named Conner. It followed the enactment in November 2003 of legislation (PL 108-105) that criminalized a procedure critics call "partial birth" abortion. (*2003 Almanac, p. 3-3*)

BoxScore

Bill:
HR 1997 — PL 108-212
Legislative Action:
House passed HR 1997
(H Rept 108-420, Part 1),
254-163, on Feb. 26.
Senate cleared HR 1997,
61-38, on March 25.
President signed April 1.

Legislative Action

House Committee Action

The House Judiciary Committee approved the bill (HR 1997 — H Rept 108-420, Part 1) by a party-line vote of 20-13 on Jan 31.

During the markup, the committee:

• Rejected, on an 11-9 party-line vote, an amendment by Zoe Lofgren, D-Calif., to create a separate offense for federal crimes against pregnant women but without recognizing fetuses as separate entities. "If we really want to punish crimes committed against pregnant women, we can do it in a way that will not entangle this issue with the abortion debate," said Democrat Tammy Baldwin of Wisconsin. Baldwin called Hart's bill a "thinly veiled attack on abortion rights."

Bill supporters said the Lofgren substitute would still recognize only one victim in attacks against pregnant women.

• Rejected, 11-20, an amendment by Baldwin to specify that nothing in the bill "shall be construed as undermining a woman's right to choose an abortion as guaranteed by the U.S. Constitution or limiting in any way the rights and freedoms of pregnant women." Chabot insisted the language was not necessary because "this particular bill has nothing to do with abortion."

• Rejected by voice vote two amendments by Robert C. Scott, D-Va. One would have directed the federal sentencing commission to amend sentencing guidelines for crimes that cause injury or death to a pregnant woman. The other would have deleted language in the bill that allowed convictions even in cases where prosecutors did not show a defendant knew the victim was pregnant or intended to cause death or injury to a fetus.

House Floor Action

The House passed the bill, 254-163, on Feb. 26. (*House vote 31, p. H-12*)

Before passage, the House rejected, 186-229, a Democratic substitute by Lofgren that did not include language defining an "unborn child." It also would have required that a defendant be convicted of a federal crime against a pregnant woman before receiving additional punishment for harming a fetus. (*House vote 30, p. H-12*)

Senate Floor Action

The Senate cleared the House bill, 61-38, on March 25, after Republicans succeeded in defeating two Democratic amendments. Majority Leader Bill Frist, R-Tenn., had tried to bring a similar measure to the Senate floor in July 2003 without allowing amendments, but Democrats objected. (*Senate vote 63, p. S-15*)

Abortion Services 'Conscience Clause'

Congress agreed to deny federal aid to states and localities that compel health care providers, facilities or insurance companies to provide, fund or refer abortion services. The language — enacted as part of the fiscal 2005 omnibus appropriations bill — significantly expanded the "conscience clause" under federal law that shields doctors and other health care providers from discrimination lawsuits when they refuse to perform abortions and cite their personal opposition to the procedure. The bill was signed into law Dec. 8 (HR 4818 — PL 108-447).

The House Appropriations Committee added the language, by Dave Weldon, R-Fla., to its version of the Labor-Health and Human Services-Education spending bill (HR 5006). Many lawmakers expected the provision to be stripped out during conference negotiations with the Senate, where a majority of members generally supported abortion rights. But the language survived at the insistence of House conservatives, whose leverage was strengthened by Election Day polls suggesting social conservatives played a pivotal role in the outcome of races nationwide.

Weldon said expanding the conscience clause would prevent situations in which cities or states denied licenses to hospitals, such as those run by the Roman Catholic Church, that refused to perform abortions. Opponents said the language marked a significant policy shift that could make it more difficult for many women to obtain abortions or other forms of reproductive health care.

Senate Democrats, led by Barbara Boxer of California, contemplated delaying action on the omnibus to protest the provision. They backed off after Republican leaders promised a vote on legislation to repeal the provision in early 2005. The vote was symbolic, since House GOP leaders were almost certain to shelve such legislation. (*Appropriations, p. 2-33*)

Lawmakers who supported the bill said it was a matter of simple justice to recognize fetuses as distinct victims under the law. Sam Brownback, R-Kan., displayed large photographs of dead fetuses to underscore that point.

The crucial vote came on a substitute by Dianne Feinstein, D-Calif., that would have enabled prosecutors to charge defendants in such criminal cases with a separate offense for interrupting or terminating a pregnancy, but would not have established a separate legal status for a fetus. The amendment was defeated, 49-50. (*Senate vote 61, p. S-15*)

"The only difference," Feinstein said, "is our substitute does not include a new, unprecedented definition of when life begins."

Mike DeWine, R-Ohio, said Feinstein's amendment would create "a legal fiction" in that it would not explicitly recognize that a crime against a pregnant woman could result in two victims. "If you believe there is a second victim, you cannot vote for the Feinstein amendment," DeWine said. The Bush administration also weighed in, releasing a statement of administration policy the day of the Senate debate opposing Feinstein's language.

Feinstein lost by a single vote after she unsuccessfully sought unanimous consent to change her amendment to clarify the language on additional criminal penalties.

John Kerry of Massachusetts, the presumed Democratic presidential nominee, interrupted his campaign and made his second appearance of the year in the Senate to vote for Feinstein's amendment and against the underlying bill.

Republicans also blocked an amendment by Patty Murray, D-Wash., to combat domestic violence. Murray proposed expanding the Family and Medical Leave Act (PL 103-3) to allow workers to take emergency leave to deal with incidents of domestic or sexual violence. The amendment also would have extended unemployment benefits to people who lost their jobs because of domestic violence or sexual assault, and allowed states to extend Medicaid benefits to cover services related to domestic violence.

Business groups, such as the U.S. Chamber of Commerce and the National Federation of Independent Business, opposed the amendment, saying it would dramatically expand workplace law and unduly burden small businesses.

Murray failed, 46-53, to overcome a procedural challenge to the amendment; she was 14 votes shy of the 60 needed to prevail. (*Senate vote 62, p. S-15*) ◆

Attempt to Ban Gay Marriage Fails

A proposed constitutional amendment to ban gay marriage, a top priority for social conservatives, failed in both the House and Senate. As a backup, the House passed a bill to bar federal courts from hearing challenges to portions of a 1996 law known as the Defense of Marriage Act, but the Senate did not take up the bill.

The proposed constitutional amendment was drafted in response to a Massachusetts Supreme Judicial Court ruling in November 2003 that same-sex couples had a right to wed under the Massachusetts Constitution. In a separate case in

June 2003, the Supreme Court had ruled in *Lawrence v. Texas* that homosexuals had a constitutional right to engage in consensual relations.

Social conservatives pointed to the rulings as evidence that the institution of marriage was under threat from an activist judiciary. They warned that the Massachusetts decision would lead to similar rulings in state and federal courts that would effectively legalize gay marriage in all 50 states. They also said they were convinced that sooner or later, the Supreme Court would rule the 1996 Defense of Marriage Act

(PL 104-199) unconstitutional. That law defined marriage as "a legal union between one man and one woman" and gave states permission not to recognize same-sex marriages performed in other states. (*1996 Almanac, p. 5-26*)

"We see the ongoing march of litigation as part of a national strategy to undermine the traditional institution of marriage that we know is the most important stabilizing influence in our society and one that functions in the best interests of our children," said Sen. John Cornyn, R-Texas.

The mostly Republican proponents of the amendment argued that the only way to safeguard the institution of marriage was by defining it in the Constitution as "a union of a man and a woman."

Opponents said that despite the fears of conservatives, the 1996 marriage law remained in effect. They said the amendment would write discrimination into the Constitution and accused GOP leaders of playing politics with a sensitive social issue that should be left to the states.

In February 2004, after months of careful hedging, President Bush endorsed a constitutional amendment. Republicans saw the issue as a chance for Bush to distinguish himself from his Democratic challenger, Sen. John Kerry of Massachusetts, and to energize the GOP's socially conservative base of supporters. Kerry's own position was somewhat nuanced: He was against gay marriage, but also against amending the Constitution to ban it, and he favored allowing civil unions.

Democrats said they were confident that the GOP would end up as the party perceived to be outside the mainstream. "The Republicans' dogged pursuit of this issue reinforces the sense that they're intolerant and divisive," said Mark S. Mellman, a Democratic pollster who advised Kerry.

Legislative Action

Senate Floor Action

Senate GOP leaders decided to bypass the Judiciary Committee, where the measure might have stalled, and bring it directly to the floor in advance of the start of the Democratic convention July 26. On July 14, the Senate rejected a motion to invoke cloture, or limit debate, on a motion to take up the resolution (S J Res 40) proposing the constitutional amendment. The vote was 48-50 — 12 short of the number needed for cloture, and 19 away from the two-thirds majority (67) needed to advance a constitutional amendment. (*Senate vote 155, p. S-34*)

Six Republicans voted against limiting debate. "The actions by jurists in one court, in one state do not represent the death knell to marriage," said John McCain of Arizona, one of the six. At least two others Republicans, Mike DeWine and George V. Voinovich, both of Ohio, said later they were prepared to vote against the amendment if it came to an up-or-down roll call.

Amendment supporters argued that allowing gays to wed so cheapened the institution that heterosexuals would aban-

---

BoxScore

Bills:
S J Res 40, H J Res 106, HR 3313

Legislative Action:
Senate rejected a motion to invoke cloture on S J Res 40, 48-50, on July 14 (60 votes required).
House passed HR 3313 (H Rept 108-614), 233-194, July 22.
House rejected H J Res 106, 227-186, on Sept. 30.

---

don it in droves. "Breakdown of the family, children being born out of wedlock, and communities and cultures in decay," said Rick Santorum of Pennsylvania, the Senate Republican Conference chairman and a main driver in the debate. "That is what I see on the horizon for America."

But Republicans were not united behind a single proposal. The resolution, by Wayne Allard, R-Colo., proposed a two-sentence addition to the Constitution. The first sentence stated, "Marriage in the United States shall consist only of the union of a man and a woman." The second mandated that "neither this Constitution, nor the constitution of any state, shall be construed to require that marriage or the legal incidents thereof be conferred upon any union other than the union of a man and a woman." The second sentence was aimed at ensuring that state legislatures — but not state courts — could create other constructs, such as civil unions or domestic partnerships

Democrats said they would not block an up-or-down vote on the resolution. But on July 12, Santorum announced that Republicans wanted to allow a vote on an amendment by Gordon H. Smith, R-Ore., that would remove the second sentence. Cornyn estimated that the shortened resolution would pick up 10 votes.

Democrats were confident that as many as 12 Republicans would vote against the Allard resolution, but they were not willing to risk a vote on the one-sentence version. Senate Minority Leader Tom Daschle, D-S.D., said that allowing changes to Allard's resolution on the floor would be tantamount to "making the Senate a constitutional convention." Frist then engineered the July 14 procedural vote.

House: Defense of Marriage Act

The House on July 22 passed a bill (HR 3313 — H Rept 108-614) to bolster the 1996 law. The measure, which passed, 233-194, sought to prevent all federal courts, including the Supreme Court, from having jurisdiction over the provision that gave states the option of not recognizing same-sex marriages performed in other states. The Judiciary Committee approved the measure, 21-13, on July 14. (*House vote 410, p. H-134*)

Republicans said the bill was urgently needed, particularly in light of the Senate's unwillingness to vote on the proposed constitutional amendment. They said the House bill would ensure that states remained the final arbiter over laws concerning marriage.

Democrats decried the measure as a back-door attempt to amend the Constitution. They also said the bill would undermine the federal judiciary by stripping courts' ability to rule on the 1996 law's constitutionality.

"This is about whether the third branch of government, the judiciary . . . will continue to be the arbiter of what is constitutional in the American system," said John Conyers Jr., D-Mich., ranking member on the House Judiciary Committee.

Bill supporters said Article III of the Constitution gives

Congress authority to regulate federal court jurisdiction. They cited a series of recently enacted laws that limited judicial review on issues ranging from the construction of the World War II memorial to fighting forest fires.

"If limiting federal court jurisdiction is good enough to protect trees, it sure ought to be good enough to protect state marriage policies," said Judiciary Committee Chairman F. James Sensenbrenner Jr., R-Wis.

House Action: Constitutional Amendment

House leaders brought the constitutional amendment (H J Res 106) to the floor Sept. 30, bypassing the Judiciary Committee and Sensenbrenner, who opposed same-sex marriage but also had reservations about amending the Constitution to achieve that end. The text was identical to the Senate resolution.

The tally was 227-186, well short of the two-thirds majority of lawmakers present and voting necessary to adopt the measure. The voting did not break cleanly along partisan lines: 27 moderate Republicans voted against the reso-

lution while 36 conservative Democrats voted for it. (*House vote 484, p. H-156*)

Though House Republican leaders predicted the result well before the vote, the occasion allowed them to again criticize "activist" judges, who they contended were unilaterally rewriting the Constitution from the bench.

Postscript

Although the issue of gay marriage did play a role in the November election, its importance remained a subject of debate. A strong Republican get-out-the-vote effort generated a big turnout among religious conservative voters that helped secure Bush's re-election, and some GOP partisans and independent analysts said he was helped especially by the 11 successful initiatives to bar gay marriage (including one in the key battleground state of Ohio) that were on state ballots Nov. 2. But Democrats and a number of outside observers contended that the impact of the issue was overstated and was small compared to voters' national security concerns. (*Election, p. 18-3*) ◆

Asbestos Compensation Fund

The efforts of top Senate leaders were not enough to break a logjam over legislation to create a no-fault compensation fund for victims of asbestos exposure. Majority Leader Bill Frist, R-Tenn., and Minority Leader Tom Daschle, D-S.D., got close to a deal on the size of the fund but remained apart on eligibility and other issues. They could not reach a deal before Election Day, when Daschle was defeated. The House did not consider an asbestos bill.

The costs of past and future lawsuits related to asbestos — a fire-resistant, cancer-causing substance used mainly in construction materials until the 1970s — had driven dozens of companies into bankruptcy. The main stakeholders — defendant corporations, their insurers and labor organizations — had agreed for more than two years that a trust fund financed by private contributions was the best solution.

The businesses and their insurers were looking for a way to pay a finite amount of money into a no-fault fund in exchange for ending their civil liability. Labor unions wanted a way for victims to receive compensation without having to go through court proceedings. But they disagreed on how large the fund should be, and they had no idea how many potential claims existed.

The Senate Judiciary Committee approved a bill (S 1125) in July 2003 to establish an asbestos compensation fund financed by contributions from businesses and insurers. In return, the companies would be shielded from lawsuits. To get the bill through, Chairman Orrin G. Hatch, R-Utah, agreed to Democratic amendments that brought the size of the fund to $153 billion. (*2003 Almanac, p. 13-7*)

BoxScore

Bill:
S 2290

Legislative Action:
Senate failed to invoke cloture, 50-47, on April 22 (60 votes needed).

Defendant businesses that would have had to foot the bill regarded the amount as too high. In late 2003, Frist intervened, making an asbestos compensation bill one of his top priorities for the 2004 session.

Frist and Hatch reworked the measure in a new bill (S 2290) introduced in April 2004. Supporters put the revised fund at $124 billion, although the Congressional Budget Office said the total was no more than $118 billion. Democrats and labor groups said that was not enough to pay all the claims that would be filed.

Although Democrats and some Republicans urged Frist to allow more time for negotiations, the majority leader brought the bill to the floor shortly after it was introduced. He was not able to muster the 60 votes needed to overcome a Democratic filibuster; his motion to invoke cloture, or limit debate, failed 50-47 on April 22. (*Senate vote 69, p. S-18*)

Hatch conceded that the bill was unlikely to succeed but said a vote could highlight Democratic obstruction of the broader GOP agenda to overhaul the civil justice system. Republicans were also pushing bills to move more class action lawsuits into federal court and to limit medical malpractice awards, as well as more limited bills to protect the fast food and gun industries. (*Class action, p. 12-7; malpractice, p. 12-12; gun liability, p. 12-13*)

When cloture failed, Frist pulled the bill and took the unusual step of agreeing with Daschle to enlist Edward R. Becker, a former chief judge of the U.S. Court of Appeals for the 3rd Circuit, to mediate negotiations among key stakeholders. When those efforts failed to produce a deal in early May, Frist

and Daschle started their own negotiations, narrowing their differences on the size of the fund to around $136 billion. That was still too low for the AFL-CIO, which insisted that $149 billion was the minimum needed to adequately compensate claimants. Defendants endorsed a fund of $128 billion.

Even if the size of the fund were settled, however, other major sticking points remained, such as how to treat the estimated 300,000 asbestos-related claims already in the courts, how much money businesses and insurers would contribute in the fund's early years and what to do if the fund was depleted.

Daschle's defeat in the Nov. 2 election ended that line of negotiations. Late in the year, Arlen Specter, R-Pa., who succeeded Hatch as Judiciary chairman, indicated that an asbestos bill would be his top priority in the 109th Congress. Specter enlisted Becker to reopen negotiating sessions with the stakeholders. ◆

Frist Withdraws Class Action Bill

Legislation aimed at limiting class action lawsuits died in the Senate after Republican leaders pulled it from the floor in July to avoid Democratic amendments, including an increase in the minimum wage. The bill was a top priority for the business community and Republicans' best hope for overhauling a portion of the civil justice system.

The Senate bill was similar to a measure (HR 1115) the House passed in June 2003. Both bills would have shifted class action cases involving at least 100 plaintiffs to federal court if at least $5 million was at stake and fewer than two-thirds of the plaintiffs lived in the same state as the defendant. Both also contained provisions to protect the rights of plaintiffs, including one to generally bar federal judges from approving settlements if the attorney fees would result in a net loss to class members. (*2003 Almanac, p. 13-10*)

Under existing law, class action suits could be heard in federal court only if each plaintiff stood to receive at least $75,000 and all the plaintiffs lived in different states from all the defendants. As a result, most class action suits were heard in state courts.

Proponents argued that the bill was needed to stop entrepreneurial attorneys who obtained huge fees by filing class action suits in venues where juries had a reputation for awarding large settlements. In some cases, the victorious plaintiffs end up with awards of little value while lawyers reaped multimillion-dollar fees.

The Senate bill (S 2062) had the support of at least 62 senators, including 11 Democrats, but the fact that it was expected to pass also made it a magnet for unrelated amendments from both sides of the aisle. Of particular concern to Majority Leader Bill Frist, R-Tenn., were Democratic proposals to raise the minimum wage, extend federal unemployment insurance and block administration rules on overtime pay.

Frist maintained that adding complex or controversial amendments would consume too much time and make it harder to push the bill through a conference with the House. After the two sides failed to agree on how many unrelated amendments to allow, Frist used his prerogative as majority leader to fill up the bill's "amendment tree," a procedural move that effectively shut off amendments from other senators. That gave him complete control, but it also angered both Democrats and Republicans, particularly Larry

BoxScore

Bills:
S 2062, HR 1115
Legislative Action:
Senate failed to invoke cloture on S 2062, 44-43, on July 8 (60 votes required).

E. Craig, R-Idaho, who intended to offer an amendment to give immigrant farm workers a path to citizenship.

"We've been closed out," said Edward M. Kennedy, D-Mass., who with Barbara Boxer, D-Calif., intended to introduce an amendment to raise the minimum wage to $7 from $5.15 an hour by 2006. (*Minimum wage, p. 8-5*)

On July 8, Frist attempted to invoke cloture, which would have limited amendments and debate, but he fell 16 short of the 60 votes needed. The tally was 44-43. Among those voting "no" were several Democratic supporters of the bill, including lead cosponsor Herb Kohl of Wisconsin and Thomas R. Carper of Delaware. Others voting against cloture included Republicans Craig, Richard C. Shelby of Alabama and John McCain of Arizona, who wanted to add an amendment to curb greenhouse gases. (*Senate vote 154, p. S-33*)

Senate Judiciary Chairman Orrin G. Hatch, R-Utah, charged that partisan politics prompted Democratic supporters to renege on a compromise that had been negotiated in November 2003 to help ensure enough minority votes to overcome a filibuster. But Carper said it was GOP leaders who doomed the bill by ignoring Democrats' advice to "let it breathe" during a few days of debate before seeking cloture. "I can't think of a strategy more likely to inflame Democrats and make it impossible to pass this bill," Carper said.

Unable to limit the debate and block unrelated amendments, Frist withdrew the bill.

The outcome was a major defeat for the GOP and its business allies, who had been pressing for changes to the legal tort system all year. But it also allowed Republicans to say that Democrats were helping trial lawyers at the expense of average Americans. Asked whether the vote might be campaign fodder, Trent Lott, R-Miss., said, "I think it's a good idea, yeah."

Democrats, too, were looking toward November, repeatedly trying to force Republicans to take uncomfortable votes on issues such as the minimum wage and unemployment insurance that were important to the Democratic base.

Even if the Senate had passed the bill, its prospects were uncertain in the House. The Senate bill was a compromise that dropped several provisions from the House version, including a ban on "bounty payments" — extra payments to named plaintiffs for testifying and having their names appear on the class action suit. ◆

DNA Testing, Victims' Rights Clear

After years of effort, sponsors won enactment of a bill to improve the quality of legal representation for defendants in capital crime cases and make it easier for inmates to get access to post-conviction DNA tests that might exonerate them. The key to their success lay in combining the initiative on defendants with popular provisions guaranteeing the rights of crime victims. Sponsors also added hundreds of millions of dollars in grants to cities and states, as well as law enforcement provisions backed by the Bush administration. President Bush signed the bill into law Oct. 30 (HR 5107 — PL 108-405).

The final bill made it easier for inmates to get access to post-conviction DNA tests and, in cases where test results indicated an inmate might not be guilty, a retrial.

It authorized about $2 billion in fiscal 2005 through 2009 for grants, mainly to state and local governments, including $755 million to speed the processing of unanalyzed biological crime evidence. It included popular provisions to authorize grants designed to defray the cost to states of post-conviction DNA testing, promote the use of forensic technology to identify missing persons and train first-responders in handling biological crime evidence. Much of the grant funding was contingent upon states preserving biological crime evidence for post-conviction DNA testing and allowing such testing in state cases.

The initiative was revised a number of times in response to conservative critics who argued that it would wrongly expand the rights of criminals and impose onerous mandates on the states. Sponsors abandoned the idea that Congress should require the states to overhaul their legal systems for capital cases, for example, and tied federal requirements to state grants to ease the problem of unfunded mandates.

The House gave overwhelming support to a bipartisan version of the bill (HR 3214) in November 2003. Judiciary Chairman F. James Sensenbrenner Jr., R-Wis., had put the bill together through months of negotiations in tandem with his Senate counterpart, Orrin G. Hatch, R-Utah. The bill included provisions to authorize post-conviction DNA testing for certain federal inmates, as well as grants to help states eliminate the backlog in testing DNA samples, train local law enforcement officials in DNA collection and improve crime labs. The measure also authorized funds for state grants to improve the prosecution of capital cases and ensure that indigent defendants would have access to competent counsel. (*2003 Almanac, p. 13-11*)

The bill brought together foes and supporters of the death penalty, who agreed that the nation's capital punishment system should be as close to flawless as possible. It also incorporated a Bush administration proposal to spend $1 billion over

BoxScore

Bill:
HR 5107 — PL 108-405

Legislative Action:

Senate passed S 2329, 96-1, on April 22.

House passed HR 5107 (H Rept 108-711), 393-14, on Oct. 6.

Senate cleared HR 5107 by voice vote Oct. 9.

President signed Oct. 30.

five years to eliminate the backlog of DNA samples.

Hatch won provisional support for the companion Senate bill (S 1700) from a bipartisan coalition of committee members, including Joseph R. Biden Jr., D-Del., and Mike DeWine, R-Ohio. But several Republicans, including Jon Kyl of Arizona, flatly opposed the bill, and Hatch was unable to get it through his committee in 2003.

After months of additional negotiations, Hatch finally won committee approval to report the bill in September 2004, but Kyl and others vowed to prevent it from reaching the Senate floor.

Meanwhile, in April 2004, the Senate overwhelmingly passed a bill (S 2329) to codify eight specific rights for federal crime victims. Victims' rights advocates — led by Kyl and Dianne Feinstein, D-Calif. — had been trying for eight years to make such rights part of the Constitution. They moved a proposed constitutional amendment (S J Res 1) through the Senate Judiciary Committee in 2003, but they lacked the votes to win on the floor. In early 2004, they decided instead to press for enactment of a bill before the end of the 108th Congress. (*2003 Almanac, p. 13-18*)

In September 2004, with the DNA bill stuck in the Senate, Sensenbrenner tried a new tack, introducing a measure (HR 5107) that combined a version of the DNA initiative with modified provisions from the Senate-passed victims' rights bill. The House passed the new bill overwhelmingly in early October and the Senate cleared it shortly thereafter.

Sensenbrenner had used a similar tactic in 2003, when he won enactment of several House-passed bills combating sex crimes against children after combining them with a popular initiative to expand AMBER alerts used to notify the public about missing children and a child-pornography bill championed by Hatch. (*2003 Almanac, p. 13-3*)

Highlights

The 2004 crime law:

● **Post-conviction DNA tests.** Established procedures to ensure that federal inmates could apply for DNA tests that could establish their innocence. A court could order testing if an inmate asserted under penalty of perjury that he was innocent, and if the test results might raise a reasonable probability that the inmate did not commit the crime.

Courts could grant new trials or resentencing if the test results and other compelling evidence showed that a new trial was likely to result in an acquittal.

● **Destruction of DNA evidence.** Barred the government from destroying DNA evidence in federal criminal cases while a defendant remained incarcerated, with some exceptions, such as when a defendant waived his right to testing.

• **DNA evidence backlog.** Authorized $151 million a year in fiscal 2005 through 2009 for grants to help states and localities improve DNA laboratories and speed the processing of biological crime scene evidence, including samples collected as part of rape investigations. If DNA testing implicated an identified person in the commission of a felony, except for certain sexual assault felonies, the person could be prosecuted even if the statute of limitations had expired.

• **Crime lab grants.** Authorized $150 million over five years for grants to state and local governments to improve the capacity of crime labs to handle DNA testing and evidence, increase research and development of new DNA-testing technologies, and provide training for police, court officials and others in the collection and use of DNA evidence. Most of the grants were contingent on the state agreeing to retain DNA evidence and to allow post-conviction tests for appropriate state inmates. The law authorized $25 million over five years for a new grant program to help states defray the costs of post-conviction DNA testing.

• **Grants for capital cases.** Authorized $75 million a year over five years for grants to help states improve the quality of the legal counsel they provide to indigent defendants in death penalty cases, as well as to improve the ability of prosecutors to effectively represent the public in such cases. States accepting the money had to allocate the funds equally between the two programs.

• **Victims' rights.** Codified eight specific rights for victims of federal crimes, including the right to be reasonably protected from the accused, to be reasonably heard at certain proceedings and to consult with government attorneys on the case and to receive full and timely restitution. It authorized more than $80 million over five years for victim assistance programs and other support services.

Legislative Action

Senate Floor Action: Victims' Rights

The Senate passed the victims' rights bill (S 2329) by a vote of 96-1 on April 22, after the chief sponsors withdrew a proposed constitutional amendment that faced almost certain defeat on the Senate floor. (*Senate vote 70, p. S-18*)

Since 2000, Kyl and Feinstein, among others, had insisted that the only way to establish the rights of crime victims in court proceedings was by amending the Constitution. They argued that judges and prosecutors did not always heed state or federal laws intended to guarantee victims' rights. But they could not overcome the reluctance of many of their colleagues, who argued that even a well-written constitutional amendment could have unintended consequences that would take years to change.

Kyl and Feinstein decided to settle for the legislation just before the Senate was to take up their constitutional amendment. "If this works out, then we are all winners, most of all [the] victims," Kyl said of the legislative approach. "If it doesn't work out, then we understand we may need to proceed at that time with a constitutional amendment."

The bill included a guarantee that victims or their representatives could be heard at public court proceedings when a defendant was brought before a judge for sentencing,

release or discussion of a plea bargain. It also required that judicial officials take victims' safety into account when deciding the fate of defendants.

Unlike the proposed constitutional amendment, however, the bill applied only to victims in federal courts, not state courts where most crimes are tried.

The bill proposed to authorize $16.3 million in fiscal 2005 and $26.5 million annually in fiscal 2006 through 2009 to improve victim notification and encourage states to protect victims' rights.

Senate Committee Action: DNA Bill

Hatch finally succeeded in muscling the DNA bill through his committee, which approved it 11-7 on Sept. 21. But critics led by Republicans Kyl, John Cornyn of Texas and Jeff Sessions of Alabama vowed to block the measure from advancing in the Senate unless much of it was rewritten. They offered nearly two dozen weakening amendments during the markup, which ran from July to September and was repeatedly interrupted when the panel could not hold its quorum. But a coalition of bill supporters, including DeWine and Biden, helped beat back their efforts.

The bill's critics were especially passionate about a portion of the legislation known as the Innocence Protection Act. In addition to ensuring access to post-conviction DNA testing for federal inmates, the section proposed $100 million a year in fiscal 2005 through 2009 for state grants to improve the quality of legal representation for indigent capital defendants, as well as the quality of the prosecution in such cases.

States that took the prosecution grants would be required to accept an equal amount of funding under the legal representation grant program. They also would have to meet certain requirements, including a mandate to create "effective" systems to ensure that defendants had access to competent legal representation.

Critics argued that cash-starved states would be tempted to put staunch death-penalty foes in charge of their capital representation programs in order to ensure that they qualified for the grants. They said the proposal amounted to an attempt to re-establish capital punishment resource centers that were stripped of funding by Congress in 1996.

"I don't want to send any of the moneys of this government . . . to these kind of programs," Sessions said.

Bill backers, led by Patrick J. Leahy, D-Vt., the author of the Innocence Protection Act, said states would not be compelled to take any money. Supporters noted that the proposal had been significantly watered down from previous versions that would have imposed such conditions on states, without tying them to federal dollars.

House Committee Action

Sensenbrenner introduced his new bill on Sept. 21 in an attempt to allow the DNA legislation to hitch a ride on the popular victims' rights bill. The Judiciary Committee approved the bill by voice vote the next day (HR 5107 — H Rept 108-711). The bill included a section stating that crime victims were entitled:

• To be reasonably protected from the accused.

• To receive reasonable, accurate and timely notice of any public court proceeding involving the crime or of any release or escape of the accused.

• To not be excluded from any such public court proceeding, unless the court determined that testimony by the victim would be materially affected if the victim heard other testimony at that proceeding.

• To be reasonably heard at any public proceeding involving release, plea or sentencing.

• To confer with the government's attorney in the case.

• To full and timely restitution as provided in law.

• To proceedings free from unreasonable delay.

• To be treated with fairness and with respect for the victim's dignity and privacy.

The victims' rights section also authorized more than $80 million over five years for grants to assist victims.

House Floor Action

The House passed Sensenbrenner's bill by a vote of 393-14 on Oct. 6, after giving voice-vote approval to a manager's amendment that made still more changes in hopes of winning over the opposition. (*House vote 497, p. H-160*)

The changes, which had the blessing of Hatch and Leahy, raised the standard for obtaining a new trial based on the outcomes of post-conviction DNA testing. The underlying bill would have allowed retrial if the test results and other factors established by a preponderance of the evidence that a new trial would result in an acquittal. The amendment raised the threshold to instances where there is "compelling evidence that a new trial would result in an acquittal."

Sensenbrenner's amendment also addressed the time frame within which federal inmates could secure post-conviction testing of biological crime evidence. The bill had proposed no limit on such tests, but Sensenbrenner said critics argued that "defendants would simply game the system, waiting until the witnesses had died and the DNA had evaporated and consequently there would not be enough evidence to conduct a retrial."

The compromise encouraged defendants to apply for DNA testing within five years of their convictions, when there would be a presumption in their favor. After five years, the burden of proof would shift to the defendants. Motions for new tests could be granted if a court found an applicant was not competent at his or her trial, if there was newly discovered DNA evidence or if denying the retest application would result in "manifest injustice."

The amendment also reduced the amount authorized for grants to improve counsel on both sides in capital trials from $100 million per year to $75 million per year.

The final bill also changed the point at which information could be entered into state and national databases of DNA profiles. The initial bill would have prohibited the entry of information about people who had been arrested but not indicted, something that was allowed in three states. The final bill allowed those states to continue that practice.

Opponents said that even with the changes, the bill would still make it too easy for certain inmates, including those who pleaded guilty, to seek DNA tests. "This would permit defendants to reopen cases — to traumatize victims — even if there is no reason to believe there will be a change in the outcome of the case," said Jeff Flake, R-Ariz.

Opponents also complained that the changes did not address concerns about states developing "effective" public defender systems to qualify for funding under the bill.

Final Action

The Senate took up the House-passed bill and cleared it by voice vote Oct. 9. But first, Kyl, Hatch and Leahy negotiated a few language changes to satisfy some of the conservatives' lingering concerns. In an unusual move, the Senate adopted the changes in the form of an enrolling resolution — usually used to correct typographical errors in a bill — and sent the resolution to the House. The House adopted the measure (H Con Res 519) by voice vote the same day in one of its last acts before heading home, and the Senate cleared it.

The main change tightened the time limit under which convicts could easily obtain DNA tests to three years after conviction. The resolution also addressed the capital defense grants. Sessions, in particular, was worried that capital defense programs would be placed under staunch death-penalty opponents. The resolution added language clarifying that with the exception of current prosecutors, anyone with "demonstrated knowledge and expertise in capital cases" could direct the programs.

While supporters hailed the bill as a major victory for victims and the wrongly accused, most were not entirely satisfied with the final product because of the compromises lawmakers on all sides had to make to get it enacted. ◆

Flag Proposal Fizzles

A proposed constitutional amendment to permit a law making desecration of the American flag a crime did not advance beyond the Senate Judiciary Committee in 2004.

Conservatives had been promoting such a change in the Constitution since the Supreme Court in 1990 struck down a federal law (PL 101-131) banning flag desecration. That law was enacted after the Supreme Court, in 1989, declared that a conviction under a Texas state law for "desecration" of a flag violated the First Amendment. (*1990 Almanac, p. 524; 1989 Almanac, p. 307*)

"There is only one United States flag, and it deserves constitutional protection," said Sen. John Cornyn, R-Texas. Opponents said that while they might not condone flag burning, they did support constitutionally protected speech. "We are talking . . . about modifying the Constitution of the United States to permit the government to criminalize conduct that, however misguided and wrong, is clearly expressive," said Russell D. Feingold, D-Wis.

The House provided the necessary two-thirds vote for the proposed constitutional amendment in 2003 (H J Res 4) — just as it had in 1995, 1997, 1999 and 2001. However, supporters had never gotten more than 63 votes in the Senate, four short of the 67 needed to reach a two-thirds majority if all senators voted. (*2003 Almanac, p. 13-14*)

The Senate Judiciary Committee approved an identical resolution (S J Res 4) by a vote of 11-7 on July 20. But Majority Leader Bill Frist, R-Tenn., never brought it to the floor because it seemed certain to come up short there once again.

If both chambers adopted the amendment, three-quarters of the states — or 38 — would have to ratify it before the language would be added to the Constitution. Supporters would have had seven years to win ratification of the proposed amendment. ◆

Lawmakers Take Aim at ID Theft

Hoping to crack down on one of the fastest growing crimes in the country, Congress cleared a bill to establish tougher criminal penalties for identity theft and make it easier for prosecutors to go after the perpetrators. The bill focused in particular on those who steal identities to commit terrorist acts and other serious crimes. President Bush signed the bill into law July 15 (HR 1731 — PL 108-275).

Identity thieves were increasingly using the personal information of others to open credit card accounts, take out loans and conceal their true identities from law enforcement.

"Federal and state officials have taken notice of this crime because of the potential threat to security," said House Judiciary Chairman F. James Sensenbrenner Jr., R-Wis., "but the cost to the consumer and corporations is equally alarming."

The Federal Trade Commission (FTC) said it had received more than 161,800 complaints from victims of identity theft in 2002. It estimated that such crimes cost businesses and financial institutions $47.6 billion that year, while the cost to consumers was $5 billion. Both the Justice Department and the FTC endorsed the bill.

In testimony before a Senate Judiciary subcommittee in 2002, Dan Collins, the Justice Department's chief privacy officer, described the rapid growth of identity theft. He said the crime "generally is not committed for the sheer thrill of impersonation. It is almost always done for the purpose of committing another state or federal offense." The effort to punish the criminal for the identity theft over and above the punishment exacted for the underlying crime was central to the bill.

The Senate passed a similar measure (S 153) in 2003 sponsored by Dianne Feinstein, D-Calif., and cosponsored by three Democrats and four Republicans.

Also in 2003, Congress cleared a financial services bill (PL 108-159) aimed at deterring the theft of identity information, for example, by allowing consumers to receive one free credit report each year, and by requiring the three national credit reporting agencies to share identity theft complaints so that a victim could notify them with a single telephone call. (*2003 Almanac, p. 4-3*)

Highlights

The following are the main components of the new identity theft law:

• **Aggravated identity theft.** The measure established new penalties for "aggravated identity theft," defined as identity theft committed in relation to a list of other serious crimes, such as mail, bank and wire fraud; posing as a U.S. citizen; and theft or embezzlement from employee benefit plans. It imposed a two-year prison sentence beyond the penalty for

BoxScore

Bill:
HR 1731 — PL 108-275

Legislative Action:
House passed HR 1731 (H Rept 108-258) by voice vote June 23.
Senate cleared the bill June 25.
President signed July 15.

the underlying crime — five years if the theft was linked to an act of terrorism.

Judges were barred from allowing the additional time to run concurrently with the underlying sentence or from giving the defendant probation. Previously, a person convicted of a felony such as those on the list was typically sentenced without regard to whether identity theft was involved.

• **Defining identity theft.** The new law made it easier to prosecute cases of identity theft by broadening the definition of the thief to include not only someone who transferred or used the the stolen information, but also someone who possessed it. The prosecutor also was required to prove only that the defendant had the information "in connection" with an unlawful activity, rather than that he intended to use it to commit a specific crime.

• **Increasing existing penalties.** The measure increased the maximum penalty for ordinary identity theft to five years from three. It also allowed prosecutors to aggregate all individual amounts of federal benefits stolen using fraudulent identities to ensure that such cases qualified for tougher penalties. Another provision instructed the U.S. Sentencing Commission to amend its guidelines to punish insider offenses that involved an "abuse of position."

Legislative Action

House Committee Action

The House Judiciary Committee approved the bill (HR 1731 — H Rept 108-258) by voice vote May 12, after voting to expand the scope of the measure to cover fraud involving federal benefits such as Social Security, Medicare, veterans' and disability payments.

The amendment, by bill sponsor John Carter, R-Texas, also permitted prosecutors to combine federal benefits stolen with the aid of identity theft to qualify for bigger penalties, and directed the U.S. Sentencing Commission to amend its guidelines to punish employees or directors who used information from their place of business to commit identity theft or fraud.

Both the amendment and the underlying measure were approved on voice votes. The panel's Crime, Terrorism and Homeland Security Subcommittee approved the measure March 30, also by voice vote.

House, Senate Final Action

The House passed the bill June 23 by voice vote under suspension of the rules, a procedure that bars amendments, limits debate and requires a two-thirds vote for passage. The Senate cleared the measure by voice vote

two days later.

Opposition to the bill came mainly from foes of mandatory minimum prison sentences.

"The bill imposes unnecessary and unproductive restrictions on the ability of the sentencing commission and judges in individual cases to ensure a rational and just system of sentencing as a whole," argued Democratic Rep. Robert C. Scott of Virginia.

Democratic Rep. Adam B. Schiff of California, a former federal prosecutor who cosponsored the measure, countered that what he called "the plague of identity theft" was one instance in which mandatory minimums were justified. Because identity theft and the resulting crime were merged for the purposes of sentencing, Schiff said, prosecutors would otherwise have little incentive to pursue the identity theft portion of such cases. ◆

No Progress on Medical Malpractice

Senate leaders failed three times in the 108th Congress to invoke cloture and end debate on legislation to cap non-economic damage awards in medical malpractice lawsuits. Attempts to win over opponents in 2004 by narrowing the bill's focus failed to garner the necessary 60 votes.

Medical liability legislation was a top priority for Senate Majority Leader Bill Frist, R-Tenn. Frist, a heart and lung transplant surgeon for most of his professional life, argued that limiting non-economic damage awards at $250,000 would achieve two objectives. He said it would help slow increases in doctors' insurance premiums, which had driven some of them into early retirement, and it would hold down health costs by limiting the practice of "defensive medicine" — ordering tests or procedures with marginal benefit because of the fear of future lawsuits.

Democrats countered that capping awards was unfair to injured plaintiffs and that high damages were not the primary reason for rising costs. They argued that insurance companies increased malpractice premiums to recoup investment losses in the stock market.

The House had passed seven medical malpractice bills since 1995, and it did so again in 2003, passing a measure (HR 5) to cap non-economic damages for all doctors at $250,000. But Republican leaders could not overcome a filibuster on the companion bill (S 11) in the Senate. (*2003 Almanac, p. 13-15*)

Senate GOP leaders changed tack in 2004. In a strategy devised by Frist and Judd Gregg of New Hampshire, they planned to bring up bills tailored to specific groups of providers and force Democrats to take repeated votes against malpractice limits. "This is very much an election-year issue," Gregg said. "The strategy is to keep the issue visible."

With strong backing from the American Medical Association lobby, they framed the issue as a matter of health for women and children. In February and again in April, Frist tried to bring up bills to protect obstetricians, gynecologists and nurse midwives. In the second try, the bill

BoxScore

Bills:
S 2061, S 2207, HR 4280

Legislative Action:

Senate failed to invoke cloture on motion to consider S 2061, 48-45, on Feb. 24 (60 votes required).

Senate failed to invoke cloture on motion to consider S 2207, 49-48, on April 7.

House passed HR 4280, 229-197, on May 12.

added emergency and trauma center personnel. But Democrats, with the support of the American Trial Lawyers Association, blocked both bills from getting to the floor.

Legislative Action

Senate Floor Action

Frist tried and failed to bring up two malpractice bills on the Senate floor in 2004.

● **February.** On Feb. 24, Republican leaders failed, 48-45, to limit debate and proceed to a bill (S 2061) that would have limited awards against obstetricians and gynecologists. The vote was largely split along party lines. Republican Sens. Michael D. Crapo of Idaho, Lindsey Graham of South Carolina and Richard C. Shelby of Alabama voted with Democrats against the motion. Robert C. Byrd of West Virginia was the only Democrat to vote for cloture. (*Senate vote 15, p. S-8*)

The bill proposed to cap non-economic damages, such as those awarded for pain and suffering, at $250,000 in suits against obstetricians, gynecologists and nurse midwives. It would have limited punitive damages to twice the amount of economic damages, or $250,000, whichever figure was larger. It also would have limited attorney fees.

As a group, obstetricians and gynecologists had some of the highest malpractice premiums in the country. Republicans argued that excessive judgments in malpractice cases were driving the premiums up, forcing specialists out of practice and threatening to restrict women's access to care.

Democrats countered that the bill would discriminate against women by capping the awards they receive and allowing other groups to recoup higher damages.

● **April.** On April 7, the leadership failed for the third time within a year to find the 60 votes needed to overcome Democratic objections to formal consideration of a medical malpractice bill. This measure (S 2207) proposed to limit damages against emergency room personnel and trauma center staff, as well as obstetricians and gynecologists. The vote failed, 49-48. (*Senate vote 66, p. S-17*)

House Floor Action

In an effort to prod the Senate, the House passed a slightly reworded version (HR 4280) of its 2003 medical malpractice bill by a vote of 229-197 on May 12. Under the rule for floor consideration, it was automatically combined with two other House-passed bills — one to expand tax-free savings accounts for health costs and the other to exempt small-business health plans from state mandates. The resulting package was HR 4279. (*House vote 166, p. H-58*)

Republicans said they hoped the tactic would intensify pressure on the Senate, but there was no further Senate action on malpractice. ◆

Senate Defeats Gun Liability Bill

Senate Republicans orchestrated the defeat of legislation they had once embraced aimed at limiting the legal liability of firearms makers and dealers. The reason for their change of heart: the addition of Democratic gun control provisions, including the renewal of a 10-year-old prohibition on certain types of assault weapons. The assault weapons ban lapsed Sept. 13.

The bill, which was the top priority of gun rights advocates in the 108th Congress, would have barred most civil lawsuits against manufacturers, distributors, dealers and importers of firearms and ammunition in a bid to stop suits aimed at making the industry liable for gun violence. Trade groups also would have been protected under the bill. Such lawsuits had been filed in more than 30 venues in recent years. While the cases generally failed, defendants still had to spend large sums on legal expenses.

Supporters, led by the National Rifle Association (NRA), said the measure would block frivolous lawsuits designed to bankrupt an industry. Critics argued that the bill would unfairly shut the courtroom door to victims of gun violence.

The Senate measure (S 1805) had the support of the Bush administration and appeared likely to pass with relative ease. The House had passed a similar bill (HR 1036) in 2003. (*2003 Almanac, p. 13-14*)

But gun control advocates succeeded in attaching a trio of amendments to the Senate bill that embodied the heart of their legislative agenda: requiring the sale of child safety locks or a storage box with every handgun, requiring criminal background checks before any firearms sale at most gun shows and renewing the 1994 ban on semi-automatic assault weapons (PL 103-322) for 10 years.

Unwilling to accept the add-ons, the NRA told its allies in the Senate to scuttle the bill. They were joined by most of the gun control advocates, who did not think their amendments would survive a House-Senate conference. As a result, the bill went down to resounding defeat.

The gun industry managed to stave off other attempts to reauthorize the assault weapons ban. Although White House officials had signaled President Bush's support for an extension of the ban, House leaders were not eager to reauthorize the statute and risk alienating the gun rights stalwarts who were an important part of the GOP base.

Majority Leader Tom DeLay, R-Texas, repeatedly said there were not enough votes to pass a stand-alone reautho-

BoxScore

Bills:
S 1805, HR 1036

Legislative Action:
Senate defeated S 1805, 8-90, on March 2.

rization bill (HR 3831) in the House, and he refused to bring the measure to the floor. Instead, two weeks after the assault weapons ban lapsed, DeLay called up, and pushed to relatively easy passage, a bill (HR 3193) that would have repealed the municipal gun control laws of the nation's capital, some of the toughest in the nation. It would have lifted a ban on private ownership of handguns and their ammunition, allowed residents to legally own semi-automatic weapons and keep loaded, unlocked guns in their homes and businesses. The Senate did not take up DeLay's bill.

Legislative Action

Senate Floor Action

The Senate defeated the gun liability bill by a vote of 8-90 on March 2. (*Senate vote 30, p. S-10*)

Knowing they could not defeat the bill outright, Democrats decided to add amendments that gun rights supporters would not stomach, mindful that the proposals probably would become sticking points in any House-Senate conference on the legislation. They insisted that GOP leaders allow votes on the amendments as their price for allowing the bill to be brought up on the floor.

Even before the floor debate began Feb. 25, the NRA drew a line in the sand, insisting that no amendments be added to the legislation. The gun lobby and bill sponsor Larry E. Craig, R-Idaho, were most concerned about the proposal to extend the assault weapons ban. They indicated they would rather see the whole bill die than send the liability measure to Bush's desk with a renewal of the ban attached. The White House took a similar stance, issuing a statement of administration policy Feb. 24 that insisted on a "clean" bill.

Nevertheless, the Senate voted 70-27 on Feb. 26 to adopt an amendment by Barbara Boxer, D-Calif., to require firearms manufacturers and dealers to provide child safety locks whenever a handgun was sold or transferred. (*Senate vote 17, p. S-8*)

Bill supporters easily turned back four other amendments that were designed to expand exemptions in the gun liability measure, including a proposal to protect any lawsuits stemming from the October 2002 sniper attacks in the Washington, D.C. area.

On March 2, Dianne Feinstein, D-Calif., won adoption of an amendment extending the 1994 assault weapons ban for 10 years. Feinstein sponsored the original 10-year ban on 19 specific guns identified as assault weapons (PL 103-322). (*1994 Almanac, p. 276*)

John Kerry of Massachusetts, who had been campaigning for the Democratic presidential nomination, returned to Washington to cast his first roll-call votes of the year in support of the assault weapons ban and the gun show amendment. In a reminder of the power of the gun lobby, Kerry gave a floor speech March 2 in which he took pains to describe himself as a hunter who supported the Second Amendment right to bear arms but nevertheless believed in reasonable safeguards on guns.

A little later, the Senate added language by Jack Reed, D-R.I., and John McCain, R-Ariz., to close what critics called a "loophole" that allowed firearms to be purchased at gun shows without background checks. The amendment required background checks at shows where at least 75 guns were sold. Gun control advocates were able to build support for the proposal by capitalizing on heightened concerns about terrorism. Reed and McCain argued that terrorists could exploit lax rules governing gun shows to acquire firearms without first passing background checks. The amendment was adopted 53-46. (*Senate vote 25, p. S-9*)

A few hours later, the NRA told its Senate allies to pull the plug on the bill. "I learned years ago, don't pass a bad bill," said Craig, who was an NRA board member. "What happened on the floor of the Senate . . . was the admission of two items that would have made this a bad bill."

Democrats also tried to use the bill to debate their election-year prescriptions for the economy and unemployment. Maria Cantwell of Washington fell two votes shy of the 60 needed to overcome a GOP point of order against an amendment to provide an additional 13 weeks of federal benefits to those who had exhausted their state unemployment aid. The vote was 58-39. Neither Kerry nor his running mate John Edwards of South Carolina were in town for that vote. (*Senate vote 18, p. S-8*) ◆

Bankruptcy Battle Continues

For the eighth straight year, Congress was unable to complete work on an overhaul of bankruptcy law despite broad bipartisan support for the core provisions. Lawmakers settled for a short-term extension of the portion of the bankruptcy code that affected farmers.

The legislation, which had changed little in five years, sought to make it more difficult for individuals to erase their debts by filing for bankruptcy protection. People with average or high incomes would be required to file under Chapter 13, which creates a payment plan for a debtor to repay most or all creditors, instead of Chapter 7, which allows the debtor to escape certain unsecured debts after the liquidation of their property and assets.

The bill remained snagged by a dispute over a Senate provision aimed at preventing protesters and demonstrators — particularly antiabortion activists — from escaping court-ordered judgments and fines by filing for bankruptcy protection. The amendment, which Sen. Charles E. Schumer, D-N.Y., began offering in 2000, would make the fines non-dischargeable, meaning they would be included among those debts that had to be repaid.

BoxScore

Bills:
HR 975, S 1920
Legislative Action:
House passed S 1920, 265-99, on Jan. 28, after substituting the text of HR 975.

As it had in the past, the House in 2003 easily passed a bill (HR 975) containing the bankruptcy overhaul without the abortion provision. Senate GOP leaders decided not to bring the bill to the floor of their chamber until they could find a way to defeat or sidestep Schumer's amendment. (*2003 Almanac, p. 13-8*)

Hoping to break the logjam, House leaders in January 2004 took up a six-month extension of special bankruptcy rules for farmers (S 1920) that the Senate had passed in 2003, substituted the text of HR 975, and passed the amended legislation, 265-99. The House then sent the bill back to the Senate with a request for a conference. (*House vote 10, p. H-6*)

But Senate Democrats declined to participate in talks on a bankruptcy bill that did not include the Schumer provision, and the legislation died at the end of the Congress.

Instead, the Senate on Oct. 6 passed a new bill to continue Chapter 12 of the federal bankruptcy code, which allows family farmers to restructure their debts without losing their land. The House cleared it two days later, and it was signed into law Oct. 25 (S 2864 — PL 108-369). ◆

Acrimony Over Judges Continues

Partisan acrimony in the Senate over President Bush's efforts to alter the ideological cast of the federal courts continued through the session. All told, in the 108th Congress Democrats used procedural votes to block 10 of Bush's appellate court nominees — six in the first session and four in the second — and threatened to block several others if their nominations were brought to the Senate floor.

Many other nominees were confirmed. At the end of his first term, Bush had filled 203 lifetime seats on federal district and appellate courts, or 24 percent of the total.

Senate Majority Leader Bill Frist, R-Tenn., tried to overcome Democrats' opposition to the 10 candidates by invoking cloture, thereby limiting the debate and forcing a vote. However, he was not able in any of the cases to muster the 60 votes needed to adopt a cloture motion, and the nominations failed. In all, there were 20 cloture votes on the 10 candidates — seven alone on Miguel A. Estrada, Bush's pick for a seat on the U.S. Court of Appeals for the District of Columbia Circuit. Estrada withdrew his name in September 2003. *(Filibustered nominees, p. 12-16; 2003 Almanac, p. 13-19)*

Republicans insisted that the Constitution required senators to give the president an up-or-down vote on each of his nominees. Democrats said they were using the Senate rules to exercise their constitutional prerogative to offer "advice and consent." They said the president was intent on packing the federal courts with right-wing ideologues.

Recess Appointments Stall Process

The second session began with a broadside from Bush, who exercised his constitutional authority to temporarily fill two judicial vacancies while Congress was in recess.

On Jan. 16, just days before the start of the second session, he appointed Charles W. Pickering Sr., a Mississippi federal district judge, to the 5th Circuit Court of Appeals. Because the appointment was made before the session, Pickering would hold the seat until the end of the 108th Congress. In blocking his nomination in 2003, Democrats had taken issue with his record on civil rights and abortion issues.

On Feb. 20, during the Presidents Day recess, Bush appointed Alabama Attorney General William H. Pryor Jr. to the 11th Circuit. Pryor, whose appointment was good until the end of the first session of the 109th Congress, had come under fire from opponents for his stands on the environment and reproductive and gay issues.

Bush also resubmitted the Pickering and Pryor nominations to the Senate for lifetime appointments.

The tactics antagonized Democrats, and on March 26, Senate Minority Leader Tom Daschle, D-S.D., vowed to block floor action on all nominees until Bush promised not to make any more recess appointments. Daschle kept his caucus united, and the stalemate dragged on for more than seven weeks.

On May 18, Bush yielded and agreed to refrain from making further such appointments through the November elections. White House Chief of Staff Andrew H. Card Jr. went to the Capitol to seal the deal with Daschle. In return, Democrats agreed to allow Senate floor votes on 25 mostly noncontroversial nominees, including five appellate court nominees, before June 25. The agreement did not cover any of the nominations that Democrats had filibustered or signaled they would hold up.

All 25 of the nominees were subsequently confirmed.

Four Cloture Votes

In early July, Senate Republicans and the White House made it clear they were intent on using the battle over judicial nominees as a campaign issue. On July 7, Bush traveled to North Carolina and Michigan to meet with several of his nominees.

In late July, days before the Democratic National Convention in Boston, Frist forced cloture votes on four controversial judicial nominees; all failed. The nominees were:

• William G. Myers III, nominated to the 9th Circuit Court of Appeals. Cloture failed 53-44. *(Senate vote 158, p. S-35)*

• Henry W. Saad, nominated for the 6th Circuit Court of Appeals. Cloture failed 52-46. *(Senate vote 160, p. S-35)*

• Richard A Griffin, nominated to the 6th Circuit Court of Appeals. Cloture failed, 54-44. *(Senate vote 161, p. S-35)*

• David W. McKeague, nominated to the 6th Circuit Court of Appeals. Cloture failed, 53-44. *(Senate vote 162, p. S-35)*

In addition to blocking some judicial nominees on ideological grounds, Democrats also opposed several officials or former officials in the Bush administration largely because of their track records in the executive branch. They signaled they would block a floor vote on Defense Department general counsel William James Haynes II for a seat on the 4th Circuit because of his role in developing administration policy on the handling of enemy combatants and detainees in military custody. They also said they would filibuster Brett M. Kavanaugh, Bush's staff secretary, who was nominated to the D.C. Circuit Court of Appeals, and Deputy Health and Human Services (HHS) Secretary Claude Allen, nominated to the 4th Circuit.

Kavanaugh had served as associate White House counsel helping to shepherd some of Bush's other contentious judicial picks, and he had worked for former independent counsel Kenneth W. Starr during the inquiry that led to the impeachment trial of President Bill Clinton. "Brett Kavanaugh's nomination to the D.C. Circuit is not just a drop of salt in the partisan wounds, it's the whole shaker," said Charles E. Schumer, D-N.Y. *(1998 Almanac, p. 12-3)*

Opponents criticized Allen for his role in HHS audits of several federally funded AIDS organizations after members heckled HHS Secretary Tommy G. Thompson at an international AIDS conference in Barcelona in 2002.

Trouble Ahead in the 109th

With the elections closing in and other pressing business in the fall, there were no further cloture votes on judicial nominees. But angry Republicans vowed that Democrats would not have the opportunity to derail a Supreme Court

Deadlock on Judicial Nominees

Democrats blocked confirmation votes on these 10 judicial nominees during the 108th Congress. Republicans could not muster the 60 votes needed to invoke cloture and move to a vote on any of the 10.

- **Janice Rogers Brown,** D.C. Circuit.
  - Nov. 14, 2003: Cloture denied, 53-43.

- **Miguel A. Estrada,** D.C. Circuit.
  - March 6, 2003: Cloture denied, 55-44.
  - March 13, 2003: Cloture denied, 55-42.
  - March 18, 2003: Cloture denied, 55-45.
  - April 2, 2003: Cloture denied, 55-44.
  - May 5, 2003: Cloture denied, 52-39.
  - May 8, 2003: Cloture denied, 54-43.
  - July 30, 2003: Cloture denied, 55-43.
  - Sept. 4, 2003: Nomination withdrawn.

- **Richard A. Griffin**, 6th Circuit.
  - July 22, 2004: Cloture denied, 54-44.

- **Carolyn Kuhl,** 9th Circuit.
  - Nov. 14, 2003: Cloture denied, 53-43.

- **David W. McKeague,** 6th Circuit.
  - July 22, 2004: Cloture denied, 53-44.

- **William G. Myers III,** 9th Circuit.
  - July 20, 2004: Cloture denied, 53-44.

- **Priscilla Owen,** 5th Circuit.
  - May 1, 2003: Cloture denied, 52-44.
  - May 8, 2003: Cloture denied, 52-45.
  - July 29, 2003: Cloture denied, 53-43.
  - Nov. 14, 2003: Cloture denied, 53-42.

- **Charles W. Pickering Sr.,** 5th Circuit.
  - Oct. 30, 2003: Cloture denied, 54-43.
  - Jan. 16, 2004: Granted recess appointment.

- **William H. Pryor Jr.,** 11th Circuit.
  - July 31, 2003: Cloture denied, 53-44.
  - Nov. 6, 2003: Cloture denied, 51-43.
  - Feb. 20, 2004: Granted recess appointment.

- **Henry W. Saad,** 6th Circuit.
  - July 22, 2004: Cloture denied, 52-46.

nomination if, as they expected, Bush won in November. With Chief Justice William H. Rehnquist absent from the court since October because of thyroid cancer, a high court vacancy appeared increasingly likely.

Conservatives pushed for a Senate rules change in the 109th Congress that would require only a simple 51-vote majority to break filibusters of judicial nominees. Frist had won approval from the Rules Committee in 2003 for a variant on that idea (S Res 138) that would allow multiple cloture motions on a judicial nominee and gradually reduce the number of votes needed to prevail until it reached 51.

Under a scenario that seemed increasingly likely — nicknamed the "nuclear option" because of the polarizing effect it was expected to have on the Senate — a Republican presiding over the Senate, perhaps Vice President Dick Cheney, would rule that a filibuster requiring 60 votes to break was beyond the Senate's advice-and-consent role. The ruling could be upheld by a simple, 51-vote majority. Some veteran Republicans said such a move would wrongly destroy generations of Senate tradition, and it could come back to haunt the GOP when they were in the minority some day. But the party picked up four seats in November, bringing the Senate Republican majority to 55 seats in the next Congress, which could allow the leadership to muster a majority even with some Republicans opposed.

On Dec. 23, the White House threw down a gauntlet before Senate Democrats, announcing that Bush intended to resubmit the names of 20 judicial nominees who failed to win confirmation during his first term — 12 for appeals court seats and eight for the district courts. Seven of the 12 appeals court nominees had been blocked on the floor by Democratic filibusters. The other five faced the same threat.

"The Senate has a constitutional obligation to vote up or down on a president's judicial nominees," White House press secretary Scott McClellan said in a statement, "and the president looks forward to working with the new Senate to ensure a well-functioning and independent judiciary." ◆

Conservatives Seek to Limit Courts

Social conservatives in Congress sought to place new restrictions on the federal courts in an effort to curb what they regarded as "activist" judges unabashedly legislating from the bench. They pressed legislation to limit judges' jurisdiction over certain types of cases and redraw appellate court maps. The House passed three such bills in 2004, but the measures died in the closely divided Senate.

Article III of the Constitution gives Congress the authority to define the jurisdiction of federal and appellate courts, and circumscribe the Supreme Court's appellate jurisdiction.

The bills were part of a longer-term effort to rein in the courts, but the immediate catalyst was a ruling by the Massachusetts high court in November 2003 that gays had a right to wed in that state. Social conservatives viewed the ruling as an egregious example of liberal judicial arrogance, describing it as an attempt by a handful of judges to devalue, and thus destroy, the institution of marriage.

Same-Sex Marriage

The House passed a bill (HR 3313) July 22 that would have barred all federal courts — including the Supreme Court — from hearing cases that challenged a provision of the 1996 Defense of Marriage Act (PL 104-199). The provision in question declared that states were not obligated to recognize any same-sex marriages that might be legally sanctioned in other states. The restriction would not have applied to another part of the law, which defined marriage as a union between a man and a woman. The vote was 233-194 and fell mostly along party lines. (*House vote 410, p. H-134; 1996 Almanac, p. 5-26*)

Conservatives were concerned that the 1996 law could be challenged in court as a result of the Massachusetts ruling. They said that same-sex couples married in Massachusetts could try to have their unions recognized in another state by citing the Constitution's guarantee that "full faith and credit shall be given in each state to the public acts, records and judicial proceedings of every other state."

Supporters saw the measure, sponsored by John Hostettler, R-Ind., as a holding action until they could get a constitutional amendment barring same-sex marriage. (*Gay marriage, p. 12-4*)

"The threat posed to traditional marriage by a handful of federal judges whose decisions can have an impact across state boundaries has renewed concern over the abuse of power by federal judges," Chairman F. James Sensenbrenner Jr., R-Wis., told the Judiciary Committee before it approved the bill July 14.

"Gay marriage doesn't threaten our future, but the eviscera-

BoxScore

Bills:
HR 2028, HR 3313, S 878

Legislative Action:

House passed HR 3313 (H Rept 108-614), 233-194, July 22.

House passed HR 2028 (H Rept 108-691), 247-173, Sept. 23.

House passed S 878 (H Rept 108-708) by voice vote Oct. 5.

tion of our Constitution and Bill of Rights does," countered Jerrold Nadler, D-N.Y., one of the bill's most outspoken critics.

Before approving the bill, the committee adopted a substitute by Sensenbrenner that narrowed the jurisdictional restriction to the single provision. As introduced, the bill also would have barred the courts from hearing cases related to the law's definition of marriage.

Pledge of Allegiance

On Sept. 23, the House passed a bill (HR 2028) that would have denied federal courts the jurisdiction over constitutional challenges to the wording of the Pledge of Allegiance. The 247-173 vote for passage was mostly along party lines. An attempt to exclude the Supreme Court from the restriction failed, 202-217. (*House votes 467, 466, p. H-152*)

The measure, by Todd Akin, R-Mo., was written in response to a 9th U.S. Circuit Court of Appeals ruling in 2002 that the phrase "under God" in the pledge was an unconstitutional establishment of religion. The Supreme Court reversed the 9th Circuit in June, but the reversal was based on a technicality rather than on constitutional grounds. Social conservatives were concerned that the high court had left the pledge open to more constitutional challenges.

As a result, Akin and Sensenbrenner agreed to insert a provision extending the restriction to the Supreme Court during the Judiciary Committee's markup of the bill. The panel approved the measure (H Rept 108-691) on a 17-10 party-line vote Sept. 15. Sensenbrenner said the amended bill would ensure that each state would be allowed to decide its own policy regarding the pledge.

Congress added "under God" to the pledge in 1954 (PL 83-396).

Splitting the 9th Circuit

The House passed a bill (S 878) by voice vote Oct. 5 that would have created more federal court judgeships. But first, the House added provisions to carve the 9th Circuit into three separate appeals courts. The 9th Circuit sprawled over nine states and had a reputation as the most liberal appellate court in the country. Its decision on the Pledge of Allegiance revived proposals by conservatives to reduce its power by splitting it up.

Mike Simpson, R-Idaho, who offered the floor amendment, insisted that he wanted to split up the 9th Circuit not because of its decisions, but because its sheer size made it too unwieldy to be efficient. "It is inevitable, inevitable, that the 9th Circuit will be split," he said.

Under his amendment, California, Hawaii, Guam and the Northern Mariana Islands would remain in the 9th Cir-

cuit. The remaining states would be divided into two new circuits: the 12th, encompassing Arizona, Nevada, Idaho and Montana; and the 13th, comprising Alaska, Oregon and Washington.

GOP leaders thought they had locked up enough support for the amendment, but during the balloting it became apparent that too many lawmakers, particularly California Republicans, were voting "no." While leaders held the vote open, Simpson and Sensenbrenner persuaded 13 Republicans, 10 from California, to switch to "yes," giving Simpson a 205-194 vote in favor of his amendment. *(House vote 492, p. H-158)*

Some California Republicans who ultimately backed the plan said they initially worried that a reduced 9th Circuit would be even more liberal without the seven states targeted for removal. Some said Sensenbrenner persuaded them to switch by reminding them that the underlying bill provided for several new judgeships for the 9th Circuit, which could serve to tilt it toward the right.

Sen. Dianne Feinstein, D-Calif., quickly announced that she would block the measure in the Senate because of the 9th Circuit provisions. She cited objections from 9th Circuit judges, lawyers and California's Republican governor, Arnold Schwarzenegger. She argued that Simpson's plan would mean added government expenses and a higher caseload for the new 9th Circuit than for either of the other two.

Even without Simpson's amendment, the legislation was imperiled in the Senate because the House Judiciary Committee had stripped dozens of federal bankruptcy judgeships before approving the bill by voice vote Sept. 9 (H Rept 108-708). The judgeships were part of a broad bankruptcy overhaul that was stalled, and Sensenbrenner did not want to pass pieces of it separately. ◆

Chapter 13

TAXES

Corporate Tax Breaks Enacted

The biggest corporate tax overhaul since 1986 became law Oct. 22, when President Bush signed what began as a bill to repeal a U.S. export subsidy that had triggered international sanctions. The legislation, which cleared on the last day of the regular session, replaced the subsidy with $137 billion in corporate tax cuts over 10 years, plus a $10 billion buyout of tobacco farmers. To help offset the lost revenue, it included curbs on tax shelters and other tax-avoidance practices. Although Bush signed the measure shortly before the election (HR 4520 — PL 108-357), he avoided a formal signing ceremony that might have made the corporate tax breaks an issue in the campaign.

The bill was driven by the need to end trade sanctions imposed by the European Union (EU) in response to the export provision. The tax break — known as the extra-territorial income exclusion (ETI) — allowed U.S. corporations to exclude 15 percent of their export earnings from their taxable income. The World Trade Organization ruled in 2001 that the exclusion was an illegal export subsidy. On March 1, 2004, the EU began imposing retaliatory tariffs of 5 percent on selected U.S. products. When the bill was enacted in October 2004, the duties had risen to 12 percent. Repeal of the tax break led the EU to announce that the sanctions would be lifted Jan. 1, 2005.

From the outset, the repeal was paired with new corporate tax breaks, including benefits for businesses that were not affected by the ETI. Business groups had watched and waited during the first three years of the Bush administration while the president won $1.8 trillion in tax cuts targeted mainly to individuals (PL 107-16, PL 107-147 and PL 108-27). Republican leaders had repeatedly assured them that their turn would come, and they expected the ETI bill to be the vehicle. (*2001 Almanac, p. 18-3; 2002 Almanac, p. 16-3; 2003 Almanac, p. 17-3*)

But Republicans also were deeply divided between those who wanted tax cuts that would help U.S.-based multinationals compete in the global market, and others who wanted to aid domestic companies that could create jobs at home.

Congressional action on the bill began in the fall of 2003. The House Ways and Means Committee approved an ETI repeal bill in October of that year that included $140 billion in corporate tax breaks over 10 years, about $80 billion of which was offset. However, Chairman Bill Thomas, R-Calif., could not win over a block of GOP critics who said the measure was too heavily weighted toward multinationals, and he was unable to get the bill to the floor in the first session.

BoxScore

Bill:
HR 4520 — PL 108-357

Legislative Action:

Senate passed S 1637 (S Rept 108-192), 92-5, on May 11.

House passed HR 4520, 251-178, on June 17.

Senate agreed, 78-15, to add tobacco provisions to S 1637 before inserting the entire text into HR 4520 and passing it by voice vote July 15.

House adopted the conference report (H Rept 108-755), 280-141, on Oct. 7.

Senate cleared the bill, 69-17, on Oct. 11.

President signed Oct. 22.

The Senate Finance Committee approved a bipartisan bill (S 1637 — S Rept 108-192) the same month with more than $60 billion in tax cuts for domestic manufacturers and almost $40 billion for the overseas operations of multinational firms. All of it was offset by revenue increases. But the Senate leadership wanted to wait until House Republicans resolved their differences before bringing the bill to the floor. (*2003 Almanac, p. 17-12*)

The Senate passed the bill May 11, 2004, after adding nearly $70 billion more in tax cuts. The House passed a version of Thomas' bill in June after he added dozens of special interest provisions, including a buyout of Southern tobacco farmers and a new deduction for state sales taxes, to garner enough support.

Despite the need to repeal the ETI, the prospects for reconciling the two bills did not seem promising over the summer. One of the biggest problems was the fact that a final bill could not get through the Senate if it increased the deficit, but to appease House leaders, its revenue-raising provisions had to be limited. The House did not even appoint conferees until late September. Meanwhile, the White House was pressing tax writers to focus on finishing a separate bill to extend popular tax breaks for families (PL 108-311) before the election.

But the two top tax writers of the House and Senate — Thomas and Senate Finance Chairman Charles E. Grassley, R-Iowa, were determined to complete the bill in the 108th Congress before sanctions rose further. Neither wanted to start from scratch in the 109th.

The final compromise came together Oct. 6, as lawmakers were preparing to leave for the fall campaign. By that point, the bill was filled with so many tax breaks tailored to benefit members' districts and states that it was impossible for most lawmakers to reject. It took the House less than two hours to adopt the conference report Oct. 7. The Senate debated it through the weekend, finally clearing it Oct. 11.

Highlights

The following are the major components of the new corporate tax law:

● **Export subsidy.** A two-year phase-out of the ETI exclusion, with full repeal in 2007. Companies could claim 80 percent of their ETI benefits in 2005 and 60 percent in 2006. Airplane makers, including the Boeing Co., were allowed to claim the subsidy for the life of long-term sales

contracts signed before Sept. 17, 2003. Over 10 years, the repeal was expected to bring in $49.2 billion in tax revenue.

- **Domestic producers.** A tax deduction for companies, including partnerships and sole proprietorships, for income resulting from domestic production. The deduction, phased in over five years, was 3 percent in 2005-06, 6 percent in 2007-09, and 9 percent in 2010. The full deduction was equivalent to a 32 percent tax rate on manufacturing activities, down from the top marginal corporate rate of 35 percent. However, the deduction could not exceed 50 percent of the wages paid by the company during the year. The estimated cost was $76.5 billion over 10 years.

- **Multinationals.** More than 20 new tax breaks, totaling $42.6 billion over 10 years, for overseas income of U.S.-based multinational corporations. The biggest was a one-time change in allocation rules for interest expenses, worth $14.4 billion to U.S. companies over 10 years. Another provision reduced nine foreign tax credit baskets to two, making it easier for companies to subtract taxes paid to foreign countries from their U.S. tax bills and saving them $7.9 billion over 10 years.

- **Small business expensing.** A two-year extension of provisions in the 2003 tax law that allowed small businesses to deduct up to $100,000 of the cost of business equipment in the year it was purchased, rather than having to depreciate it over a number of years. The full deduction was available for equipment costing up to $400,000. Without the extension, the deduction would have fallen to $25,000 and the limit on the cost of qualifying property would have decreased to $200,000. Off-the-shelf computer software qualified for the deduction. The total cost to the Treasury was $1.1 billion over 10 years.

- **Sales tax deduction.** An option for taxpayers in 2004 and 2005 to choose between deducting state sales taxes or state income taxes. Prior to enactment, state and local sales taxes were not deductible. The provision appealed to lawmakers from states such as Tennessee, Texas, Washington and Florida that had no income taxes and relied heavily on sales taxes for revenue. The 10-year cost was $5 billion.

- **Targeted provisions.** About $14 billion in tax breaks for specific interests, from fishermen to bow and arrowmakers.

- **Tax shelters.** Elimination of scores of tax shelters and tax avoidance practices. The changes were expected to increase federal revenues by about $63 billion over 10 years, partially offsetting the cost of the bill. The most lucrative was a provision expected to generate $26.6 billion over 10 years by outlawing an arrangement under which companies, primarily financial institutions, depreciated property that had been purchased from and then leased back to municipalities and other tax-exempt entities. Closing fuel-tax loopholes was estimated to raise more than $9 billion.

- **Customs fees.** A 10-year renewal of Customs' user fees, expected to bring in $18.6 billion.

- **Ethanol.** An accounting change in a tax break for ethanol producers that was credited with adding another $5.9 billion in revenue. Previously, ethanol producers had received a partial exemption from the 18.3-cents-per-gallon federal gasoline tax that fed the Highway Trust Fund. The bill replaced that with an equivalent income tax credit, which reduced Treasury revenue by the same amount. However, the credit was assumed to expire in 2010; with neither

an exemption nor a credit in 2011-14, the Treasury was assumed to net $5.9 billion. The provision had been part of the highway reauthorization bill (HR 3550), but that legislation was left unfinished at the end of the Congress. (*Surface transportation, p. 16-3*)

- **Tobacco buyout.** Repeal of the 70-year-old federal tobacco support program, including marketing quotas and non-recourse marketing loans. Instead, tobacco quota holders would receive $7 per pound times their basic quota level, paid in equal installments over 10 years. The bill also included transition payments to tobacco producers of $3 per pound times the base quota level, to be paid over 10 years. The program was estimated to cost $10.1 billion over 10 years, paid from a Tobacco Trust Fund to be financed by the tobacco companies. (*Tobacco buyout, p. 13-5*)

Legislative Action

Senate Floor Action

After three months of highly partisan debate dominated by unrelated issues such as overtime pay and unemployment benefits, the Senate passed a revised version of its corporate tax bill (S 1637) by a vote of 92-5 on May 11. To build support, senators had added more than $50 billion in corporate tax breaks to the committee-approved bill. Together with additional sweeteners added on the floor, the final bill contained $167 billion in tax cuts over 10 years. (*Senate vote 91, p. S-22*)

As passed by the Senate, the bill included the following major components. The costs are based on July 23 calculations by Congress' Joint Committee on Taxation.

- **Domestic production.** A 9 percent tax deduction, phased in over five years, for all companies that manufactured in the United States, regardless of size — including wholly domestic manufacturers, U.S.-based multinationals, foreign corporations manufacturing in the United States, S corporations (certain small businesses) and cooperatives.

An amendment by Jim Bunning, R-Ky., adopted by voice vote, accelerated the phase-in to provide reductions of 5 percent in 2004-2006, 6 percent in 2007 and 8 percent in 2008. The estimated cost was $78.7 billion over 10 years.

- **Multinationals.** $37 billion in various tax breaks on the overseas income of U.S.-based multinational corporations. Provisions included giving companies 15 extra years beyond the five they had to use foreign tax credits before they expired ($8.1 billion over 10 years), and changing the allocation rules for interest expenses ($14.4 billion over 10 years). An attempt by Ernest F. Hollings, D-S.C., to eliminate the international tax cuts and make the 9 percent deduction for domestic production effective upon enactment failed, 23-74, on May 11. (*Senate vote 90, p. S-21*)

- **Narrow tax breaks.** An $18.6 billion package of targeted tax cuts for such diverse interests as archery makers, timber companies, liquor distillers and farm cooperatives.

- **Energy.** $17.6 billion in tax cuts to promote energy production, including provisions that stalled in the 2003 energy bill (HR 6). Some of the energy provisions were added on the floor, including a proposal by Wayne Allard, R-Colo., adopted 76-23, to create a $2 billion tax-exempt bond program to finance private-sector real-estate projects involving

Tobacco Growers Offered Buyout

Congress ended the government's 70-year-old tobacco support program and replaced it with a series of fixed payments to ease farmers out of the business over 10 years. The $10.1 billion cost of the program was to be financed by the tobacco companies. The buyout was enacted as part of the corporate tax bill signed Oct. 22 (HR 4520 — PL 108-357).

The bill did not include a companion proposal advanced in the Senate to give the Food and Drug Administration (FDA) authority to regulate tobacco.

The Depression-era tobacco subsidy program used acreage allotments and marketing quotas to control supplies and prop up market prices The new law repealed those provisions and instead guaranteed tobacco quota holders $7 per pound for the quotas they owned in 2002. It also included transition payments to tobacco producers of $3 per pound, based on their basic quota levels. Both payments were to be made in installments over 10 years.

The Department of Agriculture calculated that about 437,000 quota owners and 57,000 producers would receive payments. It said most producers were quota owners and would receive both payments. The cost of the compensation was estimated at $9.6 billion over 10 years. An additional $500 million to compensate cooperatives for losses incurred in disposing of their stocks brought the total to $10.1 billion.

To pay for the costs, the law created a Tobacco Trust Fund, financed by quarterly assessments on manufacturers and importers of tobacco products.

Ending the tobacco program had become a hot political issue in several Southern states. A decrease in smoking and cheaper imported tobacco had left many tobacco farmers struggling, and they wanted the government to buy out their quotas so they could either compete on the world market or quit the business.

Legislative Action

Tobacco-state lawmakers found a vehicle to fix their constituents' problem when Republican Bill Thomas of California, chairman of the House Ways and Means Committee, needed Southern votes for his corporate tax bill (HR 4520 — H Rept 108-548). Thomas included the buyout in the bill and provided that it be paid for out of federal cigarette tax revenues. The House passed the bill easily, 251-178, June 17. (*House vote 259, p. H-88; corporate taxes, p. 13-3*)

The Senate already had passed its version of the tax bill, but before appointing conferees senators reopened the measure to insert their own tobacco provisions. The amendment combined a tobacco buyout sponsored by Mitch McConnell, R-Ky., with FDA regulation of tobacco products championed by Mike DeWine, R-Ohio, and Edward M. Kennedy, D-Mass. A number of senators opposed a buyout for tobacco growers unless it was paired with increased federal regulation of tobacco products. The amendment was adopted, 78-15, on July 15. (*Senate vote 157, p. S-34*)

The amendment proposed to dismantle the tobacco quota system and authorize $12 billion over 10 years to give farmers and quota holders time to switch crops and get out of the business. The buyout was to be financed by assessments on tobacco companies.

The amendment included provisions to

• Authorize the FDA to regulate the levels of tar, nicotine and other components of tobacco products. Congress would retain veto power over any effort to ban cigarettes or prohibit nicotine as an ingredient.

• Require tobacco companies to disclose all harmful and potentially harmful ingredients in their products to the Department of Health and Human Services (HHS), which would then publish the information for each brand in an easily available and understood format.

• Require warnings to take up at least 30 percent of tobacco labels, which would appear on the front or back of the pack.

• Prohibit the use of terms on tobacco products such as "light" and "low-tar" unless approved by the FDA.

• Ban flavored cigarettes other than menthol brands.

• Require that magazine advertisements for tobacco products appear in black and white.

• Grant the HHS secretary authority to require manufacturers to list tar and nicotine yields on packages or in advertisements.

• Require tobacco manufacturers to pay for regulation through a user fee.

Philip Morris, a Richmond, Va., division of the Altria Group Inc., was the only major tobacco company to support the proposed tobacco regulation. Lobbyists for Philip Morris and the Campaign for Tobacco-Free Kids, the lead public health group in negotiations on the bill, said the Senate language had to stay intact in conference for them to back it.

In putting together the final version of the tax bill, Thomas had to keep the buyout for tobacco farmers to gain the votes of Southern House members. But the Senate provision to allow federal regulation of tobacco products was unacceptable to House Majority Leader Tom DeLay, R-Texas.

Thomas jettisoned it, betting that the bill would include enough other sweeteners to overcome objections from senators who had insisted that the two tobacco provisions be linked.

The gamble worked. The House adopted the conference report (H Rept 108-755), 280-141, on Oct. 7. Although tobacco foes and others who did not get provisions they wanted engaged in procedural slowdowns in the Senate, that chamber cleared the bill by a vote of 69-17 on Oct. 11.

renewable fuels. (*Senate vote 84, p. S-20*)

John McCain, R-Ariz., backed down from an attempt to strip out the entire package of energy incentives. His half-hearted effort was rejected, 13-85. "I could see the handwriting on the wall," he said. "You fold your tent and fight another day." (*Senate vote 89, p. S-21*)

● **Expiring provisions.** $19.9 billion in extensions of a variety of expiring tax breaks. Many of these were added on the floor. The biggest was an $8.6 billion proposal to extend and expand the tax credit for corporate research and experimentation through 2005. The bipartisan amendment, offered by Orrin G. Hatch, R-Utah, and further expanded by Jeff Bingaman, D-N.M., was adopted 93-0. (*Senate vote 31, p. S-10*)

Many of the other extensions were added in an amendment by Grassley, which the Senate adopted by voice vote. They included a proposal to combine the work opportunity tax credit and the welfare-to-work tax credit and make them permanent at a cost of $5.9 billion over 10 years. The credits went to employers who hired workers from certain targeted groups, such as current and former welfare recipients, at-risk youth, veterans' and ex-felons.

● **Revenue offsets.** $52.1 billion from repealing the ETI exclusion, plus $106 billion over 10 years from closing tax shelters and other tax-avoidance methods. Cracking down on a single tax avoidance practice, through which financial institutions bought the right to depreciate municipal infrastructure, such as subway cars and sewer systems, on their tax returns, was projected to raise $40.6 billion. A 10-year extension of Customs fees added another $16.3 billion. The bookkeeping change in ethanol benefits contributed another $5.9 billion.

The Senate started its debate on the bill in early March, but quickly became locked in a partisan standoff over Democratic attempts to raise election-year labor issues. Majority Leader Bill Frist, R-Tenn., pulled the bill several times to avoid votes sought by Democrats and pro-labor Republicans that might have embarrassed the White House or other GOP senators.

Much of the dispute focused on an amendment by Tom Harkin, D-Iowa, to block the Labor Department from implementing a new rule on overtime pay. The administration argued that the new regulation, which revised the types of jobs eligible for time-and-a-half overtime pay under the Fair Labor Standards Act, would make 1.3 million low-income workers eligible for the first time. Democrats contended that as many as 6 million white-collar workers could lose their eligibility under the new rules; the administration put the number at 644,000. (*Overtime, p. 8-5*)

A group of Republicans led by Whip Mitch McConnell of Kentucky — whose wife, Labor Secretary Elaine L. Chao, was responsible for implementing the overtime rules — refused to allow a vote on Harkin's amendment. Harkin threatened to block the corporate tax bill and nearly every other significant action in the Senate until he got a vote.

GOP leaders added more than $27 billion in targeted tax cuts to lure Democrats to break party ranks. Though not enough Democrats took the bait, Republicans could not simply toss out breaks they had offered for ethanol, fast-food establishments and Oldsmobile dealers. Instead, they agreed by voice vote April 8 to fold the sweeteners into the bill.

Frist finally broke the logjam by agreeing to allow votes on Harkin's amendment and on a proposal to extend federal unemployment insurance. He told unhappy Republicans that it was the only way to get the export subsidy repeal through the Senate. Frist took that path after failing twice to cut off the Democrats by invoking cloture on the bill, a procedure that required 60 votes. The first cloture motion failed, 51-47, March 24; the second fell, 50-47, April 7. (*Senate votes 60, 67, pp. S-15, S-17*)

The Senate adopted Harkin's amendment, 52-47, May 4. The language exempted from the rule any employee who would lose existing overtime status; it let stand the part of the rule that allowed more workers to qualify for the extra pay. (*Senate vote 79, p. S-20*)

Maria Cantwell, D-Wash., fell one vote short of the 60 needed to overcome a procedural hurdle to extending a federal unemployment insurance program for workers who had exhausted state benefits. The vote May 11 was 59-40. (*Senate vote 88, p. S-21*)

As senators slogged their way toward passage of the bill, business lobbyists worked to protect and expand specific tax benefits.

The most threatening proposal to businesses was an amendment by Democrats Byron L. Dorgan of North Dakota and Barbara A. Mikulski of Maryland, aimed at offshore manufacturers. Dubbed the "runaway plant" provision, it would have required companies to pay federal taxes on their foreign factories when those plants produced goods that were imported into the United States. A lobbying group of 26 multinational firms, including McDonald's Corp. and Cisco Systems Inc., worked against the amendment.

A Republican motion to table (kill) the amendment prevailed, 60-39. "Big business has significant influence around here when they turn up the heat," Dorgan said after the May 5 vote. (*Senate vote 83, p. S-20*)

A politically popular amendment by Ron Wyden, D-Ore., to extend trade-adjustment assistance — a social safety net program for workers who lost their jobs because of trade — to service industry workers fell after the Blue Cross Blue Shield Association intervened. Budget Committee Chairman Don Nickles, R-Okla., sank the proposal by raising a budget point of order that required 60 votes to overcome. The amendment fell, 54-45, six votes short, May 4. (*Senate vote 80, p. S-20*)

Questioning whether any of the special-interest tax breaks loaded onto the bill would create jobs, Bob Graham, D-Fla., proposed scrapping $95 billion of the tax cuts and replacing them with a factory jobs credit that would provide manufacturers with a tax credit of as much as $35,000 per employee. Graham's amendment was defeated, 22-77, May 5. (*Senate vote 82, p. S-20*)

A proposal by Christopher J. Dodd, D-Conn., to prohibit the federal government from using offshore contractors was adopted, 70-26, after it was rewritten to limit the ban to cases where the Commerce Department certified that no U.S. jobs would be lost or economic harm would result. The amendment also included a broad national security exemption for the departments of Defense, Energy and Homeland Security, and for the intelligence agencies. Also, 27 nations, including members of the European Union and Japan, would still be able to win U.S. federal contracts. "We estab-

lished some strong principles on outsourcing. We're going to come back to this," Dodd said.

House Committee Action

In a lengthy markup session that ended just before midnight June 14, the Ways and Means Committee approved a greatly expanded version of Thomas' bill (HR 4520 — H Rept 108-548, Part 1). The vote was 27-9, with three Democrats joining all 24 Republicans in favor of the bill.

Thomas had rewritten the bill, provision by provision, to lure a few Democrats and convert some Republicans who opposed earlier versions. "There is room for purists, but none of them are chairmen of committees," Thomas said.

Among the biggest changes were the addition of a $9.6 billion buyout for tobacco farmers and a federal income tax deduction for state sales taxes. But the bill also was filled with dozens of special interest provisions tailored to attract specific members. Overall, the legislation was expected to increase the budget deficit by $35.7 billion over 10 years.

The panel rejected, 11-25, an alternative measure offered by the committee's ranking Democrat Charles B. Rangel of New York, that would have replaced the export tax break with a larger tax cut for manufacturers and included a permanent state sales tax deduction.

Major elements of the committee-approved bill included:

● **Domestic production.** A reduction from 35 percent to 32 percent in the top marginal tax rate for domestic manufacturers. The maximum would be 34 percent in 2005-2007 before falling to 32 percent beginning in 2008. The estimated cost was $63.6 billion over 10 years.

● **Small corporations.** A reduction from 35 percent to 32 percent in the top marginal rate for corporations with taxable income of $20 million or less. The new rate was to be phased in over nine years at a 10-year cost of $14.9 billion.

● **Multinationals.** $29.7 billion in new tax breaks on overseas income of U.S.-based multinational corporations. The tax benefits were similar to those in the Senate bill, though they did not include the extra time for companies to use their foreign tax credits.

● **Small business expensing.** A $1.1 billion, two-year extension of provisions in the 2003 tax law that allowed small businesses to deduct up to $100,000 of the cost of business equipment in the year it was purchased, rather than having to depreciate it over a number of years. The full deduction was available for equipment costing up to $400,000.

● **Sales tax deduction.** A $3.6 billion plan to allow individual taxpayers to deduct either state sales or state income tax payments from federal taxable income in 2004 and 2005.

The committee rejected, 8-28, an amendment by Max Sandlin, D-Texas, to make the state sales tax deduction permanent, offset by dropping proposed tax breaks for overseas income of U.S.-based multinationals.

● **Expiring provisions.** $14 billion over 11 years to extend or renew a list of expiring tax provisions. The largest was a $7.6 billion extension of the research and experimentation credit.

● **Revenue increases.** $49.6 billion from repealing the ETI, plus $18.6 billion from extending Customs fees and $40 billion from closing tax shelters and other methods of avoiding taxes. In addition, the bill counted $5.9 billion from the accounting change in ethanol benefits.

● **Tobacco buyout.** A repeal of the federal tobacco support program, combined with incentives for tobacco farmers to quit the business or switch crops. The bill proposed to repeal the existing support system of federal marketing quotas, which controlled supply, and non-recourse marketing loans, which guaranteed minimum prices. Instead tobacco quota holders would receive guaranteed payments over five years; the cost would be paid for with a portion of the federal cigarette tax.

House Floor Action

The House passed Thomas' bill, 251-178, June 17, with 48 Democrats crossing party lines to support the measure. It was a more comfortable margin than even bill proponents had expected. (*House vote 259, p. H-88*)

The rule for debate, which the House adopted 230-195, barred any amendments, although it modified portions of the bill's text. (*House vote 257, p. H-88*)

In particular, the rule automatically added language to limit the total cost of the tobacco program to $9.6 billion.

Thomas acknowledged that the bill had been loaded down with sweeteners. "I do not rise to defend the honor of Miss Piggy," he said. But the targeted provisions enabled Thomas to turn election-year pressures — which lobbyists and pundits had predicted would sink the bill — in his favor.

John M. Spratt Jr, D-S.C., a confidante of Minority Leader Nancy Pelosi of California and a noted fiscal conservative, was won over by the tobacco provision.

The federal income tax deduction for state sales taxes swayed several Texas Democrats. Martin Frost, ranking Democrat on the Rules Committee and a party loyalist, voted for the bill, as did Charles W. Stenholm, a leader of the anti-deficit Blue Dog Coalition, who had voted against all three major Bush administration tax cut bills. Both men faced tough challenges in November. Sandlin, a chief deputy whip and a Blue Dog fiscal conservative, also voted for the bill because of the benefits of the state sales tax provision for Texas residents.

In addition to 28 Democrats from tobacco districts or states without income taxes, 20 other Democrats crossed over to support the bill. Many of them were attracted by the tax cut on manufacturing income, which was important in election battleground states, such as Ohio, Pennsylvania and Michigan.

Senate Action: Round II

On July 15 the Senate took the routine step of calling up HR 4520, inserting the text of S 1637 and passing the amended House bill by voice vote. But before the vote, senators added a section on tobacco that gave them a position on the issue when the tax bill went to conference.

The amendment, by Mark DeWine, R-Ohio, and Edward M. Kennedy, D-Mass., combined a buyout of tobacco farmers similar to that in the House bill with a proposal to give the Food and Drug Administration (FDA) regulatory authority over tobacco. The two issues had been joined in the Senate since 2003; the conventional wisdom was that neither plan had enough support to get through the Senate without the other. The Senate adopted the FDA provision, 78-15, then adopted the combined amendment by voice vote. (*Senate vote 157, p. S-34; 2003 Almanac, p. 11-18*)

Conference/Final Action

After languishing for months, the corporate tax bill was revived in late September as members prepared to leave for the election campaigns. The much-delayed conference convened Sept. 29. The House adopted the conference report (H Rept 108-755) eight days later, Oct. 7, by a vote of 280-141. The Senate cleared the bill, 69-17, Oct. 11. *(House vote 509, p. H-164; Senate vote 211, p. S-44)*

House GOP leaders delayed going to conference out of concern that prolonged negotiations would allow Democrats to consume end-of-session floor time with non-binding motions to instruct conferees.

Then in early September, Grassley announced he would hold up the White House's top tax priority — a bill to extend popular middle class tax cuts — until he was confident Congress would also complete the corporate tax bill. His biggest concern was that without the repeal of the ETI, European sanctions on U.S. exports, including Midwest agricultural products, would continue to mount. *(Family taxes, this page)*

On Sept. 20, Grassley, Thomas and Frist reached a complicated agreement that freed up both tax bills. As part of the deal, Thomas agreed to shift a $12.9 billion package of about 20 expiring or soon-to-expire tax breaks for business to the family tax measure. That reduced the scope and cost of the corporate tax bill and made it easier to offset the cost.

Negotiators still had to tackle differences on more than $150 billion in core tax provisions and almost $100 billion in tax avoidance crackdowns, as well as tangential issues such as the tobacco buyout — all in the midst of a frenzy of business lobbying.

At the outset, Thomas recommended that conferees adopt the Senate position on the core manufacturing tax breaks. He gave the 41 House and Senate conferees several opportunities to submit changes, culling through more than 300 proposals and contacting senators from both parties to see what they needed to vote for the final package.

Thomas determined that he needed the tobacco buyout to gain the votes of Southern House lawmakers. But the Senate's companion provision to allow federal regulation of tobacco products was unacceptable to Majority Leader Tom DeLay, R-Texas. Thomas dropped the FDA regulation and relied on other sweeteners to win over senators who still insisted that the buyout and FDA provisions go together.

Among the other provisions dropped in conference was Harkin's amendment to bar the Bush administration from changing the rules for overtime pay.

The final 650-page bill contained billions of dollars in targeted tax breaks that Treasury Secretary John W. Snow said went "far beyond the bill's core objective." Snowe was writing to Thomas Oct. 4 to get him to eliminate numerous narrow-interest provisions.

But it was the targeted provisions that allowed tax writers to finish their work. Thomas kept them all — tax breaks for horse and dog track gambling, railroads, naval shipbuilders, restaurants, Hollywood productions and even fishing tackle boxes — luring individual lawmakers who cared about these things to support the final package. The controversial buyout for tobacco farmers, restoration of a federal income tax deduction for state sales taxes and ethanol tax breaks sealed the deal.

Although almost no one spoke favorably of the bill, including Thomas, lawmakers said they could not afford to defeat it. "In the end, Chairman Thomas had everyone in checkmate," said tax writer Ron Lewis, R-Ky. "The political pressures were [such] that they couldn't move."

In the Senate, tobacco foes and others who did not get provisions they wanted engaged in procedural slowdowns, prolonging the debate into the Columbus Day weekend. Mary L. Landrieu, D-La., vowed to use every procedural tactic available to protest exclusion of her pet provision from the conference report — a $2 billion tax credit for keeping National Guard members and military reservists on payrolls while they were fighting in Iraq or Afghanistan.

Landrieu was joined by Harkin, who was upset that a majority of senators had reneged on a pact to give the FDA authority to regulate tobacco products as a condition for the buyout for tobacco farmers.

The two were finally mollified. The Senate voted to add a scaled-back version of Landrieu's tax credit to a separate bill (HR 1779), which died at the end of the session. Harkin won passage of separate bills to require FDA regulation of tobacco (S 2974) and bar the White House from implementing new rules on overtime pay eligibility (S 2975). The House did not act on either measure.

The Senate then cleared the bill and recessed for the November elections. ◆

Middle-Class Tax Breaks Extended

Election-year politics made a Republican package of family and business tax breaks irresistible — even to Democrats who had lambasted GOP tax writers for doing too little for the poor and refusing to pay for the tax benefits. The bill cleared by overwhelming margins in both chambers Sept. 21, extending the life of the principal family tax benefits enacted in President Bush's 2001 and 2003 tax laws. The estimated cost was $146.3 billion over 10 years.

Bush signed the measure into law (HR 1308 — PL 108-311) during an Oct. 4 stop in the battleground state of Iowa, highlighting Republican efforts to showcase their tax agenda on the campaign trail.

House GOP leaders successfully resisted offsetting tax increases to pay for the bill and said they hoped their victory would be a precedent for the 109th Congress. "We're going to push for more tax cuts. You can be sure about that." said House Majority Leader Tom DeLay, R-Texas.

Democrats, too, declared victory, vowing to support further extensions of tax cuts for the middle class while pressing for tax breaks for low-income families coupled with

higher taxes for the wealthy to help reduce the deficit.

The core of the bill was the short-term renewal of four family tax breaks that were set to expire at the end of 2004: a $1,000-per-child tax credit; tax benefits for married couples; the existing upper income limit for the lowest, 10 percent tax bracket; and existing exemptions from the alternative minimum tax (AMT). At the last minute, the negotiators added a $12.9 billion package of provisions to extend expired or soon-to-expire tax breaks for businesses.

Bush had called in his fiscal 2005 budget for Congress to make the 2001 and 2003 tax cuts permanent. As a short-term measure, he asked lawmakers to extend the 2003 provisions on the child tax credit, marriage penalty relief and 10 percent bracket through 2010 at a 10-year cost that Congress' Joint Committee on Taxation put at $106.6 billion. He also proposed extending the AMT exemptions through 2005. *(Bush budget, p. 4-3)*

Republicans had wanted to make the tax cuts permanent at the time of the 2001 tax law (PL 107-16). But to comply with complex budget rules and garner the votes of wavering GOP moderates who were crucial to Senate passage, they phased in the cuts slowly and provided for them to expire in 2010. *(2001 Almanac, p. 18-3)*

Bush's second big tax package, enacted in 2003 (PL 108-27), accelerated the phase-in of several of the tax cuts. But it was set to expire at the end of 2004, at which point the tax breaks would revert to their original schedules under the 2001 law. *(2003 Almanac, p. 17-3)*

While Bush's proposal to make the tax cuts permanent enjoyed support among conservatives, concern about the gaping deficit made it unrealistic. Instead, Republicans focused on the three popular family tax breaks, which quickly became a centerpiece of the Republican election-year agenda.

House Republicans began by passing a series of separate bills to make each of the individual tax cuts permanent. Negotiations on a compromise package that could pass in the Senate did not get under way until July. House and Senate tax writers agreed on a two-year extension that had significant Democratic support, but the White House rejected the deal at the last minute, calling instead for a more generous bill closer to the November election.

After the August recess, Republican tax writers revised the bill. House leaders agreed to limit the extensions to a few years but rejected pressure from Senate Democrats and GOP deficit hawks to pay for the tax cuts with revenue-raising provisions. Helping middle-class taxpayers in an election year was widely popular, and by delaying the vote until fall, Republicans left Democrats with little choice but to back the plan.

BoxScore

Bill:
HR 1308 — PL 108-311

Legislative Action:

House passed HR 4181, 323-95, on April 28.

House passed HR 4227, 333-89, on May 5.

House passed HR 4275, 344-76, on May 13.

House passed HR 4359, 271-139, on May. 20.

House adopted the conference report on HR 1308 (H Rept 108-696), 339-65, on Sept. 23.

Senate cleared the bill, 92-3, on Sept. 23.

President signed Oct. 4.

Highlights

The following are the main components of the tax bill:

● **Child tax credit.** The $1,000-per-child tax credit was extended for five years, through 2009. Without the extension, the credit would have reverted to $700 for 2005 through 2008, increasing to $800 in 2009 and to $1,000 in 2010, before falling to $500 in 2011. The estimated cost of the change was $61.6 billion over 10 years.

The bill also accelerated to 2004 an increase, previously scheduled for 2005, in the benefits of the refundable child credit for families that earned too little to be liable for income tax. The refundable portion of the credit went to those families in the form of a check. Under the provision, the credit was refundable for up to 15 percent of a taxpayer's earned income in excess of $10,750. Without the change the limit in 2004 would have been 10 percent. The provision was expected to cost $2 billion.

The final bill did not include a House-passed plan to increase the amount a taxpayer could earn and still get at least a partial child tax credit. The House would have increased the upper limit from $110,000 to $250,000 for married couples (from $75,000 to $125,000 for individuals).

● **Marriage benefits.** Provisions intended to erase the so-called marriage penalty in the tax code were extended for four years, through 2008. For married couples filing jointly, this meant the standard deduction and the amount of income taxed at the 15 percent rate would remain twice that of a single person. Without the new law, the deduction and upper limit would have fallen in 2005, then gradually increased through 2010. The 10-year cost was $15.7 billion.

● **10 percent bracket.** The upper limit on the 10 percent tax bracket was extended through 2010. That meant the first $14,000 of income for married couples ($7,000 for individuals) would continue to be taxed at the 10 percent rate. Without the extension, the upper limit would have reverted to $12,000 for couples ($6,000 for individuals) in 2005. The 10-year cost was $29.4 billion.

● **AMT.** The law extended increased income limits for the AMT for one year, through 2005. Under the provision, married couples filing jointly with incomes below $58,000 ($40,250 for individuals) were exempt from the alternative tax, which was aimed at preventing wealthy Americans from using legitimate tax breaks to avoid paying income taxes altogether. The 10-year cost was $22.6 billion.

● **R&D.** An expired tax credit equal to 20 percent of a business' qualified research expenses was renewed through 2005 at a 10-year cost of $7.7 billion.

● **Wind and biomass.** The law extended through 2005 a tax credit for facilities that produced electricity from poultry waste, wind or biomass from plants grown specifically for that purpose. The credit was available for facilities placed in service

after 2003 and before 2006. The 10-year cost was $1.2 billion.

● **Work opportunity credit.** The law renewed through 2005 a $2,400 credit for employers who hired certain workers, including those receiving welfare benefits or food stamps. The 10-year cost was $614 million.

● **Liberty zone bonds.** Tax-exempt private activity bonds for construction and rehabilitation in New York City were extended through 2009. The bonds were created in response to the Sept. 11, 2001, terrorist attacks. The 10-year cost was $579 million.

● **District of Columbia.** Tax incentives for investment in Washington, D.C., were extended through 2005 at a 10-year cost of $522 million.

● **Welfare-to-work credit.** A tax credit to employers for wages paid during the first two years of employment to workers who were long-term family assistance recipients was renewed through 2005 at a 10-year cost of $127 million.

Legislative Action

House Action on Stand-Alone Bills

To emphasize their zeal for tax cuts, House GOP leaders began in late April with a series of stand-alone bills, passing them at a rate of one a week. Democrats insisted that the bills should do more to help the poor and that they should be paid for by reducing tax benefits for the rich. The Republican majority strenuously opposed any tax increases.

● **Marriage penalty.** The leadership began with a bill (HR 4181) to erase the so-called marriage penalty at a 10-year cost of $105 billion. The House passed it overwhelmingly, 323-95, on April 28. (*House vote 138, p. H-50*)

The GOP victory came only after Republicans agreed to the last-minute addition of Democratic-backed language on the earned income tax credit (EITC) to permanently allow qualified low-income individuals to collect refunds of the credit even if they paid no tax.

Before passing the bill, the House rejected, 189-226, a Democratic substitute offered by Charles B. Rangel of New York that would have made the marriage penalty relief permanent but specified that the tax benefits could not be reduced as a result of the AMT or affect the taxpayer's eligibility for the EITC. Rangel would have offset the tax cuts with a 3.6 percent surtax on individuals earning more than $500,000 annually and couples earning more than $1 million. (*House vote 136, p. H-50*)

The House also defeated, 199-220, a motion by Charles W. Stenholm, D-Texas, to allow the tax cuts only if the Treasury secretary certified that the money needed to pay for them could be borrowed without exceeding the statutory limit on the public debt. (*House vote 137, p. H-50*)

● **AMT.** On May 5, the House passed a one-year extension of the AMT exemptions (HR 4227), with an adjustment for inflation, by a vote of 333-89. The measure was estimated to cost $17.8 billion over 10 years. (*House vote 144, p. H-52*)

Members rejected, 197-228, a substitute by Richard E. Neal, D-Mass., that Democrats said offered a simplified way to calculate the AMT; the $19.3 billion cost would have been offset by restricting corporate bookkeeping practices aimed at reducing taxes. (*House vote 143, p. H-52*)

Critics in both parties said the AMT had evolved from a tax aimed at preventing tax avoidance by the very wealthy into a hard-to-compute extra tax on 3 million households, three times as many as in 2001. Many taxpayers had to compute their taxes twice: once using regular tax rates and rules, and a second time using the AMT rates of 26 percent for the first $175,000 of income and 28 percent for any amount above that, minus a very narrow set of allowable deductions and exemptions. The taxpayers then had to pay the amount of tax owed under the AMT or under ordinary rules, whichever was higher.

● **10 percent bracket.** The House voted, 344-76, on May 13 to make permanent the existing upper boundary of the 10 percent bracket. The bill (HR 4275) was estimated to cost $218 billion over 10 years. (*House vote 170, p. H-60*)

Lawmakers rejected, 190-227, a substitute amendment by John Tanner, D-Tenn., that would have extended the existing parameters of the 10 percent bracket only through 2010, ensured that tax breaks in the bill were not erased by the AMT, and offset the $53 billion cost with a 1.9 percent surtax on taxable income exceeding $500,000 for single taxpayers and $1 million for couples. (*House vote 169, p. H-60*)

● **Child tax credit.** The House passed a bill (HR 4359) on May 20 to make the $1,000-per-child tax credit permanent. The measure, which passed 271-139, also would have expanded the availability of the credit to parents at both ends of the income spectrum. The estimated cost was $227.9 billion over 10 years. (*House vote 209, p. H-70*)

The House rejected, 187-226, a Democratic substitute that would have extended the $1,000 credit only through 2010, indexed the benefit for inflation, and offset the cost with a surtax on taxable income exceeding $500,000 for single taxpayers and $1 million for couples. (*House vote 208, p. H-70*)

House GOP leaders seized on their success in passing the bills — particularly the lopsided vote on the 10 percent bracket — to argue for trying to make at least some of the provisions of the 2001 and 2003 laws permanent. "I want permanency. That's why you cut taxes, so that people can permanently count on it," DeLay said in mid-May. But permanent extensions were a non-starter in the Senate, where Democrats and moderate Republicans argued that any tax cuts should be offset.

Bipartisan Deal Scuttled

Over the summer, House and Senate leaders worked on assembling the tax break extensions into a package that could pass in both chambers. They were urged on by the White House, which wanted a bill before Congress left for the summer recess. In late July, they agreed on a $75 billion, two-year proposal championed by Senate Finance Chairman Charles E. Grassley, R-Iowa.

Republican leaders were hoping to force Democrats to take uncomfortable votes on the bill just before the Democratic National Convention in Boston on July 26. However, it turned out that many Democrats — including the presidential nominee, Sen. John Kerry of Massachusetts — were ready to support the two-year plan. "We think we will have a huge bipartisan vote for this on both sides of the building," said House Majority Whip Roy Blunt, R-Mo.

At that point, the White House upped the ante, demanding a more generous five-year extension package with the vote postponed until the critical fall campaign season. If

Democrats opposed the bill, they could be attacked for hurting the middle class; if they voted for it, the White House could take the victory on the campaign trail.

Negotiations, Final Action

When Congress returned in September, House Ways and Means Chairman Bill Thomas, R-Calif., and Grassley worked quickly with the leadership to produce a final bill, using the shell of a moribund bill on the child tax credit (HR 1308). The House easily adopted the conference report (H Rept 108-696), 339-65, on Sept. 23. Less than an hour later, the Senate cleared the bill, 92-3. Voicing worries about the cost and the effects on the budget deficit, Sens. Ernest F. Hollings, D-S.C.; Olympia J. Snowe, R-Maine; and Lincoln Chafee, R-R.I., voted no. (*House vote 472, p. H-152; Senate vote 188, p. S-40*)

The chief sticking point in putting together the final bill was Grassley's unwillingness to complete the job until he was confident that Congress would also clear a separate corporate tax bill (HR 4520) that had stalled over the summer. The corporate bill included the repeal of a tax subsidy for U.S. exporters that had been ruled illegal by the World Trade Organization. The European Union was imposing sanctions on U.S. exports because of the subsidy, and Grassley was concerned that Iowa farm exports would be hurt as a result. (*Corporate taxes, p. 13-3*)

The logjam was broken in late September, when Senate Majority Leader Bill Frist, R-Tenn., House Speaker J. Dennis Hastert, R-Ill., Grassley and Thomas agreed on an outline for completing the family tax bill while also getting the corporate bill moving. As part of the agreement, Thomas shifted about 20 expired or soon-to-expire tax breaks for businesses and investors from the corporate tax bill to HR 1308 — thereby reducing the scope and cost of the corporate bill and making it easier to offset with revenue-raising provision. The difficulty of finding acceptable offsets was one of the problems dogging the corporate tax bill.

Satisfied that both bills were primed for action, Grassley convened the conference on the middle-class tax bill. Thomas halted a brief stampede by Republicans who were trying to attach other unrelated items by insisting that all provisions be simple extensions, not major expansions of existing tax breaks. Republican conferees rejected an attempt by Sen. Blanche Lincoln, D-Ark., to reduce the income threshold for the refundable tax credit from $10,750 to $10,000. Republicans said the program was a form of welfare that should not be expanded.

Democrats continued to argue that the final bill would provide little tax relief to those at the bottom of the income scale and that the tax cuts should be offset. But in the end, few dared vote against the politically popular GOP package. ◆

Internet Tax Ban Extended

Congress extended the moratorium on state taxation of Internet access for another three years in a bill that cleared during the lame-duck session. The bill was retroactive to Nov. 1, 2003, when the previous moratorium expired. President Bush signed the measure into law Dec. 3 (S 150 — PL 108-435).

For most of the year, lawmakers were deadlocked on the bill, unable to resolve basic differences between supporters of a permanent tax exemption in the House and backers of a four-year tax moratorium in the Senate. In the end, the Senate prevailed.

The measure revived a moratorium that was enacted originally in 1998 (PL 105-277) and extended in 2001 (PL 107-75). Reinstating the ban was a top priority of the technology industry. Although no states had imposed new taxes since the expiration of the last law, many lawmakers and industry groups worried that it was only a matter of time. Industry groups supported a permanent ban but lined up behind the Senate bill as the end of the session neared.

Negotiations over the measure centered on three issues: the length of the new ban, whether any states should have exemptions and how to treat Internet phone calls.

The House passed a bill (HR 49) in 2003 that would have permanently banned all taxes on Internet access, including older dial-up service as well as high-speed phone

BoxScore

Bill:
S 150 — PL 108-435
Legislative Action:
Senate passed S 150 (S Rept 108-155), 93-3, on April 29.
House cleared S 150 by voice vote Nov. 19.
President signed Dec. 3.

and cable connections. It would have eliminated "grandfather" provisions that exempted 10 states from the 1998 moratorium. Similar legislation in the Senate (S 150) faltered in late 2003, when state and local governments protested that it would cost them billions of dollars in tax revenues. (*2003 Almanac, p. 17-14*)

After months of stalemate, Senate proponents of a permanent ban gave up in 2004 and supported a four-year compromise plan by John McCain, R-Ariz. It continued the exemption for states that had enacted Internet access taxes before 1998 and specified that states could tax telephone calls that were sent over the Internet.

House Judiciary Chairman F. James Sensenbrenner Jr., R-Wis., held out for a permanent access-tax ban with no exceptions for any states. But with the 108th Congress ending and potential new state Internet taxes looming, House members relented and cleared a modified version of the Senate bill.

Highlights

The following are the main provisions of the 2004 law:
● **Moratorium.** The moratorium — which prohibited states from taxing Internet access or imposing multiple or

discriminatory taxes on electronic commerce — was extended for three years, until Nov. 1, 2007, and was retroactive to Nov. 1, 2003.

● **Application.** The law clarified that the moratorium applied to all forms of consumer Internet access regardless of whether it used digital subscriber lines (DSL), cable modem, satellite or wireless service.

● **Internet phone service.** The law allowed states to tax voice calls made over the Internet, putting off the issue for the next Congress.

● **Exemptions.** The nine states that had been allowed to tax dial-up services under the old moratorium were permitted to continue doing so for the duration of the new ban. Those that taxed DSL, a service that was not covered under the old ban, were allowed to continue for two more years.

● **Study.** The law directed the comptroller general to study the impact of the Internet access tax moratorium, including its effects on state and local government revenues and on the adoption of broadband technologies for Internet access throughout the country.

Legislative Action

Senate Floor Action

After four days of often-arcane debate, the Senate passed a revised version of S 150 by a vote of 93-3 on April 29. (*Senate vote 77, p. S-19*)

The compromise was brokered by McCain, chairman of the Commerce, Science and Transportation Committee. McCain had the support of the leading sponsors of the original Senate bill, George Allen, R-Va., and Ron Wyden, D-Ore., who knew they had to make significant changes to move the bill forward. In addition to making the moratorium temporary, McCain included other significant concessions to win support from lawmakers who wanted to protect states and localities. In the crucial vote, the Senate on April 29 agreed, 64-34, to invoke cloture and thus end debate on McCain's amendment. (*Senate vote 75, p. S-19*)

The McCain compromise proposed to:

● Extend the moratorium on Internet access taxes for four years, rather than permanently, as the House preferred. The four years dated from Nov. 1, 2003.

● Exempt the nine states that taxed dial-up service before 1998 for the duration of the bill and exempt states that taxed DSL services for two years. The House bill would have required states that charged any form of Internet taxes to stop collecting those taxes immediately.

● Specify that the tax moratorium would not affect states' authority to tax Internet voice calls. The House bill made no mention of Internet phone services. House sponsors said it was unnecessary because the bill was meant to keep only Internet access tax-free, not voice applications

The four-day debate in the Senate did not break along partisan lines. Rather, it pitted parochial state and local interests against the lobbying of the technology and telecommunications industries. Much of the discussion concerned arcane details of the Internet's structure and the movement of information in an attempt to define how much of the network should be subject to taxes. Wyden described it as "eye-glazing."

A group of ex-governors in the Senate, including George V. Voinovich, R-Ohio; Lamar Alexander, R-Tenn; and Thomas R. Carper, D-Del., raised issues of states' rights and unfunded mandates.

Dianne Feinstein, D-Calif., said she had heard from people in hundreds of California cities that feared that a broadly defined version of tax-free Internet access could be interpreted to include many longstanding phone taxes and fees. Feinstein tried to get a four-year extension for states that tax DSL connections, but her amendment was tabled, or killed, by a 59-37 vote. (*Senate vote 76, p. S-19*)

Feinstein, like most senators who carried the concerns of their states and local tax commissions into the Senate debate, decided the McCain amendment had enough compromise.

The Senate also was sidetracked by partisan maneuvering over energy issues. The Senate voted against attaching unrelated amendments on ethanol production and a Republican energy bill. (*Energy policy, p. 9-4*)

What won over many undecided senators in the end was the continued exemption for nine states that had been grandfathered under the previous law.

McCain also agreed to allow taxation of Internet phone calls, a rapidly growing industry. Opponents of a broadly defined ban on Internet access taxes said they worried that unless the bill allowed taxes on Internet calls, the ban could be interpreted as taking away existing state authority to tax telephone services. Some phone companies also used the Internet for traffic over long distances.

"That's far and away the biggest issue for state and local governments," said Alexander, who had led the opposition to Allen's permanent Internet tax ban. "This has no impact on [current taxing authority for] phone calls made over the Internet."

State and local government lobbyists, who had warned of dire consequences if the moratorium was reinstated, lost on most issues in the Senate. But some of the lobbyists said they were satisfied that the Senate language would make the moratorium temporary while making it clear that telephone calls would remain taxable.

Final Action

Sensenbrenner and other backers of the House bill held out for the permanent tax ban. But as the lame-duck session drew to a close, Sensenbrenner yielded, accepting the temporary ban in exchange for a provision shortening his home state's exemption from the moratorium to two years from four. Sen. Kay Bailey Hutchison, R-Texas, requested an exemption that would allow municipalities in her state to keep collecting franchising and right-of-way fees on telecommunications infrastructure.

The Senate agreed to both requests, modifying the bill through a concurrent resolution (S Con Res 146) adopted by voice vote Nov. 17. The House adopted the resolution Nov. 19 by voice vote and went on to clear the bill, also by voice vote.

Sensenbrenner gave in, but he made it clear he was not giving up. "Let me put everyone on notice," he said during the House debate, "that in the next Congress, even though the moratorium doesn't expire during the life of the 109th Congress, I will attempt — once again — to make this permanent." ◆

Chapter 14

TECHNOLOGY & COMMUNICATIONS

Decency Debate Follows Super Bowl

Legislation to stiffen penalties for indecent television and radio broadcasts passed overwhelmingly in the House and Senate, but a dispute over an unrelated provision on media ownership blocked a final agreement between the two chambers.

Congressional interest in cleaning up lewd programming on the public airwaves was sparked by an incident at the Feb. 1 Super Bowl, which was broadcast on CBS and watched by tens of millions of Americans. During the event's halftime show, pop singer Janet Jackson's breast was exposed, igniting a firestorm on Capitol Hill and propelling the issue to the fore of the congressional agenda.

The House took the lead with a two-page bill (HR 3717) sponsored by Fred Upton, R-Mich., to increase the maximum penalties that the Federal Communications Commission (FCC) could levy on broadcasters for indecency to $275,000 from $27,500 per incident. Many lawmakers wanted tougher legislation, however, and by the time the bill emerged from the House Energy and Commerce Committee, it contained provisions to boost the maximum fine to $500,000, make it easier to fine performers rather than just their employers, and encourage the FCC to terminate a broadcast license after a company's third indecency violation.

Other proposals to extend indecency regulation to cable and satellite — media that were garnering an increasing share of the U.S. television audience — were rejected. The House passed the bill overwhelmingly in March over the fierce opposition of broadcasters and groups representing performers.

In the Senate, Sam Brownback, R-Kan., introduced a bill (S 2056) that mirrored the original House bill. Once again, however, provisions were added in committee, including a proposal to roll back FCC plans to relax media ownership rules — a potential deal breaker because of opposition from the White House, House GOP leaders and some conservative Republican senators.

Realizing that his bill would not move on its own, Brownback attached it to the must-pass defense authorization bill (S 2400). "Passing this legislation will tell the broadcasters that we are serious about protecting our airwaves, and we will give the FCC updated tools to get the job done," Brownback said.

The Senate passed the bill in June, but the language on media ownership remained the main sticking point in conference negotiations with the House. Ultimately, conferees on the defense bill decided to drop the broadcast indecency legislation.

BoxScore

Bills:
HR 3717, S 2056

Legislative Action:

Senate Commerce, Science and Transportation Committee approved S 2056 (S Rept 108-253), 23-0, March 9.

House passed HR 3717 (H Rept 108-434), 391-22, March 11.

Highlights

The following are highlights of the broadcast indecency legislation:

● **Financial penalties.** The House-passed bill allowed for the FCC to fine broadcasters up to $500,000 per indecency violation, up from $27,500. The maximum penalties on artists and performers would rise to $500,000 from $11,000, and the FCC would be able to fine artists without initial warnings.

The Senate bill included penalties on broadcasters of up to $275,000 for each incident, with a doubling of fines for "aggravated behavior," and maximum of $3 million within a 24-hour period.

● **Multiple offenses.** Both bills included greater authority for the FCC to revoke licenses for repeat offenses. Those licenses were worth billions of dollars in some cases. The "three strikes" provision in both bills required that the FCC begin license revocation hearings — the first step in the process of removing a broadcaster's license — after the third offense.

● **Review "shot clock."** The House bill provided for a "shot clock," or deadline, of 270 days for the FCC to resolve outstanding indecency complaints. Lawmakers on both sides of the aisle criticized the FCC for its backlog of complaints.

● **Small affiliate protection.** Both bills included protections for small affiliates. Lawmakers wanted to ensure the FCC would not put small stations out of business with massive fines — particularly, they said, when the stations' network parents often pressured them to air syndicated programming. The FCC would be directed under both bills to consider a company's size and ability to pay when assessing fines.

● **Media ownership.** The Senate bill included a provision that would pre-empt FCC rules issued in 2003, loosening media ownership restrictions. Those rules lifted the ban on owning a newspaper and television station in the same market, and relaxed limits on owning multiple broadcast outlets in a single local market. (*2003 Almanac, p. 2-38*)

● **TV violence.** The Senate bill called for the FCC to study the effectiveness of the "v-chip," a device in televisions that allowed consumers to block unwanted programming based on its rating. If the FCC found the system was not working as intended, it would have to issue rules to regulate violent TV content in the same way indecency or profane materials was regulated.

Legislative Action

House Subcommittee, Committee Action

The House Energy and Commerce Subcommittee on Telecommunications and the Internet approved Upton's bill proposing a tenfold increase in the maximum fine for on-air

vulgarity by voice vote Feb. 12.

The full Energy and Commerce Committee approved an expanded version of the bill (H Rept 108-434) by a vote of 49-1 on March 3, after giving voice vote approval to a package of amendments that had been worked out in two weeks of bipartisan committee negotiations.

The revised bill included provisions to:

• Increase maximum FCC fines against broadcasters to $500,000 per indecency violation.

• Increase maximum fines on individual performers from $11,000 to $500,000 with no cap for a continuing violation.

• Direct the FCC to take into account a violator's ability to pay fines, based on market size and location and whether the violator is a company or an individual.

• Direct the FCC to take into account factors such as whether the program was live or recorded, whether the indecent incident was scripted or unscripted, whether a time delay to block objectionable material was used, whether a station that did not produce the programming, was given adequate opportunity to review it or had reason to know of its content, the size of the audience and whether the incident was part of a children's television program.

• Trigger an immediate FCC license revocation hearing for broadcasters that had three or more indecency violations in a licensing term.

The only provision that inspired any serious dissension was the proposal by Republicans Christopher Cox of California and Cliff Stearns of Florida to make it easier for the FCC to fine individual artists and performers for their own indecent actions. The FCC had the power to fine individuals, but only through a cumbersome process. An attempt to strike the amendment on the grounds that it would place unconstitutional restrictions on speech failed by voice vote.

Several Democrats raised the issue of media consolidation, saying the rise in indecency violations correlated with the concentration of media ownership into fewer hands.

Senate Committee Action

The Senate Commerce, Science, and Transportation Committee approved S 2056 (S Rept 108-253) by a vote of 23-0 on March 9, after adopting a series of amendments that included controversial proposals to roll back the FCC's media ownership rules and pave the way for regulation of TV violence.

During the markup, the committee:

• Adopted, 13-10, a proposal by Byron L. Dorgan, D-N.D., to impose a yearlong moratorium on the FCC's plan to relax media ownership rules to allow the Government Accountability Office to study the issue. Republicans Trent Lott of Mississippi, Kay Bailey Hutchison of Texas and Olympia J. Snowe of Maine joined all committee Democrats

except John B. Breaux of Louisiana to back the amendment.

• Adopted, 11-10, an amendment by Ted Stevens, R-Alaska, to require the FCC to consider revoking the licenses of broadcasters after three violations of indecency rules.

• Adopted by voice vote a Stevens amendment to increase the maximum penalty for broadcasters from $275,000 in the underlying bill to $375,000 for a second violation and $500,000 for any additional violation.

• Adopted by voice vote an amendment by George Allen, R-Va., to allow the FCC to apply the same fines to individual performers.

• Adopted by voice vote a proposal by John Ensign, R-Nev., to direct the FCC to look at a broadcaster's ability to pay indecency fines based on factors such as revenues and market size when determining the amount of the penalty.

• Adopted by voice vote a proposal by Ernest F. Hollings, D-S.C., to require the FCC to study whether consumers were taking advantage of v-chip technology to block violent content on television. Congress mandated the technology in the 1996 Telecommunications Act (PL 104-104), but critics said it was not widely used and was ineffective.

• Rejected, 11-12, an amendment by Breaux that would have given the FCC the power to regulate expanded basic cable content the same way it regulated over-the-air broadcasts.

House, Senate Floor Action

The House passed HR 3717 on March 11 by a vote of 391-22. The rule for floor debate prevented Democrats from offering a media ownership amendment. The White House issued a statement the day of the vote voicing strong support for the bill. (*House vote 55, p. H-22*)

Joe L. Barton, R-Texas, Energy and Commerce Committee chairman, said the bill "answers the call of parents we heard around the country" after the edgy Super Bowl halftime show in February.

Action in the Senate was held up because Republican leaders did not want to allow the media ownership provision to stand and did not want to risk a protracted floor fight with Democrats over the issue.

Brownback then won a 99-1 Senate vote to attach a scaled-back version without the media ownership language to the Senate's fiscal 2005 defense authorization bill (S 2400). But the Senate then agreed by voice vote to add Dorgan's media ownership language as well.

When the defense bill reached conference, Brownback and his House allies again tried to strip the media ownership language, but Dorgan and other Democrats blocked the attempt. Conferees decided the entire broadcast indecency issue was too hot to handle, and dropped it from the final defense authorization bill (PL 108-375). ◆

Safety Broadcasting Left for 109th

A proposal to free up more frequencies for use by public safety agencies had broad support in Congress. The Senate included such a plan in its version of the intelligence overhaul bill, but the House refused to sign on, preferring to address the issue separately in the next Congress.

The call for Congress to improve the ability of emergency responders to radio one another was among the less-noticed recommendations of the commission that investigated the Sept. 11, 2001, terrorist attacks. The independent, bipartisan commission found that poor communications at the site of the World Trade Center attacks may have cost firefighters and police officers their lives. (*Sept. 11 commission, p. 11-8*)

Sen. John McCain, R-Ariz., and Rep. Jane Harman, D-Calif., introduced bills (S 2774, HR 1425) that would have required television broadcasters to stop using any frequencies reserved for, but not claimed by, public safety personnel. The portion of the spectrum in question, in the 700 Mhz band, was particularly valuable to first-responders because it could penetrate walls and travel long distances. It also could be used to develop more advanced, broadband-based communications systems.

The proposal had widespread support. However, McCain, who chaired the Senate Commerce panel, saw a chance to recover even more spectrum, generating billions of dollars for the Treasury and giving new technologies, such as wireless broadband, a coveted slice of the airwaves.

McCain introduced a bill (S 2820) to require television broadcasters to vacate all analog frequencies — not just the channels slated for first-responders — by 2009. Congress had tried in 1997 (PL 105-33) to mandate a full digital transition by the end of 2006, but the law allowed broadcasters to wait until 85 percent of a market's audience had digital TV equipment. That had not happened. (*1997 Almanac, p. 3-34*)

Broadcast industry supporters, led by Sen. Conrad Burns, R-Mont., argued that such a rapid changeover would force many stations off the air. Burns and McCain sparred over the issues and ultimately settled on a compromise, added to the Senate's intelligence bill in September, under which broadcasters would have to give back only channels 60-69 by the end of 2007, and only if local public safety officials specifically requested them.

The language was dropped from the final intelligence bill (PL 108-458), in part because Joe L. Barton, R-Texas, House Energy and Commerce Committee chairman, said he wanted to deal with the issue as a separate matter in 2005.

Legislative Action

Senate Committee Action

The Senate Commerce, Science and Transportation Committee approved the more wide-ranging McCain bill (S 2820 — S Rept 108-428) on Sept. 22, after adopting an amendment by Burns that reduced the portion of the spectrum broadcasters would have to vacate. The committee adopted the Burns amendment 13-9, then approved the bill by voice vote.

As introduced, McCain's bill would have required all analog broadcasters to stop using their frequencies by 2009 as they moved to a different part of the radio spectrum to offer broadcasts in a new digital format. As amended, it required that stations return the frequencies by Jan. 1, 2008, but it allowed the Federal Communications Commission (FCC) to exempt certain broadcasters to avoid "consumer disruptions" for viewers whose television sets could only receive the older type of analog programming.

McCain said the amendment "created a loophole a mile wide." He criticized the National Association of Broadcasters (NAB) for backing Burns' approach, which would force only some stations off the air. Spanish-language Univision would be among the stations targeted for a surrender of its analog frequencies, which McCain called discriminatory. The NAB said Burns' plan would turn off about 75 stations, while McCain's bill would apply to 1,700. "The deal should be, everybody should get off or no one should get off," McCain said.

The committee rejected, 9-13, a McCain amendment to let broadcasters comply with the Burns proposal through 2008, while mandating the stricter 2009 deadline in his original bill. FCC Chairman Michael K. Powell said broadcasters could delay the transition for decades unless Congress forced their hands.

In addition to setting a deadline, the bill included a provision to create a trust fund using the proceeds from auctions of the returned frequencies — which experts estimated were worth $30 billion to $40 billion — to help viewers with sets that could not process digital signals. The bill would have let the Commerce Department spend as much as $1 billion to buy set-top converters for affected viewers.

The bill also included language to authorize $117 million over five years for the Homeland Security Department's SAFECOM office, which was responsible for overseeing public safety communications infrastructure improvements.

Senate Floor Action

After watching as his bill was watered down in committee, McCain tried to strengthen it on the floor. He offered an amendment to the intelligence overhaul legislation (S 2845), similar to the bill he brought to the committee, that sought a complete handover of analog spectrum by broadcasters. (*Intelligence overhaul, p. 11-3*)

But Burns swung into action again to defend the broadcasters. After he and McCain debated the issue, McCain agreed to a compromise under which broadcasters would have to relinquish only public safety channels and only when specifically asked to do so by local first-responders.

The Senate adopted the amendment to the intelligence bill by voice vote. But the House did not include a similar provision in its intelligence bill, and it was omitted in the conference report. ◆

Bills to Halt Online Piracy Scrapped

The entertainment industry turned to Congress for help in curbing online piracy, after losing a court battle with Internet file-sharing companies. Senate Judiciary Chairman Orrin G. Hatch, R-Utah, tried without success to aid the film and song studios by brokering a compromise with the technology industry. The House and Senate passed several narrower bills, but none reached enactment.

In April 2003, a federal judge in Los Angeles ruled that two major file-sharing companies — Streamcast Networks Inc. and Grokster — could not be held liable for the songs, movies and other copyright works swapped online by their users. The entertainment companies said the practice was costing them billions of dollars in lost revenue each year. But the court said the file-sharing companies were not liable because, among other things, they did not have central servers pointing users to copyrighted material. The 9th Circuit Court of Appeals upheld the ruling in August 2004.

Hatch, the chairman of the Senate Judiciary Committee, came to the studios' aid with a bill (S 2560) to make it illegal for any company to facilitate or intentionally induce infringement by computer users. The measure quickly touched off an outcry from the technology industry, which said the wording was too broad and might undermine two decades of copyright protections emanating from a 1984 Supreme Court decision that legalized VCRs. Repeated efforts to negotiate a compromise failed.

While Hatch's bill was their biggest potential prize, the entertainment companies pushed several other proposals aimed at tightening enforcement of existing anti-piracy laws and increasing penalties on individuals who use file-sharing services to trade copyrighted songs and movies online.

The Senate passed bills in June to allow the Justice Department to file civil copyright-infringement suits and to bar the use of camcorders in movie theaters. The House passed a bill to ease the standards federal prosecutors had to meet in demonstrating that computer users had committed criminal copyright infringement.

Although those bills were seen as less radical than Hatch's legislation, some lawmakers still felt they would go too far in protecting the interests of Hollywood and the music industry. The only good news for the entertainment companies was a Supreme Court decision in December to hear an appeal of the Grokster case. The Court was expected to issue a ruling in 2005.

Legislative Action

Hatch Bill Stalls

Hatch introduced his anti-piracy bill (S 2560) in late June, but he did not begin pushing it in earnest until several months later, after the industry lost its appeal. At that point, his bill became the entertainment industry's best bet to tackle online piracy. With the support of the Senate's top two lawmakers — Majority Leader Bill Frist, R-Tenn., who sought to protect the Nashville music industry, and Minority Leader Tom Daschle, D-S.D. — the bill seemed to have a good chance of passing.

But the measure ran into stiff opposition from the technology industry. Trade organizations representing consumer electronics manufacturers, Internet service providers and other industries lined up against the bill, saying it could apply to many legitimate products and could stifle innovation. The groups said the bill would effectively overturn a 1984 Supreme Court ruling — known as *Betamax* — that legalized the VCR and underpinned innovation in the technology industry.

Hatch tried for months to find a compromise that would satisfy both the entertainment industry and the bill's opponents. But even with the help of the Library of Congress, which was asked to weigh in with its own middle-of-the-road proposal, he could not strike a deal. After scheduling and canceling several markups, he stepped back. "If we can't do it in the short term, we'll do it next year," Hatch said.

Senate Action

The Senate passed two smaller anti-piracy bills by voice vote June 25.

● **Civil suits.** The first (S 2237), by Patrick J. Leahy, D-Vt., would have given prosecutors the right to file civil suits against online pirates, sparing them the negative publicity associated with bringing criminal charges against college students and others who used Internet file-sharing systems. It also would have authorized $2 million for the Justice Department to bring federal prosecutors up to speed on the nuances of digital copyright law.

The Judiciary Committee had approved the measure by voice vote April 29. Public interest groups said the bill amounted to a handout to the entertainment industry.

● **Camcorders.** The second bill (S 1932), sponsored by John Cornyn, R-Texas, was aimed at cracking down on the distribution — either in physical form or via the Internet — of copies of movies or songs before they were officially released or fully marketed.

The bill would have made it a federal crime to use a camcorder or other recording device in a movie theater. The motion picture industry said more than 90 percent of the pirated movies online originated from camcorders.

It also would have authorized $5 million per year in fiscal years 2005 through 2009 for the Justice Department to prosecute violations of intellectual property rights.

House Action

The House passed a separate anti-piracy bill (HR 4077 — H Rept 108-700) by voice vote Sept. 28. The measure, sponsored by Lamar Smith, R-Texas, would have given the Justice Department new enforcement tools by lowering the bar prosecutors had to meet to prove criminal copyright infringement in the online world.

Supporters said existing law made it too difficult for prosecutors, forcing them to show "willful" reproduction or distribution of copyrighted works worth at least $1,000. Prov-

ing files were distributed over the Internet and determining their value was difficult.

Smith's bill sought to ease those standards by making it a criminal offense to upload and make available with "reckless disregard of the risk of further infringement" 1,000 or more copyrighted works. Offenders could get as many as five years in prison.

The House Judiciary Committee had approved the bill Sept. 8, after adding language to legalize devices designed to filter objectionable content from DVD home movies. Several Hollywood studios had sued the most prominent maker of

the technology, ClearPlay, claiming that altering the movie content amounted to copyright infringement.

Final Action

While separate online piracy bills made their way through the House and Senate, neither chamber managed to enact the other's proposals. Backers of the measures tried to bundle them into an end-of-session omnibus, but disputes over the movie-filtering language and whether too much power was being given to federal prosecutors to combat piracy combined to sink the plan. ◆

Congress Protects Rural TV Access

The prospect of roughly 2 million mostly rural Americans losing their access to network television programming prompted Congress to reauthorize the 1999 Satellite Home Viewer Improvement Act (PL 106-113), portions of which were set to expire at year's end. After last-minute negotiations that resolved the concerns of local broadcasters, the bill was cleared as part of the fiscal 2005 omnibus appropriations bill. President Bush signed the measure into law Dec. 8 (HR 4818 — PL 108-447).

There was widespread agreement within Congress that rural customers who could not receive network signals from local broadcast affiliates should continue to get analog broadcasts of NBC, CBS, ABC and Fox from other markets, through a satellite provider. The House passed a bill to that effect in October (HR 4518), reflecting an agreement between the Energy and Commerce and the Judiciary committees.

In the Senate, a similar proposal (S 2013) won approval from the Judiciary Committee. But the Commerce, Science and Transportation Committee approved a separate bill (S 2644) that added a wrinkle: a provision that would allow satellite TV providers to offer out-of-market digital network programming in markets where local broadcasters did not have full-power digital signals of their own.

Local broadcasters vigorously opposed the provision, which they saw as a competitive threat. But supporters held their ground, stalling action in the Senate and complicating the chances for a late-session deal with the House. In the November lame-duck session, opponents of the digital programming provision eventually gave way, but only after winning several additional protections for local broadcasters .

Under the final bill, satellite companies were allowed to begin beaming high-definition, digital network signals in markets where local affiliates did not broadcast digitally. Satellite companies also were allowed to show "significantly

BoxScore

Bill:
HR 4818 — PL 108-447
Legislative Action:
House passed HR 4518 (H Rept 108-660) by voice vote Oct. 6.
Senate Judiciary Committee approved S 2013 by voice vote June 17.
Senate Commerce, Science and Transportation approved S 2644 (S Rept 108-427) by voice vote July 22.
House adopted the conference report on HR 4818 (H Rept 108-792), 344-51, on Nov. 20.
Senate cleared the bill, 65-30, on Nov. 20.
President signed Dec. 8.

viewed" channels from one market to customers in a neighboring market.

Highlights

The following are the main components of the satellite TV legislation:

● **Distant network signals.** The measure extended through Dec. 31, 2009, the statutory license that allowed satellite operators to retransmit a broadcast television signal from a distant market. However, under the measure, satellite subscribers could not sign up for distant channels once their satellite provider offered local network affiliate channels, also known as "local into local" service. That was intended to protect small local broadcasters from prime time competition from larger distant network affiliates.

● **Significantly viewed channels.** Satellite operators were allowed to carry "significantly viewed" out-of-market stations, provided they first offered local-into-local service to their customers. Significantly viewed stations are stations outside a consumer's designated market area that can nonetheless be received easily over the air. Channels in Baltimore's market, for example, might be significantly viewed for consumers in the Washington, D.C., market. Under existing law, cable operators had similar authority to transmit such stations and the Federal Communications Commission (FCC) determined whether stations met certain criteria to be "significantly viewed."

● **Single-dish requirement.** All satellite companies were required to transmit all local analog broadcast channels on a single satellite dish within 18 months of enactment. This provision was intended to block a practice used by EchoStar Communications Corp. that separated programming on two dishes. The second dish was often used for religious or Spanish-language programming.

● **Royalty payments.** Under existing law, the license that

allowed satellite companies to retransmit network signals and superstations required the carriers to pay royalty fees to compensate the studios and stations that produced the programming. The new law allowed the rates to be set through voluntary negotiations rather than by a government panel. It required the Librarian of Congress to initiate, by Jan. 2, 2005, voluntary negotiation proceedings for the purpose of determining the royalty fee to be paid by satellite carriers.

• **Digital television signals.** Broadcasters were in the process of converting from analog to digital broadcast signals, and many had not completed their transition. The measure allowed satellite providers to broadcast a distant digital signal from another market to certain customers who were not able to receive digital signals from their local broadcasters. Satellite providers had to phase in the new digital offerings over a 2 1/2 year period. The FCC was charged with developing a predictive model to determine which consumers would be eligible for the digital signals.

Legislative Action

House Energy and Commerce Action

The House Energy and Commerce Committee approved its bill (HR 4501 — H Rept 108-634) by voice vote June 3. The panel's subcommittee on Telecommunications and the Internet approved a draft of the bill by voice vote April 28.

The measure reflected a bipartisan and bicameral consensus on many of the key issues. It included provisions to require satellite providers to offer all of an area's local analog programming on a single home satellite dish within a year. It also granted satellite companies the authority to provide subscribers "frequently viewed" programming from a neighboring area.

The subcommittee agreed by voice vote to amendments:

• By subcommittee Chairman Fred Upton, R-Mich., to prevent consumers from signing up for satellite broadcasts of network channels in other markets when the satellite provider offered those network stations locally.

• By Edward J. Markey, D-Mass., to extend to satellite companies many of the customer privacy rules that had been in place for digital cable providers for years. Companies would be barred from disclosing such things as a customer's viewing habits.

The subcommittee's draft did not include a provision to allow satellite providers to offer out-of-market digital programming. Senior Republicans on the committee persuaded their colleagues not to try to include it, arguing that it was too controversial with broadcasters and would slow the bill's progress.

House Judiciary Action

The House Judiciary Subcommittee on Courts, the Internet, and Intellectual Property approved its own draft version of the satellite TV bill by voice vote May 6. The full Judiciary Committee approved the bill (HR 4518 — H Rept 108-660) with minor changes by voice vote July 7.

The measure tracked closely with the Energy and Commerce bill, but it included new language proposing a tempo-

rary 12 percent increase in the royalties that satellite companies paid to holders of program copyrights. The increase was intended to account for inflation in the five years since Congress last addressed the issue. The existing rate was 15 cents per month for each distant network signal beamed to a consumer.

The new rate was to be in effect in 2005 and 2006, when a panel appointed by the Librarian of Congress was to complete an arbitration process to set a fair-market value for the content. In the meantime, the rate would get a cost-of-living increase every year, starting in 2007.

Some lawmakers said satellite carriers could pass on the royalty increases to consumers in the form of higher subscription prices. "I think members are going to hear from their constituents. It's going to seem like a huge increase," said Zoe Lofgren, D-Calif.

Others, including subcommittee ranking Democrat Howard L. Berman of California, a longtime supporter of the movie industry, said the legislation did not go far enough in requiring satellite companies to pay fair-market rates.

Senate Judiciary Action

The Senate Judiciary Committee approved its satellite TV reauthorization bill (S 2013) on June 17, adopting a substitute amendment to a skeletal proposal that was introduced by Chairman Orrin G. Hatch, R-Utah, earlier in the year. The measure fell in line with the House on most matters, but did not provide for the immediate 12 percent increase in royalties that was included in the House Judiciary bill.

The Hatch-sponsored proposal called for a copyright arbitration panel selected by the Librarian of Congress to set a fair-market royalty rate by June 1, 2005, for the network programming that satellite providers retransmitted.

Senate Commerce, Science and Transportation

The Senate Commerce, Science and Transportation Committee weighed in July 22, adding a contentious twist to an otherwise smooth legislative process. The committee approved by voice vote a bill (S 2644 — S Rept 108-427) that included a provision granting satellite providers limited authority to offer out-of-market digital programming to some consumers, in lieu of broadcasters who had not completed their transition to digital programming.

Broadcasters opposed the provision, saying it would introduce new competition in their markets for prime time viewers. Supporters said it would force broadcasters to speed up their federally mandated transition to digital broadcasting. "Exciting technologies can be developed if we can get the broadcasters off the analog spectrum they are sitting on right now," said the sponsor, John Ensign, R-Nev.

Ensign offered a substitute amendment, adopted by voice vote, that scaled back his original proposal to address concerns of broadcasters. The bill gave the FCC two years to develop a model to predict which consumers could not receive digital broadcasts. Satellite companies could not offer digital network programming until the FCC completed its model. Satellite companies also would be required to cease digital network transmissions once customers could get them from local broadcasters.

Aside from the digital programming provision, the Sen-

ate Commerce bill included nearly identical language to the House Energy and Commerce Committee bill.

House, Senate, Final Action

The House passed HR 4518 on Oct. 6 by voice vote after combining it with the Energy and Commerce bill. The manager's amendment dropped the 12 percent increase in royalties, instead allowing for private negotiations between the parties to settle on a new rate.

Final action in the Senate was stalled because of disagreements over whether to include the digital programming provision so vehemently opposed by broadcasters. After a series of last-ditch talks in the lame-duck session, negotiators agreed to a scaled-back version of the provision that phased in the authority for satellite providers.

That cleared the way for the House-Senate compromise legislation to be one of the few unrelated bills to win inclusion in the fiscal 2005 omnibus appropriations package. ◆

Electronic Privacy vs. 'Spyware'

Growing public concern about the privacy risks associated with "spyware" — computer programs that surreptitiously access hard drives to gather personal information for third parties — forced Congress to address the issue. The House passed a pair of bills by overwhelming majorities, and a separate version won committee approval in the Senate. But the issue proved too complex to resolve within a single year.

The first House bill (HR 2929), sponsored by Mary Bono, R-Calif., would have required software companies to get permission from consumers before installing programs capable of collecting personal information and sending it to third parties. Users often download spyware unknowingly as they traverse the World Wide Web and download other programs.

But the measure rankled many software makers, who said it could apply to everyday programs that rely on operating under the radar of users, such as network security programs. Many technology companies also opposed the idea of legislating how software should be built.

The second House bill (HR 4661), by Robert W. Goodlatte, R-Va., called for criminal penalties against individuals convicted of tapping into personal computers with the intent of stealing information or damaging a machine. That measure had more widespread backing in the technology industry because it avoided dictating specific technological requirements to software makers.

The Senate Commerce, Science and Transportation Committee approved a separate spyware bill (S 2145), sponsored by Conrad Burns, R-Mont. Originally similar to Bono's bill, the measure was scaled back to the liking of the technology industry, with the language on installation requirements watered down slightly and a proposal on criminal penalties similar to Goodlatte's included. The full Senate did not act on the bill.

Joe L. Barton, R-Texas, chairman of the House Energy and Commerce Committee, said he wanted to work out an agreement with Burns and House lawmakers to finish the bill before the session ended. "I am committed to try to put a bill on the president's desk for his signature this year," he

BoxScore

Bills:
HR 2929, HR 4661, S 2145
Legislative Action:
Senate Commerce Committee approved S 2145 (S Rept 108-424) by voice vote Sept. 22.
House passed HR 2929 (H Rept 108-619), 399-1, on Oct. 5.
House passed HR 4661 (H Rept 108-698), 415-0, on Oct. 7.

said. But with too many other pressing issues on the end-of-year agenda, including most of the appropriations bills, supporters of the spyware crackdown decided to put off the effort until 2005.

Legislative Action

House Energy and Commerce Committee

The House Energy and Commerce Committee approved a revised version of Bono's bill (HR 2929 — H Rept 108-619), 45-4, on June 24, after agreeing to changes that helped pacify some of the technology industry's concerns about the original version. The panel's subcommittee on Commerce, Trade and Consumer Protection approved the measure by voice vote June 17.

The bill included the following provisions

● **Unauthorized activities.** In an effort to target the specific behaviors associated with spyware, the bill included a list of off-limits practices, such as redirecting a user's browser to another Web site without permission; delivering advertisements that a computer user could not close without turning off the machine or shutting down all browser windows; collecting personally identifiable information, such as Social Security or bank account numbers, by tracking a user's keystrokes; tying up or damaging the system's resources; and inducing a user to download or execute a program by misrepresenting its identity or purpose.

● **Opt-in provision.** The distributor of any program capable of "information collection" would have to get the user's permission before the program could be installed or executed. Information collection programs were defined as those that gather personally identifiable information, track a user's Web browsing habits, and send such information to a third party.

The bill provided guidelines for the notices companies would have to give users, suggesting language such as: "This program will collect and transmit information about you and your computer use and will collect information about Web pages you access and use that information to display advertising on your computer. Do you accept?" The companies would have to provide readily accessible information

about the program and its purpose to assist users in determining whether to grant consent.

- **Enforcement.** Under the bill, the Federal Trade Commission (FTC) was charged with enforcing the measure with fines of up to $3 million for violators. The legislation would have pre-empted state laws on spyware.
- **Liability protection.** The full committee adopted by voice vote an amendment by Cliff Stearns, R-Fla., that added liability protections for several industries, including Internet service providers and network security providers. "We want to ensure that legitimate commerce is not undermined by this legislation," Stearns said. The bill also exempted law enforcement officers in the performance of their duties.

House Judiciary Committee

Rival lawmakers on the Judiciary Committee took a crack at the issue Sept. 8, approving Goodlatte's bill by voice vote (HR 4661 — H Rept 108-698).

The bill proposed to make it illegal to hack into a computer to obtain sensitive information, such as credit card numbers, Social Security numbers, or passwords, or to cause damage to the computer. Offenders would be subject to fines and up to two years in prison. Those who used their access to another's machine in furtherance of another federal crime, such as credit card fraud, could get up to five years in prison.

The committee adopted by voice vote an amendment by Goodlatte to authorize $10 million over four years for the Justice Department to prosecute cases involving spyware and "phishing" — the use of fraudulent e-mail and Internet schemes to lure consumers into disclosing sensitive financial information.

An attempt by Robert C. Scott, D-Va., to remove a provision that would have prevented victims of spyware from bringing civil suits under state laws was rejected by voice vote.

House Floor Action

Despite attempts by senior Republicans on the Energy and Commerce and Judiciary committees to merge the bills, the House took them up separately. The Bono bill passed 399-1 on Oct. 5. Two days later, the House passed the Goodlatte measure by a vote of 415-0. (*House votes 495, 503, pp. H-160, H-162*)

Senate Committee Action

The Senate Commerce, Science, and Transportation Committee approved Burns' bill (S 2145 — S Rept 108-424) by voice vote Sept. 22.

The original bill closely tracked the Bono measure, but a Burns substitute amendment, adopted by voice vote, changed the overall approach to address the concerns of software makers.

- **Software.** The amendment made it illegal to install software on a user's computer without permission, but unlike the original bill, it did not include specific technical guidelines on how software makers should get that authorization.
- **Adware.** The substitute also sought to regulate "adware" — programs that launch Internet pop-up ads. It would be illegal to serve up such ads when users were not visiting a Web site affiliated with the software company, or to launch ads "in a manner or at a time such that a reasonable user would not understand that the software is responsible for delivering the advertisements."
- **Liability protection.** The bill included liability protections for legitimate companies, including Internet service providers who unknowingly transmitted spyware programs over the Web to users, and network security providers, who often rely on software utilities that operate in the background to secure computers.
- **Civil penalties.** Enforcement was given primarily to the FTC, though the Agriculture Department, the Federal Deposit Insurance Corporation and other agencies would have some authority. No new penalties specific to spyware were mentioned.
- **Criminal penalties.** The panel also adopted by voice vote an amendment by George Allen, R-Va., to institute criminal penalties for spyware providers. The amendment, similar to Goodlatte's bill in the House, would make it illegal to gain unauthorized access to a computer in order to obtain sensitive information, such as credit card numbers, Social Security numbers, or passwords, or to cause damage to the computer. The penalties were the same as under Goodlatte's bill. ◆

School Internet Funding Protected

Congress cleared a telecommunications package just before adjourning the 108th Congress that wrapped together three separate bills. The measure included language aimed at staving off a funding crisis in the E-Rate program, which funded Internet access in schools and libraries. It also included provisions to free more government spectrum for the private sector, and to help states and localities pay for upgrades of their emergency 911 service. President Bush signed the bill into law Dec. 23 (HR 5419 — PL 108-494).

The only obstacle the legislation faced was a debate over whether it would be the vehicle for an unrelated bill on boxing safety. Senate Commerce, Science and Transportation Chairman John McCain, R-Ariz., sought to include the boxing language but was ultimately thwarted by House Republicans.

The E-Rate bill was a priority for lawmakers in both parties and helped carry the other attached measures into law. Without it, the choice would have been to increase the "universal service" fees paid by telephone companies, which in turn would be passed onto consumers, or freeze more than $1 billion in funding for schools and libraries.

Highlights

The following are the main provisions of the omnibus telecommunications legislation:

- **E-Rate funding.** The legislation exempted the E-Rate

program from the Anti-Deficiency Act, a law that barred federal agencies from committing to expenditures without having the cash on hand to meet all their obligations.

Congress created the E-Rate program under the 1996 Telecommunications Act (PL 104-104) to subsidize Internet connections for school districts, libraries and rural health centers. It was funded by a portion of the universal service fee, which was paid by the nation's telephone companies.

The Universal Service Administrative Co., which administered the program, typically sent letters of commitment before collecting all the funds needed to meet the obligations, because it often took schools many months to send back invoices. Without the exemption, the Federal Communications Commission (FCC), would have had to prohibit the practice, forcing a freeze in new E-Rate funding commitments.

● **Spectrum relocation.** The spectrum provisions aimed to provide a clear, predictable mechanism for compensating federal agencies that had to vacate radio frequencies that were being sold to wireless communications companies.

The law established the Spectrum Relocation Fund, a federal trust fund, to compensate the federal agencies. It required the FCC to notify the Commerce Department's National Telecommunications and Information Administration at least six months in advance of an auction of frequency licenses. The office was then responsible for helping any federal agency affected by the auction to find a suitable new frequency and to estimate the cost of such a move.

Under the new law, bidding in the auction could not close until it equaled at least 110 percent of the estimated cost. The money would go into the newly created spectrum fund, which the affected agency could draw upon as it shifted over to a different frequency. Previously, companies negotiated individually to reimburse agencies.

● **"E-911" services.** The law provided for the creation of a joint program — under the Commerce Department's assistant secretary for Communications and Information and the administrator of the National Highway Traffic Safety Administration — to coordinate implementation of enhanced 911 ("E-911") upgrades across the country. E-911 systems enabled public safety operators to pinpoint the location of callers who were using cell phones.

The law authorized grants of up to $250 million per year in fiscal 2005 through 2009 to help states upgrade 911 emergency services. States could use the grants to improve emergency communications planning, make infrastructure and equipment upgrades, and hire and train new personnel. The federal share of each project was limited to 50 percent.

Legislative Action

'E-911' Bill

The Senate Commerce, Science, and Transportation Committee approved its E-911 legislation (S 1250 — S Rept 108-130) on July 17, 2003, but the measure never

BoxScore

Bill:
HR 5419 — PL 108-494

Legislative Action:
House passed HR 5419 by voice vote Nov. 20.
Senate cleared the bill by voice vote Dec. 8.
President signed Dec. 23.

saw floor action. The House passed its version (HR 2898 — H Rept 108-311) by voice vote in November 2003.

The main difference between the bills was the amount to be authorized for grants to states for E-911 upgrades. The Senate measure would have authorized $500 million a year for five years, while the House bill called for $100 million a year over the same timeframe. Negotiators reached a compromise of $250 million late in the 108th Congress, in time to fold the measure into the telecommunications package.

Spectrum Relocation

The House Energy and Commerce Committee approved a spectrum relocation bill (HR 1320 — H Rept 108-137) in April 2003. The House passed the measure, 408-10, the following July. Proponents said the legislation would make it easier to free up spectrum for next-generation wireless services, providing a boost to the beleaguered telecommunications industry. "This is one area where we can immediately assist the nation's economy," said Billy Tauzin, R-La, the chairman of the Energy and Commerce Committee.

The Senate Commerce, Science and Transportation Committee approved the House bill on June 26, 2003, but with an amendment that threatened to kill it (S Rept 108-168). The amendment, sponsored by John E. Sununu, R-N.H., would have guaranteed spectrum to a terrestrial communications company, Northpoint Technology, without a traditional auction. Critics said the amendment was the result of a politically connected company peddling its influence. House Republicans said it doomed the bill's chances.

There was no further action on the bill until late in the second session, when it was rolled into the telecommunications package, with the Northpoint provision stripped out.

E-Rate and Final Action

The last piece of the end-of-session telecom package was the E-Rate measure. Without the bill, sponsors said the Universal Service Administrative Co. might have to increase the fees it charged telecom companies to raise more money. Industry experts said that could result in an increase on phone bills of as much as $12 a month. Against that backdrop, lawmakers were eager to enact the E-Rate fix before adjourning for the year.

Fred Upton, R-Mich., combined it with the E-911 and spectrum bills in a package that he introduced Saturday, Nov. 20, as Congress was rushing to finish its business for the year. The House passed the omnibus bill by voice vote later the same day. The Senate cleared it Dec. 8, also by voice vote.

Senate action was delayed by opposition from two members. McCain insisted on attaching legislation to create a safety commission to oversee professional boxing. Robert C. Byrd, D-W.Va., objected to the spectrum relocation proposal, saying it could infringe on Congress' authority over government spending. Both senators backed off in the final hours before Congress adjourned for the year, after being promised their interests would be addressed at a later date. ◆

Chapter 15

TRADE

Australia Trade Pact Endorsed

In a victory for President Bush, Congress gave overwhelming bipartisan support to a free-trade agreement with Australia — the ninth largest U.S. export market, and a country that supported U.S. efforts in the war on terrorism and in Iraq. Bush signed the bill into law Aug. 3 (HR 4759 — PL 108-286).

The accord was the third such free-trade pact approved by the 108th Congress under special fast-track procedures enacted in 2002 in the Trade Promotion Authority Act (PL 107-210). (*2002 Almanac, 18-3*)

The bill approved the U.S.-Australia Free Trade Agreement, which was signed May 18, 2004, and made the necessary changes to U.S. law. Members cited potential benefits to U.S. manufacturers, farmers and financial service providers, as well as protections for patents and other intellectual property. Free-trade advocates in Congress, however, were upset because the Bush administration sought and won exclusions and protections for U.S. agricultural interests, most notably sugar, beef and dairy producers. Some members also were unhappy that the agreement made no changes to Australia's drug-pricing program.

Highlights

The following were major elements of the U.S.-Australia trade agreement:

● **Tariffs.** Ninety-nine percent of U.S. exports of manufactured goods to Australia became duty-free immediately. Manufactured goods accounted for 93 percent of the value of U.S. exports to Australia, according to the Office of the U.S. Trade Representative (USTR), and the changes were expected to save $300 million in the first year. U.S. tariffs on Australian goods were minimal.

● **Textiles.** U.S. tariffs would be phased out over 15 years for items that met a "yarn forward" rule of origin requiring that the yarn originate in Australia or the United States. Australia produced little yarn, so the change was minimal.

● **Agriculture.** All U.S. agricultural exports gained duty-free access to the Australian market. U.S. exporters had paid $700 million in such duties to Australia in 2003.

U.S. negotiators refused to increase Australia's access to the U.S. sugar market and agreed to only modest reductions in duties on beef and dairy products.

Duties on Australian beef imports that exceeded quota would be phased out over 18 years, a provision that the USTR said would initially increase beef imports by about 0.17 percent of annual U.S. beef production. The agreement slightly increased the overall quota for imports of Australian dairy products. The additional imports were expected to amount to about 0.17 percent of the annual value of U.S.

BoxScore

Bill:
HR 4759 — PL 108-286
Legislative Action:
House passed HR 4759
(H Rept 108-597), 314-109,
on July 14.
Senate cleared the bill, 80-16,
on July 15.
President signed Aug. 3.

dairy production, and about 2 percent of the value of dairy imports. The Bush administration made it clear that without these limits, the deal would not get through Congress.

● **Intellectual property.** The agreement included protections and non-discriminatory treatment for intellectual property and other digital products, such as software, music, text, e-commerce and videos. It barred duties on digital products delivered electronically, such as music and software, and established tougher criminal penalties for end-user piracy and counterfeiting. It also contained stronger protections for copyrighted works, patents and trade secrets.

● **Pharmaceuticals.** The agreement codified an Australian ban on exporting drugs that were purchased under the country's Pharmaceuticals Benefits Scheme (PBS), which subsidizes drugs in Australia. U.S. negotiators unsuccessfully sought to modify the PBS and make Australia's drug pricing more market-based but settled for making the system more transparent by requiring analysis of its impact on drug prices and patent protections.

The U.S. pharmaceutical industry and some lawmakers argued that Australia's drug subsidies made U.S. consumers bear a huge share of research costs and created market disparities.

● **Labor, environment.** The pact included the labor and environmental objectives set out by Congress in the 2002 trade act. It required both countries to enforce their domestic labor and environmental laws, establish a dispute settlement process to enforce such obligations, and create a new enforcement mechanism that included monetary assessments.

Legislative Action

Under fast-track procedures, Congress had 90 legislative days to consider the agreement once it was formally submitted — 45 days for House committees, 15 days for House floor action, and 15 days each for Senate committee and floor votes. Congress could only accept or reject the bill. It could not amend it. The purpose for the expedited process was to assure U.S. trade partners that Congress would not alter a trade agreement once it had been signed.

In exchange for the promise of expedited action, the administration was required to consult with Congress and keep the appropriate committees informed as it negotiated the pact and wrote the bill. As part of that process, both chambers held informal "mock" markups to weigh in on the draft bill before it was formally submitted.

The House Ways and Means Committee approved the draft without amendment June 23, but the Senate Finance

Committee ran into trouble that reflected concerns over the beef and dairy provisions.

On June 23, the committee narrowly adopted an amendment by Kent Conrad, D-N.D., to make it more difficult for the president to waive a mechanism in the pact that was supposed to protect the U.S. beef industry from import surges. Olympia J. Snowe of Maine was the only Republican to support the amendment, giving Conrad a 11-10 majority. Finance Chairman Charles E. Grassley, R-Iowa, issued a statement calling the amendment "entirely unnecessary" and unconstitutional because it would violate a Supreme Court ruling against "legislative vetoes" — provisions that would allow one or both chambers of Congress to block actions of the executive branch.

The following day, the committee rejected the draft, 7-14. The vote was mainly a sign of displeasure with the Conrad amendment, but Snowe joined out of concern that even small increases in dairy imports could be detrimental to some dairy producers in her state. Conrad maintained that the trade agreement was designed more to reward Australia for supporting the U.S.-led war in Iraq than to open markets to U.S. products — an assertion flatly denied by the USTR, which said the agreement offered significant new export opportunities for U.S. manufacturers.

House, Senate Action

The Bush administration formally submitted the bill to Congress July 2, starting the 90-day timetable. The legislation did not include Conrad's amendment.

Ways and Means approved the measure (HR 4759 — H Rept 108-597) by voice vote July 8. Senate Finance approved a companion bill (S 2610 — S Rept 108-316) July 14 by a vote of 17-4, with Conrad still bitterly opposed.

The House passed the bill, 314-109, on July 14, and the Senate cleared the House measure, 80-16, on July 15. (*House vote 375, p. H-124; Senate vote 156, p. S-34*)

Despite the lopsided votes, debate continued over Australian drug pricing, agricultural products and the fast-track process itself.

A small but spirited group of House Democrats and some Senate Republicans, including John McCain of Arizona, blasted the pharmaceutical provisions saying they would tie the hands of lawmakers who might want to relax limits on importing prescription drugs as a way to reduce costs for consumers. Supporters of the pact argued that it did nothing to prevent the United States from enacting drug importation legislation and that Australian law already prohibited the export of drugs purchased within their national health care system.

The fast-track law itself became an issue during the debate, with some legislators warning that there were strains in Congress' confidence that the law was working. Conrad complained that his committee amendment had been ignored and said recent trade agreements had "undermined our jobs and undermined our economic growth."

But Grassley and others praised the administration's consultations with Congress. Sen. Craig Thomas, R-Wyo., acknowledged that he had concerns about the import of additional beef products but saluted the administration for taking those concerns into account during the negotiations. ◆

Trade Pact With Morocco Enacted

Congress in July cleared legislation to implement a free-trade agreement with Morocco. President Bush signed the measure into law Aug. 17 (HR 4842 — PL 108-302).

The U.S.-Morocco Free Trade Agreement was the second such pact endorsed by lawmakers in 2004 and the fourth approved by the 108th Congress. Lawmakers approved a free-trade agreement with Australia in July. Trade agreements with Chile and Singapore won congressional approval in 2003. (*Australia, p. 15-3; Chile, Singapore, 2003 Almanac, p. 19-3*)

Both chambers passed the bill implementing the Morocco pact by broad bipartisan margins. Free-traders said it was a sign of momentum for their goals, although many Democrats maintained that future free-trade pacts with larger countries would be much tougher to pass. Two-way trade between the United States and Morocco was valued at less than $1 billion a year.

BoxScore

Bill:
HR 4842 — PL 108-302
Legislative Action:
Senate passed S 2677, 85-13, on July 21 and deemed HR 4842 cleared, by voice vote, as soon as it was received from the House.
House passed HR 4842 (H Rept 108-627), 323-99, on July 22.
President signed Aug. 17.

The two countries concluded the trade agreement March 2 and signed it at a ceremony in Washington on June 15.

The pact was part of a broader initiative, announced by the Bush administration in May, to promote commercial relationships with certain countries in the Arab world. U.S. Trade Representative (USTR) Robert B. Zoellick laid out the administration's thinking when he notified Congress in 2002 of plans to negotiate the Morocco agreement. "Morocco was one of the first countries to condemn the Sept. 11 terrorist attacks against the United States and has stood by our side ever since," Zoellick wrote. "The administration's commitment to liberalized trade with a leading moderate Arab state supports the regional development of tolerant, open, and more prosperous Muslim societies."

The agreement gave U.S. farmers and ranchers significantly expanded access to Moroccan markets. It also eliminated tariffs on manufactured goods

and services, and updated protections for intellectual property rights.

In a possible foreshadowing of battles to come on other trade agreements, Democrats asked the administration to consider seeking more stringent labor standards than those provided for by existing law, which required trade partners to enforce their respective labor statutes. The administration, citing recent enhancements by Morocco to its labor protection laws, said the existing standard was adequate.

Highlights

The U.S.-Morocco Free Trade Agreement included the following components:

- **Tariffs.** Ninety-five percent of bilateral trade in industrial and consumer goods became duty-free immediately when the agreement became effective. Remaining duties would be lifted within the next nine years.
- **Textiles.** The agreement allowed duty-free trade in textiles and apparel made from U.S. or Moroccan yarn or fabric, with a temporary allowance for apparel containing third-country content while Morocco developed its yarn and fabric production. Morocco accounted for little more than 0.1 percent of total U.S. textiles and apparel imports in 2003.
- **Agriculture.** The pact reduced a variety of tariffs on U.S. agricultural exports to Morocco. Most Moroccan exports to the United States already enjoyed low or no tariffs. However, according to the USTR's office, the United States agreed to limit access to the Moroccan market in sensitive areas such as beef, wheat and poultry to extremely small quantities that could "in no way disrupt the Moroccan market."
- **Services.** The agreement provided market access to most service sectors, including e-commerce, financial, telecommunications, engineering and infrastructure, tourism, environmental and energy sectors.
- **Pharmaceuticals.** Intellectual property protection was strengthened for drug producers from both countries. However, the two countries agreed that this would not "affect the ability of either party to take necessary measures to protect public health by promoting access to medicines for all, in particular concerning cases such as HIV/AIDS, tuberculosis, malaria, and other epidemics as well as circumstances of extreme urgency or national emergency."
- **Labor, environment.** Both countries were required to enforce their domestic labor and environmental laws and to establish a dispute-settlement process to enforce those obligations.

Legislative Action

Congress considered the bill under so-called fast-track procedures authorized in the 2002 Trade Promotion Authority Act (PL 107-210). Fast-track rules allowed expedited action on trade bills: Congress had to accept or reject the implementing legislation and could not amend it. In return, the administration was required to consult with Congress and keep lawmakers informed. As part of that process, committees in both chambers typically held informal "mock" markups to weigh in on a draft of the bill before the White House formally submitted it. Once the bill was submitted, Congress had to complete its work within 90 days. The process was intended to assure U.S. trade partners that Congress would not alter a trade agreement once it had been signed. (*2002 Almanac, 18-3*)

The House Ways and Means Committee approved a draft of the implementing legislation for the Morocco pact by a vote of 23-1 on July 14. The Senate Finance Committee followed suit, 20-1, the same day.

During the Ways and Means session, Sander M. Levin of Michigan, the ranking Democrat on the panel's Trade Subcommittee, sought assurances that drug patent protections in the accord would not deny Moroccans access to generic drugs. He also wanted assurances that newly enacted labor laws in Morocco met international standards.

The White House formally submitted the bill, unchanged, on July 15. However, trade officials pledged to continue working with Levin to address his concerns.

Once the bill was submitted, the two committees held formal markups. Ways and Means approved it, 26-0, on July 19 (H Rept 108-627). Finance approved the same bill (S 2677 — S Rept 108-317) by a vote of 21-0 on July 20.

The Senate passed its bill by a vote of 85-13 the next day. Because the bill was considered a revenue measure, under the Constitution it had to originate in the House. So the Senate agreed by voice vote to deem HR 4842 to be cleared as soon as the House acted. The House passed the measure, 323-99, on July 22. (*Senate vote 159, p. S-35; House vote 413, p. H-134*)

Despite the strong bipartisan support for the agreement, the debate highlighted issues that seemed sure to arise in the 109th Congress, when a Central America pact and other trade agreements were expected to come before lawmakers.

Levin, for example, withheld support until he received assurances from the administration that the deal would not hinder Moroccans' access to generic drugs in emergency situations.

During the July 20 Ways and Means markup, the panel's top Democrat, Charles B. Rangel of New York, asked if the administration would be willing to seek higher labor standards than those provided for by existing law. The law stated that signatories to trade agreements with the United States had to enforce their respective labor laws. Many Democrats wanted to make the core labor standards of the International Labor Organization enforceable parts of trade agreements.

The more Rangel pressed John Veroneau, general counsel for the USTR's office, the more Veroneau demurred, saying his office took its guidance from existing trade law, which reflected a "delicate balance" with regard to labor standards. ◆

Chapter 16

TRANSPORTATION & INFRASTRUCTURE

Still No Agreement on Highways

A six-year reauthorization of the 1998 surface transportation law was left stranded in a House-Senate conference at the end of the year. Lawmakers put off to the 109th Congress the job of resolving differences with the White House over total spending and among member over the allocation of funds to state highway programs to the 109th Congress.

The bill was intended as the successor to the Transportation Equity Act for the 21st Century (PL 105-178), which expired on Sept. 30, 2003. Since then, federal highway, public transportation and road safety programs had been running on a series of temporary extensions. To give the 109th Congress time to act, lawmakers cleared a further extension good through May 31, 2005. The extension kept the program going but made it difficult for state agencies to make long-term highway and transit plans.

Lawmakers began the year on a collision course with the White House over the cost of the bill. President Bush laid down a marker in his fiscal 2005 budget of $256 billion for surface transportation over six years. The administration's proposal, with the exception of some general funds for mass transit programs, was largely based on the money expected to flow into the Highway Trust Fund, which was financed almost entirely by highway fuel taxes.

Despite veto threats, both chambers exceeded that total by veto-proof margins. The Senate bill (S 1072), which passed in February, called for $318.9 billion over six years, about 25 percent more than Bush wanted. The House passed a $283.2 billion version (HR 3550) in April; though smaller than the Senate bill, it still exceeded Bush's limit by about 11 percent.

Sponsors argued that the legislation was "paid for" — that it would use money from the Highway Trust Fund and would not dip into the general Treasury. The Bush administration disagreed. It called the legislation a test of fiscal discipline for Congress and warned that Bush would veto anything he considered excessive.

The administration also warned it would not agree with increasing the 18.4 cents-per-gallon federal tax on gasoline, nearly all of which went into the Highway Trust Fund, or with indexing it for inflation. It also opposed using long-term bonds or using money from the general fund to pay for highway and transit projects. That did not leave many options for boosting highway revenue.

But highway spending was popular in Congress. Members of both parties argued it was needed not only to untangle congestion, but also to create jobs. Some of the strongest arguments in favor of increased highway spending came from Bush's fellow Republicans. Senate Majority Leader Bill Frist, R-Tenn., said the $318.9 billion Senate bill was "an essen-

BoxScore

Bill:

HR 3550

Legislative Action:

Senate passed S 1072, 76-21, on Feb. 12; it subsequently passed HR 3550 by voice vote after substituting the text of S 1072.

House passed HR 3550 (H Rept 108-452), 357-65, on April 2.

tial investment in moving our economy forward while also making it safe for us to use our highways and our intercity rail systems."

By the end of the session, most Republicans trying to reconcile the House and Senate bills had coalesced around a bottom line of $299 billion — an amount that the White House was reportedly willing to accept.

But negotiators could not agree on a formula for allocating the highway funds to the states. The differences were regional rather than partisan, dividing areas with high traffic congestion and those with wide-open spaces. It was a battle between "donor" states mostly in the Sunbelt and the Midwest — that collected more in federal gas tax revenue than they received in highway construction aid, and the "donee" or recipient states in the Northeast and West whose federal highway aid outstripped the taxes collected at their pumps.

For most members of Congress, the deciding factor in whether to support a highway bill was how much their state or district would receive. The inability to agree on a formula sealed the bill's fate in the 108th Congress.

Highlights

The following were among the main issues as Congress debated the authorization bills:

- **Total spending.** The Senate bill called for $318.9 billion in contract authority over six years, with a $297 billion limit on actual spending, or obligations. The House-passed version totaled $283.2 billion in contract authority, with a $275 billion obligational limit. The vast majority of the spending was for core highway programs.
- **Distribution.** The Senate bill included a guarantee that by fiscal 2009 each state would receive at least 95 cents in highway aid for every dollar in taxes it collected for the Highway Trust Fund. The House bill retained the existing guarantee of a 90.5 percent return, although it included a so-called reopener clause aimed at boosting the rate to 95 percent. Most, but not all, highway aid was distributed according to formula. Much of the non-formula aid was for "high priority projects" — earmarked projects requested by individual members.
- **Reopener clause.** In an attempt to force an increase in the authorization level, the House bill included a provision to stop most highway funding at the end of fiscal 2005 unless legislation was enacted to raise the minimum federal guarantee for each state to 95 percent by fiscal 2009 — without reducing the dollar amount received by any state.
- **Revenue.** Both bills included provisions to increase the flow of revenue to the Highway Trust Fund to make more

money available for highway projects.

One of the main devices used in both bills was to restructure the existing tax break for producers of ethanol. Instead of a partial exemption from the gas tax — which came out of revenue going to the trust fund — producers would receive a tax credit paid from the general fund. The trust fund would also get about 2.5 cents-per-gallon of the tax on gasohol that had been going to the general fund.

These and other changes were estimated to add $31.6 billion to the Highway Trust Fund over 10 years under the House bill and $49.3 billion under the Senate version.

To offset the revenue loss to the general fund, the bills proposed to close loopholes and crack down on fuel fraud. An assumption — that the ethanol credit would expire after 2010 — alone was credited with bringing $4.3 billion into the Treasury. The ethanol and revenue-raising provisions eventually were enacted in the corporate tax bill (PL 108-357). (*Corporate tax bill, p. 13-3*)

Background

Transportation authorizers in both chambers began work on the six-year bill in 2003, but the legislation did not reach the floor in either chamber and all the major problems were delayed for the second session. (*2003 Almanac, p. 20-7*)

The biggest obstacle was money. A large majority of lawmakers from both parties wanted to continue or even exceed the spending growth achieved under TEA-21, the 1998 law. TEA-21 was the largest investment in transportation spending the country had ever seen. At $217.9 billion, it was 40 percent more than its predecessor, the Intermodal Surface Transportation Efficiency Act (ISTEA) of 1991 (PL 102-240). (*1991 Almanac, p. 137; 1998 Almanac, p. 24-3*)

But the situation had changed since then. Times were flush in 1998, and the budget was in the black. Gas tax revenues were pouring into the Highway Trust Fund; the challenge for transportation authorizers was to get that money released for highway projects. (The lion's share of the trust fund came from the 18.4-cents-per-gallon federal gasoline tax. A higher tax, 24.4-cents-per-gallon, was imposed on diesel fuel and kerosene. Other revenue sources included a retail sales tax on heavy highway vehicles, a manufacturers' excise tax on heavy vehicle tires and an annual use tax on heavy vehicles.)

By 2003, mostly because of the lackluster economy, gas tax revenue was flat and the trust fund did not have enough money to pay for all the projects Congress wanted to fund. Lawmakers faced a choice of authorizing a more modest expansion of highway projects or raising taxes, a solution that was anathema to the White House.

Bush's answer was to hold spending down; at the time, the White House was pushing a $247 billion plan that did not satisfy most members of either party. "There simply isn't enough funding in the administration's bill to address our efforts to address our nation's growing congestion problems," said House Transportation and Infrastructure Chairman Don Young, R-Alaska.

Young was proposing a $375 billion, six-year reauthorization that included an increase in the federal gas tax. With strong opposition from both the administration and the House GOP leadership, Young waited until the end of the

year to even introduce his bill (HR 3550). The Ways and Means Committee had yet to write the tax portion.

The Senate Environment and Public Works Committee approved a $221.7 billion package of highway provisions in November (S 1072 — S Rept 108-222). When all the pieces of the Senate bill were assembled, the total was expected to reach $311 billion. The committee promised each state a return of at least 95 percent on its contributions to the Highway Trust Fund by 2009; each donee state would see 10 percent growth in its returns over the life of the bill. The revenue provisions were left for the Finance Committee.

The other obstacle to completing the bill was agreeing on a formula for distributing core highway funds, always a hard-fought issue. TEA-21 guaranteed that each state would receive federal highway aid equal to at least 90.5 percent of the federal highway taxes it contributed. The donor states wanted a better deal, and both the House and Senate bills promised to increase the guarantee to 95 percent. Lawmakers from states that benefited under the existing system were not eager to acquiesce, however, and authorizers were not ready to provide specific formulas.

Senate Committee Action

The Senate bill was assembled in 2004 from legislation written by several committees. Some acted in 2003; others were still completing their work as the Senate started floor debate Feb. 2.

• After approving much of its bill in 2003, the Environment and Public Works Committee in January released its long-awaited state-by-state, year-by-year breakdown showing the distribution of formula highway funds. The committee said the average state would receive about 36 percent more money under the bill than under TEA-21. However some states, including Rhode Island, New Hampshire and Pennsylvania, stood to get a cut in their rate of return.

• The Finance Committee approved a package of tax provisions by a vote of 17-4 on Feb. 2 as the Senate was beginning floor action on the bill. The committee devised a plan to increase the revenue going into the Highway Trust Fund by $35 billion over six years — without raising the federal gas tax. The revenue was needed to fill the gap between the $256 billion limit on obligations in Bush's 2004 plan and the $297 billion limit that the Senate bill was proposing.

Under the Finance plan, a major part of the revenue would come from shifting the cost of some transportation tax breaks, such as the partial tax exemption for ethanol-blended fuels, from the trust fund to the general Treasury. The committee proposed to replenish the Treasury with a series of adjustments in the tax code, including curtailing certain tax shelters.

A vocal minority of senators agreed with Jon Kyl, R-Ariz., who criticized the plan as "sleight of hand."

• The Banking, Housing and Urban Affairs Committee approved $56.5 billion for public transit programs by voice vote Feb. 3. The committee included several changes in federal transit programs sought by the Bush administration, including inducements to local communities to develop bus rapid transit as an alternative to subways and light rail, increased funding for rural transit systems and changes intended to give local communities more flexibility in their use of transit funding.

Chairman Richard C. Shelby, R-Ala., won voice vote approval for an amendment that included language to modify administration efforts to streamline environmental reviews of transit construction. A summary said the committee "returned to current law for air quality conformity and environmental streamlining." The amendment also doubled, to $2.2 billion, the authorization for transit formula grants, taking $1 billion from discretionary spending accounts.

The amendment also proposed to phase out transit operating subsidies for cities of more than 200,000 people by fiscal 2007. They would receive 50 percent of their operating funds in fiscal 2005 and 25 percent in 2006.

• The Commerce, Science and Transportation Committee, which was responsible for safety programs, had given voice vote approval in June 2003 to provisions (S 1978 — S Rept 108-215) authorizing $3.5 billion over six years for the National Highway Traffic Safety Administration (NHTSA) and $12 billion for Amtrak. The measure included a provision, opposed by vehicle manufacturers, to require the NHTSA to establish rollover crashworthiness standards for SUVs and other large passenger vehicles.

Senate Floor Action

The Senate passed the combined bill (S 1072) by a vote of 76-21 on Feb. 12. The six-year measure provided $318.9 billion in contract authority with an obligational limit of $297 billion. (*Senate vote 14, p. S-7*)

The day before the vote, the White House issued a statement warning that if the bill were sent to Bush, his advisers would recommend a veto because the total exceeded the president's $256 billion limit and because the bill included Amtrak provisions, which the administration said belonged in a separate bill.

Backers said that the funding level was inextricably linked to the state allocation of highway money developed by the Environment and Public Works Committee. As long as there was enough money, even a small decline in a state's percentage could still translate into an increase in highway dollars. In addition, they said, the $318.9 billion would allow significant funding increases for programs not based on formula allocations to the states.

"As a fiscal conservative, I believe in spending more in certain areas — defense and infrastructure," said James M. Inhofe, R-Okla., chairman of the Environment and Public Works Committee. "I favor spending more money right now in this climate on roads and bridges. It's very important."

Not all senators saw their states as winners. Eight states that were paying less into the trust fund than they got in aid were slated to become donor states by 2009. They were Connecticut, Iowa, Kansas, Nebraska, New Hampshire, New York, Pennsylvania and Wisconsin. Together those states contributed eight "no" votes on the bill. Only two opponents — Larry E. Craig of Idaho and Jeff Sessions of Alabama — were from states that would be donees in 2009.

Some members objected to the bill's overall cost. "It's too much money, it's not paid for, and it sticks it to my state. So on all three counts this is a very bad bill," said Rick Santorum, R-Pa. Santorum was one of eight senators — including Budget Chairman, Judd Gregg, R-N.H., Kyl and Don Nickles, R-Okla. — who had asked the leadership to wait on the bill until "its full impact on the deficit can be determined,

considered and debated."

The leadership proceeded Feb. 2 only after winning on a cloture motion, which limited debate on whether to take up the bill. The vote was 75-11. (*Senate vote 7, p. S-6*)

During the debate that followed, the Senate:

• Rejected, 17-78, an attempt by Kay Bailey Hutchison, R-Texas, to allocate $9.25 billion to increase formula highway funding so that all states would be guaranteed a 91 percent return in fiscal 2005, rising to 95 percent by 2009. (*Senate vote 11, p. S-7*)

• Rejected, 20-78, a proposal by Kyl to reduce the total cost of the bill to $256 billion to match Bush's request. (*Senate vote 13, p. S-7*)

House Committee Action

The House bill combined provisions drafted by three committees.

• The core of the bill was written by the House Transportation and Infrastructure Committee, which approved a scaled-back version of Young's proposal by voice vote March 24 (HR 3550 — H Rept 108-452, Part 1). The measure included $283.2 billion in contract authority over six years with an obligational limit of $275 billion — a far cry from the $375 billion that Young and his colleagues had insisted on for nearly a year. But the bill also included a provision aimed at forcing Congress to revisit highway funding levels in 2005.

"This battle has just begun," Young said. "We are going to be back next Jan. 5. . . . It's just that we've been dealt a pair of deuces against a full house right now, and I've learned something about playing cards and knowing when to fold 'em and when to come back to play another hand."

Young accepted the reduced authorization level under orders from Speaker J. Dennis Hastert, R-Ill., who had grown impatient with the lengthy dispute and the need for short-term extensions to keep highway programs alive. After failing to get satisfaction from White House aides, Hastert talked directly with Bush in early March, telling him the House would move a $275 billion, six-year bill.

Hastert said the president did not endorse the figure but did not threaten to veto it either. Transportation Committee member Steven C. LaTourette, R-Ohio, who also was at the White House, said Bush reiterated his opposition to a bill that added to the deficit, increased taxes or relied on borrowing. "If you can get me a bigger number without doing those things, I'm willing to talk," LaTourette quoted the president as saying.

As a small protest, the committee also gave voice vote approval to a bill (HR 3994) that reflected Young's original $375 billion proposal.

More significant was the so-called reopener provision that would cut off funding for highway programs in fiscal 2006, unless a new law was enacted that authorized enough funding to allow each state to receive at least 95 percent of the money it contributed to the Highway Trust Fund by fiscal 2009. Supporters said the clause would be dropped in conference if the two sides agreed on the more generous, $318.9 billion funding level in the Senate bill. The provision was important in retaining the support of committee members from donor states.

Young also found enough room in the smaller bill to au-

thorize $11 billion for members' "high priority" projects. The bill listed 2,838 such projects.

"Equity" in distributing highway money was the most contentious issue during the markup. John L. Mica, R-Fla., offered — but later withdrew — an amendment on behalf of the donor states that would have enlarged the pool of money distributed by formula to include the $11 billion in earmarked projects and $6.6 billion in the bill for "projects of regional and national significance," a category that included large projects at key interstate bottlenecks.

The effect would been to reduce each state's formula allocation by the amount it received in earmarked projects, rather than using them to supplement the formula funds. Young told Mica that members from donee states would reject the bill if the amendment were included. To satisfy both sides, Young said, "What we have to do is increase the size of the pot."

• The Ways and Means Committee gave voice vote approval March 17 to a bill (HR 3971 — H Rept 108-444) that was estimated to increase revenue for highway programs by $17.7 billion in fiscal 2004 through 2009. The measure by Chairman Bill Thomas, R-Calif., proposed to increase trust fund revenue by shifting the cost of ethanol subsidies to the general Treasury, by cracking down on fuel tax evasion and through other, smaller tax adjustments.

• The Science Committee on Feb. 4 approved a bill (HR 3551 — H Rept 108-662, Part 1) authorizing surface transportation research and development grants for fiscal 2004 through 2009.

House Floor Action

The House passed the $283.2 billion bill April 2 by a vote of 357-65, despite a veto threat issued by the White House three days earlier. (*House vote 114, p. H-40*)

In warning of a veto, the Office of Management and Budget cited the bill's cost, $27 billion above the president's request, and the reopener provision, which it said was "an attempt to obtain significantly higher funding levels by threatening a shutdown of the highway program next year." The statement reiterated the administration's insistence that the bill be paid for out of the Highway Fund without increasing taxes or issuing bonds and without dipping into the general fund.

Before bringing the bill to the floor, Young and his committee added hundreds of pages of last-minute changes, including fresh earmarks, changes in the environmental review process for road projects and billions of dollars in tax breaks that had been approved by the Ways and Means Committee but had little to do with highways. The changes were made as part of the rule for floor debate (H Res 593 — H Rept 108-456).

"In less than [24 hours], the transportation bill has gained close to $1 billion in political earmarks," said Keith Ashdown, vice president of policy and communications for the group Taxpayers for Common Sense.

The tax proposals included a two-year extension of a law that allowed small businesses to deduct up to $100,000 for business equipment in the year it was purchased. The bill also proposed to exempt more small companies from the corporate alternative minimum tax.

During the floor debate, the House rejected, 170-254, an attempt by Johnny Isakson, R-Ga., and other donor state members to shift $17.7 billion into the pool of money distributed by formula to the states. "The conference committee has got to recognize that this is a serious issue," said Isakson, who had led a group of donor-state members through a week of political angling to get the funding redistributed in a way more favorable to them. (*House vote 112, p. H-40*)

Conference

Inhofe, who chaired the House-Senate conference, set out to complete the six-year bill before Congress broke in late July for the political conventions and the August recess. But the target date slipped from the summer to the fall and then vanished as conferees struggled over money issues and Congress shifted its attention to finishing the annual appropriations bills and to agreeing on a plan to overhaul the intelligence community.

It took the Senate nearly two months after the House passed its bill just to appoint conferees. Minority Leader Tom Daschle, D-S.D. — objecting that the GOP had excluded Democrats from negotiations on other key legislation — refused to cooperate until he won a pledge from Frist that Democrats would have a say in the final bill.

Conferees met in June and July, but they could not get beyond the central problem: Unless they could go well above the White House funding level, they could not meet the demand of donor states for a minimum 95 percent return without cutting the dollars going to recipient states. "It is clear that a constrained funding level produces winners and losers, pitting state against state and region against region," said Sen. James M. Jeffords, I-Vt.

Though both chambers had passed their bills by more than enough votes to override a veto, GOP leaders said that was as far as their party's defiance would go. They were not prepared to hand the president an embarrassing defeat, especially in an election year.

House GOP leaders floated several compromises, but senators of both parties, backed by transportation, business and labor groups, insisted the $318.9 billion in their bill was the minimum needed. Conferees also considered whether to change the number of programs covered by the minimum guarantee, or possibly reduce the minimum guarantee to each state, but none of the proposals satisfied both donors and donees.

Then in late July, when hopes of progress before the conventions were fading, Thomas offered a $298.9 billion bill that he said the White House would accept. That might not seem adequate to conferees, he said, but "the president will sign it." Senate conferees initially rejected the offer. "I can assure you that if we had a Senate vote on this, it will fail," said Inhofe, but he also promised to study the plan.

When Congress reconvened in September, Inhofe said he had decided to proceed with a $299 billion highway bill without Democratic backing. "I think we can get it without their support," he was quoted as saying. Infuriated Senate Democrats said Inhofe was violating Frist's agreement to strike no deals unless they were at the table.

But Inhofe pressed ahead. "When the White House comes up three times as far as we came down, I would say that is a successful negotiation," Inhofe said. "We went

down 6 percent; they came up 17 percent."

The evolving plan included a guarantee that states would get back in highway and transit aid at least 92.2 percent of the money they contributed to the Highway Trust Fund. Although the plan fell short of the 95 percent guarantee that donor-state legislators sought, it did meet their demand that funds for road projects earmarked by legislators be counted in the formula allocation to the states, rather than awarded on top of it.

House leaders had enough conferees prepared to sign onto the compromise, but Inhofe could not corral enough support in the Senate to overcome objections that Western states and public transit programs were being short-changed.

On Sept. 30, Congress cleared an eight-month extension of existing surface transportation programs — effectively conceding it was not likely to reach agreement on the six-year bill. Republican conferees continued to hope for a breakthrough in the lame-duck session, but the failure to satisfy donor states, along with partisan sniping over who was to blame for the impasse, ended the effort.

Ethanol Tax Provisions Enacted

Although the surface transportation bill did not become law, several of the main tax provisions were enacted as part of the corporate tax bill, which was signed Oct. 22.

In place of the partial exemption from the 18.4 cents-per-gallon gasoline tax, manufacturers of ethanol fuel received an equivalent tax credit, thereby shifting the burden of the tax break from the Highway Trust Fund to the General Fund. The result, according to Senate Finance Chairman Charles E. Grassley, R-Iowa, was an additional $18.9 billion for the trust fund over the coming six years. Another provision in the bill was expected to add $1 billion a year to the Trust Fund by cracking down on fuel tax evasion schemes.

Transportation authorizers hoped that with more revenue flowing into the trust fund, they would find it easier in the 109th Congress to pay for a new six-year highway bill. ◆

Hill Undecided on Amtrak's Future

Congress appropriated $1.2 billion for Amtrak in fiscal 2005, about the same as in fiscal 2004. But lawmakers once again postponed decisions about the future of the cash-strapped national passenger railroad.

The best chance for Congress to set policy for Amtrak came and went early in 2004 when some lawmakers considered trying to attach an Amtrak overhaul to the surface transportation bill (HR 3550). House Republican leaders nixed the idea, which probably would have drawn a presidential veto threat. (*Surface transportation, p. 16-3*)

The last Amtrak authorization was enacted in 1997 (PL 105-134) and expired in 2002. Attempts to enact a new authorization had failed because lawmakers could not agree on the proper direction for the government-owned corporation. Amtrak critics, including the Bush administration, wanted to see the passenger rail service privatized, forcing it to respond to market forces and survive without government aid. Others saw the railroad as a public service entity that should continue to receive federal subsidies. (*1997 Almanac, p. 3-22*)

John McCain, R-Ariz., introduced the White House plan in a bill (S 1501) that would have broken Amtrak into three operating companies, which eventually could be privatized. It would have handed much of the cost and responsibility for operating and maintaining rail lines to the states and discontinued the federal subsidies that had funded Amtrak since its creation.

A competing Senate bill (S 1505) by Republicans Kay Bailey Hutchison of Texas, Trent Lott of Mississippi, Conrad Burns of Montana and Olympia J. Snowe of Maine would have retained Amtrak's general structure, authorizing the service at $60 billion over six years — $48 billion of it from issuing tax-exempt bonds. Both bills met with lukewarm interest.

Keeping Amtrak Alive

The fiscal 2005 Transportation-Treasury bill, which cleared as part of the omnibus spending package (PL 108-447), funded Amtrak at $1.2 billion, about the same as the 2004 level but $317 million more than the House or Bush wanted. It also directed the railroad and the Transportation Department to agree on a schedule for Amtrak to repay a $100 million federal loan that had been deferred for a number of years. If Amtrak and the department could not reach a deal in 60 days, the loan was to come due. (*Appropriations, p. 2-43*)

David L. Gunn, Amtrak's president and chief executive officer, had said Amtrak needed $1.8 billion a year through fiscal 2009 to continue safe operations while starting to deal with a backlog of maintenance needs, but a spokesman said the rail service could "muddle through."

Though Amtrak got more funding than many Republicans wanted, it came with multiple strings, including a requirement for detailed financial reports to Congress. The law also directed the Transportation Department to create a procedure for states to follow if they wanted to privatize portions of Amtrak's routes; $2.5 million in Amtrak funding could be diverted to implement such a program.

On Nov. 18, two days before the Senate cleared the omnibus spending bill, the Transportation Department's inspector general issued a report warning that Amtrak could not keep postponing critical infrastructure repairs. "Continued deferral brings Amtrak closer to a major point of failure on the system, but no one knows where or when such a failure will occur," the report said. Decrying the lack of leadership from Capitol Hill, the report called for Congress "to provide clear direction for Amtrak's operating and capital investment priorities as well as federal funding levels in reauthorization legislation." ◆

Transportation Security Bills Stall

Despite warnings from the bipartisan Sept. 11 commission, efforts by Congress to improve the security of the nation's railway, public transit and port facilities were only marginally successful. Bills to enhance rail and transit security were left unfinished; the fiscal 2005 spending bill for the Department of Homeland Security included $150 million in grants for rail and train security. The Senate passed a bill to improve port security, but the measure died in the House. Several aviation security-related provisions were folded into the intelligence overhaul bill, which cleared in the lame-duck session.

In its widely read July 22 report, the National Commission on Terrorist Attacks Upon the United States found that since the Sept. 11, 2001, terrorist attacks, "about 90 percent of the nation's $5 billion annual investment in transportation security has gone to aviation, to fight the last war." The commission warned that "while commercial aviation remains a possible target, terrorists may turn their attention to other modes. Opportunities to do harm are as great, or greater, in maritime or surface transportation."

According to the Senate Banking, Housing and Urban Affairs Committee, the federal government was spending $9.16 per airline passenger per year on enhanced security measures, but less than a penny a year for each of the millions of people who used the nation's railroads, mass transit, interstate highways and seaports.

To many lawmakers, however, protecting thousands of miles of railroad tracks and highways and dozens of sprawling seaports seemed prohibitively expensive and physically impossible. Lawmakers and industries also worried about the effect that greater security might have on the flow of commerce and travel. Shipping companies, for instance, balked at paying new fees to finance port security.

Jurisdictional disputes and the time spent on the failed highway bill also slowed efforts in 2004.

Rail and Public Transit

Concern over the security of U.S. railroads was heightened by the March 11 terrorist bombing of commuter trains in Madrid that killed nearly 200 people.

● **Senate bills.** John McCain, R-Ariz., responded April 1 with a bill (S 2273) to authorize about $1.2 billion for rail security improvements through fiscal 2009, including about $670 million for Amtrak to secure rail tunnels along the populous Northeast Corridor.

McCain's Commerce, Science and Transportation Committee approved the bill by voice vote April 8 (S Rept 108-278). The Senate passed the measure by voice vote Oct. 1, but the House did not act on it.

McCain criticized what he said had been fragmented and modestly funded efforts to address rail security since Sept. 11. The Homeland Security Department, he said, "has not completed a vulnerability assessment for the rail system, nor is there an integrated security plan that reflects the unique characteristics of passenger and freight rail operations."

The bill directed the Homeland Security Department to complete an assessment of railroad security vulnerabilities within 180 days of enactment. It also called for a pilot program to determine the feasibility of screening rail passengers, baggage and cargo.

The Senate passed a separate bill Oct. 1 to enhance security on public transit systems. The measure (S 2884), introduced by Richard C. Shelby, R-Ala., passed by voice vote.

It authorized a total of $3.5 billion through fiscal 2007 for grants to public transportation agencies for security improvements. It also designated the Homeland Security Department as the lead agency in transportation security matters, with authority to distribute the grants.

The bill directed Homeland Security and the Federal Transit Administration, which was part of the Transportation Department, to draft a memorandum of understanding outlining the security responsibilities for each. Shelby hoped this would help resolve jurisdictional questions between the two departments. But those same jurisdictional issues made the bill a difficult fit in the House, where the chairmen of the Transportation and Infrastructure Committee and the Select Committee on Homeland Security were vying for control of transportation security issues.

● **House bills.** Alaska Republican Don Young, who chaired the House Transportation and Infrastructure Committee, introduced a bill that would have authorized $3.5 billion over three years for rail and bus security. But it would have given control over transit security grants to the Transportation Department. Young was fighting to keep homeland security issues related to transportation under his committee's jurisdiction.

The Transportation and Infrastructure Committee approved the bill by voice vote Sept. 29 (HR 5082 — H Rept 108-746), but the measure went no further.

Young also introduced a bill to authorize about $1.1 billion through fiscal 2009 for rail security, including more than $600 million to improve the safety of tunnels used by Amtrak and commuter railroads. No action was taken on it.

● **Intelligence law.** The intelligence overhaul law (PL 108-458) included provisions directing the Homeland Security Department to report to Congress within 180 days on its progress in completing the infrastructure vulnerability and risk assessments. The law also charged the department with developing a national transportation security strategy that identified critical transportation facilities, set priorities and prescribed the best means for defending the facilities against terrorist attacks. The department was told to report to Congress on its progress by April 1, 2005.

Port Security

The Senate passed a bill (S 2279 — S Rept 108-274) to enhance port security, but only after dropping a proposed new user fee to help pay for it. The bill, which passed by voice vote Sept. 29, provided civil penalties for vessels that violated the 2002 port security law. It required the Homeland Security Department to submit a report to Congress on

the progress made installing radiation detectors at seaports, as well as an assessment of how well foreign seaports were screening cargo. The bill also required that the department re-evaluate its method for inspecting international cargo containers and assess the quality of security on cruise ships.

As introduced by Ernest F. Hollings, D-S.C., the bill included user fees on cargo and passenger vessels as a way to help pay for enhanced port security. But the Senate Commerce Committee, where Hollings was the ranking member, dropped the user fee before approving the bill by voice vote April 8. The amendment to strip out the user fees was offered by Trent Lott, R-Miss., and adopted 13-10.

The fees would have helped pay for mandates in the 2002 port security law (PL 107-295), also chiefly written by Hollings. That law was enacted only after its user fee language was deleted in conference.

Lott said the U.S. Customs Service already collected about $15 billion in duties on cargo each year that could be dedicated to maritime programs. Hollings did not object to the idea, but the Commerce Committee did not have jurisdiction over Customs fees.

Aviation Security

The intelligence overhaul law included a title on transportation security, most of which was devoted to improving security on cargo and passenger planes. The law included provisions requiring the use of biometric screening system at airports and testing of a new passenger screening system that would run names through "no fly" lists and allow passengers to dispute their inclusion on the list. Other provisions required airport employees to undergo screening, called for a system to screen passengers and carry-on bags for explosives, and urged the president to pursue efforts to limit the easy availability of shoulder-fired missiles that could threaten airplanes on takeoff and landing. *(Intelligence, p. 11-3)* ◆

Chapter 17

NASA, POSTAL SERVICE, WELFARE

Congress Debates NASA's Future

The Senate Commerce, Science and Transportation Committee approved a five-year, $87.1 billion NASA reauthorization bill that reflected President Bush's ambitious new plans for human space exploration. But many lawmakers remained concerned about the potential cost of Bush's proposal, the lack of details and the fate of existing NASA programs that would have to be scrapped to pay for it. Without a consensus on NASA's long-term mission, the bill went no further.

Bush's space initiative, announced Jan. 14, aimed to shift NASA's long-term focus from the space shuttle and the International Space Station to the creation of a new manned space vehicle that would allow astronauts to return to the moon as early as 2015, and go on to explore Mars by 2030. Bush said the venture would cost $12 billion over the next five years, but about $11 billion of it would be reallocated from other NASA programs. Specifically, Bush proposed to:

• Complete work on the International Space Station by 2010, at which point the space shuttle would be retired.

• Develop a new manned exploration vehicle that would be ready by 2014.

• Return to the moon as soon as 2015 and no later than 2020.

• Carry out robotic missions to the moon, similar to those that sent images back to Earth from Mars, to explore the lunar surface beginning no later than 2008.

• Conduct extended lunar missions as early as 2015, with the goal of living and working there for increasingly extended periods.

• Use the moon as a jumping off point for manned exploration of Mars.

Lawmakers were slow to rally behind Bush's plan. The Senate committee approved its bill after 15 hearings and considerable debate about NASA's future. There was particular concern about the projected four-year gap in the ability to launch payloads and people into space. Members also questioned whether the space station would really be completed in 2010 when the shuttle would be retired, and some worried about protecting workers who would be laid off in their districts.

However, retiring the shuttle in 2010 was also a monetary concern. The panel that investigated the accident of the shuttle *Columbia* recommended that NASA take the costly step of re-inspecting its shuttle fleet and certifying it as safe if the vehicles were to fly beyond 2010.

In the House, lawmakers on the Science Committee, which had jurisdiction over NASA, were drafting their own bill to be introduced in 2005. A House aide said the committee "couldn't have less interest" in the Senate measure. "We think Congress and NASA need to make some tough choices about what the priorities are and what the pacing

BoxScore

Bill:
S 2541

Legislative Action:
Senate Commerce, Science and Transportation Committee approved S 2541 (S Rept 108-418) by voice vote Sept. 22.

should be," the aide said. "Just giving almost carte blanche approval to a 20-year plan at this point we don't think is the right way to proceed."

Although the reauthorization bill was stymied, Bush's Nov. 2 re-election victory, combined with support from House Majority Leader Tom DeLay, R-Texas, helped nudge appropriators in the direction the White House wanted. The fiscal 2005 year-end omnibus (PL 108-447) boosted NASA's budget to $16.2 billion, just $44 million shy of what Bush requested. The bill also gave NASA "unrestrained" authority to transfer money within its accounts, a rare exception for any agency. (*Appropriations, p. 2-47*)

Legislative Action

Senate Committee Action

The Senate Commerce, Science and Transportation Committee approved its bill embracing Bush's plan (S 2541 — S Rept 108-418) by voice vote Sept. 22.

The bill was introduced by Sam Brownback, R-Kan., who chaired the subcommittee that had jurisdiction over NASA, and committee Chairman John McCain, R-Ariz. As approved by the committee, it authorized $87.1 billion for NASA through fiscal 2009. It directed NASA to take specific steps to achieve the mileposts outlined by Bush, including plans to retire the space shuttle upon completion of the International Space Station in 2010 and to have a new space vehicle operational by 2014. The committee-approved bill included $744 million in earmarks.

The potential gap in the country's ability to transport humans to and from space worried members of the committee. Like many lawmakers, they were loath to rely on hitching rides to the space station from other nations, such as Russia. "I am not convinced that a four-year gap in U.S. manned space flight is sound policy and, more importantly, I am convinced that this time schedule is too optimistic," Sen. Christopher S. Bond, R-Mo., said at a March 11 hearing.

Sean O'Keefe, NASA's administrator, responded by saying the gap could be covered by existing technologies, including the rocket boosters that were used to propel the space shuttle into orbit and unmanned Defense Department rockets. However, O'Keefe's suggestions would only be adequate for propelling cargo — not humans — into space.

During the markup, the committee adopted several amendments by voice vote, including proposals:

• By Kay Bailey Hutchison, R-Texas, to require NASA to report to Congress on the costs of extending the space shuttle program's life past 2010. Hutchison, whose district included the Lyndon B. Johnson Space Center in Houston,

was among those concerned about the anticipated gap in U.S. capability for manned space flight.

• By Bill Nelson, D-Fla., to require NASA to report to Congress on the costs of expanding the U.S. crew compliment on the space station from two to six. Nelson's state was home to the Kennedy Space Center and its launch pads at Cape Canaveral.

• By Nelson to require that once the shuttle was retired, NASA find new jobs within the agency for workers whose

jobs were centered on the shuttle. The proposal was a subject of considerable debate. McCain criticized the amendment as micromanaging. He said he would reluctantly support it but would seek to delete it in conference if NASA disliked the language.

McCain did not get that opportunity. With the death of the bill at the end of the Congress, authorizers would have to start over, introducing and marking up a new NASA reauthorization bill in the 109th Congress. ◆

Postal Service Overhaul Dies

Despite bipartisan support in three congressional committees, legislation to overhaul U.S. Postal Service operations did not reach the floor in either chamber and died at the end of the session. The chief obstacle was a White House objection to a provision that would have transferred responsibility for about $27 billion in military retirement benefits for postal employees to the Treasury.

Proponents of the postal overhaul argued that if no action were taken, the debt-burdened Postal Service would fall into what Susan Collins, R-Maine, Senate Government Affairs chairwoman, called a "death spiral" of decreasing mail volume and increasing rates. Lawmakers said the financial decline could threaten the service's long-term ability to deliver mail at affordable rates. A presidential commission bolstered those claims in 2003.

The 730,000-employee Postal Service was struggling because of the increased use of e-mail, a decline in first-class postage sales, expensive benefits packages for employees and tough competition from private companies, such as FedEx Corp. and United Parcel Service Inc. (UPS). The agency was $5 billion in debt to the Treasury, carried $5 billion in long-term liabilities for retirement costs, had $7 billion in workers' compensation liabilities and a retiree health care liability of roughly $57 billion.

"This has to be one time when we don't wait for the free-falling crisis so often necessary to garner attention in Congress," said John M. McHugh, R-N.Y., chairman of the House Special Panel on Postal Reform. McHugh had been working on postal restructuring for a decade.

In drafting the bills, proponents brought together most of the major stakeholders, including unions, private mailers, consumer groups and even Postal Service competitors such as UPS, which had worked against earlier overhaul efforts.

Both the House and Senate bills appeared to headed for floor debate in the spring, and supporters talked hopefully about enacting the first postal overhaul since 1970 (PL 91-375).

BoxScore

Bills:
HR 4341, S 2468
Legislative Action:
House Government Reform Committee approved HR 4341 (H Rept 108-672, Part 1), 40-0, on May 12.
House Judiciary Committee approved HR 4341 (H Rept 108-672, Part 2) by voice vote on Sept. 15.
Senate Governmental Affairs Committee approved S 2468 (S Rept 108-318), 17-0, on June 2.

What stopped the legislation was Treasury Department opposition to the provision in both versions that would have transferred to Treasury the liability for pension benefits of military retirees who later worked for the Postal Service. Treasury had paid for those benefits until a law enacted in 2003 (PL 108-18) shifted the burden to the Postal Service. Treasury Secretary John W. Snow told Congress in March that the administration wanted the liability to remain there, and the White House backed him up.

Legislative Action

Both the House and Senate bills aimed to make the Postal Service operate more like a business. They proposed giving postal officials flexibility to adjust rates on products that had to compete with FedEx and UPS, and allowing the Postal Service to enter into profitable agreements with large customers. Under these "work sharing" agreements, private mailers would get rate discounts in exchange for performing some functions, such as bar coding and sorting mail, that typically were done by Postal Service workers.

Both versions proposed creating a Postal Regulatory Commission that would be a strong oversight board with subpoena powers, and called for postage rates on letters, periodicals and advertising mail to be regulated so that annual rate shifts did not exceed changes in inflation.

• **House Government Reform.** The House Government Reform Committee approved its bill (HR 4341 — H Rept 108-672, Part 1), by a vote of 40-0 on May 12. The unanimous support was in marked contrast to a vote in June 2002, when the committee rejected similar legislation, 6-20, amid objections by private delivery companies led by UPS.

Similar concerns by UPS and other companies also stalled committee consideration this time. But industry representatives, the Postal Service and committee staff eventually negotiated language aimed at ensuring that the Postal Service would not abuse its status as a government-spon-

sored monopoly for competitive advantage.

The groups' primary concern was the future rate structure for such products as Priority Mail and Express Mail, which competed directly with UPS and FedEx. The language negotiated during a postponement of the scheduled markup required that the Postal Service provide a 15- or 30-day warning period before its prices changed.

- **House Judiciary.** The House Judiciary Committee added its imprint, approving the bill by voice vote Sept. 15 (HR 4341 — Rept 108-672, Part 2). The panel adopted two amendments making relatively minor changes to the legislation before approving it.

- **Senate Governmental Affairs.** The Senate committee approved a version of the bill (S 2468 — S Rept 108-318) cosponsored by its chairwoman, Collins, and Thomas R. Carper, D-Del., by a vote of 17-0 on June 2.

One major difference between the bills appeared to be resolved when the Senate panel voted, 9-8, over Collins' objections, to adopt an amendment by ranking Democrat Joseph I. Lieberman of Connecticut. The amendment brought the bill closer to the House version by limiting to four years the period during which the Postal Service could give "excessive discounts" to private mailers who entered into the work sharing agreements.

Postmaster General John E. Potter lent his support to an overhaul May 26, but cautioned that certain provisions concerning benefits could lead to higher postal rates. Both bills required that the Postal Service pre-fund a health benefit for retirees, a $3.9 billion expense that Potter said could be recovered only through an increase in postage rates. Potter said neither bill reduced the cost of wage and benefits packages, which the Postal Service said cost $1 billion a week.

The Senate panel gave voice vote approval to two amendments. One, by John E. Sununu, R-N.H., directed the Treasury Department to consult with the Postal Service and an independent accounting firm to develop recommendations for the service's accounting practices for its competitive products. The second, by Richard J. Durbin, D-Ill., required the Government Accountability Office to study the possibility of offering rate incentives for mailers who used recycled paper. ◆

Leaders Pull Welfare Bill

For the second straight year, Congress was unable to complete legislation reauthorizing the landmark 1996 welfare overhaul law that ended more than 60 years of guaranteed assistance, ushered in new work requirements and provided more flexibility for states to operate programs. The reauthorization was a casualty of the partisanship that consumed lawmakers for much of the year.

The 1996 law (PL 104-193) imposed a five-year limit on cash assistance and required that participants work at least 30 hours a week. Most lawmakers considered the law a success because the number of individuals eligible for assistance had fallen by more than half since its enactment. But they had difficulty agreeing on the next step to help the poor go from handouts to paychecks.

The Bush administration and its congressional allies wanted to impose tougher work rules on the remaining welfare recipients and launch a sweeping marriage promotion initiative. Democrats hoped to win an increase in mandatory federal spending on child care and other forms of support, which they saw as necessary to increase the ranks of public aid beneficiaries who could become self-sufficient.

House Republicans passed a reauthorization bill (HR 4) in 2003 that called for adult participants to work up to 40 hours a week. The measure would have provided an additional $1 billion over five years in block grants to states for child care. A provision favored by the White House would have authorized $200 million annually in grants for educational and counseling programs to promote marriage, matched by $100 million in state money.

The Senate Finance Committee approved an amended version of HR 4 in September 2003 that called for recipients to work 34 hours a week — 24 hours a week for parents with children younger than 6. It retained the existing requirement that recipients be allowed to count up to 12 months of vocational education as a work activity. The House bill allowed for three months. (*2003 Almanac, p. 16-3*)

To win committee approval, Finance Chairman Charles E. Grassley, R-Iowa, promised GOP moderate Olympia J. Snowe of Maine that she could offer the first amendment during floor debate, a proposal to increase child care funding by $6 billion over five years.

The Senate easily adopted Snowe's amendment when the bill came to the floor in March 2004. But after four days, the leadership suspended debate on the bill rather than allow a vote on a Democratic amendment to increase the minimum wage. GOP leaders argued that it was pointless because Democrats would block the measure from going to conference anyway. Democrats used such a tactic a number of times during the session to protest their exclusion from conference committees.

Lawmakers were forced to continue the programs through a short-term extension, much to the frustration of state and local governments that administered the law. The short-term reauthorization (PL 108-308) was good through the end of March 2005.

Legislative Action

Senate Floor Action

The Senate began debate on the reauthorization bill March 29. Despite White House opposition, senators adopted the Snowe amendment, 78-20, the following day. (*Senate vote 64, p. S-16*)

The amendment would have provided $6 billion in additional mandatory child care funding to states over the next five years — beyond the $1 billion increase that was passed by the House. At the time, the government was providing

$4.8 billion annually for child care through a mixture of mandatory and discretionary programs.

Snowe argued that such a substantial increase was warranted because only one in seven children from families eligible to receive federal child care assistance were actually getting aid. She said the annual cost of caring for a child — $4,000 to $10,000 — was beyond the means of mothers who were trying to leave the welfare rolls. "Without good child care, a parent is left with only two choices: to leave a child in an unsafe and often unsupervised situation, or not to work, both of which are lose-lose situations," she said.

The White House Office of Management and Budget issued a statement of administration policy March 29 arguing that because welfare caseloads had fallen by more than half since 1996, states had enough money. The administration also argued that some of the extra child care money would be spent on those who had left the rolls but still met the poverty threshold to qualify for aid.

"There is no justification for that other than the fact that this is a desire to make people more dependent on government," said Rick Santorum of Pennsylvania, the chairman of the GOP Conference and a leading Republican voice on social policy.

But Snowe's amendment gave senators from both parties a chance to make a statement in favor of children and families in an election year.

Snowe proposed to offset the costs by renewing expiring Customs' user fees. That allowed her to avoid a budget point of order that would have required 60 votes to overcome, but the same offset was being used in other bills. Judd Gregg, R-N.H., called it "the ultimate shell game," saying that by his count it had been used on 17 different occasions on the Senate floor.

Grassley hoped the child care amendment would win Democratic support for the bill. Instead, Democrats planned a series of workplace and labor-related amendments that were part of a campaign to demonstrate that the administration was insensitive to the needs of working-class Americans. In particular, they insisted on a vote on an amendment by Barbara Boxer, D-Calif., to increase the minimum wage from $5.15 to $7 an hour over two years. Other Democrats including Edward M. Kennedy of Massachusetts were threatening to offer amendments to block the Labor Department from implementing new rules on overtime pay and to extend supplemental federal unemployment benefits.

GOP leaders tried to invoke cloture April 1, a move that would have limited the debate and blocked the Democratic amendments, but the motion failed, 51-47, nine votes short of the 60 required. (*Senate vote 65, p. S-16*)

At that point, the leadership pulled the bill. ◆

Chapter 18

POLITICS & ELECTIONS

Bush Wins Close Re-Election Bid

George W. Bush was elected Nov. 2 to a second term as the 43rd president of the United States. Bush's contest with the Democratic Party nominee, Sen. John Kerry of Massachusetts, was among the most competitive presidential races in history. His re-election with 286 electoral votes was not cinched until late on Election Night when it became clear that he had narrowly carried the battleground state of Ohio. But his tally of 51 percent of the vote gave a clarity that his victory lacked four years earlier, when he won a bare majority of 271 electoral votes while losing the popular vote to Al Gore, then the incumbent Democratic vice president.

Bush was the first presidential candidate to garner an absolute majority of the popular vote since his father, George Bush, won the presidency in 1988 by defeating Democrat Michael S. Dukakis.

Bush benefited greatly from an image as a strong-willed and determined leader, which emerged largely from his handling of the seminal event of his first term: the Sept. 11, 2001, terrorist attacks on the United States by Islamic extremists associated with Osama bin Laden and his al Qaeda network. Bush's job approval ratings soared to record heights as he deployed the U.S. military to Afghanistan to help local forces overthrow the Taliban regime that had harbored bin Laden.

This steadfast image helped Bush overcome slumping poll numbers, largely the result of growing dissatisfaction with his decision in March 2003 to commit a large U.S. force — in league with a small international coalition — to overthrow Saddam Hussein, the dictatorial leader of Iraq.

The Iraq engagement had evolved from a rapid victory in conventional warfare to a long occupation marked by the rise of a persistent and extremely violent insurgency. It was also marked by restiveness among much of the Iraqi population; scandals concerning the abuse of Iraqi prisoners by U.S. troops; and a failure to find an arsenal of weapons of mass destruction, allegedly amassed by the Hussein regime, the purported existence of which had been cited by Bush and his aides as a principal justification for the invasion.

Yet polls consistently showed large majorities favoring Bush as more qualified than Kerry to lead the international war on terrorism and to serve as commander in chief — the result in part of a long-held public perception that Republicans were stronger on defense than Democrats.

Bush also was able to finesse an economy that had recovered rather sluggishly from a downturn that began early in his first term and left some manufacturing-dependent regions lagging far behind the nation as a whole.

Yet the closeness of the election suggested that Bush had just barely expanded his support base during his four years as president and remained a uniquely polarizing figure. His agenda — including his assertive projection of U.S. interests abroad, an economic policy centered on tax cuts that largely benefited wealthier Americans and a conservative outlook on social issues, including stiff opposition to abortion and gay rights — made him wildly popular among the Re-publican voting base. But his policies also enraged the vast majority of people who had opposed his election in 2000, and they advocated Bush's defeat with a fervor nearly equal to that of the supporters who wanted to see him re-elected.

With the candidates' campaigns, national party organizations and allied outside groups combining to pour a record amount of money into the contest — the best estimate was that the sum of all their spending approached $1.2 billion, making it the first ever billion-dollar presidential campaign — both major party candidates received more votes than any previous candidate for president. Bush, who received 540,000 fewer votes than Gore four years earlier, outran Kerry by 3.5 million. But his 2.5 percentage-point victory margin was the smallest-ever for a re-elected president. The national political map also remained as clearly divided as it had been four years before — with the "red" Republican states sweeping across the South, Midwest and Mountain West and all the "blue" Democratic states in the Northeast, contiguous to the Great Lakes and down the West Coast. Bush added only Iowa and New Mexico to the states he won in his first race; Kerry took New Hampshire away from him.

Declaring a Mandate

Despite the close finish, Bush wasted no time declaring his victory as an affirmation of his first-term stewardship and a mandate for a second-term agenda that he said would include an overhaul of the Social Security program, more tax cuts, the indefinite extension of tax reductions enacted in 2001 (PL 107-16) and 2003 (PL 108-27) and limits on medical malpractice lawsuits.

"When you win, there is a feeling that people have spoken and embraced your point of view," Bush said at a Nov. 4 news conference. "And that's what I intend to tell the Congress: that I made it clear what I intend to do as the president and the people made it clear what they wanted." He said he had "the will of the people at my back." And — in what many opponents viewed as a slap — Bush said, "I'll reach out to everyone who shares our goals."

His critics warned that Bush was overreaching in assuming that the public had adopted his entire world view when it extended his lease on the White House. Democrats argued that the election was primarily decided on three factors: the aftereffects of the horrors of Sept. 11; the emphasis Bush placed on his opposition to abortion and gay marriage, which greatly boosted turnout among religious conservatives; and Kerry's shortcomings as a candidate.

The Democratic challenger had the stature of a senator for two decades, and his erudition gave him strengths as a campaigner that were most evident in his three nationally televised debates with Bush, in which he frequently put the president on the defensive.

But Kerry was saddled with a stolid campaign style and a weakness for rambling speeches that at times stultified even his supporters. It was a persona that contrasted poorly with the average-guy charm Bush perfected during two victorious campaigns for governor of Texas in the 1990s. Bush's folksi-

By the Numbers

- President Bush received 62.04 million votes (50.7 percent of all votes cast) to 59.03 million votes (48.3 percent) for Democratic Sen. John Kerry of Massachusetts. Other candidates took 1.23 million votes (1 percent) among them. Both of the major party nominees bested the previous record for most votes received for president — the 54.5 million that Ronald Reagan garnered when he won his second term in 1984.
- About 122.3 million Americans voted, the most in history. The turnout on Nov. 2 was 61 percent of all eligible voters, the highest percentage since the 62 percent who voted in 1968.
- Bush received 11.6 million more popular votes than he did in 2000; Kerry received 8 million more votes than the Democratic nominee of four years prior, Vice President Al Gore.
- Bush was the first presidential candidate to win a majority of the popular vote since 1988, when his father, George Bush, took 53.4 percent.
- Bush's 2.5 percentage point margin of victory in the popular vote was the smallest ever for a president who won re-election. (Harry S Truman won in 1948 with a smaller raw-vote margin, but his percentage point margin was larger than Bush's in 2004).
- Bush carried 31 states with 286 electoral votes and Kerry carried 19 states and the District of Columbia, with 252 electoral votes. But one Kerry elector from Minnesota cast his presidential vote for the Democratic vice-presidential nominee, Sen. John Edwards of North Carolina.
- Bush's 35-vote margin of victory in the Electoral College was the narrowest for a president who won re-election since 1916, when Woodrow Wilson won a second term against Republican Charles Evans Hughes by 23 electoral votes.
- Forty-seven of the 50 states voted for the same party's nominee in 2004 as they had four years before. New Hampshire backed Kerry in 2004 but Bush in 2000. Iowa and New Mexico backed Bush in 2004 but were carried by Gore in 2000.

ness may not have won him many new converts, but it captivated and energized his true believers.

Democrats hoped that the charisma gap would be filled by Kerry's vice presidential running mate, Sen. John Edwards of North Carolina. Edwards had drawn positive attention during his failed bid for the presidential nomination for his ability to connect with audiences and a populist message that many thought best encapsulated the Democrats' indictment of Bush's economic policies. But though Edwards campaigned vigorously through the fall, he appeared to have little impact on voters' decisions: Bush even carried North Carolina by 12 percentage points.

Kerry also committed stumbles that were quickly pounced on by Bush's well-oiled machine — masterminded by chief political adviser Karl Rove. Particularly harmful to Kerry was his difficulty articulating why he voted for the 2002 law (PL 107-243) that authorized Bush to use force in Iraq, but later voted against the law (PL 108-106) providing $87.5 billion in supplemental spending on the U.S. military occupations and the reconstruction of Afghanistan and Iraq. The Bush campaign wielded this as proof of their overriding theme: that Kerry was a "flip-flopper" who could not be trusted to lead at a time of war.

Perhaps most unexpected was the devaluation of what Kerry and his fellow Democrats hoped would be one of his strongest assets: his record as a decorated Navy officer during the Vietnam War, something that came under fire from a group of disgruntled fellow veterans who were determined to prevent him from becoming president.

Four Long Years

Bush's declaration of a mandate was hardly surprising. He had done the same after the 2000 election, which he won only after the Supreme Court, in a 5-4 ruling, cut off a recount in Florida, a decision that gave him a 537-vote win out of more than 2.9 million votes cast in the state.

With the party discipline invoked by House Republican leaders and a 50-50 split in a Senate in which Vice President Dick Cheney cast tie-breaking votes, Bush pushed through a tax-cutting measure early in 2001 despite protests from opponents that it was stacked in favor of the rich. And, in what would be one of his few extensively bipartisan exercises, Bush gained enactment of his major social policy initiative, dubbed No Child Left Behind (PL 107-110), which expanded the use of student testing to increase learning standards.

But Bush was saddled with a flagging economy, as the boom that coincided with the eight-year presidency of Democrat Bill Clinton ended with a downturn in the high-tech sector. A Gallup poll showed Bush with a positive job approval rating of 51 percent to 39 percent negative; the survey was completed on Sept. 10, 2001.

The destiny of the Bush presidency and of the nation changed seismically the very next day. Teams of terrorists boarded U.S. airliners posing as passengers, commandeered the planes and turned them into missiles, destroying both towers of New York's World Trade Center, severely damaging the Pentagon and killing more than 2,700 people.

Bush soon reached the apogee of his presidency with a moving memorial speech to Congress, a warning of retaliation from atop the smoldering ruins in New York and his use of force to install a pro-Western government in Afghanistan (though the failure of that campaign to capture bin Laden would haunt Bush during his re-election bid). His job approval peaked at 90 percent, the highest ever recorded by Gallup, on Sept. 22 and remained in the 80s into 2002.

Though the sputtering economy pushed Bush's approval downward, he still enjoyed strong support when he embarked on the second mission that would define his first term: the toppling of Saddam Hussein. In statements through the summer and fall of 2002, Bush, Cheney and other administration officials warned that Iraq had not destroyed biological and chemical weapons as required by U.N. resolutions following the 1991 war that ended Iraq's

Presidential Results

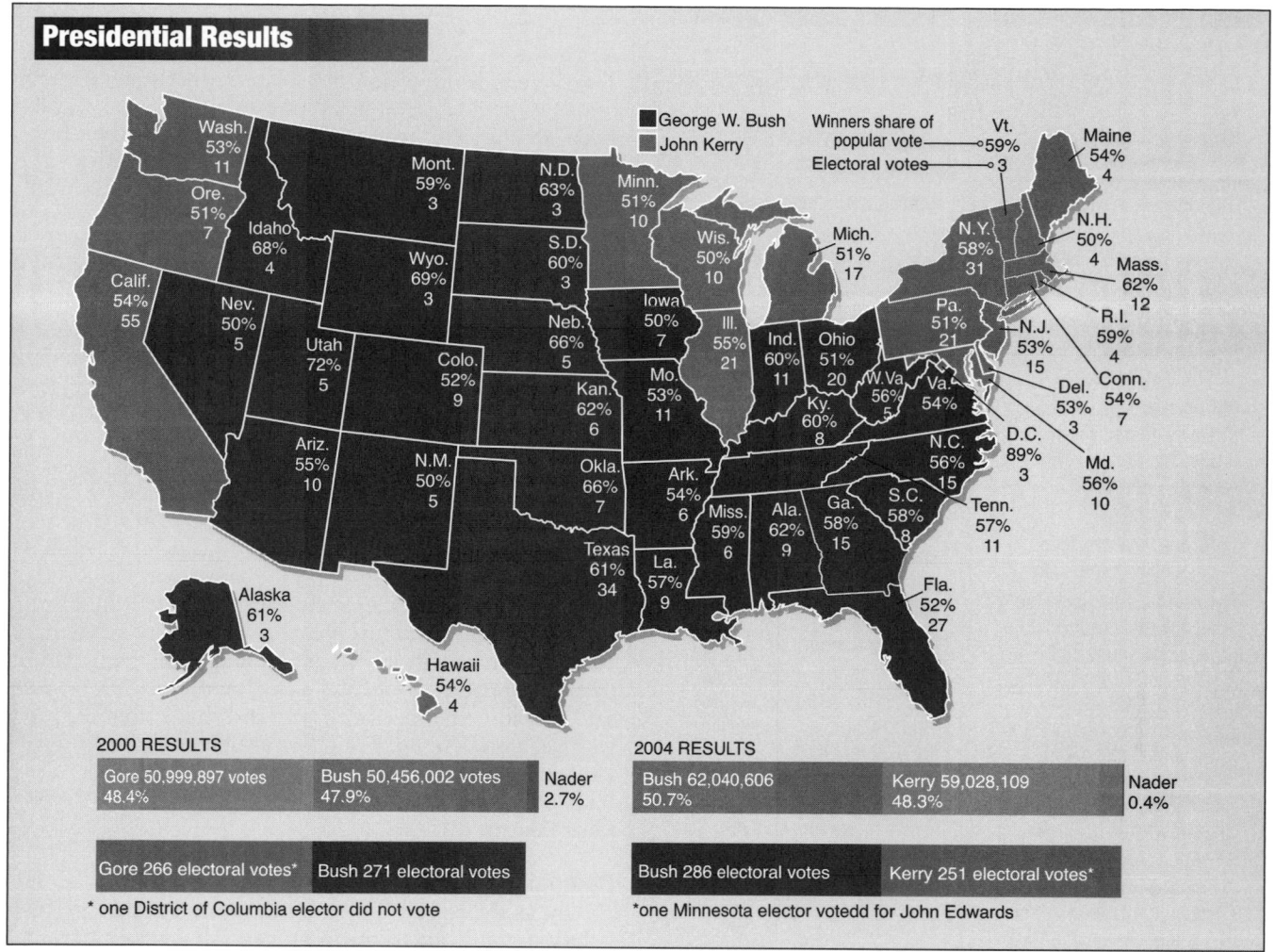

George W. Bush
John Kerry
Winners share of popular vote — 59%
Electoral votes — 3

Wash. 53% 11
Ore. 51% 7
Idaho 68% 4
Calif. 54% 55
Nev. 50% 5
Mont. 59% 3
Wyo. 69% 3
Utah 72% 5
Ariz. 55% 10
N.M. 50% 5
Colo. 52% 9
N.D. 63% 3
S.D. 60% 3
Neb. 66% 5
Kan. 62% 6
Okla. 66% 7
Texas 61% 34
Minn. 51% 10
Iowa 50% 7
Mo. 53% 11
Ark. 54% 6
La. 57% 9
Wis. 50% 10
Ill. 55% 21
Miss. 59% 6
Ala. 62% 9
Ind. 60% 11
Ky. 60% 8
Tenn. 57% 11
Ga. 58% 15
Ohio 51% 20
W.Va 56% 5
Mich. 51% 17
Va. 54%
N.C. 56% 15
S.C. 58% 8
Fla. 52% 27
Vt. 59% 3
Maine 54% 4
N.Y. 58% 31
N.H. 50% 4
Mass. 62% 12
R.I. 59% 4
N.J. 53% 15
Conn. 54% 7
Del. 53% 3
D.C. 89% 3
Md. 56% 10
Pa. 51% 21
Alaska 61% 3
Hawaii 54% 4

2000 RESULTS

| Gore 50,999,897 votes 48.4% | Bush 50,456,002 votes 47.9% | Nader 2.7% |

| Gore 266 electoral votes* | Bush 271 electoral votes |

* one District of Columbia elector did not vote

2004 RESULTS

| Bush 62,040,606 50.7% | Kerry 59,028,109 48.3% | Nader 0.4% |

| Bush 286 electoral votes | Kerry 251 electoral votes* |

*one Minnesota elector votedd for John Edwards

seizure of Kuwait. They also implied that Iraq was seeking nuclear weapons.

Bush pushed for a vote in October 2002 — just before the midterm election — on a resolution authorizing him to employ force to get Hussein to live up to his commitments. The measure would have fateful consequences in 2004. Among those voting for it were Kerry and Edwards.

After pressuring the United Nations into allowing the use of force if Hussein did not surrender his supposed arsenal, Bush set a deadline and then launched the invasion in March 2003. Despite expectations that the Iraqi military would put up a fierce resistance, opposition melted away in the face of the coalition's overwhelming power.

On May 1, 2003, Bush donned a flight suit, co-piloted a Navy jet to the deck of an aircraft carrier anchored off San Diego and — with a banner proclaiming "Mission Accomplished" draped behind him — declared that the active combat phase of the Iraq conflict was over. Democrats derided the event as stage-managed solely to provide footage for the president's 2004 campaign. But if the day was aimed to boost Bush politically, it backfired. His words rang hollow as the insurgency grew in Iraq, bolstered by the arrival of foreign Islamic jihadists drawn by the opportunity to inflict damage on U.S. forces.

From an approval rating measured by Gallup at 71 percent during the military's capture of Baghdad in April, Bush slipped to 50 percent by November. He would enjoy a brief bump up after Hussein was arrested in December. But by Feb. 1, his positive rating had slipped back to 49 percent and would stay at or just below the 50 percent mark — the danger threshold for an incumbent seeking re-election — for most of 2004.

A Challenger Emerges

Bush strategists nonetheless entered the campaign year feeling confident, in part because of early developments in the contest for the Democratic nomination. Former Gov. Howard Dean of Vermont built a movement through his vocal opposition to the Iraq war and his trailblazing use of the Internet as an organizing and fundraising tool — and for a time his lead in Democratic voter preference polls seemed irreversible. Bush backers delighted in that, believing that Dean's strongly liberal rhetoric and vituperative manner would make him an easy mark. But so, as it turned out, did Democratic voters. Kerry, after a stumbling start, found a consistent style that enabled him to win the campaign-opening Iowa caucuses and New Hampshire's primary — and he used the ensuing momentum to wrap up the nomination by early March. (*Democratic challengers, p. 18-10*)

In Kerry, the Democrats had a candidate who lacked the galvanizing activist appeal of Dean or the common touch of Clinton. Like Bush, Kerry was born into a patrician New

Republican Ticket

George Walker Bush

Hometown: Austin, Texas

Born: July 6, 1946, in New Haven, Conn.

Religion: Methodist

Family: Wife, Laura Welch Bush; twin daughters, Jenna and Barbara, 22

Education: Phillips Academy, Andover, Mass., graduated 1964; Yale U., B.A. 1968 (history); Harvard U., M.B.A. 1975

Military Service: Texas Air National Guard, 1968-73

Career: Founder and chief executive officer, Arbusto Energy Inc., later Bush Exploration Oil and Gas Co., 1975-86; paid adviser to Vice President George Bush's presidential campaign, 1987-88; managing general partner, Texas Rangers baseball team, 1989-94

Political Highlights: Lost 1978 open seat House race in Texas' 19th District, garnering 47 percent against state Sen. Kent Hance; elected governor of Texas in 1994 with 53 percent against first-term incumbent Democrat Ann Richards; re-elected in 1998 with 68 percent against Democrat Garry Mauro, the state land commissioner; elected the 43rd president of the United States in 2000 with 271 electoral votes and 47.9 percent of the popular vote.

Richard Bruce Cheney

Hometown: Casper, Wyo.

Born: Jan. 30, 1941, in Lincoln, Neb.

Religion: Methodist

Family: Wife, Lynne Vincent Cheney; daughters Elizabeth, 38, and Mary, 35

Education: Natrona County High School, Casper, graduated 1959; Yale U., attended 1959-60; Casper College, attended 1963; U. of Wyoming, B.A. 1965 (political science), M.A. 1966 (political science); Ph.D candidate, U. of Wisconsin, 1966-68 (political science)

Military Service: None

Career: Congressional fellow, Rep. William A. Steiger, R-Wis., 1968-69; special assistant to the director, Office of Economic Opportunity, 1969-70; White House staff assistant, 1971; assistant director, Cost of Living Council, 1971-73; vice president, Bradley, Woods & Co., 1973-74; deputy assistant to President Gerald R. Ford, 1974-75; White House chief of staff, 1975-77; senior fellow, American Enterprise Institute, 1993-95; chairman and chief executive, Halliburton Co., 1995-2000.

Political Highlights: Defeated Democratic attorney Bill Bagley with 59 percent to win Wyoming's at-large House seat, 1978; re-elected five times with at least 67 percent; served on the Interior, Select Intelligence, Standards of Official Conduct and Select Iran-Contra committees; defeated Marjorie S. Holt of Maryland, 99-68, to become House GOP Policy Committee chairman, 1980; unopposed for election as GOP Conference chairman, 1987; unopposed for election as minority whip, 1988; secretary of Defense, 1989-93 (confirmed 92-0); elected vice president in 2000 with 271 electoral votes and 47.9 percent of the popular vote.

England family and attended prep school and then Yale. Kerry also was married to one of the nation's wealthiest women: Teresa Heinz Kerry, widow of the late Pennsylvania Republican senator and food company heir John Heinz. And unlike Bush, who adopted the mannerisms of his adopted home state of Texas, Kerry was stuck with an aloof image.

Democrats hoped, though, that Kerry's gravitas would convince voters that he was more qualified to be president than Bush, whose malapropisms fueled both foes and comics in lampooning him as an intellectual lightweight.

Kerry's long career as a lawmaker also cut both for and against him. Supporters hoped that his deliberative approach — in which he dissected each issue and decided how to vote after long discussions with his aides — would contrast positively with Bush, who was widely viewed as approaching even the most complex policy questions with his mind made up. Detractors, though, portrayed Kerry as an opportunist with no fixed set of principles. And by plumbing Kerry's record of more than 6,300 votes in the Senate, the Bush campaign was able to find considerable ammunition to support their "flip-flopper" characterization.

Democrats hoped the trump card for Kerry would be his military record. Kerry had volunteered for duty in Vietnam, earning a Bronze Star, a Silver Star and three Purple Hearts while commanding a Navy "swift" boat. This, Democrats said, would immunize Kerry from the charge that his party was weak on defense. They also anticipated that it would keep alive an unresolved controversy over whether Bush had fulfilled his obligations as a member of the Air National Guard during the war.

Campaign Finance Ironies

One of the biggest worries for Democrats going into their primaries and caucuses was money. The party's national chairman, Terry McAuliffe, had encouraged states to bunch their primaries early in hopes — which panned out — that the process would produce an early victor. Still, party officials were concerned that the winner would emerge broke and unable to defend against an inevitable advertising onslaught by the abundantly funded Bush campaign.

The 2004 race was the first run under the campaign finance law (PL 107-155) enacted two years before; it barred large unregulated "soft money" contributions to federal candidates but doubled the amount individuals could contribute to $2,000 per campaign. Since Republicans had been better than Democrats at raising that "hard money," it was assumed that Bush would enjoy a huge money advantage.

This assumption motivated Democratic activists to invest heavily in organizations — known as 527s for the section of the Internal Revenue Code that governed them — that could accept more generous donations from individuals and groups such as labor unions. Though barred from coordinating with candidates, 527s such as Americans Coming Together and the Media Fund linked up and prepared to batter Bush while his challenger regrouped after the primaries.

The Bush campaign, also assuming a lopsided money advantage in their favor, protested unsuccessfully to the Federal Election Commission and the federal courts that Democrats were using 527s to circumvent the new finance law.

The debate had an ironic outcome: The Democratic 527s

ended up reinforcing, rather than replacing, Kerry's own message. Borrowing from the online techniques pioneered by Dean and aided by the zeal of many Democrats to defeat Bush, Kerry ended up with receipts of $345 million — just $22 million less than the incumbent. Republicans, however, took an "if you can't beat them, join them" attitude towards 527s, with consequential effects on the outcome of the race.

The Iraq Pendulum

The Iraq conflict dominated American news coverage during the general election campaign. Supporters of both candidates saw this as a plus. Citing polls that showed Bush favored over Kerry on defense-related issues, Republicans returned constantly to their theme that Bush was a strong leader. To Democrats, the Iraq drumbeat underscored what they called the president's rush to war and incompetent handling of the subsequent occupation.

Bush had some bright moments on the Iraq front, including the transfer of authority to Iraqi officials in June. But he also endured some clear setbacks. The deepening insurgency and non-violent exhibitions of dissent belied the administration's pre-war predictions that coalition forces would be warmly greeted as liberators by the Iraqi people.

There were daily reports of American deaths, hostage beheadings and incidents such as one in April in the insurgent stronghold of Fallujah, where four contractors were killed by guerrillas, mutilated and hanged from a bridge. Later that month came revelations that U.S. military personnel had abused and sexually humiliated prisoners at Iraq's Abu Ghraib prison — and photographed their actions.

Kerry, however, made a pair of crucial gaffes that neutralized his effectiveness on the Iraq issue.

During a March appearance in West Virginia, Kerry said of his vote on the wartime funding bill: "I actually did vote for the $87 billion, before I voted against it." He was trying to explain his support for an unsuccessful Democratic proposal that would have put more restrictions on how Bush could spend the money, but the phrasing perfectly captured the Bush campaign's efforts to portray Kerry as a vacillator — and the clip became the core of a particularly effective television advertisement.

And in late July, Bush challenged Kerry to say whether, knowing what he knew by then, he would still have voted for the 2002 war resolution. When a reporter relayed that question to Kerry during a photo opportunity at the Grand Canyon, the candidate said, "Yes" — dispiriting antiwar Democrats and enabling Bush to crow that Kerry had once again provided a "new nuance" on his Iraq stance.

The conventions were studies in contrast. Kerry's campaign decided that the Democrats' meeting July 26-29 in his hometown of Boston would be positive and avoid harsh attacks against Bush. The focus was to be on Kerry as a leader on the economy, but most of all on national security. Much was made of Kerry's Vietnam hero status: the candidate came out surrounded by his Navy buddies, and then opened his speech by declaring he was "reporting for duty."

The Republican convention in New York Aug. 30-Sept. 2 had a much more caustic tone. Speaker after speaker — including former New York City Mayor Rudolph Giuliani, Gov. Arnold Schwarzenegger of California, maverick conservative Democratic Sen. Zell Mill-

Democratic Ticket

John Forbes Kerry

Hometown: Boston

Born: Dec. 11, 1943, in Denver

Religion: Roman Catholic

Family: Wife, Teresa Heinz Kerry; daughters Alexandra, 30, and Vanessa, 27; stepchildren John Heinz IV, 37, Andre Heinz, 34, and Christopher Heinz, 31.

Education: St. Paul's School, Concord, N.H., graduated 1962; Yale U., B.A. 1966 (political science); Boston College, J.D. 1976

Military Service: Navy, 1966-70 (lieutenant; Bronze Star, Silver Star, three Purple Hearts)

Career: First assistant district attorney of Middlesex County (Boston), 1977-82.

Political Highlights: Lost 1972 5th District House race to Republican Paul W. Cronin, garnering 46 percent; elected lieutenant governor in 1982 on ticket headed by Democrat Michael S. Dukakis; won 1984 Senate race to succeed Democrat Paul E. Tsongas, defeating Republican Ray Shamie with 55 percent; re-elected in 1990 over Republican Jim Rappaport with 57 percent; re-elected in 1996 over Republican Gov. William F. Weld with 52 percent; re-elected in 2002 without GOP opposition.

Committees: Commerce, Science & Transportation (Oceans, Fisheries & Coast Guard, ranking Democrat); Finance; Foreign Relations (East Asian & Pacific Affairs, ranking Democrat); Small Business & Entrepreneurship, ranking Democrat

John Reid Edwards

Hometown: Raleigh, N.C.

Born: June 10, 1953, in Seneca, S.C.

Religion: Methodist

Family: Wife, Elizabeth Anania Edwards; daughters Catharine, 22, and Emma Claire, 6; son Jack, 4. Another son, Wade, died in 1996 at age 16.

Education: North Moore High School, Robbins, N.C., graduated 1971; North Carolina State U., B.S. 1974 (textiles); U. of North Carolina, J.D. 1977.

Military Service: None

Career: Clerk, U.S. District Judge Franklin T. Dupree Jr. of Raleigh, 1977-78; associate, Dearborn & Ewing of Nashville, 1978-81; associate and then partner, Tharrington, Smith & Hargrove of Raleigh, 1981-92; founding partner, Edwards & Kirby of Raleigh, 1993-98.

Political Highlights: Elected to the Senate in 1998 with 51 percent of the vote against Republican incumbent Lauch Faircloth, who was seeking a second term. Won the second largest number of delegates but just one primary (South Carolina) in his bid for the 2004 Democratic presidential nomination. Decided in September 2003 not to seek re-election to a second Senate term.

Committees: Health, Education, Labor & Pensions; Judiciary; Select Intelligence; Small Business & Entrepreneurship

2004 Presidential Election Results

George W. Bush won his second term in 2004 by the smallest Electoral College margin of any victorious incumbent since Woodrow Wilson in 1916. Still, he was the first presidential winner since 1988 to garner a popular vote majority.

	Electoral Votes			Total	George W. Bush Republican	John Kerry Democrat	Others	Percentage of total vote		
	Bush	Kerry	Other					Bush	Kerry	Others
Alabama	9	0	0	1,883,415	1,176,394	693,933	13,088	62.46	36.84	0.69
Alaska	3	0	0	312,598	190,889	111,025	10,684	61.07	35.52	3.42
Arizona	10	0	0	2,012,585	1,104,294	893,524	14,767	54.87	44.40	0.73
Arkansas	6	0	0	1,054,945	572,898	469,953	12,094	54.31	44.55	1.15
California	0	55	0	12,419,857	5,509,826	6,745,485	164,546	44.36	54.31	1.32
Colorado	9	0	0	2,129,630	1,101,255	1,001,732	26,643	51.71	47.04	1.25
Connecticut	0	7	0	1,578,769	693,826	857,488	27,455	43.95	54.31	1.74
Delaware	0	3	0	375,190	171,660	200,152	3,378	45.75	53.35	0.90
District of Columbia	0	3	0	227,586	21,256	202,970	3,360	9.34	89.18	1.48
Florida	27	0	0	7,609,810	3,964,522	3,583,544	61,744	52.10	47.09	0.81
Georgia	15	0	0	3,301,875	1,914,254	1,366,149	21,472	57.97	41.37	0.65
Hawaii	0	4	0	429,013	194,191	231,708	3,114	45.26	54.01	0.73
Idaho	4	0	0	598,376	409,235	181,098	8,043	68.39	30.26	1.34
Illinois	0	21	0	5,274,322	2,345,946	2,891,550	36,826	44.48	54.82	0.70
Indiana	11	0	0	2,468,002	1,479,438	969,011	19,553	59.94	39.26	0.79
Iowa	7	0	0	1,506,908	751,957	741,898	13,053	49.90	49.23	0.87
Kansas	6	0	0	1,187,756	736,456	434,993	16,307	62.00	36.62	1.37
Kentucky	8	0	0	1,795,860	1,069,439	712,733	13,688	59.55	39.69	0.76
Louisiana	9	0	0	1,943,106	1,102,169	820,299	20,638	56.72	42.22	1.06
Maine	0	4	0	740,752	330,201	396,842	13,709	44.58	53.57	1.85
Maryland	0	10	0	2,386,678	1,024,703	1,334,493	27,482	42.93	55.91	1.15
Massachusetts	0	12	0	2,912,388	1,071,109	1,803,800	37,479	36.78	61.94	1.29
Michigan	0	17	0	4,839,252	2,313,746	2,479,183	46,323	47.81	51.23	0.96
Minnesota *	0	9	1	2,828,387	1,346,695	1,445,014	36,678	47.61	51.09	1.30
Mississippi	6	0	0	1,161,543	684,981	457,766	18,796	58.97	39.41	1.62
Missouri	11	0	0	2,731,364	1,455,713	1,259,171	16,480	53.30	46.10	0.60
Montana	3	0	0	450,434	266,063	173,710	10,661	59.07	38.57	2.37
Nebraska	5	0	0	778,186	512,814	254,328	11,044	65.90	32.68	1.42
Nevada	5	0	0	829,587	418,690	397,190	13,707	50.47	47.88	1.65
New Hampshire	0	4	0	677,662	331,237	340,511	5,914	48.88	50.25	0.87
New Jersey	0	15	0	3,611,691	1,670,003	1,911,430	30,258	46.24	52.92	0.84
New Mexico	5	0	0	756,304	376,930	370,942	8,432	49.84	49.05	1.11
New York	0	31	0	7,391,036	2,962,567	4,314,280	114,189	40.08	58.37	1.54
North Carolina	15	0	0	3,501,007	1,961,166	1,525,849	13,992	56.02	43.58	0.40
North Dakota	3	0	0	312,833	196,651	111,052	5,130	62.86	35.50	1.64
Ohio	20	0	0	5,627,903	2,859,764	2,741,165	26,974	50.81	48.71	0.48
Oklahoma	7	0	0	1,463,758	959,792	503,966	—	65.57	34.43	0.00
Oregon	0	7	0	1,836,782	866,831	943,163	26,788	47.19	51.35	1.46
Pennsylvania	0	21	0	5,769,590	2,793,847	2,938,095	37,648	48.42	50.92	0.65
Rhode Island	0	4	0	437,134	169,046	259,760	8,328	38.67	59.42	1.91
South Carolina	8	0	0	1,617,730	937,974	661,699	18,057	57.98	40.90	1.12
South Dakota	3	0	0	388,215	232,584	149,244	6,387	59.91	38.44	1.65
Tennessee	11	0	0	2,437,319	1,384,375	1,036,477	16,467	56.80	42.53	0.68
Texas	34	0	0	7,410,749	4,526,917	2,832,704	51,128	61.09	38.22	0.69
Utah	5	0	0	927,844	663,742	241,199	22,903	71.54	26.00	2.47
Vermont	0	3	0	312,309	121,180	184,067	7,062	38.80	58.94	2.26
Virginia	13	0	0	3,198,367	1,716,959	1,454,742	26,666	53.68	45.48	0.83
Washington	0	11	0	2,859,084	1,304,894	1,510,201	43,989	45.64	52.82	1.54
West Virginia	5	0	0	755,887	423,778	326,541	5,568	56.06	43.20	0.74
Wisconsin	0	10	0	2,997,007	1,478,120	1,489,504	29,383	49.32	49.70	0.98
Wyoming	3	0	0	243,428	167,629	70,776	5,023	68.86	29.07	2.06
TOTAL	**286**	**251**	**1**	**122,301,813**	**62,040,606**	**59,028,109**	**1,233,098**	**50.73**	**48.26**	**1.01**

* One Kerry elector cast a presidential vote for the Democratic vice-presidential nominee, John Edwards.

SOURCE: State election offices

er and Cheney in his vice presidential acceptance speech — blasted Kerry as inconsistent, liberal on economics and weak on military matters.

The effectiveness of these criticisms was heightened between the conventions by the intervention of an anti-Kerry group, the Swift Boat Veterans for Truth. The group first bought time for TV ads in which veterans who served in Vietnam accused Kerry of inflating his war record. Though the charges were largely debunked, a second ad did even more serious damage. Highlighting Kerry's transition to antiwar activist after his return from Vietnam, it included excerpts of Kerry's testimony to the Senate Foreign Relations Committee in 1971 in which he related stories he had heard of American soldiers committing atrocities. These were coupled with on-screen statements from veterans associated with the Swift Boat group, including a former prisoner of war, who accused Kerry of betraying his brothers in arms.

The nation's endless divisions over the Vietnam War had one more campaign airing in September, when a CBS News report, moderated by veteran anchorman Dan Rather, presented documents purporting to prove that Bush had shirked his National Guard duties. But it was soon revealed that the documents were almost certainly fakes. The questions of what Bush had or had not done in the Guard were overshadowed by CBS's journalistic failings.

Kerry Closes, but Not Enough

Still, Kerry drew even with Bush in most polls during the fall by holding his own or better in the debates, and staged an exhausting campaign focused on a handful of states — Florida, Ohio, Pennsylvania, Michigan, Minnesota and Wisconsin — where strategists in both campaigns predicted the election would be decided.

Yet every Kerry thrust was met by a parry from the well-seasoned Bush campaign organization. Its tactical skill was never more apparent than after the first debate, which focused on Bush's supposed strong suits of defense and foreign policy. Kerry conducted himself with an ease of manner and facility for facts and figures, while Bush often appeared petulant and sensitive to Kerry's barbed criticisms; polls showed most Americans thought Kerry had "won" the debate. But during one of his answers, Kerry said U.S. foreign policy should meet a "global test." Though he was trying to suggest that the U.S. should consult with and respect the opinions of other nations, the Bush camp jumped all over the "global test" phrase, accusing Kerry of proposing to give the rest of the world veto power over American policy-making.

With the vast majority of voters holding concrete views for or against Bush, the election outcome turned on the success of the campaigns' get-out-the-vote operations. In this, Bush got a boost from a new issue: barring marriages by gay couples. The president's re-election campaign had stepped up its courting of the already important GOP constituency of religious conservatives, and the rise of this hot-button issue dovetailed perfectly with those efforts.

In 2003, the Massachusetts Supreme Court had struck down the state's ban on same-sex marriage as unconstitutional. Initially, it appeared that the Republicans would mainly be able to use the issue to stoke conservatives' anger at a liberal "activist judiciary." The court ruling, however, emboldened gay rights activists who briefly succeeded in

The Nader Non-Factor

Despite worries by Democrats that liberal consumer activist Ralph Nader would be a "spoiler" — by taking enough votes away from Democrat John Kerry to assure President Bush's re-election — Nader had virtually no impact on the 2004 outcome.

Running as an independent, Nader received just 463,653 votes in 34 states and the District of Columbia, 0.4 percent of the national total. In 2000, he tallied nearly 2.9 million votes (2.7 percent) in 48 states plus D.C. as the Green Party nominee. Democrats pointed a finger of blame at Nader after that historically close election. Nader's vote exceeded Bush's margin of victory in two states, Florida and New Hampshire; had Bush lost either state's electoral votes, Democrat Al Gore would have won the presidency.

But Nader tied his hands in 2004 by running as an independent rather than with the Green Party, which had ballot status in many states. Nader failed to meet petition thresholds in some states and was knocked off the ballots in others by Democratic challenges.

As a result, the 2004 presidential election was the first since 1988 without a significant "third-party" figure. Billionaire businessman H. Ross Perot ran in the two contests won by Democrat Bill Clinton, taking 19 percent in 1992 and 8 percent in 1996.

authorizing same-sex marriages — in contravention to their states' laws — in San Francisco and several other communities. This, in turn, spurred outrage by social conservatives that was echoed by Bush. Though the proposed constitutional amendment backed by the president, which aimed to establish marriage as only between a man and a woman, failed in the Senate, 11 similar measures (all of which would pass) were placed on state ballots across the country. The crucial battleground state of Ohio was among those that would approve an initiative to bar gay marriages.

After the election, there was considerable debate about the impact of social issues on the outcome. A CNN analysis of exit polls concluded that about 22 percent of voters identified moral values as the most important issue in the election, more than those who cited terrorism, Iraq or the economy. But the vague wording of the poll question spurred challenges to its credibility.

Election Day exit polls also caused some premature glee for Democrats by showing Kerry winning nearly all the key states. But Gov. Jeb Bush of Florida, a brother of the president and an astute observer of his state's voting trends, determined early that turnout favored the GOP. He was correct; the president carried the state by 5 percentage points. Kerry managed close wins in Pennsylvania, Michigan, Wisconsin and Minnesota — leaving Ohio to decide the presidency. Bush, who carried the state by 3 points in 2000, did so again, this time by 2 points. While some Democratic diehards complained about irregularities at Ohio polling places, Kerry determined quickly that he could not reverse the outcome, and he conceded defeat at midday Nov. 3. ◆

Quick Consensus for the Democrats

John Kerry, a senator from Massachusetts since 1985, was the early and clear favorite among political analysts to become the Democratic presidential nominee of 2004. He fulfilled that expectation by winning the party's pivotal pair of opening contests — the Iowa caucuses and the New Hampshire primary in January — which gave him sufficient momentum to dominate the "front-loaded" schedule of primaries and caucuses. By the time he essentially swept the "Super Tuesday" contests on March 2, Kerry had effectively clinched the nomination.

Yet Kerry's rise to the top of the nine-candidate Democratic field had temporarily lost its initial aura of inevitability during 2003's yearlong buildup to the actual voting, when the aggregation of endorsements, top-flight political advisors and most importantly campaign contributions defined the top tier of aspirants. It took a well-timed surge just before the Iowa and New Hampshire events to re-establish Kerry as the front-runner and to start the drive toward what, on paper, appears to have been a routine run to victory.

Bush Runs Unopposed

George W. Bush was essentially unopposed to be the Republican Party's choice, the easiest ride to the nomination for a major party candidate in two decades.

At the outset of his campaign for a second term, Bush won 98.1 percent of the overall GOP primary vote in 2004, according to returns compiled by The Rhodes Cook Letter. That share was the highest for a presidential candidate since Ronald Reagan took 98.9 percent of the aggregate GOP vote in winning the nomination for his second term in 1984.

Most votes that did not go to Bush were in the "uncommitted" category. The candidate who received the second-most number of votes was Bill Wyatt, a perennial losing candidate for public office who operated a T-shirt printing business in California. He was the choice of 11,000 primary voters in four states.

Since the growth of primary voting began in the 1970s, ease of renomination has proved to be a bellwether in predicting how an incumbent president will fare in the general election. The three presidents who won re-election since then all demonstrated rock-solid bases of support in their party. In addition to Reagan's record share in 1984, Richard M. Nixon took 97 percent of the primary ballots in 1972 and Bill Clinton took 89 percent in 1996. By contrast, the three presidents of the modern era who were defeated in November all struggled for the nomination. Gerald R. Ford took 53 percent of the primary vote in 1976, Jimmy Carter 51 percent in 1980 and George Bush 73 percent in 1992.

Slowed at the start of his campaign by surgery for prostate cancer, Kerry subsequently drew criticism for running an overly cautious campaign and for a stump speech that emphasized what many viewed as a tendency toward long-windedness. He was further hindered by an extensive roster of televised candidate debates and forums that included all the Democratic candidates — even those regarded as having no chance of winning — limiting each candidate's airtime and allowing none, including Kerry, to stand out.

Kerry was also seen as responding ineffectively to the meteoric rise of Howard Dean, the governor of Vermont from 1991 through 2002. Dean's strongly voiced opposition to the war in Iraq and his populist rhetoric on economic issues enabled him to build a sizable grass-roots movement, particularly among the liberals who make up a major part of the party's base. Dean also enjoyed staggering initial success at raising money, much of it in relatively small amounts given over the Internet. After bringing in $15 million in the three summer months of 2003, quadruple what Kerry raised in that time, he decided not to accept the public matching funds owed to him and thereby freed himself from certain federal campaign finance limits. Kerry, then on the defensive, made the risky move of eschewing public funds as well.

With Democrats who strongly opposed the war grumbling about Kerry's vote in 2002 for the law (PL 107-243) that authorized President Bush to use military force to oust Iraqi dictator Saddam Hussein, Dean zoomed to first place in many national polls of likely primary voters heading into January 2004 — leading some pundits to predict it would be he who would bull his way to a early victory for the nomination. (*2002 Almanac, p. 9-3*)

But Kerry found his balance just in time, exhibiting a more personable style in town-hall type campaign events and sharpening his indictment of Bush's handling of the economy and the massive U.S. commitment in a post-war Iraq with no clear end in sight. Kerry also got a crucial assist from the national media, which began to raise questions about Dean's temperament and "electability" after mainly according him rock-star treatment over the previous months.

A stunningly rapid collapse of Dean's campaign left one-term Sen. John Edwards of North Carolina as Kerry's last viable challenger. But Edwards, though widely credited as an attractive campaigner, rose to the attention of most voters too late for him to brake the Kerry momentum. Edwards would ultimately settle for second place on the national ticket, picked by Kerry in July to be the vice presidential nominee; after that ticket lost on Nov. 2, Dean surprised many by positioning himself to win the chairmanship of the Democratic National Committee.

Driven by the Calendar

Before 1980, primaries and caucuses were relatively spread out, culminating with decisive late-spring contests in populous states such as California and New York. But in each election cycle since, states have competed to move their events earlier and earlier, hoping to win more influ-

2004 Primary and Caucus Results

The results from the Democrats' 35 presidential primaries and 16 caucuses (shaded) underscore the dominance of Sen. John Kerry of Massachusetts, who won 47 of the official delegate-selection events in the 50 states and the District of Columbia. Percentages are rounded to the nearest whole point. The list does not include non-binding "beauty contest" primaries in the District of Columbia and Idaho. Caucus results from the District of Columbia, Hawaii, Idaho, Maine,

Minnesota, North Carolina, North Dakota and Wyoming reflect the share of the actual vote received by each candidate. For other caucus states, the results generally reflect each candidate's share of delegates elected to the next stage of the nominating process. Turnout figures for the Alaska, Colorado, Kansas, Nevada and Washington caucuses are estimates. Long dashes (—) are used when the candidate was not on the ballot.

	Date	Turnout	Wesley K. CLARK	Howard DEAN	John EDWARDS	John KERRY	Dennis J. KUCINICH	Joseph I. LIEBERMAN	Al SHARPTON	Other	Winner
Iowa	Jan. 19	124,331	0	18	32	38	1	0	0	12	Kerry
New Hampshire	Jan 27	219,787	12	26	12	38	1	9	0	1	Kerry
Arizona	Feb. 3	238,942	26	14	7	43	2	7	0	1	Kerry
Delaware	Feb. 3	33,291	9	10	11	50	1	11	6	1	Kerry
Missouri	Feb. 3	418,339	4	9	25	51	1	4	3	4	Kerry
New Mexico	Feb. 3	102,096	20	16	11	43	5	3	—	2	Kerry
North Dakota	Feb. 3	10,558	24	12	10	51	3	1	0	—	Kerry
Oklahoma	Feb. 3	302,385	30	4	30	27	1	7	1	1	Clark
South Carolina	Feb. 3	293,843	7	5	45	30	0	2	10	0	Edwards
Michigan	Feb. 7	163,769	7	17	13	52	3	0	7	1	Kerry
Washington	Feb. 7	105,000	3	30	7	49	8	0	0	3	Kerry
Maine	Feb. 8	18,259	3	28	7	44	16	0	0	1	Kerry
Tennessee	Feb. 10	369,385	23	4	27	41	1	1	2	2	Kerry
Virginia	Feb. 10	396,181	9	7	27	52	1	1	3	0	Kerry
Dist. of Columbia	Feb. 14	9,126	1	17	10	47	3	0	20	1	Kerry
Nevada	Feb. 14	9,000	—	17	10	63	7	—	1	3	Kerry
Wisconsin	Feb. 17	826,250	2	18	34	40	3	0	2	1	Kerry
Hawaii	Feb. 24	4,073	1	7	13	47	31	0	—	1	Kerry
Idaho	Feb. 24	4,920	0	11	22	54	5	0	0	7	Kerry
Utah	Feb. 24	34,854	1	4	30	55	7	1	—	1	Kerry
California	March 2	3,107,629	2	4	20	64	5	2	2	2	Kerry
Connecticut	March 2	130,023	1	4	24	58	3	5	3	2	Kerry
Georgia	March 2	626,738	1	2	41	47	1	1	6	1	Kerry
Maryland	March 2	481,476	1	3	26	60	2	1	5	4	Kerry
Massachusetts	March 2	615,188	1	3	18	72	4	1	1	2	Kerry
Minnesota	March 2	51,518	0	2	27	51	17	0	1	2	Kerry
New York	March 2	715,633	0	3	20	61	5	1	8	1	Kerry
Ohio	March 2	1,193,399	1	3	34	52	9	1	—	0	Kerry
Rhode Island	March 2	35,759	1	4	19	71	3	1	—	2	Kerry
Vermont	March 2	82,881	3	54	6	32	4	—	—	1	Dean
Florida	March 9	753,762	1	3	10	77	2	2	3	2	Kerry
Louisiana	March 9	161,653	4	5	16	70	1	—	—	3	Kerry
Mississippi	March 9	76,298	2	3	7	78	1	1	5	2	Kerry
Texas	March 9	839,231	2	5	14	67	2	3	4	3	Kerry
Kansas	March 13	2,000	1	7	9	72	10	0	0	2	Kerry
Illinois	March 16	1,217,515	2	4	11	72	2	2	3	5	Kerry
Alaska	March 20	500	0	11	3	48	26	0	0	12	Kerry
Wyoming	March 20	665	0	4	4	79	6	0	0	7	Kerry
Colorado	April 13	12,000	0	2	1	61	13	—	0	22	Kerry
North Carolina	April 17	17,809	—	6	51	27	12	—	3	1	Edwards
Pennsylvania	April 27	787,034	—	10	10	74	4	—	—	3	Kerry
Indiana	May 4	317,211	5	7	11	73	2	—	—	1	Kerry
Nebraska	May 11	71,572	—	8	14	73	2	—	2	1	Kerry
West Virginia	May 11	246,056	4	4	14	69	2	5	—	2	Kerry
Arkansas	May 18	265,849	—	—	—	66	5	—	—	28	Kerry
Kentucky	May 18	229,805	3	4	15	60	2	5	2	10	Kerry
Oregon	May 18	368,544	—	—	—	79	16	—	—	5	Kerry
Alabama	June 1	217,228	—	—	—	75	4	—	—	21	Kerry
South Dakota	June 1	84,405	—	6	—	82	2	—	—	10	Kerry
Montana	June 8	91,914	4	—	9	68	11	—	—	8	Kerry
New Jersey	June 8	208,176	—	—	—	92	4	—	—	3	Kerry

NOTE: Only Kerry and Rep. Dennis J. Kucinich, Ohio, continued to campaign through the entire primary season. The "other" category for the Jan. 19 Iowa caucuses includes 11 percent for Rep. Richard A. Gephardt, Mo., who then withdrew from the race. Sen. Joseph I. Lieberman, Conn., withdrew after the Feb. 3 contests, retired Gen. Wesley K. Clark, Ark., after the Feb. 10 primaries, former Gov. Howard Dean, Vt., after the Feb. 17 Wisconsin primary and Sen. John Edwards, N.C., after the March 2 voting. The Rev. Al Sharpton, N.Y., endorsed John Kerry on the eve of the March 16 Illinois primary.

SOURCE: The Rhodes Cook Letter. For subscription information, go to www.rhodescook.com.

Where Kerry Won the Nomination

This table reflects the delegate distribution resulting from Democratic presidential primaries and caucuses through the end of March — roughly the end of the competitive stage of the party's 2004 nominating process. The dominance of Sen. John Kerry of Massachusetts in those early campaign events virtually assured his nomination in Boston in July. (After that point, only Rep. Dennis J. Kucinich of Ohio remained an active candidate.) Altogether, 3,520 Democratic delegates were chosen to reflect the results of all the primaries and caucuses, with candidates needing to meet a threshold of 15 percent of the vote — statewide and, in most places, at the congressional district level — to qualify for a share. The totals below are for the elected delegates only: There were another 800 or so "superdelegates," prominent party and elected officials such as governors, members of Congress and members of the Democratic National Committee, who were guaranteed seats by virtue of their positions and were officially unpledged.

	Date	Elected DELEGATES	Wesley K. CLARK	Howard DEAN	John EDWARDS	John KERRY	Dennis J. KUCINICH	Joseph I. LIEBERMAN	Al SHARPTON
Iowa	Jan. 19	45	—	7	18	20	—	—	—
New Hampshire	Jan. 27	22	—	9	—	13	—	—	—
Arizona	Feb. 3	55	14	3	—	38	—	—	—
Delaware	Feb. 3	15	—	—	—	14	—	—	1
Missouri	Feb. 3	74	—	—	26	48	—	—	—
New Mexico	Feb. 3	26	8	4	—	14	—	—	—
North Dakota	Feb. 3	14	5	—	—	9	—	—	—
Oklahoma	Feb. 3	40	15	—	13	12	—	—	—
South Carolina	Feb. 3	45	—	—	28	17	—	—	—
Michigan	Feb. 7	128	—	24	6	91	—	—	7
Washington	Feb. 7	76	—	29	—	47	—	—	—
Maine	Feb. 8	24	—	9	—	15	—	—	—
Tennessee	Feb. 10	69	18	—	20	31	—	—	—
Virginia	Feb. 10	82	—	—	28	54	—	—	—
District of Columbia	Feb. 14	16	—	3	—	9	—	—	4
Nevada	Feb. 14	24	—	3	—	20	—	—	—
Wisconsin	Feb. 17	72	—	13	24	30	—	—	—
Hawaii	Feb. 24	20	—	—	—	12	8	—	—
Idaho	Feb. 24	18	—	—	6	12	—	—	—
Utah	Feb. 24	23	—	—	9	14	—	—	—
California	March 2	370	—	—	82	288	—	—	—
Connecticut	March 2	49	—	—	14	35	—	—	—
Georgia	March 2	86	—	—	32	37	—	—	—
Maryland	March 2	69	—	—	13	26	—	—	—
Massachusetts	March 2	93	—	—	13	80	—	—	—
Minnesota	March 2	72	—	—	14	26	5	—	—
New York	March 2	236	—	—	54	174	—	—	8
Ohio	March 2	140	—	—	55	81	4	—	—
Rhode Island	March 2	21	—	—	—	21	—	—	—
Vermont	March 2	15	—	9	—	6	—	—	—
Florida	March 9	177	—	—	3	174	—	—	—
Louisiana	March 9	60	—	—	10	50	—	—	—
Mississippi	March 9	33	—	—	—	33	—	—	—
Texas	March 9	195	—	—	9	118	—	—	—
Kansas	March 13	33	—	1	—	32	—	—	—
Illinois	March 16	156	—	—	—	—	—	—	—
Alaska	March 20	13	—	—	—	—	—	—	—
Wyoming	March 20	13	—	—	—	13	—	—	—
TOTAL		**2,719**	**60**	**114**	**477**	**1,714**	**17**	**—**	**20**

NOTE: Based on incomplete delegate counts from Alaska, Georgia, Illinois, Maryland, Minnesota, Nevada, Texas, Wisconsin, American Samoa and Democrats Abroad.

SOURCE: The Rhodes Cook Letter. For subscription information, go to www.rhodescook.com.

ence over the nomination and drawing the candidates' attentions. Critics say this practice inappropriately enabled a front-runner in the initial contests to gain unstoppable momentum before most of the nation could have a say — or even develop a strong impression of the candidate.

Still, neither party moved to restrict the front-loading trend. Indeed, Terry McAuliffe, the Democratic National Committee chairman in 2004, encouraged states to move up their events. His aim was to clear the field early for a single challenger largely because of one factor: money. Uncontested in his bid for the GOP nomination for a second term, Bush was well on his way to topping the fundraising record he had set in 2000, and McAuliffe worried that a prolonged Democratic nominating campaign would exhaust the winner not only physically but also financially — leaving him with few resources to combat an inevitable advertising onslaught by the president's re-election campaign.

McAuliffe got his wish. Twenty-nine states and the District of Columbia had participated in the process by March 2 — seven alone on Feb. 3, the earliest date allowed by party rules except in the traditional kickoff contests. This in turn compelled the scheduling of those contests earlier than ever: The Iowa caucuses were Jan. 19 and the New Hampshire primary was Jan. 27.

The primacy of those contests was challenged briefly by Michigan Democrats, who argued that those states were too small and demographically unrepresentative to be allowed to set the tone for the entire contest. But the Michigan protesters relented, setting their caucuses for Feb. 7 in exchange for a pledge that a commission would be empaneled in 2005 to examine the nominating process and make recommendations for the 2008 contest.

The Field Quickly Winnows

In the run-up to the first voting events, public opinion polling, fundraising and organizational presence suggested that the field could be broken into three groups:

• Running mainly symbolic candidacies from the party's left wing were Rep. Dennis J. Kucinich of Ohio; the Rev. Al Sharpton, an African-American political activist from New York; and former Sen. Carol Moseley Braun of Illinois, the only black woman ever in the Senate. Moseley Braun dropped out of the contest before the Iowa caucuses. A 10th candidate, Sen. Bob Graham of Florida, had dropped out in November 2003 and later decided to retire in 2004. (The party's 2000 nominee, Al Gore, the vice president for eight years under Bill Clinton, had announced in December 2002 that he would not seek a rematch against Bush.)

• Rep. Richard A. Gephardt of Missouri, a candidate 16 years earlier and the party's floor leader in the House from 1989 through 2002, and Sen. Joseph I. Lieberman of Connecticut, the party's 2000 vice presidential nominee, never broke out of the middle tier. Although both were highly experienced congressional figures, both were burdened with bland campaign styles and failed to gain traction among voters.

• Dean and Kerry were in the top tier with Edwards and retired Gen. Wesley K. Clark of Arkansas, the supreme allied commander of NATO from 1997 to 2000, who was the last to enter the race but gained significant public attention.

Kerry was able to re-establish his footing, and win the fa-

vor of voters with a political balancing act on defense and foreign policy issues. He used his background as a decorated Navy officer during the Vietnam War to establish his defense and foreign policy credentials, even as he blasted Bush's handling of the Iraq situation. He also reminded party liberals, including those angered by his vote for the Iraq war resolution, of his history as a war protester after he returned from Vietnam.

Kerry's decision to emphasize his Vietnam experience, which carried through the Democratic National Convention in Boston in July, would rebound against him: A group known as Swift Boat Veterans for Truth, some of whom had served in the same regions as Kerry, accused him of inflating his heroism and betraying his fellow troops by coming out against the war. But it burnished his appeal during the primaries as Democrats sought a candidate who could run credibly against Bush, whose hopes for re-election hinged greatly on his record as commander in chief in the wake of the Sept. 11, 2001 terrorist attacks.

Kerry won the Iowa caucuses with 38 percent to 32 percent for Edwards and 18 percent for Dean. The date marked Dean's unraveling: Seeking to pump up his disappointed supporters at a post-caucus rally, he rolled up his sleeves and issued a bombastic pledge to carry on — which ended with a strange yelp that turned him, almost overnight, from a legitimate contender to the butt of endless jokes.

Gephardt dropped out after drawing just 11 percent in Iowa, which he had described as "must win." Though Dean held on until finishing a distant third in the liberal redoubt of Wisconsin on Feb. 17, his fate was sealed when Kerry beat him in New Hampshire by 12 percentage points. Lieberman, whose best showing was a tie for second place in Delaware, quit the race after the Feb. 3 contests.

That left Edwards, who won South Carolina, and Clark, who won Oklahoma, jockeying to be the alternative for those who remained wary of Kerry. Each cited his Southern support in claiming he would prove more competitive against Bush than Kerry, who was derided by Republicans as a northeastern liberal. Edwards had made an impression with a stump speech laced with economic populism and his pledge to run a positive campaign; Clark argued that his military bona fides were even stronger than Kerry's, while issuing an even more scathing critique of Bush's Iraq policy.

Clark ended his campaign after finishing third in both Tennessee and Virginia on Feb. 10. Edwards kept his hopes alive by coming within 6 points of Kerry in Wisconsin a week later. But Kerry sealed the deal by winning — easily in almost every case — in nine of the 10 states holding contests on March 2. The exception was Vermont, which gave favorite son Dean his solitary primary win. Similarly, North Carolina overwhelmingly favored Edwards in its April 17 caucuses. But Kerry effortlessly swept the events in the other 20 states that voted from March 9 on.

With Sharpton ending his campaign before the March 16 Illinois primary, only Kucinich declined to concede until after the final voting on June 8. He said he was hanging in as an unvarying opponent of the Iraq war and as an advocate of poor and working class Americans — who, he argued, were getting short shrift from Kerry in his efforts to appeal to centrist voters. ◆

GOP Wins Senate Sweepstakes

The Republicans' rise to dominance in the conservative South has sustained the national success that the party has enjoyed over the past generation — including the Senate majorities the GOP has held for all but 18 months of the past decade.

That trend may have reached an apogee in 2004. A sweep of all five Southern Senate seats that were left open by Democratic incumbents boosted the Republicans to a four-seat net gain nationally, expanding their Senate majority from a tenuous 51 seats to a comfortable 55.

The gains gave Republicans 22 of the 26 seats in the South, leaving the Democrats with Arkansas' two senators and one senator each in Florida and Louisiana. Just a quarter-century before, there were only seven Republican senators from the South.

The Republicans capped Election Day 2004 with their most stunning victory, both because of its political and legislative consequences: the ouster of Tom Daschle, the Senate Democratic leader for the past decade.

Democrats were set to return for the 109th Congress in January 2005 with 44 Senate seats, the fewest for the party since Herbert Hoover was president; there was also one Democratic-leaning independent, James M. Jeffords of Vermont. In the 34 senatorial elections of 2004, the only significant bright spots for the Democrats were the takeover victories in Illinois by state Sen. Barack Obama — the party's pre-eminent rising star of the year — and in Colorado by state Attorney General Ken Salazar.

That promised to leave the Democrats severely handicapped in their quest to capture control of the Senate in the 2006 midterm elections. If Republicans maintained their 55 seats throughout the 109th Congress, Democrats would need a six-seat gain to win a majority — a feat accomplished just three times in the previous 23 elections. Another complicating factor was that more Democrats than Republicans would be defending Senate seats in 2006, as was the case in 2004. Of the 15 Republicans up for re-election, just three — Olympia J. Snowe of Maine, Lincoln Chafee of Rhode Island and Rick Santorum of Pennsylvania — were from states that Democratic Sen. John Kerry of Massachusetts carried in the 2004 presidential election. But of the 17 Democrats whose seats would be contested, five came from states that President Bush carried en route to winning his second term.

On Nov. 2, Democrats needed to dominate the closest races to reverse the Republicans' Senate majority. Instead, the pendulum swung the other way, and it did so more emphatically than even most GOP operatives expected. The party won eight of the nine most highly competitive races — a skew reminiscent of the 2000 elections, when Demo-

The Senate

109th Congress		108th Congress	
Republicans	55	Republicans	51
Democrats	44	Democrats	48
Independent	1	Independent	1

REPUBLICANS

Net Gain	4
Freshmen	7
Incumbents re-elected	12
Incumbents defeated	0

DEMOCRATS

Net Loss	4
Freshmen	2
Incumbents re-elected	13
Incumbents defeated	1

crats dominated the closest races to pull to a 50-50 tie, and the 2002 elections, in which Republicans took five of the seven closest Senate contests to reach the narrow majority that they augmented in the 2004 election.

"We exceeded all expectations," said Virginia's George Allen, the chairman of the National Republican Senatorial Committee.

The strong showing was highlighted by the GOP victory in South Dakota, where Daschle lost his campaign for a fourth term by 4,500 votes to Republican John Thune. Thune had been the state's sole House member from 1997 through 2002, when he gave up that seat to make his first run for the Senate, a narrowly unsuccessful bid to oust Democrat Tim Johnson. Daschle became the first Senate party floor leader to be defeated for re-election since Majority Leader Ernest W. McFarland, an Arizona Democrat who had held the job for just two years when he was ousted by Republican Barry Goldwater in 1952.

Daschle's status as one of the most powerful Democrats in Washington had previously helped him overcome his state's Republican leanings, but in 2004 the Republicans used his leadership role against him. They regularly branded him the Senate's "chief obstructionist," a damaging label in a state that Bush carried by a margin of 22 percentage points.

Republicans also captured the five open seats that had been held by Democrats — in North Carolina, South Carolina, Florida, Georgia and Louisiana — while fending off strong Democratic takeover bids in Oklahoma, Kentucky and Alaska. Among the competitive races, only Colorado provided a Democratic victory.

The president carried all nine states with competitive races by an average margin of 17 percentage points — from 5 points in Florida to 31 points in Oklahoma. "What we could not control was a map which was tilted decidedly in our opponent's direction and an unexpectedly strong showing by President Bush at the top of the Republican ticket," said New Jersey's Jon Corzine, chairman of the Democratic Senatorial Campaign Committee.

Democrats hoped to offset the GOP's geographical advantage by fielding candidates who had previously won statewide elections and were seen as moderate to somewhat conservative. But they got little aid from the top of the ticket, as Kerry mined for electoral votes largely outside the Senate battlegrounds.

The Republican takeovers:

● **South Carolina.** Republican Rep. Jim DeMint, who had represented part of the state's northwestern corner for six years, defeated Democrat Inez Tenenbaum, the state's superintendent of education, by 10 percentage points —

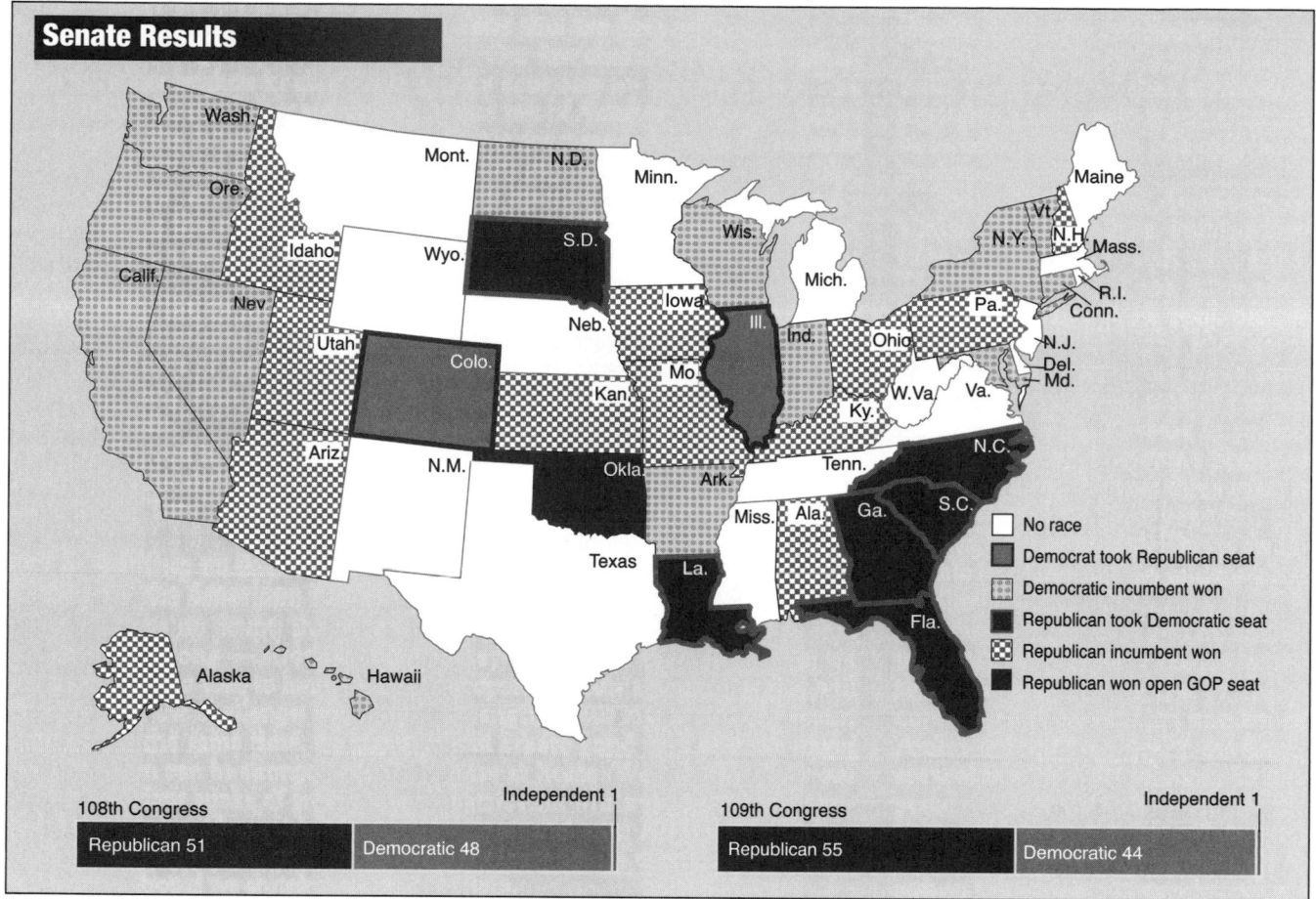

Senate Results

Wash., Ore., Calif., Nev, Idaho, Utah, Ariz., Mont., Wyo., Colo., N.M., N.D., S.D., Neb., Kan, Okla., Texas, Minn., Iowa, Mo., Ark., La., Wis, Ill., Ind., Ky., Miss., Ala., Tenn., Ga., Mich., Ohio, W.Va, Va., N.C., S.C., Fla., Pa., N.Y., Vt, N.H, Mass., R.I., Conn., N.J., Del., Md., Maine

Alaska, Hawaii

Legend:
- No race
- Democrat took Republican seat
- Democratic incumbent won
- Republican took Democratic seat
- Republican incumbent won
- Republican won open GOP seat

108th Congress
| Republican 51 | Democratic 48 | Independent 1 |

109th Congress
| Republican 55 | Democratic 44 | Independent 1 |

54 percent to 44 percent — in the race for the seat of Democrat Ernest F. Hollings, who retired after 38 years in the Senate. Bush carried the state by 17 points. "Bush's coattails here were too much to overcome," said Tenenbaum's spokesman, Adam Kovacevich. DeMint's victory put both the state's Senate seats in GOP hands for the first time since the Reconstruction era.

● **North Carolina.** Republican Rep. Richard M. Burr defeated Democrat Erskine Bowles, who had been President Bill Clinton's third White House chief of staff, with 52 percent. Burr succeeded John Edwards, the unsuccessful Democratic vice presidential nominee, who had abandoned his campaign for a second term in the Senate in the fall of 2003, when he was pursuing his party's presidential nomination.

Bowles had hoped, but ultimately failed, to improve on his respectable showing against Republican Elizabeth Dole in the state's 2002 Senate race. Burr's victory marked the fifth consecutive time that this North Carolina seat had flipped between the two parties.

● **Louisiana.** If Daschle's ouster was the sorest defeat for Democrats, the party's loss in Louisiana was probably the most embarrassing. Rep. David Vitter, who had represented the New Orleans suburbs since 1999, became the first Republican ever elected to the Senate in the history of Louisiana — the only state that had never before done so — and he did it without requiring a widely expected runoff election that his party had feared.

Vitter, a down-the-line Republican, had 51 percent of the vote, easily outdistancing Democratic Rep. Chris John

(29 percent) and Democratic state Treasurer John Kennedy (15 percent) in the race to succeed John B. Breaux, who in his three terms became synonymous with Democratic centrism and the art of senatorial compromise.

● **Florida.** In the closest of the five Southern contests, Republican Mel Martinez, Bush's initial Housing and Urban Development secretary, narrowly defeated Democrat Betty Castor, a former state education commissioner, in the contest to succeed Democrat Bob Graham, who retired after three terms. Martinez's margin of 1.1 percentage points was the closest of any Senate race in 2004.

Martinez was helped by his Hispanic ethnicity: His campaign biography emphasized that he had fled as a teenager from Fidel Castro's dictatorial regime in Cuba. The impact of his background was evident in south Florida, which leans Democratic but has a large Cuban-American constituency. Martinez narrowly won Miami-Dade; Bush lost the county by about 49,000 votes.

● **Georgia.** Republican Johnny Isakson, a House member from the Atlanta suburbs for six years, took 58 percent against Denise L. Majette, a freshman House Democrat also from the Atlanta suburbs, in the contest to succeed maverick Democrat Zell Miller, who declined to seek a full term. Isakson, a figure in state politics since the 1970s, rallied support from the Republican Party, which has been consolidating power in the conservative-leaning state. Majette emerged as the Democratic nominee only after the party failed to recruit a higher-profile candidate.

Republicans also succeeded in Southern states where

New Senators in the 109th Congress

Colorado	Ken Salazar, D	Succeeded Ben Nighthorse Campbell, R, who retired
Florida	Mel Martinez, R	Succeeded Bob Graham, D, who ran for president
Georgia	Johnny Isakson, R	Succeeded Zell Miller, D, who retired
Illinois	Barack Obama, D	Succeeded Peter G. Fitzgerald, R, who retired
Louisiana	David Vitter, R	Succeeded John B. Breaux, D, who retired
North Carolina	Richard M. Burr, R	Succeeded John Edwards, D, who ran for vice president
Oklahoma	Tom Coburn, R	Succeeded Don Nickles, R, who retired
South Carolina	Jim DeMint, R	Succeeded Ernest F. Hollings, D, who retired
South Dakota	John Thune, R	Defeated Tom Daschle, D, who sought a fourth term

they were forced to play defense:

● **Oklahoma.** The party comfortably retained the seat of Don Nickles, who rose to be party whip during his four terms. Tom Coburn, an obstetrician and prototypically conservative member of the "revolutionary" House Class of 1994 who had left the House after his self-imposed limit of three terms, took 53 percent to 41 percent for Democratic Rep. Brad Carson

Carson — seen by Democrats as a rising star — was expected to make a more competitive showing. He touted a conservative voting record and argued that Coburn's sometimes impolitic statements and iconoclastic voting record would hinder him in the Senate. But Bush's victory over Kerry by a 2-1 ratio helped seal the deal for Coburn.

● **Kentucky.** Republican incumbent Jim Bunning was initially heavily favored for a second term, but a gaffe-filled campaign plunged him into a cliffhanger race against Democratic state Sen. Daniel Mongiardo, a surgeon. Mongiardo wound up losing by fewer than 23,000 votes out of more than 1.7 million cast. Burdened by a campaign treasury that was a fraction of Bunning's, he also had to swim upstream against Bush's 20 percentage-point victory in Kentucky.

● **Alaska.** Sen. Lisa Murkowski won a full term by 3 points, an unusually weak performance for a Republican in one of the nation's most reliably Republican states. But she prevailed over tough obstacles. Her vulnerability stemmed largely from her appointment to the Senate in 2002 by her father and predecessor, GOP Gov. Frank H. Murkowski, spurring a charge of nepotism that lingered throughout her campaign. She also drew one of the Democrats' best-known challengers in Tony Knowles, a former two-term governor. Murkowski was helped by Bush's electoral dominance in Alaska and by her efforts to help pass legislation to abet construction of a natural gas pipeline in the state.

The GOP did not lose a single incumbent, a sweep that happened only twice in the previous 35 years: the party's banner years of 1980 and 1994. But Democratic takeovers of two open seats limited the damage to their party.

● **Colorado.** Salazar defeated Republican Pete Coors, a top executive in his family's brewing company, by 51 percent to 47 percent. Coors entered the contest with high name identification and a campaign treasury that was buttressed by his personal wealth, but Bush had short coattails in a state that the Kerry campaign had targeted. Ben Nighthorse Campbell, a Republican, retired after two terms.

● **Illinois.** Obama's victory over Republican Alan Keyes was so assured that he donated hundreds of thousands of dollars from his campaign treasury to other Democratic candidates and party committees. Nonetheless, Obama set a record for an Illinois Senate candidate by taking 70 percent of the vote to replace Republican Peter G. Fitzgerald, who declined to seek a second term in the face of long odds.

While the charismatic Obama was wowing a national audience with his keynote speech in July to the Democratic National Convention, Illinois Republicans were struggling to replace their original nominee, Republican businessman Jack Ryan, who quit the race after embarrassing revelations about his personal life. The GOP settled on Keyes, a conservative activist from Maryland whose hard-line ideology and lack of Illinois ties were not persuasive with voters.

The elections produced a more diverse Senate, which had no blacks or Hispanics in the previous three Congresses. Salazar and Martinez are the first Hispanics to serve in the chamber since Joseph M. Montoya, a New Mexico Democrat, was defeated for re-election in 1976. Obama became only the third black senator since the Reconstruction era — and the first since another Illinois Democrat, Carol Moseley Braun, was unseated in 1998. ◆

House GOP Strengthens Hand

Republicans in 2004 won control of the House for the sixth consecutive time, and in the process modestly fortified the relatively narrow majority they had maintained for the past decade.

They came out of the election with 232 seats in the 109th Congress, 53 percent of the total. A net gain of three seats since the previous general election, it was the largest number of seats won by Republican candidates since the first election after World War II.

The previous high-water mark was 230 seats, won in the "Republican revolution" election of 1994, which gave the party control of the House for the first time in four decades. (Because of a wave of party-switching after that contest, at one point in the 104th Congress the Republican majority amounted to 236 seats.)

Republican strategists attributed their strong showing to their candidates' efforts and, to a lesser extent, President Bush's re-election coattails. "We could not have accomplished that feat without a lot of hard work and a lot of help over the last two years, and I want to thank the president for all of his help," said Rep. Thomas M. Reynolds of New York, who took over as chairman of the National Republican Congressional Committee in the run-up to the 2004 election.

But a close look at the results of the 435 elections held across the nation revealed that the GOP gain could be attributed in its entirety to one event: The extraordinary mid-decade redistricting plan that Texas Republicans enacted in 2003 with the goal of taking control of seven Democratic seats in that state.

Republicans won six more seats in Texas on Election Day than they had won in the 2002 election, when the state used a Democratic-friendly map that was implemented by a panel of judges. That strong showing enabled Republicans to offset a small Democratic net gain elsewhere.

Democrats conceded that the broad shift in the national mood that they were counting on did not materialize by Nov. 2. Party strategists had argued throughout the 2004 campaign that any of several shifts in the attitudes of the electorate — against the president's policies, or against the way the Republican-run Congress was addressing those policies — would put them in a position to win control of the House despite the significant obstacle of the new Texas map.

Rep. Robert T. Matsui of California, the chairman of the Democratic Congressional Campaign Committee, said the hard-fought presidential campaign solidified the partisan split among the electorate — a divide which had also limited both parties' abilities to make significant House gains in

The House

109th Congress as it convened Jan. 3, 2005		108th Congress on Election Day Nov. 2, 2004	
Republicans	232	Republicans	227
Democrats	201	Democrats	205
Independent	1	Independent	1
Vacancy*	1	Vacancies	2

REPUBLICANS

Net Gain	3
Freshmen	24
Incumbents re-elected	208
Incumbents defeated	2

DEMOCRATS

Net Loss	3
Freshmen	16
Incumbents re-elected	186
Incumbents defeated	7

* Robert T. Matsui, D-Calif., died Jan. 1, 2005.

the other four elections since the watershed year of 1994.

Referring to the color-coding of the national political map that had become standard for almost all television networks and newspapers, Matsui said: "The red states, after the debates, got redder, and as a result, it made it more difficult for our candidates. The blue states, they got a little bluer, but not sufficiently bluer."

Connecticut was one prime example. John Kerry's 10 percentage-point margin of victory in the presidential contest there was significantly less than Al Gore's 18-point landslide four years earlier. That smaller cushion of support at the top of the Democratic ticket was one reason the party did not accomplish its hopes of picking up two House seats farther down the ballot. If Kerry had won by a margin approaching Gore's in 2000, those extra votes would likely have meant defeat for a pair of moderate Republicans, Christopher Shays and Rob Simmons; instead, they narrowly prevailed against well-funded opponents.

A Theme of Status Quo

The overriding theme of the House campaign, in fact, was not change, but stability — a condition reinforced by redistricting plans set before the 2002 election, which protected the incumbent party's interests in the vast majority of districts.

"The story of the House is that there was competition for only a few seats, and even those seats weren't all that competitive," said Gary C. Jacobson, a professor at the University of California-San Diego and an expert on congressional elections. He argued that all of the Republican House gains since the 2000 election, when Republicans took 221 seats to 212 for the Democrats, could be attributed to the district lines drawn for this decade.

As the campaign ended, Congressional Quarterly rated contests for 369 seats, or 85 percent of the entire House, as safe for the incumbent party, and another 29 in which one party's candidate was strongly favored. The front-runners won all of those races, most by very wide margins.

CQ rated only 37 seats (8 percent of the House) in its highly competitive categories — No Clear Favorite or Leans to one party — and even in those groups, the contests in which the winning candidate exceeded expectations outnumbered the few in which partisan turnovers occurred. In fact, excluding Texas, just six seats out of 403 changed partisan hands — a turnover rate of just 1.5 percent that had not been matched in at least half a century.

In addition, an extraordinary 99.2 percent of the non-

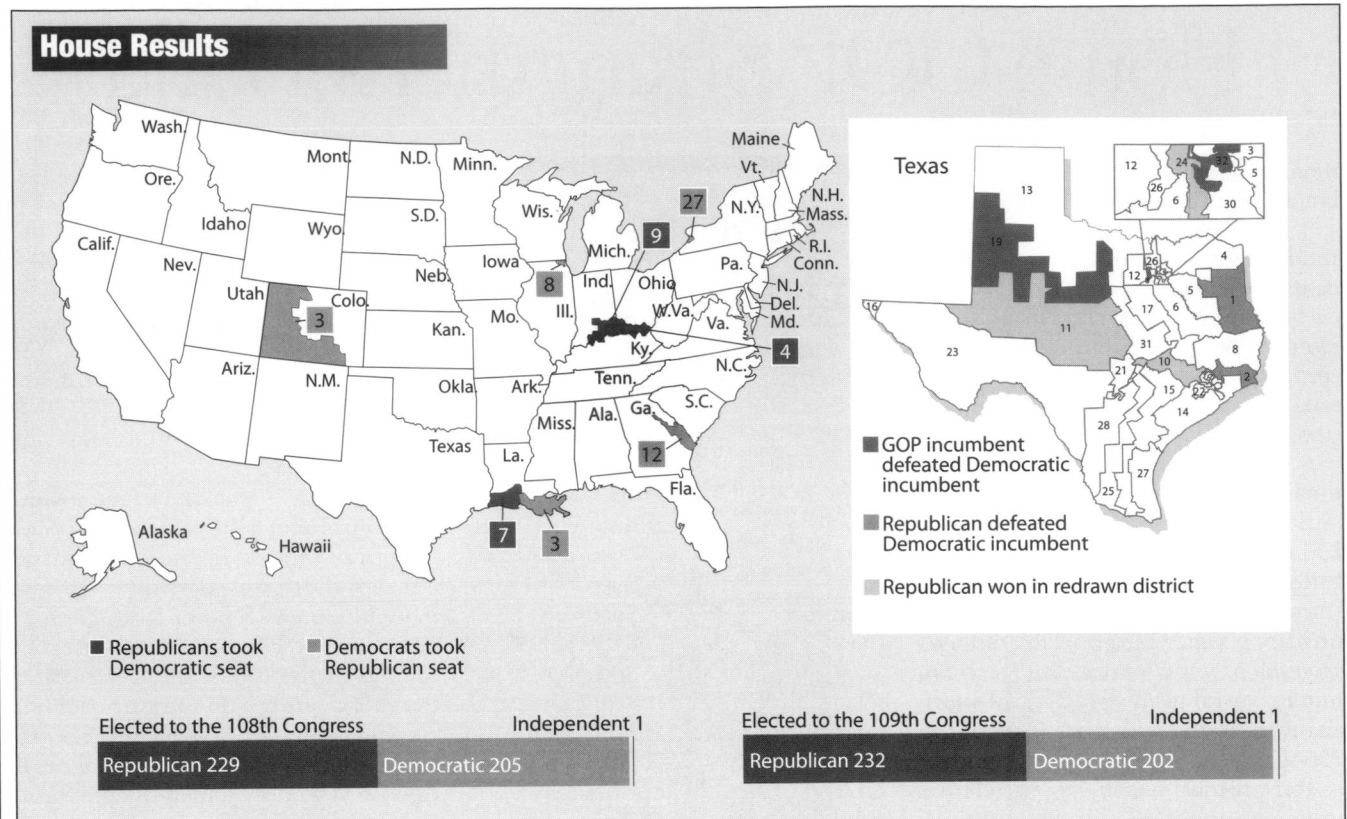

House Results

Texas

- GOP incumbent defeated Democratic incumbent
- Republican defeated Democratic incumbent
- Republican won in redrawn district

- Republicans took Democratic seat
- Democrats took Republican seat

Elected to the 108th Congress — Independent 1

| Republican 229 | Democratic 205 |

Elected to the 109th Congress — Independent 1

| Republican 232 | Democratic 202 |

Texas incumbents who sought re-election won, also the highest rate in at least 50 years. Even including Texas, 98.2 percent of incumbents were successful, up from 96 percent two years before. Only twice since 1954 had the re-election rate been higher: 98.3 percent of incumbents seeking re-election won in both 1988 and 1998.

Democrats won 202 seats but entered the 109th Congress with one fewer: Matsui died on New Year's Day 2005 of complications from a rare stem cell disorder, three days before he was to start his 14th term. Democratic-leaning Independent Bernard Sanders of Vermont was also re-elected.

Texas Redistricting Plan

The Texas redistricting plan would have been remarkable for its sweeping partisan ambitions even in the normal post-census redistricting cycle. It was even more so considering the unusual circumstances — drafted mid-decade by the newly empowered GOP majorities in the state Legislature, and spurred on by fellow Texan Tom De-Lay, the House majority leader, to replace a map drawn by judges when an earlier Legislature could not agree on a map. (*2003 Almanac, p. 14-6*)

The GOP plan paid immediate dividends. Ralph M. Hall, the dean of the delegation, reviewed the political demographics of his reconfigured district and switched to the GOP in January 2004, after an 80-year lifetime as a Democrat. In the fall he won his 13th term, and his first election as a Republican, in a landslide.

Jim Turner, the top Democrat on the Homeland Security Committee, chose to retire after four terms once his east Texas district was dismantled. The redistribution of Turner's old constituency among several other districts ef-

fectively allowed Republican legislators to create an open, Republican-dominated district linking the Houston and Austin suburbs. It was won by Republican Michael Mc-Caul, a veteran prosecutor.

Two other Democrats, each of whom had been in the House since 1979, were soundly defeated by incumbent Republicans in districts drawn with those specific outcomes in mind. Martin Frost, who chaired the House Democratic Caucus from 1999 through 2002 and the party's House campaign organization for the 1998 election, took just 44 percent of the vote in a new, suburban Dallas district against Republican Pete Sessions, an acolyte of the GOP leadership, who won a fifth term. And Charles W. Stenholm, perhaps the most influential Democratic fiscal conservative in the House and also the senior Democrat on the Agriculture Committee, took just 40 percent in a new West Texas district against Republican Randy Neugebauer, who had come to Congress only 17 months earlier as a special election winner.

The decisions by Sessions and Neugebauer to take on those incumbent-against-incumbent matchups allowed Republicans in Austin to create two more overwhelmingly Republican open seats. Kenny Marchant, who was a member of the state House redistricting committee, aided in drawing the lines of the new suburban Dallas seat he won with ease. Oil executive K. Michael Conaway won a landslide in a new district that state legislators drew with Midland as its political center.

Finally, two Democratic incumbents were defeated by GOP challengers with long resumes as judges. Nick Lampson took just 43 percent in his bid for a fifth term against Republican Ted Poe, who spent 22 years as a trial court

New House Members in the 109th Congress

California 3	Dan Lungren, R	Succeeded Doug Ose, R, who retired
California 20	Jim Costa, D	Succeeded Cal Dooley, D, who retired
Colorado 3	John Salazar, D	Succeeded Scott McInnis, R, who retired
Florida 14	Connie Mack, R	Succeeded Porter J. Goss, R, who resigned
Florida 20	Debbie Wasserman-Schultz, D	Succeeded Peter Deutsch, D, who ran for Senate
Georgia 4	Cynthia A. McKinney, D	Succeeded Denise L. Majette, D, who ran for Senate
Georgia 6	Tom Price, R	Succeeded Johnny Isakson, R, who ran for Senate
Georgia 8	Lynn Westmoreland, R	Succeeded Mac Collins, R, who ran for Senate
Georgia 12	John Barrow, D	Defeated Max Burns, R
Illinois 3	Daniel Lipinski, D	Succeeded William O. Lipinski, D, who retired
Illinois 8	Melissa Bean, D	Defeated Philip M. Crane, R
Indiana 9	Mike Sodrel, R	Defeated Baron P. Hill, D
Kentucky 4	Geoff Davis, R	Succeeded Ken Lucas, D, who retired
Louisiana 1	Bobby Jindal, R	Succeeded David Vitter, R, who ran for Senate
Louisiana 3	Charlie Melancon, D	Succeeded Billy Tauzin, R, who retired
Louisiana 7	Charles Boustany Jr., R	Succeeded Chris John, D, who ran for Senate
Michigan 7	Joe Schwarz, R	Succeeded Nick Smith, R, who retired
Missouri 3	Russ Carnahan, D	Succeeded Richard A. Gephardt, D, who ran for president
Missouri 5	Emanuel Cleaver II, D	Succeeded Karen McCarthy, D, who retired
Nebraska 1	Jeff Fortenberry, R	Succeeded Doug Bereuter, R, who resigned
New York 27	Brian Higgins, D	Succeeded Jack Quinn, R, who retired
New York 29	John R. "Randy" Kuhl Jr., R	Succeeded Amo Houghton, R, who retired
North Carolina 5	Virginia Foxx, R	Succeeded Richard M. Burr, R, who ran for Senate
North Carolina 10	Patrick T. McHenry, R	Succeeded Cass Ballenger, R, who retired
Oklahoma 2	Dan Boren, D	Succeeded Brad Carson, D, who ran for Senate
Pennsylvania 8	Michael G. Fitzpatrick, R	Succeeded James C. Greenwood, R, who retired
Pennsylvania 13	Allyson Y. Schwartz, D	Succeeded Joseph M. Hoeffel, D, who ran for Senate
Pennsylvania 15	Charlie Dent, R	Succeeded Patrick J. Toomey, R, who ran for Senate
South Carolina 4	Bob Inglis, R	Succeeded Jim DeMint, R, who ran for Senate
Texas 1	Louie Gohmert, R	Defeated Max Sandlin, D
Texas 2	Ted Poe, R	Defeated Nick Lampson, D
Texas 9	Al Green, D	Succeeded Chris Bell, D, who lost in primary
Texas 10	Michael McCaul, R	Won in newly drawn district where no incumbent ran
Texas 11	K. Michael Conaway, R	Won in newly drawn district where no incumbent ran
Texas 24	Kenny Marchant, R	Won in newly drawn district where no incumbent ran
Texas 28	Henry Cuellar, D	Succeeded Ciro D. Rodriguez, D, who lost in primary
Virginia 2	Thelma Drake, R	Succeeded Ed Schrock, R, who retired
Washington 5	Cathy McMorris, R	Succeeded George Nethercutt, R, who ran for Senate
Washington 8	Dave Reichert, R	Succeeded Jennifer Dunn, R, who retired
Wisconsin 4	Gwen Moore, D	Succeeded Gerald D. Kleczka, D, who retired

judge in Houston. Max Sandlin, also seeking a fifth term, garnered just 38 percent against Republican Louie Gohmert, who had been a trial and appeals court judge in East Texas for a decade.

The only targeted Texas incumbent who survived the redistricting onslaught was Chet Edwards, one of the most conservative House Democrats, who won an eighth term with 51 percent against GOP state Rep. Arlene Wohlgemuth.

The turnover in the delegation did not stop there. Two new Democrats from the state were also elected in November, having won the nominations in March primaries against incumbents whose fortunes were also affected by new district lines. Al Green, an attorney and former Houston NAACP leader, ousted freshman Chris Bell in a Hous-

ton district drawn to enhance the chances for an African-American Democrat. And Henry Cuellar, a former Texas secretary of state, prevailed by just 58 votes in his challenge to Ciro D. Rodriguez in a South Texas district stretching from San Antonio to Laredo.

Rodriguez, who first came to the House in 1997, spent five months contesting the outcome, the only concerted legal challenge to a federal election during the year. He and Bell were the only two congressional incumbents denied renomination in 2004.

In one ray of hope for Democrats in the state, the Supreme Court in October ordered a lower federal court to review the constitutionality of the new map. (*Redistricting, p. 18-21*)

Democrats Win All Special Elections

The Democrats asserted that the political tide was turning in their favor after taking away House seats from the Republicans in the initial pair of 2004 special elections — the first times the party had picked up seats in a special election in 13 years — but whatever trend they may have spotted faded by Election Day.

Ben Chandler, a former Kentucky attorney general and his state's 2003 Democratic gubernatorial nominee, took 55 percent of the vote against GOP state Sen. Alice Forgy Kerr in a Feb. 17 special election in the state's east-central 6th District. The seat had been held for five years by Republican Ernie Fletcher, who had defeated Chandler to win the governorship in November 2003.

Stephanie Herseth, an attorney and one-time farm union official, took 51 percent against Republican Larry Diedrich, a seven-year veteran of the state legislature, to win South Dakota's only House seat on June 1. It had become vacant Jan. 20, when Republican Bill Janklow resigned in the middle of his freshman term to prepare to serve a jail term for vehicular manslaughter. Herseth, who had lost to Janklow in 2002, became the first woman ever to represent the state in the House.

The Democrats also won the only other special election of the year, but that contest in North Carolina was in no way competitive. G. K. Butterfield, a veteran state judge, took 71 percent July 20 in the agrarian, black-majority 1st District. Freshman Democrat Frank W. Ballance Jr. had resigned June 11, citing poor health. But he was indicted Sept. 2 on money laundering and mail fraud charges stemming from his alleged use of more than $100,000 belonging to a state-funded drug counseling program — which he had operated — to benefit himself, his family and a church where he was a deacon.

Two other House vacancies occurred during the year, when Republicans who had already announced their retirements from Congress left early to pursue other careers. In both cases the departures came too late in the year to make a special election practical. Doug Bereuter of Nebraska stepped down on Aug. 31 to run the Asia Foundation, a nonprofit group that promotes economic development and improved U.S. relations with that continent. Porter J. Goss of Florida resigned Sept. 23, the day after he was confirmed by the Senate to be the director of central intelligence.

A Few Exceptions

There were only a few electoral surprises, or House incumbent losses, anywhere else in the nation.

Democrat John Barrow, a commissioner in Athens-Clarke County, took 52 percent to defeat freshman Republican Rep. Max Burns in eastern Georgia's Democratic-leaning 12th District. Democratic officials had made Burns their top Republican incumbent target this year, arguing that his 2002 victory was a fluke resulting from mid-campaign revelations that his Democratic opponent that year, Charles Walker Jr., had a prior arrest record.

The other two challenger victories outside of Texas demonstrated that persistence sometimes pays in politics: Both prevailed after losing 2002 congressional campaigns.

In Illinois, Democratic businesswoman Melissa Bean took 52 percent to unseat Republican Rep. Philip M. Crane, whose 35-year tenure representing a heavily GOP portion of suburban Chicago had made him the dean of House Republicans. Bean had garnered just 43 percent against Crane two years before, but she raised about five times as much money for her rematch and capitalized on the perception that Crane was spending little time in the district.

Aided by Bush's strong showing in southern Indiana, Republican businessman Mike Sodrel defeated Rep. Baron P. Hill, who was seeking a fourth term, by just 1,425 votes, the second closest House race of the year. Hill had won his first contest against Sodrel by 5 points two years ago.

Open-seat contests — usually the source of most partisan turnovers in each election cycle — only underscored the locked-in nature of most House seats. Only five of the 33 open seats changed party hands.

In western Colorado, Democratic state Rep. John Salazar — a brother of Ken Salazar, who won the state's open Senate seat the same day — prevailed by 4 points over Greg Walcher, a former state Department of Natural Resources director. He won the seat held for 12 years by Republican Scott McInnis, who left to become a lobbyist.

In upstate New York, Democrats took a Buffalo-area seat held for 12 years by Jack Quinn, another Republican who left for a lobbying career. State Rep. Brian Higgins defeated Republican Erie County Comptroller Nancy Naples with 51 percent.

In northern Kentucky, Republicans picked up the seat of Ken Lucas, who left after three terms as one of the most conservative Democrats in the House. Businessman Geoff Davis took 54 percent against Democrat Nick Clooney, a former local newscaster and columnist and the father of actor George Clooney.

The parties traded open seats in southern Louisiana. Democratic businessman Charles Melancon prevailed by 525 votes, the narrowest congressional margin of victory of the year. He bested Republican Billy Tauzin III, a telecommunications lobbyist who hoped to succeed his father, Republican Rep. Billy Tauzin, who retired after 12 terms to head the Pharmaceutical Research and Manufacturers of America (PhRMA). At the urging of GOP leaders, the elder Tauzin had relinquished the gavel of the Energy and Commerce Committee, which he had chaired since 2001, in February after his negotiations with PhRMA came to light.

Louisiana Republicans offset that setback in a neighboring district, where Republican physician Charles Boustany Jr. took 55 percent against Democratic state Sen. Willie

Justices Split on Redistricting

State legislators have long drawn congressional district boundaries in the hope of maximizing their party's chances for electoral success without drawing a court challenge by the rival party claiming that the new boundaries are unfair. The Supreme Court, for the first time in two decades, weighed in on the constitutional propriety of this longstanding political strategy in 2004 — but its April 28 decision in *Vieth v. Jubelier* offered an unclear path for potential challenges to maps that are politically skewed to one party.

Five justices delivered a set of fractured opinions about just how far one party could permissibly take a crusade to redistrict itself into political dominance. The other four justices held that, because of its entirely political nature, such a redistricting efforts should always be beyond the purview of the federal courts.

The court ruled, 5-4, that, in theory, a case of political gerrymandering might some day be so egregious as to be unconstitutional. But the justices also upheld — also by 5-4 — the existing congressional boundaries of Pennsylvania, which the Republican-majority General Assembly drew after the 2000 census with the principal aim of guaranteeing GOP dominance of the state's House delegation throughout this decade. Pennsylvania is vigorously competitive in statewide races, but Democrats won only seven of the state's 19 House seats under the new map in both 2002 and 2004.

The court's decision gave some new hope to Democrats wanting to kill the Texas congressional map enacted in 2003 at the urging of House Majority Leader Tom DeLay, R-Texas. The map transformed the state's House delegation from a 17-15 Democratic edge after the 2002 election to a 21-11 Republican advantage after the 2004 election. (*2003 Almanac, p. 14-6*)

In October 2004, the Supreme Court asked a federal court in Texas to consider the state's new map in light of the *Vieth* decision. Democrats said they expected to lose in that court — the same panel that rejected their original objections to the Texas map — but would appeal to the Supreme Court, which might use that case to further refine its thinking on the use of political influence of line-drawing.

Manipulating the physical shape of legislative districts to benefit a particular politician or party is a practice at least two centuries old in American politics. The shorthand for the practice, "gerrymander," was coined in 1812, when the Massachusetts legislature drew a salamander-shaped state legislative district to benefit the party of Gov. Elbridge Gerry.

Until 2004, the signature case on the issue was *Davis v. Bandemer,* in which the Supreme Court held in 1986 that political gerrymandering was subject to court review, but that claims of excessive use of political motives would need to clear a high and amorphous threshold.

The Court in *Vieth* rebuffed Democrats' argument that the frequently tortured cartography of the Pennsylvania map had deprived them of the Constitution's guarantee of equal protection. Five justices — John Paul Stevens, David H. Souter, Ruth Bader Ginsburg, Stephen G. Breyer and Anthony M. Kennedy — said such a claim could succeed in the future, but they were deeply divided over how to fashion a standard that would govern such claims.

Four justices — Chief Justice William H. Rehnquist and Justices Sandra Day O'Connor, Antonin Scalia and Clarence Thomas — called for abandoning the 1986 precedent. "No judicially discernible and manageable standards for adjudicating political gerrymandering claims have emerged" since then, Scalia wrote.

While Kennedy joined those four justices to form the majority that upheld the Pennsylvania map, he also joined the other four members of the court to form the majority that stood by *Bandemer.* Since he thereby positioned himself as the swing vote in this area, lawyers on both sides read Kennedy's opinion most carefully. He suggested that plaintiffs could mount a successful challenge to an overly political map on First Amendment grounds — by arguing that a highly partisan map unfairly punishes one group because of the political beliefs that it holds.

Kennedy summed up the difficulty that lower courts and plaintiffs face in determining when political factors become predominant in the redrawing of district lines. "Courts must be cautious about adopting a standard that turns on whether the partisan interests in the redistricting process were excessive," he wrote. "Excessiveness is not easily determined."

Landry Mount to succeed Democrat Chris John, who lost a bid for the Senate.

Both Louisiana turnovers came Dec. 4, in congressional runoffs unique to the Louisiana election system.

In November, most incumbents won with solid majorities, including several who barely won two years ago. Among them was freshman Colorado Republican Bob Beauprez, who won the closest race of 2002 but won his second term by a comfortable 12 points; Kentucky Republican Anne M. Northup, who won with 61 percent after winning her previous four races with no more than 53 percent; and Georgia Democrat Jim Marshall, who won his second term in a rematch against Republican Calder Clay by nearly 56,000 votes — after winning the first time by just 1,500 votes. ◆

Departures: The 108th Congress

Senator Defeated in General Election (1)

NAME, PARTY, STATE	AGE	BEGAN SENATE SERVICE	WINNER
Tom Daschle, D-S.D.	56	1987	John Thune

House Members Defeated in General Election (2 R, 5 D)

NAME, PARTY, STATE (DISTRICT)	AGE	BEGAN HOUSE SERVICE	WINNER
Max Burns, R-Ga. (12)	55	2003	John Barrow
Philip M. Crane, R-Ill. (8)	74	1969	Melissa Bean
Martin Frost, D-Texas (24)	62	1979	Rep. Pete Sessions *(in new 32nd District)*
Baron P. Hill, D-Ind. (9)	51	1999	Mike Sodrel
Nick Lampson, D-Texas (9)	59	1997	Ted Poe *(in new 2nd District)*
Max Sandlin, D-Texas (1)	52	1997	Louie Gohmert
Charles W. Stenholm, D-Texas (17)	66	1979	Rep. Randy Neugebauer *(in new 19th District)*

Sought Other Office (7 R, 8 D)

NAME, PARTY, STATE (DISTRICT)	AGE	BEGAN SERVICE	GOAL / OUTCOME
Rep. Richard M. Burr, R-N.C. (5)	48	1995	Senate — Won
Rep. Brad Carson, D-Okla. (2)	37	2001	Senate — Lost to Tom Coburn
Rep. Mac Collins, R-Ga. (8)	60	1993	Senate — Lost primary to Rep. Johnny Isakson
Rep. Jim DeMint, R-S.C. (4)	53	1999	Senate — Won
Rep. Peter Deutsch, D-Fla. (20)	47	1993	Senate — Lost primary to Betty Castor
Sen. John Edwards, D-N.C.	51	1999	Vice President — Lost
Rep. Richard A. Gephardt, D-Mo. (3)	63	1977	President — Dropped out during primaries
Sen. Bob Graham, D-Fla.	67	1987	President — Dropped out during primaries
Rep. Joseph M. Hoeffel, D-Pa. (13)	54	1999	Senate — Lost to Sen. Arlen Specter
Rep. Johnny Isakson, R-Ga. (6)	59	1999	Senate — Won
Rep. Chris John, D-La. (7)	44	1997	Senate — Lost to Rep. David Vitter
Rep. Denise L. Majette, D-Ga. (4)	49	2003	Senate — Lost to Rep. Johnny Isakson
Rep. George Nethercutt, R-Wash. (5)	60	1995	Senate — Lost to Sen. Patty Murray
Rep. Patrick J. Toomey, R-Pa. (15)	42	1999	Senate — Lost primary to Sen. Arlen Specter
Rep. David Vitter, R-La. (1)	43	1999	Senate — Won

NOTE: Sen. John Kerry, D-Mass., and Sen. Joseph I. Lieberman, D-Conn., also ran for president, but their Senate terms did not expire this year. Rep. Dennis J. Kucinich, D-Ohio (10) also ran for president, but he dropped his bid in time to run successfully for re-election.

Defeated in Primary (2 D)

NAME, PARTY, STATE (DISTRICT)	WINNER
Rep. Chris Bell, D-Texas (25) *(in new 9th District)*	Al Green
Rep. Ciro D. Rodriguez, D-Texas (28)	Henry Cuellar

Retiring House Members (10 R, 6 D)

NAME, PARTY, STATE (DISTRICT)	AGE	BEGAN SERVICE
Cass Ballenger, R-N.C. (10)	77	1986
Cal Dooley, D-Calif. (20)	50	1991
Jennifer Dunn, R-Wash. (8)	63	1993
James C. Greenwood, R-Pa. (8)	53	1993
Amo Houghton, R-N.Y. (29)	78	1987
Gerald D. Kleczka, D-Wis. (4)	60	1984
William O. Lipinski, D-Ill. (3)	66	1983
Ken Lucas, D-Ky. (4)	71	1999
Karen McCarthy, D-Mo. (5)	57	1995
Scott McInnis, R-Colo. (3)	51	1993
Doug Ose, R-Calif. (3)	49	1999
Jack Quinn, R-N.Y. (27)	53	1993
Ed Schrock, R-Va. (2)	63	2001
Nick Smith, R-Mich. (7)	70	1993
Billy Tauzin, R-La. (3)	61	1980
Jim Turner, D-Texas (2)	58	1997

Retiring Senators (3 R, 3 D)

NAME, PARTY, STATE (DISTRICT)	AGE	BEGAN SERVICE
John B. Breaux, D-La.	60	1987
Ben Nighthorse Campbell, R-Colo.	71	1993
Peter G. Fitzgerald, R-Ill.	44	1999
Ernest F. Hollings, D-S.C.	82	1966
Zell Miller, D-Ga.	72	2000
Don Nickles, R-Okla.	55	1981

Resigned (5 R, 1 D)

NAME, PARTY, STATE (DISTRICT)	EFFECTIVE DATE
Rep. Porter J. Goss, R-Fla. (14) *(no special election held)*	Sept. 23, 2004
Rep. Doug Bereuter, R-Neb. (1) *(no special election held)*	Aug. 31, 2004
Rep. Frank W. Ballance Jr., D-N.C. (1) *(G. K. Butterfield, D, won July 20, 2004, special election)*	June 11, 2004
Rep. Bill Janklow, R-S.D. (AL) *(Stephanie Herseth, D, won June 1, 2004, special election)*	Jan. 20, 2004
Rep. Ernie Fletcher, R-Ky. (6) *(Ben Chandler, D, won Feb. 17, 2004, special election)*	Dec. 8, 2003
Rep. Larry Combest, R-Texas (19) *(Randy Neugebauer, R, won June 3, 2003, special election)*	May 31, 2003

Bad Year for Incumbent Governors

Although most states choose to hold their elections for governor in years when there is no presidential contest, 11 states had gubernatorial races in 2004.

For incumbents in those races, it was a bad year. Of the 11 states, seven elected new chief executives. Two incumbents were defeated, and two others were denied renomination by their own parties. The other three open governors' races were created because the incumbents retired; in each case falling job approval ratings played a central role in their decisions to depart.

Only four governors were re-elected, each one to a second term: Republicans John Hoeven of North Dakota and Jim Douglas of Vermont, and Democrats Michael F. Easley of North Carolina and Ruth Ann Minner of Delaware.

The movement at the governors' mansions continued a trend begun in 2002, when a record 25 of the 36 contests produced new governors. "With the seven new governors this time around, we have hit a high-water mark for new governors out there," said Tim Storey, an elections analyst with the National Conference of State Legislatures.

Though many states were in better fiscal shape during the campaign season than they were at the height of the recession in 2002, budgetary strains nonetheless forced some outgoing governors to make politically hazardous choices involving spending restraints and tax increases. As a consequence, the new governors were certain to begin their tenures asking Washington for more cash and less interference as they worked to implement new education standards and increase health care rolls in their states.

Every state except Vermont required a balanced budget each year. With increases in broad-based income and sales taxes a politically fatal suggestion in most states, some of the 2004 candidates for governor called for "sin" taxes on products such as cigarettes or alcohol to fill in fiscal gaps. Some also proposed raising revenues by introducing various forms of gambling, such as slot machines and state lotteries.

The 64 percent turnover rate in the 2004 elections for governor had no partisan bias. The party balance after Election Day remained the same: 28 Republicans and 22 Democrats. There were two takeovers for each party, with Republicans Mitch Daniels of Indiana and Matt Blunt of Missouri capturing seats formerly held by Democrats, and Democrats John Lynch of New Hampshire and Brian Schweitzer of Montana taking over GOP seats.

One incumbent in each party was sent packing on Nov. 2. In New Hampshire, Republican Gov. Craig Benson was hurt by ethics questions that forced the resignations of several high-ranking appointees, creating an opening for Lynch, a first-time candidate who won with 51 percent of the vote.

The Governors

After 2004 Election		Before 2004 Election	
Republicans	28	Republicans	28
Democrats	22	Democrats	22

REPUBLICANS

Net gain	0
Freshmen	3
Incumbents re-elected	2
Incumbent defeated	1

DEMOCRATS

Net loss	0
Freshmen	4
Incumbents re-elected	2
Incumbent defeated	1

Daniels — President Bush's first director of the Office of Management and Budget and a rising star in the eyes of some GOP strategists — won with a comfortable 53 percent against the Democratic incumbent, Joseph E. Kernan. Kernan had moved up from lieutenant governor in 2003, when Democrat Frank L. O'Bannon died during his seventh year in office. Daniels ended one of the long-running anomalies of partisan politics: the Democrats' four-election winning streak for governor, dating to 1988, in the most reliably Republican state in the industrial midwestern area of the country.

The Republicans also picked up the governorship in Missouri, where another Democratic incumbent also was ousted — only in this case, it was by his own party. Gov. Bob Holden, who was plagued by state budget controversies during his term in office, lost the Aug. 3 primary to State Auditor Claire McCaskill. But McCaskill lost, 51 percent to 48 percent, to Republican Blunt, Missouri's secretary of State. Blunt, who turned 34 a few weeks after the election, was seen as a young Republican on the rise. He was aided by his family ties: His father, Roy, who is also from Missouri, has been the House majority whip since 2003 and was the chief deputy whip for the four previous years.

Turnovers and Long Recounts

The Democrats balanced the scales in Montana by taking advantage of the poor job approval rating of outgoing Republican incumbent Judy Martz, who was hurt by the state's economic problems. Democrats nominated a strong candidate in Schweitzer, a rancher who came within 3 percentage points of upsetting Republican Sen. Conrad Burns' bid for a third term in 2000. Schweitzer won by 50 percent to 46 percent in the Republican-leaning state, even though he drew a solid GOP opponent in Bob Brown, Montana's secretary of State.

Both of the Republican winners in turnover states were set to pursue their agendas with the benefit of consolidated partisan control in the state legislature. Republicans held on to their majorities in both halves of the Missouri General Assembly. In Indiana, voters elected a Republican-majority state House for the first time since 1994 and continued GOP control of the state Senate.

In Montana, the Democrats captured the state Senate to give Schweitzer some legislative leverage. The state House began 2005 with the membership evenly divided, though Democrats nominally controlled the chamber because state law required that the speaker and governor be of the same party if the legislature is divided.

In New Hampshire, Lynch was elected at the same time

Gubernatorial Results

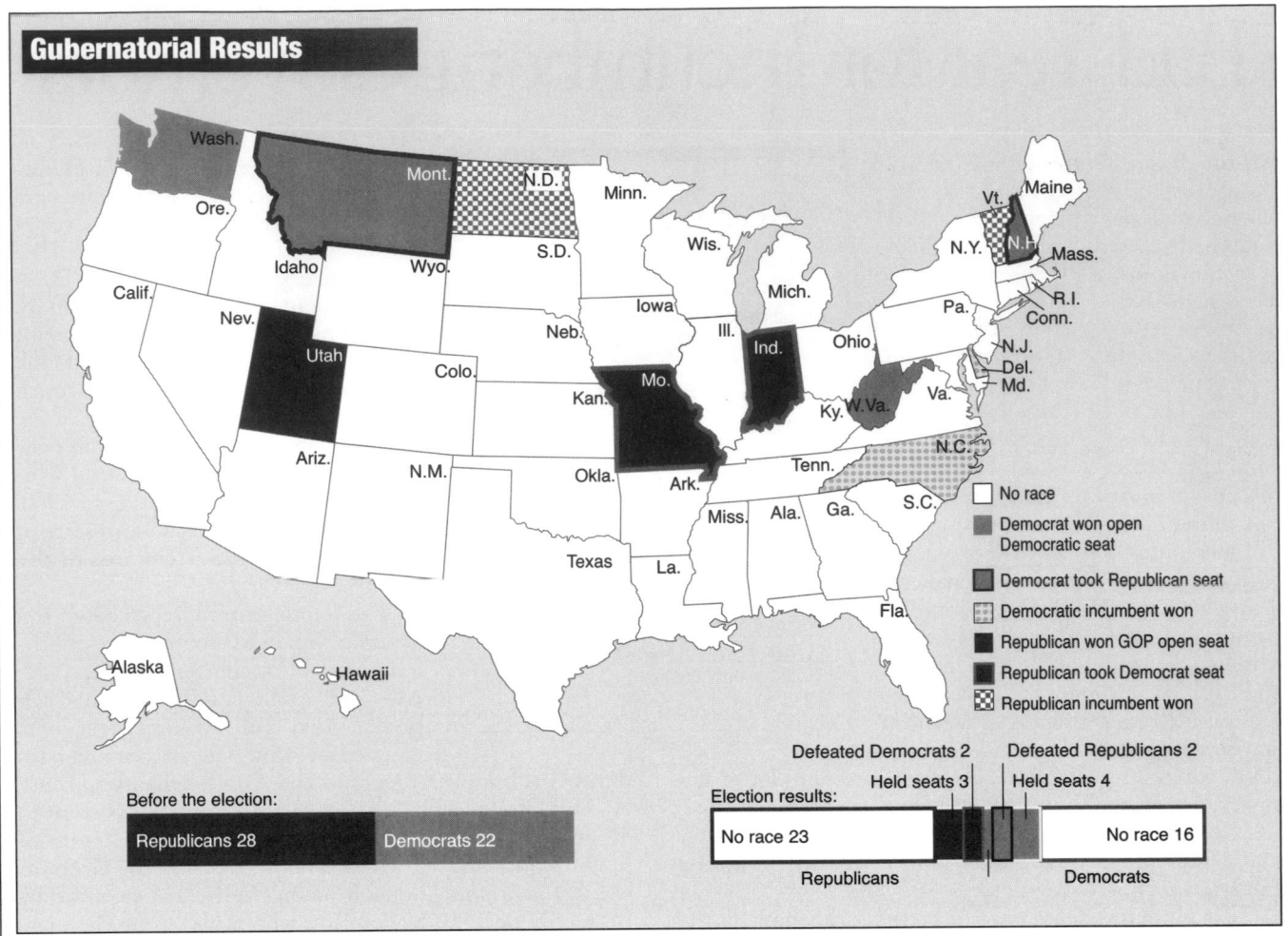

Legend:
- No race
- Democrat won open Democratic seat
- Democrat took Republican seat
- Democratic incumbent won
- Republican won GOP open seat
- Republican took Democrat seat
- Republican incumbent won

Before the election:

Republicans 28	Democrats 22

Election results:

Defeated Democrats 2 · Held seats 3 | Defeated Republicans 2 · Held seats 4

No race 23				No race 16

Republicans — Democrats

Republican majorities were retained in both halves of the state legislature.

The other three governors elected on Nov. 2 — in Washington, Utah and West Virginia — were picked to replace incumbents who chose not to seek re-election.

In Washington, where Democrat Gary Locke stepped down after two terms, Democratic state Attorney General Christine Gregoire defeated former Republican state Sen. Dino Rossi by 129 votes out of more than 2.8 million cast.

Though Gregoire was initially a strong favorite to win in the Democratic-leaning state, Rossi presented her with a tough challenge. He emphasized the state's fiscal problems, blaming them on Democrats who have held the governor's office without interruption since 1984. Gregoire held a slim lead on election night, but Rossi led by 261 votes two weeks later when all the mail-in ballots were tallied. State law triggered an automatic machine recount, which narrowed Rossi's lead to 42 votes. Democrats then sought a hand recount, and ballots in heavily Democratic King County (Seattle) put Gregoire on top to stay. Republicans pushed to delay the certification of Gregoire's election, saying there were discrepancies in the King County count. But the Democratic-controlled legislature voted to certify Gregoire as governor Jan. 11, 2005, one day before she took office.

The other new governors replaced incumbents whose problems were more personal than policy-related.

In Utah, Republican Olene S. Walker — who stepped up from lieutenant governor in 2003 when GOP Gov. Michael O. Leavitt left to head the EPA — was not expected to seek a full term. By the time she changed her mind, there was already a large field of candidates and she lost the nomination at the state GOP convention. Ultimately, primary voters chose Jon Huntsman Jr., a wealthy petrochemical businessman, who took 57 percent in the fall against Democrat Scott Matheson Jr., a law school dean whose late father was once governor and whose brother is Rep. Jim Matheson of Utah.

In West Virginia, Democrat Bob Wise dropped his plans for a second term after admitting to an extramarital affair with a woman employed by the state. But the Democrats held the governorship with ease; Joe Manchin III, well-known as the secretary of State, took 64 percent against Republican businessman Monty Warner. ◆

Congressional, Gubernatorial Returns

These are the complete and official results from the general elections for the 34 Senate seats, 435 House seats and 11 governorships contested in 2004 — as provided by the Web sites of the secretaries of state. The figures are the total votes received by, and the percentage of the vote for, each candidate.

Symbols:		
●	Incumbent	
x	Winner without opposition	
AL	At-large district	
#	2005 new member	

	Vote Total	%
ALABAMA		
Senate		
● Richard C. Shelby (R)	1,242,200	67.5
Wayne Sowell (D)	595,018	32.4
write-ins	1,848	.1
House		
1 ● Jo Bonner (R)	161,067	63.1
Judy McCain Belk (D)	93,938	36.8
write-ins	159	.1
2 ● Terry Everett (R)	177,086	71.4
Charles D "Chuck" James (D)	70,562	28.5
write-ins	299	.1
3 ● Mike D. Rogers (R)	150,411	61.2
Bill Fuller (D)	95,240	38.8
write-ins	133	—
4 ● Robert B. Aderholt (R)	191,110	74.7
Carl Cole (D)	64,278	25.1
write-ins	336	.1
5 ● Robert E. "Bud" Cramer (D)	200,999	73.0
Gerald "Gerry" Wallace (R)	74,145	26.9
write-ins	315	.1
6 ● Spencer Bachus (R)	264,819	98.8
write-ins	3,224	1.2
7 ● Artur Davis (D)	183,408	75.0
Steve F. Cameron (R)	61,019	24.9
write-ins	211	.1
ALASKA		
Senate		
● Lisa Murkowski (R)	149,773	48.6
Tony Knowles (D)	140,424	45.6
Marc J. Millican (NON)	8,885	2.9
Jerry Sanders (AKI)	3,785	1.2

	Vote Total	%
Jim Sykes (GREEN)	3,053	1.0
Scott A. Kohlhaas (LIBERT)	1,240	.4
Ted "Big" Gianoutsos (NON)	732	.2
write-ins	423	.1
House		
AL ● Don Young (R)	213,216	71.1
Thomas M. Higgins (D)	67,074	22.4
Timothy A. Feller (GREEN)	11,434	3.8
Alvin A. Anders (LIBERT)	7,157	2.4
write-ins	1,115	.4
ARIZONA		
Senate		
● John McCain (R)	1,505,372	76.7
Stuart Starky (D)	404,507	20.6
Ernest Hancock (LIBERT)	51,798	2.6
House		
1 ● Rick Renzi (R)	148,315	58.5
Paul Babbitt (D)	91,776	36.2
John Crockett (LIBERT)	13,260	5.2
2 ● Trent Franks (R)	165,260	59.2
Randy Camacho (D)	107,406	38.5
Powell Gammill (LIBERT)	6,625	2.4
write-in	12	—
3 ● John Shadegg (R)	181,012	80.1
Mark J. Yannone (LIBERT)	44,962	19.9
4 ● Ed Pastor (D)	77,150	70.1
Don Karg (R)	28,238	25.7
Gary Fallon (LIBERT)	4,639	4.2
5 ● J.D. Hayworth (R)	159,455	59.5
Elizabeth Rogers (D)	102,363	38.2
Michael Kielsky (LIBERT)	6,189	2.3
6 ● Jeff Flake (R)	202,822	79.4
Craig Stritar (LIBERT)	52,695	20.6

	Vote Total	%
7 ● Raúl M. Grijalva (D)	108,868	62.1
Joseph "Joe" Sweeney (R)	59,066	33.7
Dave Kaplan (LIBERT)	7,503	4.3
8 ● Jim Kolbe (R)	183,363	60.4
Eva Bacal (D)	109,963	36.2
Robert Anderson (LIBERT)	10,443	3.4
ARKANSAS		
Senate		
● Blanche Lincoln (D)	580,973	55.8
Jim Holt (R)	458,036	44.2
Glen A. Schwarz — write-in	212	—
Gene Mason — write-in	128	—
House		
1 ● Marion Berry (D)	162,388	66.6
Vernon Humphrey (R)	81,758	33.4
2 ● Vic Snyder (D)	160,834	58.2
Marvin Parks (R)	115,655	41.8
William Gabriel — write-in	4	—
3 ● John Boozman (R)	160,629	59.3
Jan Judy (D)	103,158	38.1
Dale Morfey (I)	7,016	2.6
4 ● Mike Ross (D)		x
CALIFORNIA		
Senate		
● Barbara Boxer (D)	6,955,728	57.7
Bill Jones (R)	4,555,922	37.8
Marsha Feinland (PFP)	243,846	2.0
James P. "Jim" Gray (LIBERT)	216,522	1.8
Don Grundmann (AMI)	81,224	.7
write-ins	53	—

Abbreviations for Party Designations

AC	—American Constitution	GREEN —Green	NL —Natural Law	S —Socialist
AKI	—Alaskan Independence	I —Independent	NON —Nonpartisan	SE —Socialist Equality
AMI	—American Independent	IA —Independent American	PAC —Politicians Are Crooks	SW —Socialist Workers
BLD	—Builders	INDC —Independence	PC —Personal Choice	UC —United Citizens
C	—Conservative	LIBERT —Libertarian	PF —Protecting Freedom	USTAX —U.S. Taxpayers
CC	—Concerned Citizens	LMP —Legalize Marijuana	PFP —Peace and Freedom	VET —Veterans
CEN	—Centrist	LU —Liberty Union	PLC —Pro Life Conservative	WFM —Working Families
CNSTP	—Constitution	M —Marijuana	PRO —Progressive	WG —Wisconsin Green
D	—Democratic	MOUNT —Mountain	R —Republican	X —Not applicable
F	—Fair	NEB —Nebraska	REF —Reform	

		Total	%
House			
1	• Mike Thompson (D)	189,366	66.9
	Lawrence Wiesner (R)	79,970	28.3
	Pamela Elizondo (GREEN)	13,635	4.8
2	• Wally Herger (R)	182,119	66.8
	Mike Johnson (D)	90,310	33.1
3	# Dan Lungren (R)	177,738	61.9
	Gabe Castillo (D)	100,025	34.8
	Douglas Tuma (LIBERT)	9,310	3.2
4	• John T. Doolittle (R)	221,926	65.4
	David L. Winters (D)	117,443	34.6
5	• Robert T. Matsui (D)	138,004	71.4
	Mike Dugas (R)	45,120	23.3
	Pat Driscoll (GREEN)	6,593	3.4
	John C. Reiger (PF)	3,670	1.9
6	• Lynn Woolsey (D)	226,423	72.7
	Paul L. Erickson (R)	85,244	27.4
7	• George Miller (D)	166,831	76.1
	Charles R. Hargrave (R)	52,446	23.9
8	• Nancy Pelosi (D)	224,017	83.0
	Jennifer Depalma (R)	31,074	11.5
	Leilani Dowell (PF)	9,527	3.5
	Terry Baum — write-in	5,446	2.0
9	• Barbara Lee (D)	215,630	84.5
	Claudia Bermudez (R)	31,278	12.3
	James M. Eyer (LIBERT)	8,131	3.2
10	• Ellen O. Tauscher (D)	182,750	65.7
	Jeff Ketelson (R)	95,349	34.3
11	• Richard W. Pombo (R)	163,582	61.2
	Gerald M. "Jerry" McNerney (D)	103,587	38.8
12	• Tom Lantos (D)	171,852	68.0
	Mike Garza (R)	52,593	20.8
	Pat Gray (GREEN)	23,038	9.1
	Harland Harrison (LIBERT)	5,116	2.0
13	• Pete Stark (D)	144,605	71.6
	George I. Bruno (R)	48,439	24.0
	Mark W. Stroberg (LIBERT)	8,877	4.4
14	• Anna G. Eshoo (D)	182,712	69.8
	John C. "Chris" Haugen (R)	69,564	26.6
	Brian Holtz (LIBERT)	9,588	3.7
	write-in	24	—
15	• Michael M. Honda (D)	154,385	72.0
	Raymond L. Chukwu (R)	59,953	28.0
16	• Zoe Lofgren (D)	129,222	70.9
	Douglas Adams McNea (R)	47,992	26.3
	Markus Welch (LIBERT)	5,067	2.8
17	• Sam Farr (D)	148,958	66.7
	Mark Risley (R)	65,117	29.2
	Ray Glock-Grueneich (GREEN)	3,645	1.6
	Joe Williams (PF)	2,823	1.3
	Jim Smolen (LIBERT)	2,607	1.2
	write-in	75	—
18	• Dennis Cardoza (D)	103,732	67.5
	Charles F. Pringle Sr. (R)	49,973	32.5
19	• George P. Radanovich (R)	155,354	66.0
	James Lex Bufford (D)	64,047	27.2
	Larry R. Mullen (GREEN)	15,863	6.7
20	# Jim Costa (D)	61,005	53.4
	Roy Ashburn (R)	53,231	46.6
21	• Devin Nunes (R)	140,721	73.2
	Fred B. Davis (D)	51,594	26.8
22	• Bill Thomas (R)	209,384	100.0
23	• Lois Capps (D)	153,980	63.0
	Donald E. Regan (R)	83,926	34.4
	Michael Favorite (LIBERT)	6,391	2.6
24	• Elton Gallegly (R)	178,660	62.8
	Brett Wagner (D)	96,397	33.9
	Stuart A. Bechman (GREEN)	9,321	3.3

		Total	%
25	• Howard P. "Buck" McKeon (R)	145,575	64.4
	Fred "Tim" Willoughby (D)	80,395	35.6
26	• David Dreier (R)	134,596	53.6
	Cynthia M. Matthews (D)	107,522	42.8
	Randall Weissbuch (LIBERT)	9,089	3.6
27	• Brad Sherman (D)	125,296	62.3
	Robert M. Levy (R)	66,946	33.3
	Eric J. Carter (GREEN)	8,956	4.5
28	• Howard L. Berman (D)	115,303	71.0
	David R. Hernandez Jr. (R)	37,868	23.3
	Kelley L. Ross (LIBERT)	9,339	5.8
29	• Adam B. Schiff (D)	133,670	64.6
	Harry Frank Scolinos (R)	62,871	30.4
	Philip Koebel (GREEN)	5,715	2.8
	Ted Brown (LIBERT)	4,570	2.2
	write-in	6	—
30	• Henry A. Waxman (D)	216,682	71.2
	Victor Elizalde (R)	87,465	28.8
31	• Xavier Becerra (D)	89,363	80.2
	Luis Vega (R)	22,048	19.8
32	• Hilda L. Solis (D)	119,144	85.0
	Leland Faegre (LIBERT)	21,002	15.0
33	• Diane Watson (D)	166,801	88.6
	Bob Weber (LIBERT)	21,513	11.4
34	• Lucille Roybal-Allard (D)	82,282	74.5
	Wayne Miller (R)	28,175	25.5
35	• Maxine Waters (D)	125,949	80.5
	Ross Moen (R)	23,591	15.1
	Gordon Michael Mego (AMI)	3,440	2.2
	Charles Tate (LIBERT)	3,427	2.2
36	• Jane Harman (D)	151,208	62.0
	Paul Whitehead (R)	81,666	33.5
	Alice Stek (PF)	6,105	2.5
	Mike Binkley (LIBERT)	5,065	2.1
37	• Juanita Millender-McDonald (D)	118,823	75.0
	Vernon Van (R)	31,960	20.2
	Herb Peters (LIBERT)	7,535	4.8
38	• Grace F. Napolitano (D)	116,851	100.0
39	• Linda T. Sánchez (D)	100,132	60.7
	Tim Escobar (R)	64,832	39.3
40	• Ed Royce (R)	147,617	67.9
	J. Tilman Williams (D)	69,684	32.1
41	• Jerry Lewis (R)	181,605	83.0
	Peymon Mottahedek (LIBERT)	37,332	17.1
42	• Gary G. Miller (R)	167,632	68.1
	Lewis Myers (D)	78,393	31.9
43	• Joe Baca (D)	86,830	66.4
	Ed Laning (R)	44,004	33.6
44	• Ken Calvert (R)	138,768	61.6
	Louis Vandenberg (D)	78,796	35.0
	Kevin Akin (PFP)	7,559	3.4
45	• Mary Bono (R)	153,523	66.6
	Richard J. Meyer (D)	76,967	33.4
46	• Dana Rohrabacher (R)	171,318	61.9
	Jim Brandt (D)	90,129	32.6
	Tom Lash (GREEN)	10,238	3.7
	Keith Gann (LIBERT)	5,005	1.8
47	• Loretta Sanchez (D)	65,684	60.4
	Alexandria A. "Alex" Coronado (R)	43,099	39.6
48	• Christopher Cox (R)	189,004	65.0
	John L. Graham (D)	93,525	32.1
	Bruce Cohen (LIBERT)	8,343	2.9
49	• Darrell Issa (R)	141,658	62.6
	Mike Byron (D)	79,057	34.9
	Lars R. Grossman (LIBERT)	5,751	2.5

		Total	%
50	• Randy "Duke" Cunningham (R)	169,025	58.4
	Francine P. Busby (D)	105,590	36.5
	Gary M. Waayers (GREEN)	6,504	2.3
	Diane Beall Templin (AMI)	4,723	1.6
	Brandon C. Osborne (LIBERT)	3,486	1.2
51	• Bob Filner (D)	111,441	61.6
	Michael Giorgino (R)	63,526	35.1
	Michael S. Metti (LIBERT)	5,912	3.3
52	• Duncan Hunter (R)	187,799	69.2
	Brian S. Keliher (D)	74,857	27.6
	Michael Benoit (LIBERT)	8,782	3.2
53	• Susan A. Davis (D)	146,449	66.1
	Darin Hunzeker (R)	63,897	28.9
	Lawrence P. Rockwood (GREEN)	7,523	3.4
	Adam Van Susteren (LIBERT)	3,567	1.6

COLORADO

		Total	%
Senate			
	# Ken Salazar (D)	1,081,188	51.3
	Pete Coors (R)	980,668	46.5
	Douglas "Dayhorse" Campbell (AC)	18,783	.9
	Richard Randall (LIBERT)	10,160	.5
	John R. Harris (I)	8,442	.4
	Victor A. Good (REF)	6,481	.3
	Finn Gotaas (X)	1,750	.1
House			
1	• Diana DeGette (D)	177,077	73.5
	Roland Chicas (R)	58,659	24.4
	George C. Lilly (AC)	5,193	2.2
2	• Mark Udall (D)	207,900	67.2
	Stephen M. Hackman (R)	94,160	30.4
	Norm Olsen (LIBERT)	7,304	2.4
3	# John Salazar (D)	153,500	50.6
	Greg Walcher (R)	141,376	46.6
	Jim Krug (X)	8,770	2.9
4	• Marilyn Musgrave (R)	155,958	51.1
	Stan Matsunaka (D)	136,812	44.8
	Bob Kinsey (GREEN)	12,739	4.2
5	• Joel Hefley (R)	193,333	70.5
	Fred Hardee (D)	74,098	27.0
	Arthur "Rob" Roberts (LIBERT)	6,627	2.4
6	• Tom Tancredo (R)	212,778	59.5
	Joanna L. Conti (D)	139,870	39.1
	Jack J. Woehr (LIBERT)	3,857	1.1
	Peter Shevchuk (AC)	1,236	.4
7	• Bob Beauprez (R)	135,571	54.7
	Dave Thomas (D)	106,026	42.8
	Clyde J. Harkins (AC)	6,167	2.5

CONNECTICUT

		Total	%
Senate			
	• Christopher J. Dodd (D)	945,347	66.3
	Jack Orchulli (R)	457,749	32.1
	Timothy A. Knibbs (CC)	12,442	.9
	Leonard H. Rasch (LIBERT)	9,188	.7
House			
1	• John B. Larson (D)	198,802	73.0
	John M. Halstead (R)	73,601	27.0
2	• Rob Simmons (R)	166,412	54.2
	Jim Sullivan (D)	140,536	45.8
	David R. Lyon — write-in	130	—

	Total	%
3 • Rosa DeLauro (D)	200,638	72.4
Richter Elser (R)	69,160	25.0
Ralph Anthony Ferrucci (GREEN)	7,182	2.6
4 • Christopher Shays (R)	152,493	52.4
Diane Farrell (D)	138,333	47.6
write-in	4	—
5 • Nancy L. Johnson (R)	168,268	59.8
Theresa B. Gerratana (D)	107,438	38.2
Fernando Ramirez (WFM)	3,196	1.1
Wildey J. Moore (CC)	2,545	.9

DELAWARE

Governor

	Total	%
• Ruth Ann Minner (D)	185,687	50.9
William Swain Lee (R)	167,115	45.8
Frank Infante (LIBERT, INDC)	12,206	3.3

House

	Total	%
AL • Michael N. Castle (R)	245,978	69.1
Paul Donnelly (D)	105,716	29.7
Maurice Barros Bud (I)	2,337	.7
William E. Morris (LIBERT)	2,014	.6

FLORIDA

Senate

	Total	%
# Mel Martinez (R)	3,672,864	49.4
Betty Castor (D)	3,590,201	48.3
Dennis F. Bradley (VET)	166,642	2.2
Mark Stufft — write-in	119	—
write-ins	68	—

House

	Total	%
1 • Jeff Miller (R)	236,604	76.5
Mark S. Coutu (D)	72,506	23.5
2 • Allen Boyd (D)	201,577	61.6
Bev Kilmer (R)	125,399	38.4
write-in	11	—
3 • Corrine Brown (D)	172,833	99.2
Johnny Brown — write-in	1,323	.8
4 • Ander Crenshaw (R)	256,157	99.5
Richard Grayson — write-in	1,170	.5
5 • Ginny Brown-Waite (R)	240,315	65.9
Robert G. Whittel (D)	124,140	34.1
write-in	33	—
6 • Cliff Stearns (R)	211,137	64.4
David E. Bruderly (D)	116,680	35.6
write-in	36	—
7 • John L. Mica (R)		x
8 • Ric Keller (R)	172,232	60.5
Stephen Murray (D)	112,343	39.5
9 • Michael Bilirakis (R)	284,035	99.9
Andrew Pasayan — write-in	243	.1
10 • C.W. Bill Young (R)	207,175	69.3
Robert D. "Bob" Derry (D)	91,658	30.7
11 • Jim Davis (D)	191,780	85.8
Robert Edward Johnson (LIBERT)	31,579	14.1
Karl M. Butts — write-in	122	.1
12 • Adam H. Putnam (R)	179,204	64.9
Bob Hagenmaier (D)	96,965	35.1
13 • Katherine Harris (R)	190,477	55.3
Jan Schneider (D)	153,961	44.7

	Total	%
14 # Connie Mack (R)	226,662	67.6
Robert M. Neeld (D)	108,672	32.4
15 • Dave Weldon (R)	210,388	65.3
Simon Pristoop (D)	111,538	34.6
16 • Mark Foley (R)	215,563	68.0
Jeff Fisher (D)	101,247	32.0
17 • Kendrick B. Meek (D)	178,690	99.6
Omari Musa — write-in	734	.4
18 • Ileana Ros-Lehtinen (R)	143,647	64.7
Sam Sheldon (D)	78,281	35.3
19 • Robert Wexler (D)		x
20 # Debbie Wasserman-Schultz (D)	191,195	70.2
Margaret Hostetter (R)	81,213	29.8
21 • Lincoln Diaz-Balart (R)	146,507	72.8
Frank J. Gonzalez (LIBERT)	54,736	27.2
22 • E. Clay Shaw Jr. (R)	192,581	62.8
Robin Rorapaugh (D)	108,258	35.3
Jack McLain (CNSTP)	5,260	1.7
Don Kennedy — write-in	627	.2
23 • Alcee L. Hastings (D)		x
24 • Tom Feeney (R)		x
25 • Mario Diaz-Balart (R)		x

GEORGIA

Senate

	Total	%
# Johnny Isakson (R)	1,864,202	57.9
Denise L. Majette (D)	1,287,690	40.0
Allen Buckley (LIBERT)	69,051	2.1
write-in	38	—

House

	Total	%
1 • Jack Kingston (R)	188,347	100.0
2 • Sanford D. Bishop Jr. (D)	129,984	66.8
Dave Eversman (R)	64,645	33.2
3 • Jim Marshall (D)	136,273	62.9
Calder Clay (R)	80,435	37.1
4 # Cynthia A. McKinney (D)	157,461	63.8
Catherine Davis (R)	89,509	36.2
5 • John Lewis (D)	201,773	100.0
6 # Tom Price (R)	267,542	100.0
write-in	77	—
7 • John Linder (R)	258,982	100.0
8 # Lynn Westmoreland (R)	227,524	75.5
Silvia Delamar (D)	73,632	24.4
9 • Charlie Norwood (R)	197,869	74.3
Bob Ellis (D)	68,462	25.7
10 • Nathan Deal (R)	219,136	100.0
11 • Phil Gingrey (R)	120,696	57.4
Rick Crawford (D)	89,591	42.6
12 # John Barrow (D)	113,036	51.8
• Max Burns (R)	105,132	48.2
13 • David Scott (D)	170,657	100.0

HAWAII

Senate

	Total	%
• Daniel K. Inouye (D)	313,629	75.5
Cam Cavasso (R)	87,172	21.0
Jim Brewer (NON)	9,269	2.2
Jeff Mallan (LIBERT)	5,277	1.3

House

	Total	%
1 • Neil Abercrombie (D)	128,567	63.0
Dalton Tanonaka (R)	69,371	34.0
Elyssa Young (LIBERT)	6,243	3.1
2 • Ed Case (D)	133,317	62.8
Mike Gabbard (R)	79,072	37.2

IDAHO

	Total	%

Senate

	Total	%
• Michael D. Crapo (R)	499,796	99.2
Scott F. McClure — write-in	4,136	.8

House

	Total	%
1 • C. L. "Butch" Otter (R)	207,662	69.5
Naomi Preston (D)	90,927	30.4
2 • Mike Simpson (R)	193,704	70.7
Lin Whitworth (D)	80,133	29.3

ILLINOIS

Senate

	Total	%
# Barack Obama (D)	3,597,456	70.0
Alan L. Keyes (R)	1,390,690	27.1
Albert J. Franzen (I)	81,164	1.6
Jerry Kohn (LIBERT)	69,253	1.4
Mark Kuhnke — write-in	2,268	—
Scott Doody — write-in	339	—
Donald McArthur-Self — write-in	134	
Kathy Campbell — write-in	129	—
write-ins	87	—

House

	Total	%
1 • Bobby L. Rush (D)	212,109	84.9
Raymond G. Wardingley (R)	37,840	15.1
2 • Jesse L. Jackson Jr. (D)	207,535	88.5
Stephanie Sailor (LIBERT)	26,990	11.5
3 # Daniel Lipinski (D)	167,034	72.6
Ryan Chlada (R)	57,845	25.2
Krista Grimm — write-in	5,077	2.2
4 • Luis V. Gutierrez (D)	104,761	83.7
Tony Cisneros (R)	15,536	12.4
Jake Whitmer (LIBERT)	4,845	3.9
5 • Rahm Emanuel (D)	158,400	76.2
Bruce Best (R)	49,530	23.8
6 • Henry J. Hyde (R)	139,627	55.8
Christine Cegelis (D)	110,470	44.2
7 • Danny K. Davis (D)	221,133	86.1
Antonio Davis-Fairman (R)	35,603	13.9
8 # Melissa Bean (D)	139,792	51.7
• Philip M. Crane (R)	130,601	48.3
9 • Jan Schakowsky (D)	175,282	75.7
Kurt J. Eckhardt (R)	56,135	24.3
10 • Mark Steven Kirk (R)	177,493	64.1
Lee Goodman (D)	99,218	35.9
11 • Jerry Weller (R)	173,057	58.7
Tari Renner (D)	121,903	41.3
12 • Jerry F. Costello (D)	198,962	69.5
Erin R. Zweigart (R)	82,677	28.9
Walter B. Steel (LIBERT)	4,794	1.7
write-in	2	—
13 • Judy Biggert (R)	200,472	65.0
Gloria Schor Andersen (D)	107,836	35.0
write-in	4	—
14 • J. Dennis Hastert (R)	191,618	68.6
Ruben K. Zamora (D)	87,590	31.4
15 • Timothy V. Johnson (R)	178,114	61.1
David Gill (D)	113,625	39.0
16 • Donald Manzullo (R)	204,350	69.1
John Kutsch (D)	91,452	30.9
write-in	4	—
17 • Lane Evans (D)	172,320	60.7
Andrea Lane Zinga (R)	111,680	39.3
18 • Ray LaHood (R)	216,047	70.2
Steve Waterworth (D)	91,548	29.8
19 • John Shimkus (R)	213,451	69.4
Tim Bagwell (D)	94,303	30.6

	Total	%

INDIANA

Governor

	Total	%
# Mitch Daniels (R)	1,302,912	53.2
• Joseph E. Kernan (D)	1,113,900	45.5
Ken Gividen (LIBERT)	31,664	1.3
write-in	22	—

Senate

• Evan Bayh (D)	1,496,976	61.6
Marvin B. Scott (R)	903,913	37.2
Albert Barger (LIBERT)	27,344	1.1

House

1	• Peter J. Visclosky (D)	178,406	68.3
	Mark J. Leyva (R)	82,858	31.7
2	• Chris Chocola (R)	140,496	54.2
	Joe Donnelly (D)	115,513	44.5
	Douglas Barnes (LIBERT)	3,346	1.3
3	• Mark Souder (R)	171,389	69.2
	Maria M. Parra (D)	76,232	30.8
4	• Steve Buyer (R)	190,445	69.5
	David Sanders (D)	77,574	28.3
	Kevin R. Fleming (LIBERT)	6,117	2.2
5	• Dan Burton (R)	228,718	71.8
	Katherine Fox Carr (D)	82,637	26.0
	Rick Hodkin (LIBERT)	7,008	2.2
6	• Mike Pence (R)	182,529	67.1
	Melina Ann "Mel" Fox (D)	85,123	31.3
	Chad "Wick" Roots (LIBERT)	4,397	1.6
7	• Julia Carson (D)	121,303	54.4
	Andrew "Andy" Horning (R)	97,491	43.7
	Barry Campbell (LIBERT)	4,381	2.0
8	• John Hostettler (R)	145,576	53.4
	Jon P. Jennings (D)	121,522	44.6
	Mark Garvin (LIBERT)	5,680	2.1
9	# Mike Sodrel (R)	142,197	49.5
	• Baron P. Hill (D)	140,772	49.0
	Al Cox (LIBERT)	4,541	1.6

IOWA

Senate

	Total	%
• Charles E. Grassley (R)	1,038,175	70.2
Arthur Small (D)	412,365	27.9
Christy Welty (LIBERT)	15,218	1.0
Darryl Northrop (GREEN)	11,121	.8
Edwin B. Fruit (SW)	1,874	.1
write-ins	475	—

House

1	• Jim Nussle (R)	159,993	55.2
	Bill Gluba (D)	125,490	43.3
	Mark Nelson (LIBERT)	2,727	.9
	Denny Heath (I)	1,756	.6
	write-ins	88	—
2	• Jim Leach (R)	176,684	58.9
	Dave Franker (D)	117,405	39.1
	Kevin Litten (LIBERT)	5,586	1.9
	write-ins	206	.1
3	• Leonard L. Boswell (D)	168,007	55.2
	Stan Thompson (R)	136,099	44.7
	write-ins	213	.1
4	• Tom Latham (R)	181,294	60.9
	Paul W. Johnson (D)	116,121	39.0
	write-ins	151	—
5	• Steve King (R)	168,583	63.3
	E. Joyce Schulte (D)	97,597	36.6
	write-ins	161	.1

KANSAS

Senate

	Total	%
• Sam Brownback (R)	780,863	69.2
Lee Jones (D)	310,337	27.5
Steven A. Rosile (LIBERT)	21,842	1.9
George Cook (REF)	15,980	1.4

House

1	• Jerry Moran (R)	239,776	90.7
	Jack W. Warner (LIBERT)	24,517	9.3
2	• Jim Ryun (R)	165,325	56.1
	Nancy Boyda (D)	121,532	41.3
	Ira Dennis "Dennis" Hawver (LIBERT)	7,579	2.6
3	• Dennis Moore (D)	184,050	54.8
	Kris Kobach (R)	145,542	43.4
	Joe Bellis (LIBERT)	3,191	1.0
	Richard Wells (REF)	2,956	.9
4	• Todd Tiahrt (R)	173,151	66.1
	Michael R. Kinard (D)	81,388	31.1
	David Loomis (LIBERT)	7,376	2.8

KENTUCKY

Senate

	Total	%
• Jim Bunning (R)	873,507	50.7
Daniel Mongiardo (D)	850,855	49.3

House

1	• Edward Whitfield (R)	175,972	67.4
	Billy R. Cartwright (D)	85,229	32.6
2	• Ron Lewis (R)	185,394	67.9
	Adam Smith (D)	87,585	32.1
3	• Anne M. Northup (R)	197,736	60.3
	Tony Miller (D)	124,040	37.8
	George C. Dick (LIBERT)	6,363	1.9
4	# Geoff Davis (R)	160,982	54.4
	Nick Clooney (D)	129,876	43.9
	Michael E. Slider (I)	5,069	1.7
5	• Harold Rogers (R)	177,579	100.0
6	• Ben Chandler (D)	175,355	58.6
	Tom Buford (R)	119,716	40.0
	Stacy Abner (CNSTP)	2,388	.8
	Mark Gailey (LIBERT)	1,758	.6

LOUISIANA

Senate

	Total	%
# David Vitter (R)	943,014	51.0
Chris John (D)	542,150	29.3
John Kennedy (D)	275,821	14.9
Arthur A. Morrell (D)	47,222	2.6
Richard M. Fontanesi (LIBERT)	15,097	.8
R.A. "Skip" Galan (X)	12,463	.7
Sam Houston Melton Jr. (D)	12,289	.7

House

1	# Bobby Jindal (R)	225,708	78.4
	Roy Armstrong (D)	19,266	6.7
	M.V. "Vinny" Mendoza (D)	12,779	4.4
	Daniel Zimmerman (D)	12,135	4.2
	Jerry Watts (D)	10,034	3.5
	Mike Rogers (R)	7,975	2.8
2	• William J. Jefferson (D)	173,510	79.0
	Arthur L. "Art" Schwertz (R)	46,097	21.0
3	**Dec. 4 runoff**		
	# Charlie Melancon (D)	57,611	50.2
	Billy Tauzin III (R)	57,042	49.8

	Total	%
3	**Nov. 2 general**		
	Billy Tauzin III (R)	84,680	32.0
	Charlie Melancon (D)	63,328	23.9
	Craig Romero (R)	61,132	23.1
	Damon J. Baldone (D)	25,783	9.7
	Charmaine Caccioppi (D)	19,347	7.3
	Kevin D. Chiasson (R)	10,350	3.9
4	• Jim McCrery (R)		x
5	• Rodney Alexander (R)	141,495	59.4
	Zelma "Tisa" Blakes (D)	58,591	24.6
	John W. "Jock" Scott (R)	37,971	16.0
6	• Richard H. Baker (R)	189,106	72.2
	Rufus Holt Craig Jr. (D)	50,732	19.4
	Edward Anthony "Scott" Galmon (D)	22,031	8.4
7	**Dec. 4 runoff**		
	# Charles Boustany Jr. (R)	75,039	55.0
	Willie Landry Mount (D)	61,493	45.0
7	**Nov. 2 general**		
	Charles Boustany Jr. (R)	105,761	38.6
	Willie Landry Mount (D)	69,079	25.2
	Don Cravins (D)	67,389	24.6
	David Thibodaux (R)	26,526	9.7
	Malcolm R. Carriere (D)	5,177	1.9

MAINE

House

1	• Tom Allen (D)	219,077	59.7
	Charles E. Summers Jr. (R)	147,663	40.3
2	• Michael H. Michaud (D)	199,303	58.0
	Brian N. Hamel (R)	135,547	39.5
	Carl Cooley (SE)	8,586	2.5

MARYLAND

Senate

	Total	%
• Barbara A. Mikulski (D)	1,504,691	64.8
E.J. Pipkin (R)	783,055	33.7
Maria Allwine (GREEN)	24,816	1.1
Thomas Trump (CNSTP)	9,009	.4
write-ins	1,299	.1
Robert Gemmill II — write-in	204	—
Ray Bly — write-in	109	—

House

1	• Wayne T. Gilchrest (R)	245,149	75.8
	Kostas Alexakis (D)	77,872	24.1
	write-ins	505	.2
2	• C.A. Dutch Ruppersberger (D)	164,751	66.6
	Jane Brooks (R)	75,812	30.7
	Keith Salkowski (GREEN)	6,508	2.6
	write-ins	224	.1
3	• Benjamin L. Cardin (D)	182,066	63.4
	Robert P. Duckworth (R)	97,008	33.8
	Patsy Allen (GREEN)	7,895	2.8
	write-ins	250	.1
4	• Albert R. Wynn (D)	196,809	75.2
	John McKinnis (R)	52,907	20.2
	Theresa Mitchell Dudley (GREEN)	11,885	4.5
	write-in	259	.1
5	• Steny H. Hoyer (D)	204,867	68.7
	Brad Jewitt (R)	87,189	29.2
	Bob S. Auerbach (GREEN)	4,224	1.4
	Steve Krukar (CNSTP)	1,849	.6
	write-ins	206	.1

	Total	%
6 • Roscoe G. Bartlett (R)	206,076	67.4
Kenneth T. Bosley (D)	90,108	29.5
Gregory J. Hemingway (GREEN)	9,324	3.1
write-ins	349	.1
7 • Elijah E. Cummings (D)	179,189	73.4
Tony Salazar (R)	60,102	24.6
Virginia T. Rodino (GREEN)	4,727	1.9
write-ins	165	.1
8 • Chris Van Hollen (D)	215,129	74.8
Chuck Floyd (R)	71,989	25.0
write-ins	562	.2

MASSACHUSETTS

House

	Total	%
1 • John W. Olver (D)	229,465	99.0
write-ins	2,282	1.0
2 • Richard E. Neal (D)	217,682	98.7
write-ins	2,802	1.3
3 • Jim McGovern (D)	192,036	70.5
Ronald A. Crews (R)	80,197	29.4
write-ins	179	.1
4 • Barney Frank (D)	219,260	77.7
Charles A. Morse (I)	62,293	22.1
write-ins	486	.2
5 • Martin T. Meehan (D)	179,652	67.0
Thomas P. Tierney (R)	88,232	32.9
write-ins	305	.1
6 • John F. Tierney (D)	213,458	69.9
Steven P. O'Malley Jr. (R)	91,597	30.0
write-ins	467	.1
7 • Edward J. Markey (D)	202,399	73.6
Kenneth G. Chase (R)	60,334	21.9
James O. Hall (I)	12,139	4.4
write-ins	227	.1
8 • Michael E. Capuano (D)	165,852	98.7
write-ins	2,229	1.3
9 • Stephen F. Lynch (D)	218,167	99.0
write-ins	2,145	1.0
10 • Bill Delahunt (D)	222,013	65.9
Michael J. Jones (R)	114,879	34.1
write-ins	178	—

MICHIGAN

House

	Total	%
1 • Bart Stupak (D)	211,571	65.6
Don Hooper (R)	105,706	32.8
David J. Newland (GREEN)	3,105	1.0
John W. Loosemore (LIBERT)	2,292	.7
2 • Peter Hoekstra (R)	225,343	69.3
Kimon Kotos (D)	94,040	28.9
Steve Van Til (LIBERT)	2,876	.9
Ronald E. Graeser (USTAX)	2,746	.8
3 • Vernon J. Ehlers (R)	214,465	66.6
Peter H. Hickey (D)	101,395	31.5
Warren Adams (LIBERT)	3,695	1.2
Marcel Sales (USTAX)	2,548	.8
4 • Dave Camp (R)	205,274	64.4
Mike Huckleberry (D)	110,885	34.8
Al Chia (LIBERT)	2,765	.9
5 • Dale E. Kildee (D)	208,163	67.2
Myrah Kirkwood (R)	96,934	31.3
Harley Mikkelson (GREEN)	2,468	.8
Clint Foster (LIBERT)	2,350	.8

	Total	%
6 • Fred Upton (R)	197,425	65.3
Scott Elliot (D)	97,978	32.4
Randall MacPhee (GREEN)	2,311	.8
Erwin J. Haas (LIBERT)	2,275	.8
W. Dennis Fitzsimons (USTAX)	2,169	.7
7 # Joe Schwarz (R)	176,053	58.4
Sharon Renier (D)	109,527	36.3
Dave Horn (USTAX)	9,032	3.0
Jason Seagraves (GREEN)	3,996	1.3
Kenneth L. Proctor (LIBERT)	3,034	1.0
8 • Mike Rogers (R)	207,925	61.1
Robert Alexander (D)	125,619	36.9
Will Tyler White (LIBERT)	3,591	1.1
John Mangopoulos (USTAX)	3,288	1.0
9 • Joe Knollenberg (R)	199,210	58.5
Steven Reifman (D)	134,764	39.5
Robert Schubring (LIBERT)	6,825	2.0
10 • Candice S. Miller (R)	227,720	68.6
Rob Casey (D)	98,029	29.5
Phoebe A. Basso (LIBERT)	3,966	1.2
Anthony America (NL)	2,153	.7
11 • Thaddeus McCotter (R)	186,431	57.0
Phillip Truran (D)	134,301	41.0
Charles I. Basso (LIBERT)	6,484	2.0
12 • Sander M. Levin (D)	210,827	69.3
Randell J. Shafer (R)	88,256	29.0
Dick Gach (LIBERT)	5,051	1.7
13 • Carolyn Cheeks Kilpatrick (D)	173,246	78.2
Cynthia Cassell (R)	40,935	18.5
Thomas Lavigne (GREEN)	4,261	1.9
Eric B. Gordon (LIBERT)	3,211	1.5
write-in	1	—
14 • John Conyers Jr. (D)	213,681	83.9
Veronica Pedraza (R)	35,089	13.8
Michael I. Donahue (LIBERT)	2,278	.9
Lisa Weltman (GREEN)	2,224	.9
Wilbert Sears (USTAX)	1,307	.5
write-in	1	—
15 • John D. Dingell (D)	218,409	70.9
Dawn Anne Reamer (R)	81,828	26.6
Gregory Stempfle (LIBERT)	3,400	1.1
Mike Eller (USTAX)	2,508	.8
Jerome S. White (X)	1,818	.6

MINNESOTA

House

	Total	%
1 • Gil Gutknecht (R)	193,132	59.6
Leigh Pomeroy (D)	115,088	35.5
Greg Mikkelson (INDC)	15,569	4.8
write-ins	266	.1
2 • John Kline (R)	206,313	56.4
Teresa Daly (D)	147,527	40.3
Doug Williams (INDC)	11,822	3.2
write-in	283	.1
3 • Jim Ramstad (R)	231,871	64.6
Deborah Watts (D)	126,665	35.3
write-in	356	.1
4 • Betty McCollum (D)	182,387	57.5
Patrice Bataglia (R)	105,467	33.2
Peter F. Vento (INDC)	29,099	9.2
write-in	346	.1
5 • Martin Olav Sabo (D)	218,434	69.7
Daniel Nielsen Mathias (R)	76,600	24.4
Jay Pond (GREEN)	17,984	5.7
write-in	508	.2

	Total	%
6 • Mark Kennedy (R)	203,669	54.0
Patty Wetterling (D)	173,309	45.9
write-in	246	.1
7 • Collin C. Peterson (D)	207,628	66.1
David E. Sturrock (R)	106,349	33.8
write-in	280	.1
8 • James L. Oberstar (D)	228,586	65.2
Mark Groettum (R)	112,693	32.1
Van Presley (GREEN)	8,933	2.6
write-in	271	.1

MISSISSIPPI

House

	Total	%
1 • Roger Wicker (R)	219,328	78.9
Barbara Dale Washer (REF)	58,256	21.1
2 • Bennie Thompson (D)	154,526	58.4
Clinton B. LeSueur (R)	107,647	40.7
Shawn O'Hara (REF)	2,596	1.0
3 • Charles W. "Chip" Pickering Jr. (R)	234,874	80.1
Jim Giles (I)	40,426	13.8
Lamonica L. Magee (REF)	18,068	6.2
4 • Gene Taylor (D)	179,979	64.2
Michael Lott (R)	96,740	34.5
Tracy Lou O'Hara Hill (REF)	3,663	1.3

MISSOURI

Governor

	Total	%
# Matt Blunt (R)	1,382,419	50.8
Claire McCaskill (D)	1,301,442	47.9
John M. Swenson (LIBERT)	24,378	.9
Robert Wells (CNSTP)	11,299	.4
Kenneth J. Johnson — write-in	61	—

Senate

	Total	%
• Christopher S. Bond (R)	1,518,089	56.1
Nancy Farmer (D)	1,158,261	42.8
Kevin J. Tull (LIBERT)	19,648	.7
Don Griffin (CNSTP)	10,404	.4

House

	Total	%
1 • William Lacy Clay (D)	213,658	75.3
Leslie L. Farr II (R)	64,791	22.8
Terry Chadwick (LIBERT)	3,937	1.4
Robert Rehbein (CNSTP)	1,385	.5
2 • Todd Akin (R)	228,725	65.4
George D. "Boots" Weber (D)	115,366	33.0
Darla R. Maloney (LIBERT)	4,822	1.4
David Leefe (CNSTP)	954	.3
3 # Russ Carnahan (D)	146,894	52.9
Bill Federer (R)	125,422	45.1
Kevin C. Babcock (LIBERT)	4,367	1.6
William J. Renaud (CNSTP)	1,222	.4
write-in	11	—
4 • Ike Skelton (D)	190,800	66.2
James A. "Jim" Noland Jr. (R)	93,334	32.4
Bill Lower (LIBERT)	2,827	1.0
Raymond Lister (CNSTP)	1,265	.4
5 # Emanuel Cleaver II (D)	161,727	55.2
Jeanne Patterson (R)	123,431	42.1
Rick Bailie (LIBERT)	5,827	2.0
Darin Rodenberg (CNSTP)	2,040	.7
6 • Sam Graves (R)	196,516	63.8
Charles S. Broomfield (D)	106,987	34.8
Erik Buck (LIBERT)	4,352	1.4

	Total	%
7 • Roy Blunt (R)	210,080	70.5
Jim Newberry (D)	84,356	28.3
Kevin Craig (LIBERT)	2,767	.9
Steve Alger (CNSTP)	1,002	.3
8 • Jo Ann Emerson (R)	194,039	72.2
Dean Henderson (D)	71,543	26.6
Stan Cuff (LIBERT)	1,810	.7
Leonard J. Davidson (CNSTP)	1,319	.5
9 • Kenny Hulshof (R)	193,429	64.6
Linda Jacobsen (D)	101,343	33.8
Tamara A. Millay (LIBERT)	3,228	1.1
Chris Earl (CNSTP)	1,447	.5

MONTANA

Governor

	Total	%
# Brian Schweitzer (D)	225,016	50.4
Bob Brown (R)	205,313	46.0
Bob Kelleher (GREEN)	8,393	1.9
Stanley R. Jones (LIBERT)	7,424	1.7

House

	Total	%
AL • Denny Rehberg (R)	286,076	64.4
Tracy Velazquez (D)	145,606	32.8
Mike Fellows (LIBERT)	12,548	2.8

NEBRASKA

House

	Total	%
1 # Jeff Fortenberry (R)	143,756	54.2
Matt Connealy (D)	113,971	43.0
Steven R. Larrick (GREEN)	7,345	2.8
2 • Lee Terry (R)	152,608	61.1
Nancy Thompson (D)	90,292	36.1
John J. Graziano (LIBERT)	4,656	1.9
Dante Salvatierra (GREEN)	2,208	.9
3 • Tom Osborne (R)	218,751	87.5
Donna J. Anderson (D)	26,434	10.6
Robert A. Rosberg (NEB)	3,396	1.4
Roy Guisinger (GREEN)	1,555	.6

NEVADA

Senate

	Total	%
• Harry Reid (D)	494,805	61.1
Richard Ziser (R)	284,640	35.1
None of these candidates	12,968	1.6
Thomas L. Hurst (LIBERT)	9,559	1.2
David K. Schumann (X)	6,001	.7
Gary Marinch (NL)	2,095	.3

House

	Total	%
1 • Shelley Berkley (D)	133,569	66.0
Russ Mickelson (R)	63,005	31.1
Jim Duensing (LIBERT)	5,862	2.9
2 • Jim Gibbons (R)	195,466	67.2
Angie G. Cochran (D)	79,978	27.5
Janine Hansen (IA)	10,638	3.7
Brendan Trainor (LIBERT)	4,997	1.7
3 • Jon Porter (R)	162,240	54.5
Tom Gallagher (D)	120,365	40.4
Joseph P. Silvestre (LIBERT)	9,260	3.1
Richard O'Dell (X)	6,053	2.0

NEW HAMPSHIRE

Governor

	Total	%
# John Lynch (D)	339,927	51.0
• Craig Benson (R)	325,514	48.9
write-ins	740	.1

Senate

	Total	%
• Judd Gregg (R)	434,847	66.2
Doris "Granny D" Haddock (D)	221,549	33.7
write-ins	588	.1
Clarence G. Blevens — write-in	102	—

House

	Total	%
1 • Jeb Bradley (R)	204,836	63.3
Justin Nadeau (D)	118,226	36.6
write-ins	310	.1
2 • Charles Bass (R)	191,188	58.3
Paul Hodes (D)	125,280	38.2
Richard B. Kahn (LIBERT)	11,311	3.5
write-ins	415	.1

NEW JERSEY

House

	Total	%
1 • Robert E. Andrews (D)	201,163	75.0
S. Daniel Hutchison (R)	66,109	24.7
Arthur Fulvio Croce (X)	931	.4
2 • Frank A. LoBiondo (R)	172,779	65.1
Timothy J. Robb (D)	86,792	32.7
Willie Norwood (JEB)	1,993	.8
Michael J. Matthews (LIBERT)	1,767	.7
Jose David Alcantara (GREEN)	1,516	.6
Constantino Rozzo (S)	595	.2
3 • H. James Saxton (R)	195,938	63.4
Herb Conaway (D)	107,034	34.6
Edward "Rob" Forchion (LMP)	4,914	1.6
Frank Orland (LIBERT)	976	.3
4 • Christopher H. Smith (R)	192,671	67.0
Amy Vasquez (D)	92,826	32.3
Richard Edgar (LIBERT)	2,056	.7
5 • Scott Garrett (R)	171,220	57.6
Dorothea Anne Wolfe (D)	122,259	41.1
Victor Kaplan (LIBERT)	1,857	.6
Thomas A. Phelan (C)	1,515	.5
Gregory Pason (S)	574	.2
6 • Frank Pallone Jr. (D)	153,981	66.9
Sylvester Fernandez (R)	70,942	30.8
Virginia A. Flynn (LIBERT)	2,829	1.2
Mac Dara Francis X. Lyden (X)	2,399	1.0
7 • Mike Ferguson (R)	162,597	56.9
Steve Brozak (D)	119,081	41.7
Thomas D. Abrams (I)	2,153	.8
Matthew Angus Williams (X)	2,016	.7
8 • Bill Pascrell Jr. (D)	152,001	69.5
George Ajjan (R)	62,747	28.7
Joseph A. Fortunato (GREEN)	4,072	1.9
9 • Steven R. Rothman (D)	146,038	67.5
Edward Trawinski (R)	68,564	31.7
Dave Daly (LIBERT)	1,649	.8
10 • Donald M. Payne (D)	155,697	96.9
Toy-Ling Washington (GREEN)	2,927	1.8
Sara J. Lobman (S)	2,089	1.3
11 • Rodney Frelinghuysen (R)	200,915	67.9
James W. Buell (D)	91,811	31.0
John Mele (IMN)	1,746	.6
Austin S. Lett (LIBERT)	1,530	.5
12 • Rush D. Holt (D)	171,691	59.3
Bill Spadea (R)	115,014	39.7
Ken Chazotte (LIBERT)	1,562	.5
Daryl M. Brooks (GREEN)	1,518	.5
13 • Robert Menendez (D)	121,018	75.9
Richard W. Piatkowski (R)	35,288	22.1
Dick Hester (PLC)	1,282	.8
Herbert H. Shaw (PAC)	1,066	.7
Angela L. Lariscy (S)	887	.6

NEW MEXICO

House

	Total	%
1 • Heather A. Wilson (R)	147,372	54.4
Richard Romero (D)	123,339	45.5
Orlin G. Cole — write-in	194	.1
2 • Steve Pearce (R)	130,498	60.2
Gary King (D)	86,292	39.8
3 • Tom Udall (D)	175,269	68.7
Gregory M. Tucker (R)	79,935	31.3

NEW YORK

Senate

	Total	%
• Charles E. Schumer (D, INDC, WFM)	4,769,824	71.2
Howard Mills (R)	1,625,069	24.2
Marilyn F. O'Grady (C)	220,960	3.3
David E. McReynolds (GREEN)	36,942	.6
Donald Silberger (LIBERT)	19,073	.3
Abraham J. Hirschfeld (BLD)	16,196	.2
Martin Koppel (SW)	14,811	.2

House

	Total	%
1 • Timothy H. Bishop (D, INDC, WFM)	156,354	56.2
Bill Manger (R, C)	121,855	43.8
2 • Steve Israel (D, INDC, WFM)	161,593	66.6
Richard Hoffmann (R, C)	80,950	33.4
3 • Peter T. King (R, INDC, C)	171,259	63.0
Blair H. Mathies Jr. (D)	100,737	37.0
4 • Carolyn McCarthy (D, INDC, WFM)	159,969	63.0
James A. Garner (R, C)	94,141	37.1
5 • Gary L. Ackerman (D, INDC, WFM)	119,726	71.3
Stephen Graves (R, C)	46,867	27.9
Gonzalo Policarpo (F)	1,248	.7
6 • Gregory W. Meeks (D, WFM)	129,688	100.0
7 • Joseph Crowley (D, WFM)	104,275	80.9
Joseph Cinquemain (R, C)	24,548	19.1
8 • Jerrold Nadler (D, WFM)	162,082	80.5
Peter Hort (R,C,INDC)	39,240	19.5
9 • Anthony Weiner (D, WFM)	113,025	71.3
Gerard J. Cronin (R, C, INDC)	45,451	28.7
10 • Edolphus Towns (D, WFM)	136,113	91.5
Harvey R. Clarke (R)	11,099	7.5
Mariana Blume (C)	1,554	1.1
11 • Major R. Owens (D, WFM)	144,999	94.0
Lorraine Stevens (INDC)	4,721	3.1
Sol Lieberman (C)	4,478	2.9
12 • Nydia M. Velazquez (D, WFM)	107,796	86.3
Paul A. Rodriguez (R, C)	17,166	13.7
13 • Vito J. Fossella (R, C)	112,934	59.0
Frank J. Barbaro (D, INDC, WFM)	78,500	41.0
14 • Carolyn B. Maloney (D, INDC, WFM)	186,688	81.1
Anton Srdanovic (R, C)	43,623	18.9
15 • Charles B. Rangel (D, WFM)	161,351	91.1
Kenneth P. Jefferson Jr. (R)	12,355	7.0
Jessie Fields (INDC)	3,345	1.9
16 • José E. Serrano (D, WFM)	111,638	95.2
Ali Mohamed (R, C)	5,610	4.8
17 • Eliot L. Engel (D, WFM)	140,530	76.2
Matthew I. Brennan (R)	40,524	22.0
Kevin Brawley (C)	3,482	1.9

	Total	%
18 • Nita M. Lowey		
(D, INDC, WFM)	170,715	69.8
Richard A. Hoffman (R)	73,975	30.2
19 • Sue W. Kelly (R, INDC, C)	175,401	66.7
Michael Jaliman (D)	87,429	33.3
20 • John E. Sweeney		
(R, INDC, C)	188,753	65.8
Doris F. Kelly (D)	96,630	33.7
Morris N. Guller (CEN)	1,353	.5
21 • Michael R. McNulty		
(D, C, INDC, WFM)	194,033	70.8
Warren Redlich (R)	80,121	29.2
22 • Maurice D. Hinchey		
(D, C, INDC, WFM)	167,489	67.2
William A. Brenner (R)	81,881	32.8
23 • John M. McHugh		
(R, C, INDC, WFM)	160,079	70.7
Robert J. Johnson (D)	66,448	29.3
24 • Sherwood Boehlert		
(R, INDC)	143,000	56.9
Jeffrey A. Miller (D)	85,140	33.9
David L. Walrath (C)	23,228	9.2
25 • James T. Walsh (R, INDC, C)	189,063	90.4
Howie Hawkins (GREEN)	20,106	9.6
26 • Thomas M. Reynolds		
(R, INDC, C)	157,466	55.6
Jack Davis (D, WFM)	125,613	44.4
27 # Brian Higgins		
(D, INDC, WFM)	143,332	50.7
Nancy Naples (R, C)	139,558	49.3
28 • Louise M. Slaughter		
(D, WFM)	159,655	72.6
Michael D. Laba (R, C)	54,543	24.8
Francina J. Cartonia (INDC)	5,678	2.6
29 # John R. "Randy" Kuhl Jr. (R)	136,883	50.7
Samara Barend (D, WFM)	110,241	40.8
Mark W. Assini (C)	17,272	6.4
John Ciampoli (INDC)	5,819	2.1

NORTH CAROLINA

	Total	%
Governor		
• Michael F. Easley (D)	1,939,154	55.6
Patrick J. Ballantine (R)	1,495,021	42.9
Barbara J. Howe (LIBERT)	52,513	1.5
Senate		
# Richard M. Burr (R)	1,791,450	51.6
Erskine Bowles (D)	1,632,527	47.0
Tom Bailey (LIBERT)	47,743	1.4
Walter F. Rucker — write-in	362	—
House		
1 • G.K. Butterfield (D)	137,667	64.0
Greg Dority (R)	77,508	36.0
2 • Bob Etheridge (D)	145,079	62.3
Billy J. Creech (R)	87,811	37.7
3 • Walter B. Jones (R)	171,863	70.7
Roger A. Eaton (D)	71,227	29.3
4 • David E. Price (D)	217,441	64.1
Todd A. Batchelor (R)	121,717	35.9
Maximilian Longley — write-in	76	—
5 # Virginia Foxx (R)	167,546	58.8
Jim A. Harrell Jr. (D)	117,271	41.2
6 • Howard Coble (R)	207,470	73.2
William W. Jordan (D)	76,153	26.9
7 • Mike McIntyre (D)	180,382	73.2
Ken Plonk (R)	66,084	26.8
8 • Robin Hayes (R)	125,070	55.5
Beth Troutman (D)	100,101	44.5

	Total	%
9 • Sue Myrick (R)	210,783	70.2
Jack Flynn (D)	89,318	29.8
10 # Patrick T. McHenry (R)	157,884	64.2
Anne N. Fischer (D)	88,233	35.9
11 • Charles H. Taylor (R)	159,709	54.9
Patsy Keever (D)	131,188	45.1
12 • Melvin Watt (D)	154,908	66.8
Ada M. Fisher (R)	76,898	33.2
13 • Brad Miller (D)	160,896	58.8
Virginia Johnson (R)	112,788	41.2

NORTH DAKOTA

	Total	%
Governor		
• John Hoeven (R)	220,803	71.3
Joseph A. Satrom (D)	84,877	27.4
Roland Riemers (I)	4,193	1.4
Senate		
• Byron L. Dorgan (D)	211,843	68.3
Mike Liffrig (R)	98,553	31.8
House		
AL • Earl Pomeroy (D)	185,130	59.6
Duane Sand (R)	125,684	40.4

OHIO

	Total	%
Senate		
• George V. Voinovich (R)	3,464,356	63.9
Eric D. Fingerhut (D)	1,961,171	36.1
Helen Meyers — write-in	296	—
House		
1 • Steve Chabot (R)	173,430	59.8
Greg Harris (D)	116,235	40.1
Rich Stevenson — write-in	198	.1
2 • Rob Portman (R)	227,102	71.7
Charles W. Sanders (D)	89,598	28.3
James Condit, Jr. — write-in	60	—
3 • Michael R. Turner (R)	197,290	62.3
Jane Mitakides (D)	119,448	37.7
4 • Michael G. Oxley (R)	167,807	58.6
Ben Konop (D)	118,538	41.4
5 • Paul E. Gillmor (R)	196,649	67.0
Robin Weirauch (D)	96,656	33.0
6 • Ted Strickland (D)	223,842	99.9
John Stephen Luchansky — write-in	145	.1
7 • David L. Hobson (R)	186,534	65.0
Kara Anastasio (D)	100,617	35.0
8 • John A. Boehner (R)	201,675	69.0
Jeff Hardenbrook (D)	90,574	31.0
9 • Marcy Kaptur (D)	205,149	68.1
Larry A. Kaczala (R)	95,983	31.9
10 • Dennis J. Kucinich (D)	172,406	60.0
Edward Fitzpatrick Herman (R)	96,463	33.6
Barbara Ann Ferris (I)	18,343	6.4
11 • Stephanie Tubbs Jones (D)	222,371	100.0
12 • Pat Tiberi (R)	198,912	62.0
Edward S. Brown (D)	122,109	38.0
write-in	22	—
13 • Sherrod Brown (D)	201,004	67.4
Robert Lucas (R)	97,090	32.6
14 • Steven C. LaTourette (R)	201,652	62.8
Capri S. Cafaro (D)	119,714	37.3
15 • Deborah Pryce (R)	166,520	60.0
Mark P. Brown (D)	110,915	40.0
16 • Ralph Regula (R)	202,544	66.5
Jeff Seemann (D)	101,817	33.5

	Total	%
17 • Tim Ryan (D)	212,800	77.2
Frank V. Cusimano (R)	62,871	22.8
18 • Bob Ney (R)	177,600	66.2
Brian R. Thomas (D)	90,820	33.8

OKLAHOMA

	Total	%
Senate		
# Tom Coburn (R)	763,433	52.8
Brad Carson (D)	596,750	41.3
Sheila Bilyeu (I)	86,663	6.0
House		
1 • John Sullivan (R)	187,145	60.2
Doug Dodd (D)	116,731	37.5
John Krymski (I)	7,058	2.3
2 # Dan Boren (D)	179,579	65.9
Wayland Smalley (R)	92,963	34.1
3 • Frank D. Lucas (R)	215,510	82.2
Gregory M. Wilson (I)	46,621	17.8
4 • Tom Cole (R)	198,985	77.8
Charlene K. Bradshaw (I)	56,869	22.2
5 • Ernest Istook (R)	180,430	66.1
Bert Smith (D)	92,719	33.9

OREGON

	Total	%
Senate		
• Ron Wyden (D)	1,128,728	63.4
Al King (R)	565,254	31.8
Teresa Keane (I)	43,053	2.4
Dan Fitzgerald (LIBERT)	29,582	1.7
David Brownlow (CNSTP)	12,397	.7
write-ins	1,536	.1
House		
1 • David Wu (D)	203,771	57.5
Goli Ameri (R)	135,164	38.1
Dean Wolf (I)	13,882	3.9
write-ins	1,521	.4
2 • Greg Walden (R)	248,461	71.6
John C. McColgan (D)	88,914	25.6
Jim Lindsay (LIBERT)	4,792	1.4
Jack Alan Brown (I)	4,060	1.2
write-ins	638	.2
3 • Earl Blumenauer (D)	245,559	70.9
Tami Mars (R)	82,045	23.7
Walter F. "Walt" Brown (S)	10,678	3.1
Dale Winegarden (I)	7,119	2.0
write-ins	1,159	.3
4 • Peter A. DeFazio (D)	228,611	61.0
Jim Feldkamp (R)	140,882	37.6
Jacob Boone (LIBERT)	3,190	.8
Michael Paul Marsh (I)	1,799	.5
write-ins	427	.1
5 • Darlene Hooley (D)	184,833	52.9
Jim Zupancic (R)	154,993	44.3
Jerry Defoe (LIBERT)	6,463	1.9
Joseph H. Bitz (I)	2,971	.8
write-ins	374	.1

PENNSYLVANIA

	Total	%
Senate		
• Arlen Specter (R)	2,925,080	52.6
Joseph M. Hoeffel (D)	2,334,126	42.0
James N. Clymer (CNSTP)	220,056	4.0
Betsy Summers (LIBERT)	79,263	1.4

	Total	%
House		
1 • Robert A. Brady (D)	214,462	86.3
Deborah L. Williams (R)	33,266	13.4
Christopher Randolf (X)	857	.4
2 • Chaka Fattah (D)	253,226	88.0
Stewart Bolno (R)	34,411	12.0
3 • Phil English (R)	166,580	60.1
Steven Porter (D)	110,684	39.9
4 • Melissa A. Hart (R)	204,329	63.1
Stevan Drobac Jr. (D)	116,303	35.9
Steven B. Larchuck (X)	3,285	1.0
5 • John E. Peterson (R)	192,852	88.0
Thomas A. Martin (LIBERT)	26,239	12.0
6 • Jim Gerlach (R)	160,348	51.0
Lois Murphy (D)	153,977	49.0
7 • Curt Weldon (R)	196,556	58.8
Paul Scoles (D)	134,932	40.3
David R. Jahn (LIBERT)	3,039	.9
8 # Michael G. Fitzpatrick (R)	183,229	55.3
Virginia Waters Schrader (D)	143,427	43.3
Arthur L. Farnsworth (LIBERT)	3,710	1.1
Erich G. Lukas (CNSTP)	898	.3
9 • Bill Shuster (R)	184,320	69.5
Paul I. Politis (D)	80,787	30.5
10 • Don Sherwood (R)	191,967	92.8
Veronica A. Hannevig (CNSTP)	14,805	7.2
11 • Paul E. Kanjorski (D)	171,147	94.4
Kenneth C. Brenneman (CNSTP)	10,105	5.6
12 • John P. Murtha (D)	204,504	100.0
13 # Allyson Y. Schwartz (D)	171,763	55.8
Melissa Brown (R)	127,205	41.3
John P. McDermott (CNSTP)	5,291	1.7
Chuck Moulton (LIBERT)	3,865	1.3
14 • Mike Doyle (D)	220,139	100.0
15 # Charlie Dent (R)	170,634	58.6
Joe Driscoll (D)	114,646	39.4
Richard J. Piotrowski (LIBERT)	3,660	1.3
Greta Browne (GREEN)	2,194	.8
16 • Joe Pitts (R)	183,620	64.4
Lois K. Herr (D)	98,410	34.5
William R. Hagen (GREEN)	3,269	1.2
17 • Tim Holden (D)	172,412	59.1
Scott Paterno (R)	113,592	38.9
Russ Diamond (LIBERT)	5,782	2.0
18 • Tim Murphy (R)	197,894	62.8
Mark G. Boles (D)	117,420	37.2
19 • Todd R. Platts (R)	224,274	91.5
Charles J. Steel (GREEN)	8,890	3.6
Michael L. Paoletta (LIBERT)	8,456	3.5
Lester B. Searer (CNSTP)	3,474	1.4

RHODE ISLAND

	Total	%
House		
1 • Patrick J. Kennedy (D)	124,923	64.1
David W. Rogers (R)	69,819	35.8
write-in	268	.1
2 • Jim Langevin (D)	154,392	74.5
Arthur "Chuck" Barton III (R)	43,139	20.8
Edward M. Morabito (I)	6,196	3.0
Dorman J. Hayes Jr. (I)	3,303	1.6
write-in	135	.1

SOUTH CAROLINA

	Total	%
Senate		
# Jim DeMint (R)	857,167	53.7
Inez Tenenbaum (D)	704,384	44.1
Patrick Tyndall (CNSTP)	13,464	.8
Rebekah Sutherland (LIBERT)	10,678	.7
Tee Ferguson (UC)	5,859	.4
Efia Nwangaza (GREEN, INDC)	4,383	.3
write-ins	1,286	.1
House		
1 • Henry E. Brown Jr. (R)	186,448	87.8
James E. Dunn (GREEN)	25,674	12.1
write-ins	186	.1
2 • Joe Wilson (R)	181,862	65.0
Michael Ray Ellisor (D)	93,249	33.3
Steve Lefemine (CNSTP)	4,447	1.6
write-ins	312	.1
3 • J. Gresham Barrett (R)	191,052	99.5
write-ins	947	.5
4 # Bob Inglis (R)	188,795	69.8
Brandon P. Brown (D)	78,376	29.0
C. Faye Walters (NL)	3,273	1.2
write-ins	150	.1
5 • John M. Spratt Jr. (D)	152,867	63.0
Albert F. Spencer (R)	89,568	36.9
write-ins	83	—
6 • James E. Clyburn (D)	161,987	67.0
Gary McLeod (R, C)	79,600	32.9
write-ins	242	.1

SOUTH DAKOTA

	Total	%
Senate		
# John Thune (R)	197,848	50.6
• Tom Daschle (D)	193,340	49.4
House		
AL • Stephanie Herseth (D)	207,837	53.4
Larry Diedrich (R)	178,823	45.9
Terry Begay (LIBERT)	2,808	.7

TENNESSEE

	Total	%
House		
1 • Bill Jenkins (R)	172,543	73.9
Graham Leonard (D)	56,361	24.1
Ralph J. Ball (X)	3,061	1.3
Michael Peavler (X)	1,595	.7
2 • John J. "Jimmy" Duncan Jr. (R)	215,575	79.0
John Greene (D)	52,155	19.1
Charles E. Howard (X)	4,978	1.8
3 • Zach Wamp (R)	166,154	64.7
John Wolfe Jr. (D)	84,295	32.9
June Griffin (X)	3,018	1.2
Doug Vandagriff (X)	1,696	.7
Jean Howard-Hill (X)	1,473	.6
4 • Lincoln Davis (D)	138,459	54.8
Janice H. Bowling (R)	109,993	43.5
Ken Martin (X)	4,194	1.7
5 • Jim Cooper (D)	168,970	69.3
Scott Knapp (R)	74,978	30.7
write-in	15	—
6 • Bart Gordon (D)	167,448	64.2
Nick Demas (R)	87,523	33.6
J. Patrick Lyons (X)	3,869	1.5
Norman R. Saliba (X)	1,802	.7

	Total	%
7 • Marsha Blackburn (R)	232,404	100.0
8 • John Tanner (D)	173,623	74.3
James L. Hart (R)	59,853	25.6
Dennis Bertrand — write-in	91	—
9 • Harold E. Ford Jr. (D)	190,648	82.0
Ruben M. Fort (R)	41,578	17.9
Jim Maynard — write-in	166	.1

TEXAS

	Total	%
House		
1 # Louie Gohmert (R)	157,068	61.5
• Max Sandlin (D)	96,281	37.7
Dean L. Tucker (LIBERT)	2,158	.8
2 # Ted Poe (R)	139,951	55.5
• Nick Lampson (D)	108,156	42.9
Sandra Leigh Saulsbury (LIBERT)	3,931	1.6
3 • Sam Johnson (R)	180,099	85.6
Paul Jenkins (I)	16,966	8.1
James Vessels (LIBERT)	13,287	6.3
4 • Ralph M. Hall (R)	182,866	68.3
Jim Nickerson (D)	81,585	30.4
Kevin D. Anderson (LIBERT)	3,491	1.3
5 • Jeb Hensarling (R)	148,816	64.5
Bill Bernstein (D)	75,911	32.9
John Gonzalez (LIBERT)	6,118	2.6
6 • Joe L. Barton (R)	168,767	66.0
Morris Meyer (D)	83,609	32.7
Stephen Schrader (LIBERT)	3,251	1.3
7 • John Culberson (R)	175,440	64.1
John Martinez (D)	91,126	33.3
Paul Staton (I)	3,713	1.4
Drew Parks (LIBERT)	3,372	1.2
8 • Kevin Brady (R)	179,599	68.9
James "Jim" Wright (D)	77,324	29.7
Paul Hansen (LIBERT)	3,705	1.4
9 # Al Green (D)	114,462	72.2
Arlette Molina (R)	42,132	26.6
Stacey Lynn Bourland (LIBERT)	1,972	1.2
10 # Michael McCaul (R)	182,113	78.6
Robert Fritsche (LIBERT)	35,569	15.4
Lorenzo Sadun (I) — write-in	13,961	6.0
11 # K. Michael Conaway (R)	177,291	76.8
Wayne Raasch (D)	50,339	21.8
Jeffrey C. Blunt (LIBERT)	3,347	1.5
12 • Kay Granger (R)	173,222	72.3
Felix Alvarado (D)	66,316	27.7
13 • William M. "Mac" Thornberry (R)	189,448	92.3
M.J. "Smitty" Smith (LIBERT)	15,793	7.7
14 • Ron Paul (R)	173,668	100.0
15 • Rubén Hinojosa (D)	96,089	57.8
Michael D. Thamm (R)	67,917	40.8
William R. Cady (LIBERT)	2,352	1.4
16 • Silvestre Reyes (D)	108,577	67.5
David Brigham (R)	49,972	31.1
Brad Clardy (LIBERT)	2,224	1.4
17 • Chet Edwards (D)	125,309	51.2
Arlene Wohlgemuth (R)	116,049	47.4
Clyde Garland (LIBERT)	3,390	1.4
18 • Sheila Jackson-Lee (D)	136,018	88.9
Tom Bazan (I)	9,787	6.4
Brent Sullivan (LIBERT)	7,183	4.7
19 • Randy Neugebauer (R)	136,459	58.4
• Charles W. Stenholm (D)	93,531	40.1
Richard Peterson (LIBERT)	3,524	1.5

	Total	%
20 • Charlie Gonzalez (D)	112,480	65.5
Roger Scott (R)	54,976	32.0
Jessie Bouley (LIBERT)	2,377	1.4
Michael Idrogo (I)	1,971	1.2
21 • Lamar Smith (R)	209,774	61.5
Rhett R. Smith (D)	121,129	35.5
Jason Pratt (LIBERT)	10,216	3.0
22 • Tom DeLay (R)	150,386	55.2
Richard R. Morrison (D)	112,034	41.1
Michael "Fjet" Fjetland (I)	5,314	2.0
Tom Morrison (LIBERT)	4,886	1.8
23 • Henry Bonilla (R)	170,716	69.3
Joseph P. "Joe" Sullivan (D)	72,480	29.4
Nazirite "Comrade" Perez (LIBERT)	3,307	1.3
24 # Kenny Marchant (R)	154,435	64.0
Gary R. Page (D)	82,599	34.2
James H. Lawrence (LIBERT)	4,340	1.8
25 • Lloyd Doggett (D)	108,309	67.6
Rebecca Armendariz Klein (R)	49,252	30.7
James Warner (LIBERT)	2,656	1.7
26 • Michael C. Burgess (R)	180,519	65.8
Lico Reyes (D)	89,809	32.7
James Gholston (LIBERT)	4,211	1.5
27 • Solomon P. Ortiz (D)	112,081	63.1
William "Willie" Vaden (R)	61,955	34.9
Christopher J. Claytor (LIBERT)	3,500	2.0
28 # Henry Cuellar (D)	106,323	59.0
James F. "Jim" Hopson (R)	69,538	38.6
Ken Ashby (LIBERT)	4,305	2.4
29 • Gene Green (D)	78,256	94.1
Clifford Lee Messina (LIBERT)	4,868	5.9
30 • Eddie Bernice Johnson (D)	144,513	93.0
John Davis (LIBERT)	10,821	7.0
31 • John Carter (R)	160,247	64.8
Jon Porter (D)	80,292	32.5
Celeste Adams (LIBERT)	6,888	2.8
32 • Pete Sessions (R)	109,859	54.3
• Martin Frost (D)	89,030	44.0
Michael D. Needleman (LIBERT)	3,347	1.7

UTAH

	Total	%
Governor		
# Jon Huntsman Jr. (R)	531,190	57.7
Scott M. Matheson Jr. (D)	380,359	41.4
Ken Larsen (PC)	8,399	.9
write-ins	12	—
Senate		
• Robert F. Bennett (R)	626,640	68.7
R. Paul Van Dam (D)	258,955	28.4
Gary R. Van Horn (C)	17,289	1.9
Joe Labonte (PC)	8,824	1.0
write-ins	18	—
House		
1 • Rob Bishop (R)	199,615	67.9
Steve Thompson (D)	85,630	29.1
Charles Johnston (C)	4,510	1.5
Richard W. Soderberg (PC)	4,206	1.4
2 • Jim Matheson (D)	187,250	54.8
John Swallow (R)	147,778	43.2
Jeremy Paul Petersen (C)	3,541	1.0
Patrick S. Diehl (GREEN)	2,189	.6
Ronald R. Amos (PC)	1,210	.4

	Total	%
3 • Chris Cannon (R)	173,010	63.4
Beau Babka (D)	88,748	32.5
Ronald Winfield (C)	5,089	1.9
Jim Dexter (LIBERT)	3,691	1.4
Curtis Darrell James (PC)	2,390	.9

VERMONT

	Total	%
Governor		
• Jim Douglas (R)	181,540	58.7
Peter Clavelle (D)	117,327	37.9
Cris Ericson (M)	4,221	1.4
Patricia Hejny (I)	2,431	.8
Hardy Machia (LIBERT)	2,263	.7
Peter Diamondstone (LU)	1,298	.4
write-ins	205	.1
Senate		
• Patrick J. Leahy (D)	216,972	70.6
John "Jack" McMullen (R)	75,398	24.5
Cris Ericson (M)	6,486	2.1
Craig Hill (GREEN)	3,999	1.3
Keith Stern (I)	3,300	1.1
Ben Mitchell (LU)	879	.3
write-ins	174	.1
House		
AL • Bernard Sanders (I, PRO)	205,774	67.5
Greg Parke (R)	74,271	24.4
Larry Drown (D)	21,684	7.1
Jane Newton (LU)	3,018	1.0
write-ins	261	.1

VIRGINIA

	Total	%
House		
1 • Jo Ann Davis (R)	225,071	78.5
William A. Lee (I)	57,434	20.0
write-ins	4,029	1.4
2 # Thelma Drake (R)	132,946	55.1
David Ashe (D)	108,180	44.8
write-ins	254	.1
3 • Robert C. Scott (D)	159,373	69.3
Winsome Sears (R)	70,194	30.5
write-ins	325	.1
4 • J. Randy Forbes (R)	182,444	64.5
Jonathan Menefee (D)	100,413	35.5
write-ins	170	.1
5 • Virgil H. Goode Jr. (R)	172,431	63.7
Al Weed (D)	98,237	36.3
write-ins	90	—
6 • Robert W. Goodlatte (R)	206,560	96.7
write-ins	7,088	3.3
7 • Eric Cantor (R)	230,765	75.5
W. Brad Blanton (I)	74,325	24.3
write-ins	568	.2
8 • James P. Moran (D)	171,986	59.7
Lisa Marie Cheney (R)	106,231	36.9
James T. Hurysz (I)	9,004	3.1
write-ins	698	.2
9 • Rick Boucher (D)	150,039	59.3
Kevin Triplett (R)	98,499	38.9
Seth Davis (I)	4,341	1.7
write-ins	68	—
10 • Frank R. Wolf (R)	205,982	63.8
James Socas (D)	116,654	36.1
write-ins	375	.1
11 • Thomas M. Davis III (R)	186,299	60.3
Ken Longmyer (D)	118,305	38.3
Joseph Oddo (I)	4,338	1.4
write-ins	291	.1

	Total	%
WASHINGTON		
Governor		
# Christine Gregoire (D)	1,373,361	48.9
Dino Rossi (R)	1,373,232	48.9
Ruth Bennett (LIBERT)	63,465	2.3
Senate		
• Patty Murray (D)	1,549,708	55.0
George Nethercutt (R)	1,204,584	42.7
J. Mills (LIBERT)	34,055	1.2
Mark B. Wilson (GREEN)	30,304	1.1
House		
1 • Jay Inslee (D)	204,121	62.3
Randy Eastwood (R)	117,850	36.0
Charles Moore (LIBERT)	5,798	1.8
2 • Rick Larsen (D)	202,383	63.9
Suzanne Sinclair (R)	106,333	33.6
Bruce Guthrie (LIBERT)	7,966	2.5
3 • Brian Baird (D)	193,626	61.9
Thomas Crowson (R)	119,027	38.1
4 • Doc Hastings (R)	154,627	62.6
Sandy Matheson (D)	92,486	37.4
5 # Cathy McMorris (R)	179,600	59.7
Don Barbieri (D)	121,333	40.3
6 • Norm Dicks (D)	202,919	69.0
Doug Cloud (R)	91,228	31.0
7 • Jim McDermott (D)	272,302	80.7
Carol Thorne Cassady (R)	65,226	19.3
8 # Dave Reichert (R)	173,298	51.5
Dave Ross (D)	157,148	46.7
Spencer Garrett (LIBERT)	6,053	1.8
9 • Adam Smith (D)	162,433	63.3
Paul J. Lord (R)	88,304	34.4
Robert F. Losey (GREEN)	5,934	2.3

	Total	%
WEST VIRGINIA		
Governor		
# Joe Manchin III (D)	472,758	63.5
Monty Warner (R)	253,131	34.0
Jesse Johnson (MOUNT)	18,430	2.5
Simon McClure — write-in	114	—
House		
1 • Alan B. Mollohan (D)	166,583	67.8
Alan Lee Parks (R)	79,196	32.2
2 • Shelley Moore Capito (R)	147,676	57.5
Erik Wells (D)	106,131	41.3
Julian Martin (I)	3,218	1.3
3 • Nick J. Rahall II (D)	142,682	65.2
Rick Snuffer (R)	76,170	34.8

	Total	%
WISCONSIN		
Senate		
• Russell D. Feingold (D)	1,632,697	55.4
Tim Michels (R)	1,301,183	44.1
Arlf Kahn (LIBERT)	8,367	.3
Eugene A. Hem (I)	6,662	.2
write-ins	834	—
House		
1 • Paul D. Ryan (R)	233,372	65.4
Jeffery Chapman Thomas (D)	116,250	32.6
Norman Aulabaugh (I)	4,252	1.2
Don Bernau (LIBERT)	2,936	.8
write-ins	166	—
2 • Tammy Baldwin (D)	251,637	63.3
David Magnum (R)	145,810	36.7
write-ins	277	.1

		Total	%
3	• Ron Kind (D)	204,856	56.4
	Dale W. Schultz (R)	157,866	43.5
	write-ins	286	.1
4	# Gwen Moore (D)	212,382	69.6
	Gerald H. Boyle (R)	85,928	28.2
	Tim Johnson (I)	3,733	1.2
	Robert R. Raymond (I)	1,861	.6
	Colin Hudson (CNSTP)	897	.3
	write-ins	341	.1
5	• F. James Sensenbrenner Jr. (R)	271,153	66.6

	Total	%
Bryan Kennedy (D)	129,384	31.8
Tim Peterson (LIBERT)	6,549	1.6
write-ins	205	—
6 • Tom Petri (R)	238,620	67.0
Jef Hall (D)	107,209	30.1
Carol Ann Rittenhouse (WG)	10,081	2.8
write-ins	148	—
7 • David R. Obey (D)	241,306	85.7
Mike Miles (WG)	26,518	9.4
Larry Oftedahl (CNSTP)	12,841	4.6
write-ins	1,087	.4

	Total	%
8 • Mark Green (R)	248,070	70.1
Dottie Le Clair (D)	105,513	29.8
write-ins	142	—

WYOMING

House

	Total	%
AL • Barbara Cubin (R)	132,107	55.3
Ted Ladd (D)	99,989	41.8
Lewis Stock (LIBERT)	6,581	2.8
write-ins	357	.1

Appendix A

CONGRESS AND ITS MEMBERS

Glossary of Congressional Terms

Act — The term for legislation once it has passed both chambers of Congress and has been signed by the president or passed over his veto, thus becoming law. Also used in parliamentary terminology for a bill that has been passed by one house and engrossed. (*Also see engrossed bill.*)

Adjournment sine die — Adjournment without a fixed day for reconvening — literally, "adjournment without a day." Usually used to connote the final adjournment of a session of Congress. A session can continue until noon Jan. 3 of the following year, when, under the 20th Amendment to the Constitution, it automatically terminates. Both chambers must agree to a concurrent resolution for either chamber to adjourn for more than three days.

Adjournment to a day certain — Adjournment under a motion or resolution that fixes the next time of meeting. Under the Constitution, neither chamber can adjourn for more than three days without the concurrence of the other. A session of Congress is not ended by adjournment to a day certain.

Amendment — A proposal by a member of Congress to alter the language, provisions or stipulations in a bill or in another amendment. An amendment usually is printed, debated and voted upon in the same manner as a bill.

Amendment in the nature of a substitute — Usually an amendment that seeks to replace the entire text of a bill by striking out everything after the enacting clause and inserting a new version of the bill. An amendment in the nature of a substitute can also refer to an amendment that replaces a large portion of the text of a bill.

Appeal — A member's challenge of a ruling or decision made by the presiding officer of the chamber. A senator can appeal to members of the Senate to override the decision. If carried by a majority vote, the appeal nullifies the chair's ruling. In the House, the decision of the Speaker traditionally has been final; seldom are there appeals to the members to reverse the Speaker's stand. To appeal a ruling is considered an attack on the Speaker.

Appropriations bill — A bill that gives legal authority to spend or obligate money from the Treasury. The Constitution disallows money to be drawn from the Treasury "but in Consequence of Appropriations made by Law."

By congressional custom, an appropriations bill originates in the House. It is not supposed to be considered by the full House or Senate until a related measure authorizing the funding is enacted. An appropriations bill grants the actual budget authority approved by the authorization bill, though not necessarily the full amount permissible under the authorization.

If the 13 regular appropriations bills are not enacted by the start of the fiscal year, Congress must pass a stopgap spending bill or the departments and agencies covered by the unfinished bills must shut down.

About half of all budget authority, notably that for Social Security and interest on the federal debt, does not require annual appropriations; those programs exist under permanent appropriations. (*Also see authorization bill, budget authority, budget process and supplemental appropriations bill.*)

Authorization bill — Basic, substantive legislation that establishes or continues the legal operation of a federal program or agency either indefinitely or for a specific period of time, or which sanctions a particular type of obligation or expenditure. Under the rules of both chambers, appropriations for a program or agency may not be considered until the program has been authorized, although this requirement is often waived.

An authorization sets the maximum amount of funds that can be given to a program or agency, although sometimes it merely authorizes "such sums as may be necessary." (*Also see backdoor spending authority.*)

Backdoor spending authority — Budget authority provided in legislation outside the normal appropriations process. The most common forms of backdoor spending are borrowing authority, contract authority, entitlements and loan guarantees that commit the government to payments of principal and interest on loans — such as guaranteed student loans — made by banks or other private lenders. Loan guarantees result in actual outlays only when there is a default by the borrower.

In some cases, such as interest on the public debt, a permanent appropriation is provided that becomes available without further action by Congress.

Bills — Most legislative proposals before Congress are in the form of bills and are designated according to the chamber in which they originate — HR in the House of Representatives or S in the Senate — and by a number assigned in the order in which they are introduced during the two-year period of a congressional term.

"Public bills" address general questions and become public laws if they are cleared by Congress and signed by the president. "Private bills" deal with individual matters, such as claims against the government, immigration and naturalization cases or land titles, and become private laws if approved and signed. (*Also see private bills, resolution.*)

Bills introduced — In both the House and Senate, any number of members may join in introducing a single bill or resolution. The first member listed is the sponsor of the bill, and all subsequent members listed are cosponsors.

Many bills are committee bills and are introduced under the name of the chairman of the committee or subcommittee. All appropriations bills fall into this category. A committee frequently holds hearings on a number of related bills and may agree to one of them or to an entirely new bill. (*Also see clean bill.*)

Bills referred — After a bill is introduced, it is referred to the committee or committees that have jurisdiction over the subject with which the bill is concerned. Under the standing rules of the House and Senate, bills are referred by the Speaker in the House and by the presiding officer in the Senate. In practice, the House and Senate parliamentarians act for these officials and refer the vast majority of bills. (*Also see discharge a committee.*)

Borrowing authority — Statutory authority that permits a federal agency to incur obligations and make payments for specified purposes with borrowed money.

Budget — The document sent to Congress by the president early each year estimating government revenue and expenditures for the ensuing fiscal year.

Budget Act — The common name for the Congressional Budget and Impoundment Control Act of 1974, which established the current budget process and created the Congressional Budget Office. The act also put limits on presidential authority to spend ap-

propriated money. It has undergone several major revisions since 1974. (*Also see budget process, impoundments.*)

Budget authority — Authority for federal agencies to enter into obligations that result in immediate or future outlays. The basic forms of budget authority are appropriations, contract authority and borrowing authority. Budget authority may be classified by (1) the period of availability (one-year, multiple-year or without a time limitation), (2) the timing of congressional action (current or permanent) or (3) the manner of determining the amount available (definite or indefinite). (*Also see appropriations, outlays.*)

Budget process — The annual budget process was created by the Congressional Budget and Impoundment Control Act of 1974, with a timetable that was modified in 1990. Under the law, the president must submit his proposed budget by the first Monday in February. Congress is supposed to complete an annual budget resolution by April 15, setting guidelines for congressional action on spending and tax measures.

Budget rules enacted in the 1990 Budget Enforcement Act and updated in 1993 and 1997 set caps on discretionary spending through fiscal 2002. The caps could be adjusted annually to account for changes in the economy and other limited factors. In addition, pay-as-you-go (PAYGO) rules required that any tax cut, new entitlement program or expansion of existing entitlement benefits that would increase a deficit be offset by an increase in taxes or a cut in entitlement spending.

The rules held Congress harmless for budget-deficit increases that lawmakers did not explicitly cause — for example, increases due to a recession or to an expansion in the number of beneficiaries qualifying for Medicare or food stamps. PAYGO did not apply when there was a budget surplus.

If Congress exceeded the discretionary spending caps in its appropriations bills, the law required an across-the-board cut — known as a sequester — in non-exempt discretionary spending accounts. If Congress violated the PAYGO rules, entitlement programs were subject to a sequester. Supplemental appropriations were subject to similar controls, with the proviso that if both Congress and the president agreed, spending designated as an emergency could exceed the caps.

Budget resolution — A concurrent resolution that is passed by both chambers of Congress but does not require the president's signature. The measure sets a strict ceiling on discretionary budget authority, along with non-binding recommendations about how the spending should be allocated. The budget resolution may also contain "reconciliation instructions" requiring authorizing and tax-writing committees to propose changes in existing law to meet deficit-reduction goals. The Budget Committee in each chamber then bundles those proposals into a reconciliation bill and sends it to the floor. (*Also see reconciliation.*)

By request — A phrase used when a senator or representative introduces a bill at the request of an executive agency or private organization but does not necessarily endorse the legislation.

Calendar — An agenda or list of business awaiting possible action by each chamber. The House uses six legislative calendars. They are the Consent, Corrections, Discharge, House, Private and Union calendars. (*Also see individual listings.*)

In the Senate, all legislative matters reported from committee go on one calendar. They are listed there in the order in which committees report them or the Senate places them on the calendar, but they may be called up out of order by the majority leader, either by obtaining unanimous consent of the Senate or by a motion to call up a bill. The Senate also has one non-legislative cal-

endar, which is used for treaties and nominations. (*Also see executive calendar.*)

Call of the calendar — Senate bills that are not brought up for debate by a motion, unanimous consent or a unanimous consent agreement are brought before the Senate for action when the calendar listing them is "called." Bills must be called in the order listed. Measures considered by this method usually are non-controversial, and debate on the bill and any proposed amendments is limited to five minutes for each senator.

Chamber — The meeting place for the membership of either the House or the Senate; also the membership of the House or Senate meeting as such.

Clean bill — Frequently after a committee has finished a major revision of a bill, one of the committee members, usually the chairman, will assemble the changes and what is left of the original bill into a new measure and introduce it as a "clean bill." The revised measure, which is given a new number, is referred back to the committee, which reports it to the floor for consideration. This often is a timesaver, as committee-recommended changes in a clean bill do not have to be considered and voted on by the chamber. Reporting a clean bill also protects committee amendments that could be subject to points of order concerning germaneness.

Clerk of the House — An officer of the House of Representatives who supervises its records and legislative business. Many former administrative duties were transferred in 1992 to a new position, the director of non-legislative and financial services.

Cloture — The process by which a filibuster can be ended in the Senate other than by unanimous consent. A motion for cloture can apply to any measure before the Senate, including a proposal to change the chamber's rules. A cloture motion requires the signatures of 16 senators to be introduced. To end a filibuster, the cloture motion must obtain the votes of three-fifths of the entire Senate membership (60 if there are no vacancies), except when the filibuster is against a proposal to amend the standing rules of the Senate and a two-thirds vote of senators present and voting is required.

The cloture request is put to a roll call vote one hour after the Senate meets on the second day following introduction of the motion. If approved, cloture limits each senator to one hour of debate. The bill or amendment in question comes to a final vote after 30 hours of consideration, including debate time and the time it takes to conduct roll calls, quorum calls and other procedural motions. (*Also see filibuster.*)

Committee — A division of the House or Senate that prepares legislation for action by the parent chamber or makes investigations as directed by the parent chamber.

There are several types of committees. Most standing committees are divided into subcommittees, which study legislation, hold hearings and report bills, with or without amendments, to the full committee. Only the full committee can report legislation for action by the House or Senate. (*Also see standing, oversight, select and special committees.*)

Committee of the Whole — The working title of what is formally "The Committee of the Whole House [of Representatives] on the State of the Union." The membership is composed of all House members sitting as a committee. Any 100 members who are present on the floor of the chamber to consider legislation comprise a quorum of the committee. Any legislation, however, must first have passed through the regular legislative or appropriations

committee and have been placed on the calendar.

Technically, the Committee of the Whole considers only bills directly or indirectly appropriating money, authorizing appropriations or involving taxes or charges on the public. Because the Committee of the Whole need number only 100 representatives, a quorum is more readily attained and legislative business is expedited. Before 1971, members' positions were not individually recorded on votes taken in the Committee of the Whole.

When the full House resolves itself into the Committee of the Whole, it replaces the Speaker with a "chairman." A measure is debated and amendments may be proposed, with votes on amendments as needed. (*Also see five-minute rule.*)

When the committee completes its work on the measure, it dissolves itself by "rising." The Speaker returns, and the chairman of the Committee of the Whole reports to the House that the committee's work has been completed. At this time, members may demand a roll call vote on any amendment adopted in the Committee of the Whole. The final vote is on passage of the legislation.

In 1993 and 1994, the four delegates from the territories and the resident commissioner of Puerto Rico were allowed to vote on questions before the Committee of the Whole. If their votes were decisive in the outcome, however, the matter was automatically re-voted, with the delegates and resident commissioner ineligible. They could vote on final passage of bills or on separate votes demanded after the Committee of the Whole rises. This limited voting right was rescinded in 1995.

Committee veto — A requirement added to a few statutes directing that certain policy directives by an executive department or agency be reviewed by certain congressional committees before they are implemented. Under common practice, the government department or agency and the committees involved are expected to reach a consensus before the directives are carried out. (*Also see legislative veto.*)

Concurrent resolution — A concurrent resolution, designated H Con Res or S Con Res, must be adopted by both chambers, but it is not sent to the president for approval and, therefore, does not have the force of law. A concurrent resolution, for example, is used to fix the time for adjournment of a Congress. It is also used to express the sense of Congress on a foreign policy or domestic issue. The annual budget resolution is a concurrent resolution.

Conference — A meeting between representatives of the House and the Senate to reconcile differences between the two chambers on provisions of a bill. Members of the conference committee are appointed by the Speaker and the presiding officer of the Senate.

A majority of the conferees for each chamber must agree on a compromise, reflected in a "conference report" before the final bill can go back to both chambers for approval. When the conference report goes to the floor, it is difficult to amend. If it is not approved by both chambers, the bill may go back to conference under certain situations, or a new conference may be convened. Many rules and informal practices govern the conduct of conference committees.

Bills that are passed by both chambers with only minor differences need not be sent to conference. Either chamber may "concur" with the other's amendments, completing action on the legislation. Sometimes leaders of the committees of jurisdiction work out an informal compromise instead of having a formal conference. (*Also see custody of the papers.*)

Confirmations — (*See nominations.*)

Congressional Record — The daily, printed account of proceedings in both the House and Senate chambers, showing substantially verbatim debate, statements and a record of floor action. Highlights of legislative and committee action are given in a Daily Digest section of the Record, and members are entitled to have their extraneous remarks printed in an appendix known as "Extension of Remarks." Members may edit and revise remarks made on the floor during debate, although the House in 1995 limited members to technical or grammatical changes.

The Congressional Record provides a way to distinguish remarks spoken on the floor of the House and Senate from undelivered speeches. In the Senate, all speeches, articles and other matter that members insert in the Record without actually reading them on the floor are set off by large black dots, or bullets. However, a loophole allows a member to avoid the bulleting if he or she delivers any portion of the speech in person. In the House, undelivered speeches and other material are printed in a distinctive typeface. The record is also available in electronic form. (*Also see Journal.*)

Congressional terms of office — Terms normally begin on Jan. 3 of the year following a general election. Terms are two years for representatives and six years for senators. Representatives elected in special elections are sworn in for the remainder of a term. Under most state laws, a person may be appointed to fill a Senate vacancy and serve until a successor is elected; the successor serves until the end of the term applying to the vacant seat.

Consent Calendar — Members of the House may place on this calendar most bills on the Union or House Calendar that are considered non-controversial. Bills on the Consent Calendar normally are called on the first and third Mondays of each month. On the first occasion that a bill is called in this manner, consideration may be blocked by the objection of any member. The second time, if there are three objections, the bill is stricken from the Consent Calendar. If fewer than three members object, the bill is given immediate consideration.

A member may also postpone action on the bill by asking that the measure be passed over "without prejudice." In that case, no objection is recorded against the bill and its status on the Consent Calendar remains unchanged. A bill stricken from the Consent Calendar remains on the Union or House Calendar. The Consent Calendar has seldom been used in recent years.

Continuing resolution — A joint resolution, cleared by Congress and signed by the president, to provide new budget authority for federal agencies and programs until the regular appropriations bills have been enacted. Also known as "CRs" or continuing appropriations, continuing resolutions are used to keep agencies operating when, as often happens, Congress fails to finish the regular appropriations process by the start of the new fiscal year.

The CR usually specifies a maximum rate at which an agency may incur obligations, based on the rate of the prior year, the president's budget request or an appropriations bill passed by either or both chambers of Congress but not yet enacted.

Contract authority — Budget authority contained in an authorization bill that permits the federal government to enter into contracts or other obligations for future payments from funds not yet appropriated by Congress. The assumption is that funds will be provided in a subsequent appropriations act. (*Also see budget authority.*)

Corrections Calendar, Corrections Day — A House calendar established in 1995 to speed consideration of bills aimed at eliminating burdensome or unnecessary regulations. Bills on the Corrections Calendar can be called up on the second and fourth Tuesday of each month, called Corrections Day. They are subject to one

hour of debate without amendment, and require a three-fifths majority for passage. (*Also see calendar.*)

Correcting recorded votes — Rules prohibit members from changing their votes after the result has been announced. Occasionally, however, a member may announce hours, days or months after a vote has been taken that he or she was "incorrectly recorded." In the Senate, a request to change one's vote almost always receives unanimous consent, as long as it does not change the outcome. In the House, members are prohibited from changing votes if they were tallied by the electronic voting system.

Cosponsor — (*See bills introduced.*)

Current services estimates — Estimated budget authority and outlays for federal programs and operations for the forthcoming fiscal year based on continuation of existing levels of service without policy changes but with adjustments for inflation and for demographic changes that affect programs. These estimates, accompanied by the underlying economic and policy assumptions upon which they are based, are transmitted by the president to Congress when the budget is submitted.

Custody of the papers — To reconcile differences between the House and Senate versions of a bill, a conference may be arranged. The chamber with "custody of the papers" — the engrossed bill, engrossed amendments, messages of transmittal — is the only body empowered to request the conference. By custom, the chamber that asks for a conference is the last to act on the conference report.

Custody of the papers sometimes is manipulated to ensure that a particular chamber acts either first or last on the conference report. (*Also see conference.*)

Deferral — Executive branch action to defer, or delay, the spending of appropriated money. The 1974 Congressional Budget and Impoundment Control Act requires a special message from the president to Congress reporting a proposed deferral of spending. Deferrals may not extend beyond the end of the fiscal year in which the message is transmitted. A federal district court in 1986 struck down the president's authority to defer spending for policy reasons; the ruling was upheld by a federal appeals court in 1987. Congress can prohibit proposed deferrals by enacting a law doing so; most often, cancellations of proposed deferrals are included in appropriations bills. (*Also see rescission.*)

Dilatory motion — A motion made for the purpose of killing time and preventing action on a bill or amendment. House rules outlaw dilatory motions, but enforcement is largely within the discretion of the Speaker or chairman of the Committee of the Whole. The Senate does not have a rule barring dilatory motions except under cloture.

Discharge a committee — Occasionally, attempts are made to relieve a committee of jurisdiction over a bill that is before it. This is attempted more often in the House than in the Senate, and the procedure rarely is successful.

In the House, if a committee does not report a bill within 30 days after the measure is referred to it, any member may file a discharge motion. Once offered, the motion is treated as a petition needing the signatures of a majority of members (218 if there are no vacancies). After the required signatures have been obtained, there is a delay of seven days.

Thereafter, on the second and fourth Mondays of each month, except during the last six days of a session, any member who has signed the petition must be recognized, if he or she so desires, to move that the committee be discharged. Debate on the motion to discharge is limited to 20 minutes. If the motion is carried, consideration of the bill becomes a matter of high privilege.

If a resolution to consider a bill is held up in the Rules Committee for more than seven legislative days, any member may enter a motion to discharge the committee. The motion is handled like any other discharge petition in the House. Occasionally, to expedite non-controversial legislative business, a committee is discharged by unanimous consent of the House, and a petition is not required. In 1993, the signatures on pending discharge petitions — previously kept secret — were made a matter of public record. (*For Senate procedure, see discharge resolution.*)

Discharge Calendar — The House calendar to which motions to discharge committees are referred when they have the required number of signatures (218) and are awaiting floor action. (*Also see calendar.*)

Discharge petition — (*See discharge a committee.*)

Discharge resolution — In the Senate, a special motion that any senator may introduce to relieve a committee from consideration of a bill before it. The resolution can be called up for Senate approval or disapproval in the same manner as any other Senate business. (*For House procedure, see discharge a committee.*)

Discretionary spending caps — (*See budget process.*)

Division of a question for voting — A practice that is more common in the Senate but also used in the House whereby a member may demand a division of an amendment or a motion for purposes of voting. Where an amendment or motion can be divided, the individual parts are voted on separately when a member demands a division. This procedure occurs most often during the consideration of conference reports.

Enacting clause — Key phrase in bills beginning, "Be it enacted by the Senate and House of Representatives . . . ." A successful motion to strike it from legislation kills the measure.

Engrossed bill — The final copy of a bill as passed by one chamber, with the text as amended by floor action and certified by the clerk of the House or the secretary of the Senate.

Enrolled bill — The final copy of a bill that has been passed in identical form by both chambers. It is certified by an officer of the chamber of origin (clerk of the House or secretary of the Senate) and then sent on for the signatures of the House Speaker, the Senate president pro tempore and the president of the United States. An enrolled bill is printed on parchment.

Entitlement program — A federal program that guarantees a certain level of benefits to people or other entities who meet requirements set by law. Examples include Social Security and unemployment benefits. Some entitlements have permanent appropriations; others are funded under annual appropriations bills. In either case, it is mandatory for Congress to provide the money.

Executive Calendar — A non-legislative calendar in the Senate that lists presidential documents such as treaties and nominations. (*Also see calendar.*)

Executive document — A document, usually a treaty, sent to the Senate by the president for consideration or approval. Executive documents are referred to committee in the same manner as other measures. Unlike legislative documents, treaties do not die at

the end of a Congress but remain "live" proposals until acted on by the Senate or withdrawn by the president.

Executive session — A meeting of a Senate or House committee (or occasionally of either chamber) that only its members may attend. Witnesses regularly appear at committee meetings in executive session — for example, Defense Department officials during presentations of classified defense information. Other members of Congress may be invited, but the public and news media are not allowed to attend.

Filibuster — A time-delaying tactic associated with the Senate and used by a minority in an effort to prevent a vote on a bill or amendment that probably would pass if voted upon directly. The most common method is to take advantage of the Senate's rules permitting unlimited debate, but other forms of parliamentary maneuvering may be used.

The stricter rules of the House make filibusters more difficult, but delaying tactics are employed occasionally through various procedural devices allowed by House rules. (*Also see cloture.*)

Fiscal year — Financial operations of the government are carried out in a 12-month fiscal year, beginning Oct. 1 and ending Sept. 30. The fiscal year carries the date of the calendar year in which it ends. (From fiscal 1844 to fiscal 1976, the fiscal year began July 1 and ended the following June 30.)

Five-minute rule — A debate-limiting rule of the House that is invoked when the House sits as the Committee of the Whole. Under the rule, a member offering an amendment and a member opposing it are each allowed to speak for five minutes. Debate is then closed. In practice, amendments regularly are debated for more than 10 minutes, with members gaining the floor by offering pro forma amendments or obtaining unanimous consent to speak longer than five minutes. (*Also see Committee of the Whole, hour rule, strike out the last word.*)

Floor manager — A member who has the task of steering legislation through floor debate and amendment to a final vote in the House or the Senate. Floor managers usually are chairmen or ranking members of the committee that reported the bill. Managers are responsible for apportioning the debate time granted to supporters of the bill. The ranking minority member of the committee normally apportions time for the minority party's participation in the debate.

Frank — A member's facsimile signature, which is used on envelopes in lieu of stamps for the member's official outgoing mail. The "franking privilege" is the right to send mail postage-free.

Germane — Pertaining to the subject matter of the measure at hand. All House amendments must be germane to the bill being considered. The Senate requires that amendments be germane when they are proposed to general appropriations bills or to bills being considered once cloture has been adopted or, frequently, when the Senate is proceeding under a unanimous consent agreement placing a time limit on consideration of a bill. The 1974 budget act also requires that amendments to concurrent budget resolutions be germane.

In the House, floor debate must be germane, and the first three hours of debate each day in the Senate must be germane to the pending business.

Gramm-Rudman-Hollings Deficit Reduction Act — (*See sequester.*)

Grandfather clause — A provision that exempts people or other entities already engaged in an activity from new rules or legislation affecting that activity.

Hearings — Committee sessions for taking testimony from witnesses. At hearings on legislation, witnesses usually include specialists, government officials and spokesmen for individuals or entities affected by the bill or bills under study. Hearings related to special investigations bring forth a variety of witnesses. Committees sometimes use their subpoena power to summon reluctant witnesses. The public and news media may attend open hearings but are barred from closed, or "executive," hearings. The vast majority of hearings are open to the public. (*Also see executive session.*)

Hold-harmless clause — A provision added to legislation to ensure that recipients of federal funds do not receive less in a future year than they did in the current year if a new formula for allocating funds authorized in the legislation would result in a reduction to the recipients. This clause has been used most often to soften the impact of sudden reductions in federal grants.

Hopper — Box on House clerk's desk into which members deposit bills and resolutions to introduce them.

Hour rule — A provision in the rules of the House that permits one hour of debate time for each member on amendments debated in the House of Representatives sitting as the House. Therefore, the House normally amends bills while sitting as the Committee of the Whole, where the five-minute rule on amendments operates.

House as in the Committee of the Whole — A procedure that can be used to expedite consideration of certain measures such as continuing resolutions and, when there is debate, private bills. The procedure can be invoked only with the unanimous consent of the House or a rule from the Rules Committee and has procedural elements of both the House sitting as the House of Representatives, such as the Speaker presiding and the previous question motion being in order, and the House sitting as the Committee of the Whole, with the five-minute rule being in order. (*See Committee of the Whole.*)

House Calendar — A listing for action by the House of public bills that do not directly or indirectly appropriate money or raise revenue. (*Also see calendar.*)

Immunity — The constitutional privilege of members of Congress to make verbal statements on the floor and in committee for which they cannot be sued or arrested for slander or libel. Also, freedom from arrest while traveling to or from sessions of Congress or on official business. Members in this status may only be arrested for treason, felonies or a breach of the peace, as defined by congressional manuals.

Joint committee — A committee composed of a specified number of members of both the House and Senate. A joint committee may be investigative or research-oriented, an example of the latter being the Joint Economic Committee. Others have housekeeping duties; examples include the joint committees on Printing and on the Library of Congress.

Joint resolution — Like a bill, a joint resolution, designated H J Res or S J Res, requires the approval of both chambers and the signature of the president, and has the force of law if approved. There is no practical difference between a bill and a joint resolution. A joint resolution generally is used to address a limited matter such as a single appropriation.

Joint resolutions are also used to propose amendments to the Constitution. In that case, they require a two-thirds majority in both chambers. They do not require a presidential signature, but they must be ratified by three-fourths of the states to become a part of the Constitution. (*Also see concurrent resolution, resolution.*)

Journal — The official record of the proceedings of the House and Senate. The Journal records the actions taken in each chamber, but, unlike the Congressional Record, it does not include the substantially verbatim report of speeches, debates, statements and the like.

Law — An act of Congress that has been signed by the president or passed, over his veto, by Congress. Public bills, when signed, become public laws and are cited by the letters PL and a hyphenated number. The number before the hyphen corresponds to the Congress, and the one or more digits after the hyphen refer to the numerical sequence in which the president signed the bills during that Congress. Private bills, when signed, become private laws. (*Also see bills, private bills.*)

Legislative day — The "day" extending from the time either chamber meets after an adjournment until the time it next adjourns. Because the House normally adjourns from day to day, legislative days and calendar days usually coincide. But in the Senate, a legislative day may, and frequently does, extend over several calendar days. (*Also see recess.*)

Line-item veto — Presidential authority to strike individual items from appropriations bills, which presidents since Ulysses S. Grant have sought. Congress gave the president a form of the power in 1996 (PL 104-130), but this "enhanced rescission authority" was struck down by the Supreme Court in 1998 as unconstitutional because it allowed the president to change laws on his own.

Loan guarantees — Loans to third parties for which the federal government guarantees the repayment of principal or interest, in whole or in part, to the lender in the event of default.

Lobby — A group seeking to influence the passage or defeat of legislation. Originally the term referred to people frequenting the lobbies or corridors of legislative chambers to speak to lawmakers.

The definition of a lobby and the activity of lobbying is a matter of differing interpretation. By some definitions, lobbying is limited to direct attempts to influence lawmakers through personal interviews and persuasion. Under other definitions, lobbying includes attempts at indirect, or "grass-roots," influence, such as persuading members of a group to write or visit their district's representative and state's senators or attempting to create a climate of opinion favorable to a desired legislative goal.

The right to attempt to influence legislation is based on the First Amendment to the Constitution, which says Congress shall make no law abridging the right of the people "to petition the government for a redress of grievances."

Majority leader — Floor leader for the majority party in each chamber. In the Senate, in consultation with the minority leader, the majority leader directs the legislative schedule for the chamber. He or she is also his party's spokesperson and chief strategist. In the House, the majority leader is second to the Speaker in the majority party's leadership and serves as the party's legislative strategist. (*Also see Speaker, whip.*)

Manual — The official handbook in each chamber prescribing in detail its organization, procedures and operations.

Marking up a bill — Going through the contents of a piece of legislation in committee or subcommittee to, for example, consider the provisions, act on amendments to provisions and proposed revisions to the language, and insert new sections and phraseology. If the bill is extensively amended, the committee's version may be introduced as a separate (or "clean") bill, with a new number, before being considered by the full House or Senate. (*Also see clean bill.*)

Minority leader — Floor leader for the minority party in each chamber.

Morning hour — The time set aside at the beginning of each legislative day for the consideration of regular, routine business. The "hour" is of indefinite duration in the House, where it is rarely used. In the Senate, it is the first two hours of a session following an adjournment, as distinguished from a recess. The morning hour can be terminated earlier if the morning business has been completed.

Business includes such matters as messages from the president, communications from the heads of departments, messages from the House, the presentation of petitions, reports of standing and select committees and the introduction of bills and resolutions.

During the first hour of the morning hour in the Senate, no motion to proceed to the consideration of any bill on the calendar is in order except by unanimous consent. During the second hour, motions can be made but must be decided without debate. Senate committees may meet while the Senate conducts the morning hour.

Motion — In the House or Senate chamber, a request by a member to institute any one of a wide array of parliamentary actions. He or she "moves" for a certain procedure, such as the consideration of a measure. The precedence of motions, and whether they are debatable, is set forth in the House and Senate manuals.

Nominations — Presidential appointments to office subject to Senate confirmation. Although most nominations win quick Senate approval, some are controversial and become the topic of hearings and debate. Sometimes senators object to appointees for patronage reasons — for example, when a nomination to a local federal job is made without consulting the senators of the state concerned. In some situations a senator may object that the nominee is "personally obnoxious" to him. Usually other senators join in blocking such appointments out of courtesy to their colleagues. (*Also see senatorial courtesy.*)

One-minute speeches — Addresses by House members at the beginning of a legislative day. The speeches may cover any subject but are limited to one minute's duration.

Outlays — Actual spending that flows from the liquidation of budget authority. Outlays associated with appropriations bills and other legislation are estimates of future spending made by the Congressional Budget Office (CBO) and the White House's Office of Management and Budget (OMB). CBO's estimates govern bills for the purpose of congressional floor debate, while OMB's numbers govern when it comes to determining whether legislation exceeds spending caps.

Outlays in a given fiscal year may result from budget authority provided in the current year or in previous years. (*Also see budget authority, budget process.*)

Override a veto — If the president vetoes a bill and sends it back to Congress with his objections, Congress may try to override his veto and enact the bill into law. Neither chamber is required to attempt to override a veto. The override of a veto requires a

recorded vote with a two-thirds majority of those present and voting in each chamber. The question put to each chamber is: "Shall the bill pass, the objections of the president to the contrary notwithstanding?" *(Also see pocket veto, veto.)*

Oversight committee — A congressional committee or designated subcommittee that is charged with general oversight of one or more federal agencies' programs and activities. Usually, the oversight panel for a particular agency is also the authorizing committee for that agency's programs and operations.

Pair — A voluntary, informal arrangement that two lawmakers, usually on opposite sides of an issue, make on recorded votes. In many cases, the result is to subtract a vote from each side, with no effect on the outcome.

Pairs are not authorized in the rules of either chamber, are not counted in tabulating the final result and have no official standing. However, members pairing are identified in the Congressional Record, along with their positions on such votes, if known. A member who expects to be absent for a vote can pair with a member who plans to vote, with the latter agreeing to withhold his or her vote.

There are three types of pairs:

(1) A live pair involves a member who is present for a vote and another who is absent. The member in attendance votes and then withdraws the vote, announcing that he or she has a live pair with colleague "X" and stating how the two members would have voted, one in favor, the other opposed. A live pair may affect the outcome of a closely contested vote, since it subtracts one "yea" or one "nay" from the final tally. A live pair may cover one or several specific issues.

(2) A general pair, widely used in the House, does not entail any arrangement between two members and does not affect the vote. Members who expect to be absent notify the clerk that they wish to make a general pair. Each member then is paired with another desiring a pair, and their names are listed in the Congressional Record. The member may or may not be paired with another taking the opposite position, and no indication of how the members would have voted is given.

(3) A specific pair is similar to a general pair, except that the opposing stands of the two members are identified and printed in the Congressional Record.

Pay-as-you go (PAYGO) rules — *(See budget process.)*

Petition — A request or plea sent to one or both chambers from an organization or private citizens' group seeking support for particular legislation or favorable consideration of a matter not yet receiving congressional attention. Petitions are referred to appropriate committees. In the House, a petition signed by a majority of members (218) can discharge a bill from a committee. *(Also see discharge a committee.)*

Pocket veto — The act of the president in withholding his approval of a bill after Congress has adjourned. When Congress is in session, a bill becomes law without the president's signature if he does not act upon it within 10 days, excluding Sundays, from the time he receives it. But if Congress adjourns sine die within that 10-day period, the bill, if unsigned, will die even if the president does not formally veto it.

The Supreme Court in 1986 agreed to decide whether the president could pocket veto a bill during recesses and between sessions of the same Congress or only between Congresses. The justices in 1987 declared the case moot, however, because the bill in question was invalid once the case reached the court. *(Also see adjournment sine die, veto.)*

Point of order — An objection raised by a member that the chamber is departing from rules governing its conduct of business. The objector cites the rule violated, with the chair sustaining his or her objection if correctly made. Order is restored by the chair's suspending proceedings of the chamber until it conforms to the prescribed "order of business."

Both chambers have procedures for overcoming a point of order, either by vote or, what is most common in the House, by including language in the rule for floor consideration that waives a point of order against a given bill. *(Also see rules.)*

President of the Senate — Under the Constitution, the vice president of the United States presides over the Senate. In his absence, the president pro tempore, or a senator designated by the president pro tempore, presides over the chamber.

President pro tempore — The chief officer of the Senate in the absence of the vice president — literally, but loosely, the president for a time. The president pro tempore is elected by his fellow senators. Recent practice has been to elect the senator of the majority party with the longest period of continuous service.

Previous question — A motion for the previous question, when carried, has the effect of cutting off all debate, preventing the offering of further amendments and forcing a vote on the pending matter. In the House, a motion for the previous question is not permitted in the Committee of the Whole, unless a rule governing debate provides otherwise. The motion for the previous question is a debate-limiting device and is not in order in the Senate.

Printed amendment — A House rule guarantees five minutes of floor debate in support and five minutes in opposition, and no other debate time, on amendments printed in the Congressional Record at least one day prior to the amendment's consideration in the Committee of the Whole.

In the Senate, while amendments may be submitted for printing, they have no parliamentary standing or status. An amendment submitted for printing in the Senate, however, may be called up by any senator.

Private bill — A bill dealing with individual matters, such as claims against the government, immigration or land titles. When a private bill is before the chamber, two members may block its consideration, thereby recommitting the bill to committee. The backers still have recourse, however. The measure can be put into an "omnibus claims bill" — several private bills rolled into one. As with any bill, no part of an omnibus claims bill may be deleted without a vote. When the private bill goes back to the House floor in this form, it can be deleted from the omnibus bill only by majority vote.

Private Calendar — The House calendar for private bills. The Private Calendar must be called on the first Tuesday of each month, and the Speaker may call it on the third Tuesday of each month as well. *(Also see calendar, private bill.)*

Privileged questions — The order in which bills, motions and other legislative measures are considered on the floor of the Senate and House is governed by strict priorities. A motion to table, for instance, is more privileged than a motion to recommit. Thus, if a member moves to recommit a bill to committee for further consideration, another member can supersede the first action by moving to table it, and a vote will occur on the motion to table (or kill) before the motion to recommit. A motion to adjourn is considered "of the highest privilege" and must be considered before virtually any other motion.

Pro forma amendment — (*See strike out the last word.*)

Public Laws — (*See law.*)

Questions of privilege — These are matters affecting members of Congress individually or collectively. Matters affecting the rights, safety, dignity and integrity of proceedings of the House or Senate as a whole are questions of privilege in both chambers.

Questions involving individual members are called questions of "personal privilege." A member rising to ask a question of personal privilege is given precedence over almost all other proceedings. For instance, if a member feels that he or she has been improperly impugned in comments by another member, he or she can immediately demand to be heard on the floor on a question of personal privilege. An annotation in the House rules points out that the privilege rests primarily on the Constitution, which gives members a conditional immunity from arrest and an unconditional freedom to speak in the House.

In 1993, the House changed its rules to allow the Speaker to delay for two legislative days the floor consideration of a question of the privileges of the House unless it is offered by the majority leader or minority leader.

Quorum — The number of members whose presence is necessary for the transaction of business. In the Senate and House, it is a majority of the membership. In the Committee of the Whole House, a quorum is 100. If a point of order is made that a quorum is not present, the only business that is in order is either a motion to adjourn or a motion to direct the sergeant-at-arms to request the attendance of absentees. In practice, however, both chambers conduct much of their business without a quorum present. (*Also see Committee of the Whole House.*)

Reading of bills — Traditional parliamentary procedure required bills to be read three times before they were passed. This custom is of little modern significance. Normally a bill is considered to have its first reading when it is introduced and printed, by title, in the Congressional Record. In the House, a bill's second reading comes when floor consideration begins. (The actual reading of a bill is most likely to occur at this point, if at all.) The second reading in the Senate is supposed to occur on the legislative day after the measure is introduced, but before it is referred to committee. The third reading (again, usually by title) takes place when floor action has been completed on amendments.

Recess — A recess, as distinguished from adjournment, does not end a legislative day and therefore does not interrupt unfinished business. (The rules in each chamber set forth certain matters to be taken up and disposed of at the beginning of each legislative day.) The House usually adjourns from day to day. The Senate often recesses, thus meeting on the same legislative day for several calendar days or even weeks at a time.

Recognition — The power of recognition of a member is lodged in the Speaker of the House and the presiding officer of the Senate. The presiding officer names the member to speak first when two or more members simultaneously request recognition. The order of recognition is governed by precedents and tradition for many situations. In the Senate, for instance, the majority leader has the right to be recognized first.

Recommit to committee — A motion, made on the floor after a bill has been debated, to return it to the committee that reported it. If approved, recommittal usually is considered a death blow to the bill. In the House, the right to offer a motion to recommit is guaranteed to the minority leader or someone he or she designates.

A motion to recommit may include instructions to the committee to report the bill again with specific amendments or by a certain date. Or the instructions may direct that a particular study be made, with no definite deadline for further action.

If the recommittal motion includes instructions to "report the bill back forthwith" and the motion is adopted, floor action on the bill continues with the changes directed by the instructions automatically incorporated into the bill; the committee does not actually reconsider the legislation.

Reconciliation — The 1974 budget act created a "reconciliation" procedure for bringing existing tax and spending laws into conformity with ceilings set in the congressional budget resolution. Under the procedure, the budget resolution sets specific deficit-reduction targets and instructs tax-writing and authorizing committees to propose changes in existing law to meet those targets. Those recommendations are consolidated without change by the Budget committees into an omnibus reconciliation bill, which then must be considered and approved by both chambers of Congress.

Special rules in the Senate limit debate on a reconciliation bill to 20 hours and bar extraneous or non-germane amendments. (*Also see budget resolution, sequester.*)

Reconsider a vote — Until it is disposed of, a motion to reconsider the vote by which an action was taken has the effect of putting the action in abeyance. In the Senate, the motion can be made only by a member who voted on the prevailing side of the original question or by a member who did not vote at all. In the House, it can be made only by a member on the prevailing side.

A common practice in the Senate after close votes on an issue is a motion to reconsider, followed by a motion to table the motion to reconsider. On this motion to table, senators vote as they voted on the original question, which allows the motion to table to prevail, assuming there are no switches. That closes the matter, and further motions to reconsider are not entertained.

In the House, as a routine precaution, a motion to reconsider usually is made every time a measure is passed. Such a motion almost always is tabled immediately, thus shutting off the possibility of future reconsideration except by unanimous consent.

Motions to reconsider must be entered in the Senate within the next two days the Senate is in session after the original vote has been taken. In the House, they must be entered either on the same day or on the next succeeding day the House is in session. Sometimes on a close vote, a member will switch his or her vote to be eligible to offer a motion to reconsider.

Recorded vote — A vote upon which each member's stand is individually made known. In the Senate, this is accomplished through a roll call of the entire membership, to which each senator on the floor must answer "yea," "nay" or "present." Since January 1973, the House has used an electronic voting system for recorded votes, including yea-and-nay votes formerly taken by roll calls.

When not required by the Constitution, a recorded vote can be obtained on questions in the House on the demand of one-fifth (44 members) of a quorum or one-fourth (25) of a quorum in the Committee of the Whole. Recorded votes are required in the House for appropriations, budget and tax bills. (*Also see yeas and nays.*)

Report — Both a verb and a noun as a congressional term. A committee that has been examining a bill referred to it by the parent chamber "reports" its findings and recommendations to the chamber when it completes consideration and returns the measure. The process is called "reporting" a bill. In some cases, a bill is reported without a written report.

A "report" is the document setting forth the committee's explanation of its action. Senate and House reports are numbered separately and are designated S Rept or H Rept. When a committee report is not unanimous, the dissenting committee members may file a statement of their views, called minority or dissenting views and referred to as a minority report. Members in disagreement with some provisions of a bill may file additional or supplementary views. Sometimes a bill is reported without a committee recommendation.

Legislative committees occasionally submit adverse reports. However, when a committee is opposed to a bill, it usually fails to report the bill at all. Some laws require that committee reports — favorable or adverse — be made.

Rescission — Cancellation of budget authority that was previously appropriated but has not yet been spent.

Resolution — A "simple" resolution, designated H Res or S Res, deals with matters entirely within the prerogatives of a single chamber. It requires neither passage by the other chamber nor approval by the president, and it does not have the force of law. Most resolutions deal with the rules or procedures of one chamber. They are also used to express the sentiments of a single chamber, such as condolences to the family of a deceased member, or to comment on foreign policy or executive business. A simple resolution is the vehicle for a "rule" from the House Rules Committee. (*Also see concurrent and joint resolutions, rules.*)

Rider — An amendment, usually not germane, that its sponsor hopes to get through more easily by including it in other legislation. A rider becomes law if the bill to which it is attached is enacted. Amendments providing legislative directives in appropriations bills are examples of riders, although technically legislation is banned from appropriations bills.

The House, unlike the Senate, has a strict germaneness rule; thus, riders usually are Senate devices to get legislation enacted quickly or to bypass lengthy House consideration and, possibly, opposition.

Rules — Each chamber has a body of rules and precedents that govern the conduct of business. These rules deal with issues such as duties of officers, the order of business, admission to the floor, parliamentary procedures on handling amendments and voting, and jurisdictions of committees. They are normally changed only at the start of each Congress.

In the House, a rule may also be a resolution reported by the Rules Committee to govern the handling of a particular bill on the floor. The committee may report a rule, also called a special order, in the form of a simple resolution. If the House adopts the resolution, the temporary rule becomes as valid as any standing rule and lapses only after action has been completed on the measure to which it pertains.

The rule sets the time limit on general debate. It may also waive points of order against provisions of the bill in question such as non-germane language or against certain amendments expected on the floor. It may even forbid all amendments or all amendments except those proposed by the legislative committee that handled the bill. In this instance, it is known as a "closed" rule as opposed to an "open" rule, which puts no limitation on floor amendments, thus leaving the bill completely open to alteration by the adoption of germane amendments. (*Also see point of order.*)

Secretary of the Senate — Chief administrative officer of the Senate, responsible for overseeing the duties of Senate employees, educating Senate pages, administering oaths, overseeing the registration of lobbyists and handling other tasks necessary for the continuing operation of the Senate. (*Also see Clerk of the House.*)

Select or special committee — A committee set up for a special purpose and, usually, for a limited time by resolution of either the House or Senate. Most special committees are investigative and lack legislative authority: Legislation is not referred to them, and they cannot report bills to their parent chambers.

Senatorial courtesy — A general practice with no written rule — sometimes referred to as "the courtesy of the Senate" — applied to consideration of executive nominations. Generally, it means that nominations from a state are not to be confirmed unless they have been approved by the senators of the president's party of that state, with other senators following their colleagues' lead in the attitude they take toward consideration of such nominations. (*Also see nominations.*)

Sequester — Automatic, across-the-board spending cuts, generally triggered after the close of a session by a report issued by the Office of Management and Budget. Under the 1985 Gramm-Rudman-Hollings anti-deficit law, modified in 1987, a year-end sequester was triggered if the deficit exceeded a pre-set maximum. However, the Budget Enforcement Act of 1990, updated in 1993 and 1997, effectively replaced that procedure through fiscal 2002.

Instead, if Congress exceeded an annual cap on discretionary budget authority or outlays, a sequester was triggered for all eligible discretionary spending to make up the difference. If Congress violated pay-as-you-go rules by allowing the net effect of legislated changes in mandatory spending and taxes to increase the deficit, a sequester was triggered for all non-exempt entitlement programs. Similar procedures applied to supplemental appropriations bills. (*Also see budget process.*)

Sine die — (*See adjournment sine die.*)

Speaker — The presiding officer of the House of Representatives, selected by his party caucus and formally elected by the whole House. While both parties nominate candidates, choice by the majority party is tantamount to election. In 1995, House rules were changed to limit the Speaker to four consecutive terms.

Special session — A session of Congress after it has adjourned sine die, completing its regular session. Special sessions are convened by the president.

Spending authority — The 1974 budget act defines spending authority as borrowing authority, contract authority and entitlement authority for which budget authority is not provided in advance by appropriation acts.

Sponsor — (*See bills introduced.*)

Standing committees — Committees that are permanently established by House and Senate rules. The standing committees of the House were reorganized in 1974, with some changes in jurisdictions and titles made when Republicans took control of the House in 1995. The last major realignment of Senate committees was in 1977. The standing committees are legislative committees: Legislation may be referred to them, and they may report bills and resolutions to their parent chambers.

Standing vote — A non-recorded vote used in both the House and Senate. (A standing vote is also called a division vote.) Members in favor of a proposal stand and are counted by the presiding officer. Then members opposed stand and are counted. There is no record of how individual members voted.

Statutes at large — A chronological arrangement of the laws enacted in each session of Congress. Though indexed, the laws are not arranged by subject matter, and there is no indication of how they changed previously enacted laws. (*Also see law, U.S. Code.*)

Strike from the Record — A member of the House who is offended by remarks made on the House floor may move that the offending words be "taken down" for the Speaker's cognizance and then expunged from the debate as published in the Congressional Record.

Strike out the last word — A motion whereby a House member is entitled to speak for five minutes on an amendment then being debated by the chamber. A member gains recognition from the chair by moving to "strike out the last word" of the amendment or section of the bill under consideration. The motion is pro forma, requires no vote and does not change the amendment being debated. (*Also see five-minute rule.*)

Substitute — A motion, amendment or entire bill introduced in place of the pending legislative business. Passage of the substitute kills the original measure by supplanting it. The substitute may also be amended. (*Also see amendment in the nature of a substitute.*)

Supplemental appropriations bill — Legislation appropriating funds after the regular annual appropriations bill for a federal department or agency has been enacted. Supplemental appropriations bills often arrive about halfway through the fiscal year, when needs that Congress and the president did not anticipate (or may not have wanted to fund) become pressing. In recent years, supplementals have been driven by spending to help victims of natural disasters and to carry out peacekeeping commitments.

Suspend the rules — A time-saving procedure for passing bills in the House. The wording of the motion, which may be made by any member recognized by the Speaker, is: "I move to suspend the rules and pass the bill . . . ." A favorable vote by two-thirds of those present is required for passage. Debate is limited to 40 minutes, and no amendments from the floor are permitted. If a two-thirds favorable vote is not attained, the bill may be considered later under regular procedures. The suspension procedure is in order every Monday and Tuesday and is intended to be reserved for non-controversial bills.

Table a bill — Motions to table, or to "lay on the table," are used to block or kill amendments or other parliamentary questions. When approved, a tabling motion is considered the final disposition of that issue. One of the most widely used parliamentary procedures, the motion to table is not debatable, and adoption requires a simple majority vote.

In the Senate, however, different language sometimes is used. The motion may be worded to let a bill "lie on the table," perhaps for subsequent "picking up." This motion is more flexible, keeping the bill pending for later action, if desired. Tabling motions on amendments are effective debate-ending devices in the Senate.

Treaties — Executive proposals — in the form of resolutions of ratification — which must be submitted to the Senate for approval by two-thirds of the senators present. Treaties are normally sent to the Foreign Relations Committee for scrutiny before the Senate takes action. Foreign Relations has jurisdiction over all treaties, regardless of the subject matter. Treaties are read three times and debated on the floor in much the same manner as legislative proposals. After approval by the Senate, treaties are formally ratified by the president.

Trust funds — Funds collected and used by the federal government for carrying out specific purposes and programs according to terms of a trust agreement or statute such as the Social Security and unemployment compensation trust funds. Such funds are administered by the government in a fiduciary capacity and are not available for the general purposes of the government.

Unanimous consent — A procedure used to expedite floor action. Proceedings of the House or Senate and action on legislation often take place upon the unanimous consent of the chamber, whether or not a rule of the chamber is being violated. It is frequently used in a routine fashion, such as by a senator requesting the unanimous consent of the Senate to have specified members of his or her staff present on the floor during debate on a specific amendment. A single member's objection blocks a unanimous consent request.

Unanimous consent agreement — A device used in the Senate to expedite legislation. Much of the Senate's legislative business, dealing with both minor and controversial issues, is conducted through unanimous consent or unanimous consent agreements. On major legislation, such agreements usually are printed and transmitted to all senators in advance of floor debate. Once agreed to, they are binding on all members unless the Senate, by unanimous consent, agrees to modify them. An agreement may list the order in which various bills are to be considered; specify the length of time for debate on bills and contested amendments and when they are to be voted upon; and, frequently, require that all amendments introduced be germane to the bill under consideration.

In this regard, unanimous consent agreements are similar to the "rules" issued by the House Rules Committee for bills pending in the House.

Union Calendar — Bills that directly or indirectly appropriate money or raise revenue are placed on this House calendar according to the date they are reported from committee. (*Also see calendar.*)

U.S. Code — A consolidation and codification of the general and permanent laws of the United States arranged by subject under 50 titles, the first six dealing with general or political subjects, and the other 44 alphabetically arranged from agriculture to war. The U.S. Code is updated annually, and a new set of bound volumes is published every six years. (*Also see law, statutes at large.*)

Veto — Disapproval by the president of a bill or joint resolution (other than one proposing an amendment to the Constitution). When Congress is in session, the president must veto a bill within 10 days, excluding Sundays, after he has received it; otherwise, it becomes law without his signature. When the president vetoes a bill, he returns it to the chamber of origin along with a message stating his objections. (*Also see pocket veto, override a veto.*)

Voice vote — In either the House or Senate, members answer "aye" or "no" in chorus, and the presiding officer decides the result. The term is also used loosely to indicate action by unanimous consent or without objection. (*Also see yeas and nays.*)

Whip — In effect, the assistant majority or minority leader, in either the House or Senate. His or her job is to help marshal votes in support of party strategy and legislation.

Without objection — Used in lieu of a vote on non-controversial motions, amendments or bills that may be passed in either chamber if no member voices an objection.

Yeas and nays — The Constitution requires that yea-and-nay votes be taken and recorded when requested by one-fifth of the members present. In the House, the Speaker determines whether one-fifth of the members present requested a vote. In the Senate, practice requires only 11 members. The Constitution requires the yeas and nays on a veto override attempt. *(Also see recorded vote.)*

Yielding — When a member has been recognized to speak, no other member may speak unless he or she obtains permission from the member recognized. This permission is called yielding and usually is requested in the form, "Will the gentleman (or gentlelady) yield to me?" While this activity occasionally is seen in the Senate, the Senate has no rule or practice to parcel out time.

In the House, the floor manager of a bill usually apportions debate time by yielding specific amounts of time to members who have requested it. ◆

Members of the 108th Congress, 2nd Session . . .

(As of Dec. 9, 2004, when the Senate adjourned sine die.)

Representatives
R 227; D 205; I 1
2 vacancies

— A —

Abercrombie, Neil, D-Hawaii (1)
Ackerman, Gary L., D-N.Y. (5)
Aderholt, Robert B., R-Ala. (4)
Akin, Todd, R-Mo. (2)
Alexander, Rodney, R-La. (5)
Allen, Tom, D-Maine (1)
Andrews, Robert E., D-N.J. (1)

— B —

Baca, Joe, D-Calif. (43)
Bachus, Spencer, R-Ala. (6)
Baird, Brian, D-Wash. (3)
Baker, Richard H., R-La. (6)
Baldwin, Tammy, D-Wis. (2)
Ballenger, Cass, R-N.C. (10)
Barrett, J. Gresham, R-S.C. (3)
Bartlett, Roscoe G., R-Md. (6)
Barton, Joe L., R-Texas (6)
Bass, Charles, R-N.H. (2)
Beauprez, Bob, R-Colo. (7)
Becerra, Xavier, D-Calif. (31)
Bell, Chris, D-Texas (25)
Berkley, Shelley, D-Nev. (1)
Berman, Howard L., D-Calif. (28)
Berry, Marion, D-Ark. (1)
Biggert, Judy, R-Ill. (13)
Bilirakis, Michael, R-Fla. (9)
Bishop, Rob, R-Utah (1)
Bishop, Sanford D. Jr., D-Ga. (2)
Bishop, Timothy H., D-N.Y. (1)
Blackburn, Marsha, R-Tenn. (7)
Blumenauer, Earl, D-Ore. (3)
Blunt, Roy, R-Mo. (7)
Boehlert, Sherwood, R-N.Y. (24)
Boehner, John A., R-Ohio (8)
Bonilla, Henry, R-Texas (23)
Bonner, Jo, R-Ala. (1)
Bono, Mary, R-Calif. (45)
Boozman, John, R-Ark. (3)
Boswell, Leonard L., D-Iowa (3)
Boucher, Rick, D-Va. (9)
Boyd, Allen, D-Fla. (2)
Bradley, Jeb, R-N.H. (1)
Brady, Kevin, R-Texas (8)
Brady, Robert A., D-Pa. (1)
Brown, Corrine, D-Fla. (3)
Brown, Henry E. Jr., R-S.C. (1)
Brown, Sherrod, D-Ohio (13)
Brown-Waite, Ginny, R-Fla. (5)
Burgess, Michael C., R-Texas (26)
Burns, Max, R-Ga. (12)
Burr, Richard M., R-N.C. (5)
Burton, Dan, R-Ind. (5)
Butterfield, G.K., D-N.C. (1)
Buyer, Steve, R-Ind. (4)

— C —

Calvert, Ken, R-Calif. (44)
Camp, Dave, R-Mich. (4)
Cannon, Chris, R-Utah (3)
Cantor, Eric, R-Va. (7)
Capito, Shelley Moore, R-W.Va. (2)
Capps, Lois, D-Calif. (23)
Capuano, Michael E., D-Mass. (8)
Cardin, Benjamin L., D-Md. (3)
Cardoza, Dennis, D-Calif. (18)
Carson, Brad, D-Okla. (2)
Carson, Julia, D-Ind. (7)
Carter, John, R-Texas (31)
Case, Ed, D-Hawaii (2)
Castle, Michael N., R-Del. (AL)
Chabot, Steve, R-Ohio (1)
Chandler, Ben, D-KY (6)
Chocola, Chris, R-Ind. (2)
Clay, William Lacy, D-Mo. (1)
Clyburn, James E., D-S.C. (6)
Coble, Howard, R-N.C. (6)
Cole, Tom, R-Okla. (4)
Collins, Mac, R-Ga. (8)
Conyers, John Jr., D-Mich. (14)

Cooper, Jim, D-Tenn. (5)
Costello, Jerry F., D-Ill. (12)
Cox, Christopher, R-Calif. (48)
Cramer, Robert E. "Bud," D-Ala. (5)
Crane, Philip M., R-Ill. (8)
Crenshaw, Ander, R-Fla. (4)
Crowley, Joseph, D-N.Y. (7)
Cubin, Barbara, R-Wyo. (AL)
Culberson, John, R-Texas (7)
Cummings, Elijah E., D-Md. (7)
Cunningham, Randy "Duke," R-Calif. (50)

— D —

Davis, Artur, D-Ala. (7)
Davis, Danny K., D-Ill. (7)
Davis, Jim, D-Fla. (11)
Davis, Jo Ann, R-Va. (1)
Davis, Lincoln, D-Tenn. (4)
Davis, Susan A., D-Calif. (53)
Davis, Thomas M. III, R-Va. (11)
Deal, Nathan, R-Ga. (10)
DeFazio, Peter A., D-Ore. (4)
DeGette, Diana, D-Colo. (1)
Delahunt, Bill, D-Mass. (10)
DeLauro, Rosa, D-Conn. (3)
DeLay, Tom, R-Texas (22)
DeMint, Jim, R-S.C. (4)
Deutsch, Peter, D-Fla. (20)
Diaz-Balart, Lincoln, R-Fla. (21)
Diaz-Balart, Mario, R-Fla. (25)
Dicks, Norm, D-Wash. (6)
Dingell, John D., D-Mich. (15)
Doggett, Lloyd, D-Texas (25)
Dooley, Cal, D-Calif. (20)
Doolittle, John T., R-Calif. (4)
Doyle, Mike, D-Pa. (14)
Dreier, David, R-Calif. (26)
Duncan, John J. "Jimmy" Jr., R-Tenn. (2)
Dunn, Jennifer, R-Wash. (8)

— E —

Edwards, Chet, D-Texas (17)
Ehlers, Vernon J., R-Mich. (3)
Emanuel, Rahm, D-Ill. (5)
Emerson, Jo Ann, R-Mo. (8)
Engel, Eliot L., D-N.Y. (17)
English, Phil, R-Pa. (3)
Eshoo, Anna G., D-Calif. (14)
Etheridge, Bob, D-N.C. (2)
Evans, Lane, D-Ill. (17)
Everett, Terry, R-Ala. (2)

— F —

Farr, Sam, D-Calif. (17)
Fattah, Chaka, D-Pa. (2)
Feeney, Tom, R-Fla. (24)
Ferguson, Mike, R-N.J. (7)
Filner, Bob, D-Calif. (51)
Flake, Jeff, R-Ariz. (6)
Foley, Mark, R-Fla. (16)
Forbes, J. Randy, R-Va. (4)
Ford, Harold E. Jr., D-Tenn. (9)
Fossella, Vito J., R-N.Y. (13)
Frank, Barney, D-Mass. (4)
Franks, Trent, R-Ariz. (2)
Frelinghuysen, Rodney, R-N.J. (11)
Frost, Martin, D-Texas (24)

— G —

Gallegly, Elton, R-Calif. (24)
Garrett, Scott, R-N.J. (5)
Gephardt, Richard A., D-Mo. (3)
Gerlach, Jim, R-Pa. (6)
Gibbons, Jim, R-Nev. (2)
Gilchrest, Wayne T., R-Md. (1)
Gillmor, Paul E., R-Ohio (5)
Gingrey, Phil, R-Ga. (11)
Gonzalez, Charlie, D-Texas (20)
Goode, Virgil H. Jr., R-Va. (5)
Goodlatte, Robert W., R-Va. (6)
Gordon, Bart, D-Tenn. (6)
Granger, Kay, R-Texas (12)
Graves, Sam, R-Mo. (6)
Green, Gene, D-Texas (29)
Green, Mark, R-Wis. (8)
Greenwood, James C., R-Pa. (8)

Grijalva, Raúl M., D-Ariz. (7)
Gutierrez, Luis V., D-Ill. (4)
Gutknecht, Gil, R-Minn. (1)

— H —

Hall, Ralph M., R-Texas (4)
Harman, Jane, D-Calif. (36)
Harris, Katherine, R-Fla. (13)
Hart, Melissa A., R-Pa. (4)
Hastert, J. Dennis, R-Ill. (14)
Hastings, Alcee L., D-Fla. (23)
Hastings, Doc, R-Wash. (4)
Hayes, Robin, R-N.C. (8)
Hayworth, J.D., R-Ariz. (5)
Hefley, Joel, R-Colo. (5)
Hensarling, Jeb, R-Texas (5)
Herger, Wally, R-Calif. (2)
Herseth, Stephanie, D-S.D. (AL)
Hill, Baron P., D-Ind. (9)
Hinchey, Maurice D., D-N.Y. (22)
Hinojosa, Rubén, D-Texas (15)
Hobson, David L., R-Ohio (7)
Hoeffel, Joseph M., D-Pa. (13)
Hoekstra, Peter, R-Mich. (2)
Holden, Tim, D-Pa. (17)
Holt, Rush D., D-N.J. (12)
Honda, Michael M., D-Calif. (15)
Hooley, Darlene, D-Ore. (5)
Hostettler, John, R-Ind. (8)
Houghton, Amo, R-N.Y. (29)
Hoyer, Steny H., D-Md. (5)
Hulshof, Kenny, R-Mo. (9)
Hunter, Duncan, R-Calif. (52)
Hyde, Henry J., R-Ill. (6)

— I, J —

Inslee, Jay, D-Wash. (1)
Isakson, Johnny, R-Ga. (6)
Israel, Steve, D-N.Y. (2)
Issa, Darrell, R-Calif. (49)
Istook, Ernest, R-Okla. (5)
Jackson, Jesse L. Jr., D-Ill. (2)
Jackson-Lee, Sheila, D-Texas (18)
Jefferson, William J., D-La. (2)
Jenkins, Bill, R-Tenn. (1)
John, Chris, D-La. (7)
Johnson, Eddie Bernice, D-Texas (30)
Johnson, Nancy L., R-Conn. (5)
Johnson, Sam, R-Texas (3)
Johnson, Timothy V., R-Ill. (15)
Jones, Stephanie Tubbs, D-Ohio (11)
Jones, Walter B., R-N.C. (3)

— K —

Kanjorski, Paul E., D-Pa. (11)
Kaptur, Marcy, D-Ohio (9)
Keller, Ric, R-Fla. (8)
Kelly, Sue W., R-N.Y. (19)
Kennedy, Mark, R-Minn. (6)
Kennedy, Patrick J., D-R.I. (1)
Kildee, Dale E., D-Mich. (5)
Kilpatrick, Carolyn Cheeks, D-Mich. (13)
Kind, Ron, D-Wis. (3)
King, Peter T., R-N.Y. (3)
King, Steve, R-Iowa (5)
Kingston, Jack, R-Ga. (1)
Kirk, Mark Steven, R-Ill. (10)
Kleczka, Gerald D., D-Wis. (4)
Kline, John, R-Minn. (2)
Knollenberg, Joe, R-Mich. (9)
Kolbe, Jim, R-Ariz. (8)
Kucinich, Dennis J., D-Ohio (10)

— L —

LaHood, Ray, R-Ill. (18)
Lampson, Nick, D-Texas (9)
Langevin, Jim, D-R.I. (2)
Lantos, Tom, D-Calif. (12)
Larsen, Rick, D-Wash. (2)
Larson, John B., D-Conn. (1)
Latham, Tom, R-Iowa (4)
LaTourette, Steven C., R-Ohio (14)
Leach, Jim, R-Iowa (2)
Lee, Barbara, D-Calif. (9)
Levin, Sander M., D-Mich. (12)
Lewis, Jerry, R-Calif. (41)
Lewis, John, D-Ga. (5)

Lewis, Ron, R-Ky. (2)
Linder, John, R-Ga. (7)
Lipinski, William O., D-Ill. (3)
LoBiondo, Frank A., R-N.J. (2)
Lofgren, Zoe, D-Calif. (16)
Lowey, Nita M., D-N.Y. (18)
Lucas, Frank D., R-Okla. (3)
Lucas, Ken, D-Ky. (4)
Lynch, Stephen F., D-Mass. (9)

— M —

Majette, Denise L., D-Ga. (4)
Maloney, Carolyn B., D-N.Y. (14)
Manzullo, Donald, R-Ill. (16)
Markey, Edward J., D-Mass. (7)
Marshall, Jim, D-Ga. (3)
Matheson, Jim, D-Utah (2)
Matsui, Robert T., D-Calif. (5)
McCarthy, Carolyn, D-N.Y. (4)
McCarthy, Karen, D-Mo. (5)
McCollum, Betty, D-Minn. (4)
McCotter, Thaddeus, R-Mich. (11)
McCrery, Jim, R-La. (4)
McDermott, Jim, D-Wash. (7)
McGovern, Jim, D-Mass. (3)
McHugh, John M., R-N.Y. (23)
McInnis, Scott, R-Colo. (3)
McIntyre, Mike, D-N.C. (7)
McKeon, Howard P. "Buck," R-Calif. (25)
McNulty, Michael R., D-N.Y. (21)
Meehan, Martin T., D-Mass. (5)
Meek, Kendrick B., D-Fla. (17)
Meeks, Gregory W., D-N.Y. (6)
Menendez, Robert, D-N.J. (13)
Mica, John L., R-Fla. (7)
Michaud, Michael H., D-Maine (2)
Millender-McDonald, Juanita, D-Calif. (37)
Miller, Brad, D-N.C. (13)
Miller, Candice S., R-Mich. (10)
Miller, Gary G., R-Calif. (42)
Miller, George, D-Calif. (7)
Miller, Jeff, R-Fla. (1)
Mollohan, Alan B., D-W.Va. (1)
Moore, Dennis, D-Kan. (3)
Moran, James P., D-Va. (8)
Moran, Jerry, R-Kan. (1)
Murphy, Tim, R-Pa. (18)
Murtha, John P., D-Pa. (12)
Musgrave, Marilyn, R-Colo. (4)
Myrick, Sue, R-N.C. (9)

— N —

Nadler, Jerrold, D-N.Y. (8)
Napolitano, Grace F., D-Calif. (38)
Neal, Richard E., D-Mass. (2)
Nethercutt, George, R-Wash. (5)
Neugebauer, Randy, R-Texas (19)
Ney, Bob, R-Ohio (18)
Northup, Anne M., R-Ky. (3)
Norwood, Charlie, R-Ga. (9)
Nunes, Devin, R-Calif. (21)
Nussle, Jim, R-Iowa (1)

— O —

Oberstar, James L., D-Minn. (8)
Obey, David R., D-Wis. (7)
Olver, John W., D-Mass. (1)
Ortiz, Solomon P., D-Texas (27)
Osborne, Tom, R-Neb. (3)
Ose, Doug, R-Calif. (3)
Otter, C. L. "Butch," R-Idaho (1)
Owens, Major R., D-N.Y. (11)
Oxley, Michael G., R-Ohio (4)

— P —

Pallone, Frank Jr., D-N.J. (6)
Pascrell, Bill Jr., D-N.J. (8)
Pastor, Ed, D-Ariz. (4)
Paul, Ron, R-Texas (14)
Payne, Donald M., D-N.J. (10)
Pearce, Steve, R-N.M. (2)
Pelosi, Nancy, D-Calif. (8)
Pence, Mike, R-Ind. (6)
Peterson, Collin C., D-Minn. (7)
Peterson, John E., R-Pa. (5)
Petri, Tom, R-Wis. (6)
Pickering, Charles W. "Chip" Jr., R-Miss. (3)

. . . Governors, Supreme Court, Cabinet-Rank Officers

Pitts, Joe, R-Pa. (16)
Platts, Todd R., R-Pa. (19)
Pombo, Richard W., R-Calif. (11)
Pomeroy, Earl, D-N.D. (AL)
Porter, Jon, R-Nev. (3)
Portman, Rob, R-Ohio (2)
Price, David E., D-N.C. (4)
Pryce, Deborah, R-Ohio (15)
Putnam, Adam H., R-Fla. (12)

— Q, R —

Quinn, Jack, R-N.Y. (27)
Radanovich, George P., R-Calif. (19)
Rahall, Nick J. II, D-W.Va. (3)
Ramstad, Jim, R-Minn. (3)
Rangel, Charles B., D-N.Y. (15)
Regula, Ralph, R-Ohio (16)
Rehberg, Denny, R-Mont. (AL)
Renzi, Rick, R-Ariz. (1)
Reyes, Silvestre, D-Texas (16)
Reynolds, Thomas M., R-N.Y. (26)
Rodriguez, Ciro D., D-Texas (28)
Rogers, Harold, R-Ky. (5)
Rogers, Mike D., R-Ala. (3)
Rogers, Mike, R-Mich. (8)
Rohrabacher, Dana, R-Calif. (46)
Ros-Lehtinen, Ileana, R-Fla. (18)
Ross, Mike, D-Ark. (4)
Rothman, Steven R., D-N.J. (9)
Roybal-Allard, Lucille, D-Calif. (34)
Royce, Ed, R-Calif. (40)
Ruppersberger, C.A. Dutch, D-Md. (2)
Rush, Bobby L., D-Ill. (1)
Ryan, Paul D., R-Wis. (1)
Ryan, Tim, D-Ohio (17)
Ryun, Jim, R-Kan. (2)

— S —

Sabo, Martin Olav, D-Minn. (5)
Sánchez, Linda T., D-Calif. (39)
Sanchez, Loretta, D-Calif. (47)
Sanders, Bernard, I-Vt. (AL)
Sandlin, Max, D-Texas (1)
Saxton, H. James, R-N.J. (3)
Schakowsky, Jan, D-Ill. (9)
Schiff, Adam B., D-Calif. (29)
Schrock, Ed, R-Va. (2)
Scott, David, D-Ga. (13)
Scott, Robert C., D-Va. (3)
Sensenbrenner, F. James Jr., R-Wis. (5)
Serrano, José E., D-N.Y. (16)
Sessions, Pete, R-Texas (32)
Shadegg, John, R-Ariz. (3)
Shaw, E. Clay Jr., R-Fla. (22)
Shays, Christopher, R-Conn. (4)
Sherman, Brad, D-Calif. (27)
Sherwood, Don, R-Pa. (10)
Shimkus, John, R-Ill. (19)
Shuster, Bill, R-Pa. (9)
Simmons, Rob, R-Conn. (2)
Simpson, Mike, R-Idaho (2)
Skelton, Ike, D-Mo. (4)
Slaughter, Louise M., D-N.Y. (28)
Smith, Adam, D-Wash. (9)
Smith, Christopher H., R-N.J. (4)
Smith, Lamar, R-Texas (21)
Smith, Nick, R-Mich. (7)
Snyder, Vic, D-Ark. (2)
Solis, Hilda L., D-Calif. (32)
Souder, Mark, R-Ind. (3)
Spratt, John M. Jr., D-S.C. (5)
Stark, Pete, D-Calif. (13)
Stearns, Cliff, R-Fla. (6)
Stenholm, Charles W., D-Texas (17)
Strickland, Ted, D-Ohio (6)
Stupak, Bart, D-Mich. (1)
Sullivan, John, R-Okla. (1)
Sweeney, John E., R-N.Y. (20)

— T —

Tancredo, Tom, R-Colo. (6)
Tanner, John, D-Tenn. (8)
Tauscher, Ellen O., D-Calif. (10)
Tauzin, Billy, R-La. (3)
Taylor, Charles H., R-N.C. (11)
Taylor, Gene, D-Miss. (4)
Terry, Lee, R-Neb. (2)
Thomas, Bill, R-Calif. (22)

Thompson, Bennie, D-Miss. (2)
Thompson, Mike, D-Calif. (1)
Thornberry, William M. "Mac," R-Texas (13)
Tiahrt, Todd, R-Kan. (4)
Tiberi, Pat, R-Ohio (12)
Tierney, John F., D-Mass. (6)
Toomey, Patrick J., R-Pa. (15)
Towns, Edolphus, D-N.Y. (10)
Turner, Jim, D-Texas (2)
Turner, Michael R., R-Ohio (3)

— U, V —

Udall, Mark, D-Colo. (2)
Udall, Tom, D-N.M. (3)
Upton, Fred, R-Mich. (6)
Van Hollen, Chris, D-Md. (8)
Velázquez, Nydia M., D-N.Y. (12)
Visclosky, Peter J., D-Ind. (1)
Vitter, David, R-La. (1)

— W —

Walden, Greg, R-Ore. (2)
Walsh, James T., R-N.Y. (25)
Wamp, Zach, R-Tenn. (3)
Waters, Maxine, D-Calif. (35)
Watson, Diane, D-Calif. (33)
Watt, Melvin, D-N.C. (12)
Waxman, Henry A., D-Calif. (30)
Weldon, Curt, R-Pa. (7)
Weldon, Dave, R-Fla. (15)
Weller, Jerry, R-Ill. (11)
Wexler, Robert, D-Fla. (19)
Whitfield, Edward, R-Ky. (1)
Wicker, Roger, R-Miss. (1)
Wilson, Heather A., R-N.M. (1)
Wilson, Joe, R-S.C. (2)
Wolf, Frank R., R-Va. (10)
Woolsey, Lynn, D-Calif. (6)
Wu, David, D-Ore. (1)
Wynn, Albert R., D-Md. (4)

— X, Y, Z —

Young, C.W. Bill, R-Fla. (10)
Young, Don, R-Alaska (AL)

Delegates

Acevedo-Vilá, Anibal, D-P.R.
Bordallo, Madeleine Z., D-Guam
Christensen, Donna M.C., D-Virgin Is.
Faleomavaega, Eni F.H., D-Am. Samoa
Norton, Eleanor Holmes, D-D.C.

Senators
R 51; D 48; I 1

Akaka, Daniel K., D-Hawaii
Alexander, Lamar, R-Tenn.
Allard, Wayne, R-Colo.
Allen, George, R-Va.
Baucus, Max, D-Mont.
Bayh, Evan, D-Ind.
Bennett, Robert F., R-Utah
Biden, Joseph R. Jr., D-Del.
Bingaman, Jeff, D-N.M.
Bond, Christopher S., R-Mo.
Boxer, Barbara, D-Calif.
Breaux, John B., D-La.
Brownback, Sam, R-Kan.
Bunning, Jim, R-Ky.
Burns, Conrad, R-Mont.
Byrd, Robert C., D-W.Va.
Campbell, Ben Nighthorse, R-Colo.
Cantwell, Maria, D-Wash.
Carper, Thomas R., D-Del.
Chafee, Lincoln, R-R.I.
Chambliss, Saxby, R-Ga.
Clinton, Hillary Rodham, D-N.Y.
Cochran, Thad, R-Miss.
Coleman, Norm, R-Minn.
Collins, Susan, R-Maine
Conrad, Kent, D-N.D.
Cornyn, John, R-Texas

Corzine, Jon, D-N.J.
Craig, Larry E., R-Idaho
Crapo, Michael D., R-Idaho
Daschle, Tom, D-S.D.
Dayton, Mark, D-Minn.
DeWine, Mike, R-Ohio
Dodd, Christopher J., D-Conn.
Dole, Elizabeth, R-N.C.
Domenici, Pete V., R-N.M.
Dorgan, Byron L., D-N.D.
Durbin, Richard J., D-Ill.
Edwards, John, D-N.C.
Ensign, John, R-Nev.
Enzi, Michael B., R-Wyo.
Feingold, Russell D., D-Wis.
Feinstein, Dianne, D-Calif.
Fitzgerald, Peter G., R-Ill.
Frist, Bill, R-Tenn.
Graham, Bob, D-Fla.
Graham, Lindsey, R-S.C.
Grassley, Charles E., R-Iowa
Gregg, Judd, R-N.H.
Hagel, Chuck, R-Neb.
Harkin, Tom, D-Iowa
Hatch, Orrin G., R-Utah
Hollings, Ernest F., D-S.C.
Hutchison, Kay Bailey, R-Texas
Inhofe, James M., R-Okla.
Inouye, Daniel K., D-Hawaii
Jeffords, James M., I-Vt.
Johnson, Tim, D-S.D.
Kennedy, Edward M., D-Mass.
Kerry, John, D-Mass.
Kohl, Herb, D-Wis.
Kyl, Jon, R-Ariz.
Landrieu, Mary L., D-La.
Lautenberg, Frank R., D-N.J.
Leahy, Patrick J., D-Vt.
Levin, Carl, D-Mich.
Lieberman, Joseph I., D-Conn.
Lincoln, Blanche, D-Ark.
Lott, Trent, R-Miss.
Lugar, Richard G., R-Ind.
McCain, John, R-Ariz.
McConnell, Mitch, R-Ky.
Mikulski, Barbara A., D-Md.
Miller, Zell, D-Ga.
Murkowski, Lisa, R-Alaska
Murray, Patty, D-Wash.
Nelson, Ben, D-Neb.
Nelson, Bill, D-Fla.
Nickles, Don, R-Okla.
Pryor, Mark, D-Ark.
Reed, Jack, D-R.I.
Reid, Harry, D-Nev.
Roberts, Pat, R-Kan.
Rockefeller, John D. IV, D-W.Va.
Santorum, Rick, R-Pa.
Sarbanes, Paul S., D-Md.
Schumer, Charles E., D-N.Y.
Sessions, Jeff, R-Ala.
Shelby, Richard C., R-Ala.
Smith, Gordon H., R-Ore.
Snowe, Olympia J., R-Maine
Specter, Arlen, R-Pa.
Stabenow, Debbie, D-Mich.
Stevens, Ted, R-Alaska
Sununu, John E., R-N.H.
Talent, Jim, R-Mo.
Thomas, Craig, R-Wyo.
Voinovich, George V., R-Ohio
Warner, John W., R-Va.
Wyden, Ron, D-Ore.

Governors
R 28; D 22

Ala. — Bob Riley, R
Alaska — Frank H. Murkowski, R
Ariz. — Janet Napolitano, D
Ark. — Mike Huckabee, R
Calif. — Arnold Schwarzenegger, R
Colo. — Bill Owens, R
Conn. — M. Jodi Rell, R
Del. — Ruth Ann Minner, D
Fla. — Jeb Bush, R
Ga. — Sonny Perdue, R
Hawaii — Linda Lingle, R

Idaho — Dirk Kempthorne, R
Ill. — Rod R. Blagojevich, D
Ind. — Joseph E. Kernan, D
Iowa — Tom Vilsack, D
Kan. — Kathleen Sebelius, D
Ky. — Ernie Fletcher, R
La. — Kathleen Babineaux Blanco, D
Maine — John Baldacci, D
Md. — Robert L. Ehrlich Jr., R
Mass. — Mitt Romney, R
Mich. — Jennifer M. Granholm, D
Minn. — Tim Pawlenty, R
Miss. — Haley Barbour, R
Mo. — Bob Holden, D
Mont. — Judy Martz, R
Neb. — Mike Johanns, R
Nev. — Kenny Guinn, R
N.H. — Craig Benson, R
N.J. — Richard J. Codey, D (acting)
N.M. — Bill Richardson, D
N.Y. — George E. Pataki, R
N.C. — Michael F. Easley, D
N.D. — John Hoeven, R
Ohio — Bob Taft, R
Okla. — Brad Henry, D
Ore. — Theodore R. Kulongoski, D
Pa. — Edward G. Rendell, D
R.I. — Donald L. Carcieri, R
S.C. — Mark Sanford, R
S.D. — Michael Rounds, R
Tenn. — Phil Bredesen, D
Texas — Rick Perry, R
Utah — Olene S. Walker, R
Vt. — Jim Douglas, R
Va. — Mark Warner, D
Wash. — Gary Locke, D
W.Va. — Bob Wise, D
Wis. — James E. Doyle, D
Wyo. — Dave Freudenthal, D

Supreme Court

Rehnquist, William H. — Va., Chief Justice
Breyer, Stephen G. — Mass.
Ginsburg, Ruth Bader — N.Y.
Kennedy, Anthony M. — Calif.
O'Connor, Sandra Day — Ariz.
Scalia, Antonin — Va.
Souter, David H. — N.H.
Stevens, John Paul — Ill.
Thomas, Clarence — Ga.

Cabinet

Abraham, Spencer — Energy
Ashcroft, John — Attorney General
Chao, Elaine L. — Labor
Evans, Donald L. — Commerce
Jackson, Alphonso R. — HUD
Mineta, Norman Y. — Transportation
Norton, Gale A. — Interior
Paige, Rod — Education
Powell, Colin L. — State
Principi, Anthony J. — Veterans Affairs
Ridge, Tom — Homeland Security
Rumsfeld, Donald H. — Defense
Snow, John W. — Treasury
Thompson, Tommy G. — HHS
Veneman, Ann M. — Agriculture

Other Executive Branch Officers

Cheney, Dick — Vice President
Bolten, Joshua B. — OMB Director
Card, Andrew H. Jr. — Chief of Staff
Friedman, Stephen — Director, National Economic Council
Leavitt, Michael O. — EPA Administrator
Negroponte, John D. — U.N. Representative
Rice, Condoleezza — Assistant to the President for National Security Affairs
Tenet, George J. — Director of Central Intelligence
Zoellick, Robert B. — U.S. Trade Representative

Appendix B

VOTE STUDIES

Bush Finds Ways to Win

When Congress gave final approval to an overhaul of the nation's intelligence system the week of Dec. 6, it was a good illustration of the George W. Bush method of legislative politics.

Bush maintained a narrow legislative agenda throughout 2004, and stayed at the periphery of House-Senate negotiations on the intelligence bill (S 2845) for months. Only in the final weeks did he take a firm stance and intervene with recalcitrant lawmakers — and then only after success looked attainable and Republican leaders, who normally handle such matters, told him it was necessary. (*Intelligence, p. 11-3*)

The victory on the most significant bill Congress passed during the year contributed to Bush's 72.6 percent success rate on congressional votes where he took an unambiguous stand in 2004. Though the lowest score of his presidency, it was the highest success rate for an incumbent seeking re-election since Jimmy Carter achieved a 75.1 percent success score in 1980.

The results reflected a divisive election year where partisan tensions remained historically high and where substantive legislative wins were not the highest priority for the president or congressional leaders. The Senate in particular did little legislating — aside from federal nominations, it took only 18 votes deemed tests of presidential persuasion by Congressional Quarterly, and supported the president 50 percent of the time. (*Party unity, p. B-8*)

And even when Bush lost, he often won in the long run.

Bush's defeats on nominations, a constitutional amendment to ban same-sex marriages and a highway bill limiting spending played to his political advantage with conservatives and may have helped his voter turnout in November. (*Elections, p. 18-3*)

When Bush lost policy votes in the House or Senate, as he did on commerce with Cuba, for instance, and opening more federal jobs to private sector competition, he usually was able to recover in conference committees controlled by Republicans. Overall, Bush's formula of remaining disengaged from Congress on many issues and using his political capital sparingly — but aggressively and to great effect — has proven advantageous, allowing him to minimize his defeats.

One way Bush has maximized his victories is by being more flexible than his reputation for stubbornness would suggest. For instance, he initially opposed creation of the Sept. 11 commission, the group that recommended many elements of the intelligence overhaul bill (S 2845 — H Rept 108-796) Bush is expected to sign into law soon.

In his four years in office, Bush has enjoyed an 81 percent success rate on congressional votes, the highest of any president since Lyndon B. Johnson and the third highest since Congressional Quarterly began measuring presidential support scores in 1953.

"The president doesn't like to lose," said Tripp Baird, director of Senate relations at the conservative Heritage Foundation. White House officials, he said, are "very attuned to which bills and legislation they should let Congress write and which ones they should write."

Perhaps most significantly, Bush has reaped the benefits of a like-minded Republican leadership bent on avoiding presidential vetoes and willing to twist arms so that the president can rack up wins and conserve his political capital for when he needs it most.

"Philosophically, we're very close," noted John Feehery, press secretary for House Speaker J. Dennis Hastert, R-Ill. "They can usually steer with a light touch."

In sum, Bush has used unified government to greater effect than most presidents, according to Theodore J. Lowi, a professor of government at Cornell University.

"He's shown a fairly rational approach that others who enjoyed their own party majority have squandered somewhat," Lowi said. "He keeps his agenda from covering everything under the sun."

Bush's challenge now is to make this formula work in a second term. His success rate has been declining for two straight years, and that could point to an erosion of his clout on Capitol Hill as his tenure as a lame duck begins.

Every second-term president since 1953 has been less successful with Congress. Academics and some lawmakers warn that Bush's need to push Congress to finish the intelligence bill foreshadows larger difficulties he may have getting his agenda through the House and Senate.

That may be particularly true due to the highly sensitive nature of one of the White House's primary goals for the second term — a partial privatization of Social Security. Already, some Republican leaders have suggested that Bush cannot expect to maintain his historically high success rate with major new proposals unless he seizes the initiative.

"Social Security and tax reform, will, by the nature of those issues, have to require a lot more leadership on the part of the president," argued one Senate GOP leadership aide, who asked to remain anonymous.

Many Decisions

But Republican leaders continue to draw huge political benefits from sticking with the president, and have shown few signs that they intend to change the way they do business.

Congressional Quarterly's calculation of presidential success measures only how often the House or Senate acts the way the president wanted. CQ looks at every House and Senate floor vote, determines whether the president took a clear position before the vote and notes the outcome.

Naturally, the CQ study has limitations. It gives equal weight to all floor votes on which the president took a stand. It does not count voice votes.

Presidential Success *History*

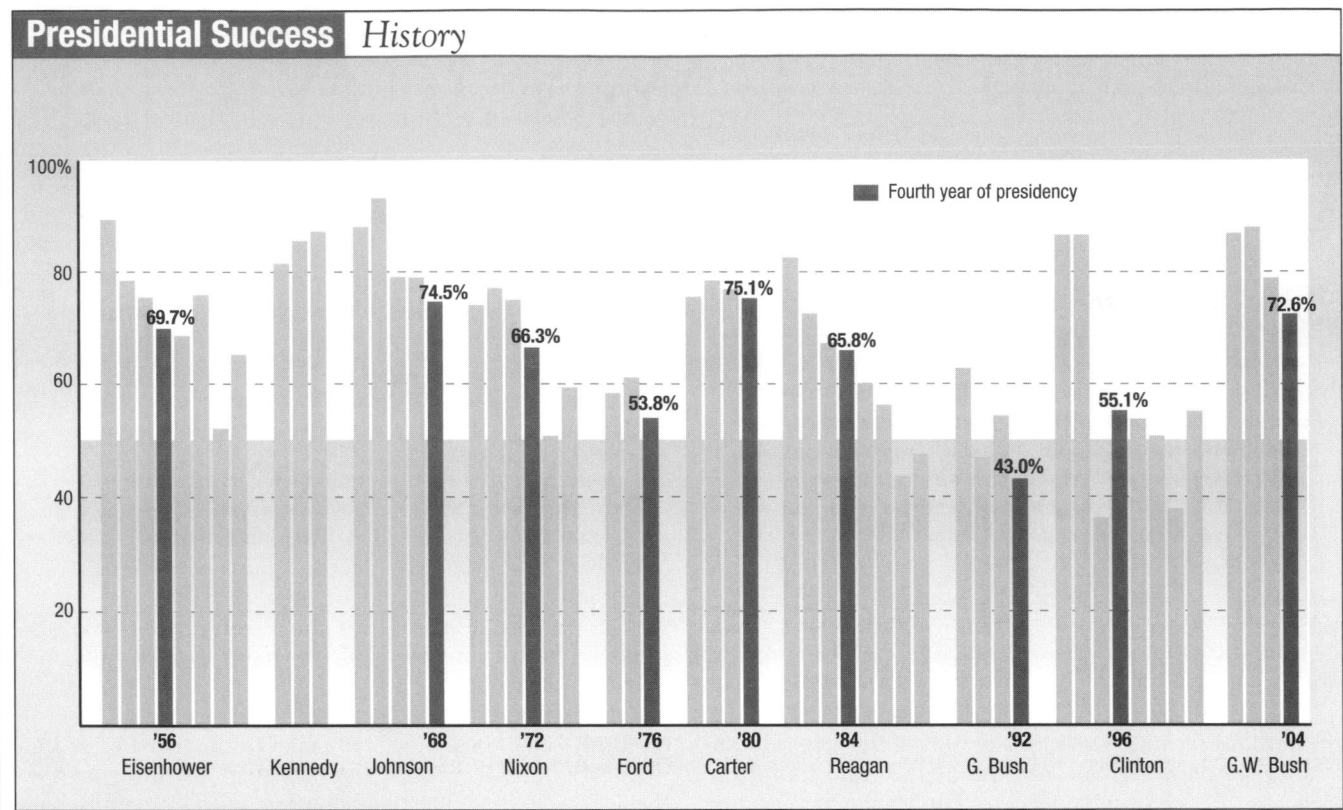

Fourth year of presidency

'56 Eisenhower Kennedy Johnson '68 '72 Nixon Ford '76 '80 Carter Reagan '84 '92 G. Bush Clinton '96 '04 G.W. Bush

2004 Data

House total	24 victories
	10 defeats
Senate total	37 victories
	13 defeats
Nominations	*28 victories*
	4 defeats
Other issues	*9 victories*
	9 defeats

Bush success rate: 72.6 percent

For More Information

And it does not reflect whether the president's proposals or legislation that he supported were enacted into law.

But the study has provided a valuable statistical snapshot of a president's year on Capitol Hill.

Bush's 2004 "batting average" is historically high. Since 1953, success rates have ranged from Johnson's high score of 93.1 percent in 1965 to Bill Clinton's low of 36.2 percent in 1995. But it is the lowest of the Bush's term. In the House, the president's 70.6 percent success rate is down from an 87.3 percent score in 2003. In the Senate, his 74.0 percent success rate reflects a drop of less than 1 percentage point from 2003.

Perhaps as significant, however, is the relative dearth of votes taken in 2004, and the low number of issues where Bush took a stand.

In 2000, for example, the last year of Clinton's second term, the Office of Management and Budget (OMB) issued formal statements of administration policy on 142 bills and resolutions. This year, OMB issued 61.

The figures reflect a year in which the president had few major legislative priorities — unlike 2003, when he lobbied heavily on Medicare legislation, tax cuts and funding for the wars in Iraq and Afghanistan.

"We were extremely busy last year," Feehery said, adding that in 2004, Bush was "busy getting himself re-elected."

Republican leaders and the White House recognized early on that an aggressive tax cut agenda would stall in the closely divided Senate, and that bolder initiatives such as Social Security would have to wait. At best, Republicans would be able to produce a budget that held down domestic spending — which they did with a nine-bill omnibus spending package (PL 108-447) and a handful of other measures. (*Appropriations, p. 2-3*)

Slowdown in the Senate

When judicial and Cabinet nominations — most of which were not controversial — are subtracted from the total, Bush's success rate in the Senate drops to exactly 50 percent, the lowest since Clinton's 39.1 percent in 2000, using the same method of calculation.

In part, the low rate on issues appears to be a function of highly partisan voting in the Senate. According to CQ's party unity study, Republicans stuck together on 90 percent of votes; Democrats on 83 percent.

Some bills supported by the president, such as legislation to limit non-economic damage awards in medical malpractice lawsuits (S 2207), followed a familiar pattern — easy passage in a House controlled by conservative Republicans; little or no action in the Senate where control is closer.

Leading Scorers: Presidential Support

Support indicates those who in 2004 voted most often for President Bush's position. **Opposition** shows those who voted most often against his position. Scores are based on actual votes cast.

Members who missed half or more of the votes are not listed. Scores are rounded to 1 decimal; those with identical scores are listed alphabetically. *(Complete scores, pp. B-17, B-18)*

Senate Support

Republicans		Democrats	
Chambliss, Ga.	100.0%	Miller, Ga.	100.0%
Ensign, Nev.	100.0	Nelson, Neb.	81.6
Kyl, Ariz.	100.0	Lincoln, Ark.	72.0
Nickles, Okla.	100.0	Biden, Del.	69.6
Santorum, Pa.	100.0	Breaux, La.	69.4
Alexander, Tenn.	98.0	Landrieu, La.	68.0
Allard, Colo.	98.0	Pryor, Ark.	68.0
Enzi, Wyo.	98.0	Cantwell, Wash.	66.0
McConnell, Ky.	98.0	Carper, Del.	66.0
Brownback, Kan.	97.9	Feingold, Wis.	66.0
Gregg, N.H.	97.9	Graham, Fla.	66.0
		Kohl, Wis.	66.0

Senate Opposition

Republicans		Democrats	
Snowe, Maine	26.0%	Harkin, Iowa	47.9%
Chafee, R.I.	24.0	Durbin, Ill.	46.0
Collins, Maine	18.0	Akaka, Hawaii	44.4
Campbell, Colo.	14.0	Baucus, Mont.	43.2
Shelby, Ala.	14.0	Corzine, N.J.	42.6
Murkowski, Alaska	13.0	Lautenberg, N.J.	42.6
Specter, Pa.	12.2	Leahy, Vt.	42.0
Crapo, Idaho	10.2	Stabenow, Mich.	42.0
Voinovich, Ohio	10.0	Inouye, Hawaii	41.3
Warner, Va.	10.2	Kennedy, Mass.	40.8
		Sarbanes, Md.	40.8
		Hollings, S.C.	40.4

House Support

Republicans		Democrats	
Blunt, Mo.	100.0%	Lucas, Ky.	68.8%
Boehner, Ohio	100.0	Skelton, Mo.	67.7
Hensarling, Texas	100.0	Cramer, Ala.	63.6
Tauzin, La.	100.0	Stenholm, Texas	62.5
Cantor, Va.	97.1	Boyd, Fla.	60.6
Kennedy, Minn.	97.1	John, La.	60.0
Oxley, Ohio	97.1	Davis, Tenn.	58.8
Thornberry, Texas	97.1	McIntyre, N.C.	58.8
Hastings, Wash.	97.0	Bishop, Ga.	57.1
Rogers, Mich.	97.0	Gordon, Tenn.	54.6
Shadegg, Ariz.	97.0	Sandlin, Texas	53.1
McCrery, La.	96.9	Marshall, Ga.	52.9
Ballenger, N.C.	96.7	Ross, Ark.	52.9

House Opposition

Republicans		Democrats	
Paul, Texas	56.3%	Conyers, Mich.	92.9%
Leach, Iowa	53.1	Payne, N.J.	90.9
Bono, Calif.	42.4	Grijalva, Ariz.	88.2
Simmons, Conn.	42.4	Schakowsky, Ill.	88.2
Houghton, N.Y.	41.4	Tierney, Mass.	88.2
Shays, Conn.	41.2	Scott, Va.	88.2
Emerson, Mo.	39.4	Serrano, N.Y.	87.9
Hostettler, Ind.	38.2	Waxman, Calif.	87.5
Johnson, Ill.	38.2	Waters, Calif.	87.1
Kirk, Ill.	36.7		
Johnson, Conn.	35.3		
Smith, N.J.	33.3		

But the more notable trend in the Senate may be its relative inactivity. The total number of roll call votes fell to 216 in 2004 from 459 in 2003. Correspondingly, the number of presidential position votes fell to 50 from 119.

Senate Majority Leader Bill Frist, R-Tenn., made a clear determination in 2004 that less was more — and Democratic leaders appeared to agree with him at times.

"A lot of it has to do with the election year," said the Senate GOP leadership aide. "There was not necessarily a desire to expose members, on both sides, to some controversial and contentious votes."

One factor in the low numbers was that only six of the 13 regular fiscal 2005 appropriations bills came up for debate in the Senate, compared with 12 the previous year. Aside from delays in the budget process and the inability of GOP leaders to push through a bicameral budget agreement, there was little enthusiasm among Republicans for letting austere domestic spending bills see the light of day and putting vulnerable incumbents on the spot. "We knew appropriations bills

were a free-for-all," the aide said.

But some of Bush's high-profile losses were open to interpretation, and ended up turning into political victories in the eyes of some conservatives.

For instance, a constitutional amendment to ban gay marriages (S J Res 40, H J Res 106) died in the Senate after lawmakers failed to invoke cloture on the bill, and in the House after backers failed to win a two-thirds majority of members present and voting. But the votes were more likely political sacrifices, allowing Bush to energize social conservatives upset by court rulings favoring of gay marriage while expending little political capital on the doomed amendments.

"It was a great issue for the president because it drew attention to what was happening in the courts," noted the Heritage Foundation's Baird, who was an aide to Sen. Trent Lott, R-Miss., when he was majority leader.

Bush also suffered three roll call losses — one in the House and two in the Senate — when both chambers voted to ap-

Presidential Success | *Excluding Nominations*

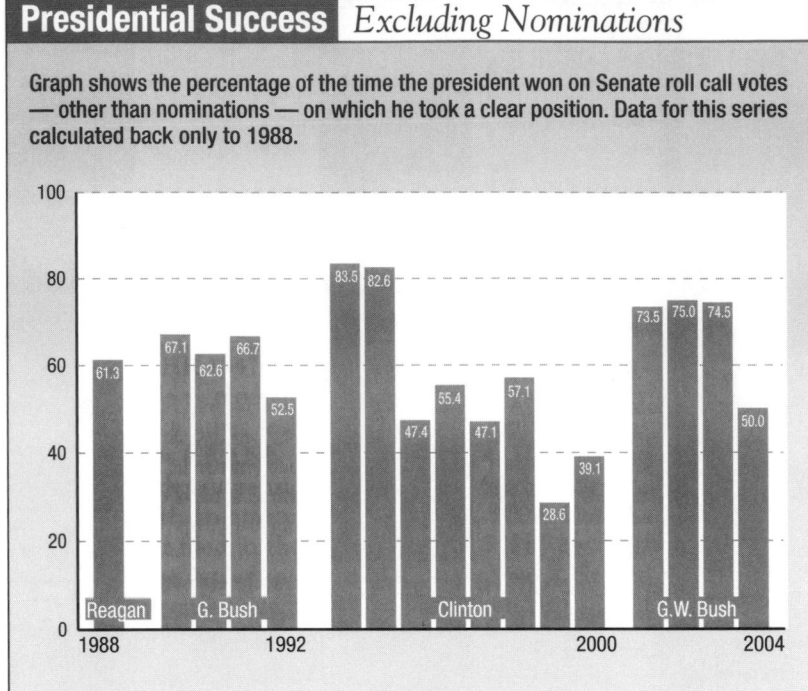

Graph shows the percentage of the time the president won on Senate roll call votes — other than nominations — on which he took a clear position. Data for this series calculated back only to 1988.

water down the Saudi Arabia language. In effect, about half of Bush's losses in the House were reversed.

The omnibus appropriations bill, in fact, has become the GOP leadership's tool of choice for dealing with spending for the last three years. By wrapping popular spending into one "must-pass" package, leaders force rank-and-file members to accept provisions that they might otherwise oppose.

One senior House Republican aide pointed to the 2003 appropriations cycle, in which lawmakers voted publicly for amendments to limit the White House's plan to shift some federal jobs to the private sector — only to see them dropped in the year-end omnibus (PL 108-199) conference. (*2003 Almanac,* p. 2-33)

"Outsourcing passed both bodies, so what do we do in the omnibus? We took it out at the behest of our leadership," the aide said. "If you had divided government, obviously, we wouldn't have done that. [White House officials] . . . have profited from the fact that they've had a united government."

prove highway reauthorization bills (HR 3550, S 1072) greatly exceeding the $256 billion price limit demanded by the White House. After Bush's position lost on the floors of both chambers, he threatened to veto the bill and remained cagey about how much highway spending he would actually support.

In the end, House-Senate talks stalled. "He won that battle," Baird argued.

Disputing Amendments

In the House, Bush's success rate dropped partly because of rebellious Republican moderates who voted with Democrats on policy amendments to fiscal 2005 appropriations bills, 12 of which made it to the floor in that chamber. But what the numbers do not show is that several of these high-profile losses were reversed in the year-end omnibus spending bill, a tactic Republican leaders used to good effect in 2003.

During the House debate on the Transportation-Treasury spending bill (HR 5025), Bush suffered defeats when the House adopted amendments that would have banned Canadian and Mexican trucks that did not comply with U.S. safety laws, lifted the Cuba travel ban, limited White House privatization plans and blocked new overtime pay regulations. Democrats also succeeded in gaining enough GOP votes to attach language to the Commerce-Justice-State bill (HR 4754) to block regulations prohibiting Cuban-Americans from mailing supplies to family members in Cuba and to limit the amount of personal baggage carried by travelers to the communist nation. In addition, the House added language to the foreign operations bill (HR 4818), over the president's objections, that would prohibit assistance to Saudi Arabia.

But in the year-end omnibus negotiations in November, Hastert, backed by a White House brandishing veto threats, forced appropriators to drop the amendments addressing privatization, overtime and Cuba, and made them significantly

Maintaining His Distance

Indeed, congressional Republicans note that on many issues, Bush can afford to maintain a wide berth, since House and Senate Republican leaders look out for his interests.

"I think the president's strength is that the similarities of the policy approaches on Capitol Hill and in the White House lets him pick his fights, because most of the time there's no need to have a fight," said Christopher Cox, R-Calif., chairman of the House Select Homeland Security Committee and a Bush loyalist.

To be sure, Bush's legislative affairs team on Capitol Hill is active and often present when major negotiations occur, especially year-end appropriations talks. But lawmakers and aides agree that Bush has shown a tendency to weigh in strongly on his few core issues, such as tax cuts and education policy, while staying on the edges of many debates, even some of the ones on which he eventually takes a decisive position.

By keeping a low profile, Bush avoids appearing overbearing to congressional Republicans, said Rep. Rob Portman, R-Ohio, who headed President George Bush's congressional lobbying team from 1989 to 1991.

"He uses his direct influence selectively. I think that's important — you can wear out your welcome on the Hill," Portman said. He added that Bush saves his energy for issues he finds "important enough to expend time, energy and capital on."

In refraining from weighing in strongly on every issue, Bush is able to keep his congressional batting average high and avoid the pitfalls inherent in the legislative process.

"If the president gets involved too early he's potentially inviting a defeat along the way. The process has got to work itself out along the way," said Charles O. Jones, a professor emeritus of political science at the University of Wisconsin-Madison. "It's almost a kind of strange situation in which

Presidential Success | *House and Senate Votes*

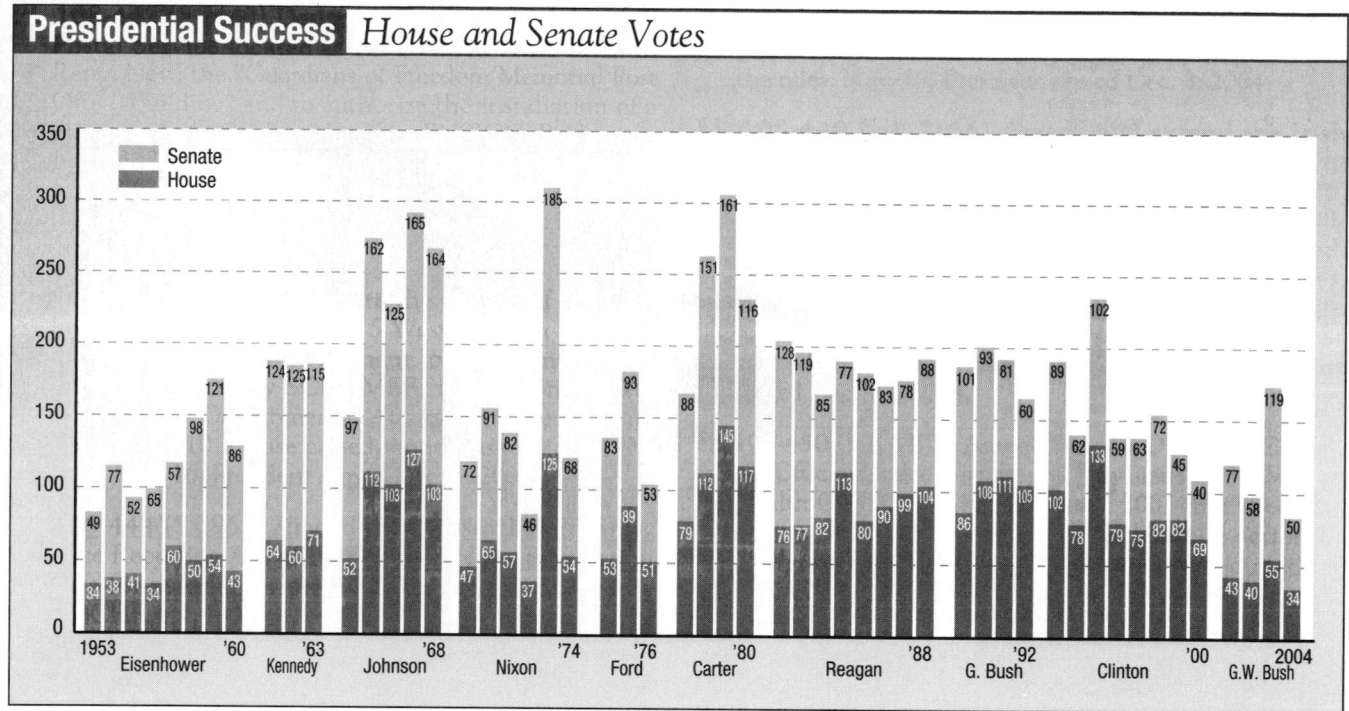

he's got to observe some dust-settling before getting too involved." Otherwise, Jones said, Bush risks a "constant drumbeat in the press of 'he's getting beat here.'"

In the House, Majority Leader Tom DeLay, R-Texas, and Majority Whip Roy Blunt, R-Mo., operate an aggressive party operation that lets few votes slip away. If the president opposes a bill or an amendment, GOP leaders almost certainly work the issue, in part to make sure the president looks good and in part to advance their own agenda.

"This whip operation is so damn good . . . it's sort of unnecessary for [the White House] to make the calls or do the hustling," said one member who does not get many calls from the GOP whip team — moderate Delaware Republican Michael N. Castle, who had the seventh highest score for voting against his party this year. "I don't think a lot passes here that the White House has not at least given its tacit consent to."

For instance, when Rep. Bernard Sanders, I-Vt., offered a popular amendment to the fiscal 2005 Commerce-Justice-State spending bill on July 8 to prevent the Justice Department from reviewing records of library and bookstore patrons under the 2001 anti-terrorism law known as the Patriot Act (PL 107-56), many observers assumed that it would be adopted and simply dropped in conference. But GOP leaders were intent on quashing any inkling of an election-year revolt. Hastert held the vote open until GOP leaders had twisted enough arms to defeat the amendment on a 210-210 tie.

Avoiding Vetoes

Underscoring the close relationship between Bush and his party leaders on Capitol Hill is the fact that he is the first president since John Quincy Adams to serve a full term without vetoing a single piece of legislation. Thomas Jefferson is the only chief executive to have gone two terms without a veto.

During his two years with a Democratic Congress, Clinton never issued a veto. But Jimmy Carter turned down 13

bills and pocket-vetoed 18 others by withholding approval after Congress had adjourned.

House Republican leaders have thus far been unwilling to send the president a bill that he might veto, partially to avoid divisions and potential Democratic charges that Republicans cannot govern effectively.

"He is very fortunate compared to his father in that he has a Congress that wants to highlight his success rather than one that wants to highlight his shortcomings," noted Kenneth R. Weinstein, vice president at the Hudson Institute, a conservative think tank.

Few doubt that Bush will continue with an aggressive agenda in 2004, including a Social Security proposal and conservative judicial nominees opposed by Democrats. But some academics and lawmakers wonder if he will be able to count on the same cooperation from House GOP leaders, as they begin to worry about their own re-elections.

"One thing that the president faces today that he didn't face prior to Nov. 2 is that his own re-election doesn't depend on his success in the Congress, and as a result in the second term the one factor of 'we've got to make sure the president positions himself as a successful incumbent for re-election' — that's gone," said Rep. Zach Wamp, a Tennessee Republican who is a strong ally of the president.

However, Bush will be working with an even larger GOP majority in the House and Senate. As a consequence, the success of his agenda will depend less on the support of a few moderates. In addition, his popularity remains high among Republicans.

"He remains wildly popular, and the House in particular will desperately need the president on our side in the '06 midterms," said Rep. Adam H. Putnam, a second-term Florida Republican who recently won a spot on the powerful Rules Committee. "He's our best campaigner. In that regard, there will continue to be a very strong working relationship between the House and Senate and the White House." ◆

Partisan Votes Echo Electoral Themes

Party Unity *Average Unity Score by Party*

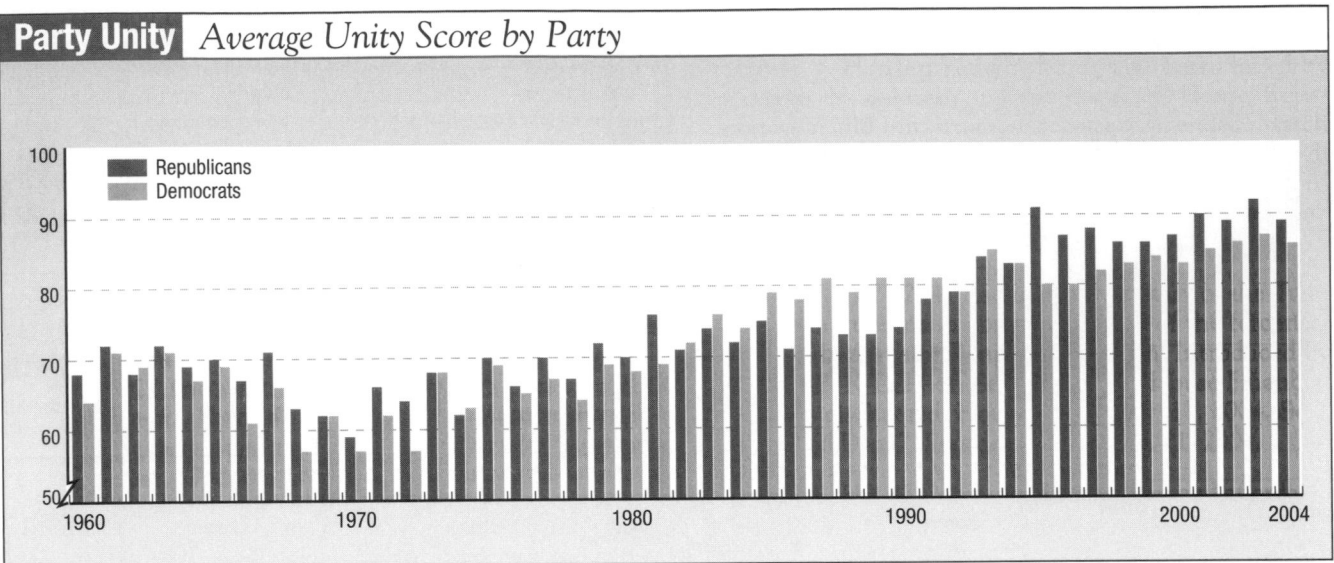

Madison Avenue would call it "building brand identity." In a tightly contested election year, Republicans and Democrats used the machinery of Congress and their members' votes to polish their images with voters and distinguish themselves from the competition.

It is part of a continuing trend away from bipartisan cooperation and toward ideological and political loyalty. On most votes, only a handful of lawmakers from either party stray across the lines into the opposition. At times, there are none.

An analysis of party unity votes by CQ shows that Republicans and Democrats retreated only slightly from the record level of polarization reflected in their votes in 2003, the most partisan year in the five decades CQ has done these annual vote studies. Party unity votes are defined by CQ as votes where a majority of one party votes against a majority of the other.

The 2004 party unity scores reflect a continuing effort by party leaders to sharpen their distinctions and to rally their troops to vote in ways that highlight those distinctions.

"When you do move into an election season, the party in control tries to shape issues in a way that works to their advantage, to unify their folks and put the other party in an awkward position," said Paul S. Herrnson, a political science professor at the University of Maryland.

Kenneth R. Weinstein, vice president and chief operating office of the Hudson Institute, a conservative research organization, said, "Because this is an election year and the president is

very popular within the party, the leadership does not put items on the agenda that are not going to get passed to begin with, and there is also the fact that no one wants to embarrass the president."

For the Republicans, the goal was to reinforce the message of the 2004 campaign: that the Republican Party was best able to keep America secure and would keep the nation's business sector humming by keeping taxes low and government unobtrusive. Republicans were able to hold themselves together most effectively when they were voting on issues related to homeland security and the war in Iraq, on tax and regulatory issues and on many issues related to controlling spending.

While congressional Democrats often found themselves unable to shape the legislative agenda, they could block or deflect — Republicans would derisively say "obstruct" — GOP initiatives to make the point that Democrats would focus on lowering the deficit, would use more targeted tax cuts and would more freely use government to protect consumers, workers and the environment.

"The most stark partisan differences remain on questions of growth, whether government should be involved in a particular area of the economy or what kind of tax code we should have," said Michael Franc, vice president for government relations at the Heritage Foundation.

The CQ analysis shows that Republicans were slightly less successful in winning their party unity votes than they were in 2003. Republicans won 83.5 percent of their House votes and

2004 Data

	AVERAGE PARTY UNITY SCORE
All Republicans	**89%**
All Democrats	**86**
House Republicans	*88*
House Democrats	*86*
Senate Republicans	*90*
Senate Democrats	*83*

	PARTISAN VOTES	TOTAL VOTES	PERCENTAGE
Senate	113	216	52.3
House	255	543	47.0

For More Information

Leading Scorers: Party Unity by the Numbers

Support indicates those who in 2004 voted most often with a majority of their party against a majority of the other party. Opposition shows those who voted most often against their party's majority on such party unity votes. Scores are based on actual votes cast. Members who missed half or more of the votes are not listed. Scores are rounded to 1 decimal point; lawmakers with identical scores are listed alphabetically. *(Complete scores: House, p. B-22, Senate, p. B-24)*

Senate Support

Republicans		Democrats	
Chambliss, Ga.	99.1%	Sarbanes, Md.	100.0%
McConnell, Ky.	99.1	Kennedy, Mass.	98.2
Roberts, Kan.	99.1	Reed, R.I.	98.2
Thomas, Wyo.	99.1	Akaka, Hawaii	96.7
Allard, Colo.	98.2	Stabenow, Mich.	96.5
Cochran, Miss.	98.2	Durbin, Ill.	96.4
Craig, Idaho	98.2	Lautenberg, N.J.	96.4
Hatch, Utah	98.2	Boxer, Calif.	96.3
Inhofe, Okla.	98.2	Corzine, N.J.	96.3
Kyl, Ariz.	98.2	Clinton, N.Y.	96.1
Bunning, Ky.	98.1	Levin, Mich.	95.6
Brownback, Kan.	98.0	Dodd, Conn.	95.5
Grassley, Iowa	97.4	Inouye, Hawaii	95.5
Stevens, Alaska	97.4	Mikulski, Md.	95.5

Senate Opposition

Republicans		Democrats	
Chafee, R.I.	35.1%	Miller, Ga.	98.2%
Specter, Pa.	29.9	Nelson, Neb.	47.8
Snowe, Maine	29.2	Baucus, Mont.	27.5
Collins, Maine	22.1	Breaux, La.	27.5
DeWine, Ohio	21.2	Bayh, Ind.	21.6
McCain, Ariz.	20.7	Lincoln, Ark.	21.2
Warner, Va.	12.5	Conrad, N.D.	19.5
Voinovich, Ohio	11.9	Landrieu, La.	19.5
Smith, Ore.	10.7	Pryor, Ark.	18.6
Hutchison, Texas	10.6	Reid, Nev.	16.7
Ensign, Nev.	9.9	Dorgan, N.D.	15.9
Fitzgerald, Ill.	9.9	Carper, Del.	14.3
Coleman, Minn.	8.9	Rockefeller, W.Va.	12.4
Murkowski, Alaska	8.5	Lieberman, Conn.	11.2

House Support

Republicans		Democrats	
Deal, Ga.	100.0%	Grijalva, Ariz.	99.6%
Akin, Mo.	99.6	Nadler, N.Y.	99.6
Barrett, S.C.	99.6	Becerra, Calif.	99.2
Myrick, N.C.	99.6	Payne, N.J.	99.2
Collins, Ga.	99.4	Solis, Calif.	99.2
Feeney, Fla.	99.2	Stark, Calif.	99.2
Pence, Ind.	99.2	Tierney, Mass.	99.2
Sessions, Texas	99.2	Fattah, Pa.	99.1
Isakson, Ga.	99.0	Hinchey, N.Y.	99.1
		Sanchez, Calif.	98.8
		Schakowsky, Ill.	98.8
		Weiner, N.Y.	98.8

House Opposition

Republicans		Democrats	
Leach, Iowa	34.2%	Stenholm, Texas	41.3%
Shays, Conn.	30.5	Cramer, Ala.	39.2
Simmons, Conn.	27.3	Lucas, Ky.	37.5
Smith, N.J.	22.6	Peterson, Minn.	37.4
Johnson, Ill.	22.5	Matheson, Utah	36.5
Castle, Del.	21.2	John, La.	34.1
Wilson, N.M.	21.2	Carson, Okla.	33.8
Boehlert, N.Y.	19.2	Boyd, Fla.	32.8
Johnson, Conn.	18.0	Taylor, Miss.	32.5
Paul, Texas	17.8	Davis, Tenn.	31.9
LoBiondo, N.J.	17.7	Marshall, Ga.	31.2
Bereuter, Neb.	17.6	Gordon, Tenn.	28.1
Houghton, N.Y.	17.3	Edwards, Texas	27.0

75.2 percent of their Senate votes. The House victory percentage dropped about five percentage points from 2003; in the Senate, the drop was more than six percentage points, but such figures have fluctuated in recent years.

On votes in which party leaders staked out clear and opposing positions, Republicans voted to support the party position on average 90 percent of the time in the Senate and 88 percent of the time in the House. Democrats lined up behind the party position 83 percent of the time in the Senate and 86 percent of the time in the House.

A handful of renegades in both parties skewed the percentages, but not by much. The most rebellious by far was Sen. Zell Miller, D-Ga., who voted with the Democrats in only two of the 113 votes analyzed by CQ. Yet if Miller had been a Republican instead of a Democrat, the Democratic party unity score would have increased only a couple of percentage points. The fact that Democratic presidential running mates John Kerry and John Edwards missed most of the Senate's roll call votes had more of an impact on the party's score.

The Republican senator who most frequently stepped out of line, Lincoln Chafee of Rhode Island, voted with his party 65 percent of the time. Five other Republicans, along with six Democrats, voted with the party majority less than 80 percent of the time. On the other hand, 26 of 51 Senate Republicans and 97 of 229 House Republicans voted with their party more than 95 percent of the time. Four out of every nine Democrats in Congress also exceeded the 95 percent threshold.

Minimizing Dissent

The voting patterns continue a transformation that accelerated in the 1990s of both parties into "much more ideological entities" than they have been in the past, said Lorenzo Morris, chairman of the political science depart-

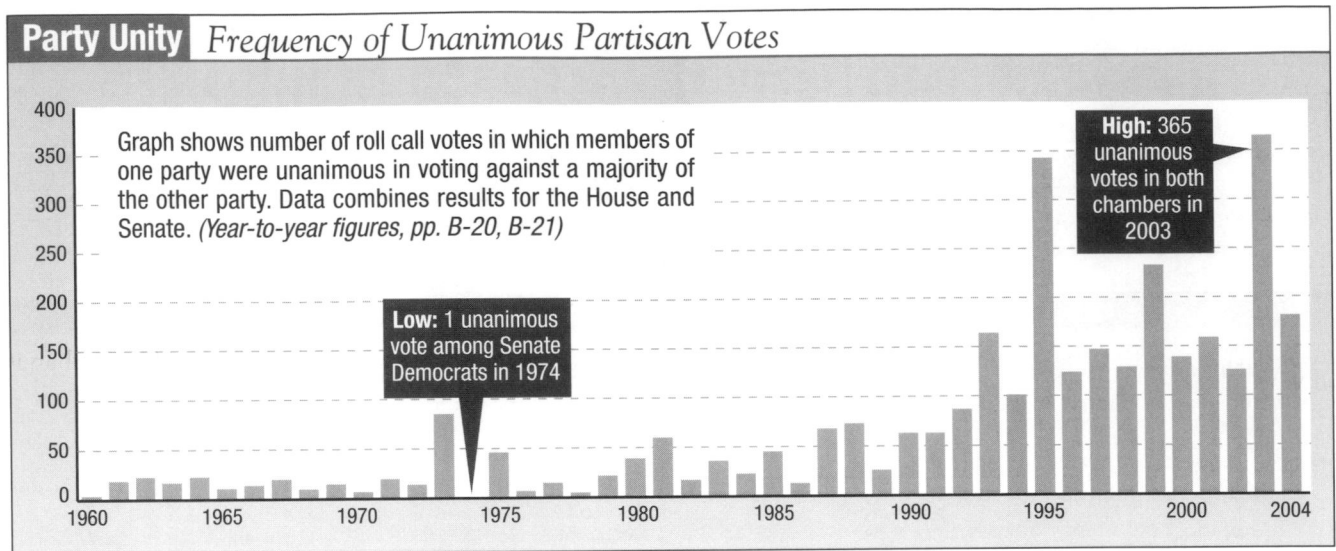

Party Unity *Frequency of Unanimous Partisan Votes*

Graph shows number of roll call votes in which members of one party were unanimous in voting against a majority of the other party. Data combines results for the House and Senate. *(Year-to-year figures, pp. B-20, B-21)*

High: 365 unanimous votes in both chambers in 2003

Low: 1 unanimous vote among Senate Democrats in 1974

ment at Howard University.

That process is further along in the Republican Party than it is in the Democratic Party, "and as a consequence they take the lead in much more ideological voting," Morris said.

Republican leaders followed a model they adopted in 2000, in which they carefully orchestrated what came to a vote and managed intraparty conflicts to minimize dissent on the floor. In both the House and the Senate, there were fewer total roll call votes than in 2000, but the percentage of total votes that were unity votes was somewhat higher in 2004 than in 2000. That is a reflection of the Republican leaders' choreography.

"The rules of the game are easy enough to manipulate by a majority party to foreclose opportunities to vote on alternatives that would attract bipartisanship," said Sarah Binder, senior fellow at the Brookings Institution. "They use the rules of the game to make sure that those party-splitting votes don't come onto the floor."

Both House party whips take pride in how their parties manage floor votes.

"We've all over the last six years . . . gotten better at listening, better at seeking early input from our members and making changes that often significantly improve legislation," said Rep. Roy Blunt, R-Mo., the House majority whip. "The best way to avoid needless conflict is to pay attention early."

"Ten years into their majority," Franc said, "the leadership is very, very comfortable and mature in managing the day-to-day legislative agenda of the House. They have a very keen sense of where the votes are, what is possible and what is not possible. That wasn't there a few years ago."

Organizing Democrats

House Minority Whip Steny H. Hoyer, D-Md., said Republicans had used their agenda-setting power to keep Democrats from winning political victories on issues such as raising the minimum wage. "They don't want their members to vote on the minimum wage, so they don't allow us an amendment," he said.

"They can simply jam us, and they do so on a regular basis and say, 'We're not going to consider these issues.' "

To counter the Republicans, Hoyer encouraged members

to start with the frame of mind that "I am going to be with the party, and if I'm not, it is because I have a very good reason not to be," such as a particular district interest.

Like the Republicans, Hoyer said he stressed Democratic unity on procedural votes. "Clearly, we have forced the Republicans to be more unified in some respects," he said.

The Senate votes reflect deliberateness in what Majority Leader Bill Frist, R-Tenn., allowed to reach the floor, according to several political observers.

"There has been a profound sense of caution that lasted throughout the Congress [that was] rooted in the narrow majority and the fact that there were six or seven swing Republican votes on any given issue," Franc said.

"There were precious few times when leader Frist could go down to the floor on anything controversial and feel with confidence that his position would prevail," Franc said. "So there is this sense he was walking on eggshells."

There was still ample evidence of internal disputes. When the Senate debated pay-as-you-go rules for the 2005 budget resolution (S Con Res 95), requiring Congress to offset tax cuts or spending increases so as to not increase the deficit, four Republicans sided with 46 Democrats to support the provision. When the language was debated in a House bill (HR 4663) in June, several roll call votes attracted significant Republican defections.

"Appropriators held firm against any kind of budget process reform and took a lot of the committee chairmen with them, while a lot of the conservative rank and file voted for the reform," Franc said.

Blunt said those votes defy the perception that the Republican caucus is becoming an ideological monolith. The budget resolution votes are "evidence of openness and diversity, not the opposite," he said.

In the end, though, the pay-as-you-go proposal died in a conference committee because "House Republicans would not sacrifice the principle of tax cuts that benefit the economy and benefit communities," he said.

No Looking Back

Political analysts generally see two parties that have moved away from the center and see no need to look back.

House members "don't worry about being outflanked by the opposition party," Herrnson said. "They don't have to worry about losing the general election. They have to worry about what happens in the primary, and that pushes them to more extreme positions."

Binder said that "there hasn't been much change in the electoral context in which these votes are taking place." Given the closely divided electorate that has not given either party a commanding advantage in Congress, "there is very little incentive for the Democrats to accommodate Republicans, or vice versa."

The Democrats, meanwhile, face continuing attrition in the South, either because party members defect, as Rodney Alexander of Louisiana did, or as they lose elections to Republicans. Seven southern Democrats and one northern Democrat who had party unity scores at or below 85 percent were replaced by Republicans in the 2004 general election.

Five of the seven Southerners — Martin Frost, Jim Turner, Nick Lampson, Charles W. Stenholm and Max Sandlin — were from Texas. "The Texas redistricting skews the re-sults," Hoyer said, referring to the successful effort by the Republican-led state legislature to redraw congressional districts to favor Republicans.

Hoyer said the dissent among House Republican conservatives over the intelligence overhaul bill (S 2845 — H Rept 108-796) foretells greater disunity among Republicans in 2005.

"I think it shows the larger your majority, the harder it is to maintain your unity," Hoyer said.

Add to the mix a lame-duck president, a growing deficit and the war in Iraq and, "I think you are going to see a Republican Party that experiences much more difficulty than it has in the past," Hoyer said.

Not surprisingly, Blunt is more optimistic. "With the president not running again, he has to work with us in a different way," making a stronger case for his proposals.

Most observers, though, see continuing polarization. "I think we are going to be stuck with this for a while," Morris said. "It may be less fun to watch in the immediate future because it will be rigid, but down the road it will be more fun to watch because there will be little brawls." ◆

Heeding the Roll Call Bell

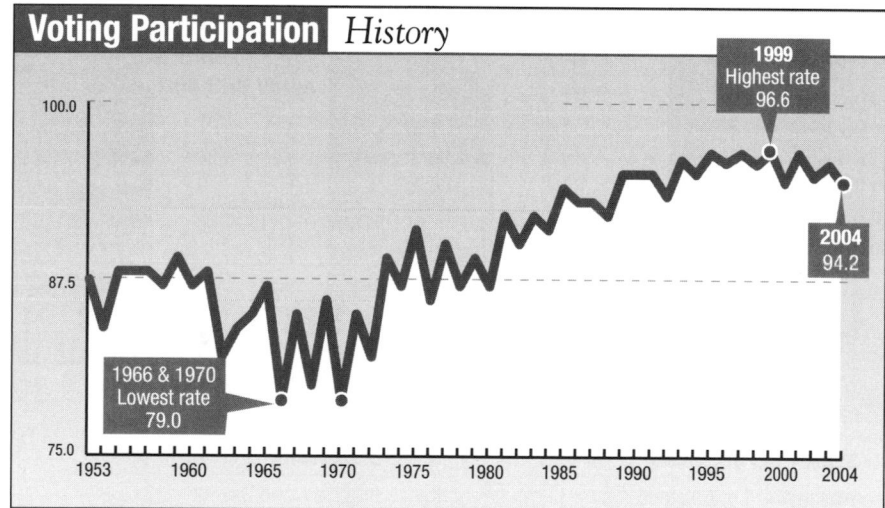

Voting Participation *History*

2004 Data

	RECORDED VOTES	PARTICIPATION RATE
Senate	216	95.5%
House	543	94.1%
Total	759	94.2%

For More Information

Historical data	B-12
Top scorers	B-12
Senators' scores	B-25
House members' scores	B-26

One clear measure of whether members of Congress are doing their jobs is how often they come to the floor of the House and Senate and cast votes.

The record of those who participate in roll call votes is tantamount to an attendance check, and while lawmakers sometimes have pressing business in their offices or even out of town that keeps them from the floor, most current members try to show up almost all of the time. That is at least partly because when they fail to do so, their constituents tend to take note.

House members collectively cast "yea" or "nay" votes an average of 94.1 percent of the time this year, and senators voted an average 95.5 percent of the time. Both figures are lower than in 2003 and lower than the chambers' averages for the past decade.

For the Congress as a whole, lawmakers made 94.2 percent of the 759 roll calls of 2004 — the lowest participation rate since 1992, when the congressional average was 93.4 percent. The low points of the last half-century were 1966 and 1970, when members voted just 79 percent of the time.

Congressional Quarterly gives credit to members for voting only when they actually take a position. On rare occasions, members will vote "present" to avoid a conflict of interest, and often such votes are not explained. Members who vote present are not counted by CQ as having participated in the vote.

Voting participation is cyclical: higher in non-election years and lower when members are on the road campaigning, as most were in 2004.

Voting Participation Historical Comparison

These tables show number of roll call votes and average participation rates for Congress as a whole and for each chamber.

Congressional Average			House Average			Senate Average		
Year	Roll Calls	Rate	Year	Roll Calls	Rate	Year	Roll Calls	Rate
2004	759	94.2%	2004	543	94.1%	2004	216	95.5%
2003	1134	95.7	2003	675	95.6	2003	459	96.1
2002	736	94.8	2002	483	94.6	2002	253	96.3
2001	887	96.5	2001	507	96.2	2001	380	98.2
2000	898	94.4	2000	600	94.1	2000	298	96.9
1999	983	96.6	1999	609	96.5	1999	374	97.9
1998	847	95.7	1998	533	95.5	1998	314	97.4
1997	931	96.5	1997	633	96.3	1997	298	98.7
1996	760	95.8	1996	454	95.5	1996	306	98.2
1995	1480	96.5	1995	867	96.4	1995	613	97.1
1994	826	95.0	1994	497	95.0	1994	329	97.0
1993	992	96.0	1993	597	96.0	1993	395	97.6
1992	743	93.4	1992	473	93.0	1992	270	95.0
1991	708	95.0	1991	428	95.0	1991	280	97.0
1990	862	95.0	1990	536	94.0	1990	326	97.0
1989	680	95.0	1989	368	94.0	1989	312	98.0
1988	830	92.0	1988	451	92.0	1988	379	92.0
1987	908	93.0	1987	488	93.0	1987	420	94.0
1986	805	93.0	1986	451	92.0	1986	354	95.0
1985	820	94.0	1985	439	94.0	1985	381	95.0
1984	683	91.0	1984	408	91.0	1984	275	91.0
1983	869	92.0	1983	498	92.0	1983	371	92.0
1982	924	90.0	1982	459	89.0	1982	465	94.0
1981	836	92.0	1981	353	91.0	1981	483	93.0
1980	1135	87.0	1980	604	88.0	1980	531	87.0
1979	1169	89.0	1979	672	89.0	1979	497	90.0
1978	1350	87.0	1978	834	87.0	1978	516	87.0
1977	1341	90.0	1977	706	91.0	1977	635	88.0
1976	1349	86.0	1976	661	87.0	1976	688	83.0
1975	1214	91.0						
1974	1081	87.0						
1973	1135	89.0						
1972	861	82.0						
1971	743	85.0						
1970	684	79.0						
1969	422	86.0						
1968	514	80.0						
1967	560	85.0						
1966	428	79.0						
1965	459	87.0						
1964	418	85.0						
1963	348	84.0						
1962	348	82.0						
1961	320	88.0						
1960	300	87.0						
1959	302	89.0						
1958	293	87.0						
1957	207	88.0						
1956	203	88.0						
1955	163	88.0						
1954	247	84.0						
1953	160	87.4						

Leading Scorers: Voting Participation

The following 18 senators and 11 House members were the only lawmakers who cast "yea" or "nay" votes on every roll call ballot conducted in 2004:

SENATE REPUBLICANS

Wayne Allard of Colorado
George Allen of Virginia
Thad Cochran of Mississippi
Susan Collins of Maine
Mike DeWine of Ohio
Charles E. Grassley of Iowa
Richard C. Shelby of Alabama
Olympia J. Snowe of Maine

SENATE DEMOCRATS

Kent Conrad of North Dakota
Maria Cantwell of Washington
Russell D. Feingold of Wisconsin
Dianne Feinstein of California
Carl Levin of Michigan
Blanche Lincoln of Arkansas
Mark Pryor of Arkansas
John D. Rockefeller IV of West Virginia
Charles E. Schumer of New York
Ron Wyden of Oregon

HOUSE REPUBLICANS

John Kline of Minnesota
Jim Ramstad of Minnesota
Frank A. LoBiondo of New Jersey
Sue W. Kelly of New York
Henry E. Brown Jr. of South Carolina
F. James Sensenbrenner Jr. of Wisconsin

HOUSE DEMOCRATS

Vic Snyder of Arkansas
Jesse L. Jackson Jr. of Illinois
Chris Van Hollen of Maryland
Dale E. Kildee of Michigan
Sander M. Levin of Michigan

Even so, House members and senators have been more available for roll calls over time as air travel has become more efficient and as congressional leaders have scheduled votes to accommodate lawmakers who want to spend time away from Washington.

In recent years, House votes have rarely been held before 6 p.m. on Tuesdays, and the chamber's week typically ends on Thursday evening. Similarly, the Senate's schedule is often negotiated.

Since 1994, House members have voted an average of 95.4 percent of the time, with an all-time high of 96.5 percent in 1999. Over the decade, senators have an average participation rate of 97.2 percent, with a peak of 98.7 percent in 1997.

The bells that signal roll calls rang 543 times in the House in 2004 (plus once for a quorum call at the start of the session Jan. 20). They rang 216 times in the Senate. For the House, the total number of roll calls in 2004 was well below the 675 in 2003, but this year's total was about average for the 31 years the chamber has used an electronic system to record votes.

Prior to 1973, when roll call votes in the House required the reading of 435 names and waiting for the members to respond, roll calls were much less frequent. In 1953, for instance, the House held only 71 roll calls. By contrast, in 1995, the year Republicans seized control of the House for the first time in 40 years and pressed an aggressive legislative agenda, the House voted 867 times.

The House managed 543 votes this year, even though it was in session only 110 days — the fewest since 1948, when it held just 79 yea-or-nay votes. The House was in session 133 days in 2003 and a whopping 168 days in 1995.

The five-votes-a-day average for 2004 was explained in part by longer workdays than when Harry S Truman was president, but also by the stacking of roll calls so that members could come to the floor and dispense with several votes in a relatively short time.

While the House kept up its pace of voting this year, the total number of Senate roll calls was the lowest since the 204 taken in 1961. Over the last 50 years, the Senate has averaged just about 350 votes a year. The Senate did meet for 133 days, about as many as is usual in an election year. ◆

CQ Vote Study Guide

Congressional Quarterly has conducted studies analyzing the voting behavior of members of Congress since 1945. This is how the studies are carried out:

● **Selecting votes.** CQ bases its vote studies on all roll call votes on which members were asked to vote "yea" or "nay." In 2004, there were 543 such votes in the House and 216 in the Senate. The totals exclude quorum calls (there was one in the House in 2004), because they require only that members vote "present."

The totals do include House votes to approve the Journal (eight in 2004) and Senate votes to instruct the sergeant at arms to request members' presence in the chamber (one in 2004).

The presidential support and party unity studies are based on votes selected from the total according to the criteria described on pages B-14 and B-20.

● **Individual scores.** Members' scores in the accompanying charts are based only on the votes each member actually cast. That has the effect of making individual support and opposition scores add to 100 percent. The same method is used for identifying the leading scorers on pages 2905 and 2909.

● **Overall scores.** For consistency with previous years, calculations of average scores by chamber, party and region are based on all yea-or-nay votes. As a result, a member's failure to vote reduces average support and opposition scores. *(Methodology, 1987 Almanac, p. 22-C)*

● **Rounding.** Scores in the tables for the full House and Senate membership are rounded to the nearest percentage point, although rounding is not used to increase any score to 100 percent or to reduce any score to zero. Scores for party and chamber support and opposition leaders are reported to 1 decimal point to better classify them.

Presidential Support Background

Congressional Quarterly selects the roll call votes used for its presidential support study based on explicit statements made by the president or his authorized spokesmen.

Support scores show the percentage of roll calls on which members voted *in agreement* with the president.

Opposition scores show the percentage of roll calls on which members voted *against* the president's position.

Success shows the percentage of the selected votes on which the president prevailed. A member's failure to vote reduces the average score for his party and chamber.

Presidential Success by Issue

"Economic affairs" includes votes on trade and on omnibus and supplemental spending bills, which may fund both domestic and defense/foreign policy programs. Senate confirmation votes are included only in the average scores.

	Defense/Foreign Policy		Domestic		Economic Affairs		Average	
	2004	2003	2004	2003	2004	2003	2004	2003
Senate	100%	69%	31%	68%	100%	92%	74%	75%
House	50	75	78	89	75	100	71	87
Congress	60	72	58	82	82	94	73	79

Average Presidential Support by Party

	Support					Opposition			
	Republicans		Democrats				Republicans		Democrats	
	2004	2003	2004	2003			2004	2003	2004	2003
Senate	91%	94%	60%	48%		**Senate**	7%	4%	35%	45%
House	80	89	30	26		**House**	16	8	66	71

Average Presidential Support by Region *

	Support									Opposition							
	East		West		South		Midwest				East		West		South		Midwest	
	2004	2003	2004	2003	2004	2003	2004	2003			2004	2003	2004	2003	2004	2003	2004	2003
Republicans										**Republicans**								
Senate	85%	87%	91%	94%	93%	95%	91%	96%		**Senate**	12%	11%	6%	3%	6%	2%	7%	2%
House	74	84	82	91	82	91	81	88		**House**	18	10	14	7	12	6	16	9
Democrats										**Democrats**								
Senate	56	41	59	48	64	51	62	52		**Senate**	35	48	37	49	27	34	38	46
House	26	23	26	21	39	35	28	24		**House**	70	75	70	76	54	61	67	70

Presidential Success-Rate History **

Annual success rate combining both chambers of Congress

Eisenhower		Johnson		Ford					
1953	89.2%	1964	87.9%	1974	58.2%	1984	65.8%	1995	36.2%
1954	78.3	1965	93.1	1975	61.0	1985	59.9	1996	55.1
1955	75.3	1966	78.9	1976	53.8	1986	56.1	1997	53.6
1956	69.7	1967	78.8	**Carter**		1987	43.5	1998	50.6
1957	68.4	1968	74.5	1977	75.4%	1988	47.4	1999	37.8
1958	75.7	**Nixon**		1978	78.3	**G. Bush**		2000	55.0
1959	52.0	1969	73.9%	1979	76.8	1989	62.6%	**G.W. Bush**	
1960	65.1	1970	76.9	1980	75.1	1990	46.8	2001	86.7%
Kennedy		1971	74.8	**Reagan**		1991	54.2	2002	87.8
1961	81.4%	1972	66.3	1981	82.4%	1992	43.0	2003	78.7
1962	85.4	1973	50.6	1982	72.4	**Clinton**		2004	72.6
1963	87.1	1974	59.6	1983	67.1	1993	86.4%		
						1994	86.4		

* **Regions:** Congressional Quarterly defines regions of the United States as follows: **East:** Conn., Del., Maine, Md., Mass., N.H., N.J., N.Y., Pa., R.I., Vt., W.Va. **West:** Alaska, Ariz., Calif., Colo., Hawaii, Idaho, Mont., Nev., N.M., Ore., Utah, Wash., Wyo. **South:** Ala., Ark., Fla., Ga., Ky., La., Miss., N.C., Okla., S.C., Tenn., Texas, Va. **Midwest:** Ill., Ind., Iowa, Kan., Mich., Minn., Mo., Neb., N.D., Ohio, S.D., Wis.

** **Revisions:** Combined presidential success scores have been adjusted back to 1953 to reflect more precise calculations and correct a longstanding error for 1954.

2004 Senate Presidential Position Votes

The following is a list of 50 Senate roll call votes in 2004 on which the president took a clear position, based on his state- ments or those of authorized spokesmen. Votes are listed by roll call number in broad categories and identified by topic.

Nominations

28 Victories

Vote Number	Description
6	Gary L. Sharpe
8	Mark R. Filip
59	Louis Guirola Jr.
85	John D. Negroponte
97	Marcia G. Cooke
102	Raymond. W. Gruender
103	Franklin S. Van Antwerpen
104	F. Dennis Saylor IV
108	Sandra L. Townes
109	Kenneth M. Karas
110	Judith C. Herrera
115	Virginia E. Hopkins
116	Ricardo S. Martinez
117	Gene E.K. Pratter
121	William S. Duffey Jr.
122	Lawrence F. Stengel
123	Paul S. Diamond
126	James L. Robart
127	Roger T. Benitez
128	Jane J. Boyle
141	Juan R. Sanchez
142	Walter D. Kelley Jr.
152	Diane S. Sykes
153	J. Leon Holmes
164	Virginia Maria Hernandez Covington
165	Michael H. Schneider Sr.
187	Porter J. Goss
212	Francis J. Harvey

4 Defeats

Vote Number	Description
158	William G. Myers III (cloture)
160	Henry W. Saad (cloture)
161	Richard A. Griffin (cloture)
162	David W. McKeague (cloture)

Defense and Foreign Policy

2 Victories

Vote Number	Description
98	Base closings
216	Intelligence overhaul

0 Defeats

Vote Number	Description

Domestic Policy

4 Victories

Vote Number	Description
61	Fetal protection
63	Fetal protection
93	Education
99	Homeland Security

9 Defeats

Vote Number	Description
13	Highway spending
14	Highway spending
15	Medical malpractice (cloture)
64	Welfare
66	Medical malpractice (cloture)
79	Labor
154	Class action suits (cloture)
155	Gay marriage constitutional amendment (cloture)
168	Federal employees

Economic Affairs and Trade

3 Victories

Vote Number	Description
156	Trade (Australia)
159	Trade (Morocco)
188	Taxes

0 Defeats

Vote Number	Description

Senate Success Score

Victories	37
Defeats	13
Total	50
Success rate	**74.0%**

2004 House Presidential Position Votes

The following is a list of 34 House roll call votes in 2004 on which the president took a clear position, based on his state- ments or those of authorized spokesmen. Votes are listed by roll call number in broad categories and identified by topic.

Domestic Policy

14 Victories

Vote Number	Description
15	Faith-based initiatives
17	Faith-based initiatives
31	Fetal protection
54	Tort reform (obesity)
55	Broadcast indecency
166	Medical malpractice
197	Abortion
225	Job training
254	Environment
263	Environment
339	Law enforcement
376	Homeland security
410	Gay marriage
452	Homeland security

4 Defeats

Vote Number	Description
114	Highway spending
434	Labor (overtime pay)
457	Federal employees
484	Gay marriage constitutional amendment

Economic Affairs and Trade

6 Victories

Vote Number	Description
138	Taxes
144	Taxes
170	Taxes
375	Trade (Australia)
413	Trade (Morocco)
472	Taxes

2 Defeats

Vote Number	Description
318	Budget
462	Trade (Mexican trucks)

Defense and Foreign Policy

4 Victories

Vote Number	Description
64	War in Iraq
381	U.S. Aid (Egypt)
461	Cuba
544	Intelligence overhaul

4 Defeats

Vote Number	Description
200	Base closings
329	Cuba
389	U.S. aid (Saudi Arabia)
460	Cuba

House Success Score

Victories	24
Defeats	10
Total	34
Success rate	70.6%

	1	2	3
ALABAMA			
Shelby	86	14	100
Sessions	96	4	98
ALASKA			
Stevens	92	8	100
Murkowski, L.	87	13	92
ARIZONA			
McCain	92	8	100
Kyl	100	0	100
ARKANSAS			
Lincoln	72	28	100
Pryor	68	32	100
CALIFORNIA			
Feinstein	62	38	100
Boxer	65	35	96
COLORADO			
Campbell	86	14	86
Allard	98	2	100
CONNECTICUT			
Dodd	60	40	100
Lieberman	63	37	92
DELAWARE			
Biden	70	30	92
Carper	66	34	100
FLORIDA			
Graham	66	34	94
Nelson	62	38	100
GEORGIA			
Miller	100	0	88
Chambliss	100	0	98
HAWAII			
Inouye	59	41	92
Akaka	56	44	90
IDAHO			
Craig	96	4	100
Crapo	90	10	98
ILLINOIS			
Fitzgerald	92	8	98
Durbin	54	46	100
INDIANA			
Lugar	93	7	92
Bayh	64	36	100

	1	2	3
IOWA			
Grassley	94	6	100
Harkin	52	48	96
KANSAS			
Brownback	98	2	96
Roberts	92	8	100
KENTUCKY			
McConnell	98	2	100
Bunning	94	6	94
LOUISIANA			
Breaux	69	31	98
Landrieu	68	32	100
MAINE			
Snowe	74	26	100
Collins	82	18	100
MARYLAND			
Sarbanes	59	41	98
Mikulski	61	39	98
MASSACHUSETTS			
Kennedy	59	41	98
Kerry	50	50	8
MICHIGAN			
Levin	60	40	100
Stabenow	58	42	100
MINNESOTA			
Dayton	60	40	100
Coleman	92	8	100
MISSISSIPPI			
Cochran	92	8	100
Lott	94	6	98
MISSOURI			
Bond	92	8	98
Talent	94	6	98
MONTANA			
Burns	94	6	100
Baucus	57	43	88
NEBRASKA			
Hagel	94	6	98
Nelson	82	18	98
NEVADA			
Reid	61	39	98
Ensign	100	0	98

	1	2	3
NEW HAMPSHIRE			
Gregg	98	2	96
Sununu	96	4	100
NEW JERSEY			
Lautenberg	57	43	94
Corzine	57	43	94
NEW MEXICO			
Domenici	94	6	94
Bingaman	64	36	100
NEW YORK			
Schumer	62	38	100
Clinton	61	39	92
NORTH CAROLINA			
Edwards	65	35	46
Dole	92	8	100
NORTH DAKOTA			
Conrad	62	38	100
Dorgan	62	38	100
OHIO			
DeWine	94	6	100
Voinovich	90	10	100
OKLAHOMA			
Nickles	100	0	96
Inhofe	92	8	100
OREGON			
Wyden	62	38	100
Smith	94	6	96
PENNSYLVANIA			
Specter	88	12	98
Santorum	100	0	88
RHODE ISLAND			
Reed	60	40	100
Chafee	76	24	100
SOUTH CAROLINA			
Hollings	60	40	94
Graham	92	8	98
SOUTH DAKOTA			
Daschle	60	40	100
Johnson	60	40	96
TENNESSEE			
Frist	92	8	100
Alexander	98	2	100

Key

Democrats   **Republicans**
Independents

	1	2	3
TEXAS			
Hutchison	94	6	98
Cornyn	96	4	100
UTAH			
Hatch	94	6	96
Bennett	94	6	96
VERMONT			
Leahy	58	42	100
Jeffords	60	40	90
VIRGINIA			
Warner	90	10	98
Allen	96	4	100
WASHINGTON			
Murray	63	37	98
Cantwell	66	34	100
WEST VIRGINIA			
Byrd	63	37	98
Rockefeller	64	36	100
WISCONSIN			
Kohl	66	34	100
Feingold	66	34	100
WYOMING			
Thomas	96	4	98
Enzi	98	2	98

Presidential Support
and Opposition: Senate

1. Presidential Support Score. Percentage of recorded votes cast in 2004 on which President Bush took a position and on which the senator voted "yea" or "nay" in agreement with the president's position. Failure to vote does not lower an individual's score.

2. Presidential Opposition Score. Percentage of recorded votes cast in 2004 on which President Bush took a position and on which the senator voted "yea" or "nay" in disagreement with the president's position. Failure to vote does not lower an individual's score.

3. Participation in Presidential Support Votes. Percentage of the 50 recorded Senate votes on which President Bush took a position and on which the senator was present and voted "yea" or "nay."

Presidential Support and Opposition: House

1. Presidential Support Score. Percentage of recorded votes cast in 2004 on which President Bush took a position and on which the member voted "yea" or "nay" in agreement with the president's position. Failure to vote does not lower an individual's score.

2. Presidential Opposition Score. Percentage of recorded votes cast in 2004 on which President Bush took a position and on which the member voted "yea" or "nay" in disagreement with the president's position. Failure to vote does not lower an individual's score.

3. Participation in Presidential Support Votes. Percentage of the 34 recorded House votes on which President Bush took a position and on which the member was present and voted "yea" or "nay."

[1] Rep. Porter J. Goss, R-Fla., resigned effective Sept. 23, 2004. The last vote for which he was eligible was vote 472. He was eligible for 32 presidential support votes in 2004.

[2] The Speaker votes only at his discretion, usually to break a tie or to emphasize the importance of a matter.

[3] Rep. Ben Chandler, D-Ky., was sworn in Feb. 24, 2004. The first vote for which he was eligible was vote 26. He was eligible for 32 presidential support votes in 2004.

[4] Rep. Rodney Alexander of Louisiana switched parties from Democrat to Republican effective Sept. 7, 2004. As a Democrat, he was eligible for 25 presidential support votes in 2004; as a Republican, he was eligible for 9 presidential support votes in 2004. His scores in the table reflect his votes as a Republican. As a Democrat, his support score was 56 percent; opposition score, 44 percent; participation rate, 100 percent.

[5] Rep. Doug Bereuter, R-Neb., resigned effective Aug. 31, 2004. The last vote for which he was eligible was vote 421. He was eligible for 25 presidential support votes in 2004.

[6] Rep. G.K. Butterfield, D-N.C., was sworn in July 21, 2004, to replace Democrat Rep. Frank W. Ballance, Jr., who resigned effective June 11. The first vote for which Butterfield was eligible was vote 405; he was eligible for 11 presidential support votes in 2004. The last vote for which Ballance was eligible was vote 231; he was eligible for 14 presidential support votes in 2004. His support score was 25 percent; opposition score, 75 percent; participation rate, 86 percent.

[7] Rep. Stephanie Herseth, D-S.D., was sworn in June 3, 2004, to replace Republican Rep. Bill Janklow, who resigned effective Jan. 20, 2004. The first vote for which Herseth was eligible was vote 224; she was eligible for 21 presidential support votes in 2004. Janklow was eligible for no presidential support votes in 2004.

Key

Democrats • **Republicans**
Independents

	1	2	3
ALABAMA			
1 Bonner	92	8	76
2 Everett	76	24	97
3 Rogers	76	24	100
4 Aderholt	85	15	100
5 Cramer	64	36	97
6 Bachus	88	12	100
7 Davis	44	56	94
ALASKA			
AL Young	87	13	88
ARIZONA			
1 Renzi	82	18	100
2 Franks	91	9	100
3 Shadegg	97	3	97
4 Pastor	18	82	100
5 Hayworth	82	18	97
6 Flake	74	26	100
7 Grijalva	12	88	100
8 Kolbe	79	21	100
ARKANSAS			
1 Berry	36	64	97
2 Snyder	41	59	100
3 Boozman	82	18	100
4 Ross	53	47	100
CALIFORNIA			
1 Thompson	24	76	97
2 Herger	88	12	100
3 Ose	82	18	100
4 Doolittle	85	15	97
5 Matsui	37	63	88
6 Woolsey	15	85	100
7 Miller, George	21	79	97
8 Pelosi	21	79	97
9 Lee	15	85	100
10 Tauscher	35	65	100
11 Pombo	79	21	100
12 Lantos	23	77	91
13 Stark	15	85	97
14 Eshoo	35	65	100
15 Honda	23	77	88
16 Lofgren	30	70	97
17 Farr	24	76	100
18 Cardoza	45	55	91
19 Radanovich	91	9	97
20 Dooley	43	57	88
21 Nunes	91	9	94
22 Thomas	91	9	100
23 Capps	21	79	100
24 Gallegly	82	18	100
25 McKeon	85	15	100
26 Dreier	94	6	100
27 Sherman	27	73	97
28 Berman	31	69	94
29 Schiff	38	62	100
30 Waxman	13	87	94
31 Becerra	18	82	97
32 Solis	18	82	97
33 Watson	23	77	91
34 Roybal-Allard	24	76	97
35 Waters	13	87	91
36 Harman	34	66	94
37 Millender-McD.	33	67	79
38 Napolitano	21	79	100
39 Sánchez, Linda	15	85	100
40 Royce	82	18	100
41 Lewis	91	9	97
42 Miller, Gary	85	15	100
43 Baca	32	68	100
44 Calvert	82	18	100
45 Bono	58	42	97
46 Rohrabacher	84	16	94
47 Sanchez, Loretta	33	67	97
48 Cox	91	9	97
49 Issa	85	15	100
50 Cunningham	85	15	100
51 Filner	23	77	91
52 Hunter	84	16	91
53 Davis	33	67	97
COLORADO			
1 DeGette	29	71	91
2 Udall	32	68	91
3 McInnis	85	15	79
4 Musgrave	85	15	100
5 Hefley	85	15	100
6 Tancredo	81	19	94
7 Beauprez	91	9	97
CONNECTICUT			
1 Larson	24	76	100
2 Simmons	58	42	97
3 DeLauro	21	79	100
4 Shays	59	41	100
5 Johnson	65	35	100
DELAWARE			
AL Castle	74	26	100
FLORIDA			
1 Miller, J.	92	8	76
2 Boyd	61	39	97
3 Brown	32	68	91
4 Crenshaw	88	12	100
5 Brown-Waite	87	13	94
6 Stearns	85	15	100
7 Mica	85	15	100
8 Keller	91	9	97
9 Bilirakis	85	15	100
10 Young	87	13	94
11 Davis	36	64	97
12 Putnam	91	9	100
13 Harris	94	6	100
14 Goss [1]	87	13	72
15 Weldon	88	12	97
16 Foley	79	21	100
17 Meek	39	61	91
18 Ros-Lehtinen	84	16	94
19 Wexler	32	68	91
20 Deutsch	42	58	76
21 Diaz-Balart, L.	91	9	94
22 Shaw	82	18	100
23 Hastings	23	77	76
24 Feeney	88	12	97
25 Diaz-Balart, M.	94	6	97
GEORGIA			
1 Kingston	91	9	97
2 Bishop	57	43	82
3 Marshall	53	47	100
4 Majette	23	77	76
5 Lewis	18	82	97
6 Isakson	89	11	79
7 Linder	94	6	94
8 Collins	87	13	68
9 Norwood	87	13	91
10 Deal	87	13	91
11 Gingrey	85	15	100
12 Burns	85	15	100
13 Scott	47	53	94
HAWAII			
1 Abercrombie	15	85	97
2 Case	30	70	97
IDAHO			
1 Otter	74	26	100
2 Simpson	79	21	100
ILLINOIS			
1 Rush	21	79	100
2 Jackson	15	85	100
3 Lipinski	39	61	91
4 Gutierrez	24	76	85
5 Emanuel	18	82	100
6 Hyde	79	21	97

	1	2	3
7 Davis	16	84	91
8 *Crane*	88	12	100
9 Schakowsky	12	88	100
10 *Kirk*	63	37	88
11 *Weller*	88	12	100
12 Costello	41	59	100
13 *Biggert*	74	26	100
14 *Hastert*[2]	100	0	21
15 *Johnson*	62	38	100
16 *Manzullo*	84	16	94
17 Evans	21	79	100
18 LaHood	75	25	94
19 *Shimkus*	76	24	100
INDIANA			
1 Visclosky	19	81	94
2 *Chocola*	91	9	100
3 *Souder*	79	21	100
4 *Buyer*	87	13	94
5 *Burton*	76	24	97
6 *Pence*	94	6	100
7 Carson	17	83	68
8 *Hostettler*	62	38	100
9 Hill	32	68	100
IOWA			
1 *Nussle*	88	12	100
2 *Leach*	47	53	94
3 Boswell	39	61	97
4 *Latham*	88	12	100
5 *King*	85	15	100
KANSAS			
1 *Moran*	68	32	100
2 *Ryun*	88	12	97
3 Moore	38	62	100
4 *Tiahrt*	85	15	100
KENTUCKY			
1 *Whitfield*	85	15	100
2 *Lewis*	82	18	100
3 *Northup*	85	15	97
4 Lucas	69	31	94
5 *Rogers*	88	12	100
6 Chandler[3]	45	55	97
LOUISIANA			
1 *Vitter*	94	6	97
2 Jefferson	32	68	100
3 *Tauzin*	100	0	35
4 *McCrery*	97	3	94
5 *Alexander*[4]	67	33	100
6 *Baker*	94	6	97
7 John	60	40	88
MAINE			
1 Allen	41	59	100
2 Michaud	38	62	100
MARYLAND			
1 *Gilchrest*	74	26	100
2 Ruppersberger	44	56	100
3 Cardin	35	65	91
4 Wynn	38	62	100
5 Hoyer	24	76	100
6 *Bartlett*	76	24	100
7 Cummings	21	79	97
8 Van Hollen	35	65	100
MASSACHUSETTS			
1 Olver	21	79	100
2 Neal	24	76	100
3 McGovern	21	79	100
4 Frank	16	84	94
5 Meehan	22	78	94
6 Tierney	12	88	100
7 Markey	15	85	100
8 Capuano	24	76	97
9 Lynch	42	58	97
10 Delahunt	19	81	94
MICHIGAN			
1 Stupak	41	59	100
2 *Hoekstra*	90	10	88
3 *Ehlers*	79	21	100
4 *Camp*	82	18	100
5 Kildee	35	65	100
6 *Upton*	82	18	100
7 *Smith*	77	23	91
8 *Rogers*	97	3	97
9 Knollenberg	88	12	100
10 Miller	85	15	100
11 McCotter	82	18	100
12 Levin	26	74	100

	1	2	3
13 Kilpatrick	28	72	94
14 Conyers	7	93	82
15 Dingell	27	73	97
MINNESOTA			
1 *Gutknecht*	82	18	100
2 *Kline*	94	6	100
3 *Ramstad*	74	26	100
4 McCollum	21	79	100
5 Sabo	18	82	97
6 *Kennedy*	97	3	100
7 Peterson	50	50	100
8 Oberstar	27	73	97
MISSISSIPPI			
1 *Wicker*	86	14	82
2 Thompson	33	67	97
3 *Pickering*	85	15	100
4 Taylor	45	55	97
MISSOURI			
1 Clay	24	76	97
2 *Akin*	94	6	100
3 Gephardt	43	57	68
4 Skelton	68	32	100
5 McCarthy	19	81	94
6 *Graves*	79	21	97
7 *Blunt*	100	0	97
8 *Emerson*	61	39	97
9 *Hulshof*	94	6	94
MONTANA			
AL *Rehberg*	76	24	100
NEBRASKA			
1 *Bereuter*[5]	83	17	92
2 *Terry*	88	12	97
3 *Osborne*	79	21	97
NEVADA			
1 Berkley	41	59	94
2 *Gibbons*	84	16	94
3 *Porter*	82	18	100
NEW HAMPSHIRE			
1 *Bradley*	85	15	100
2 *Bass*	68	32	100
NEW JERSEY			
1 Andrews	26	74	100
2 *LoBiondo*	68	32	100
3 *Saxton*	76	24	97
4 *Smith*	67	33	97
5 *Garrett*	88	12	97
6 Pallone	18	82	100
7 *Ferguson*	71	29	100
8 Pascrell	31	69	94
9 Rothman	31	69	94
10 Payne	9	91	97
11 Frelinghuysen	79	21	97
12 Holt	26	74	100
13 Menendez	34	66	94
NEW MEXICO			
1 *Wilson*	88	12	100
2 *Pearce*	91	9	100
3 Udall	21	79	100
NEW YORK			
1 Bishop	32	68	100
2 Israel	30	70	97
3 *King*	77	23	91
4 McCarthy	32	68	100
5 Ackerman	30	70	97
6 Meeks	37	63	88
7 Crowley	30	70	97
8 Nadler	18	82	100
9 Weiner	30	70	97
10 Towns	15	85	97
11 Owens	18	82	97
12 Velázquez	15	85	100
13 *Fossella*	84	16	94
14 Maloney	28	72	94
15 Rangel	19	81	91
16 Serrano	12	88	97
17 Engel	36	64	97
18 Lowey	35	65	91
19 *Kelly*	71	29	100
20 *Sweeney*	71	29	100
21 McNulty	29	71	100
22 Hinchey	20	80	88
23 *McHugh*	76	24	100
24 Boehlert	68	32	91
25 Walsh	85	15	100

	1	2	3
26 Reynolds	88	12	100
27 Quinn	75	25	71
28 Slaughter	24	76	97
29 Houghton	59	41	85
NORTH CAROLINA			
1 Butterfield[6]	27	73	100
2 Etheridge	47	53	100
3 *Jones*	75	25	94
4 Price	41	59	100
5 *Burr*	79	21	97
6 *Coble*	71	29	100
7 McIntyre	59	41	100
8 *Hayes*	76	24	97
9 *Myrick*	91	9	97
10 *Ballenger*	97	3	88
11 *Taylor*	82	18	100
12 Watt	26	74	100
13 Miller	38	62	100
NORTH DAKOTA			
AL Pomeroy	47	53	100
OHIO			
1 *Chabot*	79	21	100
2 *Portman*	94	6	97
3 *Turner*	88	12	100
4 *Oxley*	97	3	100
5 *Gillmor*	91	9	100
6 Strickland	30	70	97
7 *Hobson*	82	18	100
8 *Boehner*	100	0	100
9 Kaptur	33	67	97
10 Kucinich	22	78	79
11 Jones	29	71	91
12 *Tiberi*	82	18	100
13 Brown	26	74	100
14 *LaTourette*	82	18	97
15 *Pryce*	85	15	100
16 *Regula*	85	15	100
17 Ryan	30	70	97
18 *Ney*	82	18	100
OKLAHOMA			
1 *Sullivan*	85	15	100
2 Carson	50	50	88
3 *Lucas*	87	13	91
4 *Cole*	91	9	100
5 *Istook*	87	13	94
OREGON			
1 Wu	38	62	100
2 *Walden*	82	18	100
3 Blumenauer	23	77	88
4 DeFazio	27	73	97
5 Hooley	35	65	100
PENNSYLVANIA			
1 Brady	18	82	97
2 Fattah	20	80	88
3 *English*	76	24	100
4 *Hart*	94	6	94
5 *Peterson*	79	21	97
6 *Gerlach*	76	24	97
7 *Weldon*	85	15	97
8 *Greenwood*	71	29	71
9 *Shuster, Bill*	82	18	97
10 *Sherwood*	84	16	94
11 Kanjorski	27	73	97
12 Murtha	34	66	94
13 Hoeffel	26	74	91
14 Doyle	29	71	100
15 *Toomey*	94	6	94
16 *Pitts*	91	9	100
17 Holden	48	52	97
18 *Murphy*	84	16	94
19 *Platts*	85	15	100
RHODE ISLAND			
1 Kennedy	35	65	100
2 Langevin	42	58	91
SOUTH CAROLINA			
1 *Brown*	91	9	100
2 *Wilson*	91	9	100
3 *Barrett*	85	15	100
4 *DeMint*	92	8	71
5 Spratt	41	59	100
6 Clyburn	30	70	97
SOUTH DAKOTA			
AL Herseth[7]	45	55	95

	1	2	3
TENNESSEE			
1 *Jenkins*	81	19	91
2 *Duncan*	82	18	100
3 *Wamp*	79	21	100
4 Davis	59	41	100
5 Cooper	35	65	100
6 Gordon	55	45	97
7 *Blackburn*	91	9	100
8 Tanner	39	61	97
9 Ford	41	59	94
TEXAS			
1 Sandlin	53	47	94
2 Turner	44	56	100
3 *Johnson, Sam*	93	7	88
4 *Hall*	82	18	100
5 *Hensarling*	100	0	88
6 *Barton*	94	6	97
7 *Culberson*	90	10	88
8 *Brady*	94	6	97
9 Lampson	41	59	100
10 Doggett	27	73	88
11 Edwards	50	50	100
12 *Granger*	94	6	94
13 *Thornberry*	97	3	100
14 *Paul*	44	56	94
15 Hinojosa	36	64	97
16 Reyes	38	62	85
17 Stenholm	63	37	94
18 Jackson-Lee	21	79	97
19 *Neugebauer*	85	15	100
20 Gonzalez	35	65	100
21 *Smith*	88	12	100
22 *DeLay*	91	9	100
23 *Bonilla*	88	12	100
24 Frost	41	59	94
25 Bell	31	69	85
26 *Burgess*	88	12	100
27 Ortiz	47	53	94
28 Rodriguez	35	65	91
29 Green	27	73	97
30 Johnson, E.B.	34	66	94
31 *Carter*	94	6	97
32 *Sessions*	94	6	100
UTAH			
1 *Bishop*	85	15	97
2 Matheson	50	50	100
3 *Cannon*	87	13	71
VERMONT			
AL *Sanders*	29	71	100
VIRGINIA			
1 *Davis, Jo Ann*	76	24	100
2 *Schrock*	93	7	88
3 Scott	12	88	100
4 *Forbes*	82	18	97
5 *Goode*	76	24	100
6 *Goodlatte*	88	12	100
7 *Cantor*	97	3	100
8 Moran	41	59	100
9 Boucher	38	62	100
10 *Wolf*	85	15	100
11 *Davis, T.*	91	9	97
WASHINGTON			
1 Inslee	26	74	100
2 Larsen	29	71	100
3 Baird	37	63	88
4 *Hastings*	97	3	97
5 *Nethercutt*	80	20	88
6 Dicks	31	69	94
7 McDermott	21	79	97
8 *Dunn*	93	7	88
9 Smith	38	62	85
WEST VIRGINIA			
1 Mollohan	29	71	91
2 *Capito*	79	21	100
3 Rahall	45	55	91
WISCONSIN			
1 *Ryan*	79	21	100
2 Baldwin	32	68	100
3 Kind	41	59	94
4 Kleczka	24	76	85
5 *Sensenbrenner*	79	21	100
6 *Petri*	85	15	100
7 Obey	26	74	100
8 Green	88	12	100
WYOMING			
AL *Cubin*	82	18	100

Party Unity Background

Roll call votes used for the party unity study are those on which a majority of voting Democrats opposed a majority of voting Republicans.

Support indicates the percentage of the time that members voted *in agreement* with a majority of their party on party unity votes. **Opposition** indicates the percentage of the time members voted *against* a majority of their party.

For the **average** of members' scores by party, chamber and region, failure to vote lowers the score.

The tables also show the number of party unity votes on which each party was victorious and the number of times each party voted unanimously.

Average 2004 Party Unity Scores by Chamber

	House		Senate		Congress	
	Party Unity	Opposition	Party Unity	Opposition	Party Unity	Opposition
Republicans	88%	7%	90%	7%	89%	7%
Democrats	86	9	83	11	86	9

Average 2004 Support/Opposition Scores by Party and Region *

Senate	Support	Opposition	House	Support	Opposition
Northern Republicans	89%	8%	**Northern Republicans**	88%	8%
Southern Republicans	93	5	**Southern Republicans**	90	4
Northern Democrats	86	9	**Northern Democrats**	89	6
Southern Democrats	69	22	**Southern Democrats**	78	16

* Southern Democrats and Republicans are those from Ala., Ark., Fla., Ga., Ky., La., Miss., N.C., Okla., S.C., Tenn., Texas and Va. All others are considered Northern.

Victories in Party Unity Votes

	House		Senate		Congress	
	Republicans	Democrats	Republicans	Democrats	Republicans	Democrats
2004	213	42	85	28	298	70
2003	310	39	250	56	560	95
2002	170	39	73	42	243	81
2001	177	27	115	95	292	122
2000	182	77	114	31	296	108
1999	177	58	211	77	388	135
1998	216	80	114	61	330	141
1997	261	58	104	46	365	104
1996	208	48	132	59	340	107
1995	561	74	345	77	906	151
1994	50	257	41	129	91	386
1993	62	329	66	199	128	528
1992	54	251	61	82	115	333
1991	39	197	57	81	96	278

Unanimous Voting by Parties

	House		Senate		Congress	
	Republicans	Democrats	Republicans	Democrats	Republicans	Democrats
2004	77	70	31	3	108	73
2003	109	94	130	32	239	126
2002	54	37	23	12	77	49
2001	66	1	55	37	121	38
2000	67	1	19	52	86	53
1999	59	11	63	100	122	111
1998	42	8	33	46	75	54
1997	63	11	38	35	101	46
1996	32	10	47	35	79	45
1995	159	17	104	63	263	80
1994	38	7	19	37	57	44
1993	65	13	57	29	122	42
1992	47	18	10	12	57	30
1991	18	11	15	19	33	30

Party Unity History

These tables show how often a majority of Democrats voted against a majority of Republicans, and average support scores.

Frequency of Partisan Roll Calls			Average House Unity Scores			Average Senate Unity Scores		
Year	House	Senate	Year	Republicans	Democrats	Year	Republicans	Democrats
2004	47.0	52.3	2004	88	86	2004	90	83
2003	51.7	66.7	2003	91	87	2003	94	85
2002	43.3	45.5	2002	90	86	2002	84	83
2001	40.2	55.3	2001	91	83	2001	88	89
2000	43.2	48.7	2000	88	82	2000	89	88
1999	47.3	62.8	1999	86	83	1999	88	89
1998	55.5	55.7	1998	86	82	1998	86	87
1997	50.4	50.3	1997	88	82	1997	87	85
1996	56.4	62.4	1996	87	80	1996	89	84
1995	73.2	68.8	1995	91	80	1995	89	81
1994	61.8	51.7	1994	84	83	1994	79	84
1993	65.5	67.1	1993	84	85	1993	84	85
1992	64.5	53.0	1992	79	79	1992	79	77
1991	55.1	49.3	1991	77	81	1991	81	80
1990	49.1	54.3	1990	74	81	1990	75	80
1989	56.3	35.3	1989	72	81	1989	78	78
1988	47.0	42.5	1988	74	80	1988	68	78
1987	63.7	40.7	1987	74	81	1987	75	81
1986	56.5	52.3	1986	70	79	1986	76	72
1985	61.0	49.6	1985	75	80	1985	76	75
1984	47.1	40.0	1984	71	74	1984	78	68
1983	55.6	43.7	1983	74	76	1983	74	71
1982	36.4	43.4	1982	69	72	1982	76	72
1981	37.4	47.8	1981	74	69	1981	81	71
1980	37.6	45.8	1980	71	69	1980	65	64
1979	47.3	46.7	1979	73	69	1979	66	68
1978	33.2	45.2	1978	69	63	1978	59	66
1977	42.2	42.4	1977	71	68	1977	66	63
1976	35.9	37.2	1976	67	66	1976	61	62
1975	48.4	47.8	1975	72	69	1975	64	68
1974	29.4	44.3	1974	63	62	1974	59	63
1973	41.8	39.9	1973	68	68	1973	64	69
1972	27.1	36.5	1972	66	58	1972	61	57
1971	37.8	41.6	1971	67	61	1971	63	64
1970	27.1	35.2	1970	60	58	1970	56	55
1969	31.1	36.3	1969	62	61	1969	63	63
1968	35.2	32.0	1968	64	59	1968	60	51
1967	36.3	34.6	1967	74	67	1967	60	61
1966	41.5	50.2	1966	68	62	1966	63	57
1965	52.2	41.9	1965	71	70	1965	68	63
1964	54.9	35.7	1964	71	69	1964	65	61
1963	48.7	47.2	1963	74	73	1963	67	66
1962	46.0	41.1	1962	70	70	1962	64	65
1961	50.0	62.3						
1960	52.7	36.7						
1959	55.2	47.9						
1958	39.8	43.5						
1957	59.0	35.5						
1956	43.8	53.1						
1955	40.8	29.9						
1954	38.2	48.0						
1953	52.1	51.7						

Number of Party Unity Votes

In the House in 2004, the two parties aligned against each other on 255 of 543 roll call votes, or 47 percent. In the Senate, the parties opposed each other on 113 of 216 roll calls, or 52 percent. A list of roll call numbers that were party unity votes is available upon request from Congressional Quarterly.

In the individual member tables, Sen. James M. Jeffords, I-Vt., and Rep. Bernard Sanders, I-Vt., are treated as if they were Democrats for support and opposition scores.

Party Unity and Party Opposition: House

1. Party Unity. Percentage of recorded party unity votes in 2004 on which a member voted "yea" or "nay" in agreement with a majority of his or her party. (Party unity votes are those on which a majority of voting Democrats opposed a majority of voting Republicans.) Percentages are based on votes cast; thus, failure to vote does not lower a member's score.

2. Party Opposition. Percentage of recorded party unity votes in 2004 on which a member voted "yea" or "nay" in disagreement with a majority of his or her party. Percentages are based on votes cast; thus, failure to vote does not lower a member's score.

3. Participation in Party Unity Votes. Percentage of the 255 recorded House party unity votes in 2004 on which a member was present and voted "yea" or "nay."

[1] *Rep. Porter J. Goss, R-Fla., resigned effective Sept. 23, 2004. The last vote for which he was eligible was vote 472. He was eligible for 224 party unity votes in 2004.*

[2] *The Speaker votes only at his discretion, usually to break a tie or to emphasize the importance of a matter.*

[3] *Rep. Ben Chandler, D-Ky., was sworn in Feb. 24, 2004. The first vote for which he was eligible was vote 26. He was eligible for 246 party unity votes in 2004.*

[4] *Rep. Rodney Alexander of Louisiana switched parties from Democrat to Republican effective Sept. 7, 2004. As a Democrat, he was eligible for 194 party unity votes in 2004; as a Republican, he was eligible for 61 party unity votes in 2004. His scores in the table reflect his votes as a Republican. As a Democrat, his support score was 71 percent; opposition score, 29 percent; participation rate, 97 percent.*

[5] *Rep. Doug Bereuter, R-Neb., resigned effective Aug. 31, 2004. The last vote for which he was eligible was vote 421. He was eligible for 194 party unity votes in 2004.*

[6] *Rep. G.K. Butterfield, D-N.C., was sworn in July 21, 2004, to replace Democrat Rep. Frank W. Ballance, Jr., who resigned effective June 11. The first vote for which Butterfield was eligible was vote 405; he was eligible for 64 party unity votes in 2004. The last vote for which Ballance was eligible was vote 231; he was eligible for 90 party unity votes in 2004. His party unity score was 97 percent; party opposition score, 3 percent; participation rate, 80 percent.*

[7] *Rep. Stephanie Herseth, D-S.D., was sworn in June 3, 2004, to replace Republican Rep. Bill Janklow, who resigned effective Jan. 20, 2004. The first vote for which Herseth was eligible was vote 224; she was eligible for 167 party unity votes in 2004. Janklow was eligible for no party unity votes in 2004.*

Key

Democrats • **Republicans**
Independents

	1	2	3
ALABAMA			
1 *Bonner*	97	3	89
2 *Everett*	93	7	94
3 *Rogers*	95	5	100
4 *Aderholt*	93	7	97
5 Cramer	61	39	98
6 *Bachus*	95	5	96
7 Davis	87	13	98
ALASKA			
AL *Young*	92	8	85
ARIZONA			
1 *Renzi*	92	8	100
2 *Franks*	98	2	99
3 *Shadegg*	99	1	98
4 Pastor	93	7	99
5 *Hayworth*	96	4	96
6 *Flake*	93	7	98
7 Grijalva	99	1	98
8 *Kolbe*	85	15	98
ARKANSAS			
1 Berry	81	19	96
2 Snyder	85	15	100
3 *Boozman*	96	4	99
4 Ross	82	18	99
CALIFORNIA			
1 Thompson	91	9	99
2 *Herger*	99	1	99
3 *Ose*	90	10	99
4 *Doolittle*	96	4	99
5 Matsui	96	4	89
6 Woolsey	98	2	98
7 Miller, George	98	2	94
8 Pelosi	97	3	96
9 Lee	99	1	94
10 Tauscher	93	7	100
11 *Pombo*	96	4	97
12 Lantos	96	4	97
13 Stark	99	1	95
14 Eshoo	94	6	99
15 Honda	97	3	92
16 Lofgren	94	6	96
17 Farr	96	4	97
18 Cardoza	81	19	96
19 *Radanovich*	95	5	95
20 Dooley	81	19	90
21 *Nunes*	95	5	98
22 *Thomas*	92	8	95
23 Capps	98	2	99
24 *Gallegly*	94	6	93
25 *McKeon*	96	4	99
26 *Dreier*	92	8	99
27 Sherman	96	4	99
28 Berman	97	3	83
29 Schiff	93	7	99
30 Waxman	97	3	88
31 Becerra	99	1	98
32 Solis	99	1	98
33 Watson	98	2	92
34 Roybal-Allard	98	2	95
35 Waters	97	3	93
36 Harman	91	9	95

	1	2	3
37 Millender-McD.	95	5	85
38 Napolitano	98	2	98
39 Sánchez, Linda	99	1	99
40 *Royce*	94	6	98
41 *Lewis*	93	7	96
42 *Miller, Gary*	98	2	97
43 Baca	92	8	99
44 *Calvert*	93	7	98
45 *Bono*	86	14	95
46 *Rohrabacher*	91	9	97
47 Sanchez, Loretta	94	6	99
48 *Cox*	97	3	97
49 *Issa*	95	5	97
50 *Cunningham*	94	6	96
51 Filner	98	2	89
52 *Hunter*	95	5	91
53 Davis	95	5	100
COLORADO			
1 DeGette	97	3	93
2 Udall	94	6	96
3 *McInnis*	98	2	83
4 *Musgrave*	98	2	98
5 *Hefley*	91	9	98
6 *Tancredo*	94	6	93
7 *Beauprez*	97	3	99
CONNECTICUT			
1 Larson	95	5	99
2 *Simmons*	73	27	98
3 DeLauro	98	2	99
4 *Shays*	69	31	98
5 *Johnson*	82	18	98
DELAWARE			
AL *Castle*	79	21	100
FLORIDA			
1 *Miller, J.*	99	1	89
2 Boyd	67	33	96
3 Brown	94	6	91
4 *Crenshaw*	95	5	99
5 *Brown-Waite*	95	5	95
6 *Stearns*	96	4	99
7 *Mica*	95	5	97
8 *Keller*	98	2	99
9 *Bilirakis*	93	7	99
10 *Young*	91	9	95
11 Davis	89	11	97
12 *Putnam*	97	3	98
13 *Harris*	97	3	98
14 *Goss* [1]	92	8	83
15 *Weldon*	95	5	97
16 *Foley*	91	9	98
17 Meek	94	6	90
18 *Ros-Lehtinen*	89	11	96
19 Wexler	97	3	90
20 Deutsch	94	6	63
21 *Diaz-Balart, L.*	90	10	95
22 *Shaw*	93	7	98
23 Hastings	97	3	61
24 *Feeney*	99	1	97
25 *Diaz-Balart, M.*	94	6	98
GEORGIA			
1 *Kingston*	97	3	97
2 Bishop	78	22	93
3 Marshall	69	31	98
4 Majette	92	8	76
5 Lewis	98	2	96
6 *Isakson*	99	1	79
7 *Linder*	98	2	95
8 *Collins*	99	1	67
9 *Norwood*	99	1	79
10 *Deal*	100	0	89
11 *Gingrey*	98	2	100
12 *Burns*	95	5	100
13 Scott	79	21	96
HAWAII			
1 Abercrombie	94	6	95
2 Case	81	19	96
IDAHO			
1 *Otter*	94	6	99
2 *Simpson*	94	6	99
ILLINOIS			
1 Rush	97	3	98
2 Jackson	98	2	100
3 Lipinski	83	17	77
4 Gutierrez	99	1	89
5 Emanuel	97	3	96
6 *Hyde*	90	10	98

	1	2	3
7 Davis	98	2	96
8 Crane	99	1	97
9 Schakowsky	99	1	99
10 Kirk	84	16	95
11 Weller	92	8	97
12 Costello	82	18	98
13 Biggert	88	12	100
14 Hastert [2]	100	0	14
15 Johnson	77	23	99
16 Manzullo	93	7	99
17 Evans	97	3	99
18 LaHood	86	14	89
19 Shimkus	91	9	96
INDIANA			
1 Visclosky	90	10	98
2 Chocola	99	1	100
3 Souder	94	6	96
4 Buyer	96	4	94
5 Burton	96	4	93
6 Pence	99	1	98
7 Carson	97	3	69
8 Hostettler	93	7	99
9 Hill	83	17	99
IOWA			
1 Nussle	93	7	99
2 Leach	66	34	88
3 Boswell	83	17	99
4 Latham	92	8	99
5 King	99	1	99
KANSAS			
1 Moran	92	8	99
2 Ryun	98	2	95
3 Moore	83	17	99
4 Tiahrt	96	4	98
KENTUCKY			
1 Whitfield	91	9	96
2 Lewis	96	4	99
3 Northup	92	8	99
4 Lucas	63	37	95
5 Rogers	95	5	97
6 Chandler [3]	79	21	99
LOUISIANA			
1 Vitter	98	2	94
2 Jefferson	94	6	97
3 Tauzin	99	1	27
4 McCrery	98	2	96
5 Alexander [4]	97	3	95
6 Baker	95	5	94
7 John	66	34	82
MAINE			
1 Allen	95	5	100
2 Michaud	88	12	100
MARYLAND			
1 Gilchrest	85	15	100
2 Ruppersberger	88	12	95
3 Cardin	94	6	96
4 Wynn	88	12	98
5 Hoyer	95	5	99
6 Bartlett	93	7	100
7 Cummings	98	2	98
8 Van Hollen	96	4	100
MASSACHUSETTS			
1 Olver	98	2	99
2 Neal	98	2	98
3 McGovern	98	2	96
4 Frank	98	2	95
5 Meehan	98	2	95
6 Tierney	99	1	98
7 Markey	98	2	98
8 Capuano	96	4	98
9 Lynch	91	9	98
10 Delahunt	98	2	88
MICHIGAN			
1 Stupak	91	9	99
2 Hoekstra	98	2	98
3 Ehlers	86	14	97
4 Camp	94	6	97
5 Kildee	93	7	100
6 Upton	88	12	99
7 Smith	97	3	94
8 Rogers	95	5	99
9 Knollenberg	94	6	99
10 Miller	93	7	98
11 McCotter	91	9	100
12 Levin	95	5	100

	1	2	3
13 Kilpatrick	96	4	92
14 Conyers	98	2	88
15 Dingell	94	6	99
MINNESOTA			
1 Gutknecht	97	3	94
2 Kline	99	1	100
3 Ramstad	91	9	100
4 McCollum	97	3	100
5 Sabo	94	6	98
6 Kennedy	97	3	99
7 Peterson	63	37	99
8 Oberstar	91	9	97
MISSISSIPPI			
1 Wicker	95	5	95
2 Thompson	92	8	98
3 Pickering	94	6	98
4 Taylor	67	33	99
MISSOURI			
1 Clay	97	3	89
2 Akin	99	1	99
3 Gephardt	95	5	46
4 Skelton	80	20	98
5 McCarthy	97	3	95
6 Graves	93	7	97
7 Blunt	97	3	98
8 Emerson	89	11	96
9 Hulshof	96	4	93
MONTANA			
AL Rehberg	96	4	100
NEBRASKA			
1 Bereuter [5]	82	18	76
2 Terry	93	7	97
3 Osborne	91	9	98
NEVADA			
1 Berkley	93	7	93
2 Gibbons	95	5	95
3 Porter	83	17	100
NEW HAMPSHIRE			
1 Bradley	87	13	99
2 Bass	85	15	98
NEW JERSEY			
1 Andrews	94	6	98
2 LoBiondo	82	18	100
3 Saxton	84	16	97
4 Smith	77	23	99
5 Garrett	98	2	99
6 Pallone	96	4	99
7 Ferguson	85	15	97
8 Pascrell	94	6	95
9 Rothman	94	6	91
10 Payne	99	1	96
11 Frelinghuysen	88	12	98
12 Holt	98	2	100
13 Menendez	93	7	94
NEW MEXICO			
1 Wilson	79	21	98
2 Pearce	94	6	99
3 Udall	95	5	100
NEW YORK			
1 Bishop	95	5	96
2 Israel	92	8	93
3 King	83	17	95
4 McCarthy	94	6	97
5 Ackerman	99	1	86
6 Meeks	94	6	85
7 Crowley	93	7	96
8 Nadler	99	1	99
9 Weiner	99	1	98
10 Towns	96	4	88
11 Owens	99	1	94
12 Velázquez	96	4	97
13 Fossella	88	12	95
14 Maloney	97	3	98
15 Rangel	98	2	95
16 Serrano	98	2	95
17 Engel	96	4	91
18 Lowey	95	5	96
19 Kelly	84	16	100
20 Sweeney	88	12	98
21 McNulty	91	9	96
22 Hinchey	99	1	87
23 McHugh	87	13	99
24 Boehlert	81	19	84
25 Walsh	87	13	98

	1	2	3
26 Reynolds	96	4	97
27 Quinn	86	14	68
28 Slaughter	98	2	87
29 Houghton	83	17	88
NORTH CAROLINA			
1 Butterfield [6]	87	13	100
2 Etheridge	85	15	99
3 Jones	86	14	94
4 Price	90	10	99
5 Burr	92	8	95
6 Coble	94	6	97
7 McIntyre	74	26	97
8 Hayes	94	6	96
9 Myrick	99	1	98
10 Ballenger	97	3	79
11 Taylor	93	7	99
12 Watt	97	3	98
13 Miller	89	11	100
NORTH DAKOTA			
AL Pomeroy	82	18	100
OHIO			
1 Chabot	95	5	100
2 Portman	95	5	98
3 Turner	92	8	99
4 Oxley	94	6	96
5 Gillmor	93	7	97
6 Strickland	94	6	97
7 Hobson	92	8	98
8 Boehner	97	3	95
9 Kaptur	97	3	92
10 Kucinich	96	4	89
11 Jones	97	3	80
12 Tiberi	92	8	98
13 Brown	98	2	97
14 LaTourette	86	14	96
15 Pryce	91	9	97
16 Regula	93	7	99
17 Ryan	95	5	95
18 Ney	92	8	99
OKLAHOMA			
1 Sullivan	97	3	98
2 Carson	66	34	88
3 Lucas	94	6	97
4 Cole	97	3	99
5 Istook	96	4	92
OREGON			
1 Wu	90	10	99
2 Walden	93	7	100
3 Blumenauer	93	7	89
4 DeFazio	90	10	99
5 Hooley	87	13	100
PENNSYLVANIA			
1 Brady	96	4	99
2 Fattah	99	1	89
3 English	88	12	98
4 Hart	96	4	98
5 Peterson	92	8	93
6 Gerlach	84	16	91
7 Weldon	85	15	92
8 Greenwood	84	16	82
9 Shuster, Bill	96	4	96
10 Sherwood	92	8	99
11 Kanjorski	88	12	98
12 Murtha	80	20	96
13 Hoeffel	96	4	86
14 Doyle	93	7	98
15 Toomey	98	2	91
16 Pitts	97	3	96
17 Holden	76	24	100
18 Murphy	92	8	99
19 Platts	88	12	95
RHODE ISLAND			
1 Kennedy	95	5	98
2 Langevin	91	9	95
SOUTH CAROLINA			
1 Brown	97	3	100
2 Wilson	99	1	99
3 Barrett	99	1	99
4 DeMint	98	2	56
5 Spratt	86	14	100
6 Clyburn	93	7	98
SOUTH DAKOTA			
AL Herseth [7]	76	24	98

	1	2	3
TENNESSEE			
1 Jenkins	95	5	94
2 Duncan	92	8	98
3 Wamp	93	7	98
4 Davis	68	32	99
5 Cooper	82	18	98
6 Gordon	72	28	96
7 Blackburn	99	1	96
8 Tanner	74	26	91
9 Ford	90	10	95
TEXAS			
1 Sandlin	76	24	96
2 Turner	78	22	95
3 Johnson, Sam	99	1	92
4 Hall	92	8	98
5 Hensarling	98	2	97
6 Barton	97	3	92
7 Culberson	97	3	89
8 Brady	98	2	98
9 Lampson	85	15	96
10 Doggett	95	5	93
11 Edwards	73	27	99
12 Granger	96	4	91
13 Thornberry	98	2	100
14 Paul	82	18	86
15 Hinojosa	90	10	88
16 Reyes	86	14	80
17 Stenholm	59	41	97
18 Jackson-Lee	96	4	95
19 Neugebauer	98	2	99
20 Gonzalez	88	12	100
21 Smith	97	3	98
22 DeLay	98	2	100
23 Bonilla	94	6	99
24 Frost	84	16	98
25 Bell	92	8	86
26 Burgess	96	4	99
27 Ortiz	83	17	90
28 Rodriguez	92	8	94
29 Green	87	13	95
30 Johnson, E.B.	93	7	93
31 Carter	98	2	98
32 Sessions	99	1	99
UTAH			
1 Bishop	97	3	98
2 Matheson	64	36	100
3 Cannon	98	2	81
VERMONT			
AL Sanders	98	2	98
VIRGINIA			
1 Davis, Jo Ann	91	9	100
2 Schrock	98	2	90
3 Scott	98	2	99
4 Forbes	96	4	94
5 Goode	91	9	97
6 Goodlatte	98	2	99
7 Cantor	98	2	100
8 Moran	89	11	97
9 Boucher	81	19	99
10 Wolf	85	15	100
11 Davis, T.	88	12	93
WASHINGTON			
1 Inslee	94	6	100
2 Larsen	92	8	97
3 Baird	89	11	94
4 Hastings	96	4	94
5 Nethercutt	89	11	86
6 Dicks	90	10	92
7 McDermott	99	1	90
8 Dunn	96	4	90
9 Smith	84	16	90
WEST VIRGINIA			
1 Mollohan	81	19	84
2 Capito	89	11	99
3 Rahall	87	13	96
WISCONSIN			
1 Ryan	94	6	100
2 Baldwin	98	2	100
3 Kind	87	13	98
4 Kleczka	96	4	87
5 Sensenbrenner	94	6	100
6 Petri	89	11	99
7 Obey	93	7	99
8 Green	91	9	100
WYOMING			
AL Cubin	97	3	98

	1	2	3
ALABAMA			
Shelby	94	6	100
Sessions	97	3	95
ALASKA			
Stevens	97	3	100
Murkowski, L.	92	8	94
ARIZONA			
McCain	79	21	98
Kyl	98	2	97
ARKANSAS			
Lincoln	79	21	100
Pryor	81	19	100
CALIFORNIA			
Feinstein	95	5	100
Boxer	96	4	95
COLORADO			
Campbell	94	6	80
Allard	98	2	100
CONNECTICUT			
Dodd	95	5	98
Lieberman	89	11	95
DELAWARE			
Biden	95	5	96
Carper	86	14	99
FLORIDA			
Graham	95	5	96
Nelson	92	8	98
GEORGIA			
Miller	2	98	96
Chambliss	99	1	95
HAWAII			
Inouye	95	5	98
Akaka	97	3	81
IDAHO			
Craig	98	2	98
Crapo	96	4	99
ILLINOIS			
Fitzgerald	90	10	98
Durbin	96	4	99
INDIANA			
Lugar	94	6	98
Bayh	78	22	98

	1	2	3
IOWA			
Grassley	97	3	100
Harkin	94	6	100
KANSAS			
Brownback	98	2	90
Roberts	99	1	100
KENTUCKY			
McConnell	99	1	100
Bunning	98	2	95
LOUISIANA			
Breaux	72	28	96
Landrieu	81	19	100
MAINE			
Snowe	71	29	100
Collins	78	22	100
MARYLAND			
Sarbanes	100	0	98
Mikulski	96	4	99
MASSACHUSETTS			
Kennedy	98	2	96
Kerry	100	0	12
MICHIGAN			
Levin	96	4	100
Stabenow	96	4	100
MINNESOTA			
Dayton	91	9	99
Coleman	91	9	100
MISSISSIPPI			
Cochran	98	2	100
Lott	94	6	96
MISSOURI			
Bond	94	6	100
Talent	96	4	100
MONTANA			
Burns	97	3	97
Baucus	72	28	96
NEBRASKA			
Hagel	93	7	97
Nelson	52	48	100
NEVADA			
Reid	83	17	85
Ensign	90	10	98

	1	2	3
NEW HAMPSHIRE			
Gregg	94	6	96
Sununu	94	6	96
NEW JERSEY			
Lautenberg	96	4	97
Corzine	96	4	95
NEW MEXICO			
Domenici	97	3	89
Bingaman	90	10	97
NEW YORK			
Schumer	91	9	100
Clinton	96	4	90
NORTH CAROLINA			
Edwards	98	2	44
Dole	94	6	96
NORTH DAKOTA			
Conrad	81	19	100
Dorgan	84	16	100
OHIO			
DeWine	79	21	100
Voinovich	88	12	96
OKLAHOMA			
Nickles	97	3	98
Inhofe	98	2	96
OREGON			
Wyden	93	7	100
Smith	89	11	99
PENNSYLVANIA			
Specter	70	30	95
Santorum	96	4	98
RHODE ISLAND			
Reed	98	2	98
Chafee	65	35	98
SOUTH CAROLINA			
Hollings	92	8	95
Graham	92	8	97
SOUTH DAKOTA			
Daschle	90	10	100
Johnson	90	10	74
TENNESSEE			
Frist	96	4	100
Alexander	95	5	98

Key

Democrats • **Republicans**
Independents

	1	2	3
TEXAS			
Hutchison	89	11	100
Cornyn	97	3	98
UTAH			
Hatch	98	2	100
Bennett	97	3	96
VERMONT			
Leahy	94	6	98
Jeffords	92	8	98
VIRGINIA			
Warner	87	13	99
Allen	94	6	100
WASHINGTON			
Murray	91	9	98
Cantwell	90	10	100
WEST VIRGINIA			
Byrd	90	10	97
Rockefeller	88	12	100
WISCONSIN			
Kohl	95	5	100
Feingold	95	5	100
WYOMING			
Thomas	99	1	98
Enzi	97	3	99

ND Northern Democrats   SD Southern Democrats

Southern states - Ala., Ark., Fla., Ga., Ky., La., Miss., N.C., Okla., S.C., Tenn., Texas, Va.

Party Unity and Party Opposition: Senate

1. Party Unity. Percentage of recorded party unity votes in 2004 on which a senator voted "yea" or "nay" in agreement with a majority of his or her party. (Party unity roll calls are those on which a majority of voting Democrats opposed a majority of voting Republicans.) Percentages are based on votes cast; thus, failure to vote does not lower a member's score.

2. Party Opposition. Percentage of recorded party unity votes in 2004 on which a senator voted "yea" or "nay" in disagreement with a majority of his or her party. Percentages are based on votes cast; thus, failure to vote does not lower a member's score.

3. Participation in Party Unity Votes. Percentage of the 113 recorded Senate party unity votes in 2004 on which a senator was present and voted "yea" or "nay."

	1	2
ALABAMA		
Shelby	100	100
Sessions	96	96
ALASKA		
Stevens	99	99
Murkowski, L.	94	94
ARIZONA		
McCain	97	97
Kyl	98	98
ARKANSAS		
Lincoln	100	100
Pryor	100	100
CALIFORNIA		
Feinstein	100	100
Boxer	94	95
COLORADO		
Campbell	81	81
Allard	100	100
CONNECTICUT		
Dodd	99	99
Lieberman	94	94
DELAWARE		
Biden	92	92
Carper	99	99
FLORIDA		
Graham	90	91
Nelson	98	98
GEORGIA		
Miller	93	93
Chambliss	91	92
HAWAII		
Inouye	96	96
Akaka	83	83
IDAHO		
Craig	98	98
Crapo	99	99
ILLINOIS		
Fitzgerald	98	98
Durbin	99	99
INDIANA		
Lugar	95	95
Bayh	97	97

	1	2
IOWA		
Grassley	100	100
Harkin	98	98
KANSAS		
Brownback	93	93
Roberts	99	99
KENTUCKY		
McConnell	99	99
Bunning	96	96
LOUISIANA		
Breaux	96	96
Landrieu	99	99
MAINE		
Snowe	100	100
Collins	100	100
MARYLAND		
Sarbanes	97	97
Mikulski	99	99
MASSACHUSETTS		
Kennedy	97	97
Kerry	10	10
MICHIGAN		
Levin	100	100
Stabenow	99	99
MINNESOTA		
Dayton	99	99
Coleman	98	98
MISSISSIPPI		
Cochran	100	100
Lott	97	97
MISSOURI		
Bond	99	99
Talent	99	99
MONTANA		
Burns	98	98
Baucus	93	93
NEBRASKA		
Hagel	98	98
Nelson	99	99
NEVADA		
Reid	90	90
Ensign	98	98

	1	2
NEW HAMPSHIRE		
Gregg	96	96
Sununu	94	94
NEW JERSEY		
Lautenberg	96	96
Corzine	94	93
NEW MEXICO		
Domenici	90	90
Bingaman	98	98
NEW YORK		
Schumer	100	100
Clinton	93	93
NORTH CAROLINA		
Edwards	41	41
Dole	98	98
NORTH DAKOTA		
Conrad	100	100
Dorgan	99	99
OHIO		
DeWine	100	100
Voinovich	98	98
OKLAHOMA		
Nickles	99	99
Inhofe	95	95
OREGON		
Wyden	100	100
Smith	99	99
PENNSYLVANIA		
Specter	92	92
Santorum	96	96
RHODE ISLAND		
Reed	99	99
Chafee	99	99
SOUTH CAROLINA		
Hollings	91	92
Graham	96	97
SOUTH DAKOTA		
Daschle	99	99
Johnson	83	83
TENNESSEE		
Frist	99	99
Alexander	99	99

	1	2
TEXAS		
Hutchison	99	99
Cornyn	97	97
UTAH		
Hatch	99	99
Bennett	96	96
VERMONT		
Leahy	96	97
Jeffords	95	95
VIRGINIA		
Warner	99	99
Allen	100	100
WASHINGTON		
Murray	99	99
Cantwell	100	100
WEST VIRGINIA		
Byrd	99	99
Rockefeller	100	100
WISCONSIN		
Kohl	98	98
Feingold	100	100
WYOMING		
Thomas	99	99
Enzi	99	99

Voting Participation: Senate

1. Voting Participation. Percentage of 216 recorded votes in 2004 on which a senator voted "yea" or "nay."

2. Voting Participation (without motions to instruct). Percentage of 215 recorded votes in 2004 on which a senator voted "yea" or "nay." In this version of the study, one vote to instruct the sergeant at arms to request the attendance of absent senators was excluded.

Absences because of illness. Congressional Quarterly no longer designates members who missed votes because of illness. In the past, notations to that effect were based on official statements published in the Congressional Record, but these were found to be inconsistently used.

Rounding. Scores are rounded to the nearest percentage point, except that no scores are rounded up to 100 percent. Senators with a 100 percent score participated in all recorded votes for which they were eligible.

Key

Voting Participation: House

1. Voting Participation. Percentage of 543 recorded votes in 2004 on which a representative voted "yea" or "nay."

2. Voting Participation (without Journal votes). Percentage of 535 recorded votes in 2004 on which a member voted "yea" or "nay." In this version of the study, eight votes on approval of the House Journal were excluded.

Absences because of illness. *Congressional Quarterly no longer designates members who missed votes because of illness. In the past, notations to that effect were based on official statements published in the Congressional Record, but these were found to be inconsistently used.*

Rounding. *Scores are rounded to the nearest percentage, except that no scores are rounded up to 100 percent. Members with a 100 percent score participated in all recorded votes for which they were eligible.*

[1] *Rep. Porter J. Goss, R-Fla., resigned effective Sept. 23, 2004. The last vote for which he was eligible was vote 472.*

[2] *The Speaker votes only at his discretion, usually to break a tie or to emphasize the importance of a matter.*

[3] *Rep. Ben Chandler, D-Ky., was sworn in Feb. 24, 2004. The first vote for which he was eligible was vote 26.*

[4] *Rep. Rodney Alexander of Louisiana switched parties from Democrat to Republican effective Sept. 7, 2004.*

[5] *Rep. Doug Bereuter, R-Neb., resigned effective Aug. 31, 2004. The last vote for which he was eligible was vote 421.*

[6] *Rep. G.K. Butterfield, D-N.C., was sworn in July 21, 2004, to replace Democrat Rep. Frank W. Ballance, Jr., who resigned effective June 11. The first vote for which Butterfield was eligible was vote 405. The last vote for which Ballance was eligible was vote 231; his participation rate was 83 percent.*

[7] *Rep. Stephanie Herseth, D-S.D., was sworn in June 3, 2004, to replace Republican Rep. Bill Janklow, who resigned effective Jan. 20, 2004. The first vote for which Herseth was eligible was vote 224. Janklow was eligible for no votes in 2004.*

	1	2
ALABAMA		
1 *Bonner*	91	91
2 *Everett*	93	93
3 *Rogers*	99	99
4 *Aderholt*	95	95
5 Cramer	98	98
6 *Bachus*	93	93
7 Davis	95	95
ALASKA		
AL *Young*	88	88
ARIZONA		
1 *Renzi*	99	99
2 *Franks*	98	98
3 *Shadegg*	96	96
4 Pastor	99	99
5 *Hayworth*	97	97
6 *Flake*	97	97
7 Grijalva	97	97
8 *Kolbe*	98	98
ARKANSAS		
1 Berry	96	96
2 Snyder	100	100
3 *Boozman*	99	99
4 Ross	99	99
CALIFORNIA		
1 Thompson	99	99
2 *Herger*	98	98
3 *Ose*	97	98
4 *Doolittle*	97	97
5 Matsui	90	90
6 Woolsey	95	95
7 Miller, George	92	92
8 Pelosi	94	94
9 Lee	94	94
10 Tauscher	99	99
11 *Pombo*	96	96
12 Lantos	93	93
13 Stark	87	87
14 Eshoo	97	97
15 Honda	92	92
16 Lofgren	97	97
17 Farr	97	97
18 Cardoza	97	97
19 *Radanovich*	95	95
20 Dooley	85	85
21 *Nunes*	97	97
22 *Thomas*	97	97
23 Capps	98	98
24 *Gallegly*	93	93
25 *McKeon*	98	98
26 *Dreier*	99	99
27 Sherman	99	99
28 Berman	84	84
29 Schiff	98	98
30 Waxman	89	89
31 Becerra	94	94
32 Solis	96	96
33 Watson	92	91
34 Roybal-Allard	97	97
35 Waters	91	91
36 Harman	94	94

	1	2
37 Millender-McD.	86	86
38 Napolitano	98	98
39 Sánchez, Linda	98	98
40 *Royce*	97	97
41 *Lewis*	97	97
42 *Miller, Gary*	97	97
43 Baca	97	97
44 *Calvert*	97	96
45 *Bono*	95	95
46 *Rohrabacher*	95	96
47 Sanchez, Loretta	99	99
48 *Cox*	93	93
49 *Issa*	98	98
50 *Cunningham*	97	96
51 Filner	89	89
52 *Hunter*	90	90
53 Davis	98	98
COLORADO		
1 DeGette	91	91
2 Udall	96	96
3 *McInnis*	84	84
4 *Musgrave*	97	97
5 *Hefley*	97	97
6 *Tancredo*	94	95
7 *Beauprez*	98	98
CONNECTICUT		
1 Larson	99	99
2 *Simmons*	96	96
3 DeLauro	99	99
4 *Shays*	95	95
5 *Johnson*	97	97
DELAWARE		
AL *Castle*	99	99
FLORIDA		
1 *Miller, J.*	91	91
2 Boyd	94	94
3 Brown	90	90
4 *Crenshaw*	99	99
5 *Brown-Waite*	95	95
6 *Stearns*	99	99
7 *Mica*	98	98
8 *Keller*	99	99
9 *Bilirakis*	98	98
10 *Young*	91	91
11 Davis	95	95
12 *Putnam*	97	97
13 *Harris*	96	97
14 *Goss* [1]	86	87
15 *Weldon*	96	96
16 *Foley*	98	98
17 Meek	90	89
18 *Ros-Lehtinen*	91	91
19 Wexler	87	88
20 Deutsch	67	67
21 *Diaz-Balart, L.*	95	95
22 *Shaw*	98	98
23 Hastings	67	67
24 *Feeney*	96	96
25 *Diaz-Balart, M.*	97	97
GEORGIA		
1 *Kingston*	93	94
2 Bishop	95	95
3 Marshall	97	97
4 Majette	75	75
5 Lewis	97	97
6 *Isakson*	78	78
7 *Linder*	96	96
8 *Collins*	68	68
9 *Norwood*	82	82
10 *Deal*	92	91
11 *Gingrey*	99	99
12 *Burns*	99	99
13 Scott	96	96
HAWAII		
1 Abercrombie	93	93
2 Case	97	97
IDAHO		
1 *Otter*	99	99
2 *Simpson*	99	99
ILLINOIS		
1 Rush	93	93
2 Jackson	100	100
3 Lipinski	78	78
4 Gutierrez	84	84
5 Emanuel	96	96
6 *Hyde*	98	98

State / District	1	2
7 Davis	94	94
8 *Crane*	97	97
9 Schakowsky	98	98
10 *Kirk*	94	94
11 *Weller*	94	94
12 Costello	97	97
13 *Biggert*	99	99
14 *Hastert* [2]	10	10
15 *Johnson*	99	99
16 *Manzullo*	98	98
17 *Evans*	98	98
18 *LaHood*	92	92
19 *Shimkus*	96	96
INDIANA		
1 Visclosky	97	97
2 *Chocola*	98	98
3 *Souder*	95	95
4 *Buyer*	92	92
5 Burton	91	91
6 *Pence*	96	96
7 Carson	69	68
8 *Hostettler*	99	99
9 Hill	99	99
IOWA		
1 *Nussle*	98	98
2 *Leach*	91	91
3 Boswell	99	99
4 *Latham*	99	99
5 *King*	99	99
KANSAS		
1 *Moran*	98	98
2 *Ryun*	95	95
3 Moore	99	99
4 *Tiahrt*	96	96
KENTUCKY		
1 *Whitfield*	95	95
2 *Lewis*	99	99
3 *Northup*	99	99
4 Lucas	96	96
5 *Rogers*	97	96
6 Chandler [3]	99	99
LOUISIANA		
1 *Vitter*	92	92
2 Jefferson	96	96
3 *Tauzin*	27	27
4 *McCrery*	94	94
5 *Alexander* [4]	97	97
6 *Baker*	94	94
7 John	81	81
MAINE		
1 Allen	99	99
2 Michaud	99	99
MARYLAND		
1 *Gilchrest*	98	99
2 Ruppersberger	96	96
3 Cardin	95	95
4 Wynn	97	97
5 Hoyer	98	98
6 *Bartlett*	99	99
7 Cummings	94	95
8 Van Hollen	100	100
MASSACHUSETTS		
1 Olver	99	99
2 Neal	94	94
3 McGovern	97	97
4 Frank	95	95
5 Meehan	92	92
6 Tierney	98	98
7 Markey	97	97
8 Capuano	96	96
9 Lynch	96	96
10 Delahunt	87	87
MICHIGAN		
1 Stupak	98	98
2 *Hoekstra*	97	97
3 *Ehlers*	98	98
4 *Camp*	98	98
5 Kildee	100	100
6 *Upton*	99	99
7 *Smith*	91	91
8 *Rogers*	97	97
9 *Knollenberg*	98	98
10 *Miller*	98	98
11 *McCotter*	99	99
12 Levin	100	100

State / District	1	2
13 Kilpatrick	89	89
14 Conyers	85	86
15 Dingell	97	97
MINNESOTA		
1 *Gutknecht*	94	95
2 *Kline*	100	100
3 *Ramstad*	100	100
4 McCollum	99	99
5 Sabo	96	96
6 *Kennedy*	99	99
7 Peterson	99	99
8 Oberstar	96	96
MISSISSIPPI		
1 *Wicker*	95	95
2 Thompson	97	97
3 *Pickering*	98	98
4 Taylor	98	98
MISSOURI		
1 Clay	87	87
2 *Akin*	99	99
3 Gephardt	41	41
4 Skelton	99	99
5 McCarthy	96	96
6 *Graves*	97	97
7 *Blunt*	97	97
8 *Emerson*	95	95
9 *Hulshof*	89	89
MONTANA		
AL *Rehberg*	99	99
NEBRASKA		
1 *Bereuter* [5]	80	80
2 *Terry*	97	97
3 *Osborne*	99	99
NEVADA		
1 Berkley	95	95
2 *Gibbons*	96	96
3 *Porter*	99	99
NEW HAMPSHIRE		
1 *Bradley*	99	99
2 *Bass*	98	98
NEW JERSEY		
1 Andrews	97	96
2 *LoBiondo*	100	100
3 *Saxton*	96	96
4 *Smith*	98	98
5 *Garrett*	98	98
6 Pallone	99	99
7 *Ferguson*	96	96
8 Pascrell	95	95
9 Rothman	92	92
10 Payne	92	93
11 *Frelinghuysen*	97	96
12 Holt	99	99
13 Menendez	94	94
NEW MEXICO		
1 *Wilson*	98	98
2 *Pearce*	99	99
3 Udall	99	99
NEW YORK		
1 Bishop	98	98
2 Israel	93	93
3 *King*	94	94
4 McCarthy	96	96
5 Ackerman	87	87
6 Meeks	85	85
7 Crowley	96	96
8 Nadler	96	96
9 Weiner	95	95
10 Towns	86	86
11 Owens	92	92
12 Velázquez	96	96
13 *Fossella*	94	94
14 Maloney	96	96
15 Rangel	91	91
16 Serrano	94	94
17 Engel	91	91
18 Lowey	93	93
19 *Kelly*	100	100
20 *Sweeney*	93	93
21 McNulty	97	97
22 Hinchey	89	89
23 *McHugh*	99	99
24 *Boehlert*	84	84
25 *Walsh*	98	98

State / District	1	2
26 *Reynolds*	96	96
27 *Quinn*	73	73
28 Slaughter	85	85
29 Houghton	86	87
NORTH CAROLINA		
1 Butterfield [6]	100	100
2 Etheridge	99	99
3 *Jones*	94	94
4 Price	98	98
5 *Burr*	88	88
6 *Coble*	98	98
7 McIntyre	97	96
8 *Hayes*	97	97
9 *Myrick*	97	98
10 Ballenger	81	81
11 *Taylor*	95	95
12 Watt	96	96
13 Miller	99	99
NORTH DAKOTA		
AL Pomeroy	99	99
OHIO		
1 *Chabot*	98	98
2 *Portman*	95	95
3 *Turner*	98	98
4 *Oxley*	95	95
5 *Gillmor*	95	96
6 Strickland	97	97
7 *Hobson*	96	96
8 *Boehner*	96	96
9 Kaptur	93	93
10 Kucinich	80	80
11 Jones	81	81
12 *Tiberi*	98	98
13 Brown	94	94
14 *LaTourette*	97	97
15 *Pryce*	96	96
16 *Regula*	99	99
17 Ryan	94	94
18 *Ney*	97	97
OKLAHOMA		
1 *Sullivan*	97	96
2 Carson	85	85
3 *Lucas*	96	96
4 *Cole*	99	99
5 *Istook*	88	88
OREGON		
1 Wu	99	99
2 *Walden*	99	99
3 Blumenauer	92	92
4 DeFazio	98	98
5 Hooley	98	98
PENNSYLVANIA		
1 Brady	95	95
2 Fattah	86	87
3 *English*	96	96
4 *Hart*	98	98
5 *Peterson*	89	89
6 *Gerlach*	92	93
7 *Weldon*	91	91
8 *Greenwood*	78	78
9 *Shuster, Bill*	96	96
10 *Sherwood*	98	98
11 Kanjorski	97	97
12 Murtha	88	88
13 Hoeffel	80	80
14 Doyle	96	96
15 *Toomey*	83	83
16 *Pitts*	96	96
17 Holden	98	98
18 *Murphy*	99	99
19 *Platts*	95	95
RHODE ISLAND		
1 Kennedy	95	95
2 Langevin	95	95
SOUTH CAROLINA		
1 *Brown*	100	100
2 *Wilson*	97	97
3 *Barrett*	99	99
4 *DeMint*	56	57
5 Spratt	98	99
6 Clyburn	94	95
SOUTH DAKOTA		
AL Herseth [7]	99	99

State / District	1	2
TENNESSEE		
1 *Jenkins*	94	94
2 *Duncan*	97	97
3 *Wamp*	96	96
4 Davis	99	99
5 Cooper	98	98
6 Gordon	97	97
7 *Blackburn*	96	97
8 Tanner	92	92
9 Ford	94	94
TEXAS		
1 Sandlin	95	95
2 Turner	94	95
3 *Johnson, Sam*	93	93
4 *Hall*	97	97
5 *Hensarling*	98	98
6 *Barton*	93	93
7 *Culberson*	88	88
8 *Brady*	96	97
9 Lampson	95	96
10 Doggett	87	87
11 Edwards	97	96
12 *Granger*	92	93
13 *Thornberry*	99	99
14 Paul	86	86
15 Hinojosa	87	87
16 Reyes	79	79
17 Stenholm	97	97
18 Jackson-Lee	94	94
19 *Neugebauer*	99	99
20 Gonzalez	97	97
21 *Smith*	98	98
22 *DeLay*	99	99
23 *Bonilla*	99	99
24 Frost	94	95
25 Bell	87	87
26 *Burgess*	98	98
27 Ortiz	89	89
28 Rodriguez	90	90
29 Green	95	95
30 Johnson, E.B.	94	94
31 *Carter*	95	95
32 *Sessions*	97	98
UTAH		
1 *Bishop*	96	96
2 Matheson	99	99
3 *Cannon*	82	82
VERMONT		
AL *Sanders*	94	95
VIRGINIA		
1 *Davis, Jo Ann*	99	99
2 *Schrock*	90	90
3 Scott	99	99
4 *Forbes*	94	94
5 *Goode*	98	98
6 *Goodlatte*	99	99
7 *Cantor*	99	99
8 Moran	96	96
9 Boucher	99	99
10 *Wolf*	98	98
11 *Davis, T.*	96	96
WASHINGTON		
1 Inslee	98	98
2 Larsen	96	96
3 Baird	95	95
4 *Hastings*	95	96
5 *Nethercutt*	85	85
6 Dicks	94	93
7 McDermott	92	92
8 *Dunn*	90	90
9 Smith	91	91
WEST VIRGINIA		
1 Mollohan	85	85
2 *Capito*	99	99
3 Rahall	94	94
WISCONSIN		
1 *Ryan*	99	99
2 Baldwin	99	99
3 Kind	98	98
4 Kleczka	86	85
5 *Sensenbrenner*	100	100
6 *Petri*	99	99
7 Obey	98	98
8 *Green*	99	99
WYOMING		
AL *Cubin*	97	97

Appendix C

KEY VOTES

Partisanship Takes Its Toll

The Senate had the chance in July to pass a bill imposing limits on class action lawsuits — a premier piece of President Bush's legislative agenda. But that would have required Majority Leader Bill Frist, R-Tenn., to swallow hard and allow Democrats and some Republicans to offer amendments on labor issues, greenhouse gas emissions and other controversial subjects. Instead, Frist moved to invoke cloture and cut off the debate.

If he had succeeded, he would have blocked the amendments and allowed action on the underlying bill to proceed unimpeded. But his gambit failed when the amendments' sponsors chose to let the bill die rather than yield to the leadership. On a near-party-line split, Republicans failed to muster the necessary 60 votes for cloture and Frist pulled the bill off the floor.

At the time, Frist did not know that the GOP would increase its Senate majority on Nov. 2 — possibly improving the odds for so-called tort reform bills in the 109th Congress. So, the failed cloture vote was seen as a stunning defeat for him and for Bush, all the more so because 12 Democrats were prepared to support the bill and it was sure to pass.

The cloture vote on the class action bill was a textbook example of what happened this year on Capitol Hill: Partisanship overwhelmed consensus, the president's wishes frequently were thwarted by a minority that complained the majority was overreaching — and ultimately little was accomplished. That made the cloture vote, which might have been a procedural sideshow in many years, a sure choice by the editors of Congressional Quarterly for inclusion among the two dozen "key votes" of 2004.

For almost 60 years, CQ has identified a few dozen votes that were particularly controversial, that tested the president's ability to persuade the legislative branch and that affected Americans directly. In demonstrating the intractable politics of this election year, the cloture vote met at least two of those tests.

Two-thirds of the votes selected for 2004 were critical to the success of the president's program and he lost on half of them. Similarly, 15 of the 24 key votes pitted most Republicans against most Democrats, and the majority GOP prevailed less than a third of the time.

A few votes reflected the climaxes of significant legislative action. Congress cleared two tax bills, one (PL 108-311)

How CQ Picks Key Votes

Since 1945, Congressional Quarterly has selected a series of key votes on major issues of the year.

An issue is judged to be a key vote by the extent to which it represents:

● a matter of major controversy.
● a matter of presidential or political power.
● a matter of potentially great impact on the nation and lives of Americans.

For each group of related votes on an issue, one key vote is usually chosen — one that, in the opinion of CQ editors, was most important in determining the outcome.

a $146 billion multi-year extension of previously enacted middle-class breaks, the other (PL 108-357) a $137 billion tax cut mostly for manufacturers and multinational companies, but with plenty of other provisions to go around.

Another vote led to enactment of a law (PL 108-212) making it a federal crime to kill or injure a fetus during the commission of another violent offense — a long-sought victory for the president. And a bipartisan majority of the House handed the president an endorsement of his Iraq policy in March, on the first anniversary of the U.S. invasion, demonstrating that Bush's mantle as commander in chief would limit the ability of the Democrats to use the war as an election issue.

But there were as many tests of the president's clout that ended in defeat. Both the House and Senate voted for six-year highway bills that were far more expensive than Bush wanted. As a result, no bill was enacted. Also, despite Bush's request, neither chamber came close to providing the two-thirds majority needed to send to the states for ratification a proposed constitutional amendment that would ban gay marriages.

In the House, Bush did not win passage of a bill that would have capped discretionary spending and imposed some controls on entitlements. A third of the Republicans voted no — an overwhelming sign that members cherish their power of the purse. They joined a unanimous bloc of Democratic opponents, who not only objected to the spending constraints but complained that by exempting tax cuts from its controls the bill failed to impose fiscal discipline.

In another rebuff to Bush, the House voted to delay until 2007 a round of military base closings planned for 2005. But, by a two-vote margin, the Senate refused to join in and the closures were allowed to proceed.

One Bush victory came in the final hours of the Congress. The House had insisted on preserving the Pentagon's power over military intelligence spending, refusing to join the Senate and endorse a central recommendation of an independent commission that looked into the Sept. 11 terrorist attacks. In the end, under pressure from Bush, the House relented.

Stories of each key vote follow, the 14 in the Senate followed by the 10 in the House. They are listed in the order of their original vote numbers.

SENATE
KEY VOTES

14 Surface Transportation Spending

Passage of a bill that would authorize $318.9 billion in surface transportation spending during the next six years, 25 percent more than the Bush administration requested.

An election-year debate over federal highway and public transit spending showcased how local political interests can and will trump party alliances. In a rare affront to the Bush White House, Senate Republicans voted by a 2-to-1 ratio in February to send a generous amount of federal transportation dollars back to the states — despite administration entreaties to hold to a much harder line on spending.

The degree of overwhelming bipartisan support for the highway measure (S 1072) appeared more than sufficient to override a threatened presidential veto. But it never came to that; nettlesome policy disputes with the House meant the president never had to even consider carrying through on what was a veiled threat anyway.

That is because the $256 billion administration proposal sent to Capitol Hill in early February was dead on arrival. Politically influential states in the fast-growing South and Southwest — among them Florida, South Carolina, Texas, Arizona and Nevada — are developing a voracious appetite for transportation funds and want at least 95 cents back from each gasoline tax dollar they send to Washington.

Currently, they get a minimum of 90.5 cents to the dollar.

But under the White House plan, for these "donor" states to get more money, billions of dollars would have to shift from a number of Northeastern and northern Plains states that already use more highway dollars than they put into the Highway Trust Fund.

Although typically seen as a solid Republican fiscal conservative, James M. Inhofe of Oklahoma, the chairman of the Senate Environment and Public Works Committee, sides with pro-highway spenders, saying more infrastructure financing pays important dividends later because it boosts safety, creates jobs and helps the economy stay strong.

Bush administration officials said they did not disagree with Inhofe's premise but argued the federal budget deficit and a still tentative economy meant that for the transportation bill to win enactment, it had to meet three tests: It could not increase the deficit; it could not raise taxes, including the federal excise tax on gasoline; and it could not use borrowing.

Supporting the administration in the Senate was a small band of fiscal conservatives, including Oklahoma's other senator, Republican Budget Chairman Don Nickles.

But the fiscal conservatives were clearly in the minority. Majority Leader Bill Frist, R-Tenn., sympathetic to the argu-

ments of the dissenters but anxious to get a bill passed, ultimately succeeded in bringing the measure to a vote the evening of Feb. 12. It passed by a lopsided 76-21; R 34-17; D 41-4 (ND 35-2, SD 6-2); I 1-0. (*Senate vote 14, p. C-18*)

By the end of the year, however, the Senate's fiscal conservatives got their way, because the legislation stalled in a House-Senate conference committee; in those negotiations, lawmakers could not find a way to overcome White House objections over the spending level or the concerns of lawmakers from the donor states.

15 Medical Malpractice Liability

Defeat of an effort to limit debate on legislation that would limit punitive damages in malpractice litigation against obstetricians, gynecologists and nurse midwives.

Bill Frist of Tennessee, a heart and lung transplant surgeon for most of his professional life, wanted to make improving the health care system the signature achievement of his first term as the Senate's Republican majority leader. After shepherding the creation of a Medicare prescription drug benefit into law (PL 108-173) in 2003, he made limiting medical malpractice liability his top health care priority for 2004.

But his campaign went nowhere, even after Frist narrowed his objective to shielding some of the most politically sympathetic medical specialists — obstetricians, gynecologists and nurse midwives — from multimillion-dollar punitive damages, and framed his campaign as an effort to improve medical care for women. The denouement came on Feb. 24, when his bid to limit debate on that narrow bill (S 2061) came up a dozen votes short of the 60 required for invoking cloture. The vote was 48-45: R 47-3; D 1-41 (ND 1-34, SD 0-7); I 0-1 (*Senate vote 15, p. C-18*)

Despite Frist's efforts, the bill stalled mostly on party lines. Only one Democrat, Robert C. Byrd of West Virginia, stood with him, while three Republicans went against him: Michael D. Crapo of Idaho, Richard C. Shelby of Alabama and Lindsey Graham of South Carolina.

Frist aspires to cap non-economic damage awards in all medical malpractice lawsuits at $250,000, arguing that would achieve two objectives. He says it would help slow increases in doctors' insurance premiums, which have driven some of them into early retirement, and it would hold down health costs by limiting the practice of "defensive medicine" — ordering tests or procedures with marginal benefit because of the fear of future lawsuits.

The House passed a comprehensive bill shielding all doctors in 2003, but it stalled in the Senate when Frist won only 49 votes for his motion to limit debate and overcome a filibuster by his opponents.

After President Bush returned the issue to the spotlight by proposing a damages cap in his 2004 State of the Union address, Frist resolved to push the narrower legislation in hopes of scoring a momentum-building victory. He argued that — absent a damages cap for obstetricians and gynecologists — many more of them will soon stop practicing and many more women will be inconvenienced, if not endangered. Democrats countered that, by limiting damages in

lawsuits, Congress would wrongly discriminate against women plaintiffs wronged by their doctors and tacitly permit a certain amount of malpractice.

After his narrow proposal stalled, Frist sought to revive his campaign one more time by pressing a bill (S 2207) that would have limited punitive damages against emergency room doctors and trauma center personnel as well as obstetricians and gynecologists. But that legislation died in April as another cloture vote once again came up far short of success. That vote was 49-48.

24 Extension of Assault Weapons Ban

Adoption of an amendment, to legislation aimed at limiting the legal liability of gunmakers and gun retailers, to extend for another 10 years prohibitions on the sale of certain assault weapons that expired in September.

Gun rights advocates believed they were in position to score at least one significant success in Congress during the year. Their chief goal was enactment of legislation that would bar, with some exceptions, lawsuits against the manufacturers, distributors, dealers and importers of firearms and ammunition. The measure's aim was to limit attempts at making the gun industry financially liable for the consequences of gun violence — cases that have typically failed but nevertheless require defendants to spend large sums on legal expenses.

The House passed its version of the legislation (HR 1036) with ease in April 2003. As the Republican leaders prepared to put the companion measure (S 1805) on the Senate floor 11 months later, the National Rifle Association (NRA) pressed its senatorial allies to vote against a series of expected "killer" amendments. The White House, for its part, issued a statement of administration policy encouraging the Senate to pass the bill essentially untouched.

But that effort failed spectacularly almost from the outset. On the very first amendment offered, senators voted overwhelmingly to buck the gun lobby's wishes and require the sale of a child safety lock with every handgun transaction. When the debate resumed March 2, the Senate delivered the coup de grâce against the bill, voting to renew prohibitions against a collection of semiautomatic assault weapons that was enacted in 1994 — but due to expire in six months. The vote to add the assault weapons ban to the bill was 52-47: R 10-41; D 41-6 (ND 34-4; SD 7-2); I 1-0 *(Senate vote 24, p. C-18)*

Gun control advocates were able to build support for the amendment, eventually winning the votes of 10 Republicans, by capitalizing on the electorate's heightened concerns about terrorism in an election year. But even a few hours before the vote, the proposal's principal sponsors — Democrats Dianne Feinstein of California and Charles E. Schumer of New York — predicted they would not prevail.

Mindful that the vote would be close, they worked to ensure that everyone in their caucus was on hand — including John Kerry of Massachusetts, who by then had all-but-formally secured his party's presidential nomination, and John Edwards of North Carolina, the eventual vice presidential nominee, who abandoned his presidential bid later that night after a final series of primary and caucus losses.

On two fronts, the ballot was a high-water mark in the 108th Congress for the advocates of gun control — and their first substantive legislative success at the Capitol in five years. Soon after the language was added, the sponsors of the underlying bill turned against the measure and engineered its defeat. The vote temporarily revived efforts to keep the assault weapons ban on the books. President Bush said he would have signed an extension had it been sent to him, but Majority Leader Tom DeLay, R-Texas, made sure the House never took a vote on the matter and the ban (PL 103-322) expired in September.

The Senate vote also served to put all senators on record on the issue in an election year, and senators suggested that any measure seen as enhancing gun rights could not succeed in a closely divided Senate without offsetting provisions to tighten gun control.

But the vote also showed the continuing power of the NRA, which had helped write the underlying legislation and would itself have been shielded from lawsuits had it become law. Just hours after the assault weapons ban was added, NRA board member and bill sponsor Larry E. Craig, an Idaho Republican, served notice that the measure should be put on the legislative spike. It was defeated by a resounding 8-90.

38 'Pay As You Go' Budget Rules

Adoption of an amendment to the fiscal 2005 budget resolution to require the support of 60 senators for any tax cut or entitlement spending increase that is not offset by revenue increases or spending reductions.

From the start of the year, top Republicans warned that a fiscal 2005 budget resolution might never be finished, in large part because of disagreements between the party's moderates and conservatives over tax policy. With the Congressional Budget Office projecting a record federal deficit of $477 billion in an election year, the stage was set for a particularly bumpy budget debate.

Senate GOP leaders signaled early on that President Bush's most ambitious tax cut plans had no chance until he won a second term. Instead, leaders sought to focus their efforts on extending a trio of popular tax breaks set to expire at the end of 2004 — a $1,000 per-child tax credit, an expanded 10 percent tax bracket and tax relief for married couples. Senate Budget Chairman Don Nickles, R-Okla., proposed a budget blueprint (S Con Res 95) that would have provided procedural "reconciliation" protections for $82.6 billion in tax cuts, enough to cover extending those three breaks and little more.

The leadership's plans were relatively modest and the political stakes clearly lower than in previous years. Yet, at least several GOP moderates and deficit hawks signaled that the deepening deficit would make it difficult for them to support even that comparatively modest tax reduction.

Democrats wanted to drop the reconciliation instructions that would expedite the GOP tax-cutting agenda. But Majority Leader Bill Frist, R-Tenn., prevailed upon most of the wavering GOP moderates to oppose that approach; he wanted to have reconciliation as a fallback option, as it

would allow him to thwart potential Democratic amendments to the tax bill in the run-up to the election.

Instead, the moderates lined up behind an amendment, by Wisconsin Democrat Russell D. Feingold, to reinstate pay-as-you-go language requiring that any new tax cuts or new entitlement spending program be offset by accompanying tax increases or spending cuts — or face being struck down on the Senate floor, at least during the five-year period covered by the budget resolution, by a point of order that could be overcome only with the support of 60 or more senators.

Nickles included a less-stringent version of the pay-as-you-go requirement in his budget resolution. It would have required that new entitlement spending be offset unless 60 senators in effect voted otherwise. It would not have subjected the tax cuts called for within the budget blueprint to the same rule.

But that was not enough to win over fellow Republicans Olympia J. Snowe and Susan Collins of Maine, Lincoln Chafee of Rhode Island and John McCain of Arizona. When the Senate voted on the Feingold amendment March 10, those four joined 46 Democrats and independent James M. Jeffords of Vermont in voting for it. In a defeat that momentarily stunned GOP leaders, the amendment was adopted, 51-48: R 4-47; D 46-1 (ND 38-0, SD 8-1); I 1-0. Zell Miller of Georgia was the only Democrat to vote against it. *(Senate vote 38, p. C-18)*

The vote essentially sealed the fiscal policy impasse for the year; for only the third time in the three decades of modern budget law, no annual congressional budget resolution was adopted by Congress in 2004.

After the Senate adopted a budget measure including the Feingold language, House conservatives made clear they were adamantly opposed to placing any such restrictions on tax cuts in a compromise budget document. The pay-as-you-go issue consumed weeks of tortured conference negotiations before Senate and House GOP leaders settled on a one-year budget deal that would exempt the three proposed tax cut extensions from pay-as-you-go rules. When all four of the pivotal Senate GOP moderates spurned that language as well, the talks collapsed.

63 | Criminalization of Harm to a Fetus

Clearing a bill creating the first distinct legal status for a fetus in federal law, by making it a federal crime to harm a fetus during the course of committing another federal crime.

Social conservatives in Congress had been trying without success since 1999 to create a new category of crimes against a fetus. On the surface, proponents described the effort as a law-and-order campaign. But opponents of abortion rights quietly but fervently hoped that their cause would be strengthened if the fetus was recognized under federal law as an entity distinct from the pregnant woman.

The House passed such a bill twice by comfortable margins, in 1999 and 2001, but the Senate had never taken up the legislation. But the cause gained decisive momentum in April 2003, when the bodies of Laci Peterson and the fetus she had carried nearly to term washed ashore near San Francisco — a defining moment in one of the most celebrated

murder cases of the decade. Peterson's husband, Scott, was eventually charged under state law with two counts of murder, because California is one of 30 states with fetal homicide laws.

The exhaustive coverage of the case quickly made a federal version of such a law politically unstoppable. The only question appeared to be the timing. Because other pressing items were on their agenda in 2003 — including the enactment of the law (PL 108-105) that criminalized a procedure that its opponents described as "partial birth" abortion — social conservatives decided to wait until the election year.

The House passed the legislation (HR 1997) Feb. 26 with 254 votes, essentially the same number that had backed the measure in the House the previous two times.

Some abortion rights advocates argued for mounting an aggressive effort to once again stop the bill in the Senate. But, mindful of how the Peterson case was fueling the call for the measure, the Democrats who generally align themselves with abortion rights decided they did not want to erect too many procedural roadblocks. After just one day of substantive debate, the Senate cleared the legislation by a comfortable margin, 61-38: R 48-2; D 13-35 (ND 9-30, SD 4-5); I 0-1. *(Senate vote 63, p. C-18)*

Only two abortion rights Republicans, Lincoln Chafee of Rhode Island and Olympia J. Snowe of Maine, voted against the bill. Democrats joined them by a ratio of 2-to-1; among those voting "no" were John Kerry of Massachusetts and John Edwards of North Carolina, who later in the year became the party's national ticket. Among the 13 Democrats voting for it, however, were Minority Leader Tom Daschle of South Dakota and Minority Whip Harry Reid of Nevada.

The bill, which President Bush quickly signed (PL 108-212), defined an "unborn child" as "a member of the species homo sapiens, at any stage of development, who is carried in the womb." Opponents said that was a clear attempt to lay the legal groundwork for neutralizing *Roe v. Wade*, the 1973 Supreme Court decision that legalized abortion. In that landmark case, Supreme Court Justice Harry A. Blackmun, writing for the majority, concluded that "the unborn have never been recognized in the law as persons in the whole sense" and that the court was not ruling on "the difficult question of when life begins."

California Democrat Dianne Feinstein proposed allowing federal prosecutors to charge defendants accused of federal crimes against pregnant women with a separate offense for harming the fetus. But, unlike the GOP bill, Feinstein's language would not confer a distinct legal status on the fetus. Her amendment was defeated, 49-50.

64 | Child Care for Welfare Recipients

Adoption of an amendment to a welfare reauthorization bill that would guarantee $6 billion in additional mandatory child care funding to the states during the next five years.

Eight years after the enactment of the landmark overhaul of federal welfare programs, lawmakers continue to argue over the proper formula for helping the nation's remaining 2 million welfare families escape poverty. They reached no resolution this year, but a lopsided Senate vote in March sig-

naled the sort of balancing of "carrots" and "sticks" that must necessarily be included to get a welfare policy rewrite through the Republican-run 109th Congress.

Most lawmakers characterize the 1996 law (PL 104-193) — which ended more than 60 years of guaranteed cash assistance for recipients and ushered in new work requirements and a five-year limit on benefits — as a success. Since enactment, caseloads have fallen by more than half.

President Bush and his congressional GOP allies argue that work is the most important ingredient to help people move from a handout to a paycheck. This view was reflected in the version of the welfare reauthorization (HR 4) passed by the House in 2003; it would have increased the work requirement for adult participants to a full 40 hours a week, up from 30 hours. The House measure also contained $1 billion in additional child care funding and a $200 million White House initiative to promote healthy marriages to the poor.

But in the Senate, Democrats and some moderate Republicans contended that increasing the length of the required workweek by one-third would shortchange welfare recipients' abilities to keep in order other aspects of their lives — including child care, transportation and education — that are essential to landing and holding a job. Finance Committee Chairman Charles E. Grassley, R-Iowa, concluding that a 40-hour workweek requirement could not pass the Senate, moved a bill through his panel last fall that would have raised the threshold to only 34 hours.

To win committee approval, Grassley promised moderate Republican Olympia J. Snowe of Maine that she could offer the first amendment when the bill came to the Senate floor. Snowe wanted to provide $6 billion in additional mandatory child care funding over the next five years. She maintained that current spending — $4.8 billion per year — is enough to serve only one in seven families eligible for that type of assistance. (The cost of her amendment would have been offset by income from renewing Customs fees.)

The White House opposed Snowe's proposal, on the ground that the extra money could go not to welfare families but to families who had left the welfare rolls but continued to have incomes low enough to make them eligible for the subsidies.

But in the Senate, opposition to the amendment was muted. Rick Santorum of Pennsylvania, chairman of the GOP Conference and a leading conservative, said the plan was too generous and would make people more dependent on the government once again. Such arguments were soundly rejected March 30, when the Senate voted to adopt the amendment, 78-20: R 31-19; D 46-1 (ND 38-0; SD 8-1); I 1-0. (*Senate vote 64, p. C-18*)

Three out of every five Republicans from across the GOP ideological spectrum broke with the White House and voted for the language, including Grassley, Majority Leader Bill Frist of Tennessee and virtually every Republican then viewed as in a competitive race for re-election.

Grassley hoped the Snowe amendment would be the sweetener to win Democrats' support for the underlying bill. But Democrats refused to allow a final vote unless they were given an opportunity to vote on an amendment to raise the minimum wage. When GOP leaders rebuffed that request, the bill fell into limbo for the rest of the year.

79 | Overtime Regulations

Adoption of an amendment, to an unrelated tax bill, to block Bush administration regulations limiting some workers' eligibility for overtime pay.

Supporters of a Bush administration plan to change overtime pay rules for millions of workers knew from the start of the year that they faced a heated battle in Congress. The White House had been on the defensive on the issue since March 2003, when it first proposed a comprehensive rewrite of overtime pay rules, including a reordering of the job descriptions that would be eligible for premium pay. It would be the first overhaul in more than 50 years of the overtime provisions in the Fair Labor Standards Act, which established the basic 40-hour workweek.

Senate Democrats were able to take advantage of the support of a handful of Republicans sympathetic to labor unions and hand the Bush administration a politically embarrassing defeat on the workplace issue in May.

Although in the end Congress did not curtail the new regulations, the effort to highlight the issue was helpful to the Democrats in several ways. Sen. John Kerry of Massachusetts, the party's presidential nominee, was able to use it to solidify his support among labor union members and to portray President Bush as insensitive to the concerns of working Americans. And the party's Senate candidates were given ammunition for attacking Republicans from high-unemployment states.

It was also the second time in six months that Democrats won a Senate vote on the issue but were unable to alter the underlying policy. In September 2003, senators voted to block implementation of any Labor Department rule that would take away existing overtime eligibility from any worker. But that language — which had been added to the fiscal 2004 spending package for the department — was dropped at the last minute at the insistence of the White House.

Sensing congressional uneasiness, the Labor Department revised its proposed regulations in April, declaring that more workers would retain overtime eligibility than would have under the initial rules. But the alterations did not satisfy the labor unions. They asserted that the altered rule would take overtime eligibility away from as many as 6 million workers — a figure the administration said was wildly exaggerated.

As a condition of moving a rewrite of the corporate tax code (S 1637) through the Senate, Democrats won the right to offer an amendment, by Iowa's Tom Harkin, nearly identical to the one adopted the previous fall.

Fearing a vote against the president, Republican leaders offered a competing amendment. Judd Gregg of New Hampshire, chairman of the Health, Education, Labor and Pensions Committee, said his proposal would protect overtime pay eligibility for employees in 55 professions who were not expressly protected in the final rule. The Gregg amendment was meant to siphon the support of the six Republicans who voted for the Harkin amendment in 2003 — and, in fact, it was adopted without a single dissenting vote.

But senators nonetheless voted 52-47 on May 4 to adopt Harkin's amendment as well: R 5-46; D 46-1 (ND 38-0; SD 8-1); I 1-0. (*Senate vote 79, p. C-18*)

Republicans Lisa Murkowski of Alaska, Ben Nighthorse Campbell of Colorado, Lincoln Chafee of Rhode Island, Olympia J. Snowe of Maine and Arlen Specter of Pennsylvania crossed party lines to vote with all the Democrats except Zell Miller of Georgia. Senate Appropriations Chairman Ted Stevens of Alaska was the only Republican who voted with Harkin in 2003 but returned to the GOP fold this year.

The victory was short-lived, however: Conferees dropped the language from the final version of the corporate tax bill, and the overtime rules took effect Aug. 23.

98 Base Closure Delay

Rejection of an amendment, to the fiscal 2005 defense authorization bill, that would have postponed for at least two years the closure and realignment of domestic military installations scheduled for 2005.

When Congress agreed three years ago to President Bush's request for another round of military base closings and realignments, it did so on the condition that the decisions on the shutterings or mission reassignment be put off until 2005 — essentially requiring Bush to win re-election if he wanted to control the process. Ever since, a group of lawmakers from both parties has fought doggedly to modify or delay the process further.

But their campaign began collapsing after they narrowly lost a pivotal Senate vote in the spring, and the president is scheduled to name the next Base Realignment and Closure Commission in March 2005. As has happened four other times since the process was created in 1988, the commissions will review a Pentagon plan for proposed closures and draw up a final list, which takes effect unless Congress votes to reject it in its entirety. That has never come close to happening.

Opposition to additional base closures has generally been stronger in the House, where a small group of lawmakers must stand for re-election every two years in districts with economies dominated by the presence of military installations. But plenty of senators, in both parties, have similar concerns, and so the Senate votes on the topic have been close and the debates heated.

In the House, the Armed Services Committee wrote a fiscal 2005 defense authorization bill in May that would have delayed all base closings for two years, until 2007.

The next week, the Senate was called on to decide whether to go along with the House or side with the president, who was insisting on proceeding with base closures in 2005. By the narrowest of margins, they sided with Bush.

The vote came May 18 on an amendment to the Senate's defense authorization bill (S 2400) by Trent Lott, R-Miss. It would have limited the 2005 round to U.S. overseas bases and permitted no domestic closures before 2007, and then only under a new series of requirements. In a vote during which partisanship was replaced almost entirely by parochialism the amendment was rejected, 47-49: R 21-29; D 26-19 (ND 20-16, SD 6-3); I 0-1 (*Senate vote 98, p. C-18*)

Among the four senators absent that day was John Kerry

of Massachusetts, who by then had secured the Democratic presidential nomination and had explicitly endorsed a base closing delay.

The following day, the White House threatened to veto any defense authorization bill that delayed or blocked the 2005 round. The House emphatically ignored that warning however, when 259 lawmakers voted against an amendment that would have scratched the delaying language from the defense authorization bill and kept the base closing schedule on course.

The Senate considered its defense bill off and on for another five weeks before passing it June 23, but no further effort was made to challenge the 2005 base closures. Had Lott's amendment been adopted, negotiators on the conference agreement would have been hard-pressed to find a way not to delay the base closing round, setting up what might have been the first veto of Bush's presidency. Instead, the House language was dropped.

154 Partisan Power Struggle

Defeat of an effort to limit debate on legislation to curb class action litigation. Backers on both sides chose to kill the measure rather than cede legislative prerogatives to the opposing party.

Republicans lost their best chance to enact business-backed legislation to overhaul the civil litigation system when a cloture vote that would have sped passage of the bill (S 2062) failed this summer.

The ballot was the pivotal test of each party's ability to use Senate rules to advance its own election-year legislative agenda. By stalling the bill, the minority Democrats demonstrated that they would not be steamrolled, even though many of them supported the bill, and the majority Republicans subsequently arranged for the Democrats to offer some of their amendments as a price for moving high-profile legislation.

The bill would have shifted more class action lawsuits from state to federal courts, which advocates say would reduce the number of suits moved to jurisdictions where enormous financial judgments are commonplace.

By the time the measure reached the Senate floor, it had the support of all 51 Republicans and a dozen Democrats — taken together, more than enough senators to invoke cloture and limit debate. But the bill's breadth of support made it a magnet for unrelated amendments as the legislative year wound down. Majority Leader Bill Frist, R-Tenn., insisted that adding provisions that were not germane to the bill would consume too much of the Senate's limited time and make it harder to push the bill through a conference with the House.

Minority Leader Tom Daschle, D-S.D., saw matters entirely differently. He and other Democrats wanted to use the debate on the bill to highlight their election-year priorities, proposing amendments to raise the minimum wage, extend federal unemployment insurance and block administration-backed Labor Department rules on overtime pay. "We're running out of time," Daschle said. "We have to use the vehicles afforded to us."

Rather than permit votes on the Democratic amendments, Frist used his prerogative as majority leader to "fill

the amendment tree" — introducing enough amendments of his own to preclude any others from being offered.

The maneuver drew protests from some Republicans as well as the Democrats. Frist's last hope was a motion to invoke cloture, thereby limiting the debate to amendments germane to civil litigation. Frist pulled the bill off the floor altogether when his cloture motion fell 16 votes short of the supermajority required. The vote was 44-43: R 42-3; D 2-39 (ND 1-32, SD 1-7); I 0-1. (*Senate vote 154, p. C-19*)

Ten of the 12 Democratic supporters of the bill stuck with their party leader on this test of wills: Evan Bayh of Indiana, Jeff Bingaman of New Mexico, Maria Cantwell of Washington, Thomas R. Carper of Delaware, Christopher J. Dodd of Connecticut, Dianne Feinstein of California, Herb Kohl of Wisconsin, Mary L. Landrieu of Louisiana, Blanche Lincoln of Arkansas and Charles E. Schumer of New York. The only Democrats who broke with Daschle were Ben Nelson of Nebraska and the perpetually iconoclastic Zell Miller of Georgia.

At the same time, three Republicans who wanted to amend the bill with election-year priorities of their own broke with Frist: Larry E. Craig of Idaho, Richard C. Shelby of Alabama and John McCain of Arizona.

The vote served as an exclamation point on the Democratic Caucus' decision to stand behind Daschle, even in the face of withering campaign season criticism of the minority leader as an unalloyed "obstructionist" — a line of political attack that helped seal Daschle's defeat in his bid for a fourth term on Nov. 2.

155 Gay Marriage Prohibition

Defeat of an effort to limit debate, and thereby advance to a final vote, a proposed amendment to the Constitution banning same-sex marriages.

A pair of judicial rulings last year left social conservatives convinced that the Supreme Court would soon overturn a 1996 statute (PL 104-199) that defined marriage under federal law as "the union of a man and a woman." Their intense efforts to make gay marriage one of the defining political issues of the day led to the first-ever congressional votes on a proposed constitutional amendment to prohibit marriage of homosexual couples. But the initial test vote on the proposal, in the Senate in July, suggested that the conservatives were far short of the support they need to substantively advance their quest.

In June 2003, the Supreme Court declared unconstitutional a Texas law outlawing sodomy. Five months later, the Massachusetts Supreme Judicial Court ruled that gay people had the same right to be married under that state's constitution as straight people.

The rulings revived what had appeared to be a moribund campaign to make the definition of marriage part of the Constitution. Under intense pressure from social conservatives to make the issue a defining election-year theme, Republican leaders agreed to put it at the top of the crowded summertime legislative agenda.

On July 12, a dozen days before the opening of the Democratic National Convention in Boston, Majority Leader Bill Frist, R-Tenn., tried to call up a resolution (S J Res 40) by Wayne Allard, R-Colo., proposing a constitutional amendment defining marriage as the union of a man and a woman and specifying that neither the U.S. Constitution nor any state constitution sanctions marriages that do not comply with that definition.

Supporters cast themselves as defenders of marriage — and, by extension, allies of children and families — not as opponents of gay rights. They argued that without a constitutional amendment, "activist" judges would hijack the democratic process and legalize gay marriage everywhere. Opponents said the institution of marriage was not threatened, that the Constitution was the wrong place to have the debate over the definition of marriage, and that the debate was an unnecessary sideshow at a time when Congress should be focused on more immediate domestic and foreign policy matters.

When Republicans could not agree among themselves on the ideal language, Frist proposed votes on two versions: the one by Allard and another without the language barring judges from ruling that gays have the right to marry. When Democrats resisted, Frist moved to invoke cloture, and thereby limit debate, on his motion to consider the measure. The debate was set aside after his motion was rejected, 48-50: R 45-6; D 3-43 (ND 2-36, SD 1-7); I 0-1. (*Senate vote 155, p. C-19*)

The roster of 48 "yea" votes was a dozen short of the 60 needed to overcome a filibuster — but 19 short of the two-thirds majority needed to assure Senate endorsement of a constitutional change. Six moderate Republicans voted against Frist; only three Democrats voted with him. The two missing senators were the party's 2004 national ticket: John Kerry of Massachusetts and John Edwards of North Carolina.

In September, the House fell 49 votes short of adopting a companion resolution (H J Res 106). (*Key House vote, p. C-16*)

But by then the Senate had effectively killed the effort for the 108th Congress. Nonetheless, social conservatives say the two votes served as opening salvos, and political baselines, for what they predict will be a lengthy but ultimately successful campaign to change the Constitution.

168 Privatization of Federal Jobs

Adoption of an amendment, to a fiscal 2005 appropriations bill, barring the Bush administration from contracting with businesses for work now performed by the Bureau of Citizenship and Immigration Services.

One of President Bush's few policies that has run into significant opposition from his own party in Congress is his aspiration to turn over to private enterprise more work now performed by federal employees. When Republicans with large numbers of government workers as constituents once again sided with Democrats to oppose such privatization, the administration this fall quietly backed away from one narrow but symbolically important aspect of its plan.

In December 2003, the Homeland Security Department set in motion a competition that could have led to the privatization of more than 1,100 immigration services jobs — a relatively small slice of the estimated 23,000 positions that the ad-

ministration was considering for privatization at the time.

Before long, though, the struggle between the employees of the department's Citizenship and Immigration Services bureau and the companies that might bid for their jobs spilled over into debate on the fiscal 2005 Homeland Security funding measure (HR 4567).

In June, the House voted by a wide margin, 242-163, to adopt an amendment to the bill preventing the department from carrying out its plans to contract-out the jobs. Some of the 49 Republicans in the majority had immigration services workers as constituents; others represented districts where labor unions are a potent political force.

The Office of Management and Budget warned the Senate against following the House lead, saying the president's advisers would recommend he veto the spending bill if it restricted the administration's competitive sourcing efforts — which it said could save $1 billion over time.

But when Patrick J. Leahy, D-Vt., offered an amendment later that day mirroring the House language — he argued that the work, which included citizenship application processing, was too sensitive to be left to the private sector — the Senate voted narrowly to rebuff the president. The amendment was adopted, 49-47: R 5-46; D 43-1 (ND 36-0, SD 7-1); I 1-0. (*Senate vote 168, p. C-19*)

With the support of Pennsylvania's Arlen Specter, one of the most pro-labor Republicans in the Senate, the language was retained in the conference agreement on the bill completed Oct. 8. But, almost simultaneously, Homeland Security Secretary Tom Ridge had a letter delivered to the conferees announcing that he was canceling the jobs competition on his own authority. The Bush veto threat thereby became moot, and the president signed the bill (PL 108-334) on Oct. 18.

188 Extending Tax Cuts for the Middle Class

Clearing of a bill to extend several tax cuts enacted earlier in the decade to benefit middle-income taxpayers, although without any offsets and at a time of deepening deficits.

Republicans began the year with the idea of extending many of the tax breaks pushed into law by President Bush as part of a package protected under special budgetary rules limiting Senate debate. The demands by deficit hawks in both parties that those tax cut extensions be scaled back in order to reduce their cost won the day.

But it became apparent — and a lopsided Senate vote in September demonstrated conclusively — that some of the Bush tax cuts enjoyed a broad-based appeal in Congress this election year, despite a record federal budget deficit.

After hope of significant tax cuts collapsed with the death of the annual budget resolution (S Con Res 95), Republicans began considering a Senate floor strategy intended to benefit the GOP during the campaign season while creating a predicament for the Democrats — particularly their presidential candidate, John Kerry. To pay for some of his campaign initiatives, the Massachusetts senator advocated the repeal of many of the 2001 and 2003 tax cuts (PL 107-16, PL 108-27) for families annually earning more than $200,000.

The Republicans' strategy also promised to test the resolve of their own deficit hawks, especially in the Senate,

who had worked with the Democrats to block tax cuts they regarded as overly generous budget-busters.

At the start of the summer, the White House urged senior Republicans to move an extension of popular tax cuts in July. A midsummer vote would have forced Kerry, vice presidential candidate John Edwards of North Carolina and other Democrats to choose whether to support or oppose tax breaks right before the party's national convention.

Just before the summer recess, the White House spurned a deal on a $75 billion short-term extension of tax breaks nearly worked out by Senate Finance Committee Chairman Charles E. Grassley, R-Iowa. The deal had the backing of Minority Leader Tom Daschle, who was eager to bend on taxes while he waged his intense, and ultimately unsuccessful, bid for election to a fourth Senate term from South Dakota. And Kerry and Edwards were poised to line up behind Daschle. But the White House instead pushed for action in September on a longer extension of tax breaks.

The addition of language accelerating a scheduled increase in the refundable child tax credit helped win the support of some wavering Democratic moderates. but as the vote on the final measure (HR 1308) approached, just weeks before members were headed home to campaign, Democratic opposition collapsed altogether. Just before the roll was called Sept. 23, Kerry was on the campaign trail in Pennsylvania, where he announced his endorsement of the package as a means to help families "squeezed by the weak Bush economy."

In the end, the only dissent came from a trio of deficit hawks who objected to the measure's cost, $146 billion over 10 years, and criticized the lack of offsets to pay for it. The Senate cleared the bill by a vote of 92-3: R 49-2; D 42-1 (ND 35-0 SD 7-1): I 1-0. (*Senate vote 188, p. C-19*)

Signed into law Oct. 4 (PL 108-311), the measure extended the $1,000 per-child tax credit through 2009, the upper limit for the 10 percent income tax bracket through 2010 and tax breaks for married couples through 2008. It also extended for one year the existing income exemptions from the alternative minimum tax and extended the research and development tax credit through 2005.

199 Intelligence-Gathering Overhaul

Passage of legislation to implement most recommendations of the independent Sept. 11 commission for reorganizing the 15 U.S. intelligence agencies under a new national intelligence director.

In a rare display of bipartisan cooperation just one month before a bitterly contested presidential election, the Senate voted overwhelmingly for legislation to reorganize the nation's intelligence system along the lines proposed by an independent commission that investigated all manner of government failings in advance of the Sept. 11, 2001, terrorist attacks. The Pentagon did not like the bill, House Republican leaders pushed for a different approach and President Bush appeared ambivalent about the entire plan until late in the fall. But during the ensuing two months, the nearly unanimous support for the initial Senate measure would dictate the terms for the most important law enacted during the year.

Plenty of senators had reservations about the measure

(S 2845) when it came to the floor, but deft political maneuvering by the two moderates who were its main sponsors — Republican Susan Collins of Maine and Democrat Joseph I. Lieberman of Connecticut — helped engineer passage by 96-2 on Oct. 6: R 51-0; D 44-2 (ND 37-1, SD 7-1); I 1-0. (*Senate vote 199, p. C-19*)

Collins and Lieberman, the chairwoman and ranking Democrat on the Governmental Affairs Committee, essentially adopted the idea of a powerful national intelligence director and a national counterterrorism center that were recommended by the Sept. 11 commission, which Congress had created a year after the attacks. The two worked in tandem to overcome the concerns of Armed Services and Appropriations committee members who feared they would lose control of their leverage over the 15-agency, $40 billion intelligence system.

On the floor, the bill initially came under intense criticism from some of the most powerful figures in the Senate, among them Appropriations Chairman Ted Stevens, R-Alaska, Armed Services Chairman John W. Warner, R-Va., and Robert C. Byrd, D-W.Va., the ranking member on Appropriations.

But most senators appeared to agree that sticking close to the commission's recommendations was the best course, and Collins and Lieberman did not lose a single roll call on proposed amendments to their bill; either they engineered the defeat of the proposals they opposed, or they worked to modify amendments before accepting them. Both Byrd and Stevens proposed amendments that would have curtailed the powers of the proposed new national intelligence director, and both proposals were tabled, or killed, by comfortable margins.

That contrasted with the lengthy, partisan debate in the House, where Republican leaders demanded a weaker national intelligence director but more sweeping immigration controls. It took two months of bargaining, and eventually intense White House involvement, before the House largely gave in and agreed to send Bush a package written largely on the Senate's terms. (*Key House vote, p. C-17*)

The conference was agonizing. The Collins-Lieberman version of the legislation faced the same reservations that some senators had expressed: A powerful national intelligence director might disrupt the flow of military intelligence to battlefield commanders — 80 percent of the intelligence budget is now controlled by the Pentagon — and the bill would fail to make important safeguards unless it included strong measures against illegal immigration. A final agreement was not reached until the chairman of the Joint Chiefs of Staff, Gen. Richard B. Myers of the Air Force, withdrew his objections to a compromise plan and the president leaned on House leaders to close the deal.

211 Corporate Tax Overhaul

Clearing of legislation to revamp the taxation of business — by eliminating a tax break for exporters and providing $137 billion in tax cuts for corporations in the next decade — and authorize a $10 billion tobacco buyout.

Business groups had watched and waited through the first three years of the Bush administration while the president won $1.7 trillion in tax cuts targeted mainly to individuals.

Republican leaders repeatedly assured them that they would get their turn. It came late on the last day of the regular session, when, after a weekend of filibusters and side deals, the Senate cleared the corporate tax bill. The measure (HR 4520 — PL 108-357), which is expected to reduce business taxes by $137 billion over 10 years, is the biggest corporate tax overhaul since 1986.

The Senate had enthusiastically embraced its own version of the legislation, passing it 92-5 in May. That bill included the repeal of the $5 billion-a-year export subsidy — it was the desire to end international sanctions against U.S. goods triggered by the subsidy that created the need for the bill in the first place — and replaced it with $167 billion in business tax breaks. But to get it through the Senate, GOP leaders also included enough revenue-raising provisions and accounting maneuvers to declare that the entire cost had been offset.

In assembling the final version of the bill, House Ways and Means Chairman Bill Thomas, R-Calif., worked with lawmakers in both chambers to see what they would need to support the final product. He also managed to find ways to offset the cost — including shifting some expensive tax cuts to the middle class tax bill also moving toward enactment — without losing House conservatives who viewed such provisions as tax increases.

The final package also included a $10 billion buyout of tobacco farmers needed to secure the votes of Southerners in the House. But it did not include any new federal regulation of tobacco products, which had been viewed as a prerequisite for getting the buyout through the Senate.

Indeed, the Senate had made that point to the House in July by reopening its version of the bill and adding the buyout paired with tobacco regulation. Such regulation was unacceptable to House Majority Leader Tom DeLay, R-Texas, however, and Thomas calculated that he could leave it out and use the billions of dollars in sweeteners added to the legislation to move it through the House and then win at least the 60 votes needed to overcome any Senate filibusters and get the final package on the president's desk. That gamble paid off with ease in the House, which adopted the conference report overwhelmingly. (*Key House vote, p. C-16*)

And it did the trick in the Senate as well, although not before a weekend session of lengthy floor speeches during which disgruntled senators extracted even a few more symbolic concessions. Tom Harkin, D-Iowa, won voice vote passage of separate bills calling for tobacco regulation (S 2974) and barring implementation of Labor Department rules on overtime (S 2975).

To accommodate Mary L. Landrieu, D-La., the leadership agreed to attach to a House-passed bill (HR 1779), a tax credit for employers of reservists and National Guardsmen deployed in Iraq or Afghanistan. All of those bills died at the end of the session.

With all the haggling done, the Senate cleared the bill on a bipartisan a vote of 69-17: R 43-3; D 25-14 (ND 20-14, SD 5-0) I 1-0. (*Senate vote 211, p. C-19*)

The centerpiece was a $77 billion tax break on manufacturing income. The legislation also provided $43 billion in tax cuts on the overseas profits of U.S. multinationals, aimed at enhancing their competitive position against foreign rivals. About $14 billion in tax breaks went to a long list of beneficiaries, from fishermen to bow and arrow makers.

HOUSE
KEY VOTES

18 Unemployment Benefits Extension

Adoption of an amendment, to legislation reauthorizing an anti-poverty program, to revive a program of federal benefits for jobless people who have exhausted their unemployment insurance aid from the states.

Democrats expected that they could begin incubating a potent campaign issue at the start of the year, after the Republican-run Congress declined to renew a supplemental unemployment insurance program (PL 108-26) that expired at the end of 2003. Uneasiness about the state of the economic recovery was not confined to Democrats. Some Republicans from the industrial Midwest worried about the decline of manufacturing for their constituents.

House GOP leaders, however, would not permit a vote on a bill to continue the federal benefits, fearing that the measure would pass and send a skeptical message about the economy while President Bush was gearing up his re-election campaign. The expired program, started when the Sept. 11, 2001, terrorist attacks fueled a sharp economic downturn, had provided 13 extra weeks of benefits for those who had exhausted their 26 weeks of state benefits.

But George Miller of California, the ranking Democrat on the Education and the Workforce Committee, spotted an opportunity in early February, when a bill to reauthorize the Community Services Block Grant program (HR 3030) came to the floor under ground rules that allowed the offering of amendments without restriction. Signaling one of the year's principal Democratic legislative strategies — seeking to force the GOP to cast votes on proposals to boost the lot of the working class — Miller offered an amendment to extend the federal unemployment benefits for six months. (The amendment also would have created a duplicate unemployment insurance program in the Department of Health and Human Services, which administers Community Service Block Grants. The Labor Department normally administers unemployment insurance.)

Republican leaders opposed the proposal, arguing that it was more about scoring political points than helping the unemployed. John A. Boehner, R-Ohio, chairman of the Education and the Workforce Committee, noted that the amendment would authorize the program without appropriate any money for it.

But a majority of lawmakers — every Democrat on the House floor Feb. 4 and one-sixth of the Republican caucus — concluded that it was unwise to vote against generous federal unemployment aid at the outset of an election year. Thirty-nine Republicans broke ranks with the GOP leadership in what amounted to a rebuke of their decision to let the program expire. As a result, the amendment was adopted with ease, 227-179: R 39-179; D 187-0 (ND 132-0; SD 55-0); I 1-0. (*House vote 18, p. C-20*)

The underlying bill passed by voice vote. The Senate passed its version of the community services bill later in February, but the measure went no further.

Most Republicans who supported the Miller amendment represented states that had lost manufacturing jobs. Others were moderates or the holders of politically competitive seats. The vote embarrassed the leadership and demonstrated the level of House support for extending jobless benefits. As a result, Democrats were not allowed to repeat it for the rest of the year.

Asked why GOP leaders permitted the vote on Miller's amendment, John Feehery, the chief spokesman for Speaker J. Dennis Hastert, R-Ill., said, "That's a question a lot of us are asking ourselves."

64 Success of the War in Iraq

Adoption of a resolution praising the military 'liberation' of Iraq one year earlier and declaring that the United States and the world were made safer by the removal of Saddam Hussein from power.

One year after the U.S.-led military coalition toppled Saddam Hussein from power, Republicans commemorated the anniversary by writing a resolution — without any Democratic input — and using its adoption by the House to gain an important campaign season advantage.

At a time when the Democratic presidential candidate, Sen. John Kerry of Massachusetts, appeared ambivalent about the war in Iraq, Republicans were able to word the resolution (H Res 557) in such a way that a narrow majority of House Democrats concluded they were obliged to support it. The vote highlighted the party's mixed feelings and messages about the war, making it all the more difficult for Democrats to use the conduct of the campaign as a defining issue against President Bush and congressional Republicans. In effect, the vote helped to neutralize the war as an issue for the climactic eight months of the election year.

The resolution was brought to the floor March 17, the first anniversary of Bush's ultimatum to Saddam. At the resolution's core was a series of statements about the Iraqi dictator's barbaric regime — a human rights argument that had been only tangential to the president's rationale for invading Iraq. The resolution said nothing about the weapons of mass destruction that had been a central argument in the administration's case for war but had never been found.

The resolution affirmed that "the United States and the world have been made safer with the removal of Saddam Hussein and his regime from power in Iraq," and acclaimed the military performance that accomplished it. It also commended the Iraqi people for their courage during Saddam's reign and their adoption of an interim constitution.

The deftly written set of platitudes was something of a political trap for the Democrats, and a narrow majority of them decided it was better to embrace the language than to oppose it. As a consequence, the House adopted the resolu-

tion by a resounding 327-93: R 222-2 D 105-90 (ND 64-76, SD 41-14); I 0-1. *(House vote 64, p. C-20)*

Thirty-six of the Democrats who in 2002 voted against the law (PL 107-243) authorizing the use of force against Iraq voted in favor of the congratulatory resolution. Nine went the other way. "The only mushroom cloud resulting from the war in Iraq is that represented by the Bush administration's barrage of deception and lies," said Robert Wexler of Florida, one of those nine.

The floor debate was a microcosm of the nation's argument with itself over Iraq. Democrats tried without success to change the subject from human rights to other issues, principally the failure to find doomsday weapons in Iraq and the human and fiscal costs of the war.

"Obviously, there's one less thug in the world," said Democrat Gene Taylor of Mississippi. "But are we any safer? As a member of the Armed Services Committee, I can't say that we are. I wish I could, but I can't."

Majority Leader Tom DeLay, R-Texas, was quick to respond, asking: "What would you have us do — wait until Saddam proved that he had nuclear weapons by detonating one in New York City or wait like we waited for al Qaeda to prove that they really meant business on Sept. 11, 2001?"

Added Speaker J. Dennis Hastert, R-Ill., "When we made that decision to move into Iraq, we all made decisions based on the information we had before us, information that a previous president had. It was the best information that we could bring before us. I do not think anybody in this chamber or in this town tried to deceive anybody on that information."

114 Surface Transportation Spending

Passage of a bill that would authorize $283.2 billion in surface transportation spending during the next six years, 11 percent more than the Bush administration requested.

The vote in the House this spring for a bill to reauthorize surface transportation programs at generous levels marked a collision of three potent — and ultimately irreconcilable — political forces. There was the White House, which had a strong desire to hold down federal spending as President Bush campaigned for a second term as a fiscal conservative. There was the House GOP leadership, which had its own hopes of shielding the president from an embarrassing campaign season showdown with rank-and-file members of his own party. And there were those very Republican lawmakers, in re-election races of their own from coast to coast, whose desire was to bring home as much spending as possible for local highway and public transit projects before Election Day.

In that clash, there were no clear winners. The chairman of the House Transportation and Infrastructure Committee, Alaska Republican Don Young, led an overwhelming majority of House members April 2 in defying a strongly worded White House veto threat and passing a reauthorization bill (HR 3550) that far exceeded the bottom line set by the president. The vote was a bipartisan 357-65: R 162-59; D 194-6 (ND 144-1, SD 50-5); I 1-0. *(House vote 114, p. C-20)*

The enormous majority appeared to guarantee that any veto would easily be overridden by Congress, especially because seven weeks earlier the Senate had voted by an even more lopsided margin, 76-21, to pass a highway bill (S 1072) that would have spent even more generously than the House bill. *(Key Senate vote, p. C-4)*

Rather than force Bush to issue the first veto of his presidency, however, the House and Senate votes signaled the death knell for a long-term surface transportation policy bill in the 108th Congress. Negotiators never came close to agreeing on a funding formula or spending level, and as a consequence thousands of road projects that lawmakers had hoped to see started during the summer of 2004 were delayed.

The House bill was far less ambitious than what Young had introduced: a $375 billion, six-year bill that would have guaranteed states at least 95 cents of each gasoline tax dollar they sent to the Highway Trust Fund for road projects. Young said he based the funding level on a 2002 Department of Transportation assessment of the money needed to help states maintain and make needed improvements in the nation's highway network and to aid increasingly stressed transit systems.

But the bill immediately ran afoul of the White House because Young proposed to increase the federal gasoline tax by about 5 cents a gallon to help cover the cost. Speaker J. Dennis Hastert, R-Ill., and Majority Leader Tom DeLay, R-Texas, stood shoulder-to-shoulder with the administration's no-tax-increase pledge, and Young was forced to back down.

Without that additional revenue — and with the administration publicly refusing to support any bill larger than its own $256 billion proposal — Young reported out of his committee a bill whittled down to $283.2 billion. But that amount was as far as Young's committee members would budge; lawmakers made it clear they feared the political fallout from constituents more than from the White House.

To put on record the committee's distaste for being backed into a corner, Young put his original $375 billion bill to a symbolic voice vote in committee. It was approved without a dissenting vote. Later, Young took to the House floor and said the smaller version was not the bill he wanted, but it was the best bill possible under the circumstances.

318 Limitations on Federal Spending

Defeat of legislation that would have set caps on discretionary spending during the next two fiscal years and required that mandatory spending increases be matched by revenue increases or offsetting reductions in other spending.

It was not the House Republican leadership's idea to force a debate this summer on a bill to revive statutory caps on appropriations and curb increases in entitlement programs. GOP leaders do not like to showcase internal party divisions or schedule legislation that goes down in flames.

But that is exactly what happened during a ramshackle floor debate on legislation (HR 4663) that would have imposed a two-year appropriations cap on discretionary spending and instituted a "pay-as-you-go" requirement on new mandatory spending — although it was noticeably silent on the question of offsets for new tax cuts.

The measure came to the floor because a small band of GOP fiscal conservatives, led by Gil Gutknecht of Minnesota, demanded the debate as their price for supporting the fiscal 2005 congressional budget resolution

(S Con Res 95). The debate was intended to highlight Republicans' zeal to clamp down on spending, and to be a forum for votes on a variety of plans to "reform" the maligned congressional budget process.

Instead, the eight-hour debate on the measure — followed by its resounding defeat — was a reminder of the clout of the Appropriations panel and the lasting strength of its allies in both parties in battles against GOP spending conservatives. When the bill finally came to a vote shortly after midnight June 25, two out of three Republicans voted against it, as did every Democrat. The vote defeating the bill was 146-268: R 146-72; D 0-195 (ND 0-142, SD 0-53); I 0-1. (*House vote 318, p. C-20*)

The legislation was intended to require Congress to stick to its budget or risk across-the-board spending cuts. It would have revived statutory limits on appropriations and a pay-as-you-go law requiring offsetting spending cuts or new revenue in any legislation to increase mandatory spending.

C.W. Bill Young, R-Fla., chairman of Appropriations, led the charge against the bill, describing the proposed spending caps as an encroachment on Congress' power of the purse because the president would have a say in setting the limits.

Congress had endorsed statutory spending caps on three separate occasions — in 1990, 1993 and 1997 — which led some lawmakers to question why appropriators were so dead set against them now. "Methinks you doth protest just a little too much," Jim Nussle, R-Iowa, the Budget Committee chairman and the bill's sponsor, chided the appropriators.

For their part, Democrats unified against the bill for two reasons. They chastised the idea of not reviving pay-as-you-go requirements for tax cuts, and they considered the proposed lid on appropriations too tight.

Relatively little of the debate preceding the vote, however, focused on Nussle's bill. Instead, the discussion was dominated by a panoply of ideas on how to improve the budget process, many of which had been debated and rejected in previous years. The debate had a Keystone Kops quality to it. Because most of the sponsors of the numerous amendments had only five minutes — or at most 15 minutes — to make their case, it was plain that the debate was not a serious attempt to rewrite the Budget Act (PL 93-344), which was enacted in 1974 and has been amended several times.

Not a single substantive amendment was adopted, and, if anything, the votes on the amendments seemed to demonstrate that regardless of the merits, many lawmakers were disinclined to support anything on such a complex topic. Many privately said the entire exercise was a waste of time.

339 | Limits on Federal Search Powers

Rejection, on a tie vote, of an amendment to a fiscal 2005 appropriations bill that would have prevented the Justice Department from obtaining library and bookseller records as part of investigations of suspected terrorists.

Lawmakers sensitive to the protection of civil liberties — and they come from both ends of the ideological spectrum — have expressed deepening concern about many of the provisions of the three-year-old counterterrorism law known as the USA Patriot Act (PL 107-56). One of the provisions

they dislike the most permits federal law enforcement officers conducting terrorism investigations to obtain search warrants for "any tangible thing" without having to offer a detailed rationale for the search.

During the summer the House came within a hair's breadth of voting to effectively repeal that new power altogether. Although the effort did not quite succeed, the vote revealed that the libertarian wing of the Republican Party will have the power to combine with Democrats to reshape the Patriot Act when it comes up for reauthorization in the 109th Congress.

The American Civil Liberties Union used television advertising during the 2004 campaign season to advocate changes in the law, which they view as overly broad and invasive. Their opportunity to effect a change came on July 8, when the House took up the fiscal 2005 spending package (HR 4754) for the Justice Department. Bernard Sanders of Vermont, the one independent in the House, proposed an amendment that would have prohibited the use of funds authorized by the Foreign Intelligence Surveillance Act (PL 95-511) to acquire library circulation records, library or bookstore patron lists, Internet records or records of book purchases — the very sorts of "tangible things" the law has made it relatively easy for FBI agents to acquire.

As the roll call vote began, the number of votes in the "yea" column steadily ticked upward. Before the electronic voting system's clock had ticked down to zero, the tally briefly stood at 219-200 in favor of the amendment.

But then the Republican leadership, sensing an unexpected election-year embarrassment for President Bush in the making, stepped up its "whipping" efforts to defeat the proposal. As angry Democrats demanded "regular order" and chanted "shame, shame, shame," Republicans held the vote open for 30 minutes — double the customary time for a House floor vote, and long enough to convince eight Republicans and one Democrat to switch their votes to "nay." As soon as the tally became a tie, the presiding officer, Doc Hastings, R-Wash., gaveled the voting to an end; under the rules, the Sanders amendment was rejected on that 210-210 tie: R 18-206; D 191-4 (ND 142-2, SD 49-2); I 1-0. (*House vote 339, p. C-20*)

Several lawmakers who changed their votes said they were swayed not by leadership threats or promises, but by a letter from a Justice Department official that Frank R. Wolf, R-Va., circulated on the floor while the voting was under way. The letter, to Judiciary Committee Chairman F. James Sensenbrenner Jr., R-Wis., the sponsor of the Patriot Act, declared that the provision Sanders had targeted was essential. No information was offered on how often library or book sales information has been used or whether it has played a role in successful prosecutions.

Sanders' amendment would not necessarily have become law had it been adopted by the House. Bush had threatened to veto the legislation if it repealed any part of the Patriot Act, so majority Republicans probably would have stripped the language before the bill became law.

Nonetheless, the Sanders amendment vote was an important gauge of Republican unease with some Patriot Act provisions. Eighteen GOP lawmakers, or 8 percent of those voting that day, went against the president's position — even after the leadership arm-twisting.

452 Mexican Identification Cards

Adoption of an amendment, to the fiscal 2005 Transportation-Treasury spending bill, to preserve Bush administration regulations designed to make it easier for Mexicans residing in the United States to send money to their home country.

Immigration policy has become one of the most divisive issues within the GOP, and those differences were laid bare during House debate in September on what the federal government's posture should be toward ID cards that the Mexican government issues to its citizens living in the United States.

President Bush and some members of his party support liberalization of immigration laws as an avenue toward growing the economy, something most Democrats have long advocated. At the start of the year, the president proposed giving millions of undocumented workers in the United States a chance to legalize their status temporarily with guest worker visas.

But the proposal went nowhere — thwarted by many other Republicans, including influential members of Congress from border states such as Tom DeLay of Texas, the House majority leader. In their view, the short-term security risks, and the uncertain long-term economic effects, of illegal immigration far outweigh any benefits to relaxing the borders.

The "matricula consular" — or consular registration — cards issued by Mexican consulates to the country's citizens living in the United States are increasingly accepted by banks and other businesses, as well as by federal government agencies, as a valid form of ID. The cards include the holder's name, date and place of birth, U.S. address and photograph.

Critics say that making the cards valid for so many purposes effectively condones and perhaps encourages illegal immigration — partly, they say, because the document can be readily forged by a Mexican who is in this country illegally.

In July, the House Appropriations Committee approved language in its fiscal 2005 Transportation-Treasury spending bill (HR 5025) that would have reversed Bush administration policy and essentially prohibited banks from accepting the matricula cards as identification by those hoping to open a bank account, obtain a mortgage or other financial services.

Texas Republican John Culberson, who wrote the provision, said that state law enforcement agencies as well as officials of the Justice and Homeland Security departments had described the ID cards to him as an unjustified security risk. DeLay backed his argument.

Many security-conscious Republicans bought that argument, but in the end there were not enough of them willing to go against the White House and the banking industry, both of which lobbied intensely to leave the policy alone.

Bankers, who see immigrants as a lucrative market — Latin American immigrants send billions of dollars in remittances to families back home each year, in addition to their other banking in the United States — argued that the Culberson provision would force many consumers to use underground, unregulated financial services.

The Treasury contended that the ID cards actually enhance homeland security because they allow banks and law enforcement agents to keep an accurate watch on where money is flowing.

The combination of Bush administration and bank sup-port proved too strong for the opponents of the cards. Ohio Republican Michael G. Oxley, chairman of the Financial Services Committee, pushed an amendment to delete Culberson's provision, and it was adopted on a bipartisan vote of 222-177: R 49-161; D 172-16 (ND 128-7, SD 44-9); I 1-0. (*House vote 452, p. C-22*)

DeLay bucked the White House and was joined by three out of four Republicans; they were also joined by 16 Democrats, most of whom are conservative. The majority was made up by the remaining Democrats and 49 Republicans — including Majority Whip Roy Blunt of Missouri; his chief deputy, Eric Cantor of Virginia, and Ohio's Deborah Pryce, chairwoman of the GOP Conference.

Later in the fall, language to restrict the effectiveness of the matricula cards was inserted in the House version of the intelligence overhaul bill (S 2845), but the language was abandoned in conference negotiations.

472 Extending Tax Cuts for the Middle Class

Final passage of a bill extending several tax cuts enacted earlier in the decade to benefit middle-income taxpayers, although without offsets and at a time of deepening deficits.

By the spring, it became clear that disagreement within the Republican ranks over fiscal policy would make it impossible to write a budget resolution this year — meaning there could be no sweeping tax cut enacted under the expedited rules of reconciliation. And so, as their second choice, House GOP leaders decided to make election-year political life more difficult for the Democrats, by daring them to oppose a series of bills to extend — without revenue-raising offsets — several of this decade's more popular tax cuts beyond their scheduled expirations at the end of the year.

As it turned out, the repeated votes quickly became a wedge issue within the Democratic ranks. The leaders of the minority caucus came out against the legislation, deriding the absence of offsets as a recipe for a long-term deficit disaster. But many rank-and-file members of the party, fearing the potential wrath of their constituents, openly questioned the idea of focusing Democratic campaign season attention on the deepening deficit. Instead, they said, their party should be joining the cause of tax relief as long as it was confined to those of low and modest incomes — part of the Democratic Party's base of electoral support.

Republicans quickly recognized that they could exploit the split in order to extend three expiring tax breaks for families: the $1,000 per-child tax credit, tax breaks for married couples and the expanded 10 percent tax bracket. At the insistence of President Bush, they wrote a bill to preserve those breaks for four to six years, more than twice as long as congressional Republicans initially sought.

And, to help guarantee solid bipartisan support, the package was expanded to incorporate some items on the Democratic wish list, including an acceleration of the scheduled expansion of the refundable version of the child tax credit and a more generous version of that tax break for families of soldiers in combat. Including those provisions prompted two of the most senior Democrats on the Ways and Means Committee, Charles B. Rangel of New York and Sander M. Levin

of Michigan, to break with their leadership and back the bill.

The Democratic leaders continued to argue that the bill, by deepening the deficit, would do more harm than good to middle class families in the long run. But they also made clear that rank-and-file members were free to support it if doing so would help their campaigns. Given that choice six weeks before Election Day, Democrats backed the bill by a ratio of nearly 2-to-1, and the vote Sept. 23 to adopt the conference agreement was a resounding 339-65: R 213-0; D 125-65 (ND 83-57, SD 42-8); I 1-0. (*House vote 472, p. C-22*)

Among those voting for the measure were all five of the Texas Democrats facing tough races for re-election as a consequence of the state's redistricting at the hands of the GOP — including Charles W. Stenholm, who had long ago cemented his reputation as the pre-eminent deficit hawk among House Democrats. (He lost in November, anyway.)

GOP leaders argued that while the legislation would add to the red ink in the short term, it could spur economic growth and enhance tax revenue in the long run. Not a single House Republican rejected that argument — not even the most fiscally conservative lawmakers, who were annoyed at the expansion of the refundable child credit, which they portrayed as an unbridled new entitlement, similar to welfare.

Senators cleared the bill with only three dissenting votes, and the president signed it (HR 1308 — PL 108-311) a week later. (*Key Senate vote, p. C-10*)

484 | Gay Marriage Prohibition

Defeat of a proposed amendment to the Constitution banning same-sex marriages.

Pushed hard by social and religious conservatives and with the presidential election a month away, Republican leaders decided to take a vote on a constitutional amendment to prohibit gay marriage — knowing full well that the proposal would muster nothing close to the two-thirds House majority required to advance. Nonetheless, GOP leaders took some satisfaction when the measure drew the support of a solid 55 percent of those voting. And conservative activists said they were pleased to highlight their new marquee issue close to Election Day, and to have the tally as a baseline from which to begin the next step in their campaign.

When President Bush called on Congress in February to send such an amendment to the states for ratification, House Republican leaders reacted cautiously. "We don't want to do this in haste," Majority Leader Tom DeLay of Texas said at the time.

That stance reflected both the difficulty DeLay knew he faced in trying to pass such a measure and the reluctance of many conservative Republicans to alter the Constitution.

But social conservatives kept up a steady drumbeat of demands for a House vote. They were eager for Congress to act — and for the issue to gain prominence in the 2004 campaign — after the Massachusetts Supreme Judicial Court ruled in 2003 that homosexuals have a right to marry under the state constitution and after Mayor Gavin Newsom permitted same-sex marriages in San Francisco.

The nascent campaign for a constitutional change effectively died for the year in July, when the Senate voted to keep alive a filibuster against a gay marriage constitutional amendment (S J Res 40). (*Key Senate vote, p. C-9*)

But with the presidential general election campaign in full swing, DeLay had a change of heart. He scheduled a House vote on a resolution (H J Res 106) by Marilyn Musgrave, R-Colo., that would constitutionally define marriage as "the union of a man and a woman." To do so DeLay circumvented the Judiciary Committee, whose chairman, F. James Sensenbrenner Jr., R-Wis., was cool to the proposal and had declined to hold a markup.

With 27 Republicans voting against the idea and 36 Democrats voting for it, the Sept. 30 House ballot on the resolution came up 49 votes short of the two-thirds of lawmakers present and voting necessary for passage. The tally was 227-186: R 191-27; D 36-158 (ND 7-135, SD 29-23); I 0-1 (*House vote 484, p. C-22*)

Still, the vote demonstrated substantial support in the House for such an amendment. And it threw a spotlight on the issue of gay marriage just weeks before voters in 11 states cast ballots on whether to allow gays to wed in their state.

Supporters say the amendment is needed to protect the institutions of marriage and family against homosexual couples who wished to wed, and against courts bent on allowing them to do so. "One way or another, we know the Constitution will be amended," said Steve Chabot, R-Ohio, chairman of the House Judiciary Constitution Subcommittee. "The question is: Is it done the appropriate way, or is it done by unelected, activist judges?"

Opponents derided the amendment as constitutional overkill. Democratic Rep. Jim McGovern of Massachusetts observed that every day since gays began legally marrying in his state in May, "The world kept spinning on its axis, the sun came up the next day, people went to work, sent their kids to school and cheered for the Red Sox."

509 | Corporate Tax Overhaul

Final passage of legislation to revamp the taxation of business — by eliminating a tax break for exporters and providing $137 billion in tax cuts for corporations in the next decade — and authorize a $10 billion tobacco buyout.

It took more than two years of strategizing on Capitol Hill and K Street to the House vote in October on the biggest business tax policy change in almost two decades, as lawmakers and corporations passionately disagreed on what kinds of tax cuts should replace an export tax break other countries considered unfair. Congress was under pressure to act in 2004 because the European Union had imposed retaliatory sanctions against U.S. products for keeping the prohibited export subsidy on the books.

House Ways and Means Chairman Bill Thomas, R-Calif., who drafted the final bill (HR 4520 — PL 108-357), assembled an assortment of tax cuts that largely rewarded domestic manufacturers and the overseas operations of multinational corporations. But few lawmakers supported tax breaks for both groups of businesses or thought they were good economic policy.

Many House Democrats and Republicans from manufacturing districts complained that the overseas tax breaks,

which Thomas insisted were necessary to help U.S. multinationals compete against foreign-owned rivals, would encourage more U.S. companies to move jobs overseas.

The White House, the IRS and the Congressional Budget Office all criticized the bill's $77 billion in tax cuts over a decade for manufacturing, saying that lost revenue would not help revive the ailing manufacturing sector — but would encourage new tax avoidance practices while proving impossible to administer.

Furthermore, to accommodate senators who wanted to reduce the budget deficit, the bill included language designed to crack down on tax avoidance practices in an effort to raise billions of dollars needed to offset expensive tax cuts. That drew the ire of many House conservatives who consider these offsets tantamount to tax increases. The remainder of the tax cuts were offset by a bit of budget legerdemain — moving some effective dates to lower costs — and by extending existing Customs user fees.

To attract more than enough votes to guarantee enactment, Thomas added a host of sweeteners that appealed to lawmakers seeking re-election. Some of them were extraordinarily narrow and parochial, including special tax breaks for native Alaskan whalers and the owners of NASCAR race tracks. But by far the most politically compelling, and expensive, was a $10 billion buyout of tobacco farmers. That provision drew votes across party lines throughout the South, particularly in the Carolinas and Kentucky.

Another lure was partial restoration of the federal income tax deduction for state sales taxes that was eliminated in 1986. Under this legislation, taxpayers can deduct sales taxes in lieu of local income taxes through 2005. Lawmakers of both parties from Texas, Florida, South Dakota and Tennessee were particularly drawn to this provision because these states do not levy state income taxes.

Some blasted the "Christmas tree" approach to winning votes. "This is a blatant example of corporate welfare, full of pork for the special interests," Minority Leader Nancy Pelosi, D-Calif., said during the final House debate Oct. 7. "The oinking is so loud, the Republicans can't even think straight."

Yet the vote on the measure was the most bipartisan endorsement of a tax bill during President Bush's first term. The House adopted the conference report with the support of 73 Democrats, many from the South, and despite the opposition of 16 Republicans. The tally was 280-141: R 207-16; D 73-124 (ND 25-118, SD 48-6) I 0-1. (*House vote 509, p. C-22*)

544 Intelligence-Gathering Overhaul

Final passage of a bill to implement most recommendations of the independent Sept. 11 commission for reorganizing the 15 U.S. intelligence agencies under a new national intelligence director.

House Republican leaders found the limits of their political independence as the year came to an end, when they bowed to White House pressure and accepted a face-saving compromise on legislation to restructure the nation's intelligence system.

They had held out for two months against the Senate version of the plan, which they argued might harm military intelligence and would not do enough to slow illegal immigration.

Their resistance was stiffened by the support of the chairman of the Joint Chiefs of Staff, Air Force Gen. Richard B. Myers, and the apparent ambivalence of President Bush, who had endorsed the Senate version of the legislation but spent almost none of his political capital pushing for the enactment of a compromise bill before he stood for re-election in November.

It was not until after Thanksgiving — when the White House became actively involved in pushing for a deal and Myers mitigated his earlier opposition — that House GOP leaders agreed to a final version of the bill (S 2845) that was written largely along the lines of the Senate measure. That compromise, however, proved far more popular on the floor than the initial version of the bill that the House had passed two months before. The vote Dec. 7 to adopt the conference report was a lopsided 336-75: R 152-67; D 183-8 (ND 133-7, SD 50-1); I 1-0. Solid majorities in both parties backed the deal; only the most conservative one-third of Republicans and the most liberal handful of Democrats opposed it. (*House vote 544, p. C-22*)

The initial, strong differences between House and Senate Republicans were apparent soon after the independent Sept. 11 commission — which Congress had created two years ago with a broad mandate to probe all government failings that may have precipitated the al Qaeda attacks — recommended creation of a Cabinet-level office of national intelligence to oversee the nation's 15 spy agencies and creation of a national counterterrorism center, among dozens of other steps.

By October, the Senate had passed a bill along the lines the commission recommended. (*Key Senate vote, p. C-10*)

But House GOP leaders went their own way, writing a bill that would have given a new national intelligence director more limited powers than the Senate had endorsed and included tough measures designed to reduce illegal immigration and increase law enforcement powers.

For a time, those changes came close to transforming the House debate into another partisan spat. On Oct. 8, eight Republicans split with their party and voted with the Democrats to substitute the Senate version of the bill for the House measure. The amendment narrowly failed, 203-213.

By late November, House and Senate conferees had reached an uneasy agreement on the bill, but two House committee chairman remained adamantly opposed. Armed Services Chairman Duncan Hunter, R-Calif., said the new structure might interfere with military intelligence, and Judiciary Chairman F. James Sensenbrenner Jr. R-Wis., complained that his immigration provisions were being dropped.

Unable to gain the support of a sufficient number of Republicans, even though there were enough GOP and Democratic votes to adopt the conference report, Speaker J. Dennis Hastert, R-Ill., refused to bring the measure to the floor.

The White House responded by shifting its lobbying into high gear. The president made public appeals, and Vice President Dick Cheney lobbied recalcitrant GOP lawmakers in private. Myers announced he had backed off his initial opposition to the measure — in what appeared to be a coordinated effort by the administration to weaken Hunter's position.

Rep. Christopher Shays, a moderate Republican from Connecticut, said afterward that the compromise allowed both Hunter and the White House to claim victory: "They've been trying to work it out behind the scenes so that different people can save face." ◆

Key Senate Votes 14, 15, 24, 38, 63, 64, 79, 98

	14	15	24	38	63	64	79	98
ALABAMA								
Shelby	Y	N	N	N	Y	Y	N	N
Sessions	N	Y	N	N	Y	N	N	N
ALASKA								
Stevens	Y	Y	N	N	Y	N	Y	N
Murkowski, L.	Y	Y	N	N	Y	Y	Y	Y
ARIZONA								
McCain	N	Y	N	Y	Y	Y	N	N
Kyl	N	Y	N	N	Y	N	N	N
ARKANSAS								
Lincoln	Y	N	Y	Y	Y	Y	Y	N
Pryor	Y	N	Y	Y	Y	Y	Y	Y
CALIFORNIA								
Feinstein	Y	N	Y	Y	N	Y	Y	Y
Boxer	Y	?	Y	Y	Y	Y	Y	Y
COLORADO								
Campbell	Y	Y	N	N	Y	Y	Y	Y
Allard	Y	Y	N	N	Y	N	N	N
CONNECTICUT								
Dodd	Y	N	Y	Y	N	Y	Y	Y
Lieberman	Y	N	Y	Y	N	Y	Y	N
DELAWARE								
Biden	Y	N	Y	Y	N	Y	Y	N
Carper	Y	N	Y	Y	Y	Y	Y	N
FLORIDA								
Graham	N	N	Y	Y	N	Y	Y	N
Nelson	Y	N	Y	Y	N	Y	Y	Y
GEORGIA								
Miller	N	?	N	N	Y	N	N	N
Chambliss	N	Y	N	N	Y	N	N	N
HAWAII								
Inouye	Y	N	Y	Y	N	Y	Y	?
Akaka	Y	N	Y	Y	N	Y	N	Y
IDAHO								
Craig	N	Y	N	N	Y	N	N	N
Crapo	Y	N	N	N	Y	N	N	Y
ILLINOIS								
Fitzgerald	Y	Y	Y	N	Y	Y	Y	N
Durbin	Y	N	Y	Y	N	Y	Y	N
INDIANA								
Lugar	Y	Y	Y	N	Y	Y	N	N
Bayh	Y	N	Y	Y	N	Y	Y	Y
IOWA								
Grassley	Y	Y	N	N	Y	Y	N	N
Harkin	Y	N	Y	Y	N	Y	N	Y
KANSAS								
Brownback	N	Y	N	N	Y	N	N	N
Roberts	Y	Y	N	N	Y	N	N	N
KENTUCKY								
McConnell	N	Y	N	N	Y	N	N	N
Bunning	Y	Y	N	N	Y	N	N	+
LOUISIANA								
Breaux	Y	N	Y	Y	Y	Y	Y	N
Landrieu	Y	N	N	Y	Y	Y	Y	Y
MAINE								
Snowe	Y	Y	Y	Y	N	Y	Y	Y
Collins	Y	Y	Y	Y	N	Y	Y	N
MARYLAND								
Sarbanes	Y	N	Y	Y	N	Y	Y	Y
Mikulski	Y	N	Y	Y	N	Y	Y	Y
MASSACHUSETTS								
Kennedy	Y	N	Y	N	Y	N	Y	N
Kerry	+	–	Y	Y	N	+	?	?
MICHIGAN								
Levin	Y	N	Y	Y	N	Y	Y	Y
Stabenow	Y	N	Y	Y	N	Y	Y	Y
MINNESOTA								
Dayton	Y	N	Y	Y	N	Y	Y	Y
Coleman	Y	Y	N	N	Y	N	Y	N
MISSISSIPPI								
Cochran	Y	Y	N	N	Y	N	Y	N
Lott	Y	Y	N	N	Y	N	N	Y
MISSOURI								
Bond	Y	Y	N	N	Y	Y	N	N
Talent	Y	Y	N	N	Y	N	N	N
MONTANA								
Burns	Y	Y	N	N	Y	N	N	N
Baucus	Y	N	N	Y	N	Y	Y	Y
NEBRASKA								
Hagel	N	Y	N	N	Y	N	N	N
Nelson	+	N	N	Y	Y	Y	Y	Y
NEVADA								
Reid	Y	N	Y	Y	Y	Y	Y	N
Ensign	N	Y	N	N	Y	N	N	N
NEW HAMPSHIRE								
Gregg	N	Y	Y	N	?	N	N	Y
Sununu	N	Y	N	N	Y	N	N	Y
NEW JERSEY								
Lautenberg	Y	N	Y	Y	N	Y	Y	?
Corzine	Y	?	Y	Y	N	Y	Y	Y
NEW MEXICO								
Domenici	Y	Y	N	N	Y	?	N	Y
Bingaman	Y	N	Y	Y	Y	Y	Y	Y
NEW YORK								
Schumer	Y	N	Y	Y	N	Y	Y	Y
Clinton	Y	N	Y	Y	N	Y	Y	Y
NORTH CAROLINA								
Edwards	?	?	Y	Y	N	Y	N	N
Dole	Y	Y	N	N	Y	Y	N	N
NORTH DAKOTA								
Conrad	Y	N	Y	Y	Y	Y	Y	Y
Dorgan	Y	N	Y	Y	Y	Y	Y	Y
OHIO								
DeWine	Y	Y	Y	N	Y	Y	N	N
Voinovich	Y	Y	Y	N	Y	N	N	N
OKLAHOMA								
Nickles	N	Y	N	N	Y	N	N	N
Inhofe	Y	Y	N	N	Y	N	N	N
OREGON								
Wyden	Y	N	Y	N	Y	Y	Y	N
Smith	Y	Y	Y	N	Y	Y	N	N
PENNSYLVANIA								
Specter	N	Y	N	N	Y	Y	N	N
Santorum	N	Y	N	N	Y	N	N	N
RHODE ISLAND								
Reed	Y	N	Y	N	Y	Y	Y	N
Chafee	Y	Y	Y	N	Y	Y	Y	N
SOUTH CAROLINA								
Hollings	Y	N	Y	N	Y	Y	Y	N
Graham	N	N	N	N	Y	Y	N	N
SOUTH DAKOTA								
Daschle	Y	N	Y	Y	Y	Y	Y	Y
Johnson	Y	–	?	?	N	Y	Y	Y
TENNESSEE								
Frist	Y	Y	N	N	Y	N	N	Y
Alexander	N	Y	N	N	Y	N	N	N
TEXAS								
Hutchison	N	Y	N	N	Y	Y	N	Y
Cornyn	Y	Y	N	N	Y	N	N	N
UTAH								
Hatch	Y	Y	N	N	Y	N	N	Y
Bennett	Y	?	N	N	Y	N	N	Y
VERMONT								
Leahy	Y	N	Y	Y	N	Y	Y	N
Jeffords	Y	N	Y	Y	N	Y	Y	N
VIRGINIA								
Warner	Y	Y	Y	N	Y	Y	N	N
Allen	Y	Y	N	N	Y	N	N	N
WASHINGTON								
Murray	Y	N	Y	Y	N	Y	Y	N
Cantwell	Y	N	Y	Y	N	Y	Y	N
WEST VIRGINIA								
Byrd	Y	Y	Y	N	Y	Y	Y	N
Rockefeller	Y	N	Y	Y	Y	Y	Y	N
WISCONSIN								
Kohl	N	N	Y	Y	N	Y	Y	N
Feingold	N	N	N	Y	N	Y	Y	N
WYOMING								
Thomas	Y	Y	N	N	Y	N	N	N
Enzi	Y	Y	N	N	Y	N	N	N

Key

Y	Voted for (yea).
#	Paired for.
+	Announced for.
N	Voted against (nay).
X	Paired against.
–	Announced against.
P	Voted "present."
C	Voted "present" to avoid possible conflict of interest.
?	Did not vote or otherwise make a position known.

Democrats **Republicans**
Independents

ND Northern Democrats   SD Southern Democrats

Southern states – Ala., Ark., Fla., Ga., Ky., La., Miss., N.C., Okla., S.C., Tenn., Texas, Va.

14. S 1072. Highway Funding/Passage. Passage of the bill that would authorize $318.9 billion in federal aid for highways, highway safety programs and transit programs over six years. The total would include $255 billion for highways, $56.5 billion for transit and $6 billion for safety programs. The bill would ensure that states receive a 95 percent return on their Highway Trust Fund contributions by 2009. Passed 76-21: R 34-17; D 41-4 (ND 35-2, SD 6-2); I 1-0. Before passage, the Senate adopted the Inhofe, R-Okla., substitute amendment, as amended, by voice vote. A "nay" was a vote in support of the president's position. Feb. 12, 2004. (*Story, p. C-4*)

15. S 2061. Medical Malpractice/Cloture. Motion to invoke cloture (thus limiting debate) on the motion to proceed to consideration of the bill that would place caps on damage awards in medical malpractice lawsuits against obstetricians and gynecologists. Motion rejected 48-45: R 47-3; D 1-41 (ND 1-34, SD 0-7); I 0-1. Three-fifths of the total Senate (60) is required to invoke cloture. A "yea" was a vote in support of the president's position. Feb. 24, 2004. (*Story, p. C-4*)

24. S 1805. Gun Liability/Assault Weapons Ban. Feinstein, D-Calif., amendment that would provide a 10-year reauthorization of the assault weapons ban set to expire in September 2004. Adopted 52-47: R 10-41; D 41-6 (ND 34-4, SD 7-2); I 1-0. March 2, 2004. (*Story, p. C-5*)

38. S Con Res 95. Fiscal 2005 Budget Resolution/PAYGO Rules. Feingold, D-Wis., amendment that would restore pay-as-you-go (PAYGO) rules, which would create a 60-vote point of order against any direct spending or revenue legislation that would increase the on-budget deficit or cause an on-budget deficit. Tax cuts and new entitlement spending would have to be offset with revenue increases or spending cuts. Adopted 51-48: R 4-47; D 46-1 (ND 38-0, SD 8-1); I 1-0. March 10, 2004. (*Story, p. C-5*)

63. HR 1997. Fetal Protection/Passage. Passage of the bill that would make it a criminal offense to injure or kill a fetus during the commission of a violent crime. The measure would establish criminal penalties, equal to those that would apply if the injury or death occurred to the pregnant woman, for those who harm a fetus, regardless of the perpetrator's knowledge of the pregnancy or intent to harm the fetus. The bill states that its provisions should not be interpreted to apply to consensual abortion or to a woman's actions with respect to her pregnancy. The death penalty could not be imposed under this bill. Passed (thus cleared for the president) 61-38: R 48-2; D 13-35 (ND 9-30, SD 4-5); I 0-1. A "yea" was a vote in support of the president's position. Feb. 26, 2004. (*Story, p. C-6*)

64. HR 4. Welfare Reauthorization/Child Care Funding. Snowe, R-Maine, amendment that would increase mandatory child care funding by $6 billion over the next five years. The spending would be offset by extending expiring Customs user fees. Adopted 78-20: R 31-19; D 46-1 (ND 38-0, SD 8-1); I 1-0. A "nay" was a vote in support of the president's position. March 30, 2004. (*Story, p. C-6*)

79. S 1637. Corporate Tax Overhaul/Overtime Pay Rules. Harkin, D-Iowa, amendment that would block implementation of language in a new Labor Department rule that would cause some workers to lose their eligibility for overtime pay. Adopted 52-47: R 5-46; D 46-1 (ND 38-0, SD 8-1); I 1-0. A "nay" was a vote in support of the president's position. May 4, 2004. (*Story, p. C-7*)

98. S 2400. Fiscal 2005 Defense Authorization/Overseas Base Closures. Lott, R-Miss., amendment that would require the 2005 base realignment and closure round to apply only to U.S. military installations located overseas, delaying new U.S. domestic base closings until 2007. It also would require the Defense secretary to submit a detailed plan for reducing overseas bases. Rejected 47-49: R 21-29; D 26-19 (ND 20-16, SD 6-3); I 0-1. A "nay" was a vote in support of the president's position. May 18, 2004. (*Story, p. C-8*)

	154	155	168	188	199	211
ALABAMA						
Shelby	N	Y	N	Y	Y	Y
Sessions	Y	Y	N	Y	Y	Y
ALASKA						
Stevens	Y	Y	N	Y	Y	Y
Murkowski, L.	Y	Y	N	Y	Y	Y
ARIZONA						
McCain	N	N	N	Y	Y	?
Kyl	Y	Y	N	Y	Y	Y
ARKANSAS						
Lincoln	N	N	Y	Y	Y	Y
Pryor	N	N	Y	Y	Y	Y
CALIFORNIA						
Feinstein	N	N	Y	Y	Y	N
Boxer	?	N	Y	Y	Y	N
COLORADO						
Campbell	?	N	N	Y	Y	?
Allard	Y	Y	N	Y	Y	Y
CONNECTICUT						
Dodd	N	N	Y	Y	Y	Y
Lieberman	N	N	Y	Y	Y	Y
DELAWARE						
Biden	?	N	Y	Y	Y	N
Carper	N	N	Y	Y	Y	N
FLORIDA						
Graham	N	N	Y	Y	Y	Y
Nelson	N	N	Y	Y	Y	Y
GEORGIA						
Miller	Y	Y	N	Y	Y	?
Chambliss	Y	Y	N	Y	Y	?
HAWAII						
Inouye	N	N	Y	?	Y	Y
Akaka	N	N	?	?	Y	N
IDAHO						
Craig	N	Y	N	Y	Y	Y
Crapo	Y	Y	N	Y	Y	Y
ILLINOIS						
Fitzgerald	?	Y	N	Y	Y	Y
Durbin	N	N	Y	Y	Y	N
INDIANA						
Lugar	Y	Y	N	Y	Y	Y
Bayh	N	N	Y	Y	Y	Y

	154	155	168	188	199	211
IOWA						
Grassley	Y	Y	N	Y	Y	Y
Harkin	N	N	Y	Y	Y	Y
KANSAS						
Brownback	Y	Y	N	Y	Y	Y
Roberts	Y	Y	N	Y	Y	Y
KENTUCKY						
McConnell	Y	Y	N	Y	Y	Y
Bunning	Y	Y	N	Y	Y	Y
LOUISIANA						
Breaux	N	N	Y	Y	Y	Y
Landrieu	N	N	Y	Y	Y	Y
MAINE						
Snowe	Y	N	Y	N	Y	Y
Collins	Y	N	Y	Y	Y	N
MARYLAND						
Sarbanes	N	N	Y	Y	Y	N
Mikulski	?	N	Y	Y	Y	Y
MASSACHUSETTS						
Kennedy	N	N	Y	?	Y	N
Kerry	?	?	?	?	?	?
MICHIGAN						
Levin	N	N	Y	Y	Y	N
Stabenow	N	N	Y	Y	Y	Y
MINNESOTA						
Dayton	N	N	Y	Y	Y	Y
Coleman	Y	Y	N	Y	Y	Y
MISSISSIPPI						
Cochran	Y	Y	N	Y	Y	Y
Lott	Y	Y	N	Y	Y	Y
MISSOURI						
Bond	Y	Y	Y	Y	Y	Y
Talent	Y	Y	N	Y	Y	Y
MONTANA						
Burns	Y	Y	N	Y	Y	Y
Baucus	N	N	Y	Y	Y	Y
NEBRASKA						
Hagel	?	Y	N	Y	Y	Y
Nelson	Y	Y	Y	Y	Y	Y
NEVADA						
Reid	N	N	Y	Y	Y	Y
Ensign	?	Y	N	Y	Y	Y

	154	155	168	188	199	211
NEW HAMPSHIRE						
Gregg	Y	Y	N	Y	Y	N
Sununu	Y	N	N	Y	Y	?
NEW JERSEY						
Lautenberg	N	N	Y	Y	Y	?
Corzine	N	N	Y	Y	Y	N
NEW MEXICO						
Domenici	Y	Y	N	Y	Y	Y
Bingaman	N	N	Y	Y	Y	Y
NEW YORK						
Schumer	N	N	Y	Y	Y	Y
Clinton	?	N	?	Y	Y	Y
NORTH CAROLINA						
Edwards	?	?	?	?	?	?
Dole	Y	Y	N	Y	Y	Y
NORTH DAKOTA						
Conrad	N	N	Y	Y	Y	Y
Dorgan	N	N	Y	Y	Y	?
OHIO						
DeWine	Y	Y	N	Y	Y	N
Voinovich	Y	Y	N	Y	Y	Y
OKLAHOMA						
Nickles	Y	Y	N	Y	Y	Y
Inhofe	Y	Y	N	Y	Y	Y
OREGON						
Wyden	N	N	Y	Y	Y	Y
Smith	Y	Y	N	Y	Y	Y
PENNSYLVANIA						
Specter	Y	Y	Y	Y	Y	?
Santorum	?	Y	N	Y	Y	Y
RHODE ISLAND						
Reed	N	N	Y	Y	Y	N
Chafee	Y	N	Y	N	Y	Y
SOUTH CAROLINA						
Hollings	N	N	Y	N	N	?
Graham	Y	Y	N	Y	Y	Y
SOUTH DAKOTA						
Daschle	N	N	Y	Y	Y	Y
Johnson	N	N	Y	Y	Y	Y
TENNESSEE						
Frist	Y	Y	N	Y	Y	Y
Alexander	Y	Y	N	Y	Y	Y

	154	155	168	188	199	211
TEXAS						
Hutchison	Y	Y	N	Y	Y	Y
Cornyn	Y	Y	N	Y	Y	Y
UTAH						
Hatch	Y	Y	N	Y	Y	Y
Bennett	Y	Y	N	Y	Y	Y
VERMONT						
Leahy	N	N	Y	Y	Y	?
Jeffords	N	N	Y	Y	Y	Y
VIRGINIA						
Warner	Y	Y	N	Y	Y	Y
Allen	Y	Y	N	Y	Y	Y
WASHINGTON						
Murray	N	N	Y	Y	Y	Y
Cantwell	N	N	Y	Y	Y	Y
WEST VIRGINIA						
Byrd	?	Y	Y	Y	N	N
Rockefeller	N	N	Y	Y	N	N
WISCONSIN						
Kohl	N	N	Y	Y	Y	P
Feingold	N	N	Y	Y	Y	Y
WYOMING						
Thomas	Y	Y	N	Y	Y	Y
Enzi	?	Y	N	Y	Y	Y

Key

Y	Voted for (yea).
#	Paired for.
+	Announced for.
N	Voted against (nay).
X	Paired against.
–	Announced against.
P	Voted "present."
C	Voted "present" to avoid possible conflict of interest.
?	Did not vote or otherwise make a position known.

Democrats   **Republicans**
Independents

ND Northern Democrats   SD Southern Democrats

Southern states - Ala., Ark., Fla., Ga., Ky., La., Miss., N.C., Okla., S.C., Tenn., Texas, Va.

154. S 2062. Class Action Lawsuits/Cloture. Motion to invoke cloture (thus limiting debate) on the bill that would allow class action cases involving at least 100 plaintiffs to be sent to federal court if at least $5 million is at stake and fewer than two-thirds of the plaintiffs live in the same state as the defendant. Motion rejected 44-43: R 42-3; D 2-39 (ND 1-32, SD 1-7); I 0-1. Three-fifths of the total Senate (60) is required to invoke cloture. A "yea" was a vote in support of the president's position. July 8, 2004. (*Story, p. C-8*)

155. S J Res 40. Same-Sex Marriage Ban Constitutional Amendment/ Cloture. Motion to invoke cloture (thus limiting debate) on the motion to proceed to the joint resolution to propose a constitutional amendment that would define marriage as consisting only of the union of a man and a woman. It would provide that the U.S. Constitution or any state's constitution could not be construed to require that marriage or any other constructs of marriage be conferred to any other union. Motion rejected 48-50: R 45-6; D 3-43 (ND 2-36, SD 1-7); I 0-1. Three-fifths of the total Senate (60) is required to invoke cloture. A "yea" was a vote in support of the president's position. July 14, 2004. (*Story, p. C-9*)

168. HR 4567. Fiscal 2005 Homeland Security Appropriations/ Contract Immigration Services. Leahy, D-Vt., amendment to the Leahy amendment. The perfecting amendment would revert the base amendment to its original text, which would prohibit the use of funds to privatize or contract out services provided by the Bureau of Citizenship and Immigration Services. Adopted 49-47: R 5-46; D 43-1 (ND 36-0, SD 7-1); I 1-0. A "nay" was a vote in support of the president's position. (Subsequently, the underlying Leahy amendment was adopted by voice vote.) Sept. 8, 2004. (*Story, p. C-9*)

188. HR 1308. Family and Corporate Tax Breaks/Conference Report. Adoption of the conference report on the bill that would extend the $1,000 per-child tax credit through 2009, the upper limit for the current 10 percent bracket through 2010 and tax breaks for married couples through 2008. It also would provide a one-year extension of current income exemptions from the alternative minimum tax and extend the expiring research and development tax credit through 2005. Adopted (thus cleared for the president) 92-3: R 49-2; D 42-1 (ND 35-0, SD 7-1); I 1-0. A "yea" was a vote in support of the president's position. Sept. 23, 2004. (*Story, p. C-10*)

199. S 2845. Intelligence Overhaul/Passage. Passage of the bill that would reorganize 15 U.S. intelligence agencies and create a national intelligence director with the power to freely transfer money among the CIA, National Security Agency and other defense and civilian agencies. It also would create a counterterrorism center with operational planning capabilities and a Privacy and Civil Liberties Oversight Board to investigate use of intelligence powers and act as a watchdog for civil liberties concerns. Passed 96-2: R 51-0; D 44-2 (ND 37-1, SD 7-1); I 1-0. Oct. 6, 2004. (*Story, p. C-10*)

211. HR 4520. Corporate Tax Overhaul/Conference Report. Adoption of the conference report on the bill that would repeal an export provision in the U.S. tax code that has been ruled an unfair subsidy by the World Trade Organization and provide for $137 billion in new tax cuts for corporations over 10 years. It also includes a $10 billion buyout of tobacco farmers. The cost of the tax breaks would be offset by curbs on tax-avoidance practices. Adopted (thus cleared for the president) 69-17: R 43-3; D 25-14 (ND 20-14, SD 5-0); I 1-0. Oct. 11, 2004. (*Story, p. C-11*)

Key

Y	Voted for (yea).
#	Paired for.
+	Announced for.
N	Voted against (nay).
X	Paired against.
−	Announced against.
P	Voted "present."
C	Voted "present" to avoid possible conflict of interest.
?	Did not vote or otherwise make a position known.

Democrats **Republicans** *Independents*

---

18. HR 3030. Community Services Block Grants/Unemployment Benefits. Miller, D-Calif., amendment that would authorize such sums as necessary under the Community Services Block Grants program for a six-month federal program to provide an additional 13 weeks of unemployment benefits for people who have exhausted their state jobless benefits. Adopted 227-179: R 39-179; D 187-0 (ND 132-0, SD 55-0); I 1-0. Feb. 4, 2004. (*Story, p. C-12*)

64. H Res 557. War in Iraq and U.S. Troops/Adoption. Adoption of the resolution that would affirm the United States and the world are safer with the removal of Saddam Hussein and his regime from power in Iraq. It also would commend U.S. and coalition forces for liberating Iraq and commend the Iraqi people on the adoption of Iraq's new interim constitution. Adopted 327-93: R 222-2; D 105-90 (ND 64-76, SD 41-14); I 0-1. A "yea" was a vote in support of the president's position. March 17, 2004. (*Story, p. C-12*)

114. HR 3550. Surface Transportation/Passage. Passage of the bill that would authorize $283.2 billion for federal-aid highway, mass transit, safety and research programs from fiscal 2004 to 2009. The funding total includes $217 billion in guaranteed spending for highways, $51.5 billion for mass transit and other public transportation programs, and $11.1 billion for members' projects. It also would freeze funding in fiscal 2006 and beyond unless legislation is enacted that would ensure that states get back at least 95 percent of the dollars their motorists send to the Highway Trust Fund by fiscal 2009. Passed 357-65: R 162-59; D 194-6 (ND 144-1, SD 50-5); I 1-0. A "nay" was a vote in support of the president's position. April 2, 2004. (*Story, p. C-13*)

318. HR 4663. Budget Enforcement/Passage. Passage of the bill that would set statutory caps on discretionary spending for fiscal 2005 and 2006, and institute pay-as-you-go rules that require any mandatory spending increases to be offset. The bill, as amended, would require the Congressional Budget Office to prepare an annual analysis comparing budgeted entitlement spending to actual entitlement spending, with an account-by-account breakdown to show spending trends. Rejected 146-268: R 146-72; D 0-195 (ND 0-142, SD 0-53); I 0-1. A "yea" was a vote in support of the president's position. June 25, 2004 (in the session that began and the Congressional Record dated June 24, 2004). (*Story, p. C-13*)

339. HR 4754. Fiscal 2005 Commerce, Justice, State Appropriations/ Surveillance of Library Records. Sanders, I-Vt., amendment that would prohibit funds from being used to make an application under the Foreign Intelligence Surveillance Act to acquire library circulation records, library patron lists, library Internet records, bookseller sales records or bookseller customer lists. Rejected 210-210: R 18-206; D 191-4 (ND 142-2, SD 49-2); I 1-0. A "nay" was a vote in support of the president's position. July 8, 2004. (*Story, p. C-14*)

---

[1] *The Speaker votes only at his discretion, usually to break a tie or to emphasize the importance of a matter.*

[2] *Rep. Ben Chandler, D-Ky., was sworn in Feb. 24, 2004. The first vote for which he was eligible was vote 26.*

[3] *Rep. G.K. Butterfield, D-N.C., was sworn in July 21, 2004 to replace Democratic Rep. Frank W. Ballance, Jr., who resigned effective June 11. The first vote for which Butterfield was eligible was vote 405. The last vote for which Ballance was eligible was vote 231.*

[4] *Rep. Stephanie Herseth, D-S.D., was sworn in June 3, 2004, to fill the At Large seat vacated when Republican Rep. Bill Janklow resigned Jan. 20, 2004. The first vote for which Herseth was eligible was vote 224.*

	18	64	114	318	339
ALABAMA					
1 *Bonner*	N	Y	Y	N	N
2 *Everett*	N	Y	Y	N	N
3 *Rogers*	N	Y	Y	N	N
4 *Aderholt*	N	Y	Y	N	N
5 Cramer	Y	Y	Y	N	Y
6 *Bachus*	N	Y	Y	Y	N
7 Davis	Y	P	Y	N	Y
ALASKA					
AL *Young*	N	Y	Y	Y	Y
ARIZONA					
1 *Renzi*	N	Y	Y	N	Y
2 *Franks*	N	Y	N	Y	N
3 *Shadegg*	N	Y	N	Y	N
4 Pastor	Y	N	Y	N	Y
5 *Hayworth*	N	Y	Y	N	Y
6 *Flake*	N	Y	N	Y	Y
7 Grijalva	Y	N	Y	N	Y
8 *Kolbe*	N	Y	N	N	N
ARKANSAS					
1 Berry	Y	Y	Y	N	?
2 Snyder	Y	Y	Y	N	Y
3 *Boozman*	N	Y	Y	Y	N
4 Ross	Y	Y	Y	N	Y
CALIFORNIA					
1 Thompson	Y	N	Y	N	Y
2 *Herger*	N	Y	Y	Y	N
3 *Ose*	N	Y	Y	N	N
4 *Doolittle*	N	Y	N	N	N
5 Matsui	Y	N	Y	N	Y
6 Woolsey	Y	N	Y	N	Y
7 Miller, George	Y	N	?	N	Y
8 Pelosi	Y	N	Y	N	Y
9 Lee	Y	N	Y	N	Y
10 Tauscher	Y	N	Y	N	Y
11 *Pombo*	N	Y	Y	Y	N
12 Lantos	Y	P	Y	N	Y
13 Stark	Y	N	+	N	Y
14 Eshoo	Y	N	Y	N	Y
15 Honda	Y	N	Y	N	Y
16 Lofgren	Y	N	Y	N	P
17 Farr	Y	N	Y	N	Y
18 Cardoza	Y	Y	Y	N	Y
19 *Radanovich*	N	Y	Y	Y	N
20 Dooley	Y	Y	Y	N	Y
21 *Nunes*	N	Y	Y	Y	N
22 *Thomas*	N	Y	Y	Y	N
23 Capps	Y	N	Y	N	Y
24 *Gallegly*	N	Y	Y	N	Y
25 *McKeon*	N	Y	Y	N	N
26 *Dreier*	N	Y	Y	N	N
27 Sherman	Y	Y	Y	N	Y
28 Berman	Y	Y	Y	?	Y
29 Schiff	Y	Y	Y	N	Y
30 Waxman	Y	P	?	N	Y
31 Becerra	Y	N	Y	N	Y
32 Solis	Y	N	Y	N	Y
33 Watson	?	N	Y	N	Y
34 Roybal-Allard	Y	N	Y	N	Y
35 Waters	Y	N	Y	N	Y
36 Harman	Y	Y	Y	N	N

	18	64	114	318	339
37 Millender-McD.	?	N	Y	N	Y
38 Napolitano	?	Y	Y	N	Y
39 Sánchez, Linda	Y	N	Y	N	Y
40 *Royce*	N	Y	Y	N	N
41 *Lewis*	N	Y	Y	N	N
42 *Miller, Gary*	N	Y	Y	Y	N
43 Baca	Y	Y	Y	N	Y
44 *Calvert*	?	Y	Y	N	N
45 *Bono*	N	Y	Y	N	N
46 *Rohrabacher*	N	Y	N	N	N
47 Sanchez, Loretta	Y	N	Y	N	Y
48 *Cox*	N	Y	Y	Y	N
49 *Issa*	N	Y	Y	N	N
50 *Cunningham*	N	Y	N	N	N
51 Filner	Y	N	Y	N	Y
52 *Hunter*	N	Y	?	N	N
53 Davis	Y	P	Y	N	Y
COLORADO					
1 DeGette	?	N	Y	N	Y
2 Udall	Y	Y	Y	N	Y
3 *McInnis*	?	Y	Y	N	N
4 *Musgrave*	N	Y	Y	Y	N
5 *Hefley*	N	Y	Y	N	N
6 *Tancredo*	N	Y	N	Y	N
7 *Beauprez*	N	Y	Y	Y	N
CONNECTICUT					
1 Larson	Y	N	Y	N	Y
2 *Simmons*	Y	?	Y	N	Y
3 DeLauro	Y	N	Y	N	Y
4 *Shays*	Y	Y	Y	Y	Y
5 *Johnson*	N	Y	Y	N	Y
DELAWARE					
AL *Castle*	N	Y	N	Y	Y
FLORIDA					
1 *Miller, J.*	N	Y	N	Y	N
2 Boyd	Y	Y	N	N	Y
3 Brown	Y	N	Y	N	Y
4 *Crenshaw*	N	Y	N	N	N
5 *Brown-Waite*	?	Y	N	Y	N
6 *Stearns*	N	Y	N	Y	N
7 *Mica*	N	Y	Y	N	N
8 *Keller*	N	Y	Y	N	N
9 *Bilirakis*	N	Y	N	N	N
10 *Young*	N	Y	N	N	N
11 Davis	Y	Y	N	N	Y
12 *Putnam*	N	Y	Y	N	N
13 *Harris*	N	Y	N	N	N
14 *Goss*	−	Y	N	N	N
15 *Weldon*	N	Y	N	N	N
16 *Foley*	N	Y	N	Y	N
17 Meek	Y	N	Y	N	Y
18 *Ros-Lehtinen*	N	Y	N	N	N
19 Wexler	Y	N	N	N	Y
20 Deutsch	Y	Y	N	?	?
21 *Diaz-Balart, L.*	N	Y	N	N	N
22 *Shaw*	N	Y	N	N	N
23 Hastings	Y	N	N	?	?
24 *Feeney*	N	Y	N	Y	N
25 *Diaz-Balart, M.*	N	Y	N	Y	N
GEORGIA					
1 *Kingston*	N	Y	N	N	N
2 Bishop	Y	Y	Y	N	?
3 Marshall	Y	Y	Y	N	Y
4 Majette	Y	N	Y	N	Y
5 Lewis	Y	N	Y	N	Y
6 *Isakson*	N	Y	N	N	N
7 *Linder*	?	Y	N	Y	N
8 *Collins*	N	Y	Y	?	?
9 *Norwood*	N	Y	N	N	N
10 *Deal*	N	Y	N	N	N
11 *Gingrey*	N	Y	N	Y	N
12 *Burns*	Y	Y	Y	N	N
13 Scott	Y	Y	Y	N	Y
HAWAII					
1 Abercrombie	Y	N	Y	N	Y
2 Case	Y	Y	Y	N	Y
IDAHO					
1 *Otter*	N	Y	N	Y	Y
2 *Simpson*	N	Y	N	N	Y
ILLINOIS					
1 Rush	Y	N	Y	N	Y
2 Jackson	Y	N	Y	N	Y
3 Lipinski	?	Y	Y	N	Y
4 Gutierrez	?	N	Y	N	Y
5 Emanuel	Y	Y	Y	N	Y
6 *Hyde*	N	Y	Y	N	N

ND Northern Democrats   SD Southern Democrats

	18	64	114	318	339
7 Davis	Y	N	Y	N	Y
8 ***Crane***	N	Y	Y	Y	N
9 Schakowsky	Y	N	Y	N	Y
10 ***Kirk***	N	Y	Y	Y	Y
11 ***Weller***	N	Y	Y	N	N
12 Costello	Y	Y	Y	N	Y
13 ***Biggert***	N	Y	Y	Y	N
14 ***Hastert*** [1]	N	Y			N
15 ***Johnson***	Y	Y	Y	Y	Y
16 ***Manzullo***	N	Y	Y	Y	N
17 Evans	Y	N	Y	N	Y
18 ***LaHood***	N	Y	Y	N	?
19 ***Shimkus***	Y	Y	Y	Y	N
INDIANA					
1 Visclosky	Y	N	Y	N	Y
2 ***Chocola***	N	Y	Y	Y	N
3 ***Souder***	N	Y	N	N	N
4 ***Buyer***	N	Y	Y	Y	N
5 ***Burton***	N	Y	Y	Y	N
6 ***Pence***	N	Y	N	Y	N
7 Carson	Y	P	Y	?	?
8 ***Hostettler***	N	Y	Y	Y	N
9 Hill	Y	Y	N	N	Y
IOWA					
1 ***Nussle***	N	Y	Y	Y	N
2 ***Leach***	Y	N	Y	N	Y
3 Boswell	Y	Y	Y	N	Y
4 ***Latham***	N	Y	Y	N	N
5 ***King***	N	Y	Y	Y	N
KANSAS					
1 ***Moran***	N	Y	Y	Y	Y
2 ***Ryun***	N	Y	Y	Y	N
3 Moore	Y	Y	Y	N	Y
4 ***Tiahrt***	N	Y	Y	N	N
KENTUCKY					
1 ***Whitfield***	N	Y	Y	N	N
2 ***Lewis***	N	Y	Y	N	N
3 ***Northup***	N	Y	Y	N	N
4 Lucas	Y	Y	Y	N	Y
5 ***Rogers***	N	Y	Y	N	N
6 Chandler [2]		Y	Y	N	Y
LOUISIANA					
1 ***Vitter***	N	Y	Y	Y	N
2 Jefferson	Y	N	Y	N	Y
3 ***Tauzin***	N	?	?	?	?
4 ***McCrery***	?	Y	Y	Y	N
5 Alexander	Y	Y	Y	N	Y
6 ***Baker***	N	Y	Y	Y	N
7 John	Y	Y	Y	N	Y
MAINE					
1 Allen	Y	Y	Y	N	Y
2 Michaud	Y	Y	Y	N	Y
MARYLAND					
1 ***Gilchrest***	N	Y	Y	Y	N
2 Ruppersberger	?	Y	Y	N	Y
3 Cardin	Y	Y	Y	N	Y
4 Wynn	Y	Y	Y	N	Y
5 Hoyer	Y	Y	Y	N	Y
6 ***Bartlett***	N	Y	Y	Y	Y
7 Cummings	Y	N	Y	N	Y
8 Van Hollen	Y	N	Y	N	Y
MASSACHUSETTS					
1 Olver	Y	N	Y	N	Y
2 Neal	Y	Y	Y	N	Y
3 McGovern	Y	N	Y	N	Y
4 Frank	Y	N	Y	N	Y
5 Meehan	Y	P	Y	N	Y
6 Tierney	Y	N	Y	N	Y
7 Markey	Y	N	Y	N	Y
8 Capuano	Y	Y	Y	N	Y
9 Lynch	Y	Y	Y	N	Y
10 Delahunt	Y	N	Y	N	Y
MICHIGAN					
1 Stupak	Y	Y	Y	N	Y
2 ***Hoekstra***	N	Y	Y	Y	N
3 ***Ehlers***	N	Y	Y	Y	Y
4 ***Camp***	Y	Y	Y	Y	N
5 Kildee	Y	Y	Y	N	Y
6 ***Upton***	Y	Y	Y	Y	N
7 ***Smith***	N	Y	N	?	N
8 ***Rogers***	Y	Y	N	Y	N
9 ***Knollenberg***	N	Y	Y	N	N
10 ***Miller***	Y	Y	Y	N	N
11 ***McCotter***	Y	Y	Y	Y	N
12 Levin	Y	N	Y	N	Y

	18	64	114	318	339
13 Kilpatrick	Y	N	Y	N	Y
14 Conyers	?	N	Y	N	Y
15 Dingell	Y	Y	Y	N	Y
MINNESOTA					
1 ***Gutknecht***	N	Y	N	Y	N
2 ***Kline***	N	Y	N	Y	N
3 ***Ramstad***	N	Y	Y	Y	N
4 McCollum	Y	N	Y	N	Y
5 Sabo	Y	N	Y	N	Y
6 ***Kennedy***	N	Y	Y	Y	N
7 Peterson	Y	Y	Y	N	Y
8 Oberstar	Y	N	Y	N	Y
MISSISSIPPI					
1 ***Wicker***	N	Y	Y	N	N
2 Thompson	Y	Y	Y	N	Y
3 ***Pickering***	N	Y	Y	Y	N
4 Taylor	Y	Y	Y	N	Y
MISSOURI					
1 Clay	Y	N	Y	N	Y
2 ***Akin***	N	Y	N	Y	N
3 Gephardt	?	Y	Y	?	?
4 Skelton	Y	Y	Y	N	Y
5 McCarthy	+	N	Y	N	Y
6 ***Graves***	N	Y	Y	Y	N
7 ***Blunt***	N	Y	N	Y	N
8 ***Emerson***	Y	Y	Y	N	N
9 ***Hulshof***	N	Y	?	Y	N
MONTANA					
AL ***Rehberg***	N	Y	Y	Y	N
NEBRASKA					
1 ***Bereuter***	N	Y	Y	?	N
2 ***Terry***	N	Y	Y	Y	N
3 ***Osborne***	N	Y	Y	N	N
NEVADA					
1 Berkley	Y	Y	Y	N	Y
2 ***Gibbons***	N	Y	Y	Y	N
3 ***Porter***	N	Y	Y	N	Y
NEW HAMPSHIRE					
1 ***Bradley***	N	Y	Y	Y	N
2 ***Bass***	N	Y	Y	Y	N
NEW JERSEY					
1 Andrews	Y	Y	Y	N	Y
2 ***LoBiondo***	Y	Y	Y	N	N
3 ***Saxton***	Y	Y	?	N	N
4 ***Smith***	Y	Y	Y	N	N
5 ***Garrett***	N	Y	Y	Y	N
6 Pallone	Y	N	Y	N	Y
7 ***Ferguson***	N	Y	Y	N	N
8 Pascrell	+	Y	Y	N	Y
9 Rothman	Y	N	Y	?	Y
10 Payne	Y	N	Y	N	Y
11 ***Frelinghuysen***	N	Y	Y	N	N
12 Holt	Y	Y	Y	N	Y
13 Menendez	Y	Y	Y	N	Y
NEW MEXICO					
1 ***Wilson***	Y	Y	Y	N	N
2 ***Pearce***	N	Y	Y	Y	N
3 Udall	Y	N	Y	N	Y
NEW YORK					
1 Bishop	Y	Y	Y	N	Y
2 Israel	Y	Y	Y	N	Y
3 ***King***	Y	Y	Y	N	N
4 McCarthy	Y	Y	Y	N	Y
5 Ackerman	Y	N	Y	N	Y
6 Meeks	Y	N	Y	N	Y
7 Crowley	Y	Y	Y	N	Y
8 Nadler	Y	N	Y	N	Y
9 Weiner	Y	Y	Y	N	Y
10 Towns	Y	N	Y	N	Y
11 Owens	Y	N	Y	N	Y
12 Velázquez	Y	N	Y	N	Y
13 ***Fossella***	Y	Y	Y	Y	N
14 Maloney	Y	N	Y	N	Y
15 Rangel	Y	N	Y	N	Y
16 Serrano	Y	N	Y	N	Y
17 Engel	Y	Y	Y	N	Y
18 Lowey	Y	Y	Y	N	Y
19 ***Kelly***	Y	Y	Y	Y	N
20 ***Sweeney***	Y	Y	Y	N	N
21 McNulty	Y	Y	Y	N	Y
22 Hinchey	Y	N	Y	N	?
23 ***McHugh***	+	Y	Y	N	N
24 ***Boehlert***	Y	Y	Y	Y	N
25 ***Walsh***	Y	Y	Y	N	N

	18	64	114	318	339
26 ***Reynolds***	N	Y	Y	Y	N
27 ***Quinn***	Y	Y	Y	N	?
28 Slaughter	Y	Y	Y	N	Y
29 ***Houghton***	N	Y	Y	?	N
NORTH CAROLINA					
1 Ballance [3]	Y	N	Y		
2 Etheridge	Y	Y	Y	N	Y
3 ***Jones***	Y	Y	N	Y	N
4 Price	Y	Y	Y	N	Y
5 ***Burr***	Y	Y	Y	Y	N
6 ***Coble***	N	Y	Y	N	N
7 McIntyre	Y	Y	Y	N	Y
8 ***Hayes***	Y	Y	Y	N	N
9 ***Myrick***	N	Y	N	Y	N
10 ***Ballenger***	N	Y	Y	?	N
11 ***Taylor***	Y	Y	Y	N	N
12 Watt	Y	N	Y	N	Y
13 Miller	Y	Y	Y	N	Y
NORTH DAKOTA					
AL Pomeroy	Y	Y	Y	N	Y
OHIO					
1 ***Chabot***	N	Y	Y	Y	N
2 ***Portman***	N	Y	Y	Y	N
3 ***Turner***	Y	Y	Y	Y	N
4 ***Oxley***	N	Y	Y	Y	N
5 ***Gillmor***	N	Y	Y	Y	N
6 Strickland	Y	Y	Y	N	Y
7 ***Hobson***	N	Y	Y	N	N
8 ***Boehner***	N	Y	N	Y	N
9 Kaptur	Y	Y	Y	N	Y
10 Kucinich	?	?	Y	N	Y
11 Jones	Y	Y	Y	?	Y
12 ***Tiberi***	N	Y	Y	Y	N
13 Brown	Y	Y	Y	N	Y
14 ***LaTourette***	Y	Y	Y	N	N
15 ***Pryce***	N	Y	Y	Y	N
16 ***Regula***	N	Y	Y	N	N
17 Ryan	Y	Y	Y	N	Y
18 ***Ney***	Y	Y	Y	Y	Y
OKLAHOMA					
1 ***Sullivan***	N	Y	N	Y	N
2 Carson	Y	Y	Y	N	Y
3 ***Lucas***	?	Y	N	Y	N
4 ***Cole***	N	Y	N	Y	N
5 ***Istook***	N	Y	N	N	N
OREGON					
1 Wu	Y	Y	Y	N	Y
2 ***Walden***	Y	Y	Y	N	N
3 Blumenauer	Y	N	Y	N	?
4 DeFazio	Y	Y	Y	N	Y
5 Hooley	Y	Y	Y	N	Y
PENNSYLVANIA					
1 Brady	Y	N	Y	N	Y
2 Fattah	Y	N	Y	N	Y
3 ***English***	Y	Y	Y	N	N
4 ***Hart***	N	Y	Y	Y	N
5 ***Peterson***	Y	Y	Y	N	N
6 ***Gerlach***	N	Y	Y	N	N
7 ***Weldon***	Y	?	Y	Y	Y
8 ***Greenwood***	N	Y	Y	Y	N
9 ***Shuster, Bill***	N	Y	Y	Y	N
10 ***Sherwood***	N	?	Y	N	N
11 Kanjorski	Y	N	Y	N	Y
12 Murtha	Y	N	Y	N	Y
13 Hoeffel	Y	?	Y	N	Y
14 Doyle	Y	N	Y	N	Y
15 ***Toomey***	N	Y	N	Y	N
16 ***Pitts***	N	Y	Y	Y	N
17 Holden	Y	Y	Y	N	Y
18 ***Murphy***	Y	Y	Y	Y	N
19 ***Platts***	N	Y	Y	Y	N
RHODE ISLAND					
1 Kennedy	Y	Y	Y	N	Y
2 Langevin	?	Y	Y	N	Y
SOUTH CAROLINA					
1 ***Brown***	N	Y	Y	Y	N
2 ***Wilson***	N	Y	Y	Y	N
3 ***Barrett***	N	Y	N	Y	N
4 ***DeMint***	N	Y	?	Y	N
5 Spratt	Y	Y	Y	N	Y
6 Clyburn	Y	N	Y	N	Y
SOUTH DAKOTA					
AL Herseth [4]				N	Y

	18	64	114	318	339
TENNESSEE					
1 ***Jenkins***	N	Y	Y	Y	N
2 ***Duncan***	N	Y	Y	Y	Y
3 ***Wamp***	N	Y	Y	N	N
4 Davis	Y	Y	Y	N	Y
5 Cooper	Y	Y	Y	N	Y
6 Gordon	Y	Y	Y	?	Y
7 ***Blackburn***	N	Y	Y	Y	N
8 Tanner	Y	Y	?	N	Y
9 Ford	Y	Y	Y	N	Y
TEXAS					
1 Sandlin	Y	Y	Y	N	Y
2 Turner	Y	Y	Y	N	Y
3 ***Johnson, Sam***	N	Y	N	Y	N
4 ***Hall***	N	Y	Y	N	N
5 ***Hensarling***	N	Y	N	Y	N
6 ***Barton***	N	Y	N	?	N
7 ***Culberson***	?	Y	?	N	N
8 ***Brady***	N	Y	N	Y	N
9 Lampson	Y	Y	Y	N	Y
10 Doggett	Y	Y	Y	N	Y
11 Edwards	Y	Y	Y	N	N
12 ***Granger***	?	Y	Y	?	N
13 ***Thornberry***	N	Y	N	Y	N
14 ***Paul***	N	N	N	Y	Y
15 Hinojosa	Y	Y	Y	N	Y
16 Reyes	Y	Y	?	N	Y
17 Stenholm	Y	Y	Y	N	N
18 Jackson-Lee	Y	N	Y	N	Y
19 ***Neugebauer***	N	Y	Y	Y	N
20 Gonzalez	Y	Y	Y	N	Y
21 ***Smith***	N	Y	Y	N	N
22 ***DeLay***	N	Y	Y	Y	N
23 ***Bonilla***	N	Y	Y	N	N
24 Frost	Y	Y	Y	N	Y
25 Bell	Y	N	Y	N	?
26 ***Burgess***	N	Y	Y	Y	N
27 Ortiz	?	Y	Y	N	Y
28 Rodriguez	Y	Y	Y	N	Y
29 Green	Y	Y	Y	N	Y
30 Johnson, E.B.	Y	P	Y	N	Y
31 ***Carter***	N	Y	Y	Y	N
32 ***Sessions***	N	Y	Y	Y	N
UTAH					
1 ***Bishop***	N	Y	Y	Y	N
2 Matheson	Y	Y	Y	N	Y
3 ***Cannon***	N	Y	Y	Y	N
VERMONT					
AL *Sanders*	Y	N	Y	N	Y
VIRGINIA					
1 ***Davis, Jo Ann***	N	Y	Y	N	N
2 ***Schrock***	N	Y	Y	Y	N
3 Scott	Y	N	Y	N	Y
4 ***Forbes***	N	Y	Y	Y	N
5 ***Goode***	Y	Y	Y	Y	N
6 ***Goodlatte***	N	Y	Y	Y	N
7 ***Cantor***	N	Y	N	Y	N
8 Moran	Y	N	Y	N	Y
9 Boucher	Y	Y	Y	N	Y
10 ***Wolf***	N	Y	Y	N	N
11 ***Davis, T.***	N	Y	Y	N	N
WASHINGTON					
1 Inslee	Y	Y	Y	N	Y
2 Larsen	Y	Y	Y	N	Y
3 Baird	Y	Y	Y	N	Y
4 ***Hastings***	N	Y	Y	?	N
5 ***Nethercutt***	Y	Y	Y	N	N
6 Dicks	?	Y	Y	N	Y
7 McDermott	Y	N	Y	?	Y
8 ***Dunn***	N	Y	Y	Y	N
9 Smith	?	?	Y	N	N
WEST VIRGINIA					
1 Mollohan	Y	N	Y	?	Y
2 ***Capito***	Y	Y	Y	Y	N
3 Rahall	?	N	Y	N	Y
WISCONSIN					
1 ***Ryan***	N	Y	N	Y	N
2 Baldwin	Y	N	Y	N	Y
3 Kind	Y	Y	Y	N	Y
4 Kleczka	Y	N	Y	N	Y
5 ***Sensenbrenner***	N	Y	N	Y	N
6 ***Petri***	N	Y	Y	Y	Y
7 Obey	Y	N	Y	N	Y
8 ***Green***	Y	Y	N	Y	N
WYOMING					
AL ***Cubin***	N	Y	Y	Y	N

Southern states - Ala., Ark., Fla., Ga., Ky., La., Miss., N.C., Okla., S.C., Tenn., Texas, Va.

452. HR 5025. Fiscal 2005 Transportation-Treasury Appropriations/ Mexican Identification Cards. Oxley, R-Ohio, amendment that would strike language that would prohibit the Treasury Department from using funds in the bill to implement regulations allowing financial institutions to accept Mexican "matricula consular" identification documents. Adopted 222-177: R 49-161; D 172-16 (ND 128-7, SD 44-9); I 1-0. A "yea" was a vote in support of the president's position. Sept. 14, 2004. (*Story, p. C-15*)

472. HR 1308. Family and Corporate Tax Breaks/Conference Report. Adoption of the conference report on the bill that would extend the $1,000 per-child tax credit through 2009, the upper limit for the current 10 percent bracket through 2010 and tax breaks for married couples through 2008. It also would provide a one-year extension of current income exemptions from the alternative minimum tax and extend the expiring research and development tax credit through 2005. Adopted (thus sent to the Senate) 339-65: R 213-0; D 125-65 (ND 83-57, SD 42-8); I 1-0. A "yea" was a vote in support of the president's position. Sept. 23, 2004. (*Story, p. C-15*)

484. H J Res 106. Same-Sex Marriage Ban Constitutional Amendment/Passage. Passage of the joint resolution to propose a constitutional amendment to define marriage as consisting only of the union of a man and a woman. The U.S. Constitution or any state's constitution could not be construed to require that marriage or any other constructs of marriage be conferred to any other union. Rejected 227-186: R 191-27; D 36-158 (ND 7-135, SD 29-23); I 0-1. A two-thirds majority vote of those present and voting (276 in this case) is required to pass a joint resolution proposing an amendment to the Constitution. A "yea" was a vote in support of the president's position. Sept. 30, 2004. (*Story, p. C-16*)

509. HR 4520. Corporate Tax Overhaul/Conference Report. Adoption of the conference report on the bill that would repeal an export provision in the U.S. tax code that has been ruled an unfair subsidy by the World Trade Organization, and would provide $137 billion in new tax cuts for corporations over 10 years. It also includes a $10 billion buyout of tobacco farmers. The cost of the tax breaks would be offset by curbs on tax-avoidance practices. Adopted (thus sent to the Senate) 280-141: R 207-16; D 73-124 (ND 25-118, SD 48-6); I 0-1. Oct. 7, 2004. (*Story, p. C-16*)

544. S 2845. Intelligence Overhaul/Conference Report. Adoption of the conference report on the bill that would reorganize 15 U.S. intelligence agencies and create a new director of national intelligence to oversee all U.S. intelligence activities and determine the intelligence budget. The director would be allowed to move no more than 5 percent of an agency's budget. The National Counterterrorism Center would serve as the primary organization for analyzing and integrating all U.S. intelligence pertaining to terrorism and counterterrorism. The measure would authorize approximately 10,000 additional border patrol agents over five years, and new programs and pilot projects to upgrade airport and airplane security. The FBI would be allowed to conduct surveillance and wiretaps on suspected terrorists who have no ties to any foreign country or entity. Adopted (thus sent to the Senate) 336-75: R 152-67; D 183-8 (ND 133-7, SD 50-1); I 1-0. A "yea" was a vote in support of the president's position. Dec. 7, 2004. (*Story, p. C-17*)

[1] *Rep. Porter J. Goss, R-Fla., resigned effective Sept. 23, 2004. The last vote for which he was eligible was vote 472.*

[2] *The Speaker votes only at his discretion, usually to break a tie or to emphasize the importance of a matter.*

[3] *Rep. Rodney Alexander of Louisiana switched parties from Democrat to Republican effective Sept. 7, 2004.*

[4] *Rep. Doug Bereuter, R-Neb., resigned effective Aug. 31, 2004. The last vote for which he was eligible was vote 421.*

[5] *Rep. G.K. Butterfield, D-N.C., was sworn in July 21, 2004 to replace Democrat Rep. Frank W. Ballance, Jr., who resigned effective June 11. The first vote for which Butterfield was eligible was vote 405. The last vote for which Ballance was eligible was vote 231.*

Key

Y	Voted for (yea).
#	Paired for.
+	Announced for.
N	Voted against (nay).
X	Paired against.
−	Announced against.
P	Voted "present."
C	Voted "present" to avoid possible conflict of interest.
?	Did not vote or otherwise make a position known.

Democrats **Republicans** *Independents*

	452	472	484	509	544
ALABAMA					
1 *Bonner*	?	?	Y	Y	Y
2 *Everett*	?	Y	Y	Y	N
3 *Rogers*	N	Y	Y	Y	Y
4 *Aderholt*	N	Y	Y	Y	N
5 Cramer	N	Y	Y	Y	Y
6 *Bachus*	Y	Y	Y	Y	N
7 Davis	Y	Y	Y	Y	?
ALASKA					
AL *Young*	?	Y	Y	Y	?
ARIZONA					
1 *Renzi*	N	Y	Y	Y	Y
2 *Franks*	N	Y	Y	Y	Y
3 *Shadegg*	N	Y	Y	Y	Y
4 Pastor	Y	N	N	Y	Y
5 *Hayworth*	N	Y	Y	Y	N
6 *Flake*	Y	Y	Y	Y	N
7 *Grijalva*	Y	Y	N	N	Y
8 *Kolbe*	Y	Y	Y	Y	Y
ARKANSAS					
1 Berry	Y	N	Y	Y	Y
2 Snyder	Y	Y	N	Y	Y
3 *Boozman*	N	Y	Y	Y	N
4 Ross	Y	Y	Y	Y	Y
CALIFORNIA					
1 Thompson	Y	N	N	Y	Y
2 *Herger*	N	Y	Y	Y	N
3 *Ose*	Y	Y	N	N	N
4 *Doolittle*	N	Y	Y	Y	N
5 Matsui	Y	N	N	Y	Y
6 Woolsey	Y	N	N	N	Y
7 Miller, George	Y	N	N	Y	Y
8 Pelosi	Y	N	N	N	Y
9 Lee	Y	N	N	N	Y
10 Tauscher	Y	N	N	Y	Y
11 *Pombo*	N	Y	Y	Y	N
12 Lantos	Y	N	N	Y	Y
13 Stark	Y	N	N	N	Y
14 Eshoo	Y	N	N	Y	Y
15 Honda	Y	N	N	N	Y
16 Lofgren	Y	N	N	Y	Y
17 Farr	Y	N	N	N	Y
18 Cardoza	Y	N	N	Y	Y
19 *Radanovich*	N	Y	Y	Y	N
20 Dooley	Y	N	Y	Y	?
21 *Nunes*	N	+	Y	Y	N
22 *Thomas*	N	Y	Y	Y	N
23 Capps	Y	N	N	N	Y
24 *Gallegly*	N	Y	Y	Y	N
25 *McKeon*	N	Y	Y	Y	Y
26 *Dreier*	Y	Y	Y	Y	Y
27 Sherman	Y	Y	N	Y	Y
28 Berman	Y	Y	N	N	Y
29 Schiff	Y	Y	N	N	Y
30 Waxman	Y	N	N	Y	Y
31 Becerra	Y	N	N	N	Y
32 Solis	Y	Y	N	N	Y
33 Watson	Y	N	N	N	Y
34 Roybal-Allard	Y	Y	N	N	Y
35 Waters	Y	N	N	N	Y
36 Harman	Y	N	?	N	Y

	452	472	484	509	544
37 Millender-McD.	Y	N	N	?	Y
38 Napolitano	Y	Y	N	N	Y
39 Sánchez, Linda	Y	Y	N	N	Y
40 *Royce*	N	Y	Y	Y	N
41 *Lewis*	N	Y	Y	Y	Y
42 *Miller, Gary*	N	Y	Y	Y	N
43 Baca	Y	Y	N	N	Y
44 *Calvert*	N	Y	Y	Y	N
45 *Bono*	N	Y	N	N	Y
46 *Rohrabacher*	N	Y	Y	Y	N
47 Sanchez, Loretta	Y	Y	N	N	Y
48 *Cox*	N	Y	N	Y	Y
49 *Issa*	N	Y	Y	Y	N
50 *Cunningham*	N	Y	Y	Y	Y
51 Filner	Y	Y	N	?	Y
52 *Hunter*	N	Y	?	Y	Y
53 Davis	Y	Y	N	N	Y
COLORADO					
1 DeGette	Y	N	N	N	Y
2 Udall	Y	?	N	Y	Y
3 *McInnis*	?	Y	N	Y	N
4 *Musgrave*	N	Y	Y	Y	Y
5 *Hefley*	N	Y	Y	Y	N
6 *Tancredo*	N	Y	Y	Y	N
7 *Beauprez*	Y	Y	Y	Y	Y
CONNECTICUT					
1 Larson	Y	N	N	N	Y
2 *Simmons*	N	Y	N	Y	Y
3 DeLauro	Y	N	N	N	Y
4 *Shays*	N	Y	N	Y	Y
5 *Johnson*	N	Y	N	Y	Y
DELAWARE					
AL *Castle*	Y	Y	N	N	Y
FLORIDA					
1 *Miller, J.*	?	?	Y	Y	Y
2 Boyd	N	Y	Y	Y	Y
3 Brown	Y	N	?	Y	Y
4 *Crenshaw*	N	Y	Y	Y	Y
5 *Brown-Waite*	N	Y	Y	Y	N
6 *Stearns*	N	Y	Y	Y	N
7 *Mica*	N	Y	Y	Y	Y
8 *Keller*	N	Y	Y	Y	Y
9 *Bilirakis*	N	Y	Y	Y	Y
10 *Young*	N	Y	Y	N	Y
11 Davis	Y	Y	N	Y	Y
12 *Putnam*	N	Y	Y	Y	Y
13 *Harris*	N	Y	Y	Y	Y
14 *Goss*[1]	?	?			
15 *Weldon*	N	Y	Y	Y	N
16 *Foley*	N	Y	N	Y	Y
17 Meek	Y	Y	N	Y	Y
18 *Ros-Lehtinen*	Y	Y	?	N	Y
19 Wexler	Y	Y	N	N	Y
20 Deutsch	Y	Y	N	N	Y
21 *Diaz-Balart, L.*	Y	Y	?	N	Y
22 *Shaw*	N	Y	Y	Y	Y
23 Hastings	Y	N	?	Y	?
24 *Feeney*	N	Y	Y	Y	N
25 *Diaz-Balart, M.*	Y	Y	?	N	Y
GEORGIA					
1 *Kingston*	N	Y	Y	Y	N
2 Bishop	Y	+	Y	Y	Y
3 Marshall	N	Y	Y	Y	Y
4 *Majette*	Y	Y	N	?	Y
5 Lewis	Y	N	N	N	Y
6 *Isakson*	N	Y	Y	Y	Y
7 *Linder*	N	Y	Y	Y	N
8 *Collins*	N	?	Y	Y	N
9 *Norwood*	N	Y	Y	?	?
10 *Deal*	N	?	Y	Y	N
11 *Gingrey*	N	Y	Y	Y	N
12 *Burns*	N	Y	Y	Y	Y
13 Scott	Y	Y	Y	Y	Y
HAWAII					
1 Abercrombie	Y	Y	N	N	?
2 Case	N	Y	N	N	?
IDAHO					
1 *Otter*	N	Y	Y	Y	N
2 *Simpson*	N	Y	Y	Y	N
ILLINOIS					
1 Rush	Y	N	N	N	Y
2 Jackson	Y	N	N	N	Y
3 Lipinski	N	?	N	?	?
4 Gutierrez	Y	N	N	N	Y
5 Emanuel	Y	Y	N	N	Y
6 *Hyde*	N	Y	Y	Y	Y

ND Northern Democrats   SD Southern Democrats

	452	472	484	509	544
7 Davis	Y	N	?	Y	Y
8 *Crane*	N	Y	Y	N	Y
9 *Schakowsky*	Y	N	N	N	Y
10 *Kirk*	N	Y	N	N	Y
11 *Weller*	Y	Y	Y	Y	Y
12 Costello	Y	Y	Y	N	Y
13 *Biggert*	Y	Y	N	Y	Y
14 *Hastert*[2]		Y	Y	Y	Y
15 *Johnson*	N	Y	Y	N	Y
16 *Manzullo*	N	Y	Y	Y	N
17 Evans	Y	Y	N	N	Y
18 *LaHood*	Y	Y	Y	N	N
19 *Shimkus*	N	Y	Y	Y	Y
INDIANA					
1 Visclosky	N	N	N	N	Y
2 *Chocola*	N	Y	Y	Y	Y
3 *Souder*	N	Y	Y	Y	Y
4 *Buyer*	N	Y	Y	Y	Y
5 *Burton*	N	Y	Y	Y	Y
6 *Pence*	N	Y	Y	Y	Y
7 Carson	Y	Y	N	N	Y
8 *Hostettler*	N	Y	N	Y	N
9 Hill	Y	N	N	Y	Y
IOWA					
1 *Nussle*	Y	Y	Y	Y	Y
2 *Leach*	Y	Y	N	Y	Y
3 Boswell	Y	N	Y	N	?
4 *Latham*	Y	Y	Y	Y	Y
5 *King*	N	Y	Y	Y	N
KANSAS					
1 *Moran*	N	Y	Y	Y	Y
2 *Ryun*	N	Y	Y	Y	Y
3 Moore	Y	Y	N	Y	Y
4 *Tiahrt*	N	Y	Y	Y	Y
KENTUCKY					
1 *Whitfield*	N	Y	Y	Y	Y
2 *Lewis*	N	Y	Y	Y	N
3 *Northup*	N	Y	Y	Y	Y
4 Lucas	Y	?	Y	Y	?
5 *Rogers*	N	Y	Y	Y	Y
6 Chandler	N	Y	Y	Y	Y
LOUISIANA					
1 *Vitter*	N	?	Y	Y	Y
2 Jefferson	Y	Y	Y	Y	Y
3 *Tauzin*	?	?	?	?	Y
4 *McCrery*	Y	Y	Y	Y	Y
5 *Alexander*[3]	N	Y	Y	Y	Y
6 *Baker*	?	Y	Y	Y	Y
7 John	?	Y	Y	Y	Y
MAINE					
1 Allen	Y	Y	N	N	Y
2 Michaud	Y	Y	N	N	Y
MARYLAND					
1 *Gilchrest*	Y	Y	N	Y	Y
2 Ruppersberger	Y	Y	N	N	Y
3 Cardin	Y	Y	N	N	Y
4 Wynn	Y	N	N	N	Y
5 Hoyer	Y	N	N	N	Y
6 *Bartlett*	N	Y	Y	Y	N
7 Cummings	Y	Y	N	N	Y
8 Van Hollen	Y	Y	N	N	Y
MASSACHUSETTS					
1 Olver	Y	N	N	N	Y
2 Neal	Y	N	N	N	Y
3 McGovern	Y	N	N	N	Y
4 Frank	Y	N	N	N	Y
5 Meehan	Y	N	N	N	Y
6 Tierney	Y	N	N	N	Y
7 Markey	Y	N	N	N	Y
8 Capuano	Y	N	N	N	Y
9 Lynch	Y	Y	N	N	Y
10 Delahunt	Y	?	N	N	Y
MICHIGAN					
1 Stupak	Y	N	N	N	Y
2 *Hoekstra*	N	Y	Y	Y	Y
3 *Ehlers*	Y	Y	Y	Y	Y
4 *Camp*	N	Y	Y	Y	N
5 Kildee	Y	N	N	N	Y
6 *Upton*	N	Y	Y	N	Y
7 *Smith*	N	Y	Y	Y	?
8 *Rogers*	+	Y	N	N	Y
9 *Knollenberg*	N	Y	N	Y	Y
10 *Miller*	N	Y	Y	Y	Y
11 *McCotter*	N	Y	Y	Y	Y
12 Levin	Y	Y	N	N	Y

	452	472	484	509	544
13 Kilpatrick	Y	N	N	N	Y
14 Conyers	?	N	N	N	Y
15 Dingell	Y	Y	N	N	Y
MINNESOTA					
1 *Gutknecht*	N	Y	Y	Y	N
2 *Kline*	N	Y	Y	Y	Y
3 *Ramstad*	N	Y	Y	N	Y
4 McCollum	Y	N	N	N	Y
5 Sabo	Y	N	N	N	N
6 *Kennedy*	Y	Y	Y	Y	Y
7 Peterson	N	Y	Y	Y	Y
8 Oberstar	Y	N	?	N	N
MISSISSIPPI					
1 *Wicker*	N	Y	Y	Y	Y
2 Thompson	Y	?	Y	N	Y
3 *Pickering*	N	Y	Y	Y	Y
4 Taylor	?	N	Y	Y	Y
MISSOURI					
1 Clay	?	N	N	N	Y
2 *Akin*	N	Y	Y	Y	Y
3 Gephardt	?	Y	N	?	Y
4 Skelton	Y	Y	Y	Y	Y
5 McCarthy	Y	+	N	N	Y
6 *Graves*	N	+	Y	Y	Y
7 *Blunt*	N	Y	Y	Y	Y
8 *Emerson*	N	Y	Y	Y	Y
9 *Hulshof*	Y	Y	Y	Y	Y
MONTANA					
AL *Rehberg*	N	Y	Y	Y	N
NEBRASKA					
1 Vacant[4]					
2 *Terry*	Y	Y	Y	Y	Y
3 *Osborne*	Y	?	Y	Y	Y
NEVADA					
1 Berkley	Y	Y	N	Y	Y
2 *Gibbons*	N	Y	Y	Y	Y
3 *Porter*	Y	Y	Y	N	Y
NEW HAMPSHIRE					
1 *Bradley*	N	Y	Y	N	Y
2 *Bass*	N	Y	N	N	Y
NEW JERSEY					
1 Andrews	Y	N	N	N	Y
2 *LoBiondo*	N	Y	Y	Y	Y
3 *Saxton*	N	Y	Y	Y	Y
4 *Smith*	N	Y	Y	Y	Y
5 *Garrett*	N	?	Y	Y	Y
6 Pallone	Y	N	N	N	Y
7 *Ferguson*	N	Y	Y	Y	Y
8 Pascrell	Y	Y	N	N	Y
9 Rothman	Y	Y	N	N	Y
10 Payne	Y	N	N	N	+
11 *Frelinghuysen*	N	Y	N	Y	Y
12 Holt	Y	N	N	N	Y
13 Menendez	Y	N	?	N	Y
NEW MEXICO					
1 *Wilson*	Y	Y	Y	Y	Y
2 *Pearce*	Y	Y	Y	Y	Y
3 Udall	Y	Y	N	N	Y
NEW YORK					
1 Bishop	Y	Y	N	N	Y
2 Israel	Y	Y	N	N	Y
3 *King*	Y	Y	Y	Y	Y
4 McCarthy	Y	Y	N	N	Y
5 Ackerman	?	Y	N	N	Y
6 Meeks	Y	Y	?	N	Y
7 Crowley	Y	Y	N	N	Y
8 Nadler	Y	N	N	N	Y
9 Weiner	?	Y	N	N	Y
10 Towns	?	N	N	?	Y
11 Owens	?	N	N	N	Y
12 Velázquez	Y	N	N	N	Y
13 *Fossella*	N	Y	Y	N	Y
14 Maloney	Y	+	N	N	Y
15 Rangel	Y	Y	?	N	Y
16 Serrano	?	Y	N	N	Y
17 Engel	?	Y	N	N	Y
18 Lowey	Y	Y	N	N	Y
19 *Kelly*	N	Y	Y	Y	Y
20 *Sweeney*	N	Y	N	Y	N
21 McNulty	Y	Y	N	N	Y
22 Hinchey	Y	N	N	N	Y
23 *McHugh*	N	Y	Y	Y	Y
24 *Boehlert*	?	Y	?	?	?
25 *Walsh*	Y	Y	Y	N	Y

	452	472	484	509	544
26 *Reynolds*	N	Y	Y	Y	Y
27 *Quinn*	N	?	Y	Y	Y
28 Slaughter	+	Y	N	?	Y
29 *Houghton*	?	Y	N	Y	?
NORTH CAROLINA					
1 Butterfield[5]	Y	Y	N	Y	Y
2 Etheridge	Y	Y	Y	Y	Y
3 *Jones*	N	Y	Y	Y	N
4 Price	Y	Y	N	Y	Y
5 *Burr*	N	Y	Y	Y	?
6 *Coble*	N	Y	Y	Y	N
7 McIntyre	N	Y	Y	Y	Y
8 *Hayes*	N	Y	Y	Y	Y
9 *Myrick*	N	?	Y	Y	N
10 *Ballenger*	?	Y	Y	Y	?
11 *Taylor*	N	Y	Y	Y	N
12 Watt	Y	Y	N	N	Y
13 Miller	Y	Y	N	Y	Y
NORTH DAKOTA					
AL Pomeroy	Y	Y	N	Y	Y
OHIO					
1 *Chabot*	N	Y	Y	Y	N
2 *Portman*	N	Y	Y	Y	Y
3 *Turner*	N	Y	Y	Y	Y
4 *Oxley*	Y	Y	Y	Y	Y
5 *Gillmor*	Y	Y	Y	Y	Y
6 Strickland	Y	Y	N	N	Y
7 *Hobson*	N	Y	N	Y	Y
8 *Boehner*	N	Y	Y	Y	Y
9 Kaptur	Y	Y	N	N	Y
10 Kucinich	Y	Y	N	N	N
11 Jones	Y	Y	N	N	?
12 *Tiberi*	N	Y	Y	Y	Y
13 Brown	Y	Y	N	N	Y
14 *LaTourette*	Y	Y	Y	Y	Y
15 *Pryce*	Y	Y	N	Y	Y
16 *Regula*	N	Y	N	Y	Y
17 Ryan	N	Y	N	N	Y
18 *Ney*	N	Y	Y	Y	Y
OKLAHOMA					
1 *Sullivan*	N	Y	Y	Y	N
2 Carson	N	Y	Y	Y	Y
3 *Lucas*	Y	Y	Y	Y	N
4 *Cole*	N	Y	Y	Y	Y
5 *Istook*	N	+	Y	Y	N
OREGON					
1 Wu	Y	Y	N	Y	Y
2 *Walden*	N	Y	Y	Y	Y
3 Blumenauer	Y	N	N	N	Y
4 DeFazio	Y	N	N	N	Y
5 Hooley	Y	Y	N	Y	Y
PENNSYLVANIA					
1 Brady	Y	N	N	N	Y
2 Fattah	Y	?	N	N	?
3 *English*	Y	Y	Y	Y	Y
4 *Hart*	Y	Y	Y	Y	Y
5 *Peterson*	N	Y	Y	Y	Y
6 *Gerlach*	N	Y	N	Y	Y
7 *Weldon*	N	Y	Y	Y	Y
8 *Greenwood*	N	Y	Y	Y	Y
9 *Shuster, Bill*	Y	Y	Y	Y	Y
10 *Sherwood*	?	Y	Y	Y	Y
11 Kanjorski	Y	N	N	N	Y
12 Murtha	?	N	?	N	N
13 Hoeffel	Y	Y	N	N	Y
14 Doyle	Y	N	N	N	Y
15 *Toomey*	Y	Y	Y	Y	Y
16 *Pitts*	N	Y	Y	Y	N
17 Holden	Y	N	N	N	Y
18 *Murphy*	N	Y	Y	Y	Y
19 *Platts*	N	Y	N	Y	Y
RHODE ISLAND					
1 Kennedy	Y	Y	N	N	Y
2 Langevin	?	Y	N	N	Y
SOUTH CAROLINA					
1 *Brown*	N	Y	Y	Y	Y
2 *Wilson*	N	Y	Y	Y	Y
3 *Barrett*	N	Y	Y	Y	N
4 *DeMint*	N	Y	Y	Y	Y
5 Spratt	Y	Y	Y	N	Y
6 Clyburn	Y	Y	N	Y	Y
SOUTH DAKOTA					
AL Herseth	Y	?	Y	Y	Y

	452	472	484	509	544
TENNESSEE					
1 *Jenkins*	N	Y	Y	Y	N
2 *Duncan*	N	Y	Y	Y	N
3 *Wamp*	N	Y	Y	Y	N
4 Davis	Y	Y	Y	Y	Y
5 Cooper	Y	N	Y	Y	Y
6 Gordon	Y	N	Y	Y	Y
7 *Blackburn*	N	Y	Y	Y	N
8 Tanner	N	N	Y	Y	Y
9 Ford	Y	Y	Y	Y	Y
TEXAS					
1 Sandlin	Y	Y	Y	Y	Y
2 Turner	Y	Y	N	Y	Y
3 *Johnson, Sam*	N	Y	Y	Y	N
4 *Hall*	N	Y	Y	Y	Y
5 *Hensarling*	N	Y	Y	Y	N
6 *Barton*	N	Y	Y	Y	N
7 *Culberson*	N	Y	Y	Y	N
8 *Brady*	N	Y	Y	Y	Y
9 Lampson	Y	Y	Y	Y	Y
10 Doggett	Y	?	N	N	Y
11 Edwards	Y	Y	N	N	Y
12 *Granger*	N	Y	Y	Y	Y
13 *Thornberry*	N	Y	N	?	N
14 *Paul*	N	Y	N	?	N
15 Hinojosa	Y	Y	N	Y	Y
16 Reyes	Y	Y	?	Y	Y
17 Stenholm	N	Y	Y	Y	Y
18 Jackson-Lee	Y	Y	N	N	Y
19 *Neugebauer*	N	Y	Y	Y	N
20 Gonzalez	Y	Y	N	Y	Y
21 *Smith*	N	Y	Y	N	N
22 *DeLay*	N	Y	Y	Y	N
23 *Bonilla*	N	Y	Y	Y	Y
24 Frost	Y	Y	Y	Y	Y
25 Bell	Y	Y	N	Y	?
26 *Burgess*	N	Y	Y	Y	N
27 Ortiz	Y	Y	Y	?	Y
28 Rodriguez	Y	?	N	Y	Y
29 Green	Y	?	N	Y	Y
30 Johnson, E.B.	?	Y	N	Y	Y
31 *Carter*	N	Y	Y	Y	Y
32 *Sessions*	N	Y	Y	Y	Y
UTAH					
1 *Bishop*	N	Y	Y	Y	N
2 Matheson	Y	Y	Y	Y	Y
3 *Cannon*	?	?	?	Y	?
VERMONT					
AL *Sanders*	Y	Y	N	N	Y
VIRGINIA					
1 *Davis, Jo Ann*	N	Y	Y	Y	N
2 *Schrock*	?	Y	Y	Y	Y
3 Scott	Y	N	N	N	Y
4 *Forbes*	N	Y	Y	Y	Y
5 *Goode*	N	Y	Y	N	Y
6 *Goodlatte*	N	Y	Y	Y	Y
7 *Cantor*	N	Y	Y	Y	Y
8 Moran	Y	Y	N	N	Y
9 Boucher	N	Y	N	N	Y
10 *Wolf*	N	Y	Y	N	Y
11 *Davis, T.*	Y	Y	Y	Y	Y
WASHINGTON					
1 Inslee	Y	N	N	N	Y
2 Larsen	Y	N	N	N	Y
3 Baird	Y	Y	N	N	Y
4 *Hastings*	Y	Y	Y	Y	Y
5 *Nethercutt*	?	Y	?	Y	Y
6 Dicks	Y	N	N	N	Y
7 McDermott	Y	N	N	N	N
8 *Dunn*	?	Y	?	Y	Y
9 Smith	N	?	N	Y	Y
WEST VIRGINIA					
1 Mollohan	Y	N	N	N	N
2 *Capito*	N	Y	Y	Y	Y
3 Rahall	Y	Y	Y	N	?
WISCONSIN					
1 *Ryan*	N	Y	Y	Y	Y
2 Baldwin	Y	Y	N	N	Y
3 Kind	Y	Y	N	N	Y
4 Kleczka	?	?	N	N	Y
5 *Sensenbrenner*	N	Y	Y	N	N
6 *Petri*	N	Y	Y	Y	Y
7 Obey	Y	N	N	N	N
8 *Green*	N	Y	Y	Y	N
WYOMING					
AL *Cubin*	N	Y	Y	Y	N

Southern states - Ala., Ark., Fla., Ga., Ky., La., Miss., N.C., Okla., S.C., Tenn., Texas, Va.

Appendix D

TEXTS

Bush Defends U.S. Actions Abroad, Urges Renewal of Tax Cuts, Patriot Act

Following is a transcript of President Bush's State of the Union address delivered to a joint session of Congress the night of Jan. 20. The text was provided by the White House.

Mr. Speaker, Vice President Cheney, members of Congress, distinguished guests, and fellow citizens: America this evening is a nation called to great responsibilities. And we are rising to meet them.

As we gather tonight, hundreds of thousands of American servicemen and women are deployed across the world in the war on terror. By bringing hope to the oppressed and delivering justice to the violent, they are making America more secure.

Each day, law enforcement personnel and intelligence officers are tracking terrorist threats; analysts are examining airline passenger lists; the men and women of our new Homeland Security Department are patrolling our coasts and borders. And their vigilance is protecting America.

Americans are proving once again to be the hardest working people in the world. The American economy is growing stronger. The tax relief you passed is working.

Tonight, members of Congress can take pride in the great works of compassion and reform that skeptics had thought impossible. You're raising the standards for our public schools, and you are giving our senior citizens prescription drug coverage under Medicare.

We have faced serious challenges together, and now we face a choice: We can go forward with confidence and resolve, or we can turn back to the dangerous illusion that terrorists are not plotting and outlaw regimes are no threat to us. We can press on with economic growth, and reforms in education and Medicare, or we can turn back to old policies and old divisions.

We've not come all this way — through tragedy, and trial and war — only to falter and leave our work un-

finished. Americans are rising to the tasks of history, and they expect the same from us. In their efforts, their enterprise, and their character, the American people are showing that the state of our union is confident and strong.

Our greatest responsibility is the active defense of the American people. Twenty-eight months have passed since Sept. 11, 2001 — over two years without an attack on American soil. And it is tempting to believe that the danger is behind us. That hope is understandable, comforting — and false. The killing has continued in Bali, Jakarta, Casablanca, Riyadh, Mombasa, Jerusalem, Istanbul and Baghdad. The terrorists continue to plot against America and the civilized world. And by our will and courage, this danger will be defeated.

Inside the United States, where the war began, we must continue to give our homeland security and law enforcement personnel every tool they need to defend us. And one of those essential tools is the Patriot Act, which allows federal law enforcement to better share information, to track terrorists, to disrupt their cells, and to seize their assets. For years, we have used similar provisions to catch embezzlers and drug traffickers. If these methods are good for hunting criminals, they are even more important for hunting terrorists.

Key provisions of the Patriot Act are set to expire next year. The terrorist threat will not expire on that schedule. Our law enforcement needs this vital legislation to protect our citizens. You need to renew the Patriot Act.

Attacking Terrorism

America is on the offensive against the terrorists who started this war. Last March, Khalid Shaikh Mohammed, a mastermind of September the 11th, awoke to find himself in the custody of U.S. and Pakistani authorities. Last August the 11th brought the capture of the

terrorist Hambali, who was a key player in the attack in Indonesia that killed over 200 people. We're tracking al Qaeda around the world, and nearly two-thirds of their known leaders have now been captured or killed. Thousands of very skilled and determined military personnel are on the manhunt, going after the remaining killers who hide in cities and caves, and one by one, we will bring these terrorists to justice.

As part of the offensive against terror, we are also confronting the regimes that harbor and support terrorists, and could supply them with nuclear, chemical or biological weapons. The United States and our allies are determined: We refuse to live in the shadow of this ultimate danger.

The first to see our determination were the Taliban, who made Afghanistan the primary training base of al Qaeda killers. As of this month, that country has a new constitution, guaranteeing free elections and full participation by women. Businesses are opening, health care centers are being established, and the boys and girls of Afghanistan are back in school. With the help from the new Afghan army, our coalition is leading aggressive raids against the surviving members of the Taliban and al Qaeda. The men and women of Afghanistan are building a nation that is free and proud and fighting terror — and America is honored to be their friend.

Since we last met in this chamber, combat forces of the United States, Great Britain, Australia, Poland and other countries enforced the demands of the United Nations [and] ended the rule of Saddam Hussein, and the people of Iraq are free.

Having broken the Baathist regime, we face a remnant of violent Saddam supporters. Men who ran away from our troops in battle are now dispersed and attack from the shadows. These killers, joined by foreign terrorists, are a serious, continuing danger. Yet we're making progress against them. The

once all-powerful ruler of Iraq was found in a hole, and now sits in a prison cell.

Of the top 55 officials of the former regime, we have captured or killed 45. Our forces are on the offensive, leading over 1,600 patrols a day and conducting an average of 180 raids a week. We are dealing with these thugs in Iraq, just as surely as we dealt with Saddam Hussein's evil regime.

The work of building a new Iraq is hard, and it is right. And America has always been willing to do what it takes for what is right. Last January, Iraq's only law was the whim of one brutal man. Today our coalition is working with the Iraqi Governing Council to draft a basic law, with a bill of rights. We're working with Iraqis and the United Nations to prepare for a transition to full Iraqi sovereignty by the end of June.

As democracy takes hold in Iraq, the enemies of freedom will do all in their power to spread violence and fear. They are trying to shake the will of our country and our friends, but the United States of America will never be intimidated by thugs and assassins. The killers will fail, and the Iraqi people will live in freedom.

Month by month, Iraqis are assuming more responsibility for their own security and their own future. And tonight we are honored to welcome one of Iraq's most respected leaders: the current President of the Iraqi Governing Council, Adnan Pachachi. Sir, America stands with you and the Iraqi people as you build a free and peaceful nation.

New Threats

Because of American leadership and resolve, the world is changing for the better. Last month, the leader of Libya voluntarily pledged to disclose and dismantle all of his regime's weapons of mass destruction programs, including a uranium enrichment project for nuclear weapons. Colonel Qaddafi correctly judged that his country would be better off and far more secure without weapons of mass murder.

Nine months of intense negotiations involving the United States and Great Britain succeeded with Libya, while 12 years of diplomacy with Iraq did not. And one reason is clear: For

diplomacy to be effective, words must be credible, and no one can now doubt the word of America.

Different threats require different strategies. Along with nations in the region, we're insisting that North Korea eliminate its nuclear program. America and the international community are demanding that Iran meet its commitments and not develop nuclear weapons. America is committed to keeping the world's most dangerous weapons out of the hands of the most dangerous regimes.

When I came to this rostrum on September the 20th, 2001, I brought the police shield of a fallen officer, my reminder of lives that ended, and a task that does not end. I gave to you and to all Americans my complete commitment to securing our country and defeating our enemies. And this pledge, given by one, has been kept by many.

You in the Congress have provided the resources for our defense, and cast the difficult votes of war and peace. Our closest allies have been unwavering. America's intelligence personnel and diplomats have been skilled and tireless. And the men and women of the American military — they have taken the hardest duty. We've seen their skill and their courage in armored charges and midnight raids, and lonely hours on faithful watch. We have seen the joy when they return, and felt the sorrow when one is lost. I've had the honor of meeting our servicemen and women at many posts, from the deck of a carrier in the Pacific to a mess hall in Baghdad.

Many of our troops are listening tonight. And I want you and your families to know: America is proud of you. And my administration, and this Congress, will give you the resources you need to fight and win the war on terror.

I know that some people question if America is really in a war at all. They view terrorism more as a crime, a problem to be solved mainly with law enforcement and indictments. After the World Trade Center was first attacked in 1993, some of the guilty were indicted and tried and convicted, and sent to prison. But the matter was not settled. The terrorists were still training and plotting in other nations, and drawing up more ambitious plans. After the

chaos and carnage of September the 11th, it is not enough to serve our enemies with legal papers. The terrorists and their supporters declared war on the United States, and war is what they got.

Some in this chamber, and in our country, did not support the liberation of Iraq. Objections to war often come from principled motives. But let us be candid about the consequences of leaving Saddam Hussein in power. We're seeking all the facts. Already, the Kay Report identified dozens of weapons of mass destruction-related program activities and significant amounts of equipment that Iraq concealed from the United Nations. Had we failed to act, the dictator's weapons of mass destruction programs would continue to this day. Had we failed to act, Security Council resolutions on Iraq would have been revealed as empty threats, weakening the United Nations and encouraging defiance by dictators around the world. Iraq's torture chambers would still be filled with victims, terrified and innocent. The killing fields of Iraq — where hundreds of thousands of men and women and children vanished into the sands — would still be known only to the killers. For all who love freedom and peace, the world without Saddam Hussein's regime is a better and safer place.

Some critics have said our duties in Iraq must be internationalized. This particular criticism is hard to explain to our partners in Britain, Australia, Japan, South Korea, the Philippines, Thailand, Italy, Spain, Poland, Denmark, Hungary, Bulgaria, Ukraine, Romania, the Netherlands, Norway, El Salvador, and the 17 other countries that have committed troops to Iraq. As we debate at home, we must never ignore the vital contributions of our international partners, or dismiss their sacrifices.

Living in Freedom

From the beginning, America has sought international support for our operations in Afghanistan and Iraq, and we have gained much support. There is a difference, however, between leading a coalition of many nations, and submitting to the objections of a few. America will never seek a permission slip to defend the security of our country.

We also hear doubts that democra-

cy is a realistic goal for the greater Middle East, where freedom is rare. Yet it is mistaken, and condescending, to assume that whole cultures and great religions are incompatible with liberty and self-government. I believe that God has planted in every human heart the desire to live in freedom. And even when that desire is crushed by tyranny for decades, it will rise again.

As long as the Middle East remains a place of tyranny and despair and anger, it will continue to produce men and movements that threaten the safety of America and our friends. So America is pursuing a forward strategy of freedom in the greater Middle East. We will challenge the enemies of reform, confront the allies of terror, and expect a higher standard from our friends. To cut through the barriers of hateful propaganda, the Voice of America and other broadcast services are expanding their programming in Arabic and Persian — and soon, a new television service will begin providing reliable news and information across the region. I will send you a proposal to double the budget of the National Endowment for Democracy, and to focus its new work on the development of free elections, and free markets, free press, and free labor unions in the Middle East. And above all, we will finish the historic work of democracy in Afghanistan and Iraq, so those nations can light the way for others, and help transform a troubled part of the world.

America is a nation with a mission, and that mission comes from our most basic beliefs. We have no desire to dominate, no ambitions of empire. Our aim is a democratic peace — a peace founded upon the dignity and rights of every man and woman. America acts in this cause with friends and allies at our side, yet we understand our special calling: This great republic will lead the cause of freedom.

The Economy

In the last three years, adversity has also revealed the fundamental strengths of the American economy. We have come through recession, and terrorist attack, and corporate scandals, and the uncertainties of war. And because you acted to stimulate our economy with tax relief, this economy is strong, and growing stronger.

You have doubled the child tax credit from $500 to $1,000, reduced the marriage penalty, begun to phase out the death tax, reduced taxes on capital gains and stock dividends [and] cut taxes on small businesses, and you have lowered taxes for every American who pays income taxes.

Americans took those dollars and put them to work, driving this economy forward. The pace of economic growth in the third quarter of 2003 was the fastest in nearly 20 years; new home construction, the highest in almost 20 years; home ownership rates, the highest ever. Manufacturing activity is increasing. Inflation is low. Interest rates are low. Exports are growing. Productivity is high, and jobs are on the rise.

These numbers confirm that the American people are using their money far better than government would have — and you were right to return it.

America's growing economy is also a changing economy. As technology transforms the way almost every job is done, America becomes more productive, and workers need new skills. Much of our job growth will be found in high-skilled fields like health care and biotechnology. So we must respond by helping more Americans gain the skills to find good jobs in our new economy.

Education Goals

All skills begin with the basics of reading and math, which are supposed to be learned in the early grades of our schools. Yet for too long, for too many children, those skills were never mastered. By passing the No Child Left Behind Act, you have made the expectation of literacy the law of our country. We're providing more funding for our schools — a 36 percent increase since 2001. We're requiring higher standards. We are regularly testing every child on the fundamentals. We are reporting results to parents, and making sure they have better options when schools are not performing. We are making progress toward excellence for every child in America.

But the status quo always has defenders. Some want to undermine the No Child Left Behind Act by weakening standards and accountability. Yet the results we require are really a mat-

ter of common sense: We expect third graders to read and do math at the third-grade level — and that's not asking too much. Testing is the only way to identify and help students who are falling behind. This nation will not go back to the days of simply shuffling children along from grade to grade without them learning the basics. I refuse to give up on any child — and the No Child Left Behind Act is opening the door of opportunity to all of America's children.

At the same time, we must ensure that older students and adults can gain the skills they need to find work now. Many of the fastest growing occupations require strong math and science preparation, and training beyond the high school level. So tonight, I propose a series of measures called Jobs for the 21st Century. This program will provide extra help to middle and high school students who fall behind in reading and math, expand advanced placement programs in low-income schools, invite math and science professionals from the private sector to teach part-time in our high schools. I propose larger Pell grants for students who prepare for college with demanding courses in high school. I propose increasing our support for America's fine community colleges, so they can — I do so, so they can train workers for industries that are creating the most new jobs. By all these actions, we'll help more and more Americans to join in the growing prosperity of our country. Job training is important, and so is job creation.

Tax Business

We must continue to pursue an aggressive, pro-growth economic agenda. Congress has some unfinished business on the issue of taxes. The tax reductions you passed are set to expire. Unless you act — unless you act — unless you act, the unfair tax on marriage will go back up. Unless you act, millions of families will be charged $300 more in federal taxes for every child. Unless you act, small businesses will pay higher taxes. Unless you act, the death tax will eventually come back to life. Unless you act, Americans face a tax increase. What Congress has given, the Congress should not take away. For the sake of job growth, the tax cuts you passed should be permanent.

Our agenda for jobs and growth must help small-business owners and employees with relief from needless federal regulation, and protect them from junk and frivolous lawsuits. Consumers and businesses need reliable supplies of energy to make our economy run — so I urge you to pass legislation to modernize our electricity system, promote conservation, and make America less dependent on foreign sources of energy.

My administration is promoting free and fair trade to open up new markets for America's entrepreneurs and manufacturers and farmers — to create jobs for American workers. Younger workers should have the opportunity to build a nest egg by saving part of their Social Security taxes in a personal retirement account.

We should make the Social Security system a source of ownership for the American people. And we should limit the burden of government on this economy by acting as good stewards of taxpayers' dollars.

In two weeks, I will send you a budget that funds the war, protects the homeland, and meets important domestic needs, while limiting the growth in discretionary spending to less than 4 percent. This will require that Congress focus on priorities, cut wasteful spending, and be wise with the people's money. By doing so, we can cut the deficit in half over the next five years.

Immigration Changes

Tonight, I also ask you to reform our immigration laws so they reflect our values and benefit our economy. I propose a new temporary worker program to match willing foreign workers with willing employers when no Americans can be found to fill the job. This reform will be good for our economy because employers will find needed workers in an honest and orderly system. A temporary worker program will help protect our homeland, allowing Border Patrol and law enforcement to focus on true threats to our national security.

I oppose amnesty, because it would encourage further illegal immigration, and unfairly reward those who break our laws. My temporary worker program will preserve the citizenship path for those who respect the law, while bringing millions of hard-working men and women out from the shadows of American life.

Health Care, Prescription Drugs

Our nation's health care system, like our economy, is also in a time of change. Amazing medical technologies are improving and saving lives. This dramatic progress has brought its own challenge, in the rising costs of medical care and health insurance. Members of Congress, we must work together to help control those costs and extend the benefits of modern medicine throughout our country.

Meeting these goals requires bipartisan effort, and two months ago, you showed the way. By strengthening Medicare and adding a prescription drug benefit, you kept a basic commitment to our seniors: You are giving them the modern medicine they deserve.

Starting this year, under the law you passed, seniors can choose to receive a drug discount card, saving them 10 to 25 percent off the retail price of most prescription drugs — and millions of low-income seniors can get an additional $600 to buy medicine. Beginning next year, seniors will have new coverage for preventive screenings against diabetes and heart disease, and seniors just entering Medicare can receive wellness exams.

In January of 2006, seniors can get prescription drug coverage under Medicare. For a monthly premium of about $35, most seniors who do not have that coverage today can expect to see their drug bills cut roughly in half. Under this reform, senior citizens will be able to keep their Medicare just as it is, or they can choose a Medicare plan that fits them best — just as you, as members of Congress, can choose an insurance plan that meets your needs. And starting this year, millions of Americans will be able to save money tax-free for their medical expenses in a health savings account.

I signed this measure proudly, and any attempt to limit the choices of our seniors, or to take away their prescription drug coverage under Medicare, will meet my veto.

On the critical issue of health care, our goal is to ensure that Americans can choose and afford private health care coverage that best fits their individual needs. To make insurance more affordable, Congress must act to address rapidly rising health care costs. Small businesses should be able to band together and negotiate for lower insurance rates, so they can cover more workers with health insurance. I urge you to pass association health plans.

I ask you to give lower-income Americans a refundable tax credit that would allow millions to buy their own basic health insurance.

By computerizing health records, we can avoid dangerous medical mistakes, reduce costs, and improve care. To protect the doctor-patient relationship, and keep good doctors doing good work, we must eliminate wasteful and frivolous medical lawsuits. And tonight I propose that individuals who buy catastrophic health care coverage, as part of our new health savings accounts, be allowed to deduct 100 percent of the premiums from their taxes.

A government-run health care system is the wrong prescription. By keeping costs under control, expanding access, and helping more Americans afford coverage, we will preserve the system of private medicine that makes America's health care the best in the world.

Changes in Our Future

We are living in a time of great change — in our world, in our economy, in science and medicine. Yet some things endure: courage and compassion, reverence and integrity, respect for differences of faith and race. The values we try to live by never change. And they are instilled in us by fundamental institutions, such as families and schools and religious congregations. These institutions, these unseen pillars of civilization, must remain strong in America, and we will defend them. We must stand with our families to help them raise healthy, responsible children. When it comes to helping children make right choices, there is work for all of us to do.

One of the worst decisions our children can make is to gamble their lives and futures on drugs. Our government is helping parents confront this problem with aggressive education, treatment and law enforcement. Drug use in high school has declined by 11 percent over the last two years. Four hun-

dred thousand fewer young people are using illegal drugs than in the year 2001. In my budget, I proposed new funding to continue our aggressive, community-based strategy to reduce demand for illegal drugs. Drug testing in our schools has proven to be an effective part of this effort. So tonight I proposed an additional $23 million for schools that want to use drug testing as a tool to save children's lives. The aim here is not to punish children, but to send them this message: We love you, and we don't want to lose you.

To help children make right choices, they need good examples. Athletics play such an important role in our society, but, unfortunately, some in professional sports are not setting much of an example. The use of performance-enhancing drugs like steroids in baseball, football, and other sports is dangerous, and it sends the wrong message — that there are shortcuts to accomplishment, and that performance is more important than character. So tonight I call on team owners, union representatives, coaches and players to take the lead, to send the right signal, to get tough and to get rid of steroids now.

To encourage right choices, we must be willing to confront the dangers young people face — even when they're difficult to talk about. Each year, about 3 million teenagers contract sexually transmitted diseases that can harm them, or kill them, or prevent them from ever becoming parents. In my budget, I propose a grass-roots campaign to help inform families about these medical risks. We will double federal funding for abstinence programs, so schools can teach this fact of life: Abstinence for young people is the only certain way to avoid sexually transmitted diseases.

Decisions children now make can affect their health and character for the rest of their lives. All of us — parents and schools and government — must work together to counter the negative influence of the culture, and to send the right messages to our children.

Gay Marriage

A strong America must also value the institution of marriage. I believe we should respect individuals as we take a principled stand for one of the most fundamental, enduring institutions of our civilization. Congress has already taken a stand on this issue by passing the Defense of Marriage Act, signed in 1996 by President [Bill] Clinton. That statute protects marriage under federal law as a union of a man and a woman, and declares that one state may not redefine marriage for other states.

Activist judges, however, have begun redefining marriage by court order, without regard for the will of the people and their elected representatives. On an issue of such great consequence, the people's voice must be heard. If judges insist on forcing their arbitrary will upon the people, the only alternative left to the people would be the constitutional process. Our nation must defend the sanctity of marriage.

The outcome of this debate is important — and so is the way we conduct it. The same moral tradition that defines marriage also teaches that each individual has dignity and value in God's sight.

Religious Charities

It's also important to strengthen our communities by unleashing the compassion of America's religious institutions. Religious charities of every creed are doing some of the most vital work in our country — mentoring children, feeding the hungry, taking the hand of the lonely. Yet government has often denied social service grants and contracts to these groups, just because they have a cross or a Star of David or a crescent on the wall. By executive order, I have opened billions of dollars in grant money to competition that includes faith-based charities. Tonight, I ask you to codify this into law, so people of faith can know that the law will never discriminate against them again.

Prisoner Initiative

In the past, we've worked together to bring mentors to children of prisoners, and provide treatment for the addicted, and help for the homeless. Tonight I ask you to consider another group of Americans in need of help. This year, some 600,000 inmates will be released from prison back into society. We know from long experience that if they can't find work, or a home, or help, they are much more likely to commit crime and return to prison. So tonight, I propose a four-year, $300 million prisoner re-entry initiative to expand job training and placement services, to provide transitional housing, and to help newly released prisoners get mentoring, including from faith-based groups. America is the land of second chance, and when the gates of the prison open, the path ahead should lead to a better life.

For all Americans, the last three years have brought tests we did not ask for, and achievements shared by all. By our actions, we have shown what kind of nation we are. In grief, we have found the grace to go on. In challenge, we rediscovered the courage and daring of a free people. In victory, we have shown the noble aims and good heart of America.

And having come this far, we sense that we live in a time set apart. I've been witness to the character of the people of America, who have shown calm in times of danger, compassion for one another, and toughness for the long haul. All of us have been partners in a great enterprise. And even some of the youngest understand that we are living in historic times.

Last month a girl in Lincoln, Rhode Island, sent me a letter. It began, "Dear George W. Bush. If there's anything you know, I, Ashley Pearson, age 10, can do to help anyone, please send me a letter and tell me what I can do to save our country." She added this P.S.: "If you can send a letter to the troops, please put, 'Ashley Pearson believes in you.' "

Tonight, Ashley, your message to our troops has just been conveyed. And, yes, you have some duties yourself. Study hard in school, listen to your mom or dad, help someone in need, and when you and your friends see a man or woman in uniform, say "thank you." And, Ashley, while you do your part, all of us here in this great chamber will do our best to keep you and the rest of America safe and free.

My fellow citizens, we now move forward, with confidence and faith. Our nation is strong and steadfast. The cause we serve is right, because it is the cause of all mankind. The momentum of freedom in our world is unmistakable — and it is not carried forward by our power alone. We can trust in that greater power who guides the unfolding of the years. And in all that is to come, we can know that His purposes are just and true.

May God continue to bless America. ◆

Democrats Agree With Assessments, Differ on the Solutions Required

Following is a transcript of the Democrats' response to President Bush's State of the Union address Jan. 20. Part 1 was delivered by House Minority Leader Nancy Pelosi of California. Part 2 was delivered by Senate Minority Leader Tom Daschle of South Dakota. The text was provided by the Democratic Party.

Part 1: Protecting American Security at Home and Abroad

The state of our union is indeed strong, due to the spirit of the American people — the creativity, optimism, hard work and faith of everyday Americans.

The State of the Union address should offer a vision that unites us as a people — and priorities that move us toward the best America. For inspiration, we look to our brave young men and women in uniform, especially those in Iraq and Afghanistan. Their noble service reminds us of our mission as a nation — to build a future worthy of their sacrifice.

Tonight, from the perspective of 10 years of experience on the Intelligence Committee working on national security issues, I express the Democrats' unbending determination to make the world safer for America — for our people, our interests and our ideals.

Iraq and Afghanistan

Democrats have an unwavering commitment to ensure that America's armed forces remain the best trained, best led, best equipped force for peace the world has ever known. Never before have we been more powerful militarily. But even the most powerful nation in history must bring other nations to our side to meet common dangers.

The president's policies do not reflect that. He has pursued a go-it-alone foreign policy that leaves us isolated abroad and that steals the resources we need for education and health care here at home.

The president led us into the Iraq war on the basis of unproven assertions without evidence; he embraced a radical doctrine of pre-emptive war unprecedented in our history; and he failed to build a true international coalition.

Therefore, American taxpayers are bearing almost all the cost — a colossal $120 billion and rising. More importantly, American troops are enduring almost all the casualties — tragically, 500 killed and thousands more wounded.

Making America Safer

As a nation, we must show our greatness, not just our strength. America must be a light to the world, not just a missile.

Forty-three years ago today, as a college student standing in the freezing cold outside this Capitol Building, I heard President [John F.] Kennedy issue this challenge in his inaugural address: "My fellow citizens of the world," he said, "ask not what America will do for you, but what together we can do for the freedom of man."

There is great wisdom in that, but in it there is also greater strength for our country and the cause of a safer world.

Instead of alienating our allies, let us work with them and international institutions so that together we can prevent the proliferation of weapons of mass destruction and keep them out of the hands of terrorists.

Instead of billions of dollars in no-bid contracts for politically connected firms such as Halliburton, and an insistence on American dominance in Iraq, let us share the burden and responsibility with others, so that together we can end the sense of American occupation and bring our troops home safely when their mission is completed.

Instead of the diplomatic disengagement that almost destroyed the Middle East peace process and aggravated the danger posed by North Korea, let us seek to forge agreements and coalitions — so that, together with others, we can address challenges before they threaten the security of the world.

Terrorism and Homeland Security

We must remain focused on the greatest threat to the security of the United States — the clear and present danger of terrorism. We know what we must do to protect America, but this administration is failing to meet the challenge. Democrats have a better way to ensure our homeland security.

One hundred percent of containers coming into our ports or airports must be inspected. Today, only 3 percent are inspected. One hundred percent of chemical and nuclear plants in the United States must have high levels of security. Today, the Bush administration has tolerated a much lower standard.

One hundred percent communication in real time is needed for our police officers, firefighters, and all our first responders to prevent or respond to a terrorist attack. Today, the technology is there, but the resources are not. One hundred percent of the enriched uranium and other material for weapons of mass destruction must be secured. Today, the administration has refused to commit the resources necessary to prevent it from falling into the hands of terrorists.

America will be far safer if we reduce the chances of a terrorist attack in one of our cities than if we diminish the civil liberties of our own people.

As a nation, we must do better to keep faith with our armed forces, their families and our veterans. Our men and women in uniform show their valor every day. On the battlefield, our troops pledge to leave no soldier behind. Here at home, we must leave no veteran behind. We must ensure their health care, their pensions, and their survivors' benefits.

'Future of Our Children at Stake'

The year ahead offers great opportunity for progress and perhaps new perils still hidden in the shadows of an uncertain world. But you, the American people, have shown again and again that you are equal to any test. Now your example summons all of us in government, Republicans and Democrats, to a higher standard.

This is personal for all of us, in every community across this land. As a moth-

er of five, and now as a grandmother of five, I came into government to help make the future brighter for all of America's children. As much as at any time in my memory, the future of our country and our children is at stake.

Democrats are committed to strengthening the state of our union — to reach for a safer, more prosperous America.

Together, let us make America work for all Americans — let us restore our rightful role of leadership in the world, working with others for "the freedom of man."

I'm now proud to introduce my colleague, the outstanding Senate Democratic leader, Tom Daschle.

Part 2: Building an Opportunity Society for the American People

Let there be no doubt: the state of our union is strong — stronger than the terrorists who seek to harm us and stronger than the challenges that confront us. At the same time, we know that our union can be stronger still.

The president spoke of great goals, and America should never hesitate to push the boundaries of exploration. But neither should we shrink from the great goal of creating a more perfect union here at home.

In his speech, the president asked us to double the budget of the national endowment for democracy, to make permanent the tax cuts already passed, and he asked us to use Social Security money to pay for it.

For the last couple of weeks, I've been traveling through my home state of South Dakota, visiting the people and small towns that are America's backbone. The folks I met are good people. They're happy to help others around the world. But they're asking something, too: What about us? When do our priorities become America's priorities?

Rather than a society that restricts its rewards to a privileged few, we need an "opportunity society" that allows all Americans to succeed. Our opportunity society has at its foundation good jobs, a solid education and quality health care that is affordable and available. We believe that we have to honor the promises we've made to the millions of families who worked hard, played by the rules and have earned a retirement of dignity.

Jobs and the Economy

Our first challenge is to strengthen the economy — the right way. The true test of America's economic recovery is not measured simply in quarterly profit reports, it's measured in jobs. The massive tax cuts that were supposed to spark an economic expansion have instead led to an economic exodus. To make up for the 3 million private-sector jobs that have been lost on President Bush's watch, the economy would have to create 226,000 jobs a month through the end of his term. Last month, the economy created only 1,000 new jobs. That's not good enough.

America can't afford to keep rewarding the accumulation of wealth over the dignity of work. Instead of borrowing even more money to give more tax breaks to companies so that they can export even more jobs, we propose tax cuts and policies that will strengthen our manufacturing sector and create good jobs at good wages here at home. We can also show our patriotism while strengthening agriculture and rural America by labeling all food products with their country of origin.

Education

Education is the second key to our opportunity society. Two years ago, the president signed a new education law. The heart of that law was a promise. The federal government would set high standards for every student, and hold schools responsible for results. In exchange, schools would receive the resources to meet the new standards. America's schools are holding up their end of the bargain; the president has not held up his. Millions of children are being denied the better teachers, smaller classes and extra help they were promised.

At the same time, the president's tax cuts have put states in such a bind that they're being forced to raise the cost of college. Since President Bush took office, the average tuition at a four-year public college has increased by nearly $600. The America our parents gave us was a place in which everyone had a chance to go to a good school, and then to college, community college or vocational school, regardless of family income. Our children deserve nothing less.

Health Care and Medicare

Third, our opportunity society is built on the belief that affordable, available health care is not a luxury, but a basic foundation of a truly compassionate society.

Today, 43.6 million Americans — almost all of them from working families — have no health insurance. That's over 3.8 million more than when President Bush took office. Those Americans lucky enough to have health insurance have seen their premiums go up each of the last three years. The increase in premiums that middle-income families have seen over the past three years is larger than the four-year tax cut they've been promised. This is an invisible tax increase on middle-class families.

Tonight, three years into his administration, the president acknowledged that the rapidly rising cost of health care, and the increasing number of Americans with no health coverage, are problems. But the solutions he proposed — more tax cuts — are not the right ones. More tax cuts will do little to make health care more affordable or reduce the number of people without insurance, and they will weaken health coverage for those who now have it.

When I was driving around South Dakota this summer, I met a nurse in Sioux Falls who has cancer. She told me that she couldn't afford the $1,500 a month her drugs cost. She told me that she was going to die — that she was a lost cause. But, she said, we must solve this problem: Don't turn more people into lost causes.

We believe that the federal government should use the power of 40 million Americans to lower prescription drug prices and to allow us to get more affordable drugs from Canada — instead of forbidding both. Drug companies and insurance companies are the only ones who benefit from that restriction — not the American people — and that's why we want to change it.

Retirement

And in our vision of an "opportunity society," promises made to those who have worked a lifetime will be honored in retirement. That's why we believe that America's pension system needs to be strengthened, and that So-

cial Security's benefit should be a guarantee, not a gamble.

Only when every American who wants to work, can, when every child goes to a good school and has the opportunity to go further, only when health care is available and affordable for every American, when a lifetime of work guarantees a retirement with dignity and when America is secure at home and our strength abroad is respected and not resented — only then will we have a union as strong as the American people. That's the America we want to build, because that's the union the American people deserve. Thank you for listening, good night, and God bless America. ◆

Edwards Touches on 'Small Town' Roots, Jobs, War on Terrorism, Health Care

Following is the speech by Democratic vice presidential nominee Sen. John Edwards of North Carolina to the Democratic National Convention on July 28, as transcribed by Federal Document Clearing House Inc.:

Thank you. Now you know why Elizabeth is so amazing, right?

I am a lucky man to have the love of my life at my side. Both of us have been blessed with four extraordinary children: Wade, Cate who you heard from, Emma Claire and Jack.

We are having such an extraordinary time, myself and my entire family, at this convention.

And by the way, how great was Teresa Heinz Kerry last night?

My father and mother, Wallace and Bobbie Edwards, are also here tonight.

You taught me the values that I carry in my heart: faith, family, responsibility, opportunity for everyone. You taught me that there's dignity and honor in a hard day's work. You taught me to always look out for our neighbors, to never look down on anybody, and treat everybody with respect.

Those are the values that John Kerry and I believe in. And nothing makes me prouder than standing with him in this campaign. I am so humbled to be your candidate for vice president of the United States.

I want to talk about our next president. For those who want to know what kind of leader he'll be, I want to take you back about 30 years. When John Kerry graduated college, he volunteered for military service, volunteered to go to Vietnam, volunteered to captain a Swift boat, one of the most dangerous duties in Vietnam that you could have. As a result, he was wounded, honored for his valor.

If you have any question about what he's made of, just spend three minutes with the men who served with him then and who stand with him now. They saw up close what he's made of.

They saw him reach into the river and pull one of his men to safety and save his life. They saw him in the heat of battle make a decision in a split second to turn his boat around, drive it through an enemy position, and chase down the enemy to save his crew. Decisive, strong: Is this not what we need in a commander in chief?

You know, we hear a lot of talk about values. Where I come from, you don't judge somebody's values based upon how they use that word in a political ad. You judge their values based upon what they've spent their life doing.

So when a man volunteers to serve his country, the man volunteers and puts his life on the line for others, that's a man who represents real American values.

This is a man who is prepared to keep the American people safe, to make America stronger at home and more respected in the world.

John is a man who knows the difference between right and wrong. He wants to serve you. Your cause is his cause. And that is why we must and we will elect him the next president of the United States.

You know, for the last few months, John's been traveling around the country talking about his positive, optimistic vision for America, talking about his plan to move this country in the right direction.

But what have we seen? Relentless negative attacks against John. So in the weeks ahead, we know what's coming, don't we?

More negative attacks — aren't you sick of it?

They are doing all they can to take the campaign for the highest office in the land down the lowest possible road.

But this is where you come in: Between now and November, you, the American people, you can reject the tired, old, hateful, negative politics of the past. And instead you can embrace the politics of hope, the politics of what's possible because this is America, where everything is possible.

Growing Up

I am here tonight for a very simple reason: Because I love my country. And I have every reason to love my country. I have grown up in the bright light of America.

I grew up in a small town in rural North Carolina, a place called Robbins.

My father, he worked in a mill all his life, and I still remember vividly the men and women who worked in that mill with him. I can see them. Some of them had lint in their hair; some of them had grease on their faces. They worked hard, and they tried to put a little money away so that their kids and their grandkids could have a better life.

The truth is, they're just like the autoworkers, the office workers, the teachers and shopkeepers on main streets all across this country.

My mother had a number of jobs. She worked at the post office so she and my father could have health care. She owned her own small business. She refinished furniture to help pay for my education.

I have had such incredible opportunities in my life. I was blessed to be the first person in my family to go to college. I worked my way through, and I had opportunities beyond my wildest dreams.

And the heart of this campaign — your campaign, our campaign — is to make sure all Americans have exactly the same kind of opportunities that I had no matter where you live, no matter who your family is, no matter what the color of your skin is.

This is the America we believe in.

I have spent my life fighting for the kind of people I grew up with.

For two decades, I stood with kids and families against big HMOs and big insurance companies.

When I got to the Senate, I fought those same fights against the Washington lobbyists and for causes like the Patients' Bill of Rights.

I stand here tonight ready to work with you and John to make America stronger. And we have much work to

do, because the truth is, we still live in a country where there are two different Americas — one, for all of those people who have lived the American dream and don't have to worry, and another for most Americans, everybody else who struggles to make ends meet every single day. It doesn't have to be that way.

We can build one America where we no longer have two health care systems: one for families who get the best health care money can buy, and then one for everybody else rationed out by insurance companies, drug companies, HMOs.

Millions of Americans have no health coverage at all.

It doesn't have to be that way. We have a plan.

We have a plan that will offer all Americans the same health care that your senator has. We can give you tax breaks to help you pay for your health care. And when we're in office, we will sign a real patients' bill of rights into law so that you can make your own health care decisions.

We shouldn't have two public school systems in this country: one for the most affluent communities, and one for everybody else.

None of us believe that the quality of a child's education should be controlled by where they live or the affluence of the community they live in.

It doesn't have to be that way.

We can build one school system that works for all our kids, gives them a chance to do what they're capable of doing.

Our plan will reform our schools and raise standards. We can give our schools the resources that they need. We can provide incentives to put our best teachers in the subjects and the places where we need them the most. And we can ensure that 3 million children have a safe place to go when they leave school in the afternoon.

We can do this together, you and I.

John Kerry and I believe that we shouldn't have two different economies in America: one for people who are set for life, they know their kids and their grandkids are going to be just fine; and then one for most Americans, people who live paycheck to paycheck. You don't need me to explain this to you, do you?

You know exactly what I'm talking about. Can't save any money, can you?

Takes every dime you make just to pay your bills.

And you know what happens if something goes wrong, if you have a child that gets sick, a financial problem, a layoff in the family — you go right off the cliff. And when that happens, what's the first thing that goes? Your dreams.

It doesn't have to be that way.

We can strengthen and lift up your families. Your agenda is our agenda.

So let me give you some specifics.

Jobs, Health Care, Tax Cuts

First, we can create good-paying jobs in this country again. We're going to get rid of tax cuts for companies who are outsourcing your jobs — and, instead, we're going to give tax breaks to American companies that are keeping jobs right here in America.

And we will invest in the jobs of the future and in the technologies and innovation to ensure that America stays ahead of the competition. And we're going to do this because John and I understand that a job is about more than a paycheck; it's about dignity and self-respect.

Hard work should be valued in this country, so we're going to reward work, not just wealth.

We don't want people to just get by; we want people to get ahead.

So let me give you some specifics about what we're going to do.

First, we're going to help you pay for your health care by having a tax break and health care reform that can save you up to $1,000 on your premiums.

We're going to help you cover the rising costs of child care with a tax credit up to $1,000 so that your kids have a place to go when you're at work that they're safe and well taken care of.

If your child — if your child wants to be the first in your family to go to college, we're going to give you a tax break on up to $4,000 in tuition.

And everyone — and everybody listening here and at home is thinking one thing right now: OK, how are you going to pay for it? Right?

Well, let me tell you how we're going to pay for it. And I want to be very clear about this. We are going to keep and protect the tax cuts for 98 percent of Americans — 98 percent. We're going to roll back — we're going to roll back the tax cuts for the wealthiest Americans. And we're going to close corporate loopholes.

We're going to cut government contractors and wasteful spending. We can move this country forward without passing the burden to our children and our grandchildren.

We can also do something about 35 million Americans who live in poverty every day. And here's why we shouldn't just talk about, but do something about the millions of Americans who live in poverty: Because it is wrong. And we have a moral responsibility to lift those families up.

I mean, the very idea that in a country of our wealth and our prosperity, we have children going to bed hungry? We have children who don't have the clothes to keep them warm? We have millions of Americans who work full-time every day to support their families, working for minimum wage, and still live in poverty. It's wrong.

These are men and women who are living up to their bargain. They're working hard, they're supporting their families. Their families are doing their part; it's time we did our part.

And that's what we're going to do — that's what we're going to do when John is in the White House, because we're going to raise the minimum wage, we're going to finish the job on welfare reform, and we're going to bring good-paying jobs to the places where we need them the most.

And by doing all those things, we're going to say "no" forever to any American working full-time and living in poverty. Not in our America, not in our America, not in our America.

Let me talk about — let me talk about why we need to build one America.

Because I, like many of you, I saw up close what having two Americas can do to our country.

From the time I was very young, I saw the ugly face of segregation and discrimination. I saw young African-American kids being sent upstairs in movie theaters.

I saw "white only" signs on restaurant doors and luncheon counters.

I feel such an enormous personal responsibility when it comes to issues of race and equality and civil rights.

And I've heard some discussions

and debates around America about where and in front of what audiences we ought to talk about race and equality and civil rights. I have an answer to that question: Everywhere, everywhere, everywhere.

This is not an African-American issue. This is not a Latino issue. This is not an Asian-American issue. This is an American issue.

It is about who we are, what our values are and what kind of country we live in.

The truth is, the truth is that what John and I want, what all of us want is for our children and our grandchildren to be the first generations that grow up in an America that's no longer divided by race. We must build one America. We must be one America, strong and united for another very important reason: because we are at war.

War on Terrorism

None of us will ever forget where we were on September the 11th. We all share the same terrible images, the towers falling in New York, the Pentagon in flames, a smoldering field in Pennsylvania. We share a profound sadness for the nearly 3,000 lives that were lost.

And as a member of the Senate Intelligence Committee, I know that we have to do more to fight the war on terrorism and keep the American people safe. We can do that.

We are approaching the third anniversary of September 11th, and one thing I can tell you: When we're in office, it won't take three years to get the reforms in our intelligence that are necessary to keep the American people safe.

We will do whatever it takes, as long as it takes, to make sure this never happens again in our America.

And when John is president, we will listen to the wisdom of the September 11th commission. We will lead strong alliances. We will safeguard and secure our weapons of mass destruction. We will strengthen our homeland security, protect our ports, protect our chemical plants, and support our firefighters, police officers, EMTs.

We will always — we will always use our military might to keep the American people safe.

And we, John and I, we will have one clear unmistakable message for al Qaeda and these terrorists: You cannot run. You cannot hide. We will destroy you.

John understands personally about fighting in a war. And he knows what our brave men and women are going through right now in another war, the war in Iraq.

The human cost and the extraordinary heroism of this war, it surrounds us. It surrounds us in our cities and our towns. And we'll win this war because of the strength and courage of our own people.

Some of our friends and neighbors, they saw their last images in Baghdad. Some took their last steps outside of Fallujah. Some buttoned their uniform for the last time before they went out and saved their unit.

Men and women who used to take care of themselves, they now count on others to see them through the day. They need their mother to tie their shoe, their husband to brush their hair, their wife's arm to help them across the room.

The stars and stripes wave for them. The word "hero" was made for them. They are the best and the bravest. And they will never be left behind.

You understand that. And they deserve a president who understands that on the most personal level what they've gone through, what they've given and what they've given up for their country.

To us, the real test of patriotism is how we treat the men and women who have put their lives on the line to protect our values.

And let me tell you, the 26 million veterans in this country will not have to wonder when we're in office whether they'll have health care next week or next year. We will take care of them because they have taken care of us.

But today, our great United States military is stretched thin. We've got more than 140,000 troops in Iraq, almost 20,000 in Afghanistan. And I visited the men and women there, and we're praying as they try to give that country hope.

Like all of those brave men and women, John put his life on the line for our country. He knows that when authority is given to a president, much is expected in return.

That's why we will strengthen and modernize our military. We will double our Special Forces. We will invest in the new equipment and technologies so that our military remains the best equipped and best prepared in the world. This will make our military stronger. It'll make sure that we can defeat any enemy in this new world.

But we can't do this alone. We have got to restore our respect in the world to bring our allies to us and with us.

It is how we won the Cold War. It is how we won two world wars. And it is how we will build a stable Iraq.

With a new president who strengthens and leads our alliances, we can get NATO to help secure Iraq. We can ensure that Iraq's neighbors, like Syria and Iran, don't stand in the way of a democratic Iraq. We can help Iraq's economy by getting other countries to forgive their enormous debt and participate in the reconstruction.

We can do this for the Iraqi people. We can do it for our own soldiers. And we will get this done right.

A new president will bring the world to our side, and with it a stable Iraq, a real chance for freedom and peace in the Middle East, including a safe and secure Israel.

And John and I will bring the world together.

John and I will bring the world together to face the most dangerous threat we have: the possibility of terrorists getting their hands on a chemical, biological weapon or nuclear weapon.

With our credibility restored, we can work with other nations to secure stockpiles of the world's most dangerous weapons and safeguard this extraordinarily dangerous material. We can finish the job and secure the loose nukes in Russia. We can close the loophole in the Nuclear Nonproliferation Treaty that allows rogue nations access to the tools they need to develop these weapons.

That's how we can address the new threats we face. That's how we can keep you safe. And that's how we can restore America's respect around the world.

And together, we will ensure that the image of America — the image all of us love — America, this great shining light, this beacon of freedom, democracy and human rights that the world looks up to, is always lit.

And the truth is — the truth is, that every child, every family in

America will be safer and more secure if they grow up in a world where America is once again looked up to and respected. That is the world we can create together.

Tonight, as we celebrate in this hall, somewhere in America, a mother sits at the kitchen table. She can't sleep because she's worried she can't pay her bills. She's working hard trying to pay her rent, trying to feed her kids, but she just can't catch up.

It didn't used to be that way in her house. Her husband was called up in the Guard. Now he's been in Iraq for over a year. They thought he was going to come home last month, but now he's got to stay longer.

She thinks she's alone. But tonight in this hall and in your homes, you know what? She's got a lot of friends.

We want her to know that we hear her.

It is time to bring opportunity and an equal chance to her door.

We're here to make America stronger at home so that she can get ahead.

And we're here to make America respected in the world again so that we can bring him home. And American soldiers don't have to fight this war in Iraq or this war on terrorism alone.

So, when you return home some night, you might pass a mother on her way to work the late shift, you tell her: Hope is on the way.

When your brother calls and says he's spending his entire life at the office and he still can't get ahead, you tell him: Hope is on the way.

When your parents call and tell you their medicine's going through the roof, they can't keep up, you tell them: Hope is on the way.

And when your neighbor calls and says her daughter's worked hard and she wants to go to college, you tell her: Hope is on the way.

And when your son or daughter, who is serving this country heroically in Iraq calls, you tell them: Hope is on the way.

When you wake up and you're sitting at the kitchen table with your kids, and you're talking about the great possibilities in America, your kids should know that John and I believe, to our core, that tomorrow can be better than today.

Like all of us, I have learned a lot of lessons in my life.

Two of the most important are that, first, there will always be heartache and struggle; we can't make it go away. But the second is that people of good and strong will can make a difference.

One is a sad lesson, and the other is inspiring.

We are Americans and we choose to be inspired. We choose hope over despair, possibilities over problems, optimism over cynicism. We choose to do what's right even when those around us say, "You can't do that." We choose to be inspired, because we know that we can do better, because this is America, where everything is still possible.

What we believe — what John Kerry and I believe is that you should never look down on anybody. We ought to lift people up. We don't believe in tearing people apart. We believe in bringing them together. What we believe — what I believe — is that the family you're born into and the color of your skin in our America should never control your destiny.

Join us in this cause.

Let's make America stronger at home and more respected in the world. Let's ensure that once again, in our one America — our one America — tomorrow will always be better than today.

Thank you, God bless you, and God bless the United States of America. ◆

Kerry Accepts Democratic Nomination, Emphasizing Values, the Economy, Military Strength and Respect Abroad

Following is the speech by Democratic presidential nominee Sen. John Kerry of Massachusetts to the Democratic National Convention on July 29, as transcribed by Federal Document Clearing House Inc.

I'm John Kerry, and I'm reporting for duty.

We are here tonight because we love our country. We're proud of what America is and what it can become.

My fellow Americans, we're here tonight united in one purpose: to make America stronger at home and respected in the world.

A great American novelist wrote that you can't go home again. He could not have imagined this evening. Tonight, I am home — home where my public life began and those who made it possible live; home where our nation's history was written in blood, idealism and hope; home where my parents showed me the values of family, faith and country.

Thank you, all of you, for a welcome home I will never forget.

I wish my parents could share this moment. They went to their rest in the last few years.

But their example, their inspiration, their gift of open eyes — open eyes and open mind and endless heart and world that doesn't have an end — are bigger and more lasting than any words at all.

I was born, as some of you saw in the film, in Fitzsimmons Army Hospital in Colorado — when my dad was a pilot in World War II. Now, I am not one to read into things, but guess which wing of the hospital the maternity ward was in?

I'm not kidding. I was born in the West Wing.

My mother was the rock of our family, as so many mothers are. She stayed up late to help me with my homework. She sat by my bed when I was sick. She answered the questions of a child who, like all children, found the world full of wonders and mysteries.

She was my den mother when I was a Cub Scout, and she was so proud of her 50-year pin as a Girl Scout leader.

She gave me her passion for the environment. She taught me to see trees as the cathedrals of nature. And by the power of her example, she showed me that we can and must complete the march toward full equality for all women in the United States of America.

My dad did the things that a boy remembers. He gave me my first model airplane, my first baseball mitt, my first bicycle.

He also taught me that we are here for something bigger than ourselves. He lived out the responsibilities and the sacrifices of the "greatest generation" to whom we owe so much.

And when I was a young man, he was in the State Department, stationed in Berlin when it and the world were divided between democracy and communism.

I have unforgettable memories of being a kid mesmerized by the British, French and American troops, each of them guarding their own part of the city, and Russians standing guard on that stark line separating East from West.

On one occasion, I rode my bike into Soviet East Berlin, and when I proudly told my dad, he promptly grounded me.

But what I learned has stayed with me for a lifetime. I saw how different life was on different sides of the same city. I saw the fear in the eyes of people who were not free. I saw the gratitude of people toward the United States for all that we had done. I felt goose bumps as I got off a military train and heard the Army band strike up "Stars and Stripes Forever."

I learned what it meant to be America at our best. I learned the pride of our freedom. And I am determined now to restore that pride to all who look to America.

Mine were greatest generation parents. And as I thank them, we all join together to thank a whole generation for making America strong, for winning World War II, winning the Cold War and for the great gift of service which brought America 50 years of peace and prosperity.

My parents inspired me to serve, and when I was in high school, a junior, John Kennedy called my generation to service. It was the beginning of a great journey, a time to march for civil rights, for voting rights, for the environment, for women, for peace.

We believed we could change the world. And you know what? We did.

But we're not finished. But we're not finished.

The journey isn't complete; the march isn't over; the promise isn't perfected.

A New Chapter

Tonight, we're setting out again. And together, we're going to write the next great chapter of America's story.

We have it in our power to change the world, but only if we're true to our ideals. And that starts by telling the truth to the American people.

As president, that is my first pledge to you tonight: As president, I will restore trust and credibility to the White House.

I ask you, I ask you to judge me by my record. As a young prosecutor, I fought for victims' rights and made prosecuting violence against women a priority.

When I came to the Senate, I broke with many in my own party to vote for a balanced budget, because I thought it was the right thing to do. I fought to put 100,000 police officers on the streets of America.

And then I reached out across the aisle with John McCain to work to find the truth about our POWs and missing in action and to finally make peace in Vietnam.

I will be a commander in chief who will never mislead us into war.

I will have a vice president who will

not conduct secret meetings with polluters to rewrite our environmental laws.

I will have a secretary of Defense who will listen to the best advice of the military leaders.

And I will appoint an attorney general who will uphold the Constitution of the United States.

My fellow Americans, this is the most important election of our lifetime. The stakes are high. We are a nation at war: a global war on terror against an enemy unlike we've ever known before.

And here at home, wages are falling, health care costs are rising and our great middle class is shrinking. People are working weekends — two jobs, three jobs — and they're still not getting ahead.

We're told that outsourcing jobs is good for America. We're told that jobs that pay $9,000 less than the jobs that have been lost is the best that we can do. They say this is the best economy that we've ever had. And they say anyone who thinks otherwise is a pessimist.

Well, here is our answer: There is nothing more pessimistic than saying that America can't do better.

We can do better, and we will.

We're the optimists. For us, this is a country of the future. We're the can-do people.

And let's not forget what we did in the 1990s: We balanced the budget. We paid down the debt. We created 23 million new jobs. We lifted millions out of poverty. And we lifted the standard of living for the middle class.

We just need to believe in ourselves and we can do it again.

Acceptance

So tonight, in the city where America's freedom began, only a few blocks from where the sons and daughters of liberty gave birth to our nation, here tonight, on behalf of a new birth of freedom, on behalf of the middle class who deserve a champion, and those struggling to join it who deserve a fair shot, for the brave men and women in uniform who risk their lives every day and the families who pray for their return, for all those who believe our best days are ahead of us, with great faith in the American people, I accept your nomination for president of the United States.

I am proud —

Thank you, thank you, thank you.

Thank you. I am proud that at my side will be a running mate whose life is the story of the American dream, and who's worked every day to make that dream real for all Americans, Sen. John Edwards of North Carolina and his wife Elizabeth and their family. Thank you.

This son of a millworker is ready to lead.

And next January, Americans will be proud to have a fighter for the middle class to succeed Dick Cheney as vice president of the United States.

And what can I say about Teresa?

She has the strongest moral compass of anyone I know. She's down to earth, nurturing, courageous, wise and smart. She speaks her mind, and she speaks the truth, and I love her for that, too. And that's why America will embrace her as the next first lady of the United States.

For Teresa and me, no matter what the future holds or the past has given us, nothing will ever mean as much as our children, as you can sense listening to them. We love them, not just for who they are and what they've become, but for being themselves, making us laugh, holding our feet to the fire and never letting me get away with anything.

Thank you, Andre, Alex, Chris, Vanessa and John.

Fighting for What's Right

And in this journey, I am accompanied by an extraordinary band of brothers led by that American hero, a patriot called Max Cleland.

Our band of brothers . . .

Our band of brothers doesn't march together because of who we are as veterans, but because of what we learned as soldiers.

We fought for this nation because we loved it, and we came back with the deep belief that every day is extra. We may be a little older, we may be a little grayer, but we still know how to fight for our country.

And standing with us in that fight — standing with us in that fight are those who shared with me the long season of the primary campaign: Carol Moseley Braun, Gen. Wesley Clark, Howard Dean, Dick Gephardt, Bob Graham, Dennis Kucinich, Joe Lieberman and Al Sharpton.

To all of you, I say thank you for teaching me and testing me. But mostly, we say thank you for standing up for our country and for giving us the unity to move America forward.

My fellow Americans, the world tonight is very different from the world of four years ago. But I believe the American people are more than equal to the challenge.

Remember the hours after September 11th when we came together as one to answer the attack against our homeland. We drew strength when our firefighters ran up stairs and risked their lives so that others might live; when rescuers rushed into smoke and fire at the Pentagon; when the men and women of Flight 93 sacrificed themselves to save our nation's capital; when flags were hanging from front porches all across America, and strangers became friends. It was the worst day we have ever seen, but it brought out the best in all of us.

I am proud that after September 11th all our people rallied to President Bush's call for unity to meet the danger.

There were no Democrats. There were no Republicans. There were only Americans. And how we wish it had stayed that way.

Now, I know that there are those who criticize me for seeing complexities — and I do — because some issues just aren't all that simple. Saying there are weapons of mass destruction in Iraq doesn't make it so. Saying we can fight a war on the cheap doesn't make it so. And proclaiming "mission accomplished" certainly doesn't make it so.

As president, I will ask the hard questions and demand hard evidence. I will immediately reform the intelligence system, so policy is guided by facts, and facts are never distorted by politics.

And as president, I will bring back this nation's time-honored tradition: The United States of America never goes to war because we want to; we only go to war because we have to. That is the standard of our nation.

I know what kids go through when they are carrying — I know what kids go through when they're carrying an M-16 in a dangerous place, and they can't tell friend from foe. I know what they go through when they're out on

patrol at night and they don't know what's coming around the next bend. I know what it's like to write letters home telling your family that everything's all right, when you're not sure that that's true.

As president, I will wage this war with the lessons I learned in war. Before you go to battle, you have to be able to look a parent in the eye and truthfully say, "I tried everything possible to avoid sending your son or daughter into harm's way, but we had no choice — we had to protect the American people, fundamental American values against a threat that was real and imminent."

So, lesson No. 1, this is the only justification for going to war.

And on my first day in office, I will send a message to every man and woman in our armed forces: You will never be asked to fight a war without a plan to win the peace.

A Stronger Military

I know what we have to do in Iraq. We need a president who has the credibility to bring our allies to our side and share the burden, reduce the cost to American taxpayers, reduce the risk to American soldiers. That's the right way to get the job done and bring our troops home.

Here is the reality: That won't happen until we have a president who restores America's respect and leadership so we don't have to go it alone in the world.

And we need to rebuild our alliances so we can get the terrorists before they get us.

I defended this country as a young man, and I will defend it as president.

Let there be no mistake: I will never hesitate to use force when it is required. Any attack will be met with a swift and a certain response.

I will never give any nation or any institution a veto over our national security.

And I will build a stronger military. We will add 40,000 active duty troops, not in Iraq, but to strengthen American forces that are now overstretched, overextended and under pressure.

We will double our Special Forces to conduct terrorist operations, antiterrorist operations, and we will provide our troops with the newest weapons and technology to save their lives and win the battle. And we will end the backdoor draft of the National Guard and reservists.

To all who serve in our armed forces today, I say: Help is on the way.

As president, I will fight a smarter, more effective war on terror. We will deploy every tool in our arsenal: our economic as well as our military might, our principles as well as our firepower.

In these dangerous days, there is a right way and a wrong way to be strong. Strength is more than tough words.

After decades of experience in national security, I know the reach of our power, and I know the power of our ideals.

Strong Leaders, Allies

We need to make America once again a beacon in the world. We need to be looked up to, not just feared.

We need to lead a global effort against nuclear proliferation, to keep the most dangerous weapons in the world out of the most dangerous hands in the world.

We need a strong military, and we need to lead strong alliances.

And then, with confidence and determination, we will be able to tell the terrorists: 'You will lose, and we will win." The future doesn't belong to fear; it belongs to freedom.

And the front lines of this battle are not just far away. They're right here on our shores.

They're at our airports and potentially in any town or city.

Today, our national security begins with homeland security. The 9/11 commission has given us a path to follow, endorsed by Democrats, Republicans and the 9/11 families. As president, I will not evade or equivocate; I will immediately implement all the recommendations of that commission.

We shouldn't be letting 95 percent of our container ships come into our ports without ever being physically inspected. We shouldn't be leaving nuclear and chemical plants without enough protection. And we shouldn't be opening firehouses in Baghdad and shutting them in the United States of America.

And tonight, we have an important message for those who question the patriotism of Americans who offer a better direction for our country. Before wrapping themselves in the flag and shutting their eyes to the truth and their ears, they should remember what America is really all about. They should remember the great idea of freedom for which so many have given their lives. Our purpose now is to reclaim our democracy itself.

We are here to affirm that when Americans stand up and speak their minds and say America can do better, that is not a challenge to patriotism; it is the heart and soul of patriotism.

You see that flag up there. We call her Old Glory, the stars and stripes forever. I fought under that flag, as did so many of those people who were here tonight and all across the country. That flag flew from the gun turret right behind my head, and it was shot through and through and tattered, but it never ceased to wave in the wind. It draped the caskets of men that I served with and friends I grew up with.

For us, that flag is the most powerful symbol of who we are and what we believe in: our strength, our diversity, our love of country, all that makes America both great and good.

That flag doesn't belong to any president. It doesn't belong to any ideology.

It doesn't belong to any party. It belongs to all the American people.

My fellow citizens, elections are about choices. And choices are about values. In the end, it's not just policies and programs that matter; the president who sits at that desk must be guided by principle.

Family Values

For four years, we've heard a lot of talk about values. But values spoken without actions taken are just slogans.

Values are not just words, values are what we live by. They're about the causes that we champion and the people we fight for.

And it is time for those who talk about family values to start valuing families.

You don't value families — You don't value families by kicking kids out of after-school programs and taking cops off the streets, so that Enron can get another tax break.

We believe in the family value of caring for our children and protecting the neighborhoods where they walk and play.

And that is the choice in this election.

You don't value families by denying real prescription drug coverage to seniors so big drug companies can get another windfall.

We believe in the family value expressed in one of the oldest Commandments: "Honor thy father and thy mother."

As president, I will not privatize Social Security. I will not cut benefits. And together, we will make sure that senior citizens never have to cut their pills in half because they can't afford lifesaving medicine.

And that is the choice in this election.

You don't value families if you force them to take up a collection to buy body armor for a son or daughter in the service, if you deny veterans health care, or if you tell middle-class families to wait for a tax cut, so that the wealthiest among us can get even more.

We believe in the value of doing what's right for everyone in the American family. And that's the choice in this election.

We believe that what matters most is not narrow appeals masquerading as values, but the shared values that show the true face of America; not narrow values that divide us, but the shared values that unite us: family, faith, hard work, opportunity and responsibility for all, so that every child, every adult, every parent, every worker in America has an equal shot at living up to their God-given potential. That is the American dream and the American value.

Employment

What does it mean in America today when Dave McCune, a steelworker that I met in Canton, Ohio, saw his job sent overseas and the equipment in his factory was literally unbolted, crated up and shipped thousands of miles away, along with that job?

What does it mean when workers I've met have had to train their foreign replacements?

America can do better. And tonight we say: Help is on the way.

What does it mean when Mary Ann Knowles, a woman with breast cancer I met in New Hampshire, had to keep working day after day, right through her chemotherapy, no matter how sick she felt, because she was ter-

rified of losing her family's health insurance?

America can do better, and help is on the way.

What does it mean when Deborah Kromins from Philadelphia, Pa., works and she saves all her life, and finds out that her pension has disappeared into thin air and the executive who looted it has bailed out on a golden parachute?

America can do better, and help is on the way.

Help is on the way.

What does it mean when 25 percent of the children in Harlem have asthma because of air pollution?

We can do better, America can do better, and help is on the way.

Help is on the way.

What does it mean when people are huddled in blankets in the cold, sleeping in Lafayette Park, on the doorstep of the White House itself, and the number of families living in poverty has risen by 3 million in the last four years?

America can do better, and help is on the way.

So tonight we come here tonight to ask: Where is the conscience of our country?

I'll tell you where it is — I'll tell you where it is. It's in rural and small-town America; it's in urban neighborhoods and the suburban main streets; it's alive in the people that I've met in every single part of this land. It's bursting in the hearts of Americans who are determined to give our values and our truth back to our country.

We value jobs that actually pay you more than the job that you lost. We value jobs where, when you put in a week's work, you can actually pay your bills, provide for your children, lift up the quality of your life.

We value an America where the middle class is not being squeezed, but doing better.

The Economy

So, here is our economic plan to build a stronger America: first, new incentives to revitalize manufacturing; second, investment in technology and innovation that will create the good-paying jobs of the future; third, close the tax loopholes that reward companies for shipping jobs overseas.

Instead, we will reward the companies that create and keep good-paying jobs right where they belong, in the

good old U.S.A.

We value an America that exports products, not jobs. And we believe American workers should never have to subsidize the loss of their own job.

Next, we will trade, and we will compete in the world. But our plan calls for a fair playing field, because if you give the American worker a fair playing field, there's no one in the world that the American worker can't compete against.

And we're going to return to fiscal responsibility because it is the foundation of our economic strength. Our plan will cut the deficit in half in four years by ending tax giveaways that are nothing more than corporate welfare, and we will make government live by the rule that every family has to live by: Pay as you go.

And let me — let me tell you what we won't do: We won't raise taxes on the middle class.

You've heard a lot of false charges about this in recent months. So, let me say straight out what I will do as president: I will cut middle-class taxes. I will reduce the tax burden on small business. And I will roll back the tax cuts for the wealthiest individuals who make over $200,000 a year, so we can invest in health care, education and job creation.

Our education plan for a stronger America sets high standards and it demands accountability from parents, teachers and schools. It provides for smaller class sizes, and it treats teachers like the professionals that they are.

And it gives a tax credit to families for each and every year of college.

When I was a prosecutor, I met young kids who were in trouble, abandoned, all of them, by adults. And as president, I am determined that we stop being a nation content to spend $50,000 a year to send a young person to prison for the rest of their life, when we could invest $10,000 in Head Start, Early Start, Smart Start, a real start to the lives of our children.

And we value health care that's affordable and accessible for all Americans.

Since 2000, 4 million people have lost their health insurance. Millions more are struggling to afford it. You know what's happening.

Your premiums, your co-payments, your deductibles have all gone through the roof.

Our health care plan for a stronger America cracks down on the waste, and the greed and the abuse in our health care system, and it will save families $1,000 a year in premiums. You'll get to pick your own doctor. And patients and doctors, not insurance company bureaucrats, will make medical decisions.

Under our health care plan — Medicare will negotiate lower drug prices for seniors. And all Americans will be able to buy less-expensive prescription drugs from countries like Canada.

The story of people struggling for health care is the story of so many Americans. But you know what? It's not the story of senators and members of Congress, because we give ourselves great health care, and you get the bill.

Well, I'm here to say tonight: Your family's health care is just as important as any politician's in Washington, D.C.

And when I am president, we will stop being the only advanced nation in the world which fails to understand that health care is not a privilege for the wealthy, and the connected and the elected; it is a right for all Americans.

And we will make it so.

Energy Options

We value an America that controls its own destiny because it's finally and forever independent of Mideast oil. What does it mean for our economy and our national security when we have only 3 percent of the world's oil reserves, yet we rely on foreign countries for 53 percent of what we consume?

I want an America that relies on its ingenuity and innovation, not the Saudi royal family.

And our energy plan for a stronger America — our energy plan will invest in new technologies and alternative fuels and the cars of the future, so that no young American in uniform will ever be held hostage to our dependence on oil from the Middle East.

I've told you about our plans for the economy, for education, for health care, for energy independence. I want you to know more about them.

So now I'm going to say something that [Franklin D. Roosevelt] could never have said in his acceptance speech: Go to johnkerry.com.

I want to address these next words directly to President George W. Bush.

In the weeks ahead, let's be optimists, not just opponents. Let's build unity in the American family, not angry division. Let's honor this nation's diversity. Let's respect one another. And let's never misuse for political purposes the most precious document in American history, the Constitution of the United States.

My friends, the high road may be harder, but it leads to a better place.

And that's why Republicans and Democrats must make this election a contest of big ideas, not small-minded attacks.

This is our time to reject the kind of politics calculated to divide race from race, region from region, group from group.

Maybe some just see us divided into those red states and blue states, but I see us as one America: red, white and blue.

And when I am president, the government I lead will enlist people of talent, Republicans as well as Democrats, to find the common ground, so that no one who has something to contribute to our nation will be left on the sidelines.

And let me say it plainly: In that cause, and in this campaign, we welcome people of faith. America is not us and them.

I think of what Ron Reagan said of his father a few weeks ago, and I want to say this to you tonight: I don't wear my religion on my sleeve, but faith has given me values and hope to live by, from Vietnam to this day, from Sunday to Sunday.

I don't want to claim that God is on our side.

As Abraham Lincoln told us, I want to pray humbly that we are on God's side.

And whatever our faith — whatever our faith, one belief should bind us all: The measure of our character is our willingness to give of ourselves for others and for our country.

These aren't Democratic values. These aren't Republican values. They're American values. We believe in them. They're who we are. And if we honor them, if we believe in ourselves, we can build an America that is stronger at home and respected in the world.

So much promise stretches before us. Americans have always reached for the impossible, looked to the next horizon and asked, "What if?"

Two young bicycle mechanics from Dayton asked, "What if this airplane could take off at Kitty Hawk?" It did that, and it changed the world forever.

A young president asked, "What if we could go to the moon in 10 years?" And now we're exploring the stars and the solar systems themselves.

A young generation of entrepreneurs asked, "What if we could take all the information in a library and put it on a chip the size of a fingernail?" We did, and that, too, changed the world.

And now it's our time to ask, "What if?"

What if we find a breakthrough to cure Parkinson's, diabetes, Alzheimer's and AIDS?

What if we have a president who believes in science, so we can unleash the wonders of discovery like stem cell research and treat illness for millions of lives?

What if we do what adults should do, and make sure that all of our children are safe in the afternoons after school? What if we have a leadership that's as good as the American dream, so that bigotry and hatred never again steal the hope or future of any American?

I learned a lot about these values on that gunboat patrolling the Mekong Delta with Americans — you saw them — who come from places as different as Iowa and Oregon, Arkansas, Florida, California.

No one cared where we went to school. No one cared about our race or our backgrounds. We were literally all in the same boat. We looked out, one for the other, and we still do.

That is the kind of America that I will lead as president: an America where we are all in the same boat.

Never has there been a moment more urgent for Americans to step up and define ourselves. I will work my heart out. But, my fellow citizens, the outcome is in your hands more than mine.

It is time to reach for the next dream. It is time to look to the next horizon. For America, the hope is there. The sun is rising. Our best days are still to come.

Thank you. Good night. God bless you, and God bless the United States of America. ◆

Sept. 11 Commission Recommends Alternatives for Congressional Oversight Of Intelligence Operations

The National Commission on Terrorist Attacks Upon the United States, created by Congress in November 2002 (PL 107-306), released its 567-page report on July 22, including numerous recommendations that would require legislative action to be implemented. (Sept. 11 commission, p. 11-8; 2002 Almanac, p. 7-18)

One section of the report dealt specifically with the role of Congress and its committees in overseeing intelligence operations. Following is the text of the commission's recommendations that would affect the operations of Congress:

13.4 UNITY OF EFFORT IN THE CONGRESS

Strengthen Congressional Oversight of Intelligence and Homeland Security

Of all our recommendations, strengthening congressional oversight may be among the most difficult and important. So long as oversight is governed by current congressional rules and resolutions, we believe the American people will not get the security they want and need. The United States needs a strong, stable, and capable congressional committee structure to give America's national intelligence agencies oversight, support and leadership.

Few things are more difficult to change in Washington than congressional committee jurisdiction and prerogatives. To a member, these assignments are almost as important as the map of his or her congressional district. The American people may have to insist that these changes occur, or they may well not happen. Having interviewed numerous members of Congress from both parties, as well as congressional staff members, we found that dissatisfaction with congressional oversight remains widespread.

The future challenges of America's

intelligence agencies are daunting. They include the need to develop leading-edge technologies that give our policy-makers and war-fighters a decisive edge in any conflict where the interests of the United States are vital. Not only does good intelligence win wars, but the best intelligence enables us to prevent them from happening altogether.

Under the terms of existing rules and resolutions, the House and Senate Intelligence committees lack the power, influence and sustained capability to meet this challenge. While few members of Congress have the broad knowledge of intelligence activities or the know-how about the technologies employed, all members need to feel assured that good oversight is happening. When their unfamiliarity with the subject is combined with the need to preserve security, a mandate emerges for substantial change.

Tinkering with the existing structure is not sufficient. Either Congress should create a joint committee for intelligence, using the Joint Atomic Energy Committee as its model, or it should create House and Senate committees with combined authorizing and appropriations powers.

Whichever of these two forms [is] chosen, the goal should be a structure — codified by resolution with powers expressly granted and carefully limited — allowing a relatively small group of members of Congress, given time and reason to master the subject and the agencies, to conduct oversight of the intelligence establishment and be clearly accountable for their work. The staff of this committee should be nonpartisan and work for the entire committee and not for individual members.

The other reforms we have suggested —for a National Counterterrorism Center and a National Intelligence Director — will not work if congressional oversight does not change too. Unity of effort in executive manage-

ment can be lost if it is fractured by divided congressional oversight.

Recommendation: Congressional oversight for intelligence — and counterterrorism — is now dysfunctional. Congress should address this problem. We have considered various alternatives: A joint committee on the old model of the Joint Committee on Atomic Energy is one. A single committee in each house of Congress, combining authorizing and appropriating authorities, is another.

● The new committee or committees should conduct continuing studies of the activities of the intelligence agencies and report problems relating to the development and use of intelligence to all members of the House and Senate.

● We have already recommended that the total level of funding for intelligence be made public, and that the national intelligence program be appropriated to the National Intelligence Director, not to the secretary of Defense.

● We also recommend that the intelligence committee should have a subcommittee specifically dedicated to oversight, freed from the consuming responsibility of working on the budget.

● The resolution creating the new intelligence committee structure should grant subpoena authority to the committee or committees. The majority party's representation on this committee should never exceed the minority's representation by more than one.

● Four of the members appointed to this committee or committees should be a member who also serves on each of the following additional committees: Armed Services, Judiciary, Foreign Affairs, and the Defense Appropriations subcommittee. In this way the other major congressional interests can be brought together in the new committee's work.

- Members should serve indefinitely on the Intelligence committees, without set terms, thereby letting them accumulate expertise.

- The committees should be smaller —perhaps seven or nine members in each house — so that each member feels a greater sense of responsibility, and accountability, for the quality of the committee's work.

The leaders of the Department of Homeland Security now appear before 88 committees and subcommittees of Congress. One expert witness (not a member of the administration) told us that this is perhaps the single largest obstacle impeding the department's successful development. The one attempt to consolidate such committee authority, the House Select Committee on Homeland Security, may be eliminated. The Senate does not have even this.

Congress needs to establish for the Department of Homeland Security the kind of clear authority and responsibility that exist to enable the Justice Department to deal with crime and the Defense Department to deal with threats to national security. Through not more than one authorizing committee and one appropriating subcommittee in each house, Congress should be able to ask the secretary of Homeland Security whether he or she has the resources to provide reasonable security against major terrorist acts within the United States and to hold the secretary accountable for the department's performance.

Recommendation: Congress should create a single, principal point of oversight and review for homeland security. Congressional leaders are best able to judge what committee **should have jurisdiction over this department and its duties. But we believe that Congress does have the obligation to choose one in the House and one in the Senate, and that this committee should be a permanent standing committee with a nonpartisan staff.**

Improve the Transitions Between Administrations

In chapter 6, we described the transition of 2000-2001. Beyond the policy issues we described, the new administration did not have its deputy Cabinet officers in place until the spring of 2001, and the critical sub-Cabinet officials were not confirmed until the summer — if then. In other words, the new administration — like others before it — did not have its team on the job until at least six months after it took office.

Recommendation: Since a catastrophic attack could occur with little or no notice, we should minimize as much as possible the disruption of national security policy making during the change of administrations by accelerating the process for national security appointments. We think the process could be improved significantly so transitions can work more effectively and allow new officials to assume their new responsibilities as quickly as possible.

- Before the election, candidates should submit the names of selected members of their prospective transition teams to the FBI so that, if necessary, those team members can obtain security clearances immediately after the election is over.

- A president-elect should submit lists of possible candidates for national security positions to begin obtaining security clearances immediately after the election, so that their background investigations can be complete before January 20.

- A single federal agency should be responsible for providing and maintaining security clearances, ensuring uniform standards, including uniform security questionnaires and financial report requirements, and maintaining a single database. This agency can also be responsible for administering polygraph tests on behalf of organizations that require them.

- A president-elect should submit the nominations of the entire new national security team, through the level of under secretary of Cabinet departments, not later than January 20. The Senate, in return, should adopt special rules requiring hearings and votes to confirm or reject national security nominees within 30 days of their submission. The Senate should not require confirmation of such executive appointees below Executive Level 3.

- The outgoing administration should provide the president-elect, as soon as possible after Election Day, with a classified, compartmented list that catalogues specific, operational threats to national security; major military or covert operations; and pending decisions on the possible use of force. Such a document could provide both notice and a checklist, inviting a president-elect to inquire and learn more. ◆

President Bush Accepts Nomination, Detailing Past Four Years in Office And Next Four Years of Possibilities

Following is the speech by President Bush to the Republican National Convention on Sept. 2, as transcribed by Federal Document Clearing House Inc.

Mr. Chairman, delegates, fellow citizens, I'm honored by your support, and I accept your nomination for president of the United States.

When I said those words four years ago, none of us could have envisioned what these years would bring. In the heart of this great city, we saw tragedy arrive on a quiet morning. We saw the bravery of rescuers grow with danger. We learned of passengers on a doomed plane who died with a courage that frightened their killers.

We have seen a shaken economy rise to its feet. And we have seen Americans in uniform storming mountain strongholds and charging through sandstorms and liberating millions with acts of valor that would make the men of Normandy proud.

Since 2001, Americans have been given hills to climb and found the strength to climb them.

Now, because we have made the hard journey, we can see the valley below. Now, because we have faced challenges with resolve, we have historic goals within our reach and greatness in our future.

We will build a safer world and a more hopeful America, and nothing will hold us back.

In the work we have done and the work we will do, I am fortunate to have a superb vice president.

I have counted on Dick Cheney's calm and steady judgment in difficult days, and I'm honored to have him at my side.

I am grateful to share my walk in life with Laura Bush.

Americans have come to see the goodness and kindness and strength I first saw 26 years ago, and we love our first lady.

I'm a fortunate father of two spirited, intelligent and lovely young women.

I'm blessed with a sister and brothers who are my closest friends.

And I will always be the proud and grateful son of George and Barbara Bush.

My father served eight years at the side of another great American, Ronald Reagan.

His spirit of optimism and good will and decency are in this hall and are in our hearts and will always define our party.

Two months from today, voters will make a choice based on the records we have built, the convictions we hold and the vision that guides us forward.

A presidential election is a contest for the future. Tonight, I will tell you where I stand, what I believe, and where I will lead this country in the next four years.

The Agenda

I believe every child can learn and every school must teach, so we passed the most important federal education reform in history. Because we acted, children are making sustained progress in reading and math, America's schools are getting better, and nothing will hold us back.

I believe we have a moral responsibility to honor America's seniors, so I brought Republicans and Democrats together to strengthen Medicare. Now seniors are getting immediate help buying medicine. Soon every senior will be able to get prescription drug coverage, and nothing will hold us back.

I believe in the energy and innovative spirit of America's workers, entrepreneurs, farmers and ranchers, so we unleashed that energy with the largest tax relief in a generation.

Because we acted, our economy is growing again and creating jobs, and nothing will hold us back.

I believe the most solemn duty of the American president is to protect the American people.

If America shows uncertainty or weakness in this decade, the world will drift toward tragedy.

This will not happen on my watch.

I am running for president with a clear and positive plan to build a safer world and a more hopeful America. I am running with a compassionate conservative philosophy: that government should help people improve their lives, not try to run their lives.

I believe this nation wants steady, consistent, principled leadership. And that is why, with your help, we will win this election.

The story of America is the story of expanding liberty, an ever-widening circle, constantly growing to reach further and include more.

Our nation's founding commitment is still our deepest commitment: In our world, and here at home, we will extend the frontiers of freedom.

Transforming the System

The times in which we work and live are changing dramatically. The workers of our parents' generation typically had one job, one skill, one career, often with one company that provided health care and a pension. And most of those workers were men.

Today, workers change jobs, even careers, many times during their lives. And in one of the most dramatic shifts our society has seen, two-thirds of all moms also work outside the home.

This changed world can be a time of great opportunity for all Americans to earn a better living, support your family, and have a rewarding career. And government must take your side.

Many of our most fundamental systems — the tax code, health coverage, pension plans, worker training — were created for the world of yesterday, not tomorrow. We will transform these systems so that all citizens are equipped, prepared, and thus truly free to make your own choices and pursue your own dreams.

My plan begins with providing the security and opportunity of a growing economy. We now compete in a global

market that provides new buyers for our goods, but new competition for our workers. To create more jobs in America, America must be the best place in the world to do business.

To create jobs, my plan will encourage investment and expansion by restraining federal spending, reducing regulation and making the tax relief permanent.

To create jobs, we will make our country less dependent on foreign sources of energy.

To create jobs, we will expand trade and level the playing field to sell American goods and services across the globe.

And we must protect small-business owners and workers from the explosion of frivolous lawsuits that threaten jobs across our country.

Another drag on our economy is the current tax code, which is a complicated mess, filled with special interest loopholes, saddling our people with more than 6 billion hours of paperwork and headache every year. The American people deserve — and our economic future demands — a simpler, fairer, pro-growth system.

In a new term, I will lead a bipartisan effort to reform and simplify the federal tax code.

Another priority in a new term will be to help workers take advantage of the expanding economy to find better and higher-paying jobs. In this time of change, many workers want to go back to school to learn different or higher-level skills. So we will double the number of people served by our principal job training program and increase funding for community colleges.

I know that with the right skills, American workers can compete with anyone, anywhere in the world.

In this time of change, opportunity in some communities is more distant than in others. To stand with workers in poor communities and those that have lost manufacturing, textile, and other jobs, we will create American opportunity zones.

In these areas, we'll provide tax relief and other incentives to attract new business and improve housing and job training to bring hope and work throughout all of America.

As I've traveled the country, I've met many workers and small-business owners who have told me that they are

worried they cannot afford health care. More than half of the uninsured are small-business employees and their families.

In a new term, we must allow small firms to join together to purchase insurance at the discounts available to big companies.

We will offer a tax credit to encourage small businesses and their employees to set up health savings accounts and provide direct help for low-income Americans to purchase them. These accounts give workers the security of insurance against major illness, the opportunity to save tax-free for routine health expenses, and the freedom of knowing you can take your account with you whenever you change jobs.

We will provide low-income Americans with better access to health care. In a new term, I will ensure every poor county in America has a community or rural health center.

As I have traveled our country, I've met too many good doctors, especially OB/GYNs, who are being forced out of practice because of the high cost of lawsuits.

To make health care more affordable and accessible, we must pass medical liability reform now.

And in all we do to improve health care in America, we will make sure that health decisions are made by doctors and patients, not by bureaucrats in Washington, D.C.

In this time of change, government must take the side of working families.

In a new term we will change outdated labor laws to offer comp-time and flex-time. Our laws should never stand in the way of a more family-friendly workplace.

Another priority for a new term is to build an ownership society, because ownership brings security and dignity and independence.

Thanks to our policies, home ownership in America is at an all-time high.

Tonight, we set a new goal: 7 million more affordable homes in the next 10 years, so more American families will be able to open the door and say, "Welcome to my home."

In an ownership society, more people will own their health plans and have the confidence of owning a piece of their retirement.

We'll always keep the promise of

Social Security for our older workers.

With the huge baby boom generation approaching retirement, many of our children and grandchildren understandably worry whether Social Security will be there when they need it.

We must strengthen Social Security by allowing younger workers to save some of their taxes in a personal account, a nest egg you can call your own and government can never take away.

Education Overhaul

In all these proposals, we seek to provide not just a government program, but a path, a path to greater opportunity, more freedom and more control over your own life.

And the path begins with our youngest Americans.

To build a more hopeful America, we must help our children reach as far as their vision and character can take them.

Tonight, I remind every parent and every teacher, I say to every child: No matter what your circumstance, no matter where you live, your school will be the path to promise of America.

We are transforming our schools by raising standards and focusing on results. We are insisting on accountability, empowering parents and teachers, and making sure that local people are in charge of their schools.

By testing every child, we are identifying those who need help, and we're providing a record level of funding to get them that help.

In northeast Georgia, Gainesville Elementary School is mostly Hispanic and 90 percent poor. And this year, 90 percent of its students passed state tests in reading and math.

The principal — the principal expresses the philosophy of his school this way: "We don't focus on what we can't do at this school; we focus on what we can do. And we do whatever it takes to get kids across the finish line."

See, this principal is challenging the soft bigotry of low expectations.

And that is the spirit of our education reform and the commitment of our country: No dejaremos a ningun niño atras. We will leave no child behind.

We are making progress. We are making progress. And there is more to do.

In this time of change, most new jobs are filled by people with at least

two years of college, yet only about one in four students gets there. In our high schools, we will fund early intervention programs to help students at risk. We will place a new focus on math and science.

As we make progress, we will require a rigorous exam before graduation. By raising performance in our high schools and expanding Pell Grants for low and middle income families, we will help more Americans start their career with a college diploma.

America's children must also have a healthy start in life. In a new term, we will lead an aggressive effort to enroll millions of poor children who are eligible but not signed up for the government's health insurance programs. We will not allow a lack of attention or information to stand between these children and the health care they need.

Anyone who wants more details on my agenda can find them online. The Web address is not very imaginative, but it's easy to remember: georgewbush.com.

These changing times can be exciting times of expanded opportunity.

And here, you face a choice. My opponent's policies are dramatically different from ours.

Sen. Kerry opposed Medicare reform and health savings accounts. After supporting my education reforms, he now wants to dilute them. He opposes legal and medical liability reform. He opposed reducing the marriage penalty, opposed doubling the child credit, opposed lowering income taxes for all who pay them.

To be fair, there are some things my opponent is for.

He's proposed more than $2 trillion in new federal spending so far, and that's a lot, even for a senator from Massachusetts.

And to pay for that spending, he is running on a platform of increasing taxes. And that's the kind of promise a politician usually keeps.

His policies of tax and spend, of expanding government rather than expanding opportunity, are the politics of the past. We are on the path to the future, and we're not turning back.

In this world of change, some things do not change: the values we try to live by, the institutions that give our lives meaning and purpose. Our society rests on a foundation of responsibility and character and family commitment.

Because family and work are sources of stability and dignity, I support welfare reform that strengthens family and requires work.

Because a caring society will value its weakest members, we must make a place for the unborn child.

Because religious charities provide a safety net of mercy and compassion, our government must never discriminate against them.

Because the union of a man and woman deserves an honored place in our society, I support the protection of marriage against activist judges.

And I will continue to appoint federal judges who know the difference between personal opinion and the strict interpretation of the law.

My opponent recently announced that he is the candidate of "conservative values," which must have come as a surprise to a lot of his supporters.

Now, there are some problems with this claim. If you say the heart and soul of America is found in Hollywood, I'm afraid you are not the candidate of conservative values.

If you voted against the bipartisan Defense of Marriage Act, which President [Bill] Clinton signed, you are not the candidate of conservative values.

If you gave a speech, as my opponent did, calling the Reagan presidency eight years of "moral darkness," then you may be a lot of things, but the candidate of conservative values is not one of them.

Protecting America

This election will also determine how America responds to the continuing danger of terrorism, and you know where I stand.

Three days after September the 11th, I stood where Americans died, in the ruins of the twin towers.

Workers in hard hats were shouting to me, "Whatever it takes." A fellow grabbed me by the arm, and he said, "Do not let me down." Since that day, I wake up every morning thinking about how to better protect our country. I will never relent in defending America — whatever it takes.

So we have fought the terrorists across the Earth, not for pride, not for power, but because the lives of our citizens are at stake.

Our strategy is clear. We have tripled funding for homeland security and trained half a million first responders because we are determined to protect our homeland.

We are transforming our military and reforming and strengthening our intelligence services. We are staying on the offensive, striking terrorists abroad so we do not have to face them here at home.

And we are working to advance liberty in the broader Middle East, because freedom will bring a future of hope and the peace we all want. And we will prevail.

Our strategy is succeeding. Four years ago, Afghanistan was the home base of al Qaeda.

Pakistan was a transit point for terrorist groups. Saudi Arabia was fertile ground for terrorist fundraising. Libya was secretly pursuing nuclear weapons, Iraq was a gathering threat. And al Qaeda was largely unchallenged as it planned attacks.

Today, the government of a free Afghanistan is fighting terror. Pakistan is capturing terrorist leaders. Saudi Arabia is making raids and arrests. Libya is dismantling its weapons programs. The army of a free Iraq is fighting for freedom. And more than three-quarters of al Qaeda's key members and associates have been detained or killed.

We have led, many have joined, and America and the world are safer.

This progress involved careful diplomacy, clear moral purpose and some tough decisions.

And the toughest came on Iraq. We knew Saddam Hussein's record of aggression and support for terror. We knew his long history of pursuing, even using, weapons of mass destruction. And we know that September the 11th requires our country to think differently. We must, and we will, confront threats to America before it is too late.

In Saddam Hussein, we saw a threat. Members of both political parties, including. . . . Members of both political parties, including my opponent and his running mate, saw the threat, and voted to authorize the use of force. We went to the United Nations Security Council, which passed a unanimous resolution demanding the dictator disarm, or face serious consequences. Leaders in the Middle East

urged him to comply.

After more than a decade of diplomacy, we gave Saddam Hussein another chance, a final chance, to meet his responsibilities to the civilized world. He again refused.

And I faced the kind of decision that comes only to the Oval Office, a decision no president would ask for, but must be prepared to make: Do I forget the lessons of September 11th and take the word of a madman or do I take action to defend our country?

Faced with that choice, I will defend America every time.

Because we acted to defend our country, the murderous regimes of Saddam Hussein and the Taliban are history; more than 50 million people have been liberated, and democracy is coming to the broader Middle East.

In Afghanistan, terrorists have done everything they can to intimidate people, yet more than 10 million citizens have registered to vote in the October presidential election, a resounding endorsement for democracy.

Despite ongoing acts of violence, Iraq now has a strong prime minister, a national council, and national elections are scheduled for January.

Our nation is standing with the people of Afghanistan and Iraq, because when America gives its word, America must keep its word.

Military Mission

As importantly, we are serving a vital and historic cause that will make our country safer. Free societies in the Middle East will be hopeful societies which no longer feed resentments and breed violence for export. Free governments in the Middle East will fight terrorists instead of harboring them.

And that helps us keep the peace.

So our mission in Afghanistan and Iraq is clear. We will help new leaders to train their armies, and move toward elections, and get on the path of stability and democracy as quickly as possible. And then our troops will return home with the honor they have earned.

Our troops know the historic importance of our work. One Army specialist wrote home, "We are transforming a once-sick society into a hopeful place. The various terrorist enemies we are facing in Iraq," he continued, "are really aiming at you back in the United States. This is a test of will for our country. We soldiers of yours are doing great and scoring victories in confronting the evil terrorists."

That young man is right. Our men and women in uniform are doing a superb job for America.

Tonight, I want to speak to all of them and to their families: You are involved in a struggle of historic proportion. Because of your service and sacrifice, we are defeating the terrorists where they live and plan, and you're making America safer.

Because of you, women in Afghanistan are no longer shot in a sports stadium. Because of you, the people of Iraq no longer fear being executed and left in mass graves.

Because of you, the world is more just and will be more peaceful.

We owe you our thanks. And we owe you something more. We will give you all the resources, all the tools, and all the support you need for victory.

Again, my opponent and I have different approaches. I proposed, and the Congress overwhelmingly passed, $87 billion in funding needed by our troops doing battle in Afghanistan and Iraq. My opponent and his running mate voted against this money for bullets and fuel and vehicles and body armor.

When asked to explain his vote, the senator said, "I actually did vote for the $87 billion, before I voted against it."

Then he said he was "proud" of his vote. Then, when pressed, he said it was a "complicated" matter.

There's nothing complicated about supporting our troops in combat.

Our allies also know the historic importance of our work. About 40 nations stand beside us in Afghanistan, and some 30 in Iraq. I deeply appreciate the courage and wise counsel of leaders like [Australian] Prime Minister Howard, [Polish] President Kwasniewski, [Italian] Prime Minister Berlusconi and, of course, [British] Prime Minister Tony Blair.

Again, my opponent takes a different approach. In the midst of war, he has called American allies, quote, a "coalition of the coerced and the bribed."

That would be nations like Great Britain, Poland, Italy, Japan, the Netherlands, Denmark, El Salvador, Australia and others — allies that deserve the respect of all Americans, not the scorn of a politician.

I respect every soldier, from every country, who serves beside us in the hard work of history. America is grateful, and America will not forget.

The people we have freed won't forget either. Not long ago, seven Iraqi men came to see me in the Oval Office. They had Xs branded into their foreheads and their right hands had been cut off by Saddam Hussein's secret police, the sadistic punishment for imaginary crimes.

During our emotional visit one of the Iraqi men used his new prosthetic hand to slowly write out, in Arabic, a prayer for God to bless America.

I am proud that our country remains the hope of the oppressed and the greatest force for good on this Earth.

Others understand the historic importance of our work. The terrorists know. They know that a vibrant, successful democracy at the heart of the Middle East will discredit their radical ideology of hate.

They know that men and women with hope and purpose and dignity do not strap bombs on their bodies and kill the innocent.

The terrorists are fighting freedom with all their cunning and cruelty because freedom is their greatest fear. And they should be afraid, because freedom is on the march.

Democracy Within Reach

I believe in the transformational power of liberty. The wisest use of American strength is to advance freedom.

As the citizens of Afghanistan and Iraq seize the moment, their example will send a message of hope throughout a vital region.

Palestinians will hear the message that democracy and reform are within their reach and so is peace with our good friend, Israel.

Young women across the Middle East will hear the message that their day of equality and justice is coming. Young men will hear the message that national progress and dignity are found in liberty, not tyranny and terror.

Reformers and political prisoners and exiles will hear the message that their dream of freedom cannot be denied forever. And as freedom ad-

vances, heart by heart, and nation by nation, America will be more secure and the world more peaceful.

America has done this kind of work before, and there have always been doubters. In 1946, 18 months after the fall of Berlin to allied forces, a journalist in The New York Times wrote this: "Germany is a land in an acute stage of economic, political and moral crisis. European capitals are frightened. In every military headquarters, one meets alarmed officials doing their utmost to deal with the consequences of the occupation policy that they admit has failed," end quote.

Maybe that same person is still around, writing editorials.

Fortunately, we had a resolute president named Truman who, with the American people, persevered, knowing that a new democracy at the center of Europe would lead to stability and peace. And because that generation of Americans held firm in the cause of liberty, we live in a better and safer world today.

The progress we and our friends and allies seek in the broader Middle East will not come easily or all at once.

Yet Americans, of all people, should never be surprised by the power of liberty to transform lives and nations. That power brought settlers on perilous journeys, inspired colonies to rebellion, ended the sin of slavery, and set our nation against the tyrannies of the 20th century.

We were honored to aid the rise of democracy in Germany and Japan, Nicaragua and Central Europe and the Baltics, and that noble story goes on.

Freedom: America's Gift

I believe that America is called to lead the cause of freedom in a new century. I believe that millions in the Middle East plead in silence for their liberty. I believe that given the chance, they will embrace the most honorable form of government ever devised by man.

I believe all these things because freedom is not America's gift to the world; it is the almighty God's gift to every man and woman in this world.

This moment in the life of our country will be remembered. Generations will know if we kept our faith and kept our word. Generations will know if we seized this moment and used it to build a future of safety and peace. The freedom of many and the future security of our nation now depend on us.

And tonight, my fellow Americans, I ask you to stand with me.

In the last four years — in the last four years, you and I have come to know each other. Even when we don't agree, at least you know what I believe and where I stand.

You may have noticed I have a few flaws, too. People sometimes have to correct my English.

I knew I had a problem when Arnold Schwarzenegger started doing it.

Some folks look at me and see a certain swagger, which in Texas is called "walking."

Now and then I come across as a little too blunt, and for that we can all thank the white-haired lady sitting right up there.

One thing I have learned about the presidency is that whatever shortcomings you have, people are going to notice them; and whatever strengths you have, you're going to need them.

These four years have brought moments I could not foresee and will not forget. I've tried to comfort Americans who lost the most on September the 11th: people who showed me a picture or told me a story so I would know how much was taken from them.

I have learned first-hand that ordering Americans into battle is the hardest decision even when it is right. I have returned the salute of wounded soldiers, some with a very tough road ahead, who say they were just doing their job. I've held the children of the fallen who are told their dad or mom is a hero, but would rather just have their dad or mom.

I've met with parents and wives and husbands who have received a folded flag and said a final goodbye to a soldier they loved. I am awed that so many have used those meetings to say that I am in their prayers and to offer encouragement to me.

Where does that strength like that come from? How can people so burdened with sorrow also feel such pride? It is because they know their loved one was last seen doing good because they know that liberty was precious to the one they lost.

And in those military families, I have seen the character of a great nation: decent and idealistic and strong.

The world saw that spirit three miles from here, when the people of this city faced peril together and lifted a flag over the ruins and defied the enemy with their courage.

My fellow Americans, for as long as our country stands, people will look to the resurrection of New York City and they will say: Here buildings fell, and here a nation rose.

We see America's character in our military, which finds a way or makes one. We see it in our veterans, who are supporting military families in their days of worry. We see it in our young people, who have found heroes once again.

We see that character in workers and entrepreneurs, who are renewing our economy with their effort and optimism.

And all of this has confirmed one belief beyond doubt: Having come this far, our tested and confident nation can achieve anything.

To everything we know there is a season — a time for sadness, a time for struggle, a time for rebuilding.

And now we have reached a time for hope. This young century will be liberty's century.

By promoting liberty abroad, we will build a safer world. By encouraging liberty at home, we will build a more hopeful America.

Like generations before us, we have a calling from beyond the stars to stand for freedom. This is the everlasting dream of America. And tonight, in this place, that dream is renewed.

Now we go forward, grateful for our freedom, faithful to our cause, and confident in the future of the greatest nation on Earth.

May God bless you, and may God continue to bless our great country. ◆

'America Is in Need of Unity and Longing For a Larger Measure of Compassion'

Following is the speech that Sen. John Kerry of Massachusetts, the 2004 Democratic presidential nominee, delivered at Faneuil Hall in Boston on Nov. 3 in which he conceded his defeat — as transcribed by Federal Document Clearing House Inc.

Thank you so much. Thank you, thank you. I love you. I love you, thank you. Thank you, thank you so much. Thank you so much. You just have no idea how warming and how generous that welcome is, your love is, your affection. And I'm gratified by it.

I'm sorry that we got here a little bit late — and little bit short.

I spoke to President Bush and I offered him and Laura our congratulations on their victory. We had a good conversation, and we talked about the danger of division in our country and the need — the desperate need for unity, for finding the common ground, coming together.

Today, I hope that we can begin the healing.

In America, it is vital that every vote count, and that every vote be counted. But the outcome should be decided by voters, not a protracted legal process. I would not give up this fight if there was a chance that we would prevail. But it is now clear that even when all the provisional ballots are counted, which they will be, there won't be enough outstanding votes for us to be able to win Ohio.

And therefore we cannot win this election.

My friends, it was here that we began our campaign for the presidency and all we had was hope and vision for a better America. It was a privilege and a gift to spend two years traveling this country, coming to know so many of you.

I wish that I could just wrap you up in my arms and embrace each and every one of you individually all across this nation. I thank you from the bottom of my heart.

Thank you. Thank you.

(Audience member: "We still got your back.")

Thank you, man. And I'm. . . . And I assure you, you watch, I'll still love yours. So hang in there.

I will always be particularly grateful to the colleague that you just heard from who became my partner, my very close friend, an extraordinary leader, John Edwards. And I thank him for everything he did. Thank you, sir.

John and I would be the first to tell you that we owe so much to our families. They're here with us today. They were with us every single step of the way. They sustained us. They went out on their own and they multiplied our campaign all across this country.

No one did this more with grace and with courage and candor, that I love, than my wife Teresa, and I thank her.

And our children were there every single step of the way. It was unbelievable. Vanessa, Alex, Chris, Andre and John from my family. And Elizabeth Edwards, who is so remarkable and so strong and so smart.

And Johnny and Kate, who went out there on their own, just like my daughters did. And also Emma Claire and Jack, who were up beyond their bedtime last night, like a lot of us.

I want to thank my crewmates and my friends from 35 years ago, that great band of brothers who crisscrossed this country on my behalf for 2004. They had the courage to speak the truth back then and they spoke it again this year. And for that, I will forever be grateful.

And thanks also, as I look around here, to friends and family of a lifetime, some from college, friends made all across the years, and then all across the miles of this campaign. You are so special. You brought the gift of your passion for our country and the possibilities of change. And that will stay with us and with this country forever.

Thanks to Democrats and Republicans and independents who stood with us, and everyone who voted, no matter who their candidate was.

And thanks to my absolutely unbelievable, dedicated staff lead by a wonderful campaign manager, Mary Beth Cahill, who did an extraordinary job.

There's so much written about campaigns and there's so much that Americans never get to see.

Volunteers, Big and Small

I wish they could all spend a day on a campaign and see how hard these folks work to make America better. It is its own unbelievable contribution to our democracy and it's a gift to everybody, but especially to me, and I'm grateful to each and every one of you.

And I thank your families and I thank you for the sacrifices you've made. And to all the volunteers all across this country who gave so much of themselves. You know, thanks to William Field, a six-year-old who collected $680 — a quarter and a dollar at a time — selling bracelets during the summer to help change America.

Thanks to Michael Benson from Florida, who I spied in a rope line holding a container of money and it turned out he had raided his piggy bank and wanted to contribute.

And thanks to Ilana Wexler, 11 years old, who started Kids for Kerry all across our country.

I think of the brigades of students and people, young and old, who took time to travel, time off from work, their own vacation time, to work in states far and wide. They braved the hot days of and the winter to knock on doors because they were determined to open the doors of opportunity to all Americans.

They worked their hearts out. And I wish, you don't know how much, that I could have brought this race home for you, for them.

'I Will Never Forget You'

And I say to them now: Don't lose faith. What you did made a difference.

And building on itself, we go on to make a difference another day.

I promise you, that time will come, the time will come, the election will come, when your work and your ballots will change the world. And it's worth fighting for.

I want to especially say to the American people: In this journey, you have given me the honor and the gift of listening and learning from you.

I have visited your homes, I visited your churches, I visited your community halls, I've heard your stories. I know your struggles, I know your hopes. They are part of me now. And I will never forget you and I'll never stop fighting for you.

You may not understand completely in what ways, but it is true when I say to you that you have taught me and you have tested me and you've lifted me up and you've made me stronger.

I did my best to express my vision and my hopes for America. We worked hard and we fought hard, and I wish that things had turned out a little differently. But in an American election, there are no losers — because whether or not our candidates are successful, the next morning we all wake up as Americans.

That is the greatest privilege and the most remarkable good fortune that can come to us on Earth.

With that gift also comes obligation. We are required now to work together for the good of our country.

In the days ahead, we must find common cause. We must join in common effort, without remorse or recrimination, without anger or rancor. America is in need of unity and longing for a larger measure of compassion.

I hope President Bush will advance those values in the coming years.

I pledge to do my part to try to bridge the partisan divide.

I know this is a difficult time for my supporters, but I ask them, all of you, to join me in doing that. Now, more than ever, with our soldiers in harm's way, we must stand together and succeed in Iraq and win the war on terror.

I will also do everything in my power to ensure that my party, a proud Democratic Party, stands true to our best hopes and ideals.

I believe that what we started in this campaign will not end here.

Our fight goes on to put America back to work and to make our economy a great engine of job growth.

Our fight goes on to make affordable health care an accessible right for all Americans, not privilege.

Our fight goes on to protect the environment, to achieve equality, to push the frontiers of science and discovery and to restore America's reputation in the world.

I believe that all of this will happen, and sooner than we may think, because we're America, and America always moves forward.

I've been honored to represent the citizens of this commonwealth in the United States Senate now for 20 years. And I pledge to them that in the years ahead, I'm going to fight on for the people and for the principles that I've learned and lived with here in Massachusetts.

I'm proud of what we stood for in this campaign and of what we accomplished. When we began, no one thought it was possible to even make this a close race. But we stood for real change, change that would make a real difference in the life of our nation and the lives of our families. And we defined that choice to America.

I'll never forget the wonderful people who came to our rallies, who stood in our rope lines, who put their hopes in our hands, who invested in each and every one of us. I saw in them the truth that America is not only great, but it is good.

So with a grateful heart, I leave this campaign with a prayer that has even greater meaning to me now that I've come to know our vast country so much better thanks to all of you and what a privilege it has been to do so.

And that prayer is very simple: God bless America.

Thank you. ◆

Bush Thanks Supporters, Vows to Earn Trust of Those Who Opposed Him

Following is the speech that George W. Bush delivered at the Ronald Reagan Federal Building in Washington on Nov. 3 in which he claimed victory in his bid for a second term as president — as transcribed by Federal Document Clearing House Inc.

Thank you all. Thank you all for coming. We had a long night. . . .

The voters turned out in record numbers and delivered an historic victory.

Earlier today, Sen. Kerry called with his congratulations. We had a really good phone call. He was very gracious. Sen. Kerry waged a spirited campaign, and he and his supporters can be proud of their efforts. Laura and I wish Sen. Kerry and Teresa and their whole family all our best wishes.

America has spoken, and I'm humbled by the trust and the confidence of my fellow citizens.

With that trust comes a duty to serve all Americans. And I will do my best to fulfill that duty every day as your president.

There are many people to thank, and my family comes first. Laura is the love of my life. I'm glad you love her, too. I want to thank our daughters, who joined their dad for his last campaign. I appreciate the hard work of my sister and brothers. I especially want to thank my parents for their loving support.

I'm grateful to the vice president and Lynne and their daughters who have worked so hard and been such a vital part of our team. The vice president serves America with wisdom and honor, and I'm proud to serve beside him.

I want to thank my superb campaign team. I want to thank you all for your hard work. I was impressed every day by how hard and how skillful our team was.

I want to thank Chairman Marc Racicot and the campaign manager, Ken Mehlman; the architect, Karl Rove. I want to thank Ed Gillespie for leading our party so well.

I want to thank the thousands of our supporters across our country. I want to thank you for your hugs on the rope lines. I want thank you for your prayers on the rope lines. I want to thank you for your kind words on the rope lines.

I want to thank you for everything you did to make the calls and to put up the signs, to talk to your neighbors and to get out the vote.

And because you did the incredible work, we are celebrating today.

There is an old saying: "Do not pray for tasks equal to your powers; pray for powers equal to your tasks." In four historic years, America has been given great tasks and faced them with strength and courage.

Our people have restored the vigor of this economy and shown resolve and patience in a new kind of war.

Our military has brought justice to the enemy and honor to America.

Our nation has defended itself and served the freedom of all mankind.

I'm proud to lead such an amazing country, and I'm proud to lead it forward. Because we have done the hard work, we are entering a season of hope.

We will continue our economic progress. We'll reform our outdated tax code. We'll strengthen Social Security for the next generation. We'll make public schools all they can be. And we will uphold our deepest values of family and faith.

We'll help the emerging democracies of Iraq and Afghanistan so they can grow in strength and defend their freedom. And then our service men and women will come home with the honor they have earned.

With good allies at our side, we will fight this war on terror with every resource of our national power so our children can live in freedom and in peace.

Reaching these goals will require the broad support of Americans.

So today, I want to speak to every person who voted for my opponent. To make this nation stronger and better, I will need your support, and I will work to earn it. I will do all I can do to deserve your trust.

A new term is a new opportunity to reach out to the whole nation. We have one country, one Constitution, and one future that binds us. And when we come together and work together, there is no limit to the greatness of America.

Let me close with a word for the people of the state of Texas.

We have known each other the longest, and you started me on this journey. On the open plains of Texas, I first learned the character of our country: sturdy and honest, and as hopeful as the break of day. I will always be grateful to the good people of my state. And whatever the road that lies ahead, that road will take me home.

The campaign has ended, and the United States of America goes forward with confidence and faith. I see a great day coming for our country, and I am eager for the work ahead.

God bless you and may God bless America. ◆

PUBLIC LAWS

Public Laws

Public laws 108-101 through 108-198, enacted in the first session of the 108th Congress, were published in the previous edition of the CQ Almanac. (2003 Almanac, p. E-3)

PL 108-199 (HR 2673) Make consolidated appropriations for the fiscal year ending Sept. 30, 2004. Introduced by BONILLA, R-Texas, on July 9, 2003. House Appropriations reported July 9 (H Rept 108-193). House passed, amended, July 14. Senate passed, with amendments, Nov. 6. Conference report filed in the House on Nov. 25 (H Rept 108-401). House agreed to the conference report Dec. 8. Senate agreed to the conference report Jan. 22, 2004. President signed Jan. 23, 2004.

PL 108-200 (HR 2264) Authorize appropriations for fiscal 2004 to carry out the Congo Basin Forest Partnership program. Introduced by SHAW, R-Fla., on May 22, 2003. House passed, under suspension of the rules, Oct. 7. Senate Foreign Relations discharged. Senate passed, with amendments, Dec. 9. House agreed to Senate amendments, under suspension of the rules, Feb. 3, 2004. President signed Feb. 13, 2004.

PL 108-201 (S 610) Amend the provisions of Title 5, U.S. Code, to provide for workforce flexibilities and certain federal personnel provisions relating to NASA. Introduced by VOINOVICH, R-Ohio, on March 13, 2003. Senate Governmental Affairs reported, amended, July 28 (S Rept 108-113). Senate passed, amended, Nov. 24. House passed Jan. 28, 2004. President signed Feb. 24, 2004.

PL 108-202 (HR 3850) Provide an extension of highway, highway safety, motor carrier safety, transit and other programs funded out of the Highway Trust Fund, pending enactment of a law reauthorizing the Transportation Equity Act for the 21st Century (TEA-21). Introduced by YOUNG, R-Alaska, on Feb. 26, 2004. House Resources, Science, Transportation and Infrastructure, and Ways and Means discharged. House passed Feb. 26. Senate passed Feb. 27. President signed Feb. 29, 2004.

PL 108-203 (HR 743) Amend the Social Security Act and the Internal Revenue Code of 1986 to provide additional safeguards for Social Security and Supplemental Security Income beneficiaries with representative payees. Introduced by SHAW, R-Fla., on Feb 12, 2003. House defeated, under suspension of the rules, March 5. House Ways and Means reported, amended, March 24 (H Rept 108-46). House passed April 2. Senate Finance reported, with amendment, Oct. 29 (S Rept 108-176). Senate passed, with amendment, Dec. 9. House agreed to Senate amendment Feb. 11, 2004. President signed March 2, 2004.

PL 108-204 (S 523) Make technical corrections to law relating to Native Americans. Introduced by CAMPBELL, R-Colo., on March 5, 2003. Senate Indian Affairs reported, amended, May 15 (S Rept 108-49). Senate passed, amended, July 30. House Resources reported Nov. 17 (H Rept 108-374, Part 1). House Agriculture discharged. House passed, under suspension of the rules, Feb. 11, 2004. President signed March 2, 2004.

PL 108-205 (HR 3915) Provide for an additional temporary extension of programs under the Small Business Act and the Small Business Investment Act of 1958. Introduced by MANZULLO, R-Ill., on March 9, 2004. House passed, amended, under suspension of the rules, March 10. Senate passed March 12. President signed March 15, 2004.

PL 108-206 (S 714) Provide for the conveyance of a small parcel of Bureau of Land Management land in Douglas County, Ore., to the county to improve management of and recreational access to the Oregon Dunes National Recreation Area. Introduced by WYDEN, D-Ore., on March 26, 2003. Senate Energy and Natural Resources reported, amended, Aug. 26 (S Rept 108-135). Senate passed, with amendments, Nov. 24. House passed, under suspension of the rules, Feb. 24, 2004. President signed March 15, 2004.

PL 108-207 (S 2136) Extend the final report and termination date of the National Commission on Terrorist Attacks Upon the United States and provide additional funding for the commission. Introduced by ROBERTS, R-Kan., on Feb. 26, 2004. Senate Intelligence reported Feb. 26 (no written report). Senate passed Feb. 27. House passed March 3. President signed March 16, 2004.

PL 108-208 (HR 506) Provide for the protection of archaeological sites in the Galisteo Basin in New Mexico. Introduced by UDALL, D-N.M., on Jan. 29, 2003. House Resources reported, amended, Nov. 4 (H Rept 108-346). House passed, amended, under suspension of the rules, Nov. 4. Senate passed March 4, 2004. President signed March 19, 2004.

PL 108-209 (HR 2059) Designate Fort Bayard Historic District in New Mexico as a National Historic Landmark. Introduced by PEARCE, R-N.M., on May 9, 2003. House Resources reported Sept. 3 (H Rept 108-257). House passed, under suspension of the rules, Sept. 23. Senate passed March 4, 2004. President signed March 19, 2004.

PL 108-210 (S 2231) Reauthorize the Temporary Assistance for Needy Families block grant program through June 30, 2004. Introduced by GRASSLEY, R-Iowa, on

March 25, 2004. Senate passed March 25. House passed, under suspension of the rules, March 30. President signed March 31, 2004.

PL 108-211 (S 2241) Reauthorize certain school lunch and child nutrition programs through June 30, 2004. Introduced by COCHRAN, R-Miss., on March 26, 2004. Senate passed March 26. House passed, under suspension of the rules, March 30. President signed March 31, 2004.

PL 108-212 (HR 1997) Amend Title 18, U.S. Code, and the Uniform Code of Military Justice to create a separate federal offense for harming a fetus during the commission of a federal crime. Introduced by HART, R-Pa., on May 7, 2003. House Judiciary reported, amended, Feb. 11, 2004 (H Rept 108-420, Part 1). House Armed Services discharged. House passed, amended, Feb. 26. Senate passed March 25. President signed April 1, 2004.

PL 108-213 (HR 3724) Amend the National Housing Act to make a technical correction to restore allowable increases in the maximum mortgage limits for Federal Housing Administration-insured mortgages for multifamily housing projects to cover increased costs of installing a solar energy system or residential energy conservation measures. Introduced by SHAYS, R-Conn., on Jan. 21, 2004. House passed, under suspension of the rules, Feb. 3. Senate Banking, Housing and Urban Affairs discharged. Senate passed March 12. President signed April 1, 2004.

PL 108-214 (S 1881) Amend the Federal Food, Drug, and Cosmetic Act to make technical corrections relating to amendments made by the Medical Device User Fee and Modernization Act of 2002. Introduced by ALEXANDER, R-Tenn., on Nov. 18, 2003. Senate Health, Education, Labor and Pensions reported, amended, Nov. 24 (no written report). Senate passed, with an amendment, Nov. 25. House Energy and Commerce reported, amended, March 9, 2004 (H Rept 108-433). House passed, with an amendment, under suspension of the rules, March 10. Senate agreed to House amendment March 12. President signed April 1, 2004.

PL 108-215 (HR 254) Authorize the president to agree to certain amendments to a U.S.-Mexico agreement concerning the establishment of a Border Environment Cooperation Commission and a North American Development Bank. Introduced by BEREUTER, R-Neb., on Jan. 8, 2003. House Financial Services reported Feb. 25 (H Rept 108-17). House passed, under suspension of the rules, Feb. 26. Senate Foreign Relations discharged. Senate passed, with amendment, March 12, 2004. House agreed to Senate amendment, under suspension of the rules, March 25. President signed April 5, 2004.

PL 108-216 (HR 3926) Amend the Public Health Service Act to promote organ donation. Introduced by BILIRAKIS, R-Fla., on March 10, 2004. House passed, under suspension of the rules, March 24. Senate passed March 25. President signed April 5, 2004.

PL 108-217 (HR 4026) Provide for an additional temporary extension of programs under the Small Business Act and the Small Business Investment Act of 1958 through June 4, 2004. Introduced by MANZULLO, R-Ill., on March 30, 2004. House passed, under suspension of the rules, March 30. Senate passed April 1. President signed April 5, 2004.

PL 108-218 (HR 3108) Amend the Employee Retirement Income Security Act of 1974 and the Internal Revenue Code of 1986 to temporarily replace the rate on the 30-year Treasury bond with a rate based on long-term corporate bonds for certain pension plan funding requirements and other provisions. Introduced by BOEHNER, R-Ohio, on Sept. 17, 2003. House passed, amended, Oct. 8. Senate Finance discharged. Senate passed, with amendment, Jan. 28, 2004. Conference report filed in the House April 1 (H Rept 108-457). House agreed to the conference report April 2. Senate agreed to the conference report April 8. President signed April 10, 2004.

PL 108-219 (HR 2584) Provide for the conveyance to the Utrok Atoll local government of a decommissioned National Oceanic and Atmospheric Administration ship. Introduced by FALEOMAVAEGA, D-Am. Samoa, on June 24, 2003. House Resources reported Nov. 18 (H Rept 108-378). House passed, amended, under suspension of the rules, Nov. 21. Senate Energy and Natural Resources discharged. Senate Commerce, Science and Transportation discharged. Senate passed, with amendments, March 24, 2004. House agreed to Senate amendments, under suspension of the rules, March 29. President signed April 13, 2004.

PL 108-220 (S 2057) Require the secretary of Defense to reimburse members of the Armed Forces for domestic travel expenses incurred as part of the rest and recuperation program, retroactive, to the expansion of the program. Introduced by COLEMAN, R-Minn., on Feb. 9, 2004. Senate Armed Services discharged. Senate passed March 3. House passed, under suspension of the rules, March 30. President signed April 22, 2004.

PL 108-221 (HR 1274) Direct the administrator of the General Services Administration to convey to Fresno County, Calif., the existing federal courthouse. Introduced by DOOLEY, D-Calif., on March 13, 2003. House Transportation and Infrastructure reported, amended, Nov. 4 (H Rept 108-341). House passed, under suspension of the rules, Nov. 18. Senate passed April 20, 2004. President signed April 30, 2004.

PL 108-222 (HR 2489) Provide for the distribution of judgment funds to the Cowlitz Indian Tribe in the state of Washington. Introduced by BAIRD, D-Wash., on June 17, 2003. House Resources reported, amended, Nov. 17 (H Rept 108-368). House passed, under suspension of the rules, March 23, 2004. Senate passed April 20. President signed April 30, 2004.

PL 108-223 (HR 3118) Designate the Orville Wright Fed-

eral Building and the Wilbur Wright Federal Building in Washington, D.C. Introduced by HAYES, R-N.C., on Sept. 17, 2003. House Transportation and Infrastructure reported Oct. 15 (H Rept 108-317). House passed, under suspension of the rules, Nov. 4. Senate Environment and Public Works discharged. Senate passed April 20, 2004. President signed April 30, 2004.

PL 108-224 (HR 4219) Provide an extension of highway, highway safety, motor carrier safety, transit and other programs funded out of the Highway Trust Fund pending enactment of a law reauthorizing the Transportation Equity Act for the 21st Century through June 30, 2004. Introduced by PETRI, R-Wis. on April 27, 2004. House passed, under suspension of the rules, April 28. Senate passed April 29. President signed April 30, 2004.

PL 108-225 (S 1904) Designate the U.S. courthouse at 400 North Miami Ave. in Miami, Fla., as the "Wilkie D. Ferguson Jr. United States Courthouse." Introduced by GRAHAM, D-Fla., on Nov. 20, 2003. Senate Environment and Public Works reported on March 10, 2004 (no written report). Senate passed March 12. House passed, under suspension of the rules, April 28. President signed May 7, 2004.

PL 108-226 (S 2022) Designate the federal building located at 250 West Cherry St. in Carbondale, Ill., the "Senator Paul Simon Federal Building." Introduced by DURBIN, D-Ill., on Jan. 22, 2004. Senate Environment and Public Works reported March 10 (no written report). Senate passed March 12. House passed, under suspension of the rules, April 21. President signed May 7, 2004.

PL 108-227 (S 2043) Designate a federal building in Harrisburg, Pa., as the "Ronald Reagan Federal Building." Introduced by SPECTER, R-Pa., on Feb. 2, 2004. Senate Environment and Public Works reported March 10 (no written report). Senate passed March 12. House passed, under suspension of the rules, April 28. President signed May 7, 2004.

PL 108-228 (S 2315) Amend the Communications Satellite Act of 1962 to extend the deadline for the INTELSAT initial public offering. Introduced by BURNS, R-Mont., on April 8, 2004. Senate Commerce, Science and Transportation discharged. Senate passed April 27. House Energy and Commerce discharged. House passed May 5. President signed May 18, 2004.

PL 108-229 (HR 408) Provide for expansion of Sleeping Bear Dunes National Lakeshore in Michigan. Introduced by CAMP, R-Mich., on Jan. 28, 2003. House Resources reported, amended, Oct. 2 (H Rept 108-292). House passed, under suspension of the rules, Oct. 8. Senate Energy and Natural Resources reported March 9, 2004 (S Rept 108-240). Senate passed May 19. President signed May 28, 2004.

PL 108-230 (HR 708) Require the conveyance of certain National Forest System lands in Mendocino National Forest, Calif., and provide for the use of the proceeds for National Forest purposes. Introduced by THOMPSON, D-Calif., on Feb. 11, 2003. House Resources reported, Oct. 2 (H Rept 108-293). House passed, under suspension of the rules, Oct. 8. Senate Energy and Natural Resources reported March 9, 2004 (S Rept 108-242). Senate passed May 19. President signed May 28, 2004.

PL 108-231 (HR 856) Authorize the secretary of the Interior to revise a repayment contract with the Tom Green County Water Control and Improvement District No. 1, San Angelo project, Texas. Introduced by STENHOLM, D-Texas, on Feb. 13, 2003. House passed, under suspension of the rules, May 14. Senate Energy and Natural Resources reported March 9, 2004 (S Rept 108-243). Senate passed May 19. President signed May 28, 2004.

PL 108-232 (HR 923) Amend the Small Business Investment Act of 1958 to allow certain premier certified lenders to elect to maintain an alternative loss reserve. Introduced by DOOLITTLE, R-Calif., on Feb. 26, 2003. House Small Business reported, amended, June 12 (H Rept 108-153). House passed, under suspension of the rules, June 24. Senate Small Business and Entrepreneurship discharged. Senate passed May 18, 2004. President signed May 28, 2004.

PL 108-233 (HR 1598) Amend the Reclamation Wastewater and Groundwater Study and Facilities Act to authorize the secretary of the Interior to participate in projects within the San Diego Creek Watershed, Calif. Introduced by COX, R-Calif., on April 3, 2003. House Resources reported, Oct. 8 (H Rept 108-306). House passed, under suspension of the rules, Oct. 15. Senate Energy and Natural Resources reported March 9, 2004 (S Rept 108-244). Senate passed May 19. President signed May 28, 2004.

PL 108-234 (HR 3104) Provide for the establishment of separate campaign medals to be awarded to members of the uniformed services who participate in Operation Enduring Freedom and in Operation Iraqi Freedom. Introduced by SNYDER, D-Ark., on Sept. 16, 2003. House passed, amended, under suspension of the rules, March 30, 2004. Senate Armed Services reported May 11 (no written report). Senate passed May 18. President signed May 28, 2004.

PL 108-235 (S 2092) Address the participation of Taiwan in the World Health Organization. Introduced by ALLEN, R-Va., on Feb. 12, 2004. Senate Foreign Relations reported, amended, April 29 (no written report). Senate passed May 6. House passed May 20. President signed June 14, 2004.

PL 108-236 (S J Res 28) Recognize the 60th anniversary of the Allied landing at Normandy during World War II. Introduced by CAMPBELL, R-Colo., on Feb. 25, 2004. Senate Judiciary discharged. Senate passed April 1. House passed, under suspension of the rules, June 2. President signed June 15, 2004.

PL 108-237 (HR 1086) Encourage the development and promulgation of voluntary consensus standards for industry and various levels of government by providing relief under the antitrust laws to organizations that develop the standards. Introduced by SENSENBRENNER, R-Wis., on March 5, 2003. House Judiciary reported May 22 (H Rept 108-125, Part 1). House Judiciary supplemental report filed June 4 (H Rept 108-125, Part 2). House passed, under suspension of the rules, June 10. Senate Judiciary reported, amended, Nov. 6 (no written report). Senate passed, with an amendment, April 2, 2004. House agreed to Senate amendment, under suspension of the rules, June 2. President signed June 22, 2004.

PL 108-238 (S 1233) Authorize assistance for the National Great Blacks in Wax Museum and Justice Learning Center in Baltimore, Md. Introduced by MIKULSKI, D-Md., on June 11, 2003. Senate Judiciary reported June 19 (no written report). Senate passed July 14. House Resources reported, Nov. 17 (H Rept 108-372, Part 1). House Judiciary discharged. House passed, with an amendment, under suspension of the rules, June 1, 2004. Senate agreed to House amendment, June 3. President signed June 22, 2004.

PL 108-239 (HR 1822) Designate the facility of the U.S. Postal Service located at 3751 West 6th St., Los Angeles, Calif., as the "Dosan Ahn Chang Ho Post Office." Introduced by WATSON, D-Calif., on April 11, 2003. House passed, under suspension of the rules, April 20, 2004. Senate Governmental Affairs reported June 7 (no written report). Senate passed June 9. President signed June 25, 2004.

PL 108-240 (HR 2130) Redesignate the facility of the U.S. Postal Service located at 121 Kinderkamack Road in River Edge, N.J., as the "New Bridge Landing Post Office." Introduced by GARRETT, R-N.J., on May 15, 2003. House passed, amended, under suspension of the rules, Nov. 18. Senate Governmental Affairs reported June 7, 2004 (no written report). Senate passed June 9. President signed June 25, 2004.

PL 108-241 (HR 2438) Designate the facility of the U.S. Postal Service located at 115 West Pine St. in Hattiesburg, Miss., as the "Major Henry A. Commiskey Sr. Post Office Building." Introduced by TAYLOR, D-Miss., on June 11, 2003. House passed, under suspension of the rules, Nov. 4. Senate Governmental Affairs reported June 7, 2004 (no written report). Senate passed June 9. President signed June 25, 2004.

PL 108-242 (HR 3029) Designate the facility of the U.S. Postal Service located at 255 North Main St. in Jonesboro, Ga., as the "S. Truett Cathy Post Office Building." Introduced by SCOTT, D-Ga., on Sept. 5, 2003. House passed, under suspension of the rules, Nov. 4. Senate Governmental Affairs reported June 7, 2004 (no written report). Senate passed June 9. President signed June 25, 2004.

PL 108-243 (HR 3059) Designate the facility of the U.S. Postal Service located at 304 West Michigan St. in Stuttgart, Ark., as the "Lloyd L. Burke Post Office." Introduced by BERRY, D-Ark., on Sept. 10, 2003. House passed, under suspension of the rules, March 24, 2004. Senate Governmental Affairs reported June 7 (no written report). Senate passed June 9. President signed June 25, 2004.

PL 108-244 (HR 3068) Designate the facility of the U.S. Postal Service located at 2055 Siesta Drive in Sarasota, Fla., as the "Brigadier General (AUS-Ret.) John H. McLain Post Office." Introduced by HARRIS, R-Fla., on Sept. 10, 2003. House passed, under suspension of the rules, Oct. 20. Senate Governmental Affairs reported June 7, 2004 (no written report). Senate passed June 9. President signed June 25, 2004.

PL 108-245 (HR 3234) Designate the facility of the U.S. Postal Service located at 14 Chestnut St. in Liberty, N.Y., as the "Ben R. Gerow Post Office Building." Introduced by HINCHEY, D-N.Y., on Oct. 2, 2003. House passed, under suspension of the rules, Oct. 28. Senate Governmental Affairs reported June 7, 2004 (no written report). Senate passed June 9. President signed June 25, 2004.

PL 108-246 (HR 3300) Designate the facility of the U.S. Postal Service located at 15500 Pearl Road in Strongsville, Ohio, as the "Walter F. Ehrnfelt Jr. Post Office Building." Introduced by LATOURETTE, R-Ohio, on Oct. 15, 2003. House passed, under suspension of the rules, Nov. 18. Senate Governmental Affairs reported June 7, 2004 (no written report). Senate passed June 9. President signed June 25, 2004.

PL 108-247 (HR 3353) Designate the facility of the U.S. Postal Service located at 525 Main St. in Tarboro, N.C., as the "George Henry White Post Office Building." Introduced by BALLANCE, D-N.C., on Oct. 21, 2003. House passed, under suspension of the rules, Nov. 17. Senate Governmental Affairs reported June 7, 2004 (no written report). Senate passed June 9. President signed June 25, 2004.

PL 108-248 (HR 3536) Designate the facility of the U.S. Postal Service located at 210 Main St. in Malden, Ill., as the "Army Staff Sgt. Lincoln Hollinsaid Malden Post Office." Introduced by WELLER, R-Ill., on Nov. 19, 2003. House passed, under suspension of the rules, March 9, 2004. Senate Governmental Affairs reported June 7 (no written report). Senate passed June 9. President signed June 25, 2004.

PL 108-249 (HR 3537) Designate the facility of the U.S. Postal Service located at 185 State St. in Manhattan, Ill., as the "Army Pvt. Shawn Pahnke Manhattan Post Office." Introduced by WELLER, R-Ill., on Nov. 19, 2003. House passed, under suspension of the rules, March 9, 2004. Senate Governmental Affairs reported June 7 (no written report). Senate passed June 9. President signed June 25, 2004.

PL 108-250 (HR 3538) Designate the facility of the U.S. Postal Service located at 201 South Chicago Ave. in Saint Anne, Ill., as the "Marine Capt. Ryan Beaupre Saint Anne Post Office." Introduced by WELLER, R-Ill., on Nov. 19, 2003. House passed, under suspension of the rules, March 9, 2004. Senate Governmental Affairs reported June 7 (no written report). Senate passed June 9. President signed June 25, 2004.

PL 108-251 (HR 3690) Designate the facility of the U.S. Postal Service located at 2 West Main St. in Batavia, N.Y., as the "Barber Conable Post Office Building." Introduced by REYNOLDS, R-N.Y., on Dec. 8, 2003. House passed, under suspension of the rules, Feb. 25, 2004. Senate Governmental Affairs reported June 7 (no written report). Senate passed June 9. President signed June 25, 2004.

PL 108-252 (HR 3733) Designate the facility of the U.S. Postal Service located at 410 Huston St. in Altamont, Kan., as the "Myron V. George Post Office." Introduced by RYUN, R-Kan., on Jan. 27, 2004. House passed, under suspension of the rules, March 16. Senate Governmental Affairs reported June 7 (no written report). Senate passed June 9. President signed June 25, 2004.

PL 108-253 (HR 3740) Designate the facility of the U.S. Postal Service located at 223 South Main St. in Roxboro, N.C., as the "Oscar Scott Woody Post Office Building." Introduced by MILLER, D-N.C., on Jan. 28, 2004. House passed, under suspension of the rules, May 18. Senate Governmental Affairs reported June 7 (no written report). Senate passed June 9. President signed June 25, 2004.

PL 108-254 (HR 3769) Designate the facility of the U.S. Postal Service located at 137 East Young High Pike in Knoxville, Tenn., as the "Ben Atchley Post Office Building." Introduced by DUNCAN, R-Tenn., on Feb. 4, 2004. House passed, under suspension of the rules, March 2. Senate Governmental Affairs reported June 7 (no written report). Senate passed June 9. President signed June 25, 2004.

PL 108-255 (HR 3855) Designate the facility of the U.S. Postal Service located at 607 Pershing Drive in Laclede, Mo., as the "General John J. Pershing Post Office." Introduced by GRAVES, R-Mo., on Feb. 26, 2004. House passed, under suspension of the rules, April 20. Senate Governmental Affairs reported June 7 (no written report). Senate passed June 9. President signed June 25, 2004.

PL 108-256 (HR 3917) Designate the facility of the U.S. Postal Service located at 695 Marconi Blvd. in Copiague, N.Y., as the "Maxine S. Postal United States Post Office." Introduced by ISRAEL, D-N.Y, on March 9, 2004. House passed, under suspension of the rules, March 29. Senate Governmental Affairs reported June 7 (no written report). Senate passed June 9. President signed June 25, 2004.

PL 108-257 (HR 3939) Redesignate the facility of the U.S. Postal Service located at 14-24 Abbott Road in Fair Lawn, N.J., as the "Mary Ann Collura Post Office Building." Introduced by ROTHMAN, D-N.J., on March 11, 2004. House passed, under suspension of the rules, May 11. Senate Governmental Affairs reported June 7 (no written report). Senate passed June 9. President signed June 25, 2004.

PL 108-258 (HR 3942) Redesignate the facility of the U.S. Postal Service located at 7 Commercial Blvd. in Middletown, R.I., as the "Rhode Island Veterans Post Office Building." Introduced by KENNEDY, D-R.I., on March 11, 2004. House passed, under suspension of the rules, April 27. Senate Governmental Affairs reported June 7 (no written report). Senate passed June 9. President signed June 25, 2004.

PL 108-259 (HR 4037) Designate the facility of the U.S. Postal Service located at 475 Kell Farm Drive in Cape Girardeau, Mo., as the "Richard G. Wilson Processing and Distribution Facility." Introduced by EMERSON, R-Mo., on March 25, 2004. House passed, under suspension of the rules, April 20. Senate Governmental Affairs reported June 7 (no written report). Senate passed June 9. President signed June 25, 2004.

PL 108-260 (HR 4176) Designate the facility of the U.S. Postal Service located at 122 West Elwood Ave. in Raeford, N.C., as the "Bobby Marshall Gentry Post Office Building." Introduced by HAYES, R-N.C., on April 20, 2004. House passed, under suspension of the rules, May 18. Senate Governmental Affairs reported June 7 (no written report). Senate passed June 9. President signed June 25, 2004.

PL 108-261 (HR 4299) Designate the facility of the U.S. Postal Service located at 410 South Jackson Road in Edinburg, Texas, as the "Dr. Miguel A. Nevarez Post Office Building." Introduced by HINOJOSA, D-Texas, on May 6, 2004. House passed, under suspension of the rules, May 11. Senate Governmental Affairs reported June 7 (no written report). Senate passed June 9. President signed June 25, 2004.

PL 108-262 (HR 4589) Reauthorize the Temporary Assistance for Needy Families block grant program through Sept. 30, 2004. Introduced by HERGER, R-Calif., on June 16, 2004. House passed, under suspension of the rules, June 22. Senate passed June 22. President signed June 30, 2004.

PL 108-263 (HR 4635) Provide an extension through July 31, 2004, of highway, highway safety, motor carrier safety, transit and other programs funded out of the Highway Trust Fund pending enactment of a law reauthorizing the Transportation Equity Act for the 21st Century. Introduced by YOUNG, R-Alaska, on June 22, 2004. House passed, under suspension of the rules, June 23. Senate passed June 23. President signed June 30, 2004.

PL 108-264 (S 2238) Amend the National Flood Insurance Act of 1968 to reduce losses to properties for which repetitive flood insurance claim payments have been made. Introduced by BUNNING, R-Ky., on March 25, 2004. Senate Banking, Housing and Urban Affairs reported May 13 (S Rept 108-262). Senate passed, amended, June 15. House passed, under suspension of the rules, June 21. President signed June 30, 2004.

PL 108-265 (S 2507) Amend the Richard B. Russell National School Lunch Act and the Child Nutrition Act of 1966 to provide children with increased access to food and nutrition assistance, to simplify program operations and improve program management and to reauthorize child nutrition programs. Introduced by COCHRAN, R-Miss., on June 7, 2004. Senate Agriculture, Nutrition and Forestry reported June 7 (S Rept 108-279). Senate passed, amended, June 23. House passed June 24. President signed June 30, 2004.

PL 108-266 (HR 3378) Assist in the conservation of marine turtles and the nesting habitats of marine turtles in foreign countries. Introduced by GILCHREST, R-Md., on Oct. 28, 2003. House Resources reported, amended, May 20, 2004 (H Rept 108-507). House passed, under suspension of the rules, June 14. Senate passed June 18. President signed July 2, 2004.

PL 108-267 (HR 3504) Amend the Indian Self-Determination and Education Assistance Act to redesignate the American Indian Education Foundation as the National Fund for Excellence in American Indian Education. Introduced by RENZI, R-Ariz., on Nov. 17, 2003. House Resources reported May 20, 2004 (H Rept 108-510, Part 1). House passed, under suspension of the rules, June 14. Senate passed June 18. President signed July 2, 2004.

PL 108-268 (HR 4322) Provide for the transfer of the Nebraska Ave. Naval Complex in the District of Columbia to facilitate the establishment of the headquarters for the Department of Homeland Security and provide for the acquisition by the Department of the Navy of suitable replacement facilities. Introduced by HUNTER, R-Calif., on May 11, 2004. House Armed Services reported, amended, May 13 (no written report). House passed, under suspension of the rules, June 14. Senate passed June 21. President signed July 2, 2004.

PL 108-269 (S 1848) Amend the Bend Pine Nursery Land Conveyance Act to direct the secretary of Agriculture to sell the Bend Pine Nursery Administration Site in the state of Oregon. Introduced by WYDEN, D-Ore., on Nov. 11, 2003. Senate Energy and Natural Resources reported, amended, March 9, 2004 (S Rept 108-238). Senate passed, with amendment, May 19. House passed, under suspension of the rules, June 21. President signed July 2, 2004.

PL 108-270 (HR 884) Provide for the use and distribution of the funds awarded to the Western Shoshone identifiable group under Indian Claims Commission Docket Numbers 326-A-1, 326-A-3, and 326-K. Introduced by GIBBONS, R-Nev., on Feb. 25, 2003. House Resources reported, amended, Oct. 7 (H Rept 108-299). House passed, under suspension of the rules, June 21, 2004. Senate passed June 24. President signed July 7, 2004.

PL 108-271 (HR 2751) Change the name of the General Accounting Office to the Government Accountability Office and alter the agency's personnel rules. Introduced by J. DAVIS, R-Va., on July 16, 2003. House Government Reform reported, amended, Nov. 19 (H Rept 108-380). House passed, amended, Feb. 25, 2004. Senate Governmental Affairs discharged. Senate passed June 24. President signed July 7, 2004.

PL 108-272 (H J Res 97) Approve the renewal of import restrictions contained in the Burmese Freedom and Democracy Act of 2003. Introduced by LANTOS, D-Calif., on June 3, 2004. House passed, under suspension of the rules, June 14. Senate passed June 24. President signed July 7, 2004.

PL 108-273 (S 2017) Designate the U.S. courthouse and post office building located at 93 Atocha St. in Ponce, Puerto Rico, as the "Luis A. Ferre United States Courthouse and Post Office Building." Introduced by SANTORUM, R-Pa., on Jan. 22, 2004. Senate Governmental Affairs reported June 7 (no written report). Senate passed June 9. House passed, under suspension of the rules, June 22. President signed July 7, 2004.

PL 108-274 (HR 4103) Extend and modify trade benefits under the African Growth and Opportunity Act. Introduced by THOMAS, R-Calif., on April 1, 2004. House Ways and Means reported, amended, May 19 (H Rept 108-501). House passed, under suspension of the rules, June 14. Senate passed June 24. President signed July 13, 2004.

PL 108-275 (HR 1731) Amend Title 18, U.S. Code, to establish penalties for aggravated identity theft. Introduced by CARTER, R-Texas, on April 10, 2003. House Judiciary reported, amended, June 8, 2004 (H Rept 108-528). House passed, under suspension of the rules, June 23. Senate passed June 25. President signed July 15, 2004.

PL 108-276 (S 15) Amend the Public Health Service Act to provide protections and countermeasures against chemical, radiological or nuclear agents that may be used in a terrorist attack against the United States by giving the National Institutes of Health contracting flexibility, infrastructure improvements and expedited scientific peer review procedures, and by streamlining the Food and Drug Administration approval process for countermeasures. Introduced by GREGG, R-N.H., on March 11, 2003. Senate Health, Education, Labor and Pensions reported, amended, March 25 (no written report). Senate passed, amended, May 19, 2004. House passed July 14. President signed July 21, 2004.

PL 108-277 (HR 218) Amend Title 18, U.S. Code, to exempt qualified current and former law enforcement offi-

cers from state laws prohibiting the carrying of concealed handguns. Introduced by CUNNINGHAM, R-Calif., on Jan. 7, 2003. House Judiciary reported, amended, June 22, 2004 (H Rept 108-560). House passed, under suspension of the rules, June 23. Senate passed July 7. President signed July 22, 2004.

PL 108-278 (HR 3846) Authorize the secretary of Agriculture and the secretary of the Interior to enter into an agreement or contract with Indian tribes meeting certain criteria to carry out projects to protect Indian forest land. Introduced by POMBO, R-Calif., on Feb. 26, 2004. House Resources reported, amended, May 20, 2004 (H Rept 108-509, Part 1). House Agriculture discharged. House passed, under suspension of the rules, June 21. Senate passed June 25. President signed July 22, 2004.

PL 108-279 (S 1167) Resolve the boundary conflicts in Barry and Stone counties in the state of Missouri. Introduced by BOND, R-Mo., on June 2, 2003. Senate Energy and Natural Resources reported, amended, March 9, 2004 (S Rept 108-234). Senate passed, amended, May 19. House passed, under suspension of the rules, July 12. President signed July 22, 2004.

PL 108-280 (HR 4916) Provide an extension of highway, highway safety, motor carrier safety, transit and other programs funded out of the Highway Trust Fund pending enactment of a law reauthorizing the Transportation Equity Act for the 21st Century. The extension goes through Sept. 24 for highways and through Sept. 30 for transit and other activities. Introduced by YOUNG, R-Alaska, on July 22, 2004. House Resources, House Science, House Transportation and Infrastructure, and House Ways and Means discharged. House passed July 22. Senate passed July 22. President signed July 30, 2004.

PL 108-281 (HR 1303) Amend the E-Government Act of 2002 with respect to rulemaking authority of the Judicial Conference. Introduced by SMITH, R-Texas, on March 18, 2003. House Judiciary reported, amended, July 25 (H Rept 108-239). House passed, under suspension of the rules, Oct 7. Senate Governmental Affairs reported July 7, 2004 (no written report). Senate passed July 9. Senate vitiated reporting of HR 1303, July 14. Senate vitiated passage of HR 1303, July 14. Senate Governmental Affairs discharged. Senate passed July 15. President signed Aug. 2, 2004.

PL 108-282 (S 741) Amend the Federal Food, Drug and Cosmetic Act with regard to new animal drugs. Introduced by SESSIONS, R-Ala., on March 27, 2003. Senate Health, Education, Labor and Pensions reported, amended, Feb. 18, 2004 (S Rept 108-226). Senate passed, amended, March 8. House Energy and Commerce reported July 15 (H Rept 108-608). House passed, under suspension of the rules, July 20. President signed Aug. 2, 2004.

PL 108-283 (S 2264) Require a report on the conflict in Uganda. Introduced by FEINGOLD, D-Wis., on March

31, 2004. Senate Foreign Relations reported April 29 (no written report). Senate passed May 7. House passed, under suspension of the rules, July 19. President signed Aug. 2, 2004.

PL 108-284 (S J Res 38) Provide for the appointment of Eli Broad as a citizen regent of the Board of Regents of the Smithsonian Institution. Introduced by COCHRAN, R-Miss., on June 3, 2004. Senate Rules and Administration discharged. Senate passed June 9. House passed, under suspension of the rules, July 20. President signed Aug. 2, 2004.

PL 108-285 (HR 4363) Facilitate self-help housing homeownership opportunities. Introduced by GREEN, R-Wis., on May 13, 2004. House Financial Services reported, amended, June 16 (H Rept 108-546). House passed, under suspension of the rules, June 21. Senate Banking, Housing and Urban Affairs discharged. Senate passed July 14. President signed Aug. 2, 2004.

PL 108-286 (HR 4759) Implement the United States-Australia Free Trade Agreement. Introduced by DELAY, R-Texas, on July 6, 2004. House Ways and Means reported July 12 (H Rept 108-597). House passed July 14. Senate passed July 15. President signed Aug. 3, 2004.

PL 108-287 (HR 4613) Make appropriations for the Department of Defense for the fiscal year ending Sept. 30, 2005. Introduced by LEWIS, R-Calif., on June 18, 2004. House Appropriations reported June 18 (H Rept 108-553). House passed, amended, June 22. Senate passed, amended, June 24. Conference report filed in the House on July 20 (H Rept 108-622). House agreed to the conference report July 22. Senate agreed to the conference report July 22. President signed Aug. 5, 2004.

PL 108-288 (HR 1572) Designate the U.S. courthouse located at 100 North Palafox St. in Pensacola, Fla., as the "Winston E. Arnow United States Courthouse." Introduced by MILLER, R-Fla., on April 2, 2003. House Transportation and Infrastructure reported, amended, July 17, 2003 (H Rept 108-216). House passed, under suspension of the rules, Sept. 3. Senate Environment and Public Works reported June 24, 2004 (no written report). Senate passed July 19. President signed Aug. 6, 2004.

PL 108-289 (HR 1914) Provide for the issuance of a coin to commemorate the 400th anniversary of the Jamestown settlement. Introduced by J. DAVIS, R-Va., on May 1, 2003. House Financial Services reported April 27, 2004 (H Rept 108-472, Part 1). House Ways and Means reported, amended, July 6 (H Rept 108-472, Part 2). House passed, under suspension of the rules, July 14. Senate passed July 20. President signed Aug. 6, 2004.

PL 108-290 (HR 2768) Require the secretary of the Treasury to mint coins in commemoration of Chief Justice John Marshall. Introduced by BACHUS, R-Ala., on July 17, 2003. House Financial Services reported April 27, 2004 (H Rept 108-473, Part 1). House Ways and

Means reported, amended, July 6 (H Rept 108-473, Part 2). House passed, under suspension of the rules, July 14. Senate passed July 20. President signed Aug. 6, 2004.

PL 108-291 (HR 3277) Require the secretary of the Treasury to mint coins in commemoration of the 230th anniversary of the U.S. Marine Corps and to support construction of the Marine Corps Heritage Center. Introduced by MURTHA, D-Pa., on Oct. 8, 2003. House Financial Services reported April 27, 2004 (H Rept 108-474, Part 1). House Ways and Means reported, amended, July 6 (H Rept 108-474, Part 2). House passed, under suspension of the rules, July 14. Senate passed July 20. President signed Aug. 6, 2004.

PL 108-292 (HR 4380) Designate the facility of the U.S. Postal Service located at 4737 Mile Stretch Drive in Holiday, Fla., as the "Sergeant First Class Paul Ray Smith Post Office Building." Introduced by BILIRAKIS, R-Fla., on May 18, 2004. House passed, under suspension of the rules, July 12. Senate Governmental Affairs discharged. Senate passed July 19. President signed Aug. 6, 2004.

PL 108-293 (HR 2443) Authorize appropriations for fiscal 2004 and 2005 for the U.S. Coast Guard. Introduced by YOUNG, R-Alaska, on June 12, 2003. House Transportation and Infrastructure reported, amended, July 24 (H Rept 108-233). House passed Nov. 5. Senate Commerce, Science and Transportation discharged. Senate passed with an amendment March 30, 2004. Conference report filed in the House on July 20 (H Rept 108-617). House agreed to the conference report July 21. Senate agreed to the conference report July 22. President signed Aug. 9, 2004.

PL 108-294 (HR 3340) Redesignate the facilities of the U.S. Postal Service located at 7715 and 7748 S. Cottage Grove Ave. in Chicago, Ill., as the "James E. Worsham Post Office" and the "James E. Worsham Carrier Annex Building," respectively. Introduced by RUSH, D-Ill., on Oct. 20. 2003. House passed, under suspension of the rules, July 6, 2004. Senate Governmental Affairs reported July 22 (no written report). Senate passed July 22. President signed Aug. 9, 2004.

PL 108-295 (HR 3463) Amend titles III and IV of the Social Security Act to improve the administration of unemployment taxes and benefits. Introduced by HERGER, R-Calif., on Nov. 16, 2003. House passed, under suspension of the rules, July 14, 2004. Senate passed July 22. President signed Aug. 9, 2004.

PL 108-296 (HR 4222) Designate the facility of the U.S. Postal Service located at 550 Nebraska Ave. in Kansas City, Kan., as the "Newell George Post Office Building." Introduced by MOORE, D-Kan., on April 27, 2004. House passed, under suspension of the rules, June 21. Senate Governmental Affairs reported July 22 (no written report). Senate passed July 22. President signed Aug. 9, 2004.

PL 108-297 (HR 4226) Make conforming changes to provisions governing the registration of aircraft and the recordification of instruments in order to implement the Cape Town Treaty. Introduced by YOUNG, R-Alaska, on April 28, 2004. House Transportation and Infrastructure reported, amended, June 8 (H Rept 108-526). House passed, under suspension of the rules, June 22. Senate Commerce, Science and Transportation discharged. Senate passed July 21. President signed Aug. 9, 2004.

PL 108-298 (HR 4327) Designate the facility of the U.S. Postal Service located at 7450 Natural Bridge Road in St. Louis, Mo., as the "Vitilas 'Veto' Reid Post Office Building." Introduced by CLAY, D-Mo., on May 11, 2004. House passed, under suspension of the rules, July 6. Senate Governmental Affairs reported July 22 (no written report). Senate passed July 22. President signed Aug. 9, 2004.

PL 108-299 (HR 4417) Modify certain deadlines pertaining to machine-readable, tamper-resistant entry and exit documents and passports that contain biometric identifiers. Introduced by SENSENBRENNER, R-Wis., on May 20, 2004. House passed, under suspension of the rules, June 14. Senate Judiciary discharged. Senate passed July 22. President signed Aug. 9, 2004.

PL 108-300 (HR 4427) Designate the facility of the U.S. Postal Service located at 73 South Euclid Ave. in Montauk, N.Y., as the "Perry B. Duryea Jr. Post Office." Introduced by BISHOP, D-N.Y., on May 20, 2004. House passed, under suspension of the rules, July 6. Senate Governmental Affairs reported July 22 (no written report). Senate passed July 22. President signed Aug. 9, 2004.

PL 108-301 (S 2712) Preserve the ability of the Federal Housing Administration to insure mortgages under sections 238 and 519 of the National Housing Act. Introduced by REED, D-R.I., on July 21, 2004. Senate Banking, Housing and Urban Affairs discharged. Senate passed July 22. House passed July 22. President signed Aug. 9, 2004.

PL 108-302 (HR 4842) Implement the U.S.-Morocco Free Trade Agreement. Introduced by DELAY, R-Texas, on July 15, 2004. House Ways and Means reported, July 21 (H Rept 108-627). House passed July 22. Senate passed July 22. President signed Aug. 17, 2004.

PL 108-303 (HR 5005) Make emergency supplemental appropriations for the fiscal year ending Sept. 30, 2004. Introduced by YOUNG, R-Fla., on Sept. 7, 2004. House passed, under suspension of the rules, Sept. 7. Senate passed Sept. 7. President signed Sept. 8, 2004.

PL 108-304 (HR 361) Designate certain conduct by sports agents relating to the signing of contracts with student athletes as unfair and deceptive acts or practices to be regulated by the Federal Trade Commission. Introduced by GORDON, D-Tenn., on Jan. 27, 2003. House Energy and Commerce reported March 5 (H Rept 108-24, Part 1). House Judiciary reported, amended, June 2 (H Rept 108-24, Part 2). House passed, under suspension of the

rules, June 4. Senate Commerce, Science and Transportation discharged. Senate passed Sept. 9, 2004. President signed Sept. 24, 2004.

PL 108-305 (HR 3908) Provide for the conveyance of the real property located at 1081 West Main St. in Ravenna, Ohio. Introduced by RYAN, D-Ohio, on March 4, 2004. House passed, under suspension of the rules, June 2. Senate Health, Education, Labor and Pensions discharged. Senate passed Sept. 10. President signed Sept. 24, 2004.

PL 108-306 (HR 5008) Provide an additional temporary extension through Sept. 30, 2004, of programs under the Small Business Act and the Small Business Investment Act of 1958. Introduced by MANZULLO, R-Ill., on Sept. 7, 2004. House passed, under suspension of the rules, Sept. 13. Senate passed Sept. 14. President signed Sept. 24, 2004.

PL 108-307 (S 1576) Revise the boundary of Harpers Ferry National Historical Park. Introduced by BYRD, D-W.Va., on Sept. 3, 2003. Senate Energy and Natural Resources reported March 9, 2004 (S Rept 108-236). Senate passed May 19. House Resources reported Sept. 7 (H Rept 108-655). House passed, under suspension of the rules, Sept. 13. President signed Sept. 24, 2004.

PL 108-308 (HR 5149) Reauthorize the Temporary Assistance for Needy Families block grant program through March 31, 2005. Introduced by HERGER, R-Calif., on Sept. 24, 2004. House passed, under suspension of the rules, Sept. 30. Senate passed Sept. 30. President signed Sept. 30, 2004.

PL 108-309 (H J Res 107) Make continuing appropriations for fiscal 2005. Introduced by YOUNG, R-Fla., on Sept. 28, 2004. House passed Sept. 29. Senate passed Sept. 29. President signed Sept. 30, 2004.

PL 108-310 (HR 5183) Extend highway, highway safety, motor carrier safety, transit and other programs funded out of the Highway Trust Fund through May 31, 2005, pending enactment of a law reauthorizing the Transportation Equity Act for the 21st Century. Introduced by YOUNG, R-Alaska, on Sept. 29, 2004. House passed Sept. 30. Senate passed Sept. 30. President signed Sept. 30, 2004.

PL 108-311(HR 1308) Amend the Internal Revenue Code to provide tax relief for working families. Introduced by THOMAS, R-Calif., on March 18, 2003. House passed March 19. Senate passed, with an amendment, June 5. Conference report filed in the House on Sept. 23, 2004 (H Rept 108-696). House agreed to the conference report Sept. 23. Senate agreed to the conference report Sept. 23 President signed Oct. 4, 2004.

PL 108-312 (HR 265) Provide for an adjustment of the boundaries of Mount Rainier National Park. Introduced by DUNN, R-Wash., on Jan. 8, 2003. House Resources reported, amended, May 17, 2004 (H Rept 108-495). House passed, under suspension of the rules, June 1.

Senate Energy and Natural Resources reported Aug. 25 (S Rept 108-330). Senate passed Sept. 15. President signed Oct. 5, 2004.

PL 108-313 (HR 1521) Provide for additional lands to be included within the boundary of the Johnstown Flood National Memorial in Pennsylvania. Introduced by MURTHA, D-Pa., on March 31, 2003. House Resources reported, amended, Oct. 7 (H Rept 108-301). House passed, under suspension of the rules, Oct. 15. Senate Energy and Natural Resources reported May 20 (S Rept 108-276). Senate passed Sept. 15. President signed Oct. 5, 2004.

PL 108-314 (HR 1616) Authorize the exchange of certain lands within the Martin Luther King Jr. National Historic Site for lands owned by the City of Atlanta, Ga. Introduced by LEWIS, D-Ga., on April 3, 2003. House Resources reported Sept. 3 (H Rept 108-255). House passed, under suspension of the rules, Oct. 28. Senate Energy and Natural Resources reported Aug. 25, 2004 (S Rept 108-332). Senate passed Sept. 15. President signed Oct. 5, 2004.

PL 108-315 (HR 1648) Authorize the secretary of the Interior to convey certain water distribution systems of the Cachuma Project in California, to the Carpinteria Valley Water District and the Montecito Water District. Introduced by CAPPS, D-Calif., on April 7, 2003. House Resources reported Nov. 17 (H Rept 108-363). House passed, under suspension of the rules, Nov. 17. Senate Energy and Natural Resources reported June 25, 2004 (S Rept 108-287). Senate passed Sept. 15. President signed Oct. 5, 2004.

PL 108-316 (HR 1732) Amend the Reclamation Wastewater and Groundwater Study and Facilities Act to authorize the secretary of the Interior to participate in the Williamson County, Texas, Water Recycling and Reuse Project. Introduced by CARTER, R-Texas, on April 10, 2003. House Resources reported Nov. 17 (H Rept 108-364). House passed, under suspension of the rules, Nov. 17. Senate Energy and Natural Resources reported June 25, 2004 (S Rept 108-288). Senate passed Sept. 15. President signed Oct. 5, 2004.

PL 108-317 (HR 2696) Establish institutes to demonstrate and promote the use of adaptive ecosystem management to reduce the risk of wildfires, and to restore the health of fire-adapted forest and woodland ecosystems of the interior West. Introduced by RENZI, R-Ariz., on July 10, 2003. House Resources reported, amended, Nov. 21 (H Rept 108-397, Part 1). House Agriculture discharged. House passed, under suspension of the rules, Feb. 24, 2004. Senate Energy and Natural Resources reported March 29 (S Rept 108-252). Senate passed Sept. 15. President signed Oct. 5, 2004.

PL 108-318 (HR 3209) Amend the Reclamation Project Authorization Act of 1972 to clarify the acreage for which the North Loup division is authorized to provide irrigation water under the Missouri River Basin project. Introduced by OSBORNE, R-Neb., on Sept. 30, 2003.

House Resources reported Nov. 7 (H Rept 108-356). House passed, under suspension of the rules, Nov. 17. Senate Energy and Natural Resources reported June 25, 2004 (S Rept 108-289). Senate passed Sept. 15. President signed Oct. 5, 2004.

PL 108-319 (HR 3249) Extend the term of the Forest Counties Payments Committee. Introduced by WALDEN, R-Ore., on Oct. 3, 2003. House passed, under suspension of the rules, Oct. 28. Senate Energy and Natural Resources reported May 20, 2004 (S Rept 108-277). Senate passed Sept. 15. President signed Oct. 5, 2004.

PL 108-320 (HR 3389) Amend the Stevenson-Wydler Technology Innovation Act of 1980 to permit Malcolm Baldrige National Quality Awards to be made to nonprofit organizations. Introduced by MILLER, D-N.C., on Oct. 29, 2003. House Science reported, Feb. 11, 2004 (H Rept 108-419). House passed, under suspension of the rules, March 3. Senate Commerce, Science and Transportation discharged. Senate passed Sept. 23. President signed Oct. 5, 2004.

PL 108-321 (HR 3768) Expand the Timucuan Ecological and Historic Preserve in St. Johns River Valley, Jacksonville, Fla. Introduced by CRENSHAW, R-Fla., on Feb. 4, 2004. House Resources reported, amended, May 17 (H Rept 108-493). House passed, under suspension of the rules, May 17. Senate Energy and Natural Resources reported Aug. 25 (S Rept 108-333). Senate passed Sept. 15. President signed Oct. 5, 2004.

PL 108-322 (S J Res 41) Commemorate the opening of the National Museum of the American Indian. Introduced by CAMPBELL, R-Colo., on July 7, 2004. Senate Indian Affairs reported, amended, July 16 (no written report). Senate passed July 22. House passed, under suspension of the rules, Sept. 21. President signed Oct. 5, 2004.

PL 108-323 (HR 4654) Reauthorize the Tropical Forest Conservation Act of 1998 through fiscal 2007. Introduced by PORTMAN, R-Ohio, on June 23, 2004. House International Relations reported July 14 (H Rept 108-603). House passed, under suspension of the rules, Sept. 7. Senate Foreign Relations discharged. Senate passed Sept. 28. President signed Oct. 6, 2004.

PL 108-324 (HR 4837) Make appropriations for military construction, family housing, and base realignment and closure for the Department of Defense for the fiscal year ending Sept. 30, 2005. Introduced by KNOLLENBERG, R-Mich., on July 15, 2004. House Appropriations reported July 15 (H Rept 108-607). House passed July 22. Senate passed, amended, Sept. 20. Conference report filed in the House Oct. 9 (H Rept 108-773). House agreed to the conference report Oct. 9. Senate agreed to the conference report Oct. 11. President signed Oct. 13, 2004.

PL 108-325 (S 1778) Authorize a land conveyance between the United States and the City of Craig, Alaska. Introduced by MURKOWSKI, R-Alaska, on Oct. 23, 2003. Senate Energy and Natural Resources reported, amended, May 20, 2004 (S Rept 108-271). Senate passed Sept. 15. House passed, under suspension of the rules, Sept. 28. President signed Oct. 13, 2004.

PL 108-326 (HR 982) Clarify the tax treatment of bonds and other obligations issued by the government of American Samoa. Introduced by FALEOMAVAEGA, D-Am. Samoa, on Feb. 27, 2003. House Judiciary reported May 15 (H Rept 108-102, Part 1). House Resources reported Oct. 7 (H Rept 108-102, Part 2). House passed, under suspension of the rules, Nov. 4. Senate Finance reported July 20, 2004 (no written report). Senate passed Sept. 29. President signed Oct. 16, 2004.

PL 108-327 (HR 2408) Amend the Fish and Wildlife Act of 1956 to reauthorize volunteer programs and community partnerships for national wildlife refuges. Introduced by SAXTON, R-N.J., on June 10, 2003. House Resources reported, amended, Nov. 20 (H Rept 108-385). House passed, under suspension of the rules, March 23, 2004. Senate Environment and Public Works reported Aug. 25 (S Rept 108-315). Senate passed Sept. 30. President signed Oct. 16, 2004.

PL 108-328 (HR 2771) Amend the Safe Drinking Water Act to reauthorize the New York City Watershed Protection Program. Introduced by FOSSELLA, R-N.Y., on July 17, 2003. House Energy and Commerce reported April 28, 2004 (H Rept 108-476). House passed, under suspension of the rules, May 5. Senate passed Sept. 30. President signed Oct. 16, 2004.

PL 108-329 (HR 4115) Amend federal law to allow binding arbitration clauses to be included in all contracts affecting the land within the Salt River Pima-Maricopa Indian Reservation. Introduced by HAYWORTH, R-Ariz., on April 1, 2004. House Resources reported June 9 (H Rept 108-535). House passed, under suspension of the rules, July 19. Senate passed Sept. 29. President signed Oct. 16, 2004.

PL 108-330 (HR 4259) Improve the financial accountability requirements applicable to the Department of Homeland Security and establish requirements for the department's Future Years Homeland Security Program. Introduced by PLATTS, R-Pa., on May 4, 2004. House Government Reform reported June 9 (H Rept 108-533, Part 1). House Select Homeland Security discharged. House passed, under suspension of the rules, July 20. Senate Governmental Affairs discharged. Senate passed Sept. 29. President signed Oct. 16, 2004.

PL 108-331 (HR 5105) Authorize the Board of Regents of the Smithsonian Institution to carry out construction and related activities in support of the collaborative Very Energetic Radiation Imaging Telescope Array System (VERITAS) project on Kitt Peak near Tucson, Ariz. Introduced by NEY, R-Ohio, on Sept. 17, 2004. House passed, under suspension of the rules, Sept. 29. Senate passed Oct. 1. President signed Oct. 16, 2004.

PL 108-332 (S 2292) Require a report on acts of anti-semitism around the world. Introduced by VOINOVICH, R-Ohio, on April 7, 2004. Senate Foreign Relations re-

ported, amended, April 29 (no written report). Senate passed May 7. House International Relations discharged. House passed, amended, Oct. 8 . Senate agreed to House amendments, Oct. 10. President signed Oct. 16, 2004.

PL 108-333 (HR 4011) Promote human rights and freedom in the Democratic People's Republic of Korea. Introduced by LEACH, R-Iowa, on March 23, 2004. House International Relations reported, amended, May 4 (H Rept 108-478, Part 1). House Judiciary discharged. House passed, under suspension of the rules, July 21. Senate Foreign Relations discharged. Senate passed, amended, Sept. 28. House agreed to Senate amendments, under suspension of the rules, Oct. 4. President signed Oct. 18, 2004.

PL 108-334 (HR 4567) Make appropriations for the Department of Homeland Security for the fiscal year ending Sept. 30, 2005. Introduced by ROGERS, R-Ky., on June 15, 2004. House Appropriations reported June 15 (H Rept 108-541). House passed, amended, June 18. Senate passed, amended, Sept. 14. Conference report filed in the House Oct. 9 (H Rept 108-774). House agreed to the conference report Oct. 9. Senate agreed to the conference report Oct. 11. President signed Oct. 18, 2004.

PL 108-335 (HR 4850) Make appropriations for the government of the District of Columbia and other activities chargeable in whole or in part against the revenues of the District for the fiscal year ending Sept. 30, 2005. Introduced by FRELINGHUYSEN, R-N.J., on July 19, 2004. House Appropriations reported July 19 (H Rept 108-610). House passed July 20. Senate Appropriations discharged. Senate passed, amended, Sept. 22. Conference report filed in the House Oct. 5 (H Rept 108-734). House agreed to the conference report Oct. 6. Senate agreed to the conference report Oct. 6. President signed Oct. 18, 2004.

PL 108-336 (S 551) Provide for the implementation of air quality programs developed in accordance with an intergovernmental agreement between the Southern Ute Indian Tribe and the State of Colorado concerning air quality control on the Southern Ute Indian Reservation. Introduced by CAMPBELL, R-Colo., on March 16, 2003. Senate Environment and Public Works reported, amended, Nov. 19 (S Rept 108-201). Senate passed Nov. 21. House Resources reported Sept. 30, 2004 (H Rept 108-712, Part 1). House Energy and Commerce reported Oct. 4 (H Rept 108-712, Part 2). House passed, under suspension of the rules, Oct. 4. President signed Oct. 18, 2004.

PL 108-337 (S 1421) Authorize the subdivision and dedication of restricted land owned by Alaska natives. Introduced by MURKOWSKI, R-Alaska, on July 16, 2003. Senate Energy and Natural Resources reported, amended, March 29, 2004(S Rept 108-251). Senate passed Sept. 15. House passed, under suspension of the rules, Oct. 4. President signed Oct. 18, 2004.

PL 108-338 (S 1537) Direct the secretary of Agriculture to convey to the New Hope Cemetery Association certain land in Arkansas for use as a cemetery. Introduced by LINCOLN, D-Ark., on July 31, 2003. Senate Agriculture, Nutrition and Forestry discharged. Senate passed Nov. 24. House Resources reported Sept. 7, 2004 (H Rept 108-654). House passed, under suspension of the rules, Sept. 28. President signed Oct. 18, 2004.

PL 108-339 (S 1663) Replace certain Coastal Barrier Resources System maps. Introduced by DOLE, R-N.C., on Sept. 25, 2003. Senate Environment and Public Works reported Oct. 30 (S Rept 108-179). Senate passed Nov. 6. House passed, amended, under suspension of the rules, June 14, 2004. Senate agreed to House amendments Sept. 28. President signed Oct. 18, 2004.

PL 108-340 (S 1687) Direct the secretary of the Interior to conduct a study on the preservation and interpretation of the historic sites of the Manhattan Project for potential inclusion in the National Park System. Introduced by BINGAMAN, D-N.M., on Sept. 30, 2003. Senate Energy and Natural Resources reported, amended, May 20, 2004 (S Rept 108-270). Senate passed Sept. 15. House passed, under suspension of the rules, Sept. 28. President signed Oct. 18, 2004.

PL 108-341 (S 1814) Transfer control of the Mingo Job Corps Center in southern Missouri from the secretary of Interior to the secretary of Agriculture. Introduced by BOND, R-Mo., on Nov. 3, 2003. Senate Environment and Public Works discharged. Senate passed April 20, 2004. House Resources reported Oct. 4 (H Rept 108-716, Part 1). House Agriculture discharged. House Education and the Workforce discharged. House passed, under suspension of the rules, Oct. 4. President signed Oct. 18, 2004.

PL 108-342 (S 2052) Amend the National Trails System Act to designate El Camino Real de los Tejas as a National Historic Trail. Introduced by HUTCHISON, R-Texas, on Feb. 5, 2004. Senate Energy and Natural Resources reported, amended, Aug. 25 (S Rept 108-321). Senate passed Sept. 15. House passed, under suspension of the rules, Sept. 28. President signed Oct. 18, 2004.

PL 108-343 (S 2319) Authorize and facilitate hydroelectric power licensing of the Tapoco Project. Introduced by ALEXANDER, R-Tenn., on April 19, 2004. Senate Energy and Natural Resources reported, amended, July 7 (S Rept 108-299). Senate passed Sept. 15. House passed, under suspension of the rules, Oct. 4. President signed Oct. 18, 2004.

PL 108-344 (S 2363) Revise and extend the Boys and Girls Clubs of America. Introduced by HATCH, R-Utah, on April 29, 2004. Senate Judiciary reported June 3 (no written report). Senate passed June 3. House Judiciary reported July 13 (H Rept 108-601). House passed, under suspension of the rules, Sept. 28. President signed Oct. 18, 2004.

PL 108-345 (S 2508) Redesignate the Ridges Basin

Reservoir, Colo., as Lake Nighthorse. Introduced by DOMENICI, R-N.M., on June 7, 2004. Senate Energy and Natural Resources reported, amended, Aug. 25 (S Rept 108-327). Senate passed Sept. 15. House passed, under suspension of the rules, Sept. 28. President signed Oct. 18, 2004.

PL 108-346 (S 2180) Direct the secretary of Agriculture to exchange certain lands in the Arapaho and Roosevelt national forests in Colorado. Introduced by CAMPBELL, R-Colo., on March 9, 2004. Senate Energy and Natural Resources reported, amended, June 25 (S Rept 108-285). Senate passed Sept. 15. House passed, under suspension of the rules, Sept. 28. President signed Oct. 18, 2004.

PL 108-347 (HR 854) Provide for the promotion of democracy, human rights and rule of law in the Republic of Belarus and for the consolidation and strengthening of Belarus sovereignty and independence. Introduced by SMITH, R-N.J., on Feb. 13, 2003. House passed, amended, under suspension of the rules, Oct. 4, 2004. Senate passed Oct. 6. President signed Oct. 20, 2004.

PL 108-348 (S 2895) Authorize the Gateway Arch in St. Louis, Mo., to be illuminated by pink lights in honor of breast cancer awareness month. Introduced by TALENT, R-Mo., on Oct. 5, 2004. Senate passed Oct. 5. House passed Oct. 8. President signed Oct. 20, 2004.

PL 108-349 (HR 5122) Amend the Congressional Accountability Act of 1995 to permit members of the board of directors of the Office of Compliance to serve for two terms. Introduced by NEY, R-Ohio, on Sept. 22, 2004. House Administration discharged. House passed Sept. 28. Senate passed, with an amendment, Oct. 4. House agreed to Senate amendment Oct. 7. President signed Oct. 21, 2004.

PL 108-350 (S 33) Authorize the secretary of Agriculture to sell or exchange all or part of certain administrative sites and other land in the Ozark-St. Francis and Ouachita National Forests and to use funds derived from the sale or exchange to acquire, construct or improve administrative sites. Introduced by LINCOLN, D-Ark., on Jan. 7, 2003. Senate passed Nov. 24. House passed, under suspension of the rules, Oct. 5, 2004. President signed Oct. 21 2004.

PL 108-351 (S 1791) Amend the Lease Lot Conveyance Act of 2002 to provide that the amounts received by the United States under that act be deposited in the reclamation fund. Introduced by DOMENICI, R-N.M., on Oct. 28, 2003. Senate Energy and Natural Resources reported May 20, 2004 (S Rept 108-272). Senate passed Sept. 15. House passed, under suspension of the rules, Oct. 7. President signed Oct. 21, 2004.

PL 108-352 (S 2178) Make technical corrections to laws relating to certain units of the National Park System and to National Park programs. Introduced by DOMENICI, R-N.M., on March 9, 2004. Senate Energy and Natural Resources reported March 9, 2004 (S Rept 108-239).

Senate passed May 19. House passed, under suspension of the rules, Oct. 7. President signed Oct. 21, 2004.

PL 108-353 (S 2415) Designate the facility of the U.S. Postal Service located at 4141 Postmark Drive, Anchorage, Alaska, as the "Robert J. Opinsky Post Office Building." Introduced by STEVENS, R-Alaska, on May 13, 2004. Senate Governmental Affairs reported June 7 (no written report). Senate passed June 9. House passed, under suspension of the rules, Oct. 6. President signed Oct. 21, 2004.

PL 108-354 (S 2511) Direct the secretary of the Interior to conduct a feasibility study of a Chimayo water supply system and to provide for the planning, design and construction of a water supply, reclamation and filtration facility for Espanola, N.M. Introduced by DOMENICI, R-N.M., on June 8, 2004. Senate Energy and Natural Resources reported, amended, Aug. 25 (S Rept 108-328). Senate passed Sept. 15. House passed, under suspension of the rules, Oct. 7. President signed Oct. 21, 2004.

PL 108-355 (S 2634) Amend the Public Health Service Act to support the planning, implementation and evaluation of organized activities involving statewide youth suicide early intervention and prevention strategies, and authorize grants to institutions of higher education to reduce student mental and behavioral health problems. Introduced by DODD, D-Conn., on July 8, 2004. Senate passed July 8. House passed, amended, under suspension of the rules, Sept. 8. Senate agreed to House amendments Sept. 9. President signed Oct. 21, 2004.

PL 108-356 (S 2742) Extend certain authority of the Supreme Court Police, modify the venue of prosecutions relating to the Supreme Court building and grounds, and authorize the acceptance of gifts to the U.S. Supreme Court. Introduced by HATCH, R-Utah, on July 22, 2004. Senate Judiciary reported Sept. 21 (no written report). Senate passed, with an amendment, Sept. 28. House passed, under suspension of the rules, Oct. 6. President signed Oct. 21, 2004.

PL 108-357 (HR 4520) Amend the Internal Revenue Code to repeal the tax exclusion for extraterritorial income and reduce corporate taxes. Introduced by THOMAS, R-Calif., on June 4, 2004. House Ways and Means reported, amended, June 16 (H Rept 108-548, Part 1). House Agriculture discharged. House passed June 17. Senate passed, with amendments, July 15. Conference report filed in the House on Oct. 7 (H Rept 108-755). House agreed to the conference report Oct. 7. Senate agreed to the conference report Oct. 11. President signed Oct. 22, 2004.

PL 108-358 (S 2195) Amend the Controlled Substances Act to clarify the definition of anabolic steroids and to provide for research and education activities relating to steroids and steroid precursors. Introduced by BIDEN, D-Del., on March 11, 2004. Senate Judiciary reported Sept. 30 (no written report). Senate passed, with an amendment, Oct. 6. House passed Oct. 8. President signed Oct. 22, 2004.

PL 108-359 (HR 1533) Amend securities law to permit church pension plans to be invested in collective trusts. Introduced by BIGGERT, R-Ill., on April 1, 2003. House Financial Services reported Sept. 3 (H Rept 108-248). House passed, amended, under suspension of the rules, Sept. 3. Senate Banking, Housing and Urban Affairs discharged. Senate passed, with an amendment, Oct. 1, 2004. House agreed to Senate amendment, Oct. 8. President signed Oct. 25, 2004.

PL 108-360 (HR 2608) Reauthorize the National Earthquake Hazards Reduction Program. Introduced by SMITH, R-Mich., on June 26, 2003. House Science reported, amended, Aug. 14 (H Rept 108-246, Part 1). House Resources discharged. House passed, under suspension of the rules, Oct. 1. Senate Commerce, Science and Transportation reported Oct. 5, 2004 (H Rept 108-385). Senate passed, with an amendment, Oct. 6. House agreed to Senate amendment, Oct. 8. President signed Oct. 25, 2004.

PL 108-361 (HR 2828) Authorize the secretary of the Interior to implement water supply technology and infrastructure programs aimed at increasing and diversifying domestic water resources, primarily in California. Introduced by CALVERT, R-Calif., on July 23, 2003. House Resources reported June 25, 2004 (H Rept 108-573, Part 1). House Transportation and Infrastructure discharged. House passed, amended, July 9. Senate passed, with an amendment, Sept. 15. House agreed to Senate amendment, under suspension of the rules, Oct. 6. President signed Oct. 25, 2004.

PL 108-362 (HR 3858) Amend the Public Health Service Act to increase the supply of pancreatic islet cells for research, and to provide for better coordination of federal efforts and information on islet cell transplantation. Introduced by NETHERCUTT, R-Wash., on Feb. 26, 2004. House Energy and Commerce reported Oct. 5 (H Rept 108-726). House passed, under suspension of the rules, Oct. 5. Senate passed Oct. 8. President signed Oct. 25, 2004.

PL 108-363 (HR 4175) Increase, effective Dec. 1, 2004, the rates of disability compensation for veterans with service-connected disabilities and the rates of dependency and indemnity compensation for survivors of certain veterans with service-connected disabilities. Introduced by SMITH, R-N.J., on April 20, 2004. House Veterans' Affairs reported, amended, June 3 (H Rept 108-524). House passed, amended, under suspension of the rules, July 22. Senate Veterans' Affairs discharged. Senate passed, with an amendment, Oct. 5. House agreed to Senate amendment, Oct. 8. President signed Oct. 25, 2004.

PL 108-364 (HR 4278) Amend the Assistive Technology Act of 1998 to support grants to states to address the assistive technology needs of individuals with disabilities. Introduced by MCKEON, R-Calif., on May 5, 2004. House Education and the Workforce reported, amended, June 1 (H Rept 108-514). House passed, amended, un-

der suspension of the rules, June 14. Senate passed, with an amendment, Sept. 30. House agreed to Senate amendment Oct. 8. President signed Oct. 25, 2004.

PL 108-365 (HR 4555) Amend the Public Health Service Act to revise and extend provisions relating to mammography quality standards. Introduced by DINGELL, D-Mich., on June 14, 2004. House Energy and Commerce reported, amended, Sept. 22 (H Rept 108-694). House passed, amended, under suspension of the rules, Oct. 5. Senate passed Oct. 9. President signed Oct. 25, 2004.

PL 108-366 (HR 5185) Temporarily extend the programs under the Higher Education Act of 1965. Introduced by BOEHNER, R-Ohio, on Sept. 30, 2004. House passed, amended, under suspension of the rules, Oct. 6. Senate passed Oct. 9. President signed Oct. 25, 2004.

PL 108-367 (S 524) Expand the boundaries of the Fort Donelson National Battlefield to authorize the acquisition and interpretation of lands associated with the campaign that resulted in the capture of the fort in 1862. Introduced by BUNNING, R-Ky., on March 5, 2003. Senate Energy and Natural Resources, reported, amended, March 9, 2004 (S Rept 108-230). Senate passed May 19. House Resources discharged. House passed Oct. 8. President signed Oct. 25, 2004.

PL 108-368 (S 1368) Authorize the president to award a gold medal on behalf of the Congress to Rev. Dr. Martin Luther King Jr. and his widow Coretta Scott King in recognition of their contributions to the nation on behalf of the civil rights movement. Introduced by LEVIN, D-Mich., on June 27, 2003. Senate Banking, Housing and Urban Affairs discharged. Senate passed Sept. 9, 2004. House Financial Services discharged. House passed Oct. 8. President signed Oct. 25, 2004.

PL 108-369 (S 2864) Extend family farmer bankruptcy protection through June 30, 2005. Introduced by GRASSLEY, R-Iowa, on Sept. 29, 2004. Senate Judiciary discharged. Senate passed Oct. 6. House Judiciary discharged. House passed Oct. 8. President signed Oct. 25, 2004.

PL 108-370 (S 2883) Amend the International Child Abduction Remedies Act to limit the tort liability of private entities or organizations that carry out responsibilities of United States Central Authority under the act. Introduced by HATCH, R-Utah, on Oct. 1, 2004. Senate passed Oct. 1. House passed Oct. 8. President signed Oct. 25, 2004.

PL 108-371 (S 2896) Modify and extend certain privatization requirements of the Communications Satellite Act of 1962. Introduced by BURNS, R-Mont. on Oct. 5, 2004. Senate passed Oct. 5. House passed Oct. 8. President signed Oct. 25, 2004.

PL 108-372 (HR 2714) Reauthorize the State Justice Institute. Introduced by SMITH, R-Texas, on July 14, 2003. House Judiciary reported Sept. 25 (H Rept 108-285). House passed, amended, under suspension of the

rules, March 10, 2004. Senate Judiciary discharged. Senate passed with an amendment Sept. 30. House agreed to Senate amendment Oct. 8. President signed Oct. 25, 2004.

PL 108-373 (S 1134) Reauthorize and improve the programs authorized by the Public Works and Economic Development Act of 1965. Introduced by BOND, R-Mo., on May 22, 2003. Senate Environment and Public Works, reported, amended, Oct. 1, 2004 (S Rept 108-382). Senate passed, with an amendment, Oct. 6. House passed, under suspension of the rules, Oct. 7. President signed Oct. 27, 2004.

PL 108-374 (S 1721) Amend the Indian Land Consolidation Act to improve provisions relating to probate of trust and restricted land. Introduced by CAMPBELL, R-Colo., on Oct. 14, 2003. Senate Indian Affairs, reported, amended, May 13, 2004 (S Rept 108-264). Senate passed, June 2. House Resources reported Sept. 7 (H Rept 108-656). House passed, under suspension of the rules, Oct. 7. President signed Oct. 27, 2004.

PL 108-375 (HR 4200) Authorize appropriations for fiscal 2005 for military activities of the Department of Defense, for military construction and for defense activities of the Department of Energy, and prescribe personnel strengths for the Armed Forces. Introduced by HUNTER, R-Calif., on April 22, 2004. House Armed Services, reported, amended, May 14 (H Rept 108-491). House passed, amended, May 20. Senate passed, with an amendment, June 23. Conference report filed in the House, Oct. 8 (H Rept 108-767). House agreed to conference report, Oct. 9. Senate agreed to conference report, Oct. 9. President signed Oct. 28, 2004.

PL 108-376 (HR 2010) Protect the voting rights of members of the Armed Services in elections for the delegate representing American Samoa in the U.S. House of Representatives. Introduced by FALEOMAVAEGA, D-Am. Samoa, on May 7, 2003. House Resources reported, amended, June 1, 2004 (H Rept 108-515). House passed, amended, under suspension of the rules, June 14. Senate Energy and Natural Resources reported, Sept. 28 (S Rept 108-377). Senate passed Oct. 10. President signed Oct. 30, 2004.

PL 108-377 (HR 2023) Give a preference regarding states that require schools to allow students to self-administer medication to treat their asthma or anaphylaxis. Introduced by STEARNS, R-Fla., on May 7, 2003. House Energy and Commerce reported, amended, July 14, 2004 (H Rept 108-606, Part 1). House Education and the Workforce discharged. House passed, amended, under suspension of the rules, Oct. 5. Senate passed Oct. 11. President signed Oct. 30, 2004.

PL 108-378 (HR 2400) Amend the Organic Act of Guam for the purposes of clarifying the local judicial structure of Guam. Introduced by BORDALLO, D-Guam, on June 10, 2003. House Resources reported, amended, Sept. 7, 2004 (H Rept 108-638). House passed, under suspension of the rules, Sept. 13. Senate Energy and Natural Resources discharged. Senate passed Oct. 10. President signed Oct. 30, 2004.

PL 108-379 (HR 2984) Amend the Agricultural Adjustment Act to remove the requirement that processors be members of an agency administering a marketing order applicable to pears. Introduced by WALDEN, R-Ore., on July 25, 2003. House passed, under suspension of the rules, Oct. 5, 2004. Senate passed Oct. 11. President signed Oct. 30, 2004.

PL 108-380 (HR 3056) Clarify the boundaries of the John H. Chafee Coast Barrier Resources System Cedar Keys Unit P25 on Otherwise Protected Area P25P. Introduced by BROWN-WAITE, R-Fla., on Sept. 10, 2003. House Resources reported, amended, Sept. 7, 2004 (H Rept 108-641). House passed, amended, under suspension of the rules, Sept. 13. Senate Environment and Public Works discharged. Senate passed Oct. 11. President signed Oct. 30, 2004.

PL 108-381 (HR 3217) Provide for the conveyance of several small parcels of National Forest System land in the Apalachicola National Forest in Florida, to resolve boundary discrepancies involving the Mt. Trial Primitive Baptist Church of Wakulla County, Fla. Introduced by BOYD, D-Fla., on Oct. 1, 2003. House passed, under suspension of the rules, Nov. 17. Senate Agriculture, Nutrition and Forestry discharged. Senate passed Oct. 11, 2004. President signed Oct. 30, 2004.

PL 108-382 (HR 3391) Authorize the secretary of the Interior to convey certain lands and facilities of the Provo River Project. Introduced by CANNON, R-Utah, on Oct. 29, 2003. House Resources reported, amended, Oct. 4, 2004 (H Rept 108-719). House passed, amended, under suspension of the rules, Oct. 4. Senate passed Oct. 10. President signed Oct. 30, 2004.

PL 108-383 (HR 3478) Amend Title 44, U.S. Code, to improve the efficiency of operations by the National Archives and Records Administration and to reauthorize the National Historical Publications and Records Commission. Introduced by PUTNAM, R-Fla., on Nov. 7, 2003. House Government Reform reported Dec. 8 (H Rept 108-403). House passed, amended, under suspension of the rules, Sept. 13, 2004. Senate Governmental Affairs discharged. Senate passed Oct. 11. President signed Oct. 30, 2004.

PL 108-384 (HR 3479) Provide for the control and eradication of the brown tree snake on the island of Guam and the prevention of the introduction of the brown tree snake to other areas of the United States. Introduced by BORDALLO, D-Guam, on Nov. 7, 2003. House Resources reported, amended, Sept. 15, 2004 (H Rept 108-687, Part 1). House Agriculture discharged. House passed, amended, under suspension of the rules, Sept. 28. Senate passed Oct. 10. President signed Oct. 30, 2004.

PL 108-385 (HR 3706) Adjust the boundary of the John Muir National Historic Site. Introduced by MILLER, D-Calif. on Jan. 20, 2004. House Resources reported June

18 (H Rept 108-555). House passed, under suspension of the rules, June 21. Senate Energy and Natural Resources reported Sept. 28 (S Rept 108-378). Senate passed Oct. 10. President signed Oct. 30, 2004.

PL 108-386 (HR 3797) Authorize improvements in the operations of the government of the District of Columbia. Introduced by T. DAVIS, R-Va., on Feb. 11, 2004. House Government Reform reported June 17 (H Rept 108-551, Part 1). House Education and the Workforce discharged. House Financial Services discharged. House passed, under suspension of the rules, June 21. Senate Governmental Affairs discharged. Senate passed Oct. 11. President signed Oct. 30, 2004.

PL 108-387 (HR 3819) Redesignate Fort Clatsop National Memorial as the Lewis and Clark National Historical Park and include in the park sites in the state of Washington and Oregon. Introduced by BAIRD, D-Wash., on Feb. 24, 2004. House Resources reported, amended, June 25 (H Rept 108-570). House passed, amended, under suspension of the rules, July 19. Senate Energy and Natural Resources discharged. Senate passed Oct. 10. President signed Oct. 30, 2004.

PL 108-388 (HR 4046) Designate the facility of the U.S. Postal Service located at 555 West 180th St. in New York as the "Sergeant Riayan A. Tejeda Post Office." Introduced by RANGEL, D-N.Y., on March 25, 2004. House passed, amended, under suspension of the rules, Sept. 28. Senate passed Oct. 10. President signed Oct. 30, 2004.

PL 108-389 (HR 4066) Provide for the conveyance of certain land to the United States and revise the boundary of Chickasaw National Recreation Area in Oklahoma. Introduced by COLE, R-Okla., on March 30, 2004. House Resources reported, amended, Sept. 28 (H Rept 108-702). House passed, amended, under suspension of the rules, Sept. 28. Senate passed Oct. 10. President signed Oct. 30, 2004.

PL 108-390 (HR 4306) Amend Section 274A of the Immigration and Nationality Act to improve the process for verifying an individual's eligibility for employment. Introduced by CANNON, R-Utah, on May 6, 2004. House Judiciary reported, amended, Oct. 5 (H Rept 108-731). House passed, amended, under suspension of the rules, Oct. 6. Senate passed Oct. 11. President signed Oct. 30, 2004.

PL 108-391 (H J Res 57) Express the sense of the Congress in recognition of the contributions of the seven Columbia astronauts by supporting establishment of a Columbia Memorial Space Science Learning Center. Introduced by ROYBAL-ALLARD, D-Calif., on May 22, 2003. House passed, amended, under suspension of the rules, Oct. 5, 2004. Senate passed Oct. 10. President signed Oct. 30, 2004.

PL 108-392 (HR 4381) Designate the facility of the U.S. Postal Service located at 2811 Springdale Ave., Springdale, Ark., as the "Harvey and Bernice Jones Post Office Building." Introduced by BOOZMAN, R-Ark., on May 18, 2004. House passed, under suspension of the rules, Sept. 7. Senate Governmental Affairs discharged. Senate passed Oct. 10. President signed Oct. 30, 2004.

PL 108-393 (HR 4471) Clarify the loan guarantee authority under Title VI of the Native American Housing Assistance and Self-Determination Act of 1996. Introduced by RENZI, R-Ariz., on June 1, 2004. House Financial Services reported June 17 (H Rept 108-550). House passed, under suspension of the rules, June 21. Senate Indian Affairs discharged. Senate passed Oct. 11. President signed Oct. 30, 2004.

PL 108-394 (HR 4481) Amend Public Law 86-434 establishing Wilson's Creek National Battlefield in the state of Missouri to expand the boundaries of the park. Introduced by BLUNT, R-Mo., on June 2, 2004. House Resources reported, amended, Sept. 7 (H Rept 108-651). House passed, amended, under suspension of the rules, Sept. 13. Senate Energy and Natural Resources discharged. Senate passed Oct. 10. President signed Oct. 30, 2004.

PL 108-395 (HR 4556) Designate the facility of the U.S. Postal Service located at 1115 South Clinton Ave. in Dunn, N.C., as the "Gen. William Carey Lee Post Office Building." Introduced by ETHERIDGE, D-N.C., on June 14, 2004. House passed, under suspension of the rules, Sept. 7. Senate Governmental Affairs discharged. Senate passed Oct. 10. President signed Oct. 30, 2004.

PL 108-396 (HR 4579) Modify the boundary of the Harry S Truman National Historic Site in Missouri. Introduced by MCCARTHY, D-Mo., on June 15, 2004. House Resources reported Sept. 28 (H Rept 108-703). House passed, under suspension of the rules, Sept. 28. Senate passed Oct. 10. President signed Oct. 30, 2004.

PL 108-397 (HR 4618) Designate the facility of the U.S. Postal Service located at 10 West Prospect St., Nanuet, N.Y., as the "Anthony I. Lombardi Memorial Post Office Building." Introduced by ENGEL, D-N.Y., on June 18, 2004. House passed, under suspension of the rules, Sept. 7. Senate Governmental Affairs discharged. Senate passed Oct. 10. President signed Oct. 30, 2004.

PL 108-398 (HR 4632) Designate the facility of the U.S. Postal Service located at 19504 Linden Blvd., St. Albans, N.Y., as the "Archie Spigner Post Office Building." Introduced by MEEKS, D-N.Y., on June 21, 2004. House passed, under suspension of the rules, Sept. 13. Senate Governmental Affairs discharged. Senate passed Oct. 10. President signed Oct. 30, 2004.

PL 108-399 (HR 4731) Amend the Federal Water Pollution Control Act to reauthorize the National Estuary Program. Introduced by GERLACH, R-Pa., on June 25, 2004. House Transportation and Infrastructure reported Sept. 13 (H Rept 108-678). House passed, under suspension of the rules, Sept. 29. Senate passed Oct. 11. President signed Oct. 30, 2004.

PL 108-400 (HR 4827) Amend the Colorado Canyons National Conservation Area and Black Ridge Canyons Wilderness Act of 2000 to rename the Colorado Canyons National Conservation Area as the McInnis Canyons National Conservation Area. Introduced by WALDEN, R-Ore., on July 13, 2004. House passed, under suspension of the rules, Sept. 28. Senate passed Oct. 10. President signed Oct. 30, 2004.

PL 108-401 (HR 4917) Amend Title 5, U.S. Code, to authorize appropriations for the Administrative Conference of the United States for fiscal years 2005, 2006 and 2007. Introduced by CANNON, R-Utah, on July 22, 2004. House Judiciary discharged. House passed Oct. 8. Senate passed Oct. 11. President signed Oct. 30, 2004.

PL 108-402 (HR 5027) Designate the facility of the U.S. Postal Service located at 411 Midway Ave., Mascotte, Fla., as the "Specialist Eric Ramirez Post Office." Introduced by BROWN-WAITE, R-Fla., on Sept. 8, 2004. House passed, under suspension of the rules, Sept. 28. Senate passed Oct. 10. President signed Oct. 30, 2004.

PL 108-403 (HR 5039) Designate the facility of the U.S. Postal Service located at U.S. Route 1 in Ridgeway, N.C., as the "Eva Holtzman Post Office." Introduced by BUTTERFIELD, D-N.C., on Sept. 9, 2004. House passed, under suspension of the rules, Sept. 22. Senate Governmental Affairs discharged. Senate passed Oct. 10. President signed Oct. 30, 2004.

PL 108-404 (HR 5051) Designate the facility of the U.S. Postal Service located at 1001 Williams St., Ignacio, Colo., as the "Leonard C. Burch Post Office Building." Introduced by MCINNIS, R-Colo., on Sept. 9, 2004. House passed, under suspension of the rules, Oct. 6. Senate passed Oct. 10. President signed Oct. 30, 2004.

PL 108-405 (HR 5107) Protect crime victims' rights; eliminate the substantial backlog of DNA samples collected from crime scenes and convicted offenders; improve and expand the DNA testing capacity of federal, state and local crime laboratories; increase research and development of new DNA testing technologies; develop new training programs regarding the collection and use of DNA evidence; provide post-conviction testing of DNA evidence to exonerate the innocent; and improve the performance of counsel in state capital cases. Introduced by SENSENBRENNER, R-Wis., on Sept. 21, 2004. House Judiciary reported Sept. 30 (H Rept 108-711). House passed, amended, Oct. 6. Senate passed Oct. 9. President signed Oct. 30, 2004.

PL 108-406 (HR 5131) Provide assistance to support expansion of Special Olympics and development of education programs and a Healthy Athletes Program. Introduced by BLUNT, R-Mo., on Sept. 23, 2004. House passed, under suspension of the rules, Oct. 6. Senate passed Oct. 10. President signed Oct. 30, 2004.

PL 108-407 (HR 5133) Designate the facility of the U.S. Postal Service located at 11110 Sunset Hills Rd., Reston, Va., as the "Martha Pennino Post Office Building." Introduced by MORAN, D-Va., on Sept. 23, 2004. House passed, under suspension of the rules, Sept. 28. Senate passed Oct. 10. President signed Oct. 30, 2004.

PL 108-408 (HR 5147) Designate the facility of the U.S. Postal Service located at 23055 Sherman Way, West Hills, Calif., as the "Evan Asa Ashcraft Post Office Building." Introduced by WAXMAN, D-Calif., on Sept. 24, 2004. House passed, under suspension of the rules, Sept. 28. Senate passed Oct. 10. President signed Oct. 30, 2004.

PL 108-409 (HR 5186) Reduce certain special allowance payments and provide additional teacher loan forgiveness on federal student loans. Introduced by BOEHNER, R-Ohio, on Sept. 30, 2004. House passed, amended, under suspension of the rules, Oct. 7. Senate passed Oct. 9. President signed Oct. 30, 2004.

PL 108-410 (HR 5294) Amend the John F. Kennedy Center Act to authorize appropriations for the John F. Kennedy Center for the Performing Arts. Introduced by YOUNG, R-Alaska, on Oct. 8, 2004. House Transportation and Infrastructure discharged. House passed Oct. 8. Senate passed Oct. 11. President signed Oct. 30, 2004.

PL 108-411 (S 129) Provide for reform relating to federal employment. Introduced by VOINOVICH, R-Ohio, on Jan. 9, 2003. Senate Governmental Affairs reported, amended, Jan. 27, 2004 (S Rept 108-223). Senate passed, with an amendment, April 8. House Government Reform reported, amended, Oct. 5 (H Rept 108-733). House passed, amended, under suspension of the rules, Oct. 6. Senate agreed to House amendment, Oct. 11. President signed Oct. 30, 2004.

PL 108-412 (S 144) Require the secretary of Agriculture to establish a program to assist eligible weed management entities to control or eradicate noxious weeds on public and private land. Introduced by CRAIG, R-Idaho, on Jan. 13, 2003. Senate Energy and Natural Resources reported, amended, Feb. 11 (S Rept 108-6). Senate passed, with an amendment, March 4. House Resources reported, amended, June 1, 2004 (H Rept 108-517, Part 1). House Agriculture discharged. House passed, amended, under suspension of the rules, Oct. 4. Senate agreed to House amendment, Oct. 10. President signed Oct. 30, 2004.

PL 108-413 (S 643) Authorize the secretary of the Interior, in cooperation with the University of New Mexico, to construct and occupy a portion of the Hibben Center for Archaeological Research at the University of New Mexico. Introduced by DOMENICI, R-N.M. on March 18, 2003. Senate Energy and Natural Resources reported, amended, July 11 (S Rept 108-94). Senate passed, with an amendment, July 17. House passed, amended, under suspension of the rules, Sept. 28. Senate agreed to House amendment, Oct. 10. President signed Oct. 30, 2004.

PL 108-414 (S 1194) Foster local collaborations to ensure that resources are effectively and efficiently used within the criminal and juvenile justice systems. Introduced by

DEWINE, R-Ohio, on June 5, 2003. Senate Judiciary reported, amended, Oct. 23 (no written report). Senate passed, with an amendment, Oct. 27. House Judiciary reported, amended, Oct. 5, 2004 (H Rept 108-732). House passed, amended, under suspension of the rules, Oct. 6. Senate agreed to House amendment, Oct. 11. President signed Oct. 30, 2004.

PL 108-415 (S 2986) Amend Title 31 of the U.S. Code to increase the public debt limit. Introduced by FRIST, R-Tenn., on Nov. 16, 2004. Senate passed Nov. 17. House passed Nov. 18. President signed Nov. 19, 2004.

PL 108-416 (H J Res 114) Make further continuing appropriations for fiscal 2005. Introduced by YOUNG, R-Fla., on Nov. 19, 2004. House passed Nov. 20. Senate passed Nov. 20. President signed Nov. 21, 2004.

PL 108-417 (HR 1113) Authorize an exchange of land at Fort Frederica National Monument. Introduced by KINGSTON, R-Ga., on March 6, 2003. House Resources reported, amended, July 14 (H Rept 108-201). House passed, amended, under suspension of the rules, Sept. 23. Senate Energy and Natural Resources reported, amended, Sept. 28, 2004 (S Rept 108-374). Senate passed, amended, Oct. 10. House agreed to Senate amendment, under suspension of the rules, Nov. 17. President signed Nov. 30, 2004.

PL 108-418 (HR 1284) Amend the Reclamation Projects Authorization and Adjustment Act of 1992 to increase the federal share of the costs of the San Gabriel Basin demonstration project. Introduced by NAPOLITANO, D-Calif., on March 13, 2003. House Resources reported July 14 (H Rept 108-204). House passed, under suspension of the rules, Sept. 16. Senate Energy and Natural Resources reported, amended, July 22, 2004 (S Rept 108-331). Senate passed, amended, Sept. 15. House agreed to Senate amendment, under suspension of the rules, Nov. 17. President signed Nov. 30, 2004.

PL 108-419 (HR 1417) Amend Title 17, U.S. Code, to replace copyright arbitration royalty panels with copyright royalty judges. Introduced by SMITH, R-Texas, on March 25, 2003. House Judiciary reported, amended, Jan. 30, 2004 (H Rept 108-408). House passed, under suspension of the rules, March 3. Senate Judiciary reported, amended, Sept. 29 (no written report). Senate passed with an amendment, Oct. 6. House agreed to Senate amendment, under suspension of the rules, Nov. 17. President signed Nov. 30, 2004.

PL 108-420 (HR 1446) Support the efforts of the California Missions Foundation to restore and repair the Spanish colonial and mission-era missions in California and to preserve the artwork and artifacts of these missions. Introduced by FARR, D-Calif., on March 26, 2003. House passed, under suspension of the rules, Oct. 20. Senate Energy and Natural Resources reported, amended, Sept. 28, 2004 (S Rept 108-375). Senate passed, amended, Oct. 10. House agreed to Senate amendment, under suspension of the rules, Nov. 17. President signed Nov. 30, 2004.

PL 108-421 (HR 1964) Assist Connecticut, New Jersey, New York and Pennsylvania in conserving priority lands and natural resources in the Highlands region. Introduced by FRELINGHUYSEN, R-N.J., on May 6, 2003. House Resources reported, amended, Nov. 17 (H Rept 108-373, Part 1). House passed, under suspension of the rules, Nov. 21. Senate Energy and Natural Resources reported, amended, Sept. 28, 2004 (S Rept 108-376). Senate passed, amended, Oct. 10. House agreed to Senate amendment, under suspension of the rules, Nov. 17. President signed Nov. 30, 2004.

PL 108-422 (HR 3936) Amend Title 38, U.S. Code, to increase the authorization for grants to benefit homeless veterans and improve management and administration of veterans' facilities and health care programs. Introduced by SMITH, R-N.J., on March 11, 2004. House Veterans' Affairs reported June 25 (H Rept 108-574, Part 1). House Armed Services discharged. House passed, under suspension of the rules, July 20. Senate Veterans' Affairs discharged. Senate passed with an amendment Oct. 9. House agreed to Senate amendment, under suspension of the rules, Nov. 17. President signed Nov. 30, 2004.

PL 108-423 (HR 4516) Require the secretary of Energy to carry out a program of research and development to advance high-end computing. Introduced by BIGGERT, R-Ill., on June 4, 2004. House Science reported, amended, July 1 (H Rept 108-578). House passed, amended, under suspension of the rules, July 7. Senate Energy and Natural Resources reported, amended, Sept. 28 (S Rept 108-379). Senate passed with an amendment, Oct. 10. House agreed to Senate amendment, under suspension of the rules, Nov. 17. President signed Nov. 30, 2004.

PL 108-424 (HR 4593) Establish wilderness areas, promote conservation, improve public land and provide for development in Lincoln County, Nev. Introduced by GIBBONS, R-Nev., on June 16, 2004. House Resources reported, amended, Oct. 4 (H Rept 108-720). House passed, under suspension of the rules, Oct. 4. Senate passed with an amendment, Oct. 10. House agreed to Senate amendment, under suspension of the rules, Nov. 17. President signed Nov. 30, 2004.

PL 108-425 (HR 4794) Amend the Tijuana River Valley Estuary and Beach Sewage Cleanup Act of 2000 to extend the authorization. Introduced by HUNTER, R-Calif., on July 9, 2004. House Transportation and Infrastructure reported Sept. 15 (H Rept 108-688, Part 1). House passed, under suspension of the rules, Oct. 7. Senate passed Nov. 16. President signed Nov. 30, 2004.

PL 108-426 (HR 5163) Amend Title 49, U.S. Code, to reorganize Department of Transportation research activities. Introduced by YOUNG, R-Alaska, on Sept. 29, 2004. House Transportation and Infrastructure reported Oct. 6 (H Rept 108-749, Part 1). House Energy and Commerce, and House Science discharged. House passed, amended, under suspension of the rules, Oct. 7. Senate passed Nov. 16. President signed Nov. 30, 2004.

PL 108-427 (HR 5213) Expand research information regarding multidisciplinary research projects and epidemiological studies. Introduced by BILIRAKIS, R-Fla., on Oct. 5, 2004. House passed, amended, under suspension of the rules, Oct. 7. Senate passed Nov. 16. President signed Nov. 30, 2004.

PL 108-428 (HR 5245) Extend the liability indemnification regime for the commercial space transportation industry. Introduced by BOEHLERT, R-N.Y., on Oct. 7, 2004. House Science discharged. House passed Oct. 8. Senate passed Nov. 16. President signed Nov. 30, 2004.

PL 108-429 (HR 1047) Amend the U.S. Harmonized Tariff Schedule to modify temporarily certain rates of duty and to make other technical changes to trade laws. Introduced by CRANE, R-Ill., on March 4, 2003. House passed, under suspension of the rules, March 5. Senate passed, with an amendment, March 4, 2004. Conference report filed in the House on Oct. 8 (H Rept 108-771). House agreed to conference report Oct. 8. Senate agreed to conference report Nov. 19. President signed Dec. 3, 2004.

PL 108-430 (HR 1630) Revise the boundary of the Petrified Forest National Park in Arizona. Introduced by RENZI, R-Ariz., on April 3, 2003. House Resources reported, amended, Sept. 30, 2004 (H Rept 108-713). House passed, under suspension of the rules, Oct. 4. Senate passed, with an amendment, Oct. 10. House agreed to Senate amendment Nov. 19. President signed Dec. 3, 2004.

PL 108-431 (HR 2912) Reaffirm the inherent sovereign rights of the Osage Tribe to determine its membership and form of government. Introduced by LUCAS, R-Okla., on July 25, 2003. House Resources reported May 19, 2004 (H Rept 108-502). House passed, under suspension of the rules, June 1. Senate Indian Affairs reported Sept. 15 (S Rept 108-343). Senate passed Nov. 19. President signed Dec. 3, 2004.

PL 108-432 (H J Res 110) Recognize the 60th anniversary of the Battle of the Bulge during World War II. Introduced by HASTERT, R-Ill., on Oct. 8, 2004. House passed, under suspension of the rules, Nov. 16. Senate passed Nov. 19. President signed Dec. 3, 2004.

PL 108-433 (H J Res 111) Appoint the day for convening of the first session of the 109th Congress. Introduced by BOEHNER, R-Ohio, on Nov. 17, 2004. House passed Nov. 17. Senate passed Nov. 19. President signed Dec. 3, 2004.

PL 108-434 (H J Res 115) Make further continuing appropriations for fiscal 2005 through Dec. 8, 2004. Introduced by WOLF, R-Va., on Nov. 24, 2004. House Appropriations discharged. House passed Nov. 24. Senate passed Nov. 24. President signed Dec. 3, 2004.

PL 108-435 (S 150) Amend the Internet Tax Freedom Act to extend for four years the moratorium on taxes on Internet access and multiple and discriminatory taxes on electronic commerce. Introduced by ALLEN, R-Va., on Jan. 13, 2003. Senate Commerce, Science and Transportation reported, amended, Sept. 29 (S Rept 108-155). Senate Finance discharged. Senate passed, with amendments, April 29, 2004. House passed, under suspension of the rules, Nov. 19. President signed Dec. 3, 2004.

PL 108-436 (S 434) Authorize the secretary of Agriculture to sell or exchange all or part of certain parcels of National Forest System land in Idaho and use the proceeds derived from the sale or exchange for National Forest System purposes. Introduced by CRAIG, R-Idaho, on Feb. 25, 2003. Senate Energy and Natural Resources reported, amended, July 21 (S Rept 108-132). Senate passed, with an amendment, Nov. 24. House Resources reported Oct. 6, 2004 (H Rept 108-740). House passed, under suspension of the rules, Nov. 17. President signed Dec. 3, 2004.

PL 108-437 (S 1146) Implement the recommendations of the Garrison Unit Joint Tribal Advisory Committee by authorizing the construction of a rural health care facility on the Fort Berthold Indian Reservation, N.D. Introduced by CONRAD, D-N.D., on May 23, 2003. Senate Indian Affairs reported, amended, Oct. 15 (S Rept 108-165). Senate passed, amended, Oct. 27. House Resources reported June 3, 2004 (H Rept 108-523, Part 1). House Energy and Commerce discharged. House passed, under suspension of the rules, Nov. 17. President signed Dec. 3, 2004.

PL 108-438 (S 1241) Establish the Kate Mullany National Historic Site in New York. Introduced by CLINTON, D-N.Y., on June 11, 2003. Senate Energy and Natural Resources reported, amended, July 7, 2004 (S Rept 108-295). Senate passed, amended, Sept. 15. House passed, under suspension of the rules, Nov. 17. President signed Dec. 3, 2004.

PL 108-439 (S 1727) Authorize additional appropriations for the Reclamation Safety of Dams Act of 1978. Introduced by DOMENICI, R-N.M., on Oct. 14, 2003. Senate Energy and Natural Resources reported, amended, July 7, 2004 (S Rept 108-296). Senate passed, amended, Sept. 15. House passed, under suspension of the rules, Nov. 17. President signed Dec. 3, 2004.

PL 108-440 (S 2214) Designate the facility of the U.S. Postal Service located at 3150 Great Northern Ave. in Missoula, Mont., the "Mike Mansfield Post Office." Introduced by BURNS, R-Mont., on March 12, 2004. Senate Governmental Affairs reported June 7 (no written report). Senate passed June 9. House passed, under suspension of the rules, Nov. 16. President signed Dec. 3, 2004.

PL 108-441 (S 2302) Improve access to physicians in medically underserved areas. Introduced by CONRAD, D-N.D., on April 7, 2004. Senate Judiciary reported, amended, Oct. 7 (no written report). Senate passed, amended, Oct. 11. House passed, under suspension of the rules, Nov. 17. President signed Dec. 3, 2004.

PL 108-442 (S 2640) Designate the facility of the U.S. Postal Service located at 1050 North Hills Blvd. in Reno, Nev., the "Guardians of Freedom Memorial Post Office Building" and to authorize the installation of a plaque at such site. Introduced by ENSIGN, R-Nev., on July 13, 2004. Senate Governmental Affairs reported July 22 (no written report). Senate passed July 22. House passed, under suspension of the rules, Nov. 16. President signed Dec. 3, 2004.

PL 108-443 (S 2693) Designate the facility of the U.S. Postal Service located at 1475 Western Ave., Suite 45, in Albany, N.Y., the "Lieutenant John F. Finn Post Office." Introduced by SCHUMER, D-N.Y., on July 20, 2004. Senate Governmental Affairs discharged. Senate passed Oct. 10. House passed, under suspension of the rules, Nov. 16. President signed Dec. 3, 2004.

PL 108-444 (S 2965) Amend the Livestock Mandatory Price Reporting Act of 1999 to modify the termination date for mandatory price reporting. Introduced by COCHRAN, R-Miss., on Oct. 8, 2004. Senate passed Oct. 8. House passed, under suspension of the rules, Nov. 17. President signed Dec. 3, 2004.

PL 108-445 (S 2484) Amend Title 38, U.S. Code, to simplify and improve pay provisions for physicians and dentists in VA facilities and to authorize alternate work schedules and executive pay for nurses. Introduced by SPECTER, R-Pa., on June 1, 2004. Senate Veterans' Affairs reported, amended, Sept. 23 (S Rept 108-357). Senate passed, with an amendment, Oct. 5. House passed, under suspension of the rules, Nov. 17. President signed Dec. 3, 2004.

PL 108-446 (HR 1350) Reauthorize the Individuals with Disabilities Education Act. Introduced by CASTLE, R-Del., on March 19, 2003. House Education and the Workforce reported, amended, April 29 (H Rept 108-77). House passed, with amendments, April 30. Senate Health, Education, Labor and Pensions discharged. Senate passed, amended, May 13, 2004. Conference report filed Nov. 17 (H Rept 108-779). House agreed to conference report Nov. 19. Senate agreed to conference report Nov. 19. President signed Dec. 3, 2004.

PL 108-447 (HR 4818) Make appropriations for foreign operations, export financing and related programs for the fiscal year ending Sept. 30, 2005. (The conference report also incorporated eight other fiscal 2005 appropriations bills.) Introduced by KOLBE, R-Ariz., on July 13, 2004. House Appropriations reported July 13 (H Rept 108-599). House passed, with amendments, July 15. Senate Appropriations discharged. Senate passed, with amendments, Sept. 23. Conference report filed in the House on Nov. 20 (H Rept 108-792). House agreed to the conference report Nov. 20. Senate agreed to the conference report Nov. 20. President signed Dec. 8, 2004.

PL 108-448 (S 2618) Amend Title XIX of the Social Security Act to extend Medicare cost-sharing for the Medicare part B premium for qualifying individuals through September 2005. Introduced by GRASSLEY, R-Iowa,

on July 7, 2004. Senate Finance discharged. Senate passed Nov. 16, 2004. House passed, under suspension of the rules, Nov. 19. President signed Dec. 8, 2004.

PL 108-449 (HR 2655) Amend and extend the Irish Peace Process Cultural and Training Program Act of 1998. Introduced by WALSH, R-N.Y., on June 26, 2003. House Judiciary reported Sept. 4 (H Rept 108-260, Part 1). House International Relations discharged. House passed, amended, under suspension of the rules, Oct. 7. Senate Foreign Relations discharged. Senate passed, with an amendment, Nov. 19, 2004. House agreed to Senate amendment, Nov. 20. President signed Dec. 10, 2004.

PL 108-450 (HR 4302) Amend Title 21, District of Columbia Official Code, to enact the provisions of the Mental Health Civil Commitment Act of 2002 that affect the Commission on Mental Health and require action by Congress in order to take effect. Introduced by T. DAVIS, R-Va., on May 6, 2004. House Government Reform reported Oct. 5 (H Rept 108-729). House passed, amended, under suspension of the rules, Oct. 6. Senate passed Nov. 20. President signed Dec. 10, 2004.

PL 108-451 (S 437) Provide for adjustments to the Central Arizona Project, authorize the Gila River Indian Community water rights settlement, and reauthorize and amend the Southern Arizona Water Rights Settlement Act of 1982. Introduced by KYL, R-Ariz., on Feb. 25, 2003. Senate Energy and Natural Resources reported, amended, Sept. 28, 2004 (S Rept 108-360). Senate passed, with an amendment, Oct. 10. House passed, under suspension of the rules, Nov. 17. President signed Dec. 10, 2004.

PL 108-452 (S 1466) Facilitate the transfer of land in the state of Alaska. Introduced by MURKOWSKI, R-Alaska, on July 25, 2003. Senate Energy and Natural Resources discharged. Senate passed, with an amendment, Oct. 10, 2004. House passed, under suspension of the rules, Nov. 17. President signed Dec. 10, 2004.

PL 108-453 (S 2192) Amend Title 35, U.S. Code, to promote cooperative research involving universities, the public sector, and private enterprises. Introduced by HATCH, R-Utah, on March 10, 2004. Senate Judiciary reported April 29 (no written report). Senate passed June 25. House passed Nov. 20. President signed Dec. 10, 2004.

PL 108-454 (S 2486) Amend Title 38, U.S. Code, to improve and enhance housing, education and other benefits under the laws administered by the secretary of Veterans Affairs. Introduced by SPECTER, R-Pa., on June 1, 2004. Senate Veterans' Affairs reported, amended, Sept. 20 (S Rept 108-352). Senate passed, with an amendment, Oct. 8. House passed, under suspension of the rules, Nov. 17. President signed Dec. 10, 2004.

PL 108-455 (S 2873) Extend the authority of the U.S. District Court for the Southern District of Iowa to hold court in Rock Island, Ill. Introduced by GRASSLEY, R-

Iowa, on Sept. 30, 2004. Senate Judiciary discharged. Senate passed, with an amendment, Nov. 19. House passed Nov. 20. President signed Dec. 10, 2004.

PL 108-456 (S 3014) Reauthorize the Harmful Algal Bloom and Hypoxia Research and Control Act of 1998. Introduced by SNOWE, R-Maine, on Nov. 19, 2004. Senate passed Nov. 19. House passed Nov. 20. President signed Dec. 10, 2004.

PL 108-457 (HR 4012) Amend the District of Columbia College Access Act of 1999 to reauthorize for two additional years the public school and private school tuition assistance programs established under the act. Introduced by T. DAVIS, R-Va., on March 23, 2004. House Government Reform reported June 8 (H Rept 108-527). House passed, amended, under suspension of the rules, July 14. Senate Governmental Affairs reported July 22 (no written report). Senate passed with amendments, Nov. 24. House agreed to Senate amendments, under suspension of the rules, Dec. 6. President signed Dec. 17, 2004.

PL 108-458 (S 2845) Reform the intelligence community and the intelligence and intelligence-related activities of the United States government. Introduced by COLLINS, R-Maine, on Sept. 23, 2004. Senate passed with amendments, Oct. 6. House passed, amended, Oct. 16. Conference report filed in the House on Dec. 7 (H Rept 108-796). House agreed to the conference report Dec. 7. Senate agreed to the conference report Dec. 8. President signed Dec. 17, 2004.

PL 108-459 (HR 480) Redesignate the facility of the United States Postal Service located at 747 Broadway in Albany, N.Y., the "United States Postal Service Henry Johnson Annex." Introduced by MCNULTY, D-N.Y., on Jan. 29, 2003. House passed, under suspension of the rules, Sept. 22, 2004. Senate passed Dec. 7. President signed Dec. 21, 2004.

PL 108-460 (HR 2119) Provide for the conveyance of Federal lands, improvements, equipment and resource materials at the Oxford Research Station in Granville County, N.C., to the State of North Carolina. Introduced by BALLANCE, D-N.C., on May 15, 2003. House passed, amended, under suspension of the rules, Oct. 5, 2004. Senate passed Dec. 7. President signed Dec. 21, 2004.

PL 108-461 (HR 2523) Designate the United States courthouse located at 125 Bull Street in Savannah, Ga., the "Tomochichi United States Courthouse." Introduced by BURNS, R-Ga., on June 19, 2003. House Transportation and Infrastructure reported March 25, 2004 (H Rept 108-447). House passed, under suspension of the rules, May 11. Senate Environment and Public Works discharged. Senate passed Dec. 7. President signed Dec. 21, 2004.

PL 108-462 (HR 3124) Designate the facility of the United States Geological Survey and the United States Bureau of Reclamation located at 230 Collins Road, Boise,

Idaho, the "F.H. Newell Building." Introduced by OTTER, R-Idaho, on Sept. 17, 2003. House passed, under suspension of the rules, Sept. 29, 2004. Senate passed Dec. 7. President signed Dec. 21, 2004.

PL 108-463 (HR 3147) Designate the federal building located at 324 Twenty-Fifth Street in Ogden, Utah, the "James V. Hansen Federal Building." Introduced by CANNON, R-Utah, on Sept. 23, 2003. House Transportation and Infrastructure reported, amended, March 25, 2004 (H Rept 108-449). House passed, amended, under suspension of the rules, April 21. Senate Environment and Public Works discharged. Senate passed Dec. 7. President signed Dec. 21, 2004.

PL 108-464 (HR 3204) Require the secretary of the Treasury to mint coins in commemoration of the tercentenary of the birth of Benjamin Franklin. Introduced by CASTLE, R-Del., on Sept. 30, 2003. House Financial Services discharged. House passed Nov. 17, 2004. Senate passed Dec. 7. President signed Dec. 21, 2004.

PL 108-465 (HR 3242) Ensure an abundant and affordable supply of highly nutritious fruits, vegetables and other specialty crops for American consumers and international markets by enhancing the competitiveness of U.S.-grown specialty crops. Introduced by OSE, R-Calif., on Oct. 2, 2003. House Agriculture reported, amended, Oct. 6, 2004 (H Rept 108-750, Part 1). House Ways and Means discharged. House passed, amended, under suspension of the rules, Oct. 7. Senate passed Dec. 7. President signed Dec. 21, 2004.

PL 108-466 (HR 3734) Designate the federal building located at Fifth and Richardson Avenues in Roswell, N.M., the "Joe Skeen Federal Building." Introduced by WILSON, R-N.M., on Jan. 27, 2004. House Transportation and Infrastructure reported July 12 (H Rept 108-596). House passed, under suspension of the rules, Sept. 22. Senate passed Dec. 7. President signed Dec. 21, 2004.

PL 108-467 (HR 3884) Designate the Federal building and United States courthouse located at 615 East Houston Street in San Antonio the "Hipolito F. Garcia Federal Building and United States Courthouse." Introduced by GONZALEZ, D-Texas, on March 3, 2004. House Transportation and Infrastructure reported June 21 (H Rept 108-557). House passed, under suspension of the rules, July 21. Senate Environment and Public Works discharged. Senate passed Dec. 7. President signed Dec. 21, 2004.

PL 108-468 (HR 4232) Redesignate the facility of the United States Postal Service located at 4025 Feather Lakes Way in Kingwood, Texas, the "Congressman Jack Fields Post Office." Introduced by BRADY, R-Texas, on April 28, 2004. House passed, under suspension of the rules, Oct. 6. Senate passed Dec. 7. President signed Dec. 21, 2004.

PL 108-469 (HR 4324) Amend chapter 84 of title 5, U.S. Code, to provide for federal employees to make, modify

and terminate contributions to the Thrift Savings Fund at any time. Introduced by T. DAVIS, R-Va., on May 11, 2004. House passed, under suspension of the rules, amended, Nov. 19. Senate passed Dec. 7. President signed Dec. 21, 2004.

PL 108-470 (HR 4620) Confirm the authority of the secretary of Agriculture to collect approved state commodity assessments on behalf of the state from the proceeds of marketing assistance loans. Introduced by NETHERCUTT, R-Wash., on June 18, 2004. House passed, under suspension of the rules, amended, Oct. 5. Senate passed Dec. 7. President signed Dec. 21, 2004.

PL 108-471 (HR 4807) Designate the facility of the United States Postal Service located at 140 Sacramento Street in Rio Vista, Calif., the "Adam G. Kinser Post Office Building." Introduced by OSE, R-Calif., on July 9, 2004. House passed, under suspension of the rules, Oct. 6. Senate passed Dec. 7. President signed Dec. 21, 2004.

PL 108-472 (HR 4847) Designate the facility of the United States Postal Service located at 560 Bay Isles Road in Longboat Key, Fla., the "Lieutenant General James V. Edmundson Post Office Building." Introduced by HARRIS, R-Fla., on July 15, 2004. House passed, under suspension of the rules, Oct. 6. Senate passed Dec. 7. President signed Dec. 21, 2004.

PL 108-473 (HR 4968) Designate the facility of the United States Postal Service located at 25 McHenry Street in Rosine, Ky., the "Bill Monroe Post Office." Introduced by LEWIS, R-Ky., on July 22, 2004. House passed, under suspension of the rules, Oct. 6. Senate passed Dec. 7. President signed Dec. 21, 2004.

PL 108-474 (HR 5360) Authorize grants to establish academies for teachers and students of American history and civics. Introduced by WICKER, R-Miss., on Nov. 16, 2004. House passed, under suspension of the rules, amended, Nov. 19. Senate passed Dec. 7. President signed Dec. 21, 2004.

PL 108-475 (HR 5364) Designate the facility of the United States Postal Service located at 5505 Stevens Way in San Diego the "Earl B. Gilliam/Imperial Avenue Post Office Building." Introduced by FILNER, D-Calif., on Nov. 16, 2004. House passed, under suspension of the rules, Nov. 17. Senate passed Dec. 7. President signed Dec. 21, 2004.

PL 108-476 (HR 5365) Treat certain arrangements maintained by the YMCA Retirement Fund as church plans for the purposes of certain provisions of the Internal Revenue Code of 1986. Introduced by ENGLISH, R-Pa., on Nov. 16, 2004. House passed, under suspension of the rules, Nov. 19. Senate passed Dec. 7. President signed Dec. 21, 2004.

PL 108-477 (HR 5370) Designate the facility of the United States Postal Service located at 4985 Moorhead Avenue in Boulder, Colo., the "Donald G. Brotzman Post Office Building." Introduced by UDALL, D-Colo., on Nov. 16, 2004. House Government Reform discharged. House passed Nov. 19. Senate passed Dec. 7. President signed Dec. 21, 2004.

PL 108-478 (HR 4829) Designate the facility of the United States Postal Service located at 103 East Kleberg in Kingsville, Texas, the "Irma Rangel Post Office Building." Introduced by HINOJOSA, D-Texas, on July 14, 2004. House passed, under suspension of the rules, Oct. 6. Senate passed Dec. 7. President signed Dec. 21, 2004.

PL 108-479 (H J Res 102) Recognize the 60th anniversary of the Battle of Peleliu and the end of Imperial Japanese control of Palau during World War II and urging the secretary of the Interior to work to protect the historic sites of the Peleliu Battlefield National Historic Landmark and to establish commemorative programs honoring the Americans who fought there. Introduced by FLAKE, R-Ariz., on Sept. 9, 2004. House passed, under suspension of the rules, Sept. 28. Senate passed Dec. 7. President signed Dec. 21, 2004.

PL 108-480 (HR 2457) Authorize funds for an educational center for the Castillo de San Marcos National Monument. Introduced by MICA, R-Fla., on June 12, 2003. House Resources reported, amended, Sept. 7, 2004 (H Rept 108-639). House passed, under suspension of the rules, Sept. 13. Senate Energy and Natural Resources discharged. Senate passed Dec. 8. President signed Dec. 23, 2004.

PL 108-481 (HR 2619) Provide for the expansion of Kilauea Point National Wildlife Refuge. Introduced by CASE, D-Hawaii, on June 26, 2003. House Resources reported, amended, June 3, 2004 (H Rept 108-522). House passed, under suspension of the rules, July 19. Senate Environment and Public Works discharged. Senate passed Dec. 8. President signed Dec. 23, 2004.

PL 108-482 (HR 3632) Prevent and punish counterfeiting of copyrighted copies and phono records. Introduced by SMITH, R-Texas, on Nov. 21, 2003. House Judiciary reported, amended, July 13, 2004 (H Rept 108-600). House passed, under suspension of the rules, Sept. 21. Senate Judiciary discharged. Senate passed Dec. 8. President signed Dec. 23, 2004.

PL 108-483 (HR 3785) Authorize the exchange of certain land in the Everglades National Park. Introduced by DIAZ-BALART, M., R-Fla., on Feb. 10, 2004. House Resources reported, amended, June 1 (H Rept 108-516). House passed, under suspension of the rules, July 19. Senate passed Dec. 8. President signed Dec. 23, 2004.

PL 108-484 (HR 3818) Amend the Foreign Assistance Act of 1961 to improve the results and accountability of microenterprise development assistance programs. Introduced by SMITH, R-N.J., on Feb. 24, 2004. House International Relations reported, amended, April 2 (H Rept 108-459). House passed, amended, Nov. 20. Senate passed Dec. 8. President signed Dec. 23, 2004.

PL 108-485 (HR 4027) Authorize the secretary of Commerce to make available to the University of Miami property under the administrative jurisdiction of the National Oceanic and Atmospheric Administration on Virginia Key, Fla., for use as a Marine Life Science Center. Introduced by ROS-LEHTINEN, R-Fla., on March 24, 2004. House Resources reported, amended, Sept. 8 (H Rept 108-665). House passed, under suspension of the rules, Sept. 13. Senate Commerce, Science and Transportation discharged. Senate passed Dec. 8. President signed Dec. 23, 2004.

PL 108-486 (HR 4116) Require the secretary of the Treasury to mint coins celebrating the recovery and restoration of the American bald eagle. Introduced by JENKINS, R-Tenn., on April 1, 2004. House Financial Services discharged. House passed, amended, Dec. 7. Senate passed Dec. 8. President signed Dec. 23, 2004.

PL 108-487 (HR 4548) Authorize appropriations for fiscal 2005 for U.S. intelligence and intelligence-related activities, and for the CIA Retirement and Disability System. Introduced by GOSS, R-Fla., on June 14, 2004. House Intelligence reported, amended, June 21 (H Rept 108-558). House passed, amended, June 23. Senate Intelligence discharged. Senate passed, with an amendment, Oct. 11. Conference report filed in the House on Dec. 7 (H Rept 108-798). House agreed to the conference report Dec. 7. Senate agreed to the conference report Dec. 8. President signed Dec. 23, 2004.

PL 108-488 (HR 4569) Provide for the development of a national plan for the control and management of Sudden Oak Death, a tree disease caused by the fungus-like pathogen Phytophthora ramorum. Introduced by BURNS, R-Ga., on June 15, 2004. House passed, under suspension of the rules, Oct. 5. Senate passed Dec. 8. President signed Dec. 23, 2004.

PL 108-489 (HR 4657) Amend the Balanced Budget Act of 1997 to improve the administration of federal pension benefit payments for District of Columbia teachers, police officers and fire fighters. Introduced by T. DAVIS, R-Va., on June 23, 2004. House passed, amended, under suspension of the rules, Sept. 28. Senate passed Dec. 8. President signed Dec. 23, 2004.

PL 108-490 (HR 5204) Amend the Public Health Service Act to modify provisions regarding the determination of the amount of payments for indirect expenses associated with operating approved graduate medical residency training programs. Introduced by ESHOO, D-Calif., on Oct. 4, 2004. House passed, under suspension of the rules, Oct. 6. Senate passed Dec. 8. President signed Dec. 23, 2004.

PL 108-491 (HR 5363) Authorize salary adjustments for justices and judges of the United States for fiscal 2005. Introduced by SENSENBRENNER, R-Wis., on Nov. 16, 2004. House passed, under suspension of the rules,

Nov. 17. Senate passed Dec. 8. President signed Dec. 23, 2004.

PL 108-492 (HR 5382) Promote the development of the emerging commercial human space flight industry. Introduced by ROHRABACHER, R-Calif., on Nov. 18, 2004. House passed, under suspension of the rules, Nov. 20. Senate passed Dec. 8. President signed Dec. 23, 2004.

PL 108-493 (HR 5394) Amend the Internal Revenue Code to modify the taxation of arrow components. Introduced by RYAN, R-Wis., on Nov. 19, 2004. House passed, under suspension of the rules, Dec. 6. Senate passed Dec. 8. President signed Dec. 23, 2004.

PL 108-494 (HR 5419) Facilitate the reallocation of spectrum from government to commercial users, and improve the nation's homeland security, public safety and citizen activated emergency response capabilities through the use of enhanced 911 services. Introduced by UPTON, R-Mich., on Nov. 20, 2004. House Energy and Commerce discharged. House passed Nov. 20. Senate passed Dec. 8. President signed Dec. 23, 2004.

PL 108-495 (S 1301) Prohibit video voyeurism at locations under federal jurisdiction. Introduced by DEWINE, R-Ohio, on June 19, 2003. Senate Judiciary reported, amended, July 24 (no written report). Senate passed Sept. 25. House Judiciary reported, amended, May 20, 2004 (H Rept 108-504). House passed, under suspension of the rules, Sept. 21. Senate agreed to House amendment, Dec. 7. President signed Dec. 23, 2004.

PL 108-496 (S 2657) Establish programs under which supplemental dental and vision benefits are made available to federal employees, retirees and their dependents, and expand the contracting authority of the Office of Personnel Management. Introduced by COLLINS, R-Maine, on July 14, 2004. Senate Governmental Affairs reported, amended, Oct. 8 (S Rept 108-393). Senate passed, with an amendment, Nov. 20. House passed, under suspension of the rules, Dec. 6. President signed Dec. 23, 2004.

PL 108-497 (S 2781) Express the sense of Congress regarding the conflict in Darfur, Sudan, and authorize assistance to Sudanese refugees in Darfur and eastern Chad. Introduced by LUGAR, R-Ind., on Sept. 9, 2004. Senate Foreign Relations discharged. Senate passed, amended, Sept. 23. House passed, with an amendment, under suspension of the rules, Nov. 19. Senate agreed to House amendment, Dec. 7. President signed Dec. 23, 2004.

PL 108-498 (S 2856) Limit the transfer of certain Commodity Credit Corporation funds between conservation programs for technical assistance. Introduced by COCHRAN, R-Miss., on Sept. 28, 2004. Senate Agriculture, Nutrition and Forestry discharged. Senate passed Oct. 11. House passed, under suspension of the rules, Dec. 6. President signed Dec. 23, 2004. ◆

Appendix H

HOUSE ROLL CALL VOTES

House Roll Call Votes By Bill Number

House Bills

H Con Res 13, H-96
H Con Res 15, H-22
H Con Res 189, H-30
H Con Res 257, H-110
H Con Res 264, H-10
H Con Res 287, H-12
H Con Res 295, H-72
H Con Res 326, H-54
H Con Res 328, H-30
H Con Res 352, H-58
H Con Res 358, H-10
H Con Res 359, H-10
H Con Res 363, H-144
H Con Res 364, H-26
H Con Res 373, H-18
H Con Res 378, H-58
H Con Res 380, H-52
H Con Res 386, H-38
H Con Res 393, H-32, H-34
H Con Res 398, H-54
H Con Res 403, H-62
H Con Res 404, H-42
H Con Res 409, H-58
H Con Res 410, H-110
H Con Res 413, H-74
H Con Res 414, H-60
H Con Res 417, H-72
H Con Res 418, H-136
H Con Res 420, H-62
H Con Res 423, H-62
H Con Res 424, H-66
H Con Res 432, H-70
H Con Res 436, H-134
H Con Res 449, H-96
H Con Res 460, H-98
H Con Res 462, H-126
H Con Res 467, H-136
H Con Res 469, H-136
H Con Res 501, H-156
H Con Res 518, H-170

H J Res 83, H-72, H-74
H J Res 87, H-24
H J Res 91, H-60
H J Res 97, H-80
H J Res 106, H-156
H J Res 107, H-154
H J Res 110, H-172

H Res 56, H-16
H Res 84, H-8
H Res 114, H-174
H Res 157, H-8
H Res 392, H-18
H Res 399, H-50
H Res 402, H-54
H Res 412, H-16
H Res 433, H-24
H Res 475, H-18
H Res 489, H-4
H Res 490, H-4
H Res 491, H-4
H Res 492, H-4
H Res 507, H-8
H Res 519, H-18
H Res 522, H-28
H Res 526, H-14
H Res 530, H-14
H Res 540, H-22
H Res 551, H-24
H Res 557, H-24
H Res 558, H-36
H Res 567, H-158
H Res 576, H-124
H Res 577, H-56
H Res 578, H-50
H Res 581, H-38
H Res 591, H-94
H Res 599, H-52
H Res 600, H-52
H Res 605, H-52
H Res 608, H-56
H Res 612, H-72
H Res 615, H-124
H Res 622, H-56
H Res 627, H-54
H Res 652, H-134
H Res 653, H-80
H Res 655, H-76
H Res 658, H-96
H Res 660, H-94
H Res 663, H-78
H Res 664, H-78
H Res 667, H-144
H Res 669, H-80
H Res 676, H-102
H Res 685, H-100
H Res 691, H-106
H Res 705, H-122
H Res 713, H-124
H Res 723, H-132
H Res 728, H-134
H Res 757, H-140
H Res 760, H-144
H Res 792, H-156
H Res 845, H-170
H Res 853, H-174

HR 10, H-164, H-166, H-168
HR 163, H-160
HR 254, H-32
HR 339, H-22
HR 444, H-74, H-76
HR 743, H-10
HR 912, H-14
HR 958, H-28
HR 1057, H-152
HR 1084, H-146
HR 1308, H-136, H-140, H-152
HR 1350, H-174
HR 1375, H-26
HR 1385, H-6
HR 1417, H-16, H-172
HR 1561, H-16
HR 1587, H-130
HR 1768, H-30
HR 1779, H-46
HR 1787, H-144
HR 1822, H-44
HR 1997, H-12
HR 2028, H-152
HR 2408, H-28
HR 2432, H-64
HR 2443, H-54, H-132
HR 2489, H-28
HR 2584, H-36
HR 2660, H-56, H-62
HR 2707, H-12
HR 2728, H-62
HR 2729, H-62, H-64
HR 2730, H-62, H-64
HR 2731, H-62, H-64
HR 2732, H-62
HR 2751, H-12
HR 2828, H-116
HR 2844, H-46, H-48
HR 2929, H-160
HR 2993, H-32
HR 3030, H-8
HR 3059, H-30
HR 3095, H-34
HR 3104, H-38
HR 3108, H-42
HR 3147, H-46
HR 3193, H-154
HR 3313, H-134
HR 3369, H-144
HR 3389, H-14
HR 3493, H-6
HR 3550, H-38, H-40, H-76
HR 3574, H-130
HR 3598, H-112, H-118
HR 3717, H-22
HR 3722, H-62
HR 3723, H-36
HR 3733, H-24
HR 3740, H-64
HR 3752, H-16
HR 3769, H-14

HR 3782, H-26
HR 3783, H-10
HR 3786, H-32
HR 3855, H-44
HR 3866, H-76
HR 3873, H-30
HR 3926, H-28
HR 3942, H-50
HR 3966, H-36
HR 3970, H-44
HR 3980, H-112
HR 4019, H-46
HR 4030, H-44
HR 4037, H-44
HR 4053, H-98
HR 4056, H-134
HR 4109, H-74
HR 4175, H-134
HR 4176, H-64
HR 4181, H-50
HR 4200, H-66, H-68, H-70, H-154, H-168, H-170
HR 4219, H-50
HR 4227, H-52
HR 4231, H-156
HR 4275, H-56, H-60
HR 4279, H-56, H-58
HR 4280, H-56, H-58
HR 4281, H-56, H-60
HR 4299, H-56
HR 4323, H-80
HR 4359, H-70
HR 4363, H-94
HR 4381, H-138
HR 4418, H-124
HR 4503, H-80, H-82
HR 4513, H-82
HR 4517, H-80, H-84
HR 4520, H-88, H-154, H-164
HR 4529, H-82
HR 4545, H-84
HR 4548, H-96, H-98, H-100
HR 4556, H-138
HR 4567, H-82, H-84, H-90, H-92, H-94, H-162, H-170
HR 4568, H-84, H-86, H-88, H-90
HR 4571, H-144, H-146
HR 4608, H-132
HR 4613, H-94, H-96, H-120, H-136
HR 4614, H-108
HR 4635, H-98
HR 4661, H-162
HR 4663, H-102, H-104, H-106
HR 4754, H-110, H-112, H-114
HR 4755, H-112, H-118, H-120

HR 4759, H-122, H-124
HR 4766, H-120, H-122
HR 4818, H-126, H-128, H-174, H-176
HR 4837, H-132, H-136, H-170
HR 4840, H-132
HR 4842, H-134
HR 4850, H-130, H-132, H-160
HR 4879, H-132
HR 5006, H-138, H-140, H-142
HR 5011, H-160
HR 5025, H-146, H-148, H-150, H-152
HR 5061, H-164
HR 5107, H-160
HR 5149, H-156
HR 5183, H-154, H-156
HR 5186, H-162
HR 5212, H-160, H-162
HR 5213, H-162
HR 5382, H-174

Senate Bills

S 15, H-124
S 714, H-12
S 878, H-158
S 1134, H-164
S 1814, H-158
S 1881, H-18
S 1904, H-50
S 1920, H-6
S 2057, H-36
S 2264, H-130
S 2302, H-172
S 2363, H-154
S 2634, H-140
S 2845, H-170, H-176
S 2986, H-172

S Con Res 76, H-158
S Con Res 95, H-36, H-52, H-60, H-66, H-68
S Con Res 114, H-130

S J Res 28, H-74

Key

Y	Voted for (yea).
#	Paired for.
+	Announced for.
N	Voted against (nay).
X	Paired against.
–	Announced against.
P	Voted "present."
C	Voted "present" to avoid possible conflict of interest.
?	Did not vote or otherwise make a position known.

Democrats **Republicans**
Independents

1.* Quorum Call. 321 members responded. (113 members did not respond.) Jan. 20, 2004.

2. H Res 492. Catholic Schools Tribute/Adoption. Boehner, R-Ohio, motion to suspend the rules and adopt the resolution that would express support for Catholic Schools Week and honor Catholic schools for their contributions to American education. Motion agreed to 398-1: R 216-0; D 181-1 (ND 129-1, SD 52-0); I 1-0. A two-thirds majority of those present and voting (265 in this case) is required for adoption under suspension of the rules. Jan. 21, 2004.

3. H Res 491. Benefits of Mentoring/Adoption. Osborne, R-Neb., motion to suspend the rules and adopt the resolution that would commend people who mentor children and support efforts to recruit more mentors in the United States. Motion agreed to 397-0: R 214-0; D 182-0 (ND 130-0, SD 52-0); I 1-0. A two-thirds majority of those present and voting (265 in this case) is required for adoption under suspension of the rules. Jan. 21, 2004.

4. H Res 490. Mars Space Probe Recognition/Adoption. Rohrabacher, R-Calif., motion to suspend the rules and adopt the resolution that would recognize and commend the achievements of NASA, the Jet Propulsion Laboratory and Cornell University in conducting the Mars Exploration Rover mission, and to recognize the importance of space exploration. Motion agreed to 389-0: R 209-0; D 179-0 (ND 129-0, SD 50-0); I 1-0. A two-thirds majority of those present and voting (259 in this case) is required for adoption under suspension of the rules. Jan. 21, 2004.

5. H Res 489. Paul Simon Tribute/Adoption. Doolittle, R-Calif., D-Ill., motion to suspend the rules and adopt the resolution that concurs with S Res 281, which honored former Sen. Paul Simon, D-Ill., and expressed sorrow and regret over the announcement of his death. Motion agreed to 394-0: R 213-0; D 180-0 (ND 129-0, SD 51-0); I 1-0. A two-thirds majority of those present and voting (263 in this case) is required for adoption under suspension of the rules. Jan. 21, 2004.

* CQ does not include quorum calls in its vote charts.

[1] Rep. Ernie Fletcher, R-Ky., resigned effective 11:59 p.m., Dec. 8, 2003. He was sworn in as governor of Kentucky the next day. A special election for the 6th District seat was scheduled for Feb. 17.

[2] Rep. Bill Janklow, R-S.D., resigned effective 11:59 p.m., Jan. 20. A special election to fill the At Large seat was scheduled for June 1.

	2	3	4	5
ALABAMA				
1 *Bonner*	Y	Y	Y	Y
2 *Everett*	?	?	?	?
3 *Rogers*	Y	Y	Y	Y
4 *Aderholt*	Y	Y	Y	Y
5 Cramer	Y	Y	Y	Y
6 *Bachus*	Y	Y	Y	Y
7 Davis	Y	Y	Y	Y
ALASKA				
AL *Young*	Y	Y	Y	Y
ARIZONA				
1 *Renzi*	Y	Y	Y	Y
2 *Franks*	?	?	?	?
3 *Shadegg*	Y	Y	Y	Y
4 Pastor	Y	Y	Y	Y
5 *Hayworth*	?	?	?	?
6 *Flake*	+	+	+	+
7 Grijalva	Y	Y	Y	Y
8 *Kolbe*	Y	Y	Y	Y
ARKANSAS				
1 Berry	Y	Y	Y	Y
2 Snyder	Y	Y	Y	Y
3 *Boozman*	Y	Y	Y	Y
4 Ross	Y	Y	Y	Y
CALIFORNIA				
1 Thompson	Y	Y	Y	Y
2 *Herger*	Y	Y	?	Y
3 *Ose*	Y	Y	Y	Y
4 *Doolittle*	Y	Y	Y	Y
5 Matsui	Y	Y	Y	Y
6 Woolsey	Y	Y	Y	Y
7 Miller, George	?	?	?	?
8 Pelosi	Y	Y	Y	Y
9 Lee	Y	Y	Y	Y
10 Tauscher	Y	Y	Y	Y
11 *Pombo*	Y	Y	Y	Y
12 Lantos	Y	Y	Y	Y
13 Stark	Y	Y	Y	Y
14 Eshoo	Y	Y	?	?
15 Honda	Y	Y	Y	Y
16 Lofgren	Y	Y	Y	Y
17 Farr	Y	Y	Y	Y
18 Cardoza	Y	Y	Y	Y
19 *Radanovich*	Y	Y	Y	Y
20 Dooley	Y	Y	Y	Y
21 *Nunes*	Y	Y	Y	Y
22 *Thomas*	Y	Y	Y	Y
23 Capps	Y	Y	Y	Y
24 *Gallegly*	Y	Y	Y	Y
25 *McKeon*	Y	Y	Y	Y
26 *Dreier*	Y	Y	Y	Y
27 Sherman	?	?	?	?
28 Berman	?	?	?	?
29 Schiff	Y	Y	Y	Y
30 Waxman	?	?	?	?
31 Becerra	Y	Y	Y	Y
32 Solis	Y	Y	Y	Y
33 Watson	+	+	+	+
34 Roybal-Allard	Y	Y	Y	Y
35 Waters	Y	Y	Y	Y
36 Harman	Y	Y	Y	Y

	2	3	4	5
37 Millender McD.	Y	Y	Y	Y
38 Napolitano	Y	Y	Y	Y
39 Sánchez, Linda	Y	Y	Y	Y
40 *Royce*	Y	Y	Y	Y
41 *Lewis*	Y	Y	Y	Y
42 *Miller, Gary*	Y	Y	Y	Y
43 Baca	Y	Y	Y	Y
44 *Calvert*	Y	+	Y	Y
45 *Bono*	Y	Y	Y	Y
46 *Rohrabacher*	Y	Y	Y	Y
47 Sanchez, Loretta	Y	Y	Y	Y
48 *Cox*	Y	Y	Y	Y
49 *Issa*	Y	Y	Y	Y
50 *Cunningham*	Y	?	?	?
51 Filner	Y	Y	Y	Y
52 *Hunter*	Y	Y	Y	Y
53 Davis	?	?	?	?
COLORADO				
1 DeGette	?	?	?	?
2 Udall	Y	Y	Y	Y
3 *McInnis*	Y	Y	Y	Y
4 *Musgrave*	Y	Y	Y	Y
5 *Hefley*	Y	Y	Y	Y
6 *Tancredo*	Y	Y	Y	Y
7 *Beauprez*	Y	Y	Y	Y
CONNECTICUT				
1 Larson	Y	Y	Y	Y
2 *Simmons*	Y	Y	Y	Y
3 DeLauro	Y	Y	Y	Y
4 *Shays*	Y	Y	Y	Y
5 *Johnson*	Y	Y	Y	Y
DELAWARE				
AL *Castle*	Y	Y	Y	Y
FLORIDA				
1 *Miller, J.*	Y	Y	Y	Y
2 Boyd	Y	Y	Y	Y
3 Brown	Y	Y	Y	Y
4 *Crenshaw*	Y	Y	Y	Y
5 *Brown-Waite*	Y	Y	Y	Y
6 *Stearns*	Y	Y	Y	Y
7 *Mica*	Y	Y	Y	Y
8 *Keller*	Y	Y	Y	Y
9 *Bilirakis*	Y	Y	Y	Y
10 *Young*	Y	Y	Y	Y
11 Davis	Y	Y	Y	Y
12 *Putnam*	Y	Y	Y	Y
13 *Harris*	Y	Y	Y	?
14 *Goss*	Y	Y	Y	Y
15 *Weldon*	Y	Y	Y	Y
16 *Foley*	Y	Y	Y	Y
17 Meek	Y	Y	Y	Y
18 *Ros-Lehtinen*	Y	Y	Y	Y
19 Wexler	Y	Y	Y	Y
20 Deutsch	Y	Y	Y	Y
21 *Diaz-Balart, L.*	Y	Y	Y	Y
22 *Shaw*	Y	Y	Y	Y
23 Hastings	Y	Y	Y	Y
24 *Feeney*	Y	Y	Y	Y
25 *Diaz-Balart, M.*	Y	Y	Y	Y
GEORGIA				
1 *Kingston*	Y	Y	Y	Y
2 Bishop	Y	Y	Y	Y
3 Marshall	+	+	+	+
4 Majette	Y	Y	Y	Y
5 Lewis	Y	Y	Y	Y
6 *Isakson*	Y	Y	Y	Y
7 *Linder*	Y	Y	Y	Y
8 *Collins*	Y	Y	Y	Y
9 *Norwood*	Y	Y	Y	Y
10 *Deal*	Y	Y	Y	Y
11 *Gingrey*	Y	Y	Y	Y
12 *Burns*	Y	Y	Y	Y
13 Scott	Y	Y	Y	Y
HAWAII				
1 Abercrombie	+	+	+	+
2 Case	Y	Y	Y	Y
IDAHO				
1 *Otter*	Y	Y	Y	Y
2 *Simpson*	Y	Y	Y	Y
ILLINOIS				
1 Rush	Y	Y	Y	Y
2 Jackson	Y	Y	Y	Y
3 Lipinski	Y	Y	Y	Y
4 Gutierrez	Y	Y	?	Y
5 Emanuel	Y	Y	Y	Y
6 *Hyde*	Y	Y	Y	Y

ND Northern Democrats   SD Southern Democrats

Member	2	3	4	5
7 Davis	Y	Y	Y	Y
8 *Crane*	Y	Y	Y	Y
9 Schakowsky	Y	Y	Y	Y
10 *Kirk*	Y	Y	Y	Y
11 *Weller*	Y	Y	Y	Y
12 Costello	Y	Y	Y	Y
13 *Biggert*	Y	Y	Y	Y
14 *Hastert*				Y
15 *Johnson*	Y	Y	Y	Y
16 *Manzullo*	Y	Y	Y	Y
17 Evans	Y	Y	Y	Y
18 *LaHood*	Y	Y	Y	Y
19 *Shimkus*	Y	Y	Y	Y

INDIANA

Member	2	3	4	5
1 Visclosky	Y	Y	Y	Y
2 *Chocola*	Y	Y	Y	Y
3 *Souder*	Y	Y	Y	Y
4 *Buyer*	Y	Y	Y	Y
5 *Burton*	+	+	+	+
6 *Pence*	Y	Y	Y	Y
7 Carson	?	?	?	?
8 *Hostettler*	Y	Y	Y	Y
9 Hill	Y	Y	Y	Y

IOWA

Member	2	3	4	5
1 *Nussle*	Y	Y	Y	Y
2 *Leach*	Y	Y	Y	Y
3 Boswell	Y	Y	Y	Y
4 *Latham*	Y	Y	Y	Y
5 *King*	Y	Y	Y	Y

KANSAS

Member	2	3	4	5
1 *Moran*	Y	Y	Y	Y
2 *Ryun*	Y	Y	Y	Y
3 Moore	Y	Y	Y	Y
4 *Tiahrt*	Y	Y	Y	Y

KENTUCKY

Member	2	3	4	5
1 *Whitfield*	Y	Y	Y	Y
2 *Lewis*	Y	Y	Y	Y
3 *Northup*	Y	Y	Y	Y
4 Lucas	Y	Y	?	Y
5 *Rogers*	Y	Y	Y	Y
6 Vacant [1]				

LOUISIANA

Member	2	3	4	5
1 *Vitter*	Y	Y	Y	Y
2 Jefferson	Y	Y	Y	?
3 *Tauzin*	?	?	?	?
4 *McCrery*	Y	Y	Y	Y
5 Alexander	Y	Y	Y	Y
6 *Baker*	Y	Y	Y	Y
7 John	Y	Y	Y	Y

MAINE

Member	2	3	4	5
1 Allen	Y	Y	Y	Y
2 Michaud	Y	Y	Y	Y

MARYLAND

Member	2	3	4	5
1 *Gilchrest*	Y	Y	Y	Y
2 Ruppersberger	Y	Y	Y	Y
3 Cardin	Y	Y	Y	Y
4 Wynn	Y	Y	Y	Y
5 Hoyer	?	?	?	?
6 *Bartlett*	Y	Y	Y	Y
7 Cummings	Y	Y	Y	Y
8 Van Hollen	Y	Y	Y	Y

MASSACHUSETTS

Member	2	3	4	5
1 Olver	Y	Y	Y	Y
2 Neal	Y	Y	Y	Y
3 McGovern	?	?	?	?
4 Frank	?	?	?	?
5 Meehan	Y	Y	Y	Y
6 Tierney	Y	Y	Y	Y
7 Markey	Y	Y	Y	Y
8 Capuano	Y	Y	Y	Y
9 Lynch	Y	Y	Y	Y
10 Delahunt	?	?	?	?

MICHIGAN

Member	2	3	4	5
1 Stupak	Y	Y	Y	Y
2 *Hoekstra*	Y	Y	Y	Y
3 *Ehlers*	Y	Y	Y	Y
4 *Camp*	Y	Y	Y	Y
5 Kildee	Y	Y	Y	Y
6 *Upton*	Y	Y	Y	Y
7 *Smith*	Y	Y	Y	Y
8 *Rogers*	Y	Y	Y	Y
9 *Knollenberg*	Y	Y	Y	Y
10 *Miller*	Y	Y	Y	Y
11 *McCotter*	Y	Y	Y	Y
12 Levin	Y	Y	Y	Y

Member	2	3	4	5
13 Kilpatrick	Y	Y	Y	Y
14 Conyers	Y	Y	Y	Y
15 Dingell	Y	Y	Y	Y

MINNESOTA

Member	2	3	4	5
1 *Gutknecht*	Y	Y	Y	Y
2 *Kline*	Y	Y	Y	Y
3 *Ramstad*	Y	Y	Y	Y
4 McCollum	Y	Y	Y	Y
5 Sabo	Y	Y	Y	Y
6 *Kennedy*	Y	Y	Y	Y
7 Peterson	Y	Y	Y	Y
8 Oberstar	Y	Y	Y	Y

MISSISSIPPI

Member	2	3	4	5
1 *Wicker*	Y	Y	Y	Y
2 Thompson	Y	Y	Y	Y
3 *Pickering*	Y	Y	Y	Y
4 Taylor	Y	Y	Y	Y

MISSOURI

Member	2	3	4	5
1 Clay	Y	Y	Y	Y
2 *Akin*	Y	Y	?	Y
3 Gephardt	?	?	?	?
4 Skelton	Y	Y	Y	Y
5 McCarthy	Y	Y	Y	Y
6 *Graves*	Y	Y	?	Y
7 *Blunt*	Y	Y	Y	Y
8 *Emerson*	Y	Y	Y	Y
9 *Hulshof*	Y	Y	Y	Y

MONTANA

Member	2	3	4	5
AL *Rehberg*	Y	Y	Y	Y

NEBRASKA

Member	2	3	4	5
1 *Bereuter*	Y	Y	Y	Y
2 *Terry*	Y	Y	Y	Y
3 *Osborne*	Y	Y	Y	Y

NEVADA

Member	2	3	4	5
1 Berkley	Y	Y	Y	Y
2 *Gibbons*	Y	Y	Y	Y
3 *Porter*	Y	Y	Y	Y

NEW HAMPSHIRE

Member	2	3	4	5
1 *Bradley*	Y	Y	Y	Y
2 *Bass*	Y	Y	Y	Y

NEW JERSEY

Member	2	3	4	5
1 Andrews	Y	Y	Y	Y
2 *LoBiondo*	Y	Y	Y	Y
3 *Saxton*	Y	Y	Y	Y
4 *Smith*	Y	Y	Y	Y
5 *Garrett*	Y	Y	Y	Y
6 Pallone	Y	Y	Y	Y
7 *Ferguson*	Y	Y	Y	Y
8 Pascrell	Y	Y	Y	Y
9 Rothman	Y	Y	Y	Y
10 Payne	Y	Y	Y	Y
11 *Frelinghuysen*	Y	Y	Y	Y
12 Holt	Y	Y	Y	Y
13 Menendez	Y	Y	Y	Y

NEW MEXICO

Member	2	3	4	5
1 *Wilson*	Y	Y	Y	Y
2 *Pearce*	Y	Y	Y	Y
3 Udall	Y	Y	Y	Y

NEW YORK

Member	2	3	4	5
1 Bishop	Y	Y	Y	Y
2 Israel	Y	Y	Y	Y
3 *King*	Y	Y	Y	Y
4 McCarthy	Y	Y	Y	Y
5 Ackerman	Y	Y	Y	Y
6 Meeks	Y	Y	Y	Y
7 Crowley	Y	Y	Y	Y
8 Nadler	?	?	?	?
9 Weiner	Y	Y	Y	Y
10 Towns	Y	Y	Y	Y
11 Owens	Y	Y	Y	Y
12 Velázquez	Y	Y	Y	Y
13 *Fossella*	Y	Y	Y	Y
14 Maloney	Y	Y	Y	Y
15 Rangel	Y	Y	Y	Y
16 Serrano	?	?	?	?
17 Engel	Y	Y	Y	Y
18 Lowey	Y	Y	Y	Y
19 *Kelly*	Y	Y	Y	Y
20 *Sweeney*	Y	Y	Y	Y
21 McNulty	Y	Y	Y	Y
22 Hinchey	N	Y	Y	Y
23 *McHugh*	Y	Y	Y	Y
24 *Boehlert*	Y	Y	Y	Y
25 *Walsh*	Y	Y	Y	Y

Member	2	3	4	5
26 *Reynolds*	Y	Y	?	Y
27 *Quinn*	Y	Y	Y	Y
28 Slaughter	Y	Y	Y	Y
29 Houghton	Y	Y	Y	?

NORTH CAROLINA

Member	2	3	4	5
1 Ballance	Y	Y	Y	Y
2 Etheridge	Y	Y	Y	Y
3 *Jones*	Y	Y	Y	Y
4 Price	Y	Y	Y	Y
5 *Burr*	?	?	?	?
6 *Coble*	Y	Y	Y	Y
7 McIntyre	Y	Y	Y	Y
8 *Hayes*	Y	Y	Y	Y
9 *Myrick*	Y	Y	Y	Y
10 *Ballenger*	Y	Y	Y	Y
11 *Taylor*	Y	Y	Y	Y
12 Watt	Y	Y	Y	Y
13 Miller	Y	Y	Y	Y

NORTH DAKOTA

Member	2	3	4	5
AL Pomeroy	Y	Y	Y	Y

OHIO

Member	2	3	4	5
1 *Chabot*	Y	Y	Y	Y
2 *Portman*	Y	Y	Y	Y
3 *Turner*	Y	Y	Y	Y
4 *Oxley*	Y	Y	Y	Y
5 *Gillmor*	?	?	?	?
6 Strickland	Y	Y	Y	Y
7 *Hobson*	Y	Y	Y	Y
8 *Boehner*	Y	Y	Y	Y
9 Kaptur	Y	Y	Y	Y
10 Kucinich	?	?	?	?
11 Jones	Y	Y	Y	Y
12 *Tiberi*	Y	Y	Y	Y
13 Brown	Y	Y	Y	Y
14 *LaTourette*	Y	Y	Y	Y
15 *Pryce*	Y	Y	Y	Y
16 *Regula*	Y	Y	Y	Y
17 Ryan	Y	Y	Y	Y
18 *Ney*	Y	Y	Y	Y

OKLAHOMA

Member	2	3	4	5
1 *Sullivan*	Y	Y	Y	Y
2 Carson	Y	Y	Y	Y
3 *Lucas*	Y	Y	Y	Y
4 *Cole*	Y	Y	Y	Y
5 *Istook*	?	?	?	?

OREGON

Member	2	3	4	5
1 Wu	Y	Y	Y	Y
2 *Walden*	Y	Y	Y	?
3 Blumenauer	Y	Y	Y	Y
4 DeFazio	Y	Y	Y	Y
5 Hooley	Y	Y	Y	Y

PENNSYLVANIA

Member	2	3	4	5
1 Brady	Y	Y	Y	Y
2 Fattah	Y	Y	Y	Y
3 *English*	Y	Y	Y	Y
4 *Hart*	Y	Y	Y	Y
5 *Peterson*	Y	Y	Y	Y
6 *Gerlach*	Y	Y	Y	Y
7 *Weldon*	Y	Y	Y	Y
8 *Greenwood*	Y	Y	Y	Y
9 *Shuster, Bill*	Y	Y	Y	Y
10 *Sherwood*	Y	Y	Y	Y
11 Kanjorski	Y	Y	Y	Y
12 Murtha	Y	Y	Y	Y
13 Hoeffel	Y	Y	Y	Y
14 Doyle	?	?	?	?
15 *Toomey*	Y	Y	Y	Y
16 *Pitts*	Y	Y	Y	Y
17 Holden	Y	Y	Y	Y
18 *Murphy*	Y	Y	Y	Y
19 *Platts*	?	?	?	?

RHODE ISLAND

Member	2	3	4	5
1 Kennedy	Y	Y	Y	Y
2 Langevin	Y	Y	Y	Y

SOUTH CAROLINA

Member	2	3	4	5
1 *Brown*	Y	Y	Y	Y
2 *Wilson*	Y	Y	Y	Y
3 *Barrett*	Y	Y	Y	Y
4 *DeMint*	Y	Y	Y	Y
5 Spratt	Y	Y	Y	Y
6 Clyburn	Y	Y	Y	Y

SOUTH DAKOTA

Member	2	3	4	5
AL Vacant [2]				

TENNESSEE

Member	2	3	4	5
1 *Jenkins*	Y	Y	Y	Y
2 *Duncan*	Y	Y	?	Y
3 *Wamp*	Y	Y	Y	Y
4 Davis	Y	Y	Y	Y
5 Cooper	Y	Y	Y	Y
6 Gordon	Y	Y	Y	Y
7 *Blackburn*	Y	Y	Y	Y
8 Tanner	Y	Y	Y	Y
9 Ford	Y	Y	Y	Y

TEXAS

Member	2	3	4	5
1 Sandlin	Y	Y	Y	Y
2 Turner	Y	Y	Y	Y
3 *Johnson, Sam*	Y	Y	Y	Y
4 *Hall*	Y	Y	Y	Y
5 *Hensarling*	Y	Y	Y	Y
6 *Barton*	Y	Y	Y	Y
7 *Culberson*	Y	Y	Y	Y
8 *Brady*	Y	Y	Y	Y
9 Lampson	Y	Y	Y	Y
10 Doggett	?	?	?	?
11 Edwards	?	?	?	?
12 *Granger*	Y	Y	Y	Y
13 *Thornberry*	Y	Y	Y	Y
14 *Paul*	Y	Y	Y	Y
15 Hinojosa	Y	Y	Y	Y
16 Reyes	?	?	?	?
17 Stenholm	Y	Y	Y	Y
18 Jackson-Lee	Y	Y	Y	Y
19 *Neugebauer*	Y	Y	Y	Y
20 Gonzalez	Y	Y	Y	Y
21 *Smith*	Y	Y	Y	Y
22 *DeLay*	Y	Y	Y	Y
23 *Bonilla*	Y	Y	Y	Y
24 Frost	Y	Y	Y	Y
25 Bell	Y	Y	Y	Y
26 *Burgess*	Y	Y	Y	Y
27 Ortiz	Y	Y	Y	Y
28 Rodriguez	Y	Y	Y	Y
29 Green	Y	Y	Y	Y
30 Johnson, E.B.	Y	Y	Y	Y
31 *Carter*	Y	Y	Y	Y
32 *Sessions*	Y	Y	Y	Y

UTAH

Member	2	3	4	5
1 *Bishop*	Y	Y	Y	Y
2 *Matheson*	Y	Y	Y	Y
3 *Cannon*	Y	Y	Y	Y

VERMONT

Member	2	3	4	5
AL *Sanders*	Y	Y	Y	Y

VIRGINIA

Member	2	3	4	5
1 *Davis, Jo Ann*	Y	Y	Y	Y
2 *Schrock*	Y	Y	Y	Y
3 Scott	Y	Y	Y	Y
4 *Forbes*	Y	Y	Y	Y
5 *Goode*	Y	Y	?	Y
6 *Goodlatte*	Y	Y	Y	Y
7 *Cantor*	Y	Y	Y	Y
8 Moran	Y	Y	Y	Y
9 Boucher	Y	Y	Y	Y
10 *Wolf*	Y	Y	Y	Y
11 *Davis, T.*	Y	Y	Y	Y

WASHINGTON

Member	2	3	4	5
1 Inslee	Y	Y	Y	Y
2 Larsen	Y	Y	Y	Y
3 Baird	Y	Y	Y	Y
4 *Hastings*	Y	Y	Y	Y
5 *Nethercutt*	Y	Y	Y	Y
6 Dicks	Y	Y	Y	Y
7 McDermott	Y	Y	Y	Y
8 *Dunn*	+	+	+	+
9 Smith	Y	Y	Y	Y

WEST VIRGINIA

Member	2	3	4	5
1 Mollohan	Y	Y	Y	Y
2 *Capito*	Y	Y	Y	Y
3 Rahall	?	?	?	?

WISCONSIN

Member	2	3	4	5
1 *Ryan*	Y	Y	Y	Y
2 Baldwin	Y	Y	Y	Y
3 Kind	Y	Y	Y	Y
4 Kleczka	Y	Y	Y	Y
5 *Sensenbrenner*	Y	Y	Y	Y
6 *Petri*	Y	Y	Y	Y
7 Obey	Y	Y	Y	Y
8 *Green*	Y	Y	Y	Y

WYOMING

Member	2	3	4	5
AL *Cubin*	Y	Y	Y	Y

Southern states - Ala., Ark., Fla., Ga., Ky., La., Miss., N.C., Okla., S.C., Tenn., Texas, Va.

Key

6. HR 1385. Breast Cancer Stamp Extension/Passage. Ose, R-Calif., motion to suspend the rules and pass the bill that would extend through 2006 the authority of the Postal Service to issue a special postage stamp that benefits breast cancer research. Motion agreed to 331-1: R 182-1; D 148-0 (ND 111-0, SD 37-0); I 1-0. A two-thirds majority of those present and voting (222 in this case) is required for passage under suspension of the rules. Jan. 27, 2004.

7. HR 3493. Medical Devices Technical Corrections/Passage. Greenwood, R-Pa., motion to suspend the rules and pass the bill that would make technical corrections and clarifications to the Medical Device User Fee and Modernization Act of 2002, including clarifying the types of fees applicable under the act. Motion agreed to 333-0: R 183-0; D 149-0 (ND 112-0, SD 37-0); I 1-0. A two-thirds majority of those present and voting (222 in this case) is required for passage under suspension of the rules. Jan. 27, 2004.

8. S 1920. Bankruptcy Extension and Overhaul/Democratic Substitute. Baldwin, D-Wis., substitute amendment that would make permanent Chapter 12 bankruptcy protection for family farmers and would expand eligibility requirements for Chapter 12, including permitting family fishermen to file for bankruptcy. Rejected 158-204: R 0-193; D 157-11 (ND 125-3, SD 32-8); I 1-0. Jan. 28, 2004.

9. S 1920. Bankruptcy Extension and Overhaul/Recommit. Schakowsky, D-Ill., motion to recommit the bill to the House Judiciary Committee with instructions to include a new section in the bill that would increase bankruptcy protection for members of the military, veterans, and their families. Motion rejected 170-198: R 1-197; D 168-1 (ND 128-0, SD 40-1); I 1-0. Jan. 28, 2004.

10. S 1920. Bankruptcy Extension and Overhaul/Passage. Passage of the bill that would require debtors who are able to repay $10,000 or 25 percent of their debts over five years to file under Chapter 13, which requires a reorganization of debts under a repayment plan, instead of seeking to discharge their debts under Chapter 7. A debtor would be limited to a total exemption of $125,000 in home equity for residences purchased within 40 months of a bankruptcy filing. The bill also would make permanent and retroactive Chapter 12 bankruptcy relief for farmers. Passed 265-99: R 195-0; D 70-98 (ND 41-87, SD 29-11); I 0-1. (Previously, the House adopted by voice vote a rule that substituted the text of the House-passed bill HR 975.) Jan. 28, 2004.

11. S 1920. Bankruptcy Extension and Overhaul/Motion to Instruct. Nadler, D-N.Y., motion to instruct conferees to strike parts of the bill that would repeal an element of the bankruptcy code designed to prevent conflicts of interest for investment bankers. Motion rejected 146-203: R 6-182; D 139-21 (ND 111-9, SD 28-12); I 1-0. Jan. 28, 2004.

	6	7	8	9	10	11
ALABAMA						
1 *Bonner*	Y	Y	N	N	Y	N
2 *Everett*	Y	Y	?	?	?	?
3 *Rogers*	Y	Y	N	N	Y	N
4 *Aderholt*	Y	Y	N	N	Y	N
5 Cramer	Y	Y	N	Y	N	N
6 *Bachus*	?	?	?	N	Y	Y
7 Davis	Y	Y	Y	Y	Y	N
ALASKA						
AL *Young*	Y	Y	?	?	?	?
ARIZONA						
1 *Renzi*	Y	Y	N	N	Y	N
2 *Franks*	Y	Y	N	N	Y	N
3 *Shadegg*	Y	Y	N	N	Y	N
4 Pastor	Y	Y	Y	Y	Y	Y
5 *Hayworth*	Y	Y	N	N	Y	Y
6 *Flake*	Y	Y	N	N	Y	N
7 Grijalva	Y	Y	Y	Y	N	Y
8 *Kolbe*	Y	Y	?	N	Y	N
ARKANSAS						
1 Berry	Y	Y	Y	Y	Y	?
2 Snyder	Y	Y	Y	Y	N	Y
3 *Boozman*	?	?	N	N	Y	N
4 Ross	Y	Y	Y	Y	Y	Y
CALIFORNIA						
1 Thompson	Y	Y	Y	Y	Y	Y
2 *Herger*	Y	Y	N	N	Y	N
3 *Ose*	Y	Y	N	N	Y	N
4 *Doolittle*	?	?	N	N	Y	N
5 Matsui	Y	Y	Y	Y	N	Y
6 Woolsey	Y	Y	Y	Y	N	Y
7 Miller, George	?	?	?	?	?	?
8 Pelosi	Y	Y	Y	Y	N	Y
9 Lee	Y	Y	Y	Y	N	Y
10 Tauscher	?	?	Y	Y	Y	N
11 *Pombo*	?	?	?	?	?	?
12 Lantos	?	?	Y	Y	N	Y
13 Stark	?	?	Y	Y	N	?
14 Eshoo	Y	Y	Y	Y	N	Y
15 Honda	?	?	?	?	?	?
16 Lofgren	Y	Y	Y	Y	N	Y
17 Farr	Y	Y	Y	Y	N	Y
18 Cardoza	Y	Y	Y	Y	Y	N
19 *Radanovich*	Y	Y	N	N	Y	N
20 Dooley	Y	Y	Y	Y	Y	N
21 *Nunes*	Y	Y	N	N	Y	N
22 *Thomas*	Y	Y	?	?	?	?
23 Capps	Y	Y	Y	Y	N	Y
24 *Gallegly*	?	?	?	?	?	?
25 *McKeon*	Y	Y	N	N	Y	N
26 *Dreier*	Y	Y	N	N	Y	N
27 Sherman	Y	Y	Y	Y	N	Y
28 Berman	Y	Y	Y	Y	N	?
29 Schiff	Y	Y	Y	Y	Y	N
30 Waxman	Y	Y	Y	Y	N	Y
31 Becerra	Y	Y	Y	Y	N	Y
32 Solis	Y	Y	Y	Y	N	Y
33 Watson	?	?	?	?	?	?
34 Roybal-Allard	?	?	?	?	?	?
35 Waters	?	?	?	?	?	?
36 Harman	Y	Y	Y	Y	Y	Y

	6	7	8	9	10	11
37 Millender-McD.	Y	Y	Y	Y	N	Y
38 Napolitano	Y	Y	Y	Y	N	?
39 Sánchez, Linda	?	?	Y	Y	N	Y
40 *Royce*	?	?	?	?	?	?
41 *Lewis*	?	?	?	?	?	?
42 *Miller, Gary*	Y	Y	N	N	Y	Y
43 Baca	Y	Y	N	Y	Y	Y
44 *Calvert*	?	?	N	N	Y	N
45 *Bono*	?	?	?	?	?	?
46 *Rohrabacher*	?	?	N	N	Y	Y
47 Sanchez, Loretta	Y	Y	Y	Y	N	Y
48 *Cox*	Y	Y	N	N	Y	N
49 *Issa*	Y	Y	N	N	Y	N
50 *Cunningham*	?	?	?	?	?	?
51 Filner	Y	Y	Y	Y	N	Y
52 *Hunter*	?	?	?	?	?	?
53 Davis	Y	Y	Y	Y	N	Y
COLORADO						
1 DeGette	?	?	?	?	?	?
2 Udall	Y	Y	Y	Y	N	Y
3 *McInnis*	Y	Y	?	?	?	?
4 *Musgrave*	Y	Y	N	N	Y	N
5 *Hefley*	Y	Y	?	?	?	?
6 *Tancredo*	Y	Y	N	N	Y	N
7 *Beauprez*	Y	Y	N	N	Y	N
CONNECTICUT						
1 Larson	Y	Y	Y	Y	Y	Y
2 *Simmons*	Y	?	N	Y	Y	N
3 DeLauro	Y	Y	Y	Y	N	Y
4 *Shays*	Y	Y	N	N	Y	N
5 *Johnson*	Y	Y	N	N	Y	N
DELAWARE						
AL *Castle*	Y	Y	N	N	Y	N
FLORIDA						
1 *Miller, J.*	Y	Y	N	N	Y	N
2 Boyd	Y	Y	N	Y	Y	Y
3 Brown	?	?	?	?	?	?
4 *Crenshaw*	Y	Y	N	N	Y	N
5 *Brown-Waite*	Y	Y	?	?	?	?
6 *Stearns*	Y	Y	N	N	Y	N
7 *Mica*	Y	Y	N	N	Y	N
8 *Keller*	Y	Y	N	N	Y	N
9 *Bilirakis*	Y	Y	N	N	Y	N
10 *Young*	?	?	N	N	Y	N
11 Davis	Y	Y	Y	Y	Y	N
12 *Putnam*	Y	Y	N	N	Y	N
13 *Harris*	Y	Y	N	N	Y	N
14 *Goss*	Y	Y	N	N	Y	N
15 *Weldon*	Y	Y	N	N	Y	N
16 *Foley*	Y	Y	N	N	Y	N
17 Meek	Y	Y	N	Y	N	Y
18 *Ros-Lehtinen*	Y	Y	N	N	Y	N
19 Wexler	?	?	Y	Y	?	Y
20 Deutsch	Y	Y	Y	Y	Y	Y
21 *Diaz-Balart, L.*	Y	Y	N	N	Y	N
22 *Shaw*	Y	Y	N	N	Y	N
23 Hastings	?	?	?	?	?	?
24 *Feeney*	Y	Y	N	N	Y	N
25 *Diaz-Balart, M.*	Y	Y	N	N	Y	?
GEORGIA						
1 *Kingston*	?	?	N	N	Y	N
2 Bishop	Y	Y	?	Y	Y	Y
3 Marshall	Y	Y	Y	Y	N	N
4 Majette	Y	Y	Y	Y	N	Y
5 Lewis	Y	Y	Y	Y	N	Y
6 *Isakson*	Y	Y	N	N	Y	N
7 *Linder*	Y	Y	N	N	Y	N
8 *Collins*	Y	Y	N	N	Y	?
9 *Norwood*	Y	Y	N	N	Y	N
10 *Deal*	Y	Y	N	N	Y	?
11 *Gingrey*	Y	Y	N	N	Y	N
12 *Burns*	Y	Y	N	N	Y	N
13 Scott	?	?	Y	Y	Y	Y
HAWAII						
1 Abercrombie	+	+	+	+	–	+
2 Case	Y	Y	Y	Y	Y	Y
IDAHO						
1 *Otter*	Y	Y	N	N	Y	N
2 *Simpson*	Y	Y	N	N	Y	N
ILLINOIS						
1 Rush	?	?	Y	Y	N	Y
2 Jackson	Y	Y	Y	Y	N	Y
3 Lipinski	?	?	?	?	?	?
4 Gutierrez	Y	Y	?	?	?	?
5 Emanuel	Y	Y	Y	Y	N	Y
6 *Hyde*	?	?	?	?	?	?

ND Northern Democrats   SD Southern Democrats

	6	7	8	9	10	11
7 Davis	Y	Y	Y	Y	N	Y
8 ***Crane***	Y	Y	?	?	?	?
9 Schakowsky	Y	Y	Y	Y	N	Y
10 ***Kirk***	Y	Y	N	N	Y	N
11 ***Weller***	Y	Y	N	N	Y	N
12 Costello	?	?	Y	Y	N	Y
13 ***Biggert***	Y	Y	N	N	Y	N
14 ***Hastert***			N			
15 ***Johnson***	?	?	N	N	Y	N
16 ***Manzullo***	Y	Y	N	N	Y	N
17 Evans	Y	Y	Y	Y	N	Y
18 ***LaHood***	Y	Y	N	N	Y	N
19 ***Shimkus***	Y	Y	?	?	?	?
INDIANA						
1 Visclosky	Y	Y	Y	Y	N	Y
2 ***Chocola***	Y	Y	N	N	Y	N
3 ***Souder***	?	?	?	?	?	?
4 ***Buyer***	?	?	?	?	?	?
5 ***Burton***	Y	Y	N	N	Y	N
6 ***Pence***	Y	Y	N	N	Y	N
7 Carson	Y	Y	Y	Y	N	Y
8 ***Hostettler***	Y	Y	N	N	Y	N
9 Hill	Y	Y	Y	Y	Y	Y
IOWA						
1 ***Nussle***	Y	Y	N	N	Y	N
2 ***Leach***	?	?	?	?	?	?
3 Boswell	Y	Y	Y	Y	Y	N
4 ***Latham***	Y	Y	N	N	Y	N
5 ***King***	Y	Y	N	N	Y	N
KANSAS						
1 ***Moran***	Y	Y	N	N	Y	N
2 ***Ryun***	Y	Y	?	?	?	?
3 Moore	Y	Y	Y	Y	Y	Y
4 ***Tiahrt***	Y	Y	N	N	Y	N
KENTUCKY						
1 ***Whitfield***	Y	Y	N	N	Y	N
2 ***Lewis***	Y	Y	N	N	Y	N
3 ***Northup***	?	?	N	N	Y	N
4 Lucas	Y	Y	N	Y	Y	N
5 ***Rogers***	?	?	?	?	?	?
6 Vacant						
LOUISIANA						
1 ***Vitter***	Y	Y	N	N	Y	N
2 Jefferson	Y	Y	Y	Y	Y	Y
3 ***Tauzin***	?	?	N	N	Y	N
4 ***McCrery***	Y	Y	N	N	Y	N
5 Alexander	?	?	?	?	?	?
6 ***Baker***	Y	Y	N	N	?	?
7 John	Y	Y	Y	Y	Y	N
MAINE						
1 Allen	Y	Y	Y	Y	N	Y
2 Michaud	Y	Y	Y	Y	Y	Y
MARYLAND						
1 ***Gilchrest***	Y	Y	N	N	Y	N
2 Ruppersberger	Y	Y	C	C	C	C
3 Cardin	Y	Y	Y	Y	N	Y
4 Wynn	Y	Y	Y	Y	Y	?
5 Hoyer	Y	Y	Y	Y	Y	Y
6 ***Bartlett***	Y	Y	N	N	Y	N
7 Cummings	?	Y	Y	Y	N	Y
8 Van Hollen	Y	Y	Y	Y	N	Y
MASSACHUSETTS						
1 Olver	Y	Y	Y	Y	N	Y
2 Neal	Y	Y	Y	Y	N	Y
3 McGovern	Y	Y	Y	Y	N	Y
4 Frank	Y	Y	Y	Y	N	Y
5 Meehan	Y	Y	Y	Y	N	Y
6 Tierney	Y	Y	Y	Y	N	Y
7 Markey	Y	Y	Y	Y	N	Y
8 Capuano	?	?	Y	Y	N	Y
9 Lynch	Y	Y	Y	Y	N	Y
10 Delahunt	?	?	?	?	?	?
MICHIGAN						
1 Stupak	Y	Y	Y	Y	N	Y
2 ***Hoekstra***	Y	Y	N	N	Y	N
3 ***Ehlers***	Y	Y	N	N	Y	N
4 ***Camp***	?	?	?	?	?	?
5 Kildee	Y	Y	Y	Y	N	Y
6 ***Upton***	Y	Y	N	N	Y	N
7 ***Smith***	Y	Y	N	N	?	N
8 ***Rogers***	Y	Y	N	N	Y	N
9 ***Knollenberg***	Y	Y	N	N	Y	N
10 ***Miller***	?	?	?	?	?	?
11 ***McCotter***	Y	Y	N	N	Y	N
12 Levin	Y	Y	Y	Y	N	Y
13 Kilpatrick	Y	Y	Y	Y	N	Y
14 Conyers	Y	Y	Y	Y	N	Y
15 Dingell	?	?	Y	Y	Y	Y
MINNESOTA						
1 ***Gutknecht***	?	?	N	N	Y	N
2 ***Kline***	Y	Y	N	N	Y	N
3 ***Ramstad***	Y	Y	N	N	Y	N
4 McCollum	Y	Y	Y	Y	N	Y
5 Sabo	?	?	Y	Y	N	Y
6 ***Kennedy***	Y	Y	N	N	Y	N
7 Peterson	Y	Y	N	Y	Y	Y
8 Oberstar	Y	Y	Y	Y	N	Y
MISSISSIPPI						
1 ***Wicker***	Y	Y	N	N	Y	N
2 Thompson	Y	Y	Y	Y	Y	Y
3 ***Pickering***	Y	Y	N	N	Y	N
4 Taylor	Y	Y	Y	Y	Y	N
MISSOURI						
1 Clay	Y	Y	Y	Y	N	?
2 ***Akin***	Y	Y	N	N	Y	N
3 Gephardt	?	?	?	?	?	?
4 Skelton	Y	Y	Y	Y	Y	Y
5 McCarthy	Y	Y	Y	Y	N	Y
6 ***Graves***	Y	Y	N	N	Y	N
7 ***Blunt***	Y	Y	N	N	Y	N
8 ***Emerson***	Y	Y	N	N	Y	N
9 ***Hulshof***	Y	Y	N	N	Y	N
MONTANA						
AL ***Rehberg***	Y	Y	N	N	Y	N
NEBRASKA						
1 ***Bereuter***	Y	Y	–	N	Y	N
2 ***Terry***	Y	Y	N	N	Y	N
3 ***Osborne***	Y	Y	N	N	Y	N
NEVADA						
1 Berkley	Y	Y	Y	Y	Y	Y
2 ***Gibbons***	Y	Y	N	N	Y	N
3 ***Porter***	Y	Y	N	N	Y	N
NEW HAMPSHIRE						
1 ***Bradley***	Y	Y	N	N	Y	N
2 ***Bass***	Y	Y	N	N	Y	N
NEW JERSEY						
1 Andrews	Y	Y	Y	Y	Y	Y
2 ***LoBiondo***	Y	Y	N	N	Y	N
3 ***Saxton***	Y	Y	N	N	Y	N
4 ***Smith***	Y	Y	N	N	Y	Y
5 ***Garrett***	Y	Y	N	N	Y	N
6 Pallone	Y	Y	Y	Y	Y	Y
7 ***Ferguson***	Y	Y	N	N	Y	N
8 Pascrell	Y	Y	Y	Y	Y	Y
9 Rothman	?	?	Y	Y	Y	Y
10 Payne	?	?	Y	Y	N	Y
11 ***Frelinghuysen***	Y	Y	N	N	Y	N
12 Holt	Y	Y	Y	Y	N	Y
13 Menendez	Y	Y	Y	Y	Y	Y
NEW MEXICO						
1 ***Wilson***	Y	Y	N	N	Y	N
2 ***Pearce***	Y	Y	N	N	Y	N
3 Udall	Y	Y	Y	Y	N	Y
NEW YORK						
1 Bishop	Y	Y	Y	Y	Y	Y
2 Israel	?	?	?	?	?	?
3 ***King***	Y	Y	N	N	Y	?
4 McCarthy	Y	Y	Y	Y	Y	N
5 Ackerman	?	?	?	?	?	?
6 Meeks	?	?	?	?	?	?
7 Crowley	Y	Y	Y	Y	Y	N
8 Nadler	?	?	Y	Y	N	Y
9 Weiner	Y	Y	Y	Y	N	N
10 Towns	Y	Y	Y	Y	N	Y
11 Owens	?	?	Y	Y	N	Y
12 Velázquez	Y	Y	Y	Y	N	Y
13 ***Fossella***	Y	Y	N	N	Y	N
14 Maloney	Y	Y	Y	Y	N	Y
15 Rangel	Y	Y	Y	Y	N	Y
16 Serrano	?	?	?	Y	N	Y
17 Engel	Y	Y	Y	Y	N	Y
18 Lowey	Y	Y	Y	Y	N	?
19 ***Kelly***	Y	Y	N	N	Y	N
20 ***Sweeney***	Y	Y	N	N	Y	N
21 McNulty	Y	Y	Y	Y	N	?
22 Hinchey	Y	Y	Y	Y	N	?
23 ***McHugh***	Y	Y	N	N	Y	N
24 ***Boehlert***	Y	Y	N	N	Y	N
25 ***Walsh***	Y	Y	N	N	Y	N
26 ***Reynolds***	Y	Y	–	N	?	N
27 ***Quinn***	Y	Y	N	N	Y	N
28 Slaughter	?	?	?	?	?	?
29 ***Houghton***	Y	?	?	N	Y	N
NORTH CAROLINA						
1 Ballance	?	?	Y	Y	N	Y
2 Etheridge	Y	Y	Y	Y	Y	Y
3 ***Jones***	?	?	?	?	?	?
4 Price	?	?	Y	Y	Y	Y
5 ***Burr***	?	?	N	N	Y	N
6 ***Coble***	Y	Y	N	N	Y	N
7 McIntyre	?	?	?	?	?	?
8 ***Hayes***	Y	Y	N	N	Y	N
9 ***Myrick***	Y	Y	N	N	Y	N
10 ***Ballenger***	?	?	?	?	?	?
11 ***Taylor***	Y	Y	N	N	Y	N
12 Watt	Y	Y	Y	Y	N	Y
13 Miller	?	?	Y	Y	N	Y
NORTH DAKOTA						
AL Pomeroy	Y	Y	Y	Y	Y	Y
OHIO						
1 ***Chabot***	Y	Y	N	N	Y	N
2 ***Portman***	Y	Y	N	N	Y	N
3 ***Turner***	Y	Y	N	N	Y	N
4 ***Oxley***	Y	Y	N	N	Y	N
5 ***Gillmor***	Y	Y	N	N	Y	N
6 Strickland	Y	Y	Y	Y	Y	Y
7 ***Hobson***	?	?	N	N	Y	N
8 ***Boehner***	Y	Y	N	N	Y	?
9 Kaptur	Y	Y	Y	Y	N	Y
10 Kucinich	?	?	?	?	?	?
11 Jones	Y	Y	Y	Y	N	Y
12 ***Tiberi***	?	?	N	N	Y	N
13 Brown	Y	Y	Y	Y	N	Y
14 ***LaTourette***	?	?	N	N	Y	N
15 ***Pryce***	Y	Y	N	N	Y	N
16 ***Regula***	Y	Y	N	N	Y	N
17 Ryan	?	?	Y	Y	N	Y
18 ***Ney***	Y	Y	N	N	Y	N
OKLAHOMA						
1 ***Sullivan***	?	?	N	N	Y	N
2 Carson	?	?	?	?	?	?
3 ***Lucas***	Y	Y	N	N	Y	N
4 ***Cole***	Y	Y	N	N	Y	N
5 ***Istook***	Y	Y	N	N	Y	N
OREGON						
1 Wu	Y	Y	Y	?	?	?
2 ***Walden***	Y	Y	N	N	Y	N
3 Blumenauer	Y	Y	Y	Y	Y	N
4 DeFazio	?	?	Y	Y	N	Y
5 Hooley	Y	Y	Y	Y	Y	Y
PENNSYLVANIA						
1 Brady	?	?	Y	Y	N	Y
2 Fattah	?	?	?	?	?	?
3 ***English***	?	?	N	N	Y	N
4 ***Hart***	Y	Y	N	N	Y	N
5 ***Peterson***	Y	Y	N	N	Y	N
6 ***Gerlach***	Y	Y	?	?	?	?
7 ***Weldon***	?	?	?	?	?	?
8 ***Greenwood***	Y	Y	N	N	Y	N
9 ***Shuster, Bill***	Y	Y	N	N	Y	N
10 ***Sherwood***	Y	Y	N	N	Y	N
11 Kanjorski	Y	Y	Y	Y	N	Y
12 Murtha	?	?	Y	Y	Y	Y
13 Hoeffel	Y	Y	Y	Y	N	Y
14 Doyle	Y	Y	Y	Y	Y	Y
15 ***Toomey***	Y	Y	N	N	Y	N
16 ***Pitts***	Y	Y	N	N	Y	N
17 Holden	Y	Y	Y	Y	N	Y
18 ***Murphy***	Y	Y	N	N	Y	N
19 ***Platts***	Y	Y	N	N	Y	N
RHODE ISLAND						
1 Kennedy	Y	Y	Y	Y	N	Y
2 Langevin	Y	Y	Y	Y	N	Y
SOUTH CAROLINA						
1 ***Brown***	Y	Y	N	N	Y	N
2 ***Wilson***	?	?	N	N	Y	N
3 ***Barrett***	Y	Y	N	N	Y	–
4 ***DeMint***	?	Y	N	N	Y	N
5 Spratt	Y	Y	Y	Y	Y	N
6 Clyburn	?	?	Y	Y	Y	Y
SOUTH DAKOTA						
AL Vacant						
TENNESSEE						
1 ***Jenkins***	?	?	?	?	?	?
2 ***Duncan***	?	?	N	N	Y	N
3 ***Wamp***	?	?	N	N	Y	N
4 Davis	Y	Y	Y	Y	Y	N
5 Cooper	Y	Y	Y	Y	N	Y
6 Gordon	Y	Y	N	Y	Y	N
7 ***Blackburn***	Y	Y	N	N	Y	?
8 Tanner	Y	Y	?	?	?	?
9 Ford	?	?	Y	Y	Y	Y
TEXAS						
1 Sandlin	?	?	?	?	?	?
2 Turner	Y	Y	?	?	?	?
3 ***Johnson, Sam***	Y	Y	N	N	Y	N
4 ***Hall***	Y	Y	N	N	Y	N
5 ***Hensarling***	Y	Y	N	N	Y	N
6 ***Barton***	Y	Y	N	N	Y	N
7 ***Culberson***	?	?	N	N	Y	N
8 ***Brady***	Y	Y	N	N	Y	N
9 Lampson	Y	Y	Y	Y	Y	Y
10 Doggett	?	?	?	?	?	?
11 Edwards	Y	Y	N	Y	Y	Y
12 ***Granger***	Y	Y	N	N	Y	N
13 ***Thornberry***	Y	Y	N	N	Y	N
14 ***Paul***	N	Y	N	N	Y	?
15 Hinojosa	Y	Y	Y	Y	Y	Y
16 Reyes	?	?	?	?	?	?
17 Stenholm	Y	Y	Y	Y	Y	N
18 Jackson-Lee	Y	Y	?	?	?	?
19 ***Neugebauer***	Y	Y	N	N	Y	N
20 Gonzalez	Y	Y	Y	Y	N	Y
21 ***Smith***	Y	Y	N	N	Y	N
22 ***DeLay***	Y	Y	N	N	Y	N
23 ***Bonilla***	Y	Y	N	N	Y	N
24 Frost	?	?	Y	Y	Y	Y
25 Bell	Y	Y	?	?	?	?
26 ***Burgess***	Y	Y	N	N	Y	N
27 Ortiz	?	?	?	?	?	?
28 Rodriguez	?	?	?	?	?	?
29 Green	Y	Y	Y	Y	N	Y
30 Johnson, E.B.	Y	Y	+	+	+	+
31 ***Carter***	?	Y	N	N	Y	N
32 ***Sessions***	Y	Y	N	N	Y	N
UTAH						
1 ***Bishop***	Y	Y	N	N	Y	N
2 Matheson	Y	Y	N	Y	Y	N
3 ***Cannon***	Y	Y	N	N	Y	N
VERMONT						
AL *Sanders*	Y	Y	Y	Y	N	Y
VIRGINIA						
1 ***Davis, Jo Ann***	?	?	N	N	Y	Y
2 ***Schrock***	Y	Y	N	N	Y	N
3 Scott	Y	Y	Y	Y	N	Y
4 ***Forbes***	?	?	?	?	?	?
5 ***Goode***	Y	Y	N	N	Y	N
6 ***Goodlatte***	Y	Y	N	N	Y	N
7 ***Cantor***	Y	Y	N	N	Y	N
8 Moran	Y	Y	Y	Y	Y	Y
9 Boucher	?	?	N	N	Y	N
10 ***Wolf***	?	?	N	N	Y	N
11 ***Davis, T.***	Y	Y	N	N	Y	N
WASHINGTON						
1 Inslee	Y	Y	Y	Y	Y	Y
2 Larsen	Y	Y	Y	Y	Y	Y
3 Baird	Y	Y	Y	Y	Y	Y
4 ***Hastings***	Y	Y	N	N	Y	N
5 ***Nethercutt***	Y	Y	N	N	Y	N
6 Dicks	Y	Y	Y	Y	Y	Y
7 McDermott	Y	Y	Y	Y	N	Y
8 ***Dunn***	Y	Y	N	N	Y	N
9 Smith	Y	Y	Y	Y	Y	Y
WEST VIRGINIA						
1 Mollohan	?	?	?	?	?	?
2 ***Capito***	Y	Y	N	N	Y	N
3 Rahall	Y	Y	Y	Y	Y	Y
WISCONSIN						
1 ***Ryan***	Y	Y	N	N	Y	N
2 Baldwin	Y	Y	Y	Y	N	Y
3 Kind	Y	Y	Y	Y	Y	Y
4 Kleczka	?	?	Y	Y	N	Y
5 ***Sensenbrenner***	Y	Y	N	N	Y	N
6 ***Petri***	Y	Y	?	N	Y	N
7 Obey	Y	Y	Y	Y	N	Y
8 ***Green***	Y	Y	N	N	Y	N
WYOMING						
AL ***Cubin***	Y	Y	N	N	Y	N

Southern states - Ala., Ark., Fla., Ga., Ky., La., Miss., N.C., Okla., S.C., Tenn., Texas, Va.

12. H Res 507. First Anniversary of the *Columbia* Tragedy/Adoption. Burgess, R-Texas, motion to suspend the rules and adopt the resolution that would express the profound sorrow of the House on the anniversary of the space shuttle *Columbia* accident and offer condolences to the families of the seven astronauts killed in the disaster. Motion agreed to 397-0: R 217-0; D 179-0 (ND 127-0, SD 52-0); I 1-0. A two-thirds majority of those present and voting (265 in this case) is required for adoption under suspension of the rules. Feb. 2, 2004.

13. H Res 157. Prisoners of Conscience in China/Adoption. Royce, R-Calif., motion to suspend the rules and adopt the resolution that would express the sense of the House that the Chinese government should immediately release all prisoners of conscience, including Phuntsog Nyidron, a Tibetan Buddhist nun. Motion agreed to 398-0: R 215-0; D 182-0 (ND 128-0, SD 54-0); I 1-0. A two-thirds majority of those present and voting (266 in this case) is required for adoption under suspension of the rules. Feb. 3, 2004.

14. H J Res 84. Ronald Reagan's 93rd Birthday/Passage. Shays, R-Conn., motion to suspend the rules and pass the joint resolution that would extend birthday greetings and best wishes to former President Ronald Reagan on his 93rd birthday. Motion agreed to 394-0: R 217-0; D 176-0 (ND 125-0, SD 51-0); I 1-0. A two-thirds majority of those present and voting (263 in this case) is required for passage under suspension of the rules. Feb. 3, 2004.

15. HR 3030. Community Services Block Grants/Non-Discrimination. Scott, D-Va., amendment that would add religion as a non-discrimination criteria for hiring by organizations receiving federal Community Services Block Grant (CSBG) funds. The amendment also would strike language in current law that allows organizations receiving CSBG funds to hire on a religious basis. Rejected 182-231: R 3-218; D 178-13 (ND 133-3, SD 45-10); I 1-0. A "nay" was a vote in support of the president's position. Feb. 4, 2004.

16. HR 3030. Community Services Block Grants/Religious Activity. Scott, D-Va., amendment that would require religious groups that receive Community Services Block Grant funds to conduct religious activities separately and make them voluntary for program participants. Rejected 180-233: R 2-219; D 177-14 (ND 132-4, SD 45-10); I 1-0. Feb. 4, 2004.

17. HR 3030. Community Services Block Grants/Democratic Substitute. Woolsey, D-Calif., substitute amendment that would prohibit organizations that receive federal Community Services Block Grant funds from hiring on a religious basis and require them to operate in a "lawful and secular" manner when using the funds. Rejected 183-232: R 3-219; D 179-13 (ND 133-4, SD 46-9); I 1-0. A "nay" was a vote in support of the president's position. Feb. 4, 2004.

18. HR 3030. Community Services Block Grants/Unemployment Benefits. Miller, D-Calif., amendment that would authorize such sums as necessary under the Community Services Block Grants program for a six-month federal program to provide an additional 13 weeks of unemployment benefits for people who have exhausted their state jobless benefits. Adopted 227-179: R 39-179; D 187-0 (ND 132-0, SD 55-0); I 1-0. Feb. 4, 2004.

Key

Y	Voted for (yea).
#	Paired for.
+	Announced for.
N	Voted against (nay).
X	Paired against.
−	Announced against.
P	Voted "present."
C	Voted "present" to avoid possible conflict of interest.
?	Did not vote or otherwise make a position known.

Democrats   **Republicans**
Independents

	12	13	14	15	16	17	18
ALABAMA							
1 *Bonner*	Y	Y	Y	N	N	N	N
2 *Everett*	Y	Y	Y	N	N	N	N
3 *Rogers*	Y	Y	Y	N	N	N	N
4 *Aderholt*	Y	Y	Y	N	N	N	N
5 Cramer	Y	Y	Y	N	N	N	Y
6 *Bachus*	Y	Y	Y	N	N	N	N
7 Davis	Y	Y	Y	Y	Y	Y	Y
ALASKA							
AL *Young*	Y	Y	Y	N	N	N	N
ARIZONA							
1 *Renzi*	Y	Y	Y	N	N	N	N
2 *Franks*	Y	Y	Y	N	N	N	N
3 *Shadegg*	Y	Y	Y	N	N	N	N
4 Pastor	Y	Y	Y	Y	Y	Y	Y
5 *Hayworth*	Y	Y	Y	N	N	N	N
6 *Flake*	Y	Y	Y	N	N	N	N
7 Grijalva	?	?	?	Y	Y	Y	Y
8 *Kolbe*	Y	Y	Y	N	N	N	N
ARKANSAS							
1 Berry	Y	Y	Y	Y	N	Y	Y
2 Snyder	Y	Y	Y	Y	Y	Y	Y
3 *Boozman*	Y	Y	Y	N	N	N	N
4 Ross	Y	Y	Y	N	Y	Y	Y
CALIFORNIA							
1 Thompson	Y	Y	Y	Y	Y	Y	Y
2 *Herger*	Y	Y	Y	N	N	N	N
3 *Ose*	Y	Y	Y	N	N	N	N
4 *Doolittle*	Y	Y	Y	N	N	N	N
5 Matsui	Y	Y	Y	Y	Y	Y	Y
6 Woolsey	Y	Y	Y	Y	Y	Y	Y
7 Miller, George	Y	Y	Y	Y	Y	Y	Y
8 Pelosi	Y	Y	Y	Y	Y	Y	Y
9 Lee	Y	Y	P	Y	Y	Y	Y
10 Tauscher	Y	Y	Y	Y	Y	Y	Y
11 *Pombo*	?	?	?	N	N	N	N
12 Lantos	Y	Y	Y	Y	Y	Y	Y
13 Stark	?	?	?	Y	Y	Y	Y
14 Eshoo	?	?	?	Y	Y	Y	Y
15 Honda	?	?	?	Y	Y	Y	Y
16 Lofgren	Y	Y	Y	Y	Y	Y	Y
17 Farr	?	?	?	Y	Y	Y	Y
18 Cardoza	Y	Y	Y	N	Y	N	Y
19 *Radanovich*	Y	Y	Y	N	N	N	N
20 Dooley	?	?	?	Y	Y	Y	Y
21 *Nunes*	Y	Y	Y	N	N	N	N
22 *Thomas*	Y	Y	Y	N	N	N	N
23 Capps	Y	Y	Y	Y	Y	Y	Y
24 *Gallegly*	Y	Y	Y	N	N	N	N
25 *McKeon*	Y	Y	Y	N	N	N	N
26 *Dreier*	Y	Y	Y	N	N	N	N
27 Sherman	Y	Y	Y	Y	Y	Y	Y
28 Berman	Y	?	Y	Y	Y	Y	Y
29 Schiff	Y	Y	Y	Y	Y	Y	Y
30 Waxman	Y	Y	Y	Y	Y	Y	Y
31 Becerra	Y	Y	Y	Y	Y	Y	Y
32 Solis	Y	Y	Y	Y	Y	Y	Y
33 Watson	?	?	?	?	?	?	?
34 Roybal-Allard	Y	Y	Y	Y	Y	Y	Y
35 Waters	Y	Y	P	Y	Y	Y	Y
36 Harman	Y	Y	Y	Y	Y	Y	Y

	12	13	14	15	16	17	18
37 Millender-McD.	?	?	?	?	?	?	?
38 Napolitano	Y	Y	Y	Y	Y	Y	Y
39 Sánchez, Linda	Y	Y	Y	Y	Y	Y	Y
40 *Royce*	Y	Y	Y	N	N	N	N
41 *Lewis*	Y	Y	Y	N	N	N	N
42 *Miller, Gary*	Y	Y	Y	N	N	N	N
43 Baca	Y	Y	Y	Y	Y	Y	Y
44 *Calvert*	Y	Y	Y	N	N	N	Y
45 *Bono*	Y	Y	Y	N	N	N	N
46 *Rohrabacher*	Y	Y	Y	N	N	N	N
47 Sanchez, Lorotta	Y	Y	Y	Y	Y	Y	Y
48 *Cox*	?	?	?	N	N	N	N
49 *Issa*	Y	Y	Y	N	N	N	N
50 *Cunningham*	Y	Y	Y	N	N	N	N
51 Filner	Y	Y	Y	Y	Y	Y	Y
52 *Hunter*	Y	Y	Y	?	?	N	N
53 Davis	Y	Y	Y	Y	Y	Y	Y
COLORADO							
1 DeGette	?	?	?	?	?	?	?
2 Udall	Y	Y	Y	Y	Y	Y	Y
3 *McInnis*	Y	Y	Y	N	N	N	?
4 *Musgrave*	Y	Y	Y	N	N	N	N
5 *Hefley*	Y	Y	Y	N	N	N	N
6 *Tancredo*	Y	Y	Y	N	N	N	N
7 *Beauprez*	Y	Y	Y	N	N	N	N
CONNECTICUT							
1 Larson	Y	Y	Y	Y	Y	Y	Y
2 *Simmons*	Y	Y	Y	N	N	N	Y
3 DeLauro	Y	Y	Y	Y	Y	Y	Y
4 *Shays*	Y	Y	Y	Y	Y	Y	Y
5 *Johnson*	Y	Y	Y	N	N	N	N
DELAWARE							
AL *Castle*	Y	Y	Y	N	N	N	N
FLORIDA							
1 *Miller, J.*	Y	Y	Y	N	N	N	N
2 Boyd	Y	Y	Y	Y	N	Y	Y
3 Brown	Y	Y	P	Y	Y	Y	Y
4 *Crenshaw*	Y	Y	Y	N	N	N	N
5 *Brown-Waite*	?	?	?	?	?	?	?
6 *Stearns*	Y	Y	Y	N	N	N	N
7 *Mica*	Y	Y	Y	N	N	N	N
8 *Keller*	Y	Y	Y	N	N	N	N
9 *Bilirakis*	Y	Y	Y	N	N	N	N
10 *Young*	Y	Y	Y	N	N	N	N
11 Davis	Y	Y	Y	Y	Y	Y	Y
12 *Putnam*	Y	Y	Y	N	N	N	N
13 *Harris*	Y	Y	Y	N	N	N	N
14 *Goss*	Y	Y	Y	N	N	N	—
15 *Weldon*	Y	Y	Y	N	N	N	N
16 *Foley*	Y	Y	Y	N	N	N	N
17 Meek	Y	Y	Y	Y	Y	Y	Y
18 *Ros-Lehtinen*	Y	Y	Y	N	N	N	N
19 Wexler	Y	Y	Y	Y	Y	Y	Y
20 Deutsch	Y	Y	Y	Y	Y	Y	Y
21 *Diaz-Balart, L.*	Y	Y	Y	N	N	N	N
22 *Shaw*	Y	Y	Y	N	N	N	N
23 Hastings	Y	Y	Y	Y	Y	Y	Y
24 *Feeney*	Y	Y	Y	N	N	N	N
25 *Diaz-Balart, M.*	Y	Y	Y	N	N	N	N
GEORGIA							
1 *Kingston*	Y	Y	Y	N	N	N	N
2 Bishop	Y	Y	Y	Y	Y	Y	Y
3 Marshall	Y	Y	Y	N	Y	Y	Y
4 Majette	Y	Y	Y	Y	Y	Y	Y
5 Lewis	Y	Y	Y	Y	Y	Y	Y
6 *Isakson*	Y	Y	Y	N	N	N	N
7 *Linder*	Y	Y	Y	?	?	?	?
8 *Collins*	Y	Y	Y	N	N	N	N
9 *Norwood*	Y	Y	Y	N	N	N	N
10 *Deal*	Y	Y	Y	N	N	N	N
11 *Gingrey*	Y	Y	Y	N	N	N	N
12 *Burns*	Y	Y	Y	N	N	N	Y
13 Scott	Y	Y	Y	Y	Y	Y	Y
HAWAII							
1 Abercrombie	Y	Y	Y	Y	Y	Y	Y
2 Case	Y	Y	Y	Y	Y	Y	Y
IDAHO							
1 *Otter*	Y	Y	Y	N	N	N	N
2 *Simpson*	Y	Y	Y	N	N	N	N
ILLINOIS							
1 Rush	Y	Y	Y	Y	Y	Y	Y
2 Jackson	Y	Y	Y	Y	Y	Y	Y
3 Lipinski	Y	Y	Y	N	N	N	?
4 Gutierrez	?	?	?	?	?	?	?
5 Emanuel	Y	Y	Y	Y	Y	Y	Y
6 *Hyde*	Y	Y	Y	N	N	N	N

ND Northern Democrats   SD Southern Democrats

	12	13	14	15	16	17	18
7 Davis	Y	Y	Y	Y	Y	Y	Y
8 ***Crane***	Y	Y	Y	N	N	N	N
9 Schakowsky	Y	Y	Y	Y	Y	Y	Y
10 ***Kirk***	Y	Y	Y	Y	N	Y	N
11 ***Weller***	Y	Y	Y	N	N	N	N
12 Costello	Y	Y	Y	Y	Y	Y	Y
13 ***Biggert***	Y	Y	Y	N	N	N	N
14 ***Hastert***							N
15 ***Johnson***	Y	Y	Y	N	N	N	Y
16 ***Manzullo***	Y	Y	Y	N	N	N	N
17 Evans	Y	Y	Y	Y	Y	Y	Y
18 ***LaHood***	Y	Y	Y	N	N	N	N
19 ***Shimkus***	Y	Y	Y	N	N	N	Y
INDIANA							
1 Visclosky	Y	Y	Y	Y	Y	Y	Y
2 ***Chocola***	Y	Y	Y	N	N	N	N
3 ***Souder***	Y	Y	Y	N	N	N	N
4 ***Buyer***	Y	Y	Y	N	N	N	N
5 ***Burton***	Y	Y	Y	N	N	N	N
6 ***Pence***	Y	Y	Y	N	N	N	N
7 Carson	Y	Y	Y	Y	Y	Y	Y
8 ***Hostettler***	Y	Y	Y	N	N	N	N
9 Hill	Y	Y	Y	Y	Y	Y	Y
IOWA							
1 ***Nussle***	Y	Y	Y	N	N	N	N
2 ***Leach***	Y	Y	Y	Y	Y	Y	Y
3 Boswell	Y	Y	Y	Y	Y	Y	Y
4 ***Latham***	Y	Y	Y	N	N	N	N
5 ***King***	Y	Y	Y	N	N	N	N
KANSAS							
1 ***Moran***	Y	Y	Y	N	N	N	N
2 ***Ryun***	?	?	?	N	N	N	N
3 Moore	Y	Y	Y	Y	Y	Y	Y
4 ***Tiahrt***	Y	Y	Y	N	N	N	N
KENTUCKY							
1 ***Whitfield***	Y	Y	Y	N	N	N	N
2 ***Lewis***	Y	Y	Y	N	N	N	N
3 ***Northup***	Y	Y	Y	N	N	N	N
4 Lucas	Y	Y	Y	N	N	N	Y
5 ***Rogers***	Y	Y	Y	N	N	N	N
6 Vacant							
LOUISIANA							
1 ***Vitter***	Y	Y	Y	N	N	N	N
2 Jefferson	Y	Y	Y	Y	Y	Y	Y
3 ***Tauzin***	?	Y	Y	N	N	N	N
4 ***McCrery***	?	?	?	?	?	?	?
5 Alexander	Y	Y	Y	N	Y	Y	Y
6 ***Baker***	Y	Y	Y	N	N	N	N
7 John	Y	Y	Y	Y	Y	Y	Y
MAINE							
1 Allen	Y	Y	Y	Y	Y	Y	Y
2 Michaud	Y	Y	Y	Y	Y	Y	Y
MARYLAND							
1 ***Gilchrest***	Y	Y	Y	N	N	N	N
2 Ruppersberger	Y	Y	Y	Y	Y	Y	?
3 Cardin	Y	Y	Y	Y	Y	Y	Y
4 Wynn	?	?	?	Y	Y	Y	Y
5 Hoyer	Y	Y	Y	Y	Y	Y	Y
6 ***Bartlett***	Y	Y	Y	N	N	N	N
7 Cummings	Y	Y	Y	Y	Y	Y	Y
8 Van Hollen	Y	Y	Y	Y	Y	Y	Y
MASSACHUSETTS							
1 Olver	Y	Y	Y	Y	Y	Y	Y
2 Neal	Y	Y	Y	Y	Y	Y	Y
3 McGovern	Y	Y	Y	Y	Y	Y	Y
4 Frank	Y	Y	Y	Y	Y	Y	Y
5 Meehan	Y	Y	Y	Y	Y	Y	Y
6 Tierney	Y	Y	Y	Y	Y	Y	Y
7 Markey	Y	Y	Y	Y	Y	Y	Y
8 Capuano	Y	Y	Y	Y	Y	Y	Y
9 Lynch	Y	Y	Y	Y	Y	Y	Y
10 Delahunt	Y	Y	Y	Y	Y	Y	Y
MICHIGAN							
1 Stupak	Y	Y	Y	Y	Y	Y	Y
2 ***Hoekstra***	Y	Y	Y	N	N	N	N
3 ***Ehlers***	Y	Y	Y	N	N	N	N
4 ***Camp***	Y	Y	Y	N	N	N	Y
5 Kildee	Y	Y	Y	Y	Y	Y	Y
6 ***Upton***	Y	Y	Y	N	N	N	Y
7 ***Smith***	Y	Y	Y	N	N	N	N
8 ***Rogers***	Y	Y	Y	N	N	N	Y
9 ***Knollenberg***	Y	Y	Y	N	N	N	N
10 ***Miller***	Y	Y	Y	N	N	N	N
11 ***McCotter***	Y	Y	Y	N	N	N	Y
12 Levin	Y	Y	Y	Y	Y	Y	Y

	12	13	14	15	16	17	18
13 Kilpatrick	Y	Y	Y	Y	Y	Y	Y
14 Conyers	?	Y	?	Y	Y	Y	?
15 Dingell	Y	Y	Y	Y	Y	Y	Y
MINNESOTA							
1 ***Gutknecht***	Y	Y	Y	N	N	N	N
2 ***Kline***	Y	Y	Y	N	N	N	N
3 ***Ramstad***	Y	Y	Y	N	N	N	N
4 McCollum	Y	Y	Y	Y	Y	Y	Y
5 Sabo	Y	Y	Y	?	?	Y	Y
6 ***Kennedy***	Y	Y	Y	N	N	N	N
7 Peterson	Y	Y	Y	Y	N	Y	Y
8 Oberstar	Y	Y	Y	Y	Y	Y	Y
MISSISSIPPI							
1 ***Wicker***	Y	Y	Y	N	N	N	N
2 Thompson	Y	Y	Y	Y	Y	Y	Y
3 ***Pickering***	Y	Y	Y	N	N	N	N
4 Taylor	Y	Y	Y	N	N	N	Y
MISSOURI							
1 Clay	?	?	?	Y	Y	Y	Y
2 ***Akin***	Y	Y	Y	N	N	N	N
3 Gephardt	?	?	?	?	?	?	?
4 Skelton	Y	Y	Y	N	Y	N	Y
5 McCarthy	Y	Y	Y	Y	Y	Y	+
6 ***Graves***	Y	Y	Y	N	N	N	N
7 ***Blunt***	Y	Y	Y	N	N	N	N
8 ***Emerson***	Y	Y	Y	N	N	N	Y
9 ***Hulshof***	Y	Y	Y	N	N	N	N
MONTANA							
AL ***Rehberg***	Y	Y	Y	N	N	N	N
NEBRASKA							
1 ***Bereuter***	Y	Y	?	N	N	N	N
2 ***Terry***	Y	Y	Y	N	N	N	N
3 ***Osborne***	Y	Y	Y	N	N	N	N
NEVADA							
1 Berkley	Y	Y	Y	Y	Y	Y	Y
2 ***Gibbons***	Y	Y	Y	N	N	N	N
3 ***Porter***	Y	Y	Y	N	N	N	N
NEW HAMPSHIRE							
1 ***Bradley***	Y	Y	Y	N	N	N	N
2 ***Bass***	Y	Y	Y	N	N	N	N
NEW JERSEY							
1 Andrews	Y	Y	Y	Y	Y	Y	Y
2 ***LoBiondo***	Y	Y	Y	N	N	N	Y
3 ***Saxton***	Y	Y	Y	N	N	N	Y
4 ***Smith***	Y	Y	Y	N	N	N	Y
5 ***Garrett***	Y	Y	Y	N	N	N	N
6 Pallone	Y	Y	Y	Y	Y	Y	Y
7 ***Ferguson***	Y	Y	Y	N	N	N	N
8 Pascrell	Y	Y	Y	+	+	+	+
9 Rothman	Y	Y	Y	Y	Y	Y	Y
10 Payne	Y	Y	Y	Y	Y	Y	Y
11 ***Frelinghuysen***	Y	Y	Y	N	N	N	N
12 Holt	Y	Y	Y	Y	Y	Y	Y
13 Menendez	Y	Y	Y	Y	Y	Y	Y
NEW MEXICO							
1 ***Wilson***	Y	Y	Y	N	N	N	Y
2 ***Pearce***	Y	Y	Y	N	N	N	N
3 Udall	Y	Y	Y	Y	Y	Y	Y
NEW YORK							
1 Bishop	Y	Y	Y	Y	Y	Y	Y
2 Israel	Y	Y	Y	Y	Y	Y	Y
3 ***King***	Y	Y	Y	N	N	N	Y
4 McCarthy	Y	Y	Y	Y	Y	Y	Y
5 Ackerman	Y	Y	Y	Y	Y	Y	Y
6 Meeks	Y	Y	Y	Y	Y	Y	Y
7 Crowley	Y	Y	Y	Y	Y	Y	Y
8 Nadler	Y	Y	Y	Y	Y	Y	Y
9 Weiner	Y	Y	Y	Y	Y	Y	Y
10 Towns	Y	Y	Y	Y	Y	Y	Y
11 Owens	Y	Y	Y	Y	Y	Y	Y
12 Velázquez	Y	Y	Y	Y	Y	Y	Y
13 ***Fossella***	Y	Y	Y	N	N	N	Y
14 Maloney	Y	Y	Y	Y	Y	Y	Y
15 Rangel	Y	Y	Y	Y	Y	Y	Y
16 Serrano	Y	Y	Y	Y	Y	Y	Y
17 Engel	Y	Y	Y	Y	Y	Y	Y
18 Lowey	Y	Y	Y	Y	Y	Y	Y
19 ***Kelly***	Y	Y	Y	N	N	N	Y
20 ***Sweeney***	Y	Y	Y	N	N	N	Y
21 McNulty	Y	Y	Y	Y	Y	Y	Y
22 Hinchey	Y	Y	Y	Y	Y	Y	Y
23 ***McHugh***	Y	Y	Y	N	N	N	+
24 ***Boehlert***	Y	Y	Y	N	N	N	Y
25 ***Walsh***	Y	Y	Y	N	N	N	Y

	12	13	14	15	16	17	18
26 ***Reynolds***	Y	Y	Y	N	N	N	N
27 ***Quinn***	Y	Y	Y	N	N	N	Y
28 Slaughter	Y	Y	Y	Y	Y	Y	Y
29 ***Houghton***	Y	Y	Y	N	N	N	N
NORTH CAROLINA							
1 Ballance	Y	Y	Y	Y	Y	Y	Y
2 Etheridge	+	Y	Y	Y	Y	Y	Y
3 ***Jones***	Y	Y	Y	N	N	N	Y
4 Price	Y	Y	Y	Y	Y	Y	Y
5 ***Burr***	Y	Y	Y	N	N	N	Y
6 ***Coble***	Y	Y	Y	N	N	N	N
7 McIntyre	Y	Y	Y	N	N	N	Y
8 ***Hayes***	Y	Y	Y	N	N	N	Y
9 ***Myrick***	?	?	?	N	N	N	N
10 ***Ballenger***	Y	Y	Y	N	N	N	N
11 ***Taylor***	Y	Y	Y	N	N	N	Y
12 Watt	Y	Y	P	Y	Y	Y	Y
13 Miller	Y	Y	Y	Y	Y	Y	Y
NORTH DAKOTA							
AL Pomeroy	Y	Y	Y	Y	Y	Y	Y
OHIO							
1 ***Chabot***	Y	Y	Y	N	N	N	N
2 ***Portman***	Y	Y	Y	N	N	N	N
3 ***Turner***	Y	Y	Y	N	N	N	Y
4 ***Oxley***	Y	Y	Y	N	N	N	N
5 ***Gillmor***	Y	Y	Y	N	N	N	N
6 Strickland	Y	Y	Y	Y	Y	Y	Y
7 ***Hobson***	Y	Y	Y	N	N	N	N
8 ***Boehner***	Y	Y	Y	N	N	N	N
9 Kaptur	Y	Y	Y	Y	Y	Y	Y
10 Kucinich	?	?	?	?	?	?	?
11 Jones	Y	Y	Y	Y	Y	Y	Y
12 ***Tiberi***	Y	Y	Y	N	N	N	N
13 Brown	Y	Y	Y	Y	Y	Y	Y
14 ***LaTourette***	Y	Y	Y	N	N	N	Y
15 ***Pryce***	Y	Y	Y	N	N	N	N
16 ***Regula***	Y	Y	Y	N	N	N	N
17 Ryan	?	Y	Y	Y	Y	Y	Y
18 ***Ney***	Y	Y	Y	N	N	N	Y
OKLAHOMA							
1 ***Sullivan***	Y	Y	Y	N	N	N	N
2 Carson	Y	Y	Y	Y	Y	Y	Y
3 ***Lucas***	?	?	?	?	?	?	?
4 ***Cole***	Y	Y	Y	N	N	N	N
5 ***Istook***	Y	?	Y	N	N	N	N
OREGON							
1 Wu	Y	Y	Y	Y	Y	Y	Y
2 ***Walden***	Y	Y	Y	N	N	N	Y
3 Blumenauer	Y	Y	Y	Y	Y	Y	Y
4 DeFazio	Y	Y	Y	Y	Y	Y	Y
5 Hooley	Y	Y	Y	Y	Y	Y	Y
PENNSYLVANIA							
1 Brady	Y	Y	Y	Y	Y	Y	Y
2 Fattah	Y	Y	?	Y	Y	Y	Y
3 ***English***	+	+	+	N	N	N	Y
4 ***Hart***	Y	Y	Y	N	N	N	N
5 ***Peterson***	Y	Y	Y	N	N	N	Y
6 ***Gerlach***	Y	Y	Y	N	N	N	N
7 ***Weldon***	Y	Y	Y	N	N	N	Y
8 ***Greenwood***	Y	Y	Y	N	N	N	N
9 ***Shuster, Bill***	Y	Y	Y	N	N	N	N
10 ***Sherwood***	Y	Y	Y	N	N	N	N
11 Kanjorski	Y	Y	Y	Y	Y	Y	Y
12 Murtha	Y	Y	Y	Y	Y	Y	Y
13 Hoeffel	Y	Y	Y	Y	Y	Y	Y
14 Doyle	Y	Y	Y	Y	Y	Y	Y
15 ***Toomey***	Y	Y	Y	N	N	N	N
16 ***Pitts***	Y	Y	Y	N	N	N	N
17 Holden	Y	Y	Y	Y	Y	Y	Y
18 ***Murphy***	Y	Y	Y	N	N	N	Y
19 ***Platts***	Y	Y	Y	N	N	N	N
RHODE ISLAND							
1 Kennedy	Y	Y	Y	Y	Y	Y	Y
2 Langevin	?	?	?	?	?	?	?
SOUTH CAROLINA							
1 ***Brown***	Y	Y	Y	N	N	N	N
2 ***Wilson***	Y	Y	Y	N	N	N	N
3 ***Barrett***	Y	Y	Y	N	N	N	N
4 ***DeMint***	Y	Y	Y	N	N	N	N
5 Spratt	Y	Y	Y	Y	Y	Y	Y
6 Clyburn	?	?	?	Y	Y	Y	Y
SOUTH DAKOTA							
AL Vacant							

	12	13	14	15	16	17	18
TENNESSEE							
1 ***Jenkins***	Y	Y	Y	N	N	N	N
2 ***Duncan***	Y	Y	Y	N	N	N	N
3 ***Wamp***	Y	Y	Y	N	N	N	N
4 Davis	Y	Y	Y	N	N	N	Y
5 Cooper	Y	Y	Y	N	N	N	Y
6 Gordon	Y	Y	Y	N	N	N	Y
7 ***Blackburn***	Y	Y	Y	N	N	N	N
8 Tanner	Y	Y	Y	Y	Y	Y	Y
9 Ford	Y	Y	Y	Y	Y	Y	Y
TEXAS							
1 Sandlin	Y	Y	Y	Y	Y	Y	Y
2 Turner	Y	Y	Y	Y	Y	Y	Y
3 ***Johnson, Sam***	Y	Y	Y	N	N	N	N
4 ***Hall***	Y	Y	Y	N	N	N	N
5 ***Hensarling***	Y	Y	Y	N	N	N	N
6 ***Barton***	Y	Y	Y	N	N	N	N
7 ***Culberson***	?	?	?	?	?	?	?
8 ***Brady***	Y	Y	Y	N	N	N	N
9 Lampson	Y	Y	Y	Y	Y	Y	Y
10 Doggett	Y	Y	Y	Y	Y	Y	Y
11 Edwards	Y	Y	Y	Y	Y	Y	Y
12 ***Granger***	Y	Y	Y	N	N	N	?
13 ***Thornberry***	Y	Y	Y	N	N	N	N
14 ***Paul***	Y	Y	Y	N	N	N	N
15 Hinojosa	+	Y	Y	Y	Y	Y	Y
16 Reyes	Y	Y	Y	Y	Y	Y	Y
17 Stenholm	Y	Y	Y	Y	N	Y	Y
18 Jackson-Lee	Y	Y	Y	Y	Y	Y	Y
19 ***Neugebauer***	Y	Y	Y	N	N	N	N
20 Gonzalez	Y	Y	Y	Y	Y	Y	Y
21 ***Smith***	Y	Y	Y	N	N	N	N
22 ***DeLay***	Y	Y	Y	N	N	N	N
23 ***Bonilla***	Y	Y	Y	N	N	N	N
24 Frost	Y	Y	Y	Y	Y	Y	Y
25 Bell	Y	Y	Y	Y	Y	Y	Y
26 ***Burgess***	Y	Y	Y	N	N	N	N
27 Ortiz	?	?	?	?	?	?	?
28 Rodriguez	Y	Y	Y	Y	Y	Y	Y
29 Green	Y	Y	Y	Y	Y	Y	Y
30 Johnson, E.B.	Y	Y	P	Y	Y	Y	Y
31 ***Carter***	Y	Y	Y	N	N	N	N
32 ***Sessions***	Y	?	Y	N	N	N	N
UTAH							
1 ***Bishop***	Y	Y	Y	N	N	N	N
2 Matheson	Y	Y	Y	Y	Y	Y	Y
3 ***Cannon***	Y	Y	Y	N	N	N	N
VERMONT							
AL *Sanders*	Y	Y	Y	Y	Y	Y	Y
VIRGINIA							
1 ***Davis, Jo Ann***	Y	Y	Y	N	N	N	N
2 ***Schrock***	Y	Y	Y	N	N	N	N
3 Scott	Y	Y	Y	Y	Y	Y	Y
4 ***Forbes***	Y	Y	Y	N	N	N	N
5 ***Goode***	Y	Y	Y	N	N	N	Y
6 ***Goodlatte***	Y	Y	Y	N	N	N	N
7 ***Cantor***	Y	Y	Y	N	N	N	N
8 Moran	Y	Y	Y	Y	Y	Y	Y
9 Boucher	Y	Y	Y	Y	Y	Y	Y
10 ***Wolf***	Y	Y	Y	N	N	N	N
11 ***Davis, T.***	Y	Y	Y	N	N	N	N
WASHINGTON							
1 Inslee	?	?	?	Y	Y	Y	Y
2 Larsen	Y	Y	Y	Y	Y	Y	Y
3 Baird	Y	Y	Y	Y	N	Y	Y
4 ***Hastings***	Y	Y	Y	N	N	N	N
5 ***Nethercutt***	Y	Y	Y	N	N	N	N
6 Dicks	?	?	?	?	?	?	?
7 McDermott	Y	Y	Y	Y	Y	Y	Y
8 ***Dunn***	Y	Y	Y	N	N	N	N
9 Smith	?	?	?	?	?	?	?
WEST VIRGINIA							
1 Mollohan	Y	Y	Y	Y	N	N	Y
2 ***Capito***	Y	Y	Y	N	N	N	Y
3 Rahall	?	?	?	?	?	?	?
WISCONSIN							
1 ***Ryan***	Y	?	Y	N	N	N	N
2 Baldwin	Y	Y	Y	Y	Y	Y	Y
3 Kind	Y	Y	Y	Y	Y	Y	Y
4 Kleczka	Y	Y	Y	Y	Y	Y	Y
5 ***Sensenbrenner***	Y	Y	Y	N	N	N	N
6 ***Petri***	Y	Y	Y	N	N	N	N
7 Obey	Y	Y	Y	Y	Y	Y	Y
8 ***Green***	Y	Y	Y	N	N	N	Y
WYOMING							
AL ***Cubin***	Y	Y	Y	N	N	N	N

Southern states - Ala., Ark., Fla., Ga., Ky., La., Miss., N.C., Okla., S.C., Tenn., Texas, Va.

19. H Con Res 358. History of the Capitol/Adoption. Mica, R-Fla., motion to suspend the rules and adopt the concurrent resolution that would authorize the printing of "History of the United States Capitol" as a House document. Motion agreed to 402-1: R 219-1; D 182-0 (ND 131-0, SD 51-0); I 1-0. A two-thirds majority of those present and voting (269 in this case) is required for adoption under suspension of the rules. Feb. 10, 2004.

20. H Con Res 359. Holocaust Remembrance/Adoption. Mica, R-Fla., motion to suspend the rules and adopt the concurrent resolution that would authorize the use of the Capitol Rotunda for a ceremony on April 22, 2004, as part of the commemoration of the days of remembrance of victims of the Holocaust. Motion agreed to 402-0: R 217-0; D 184-0 (ND 133-0, SD 51-0); I 1-0. A two-thirds majority of those present and voting (268 in this case) is required for adoption under suspension of the rules. Feb. 10, 2004.

21. H Con Res 264. Constantino Brumidi Tribute/Adoption. Mica, R-Fla., motion to suspend the rules and adopt the concurrent resolution that would authorize and request that the president issue a proclamation to commemorate the 200th anniversary of the birth of Constantino Brumidi, who spent more than 25 years of his life painting and decorating the Capitol. Motion agreed to 404-0: R 218-0; D 185-0 (ND 133-0, SD 52-0); I 1-0. A two-thirds majority of those present and voting (270 in this case) is required for adoption under suspension of the rules. Feb. 10, 2004.

22. HR 743. Social Security Fraud/Previous Question. Linder, R-Ga., motion to order the previous question (thus ending debate and possibility of amendment) on adoption of the rule (H Res 520) to provide for House floor consideration of the motion to concur with the Senate amendments to the bill that would require the Social Security Administration to re-issue benefits when a "representative payee" misuses funds. Motion agreed to 226-197: R 225-1; D 1-195 (ND 1-141, SD 0-54); I 0-1. Feb. 11, 2004.

23. HR 743. Social Security Fraud/Concur with Senate Amendments. Shaw, R-Fla., motion to concur with the Senate amendments to the bill that would require the Social Security Administration to re-issue benefits when a "representative payee" misuses funds. It also would require state or local government employees to work in a job that pays into Social Security for five years before they could qualify for an exemption under the government pension offset. Illegal immigrants would not be able to collect Social Security benefits for the time they worked in the country illegally unless they were later granted legal status. Motion agreed to, 402-19: R 221-4; D 180-15 (ND 140-1, SD 40-14); I 1-0. Feb. 11, 2004.

24. HR 3783. Highway Funds Extension/Passage. Young, R-Alaska, motion to suspend the rules and pass the bill that would extend funding for highway, transit and transportation safety programs for an additional four months, through June 30, 2004. Funding was originally set to expire Oct. 1, 2003, but Congress enacted a five-month extension through Feb. 29, 2004. The measure includes $25.2 billion in contract authority for federal-aid highway programs. Motion agreed to 421-0: R 224-0; D 196-0 (ND 141-0, SD 55-0); I 1-0. A two-thirds majority of those present and voting (281 in this case) is required for passage under suspension of the rules. Feb. 11, 2004.

Key

Y	Voted for (yea).
#	Paired for.
+	Announced for.
N	Voted against (nay).
X	Paired against.
–	Announced against.
P	Voted "present."
C	Voted "present" to avoid possible conflict of interest.
?	Did not vote or otherwise make a position known.

Democrats **Republicans**
Independents

		19	20	21	22	23	24
ALABAMA							
1	*Bonner*	Y	Y	Y	Y	Y	Y
2	*Everett*	Y	Y	Y	Y	Y	Y
3	*Rogers*	Y	Y	Y	Y	Y	Y
4	*Aderholt*	Y	Y	Y	Y	Y	Y
5	Cramer	Y	Y	Y	N	Y	Y
6	*Bachus*	Y	Y	Y	Y	Y	Y
7	Davis	Y	Y	Y	N	Y	Y
ALASKA							
AL	*Young*	Y	Y	Y	Y	Y	Y
ARIZONA							
1	*Renzi*	Y	Y	Y	Y	Y	?
2	*Franks*	Y	Y	Y	Y	Y	Y
3	*Shadegg*	Y	Y	Y	Y	Y	Y
4	Pastor	Y	Y	Y	N	Y	Y
5	*Hayworth*	Y	Y	Y	Y	Y	Y
6	*Flake*	Y	Y	Y	Y	Y	Y
7	Grijalva	Y	Y	Y	N	Y	Y
8	*Kolbe*	Y	Y	Y	Y	Y	Y
ARKANSAS							
1	Berry	Y	Y	Y	N	Y	Y
2	Snyder	Y	Y	Y	N	Y	Y
3	*Boozman*	Y	Y	Y	Y	Y	Y
4	Ross	Y	Y	Y	N	Y	Y
CALIFORNIA							
1	Thompson	Y	Y	Y	N	Y	Y
2	*Herger*	Y	Y	Y	Y	Y	Y
3	*Ose*	N	Y	Y	Y	Y	Y
4	*Doolittle*	Y	Y	Y	Y	Y	Y
5	Matsui	Y	Y	Y	N	Y	Y
6	Woolsey	Y	Y	Y	N	Y	Y
7	Miller, George	Y	Y	Y	N	Y	Y
8	Pelosi	Y	Y	Y	N	Y	Y
9	Lee	Y	Y	Y	N	Y	Y
10	Tauscher	Y	Y	Y	N	Y	Y
11	*Pombo*	Y	Y	Y	N	Y	Y
12	Lantos	Y	Y	Y	N	Y	Y
13	Stark	?	?	?	N	Y	Y
14	Eshoo	?	Y	Y	N	Y	Y
15	Honda	?	?	?	?	?	?
16	Lofgren	Y	Y	Y	N	Y	Y
17	Farr	Y	Y	Y	N	Y	Y
18	Cardoza	Y	Y	Y	N	Y	Y
19	*Radanovich*	Y	Y	?	Y	Y	Y
20	Dooley	Y	Y	Y	N	Y	Y
21	*Nunes*	Y	Y	Y	Y	Y	Y
22	*Thomas*	Y	Y	Y	N	Y	Y
23	Capps	Y	Y	Y	N	Y	Y
24	*Gallegly*	Y	Y	Y	Y	Y	Y
25	*McKeon*	Y	Y	Y	Y	Y	Y
26	*Dreier*	Y	Y	Y	Y	Y	Y
27	Sherman	Y	Y	Y	N	Y	Y
28	Berman	Y	Y	Y	N	Y	Y
29	Schiff	Y	Y	Y	N	Y	Y
30	Waxman	Y	Y	Y	N	Y	Y
31	Becerra	Y	Y	Y	N	Y	Y
32	Solis	Y	Y	Y	N	+	+
33	Watson	?	?	?	?	?	?
34	Roybal-Allard	Y	Y	Y	N	Y	Y
35	Waters	Y	Y	Y	N	Y	Y
36	Harman	Y	Y	Y	N	Y	Y

		19	20	21	22	23	24
37	Millender-McD.	Y	Y	Y	N	Y	Y
38	Napolitano	Y	Y	Y	N	Y	Y
39	Sánchez, Linda	Y	Y	Y	N	Y	Y
40	*Royce*	Y	Y	Y	Y	Y	Y
41	*Lewis*	Y	Y	Y	Y	Y	Y
42	*Miller, Gary*	Y	Y	Y	Y	Y	Y
43	Baca	Y	Y	Y	N	Y	Y
44	*Calvert*	Y	Y	Y	Y	Y	Y
45	*Bono*	Y	Y	Y	Y	Y	Y
46	*Rohrabacher*	Y	Y	Y	Y	Y	Y
47	Sanchez, Loretta	Y	Y	Y	N	Y	Y
48	*Cox*	Y	?	Y	Y	Y	Y
49	*Issa*	Y	Y	Y	Y	Y	Y
50	*Cunningham*	Y	Y	Y	Y	Y	Y
51	Filner	Y	Y	Y	–	Y	Y
52	*Hunter*	Y	Y	Y	Y	Y	Y
53	Davis	Y	Y	Y	N	Y	Y
COLORADO							
1	DeGette	?	?	?	?	?	?
2	Udall	Y	Y	Y	N	Y	Y
3	*McInnis*	Y	Y	Y	Y	Y	Y
4	*Musgrave*	Y	Y	Y	Y	Y	Y
5	*Hefley*	Y	Y	Y	Y	Y	Y
6	*Tancredo*	Y	Y	Y	Y	Y	Y
7	*Beauprez*	Y	Y	Y	Y	Y	Y
CONNECTICUT							
1	Larson	Y	Y	Y	N	Y	Y
2	*Simmons*	Y	Y	Y	Y	Y	Y
3	DeLauro	Y	Y	Y	N	Y	Y
4	*Shays*	Y	Y	Y	Y	Y	Y
5	*Johnson*	Y	Y	Y	Y	Y	Y
DELAWARE							
AL	*Castle*	Y	Y	Y	Y	Y	Y
FLORIDA							
1	*Miller, J.*	Y	Y	Y	Y	Y	Y
2	Boyd	?	?	?	N	Y	Y
3	Brown	Y	Y	Y	N	Y	Y
4	*Crenshaw*	Y	Y	Y	Y	Y	Y
5	*Brown-Waite*	Y	Y	Y	Y	Y	Y
6	*Stearns*	Y	Y	Y	Y	Y	Y
7	*Mica*	Y	Y	Y	Y	Y	Y
8	*Keller*	Y	?	Y	Y	Y	Y
9	*Bilirakis*	Y	Y	Y	Y	Y	Y
10	*Young*	?	?	?	?	Y	Y
11	Davis	Y	Y	Y	N	Y	Y
12	*Putnam*	Y	Y	Y	Y	Y	Y
13	*Harris*	Y	Y	Y	Y	Y	Y
14	*Goss*	Y	Y	Y	Y	Y	Y
15	*Weldon*	Y	Y	Y	Y	Y	Y
16	*Foley*	Y	Y	Y	Y	Y	Y
17	Meek	Y	Y	Y	N	Y	Y
18	*Ros-Lehtinen*	Y	Y	Y	Y	Y	Y
19	Wexler	Y	Y	Y	N	Y	Y
20	Deutsch	Y	Y	Y	N	Y	Y
21	*Diaz-Balart, L.*	Y	Y	Y	Y	Y	Y
22	*Shaw*	Y	Y	Y	Y	Y	Y
23	Hastings	Y	Y	Y	N	Y	Y
24	*Feeney*	Y	Y	Y	Y	Y	Y
25	*Diaz-Balart, M.*	Y	Y	Y	Y	?	?
GEORGIA							
1	*Kingston*	Y	Y	Y	Y	Y	Y
2	Bishop	Y	Y	Y	N	Y	Y
3	Marshall	Y	Y	Y	N	Y	Y
4	Majette	Y	Y	Y	N	Y	Y
5	Lewis	Y	Y	Y	N	Y	Y
6	*Isakson*	Y	Y	Y	Y	Y	Y
7	*Linder*	Y	Y	Y	Y	Y	?
8	*Collins*	Y	Y	Y	Y	Y	Y
9	*Norwood*	Y	Y	Y	Y	Y	Y
10	*Deal*	Y	Y	Y	Y	Y	Y
11	*Gingrey*	Y	Y	Y	Y	Y	Y
12	*Burns*	Y	Y	Y	Y	Y	Y
13	Scott	Y	Y	Y	N	Y	Y
HAWAII							
1	Abercrombie	Y	Y	Y	N	Y	Y
2	Case	Y	Y	Y	N	Y	Y
IDAHO							
1	*Otter*	Y	Y	Y	Y	Y	Y
2	*Simpson*	Y	Y	Y	Y	Y	Y
ILLINOIS							
1	Rush	Y	Y	Y	N	Y	Y
2	Jackson	Y	Y	Y	N	Y	Y
3	Lipinski	Y	Y	Y	N	Y	Y
4	Gutierrez	Y	Y	Y	N	Y	Y
5	Emanuel	Y	Y	Y	N	Y	Y
6	*Hyde*	Y	Y	Y	Y	Y	Y

ND Northern Democrats SD Southern Democrats

Southern states - Ala., Ark., Fla., Ga., Ky., La., Miss., N.C., Okla., S.C., Tenn., Texas, Va.

Key

Y	Voted for (yea).
#	Paired for.
+	Announced for.
N	Voted against (nay).
X	Paired against.
–	Announced against.
P	Voted "present."
C	Voted "present" to avoid possible conflict of interest.
?	Did not vote or otherwise make a position known.

Democrats **Republicans**
Independents

---

25. Procedural Motion/Journal. Approval of the House Journal of Wednesday, Feb. 11, 2004. Approved 381-32: R 211-10; D 169-22 (ND 119-20, SD 50-2); I 1-0. Feb. 24, 2004.

26. HR 2707. Salt Cedar and Russian Olive Control/Passage. Pearce, R-N.M., motion to suspend the rules and pass the bill that would direct the Forest Service to create a trial program to control salt cedar and Russian olive trees in the western United States. The measure would authorize $5 million in fiscal 2005 for assessing ways to control the trees and $18 million annually in fiscal 2005 through fiscal 2009 to carry out demonstration projects. Motion agreed to 367-40: R 180-39; D 186-1 (ND 135-0, SD 51-1); I 1-0. A two-thirds majority of those present and voting (272 in this case) is required for passage under suspension of the rules. Feb. 24, 2004.

27. S 714. Oregon Land Conveyance/Passage. Renzi, R-Ariz., motion to suspend the rules and pass the bill that would authorize the Bureau of Land Management to convey, without costs, approximately 68.8 acres of land to Douglas County, Ore. The conveyance is intended to provide improved access to the Oregon Dunes National Recreational Area for off-road vehicles and other visitors. Motion agreed to 397-0: R 209-0; D 187-0 (ND 136-0, SD 51-0); I 1-0. A two-thirds majority of those present and voting (265 in this case) is required for passage under suspension of the rules. Feb. 24, 2004.

28. HR 2751. GAO Personnel Management/Passage. Passage of the bill that would provide the General Accounting Office (GAO) with additional discretion to manage its workforce, including tying employee raises to a minimum performance standard and making permanent the agency's authority to offer early retirement. The bill also would change the name of the agency to the Government Accountability Office. Passed 382-43: R 183-42; D 198-1 (ND 143-1, SD 55-0); I 1-0. Feb. 25, 2004.

29. H Con Res 287. Raul Julia Tribute/Adoption. Miller, R-Mich., motion to suspend the rules and adopt the concurrent resolution that would honor the late actor Raul Julia for his contributions to the performing arts and the Latino community as well as his commitment to ending world hunger. Motion agreed to 422-0: R 223-0; D 198-0 (ND 143-0, SD 55-0); I 1-0. A two-thirds majority of those present and voting (282 in this case) is required for adoption under suspension of the rules. Feb. 25, 2004.

30. HR 1997. Fetal Protection/Democratic Substitute. Lofgren, D-Calif., substitute amendment that would make assault on a pregnant woman a federal crime. Under the substitute, a perpetrator could be subject to up to 20 years' imprisonment for an assault causing pre-natal injury and up to life imprisonment for an assault causing termination of the pregnancy. Rejected 186-229: R 22-197; D 163-32 (ND 121-19, SD 42-13); I 1-0. Feb. 26, 2004.

31. HR 1997. Fetal Protection/Passage. Passage of the bill that would make it a criminal offense to injure or kill a fetus during the commission of a violent crime. The measure would establish criminal penalties, equal to those that would apply if the injury or death occurred to the pregnant woman, for those who harm a fetus, regardless of the perpetrator's knowledge of the pregnancy or intent to harm the fetus. The bill states that its provisions should not be interpreted to apply to consensual abortion or to a woman's actions with respect to her pregnancy. The death penalty could not be imposed under this bill. Passed 254-163: R 207-13; D 47-149 (ND 26-115, SD 21-34); I 0-1. A "yea" was a vote in support of the president's position. Feb. 26, 2004.

[1] Rep. Ben Chandler, D-Ky., was sworn in Feb. 24, 2004. The first vote for which he was eligible was vote 26.

		25	26	27	28	29	30	31
ALABAMA								
1	*Bonner*	Y	Y	Y	Y	Y	N	Y
2	*Everett*	Y	N	Y	Y	Y	N	Y
3	*Rogers*	Y	Y	Y	Y	Y	N	Y
4	*Aderholt*	N	Y	Y	Y	Y	N	Y
5	Cramer	Y	Y	Y	Y	Y	N	Y
6	*Bachus*	Y	Y	Y	Y	Y	N	Y
7	Davis	Y	Y	Y	Y	Y	Y	N
ALASKA								
AL	*Young*	Y	Y	Y	Y	Y	N	Y
ARIZONA								
1	*Renzi*	Y	Y	Y	Y	Y	N	Y
2	*Franks*	Y	N	Y	N	Y	N	Y
3	*Shadegg*	Y	Y	Y	N	?	N	Y
4	Pastor	Y	Y	Y	Y	Y	Y	N
5	*Hayworth*	Y	Y	Y	Y	Y	N	Y
6	*Flake*	Y	N	Y	N	Y	N	Y
7	Grijalva	Y	Y	Y	Y	Y	Y	N
8	*Kolbe*	Y	Y	Y	Y	Y	Y	N
ARKANSAS								
1	Berry	Y	Y	Y	Y	Y	N	Y
2	Snyder	Y	Y	Y	Y	Y	Y	N
3	*Boozman*	Y	Y	Y	Y	Y	N	Y
4	Ross	Y	Y	Y	Y	Y	Y	Y
CALIFORNIA								
1	Thompson	N	Y	Y	Y	Y	Y	N
2	*Herger*	Y	N	Y	Y	Y	N	Y
3	*Ose*	?	?	?	N	Y	Y	Y
4	*Doolittle*	Y	N	Y	Y	Y	N	Y
5	Matsui	Y	Y	Y	Y	Y	N	Y
6	Woolsey	Y	Y	Y	Y	Y	Y	N
7	Miller, George	Y	Y	Y	Y	Y	Y	N
8	Pelosi	Y	Y	Y	Y	Y	Y	N
9	Lee	Y	Y	Y	Y	Y	Y	N
10	Tauscher	Y	Y	Y	Y	Y	Y	N
11	*Pombo*	Y	Y	?	Y	Y	N	Y
12	Lantos	?	?	?	?	?	?	?
13	Stark	?	?	?	Y	Y	Y	N
14	Eshoo	Y	Y	Y	Y	Y	Y	N
15	Honda	?	?	?	?	?	?	?
16	Lofgren	Y	Y	Y	Y	Y	Y	N
17	Farr	Y	Y	Y	Y	Y	Y	N
18	Cardoza	Y	Y	Y	Y	Y	N	Y
19	*Radanovich*	Y	Y	Y	Y	Y	N	Y
20	Dooley	Y	Y	Y	Y	Y	N	Y
21	*Nunes*	Y	Y	Y	Y	Y	N	Y
22	*Thomas*	Y	Y	Y	Y	Y	N	Y
23	Capps	Y	Y	?	Y	Y	Y	N
24	*Gallegly*	Y	Y	Y	Y	Y	N	Y
25	*McKeon*	Y	Y	Y	Y	Y	N	Y
26	*Dreier*	Y	Y	?	Y	Y	N	Y
27	Sherman	Y	Y	Y	Y	Y	Y	N
28	Berman	Y	Y	Y	Y	Y	Y	N
29	Schiff	Y	Y	Y	Y	Y	Y	N
30	Waxman	Y	Y	Y	Y	Y	Y	N
31	Becerra	Y	Y	Y	Y	Y	Y	N
32	Solis	Y	Y	Y	Y	Y	Y	N
33	Watson	Y	Y	Y	Y	Y	Y	N
34	Roybal-Allard	Y	Y	Y	Y	Y	Y	N
35	Waters	N	Y	Y	Y	Y	Y	N
36	Harman	Y	Y	Y	Y	Y	N	Y

		25	26	27	28	29	30	31
37	Millender-McD.	Y	Y	Y	Y	Y	?	?
38	Napolitano	Y	Y	Y	Y	Y	Y	N
39	Sánchez, Linda	Y	Y	Y	Y	Y	Y	N
40	*Royce*	Y	N	Y	N	Y	N	Y
41	*Lewis*	Y	Y	Y	Y	Y	N	Y
42	*Miller, Gary*	Y	Y	Y	Y	Y	N	Y
43	Baca	Y	Y	Y	Y	Y	Y	N
44	*Calvert*	Y	Y	Y	Y	Y	N	Y
45	*Bono*	Y	Y	Y	Y	Y	N	Y
46	*Rohrabacher*	Y	N	Y	N	Y	N	Y
47	Sanchez, Loretta	Y	Y	Y	Y	Y	Y	N
48	*Cox*	Y	Y	?	Y	Y	N	Y
49	*Issa*	Y	Y	Y	Y	Y	N	Y
50	*Cunningham*	Y	Y	Y	Y	Y	N	Y
51	Filner	N	Y	N	Y	Y	Y	N
52	*Hunter*	Y	Y	Y	Y	Y	N	Y
53	Davis	Y	Y	Y	Y	Y	Y	N
COLORADO								
1	DeGette	Y	Y	Y	Y	Y	Y	N
2	Udall	Y	Y	Y	Y	Y	Y	N
3	*McInnis*	Y	Y	Y	Y	Y	?	?
4	*Musgrave*	Y	?	?	Y	Y	N	Y
5	*Hefley*	N	N	N	N	Y	N	Y
6	*Tancredo*	Y	N	Y	N	Y	N	Y
7	*Beauprez*	Y	Y	Y	Y	Y	N	Y
CONNECTICUT								
1	Larson	Y	Y	Y	Y	Y	Y	N
2	*Simmons*	Y	Y	Y	Y	Y	Y	N
3	DeLauro	Y	Y	Y	Y	Y	Y	N
4	*Shays*	Y	Y	Y	Y	Y	Y	N
5	*Johnson*	Y	Y	Y	Y	Y	Y	N
DELAWARE								
AL	*Castle*	Y	Y	Y	Y	Y	Y	Y
FLORIDA								
1	*Miller, J.*	Y	N	Y	N	Y	N	Y
2	Boyd	Y	Y	Y	Y	Y	Y	N
3	Brown	Y	Y	Y	Y	Y	Y	N
4	*Crenshaw*	Y	Y	Y	Y	Y	N	Y
5	*Brown-Waite*	Y	Y	Y	Y	Y	N	Y
6	*Stearns*	Y	N	Y	N	Y	N	Y
7	*Mica*	Y	Y	Y	Y	Y	N	Y
8	*Keller*	Y	Y	Y	Y	Y	N	Y
9	*Bilirakis*	Y	Y	Y	Y	Y	N	Y
10	*Young*	?	?	?	Y	Y	N	Y
11	Davis	Y	Y	Y	Y	Y	Y	N
12	*Putnam*	Y	Y	Y	Y	Y	N	Y
13	*Harris*	Y	Y	Y	Y	Y	N	Y
14	*Goss*	Y	Y	Y	Y	Y	N	Y
15	*Weldon*	Y	Y	Y	Y	Y	N	Y
16	*Foley*	Y	Y	Y	Y	Y	N	Y
17	Meek	Y	Y	Y	Y	Y	Y	N
18	*Ros-Lehtinen*	Y	Y	Y	Y	Y	N	Y
19	Wexler	?	?	?	Y	Y	Y	N
20	Deutsch	Y	Y	Y	Y	Y	Y	N
21	*Diaz-Balart, L.*	Y	Y	Y	Y	Y	N	Y
22	*Shaw*	Y	Y	Y	Y	Y	N	Y
23	Hastings	Y	Y	Y	Y	Y	Y	N
24	*Feeney*	Y	N	Y	N	Y	N	Y
25	*Diaz-Balart, M.*	Y	Y	Y	Y	Y	N	Y
GEORGIA								
1	*Kingston*	Y	Y	Y	Y	Y	N	Y
2	Bishop	Y	Y	Y	Y	Y	Y	Y
3	Marshall	Y	Y	Y	Y	Y	N	Y
4	Majette	Y	Y	Y	Y	Y	Y	N
5	Lewis	Y	Y	Y	Y	Y	Y	N
6	*Isakson*	Y	Y	Y	Y	Y	N	Y
7	*Linder*	Y	Y	Y	Y	Y	N	Y
8	*Collins*	?	?	?	?	?	?	?
9	*Norwood*	Y	N	Y	Y	Y	N	Y
10	*Deal*	Y	N	Y	Y	Y	N	Y
11	*Gingrey*	Y	N	?	Y	Y	N	Y
12	*Burns*	Y	Y	Y	Y	Y	N	Y
13	Scott	Y	Y	Y	Y	Y	Y	N
HAWAII								
1	Abercrombie	Y	Y	Y	Y	Y	Y	N
2	Case	Y	Y	Y	Y	Y	Y	N
IDAHO								
1	*Otter*	Y	Y	?	Y	Y	N	Y
2	*Simpson*	Y	Y	Y	Y	Y	N	Y
ILLINOIS								
1	Rush	N	Y	Y	Y	Y	Y	N
2	Jackson	Y	Y	Y	Y	Y	Y	N
3	Lipinski	Y	Y	Y	Y	Y	Y	N
4	Gutierrez	Y	Y	Y	Y	Y	Y	N
5	Emanuel	Y	Y	Y	Y	Y	Y	N
6	*Hyde*	Y	Y	Y	Y	Y	N	Y

ND Northern Democrats   SD Southern Democrats

	25	26	27	28	29	30	31
7 Davis	Y	Y	Y	Y	Y	Y	N
8 ***Crane***	N	Y	Y	Y	Y	N	Y
9 Schakowsky	Y	Y	Y	Y	Y	Y	N
10 ***Kirk***	Y	Y	Y	Y	Y	+	N
11 ***Weller***	N	Y	?	Y	Y	N	Y
12 Costello	N	Y	Y	Y	Y	N	Y
13 ***Biggert***	Y	Y	Y	Y	Y	Y	N
14 ***Hastert***							
15 ***Johnson***	Y	Y	Y	Y	Y	N	Y
16 ***Manzullo***	Y	Y	Y	N	Y	N	Y
17 Evans	Y	Y	Y	Y	Y	Y	N
18 ***LaHood***	Y	Y	Y	Y	Y	N	Y
19 ***Shimkus***	Y	N	Y	N	Y	N	Y
INDIANA							
1 Visclosky	N	Y	Y	Y	Y	N	N
2 ***Chocola***	Y	Y	Y	Y	Y	N	Y
3 ***Souder***	Y	Y	Y	Y	Y	N	Y
4 ***Buyer***	Y	Y	Y	Y	Y	?	?
5 ***Burton***	Y	Y	Y	N	Y	N	Y
6 ***Pence***	Y	Y	Y	N	Y	N	Y
7 Carson	Y	Y	Y	Y	Y	Y	N
8 ***Hostettler***	Y	N	Y	N	Y	N	Y
9 Hill	Y	Y	Y	Y	Y	Y	Y
IOWA							
1 ***Nussle***	Y	N	Y	N	Y	N	Y
2 ***Leach***	Y	Y	Y	Y	Y	Y	Y
3 Boswell	Y	Y	Y	Y	Y	Y	N
4 ***Latham***	Y	Y	Y	Y	Y	N	Y
5 ***King***	Y	Y	Y	N	Y	N	Y
KANSAS							
1 ***Moran***	Y	Y	Y	N	Y	N	Y
2 ***Ryun***	Y	Y	Y	Y	Y	N	Y
3 Moore	Y	Y	Y	Y	Y	Y	N
4 ***Tiahrt***	Y	Y	Y	Y	Y	N	Y
KENTUCKY							
1 ***Whitfield***	Y	Y	Y	Y	Y	N	Y
2 ***Lewis***	Y	Y	Y	Y	Y	N	Y
3 ***Northup***	Y	Y	Y	Y	Y	?	?
4 Lucas	Y	Y	Y	Y	Y	N	Y
5 ***Rogers***	Y	Y	Y	Y	Y	N	Y
6 Chandler [1]		Y	Y	Y	Y	N	Y
LOUISIANA							
1 ***Vitter***	Y	Y	Y	Y	Y	N	Y
2 Jefferson	Y	Y	Y	Y	Y	Y	Y
3 ***Tauzin***	Y	Y	Y	Y	Y	N	Y
4 ***McCrery***	Y	Y	Y	Y	Y	N	Y
5 Alexander	Y	Y	Y	Y	Y	N	Y
6 ***Baker***	Y	Y	Y	Y	Y	N	Y
7 John	Y	Y	Y	Y	Y	N	Y
MAINE							
1 Allen	Y	Y	Y	Y	Y	Y	N
2 Michaud	Y	Y	Y	Y	Y	N	N
MARYLAND							
1 ***Gilchrest***	Y	Y	Y	Y	Y	N	Y
2 Ruppersberger	Y	Y	Y	Y	Y	Y	N
3 Cardin	Y	Y	Y	Y	Y	Y	N
4 Wynn	Y	Y	Y	Y	Y	Y	N
5 Hoyer	Y	Y	Y	Y	Y	Y	N
6 ***Bartlett***	Y	N	Y	N	Y	N	Y
7 Cummings	Y	Y	Y	Y	Y	Y	N
8 Van Hollen	Y	Y	Y	Y	Y	Y	N
MASSACHUSETTS							
1 Olver	N	Y	Y	Y	Y	+	N
2 Neal	Y	Y	Y	Y	Y	Y	Y
3 McGovern	Y	Y	Y	Y	Y	Y	N
4 Frank	Y	Y	Y	Y	Y	Y	N
5 Meehan	Y	Y	Y	Y	Y	Y	N
6 Tierney	Y	Y	Y	Y	Y	Y	N
7 Markey	Y	Y	Y	Y	Y	Y	N
8 Capuano	N	Y	Y	Y	Y	Y	N
9 Lynch	Y	Y	Y	Y	Y	Y	Y
10 Delahunt	Y	Y	Y	Y	Y	Y	N
MICHIGAN							
1 Stupak	N	Y	Y	Y	Y	N	Y
2 ***Hoekstra***	Y	Y	Y	Y	Y	N	Y
3 ***Ehlers***	Y	Y	Y	Y	Y	N	Y
4 ***Camp***	Y	Y	Y	Y	Y	N	Y
5 Kildee	Y	Y	Y	Y	Y	N	Y
6 ***Upton***	Y	Y	Y	Y	Y	N	Y
7 ***Smith***	Y	N	Y	N	Y	N	Y
8 ***Rogers***	Y	Y	?	Y	Y	N	Y
9 ***Knollenberg***	Y	Y	Y	Y	Y	N	Y
10 ***Miller***	Y	Y	?	Y	Y	N	Y
11 ***McCotter***	Y	Y	Y	Y	Y	N	Y
12 Levin	Y	Y	Y	Y	Y	Y	N
13 Kilpatrick	+	+	+	Y	Y	Y	N
14 Conyers	Y	?	Y	Y	Y	Y	N
15 Dingell	Y	Y	Y	Y	Y	Y	N
MINNESOTA							
1 ***Gutknecht***	N	Y	Y	N	Y	N	Y
2 ***Kline***	Y	Y	Y	Y	Y	N	Y
3 ***Ramstad***	N	Y	Y	Y	Y	N	Y
4 McCollum	Y	Y	Y	Y	Y	Y	N
5 Sabo	Y	?	?	Y	Y	Y	N
6 ***Kennedy***	N	Y	Y	Y	Y	N	Y
7 Peterson	N	Y	Y	Y	Y	N	Y
8 Oberstar	N	Y	Y	Y	Y	N	Y
MISSISSIPPI							
1 ***Wicker***	Y	Y	Y	Y	Y	N	Y
2 Thompson	N	Y	Y	Y	Y	Y	N
3 ***Pickering***	Y	Y	Y	Y	Y	N	Y
4 Taylor	N	N	Y	Y	Y	N	Y
MISSOURI							
1 Clay	Y	Y	Y	Y	Y	Y	N
2 ***Akin***	Y	N	Y	N	Y	N	Y
3 Gephardt	?	?	?	Y	Y	Y	N
4 Skelton	Y	Y	Y	Y	Y	N	Y
5 McCarthy	Y	Y	Y	Y	Y	Y	N
6 ***Graves***	Y	Y	Y	Y	Y	N	Y
7 ***Blunt***	Y	Y	Y	Y	Y	N	Y
8 ***Emerson***	Y	Y	Y	Y	Y	N	Y
9 ***Hulshof***	?	?	?	Y	Y	N	Y
MONTANA							
AL ***Rehberg***	Y	Y	Y	Y	Y	N	Y
NEBRASKA							
1 ***Bereuter***	Y	Y	Y	Y	Y	N	Y
2 ***Terry***	Y	Y	Y	Y	Y	N	Y
3 ***Osborne***	Y	Y	Y	Y	Y	N	Y
NEVADA							
1 Berkley	Y	Y	Y	Y	Y	Y	N
2 ***Gibbons***	Y	Y	Y	Y	Y	N	Y
3 ***Porter***	Y	Y	Y	Y	Y	N	Y
NEW HAMPSHIRE							
1 ***Bradley***	Y	Y	Y	Y	Y	Y	Y
2 ***Bass***	Y	Y	Y	Y	Y	Y	N
NEW JERSEY							
1 Andrews	Y	Y	Y	Y	Y	Y	N
2 ***LoBiondo***	N	Y	Y	Y	Y	N	Y
3 ***Saxton***	Y	Y	Y	Y	Y	N	Y
4 ***Smith***	Y	Y	Y	Y	Y	N	Y
5 ***Garrett***	Y	N	Y	N	Y	N	Y
6 Pallone	Y	Y	Y	Y	Y	Y	N
7 ***Ferguson***	Y	Y	Y	Y	Y	N	Y
8 Pascrell	Y	Y	Y	Y	Y	Y	N
9 Rothman	Y	Y	Y	Y	Y	Y	N
10 Payne	Y	Y	Y	Y	Y	Y	N
11 ***Frelinghuysen***	Y	Y	Y	Y	Y	Y	Y
12 Holt	Y	Y	Y	Y	Y	Y	N
13 Menendez	Y	Y	Y	Y	Y	?	?
NEW MEXICO							
1 ***Wilson***	Y	Y	Y	Y	Y	N	Y
2 ***Pearce***	Y	Y	Y	Y	Y	N	Y
3 Udall	N	Y	Y	Y	Y	Y	N
NEW YORK							
1 Bishop	Y	Y	Y	Y	Y	Y	N
2 Israel	Y	Y	Y	Y	Y	Y	N
3 ***King***	Y	Y	Y	Y	Y	N	Y
4 McCarthy	Y	Y	Y	Y	Y	Y	N
5 Ackerman	Y	Y	Y	Y	Y	Y	N
6 Meeks	Y	Y	Y	Y	Y	?	?
7 Crowley	Y	Y	Y	Y	Y	Y	Y
8 Nadler	Y	Y	Y	Y	Y	Y	N
9 Weiner	Y	Y	Y	Y	Y	Y	N
10 Towns	Y	Y	Y	Y	Y	Y	N
11 Owens	Y	Y	Y	Y	Y	Y	N
12 Velázquez	Y	Y	Y	Y	Y	Y	N
13 ***Fossella***	N	Y	Y	N	Y	N	Y
14 Maloney	Y	Y	Y	Y	Y	Y	N
15 Rangel	Y	Y	Y	Y	Y	Y	N
16 Serrano	Y	Y	Y	Y	Y	Y	N
17 Engel	?	?	Y	Y	Y	Y	N
18 Lowey	?	?	?	Y	Y	Y	N
19 ***Kelly***	Y	Y	Y	Y	Y	Y	N
20 ***Sweeney***	Y	Y	Y	N	Y	Y	Y
21 McNulty	Y	Y	Y	Y	Y	N	Y
22 Hinchey	Y	Y	Y	Y	Y	Y	N
23 ***McHugh***	Y	Y	Y	Y	Y	N	Y
24 ***Boehlert***	Y	Y	Y	Y	Y	Y	N
25 ***Walsh***	Y	Y	Y	Y	Y	N	Y
26 ***Reynolds***	Y	Y	?	Y	Y	N	Y
27 ***Quinn***	Y	Y	Y	Y	Y	?	?
28 Slaughter	Y	Y	Y	Y	Y	Y	N
29 ***Houghton***	Y	Y	Y	Y	Y	Y	N
NORTH CAROLINA							
1 Ballance	Y	Y	Y	Y	Y	Y	N
2 Etheridge	Y	Y	Y	Y	Y	Y	N
3 ***Jones***	Y	N	Y	N	?	N	Y
4 Price	Y	Y	Y	Y	Y	Y	N
5 ***Burr***	Y	Y	Y	Y	Y	N	Y
6 ***Coble***	Y	N	Y	N	Y	N	Y
7 McIntyre	Y	Y	Y	Y	Y	N	Y
8 ***Hayes***	Y	N	Y	Y	Y	N	Y
9 ***Myrick***	Y	N	Y	Y	Y	N	Y
10 ***Ballenger***	Y	Y	Y	Y	Y	N	Y
11 ***Taylor***	Y	N	Y	N	Y	N	Y
12 Watt	Y	Y	Y	Y	Y	Y	N
13 Miller	Y	Y	Y	Y	Y	Y	N
NORTH DAKOTA							
AL Pomeroy	Y	Y	Y	Y	Y	Y	Y
OHIO							
1 ***Chabot***	Y	Y	Y	Y	Y	N	Y
2 ***Portman***	Y	Y	Y	Y	Y	N	Y
3 ***Turner***	Y	Y	Y	Y	Y	N	Y
4 ***Oxley***	Y	Y	Y	Y	Y	N	Y
5 ***Gillmor***	Y	Y	Y	Y	Y	N	Y
6 Strickland	N	Y	Y	Y	Y	Y	N
7 ***Hobson***	Y	Y	Y	Y	Y	Y	Y
8 ***Boehner***	Y	Y	Y	Y	Y	N	Y
9 Kaptur	Y	Y	Y	Y	Y	Y	Y
10 Kucinich	?	?	?	?	?	?	?
11 Jones	N	Y	Y	Y	Y	Y	N
12 ***Tiberi***	Y	Y	Y	Y	Y	N	Y
13 Brown	Y	Y	Y	Y	Y	Y	N
14 ***LaTourette***	Y	Y	Y	Y	Y	N	Y
15 ***Pryce***	Y	Y	Y	Y	Y	Y	Y
16 ***Regula***	Y	Y	Y	Y	Y	N	Y
17 Ryan	Y	Y	Y	Y	Y	N	Y
18 ***Ney***	Y	Y	Y	Y	Y	N	Y
OKLAHOMA							
1 ***Sullivan***	Y	Y	Y	Y	Y	N	Y
2 Carson	Y	Y	Y	Y	Y	N	Y
3 ***Lucas***	Y	Y	Y	Y	Y	N	Y
4 ***Cole***	Y	Y	Y	Y	Y	N	Y
5 ***Istook***	Y	Y	Y	N	Y	N	Y
OREGON							
1 Wu	N	Y	Y	Y	Y	Y	N
2 ***Walden***	Y	Y	Y	Y	Y	N	Y
3 Blumenauer	Y	Y	Y	Y	Y	Y	N
4 DeFazio	N	Y	Y	Y	Y	Y	N
5 Hooley	Y	Y	Y	Y	Y	Y	N
PENNSYLVANIA							
1 Brady	N	Y	Y	Y	Y	Y	N
2 Fattah	Y	Y	Y	Y	Y	Y	N
3 ***English***	N	Y	Y	Y	Y	N	Y
4 ***Hart***	Y	Y	Y	Y	Y	N	Y
5 ***Peterson***	Y	Y	?	Y	Y	N	Y
6 ***Gerlach***	Y	Y	Y	Y	Y	N	Y
7 ***Weldon***	Y	Y	Y	Y	Y	N	Y
8 ***Greenwood***	Y	?	?	Y	Y	Y	N
9 ***Shuster, Bill***	Y	Y	Y	Y	Y	N	Y
10 ***Sherwood***	Y	Y	Y	Y	Y	N	Y
11 Kanjorski	Y	Y	Y	Y	Y	N	Y
12 Murtha	?	?	?	Y	Y	N	Y
13 Hoeffel	Y	Y	Y	Y	Y	Y	N
14 Doyle	Y	?	?	Y	Y	N	Y
15 ***Toomey***	Y	N	Y	N	Y	N	Y
16 ***Pitts***	Y	Y	Y	Y	Y	N	Y
17 Holden	Y	?	?	Y	Y	N	Y
18 ***Murphy***	Y	Y	Y	Y	Y	N	Y
19 ***Platts***	Y	N	Y	Y	Y	N	Y
RHODE ISLAND							
1 Kennedy	Y	Y	Y	Y	Y	Y	N
2 Langevin	Y	Y	Y	Y	Y	N	Y
SOUTH CAROLINA							
1 ***Brown***	Y	Y	Y	Y	Y	N	Y
2 ***Wilson***	Y	Y	Y	Y	Y	N	Y
3 ***Barrett***	Y	N	Y	N	Y	N	Y
4 ***DeMint***	Y	Y	Y	Y	Y	N	Y
5 Spratt	Y	Y	Y	Y	Y	Y	Y
6 Clyburn	Y	Y	Y	?	?	Y	N
SOUTH DAKOTA							
AL Vacant							
TENNESSEE							
1 ***Jenkins***	Y	Y	Y	Y	Y	N	Y
2 ***Duncan***	Y	N	Y	N	Y	N	Y
3 ***Wamp***	Y	Y	Y	Y	Y	N	Y
4 Davis	Y	Y	Y	Y	Y	N	Y
5 Cooper	Y	Y	Y	Y	Y	Y	N
6 Gordon	Y	Y	Y	Y	Y	Y	Y
7 ***Blackburn***	Y	N	Y	Y	Y	N	Y
8 Tanner	Y	Y	Y	Y	Y	Y	Y
9 Ford	Y	Y	Y	Y	Y	Y	N
TEXAS							
1 Sandlin	Y	Y	Y	Y	Y	Y	N
2 Turner	Y	Y	Y	Y	Y	Y	Y
3 ***Johnson, Sam***	Y	N	Y	Y	Y	N	Y
4 ***Hall***	Y	Y	Y	Y	Y	N	Y
5 ***Hensarling***	Y	Y	Y	N	Y	N	Y
6 ***Barton***	Y	Y	Y	Y	Y	N	Y
7 ***Culberson***	Y	N	Y	N	Y	N	Y
8 ***Brady***	?	?	?	Y	Y	?	?
9 Lampson	Y	Y	Y	Y	Y	Y	N
10 Doggett	?	?	?	?	?	?	?
11 Edwards	Y	Y	Y	Y	Y	Y	N
12 ***Granger***	Y	Y	Y	Y	Y	Y	Y
13 ***Thornberry***	Y	Y	Y	Y	Y	N	Y
14 ***Paul***	Y	N	Y	N	Y	N	N
15 Hinojosa	Y	Y	Y	Y	Y	Y	N
16 Reyes	Y	Y	Y	Y	Y	Y	N
17 Stenholm	Y	Y	Y	Y	Y	N	Y
18 Jackson-Lee	Y	Y	Y	Y	Y	Y	N
19 ***Neugebauer***	Y	Y	Y	Y	Y	N	Y
20 Gonzalez	?	?	?	Y	Y	Y	N
21 ***Smith***	Y	Y	Y	Y	Y	N	Y
22 ***DeLay***	Y	Y	Y	Y	Y	N	Y
23 ***Bonilla***	Y	Y	Y	Y	Y	N	Y
24 Frost	Y	Y	Y	Y	Y	Y	N
25 Bell	Y	Y	Y	Y	Y	?	?
26 ***Burgess***	Y	Y	Y	N	Y	N	Y
27 Ortiz	?	?	?	Y	Y	N	Y
28 Rodriguez	Y	Y	Y	Y	Y	Y	N
29 Green	Y	Y	Y	Y	Y	Y	N
30 Johnson, E.B.	Y	Y	Y	Y	Y	Y	N
31 ***Carter***	Y	Y	Y	Y	Y	N	Y
32 ***Sessions***	Y	N	Y	Y	Y	N	Y
UTAH							
1 ***Bishop***	Y	Y	Y	Y	Y	N	Y
2 Matheson	Y	Y	Y	Y	Y	Y	Y
3 ***Cannon***	Y	Y	Y	N	Y	N	Y
VERMONT							
AL *Sanders*	Y	Y	Y	Y	Y	Y	N
VIRGINIA							
1 ***Davis, Jo Ann***	Y	N	Y	Y	Y	N	Y
2 ***Schrock***	Y	Y	Y	Y	Y	N	Y
3 Scott	Y	?	?	Y	Y	Y	N
4 ***Forbes***	?	?	?	?	?	?	?
5 ***Goode***	Y	Y	Y	N	Y	N	Y
6 ***Goodlatte***	Y	Y	Y	Y	Y	N	Y
7 ***Cantor***	Y	Y	Y	Y	Y	N	Y
8 Moran	Y	Y	?	Y	Y	Y	N
9 Boucher	Y	Y	Y	Y	Y	Y	N
10 ***Wolf***	Y	Y	Y	Y	Y	N	Y
11 ***Davis, T.***	Y	Y	Y	Y	Y	N	Y
WASHINGTON							
1 Inslee	Y	Y	Y	Y	Y	Y	N
2 Larsen	N	Y	Y	Y	Y	Y	N
3 Baird	Y	Y	Y	?	?	Y	N
4 ***Hastings***	Y	Y	Y	Y	Y	N	Y
5 ***Nethercutt***	Y	Y	Y	Y	Y	N	Y
6 Dicks	Y	Y	Y	Y	?	Y	N
7 McDermott	N	Y	Y	Y	Y	Y	N
8 ***Dunn***	Y	Y	Y	Y	Y	Y	Y
9 Smith	Y	Y	Y	Y	Y	Y	N
WEST VIRGINIA							
1 Mollohan	Y	Y	Y	Y	Y	N	Y
2 ***Capito***	Y	Y	Y	Y	Y	N	Y
3 Rahall	Y	Y	Y	Y	Y	N	Y
WISCONSIN							
1 ***Ryan***	Y	Y	Y	Y	Y	N	Y
2 Baldwin	N	Y	Y	Y	Y	Y	N
3 Kind	Y	Y	Y	Y	Y	Y	Y
4 Kleczka	Y	Y	Y	Y	Y	+	–
5 ***Sensenbrenner***	Y	N	Y	N	Y	N	Y
6 ***Petri***	Y	N	Y	N	Y	N	Y
7 Obey	Y	Y	Y	Y	Y	Y	Y
8 ***Green***	Y	Y	Y	Y	Y	N	Y
WYOMING							
AL ***Cubin***	Y	Y	Y	N	Y	N	Y

Southern states - Ala., Ark., Fla., Ga., Ky., La., Miss., N.C., Okla., S.C., Tenn., Texas, Va.

Key

Y	Voted for (yea).
#	Paired for.
+	Announced for.
N	Voted against (nay).
X	Paired against.
−	Announced against.
P	Voted "present."
C	Voted "present" to avoid possible conflict of interest.
?	Did not vote or otherwise make a position known.

Democrats **Republicans**
Independents

32. HR 3769. Ben Atchley Post Office/Passage. Duncan, R-Tenn., motion to suspend the rules and pass the bill that would name a post office building in Knoxville, Tenn., after Republican State Sen. Ben Atchley. Motion agreed to 383-0: R 208-0; D 174-0 (ND 125-0, SD 49-0); I 1-0. A two-thirds majority of those present and voting (256 in this case) is required for passage under suspension of the rules. March 2, 2004.

33. H Res 526. Iranian Earthquake/Adoption. Hyde, R-Ill., motion to suspend the rules and adopt the resolution that would express the sympathy of the House of Representatives for the victims of the Dec. 26, 2003, earthquake in Bam, Iran. The resolution also would honor the life-saving work of U.S. and international aid personnel in Iran. Motion agreed to 381-0: R 209-0; D 171-0 (ND 123-0, SD 48-0); I 1-0. A two-thirds majority of those present and voting (254 in this case) is required for adoption under suspension of the rules. March 2, 2004.

34. H Res 530. Human Rights in China/Adoption. Smith, R-N.J., motion to suspend the rules and adopt the resolution that would express the sense of Congress that the U.S. government should continue to insist that China adhere to fundamental human rights principles. The measure also would urge the U.S. government to introduce a resolution at the 60th session of the U.N. Human Rights Commission in Geneva, Switzerland, calling on China to end its human rights violations and meet internationally recognized standards for human rights. Motion agreed to 402-2: R 214-1; D 187-1 (ND 136-1, SD 51-0); I 1-0. A two-thirds majority of those present and voting (270 in this case) is required for adoption under suspension of the rules. March 3, 2004.

35. HR 912. Amateur Astronomy Awards/Passage. Rohrabacher, R-Calif., motion to suspend the rules and pass the bill that would authorize NASA and the Minor Planet Center of the Smithsonian Astrophysical Observatory to establish two annual Charles "Pete" Conrad Astronomy Awards of $3,000 each for amateur astronomers. Motion agreed to 404-1: R 213-1; D 190-0 (ND 139-0, SD 51-0); I 1-0. A two-thirds majority of those present and voting (270 in this case) is required for passage under suspension of the rules. March 3, 2004.

36. HR 3389. Nonprofit Management Awards/Passage. Hart, R-Pa., motion to suspend the rules and pass the bill that would make nonprofit entities eligible to apply for and receive Malcolm Baldrige National Quality Awards, which recognize organizations that have provided substantial economic or social benefits through improvements in their goods or services that result from effective management practices. Motion agreed to 408-0: R 217-0; D 190-0 (ND 139-0, SD 51-0); I 1-0. A two-thirds majority of those present and voting (272 in this case) is required for passage under suspension of the rules. March 3, 2004.

	32	33	34	35	36
ALABAMA					
1 *Bonner*	Y	Y	Y	Y	Y
2 *Everett*	Y	Y	Y	Y	Y
3 *Rogers*	Y	Y	Y	Y	Y
4 *Aderholt*	?	?	?	?	?
5 Cramer	Y	Y	Y	Y	Y
6 *Bachus*	Y	Y	Y	Y	Y
7 Davis	Y	Y	Y	Y	Y
ALASKA					
AL *Young*	Y	Y	Y	Y	Y
ARIZONA					
1 *Renzi*	Y	Y	Y	Y	Y
2 *Franks*	Y	Y	Y	Y	Y
3 *Shadegg*	Y	Y	Y	Y	Y
4 Pastor	Y	Y	Y	Y	Y
5 *Hayworth*	Y	Y	Y	Y	Y
6 *Flake*	Y	Y	Y	Y	Y
7 Grijalva	Y	Y	Y	Y	Y
8 *Kolbe*	Y	Y	Y	Y	Y
ARKANSAS					
1 Berry	?	?	?	?	?
2 Snyder	Y	Y	Y	Y	Y
3 *Boozman*	Y	Y	Y	Y	Y
4 Ross	Y	Y	Y	Y	Y
CALIFORNIA					
1 Thompson	Y	Y	Y	Y	Y
2 *Herger*	?	?	Y	Y	Y
3 *Ose*	?	?	Y	Y	Y
4 *Doolittle*	Y	Y	Y	Y	Y
5 Matsui	Y	Y	Y	Y	Y
6 Woolsey	?	?	?	Y	Y
7 Miller, George	?	?	Y	Y	Y
8 Pelosi	?	?	Y	Y	Y
9 Lee	Y	Y	Y	Y	Y
10 Tauscher	Y	Y	Y	Y	Y
11 *Pombo*	Y	Y	Y	Y	Y
12 Lantos	?	?	?	?	?
13 Stark	Y	Y	Y	Y	Y
14 Eshoo	Y	Y	Y	Y	Y
15 Honda	Y	Y	Y	Y	Y
16 Lofgren	Y	Y	Y	Y	Y
17 Farr	Y	Y	Y	Y	Y
18 Cardoza	Y	Y	Y	Y	Y
19 *Radanovich*	Y	Y	Y	Y	Y
20 Dooley	?	?	?	?	?
21 *Nunes*	Y	Y	Y	Y	Y
22 *Thomas*	Y	Y	Y	Y	Y
23 Capps	Y	Y	Y	Y	Y
24 *Gallegly*	Y	Y	Y	Y	Y
25 *McKeon*	Y	Y	Y	Y	Y
26 *Dreier*	Y	Y	Y	Y	Y
27 Sherman	Y	Y	Y	Y	Y
28 Berman	Y	Y	Y	Y	Y
29 Schiff	?	?	?	?	?
30 Waxman	Y	Y	Y	Y	Y
31 Becerra	Y	Y	Y	Y	Y
32 Solis	Y	Y	Y	Y	Y
33 Watson	Y	Y	Y	Y	Y
34 Roybal-Allard	Y	Y	Y	Y	Y
35 Waters	?	?	Y	Y	Y
36 Harman	?	?	Y	Y	Y

	32	33	34	35	36
37 Millender-McD.	?	?	Y	Y	Y
38 Napolitano	?	?	Y	Y	Y
39 Sánchez, Linda	Y	Y	?	Y	Y
40 *Royce*	?	?	?	?	?
41 *Lewis*	Y	Y	Y	Y	Y
42 *Miller, Gary*	Y	Y	Y	Y	Y
43 Baca	+	+	+	+	+
44 *Calvert*	?	?	?	?	?
45 *Bono*	Y	Y	Y	Y	Y
46 *Rohrabacher*	Y	Y	Y	Y	Y
47 Sanchez, Loretta	?	?	Y	Y	Y
48 *Cox*	Y	Y	Y	Y	Y
49 *Issa*	Y	Y	Y	Y	Y
50 *Cunningham*	Y	Y	Y	Y	Y
51 Filner	+	+	+	+	+
52 *Hunter*	Y	Y	Y	Y	Y
53 Davis	?	?	?	?	?
COLORADO					
1 DeGette	Y	Y	Y	Y	Y
2 Udall	Y	Y	Y	Y	Y
3 *McInnis*	Y	Y	Y	Y	Y
4 *Musgrave*	Y	Y	Y	Y	Y
5 *Hefley*	Y	Y	Y	Y	Y
6 *Tancredo*	Y	Y	Y	Y	Y
7 *Beauprez*	Y	Y	Y	Y	Y
CONNECTICUT					
1 Larson	Y	Y	Y	Y	Y
2 *Simmons*	Y	Y	Y	Y	Y
3 DeLauro	Y	Y	Y	Y	Y
4 *Shays*	Y	Y	Y	Y	Y
5 *Johnson*	?	Y	Y	Y	Y
DELAWARE					
AL *Castle*	?	?	?	?	?
FLORIDA					
1 *Miller, J.*	Y	Y	Y	Y	Y
2 Boyd	Y	Y	Y	Y	Y
3 Brown	Y	Y	Y	Y	Y
4 *Crenshaw*	Y	Y	Y	Y	Y
5 *Brown-Waite*	Y	Y	Y	Y	Y
6 *Stearns*	Y	Y	+	Y	Y
7 *Mica*	Y	Y	Y	Y	Y
8 *Keller*	Y	Y	Y	Y	Y
9 *Bilirakis*	Y	Y	Y	Y	Y
10 *Young*	?	?	Y	Y	Y
11 Davis	Y	Y	Y	Y	Y
12 *Putnam*	Y	Y	Y	Y	Y
13 *Harris*	Y	Y	Y	Y	Y
14 *Goss*	Y	Y	Y	Y	Y
15 *Weldon*	Y	Y	Y	+	Y
16 *Foley*	Y	Y	Y	Y	Y
17 Meek	Y	Y	Y	Y	Y
18 *Ros-Lehtinen*	Y	Y	Y	Y	Y
19 Wexler	Y	Y	Y	Y	Y
20 Deutsch	Y	Y	Y	Y	Y
21 *Diaz-Balart, L.*	Y	Y	Y	Y	Y
22 *Shaw*	Y	Y	Y	Y	Y
23 Hastings	Y	Y	Y	Y	Y
24 *Feeney*	Y	Y	Y	Y	Y
25 *Diaz-Balart, M.*	Y	Y	Y	Y	Y
GEORGIA					
1 *Kingston*	?	?	Y	Y	Y
2 Bishop	Y	Y	Y	Y	Y
3 Marshall	?	?	Y	Y	Y
4 Majette	Y	Y	Y	Y	Y
5 Lewis	Y	Y	Y	Y	Y
6 *Isakson*	Y	Y	Y	Y	Y
7 *Linder*	Y	Y	Y	Y	Y
8 *Collins*	Y	Y	Y	Y	Y
9 *Norwood*	Y	Y	Y	Y	Y
10 *Deal*	Y	Y	Y	Y	Y
11 *Gingrey*	Y	Y	Y	Y	Y
12 *Burns*	Y	Y	Y	Y	Y
13 Scott	Y	Y	Y	Y	Y
HAWAII					
1 Abercrombie	Y	Y	Y	Y	Y
2 Case	Y	Y	Y	Y	Y
IDAHO					
1 *Otter*	Y	Y	Y	Y	Y
2 *Simpson*	Y	Y	Y	Y	Y
ILLINOIS					
1 Rush	Y	Y	Y	Y	Y
2 Jackson	Y	Y	Y	Y	Y
3 Lipinski	Y	Y	Y	Y	Y
4 Gutierrez	?	?	Y	Y	Y
5 Emanuel	Y	Y	Y	Y	Y
6 *Hyde*	Y	Y	Y	Y	Y

ND Northern Democrats   SD Southern Democrats

Member	32	33	34	35	36
7 Davis	Y	Y	Y	Y	Y
8 *Crane*	Y	Y	Y	Y	Y
9 *Schakowsky*	Y	Y	Y	Y	Y
10 *Kirk*	Y	Y	Y	Y	Y
11 *Weller*	Y	Y	Y	Y	Y
12 Costello	Y	Y	Y	Y	Y
13 *Biggert*	Y	Y	Y	Y	Y
14 *Hastert*					
15 *Johnson*	Y	Y	Y	Y	Y
16 *Manzullo*	Y	Y	Y	Y	Y
17 Evans	Y	?	Y	Y	Y
18 *LaHood*	Y	Y	Y	Y	Y
19 *Shimkus*	Y	Y	Y	Y	Y
INDIANA					
1 Visclosky	Y	Y	Y	Y	Y
2 *Chocola*	?	?	?	?	?
3 *Souder*	Y	Y	Y	Y	Y
4 *Buyer*	Y	Y	Y	Y	Y
5 *Burton*	+	+	Y	Y	Y
6 *Pence*	?	?	?	?	?
7 Carson	Y	Y	Y	Y	Y
8 *Hostettler*	Y	Y	Y	Y	Y
9 Hill	Y	Y	Y	Y	Y
IOWA					
1 *Nussle*	Y	Y	Y	Y	Y
2 *Leach*	Y	Y	Y	Y	Y
3 Boswell	Y	Y	Y	Y	Y
4 *Latham*	Y	Y	Y	Y	Y
5 *King*	?	?	Y	?	Y
KANSAS					
1 *Moran*	Y	Y	Y	Y	Y
2 *Ryun*	Y	Y	Y	Y	Y
3 Moore	Y	Y	Y	Y	Y
4 *Tiahrt*	Y	Y	Y	Y	Y
KENTUCKY					
1 *Whitfield*	Y	Y	Y	Y	Y
2 *Lewis*	Y	Y	Y	Y	Y
3 *Northup*	Y	Y	Y	Y	Y
4 Lucas	Y	Y	Y	Y	Y
5 *Rogers*	Y	Y	Y	Y	Y
6 Chandler	Y	Y	Y	Y	Y
LOUISIANA					
1 *Vitter*	Y	Y	Y	Y	Y
2 Jefferson	Y	Y	Y	Y	Y
3 *Tauzin*	Y	Y	Y	Y	Y
4 *McCrery*	Y	Y	Y	Y	Y
5 Alexander	Y	Y	Y	Y	Y
6 *Baker*	Y	Y	Y	Y	Y
7 John	Y	Y	Y	Y	Y
MAINE					
1 Allen	Y	Y	Y	Y	Y
2 Michaud	Y	Y	Y	Y	Y
MARYLAND					
1 *Gilchrest*	?	?	Y	Y	Y
2 Ruppersberger	Y	Y	Y	Y	Y
3 Cardin	Y	Y	Y	Y	Y
4 Wynn	?	?	Y	Y	Y
5 Hoyer	Y	Y	Y	Y	Y
6 *Bartlett*	Y	Y	Y	Y	Y
7 Cummings	?	?	Y	Y	Y
8 Van Hollen	Y	Y	Y	Y	Y
MASSACHUSETTS					
1 Olver	Y	Y	Y	Y	Y
2 Neal	Y	Y	Y	Y	Y
3 McGovern	Y	Y	Y	Y	Y
4 Frank	Y	Y	?	Y	Y
5 Meehan	Y	Y	Y	Y	Y
6 Tierney	Y	Y	Y	Y	Y
7 Markey	?	?	Y	Y	Y
8 Capuano	Y	Y	Y	Y	Y
9 Lynch	Y	Y	Y	Y	Y
10 Delahunt	Y	Y	Y	Y	Y
MICHIGAN					
1 Stupak	Y	Y	Y	Y	Y
2 *Hoekstra*	Y	Y	Y	Y	Y
3 *Ehlers*	Y	Y	Y	Y	Y
4 *Camp*	Y	Y	Y	Y	Y
5 Kildee	Y	Y	Y	Y	Y
6 *Upton*	Y	Y	Y	Y	Y
7 *Smith*	?	?	?	?	?
8 *Rogers*	Y	Y	Y	Y	Y
9 *Knollenberg*	Y	Y	Y	Y	Y
10 *Miller*	Y	Y	Y	Y	Y
11 *McCotter*	?	?	?	?	?
12 Levin	Y	Y	Y	Y	Y

Member	32	33	34	35	36
13 Kilpatrick	Y	Y	Y	Y	Y
14 Conyers	Y	Y	Y	Y	Y
15 Dingell	Y	Y	Y	Y	Y
MINNESOTA					
1 *Gutknecht*	Y	Y	Y	Y	Y
2 *Kline*	Y	Y	Y	Y	Y
3 *Ramstad*	Y	Y	Y	Y	Y
4 McCollum	Y	Y	Y	Y	Y
5 Sabo	Y	Y	Y	Y	Y
6 *Kennedy*	Y	Y	Y	Y	Y
7 Peterson	Y	Y	Y	Y	Y
8 Oberstar	Y	Y	Y	Y	Y
MISSISSIPPI					
1 *Wicker*	Y	Y	Y	Y	Y
2 Thompson	Y	Y	Y	Y	Y
3 *Pickering*	Y	Y	Y	Y	Y
4 Taylor	Y	Y	Y	Y	Y
MISSOURI					
1 Clay	Y	Y	Y	Y	Y
2 *Akin*	Y	Y	?	Y	Y
3 Gephardt	Y	Y	Y	Y	Y
4 Skelton	Y	Y	Y	Y	Y
5 McCarthy	Y	Y	Y	Y	Y
6 *Graves*	Y	Y	Y	Y	Y
7 *Blunt*	Y	Y	Y	Y	Y
8 *Emerson*	Y	Y	Y	Y	Y
9 *Hulshof*	Y	Y	Y	Y	Y
MONTANA					
AL *Rehberg*	Y	Y	Y	Y	Y
NEBRASKA					
1 *Bereuter*	Y	Y	Y	Y	Y
2 *Terry*	Y	Y	Y	Y	Y
3 *Osborne*	Y	Y	Y	Y	Y
NEVADA					
1 Berkley	Y	Y	Y	Y	Y
2 *Gibbons*	Y	Y	Y	Y	Y
3 *Porter*	Y	Y	Y	Y	Y
NEW HAMPSHIRE					
1 *Bradley*	Y	Y	Y	Y	Y
2 *Bass*	Y	Y	Y	Y	Y
NEW JERSEY					
1 Andrews	Y	Y	Y	Y	Y
2 *LoBiondo*	Y	Y	Y	Y	Y
3 *Saxton*	Y	Y	Y	Y	Y
4 *Smith*	Y	Y	Y	Y	Y
5 *Garrett*	Y	Y	Y	Y	Y
6 Pallone	Y	Y	Y	Y	Y
7 *Ferguson*	Y	Y	Y	Y	Y
8 Pascrell	Y	Y	Y	Y	Y
9 Rothman	Y	Y	Y	Y	Y
10 Payne	Y	Y	Y	Y	Y
11 *Frelinghuysen*	Y	Y	Y	Y	Y
12 Holt	Y	Y	Y	Y	Y
13 Menendez	Y	Y	Y	Y	Y
NEW MEXICO					
1 *Wilson*	Y	Y	Y	Y	Y
2 *Pearce*	Y	Y	Y	Y	Y
3 Udall	Y	Y	Y	Y	Y
NEW YORK					
1 Bishop	Y	Y	Y	Y	Y
2 Israel	Y	Y	Y	Y	Y
3 *King*	Y	Y	Y	Y	Y
4 McCarthy	Y	Y	Y	Y	Y
5 Ackerman	Y	Y	Y	Y	Y
6 Meeks	?	?	Y	Y	Y
7 Crowley	Y	Y	Y	Y	Y
8 Nadler	Y	Y	Y	Y	Y
9 Weiner	Y	Y	Y	Y	Y
10 Towns	?	?	Y	Y	Y
11 Owens	Y	Y	Y	Y	Y
12 Velázquez	Y	Y	Y	Y	Y
13 *Fossella*	Y	Y	Y	Y	Y
14 Maloney	Y	Y	Y	Y	Y
15 Rangel	Y	Y	Y	Y	Y
16 Serrano	Y	Y	Y	Y	Y
17 Engel	Y	Y	Y	Y	Y
18 Lowey	Y	Y	Y	Y	Y
19 *Kelly*	Y	Y	Y	Y	Y
20 *Sweeney*	Y	Y	Y	Y	Y
21 McNulty	Y	Y	Y	Y	Y
22 Hinchey	Y	Y	Y	Y	Y
23 *McHugh*	Y	Y	Y	Y	Y
24 *Boehlert*	Y	Y	Y	Y	Y
25 Walsh	Y	Y	Y	Y	Y

Member	32	33	34	35	36
26 *Reynolds*	Y	Y	Y	Y	Y
27 *Quinn*	Y	Y	Y	Y	Y
28 Slaughter	Y	Y	Y	Y	Y
29 Houghton	Y	Y	Y	Y	
NORTH CAROLINA					
1 Ballance	Y	Y	Y	Y	Y
2 Etheridge	Y	Y	Y	Y	Y
3 *Jones*	Y	Y	Y	Y	Y
4 Price	Y	Y	Y	Y	Y
5 *Burr*	Y	Y	Y	Y	Y
6 *Coble*	Y	Y	Y	Y	Y
7 McIntyre	Y	Y	Y	Y	Y
8 *Hayes*	Y	Y	Y	Y	Y
9 *Myrick*	Y	Y	Y	Y	Y
10 *Ballenger*	Y	Y	Y	Y	Y
11 *Taylor*	Y	Y	Y	Y	Y
12 Watt	Y	Y	Y	Y	Y
13 Miller	Y	Y	Y	Y	Y
NORTH DAKOTA					
AL Pomeroy	Y	Y	Y	Y	Y
OHIO					
1 *Chabot*	Y	Y	Y	Y	Y
2 *Portman*	Y	Y	Y	Y	Y
3 *Turner*	Y	Y	Y	Y	Y
4 *Oxley*	Y	Y	Y	Y	Y
5 *Gillmor*	Y	Y	Y	Y	Y
6 Strickland	Y	Y	Y	Y	Y
7 *Hobson*	Y	Y	Y	Y	Y
8 *Boehner*	Y	Y	Y	Y	Y
9 Kaptur	Y	Y	Y	Y	Y
10 Kucinich	?	?	?	?	?
11 Jones	?	?	Y	Y	Y
12 *Tiberi*	Y	Y	Y	Y	Y
13 Brown	Y	Y	Y	Y	Y
14 *LaTourette*	Y	Y	Y	Y	Y
15 *Pryce*	Y	Y	Y	Y	Y
16 *Regula*	Y	Y	Y	Y	Y
17 Ryan	Y	Y	Y	Y	Y
18 *Ney*	Y	Y	Y	Y	Y
OKLAHOMA					
1 *Sullivan*	Y	Y	Y	Y	Y
2 Carson	Y	Y	Y	Y	Y
3 *Lucas*	Y	Y	Y	Y	Y
4 *Cole*	Y	Y	Y	Y	Y
5 *Istook*	Y	Y	Y	Y	Y
OREGON					
1 Wu	Y	Y	Y	Y	Y
2 *Walden*	Y	Y	Y	Y	Y
3 Blumenauer	Y	Y	Y	Y	Y
4 DeFazio	Y	Y	Y	Y	Y
5 Hooley	?	?	?	?	?
PENNSYLVANIA					
1 Brady	Y	Y	Y	Y	Y
2 Fattah	Y	Y	Y	Y	Y
3 *English*	Y	Y	Y	Y	Y
4 *Hart*	Y	Y	Y	Y	Y
5 *Peterson*	Y	Y	Y	?	Y
6 *Gerlach*	Y	Y	Y	Y	Y
7 *Weldon*	?	?	?	?	?
8 *Greenwood*	Y	Y	Y	Y	Y
9 *Shuster, Bill*	Y	Y	Y	Y	Y
10 *Sherwood*	Y	Y	Y	Y	Y
11 Kanjorski	Y	Y	Y	Y	Y
12 Murtha	Y	?	Y	Y	Y
13 Hoeffel	Y	Y	Y	Y	Y
14 Doyle	Y	Y	Y	Y	Y
15 *Toomey*	?	?	?	?	?
16 *Pitts*	Y	Y	Y	Y	Y
17 Holden	Y	Y	Y	Y	Y
18 *Murphy*	Y	Y	Y	Y	Y
19 *Platts*	Y	Y	Y	Y	Y
RHODE ISLAND					
1 Kennedy	Y	Y	Y	Y	Y
2 Langevin	Y	Y	Y	Y	Y
SOUTH CAROLINA					
1 *Brown*	Y	Y	Y	Y	Y
2 *Wilson*	Y	Y	Y	Y	Y
3 *Barrett*	Y	Y	Y	Y	Y
4 *DeMint*	+	+	Y	Y	Y
5 Spratt	Y	Y	Y	Y	Y
6 Clyburn	Y	Y	Y	Y	Y
SOUTH DAKOTA					
AL Vacant					

Member	32	33	34	35	36
TENNESSEE					
1 *Jenkins*	Y	Y	Y	Y	Y
2 *Duncan*	Y	Y	Y	Y	Y
3 *Wamp*	Y	Y	Y	Y	Y
4 Davis	Y	Y	Y	Y	Y
5 Cooper	Y	Y	Y	Y	Y
6 Gordon	Y	Y	Y	Y	Y
7 *Blackburn*	Y	Y	Y	Y	Y
8 Tanner	Y	Y	Y	Y	Y
9 Ford	Y	Y	Y	Y	Y
TEXAS					
1 Sandlin	?	?	Y	Y	Y
2 Turner	Y	Y	Y	Y	Y
3 *Johnson, Sam*	Y	Y	Y	Y	Y
4 *Hall*	Y	Y	Y	Y	Y
5 *Hensarling*	Y	Y	Y	Y	Y
6 *Barton*	Y	Y	Y	Y	Y
7 *Culberson*	Y	Y	Y	Y	Y
8 *Brady*	Y	Y	Y	Y	Y
9 Lampson	Y	Y	Y	Y	Y
10 Doggett	?	?	?	?	?
11 Edwards	Y	Y	Y	Y	Y
12 *Granger*	Y	Y	Y	Y	Y
13 *Thornberry*	Y	Y	Y	Y	Y
14 *Paul*	Y	Y	N	N	Y
15 Hinojosa	?	?	?	?	?
16 Reyes	?	?	?	?	?
17 Stenholm	Y	Y	Y	Y	Y
18 Jackson-Lee	Y	Y	Y	Y	Y
19 *Neugebauer*	Y	Y	Y	Y	Y
20 Gonzalez	Y	Y	Y	Y	Y
21 *Smith*	Y	Y	Y	Y	Y
22 *DeLay*	Y	Y	Y	Y	Y
23 *Bonilla*	Y	Y	Y	Y	Y
24 Frost	Y	Y	Y	Y	Y
25 Bell	?	?	Y	Y	Y
26 *Burgess*	Y	Y	Y	Y	Y
27 Ortiz	?	?	?	?	?
28 Rodriguez	?	?	?	?	?
29 Green	Y	Y	Y	Y	Y
30 Johnson, E.B.	Y	Y	Y	Y	Y
31 *Carter*	Y	Y	Y	Y	Y
32 *Sessions*	Y	Y	Y	Y	Y
UTAH					
1 *Bishop*	Y	Y	Y	Y	Y
2 Matheson	Y	Y	Y	Y	Y
3 *Cannon*	Y	Y	Y	Y	Y
VERMONT					
AL *Sanders*	Y	Y	Y	Y	Y
VIRGINIA					
1 *Davis, Jo Ann*	Y	Y	Y	Y	Y
2 *Schrock*	Y	Y	Y	Y	Y
3 Scott	Y	Y	Y	Y	Y
4 *Forbes*	Y	Y	Y	Y	Y
5 *Goode*	Y	Y	Y	Y	Y
6 *Goodlatte*	Y	Y	Y	Y	Y
7 *Cantor*	Y	Y	Y	Y	Y
8 Moran	Y	Y	Y	Y	Y
9 Boucher	Y	Y	Y	Y	Y
10 *Wolf*	Y	Y	Y	Y	Y
11 *Davis, T.*	Y	Y	Y	Y	Y
WASHINGTON					
1 Inslee	Y	Y	Y	Y	Y
2 Larsen	Y	Y	Y	Y	Y
3 Baird	Y	Y	Y	Y	Y
4 *Hastings*	Y	Y	Y	Y	Y
5 *Nethercutt*	Y	Y	Y	Y	Y
6 Dicks	Y	Y	Y	Y	Y
7 McDermott	Y	Y	N	Y	Y
8 *Dunn*	Y	Y	Y	Y	Y
9 Smith	Y	Y	Y	Y	Y
WEST VIRGINIA					
1 Mollohan	?	?	Y	Y	Y
2 *Capito*	Y	Y	Y	Y	Y
3 Rahall	Y	Y	Y	Y	Y
WISCONSIN					
1 *Ryan*	Y	Y	Y	Y	Y
2 Baldwin	Y	Y	Y	Y	Y
3 Kind	Y	Y	Y	Y	Y
4 Kleczka	Y	Y	Y	Y	Y
5 *Sensenbrenner*	Y	Y	Y	Y	Y
6 *Petri*	Y	Y	Y	Y	Y
7 Obey	Y	Y	Y	Y	Y
8 *Green*	Y	Y	Y	Y	Y
WYOMING					
AL *Cubin*	Y	Y	Y	Y	Y

Southern states - Ala., Ark., Fla., Ga., Ky., La., Miss., N.C., Okla., S.C., Tenn., Texas, Va.

Key

Y	Voted for (yea).
#	Paired for.
+	Announced for.
N	Voted against (nay).
X	Paired against.
−	Announced against.
P	Voted "present."
C	Voted "present" to avoid possible conflict of interest.
?	Did not vote or otherwise make a position known.

Democrats ***Republicans***
Independents

37. HR 1417. Copyright Royalty Regulation/Passage. Sensenbrenner, R-Wis., motion to suspend the rules and pass the bill that would establish three judgeships, called copyright royalty judges, to determine copyright royalty rates and the distribution of royalties. The Librarian of Congress — in consultation with the Register of Copyrights — would appoint the three full-time copyright royalty judges to serve six-year, staggered terms. Motion agreed to 406-0: R 216-0; D 189-0 (ND 138-0, SD 51-0); I 1-0. A two-thirds majority of those present and voting (271 in this case) is required for passage under suspension of the rules. March 3, 2004.

38. HR 1561. Patent and Trademark Fees/Passage. Passage of the bill that would increase most patent application fees by approximately 15 percent. Fees in excess of the amount appropriated to the agency in a fiscal year would be deposited in a special Treasury fund and could be refunded. The bill, as amended, also would reduce the filing fee charged to small businesses, independent investors and nonprofit organizations by 75 percent if the application is filed electronically. Passed 379-28: R 210-4; D 169-23 (ND 122-19, SD 47-4); I 0-1. March 3, 2004.

39. HR 3752. Space Tourism/Passage. Passage of the bill that would give the Federal Aviation Administration (FAA) regulatory authority over space tourism. The bill would streamline FAA regulations for issuing experimental permits to companies that want to test new flight vehicles. Passed 402-1: R 211-1; D 190-0 (ND 138-0, SD 52-0); I 1-0. March 4, 2004.

40. H Res 412. Drug Enforcement Administration Anniversary/Adoption. Sensenbrenner, R-Wis., motion to suspend the rules and adopt the resolution that would congratulate the Drug Enforcement Administration (DEA) on its 30th anniversary and honor DEA employees who have been killed or wounded in the line of duty. Motion agreed to 402-1: R 209-1; D 192-0 (ND 140-0, SD 52-0); I 1-0. A two-thirds majority of those present and voting (269 in this case) is required for adoption under suspension of the rules. March 4, 2004.

41. H Res 56. Day of Remembrance/Adoption. Sensenbrenner, R-Wis., motion to suspend the rules and adopt the resolution that would recognize the historical significance of an Executive Order signed by President Franklin D. Roosevelt on Feb. 19, 1942, which restricted the freedom of Japanese-Americans, German-Americans, Italian-Americans, and legal resident aliens by requiring identification cards and imposing travel restrictions, personal property seizures and internment. The bill also would support the efforts of Japanese-American, German-American, and Italian-American communities to recognize a National Day of Remembrance to increase awareness of these events. Motion agreed to 404-0: R 213-0; D 190-0 (ND 142-0, SD 48-0); I 1-0. A two-thirds majority of those present and voting (270 in this case) is required for adoption under suspension of the rules. March 4, 2004.

	37	38	39	40	41
ALABAMA					
1 *Bonner*	Y	Y	Y	Y	Y
2 *Everett*	Y	Y	Y	Y	Y
3 *Rogers*	Y	Y	Y	Y	Y
4 *Aderholt*	?	?	?	?	?
5 Cramer	Y	Y	Y	Y	Y
6 *Bachus*	Y	Y	Y	Y	Y
7 Davis	Y	Y	Y	Y	Y
ALASKA					
AL *Young*	Y	Y	Y	Y	Y
ARIZONA					
1 *Renzi*	Y	Y	Y	Y	Y
2 *Franks*	Y	Y	Y	Y	Y
3 *Shadegg*	Y	Y	Y	Y	Y
4 Pastor	Y	Y	Y	Y	Y
5 *Hayworth*	Y	Y	Y	Y	Y
6 *Flake*	Y	Y	Y	Y	Y
7 Grijalva	Y	Y	Y	Y	Y
8 *Kolbe*	Y	Y	?	Y	Y
ARKANSAS					
1 Berry	?	?	?	?	?
2 Snyder	Y	Y	Y	Y	Y
3 *Boozman*	Y	Y	Y	Y	Y
4 Ross	Y	Y	Y	Y	Y
CALIFORNIA					
1 Thompson	Y	Y	Y	Y	Y
2 *Herger*	Y	Y	Y	Y	Y
3 *Ose*	Y	Y	Y	Y	Y
4 *Doolittle*	Y	Y	Y	Y	Y
5 Matsui	Y	Y	Y	Y	Y
6 Woolsey	?	?	Y	Y	Y
7 Miller, George	Y	Y	Y	Y	Y
8 Pelosi	Y	Y	Y	Y	Y
9 Lee	Y	Y	Y	Y	Y
10 Tauscher	Y	Y	Y	Y	Y
11 *Pombo*	Y	Y	Y	Y	Y
12 Lantos	?	?	?	?	?
13 Stark	Y	Y	Y	Y	Y
14 Eshoo	Y	Y	Y	Y	Y
15 Honda	Y	Y	Y	Y	Y
16 Lofgren	Y	Y	Y	Y	Y
17 Farr	Y	Y	Y	Y	Y
18 Cardoza	Y	Y	Y	Y	Y
19 *Radanovich*	Y	Y	Y	Y	Y
20 Dooley	?	?	?	?	?
21 *Nunes*	Y	Y	Y	Y	Y
22 *Thomas*	Y	Y	Y	Y	Y
23 Capps	Y	Y	Y	Y	Y
24 *Gallegly*	Y	Y	Y	Y	Y
25 *McKeon*	Y	Y	Y	Y	Y
26 *Dreier*	Y	Y	Y	Y	Y
27 Sherman	Y	Y	Y	Y	Y
28 Berman	Y	Y	Y	Y	Y
29 Schiff	?	Y	Y	Y	Y
30 Waxman	Y	Y	Y	Y	Y
31 Becerra	Y	Y	Y	Y	Y
32 Solis	Y	Y	Y	Y	Y
33 Watson	Y	Y	N	Y	Y
34 Roybal-Allard	Y	Y	Y	Y	Y
35 Waters	Y	N	Y	Y	Y
36 Harman	Y	Y	Y	Y	Y

	37	38	39	40	41
37 Millender-McD.	Y	Y	Y	Y	Y
38 Napolitano	Y	Y	Y	Y	Y
39 Sánchez, Linda	Y	?	Y	Y	Y
40 *Royce*	?	Y	Y	Y	Y
41 *Lewis*	Y	Y	Y	Y	Y
42 *Miller, Gary*	Y	Y	Y	Y	Y
43 Baca	+	Y	Y	Y	Y
44 *Calvert*	?	?	?	?	?
45 *Bono*	Y	Y	Y	Y	Y
46 *Rohrabacher*	Y	Y	Y	Y	Y
47 Sanchez, Loretta	Y	Y	Y	Y	Y
48 *Cox*	Y	Y	Y	Y	Y
49 *Issa*	Y	Y	Y	Y	Y
50 *Cunningham*	Y	Y	Y	Y	Y
51 Filner	+	Y	Y	Y	Y
52 *Hunter*	Y	N	Y	Y	Y
53 Davis	?	Y	Y	Y	Y
COLORADO					
1 DeGette	Y	Y	Y	Y	Y
2 Udall	Y	Y	Y	Y	Y
3 *McInnis*	Y	Y	Y	Y	Y
4 *Musgrave*	Y	Y	Y	Y	Y
5 *Hefley*	Y	Y	Y	Y	Y
6 *Tancredo*	Y	Y	Y	Y	Y
7 *Beauprez*	Y	Y	Y	Y	Y
CONNECTICUT					
1 Larson	Y	Y	Y	Y	Y
2 *Simmons*	Y	Y	Y	Y	Y
3 DeLauro	Y	Y	Y	Y	Y
4 *Shays*	Y	Y	Y	Y	Y
5 *Johnson*	Y	Y	Y	Y	Y
DELAWARE					
AL *Castle*	?	?	Y	Y	Y
FLORIDA					
1 *Miller, J.*	Y	Y	Y	Y	Y
2 Boyd	Y	Y	Y	Y	Y
3 Brown	Y	Y	Y	Y	Y
4 *Crenshaw*	Y	Y	Y	Y	Y
5 *Brown-Waite*	Y	Y	Y	Y	Y
6 *Stearns*	Y	Y	Y	Y	Y
7 *Mica*	Y	Y	Y	Y	Y
8 *Keller*	Y	Y	Y	Y	Y
9 *Bilirakis*	Y	Y	Y	Y	Y
10 *Young*	Y	?	Y	Y	Y
11 Davis	Y	Y	Y	Y	Y
12 *Putnam*	Y	Y	Y	Y	Y
13 *Harris*	Y	Y	Y	Y	Y
14 *Goss*	Y	Y	Y	Y	Y
15 *Weldon*	Y	Y	Y	Y	Y
16 *Foley*	Y	Y	Y	Y	Y
17 Meek	Y	N	Y	Y	Y
18 *Ros-Lehtinen*	Y	Y	Y	Y	Y
19 Wexler	Y	Y	Y	Y	Y
20 Deutsch	Y	Y	Y	Y	Y
21 *Diaz-Balart, L.*	Y	Y	Y	Y	Y
22 *Shaw*	Y	Y	Y	Y	Y
23 Hastings	Y	N	Y	Y	Y
24 *Feeney*	Y	Y	Y	Y	Y
25 *Diaz-Balart, M.*	Y	Y	Y	Y	Y
GEORGIA					
1 *Kingston*	Y	Y	Y	Y	Y
2 Bishop	Y	Y	Y	Y	Y
3 Marshall	Y	Y	Y	Y	?
4 Majette	Y	Y	Y	Y	Y
5 Lewis	Y	N	Y	Y	Y
6 *Isakson*	Y	Y	?	?	?
7 *Linder*	Y	Y	Y	Y	Y
8 *Collins*	Y	Y	Y	Y	Y
9 *Norwood*	Y	Y	Y	Y	Y
10 *Deal*	Y	Y	Y	Y	Y
11 *Gingrey*	Y	Y	Y	Y	Y
12 *Burns*	Y	Y	Y	Y	Y
13 Scott	Y	Y	Y	Y	Y
HAWAII					
1 Abercrombie	Y	Y	Y	Y	Y
2 Case	Y	Y	Y	Y	Y
IDAHO					
1 *Otter*	Y	Y	Y	Y	Y
2 *Simpson*	Y	Y	Y	Y	Y
ILLINOIS					
1 Rush	Y	Y	?	?	?
2 Jackson	Y	N	Y	Y	Y
3 Lipinski	Y	Y	Y	Y	Y
4 Gutierrez	Y	Y	Y	Y	Y
5 Emanuel	Y	Y	Y	Y	Y
6 *Hyde*	Y	Y	Y	Y	Y

ND Northern Democrats   SD Southern Democrats

	37	38	39	40	41
7 Davis	Y	Y	?	Y	Y
8 Crane	Y	Y	Y	Y	Y
9 Schakowsky	Y	N	Y	Y	Y
10 *Kirk*	Y	Y	Y	Y	Y
11 *Weller*	?	Y	?	?	?
12 Costello	Y	N	Y	Y	Y
13 *Biggert*	Y	Y	Y	Y	Y
14 Hastert					
15 *Johnson*	Y	Y	Y	Y	Y
16 *Manzullo*	Y	Y	Y	?	?
17 Evans	Y	N	Y	Y	Y
18 *LaHood*	Y	Y	Y	Y	Y
19 *Shimkus*	Y	Y	Y	Y	Y

INDIANA

	37	38	39	40	41
1 Visclosky	Y	N	Y	Y	Y
2 *Chocola*	?	Y	Y	Y	Y
3 *Souder*	Y	Y	Y	Y	Y
4 *Buyer*	Y	Y	Y	Y	Y
5 *Burton*	Y	Y	Y	Y	Y
6 *Pence*	?	?	?	?	?
7 Carson	Y	N	Y	Y	Y
8 *Hostettler*	Y	Y	Y	Y	Y
9 Hill	Y	Y	Y	Y	Y

IOWA

	37	38	39	40	41
1 *Nussle*	Y	Y	Y	Y	Y
2 *Leach*	Y	Y	Y	Y	Y
3 Boswell	Y	Y	Y	Y	Y
4 *Latham*	Y	Y	Y	Y	Y
5 *King*	Y	Y	Y	Y	Y

KANSAS

	37	38	39	40	41
1 *Moran*	Y	Y	Y	Y	Y
2 *Ryun*	Y	Y	Y	Y	Y
3 Moore	Y	Y	Y	Y	Y
4 *Tiahrt*	Y	Y	Y	Y	Y

KENTUCKY

	37	38	39	40	41
1 *Whitfield*	Y	Y	?	?	?
2 *Lewis*	Y	Y	Y	Y	Y
3 *Northup*	Y	Y	Y	Y	Y
4 Lucas	Y	Y	Y	Y	Y
5 *Rogers*	Y	Y	Y	Y	Y
6 Chandler	Y	Y	Y	Y	Y

LOUISIANA

	37	38	39	40	41
1 *Vitter*	Y	Y	Y	Y	Y
2 Jefferson	Y	Y	Y	Y	Y
3 *Tauzin*	Y	Y	Y	Y	Y
4 *McCrery*	Y	Y	Y	Y	Y
5 Alexander	Y	Y	Y	Y	Y
6 *Baker*	Y	Y	Y	Y	Y
7 John	Y	Y	Y	Y	Y

MAINE

	37	38	39	40	41
1 Allen	Y	Y	Y	Y	Y
2 Michaud	Y	Y	Y	Y	Y

MARYLAND

	37	38	39	40	41
1 *Gilchrest*	Y	Y	Y	Y	Y
2 Ruppersberger	Y	N	Y	Y	Y
3 Cardin	Y	Y	Y	Y	Y
4 Wynn	Y	N	Y	Y	Y
5 Hoyer	Y	Y	Y	Y	Y
6 *Bartlett*	Y	N	Y	Y	Y
7 Cummings	Y	N	?	Y	Y
8 Van Hollen	Y	Y	Y	Y	Y

MASSACHUSETTS

	37	38	39	40	41
1 Olver	Y	Y	Y	Y	Y
2 Neal	Y	Y	Y	Y	Y
3 McGovern	Y	Y	Y	Y	Y
4 Frank	Y	Y	Y	Y	Y
5 Meehan	Y	Y	Y	Y	Y
6 Tierney	Y	Y	Y	Y	Y
7 Markey	Y	Y	Y	Y	Y
8 Capuano	Y	Y	Y	Y	Y
9 Lynch	Y	Y	Y	Y	Y
10 Delahunt	Y	Y	Y	Y	Y

MICHIGAN

	37	38	39	40	41
1 Stupak	Y	Y	Y	Y	Y
2 *Hoekstra*	Y	Y	Y	Y	Y
3 *Ehlers*	Y	Y	Y	Y	Y
4 *Camp*	Y	Y	Y	Y	Y
5 Kildee	Y	Y	Y	Y	Y
6 *Upton*	Y	Y	Y	Y	Y
7 *Smith*	?	Y	Y	Y	Y
8 *Rogers*	Y	Y	Y	Y	Y
9 *Knollenberg*	Y	Y	Y	Y	Y
10 *Miller*	Y	Y	Y	Y	Y
11 *McCotter*	?	Y	Y	Y	Y
12 Levin	Y	Y	Y	Y	Y

	37	38	39	40	41
13 Kilpatrick	Y	Y	Y	Y	Y
14 Conyers	Y	Y	Y	Y	Y
15 Dingell	Y	Y	Y	Y	Y

MINNESOTA

	37	38	39	40	41
1 *Gutknecht*	Y	Y	Y	Y	Y
2 *Kline*	Y	Y	Y	Y	Y
3 *Ramstad*	Y	Y	Y	Y	Y
4 McCollum	Y	Y	Y	Y	Y
5 Sabo	Y	Y	Y	Y	Y
6 *Kennedy*	Y	Y	Y	Y	Y
7 Peterson	Y	Y	Y	Y	Y
8 Oberstar	Y	N	Y	Y	Y

MISSISSIPPI

	37	38	39	40	41
1 *Wicker*	Y	Y	Y	Y	Y
2 Thompson	Y	Y	Y	Y	Y
3 *Pickering*	Y	Y	Y	Y	Y
4 Taylor	Y	Y	Y	Y	Y

MISSOURI

	37	38	39	40	41
1 Clay	Y	N	Y	Y	Y
2 *Akin*	Y	Y	Y	Y	Y
3 Gephardt	Y	Y	Y	Y	Y
4 Skelton	Y	Y	Y	Y	Y
5 McCarthy	Y	Y	Y	Y	Y
6 *Graves*	Y	Y	Y	Y	Y
7 *Blunt*	Y	Y	?	?	?
8 *Emerson*	Y	Y	Y	Y	Y
9 *Hulshof*	Y	Y	Y	Y	Y

MONTANA

	37	38	39	40	41
AL *Rehberg*	Y	Y	Y	Y	Y

NEBRASKA

	37	38	39	40	41
1 *Bereuter*	Y	Y	Y	Y	Y
2 *Terry*	Y	Y	Y	Y	Y
3 *Osborne*	Y	Y	Y	Y	Y

NEVADA

	37	38	39	40	41
1 Berkley	Y	Y	Y	Y	Y
2 *Gibbons*	Y	Y	Y	Y	Y
3 *Porter*	Y	Y	Y	Y	Y

NEW HAMPSHIRE

	37	38	39	40	41
1 *Bradley*	Y	Y	Y	Y	Y
2 *Bass*	Y	Y	Y	Y	Y

NEW JERSEY

	37	38	39	40	41
1 Andrews	Y	Y	Y	Y	Y
2 *LoBiondo*	Y	Y	Y	Y	Y
3 *Saxton*	Y	Y	Y	Y	Y
4 *Smith*	Y	Y	Y	Y	Y
5 *Garrett*	Y	Y	Y	Y	Y
6 Pallone	Y	Y	Y	Y	Y
7 *Ferguson*	Y	Y	Y	Y	Y
8 Pascrell	Y	Y	Y	Y	Y
9 Rothman	Y	Y	Y	Y	Y
10 Payne	Y	Y	Y	Y	Y
11 *Frelinghuysen*	Y	Y	Y	Y	Y
12 Holt	Y	N	Y	Y	Y
13 Menendez	Y	?	Y	Y	Y

NEW MEXICO

	37	38	39	40	41
1 *Wilson*	Y	Y	Y	Y	Y
2 *Pearce*	Y	Y	Y	Y	Y
3 Udall	Y	Y	Y	Y	Y

NEW YORK

	37	38	39	40	41
1 Bishop	Y	Y	Y	Y	Y
2 Israel	Y	Y	Y	Y	Y
3 *King*	Y	Y	?	?	?
4 McCarthy	Y	Y	Y	Y	Y
5 Ackerman	Y	Y	Y	Y	Y
6 Meeks	Y	Y	Y	Y	Y
7 Crowley	Y	Y	Y	Y	Y
8 Nadler	Y	Y	Y	Y	Y
9 Weiner	Y	Y	Y	Y	Y
10 Towns	Y	Y	Y	Y	Y
11 Owens	Y	Y	Y	Y	Y
12 Velázquez	Y	Y	Y	Y	Y
13 *Fossella*	Y	Y	Y	Y	Y
14 Maloney	Y	Y	Y	Y	Y
15 Rangel	Y	Y	Y	Y	Y
16 Serrano	Y	Y	Y	Y	Y
17 Engel	Y	Y	?	?	?
18 Lowey	Y	Y	Y	Y	Y
19 *Kelly*	Y	Y	Y	Y	Y
20 *Sweeney*	Y	Y	Y	Y	Y
21 McNulty	Y	Y	Y	Y	Y
22 Hinchey	Y	Y	Y	Y	Y
23 *McHugh*	Y	Y	Y	Y	Y
24 *Boehlert*	Y	Y	Y	Y	Y
25 Walsh	Y	Y	Y	?	Y

	37	38	39	40	41
26 *Reynolds*	Y	Y	Y	Y	Y
27 *Quinn*	Y	Y	Y	Y	Y
28 Slaughter	Y	Y	Y	Y	Y
29 Houghton	Y	Y	?	?	?

NORTH CAROLINA

	37	38	39	40	41
1 Ballance	Y	Y	Y	Y	Y
2 Etheridge	Y	Y	Y	Y	Y
3 *Jones*	Y	N	Y	Y	Y
4 Price	Y	Y	Y	Y	Y
5 *Burr*	Y	Y	Y	Y	Y
6 *Coble*	Y	Y	Y	Y	Y
7 McIntyre	Y	Y	Y	Y	Y
8 *Hayes*	Y	Y	Y	Y	Y
9 *Myrick*	Y	Y	Y	Y	Y
10 *Ballenger*	Y	?	Y	Y	Y
11 *Taylor*	Y	Y	Y	Y	Y
12 Watt	Y	Y	Y	Y	Y
13 Miller	Y	Y	Y	Y	Y

NORTH DAKOTA

	37	38	39	40	41
AL Pomeroy	Y	Y	Y	Y	Y

OHIO

	37	38	39	40	41
1 *Chabot*	Y	Y	Y	Y	Y
2 *Portman*	Y	Y	Y	Y	Y
3 *Turner*	Y	Y	Y	Y	Y
4 *Oxley*	Y	Y	Y	Y	Y
5 *Gillmor*	Y	Y	Y	Y	Y
6 Strickland	Y	N	Y	Y	Y
7 *Hobson*	Y	Y	Y	Y	Y
8 *Boehner*	Y	Y	Y	Y	Y
9 Kaptur	Y	N	Y	Y	Y
10 Kucinich	?	?	?	?	?
11 Jones	Y	Y	Y	Y	Y
12 *Tiberi*	Y	Y	Y	Y	Y
13 Brown	?	N	Y	Y	Y
14 *LaTourette*	Y	Y	Y	Y	Y
15 *Pryce*	Y	Y	Y	Y	Y
16 *Regula*	Y	Y	Y	Y	Y
17 Ryan	Y	Y	Y	Y	Y
18 *Ney*	Y	Y	Y	Y	Y

OKLAHOMA

	37	38	39	40	41
1 *Sullivan*	Y	?	Y	Y	Y
2 Carson	Y	?	Y	Y	Y
3 *Lucas*	Y	?	Y	Y	Y
4 *Cole*	Y	?	Y	Y	Y
5 *Istook*	Y	?	Y	Y	Y

OREGON

	37	38	39	40	41
1 Wu	Y	Y	Y	Y	Y
2 *Walden*	Y	Y	Y	Y	Y
3 Blumenauer	Y	Y	Y	Y	Y
4 DeFazio	Y	Y	Y	Y	Y
5 Hooley	?	?	?	?	?

PENNSYLVANIA

	37	38	39	40	41
1 Brady	Y	Y	Y	Y	Y
2 Fattah	Y	Y	Y	?	Y
3 *English*	Y	Y	Y	Y	Y
4 *Hart*	Y	Y	Y	Y	Y
5 *Peterson*	Y	Y	Y	Y	Y
6 *Gerlach*	Y	Y	+	+	Y
7 *Weldon*	?	?	Y	Y	Y
8 *Greenwood*	Y	Y	Y	Y	Y
9 *Shuster, Bill*	Y	Y	Y	Y	Y
10 *Sherwood*	Y	Y	Y	Y	Y
11 Kanjorski	Y	N	Y	Y	Y
12 Murtha	Y	Y	Y	Y	Y
13 Hoeffel	Y	Y	Y	Y	Y
14 Doyle	Y	Y	Y	Y	Y
15 *Toomey*	?	?	?	?	?
16 *Pitts*	Y	Y	Y	Y	Y
17 Holden	Y	Y	Y	Y	Y
18 *Murphy*	Y	Y	Y	Y	Y
19 *Platts*	Y	Y	Y	Y	Y

RHODE ISLAND

	37	38	39	40	41
1 Kennedy	Y	Y	+	Y	Y
2 Langevin	Y	Y	Y	Y	Y

SOUTH CAROLINA

	37	38	39	40	41
1 *Brown*	Y	Y	Y	Y	Y
2 *Wilson*	Y	Y	Y	Y	Y
3 *Barrett*	Y	Y	Y	Y	Y
4 *DeMint*	Y	Y	Y	Y	Y
5 Spratt	Y	Y	Y	Y	Y
6 Clyburn	Y	Y	Y	Y	Y

SOUTH DAKOTA

	37	38	39	40	41
AL Vacant					

TENNESSEE

	37	38	39	40	41
1 *Jenkins*	Y	Y	Y	Y	Y
2 *Duncan*	Y	Y	Y	Y	Y
3 *Wamp*	Y	Y	Y	Y	Y
4 Davis	Y	Y	Y	Y	Y
5 Cooper	Y	Y	Y	Y	Y
6 Gordon	Y	Y	Y	Y	Y
7 *Blackburn*	Y	Y	Y	Y	Y
8 Tanner	Y	Y	Y	Y	Y
9 Ford	Y	Y	Y	Y	?

TEXAS

	37	38	39	40	41
1 Sandlin	Y	?	Y	Y	Y
2 Turner	Y	Y	Y	Y	Y
3 *Johnson, Sam*	Y	Y	Y	Y	Y
4 *Hall*	Y	?	Y	Y	Y
5 *Hensarling*	Y	Y	Y	Y	Y
6 *Barton*	Y	Y	Y	Y	Y
7 *Culberson*	Y	Y	?	?	?
8 *Brady*	Y	Y	Y	Y	Y
9 Lampson	Y	Y	Y	Y	Y
10 Doggett	?	?	?	?	?
11 Edwards	Y	Y	Y	?	Y
12 *Granger*	Y	Y	Y	Y	Y
13 *Thornberry*	Y	Y	Y	Y	Y
14 *Paul*	Y	N	N	N	Y
15 Hinojosa	?	?	?	?	?
16 Reyes	?	Y	Y	Y	Y
17 Stenholm	Y	Y	Y	Y	Y
18 Jackson-Lee	Y	N	Y	Y	Y
19 *Neugebauer*	Y	Y	Y	Y	Y
20 Gonzalez	Y	Y	Y	Y	Y
21 *Smith*	Y	Y	Y	Y	Y
22 *DeLay*	Y	Y	Y	Y	Y
23 *Bonilla*	Y	Y	Y	Y	Y
24 Frost	Y	Y	Y	Y	Y
25 Bell	Y	Y	?	?	?
26 *Burgess*	Y	Y	Y	Y	Y
27 Ortiz	?	Y	Y	Y	Y
28 Rodriguez	?	?	?	?	?
29 Green	Y	Y	Y	Y	?
30 Johnson, E.B.	Y	Y	Y	Y	Y
31 *Carter*	Y	Y	Y	Y	Y
32 *Sessions*	Y	Y	?	?	?

UTAH

	37	38	39	40	41
1 *Bishop*	Y	Y	Y	Y	Y
2 Matheson	Y	Y	Y	Y	Y
3 *Cannon*	Y	Y	Y	Y	Y

VERMONT

	37	38	39	40	41
AL *Sanders*	Y	N	Y	Y	Y

VIRGINIA

	37	38	39	40	41
1 *Davis, Jo Ann*	Y	Y	Y	Y	Y
2 *Schrock*	Y	Y	Y	?	Y
3 Scott	Y	Y	Y	Y	Y
4 *Forbes*	Y	Y	Y	Y	Y
5 *Goode*	Y	Y	Y	Y	Y
6 *Goodlatte*	Y	Y	Y	Y	Y
7 *Cantor*	Y	Y	Y	Y	Y
8 Moran	Y	Y	Y	Y	Y
9 Boucher	Y	Y	Y	Y	Y
10 *Wolf*	Y	Y	?	?	?
11 *Davis, T.*	Y	Y	Y	Y	Y

WASHINGTON

	37	38	39	40	41
1 Inslee	Y	Y	Y	Y	Y
2 Larsen	Y	Y	Y	Y	Y
3 Baird	Y	Y	Y	Y	Y
4 *Hastings*	Y	Y	Y	Y	Y
5 *Nethercutt*	Y	Y	Y	Y	Y
6 Dicks	Y	Y	Y	Y	Y
7 McDermott	Y	Y	Y	Y	Y
8 *Dunn*	Y	Y	Y	Y	Y
9 Smith	Y	Y	Y	Y	Y

WEST VIRGINIA

	37	38	39	40	41
1 Mollohan	Y	Y	Y	Y	Y
2 *Capito*	Y	Y	Y	Y	Y
3 Rahall	Y	Y	Y	Y	Y

WISCONSIN

	37	38	39	40	41
1 *Ryan*	Y	Y	Y	Y	Y
2 Baldwin	Y	Y	Y	Y	Y
3 Kind	Y	Y	Y	Y	Y
4 Kleczka	Y	Y	?	?	Y
5 *Sensenbrenner*	Y	Y	Y	Y	Y
6 *Petri*	Y	Y	Y	Y	Y
7 Obey	Y	N	Y	Y	Y
8 *Green*	Y	Y	Y	Y	Y

WYOMING

	37	38	39	40	41
AL *Cubin*	Y	Y	Y	Y	Y

Southern states - Ala., Ark., Fla., Ga., Ky., La., Miss., N.C., Okla., S.C., Tenn., Texas, Va.

Key

42. H Res 519. California Earthquake/Adoption. T. Davis, R-Va., motion to suspend the rules and adopt the resolution that would express sadness at the loss of life and property caused by the Dec. 22, 2003, earthquake in San Luis Obispo County, Calif., and recognize the local officials and personnel who aided the earthquake victims and their families. Motion agreed to 404-0: R 215-0; D 188-0 (ND 140-0, SD 48-0); I 1-0. A two-thirds majority of those present and voting (270 in this case) is required for adoption under suspension of the rules. March 9, 2004.

43. H Res 392. Detroit Shock Basketball Tribute/Adoption. Miller, R-Mich., motion to suspend the rules and adopt the resolution that would congratulate the Detroit Shock for winning the 2003 Women's National Basketball Association Championship. Motion agreed to 401-0: R 213-0; D 187-0 (ND 139-0, SD 48-0); I 1-0. A two-thirds majority of those present and voting (268 in this case) is required for adoption under suspension of the rules. March 9, 2004.

44. H Res 475. San Jose Earthquakes Soccer Tribute/Adoption. Miller, R-Mich., motion to suspend the rules and adopt the resolution that would congratulate the San Jose Earthquakes for winning the 2003 Major League Soccer Cup. Motion agreed to 399-0: R 212-0; D 186-0 (ND 138-0, SD 48-0); I 1-0. A two-thirds majority of those present and voting (266 in this case) is required for adoption under suspension of the rules. March 9, 2004.

45. Procedural Motion/Journal. Approval of the House Journal of Tuesday, March 9, 2004. Approved 353-41: R 197-12; D 155-29 (ND 112-25, SD 43-4); I 1-0. March 10, 2004.

46. S 1881. Medical Devices Technical Corrections/Passage. Greenwood, R-Pa., motion to suspend the rules and pass the bill that would make technical corrections and clarifications to the Medical Device User Fee and Modernization Act of 2002, including clarifying the types of fees applicable under the act. Motion agreed to 396-0: R 211-0; D 184-0 (ND 137-0, SD 47-0); I 1-0. A two-thirds majority of those present and voting (264 in this case) is required for passage under suspension of the rules. March 10, 2004.

47. H Con Res 373. "Kids Love a Mystery" Program/Adoption. Gingrey, R-Ga., motion to suspend the rules and adopt the concurrent resolution that would express the sense of Congress that "Kids Love a Mystery" — a program that promotes children's reading and literacy — should be supported and encouraged. Motion agreed to 388-11: R 203-11; D 184-0 (ND 136-0, SD 48-0); I 1-0. A two-thirds majority of those present and voting (266 in this case) is required for adoption under suspension of the rules. March 10, 2004.

	42	43	44	45	46	47
ALABAMA						
1 *Bonner*	Y	Y	Y	Y	Y	Y
2 *Everett*	Y	Y	Y	Y	Y	N
3 *Rogers*	Y	Y	Y	Y	Y	Y
4 *Aderholt*	Y	Y	Y	N	Y	Y
5 Cramer	Y	Y	Y	Y	Y	Y
6 *Bachus*	Y	Y	Y	Y	Y	Y
7 Davis	Y	Y	Y	Y	Y	Y
ALASKA						
AL *Young*	Y	Y	Y	Y	Y	Y
ARIZONA						
1 *Renzi*	Y	Y	Y	Y	Y	Y
2 *Franks*	Y	Y	Y	Y	Y	Y
3 *Shadegg*	?	?	?	Y	Y	Y
4 Pastor	Y	Y	Y	Y	Y	Y
5 *Hayworth*	Y	Y	Y	Y	Y	Y
6 *Flake*	Y	Y	Y	Y	Y	N
7 Grijalva	Y	Y	Y	Y	Y	Y
8 *Kolbe*	Y	Y	Y	Y	Y	Y
ARKANSAS						
1 Berry	Y	Y	Y	Y	Y	Y
2 Snyder	Y	Y	Y	Y	Y	Y
3 *Boozman*	Y	Y	Y	Y	Y	Y
4 Ross	Y	Y	Y	Y	Y	Y
CALIFORNIA						
1 Thompson	Y	Y	Y	N	Y	Y
2 *Herger*	Y	Y	Y	Y	Y	Y
3 *Ose*	Y	Y	Y	Y	Y	Y
4 *Doolittle*	Y	Y	Y	Y	Y	Y
5 Matsui	Y	Y	Y	Y	Y	Y
6 Woolsey	Y	Y	Y	Y	Y	Y
7 Miller, George	Y	Y	Y	N	Y	Y
8 Pelosi	Y	Y	Y	Y	Y	Y
9 Lee	Y	Y	Y	Y	Y	Y
10 Tauscher	Y	Y	Y	N	Y	Y
11 *Pombo*	Y	Y	Y	Y	Y	Y
12 Lantos	Y	Y	Y	Y	Y	Y
13 Stark	Y	Y	Y	Y	Y	Y
14 Eshoo	Y	Y	Y	Y	Y	Y
15 Honda	Y	Y	Y	Y	Y	Y
16 Lofgren	Y	Y	Y	?	?	?
17 Farr	Y	Y	Y	Y	Y	Y
18 Cardoza	Y	Y	Y	Y	Y	Y
19 *Radanovich*	Y	Y	Y	Y	Y	Y
20 Dooley	Y	Y	Y	Y	Y	Y
21 *Nunes*	Y	Y	Y	Y	Y	Y
22 *Thomas*	Y	Y	Y	Y	Y	Y
23 *Capps*	Y	?	Y	Y	Y	Y
24 *Gallegly*	Y	Y	Y	Y	Y	Y
25 *McKeon*	Y	Y	Y	Y	Y	Y
26 *Dreier*	Y	Y	Y	Y	Y	Y
27 Sherman	Y	Y	Y	Y	Y	Y
28 Berman	Y	Y	Y	Y	Y	Y
29 Schiff	Y	Y	Y	?	?	?
30 Waxman	Y	Y	Y	Y	Y	Y
31 Becerra	Y	Y	Y	Y	Y	Y
32 Solis	Y	Y	Y	Y	Y	Y
33 Watson	Y	Y	Y	Y	Y	Y
34 Roybal-Allard	Y	Y	Y	Y	Y	Y
35 Waters	Y	Y	Y	N	Y	Y
36 Harman	Y	Y	Y	Y	Y	Y

	42	43	44	45	46	47
37 Millender-McD.	Y	Y	Y	Y	Y	Y
38 Napolitano	Y	Y	Y	Y	Y	Y
39 Sánchez, Linda	Y	Y	Y	Y	Y	Y
40 *Royce*	Y	Y	Y	Y	Y	N
41 *Lewis*	Y	Y	Y	Y	Y	Y
42 *Miller, Gary*	Y	Y	Y	Y	Y	Y
43 Baca	Y	Y	Y	Y	Y	Y
44 *Calvert*	Y	Y	Y	Y	Y	Y
45 *Bono*	Y	Y	Y	Y	Y	Y
46 *Rohrabacher*	Y	Y	Y	Y	Y	Y
47 Sanchez, Loretta	Y	Y	Y	Y	Y	Y
48 *Cox*	Y	Y	Y	?	?	Y
49 *Issa*	Y	Y	Y	Y	Y	Y
50 *Cunningham*	Y	Y	Y	Y	Y	Y
51 Filner	Y	Y	Y	N	Y	Y
52 *Hunter*	Y	Y	Y	Y	Y	Y
53 Davis	Y	Y	Y	Y	Y	Y
COLORADO						
1 DeGette	Y	Y	Y	Y	Y	Y
2 Udall	?	?	?	?	?	?
3 *McInnis*	Y	Y	Y	Y	Y	Y
4 *Musgrave*	Y	Y	Y	Y	Y	Y
5 *Hefley*	Y	Y	Y	N	Y	N
6 *Tancredo*	Y	Y	Y	P	Y	N
7 *Beauprez*	Y	Y	Y	Y	Y	Y
CONNECTICUT						
1 Larson	Y	Y	Y	Y	Y	Y
2 *Simmons*	Y	Y	Y	Y	Y	Y
3 DeLauro	Y	Y	Y	Y	Y	Y
4 *Shays*	Y	Y	Y	Y	Y	Y
5 Johnson	Y	Y	Y	Y	Y	Y
DELAWARE						
AL *Castle*	Y	Y	Y	Y	Y	Y
FLORIDA						
1 *Miller, J.*	?	?	?	?	?	?
2 Boyd	Y	Y	Y	Y	Y	Y
3 Brown	Y	Y	Y	Y	Y	Y
4 *Crenshaw*	Y	Y	Y	Y	Y	Y
5 *Brown-Waite*	Y	Y	Y	Y	Y	Y
6 *Stearns*	Y	Y	Y	Y	Y	Y
7 *Mica*	Y	Y	Y	Y	Y	Y
8 *Keller*	Y	Y	Y	Y	Y	Y
9 *Bilirakis*	Y	Y	Y	Y	Y	Y
10 *Young*	Y	Y	Y	Y	Y	Y
11 Davis	Y	Y	Y	Y	Y	Y
12 *Putnam*	Y	Y	Y	Y	Y	Y
13 *Harris*	Y	Y	Y	Y	Y	Y
14 *Goss*	?	?	?	Y	Y	Y
15 *Weldon*	?	?	Y	Y	Y	Y
16 *Foley*	Y	Y	Y	Y	Y	Y
17 Meek	Y	Y	Y	Y	Y	Y
18 *Ros-Lehtinen*	Y	?	Y	Y	Y	Y
19 Wexler	?	?	Y	Y	Y	Y
20 Deutsch	Y	Y	Y	Y	Y	Y
21 *Diaz-Balart, L.*	Y	Y	Y	Y	Y	Y
22 *Shaw*	Y	Y	Y	Y	Y	Y
23 Hastings	Y	Y	Y	Y	Y	Y
24 *Feeney*	Y	Y	Y	Y	Y	Y
25 *Diaz-Balart, M.*	Y	Y	Y	?	?	Y
GEORGIA						
1 *Kingston*	Y	Y	Y	Y	Y	N
2 Bishop	Y	Y	Y	Y	?	Y
3 Marshall	Y	Y	Y	Y	Y	Y
4 Majette	Y	Y	Y	Y	Y	Y
5 Lewis	Y	Y	Y	N	Y	Y
6 *Isakson*	Y	Y	Y	Y	Y	Y
7 *Linder*	Y	Y	Y	Y	Y	Y
8 *Collins*	Y	Y	Y	Y	Y	N
9 *Norwood*	Y	Y	Y	Y	Y	Y
10 *Deal*	Y	Y	Y	Y	Y	Y
11 *Gingrey*	Y	Y	Y	Y	Y	Y
12 *Burns*	Y	Y	Y	Y	Y	Y
13 Scott	Y	Y	Y	Y	Y	Y
HAWAII						
1 Abercrombie	Y	Y	Y	Y	Y	Y
2 Case	Y	Y	Y	Y	Y	Y
IDAHO						
1 *Otter*	Y	Y	Y	N	Y	Y
2 *Simpson*	Y	Y	Y	Y	Y	Y
ILLINOIS						
1 Rush	?	?	?	Y	Y	Y
2 Jackson	Y	Y	Y	Y	Y	Y
3 Lipinski	Y	Y	Y	Y	Y	Y
4 Gutierrez	?	?	?	Y	Y	Y
5 Emanuel	Y	Y	Y	Y	Y	Y
6 *Hyde*	Y	Y	Y	Y	Y	Y

ND Northern Democrats   SD Southern Democrats

	42	43	44	45	46	47
7 Davis	?	?	?	?	?	?
8 ***Crane***	Y	Y	Y	?	?	?
9 Schakowsky	Y	Y	Y	N	Y	Y
10 ***Kirk***	Y	Y	Y	Y	Y	Y
11 ***Weller***	Y	Y	Y	N	Y	Y
12 Costello	Y	Y	Y	N	Y	Y
13 ***Biggert***	Y	Y	Y	Y	Y	Y
14 ***Hastert***						
15 ***Johnson***	Y	Y	Y	Y	Y	Y
16 ***Manzullo***	Y	Y	Y	Y	Y	Y
17 Evans	Y	Y	Y	Y	Y	Y
18 ***LaHood***	Y	Y	Y	Y	Y	Y
19 ***Shimkus***	Y	Y	Y	Y	Y	Y
INDIANA						
1 Visclosky	Y	Y	Y	N	Y	Y
2 ***Chocola***	Y	Y	Y	Y	Y	Y
3 ***Souder***	Y	Y	Y	Y	Y	P
4 ***Buyer***	Y	Y	?	Y	Y	Y
5 ***Burton***	Y	Y	Y	Y	Y	Y
6 ***Pence***	Y	Y	Y	Y	Y	Y
7 Carson	Y	Y	Y	Y	Y	Y
8 ***Hostettler***	Y	Y	Y	Y	Y	Y
9 Hill	Y	Y	Y	Y	Y	Y
IOWA						
1 ***Nussle***	Y	Y	Y	Y	Y	Y
2 ***Leach***	Y	Y	Y	Y	Y	Y
3 Boswell	Y	Y	Y	Y	Y	Y
4 ***Latham***	Y	Y	Y	N	Y	Y
5 ***King***	Y	Y	Y	Y	Y	Y
KANSAS						
1 ***Moran***	Y	Y	Y	N	Y	Y
2 ***Ryun***	Y	Y	Y	Y	Y	Y
3 Moore	Y	Y	Y	Y	Y	Y
4 ***Tiahrt***	Y	?	Y	Y	Y	Y
KENTUCKY						
1 ***Whitfield***	Y	Y	Y	Y	Y	Y
2 ***Lewis***	Y	Y	Y	Y	Y	Y
3 ***Northup***	Y	Y	Y	Y	Y	Y
4 Lucas	Y	Y	Y	Y	Y	Y
5 ***Rogers***	Y	Y	Y	Y	Y	Y
6 Chandler	Y	Y	Y	Y	Y	Y
LOUISIANA						
1 ***Vitter***	Y	Y	Y	Y	Y	Y
2 Jefferson	Y	Y	Y	Y	Y	Y
3 ***Tauzin***	?	?	?	?	?	?
4 ***McCrery***	Y	Y	Y	Y	Y	Y
5 Alexander	Y	Y	Y	Y	Y	Y
6 ***Baker***	Y	Y	Y	Y	Y	Y
7 John	Y	Y	Y	Y	Y	Y
MAINE						
1 Allen	Y	Y	Y	Y	Y	Y
2 Michaud	Y	Y	Y	Y	Y	Y
MARYLAND						
1 ***Gilchrest***	Y	Y	Y	Y	Y	Y
2 Ruppersberger	Y	Y	Y	Y	Y	Y
3 Cardin	Y	Y	Y	Y	Y	Y
4 Wynn	Y	Y	Y	Y	Y	Y
5 Hoyer	Y	Y	Y	Y	Y	Y
6 ***Bartlett***	Y	Y	Y	Y	Y	Y
7 Cummings	Y	Y	Y	?	?	?
8 Van Hollen	Y	Y	Y	Y	Y	Y
MASSACHUSETTS						
1 Olver	Y	Y	Y	N	Y	Y
2 Neal	Y	Y	Y	Y	Y	Y
3 McGovern	Y	Y	Y	Y	Y	Y
4 Frank	Y	Y	Y	Y	Y	Y
5 Meehan	Y	Y	?	Y	Y	Y
6 Tierney	Y	Y	Y	Y	Y	Y
7 Markey	Y	Y	Y	Y	Y	Y
8 Capuano	Y	Y	Y	N	Y	Y
9 Lynch	Y	Y	Y	Y	Y	Y
10 Delahunt	Y	Y	Y	Y	Y	Y
MICHIGAN						
1 Stupak	Y	Y	?	N	Y	Y
2 ***Hoekstra***	Y	Y	Y	Y	Y	Y
3 ***Ehlers***	Y	Y	Y	Y	Y	Y
4 ***Camp***	Y	Y	Y	Y	Y	Y
5 Kildee	Y	Y	Y	Y	Y	Y
6 ***Upton***	Y	Y	Y	Y	Y	Y
7 ***Smith***	Y	Y	Y	Y	Y	Y
8 ***Rogers***	Y	Y	Y	Y	Y	Y
9 ***Knollenberg***	Y	Y	Y	Y	Y	Y
10 ***Miller***	Y	Y	Y	Y	Y	Y
11 ***McCotter***	Y	Y	Y	Y	Y	Y
12 Levin	Y	Y	Y	Y	Y	Y
13 Kilpatrick	Y	Y	Y	Y	Y	Y
14 Conyers	Y	Y	Y	Y	Y	Y
15 Dingell	Y	Y	Y	Y	Y	Y
MINNESOTA						
1 ***Gutknecht***	Y	Y	Y	Y	Y	Y
2 ***Kline***	Y	Y	Y	Y	Y	Y
3 ***Ramstad***	Y	Y	Y	N	Y	Y
4 McCollum	Y	Y	Y	Y	Y	Y
5 Sabo	Y	Y	Y	N	Y	Y
6 ***Kennedy***	Y	Y	Y	Y	Y	Y
7 Peterson	Y	Y	Y	N	Y	Y
8 Oberstar	Y	Y	Y	N	Y	Y
MISSISSIPPI						
1 ***Wicker***	Y	Y	Y	?	?	?
2 Thompson	Y	Y	Y	N	Y	Y
3 ***Pickering***	Y	Y	Y	Y	Y	Y
4 Taylor	Y	Y	Y	N	Y	Y
MISSOURI						
1 Clay	Y	Y	Y	?	?	?
2 ***Akin***	Y	Y	Y	Y	Y	Y
3 Gephardt	?	?	?	?	?	?
4 Skelton	Y	Y	Y	Y	Y	Y
5 McCarthy	Y	Y	Y	Y	Y	Y
6 ***Graves***	Y	Y	Y	N	Y	Y
7 ***Blunt***	Y	Y	Y	Y	Y	Y
8 ***Emerson***	Y	Y	Y	Y	Y	Y
9 ***Hulshof***	Y	Y	Y	N	Y	Y
MONTANA						
AL ***Rehberg***	Y	Y	Y	Y	Y	Y
NEBRASKA						
1 ***Bereuter***	?	?	?	Y	Y	Y
2 ***Terry***	Y	Y	Y	Y	Y	Y
3 ***Osborne***	Y	Y	Y	Y	Y	Y
NEVADA						
1 Berkley	Y	Y	Y	Y	Y	Y
2 ***Gibbons***	Y	Y	Y	Y	Y	Y
3 ***Porter***	Y	Y	Y	Y	Y	Y
NEW HAMPSHIRE						
1 ***Bradley***	Y	Y	Y	Y	Y	Y
2 ***Bass***	Y	Y	Y	Y	Y	Y
NEW JERSEY						
1 Andrews	Y	Y	Y	Y	Y	Y
2 ***LoBiondo***	Y	Y	Y	N	Y	Y
3 ***Saxton***	Y	Y	Y	Y	Y	Y
4 ***Smith***	Y	Y	Y	Y	Y	Y
5 ***Garrett***	Y	Y	Y	Y	Y	Y
6 Pallone	Y	Y	Y	Y	Y	Y
7 ***Ferguson***	Y	Y	Y	Y	Y	Y
8 Pascrell	Y	Y	Y	Y	Y	Y
9 Rothman	Y	Y	Y	Y	Y	Y
10 Payne	Y	Y	Y	Y	Y	Y
11 ***Frelinghuysen***	Y	Y	Y	Y	Y	Y
12 Holt	Y	Y	Y	N	Y	Y
13 Menendez	Y	Y	Y	Y	Y	Y
NEW MEXICO						
1 ***Wilson***	Y	Y	Y	Y	Y	Y
2 ***Pearce***	Y	Y	Y	Y	Y	Y
3 Udall	Y	Y	Y	N	Y	Y
NEW YORK						
1 Bishop	Y	Y	Y	Y	Y	Y
2 Israel	Y	Y	Y	Y	Y	Y
3 ***King***	Y	Y	Y	Y	Y	Y
4 McCarthy	Y	Y	Y	Y	Y	Y
5 Ackerman	Y	Y	Y	Y	Y	?
6 Meeks	Y	Y	Y	Y	Y	Y
7 Crowley	Y	Y	Y	Y	Y	Y
8 Nadler	Y	Y	Y	Y	Y	Y
9 Weiner	Y	Y	Y	Y	Y	Y
10 Towns	Y	Y	Y	Y	Y	Y
11 Owens	Y	Y	Y	?	?	?
12 Velázquez	Y	Y	Y	N	Y	Y
13 ***Fossella***	Y	Y	Y	?	?	Y
14 Maloney	Y	Y	Y	Y	Y	Y
15 Rangel	Y	Y	Y	Y	Y	Y
16 Serrano	Y	Y	Y	Y	Y	Y
17 Engel	Y	Y	Y	Y	Y	Y
18 Lowey	Y	Y	Y	Y	Y	Y
19 ***Kelly***	Y	Y	Y	Y	Y	Y
20 ***Sweeney***	Y	Y	Y	?	?	Y
21 McNulty	Y	Y	Y	N	Y	Y
22 Hinchey	Y	Y	Y	?	?	?
23 ***McHugh***	Y	Y	Y	Y	Y	Y
24 ***Boehlert***	Y	Y	Y	Y	Y	Y
25 ***Walsh***	Y	Y	Y	Y	Y	Y
26 ***Reynolds***	Y	Y	Y	Y	Y	Y
27 ***Quinn***	Y	Y	Y	Y	Y	Y
28 Slaughter	Y	Y	Y	Y	Y	Y
29 ***Houghton***	Y	Y	Y	Y	Y	Y
NORTH CAROLINA						
1 Ballance	Y	Y	Y	Y	Y	Y
2 Etheridge	Y	Y	Y	Y	Y	Y
3 ***Jones***	Y	Y	Y	Y	Y	N
4 Price	Y	Y	Y	Y	Y	Y
5 ***Burr***	Y	Y	Y	Y	Y	Y
6 ***Coble***	Y	Y	Y	Y	Y	Y
7 McIntyre	Y	Y	Y	Y	Y	Y
8 ***Hayes***	Y	Y	Y	Y	Y	Y
9 ***Myrick***	Y	Y	Y	Y	Y	Y
10 ***Ballenger***	Y	Y	Y	Y	Y	Y
11 ***Taylor***	Y	Y	Y	Y	Y	Y
12 Watt	Y	Y	Y	Y	Y	Y
13 Miller	Y	Y	Y	Y	Y	Y
NORTH DAKOTA						
AL Pomeroy	Y	Y	Y	Y	Y	Y
OHIO						
1 ***Chabot***	Y	Y	Y	Y	Y	Y
2 ***Portman***	Y	Y	Y	Y	Y	Y
3 ***Turner***	Y	Y	Y	Y	Y	Y
4 ***Oxley***	Y	Y	Y	Y	Y	Y
5 ***Gillmor***	Y	Y	Y	N	Y	Y
6 Strickland	Y	Y	Y	N	Y	Y
7 ***Hobson***	Y	Y	Y	Y	Y	Y
8 ***Boehner***	Y	Y	Y	Y	Y	Y
9 Kaptur	Y	Y	Y	Y	Y	Y
10 Kucinich	?	?	?	?	?	?
11 Jones	Y	Y	Y	Y	Y	Y
12 ***Tiberi***	Y	Y	Y	Y	Y	Y
13 Brown	Y	Y	Y	Y	Y	Y
14 ***LaTourette***	Y	Y	Y	?	?	?
15 ***Pryce***	Y	Y	Y	Y	Y	Y
16 ***Regula***	Y	Y	Y	Y	Y	Y
17 Ryan	Y	Y	Y	Y	Y	Y
18 ***Ney***	Y	Y	Y	Y	Y	Y
OKLAHOMA						
1 ***Sullivan***	Y	Y	Y	Y	Y	Y
2 Carson	Y	Y	Y	Y	Y	Y
3 ***Lucas***	Y	Y	Y	Y	Y	Y
4 ***Cole***	Y	Y	Y	Y	Y	Y
5 ***Istook***	Y	Y	Y	Y	Y	Y
OREGON						
1 Wu	Y	Y	Y	Y	Y	Y
2 ***Walden***	Y	Y	Y	Y	Y	Y
3 Blumenauer	Y	Y	Y	Y	Y	Y
4 DeFazio	Y	Y	Y	N	Y	Y
5 Hooley	Y	Y	Y	Y	Y	Y
PENNSYLVANIA						
1 Brady	Y	Y	Y	N	Y	Y
2 Fattah	Y	Y	Y	Y	Y	Y
3 ***English***	Y	Y	Y	N	Y	Y
4 ***Hart***	Y	Y	Y	Y	Y	Y
5 ***Peterson***	Y	Y	Y	Y	Y	Y
6 ***Gerlach***	Y	Y	Y	Y	Y	Y
7 ***Weldon***	Y	Y	Y	Y	Y	Y
8 ***Greenwood***	Y	Y	Y	?	?	Y
9 ***Shuster, Bill***	Y	Y	Y	Y	Y	Y
10 ***Sherwood***	Y	Y	Y	Y	Y	Y
11 Kanjorski	Y	Y	Y	Y	Y	Y
12 Murtha	?	?	?	Y	Y	Y
13 Hoeffel	?	?	?	Y	Y	Y
14 Doyle	Y	Y	Y	Y	Y	Y
15 ***Toomey***	?	?	?	?	?	?
16 ***Pitts***	Y	Y	Y	Y	Y	Y
17 Holden	Y	Y	Y	Y	Y	Y
18 ***Murphy***	Y	Y	Y	Y	Y	Y
19 ***Platts***	Y	Y	Y	Y	Y	Y
RHODE ISLAND						
1 Kennedy	Y	Y	Y	?	?	?
2 Langevin	Y	Y	Y	Y	Y	Y
SOUTH CAROLINA						
1 ***Brown***	Y	Y	Y	Y	Y	Y
2 ***Wilson***	Y	Y	Y	Y	Y	Y
3 ***Barrett***	Y	Y	Y	Y	Y	Y
4 ***DeMint***	?	?	?	Y	Y	Y
5 Spratt	Y	Y	Y	?	Y	Y
6 Clyburn	Y	Y	Y	Y	Y	Y
SOUTH DAKOTA						
AL Vacant						
TENNESSEE						
1 ***Jenkins***	Y	Y	Y	Y	Y	Y
2 ***Duncan***	Y	Y	Y	Y	Y	Y
3 ***Wamp***	Y	Y	Y	Y	Y	Y
4 Davis	Y	Y	Y	Y	Y	Y
5 Cooper	Y	Y	Y	Y	Y	Y
6 Gordon	Y	Y	Y	Y	Y	Y
7 ***Blackburn***	Y	Y	Y	?	Y	Y
8 Tanner	Y	Y	Y	Y	Y	Y
9 Ford	Y	Y	Y	Y	Y	Y
TEXAS						
1 Sandlin	Y	Y	Y	Y	Y	Y
2 Turner	Y	Y	Y	Y	Y	Y
3 ***Johnson, Sam***	?	?	?	?	?	?
4 ***Hall***	?	?	?	?	?	?
5 ***Hensarling***	Y	Y	Y	Y	Y	Y
6 ***Barton***	?	?	?	?	?	?
7 ***Culberson***	?	?	?	Y	Y	Y
8 ***Brady***	Y	Y	Y	Y	Y	Y
9 Lampson	Y	Y	Y	Y	Y	Y
10 Doggett	?	?	?	?	?	?
11 Edwards	Y	Y	Y	Y	Y	Y
12 ***Granger***	Y	Y	Y	?	?	?
13 ***Thornberry***	Y	Y	?	Y	Y	Y
14 ***Paul***	Y	Y	Y	Y	Y	N
15 Hinojosa	?	?	?	?	?	?
16 Reyes	?	?	?	?	?	?
17 Stenholm	Y	Y	Y	Y	Y	Y
18 Jackson-Lee	?	?	?	?	?	?
19 ***Neugebauer***	Y	Y	Y	Y	Y	Y
20 Gonzalez	?	?	?	?	?	?
21 ***Smith***	Y	Y	Y	Y	Y	Y
22 ***DeLay***	Y	Y	Y	Y	Y	Y
23 ***Bonilla***	Y	Y	Y	Y	Y	Y
24 Frost	Y	Y	Y	Y	Y	Y
25 Bell	?	?	?	?	?	?
26 ***Burgess***	Y	Y	Y	Y	Y	N
27 Ortiz	?	?	?	?	?	?
28 Rodriguez	?	?	?	?	?	?
29 Green	Y	Y	Y	N	Y	Y
30 Johnson, E.B.	Y	Y	Y	Y	Y	Y
31 ***Carter***	?	?	?	?	?	?
32 ***Sessions***	Y	Y	Y	Y	Y	Y
UTAH						
1 ***Bishop***	Y	Y	Y	Y	Y	Y
2 Matheson	Y	Y	Y	Y	Y	Y
3 ***Cannon***	Y	Y	Y	Y	Y	Y
VERMONT						
AL *Sanders*	Y	Y	Y	Y	Y	Y
VIRGINIA						
1 ***Davis, Jo Ann***	Y	Y	Y	Y	Y	Y
2 ***Schrock***	Y	Y	Y	Y	Y	Y
3 Scott	Y	Y	Y	Y	Y	Y
4 ***Forbes***	Y	Y	Y	Y	Y	Y
5 ***Goode***	Y	Y	Y	Y	Y	N
6 ***Goodlatte***	Y	Y	Y	Y	Y	Y
7 ***Cantor***	Y	Y	Y	Y	Y	Y
8 Moran	Y	Y	Y	?	?	?
9 Boucher	Y	Y	Y	Y	Y	Y
10 ***Wolf***	Y	Y	Y	Y	Y	Y
11 ***Davis, T.***	Y	Y	Y	Y	Y	Y
WASHINGTON						
1 Inslee	Y	Y	Y	Y	Y	Y
2 Larsen	Y	Y	Y	N	Y	Y
3 Baird	Y	Y	Y	N	Y	Y
4 ***Hastings***	Y	Y	Y	Y	Y	Y
5 ***Nethercutt***	Y	Y	Y	Y	Y	Y
6 Dicks	Y	Y	Y	Y	Y	Y
7 McDermott	Y	Y	Y	N	Y	Y
8 ***Dunn***	Y	Y	Y	Y	Y	Y
9 Smith	Y	Y	Y	Y	Y	Y
WEST VIRGINIA						
1 Mollohan	Y	Y	Y	Y	Y	Y
2 ***Capito***	Y	Y	Y	Y	Y	Y
3 Rahall	Y	Y	Y	Y	Y	Y
WISCONSIN						
1 ***Ryan***	Y	Y	Y	Y	Y	Y
2 Baldwin	Y	Y	Y	N	Y	Y
3 Kind	Y	Y	Y	Y	Y	Y
4 Kleczka	Y	Y	Y	Y	Y	Y
5 ***Sensenbrenner***	Y	Y	Y	Y	Y	Y
6 ***Petri***	Y	Y	Y	Y	Y	Y
7 Obey	Y	Y	Y	Y	Y	Y
8 ***Green***	Y	Y	Y	Y	Y	Y
WYOMING						
AL ***Cubin***	Y	Y	Y	Y	Y	Y

Southern states - Ala., Ark., Fla., Ga., Ky., La., Miss., N.C., Okla., S.C., Tenn., Texas, Va.

Key

Y	Voted for (yea).
#	Paired for.
+	Announced for.
N	Voted against (nay).
X	Paired against.
–	Announced against.
P	Voted "present."
C	Voted "present" to avoid possible conflict of interest.
?	Did not vote or otherwise make a position known.

Democrats **Republicans**
Independents

48. HR 339. Food Industry Lawsuits/State Consumer Protection Laws. Scott, D-Va., amendment that would exempt from the bill an action brought by a state agency to enforce state consumer protection laws concerning mislabeling or other "unfair and deceptive trade practices." Rejected 177-241: R 2-222; D 174-19 (ND 134-6, SD 40-13); I 1-0. March 10, 2004.

49. HR 339. Food Industry Lawsuits/Federal Court Restrictions. Watt, D-N.C., amendment that would restrict the provisions of the bill to lawsuits filed in federal courts, allowing weight-related civil liability suits to be brought in state courts. Rejected 158-261: R 1-223; D 156-38 (ND 123-18, SD 33-20); I 1-0. March 10, 2004.

50. HR 339. Food Industry Lawsuits/Genetically Modified Foods. Andrews, D-N.J., amendment that would permit civil liability suits in cases related to food that contains genetically engineered material, unless the food's labeling explicitly states that it contains genetically engineered material. Rejected 129-285: R 0-220; D 128-65 (ND 107-32, SD 21-33); I 1-0. March 10, 2004.

51. HR 339. Food Industry Lawsuits/"Downed" Animal Meat. Ackerman, D-N.Y., amendment that would change the bill's definition of a "manufacturer" and "seller" so that it does not apply to meat slaughtering, packing, canning or rendering establishments that provide meat for human consumption that comes from "downed" animals, or those that cannot stand or walk. Rejected 141-276: R 2-219; D 138-57 (ND 119-22, SD 19-35); I 1-0. March 10, 2004.

52. HR 339. Food Industry Lawsuits/Weight Loss Products. Jackson-Lee, D-Texas, amendment that would exempt from the bill civil actions that allege a weight loss product caused health problems or any other complication that might be associated with a person's weight gain. Rejected 166-250: R 1-221; D 164-29 (ND 126-13, SD 38-16); I 1-0. March 10, 2004.

	48	49	50	51	52
ALABAMA					
1 *Bonner*	N	N	N	N	N
2 *Everett*	N	N	N	N	N
3 *Rogers*	N	N	N	N	N
4 *Aderholt*	N	N	N	N	N
5 Cramer	N	N	N	N	N
6 *Bachus*	N	N	N	N	N
7 Davis	Y	N	N	N	Y
ALASKA					
AL *Young*	N	N	N	N	N
ARIZONA					
1 *Renzi*	N	N	N	N	N
2 *Franks*	N	N	N	N	N
3 *Shadegg*	N	N	N	N	N
4 Pastor	Y	Y	Y	N	Y
5 *Hayworth*	N	N	N	N	N
6 *Flake*	N	N	N	N	N
7 Grijalva	Y	Y	Y	Y	Y
8 *Kolbe*	N	N	N	N	N
ARKANSAS					
1 Berry	Y	N	N	N	Y
2 Snyder	Y	Y	N	Y	Y
3 *Boozman*	N	N	N	N	N
4 Ross	N	Y	N	N	Y
CALIFORNIA					
1 Thompson	Y	Y	Y	Y	N
2 *Herger*	N	N	N	N	N
3 *Ose*	N	N	N	N	N
4 *Doolittle*	N	N	N	N	N
5 Matsui	Y	Y	Y	Y	Y
6 Woolsey	Y	Y	?	Y	Y
7 Miller, George	Y	Y	Y	Y	Y
8 Pelosi	Y	Y	Y	Y	?
9 Lee	Y	Y	Y	Y	Y
10 Tauscher	Y	N	N	Y	Y
11 *Pombo*	N	N	N	N	N
12 Lantos	Y	Y	Y	Y	Y
13 Stark	Y	Y	Y	Y	Y
14 Eshoo	Y	Y	Y	Y	Y
15 Honda	Y	Y	Y	Y	Y
16 Lofgren	Y	Y	Y	Y	Y
17 Farr	Y	Y	Y	Y	Y
18 Cardoza	N	N	N	N	?
19 *Radanovich*	N	N	?	N	N
20 Dooley	N	N	N	N	Y
21 *Nunes*	N	N	N	N	N
22 *Thomas*	N	N	N	N	N
23 Capps	Y	Y	Y	Y	Y
24 *Gallegly*	N	N	N	N	N
25 *McKeon*	N	N	N	N	N
26 *Dreier*	N	N	N	N	N
27 Sherman	Y	Y	Y	Y	Y
28 Berman	Y	Y	N	Y	Y
29 Schiff	Y	Y	Y	Y	Y
30 Waxman	Y	Y	N	Y	Y
31 Becerra	Y	Y	Y	Y	Y
32 Solis	Y	Y	Y	Y	Y
33 Watson	Y	Y	Y	Y	Y
34 Roybal-Allard	Y	Y	Y	Y	Y
35 Waters	Y	Y	Y	Y	Y
36 Harman	Y	N	Y	Y	?

	48	49	50	51	52
37 Millender-McD.	Y	Y	Y	Y	Y
38 Napolitano	Y	Y	Y	Y	Y
39 Sánchez, Linda	Y	Y	Y	Y	Y
40 *Royce*	N	N	N	N	N
41 *Lewis*	N	N	N	N	N
42 *Miller, Gary*	N	N	N	N	N
43 Baca	Y	Y	N	Y	Y
44 *Calvert*	N	N	N	N	N
45 *Bono*	N	N	N	N	N
46 *Rohrabacher*	N	N	N	N	N
47 Sanchez, Loretta	Y	Y	Y	Y	Y
48 *Cox*	N	N	N	N	N
49 *Issa*	N	N	N	N	N
50 *Cunningham*	N	N	N	N	N
51 Filner	Y	Y	Y	Y	Y
52 *Hunter*	N	N	N	N	N
53 Davis	Y	Y	Y	Y	Y
COLORADO					
1 DeGette	Y	Y	Y	Y	Y
2 Udall	?	?	?	?	?
3 *McInnis*	N	N	N	N	N
4 *Musgrave*	N	N	N	N	N
5 *Hefley*	N	N	N	N	N
6 *Tancredo*	N	N	N	Y	N
7 *Beauprez*	N	N	N	N	N
CONNECTICUT					
1 Larson	Y	Y	Y	Y	Y
2 *Simmons*	N	N	N	N	N
3 DeLauro	Y	Y	Y	Y	Y
4 *Shays*	N	N	N	N	N
5 *Johnson*	N	N	N	N	N
DELAWARE					
AL *Castle*	N	N	N	N	N
FLORIDA					
1 *Miller, J.*	?	?	?	?	?
2 Boyd	Y	N	N	N	N
3 Brown	Y	Y	Y	Y	Y
4 *Crenshaw*	N	N	N	N	N
5 *Brown-Waite*	N	N	N	N	N
6 *Stearns*	N	N	N	N	N
7 *Mica*	N	N	N	N	N
8 *Keller*	N	N	N	N	N
9 *Bilirakis*	N	N	N	N	N
10 *Young*	N	N	N	N	N
11 Davis	Y	N	Y	N	Y
12 *Putnam*	N	N	N	N	N
13 *Harris*	N	N	N	N	N
14 *Goss*	N	N	N	N	?
15 *Weldon*	N	N	N	N	N
16 *Foley*	N	N	N	N	N
17 Meek	Y	Y	Y	Y	Y
18 *Ros-Lehtinen*	N	N	N	N	N
19 Wexler	Y	Y	Y	Y	Y
20 Deutsch	Y	N	Y	Y	N
21 *Diaz-Balart, L.*	N	N	N	N	N
22 *Shaw*	N	N	N	N	N
23 Hastings	Y	Y	Y	Y	Y
24 *Feeney*	N	N	N	N	N
25 *Diaz-Balart, M.*	N	N	N	N	N
GEORGIA					
1 *Kingston*	N	N	N	N	N
2 Bishop	Y	N	N	N	Y
3 Marshall	Y	N	N	N	Y
4 Majette	Y	Y	Y	N	Y
5 Lewis	Y	Y	Y	Y	Y
6 *Isakson*	N	N	N	N	N
7 *Linder*	N	N	N	N	N
8 *Collins*	N	N	N	N	N
9 *Norwood*	N	N	N	N	N
10 *Deal*	N	N	N	N	N
11 *Gingrey*	N	N	N	N	N
12 *Burns*	N	N	N	N	N
13 Scott	N	N	N	N	N
HAWAII					
1 Abercrombie	Y	Y	Y	Y	Y
2 Case	Y	Y	Y	Y	Y
IDAHO					
1 *Otter*	N	N	N	N	N
2 *Simpson*	N	N	N	?	N
ILLINOIS					
1 Rush	Y	Y	Y	Y	Y
2 Jackson	Y	Y	Y	Y	Y
3 Lipinski	Y	Y	Y	N	Y
4 Gutierrez	Y	Y	Y	Y	Y
5 Emanuel	Y	Y	Y	Y	Y
6 *Hyde*	N	N	N	N	N

ND Northern Democrats   SD Southern Democrats

		48	49	50	51	52
7	Davis	?	?	?	?	?
8	**Crane**	N	N	N	N	N
9	Schakowsky	Y	Y	Y	Y	Y
10	**Kirk**	N	N	N	N	N
11	**Weller**	N	N	N	N	N
12	Costello	Y	Y	Y	Y	N
13	**Biggert**	N	N	N	N	N
14	**Hastert**					
15	**Johnson**	N	N	N	N	N
16	**Manzullo**	N	N	N	N	N
17	Evans	Y	Y	Y	Y	Y
18	**LaHood**	N	N	N	N	N
19	**Shimkus**	N	N	N	N	N
INDIANA						
1	Visclosky	Y	Y	Y	Y	Y
2	**Chocola**	N	N	N	N	N
3	**Souder**	N	N	?	N	N
4	**Buyer**	N	N	N	N	N
5	**Burton**	N	N	N	N	N
6	**Pence**	N	N	N	N	N
7	Carson	Y	Y	Y	Y	Y
8	**Hostettler**	N	N	N	N	N
9	Hill	Y	Y	N	N	Y
IOWA						
1	**Nussle**	N	N	N	N	N
2	**Leach**	Y	N	N	N	Y
3	Boswell	Y	Y	N	N	Y
4	**Latham**	N	N	N	N	N
5	**King**	N	N	N	N	N
KANSAS						
1	**Moran**	N	N	N	N	N
2	**Ryun**	N	N	N	N	N
3	Moore	Y	Y	N	Y	Y
4	**Tiahrt**	N	N	N	N	N
KENTUCKY						
1	**Whitfield**	N	N	N	N	N
2	**Lewis**	N	N	N	N	N
3	**Northup**	N	N	N	N	N
4	Lucas	N	N	N	N	N
5	**Rogers**	N	N	N	N	N
6	Chandler	Y	Y	N	N	Y
LOUISIANA						
1	**Vitter**	N	N	N	N	N
2	Jefferson	Y	Y	Y	Y	Y
3	**Tauzin**	?	?	?	?	?
4	**McCrery**	N	N	N	N	N
5	Alexander	N	N	N	N	N
6	**Baker**	N	N	N	N	N
7	John	N	N	N	N	N
MAINE						
1	Allen	Y	Y	Y	Y	Y
2	Michaud	Y	N	N	Y	Y
MARYLAND						
1	**Gilchrest**	N	N	N	N	N
2	Ruppersberger	N	N	N	N	N
3	Cardin	Y	Y	N	Y	Y
4	Wynn	Y	N	N	N	Y
5	Hoyer	Y	Y	N	Y	Y
6	**Bartlett**	N	N	N	N	N
7	Cummings	Y	Y	Y	Y	Y
8	Van Hollen	Y	Y	Y	Y	Y
MASSACHUSETTS						
1	Olver	Y	Y	Y	Y	Y
2	Neal	Y	Y	Y	Y	Y
3	McGovern	Y	Y	Y	Y	Y
4	Frank	?	?	?	?	?
5	Meehan	Y	Y	Y	Y	Y
6	Tierney	Y	Y	Y	Y	Y
7	Markey	Y	Y	Y	Y	Y
8	Capuano	Y	Y	N	Y	Y
9	Lynch	Y	Y	Y	N	N
10	Delahunt	Y	Y	Y	Y	Y
MICHIGAN						
1	Stupak	Y	Y	Y	Y	Y
2	**Hoekstra**	N	N	N	N	N
3	**Ehlers**	N	N	N	N	N
4	**Camp**	N	N	N	N	N
5	Kildee	Y	Y	Y	Y	Y
6	**Upton**	N	N	N	N	N
7	**Smith**	N	N	N	N	N
8	**Rogers**	N	N	N	N	N
9	**Knollenberg**	N	N	N	N	N
10	**Miller**	N	N	N	N	N
11	**McCotter**	N	N	N	N	N
12	Levin	Y	Y	N	Y	Y

		48	49	50	51	52
13	Kilpatrick	Y	Y	Y	Y	Y
14	Conyers	?	?	?	?	Y
15	Dingell	Y	Y	Y	Y	Y
MINNESOTA						
1	**Gutknecht**	N	N	N	N	N
2	**Kline**	N	N	N	N	N
3	**Ramstad**	N	N	N	N	N
4	McCollum	Y	Y	Y	Y	Y
5	Sabo	Y	Y	Y	Y	Y
6	**Kennedy**	N	N	N	N	N
7	Peterson	N	N	N	N	N
8	Oberstar	Y	Y	Y	N	Y
MISSISSIPPI						
1	**Wicker**	?	?	?	?	?
2	Thompson	Y	Y	Y	N	Y
3	**Pickering**	N	N	N	N	N
4	Taylor	N	N	N	Y	N
MISSOURI						
1	Clay	Y	Y	N	Y	Y
2	**Akin**	N	N	N	N	N
3	Gephardt	?	?	?	?	?
4	Skelton	Y	Y	N	N	Y
5	McCarthy	Y	Y	Y	Y	Y
6	**Graves**	N	N	N	N	N
7	**Blunt**	N	N	N	N	N
8	**Emerson**	N	N	N	N	N
9	**Hulshof**	N	N	N	N	N
MONTANA						
AL	**Rehberg**	N	N	N	N	N
NEBRASKA						
1	**Bereuter**	N	N	N	N	N
2	**Terry**	N	N	N	N	N
3	**Osborne**	N	N	N	N	N
NEVADA						
1	Berkley	?	?	?	?	?
2	**Gibbons**	N	N	N	N	?
3	**Porter**	N	N	N	N	N
NEW HAMPSHIRE						
1	**Bradley**	N	N	N	N	N
2	**Bass**	N	N	N	N	N
NEW JERSEY						
1	Andrews	Y	Y	Y	Y	Y
2	**LoBiondo**	N	N	N	N	N
3	**Saxton**	N	N	N	N	N
4	**Smith**	N	N	N	?	N
5	**Garrett**	N	N	N	N	N
6	Pallone	Y	Y	Y	Y	Y
7	**Ferguson**	N	N	N	N	N
8	Pascrell	Y	Y	Y	Y	Y
9	Rothman	Y	Y	Y	Y	Y
10	Payne	Y	Y	Y	Y	Y
11	**Frelinghuysen**	N	N	N	N	N
12	Holt	Y	Y	Y	Y	Y
13	Menendez	Y	Y	N	N	N
NEW MEXICO						
1	**Wilson**	N	N	N	N	N
2	**Pearce**	N	N	N	N	N
3	Udall	Y	Y	Y	Y	Y
NEW YORK						
1	Bishop	Y	Y	Y	Y	Y
2	Israel	Y	Y	Y	Y	Y
3	**King**	N	N	N	N	N
4	McCarthy	Y	Y	Y	Y	Y
5	Ackerman	Y	Y	Y	Y	Y
6	Meeks	Y	Y	N	Y	Y
7	Crowley	Y	Y	Y	Y	Y
8	Nadler	Y	Y	Y	Y	Y
9	Weiner	Y	Y	Y	Y	Y
10	Towns	Y	Y	N	Y	Y
11	Owens	Y	Y	Y	Y	Y
12	Velázquez	Y	Y	Y	Y	Y
13	**Fossella**	N	N	N	N	N
14	Maloney	Y	Y	Y	Y	Y
15	Rangel	Y	Y	Y	Y	Y
16	Serrano	Y	Y	Y	Y	Y
17	Engel	Y	Y	Y	Y	Y
18	Lowey	Y	Y	Y	Y	Y
19	**Kelly**	N	N	N	Y	N
20	**Sweeney**	N	N	N	N	N
21	McNulty	Y	Y	Y	Y	Y
22	Hinchey	Y	Y	Y	Y	Y
23	**McHugh**	N	N	N	N	N
24	**Boehlert**	N	N	N	N	N
25	**Walsh**	N	N	N	N	N

		48	49	50	51	52
26	**Reynolds**	N	N	N	N	N
27	**Quinn**	N	N	N	N	N
28	Slaughter	Y	Y	Y	Y	Y
29	**Houghton**	N	N	N	N	N
NORTH CAROLINA						
1	Ballance	?	?	Y	N	Y
2	Etheridge	Y	Y	N	N	Y
3	**Jones**	N	N	?	N	N
4	Price	Y	Y	N	Y	Y
5	**Burr**	N	N	N	N	N
6	**Coble**	N	N	N	N	N
7	McIntyre	Y	Y	Y	N	Y
8	**Hayes**	N	N	N	N	N
9	**Myrick**	N	N	N	N	N
10	**Ballenger**	N	N	N	N	N
11	**Taylor**	N	N	N	N	N
12	Watt	Y	Y	Y	Y	Y
13	Miller	Y	Y	N	N	Y
NORTH DAKOTA						
AL	Pomeroy	Y	N	N	N	N
OHIO						
1	**Chabot**	N	N	N	N	N
2	**Portman**	N	N	N	N	N
3	**Turner**	N	N	N	N	N
4	**Oxley**	N	N	N	?	N
5	**Gillmor**	N	N	N	N	N
6	Strickland	Y	Y	?	N	Y
7	**Hobson**	N	N	N	N	N
8	**Boehner**	N	N	N	N	N
9	Kaptur	Y	Y	Y	Y	Y
10	Kucinich	?	?	?	?	?
11	Jones	Y	Y	Y	Y	Y
12	**Tiberi**	N	N	N	N	N
13	Brown	Y	Y	Y	Y	Y
14	**LaTourette**	N	N	N	N	N
15	**Pryce**	N	N	N	N	N
16	**Regula**	N	N	N	N	N
17	Ryan	Y	Y	Y	Y	N
18	**Ney**	N	N	N	N	N
OKLAHOMA						
1	**Sullivan**	N	N	N	N	N
2	Carson	Y	N	N	N	Y
3	**Lucas**	N	N	N	N	N
4	**Cole**	N	N	N	N	N
5	**Istook**	N	N	?	N	N
OREGON						
1	Wu	Y	Y	Y	Y	Y
2	**Walden**	N	N	N	N	N
3	Blumenauer	Y	Y	Y	Y	Y
4	DeFazio	Y	Y	Y	Y	Y
5	Hooley	Y	N	N	Y	Y
PENNSYLVANIA						
1	Brady	Y	Y	Y	Y	Y
2	Fattah	?	Y	Y	Y	Y
3	**English**	N	N	N	N	N
4	**Hart**	N	N	N	N	N
5	**Peterson**	N	N	N	N	N
6	**Gerlach**	N	N	N	N	N
7	**Weldon**	N	N	N	N	N
8	**Greenwood**	N	N	N	N	N
9	**Shuster, Bill**	N	N	N	N	N
10	**Sherwood**	N	N	N	N	N
11	Kanjorski	Y	Y	Y	Y	Y
12	Murtha	Y	Y	Y	Y	Y
13	Hoeffel	Y	Y	Y	Y	Y
14	Doyle	Y	Y	Y	Y	Y
15	**Toomey**	N	N	N	N	N
16	**Pitts**	N	N	N	N	N
17	Holden	N	N	N	N	N
18	**Murphy**	N	N	N	N	N
19	**Platts**	N	N	N	N	N
RHODE ISLAND						
1	Kennedy	Y	Y	Y	Y	Y
2	Langevin	Y	Y	Y	Y	Y
SOUTH CAROLINA						
1	**Brown**	N	N	N	N	N
2	**Wilson**	N	N	N	N	N
3	**Barrett**	N	N	N	N	N
4	**DeMint**	N	N	N	N	N
5	Spratt	Y	N	N	N	Y
6	Clyburn	Y	Y	Y	Y	Y
SOUTH DAKOTA						
AL	Vacant					

		48	49	50	51	52
TENNESSEE						
1	**Jenkins**	N	N	N	N	N
2	**Duncan**	N	N	N	N	N
3	**Wamp**	N	N	N	N	N
4	Davis	N	N	N	N	N
5	Cooper	N	N	N	N	N
6	Gordon	N	N	N	N	N
7	**Blackburn**	N	N	N	N	N
8	Tanner	N	N	N	N	N
9	Ford	Y	Y	Y	N	N
TEXAS						
1	Sandlin	Y	Y	N	N	Y
2	Turner	Y	Y	N	N	Y
3	**Johnson, Sam**	N	N	N	N	N
4	**Hall**	N	N	N	N	N
5	**Hensarling**	N	N	N	N	N
6	**Barton**	N	N	N	N	N
7	**Culberson**	N	N	N	N	N
8	**Brady**	N	N	N	N	N
9	Lampson	Y	Y	Y	Y	Y
10	Doggett	Y	Y	Y	Y	Y
11	Edwards	N	N	N	N	N
12	**Granger**	N	N	N	N	N
13	**Thornberry**	N	N	N	N	N
14	**Paul**	Y	Y	N	N	N
15	Hinojosa	?	?	?	?	?
16	Reyes	Y	Y	N	N	Y
17	Stenholm	N	N	N	N	N
18	Jackson-Lee	Y	Y	Y	Y	Y
19	**Neugebauer**	N	N	N	N	N
20	Gonzalez	Y	Y	N	N	Y
21	**Smith**	N	N	N	N	N
22	**DeLay**	N	N	N	N	N
23	**Bonilla**	N	N	N	N	N
24	Frost	Y	Y	Y	N	Y
25	Bell	?	?	?	?	?
26	**Burgess**	N	N	N	N	N
27	Ortiz	Y	Y	N	N	Y
28	Rodriguez	?	?	?	?	?
29	Green	Y	Y	Y	Y	Y
30	Johnson, E.B.	Y	Y	Y	Y	Y
31	**Carter**	N	N	N	N	N
32	**Sessions**	N	N	N	N	N
UTAH						
1	**Bishop**	N	N	N	N	N
2	Matheson	N	N	N	N	N
3	**Cannon**	N	N	N	N	N
VERMONT						
AL	Sanders	Y	Y	Y	Y	Y
VIRGINIA						
1	**Davis, Jo Ann**	N	N	N	N	N
2	**Schrock**	N	N	N	N	N
3	Scott	Y	Y	Y	Y	Y
4	**Forbes**	N	N	N	N	N
5	**Goode**	N	N	N	N	N
6	**Goodlatte**	N	N	N	N	N
7	**Cantor**	N	N	N	N	N
8	Moran	Y	N	N	N	Y
9	Boucher	Y	N	N	N	N
10	**Wolf**	N	N	N	N	N
11	**Davis, T.**	N	N	N	N	N
WASHINGTON						
1	Inslee	Y	Y	N	Y	Y
2	Larsen	Y	N	N	N	N
3	Baird	Y	N	N	N	N
4	**Hastings**	N	N	N	N	N
5	**Nethercutt**	N	N	N	N	N
6	Dicks	Y	N	N	Y	Y
7	McDermott	Y	Y	Y	Y	Y
8	**Dunn**	N	N	N	N	N
9	Smith	Y	N	N	N	Y
WEST VIRGINIA						
1	Mollohan	Y	Y	Y	Y	Y
2	**Capito**	N	N	N	N	N
3	Rahall	Y	N	Y	Y	Y
WISCONSIN						
1	**Ryan**	N	N	N	N	N
2	Baldwin	Y	Y	Y	Y	Y
3	Kind	Y	N	N	N	Y
4	Kleczka	Y	Y	Y	Y	Y
5	**Sensenbrenner**	N	N	N	N	N
6	**Petri**	N	N	N	N	N
7	Obey	Y	Y	Y	N	Y
8	**Green**	N	N	N	N	N
WYOMING						
AL	**Cubin**	N	N	N	N	N

Southern states - Ala., Ark., Fla., Ga., Ky., La., Miss., N.C., Okla., S.C., Tenn., Texas, Va.

Key

Y	Voted for (yea).
#	Paired for.
+	Announced for.
N	Voted against (nay).
X	Paired against.
−	Announced against.
P	Voted "present."
C	Voted "present" to avoid possible conflict of interest.
?	Did not vote or otherwise make a position known.

Democrats   ***Republicans***
Independents

---

53. HR 339. Food Industry Lawsuits/Pending Civil Actions. Watt, D-N.C., amendment that would strike the section of the bill that dismisses all qualified weight-related civil liability actions pending at the time of the bill's enactment. Rejected 164-249: R 1-218; D 162-31 (ND 122-17, SD 40-14); I 1-0. March 10, 2004.

54. HR 339. Food Industry Lawsuits/Passage. Passage of the bill that would prohibit lawsuits in federal or state courts against restaurants, food manufacturers and distributors based on claims that the food contributed to the plaintiff's obesity or weight gain. The bill would allow suits if the defendant knowingly and willfully violated federal or state laws governing the labeling, advertising or selling of food products. Passed 276-139: R 221-1; D 55-137 (ND 27-111, SD 28-26); I 0-1. A "yea" was a vote in support of the president's position. March 10, 2004.

55. HR 3717. Broadcast Indecency/Passage. Passage of the bill that would increase to $500,000 per violation the maximum fines that the Federal Communications Commission (FCC) could levy on broadcasters for airing indecent, obscene or profane material. The bill would make it easier for the FCC to fine individuals for indecent actions and make them subject to the same fines as broadcasters. It would require that the FCC consider revoking a license after a broadcaster committed three or more indecency-related offenses. The bill also would establish a 180-day window for the FCC to make indecency enforcement decisions. Passed 391-22: R 218-1; D 172-21 (ND 121-18, SD 51-3); I 1-0. A "yea" was a vote in support of the president's position. March 11, 2004.

56. H Con Res 15. India's Republic Day/Adoption. Leach, R-Iowa, motion to suspend the rules and adopt the concurrent resolution that would commend India on its celebration of Republic Day, and reiterate Congress' support for continued strong relations between the United States and India. Motion agreed to 418-0: R 220-0; D 197-0 (ND 143-0, SD 54-0); I 1-0. A two-thirds majority of those present and voting (279 in this case) is required for adoption under suspension of the rules. March 11, 2004.

57. H Res 540. Boris Trajkovski Remembrance/Adoption. Bereuter, R-Neb., motion to suspend the rules and adopt the resolution that would express the condolences and deepest sympathies of the House of Representatives for the death of Macedonian President Boris Trajkovski, who was killed in a plane crash Feb. 26. Motion agreed to 411-0: R 215-0; D 195-0 (ND 142-0, SD 53-0); I 1-0. A two-thirds majority of those present and voting (274 in this case) is required for adoption under suspension of the rules. March 11, 2004.

	53	54	55	56	57
ALABAMA					
1 *Bonner*	N	Y	Y	Y	Y
2 *Everett*	N	Y	Y	Y	Y
3 *Rogers*	N	Y	Y	Y	Y
4 *Aderholt*	N	Y	Y	Y	Y
5 Cramer	N	Y	Y	Y	Y
6 *Bachus*	N	Y	Y	Y	Y
7 Davis	Y	Y	Y	Y	Y
ALASKA					
AL *Young*	N	Y	Y	Y	Y
ARIZONA					
1 *Renzi*	N	Y	Y	Y	Y
2 *Franks*	N	Y	Y	Y	Y
3 *Shadegg*	N	Y	Y	Y	Y
4 Pastor	Y	N	Y	Y	Y
5 *Hayworth*	N	Y	Y	Y	Y
6 *Flake*	N	Y	Y	Y	Y
7 Grijalva	Y	N	N	Y	Y
8 *Kolbe*	N	Y	Y	Y	Y
ARKANSAS					
1 Berry	Y	Y	Y	Y	Y
2 Snyder	Y	N	Y	Y	Y
3 *Boozman*	N	Y	Y	Y	Y
4 Ross	Y	Y	Y	Y	Y
CALIFORNIA					
1 Thompson	Y	Y	Y	Y	Y
2 *Herger*	N	Y	Y	Y	Y
3 *Ose*	N	Y	Y	Y	Y
4 *Doolittle*	N	Y	?	Y	Y
5 Matsui	Y	N	Y	Y	Y
6 Woolsey	Y	N	Y	Y	Y
7 Miller, George	Y	N	Y	Y	Y
8 Pelosi	?	?	Y	Y	?
9 Lee	Y	N	N	Y	Y
10 Tauscher	Y	Y	Y	Y	Y
11 *Pombo*	N	Y	Y	Y	Y
12 Lantos	Y	N	Y	Y	Y
13 Stark	Y	N	N	Y	Y
14 Eshoo	Y	N	Y	Y	Y
15 Honda	Y	N	N	Y	Y
16 Lofgren	Y	N	N	Y	Y
17 Farr	Y	N	Y	Y	Y
18 Cardoza	?	?	?	?	?
19 *Radanovich*	N	Y	Y	Y	Y
20 Dooley	N	Y	Y	Y	Y
21 *Nunes*	N	Y	Y	Y	?
22 *Thomas*	N	Y	Y	Y	Y
23 Capps	Y	N	Y	Y	Y
24 *Gallegly*	N	Y	Y	Y	Y
25 *McKeon*	N	Y	Y	Y	Y
26 *Dreier*	N	Y	Y	Y	Y
27 Sherman	Y	N	P	Y	Y
28 Berman	Y	N	N	Y	Y
29 Schiff	Y	N	Y	Y	Y
30 Waxman	Y	N	N	Y	Y
31 Becerra	Y	N	Y	Y	Y
32 Solis	Y	N	Y	Y	Y
33 Watson	Y	N	Y	Y	Y
34 Roybal-Allard	Y	N	Y	Y	Y
35 Waters	Y	N	Y	Y	Y
36 Harman	?	?	N	Y	Y

	53	54	55	56	57
37 Millender-McD.	Y	N	Y	Y	Y
38 Napolitano	Y	N	Y	Y	Y
39 Sánchez, Linda	Y	N	Y	Y	Y
40 *Royce*	N	Y	Y	Y	Y
41 *Lewis*	N	Y	?	?	?
42 *Miller, Gary*	N	Y	Y	Y	Y
43 Baca	Y	N	Y	Y	Y
44 *Calvert*	N	Y	Y	Y	Y
45 *Bono*	?	Y	Y	Y	Y
46 *Rohrabacher*	N	Y	Y	Y	Y
47 Sanchez, Loretta	Y	N	?	Y	Y
48 *Cox*	N	Y	Y	Y	Y
49 *Issa*	N	Y	Y	Y	Y
50 *Cunningham*	N	Y	Y	Y	Y
51 Filner	Y	N	Y	Y	Y
52 *Hunter*	?	Y	Y	Y	Y
53 Davis	Y	N	Y	Y	Y
COLORADO					
1 DeGette	Y	N	Y	Y	Y
2 Udall	?	?	?	?	?
3 *McInnis*	N	Y	Y	Y	Y
4 *Musgrave*	N	Y	Y	Y	Y
5 *Hefley*	N	Y	Y	Y	Y
6 *Tancredo*	N	Y	Y	Y	Y
7 *Beauprez*	N	Y	Y	Y	Y
CONNECTICUT					
1 Larson	Y	Y	Y	Y	Y
2 *Simmons*	N	Y	Y	Y	Y
3 DeLauro	Y	N	Y	Y	Y
4 *Shays*	N	Y	Y	Y	Y
5 Johnson	N	Y	Y	Y	Y
DELAWARE					
AL *Castle*	N	Y	Y	Y	Y
FLORIDA					
1 *Miller, J.*	?	?	?	?	?
2 Boyd	Y	Y	Y	Y	Y
3 Brown	Y	N	Y	Y	Y
4 *Crenshaw*	N	Y	Y	Y	Y
5 *Brown-Waite*	N	Y	Y	Y	Y
6 *Stearns*	N	Y	Y	Y	Y
7 *Mica*	N	Y	Y	Y	Y
8 *Keller*	N	Y	Y	Y	Y
9 *Bilirakis*	N	Y	Y	Y	Y
10 *Young*	N	Y	Y	Y	Y
11 Davis	Y	N	Y	Y	Y
12 *Putnam*	N	Y	Y	Y	Y
13 *Harris*	N	Y	Y	Y	Y
14 *Goss*	?	?	Y	Y	Y
15 *Weldon*	N	Y	Y	Y	Y
16 *Foley*	N	Y	Y	Y	Y
17 Meek	Y	N	Y	Y	Y
18 *Ros-Lehtinen*	N	Y	Y	Y	Y
19 Wexler	Y	N	Y	Y	Y
20 Deutsch	Y	N	Y	Y	Y
21 *Diaz-Balart, L.*	N	Y	Y	Y	Y
22 *Shaw*	N	Y	Y	Y	Y
23 Hastings	Y	N	Y	Y	Y
24 *Feeney*	N	Y	Y	Y	Y
25 *Diaz-Balart, M.*	N	Y	Y	Y	Y
GEORGIA					
1 *Kingston*	N	Y	Y	Y	Y
2 Bishop	Y	Y	Y	Y	Y
3 Marshall	Y	Y	Y	Y	?
4 Majette	Y	N	Y	Y	Y
5 Lewis	Y	N	N	Y	Y
6 *Isakson*	N	Y	Y	Y	Y
7 *Linder*	N	Y	Y	Y	Y
8 *Collins*	N	Y	Y	Y	Y
9 *Norwood*	N	Y	Y	Y	?
10 *Deal*	N	Y	Y	Y	Y
11 *Gingrey*	N	Y	Y	Y	Y
12 *Burns*	N	Y	Y	Y	Y
13 Scott	N	Y	Y	Y	Y
HAWAII					
1 Abercrombie	Y	N	Y	Y	Y
2 Case	Y	N	Y	Y	Y
IDAHO					
1 *Otter*	N	Y	Y	Y	Y
2 *Simpson*	N	Y	Y	Y	Y
ILLINOIS					
1 Rush	Y	N	Y	Y	Y
2 Jackson	Y	N	Y	Y	Y
3 Lipinski	Y	N	Y	Y	Y
4 Gutierrez	Y	N	Y	Y	Y
5 Emanuel	Y	N	Y	Y	Y
6 *Hyde*	N	Y	Y	Y	Y

ND Northern Democrats   SD Southern Democrats

	53	54	55	56	57
7 Davis	?	?	?	?	?
8 ***Crane***	N	Y	Y	Y	Y
9 Schakowsky	Y	N	N	Y	Y
10 ***Kirk***	N	Y	Y	Y	Y
11 ***Weller***	N	Y	Y	Y	Y
12 Costello	Y	N	Y	Y	Y
13 ***Biggert***	N	Y	Y	Y	Y
14 ***Hastert***					
15 ***Johnson***	N	Y	Y	Y	Y
16 ***Manzullo***	N	Y	Y	Y	Y
17 Evans	Y	N	Y	Y	Y
18 ***LaHood***	N	Y	Y	Y	Y
19 ***Shimkus***	N	Y	Y	Y	Y
INDIANA					
1 Visclosky	Y	N	Y	Y	Y
2 ***Chocola***	N	Y	Y	Y	Y
3 ***Souder***	N	Y	Y	Y	?
4 ***Buyer***	N	Y	Y	Y	Y
5 ***Burton***	N	Y	Y	Y	Y
6 ***Pence***	N	Y	Y	Y	Y
7 Carson	Y	?	Y	Y	Y
8 ***Hostettler***	N	Y	Y	Y	Y
9 Hill	Y	Y	Y	Y	Y
IOWA					
1 ***Nussle***	N	Y	Y	Y	Y
2 ***Leach***	N	Y	Y	Y	Y
3 Boswell	Y	N	Y	Y	Y
4 ***Latham***	N	Y	Y	Y	Y
5 ***King***	N	Y	Y	Y	Y
KANSAS					
1 ***Moran***	N	Y	Y	Y	Y
2 ***Ryun***	N	Y	Y	Y	Y
3 Moore	Y	Y	Y	Y	Y
4 ***Tiahrt***	N	Y	Y	Y	Y
KENTUCKY					
1 ***Whitfield***	N	Y	Y	Y	Y
2 ***Lewis***	N	Y	Y	Y	Y
3 ***Northup***	N	Y	Y	Y	Y
4 Lucas	N	Y	Y	Y	Y
5 ***Rogers***	N	Y	Y	Y	Y
6 Chandler	Y	N	Y	Y	Y
LOUISIANA					
1 ***Vitter***	N	Y	Y	Y	Y
2 Jefferson	Y	N	Y	Y	Y
3 ***Tauzin***	?	?	?	?	?
4 ***McCrery***	N	Y	Y	Y	Y
5 Alexander	N	Y	Y	Y	Y
6 ***Baker***	N	Y	Y	Y	Y
7 John	N	Y	?	?	?
MAINE					
1 Allen	Y	N	Y	Y	Y
2 Michaud	N	Y	Y	Y	Y
MARYLAND					
1 ***Gilchrest***	N	Y	Y	Y	Y
2 Ruppersberger	N	Y	Y	Y	Y
3 Cardin	Y	N	Y	Y	Y
4 Wynn	N	Y	Y	Y	Y
5 Hoyer	Y	N	Y	Y	Y
6 ***Bartlett***	N	Y	Y	Y	Y
7 Cummings	Y	N	Y	Y	Y
8 Van Hollen	Y	N	Y	Y	Y
MASSACHUSETTS					
1 Olver	Y	N	Y	Y	Y
2 Neal	Y	N	Y	Y	Y
3 McGovern	Y	N	Y	Y	Y
4 Frank	?	?	Y	Y	Y
5 Meehan	Y	N	Y	Y	Y
6 Tierney	Y	N	Y	Y	Y
7 Markey	Y	N	Y	Y	Y
8 Capuano	Y	N	Y	Y	Y
9 Lynch	N	Y	Y	Y	Y
10 Delahunt	Y	N	Y	Y	Y
MICHIGAN					
1 Stupak	Y	N	Y	Y	Y
2 ***Hoekstra***	N	Y	Y	Y	Y
3 ***Ehlers***	N	Y	Y	Y	Y
4 ***Camp***	N	Y	Y	Y	?
5 Kildee	Y	N	Y	Y	Y
6 ***Upton***	N	Y	Y	Y	Y
7 ***Smith***	N	Y	Y	Y	Y
8 ***Rogers***	N	Y	Y	Y	Y
9 ***Knollenberg***	N	Y	Y	Y	Y
10 ***Miller***	N	Y	Y	Y	Y
11 ***McCotter***	N	Y	Y	Y	Y
12 Levin	Y	N	Y	Y	Y
13 Kilpatrick	Y	N	Y	Y	Y
14 Conyers	Y	N	?	Y	Y
15 Dingell	Y	N	Y	Y	Y
MINNESOTA					
1 ***Gutknecht***	N	Y	Y	Y	Y
2 ***Kline***	N	Y	Y	Y	Y
3 ***Ramstad***	N	Y	Y	Y	Y
4 McCollum	Y	N	Y	Y	Y
5 Sabo	Y	N	Y	Y	Y
6 ***Kennedy***	N	Y	Y	Y	Y
7 Peterson	N	Y	Y	Y	Y
8 Oberstar	Y	N	Y	Y	Y
MISSISSIPPI					
1 ***Wicker***	?	?	?	?	?
2 Thompson	Y	N	Y	Y	Y
3 ***Pickering***	N	Y	Y	Y	Y
4 Taylor	N	Y	Y	Y	Y
MISSOURI					
1 Clay	Y	N	N	Y	Y
2 ***Akin***	N	Y	Y	Y	Y
3 Gephardt	?	?	Y	Y	Y
4 Skelton	Y	Y	Y	Y	Y
5 McCarthy	Y	N	Y	Y	Y
6 ***Graves***	N	Y	Y	Y	Y
7 ***Blunt***	N	Y	Y	Y	Y
8 ***Emerson***	N	Y	Y	Y	Y
9 ***Hulshof***	N	Y	Y	Y	Y
MONTANA					
AL ***Rehberg***	N	Y	Y	Y	Y
NEBRASKA					
1 ***Bereuter***	N	Y	Y	Y	Y
2 ***Terry***	N	Y	Y	Y	Y
3 ***Osborne***	N	Y	Y	Y	Y
NEVADA					
1 Berkley	?	?	?	?	?
2 ***Gibbons***	?	?	?	?	?
3 ***Porter***	N	Y	Y	Y	Y
NEW HAMPSHIRE					
1 ***Bradley***	N	Y	Y	Y	Y
2 ***Bass***	N	Y	Y	Y	Y
NEW JERSEY					
1 Andrews	Y	N	Y	Y	Y
2 ***LoBiondo***	N	Y	Y	Y	Y
3 ***Saxton***	N	Y	Y	Y	Y
4 ***Smith***	N	Y	Y	Y	Y
5 ***Garrett***	N	Y	Y	Y	Y
6 Pallone	Y	N	Y	Y	Y
7 ***Ferguson***	N	Y	Y	Y	Y
8 Pascrell	Y	N	Y	Y	Y
9 Rothman	Y	N	Y	Y	Y
10 Payne	Y	N	Y	Y	Y
11 ***Frelinghuysen***	N	Y	Y	Y	Y
12 Holt	Y	N	Y	Y	Y
13 Menendez	Y	Y	Y	Y	Y
NEW MEXICO					
1 ***Wilson***	N	Y	Y	Y	Y
2 ***Pearce***	N	Y	Y	Y	Y
3 Udall	Y	N	Y	Y	Y
NEW YORK					
1 Bishop	Y	N	Y	Y	Y
2 Israel	Y	N	Y	Y	Y
3 ***King***	N	Y	?	?	?
4 McCarthy	Y	N	Y	Y	Y
5 Ackerman	Y	N	N	Y	Y
6 Meeks	Y	N	Y	Y	Y
7 Crowley	Y	N	Y	Y	Y
8 Nadler	Y	N	N	Y	Y
9 Weiner	Y	N	Y	Y	Y
10 Towns	Y	N	Y	Y	Y
11 Owens	Y	N	Y	Y	Y
12 Velázquez	Y	N	N	Y	Y
13 ***Fossella***	N	Y	?	?	?
14 Maloney	Y	N	?	Y	Y
15 Rangel	Y	N	Y	Y	Y
16 Serrano	Y	N	N	Y	Y
17 Engel	Y	N	Y	Y	Y
18 Lowey	Y	N	Y	Y	Y
19 ***Kelly***	N	Y	Y	Y	Y
20 ***Sweeney***	N	Y	Y	Y	Y
21 McNulty	Y	Y	Y	Y	Y
22 Hinchey	Y	N	Y	Y	Y
23 ***McHugh***	N	Y	Y	Y	Y
24 ***Boehlert***	N	Y	Y	Y	Y
25 ***Walsh***	N	Y	Y	Y	Y
26 ***Reynolds***	N	Y	Y	Y	Y
27 ***Quinn***	N	Y	Y	Y	Y
28 Slaughter	Y	N	Y	Y	Y
29 ***Houghton***	N	Y	Y	Y	Y
NORTH CAROLINA					
1 Ballance	Y	N	Y	Y	Y
2 Etheridge	Y	N	Y	Y	Y
3 ***Jones***	N	Y	Y	Y	Y
4 Price	Y	N	Y	Y	Y
5 ***Burr***	N	Y	Y	Y	Y
6 ***Coble***	Y	Y	Y	Y	Y
7 McIntyre	Y	Y	Y	Y	Y
8 ***Hayes***	N	Y	Y	Y	Y
9 ***Myrick***	N	Y	Y	Y	Y
10 ***Ballenger***	N	Y	Y	Y	Y
11 ***Taylor***	N	Y	Y	Y	Y
12 Watt	Y	N	Y	Y	Y
13 Miller	Y	N	Y	Y	Y
NORTH DAKOTA					
AL Pomeroy	N	Y	Y	Y	Y
OHIO					
1 ***Chabot***	N	Y	Y	Y	Y
2 ***Portman***	N	Y	Y	Y	Y
3 ***Turner***	N	Y	Y	Y	Y
4 ***Oxley***	N	Y	Y	Y	Y
5 ***Gillmor***	N	Y	Y	Y	Y
6 Strickland	Y	N	Y	Y	Y
7 ***Hobson***	N	Y	Y	Y	Y
8 ***Boehner***	N	Y	Y	Y	Y
9 Kaptur	Y	N	Y	Y	Y
10 Kucinich	?	?	N	Y	Y
11 Jones	Y	N	N	Y	Y
12 ***Tiberi***	N	Y	Y	Y	Y
13 Brown	Y	N	Y	Y	Y
14 ***LaTourette***	N	Y	Y	Y	Y
15 ***Pryce***	N	Y	Y	Y	Y
16 ***Regula***	N	Y	Y	Y	Y
17 Ryan	Y	N	Y	Y	Y
18 ***Ney***	N	Y	Y	Y	Y
OKLAHOMA					
1 ***Sullivan***	N	Y	Y	Y	Y
2 Carson	Y	Y	Y	Y	Y
3 ***Lucas***	N	Y	Y	Y	Y
4 ***Cole***	N	Y	Y	Y	Y
5 ***Istook***	?	Y	Y	Y	?
OREGON					
1 Wu	N	Y	Y	Y	Y
2 ***Walden***	N	Y	Y	Y	Y
3 Blumenauer	Y	N	Y	Y	Y
4 DeFazio	N	Y	?	?	?
5 Hooley	Y	Y	Y	Y	Y
PENNSYLVANIA					
1 Brady	Y	N	Y	Y	Y
2 Fattah	Y	N	Y	Y	Y
3 ***English***	N	Y	Y	Y	Y
4 ***Hart***	N	Y	Y	Y	Y
5 ***Peterson***	N	Y	Y	Y	Y
6 ***Gerlach***	N	Y	Y	Y	Y
7 ***Weldon***	N	Y	Y	Y	Y
8 ***Greenwood***	N	Y	Y	Y	Y
9 ***Shuster, Bill***	N	Y	Y	Y	Y
10 ***Sherwood***	N	Y	Y	Y	Y
11 Kanjorski	Y	N	Y	Y	Y
12 Murtha	Y	N	Y	Y	Y
13 Hoeffel	Y	N	Y	Y	Y
14 Doyle	Y	Y	Y	Y	Y
15 ***Toomey***	N	Y	Y	Y	Y
16 ***Pitts***	N	Y	Y	Y	Y
17 Holden	N	Y	Y	Y	Y
18 ***Murphy***	N	Y	Y	Y	Y
19 ***Platts***	N	Y	Y	Y	Y
RHODE ISLAND					
1 Kennedy	Y	N	Y	Y	Y
2 Langevin	N	Y	Y	Y	Y
SOUTH CAROLINA					
1 ***Brown***	N	Y	Y	Y	Y
2 ***Wilson***	N	Y	Y	Y	Y
3 ***Barrett***	N	Y	Y	Y	Y
4 ***DeMint***	N	Y	Y	Y	Y
5 Spratt	Y	Y	Y	Y	Y
6 Clyburn	Y	N	Y	Y	Y
SOUTH DAKOTA					
AL Vacant					
TENNESSEE					
1 ***Jenkins***	N	Y	Y	Y	Y
2 ***Duncan***	N	Y	Y	Y	Y
3 ***Wamp***	N	Y	Y	Y	Y
4 Davis	N	Y	Y	Y	Y
5 Cooper	N	Y	Y	Y	Y
6 Gordon	N	Y	Y	Y	Y
7 ***Blackburn***	N	Y	Y	Y	Y
8 Tanner	N	Y	Y	Y	Y
9 Ford	Y	Y	Y	Y	Y
TEXAS					
1 Sandlin	Y	Y	Y	Y	Y
2 Turner	Y	Y	Y	Y	Y
3 ***Johnson, Sam***	N	Y	Y	Y	Y
4 ***Hall***	N	Y	Y	Y	Y
5 ***Hensarling***	N	Y	Y	Y	Y
6 ***Barton***	N	Y	Y	Y	Y
7 ***Culberson***	N	Y	Y	Y	Y
8 ***Brady***	N	Y	Y	Y	Y
9 Lampson	Y	Y	Y	Y	Y
10 Doggett	Y	N	Y	Y	Y
11 Edwards	N	Y	Y	Y	Y
12 ***Granger***	N	Y	Y	Y	Y
13 ***Thornberry***	N	Y	Y	Y	Y
14 ***Paul***	N	N	N	Y	Y
15 Hinojosa	?	?	Y	Y	Y
16 Reyes	Y	N	Y	Y	Y
17 Stenholm	N	Y	Y	Y	Y
18 Jackson-Lee	Y	N	N	Y	Y
19 ***Neugebauer***	N	Y	Y	Y	Y
20 Gonzalez	Y	N	Y	Y	Y
21 ***Smith***	N	Y	Y	Y	Y
22 ***DeLay***	N	Y	Y	Y	Y
23 ***Bonilla***	N	Y	Y	Y	Y
24 Frost	Y	N	Y	Y	Y
25 Bell	?	?	?	?	?
26 ***Burgess***	N	Y	Y	Y	Y
27 Ortiz	Y	N	Y	Y	Y
28 Rodriguez	?	?	?	?	?
29 Green	Y	Y	Y	Y	Y
30 Johnson, E.B.	Y	N	Y	Y	Y
31 ***Carter***	N	Y	Y	Y	Y
32 ***Sessions***	N	Y	Y	Y	Y
UTAH					
1 ***Bishop***	N	Y	Y	Y	Y
2 Matheson	N	Y	Y	Y	Y
3 ***Cannon***	N	Y	Y	Y	Y
VERMONT					
AL *Sanders*	Y	N	Y	Y	Y
VIRGINIA					
1 ***Davis, Jo Ann***	N	Y	Y	Y	Y
2 ***Schrock***	N	Y	Y	Y	Y
3 Scott	Y	N	N	Y	Y
4 ***Forbes***	N	Y	Y	Y	Y
5 ***Goode***	N	Y	Y	Y	Y
6 ***Goodlatte***	N	Y	Y	Y	Y
7 ***Cantor***	N	Y	Y	Y	Y
8 Moran	N	Y	Y	Y	Y
9 Boucher	N	Y	Y	Y	Y
10 ***Wolf***	N	Y	Y	Y	Y
11 ***Davis, T.***	N	Y	Y	Y	Y
WASHINGTON					
1 Inslee	Y	N	Y	Y	Y
2 Larsen	N	Y	Y	Y	Y
3 Baird	N	Y	N	Y	Y
4 ***Hastings***	N	Y	Y	Y	Y
5 ***Nethercutt***	N	Y	Y	Y	Y
6 Dicks	N	Y	Y	Y	Y
7 McDermott	Y	N	Y	Y	Y
8 ***Dunn***	N	Y	Y	Y	Y
9 Smith	N	Y	Y	Y	Y
WEST VIRGINIA					
1 Mollohan	Y	N	Y	Y	Y
2 ***Capito***	N	Y	Y	Y	Y
3 Rahall	Y	N	Y	Y	Y
WISCONSIN					
1 ***Ryan***	N	Y	Y	Y	Y
2 Baldwin	Y	N	Y	Y	Y
3 Kind	N	Y	Y	Y	Y
4 Kleczka	Y	N	Y	Y	Y
5 ***Sensenbrenner***	N	Y	Y	Y	Y
6 ***Petri***	N	Y	Y	Y	Y
7 Obey	Y	N	Y	Y	Y
8 ***Green***	N	Y	Y	Y	Y
WYOMING					
AL ***Cubin***	N	Y	Y	Y	Y

Southern states - Ala., Ark., Fla., Ga., Ky., La., Miss., N.C., Okla., S.C., Tenn., Texas, Va.

58. H Res 551. C-SPAN Anniversary/Adoption. Ney, R-Ohio, motion to suspend the rules and adopt the resolution that would recognize the 25th anniversary of the Cable-Satellite Public Affairs Network (C-SPAN) and its coverage of the House of Representatives' proceedings. The resolution also would commend the network and its employees for providing outstanding coverage that benefits the government and the public. Motion agreed to 392-0: R 209-0; D 182-0 (ND 129-0, SD 53-0); I 1-0. A two-thirds majority of those present and voting (262 in this case) is required for adoption under suspension of the rules. March 16, 2004.

59. HR 3733. Myron V. George Post Office/Passage. Miller, R-Mich., motion to suspend the rules and pass the bill that would name a post office building in Altamont, Kan., after the late, former Rep. Myron V. George, R-Kan. (1950-59). Motion agreed to 394-0: R 211-0; D 182-0 (ND 127-0, SD 55-0); I 1-0. A two-thirds majority of those present and voting (263 in this case) is required for passage under suspension of the rules. March 16, 2004.

60. H Res 433. Luis A. Ferre Tribute/Adoption. Miller, R-Mich., motion to suspend the rules and adopt the resolution that would honor the late Luis A. Ferre — former governor of Puerto Rico and recipient of the Presidential Medal of Freedom — for his outstanding political leadership, business savvy, advocacy for social justice, and love and support of the arts. Motion agreed to 398-0: R 212-0; D 185-0 (ND 129-0, SD 56-0); I 1-0. A two-thirds majority of those present and voting (266 in this case) is required for adoption under suspension of the rules. March 16, 2004.

61. Procedural Motion/Adjourn. Hastings, D-Fla., motion to adjourn. Motion rejected 36-377: R 1-219; D 34-158 (ND 28-110, SD 6-48); I 1-0. March 17, 2004.

62. H Res 557. War in Iraq and U.S. Troops/Previous Question. Dreier, R-Calif., motion to order the previous question (thus ending debate and possibility of amendment) on adoption of the rule (H Res 561) to provide for House floor consideration of the resolution that would affirm that the United States and the world are safer with the removal of Saddam Hussein and his regime from power in Iraq. It also would commend U.S. and coalition forces for liberating Iraq. Motion agreed to 217-197: R 217-0; D 0-196 (ND 0-139, SD 0-57); I 0-1. March 17, 2004.

63. H Res 557. War in Iraq and U.S. Troops/Rule. Adoption of the rule (H Res 561) to provide for House floor consideration of the resolution that would affirm the United States and the world are safer with the removal of Saddam Hussein and his regime from power in Iraq. It also would commend U.S. and coalition forces for liberating Iraq. Adopted 228-195: R 226-0; D 2-194 (ND 0-139, SD 2-55); I 0-1. March 17, 2004.

64. H Res 557. War in Iraq and U.S. Troops/Adoption. Adoption of the resolution that would affirm the United States and the world are safer with the removal of Saddam Hussein and his regime from power in Iraq. It also would commend U.S. and coalition forces for liberating Iraq and commend the Iraqi people on the adoption of Iraq's new interim constitution. Adopted 327-93: R 222-2; D 105-90 (ND 64-76, SD 41-14); I 0-1. A "yea" was a vote in support of the president's position. March 17, 2004.

65. H J Res 87. Franklin Delano Roosevelt Tribute/Passage. Miller, R-Mich., motion to suspend the rules and pass the joint resolution that would honor the life and legacy of President Franklin D. Roosevelt and recognize his contributions to the United States and the world on the anniversary of his birthday. Motion agreed to 398-5: R 199-5; D 198-0 (ND 141-0, SD 57-0); I 1-0. A two-thirds majority of those present and voting (269 in this case) is required for passage under suspension of the rules. March 17, 2004.

Key

Y	Voted for (yea).
#	Paired for.
+	Announced for.
N	Voted against (nay).
X	Paired against.
−	Announced against.
P	Voted "present."
C	Voted "present" to avoid possible conflict of interest.
?	Did not vote or otherwise make a position known.

Democrats **Republicans**
Independents

	58	59	60	61	62	63	64	65
ALABAMA								
1 *Bonner*	Y	Y	Y	N	Y	Y	Y	Y
2 *Everett*	?	?	?	N	Y	Y	Y	P
3 *Rogers*	Y	Y	Y	N	Y	Y	Y	Y
4 *Aderholt*	Y	Y	Y	N	Y	Y	Y	Y
5 Cramer	Y	Y	Y	N	N	N	Y	Y
6 *Bachus*	Y	Y	Y	N	Y	Y	Y	Y
7 Davis	Y	Y	Y	N	N	N	P	Y
ALASKA								
AL *Young*	Y	Y	Y	N	Y	Y	Y	Y
ARIZONA								
1 *Renzi*	Y	Y	Y	N	Y	Y	Y	Y
2 *Franks*	Y	Y	N	Y	Y	Y	Y	Y
3 *Shadegg*	?	?	?	N	Y	Y	Y	Y
4 Pastor	Y	Y	Y	N	N	N	N	Y
5 *Hayworth*	Y	Y	Y	N	Y	Y	Y	Y
6 *Flake*	Y	Y	Y	N	Y	Y	Y	N
7 Grijalva	Y	Y	N	Y	N	N	N	Y
8 *Kolbe*	?	?	?	N	Y	Y	Y	Y
ARKANSAS								
1 Berry	Y	Y	Y	N	N	N	Y	Y
2 Snyder	Y	Y	Y	N	N	N	Y	Y
3 *Boozman*	Y	Y	Y	N	Y	Y	Y	Y
4 Ross	Y	Y	Y	N	N	N	Y	Y
CALIFORNIA								
1 Thompson	Y	Y	Y	N	N	N	N	Y
2 *Herger*	Y	Y	Y	N	Y	Y	Y	Y
3 *Ose*	Y	Y	Y	N	Y	Y	Y	Y
4 *Doolittle*	Y	Y	Y	N	Y	Y	Y	?
5 Matsui	Y	Y	Y	N	N	N	N	?
6 Woolsey	Y	Y	Y	N	N	N	N	Y
7 Miller, George	Y	Y	Y	N	N	N	N	Y
8 Pelosi	Y	Y	Y	N	N	N	N	Y
9 Lee	Y	Y	Y	N	N	N	N	Y
10 Tauscher	Y	Y	Y	N	N	N	N	Y
11 *Pombo*	Y	Y	Y	N	Y	Y	Y	Y
12 Lantos	Y	Y	Y	N	N	P	Y	Y
13 Stark	Y	Y	Y	N	N	N	N	Y
14 Eshoo	Y	Y	Y	N	N	N	N	Y
15 Honda	Y	Y	Y	N	N	N	N	Y
16 Lofgren	Y	Y	Y	N	N	N	N	Y
17 Farr	Y	Y	Y	N	N	N	N	Y
18 Cardoza	Y	Y	Y	N	N	N	Y	Y
19 *Radanovich*	Y	Y	Y	N	Y	Y	Y	Y
20 Dooley	Y	Y	Y	N	N	N	N	?
21 *Nunes*	Y	Y	Y	N	Y	Y	Y	Y
22 *Thomas*	Y	Y	Y	N	Y	Y	Y	Y
23 Capps	Y	Y	Y	N	N	N	N	Y
24 *Gallegly*	Y	Y	Y	N	Y	Y	Y	Y
25 *McKeon*	Y	Y	Y	N	Y	Y	Y	Y
26 *Dreier*	Y	Y	Y	N	Y	Y	Y	Y
27 Sherman	Y	Y	Y	N	N	N	N	Y
28 Berman	Y	Y	Y	N	N	N	N	Y
29 Schiff	Y	Y	Y	N	N	N	N	Y
30 Waxman	Y	Y	Y	N	N	P	N	Y
31 Becerra	?	?	?	N	N	N	N	Y
32 Solis	Y	Y	Y	N	N	N	N	Y
33 Watson	Y	Y	Y	N	N	N	N	Y
34 Roybal-Allard	Y	Y	Y	N	N	N	N	Y
35 Waters	Y	Y	Y	N	N	N	N	Y
36 Harman	Y	Y	Y	N	N	N	Y	?

	58	59	60	61	62	63	64	65
37 Millender-McD.	Y	Y	Y	N	N	N	N	Y
38 Napolitano	Y	Y	Y	N	N	N	N	Y
39 Sánchez, Linda	Y	Y	Y	N	N	N	N	Y
40 *Royce*	Y	Y	Y	N	Y	Y	Y	?
41 *Lewis*	Y	Y	Y	N	Y	Y	Y	Y
42 *Miller, Gary*	Y	Y	Y	N	N	N	Y	Y
43 Baca	Y	Y	Y	N	N	N	N	Y
44 *Calvert*	Y	Y	Y	N	Y	Y	Y	Y
45 *Bono*	Y	Y	Y	N	Y	Y	Y	Y
46 *Rohrabacher*	Y	Y	Y	?	Y	Y	Y	?
47 Sanchez, Loretta	Y	Y	Y	Y	N	N	N	Y
48 *Cox*	Y	Y	?	N	Y	Y	Y	Y
49 *Issa*	Y	Y	Y	N	Y	Y	Y	Y
50 *Cunningham*	Y	Y	Y	N	Y	Y	Y	P
51 Filner	Y	Y	Y	N	N	N	N	Y
52 *Hunter*	Y	Y	Y	?	Y	Y	Y	Y
53 Davis	Y	Y	Y	N	N	N	P	Y
COLORADO								
1 DeGette	Y	Y	Y	N	N	N	N	Y
2 Udall	Y	Y	N	N	N	Y	Y	Y
3 *McInnis*	Y	Y	Y	N	Y	Y	Y	Y
4 *Musgrave*	Y	Y	Y	N	Y	Y	Y	Y
5 *Hefley*	Y	Y	Y	N	Y	Y	Y	N
6 *Tancredo*	Y	Y	Y	N	Y	Y	Y	Y
7 *Beauprez*	?	?	?	N	Y	Y	Y	Y
CONNECTICUT								
1 Larson	Y	Y	Y	N	N	N	N	Y
2 *Simmons*	Y	Y	Y	N	Y	Y	?	?
3 DeLauro	Y	Y	Y	N	N	N	N	Y
4 *Shays*	Y	Y	Y	N	Y	Y	Y	Y
5 *Johnson*	Y	Y	Y	N	Y	Y	Y	Y
DELAWARE								
AL *Castle*	Y	Y	Y	N	Y	Y	Y	Y
FLORIDA								
1 *Miller, J.*	Y	Y	Y	N	Y	Y	Y	Y
2 Boyd	Y	Y	Y	N	N	N	Y	Y
3 Brown	Y	Y	Y	N	N	N	N	Y
4 *Crenshaw*	Y	Y	Y	N	Y	Y	Y	Y
5 *Brown-Waite*	Y	Y	Y	N	Y	Y	Y	Y
6 *Stearns*	Y	Y	Y	N	Y	Y	Y	Y
7 *Mica*	Y	Y	Y	N	Y	Y	Y	Y
8 *Keller*	Y	Y	Y	N	Y	Y	Y	Y
9 *Bilirakis*	Y	Y	Y	N	Y	Y	Y	Y
10 *Young*	?	?	?	N	Y	Y	Y	Y
11 Davis	Y	Y	Y	N	N	N	Y	Y
12 *Putnam*	Y	Y	Y	N	Y	Y	Y	Y
13 *Harris*	Y	Y	Y	N	Y	Y	Y	Y
14 *Goss*	Y	Y	Y	N	Y	Y	Y	Y
15 *Weldon*	Y	Y	Y	N	Y	Y	Y	Y
16 *Foley*	Y	Y	Y	N	Y	Y	Y	?
17 Meek	Y	Y	Y	N	N	N	N	Y
18 *Ros-Lehtinen*	Y	Y	Y	N	N	N	Y	Y
19 Wexler	?	?	?	Y	N	N	N	Y
20 Deutsch	?	Y	Y	N	N	N	N	Y
21 *Diaz-Balart, L.*	Y	Y	Y	N	Y	Y	Y	Y
22 *Shaw*	Y	Y	Y	N	Y	Y	Y	Y
23 Hastings	Y	Y	Y	N	N	N	N	Y
24 *Feeney*	Y	Y	Y	N	Y	Y	Y	Y
25 *Diaz-Balart, M.*	Y	Y	Y	N	Y	Y	Y	Y
GEORGIA								
1 *Kingston*	Y	Y	Y	N	Y	Y	Y	P
2 Bishop	Y	Y	Y	N	N	N	Y	Y
3 Marshall	Y	?	Y	N	N	N	Y	Y
4 Majette	Y	Y	Y	N	N	N	N	Y
5 Lewis	Y	Y	Y	N	N	N	N	Y
6 *Isakson*	Y	Y	Y	N	Y	Y	Y	Y
7 *Linder*	Y	Y	Y	N	Y	Y	Y	Y
8 *Collins*	Y	Y	Y	N	Y	Y	Y	?
9 *Norwood*	Y	Y	Y	N	Y	Y	Y	Y
10 *Deal*	Y	Y	Y	N	Y	Y	Y	Y
11 *Gingrey*	Y	Y	Y	N	Y	Y	Y	Y
12 *Burns*	Y	Y	Y	N	Y	Y	Y	Y
13 Scott	Y	Y	Y	N	N	N	N	Y
HAWAII								
1 Abercrombie	Y	Y	Y	N	N	N	Y	Y
2 Case	Y	Y	Y	N	N	N	Y	Y
IDAHO								
1 *Otter*	Y	Y	Y	N	Y	Y	Y	?
2 *Simpson*	Y	Y	Y	N	Y	Y	Y	Y
ILLINOIS								
1 Rush	?	?	?	?	?	?	N	Y
2 Jackson	?	?	?	N	N	N	N	Y
3 Lipinski	?	?	Y	N	N	N	N	Y
4 Gutierrez	?	?	Y	N	N	N	N	Y
5 Emanuel	?	?	Y	N	N	N	N	Y
6 *Hyde*	Y	Y	Y	N	Y	Y	Y	Y

ND Northern Democrats   SD Southern Democrats

	58	59	60	61	62	63	64	65
7 Davis	?	?	?	N	N	N	N	Y
8 ***Crane***	?	?	?	N	Y	Y	Y	P
9 Schakowsky	?	?	?	Y	N	N	N	Y
10 ***Kirk***	?	?	?	N	?	Y	Y	Y
11 ***Weller***	Y	Y	Y	N	Y	Y	Y	?
12 Costello	Y	Y	Y	N	N	N	Y	Y
13 ***Biggert***	Y	Y	Y	N	Y	Y	Y	Y
14 ***Hastert***							Y	
15 ***Johnson***	Y	Y	Y	N	Y	Y	Y	Y
16 ***Manzullo***	Y	Y	Y	N	Y	Y	Y	?
17 Evans	Y	Y	Y	N	N	N	N	Y
18 ***LaHood***	Y	Y	Y	N	Y	Y	Y	Y
19 ***Shimkus***	Y	Y	Y	Y	Y	Y	Y	Y
INDIANA								
1 Visclosky	Y	Y	Y	N	N	N	N	Y
2 ***Chocola***	Y	Y	Y	N	Y	Y	Y	Y
3 ***Souder***	Y	Y	Y	?	?	Y	Y	Y
4 ***Buyer***	Y	Y	Y	N	Y	Y	Y	Y
5 ***Burton***	Y	Y	Y	N	Y	Y	Y	Y
6 ***Pence***	Y	Y	Y	N	Y	Y	Y	P
7 Carson	Y	Y	Y	N	N	N	P	Y
8 ***Hostettler***	Y	Y	Y	N	Y	Y	Y	Y
9 Hill	Y	Y	Y	N	N	N	Y	Y
IOWA								
1 ***Nussle***	Y	Y	Y	N	Y	Y	Y	Y
2 ***Leach***	Y	Y	Y	N	?	Y	N	Y
3 Boswell	Y	Y	Y	N	N	N	Y	Y
4 ***Latham***	Y	Y	Y	N	Y	Y	Y	Y
5 ***King***	Y	Y	Y	N	Y	Y	Y	N
KANSAS								
1 ***Moran***	Y	Y	Y	N	Y	Y	Y	Y
2 ***Ryun***	Y	Y	Y	N	Y	Y	Y	Y
3 Moore	Y	Y	Y	N	N	N	Y	Y
4 ***Tiahrt***	Y	Y	Y	N	+	Y	Y	Y
KENTUCKY								
1 ***Whitfield***	Y	Y	Y	N	Y	Y	Y	Y
2 ***Lewis***	Y	Y	Y	N	Y	Y	Y	Y
3 ***Northup***	Y	Y	Y	N	Y	Y	Y	Y
4 Lucas	Y	Y	Y	N	N	N	Y	Y
5 ***Rogers***	Y	Y	Y	N	Y	Y	Y	Y
6 Chandler	Y	Y	Y	N	N	N	Y	Y
LOUISIANA								
1 ***Vitter***	Y	Y	Y	N	Y	Y	Y	Y
2 Jefferson	Y	Y	Y	?	N	N	N	Y
3 ***Tauzin***	?	?	?	?	?	?	?	?
4 ***McCrery***	Y	Y	Y	N	Y	Y	Y	Y
5 Alexander	Y	Y	Y	N	N	Y	Y	Y
6 ***Baker***	Y	Y	Y	N	Y	Y	Y	Y
7 John	Y	Y	Y	N	N	N	Y	Y
MAINE								
1 Allen	Y	Y	Y	Y	N	N	Y	Y
2 Michaud	Y	Y	Y	N	N	N	Y	Y
MARYLAND								
1 ***Gilchrest***	Y	Y	Y	N	Y	Y	Y	Y
2 Ruppersberger	Y	Y	Y	N	N	N	Y	Y
3 Cardin	Y	Y	Y	N	N	N	Y	Y
4 Wynn	Y	Y	Y	N	N	N	Y	Y
5 Hoyer	Y	Y	Y	N	N	N	Y	Y
6 ***Bartlett***	Y	Y	Y	N	Y	Y	Y	N
7 Cummings	Y	Y	Y	N	N	N	N	Y
8 Van Hollen	Y	Y	Y	N	N	N	N	Y
MASSACHUSETTS								
1 Olver	Y	Y	Y	Y	N	N	N	Y
2 Neal	Y	Y	Y	N	N	N	Y	Y
3 McGovern	Y	Y	Y	Y	N	N	N	Y
4 Frank	Y	Y	Y	?	N	N	N	Y
5 Meehan	Y	Y	Y	N	N	N	P	Y
6 Tierney	Y	Y	Y	Y	N	N	N	Y
7 Markey	Y	Y	Y	N	N	N	N	Y
8 Capuano	Y	Y	Y	Y	N	N	Y	Y
9 Lynch	Y	Y	Y	?	?	N	Y	Y
10 Delahunt	Y	Y	Y	Y	N	N	N	Y
MICHIGAN								
1 Stupak	Y	Y	Y	N	N	N	Y	Y
2 ***Hoekstra***	Y	Y	Y	N	Y	Y	Y	Y
3 ***Ehlers***	Y	Y	Y	N	Y	Y	Y	Y
4 ***Camp***	Y	Y	Y	N	Y	Y	Y	Y
5 Kildee	Y	Y	Y	N	N	N	Y	Y
6 ***Upton***	Y	Y	Y	N	Y	Y	Y	Y
7 ***Smith***	Y	Y	Y	N	Y	Y	Y	Y
8 ***Rogers***	Y	Y	Y	N	Y	Y	Y	Y
9 ***Knollenberg***	Y	Y	Y	N	Y	Y	Y	Y
10 ***Miller***	Y	Y	Y	N	Y	Y	Y	Y
11 ***McCotter***	Y	Y	Y	N	Y	Y	Y	Y
12 Levin	Y	Y	Y	N	N	N	N	Y

	58	59	60	61	62	63	64	65
13 Kilpatrick	Y	?	Y	Y	N	N	N	Y
14 Conyers	Y	Y	Y	Y	N	N	N	Y
15 Dingell	Y	Y	Y	Y	N	N	Y	Y
MINNESOTA								
1 ***Gutknecht***	Y	Y	Y	N	Y	Y	Y	Y
2 ***Kline***	Y	Y	Y	N	Y	Y	Y	Y
3 ***Ramstad***	Y	Y	Y	N	Y	Y	Y	Y
4 McCollum	Y	Y	Y	N	N	N	N	Y
5 Sabo	Y	Y	Y	N	N	N	N	Y
6 ***Kennedy***	Y	Y	Y	N	Y	Y	Y	Y
7 Peterson	Y	Y	Y	N	N	N	Y	Y
8 Oberstar	?	?	?	N	N	N	N	Y
MISSISSIPPI								
1 ***Wicker***	?	Y	Y	N	Y	Y	Y	Y
2 Thompson	Y	Y	Y	Y	N	N	Y	Y
3 ***Pickering***	Y	Y	Y	N	Y	Y	Y	Y
4 Taylor	Y	Y	Y	N	N	N	Y	Y
MISSOURI								
1 Clay	Y	Y	Y	?	N	N	N	Y
2 ***Akin***	Y	Y	Y	N	Y	Y	Y	?
3 Gephardt	?	?	?	N	N	N	Y	?
4 Skelton	Y	Y	Y	N	N	N	Y	Y
5 McCarthy	Y	Y	Y	N	N	N	N	Y
6 ***Graves***	Y	Y	Y	N	Y	Y	Y	Y
7 ***Blunt***	Y	Y	Y	N	Y	Y	Y	?
8 ***Emerson***	Y	Y	Y	N	Y	Y	Y	Y
9 ***Hulshof***	Y	Y	Y	N	Y	Y	Y	Y
MONTANA								
AL ***Rehberg***	Y	Y	Y	N	Y	Y	Y	Y
NEBRASKA								
1 ***Bereuter***	Y	Y	Y	N	?	Y	Y	Y
2 ***Terry***	Y	Y	Y	N	Y	Y	Y	Y
3 ***Osborne***	Y	Y	Y	N	Y	Y	Y	Y
NEVADA								
1 Berkley	Y	Y	Y	N	N	N	Y	Y
2 ***Gibbons***	Y	Y	Y	N	+	Y	Y	Y
3 ***Porter***	Y	Y	Y	N	Y	Y	Y	Y
NEW HAMPSHIRE								
1 ***Bradley***	Y	Y	Y	N	Y	Y	Y	Y
2 ***Bass***	Y	Y	Y	N	Y	Y	Y	Y
NEW JERSEY								
1 Andrews	Y	Y	Y	N	N	N	Y	Y
2 ***LoBiondo***	Y	Y	Y	N	Y	Y	Y	Y
3 ***Saxton***	Y	Y	Y	N	Y	Y	Y	Y
4 ***Smith***	Y	Y	Y	N	Y	Y	Y	Y
5 ***Garrett***	Y	Y	Y	N	Y	Y	Y	?
6 Pallone	Y	Y	Y	N	N	N	N	Y
7 ***Ferguson***	Y	Y	Y	N	Y	Y	Y	Y
8 Pascrell	Y	Y	Y	N	N	N	Y	Y
9 Rothman	Y	Y	Y	Y	N	N	N	Y
10 Payne	Y	Y	Y	Y	N	N	N	Y
11 ***Frelinghuysen***	Y	Y	Y	N	Y	Y	Y	Y
12 Holt	Y	Y	Y	Y	N	N	Y	Y
13 Menendez	Y	Y	Y	N	N	N	Y	Y
NEW MEXICO								
1 ***Wilson***	Y	Y	Y	N	Y	Y	Y	Y
2 ***Pearce***	Y	Y	Y	N	Y	Y	Y	Y
3 Udall	Y	Y	Y	N	N	N	N	Y
NEW YORK								
1 Bishop	Y	Y	Y	N	N	N	Y	Y
2 Israel	?	?	?	?	?	?	Y	Y
3 ***King***	Y	Y	Y	?	Y	Y	Y	Y
4 McCarthy	Y	Y	Y	N	N	N	Y	Y
5 Ackerman	Y	Y	Y	N	N	N	N	Y
6 Meeks	?	?	?	N	N	N	N	Y
7 Crowley	Y	Y	Y	N	N	N	Y	Y
8 Nadler	Y	Y	Y	N	N	N	N	Y
9 Weiner	Y	Y	Y	N	N	N	N	Y
10 Towns	Y	Y	Y	N	N	N	N	Y
11 Owens	Y	Y	Y	Y	N	N	N	Y
12 Velázquez	Y	Y	Y	N	N	N	N	Y
13 ***Fossella***	Y	Y	Y	N	Y	Y	Y	Y
14 Maloney	?	?	?	?	?	?	N	Y
15 Rangel	Y	Y	Y	N	N	N	N	Y
16 Serrano	Y	Y	Y	N	N	N	N	Y
17 Engel	Y	Y	Y	N	N	N	Y	Y
18 Lowey	Y	Y	Y	N	N	?	Y	Y
19 ***Kelly***	Y	Y	Y	N	Y	Y	Y	Y
20 ***Sweeney***	Y	Y	Y	N	Y	Y	Y	Y
21 McNulty	Y	Y	Y	N	N	N	Y	Y
22 Hinchey	Y	Y	Y	Y	N	N	N	Y
23 ***McHugh***	Y	Y	Y	N	Y	Y	Y	Y
24 ***Boehlert***	Y	Y	Y	N	Y	Y	Y	Y
25 ***Walsh***	Y	Y	Y	?	Y	Y	Y	Y

	58	59	60	61	62	63	64	65
26 ***Reynolds***	Y	Y	Y	?	Y	Y	Y	Y
27 ***Quinn***	Y	Y	Y	?	Y	Y	Y	Y
28 Slaughter	Y	Y	Y	N	N	N	Y	Y
29 ***Houghton***	Y	Y	Y	N	Y	Y	Y	Y
NORTH CAROLINA								
1 Ballance	Y	Y	Y	N	N	N	N	Y
2 Etheridge	Y	Y	Y	N	N	N	Y	Y
3 ***Jones***	Y	Y	Y	N	Y	Y	Y	Y
4 Price	Y	Y	Y	N	N	N	Y	Y
5 ***Burr***	?	?	?	N	Y	Y	Y	Y
6 ***Coble***	Y	Y	Y	N	Y	Y	Y	Y
7 McIntyre	Y	Y	Y	N	N	N	Y	Y
8 ***Hayes***	Y	Y	Y	N	Y	Y	Y	Y
9 ***Myrick***	Y	Y	Y	N	Y	Y	Y	Y
10 ***Ballenger***	Y	Y	Y	N	Y	Y	Y	?
11 ***Taylor***	Y	Y	Y	N	Y	Y	Y	Y
12 Watt	Y	Y	Y	N	N	N	N	Y
13 Miller	Y	Y	Y	Y	N	N	Y	Y
NORTH DAKOTA								
AL Pomeroy	Y	Y	Y	N	N	N	Y	Y
OHIO								
1 ***Chabot***	Y	Y	Y	N	Y	Y	Y	Y
2 ***Portman***	Y	Y	Y	N	Y	Y	Y	Y
3 ***Turner***	Y	Y	Y	N	+	Y	Y	Y
4 ***Oxley***	Y	Y	Y	N	Y	Y	Y	Y
5 ***Gillmor***	Y	Y	Y	N	Y	Y	Y	Y
6 Strickland	Y	?	Y	N	N	N	Y	Y
7 ***Hobson***	Y	Y	Y	N	Y	Y	Y	Y
8 ***Boehner***	Y	Y	Y	N	Y	Y	Y	Y
9 Kaptur	Y	Y	Y	N	N	?	Y	Y
10 Kucinich	?	?	?	?	?	?	?	?
11 Jones	Y	Y	Y	N	N	N	Y	Y
12 ***Tiberi***	Y	Y	Y	N	Y	Y	Y	Y
13 Brown	Y	Y	Y	N	N	N	Y	Y
14 ***LaTourette***	Y	Y	Y	N	Y	Y	Y	Y
15 ***Pryce***	Y	?	Y	N	Y	Y	Y	Y
16 ***Regula***	Y	Y	Y	N	Y	Y	Y	Y
17 Ryan	?	?	?	?	?	?	Y	Y
18 ***Ney***	Y	Y	Y	N	Y	Y	Y	Y
OKLAHOMA								
1 ***Sullivan***	Y	Y	Y	N	Y	Y	Y	Y
2 Carson	Y	Y	Y	N	N	N	Y	Y
3 ***Lucas***	Y	Y	Y	N	Y	Y	Y	Y
4 ***Cole***	Y	Y	Y	N	Y	Y	Y	Y
5 ***Istook***	?	?	?	N	Y	Y	Y	Y
OREGON								
1 Wu	Y	Y	Y	N	N	N	Y	Y
2 ***Walden***	Y	Y	Y	N	Y	Y	Y	Y
3 Blumenauer	Y	Y	Y	N	N	N	N	Y
4 DeFazio	Y	Y	Y	N	N	N	Y	Y
5 Hooley	Y	Y	Y	N	N	N	Y	Y
PENNSYLVANIA								
1 Brady	Y	Y	Y	N	N	N	N	Y
2 Fattah	?	?	?	N	N	N	N	Y
3 ***English***	Y	Y	Y	N	Y	Y	Y	Y
4 ***Hart***	Y	Y	Y	N	Y	Y	Y	Y
5 ***Peterson***	Y	Y	Y	N	Y	Y	Y	Y
6 ***Gerlach***	Y	Y	Y	N	Y	Y	Y	Y
7 ***Weldon***	Y	Y	Y	N	?	Y	?	?
8 ***Greenwood***	Y	Y	Y	N	Y	Y	Y	Y
9 ***Shuster, Bill***	Y	Y	Y	N	Y	Y	Y	Y
10 ***Sherwood***	Y	Y	Y	N	Y	Y	?	?
11 Kanjorski	Y	Y	Y	N	N	N	N	Y
12 Murtha	Y	Y	Y	N	N	N	N	Y
13 Hoeffel	Y	Y	Y	?	?	?	?	?
14 Doyle	Y	Y	Y	N	N	N	N	Y
15 ***Toomey***	?	?	Y	N	Y	Y	Y	Y
16 ***Pitts***	Y	Y	Y	N	Y	Y	Y	Y
17 Holden	Y	Y	Y	N	N	N	Y	Y
18 ***Murphy***	Y	Y	Y	N	Y	Y	Y	Y
19 ***Platts***	?	Y	Y	N	Y	Y	Y	Y
RHODE ISLAND								
1 Kennedy	Y	Y	Y	N	N	N	Y	Y
2 Langevin	Y	Y	Y	N	N	N	Y	Y
SOUTH CAROLINA								
1 ***Brown***	Y	Y	Y	N	Y	Y	Y	Y
2 ***Wilson***	Y	Y	Y	N	Y	Y	Y	Y
3 ***Barrett***	Y	Y	Y	N	Y	Y	Y	Y
4 ***DeMint***	?	?	?	N	Y	Y	Y	Y
5 Spratt	Y	Y	Y	N	N	N	Y	Y
6 Clyburn	Y	Y	Y	N	N	N	N	Y
SOUTH DAKOTA								
AL Vacant								

	58	59	60	61	62	63	64	65
TENNESSEE								
1 ***Jenkins***	Y	Y	Y	N	Y	Y	Y	Y
2 ***Duncan***	Y	Y	Y	N	Y	Y	Y	Y
3 ***Wamp***	Y	Y	Y	N	Y	Y	Y	Y
4 Davis	Y	Y	Y	N	N	Y	Y	Y
5 Cooper	Y	Y	Y	N	N	N	Y	Y
6 Gordon	Y	Y	Y	N	N	N	Y	Y
7 ***Blackburn***	Y	Y	Y	N	Y	Y	Y	Y
8 Tanner	Y	Y	Y	N	N	N	Y	Y
9 Ford	Y	Y	Y	N	N	N	Y	Y
TEXAS								
1 Sandlin	?	Y	Y	N	N	N	Y	Y
2 Turner	Y	Y	Y	N	N	N	Y	Y
3 ***Johnson, Sam***	Y	Y	Y	N	Y	Y	Y	P
4 ***Hall***	?	?	?	N	Y	Y	Y	Y
5 ***Hensarling***	Y	Y	Y	N	Y	Y	Y	Y
6 ***Barton***	Y	Y	Y	N	?	Y	Y	Y
7 ***Culberson***	Y	Y	Y	N	Y	Y	Y	Y
8 ***Brady***	Y	Y	Y	N	Y	Y	Y	Y
9 Lampson	Y	Y	Y	N	N	N	Y	Y
10 Doggett	Y	Y	Y	Y	N	N	Y	Y
11 Edwards	?	Y	Y	N	N	N	Y	Y
12 ***Granger***	Y	Y	Y	N	Y	Y	Y	Y
13 ***Thornberry***	Y	Y	Y	N	Y	Y	Y	Y
14 ***Paul***	Y	Y	Y	N	Y	Y	N	N
15 Hinojosa	Y	Y	Y	N	N	N	Y	Y
16 Reyes	Y	Y	Y	?	N	N	Y	Y
17 Stenholm	Y	Y	Y	N	N	N	Y	Y
18 Jackson-Lee	Y	Y	Y	N	N	N	N	Y
19 ***Neugebauer***	Y	Y	Y	N	Y	Y	Y	Y
20 Gonzalez	Y	Y	Y	N	N	N	Y	Y
21 ***Smith***	Y	Y	Y	N	Y	Y	Y	Y
22 ***DeLay***	Y	Y	Y	N	Y	Y	Y	Y
23 ***Bonilla***	Y	Y	Y	N	Y	Y	Y	Y
24 Frost	Y	Y	Y	?	N	N	Y	Y
25 Bell	Y	Y	Y	N	N	N	N	Y
26 ***Burgess***	Y	Y	Y	N	Y	Y	Y	Y
27 Ortiz	Y	Y	Y	N	N	N	Y	Y
28 Rodriguez	Y	Y	Y	N	N	N	Y	Y
29 Green	Y	Y	Y	N	N	N	Y	Y
30 Johnson, E.B.	Y	Y	Y	Y	N	N	P	Y
31 ***Carter***	Y	Y	Y	N	Y	Y	Y	Y
32 ***Sessions***	?	?	?	N	Y	Y	Y	Y
UTAH								
1 ***Bishop***	?	?	?	N	Y	Y	Y	Y
2 Matheson	Y	Y	Y	N	N	N	Y	Y
3 ***Cannon***	Y	Y	Y	N	Y	Y	Y	Y
VERMONT								
AL *Sanders*	Y	Y	Y	Y	N	N	N	Y
VIRGINIA								
1 ***Davis, Jo Ann***	Y	Y	Y	N	Y	Y	Y	Y
2 ***Schrock***	Y	Y	Y	N	Y	Y	Y	Y
3 Scott	Y	Y	Y	N	N	N	N	Y
4 ***Forbes***	Y	Y	Y	N	Y	Y	Y	Y
5 ***Goode***	Y	Y	Y	N	Y	Y	Y	Y
6 ***Goodlatte***	Y	Y	Y	N	Y	Y	Y	Y
7 ***Cantor***	Y	Y	Y	N	Y	Y	Y	Y
8 Moran	Y	Y	Y	N	N	N	N	Y
9 Boucher	Y	Y	Y	N	N	N	Y	Y
10 ***Wolf***	Y	Y	Y	N	Y	Y	Y	Y
11 ***Davis, T.***	Y	Y	Y	N	Y	Y	Y	Y
WASHINGTON								
1 Inslee	Y	Y	Y	N	N	N	Y	Y
2 Larsen	?	?	?	N	N	N	Y	Y
3 Baird	Y	Y	Y	N	N	N	Y	Y
4 ***Hastings***	Y	Y	Y	N	Y	Y	Y	Y
5 ***Nethercutt***	Y	Y	Y	N	Y	Y	Y	Y
6 Dicks	Y	Y	Y	Y	N	N	Y	Y
7 McDermott	Y	Y	Y	Y	N	N	N	Y
8 ***Dunn***	Y	Y	Y	N	Y	Y	Y	Y
9 Smith	?	?	?	?	?	?	?	?
WEST VIRGINIA								
1 Mollohan	Y	Y	Y	N	N	N	N	Y
2 ***Capito***	Y	Y	Y	N	Y	Y	Y	Y
3 Rahall	?	?	?	N	N	N	N	Y
WISCONSIN								
1 ***Ryan***	Y	Y	Y	N	Y	Y	Y	Y
2 Baldwin	Y	Y	Y	N	N	N	N	Y
3 Kind	Y	Y	Y	N	N	N	Y	Y
4 Kleczka	Y	Y	Y	N	N	N	N	Y
5 ***Sensenbrenner***	Y	Y	Y	N	Y	Y	Y	Y
6 ***Petri***	Y	Y	Y	N	Y	Y	Y	Y
7 Obey	?	?	?	N	N	N	N	Y
8 ***Green***	Y	Y	Y	N	Y	Y	Y	Y
WYOMING								
AL ***Cubin***	Y	Y	Y	N	Y	Y	Y	Y

Southern states - Ala., Ark., Fla., Ga., Ky., La., Miss., N.C., Okla., S.C., Tenn., Texas, Va.

Key

Y	Voted for (yea).
#	Paired for.
+	Announced for.
N	Voted against (nay).
X	Paired against.
–	Announced against.
P	Voted "present."
C	Voted "present" to avoid possible conflict of interest.
?	Did not vote or otherwise make a position known.

Democrats **Republicans**
Independents

66. HR 1375. Financial Services Regulation/Returned Checks. Weiner, D-N.Y., amendment that would prohibit commercial banks from charging a fee to the depositor of a check that is returned for insufficient funds. Rejected 167-255: R 8-212; D 158-43 (ND 124-21, SD 34-22); I 1-0. March 18, 2004.

67. HR 1375. Financial Services Regulation/Impact of Bank Mergers. Jackson-Lee, D-Texas, amendment that would express the sense of Congress that when a banking agency requests expedited action on a merger application, the merger's impact on corporate and individual customers should be considered. Rejected 194-225: R 13-205; D 180-20 (ND 135-9, SD 45-11); I 1-0. March 18, 2004.

68. HR 1375. Financial Services Regulation/Interest Restriction Removal. Kelly, R-N.Y., amendment that would allow banks to pay interest on business checking accounts and allow the Federal Reserve to pay interest on "sterile" accounts that banks must maintain under federal law. Adopted 418-0: R 217-0; D 200-0 (ND 144-0, SD 56-0); I 1-0. March 18, 2004.

69. HR 1375. Financial Services Regulation/Passage. Passage of the bill that would ease dozens of banking regulations, including expanding the ability of banks and thrifts to open new branches or merge with other institutions. It would provide banks with greater flexibility to manage their operations, such as providing greater leeway in the calculation of dividend payments. The bill, as amended, would ban any company with less than 85 percent of its business in financial services from using an industrial loan company to branch across state lines. It also would allow credit unions to expand their investment opportunities and their service offerings, such as wire transfers, while streamlining merger procedures. Passed 392-25: R 207-11; D 185-13 (ND 132-10, SD 53-3); I 0-1. March 18, 2004.

70. HR 3782. Terrorism Informant Rewards/Passage. Harris, R-Fla., motion to suspend the rules and pass the bill that would raise the maximum reward available under the Department of State rewards program from $5 million to $25 million for information leading to the arrest or conviction of foreign terrorists or narco-terrorists. Any information that leads to the disruption of terrorist financing networks would also be eligible for a reward. The bill would authorize up to $50 million for the capture of a leader of a foreign terrorist organization. Motion agreed to 414-0: R 216-0; D 197-0 (ND 142-0, SD 55-0); I 1-0. A two-thirds majority of those present and voting (276 in this case) is required for passage under suspension of the rules. March 18, 2004.

71. H Con Res 364. Marshall Islands Partnership/Adoption. Harris, R-Fla., motion to suspend the rules and adopt the concurrent resolution that would express Congress' recognition of more than 50 years of strategic partnership between the United States and the people of the Marshall Islands. The resolution also would recognize the importance of the nuclear weapon test code-named Bravo at Bikini Atoll in the Marshall Islands on March 1, 1954. Motion agreed to 408-0: R 214-0; D 193-0 (ND 140-0, SD 53-0); I 1-0. A two-thirds majority of those present and voting (272 in this case) is required for adoption under suspension of the rules. March 18, 2004.

	66	67	68	69	70	71
ALABAMA						
1 *Bonner*	N	N	Y	Y	Y	Y
2 *Everett*	N	N	Y	Y	Y	Y
3 *Rogers*	N	N	Y	Y	Y	Y
4 *Aderholt*	N	Y	Y	?	Y	Y
5 Cramer	N	N	Y	Y	Y	Y
6 *Bachus*	N	N	Y	Y	Y	Y
7 Davis	Y	Y	Y	Y	Y	?
ALASKA						
AL *Young*	N	N	Y	Y	Y	Y
ARIZONA						
1 *Renzi*	N	N	Y	Y	Y	Y
2 *Franks*	N	N	Y	Y	Y	Y
3 *Shadegg*	N	N	Y	Y	Y	Y
4 Pastor	Y	Y	Y	Y	Y	Y
5 *Hayworth*	N	N	Y	Y	Y	Y
6 *Flake*	N	N	Y	Y	Y	Y
7 Grijalva	Y	Y	Y	Y	Y	Y
8 *Kolbe*	N	N	Y	Y	Y	Y
ARKANSAS						
1 Berry	N	Y	Y	Y	Y	Y
2 Snyder	Y	Y	Y	Y	Y	Y
3 *Boozman*	N	N	Y	Y	Y	Y
4 Ross	N	Y	Y	Y	Y	Y
CALIFORNIA						
1 Thompson	N	Y	Y	Y	Y	Y
2 *Herger*	N	N	Y	Y	Y	Y
3 *Ose*	N	N	Y	Y	Y	Y
4 *Doolittle*	N	N	Y	Y	Y	Y
5 Matsui	Y	Y	Y	Y	Y	Y
6 Woolsey	Y	Y	Y	Y	Y	Y
7 Miller, George	Y	Y	Y	Y	Y	?
8 Pelosi	Y	Y	Y	Y	Y	Y
9 Lee	Y	Y	Y	Y	Y	Y
10 Tauscher	Y	Y	Y	Y	Y	Y
11 *Pombo*	N	N	Y	Y	Y	Y
12 Lantos	Y	Y	Y	Y	Y	Y
13 Stark	Y	Y	Y	Y	Y	?
14 Eshoo	Y	Y	Y	Y	Y	Y
15 Honda	Y	Y	Y	Y	Y	Y
16 Lofgren	Y	Y	Y	Y	Y	Y
17 Farr	Y	Y	Y	Y	Y	Y
18 Cardoza	Y	Y	Y	Y	Y	Y
19 *Radanovich*	N	N	Y	Y	Y	?
20 Dooley	N	Y	Y	Y	Y	Y
21 *Nunes*	N	N	Y	Y	Y	Y
22 *Thomas*	N	N	Y	Y	Y	Y
23 Capps	Y	Y	Y	Y	Y	Y
24 *Gallegly*	N	N	Y	Y	Y	Y
25 *McKeon*	N	N	Y	Y	Y	Y
26 *Dreier*	N	N	Y	Y	Y	Y
27 Sherman	N	Y	Y	Y	Y	Y
28 Berman	Y	Y	Y	Y	Y	Y
29 Schiff	Y	Y	Y	Y	Y	Y
30 Waxman	Y	Y	Y	Y	Y	Y
31 Becerra	Y	Y	Y	Y	Y	Y
32 Solis	Y	Y	Y	Y	Y	Y
33 Watson	Y	Y	Y	Y	Y	Y
34 Roybal-Allard	Y	Y	Y	Y	Y	Y
35 Waters	Y	Y	Y	Y	Y	Y
36 Harman	?	?	?	?	?	?

	66	67	68	69	70	71
37 Millender-McD.	Y	Y	Y	Y	Y	Y
38 Napolitano	Y	Y	Y	Y	Y	Y
39 Sánchez, Linda	Y	Y	Y	Y	Y	Y
40 *Royce*	N	N	Y	N	Y	Y
41 *Lewis*	N	?	Y	Y	Y	Y
42 *Miller, Gary*	N	N	Y	Y	Y	Y
43 Baca	Y	Y	Y	Y	Y	Y
44 *Calvert*	N	N	Y	Y	Y	Y
45 *Bono*	N	N	Y	Y	Y	Y
46 *Rohrabacher*	N	N	Y	Y	Y	Y
47 Sanchez, Loretta	Y	Y	Y	Y	Y	Y
48 *Cox*	N	N	Y	Y	?	Y
49 *Issa*	N	N	Y	Y	Y	Y
50 *Cunningham*	N	N	Y	Y	Y	Y
51 Filner	Y	Y	Y	Y	Y	Y
52 *Hunter*	N	?	Y	Y	Y	Y
53 Davis	Y	Y	Y	Y	Y	Y
COLORADO						
1 DeGette	Y	Y	Y	Y	Y	Y
2 Udall	Y	Y	Y	Y	Y	Y
3 *McInnis*	N	N	Y	Y	Y	Y
4 *Musgrave*	N	N	Y	N	Y	Y
5 *Hefley*	N	N	Y	Y	Y	Y
6 *Tancredo*	N	N	Y	Y	Y	Y
7 *Beauprez*	N	N	Y	Y	Y	Y
CONNECTICUT						
1 Larson	Y	Y	Y	Y	Y	Y
2 *Simmons*	N	N	Y	Y	Y	Y
3 DeLauro	Y	Y	Y	Y	Y	Y
4 *Shays*	N	Y	Y	Y	Y	Y
5 *Johnson*	N	N	Y	Y	Y	Y
DELAWARE						
AL *Castle*	N	N	Y	Y	Y	Y
FLORIDA						
1 *Miller, J.*	N	N	Y	Y	Y	Y
2 Boyd	Y	N	Y	Y	Y	Y
3 Brown	Y	Y	Y	Y	Y	Y
4 *Crenshaw*	N	N	Y	Y	Y	Y
5 *Brown-Waite*	N	N	Y	Y	Y	Y
6 *Stearns*	N	N	Y	Y	Y	Y
7 *Mica*	N	N	Y	Y	Y	Y
8 *Keller*	N	N	Y	Y	Y	Y
9 *Bilirakis*	N	N	Y	Y	Y	Y
10 *Young*	N	N	Y	Y	Y	Y
11 Davis	N	Y	Y	Y	Y	?
12 *Putnam*	N	N	Y	Y	Y	Y
13 *Harris*	N	N	Y	Y	Y	Y
14 *Goss*	N	N	?	Y	Y	Y
15 *Weldon*	N	N	Y	Y	Y	Y
16 *Foley*	N	N	Y	Y	Y	Y
17 Meek	Y	Y	Y	Y	Y	Y
18 *Ros-Lehtinen*	N	N	Y	Y	Y	Y
19 Wexler	Y	Y	Y	Y	Y	Y
20 Deutsch	Y	Y	Y	Y	Y	Y
21 *Diaz-Balart, L.*	N	N	Y	Y	Y	Y
22 *Shaw*	N	N	Y	Y	Y	Y
23 Hastings	Y	Y	Y	Y	Y	Y
24 *Feeney*	N	N	Y	Y	Y	Y
25 *Diaz-Balart, M.*	N	N	Y	Y	Y	Y
GEORGIA						
1 *Kingston*	N	N	Y	Y	Y	Y
2 Bishop	N	Y	Y	Y	Y	Y
3 Marshall	N	N	Y	Y	Y	Y
4 Majette	Y	Y	Y	Y	Y	Y
5 Lewis	Y	Y	Y	N	Y	Y
6 *Isakson*	N	N	Y	Y	Y	Y
7 *Linder*	N	N	Y	Y	Y	Y
8 *Collins*	N	N	Y	Y	Y	Y
9 *Norwood*	N	N	Y	Y	Y	Y
10 *Deal*	N	N	Y	Y	?	?
11 *Gingrey*	N	N	Y	Y	Y	Y
12 *Burns*	N	N	Y	Y	Y	Y
13 Scott	N	Y	Y	Y	Y	Y
HAWAII						
1 Abercrombie	Y	Y	Y	?	Y	Y
2 Case	N	Y	Y	Y	Y	Y
IDAHO						
1 *Otter*	Y	N	Y	Y	Y	Y
2 *Simpson*	Y	N	Y	Y	Y	Y
ILLINOIS						
1 Rush	Y	Y	Y	Y	Y	Y
2 Jackson	Y	Y	Y	Y	Y	Y
3 Lipinski	Y	N	Y	Y	Y	Y
4 Gutierrez	Y	Y	Y	Y	Y	Y
5 Emanuel	Y	Y	Y	Y	Y	Y
6 *Hyde*	N	N	Y	Y	Y	Y

ND Northern Democrats   SD Southern Democrats

	66	67	68	69	70	71
7 Davis	Y	Y	Y	Y	Y	Y
8 ***Crane***	N	N	Y	Y	Y	Y
9 Schakowsky	Y	Y	Y	Y	Y	Y
10 ***Kirk***	N	N	Y	Y	Y	Y
11 ***Weller***	N	N	Y	Y	Y	Y
12 Costello	Y	Y	Y	Y	Y	Y
13 ***Biggert***	N	N	Y	Y	Y	Y
14 ***Hastert***						
15 ***Johnson***	N	N	Y	Y	Y	Y
16 ***Manzullo***	N	N	Y	Y	Y	Y
17 Evans	Y	Y	Y	N	Y	Y
18 ***LaHood***	N	N	Y	Y	Y	Y
19 ***Shimkus***	?	?	?	?	?	?
INDIANA						
1 Visclosky	N	Y	Y	Y	Y	Y
2 ***Chocola***	N	N	Y	Y	Y	Y
3 ***Souder***	N	N	Y	Y	Y	Y
4 ***Buyer***	N	N	Y	Y	Y	Y
5 ***Burton***	N	N	Y	Y	Y	Y
6 ***Pence***	N	Y	Y	Y	Y	Y
7 Carson	Y	Y	Y	Y	Y	Y
8 ***Hostettler***	N	N	Y	Y	?	?
9 Hill	Y	Y	Y	Y	Y	Y
IOWA						
1 ***Nussle***	N	N	Y	N	Y	Y
2 ***Leach***	N	Y	Y	N	Y	Y
3 Boswell	N	Y	Y	N	Y	Y
4 ***Latham***	N	N	Y	N	Y	Y
5 ***King***	N	N	Y	N	Y	Y
KANSAS						
1 ***Moran***	N	N	Y	Y	Y	Y
2 ***Ryun***	N	N	Y	Y	Y	Y
3 Moore	N	Y	Y	Y	Y	Y
4 ***Tiahrt***	N	N	Y	Y	Y	Y
KENTUCKY						
1 ***Whitfield***	?	?	?	?	?	?
2 ***Lewis***	N	N	Y	Y	Y	Y
3 ***Northup***	N	N	Y	Y	Y	Y
4 Lucas	N	N	Y	Y	Y	Y
5 ***Rogers***	N	N	Y	Y	Y	Y
6 Chandler	Y	Y	Y	Y	Y	Y
LOUISIANA						
1 ***Vitter***	N	N	Y	Y	Y	Y
2 Jefferson	Y	Y	Y	Y	Y	Y
3 ***Tauzin***	?	?	?	?	?	?
4 ***McCrery***	N	N	Y	Y	Y	Y
5 Alexander	N	Y	Y	Y	Y	Y
6 ***Baker***	N	N	Y	Y	Y	Y
7 John	?	?	?	?	?	?
MAINE						
1 Allen	N	Y	Y	Y	Y	Y
2 Michaud	N	N	Y	Y	Y	Y
MARYLAND						
1 ***Gilchrest***	N	N	Y	N	Y	Y
2 Ruppersberger	N	N	Y	Y	Y	Y
3 Cardin	Y	Y	Y	Y	Y	Y
4 Wynn	Y	Y	Y	Y	Y	Y
5 Hoyer	Y	Y	Y	Y	Y	Y
6 ***Bartlett***	N	N	Y	Y	Y	Y
7 Cummings	Y	Y	Y	Y	Y	Y
8 Van Hollen	Y	Y	Y	Y	Y	Y
MASSACHUSETTS						
1 Olver	Y	Y	Y	Y	Y	Y
2 Neal	Y	Y	Y	Y	Y	Y
3 McGovern	Y	Y	Y	Y	Y	Y
4 Frank	Y	Y	Y	Y	Y	Y
5 Meehan	Y	Y	Y	Y	Y	Y
6 Tierney	Y	Y	Y	Y	Y	Y
7 Markey	Y	N	Y	N	?	Y
8 Capuano	Y	Y	Y	Y	Y	Y
9 Lynch	Y	Y	Y	Y	Y	Y
10 Delahunt	Y	Y	Y	N	Y	Y
MICHIGAN						
1 Stupak	Y	Y	Y	Y	Y	Y
2 ***Hoekstra***	N	Y	Y	Y	Y	Y
3 ***Ehlers***	N	Y	Y	Y	Y	Y
4 ***Camp***	N	Y	Y	Y	Y	Y
5 Kildee	Y	Y	Y	Y	Y	Y
6 ***Upton***	N	Y	Y	Y	Y	Y
7 ***Smith***	N	N	Y	Y	Y	Y
8 ***Rogers***	N	N	Y	Y	Y	?
9 ***Knollenberg***	N	N	Y	Y	Y	Y
10 ***Miller***	N	N	Y	Y	Y	Y
11 ***McCotter***	N	N	Y	Y	Y	Y
12 Levin	Y	Y	Y	Y	Y	Y
13 Kilpatrick	Y	Y	Y	Y	Y	Y
14 Conyers	Y	?	?	?	?	?
15 Dingell	Y	Y	Y	Y	Y	Y
MINNESOTA						
1 ***Gutknecht***	N	N	Y	Y	Y	Y
2 ***Kline***	N	N	Y	Y	Y	Y
3 ***Ramstad***	N	N	Y	Y	Y	Y
4 McCollum	Y	Y	Y	Y	Y	Y
5 Sabo	Y	Y	Y	Y	Y	Y
6 ***Kennedy***	N	N	Y	Y	Y	Y
7 Peterson	N	N	Y	Y	Y	Y
8 Oberstar	Y	Y	Y	Y	Y	Y
MISSISSIPPI						
1 ***Wicker***	N	N	Y	Y	Y	Y
2 Thompson	Y	Y	Y	Y	Y	Y
3 ***Pickering***	N	N	Y	Y	Y	Y
4 Taylor	N	Y	Y	N	Y	Y
MISSOURI						
1 Clay	Y	Y	Y	Y	Y	Y
2 ***Akin***	N	N	Y	Y	Y	Y
3 Gephardt	Y	Y	Y	Y	Y	Y
4 Skelton	N	Y	Y	Y	Y	Y
5 McCarthy	N	Y	Y	Y	Y	Y
6 ***Graves***	N	N	Y	Y	Y	Y
7 ***Blunt***	N	N	Y	Y	Y	Y
8 ***Emerson***	N	N	Y	Y	Y	Y
9 ***Hulshof***	N	N	Y	Y	Y	Y
MONTANA						
AL ***Rehberg***	N	N	Y	Y	Y	Y
NEBRASKA						
1 ***Bereuter***	N	Y	Y	N	Y	Y
2 ***Terry***	N	N	Y	N	?	?
3 ***Osborne***	N	N	Y	N	Y	Y
NEVADA						
1 Berkley	Y	Y	Y	Y	Y	Y
2 ***Gibbons***	N	N	Y	Y	Y	Y
3 ***Porter***	N	Y	Y	Y	Y	Y
NEW HAMPSHIRE						
1 ***Bradley***	N	N	Y	Y	Y	Y
2 ***Bass***	N	N	Y	Y	Y	Y
NEW JERSEY						
1 Andrews	Y	Y	Y	Y	Y	Y
2 ***LoBiondo***	N	N	Y	Y	Y	Y
3 ***Saxton***	N	N	Y	Y	Y	Y
4 ***Smith***	Y	N	?	Y	Y	Y
5 ***Garrett***	N	N	Y	Y	Y	Y
6 Pallone	Y	Y	Y	Y	Y	Y
7 ***Ferguson***	N	N	Y	Y	Y	Y
8 Pascrell	Y	Y	Y	Y	Y	Y
9 Rothman	Y	Y	Y	Y	Y	Y
10 Payne	Y	Y	Y	Y	Y	Y
11 ***Frelinghuysen***	N	N	Y	Y	Y	Y
12 Holt	Y	Y	Y	Y	Y	Y
13 Menendez	Y	Y	Y	Y	Y	Y
NEW MEXICO						
1 ***Wilson***	N	N	Y	Y	Y	Y
2 ***Pearce***	N	N	Y	Y	Y	Y
3 Udall	Y	Y	Y	Y	Y	Y
NEW YORK						
1 Bishop	Y	Y	Y	Y	Y	Y
2 Israel	Y	Y	Y	Y	Y	Y
3 ***King***	N	N	Y	Y	Y	Y
4 McCarthy	Y	Y	Y	Y	Y	Y
5 Ackerman	Y	Y	Y	Y	Y	Y
6 Meeks	Y	Y	Y	Y	Y	Y
7 Crowley	Y	Y	Y	?	Y	Y
8 Nadler	Y	Y	Y	Y	Y	Y
9 Weiner	Y	Y	Y	Y	Y	Y
10 Towns	Y	Y	Y	Y	Y	Y
11 Owens	Y	Y	Y	Y	Y	Y
12 Velázquez	Y	Y	Y	Y	Y	?
13 ***Fossella***	N	N	Y	Y	?	Y
14 Maloney	Y	N	Y	Y	Y	Y
15 Rangel	Y	Y	Y	Y	Y	Y
16 Serrano	Y	Y	Y	Y	Y	Y
17 Engel	Y	Y	Y	Y	Y	Y
18 Lowey	Y	Y	Y	Y	Y	Y
19 ***Kelly***	N	N	Y	Y	Y	Y
20 ***Sweeney***	N	N	Y	Y	Y	Y
21 McNulty	Y	Y	Y	Y	Y	Y
22 Hinchey	Y	Y	Y	N	?	?
23 ***McHugh***	N	N	Y	Y	Y	Y
24 ***Boehlert***	N	N	Y	Y	Y	Y
25 ***Walsh***	N	N	Y	Y	Y	Y
26 ***Reynolds***	N	N	Y	Y	Y	Y
27 ***Quinn***	N	N	Y	Y	Y	Y
28 Slaughter	Y	Y	Y	N	Y	Y
29 ***Houghton***	N	N	Y	Y	Y	Y
NORTH CAROLINA						
1 Ballance	Y	Y	Y	Y	Y	Y
2 Etheridge	Y	Y	Y	Y	Y	Y
3 ***Jones***	N	Y	Y	Y	Y	Y
4 Price	Y	Y	Y	Y	Y	Y
5 ***Burr***	N	N	Y	Y	Y	Y
6 ***Coble***	N	N	Y	Y	Y	Y
7 McIntyre	Y	Y	Y	Y	Y	Y
8 ***Hayes***	N	N	Y	Y	Y	Y
9 ***Myrick***	N	N	Y	Y	Y	Y
10 ***Ballenger***	N	N	Y	Y	Y	Y
11 ***Taylor***	N	N	Y	Y	Y	Y
12 Watt	Y	Y	Y	Y	Y	Y
13 Miller	N	Y	Y	Y	Y	Y
NORTH DAKOTA						
AL Pomeroy	N	Y	Y	Y	Y	Y
OHIO						
1 ***Chabot***	N	N	Y	Y	Y	Y
2 ***Portman***	N	N	Y	Y	Y	Y
3 ***Turner***	N	N	Y	Y	Y	Y
4 ***Oxley***	N	N	Y	Y	Y	Y
5 ***Gillmor***	N	N	Y	Y	Y	Y
6 Strickland	Y	Y	Y	Y	Y	Y
7 ***Hobson***	N	N	Y	Y	Y	Y
8 ***Boehner***	?	?	?	?	?	?
9 Kaptur	Y	Y	Y	Y	Y	Y
10 Kucinich	?	?	?	?	?	?
11 Jones	N	Y	Y	Y	Y	Y
12 ***Tiberi***	?	?	?	?	?	?
13 Brown	Y	Y	Y	Y	Y	Y
14 ***LaTourette***	N	N	Y	Y	Y	Y
15 ***Pryce***	N	N	Y	Y	Y	Y
16 ***Regula***	N	N	Y	Y	Y	Y
17 Ryan	Y	Y	Y	Y	Y	Y
18 ***Ney***	N	N	Y	Y	Y	Y
OKLAHOMA						
1 ***Sullivan***	N	N	Y	Y	Y	Y
2 Carson	Y	Y	Y	Y	?	Y
3 ***Lucas***	N	N	Y	Y	Y	Y
4 ***Cole***	N	N	Y	Y	Y	Y
5 ***Istook***	N	N	Y	Y	Y	Y
OREGON						
1 Wu	Y	Y	Y	Y	Y	Y
2 ***Walden***	N	N	Y	Y	Y	Y
3 Blumenauer	Y	N	Y	Y	Y	Y
4 DeFazio	Y	Y	Y	N	Y	Y
5 Hooley	N	Y	Y	Y	Y	Y
PENNSYLVANIA						
1 Brady	Y	Y	Y	Y	Y	Y
2 Fattah	Y	Y	Y	Y	Y	Y
3 ***English***	N	N	Y	Y	Y	Y
4 ***Hart***	N	N	Y	Y	Y	Y
5 ***Peterson***	Y	N	Y	Y	Y	Y
6 ***Gerlach***	N	N	Y	Y	Y	Y
7 ***Weldon***	?	?	?	?	Y	Y
8 ***Greenwood***	Y	N	Y	Y	Y	Y
9 ***Shuster, Bill***	N	N	Y	Y	Y	Y
10 ***Sherwood***	N	N	Y	Y	Y	Y
11 Kanjorski	N	Y	Y	N	Y	Y
12 Murtha	Y	Y	Y	Y	Y	Y
13 Hoeffel	Y	Y	Y	Y	Y	Y
14 Doyle	Y	Y	Y	Y	Y	Y
15 ***Toomey***	N	N	Y	Y	Y	?
16 ***Pitts***	N	N	Y	Y	Y	Y
17 Holden	Y	Y	Y	Y	Y	Y
18 ***Murphy***	N	N	Y	Y	Y	Y
19 ***Platts***	Y	N	Y	Y	Y	Y
RHODE ISLAND						
1 Kennedy	Y	Y	Y	Y	Y	Y
2 Langevin	Y	Y	Y	Y	Y	Y
SOUTH CAROLINA						
1 ***Brown***	N	N	Y	Y	Y	Y
2 ***Wilson***	N	N	Y	Y	Y	Y
3 ***Barrett***	N	N	Y	Y	Y	Y
4 ***DeMint***	N	N	Y	Y	Y	Y
5 Spratt	Y	Y	Y	Y	Y	Y
6 Clyburn	Y	Y	Y	Y	Y	Y
SOUTH DAKOTA						
AL Vacant						
TENNESSEE						
1 ***Jenkins***	N	N	Y	Y	Y	Y
2 ***Duncan***	N	Y	Y	Y	Y	Y
3 ***Wamp***	N	Y	Y	Y	Y	Y
4 Davis	N	N	Y	Y	Y	Y
5 Cooper	N	N	Y	N	Y	Y
6 Gordon	N	N	Y	Y	Y	Y
7 ***Blackburn***	?	?	?	?	?	?
8 Tanner	N	N	Y	Y	Y	Y
9 Ford	Y	Y	Y	Y	Y	Y
TEXAS						
1 Sandlin	N	N	Y	Y	Y	Y
2 Turner	Y	Y	Y	Y	Y	Y
3 ***Johnson, Sam***	N	N	Y	Y	Y	Y
4 ***Hall***	N	N	Y	Y	Y	Y
5 ***Hensarling***	N	N	Y	Y	Y	Y
6 ***Barton***	Y	N	Y	Y	Y	Y
7 ***Culberson***	N	N	Y	Y	Y	?
8 ***Brady***	N	N	Y	Y	Y	Y
9 Lampson	Y	Y	Y	Y	Y	Y
10 Doggett	Y	Y	Y	Y	Y	Y
11 Edwards	N	Y	Y	Y	Y	Y
12 ***Granger***	N	N	Y	Y	Y	Y
13 ***Thornberry***	N	N	Y	Y	Y	Y
14 ***Paul***	N	N	Y	Y	Y	Y
15 Hinojosa	Y	Y	Y	Y	Y	Y
16 Reyes	Y	Y	Y	Y	Y	Y
17 Stenholm	N	N	Y	Y	Y	Y
18 Jackson-Lee	Y	Y	Y	Y	Y	?
19 ***Neugebauer***	N	N	Y	Y	Y	Y
20 Gonzalez	N	Y	Y	Y	Y	Y
21 ***Smith***	N	N	Y	Y	Y	Y
22 ***DeLay***	N	N	Y	Y	Y	Y
23 ***Bonilla***	N	N	Y	Y	Y	Y
24 Frost	Y	Y	Y	Y	Y	Y
25 Bell	Y	Y	Y	Y	Y	Y
26 ***Burgess***	N	N	Y	Y	Y	Y
27 Ortiz	Y	Y	Y	Y	Y	Y
28 Rodriguez	Y	Y	Y	Y	Y	Y
29 Green	Y	Y	Y	Y	Y	Y
30 Johnson, E.B.	Y	Y	Y	Y	Y	Y
31 ***Carter***	N	N	?	Y	Y	Y
32 ***Sessions***	N	N	Y	Y	Y	Y
UTAH						
1 ***Bishop***	N	N	Y	N	Y	Y
2 Matheson	Y	Y	Y	N	Y	Y
3 ***Cannon***	N	N	Y	Y	Y	Y
VERMONT						
AL *Sanders*	Y	Y	Y	N	Y	Y
VIRGINIA						
1 ***Davis, Jo Ann***	Y	N	Y	Y	Y	Y
2 ***Schrock***	N	N	Y	Y	Y	Y
3 Scott	Y	Y	Y	Y	Y	Y
4 ***Forbes***	N	N	Y	Y	Y	Y
5 ***Goode***	N	N	Y	Y	Y	Y
6 ***Goodlatte***	N	N	Y	Y	Y	Y
7 ***Cantor***	N	N	Y	Y	Y	Y
8 Moran	Y	Y	Y	Y	Y	Y
9 Boucher	N	N	Y	Y	Y	Y
10 ***Wolf***	N	N	Y	Y	Y	Y
11 ***Davis, T.***	N	N	Y	Y	Y	Y
WASHINGTON						
1 Inslee	N	Y	Y	Y	Y	Y
2 Larsen	N	Y	Y	Y	Y	Y
3 Baird	Y	Y	Y	Y	Y	Y
4 ***Hastings***	N	N	Y	Y	Y	Y
5 ***Nethercutt***	N	N	Y	Y	Y	Y
6 Dicks	Y	Y	Y	Y	Y	Y
7 McDermott	Y	Y	Y	N	Y	Y
8 ***Dunn***	N	N	Y	?	Y	Y
9 Smith	?	?	?	?	?	?
WEST VIRGINIA						
1 Mollohan	Y	Y	Y	Y	Y	Y
2 ***Capito***	N	N	Y	Y	Y	Y
3 Rahall	N	Y	Y	Y	Y	Y
WISCONSIN						
1 ***Ryan***	N	N	Y	Y	Y	Y
2 Baldwin	Y	Y	Y	Y	Y	Y
3 Kind	N	Y	Y	Y	Y	Y
4 Kleczka	Y	N	Y	Y	Y	Y
5 ***Sensenbrenner***	N	N	Y	Y	Y	Y
6 ***Petri***	N	N	Y	Y	Y	Y
7 Obey	Y	Y	Y	Y	Y	Y
8 ***Green***	N	N	Y	Y	Y	Y
WYOMING						
AL ***Cubin***	N	N	Y	Y	Y	Y

Southern states - Ala., Ark., Fla., Ga., Ky., La., Miss., N.C., Okla., S.C., Tenn., Texas, Va.

Key

Y	Voted for (yea).
#	Paired for.
+	Announced for.
N	Voted against (nay).
X	Paired against.
–	Announced against.
P	Voted "present."
C	Voted "present" to avoid possible conflict of interest.
?	Did not vote or otherwise make a position known.

Democrats **Republicans**
Independents

---

72. Procedural Motion/Journal. Approval of the House Journal of Thursday, March 18, 2004. Approved 380-26: R 204-10; D 175-16 (ND 125-14, SD 50-2); I 1-0. March 23, 2004.

73. HR 958. Navigational Safety/Passage. Saxton, R-N.J., motion to suspend the rules and pass the bill that would require the National Oceanic and Atmospheric Administration (NOAA) to maintain four navigation response teams in priority coastal areas to conduct navigational safety activities and to verify hydrographic data, which helps chart or map bodies of water. The bill also would extend the 2000 Fisheries Survey Vessel Authorization Act, which allows NOAA to acquire or lease up to six fishery research vessels. Motion agreed to 384-23: R 192-23; D 191-0 (ND 137-0, SD 54-0); I 1-0. A two-thirds majority of those present and voting (272 in this case) is required for passage under suspension of the rules. March 23, 2004.

74. HR 2408. U.S. Fish and Wildlife Volunteers/Passage. Saxton, R-N.J., motion to suspend the rules and pass the bill that would reauthorize funding for the U.S. Fish and Wildlife Service's volunteer programs, which allow the agency to recruit volunteers and enter into cooperative agreements with partner organizations, such as academic institutions. Motion agreed to 401-10: R 207-10; D 193-0 (ND 139-0, SD 54-0); I 1-0. A two-thirds majority of those present and voting (274 in this case) is required for passage under suspension of the rules. March 23, 2004.

75. HR 2489. Cowlitz Indian Settlement/Passage. Saxton, R-N.J., motion to suspend the rules and pass the bill that would set aside 20 percent of the funds from a government settlement owed to the Cowlitz Indian Tribe of Washington for a tribal elderly assistance program, with the remainder distributed among eight other assistance programs. Motion agreed to 404-0: R 215-0; D 188-0 (ND 136-0, SD 52-0); I 1-0. A two-thirds majority of those present and voting (270 in this case) is required for passage under suspension of the rules. March 23, 2004.

76. HR 3926. Organ Donations/Passage. Rogers, R-Mich., motion to suspend the rules and pass the bill that would authorize the Health and Human Services Department to provide reimbursement for travel and other incidental non-medical expenses incurred by individuals making living organ donations. Motion agreed to 414-2: R 211-2; D 202-0 (ND 146-0, SD 56-0); I 1-0. A two-thirds majority of those present and voting (278 in this case) is required for passage under suspension of the rules. March 24, 2004.

77. H Res 522. Women and Heart Disease/Adoption. Rogers, R-Mich., motion to suspend the rules and adopt the resolution that would express the sense of the House that there is a critical need to increase awareness and education about the risk factors for heart disease among women. It would commend first lady Laura Bush and the National Heart, Lung, and Blood Institute for their efforts to raise public awareness about heart disease and women. Motion agreed to 420-0: R 215-0; D 204-0 (ND 148-0, SD 56-0); I 1-0. A two-thirds majority of those present and voting (280 in this case) is required for adoption under suspension of the rules. March 24, 2004.

78. Procedural Motion/Journal. Approval of the House Journal of Tuesday, March 23, 2004. Approved 377-35: R 197-12; D 179-23 (ND 128-19, SD 51-4); I 1-0. March 24, 2004.

	72	73	74	75	76	77	78
ALABAMA							
1 *Bonner*	Y	Y	Y	Y	Y	Y	Y
2 *Everett*	Y	N	Y	Y	Y	Y	Y
3 *Rogers*	Y	Y	Y	Y	Y	Y	Y
4 *Aderholt*	Y	Y	Y	Y	Y	Y	Y
5 Cramer	Y	Y	Y	Y	Y	Y	Y
6 *Bachus*	?	?	Y	Y	Y	Y	Y
7 Davis	Y	Y	Y	Y	Y	Y	Y
ALASKA							
AL *Young*	Y	Y	Y	Y	Y	Y	Y
ARIZONA							
1 *Renzi*	Y	Y	Y	Y	Y	Y	Y
2 *Franks*	Y	N	N	Y	Y	Y	Y
3 *Shadegg*	Y	N	Y	Y	Y	Y	Y
4 Pastor	Y	Y	Y	Y	Y	Y	Y
5 *Hayworth*	Y	Y	Y	Y	Y	Y	Y
6 *Flake*	Y	N	N	Y	N	Y	Y
7 Grijalva	Y	Y	Y	Y	Y	Y	Y
8 *Kolbe*	Y	Y	Y	+	Y	Y	
ARKANSAS							
1 Berry	Y	Y	Y	Y	Y	Y	Y
2 Snyder	Y	Y	Y	Y	Y	Y	Y
3 *Boozman*	Y	Y	Y	Y	Y	Y	Y
4 Ross	Y	Y	Y	Y	Y	Y	Y
CALIFORNIA							
1 Thompson	N	Y	Y	Y	Y	Y	N
2 *Herger*	Y	N	Y	Y	Y	Y	Y
3 *Ose*	Y	Y	Y	Y	Y	Y	Y
4 *Doolittle*	Y	Y	Y	Y	Y	Y	Y
5 Matsui	?	?	?	?	Y	Y	Y
6 Woolsey	Y	Y	Y	Y	Y	Y	Y
7 Miller, George	Y	Y	Y	Y	Y	Y	N
8 Pelosi	Y	Y	Y	Y	Y	Y	Y
9 Lee	N	Y	Y	Y	Y	Y	Y
10 Tauscher	Y	Y	Y	Y	Y	Y	Y
11 *Pombo*	Y	Y	Y	Y	Y	Y	Y
12 Lantos	Y	Y	Y	Y	Y	Y	Y
13 Stark	?	?	?	?	Y	Y	Y
14 Eshoo	?	?	?	?	Y	Y	Y
15 Honda	Y	Y	Y	Y	Y	Y	Y
16 Lofgren	Y	Y	Y	Y	Y	Y	Y
17 Farr	Y	Y	Y	Y	Y	Y	Y
18 Cardoza	Y	Y	Y	Y	Y	Y	Y
19 *Radanovich*	Y	Y	Y	Y	?	?	?
20 Dooley	Y	Y	Y	Y	Y	Y	Y
21 *Nunes*	Y	Y	Y	Y	Y	Y	Y
22 *Thomas*	Y	Y	Y	Y	Y	Y	Y
23 Capps	Y	Y	Y	Y	Y	Y	Y
24 *Gallegly*	Y	Y	Y	Y	Y	Y	Y
25 *McKeon*	?	?	?	?	Y	Y	Y
26 *Dreier*	Y	Y	Y	Y	Y	Y	Y
27 Sherman	Y	Y	Y	Y	Y	Y	Y
28 Berman	Y	Y	Y	Y	Y	Y	Y
29 Schiff	Y	Y	Y	Y	Y	Y	Y
30 Waxman	Y	Y	Y	Y	Y	Y	Y
31 Becerra	Y	Y	Y	Y	Y	Y	Y
32 Solis	Y	Y	Y	Y	Y	Y	Y
33 Watson	Y	Y	Y	Y	Y	Y	Y
34 Roybal-Allard	Y	Y	Y	Y	Y	Y	Y
35 Waters	?	?	?	?	Y	Y	?
36 Harman	Y	Y	Y	Y	Y	Y	Y

	72	73	74	75	76	77	78
37 Millender-McD.	Y	Y	Y	Y	Y	Y	Y
38 Napolitano	Y	Y	Y	Y	Y	Y	Y
39 Sánchez, Linda	Y	Y	Y	Y	Y	Y	Y
40 *Royce*	Y	N	Y	Y	Y	Y	Y
41 *Lewis*	Y	Y	Y	Y	Y	Y	Y
42 *Miller, Gary*	Y	Y	Y	Y	Y	Y	Y
43 Baca	Y	Y	Y	Y	Y	Y	Y
44 *Calvert*	Y	Y	Y	Y	Y	Y	Y
45 *Bono*	Y	Y	Y	Y	Y	Y	?
46 *Rohrabacher*	Y	Y	Y	Y	Y	Y	Y
47 Sanchez, Loretta	Y	Y	Y	Y	Y	Y	Y
48 *Cox*	Y	?	Y	Y	Y	Y	Y
49 *Issa*	Y	Y	Y	Y	Y	Y	Y
50 *Cunningham*	Y	Y	Y	Y	Y	Y	Y
51 Filner	N	Y	Y	Y	Y	Y	N
52 *Hunter*	Y	Y	Y	?	Y	Y	Y
53 Davis	Y	Y	Y	Y	Y	Y	Y
COLORADO							
1 DeGette	Y	Y	Y	Y	Y	Y	Y
2 Udall	Y	Y	Y	Y	Y	Y	N
3 *McInnis*	Y	Y	Y	Y	Y	Y	Y
4 *Musgrave*	Y	Y	Y	Y	Y	Y	Y
5 *Hefley*	N	Y	Y	Y	Y	Y	N
6 *Tancredo*	P	N	Y	Y	?	?	Y
7 *Beauprez*	Y	Y	Y	Y	Y	Y	Y
CONNECTICUT							
1 Larson	Y	Y	Y	Y	Y	Y	Y
2 *Simmons*	?	?	?	?	?	?	?
3 DeLauro	Y	Y	Y	Y	Y	Y	Y
4 *Shays*	Y	Y	Y	Y	Y	Y	Y
5 *Johnson*	Y	Y	Y	Y	Y	Y	Y
DELAWARE							
AL *Castle*	Y	Y	Y	Y	Y	Y	Y
FLORIDA							
1 *Miller, J.*	Y	N	Y	Y	Y	Y	Y
2 Boyd	Y	Y	Y	Y	Y	Y	Y
3 Brown	Y	Y	Y	Y	Y	Y	Y
4 *Crenshaw*	Y	Y	Y	Y	Y	Y	Y
5 *Brown-Waite*	Y	Y	Y	Y	?	?	?
6 *Stearns*	Y	N	N	Y	Y	Y	Y
7 *Mica*	Y	Y	Y	Y	Y	Y	Y
8 *Keller*	Y	Y	Y	Y	Y	Y	Y
9 *Bilirakis*	Y	Y	Y	Y	Y	Y	Y
10 *Young*	Y	Y	Y	Y	Y	Y	Y
11 Davis	Y	Y	Y	?	Y	Y	Y
12 *Putnam*	Y	Y	Y	Y	Y	Y	Y
13 *Harris*	Y	Y	Y	Y	Y	Y	Y
14 *Goss*	Y	Y	Y	Y	Y	+	
15 *Weldon*	Y	Y	Y	Y	Y	Y	Y
16 *Foley*	Y	Y	Y	Y	Y	Y	Y
17 Meek	Y	Y	Y	Y	Y	Y	Y
18 *Ros-Lehtinen*	Y	Y	Y	Y	Y	Y	Y
19 Wexler	?	?	?	?	Y	Y	Y
20 Deutsch	Y	Y	Y	Y	Y	Y	Y
21 *Diaz-Balart, L.*	Y	Y	Y	Y	Y	Y	Y
22 *Shaw*	Y	Y	Y	Y	Y	Y	Y
23 Hastings	Y	Y	Y	Y	Y	Y	N
24 *Feeney*	Y	Y	Y	Y	Y	Y	?
25 *Diaz-Balart, M.*	Y	Y	Y	Y	Y	Y	Y
GEORGIA							
1 *Kingston*	Y	Y	Y	Y	Y	Y	Y
2 Bishop	Y	Y	Y	Y	Y	Y	Y
3 Marshall	Y	Y	Y	Y	Y	Y	Y
4 Majette	Y	Y	Y	Y	Y	Y	P
5 Lewis	Y	Y	Y	Y	Y	Y	N
6 *Isakson*	Y	Y	Y	Y	Y	Y	Y
7 *Linder*	Y	Y	Y	Y	Y	Y	Y
8 *Collins*	Y	N	Y	?	Y	Y	Y
9 *Norwood*	Y	Y	Y	Y	Y	?	?
10 *Deal*	Y	N	Y	Y	Y	Y	Y
11 *Gingrey*	Y	Y	Y	Y	Y	Y	Y
12 *Burns*	Y	Y	Y	Y	Y	Y	Y
13 Scott	Y	Y	Y	Y	Y	Y	Y
HAWAII							
1 Abercrombie	Y	Y	Y	Y	Y	Y	Y
2 Case	Y	Y	Y	Y	Y	Y	Y
IDAHO							
1 *Otter*	Y	Y	Y	Y	Y	Y	N
2 *Simpson*	Y	Y	Y	Y	?	Y	Y
ILLINOIS							
1 Rush	Y	Y	Y	Y	Y	Y	Y
2 Jackson	Y	Y	Y	Y	Y	Y	Y
3 Lipinski	Y	Y	Y	Y	Y	Y	Y
4 Gutierrez	Y	Y	Y	Y	Y	Y	Y
5 Emanuel	Y	Y	Y	Y	Y	Y	Y
6 *Hyde*	Y	Y	Y	Y	Y	Y	Y

ND Northern Democrats   SD Southern Democrats

	72	73	74	75	76	77	78
7 Davis	Y	Y	Y	Y	Y	Y	Y
8 ***Crane***	N	Y	Y	Y	Y	Y	N
9 Schakowsky	Y	Y	Y	Y	Y	Y	N
10 ***Kirk***	Y	Y	Y	Y	Y	Y	Y
11 ***Weller***	N	Y	Y	Y	Y	Y	N
12 Costello	N	Y	Y	Y	Y	Y	Y
13 ***Biggert***	Y	Y	Y	Y	Y	Y	Y
14 ***Hastert***							
15 ***Johnson***	Y	Y	Y	Y	Y	Y	Y
16 ***Manzullo***	Y	Y	Y	Y	Y	Y	Y
17 Evans	Y	Y	Y	?	Y	Y	Y
18 ***LaHood***	Y	Y	Y	Y	Y	Y	Y
19 ***Shimkus***	Y	N	Y	Y	Y	Y	?
INDIANA							
1 Visclosky	N	Y	Y	Y	Y	Y	N
2 ***Chocola***	Y	Y	Y	Y	Y	Y	Y
3 ***Souder***	Y	Y	Y	Y	Y	Y	Y
4 ***Buyer***	Y	Y	Y	Y	Y	Y	Y
5 ***Burton***	Y	Y	Y	Y	Y	Y	Y
6 ***Pence***	Y	Y	Y	Y	Y	Y	Y
7 Carson	Y	Y	Y	Y	Y	Y	Y
8 ***Hostettler***	Y	Y	Y	Y	Y	Y	Y
9 Hill	Y	Y	Y	Y	Y	Y	Y
IOWA							
1 ***Nussle***	?	Y	Y	Y	Y	Y	Y
2 ***Leach***	Y	Y	Y	Y	Y	Y	Y
3 Boswell	Y	?	Y	Y	Y	Y	Y
4 ***Latham***	N	Y	Y	Y	Y	Y	N
5 ***King***	Y	Y	Y	Y	Y	Y	Y
KANSAS							
1 ***Moran***	N	Y	Y	Y	Y	Y	N
2 ***Ryun***	Y	Y	Y	Y	Y	Y	Y
3 Moore	Y	Y	Y	Y	Y	Y	Y
4 ***Tiahrt***	Y	Y	Y	Y	Y	Y	Y
KENTUCKY							
1 ***Whitfield***	Y	Y	Y	Y	Y	Y	Y
2 ***Lewis***	Y	Y	Y	Y	Y	Y	Y
3 ***Northup***	Y	Y	Y	Y	Y	Y	Y
4 Lucas	Y	Y	Y	Y	Y	Y	Y
5 ***Rogers***	Y	Y	Y	Y	Y	Y	Y
6 Chandler	Y	Y	Y	?	Y	Y	Y
LOUISIANA							
1 ***Vitter***	Y	Y	Y	Y	Y	Y	Y
2 Jefferson	Y	Y	Y	Y	Y	Y	Y
3 ***Tauzin***	?	?	?	?	?	?	?
4 ***McCrery***	Y	Y	Y	Y	Y	Y	Y
5 Alexander	Y	Y	Y	Y	Y	Y	Y
6 ***Baker***	Y	Y	Y	Y	Y	Y	Y
7 John	Y	Y	Y	Y	Y	Y	Y
MAINE							
1 Allen	Y	Y	Y	Y	Y	Y	Y
2 Michaud	Y	Y	Y	Y	Y	Y	Y
MARYLAND							
1 ***Gilchrest***	Y	Y	Y	Y	Y	Y	Y
2 Ruppersberger	Y	Y	Y	Y	Y	Y	Y
3 Cardin	Y	Y	Y	Y	Y	Y	Y
4 Wynn	?	?	?	?	Y	Y	Y
5 Hoyer	Y	Y	Y	Y	Y	Y	Y
6 ***Bartlett***	Y	N	Y	Y	Y	Y	Y
7 Cummings	Y	Y	Y	Y	Y	Y	Y
8 Van Hollen	Y	Y	Y	Y	Y	Y	Y
MASSACHUSETTS							
1 Olver	Y	Y	Y	Y	Y	Y	N
2 Neal	Y	Y	Y	Y	Y	Y	Y
3 McGovern	Y	Y	Y	Y	Y	Y	Y
4 Frank	N	Y	Y	Y	Y	Y	Y
5 Meehan	Y	Y	Y	Y	Y	Y	Y
6 Tierney	Y	Y	Y	Y	Y	Y	Y
7 Markey	Y	Y	Y	Y	Y	Y	Y
8 Capuano	N	Y	Y	Y	Y	Y	N
9 Lynch	Y	Y	Y	Y	Y	Y	Y
10 Delahunt	Y	Y	Y	Y	Y	Y	Y
MICHIGAN							
1 Stupak	N	Y	Y	Y	Y	Y	N
2 ***Hoekstra***	Y	Y	Y	Y	Y	Y	Y
3 ***Ehlers***	Y	Y	Y	Y	Y	Y	Y
4 ***Camp***	Y	Y	Y	Y	Y	Y	Y
5 Kildee	Y	Y	Y	Y	Y	Y	Y
6 ***Upton***	Y	Y	Y	Y	Y	Y	Y
7 ***Smith***	Y	Y	Y	?	Y	Y	Y
8 ***Rogers***	Y	Y	Y	Y	Y	Y	Y
9 ***Knollenberg***	Y	Y	Y	Y	Y	Y	Y
10 ***Miller***	Y	Y	Y	Y	Y	Y	Y
11 ***McCotter***	Y	Y	Y	Y	Y	Y	Y
12 Levin	Y	Y	Y	Y	Y	Y	Y
13 Kilpatrick	Y	Y	Y	Y	Y	Y	Y
14 Conyers	Y	Y	Y	Y	?	Y	Y
15 Dingell	Y	Y	Y	Y	Y	Y	Y
MINNESOTA							
1 ***Gutknecht***	N	Y	Y	Y	Y	Y	Y
2 ***Kline***	Y	Y	Y	Y	Y	Y	Y
3 ***Ramstad***	N	Y	Y	Y	Y	Y	N
4 McCollum	Y	Y	Y	Y	Y	Y	Y
5 Sabo	N	Y	Y	Y	Y	Y	N
6 ***Kennedy***	N	Y	Y	Y	Y	Y	Y
7 Peterson	N	Y	Y	Y	Y	Y	N
8 Oberstar	N	Y	Y	Y	Y	Y	N
MISSISSIPPI							
1 ***Wicker***	Y	Y	Y	Y	Y	Y	Y
2 Thompson	N	Y	Y	Y	Y	Y	N
3 ***Pickering***	Y	Y	Y	Y	Y	Y	Y
4 Taylor	Y	Y	Y	Y	Y	Y	N
MISSOURI							
1 Clay	Y	Y	Y	Y	Y	Y	Y
2 ***Akin***	Y	N	Y	Y	Y	Y	Y
3 Gephardt	?	?	?	?	Y	Y	Y
4 Skelton	Y	Y	Y	Y	Y	Y	Y
5 McCarthy	Y	Y	Y	Y	Y	Y	Y
6 ***Graves***	Y	Y	Y	Y	Y	Y	Y
7 ***Blunt***	Y	Y	Y	Y	Y	Y	Y
8 ***Emerson***	Y	Y	Y	Y	Y	Y	Y
9 ***Hulshof***	?	?	?	?	Y	Y	Y
MONTANA							
AL ***Rehberg***	Y	Y	Y	Y	Y	Y	Y
NEBRASKA							
1 ***Bereuter***	Y	Y	Y	Y	Y	Y	Y
2 ***Terry***	Y	Y	Y	Y	Y	Y	Y
3 ***Osborne***	Y	Y	Y	Y	Y	Y	Y
NEVADA							
1 Berkley	Y	Y	Y	Y	Y	Y	Y
2 ***Gibbons***	Y	Y	Y	Y	+	+	+
3 ***Porter***	Y	Y	Y	Y	Y	Y	Y
NEW HAMPSHIRE							
1 ***Bradley***	Y	Y	Y	Y	Y	Y	Y
2 ***Bass***	Y	Y	Y	Y	Y	Y	Y
NEW JERSEY							
1 Andrews	Y	Y	Y	Y	Y	Y	Y
2 ***LoBiondo***	Y	Y	Y	Y	Y	Y	N
3 ***Saxton***	Y	Y	Y	Y	Y	Y	Y
4 ***Smith***	Y	Y	Y	Y	Y	Y	Y
5 ***Garrett***	Y	Y	Y	Y	Y	Y	Y
6 Pallone	Y	Y	Y	Y	Y	Y	Y
7 ***Ferguson***	Y	Y	Y	Y	Y	Y	Y
8 Pascrell	Y	Y	Y	Y	Y	Y	Y
9 Rothman	Y	Y	Y	Y	Y	Y	Y
10 Payne	Y	Y	Y	Y	Y	Y	Y
11 ***Frelinghuysen***	Y	Y	Y	Y	Y	Y	Y
12 Holt	Y	Y	Y	Y	Y	Y	Y
13 Menendez	Y	Y	Y	Y	Y	Y	Y
NEW MEXICO							
1 ***Wilson***	Y	Y	Y	Y	Y	Y	Y
2 ***Pearce***	Y	Y	Y	Y	Y	Y	Y
3 Udall	N	Y	Y	Y	Y	Y	N
NEW YORK							
1 Bishop	Y	Y	Y	Y	Y	Y	Y
2 Israel	Y	Y	Y	Y	Y	Y	Y
3 ***King***	Y	Y	Y	Y	Y	Y	Y
4 McCarthy	Y	Y	Y	Y	Y	Y	Y
5 Ackerman	Y	Y	Y	Y	Y	Y	Y
6 Meeks	Y	?	Y	Y	Y	Y	Y
7 Crowley	Y	Y	Y	Y	Y	Y	Y
8 Nadler	Y	Y	Y	Y	Y	Y	Y
9 Weiner	Y	Y	Y	Y	Y	Y	Y
10 Towns	Y	Y	Y	Y	Y	Y	Y
11 Owens	Y	Y	Y	Y	Y	Y	Y
12 Velázquez	Y	Y	Y	Y	Y	Y	Y
13 ***Fossella***	Y	Y	Y	Y	Y	Y	N
14 Maloney	Y	Y	Y	Y	Y	Y	Y
15 Rangel	Y	Y	Y	Y	Y	Y	Y
16 Serrano	Y	Y	Y	Y	Y	Y	Y
17 Engel	Y	Y	Y	Y	Y	Y	Y
18 Lowey	Y	Y	Y	Y	Y	Y	Y
19 ***Kelly***	Y	Y	Y	Y	Y	Y	Y
20 ***Sweeney***	Y	Y	Y	Y	Y	Y	N
21 McNulty	Y	Y	Y	Y	Y	Y	N
22 Hinchey	Y	Y	Y	Y	Y	Y	Y
23 ***McHugh***	Y	Y	Y	Y	Y	Y	Y
24 ***Boehlert***	Y	Y	Y	Y	Y	Y	Y
25 ***Walsh***	Y	Y	Y	Y	Y	Y	Y
26 ***Reynolds***	Y	Y	Y	Y	Y	Y	Y
27 ***Quinn***	Y	Y	Y	Y	Y	Y	Y
28 Slaughter	Y	Y	Y	Y	Y	Y	Y
29 ***Houghton***	Y	Y	Y	Y	Y	Y	?
NORTH CAROLINA							
1 Ballance	Y	Y	Y	Y	Y	Y	Y
2 Etheridge	Y	Y	Y	Y	Y	Y	Y
3 ***Jones***	Y	Y	N	Y	Y	Y	Y
4 Price	Y	Y	Y	Y	Y	Y	Y
5 ***Burr***	?	?	?	?	Y	Y	Y
6 ***Coble***	Y	N	N	Y	Y	Y	Y
7 McIntyre	Y	Y	Y	Y	Y	Y	Y
8 ***Hayes***	Y	Y	Y	Y	Y	Y	Y
9 ***Myrick***	Y	Y	Y	Y	Y	Y	Y
10 ***Ballenger***	Y	Y	Y	Y	Y	Y	Y
11 ***Taylor***	Y	Y	Y	Y	Y	Y	?
12 Watt	Y	Y	Y	Y	Y	Y	Y
13 Miller	Y	Y	Y	Y	Y	Y	Y
NORTH DAKOTA							
AL Pomeroy	Y	Y	Y	Y	Y	Y	Y
OHIO							
1 ***Chabot***	Y	Y	Y	Y	Y	Y	Y
2 ***Portman***	Y	Y	Y	Y	Y	Y	Y
3 ***Turner***	Y	Y	Y	Y	Y	Y	Y
4 ***Oxley***	Y	Y	Y	Y	Y	Y	Y
5 ***Gillmor***	?	?	?	?	?	?	?
6 Strickland	Y	Y	Y	Y	Y	Y	N
7 ***Hobson***	Y	Y	Y	Y	Y	Y	Y
8 ***Boehner***	Y	Y	Y	Y	Y	?	Y
9 Kaptur	Y	Y	Y	Y	Y	Y	Y
10 Kucinich	Y	Y	Y	Y	Y	Y	Y
11 Jones	Y	Y	Y	Y	?	Y	Y
12 ***Tiberi***	Y	Y	Y	Y	Y	Y	Y
13 Brown	Y	Y	Y	Y	Y	Y	Y
14 ***LaTourette***	Y	Y	Y	Y	Y	Y	Y
15 ***Pryce***	Y	Y	Y	Y	Y	Y	Y
16 ***Regula***	Y	Y	Y	Y	Y	Y	Y
17 Ryan	Y	Y	Y	Y	Y	Y	Y
18 ***Ney***	Y	Y	Y	Y	Y	Y	Y
OKLAHOMA							
1 ***Sullivan***	Y	N	Y	Y	Y	Y	Y
2 Carson	Y	Y	Y	Y	Y	Y	Y
3 ***Lucas***	Y	Y	Y	Y	Y	Y	Y
4 ***Cole***	Y	Y	Y	Y	Y	Y	Y
5 ***Istook***	Y	Y	Y	Y	?	Y	Y
OREGON							
1 Wu	Y	Y	Y	Y	Y	Y	Y
2 ***Walden***	Y	Y	Y	Y	Y	Y	Y
3 Blumenauer	Y	Y	Y	Y	Y	Y	Y
4 DeFazio	N	Y	Y	Y	Y	Y	Y
5 Hooley	Y	Y	Y	?	Y	Y	Y
PENNSYLVANIA							
1 Brady	Y	Y	Y	Y	Y	Y	N
2 Fattah	?	?	?	?	Y	Y	Y
3 ***English***	N	Y	Y	Y	Y	Y	N
4 ***Hart***	N	Y	Y	Y	Y	Y	N
5 ***Peterson***	?	?	?	?	Y	Y	Y
6 ***Gerlach***	Y	Y	Y	Y	Y	Y	Y
7 ***Weldon***	Y	Y	Y	Y	Y	Y	Y
8 ***Greenwood***	Y	Y	Y	Y	Y	Y	Y
9 ***Shuster, Bill***	Y	Y	Y	Y	Y	Y	Y
10 ***Sherwood***	Y	Y	Y	Y	Y	Y	Y
11 Kanjorski	Y	Y	Y	Y	Y	Y	Y
12 Murtha	Y	Y	Y	?	Y	Y	Y
13 Hoeffel	?	?	?	?	Y	Y	Y
14 Doyle	Y	Y	Y	Y	Y	Y	Y
15 ***Toomey***	?	?	?	?	Y	Y	Y
16 ***Pitts***	Y	Y	Y	Y	Y	Y	Y
17 Holden	Y	Y	Y	Y	Y	Y	Y
18 ***Murphy***	Y	Y	Y	Y	Y	Y	Y
19 ***Platts***	Y	Y	Y	Y	Y	Y	Y
RHODE ISLAND							
1 Kennedy	Y	Y	Y	Y	Y	Y	Y
2 Langevin	Y	Y	Y	Y	Y	Y	Y
SOUTH CAROLINA							
1 ***Brown***	Y	Y	Y	Y	Y	Y	Y
2 ***Wilson***	Y	Y	Y	Y	Y	Y	Y
3 ***Barrett***	Y	Y	Y	Y	Y	Y	Y
4 ***DeMint***	Y	Y	Y	Y	+	+	+
5 Spratt	Y	Y	Y	Y	Y	Y	Y
6 Clyburn	?	?	?	?	?	?	?
SOUTH DAKOTA							
AL Vacant							
TENNESSEE							
1 ***Jenkins***	Y	Y	Y	Y	Y	Y	Y
2 ***Duncan***	Y	N	N	Y	Y	Y	Y
3 ***Wamp***	Y	N	Y	Y	Y	Y	Y
4 Davis	Y	Y	Y	Y	Y	Y	Y
5 Cooper	Y	Y	Y	Y	Y	Y	Y
6 Gordon	Y	Y	Y	Y	Y	Y	Y
7 ***Blackburn***	Y	N	Y	Y	Y	Y	?
8 Tanner	Y	Y	Y	Y	Y	Y	Y
9 Ford	Y	Y	Y	Y	Y	Y	Y
TEXAS							
1 Sandlin	Y	Y	Y	Y	Y	Y	Y
2 Turner	Y	Y	Y	Y	Y	Y	Y
3 ***Johnson, Sam***	Y	N	N	Y	Y	Y	Y
4 ***Hall***	Y	Y	Y	Y	Y	Y	Y
5 ***Hensarling***	Y	Y	N	Y	Y	Y	Y
6 ***Barton***	Y	Y	Y	Y	Y	?	Y
7 ***Culberson***	?	?	?	?	Y	Y	Y
8 ***Brady***	Y	Y	Y	Y	Y	Y	?
9 Lampson	Y	Y	Y	Y	Y	Y	Y
10 Doggett	Y	Y	Y	Y	Y	Y	Y
11 Edwards	Y	Y	Y	Y	Y	Y	Y
12 ***Granger***	Y	Y	Y	Y	Y	Y	Y
13 ***Thornberry***	Y	Y	Y	Y	Y	Y	Y
14 ***Paul***	Y	N	N	Y	N	Y	Y
15 Hinojosa	+	Y	Y	Y	Y	Y	Y
16 Reyes	?	Y	Y	Y	Y	Y	Y
17 Stenholm	Y	Y	Y	Y	Y	Y	Y
18 Jackson-Lee	Y	Y	Y	Y	Y	Y	Y
19 ***Neugebauer***	Y	N	Y	Y	Y	Y	?
20 Gonzalez	Y	Y	Y	Y	Y	Y	Y
21 ***Smith***	Y	Y	Y	Y	Y	Y	Y
22 ***DeLay***	Y	Y	Y	Y	Y	Y	Y
23 ***Bonilla***	Y	Y	Y	Y	?	Y	Y
24 Frost	Y	Y	Y	Y	Y	Y	Y
25 Bell	Y	Y	Y	Y	Y	Y	Y
26 ***Burgess***	Y	Y	Y	Y	Y	Y	Y
27 Ortiz	Y	Y	Y	Y	Y	Y	Y
28 Rodriguez	?	?	?	?	Y	Y	Y
29 Green	N	Y	Y	Y	Y	Y	Y
30 Johnson, E.B.	Y	Y	Y	Y	Y	Y	Y
31 ***Carter***	Y	Y	Y	Y	Y	Y	Y
32 ***Sessions***	Y	Y	Y	Y	Y	Y	Y
UTAH							
1 ***Bishop***	Y	Y	Y	Y	Y	Y	Y
2 Matheson	Y	Y	Y	Y	Y	Y	Y
3 ***Cannon***	Y	Y	Y	Y	?	?	?
VERMONT							
AL *Sanders*	Y	Y	Y	Y	Y	Y	Y
VIRGINIA							
1 ***Davis, Jo Ann***	Y	Y	Y	Y	Y	Y	Y
2 ***Schrock***	Y	Y	Y	Y	Y	Y	Y
3 Scott	Y	Y	Y	Y	Y	Y	Y
4 ***Forbes***	Y	Y	Y	Y	Y	Y	Y
5 ***Goode***	Y	Y	N	Y	Y	Y	Y
6 ***Goodlatte***	Y	Y	Y	Y	Y	Y	Y
7 ***Cantor***	Y	Y	Y	Y	Y	Y	Y
8 Moran	Y	Y	Y	Y	Y	Y	Y
9 Boucher	Y	Y	Y	Y	Y	Y	Y
10 ***Wolf***	Y	Y	Y	Y	Y	Y	Y
11 ***Davis, T.***	Y	Y	Y	Y	Y	Y	Y
WASHINGTON							
1 Inslee	Y	Y	Y	Y	Y	Y	Y
2 Larsen	Y	Y	Y	Y	Y	Y	N
3 Baird	Y	Y	Y	Y	Y	Y	Y
4 ***Hastings***	Y	Y	Y	Y	Y	Y	Y
5 ***Nethercutt***	?	?	?	?	Y	Y	Y
6 Dicks	Y	Y	Y	Y	Y	Y	Y
7 McDermott	N	Y	Y	Y	Y	Y	N
8 ***Dunn***	Y	Y	Y	Y	Y	Y	Y
9 Smith	Y	Y	Y	Y	Y	Y	Y
WEST VIRGINIA							
1 Mollohan	?	?	?	?	Y	Y	Y
2 ***Capito***	Y	Y	Y	Y	Y	Y	Y
3 Rahall	Y	Y	Y	Y	Y	Y	Y
WISCONSIN							
1 ***Ryan***	Y	Y	Y	Y	Y	Y	Y
2 Baldwin	Y	Y	Y	Y	Y	Y	N
3 Kind	Y	Y	Y	Y	Y	Y	Y
4 Kleczka	Y	Y	Y	Y	Y	Y	Y
5 ***Sensenbrenner***	Y	N	Y	Y	Y	Y	Y
6 ***Petri***	Y	Y	Y	Y	Y	Y	Y
7 Obey	Y	Y	Y	Y	Y	Y	Y
8 ***Green***	Y	Y	Y	Y	Y	Y	Y
WYOMING							
AL ***Cubin***	Y	Y	Y	Y	Y	Y	Y

Southern states - Ala., Ark., Fla., Ga., Ky., La., Miss., N.C., Okla., S.C., Tenn., Texas, Va.

Key

Y	Voted for (yea).
#	Paired for.
+	Announced for.
N	Voted against (nay).
X	Paired against.
–	Announced against.
P	Voted "present."
C	Voted "present" to avoid possible conflict of interest.
?	Did not vote or otherwise make a position known.

Democrats   **Republicans**
Independents

79. HR 1768. Multidistrict Litigation/Passage. Sensenbrenner, R-Wis., motion to suspend the rules and pass the bill that would allow federal judges to retain jurisdiction over lawsuits that have been filed in multiple federal district courts by plaintiffs but consolidated in one district. Motion agreed to 418-0: R 213-0; D 204-0 (ND 148-0, SD 56-0); I 1-0. A two-thirds majority of those present and voting (279 in this case) is required for passage under suspension of the rules. March 24, 2004.

80. H Con Res 328. National Military Appreciation Month/Adoption. Miller, R-Mich., motion to suspend the rules and adopt the concurrent resolution that would express Congress' support for the designation of a National Military Appreciation Month that honors members of the armed forces, including those who have died in the line of duty. Motion agreed to 424-0: R 223-0; D 200-0 (ND 143-0, SD 57-0); I 1-0. A two-thirds majority of those present and voting (283 in this case) is required for adoption under suspension of the rules. March 24, 2004.

81. HR 3059. Lloyd L. Burke Post Office/Passage. Miller, R-Mich., motion to suspend the rules and pass the bill that would name a post office building in Stuttgart, Ark., after the late Col. Lloyd L. Burke, a veteran of three wars and winner of the Congressional Medal of Honor. Motion agreed to 425-0: R 222-0; D 202-0 (ND 145-0, SD 57-0); I 1-0. A two-thirds majority of those present and voting (284 in this case) is required for passage under suspension of the rules. March 24, 2004.

82. HR 3873. Child Nutrition Programs/Passage. Boehner, R-Ohio, motion to suspend the rules and pass the bill that would reauthorize such sums as necessary through fiscal year 2008 for a number of child nutrition programs, including the National School Lunch and Breakfast programs, Child and Adult Care Food Program and After-School Snack Program. It also would require schools to develop "wellness policies" setting standards for nutrition education and physical activity and to set guidelines for food sold on campus. Motion agreed to 419-5: R 217-5; D 201-0 (ND 145-0, SD 56-0); I 1-0. A two-thirds majority of those present and voting (283 in this case) is required for passage under suspension of the rules. March 24, 2004.

83. H Con Res 189. International Geophysical Year/Adoption. Bonner, R-Ala., motion to suspend the rules and adopt the concurrent resolution that would express the sense of Congress that the president should endorse an International Geophysical Year 2 (IGY-2) for 2007 to 2008, which would promote global scientific cooperation. Motion agreed to 420-3: R 221-3; D 198-0 (ND 141-0, SD 57-0); I 1-0. A two-thirds majority of those present and voting (282 in this case) is required for adoption under suspension of the rules. March 25, 2004.

	79	80	81	82	83
ALABAMA					
1 *Bonner*	Y	Y	Y	Y	Y
2 *Everett*	Y	Y	Y	Y	Y
3 *Rogers*	Y	Y	Y	Y	Y
4 *Aderholt*	Y	Y	Y	Y	Y
5 Cramer	Y	Y	Y	Y	Y
6 *Bachus*	Y	Y	Y	Y	Y
7 Davis	Y	Y	Y	Y	Y
ALASKA					
AL *Young*	Y	Y	Y	Y	Y
ARIZONA					
1 *Renzi*	Y	Y	Y	Y	Y
2 *Franks*	Y	Y	Y	Y	Y
3 *Shadegg*	Y	Y	Y	N	Y
4 Pastor	Y	Y	Y	Y	Y
5 *Hayworth*	Y	Y	Y	Y	Y
6 *Flake*	Y	Y	Y	N	N
7 Grijalva	Y	Y	Y	Y	Y
8 *Kolbe*	Y	Y	Y	Y	Y
ARKANSAS					
1 Berry	Y	Y	Y	Y	Y
2 Snyder	Y	Y	Y	Y	Y
3 *Boozman*	Y	Y	Y	Y	Y
4 Ross	Y	Y	Y	Y	Y
CALIFORNIA					
1 Thompson	Y	Y	Y	Y	Y
2 *Herger*	Y	Y	Y	Y	Y
3 *Ose*	Y	Y	Y	Y	Y
4 *Doolittle*	Y	Y	Y	Y	Y
5 Matsui	Y	Y	Y	Y	Y
6 Woolsey	Y	?	Y	Y	Y
7 Miller, George	Y	Y	Y	Y	Y
8 Pelosi	Y	Y	Y	Y	Y
9 Lee	Y	Y	Y	Y	Y
10 Tauscher	Y	Y	Y	Y	Y
11 *Pombo*	Y	Y	Y	Y	Y
12 Lantos	Y	Y	Y	Y	Y
13 Stark	Y	Y	Y	Y	Y
14 Eshoo	Y	Y	Y	Y	Y
15 Honda	Y	Y	Y	Y	Y
16 Lofgren	Y	Y	Y	Y	Y
17 Farr	Y	Y	Y	Y	?
18 Cardoza	Y	Y	Y	Y	Y
19 *Radanovich*	Y	Y	Y	Y	Y
20 Dooley	Y	?	?	?	?
21 *Nunes*	Y	Y	Y	Y	Y
22 *Thomas*	Y	Y	Y	Y	Y
23 Capps	Y	Y	Y	Y	Y
24 *Gallegly*	Y	Y	Y	Y	Y
25 *McKeon*	Y	Y	Y	Y	Y
26 *Dreier*	Y	Y	Y	Y	Y
27 Sherman	Y	Y	Y	Y	Y
28 Berman	Y	Y	Y	Y	Y
29 Schiff	Y	Y	Y	Y	Y
30 Waxman	Y	Y	Y	Y	Y
31 Becerra	Y	Y	Y	Y	Y
32 Solis	Y	Y	Y	Y	Y
33 Watson	Y	Y	Y	Y	Y
34 Roybal-Allard	Y	Y	Y	Y	Y
35 Waters	Y	Y	Y	Y	Y
36 Harman	Y	Y	Y	Y	Y

	79	80	81	82	83
37 Millender-McD.	Y	Y	Y	Y	Y
38 Napolitano	Y	Y	Y	Y	Y
39 Sánchez, Linda	Y	Y	Y	Y	Y
40 *Royce*	Y	Y	Y	Y	Y
41 *Lewis*	Y	Y	Y	Y	Y
42 *Miller, Gary*	Y	Y	Y	Y	Y
43 Baca	Y	Y	Y	Y	Y
44 *Calvert*	Y	Y	Y	Y	Y
45 *Bono*	Y	Y	Y	Y	Y
46 *Rohrabacher*	Y	Y	Y	Y	Y
47 Sanchez, Loretta	Y	Y	Y	Y	Y
48 *Cox*	Y	Y	Y	Y	Y
49 *Issa*	Y	Y	Y	Y	Y
50 *Cunningham*	Y	Y	Y	Y	Y
51 Filner	Y	Y	Y	Y	Y
52 *Hunter*	Y	Y	Y	Y	Y
53 Davis	Y	Y	Y	Y	Y
COLORADO					
1 DeGette	Y	Y	Y	Y	Y
2 Udall	Y	Y	Y	Y	Y
3 *McInnis*	Y	Y	Y	Y	Y
4 *Musgrave*	Y	Y	Y	Y	Y
5 *Hefley*	Y	Y	Y	?	Y
6 *Tancredo*	Y	Y	Y	Y	Y
7 *Beauprez*	Y	Y	Y	Y	Y
CONNECTICUT					
1 Larson	Y	Y	Y	Y	Y
2 *Simmons*	?	?	?	Y	Y
3 DeLauro	Y	Y	Y	Y	Y
4 *Shays*	Y	Y	Y	Y	Y
5 *Johnson*	Y	Y	Y	Y	Y
DELAWARE					
AL *Castle*	Y	Y	Y	Y	Y
FLORIDA					
1 *Miller, J.*	?	Y	Y	Y	Y
2 Boyd	Y	Y	Y	Y	Y
3 Brown	Y	Y	Y	Y	Y
4 *Crenshaw*	Y	Y	Y	Y	Y
5 *Brown-Waite*	?	Y	Y	Y	Y
6 *Stearns*	Y	Y	Y	Y	Y
7 *Mica*	Y	Y	Y	Y	Y
8 *Keller*	Y	Y	Y	Y	Y
9 *Bilirakis*	Y	Y	Y	Y	Y
10 *Young*	Y	?	?	?	?
11 Davis	Y	Y	Y	Y	Y
12 *Putnam*	Y	Y	Y	Y	Y
13 *Harris*	Y	Y	Y	Y	Y
14 *Goss*	Y	Y	Y	Y	Y
15 *Weldon*	Y	Y	Y	Y	Y
16 *Foley*	Y	Y	Y	Y	Y
17 Meek	Y	Y	Y	Y	Y
18 *Ros-Lehtinen*	Y	Y	Y	Y	Y
19 Wexler	Y	Y	Y	Y	Y
20 Deutsch	Y	Y	Y	Y	Y
21 *Diaz-Balart, L.*	Y	Y	Y	Y	Y
22 *Shaw*	Y	Y	Y	Y	Y
23 Hastings	Y	Y	Y	Y	Y
24 *Feeney*	Y	Y	Y	Y	Y
25 *Diaz-Balart, M.*	?	Y	Y	Y	Y
GEORGIA					
1 *Kingston*	Y	Y	Y	Y	Y
2 Bishop	Y	Y	Y	Y	Y
3 Marshall	Y	Y	Y	Y	Y
4 Majette	Y	Y	Y	Y	Y
5 Lewis	Y	Y	Y	Y	Y
6 *Isakson*	Y	Y	Y	Y	Y
7 *Linder*	Y	Y	Y	Y	Y
8 *Collins*	Y	Y	Y	Y	Y
9 *Norwood*	?	Y	Y	Y	Y
10 *Deal*	Y	Y	Y	Y	Y
11 *Gingrey*	Y	Y	Y	Y	Y
12 *Burns*	Y	Y	Y	Y	Y
13 Scott	Y	Y	Y	Y	Y
HAWAII					
1 Abercrombie	Y	Y	Y	Y	Y
2 Case	Y	Y	Y	Y	Y
IDAHO					
1 *Otter*	Y	Y	Y	Y	N
2 *Simpson*	Y	Y	Y	Y	Y
ILLINOIS					
1 Rush	Y	Y	Y	Y	Y
2 Jackson	Y	Y	Y	Y	Y
3 Lipinski	Y	Y	Y	Y	Y
4 Gutierrez	Y	Y	Y	Y	Y
5 Emanuel	Y	Y	Y	Y	Y
6 *Hyde*	Y	Y	Y	Y	Y

ND Northern Democrats   SD Southern Democrats

	79	80	81	82	83
7 Davis	Y	Y	Y	Y	Y
8 *Crane*	Y	Y	Y	Y	Y
9 Schakowsky	Y	Y	Y	Y	Y
10 *Kirk*	Y	Y	Y	Y	Y
11 *Weller*	Y	Y	Y	Y	Y
12 Costello	Y	Y	Y	Y	Y
13 *Biggert*	Y	Y	Y	Y	Y
14 *Hastert*					
15 *Johnson*	Y	Y	Y	Y	Y
16 *Manzullo*	Y	Y	Y	Y	Y
17 Evans	Y	Y	Y	Y	?
18 *LaHood*	Y	Y	Y	Y	Y
19 *Shimkus*	Y	Y	Y	Y	
INDIANA					
1 Visclosky	Y	Y	Y	Y	Y
2 *Chocola*	Y	Y	Y	Y	Y
3 *Souder*	Y	Y	Y	Y	Y
4 *Buyer*	Y	Y	Y	Y	Y
5 *Burton*	Y	Y	Y	Y	Y
6 *Pence*	Y	Y	Y	Y	Y
7 Carson	Y	Y	Y	Y	Y
8 *Hostettler*	Y	Y	Y	Y	Y
9 Hill	Y	Y	Y	Y	Y
IOWA					
1 *Nussle*	Y	Y	Y	Y	Y
2 *Leach*	Y	Y	Y	Y	Y
3 Boswell	Y	Y	Y	Y	Y
4 *Latham*	Y	Y	Y	Y	Y
5 *King*	Y	Y	+	Y	Y
KANSAS					
1 *Moran*	Y	Y	Y	Y	Y
2 *Ryun*	Y	Y	Y	Y	Y
3 Moore					
4 *Tiahrt*	Y	Y	Y	Y	Y
KENTUCKY					
1 *Whitfield*	Y	Y	Y	Y	Y
2 *Lewis*	Y	Y	Y	Y	Y
3 *Northup*	Y	Y	Y	Y	Y
4 Lucas	Y	Y	Y	Y	Y
5 *Rogers*	Y	Y	Y	Y	Y
6 Chandler	Y	Y	Y	Y	Y
LOUISIANA					
1 *Vitter*	Y	Y	Y	Y	Y
2 Jefferson	Y	Y	Y	Y	Y
3 *Tauzin*	?	?	?	?	?
4 *McCrery*	Y	Y	Y	Y	Y
5 Alexander	Y	Y	Y	Y	Y
6 *Baker*	Y	Y	Y	Y	Y
7 John	Y	Y	Y	Y	Y
MAINE					
1 Allen	Y	Y	Y	Y	Y
2 Michaud	Y	Y	Y	Y	Y
MARYLAND					
1 *Gilchrest*	Y	Y	?	Y	Y
2 Ruppersberger	Y	Y	Y	Y	Y
3 Cardin	Y	Y	Y	Y	Y
4 Wynn	Y	Y	Y	Y	Y
5 Hoyer	Y	Y	Y	Y	Y
6 *Bartlett*	Y	Y	Y	Y	Y
7 Cummings	Y	Y	Y	Y	Y
8 Van Hollen	Y	Y	Y	Y	Y
MASSACHUSETTS					
1 Olver	Y	Y	Y	Y	Y
2 Neal	Y	Y	Y	Y	Y
3 McGovern	Y	Y	Y	Y	Y
4 Frank	Y	Y	Y	Y	Y
5 Meehan	Y	Y	Y	Y	Y
6 Tierney	Y	Y	Y	Y	Y
7 Markey	Y	Y	Y	Y	Y
8 Capuano	Y	Y	Y	Y	Y
9 Lynch	Y	Y	Y	Y	Y
10 Delahunt	Y	Y	Y	Y	Y
MICHIGAN					
1 Stupak	Y	Y	Y	Y	Y
2 *Hoekstra*	Y	Y	Y	Y	Y
3 *Ehlers*	Y	Y	Y	Y	Y
4 *Camp*	Y	Y	Y	Y	Y
5 Kildee	Y	Y	Y	Y	Y
6 *Upton*	Y	Y	Y	Y	Y
7 *Smith*	?	?	Y	Y	Y
8 *Rogers*	Y	Y	Y	Y	Y
9 *Knollenberg*	Y	Y	Y	Y	Y
10 *Miller*	Y	Y	Y	?	Y
11 *McCotter*	Y	Y	Y	Y	Y
12 Levin	Y	Y	Y	Y	Y

	79	80	81	82	83
13 Kilpatrick	Y	Y	Y	Y	Y
14 Conyers	Y	Y	Y	Y	Y
15 Dingell	Y	?	?	?	?
MINNESOTA					
1 *Gutknecht*	Y	Y	Y	Y	Y
2 *Kline*	Y	Y	Y	Y	Y
3 *Ramstad*	Y	Y	Y	Y	Y
4 McCollum	Y	Y	Y	Y	Y
5 Sabo	Y	Y	Y	Y	Y
6 *Kennedy*	Y	Y	Y	Y	Y
7 Peterson	Y	Y	Y	Y	Y
8 Oberstar	Y	Y	Y	Y	Y
MISSISSIPPI					
1 *Wicker*	Y	Y	Y	Y	Y
2 Thompson	Y	Y	Y	Y	Y
3 *Pickering*	Y	Y	Y	Y	?
4 Taylor	Y	Y	Y	Y	Y
MISSOURI					
1 Clay	Y	Y	Y	Y	Y
2 *Akin*	Y	Y	Y	N	Y
3 Gephardt	Y	Y	Y	Y	Y
4 Skelton	Y	Y	Y	Y	Y
5 McCarthy	Y	Y	Y	Y	Y
6 *Graves*	Y	Y	Y	Y	Y
7 *Blunt*	Y	Y	Y	Y	Y
8 *Emerson*	Y	Y	Y	Y	Y
9 *Hulshof*	Y	Y	Y	Y	Y
MONTANA					
AL *Rehberg*	Y	Y	Y	Y	Y
NEBRASKA					
1 *Bereuter*	Y	Y	Y	Y	Y
2 *Terry*	Y	Y	Y	Y	Y
3 *Osborne*	Y	Y	Y	Y	Y
NEVADA					
1 Berkley	Y	Y	Y	Y	Y
2 *Gibbons*	Y	Y	Y	Y	Y
3 *Porter*	Y	Y	Y	Y	Y
NEW HAMPSHIRE					
1 *Bradley*	Y	Y	Y	Y	Y
2 *Bass*	Y	Y	Y	Y	Y
NEW JERSEY					
1 Andrews	Y	Y	Y	Y	Y
2 *LoBiondo*	Y	Y	Y	Y	Y
3 *Saxton*	Y	Y	Y	Y	Y
4 *Smith*	Y	Y	Y	Y	Y
5 *Garrett*	Y	Y	Y	Y	Y
6 Pallone	Y	Y	Y	Y	Y
7 *Ferguson*	Y	Y	Y	Y	Y
8 Pascrell	Y	Y	Y	Y	Y
9 Rothman	Y	Y	Y	Y	Y
10 Payne	Y	Y	Y	Y	Y
11 *Frelinghuysen*	Y	Y	Y	Y	Y
12 Holt	Y	Y	Y	Y	Y
13 Menendez	Y	Y	Y	Y	Y
NEW MEXICO					
1 *Wilson*	Y	Y	Y	Y	Y
2 *Pearce*	Y	Y	Y	Y	Y
3 Udall	Y	Y	Y	Y	Y
NEW YORK					
1 Bishop	Y	Y	Y	Y	Y
2 Israel	Y	Y	Y	Y	Y
3 *King*	Y	Y	Y	Y	Y
4 McCarthy	Y	Y	Y	Y	Y
5 Ackerman	Y	Y	Y	Y	Y
6 Meeks	Y	Y	Y	Y	Y
7 Crowley	Y	Y	Y	Y	Y
8 Nadler	Y	Y	Y	Y	Y
9 Weiner	Y	Y	Y	Y	Y
10 Towns	Y	Y	Y	Y	Y
11 Owens	Y	Y	Y	Y	Y
12 Velázquez	Y	Y	Y	Y	Y
13 *Fossella*	Y	Y	Y	Y	Y
14 Maloney	Y	Y	Y	Y	Y
15 Rangel	Y	Y	Y	Y	Y
16 Serrano	Y	Y	Y	Y	Y
17 Engel	Y	Y	Y	Y	Y
18 Lowey	Y	Y	Y	Y	Y
19 *Kelly*	Y	Y	Y	Y	Y
20 *Sweeney*	Y	Y	Y	Y	Y
21 McNulty	Y	Y	Y	Y	Y
22 Hinchey	Y	Y	Y	Y	Y
23 *McHugh*	Y	Y	Y	Y	Y
24 *Boehlert*	Y	Y	Y	Y	Y
25 *Walsh*	Y	Y	Y	Y	Y

	79	80	81	82	83
26 *Reynolds*	Y	Y	Y	Y	Y
27 *Quinn*	Y	Y	Y	Y	Y
28 Slaughter	Y	Y	Y	Y	Y
29 *Houghton*	?	Y	Y	Y	Y
NORTH CAROLINA					
1 Ballance	Y	Y	Y	Y	Y
2 Etheridge	Y	Y	Y	Y	Y
3 *Jones*	Y	Y	Y	Y	Y
4 Price	Y	Y	Y	Y	Y
5 *Burr*	Y	Y	Y	Y	Y
6 *Coble*	Y	Y	Y	Y	Y
7 McIntyre	Y	Y	Y	Y	Y
8 *Hayes*	Y	Y	Y	Y	Y
9 *Myrick*	Y	Y	Y	Y	Y
10 *Ballenger*	Y	Y	Y	Y	Y
11 *Taylor*	?	Y	Y	Y	Y
12 Watt	Y	Y	Y	Y	Y
13 Miller	Y	Y	Y	Y	Y
NORTH DAKOTA					
AL Pomeroy	Y	Y	Y	Y	Y
OHIO					
1 *Chabot*	Y	Y	Y	Y	Y
2 *Portman*	Y	Y	Y	Y	Y
3 *Turner*	Y	Y	Y	Y	Y
4 *Oxley*	Y	Y	Y	Y	Y
5 *Gillmor*	?	Y	Y	Y	Y
6 Strickland	Y	Y	Y	Y	Y
7 *Hobson*	Y	Y	Y	Y	Y
8 *Boehner*	Y	Y	Y	Y	Y
9 Kaptur	Y	Y	Y	Y	Y
10 Kucinich	Y	P	Y	Y	Y
11 Jones	Y	Y	Y	Y	Y
12 *Tiberi*	Y	Y	Y	Y	Y
13 Brown	Y	Y	Y	Y	Y
14 *LaTourette*	Y	Y	Y	Y	Y
15 *Pryce*	Y	Y	Y	Y	Y
16 *Regula*	Y	Y	Y	Y	Y
17 Ryan	Y	Y	Y	Y	Y
18 *Ney*	Y	Y	Y	Y	Y
OKLAHOMA					
1 *Sullivan*	Y	Y	Y	Y	Y
2 Carson	Y	Y	Y	?	Y
3 *Lucas*	Y	Y	Y	Y	Y
4 *Cole*	Y	Y	Y	Y	Y
5 *Istook*	Y	Y	Y	Y	Y
OREGON					
1 Wu	Y	Y	Y	Y	Y
2 *Walden*	Y	Y	Y	Y	Y
3 Blumenauer	Y	Y	Y	Y	Y
4 DeFazio	Y	Y	Y	Y	Y
5 Hooley	Y	Y	Y	Y	Y
PENNSYLVANIA					
1 Brady	Y	Y	Y	Y	Y
2 Fattah	Y	Y	Y	Y	Y
3 *English*	Y	Y	Y	Y	Y
4 *Hart*	Y	Y	Y	Y	Y
5 *Peterson*	Y	Y	Y	Y	Y
6 *Gerlach*	Y	Y	Y	Y	Y
7 *Weldon*	Y	Y	Y	Y	Y
8 *Greenwood*	Y	Y	Y	Y	Y
9 *Shuster, Bill*	Y	Y	Y	Y	Y
10 *Sherwood*	Y	Y	Y	Y	Y
11 Kanjorski	Y	Y	Y	Y	Y
12 Murtha	Y	Y	Y	Y	?
13 Hoeffel	Y	?	?	?	?
14 Doyle	Y	Y	Y	Y	?
15 *Toomey*	Y	Y	Y	Y	Y
16 *Pitts*	Y	Y	Y	Y	Y
17 Holden	Y	Y	Y	Y	Y
18 *Murphy*	Y	Y	Y	Y	Y
19 *Platts*	Y	Y	Y	Y	Y
RHODE ISLAND					
1 Kennedy	Y	Y	Y	Y	Y
2 Langevin	Y	Y	Y	Y	Y
SOUTH CAROLINA					
1 *Brown*	Y	Y	Y	Y	Y
2 *Wilson*	Y	Y	Y	Y	Y
3 *Barrett*	?	Y	Y	Y	Y
4 *DeMint*	+	Y	Y	Y	Y
5 Spratt	Y	Y	Y	Y	Y
6 Clyburn	?	Y	Y	Y	Y
SOUTH DAKOTA					
AL Vacant					

	79	80	81	82	83
TENNESSEE					
1 *Jenkins*	Y	Y	Y	Y	Y
2 *Duncan*	Y	Y	Y	Y	Y
3 *Wamp*	Y	Y	Y	Y	Y
4 *Davis*	Y	Y	Y	Y	Y
5 Cooper	Y	Y	Y	Y	Y
6 Gordon	Y	Y	Y	Y	Y
7 *Blackburn*	?	Y	Y	Y	Y
8 Tanner	Y	Y	Y	Y	Y
9 Ford	Y	Y	Y	Y	
TEXAS					
1 Sandlin	Y	Y	Y	Y	Y
2 Turner	Y	Y	Y	Y	Y
3 *Johnson, Sam*	Y	Y	Y	Y	Y
4 *Hall*	Y	Y	Y	Y	Y
5 *Hensarling*	Y	Y	Y	N	Y
6 *Barton*	Y	Y	Y	Y	Y
7 *Culberson*	Y	Y	Y	Y	Y
8 *Brady*	Y	Y	Y	Y	Y
9 Lampson	Y	Y	Y	Y	Y
10 Doggett	Y	Y	Y	Y	Y
11 Edwards	Y	Y	Y	Y	Y
12 *Granger*	Y	Y	Y	Y	Y
13 *Thornberry*	Y	Y	Y	Y	Y
14 *Paul*	Y	Y	Y	N	N
15 Hinojosa	Y	Y	Y	Y	Y
16 Reyes	Y	Y	Y	Y	Y
17 Stenholm	Y	Y	Y	Y	Y
18 Jackson-Lee	Y	Y	Y	Y	Y
19 *Neugebauer*	Y	Y	Y	Y	Y
20 Gonzalez	Y	Y	Y	Y	Y
21 *Smith*	Y	Y	Y	Y	Y
22 *DeLay*	Y	Y	Y	Y	Y
23 *Bonilla*	Y	Y	Y	Y	Y
24 Frost	Y	Y	Y	Y	Y
25 Bell	Y	Y	Y	Y	Y
26 *Burgess*	Y	Y	Y	Y	Y
27 Ortiz	Y	Y	Y	Y	Y
28 Rodriguez	Y	Y	Y	Y	Y
29 Green	Y	Y	Y	Y	Y
30 Johnson, E.B.	Y	Y	Y	Y	Y
31 *Carter*	Y	Y	Y	?	Y
32 *Sessions*	Y	Y	Y	Y	Y
UTAH					
1 *Bishop*	Y	Y	Y	Y	Y
2 Matheson	Y	Y	Y	Y	Y
3 *Cannon*	?	Y	Y	Y	Y
VERMONT					
AL *Sanders*	Y	Y	Y	Y	Y
VIRGINIA					
1 *Davis, Jo Ann*	Y	Y	Y	Y	Y
2 *Schrock*	Y	Y	Y	Y	Y
3 Scott	Y	Y	Y	Y	Y
4 *Forbes*	Y	Y	Y	Y	Y
5 *Goode*	Y	Y	Y	Y	Y
6 *Goodlatte*	Y	Y	Y	Y	Y
7 *Cantor*	Y	Y	Y	Y	Y
8 Moran	Y	Y	Y	Y	Y
9 Boucher	Y	Y	Y	Y	Y
10 *Wolf*	Y	Y	Y	Y	Y
11 *Davis, T.*	Y	Y	Y	Y	Y
WASHINGTON					
1 Inslee	Y	Y	Y	Y	Y
2 Larsen	Y	Y	Y	Y	Y
3 Baird	Y	Y	Y	Y	Y
4 *Hastings*	Y	Y	Y	Y	Y
5 *Nethercutt*	Y	Y	Y	Y	Y
6 Dicks	Y	Y	Y	Y	Y
7 McDermott	Y	Y	Y	Y	Y
8 *Dunn*	Y	Y	Y	Y	Y
9 Smith	Y	Y	Y	Y	Y
WEST VIRGINIA					
1 Mollohan	Y	Y	Y	Y	Y
2 *Capito*	Y	Y	Y	Y	Y
3 Rahall	Y	Y	Y	Y	Y
WISCONSIN					
1 *Ryan*	Y	Y	Y	Y	Y
2 Baldwin	Y	Y	Y	Y	Y
3 Kind	Y	Y	Y	Y	Y
4 Kleczka	Y	Y	Y	Y	Y
5 *Sensenbrenner*	Y	Y	Y	Y	Y
6 *Petri*	Y	Y	Y	Y	Y
7 Obey	Y	Y	Y	Y	Y
8 *Green*	Y	Y	Y	Y	Y
WYOMING					
AL *Cubin*	Y	Y	Y	Y	Y

Southern states - Ala., Ark., Fla., Ga., Ky., La., Miss., N.C., Okla., S.C., Tenn., Texas, Va.

Key

Y	Voted for (yea).
#	Paired for.
+	Announced for.
N	Voted against (nay).
X	Paired against.
−	Announced against.
P	Voted "present."
C	Voted "present" to avoid possible conflict of interest.
?	Did not vote or otherwise make a position known.

Democrats **Republicans**
Independents

84. H Con Res 393. Fiscal 2005 Budget Resolution/Previous Question. Hastings, R-Wash., motion to order the previous question (thus ending debate and possibility of amendment) on adoption of the rule (H Res 574) to provide for House floor consideration of the concurrent resolution that would set broad spending and revenue targets over the next five years. Motion agreed to 222-201: R 222-0; D 0-200 (ND 0-144, SD 0-56); I 0-1. March 25, 2004.

85. HR 3786. Printing Foreign Documents/Passage. Castle, R-Del., motion to suspend the rules and pass the bill that would authorize the secretary of the Treasury to produce currency, postage stamps and other security documents for foreign governments — provided that the foreign government reimburses the United States for the costs of production. Motion agreed to 422-2: R 221-2; D 200-0 (ND 144-0, SD 56-0); I 1-0. A two-thirds majority of those present and voting (283 in this case) is required for passage under suspension of the rules. March 25, 2004.

86. HR 2993. Commemorative Coins/Passage. Castle, R-Del., motion to suspend the rules and pass the bill that would extend the Commemorative Coin Program — which issues a commemorative quarter for each state — for an additional year, through 2009, and would add the District of Columbia and five U.S. territories to the program. Motion agreed to 411-14: R 208-14; D 202-0 (ND 145-0, SD 57-0); I 1-0. A two-thirds majority of those present and voting (284 in this case) is required for passage under suspension of the rules. March 25, 2004.

87. HR 254. North American Development Bank/Concur with Senate Amendments. Bereuter, R-Neb., motion to suspend the rules and concur with Senate amendments to the bill that would revamp the North American Development Bank, including codifying a U.S.-Mexico agreement that would allow the bank to make below-market-rate loans and extend the zone in Mexico served by the bank. The bill, as amended, would limit the bank's new authority to make grants. Motion agreed to (thus clearing the measure for the president) 377-48: R 176-47; D 200-1 (ND 144-0, SD 56-1); I 1-0. A two-thirds majority of those present and voting (284 in this case) is required for passage under suspension of the rules. March 25, 2004.

88. H Con Res 393. Fiscal 2005 Budget Resolution/Congressional Black Caucus Substitute. Cummings, D-Md., amendment that would call for $43.3 billion in additional spending and $5 billion for deficit reduction in fiscal 2005. It would call for action to rescind tax cuts for individuals making more than $200,000 in gross income, close several tax loopholes and reduce funding for the ballistic missile defense program. Spending increases would include $30.5 billion more for non-defense programs and an additional $12.8 billion for defense, homeland security and veterans' programs. Rejected 119-302: R 0-220; D 118-82 (ND 95-51, SD 23-31); I 1-0. March 25, 2004.

		84	85	86	87	88
ALABAMA						
1	*Bonner*	Y	Y	Y	Y	?
2	*Everett*	Y	Y	N	N	N
3	*Rogers*	Y	Y	Y	Y	N
4	*Aderholt*	Y	Y	Y	Y	N
5	Cramer	N	Y	Y	Y	N
6	*Bachus*	Y	Y	Y	Y	N
7	Davis	N	Y	Y	Y	Y
ALASKA						
AL	*Young*	Y	Y	Y	Y	N
ARIZONA						
1	*Renzi*	Y	Y	Y	Y	N
2	*Franks*	Y	Y	N	N	N
3	*Shadegg*	Y	Y	Y	N	N
4	Pastor	N	Y	Y	Y	Y
5	*Hayworth*	Y	Y	Y	N	N
6	*Flake*	Y	Y	Y	N	N
7	Grijalva	N	Y	Y	Y	Y
8	*Kolbe*	Y	Y	Y	Y	N
ARKANSAS						
1	Berry	N	Y	Y	Y	N
2	Snyder	N	Y	Y	Y	N
3	*Boozman*	Y	Y	Y	Y	N
4	Ross	N	Y	Y	Y	N
CALIFORNIA						
1	Thompson	N	Y	Y	Y	N
2	*Herger*	Y	Y	Y	Y	N
3	*Ose*	Y	Y	Y	Y	N
4	*Doolittle*	Y	Y	Y	Y	N
5	Matsui	N	Y	Y	Y	Y
6	Woolsey	N	Y	Y	Y	Y
7	Miller, George	N	Y	Y	Y	Y
8	Pelosi	N	Y	Y	Y	Y
9	Lee	N	Y	Y	Y	Y
10	Tauscher	N	Y	Y	Y	Y
11	*Pombo*	Y	Y	Y	Y	N
12	Lantos	N	Y	Y	Y	Y
13	Stark	N	Y	Y	Y	Y
14	Eshoo	N	Y	Y	Y	Y
15	Honda	N	Y	Y	Y	Y
16	Lofgren	N	Y	Y	Y	Y
17	Farr	N	Y	Y	Y	Y
18	Cardoza	N	Y	Y	Y	N
19	*Radanovich*	Y	Y	Y	Y	N
20	Dooley	N	Y	Y	Y	N
21	*Nunes*	Y	Y	Y	Y	N
22	*Thomas*	Y	Y	Y	Y	N
23	Capps	N	Y	Y	Y	Y
24	*Gallegly*	Y	Y	Y	Y	N
25	*McKeon*	Y	Y	Y	Y	N
26	*Dreier*	Y	Y	Y	Y	N
27	Sherman	N	Y	Y	Y	Y
28	Berman	N	Y	Y	Y	Y
29	Schiff	N	Y	Y	Y	Y
30	Waxman	N	Y	Y	Y	Y
31	Becerra	N	Y	Y	Y	Y
32	Solis	N	Y	Y	Y	Y
33	Watson	N	Y	Y	Y	Y
34	Roybal-Allard	N	Y	Y	Y	Y
35	Waters	N	Y	Y	Y	Y
36	Harman	N	Y	Y	Y	N

		84	85	86	87	88
37	Millender-McD.	N	Y	Y	Y	Y
38	Napolitano	N	Y	Y	Y	Y
39	Sánchez, Linda	N	Y	Y	Y	Y
40	*Royce*	Y	Y	N	Y	N
41	*Lewis*	Y	Y	Y	Y	N
42	*Miller, Gary*	Y	Y	N	Y	N
43	Baca	N	Y	Y	Y	Y
44	*Calvert*	Y	Y	Y	Y	N
45	*Bono*	Y	Y	Y	Y	N
46	*Rohrabacher*	Y	Y	Y	Y	N
47	Sanchez, Loretta	N	Y	Y	Y	Y
48	*Cox*	Y	?	Y	Y	N
49	*Issa*	Y	Y	Y	Y	N
50	*Cunningham*	Y	Y	Y	Y	N
51	Filner	N	Y	Y	Y	Y
52	*Hunter*	Y	Y	Y	Y	N
53	Davis	N	Y	Y	Y	N
COLORADO						
1	DeGette	N	Y	Y	Y	N
2	Udall	N	Y	Y	Y	N
3	*McInnis*	?	?	?	?	?
4	*Musgrave*	Y	Y	Y	N	N
5	*Hefley*	Y	Y	Y	Y	N
6	*Tancredo*	Y	Y	Y	N	N
7	*Beauprez*	Y	Y	Y	Y	N
CONNECTICUT						
1	Larson	N	Y	Y	Y	Y
2	*Simmons*	Y	Y	Y	Y	N
3	DeLauro	N	Y	Y	Y	Y
4	*Shays*	Y	Y	Y	Y	N
5	*Johnson*	Y	Y	?	Y	N
DELAWARE						
AL	*Castle*	Y	Y	Y	Y	N
FLORIDA						
1	*Miller, J.*	Y	Y	N	N	N
2	Boyd	N	Y	Y	Y	N
3	Brown	N	Y	Y	Y	Y
4	*Crenshaw*	Y	Y	N	N	N
5	*Brown-Waite*	Y	Y	N	N	N
6	*Stearns*	Y	Y	Y	Y	N
7	*Mica*	Y	Y	Y	Y	N
8	*Keller*	Y	Y	Y	Y	N
9	*Bilirakis*	Y	Y	Y	Y	N
10	*Young*	Y	Y	Y	Y	N
11	Davis	N	Y	Y	Y	N
12	*Putnam*	Y	Y	N	Y	N
13	*Harris*	Y	Y	Y	Y	N
14	*Goss*	Y	Y	N	Y	N
15	*Weldon*	Y	Y	Y	Y	N
16	*Foley*	Y	Y	Y	Y	N
17	Meek	N	Y	Y	Y	Y
18	*Ros-Lehtinen*	Y	Y	Y	Y	N
19	Wexler	N	Y	Y	Y	?
20	Deutsch	N	Y	Y	Y	Y
21	*Diaz-Balart, L.*	Y	Y	Y	Y	N
22	*Shaw*	Y	Y	Y	Y	N
23	Hastings	N	Y	Y	Y	Y
24	*Feeney*	Y	Y	Y	N	N
25	*Diaz-Balart, M.*	Y	Y	Y	Y	N
GEORGIA						
1	*Kingston*	Y	Y	N	Y	N
2	Bishop	N	Y	Y	Y	Y
3	Marshall	N	Y	Y	Y	Y
4	Majette	N	Y	Y	Y	Y
5	Lewis	N	Y	Y	Y	Y
6	*Isakson*	Y	Y	Y	N	N
7	*Linder*	Y	Y	Y	Y	?
8	*Collins*	Y	N	Y	N	N
9	*Norwood*	Y	N	N	N	N
10	*Deal*	Y	Y	N	N	N
11	*Gingrey*	Y	Y	Y	Y	N
12	*Burns*	Y	Y	Y	Y	N
13	Scott	N	Y	Y	Y	Y
HAWAII						
1	Abercrombie	?	?	?	?	?
2	Case	N	Y	Y	Y	N
IDAHO						
1	*Otter*	Y	Y	N	N	N
2	*Simpson*	Y	Y	Y	Y	N
ILLINOIS						
1	Rush	N	Y	Y	Y	Y
2	Jackson	N	Y	Y	Y	Y
3	Lipinski	N	Y	Y	Y	N
4	Gutierrez	N	Y	Y	?	Y
5	Emanuel	N	Y	Y	Y	N
6	*Hyde*	Y	Y	Y	Y	N

ND Northern Democrats   SD Southern Democrats

Member	84	85	86	87	88
7 Davis	?	?	Y	Y	Y
8 ***Crane***	Y	Y	Y	Y	N
9 Schakowsky	N	Y	Y	Y	Y
10 ***Kirk***	Y	Y	Y	Y	N
11 ***Weller***	Y	Y	Y	Y	N
12 Costello	N	Y	Y	Y	N
13 ***Biggert***	Y	Y	Y	Y	N
14 ***Hastert***					
15 ***Johnson***	Y	Y	Y	Y	N
16 ***Manzullo***	Y	Y	Y	?	N
17 Evans	N	Y	Y	Y	Y
18 ***LaHood***	Y	Y	Y	Y	N
19 ***Shimkus***	Y	Y	Y	Y	N
INDIANA					
1 Visclosky	N	Y	Y	Y	N
2 ***Chocola***	Y	Y	Y	Y	N
3 ***Souder***	Y	Y	Y	Y	N
4 ***Buyer***	Y	Y	Y	Y	N
5 ***Burton***	Y	Y	Y	Y	N
6 ***Pence***	+	+	+	+	–
7 Carson	N	Y	Y	Y	Y
8 ***Hostettler***	Y	Y	Y	N	N
9 Hill	N	Y	Y	Y	N
IOWA					
1 ***Nussle***	Y	Y	Y	Y	N
2 ***Leach***	Y	Y	Y	Y	N
3 Boswell	N	Y	Y	Y	N
4 ***Latham***	Y	Y	Y	Y	N
5 ***King***	Y	Y	Y	N	N
KANSAS					
1 ***Moran***	Y	Y	Y	N	N
2 ***Ryun***	Y	Y	Y	Y	N
3 Moore	N	Y	Y	Y	N
4 ***Tiahrt***	Y	Y	Y	Y	N
KENTUCKY					
1 ***Whitfield***	Y	Y	Y	Y	N
2 ***Lewis***	Y	Y	Y	N	N
3 ***Northup***	Y	Y	Y	Y	N
4 Lucas	N	Y	Y	Y	?
5 ***Rogers***	Y	Y	Y	N	N
6 Chandler	N	Y	Y	Y	N
LOUISIANA					
1 ***Vitter***	Y	Y	Y	Y	N
2 Jefferson	N	Y	Y	Y	Y
3 ***Tauzin***	?	?	?	?	?
4 ***McCrery***	Y	Y	Y	Y	N
5 Alexander	N	Y	Y	Y	N
6 ***Baker***	Y	Y	Y	Y	N
7 John	N	Y	Y	Y	N
MAINE					
1 Allen	N	Y	Y	Y	N
2 Michaud	N	Y	Y	Y	N
MARYLAND					
1 ***Gilchrest***	Y	Y	Y	Y	N
2 Ruppersberger	N	Y	Y	Y	Y
3 Cardin	N	Y	Y	Y	N
4 Wynn	N	Y	Y	Y	Y
5 Hoyer	N	Y	Y	Y	N
6 ***Bartlett***	Y	Y	Y	N	N
7 Cummings	N	Y	Y	Y	Y
8 Van Hollen	N	Y	Y	Y	Y
MASSACHUSETTS					
1 Olver	N	Y	Y	Y	Y
2 Neal	N	Y	Y	Y	Y
3 McGovern	N	Y	Y	Y	Y
4 Frank	N	Y	Y	Y	Y
5 Meehan	N	Y	Y	Y	Y
6 Tierney	N	Y	Y	Y	Y
7 Markey	N	Y	Y	Y	Y
8 Capuano	N	Y	Y	Y	Y
9 Lynch	N	Y	Y	Y	Y
10 Delahunt	N	Y	Y	Y	Y
MICHIGAN					
1 Stupak	N	Y	Y	Y	N
2 ***Hoekstra***	Y	Y	Y	N	N
3 ***Ehlers***	Y	Y	Y	Y	N
4 ***Camp***	Y	Y	Y	Y	N
5 Kildee	N	Y	Y	Y	N
6 ***Upton***	Y	Y	Y	Y	N
7 ***Smith***	Y	Y	Y	N	N
8 ***Rogers***	Y	Y	Y	Y	N
9 ***Knollenberg***	Y	Y	Y	Y	N
10 ***Miller***	Y	Y	Y	Y	N
11 ***McCotter***	Y	Y	Y	Y	N
12 Levin	N	Y	Y	Y	N
13 Kilpatrick	N	Y	Y	Y	Y
14 Conyers	N	Y	Y	Y	Y
15 Dingell	N	Y	Y	Y	Y
MINNESOTA					
1 ***Gutknecht***	Y	Y	Y	N	N
2 ***Kline***	Y	Y	Y	Y	N
3 ***Ramstad***	Y	Y	Y	N	N
4 McCollum	N	Y	Y	Y	Y
5 Sabo	N	Y	Y	Y	Y
6 ***Kennedy***	Y	Y	Y	Y	N
7 Peterson	N	Y	Y	Y	N
8 Oberstar	N	Y	Y	Y	Y
MISSISSIPPI					
1 ***Wicker***	Y	Y	Y	Y	N
2 Thompson	N	Y	Y	Y	Y
3 ***Pickering***	Y	Y	Y	Y	N
4 Taylor	N	Y	Y	N	N
MISSOURI					
1 Clay	?	?	?	?	Y
2 ***Akin***	Y	Y	Y	Y	N
3 Gephardt	N	Y	Y	Y	Y
4 Skelton	N	Y	Y	Y	N
5 McCarthy	N	Y	Y	Y	N
6 ***Graves***	Y	Y	Y	Y	N
7 ***Blunt***	Y	Y	Y	Y	N
8 ***Emerson***	Y	Y	Y	Y	N
9 ***Hulshof***	Y	Y	Y	Y	N
MONTANA					
AL ***Rehberg***	Y	Y	Y	Y	N
NEBRASKA					
1 ***Bereuter***	Y	Y	Y	Y	N
2 ***Terry***	Y	Y	Y	Y	N
3 ***Osborne***	Y	Y	Y	Y	N
NEVADA					
1 Berkley	N	Y	Y	Y	N
2 ***Gibbons***	Y	Y	Y	Y	N
3 ***Porter***	Y	Y	Y	Y	N
NEW HAMPSHIRE					
1 ***Bradley***	Y	Y	Y	Y	N
2 ***Bass***	Y	Y	Y	Y	N
NEW JERSEY					
1 Andrews	N	Y	Y	Y	N
2 ***LoBiondo***	Y	Y	Y	Y	N
3 ***Saxton***	Y	Y	Y	Y	N
4 ***Smith***	Y	Y	Y	Y	N
5 ***Garrett***	Y	Y	Y	Y	N
6 Pallone	N	Y	Y	Y	Y
7 ***Ferguson***	Y	Y	Y	Y	N
8 Pascrell	N	Y	Y	Y	Y
9 Rothman	N	Y	Y	Y	Y
10 Payne	N	Y	Y	Y	Y
11 ***Frelinghuysen***	Y	Y	Y	Y	N
12 Holt	N	Y	Y	Y	Y
13 Menendez	N	Y	Y	Y	Y
NEW MEXICO					
1 ***Wilson***	Y	Y	Y	Y	N
2 ***Pearce***	Y	Y	Y	N	N
3 Udall	N	Y	Y	Y	N
NEW YORK					
1 Bishop	N	Y	Y	Y	N
2 Israel	N	Y	Y	Y	N
3 ***King***	Y	Y	Y	Y	N
4 McCarthy	N	Y	Y	Y	N
5 Ackerman	N	Y	Y	Y	Y
6 Meeks	N	Y	Y	Y	Y
7 Crowley	N	Y	Y	Y	Y
8 Nadler	N	Y	Y	Y	Y
9 Weiner	N	Y	Y	Y	Y
10 Towns	N	Y	Y	Y	Y
11 Owens	N	Y	Y	Y	Y
12 Velázquez	N	Y	Y	Y	Y
13 ***Fossella***	Y	Y	Y	Y	N
14 Maloney	N	Y	Y	Y	Y
15 Rangel	N	Y	Y	Y	Y
16 Serrano	N	Y	Y	Y	Y
17 Engel	N	Y	Y	Y	Y
18 Lowey	N	Y	Y	Y	Y
19 ***Kelly***	Y	Y	Y	Y	N
20 ***Sweeney***	Y	Y	Y	Y	N
21 McNulty	N	Y	Y	Y	Y
22 Hinchey	N	Y	Y	Y	Y
23 ***McHugh***	Y	Y	Y	Y	N
24 ***Boehlert***	Y	Y	Y	Y	N
25 ***Walsh***	Y	Y	Y	Y	N
26 ***Reynolds***	Y	Y	Y	Y	N
27 ***Quinn***	Y	Y	Y	Y	?
28 Slaughter	N	Y	Y	Y	N
29 ***Houghton***	Y	Y	Y	Y	N
NORTH CAROLINA					
1 Ballance	N	Y	Y	Y	Y
2 Etheridge	N	Y	Y	Y	N
3 ***Jones***	Y	Y	Y	N	N
4 Price	?	?	Y	Y	?
5 ***Burr***	Y	Y	Y	Y	N
6 ***Coble***	Y	Y	Y	Y	N
7 McIntyre	N	Y	Y	Y	N
8 ***Hayes***	Y	Y	Y	N	N
9 ***Myrick***	Y	Y	Y	Y	N
10 ***Ballenger***	Y	Y	Y	Y	N
11 ***Taylor***	Y	Y	N	N	N
12 Watt	N	Y	Y	Y	Y
13 Miller	N	Y	Y	Y	N
NORTH DAKOTA					
AL Pomeroy	N	Y	Y	Y	N
OHIO					
1 ***Chabot***	Y	Y	Y	N	N
2 ***Portman***	Y	Y	Y	Y	N
3 ***Turner***	Y	Y	Y	Y	N
4 ***Oxley***	Y	Y	Y	Y	N
5 ***Gillmor***	Y	Y	Y	Y	N
6 Strickland	N	Y	Y	Y	N
7 ***Hobson***	Y	Y	?	Y	N
8 ***Boehner***	?	Y	Y	Y	N
9 Kaptur	N	Y	Y	Y	Y
10 Kucinich	N	Y	Y	Y	Y
11 Jones	N	Y	Y	Y	Y
12 ***Tiberi***	Y	Y	Y	Y	N
13 Brown	N	Y	Y	Y	Y
14 ***LaTourette***	Y	Y	Y	Y	N
15 ***Pryce***	Y	Y	Y	Y	N
16 ***Regula***	Y	Y	Y	Y	N
17 Ryan	N	Y	Y	Y	Y
18 ***Ney***	Y	Y	Y	Y	N
OKLAHOMA					
1 ***Sullivan***	Y	Y	Y	N	N
2 Carson	N	Y	Y	Y	N
3 ***Lucas***	Y	Y	Y	Y	N
4 ***Cole***	Y	Y	Y	Y	N
5 ***Istook***	Y	Y	Y	Y	N
OREGON					
1 Wu	N	Y	Y	Y	N
2 ***Walden***	Y	Y	Y	Y	N
3 Blumenauer	N	Y	Y	Y	Y
4 DeFazio	N	Y	Y	Y	Y
5 Hooley	N	Y	Y	Y	N
PENNSYLVANIA					
1 Brady	N	Y	Y	Y	Y
2 Fattah	N	Y	Y	Y	Y
3 ***English***	Y	Y	Y	Y	N
4 ***Hart***	Y	Y	Y	Y	N
5 ***Peterson***	Y	Y	Y	Y	N
6 ***Gerlach***	Y	Y	Y	Y	N
7 ***Weldon***	?	Y	Y	Y	N
8 ***Greenwood***	Y	Y	Y	Y	N
9 ***Shuster, Bill***	Y	Y	Y	N	N
10 ***Sherwood***	Y	Y	Y	N	N
11 Kanjorski	N	Y	Y	Y	N
12 Murtha	N	Y	Y	Y	N
13 Hoeffel	?	?	?	?	?
14 Doyle	N	Y	Y	Y	Y
15 ***Toomey***	Y	Y	Y	N	N
16 ***Pitts***	Y	Y	Y	Y	N
17 Holden	N	Y	Y	Y	N
18 ***Murphy***	Y	Y	Y	Y	N
19 ***Platts***	Y	Y	Y	N	N
RHODE ISLAND					
1 Kennedy	N	Y	Y	Y	Y
2 Langevin	N	Y	Y	Y	N
SOUTH CAROLINA					
1 ***Brown***	Y	Y	Y	Y	N
2 ***Wilson***	Y	Y	Y	Y	N
3 ***Barrett***	Y	Y	Y	Y	N
4 ***DeMint***	Y	Y	Y	Y	?
5 Spratt	N	Y	Y	Y	N
6 Clyburn	N	Y	Y	Y	Y
SOUTH DAKOTA					
AL Vacant					
TENNESSEE					
1 ***Jenkins***	Y	Y	Y	N	N
2 ***Duncan***	Y	N	Y	N	N
3 ***Wamp***	Y	Y	Y	Y	N
4 Davis	N	Y	Y	Y	N
5 Cooper	N	Y	Y	Y	Y
6 Gordon	N	Y	Y	Y	N
7 ***Blackburn***	Y	Y	Y	N	N
8 Tanner	N	Y	Y	Y	N
9 Ford	N	Y	Y	Y	Y
TEXAS					
1 Sandlin	N	Y	Y	Y	N
2 Turner	N	Y	Y	Y	N
3 ***Johnson, Sam***	Y	Y	Y	Y	N
4 ***Hall***	Y	Y	Y	Y	N
5 ***Hensarling***	Y	Y	Y	Y	N
6 ***Barton***	Y	Y	Y	Y	N
7 ***Culberson***	Y	Y	N	N	N
8 ***Brady***	Y	Y	Y	Y	N
9 Lampson	N	Y	Y	Y	N
10 Doggett	N	Y	Y	Y	Y
11 Edwards	N	Y	Y	Y	N
12 ***Granger***	Y	Y	Y	Y	N
13 ***Thornberry***	Y	Y	N	Y	N
14 ***Paul***	Y	N	Y	N	N
15 Hinojosa	N	Y	Y	Y	Y
16 Reyes	N	Y	Y	Y	N
17 Stenholm	N	Y	Y	Y	N
18 Jackson-Lee	N	Y	Y	Y	Y
19 ***Neugebauer***	Y	Y	Y	Y	N
20 Gonzalez	N	Y	Y	Y	N
21 ***Smith***	Y	Y	Y	Y	N
22 ***DeLay***	Y	Y	Y	Y	N
23 ***Bonilla***	Y	Y	Y	Y	N
24 Frost	N	Y	Y	Y	N
25 Bell	N	Y	Y	Y	N
26 ***Burgess***	Y	Y	Y	N	N
27 Ortiz	N	Y	Y	Y	N
28 Rodriguez	N	Y	Y	Y	N
29 Green	N	Y	Y	Y	Y
30 Johnson, E.B.	N	Y	Y	Y	Y
31 ***Carter***	Y	Y	Y	Y	N
32 ***Sessions***	Y	Y	Y	Y	N
UTAH					
1 ***Bishop***	Y	Y	Y	N	N
2 Matheson	N	Y	Y	Y	N
3 ***Cannon***	Y	Y	Y	Y	N
VERMONT					
AL *Sanders*	N	Y	Y	Y	Y
VIRGINIA					
1 ***Davis, Jo Ann***	Y	Y	Y	N	N
2 ***Schrock***	Y	Y	Y	Y	N
3 Scott	N	Y	Y	Y	Y
4 ***Forbes***	Y	Y	Y	N	N
5 ***Goode***	Y	Y	Y	N	N
6 ***Goodlatte***	Y	Y	Y	N	N
7 ***Cantor***	Y	Y	Y	Y	N
8 Moran	N	Y	Y	Y	Y
9 Boucher	N	Y	Y	Y	N
10 ***Wolf***	Y	Y	Y	Y	N
11 ***Davis, T.***	Y	Y	Y	Y	N
WASHINGTON					
1 Inslee	N	Y	Y	Y	N
2 Larsen	N	Y	Y	Y	N
3 Baird	N	Y	Y	Y	N
4 ***Hastings***	Y	Y	Y	Y	N
5 ***Nethercutt***	Y	Y	Y	Y	N
6 Dicks	N	Y	Y	Y	N
7 McDermott	N	Y	Y	Y	Y
8 ***Dunn***	Y	Y	Y	Y	N
9 Smith	N	Y	Y	Y	N
WEST VIRGINIA					
1 Mollohan	N	Y	Y	Y	N
2 ***Capito***	Y	Y	Y	Y	N
3 Rahall	N	Y	Y	Y	Y
WISCONSIN					
1 ***Ryan***	Y	Y	Y	Y	N
2 Baldwin	N	Y	Y	Y	Y
3 Kind	N	Y	Y	Y	N
4 Kleczka	N	Y	Y	Y	Y
5 ***Sensenbrenner***	Y	Y	Y	N	N
6 ***Petri***	Y	Y	Y	Y	N
7 Obey	N	Y	Y	Y	N
8 ***Green***	Y	Y	Y	Y	N
WYOMING					
AL ***Cubin***	Y	Y	N	Y	N

Southern states - Ala., Ark., Fla., Ga., Ky., La., Miss., N.C., Okla., S.C., Tenn., Texas, Va.

Key

Y	Voted for (yea).
#	Paired for.
+	Announced for.
N	Voted against (nay).
X	Paired against.
–	Announced against.
P	Voted "present."
C	Voted "present" to avoid possible conflict of interest.
?	Did not vote or otherwise make a position known.

Democrats **Republicans** *Independents*

89. H Con Res 393. Fiscal 2005 Budget Resolution/Blue Dog Substitute. Stenholm, D-Texas, amendment that would provide for a balanced budget by fiscal 2012 and reduce the deficit by half over the next two years. Action on additional tax cuts or other proposals that would create additional budgetary obligations would be deferred until Congress and the president have taken action to reduce the deficit. It would allow for a one-year extension of the $1,000 child tax credit, so-called marriage penalty relief, and the 10 percent tax bracket and allow for an extension of the tax cuts after 2010 subject to pay-as-you-go rules. Rejected 183-243: R 12-211; D 171-31 (ND 120-26, SD 51-5); I 0-1. March 25, 2004.

90. H Con Res 393. Fiscal 2005 Budget Resolution/Republican Study Committee Substitute. Hensarling, R-Texas, amendment that would provide procedural protection for $182.6 billion in tax cuts over five years, while reducing the deficit by half in three years. It would call for reducing non-defense, non-homeland security discretionary spending by 1 percent from fiscal 2004 levels and scaling back the growth of non-Social Security mandatory spending by 1 percent in fiscal 2005. Rejected 116-309: R 115-108; D 1-200 (ND 0-146, SD 1-54); I 0-1. March 25, 2004.

91. H Con Res 393. Fiscal 2005 Budget Resolution/Democratic Substitute. Spratt, D-S.C., amendment that would provide for a balanced budget by fiscal 2012 and allow discretionary spending to keep pace with inflation. It would allow for an extension of certain tax cuts, such as the $1,000 child tax credit, while reducing tax cuts for those who make more than $500,000 a year. It also would establish a "pay-as-you-go" point of order that could be raised against any tax cuts or spending increases that are not offset. Rejected 194-232: R 0-224; D 193-8 (ND 142-5, SD 51-3); I 1-0. March 25, 2004.

92. H Con Res 393. Fiscal 2005 Budget Resolution/Adoption. Adoption of the concurrent resolution that would set broad spending and revenue targets over the next five years. The resolution would call for $821.3 billion in discretionary spending for fiscal 2005, and assumes $50 billion in additional fiscal 2005 spending to support military operations in Iraq. It would call for $152.6 billion in tax cuts over five years and provide reconciliation protection for $137.6 billion of that total. It also would call for the budget deficit to be reduced by approximately half by fiscal 2009. Mandatory spending would rise by 5 percent in fiscal 2005. It would allow for a 7 percent increase in defense spending in fiscal 2005 and a 12 percent increase in homeland security spending. Adopted 215-212: R 215-10; D 0-201 (ND 0-147, SD 0-54); I 0-1. March 25, 2004.

93. HR 3095. Lowering of Flags/Passage. Sensenbrenner, R-Wis., motion to suspend the rules and pass the bill that would explicitly authorize top local government officials to order the lowering of the U.S. flag to half-staff to honor the deaths of current and past local government employees. Motion agreed to 374-2: R 200-2; D 173-0 (ND 129-0, SD 44-0); I 1-0. A two-thirds majority of those present and voting (251 in this case) is required for passage under suspension of the rules. March 25, 2004.

	89	90	91	92	93
ALABAMA					
1 *Bonner*	N	Y	N	Y	?
2 *Everett*	N	N	N	Y	?
3 *Rogers*	N	N	N	Y	Y
4 *Aderholt*	N	N	N	Y	Y
5 Cramer	Y	N	Y	N	Y
6 *Bachus*	N	Y	N	Y	Y
7 Davis	Y	N	Y	N	Y
ALASKA					
AL *Young*	N	N	N	Y	Y
ARIZONA					
1 *Renzi*	N	N	N	N	Y
2 *Franks*	N	Y	N	Y	Y
3 *Shadegg*	N	Y	N	Y	Y
4 Pastor	Y	N	Y	N	Y
5 *Hayworth*	N	Y	N	Y	Y
6 *Flake*	N	Y	N	Y	Y
7 Grijalva	Y	N	Y	N	Y
8 *Kolbe*	N	N	N	Y	Y
ARKANSAS					
1 Berry	Y	N	Y	N	?
2 Snyder	Y	N	Y	N	Y
3 *Boozman*	N	Y	N	Y	Y
4 Ross	Y	N	Y	N	Y
CALIFORNIA					
1 Thompson	Y	N	Y	N	Y
2 *Herger*	N	Y	N	Y	Y
3 *Ose*	N	Y	N	Y	Y
4 *Doolittle*	N	Y	N	Y	Y
5 Matsui	Y	N	Y	N	Y
6 Woolsey	Y	N	Y	N	Y
7 Miller, George	Y	N	Y	N	Y
8 Pelosi	Y	N	Y	N	?
9 Lee	N	N	N	N	Y
10 Tauscher	Y	N	Y	N	Y
11 *Pombo*	N	Y	N	Y	Y
12 Lantos	Y	N	Y	N	Y
13 Stark	Y	N	Y	N	?
14 Eshoo	Y	N	Y	N	Y
15 Honda	Y	N	Y	N	Y
16 Lofgren	Y	N	Y	N	Y
17 Farr	Y	N	Y	N	Y
18 Cardoza	Y	N	Y	N	Y
19 *Radanovich*	N	Y	N	Y	Y
20 Dooley	Y	N	Y	N	?
21 *Nunes*	N	Y	N	Y	Y
22 *Thomas*	N	N	N	Y	Y
23 Capps	Y	N	Y	N	Y
24 *Gallegly*	N	Y	N	Y	Y
25 *McKeon*	N	Y	N	Y	Y
26 *Dreier*	N	N	N	Y	Y
27 Sherman	Y	N	Y	N	Y
28 Berman	N	N	Y	N	Y
29 Schiff	Y	N	Y	N	Y
30 Waxman	Y	N	Y	N	Y
31 Becerra	Y	N	Y	N	Y
32 Solis	Y	N	Y	N	Y
33 Watson	Y	N	Y	N	Y
34 Roybal-Allard	Y	N	Y	N	Y
35 Waters	Y	N	Y	N	Y
36 Harman	Y	N	Y	N	Y

	89	90	91	92	93
37 Millender-McD.	Y	N	Y	N	Y
38 Napolitano	Y	N	Y	N	Y
39 Sánchez, Linda	Y	N	Y	N	Y
40 *Royce*	N	Y	N	Y	Y
41 *Lewis*	N	N	N	Y	Y
42 *Miller, Gary*	N	Y	N	Y	Y
43 Baca	Y	N	Y	N	Y
44 *Calvert*	N	N	N	Y	Y
45 *Bono*	N	N	N	Y	Y
46 *Rohrabacher*	N	Y	N	Y	Y
47 Sanchez, Loretta	Y	N	Y	N	Y
48 *Cox*	N	Y	N	Y	?
49 *Issa*	N	N	N	Y	Y
50 *Cunningham*	N	Y	N	Y	Y
51 Filner	Y	N	Y	N	Y
52 *Hunter*	N	Y	N	Y	Y
53 Davis	Y	N	Y	N	Y
COLORADO					
1 DeGette	Y	N	Y	N	Y
2 Udall	Y	N	Y	N	Y
3 *McInnis*	?	?	?	?	?
4 *Musgrave*	N	Y	N	Y	Y
5 *Hefley*	N	Y	N	N	Y
6 *Tancredo*	N	Y	N	Y	Y
7 *Beauprez*	N	Y	N	Y	Y
CONNECTICUT					
1 Larson	Y	N	Y	N	Y
2 *Simmons*	N	N	N	Y	Y
3 DeLauro	Y	N	Y	N	Y
4 *Shays*	N	N	N	N	Y
5 *Johnson*	N	N	N	Y	Y
DELAWARE					
AL *Castle*	N	N	N	N	Y
FLORIDA					
1 *Miller, J.*	N	Y	N	Y	Y
2 Boyd	Y	N	Y	N	?
3 Brown	Y	N	Y	N	Y
4 *Crenshaw*	N	Y	N	Y	Y
5 *Brown-Waite*	N	Y	N	Y	Y
6 *Stearns*	N	Y	N	Y	Y
7 *Mica*	N	N	N	Y	Y
8 *Keller*	N	Y	N	Y	Y
9 *Bilirakis*	Y	N	Y	Y	Y
10 *Young*	N	N	N	Y	Y
11 Davis	Y	N	Y	N	Y
12 *Putnam*	N	Y	N	Y	Y
13 *Harris*	N	Y	N	Y	?
14 *Goss*	N	N	N	Y	Y
15 *Weldon*	N	Y	N	Y	Y
16 *Foley*	N	N	N	Y	Y
17 Meek	Y	N	Y	N	Y
18 *Ros-Lehtinen*	N	N	N	Y	Y
19 Wexler	Y	N	Y	N	Y
20 Deutsch	Y	N	Y	N	Y
21 *Diaz-Balart, L.*	N	N	N	Y	Y
22 *Shaw*	N	N	N	Y	Y
23 Hastings	Y	N	Y	N	Y
24 *Feeney*	N	Y	N	Y	?
25 *Diaz-Balart, M.*	N	Y	N	Y	Y
GEORGIA					
1 *Kingston*	N	Y	N	Y	Y
2 Bishop	Y	N	Y	N	Y
3 Marshall	Y	N	N	N	?
4 Majette	Y	N	Y	N	Y
5 Lewis	Y	N	Y	N	Y
6 *Isakson*	N	Y	N	Y	?
7 *Linder*	N	Y	N	Y	Y
8 *Collins*	N	Y	N	Y	Y
9 *Norwood*	N	Y	N	Y	Y
10 *Deal*	N	Y	N	Y	Y
11 *Gingrey*	N	Y	N	Y	Y
12 *Burns*	N	N	N	Y	Y
13 Scott	Y	Y	Y	N	Y
HAWAII					
1 Abercrombie	?	?	?	?	?
2 Case	Y	N	Y	N	Y
IDAHO					
1 *Otter*	N	Y	N	Y	Y
2 *Simpson*	N	Y	N	Y	Y
ILLINOIS					
1 Rush	N	N	N	Y	Y
2 Jackson	N	N	Y	N	Y
3 Lipinski	Y	N	Y	N	?
4 Gutierrez	Y	N	Y	N	Y
5 Emanuel	Y	N	Y	N	Y
6 *Hyde*	N	N	N	Y	Y

ND Northern Democrats   SD Southern Democrats

	89	90	91	92	93
7 Davis	Y	N	Y	N	Y
8 ***Crane***	N	Y	N	Y	Y
9 Schakowsky	N	N	Y	N	Y
10 ***Kirk***	N	N	N	Y	Y
11 ***Weller***	N	Y	N	Y	Y
12 Costello	N	N	Y	N	Y
13 ***Biggert***	N	Y	N	Y	?
14 ***Hastert***				Y	
15 ***Johnson***	N	N	N	Y	Y
16 ***Manzullo***	N	Y	N	Y	Y
17 Evans	N	N	Y	N	?
18 ***LaHood***	Y	N	N	Y	?
19 ***Shimkus***	Y	Y	N	Y	Y
INDIANA					
1 Visclosky	N	N	N	N	Y
2 ***Chocola***	N	Y	N	Y	Y
3 ***Souder***	N	N	N	Y	Y
4 ***Buyer***	N	N	N	Y	?
5 ***Burton***	N	Y	N	Y	Y
6 ***Pence***	–	+	N	Y	Y
7 Carson	Y	N	Y	N	Y
8 ***Hostettler***	N	N	N	N	Y
9 Hill	Y	N	Y	N	Y
IOWA					
1 ***Nussle***	N	N	N	Y	Y
2 ***Leach***	N	N	N	Y	?
3 Boswell	Y	N	Y	N	Y
4 ***Latham***	N	N	N	Y	Y
5 ***King***	N	Y	N	Y	Y
KANSAS					
1 ***Moran***	Y	Y	N	Y	Y
2 ***Ryun***	N	Y	N	Y	Y
3 Moore	Y	N	Y	N	Y
4 ***Tiahrt***	N	Y	N	Y	Y
KENTUCKY					
1 ***Whitfield***	N	N	N	Y	Y
2 ***Lewis***	N	N	N	Y	Y
3 ***Northup***	N	N	N	Y	Y
4 Lucas	?	?	?	?	?
5 ***Rogers***	N	N	N	Y	Y
6 Chandler	Y	N	Y	N	Y
LOUISIANA					
1 ***Vitter***	N	Y	N	Y	?
2 Jefferson	Y	N	Y	N	?
3 ***Tauzin***	?	?	?	?	?
4 ***McCrery***	N	Y	N	Y	Y
5 Alexander	Y	N	Y	N	?
6 ***Baker***	N	N	N	Y	Y
7 John	Y	N	Y	N	Y
MAINE					
1 Allen	Y	N	Y	N	Y
2 Michaud	Y	N	Y	N	Y
MARYLAND					
1 ***Gilchrest***	N	N	N	Y	Y
2 Ruppersberger	Y	N	Y	N	Y
3 Cardin	Y	N	Y	N	Y
4 Wynn	Y	N	Y	N	Y
5 Hoyer	Y	N	Y	N	Y
6 ***Bartlett***	N	Y	N	Y	Y
7 Cummings	Y	N	Y	N	Y
8 Van Hollen	Y	N	Y	N	Y
MASSACHUSETTS					
1 Olver	Y	N	Y	N	Y
2 Neal	Y	N	Y	N	Y
3 McGovern	Y	N	Y	N	Y
4 Frank	Y	N	Y	N	Y
5 Meehan	Y	N	Y	N	?
6 Tierney	Y	N	Y	N	Y
7 Markey	Y	N	Y	N	Y
8 Capuano	Y	N	Y	N	Y
9 Lynch	Y	N	Y	N	Y
10 Delahunt	Y	N	Y	N	Y
MICHIGAN					
1 Stupak	Y	N	Y	N	Y
2 ***Hoekstra***	N	Y	N	Y	Y
3 ***Ehlers***	N	N	N	Y	Y
4 ***Camp***	N	N	N	Y	Y
5 Kildee	N	N	Y	N	Y
6 ***Upton***	Y	N	N	Y	Y
7 ***Smith***	N	Y	N	Y	?
8 ***Rogers***	N	N	N	Y	Y
9 ***Knollenberg***	N	N	N	Y	Y
10 ***Miller***	N	N	N	Y	Y
11 ***McCotter***	N	N	N	Y	Y
12 Levin	Y	N	Y	N	Y

	89	90	91	92	93
13 Kilpatrick	Y	N	Y	N	Y
14 Conyers	Y	N	Y	N	Y
15 Dingell	Y	N	Y	N	Y
MINNESOTA					
1 ***Gutknecht***	N	Y	N	Y	N
2 ***Kline***	N	Y	N	Y	N
3 ***Ramstad***	N	Y	N	Y	Y
4 McCollum	Y	N	Y	N	Y
5 Sabo	Y	N	Y	N	Y
6 ***Kennedy***	N	Y	N	Y	Y
7 Peterson	Y	N	N	N	Y
8 Oberstar	Y	N	Y	N	Y
MISSISSIPPI					
1 ***Wicker***	N	N	N	Y	Y
2 Thompson	N	N	Y	N	Y
3 ***Pickering***	N	N	N	Y	Y
4 Taylor	Y	N	N	N	Y
MISSOURI					
1 Clay	Y	N	Y	N	?
2 ***Akin***	N	Y	N	Y	Y
3 Gephardt	Y	N	Y	N	?
4 Skelton	Y	N	Y	N	Y
5 McCarthy	Y	N	Y	N	+
6 ***Graves***	N	N	N	Y	Y
7 ***Blunt***	N	Y	N	Y	Y
8 ***Emerson***	Y	N	N	Y	Y
9 ***Hulshof***	N	N	N	Y	?
MONTANA					
AL ***Rehberg***	N	Y	N	Y	Y
NEBRASKA					
1 ***Bereuter***	Y	N	N	Y	Y
2 ***Terry***	N	Y	N	Y	Y
3 ***Osborne***	Y	N	N	Y	Y
NEVADA					
1 Berkley	Y	N	Y	N	Y
2 ***Gibbons***	N	Y	N	Y	Y
3 ***Porter***	N	N	N	Y	Y
NEW HAMPSHIRE					
1 ***Bradley***	N	N	N	Y	Y
2 ***Bass***	Y	N	N	Y	?
NEW JERSEY					
1 Andrews	Y	N	Y	N	Y
2 ***LoBiondo***	N	N	N	Y	Y
3 ***Saxton***	N	N	N	Y	Y
4 ***Smith***	N	N	N	N	Y
5 ***Garrett***	N	Y	N	Y	Y
6 Pallone	Y	N	Y	N	Y
7 ***Ferguson***	N	N	N	Y	Y
8 Pascrell	Y	N	Y	N	Y
9 Rothman	N	N	Y	N	Y
10 Payne	N	N	Y	N	Y
11 ***Frelinghuysen***	N	N	N	Y	Y
12 Holt	Y	N	Y	N	Y
13 Menendez	Y	N	Y	N	Y
NEW MEXICO					
1 ***Wilson***	N	N	N	Y	Y
2 ***Pearce***	N	N	N	Y	Y
3 Udall	N	N	Y	N	Y
NEW YORK					
1 Bishop	Y	N	Y	N	Y
2 Israel	Y	N	Y	N	Y
3 ***King***	N	N	N	Y	Y
4 McCarthy	Y	N	Y	N	Y
5 Ackerman	Y	N	Y	N	?
6 Meeks	Y	N	Y	N	Y
7 Crowley	N	N	Y	N	Y
8 Nadler	Y	N	Y	N	Y
9 Weiner	Y	N	Y	N	Y
10 Towns	Y	N	Y	N	Y
11 Owens	N	N	Y	N	Y
12 Velázquez	Y	N	Y	N	Y
13 ***Fossella***	N	N	N	Y	Y
14 Maloney	Y	N	Y	N	Y
15 Rangel	Y	N	Y	N	?
16 Serrano	Y	N	Y	N	Y
17 Engel	Y	N	Y	N	?
18 Lowey	N	N	Y	N	?
19 ***Kelly***	N	N	N	Y	Y
20 ***Sweeney***	N	N	N	Y	Y
21 McNulty	Y	N	Y	N	Y
22 Hinchey	Y	N	Y	N	?
23 ***McHugh***	N	N	N	Y	Y
24 ***Boehlert***	N	N	N	Y	Y
25 ***Walsh***	N	N	N	Y	Y

	89	90	91	92	93
26 ***Reynolds***	N	N	N	Y	Y
27 ***Quinn***	?	?	?	?	?
28 Slaughter	Y	N	Y	N	Y
29 ***Houghton***	N	N	N	Y	Y
NORTH CAROLINA					
1 Ballance	Y	N	Y	N	Y
2 Etheridge	Y	N	Y	N	Y
3 ***Jones***	N	Y	N	N	?
4 Price	Y	N	Y	N	Y
5 ***Burr***	N	N	N	Y	Y
6 ***Coble***	N	Y	N	Y	Y
7 McIntyre	Y	N	Y	N	Y
8 ***Hayes***	Y	N	N	Y	Y
9 ***Myrick***	N	Y	N	Y	Y
10 ***Ballenger***	N	Y	N	Y	Y
11 ***Taylor***	N	Y	N	Y	Y
12 Watt	Y	N	Y	N	Y
13 Miller	Y	N	Y	N	Y
NORTH DAKOTA					
AL Pomeroy	Y	N	Y	N	Y
OHIO					
1 ***Chabot***	N	Y	N	Y	Y
2 ***Portman***	N	N	N	Y	Y
3 ***Turner***	N	N	N	Y	?
4 ***Oxley***	N	Y	N	Y	Y
5 ***Gillmor***	N	N	N	Y	?
6 Strickland	N	N	Y	N	Y
7 ***Hobson***	N	N	N	Y	Y
8 ***Boehner***	N	Y	N	Y	Y
9 Kaptur	Y	N	Y	N	Y
10 Kucinich	N	N	N	N	Y
11 Jones	N	N	Y	N	Y
12 ***Tiberi***	N	N	N	Y	Y
13 Brown	Y	N	Y	N	Y
14 ***LaTourette***	N	N	N	Y	Y
15 ***Pryce***	N	N	N	Y	Y
16 ***Regula***	N	N	N	Y	Y
17 Ryan	Y	N	Y	N	Y
18 ***Ney***	N	N	N	Y	Y
OKLAHOMA					
1 ***Sullivan***	N	Y	N	Y	?
2 Carson	N	N	N	N	?
3 ***Lucas***	N	N	N	Y	Y
4 ***Cole***	N	Y	N	Y	Y
5 ***Istook***	N	Y	N	Y	Y
OREGON					
1 Wu	Y	N	Y	N	Y
2 ***Walden***	N	N	N	Y	Y
3 Blumenauer	Y	N	Y	N	Y
4 DeFazio	Y	N	Y	N	Y
5 Hooley	Y	N	Y	N	Y
PENNSYLVANIA					
1 Brady	Y	N	Y	N	Y
2 Fattah	Y	N	Y	N	Y
3 ***English***	N	Y	N	Y	Y
4 ***Hart***	N	Y	N	Y	Y
5 ***Peterson***	N	N	N	Y	Y
6 ***Gerlach***	N	N	N	Y	Y
7 ***Weldon***	N	N	N	Y	Y
8 ***Greenwood***	N	N	N	Y	Y
9 ***Shuster, Bill***	N	Y	N	Y	Y
10 ***Sherwood***	N	N	N	Y	Y
11 Kanjorski	N	N	Y	N	Y
12 Murtha	N	N	Y	N	?
13 Hoeffel	?	?	Y	N	Y
14 Doyle	Y	N	Y	N	?
15 ***Toomey***	N	Y	N	Y	Y
16 ***Pitts***	N	Y	N	Y	Y
17 Holden	Y	N	Y	N	?
18 ***Murphy***	N	Y	N	Y	Y
19 ***Platts***	N	N	N	Y	Y
RHODE ISLAND					
1 Kennedy	N	N	Y	N	Y
2 Langevin	Y	N	Y	N	Y
SOUTH CAROLINA					
1 ***Brown***	N	N	N	Y	Y
2 ***Wilson***	N	Y	N	Y	Y
3 ***Barrett***	N	Y	N	Y	Y
4 ***DeMint***	N	Y	N	Y	Y
5 Spratt	Y	N	Y	N	Y
6 Clyburn	Y	N	Y	N	Y
SOUTH DAKOTA					
AL Vacant					

	89	90	91	92	93
TENNESSEE					
1 ***Jenkins***	N	N	N	Y	Y
2 ***Duncan***	N	N	N	N	Y
3 ***Wamp***	N	N	N	Y	Y
4 Davis	Y	N	Y	N	?
5 Cooper	Y	N	Y	N	Y
6 Gordon	N	N	Y	N	Y
7 ***Blackburn***	N	Y	N	Y	Y
8 Tanner	Y	?	?	?	?
9 Ford	Y	N	?	?	?
TEXAS					
1 Sandlin	Y	N	Y	N	Y
2 Turner	Y	N	Y	N	Y
3 ***Johnson, Sam***	N	Y	N	Y	Y
4 ***Hall***	Y	N	N	Y	?
5 ***Hensarling***	N	Y	N	Y	Y
6 ***Barton***	N	Y	N	Y	Y
7 ***Culberson***	N	Y	N	Y	Y
8 ***Brady***	N	Y	N	Y	Y
9 Lampson	Y	N	Y	N	Y
10 Doggett	Y	N	Y	N	Y
11 Edwards	Y	N	Y	N	Y
12 ***Granger***	N	N	N	Y	Y
13 ***Thornberry***	N	Y	N	Y	Y
14 ***Paul***	N	Y	N	N	Y
15 Hinojosa	Y	N	Y	N	+
16 Reyes	Y	N	Y	N	?
17 Stenholm	Y	N	Y	N	Y
18 Jackson-Lee	Y	N	Y	N	Y
19 ***Neugebauer***	N	Y	N	Y	Y
20 Gonzalez	Y	N	Y	N	Y
21 ***Smith***	N	Y	N	Y	Y
22 ***DeLay***	N	Y	N	Y	Y
23 ***Bonilla***	N	N	N	Y	Y
24 Frost	Y	N	Y	N	Y
25 Bell	Y	N	Y	N	Y
26 ***Burgess***	N	Y	N	Y	Y
27 Ortiz	Y	N	Y	N	Y
28 Rodriguez	Y	N	Y	N	Y
29 Green	Y	N	Y	N	Y
30 Johnson, E.B.	Y	N	Y	N	Y
31 ***Carter***	N	Y	N	Y	Y
32 ***Sessions***	N	Y	N	Y	?
UTAH					
1 ***Bishop***	N	Y	N	Y	Y
2 Matheson	N	N	N	N	Y
3 ***Cannon***	N	Y	N	Y	Y
VERMONT					
AL *Sanders*	N	N	Y	N	Y
VIRGINIA					
1 ***Davis, Jo Ann***	N	Y	N	Y	Y
2 ***Schrock***	N	Y	N	Y	?
3 Scott	Y	N	Y	N	Y
4 ***Forbes***	N	Y	N	Y	Y
5 ***Goode***	N	Y	N	N	Y
6 ***Goodlatte***	N	Y	N	Y	Y
7 ***Cantor***	N	Y	N	Y	Y
8 Moran	Y	N	Y	N	?
9 Boucher	N	N	Y	N	Y
10 ***Wolf***	N	N	N	Y	Y
11 ***Davis, T.***	N	N	N	Y	Y
WASHINGTON					
1 Inslee	Y	N	Y	N	Y
2 Larsen	Y	N	Y	N	Y
3 Baird	Y	N	Y	N	Y
4 ***Hastings***	N	Y	N	Y	Y
5 ***Nethercutt***	N	N	N	Y	Y
6 Dicks	Y	N	Y	N	Y
7 McDermott	Y	N	Y	N	Y
8 ***Dunn***	N	Y	N	Y	Y
9 Smith	Y	N	Y	N	Y
WEST VIRGINIA					
1 Mollohan	N	N	Y	N	Y
2 ***Capito***	N	N	N	Y	Y
3 Rahall	N	N	Y	N	Y
WISCONSIN					
1 ***Ryan***	N	Y	N	Y	Y
2 Baldwin	Y	N	Y	N	Y
3 Kind	Y	N	Y	N	Y
4 Kleczka	Y	N	Y	N	Y
5 ***Sensenbrenner***	N	Y	N	Y	Y
6 ***Petri***	Y	N	N	Y	Y
7 Obey	N	N	Y	N	?
8 ***Green***	N	N	N	Y	Y
WYOMING					
AL ***Cubin***	N	Y	N	Y	Y

Southern states - Ala., Ark., Fla., Ga., Ky., La., Miss., N.C., Okla., S.C., Tenn., Texas, Va.

94. HR 2584. Utrok Atoll Monitoring/Concur with Senate Amendments. Gilchrest, R-Md., motion to suspend the rules and concur with the Senate amendments to the bill that would convey a decommissioned ship to the Utrok Atoll in the Marshall Islands to support radiological monitoring and resettlement of the atoll, whose residents were affected by U.S. nuclear testing. Motion agreed to 379-1: R 203-1; D 176-0 (ND 130-0, SD 46-0); I 0-0. A two-thirds majority of those present and voting (254 in this case) is required for passage under suspension of the rules. March 29, 2004.

95. HR 3723. Vaughn Gross Post Office/Passage. Carter, R-Texas, motion to suspend the rules and pass the bill that would name a post office building in Dallas after Vaughn Gross, the assistant superintendent of the Richardson Independent School District, located just outside of Dallas. Motion agreed to 379-0: R 204-0; D 175-0 (ND 130-0, SD 45-0); I 0-0. A two-thirds majority of those present and voting (253 in this case) is required for passage under suspension of the rules. March 29, 2004.

96. Procedural Motion/Journal. Approval of the House Journal of Monday, March 29, 2004. Approved 353-55: R 200-14; D 153-41 (ND 108-31, SD 45-10); I 0-0. March 30, 2004.

97. S Con Res 95. Fiscal 2005 Budget Resolution/Motion to Instruct. Thompson, D-Calif., motion to instruct House conferees to accept provisions in the Senate version of the budget resolution that would subject any tax cut or mandatory spending expansion to either a pay-as-you-go offset or a 60-vote point of order in the Senate. Motion rejected 209-209: R 11-209; D 197-0 (ND 142-0, SD 55-0); I 1-0. March 30, 2004.

98. HR 3966. Access for Military Recruiters/Previous Question. Myrick, R-N.C., motion to order the previous question (thus ending debate and possibility of amendment) on adoption of the rule (H Res 580) to provide for House floor consideration of the bill that would prohibit universities that bar access to Reserve Officer Training Corps or military recruiters from receiving certain federal funding. Motion agreed to 223-202: R 223-0; D 0-201 (ND 0-145, SD 0-56); I 0-1. March 30, 2004.

99. H Res 558. New NATO Members/Adoption. Bereuter, R-Neb., motion to suspend the rules and adopt the resolution that would express the sense of the House in welcoming the accession of Bulgaria, Estonia, Latvia, Lithuania, Romania, Slovakia and Slovenia to the North Atlantic Treaty Organization (NATO) and reaffirming that NATO expansion enhances the security of the United States and the North Atlantic area. Motion agreed to 422-2: R 220-2; D 201-0 (ND 145-0, SD 56-0); I 1-0, A two-thirds majority of those present and voting (283 in this case) is required for adoption under suspension of the rules. March 30, 2004.

100. S 2057. Military Travel Reimbursement/Passage. Bradley, R-N.H., motion to suspend the rules and pass the bill that would require the Defense Department to reimburse members of the armed services for one domestic round trip between Sept. 25, 2003, and Dec. 18, 2003, related to their leave from Iraq and Afghanistan. Motion agreed to 423-0: R 222-0; D 200-0 (ND 144-0, SD 56-0); I 1-0. A two-thirds majority of those present and voting (282 in this case) is required for passage under suspension of the rules. March 30, 2004.

101. HR 3966. Access for Military Recruiters/Passage. Passage of the bill that would prohibit universities that bar access to Reserve Officer Training Corps or military recruiters from receiving certain federal funding. Schools that receive federal funding would be required to provide military recruiters the same access to students as they offer other groups. Passed 343-81: R 220-2; D 123-78 (ND 75-71, SD 48-7); I 0-1. March 30, 2004.

Key

Y	Voted for (yea).
#	Paired for.
+	Announced for.
N	Voted against (nay).
X	Paired against.
–	Announced against.
P	Voted "present."
C	Voted "present" to avoid possible conflict of interest.
?	Did not vote or otherwise make a position known.

Democrats   ***Republicans***
Independents

	94	95	96	97	98	99	100	101
ALABAMA								
1 *Bonner*	Y	Y	Y	N	Y	Y	Y	Y
2 *Everett*	?	?	Y	N	Y	Y	Y	Y
3 *Rogers*	Y	Y	Y	N	Y	Y	Y	Y
4 *Aderholt*	Y	Y	Y	N	Y	Y	Y	Y
5 Cramer	Y	Y	Y	N	Y	Y	Y	Y
6 *Bachus*	?	?	Y	N	Y	Y	Y	Y
7 Davis	?	?	Y	Y	N	Y	Y	Y
ALASKA								
AL *Young*	Y	Y	Y	N	Y	Y	Y	Y
ARIZONA								
1 *Renzi*	Y	Y	Y	N	Y	Y	Y	Y
2 *Franks*	Y	Y	Y	N	Y	Y	Y	Y
3 *Shadegg*	Y	Y	Y	N	Y	Y	Y	Y
4 Pastor	Y	Y	N	Y	N	Y	Y	N
5 *Hayworth*	Y	Y	Y	N	Y	Y	Y	N
6 *Flake*	Y	Y	Y	N	Y	Y	Y	Y
7 Grijalva	Y	Y	Y	Y	N	Y	Y	N
8 *Kolbe*	Y	Y	Y	Y	Y	Y	Y	Y
ARKANSAS								
1 Berry	Y	Y	Y	Y	N	Y	Y	Y
2 Snyder	Y	Y	Y	Y	N	Y	Y	Y
3 *Boozman*	Y	Y	Y	N	Y	Y	Y	Y
4 Ross	Y	Y	Y	Y	N	Y	Y	Y
CALIFORNIA								
1 Thompson	Y	Y	N	Y	N	Y	N	N
2 *Herger*	Y	Y	Y	N	Y	Y	Y	Y
3 *Ose*	?	?	Y	N	Y	Y	Y	Y
4 *Doolittle*	?	?	Y	N	Y	Y	Y	Y
5 Matsui	Y	Y	Y	Y	N	Y	Y	N
6 Woolsey	Y	Y	Y	Y	N	Y	Y	N
7 Miller, George	Y	Y	N	Y	N	Y	Y	N
8 Pelosi	Y	Y	Y	Y	N	Y	Y	N
9 Lee	Y	Y	Y	Y	N	Y	Y	N
10 Tauscher	Y	Y	Y	Y	N	Y	Y	N
11 *Pombo*	Y	Y	Y	N	Y	Y	Y	Y
12 Lantos	Y	Y	Y	Y	N	Y	Y	N
13 Stark	?	?	?	Y	N	Y	Y	N
14 Eshoo	Y	Y	Y	Y	N	Y	Y	N
15 Honda	Y	Y	Y	Y	N	Y	Y	N
16 Lofgren	Y	Y	Y	Y	N	Y	Y	N
17 Farr	Y	Y	Y	Y	N	Y	Y	N
18 Cardoza	Y	Y	N	Y	N	Y	?	Y
19 *Radanovich*	Y	Y	Y	N	Y	Y	Y	Y
20 Dooley	Y	Y	Y	Y	N	Y	Y	N
21 *Nunes*	Y	Y	Y	N	Y	Y	Y	Y
22 *Thomas*	Y	Y	Y	N	Y	Y	Y	Y
23 Capps	Y	Y	Y	Y	N	Y	Y	N
24 *Gallegly*	+	+	Y	N	Y	Y	Y	Y
25 *McKeon*	Y	Y	Y	N	Y	Y	Y	Y
26 *Dreier*	Y	Y	Y	N	Y	Y	Y	Y
27 Sherman	Y	Y	Y	Y	N	Y	Y	Y
28 Berman	?	?	?	?	N	Y	Y	N
29 Schiff	Y	Y	Y	Y	N	Y	Y	N
30 Waxman	Y	Y	?	Y	N	Y	Y	N
31 Becerra	+	+	Y	Y	N	Y	Y	N
32 Solis	Y	Y	Y	Y	N	Y	Y	N
33 Watson	Y	Y	Y	Y	N	Y	Y	N
34 Roybal-Allard	Y	Y	Y	Y	N	Y	Y	N
35 Waters	Y	Y	N	Y	N	Y	Y	N
36 Harman	Y	Y	Y	Y	N	Y	Y	N

	94	95	96	97	98	99	100	101
37 Millendor McD.	Y	Y	Y	Y	N	Y	Y	Y
38 Napolitano	Y	Y	Y	N	Y	Y	Y	Y
39 Sánchez, Linda	Y	Y	Y	Y	N	Y	Y	N
40 *Royce*	Y	Y	Y	N	Y	Y	Y	Y
41 *Lewis*	Y	Y	Y	N	Y	Y	Y	Y
42 *Miller, Gary*	Y	Y	Y	N	Y	Y	Y	Y
43 Baca	Y	Y	Y	Y	N	Y	Y	Y
44 *Calvert*	Y	Y	Y	N	Y	Y	Y	Y
45 *Bono*	Y	Y	Y	N	Y	Y	Y	Y
46 *Rohrabacher*	Y	Y	Y	N	Y	Y	Y	Y
47 Sanchez, Loretta	Y	Y	Y	N	Y	Y	Y	Y
48 *Cox*	Y	Y	Y	N	Y	Y	Y	Y
49 *Issa*	Y	Y	Y	N	Y	Y	Y	Y
50 *Cunningham*	Y	Y	Y	N	Y	Y	Y	Y
51 Filner	Y	Y	N	Y	N	Y	Y	N
52 *Hunter*	?	?	Y	N	Y	Y	Y	Y
53 Davis	Y	Y	Y	N	Y	Y	Y	Y
COLORADO								
1 DeGette	Y	Y	Y	Y	N	Y	Y	N
2 Udall	Y	Y	N	Y	N	Y	Y	Y
3 *McInnis*	Y	Y	Y	N	Y	Y	Y	Y
4 *Musgrave*	Y	Y	Y	N	Y	Y	Y	Y
5 *Hefley*	?	?	N	N	Y	Y	Y	Y
6 *Tancredo*	Y	Y	P	N	Y	Y	Y	Y
7 *Beauprez*	Y	Y	Y	N	Y	Y	Y	Y
CONNECTICUT								
1 Larson	Y	Y	N	Y	N	Y	Y	N
2 *Simmons*	Y	Y	Y	N	Y	Y	Y	N
3 DeLauro	Y	Y	Y	Y	N	Y	Y	N
4 *Shays*	+	+	Y	Y	Y	Y	Y	Y
5 *Johnson*	Y	Y	Y	N	Y	Y	Y	Y
DELAWARE								
AL *Castle*	Y	Y	Y	Y	Y	Y	Y	Y
FLORIDA								
1 *Miller, J.*	Y	Y	Y	N	Y	Y	Y	Y
2 Boyd	Y	Y	Y	Y	N	Y	Y	Y
3 Brown	?	?	Y	Y	N	Y	Y	Y
4 *Crenshaw*	Y	Y	Y	N	Y	Y	Y	Y
5 *Brown-Waite*	Y	Y	Y	N	Y	Y	Y	Y
6 *Stearns*	Y	Y	Y	N	Y	Y	Y	Y
7 *Mica*	Y	Y	Y	N	Y	Y	Y	Y
8 *Keller*	Y	Y	Y	N	Y	Y	Y	Y
9 *Bilirakis*	Y	Y	Y	N	Y	Y	Y	Y
10 *Young*	?	?	Y	N	Y	Y	Y	Y
11 Davis	Y	Y	Y	Y	N	Y	Y	Y
12 *Putnam*	Y	Y	Y	N	Y	Y	Y	Y
13 *Harris*	Y	Y	?	N	Y	Y	Y	Y
14 *Goss*	Y	Y	Y	N	Y	Y	Y	Y
15 *Weldon*	Y	Y	Y	N	Y	Y	Y	Y
16 *Foley*	?	?	Y	N	Y	Y	Y	Y
17 Meek	Y	Y	Y	Y	N	Y	Y	N
18 *Ros-Lehtinen*	?	?	Y	N	Y	Y	Y	Y
19 Wexler	Y	Y	Y	Y	N	Y	Y	N
20 Deutsch	Y	Y	Y	Y	N	Y	Y	Y
21 *Diaz-Balart, L.*	Y	Y	Y	N	Y	Y	Y	Y
22 *Shaw*	Y	Y	Y	N	Y	Y	Y	Y
23 Hastings	Y	Y	Y	Y	N	Y	Y	N
24 *Feeney*	Y	Y	Y	N	Y	Y	Y	Y
25 *Diaz-Balart, M.*	Y	Y	Y	N	Y	Y	Y	Y
GEORGIA								
1 *Kingston*	Y	Y	Y	N	Y	Y	Y	Y
2 Bishop	Y	Y	Y	Y	N	Y	Y	Y
3 Marshall	Y	Y	Y	Y	N	Y	Y	Y
4 *Majette*	Y	Y	Y	N	Y	Y	Y	Y
5 Lewis	?	?	Y	N	Y	Y	Y	N
6 *Isakson*	Y	Y	Y	N	Y	Y	Y	Y
7 *Linder*	Y	Y	Y	N	Y	Y	Y	?
8 *Collins*	Y	Y	Y	N	Y	Y	Y	Y
9 *Norwood*	Y	Y	Y	N	Y	Y	Y	Y
10 *Deal*	Y	Y	Y	N	Y	Y	Y	Y
11 *Gingrey*	Y	Y	Y	N	Y	Y	Y	Y
12 *Burns*	Y	Y	Y	N	Y	Y	Y	Y
13 Scott	Y	Y	Y	Y	N	Y	Y	Y
HAWAII								
1 Abercrombie	Y	Y	Y	Y	N	Y	Y	N
2 Case	Y	Y	Y	Y	N	Y	Y	Y
IDAHO								
1 *Otter*	Y	Y	N	N	Y	Y	Y	Y
2 *Simpson*	Y	Y	Y	N	Y	Y	Y	Y
ILLINOIS								
1 Rush	Y	Y	Y	Y	N	Y	Y	N
2 Jackson	Y	Y	Y	Y	N	Y	Y	N
3 Lipinski	?	?	Y	Y	N	Y	Y	Y
4 Gutierrez	?	?	Y	Y	N	Y	Y	N
5 Emanuel	Y	Y	Y	Y	N	Y	Y	N
6 *Hyde*	Y	Y	Y	N	Y	Y	Y	Y

ND Northern Democrats   SD Southern Democrats

	94	95	96	97	98	99	100	101
7 Davis	Y	Y	Y	Y	N	Y	Y	N
8 ***Crane***	Y	Y	N	N	Y	Y	Y	Y
9 Schakowsky	Y	Y	N	Y	N	Y	Y	N
10 ***Kirk***	Y	Y	Y	N	Y	Y	Y	Y
11 ***Weller***	Y	Y	N	N	Y	Y	Y	Y
12 Costello	Y	Y	N	Y	N	Y	Y	Y
13 ***Biggert***	Y	Y	Y	N	Y	Y	Y	Y
14 ***Hastert***				N				
15 ***Johnson***	Y	Y	Y	N	Y	Y	Y	Y
16 ***Manzullo***	Y	Y	Y	N	Y	Y	Y	Y
17 Evans	Y	Y	Y	Y	N	Y	Y	Y
18 ***LaHood***	Y	Y	Y	N	Y	Y	Y	Y
19 ***Shimkus***	Y	Y	Y	N	Y	Y	Y	Y
INDIANA								
1 Visclosky	Y	Y	N	Y	N	Y	Y	Y
2 ***Chocola***	Y	Y	Y	N	Y	Y	?	Y
3 ***Souder***	Y	Y	Y	N	Y	Y	Y	Y
4 ***Buyer***	Y	Y	Y	N	Y	Y	Y	Y
5 ***Burton***	Y	Y	Y	?	Y	Y	Y	Y
6 ***Pence***	Y	Y	Y	N	Y	Y	Y	Y
7 Carson	Y	Y	Y	Y	N	Y	Y	Y
8 ***Hostettler***	Y	Y	Y	N	Y	Y	Y	Y
9 Hill	Y	Y	Y	Y	N	Y	Y	Y
IOWA								
1 ***Nussle***	Y	Y	Y	N	Y	Y	Y	Y
2 ***Leach***	Y	Y	Y	Y	Y	Y	Y	Y
3 Boswell	Y	Y	Y	Y	N	Y	Y	Y
4 ***Latham***	Y	Y	N	N	Y	Y	Y	Y
5 ***King***	Y	Y	Y	N	Y	Y	Y	Y
KANSAS								
1 ***Moran***	Y	Y	Y	N	Y	Y	Y	Y
2 ***Ryun***	Y	Y	Y	N	Y	Y	Y	Y
3 Moore	Y	Y	N	Y	N	Y	Y	Y
4 ***Tiahrt***	Y	Y	Y	N	Y	Y	Y	Y
KENTUCKY								
1 ***Whitfield***	Y	Y	Y	N	Y	Y	Y	Y
2 ***Lewis***	Y	Y	Y	N	Y	Y	Y	Y
3 ***Northup***	Y	Y	Y	N	Y	Y	Y	Y
4 Lucas	Y	Y	Y	Y	N	Y	Y	Y
5 ***Rogers***	Y	Y	Y	N	Y	Y	Y	Y
6 Chandler	Y	Y	Y	Y	N	Y	Y	Y
LOUISIANA								
1 ***Vitter***	Y	Y	Y	N	Y	Y	Y	Y
2 Jefferson	Y	Y	Y	Y	N	Y	Y	Y
3 ***Tauzin***	?	?	?	?	?	?	?	?
4 ***McCrery***	Y	Y	Y	N	Y	Y	Y	Y
5 Alexander	Y	Y	Y	Y	N	Y	Y	Y
6 ***Baker***	Y	Y	Y	N	Y	Y	Y	Y
7 John	?	?	Y	Y	N	Y	Y	Y
MAINE								
1 Allen	Y	Y	Y	Y	N	Y	Y	Y
2 Michaud	Y	Y	Y	Y	N	Y	Y	Y
MARYLAND								
1 ***Gilchrest***	Y	Y	Y	N	Y	Y	Y	Y
2 Ruppersberger	Y	Y	Y	Y	N	Y	Y	Y
3 Cardin	Y	Y	Y	Y	N	Y	Y	Y
4 Wynn	Y	Y	Y	Y	N	Y	Y	Y
5 Hoyer	Y	Y	?	+	N	Y	Y	Y
6 ***Bartlett***	Y	Y	Y	N	Y	N	Y	Y
7 Cummings	Y	Y	Y	Y	N	Y	Y	N
8 Van Hollen	Y	Y	Y	Y	N	Y	Y	Y
MASSACHUSETTS								
1 Olver	Y	Y	N	Y	N	Y	Y	N
2 Neal	?	?	?	?	N	Y	Y	N
3 McGovern	Y	Y	N	Y	N	Y	Y	N
4 Frank	?	?	?	?	N	Y	Y	N
5 Meehan	Y	Y	Y	Y	N	Y	Y	N
6 Tierney	Y	Y	Y	Y	N	Y	Y	N
7 Markey	Y	Y	Y	Y	N	Y	Y	N
8 Capuano	Y	Y	N	Y	N	Y	Y	N
9 Lynch	Y	Y	Y	Y	N	Y	Y	N
10 Delahunt	Y	Y	Y	Y	N	Y	Y	N
MICHIGAN								
1 Stupak	Y	Y	N	Y	N	Y	Y	Y
2 ***Hoekstra***	Y	Y	Y	N	Y	Y	Y	Y
3 ***Ehlers***	Y	Y	Y	N	Y	Y	Y	Y
4 ***Camp***	Y	Y	Y	N	Y	Y	Y	Y
5 Kildee	Y	Y	Y	Y	N	Y	Y	Y
6 ***Upton***	Y	Y	Y	N	Y	Y	Y	Y
7 ***Smith***	Y	Y	Y	N	Y	Y	Y	Y
8 ***Rogers***	Y	Y	Y	N	Y	Y	Y	Y
9 ***Knollenberg***	+	+	+	N	Y	Y	Y	Y
10 ***Miller***	Y	Y	Y	N	Y	Y	Y	Y
11 ***McCotter***	Y	Y	Y	N	Y	Y	Y	Y
12 Levin	Y	Y	Y	Y	N	Y	Y	Y

	94	95	96	97	98	99	100	101
13 Kilpatrick	+	+	Y	Y	N	Y	Y	Y
14 Conyers	Y	Y	?	?	N	Y	?	N
15 Dingell	Y	Y	?	Y	N	Y	Y	Y
MINNESOTA								
1 ***Gutknecht***	Y	Y	N	N	Y	Y	Y	?
2 ***Kline***	Y	Y	Y	N	Y	Y	Y	Y
3 ***Ramstad***	Y	Y	N	N	Y	Y	Y	Y
4 McCollum	Y	Y	Y	Y	N	Y	Y	Y
5 Sabo	Y	Y	N	Y	N	Y	Y	Y
6 ***Kennedy***	Y	Y	Y	N	Y	Y	Y	Y
7 Peterson	Y	Y	N	Y	N	Y	Y	Y
8 Oberstar	Y	Y	N	Y	N	Y	Y	N
MISSISSIPPI								
1 ***Wicker***	Y	Y	Y	N	Y	Y	Y	Y
2 Thompson	Y	Y	N	Y	N	Y	Y	Y
3 ***Pickering***	Y	Y	Y	N	Y	Y	Y	Y
4 Taylor	+	+	N	Y	N	Y	Y	Y
MISSOURI								
1 Clay	Y	Y	Y	Y	N	Y	Y	N
2 ***Akin***	Y	Y	Y	N	Y	Y	Y	Y
3 Gephardt	?	?	?	?	?	?	?	?
4 Skelton	Y	Y	Y	Y	N	Y	Y	Y
5 McCarthy	Y	Y	Y	Y	N	Y	Y	N
6 ***Graves***	Y	Y	N	N	Y	Y	Y	Y
7 ***Blunt***	Y	Y	Y	N	Y	Y	Y	Y
8 ***Emerson***	Y	Y	Y	Y	Y	Y	Y	Y
9 ***Hulshof***	?	?	?	?	?	?	?	?
MONTANA								
AL ***Rehberg***	Y	Y	Y	N	Y	Y	Y	Y
NEBRASKA								
1 ***Bereuter***	Y	Y	Y	Y	Y	Y	Y	Y
2 ***Terry***	?	?	Y	N	Y	Y	Y	Y
3 ***Osborne***	Y	Y	Y	N	Y	Y	Y	Y
NEVADA								
1 Berkley	Y	Y	Y	Y	N	Y	Y	Y
2 ***Gibbons***	Y	Y	Y	N	Y	Y	Y	Y
3 ***Porter***	Y	Y	Y	N	Y	Y	Y	Y
NEW HAMPSHIRE								
1 ***Bradley***	Y	Y	Y	N	Y	Y	Y	Y
2 ***Bass***	Y	Y	Y	Y	Y	Y	Y	Y
NEW JERSEY								
1 Andrews	Y	Y	Y	Y	N	Y	Y	Y
2 ***LoBiondo***	Y	Y	N	N	Y	Y	Y	Y
3 ***Saxton***	Y	Y	Y	N	Y	Y	Y	Y
4 ***Smith***	Y	Y	Y	N	Y	Y	Y	Y
5 ***Garrett***	Y	Y	Y	N	Y	Y	Y	Y
6 Pallone	Y	Y	Y	Y	N	Y	Y	N
7 ***Ferguson***	Y	Y	Y	N	Y	Y	Y	Y
8 Pascrell	Y	Y	Y	Y	N	Y	Y	N
9 Rothman	Y	Y	Y	Y	N	Y	Y	N
10 Payne	?	?	Y	Y	N	Y	Y	N
11 ***Frelinghuysen***	Y	Y	Y	N	Y	Y	Y	Y
12 Holt	Y	Y	Y	Y	N	Y	Y	N
13 Menendez	Y	Y	Y	Y	N	Y	Y	Y
NEW MEXICO								
1 ***Wilson***	Y	Y	Y	N	Y	Y	Y	Y
2 ***Pearce***	Y	Y	Y	N	Y	Y	Y	Y
3 Udall	Y	Y	N	Y	N	Y	Y	Y
NEW YORK								
1 Bishop	Y	Y	Y	Y	N	Y	Y	Y
2 Israel	Y	Y	Y	Y	N	Y	Y	Y
3 ***King***	Y	Y	Y	N	Y	Y	Y	Y
4 McCarthy	Y	Y	Y	Y	N	Y	Y	Y
5 Ackerman	?	?	N	Y	N	Y	Y	N
6 Meeks	Y	Y	Y	Y	N	Y	Y	N
7 Crowley	Y	Y	Y	Y	N	Y	Y	N
8 Nadler	Y	Y	Y	Y	N	Y	Y	N
9 Weiner	Y	Y	Y	Y	N	Y	Y	N
10 Towns	Y	Y	Y	Y	N	Y	Y	Y
11 Owens	Y	Y	Y	Y	N	Y	Y	N
12 Velázquez	Y	Y	Y	Y	N	Y	Y	N
13 ***Fossella***	Y	Y	?	?	Y	Y	Y	Y
14 Maloney	+	+	Y	Y	N	Y	Y	N
15 Rangel	Y	Y	Y	Y	N	Y	Y	N
16 Serrano	Y	Y	Y	Y	?	?	Y	N
17 Engel	Y	Y	Y	Y	N	Y	Y	Y
18 Lowey	Y	Y	Y	Y	N	Y	Y	Y
19 ***Kelly***	Y	Y	Y	N	Y	Y	Y	Y
20 ***Sweeney***	Y	Y	Y	N	Y	Y	Y	Y
21 McNulty	Y	Y	N	Y	N	Y	Y	Y
22 Hinchey	Y	Y	N	Y	N	Y	Y	N
23 ***McHugh***	Y	Y	Y	N	Y	Y	Y	Y
24 ***Boehlert***	Y	Y	Y	N	Y	Y	Y	Y
25 ***Walsh***	Y	Y	Y	N	Y	Y	Y	Y

	94	95	96	97	98	99	100	101
26 ***Reynolds***	Y	Y	Y	N	Y	Y	Y	Y
27 ***Quinn***	Y	Y	Y	N	Y	Y	Y	Y
28 Slaughter	Y	Y	Y	Y	N	Y	Y	Y
29 ***Houghton***	Y	Y	?	?	Y	Y	Y	Y
NORTH CAROLINA								
1 Ballance	Y	Y	N	Y	N	Y	Y	Y
2 Etheridge	+	+	Y	Y	N	Y	Y	Y
3 ***Jones***	Y	Y	Y	N	Y	Y	Y	Y
4 Price	Y	Y	Y	Y	N	Y	Y	Y
5 ***Burr***	?	?	Y	N	Y	Y	Y	Y
6 ***Coble***	Y	Y	Y	N	Y	Y	Y	Y
7 McIntyre	?	?	Y	Y	N	Y	Y	Y
8 ***Hayes***	Y	Y	Y	N	Y	Y	Y	Y
9 ***Myrick***	Y	Y	Y	N	Y	Y	Y	Y
10 ***Ballenger***	Y	Y	Y	N	Y	Y	Y	Y
11 ***Taylor***	?	?	?	?	Y	Y	Y	Y
12 Watt	Y	Y	Y	Y	N	Y	Y	N
13 MIller	Y	Y	Y	Y	N	Y	Y	Y
NORTH DAKOTA								
AL Pomeroy	?	Y	Y	Y	N	Y	Y	Y
OHIO								
1 ***Chabot***	Y	Y	Y	N	Y	Y	Y	Y
2 ***Portman***	+	+	Y	N	Y	Y	Y	Y
3 ***Turner***	Y	Y	Y	N	Y	Y	Y	Y
4 ***Oxley***	+	+	Y	N	Y	Y	Y	Y
5 ***Gillmor***	Y	Y	N	N	Y	Y	Y	Y
6 Strickland	Y	Y	N	Y	N	Y	Y	Y
7 ***Hobson***	Y	Y	Y	N	Y	Y	Y	Y
8 ***Boehner***	Y	Y	Y	N	Y	Y	Y	Y
9 Kaptur	Y	Y	Y	Y	N	Y	Y	Y
10 Kucinich	?	?	Y	Y	N	Y	Y	N
11 Jones	Y	Y	Y	Y	?	?	?	?
12 ***Tiberi***	Y	Y	Y	N	Y	Y	Y	Y
13 Brown	Y	Y	Y	Y	N	Y	Y	N
14 ***LaTourette***	Y	Y	Y	N	Y	Y	Y	Y
15 ***Pryce***	Y	Y	Y	N	Y	Y	Y	Y
16 ***Regula***	Y	Y	Y	N	Y	Y	Y	Y
17 Ryan	?	?	Y	Y	N	Y	Y	Y
18 ***Ney***	Y	Y	Y	N	Y	Y	Y	Y
OKLAHOMA								
1 ***Sullivan***	Y	Y	Y	N	Y	Y	Y	Y
2 Carson	?	?	Y	Y	N	Y	Y	Y
3 ***Lucas***	Y	Y	Y	N	Y	Y	Y	Y
4 ***Cole***	Y	Y	Y	N	Y	Y	Y	Y
5 ***Istook***	Y	Y	Y	N	Y	Y	Y	Y
OREGON								
1 Wu	Y	Y	N	Y	N	Y	Y	Y
2 ***Walden***	Y	Y	Y	N	Y	Y	Y	Y
3 Blumenauer	Y	Y	Y	Y	N	Y	Y	N
4 DeFazio	Y	Y	N	Y	N	Y	Y	Y
5 Hooley	Y	Y	Y	Y	N	Y	Y	Y
PENNSYLVANIA								
1 Brady	Y	Y	N	Y	N	Y	Y	N
2 Fattah	?	?	Y	Y	N	Y	Y	N
3 ***English***	Y	Y	N	N	Y	Y	Y	Y
4 ***Hart***	Y	Y	N	N	Y	Y	Y	Y
5 ***Peterson***	Y	Y	Y	N	Y	Y	Y	Y
6 ***Gerlach***	Y	Y	Y	N	Y	Y	Y	Y
7 ***Weldon***	Y	Y	Y	N	Y	Y	Y	Y
8 ***Greenwood***	?	?	Y	Y	Y	Y	Y	Y
9 ***Shuster, Bill***	Y	Y	Y	N	Y	Y	Y	Y
10 ***Sherwood***	Y	Y	N	N	Y	Y	Y	Y
11 Kanjorski	Y	Y	Y	Y	N	Y	Y	Y
12 Murtha	Y	?	Y	Y	N	Y	Y	Y
13 Hoeffel	?	?	Y	Y	N	Y	Y	Y
14 Doyle	Y	Y	Y	Y	N	Y	Y	Y
15 ***Toomey***	?	?	Y	N	Y	Y	Y	Y
16 ***Pitts***	Y	Y	Y	N	Y	Y	Y	Y
17 Holden	Y	Y	Y	Y	N	Y	Y	Y
18 ***Murphy***	Y	Y	Y	N	Y	Y	Y	Y
19 ***Platts***	Y	Y	N	N	Y	Y	Y	Y
RHODE ISLAND								
1 Kennedy	Y	Y	Y	Y	N	Y	Y	Y
2 Langevin	Y	Y	Y	Y	N	Y	Y	Y
SOUTH CAROLINA								
1 ***Brown***	Y	Y	Y	N	Y	Y	Y	Y
2 ***Wilson***	Y	Y	Y	N	Y	Y	Y	Y
3 ***Barrett***	+	+	Y	N	Y	Y	Y	Y
4 ***DeMint***	+	+	?	?	?	?	?	?
5 Spratt	Y	Y	Y	Y	N	Y	Y	Y
6 Clyburn	Y	Y	Y	Y	N	Y	Y	Y
SOUTH DAKOTA								
AL Vacant								

	94	95	96	97	98	99	100	101
TENNESSEE								
1 ***Jenkins***	Y	Y	Y	N	Y	Y	Y	Y
2 ***Duncan***	Y	Y	Y	N	Y	Y	Y	Y
3 ***Wamp***	Y	Y	Y	Y	Y	Y	Y	Y
4 Davis	Y	Y	N	Y	N	Y	Y	Y
5 Cooper	Y	Y	N	Y	N	Y	Y	Y
6 Gordon	Y	Y	Y	Y	N	Y	Y	Y
7 ***Blackburn***	Y	Y	?	N	Y	Y	Y	Y
8 Tanner	?	?	?	?	?	?	?	?
9 Ford	Y	Y	N	Y	N	Y	Y	Y
TEXAS								
1 Sandlin	Y	Y	Y	Y	N	Y	Y	Y
2 Turner	Y	Y	N	Y	N	Y	Y	Y
3 ***Johnson, Sam***	Y	Y	Y	N	Y	Y	Y	Y
4 ***Hall***	Y	Y	Y	N	Y	Y	Y	Y
5 ***Hensarling***	Y	Y	Y	N	Y	Y	Y	Y
6 ***Barton***	Y	Y	?	N	Y	Y	Y	Y
7 ***Culberson***	Y	Y	?	?	?	?	?	Y
8 ***Brady***	Y	Y	Y	N	Y	Y	Y	Y
9 Lampson	Y	Y	Y	Y	N	Y	Y	Y
10 Doggett	Y	Y	Y	Y	N	Y	Y	Y
11 Edwards	Y	Y	Y	Y	N	Y	Y	Y
12 ***Granger***	Y	Y	Y	N	Y	Y	Y	Y
13 ***Thornberry***	Y	Y	?	N	Y	Y	Y	Y
14 ***Paul***	N	Y	Y	N	Y	N	Y	N
15 Hinojosa	Y	Y	Y	Y	N	Y	Y	Y
16 Reyes	Y	Y	Y	Y	N	Y	Y	Y
17 Stenholm	Y	Y	N	Y	N	Y	Y	Y
18 Jackson-Lee	?	?	Y	Y	N	Y	Y	Y
19 ***Neugebauer***	Y	Y	Y	N	Y	Y	Y	Y
20 Gonzalez	Y	Y	Y	Y	N	Y	Y	Y
21 ***Smith***	Y	Y	Y	N	Y	Y	Y	Y
22 ***DeLay***	Y	Y	Y	N	Y	Y	Y	Y
23 ***Bonilla***	Y	Y	Y	N	Y	Y	Y	Y
24 Frost	Y	Y	Y	Y	N	Y	Y	Y
25 Bell	?	?	?	?	N	Y	Y	Y
26 ***Burgess***	Y	Y	Y	N	Y	Y	Y	Y
27 Ortiz	Y	Y	Y	Y	N	Y	Y	Y
28 Rodriguez	Y	Y	Y	Y	N	Y	Y	?
29 Green	Y	Y	N	Y	N	Y	Y	Y
30 Johnson, E.B.	Y	?	N	Y	N	Y	Y	Y
31 ***Carter***	Y	Y	Y	N	Y	?	?	Y
32 ***Sessions***	Y	Y	Y	N	Y	Y	Y	Y
UTAH								
1 ***Bishop***	Y	Y	Y	N	Y	Y	Y	Y
2 Matheson	Y	Y	Y	Y	N	Y	Y	Y
3 ***Cannon***	Y	Y	Y	N	Y	Y	Y	Y
VERMONT								
AL *Sanders*	?	?	?	Y	N	Y	Y	N
VIRGINIA								
1 ***Davis, Jo Ann***	Y	Y	Y	N	Y	Y	Y	Y
2 ***Schrook***	Y	Y	Y	N	Y	Y	Y	Y
3 Scott	Y	Y	Y	Y	N	Y	Y	N
4 ***Forbes***	Y	Y	Y	N	Y	Y	Y	Y
5 ***Goode***	Y	Y	Y	N	Y	Y	Y	Y
6 ***Goodlatte***	Y	Y	Y	N	Y	Y	Y	Y
7 ***Cantor***	Y	Y	Y	N	Y	Y	Y	Y
8 Moran	Y	Y	Y	Y	N	Y	Y	Y
9 Boucher	Y	Y	Y	Y	N	Y	Y	Y
10 ***Wolf***	Y	Y	Y	N	Y	Y	Y	Y
11 ***Davis, T.***	Y	Y	Y	N	Y	Y	Y	Y
WASHINGTON								
1 Inslee	Y	Y	Y	Y	N	Y	Y	Y
2 Larsen	Y	Y	N	Y	N	Y	Y	Y
3 Baird	Y	Y	N	Y	N	Y	Y	Y
4 ***Hastings***	Y	Y	Y	N	Y	Y	Y	Y
5 ***Nethercutt***	Y	Y	Y	N	Y	Y	Y	Y
6 Dicks	Y	Y	Y	Y	N	Y	Y	Y
7 McDermott	Y	Y	N	Y	N	Y	Y	N
8 ***Dunn***	Y	Y	Y	N	Y	Y	Y	Y
9 Smith	Y	Y	Y	Y	N	Y	Y	Y
WEST VIRGINIA								
1 Mollohan	Y	Y	Y	Y	N	Y	Y	Y
2 ***Capito***	Y	Y	Y	N	Y	Y	Y	Y
3 Rahall	?	?	Y	Y	N	Y	Y	Y
WISCONSIN								
1 ***Ryan***	Y	Y	Y	N	Y	Y	Y	Y
2 Baldwin	Y	Y	N	Y	N	Y	Y	N
3 Kind	Y	Y	Y	Y	N	Y	Y	Y
4 Kleczka	Y	Y	Y	Y	N	Y	Y	Y
5 ***Sensenbrenner***	Y	Y	Y	N	Y	Y	Y	N
6 ***Petri***	Y	Y	Y	Y	Y	Y	Y	Y
7 Obey	Y	Y	Y	Y	N	Y	Y	Y
8 ***Green***	Y	Y	Y	N	Y	Y	Y	Y
WYOMING								
AL ***Cubin***	Y	Y	Y	N	Y	Y	Y	Y

Southern states - Ala., Ark., Fla., Ga., Ky., La., Miss., N.C., Okla., S.C., Tenn., Texas, Va.

102. HR 3104. Military Medals/Passage. Simmons, R-Conn., motion to suspend the rules and pass the bill that would require the president to establish a campaign medal specifically to recognize service by members of the armed forces in Afghanistan and Iraq. Motion agreed to 423-0: R 222-0; D 200-0 (ND 145-0, SD 55-0); I 1-0. A two-thirds majority of those present and voting (282 in this case) is required for passage under suspension of the rules. March 30, 2004.

103. H Con Res 386. Air Force Academy Anniversary/Adoption. Wilson, R-N.M., motion to suspend the rules and adopt the concurrent resolution that would congratulate the U.S. Air Force Academy on its 50th anniversary, acknowledge the academy's role in U.S. defense and recognize the service provided by the academy's graduates. Motion agreed to 420-0: R 219-0; D 200-0 (ND 145-0, SD 55-0); I 1-0. A two-thirds majority of those present and voting (280 in this case) is required for adoption under suspension of the rules. March 30, 2004.

104. H Res 581. Federal Employee Pay Parity/Adoption. Adoption of the resolution that would express the sense of the House that federal civilian employees and military personnel should receive the same percentage pay increases in fiscal 2005, and that compensation must be sufficient to retain "quality" government employees. Adopted 299-126: R 95-126; D 203-0 (ND 148-0, SD 55-0); I 1-0. March 31, 2004.

105. HR 3550. Surface Transportation/Previous Question. Dreier, R-Calif., motion to order the previous question (thus ending debate and possibility of amendment) on adoption of the rule (H Res 593) to provide for House floor consideration of the bill that would authorize $275 billion for federal-aid highway, mass transit, safety and research programs from fiscal 2004 to 2009. Motion agreed to 229-194: R 215-5; D 14-188 (ND 13-133, SD 1-55); I 0-1. April 1, 2004.

106. HR 3550. Surface Transportation/Earmarked Funding. Flake, R-Ariz., amendment that would subtract the amount that states receive in high priority program earmarks from their formula totals for the Surface Transportation Program. Rejected 60-367: R 55-169; D 5-197 (ND 3-143, SD 2-54); I 0-1. April 1, 2004.

107. HR 3550. Surface Transportation/Toll Credits. Jackson-Lee, D-Texas, amendment that would allow states to receive toll credits — government credits that match toll revenues — for any local, state or private funds contributed to a toll project that exceed the minimum non-federal 20 percent threshold required for federal matching funds. Rejected 50-376: R 27-196; D 23-179 (ND 7-139, SD 16-40); I 0-1. April 1, 2004.

108. HR 3550. Surface Transportation/Truck Weight Limit Exclusion. Chocola, R-Ind., amendment that would provide for a 400-pound weight limit exclusion for any heavy-duty motor vehicle equipped with EPA-approved "idling reduction technology," which is intended to reduce emissions and fuel consumption. Rejected 198-228: R 182-41; D 16-186 (ND 7-139, SD 9-47); I 0-1. April 1, 2004.

109. HR 3550. Surface Transportation/Trucking Rest Periods. Bachus, R-Ala., amendment that would exempt motion picture and television production truck drivers from new hours-of-service regulations, which increased required rest periods for truck drivers by two hours. Adopted 365-62: R 209-15; D 155-47 (ND 106-40, SD 49-7); I 1-0. April 1, 2004.

Key

Y	Voted for (yea).
#	Paired for.
+	Announced for.
N	Voted against (nay).
X	Paired against.
–	Announced against.
P	Voted "present."
C	Voted "present" to avoid possible conflict of interest.
?	Did not vote or otherwise make a position known.

Democrats **Republicans**
Independents

	102	103	104	105	106	107	108	109
ALABAMA								
1 *Bonner*	Y	Y	N	Y	N	N	Y	Y
2 *Everett*	Y	Y	Y	Y	N	Y	N	Y
3 *Rogers*	Y	?	Y	Y	N	N	Y	Y
4 *Aderholt*	Y	Y	N	Y	N	N	Y	Y
5 Cramer	Y	Y	Y	N	N	N	Y	Y
6 *Bachus*	Y	Y	N	Y	N	N	Y	Y
7 Davis	Y	Y	Y	N	N	Y	N	Y
ALASKA								
AL *Young*	Y	Y	Y	Y	N	N	?	N
ARIZONA								
1 *Renzi*	Y	Y	Y	Y	Y	N	Y	Y
2 *Franks*	Y	Y	N	Y	Y	N	Y	Y
3 *Shadegg*	Y	Y	N	Y	Y	Y	Y	Y
4 Pastor	Y	Y	Y	N	N	N	N	Y
5 *Hayworth*	Y	Y	N	Y	N	N	Y	Y
6 *Flake*	Y	Y	N	Y	Y	Y	Y	Y
7 Grijalva	Y	Y	Y	N	N	N	N	Y
8 *Kolbe*	Y	Y	Y	Y	N	Y	Y	Y
ARKANSAS								
1 Berry	Y	Y	Y	N	N	N	N	N
2 Snyder	Y	Y	Y	N	N	N	N	N
3 *Boozman*	Y	Y	N	Y	N	N	Y	Y
4 Ross	Y	Y	Y	N	N	N	N	Y
CALIFORNIA								
1 Thompson	Y	Y	Y	N	N	N	N	Y
2 *Herger*	Y	Y	N	Y	N	N	Y	Y
3 *Ose*	Y	Y	N	Y	N	N	Y	Y
4 *Doolittle*	Y	Y	N	Y	N	N	Y	Y
5 Matsui	Y	?	Y	N	N	N	N	Y
6 Woolsey	Y	Y	Y	N	N	N	N	Y
7 Miller, George	Y	Y	Y	N	N	N	N	Y
8 Pelosi	Y	Y	Y	N	N	N	N	Y
9 Lee	Y	Y	Y	N	N	N	N	Y
10 Tauscher	Y	Y	Y	N	N	N	N	Y
11 *Pombo*	Y	Y	N	Y	N	N	Y	Y
12 Lantos	?	Y	Y	N	N	N	N	Y
13 Stark	Y	Y	Y	N	N	N	N	N
14 Eshoo	Y	Y	Y	N	N	N	N	Y
15 Honda	Y	Y	Y	?	N	N	N	Y
16 Lofgren	Y	Y	Y	N	N	N	N	Y
17 Farr	Y	Y	Y	N	N	N	N	Y
18 Cardoza	Y	Y	Y	N	N	N	Y	Y
19 *Radanovich*	Y	Y	Y	N	N	N	Y	Y
20 Dooley	Y	Y	Y	N	N	N	N	Y
21 *Nunes*	Y	Y	Y	Y	N	Y	Y	Y
22 *Thomas*	Y	Y	Y	Y	N	N	Y	Y
23 Capps	Y	Y	Y	N	N	N	N	Y
24 *Gallegly*	Y	Y	Y	Y	N	N	N	Y
25 *McKeon*	Y	Y	N	Y	N	N	Y	Y
26 *Dreier*	Y	Y	Y	Y	N	Y	Y	Y
27 Sherman	Y	Y	Y	N	N	N	N	Y
28 Berman	Y	Y	Y	N	N	N	N	Y
29 Schiff	Y	Y	Y	N	N	N	N	Y
30 Waxman	Y	Y	Y	N	?	?	?	?
31 Becerra	Y	Y	Y	N	N	N	N	Y
32 Solis	Y	Y	Y	N	N	N	N	Y
33 Watson	Y	Y	Y	N	N	N	N	Y
34 Roybal-Allard	Y	Y	Y	N	N	N	N	Y
35 Waters	Y	Y	Y	N	N	N	N	Y
36 Harman	Y	Y	Y	N	N	N	N	Y
COLORADO								
1 DeGette	Y	Y	Y	N	N	N	N	Y
2 Udall	Y	Y	Y	N	N	Y	N	Y
3 *McInnis*	Y	Y	N	Y	N	N	Y	Y
4 *Musgrave*	Y	Y	Y	Y	N	N	Y	Y
5 *Hefley*	Y	Y	N	Y	N	N	Y	Y
6 *Tancredo*	Y	?	N	N	Y	N	Y	Y
7 *Beauprez*	Y	Y	N	Y	N	N	Y	Y
CONNECTICUT								
1 Larson	Y	Y	Y	N	N	N	N	Y
2 *Simmons*	Y	Y	Y	N	N	N	N	Y
3 DeLauro	Y	Y	Y	N	N	N	N	Y
4 *Shays*	Y	Y	N	Y	N	N	N	Y
5 *Johnson*	Y	Y	N	Y	N	N	N	Y
DELAWARE								
AL *Castle*	Y	Y	Y	N	N	N	N	Y
FLORIDA								
1 *Miller, J.*	Y	Y	Y	Y	N	Y	Y	Y
2 Boyd	Y	Y	Y	N	N	N	N	Y
3 Brown	Y	Y	Y	N	N	N	N	Y
4 *Crenshaw*	Y	Y	Y	Y	N	N	Y	Y
5 *Brown-Waite*	Y	Y	N	?	N	N	Y	Y
6 *Stearns*	Y	Y	Y	Y	Y	Y	Y	N
7 *Mica*	Y	Y	N	Y	N	N	Y	Y
8 *Keller*	Y	Y	N	Y	N	N	Y	Y
9 *Bilirakis*	Y	Y	N	Y	N	N	Y	Y
10 *Young*	Y	Y	Y	N	N	N	N	Y
11 Davis	Y	Y	Y	N	Y	N	N	Y
12 *Putnam*	Y	Y	N	Y	N	N	Y	Y
13 *Harris*	Y	Y	?	Y	N	Y	Y	Y
14 *Goss*	Y	Y	Y	N	N	N	Y	Y
15 *Weldon*	Y	Y	N	Y	N	Y	N	N
16 *Foley*	Y	Y	Y	N	N	N	Y	Y
17 Meek	Y	Y	Y	N	N	N	N	Y
18 *Ros-Lehtinen*	Y	Y	N	Y	N	N	Y	Y
19 Wexler	Y	Y	Y	N	N	N	N	Y
20 Deutsch	Y	Y	Y	N	N	N	N	Y
21 *Diaz-Balart, L.*	Y	Y	Y	N	N	N	Y	Y
22 *Shaw*	Y	Y	Y	N	N	N	Y	Y
23 Hastings	Y	Y	Y	N	N	Y	N	N
24 *Feeney*	Y	Y	N	Y	N	N	N	Y
25 *Diaz-Balart, M.*	Y	Y	N	Y	N	N	Y	Y
GEORGIA								
1 *Kingston*	Y	Y	N	Y	N	Y	N	Y
2 Bishop	Y	Y	Y	N	N	N	N	Y
3 Marshall	Y	Y	Y	N	N	N	Y	Y
4 Majette	Y	Y	N	Y	N	Y	N	Y
5 Lewis	Y	Y	Y	N	N	N	N	Y
6 *Isakson*	Y	Y	N	Y	N	Y	Y	Y
7 *Linder*	Y	Y	N	Y	N	Y	N	Y
8 *Collins*	Y	Y	Y	Y	N	N	Y	N
9 *Norwood*	Y	Y	Y	N	N	N	Y	Y
10 *Deal*	Y	Y	N	Y	N	Y	Y	Y
11 *Gingrey*	Y	Y	N	Y	N	N	Y	Y
12 *Burns*	Y	Y	Y	Y	N	Y	Y	Y
13 Scott	Y	Y	Y	N	N	N	N	Y
HAWAII								
1 Abercrombie	Y	Y	Y	N	N	N	N	Y
2 Case	Y	Y	Y	N	N	N	N	N
IDAHO								
1 *Otter*	Y	Y	N	Y	Y	Y	Y	Y
2 *Simpson*	Y	Y	N	Y	Y	N	N	Y
ILLINOIS								
1 Rush	Y	Y	Y	N	N	N	N	Y
2 Jackson	Y	Y	Y	N	N	N	N	Y
3 Lipinski	Y	Y	Y	N	N	N	N	Y
4 Gutierrez	Y	Y	Y	N	N	N	N	Y
5 Emanuel	Y	Y	Y	N	N	N	N	Y
6 *Hyde*	Y	Y	Y	N	N	N	Y	Y

	102	103	104	105	106	107	108	109
37 Millender-McD.	Y	Y	Y	N	N	N	N	Y
38 Napolitano	Y	Y	Y	N	N	N	N	Y
39 Sánchez, Linda	Y	Y	Y	N	N	N	N	Y
40 *Royce*	Y	Y	N	Y	N	Y	Y	Y
41 *Lewis*	Y	Y	Y	Y	N	Y	Y	Y
42 *Miller, Gary*	Y	N	N	N	N	Y	Y	Y
43 Baca	Y	Y	Y	N	N	N	N	Y
44 *Calvert*	Y	Y	Y	N	N	N	Y	Y
45 *Bono*	Y	Y	Y	N	N	N	Y	Y
46 *Rohrabacher*	Y	Y	N	Y	N	N	N	Y
47 Sanchez, Loretta	Y	Y	Y	N	N	N	N	Y
48 *Cox*	?	Y	N	Y	N	N	Y	Y
49 *Issa*	Y	Y	N	Y	N	N	Y	Y
50 *Cunningham*	Y	Y	N	Y	N	N	Y	Y
51 Filner	Y	Y	Y	N	N	N	N	N
52 *Hunter*	Y	Y	N	Y	N	Y	Y	Y
53 Davis	Y	Y	Y	N	N	N	N	Y

ND Northern Democrats SD Southern Democrats

Member	102	103	104	105	106	107	108	109
7 Davis	Y	Y	Y	N	N	N	N	Y
8 ***Crane***	Y	Y	N	Y	N	N	Y	Y
9 Schakowsky	Y	Y	Y	N	N	N	N	Y
10 ***Kirk***	Y	Y	?	Y	N	N	Y	Y
11 ***Weller***	Y	Y	N	Y	N	N	Y	Y
12 Costello	Y	Y	Y	Y	N	N	N	N
13 ***Biggert***	Y	Y	N	Y	N	N	Y	Y
14 ***Hastert***								
15 ***Johnson***	Y	Y	Y	Y	N	N	N	Y
16 ***Manzullo***	Y	Y	Y	Y	N	N	Y	Y
17 Evans	Y	Y	Y	N	N	N	N	Y
18 ***LaHood***	Y	Y	Y	Y	N	N	Y	Y
19 ***Shimkus***	Y	Y	Y	Y	N	N	Y	Y
INDIANA								
1 Visclosky	Y	Y	Y	N	N	N	Y	N
2 ***Chocola***	Y	Y	N	Y	N	N	Y	Y
3 ***Souder***	Y	Y	N	Y	N	N	Y	Y
4 ***Buyer***	Y	Y	N	Y	N	N	Y	Y
5 ***Burton***	Y	Y	N	Y	N	N	Y	Y
6 ***Pence***	Y	Y	N	Y	Y	Y	Y	Y
7 Carson	Y	Y	Y	N	N	Y	Y	Y
8 ***Hostettler***	Y	Y	Y	Y	N	N	Y	N
9 Hill	Y	Y	Y	N	N	N	Y	Y
IOWA								
1 ***Nussle***	Y	Y	N	Y	N	N	Y	Y
2 ***Leach***	Y	Y	Y	Y	N	N	Y	Y
3 Boswell	Y	Y	Y	N	N	N	N	Y
4 ***Latham***	Y	Y	Y	Y	N	N	Y	Y
5 ***King***	Y	Y	N	Y	Y	N	Y	Y
KANSAS								
1 ***Moran***	Y	Y	N	Y	N	N	Y	Y
2 ***Ryun***	Y	Y	N	Y	N	N	Y	Y
3 Moore	Y	Y	Y	N	N	N	N	Y
4 ***Tiahrt***	Y	Y	N	Y	N	N	Y	Y
KENTUCKY								
1 ***Whitfield***	Y	Y	Y	Y	N	N	Y	Y
2 ***Lewis***	Y	Y	Y	Y	N	?	Y	Y
3 ***Northup***	Y	?	N	Y	N	N	Y	Y
4 Lucas	Y	Y	Y	N	N	N	N	Y
5 ***Rogers***	Y	Y	N	Y	N	N	Y	Y
6 Chandler	Y	Y	Y	N	N	N	N	Y
LOUISIANA								
1 ***Vitter***	Y	Y	N	Y	N	Y	Y	Y
2 Jefferson	Y	Y	Y	N	N	N	N	Y
3 ***Tauzin***	?	?	?	?	?	?	?	?
4 ***McCrery***	Y	Y	N	Y	N	N	Y	Y
5 Alexander	Y	Y	Y	N	N	N	N	N
6 ***Baker***	Y	Y	N	Y	N	N	N	Y
7 John	Y	Y	Y	N	N	N	Y	Y
MAINE								
1 Allen	Y	Y	Y	N	N	N	N	Y
2 Michaud	Y	Y	Y	N	N	N	N	Y
MARYLAND								
1 ***Gilchrest***	Y	Y	Y	Y	N	N	Y	Y
2 Ruppersberger	Y	Y	Y	N	N	N	N	Y
3 Cardin	Y	Y	Y	N	N	N	N	Y
4 Wynn	Y	Y	Y	N	N	Y	N	Y
5 Hoyer	Y	Y	Y	N	N	N	N	Y
6 ***Bartlett***	Y	Y	N	Y	Y	N	Y	Y
7 Cummings	Y	Y	Y	N	N	Y	N	Y
8 Van Hollen	Y	Y	Y	N	N	N	N	Y
MASSACHUSETTS								
1 Olver	Y	Y	Y	N	N	N	N	Y
2 Neal	Y	Y	Y	N	N	N	N	Y
3 McGovern	Y	Y	Y	N	N	N	N	Y
4 Frank	Y	Y	Y	N	N	N	N	N
5 Meehan	Y	Y	Y	N	N	N	N	Y
6 Tierney	Y	Y	Y	N	N	N	N	N
7 Markey	Y	Y	Y	N	N	N	N	N
8 Capuano	Y	Y	Y	Y	N	N	N	N
9 Lynch	Y	Y	Y	N	N	N	N	Y
10 Delahunt	Y	Y	Y	Y	N	N	N	N
MICHIGAN								
1 Stupak	Y	Y	Y	N	N	N	N	N
2 ***Hoekstra***	Y	Y	N	Y	N	N	Y	Y
3 ***Ehlers***	Y	Y	N	Y	N	N	Y	Y
4 ***Camp***	Y	Y	N	Y	N	N	N	Y
5 Kildee	Y	Y	Y	N	N	N	N	N
6 ***Upton***	Y	Y	Y	Y	N	N	Y	Y
7 ***Smith***	Y	Y	N	Y	Y	N	Y	Y
8 ***Rogers***	Y	Y	N	Y	N	N	N	Y
9 ***Knollenberg***	Y	Y	N	Y	N	N	Y	Y
10 ***Miller***	Y	Y	Y	Y	N	N	Y	Y
11 ***McCotter***	Y	Y	Y	Y	N	N	Y	Y
12 Levin	Y	Y	Y	N	N	N	N	N
13 Kilpatrick	Y	Y	Y	N	N	N	N	N
14 Conyers	Y	Y	Y	N	N	Y	N	N
15 Dingell	Y	Y	Y	N	N	N	N	N
MINNESOTA								
1 ***Gutknecht***	?	?	N	Y	Y	N	Y	Y
2 ***Kline***	Y	Y	N	Y	Y	N	Y	Y
3 ***Ramstad***	Y	Y	N	Y	Y	N	Y	Y
4 McCollum	Y	Y	Y	N	N	N	N	N
5 Sabo	Y	Y	Y	N	N	N	N	N
6 ***Kennedy***	Y	Y	N	Y	Y	N	Y	Y
7 Peterson	Y	Y	Y	Y	N	N	N	Y
8 Oberstar	Y	Y	Y	N	N	N	N	N
MISSISSIPPI								
1 ***Wicker***	Y	Y	N	Y	N	N	Y	Y
2 Thompson	Y	Y	Y	N	N	N	N	Y
3 ***Pickering***	Y	Y	?	Y	N	N	Y	Y
4 Taylor	Y	Y	Y	N	N	N	N	Y
MISSOURI								
1 Clay	Y	Y	Y	N	N	N	N	Y
2 ***Akin***	Y	Y	N	Y	Y	N	Y	Y
3 Gephardt	?	?	Y	?	?	?	?	?
4 Skelton	Y	Y	Y	N	N	N	N	N
5 McCarthy	Y	Y	Y	N	N	N	N	Y
6 ***Graves***	Y	Y	Y	Y	N	N	Y	Y
7 ***Blunt***	Y	Y	N	Y	N	N	Y	Y
8 ***Emerson***	Y	Y	Y	Y	N	N	N	Y
9 ***Hulshof***	?	?	?	?	?	?	?	?
MONTANA								
AL ***Rehberg***	Y	Y	N	Y	N	N	Y	Y
NEBRASKA								
1 ***Bereuter***	Y	Y	Y	Y	N	N	Y	Y
2 ***Terry***	Y	Y	N	Y	N	N	Y	Y
3 ***Osborne***	Y	Y	N	Y	N	N	N	Y
NEVADA								
1 Berkley	Y	Y	Y	N	N	N	N	Y
2 ***Gibbons***	Y	Y	N	?	N	N	Y	Y
3 ***Porter***	Y	Y	Y	Y	N	N	Y	Y
NEW HAMPSHIRE								
1 ***Bradley***	Y	Y	Y	?	Y	N	Y	Y
2 ***Bass***	Y	Y	N	Y	Y	N	Y	Y
NEW JERSEY								
1 Andrews	Y	Y	Y	Y	N	N	N	N
2 ***LoBiondo***	Y	Y	Y	Y	N	N	Y	Y
3 ***Saxton***	Y	Y	N	Y	N	N	Y	Y
4 ***Smith***	Y	Y	Y	Y	N	N	Y	Y
5 ***Garrett***	Y	Y	N	Y	Y	N	Y	Y
6 Pallone	Y	Y	Y	N	N	N	N	N
7 ***Ferguson***	Y	Y	Y	Y	N	N	Y	Y
8 Pascrell	Y	Y	Y	Y	N	N	N	Y
9 Rothman	Y	Y	Y	N	N	N	N	Y
10 Payne	Y	Y	Y	N	N	N	N	Y
11 ***Frelinghuysen***	Y	Y	Y	Y	N	N	N	Y
12 Holt	Y	Y	Y	N	N	N	N	N
13 Menendez	Y	Y	Y	N	N	N	N	Y
NEW MEXICO								
1 ***Wilson***	Y	Y	Y	Y	N	N	Y	Y
2 ***Pearce***	Y	Y	Y	Y	N	N	Y	Y
3 Udall	Y	Y	Y	N	N	N	N	Y
NEW YORK								
1 Bishop	Y	Y	Y	N	N	N	N	Y
2 Israel	Y	Y	Y	N	N	N	N	Y
3 ***King***	Y	Y	Y	Y	N	N	Y	Y
4 McCarthy	Y	Y	Y	N	N	N	N	Y
5 Ackerman	Y	Y	Y	N	N	N	N	Y
6 Meeks	Y	Y	Y	N	N	N	N	Y
7 Crowley	Y	Y	Y	Y	N	N	N	N
8 Nadler	Y	Y	Y	Y	N	N	N	Y
9 Weiner	Y	Y	Y	N	N	N	N	Y
10 Towns	Y	Y	Y	N	N	N	N	Y
11 Owens	Y	Y	Y	N	N	N	N	N
12 Velázquez	Y	Y	Y	N	N	N	N	Y
13 ***Fossella***	Y	Y	Y	Y	N	Y	Y	Y
14 Maloney	Y	Y	Y	N	N	N	N	Y
15 Rangel	Y	Y	Y	N	N	N	Y	Y
16 Serrano	Y	Y	Y	N	N	N	N	Y
17 Engel	Y	Y	Y	N	N	N	N	Y
18 Lowey	Y	Y	Y	N	N	N	N	Y
19 ***Kelly***	Y	Y	Y	Y	N	N	Y	Y
20 ***Sweeney***	Y	Y	Y	Y	N	N	Y	Y
21 McNulty	Y	Y	Y	N	N	N	N	Y
22 Hinchey	Y	Y	Y	N	N	N	N	Y
23 ***McHugh***	Y	Y	?	Y	N	N	Y	Y
24 ***Boehlert***	Y	Y	Y	Y	N	N	Y	Y
25 ***Walsh***	Y	Y	Y	Y	N	N	Y	N
26 ***Reynolds***	Y	Y	N	Y	N	N	Y	Y
27 ***Quinn***	Y	Y	Y	?	N	N	Y	Y
28 Slaughter	Y	Y	Y	N	N	N	N	Y
29 ***Houghton***	Y	Y	Y	Y	N	N	N	Y
NORTH CAROLINA								
1 Ballance	Y	Y	Y	N	N	Y	N	Y
2 Etheridge	Y	Y	Y	N	N	N	N	Y
3 ***Jones***	Y	Y	Y	N	N	N	Y	Y
4 Price	Y	Y	Y	N	N	N	N	Y
5 ***Burr***	Y	Y	Y	Y	N	N	Y	Y
6 ***Coble***	Y	Y	N	Y	N	N	Y	Y
7 McIntyre	Y	Y	Y	N	N	N	N	Y
8 ***Hayes***	Y	Y	N	Y	N	N	Y	Y
9 ***Myrick***	Y	Y	N	Y	Y	N	Y	Y
10 ***Ballenger***	Y	Y	N	Y	N	N	N	Y
11 ***Taylor***	Y	Y	N	Y	N	N	N	Y
12 Watt	Y	Y	Y	N	N	N	N	Y
13 Miller	Y	Y	Y	N	N	N	N	Y
NORTH DAKOTA								
AL Pomeroy	Y	Y	Y	N	N	N	N	Y
OHIO								
1 ***Chabot***	Y	Y	N	Y	Y	N	Y	Y
2 ***Portman***	Y	Y	N	Y	N	N	Y	Y
3 ***Turner***	Y	Y	Y	Y	N	N	Y	Y
4 ***Oxley***	Y	Y	N	Y	N	N	Y	Y
5 ***Gillmor***	Y	Y	Y	Y	N	N	N	Y
6 Strickland	Y	Y	Y	N	N	N	N	Y
7 ***Hobson***	Y	Y	Y	Y	N	N	Y	Y
8 ***Boehner***	Y	Y	Y	Y	Y	N	Y	Y
9 Kaptur	Y	Y	Y	N	N	N	N	Y
10 Kucinich	Y	Y	Y	N	N	N	N	N
11 Jones	?	?	Y	N	N	N	N	Y
12 ***Tiberi***	Y	Y	Y	Y	N	N	Y	Y
13 Brown	Y	Y	Y	N	N	N	N	Y
14 ***LaTourette***	Y	Y	Y	Y	N	N	Y	Y
15 ***Pryce***	Y	Y	Y	Y	N	N	Y	Y
16 ***Regula***	Y	Y	Y	Y	N	N	Y	Y
17 Ryan	Y	Y	Y	N	N	N	N	N
18 ***Ney***	Y	Y	N	Y	N	N	Y	Y
OKLAHOMA								
1 ***Sullivan***	Y	Y	N	Y	Y	N	Y	Y
2 Carson	Y	Y	Y	N	N	N	N	Y
3 ***Lucas***	Y	Y	Y	Y	N	N	Y	Y
4 ***Cole***	Y	Y	Y	Y	N	N	Y	Y
5 ***Istook***	Y	Y	N	Y	N	N	N	Y
OREGON								
1 Wu	Y	Y	Y	N	N	N	N	N
2 ***Walden***	Y	Y	Y	Y	N	Y	Y	Y
3 Blumenauer	Y	Y	Y	N	N	N	N	Y
4 DeFazio	Y	Y	Y	Y	N	N	N	N
5 Hooley	Y	Y	Y	N	N	N	N	Y
PENNSYLVANIA								
1 Brady	Y	Y	Y	N	N	N	N	Y
2 Fattah	Y	Y	Y	N	N	N	N	Y
3 ***English***	Y	Y	Y	Y	N	N	N	Y
4 ***Hart***	Y	Y	N	Y	N	N	Y	Y
5 ***Peterson***	Y	Y	N	Y	N	N	Y	Y
6 ***Gerlach***	Y	Y	Y	Y	N	N	Y	Y
7 ***Weldon***	Y	Y	Y	Y	N	N	Y	Y
8 ***Greenwood***	Y	Y	Y	Y	N	N	Y	Y
9 ***Shuster, Bill***	Y	Y	N	Y	N	N	Y	Y
10 ***Sherwood***	Y	Y	N	Y	N	N	N	N
11 Kanjorski	Y	Y	Y	N	N	N	N	Y
12 Murtha	Y	Y	Y	N	N	N	N	Y
13 Hoeffel	Y	Y	Y	Y	N	N	N	Y
14 Doyle	Y	Y	Y	N	N	N	N	Y
15 ***Toomey***	Y	Y	N	Y	N	Y	Y	Y
16 ***Pitts***	Y	Y	Y	Y	N	Y	Y	Y
17 Holden	Y	Y	Y	Y	N	N	N	Y
18 ***Murphy***	Y	?	Y	Y	N	N	N	Y
19 ***Platts***	Y	Y	Y	Y	N	N	N	Y
RHODE ISLAND								
1 Kennedy	Y	Y	Y	N	N	N	N	N
2 Langevin	Y	Y	Y	N	N	N	N	N
SOUTH CAROLINA								
1 ***Brown***	Y	Y	N	Y	N	N	Y	Y
2 ***Wilson***	Y	Y	N	Y	Y	N	Y	Y
3 ***Barrett***	Y	Y	N	Y	Y	N	Y	Y
4 ***DeMint***	?	?	N	Y	?	?	?	?
5 Spratt	Y	Y	Y	N	N	N	Y	Y
6 Clyburn	Y	Y	Y	N	N	N	N	Y
SOUTH DAKOTA								
AL Vacant								
TENNESSEE								
1 ***Jenkins***	Y	Y	N	Y	N	N	N	Y
2 ***Duncan***	Y	Y	N	Y	N	N	N	Y
3 ***Wamp***	Y	Y	N	Y	N	N	N	Y
4 Davis	Y	Y	Y	N	N	N	N	Y
5 Cooper	Y	Y	Y	N	N	N	N	Y
6 Gordon	Y	Y	Y	N	N	N	Y	Y
7 ***Blackburn***	Y	Y	N	Y	N	N	N	Y
8 Tanner	?	?	?	N	?	?	?	?
9 Ford	Y	Y	Y	N	N	N	N	Y
TEXAS								
1 Sandlin	Y	Y	Y	N	N	Y	N	Y
2 Turner	Y	Y	Y	N	N	Y	Y	Y
3 ***Johnson, Sam***	Y	Y	N	Y	N	Y	N	N
4 ***Hall***	Y	Y	N	Y	N	Y	Y	Y
5 ***Hensarling***	Y	Y	N	Y	Y	Y	Y	Y
6 ***Barton***	Y	Y	N	Y	N	N	Y	Y
7 ***Culberson***	Y	Y	N	Y	N	Y	Y	Y
8 ***Brady***	Y	Y	N	Y	Y	Y	Y	Y
9 Lampson	Y	Y	Y	N	N	Y	N	Y
10 Doggett	Y	Y	Y	N	N	Y	N	Y
11 Edwards	Y	Y	Y	N	N	N	N	Y
12 ***Granger***	Y	Y	Y	Y	N	Y	Y	Y
13 ***Thornberry***	Y	Y	N	Y	Y	Y	Y	N
14 ***Paul***	Y	Y	N	Y	Y	Y	Y	Y
15 Hinojosa	Y	Y	Y	N	N	Y	N	Y
16 Reyes	Y	Y	Y	N	N	N	N	Y
17 Stenholm	Y	Y	Y	Y	N	Y	Y	Y
18 Jackson-Lee	Y	Y	Y	N	N	Y	N	Y
19 ***Neugebauer***	Y	Y	N	Y	N	Y	Y	Y
20 Gonzalez	Y	Y	Y	N	N	Y	N	N
21 ***Smith***	Y	Y	Y	Y	N	N	Y	Y
22 ***DeLay***	Y	Y	N	Y	N	Y	Y	Y
23 ***Bonilla***	Y	Y	Y	Y	N	Y	Y	N
24 Frost	Y	Y	Y	N	N	Y	N	Y
25 Bell	Y	Y	Y	N	N	Y	N	Y
26 ***Burgess***	Y	Y	N	Y	N	Y	N	Y
27 Ortiz	Y	Y	Y	N	N	N	N	N
28 Rodriguez	?	?	?	N	N	N	N	Y
29 Green	Y	Y	Y	N	N	Y	N	Y
30 Johnson, E.B.	Y	Y	Y	N	N	Y	N	Y
31 ***Carter***	Y	Y	N	Y	Y	Y	Y	N
32 ***Sessions***	Y	Y	N	?	N	Y	Y	Y
UTAH								
1 ***Bishop***	Y	Y	Y	Y	Y	N	Y	Y
2 Matheson	Y	Y	Y	N	N	N	N	Y
3 ***Cannon***	Y	Y	N	Y	N	N	Y	Y
VERMONT								
AL *Sanders*	Y	Y	Y	N	N	N	N	Y
VIRGINIA								
1 ***Davis, Jo Ann***	Y	Y	Y	Y	N	N	Y	N
2 ***Schrock***	Y	Y	Y	Y	N	N	N	Y
3 Scott	Y	Y	Y	N	N	Y	N	N
4 ***Forbes***	Y	Y	Y	Y	N	N	Y	Y
5 ***Goode***	Y	Y	Y	N	N	N	Y	Y
6 ***Goodlatte***	Y	Y	Y	Y	N	N	Y	Y
7 ***Cantor***	Y	Y	Y	Y	Y	N	Y	Y
8 Moran	Y	Y	Y	?	N	N	N	Y
9 Boucher	Y	Y	Y	N	N	N	N	Y
10 ***Wolf***	Y	Y	Y	Y	N	N	N	N
11 ***Davis, T.***	Y	Y	Y	Y	N	Y	N	Y
WASHINGTON								
1 Inslee	Y	Y	Y	N	N	N	N	N
2 Larsen	Y	Y	Y	N	N	N	N	Y
3 Baird	Y	Y	Y	N	N	N	Y	Y
4 ***Hastings***	Y	Y	Y	Y	Y	N	Y	Y
5 ***Nethercutt***	Y	Y	Y	Y	N	N	Y	Y
6 Dicks	Y	Y	Y	N	N	N	N	N
7 McDermott	Y	Y	Y	N	N	N	N	Y
8 ***Dunn***	Y	Y	Y	Y	N	N	Y	Y
9 Smith	Y	Y	Y	N	N	N	Y	Y
WEST VIRGINIA								
1 Mollohan	Y	Y	Y	N	N	N	N	N
2 ***Capito***	Y	Y	Y	Y	N	N	Y	Y
3 Rahall	Y	Y	Y	N	N	N	N	N
WISCONSIN								
1 ***Ryan***	Y	Y	N	Y	N	N	Y	Y
2 Baldwin	Y	Y	Y	N	N	N	N	Y
3 Kind	Y	Y	Y	N	N	N	N	Y
4 Kleczka	Y	Y	Y	N	N	N	N	N
5 ***Sensenbrenner***	Y	Y	N	Y	Y	N	Y	Y
6 ***Petri***	Y	Y	N	Y	N	N	N	N
7 Obey	Y	Y	Y	N	N	N	N	N
8 ***Green***	Y	Y	N	Y	N	N	Y	Y
WYOMING								
AL ***Cubin***	Y	Y	N	Y	N	N	N	Y

Southern states - Ala., Ark., Fla., Ga., Ky., La., Miss., N.C., Okla., S.C., Tenn., Texas, Va.

Key

Y   Voted for (yea).
\#   Paired for.
\+   Announced for.
N   Voted against (nay).
X   Paired against.
−   Announced against.
P   Voted "present."
C   Voted "present" to avoid possible conflict of interest.
?   Did not vote or otherwise make a position known.

•

Democrats   **Republicans**
Independents

110. HR 3550. Surface Transportation/New Hampshire Weight Limits. Bradley, R-N.H., amendment that would increase the allowable weight of vehicles permitted to travel on Interstate highways 93 and 89 in New Hampshire from 80,000 to 99,000 pounds, while also instructing the New Hampshire Transportation Department to study the impact of the changes. Rejected 90-334: R 86-137; D 4-196 (ND 2-143, SD 2-53); I 0-1. April 2, 2004.

111. HR 3550. Surface Transportation/New Tolls. Kennedy, R-Minn., amendment that would replace a provision in the bill to implement new tolls on existing highway lanes and continue charging tolls indefinitely, with language that would permit tolls only on new voluntary-use lanes until the new lanes are paid for. Adopted 231-193: R 198-25; D 33-167 (ND 14-131, SD 19-36); I 0-1. April 2, 2004.

112. HR 3550. Surface Transportation/High Priority Project Funding. Isakson, R-Ga., amendment that would include high priority projects and projects of "regional and national significance" within the minimum guarantee of funds provided to each state, making the bill consistent with current law. Money saved by the calculation change would be returned to core highway programs, including Interstate highway maintenance, the National Highway System, surface transportation and bridges. Rejected 170-254: R 121-102; D 49-151 (ND 12-133, SD 37-18); I 0-1. April 2, 2004.

113. HR 3550. Surface Transportation/Recommit. Davis, D-Tenn., motion to recommit the bill to the House Transportation and Infrastructure Committee with instructions to increase funding for the bill to the Senate-passed level of $318 billion. Motion rejected 198-225: R 0-222; D 197-3 (ND 144-1, SD 53-2); I 1-0. April 2, 2004.

114. HR 3550. Surface Transportation/Passage. Passage of the bill that would authorize $283.2 billion for federal-aid highway, mass transit, safety and research programs from fiscal 2004 to 2009. The funding total includes $217 billion in guaranteed spending for highways, $51.5 billion for mass transit and other public transportation programs, and $11.1 billion for members' projects. It also would freeze funding in fiscal 2006 and beyond unless legislation is enacted that would ensure that states get back at least 95 percent of the dollars their motorists send to the Highway Trust Fund by fiscal 2009. Passed 357-65: R 162-59; D 194-6 (ND 144-1, SD 50-5); I 1-0. A "nay" was a vote in support of the president's position. April 2, 2004.

	110	111	112	113	114
ALABAMA					
1 *Bonner*	Y	Y	N	N	Y
2 *Everett*	Y	Y	N	N	Y
3 *Rogers*	Y	Y	N	N	Y
4 *Aderholt*	Y	Y	N	N	Y
5 Cramer	N	N	N	Y	Y
6 *Bachus*	N	Y	N	N	Y
7 Davis	N	N	Y	Y	Y
ALASKA					
AL *Young*	N	N	N	N	Y
ARIZONA					
1 *Renzi*	N	Y	Y	N	Y
2 *Franks*	Y	Y	Y	N	N
3 *Shadegg*	Y	Y	Y	N	N
4 Pastor	N	N	N	Y	Y
5 *Hayworth*	Y	Y	Y	N	Y
6 *Flake*	Y	Y	Y	N	N
7 Grijalva	N	N	N	Y	Y
8 *Kolbe*	N	Y	Y	N	N
ARKANSAS					
1 Berry	N	N	N	Y	Y
2 Snyder	N	N	N	Y	Y
3 *Boozman*	N	Y	N	N	Y
4 Ross	N	Y	N	Y	Y
CALIFORNIA					
1 Thompson	N	N	N	Y	Y
2 *Herger*	Y	Y	N	N	Y
3 *Ose*	N	Y	N	N	Y
4 *Doolittle*	N	Y	N	N	Y
5 Matsui	N	N	N	Y	Y
6 Woolsey	N	N	N	Y	Y
7 Miller, George	?	?	?	?	?
8 Pelosi	N	N	N	Y	Y
9 Lee	N	N	N	Y	Y
10 Tauscher	N	N	N	Y	Y
11 *Pombo*	N	Y	N	N	Y
12 Lantos	N	N	N	Y	Y
13 Stark	N	N	N	Y	+
14 Eshoo	N	N	N	Y	Y
15 Honda	N	N	N	Y	Y
16 Lofgren	N	N	N	Y	Y
17 Farr	N	N	N	Y	Y
18 Cardoza	N	Y	N	Y	Y
19 *Radanovich*	N	Y	N	N	Y
20 Dooley	N	N	N	Y	Y
21 *Nunes*	Y	Y	N	N	Y
22 *Thomas*	N	N	N	N	Y
23 Capps	N	N	N	Y	Y
24 *Gallegly*	N	Y	N	N	Y
25 *McKeon*	N	N	N	N	Y
26 *Dreier*	Y	Y	N	N	Y
27 Sherman	N	N	N	Y	Y
28 Berman	N	N	N	Y	Y
29 Schiff	N	N	N	Y	Y
30 Waxman	?	?	?	?	?
31 Becerra	N	N	N	Y	Y
32 Solis	N	N	N	Y	Y
33 Watson	N	N	N	Y	Y
34 Roybal-Allard	N	N	N	Y	Y
35 Waters	N	N	N	Y	Y
36 Harman	N	N	N	Y	Y

	110	111	112	113	114
37 Millender-McD.	N	N	N	Y	Y
38 Napolitano	N	N	N	Y	Y
39 Sánchez, Linda	N	N	N	Y	Y
40 *Royce*	N	Y	N	N	Y
41 *Lewis*	N	N	N	N	Y
42 *Miller, Gary*	N	Y	N	Y	Y
43 Baca	N	N	N	Y	Y
44 *Calvert*	Y	Y	N	N	Y
45 *Bono*	N	Y	N	N	Y
46 *Rohrabacher*	N	N	N	N	Y
47 Sanchez, Loretta	N	N	N	Y	Y
48 *Cox*	Y	Y	N	N	Y
49 *Issa*	N	Y	N	?	Y
50 *Cunningham*	N	Y	Y	N	Y
51 Filner	N	N	N	Y	Y
52 *Hunter*	Y	Y	Y	N	?
53 Davis	N	N	N	Y	Y
COLORADO					
1 DeGette	N	N	Y	Y	Y
2 Udall	N	N	Y	Y	Y
3 *McInnis*	N	N	Y	N	Y
4 *Musgrave*	Y	Y	Y	N	Y
5 *Hefley*	N	Y	N	N	Y
6 *Tancredo*	Y	Y	N	N	N
7 *Beauprez*	Y	Y	Y	N	Y
CONNECTICUT					
1 Larson	N	N	N	Y	Y
2 *Simmons*	Y	N	N	N	Y
3 DeLauro	N	N	N	Y	Y
4 *Shays*	N	N	N	N	Y
5 *Johnson*	Y	N	N	N	Y
DELAWARE					
AL *Castle*	Y	N	N	N	N
FLORIDA					
1 *Miller, J.*	Y	Y	Y	N	N
2 Boyd	N	Y	Y	Y	N
3 Brown	N	N	N	Y	Y
4 *Crenshaw*	N	Y	N	N	Y
5 *Brown-Waite*	N	Y	Y	N	Y
6 *Stearns*	N	Y	Y	N	Y
7 *Mica*	N	Y	Y	N	Y
8 *Keller*	Y	Y	Y	N	Y
9 *Bilirakis*	Y	Y	Y	N	Y
10 *Young*	N	N	N	N	N
11 Davis	N	N	Y	Y	Y
12 *Putnam*	N	Y	Y	N	Y
13 *Harris*	Y	Y	Y	N	Y
14 *Goss*	N	N	Y	N	N
15 *Weldon*	?	?	Y	N	Y
16 *Foley*	N	Y	Y	N	Y
17 Meek	N	N	Y	Y	Y
18 *Ros-Lehtinen*	N	Y	N	N	Y
19 Wexler	N	N	N	Y	Y
20 Deutsch	N	N	N	Y	Y
21 *Diaz-Balart, L.*	N	Y	N	N	Y
22 *Shaw*	N	Y	N	N	Y
23 Hastings	N	N	N	Y	Y
24 *Feeney*	Y	Y	N	N	N
25 *Diaz-Balart, M.*	Y	Y	N	N	N
GEORGIA					
1 *Kingston*	N	Y	N	N	N
2 Bishop	N	Y	Y	Y	Y
3 Marshall	N	N	Y	Y	Y
4 Majette	N	N	Y	Y	Y
5 Lewis	N	Y	Y	Y	Y
6 *Isakson*	N	Y	N	N	Y
7 *Linder*	N	Y	N	N	N
8 *Collins*	N	Y	N	Y	Y
9 *Norwood*	Y	Y	N	N	N
10 *Deal*	Y	Y	Y	N	N
11 *Gingrey*	Y	Y	N	N	N
12 *Burns*	Y	Y	Y	N	N
13 Scott	N	Y	Y	Y	Y
HAWAII					
1 Abercrombie	N	N	N	Y	Y
2 Case	N	N	N	Y	Y
IDAHO					
1 *Otter*	N	Y	Y	N	N
2 *Simpson*	Y	Y	Y	N	N
ILLINOIS					
1 Rush	N	N	N	Y	Y
2 Jackson	N	N	N	Y	Y
3 Lipinski	N	N	N	Y	Y
4 Gutierrez	N	N	N	Y	Y
5 Emanuel	N	N	N	Y	Y
6 *Hyde*	N	Y	N	N	Y

ND Northern Democrats   SD Southern Democrats

	110	111	112	113	114
7 Davis	N	N	N	Y	Y
8 ***Crane***	N	Y	N	N	Y
9 Schakowsky	N	N	N	Y	Y
10 ***Kirk***	N	N	N	N	Y
11 ***Weller***	N	Y	N	N	Y
12 Costello	N	N	N	Y	Y
13 ***Biggert***	N	N	N	N	Y
14 ***Hastert***	Y	Y			
15 ***Johnson***	N	Y	N	N	Y
16 ***Manzullo***	Y	Y	N	N	Y
17 Evans	N	N	N	Y	Y
18 ***LaHood***	N	Y	N	N	Y
19 ***Shimkus***	Y	Y	N	N	Y
INDIANA					
1 Visclosky	N	N	Y	Y	Y
2 ***Chocola***	Y	Y	Y	N	Y
3 ***Souder***	Y	Y	Y	N	N
4 ***Buyer***	Y	Y	Y	N	Y
5 ***Burton***	N	Y	Y	N	Y
6 ***Pence***	Y	Y	Y	N	N
7 Carson	N	N	Y	Y	Y
8 ***Hostettler***	Y	Y	N	N	Y
9 Hill	N	Y	Y	Y	N
IOWA					
1 ***Nussle***	N	Y	Y	N	Y
2 ***Leach***	N	Y	Y	N	Y
3 Boswell	N	N	N	Y	Y
4 ***Latham***	Y	Y	N	N	Y
5 ***King***	Y	Y	Y	N	Y
KANSAS					
1 ***Moran***	N	Y	N	N	Y
2 ***Ryun***	Y	Y	N	N	Y
3 Moore	N	Y	N	Y	Y
4 ***Tiahrt***	N	Y	Y	N	Y
KENTUCKY					
1 ***Whitfield***	Y	Y	Y	N	Y
2 ***Lewis***	Y	Y	Y	N	Y
3 ***Northup***	N	Y	Y	N	Y
4 Lucas	N	Y	Y	Y	Y
5 ***Rogers***	N	Y	Y	N	Y
6 Chandler	N	N	Y	Y	Y
LOUISIANA					
1 ***Vitter***	N	Y	N	N	Y
2 Jefferson	N	N	Y	Y	Y
3 ***Tauzin***	?	?	?	?	?
4 ***McCrery***	N	N	N	N	Y
5 Alexander	N	Y	N	Y	Y
6 ***Baker***	N	Y	N	N	Y
7 John	N	Y	N	Y	Y
MAINE					
1 Allen	Y	N	N	Y	Y
2 Michaud	Y	N	N	Y	Y
MARYLAND					
1 ***Gilchrest***	N	Y	N	N	Y
2 Ruppersberger	N	N	N	Y	Y
3 Cardin	N	N	N	Y	Y
4 Wynn	N	N	N	Y	Y
5 Hoyer	N	N	N	Y	Y
6 ***Bartlett***	Y	Y	Y	N	Y
7 Cummings	N	N	N	Y	Y
8 Van Hollen	N	N	N	Y	Y
MASSACHUSETTS					
1 Olver	N	N	N	Y	Y
2 Neal	N	N	N	Y	Y
3 McGovern	N	N	N	Y	Y
4 Frank	N	N	N	Y	Y
5 Meehan	N	N	N	Y	Y
6 Tierney	N	N	N	Y	Y
7 Markey	N	N	N	Y	Y
8 Capuano	N	N	N	Y	Y
9 Lynch	N	N	N	Y	Y
10 Delahunt	N	N	N	Y	Y
MICHIGAN					
1 Stupak	N	Y	Y	Y	Y
2 ***Hoekstra***	N	Y	Y	N	Y
3 ***Ehlers***	N	Y	Y	N	Y
4 ***Camp***	N	Y	Y	N	Y
5 Kildee	N	N	Y	Y	Y
6 ***Upton***	N	Y	Y	N	Y
7 ***Smith***	Y	Y	Y	N	N
8 ***Rogers***	N	Y	Y	N	N
9 ***Knollenberg***	N	Y	Y	N	Y
10 ***Miller***	N	Y	Y	N	Y
11 ***McCotter***	N	Y	Y	N	Y
12 Levin	N	N	Y	Y	Y

	110	111	112	113	114
13 Kilpatrick	N	N	Y	Y	Y
14 Conyers	N	N	Y	Y	Y
15 Dingell	N	N	Y	Y	Y
MINNESOTA					
1 ***Gutknecht***	N	Y	Y	N	N
2 ***Kline***	Y	Y	Y	N	N
3 ***Ramstad***	N	Y	Y	N	Y
4 McCollum	N	N	N	Y	Y
5 Sabo	N	N	N	Y	Y
6 ***Kennedy***	Y	Y	Y	N	Y
7 Peterson	N	N	N	N	Y
8 Oberstar	N	N	N	Y	Y
MISSISSIPPI					
1 ***Wicker***	N	Y	N	N	Y
2 Thompson	N	N	N	Y	Y
3 ***Pickering***	N	Y	N	N	Y
4 Taylor	N	N	N	Y	Y
MISSOURI					
1 Clay	N	N	N	Y	Y
2 ***Akin***	Y	Y	Y	N	N
3 Gephardt	?	?	?	Y	Y
4 Skelton	N	N	N	Y	Y
5 McCarthy	N	N	N	Y	Y
6 ***Graves***	N	Y	N	N	Y
7 ***Blunt***	Y	Y	Y	N	N
8 ***Emerson***	N	Y	Y	N	Y
9 ***Hulshof***	?	?	?	?	?
MONTANA					
AL ***Rehberg***	Y	Y	N	N	Y
NEBRASKA					
1 ***Bereuter***	N	Y	N	N	Y
2 ***Terry***	Y	Y	Y	N	Y
3 ***Osborne***	N	Y	N	N	Y
NEVADA					
1 Berkley	N	Y	N	Y	Y
2 ***Gibbons***	N	Y	N	N	Y
3 ***Porter***	N	Y	N	N	Y
NEW HAMPSHIRE					
1 ***Bradley***	Y	Y	N	N	Y
2 ***Bass***	Y	Y	N	N	Y
NEW JERSEY					
1 Andrews	N	N	N	Y	Y
2 ***LoBiondo***	N	Y	N	N	Y
3 ***Saxton***	N	Y	N	N	?
4 ***Smith***	N	Y	N	N	Y
5 ***Garrett***	Y	Y	Y	N	Y
6 Pallone	N	N	N	Y	Y
7 ***Ferguson***	N	Y	Y	N	Y
8 Pascrell	N	N	N	Y	Y
9 Rothman	N	N	N	Y	Y
10 Payne	N	N	N	Y	Y
11 ***Frelinghuysen***	Y	Y	Y	N	Y
12 Holt	N	N	N	Y	Y
13 Menendez	N	N	N	Y	Y
NEW MEXICO					
1 ***Wilson***	N	Y	N	N	Y
2 ***Pearce***	Y	Y	N	N	Y
3 Udall	N	N	N	Y	Y
NEW YORK					
1 Bishop	N	N	N	Y	Y
2 Israel	N	N	N	Y	Y
3 ***King***	N	Y	N	N	Y
4 McCarthy	N	N	N	Y	Y
5 Ackerman	N	N	N	Y	Y
6 Meeks	N	N	N	Y	Y
7 Crowley	N	N	N	Y	Y
8 Nadler	N	N	N	Y	Y
9 Weiner	N	N	N	Y	Y
10 Towns	N	N	N	Y	Y
11 Owens	N	N	N	Y	Y
12 Velázquez	N	N	N	Y	Y
13 ***Fossella***	Y	Y	N	N	Y
14 Maloney	N	N	N	Y	Y
15 Rangel	N	N	N	Y	Y
16 Serrano	N	N	N	?	Y
17 Engel	N	Y	N	Y	Y
18 Lowey	N	N	N	Y	Y
19 ***Kelly***	N	Y	N	N	Y
20 ***Sweeney***	Y	Y	N	N	Y
21 McNulty	N	N	N	Y	Y
22 Hinchey	N	Y	N	Y	Y
23 ***McHugh***	N	Y	N	N	Y
24 ***Boehlert***	N	Y	N	N	Y
25 ***Walsh***	Y	Y	N	N	Y

	110	111	112	113	114
26 ***Reynolds***	N	Y	N	N	Y
27 ***Quinn***	N	Y	N	N	Y
28 Slaughter	N	N	N	Y	Y
29 ***Houghton***	Y	Y	N	N	Y
NORTH CAROLINA					
1 Ballance	N	N	Y	Y	Y
2 Etheridge	N	N	Y	Y	Y
3 ***Jones***	N	Y	Y	N	N
4 Price	N	N	Y	Y	Y
5 ***Burr***	Y	Y	Y	N	Y
6 ***Coble***	N	Y	Y	N	Y
7 McIntyre	Y	Y	Y	Y	Y
8 ***Hayes***	Y	Y	Y	N	Y
9 ***Myrick***	Y	Y	Y	N	N
10 ***Ballenger***	N	Y	Y	N	Y
11 ***Taylor***	Y	Y	Y	N	Y
12 Watt	N	N	Y	Y	Y
13 Miller	N	N	Y	Y	Y
NORTH DAKOTA					
AL Pomeroy	N	N	N	Y	Y
OHIO					
1 ***Chabot***	N	Y	Y	N	Y
2 ***Portman***	N	Y	Y	N	Y
3 ***Turner***	N	Y	N	N	Y
4 ***Oxley***	N	Y	N	N	Y
5 ***Gillmor***	N	Y	N	N	Y
6 Strickland	N	Y	Y	Y	Y
7 ***Hobson***	N	Y	N	N	Y
8 ***Boehner***	Y	Y	Y	N	N
9 Kaptur	N	N	N	Y	Y
10 Kucinich	N	N	N	Y	Y
11 Jones	N	Y	N	Y	Y
12 ***Tiberi***	N	Y	Y	N	Y
13 Brown	N	Y	N	Y	Y
14 ***LaTourette***	N	Y	N	N	Y
15 ***Pryce***	Y	Y	N	N	Y
16 ***Regula***	N	Y	N	N	Y
17 Ryan	N	N	N	Y	Y
18 ***Ney***	N	Y	N	N	Y
OKLAHOMA					
1 ***Sullivan***	N	Y	Y	N	N
2 Carson	N	N	Y	Y	Y
3 ***Lucas***	N	N	Y	N	N
4 ***Cole***	N	Y	Y	N	N
5 ***Istook***	N	Y	Y	N	N
OREGON					
1 Wu	N	N	N	Y	Y
2 ***Walden***	N	Y	N	N	Y
3 Blumenauer	N	N	N	Y	Y
4 DeFazio	N	N	N	Y	Y
5 Hooley	N	N	N	Y	Y
PENNSYLVANIA					
1 Brady	N	N	N	Y	Y
2 Fattah	N	N	N	Y	Y
3 ***English***	N	Y	N	N	Y
4 ***Hart***	N	Y	N	N	Y
5 ***Peterson***	N	Y	N	N	Y
6 ***Gerlach***	N	Y	N	N	Y
7 ***Weldon***	N	Y	N	N	Y
8 ***Greenwood***	Y	N	N	N	Y
9 ***Shuster, Bill***	N	Y	N	N	Y
10 ***Sherwood***	Y	Y	N	N	Y
11 Kanjorski	N	N	N	Y	Y
12 Murtha	N	N	N	Y	Y
13 Hoeffel	N	N	N	Y	Y
14 Doyle	N	N	N	Y	Y
15 ***Toomey***	N	Y	N	N	N
16 ***Pitts***	Y	Y	N	N	Y
17 Holden	N	N	N	Y	Y
18 ***Murphy***	N	Y	N	N	Y
19 ***Platts***	N	Y	N	N	Y
RHODE ISLAND					
1 Kennedy	N	N	N	Y	Y
2 Langevin	N	N	N	Y	Y
SOUTH CAROLINA					
1 ***Brown***	N	Y	Y	N	Y
2 ***Wilson***	Y	Y	Y	N	Y
3 ***Barrett***	Y	Y	Y	N	N
4 ***DeMint***	?	?	?	?	?
5 Spratt	N	N	Y	Y	Y
6 Clyburn	N	N	N	Y	Y
SOUTH DAKOTA					
AL Vacant					

	110	111	112	113	114
TENNESSEE					
1 ***Jenkins***	N	Y	Y	N	Y
2 ***Duncan***	N	Y	Y	N	Y
3 ***Wamp***	N	Y	Y	N	Y
4 Davis	N	Y	N	Y	Y
5 Cooper	N	N	N	Y	Y
6 Gordon	N	N	N	Y	Y
7 ***Blackburn***	Y	Y	Y	N	Y
8 Tanner	?	?	?	?	?
9 Ford	N	N	N	Y	Y
TEXAS					
1 Sandlin	N	Y	Y	Y	Y
2 Turner	N	Y	Y	Y	Y
3 ***Johnson, Sam***	N	Y	Y	N	N
4 ***Hall***	Y	Y	Y	N	Y
5 ***Hensarling***	Y	Y	Y	N	N
6 ***Barton***	N	N	Y	N	N
7 ***Culberson***	?	?	?	?	?
8 ***Brady***	N	Y	Y	N	N
9 Lampson	N	N	Y	Y	Y
10 Doggett	N	Y	Y	Y	Y
11 Edwards	N	N	Y	Y	Y
12 ***Granger***	Y	N	Y	N	Y
13 ***Thornberry***	Y	Y	Y	N	N
14 ***Paul***	Y	Y	Y	N	N
15 Hinojosa	N	Y	N	Y	Y
16 Reyes	?	?	?	?	?
17 Stenholm	Y	Y	Y	N	Y
18 Jackson-Lee	N	N	Y	Y	Y
19 ***Neugebauer***	Y	Y	Y	N	Y
20 Gonzalez	N	Y	Y	Y	Y
21 ***Smith***	N	Y	Y	N	Y
22 ***DeLay***	Y	Y	Y	N	Y
23 ***Bonilla***	N	N	Y	N	Y
24 Frost	N	N	Y	Y	Y
25 Bell	N	N	Y	Y	Y
26 ***Burgess***	N	N	Y	N	Y
27 Ortiz	N	Y	N	Y	Y
28 Rodriguez	N	N	Y	Y	Y
29 Green	N	Y	Y	Y	Y
30 Johnson, E.B.	N	N	Y	Y	Y
31 ***Carter***	N	Y	Y	N	Y
32 ***Sessions***	Y	Y	Y	N	Y
UTAH					
1 ***Bishop***	Y	Y	N	N	Y
2 Matheson	N	N	N	Y	Y
3 ***Cannon***	Y	Y	N	N	Y
VERMONT					
AL *Sanders*	N	N	N	Y	Y
VIRGINIA					
1 ***Davis, Jo Ann***	N	N	Y	N	Y
2 ***Schrock***	N	Y	Y	N	Y
3 Scott	N	N	Y	Y	Y
4 ***Forbes***	N	Y	Y	N	Y
5 ***Goode***	Y	Y	Y	N	Y
6 ***Goodlatte***	N	N	Y	N	Y
7 ***Cantor***	Y	Y	Y	N	N
8 Moran	N	N	N	Y	Y
9 Boucher	N	N	N	Y	Y
10 ***Wolf***	N	N	Y	N	Y
11 ***Davis, T.***	N	Y	Y	N	Y
WASHINGTON					
1 Inslee	N	N	N	Y	Y
2 Larsen	N	N	N	Y	Y
3 Baird	N	N	N	Y	Y
4 ***Hastings***	N	Y	N	N	Y
5 ***Nethercutt***	Y	Y	N	N	Y
6 Dicks	N	N	N	Y	Y
7 McDermott	N	N	N	Y	Y
8 ***Dunn***	N	Y	N	N	Y
9 Smith	N	Y	N	Y	Y
WEST VIRGINIA					
1 Mollohan	N	N	N	Y	Y
2 ***Capito***	N	Y	N	N	Y
3 Rahall	N	N	N	Y	Y
WISCONSIN					
1 ***Ryan***	N	Y	N	N	N
2 Baldwin	N	N	N	Y	Y
3 Kind	N	Y	N	Y	Y
4 Kleczka	N	N	N	Y	Y
5 ***Sensenbrenner***	N	Y	N	N	N
6 ***Petri***	N	N	N	N	Y
7 Obey	N	Y	N	Y	Y
8 ***Green***	N	Y	N	N	N
WYOMING					
AL ***Cubin***	N	Y	N	N	Y

Southern states - Ala., Ark., Fla., Ga., Ky., La., Miss., N.C., Okla., S.C., Tenn., Texas, Va.

Key

Y	Voted for (yea).
#	Paired for.
+	Announced for.
N	Voted against (nay).
X	Paired against.
–	Announced against.
P	Voted "present."
C	Voted "present" to avoid possible conflict of interest.
?	Did not vote or otherwise make a position known.

Democrats **Republicans**
Independents

115. H Con Res 404. Adjournment/Adoption. Adoption of the concurrent resolution that would provide for an adjournment of the House until 2 p.m., Tuesday, April 20. Adopted 211-201: R 211-2; D 0-198 (ND 0-144, SD 0-54); I 0-1. April 2, 2004.

116. HR 3108. Pension Funding/Recommit. Andrews, D-N.J., motion to recommit the conference report to the conference committee with instructions that it be reported back to the House with a provision that would allow 20 percent of multi-employer pension plans to reduce contributions to their plans, an increase from about 4 percent. Motion rejected 195-217: R 3-212; D 191-5 (ND 140-2, SD 51-3); I 1-0. April 2, 2004.

117. HR 3108. Pension Funding/Conference Report. Adoption of the conference report on the bill that would allow companies to reduce contributions to their pension plans by temporarily altering the formula used to calculate whether those contributions are sufficient to cover liabilities. The new formula would use a rate based on yields on a corporate bond index. The bill also would ease funding rules for about 4 percent of multi-employer pension plans, giving them a grace period to account for losses. Adopted (thus sent to the Senate) 336-69: R 199-7; D 137-61 (ND 94-49, SD 43-12); I 0-1. A "yea" was a vote in support of the president's position. April 2, 2004.

	115	116	117
ALABAMA			
1 *Bonner*	Y	N	Y
2 *Everett*	Y	N	Y
3 *Rogers*	Y	N	Y
4 *Aderholt*	Y	N	Y
5 Cramer	N	Y	Y
6 *Bachus*	Y	N	Y
7 Davis	N	Y	Y
ALASKA			
AL *Young*	Y	N	Y
ARIZONA			
1 *Renzi*	Y	N	Y
2 *Franks*	Y	N	Y
3 *Shadegg*	Y	N	Y
4 Pastor	N	Y	Y
5 *Hayworth*	Y	N	Y
6 *Flake*	Y	N	N
7 Grijalva	N	Y	N
8 *Kolbe*	Y	N	Y
ARKANSAS			
1 Berry	N	Y	Y
2 Snyder	N	Y	Y
3 *Boozman*	Y	N	Y
4 Ross	N	Y	Y
CALIFORNIA			
1 Thompson	N	Y	Y
2 *Herger*	Y	N	Y
3 *Ose*	Y	N	N
4 *Doolittle*	Y	N	Y
5 Matsui	N	Y	Y
6 Woolsey	N	Y	N
7 Miller, George	?	?	?
8 Pelosi	N	Y	Y
9 Lee	N	Y	N
10 Tauscher	N	Y	Y
11 *Pombo*	Y	N	Y
12 Lantos	N	Y	Y
13 Stark	N	Y	N
14 Eshoo	N	Y	N
15 Honda	N	Y	N
16 Lofgren	N	Y	N
17 Farr	N	Y	Y
18 Cardoza	N	Y	Y
19 *Radanovich*	Y	N	Y
20 Dooley	N	Y	Y
21 *Nunes*	Y	N	Y
22 *Thomas*	Y	N	Y
23 Capps	N	Y	Y
24 *Gallegly*	Y	N	?
25 *McKeon*	Y	N	Y
26 *Dreier*	Y	N	Y
27 Sherman	N	Y	Y
28 Berman	N	Y	N
29 Schiff	N	Y	Y
30 Waxman	?	?	?
31 Becerra	N	Y	N
32 Solis	N	Y	N
33 Watson	N	Y	N
34 Roybal-Allard	N	Y	N
35 Waters	N	Y	Y
36 Harman	N	Y	Y

	115	116	117
37 Millender-McD.	N	Y	Y
38 Napolitano	N	Y	N
39 Sánchez, Linda	N	Y	N
40 *Royce*	Y	N	Y
41 *Lewis*	Y	N	Y
42 *Miller, Gary*	Y	N	Y
43 Baca	N	Y	N
44 *Calvert*	Y	N	Y
45 *Bono*	Y	N	Y
46 *Rohrabacher*	Y	N	Y
47 Sanchez, Loretta	N	+	+
48 *Cox*	Y	N	Y
49 *Issa*	Y	N	Y
50 *Cunningham*	Y	N	Y
51 Filner	N	Y	N
52 *Hunter*	Y	N	Y
53 Davis	N	Y	Y
COLORADO			
1 DeGette	N	Y	Y
2 Udall	N	Y	Y
3 *McInnis*	Y	N	Y
4 *Musgrave*	Y	N	Y
5 *Hefley*	Y	N	Y
6 *Tancredo*	Y	N	Y
7 *Beauprez*	Y	N	Y
CONNECTICUT			
1 Larson	N	Y	Y
2 *Simmons*	Y	N	Y
3 DeLauro	N	Y	Y
4 *Shays*	Y	N	Y
5 *Johnson*	Y	N	Y
DELAWARE			
AL *Castle*	Y	N	Y
FLORIDA			
1 *Miller, J.*	?	N	Y
2 Boyd	N	N	Y
3 Brown	N	Y	N
4 *Crenshaw*	Y	N	Y
5 *Brown-Waite*	Y	N	Y
6 *Stearns*	Y	N	Y
7 *Mica*	Y	N	Y
8 *Keller*	Y	N	Y
9 *Bilirakis*	Y	N	?
10 *Young*	Y	N	Y
11 Davis	N	Y	Y
12 *Putnam*	Y	N	Y
13 *Harris*	Y	N	Y
14 *Goss*	?	N	Y
15 *Weldon*	Y	N	Y
16 *Foley*	?	N	Y
17 Meek	N	Y	Y
18 *Ros-Lehtinen*	?	?	?
19 Wexler	N	Y	N
20 Deutsch	N	Y	Y
21 *Diaz-Balart, L.*	Y	?	?
22 *Shaw*	Y	N	Y
23 Hastings	N	Y	N
24 *Feeney*	Y	N	Y
25 *Diaz-Balart, M.*	Y	N	Y
GEORGIA			
1 *Kingston*	Y	N	Y
2 Bishop	N	Y	Y
3 Marshall	N	N	Y
4 Majette	?	Y	N
5 Lewis	N	Y	N
6 *Isakson*	Y	N	Y
7 *Linder*	Y	N	Y
8 *Collins*	Y	N	?
9 *Norwood*	Y	?	?
10 *Deal*	Y	?	?
11 *Gingrey*	Y	N	Y
12 *Burns*	Y	N	Y
13 Scott	N	Y	Y
HAWAII			
1 Abercrombie	N	Y	N
2 Case	N	Y	Y
IDAHO			
1 *Otter*	Y	N	?
2 *Simpson*	Y	N	Y
ILLINOIS			
1 Rush	N	Y	Y
2 Jackson	N	Y	Y
3 Lipinski	N	Y	Y
4 Gutierrez	?	?	?
5 Emanuel	N	Y	Y
6 *Hyde*	Y	N	Y

ND Northern Democrats   SD Southern Democrats

Member	115	116	117
7 Davis	N	Y	Y
8 Crane	Y	Y	Y
9 Schakowsky	N	Y	Y
10 *Kirk*	Y	N	Y
11 Weller	Y	N	Y
12 Costello	N	Y	N
13 *Biggert*	Y	N	Y
14 Hastert		N	
15 *Johnson*	Y	N	Y
16 *Manzullo*	Y	N	Y
17 Evans	N	Y	Y
18 *LaHood*	?	?	?
19 *Shimkus*	Y	N	Y
INDIANA			
1 Visclosky	N	Y	N
2 *Chocola*	Y	N	Y
3 *Souder*	Y	N	Y
4 *Buyer*	Y	N	Y
5 *Burton*	Y	N	Y
6 *Pence*	Y	N	Y
7 Carson	N	Y	Y
8 *Hostettler*	Y	N	Y
9 Hill	N	Y	Y
IOWA			
1 *Nussle*	Y	N	Y
2 *Leach*	Y	N	Y
3 Boswell	N	Y	Y
4 *Latham*	Y	N	Y
5 *King*	Y	N	Y
KANSAS			
1 *Moran*	Y	N	Y
2 *Ryun*	Y	N	Y
3 Moore	N	Y	Y
4 *Tiahrt*	Y	N	Y
KENTUCKY			
1 *Whitfield*	Y	N	?
2 *Lewis*	Y	N	Y
3 *Northup*	Y	N	Y
4 Lucas	N	Y	Y
5 *Rogers*	Y	N	Y
6 Chandler	N	Y	Y
LOUISIANA			
1 *Vitter*	Y	N	?
2 Jefferson	N	Y	Y
3 *Tauzin*	?	?	?
4 *McCrery*	Y	N	Y
5 Alexander	Y	N	Y
6 *Baker*	Y	N	Y
7 John	N	Y	Y
MAINE			
1 Allen	N	Y	Y
2 Michaud	N	Y	Y
MARYLAND			
1 *Gilchrest*	Y	N	Y
2 Ruppersberger	N	Y	Y
3 Cardin	N	Y	Y
4 Wynn	N	Y	Y
5 Hoyer	N	Y	Y
6 *Bartlett*	Y	N	Y
7 Cummings	?	Y	Y
8 Van Hollen	N	Y	Y
MASSACHUSETTS			
1 Olver	N	Y	N
2 Neal	N	Y	Y
3 McGovern	N	+	Y
4 Frank	N	Y	N
5 Meehan	N	Y	Y
6 Tierney	N	Y	Y
7 Markey	N	Y	Y
8 Capuano	N	Y	Y
9 Lynch	N	Y	Y
10 Delahunt	N	Y	Y
MICHIGAN			
1 Stupak	N	Y	Y
2 *Hoekstra*	Y	N	Y
3 *Ehlers*	Y	N	Y
4 *Camp*	Y	N	Y
5 Kildee	N	Y	Y
6 *Upton*	Y	N	Y
7 *Smith*	Y	N	Y
8 *Rogers*	Y	N	Y
9 *Knollenberg*	Y	N	Y
10 *Miller*	Y	N	Y
11 *McCotter*	Y	N	Y
12 Levin	N	Y	Y

Member	115	116	117
13 Kilpatrick	N	Y	Y
14 Conyers	N	Y	Y
15 Dingell	N	Y	Y
MINNESOTA			
1 *Gutknecht*	Y	N	Y
2 *Kline*	Y	N	Y
3 *Ramstad*	Y	N	Y
4 McCollum	N	Y	Y
5 Sabo	N	Y	Y
6 *Kennedy*	Y	N	Y
7 Peterson	N	Y	Y
8 Oberstar	N	Y	Y
MISSISSIPPI			
1 *Wicker*	Y	N	Y
2 Thompson	N	Y	N
3 *Pickering*	Y	N	Y
4 Taylor	N	Y	N
MISSOURI			
1 Clay	N	Y	Y
2 *Akin*	Y	N	Y
3 Gephardt	N	?	Y
4 Skelton	N	Y	Y
5 McCarthy	N	Y	N
6 *Graves*	Y	N	Y
7 *Blunt*	Y	N	Y
8 *Emerson*	Y	N	Y
9 *Hulshof*	?	?	?
MONTANA			
AL *Rehberg*	Y	N	?
NEBRASKA			
1 *Bereuter*	Y	N	Y
2 *Terry*	Y	N	Y
3 *Osborne*	?	N	Y
NEVADA			
1 Berkley	N	Y	Y
2 *Gibbons*	Y	N	Y
3 *Porter*	Y	N	Y
NEW HAMPSHIRE			
1 *Bradley*	Y	N	Y
2 *Bass*	Y	N	Y
NEW JERSEY			
1 Andrews	N	Y	N
2 *LoBiondo*	Y	Y	N
3 *Saxton*	Y	Y	N
4 *Smith*	Y	N	Y
5 *Garrett*	Y	N	Y
6 Pallone	N	Y	N
7 *Ferguson*	Y	N	Y
8 Pascrell	N	Y	N
9 Rothman	N	Y	N
10 Payne	N	Y	N
11 *Frelinghuysen*	Y	N	Y
12 Holt	N	Y	N
13 Menendez	N	Y	N
NEW MEXICO			
1 *Wilson*	Y	N	Y
2 *Pearce*	Y	N	Y
3 Udall	N	Y	N
NEW YORK			
1 Bishop	N	Y	Y
2 Israel	N	Y	Y
3 *King*	Y	N	Y
4 McCarthy	N	Y	Y
5 Ackerman	N	Y	Y
6 Meeks	N	Y	Y
7 Crowley	N	Y	Y
8 Nadler	N	Y	Y
9 Weiner	N	Y	Y
10 Towns	N	Y	Y
11 Owens	N	Y	N
12 Velázquez	N	Y	?
13 *Fossella*	Y	?	?
14 Maloney	N	Y	Y
15 Rangel	N	Y	Y
16 Serrano	N	Y	Y
17 Engel	N	Y	Y
18 Lowey	N	Y	Y
19 *Kelly*	Y	N	Y
20 *Sweeney*	N	N	N
21 McNulty	N	Y	N
22 Hinchey	N	Y	Y
23 *McHugh*	Y	N	Y
24 *Boehlert*	Y	N	Y
25 *Walsh*	Y	N	N

Member	115	116	117
26 *Reynolds*	Y	N	Y
27 *Quinn*	Y	N	Y
28 Slaughter	N	Y	Y
29 *Houghton*	Y	N	?
NORTH CAROLINA			
1 Ballance	N	Y	N
2 Etheridge	N	Y	Y
3 *Jones*	Y	N	Y
4 Price	N	Y	Y
5 *Burr*	Y	N	?
6 *Coble*	Y	N	Y
7 McIntyre	Y	N	Y
8 *Hayes*	Y	N	Y
9 *Myrick*	Y	N	N
10 *Ballenger*	N	N	N
11 *Taylor*	Y	N	Y
12 Watt	N	Y	Y
13 Miller	N	Y	N
NORTH DAKOTA			
AL Pomeroy	N	Y	Y
OHIO			
1 *Chabot*	Y	N	Y
2 *Portman*	Y	N	+
3 *Turner*	Y	N	Y
4 *Oxley*	Y	N	Y
5 *Gillmor*	Y	N	Y
6 Strickland	N	Y	Y
7 *Hobson*	Y	N	Y
8 *Boehner*	Y	N	Y
9 Kaptur	N	Y	N
10 Kucinich	N	Y	Y
11 Jones	N	Y	Y
12 *Tiberi*	Y	N	Y
13 Brown	N	Y	Y
14 *LaTourette*	Y	N	Y
15 *Pryce*	?	N	Y
16 *Regula*	Y	N	Y
17 Ryan	N	Y	N
18 *Ney*	Y	N	Y
OKLAHOMA			
1 *Sullivan*	?	N	Y
2 Carson	N	Y	Y
3 *Lucas*	Y	N	Y
4 *Cole*	Y	N	Y
5 *Istook*	Y	N	Y
OREGON			
1 Wu	N	Y	Y
2 *Walden*	Y	N	Y
3 Blumenauer	N	Y	Y
4 DeFazio	N	Y	Y
5 Hooley	N	Y	Y
PENNSYLVANIA			
1 Brady	N	Y	N
2 Fattah	N	Y	N
3 *English*	Y	N	Y
4 *Hart*	Y	N	Y
5 *Peterson*	Y	N	Y
6 *Gerlach*	Y	N	Y
7 *Weldon*	Y	N	Y
8 *Greenwood*	Y	N	Y
9 *Shuster, Bill*	Y	N	Y
10 *Sherwood*	Y	N	Y
11 Kanjorski	N	Y	Y
12 Murtha	N	Y	Y
13 Hoeffel	N	Y	Y
14 Doyle	N	Y	Y
15 *Toomey*	Y	N	Y
16 *Pitts*	Y	N	Y
17 Holden	N	Y	Y
18 *Murphy*	Y	N	Y
19 *Platts*	Y	N	Y
RHODE ISLAND			
1 Kennedy	N	Y	N
2 Langevin	N	Y	N
SOUTH CAROLINA			
1 *Brown*	Y	N	Y
2 *Wilson*	Y	N	Y
3 *Barrett*	Y	N	Y
4 *DeMint*	?	?	?
5 Spratt	N	Y	Y
6 Clyburn	N	Y	N
SOUTH DAKOTA			
AL Vacant			

Member	115	116	117
TENNESSEE			
1 *Jenkins*	Y	N	Y
2 *Duncan*	Y	N	Y
3 *Wamp*	Y	N	Y
4 Davis	N	Y	Y
5 Cooper	N	Y	Y
6 Gordon	N	Y	Y
7 *Blackburn*	Y	N	Y
8 Tanner	?	?	?
9 Ford	N	Y	Y
TEXAS			
1 Sandlin	N	Y	Y
2 Turner	N	Y	Y
3 *Johnson, Sam*	Y	N	Y
4 *Hall*	Y	N	Y
5 *Hensarling*	Y	N	Y
6 *Barton*	Y	N	Y
7 *Culberson*	?	?	?
8 *Brady*	Y	?	Y
9 Lampson	N	Y	Y
10 Doggett	N	Y	Y
11 Edwards	N	Y	Y
12 *Granger*	?	N	Y
13 *Thornberry*	Y	N	Y
14 *Paul*	?	?	?
15 Hinojosa	N	Y	Y
16 Reyes	?	?	?
17 Stenholm	N	N	Y
18 Jackson-Lee	N	Y	Y
19 *Neugebauer*	Y	N	Y
20 Gonzalez	N	Y	Y
21 *Smith*	Y	N	Y
22 *DeLay*	Y	N	Y
23 *Bonilla*	Y	N	Y
24 Frost	N	Y	Y
25 Bell	N	Y	Y
26 *Burgess*	Y	N	Y
27 Ortiz	N	Y	Y
28 Rodriguez	N	Y	Y
29 Green	N	Y	N
30 Johnson, E.B.	N	Y	Y
31 *Carter*	Y	N	Y
32 *Sessions*	Y	N	Y
UTAH			
1 *Bishop*	Y	?	?
2 Matheson	N	N	Y
3 *Cannon*	Y	N	Y
VERMONT			
AL *Sanders*	N	Y	N
VIRGINIA			
1 *Davis, Jo Ann*	Y	N	Y
2 *Schrock*	Y	N	Y
3 Scott	N	Y	Y
4 *Forbes*	Y	N	Y
5 *Goode*	Y	N	Y
6 *Goodlatte*	Y	N	Y
7 *Cantor*	Y	N	Y
8 Moran	N	?	Y
9 Boucher	N	Y	Y
10 *Wolf*	Y	N	Y
11 *Davis, T.*	Y	N	Y
WASHINGTON			
1 Inslee	N	Y	Y
2 Larsen	N	Y	Y
3 Baird	N	Y	Y
4 *Hastings*	Y	N	Y
5 *Nethercutt*	Y	N	Y
6 Dicks	N	Y	Y
7 McDermott	N	Y	Y
8 *Dunn*	Y	N	Y
9 Smith	N	Y	Y
WEST VIRGINIA			
1 Mollohan	N	Y	Y
2 *Capito*	Y	N	Y
3 Rahall	N	Y	Y
WISCONSIN			
1 *Ryan*	Y	N	Y
2 Baldwin	N	Y	Y
3 Kind	N	Y	Y
4 Kleczka	N	Y	Y
5 *Sensenbrenner*	Y	N	Y
6 *Petri*	Y	N	Y
7 Obey	N	Y	Y
8 *Green*	Y	N	Y
WYOMING			
AL *Cubin*	Y	N	Y

Southern states - Ala., Ark., Fla., Ga., Ky., La., Miss., N.C., Okla., S.C., Tenn., Texas, Va.

Key

Y	Voted for (yea).
#	Paired for.
+	Announced for.
N	Voted against (nay).
X	Paired against.
–	Announced against.
P	Voted "present."
C	Voted "present" to avoid possible conflict of interest.
?	Did not vote or otherwise make a position known.

Democrats **Republicans**
Independents

118. HR 4037. Richard G. Wilson Postal Facility/Passage. Miller, R-Mich., motion to suspend the rules and pass the bill that would name a postal facility in Cape Girardeau, Mo., after Army Pfc. Richard G. Wilson, who was killed in the Korean War and posthumously awarded the Congressional Medal of Honor in 1951. Motion agreed to 392-0: R 205-0; D 186-0 (ND 138-0, SD 48-0); I 1-0. A two-thirds majority of those present and voting (262 in this case) is required for passage under suspension of the rules. April 20, 2004.

119. HR 3855. Gen. John J. Pershing Post Office/Passage. Miller, R-Mich., motion to suspend the rules and pass the bill that would name a post office building in Laclede, Mo., after the late Gen. John J. Pershing, who led U.S. forces during World War I. Motion agreed to 389-0: R 202-0; D 186-0 (ND 138-0, SD 48-0); I 1-0. A two-thirds majority of those present and voting (260 in this case) is required for passage under suspension of the rules. April 20, 2004.

120. HR 1822. Dosan Ahn Chang Ho Post Office/Passage. Miller, R-Mich., motion to suspend the rules and pass the bill that would name a post office building in Los Angeles after the late Dosan Ahn Chang Ho, who founded the Young Korean Academy in Los Angeles and played a significant role in the growth of the Korean-American community in the city. Motion agreed to 399-0: R 213-0; D 185-0 (ND 137-0, SD 48-0); I 1-0. A two-thirds majority of those present and voting (266 in this case) is required for passage under suspension of the rules. April 20, 2004.

121. HR 3970. "Green" Chemistry/Passage. Gingrey, R-Ga., motion to suspend the rules and pass the bill that would direct several federal agencies to promote research and development of "green" chemistry — the use of chemistry to reduce pollution. The bill would authorize $84 million through fiscal 2007 for programs such as competitive grants to researchers from universities, industry and nonprofit organizations, and for research at federal laboratories. Motion agreed to 402-14: R 202-14; D 199-0 (ND 145-0, SD 54-0); I 1-0. A two-thirds majority of those present and voting (278 in this case) is required for passage under suspension of the rules. April 21, 2004.

122. HR 4030. Math and Science Medals/Passage. Smith, R-Mich., motion to suspend the rules and pass the bill that would direct the National Science Foundation to award 10 annual congressional medals to private companies that have supported student achievement in science, technology, engineering and mathematics at elementary and secondary schools. Motion agreed to 411-7: R 210-7; D 200-0 (ND 145-0, SD 55-0); I 1-0. A two-thirds majority of those present and voting (279 in this case) is required for passage under suspension of the rules. April 21, 2004.

	118	119	120	121	122
ALABAMA					
1 *Bonner*	Y	Y	Y	Y	Y
2 *Everett*	Y	Y	Y	N	Y
3 *Rogers*	Y	Y	Y	Y	Y
4 *Aderholt*	Y	Y	Y	Y	Y
5 Cramer	Y	Y	Y	Y	Y
6 *Bachus*	Y	Y	Y	Y	Y
7 Davis	?	?	?	Y	Y
ALASKA					
AL *Young*	Y	Y	Y	Y	Y
ARIZONA					
1 *Renzi*	Y	Y	Y	Y	Y
2 *Franks*	Y	Y	Y	Y	N
3 *Shadegg*	Y	Y	Y	Y	N
4 Pastor	Y	Y	Y	Y	Y
5 *Hayworth*	Y	Y	Y	Y	Y
6 *Flake*	Y	Y	Y	N	N
7 Grijalva	Y	Y	Y	Y	Y
8 *Kolbe*	Y	Y	Y	Y	Y
ARKANSAS					
1 Berry	Y	Y	Y	Y	Y
2 Snyder	Y	Y	Y	Y	Y
3 *Boozman*	Y	Y	Y	Y	Y
4 Ross	Y	Y	Y	Y	Y
CALIFORNIA					
1 Thompson	Y	Y	Y	Y	Y
2 *Herger*	Y	Y	Y	Y	Y
3 *Ose*	Y	Y	Y	Y	Y
4 *Doolittle*	?	?	Y	Y	Y
5 Matsui	Y	Y	Y	Y	Y
6 Woolsey	Y	Y	Y	Y	Y
7 Miller, George	Y	Y	Y	Y	Y
8 Pelosi	Y	Y	Y	Y	Y
9 Lee	Y	Y	Y	Y	Y
10 Tauscher	Y	Y	Y	Y	Y
11 *Pombo*	Y	Y	Y	Y	Y
12 Lantos	Y	Y	Y	Y	Y
13 Stark	Y	Y	Y	Y	Y
14 Eshoo	Y	Y	Y	Y	Y
15 Honda	Y	Y	Y	Y	Y
16 Lofgren	Y	Y	Y	Y	Y
17 Farr	Y	Y	Y	Y	Y
18 Cardoza	Y	Y	Y	Y	Y
19 *Radanovich*	?	?	?	Y	Y
20 Dooley	?	?	Y	Y	Y
21 *Nunes*	Y	?	Y	Y	Y
22 *Thomas*	Y	Y	Y	Y	Y
23 Capps	Y	Y	Y	Y	Y
24 *Gallegly*	Y	Y	Y	Y	Y
25 *McKeon*	Y	Y	Y	Y	Y
26 *Dreier*	?	?	Y	Y	Y
27 Sherman	Y	Y	Y	Y	Y
28 Berman	Y	Y	Y	Y	Y
29 Schiff	Y	Y	Y	Y	Y
30 Waxman	Y	Y	Y	Y	Y
31 Becerra	Y	Y	Y	Y	Y
32 Solis	Y	Y	Y	Y	Y
33 Watson	Y	Y	Y	Y	Y
34 Roybal-Allard	Y	Y	Y	Y	Y
35 Waters	Y	Y	Y	Y	Y
36 Harman	Y	Y	Y	Y	Y

	118	119	120	121	122
37 Millender-McD.	Y	Y	Y	Y	Y
38 Napolitano	Y	Y	Y	Y	Y
39 Sánchez, Linda	Y	Y	Y	Y	Y
40 *Royce*	Y	Y	Y	Y	Y
41 *Lewis*	Y	Y	Y	Y	Y
42 *Miller, Gary*	Y	Y	Y	Y	Y
43 Baca	Y	Y	Y	Y	Y
44 *Calvert*	Y	Y	Y	Y	Y
45 *Bono*	Y	Y	Y	Y	Y
46 *Rohrabacher*	Y	Y	Y	Y	Y
47 Sanchez, Loretta	Y	Y	Y	Y	Y
48 *Cox*	?	?	Y	Y	Y
49 *Issa*	Y	Y	Y	Y	Y
50 *Cunningham*	Y	Y	Y	Y	Y
51 Filner	Y	Y	Y	Y	Y
52 *Hunter*	Y	Y	Y	Y	Y
53 Davis	Y	Y	Y	Y	Y
COLORADO					
1 DeGette	Y	Y	Y	Y	Y
2 Udall	Y	Y	Y	Y	Y
3 *McInnis*	Y	Y	Y	Y	Y
4 *Musgrave*	Y	Y	Y	N	Y
5 *Hefley*	Y	Y	Y	Y	Y
6 *Tancredo*	Y	Y	Y	N	Y
7 *Beauprez*	Y	?	Y	Y	Y
CONNECTICUT					
1 Larson	Y	Y	Y	Y	Y
2 *Simmons*	Y	Y	Y	Y	Y
3 DeLauro	Y	Y	Y	Y	Y
4 *Shays*	Y	Y	Y	Y	Y
5 *Johnson*	Y	Y	Y	Y	Y
DELAWARE					
AL *Castle*	Y	Y	Y	Y	Y
FLORIDA					
1 *Miller, J.*	Y	Y	Y	N	Y
2 Boyd	Y	Y	Y	Y	Y
3 Brown	Y	Y	Y	Y	Y
4 *Crenshaw*	Y	Y	Y	Y	Y
5 *Brown-Waite*	Y	Y	Y	Y	Y
6 *Stearns*	Y	Y	Y	Y	Y
7 *Mica*	Y	Y	Y	Y	Y
8 *Keller*	Y	Y	Y	Y	Y
9 *Bilirakis*	Y	Y	Y	Y	Y
10 *Young*	Y	Y	Y	Y	Y
11 Davis	?	?	Y	Y	Y
12 *Putnam*	Y	Y	Y	Y	Y
13 *Harris*	Y	Y	Y	+	+
14 *Goss*	Y	Y	Y	Y	Y
15 *Weldon*	Y	Y	Y	Y	Y
16 *Foley*	Y	Y	Y	Y	Y
17 Meek	?	?	?	Y	Y
18 *Ros-Lehtinen*	?	?	?	?	?
19 Wexler	Y	Y	Y	Y	Y
20 Deutsch	+	+	+	Y	Y
21 *Diaz-Balart, L.*	Y	Y	Y	Y	Y
22 *Shaw*	Y	Y	Y	Y	Y
23 Hastings	?	?	?	?	?
24 *Feeney*	Y	Y	Y	Y	Y
25 *Diaz-Balart, M.*	Y	Y	Y	Y	Y
GEORGIA					
1 *Kingston*	?	?	Y	?	?
2 Bishop	Y	Y	Y	Y	Y
3 Marshall	Y	Y	Y	Y	Y
4 Majette	Y	Y	Y	Y	Y
5 Lewis	Y	Y	Y	Y	Y
6 *Isakson*	?	?	?	Y	Y
7 *Linder*	Y	Y	Y	Y	Y
8 *Collins*	Y	Y	?	Y	Y
9 *Norwood*	Y	Y	Y	Y	Y
10 *Deal*	Y	Y	Y	Y	Y
11 *Gingrey*	Y	Y	Y	Y	Y
12 *Burns*	Y	Y	Y	Y	Y
13 Scott	Y	Y	Y	Y	Y
HAWAII					
1 Abercrombie	Y	Y	Y	Y	Y
2 Case	Y	Y	Y	Y	Y
IDAHO					
1 *Otter*	Y	Y	Y	N	Y
2 *Simpson*	Y	Y	Y	Y	Y
ILLINOIS					
1 Rush	Y	Y	Y	Y	Y
2 Jackson	Y	Y	Y	Y	Y
3 Lipinski	Y	Y	Y	Y	Y
4 Gutierrez	?	?	?	Y	Y
5 Emanuel	Y	Y	Y	Y	Y
6 *Hyde*	Y	Y	Y	Y	Y

ND Northern Democrats   SD Southern Democrats

	118	119	120	121	122
7 Davis	Y	Y	Y	Y	Y
8 *Crane*	Y	Y	Y	Y	Y
9 Schakowsky	Y	Y	Y	Y	Y
10 *Kirk*	Y	Y	Y	Y	Y
11 *Weller*	Y	Y	Y	?	?
12 Costello	Y	Y	Y	Y	Y
13 *Biggert*	Y	Y	Y	Y	Y
14 *Hastert*					
15 *Johnson*	Y	Y	Y	Y	Y
16 *Manzullo*	Y	Y	Y	Y	Y
17 Evans	Y	Y	Y	Y	Y
18 *LaHood*	Y	Y	Y	Y	Y
19 *Shimkus*	Y	Y	Y	Y	Y
INDIANA					
1 Visclosky	Y	Y	Y	Y	Y
2 *Chocola*	Y	Y	Y	Y	Y
3 *Souder*	Y	Y	Y	Y	Y
4 *Buyer*	?	?	?	Y	Y
5 *Burton*	Y	Y	Y	Y	Y
6 *Pence*	Y	Y	Y	N	N
7 Carson	Y	Y	Y	Y	Y
8 *Hostettler*	Y	Y	Y	N	Y
9 Hill	Y	Y	Y	Y	Y
IOWA					
1 *Nussle*	Y	Y	Y	Y	Y
2 *Leach*	Y	Y	Y	Y	Y
3 Boswell	Y	Y	Y	Y	Y
4 *Latham*	Y	Y	Y	Y	Y
5 *King*	Y	Y	Y	Y	Y
KANSAS					
1 *Moran*	Y	Y	Y	Y	Y
2 *Ryun*	Y	Y	Y	Y	Y
3 Moore	Y	Y	Y	Y	Y
4 *Tiahrt*	Y	Y	Y	Y	Y
KENTUCKY					
1 *Whitfield*	Y	Y	Y	Y	Y
2 *Lewis*	Y	Y	Y	?	Y
3 *Northup*	Y	Y	Y	Y	Y
4 Lucas	Y	Y	Y	Y	Y
5 *Rogers*	Y	Y	Y	Y	Y
6 Chandler	Y	Y	Y	Y	Y
LOUISIANA					
1 *Vitter*	Y	Y	Y	Y	Y
2 Jefferson	?	?	?	?	?
3 *Tauzin*	?	?	?	?	?
4 *McCrery*	?	?	?	Y	Y
5 Alexander	Y	Y	Y	Y	Y
6 *Baker*	Y	Y	Y	Y	Y
7 John	Y	Y	Y	?	Y
MAINE					
1 Allen	Y	Y	Y	Y	
2 Michaud	Y	Y	Y	Y	
MARYLAND					
1 *Gilchrest*	Y	Y	Y	Y	Y
2 Ruppersberger	Y	Y	Y	Y	Y
3 Cardin	Y	Y	Y	Y	Y
4 Wynn	Y	Y	Y	Y	Y
5 Hoyer	Y	Y	Y	Y	Y
6 *Bartlett*	Y	Y	Y	Y	Y
7 Cummings	Y	Y	Y	Y	Y
8 Van Hollen	Y	Y	Y	Y	Y
MASSACHUSETTS					
1 Olver	Y	Y	Y	Y	Y
2 Neal	Y	Y	Y	Y	Y
3 McGovern	Y	Y	Y	Y	Y
4 Frank	Y	Y	Y	Y	Y
5 Meehan	Y	Y	Y	Y	Y
6 Tierney	Y	Y	Y	Y	Y
7 Markey	Y	Y	Y	Y	Y
8 Capuano	Y	Y	Y	Y	Y
9 Lynch	Y	Y	Y	Y	Y
10 Delahunt	Y	Y	Y	Y	Y
MICHIGAN					
1 Stupak	Y	Y	Y	Y	Y
2 *Hoekstra*	Y	Y	Y	Y	N
3 *Ehlers*	Y	Y	Y	Y	Y
4 *Camp*	Y	Y	Y	Y	Y
5 Kildee	Y	Y	Y	Y	Y
6 *Upton*	Y	Y	Y	Y	Y
7 *Smith*	Y	Y	Y	Y	Y
8 *Rogers*	Y	Y	Y	Y	Y
9 *Knollenberg*	Y	Y	Y	Y	Y
10 *Miller*	Y	Y	Y	Y	Y
11 *McCotter*	Y	Y	Y	Y	Y
12 Levin	Y	Y	Y	Y	Y

	118	119	120	121	122
13 Kilpatrick	Y	Y	Y	Y	Y
14 Conyers	Y	Y	Y	Y	Y
15 Dingell	Y	Y	Y	Y	Y
MINNESOTA					
1 *Gutknecht*	Y	Y	Y	Y	Y
2 *Kline*	Y	Y	Y	Y	Y
3 *Ramstad*	Y	Y	Y	Y	Y
4 McCollum	Y	Y	Y	Y	Y
5 Sabo	Y	Y	Y	Y	Y
6 *Kennedy*	Y	Y	Y	Y	Y
7 Peterson	Y	Y	Y	Y	Y
8 Oberstar	Y	Y	Y	Y	Y
MISSISSIPPI					
1 *Wicker*	Y	Y	Y	Y	Y
2 Thompson	Y	Y	Y	Y	Y
3 *Pickering*	Y	Y	Y	Y	Y
4 Taylor	Y	Y	Y	Y	Y
MISSOURI					
1 Clay	Y	Y	Y	Y	Y
2 *Akin*	Y	Y	Y	Y	Y
3 Gephardt	?	?	?	?	?
4 Skelton	Y	Y	Y	Y	Y
5 McCarthy	Y	Y	Y	Y	Y
6 *Graves*	Y	Y	Y	Y	Y
7 *Blunt*	?	?	Y	Y	Y
8 *Emerson*	Y	Y	Y	Y	Y
9 *Hulshof*	Y	Y	Y	?	?
MONTANA					
AL *Rehberg*	Y	Y	Y	Y	Y
NEBRASKA					
1 *Bereuter*	Y	Y	Y	Y	Y
2 *Terry*	Y	Y	Y	Y	Y
3 *Osborne*	Y	Y	Y	Y	Y
NEVADA					
1 Berkley	Y	Y	Y	Y	Y
2 *Gibbons*	Y	Y	Y	Y	Y
3 *Porter*	Y	Y	Y	Y	Y
NEW HAMPSHIRE					
1 *Bradley*	Y	Y	Y	Y	Y
2 *Bass*	Y	Y	Y	Y	Y
NEW JERSEY					
1 Andrews	?	?	?	Y	Y
2 *LoBiondo*	Y	Y	Y	Y	Y
3 *Saxton*	Y	Y	Y	Y	Y
4 *Smith*	Y	Y	Y	Y	Y
5 *Garrett*	Y	Y	Y	Y	Y
6 Pallone	Y	Y	Y	Y	Y
7 *Ferguson*	Y	Y	Y	Y	Y
8 Pascrell	Y	Y	Y	Y	Y
9 Rothman	Y	Y	Y	Y	Y
10 Payne	Y	Y	Y	Y	Y
11 *Frelinghuysen*	?	?	?	+	+
12 Holt	Y	Y	Y	Y	Y
13 Menendez	Y	Y	Y	Y	Y
NEW MEXICO					
1 *Wilson*	Y	Y	Y	Y	Y
2 *Pearce*	Y	Y	Y	Y	Y
3 Udall	Y	Y	Y	Y	Y
NEW YORK					
1 Bishop	Y	Y	Y	Y	Y
2 Israel	Y	Y	Y	Y	Y
3 *King*	Y	Y	Y	Y	Y
4 McCarthy	Y	Y	Y	Y	Y
5 Ackerman	Y	Y	Y	Y	Y
6 Meeks	?	?	?	Y	Y
7 Crowley	Y	Y	Y	Y	Y
8 Nadler	Y	Y	Y	Y	Y
9 Weiner	?	?	?	Y	Y
10 Towns	Y	Y	Y	Y	Y
11 Owens	Y	Y	Y	Y	Y
12 Velázquez	Y	Y	Y	?	?
13 *Fossella*	Y	Y	Y	Y	Y
14 Maloney	Y	Y	Y	Y	Y
15 Rangel	Y	Y	Y	Y	Y
16 Serrano	Y	Y	Y	Y	Y
17 Engel	Y	Y	Y	Y	Y
18 Lowey	Y	Y	Y	Y	Y
19 *Kelly*	Y	Y	Y	Y	Y
20 *Sweeney*	?	?	?	Y	Y
21 McNulty	Y	Y	Y	Y	Y
22 Hinchey	Y	Y	Y	Y	Y
23 *McHugh*	Y	Y	Y	Y	Y
24 *Boehlert*	Y	Y	Y	Y	Y
25 *Walsh*	Y	Y	Y	Y	Y

	118	119	120	121	122
26 *Reynolds*	?	?	Y	Y	Y
27 *Quinn*	Y	Y	Y	?	Y
28 Slaughter	Y	Y	Y	Y	Y
29 Houghton	Y	Y	Y	Y	Y
NORTH CAROLINA					
1 Ballance	Y	Y	Y	Y	Y
2 Etheridge	Y	Y	Y	Y	Y
3 *Jones*	Y	Y	Y	N	Y
4 Price	Y	Y	Y	Y	Y
5 *Burr*	Y	Y	Y	Y	Y
6 *Coble*	Y	Y	Y	Y	Y
7 McIntyre	Y	Y	Y	Y	Y
8 *Hayes*	Y	Y	Y	Y	Y
9 *Myrick*	Y	Y	Y	Y	Y
10 *Ballenger*	Y	Y	Y	Y	Y
11 *Taylor*	Y	Y	Y	Y	Y
12 Watt	Y	Y	Y	Y	Y
13 Miller	Y	Y	Y	Y	Y
NORTH DAKOTA					
AL Pomeroy	Y	Y	Y	Y	Y
OHIO					
1 *Chabot*	Y	Y	Y	Y	Y
2 *Portman*	?	?	Y	Y	Y
3 *Turner*	Y	Y	Y	Y	Y
4 *Oxley*	Y	Y	Y	Y	Y
5 *Gillmor*	Y	Y	Y	Y	Y
6 Strickland	Y	Y	Y	Y	Y
7 *Hobson*	Y	Y	Y	Y	Y
8 *Boehner*	Y	Y	Y	Y	Y
9 Kaptur	Y	Y	Y	Y	Y
10 Kucinich	?	?	Y	Y	Y
11 Jones	Y	Y	Y	Y	Y
12 *Tiberi*	Y	Y	Y	Y	Y
13 Brown	Y	Y	Y	Y	Y
14 *LaTourette*	Y	Y	Y	Y	Y
15 *Pryce*	?	?	Y	Y	Y
16 *Regula*	Y	Y	Y	Y	Y
17 Ryan	Y	Y	Y	Y	Y
18 *Ney*	Y	Y	Y	Y	Y
OKLAHOMA					
1 *Sullivan*	Y	Y	Y	Y	Y
2 Carson	Y	Y	Y	Y	Y
3 *Lucas*	Y	Y	Y	Y	Y
4 *Cole*	Y	Y	Y	Y	Y
5 *Istook*	Y	Y	Y	Y	Y
OREGON					
1 Wu	Y	Y	Y	Y	Y
2 *Walden*	Y	Y	Y	Y	Y
3 Blumenauer	Y	Y	Y	Y	Y
4 DeFazio	Y	Y	Y	Y	Y
5 Hooley	Y	Y	Y	Y	Y
PENNSYLVANIA					
1 Brady	Y	Y	Y	Y	Y
2 Fattah	Y	Y	Y	Y	Y
3 *English*	Y	Y	Y	Y	Y
4 *Hart*	Y	Y	Y	Y	Y
5 *Peterson*	Y	Y	Y	Y	Y
6 *Gerlach*	Y	Y	Y	Y	Y
7 *Weldon*	Y	Y	Y	Y	Y
8 *Greenwood*	Y	Y	Y	?	?
9 *Shuster, Bill*	Y	Y	Y	Y	Y
10 *Sherwood*	Y	Y	Y	Y	Y
11 Kanjorski	Y	Y	Y	Y	Y
12 Murtha	Y	Y	Y	Y	Y
13 Hoeffel	?	?	?	?	?
14 Doyle	Y	Y	Y	Y	Y
15 *Toomey*	?	?	?	?	?
16 *Pitts*	Y	Y	Y	Y	Y
17 Holden	Y	Y	Y	Y	Y
18 *Murphy*	Y	Y	Y	Y	Y
19 *Platts*	Y	Y	Y	Y	Y
RHODE ISLAND					
1 Kennedy	Y	Y	Y	Y	Y
2 Langevin	Y	Y	Y	Y	Y
SOUTH CAROLINA					
1 *Brown*	Y	Y	Y	Y	Y
2 *Wilson*	Y	Y	Y	Y	Y
3 *Barrett*	Y	Y	Y	Y	Y
4 *DeMint*	Y	Y	Y	Y	Y
5 Spratt	Y	Y	Y	Y	Y
6 Clyburn	Y	Y	Y	Y	Y
SOUTH DAKOTA					
AL Vacant					

	118	119	120	121	122
TENNESSEE					
1 *Jenkins*	Y	Y	Y	Y	Y
2 *Duncan*	Y	Y	Y	N	Y
3 *Wamp*	Y	Y	Y	Y	Y
4 Davis	Y	Y	Y	Y	Y
5 Cooper	Y	Y	Y	Y	Y
6 Gordon	Y	Y	Y	Y	Y
7 *Blackburn*	Y	Y	Y	Y	Y
8 Tanner	Y	Y	Y	Y	Y
9 Ford	?	?	?	Y	Y
TEXAS					
1 Sandlin	Y	Y	Y	Y	Y
2 Turner	Y	Y	Y	Y	Y
3 *Johnson, Sam*	Y	Y	Y	Y	Y
4 Hall	Y	Y	Y	Y	Y
5 *Hensarling*	Y	Y	Y	N	N
6 *Barton*	Y	Y	Y	Y	Y
7 *Culberson*	Y	Y	Y	Y	Y
8 *Brady*	Y	Y	Y	Y	Y
9 Lampson	Y	Y	Y	Y	Y
10 Doggett	Y	Y	Y	Y	Y
11 Edwards	Y	Y	Y	Y	Y
12 *Granger*	Y	Y	?	Y	Y
13 *Thornberry*	Y	Y	Y	Y	Y
14 *Paul*	Y	Y	Y	N	N
15 Hinojosa	Y	Y	Y	Y	Y
16 Reyes	Y	Y	Y	Y	Y
17 Stenholm	Y	Y	Y	Y	Y
18 Jackson-Lee	Y	Y	Y	Y	Y
19 *Neugebauer*	Y	Y	Y	Y	Y
20 Gonzalez	?	?	?	Y	Y
21 *Smith*	Y	Y	Y	Y	Y
22 *DeLay*	?	?	?	Y	Y
23 *Bonilla*	Y	Y	Y	Y	Y
24 Frost	Y	Y	Y	Y	Y
25 Bell	Y	Y	Y	Y	Y
26 *Burgess*	Y	Y	Y	Y	Y
27 Ortiz	Y	Y	Y	Y	Y
28 Rodriguez	Y	Y	Y	Y	Y
29 Green	Y	Y	Y	Y	Y
30 Johnson, E.B.	Y	Y	Y	Y	Y
31 *Carter*	Y	Y	Y	Y	Y
32 *Sessions*	Y	Y	Y	Y	Y
UTAH					
1 *Bishop*	?	?	?	Y	Y
2 Matheson	Y	Y	Y	Y	Y
3 *Cannon*	Y	Y	Y	Y	Y
VERMONT					
AL *Sanders*	Y	Y	Y	Y	Y
VIRGINIA					
1 *Davis, Jo Ann*	Y	Y	Y	N	Y
2 *Schrock*	Y	Y	Y	Y	?
3 Scott	Y	Y	Y	Y	Y
4 *Forbes*	Y	Y	Y	Y	Y
5 *Goode*	Y	Y	Y	Y	Y
6 *Goodlatte*	Y	Y	Y	Y	Y
7 *Cantor*	Y	Y	Y	Y	Y
8 Moran	Y	Y	Y	Y	Y
9 Boucher	Y	Y	Y	Y	Y
10 *Wolf*	?	?	?	Y	Y
11 *Davis, T.*	Y	Y	Y	Y	Y
WASHINGTON					
1 Inslee	?	?	?	Y	Y
2 Larsen	Y	Y	Y	Y	Y
3 Baird	Y	Y	Y	Y	Y
4 *Hastings*	Y	Y	Y	Y	Y
5 *Nethercutt*	Y	Y	Y	Y	Y
6 Dicks	Y	Y	Y	Y	Y
7 McDermott	Y	Y	Y	Y	Y
8 *Dunn*	?	?	?	Y	Y
9 Smith	Y	Y	Y	Y	Y
WEST VIRGINIA					
1 Mollohan	Y	Y	Y	Y	Y
2 *Capito*	Y	Y	Y	Y	Y
3 Rahall	Y	Y	Y	Y	Y
WISCONSIN					
1 *Ryan*	Y	Y	Y	Y	Y
2 Baldwin	Y	Y	?	Y	Y
3 Kind	Y	Y	Y	Y	Y
4 Kleczka	?	?	?	Y	Y
5 *Sensenbrenner*	Y	Y	Y	Y	Y
6 *Petri*	Y	Y	Y	Y	Y
7 Obey	Y	Y	Y	Y	Y
8 *Green*	Y	Y	Y	Y	Y
WYOMING					
AL *Cubin*	Y	Y	Y	N	Y

Southern states - Ala., Ark., Fla., Ga., Ky., La., Miss., N.C., Okla., S.C., Tenn., Texas, Va.

Key

Y	Voted for (yea).
#	Paired for.
+	Announced for.
N	Voted against (nay).
X	Paired against.
−	Announced against.
P	Voted "present."
C	Voted "present" to avoid possible conflict of interest.
?	Did not vote or otherwise make a position known.

Democrats   **Republicans**
Independents

123. HR 3147. James V. Hansen Building/Passage. LaTourette, R-Ohio, motion to suspend the rules and pass the bill that would name a federal building in Ogden, Utah, after former Rep. James V. Hansen, R-Utah, who served in the House from 1981 to 2003. Motion agreed to 418-0: R 217-0; D 200-0 (ND 145-0, SD 55-0); I 1-0. A two-thirds majority of those present and voting (279 in this case) is required for passage under suspension of the rules. April 21, 2004.

124. HR 4019. World Health Organization and Taiwan/Passage. Chabot, R-Ohio, motion to suspend the rules and pass the bill that would authorize the secretary of State to endorse and obtain observer status for Taiwan at the annual weeklong summit of the World Health Assembly in May 2004 in Geneva. Motion agreed to 416-0: R 215-0; D 200-0 (ND 146-0, SD 54-0); I 1-0. A two-thirds majority of those present and voting (278 in this case) is required for passage under suspension of the rules. April 21, 2004.

125. HR 1779. Reservist Retirement Withdrawals/Passage. Shaw, R-Fla., motion to suspend the rules and pass the bill that would allow members of the active-duty National Guard and reserves to make penalty-free early withdrawals from retirement plans. The bill would limit the withdrawals to members of the military activated between Sept. 11, 2001, and Sept. 12, 2005, and who serve in excess of 179 days. Motion agreed to 415-0: R 214-0; D 200-0 (ND 146-0, SD 54-0); I 1-0. A two-thirds majority of those present and voting (277 in this case) is required for passage under suspension of the rules. April 21, 2004.

126. HR 2844. Continuity of Congress/Previous Question. Hastings, R-Wash., motion to order the previous question (thus ending debate and possibility of amendment) on adoption of the rule (H Res 602) to provide for House floor consideration of the bill that would require special elections to fill vacant House seats within 45 days of a catastrophe that kills at least 100 House members. Motion agreed to 210-198: R 210-0; D 0-197 (ND 0-145, SD 0-52); I 0-1. April 22, 2004.

	123	124	125	126
ALABAMA				
1 *Bonner*	Y	Y	Y	Y
2 *Everett*	Y	Y	Y	Y
3 *Rogers*	Y	Y	Y	Y
4 *Aderholt*	Y	Y	Y	Y
5 Cramer	Y	Y	Y	N
6 *Bachus*	Y	Y	Y	Y
7 Davis	Y	Y	Y	N
ALASKA				
AL *Young*	Y	Y	Y	Y
ARIZONA				
1 *Renzi*	Y	Y	Y	Y
2 *Franks*	Y	Y	Y	Y
3 *Shadegg*	Y	Y	Y	Y
4 Pastor	Y	Y	Y	N
5 *Hayworth*	Y	Y	Y	Y
6 *Flake*	Y	Y	Y	Y
7 Grijalva	Y	Y	Y	N
8 *Kolbe*	Y	Y	Y	Y
ARKANSAS				
1 Berry	Y	Y	Y	N
2 Snyder	Y	Y	Y	N
3 *Boozman*	Y	Y	Y	Y
4 Ross	Y	Y	Y	N
CALIFORNIA				
1 Thompson	Y	Y	Y	N
2 *Herger*	Y	Y	Y	Y
3 *Ose*	Y	Y	Y	Y
4 *Doolittle*	?	Y	Y	Y
5 Matsui	Y	Y	Y	N
6 Woolsey	Y	Y	Y	N
7 Miller, George	Y	Y	Y	N
8 Pelosi	Y	Y	Y	N
9 Lee	Y	Y	Y	N
10 Tauscher	Y	Y	Y	N
11 *Pombo*	Y	Y	Y	?
12 Lantos	Y	Y	Y	N
13 Stark	Y	Y	Y	N
14 Eshoo	Y	Y	Y	N
15 Honda	Y	Y	Y	N
16 Lofgren	Y	Y	Y	N
17 Farr	Y	Y	Y	N
18 Cardoza	Y	Y	Y	N
19 *Radanovich*	Y	?	?	Y
20 Dooley	Y	Y	Y	N
21 *Nunes*	Y	Y	Y	Y
22 *Thomas*	Y	Y	Y	Y
23 Capps	Y	Y	Y	N
24 *Gallegly*	Y	Y	Y	?
25 *McKeon*	Y	Y	Y	Y
26 *Dreier*	Y	Y	Y	Y
27 Sherman	Y	Y	Y	N
28 Berman	Y	Y	Y	N
29 Schiff	Y	Y	Y	N
30 Waxman	Y	Y	Y	N
31 Becerra	Y	Y	Y	N
32 Solis	Y	Y	Y	N
33 Watson	Y	Y	Y	N
34 Roybal-Allard	Y	Y	Y	N
35 Waters	Y	Y	Y	N
36 Harman	Y	Y	Y	N

	123	124	125	126
37 Millender-McD.	Y	Y	Y	?
38 Napolitano	Y	Y	Y	N
39 Sánchez, Linda	Y	Y	Y	N
40 *Royce*	Y	Y	Y	Y
41 *Lewis*	Y	Y	Y	Y
42 *Miller, Gary*	Y	Y	Y	Y
43 Baca	Y	Y	Y	N
44 *Calvert*	Y	Y	Y	Y
45 *Bono*	Y	Y	Y	Y
46 *Rohrabacher*	Y	Y	Y	Y
47 Sanchez, Loretta	Y	Y	Y	N
48 *Cox*	Y	Y	Y	Y
49 *Issa*	Y	Y	Y	Y
50 *Cunningham*	Y	Y	Y	Y
51 Filner	Y	Y	Y	N
52 *Hunter*	Y	Y	Y	?
53 Davis	Y	Y	Y	N
COLORADO				
1 DeGette	Y	Y	Y	N
2 Udall	Y	Y	Y	N
3 *McInnis*	Y	Y	Y	Y
4 *Musgrave*	Y	Y	Y	Y
5 *Hefley*	Y	Y	Y	Y
6 *Tancredo*	Y	Y	Y	Y
7 *Beauprez*	Y	Y	Y	Y
CONNECTICUT				
1 Larson	Y	Y	Y	N
2 *Simmons*	Y	Y	Y	Y
3 DeLauro	Y	Y	Y	N
4 *Shays*	Y	Y	Y	Y
5 *Johnson*	Y	Y	Y	Y
DELAWARE				
AL *Castle*	Y	Y	Y	Y
FLORIDA				
1 *Miller, J.*	Y	Y	Y	?
2 Boyd	Y	Y	Y	N
3 Brown	Y	Y	Y	N
4 *Crenshaw*	Y	Y	Y	Y
5 *Brown-Waite*	Y	Y	Y	Y
6 *Stearns*	Y	Y	Y	Y
7 *Mica*	Y	Y	Y	Y
8 *Keller*	Y	Y	Y	Y
9 *Bilirakis*	Y	Y	Y	Y
10 *Young*	Y	Y	Y	Y
11 Davis	Y	Y	Y	N
12 *Putnam*	Y	Y	Y	Y
13 *Harris*	+	+	+	Y
14 *Goss*	Y	Y	Y	Y
15 *Weldon*	Y	Y	Y	Y
16 *Foley*	Y	Y	Y	Y
17 Meek	Y	Y	Y	N
18 *Ros-Lehtinen*	?	?	?	Y
19 Wexler	Y	Y	Y	N
20 Deutsch	Y	Y	Y	N
21 *Diaz-Balart, L.*	Y	Y	Y	Y
22 *Shaw*	Y	Y	Y	Y
23 Hastings	?	?	?	?
24 *Feeney*	Y	?	?	Y
25 *Diaz-Balart, M.*	Y	Y	Y	Y
GEORGIA				
1 *Kingston*	?	?	?	Y
2 Bishop	Y	Y	Y	N
3 Marshall	Y	Y	Y	N
4 Majette	Y	Y	Y	N
5 Lewis	Y	Y	Y	N
6 *Isakson*	Y	Y	Y	Y
7 *Linder*	Y	Y	Y	Y
8 *Collins*	Y	Y	Y	Y
9 *Norwood*	Y	Y	Y	Y
10 *Deal*	Y	Y	Y	Y
11 *Gingrey*	Y	Y	Y	Y
12 *Burns*	Y	Y	Y	Y
13 Scott	Y	Y	Y	N
HAWAII				
1 Abercrombie	Y	Y	Y	N
2 Case	Y	Y	Y	N
IDAHO				
1 *Otter*	Y	Y	+	Y
2 *Simpson*	Y	Y	Y	Y
ILLINOIS				
1 Rush	Y	Y	Y	N
2 Jackson	Y	Y	Y	N
3 Lipinski	Y	Y	Y	N
4 Gutierrez	Y	Y	Y	N
5 Emanuel	Y	Y	Y	N
6 *Hyde*	Y	Y	Y	Y

ND Northern Democrats   SD Southern Democrats

	123	124	125	126
7 Davis	Y	Y	Y	N
8 Crane	Y	Y	Y	N
9 Schakowsky	Y	Y	Y	N
10 Kirk	Y	Y	Y	Y
11 Weller	?	?	?	Y
12 Costello	Y	Y	Y	N
13 Biggert	Y	Y	Y	Y
14 Hastert				
15 Johnson	Y	Y	Y	Y
16 Manzullo	Y	Y	Y	Y
17 Evans	Y	Y	Y	N
18 LaHood	Y	Y	Y	Y
19 Shimkus	Y	Y	Y	Y
INDIANA				
1 Visclosky	Y	Y	Y	N
2 Chocola	Y	Y	Y	Y
3 Souder	Y	Y	Y	Y
4 Buyer	Y	Y	Y	Y
5 Burton	Y	Y	Y	Y
6 Pence	Y	Y	Y	Y
7 Carson	Y	Y	Y	N
8 Hostettler	Y	Y	Y	Y
9 Hill	Y	Y	Y	N
IOWA				
1 Nussle	Y	Y	Y	Y
2 Leach	Y	Y	Y	Y
3 Boswell	Y	Y	Y	N
4 Latham	Y	Y	Y	Y
5 King	Y	Y	Y	Y
KANSAS				
1 Moran	Y	Y	Y	Y
2 Ryun	Y	Y	Y	Y
3 Moore	Y	Y	Y	N
4 Tiahrt	Y	Y	Y	Y
KENTUCKY				
1 Whitfield	Y	Y	?	Y
2 Lewis	Y	Y	Y	Y
3 Northup	Y	Y	Y	Y
4 Lucas	Y	Y	Y	?
5 Rogers	Y	Y	Y	Y
6 Chandler	Y	Y	Y	N
LOUISIANA				
1 Vitter	Y	Y	Y	Y
2 Jefferson	?	?	?	N
3 Tauzin	?	?	?	?
4 McCrery	Y	Y	Y	Y
5 Alexander	Y	Y	Y	Y
6 Baker	Y	Y	Y	Y
7 John	Y	Y	Y	N
MAINE				
1 Allen	Y	Y	Y	N
2 Michaud	Y	Y	Y	N
MARYLAND				
1 Gilchrest	Y	Y	Y	Y
2 Ruppersberger	Y	Y	?	N
3 Cardin	Y	Y	Y	N
4 Wynn	Y	Y	Y	N
5 Hoyer	Y	Y	Y	N
6 Bartlett	Y	Y	Y	Y
7 Cummings	Y	Y	Y	N
8 Van Hollen	Y	Y	Y	N
MASSACHUSETTS				
1 Olver	Y	Y	Y	N
2 Neal	Y	Y	Y	N
3 McGovern	Y	Y	Y	N
4 Frank	Y	Y	Y	N
5 Meehan	Y	Y	Y	N
6 Tierney	Y	Y	Y	N
7 Markey	Y	Y	Y	N
8 Capuano	Y	Y	Y	N
9 Lynch	Y	Y	Y	N
10 Delahunt	Y	Y	Y	N
MICHIGAN				
1 Stupak	Y	Y	Y	N
2 Hoekstra	Y	Y	Y	Y
3 Ehlers	Y	Y	Y	Y
4 Camp	Y	Y	Y	Y
5 Kildee	Y	Y	Y	N
6 Upton	Y	Y	Y	Y
7 Smith	Y	Y	Y	Y
8 Rogers	Y	Y	Y	Y
9 Knollenberg	Y	Y	Y	Y
10 Miller	Y	Y	Y	Y
11 McCotter	Y	Y	Y	Y
12 Levin	Y	Y	Y	N

	123	124	125	126
13 Kilpatrick	Y	Y	Y	N
14 Conyers	Y	?	Y	N
15 Dingell	Y	Y	Y	N
MINNESOTA				
1 Gutknecht	Y	Y	Y	Y
2 Kline	Y	Y	Y	Y
3 Ramstad	Y	Y	Y	Y
4 McCollum	Y	Y	Y	N
5 Sabo	Y	Y	Y	N
6 Kennedy	Y	Y	Y	Y
7 Peterson	Y	Y	Y	N
8 Oberstar	Y	Y	Y	N
MISSISSIPPI				
1 Wicker	Y	Y	Y	Y
2 Thompson	Y	Y	Y	N
3 Pickering	Y	Y	Y	Y
4 Taylor	Y	Y	Y	N
MISSOURI				
1 Clay	Y	Y	Y	N
2 Akin	Y	Y	Y	Y
3 Gephardt	?	?	?	?
4 Skelton	Y	Y	Y	N
5 McCarthy	Y	Y	Y	N
6 Graves	Y	Y	Y	Y
7 Blunt	Y	Y	Y	Y
8 Emerson	Y	Y	Y	Y
9 Hulshof	?	?	?	?
MONTANA				
AL Rehberg	Y	Y	Y	Y
NEBRASKA				
1 Bereuter	Y	Y	Y	Y
2 Terry	Y	Y	Y	Y
3 Osborne	Y	Y	Y	Y
NEVADA				
1 Berkley	Y	Y	Y	N
2 Gibbons	Y	Y	Y	Y
3 Porter	Y	Y	Y	N
NEW HAMPSHIRE				
1 Bradley	Y	Y	Y	Y
2 Bass	Y	Y	Y	Y
NEW JERSEY				
1 Andrews	Y	Y	Y	N
2 LoBiondo	Y	Y	Y	N
3 Saxton	Y	Y	Y	N
4 Smith	Y	Y	Y	N
5 Garrett	Y	Y	Y	N
6 Pallone	Y	Y	Y	N
7 Ferguson	Y	Y	Y	N
8 Pascrell	Y	Y	Y	N
9 Rothman	Y	Y	Y	N
10 Payne	Y	Y	Y	N
11 Frelinghuysen	+	+	+	Y
12 Holt	Y	Y	Y	N
13 Menendez	Y	Y	Y	N
NEW MEXICO				
1 Wilson	Y	Y	Y	Y
2 Pearce	Y	Y	Y	Y
3 Udall	Y	Y	Y	N
NEW YORK				
1 Bishop	Y	Y	Y	N
2 Israel	Y	Y	Y	N
3 King	Y	Y	Y	N
4 McCarthy	Y	Y	Y	N
5 Ackerman	Y	Y	Y	N
6 Meeks	Y	Y	Y	N
7 Crowley	Y	Y	Y	N
8 Nadler	Y	Y	Y	N
9 Weiner	Y	Y	Y	N
10 Towns	Y	Y	Y	N
11 Owens	Y	Y	Y	N
12 Velázquez	Y	Y	Y	N
13 Fossella	Y	Y	Y	?
14 Maloney	Y	Y	Y	N
15 Rangel	Y	Y	Y	N
16 Serrano	Y	Y	Y	N
17 Engel	Y	Y	Y	N
18 Lowey	Y	Y	Y	N
19 Kelly	Y	Y	Y	Y
20 Sweeney	Y	Y	Y	Y
21 McNulty	Y	Y	Y	N
22 Hinchey	Y	Y	Y	N
23 McHugh	Y	Y	Y	Y
24 Boehlert	Y	Y	Y	Y
25 Walsh	Y	Y	Y	Y

	123	124	125	126
26 Reynolds	Y	Y	Y	Y
27 Quinn	Y	Y	Y	Y
28 Slaughter	?	Y	Y	N
29 Houghton	Y	Y	Y	Y
NORTH CAROLINA				
1 Ballance	Y	Y	Y	N
2 Etheridge	Y	Y	Y	N
3 Jones	Y	Y	Y	N
4 Price	Y	Y	Y	N
5 Burr	Y	Y	Y	Y
6 Coble	Y	Y	Y	Y
7 McIntyre	Y	Y	Y	N
8 Hayes	Y	Y	Y	Y
9 Myrick	Y	Y	Y	Y
10 Ballenger	Y	Y	Y	Y
11 Taylor	Y	Y	Y	Y
12 Watt	Y	Y	Y	N
13 Miller	Y	Y	Y	N
NORTH DAKOTA				
AL Pomeroy	Y	Y	Y	N
OHIO				
1 Chabot	Y	Y	Y	Y
2 Portman	Y	Y	Y	Y
3 Turner	Y	Y	Y	Y
4 Oxley	Y	Y	Y	Y
5 Gillmor	Y	Y	Y	Y
6 Strickland	Y	Y	Y	N
7 Hobson	Y	Y	Y	Y
8 Boehner	Y	Y	Y	Y
9 Kaptur	Y	Y	Y	N
10 Kucinich	Y	Y	Y	N
11 Jones	Y	Y	Y	N
12 Tiberi	Y	Y	Y	Y
13 Brown	Y	Y	Y	N
14 LaTourette	Y	Y	Y	Y
15 Pryce	Y	Y	Y	Y
16 Regula	Y	Y	Y	Y
17 Ryan	Y	Y	Y	N
18 Ney	Y	Y	Y	Y
OKLAHOMA				
1 Sullivan	Y	Y	Y	Y
2 Carson	Y	Y	Y	N
3 Lucas	Y	Y	Y	Y
4 Cole	Y	Y	Y	Y
5 Istook	Y	Y	Y	Y
OREGON				
1 Wu	Y	Y	Y	N
2 Walden	Y	Y	Y	N
3 Blumenauer	Y	Y	Y	N
4 DeFazio	Y	Y	Y	N
5 Hooley	Y	Y	Y	N
PENNSYLVANIA				
1 Brady	Y	Y	Y	N
2 Fattah	Y	Y	Y	N
3 English	Y	Y	Y	Y
4 Hart	Y	Y	Y	Y
5 Peterson	Y	Y	Y	?
6 Gerlach	Y	Y	Y	Y
7 Weldon	Y	Y	Y	Y
8 Greenwood	?	?	?	?
9 Shuster, Bill	Y	Y	Y	?
10 Sherwood	Y	Y	Y	Y
11 Kanjorski	Y	Y	Y	N
12 Murtha	Y	Y	Y	N
13 Hoeffel	?	Y	Y	N
14 Doyle	Y	Y	Y	N
15 Toomey	?	?	?	?
16 Pitts	Y	Y	Y	Y
17 Holden	Y	Y	Y	N
18 Murphy	Y	Y	Y	Y
19 Platts	Y	Y	Y	Y
RHODE ISLAND				
1 Kennedy	Y	Y	Y	N
2 Langevin	Y	Y	Y	N
SOUTH CAROLINA				
1 Brown	Y	Y	Y	Y
2 Wilson	Y	Y	Y	Y
3 Barrett	Y	Y	Y	Y
4 DeMint	Y	Y	Y	?
5 Spratt	Y	Y	Y	N
6 Clyburn	Y	Y	Y	N
SOUTH DAKOTA				
AL Vacant				

	123	124	125	126
TENNESSEE				
1 Jenkins	Y	Y	Y	Y
2 Duncan	Y	Y	Y	?
3 Wamp	Y	Y	Y	Y
4 Davis	Y	Y	Y	N
5 Cooper	Y	Y	Y	N
6 Gordon	Y	Y	Y	N
7 Blackburn	Y	Y	Y	Y
8 Tanner	Y	Y	Y	N
9 Ford	Y	Y	Y	N
TEXAS				
1 Sandlin	Y	Y	Y	N
2 Turner	Y	Y	Y	N
3 Johnson, Sam	Y	Y	Y	Y
4 Hall	Y	Y	Y	?
5 Hensarling	Y	Y	Y	Y
6 Barton	Y	Y	Y	Y
7 Culberson	Y	Y	Y	Y
8 Brady	Y	Y	Y	Y
9 Lampson	Y	Y	Y	N
10 Doggett	Y	Y	Y	N
11 Edwards	Y	Y	Y	?
12 Granger	Y	Y	Y	Y
13 Thornberry	Y	Y	Y	Y
14 Paul	Y	Y	Y	Y
15 Hinojosa	Y	+	+	?
16 Reyes	Y	Y	Y	N
17 Stenholm	Y	Y	Y	N
18 Jackson-Lee	Y	Y	Y	?
19 Neugebauer	Y	Y	Y	Y
20 Gonzalez	Y	Y	Y	N
21 Smith	Y	Y	Y	Y
22 DeLay	Y	Y	Y	Y
23 Bonilla	Y	Y	Y	Y
24 Frost	Y	Y	Y	N
25 Bell	Y	Y	Y	N
26 Burgess	Y	Y	Y	Y
27 Ortiz	Y	Y	Y	N
28 Rodriguez	Y	Y	Y	N
29 Green	Y	Y	Y	N
30 Johnson, E.B.	Y	Y	Y	N
31 Carter	Y	Y	Y	+
32 Sessions	Y	Y	Y	Y
UTAH				
1 Bishop	Y	Y	Y	Y
2 Matheson	Y	Y	Y	N
3 Cannon	Y	?	Y	Y
VERMONT				
AL Sanders	Y	Y	Y	N
VIRGINIA				
1 Davis, Jo Ann	Y	Y	Y	Y
2 Schrock	Y	Y	Y	Y
3 Scott	Y	Y	Y	N
4 Forbes	Y	Y	Y	?
5 Goode	Y	Y	Y	Y
6 Goodlatte	Y	Y	Y	Y
7 Cantor	Y	Y	Y	Y
8 Moran	Y	Y	Y	N
9 Boucher	Y	Y	Y	N
10 Wolf	Y	Y	Y	Y
11 Davis, T.	Y	Y	Y	?
WASHINGTON				
1 Inslee	Y	Y	Y	N
2 Larsen	Y	Y	Y	N
3 Baird	Y	Y	Y	N
4 Hastings	Y	Y	Y	Y
5 Nethercutt	Y	Y	Y	Y
6 Dicks	Y	Y	Y	N
7 McDermott	Y	Y	Y	N
8 Dunn	Y	Y	Y	Y
9 Smith	Y	Y	Y	N
WEST VIRGINIA				
1 Mollohan	Y	Y	Y	?
2 Capito	Y	Y	Y	Y
3 Rahall	Y	Y	Y	N
WISCONSIN				
1 Ryan	Y	Y	Y	Y
2 Baldwin	Y	Y	Y	N
3 Kind	Y	Y	Y	N
4 Kleczka	Y	Y	Y	N
5 Sensenbrenner	Y	Y	Y	Y
6 Petri	Y	Y	Y	Y
7 Obey	Y	Y	Y	N
8 Green	Y	Y	Y	Y
WYOMING				
AL Cubin	Y	Y	Y	Y

Southern states - Ala., Ark., Fla., Ga., Ky., La., Miss., N.C., Okla., S.C., Tenn., Texas, Va.

Key

Y	Voted for (yea).
#	Paired for.
+	Announced for.
N	Voted against (nay).
X	Paired against.
−	Announced against.
P	Voted "present."
C	Voted "present" to avoid possible conflict of interest.
?	Did not vote or otherwise make a position known.

Democrats **Republicans**
Independents

127. HR 2844. Continuity of Congress/Rule. Adoption of the rule (H Res 602) to provide for House floor consideration of the bill that would require special elections to fill vacant House seats within 45 days of a catastrophe that kills at least 100 House members. Adopted 212-197: R 212-0; D 0-196 (ND 0-144, SD 0-52); I 0-1. April 22, 2004.

128. HR 2844. Continuity of Congress/Deadline Extension. Larson, D-Conn., amendment that would extend the time frame for conducting special elections from 45 to 75 days. Rejected 179-229: R 0-212; D 178-17 (ND 130-12, SD 48-5); I 1-0. April 22, 2004.

129. HR 2844. Continuity of Congress/Candidate Selection. Larson, D-Conn., amendment that would strike the bill's 10-day deadline for political parties to select nominees and substitute language that would require a potential candidate to meet the requirements to get on the ballot as set by state law. Rejected 188-217: R 2-207; D 185-10 (ND 135-7, SD 50-3); I 1-0. April 22, 2004.

130. HR 2844. Continuity of Congress/Passage. Passage of the bill that would require special elections to fill vacant House seats within 45 days of a catastrophe that kills at least 100 House members. If a regularly scheduled election is planned to fill a vacant House seat within 75 days of the House Speaker's announcement of the vacancies, then no special election for that seat is required. It also would require parties to nominate their candidates within 10 days of the House Speaker's announcement. Passed 306-97: R 202-7; D 104-89 (ND 65-75, SD 39-14); I 0-1. April 22, 2004.

	127	128	129	130
ALABAMA				
1 *Bonner*	Y	N	N	Y
2 *Everett*	Y	N	N	Y
3 *Rogers*	Y	N	N	Y
4 *Aderholt*	Y	N	N	Y
5 Cramer	N	Y	Y	N
6 *Bachus*	Y	N	N	Y
7 Davis	N	Y	Y	N
ALASKA				
AL *Young*	Y	?	?	?
ARIZONA				
1 *Renzi*	Y	N	N	Y
2 *Franks*	Y	N	N	Y
3 *Shadegg*	Y	N	N	Y
4 Pastor	N	Y	Y	Y
5 *Hayworth*	Y	N	N	Y
6 *Flake*	Y	N	N	Y
7 Grijalva	N	Y	Y	N
8 *Kolbe*	Y	N	N	Y
ARKANSAS				
1 Berry	N	Y	Y	N
2 Snyder	N	N	N	Y
3 *Boozman*	Y	N	N	Y
4 Ross	N	Y	Y	N
CALIFORNIA				
1 Thompson	N	Y	Y	N
2 *Herger*	Y	N	N	Y
3 *Ose*	Y	N	N	Y
4 *Doolittle*	Y	N	N	Y
5 Matsui	N	Y	Y	N
6 Woolsey	N	Y	Y	N
7 Miller, George	N	Y	Y	N
8 Pelosi	N	Y	Y	N
9 Lee	N	Y	Y	N
10 Tauscher	N	Y	Y	N
11 *Pombo*	?	?	?	?
12 Lantos	N	Y	Y	Y
13 Stark	N	Y	Y	N
14 Eshoo	N	Y	Y	N
15 Honda	N	Y	Y	N
16 Lofgren	N	Y	Y	Y
17 Farr	N	Y	Y	N
18 Cardoza	N	Y	Y	Y
19 *Radanovich*	Y	N	N	Y
20 Dooley	N	Y	Y	N
21 *Nunes*	Y	N	N	?
22 *Thomas*	Y	N	N	N
23 Capps	N	Y	Y	Y
24 *Gallegly*	?	?	?	?
25 *McKeon*	Y	N	N	Y
26 *Dreier*	Y	N	N	Y
27 Sherman	N	Y	Y	N
28 Berman	N	Y	Y	N
29 Schiff	N	Y	Y	N
30 Waxman	N	Y	Y	N
31 Becerra	N	Y	Y	Y
32 Solis	N	Y	Y	N
33 Watson	N	Y	Y	N
34 Roybal-Allard	N	Y	Y	Y
35 Waters	N	Y	Y	N
36 Harman	N	Y	Y	Y

	127	128	129	130
37 Millender-McD.	?	?	?	?
38 Napolitano	N	Y	Y	Y
39 Sánchez, Linda	N	Y	Y	N
40 *Royce*	Y	N	N	Y
41 *Lewis*	Y	N	N	Y
42 *Miller, Gary*	Y	N	N	Y
43 Baca	N	Y	Y	Y
44 *Calvert*	Y	N	N	Y
45 *Bono*	Y	N	N	Y
46 *Rohrabacher*	Y	N	N	N
47 Sanchez, Loretta	N	N	N	Y
48 *Cox*	Y	N	?	Y
49 *Issa*	Y	N	N	Y
50 *Cunningham*	Y	N	N	Y
51 Filner	N	Y	Y	N
52 *Hunter*	?	N	N	Y
53 Davis	N	Y	Y	N
COLORADO				
1 DeGette	N	Y	Y	N
2 Udall	N	Y	Y	Y
3 *McInnis*	Y	N	N	N
4 *Musgrave*	Y	N	N	Y
5 *Hefley*	Y	N	Y	N
6 *Tancredo*	Y	N	N	Y
7 *Beauprez*	Y	N	N	Y
CONNECTICUT				
1 Larson	N	Y	Y	N
2 *Simmons*	Y	N	N	Y
3 DeLauro	N	Y	Y	N
4 *Shays*	Y	N	N	Y
5 *Johnson*	Y	N	N	N
DELAWARE				
AL *Castle*	Y	N	N	Y
FLORIDA				
1 *Miller, J.*	Y	N	N	Y
2 Boyd	N	Y	Y	Y
3 Brown	N	Y	Y	Y
4 *Crenshaw*	Y	N	N	Y
5 *Brown-Waite*	Y	N	N	Y
6 *Stearns*	Y	N	N	Y
7 *Mica*	Y	N	Y	Y
8 *Keller*	Y	N	N	Y
9 *Bilirakis*	Y	N	N	Y
10 *Young*	Y	N	N	Y
11 Davis	N	Y	Y	Y
12 *Putnam*	Y	N	N	Y
13 *Harris*	Y	N	N	Y
14 *Goss*	Y	−	−	Y
15 *Weldon*	Y	N	N	Y
16 *Foley*	Y	N	N	Y
17 Meek	N	Y	Y	N
18 *Ros-Lehtinen*	Y	N	N	Y
19 Wexler	N	N	N	Y
20 Deutsch	N	Y	Y	N
21 *Diaz-Balart, L.*	Y	N	N	Y
22 *Shaw*	Y	N	N	Y
23 Hastings	?	?	?	?
24 *Feeney*	Y	N	N	Y
25 *Diaz-Balart, M.*	Y	N	N	Y
GEORGIA				
1 *Kingston*	Y	N	N	Y
2 Bishop	N	Y	Y	Y
3 Marshall	N	Y	Y	Y
4 Majette	N	Y	Y	N
5 Lewis	N	Y	Y	Y
6 *Isakson*	Y	N	N	Y
7 *Linder*	Y	N	N	Y
8 *Collins*	Y	N	?	?
9 *Norwood*	Y	N	N	Y
10 *Deal*	Y	N	N	Y
11 *Gingrey*	Y	N	N	Y
12 *Burns*	Y	N	N	Y
13 Scott	N	N	Y	Y
HAWAII				
1 Abercrombie	N	Y	Y	Y
2 Case	N	N	N	Y
IDAHO				
1 *Otter*	Y	N	N	Y
2 *Simpson*	Y	N	N	Y
ILLINOIS				
1 Rush	N	Y	Y	Y
2 Jackson	N	Y	Y	N
3 Lipinski	N	Y	N	Y
4 Gutierrez	N	Y	Y	N
5 Emanuel	N	Y	Y	Y
6 *Hyde*	Y	N	N	Y

ND Northern Democrats   SD Southern Democrats

	127	128	129	130
7 Davis	N	Y	Y	N
8 *Crane*	Y	N	N	N
9 Schakowsky	N	Y	Y	N
10 *Kirk*	Y	N	N	Y
11 *Weller*	Y	N	N	Y
12 Costello	N	Y	Y	Y
13 *Biggert*	Y	N	N	Y
14 *Hastert*				
15 *Johnson*	Y	N	N	Y
16 *Manzullo*	Y	N	N	Y
17 Evans	N	Y	Y	Y
18 *LaHood*	Y	N	N	Y
19 *Shimkus*	Y	N	N	Y
INDIANA				
1 Visclosky	N	Y	Y	N
2 *Chocola*	Y	N	N	Y
3 *Souder*	Y	N	N	Y
4 *Buyer*	Y	N	N	Y
5 *Burton*	Y	N	N	Y
6 *Pence*	Y	N	N	Y
7 Carson	N	Y	Y	Y
8 *Hostettler*	Y	N	N	Y
9 Hill	N	Y	Y	N
IOWA				
1 *Nussle*	Y	N	N	Y
2 *Leach*	Y	N	N	Y
3 Boswell	N	Y	Y	Y
4 *Latham*	Y	N	N	Y
5 *King*	Y	N	N	Y
KANSAS				
1 *Moran*	Y	N	N	Y
2 *Ryun*	Y	N	N	Y
3 Moore	N	Y	Y	Y
4 *Tiahrt*	Y	N	N	Y
KENTUCKY				
1 *Whitfield*	Y	N	N	Y
2 *Lewis*	Y	N	N	Y
3 *Northup*	Y	N	N	Y
4 Lucas	?	Y	N	Y
5 *Rogers*	Y	N	N	Y
6 Chandler	N	Y	Y	Y
LOUISIANA				
1 *Vitter*	Y	N	N	Y
2 Jefferson	N	Y	Y	Y
3 *Tauzin*	?	?	?	?
4 *McCrery*	Y	N	N	Y
5 Alexander	N	Y	Y	Y
6 *Baker*	Y	N	N	Y
7 John	N	Y	Y	N
MAINE				
1 Allen	N	Y	Y	N
2 Michaud	N	N	Y	N
MARYLAND				
1 *Gilchrest*	Y	N	N	Y
2 Ruppersberger	N	Y	Y	Y
3 Cardin	N	?	?	?
4 Wynn	N	Y	Y	Y
5 Hoyer	N	Y	Y	Y
6 *Bartlett*	Y	N	N	Y
7 Cummings	N	Y	Y	Y
8 Van Hollen	N	Y	Y	N
MASSACHUSETTS				
1 Olver	N	Y	Y	Y
2 Neal	N	Y	Y	N
3 McGovern	N	Y	Y	Y
4 Frank	N	Y	Y	Y
5 Meehan	N	Y	Y	Y
6 Tierney	N	Y	Y	Y
7 Markey	N	Y	Y	Y
8 Capuano	N	Y	Y	Y
9 Lynch	N	Y	Y	Y
10 Delahunt	N	Y	Y	?
MICHIGAN				
1 Stupak	N	Y	Y	Y
2 *Hoekstra*	Y	N	N	Y
3 *Ehlers*	Y	N	N	Y
4 *Camp*	Y	N	N	Y
5 Kildee	N	Y	Y	Y
6 *Upton*	Y	N	N	Y
7 *Smith*	Y	?	?	?
8 *Rogers*	Y	N	N	Y
9 *Knollenberg*	Y	N	N	Y
10 *Miller*	Y	N	N	Y
11 *McCotter*	Y	N	N	Y
12 Levin	N	Y	Y	Y

	127	128	129	130
13 Kilpatrick	N	Y	Y	N
14 Conyers	N	Y	Y	Y
15 Dingell	N	N	N	N
MINNESOTA				
1 *Gutknecht*	Y	N	N	Y
2 *Kline*	Y	N	N	Y
3 *Ramstad*	Y	N	N	Y
4 McCollum	N	Y	Y	Y
5 Sabo	N	Y	Y	Y
6 *Kennedy*	Y	N	N	Y
7 Peterson	N	N	N	Y
8 Oberstar	N	N	Y	N
MISSISSIPPI				
1 *Wicker*	Y	N	N	Y
2 Thompson	N	Y	Y	Y
3 *Pickering*	Y	N	N	Y
4 Taylor	N	Y	Y	N
MISSOURI				
1 Clay	N	Y	Y	N
2 *Akin*	Y	N	N	Y
3 Gephardt	?	?	?	?
4 Skelton	N	Y	Y	Y
5 McCarthy	N	Y	Y	Y
6 *Graves*	Y	N	N	Y
7 *Blunt*	Y	N	N	Y
8 *Emerson*	Y	N	?	Y
9 *Hulshof*	?	?	?	?
MONTANA				
AL *Rehberg*	Y	N	N	Y
NEBRASKA				
1 *Bereuter*	Y	N	N	Y
2 *Terry*	Y	N	N	Y
3 *Osborne*	Y	N	N	Y
NEVADA				
1 Berkley	N	Y	Y	N
2 *Gibbons*	Y	N	N	Y
3 *Porter*	Y	N	N	Y
NEW HAMPSHIRE				
1 *Bradley*	Y	N	N	Y
2 *Bass*	Y	N	N	Y
NEW JERSEY				
1 Andrews	N	Y	Y	N
2 *LoBiondo*	Y	N	N	Y
3 *Saxton*	Y	N	N	Y
4 *Smith*	Y	N	N	Y
5 *Garrett*	Y	N	N	Y
6 Pallone	N	Y	Y	N
7 *Ferguson*	Y	N	N	Y
8 Pascrell	N	Y	Y	Y
9 Rothman	N	Y	Y	Y
10 Payne	N	Y	Y	?
11 *Frelinghuysen*	Y	N	N	Y
12 Holt	N	Y	Y	N
13 Menendez	N	Y	Y	N
NEW MEXICO				
1 *Wilson*	Y	N	N	Y
2 *Pearce*	Y	N	N	Y
3 Udall	N	Y	Y	Y
NEW YORK				
1 Bishop	N	Y	Y	Y
2 Israel	N	Y	Y	Y
3 *King*	Y	N	N	Y
4 McCarthy	N	Y	Y	Y
5 Ackerman	N	Y	Y	Y
6 Meeks	N	Y	Y	Y
7 Crowley	N	N	Y	Y
8 Nadler	N	Y	Y	N
9 Weiner	N	Y	Y	Y
10 Towns	N	Y	Y	Y
11 Owens	N	Y	Y	Y
12 Velázquez	N	Y	Y	Y
13 *Fossella*	Y	N	N	Y
14 Maloney	N	Y	Y	Y
15 Rangel	N	Y	Y	Y
16 Serrano	N	Y	Y	Y
17 Engel	N	Y	Y	Y
18 Lowey	N	Y	Y	Y
19 *Kelly*	Y	N	N	Y
20 *Sweeney*	Y	N	N	Y
21 McNulty	N	Y	Y	Y
22 Hinchey	N	?	?	?
23 *McHugh*	Y	N	N	Y
24 *Boehlert*	Y	N	N	?
25 *Walsh*	Y	N	N	Y

	127	128	129	130
26 *Reynolds*	Y	N	N	Y
27 *Quinn*	Y	N	N	Y
28 Slaughter	N	Y	Y	N
29 *Houghton*	Y	N	N	?
NORTH CAROLINA				
1 Ballance	N	Y	Y	Y
2 Etheridge	N	Y	Y	Y
3 *Jones*	Y	N	N	Y
4 Price	N	Y	Y	Y
5 *Burr*	Y	N	N	Y
6 *Coble*	Y	N	N	Y
7 McIntyre	N	Y	Y	Y
8 *Hayes*	Y	N	N	Y
9 *Myrick*	Y	N	N	Y
10 *Ballenger*	Y	N	N	Y
11 *Taylor*	Y	N	N	?
12 Watt	N	Y	Y	Y
13 Miller	N	Y	Y	Y
NORTH DAKOTA				
AL Pomeroy	N	Y	Y	N
OHIO				
1 *Chabot*	Y	N	N	Y
2 *Portman*	Y	N	N	Y
3 *Turner*	Y	N	N	Y
4 *Oxley*	Y	N	N	Y
5 *Gillmor*	Y	N	N	Y
6 Strickland	?	Y	Y	Y
7 *Hobson*	Y	N	N	Y
8 *Boehner*	Y	N	N	Y
9 Kaptur	N	Y	Y	N
10 Kucinich	N	Y	Y	Y
11 Jones	N	+	+	−
12 *Tiberi*	Y	N	N	Y
13 Brown	N	Y	Y	Y
14 *LaTourette*	Y	N	N	Y
15 *Pryce*	Y	N	N	Y
16 *Regula*	Y	N	N	Y
17 Ryan	N	Y	Y	Y
18 *Ney*	Y	N	N	Y
OKLAHOMA				
1 *Sullivan*	Y	?	N	Y
2 Carson	N	Y	Y	Y
3 *Lucas*	Y	N	N	Y
4 *Cole*	Y	N	N	Y
5 *Istook*	Y	N	N	Y
OREGON				
1 Wu	N	Y	Y	Y
2 *Walden*	Y	N	N	Y
3 Blumenauer	N	Y	Y	Y
4 DeFazio	N	Y	Y	Y
5 Hooley	N	Y	Y	Y
PENNSYLVANIA				
1 Brady	N	Y	Y	N
2 Fattah	N	Y	Y	Y
3 *English*	Y	N	N	Y
4 *Hart*	Y	N	N	Y
5 *Peterson*	?	?	?	?
6 *Gerlach*	Y	N	N	Y
7 *Weldon*	Y	N	N	Y
8 *Greenwood*	?	N	N	Y
9 *Shuster, Bill*	?	?	?	?
10 *Sherwood*	Y	N	N	Y
11 Kanjorski	N	Y	Y	Y
12 Murtha	N	Y	Y	Y
13 Hoeffel	N	Y	Y	Y
14 Doyle	N	Y	Y	Y
15 *Toomey*	?	?	?	?
16 *Pitts*	Y	N	N	Y
17 Holden	N	Y	Y	Y
18 *Murphy*	Y	N	N	Y
19 *Platts*	Y	N	N	Y
RHODE ISLAND				
1 Kennedy	N	Y	Y	N
2 Langevin	N	Y	Y	N
SOUTH CAROLINA				
1 *Brown*	Y	N	N	Y
2 *Wilson*	Y	N	N	Y
3 *Barrett*	Y	N	N	Y
4 *DeMint*	?	?	?	?
5 Spratt	N	Y	Y	Y
6 Clyburn	N	?	?	?
SOUTH DAKOTA				
AL Vacant				

	127	128	129	130
TENNESSEE				
1 *Jenkins*	Y	N	N	Y
2 *Duncan*	?	?	?	?
3 *Wamp*	Y	N	N	Y
4 Davis	N	Y	Y	Y
5 Cooper	N	Y	Y	Y
6 Gordon	N	Y	Y	Y
7 *Blackburn*	Y	N	N	Y
8 Tanner	N	Y	Y	Y
9 Ford	N	Y	Y	Y
TEXAS				
1 Sandlin	N	Y	Y	Y
2 Turner	N	Y	Y	Y
3 *Johnson, Sam*	Y	N	N	Y
4 *Hall*	Y	N	N	Y
5 *Hensarling*	Y	N	N	Y
6 *Barton*	Y	N	N	Y
7 *Culberson*	Y	N	N	Y
8 *Brady*	Y	N	N	Y
9 Lampson	N	Y	Y	Y
10 Doggett	N	Y	Y	N
11 Edwards	?	Y	Y	Y
12 *Granger*	Y	N	N	Y
13 *Thornberry*	Y	N	N	Y
14 *Paul*	Y	N	N	Y
15 Hinojosa	?	?	?	?
16 Reyes	N	Y	Y	Y
17 Stenholm	N	Y	Y	Y
18 Jackson-Lee	?	?	?	?
19 *Neugebauer*	Y	N	—	Y
20 Gonzalez	N	Y	Y	Y
21 *Smith*	Y	N	N	Y
22 *DeLay*	Y	N	N	Y
23 *Bonilla*	Y	N	N	Y
24 Frost	N	Y	Y	N
25 Bell	N	Y	Y	N
26 *Burgess*	Y	N	N	Y
27 Ortiz	N	Y	Y	Y
28 Rodriguez	N	Y	Y	Y
29 Green	N	Y	Y	Y
30 Johnson, E.B.	N	Y	Y	N
31 *Carter*	+	−	−	+
32 *Sessions*	Y	N	N	Y
UTAH				
1 *Bishop*	Y	N	N	Y
2 Matheson	N	Y	Y	Y
3 *Cannon*	?	N	N	Y
VERMONT				
AL *Sanders*	N	Y	Y	N
VIRGINIA				
1 *Davis, Jo Ann*	Y	N	N	Y
2 *Schrock*	Y	N	N	Y
3 Scott	N	Y	Y	Y
4 *Forbes*	?	?	?	?
5 *Goode*	Y	N	N	Y
6 *Goodlatte*	Y	N	N	Y
7 *Cantor*	Y	N	N	Y
8 Moran	N	Y	Y	Y
9 Boucher	N	Y	Y	Y
10 *Wolf*	Y	N	N	Y
11 *Davis, T.*	?	N	N	Y
WASHINGTON				
1 Inslee	N	Y	Y	N
2 Larsen	N	Y	Y	N
3 Baird	N	Y	Y	N
4 *Hastings*	Y	N	N	Y
5 *Nethercutt*	Y	N	N	Y
6 Dicks	N	Y	Y	N
7 McDermott	N	Y	Y	N
8 *Dunn*	Y	N	N	Y
9 Smith	N	Y	Y	Y
WEST VIRGINIA				
1 Mollohan	?	?	?	?
2 *Capito*	Y	N	N	Y
3 Rahall	N	Y	Y	Y
WISCONSIN				
1 *Ryan*	Y	N	N	Y
2 Baldwin	N	Y	Y	N
3 Kind	N	Y	Y	Y
4 Kleczka	N	N	N	Y
5 *Sensenbrenner*	Y	N	N	Y
6 *Petri*	Y	N	N	Y
7 Obey	N	N	Y	Y
8 *Green*	Y	N	N	Y
WYOMING				
AL *Cubin*	Y	N	N	Y

Southern states - Ala., Ark., Fla., Ga., Ky., La., Miss., N.C., Okla., S.C., Tenn., Texas, Va.

131. HR 3942. Rhode Island Veterans Post Office/Passage. Cannon, R-Utah, motion to suspend the rules and pass the bill that would rename a post office building in Middletown, R.I., as the Rhode Island Veterans Post Office Building. Motion agreed to 395-0: R 210-0; D 184-0 (ND 129-0, SD 55-0); I 1-0. A two-thirds majority of those present and voting (264 in this case) is required for passage under suspension of the rules. April 27, 2004.

132. H Res 399. Melvin Jones Tribute/Adoption. Cannon, R-Utah, motion to suspend the rules and adopt the resolution that would honor the late Melvin Jones, founder of the Association of Lions Clubs, and recognize the contributions of Lions Clubs International to communities in need. Motion agreed to 395-0: R 209-0; D 185-0 (ND 130-0, SD 55-0); I 1-0. A two-thirds majority of those present and voting (264 in this case) is required for adoption under suspension of the rules. April 27, 2004.

133. H Res 578. Financial Literacy Month/Adoption. Cannon, R-Utah, motion to suspend the rules and adopt the resolution that would support the goals and ideals of Financial Literacy Month. Motion agreed to 391-0: R 208-0; D 182-0 (ND 127-0, SD 55-0); I 1-0. A two-thirds majority of those present and voting (261 in this case) is required for adoption under suspension of the rules. April 27, 2004.

134. HR 4219. Surface Transportation Extension/Passage. Petri, R-Wis., motion to suspend the rules and pass the bill that would extend funding for highway, transit and transportation safety programs for an additional two months, through June 30, 2004. The bill includes $24.3 billion in contract authority for federal-aid highway programs. Motion agreed to 410-0: R 218-0; D 191-0 (ND 137-0, SD 54-0); I 1-0. A two-thirds majority of those present and voting (274 in this case) is required for passage under suspension of the rules. April 28, 2004.

135. S 1904. Wilkie D. Ferguson Jr. Courthouse/Passage. LaTourette, R-Ohio, motion to suspend the rules and pass the bill that would name a federal courthouse in Miami after the late Judge Wilkie D. Ferguson Jr., who served on the U.S. District Court for the Southern District of Florida. Motion agreed to 408-0: R 216-0; D 191-0 (ND 137-0, SD 54-0); I 1-0. A two-thirds majority of those present and voting (272 in this case) is required for passage under suspension of the rules. April 28, 2004.

136. HR 4181. "Marriage Penalty" Relief/Rangel Substitute. Rangel, D-N.Y., substitute amendment that would permanently extend tax provisions eliminating the so-called marriage penalty. It also would prevent the alternative minimum tax from negating the benefits of the bill for married couples, and it would offset the cost of the bill by imposing a 3.6 percent surtax on taxpayers earning more than $500,000 a year and married couples with annual incomes of more than $1 million. Rejected 189-226: R 1-216; D 187-10 (ND 138-4, SD 49-6); I 1-0. April 28, 2004.

137. HR 4181. "Marriage Penalty" Relief/Recommit. Stenholm, D-Texas, motion to recommit the bill to the House Ways and Means Committee with instructions to add language that would require the Treasury secretary to certify that there is sufficient room under the current debt ceiling to provide funds for the bill. Motion rejected 199-220: R 0-220; D 198-0 (ND 143-0, SD 55-0); I 1-0. April 28, 2004.

138. HR 4181. "Marriage Penalty" Relief/Passage. Passage of the bill that would permanently extend tax provisions eliminating the so-called marriage penalty by making the standard deduction for married couples double that of single taxpayers and increasing the upper limit of the 15 percent tax bracket for married couples to twice that of singles. It also would make permanent higher income limits for married couples eligible to receive the refundable earned-income tax credit. Passed 323-95: R 220-0; D 102-95 (ND 62-80, SD 40-15); I 1-0. A "yea" was a vote in support of the president's position. April 28, 2004.

Key

Y	Voted for (yea).
#	Paired for.
+	Announced for.
N	Voted against (nay).
X	Paired against.
–	Announced against.
P	Voted "present."
C	Voted "present" to avoid possible conflict of interest.
?	Did not vote or otherwise make a position known.

Democrats   **Republicans**
Independents

	131	132	133	134	135	136	137	138
ALABAMA								
1 *Bonner*	?	?	?	?	?	?	?	?
2 *Everett*	Y	Y	Y	Y	Y	N	N	Y
3 *Rogers*	Y	Y	Y	Y	Y	N	N	Y
4 *Aderholt*	Y	Y	Y	Y	Y	N	N	Y
5 Cramer	Y	Y	Y	Y	Y	N	Y	Y
6 *Bachus*	Y	Y	Y	Y	Y	N	N	Y
7 Davis	Y	Y	Y	Y	Y	Y	Y	Y
ALASKA								
AL *Young*	?	?	?	Y	Y	N	N	Y
ARIZONA								
1 *Renzi*	Y	Y	Y	Y	Y	N	N	Y
2 *Franks*	Y	Y	Y	Y	Y	N	N	Y
3 *Shadegg*	Y	Y	Y	Y	Y	N	N	Y
4 Pastor	Y	Y	Y	Y	Y	Y	Y	N
5 *Hayworth*	Y	Y	Y	Y	Y	N	N	Y
6 *Flake*	Y	Y	Y	Y	Y	N	N	Y
7 Grijalva	Y	Y	Y	Y	Y	Y	Y	N
8 *Kolbe*	Y	Y	Y	Y	Y	N	N	Y
ARKANSAS								
1 Berry	Y	Y	Y	Y	Y	Y	Y	N
2 Snyder	Y	Y	Y	Y	Y	Y	Y	Y
3 *Boozman*	Y	Y	Y	Y	Y	N	N	Y
4 Ross	Y	Y	Y	Y	Y	Y	Y	Y
CALIFORNIA								
1 Thompson	Y	Y	Y	Y	Y	+	+	–
2 *Herger*	Y	Y	Y	Y	Y	N	N	Y
3 *Ose*	+	+	Y	Y	Y	N	N	Y
4 *Doolittle*	Y	Y	Y	Y	Y	N	N	Y
5 Matsui	Y	Y	Y	Y	Y	Y	Y	Y
6 Woolsey	Y	Y	Y	Y	Y	Y	Y	N
7 Miller, George	Y	Y	?	Y	Y	Y	Y	N
8 Pelosi	Y	Y	Y	Y	Y	Y	Y	N
9 Lee	Y	Y	Y	Y	Y	Y	Y	N
10 Tauscher	Y	Y	Y	Y	Y	Y	Y	Y
11 *Pombo*	Y	Y	Y	Y	Y	N	N	Y
12 Lantos	Y	Y	Y	Y	Y	Y	Y	N
13 Stark	?	?	Y	Y	Y	Y	Y	N
14 Eshoo	Y	Y	Y	Y	Y	Y	Y	N
15 Honda	Y	Y	Y	Y	Y	Y	Y	N
16 Lofgren	Y	Y	Y	Y	Y	Y	Y	Y
17 Farr	Y	Y	Y	Y	Y	Y	Y	N
18 Cardoza	Y	Y	Y	Y	Y	Y	Y	Y
19 *Radanovich*	Y	Y	Y	Y	Y	N	N	Y
20 Dooley	?	?	?	Y	Y	Y	Y	Y
21 *Nunes*	Y	Y	Y	Y	Y	N	N	Y
22 *Thomas*	Y	Y	Y	Y	Y	N	N	Y
23 Capps	Y	Y	Y	Y	Y	Y	Y	N
24 *Gallegly*	Y	Y	Y	Y	Y	N	N	Y
25 *McKeon*	Y	Y	Y	Y	Y	N	N	Y
26 *Dreier*	Y	Y	Y	Y	Y	N	N	Y
27 Sherman	Y	Y	Y	Y	Y	Y	Y	N
28 Berman	?	?	Y	Y	Y	Y	Y	N
29 Schiff	Y	Y	Y	Y	+	Y	Y	Y
30 Waxman	Y	Y	Y	Y	Y	Y	Y	N
31 Becerra	Y	Y	?	Y	Y	Y	Y	N
32 Solis	Y	Y	Y	Y	Y	Y	Y	N
33 Watson	Y	Y	Y	Y	Y	Y	Y	N
34 Roybal-Allard	Y	Y	Y	Y	Y	Y	Y	N
35 Waters	?	?	?	?	?	?	?	?
36 Harman	Y	Y	Y	Y	Y	Y	Y	Y

	131	132	133	134	135	136	137	138
37 Millender-McD.	Y	Y	Y	+	Y	Y	Y	N
38 Napolitano	Y	Y	Y	Y	Y	Y	Y	N
39 Sánchez, Linda	Y	Y	Y	Y	Y	Y	Y	N
40 *Royce*	Y	Y	Y	Y	Y	N	N	Y
41 *Lewis*	Y	Y	Y	Y	Y	N	N	Y
42 *Miller, Gary*	Y	Y	Y	Y	Y	N	N	Y
43 Baca	Y	Y	Y	Y	Y	Y	Y	N
44 *Calvert*	Y	Y	Y	Y	Y	N	N	Y
45 *Bono*	Y	Y	Y	Y	Y	N	N	Y
46 *Rohrabacher*	?	?	?	?	?	?	?	?
47 Sanchez, Loretta	Y	Y	Y	Y	Y	Y	Y	N
48 *Cox*	Y	Y	Y	Y	Y	N	N	Y
49 *Issa*	Y	Y	Y	Y	Y	N	N	Y
50 *Cunningham*	Y	Y	Y	Y	Y	N	N	Y
51 Filner	Y	Y	Y	Y	Y	Y	Y	N
52 *Hunter*	Y	Y	Y	Y	Y	N	N	Y
53 Davis	Y	Y	Y	Y	Y	Y	Y	Y
COLORADO								
1 DeGette	Y	Y	Y	Y	Y	Y	Y	N
2 Udall	Y	Y	Y	Y	Y	Y	Y	Y
3 *McInnis*	Y	Y	Y	Y	Y	N	N	Y
4 *Musgrave*	Y	Y	Y	Y	Y	N	N	Y
5 *Hefley*	Y	Y	Y	Y	Y	N	N	Y
6 *Tancredo*	Y	Y	Y	Y	Y	N	?	Y
7 *Beauprez*	Y	Y	Y	Y	Y	N	N	Y
CONNECTICUT								
1 Larson	Y	Y	Y	Y	Y	Y	Y	N
2 *Simmons*	Y	Y	Y	Y	Y	N	N	Y
3 DeLauro	Y	Y	Y	Y	Y	Y	Y	N
4 *Shays*	Y	Y	Y	Y	Y	N	N	Y
5 *Johnson*	Y	Y	Y	Y	Y	N	N	Y
DELAWARE								
AL *Castle*	Y	Y	Y	Y	Y	N	N	Y
FLORIDA								
1 *Miller, J.*	Y	Y	Y	Y	Y	N	N	Y
2 Boyd	Y	Y	Y	Y	Y	Y	Y	Y
3 Brown	Y	Y	Y	Y	Y	Y	Y	N
4 *Crenshaw*	+	+	+	Y	Y	N	N	Y
5 *Brown-Waite*	Y	Y	?	Y	Y	N	N	Y
6 *Stearns*	Y	Y	Y	Y	Y	N	N	Y
7 *Mica*	Y	Y	Y	Y	Y	N	N	Y
8 *Keller*	Y	Y	Y	Y	Y	N	N	Y
9 *Bilirakis*	Y	Y	Y	Y	Y	N	N	Y
10 *Young*	Y	Y	Y	Y	Y	N	N	Y
11 Davis	Y	Y	Y	Y	Y	Y	Y	Y
12 *Putnam*	Y	Y	Y	Y	Y	N	N	Y
13 *Harris*	Y	Y	Y	Y	Y	N	N	Y
14 *Goss*	Y	Y	Y	Y	Y	N	N	Y
15 *Weldon*	Y	Y	Y	Y	Y	N	N	?
16 *Foley*	Y	Y	Y	Y	Y	N	N	Y
17 Meek	Y	Y	Y	Y	Y	Y	Y	N
18 *Ros-Lehtinen*	Y	Y	Y	Y	Y	N	N	Y
19 Wexler	?	?	?	?	?	?	?	?
20 Deutsch	Y	Y	Y	Y	Y	Y	Y	Y
21 *Diaz-Balart, L.*	Y	Y	Y	Y	Y	N	N	Y
22 *Shaw*	Y	Y	Y	Y	Y	N	N	Y
23 Hastings	?	?	?	?	?	?	?	?
24 *Feeney*	Y	Y	Y	Y	Y	N	N	Y
25 *Diaz-Balart, M.*	Y	Y	Y	Y	Y	N	N	Y
GEORGIA								
1 *Kingston*	Y	Y	Y	Y	Y	N	N	Y
2 Bishop	Y	Y	Y	Y	Y	Y	Y	Y
3 Marshall	Y	Y	Y	Y	Y	N	Y	Y
4 *Majette*	Y	Y	Y	Y	Y	Y	Y	N
5 Lewis	Y	Y	Y	Y	Y	Y	Y	N
6 *Isakson*	Y	Y	Y	Y	Y	N	N	Y
7 *Linder*	Y	Y	Y	Y	Y	N	N	Y
8 *Collins*	+	+	+	Y	Y	N	N	Y
9 *Norwood*	Y	Y	Y	Y	Y	N	N	Y
10 *Deal*	Y	Y	Y	Y	Y	N	N	Y
11 *Gingrey*	Y	Y	Y	Y	Y	N	N	Y
12 *Burns*	Y	Y	Y	Y	Y	N	N	Y
13 Scott	Y	Y	Y	Y	Y	Y	Y	Y
HAWAII								
1 Abercrombie	Y	Y	Y	Y	Y	Y	Y	N
2 Case	Y	Y	Y	Y	Y	Y	Y	Y
IDAHO								
1 *Otter*	Y	Y	Y	Y	Y	N	N	Y
2 *Simpson*	Y	Y	Y	Y	Y	N	N	Y
ILLINOIS								
1 Rush	?	Y	Y	Y	Y	Y	Y	N
2 Jackson	Y	Y	Y	Y	Y	Y	Y	N
3 Lipinski	?	?	Y	Y	Y	Y	Y	?
4 Gutierrez	Y	Y	Y	Y	Y	Y	Y	N
5 Emanuel	Y	Y	Y	Y	Y	Y	Y	N
6 *Hyde*	Y	Y	Y	Y	Y	N	N	Y

ND Northern Democrats   SD Southern Democrats

	131	132	133	134	135	136	137	138
7 Davis	Y	Y	Y	?	?	Y	Y	N
8 ***Crane***	Y	Y	Y	Y	Y	N	N	Y
9 Schakowsky	Y	Y	Y	Y	Y	Y	Y	N
10 ***Kirk***	Y	Y	Y	Y	Y	N	N	Y
11 ***Weller***	Y	Y	Y	Y	Y	N	N	Y
12 Costello	Y	Y	Y	Y	Y	Y	Y	Y
13 ***Biggert***	Y	Y	Y	Y	Y	N	N	Y
14 ***Hastert***								
15 ***Johnson***	Y	Y	Y	Y	Y	N	N	Y
16 ***Manzullo***	Y	Y	Y	Y	Y	N	N	Y
17 Evans	Y	Y	Y	Y	Y	Y	Y	N
18 ***LaHood***	Y	Y	Y	Y	Y	N	N	Y
19 ***Shimkus***	Y	Y	Y	Y	Y	N	N	Y
INDIANA								
1 Visclosky	Y	Y	Y	Y	Y	Y	Y	N
2 ***Chocola***	Y	Y	Y	Y	Y	N	N	Y
3 ***Souder***	?	?	?	Y	Y	N	N	Y
4 ***Buyer***	?	?	?	Y	Y	N	N	Y
5 ***Burton***	Y	Y	Y	Y	+	N	N	Y
6 ***Pence***	Y	Y	Y	Y	Y	N	N	Y
7 Carson	Y	Y	Y	Y	Y	Y	Y	N
8 ***Hostettler***	Y	Y	Y	Y	Y	N	N	Y
9 Hill	Y	Y	Y	Y	Y	Y	Y	N
IOWA								
1 ***Nussle***	Y	Y	Y	Y	Y	?	N	Y
2 ***Leach***	Y	Y	Y	Y	Y	N	N	Y
3 Boswell	Y	Y	Y	Y	Y	Y	Y	Y
4 ***Latham***	Y	Y	Y	Y	Y	N	N	Y
5 ***King***	Y	Y	Y	Y	Y	N	N	Y
KANSAS								
1 ***Moran***	Y	Y	Y	Y	Y	N	N	Y
2 ***Ryun***	Y	Y	Y	Y	Y	–	N	Y
3 Moore	Y	Y	Y	Y	Y	Y	Y	Y
4 ***Tiahrt***	Y	Y	Y	?	?	N	N	Y
KENTUCKY								
1 ***Whitfield***	Y	Y	Y	Y	Y	N	N	Y
2 ***Lewis***	Y	Y	Y	Y	Y	N	N	Y
3 ***Northup***	Y	Y	Y	Y	Y	N	N	Y
4 Lucas	Y	Y	Y	Y	Y	Y	Y	Y
5 ***Rogers***	Y	Y	Y	Y	Y	N	N	Y
6 Chandler	Y	Y	Y	Y	Y	N	Y	Y
LOUISIANA								
1 ***Vitter***	Y	Y	Y	Y	Y	N	N	Y
2 Jefferson	Y	Y	Y	Y	Y	Y	Y	N
3 ***Tauzin***	?	?	?	?	?	?	?	?
4 ***McCrery***	Y	Y	Y	Y	Y	N	N	Y
5 Alexander	Y	Y	Y	Y	Y	N	Y	Y
6 ***Baker***	Y	Y	Y	Y	Y	N	N	Y
7 John	Y	Y	Y	Y	Y	Y	Y	Y
MAINE								
1 Allen	Y	Y	Y	Y	Y	Y	Y	Y
2 Michaud	Y	Y	Y	Y	Y	Y	Y	Y
MARYLAND								
1 ***Gilchrest***	Y	Y	Y	Y	Y	N	N	Y
2 Ruppersberger	Y	Y	?	Y	Y	Y	Y	Y
3 Cardin	?	?	?	?	?	?	?	?
4 Wynn	Y	Y	Y	Y	Y	Y	Y	Y
5 Hoyer	Y	Y	Y	Y	Y	Y	Y	N
6 ***Bartlett***	Y	Y	Y	Y	Y	N	N	Y
7 Cummings	Y	Y	Y	Y	Y	Y	Y	N
8 Van Hollen	Y	Y	Y	Y	Y	Y	Y	Y
MASSACHUSETTS								
1 Olver	Y	Y	Y	Y	Y	Y	Y	N
2 Neal	Y	Y	Y	Y	Y	Y	Y	N
3 McGovern	Y	Y	Y	Y	Y	Y	Y	N
4 Frank	?	?	?	Y	Y	Y	Y	N
5 Meehan	Y	Y	Y	Y	Y	Y	Y	N
6 Tierney	Y	Y	Y	Y	Y	Y	Y	N
7 Markey	Y	Y	Y	Y	Y	Y	Y	N
8 Capuano	Y	Y	Y	Y	Y	Y	Y	N
9 Lynch	Y	Y	Y	Y	Y	Y	Y	Y
10 Delahunt	?	?	?	Y	Y	Y	Y	N
MICHIGAN								
1 Stupak	Y	Y	Y	Y	Y	Y	Y	Y
2 ***Hoekstra***	Y	Y	Y	Y	Y	N	N	Y
3 ***Ehlers***	Y	Y	Y	Y	Y	N	N	Y
4 ***Camp***	Y	Y	Y	Y	Y	N	N	Y
5 Kildee	Y	Y	Y	Y	Y	Y	Y	Y
6 ***Upton***	Y	Y	Y	Y	Y	N	N	Y
7 ***Smith***	Y	Y	Y	Y	Y	N	N	Y
8 ***Rogers***	Y	Y	Y	Y	Y	N	N	Y
9 ***Knollenberg***	Y	Y	Y	Y	Y	N	N	Y
10 ***Miller***	Y	Y	Y	Y	Y	N	N	Y
11 ***McCotter***	Y	Y	Y	Y	Y	N	N	Y
12 Levin	Y	Y	Y	Y	Y	Y	Y	N

	131	132	133	134	135	136	137	138
13 Kilpatrick	Y	Y	Y	+	+	+	+	–
14 Conyers	Y	Y	Y	Y	Y	Y	Y	N
15 Dingell	Y	Y	Y	Y	Y	Y	Y	N
MINNESOTA								
1 ***Gutknecht***	Y	Y	Y	Y	Y	N	N	Y
2 ***Kline***	Y	Y	Y	Y	Y	N	N	Y
3 ***Ramstad***	Y	Y	Y	Y	Y	N	N	Y
4 McCollum	Y	Y	Y	Y	Y	Y	Y	N
5 Sabo	Y	Y	Y	Y	Y	Y	Y	N
6 ***Kennedy***	Y	Y	Y	Y	Y	N	N	Y
7 Peterson	Y	Y	Y	Y	Y	N	Y	Y
8 Oberstar	Y	Y	Y	Y	Y	Y	Y	N
MISSISSIPPI								
1 ***Wicker***	Y	Y	Y	Y	Y	N	N	Y
2 Thompson	Y	Y	Y	Y	Y	Y	Y	Y
3 ***Pickering***	Y	Y	Y	Y	Y	N	N	Y
4 Taylor	Y	Y	Y	Y	Y	Y	Y	N
MISSOURI								
1 Clay	Y	Y	Y	Y	Y	Y	Y	Y
2 ***Akin***	Y	Y	Y	Y	Y	N	N	Y
3 Gephardt	?	?	?	?	?	?	?	Y
4 Skelton	Y	Y	Y	Y	Y	Y	Y	Y
5 McCarthy	Y	Y	Y	Y	Y	Y	Y	N
6 ***Graves***	Y	Y	Y	Y	Y	N	N	Y
7 ***Blunt***	Y	Y	Y	Y	?	N	N	Y
8 ***Emerson***	Y	Y	Y	Y	Y	N	N	Y
9 ***Hulshof***	Y	Y	Y	Y	Y	N	N	Y
MONTANA								
AL ***Rehberg***	Y	Y	Y	Y	Y	N	N	Y
NEBRASKA								
1 ***Bereuter***	Y	Y	Y	Y	Y	N	N	Y
2 ***Terry***	Y	Y	Y	Y	Y	N	N	Y
3 ***Osborne***	Y	Y	Y	Y	Y	N	N	Y
NEVADA								
1 Berkley	Y	Y	Y	Y	Y	Y	Y	Y
2 ***Gibbons***	Y	Y	Y	Y	Y	N	N	Y
3 ***Porter***	Y	Y	Y	Y	Y	N	N	Y
NEW HAMPSHIRE								
1 ***Bradley***	Y	Y	Y	Y	Y	N	N	Y
2 ***Bass***	Y	Y	Y	Y	Y	N	N	Y
NEW JERSEY								
1 Andrews	Y	Y	Y	Y	Y	Y	Y	N
2 ***LoBiondo***	Y	Y	Y	Y	Y	N	N	Y
3 ***Saxton***	Y	Y	Y	Y	Y	N	N	Y
4 ***Smith***	?	?	?	?	?	?	?	?
5 ***Garrett***	Y	Y	Y	Y	Y	N	N	Y
6 Pallone	Y	Y	Y	Y	Y	Y	Y	N
7 ***Ferguson***	Y	Y	Y	Y	Y	N	N	Y
8 Pascrell	Y	Y	Y	+	Y	Y	Y	N
9 Rothman	?	?	?	?	?	?	?	?
10 Payne	Y	Y	Y	Y	Y	Y	Y	N
11 ***Frelinghuysen***	Y	Y	Y	Y	Y	N	N	Y
12 Holt	Y	Y	Y	Y	Y	Y	Y	Y
13 Menendez	Y	Y	Y	Y	Y	Y	Y	N
NEW MEXICO								
1 ***Wilson***	Y	Y	Y	Y	Y	Y	N	Y
2 ***Pearce***	Y	Y	Y	Y	Y	N	N	Y
3 Udall	Y	Y	Y	Y	Y	Y	Y	N
NEW YORK								
1 Bishop	Y	Y	Y	Y	Y	Y	Y	Y
2 Israel	Y	Y	Y	Y	Y	Y	Y	Y
3 ***King***	Y	Y	Y	Y	Y	N	N	Y
4 McCarthy	Y	Y	Y	Y	Y	Y	Y	Y
5 Ackerman	Y	Y	Y	Y	Y	Y	Y	Y
6 Meeks	Y	Y	Y	Y	Y	Y	Y	Y
7 Crowley	Y	Y	Y	Y	Y	Y	Y	N
8 Nadler	?	?	?	Y	Y	Y	Y	N
9 Weiner	Y	Y	Y	Y	Y	Y	Y	Y
10 Towns	Y	Y	Y	Y	Y	Y	Y	N
11 Owens	Y	Y	Y	Y	Y	Y	Y	N
12 Velázquez	Y	Y	Y	Y	Y	Y	Y	N
13 ***Fossella***	Y	Y	Y	Y	Y	N	N	Y
14 Maloney	Y	Y	Y	Y	Y	Y	Y	Y
15 Rangel	Y	Y	Y	Y	Y	Y	Y	N
16 Serrano	Y	Y	Y	Y	Y	Y	Y	N
17 Engel	Y	Y	Y	Y	Y	Y	Y	Y
18 Lowey	Y	Y	Y	Y	Y	Y	Y	Y
19 ***Kelly***	Y	Y	Y	Y	Y	N	N	Y
20 ***Sweeney***	Y	Y	Y	Y	Y	N	N	Y
21 McNulty	Y	Y	Y	Y	Y	Y	Y	N
22 Hinchey	Y	Y	Y	Y	Y	Y	Y	N
23 ***McHugh***	Y	Y	Y	Y	Y	N	N	Y
24 ***Boehlert***	Y	Y	Y	Y	Y	N	N	Y
25 ***Walsh***	Y	Y	Y	Y	Y	N	N	Y

	131	132	133	134	135	136	137	138
26 ***Reynolds***	Y	Y	Y	Y	Y	N	N	Y
27 ***Quinn***	Y	Y	Y	Y	Y	N	N	Y
28 Slaughter	Y	Y	Y	Y	Y	Y	Y	N
29 ***Houghton***	Y	Y	Y	Y	Y	N	N	Y
NORTH CAROLINA								
1 Ballance	Y	Y	Y	Y	Y	Y	Y	Y
2 Etheridge	Y	Y	Y	Y	Y	Y	Y	Y
3 ***Jones***	Y	Y	Y	Y	Y	N	N	Y
4 Price	Y	Y	Y	Y	Y	Y	Y	Y
5 ***Burr***	?	?	?	Y	Y	N	N	Y
6 ***Coble***	Y	Y	Y	Y	Y	N	N	Y
7 McIntyre	Y	Y	Y	Y	Y	Y	Y	Y
8 ***Hayes***	Y	Y	Y	Y	Y	N	N	Y
9 ***Myrick***	Y	Y	Y	Y	Y	N	N	Y
10 ***Ballenger***	Y	Y	Y	Y	Y	N	N	Y
11 ***Taylor***	Y	Y	Y	Y	Y	N	N	Y
12 Watt	Y	Y	Y	Y	Y	Y	Y	N
13 Miller	Y	Y	Y	Y	Y	Y	Y	Y
NORTH DAKOTA								
AL Pomeroy	Y	Y	Y	Y	Y	Y	Y	Y
OHIO								
1 ***Chabot***	Y	Y	Y	Y	Y	N	N	Y
2 ***Portman***	Y	Y	Y	Y	Y	N	N	Y
3 ***Turner***	Y	Y	Y	Y	Y	N	N	Y
4 ***Oxley***	Y	Y	Y	Y	Y	N	N	Y
5 ***Gillmor***	Y	Y	Y	Y	Y	N	N	Y
6 Strickland	?	?	?	Y	Y	Y	Y	Y
7 ***Hobson***	Y	Y	Y	Y	Y	N	N	Y
8 ***Boehner***	Y	Y	Y	Y	Y	N	N	Y
9 Kaptur	Y	Y	Y	Y	Y	Y	Y	Y
10 Kucinich	?	?	?	Y	Y	Y	Y	N
11 Jones	+	+	+	Y	Y	Y	Y	N
12 ***Tiberi***	Y	Y	Y	Y	Y	N	N	Y
13 Brown	?	?	?	Y	Y	Y	Y	Y
14 ***LaTourette***	Y	Y	Y	Y	Y	N	N	Y
15 ***Pryce***	Y	Y	Y	Y	Y	N	N	Y
16 ***Regula***	Y	Y	Y	Y	Y	N	N	Y
17 Ryan	Y	Y	Y	Y	Y	Y	Y	Y
18 ***Ney***	Y	Y	Y	Y	Y	N	N	Y
OKLAHOMA								
1 ***Sullivan***	Y	Y	Y	Y	Y	N	N	Y
2 Carson	Y	Y	Y	Y	Y	N	Y	Y
3 ***Lucas***	?	?	?	Y	Y	N	N	Y
4 ***Cole***	Y	Y	Y	Y	Y	N	N	Y
5 ***Istook***	Y	Y	Y	Y	Y	N	N	Y
OREGON								
1 Wu	Y	Y	Y	Y	Y	Y	Y	Y
2 ***Walden***	Y	Y	Y	Y	Y	N	N	Y
3 Blumenauer	Y	Y	Y	Y	Y	Y	Y	N
4 DeFazio	Y	Y	Y	Y	Y	Y	Y	Y
5 Hooley	Y	Y	Y	Y	Y	Y	Y	Y
PENNSYLVANIA								
1 Brady	?	?	?	Y	Y	Y	Y	N
2 Fattah	Y	Y	Y	?	?	Y	Y	N
3 ***English***	Y	Y	Y	Y	Y	N	N	Y
4 ***Hart***	?	?	?	Y	Y	N	N	Y
5 ***Peterson***	Y	Y	Y	Y	Y	N	N	Y
6 ***Gerlach***	Y	Y	Y	Y	Y	N	N	Y
7 ***Weldon***	Y	Y	Y	Y	Y	N	N	Y
8 ***Greenwood***	?	?	?	?	?	N	N	Y
9 ***Shuster, Bill***	?	?	?	?	?	N	N	Y
10 ***Sherwood***	Y	Y	Y	Y	Y	N	N	Y
11 Kanjorski	Y	Y	Y	Y	Y	Y	Y	N
12 Murtha	Y	Y	Y	Y	Y	N	Y	N
13 Hoeffel	?	?	?	?	?	Y	Y	Y
14 Doyle	Y	Y	Y	Y	Y	Y	Y	N
15 ***Toomey***	?	?	?	?	?	?	?	?
16 ***Pitts***	Y	Y	Y	Y	Y	N	N	Y
17 Holden	Y	Y	Y	Y	Y	Y	Y	Y
18 ***Murphy***	Y	Y	Y	Y	Y	N	N	Y
19 ***Platts***	?	?	?	Y	Y	N	N	Y
RHODE ISLAND								
1 Kennedy	Y	Y	Y	Y	Y	Y	Y	Y
2 Langevin	Y	Y	Y	Y	Y	Y	Y	Y
SOUTH CAROLINA								
1 ***Brown***	Y	Y	Y	Y	Y	N	N	Y
2 ***Wilson***	Y	Y	Y	Y	Y	N	N	Y
3 ***Barrett***	Y	Y	Y	Y	Y	N	N	Y
4 ***DeMint***	Y	Y	Y	+	+	–	–	+
5 Spratt	Y	Y	Y	Y	Y	Y	Y	Y
6 Clyburn	Y	Y	Y	Y	Y	Y	Y	Y
SOUTH DAKOTA								
AL Vacant								

	131	132	133	134	135	136	137	138
TENNESSEE								
1 ***Jenkins***	Y	Y	Y	Y	Y	N	N	Y
2 ***Duncan***	Y	Y	Y	Y	Y	N	N	Y
3 ***Wamp***	Y	Y	Y	Y	Y	N	N	Y
4 Davis	Y	Y	Y	Y	Y	Y	Y	Y
5 Cooper	Y	Y	Y	Y	Y	Y	Y	N
6 Gordon	Y	Y	Y	?	?	Y	Y	Y
7 ***Blackburn***	Y	Y	Y	Y	Y	N	N	Y
8 Tanner	Y	Y	Y	Y	Y	Y	Y	N
9 Ford	Y	Y	Y	Y	Y	Y	Y	Y
TEXAS								
1 Sandlin	Y	Y	Y	Y	Y	N	Y	Y
2 Turner	Y	Y	Y	Y	Y	Y	Y	N
3 ***Johnson, Sam***	Y	Y	Y	Y	Y	N	N	Y
4 ***Hall***	Y	Y	Y	Y	Y	N	N	Y
5 ***Hensarling***	Y	Y	Y	Y	Y	N	N	Y
6 ***Barton***	Y	Y	Y	Y	Y	N	N	Y
7 ***Culberson***	Y	Y	Y	Y	Y	N	N	Y
8 ***Brady***	Y	Y	Y	Y	Y	N	N	Y
9 Lampson	Y	Y	Y	Y	Y	Y	Y	Y
10 Doggett	Y	Y	Y	Y	Y	Y	Y	N
11 Edwards	Y	Y	Y	Y	Y	Y	Y	Y
12 ***Granger***	Y	Y	Y	Y	Y	?	N	Y
13 ***Thornberry***	Y	Y	Y	Y	Y	N	N	Y
14 ***Paul***	Y	Y	Y	Y	Y	N	N	Y
15 Hinojosa	Y	Y	Y	Y	Y	Y	Y	Y
16 Reyes	Y	Y	Y	Y	Y	Y	Y	Y
17 Stenholm	Y	Y	Y	Y	Y	Y	Y	N
18 Jackson-Lee	Y	Y	Y	Y	Y	Y	Y	N
19 ***Neugebauer***	Y	Y	Y	Y	Y	N	N	Y
20 Gonzalez	Y	Y	Y	Y	Y	Y	Y	Y
21 ***Smith***	Y	Y	Y	Y	Y	N	N	Y
22 ***DeLay***	Y	Y	Y	Y	Y	N	N	Y
23 ***Bonilla***	Y	Y	Y	Y	Y	?	N	Y
24 Frost	Y	Y	Y	Y	Y	Y	Y	Y
25 Bell	Y	Y	Y	Y	Y	Y	Y	Y
26 ***Burgess***	Y	Y	Y	Y	Y	N	N	Y
27 Ortiz	Y	Y	Y	Y	Y	Y	Y	N
28 Rodriguez	Y	Y	Y	Y	Y	Y	Y	Y
29 Green	Y	Y	Y	Y	Y	Y	Y	N
30 Johnson, E.B.	Y	Y	Y	Y	Y	Y	Y	Y
31 ***Carter***	Y	Y	Y	Y	Y	N	N	Y
32 ***Sessions***	Y	Y	?	Y	Y	N	N	Y
UTAH								
1 ***Bishop***	Y	Y	Y	Y	Y	N	N	Y
2 Matheson	Y	Y	Y	Y	Y	N	Y	Y
3 ***Cannon***	Y	?	Y	Y	Y	N	N	Y
VERMONT								
AL *Sanders*	Y	Y	Y	Y	Y	Y	Y	Y
VIRGINIA								
1 ***Davis, Jo Ann***	Y	Y	Y	Y	Y	N	N	Y
2 ***Schrock***	Y	Y	Y	Y	Y	N	N	Y
3 Scott	Y	Y	Y	Y	Y	Y	Y	N
4 ***Forbes***	Y	Y	Y	Y	Y	N	N	Y
5 ***Goode***	Y	Y	Y	Y	Y	N	N	Y
6 ***Goodlatte***	Y	Y	Y	Y	Y	N	N	Y
7 ***Cantor***	Y	Y	Y	Y	Y	N	N	Y
8 Moran	Y	Y	Y	Y	Y	Y	Y	Y
9 Boucher	Y	Y	Y	Y	Y	Y	Y	Y
10 ***Wolf***	Y	Y	Y	Y	Y	N	N	Y
11 ***Davis, T.***	Y	Y	Y	Y	Y	N	N	Y
WASHINGTON								
1 Inslee	Y	Y	Y	Y	Y	Y	Y	N
2 Larsen	Y	Y	Y	Y	Y	Y	Y	N
3 Baird	Y	Y	Y	Y	Y	Y	Y	N
4 ***Hastings***	Y	Y	Y	Y	Y	N	N	Y
5 ***Nethercutt***	Y	Y	Y	Y	Y	N	N	Y
6 Dicks	Y	Y	Y	Y	Y	Y	Y	N
7 McDermott	Y	Y	Y	Y	Y	Y	Y	N
8 ***Dunn***	Y	Y	Y	Y	Y	N	N	Y
9 Smith	Y	Y	Y	Y	Y	Y	Y	N
WEST VIRGINIA								
1 Mollohan	?	?	?	Y	?	N	Y	N
2 ***Capito***	Y	Y	Y	Y	Y	N	N	Y
3 Rahall	Y	Y	Y	Y	Y	Y	Y	Y
WISCONSIN								
1 ***Ryan***	Y	Y	Y	Y	Y	N	N	Y
2 Baldwin	Y	Y	Y	Y	Y	Y	Y	Y
3 Kind	Y	Y	Y	Y	Y	Y	Y	Y
4 Kleczka	Y	Y	Y	?	?	Y	Y	Y
5 ***Sensenbrenner***	Y	Y	Y	Y	Y	N	N	Y
6 ***Petri***	Y	Y	Y	Y	Y	N	N	Y
7 Obey	Y	Y	Y	Y	Y	Y	Y	N
8 ***Green***	Y	Y	Y	Y	Y	N	N	Y
WYOMING								
AL ***Cubin***	Y	Y	Y	Y	Y	N	N	Y

Southern states - Ala., Ark., Fla., Ga., Ky., La., Miss., N.C., Okla., S.C., Tenn., Texas, Va.

139. H Res 600. Charter Schools Tribute/Adoption. Porter, R-Nev., motion to suspend the rules and adopt the resolution that would commend charter schools and their students, parents, teachers and administrators for their contributions to education and public school systems. It also would urge the president to call on the public to support National Charter Schools week. Motion agreed to 396-0: R 207-0; D 188-0 (ND 136-0, SD 52-0); I 1-0. A two-thirds majority of those present and voting (264 in this case) is required for adoption under suspension of the rules. May 4, 2004.

140. H Con Res 380. Music Education/Adoption. Porter, R-Nev., motion to suspend the rules and adopt the concurrent resolution that would express the sense of the Congress that music education is an important component of an academic curriculum and should be available to every student. Motion agreed to 402-0: R 207-0; D 194-0 (ND 141-0, SD 53-0); I 1-0. A two-thirds majority of those present and voting (268 in this case) is required for adoption under suspension of the rules. May, 4, 2004.

141. H Res 599. University of Connecticut Basketball Tribute/Adoption. Simmons, R-Conn., motion to suspend the rules and adopt the resolution that would congratulate the University of Connecticut men's and women's basketball teams for winning the 2004 NCAA Championships. Motion agreed to 401-0: R 208-0; D 192-0 (ND 138-0, SD 54-0); I 1-0. A two-thirds majority of those present and voting (268 in this case) is required for adoption under suspension of the rules. May 4, 2004.

142. HR 4227. Alternative Minimum Tax/Previous Question. Linder, R-Ga., motion to order the previous question (thus ending debate and possibility of amendment) on adoption of the rule (H Res 619) to provide for House floor consideration of the bill that would extend for one year the current income exemptions from the alternative minimum tax. Motion agreed to 220-201: R 220-0; D 0-200 (ND 0-145, SD 0-55); I 0-1. May 5, 2004.

143. HR 4227. Alternative Minimum Tax/Democratic Substitute. Neal, D-Mass., substitute amendment that would exempt individuals with adjusted gross incomes of less than $125,000 and married couples with incomes below $250,000 from the alternative minimum tax (AMT) in 2005. It would phase in AMT liability for individuals with income of $125,000 to $145,000, and married taxpayers with income of $250,000 to $290,000. The cost would be offset by restricting certain tax shelter transactions. Rejected 197-228: R 0-223; D 196-5 (ND 141-4, SD 55-1); I 1-0. May 5, 2004.

144. HR 4227. Alternative Minimum Tax/Passage. Passage of the bill that would extend for one year the current income exemptions — up to $40,250 for individual taxpayers and $58,000 for married couples — from the alternative minimum tax. Passed 333-89: R 223-0; D 109-89 (ND 69-74, SD 40-15); I 1-0. A "yea" was a vote in support of the president's position. May 5, 2004.

145. S Con Res 95. Fiscal 2005 Budget Resolution/Motion to Instruct. Moore, D-Kan., motion to instruct House conferees to accept provisions in the Senate version of the budget resolution that would subject any tax cut or mandatory spending expansion to either a pay-as-you-go offset or a 60-vote point of order in the Senate. Motion rejected 208-215: R 7-215; D 200-0 (ND 145-0, SD 55-0); I 1-0. May 5, 2004.

146. H Res 605. Autism Awareness/Adoption. Bilirakis, R-Fla., motion to suspend the rules and adopt the resolution that would support the designation of a "National Autism Awareness Month." It also would commend parents and relatives of children with autism for providing for their special needs and support increased federal funding for research to determine the causes of autism. Motion agreed to 421-0: R 220-0; D 200-0 (ND 145-0, SD 55-0); I 1-0. A two-thirds majority of those present and voting (281 in this case) is required for adoption under suspension of the rules. May 5, 2004.

Key

Y	Voted for (yea).
#	Paired for.
+	Announced for.
N	Voted against (nay).
X	Paired against.
−	Announced against.
P	Voted "present."
C	Voted "present" to avoid possible conflict of interest.
?	Did not vote or otherwise make a position known.

Democrats **Republicans**
Independents

	139	140	141	142	143	144	145	146
ALABAMA								
1 *Bonner*	Y	Y	Y	Y	N	Y	N	Y
2 *Everett*	Y	Y	Y	Y	N	Y	N	Y
3 *Rogers*	Y	Y	Y	Y	N	Y	N	Y
4 *Aderholt*	Y	Y	Y	Y	N	Y	N	Y
5 Cramer	Y	Y	Y	N	Y	Y	Y	Y
6 Bachus	Y	Y	Y	Y	N	Y	N	Y
7 Davis	Y	Y	Y	N	Y	Y	Y	Y
ALASKA								
AL *Young*	Y	?	Y	Y	N	Y	N	Y
ARIZONA								
1 *Renzi*	Y	Y	Y	Y	N	Y	N	Y
2 *Franks*	Y	Y	Y	Y	N	Y	N	Y
3 *Shadegg*	Y	Y	Y	Y	N	Y	N	Y
4 Pastor	Y	Y	Y	N	Y	N	Y	Y
5 *Hayworth*	Y	Y	Y	Y	N	Y	N	Y
6 *Flake*	Y	Y	Y	Y	N	Y	N	Y
7 Grijalva	Y	Y	Y	N	Y	N	Y	Y
8 *Kolbe*	Y	Y	Y	Y	N	Y	Y	Y
ARKANSAS								
1 Berry	Y	Y	Y	N	Y	N	Y	Y
2 Snyder	Y	Y	Y	N	Y	Y	Y	Y
3 *Boozman*	Y	Y	Y	Y	N	Y	N	Y
4 Ross	Y	Y	Y	N	Y	Y	Y	Y
CALIFORNIA								
1 Thompson	Y	Y	Y	N	Y	N	Y	Y
2 *Herger*	Y	Y	Y	Y	N	Y	N	Y
3 *Ose*	Y	Y	Y	Y	N	Y	?	Y
4 *Doolittle*	Y	Y	Y	Y	N	Y	N	Y
5 Matsui	Y	Y	Y	N	?	N	Y	Y
6 Woolsey	Y	Y	Y	N	Y	N	Y	Y
7 Miller, George	Y	Y	Y	N	Y	N	Y	Y
8 Pelosi	Y	Y	Y	N	Y	N	Y	Y
9 Lee	Y	Y	Y	N	Y	N	Y	Y
10 Tauscher	Y	Y	Y	N	Y	Y	Y	Y
11 *Pombo*	Y	Y	Y	Y	N	Y	N	Y
12 Lantos	Y	Y	Y	N	Y	N	Y	Y
13 Stark	Y	Y	Y	N	Y	N	Y	Y
14 Eshoo	Y	Y	Y	N	Y	N	Y	Y
15 Honda	Y	Y	Y	N	Y	+	Y	Y
16 Lofgren	Y	Y	Y	N	Y	Y	Y	Y
17 Farr	Y	Y	Y	N	Y	N	Y	Y
18 Cardoza	Y	Y	Y	N	Y	Y	Y	Y
19 *Radanovich*	Y	Y	Y	Y	N	Y	N	Y
20 Dooley	Y	Y	Y	N	Y	Y	N	Y
21 *Nunes*	Y	Y	Y	Y	N	Y	N	Y
22 *Thomas*	Y	Y	Y	Y	N	Y	N	Y
23 Capps	Y	Y	Y	N	Y	N	Y	Y
24 *Gallegly*	Y	Y	Y	Y	N	Y	N	Y
25 *McKeon*	Y	Y	Y	Y	N	Y	N	Y
26 *Dreier*	Y	Y	Y	Y	N	Y	N	Y
27 Sherman	Y	Y	Y	N	Y	N	Y	Y
28 Berman	Y	Y	?	N	Y	N	Y	Y
29 Schiff	Y	Y	Y	N	Y	N	Y	Y
30 Waxman	Y	Y	Y	N	Y	N	Y	Y
31 Becerra	Y	Y	Y	N	Y	N	Y	Y
32 Solis	?	?	?	?	?	−	+	?
33 Watson	Y	Y	Y	N	Y	N	Y	Y
34 Roybal-Allard	Y	Y	Y	N	Y	N	Y	Y
35 Waters	Y	Y	Y	N	Y	?	Y	Y
36 Harman	Y	Y	Y	N	Y	Y	Y	Y

	139	140	141	142	143	144	145	146
37 Millender-McD.	Y	Y	Y	N	Y	Y	Y	Y
38 Napolitano	Y	Y	Y	N	Y	Y	Y	Y
39 Sánchez, Linda	Y	Y	Y	N	Y	N	Y	Y
40 *Royce*	Y	Y	Y	Y	N	Y	N	Y
41 *Lewis*	Y	Y	Y	Y	N	Y	N	Y
42 *Miller, Gary*	Y	Y	Y	Y	N	Y	N	Y
43 Baca	Y	Y	Y	N	Y	N	Y	Y
44 *Calvert*	Y	Y	Y	Y	N	Y	N	Y
45 *Bono*	?	?	?	?	?	?	?	?
46 *Rohrabacher*	?	?	?	Y	N	Y	N	Y
47 Sanchez, Loretta	Y	Y	Y	N	Y	Y	Y	Y
48 *Cox*	Y	Y	Y	Y	N	Y	N	Y
49 *Issa*	Y	Y	Y	Y	N	Y	N	Y
50 *Cunningham*	Y	Y	Y	Y	N	Y	N	Y
51 Filner	Y	Y	Y	−	+	+	+	+
52 *Hunter*	Y	Y	Y	Y	N	Y	N	Y
53 Davis	Y	Y	Y	N	Y	Y	Y	Y
COLORADO								
1 DeGette	Y	Y	Y	N	Y	Y	Y	Y
2 Udall	Y	Y	Y	N	Y	N	Y	Y
3 *McInnis*	?	?	?	Y	N	Y	N	Y
4 *Musgrave*	?	Y	Y	Y	N	Y	N	Y
5 *Hefley*	Y	Y	Y	Y	N	Y	N	Y
6 *Tancredo*	Y	Y	Y	Y	N	Y	N	Y
7 *Beauprez*	Y	Y	Y	Y	N	Y	N	Y
CONNECTICUT								
1 Larson	Y	Y	Y	N	Y	N	Y	Y
2 *Simmons*	Y	Y	Y	Y	N	Y	N	Y
3 DeLauro	Y	Y	Y	N	Y	N	Y	Y
4 *Shays*	Y	Y	Y	Y	N	Y	N	Y
5 *Johnson*	Y	Y	Y	Y	N	Y	N	Y
DELAWARE								
AL *Castle*	Y	Y	Y	Y	N	Y	N	Y
FLORIDA								
1 *Miller, J.*	Y	Y	Y	Y	N	Y	N	Y
2 Boyd	?	?	?	?	?	?	?	?
3 Brown	?	?	?	N	Y	Y	Y	Y
4 *Crenshaw*	Y	Y	Y	Y	N	Y	N	Y
5 *Brown-Waite*	Y	Y	Y	Y	N	Y	N	Y
6 *Stearns*	Y	Y	Y	Y	N	Y	N	Y
7 *Mica*	Y	Y	Y	Y	N	Y	N	Y
8 *Keller*	Y	Y	Y	Y	N	Y	N	Y
9 *Bilirakis*	Y	Y	Y	Y	N	Y	N	Y
10 *Young*	Y	Y	Y	Y	N	Y	N	Y
11 Davis	Y	Y	Y	N	Y	Y	N	Y
12 *Putnam*	Y	Y	Y	Y	N	Y	N	Y
13 *Harris*	Y	Y	Y	Y	N	Y	N	Y
14 *Goss*	Y	Y	Y	Y	N	Y	N	Y
15 *Weldon*	Y	Y	Y	Y	N	Y	N	Y
16 *Foley*	Y	Y	Y	Y	N	Y	N	Y
17 Meek	Y	Y	Y	N	Y	Y	?	?
18 *Ros-Lehtinen*	Y	Y	Y	Y	N	Y	N	Y
19 Wexler	Y	Y	Y	N	Y	N	Y	Y
20 Deutsch	Y	Y	Y	Y	Y	Y	Y	Y
21 *Diaz-Balart, L.*	Y	Y	Y	Y	N	Y	N	Y
22 *Shaw*	Y	Y	Y	Y	N	Y	N	Y
23 Hastings	Y	Y	Y	N	Y	N	Y	Y
24 *Feeney*	Y	Y	Y	Y	N	Y	N	Y
25 *Diaz-Balart, M.*	Y	Y	Y	Y	N	Y	N	Y
GEORGIA								
1 *Kingston*	Y	Y	Y	Y	N	Y	N	Y
2 Bishop	Y	Y	Y	N	Y	Y	Y	Y
3 Marshall	Y	Y	Y	N	Y	Y	Y	Y
4 Majette	Y	Y	Y	N	Y	N	Y	Y
5 Lewis	Y	Y	Y	N	Y	N	Y	Y
6 *Isakson*	Y	Y	Y	Y	N	Y	N	Y
7 *Linder*	Y	Y	Y	Y	N	Y	N	Y
8 *Collins*	Y	Y	Y	Y	N	Y	N	Y
9 *Norwood*	Y	Y	Y	Y	N	Y	N	Y
10 *Deal*	Y	Y	Y	Y	N	Y	N	Y
11 *Gingrey*	Y	Y	P	Y	N	Y	N	Y
12 *Burns*	Y	Y	Y	Y	N	Y	N	Y
13 Scott	Y	Y	Y	N	Y	Y	Y	Y
HAWAII								
1 Abercrombie	Y	Y	Y	N	Y	N	Y	Y
2 Case	Y	Y	Y	N	Y	N	Y	Y
IDAHO								
1 *Otter*	Y	Y	Y	Y	N	Y	N	Y
2 *Simpson*	Y	Y	Y	Y	N	Y	N	Y
ILLINOIS								
1 Rush	Y	Y	Y	N	Y	N	Y	Y
2 Jackson	Y	Y	Y	N	Y	N	Y	Y
3 Lipinski	Y	Y	Y	N	Y	Y	Y	Y
4 Gutierrez	Y	Y	Y	N	Y	N	Y	Y
5 Emanuel	Y	Y	Y	N	Y	Y	Y	Y
6 *Hyde*	Y	Y	Y	N	Y	N	Y	Y

ND Northern Democrats   SD Southern Democrats

	139	140	141	142	143	144	145	146
7 Davis	Y	Y	Y	N	Y	N	Y	Y
8 ***Crane***	Y	Y	Y	Y	N	Y	N	Y
9 Schakowsky	Y	Y	Y	N	Y	N	Y	Y
10 ***Kirk***	Y	Y	Y	Y	N	Y	N	Y
11 ***Weller***	Y	Y	Y	Y	N	Y	N	Y
12 Costello	Y	Y	Y	N	Y	Y	Y	Y
13 ***Biggert***	Y	Y	Y	Y	N	Y	N	Y
14 ***Hastert***							N	
15 ***Johnson***	Y	Y	Y	Y	N	Y	N	Y
16 ***Manzullo***	Y	Y	Y	Y	N	Y	N	Y
17 Evans	Y	Y	Y	N	Y	Y	Y	Y
18 ***LaHood***	Y	Y	Y	Y	N	Y	N	Y
19 ***Shimkus***	Y	Y	Y	Y	N	Y	N	Y
INDIANA								
1 Visclosky	?	?	?	N	Y	N	Y	Y
2 ***Chocola***	Y	Y	Y	Y	N	Y	N	Y
3 ***Souder***	Y	Y	Y	Y	N	Y	N	Y
4 ***Buyer***	?	?	?	Y	N	Y	N	Y
5 ***Burton***	?	?	?	Y	N	Y	N	Y
6 ***Pence***	Y	Y	Y	Y	N	Y	N	Y
7 Carson	?	Y	?	N	Y	N	Y	Y
8 ***Hostettler***	Y	Y	Y	Y	N	Y	N	Y
9 Hill	Y	Y	Y	N	Y	N	Y	Y
IOWA								
1 ***Nussle***	Y	Y	Y	Y	N	Y	N	Y
2 ***Leach***	Y	Y	Y	Y	N	Y	Y	Y
3 Boswell	Y	Y	Y	N	Y	Y	Y	Y
4 ***Latham***	Y	Y	Y	Y	N	Y	N	Y
5 ***King***	Y	Y	Y	Y	N	Y	N	Y
KANSAS								
1 ***Moran***	Y	Y	Y	Y	N	Y	N	Y
2 ***Ryun***	Y	Y	Y	Y	N	Y	N	Y
3 Moore	Y	Y	Y	N	Y	Y	Y	Y
4 ***Tiahrt***	Y	Y	Y	Y	N	Y	N	Y
KENTUCKY								
1 ***Whitfield***	Y	Y	Y	Y	N	Y	N	Y
2 ***Lewis***	Y	Y	Y	Y	N	Y	N	Y
3 ***Northup***	Y	Y	Y	Y	N	Y	N	Y
4 Lucas	Y	Y	Y	N	Y	Y	Y	Y
5 ***Rogers***	Y	Y	Y	Y	N	Y	N	Y
6 Chandler	Y	Y	Y	N	Y	Y	Y	Y
LOUISIANA								
1 ***Vitter***	Y	Y	Y	Y	N	Y	N	Y
2 Jefferson	Y	Y	Y	N	Y	Y	Y	Y
3 ***Tauzin***	?	?	?	?	?	?	?	?
4 ***McCrery***	Y	Y	Y	Y	N	Y	N	Y
5 Alexander	Y	Y	Y	N	Y	Y	Y	Y
6 ***Baker***	Y	Y	Y	Y	N	Y	N	Y
7 John	Y	Y	Y	N	Y	Y	Y	Y
MAINE								
1 Allen	Y	Y	Y	N	Y	Y	Y	Y
2 Michaud	Y	Y	Y	N	Y	Y	Y	Y
MARYLAND								
1 ***Gilchrest***	Y	Y	Y	Y	N	Y	N	Y
2 Ruppersberger	Y	Y	Y	N	Y	Y	Y	Y
3 Cardin	Y	Y	Y	N	Y	Y	Y	Y
4 Wynn	Y	Y	Y	N	Y	Y	Y	Y
5 Hoyer	Y	Y	Y	N	Y	N	Y	Y
6 ***Bartlett***	Y	Y	Y	Y	N	Y	N	Y
7 Cummings	Y	Y	Y	N	Y	?	Y	Y
8 Van Hollen	Y	Y	Y	N	Y	Y	Y	Y
MASSACHUSETTS								
1 Olver	Y	Y	Y	N	Y	N	Y	Y
2 Neal	Y	Y	Y	N	Y	N	Y	Y
3 McGovern	Y	Y	Y	N	Y	N	Y	Y
4 Frank	Y	Y	Y	N	Y	N	Y	Y
5 Meehan	Y	Y	Y	N	Y	Y	Y	Y
6 Tierney	P	Y	Y	N	Y	N	Y	Y
7 Markey	Y	Y	Y	N	Y	N	Y	Y
8 Capuano	Y	Y	Y	N	Y	N	Y	Y
9 Lynch	Y	Y	Y	N	Y	Y	Y	Y
10 Delahunt	?	?	?	N	Y	Y	Y	Y
MICHIGAN								
1 Stupak	Y	Y	Y	N	Y	Y	Y	Y
2 ***Hoekstra***	Y	Y	Y	Y	N	Y	N	Y
3 ***Ehlers***	Y	Y	Y	Y	N	Y	N	Y
4 ***Camp***	Y	Y	Y	Y	N	Y	N	Y
5 Kildee	Y	Y	Y	N	Y	Y	Y	Y
6 ***Upton***	Y	Y	Y	Y	N	Y	Y	Y
7 ***Smith***	Y	?	Y	Y	N	Y	N	Y
8 ***Rogers***	Y	Y	Y	Y	N	Y	N	Y
9 ***Knollenberg***	?	Y	Y	Y	N	Y	N	Y
10 ***Miller***	Y	Y	Y	Y	N	Y	N	Y
11 ***McCotter***	Y	Y	Y	Y	N	Y	N	Y
12 Levin	Y	Y	Y	N	Y	N	Y	Y
13 Kilpatrick	Y	Y	Y	N	Y	N	+	+
14 Conyers	Y	Y	Y	N	Y	N	Y	Y
15 Dingell	Y	Y	Y	N	Y	N	Y	Y
MINNESOTA								
1 ***Gutknecht***	Y	Y	Y	Y	N	Y	N	Y
2 ***Kline***	Y	Y	Y	Y	N	Y	N	Y
3 ***Ramstad***	Y	Y	Y	Y	N	Y	N	Y
4 McCollum	Y	Y	Y	N	Y	N	Y	Y
5 Sabo	Y	Y	Y	N	Y	N	Y	Y
6 ***Kennedy***	Y	Y	Y	Y	N	Y	N	Y
7 Peterson	Y	Y	Y	N	Y	Y	Y	Y
8 Oberstar	Y	Y	Y	N	Y	N	Y	Y
MISSISSIPPI								
1 ***Wicker***	Y	Y	Y	Y	N	Y	N	Y
2 Thompson	Y	Y	Y	N	Y	Y	Y	Y
3 ***Pickering***	Y	Y	Y	Y	N	Y	N	Y
4 Taylor	Y	Y	Y	N	Y	N	Y	Y
MISSOURI								
1 Clay	Y	Y	Y	N	Y	Y	Y	Y
2 ***Akin***	Y	Y	Y	Y	N	Y	N	Y
3 Gephardt	?	?	?	N	Y	Y	Y	Y
4 Skelton	Y	Y	Y	N	Y	Y	Y	Y
5 McCarthy	Y	Y	Y	N	Y	N	Y	Y
6 ***Graves***	Y	Y	Y	Y	N	Y	N	Y
7 ***Blunt***	Y	Y	Y	Y	N	Y	N	Y
8 ***Emerson***	Y	Y	Y	Y	N	Y	?	?
9 ***Hulshof***	?	?	?	Y	N	Y	N	Y
MONTANA								
AL ***Rehberg***	Y	Y	Y	Y	N	Y	N	Y
NEBRASKA								
1 ***Bereuter***	Y	Y	Y	Y	N	Y	Y	?
2 ***Terry***	Y	Y	Y	Y	N	Y	N	Y
3 ***Osborne***	Y	Y	Y	Y	N	Y	N	Y
NEVADA								
1 Berkley	Y	Y	Y	N	Y	Y	Y	Y
2 ***Gibbons***	Y	Y	Y	Y	N	Y	N	Y
3 ***Porter***	Y	Y	Y	Y	N	Y	N	Y
NEW HAMPSHIRE								
1 ***Bradley***	Y	Y	Y	Y	N	Y	N	Y
2 ***Bass***	Y	Y	Y	Y	N	Y	Y	Y
NEW JERSEY								
1 Andrews	Y	Y	Y	N	Y	N	Y	Y
2 ***LoBiondo***	Y	Y	Y	Y	N	Y	N	Y
3 ***Saxton***	Y	Y	Y	Y	N	Y	N	Y
4 ***Smith***	Y	Y	Y	Y	N	Y	N	Y
5 ***Garrett***	Y	Y	Y	Y	N	Y	N	Y
6 Pallone	Y	Y	Y	N	Y	N	Y	Y
7 ***Ferguson***	Y	Y	Y	Y	N	Y	N	Y
8 Pascrell	Y	Y	Y	N	Y	Y	Y	Y
9 Rothman	Y	Y	Y	N	Y	N	Y	Y
10 Payne	Y	Y	Y	N	Y	N	Y	Y
11 ***Frelinghuysen***	Y	Y	Y	Y	N	Y	N	Y
12 Holt	Y	Y	Y	N	Y	N	Y	Y
13 Menendez	Y	Y	Y	N	Y	N	Y	Y
NEW MEXICO								
1 ***Wilson***	Y	Y	Y	Y	N	Y	N	Y
2 ***Pearce***	Y	Y	Y	Y	N	Y	N	Y
3 Udall	Y	Y	Y	N	Y	N	Y	Y
NEW YORK								
1 Bishop	Y	Y	Y	N	Y	Y	Y	Y
2 Israel	Y	Y	Y	N	Y	Y	Y	Y
3 ***King***	Y	Y	Y	Y	N	Y	N	Y
4 McCarthy	Y	Y	Y	N	Y	Y	Y	Y
5 Ackerman	P	Y	Y	N	Y	Y	Y	Y
6 Meeks	Y	Y	Y	N	Y	Y	Y	Y
7 Crowley	Y	Y	Y	N	Y	Y	Y	Y
8 Nadler	Y	Y	Y	N	Y	Y	Y	Y
9 Weiner	Y	Y	Y	N	Y	Y	Y	Y
10 Towns	Y	Y	Y	N	Y	N	Y	Y
11 Owens	Y	Y	Y	N	Y	Y	Y	Y
12 Velázquez	Y	Y	Y	N	Y	N	Y	Y
13 ***Fossella***	Y	Y	Y	Y	N	Y	N	Y
14 Maloney	Y	Y	Y	N	Y	Y	Y	Y
15 Rangel	Y	Y	?	N	Y	N	Y	Y
16 Serrano	Y	Y	Y	N	Y	N	Y	Y
17 Engel	Y	Y	Y	N	Y	Y	Y	Y
18 Lowey	Y	Y	Y	N	Y	Y	Y	Y
19 ***Kelly***	Y	Y	Y	Y	N	Y	N	Y
20 ***Sweeney***	Y	Y	Y	Y	N	Y	N	Y
21 McNulty	Y	Y	Y	N	Y	N	Y	Y
22 Hinchey	Y	Y	Y	N	Y	N	Y	Y
23 ***McHugh***	Y	Y	Y	Y	N	Y	N	Y
24 ***Boehlert***	Y	Y	Y	Y	N	Y	N	Y
25 ***Walsh***	Y	Y	Y	?	N	Y	N	Y
26 ***Reynolds***	?	?	?	?	N	Y	N	Y
27 ***Quinn***	Y	Y	Y	Y	N	Y	N	Y
28 Slaughter	?	Y	Y	N	Y	Y	Y	Y
29 ***Houghton***	Y	Y	Y	Y	N	Y	N	Y
NORTH CAROLINA								
1 Ballance	Y	Y	Y	+	Y	Y	Y	Y
2 Etheridge	Y	Y	Y	N	Y	Y	Y	Y
3 ***Jones***	Y	Y	Y	Y	N	Y	N	Y
4 Price	Y	Y	Y	N	Y	Y	Y	Y
5 ***Burr***	?	?	?	Y	N	Y	N	Y
6 ***Coble***	Y	Y	Y	Y	N	Y	N	Y
7 McIntyre	Y	Y	Y	N	Y	Y	Y	Y
8 ***Hayes***	Y	Y	P	Y	N	Y	N	Y
9 ***Myrick***	Y	Y	Y	Y	N	Y	N	Y
10 ***Ballenger***	Y	Y	Y	Y	N	Y	N	Y
11 ***Taylor***	Y	Y	Y	Y	N	Y	N	Y
12 Watt	Y	Y	Y	N	Y	N	Y	Y
13 Miller	Y	Y	Y	N	Y	Y	Y	Y
NORTH DAKOTA								
AL Pomeroy	Y	Y	Y	N	Y	Y	Y	Y
OHIO								
1 ***Chabot***	?	?	?	Y	N	Y	N	Y
2 ***Portman***	?	?	?	Y	N	Y	N	Y
3 ***Turner***	?	?	?	Y	N	Y	N	Y
4 ***Oxley***	Y	Y	Y	Y	N	Y	N	Y
5 ***Gillmor***	Y	Y	Y	Y	N	Y	N	Y
6 Strickland	P	Y	Y	N	Y	Y	Y	Y
7 ***Hobson***	Y	Y	Y	Y	N	Y	N	Y
8 ***Boehner***	Y	Y	Y	Y	N	Y	N	Y
9 Kaptur	Y	Y	Y	?	Y	Y	Y	Y
10 Kucinich	?	?	?	N	Y	N	Y	Y
11 Jones	Y	Y	Y	N	Y	Y	Y	Y
12 ***Tiberi***	Y	Y	Y	Y	N	Y	N	Y
13 Brown	Y	Y	Y	N	Y	Y	Y	Y
14 ***LaTourette***	Y	Y	Y	Y	N	Y	N	Y
15 ***Pryce***	Y	Y	Y	Y	N	Y	N	Y
16 ***Regula***	Y	Y	Y	Y	N	Y	N	Y
17 Ryan	Y	Y	Y	N	Y	Y	Y	Y
18 ***Ney***	Y	Y	Y	Y	N	Y	N	Y
OKLAHOMA								
1 ***Sullivan***	Y	?	Y	Y	N	Y	N	Y
2 Carson	Y	?	Y	N	N	Y	Y	Y
3 ***Lucas***	Y	Y	Y	Y	N	Y	N	Y
4 ***Cole***	Y	Y	Y	Y	N	Y	N	Y
5 ***Istook***	Y	Y	Y	Y	N	Y	N	Y
OREGON								
1 Wu	Y	Y	Y	N	Y	Y	Y	Y
2 ***Walden***	Y	Y	Y	Y	N	Y	N	Y
3 Blumenauer	Y	Y	Y	N	Y	N	Y	Y
4 DeFazio	Y	Y	Y	N	Y	Y	Y	Y
5 Hooley	Y	Y	Y	N	Y	Y	Y	Y
PENNSYLVANIA								
1 Brady	Y	Y	Y	N	Y	N	Y	Y
2 Fattah	Y	Y	Y	N	Y	N	Y	Y
3 ***English***	?	?	?	Y	N	Y	N	Y
4 ***Hart***	Y	Y	Y	Y	N	Y	N	Y
5 ***Peterson***	Y	Y	Y	Y	N	Y	N	Y
6 ***Gerlach***	Y	Y	Y	Y	N	Y	N	Y
7 ***Weldon***	Y	Y	Y	Y	N	Y	N	Y
8 ***Greenwood***	Y	Y	Y	?	?	?	?	?
9 ***Shuster, Bill***	Y	Y	Y	Y	N	Y	N	Y
10 ***Sherwood***	Y	Y	Y	Y	N	Y	N	Y
11 Kanjorski	?	?	?	N	N	N	Y	Y
12 Murtha	?	?	?	N	N	N	Y	Y
13 Hoeffel	Y	Y	Y	N	Y	Y	Y	Y
14 Doyle	Y	Y	Y	N	Y	N	Y	Y
15 ***Toomey***	?	Y	Y	Y	N	Y	N	Y
16 ***Pitts***	Y	Y	Y	Y	N	Y	N	Y
17 Holden	Y	Y	Y	N	Y	Y	Y	Y
18 ***Murphy***	Y	Y	Y	Y	N	Y	N	Y
19 ***Platts***	?	Y	Y	Y	N	Y	N	Y
RHODE ISLAND								
1 Kennedy	Y	Y	Y	N	Y	Y	Y	Y
2 Langevin	Y	Y	Y	N	Y	Y	Y	Y
SOUTH CAROLINA								
1 ***Brown***	Y	Y	Y	Y	N	Y	N	Y
2 ***Wilson***	Y	Y	Y	Y	N	Y	N	Y
3 ***Barrett***	Y	Y	Y	Y	N	Y	N	Y
4 ***DeMint***	?	?	?	?	?	?	?	?
5 Spratt	Y	Y	Y	N	Y	N	Y	Y
6 Clyburn	Y	Y	Y	N	Y	N	Y	Y
SOUTH DAKOTA								
AL Vacant								
TENNESSEE								
1 ***Jenkins***	Y	Y	Y	Y	N	Y	N	Y
2 ***Duncan***	Y	Y	Y	Y	N	Y	N	Y
3 ***Wamp***	Y	Y	Y	Y	N	Y	N	Y
4 Davis	Y	Y	Y	N	Y	Y	Y	Y
5 Cooper	Y	Y	Y	N	Y	N	Y	Y
6 Gordon	Y	Y	Y	N	Y	Y	Y	Y
7 ***Blackburn***	Y	Y	Y	Y	N	Y	N	Y
8 Tanner	Y	Y	Y	N	Y	Y	Y	Y
9 Ford	Y	Y	Y	N	Y	Y	Y	Y
TEXAS								
1 Sandlin	Y	Y	Y	N	Y	Y	Y	Y
2 Turner	Y	Y	Y	N	Y	N	Y	Y
3 ***Johnson, Sam***	Y	Y	Y	Y	N	Y	N	Y
4 ***Hall***	Y	Y	Y	Y	N	Y	N	Y
5 ***Hensarling***	Y	Y	Y	Y	N	Y	N	Y
6 ***Barton***	Y	Y	Y	?	N	Y	N	Y
7 ***Culberson***	?	?	?	Y	N	Y	N	Y
8 ***Brady***	Y	Y	Y	Y	N	Y	N	Y
9 Lampson	Y	Y	Y	N	Y	Y	Y	Y
10 Doggett	?	?	?	N	Y	Y	Y	Y
11 Edwards	?	Y	Y	N	Y	Y	Y	Y
12 ***Granger***	Y	Y	Y	Y	N	Y	N	Y
13 ***Thornberry***	Y	Y	Y	Y	N	Y	N	Y
14 ***Paul***	Y	Y	Y	Y	N	Y	N	Y
15 Hinojosa	Y	Y	Y	N	Y	Y	Y	Y
16 Reyes	Y	Y	Y	N	Y	Y	Y	Y
17 Stenholm	Y	Y	Y	N	Y	N	Y	Y
18 Jackson-Lee	Y	Y	Y	N	Y	–	Y	Y
19 ***Neugebauer***	Y	Y	Y	Y	N	Y	N	Y
20 Gonzalez	Y	Y	Y	N	Y	Y	Y	Y
21 ***Smith***	Y	Y	Y	Y	N	Y	N	Y
22 ***DeLay***	Y	Y	Y	Y	N	Y	N	Y
23 ***Bonilla***	Y	Y	Y	Y	N	Y	N	Y
24 Frost	Y	Y	Y	N	Y	Y	Y	Y
25 Bell	?	Y	Y	N	Y	Y	Y	Y
26 ***Burgess***	Y	Y	Y	Y	N	Y	N	Y
27 Ortiz	Y	Y	Y	N	Y	N	Y	Y
28 Rodriguez	Y	Y	Y	N	Y	Y	Y	Y
29 Green	Y	Y	Y	N	Y	N	Y	Y
30 Johnson, E.B.	Y	Y	Y	N	Y	Y	Y	Y
31 ***Carter***	Y	Y	Y	Y	N	Y	N	Y
32 ***Sessions***	Y	Y	Y	Y	N	Y	N	Y
UTAH								
1 ***Bishop***	Y	Y	?	Y	N	Y	N	Y
2 Matheson	Y	Y	Y	N	N	Y	Y	Y
3 ***Cannon***	Y	?	Y	Y	N	Y	N	Y
VERMONT								
AL *Sanders*	Y	Y	Y	N	Y	Y	Y	Y
VIRGINIA								
1 ***Davis, Jo Ann***	Y	Y	Y	Y	N	Y	N	Y
2 ***Schrock***	Y	Y	Y	Y	N	Y	N	Y
3 Scott	Y	Y	Y	N	Y	N	Y	Y
4 ***Forbes***	Y	Y	Y	Y	N	Y	N	Y
5 ***Goode***	Y	Y	Y	Y	N	Y	N	Y
6 ***Goodlatte***	Y	Y	Y	Y	N	Y	N	Y
7 ***Cantor***	Y	Y	Y	Y	N	Y	N	Y
8 Moran	Y	Y	Y	N	Y	Y	Y	Y
9 Boucher	Y	Y	Y	N	Y	Y	Y	Y
10 ***Wolf***	Y	Y	Y	Y	N	Y	N	Y
11 ***Davis, T.***	Y	Y	Y	Y	N	Y	N	Y
WASHINGTON								
1 Inslee	Y	Y	Y	N	Y	N	Y	Y
2 Larsen	Y	Y	Y	N	Y	N	Y	Y
3 Baird	Y	Y	Y	N	Y	N	Y	Y
4 ***Hastings***	Y	Y	Y	Y	N	Y	N	Y
5 ***Nethercutt***	?	?	?	Y	N	Y	N	Y
6 Dicks	Y	Y	Y	N	Y	N	Y	Y
7 McDermott	Y	Y	Y	N	Y	N	Y	Y
8 ***Dunn***	Y	Y	Y	Y	N	Y	N	Y
9 Smith	Y	Y	Y	N	Y	N	Y	Y
WEST VIRGINIA								
1 Mollohan	Y	Y	Y	N	N	N	Y	Y
2 ***Capito***	Y	Y	Y	Y	N	Y	N	Y
3 Rahall	Y	Y	Y	N	Y	Y	Y	Y
WISCONSIN								
1 ***Ryan***	Y	Y	Y	Y	N	Y	N	?
2 Baldwin	Y	Y	Y	N	Y	Y	Y	Y
3 Kind	Y	Y	Y	N	Y	Y	Y	Y
4 Kleczka	Y	Y	Y	N	Y	Y	Y	Y
5 ***Sensenbrenner***	Y	Y	Y	Y	N	Y	N	Y
6 ***Petri***	Y	Y	Y	Y	N	Y	N	Y
7 Obey	Y	Y	Y	N	Y	N	Y	Y
8 ***Green***	Y	Y	Y	Y	N	Y	N	Y
WYOMING								
AL ***Cubin***	Y	Y	Y	Y	N	Y	N	Y

Southern states - Ala., Ark., Fla., Ga., Ky., La., Miss., N.C., Okla., S.C., Tenn., Texas, Va.

Key

Y	Voted for (yea).
#	Paired for.
+	Announced for.
N	Voted against (nay).
X	Paired against.
−	Announced against.
P	Voted "present."
C	Voted "present" to avoid possible conflict of interest.
?	Did not vote or otherwise make a position known.

Democrats   **Republicans**
Independents

147. H Res 627. Treatment of Iraqi Prisoners/Previous Question. Hastings, R-Wash., motion to order the previous question (thus ending debate and possibility of amendment) on adoption of the rule (H Res 628) to provide for House floor consideration of the resolution that would condemn the abuse of Iraqi prisoners in U.S. custody, regardless of the circumstances of their detention. Motion agreed to 218-201: R 218-0; D 0-200 (ND 0-144, SD 0-56); I 0-1. May 6, 2004.

148. HR 2443. Coast Guard Reauthorization/Motion to Instruct. Filner, D-Calif., motion to instruct House conferees to insist on a provision in the House-passed bill requiring foreign-flag vessels to have their vessel security plans approved by the Coast Guard before entering the United States. Motion agreed to 395-19: R 197-19; D 197-0 (ND 143-0, SD 54-0); I 1-0. May 6, 2004.

149. H Res 402. Democracy in Laos/Adoption. Burton, R-Ind., motion to suspend the rules and adopt the resolution that would urge the Lao People's Democratic Republic, the United Nations, the European Union and the Association of South East Asian Nations to work to provide unrestricted access to Laos for international election monitors and humanitarian aid workers. Motion agreed to 408-1: R 210-1; D 197-0 (ND 141-0, SD 56-0); I 1-0. A two-thirds majority of those present and voting (273 in this case) is required for adoption under suspension of the rules. May 6, 2004.

150. H Res 627. Treatment of Iraqi Prisoners/Adoption. Adoption of the resolution that would condemn abuse of Iraqi prisoners in U.S. custody, regardless of the circumstances of their detention. It also would urge the secretary of the Army to investigate any allegations of abuse and bring to justice any member of the armed forces who violated the Uniform Code of Military Justice. Adopted 365-50: R 213-1; D 151-49 (ND 102-43, SD 49-6); I 1-0. May 6, 2004.

151. H Con Res 326. Chinese Prisoner Wang Bingzhang/Adoption. Burton, R-Ind., motion to suspend the rules and adopt the concurrent resolution that would express the sense of Congress that Dr. Wang Bingzhang, a permanent resident of the United States, is being detained in China in violation of international law and should be released. Motion agreed to 399-0: R 207-0; D 191-0 (ND 138-0, SD 53-0); I 1-0. A two-thirds majority of those present and voting (266 in this case) is required for adoption under suspension of the rules. May 6, 2004.

152. H Con Res 398. Iran's Nuclear Program/Adoption. Burton, R-Ind., motion to suspend the rules and adopt the concurrent resolution that would condemn Iran's continuing deceptions and falsehoods about its nuclear programs. It also would call upon all parties to the Non-Proliferation of Nuclear Weapons Treaty, including the United States, to use all appropriate means to prevent Iran from acquiring nuclear weapons. Motion agreed to 376-3: R 203-1; D 172-2 (ND 120-2, SD 52-0); I 1-0. A two-thirds majority of those present and voting (253 in this case) is required for adoption under suspension of the rules. May 6, 2004.

	147	148	149	150	151	152
ALABAMA						
1 *Bonner*	Y	Y	Y	Y	Y	Y
2 *Everett*	Y	Y	Y	Y	Y	Y
3 *Rogers*	Y	Y	Y	Y	Y	Y
4 *Aderholt*	Y	Y	Y	Y	Y	Y
5 Cramer	N	Y	Y	Y	Y	Y
6 *Bachus*	Y	Y	Y	Y	Y	Y
7 Davis	N	Y	Y	Y	Y	Y
ALASKA						
AL *Young*	Y	Y	Y	Y	Y	Y
ARIZONA						
1 *Renzi*	Y	Y	Y	Y	Y	Y
2 *Franks*	Y	Y	Y	Y	Y	Y
3 *Shadegg*	Y	Y	Y	Y	Y	Y
4 Pastor	N	Y	Y	Y	Y	Y
5 *Hayworth*	Y	Y	Y	Y	Y	Y
6 *Flake*	Y	Y	Y	Y	Y	Y
7 Grijalva	N	Y	N	Y	N	Y
8 *Kolbe*	Y	Y	Y	Y	Y	Y
ARKANSAS						
1 Berry	N	Y	Y	Y	Y	Y
2 Snyder	N	Y	Y	Y	Y	Y
3 *Boozman*	Y	Y	Y	Y	Y	Y
4 Ross	N	Y	Y	Y	Y	Y
CALIFORNIA						
1 Thompson	N	Y	Y	Y	Y	Y
2 *Herger*	Y	Y	Y	Y	Y	Y
3 *Ose*	Y	Y	Y	Y	Y	Y
4 *Doolittle*	Y	Y	Y	Y	Y	Y
5 Matsui	N	Y	Y	Y	Y	Y
6 Woolsey	N	Y	Y	N	Y	P
7 Miller, George	N	?	P	N	Y	P
8 Pelosi	N	Y	N	Y	Y	Y
9 Lee	N	Y	N	Y	N	P
10 Tauscher	N	Y	Y	Y	Y	Y
11 *Pombo*	Y	Y	Y	Y	Y	Y
12 Lantos	N	Y	Y	Y	Y	Y
13 Stark	N	Y	N	Y	N	P
14 Eshoo	N	Y	Y	Y	Y	Y
15 Honda	N	Y	Y	Y	Y	Y
16 Lofgren	N	Y	?	Y	Y	Y
17 Farr	N	Y	Y	Y	Y	?
18 Cardoza	N	Y	Y	Y	Y	Y
19 *Radanovich*	Y	Y	Y	Y	Y	Y
20 Dooley	N	Y	?	Y	Y	Y
21 *Nunes*	Y	Y	Y	Y	Y	Y
22 *Thomas*	Y	N	Y	Y	Y	Y
23 Capps	N	Y	Y	Y	Y	Y
24 *Gallegly*	Y	Y	Y	Y	Y	Y
25 *McKeon*	Y	Y	Y	Y	Y	Y
26 *Dreier*	Y	Y	Y	Y	Y	Y
27 Sherman	N	Y	Y	Y	Y	Y
28 Berman	N	Y	Y	Y	Y	Y
29 Schiff	N	Y	Y	Y	Y	Y
30 Waxman	N	Y	N	N	Y	Y
31 Becerra	N	Y	Y	Y	Y	Y
32 Solis	?	+	+	?	+	?
33 Watson	N	Y	N	N	Y	P
34 Roybal-Allard	N	Y	Y	Y	Y	Y
35 Waters	N	Y	N	N	Y	P
36 Harman	N	Y	Y	Y	Y	Y

	147	148	149	150	151	152
37 Millender-McD.	N	Y	Y	N	Y	Y
38 Napolitano	N	Y	Y	Y	Y	Y
39 Sánchez, Linda	N	Y	Y	Y	Y	Y
40 *Royce*	Y	Y	Y	Y	Y	Y
41 *Lewis*	Y	Y	Y	Y	Y	Y
42 *Miller, Gary*	Y	Y	Y	Y	Y	Y
43 Baca	?	?	?	?	?	?
44 *Calvert*	Y	Y	Y	Y	Y	Y
45 *Bono*	?	?	?	?	?	?
46 *Rohrabacher*	Y	Y	Y	Y	Y	Y
47 Sanchez, Loretta	N	Y	Y	Y	Y	Y
48 *Cox*	Y	Y	Y	?	Y	Y
49 *Issa*	Y	Y	Y	Y	Y	Y
50 *Cunningham*	Y	Y	Y	Y	Y	Y
51 Filner	N	Y	Y	Y	Y	P
52 *Hunter*	Y	?	Y	Y	Y	?
53 Davis	N	Y	Y	Y	Y	Y
COLORADO						
1 DeGette	N	Y	Y	Y	Y	Y
2 Udall	N	Y	Y	Y	Y	Y
3 *McInnis*	Y	Y	Y	Y	Y	Y
4 *Musgrave*	Y	Y	Y	Y	Y	Y
5 *Hefley*	Y	Y	Y	Y	Y	Y
6 *Tancredo*	Y	N	Y	Y	Y	Y
7 *Beauprez*	Y	Y	Y	Y	Y	Y
CONNECTICUT						
1 Larson	N	Y	Y	Y	Y	Y
2 *Simmons*	Y	Y	Y	Y	Y	Y
3 DeLauro	N	Y	Y	Y	Y	Y
4 *Shays*	Y	Y	Y	Y	Y	Y
5 *Johnson*	Y	Y	?	Y	Y	Y
DELAWARE						
AL *Castle*	Y	Y	Y	Y	Y	Y
FLORIDA						
1 *Miller, J.*	Y	Y	Y	Y	Y	Y
2 Boyd	?	?	?	?	?	?
3 Brown	N	Y	Y	Y	Y	Y
4 *Crenshaw*	Y	Y	Y	Y	Y	Y
5 *Brown-Waite*	Y	Y	Y	Y	Y	Y
6 *Stearns*	Y	Y	Y	Y	Y	Y
7 *Mica*	Y	Y	Y	Y	Y	Y
8 *Keller*	Y	Y	Y	Y	Y	Y
9 *Bilirakis*	Y	Y	Y	Y	Y	Y
10 *Young*	Y	Y	Y	Y	Y	?
11 Davis	N	Y	Y	Y	Y	Y
12 *Putnam*	Y	N	Y	Y	Y	Y
13 *Harris*	Y	Y	Y	Y	Y	Y
14 *Goss*	Y	Y	Y	Y	Y	Y
15 *Weldon*	Y	Y	Y	Y	Y	Y
16 *Foley*	Y	Y	Y	Y	Y	Y
17 Meek	N	Y	N	N	Y	Y
18 *Ros-Lehtinen*	Y	Y	Y	Y	Y	Y
19 Wexler	N	Y	Y	Y	Y	Y
20 Deutsch	N	Y	Y	Y	Y	Y
21 *Diaz-Balart, L.*	Y	Y	?	Y	Y	Y
22 *Shaw*	Y	Y	Y	Y	Y	Y
23 Hastings	N	Y	N	N	Y	Y
24 *Feeney*	Y	Y	Y	Y	Y	?
25 *Diaz-Balart, M.*	Y	Y	Y	Y	Y	Y
GEORGIA						
1 *Kingston*	Y	N	Y	Y	Y	Y
2 Bishop	N	Y	Y	Y	Y	Y
3 Marshall	N	Y	Y	Y	Y	Y
4 Majette	N	Y	Y	Y	Y	Y
5 Lewis	N	Y	N	N	Y	Y
6 *Isakson*	Y	Y	Y	Y	Y	Y
7 *Linder*	Y	Y	Y	Y	Y	Y
8 *Collins*	Y	Y	Y	Y	Y	Y
9 *Norwood*	Y	Y	Y	Y	Y	Y
10 *Deal*	Y	Y	Y	Y	Y	Y
11 *Gingrey*	Y	Y	Y	Y	Y	Y
12 *Burns*	Y	Y	Y	Y	Y	Y
13 Scott	N	Y	Y	Y	Y	Y
HAWAII						
1 Abercrombie	N	Y	Y	N	Y	Y
2 Case	N	Y	Y	Y	Y	Y
IDAHO						
1 *Otter*	Y	Y	Y	Y	Y	Y
2 *Simpson*	Y	Y	Y	Y	Y	Y
ILLINOIS						
1 Rush	N	Y	Y	Y	Y	Y
2 Jackson	N	Y	Y	Y	Y	Y
3 Lipinski	N	Y	Y	Y	Y	Y
4 Gutierrez	N	Y	Y	N	Y	?
5 Emanuel	N	Y	Y	Y	Y	Y
6 *Hyde*	Y	Y	Y	Y	Y	Y

ND Northern Democrats   SD Southern Democrats

	147	148	149	150	151	152
7 Davis	N	Y	Y	Y	Y	Y
8 ***Crane***	Y	Y	Y	Y	Y	Y
9 Schakowsky	N	Y	Y	N	Y	Y
10 ***Kirk***	Y	Y	Y	Y	Y	Y
11 ***Weller***	Y	Y	Y	Y	Y	Y
12 Costello	N	Y	Y	Y	Y	Y
13 ***Biggert***	Y	Y	Y	Y	Y	Y
14 ***Hastert***				Y		
15 ***Johnson***	+	Y	Y	Y	Y	Y
16 ***Manzullo***	Y	Y	Y	Y	Y	Y
17 Evans	N	Y	Y	Y	Y	Y
18 ***LaHood***	Y	Y	Y	Y	Y	Y
19 ***Shimkus***	Y	Y	Y	Y	Y	Y
INDIANA						
1 Visclosky	N	Y	Y	Y	Y	Y
2 ***Chocola***	Y	N	Y	Y	Y	Y
3 ***Souder***	Y	Y	Y	Y	Y	Y
4 ***Buyer***	Y	Y	Y	Y	?	Y
5 ***Burton***	Y	Y	Y	Y	Y	Y
6 ***Pence***	Y	Y	Y	Y	Y	Y
7 Carson	N	Y	Y	Y	Y	Y
8 ***Hostettler***	Y	Y	Y	Y	Y	Y
9 Hill	N	Y	Y	Y	Y	Y
IOWA						
1 ***Nussle***	Y	Y	Y	Y	Y	Y
2 ***Leach***	Y	Y	Y	Y	Y	Y
3 Boswell	N	Y	Y	Y	Y	Y
4 ***Latham***	Y	?	?	?	?	?
5 ***King***	Y	Y	Y	Y	Y	Y
KANSAS						
1 ***Moran***	Y	Y	Y	Y	Y	Y
2 ***Ryun***	Y	Y	Y	Y	Y	Y
3 Moore	N	Y	Y	Y	Y	Y
4 ***Tiahrt***	Y	Y	Y	Y	Y	Y
KENTUCKY						
1 ***Whitfield***	Y	Y	Y	Y	Y	Y
2 ***Lewis***	?	?	?	?	?	?
3 ***Northup***	Y	Y	Y	Y	Y	Y
4 Lucas	N	Y	Y	Y	Y	Y
5 ***Rogers***	Y	Y	Y	Y	Y	Y
6 Chandler	N	Y	Y	Y	Y	Y
LOUISIANA						
1 ***Vitter***	Y	Y	Y	Y	Y	Y
2 Jefferson	N	Y	Y	Y	Y	Y
3 ***Tauzin***	?	?	?	?	?	?
4 ***McCrery***	Y	Y	Y	?	?	?
5 Alexander	N	Y	Y	Y	Y	Y
6 ***Baker***	Y	Y	Y	Y	Y	Y
7 John	N	Y	Y	?	?	?
MAINE						
1 Allen	N	Y	Y	Y	Y	Y
2 Michaud	N	Y	Y	Y	Y	Y
MARYLAND						
1 ***Gilchrest***	Y	N	Y	Y	Y	Y
2 Ruppersberger	N	Y	Y	Y	Y	Y
3 Cardin	N	Y	Y	Y	Y	Y
4 Wynn	N	Y	Y	Y	Y	Y
5 Hoyer	N	Y	Y	N	Y	Y
6 ***Bartlett***	Y	N	Y	Y	Y	Y
7 Cummings	N	Y	Y	N	Y	Y
8 Van Hollen	N	Y	Y	Y	Y	Y
MASSACHUSETTS						
1 Olver	N	Y	Y	N	Y	Y
2 Neal	N	Y	Y	Y	?	?
3 McGovern	N	Y	Y	N	Y	Y
4 Frank	N	Y	Y	N	Y	Y
5 Meehan	N	Y	Y	Y	Y	Y
6 Tierney	N	Y	Y	Y	Y	Y
7 Markey	N	Y	Y	N	Y	Y
8 Capuano	N	Y	Y	Y	Y	P
9 Lynch	N	Y	Y	Y	Y	Y
10 Delahunt	N	Y	Y	Y	?	?
MICHIGAN						
1 Stupak	N	Y	Y	Y	Y	Y
2 ***Hoekstra***	Y	Y	Y	Y	Y	Y
3 ***Ehlers***	Y	Y	Y	Y	Y	Y
4 ***Camp***	Y	Y	Y	Y	Y	Y
5 Kildee	N	Y	Y	Y	Y	Y
6 ***Upton***	Y	Y	Y	Y	Y	Y
7 ***Smith***	Y	Y	Y	Y	Y	Y
8 ***Rogers***	Y	Y	?	Y	Y	Y
9 ***Knollenberg***	Y	Y	Y	Y	Y	Y
10 ***Miller***	Y	Y	Y	Y	Y	Y
11 ***McCotter***	Y	Y	Y	Y	Y	Y
12 Levin	N	Y	Y	Y	Y	Y

	147	148	149	150	151	152
13 Kilpatrick	N	Y	Y	N	Y	Y
14 Conyers	N	Y	Y	N	Y	N
15 Dingell	N	Y	Y	Y	Y	Y
MINNESOTA						
1 ***Gutknecht***	Y	Y	Y	Y	Y	Y
2 ***Kline***	Y	Y	Y	Y	Y	Y
3 ***Ramstad***	Y	Y	Y	Y	Y	Y
4 McCollum	N	Y	Y	N	?	?
5 Sabo	N	Y	Y	N	Y	Y
6 ***Kennedy***	Y	Y	Y	Y	Y	Y
7 Peterson	N	Y	Y	Y	Y	Y
8 Oberstar	N	Y	Y	N	Y	Y
MISSISSIPPI						
1 ***Wicker***	Y	Y	Y	Y	Y	Y
2 Thompson	N	Y	Y	Y	Y	Y
3 ***Pickering***	Y	Y	Y	Y	Y	Y
4 Taylor	N	Y	Y	Y	Y	Y
MISSOURI						
1 Clay	N	Y	Y	Y	Y	Y
2 ***Akin***	Y	Y	Y	Y	Y	Y
3 Gephardt	N	Y	Y	Y	?	?
4 Skelton	N	Y	Y	Y	Y	Y
5 McCarthy	N	Y	Y	Y	Y	Y
6 ***Graves***	Y	N	Y	Y	Y	Y
7 ***Blunt***	Y	N	Y	?	?	?
8 ***Emerson***	Y	Y	Y	Y	Y	Y
9 ***Hulshof***	Y	Y	Y	Y	Y	Y
MONTANA						
AL ***Rehberg***	Y	Y	Y	Y	Y	Y
NEBRASKA						
1 ***Bereuter***	Y	Y	Y	Y	Y	Y
2 ***Terry***	Y	Y	Y	Y	Y	Y
3 ***Osborne***	Y	Y	Y	Y	Y	Y
NEVADA						
1 Berkley	N	Y	Y	Y	?	?
2 ***Gibbons***	Y	Y	Y	Y	Y	Y
3 ***Porter***	Y	Y	Y	Y	Y	Y
NEW HAMPSHIRE						
1 ***Bradley***	Y	Y	Y	Y	Y	Y
2 ***Bass***	Y	Y	Y	Y	Y	Y
NEW JERSEY						
1 Andrews	N	Y	Y	Y	Y	Y
2 ***LoBiondo***	Y	Y	Y	Y	Y	Y
3 ***Saxton***	?	Y	Y	Y	Y	Y
4 ***Smith***	Y	Y	Y	Y	Y	Y
5 ***Garrett***	Y	Y	Y	Y	Y	Y
6 Pallone	N	Y	Y	N	Y	Y
7 ***Ferguson***	Y	Y	?	Y	Y	Y
8 Pascrell	N	Y	Y	Y	Y	Y
9 Rothman	N	Y	Y	Y	Y	Y
10 Payne	N	Y	Y	N	Y	Y
11 ***Frelinghuysen***	Y	Y	?	Y	Y	Y
12 Holt	N	Y	Y	Y	Y	Y
13 Menendez	?	+	+	Y	Y	Y
NEW MEXICO						
1 ***Wilson***	Y	Y	Y	Y	Y	Y
2 ***Pearce***	Y	Y	Y	Y	Y	Y
3 Udall	N	Y	Y	Y	Y	Y
NEW YORK						
1 Bishop	N	Y	Y	Y	Y	Y
2 Israel	N	Y	Y	Y	Y	Y
3 ***King***	Y	Y	Y	Y	Y	Y
4 McCarthy	N	Y	Y	Y	Y	Y
5 Ackerman	N	Y	Y	Y	Y	Y
6 Meeks	?	?	?	?	?	?
7 Crowley	N	Y	Y	Y	Y	Y
8 Nadler	N	Y	Y	Y	Y	Y
9 Weiner	N	Y	Y	Y	Y	Y
10 Towns	N	Y	Y	N	Y	Y
11 Owens	N	Y	Y	N	Y	Y
12 Velázquez	N	Y	Y	N	Y	Y
13 ***Fossella***	Y	Y	Y	Y	Y	Y
14 Maloney	N	Y	Y	Y	Y	Y
15 Rangel	N	Y	Y	N	Y	Y
16 Serrano	N	Y	Y	N	Y	P
17 Engel	N	Y	Y	Y	Y	Y
18 Lowey	N	Y	Y	Y	Y	Y
19 ***Kelly***	Y	Y	Y	Y	Y	Y
20 ***Sweeney***	Y	Y	Y	Y	Y	Y
21 McNulty	N	Y	Y	Y	?	?
22 Hinchey	N	Y	Y	N	Y	P
23 ***McHugh***	Y	Y	Y	?	?	?
24 ***Boehlert***	Y	Y	Y	Y	Y	Y
25 ***Walsh***	Y	Y	Y	Y	Y	Y

	147	148	149	150	151	152
26 ***Reynolds***	Y	Y	Y	Y	Y	Y
27 ***Quinn***	Y	Y	Y	Y	Y	Y
28 Slaughter	N	Y	Y	Y	Y	Y
29 ***Houghton***	Y	Y	Y	Y	Y	Y
NORTH CAROLINA						
1 Ballance	N	Y	Y	Y	Y	Y
2 Etheridge	N	Y	Y	Y	Y	Y
3 ***Jones***	Y	Y	Y	Y	Y	Y
4 Price	N	Y	Y	Y	Y	Y
5 ***Burr***	Y	Y	Y	Y	Y	Y
6 ***Coble***	Y	Y	Y	Y	Y	Y
7 McIntyre	N	Y	Y	Y	Y	Y
8 ***Hayes***	Y	Y	Y	Y	Y	Y
9 ***Myrick***	Y	Y	Y	Y	Y	Y
10 ***Ballenger***	Y	?	Y	Y	?	?
11 ***Taylor***	Y	N	Y	Y	Y	Y
12 Watt	N	Y	Y	N	Y	Y
13 Miller	N	Y	Y	Y	Y	Y
NORTH DAKOTA						
AL Pomeroy	N	Y	Y	Y	Y	Y
OHIO						
1 ***Chabot***	Y	Y	Y	Y	Y	Y
2 ***Portman***	Y	N	Y	Y	Y	Y
3 ***Turner***	Y	Y	Y	Y	Y	Y
4 ***Oxley***	Y	Y	Y	?	+	+
5 ***Gillmor***	Y	Y	Y	Y	Y	Y
6 Strickland	N	Y	Y	N	Y	Y
7 ***Hobson***	Y	Y	Y	Y	Y	Y
8 ***Boehner***	Y	Y	Y	Y	?	?
9 Kaptur	N	Y	Y	N	Y	Y
10 Kucinich	N	Y	Y	N	Y	N
11 Jones	N	Y	Y	N	Y	Y
12 ***Tiberi***	Y	N	Y	Y	Y	Y
13 Brown	N	Y	Y	N	Y	Y
14 ***LaTourette***	Y	Y	Y	Y	Y	Y
15 ***Pryce***	Y	Y	Y	Y	Y	Y
16 ***Regula***	Y	Y	Y	Y	Y	Y
17 Ryan	N	Y	Y	N	Y	Y
18 ***Ney***	Y	Y	Y	Y	Y	Y
OKLAHOMA						
1 ***Sullivan***	Y	N	Y	Y	Y	Y
2 Carson	N	Y	Y	Y	Y	Y
3 ***Lucas***	Y	Y	Y	Y	Y	Y
4 ***Cole***	Y	Y	Y	Y	Y	?
5 ***Istook***	Y	Y	Y	Y	Y	Y
OREGON						
1 Wu	N	Y	Y	Y	Y	Y
2 ***Walden***	Y	Y	Y	Y	Y	Y
3 Blumenauer	N	Y	Y	N	Y	Y
4 DeFazio	N	Y	Y	Y	Y	Y
5 Hooley	N	Y	Y	Y	Y	Y
PENNSYLVANIA						
1 Brady	N	Y	Y	Y	Y	Y
2 Fattah	N	Y	Y	N	Y	Y
3 ***English***	Y	Y	Y	Y	Y	Y
4 ***Hart***	Y	Y	Y	Y	Y	Y
5 ***Peterson***	Y	Y	Y	Y	?	?
6 ***Gerlach***	Y	Y	Y	Y	Y	Y
7 ***Weldon***	Y	Y	Y	Y	Y	Y
8 ***Greenwood***	?	?	?	?	?	?
9 ***Shuster, Bill***	Y	Y	Y	Y	Y	Y
10 ***Sherwood***	Y	Y	Y	Y	Y	Y
11 Kanjorski	N	Y	Y	Y	Y	P
12 Murtha	N	Y	Y	Y	Y	Y
13 Hoeffel	N	Y	Y	Y	Y	Y
14 Doyle	N	Y	Y	Y	?	?
15 ***Toomey***	Y	Y	Y	Y	Y	Y
16 ***Pitts***	Y	Y	Y	Y	Y	Y
17 Holden	N	Y	Y	Y	Y	Y
18 ***Murphy***	Y	Y	Y	Y	Y	Y
19 ***Platts***	Y	Y	Y	Y	Y	Y
RHODE ISLAND						
1 Kennedy	N	Y	Y	Y	Y	Y
2 Langevin	N	Y	Y	Y	Y	Y
SOUTH CAROLINA						
1 ***Brown***	Y	Y	Y	Y	Y	Y
2 ***Wilson***	?	?	?	?	?	?
3 ***Barrett***	Y	Y	?	Y	Y	Y
4 ***DeMint***	?	?	?	?	?	?
5 Spratt	N	Y	Y	Y	Y	?
6 Clyburn	N	Y	Y	N	Y	Y
SOUTH DAKOTA						
AL Vacant						

	147	148	149	150	151	152
TENNESSEE						
1 ***Jenkins***	?	?	?	?	?	?
2 ***Duncan***	Y	Y	Y	Y	Y	Y
3 ***Wamp***	Y	Y	Y	Y	Y	Y
4 Davis	N	Y	Y	Y	Y	Y
5 Cooper	N	Y	Y	Y	Y	Y
6 Gordon	N	Y	Y	Y	Y	Y
7 ***Blackburn***	Y	Y	Y	Y	Y	Y
8 Tanner	N	Y	Y	Y	Y	Y
9 Ford	N	?	Y	Y	Y	Y
TEXAS						
1 Sandlin	N	Y	Y	Y	Y	Y
2 Turner	N	Y	Y	Y	?	?
3 ***Johnson, Sam***	Y	N	Y	Y	Y	Y
4 ***Hall***	Y	Y	Y	Y	Y	Y
5 ***Hensarling***	Y	N	Y	Y	Y	Y
6 ***Barton***	Y	Y	Y	Y	Y	Y
7 ***Culberson***	Y	Y	Y	Y	Y	Y
8 ***Brady***	Y	?	?	Y	?	Y
9 Lampson	N	Y	Y	Y	Y	Y
10 Doggett	N	Y	Y	Y	Y	Y
11 Edwards	N	Y	Y	Y	Y	Y
12 ***Granger***	Y	Y	Y	Y	Y	?
13 ***Thornberry***	Y	Y	Y	Y	Y	Y
14 ***Paul***	Y	Y	N	N	Y	N
15 Hinojosa	N	Y	Y	Y	Y	Y
16 Reyes	N	Y	Y	Y	?	?
17 Stenholm	N	Y	Y	Y	Y	Y
18 Jackson-Lee	N	Y	Y	N	Y	Y
19 ***Neugebauer***	Y	Y	Y	Y	Y	Y
20 Gonzalez	N	Y	Y	Y	Y	Y
21 ***Smith***	Y	Y	Y	Y	Y	Y
22 ***DeLay***	Y	N	Y	Y	Y	Y
23 ***Bonilla***	Y	N	Y	Y	Y	Y
24 Frost	N	Y	Y	Y	Y	Y
25 Bell	N	Y	Y	Y	Y	Y
26 ***Burgess***	Y	Y	Y	Y	?	?
27 Ortiz	N	Y	Y	Y	Y	Y
28 Rodriguez	N	Y	Y	Y	Y	Y
29 Green	N	?	Y	Y	Y	Y
30 Johnson, E.B.	N	Y	Y	Y	Y	Y
31 ***Carter***	Y	Y	?	Y	Y	Y
32 ***Sessions***	Y	Y	Y	Y	Y	Y
UTAH						
1 ***Bishop***	Y	Y	Y	Y	Y	Y
2 Matheson	N	Y	Y	Y	Y	Y
3 ***Cannon***	Y	Y	Y	Y	Y	Y
VERMONT						
AL *Sanders*	N	Y	Y	Y	Y	Y
VIRGINIA						
1 ***Davis, Jo Ann***	Y	Y	Y	?	?	?
2 ***Schrock***	Y	Y	Y	Y	Y	Y
3 Scott	N	Y	Y	Y	Y	Y
4 ***Forbes***	Y	Y	Y	Y	Y	Y
5 ***Goode***	Y	Y	Y	Y	Y	Y
6 ***Goodlatte***	Y	Y	Y	Y	Y	Y
7 ***Cantor***	Y	N	Y	Y	Y	Y
8 Moran	N	Y	Y	Y	Y	Y
9 Boucher	N	Y	Y	Y	Y	Y
10 ***Wolf***	Y	Y	Y	Y	Y	Y
11 ***Davis, T.***	Y	Y	Y	Y	Y	Y
WASHINGTON						
1 Inslee	N	Y	Y	N	Y	Y
2 Larsen	N	Y	Y	Y	Y	Y
3 Baird	N	Y	Y	Y	Y	Y
4 ***Hastings***	Y	Y	Y	Y	?	?
5 ***Nethercutt***	Y	Y	Y	Y	Y	Y
6 Dicks	N	Y	Y	Y	Y	Y
7 McDermott	N	Y	Y	N	Y	P
8 ***Dunn***	Y	Y	Y	Y	Y	Y
9 Smith	N	Y	Y	Y	Y	Y
WEST VIRGINIA						
1 Mollohan	N	Y	Y	N	Y	P
2 ***Capito***	Y	Y	Y	Y	Y	Y
3 Rahall	N	Y	Y	Y	Y	P
WISCONSIN						
1 ***Ryan***	Y	Y	Y	Y	Y	Y
2 Baldwin	N	Y	Y	Y	Y	Y
3 Kind	N	Y	Y	Y	Y	Y
4 Kleczka	N	Y	Y	Y	Y	Y
5 ***Sensenbrenner***	Y	Y	Y	Y	Y	Y
6 ***Petri***	Y	Y	Y	Y	Y	Y
7 Obey	N	Y	Y	Y	Y	Y
8 ***Green***	Y	Y	Y	Y	Y	Y
WYOMING						
AL ***Cubin***	Y	Y	Y	Y	Y	Y

Southern states - Ala., Ark., Fla., Ga., Ky., La., Miss., N.C., Okla., S.C., Tenn., Texas, Va.

153. HR 1299. Miguel A. Nevarez Post Office/Passage. Miller, R-Mich., motion to suspend the rules and pass the bill that would name a post office building in Edinburg, Texas, after Dr. Miguel A. Nevarez, the first Hispanic president of the University of Texas-Pan American. Motion agreed to 405-0: R 216-0; D 188-0 (ND 136-0, SD 52-0); I 1-0. A two-thirds majority of those present and voting (270 in this case) is required for passage under suspension of the rules. May 11, 2004.

154. H Res 622. Peace Officers Memorial Day/Adoption. Miller, R-Mich., motion to suspend the rules and adopt the resolution that would support Peace Officers Memorial Day to honor federal, state and local peace officers killed or disabled in the line of duty. Motion agreed to 404-0: R 216-0; D 187-0 (ND 136-0, SD 51-0); I 1-0. A two-thirds majority of those present and voting (270 in this case) is required for adoption under suspension of the rules. May 11, 2004.

155. H Res 577. U.S.-European Relations/Adoption. Bereuter, R-Neb., motion to suspend the rules and adopt the resolution that would mark the 50th anniversary of relations between the United States and the European Union (EU). It also would recognize that continued cooperation between the United States and the EU is essential to resolving international disputes and combating global threats. Motion agreed to 397-7: R 208-7; D 188-0 (ND 136-0, SD 52-0); I 1-0. A two-thirds majority of those present and voting (270 in this case) is required for adoption under suspension of the rules. May 11, 2004.

156. HR 4275. Ten Percent Tax Bracket/Previous Question. Sessions, R-Texas, motion to order the previous question (thus ending debate and possibility of amendment) on adoption of the rule (H Res 637) to provide for House floor consideration of the bill that would make permanent the current upper limit of the 10 percent income tax bracket. Motion agreed to 221-203: R 221-2; D 0-200 (ND 0-146, SD 0-54); I 0-1. May 12, 2004.

157. HR 4279, HR 4280, HR 4281. Health Care Bills/Previous Question. Pryce, R-Ohio, motion to order the previous question (thus ending debate and possibility of amendment) on adoption of the rule (H Res 638) to provide for House floor consideration of three health care-related bills. Motion agreed to 222-202: R 222-0; D 0-201 (ND 0-147, SD 0-54); I 0-1. May 12, 2004.

158. HR 4279, HR 4280, HR 4281. Health Care Bills/Rule. Adoption of the rule (H Res 638) to provide for House floor consideration of three health care-related bills. The rule specifies that if more than one bill passes the House, the texts will be combined into one measure. Adopted 224-203: R 223-0; D 1-202 (ND 0-147, SD 1-55); I 0-1. May 12, 2004.

159. HR 2660. Fiscal 2004 Labor-HHS-Education Appropriations/ Motion to Instruct. DeLay, R-Texas, motion to table (kill) the Miller, D-Calif., motion to instruct House conferees to keep the Senate language that would block the Labor Department from implementing any portion of the new overtime pay rules that would deny premium pay to an employee who would otherwise qualify for such pay. Motion agreed to 222-205: R 222-2; D 0-202 (ND 0-147, SD 0-55); I 0-1. May 12, 2004.

160. H Res 608. Overseas Military Voting/Adoption. Forbes, R-Va., motion to suspend the rules and adopt the resolution that would express the sense of the House that the Defense secretary should ensure that the military expedites the delivery of election ballots to armed services members so they may be counted in the election. Motion agreed to 421-0: R 221-0; D 199-0 (ND 143-0, SD 56-0); I 1-0. A two-thirds majority of those present and voting (281 in this case) is required for adoption under suspension of the rules. May 12, 2004.

Key

Y	Voted for (yea).
#	Paired for.
+	Announced for.
N	Voted against (nay).
X	Paired against.
–	Announced against.
P	Voted "present."
C	Voted "present" to avoid possible conflict of interest.
?	Did not vote or otherwise make a position known.

Democrats · **Republicans**
Independents

	153	154	155	156	157	158	159	160
ALABAMA								
1 *Bonner*	Y	Y	Y	Y	Y	Y	Y	Y
2 *Everett*	Y	Y	Y	Y	Y	Y	Y	Y
3 *Rogers*	Y	Y	Y	Y	Y	Y	Y	Y
4 *Aderholt*	Y	Y	Y	Y	Y	Y	Y	Y
5 Cramer	Y	Y	Y	N	N	N	N	Y
6 *Bachus*	Y	Y	Y	Y	Y	Y	Y	Y
7 Davis	Y	Y	Y	N	N	N	N	Y
ALASKA								
AL *Young*	Y	Y	Y	Y	Y	Y	Y	Y
ARIZONA								
1 *Renzi*	Y	Y	Y	Y	Y	Y	Y	Y
2 *Franks*	Y	Y	Y	Y	Y	Y	Y	Y
3 *Shadegg*	Y	Y	Y	Y	Y	Y	Y	Y
4 Pastor	Y	Y	Y	N	N	N	N	Y
5 *Hayworth*	Y	Y	Y	Y	Y	Y	Y	Y
6 *Flake*	Y	Y	Y	Y	Y	Y	Y	Y
7 Grijalva	Y	Y	Y	N	N	N	N	Y
8 *Kolbe*	Y	Y	Y	Y	Y	Y	Y	Y
ARKANSAS								
1 Berry	Y	Y	Y	N	N	N	N	Y
2 Snyder	Y	Y	Y	N	N	N	N	Y
3 *Boozman*	Y	Y	Y	Y	Y	Y	Y	Y
4 Ross	Y	Y	Y	N	N	N	?	Y
CALIFORNIA								
1 Thompson	Y	Y	Y	N	N	N	N	Y
2 *Herger*	Y	Y	Y	Y	Y	Y	Y	Y
3 *Ose*	Y	Y	Y	Y	Y	Y	Y	Y
4 *Doolittle*	Y	Y	Y	Y	Y	Y	Y	Y
5 Matsui	Y	Y	Y	N	N	N	N	Y
6 Woolsey	Y	Y	Y	N	N	N	N	Y
7 Miller, George	Y	Y	Y	N	N	N	N	Y
8 Pelosi	Y	Y	Y	N	N	N	N	Y
9 Lee	Y	Y	Y	N	N	N	N	Y
10 Tauscher	Y	Y	Y	N	N	N	N	Y
11 *Pombo*	Y	Y	Y	Y	Y	Y	Y	Y
12 Lantos	Y	Y	Y	N	N	N	N	Y
13 Stark	?	?	?	N	N	N	N	Y
14 Eshoo	Y	Y	Y	N	N	N	N	Y
15 Honda	Y	Y	Y	N	N	N	N	Y
16 Lofgren	Y	Y	Y	N	N	N	N	Y
17 Farr	Y	Y	Y	N	N	N	N	Y
18 Cardoza	Y	Y	Y	N	N	N	N	Y
19 *Radanovich*	Y	Y	Y	Y	Y	Y	Y	Y
20 Dooley	Y	Y	Y	N	N	N	N	Y
21 *Nunes*	Y	Y	Y	Y	Y	Y	Y	Y
22 *Thomas*	Y	Y	Y	Y	Y	Y	Y	Y
23 Capps	Y	Y	Y	N	N	N	N	Y
24 *Gallegly*	Y	Y	Y	?	?	Y	Y	Y
25 *McKeon*	Y	Y	Y	Y	Y	Y	Y	Y
26 *Dreier*	Y	Y	Y	Y	Y	Y	Y	Y
27 Sherman	Y	Y	Y	N	N	N	N	Y
28 Berman	Y	Y	Y	N	N	N	N	Y
29 Schiff	Y	Y	Y	N	N	N	N	Y
30 Waxman	Y	Y	Y	N	N	N	N	Y
31 Becerra	Y	Y	Y	N	N	N	N	Y
32 Solis	Y	Y	Y	N	N	N	N	Y
33 Watson	Y	Y	Y	N	N	N	N	Y
34 Roybal-Allard	Y	Y	Y	N	N	N	N	Y
35 Waters	Y	Y	Y	N	N	N	N	Y
36 Harman	Y	Y	Y	N	N	N	N	Y

	153	154	155	156	157	158	159	160
37 Millender-McD.	Y	Y	Y	N	N	N	N	Y
38 Napolitano	Y	Y	Y	N	N	N	N	Y
39 Sánchez, Linda	Y	Y	Y	N	N	N	N	Y
40 *Royce*	Y	Y	Y	Y	Y	Y	Y	Y
41 *Lewis*	Y	Y	Y	Y	Y	Y	Y	Y
42 *Miller, Gary*	Y	Y	Y	Y	Y	Y	Y	Y
43 Baca	Y	Y	Y	N	N	N	N	Y
44 *Calvert*	Y	Y	Y	Y	Y	Y	Y	Y
45 *Bono*	Y	Y	Y	Y	Y	Y	Y	Y
46 *Rohrabacher*	?	?	?	Y	Y	Y	Y	Y
47 Sanchez, Loretta	Y	Y	Y	N	N	N	N	Y
48 *Cox*	Y	Y	Y	Y	Y	Y	Y	Y
49 *Issa*	Y	Y	Y	Y	Y	Y	Y	+
50 *Cunningham*	Y	Y	Y	Y	Y	Y	Y	Y
51 Filner	Y	Y	Y	N	N	N	N	Y
52 *Hunter*	Y	Y	Y	Y	Y	Y	Y	Y
53 Davis	Y	Y	Y	N	N	N	N	Y
COLORADO								
1 DeGette	Y	Y	Y	N	N	N	N	Y
2 Udall	Y	Y	Y	N	N	N	N	Y
3 *McInnis*	Y	Y	Y	Y	Y	Y	Y	Y
4 *Musgrave*	Y	Y	N	Y	Y	Y	Y	Y
5 *Hefley*	Y	Y	Y	Y	Y	Y	Y	Y
6 *Tancredo*	Y	Y	Y	Y	Y	Y	Y	Y
7 *Beauprez*	Y	Y	Y	Y	Y	Y	Y	Y
CONNECTICUT								
1 Larson	Y	Y	Y	N	N	N	N	?
2 *Simmons*	Y	Y	Y	Y	Y	Y	Y	Y
3 DeLauro	Y	Y	Y	N	N	N	N	Y
4 *Shays*	Y	Y	Y	Y	Y	Y	Y	Y
5 *Johnson*	Y	Y	Y	Y	Y	Y	Y	Y
DELAWARE								
AL *Castle*	Y	Y	Y	Y	Y	Y	Y	Y
FLORIDA								
1 *Miller, J.*	Y	Y	N	Y	Y	Y	Y	Y
2 Boyd	Y	Y	N	N	N	N	N	Y
3 Brown	?	?	N	N	N	N	N	Y
4 *Crenshaw*	Y	Y	Y	Y	Y	Y	Y	Y
5 *Brown-Waite*	Y	Y	Y	Y	Y	Y	Y	Y
6 *Stearns*	Y	Y	Y	Y	Y	Y	Y	Y
7 *Mica*	Y	Y	Y	Y	Y	Y	Y	Y
8 *Keller*	Y	Y	Y	Y	Y	Y	Y	Y
9 *Bilirakis*	Y	Y	Y	Y	Y	Y	Y	Y
10 *Young*	Y	Y	Y	Y	Y	Y	Y	Y
11 Davis	Y	Y	Y	?	?	N	N	Y
12 *Putnam*	Y	Y	Y	Y	Y	Y	Y	Y
13 *Harris*	Y	Y	Y	Y	Y	Y	Y	Y
14 *Goss*	Y	Y	Y	Y	Y	Y	Y	Y
15 *Weldon*	Y	Y	Y	Y	Y	Y	Y	Y
16 *Foley*	Y	Y	Y	Y	Y	Y	Y	Y
17 Meek	Y	Y	Y	N	N	N	N	Y
18 *Ros-Lehtinen*	Y	Y	Y	Y	Y	Y	Y	Y
19 Wexler	Y	Y	Y	N	N	N	N	Y
20 Deutsch	Y	Y	Y	N	N	N	N	Y
21 *Diaz-Balart, L.*	Y	Y	Y	Y	Y	Y	Y	Y
22 *Shaw*	Y	Y	Y	Y	Y	Y	Y	Y
23 Hastings	Y	Y	Y	N	N	N	N	Y
24 *Feeney*	Y	Y	Y	Y	Y	Y	Y	Y
25 *Diaz-Balart, M.*	Y	Y	Y	Y	Y	Y	Y	Y
GEORGIA								
1 *Kingston*	?	?	?	Y	Y	Y	Y	Y
2 Bishop	Y	Y	N	N	N	N	N	Y
3 Marshall	Y	Y	Y	N	N	N	N	Y
4 Majette	Y	Y	N	N	N	N	N	Y
5 Lewis	Y	Y	N	N	N	N	N	Y
6 *Isakson*	?	Y	Y	Y	Y	Y	Y	Y
7 *Linder*	Y	Y	Y	Y	Y	Y	Y	Y
8 *Collins*	Y	Y	Y	Y	Y	Y	Y	Y
9 *Norwood*	Y	Y	Y	Y	Y	Y	Y	Y
10 *Deal*	Y	Y	Y	Y	Y	Y	Y	Y
11 *Gingrey*	Y	Y	Y	Y	Y	Y	Y	Y
12 *Burns*	Y	Y	Y	Y	Y	Y	Y	Y
13 Scott	Y	Y	N	N	N	N	N	Y
HAWAII								
1 Abercrombie	Y	Y	N	N	N	N	N	Y
2 Case	Y	Y	N	N	N	N	N	Y
IDAHO								
1 *Otter*	Y	Y	Y	Y	Y	Y	Y	Y
2 *Simpson*	Y	Y	Y	Y	Y	Y	Y	Y
ILLINOIS								
1 Rush	Y	Y	N	N	N	N	N	Y
2 Jackson	Y	Y	N	N	N	N	N	Y
3 Lipinski	?	?	N	N	N	N	N	?
4 Gutierrez	Y	Y	N	N	N	N	N	?
5 Emanuel	Y	Y	Y	N	N	N	N	Y
6 *Hyde*	Y	Y	Y	Y	Y	Y	Y	Y

ND Northern Democrats   SD Southern Democrats

	153	154	155	156	157	158	159	160
7 Davis	Y	Y	Y	N	N	N	N	Y
8 ***Crane***	Y	Y	Y	Y	Y	Y	Y	Y
9 Schakowsky	Y	Y	Y	N	N	N	N	Y
10 ***Kirk***	Y	Y	Y	Y	Y	Y	Y	Y
11 ***Weller***	Y	Y	?	Y	Y	Y	Y	Y
12 Costello	Y	Y	Y	N	N	N	N	Y
13 ***Biggert***	Y	Y	Y	Y	Y	Y	Y	Y
14 ***Hastert***								
15 ***Johnson***	Y	Y	Y	Y	Y	Y	N	Y
16 ***Manzullo***	Y	Y	Y	Y	Y	Y	Y	Y
17 Evans	Y	Y	Y	N	N	N	N	Y
18 ***LaHood***	Y	Y	N	Y	Y	Y	Y	Y
19 ***Shimkus***	Y	Y	Y	Y	Y	Y	Y	Y
INDIANA								
1 Visclosky	?	?	?	N	N	N	N	Y
2 ***Chocola***	Y	Y	Y	Y	Y	Y	Y	Y
3 ***Souder***	?	?	?	Y	Y	Y	Y	Y
4 ***Buyer***	?	?	?	Y	Y	Y	Y	Y
5 ***Burton***	Y	Y	Y	?	Y	Y	Y	Y
6 ***Pence***	Y	Y	Y	Y	Y	Y	Y	Y
7 Carson	Y	Y	Y	N	N	N	N	Y
8 ***Hostettler***	Y	Y	Y	Y	Y	Y	Y	Y
9 Hill	Y	Y	Y	N	N	N	N	Y
IOWA								
1 ***Nussle***	Y	Y	Y	Y	Y	Y	Y	Y
2 ***Leach***	Y	Y	Y	Y	Y	Y	N	Y
3 Boswell	Y	Y	Y	N	N	N	N	Y
4 ***Latham***	Y	Y	Y	Y	Y	Y	Y	Y
5 ***King***	Y	Y	Y	Y	Y	Y	Y	Y
KANSAS								
1 ***Moran***	Y	Y	Y	Y	Y	Y	Y	Y
2 ***Ryun***	Y	Y	Y	Y	Y	Y	Y	Y
3 Moore	Y	Y	Y	N	N	N	N	Y
4 ***Tiahrt***	Y	Y	Y	Y	?	Y	Y	?
KENTUCKY								
1 ***Whitfield***	Y	Y	Y	Y	Y	Y	Y	Y
2 ***Lewis***	Y	Y	Y	Y	Y	Y	Y	Y
3 ***Northup***	Y	Y	Y	Y	Y	Y	Y	Y
4 Lucas	Y	Y	Y	N	N	N	N	Y
5 ***Rogers***	Y	Y	Y	Y	Y	Y	Y	Y
6 Chandler	Y	Y	Y	N	N	N	N	Y
LOUISIANA								
1 ***Vitter***	Y	Y	Y	Y	Y	Y	Y	Y
2 Jefferson	Y	Y	Y	N	N	N	N	Y
3 ***Tauzin***	?	?	?	?	?	?	?	?
4 ***McCrery***	Y	Y	Y	Y	Y	Y	Y	Y
5 Alexander	Y	Y	Y	N	N	N	N	Y
6 ***Baker***	Y	Y	Y	Y	Y	Y	Y	Y
7 John	?	?	?	?	N	N	N	Y
MAINE								
1 Allen	Y	Y	Y	N	N	N	N	Y
2 Michaud	Y	Y	Y	N	N	N	N	Y
MARYLAND								
1 ***Gilchrest***	Y	Y	Y	Y	Y	Y	Y	Y
2 Ruppersberger	Y	Y	Y	N	N	N	N	Y
3 Cardin	Y	Y	Y	N	N	N	N	Y
4 Wynn	Y	Y	Y	N	N	N	N	Y
5 Hoyer	Y	Y	Y	N	N	N	N	Y
6 ***Bartlett***	Y	Y	Y	Y	Y	Y	Y	Y
7 Cummings	Y	Y	Y	N	N	N	N	Y
8 Van Hollen	Y	Y	Y	N	N	N	N	Y
MASSACHUSETTS								
1 Olver	Y	Y	Y	N	N	N	N	Y
2 Neal	Y	Y	Y	N	N	N	N	Y
3 McGovern	Y	Y	Y	N	N	N	N	Y
4 Frank	Y	Y	Y	N	N	N	N	Y
5 Meehan	Y	Y	Y	N	N	N	N	Y
6 Tierney	Y	Y	Y	N	N	N	N	Y
7 Markey	Y	Y	Y	N	N	N	N	Y
8 Capuano	Y	Y	Y	N	N	N	N	Y
9 Lynch	Y	Y	?	N	N	N	N	Y
10 Delahunt	Y	Y	Y	N	N	N	N	Y
MICHIGAN								
1 Stupak	?	?	?	N	N	N	N	Y
2 ***Hoekstra***	Y	Y	Y	Y	Y	Y	Y	Y
3 ***Ehlers***	Y	Y	Y	Y	Y	Y	Y	Y
4 ***Camp***	Y	Y	Y	Y	Y	Y	Y	Y
5 Kildee	Y	Y	Y	N	N	N	N	Y
6 ***Upton***	Y	Y	Y	Y	Y	Y	Y	Y
7 ***Smith***	Y	Y	Y	Y	Y	Y	Y	Y
8 ***Rogers***	Y	Y	Y	Y	Y	Y	Y	Y
9 ***Knollenberg***	Y	Y	Y	Y	Y	Y	Y	Y
10 ***Miller***	Y	Y	Y	Y	Y	Y	Y	Y
11 ***McCotter***	Y	Y	Y	Y	Y	Y	Y	Y
12 Levin	Y	Y	Y	N	N	N	N	Y

	153	154	155	156	157	158	159	160
13 Kilpatrick	Y	Y	Y	N	N	N	N	Y
14 Conyers	Y	Y	Y	N	N	N	N	Y
15 Dingell	?	?	?	N	N	N	N	Y
MINNESOTA								
1 ***Gutknecht***	Y	Y	Y	Y	Y	?	Y	Y
2 ***Kline***	Y	Y	Y	Y	Y	Y	Y	Y
3 ***Ramstad***	Y	Y	Y	Y	Y	Y	Y	Y
4 McCollum	Y	Y	Y	N	N	N	N	Y
5 Sabo	Y	Y	Y	N	N	N	N	Y
6 ***Kennedy***	Y	Y	Y	Y	Y	Y	Y	Y
7 Peterson	Y	Y	Y	N	N	N	N	Y
8 Oberstar	Y	Y	Y	N	N	N	N	?
MISSISSIPPI								
1 ***Wicker***	Y	Y	Y	Y	Y	Y	Y	Y
2 Thompson	Y	Y	Y	N	N	N	N	Y
3 ***Pickering***	Y	Y	Y	Y	Y	Y	Y	Y
4 Taylor	Y	Y	Y	N	N	Y	N	Y
MISSOURI								
1 Clay	Y	Y	Y	N	N	N	N	Y
2 ***Akin***	Y	Y	N	Y	Y	Y	Y	Y
3 Gephardt	Y	Y	Y	N	N	N	N	Y
4 Skelton	Y	Y	Y	N	N	N	N	Y
5 McCarthy	Y	Y	Y	N	N	N	N	Y
6 ***Graves***	Y	Y	Y	Y	Y	Y	Y	Y
7 ***Blunt***	Y	Y	Y	Y	Y	Y	Y	Y
8 ***Emerson***	Y	Y	Y	Y	?	Y	Y	Y
9 ***Hulshof***	Y	Y	Y	Y	Y	Y	Y	Y
MONTANA								
AL ***Rehberg***	Y	Y	Y	Y	Y	Y	Y	Y
NEBRASKA								
1 ***Bereuter***	Y	Y	Y	Y	Y	Y	Y	Y
2 ***Terry***	Y	Y	Y	Y	Y	Y	Y	Y
3 ***Osborne***	Y	Y	Y	Y	Y	Y	Y	Y
NEVADA								
1 Berkley	Y	Y	Y	N	N	N	N	Y
2 ***Gibbons***	Y	Y	Y	Y	Y	Y	Y	Y
3 ***Porter***	Y	Y	Y	Y	Y	Y	Y	Y
NEW HAMPSHIRE								
1 ***Bradley***	Y	Y	Y	Y	Y	Y	Y	Y
2 ***Bass***	Y	Y	Y	Y	Y	Y	Y	Y
NEW JERSEY								
1 Andrews	Y	Y	Y	N	N	N	N	Y
2 ***LoBiondo***	Y	Y	Y	Y	Y	Y	Y	Y
3 ***Saxton***	Y	Y	Y	Y	Y	Y	Y	Y
4 ***Smith***	Y	Y	Y	Y	Y	Y	Y	Y
5 ***Garrett***	Y	Y	Y	Y	Y	Y	Y	Y
6 Pallone	Y	Y	Y	N	N	N	N	Y
7 ***Ferguson***	Y	Y	Y	Y	Y	Y	Y	Y
8 Pascrell	Y	Y	Y	N	N	N	N	Y
9 Rothman	Y	Y	Y	N	N	N	N	Y
10 Payne	Y	Y	Y	N	N	N	N	Y
11 ***Frelinghuysen***	Y	Y	Y	Y	Y	Y	Y	Y
12 Holt	Y	Y	Y	N	N	N	N	Y
13 Menendez	Y	Y	Y	N	N	N	N	Y
NEW MEXICO								
1 ***Wilson***	Y	Y	Y	Y	Y	Y	Y	Y
2 ***Pearce***	Y	Y	Y	Y	Y	Y	Y	Y
3 Udall	Y	Y	Y	N	N	N	N	Y
NEW YORK								
1 Bishop	Y	Y	Y	N	N	N	N	Y
2 Israel	Y	Y	Y	N	N	N	N	Y
3 ***King***	Y	Y	Y	Y	Y	Y	Y	Y
4 McCarthy	Y	Y	Y	N	N	N	N	Y
5 Ackerman	Y	Y	Y	N	N	N	N	Y
6 Meeks	Y	Y	Y	N	N	N	N	Y
7 Crowley	Y	Y	Y	N	N	N	N	Y
8 Nadler	Y	Y	Y	N	N	N	N	Y
9 Weiner	Y	Y	Y	N	N	N	N	Y
10 Towns	Y	Y	Y	N	N	N	N	Y
11 Owens	Y	Y	Y	N	N	N	N	Y
12 Velázquez	Y	Y	Y	N	N	N	N	Y
13 ***Fossella***	Y	Y	Y	Y	Y	Y	Y	Y
14 Maloney	?	?	Y	N	N	N	N	Y
15 Rangel	Y	Y	Y	N	N	N	N	Y
16 Serrano	Y	Y	Y	N	N	N	N	Y
17 Engel	Y	Y	Y	N	N	N	N	Y
18 Lowey	Y	Y	Y	N	N	N	N	Y
19 ***Kelly***	Y	Y	Y	Y	Y	Y	Y	Y
20 ***Sweeney***	?	?	?	Y	Y	Y	Y	Y
21 McNulty	?	?	?	?	?	?	?	?
22 Hinchey	Y	Y	Y	N	N	N	N	Y
23 ***McHugh***	Y	Y	Y	Y	Y	Y	Y	Y
24 ***Boehlert***	Y	Y	Y	Y	Y	Y	Y	Y
25 ***Walsh***	Y	Y	Y	Y	Y	Y	Y	Y

	153	154	155	156	157	158	159	160
26 ***Reynolds***	Y	Y	Y	Y	Y	Y	Y	Y
27 ***Quinn***	Y	Y	Y	Y	Y	Y	Y	Y
28 Slaughter	Y	Y	Y	N	N	N	N	Y
29 ***Houghton***	Y	Y	Y	Y	Y	Y	Y	Y
NORTH CAROLINA								
1 Ballance	Y	Y	Y	N	N	N	N	Y
2 Etheridge	Y	Y	Y	N	N	N	N	Y
3 ***Jones***	Y	Y	N	Y	Y	Y	Y	Y
4 Price	Y	Y	Y	N	N	N	N	Y
5 ***Burr***	Y	Y	Y	Y	Y	Y	Y	Y
6 ***Coble***	Y	Y	Y	Y	Y	Y	Y	Y
7 McIntyre	Y	Y	Y	N	N	N	N	Y
8 ***Hayes***	Y	Y	Y	Y	Y	Y	Y	Y
9 ***Myrick***	Y	Y	Y	Y	Y	Y	Y	Y
10 ***Ballenger***	Y	Y	Y	Y	Y	Y	Y	Y
11 ***Taylor***	Y	Y	Y	Y	Y	Y	Y	Y
12 Watt	Y	Y	Y	N	N	N	N	Y
13 Miller	Y	Y	Y	N	N	N	N	Y
NORTH DAKOTA								
AL Pomeroy	Y	Y	Y	N	N	N	N	Y
OHIO								
1 ***Chabot***	Y	Y	Y	Y	Y	Y	Y	Y
2 ***Portman***	Y	Y	Y	Y	Y	Y	Y	Y
3 ***Turner***	Y	Y	Y	Y	Y	Y	Y	Y
4 ***Oxley***	Y	Y	Y	Y	Y	Y	Y	Y
5 ***Gillmor***	Y	Y	Y	Y	Y	Y	Y	Y
6 Strickland	?	?	?	N	N	N	N	Y
7 ***Hobson***	Y	Y	Y	Y	Y	Y	Y	Y
8 ***Boehner***	Y	Y	Y	Y	Y	Y	Y	Y
9 Kaptur	Y	Y	Y	N	N	N	N	Y
10 Kucinich	?	?	?	N	N	N	N	Y
11 Jones	Y	Y	Y	N	N	N	N	Y
12 ***Tiberi***	Y	Y	Y	Y	Y	Y	Y	Y
13 Brown	Y	Y	Y	N	N	N	N	Y
14 ***LaTourette***	Y	Y	Y	Y	Y	Y	Y	Y
15 ***Pryce***	Y	Y	Y	Y	Y	Y	Y	Y
16 ***Regula***	Y	Y	Y	Y	Y	Y	Y	?
17 Ryan	Y	Y	Y	N	N	N	N	Y
18 ***Ney***	Y	Y	Y	Y	Y	Y	Y	Y
OKLAHOMA								
1 ***Sullivan***	Y	Y	Y	Y	Y	Y	Y	Y
2 Carson	Y	Y	Y	N	N	N	N	Y
3 ***Lucas***	Y	Y	Y	Y	Y	Y	Y	Y
4 ***Cole***	Y	Y	Y	Y	Y	Y	Y	Y
5 ***Istook***	Y	Y	Y	Y	Y	Y	Y	Y
OREGON								
1 Wu	Y	Y	Y	N	N	N	N	Y
2 ***Walden***	Y	Y	Y	Y	Y	Y	Y	Y
3 Blumenauer	Y	Y	Y	N	N	N	N	Y
4 DeFazio	Y	Y	Y	?	N	N	N	Y
5 Hooley	Y	Y	Y	N	N	N	N	Y
PENNSYLVANIA								
1 Brady	Y	Y	Y	N	N	N	N	Y
2 Fattah	Y	Y	Y	N	N	N	N	Y
3 ***English***	Y	Y	Y	Y	Y	Y	?	Y
4 ***Hart***	Y	Y	Y	Y	Y	Y	Y	Y
5 ***Peterson***	Y	Y	Y	Y	Y	Y	Y	Y
6 ***Gerlach***	?	?	?	Y	Y	Y	Y	Y
7 ***Weldon***	Y	Y	Y	Y	Y	Y	Y	Y
8 ***Greenwood***	Y	Y	Y	Y	Y	Y	Y	Y
9 ***Shuster, Bill***	Y	Y	Y	Y	Y	Y	Y	Y
10 ***Sherwood***	Y	Y	Y	Y	Y	Y	Y	Y
11 Kanjorski	Y	Y	Y	N	N	N	N	Y
12 Murtha	?	?	?	N	N	N	N	Y
13 Hoeffel	?	?	?	N	N	N	N	Y
14 Doyle	Y	Y	Y	N	N	N	N	Y
15 ***Toomey***	Y	Y	Y	Y	Y	Y	Y	Y
16 ***Pitts***	Y	Y	Y	Y	Y	Y	Y	Y
17 Holden	Y	Y	Y	N	N	N	N	Y
18 ***Murphy***	Y	Y	Y	Y	Y	Y	Y	Y
19 ***Platts***	Y	Y	Y	Y	Y	Y	Y	Y
RHODE ISLAND								
1 Kennedy	Y	Y	Y	N	N	N	N	Y
2 Langevin	Y	Y	Y	N	N	N	N	Y
SOUTH CAROLINA								
1 ***Brown***	Y	Y	Y	Y	Y	Y	Y	Y
2 ***Wilson***	Y	Y	Y	Y	Y	Y	Y	Y
3 ***Barrett***	Y	Y	Y	Y	Y	Y	Y	Y
4 ***DeMint***	+	+	+	?	?	?	?	?
5 Spratt	Y	Y	Y	N	N	N	N	Y
6 Clyburn	Y	Y	Y	N	N	N	N	Y
SOUTH DAKOTA								
AL Vacant								

	153	154	155	156	157	158	159	160
TENNESSEE								
1 ***Jenkins***	Y	Y	Y	N	Y	Y	Y	Y
2 ***Duncan***	Y	Y	Y	N	Y	Y	Y	Y
3 ***Wamp***	Y	Y	Y	Y	Y	Y	Y	Y
4 Davis	Y	?	Y	N	N	N	N	Y
5 Cooper	Y	Y	Y	N	?	N	N	Y
6 Gordon	Y	Y	Y	N	N	N	N	Y
7 ***Blackburn***	Y	Y	?	Y	Y	Y	Y	Y
8 Tanner	Y	Y	Y	N	N	N	N	Y
9 Ford	Y	Y	Y	N	N	N	N	Y
TEXAS								
1 Sandlin	Y	Y	Y	N	N	N	N	Y
2 Turner	Y	Y	Y	N	N	N	N	Y
3 ***Johnson, Sam***	Y	Y	N	Y	Y	Y	Y	Y
4 ***Hall***	Y	Y	Y	Y	Y	Y	Y	Y
5 ***Hensarling***	Y	Y	Y	Y	Y	Y	Y	Y
6 ***Barton***	Y	Y	Y	Y	Y	Y	Y	Y
7 ***Culberson***	Y	Y	Y	Y	Y	Y	Y	Y
8 ***Brady***	Y	Y	Y	Y	Y	Y	Y	Y
9 Lampson	Y	Y	Y	N	N	N	N	Y
10 Doggett	Y	Y	Y	N	N	N	N	Y
11 Edwards	?	?	?	N	N	N	N	Y
12 ***Granger***	Y	Y	Y	Y	Y	Y	Y	Y
13 ***Thornberry***	Y	Y	Y	Y	Y	Y	Y	Y
14 ***Paul***	Y	Y	N	Y	Y	Y	Y	Y
15 Hinojosa	Y	Y	Y	N	N	N	N	Y
16 Reyes	?	?	?	?	?	?	?	?
17 Stenholm	Y	Y	Y	N	N	N	N	Y
18 Jackson-Lee	Y	Y	Y	N	N	N	N	Y
19 ***Neugebauer***	Y	Y	Y	Y	Y	Y	Y	Y
20 Gonzalez	?	?	?	N	N	N	N	Y
21 ***Smith***	Y	Y	Y	Y	Y	Y	Y	Y
22 ***DeLay***	Y	Y	Y	Y	Y	Y	Y	Y
23 ***Bonilla***	Y	Y	Y	Y	Y	Y	Y	Y
24 Frost	Y	Y	Y	N	N	N	N	Y
25 Bell	Y	Y	Y	N	N	N	N	Y
26 ***Burgess***	Y	Y	Y	Y	Y	Y	Y	Y
27 Ortiz	Y	Y	Y	N	N	N	N	Y
28 Rodriguez	Y	Y	Y	N	N	N	N	Y
29 Green	Y	Y	Y	N	N	N	N	Y
30 Johnson, E.B.	Y	Y	Y	N	N	N	N	Y
31 ***Carter***	?	?	?	Y	Y	Y	Y	Y
32 ***Sessions***	Y	Y	Y	Y	Y	Y	Y	?
UTAH								
1 ***Bishop***	Y	Y	Y	Y	Y	Y	Y	Y
2 Matheson	Y	Y	Y	N	N	N	N	Y
3 ***Cannon***	Y	Y	Y	Y	Y	Y	Y	Y
VERMONT								
AL *Sanders*	Y	Y	Y	N	N	N	N	Y
VIRGINIA								
1 ***Davis, Jo Ann***	Y	Y	Y	Y	Y	Y	Y	Y
2 ***Schrock***	Y	Y	Y	Y	Y	Y	Y	Y
3 Scott	Y	Y	Y	N	N	N	N	Y
4 ***Forbes***	Y	Y	Y	Y	Y	Y	Y	Y
5 ***Goode***	Y	Y	Y	Y	Y	Y	Y	Y
6 ***Goodlatte***	Y	Y	Y	Y	Y	Y	Y	Y
7 ***Cantor***	Y	Y	Y	Y	Y	Y	Y	Y
8 Moran	Y	Y	Y	N	N	N	N	Y
9 Boucher	Y	Y	Y	N	N	N	N	Y
10 ***Wolf***	Y	Y	Y	Y	Y	Y	Y	Y
11 ***Davis, T.***	Y	Y	Y	Y	Y	Y	Y	Y
WASHINGTON								
1 Inslee	Y	Y	Y	N	N	N	N	Y
2 Larsen	Y	Y	Y	N	N	N	N	Y
3 Baird	Y	Y	Y	N	N	N	N	Y
4 ***Hastings***	Y	Y	Y	Y	Y	Y	Y	Y
5 ***Nethercutt***	Y	Y	Y	Y	Y	Y	Y	Y
6 Dicks	Y	Y	Y	N	N	N	N	Y
7 McDermott	Y	Y	Y	N	N	N	N	Y
8 ***Dunn***	Y	Y	Y	Y	Y	?	Y	Y
9 Smith	Y	Y	Y	N	N	N	N	Y
WEST VIRGINIA								
1 Mollohan	?	?	?	N	N	N	N	Y
2 ***Capito***	Y	Y	Y	Y	Y	Y	Y	Y
3 Rahall	Y	Y	Y	N	N	N	N	Y
WISCONSIN								
1 ***Ryan***	Y	Y	Y	Y	Y	Y	Y	Y
2 Baldwin	Y	Y	Y	N	N	N	N	Y
3 Kind	Y	Y	Y	N	N	N	N	Y
4 Kleczka	Y	Y	Y	N	N	N	N	Y
5 ***Sensenbrenner***	Y	Y	Y	Y	Y	Y	Y	Y
6 ***Petri***	Y	Y	Y	Y	Y	Y	Y	Y
7 Obey	Y	Y	Y	N	N	N	N	Y
8 ***Green***	?	?	?	Y	Y	Y	Y	Y
WYOMING								
AL ***Cubin***	Y	Y	Y	Y	Y	Y	Y	Y

Southern states - Ala., Ark., Fla., Ga., Ky., La., Miss., N.C., Okla., S.C., Tenn., Texas, Va.

161. HR 4279. Unused Health Benefits/Democratic Substitute. Stark, D-Calif., substitute amendment that would allow up to $500 of unused benefits in an employee's health flexible spending account (FSA) to be carried over to the next year's FSA. The cost would be offset by eliminating certain tax provisions, including denying some tax benefits to domestic corporations that reincorporate overseas to avoid U.S. income taxes. Rejected 197-230: R 0-222; D 196-8 (ND 143-5, SD 53-3); I 1-0. May 12, 2004.

162. HR 4279. Unused Health Benefits/Recommit. Stark, D-Calif., motion to recommit the bill to the House Ways and Means Committee with instructions to ensure that the bill would not affect the Social Security or Medicare trust funds. Motion rejected 202-224: R 0-224; D 201-0 (ND 146-0, SD 55-0); I 1-0. May 12, 2004.

163. HR 4279. Unused Health Benefits/Passage. Passage of the bill that would permit up to $500 of unused funds in an employee's health flexible spending account (FSA) to be carried over to the next year's FSA or transferred to the employee's health savings account. Passed 273-152: R 223-0; D 50-151 (ND 28-119, SD 22-32); I 0-1. May 12, 2004.

164. H Con Res 352. Indian-American Tribute/Adoption. Bereuter, R-Neb., motion to suspend the rules and adopt the concurrent resolution that would honor the contributions of Indian-Americans to the United States, and would express Congress' commitment to working together with India to promote peace, prosperity and freedom among all countries. Motion agreed to 415-2: R 217-2; D 198-0 (ND 143-0, SD 55-0); I 0-0. A two-thirds majority of those present and voting (278 in this case) is required for adoption under suspension of the rules. May 12, 2004.

165. HR 4280. Medical Malpractice/Recommit. Conyers, D-Mich., motion to recommit the bill to the House Judiciary and Energy and Commerce committees with instructions to include language that would establish an independent advisory commission, and require plaintiff attorneys in medical malpractice cases to file a certificate of merit. Motion rejected 193-231: R 3-219; D 189-12 (ND 139-7, SD 50-5); I 1-0. May 12, 2004.

166. HR 4280. Medical Malpractice/Passage. Passage of the bill that would cap the awards that plaintiffs and their attorneys could receive in medical malpractice cases. The bill would limit non-economic damages to $250,000 and cap punitive damages at $250,000 or double economic damages, whichever is greater. Punitive damages would be barred against makers and distributors of medical products that were approved by the Food and Drug Administration. The bill would not pre-empt state damage caps but would impose federal caps on any states that do not have their own. Attorneys' contingent fees would be limited. Passed 229-197: R 214-10; D 15-186 (ND 8-138, SD 7-48); I 0-1. A "yea" was a vote in support of the president's position. May 12, 2004.

167. H Con Res 378. Vietnamese Prisoner Thaddeus Nguyen Van Ly/Adoption. Smith, R-N.J., motion to suspend the rules and adopt the concurrent resolution that would condemn the detention of Thaddeus Nguyen Van Ly, a Roman Catholic priest, by the government of Vietnam and call for his immediate release. Motion agreed to 424-1: R 223-1; D 200-0 (ND 145-0, SD 55-0); I 1-0. A two-thirds majority of those present and voting (284 in this case) is required for adoption under suspension of the rules. May 12, 2004.

168. H Con Res 409. World War II Veterans Tribute/Adoption. Smith, R-N.J., motion to suspend the rules and adopt the concurrent resolution that would recognize the more than 16 million U.S. veterans who served during World War II, the 400,000 U.S. service members who died in the war and the Americans who supported the war effort at home. Motion agreed to 422-0: R 221-0; D 200-0 (ND 146-0, SD 54-0); I 1-0. A two-thirds majority of those present and voting (282 in this case) is required for adoption under suspension of the rules. May 12, 2004.

Key

Y	Voted for (yea).
#	Paired for.
+	Announced for.
N	Voted against (nay).
X	Paired against.
–	Announced against.
P	Voted "present."
C	Voted "present" to avoid possible conflict of interest.
?	Did not vote or otherwise make a position known.

Democrats **Republicans**
Independents

	161	162	163	164	165	166	167	168
ALABAMA								
1 *Bonner*	N	N	Y	N	Y	Y	Y	Y
2 *Everett*	N	N	Y	Y	N	Y	Y	Y
3 *Rogers*	N	N	Y	Y	N	Y	Y	Y
4 *Aderholt*	N	?	?	Y	N	Y	Y	Y
5 Cramer	Y	Y	Y	Y	N	Y	Y	Y
6 *Bachus*	N	N	Y	Y	N	Y	Y	Y
7 Davis	Y	Y	Y	Y	N	Y	Y	Y
ALASKA								
AL *Young*	N	N	Y	N	Y	Y	Y	Y
ARIZONA								
1 *Renzi*	N	N	Y	N	Y	Y	Y	Y
2 *Franks*	N	N	Y	N	Y	Y	Y	Y
3 *Shadegg*	N	N	Y	N	Y	Y	Y	Y
4 Pastor	Y	Y	N	Y	N	Y	N	Y
5 *Hayworth*	N	N	Y	N	Y	Y	Y	Y
6 *Flake*	N	N	Y	N	Y	N	Y	Y
7 Grijalva	Y	Y	N	Y	N	Y	N	Y
8 *Kolbe*	?	N	Y	Y	N	Y	Y	Y
ARKANSAS								
1 Berry	Y	Y	N	Y	N	Y	N	Y
2 Snyder	Y	Y	Y	Y	N	Y	N	Y
3 *Boozman*	N	N	Y	N	Y	Y	Y	Y
4 Ross	Y	Y	N	Y	N	Y	N	Y
CALIFORNIA								
1 Thompson	Y	Y	N	Y	N	Y	Y	Y
2 *Herger*	N	N	Y	N	Y	Y	Y	Y
3 *Ose*	N	N	Y	Y	N	Y	Y	Y
4 *Doolittle*	N	N	Y	N	Y	N	Y	Y
5 Matsui	Y	Y	N	Y	N	Y	N	Y
6 Woolsey	Y	?	N	Y	N	Y	N	Y
7 Miller, George	Y	Y	N	?	N	Y	N	Y
8 Pelosi	Y	Y	N	Y	N	Y	N	Y
9 Lee	Y	Y	N	Y	N	Y	N	Y
10 Tauscher	Y	Y	N	Y	N	Y	N	Y
11 *Pombo*	N	N	Y	N	Y	N	Y	Y
12 Lantos	Y	Y	N	?	?	?	?	?
13 Stark	Y	Y	N	Y	N	Y	N	Y
14 Eshoo	Y	Y	N	Y	N	Y	N	Y
15 Honda	Y	Y	Y	Y	N	Y	N	Y
16 Lofgren	Y	Y	N	Y	N	Y	N	Y
17 Farr	Y	Y	N	Y	N	Y	N	Y
18 Cardoza	Y	Y	Y	Y	N	Y	Y	Y
19 *Radanovich*	N	N	?	Y	N	Y	Y	Y
20 Dooley	Y	Y	Y	Y	Y	Y	Y	Y
21 *Nunes*	N	N	Y	N	Y	Y	Y	Y
22 *Thomas*	N	N	Y	N	Y	Y	Y	Y
23 Capps	Y	Y	N	Y	N	Y	N	Y
24 *Gallegly*	N	N	Y	N	Y	Y	Y	Y
25 *McKeon*	N	N	Y	N	Y	Y	Y	Y
26 *Dreier*	N	N	Y	N	Y	Y	Y	Y
27 Sherman	Y	Y	N	Y	N	Y	N	Y
28 Berman	Y	Y	N	Y	N	Y	N	Y
29 Schiff	Y	Y	N	Y	N	Y	N	Y
30 Waxman	Y	Y	N	Y	N	Y	N	Y
31 Becerra	Y	Y	N	Y	N	Y	N	Y
32 Solis	Y	Y	N	Y	N	Y	N	Y
33 Watson	Y	Y	N	Y	N	Y	N	Y
34 Roybal-Allard	Y	Y	N	?	N	Y	N	Y
35 Waters	Y	Y	N	Y	N	Y	N	Y
36 Harman	Y	Y	N	Y	N	Y	N	Y

	161	162	163	164	165	166	167	168
37 Millender-McD.	Y	Y	N	Y	N	Y	N	Y
38 Napolitano	Y	Y	N	Y	N	Y	N	Y
39 Sánchez, Linda	Y	Y	N	Y	N	Y	N	Y
40 *Royce*	N	N	Y	N	Y	Y	Y	Y
41 *Lewis*	N	N	Y	N	Y	Y	Y	Y
42 *Miller, Gary*	N	N	Y	N	Y	Y	Y	Y
43 Baca	Y	Y	N	Y	N	Y	N	Y
44 *Calvert*	N	N	Y	N	Y	Y	Y	Y
45 *Bono*	N	N	Y	N	Y	Y	Y	Y
46 *Rohrabacher*	N	N	Y	N	Y	N	Y	Y
47 Sanchez, Loretta	Y	Y	N	Y	N	Y	N	Y
48 *Cox*	N	N	Y	N	Y	Y	Y	Y
49 *Issa*	N	N	Y	N	Y	Y	Y	Y
50 *Cunningham*	Y	N	Y	N	Y	Y	Y	Y
51 Filner	Y	Y	N	Y	N	Y	N	Y
52 *Hunter*	N	N	Y	N	Y	Y	Y	Y
53 Davis	Y	Y	N	Y	N	Y	N	Y
COLORADO								
1 DeGette	Y	Y	N	Y	N	Y	N	Y
2 Udall	Y	Y	N	Y	N	Y	N	Y
3 *McInnis*	N	N	Y	N	Y	Y	Y	Y
4 *Musgrave*	N	N	Y	N	Y	Y	Y	Y
5 *Hefley*	N	N	Y	N	Y	Y	Y	Y
6 *Tancredo*	N	N	Y	N	Y	Y	Y	Y
7 *Beauprez*	N	N	Y	N	Y	Y	Y	Y
CONNECTICUT								
1 Larson	Y	Y	N	Y	N	Y	N	Y
2 *Simmons*	?	N	Y	N	Y	Y	Y	Y
3 DeLauro	Y	Y	N	Y	N	Y	N	Y
4 *Shays*	N	N	Y	Y	N	Y	Y	Y
5 *Johnson*	N	N	Y	Y	N	Y	Y	Y
DELAWARE								
AL *Castle*	N	N	Y	N	Y	Y	Y	Y
FLORIDA								
1 *Miller, J.*	N	N	Y	N	Y	Y	Y	Y
2 Boyd	Y	Y	Y	N	Y	Y	Y	Y
3 Brown	Y	Y	N	Y	N	Y	Y	Y
4 *Crenshaw*	N	N	Y	N	Y	Y	Y	Y
5 *Brown-Waite*	N	N	Y	–	Y	Y	Y	Y
6 *Stearns*	N	N	Y	N	Y	Y	Y	Y
7 *Mica*	N	N	Y	N	Y	Y	Y	Y
8 *Keller*	N	N	Y	N	Y	Y	Y	Y
9 *Bilirakis*	N	N	Y	N	Y	Y	Y	Y
10 *Young*	N	N	Y	N	Y	Y	Y	Y
11 Davis	Y	Y	N	Y	N	Y	Y	Y
12 *Putnam*	N	N	Y	N	Y	Y	Y	Y
13 *Harris*	N	N	Y	N	Y	Y	Y	Y
14 *Goss*	N	N	Y	N	Y	Y	Y	Y
15 *Weldon*	N	N	Y	N	Y	Y	Y	Y
16 *Foley*	N	N	Y	N	Y	Y	Y	Y
17 Meek	Y	Y	N	Y	N	Y	N	Y
18 *Ros-Lehtinen*	N	N	Y	N	Y	Y	Y	Y
19 Wexler	Y	Y	?	Y	Y	Y	Y	Y
20 Deutsch	Y	Y	Y	Y	N	Y	Y	Y
21 *Diaz-Balart, L.*	N	N	Y	N	Y	Y	Y	Y
22 *Shaw*	N	N	Y	N	Y	Y	Y	Y
23 Hastings	Y	Y	N	Y	N	Y	Y	Y
24 *Feeney*	N	N	Y	?	Y	Y	Y	Y
25 *Diaz-Balart, M.*	N	N	Y	N	Y	Y	Y	Y
GEORGIA								
1 *Kingston*	N	N	Y	N	Y	Y	Y	Y
2 Bishop	Y	Y	Y	Y	N	Y	Y	Y
3 Marshall	Y	Y	N	Y	N	Y	Y	Y
4 Majette	Y	Y	Y	Y	N	Y	Y	Y
5 Lewis	Y	Y	N	Y	N	Y	N	Y
6 *Isakson*	N	N	Y	N	Y	Y	Y	Y
7 *Linder*	N	N	Y	N	Y	Y	Y	Y
8 *Collins*	N	N	Y	N	Y	Y	Y	Y
9 *Norwood*	N	N	Y	N	Y	Y	Y	Y
10 *Deal*	N	N	Y	N	Y	Y	Y	Y
11 *Gingrey*	N	N	Y	N	Y	Y	Y	Y
12 *Burns*	N	N	Y	N	Y	Y	Y	Y
13 Scott	Y	?	?	?	?	?	?	?
HAWAII								
1 Abercrombie	Y	Y	N	Y	N	Y	N	?
2 Case	Y	Y	Y	Y	N	Y	Y	Y
IDAHO								
1 *Otter*	N	N	Y	N	Y	N	Y	+
2 *Simpson*	N	N	Y	N	Y	N	Y	Y
ILLINOIS								
1 Rush	Y	Y	N	Y	Y	N	Y	Y
2 Jackson	Y	Y	N	Y	Y	N	Y	Y
3 Lipinski	Y	Y	Y	Y	N	Y	N	Y
4 Gutierrez	Y	Y	N	Y	N	Y	N	Y
5 Emanuel	Y	Y	N	Y	N	Y	N	Y
6 *Hyde*	N	N	Y	Y	?	?	?	Y

ND Northern Democrats   SD Southern Democrats

	161	162	163	164	165	166	167	168
7 Davis	Y	Y	N	Y	Y	N	Y	Y
8 ***Crane***	N	N	Y	Y	N	Y	Y	Y
9 Schakowsky	Y	Y	N	Y	Y	N	Y	Y
10 ***Kirk***	N	N	Y	Y	N	Y	Y	Y
11 ***Weller***	N	N	Y	?	N	Y	Y	Y
12 Costello	Y	Y	Y	Y	Y	N	Y	Y
13 ***Biggert***	N	N	Y	Y	N	Y	Y	Y
14 ***Hastert***								
15 ***Johnson***	N	N	Y	Y	Y	N	Y	Y
16 ***Manzullo***	N	N	Y	Y	N	Y	Y	Y
17 Evans	Y	Y	N	Y	Y	N	Y	Y
18 ***LaHood***	N	N	Y	Y	N	Y	Y	Y
19 ***Shimkus***	N	N	Y	Y	N	Y	Y	Y
INDIANA								
1 Visclosky	Y	Y	Y	Y	Y	N	Y	Y
2 ***Chocola***	N	N	Y	Y	N	Y	Y	Y
3 ***Souder***	N	N	Y	Y	N	Y	Y	Y
4 ***Buyer***	N	N	Y	?	N	Y	Y	Y
5 ***Burton***	N	N	Y	Y	N	Y	Y	Y
6 ***Pence***	N	N	Y	Y	N	Y	Y	Y
7 Carson	Y	Y	N	Y	Y	N	Y	Y
8 ***Hostettler***	N	N	Y	Y	N	Y	Y	Y
9 Hill	Y	Y	N	Y	Y	N	Y	Y
IOWA								
1 ***Nussle***	N	N	Y	Y	N	Y	Y	Y
2 ***Leach***	N	N	Y	Y	N	Y	Y	Y
3 Boswell	Y	Y	N	Y	Y	N	Y	Y
4 ***Latham***	N	N	Y	Y	N	Y	Y	Y
5 ***King***	N	N	Y	Y	N	Y	Y	Y
KANSAS								
1 ***Moran***	N	N	Y	Y	N	Y	Y	Y
2 ***Ryun***	N	N	Y	Y	N	Y	Y	Y
3 Moore	Y	Y	Y	Y	Y	N	Y	Y
4 ***Tiahrt***	N	N	Y	Y	N	Y	Y	Y
KENTUCKY								
1 ***Whitfield***	N	N	Y	Y	N	Y	Y	Y
2 ***Lewis***	N	N	Y	Y	N	Y	Y	Y
3 ***Northup***	N	N	Y	Y	N	Y	Y	Y
4 Lucas	N	Y	Y	Y	N	Y	Y	Y
5 ***Rogers***	N	N	Y	Y	N	Y	Y	Y
6 Chandler	Y	Y	Y	Y	Y	N	Y	Y
LOUISIANA								
1 ***Vitter***	N	N	Y	Y	N	Y	Y	Y
2 Jefferson	Y	Y	N	Y	Y	N	Y	Y
3 ***Tauzin***	?	?	?	?	?	?	?	?
4 ***McCrery***	N	N	Y	Y	N	Y	Y	Y
5 Alexander	Y	Y	Y	Y	Y	N	Y	Y
6 ***Baker***	N	N	Y	Y	N	Y	Y	Y
7 John	Y	Y	Y	Y	Y	N	Y	Y
MAINE								
1 Allen	Y	Y	N	Y	Y	N	Y	Y
2 Michaud	Y	Y	N	Y	Y	N	Y	Y
MARYLAND								
1 ***Gilchrest***	N	N	Y	Y	N	Y	Y	Y
2 Ruppersberger	Y	Y	Y	Y	Y	N	Y	Y
3 Cardin	Y	Y	N	Y	Y	N	Y	Y
4 Wynn	Y	Y	Y	Y	Y	N	Y	Y
5 Hoyer	Y	Y	N	Y	Y	N	Y	Y
6 ***Bartlett***	N	N	Y	Y	N	Y	Y	Y
7 Cummings	Y	Y	N	Y	Y	N	Y	Y
8 Van Hollen	Y	Y	N	Y	Y	N	Y	Y
MASSACHUSETTS								
1 Olver	Y	Y	N	Y	Y	N	Y	Y
2 Neal	Y	Y	N	Y	Y	N	Y	Y
3 McGovern	Y	Y	N	Y	Y	N	Y	Y
4 Frank	Y	Y	N	Y	Y	Y	Y	Y
5 Meehan	Y	Y	N	Y	Y	N	Y	Y
6 Tierney	Y	Y	N	Y	Y	N	Y	Y
7 Markey	Y	Y	N	Y	Y	N	Y	Y
8 Capuano	Y	Y	N	Y	Y	N	Y	Y
9 Lynch	Y	Y	N	Y	Y	N	Y	Y
10 Delahunt	Y	Y	N	Y	Y	N	Y	Y
MICHIGAN								
1 Stupak	Y	Y	N	Y	Y	N	Y	Y
2 ***Hoekstra***	N	N	Y	Y	N	Y	Y	Y
3 ***Ehlers***	N	N	Y	Y	N	Y	Y	Y
4 ***Camp***	N	N	Y	Y	N	Y	Y	Y
5 Kildee	Y	Y	N	Y	Y	N	Y	Y
6 ***Upton***	N	N	Y	Y	N	Y	Y	Y
7 ***Smith***	N	N	Y	Y	N	Y	Y	Y
8 ***Rogers***	N	N	Y	Y	N	Y	Y	Y
9 ***Knollenberg***	N	N	Y	Y	N	Y	Y	Y
10 ***Miller***	N	N	Y	Y	N	Y	Y	Y
11 ***McCotter***	N	N	Y	Y	N	Y	Y	Y
12 Levin	Y	Y	N	Y	Y	N	Y	Y
13 Kilpatrick	Y	Y	N	Y	Y	N	Y	Y
14 Conyers	Y	Y	N	Y	Y	N	Y	Y
15 Dingell	Y	Y	N	Y	Y	N	Y	Y
MINNESOTA								
1 ***Gutknecht***	N	N	Y	Y	N	Y	Y	Y
2 ***Kline***	N	N	Y	Y	N	Y	Y	Y
3 ***Ramstad***	N	N	Y	Y	N	Y	Y	Y
4 McCollum	Y	Y	N	Y	Y	N	Y	Y
5 Sabo	Y	Y	N	Y	Y	N	Y	Y
6 ***Kennedy***	N	N	Y	Y	N	Y	Y	Y
7 Peterson	N	Y	Y	Y	N	Y	Y	Y
8 Oberstar	Y	Y	N	Y	Y	N	Y	Y
MISSISSIPPI								
1 ***Wicker***	N	N	Y	Y	N	Y	Y	?
2 Thompson	Y	Y	N	Y	Y	N	Y	Y
3 ***Pickering***	N	N	Y	Y	N	Y	Y	Y
4 Taylor	Y	Y	N	Y	N	Y	Y	Y
MISSOURI								
1 Clay	Y	Y	N	Y	Y	N	Y	Y
2 ***Akin***	N	N	Y	Y	N	Y	Y	Y
3 Gephardt	Y	Y	N	Y	Y	N	Y	Y
4 Skelton	Y	Y	N	Y	Y	N	Y	Y
5 McCarthy	Y	Y	N	Y	Y	N	Y	Y
6 ***Graves***	N	N	Y	Y	N	Y	Y	Y
7 ***Blunt***	N	N	Y	Y	N	Y	Y	Y
8 ***Emerson***	N	N	Y	Y	N	Y	Y	Y
9 ***Hulshof***	N	N	Y	Y	N	Y	Y	Y
MONTANA								
AL ***Rehberg***	N	N	Y	Y	N	Y	Y	Y
NEBRASKA								
1 ***Bereuter***	N	N	Y	Y	N	Y	Y	Y
2 ***Terry***	N	N	Y	Y	N	N	Y	Y
3 ***Osborne***	N	N	Y	Y	N	Y	Y	Y
NEVADA								
1 Berkley	Y	Y	Y	Y	N	N	Y	Y
2 ***Gibbons***	N	N	Y	Y	N	Y	Y	Y
3 ***Porter***	N	N	Y	Y	N	Y	Y	Y
NEW HAMPSHIRE								
1 ***Bradley***	N	N	Y	Y	N	Y	Y	Y
2 ***Bass***	N	N	Y	Y	N	Y	Y	Y
NEW JERSEY								
1 Andrews	Y	Y	N	Y	Y	N	Y	Y
2 ***LoBiondo***	N	N	Y	Y	N	Y	Y	Y
3 ***Saxton***	N	N	Y	Y	N	Y	Y	Y
4 ***Smith***	N	N	Y	Y	N	Y	Y	Y
5 ***Garrett***	N	N	Y	Y	N	Y	Y	Y
6 Pallone	Y	Y	N	Y	Y	N	Y	Y
7 ***Ferguson***	N	N	Y	Y	N	Y	Y	Y
8 Pascrell	Y	Y	N	Y	Y	N	Y	Y
9 Rothman	Y	Y	N	Y	Y	N	Y	Y
10 Payne	Y	Y	N	Y	Y	N	Y	Y
11 ***Frelinghuysen***	N	N	Y	Y	N	Y	Y	Y
12 Holt	Y	Y	N	Y	Y	N	Y	Y
13 Menendez	Y	Y	N	Y	Y	N	Y	Y
NEW MEXICO								
1 ***Wilson***	N	N	Y	Y	N	Y	Y	Y
2 ***Pearce***	N	N	Y	Y	N	Y	Y	Y
3 Udall	Y	Y	N	Y	Y	N	Y	Y
NEW YORK								
1 Bishop	Y	Y	N	Y	Y	N	Y	Y
2 Israel	Y	Y	N	Y	Y	N	Y	Y
3 ***King***	N	N	Y	Y	N	N	Y	Y
4 McCarthy	Y	Y	Y	Y	Y	N	Y	Y
5 Ackerman	Y	Y	N	Y	Y	N	Y	Y
6 Meeks	Y	Y	Y	Y	Y	N	Y	Y
7 Crowley	Y	Y	N	Y	Y	N	Y	Y
8 Nadler	Y	Y	N	Y	Y	N	Y	Y
9 Weiner	Y	Y	N	Y	Y	N	Y	Y
10 Towns	Y	Y	N	Y	Y	N	Y	Y
11 Owens	Y	?	N	Y	Y	N	Y	Y
12 Velázquez	Y	Y	N	Y	Y	N	Y	Y
13 ***Fossella***	N	N	Y	Y	N	Y	Y	Y
14 Maloney	Y	Y	Y	Y	Y	N	Y	Y
15 Rangel	Y	Y	N	?	Y	N	Y	Y
16 Serrano	Y	Y	N	Y	Y	N	Y	Y
17 Engel	Y	Y	N	Y	Y	N	Y	Y
18 Lowey	Y	Y	Y	Y	?	?	?	?
19 ***Kelly***	N	N	Y	Y	N	Y	Y	Y
20 ***Sweeney***	N	N	Y	Y	N	Y	Y	Y
21 McNulty	Y	Y	N	Y	Y	N	Y	Y
22 Hinchey	Y	Y	N	Y	Y	N	Y	Y
23 ***McHugh***	N	N	Y	Y	N	Y	Y	Y
24 ***Boehlert***	N	N	Y	Y	N	Y	Y	Y
25 ***Walsh***	N	N	Y	Y	N	Y	Y	Y
26 ***Reynolds***	N	N	Y	Y	N	Y	Y	Y
27 ***Quinn***	N	N	Y	Y	N	Y	Y	Y
28 Slaughter	Y	Y	Y	Y	Y	N	Y	Y
29 ***Houghton***	N	N	Y	Y	N	Y	Y	Y
NORTH CAROLINA								
1 Ballance	Y	Y	N	Y	Y	N	Y	Y
2 Etheridge	Y	Y	N	Y	Y	N	Y	Y
3 ***Jones***	N	N	Y	Y	N	Y	Y	Y
4 Price	Y	Y	N	Y	Y	N	Y	Y
5 ***Burr***	N	N	Y	Y	N	Y	Y	Y
6 ***Coble***	N	N	Y	Y	N	N	Y	Y
7 McIntyre	Y	Y	N	Y	Y	N	Y	Y
8 ***Hayes***	N	N	Y	Y	N	Y	Y	Y
9 ***Myrick***	N	N	Y	Y	N	Y	Y	Y
10 ***Ballenger***	N	N	Y	Y	N	Y	Y	Y
11 ***Taylor***	N	N	Y	Y	N	Y	Y	Y
12 Watt	Y	Y	N	Y	Y	N	Y	Y
13 Miller	Y	Y	N	Y	Y	N	Y	Y
NORTH DAKOTA								
AL Pomeroy	Y	Y	Y	Y	Y	Y	Y	Y
OHIO								
1 ***Chabot***	N	N	Y	Y	N	Y	Y	Y
2 ***Portman***	N	N	Y	Y	N	Y	Y	Y
3 ***Turner***	N	N	Y	Y	N	Y	Y	Y
4 ***Oxley***	N	N	Y	Y	N	Y	Y	Y
5 ***Gillmor***	N	N	Y	Y	N	Y	Y	Y
6 Strickland	Y	Y	Y	Y	Y	N	Y	Y
7 ***Hobson***	N	N	Y	Y	N	Y	Y	Y
8 ***Boehner***	N	N	Y	Y	N	Y	Y	Y
9 Kaptur	Y	Y	N	Y	Y	N	Y	Y
10 Kucinich	Y	Y	N	Y	Y	N	Y	Y
11 Jones	Y	Y	N	Y	Y	N	Y	Y
12 ***Tiberi***	N	N	Y	Y	N	Y	Y	Y
13 Brown	Y	Y	N	Y	Y	N	Y	Y
14 ***LaTourette***	N	N	Y	Y	N	Y	Y	Y
15 ***Pryce***	N	N	Y	Y	N	Y	Y	Y
16 ***Regula***	?	N	Y	Y	N	Y	Y	Y
17 Ryan	Y	Y	N	Y	Y	N	Y	Y
18 ***Ney***	N	N	Y	Y	N	Y	Y	Y
OKLAHOMA								
1 ***Sullivan***	N	N	Y	Y	N	Y	Y	Y
2 Carson	N	Y	Y	Y	Y	N	Y	Y
3 ***Lucas***	N	N	Y	Y	N	Y	Y	Y
4 ***Cole***	N	N	Y	Y	N	Y	Y	Y
5 ***Istook***	N	N	Y	?	?	N	Y	Y
OREGON								
1 Wu	Y	Y	Y	Y	Y	N	Y	Y
2 ***Walden***	N	N	Y	Y	N	Y	Y	Y
3 Blumenauer	Y	Y	N	Y	Y	N	Y	Y
4 DeFazio	Y	Y	Y	P	Y	N	Y	Y
5 Hooley	Y	Y	Y	Y	Y	N	Y	Y
PENNSYLVANIA								
1 Brady	Y	Y	N	Y	Y	N	Y	Y
2 Fattah	Y	Y	N	Y	Y	N	Y	Y
3 ***English***	N	N	Y	Y	N	Y	Y	Y
4 ***Hart***	N	N	Y	Y	N	Y	Y	Y
5 ***Peterson***	N	N	Y	Y	N	Y	Y	Y
6 ***Gerlach***	N	N	Y	Y	N	Y	Y	Y
7 ***Weldon***	N	N	Y	Y	N	Y	Y	Y
8 ***Greenwood***	N	N	Y	Y	N	Y	Y	Y
9 ***Shuster, Bill***	N	N	Y	Y	N	Y	Y	Y
10 ***Sherwood***	N	N	Y	Y	N	Y	Y	Y
11 Kanjorski	N	Y	N	Y	Y	N	Y	Y
12 Murtha	N	Y	N	Y	N	Y	Y	Y
13 Hoeffel	Y	Y	N	Y	Y	N	Y	Y
14 Doyle	Y	Y	N	Y	Y	N	Y	Y
15 ***Toomey***	N	N	Y	Y	N	Y	Y	Y
16 ***Pitts***	N	N	Y	Y	N	Y	Y	Y
17 Holden	Y	Y	Y	Y	N	Y	Y	Y
18 ***Murphy***	N	N	Y	Y	N	Y	Y	Y
19 ***Platts***	N	N	Y	Y	N	Y	Y	Y
RHODE ISLAND								
1 Kennedy	Y	Y	N	?	Y	N	Y	Y
2 Langevin	Y	Y	N	Y	Y	N	Y	Y
SOUTH CAROLINA								
1 ***Brown***	N	N	Y	Y	N	Y	Y	Y
2 ***Wilson***	N	N	Y	Y	N	Y	Y	Y
3 ***Barrett***	N	N	Y	Y	N	Y	Y	Y
4 ***DeMint***	?	?	?	?	?	?	?	?
5 Spratt	Y	Y	N	Y	Y	N	Y	Y
6 Clyburn	Y	Y	N	Y	Y	N	Y	Y
SOUTH DAKOTA								
AL Vacant								
TENNESSEE								
1 ***Jenkins***	N	N	Y	Y	N	N	Y	Y
2 ***Duncan***	N	N	Y	?	Y	Y	Y	Y
3 ***Wamp***	N	N	Y	Y	N	Y	Y	Y
4 Davis	Y	Y	Y	Y	Y	Y	Y	Y
5 Cooper	N	Y	Y	Y	Y	N	Y	Y
6 Gordon	Y	Y	Y	Y	Y	Y	Y	Y
7 ***Blackburn***	N	N	Y	Y	N	Y	Y	Y
8 Tanner	Y	Y	N	Y	Y	N	Y	Y
9 Ford	Y	Y	N	Y	Y	N	Y	Y
TEXAS								
1 Sandlin	Y	Y	N	Y	Y	N	Y	Y
2 Turner	Y	Y	N	Y	Y	N	Y	Y
3 ***Johnson, Sam***	N	N	Y	N	N	Y	Y	Y
4 ***Hall***	N	N	Y	Y	N	Y	Y	Y
5 ***Hensarling***	N	N	Y	Y	N	Y	Y	Y
6 ***Barton***	N	N	Y	Y	N	Y	Y	Y
7 ***Culberson***	N	N	Y	Y	N	Y	Y	Y
8 ***Brady***	N	N	Y	Y	N	Y	Y	Y
9 Lampson	Y	Y	N	Y	Y	N	Y	Y
10 Doggett	Y	Y	N	Y	Y	N	Y	Y
11 Edwards	Y	Y	Y	Y	Y	N	Y	Y
12 ***Granger***	N	N	Y	Y	N	Y	Y	Y
13 ***Thornberry***	N	N	Y	Y	N	Y	Y	Y
14 ***Paul***	N	N	Y	N	N	N	N	Y
15 Hinojosa	Y	Y	Y	Y	Y	N	Y	Y
16 Reyes	?	?	?	?	?	?	?	?
17 Stenholm	Y	Y	N	Y	Y	Y	Y	?
18 Jackson-Lee	Y	Y	N	Y	Y	N	Y	Y
19 ***Neugebauer***	N	N	Y	Y	N	Y	Y	Y
20 Gonzalez	Y	Y	Y	Y	Y	N	Y	Y
21 ***Smith***	N	N	Y	Y	N	Y	Y	Y
22 ***DeLay***	N	N	Y	Y	N	Y	Y	Y
23 ***Bonilla***	N	N	Y	Y	N	Y	Y	Y
24 Frost	Y	Y	Y	Y	Y	N	Y	Y
25 Bell	Y	Y	N	Y	Y	N	Y	Y
26 ***Burgess***	N	N	Y	Y	N	Y	Y	Y
27 Ortiz	Y	Y	N	Y	Y	N	Y	Y
28 Rodriguez	Y	Y	N	Y	Y	N	Y	Y
29 Green	Y	Y	N	Y	Y	N	Y	Y
30 Johnson, E.B.	Y	Y	Y	Y	Y	N	Y	Y
31 ***Carter***	N	N	Y	Y	N	Y	Y	Y
32 ***Sessions***	N	N	Y	Y	N	Y	Y	Y
UTAH								
1 ***Bishop***	N	N	Y	Y	N	Y	Y	Y
2 Matheson	N	Y	Y	Y	N	Y	Y	Y
3 ***Cannon***	N	N	Y	Y	N	Y	Y	Y
VERMONT								
AL *Sanders*	Y	Y	N	P	Y	N	Y	Y
VIRGINIA								
1 ***Davis, Jo Ann***	N	N	Y	Y	N	Y	Y	Y
2 ***Schrock***	N	N	Y	Y	N	Y	Y	Y
3 Scott	Y	Y	N	Y	Y	N	Y	Y
4 ***Forbes***	N	N	Y	Y	N	Y	Y	Y
5 ***Goode***	N	N	Y	Y	N	Y	Y	Y
6 ***Goodlatte***	N	N	Y	Y	N	Y	Y	Y
7 ***Cantor***	N	N	Y	Y	N	Y	Y	?
8 Moran	Y	Y	Y	Y	Y	N	Y	Y
9 Boucher	Y	Y	Y	Y	Y	N	Y	Y
10 ***Wolf***	N	N	Y	Y	N	Y	Y	Y
11 ***Davis, T.***	N	N	Y	Y	N	Y	Y	Y
WASHINGTON								
1 Inslee	Y	Y	Y	Y	Y	N	Y	Y
2 Larsen	Y	Y	N	Y	Y	N	Y	Y
3 Baird	Y	Y	N	Y	Y	N	Y	Y
4 ***Hastings***	N	N	Y	Y	N	Y	Y	Y
5 ***Nethercutt***	N	N	Y	Y	N	Y	Y	Y
6 Dicks	Y	Y	N	Y	Y	N	Y	Y
7 McDermott	Y	Y	N	Y	Y	N	Y	Y
8 ***Dunn***	N	N	Y	Y	N	Y	Y	Y
9 Smith	Y	Y	N	Y	Y	N	Y	Y
WEST VIRGINIA								
1 Mollohan	N	Y	Y	Y	N	N	Y	Y
2 ***Capito***	N	N	Y	Y	N	Y	Y	Y
3 Rahall	Y	Y	N	Y	Y	N	Y	Y
WISCONSIN								
1 ***Ryan***	N	N	Y	Y	N	Y	Y	Y
2 Baldwin	Y	Y	N	Y	Y	N	Y	Y
3 Kind	Y	Y	N	Y	Y	N	Y	Y
4 Kleczka	Y	Y	N	Y	Y	N	Y	Y
5 ***Sensenbrenner***	N	N	Y	Y	N	Y	Y	Y
6 ***Petri***	N	N	Y	Y	N	Y	Y	Y
7 Obey	Y	Y	?	Y	Y	N	Y	Y
8 ***Green***	N	N	Y	Y	N	Y	Y	Y
WYOMING								
AL ***Cubin***	N	N	Y	?	N	Y	Y	Y

Southern states - Ala., Ark., Fla., Ga., Ky., La., Miss., N.C., Okla., S.C., Tenn., Texas, Va.

169. HR 4275. Ten Percent Tax Bracket/Democratic Substitute. Tanner, D-Tenn., substitute amendment that would extend through 2010 the current upper limit of the 10 percent income tax bracket, while ensuring that the bill's tax provisions would not be affected by the alternative minimum tax. It would condition a permanent extension on passage of legislation that balances the budget by fiscal 2014 without using the Social Security and Medicare trust funds. The cost of the substitute would be offset by applying an additional tax of 1.9 percent for 2005 through 2010 on individuals with incomes of more than $500,000 a year and married taxpayers with incomes of more than $1 million. Rejected 190-227: R 1-216; D 188-11 (ND 141-5, SD 47-6); I 1-0. May 13, 2004.

170. HR 4275. Ten Percent Tax Bracket/Passage. Passage of the bill that would make permanent the current upper limit of the 10 percent income tax bracket. The current limits of $7,000 for individuals and $14,000 for couples are set to revert to $6,000 and $12,000 in 2005. Passed 344-76: R 219-1; D 124-75 (ND 85-61, SD 39-14); I 1-0. A "yea" was a vote in support of the president's position. May 13, 2004.

171. S Con Res 95. Fiscal 2005 Budget Resolution/Motion to Instruct. Pomeroy, D-N.D., motion to instruct House conferees to accept provisions in the Senate version of the budget resolution that would subject any tax cut or mandatory spending expansion to either a pay-as-you-go offset or a 60-vote point of order in the Senate. Motion rejected 207-211: R 8-211; D 198-0 (ND 145-0, SD 53-0); I 1-0. May 13, 2004.

172. HR 4281. Health Plans for Small Businesses/Democratic Substitute. Kind, D-Wis., substitute amendment that would allow employers with fewer than 100 employees to participate in a Small Employer Health Benefits program that would be similar to the Federal Employees Health Benefits program. Employers would be required to pay at least half of their employees' premium costs and to offer coverage to all employees who have completed three months of service. Rejected 193-224: R 0-218; D 192-6 (ND 142-3, SD 50-3); I 1-0. May 13, 2004.

173. HR 4281. Health Plans for Small Businesses/Recommit. McCarthy, D-N.Y., motion to recommit the bill to the Education and the Workforce Committee with instructions to add language that would prohibit employers from joining a health plan if it allows for a reduction in breast cancer coverage. Motion rejected 196-218: R 0-215; D 195-3 (ND 141-3, SD 54-0); I 1-0. May 13, 2004.

174. HR 4281. Health Plans for Small Businesses/Passage. Passage of the bill that would allow for the creation of association health plans through which small companies could band together to buy insurance for their employees. Association health plans that cover employees in multiple states would be exempt from many individual state insurance regulations but would be regulated by the Labor Department. Passed 252-162: R 215-0; D 37-161 (ND 12-132, SD 25-29); I 0-1. May 13, 2004.

175. H J Res 91. 60th Anniversary of "G.I. Bill of Rights"/Passage. Smith, R-N.J., motion to suspend the rules and pass the joint resolution that would recognize the 60th anniversary of the Servicemen's Readjustment Act of 1944, also known as the G.I. Bill of Rights. Motion agreed to 409-0: R 214-0; D 194-0 (ND 142-0, SD 52-0); I 1-0. A two-thirds majority of those present and voting (273 in this case) is required for passage under suspension of the rules. May 13, 2004.

176. H Con Res 414. School Desegregation Ruling/Adoption. Adoption of the concurrent resolution that would mark the 50th anniversary of the Supreme Court's *Brown v. Board of Education* ruling that racial segregation in public schools is unconstitutional. It also would renew the commitment of Congress to continue and build on the legacy of the *Brown* decision. Adopted 406-1: R 212-1; D 194-0 (ND 142-0, SD 52-0); I 0-0. May 13, 2004.

Key

Y	Voted for (yea).
#	Paired for.
+	Announced for.
N	Voted against (nay).
X	Paired against.
–	Announced against.
P	Voted "present."
C	Voted "present" to avoid possible conflict of interest.
?	Did not vote or otherwise make a position known.

Democrats **Republicans**
Independents

		169	170	171	172	173	174	175	176
ALABAMA									
1	*Bonner*	N	Y	N	N	N	Y	Y	Y
2	*Everett*	N	Y	N	N	N	Y	Y	Y
3	*Rogers*	N	Y	N	N	N	Y	Y	Y
4	*Aderholt*	N	Y	N	?	?	?	?	?
5	Cramer	N	Y	Y	N	N	Y	Y	Y
6	*Bachus*	N	Y	N	N	N	Y	Y	Y
7	Davis	Y	Y	Y	Y	Y	Y	Y	Y
ALASKA									
AL	*Young*	?	Y	N	N	N	Y	Y	Y
ARIZONA									
1	*Renzi*	N	Y	N	N	N	Y	Y	Y
2	*Franks*	N	Y	N	N	N	Y	Y	Y
3	*Shadegg*	?	?	?	?	?	?	?	?
4	Pastor	Y	N	Y	Y	Y	N	Y	Y
5	*Hayworth*	N	Y	N	N	N	Y	Y	Y
6	*Flake*	N	Y	N	N	N	Y	Y	Y
7	Grijalva	Y	N	Y	Y	Y	N	Y	Y
8	*Kolbe*	N	Y	Y	N	N	Y	Y	Y
ARKANSAS									
1	Berry	Y	N	Y	Y	Y	N	Y	Y
2	Snyder	Y	Y	Y	Y	Y	Y	Y	Y
3	*Boozman*	N	Y	N	N	N	Y	Y	Y
4	Ross	Y	Y	Y	Y	Y	N	Y	Y
CALIFORNIA									
1	Thompson	Y	N	Y	Y	Y	N	Y	Y
2	*Herger*	N	Y	N	N	N	Y	Y	Y
3	*Ose*	N	Y	N	N	N	Y	Y	Y
4	*Doolittle*	N	Y	N	N	N	Y	Y	?
5	Matsui	Y	Y	Y	Y	Y	N	Y	Y
6	Woolsey	Y	N	Y	Y	Y	N	Y	Y
7	Miller, George	Y	Y	Y	Y	Y	N	Y	Y
8	Pelosi	Y	N	Y	Y	Y	N	Y	Y
9	Lee	Y	N	Y	Y	Y	N	Y	Y
10	Tauscher	Y	Y	Y	Y	Y	N	Y	Y
11	*Pombo*	N	Y	N	N	N	Y	Y	Y
12	Lantos	Y	Y	Y	Y	Y	N	Y	Y
13	Stark	Y	N	Y	Y	Y	N	Y	Y
14	Eshoo	Y	Y	Y	Y	Y	N	Y	Y
15	Honda	Y	Y	Y	Y	Y	N	Y	Y
16	Lofgren	Y	Y	Y	Y	Y	N	Y	Y
17	Farr	Y	Y	Y	Y	Y	N	Y	Y
18	Cardoza	Y	Y	Y	Y	Y	N	Y	Y
19	*Radanovich*	N	Y	N	N	N	Y	Y	Y
20	Dooley	Y	Y	Y	Y	Y	Y	Y	Y
21	*Nunes*	N	Y	N	N	N	Y	Y	Y
22	*Thomas*	N	Y	N	N	N	Y	Y	Y
23	Capps	Y	N	Y	Y	Y	N	Y	Y
24	*Gallegly*	N	Y	N	N	N	Y	Y	Y
25	*McKeon*	N	Y	N	N	N	Y	Y	Y
26	*Dreier*	N	Y	N	N	N	Y	Y	Y
27	Sherman	Y	N	Y	Y	Y	N	Y	Y
28	Berman	Y	Y	Y	Y	Y	N	?	?
29	Schiff	Y	Y	Y	Y	Y	N	Y	Y
30	Waxman	Y	N	Y	Y	Y	N	Y	Y
31	Becerra	Y	N	Y	Y	Y	N	Y	Y
32	Solis	Y	N	Y	Y	Y	N	Y	Y
33	Watson	Y	N	Y	Y	Y	N	Y	Y
34	Roybal-Allard	Y	N	Y	Y	Y	N	Y	Y
35	Waters	Y	N	Y	Y	Y	N	Y	Y
36	Harman	Y	Y	Y	Y	Y	Y	Y	Y

		169	170	171	172	173	174	175	176
37	Millender-McD.	Y	Y	Y	Y	Y	N	Y	Y
38	Napolitano	Y	N	Y	Y	Y	N	Y	Y
39	Sánchez, Linda	Y	N	Y	Y	Y	N	Y	Y
40	*Royce*	N	Y	N	N	N	Y	Y	Y
41	*Lewis*	N	Y	N	N	N	Y	Y	Y
42	*Miller, Gary*	N	Y	N	N	N	Y	Y	Y
43	Baca	N	Y	Y	Y	Y	N	Y	Y
44	*Calvert*	N	Y	N	N	N	Y	Y	Y
45	*Bono*	N	Y	N	N	N	Y	Y	Y
46	*Rohrabacher*	N	Y	N	N	N	Y	Y	Y
47	Sánchez, Loretta	Y	N	Y	Y	Y	N	Y	Y
48	*Cox*	N	Y	N	N	N	Y	Y	Y
49	*Issa*	N	Y	N	N	N	Y	Y	Y
50	*Cunningham*	N	Y	N	N	N	Y	Y	Y
51	Filner	?	?	?	?	?	?	?	?
52	*Hunter*	N	Y	N	N	N	Y	Y	Y
53	Davis	Y	Y	Y	Y	Y	N	Y	Y
COLORADO									
1	DeGette	Y	N	Y	?	?	?	?	?
2	Udall	Y	Y	Y	Y	Y	N	Y	Y
3	*McInnis*	N	Y	N	?	?	?	?	?
4	*Musgrave*	N	Y	N	N	N	Y	Y	Y
5	*Hefley*	Y	Y	N	N	N	Y	Y	Y
6	*Tancredo*	N	Y	N	N	N	Y	Y	Y
7	*Beauprez*	N	Y	N	N	N	Y	Y	Y
CONNECTICUT									
1	Larson	Y	Y	Y	Y	Y	N	Y	Y
2	*Simmons*	N	Y	N	N	N	Y	Y	Y
3	DeLauro	Y	Y	Y	Y	Y	N	Y	Y
4	*Shays*	N	Y	Y	Y	Y	N	Y	Y
5	*Johnson*	N	Y	N	N	N	Y	Y	Y
DELAWARE									
AL	*Castle*	N	Y	Y	N	N	Y	Y	Y
FLORIDA									
1	*Miller, J.*	N	Y	N	N	N	Y	Y	Y
2	Boyd	Y	Y	Y	Y	Y	N	Y	Y
3	Brown	Y	Y	Y	Y	Y	N	Y	Y
4	*Crenshaw*	N	Y	N	N	N	Y	Y	Y
5	*Brown-Waite*	N	Y	N	N	N	Y	Y	Y
6	*Stearns*	N	Y	N	N	N	Y	Y	?
7	*Mica*	N	Y	N	N	N	Y	Y	Y
8	*Keller*	N	Y	N	N	N	Y	Y	Y
9	*Bilirakis*	N	Y	N	N	N	Y	Y	Y
10	*Young*	N	Y	N	N	N	Y	Y	Y
11	Davis	Y	N	Y	Y	Y	N	Y	Y
12	*Putnam*	N	Y	N	N	N	Y	Y	Y
13	*Harris*	N	Y	N	N	N	Y	Y	Y
14	*Goss*	?	?	N	N	N	Y	Y	Y
15	*Weldon*	N	Y	N	N	N	Y	Y	Y
16	*Foley*	N	Y	N	N	N	Y	Y	Y
17	Meek	Y	Y	Y	Y	Y	N	Y	Y
18	*Ros-Lehtinen*	N	N	N	N	N	Y	Y	Y
19	Wexler	Y	N	Y	Y	Y	N	Y	Y
20	Deutsch	Y	Y	Y	Y	Y	N	Y	Y
21	*Diaz-Balart, L.*	N	Y	N	N	N	Y	Y	Y
22	*Shaw*	N	Y	N	N	N	Y	Y	Y
23	Hastings	Y	N	Y	Y	Y	N	Y	Y
24	*Feeney*	N	Y	N	N	N	Y	Y	Y
25	*Diaz-Balart, M.*	N	Y	N	N	N	Y	Y	Y
GEORGIA									
1	*Kingston*	N	Y	N	N	N	Y	Y	Y
2	Bishop	Y	Y	Y	Y	Y	Y	Y	Y
3	Marshall	N	Y	Y	Y	Y	Y	Y	Y
4	*Majette*	?	?	?	?	?	?	?	?
5	Lewis	?	?	?	Y	Y	N	Y	Y
6	*Isakson*	N	Y	N	N	N	Y	Y	Y
7	*Linder*	N	Y	N	N	?	Y	?	?
8	*Collins*	N	Y	N	N	N	Y	Y	Y
9	*Norwood*	N	Y	N	N	N	P	Y	Y
10	*Deal*	?	?	?	?	?	?	?	?
11	*Gingrey*	N	Y	N	N	N	Y	Y	Y
12	*Burns*	N	Y	N	N	N	Y	Y	Y
13	Scott	?	?	?	?	?	?	?	?
HAWAII									
1	Abercrombie	Y	N	Y	Y	Y	N	Y	Y
2	Case	Y	Y	N	Y	N	N	Y	Y
IDAHO									
1	*Otter*	N	Y	N	N	N	Y	Y	Y
2	*Simpson*	N	Y	N	N	N	Y	Y	Y
ILLINOIS									
1	Rush	Y	Y	Y	Y	Y	N	Y	Y
2	Jackson	Y	N	Y	Y	Y	N	Y	Y
3	Lipinski	Y	Y	Y	Y	Y	N	Y	Y
4	Gutierrez	Y	Y	Y	Y	Y	N	Y	Y
5	Emanuel	Y	N	Y	Y	Y	N	Y	Y
6	*Hyde*	N	Y	N	N	N	Y	Y	Y

ND Northern Democrats   SD Southern Democrats

	169	170	171	172	173	174	175	176
7 Davis	Y	N	Y	Y	Y	N	Y	Y
8 *Crane*	N	Y	N	N	N	Y	Y	Y
9 Schakowsky	Y	N	Y	Y	Y	N	Y	Y
10 *Kirk*	N	Y	N	N	N	Y	Y	Y
11 *Weller*	N	Y	N	N	N	Y	Y	Y
12 Costello	Y	Y	Y	Y	Y	Y	Y	Y
13 *Biggert*	N	Y	N	N	N	Y	Y	Y
14 *Hastert*								
15 *Johnson*	N	Y	N	N	N	Y	Y	Y
16 *Manzullo*	N	Y	N	N	N	Y	Y	Y
17 Evans	Y	Y	Y	Y	Y	N	Y	Y
18 *LaHood*	N	Y	N	N	N	Y	Y	Y
19 *Shimkus*	N	Y	N	?	?	?	?	?
INDIANA								
1 Visclosky	Y	N	Y	Y	Y	N	Y	Y
2 *Chocola*	N	Y	N	N	N	Y	Y	Y
3 *Souder*	N	Y	N	N	N	Y	Y	Y
4 *Buyer*	N	Y	N	N	N	Y	Y	Y
5 *Burton*	N	Y	N	N	N	Y	Y	Y
6 *Pence*	N	Y	N	N	N	Y	Y	Y
7 Carson	Y	N	Y	Y	Y	N	Y	Y
8 *Hostettler*	N	Y	N	N	N	Y	Y	Y
9 Hill	Y	N	Y	Y	Y	N	Y	Y
IOWA								
1 *Nussle*	N	Y	N	N	N	Y	Y	Y
2 *Leach*	N	Y	Y	N	N	Y	Y	Y
3 Boswell	Y	Y	Y	Y	Y	N	Y	Y
4 *Latham*	N	Y	N	N	N	Y	Y	Y
5 *King*	N	Y	?	N	N	Y	Y	Y
KANSAS								
1 *Moran*	N	Y	N	N	N	Y	Y	Y
2 *Ryun*	N	Y	N	N	N	Y	Y	Y
3 Moore	Y	Y	Y	Y	Y	N	Y	Y
4 *Tiahrt*	N	Y	N	N	N	Y	Y	Y
KENTUCKY								
1 *Whitfield*	N	Y	N	N	N	Y	Y	Y
2 *Lewis*	N	Y	N	N	N	Y	Y	Y
3 *Northup*	N	Y	N	N	N	Y	Y	Y
4 Lucas	Y	Y	Y	Y	Y	Y	Y	Y
5 *Rogers*	N	Y	N	N	N	Y	Y	Y
6 Chandler	N	Y	Y	Y	Y	N	Y	Y
LOUISIANA								
1 *Vitter*	N	Y	N	N	N	Y	Y	Y
2 Jefferson	Y	N	Y	Y	Y	Y	Y	Y
3 *Tauzin*	?	?	?	?	?	?	?	?
4 *McCrery*	N	Y	N	N	N	Y	Y	Y
5 Alexander	N	Y	Y	Y	Y	N	Y	Y
6 *Baker*	N	Y	N	N	N	Y	Y	Y
7 John	Y	Y	Y	Y	Y	Y	Y	Y
MAINE								
1 Allen	Y	Y	Y	Y	Y	N	Y	Y
2 Michaud	Y	Y	Y	Y	Y	N	Y	Y
MARYLAND								
1 *Gilchrest*	N	Y	N	N	N	Y	Y	Y
2 Ruppersberger	Y	N	Y	Y	Y	N	Y	Y
3 Cardin	Y	Y	Y	Y	Y	N	Y	Y
4 Wynn	Y	Y	Y	Y	Y	Y	Y	Y
5 Hoyer	Y	N	Y	Y	Y	N	Y	Y
6 *Bartlett*	N	Y	N	N	N	Y	Y	Y
7 Cummings	Y	N	Y	Y	Y	N	?	Y
8 Van Hollen	Y	Y	Y	Y	Y	N	Y	Y
MASSACHUSETTS								
1 Olver	Y	Y	Y	Y	Y	N	Y	Y
2 Neal	Y	N	Y	Y	Y	N	Y	Y
3 McGovern	Y	N	Y	Y	Y	N	Y	Y
4 Frank	Y	N	Y	Y	Y	N	Y	Y
5 Meehan	Y	Y	Y	Y	?	?	?	?
6 Tierney	Y	N	Y	Y	Y	N	Y	Y
7 Markey	Y	Y	Y	Y	Y	N	Y	Y
8 Capuano	Y	Y	Y	Y	Y	N	Y	Y
9 Lynch	Y	Y	Y	Y	Y	N	Y	Y
10 Delahunt	Y	Y	Y	Y	Y	N	Y	Y
MICHIGAN								
1 Stupak	Y	Y	Y	Y	Y	N	Y	Y
2 *Hoekstra*	N	Y	N	N	N	Y	Y	Y
3 *Ehlers*	N	Y	N	N	N	Y	Y	Y
4 *Camp*	N	Y	N	N	N	Y	Y	Y
5 Kildee	Y	Y	Y	Y	Y	N	Y	Y
6 *Upton*	N	Y	Y	N	N	Y	Y	Y
7 *Smith*	N	Y	N	N	?	?	?	?
8 *Rogers*	N	Y	N	N	N	Y	Y	Y
9 *Knollenberg*	N	Y	N	N	N	Y	Y	Y
10 *Miller*	N	Y	N	N	N	Y	Y	Y
11 *McCotter*	N	Y	N	N	N	Y	Y	Y
12 Levin	Y	Y	Y	Y	Y	N	Y	Y

	169	170	171	172	173	174	175	176
13 Kilpatrick	Y	Y	Y	Y	Y	N	Y	Y
14 Conyers	Y	N	Y	Y	Y	N	Y	Y
15 Dingell	Y	N	Y	Y	Y	N	Y	Y
MINNESOTA								
1 *Gutknecht*	N	Y	N	N	N	Y	Y	Y
2 *Kline*	N	Y	N	N	N	Y	Y	Y
3 *Ramstad*	N	Y	N	N	N	Y	Y	Y
4 McCollum	Y	Y	Y	Y	Y	N	Y	Y
5 Sabo	Y	Y	Y	Y	Y	N	Y	Y
6 *Kennedy*	N	Y	N	N	N	Y	Y	Y
7 Peterson	Y	Y	Y	Y	Y	Y	Y	Y
8 Oberstar	Y	Y	Y	Y	Y	N	Y	Y
MISSISSIPPI								
1 *Wicker*	N	Y	N	N	N	Y	Y	Y
2 Thompson	Y	Y	Y	Y	Y	Y	Y	Y
3 *Pickering*	N	Y	N	N	N	Y	Y	Y
4 Taylor	Y	N	Y	Y	Y	Y	Y	Y
MISSOURI								
1 Clay	Y	Y	Y	Y	Y	Y	Y	Y
2 *Akin*	N	Y	N	N	N	Y	Y	Y
3 Gephardt	Y	Y	Y	Y	Y	N	Y	Y
4 Skelton	Y	Y	Y	Y	Y	N	Y	Y
5 McCarthy	Y	N	Y	Y	Y	N	Y	Y
6 *Graves*	N	Y	N	N	N	Y	Y	Y
7 *Blunt*	?	Y	N	N	N	Y	Y	Y
8 *Emerson*	N	Y	N	N	N	Y	Y	Y
9 *Hulshof*	?	?	?	?	?	?	?	?
MONTANA								
AL *Rehberg*	N	Y	N	N	N	Y	Y	Y
NEBRASKA								
1 *Bereuter*	N	Y	Y	N	N	Y	Y	Y
2 *Terry*	N	Y	N	N	N	Y	Y	Y
3 *Osborne*	N	Y	N	N	N	Y	Y	Y
NEVADA								
1 Berkley	Y	Y	Y	Y	Y	N	Y	Y
2 *Gibbons*	N	Y	N	N	N	Y	Y	Y
3 *Porter*	N	Y	N	N	N	Y	Y	Y
NEW HAMPSHIRE								
1 *Bradley*	N	Y	N	N	N	Y	Y	Y
2 *Bass*	N	Y	Y	N	N	Y	Y	Y
NEW JERSEY								
1 Andrews	Y	N	Y	Y	Y	N	Y	Y
2 *LoBiondo*	N	Y	N	N	N	Y	Y	Y
3 *Saxton*	N	Y	N	N	N	Y	Y	Y
4 *Smith*	N	Y	N	N	N	Y	Y	Y
5 *Garrett*	N	Y	N	N	N	Y	Y	Y
6 Pallone	Y	N	Y	Y	Y	N	Y	Y
7 *Ferguson*	N	Y	N	N	N	Y	Y	Y
8 Pascrell	Y	N	Y	Y	Y	N	Y	Y
9 Rothman	Y	Y	Y	Y	Y	N	Y	Y
10 Payne	Y	N	Y	Y	Y	N	Y	Y
11 *Frelinghuysen*	N	Y	N	N	N	Y	Y	Y
12 Holt	Y	N	Y	Y	Y	N	Y	Y
13 Menendez	Y	N	Y	Y	Y	N	Y	Y
NEW MEXICO								
1 *Wilson*	N	Y	N	N	N	Y	Y	Y
2 *Pearce*	N	Y	N	N	N	Y	Y	Y
3 Udall	Y	Y	Y	Y	Y	N	Y	Y
NEW YORK								
1 Bishop	Y	Y	Y	Y	Y	N	Y	Y
2 Israel	?	?	?	?	?	?	?	?
3 *King*	N	Y	N	N	N	Y	Y	Y
4 McCarthy	Y	Y	Y	Y	Y	N	Y	Y
5 Ackerman	Y	Y	Y	Y	Y	N	Y	Y
6 Meeks	Y	Y	Y	Y	Y	N	Y	Y
7 Crowley	Y	Y	Y	Y	Y	N	Y	Y
8 Nadler	Y	Y	Y	Y	Y	N	Y	Y
9 Weiner	Y	Y	Y	Y	Y	N	Y	Y
10 Towns	Y	N	Y	Y	Y	N	Y	Y
11 Owens	Y	Y	Y	Y	Y	N	Y	Y
12 Velázquez	Y	N	Y	N	N	N	Y	Y
13 *Fossella*	N	Y	N	N	N	Y	Y	Y
14 Maloney	Y	Y	Y	Y	Y	N	Y	Y
15 Rangel	Y	N	Y	Y	Y	N	Y	Y
16 Serrano	Y	N	Y	Y	Y	N	Y	Y
17 Engel	Y	Y	Y	Y	Y	N	Y	Y
18 Lowey	Y	Y	Y	Y	Y	N	Y	Y
19 *Kelly*	N	Y	N	N	N	Y	Y	Y
20 *Sweeney*	N	Y	N	N	N	Y	Y	Y
21 McNulty	Y	Y	Y	Y	Y	N	Y	Y
22 Hinchey	Y	N	Y	Y	Y	N	Y	Y
23 *McHugh*	N	Y	N	N	N	Y	Y	Y
24 *Boehlert*	N	Y	N	N	N	Y	Y	Y
25 *Walsh*	N	Y	N	N	N	Y	Y	Y

	169	170	171	172	173	174	175	176
26 *Reynolds*	N	Y	N	N	N	Y	Y	Y
27 *Quinn*	?	?	?	N	N	Y	Y	Y
28 Slaughter	Y	Y	Y	Y	Y	N	Y	Y
29 *Houghton*	N	N	N	N	N	Y	Y	Y
NORTH CAROLINA								
1 Ballance	Y	N	Y	Y	Y	N	Y	Y
2 Etheridge	Y	Y	Y	Y	Y	N	Y	Y
3 *Jones*	N	Y	N	N	N	Y	Y	Y
4 Price	Y	Y	Y	Y	Y	N	Y	Y
5 *Burr*	N	Y	N	N	N	Y	Y	Y
6 *Coble*	N	Y	N	N	N	Y	Y	Y
7 McIntyre	Y	Y	Y	N	Y	Y	Y	Y
8 *Hayes*	N	Y	N	N	N	Y	Y	Y
9 *Myrick*	N	Y	N	N	N	Y	Y	Y
10 *Ballenger*	N	Y	N	N	N	Y	Y	Y
11 *Taylor*	N	Y	N	N	N	Y	Y	Y
12 Watt	Y	N	Y	Y	Y	N	Y	Y
13 Miller	Y	Y	Y	Y	Y	N	Y	Y
NORTH DAKOTA								
AL Pomeroy	Y	Y	Y	Y	Y	N	Y	Y
OHIO								
1 *Chabot*	N	Y	N	N	N	Y	Y	Y
2 *Portman*	N	Y	N	N	N	Y	Y	Y
3 *Turner*	N	Y	N	N	N	Y	Y	Y
4 *Oxley*	N	Y	N	N	N	Y	Y	Y
5 *Gillmor*	N	Y	N	N	N	Y	Y	Y
6 Strickland	Y	Y	Y	Y	Y	N	Y	Y
7 *Hobson*	N	Y	N	N	N	Y	Y	Y
8 *Boehner*	N	Y	N	N	N	Y	Y	Y
9 Kaptur	Y	Y	Y	Y	Y	N	Y	Y
10 Kucinich	Y	N	Y	N	Y	N	Y	Y
11 Jones	Y	Y	Y	Y	Y	N	Y	?
12 *Tiberi*	N	Y	N	N	N	Y	Y	Y
13 Brown	Y	Y	Y	Y	Y	N	Y	Y
14 *LaTourette*	N	Y	N	N	N	Y	Y	Y
15 *Pryce*	N	Y	N	N	N	Y	Y	Y
16 *Regula*	N	Y	N	N	N	Y	Y	Y
17 Ryan	Y	Y	Y	Y	Y	N	Y	Y
18 *Ney*	N	Y	N	N	N	Y	Y	Y
OKLAHOMA								
1 *Sullivan*	N	Y	N	N	N	Y	Y	Y
2 Carson	N	Y	Y	N	Y	Y	Y	Y
3 *Lucas*	N	Y	N	N	N	Y	Y	Y
4 *Cole*	N	Y	N	N	N	Y	Y	Y
5 *Istook*	N	Y	N	N	N	Y	Y	Y
OREGON								
1 Wu	Y	Y	Y	Y	Y	N	Y	Y
2 *Walden*	N	Y	N	N	N	Y	Y	Y
3 Blumenauer	Y	N	Y	Y	Y	N	Y	Y
4 DeFazio	Y	Y	Y	Y	Y	N	Y	Y
5 Hooley	N	Y	Y	Y	Y	N	Y	Y
PENNSYLVANIA								
1 Brady	Y	N	Y	Y	Y	N	Y	Y
2 Fattah	Y	N	Y	Y	Y	N	Y	Y
3 *English*	N	Y	N	N	N	Y	Y	Y
4 *Hart*	N	Y	N	N	N	Y	Y	Y
5 *Peterson*	N	Y	N	N	N	Y	Y	Y
6 *Gerlach*	N	Y	N	N	N	Y	Y	Y
7 *Weldon*	N	Y	N	N	N	Y	Y	Y
8 *Greenwood*	N	Y	Y	N	N	Y	Y	Y
9 *Shuster, Bill*	N	Y	N	N	N	Y	Y	Y
10 *Sherwood*	N	Y	N	N	N	Y	Y	Y
11 Kanjorski	N	N	Y	Y	Y	N	Y	Y
12 Murtha	N	N	?	Y	Y	N	Y	Y
13 Hoeffel	Y	Y	Y	Y	Y	N	Y	Y
14 Doyle	Y	N	Y	Y	Y	N	Y	Y
15 *Toomey*	N	Y	N	N	N	Y	Y	Y
16 *Pitts*	N	Y	N	N	N	Y	Y	Y
17 Holden	Y	Y	Y	Y	Y	N	Y	Y
18 *Murphy*	N	Y	N	N	N	Y	Y	Y
19 *Platts*	N	Y	N	N	N	Y	Y	Y
RHODE ISLAND								
1 Kennedy	Y	Y	Y	Y	Y	N	Y	Y
2 Langevin	Y	Y	Y	Y	Y	N	Y	Y
SOUTH CAROLINA								
1 *Brown*	N	Y	N	N	N	Y	Y	Y
2 *Wilson*	N	Y	N	N	N	Y	Y	Y
3 *Barrett*	N	Y	N	N	N	Y	Y	Y
4 *DeMint*	?	?	?	?	?	?	?	?
5 Spratt	Y	Y	Y	Y	Y	N	Y	Y
6 Clyburn	Y	Y	Y	Y	Y	Y	Y	Y
SOUTH DAKOTA								
AL Vacant								

	169	170	171	172	173	174	175	176
TENNESSEE								
1 *Jenkins*	N	Y	N	N	N	Y	Y	Y
2 *Duncan*	N	Y	N	N	N	Y	Y	Y
3 *Wamp*	N	Y	N	N	N	Y	Y	Y
4 Davis	Y	Y	Y	Y	Y	Y	Y	Y
5 Cooper	Y	N	Y	Y	Y	Y	Y	Y
6 Gordon	Y	Y	Y	Y	Y	N	Y	Y
7 *Blackburn*	N	Y	N	N	N	Y	Y	Y
8 Tanner	Y	N	Y	Y	Y	N	Y	Y
9 Ford	Y	Y	Y	?	Y	N	Y	Y
TEXAS								
1 Sandlin	N	Y	Y	Y	Y	N	Y	Y
2 Turner	Y	N	Y	Y	Y	Y	Y	Y
3 *Johnson, Sam*	N	Y	N	N	N	Y	Y	Y
4 *Hall*	N	Y	N	N	N	Y	Y	Y
5 *Hensarling*	N	Y	N	N	N	Y	Y	Y
6 *Barton*	N	Y	N	N	N	Y	Y	Y
7 *Culberson*	N	Y	N	N	N	Y	Y	Y
8 *Brady*	N	Y	N	N	N	Y	Y	Y
9 Lampson	Y	Y	Y	Y	Y	N	Y	Y
10 Doggett	Y	N	Y	Y	Y	N	Y	Y
11 Edwards	Y	Y	Y	Y	Y	Y	Y	Y
12 *Granger*	N	Y	N	N	?	?	?	?
13 *Thornberry*	N	Y	N	N	N	Y	Y	Y
14 *Paul*	N	Y	N	N	N	Y	Y	N
15 Hinojosa	Y	Y	Y	Y	Y	N	Y	Y
16 Reyes	?	?	?	?	?	?	?	?
17 Stenholm	Y	N	Y	Y	Y	Y	Y	Y
18 Jackson-Lee	Y	Y	Y	Y	Y	Y	Y	Y
19 *Neugebauer*	N	Y	N	N	N	Y	Y	Y
20 Gonzalez	Y	Y	Y	Y	Y	Y	Y	Y
21 *Smith*	N	Y	N	N	N	Y	Y	Y
22 *DeLay*	N	Y	N	N	N	Y	Y	Y
23 *Bonilla*	N	Y	N	N	N	Y	Y	Y
24 Frost	Y	Y	Y	Y	Y	Y	Y	Y
25 Bell	Y	Y	Y	Y	Y	Y	Y	Y
26 *Burgess*	N	Y	N	N	N	Y	Y	Y
27 Ortiz	Y	Y	Y	Y	Y	N	Y	Y
28 Rodriguez	Y	Y	Y	Y	Y	N	?	?
29 Green	Y	Y	Y	Y	Y	N	?	?
30 Johnson, E.B.	Y	Y	Y	Y	Y	Y	Y	Y
31 *Carter*	N	Y	N	N	N	Y	Y	Y
32 *Sessions*	N	Y	N	N	N	Y	Y	Y
UTAH								
1 *Bishop*	N	Y	N	N	N	Y	Y	Y
2 Matheson	N	Y	Y	Y	Y	Y	Y	Y
3 *Cannon*	N	Y	N	N	N	Y	Y	Y
VERMONT								
AL *Sanders*	Y	Y	Y	Y	Y	N	Y	?
VIRGINIA								
1 *Davis, Jo Ann*	N	Y	N	N	N	Y	Y	Y
2 *Schrock*	N	Y	N	N	N	Y	Y	Y
3 Scott	Y	N	Y	Y	Y	N	Y	Y
4 *Forbes*	N	Y	N	N	N	Y	Y	Y
5 *Goode*	N	Y	?	N	N	Y	Y	Y
6 *Goodlatte*	N	Y	N	N	N	Y	Y	Y
7 *Cantor*	N	Y	N	N	N	Y	Y	Y
8 Moran	Y	Y	Y	Y	Y	Y	Y	Y
9 Boucher	Y	Y	Y	Y	Y	Y	Y	Y
10 *Wolf*	N	Y	N	N	N	Y	Y	Y
11 *Davis, T.*	N	Y	N	N	N	Y	Y	Y
WASHINGTON								
1 Inslee	Y	N	Y	Y	Y	N	Y	Y
2 Larsen	Y	N	Y	Y	Y	N	Y	Y
3 Baird	Y	Y	Y	Y	Y	N	Y	Y
4 *Hastings*	N	Y	N	N	N	Y	Y	Y
5 *Nethercutt*	N	Y	N	?	?	?	?	?
6 Dicks	Y	N	Y	Y	Y	N	Y	Y
7 McDermott	Y	N	Y	Y	Y	N	Y	Y
8 *Dunn*	N	Y	N	N	N	Y	Y	Y
9 Smith	Y	N	Y	Y	Y	N	Y	Y
WEST VIRGINIA								
1 Mollohan	N	N	Y	Y	Y	N	Y	Y
2 *Capito*	?	Y	N	N	N	Y	Y	Y
3 Rahall	Y	Y	Y	Y	N	Y	Y	Y
WISCONSIN								
1 *Ryan*	N	Y	N	N	N	Y	Y	Y
2 Baldwin	Y	Y	Y	Y	Y	N	Y	Y
3 Kind	Y	Y	Y	Y	Y	N	Y	Y
4 Kleczka	Y	Y	Y	Y	Y	N	Y	Y
5 *Sensenbrenner*	N	Y	N	N	N	Y	Y	Y
6 *Petri*	N	Y	N	N	N	Y	Y	Y
7 Obey	Y	Y	Y	Y	Y	N	Y	Y
8 *Green*	N	Y	N	N	N	Y	Y	Y
WYOMING								
AL *Cubin*	N	Y	N	N	N	Y	Y	Y

Southern states - Ala., Ark., Fla., Ga., Ky., La., Miss., N.C., Okla., S.C., Tenn., Texas, Va.

Key

		177	178	179	180	181	182	183
37	Millender-McD.	Y	Y	Y	N	N	N	N
38	Napolitano	Y	Y	Y	N	N	N	N
39	Sánchez, Linda	Y	Y	Y	N	N	N	N
40	*Royce*	Y	Y	Y	Y	Y	N	Y
41	*Lewis*	Y	Y	Y	Y	Y	N	Y
42	*Miller, Gary*	Y	Y	Y	Y	Y	N	Y
43	Baca	Y	Y	Y	N	N	N	Y
44	*Calvert*	Y	Y	Y	Y	Y	N	Y
45	*Bono*	Y	Y	Y	Y	Y	N	Y
46	*Rohrabacher*	Y	Y	Y	Y	Y	Y	Y
47	Sánchez, Loretta	Y	Y	Y	N	N	N	Y
48	*Cox*	Y	Y	Y	Y	Y	N	Y
49	*Issa*	Y	Y	Y	Y	Y	N	Y
50	*Cunningham*	Y	Y	Y	Y	Y	N	Y
51	Filner	Y	Y	Y	N	N	N	N
52	*Hunter*	Y	Y	Y	Y	Y	Y	Y
53	Davis	Y	Y	Y	N	N	N	N

COLORADO
		177	178	179	180	181	182	183
1	DeGette	Y	Y	Y	N	N	N	N
2	Udall	Y	Y	Y	N	N	N	N
3	*McInnis*	Y	Y	Y	Y	Y	N	Y
4	*Musgrave*	Y	Y	Y	Y	Y	Y	Y
5	*Hefley*	Y	Y	Y	Y	Y	Y	Y
6	*Tancredo*	Y	Y	Y	Y	Y	Y	Y
7	*Beauprez*	Y	Y	Y	Y	Y	N	Y

CONNECTICUT
		177	178	179	180	181	182	183
1	Larson	Y	Y	Y	N	N	N	N
2	*Simmons*	Y	Y	Y	Y	Y	N	N
3	DeLauro	Y	Y	Y	N	N	N	N
4	*Shays*	?	?	?	?	?	?	Y
5	*Johnson*	Y	Y	Y	Y	Y	N	N

DELAWARE
		177	178	179	180	181	182	183
AL	*Castle*	Y	Y	Y	Y	Y	N	Y

FLORIDA
		177	178	179	180	181	182	183
1	*Miller, J.*	Y	Y	Y	Y	Y	Y	Y
2	Boyd	Y	Y	Y	N	N	N	N
3	Brown	?	?	?	?	?	?	N
4	*Crenshaw*	Y	Y	Y	Y	Y	N	Y
5	*Brown-Waite*	Y	Y	Y	Y	Y	N	Y
6	*Stearns*	Y	Y	Y	Y	Y	N	Y
7	*Mica*	Y	Y	Y	Y	Y	Y	Y
8	*Keller*	Y	Y	Y	Y	Y	N	Y
9	*Bilirakis*	Y	Y	Y	Y	Y	N	Y
10	*Young*	Y	Y	Y	N	N	N	Y
11	Davis	Y	Y	Y	N	N	N	N
12	*Putnam*	Y	Y	Y	Y	Y	N	Y
13	*Harris*	Y	Y	Y	Y	Y	N	Y
14	*Goss*	Y	Y	Y	Y	Y	N	Y
15	*Weldon*	Y	Y	Y	Y	Y	Y	Y
16	*Foley*	Y	Y	Y	Y	Y	N	Y
17	Meek	Y	Y	Y	N	N	N	N
18	*Ros-Lehtinen*	?	?	?	Y	Y	N	Y
19	Wexler	Y	Y	Y	?	?	?	Y
20	Deutsch	Y	Y	Y	?	?	?	?
21	*Diaz-Balart, L.*	Y	Y	Y	Y	Y	N	Y
22	*Shaw*	Y	Y	Y	Y	Y	N	Y
23	Hastings	Y	Y	Y	N	N	N	N
24	*Feeney*	Y	Y	Y	Y	Y	Y	Y
25	*Diaz-Balart, M.*	Y	Y	Y	Y	Y	N	Y

GEORGIA
		177	178	179	180	181	182	183
1	*Kingston*	Y	Y	Y	Y	Y	Y	Y
2	Bishop	Y	Y	Y	N	N	N	N
3	Marshall	Y	Y	Y	N	N	N	N
4	Majette	Y	Y	Y	N	N	N	N
5	Lewis	Y	Y	Y	?	N	N	N
6	*Isakson*	?	?	?	Y	Y	Y	Y
7	*Linder*	Y	Y	Y	Y	Y	Y	Y
8	*Collins*	?	?	?	Y	Y	Y	Y
9	*Norwood*	Y	Y	Y	Y	Y	Y	Y
10	*Deal*	Y	Y	Y	Y	Y	Y	Y
11	*Gingrey*	?	?	?	Y	Y	Y	Y
12	*Burns*	Y	Y	Y	Y	Y	N	Y
13	Scott	Y	Y	Y	N	N	N	N

HAWAII
		177	178	179	180	181	182	183
1	Abercrombie	Y	Y	Y	N	N	N	N
2	Case	Y	Y	Y	N	N	N	N

IDAHO
		177	178	179	180	181	182	183
1	*Otter*	Y	Y	Y	Y	Y	Y	Y
2	*Simpson*	Y	Y	Y	Y	Y	Y	Y

ILLINOIS
		177	178	179	180	181	182	183
1	Rush	?	?	?	N	N	N	N
2	Jackson	?	?	?	N	N	N	N
3	Lipinski	?	?	?	N	N	N	N
4	Gutierrez	?	?	?	N	N	N	N
5	Emanuel	Y	Y	Y	N	N	N	N
6	*Hyde*	Y	Y	Y	Y	Y	N	Y

ND Northern Democrats   SD Southern Democrats

---

177. H Con Res 420. National Transportation Week/Adoption. Porter, R-Nev., motion to suspend the rules and adopt the concurrent resolution that would recognize National Transportation Week and urge Americans to be more aware of the benefits that transportation provides to the U.S. economy. Motion agreed to 360-0: R 195-0; D 165-0 (ND 117-0, SD 48-0), I 0-0. A two-thirds majority of those present and voting (240 in this case) is required for adoption under suspension of the rules. May 17, 2004.

178. H Con Res 423. World War II Memorial/Adoption. Porter, R-Nev., motion to suspend the rules and adopt the concurrent resolution that would authorize the use of the U.S. Capitol for an event in conjunction with the dedication of the World War II Memorial on May 29. Motion agreed to 364-0: R 198-0; D 166-0 (ND 118-0, SD 48-0); I 0-0. A two-thirds majority of those present and voting (243 in this case) is required for adoption under suspension of the rules. May 17, 2004.

179. H Con Res 403. Condemnation of Attacks in Sudan/Adoption. Green, R-Wis., motion to suspend the rules and adopt the concurrent resolution that would condemn the Sudanese government for its attacks against civilians in the Darfur region of western Sudan and demand an immediate stop to the attacks. Motion agreed to 360-1: R 195-1; D 165-0 (ND 118-0, SD 47-0); I 0-0. A two-thirds majority of those present and voting (241 in this case) is required for adoption under suspension of the rules. May 17, 2004.

180. HR 2728, HR 2729, HR 2730, HR 2731, HR 2432. Workplace Safety Bills/Rule. Adoption of the rule (H Res 645) to provide for House floor consideration of four bills that would change the way the Occupational Safety and Health Administration (OSHA) regulates companies and a bill aimed at reducing the paperwork required by federal agencies, such as the IRS. The rule specifies that if more than one of the bills passes the House, the text of those bills will be combined into a single measure. Adopted 219-195: R 219-0; D 0-194 (ND 0-142, SD 0-52); I 0-1. May 18, 2004.

181. HR 2660. Fiscal 2004 Labor-HHS-Education Appropriations/ Motion to Instruct. DeLay, R-Texas, motion to table (kill) the Miller, D-Calif., motion to instruct House conferees to keep the Senate language that would block the Labor Department from implementing any portion of the new overtime pay rules that would deny premium pay to an employee who would otherwise qualify for such pay. Motion agreed to 216-199: R 216-1; D 0-197 (ND 0-143, SD 0-54); I 0-1. May 18, 2004.

182. HR 3722. Emergency Medical Care for Illegal Aliens/Passage. Barton, R-Texas, motion to suspend the rules and pass the bill that would require hospitals to collect and report information on potential illegal aliens before being reimbursed for treating them. Employers would be liable for the reimbursements if an undocumented employee seeks medical attention, unless the employer meets certain conditions for exemption. Hospitals would not be required to provide care to undocumented aliens if they could be transported to their home country without significant likelihood of making their condition worse. Motion rejected 88-331: R 86-133; D 2-197 (ND 0-145, SD 2-52); I 0-1. A two-thirds majority of those present and voting (280 in this case) is required for passage under suspension of the rules. May 18, 2004.

183. HR 2728. Workplace Safety Citations/Passage. Passage of the bill that would allow the Occupational Safety and Health Review Commission to make exceptions to the 15-day deadline for employers to respond to a citation from OSHA. Passed 251-177: R 224-0; D 27-176 (ND 8-139, SD 19-37); I 0-1. May 18, 2004.

Key

Y Voted for (yea).
\# Paired for.
\+ Announced for.
N Voted against (nay).
X Paired against.
\– Announced against.
P Voted "present."
C Voted "present" to avoid possible conflict of interest.
? Did not vote or otherwise make a position known.

Democrats **Republicans**
Independents

		177	178	179	180	181	182	183
ALABAMA								
1	*Bonner*	Y	Y	Y	Y	Y	N	Y
2	*Everett*	Y	Y	Y	Y	Y	Y	Y
3	*Rogers*	Y	Y	Y	Y	Y	Y	Y
4	*Aderholt*	Y	Y	Y	Y	Y	Y	Y
5	Cramer	Y	Y	Y	N	N	N	Y
6	*Bachus*	?	?	?	Y	Y	Y	Y
7	Davis	?	?	?	N	N	N	N

		177	178	179	180	181	182	183
ALASKA								
AL	*Young*	Y	Y	Y	?	?	?	Y

		177	178	179	180	181	182	183
ARIZONA								
1	*Renzi*	Y	Y	Y	Y	Y	N	Y
2	*Franks*	Y	Y	Y	Y	?	Y	Y
3	*Shadegg*	Y	Y	Y	Y	Y	N	Y
4	Pastor	Y	Y	Y	N	N	N	N
5	*Hayworth*	Y	Y	Y	Y	Y	Y	Y
6	*Flake*	?	?	?	Y	Y	N	Y
7	Grijalva	Y	Y	Y	N	N	N	N
8	*Kolbe*	Y	Y	Y	Y	Y	N	Y

		177	178	179	180	181	182	183
ARKANSAS								
1	Berry	Y	Y	Y	N	N	N	N
2	Snyder	Y	Y	Y	N	N	N	N
3	*Boozman*	Y	Y	Y	Y	Y	Y	Y
4	Ross	Y	Y	Y	N	N	N	N

		177	178	179	180	181	182	183
CALIFORNIA								
1	Thompson	Y	Y	Y	N	N	N	N
2	*Herger*	Y	Y	Y	Y	Y	?	Y
3	*Ose*	Y	Y	Y	Y	Y	N	Y
4	*Doolittle*	Y	Y	Y	Y	Y	Y	Y
5	Matsui	Y	Y	Y	N	N	N	N
6	Woolsey	?	?	?	N	N	N	N
7	Miller, George	Y	Y	Y	N	N	N	N
8	Pelosi	Y	Y	Y	N	N	N	N
9	Lee	Y	Y	Y	N	N	N	N
10	Tauscher	Y	Y	Y	N	N	N	N
11	*Pombo*	Y	Y	Y	Y	Y	N	Y
12	Lantos	Y	Y	Y	N	N	N	N
13	Stark	Y	Y	Y	N	N	N	N
14	Eshoo	Y	Y	Y	N	N	N	N
15	Honda	Y	Y	Y	N	N	N	N
16	Lofgren	Y	Y	Y	N	N	N	N
17	Farr	Y	Y	Y	N	N	N	N
18	Cardoza	Y	Y	Y	N	N	N	N
19	*Radanovich*	Y	Y	Y	Y	Y	Y	Y
20	Dooley	Y	Y	Y	N	N	N	Y
21	*Nunes*	Y	Y	Y	Y	Y	N	Y
22	*Thomas*	Y	Y	Y	Y	Y	N	Y
23	Capps	Y	Y	Y	N	N	N	N
24	*Gallegly*	Y	Y	Y	Y	Y	Y	Y
25	*McKeon*	Y	Y	Y	Y	Y	N	Y
26	*Dreier*	Y	Y	Y	Y	Y	N	Y
27	Sherman	Y	Y	Y	N	N	N	N
28	Berman	Y	Y	Y	?	?	N	N
29	Schiff	Y	Y	Y	N	N	N	N
30	Waxman	Y	Y	Y	N	N	N	N
31	Becerra	?	?	?	N	N	N	N
32	Solis	Y	Y	Y	N	N	N	N
33	Watson	Y	Y	Y	N	N	N	N
34	Roybal-Allard	Y	Y	Y	N	N	N	N
35	Waters	Y	Y	Y	N	N	N	N
36	Harman	Y	Y	Y	N	N	N	Y

	177	178	179	180	181	182	183
7 Davis	Y	Y	Y	N	N	N	N
8 **Crane**	Y	Y	Y	Y	Y	N	Y
9 Schakowsky	Y	Y	Y	N	N	N	N
10 **Kirk**	Y	Y	Y	Y	Y	N	Y
11 **Weller**	Y	Y	Y	Y	Y	N	Y
12 Costello	Y	Y	Y	N	N	N	N
13 **Biggert**	Y	Y	Y	Y	Y	N	Y
14 **Hastert**							
15 **Johnson**	?	Y	Y	Y	N	N	Y
16 **Manzullo**	Y	Y	Y	Y	Y	Y	Y
17 Evans	Y	Y	Y	N	N	N	N
18 **LaHood**	Y	Y	Y	Y	Y	N	Y
19 **Shimkus**	Y	Y	Y	Y	Y	Y	Y
INDIANA							
1 Visclosky	Y	Y	Y	N	N	N	N
2 **Chocola**	Y	Y	Y	Y	Y	N	Y
3 **Souder**	Y	Y	Y	Y	Y	N	Y
4 **Buyer**	Y	Y	Y	Y	Y	Y	Y
5 **Burton**	?	?	?	Y	Y	Y	Y
6 **Pence**	Y	Y	Y	Y	Y	Y	Y
7 Carson	?	?	?	N	N	N	N
8 **Hostettler**	Y	Y	Y	Y	Y	Y	Y
9 Hill	Y	Y	Y	N	N	N	N
IOWA							
1 **Nussle**	Y	Y	Y	Y	Y	N	Y
2 **Leach**	?	?	?	?	?	?	?
3 Boswell	Y	Y	Y	N	N	N	N
4 **Latham**	Y	Y	Y	Y	Y	N	Y
5 **King**	Y	Y	Y	Y	Y	Y	Y
KANSAS							
1 **Moran**	?	?	?	Y	Y	N	Y
2 **Ryun**	?	?	?	Y	Y	N	Y
3 Moore	?	?	?	N	N	N	N
4 **Tiahrt**	?	?	?	Y	Y	N	Y
KENTUCKY							
1 **Whitfield**	Y	Y	Y	Y	Y	Y	Y
2 **Lewis**	Y	Y	Y	Y	Y	N	Y
3 **Northup**	Y	Y	Y	Y	Y	N	Y
4 Lucas	Y	Y	Y	N	N	N	Y
5 **Rogers**	Y	Y	Y	Y	Y	N	Y
6 Chandler	Y	Y	Y	N	N	N	N
LOUISIANA							
1 **Vitter**	Y	Y	Y	Y	Y	Y	Y
2 Jefferson	Y	Y	Y	N	N	N	N
3 **Tauzin**	?	?	?	?	?	?	?
4 **McCrery**	Y	Y	Y	Y	Y	Y	Y
5 Alexander	Y	Y	Y	N	N	N	N
6 **Baker**	Y	Y	Y	Y	Y	N	Y
7 John	Y	Y	Y	N	N	N	Y
MAINE							
1 Allen	?	?	?	N	N	N	N
2 Michaud	Y	Y	Y	N	N	N	N
MARYLAND							
1 **Gilchrest**	Y	Y	Y	Y	Y	N	Y
2 Ruppersberger	Y	Y	Y	N	N	N	N
3 Cardin	Y	Y	Y	N	N	N	Y
4 Wynn	Y	Y	Y	N	N	N	Y
5 Hoyer	Y	Y	Y	N	N	N	N
6 **Bartlett**	Y	Y	Y	Y	Y	N	Y
7 Cummings	?	?	?	N	N	N	N
8 Van Hollen	Y	Y	Y	N	N	N	N
MASSACHUSETTS							
1 Olver	Y	Y	Y	N	N	N	N
2 Neal	?	?	?	N	N	N	N
3 McGovern	Y	Y	Y	N	N	N	N
4 Frank	Y	Y	Y	N	N	N	N
5 Meehan	Y	Y	Y	N	N	N	N
6 Tierney	Y	Y	Y	N	N	N	N
7 Markey	Y	Y	Y	N	N	N	N
8 Capuano	Y	Y	Y	N	N	N	N
9 Lynch	Y	Y	Y	N	N	N	N
10 Delahunt	Y	Y	Y	N	N	N	N
MICHIGAN							
1 Stupak	Y	Y	Y	N	N	N	N
2 **Hoekstra**	Y	Y	Y	Y	Y	Y	Y
3 **Ehlers**	Y	Y	Y	Y	Y	N	Y
4 **Camp**	Y	Y	Y	Y	Y	N	Y
5 Kildee	Y	Y	Y	N	N	N	N
6 **Upton**	Y	Y	Y	Y	Y	N	Y
7 **Smith**	Y	Y	Y	Y	?	N	Y
8 **Rogers**	?	?	?	Y	Y	N	Y
9 **Knollenberg**	?	?	?	Y	Y	N	Y
10 **Miller**	Y	Y	Y	Y	Y	N	Y
11 **McCotter**	Y	Y	Y	Y	Y	Y	Y
12 Levin	Y	Y	Y	N	N	N	N
13 Kilpatrick	?	?	?	N	N	N	N
14 Conyers	Y	Y	Y	N	N	N	N
15 Dingell	Y	Y	Y	N	N	N	N
MINNESOTA							
1 **Gutknecht**	?	Y	Y	Y	Y	Y	Y
2 **Kline**	Y	Y	Y	Y	Y	Y	Y
3 **Ramstad**	Y	Y	Y	Y	Y	Y	Y
4 McCollum	Y	Y	Y	N	N	N	N
5 Sabo	Y	Y	Y	N	N	N	N
6 **Kennedy**	Y	Y	Y	Y	Y	N	Y
7 Peterson	Y	Y	Y	N	N	N	N
8 Oberstar	?	?	?	?	?	?	N
MISSISSIPPI							
1 **Wicker**	Y	Y	Y	Y	Y	Y	Y
2 Thompson	Y	Y	Y	N	N	N	N
3 **Pickering**	Y	Y	Y	Y	Y	N	Y
4 Taylor	Y	Y	Y	N	N	Y	Y
MISSOURI							
1 Clay	?	?	?	N	N	N	N
2 **Akin**	Y	Y	Y	Y	Y	Y	Y
3 Gephardt	?	?	?	N	N	N	?
4 Skelton	Y	Y	Y	N	N	N	Y
5 McCarthy	Y	Y	Y	N	N	N	N
6 **Graves**	Y	Y	Y	Y	Y	N	Y
7 **Blunt**	Y	Y	Y	Y	Y	N	Y
8 **Emerson**	Y	Y	Y	Y	Y	N	Y
9 **Hulshof**	Y	Y	Y	Y	Y	Y	Y
MONTANA							
AL **Rehberg**	Y	Y	Y	Y	Y	Y	Y
NEBRASKA							
1 **Bereuter**	Y	Y	Y	Y	Y	Y	Y
2 **Terry**	Y	Y	Y	Y	Y	N	Y
3 **Osborne**	Y	Y	Y	Y	Y	N	Y
NEVADA							
1 Berkley	Y	Y	Y	N	N	N	N
2 **Gibbons**	Y	Y	Y	Y	Y	Y	Y
3 **Porter**	Y	Y	Y	Y	Y	N	Y
NEW HAMPSHIRE							
1 **Bradley**	Y	Y	Y	Y	Y	Y	Y
2 **Bass**	Y	Y	Y	Y	Y	Y	Y
NEW JERSEY							
1 Andrews	?	?	?	?	?	?	N
2 **LoBiondo**	Y	Y	Y	Y	Y	N	Y
3 **Saxton**	Y	Y	Y	Y	Y	N	Y
4 **Smith**	Y	Y	Y	Y	Y	N	Y
5 **Garrett**	Y	Y	Y	Y	Y	Y	Y
6 Pallone	Y	Y	Y	N	N	N	N
7 **Ferguson**	Y	Y	Y	Y	Y	N	Y
8 Pascrell	Y	Y	Y	N	N	N	N
9 Rothman	Y	Y	Y	N	N	N	N
10 Payne	?	?	?	N	N	N	N
11 **Frelinghuysen**	Y	Y	Y	Y	Y	N	Y
12 Holt	Y	Y	Y	N	N	N	N
13 Menendez	Y	Y	Y	N	N	N	N
NEW MEXICO							
1 **Wilson**	Y	Y	Y	Y	Y	N	Y
2 **Pearce**	Y	Y	Y	Y	Y	N	Y
3 Udall	Y	Y	Y	N	N	N	N
NEW YORK							
1 Bishop	Y	Y	Y	N	N	N	N
2 Israel	Y	Y	Y	N	N	N	N
3 **King**	Y	Y	Y	Y	Y	N	Y
4 McCarthy	Y	Y	Y	N	N	N	N
5 Ackerman	Y	Y	Y	N	N	N	N
6 Meeks	?	?	?	N	N	N	N
7 Crowley	Y	Y	Y	N	N	N	N
8 Nadler	Y	Y	Y	N	N	N	N
9 Weiner	?	?	?	N	N	N	N
10 Towns	?	?	?	?	?	N	N
11 Owens	?	?	?	N	N	N	N
12 Velázquez	?	?	?	N	N	N	N
13 **Fossella**	?	?	?	Y	Y	N	Y
14 Maloney	?	Y	Y	N	N	N	N
15 Rangel	?	?	?	?	?	?	N
16 Serrano	Y	Y	Y	N	N	N	N
17 Engel	Y	Y	Y	N	N	N	N
18 Lowey	?	?	?	?	N	N	N
19 **Kelly**	Y	Y	Y	Y	Y	Y	Y
20 **Sweeney**	?	?	?	Y	Y	N	Y
21 McNulty	Y	Y	Y	N	N	N	N
22 Hinchey	Y	Y	Y	N	N	N	N
23 **McHugh**	Y	Y	Y	Y	Y	Y	Y
24 **Boehlert**	Y	Y	Y	Y	Y	N	Y
25 **Walsh**	Y	Y	Y	Y	Y	N	Y
26 **Reynolds**	Y	Y	Y	Y	Y	N	Y
27 **Quinn**	Y	Y	Y	Y	Y	N	Y
28 Slaughter	?	?	?	N	N	N	N
29 **Houghton**	Y	Y	Y	Y	Y	N	Y
NORTH CAROLINA							
1 Ballance	Y	Y	Y	N	N	N	N
2 Etheridge	Y	Y	Y	N	N	N	N
3 **Jones**	Y	Y	Y	Y	Y	Y	Y
4 Price	?	?	?	N	N	N	N
5 **Burr**	?	?	?	Y	Y	N	Y
6 **Coble**	Y	Y	Y	Y	Y	Y	Y
7 McIntyre	Y	Y	Y	N	N	N	Y
8 **Hayes**	Y	Y	Y	Y	Y	Y	Y
9 **Myrick**	Y	Y	Y	Y	Y	Y	Y
10 **Ballenger**	Y	Y	Y	Y	Y	N	Y
11 **Taylor**	?	?	?	Y	Y	Y	Y
12 Watt	Y	Y	Y	N	N	N	N
13 Miller	?	?	?	N	N	N	N
NORTH DAKOTA							
AL Pomeroy	?	?	?	N	N	N	N
OHIO							
1 **Chabot**	Y	Y	Y	Y	Y	N	Y
2 **Portman**	Y	Y	Y	Y	Y	N	Y
3 **Turner**	Y	Y	Y	Y	Y	N	Y
4 **Oxley**	Y	Y	?	Y	Y	N	Y
5 **Gillmor**	Y	Y	Y	Y	Y	N	Y
6 Strickland	Y	Y	Y	N	N	N	N
7 **Hobson**	Y	Y	Y	Y	Y	N	Y
8 **Boehner**	Y	Y	Y	Y	Y	N	Y
9 Kaptur	Y	Y	Y	N	N	N	N
10 Kucinich	?	?	?	N	N	N	N
11 Jones	Y	Y	Y	N	N	N	N
12 **Tiberi**	Y	Y	Y	Y	Y	N	Y
13 Brown	Y	Y	Y	N	N	N	N
14 **LaTourette**	Y	Y	Y	Y	Y	N	Y
15 **Pryce**	?	?	?	Y	Y	N	Y
16 **Regula**	Y	Y	Y	Y	Y	N	Y
17 Ryan	Y	Y	Y	N	N	N	N
18 **Ney**	?	?	?	Y	Y	N	Y
OKLAHOMA							
1 **Sullivan**	Y	Y	Y	Y	Y	Y	Y
2 Carson	?	?	?	N	N	N	N
3 **Lucas**	Y	Y	Y	Y	Y	N	Y
4 **Cole**	Y	Y	Y	Y	Y	N	Y
5 **Istook**	?	?	?	?	?	?	Y
OREGON							
1 Wu	Y	Y	Y	N	N	N	N
2 **Walden**	Y	Y	Y	Y	Y	N	Y
3 Blumenauer	?	?	?	N	N	N	N
4 DeFazio	?	?	?	N	N	N	N
5 Hooley	Y	Y	Y	N	N	N	N
PENNSYLVANIA							
1 Brady	?	?	?	N	N	N	N
2 Fattah	Y	Y	Y	N	N	N	N
3 **English**	?	?	?	Y	Y	N	Y
4 **Hart**	Y	Y	Y	Y	Y	N	Y
5 **Peterson**	?	?	?	Y	?	N	Y
6 **Gerlach**	Y	Y	Y	Y	Y	Y	Y
7 **Weldon**	Y	Y	Y	Y	Y	N	Y
8 **Greenwood**	Y	Y	Y	Y	Y	N	Y
9 **Shuster, Bill**	Y	Y	Y	Y	Y	Y	Y
10 **Sherwood**	Y	Y	Y	Y	Y	N	Y
11 Kanjorski	Y	Y	Y	N	N	N	N
12 Murtha	?	?	?	N	N	N	N
13 Hoeffel	Y	Y	Y	N	N	N	N
14 Doyle	Y	Y	Y	N	N	N	N
15 **Toomey**	Y	Y	Y	Y	Y	Y	Y
16 **Pitts**	Y	Y	Y	Y	Y	Y	Y
17 Holden	Y	Y	Y	N	N	N	N
18 **Murphy**	Y	Y	Y	Y	Y	N	Y
19 **Platts**	?	Y	Y	Y	Y	Y	Y
RHODE ISLAND							
1 Kennedy	Y	Y	Y	N	N	N	N
2 Langevin	Y	Y	Y	N	N	N	N
SOUTH CAROLINA							
1 **Brown**	Y	Y	Y	Y	Y	N	Y
2 **Wilson**	Y	Y	Y	Y	Y	Y	Y
3 **Barrett**	Y	Y	Y	Y	Y	Y	Y
4 **DeMint**	?	?	?	?	?	?	?
5 Spratt	Y	Y	Y	N	N	N	Y
6 Clyburn	?	?	?	N	N	N	N
SOUTH DAKOTA							
AL Vacant							
TENNESSEE							
1 **Jenkins**	?	?	?	Y	Y	Y	Y
2 **Duncan**	Y	Y	Y	Y	Y	Y	Y
3 **Wamp**	?	?	?	Y	Y	Y	Y
4 Davis	Y	Y	Y	N	N	N	Y
5 Cooper	Y	Y	Y	N	N	N	Y
6 Gordon	Y	Y	Y	N	N	N	Y
7 **Blackburn**	Y	Y	Y	Y	Y	Y	Y
8 Tanner	?	?	?	N	N	N	Y
9 Ford	Y	Y	Y	N	N	N	N
TEXAS							
1 Sandlin	Y	Y	Y	N	N	N	Y
2 Turner	Y	Y	Y	N	N	N	Y
3 **Johnson, Sam**	Y	Y	Y	Y	Y	Y	Y
4 **Hall**	Y	Y	Y	Y	Y	Y	Y
5 **Hensarling**	Y	Y	?	Y	Y	N	Y
6 **Barton**	Y	Y	Y	Y	Y	N	Y
7 **Culberson**	Y	Y	Y	Y	Y	Y	Y
8 **Brady**	Y	Y	Y	Y	Y	N	Y
9 Lampson	Y	Y	?	N	N	N	N
10 Doggett	Y	Y	Y	N	N	N	N
11 Edwards	Y	Y	Y	N	N	N	Y
12 **Granger**	Y	Y	Y	Y	Y	N	Y
13 **Thornberry**	Y	Y	Y	Y	Y	N	Y
14 **Paul**	Y	Y	N	Y	Y	Y	Y
15 Hinojosa	Y	Y	Y	N	N	N	N
16 Reyes	?	?	?	N	N	N	N
17 Stenholm	Y	Y	Y	N	N	N	Y
18 Jackson-Lee	Y	Y	Y	N	N	N	N
19 **Neugebauer**	Y	Y	Y	Y	Y	N	Y
20 Gonzalez	Y	Y	Y	N	N	N	Y
21 **Smith**	?	?	?	Y	Y	Y	Y
22 **DeLay**	Y	Y	Y	Y	Y	N	Y
23 **Bonilla**	Y	Y	Y	Y	Y	N	Y
24 Frost	Y	Y	Y	N	N	N	N
25 Bell	?	?	?	N	N	N	N
26 **Burgess**	Y	Y	Y	Y	Y	Y	Y
27 Ortiz	Y	Y	Y	N	N	N	N
28 Rodriguez	Y	Y	Y	N	N	N	N
29 Green	Y	Y	Y	N	N	N	N
30 Johnson, E.B.	Y	Y	Y	N	N	N	N
31 **Carter**	Y	Y	Y	Y	Y	Y	Y
32 **Sessions**	Y	Y	Y	Y	Y	N	Y
UTAH							
1 **Bishop**	Y	Y	Y	Y	Y	Y	Y
2 Matheson	Y	Y	Y	N	N	N	Y
3 **Cannon**	Y	Y	Y	Y	Y	N	Y
VERMONT							
AL Sanders	?	?	?	N	N	N	N
VIRGINIA							
1 **Davis, Jo Ann**	Y	Y	Y	Y	Y	N	Y
2 **Schrock**	Y	Y	Y	Y	Y	Y	Y
3 Scott	Y	Y	Y	N	N	N	N
4 **Forbes**	?	?	?	?	?	?	Y
5 **Goode**	Y	Y	Y	Y	Y	Y	Y
6 **Goodlatte**	Y	Y	Y	Y	Y	Y	Y
7 **Cantor**	Y	Y	Y	Y	Y	Y	Y
8 Moran	Y	Y	Y	N	N	N	N
9 Boucher	Y	Y	Y	?	N	Y	N
10 **Wolf**	Y	Y	Y	Y	Y	N	Y
11 **Davis, T.**	Y	Y	Y	Y	Y	N	Y
WASHINGTON							
1 Inslee	Y	Y	Y	N	N	N	N
2 Larsen	Y	Y	Y	N	N	N	N
3 Baird	Y	Y	Y	N	N	N	N
4 **Hastings**	Y	Y	Y	Y	Y	N	Y
5 **Nethercutt**	Y	Y	Y	Y	Y	N	Y
6 Dicks	Y	Y	Y	N	N	N	N
7 McDermott	Y	Y	Y	N	N	N	N
8 **Dunn**	Y	Y	Y	?	Y	N	Y
9 Smith	Y	Y	Y	N	N	N	N
WEST VIRGINIA							
1 Mollohan	Y	Y	Y	N	N	N	N
2 **Capito**	Y	Y	Y	Y	Y	N	Y
3 Rahall	Y	Y	Y	N	N	N	Y
WISCONSIN							
1 **Ryan**	Y	Y	Y	Y	Y	N	Y
2 Baldwin	Y	Y	Y	N	N	N	N
3 Kind	Y	Y	Y	N	N	N	N
4 Kleczka	Y	Y	Y	N	N	N	N
5 **Sensenbrenner**	Y	Y	Y	Y	Y	Y	Y
6 **Petri**	Y	Y	Y	Y	Y	N	Y
7 Obey	Y	Y	Y	N	N	N	N
8 **Green**	Y	Y	Y	Y	Y	N	Y
WYOMING							
AL **Cubin**	Y	Y	Y	Y	Y	N	Y

Southern states - Ala., Ark., Fla., Ga., Ky., La., Miss., N.C., Okla., S.C., Tenn., Texas, Va.

Key

Y	Voted for (yea).
#	Paired for.
+	Announced for.
N	Voted against (nay).
X	Paired against.
–	Announced against.
P	Voted "present."
C	Voted "present" to avoid possible conflict of interest.
?	Did not vote or otherwise make a position known.

Democrats   ***Republicans***

Independents

184. HR 2729. Occupational Safety and Health Review Commission/Passage. Passage of the bill that would expand the membership of the Occupational Safety and Health Review Commission from three to five members. Passed 228-199: R 222-0; D 6-198 (ND 1-147, SD 5-51); I 0-1. May 18, 2004.

185. HR 2730. Occupational Safety and Health Review Commission Rulings/Passage. Passage of the bill that would require courts and judges to defer to Occupational Safety and Health Review Commission rulings when interpreting questions of law. The commission hears appeals of OSHA violations. Passed 224-204: R 215-8; D 9-195 (ND 2-146, SD 7-49); I 0-1. May 18, 2004.

186. HR 3740. Oscar Scott Woody Post Office/Passage. Murphy, R-Pa., motion to suspend the rules and pass the bill that would name a post office building in Roxboro, N.C., after the late Oscar Scott Woody, a post office employee who died when the R.M.S. *Titanic* sank in 1912. Motion agreed to 422-0: R 220-0; D 201-0 (ND 145-0, SD 56-0); I 1-0. A two-thirds majority of those present and voting (282 in this case) is required for passage under suspension of the rules. May 18, 2004.

187. HR 2432. Paperwork Reduction/Politicization of Science. Waxman, D-Calif., amendment that would establish a commission to evaluate executive branch regulatory activities and decisions to determine whether political considerations have undermined the quality and use of science. It would authorize $5 million for the commission to carry out its duties. Rejected 201-226: R 1-221; D 199-5 (ND 147-1, SD 52-4); I 1-0. May 18, 2004.

188. HR 2432. Paperwork Reduction/Passage. Passage of the bill that would require each federal agency to provide the Office of Management and Budget (OMB) an annual cost-benefit estimate of all its required paperwork. It also would require the IRS to identify ways that it could reduce the paperwork burden on small businesses. Passed 373-54: R 222-0; D 150-54 (ND 96-52, SD 54-2); I 1-0. May 18, 2004.

189. HR 2731. Small-Business Attorneys' Fees/Passage. Passage of the bill that would allow courts to reimburse small businesses for their attorney fees if they successfully contest an OSHA ruling. Current law permits such reimbursement only if the court finds that OSHA was not "substantially justified" in its ruling. Passed 233-194: R 217-5; D 16-188 (ND 4-144, SD 12-44); I 0-1. May 18, 2004.

190. HR 4176. Bobby Marshall Gentry Post Office/Passage. Murphy, R-Pa., motion to suspend the rules and pass the bill that would name a post office building in Raeford, N.C., after the late Bobby Marshall Gentry, the former mayor of Raeford. Motion agreed to 421-0: R 220-0; D 200-0 (ND 146-0, SD 54-0); I 1-0. A two-thirds majority of those present and voting (281 in this case) is required for passage under suspension of the rules. May 18, 2004.

	184	185	186	187	188	189	190
ALABAMA							
1 *Bonner*	Y	Y	Y	N	Y	Y	Y
2 *Everett*	Y	Y	Y	N	Y	Y	Y
3 *Rogers*	Y	Y	Y	N	Y	Y	Y
4 *Aderholt*	Y	Y	Y	N	Y	Y	Y
5 Cramer	Y	Y	Y	N	Y	Y	Y
6 *Bachus*	Y	Y	Y	N	Y	Y	Y
7 Davis	N	N	Y	Y	Y	N	?
ALASKA							
AL *Young*	Y	Y	Y	N	Y	Y	Y
ARIZONA							
1 *Renzi*	Y	Y	Y	N	Y	Y	Y
2 *Franks*	Y	Y	Y	N	Y	Y	Y
3 *Shadegg*	Y	Y	Y	N	Y	Y	Y
4 Pastor	N	N	Y	Y	N	N	Y
5 *Hayworth*	Y	Y	Y	?	?	?	?
6 *Flake*	Y	Y	Y	N	Y	N	Y
7 Grijalva	N	N	Y	Y	N	N	Y
8 *Kolbe*	Y	Y	Y	N	Y	Y	Y
ARKANSAS							
1 Berry	N	N	Y	Y	Y	N	Y
2 Snyder	N	N	Y	Y	N	N	Y
3 *Boozman*	Y	Y	Y	N	Y	Y	Y
4 Ross	N	N	Y	Y	Y	N	Y
CALIFORNIA							
1 Thompson	N	N	Y	Y	Y	N	Y
2 *Herger*	Y	Y	Y	N	Y	Y	Y
3 *Ose*	Y	Y	Y	N	Y	Y	Y
4 *Doolittle*	Y	Y	Y	N	Y	Y	Y
5 Matsui	N	N	Y	Y	N	N	Y
6 Woolsey	N	N	Y	Y	N	N	Y
7 Miller, George	N	N	Y	Y	N	N	Y
8 Pelosi	N	N	Y	Y	N	N	Y
9 Lee	N	N	Y	Y	N	N	Y
10 Tauscher	N	N	Y	Y	N	N	Y
11 *Pombo*	Y	Y	Y	N	Y	Y	Y
12 Lantos	N	N	Y	Y	N	N	Y
13 Stark	N	N	Y	Y	N	N	Y
14 Eshoo	N	N	Y	Y	N	N	Y
15 Honda	N	N	Y	Y	N	N	Y
16 Lofgren	N	N	Y	Y	N	N	Y
17 Farr	N	N	Y	Y	N	N	Y
18 Cardoza	N	N	Y	Y	Y	N	Y
19 *Radanovich*	Y	Y	Y	N	Y	Y	Y
20 Dooley	N	N	Y	Y	Y	N	Y
21 *Nunes*	Y	Y	Y	N	Y	Y	Y
22 *Thomas*	Y	Y	Y	N	Y	Y	Y
23 Capps	N	N	Y	Y	N	N	Y
24 *Gallegly*	Y	Y	Y	N	Y	Y	Y
25 *McKeon*	Y	Y	Y	N	Y	Y	Y
26 *Dreier*	Y	Y	Y	N	Y	Y	Y
27 Sherman	N	N	Y	Y	N	N	Y
28 Berman	N	N	Y	Y	N	N	Y
29 Schiff	N	N	Y	Y	N	N	Y
30 Waxman	N	N	Y	Y	N	N	Y
31 Becerra	N	N	Y	Y	N	N	Y
32 Solis	N	N	Y	Y	N	N	Y
33 Watson	N	N	Y	Y	N	N	Y
34 Roybal-Allard	N	N	Y	Y	N	N	Y
35 Waters	N	N	Y	Y	N	N	Y
36 Harman	N	N	Y	Y	N	N	Y

	184	185	186	187	188	189	190
37 Millender-McD.	N	N	Y	Y	Y	N	Y
38 Napolitano	N	N	Y	Y	N	N	Y
39 Sánchez, Linda	N	N	Y	Y	N	N	Y
40 *Royce*	Y	Y	Y	N	Y	Y	Y
41 *Lewis*	Y	Y	Y	N	Y	Y	Y
42 *Miller, Gary*	Y	Y	Y	N	Y	Y	Y
43 Baca	N	N	Y	Y	N	N	Y
44 *Calvert*	Y	Y	Y	N	Y	Y	Y
45 *Bono*	Y	Y	Y	N	Y	Y	Y
46 *Rohrabacher*	Y	Y	Y	N	Y	Y	Y
47 Sanchez, Loretta	N	N	Y	Y	N	N	Y
48 *Cox*	Y	Y	Y	N	Y	Y	Y
49 *Issa*	Y	Y	Y	N	Y	Y	Y
50 *Cunningham*	Y	Y	Y	N	Y	Y	Y
51 Filner	N	N	Y	Y	N	N	Y
52 *Hunter*	Y	Y	Y	?	Y	Y	Y
53 Davis	N	N	Y	Y	N	Y	Y
COLORADO							
1 DeGette	N	N	Y	Y	N	N	Y
2 Udall	N	N	Y	Y	N	N	Y
3 *McInnis*	Y	Y	Y	N	Y	Y	Y
4 *Musgrave*	Y	Y	Y	N	Y	Y	Y
5 *Hefley*	Y	Y	Y	N	Y	Y	Y
6 *Tancredo*	Y	Y	Y	N	Y	Y	Y
7 *Beauprez*	Y	Y	Y	N	Y	Y	Y
CONNECTICUT							
1 Larson	N	N	Y	Y	Y	N	?
2 *Simmons*	Y	Y	Y	N	Y	Y	Y
3 DeLauro	N	N	Y	Y	N	N	Y
4 *Shays*	Y	Y	Y	Y	Y	N	Y
5 *Johnson*	Y	Y	Y	N	Y	Y	Y
DELAWARE							
AL *Castle*	Y	Y	Y	N	Y	Y	Y
FLORIDA							
1 *Miller, J.*	Y	Y	Y	N	Y	Y	Y
2 Boyd	Y	Y	Y	Y	Y	Y	Y
3 Brown	N	N	Y	Y	Y	N	Y
4 *Crenshaw*	Y	Y	Y	N	Y	Y	Y
5 *Brown-Waite*	Y	Y	Y	N	Y	Y	Y
6 *Stearns*	Y	Y	Y	N	Y	Y	Y
7 *Mica*	Y	Y	Y	N	Y	Y	Y
8 *Keller*	Y	Y	Y	N	Y	Y	Y
9 *Bilirakis*	Y	Y	Y	N	Y	Y	Y
10 *Young*	Y	Y	Y	N	Y	Y	Y
11 Davis	N	N	Y	Y	Y	N	Y
12 *Putnam*	Y	Y	Y	N	Y	Y	Y
13 *Harris*	Y	Y	Y	N	Y	Y	Y
14 *Goss*	Y	Y	Y	N	Y	Y	Y
15 *Weldon*	Y	Y	Y	N	Y	Y	Y
16 *Foley*	Y	Y	Y	N	Y	Y	Y
17 Meek	N	N	Y	Y	N	N	Y
18 *Ros-Lehtinen*	Y	Y	Y	N	Y	Y	Y
19 Wexler	N	N	Y	Y	N	N	Y
20 Deutsch	?	?	?	?	?	?	?
21 *Diaz-Balart, L.*	Y	Y	Y	N	Y	Y	Y
22 *Shaw*	Y	Y	Y	N	Y	Y	Y
23 Hastings	N	N	Y	Y	N	N	Y
24 *Feeney*	Y	Y	Y	N	Y	Y	Y
25 *Diaz-Balart, M.*	Y	Y	Y	N	Y	Y	Y
GEORGIA							
1 *Kingston*	Y	Y	Y	N	Y	Y	Y
2 Bishop	N	N	Y	Y	Y	Y	Y
3 Marshall	N	N	Y	Y	Y	Y	Y
4 Majette	N	N	Y	Y	N	N	Y
5 Lewis	N	N	Y	Y	N	N	Y
6 *Isakson*	Y	Y	Y	N	Y	Y	Y
7 *Linder*	Y	Y	Y	N	Y	Y	Y
8 *Collins*	Y	Y	Y	N	Y	Y	Y
9 *Norwood*	Y	Y	Y	N	Y	Y	Y
10 *Deal*	Y	Y	Y	N	Y	Y	Y
11 *Gingrey*	Y	Y	Y	N	Y	Y	Y
12 *Burns*	Y	Y	Y	N	Y	Y	Y
13 Scott	N	N	Y	Y	N	N	Y
HAWAII							
1 Abercrombie	N	N	Y	Y	Y	N	Y
2 Case	N	Y	Y	Y	Y	N	Y
IDAHO							
1 *Otter*	Y	Y	Y	N	Y	Y	Y
2 *Simpson*	Y	Y	Y	N	Y	Y	Y
ILLINOIS							
1 Rush	N	N	Y	N	N	N	Y
2 Jackson	N	N	Y	Y	N	N	Y
3 Lipinski	N	N	Y	Y	N	N	Y
4 Gutierrez	N	N	Y	Y	N	N	Y
5 Emanuel	N	N	Y	Y	N	N	Y
6 *Hyde*	Y	Y	Y	N	Y	Y	Y

ND Northern Democrats   SD Southern Democrats

	184	185	186	187	188	189	190
7 Davis	N	N	Y	Y	N	N	Y
8 ***Crane***	Y	Y	Y	N	Y	Y	Y
9 Schakowsky	N	N	Y	Y	N	N	Y
10 ***Kirk***	Y	Y	Y	N	Y	Y	Y
11 ***Weller***	Y	Y	Y	N	Y	Y	Y
12 Costello	N	N	Y	Y	Y	N	Y
13 ***Biggert***	Y	Y	Y	N	Y	Y	Y
14 ***Hastert***							
15 ***Johnson***	Y	Y	Y	N	Y	Y	Y
16 ***Manzullo***	Y	Y	Y	N	Y	Y	Y
17 Evans	N	N	?	Y	Y	N	Y
18 ***LaHood***	Y	Y	Y	N	Y	Y	Y
19 ***Shimkus***	Y	Y	Y	N	Y	Y	Y
INDIANA							
1 Visclosky	N	N	Y	Y	Y	N	Y
2 ***Chocola***	Y	Y	Y	N	Y	Y	Y
3 ***Souder***	Y	Y	Y	N	Y	Y	Y
4 ***Buyer***	Y	Y	Y	N	Y	Y	Y
5 ***Burton***	?	Y	Y	N	Y	Y	Y
6 ***Pence***	Y	Y	Y	N	Y	Y	Y
7 Carson	N	N	Y	Y	Y	N	Y
8 ***Hostettler***	Y	Y	Y	N	Y	Y	Y
9 Hill	N	N	Y	Y	Y	N	Y
IOWA							
1 ***Nussle***	Y	Y	Y	N	Y	Y	Y
2 ***Leach***	?	?	?	?	?	?	?
3 Boswell	N	N	Y	Y	Y	N	Y
4 ***Latham***	Y	Y	Y	N	Y	Y	Y
5 ***King***	Y	Y	Y	N	Y	Y	Y
KANSAS							
1 ***Moran***	Y	Y	Y	N	Y	Y	Y
2 ***Ryun***	Y	Y	Y	N	Y	Y	Y
3 Moore	N	N	Y	Y	Y	N	Y
4 ***Tiahrt***	Y	Y	Y	N	Y	Y	Y
KENTUCKY							
1 ***Whitfield***	Y	Y	Y	N	Y	Y	Y
2 ***Lewis***	Y	Y	Y	N	Y	Y	Y
3 ***Northup***	Y	Y	Y	N	Y	Y	Y
4 Lucas	Y	Y	Y	Y	Y	Y	Y
5 ***Rogers***	Y	Y	Y	N	Y	Y	Y
6 Chandler	N	N	Y	Y	Y	N	Y
LOUISIANA							
1 ***Vitter***	Y	Y	Y	N	Y	Y	Y
2 Jefferson	N	N	Y	Y	Y	N	Y
3 ***Tauzin***	?	?	?	?	?	?	?
4 ***McCrery***	Y	Y	Y	N	Y	Y	Y
5 Alexander	N	N	Y	Y	Y	N	Y
6 ***Baker***	Y	Y	Y	N	Y	Y	Y
7 John	N	N	Y	N	Y	Y	Y
MAINE							
1 Allen	N	N	Y	Y	N	N	Y
2 Michaud	N	N	Y	Y	Y	N	Y
MARYLAND							
1 ***Gilchrest***	Y	Y	Y	N	Y	Y	Y
2 Ruppersberger	N	N	Y	Y	Y	N	Y
3 Cardin	N	N	Y	Y	Y	N	Y
4 Wynn	N	N	Y	Y	Y	Y	Y
5 Hoyer	N	N	Y	Y	Y	N	Y
6 ***Bartlett***	Y	Y	Y	N	Y	Y	Y
7 Cummings	N	N	Y	Y	Y	N	Y
8 Van Hollen	N	N	Y	Y	N	N	Y
MASSACHUSETTS							
1 Olver	N	N	Y	Y	N	N	Y
2 Neal	N	N	Y	Y	Y	N	Y
3 McGovern	N	N	Y	Y	Y	N	Y
4 Frank	N	N	Y	Y	N	N	Y
5 Meehan	N	N	Y	Y	N	N	Y
6 Tierney	N	N	Y	Y	N	N	Y
7 Markey	N	N	Y	Y	N	N	Y
8 Capuano	N	N	Y	Y	N	N	Y
9 Lynch	N	N	Y	Y	Y	N	Y
10 Delahunt	N	N	Y	Y	Y	N	Y
MICHIGAN							
1 Stupak	N	N	Y	Y	Y	N	Y
2 ***Hoekstra***	Y	Y	Y	N	Y	Y	Y
3 ***Ehlers***	Y	Y	Y	N	Y	Y	Y
4 ***Camp***	Y	Y	Y	N	Y	Y	Y
5 Kildee	N	N	Y	Y	Y	N	Y
6 ***Upton***	Y	Y	Y	N	Y	Y	Y
7 ***Smith***	Y	Y	Y	N	?	Y	Y
8 ***Rogers***	Y	Y	Y	N	Y	Y	Y
9 ***Knollenberg***	Y	Y	Y	N	Y	Y	Y
10 ***Miller***	Y	Y	Y	N	Y	Y	Y
11 ***McCotter***	Y	Y	Y	N	Y	Y	Y
12 Levin	N	N	Y	Y	Y	N	Y
13 Kilpatrick	N	N	Y	Y	Y	N	Y
14 Conyers	N	N	Y	Y	N	N	Y
15 Dingell	N	N	Y	Y	N	N	Y
MINNESOTA							
1 ***Gutknecht***	Y	Y	Y	N	Y	Y	Y
2 ***Kline***	Y	Y	Y	N	Y	Y	Y
3 ***Ramstad***	Y	Y	Y	N	Y	Y	Y
4 McCollum	N	N	Y	Y	N	N	Y
5 Sabo	N	N	Y	Y	N	N	Y
6 ***Kennedy***	Y	Y	Y	N	Y	Y	Y
7 Peterson	N	N	?	N	Y	N	Y
8 Oberstar	N	N	Y	Y	N	N	Y
MISSISSIPPI							
1 ***Wicker***	Y	Y	Y	N	Y	Y	Y
2 Thompson	N	N	Y	Y	Y	N	Y
3 ***Pickering***	Y	Y	Y	N	Y	Y	Y
4 Taylor	Y	Y	Y	N	Y	Y	Y
MISSOURI							
1 Clay	N	N	Y	Y	Y	N	Y
2 ***Akin***	Y	Y	Y	N	Y	Y	Y
3 Gephardt	N	N	Y	Y	Y	N	?
4 Skelton	N	N	Y	Y	Y	N	Y
5 McCarthy	N	N	Y	Y	Y	N	Y
6 ***Graves***	Y	Y	Y	N	Y	Y	Y
7 ***Blunt***	Y	Y	Y	N	Y	Y	Y
8 ***Emerson***	Y	Y	Y	N	Y	Y	Y
9 ***Hulshof***	Y	Y	Y	N	Y	Y	Y
MONTANA							
AL ***Rehberg***	Y	Y	Y	N	Y	Y	Y
NEBRASKA							
1 ***Bereuter***	Y	Y	Y	N	Y	Y	Y
2 ***Terry***	Y	Y	Y	N	Y	Y	Y
3 ***Osborne***	Y	Y	Y	N	Y	Y	Y
NEVADA							
1 Berkley	N	N	Y	Y	Y	N	Y
2 ***Gibbons***	Y	Y	Y	N	Y	Y	Y
3 ***Porter***	Y	Y	Y	N	Y	Y	Y
NEW HAMPSHIRE							
1 ***Bradley***	Y	Y	Y	N	Y	Y	Y
2 ***Bass***	Y	Y	Y	N	Y	Y	Y
NEW JERSEY							
1 Andrews	N	N	Y	Y	N	N	Y
2 ***LoBiondo***	Y	N	Y	N	Y	N	Y
3 ***Saxton***	Y	N	Y	N	Y	N	Y
4 ***Smith***	Y	N	Y	N	Y	N	Y
5 ***Garrett***	Y	Y	Y	N	Y	Y	Y
6 Pallone	N	N	Y	Y	N	N	Y
7 ***Ferguson***	Y	Y	Y	N	Y	Y	Y
8 Pascrell	N	N	Y	Y	Y	N	Y
9 Rothman	N	N	Y	Y	N	N	Y
10 Payne	N	N	Y	Y	N	N	Y
11 ***Frelinghuysen***	Y	Y	Y	N	Y	Y	Y
12 Holt	N	N	Y	Y	N	N	Y
13 Menendez	N	N	Y	Y	Y	N	Y
NEW MEXICO							
1 ***Wilson***	Y	Y	Y	N	Y	Y	Y
2 ***Pearce***	Y	Y	Y	N	Y	Y	?
3 Udall	N	N	Y	Y	Y	N	Y
NEW YORK							
1 Bishop	N	N	Y	Y	Y	N	Y
2 Israel	N	N	Y	Y	Y	N	Y
3 ***King***	Y	N	Y	N	Y	Y	Y
4 McCarthy	N	N	Y	Y	Y	N	Y
5 Ackerman	N	N	Y	Y	Y	N	Y
6 Meeks	N	N	Y	Y	Y	N	Y
7 Crowley	N	N	Y	Y	Y	N	Y
8 Nadler	N	N	Y	Y	N	N	Y
9 Weiner	N	N	Y	Y	Y	N	Y
10 Towns	N	N	Y	Y	Y	N	Y
11 Owens	N	N	Y	Y	N	N	Y
12 Velázquez	N	N	Y	Y	Y	N	Y
13 ***Fossella***	Y	Y	Y	N	Y	Y	Y
14 Maloney	N	N	Y	Y	Y	N	Y
15 Rangel	N	N	Y	Y	Y	N	Y
16 Serrano	N	N	Y	Y	Y	N	Y
17 Engel	N	N	Y	Y	N	N	Y
18 Lowey	N	N	Y	Y	Y	N	Y
19 ***Kelly***	Y	Y	Y	N	Y	Y	Y
20 ***Sweeney***	Y	N	Y	N	Y	Y	Y
21 McNulty	N	N	Y	Y	Y	N	Y
22 Hinchey	N	N	Y	Y	N	N	Y
23 ***McHugh***	Y	N	Y	N	Y	Y	Y
24 ***Boehlert***	Y	N	Y	N	Y	Y	Y
25 ***Walsh***	Y	Y	Y	N	Y	Y	Y
26 ***Reynolds***	Y	Y	Y	N	Y	Y	Y
27 ***Quinn***	Y	Y	Y	N	Y	Y	Y
28 Slaughter	N	N	Y	Y	N	N	Y
29 ***Houghton***	Y	Y	Y	N	Y	Y	Y
NORTH CAROLINA							
1 Ballance	N	N	Y	Y	Y	N	Y
2 Etheridge	N	N	Y	Y	Y	N	Y
3 ***Jones***	Y	Y	Y	N	Y	Y	Y
4 Price	N	N	Y	Y	Y	N	Y
5 ***Burr***	Y	Y	Y	N	Y	Y	Y
6 ***Coble***	Y	Y	Y	N	Y	Y	Y
7 McIntyre	N	N	Y	Y	Y	N	Y
8 ***Hayes***	Y	?	Y	N	Y	Y	Y
9 ***Myrick***	Y	Y	Y	N	Y	Y	Y
10 ***Ballenger***	Y	Y	Y	N	Y	Y	Y
11 ***Taylor***	Y	Y	Y	N	Y	Y	Y
12 Watt	N	N	Y	Y	Y	N	Y
13 Miller	N	N	Y	Y	Y	N	Y
NORTH DAKOTA							
AL Pomeroy	N	N	Y	Y	Y	N	Y
OHIO							
1 ***Chabot***	Y	Y	Y	N	Y	Y	Y
2 ***Portman***	Y	Y	Y	N	Y	Y	Y
3 ***Turner***	Y	Y	Y	N	Y	Y	Y
4 ***Oxley***	Y	Y	Y	N	Y	Y	Y
5 ***Gillmor***	Y	Y	Y	N	Y	Y	Y
6 Strickland	N	N	Y	Y	Y	N	Y
7 ***Hobson***	Y	Y	Y	N	Y	Y	Y
8 ***Boehner***	Y	Y	Y	N	Y	Y	Y
9 Kaptur	N	N	Y	Y	Y	N	Y
10 Kucinich	N	N	Y	Y	N	N	Y
11 Jones	N	N	Y	Y	N	N	Y
12 ***Tiberi***	Y	Y	Y	N	Y	Y	Y
13 Brown	N	N	Y	Y	N	N	Y
14 ***LaTourette***	Y	Y	Y	N	Y	N	Y
15 ***Pryce***	Y	Y	Y	N	Y	?	Y
16 ***Regula***	Y	Y	Y	N	Y	Y	Y
17 Ryan	N	N	Y	Y	Y	N	Y
18 ***Ney***	Y	Y	Y	N	Y	Y	Y
OKLAHOMA							
1 ***Sullivan***	Y	Y	Y	N	Y	Y	Y
2 Carson	N	N	Y	Y	Y	N	Y
3 ***Lucas***	Y	Y	?	N	Y	Y	Y
4 ***Cole***	Y	Y	Y	N	Y	Y	Y
5 ***Istook***	Y	Y	Y	N	Y	Y	Y
OREGON							
1 Wu	N	N	Y	Y	Y	N	Y
2 ***Walden***	Y	Y	Y	N	Y	Y	Y
3 Blumenauer	N	N	Y	Y	N	N	Y
4 DeFazio	N	N	Y	Y	N	N	Y
5 Hooley	N	N	Y	Y	Y	N	Y
PENNSYLVANIA							
1 Brady	N	N	Y	Y	N	N	Y
2 Fattah	N	N	Y	Y	Y	N	Y
3 ***English***	Y	Y	Y	N	Y	Y	Y
4 ***Hart***	Y	Y	Y	N	Y	Y	Y
5 ***Peterson***	Y	Y	Y	N	Y	Y	Y
6 ***Gerlach***	Y	Y	Y	N	Y	Y	Y
7 ***Weldon***	Y	Y	Y	N	Y	Y	Y
8 ***Greenwood***	Y	Y	Y	N	Y	Y	Y
9 ***Shuster, Bill***	Y	Y	Y	N	Y	Y	Y
10 ***Sherwood***	Y	Y	Y	N	Y	Y	Y
11 Kanjorski	N	N	Y	Y	Y	N	Y
12 Murtha	N	N	Y	Y	Y	N	Y
13 Hoeffel	N	N	Y	Y	Y	N	Y
14 Doyle	N	N	Y	Y	Y	N	Y
15 ***Toomey***	Y	Y	Y	N	Y	Y	Y
16 ***Pitts***	?	Y	?	N	Y	Y	Y
17 Holden	N	N	Y	Y	Y	N	Y
18 ***Murphy***	Y	Y	?	N	Y	Y	Y
19 ***Platts***	Y	Y	Y	N	Y	Y	Y
RHODE ISLAND							
1 Kennedy	N	N	?	Y	Y	N	Y
2 Langevin	N	N	Y	Y	Y	N	Y
SOUTH CAROLINA							
1 ***Brown***	Y	Y	Y	N	Y	Y	Y
2 ***Wilson***	Y	Y	Y	N	Y	Y	Y
3 ***Barrett***	Y	Y	Y	N	Y	Y	Y
4 ***DeMint***	?	?	?	?	?	?	?
5 Spratt	N	N	Y	Y	Y	N	Y
6 Clyburn	N	N	Y	Y	Y	N	Y
SOUTH DAKOTA							
AL Vacant							
TENNESSEE							
1 ***Jenkins***	Y	Y	Y	N	Y	Y	Y
2 ***Duncan***	Y	Y	Y	N	Y	Y	Y
3 ***Wamp***	Y	Y	Y	N	Y	Y	Y
4 Davis	N	Y	Y	Y	Y	Y	Y
5 Cooper	N	N	Y	Y	Y	Y	Y
6 Gordon	N	N	Y	Y	Y	N	Y
7 ***Blackburn***	Y	Y	Y	N	Y	Y	Y
8 Tanner	N	N	Y	Y	Y	Y	Y
9 Ford	N	N	Y	Y	Y	N	Y
TEXAS							
1 Sandlin	N	N	Y	Y	Y	Y	Y
2 Turner	N	N	Y	N	Y	N	Y
3 ***Johnson, Sam***	Y	Y	Y	N	Y	Y	Y
4 ***Hall***	Y	Y	Y	N	Y	Y	Y
5 ***Hensarling***	Y	Y	?	N	Y	Y	Y
6 ***Barton***	Y	Y	Y	N	Y	Y	Y
7 ***Culberson***	Y	Y	Y	N	Y	Y	Y
8 ***Brady***	Y	Y	Y	N	Y	Y	?
9 Lampson	N	N	Y	Y	Y	N	Y
10 Doggett	N	N	Y	Y	Y	N	Y
11 Edwards	N	N	Y	Y	Y	Y	Y
12 ***Granger***	Y	Y	Y	N	Y	Y	Y
13 ***Thornberry***	Y	Y	Y	N	Y	Y	Y
14 ***Paul***	Y	Y	Y	N	Y	Y	Y
15 Hinojosa	N	N	Y	Y	Y	N	Y
16 Reyes	N	N	Y	Y	Y	N	Y
17 Stenholm	Y	Y	Y	Y	Y	Y	Y
18 Jackson-Lee	N	N	Y	Y	Y	N	Y
19 ***Neugebauer***	Y	Y	Y	N	Y	Y	Y
20 Gonzalez	N	N	Y	Y	Y	N	Y
21 ***Smith***	Y	Y	Y	N	Y	Y	Y
22 ***DeLay***	Y	Y	Y	N	Y	Y	Y
23 ***Bonilla***	Y	Y	Y	N	Y	Y	Y
24 Frost	N	N	Y	Y	Y	N	Y
25 Bell	N	N	Y	Y	Y	N	Y
26 ***Burgess***	Y	Y	Y	N	Y	Y	Y
27 Ortiz	N	N	Y	Y	Y	N	Y
28 Rodriguez	N	N	Y	Y	Y	N	Y
29 Green	N	N	Y	Y	Y	N	Y
30 Johnson, E.B.	N	N	Y	Y	Y	N	Y
31 ***Carter***	Y	Y	Y	N	Y	Y	Y
32 ***Sessions***	Y	Y	Y	N	Y	Y	Y
UTAH							
1 ***Bishop***	Y	Y	Y	N	Y	Y	Y
2 Matheson	Y	Y	Y	Y	Y	Y	Y
3 ***Cannon***	Y	Y	Y	N	Y	Y	Y
VERMONT							
AL *Sanders*	N	N	Y	Y	Y	N	Y
VIRGINIA							
1 ***Davis, Jo Ann***	Y	Y	Y	N	Y	Y	Y
2 ***Schrock***	Y	Y	Y	N	Y	Y	Y
3 Scott	N	N	Y	Y	Y	N	Y
4 ***Forbes***	Y	Y	Y	N	Y	Y	Y
5 ***Goode***	Y	Y	Y	N	Y	Y	Y
6 ***Goodlatte***	Y	Y	Y	N	Y	Y	Y
7 ***Cantor***	Y	Y	Y	N	Y	Y	Y
8 Moran	N	N	Y	Y	Y	N	?
9 Boucher	N	N	Y	Y	Y	N	Y
10 ***Wolf***	Y	Y	Y	N	Y	Y	Y
11 ***Davis, T.***	Y	Y	Y	N	Y	Y	Y
WASHINGTON							
1 Inslee	N	N	Y	Y	Y	N	Y
2 Larsen	N	N	Y	Y	Y	N	Y
3 Baird	N	N	Y	Y	Y	N	Y
4 ***Hastings***	Y	Y	Y	N	Y	Y	?
5 ***Nethercutt***	Y	Y	Y	N	Y	Y	Y
6 Dicks	N	N	Y	Y	Y	N	Y
7 McDermott	N	N	Y	Y	N	N	Y
8 ***Dunn***	Y	Y	Y	N	Y	Y	Y
9 Smith	N	N	Y	Y	Y	N	Y
WEST VIRGINIA							
1 Mollohan	N	N	Y	Y	N	N	Y
2 ***Capito***	Y	Y	Y	N	Y	Y	Y
3 Rahall	N	N	Y	Y	Y	Y	Y
WISCONSIN							
1 ***Ryan***	Y	Y	Y	N	Y	Y	Y
2 Baldwin	N	N	Y	Y	N	N	Y
3 Kind	N	N	Y	Y	Y	N	Y
4 Kleczka	N	N	Y	Y	N	N	Y
5 ***Sensenbrenner***	Y	N	Y	N	Y	Y	Y
6 ***Petri***	Y	Y	Y	N	Y	Y	Y
7 Obey	N	N	Y	Y	Y	N	Y
8 ***Green***	Y	Y	Y	N	Y	Y	Y
WYOMING							
AL ***Cubin***	Y	Y	Y	N	Y	Y	Y

Southern states - Ala., Ark., Fla., Ga., Ky., La., Miss., N.C., Okla., S.C., Tenn., Texas, Va.

Key

Y	Voted for (yea).
#	Paired for.
+	Announced for.
N	Voted against (nay).
X	Paired against.
–	Announced against.
P	Voted "present."
C	Voted "present" to avoid possible conflict of interest.
?	Did not vote or otherwise make a position known.

Democrats **Republicans**
Independents

191. S Con Res 95. Fiscal 2005 Budget Resolution/Previous Question. Hastings, R-Wash., motion to order the previous question (thus ending debate and possibility of amendment) on adoption of the rule (H Res 649) to provide for House floor consideration of the conference report on the concurrent resolution that would set broad spending and revenue targets, including $821.4 billion in discretionary spending, for fiscal 2005. Motion agreed to 220-204: R 220-0; D 0-203 (ND 0-148, SD 0-55); I 0-1. May 19, 2004.

192. S Con Res 95. Fiscal 2005 Budget Resolution/Rule. Adoption of the rule (H Res 649) to provide for House floor consideration of the conference report on the concurrent resolution that would set broad spending and revenue targets, including $821.4 billion in discretionary spending, for fiscal 2005. Adopted 220-204: R 220-0; D 0-203 (ND 0-148, SD 0-55); I 0-1. May 19, 2004.

193. HR 4200. Fiscal 2005 Defense Authorization/Previous Question. Myrick, R-N.C., motion to order the previous question (thus ending debate and possibility of amendment) on adoption of the rule (H Res 648) to provide for House floor consideration of the bill that would authorize $422.2 billion for defense programs for fiscal 2005 and an additional $25 billion for operations in Iraq. Motion agreed to 220-204: R 220-0; D 0-203 (ND 0-148, SD 0-55); I 0-1. May 19, 2004.

194. HR 4200. Fiscal 2005 Defense Authorization/Rule. Adoption of the rule (H Res 648) to provide for House floor consideration of the bill that would authorize $422.2 billion for defense programs for fiscal 2005 and an additional $25 billion for operations in Iraq. Adopted 220-205: R 220-1; D 0-203 (ND 0-148, SD 0-55); I 0-1. May 19, 2004.

195. H Con Res 424. Memorial Day/Adoption. Schrock, R-Va., motion to suspend the rules and adopt the concurrent resolution that would honor members of the U.S. armed forces by encouraging every American to wear a red poppy on Memorial Day as a sign of thanks to service members who have died. Motion agreed to 419-0: R 217-0; D 201-0 (ND 146-0, SD 55-0); I 1-0. A two-thirds majority of those present and voting (280 in this case) is required for adoption under suspension of the rules. May 19, 2004.

196. HR 4200. Fiscal 2005 Defense Authorization/Border Security. Goode, R-Va., amendment that would authorize the Defense secretary to assign military personnel to assist the Homeland Security Department with border security under certain circumstances such as a threat to national security. Adopted 231-191: R 200-20; D 31-170 (ND 17-128, SD 14-42); I 0-1. May 19, 2004.

197. HR 4200. Fiscal 2005 Defense Authorization/Abortion at Military Facilities. Davis, D-Calif., amendment that would allow overseas military facilities to provide privately funded abortions for women who are in the military or are military dependents. Rejected 202-221: R 27-193; D 174-28 (ND 129-17, SD 45-11); I 1-0. A "nay" was a vote in support of the president's position. May 19, 2004.

		191	192	193	194	195	196	197
ALABAMA								
1	*Bonner*	Y	Y	Y	Y	Y	Y	N
2	*Everett*	Y	Y	Y	Y	Y	Y	N
3	*Rogers*	Y	Y	Y	Y	Y	Y	N
4	*Aderholt*	Y	Y	Y	Y	Y	Y	N
5	Cramer	N	N	N	N	Y	Y	Y
6	*Bachus*	Y	Y	Y	Y	Y	Y	N
7	Davis	?	?	?	?	?	N	Y
ALASKA								
AL	*Young*	Y	Y	Y	Y	Y	Y	N
ARIZONA								
1	*Renzi*	Y	Y	Y	Y	Y	Y	N
2	*Franks*	Y	Y	Y	Y	Y	Y	N
3	*Shadegg*	Y	Y	Y	Y	Y	Y	N
4	Pastor	N	N	N	N	Y	N	Y
5	*Hayworth*	?	?	?	?	?	?	?
6	*Flake*	Y	Y	Y	Y	Y	N	N
7	Grijalva	N	N	N	N	Y	N	Y
8	*Kolbe*	Y	Y	Y	Y	Y	N	Y
ARKANSAS								
1	Berry	N	N	N	N	Y	N	N
2	Snyder	N	N	N	N	Y	N	Y
3	*Boozman*	Y	Y	Y	Y	Y	Y	N
4	Ross	N	N	N	N	Y	N	N
CALIFORNIA								
1	Thompson	N	N	N	N	Y	N	Y
2	*Herger*	Y	Y	Y	Y	Y	Y	N
3	*Ose*	Y	Y	Y	Y	Y	Y	Y
4	*Doolittle*	Y	Y	Y	Y	Y	Y	N
5	Matsui	N	N	N	N	Y	N	Y
6	Woolsey	N	N	N	N	Y	N	Y
7	Miller, George	N	N	N	N	Y	N	Y
8	Pelosi	N	N	N	N	Y	N	Y
9	Lee	N	N	N	N	Y	N	Y
10	Tauscher	N	N	N	N	Y	N	Y
11	*Pombo*	Y	Y	Y	Y	Y	Y	N
12	Lantos	N	N	N	N	Y	N	Y
13	Stark	N	N	N	N	Y	N	Y
14	Eshoo	N	N	N	N	Y	N	Y
15	Honda	N	N	N	N	Y	N	Y
16	Lofgren	N	N	N	N	Y	N	Y
17	Farr	N	N	N	N	Y	N	Y
18	Cardoza	N	N	N	N	Y	N	Y
19	*Radanovich*	Y	Y	Y	?	Y	Y	N
20	Dooley	N	N	N	N	Y	N	Y
21	*Nunes*	Y	Y	Y	Y	Y	Y	N
22	*Thomas*	Y	Y	Y	Y	Y	Y	Y
23	Capps	N	N	N	N	Y	N	Y
24	*Gallegly*	Y	Y	Y	Y	Y	Y	N
25	*McKeon*	Y	Y	Y	Y	Y	Y	N
26	*Dreier*	Y	Y	Y	Y	Y	Y	N
27	Sherman	N	N	N	N	Y	N	Y
28	Berman	N	N	N	N	Y	N	Y
29	Schiff	N	N	N	N	Y	N	Y
30	Waxman	N	N	N	N	Y	N	Y
31	Becerra	N	N	N	N	Y	N	Y
32	Solis	N	N	N	N	Y	N	Y
33	Watson	N	N	N	N	Y	N	Y
34	Roybal-Allard	N	N	N	N	Y	N	Y
35	Waters	N	N	N	N	Y	N	Y
36	Harman	N	N	N	N	Y	N	Y
37	Millender-McD.	N	N	N	N	Y	N	Y
38	Napolitano	N	N	N	N	Y	N	Y
39	Sánchez, Linda	N	N	N	N	Y	N	Y
40	*Royce*	Y	Y	Y	Y	Y	Y	N
41	*Lewis*	Y	Y	Y	Y	Y	Y	N
42	*Miller, Gary*	Y	Y	Y	Y	Y	Y	N
43	Baca	N	N	N	N	Y	N	Y
44	*Calvert*	Y	Y	Y	Y	Y	Y	N
45	*Bono*	Y	Y	Y	Y	Y	Y	N
46	*Rohrabacher*	Y	Y	Y	Y	Y	Y	N
47	Sanchez, Loretta	N	N	N	N	Y	N	Y
48	*Cox*	Y	Y	Y	Y	Y	Y	N
49	*Issa*	Y	Y	Y	Y	Y	Y	N
50	*Cunningham*	Y	Y	Y	Y	Y	Y	N
51	Filner	N	N	N	N	Y	N	Y
52	*Hunter*	Y	Y	Y	Y	Y	Y	N
53	Davis	N	N	N	N	Y	N	Y
COLORADO								
1	DeGette	N	N	N	N	Y	N	Y
2	Udall	N	N	N	N	Y	N	Y
3	*McInnis*	Y	Y	Y	Y	Y	Y	N
4	*Musgrave*	Y	Y	Y	Y	Y	Y	N
5	*Hefley*	Y	Y	Y	Y	Y	Y	N
6	*Tancredo*	Y	Y	Y	Y	Y	Y	N
7	*Beauprez*	Y	Y	Y	Y	Y	Y	N
CONNECTICUT								
1	Larson	N	N	N	N	Y	N	Y
2	*Simmons*	?	Y	Y	Y	Y	Y	Y
3	DeLauro	N	N	N	N	Y	N	Y
4	*Shays*	Y	Y	Y	Y	Y	Y	Y
5	*Johnson*	Y	Y	Y	Y	Y	Y	Y
DELAWARE								
AL	*Castle*	Y	Y	Y	Y	Y	Y	Y
FLORIDA								
1	*Miller, J.*	Y	Y	Y	Y	Y	Y	N
2	Boyd	N	N	N	N	Y	N	Y
3	Brown	N	N	N	N	Y	N	Y
4	*Crenshaw*	Y	Y	Y	Y	Y	Y	N
5	*Brown-Waite*	Y	Y	Y	Y	Y	Y	N
6	*Stearns*	Y	Y	Y	Y	Y	Y	N
7	*Mica*	Y	Y	Y	Y	Y	Y	N
8	*Keller*	Y	Y	Y	Y	Y	Y	N
9	*Bilirakis*	Y	Y	Y	Y	Y	Y	N
10	*Young*	Y	Y	Y	Y	Y	Y	N
11	Davis	N	N	N	N	Y	N	Y
12	*Putnam*	Y	Y	Y	Y	Y	Y	N
13	*Harris*	Y	Y	Y	Y	Y	Y	N
14	*Goss*	Y	Y	Y	Y	Y	Y	N
15	*Weldon*	Y	Y	Y	Y	Y	Y	N
16	*Foley*	N	N	N	N	Y	N	Y
17	Meek	N	N	N	N	Y	N	Y
18	*Ros-Lehtinen*	Y	Y	Y	Y	Y	Y	N
19	Wexler	N	N	N	N	Y	N	Y
20	Deutsch	?	?	?	?	?	N	Y
21	*Diaz-Balart, L.*	Y	Y	Y	Y	Y	Y	N
22	*Shaw*	Y	Y	Y	Y	Y	Y	N
23	Hastings	N	N	N	N	Y	N	Y
24	*Feeney*	Y	Y	Y	Y	Y	Y	N
25	*Diaz-Balart, M.*	Y	Y	Y	Y	Y	Y	N
GEORGIA								
1	*Kingston*	Y	Y	Y	Y	?	?	?
2	Bishop	N	N	N	N	Y	N	Y
3	Marshall	N	N	N	N	Y	N	Y
4	Majette	N	N	N	N	Y	N	Y
5	Lewis	N	N	N	N	Y	N	Y
6	*Isakson*	Y	Y	Y	Y	Y	Y	N
7	*Linder*	Y	Y	Y	Y	Y	Y	N
8	*Collins*	Y	Y	Y	Y	Y	Y	N
9	*Norwood*	?	?	?	?	?	?	?
10	*Deal*	Y	Y	Y	Y	Y	Y	N
11	*Gingrey*	Y	Y	Y	Y	Y	Y	N
12	*Burns*	Y	Y	Y	Y	Y	Y	N
13	Scott	N	N	N	N	Y	N	Y
HAWAII								
1	Abercrombie	N	N	N	N	Y	N	Y
2	Case	N	N	N	N	Y	Y	Y
IDAHO								
1	*Otter*	Y	Y	Y	Y	Y	Y	N
2	*Simpson*	Y	Y	Y	Y	Y	Y	N
ILLINOIS								
1	Rush	N	N	N	N	Y	N	Y
2	Jackson	N	N	N	N	Y	N	Y
3	Lipinski	N	N	N	N	Y	N	Y
4	Gutierrez	N	N	N	N	Y	N	Y
5	Emanuel	N	N	N	N	Y	N	Y
6	*Hyde*	Y	Y	Y	Y	Y	N	Y

ND Northern Democrats   SD Southern Democrats

	191	192	193	194	195	196	197
7 Davis	N	N	N	N	Y	N	Y
8 ***Crane***	Y	Y	Y	Y	Y	Y	N
9 Schakowsky	N	N	N	N	Y	N	Y
10 ***Kirk***	Y	Y	Y	Y	Y	Y	Y
11 ***Weller***	Y	Y	Y	Y	Y	N	N
12 Costello	N	N	N	N	Y	Y	N
13 ***Biggert***	Y	Y	Y	Y	Y	Y	Y
14 ***Hastert***							
15 ***Johnson***	Y	Y	Y	Y	Y	Y	N
16 ***Manzullo***	Y	Y	Y	Y	Y	Y	N
17 Evans	N	N	N	N	Y	N	Y
18 ***LaHood***	Y	Y	Y	Y	Y	Y	N
19 ***Shimkus***	Y	Y	Y	Y	Y	Y	N
INDIANA							
1 Visclosky	N	N	N	N	Y	N	Y
2 ***Chocola***	Y	Y	Y	Y	Y	Y	N
3 ***Souder***	Y	Y	Y	Y	Y	N	N
4 ***Buyer***	Y	Y	Y	Y	Y	Y	N
5 ***Burton***	Y	Y	Y	Y	Y	Y	N
6 ***Pence***	Y	Y	Y	Y	Y	Y	N
7 Carson	N	N	N	N	Y	N	Y
8 ***Hostettler***	Y	Y	Y	Y	Y	Y	N
9 Hill	N	N	N	N	Y	N	Y
IOWA							
1 ***Nussle***	Y	Y	Y	Y	?	Y	N
2 ***Leach***	?	?	?	?	?	?	?
3 Boswell	N	N	N	N	Y	Y	N
4 ***Latham***	Y	Y	Y	Y	Y	Y	N
5 ***King***	Y	Y	Y	Y	Y	Y	N
KANSAS							
1 ***Moran***	Y	Y	Y	Y	Y	Y	N
2 ***Ryun***	Y	Y	Y	Y	Y	Y	N
3 Moore	N	N	N	N	Y	N	Y
4 ***Tiahrt***	Y	Y	Y	Y	Y	Y	N
KENTUCKY							
1 ***Whitfield***	Y	Y	Y	Y	Y	N	N
2 ***Lewis***	Y	Y	Y	Y	Y	Y	N
3 ***Northup***	Y	Y	Y	Y	Y	Y	N
4 Lucas	N	N	N	N	Y	Y	N
5 ***Rogers***	Y	Y	Y	Y	Y	Y	N
6 Chandler	N	N	N	N	Y	N	Y
LOUISIANA							
1 ***Vitter***	Y	Y	Y	Y	Y	Y	N
2 Jefferson	N	N	N	N	N	Y	Y
3 ***Tauzin***	?	?	?	?	?	?	?
4 ***McCrery***	Y	Y	Y	Y	Y	Y	N
5 Alexander	N	N	N	N	Y	Y	N
6 ***Baker***	Y	Y	Y	Y	Y	Y	N
7 John	N	N	N	N	Y	N	N
MAINE							
1 Allen	N	N	N	N	Y	N	Y
2 Michaud	N	N	N	N	Y	N	N
MARYLAND							
1 ***Gilchrest***	Y	Y	Y	Y	Y	Y	Y
2 Ruppersberger	N	N	N	N	Y	N	Y
3 Cardin	N	N	N	N	Y	N	Y
4 Wynn	N	N	N	N	Y	N	Y
5 Hoyer	N	N	N	N	Y	N	Y
6 ***Bartlett***	Y	Y	Y	Y	Y	Y	N
7 Cummings	N	N	N	N	Y	N	Y
8 Van Hollen	N	N	N	N	Y	N	Y
MASSACHUSETTS							
1 Olver	N	N	N	N	Y	N	Y
2 Neal	N	N	N	N	Y	N	Y
3 McGovern	N	N	N	N	Y	N	Y
4 Frank	N	N	N	N	Y	N	Y
5 Meehan	N	N	N	N	Y	N	Y
6 Tierney	N	N	N	N	Y	N	Y
7 Markey	N	N	N	N	Y	N	Y
8 Capuano	N	N	N	N	Y	N	Y
9 Lynch	N	N	N	N	Y	N	N
10 Delahunt	N	N	N	N	Y	?	?
MICHIGAN							
1 Stupak	N	N	N	N	Y	N	N
2 ***Hoekstra***	Y	Y	Y	Y	Y	Y	N
3 ***Ehlers***	Y	Y	Y	Y	Y	N	N
4 ***Camp***	Y	Y	Y	Y	Y	Y	N
5 Kildee	N	N	N	N	Y	N	N
6 ***Upton***	Y	Y	Y	Y	Y	Y	N
7 ***Smith***	Y	Y	Y	Y	Y	Y	N
8 ***Rogers***	Y	Y	Y	Y	Y	Y	N
9 ***Knollenberg***	Y	Y	Y	Y	Y	Y	N
10 ***Miller***	Y	Y	Y	Y	Y	Y	N
11 ***McCotter***	Y	Y	Y	Y	Y	Y	N
12 Levin	N	N	N	N	Y	Y	Y
13 Kilpatrick	N	N	N	N	Y	N	Y
14 Conyers	N	N	N	N	?	N	Y
15 Dingell	N	N	N	N	Y	Y	Y
MINNESOTA							
1 ***Gutknecht***	Y	Y	Y	Y	Y	Y	N
2 ***Kline***	Y	Y	Y	Y	Y	Y	N
3 ***Ramstad***	Y	Y	Y	Y	Y	Y	Y
4 McCollum	N	N	N	N	Y	N	Y
5 Sabo	N	N	N	N	Y	N	Y
6 ***Kennedy***	Y	Y	Y	Y	Y	Y	N
7 Peterson	N	N	N	N	Y	Y	N
8 Oberstar	N	N	N	N	Y	N	N
MISSISSIPPI							
1 ***Wicker***	Y	Y	Y	Y	Y	Y	N
2 Thompson	N	N	N	N	Y	N	Y
3 ***Pickering***	Y	Y	Y	Y	Y	Y	N
4 Taylor	N	N	N	N	Y	N	N
MISSOURI							
1 Clay	N	N	N	N	Y	N	Y
2 ***Akin***	Y	Y	Y	Y	Y	Y	N
3 Gephardt	N	N	N	N	Y	N	Y
4 Skelton	N	N	N	N	Y	N	N
5 McCarthy	N	N	N	N	Y	N	Y
6 ***Graves***	Y	Y	Y	Y	Y	Y	N
7 ***Blunt***	Y	Y	Y	Y	Y	Y	N
8 ***Emerson***	Y	Y	?	Y	Y	Y	N
9 ***Hulshof***	Y	Y	Y	Y	Y	Y	N
MONTANA							
AL ***Rehberg***	Y	Y	Y	Y	Y	Y	N
NEBRASKA							
1 ***Bereuter***	Y	Y	Y	Y	Y	N	N
2 ***Terry***	Y	Y	Y	Y	Y	N	N
3 ***Osborne***	Y	Y	Y	Y	Y	Y	N
NEVADA							
1 Berkley	N	N	N	N	Y	N	Y
2 ***Gibbons***	Y	Y	Y	Y	Y	Y	N
3 ***Porter***	Y	Y	Y	Y	Y	Y	N
NEW HAMPSHIRE							
1 ***Bradley***	Y	Y	Y	Y	Y	Y	Y
2 ***Bass***	Y	Y	Y	Y	Y	Y	Y
NEW JERSEY							
1 Andrews	N	N	N	N	Y	N	Y
2 ***LoBiondo***	Y	Y	Y	Y	Y	Y	N
3 ***Saxton***	Y	Y	Y	Y	Y	Y	N
4 ***Smith***	Y	Y	Y	Y	Y	Y	N
5 ***Garrett***	Y	Y	Y	Y	Y	Y	N
6 Pallone	N	N	N	N	Y	N	Y
7 ***Ferguson***	Y	Y	Y	Y	Y	Y	N
8 Pascrell	N	N	N	N	Y	N	Y
9 Rothman	N	N	N	N	Y	N	Y
10 Payne	N	N	N	N	Y	N	Y
11 ***Frelinghuysen***	Y	Y	Y	Y	Y	Y	Y
12 Holt	N	N	N	N	Y	N	Y
13 Menendez	N	N	N	N	Y	N	Y
NEW MEXICO							
1 ***Wilson***	Y	Y	Y	Y	Y	N	N
2 ***Pearce***	Y	Y	Y	Y	Y	N	N
3 Udall	N	N	N	N	Y	N	Y
NEW YORK							
1 Bishop	N	N	N	N	Y	Y	Y
2 Israel	N	N	N	N	Y	N	Y
3 ***King***	Y	Y	Y	Y	Y	Y	N
4 McCarthy	N	N	N	N	Y	N	Y
5 Ackerman	N	N	N	N	Y	N	Y
6 Meeks	N	N	N	N	Y	N	Y
7 Crowley	N	N	N	N	Y	N	Y
8 Nadler	N	N	N	N	Y	N	Y
9 Weiner	N	N	N	N	Y	N	Y
10 Towns	N	N	N	N	Y	N	Y
11 Owens	N	N	N	N	Y	N	Y
12 Velázquez	N	N	N	N	Y	N	Y
13 ***Fossella***	Y	Y	Y	Y	Y	Y	N
14 Maloney	N	N	N	N	Y	N	Y
15 Rangel	N	N	N	N	Y	N	Y
16 Serrano	N	N	N	N	Y	N	Y
17 Engel	N	N	N	N	Y	N	Y
18 Lowey	N	N	N	N	Y	Y	Y
19 ***Kelly***	Y	Y	Y	Y	Y	Y	Y
20 ***Sweeney***	Y	Y	Y	Y	Y	Y	N
21 McNulty	N	N	N	N	Y	N	N
22 Hinchey	N	N	N	N	Y	N	Y
23 ***McHugh***	Y	Y	Y	Y	Y	Y	Y
24 ***Boehlert***	Y	Y	Y	Y	Y	Y	Y
25 ***Walsh***	Y	Y	Y	Y	Y	Y	N
26 ***Reynolds***	Y	Y	Y	Y	?	Y	N
27 ***Quinn***	Y	Y	Y	Y	Y	Y	N
28 Slaughter	N	N	N	N	Y	N	Y
29 ***Houghton***	Y	Y	Y	Y	Y	Y	Y
NORTH CAROLINA							
1 Ballance	N	N	N	N	Y	N	Y
2 Etheridge	N	N	N	N	Y	Y	Y
3 ***Jones***	Y	Y	Y	Y	Y	Y	N
4 Price	N	N	N	N	Y	N	Y
5 ***Burr***	Y	Y	Y	Y	Y	N	N
6 ***Coble***	Y	Y	Y	Y	Y	Y	N
7 McIntyre	N	N	N	N	Y	Y	N
8 ***Hayes***	Y	Y	Y	Y	Y	Y	N
9 ***Myrick***	Y	Y	Y	Y	Y	Y	N
10 ***Ballenger***	Y	Y	Y	Y	Y	Y	N
11 ***Taylor***	Y	Y	Y	Y	Y	Y	N
12 Watt	N	N	N	N	Y	N	Y
13 Miller	N	N	N	N	Y	N	Y
NORTH DAKOTA							
AL Pomeroy	N	N	N	N	Y	Y	Y
OHIO							
1 ***Chabot***	Y	Y	Y	Y	Y	Y	N
2 ***Portman***	Y	Y	Y	Y	Y	?	?
3 ***Turner***	Y	Y	Y	Y	Y	Y	N
4 ***Oxley***	Y	Y	Y	Y	Y	Y	N
5 ***Gillmor***	Y	Y	Y	Y	Y	Y	N
6 Strickland	N	N	N	N	Y	N	Y
7 ***Hobson***	Y	Y	Y	Y	Y	Y	N
8 ***Boehner***	Y	Y	Y	Y	Y	Y	N
9 Kaptur	N	N	N	N	Y	Y	Y
10 Kucinich	N	N	N	N	Y	N	Y
11 Jones	N	N	N	N	Y	?	Y
12 ***Tiberi***	Y	Y	Y	Y	Y	Y	N
13 Brown	N	N	N	N	Y	Y	Y
14 ***LaTourette***	Y	Y	Y	Y	Y	Y	Y
15 ***Pryce***	Y	Y	Y	Y	Y	Y	Y
16 ***Regula***	Y	Y	Y	Y	Y	Y	N
17 Ryan	N	N	N	N	Y	N	Y
18 ***Ney***	Y	Y	Y	Y	Y	Y	N
OKLAHOMA							
1 ***Sullivan***	Y	Y	Y	Y	Y	Y	N
2 Carson	N	N	N	N	Y	Y	Y
3 ***Lucas***	Y	Y	Y	Y	Y	N	N
4 ***Cole***	Y	Y	Y	Y	Y	Y	N
5 ***Istook***	Y	Y	Y	Y	Y	Y	N
OREGON							
1 Wu	N	N	N	N	Y	N	Y
2 ***Walden***	Y	Y	Y	Y	Y	Y	Y
3 Blumenauer	N	N	N	N	Y	N	Y
4 DeFazio	N	N	N	N	Y	Y	Y
5 Hooley	N	N	N	N	Y	Y	Y
PENNSYLVANIA							
1 Brady	N	N	N	N	Y	N	Y
2 Fattah	N	N	N	N	Y	?	?
3 ***English***	Y	Y	Y	Y	Y	Y	N
4 ***Hart***	Y	Y	Y	Y	Y	Y	N
5 ***Peterson***	Y	?	Y	Y	Y	Y	N
6 ***Gerlach***	Y	Y	Y	Y	Y	Y	N
7 ***Weldon***	+	+	+	+	+	Y	N
8 ***Greenwood***	Y	Y	Y	Y	Y	Y	Y
9 ***Shuster, Bill***	Y	Y	Y	Y	Y	Y	N
10 ***Sherwood***	Y	Y	Y	Y	Y	Y	N
11 Kanjorski	N	N	N	N	Y	N	N
12 Murtha	N	N	N	N	Y	N	N
13 Hoeffel	N	N	N	N	Y	N	Y
14 Doyle	N	N	N	N	Y	N	N
15 ***Toomey***	Y	Y	Y	Y	Y	Y	N
16 ***Pitts***	Y	Y	Y	Y	Y	Y	N
17 Holden	N	N	N	N	Y	N	N
18 ***Murphy***	Y	Y	Y	Y	Y	Y	N
19 ***Platts***	Y	Y	Y	Y	Y	Y	N
RHODE ISLAND							
1 Kennedy	N	N	N	N	Y	N	Y
2 Langevin	N	N	N	N	Y	N	N
SOUTH CAROLINA							
1 ***Brown***	Y	Y	Y	Y	Y	Y	N
2 ***Wilson***	Y	Y	Y	Y	Y	Y	N
3 ***Barrett***	Y	Y	Y	Y	Y	Y	N
4 ***DeMint***	Y	Y	Y	Y	Y	Y	N
5 Spratt	N	N	N	N	Y	Y	Y
6 Clyburn	N	N	N	N	Y	Y	Y
SOUTH DAKOTA							
AL Vacant							
TENNESSEE							
1 ***Jenkins***	Y	Y	Y	Y	Y	Y	N
2 ***Duncan***	Y	Y	Y	Y	Y	Y	N
3 ***Wamp***	Y	Y	Y	Y	Y	Y	N
4 Davis	N	N	N	N	Y	Y	N
5 Cooper	N	N	N	N	Y	N	Y
6 Gordon	N	N	N	N	Y	Y	Y
7 ***Blackburn***	Y	Y	Y	Y	Y	Y	N
8 Tanner	N	N	N	N	Y	Y	Y
9 Ford	N	N	N	N	Y	?	?
TEXAS							
1 Sandlin	N	N	N	N	Y	N	Y
2 Turner	N	N	N	N	Y	N	Y
3 ***Johnson, Sam***	?	?	?	?	?	?	?
4 ***Hall***	Y	Y	Y	Y	Y	Y	N
5 ***Hensarling***	Y	Y	Y	Y	Y	Y	N
6 ***Barton***	Y	Y	Y	Y	Y	Y	N
7 ***Culberson***	Y	Y	Y	Y	Y	Y	N
8 ***Brady***	Y	Y	Y	Y	Y	Y	N
9 Lampson	N	N	N	N	Y	N	Y
10 Doggett	N	N	N	N	Y	N	Y
11 Edwards	N	N	N	N	Y	N	Y
12 ***Granger***	Y	Y	Y	Y	Y	Y	N
13 ***Thornberry***	Y	Y	Y	Y	Y	Y	N
14 ***Paul***	Y	Y	Y	Y	Y	N	N
15 Hinojosa	N	N	N	N	Y	N	Y
16 Reyes	N	N	N	N	Y	N	Y
17 Stenholm	N	N	N	N	Y	N	N
18 Jackson-Lee	N	N	N	N	Y	N	Y
19 ***Neugebauer***	Y	Y	Y	Y	Y	Y	N
20 Gonzalez	N	N	N	N	Y	N	Y
21 ***Smith***	Y	Y	Y	Y	Y	Y	N
22 ***DeLay***	Y	Y	Y	Y	Y	Y	N
23 ***Bonilla***	Y	Y	Y	Y	Y	Y	N
24 Frost	N	N	N	N	Y	N	Y
25 Bell	N	N	N	N	Y	N	Y
26 ***Burgess***	Y	Y	Y	Y	Y	N	N
27 Ortiz	N	N	N	N	Y	N	N
28 Rodriguez	N	N	N	N	Y	N	Y
29 Green	N	N	N	N	Y	N	Y
30 Johnson, E.B.	N	N	N	N	Y	N	Y
31 ***Carter***	Y	Y	Y	Y	Y	Y	N
32 ***Sessions***	Y	Y	Y	Y	Y	Y	N
UTAH							
1 ***Bishop***	Y	Y	Y	Y	Y	Y	N
2 Matheson	N	N	N	N	Y	Y	Y
3 ***Cannon***	Y	Y	Y	Y	Y	Y	N
VERMONT							
AL *Sanders*	N	N	N	N	Y	N	Y
VIRGINIA							
1 ***Davis, Jo Ann***	Y	Y	Y	Y	Y	Y	N
2 ***Schrock***	Y	Y	Y	Y	Y	Y	N
3 Scott	N	N	N	N	Y	N	Y
4 ***Forbes***	Y	Y	Y	Y	Y	Y	N
5 ***Goode***	Y	Y	Y	Y	Y	Y	N
6 ***Goodlatte***	Y	Y	Y	Y	Y	Y	N
7 ***Cantor***	Y	Y	Y	Y	Y	Y	N
8 Moran	N	N	N	N	Y	N	Y
9 Boucher	N	N	N	N	Y	Y	Y
10 ***Wolf***	Y	Y	Y	Y	Y	Y	N
11 ***Davis, T.***	Y	Y	Y	Y	Y	N	N
WASHINGTON							
1 Inslee	N	N	N	N	Y	N	Y
2 Larsen	N	N	N	N	Y	N	Y
3 Baird	N	N	N	N	?	N	Y
4 ***Hastings***	Y	Y	Y	Y	Y	Y	N
5 ***Nethercutt***	Y	Y	Y	Y	Y	Y	N
6 Dicks	N	N	N	N	Y	N	Y
7 McDermott	N	N	N	N	Y	N	Y
8 ***Dunn***	Y	Y	Y	Y	Y	Y	Y
9 Smith	N	N	N	N	Y	N	Y
WEST VIRGINIA							
1 Mollohan	N	N	N	N	Y	N	N
2 ***Capito***	Y	Y	Y	Y	Y	Y	Y
3 Rahall	N	N	N	N	Y	N	N
WISCONSIN							
1 ***Ryan***	Y	Y	Y	Y	Y	Y	N
2 Baldwin	N	N	N	N	Y	N	Y
3 Kind	N	N	N	N	Y	Y	Y
4 Kleczka	N	N	N	N	Y	N	Y
5 ***Sensenbrenner***	Y	Y	Y	Y	Y	Y	N
6 ***Petri***	Y	Y	Y	Y	Y	Y	N
7 Obey	N	N	N	N	Y	N	Y
8 ***Green***	Y	Y	Y	Y	Y	Y	N
WYOMING							
AL ***Cubin***	Y	Y	Y	Y	Y	Y	N

Southern states - Ala., Ark., Fla., Ga., Ky., La., Miss., N.C., Okla., S.C., Tenn., Texas, Va.

Key

Y	Voted for (yea).
#	Paired for.
+	Announced for.
N	Voted against (nay).
X	Paired against.
–	Announced against.
P	Voted "present."
C	Voted "present" to avoid possible conflict of interest.
?	Did not vote or otherwise make a position known.

Democrats *Republicans*
Independents

198. S Con Res 95. Fiscal 2005 Budget Resolution/Conference Report. Adoption of the conference report on the concurrent resolution that would set broad spending and revenue targets for fiscal 2005, including $821.4 billion in discretionary spending and an additional $50 billion for operations in Iraq. It would apply pay-as-you-go rules to both spending and tax cuts until April 15, 2005, while exempting tax cuts contained in a reconciliation bill. Adopted (thus sent to the Senate) 216-213: R 216-9; D 0-203 (ND 0-147, SD 0-56); I 0-1. May 19, 2004.

199. HR 4200. Fiscal 2005 Defense Authorization/Iraqi Prisoner Abuse. Hunter, R-Calif., amendment that would express the sense of Congress that the abuse of Iraqi prisoners at Abu Ghraib prison is offensive and that the majority of U.S. personnel have performed admirably. Adopted 416-4: R 221-0; D 194-4 (ND 138-4, SD 56-0); I 1-0. May 19, 2004.

200. HR 4200. Fiscal 2005 Defense Authorization/Base Closings. Kennedy, R-Minn., amendment that would strike provisions in the bill that would delay for two years the military Base Realignment and Closure process, from 2005 to 2007. It would require the Defense Department to prepare reports on military infrastructure needs before Congress is required to vote on proposed base-closings. Rejected 162-259: R 118-103; D 44-155 (ND 31-114, SD 13-41); I 0-1. A "yea" was a vote in support of the president's position. May 20, 2004.

201. HR 4200. Fiscal 2005 Defense Authorization/Abu Ghraib Prison Demolition. Weldon, R-Pa., amendment that would express the sense of Congress that the Defense secretary should assist the Iraqi government in destroying the Abu Ghraib prison and replacing it with a modern detention facility. Adopted 308-114: R 129-94; D 178-20 (ND 136-8, SD 42-12); I 1-0. May 20, 2004.

202. HR 4200. Fiscal 2005 Defense Authorization/Sexual Assault Policy. Skelton, D-Mo., amendment that would direct the Defense Department to develop a comprehensive policy for the prevention of, and response to, sexual assaults involving members of the armed forces. Adopted 410-0: R 216-0; D 193-0 (ND 140-0, SD 53-0); I 1-0. May 20, 2004.

203. HR 4200. Fiscal 2005 Defense Authorization/Nuclear Bunker Busters. Tauscher, D-Calif., amendment that would transfer $36.6 million from the Energy Department's Robust Nuclear Earth Penetrator "bunkerbuster" and Advanced Concepts programs to various intelligence programs focusing on improving conventional bunker-busting capabilities. Rejected 204-214: R 11-207; D 192-7 (ND 142-2, SD 50-5); I 1-0. May 20, 2004.

	198	199	200	201	202	203
ALABAMA						
1 *Bonner*	Y	Y	Y	N	Y	N
2 *Everett*	Y	Y	N	N	Y	N
3 *Rogers*	Y	Y	N	N	Y	N
4 *Aderholt*	Y	Y	Y	N	Y	N
5 Cramer	N	Y	Y	Y	Y	Y
6 *Bachus*	Y	Y	Y	Y	Y	N
7 Davis	N	Y	N	Y	Y	Y
ALASKA						
AL *Young*	Y	Y	N	N	Y	N
ARIZONA						
1 *Renzi*	Y	Y	Y	Y	Y	N
2 *Franks*	N	Y	N	N	Y	N
3 *Shadegg*	Y	Y	Y	Y	Y	N
4 Pastor	N	Y	N	Y	Y	Y
5 *Hayworth*	?	?	Y	Y	Y	N
6 *Flake*	Y	Y	N	Y	N	N
7 Grijalva	N	Y	N	Y	Y	Y
8 *Kolbe*	Y	Y	Y	Y	Y	N
ARKANSAS						
1 Berry	N	Y	N	Y	Y	Y
2 Snyder	N	Y	Y	N	Y	Y
3 *Boozman*	Y	Y	Y	N	Y	N
4 Ross	N	Y	N	Y	Y	Y
CALIFORNIA						
1 Thompson	N	Y	N	Y	Y	Y
2 *Herger*	Y	Y	Y	N	Y	N
3 *Ose*	Y	Y	Y	N	Y	N
4 *Doolittle*	Y	Y	Y	N	Y	?
5 Matsui	N	Y	?	?	?	Y
6 Woolsey	N	N	N	Y	Y	Y
7 Miller, George	N	Y	N	Y	?	Y
8 Pelosi	N	Y	N	Y	?	Y
9 Lee	N	N	Y	Y	Y	Y
10 Tauscher	N	Y	N	Y	Y	Y
11 *Pombo*	Y	Y	N	N	Y	N
12 Lantos	N	Y	N	Y	Y	Y
13 Stark	N	Y	Y	Y	Y	Y
14 Eshoo	N	Y	Y	Y	Y	Y
15 Honda	N	Y	N	N	Y	Y
16 Lofgren	N	Y	N	Y	Y	Y
17 Farr	N	Y	N	Y	Y	Y
18 Cardoza	N	Y	N	Y	Y	Y
19 *Radanovich*	Y	Y	N	?	Y	N
20 Dooley	N	?	?	?	?	Y
21 *Nunes*	Y	Y	N	N	Y	N
22 *Thomas*	Y	Y	Y	Y	Y	N
23 Capps	N	Y	Y	Y	Y	Y
24 *Gallegly*	Y	Y	N	N	Y	N
25 *McKeon*	Y	Y	N	N	Y	N
26 *Dreier*	Y	Y	Y	Y	Y	N
27 Sherman	N	Y	Y	Y	Y	Y
28 Berman	N	Y	Y	Y	Y	Y
29 Schiff	N	Y	N	Y	Y	Y
30 Waxman	N	Y	Y	Y	Y	Y
31 Becerra	N	Y	N	Y	Y	?
32 Solis	N	Y	N	Y	Y	Y
33 Watson	N	Y	N	Y	Y	Y
34 Roybal-Allard	N	Y	N	Y	Y	Y
35 Waters	N	N	N	Y	Y	Y
36 Harman	N	Y	N	Y	Y	Y

	198	199	200	201	202	203
37 Millender-McD.	N	Y	N	Y	Y	Y
38 Napolitano	N	Y	N	Y	Y	Y
39 Sánchez, Linda	N	Y	N	Y	Y	Y
40 *Royce*	Y	Y	Y	Y	Y	N
41 *Lewis*	Y	Y	Y	Y	Y	N
42 *Miller, Gary*	Y	Y	N	N	Y	N
43 Baca	N	Y	N	Y	Y	Y
44 *Calvert*	Y	Y	N	N	Y	N
45 *Bono*	Y	Y	N	N	Y	N
46 *Rohrabacher*	Y	Y	N	N	Y	N
47 Sanchez, Loretta	N	Y	Y	Y	Y	Y
48 *Cox*	Y	Y	N	N	Y	N
49 *Issa*	Y	Y	N	N	Y	N
50 *Cunningham*	Y	Y	N	N	Y	N
51 Filner	N	Y	N	Y	Y	Y
52 *Hunter*	Y	Y	N	N	Y	N
53 Davis	N	Y	N	Y	Y	Y
COLORADO						
1 DeGette	N	Y	Y	Y	Y	Y
2 Udall	N	Y	N	Y	Y	Y
3 *McInnis*	Y	Y	N	N	Y	N
4 *Musgrave*	N	Y	N	N	Y	N
5 *Hefley*	Y	Y	N	N	Y	N
6 *Tancredo*	Y	Y	N	N	Y	N
7 *Beauprez*	Y	Y	–	N	Y	N
CONNECTICUT						
1 Larson	N	Y	N	Y	Y	Y
2 *Simmons*	N	Y	N	Y	Y	Y
3 DeLauro	N	Y	N	Y	Y	Y
4 *Shays*	Y	Y	Y	Y	Y	Y
5 *Johnson*	Y	Y	Y	Y	Y	Y
DELAWARE						
AL *Castle*	Y	Y	Y	Y	Y	N
FLORIDA						
1 *Miller, J.*	Y	Y	N	N	Y	N
2 Boyd	N	Y	Y	Y	Y	Y
3 Brown	N	Y	Y	Y	Y	Y
4 *Crenshaw*	Y	Y	N	N	Y	N
5 *Brown-Waite*	Y	Y	N	N	Y	N
6 *Stearns*	Y	Y	N	N	Y	N
7 *Mica*	Y	Y	N	N	Y	N
8 *Keller*	Y	Y	N	N	Y	N
9 *Bilirakis*	Y	Y	N	N	Y	N
10 *Young*	Y	Y	N	N	Y	N
11 Davis	N	Y	Y	Y	Y	Y
12 *Putnam*	Y	Y	Y	Y	Y	N
13 *Harris*	Y	Y	Y	N	Y	N
14 *Goss*	Y	Y	N	N	Y	N
15 *Weldon*	Y	Y	N	N	Y	N
16 *Foley*	N	Y	N	N	Y	N
17 Meek	N	N	N	Y	Y	Y
18 *Ros-Lehtinen*	Y	Y	N	Y	Y	N
19 Wexler	N	Y	N	Y	Y	Y
20 Deutsch	N	Y	?	?	?	?
21 *Diaz-Balart, L.*	Y	Y	N	N	Y	N
22 *Shaw*	Y	Y	N	N	Y	N
23 Hastings	N	Y	N	Y	Y	Y
24 *Feeney*	Y	Y	N	N	Y	N
25 *Diaz-Balart, M.*	Y	Y	N	Y	Y	N
GEORGIA						
1 *Kingston*	Y	Y	Y	N	Y	N
2 Bishop	N	Y	N	Y	Y	Y
3 Marshall	N	N	N	Y	Y	Y
4 Majette	N	N	N	Y	Y	Y
5 Lewis	N	Y	N	Y	Y	Y
6 *Isakson*	Y	Y	N	N	Y	N
7 *Linder*	Y	Y	N	N	Y	N
8 *Collins*	Y	Y	?	?	?	?
9 *Norwood*	Y	Y	?	?	?	?
10 *Deal*	Y	Y	N	N	Y	N
11 *Gingrey*	Y	Y	N	N	Y	N
12 *Burns*	Y	Y	N	N	Y	N
13 Scott	N	Y	N	Y	Y	Y
HAWAII						
1 Abercrombie	N	Y	N	Y	Y	Y
2 Case	N	Y	Y	N	Y	Y
IDAHO						
1 *Otter*	Y	Y	Y	N	Y	N
2 *Simpson*	Y	Y	Y	N	Y	N
ILLINOIS						
1 Rush	N	Y	Y	Y	Y	Y
2 Jackson	N	Y	Y	Y	Y	Y
3 Lipinski	N	Y	N	Y	Y	Y
4 Gutierrez	N	Y	N	Y	Y	Y
5 Emanuel	N	Y	N	Y	Y	Y
6 *Hyde*	Y	Y	N	Y	Y	N

ND Northern Democrats   SD Southern Democrats

	198	199	200	201	202	203
7 Davis	N	Y	Y	Y	Y	Y
8 ***Crane***	Y	Y	Y	Y	Y	N
9 Schakowsky	N	Y	N	Y	Y	Y
10 ***Kirk***	Y	Y	Y	Y	Y	N
11 ***Weller***	Y	Y	Y	Y	Y	N
12 Costello	N	Y	N	Y	Y	Y
13 ***Biggert***	Y	Y	Y	Y	Y	N
14 ***Hastert***	Y					N
15 ***Johnson***	Y	Y	Y	Y	Y	N
16 ***Manzullo***	Y	Y	N	Y	Y	N
17 Evans	N	Y	N	Y	Y	Y
18 ***LaHood***	Y	Y	N	Y	Y	N
19 ***Shimkus***	Y	Y	N	Y	Y	N
INDIANA						
1 Visclosky	N	Y	N	Y	Y	Y
2 ***Chocola***	Y	Y	Y	Y	Y	N
3 ***Souder***	Y	Y	N	Y	Y	N
4 ***Buyer***	Y	Y	N	Y	Y	N
5 ***Burton***	Y	Y	N	Y	Y	N
6 ***Pence***	Y	Y	Y	Y	?	N
7 Carson	N	Y	N	Y	Y	Y
8 ***Hostettler***	N	Y	N	Y	Y	N
9 Hill	N	Y	N	Y	Y	Y
IOWA						
1 ***Nussle***	Y	Y	Y	Y	Y	N
2 ***Leach***	?	?	?	?	?	?
3 Boswell	N	Y	Y	Y	Y	Y
4 ***Latham***	Y	Y	Y	Y	Y	N
5 ***King***	Y	Y	Y	N	Y	N
KANSAS						
1 ***Moran***	Y	Y	N	N	Y	N
2 ***Ryun***	Y	Y	N	Y	Y	N
3 Moore	N	Y	N	Y	Y	Y
4 ***Tiahrt***	Y	Y	N	N	Y	N
KENTUCKY						
1 ***Whitfield***	Y	Y	Y	Y	Y	N
2 ***Lewis***	Y	Y	Y	Y	Y	N
3 ***Northup***	Y	Y	Y	N	Y	N
4 Lucas	N	Y	Y	Y	Y	Y
5 ***Rogers***	Y	Y	Y	Y	Y	N
6 Chandler	N	Y	N	Y	Y	Y
LOUISIANA						
1 ***Vitter***	Y	Y	Y	N	Y	N
2 Jefferson	N	Y	N	N	Y	Y
3 ***Tauzin***	?	?	?	?	?	?
4 ***McCrery***	Y	Y	Y	N	?	N
5 Alexander	N	Y	N	Y	Y	Y
6 ***Baker***	Y	Y	Y	N	Y	N
7 John	N	Y	N	N	Y	Y
MAINE						
1 Allen	N	Y	N	Y	Y	Y
2 Michaud	N	Y	N	Y	Y	Y
MARYLAND						
1 ***Gilchrest***	Y	Y	Y	Y	Y	Y
2 Ruppersberger	N	Y	Y	Y	Y	Y
3 Cardin	N	Y	N	Y	Y	Y
4 Wynn	N	Y	N	Y	Y	Y
5 Hoyer	N	Y	N	?	?	Y
6 ***Bartlett***	Y	Y	N	N	Y	N
7 Cummings	N	Y	N	Y	Y	Y
8 Van Hollen	N	Y	Y	Y	Y	Y
MASSACHUSETTS						
1 Olver	N	Y	N	Y	Y	Y
2 Neal	N	Y	N	Y	Y	Y
3 McGovern	N	Y	N	Y	Y	Y
4 Frank	N	Y	N	Y	Y	Y
5 Meehan	N	Y	N	Y	Y	Y
6 Tierney	N	Y	N	Y	Y	Y
7 Markey	N	Y	N	Y	Y	Y
8 Capuano	N	Y	N	Y	Y	Y
9 Lynch	N	Y	N	Y	Y	Y
10 Delahunt	?	?	N	Y	Y	Y
MICHIGAN						
1 Stupak	N	Y	N	Y	+	Y
2 ***Hoekstra***	Y	Y	Y	N	Y	N
3 ***Ehlers***	Y	Y	Y	Y	Y	Y
4 ***Camp***	Y	Y	Y	Y	Y	N
5 Kildee	N	Y	N	Y	Y	Y
6 ***Upton***	Y	Y	Y	N	Y	Y
7 ***Smith***	Y	Y	Y	N	Y	N
8 ***Rogers***	Y	Y	Y	Y	Y	N
9 ***Knollenberg***	Y	Y	Y	Y	Y	N
10 ***Miller***	Y	Y	N	N	Y	N
11 ***McCotter***	Y	Y	N	N	Y	N
12 Levin	N	Y	N	Y	Y	Y

	198	199	200	201	202	203
13 Kilpatrick	N	Y	N	Y	Y	Y
14 Conyers	N	N	N	N	Y	Y
15 Dingell	N	Y	N	Y	Y	Y
MINNESOTA						
1 ***Gutknecht***	Y	Y	Y	Y	Y	N
2 ***Kline***	Y	Y	Y	Y	Y	N
3 ***Ramstad***	Y	Y	Y	Y	Y	N
4 McCollum	N	Y	Y	Y	Y	Y
5 Sabo	N	Y	Y	Y	Y	Y
6 ***Kennedy***	Y	Y	Y	Y	Y	N
7 Peterson	N	Y	N	N	Y	N
8 Oberstar	N	Y	Y	Y	Y	Y
MISSISSIPPI						
1 ***Wicker***	Y	Y	N	Y	Y	N
2 Thompson	N	Y	N	Y	Y	Y
3 ***Pickering***	Y	Y	N	Y	Y	N
4 Taylor	N	Y	N	Y	Y	Y
MISSOURI						
1 Clay	N	Y	N	Y	Y	Y
2 ***Akin***	Y	Y	Y	Y	Y	N
3 Gephardt	N	?	N	Y	Y	?
4 Skelton	N	Y	N	Y	Y	Y
5 McCarthy	N	Y	N	Y	Y	Y
6 ***Graves***	Y	Y	Y	N	Y	N
7 ***Blunt***	Y	Y	Y	N	Y	N
8 ***Emerson***	Y	?	N	Y	Y	N
9 ***Hulshof***	Y	Y	N	Y	Y	N
MONTANA						
AL ***Rehberg***	Y	Y	N	Y	Y	N
NEBRASKA						
1 ***Bereuter***	Y	Y	N	Y	Y	N
2 ***Terry***	Y	Y	Y	Y	Y	N
3 ***Osborne***	Y	Y	N	Y	Y	N
NEVADA						
1 Berkley	N	Y	Y	Y	Y	Y
2 ***Gibbons***	Y	Y	N	Y	Y	N
3 ***Porter***	Y	Y	Y	Y	Y	N
NEW HAMPSHIRE						
1 ***Bradley***	Y	Y	N	Y	Y	N
2 ***Bass***	Y	Y	N	Y	Y	N
NEW JERSEY						
1 Andrews	N	Y	Y	Y	Y	Y
2 ***LoBiondo***	Y	Y	N	Y	Y	N
3 ***Saxton***	Y	Y	N	N	Y	N
4 ***Smith***	N	Y	N	Y	Y	N
5 ***Garrett***	Y	Y	Y	N	Y	N
6 Pallone	N	Y	N	Y	Y	Y
7 ***Ferguson***	Y	Y	N	Y	Y	N
8 Pascrell	N	Y	N	Y	Y	Y
9 Rothman	N	Y	N	Y	Y	Y
10 Payne	N	Y	N	N	Y	Y
11 ***Frelinghuysen***	Y	Y	N	Y	Y	N
12 Holt	N	Y	N	Y	Y	Y
13 Menendez	N	Y	N	Y	Y	Y
NEW MEXICO						
1 ***Wilson***	Y	Y	N	Y	Y	N
2 ***Pearce***	Y	Y	N	Y	Y	N
3 Udall	N	Y	N	Y	Y	Y
NEW YORK						
1 Bishop	N	Y	N	Y	Y	Y
2 Israel	N	Y	N	Y	Y	Y
3 ***King***	Y	Y	N	N	Y	N
4 McCarthy	N	Y	N	Y	Y	Y
5 Ackerman	N	Y	N	Y	Y	Y
6 Meeks	N	Y	N	N	Y	Y
7 Crowley	N	Y	N	Y	Y	?
8 Nadler	N	Y	N	Y	Y	Y
9 Weiner	N	Y	N	Y	Y	Y
10 Towns	N	Y	N	Y	Y	Y
11 Owens	N	Y	N	Y	Y	Y
12 Velázquez	N	Y	N	Y	Y	Y
13 ***Fossella***	Y	Y	N	N	Y	?
14 Maloney	N	Y	N	Y	Y	Y
15 Rangel	N	Y	N	N	Y	Y
16 Serrano	N	Y	N	Y	Y	Y
17 Engel	N	Y	N	Y	Y	Y
18 Lowey	N	Y	N	Y	Y	Y
19 ***Kelly***	Y	Y	Y	Y	Y	N
20 ***Sweeney***	Y	Y	N	N	Y	N
21 McNulty	N	Y	N	Y	Y	Y
22 Hinchey	N	Y	N	Y	Y	Y
23 ***McHugh***	Y	Y	Y	Y	Y	N
24 ***Boehlert***	Y	Y	N	Y	Y	Y
25 ***Walsh***	Y	Y	Y	Y	Y	?

	198	199	200	201	202	203
26 ***Reynolds***	Y	Y	Y	Y	Y	N
27 ***Quinn***	Y	Y	N	Y	Y	?
28 Slaughter	N	Y	N	Y	Y	Y
29 ***Houghton***	Y	Y	N	N	Y	N
NORTH CAROLINA						
1 Ballance	?	?	?	?	?	?
2 Etheridge	N	Y	N	Y	Y	Y
3 ***Jones***	N	?	N	N	Y	N
4 Price	N	Y	Y	Y	Y	Y
5 ***Burr***	Y	?	N	Y	Y	?
6 ***Coble***	Y	Y	Y	N	Y	N
7 McIntyre	N	Y	N	Y	Y	Y
8 ***Hayes***	Y	Y	N	N	Y	N
9 ***Myrick***	Y	Y	Y	Y	Y	N
10 ***Ballenger***	Y	Y	Y	Y	Y	N
11 ***Taylor***	Y	Y	Y	Y	Y	N
12 Watt	N	Y	N	N	Y	Y
13 Miller	N	Y	Y	Y	Y	Y
NORTH DAKOTA						
AL Pomeroy	N	Y	N	Y	Y	Y
OHIO						
1 ***Chabot***	Y	Y	Y	N	Y	N
2 ***Portman***	Y	Y	Y	Y	Y	N
3 ***Turner***	Y	Y	N	Y	Y	N
4 ***Oxley***	Y	Y	Y	Y	Y	N
5 ***Gillmor***	Y	Y	Y	Y	Y	N
6 Strickland	N	Y	N	Y	Y	Y
7 ***Hobson***	Y	Y	N	Y	Y	N
8 ***Boehner***	Y	Y	Y	Y	Y	N
9 Kaptur	N	Y	N	Y	Y	Y
10 Kucinich	N	N	Y	Y	Y	Y
11 Jones	N	Y	N	Y	Y	Y
12 ***Tiberi***	Y	Y	N	Y	Y	N
13 Brown	N	Y	N	Y	+	Y
14 ***LaTourette***	Y	Y	N	Y	Y	?
15 ***Pryce***	Y	Y	N	Y	Y	N
16 ***Regula***	Y	Y	N	Y	Y	N
17 Ryan	N	Y	N	Y	Y	Y
18 ***Ney***	Y	Y	N	N	Y	N
OKLAHOMA						
1 ***Sullivan***	Y	Y	N	N	Y	N
2 Carson	N	Y	–	+	+	N
3 ***Lucas***	Y	Y	N	N	Y	N
4 ***Cole***	Y	Y	N	Y	+	N
5 ***Istook***	Y	Y	Y	N	Y	N
OREGON						
1 Wu	N	Y	N	Y	Y	Y
2 ***Walden***	Y	Y	Y	Y	Y	N
3 Blumenauer	N	Y	Y	Y	Y	Y
4 DeFazio	N	Y	Y	Y	Y	Y
5 Hooley	N	Y	N	Y	Y	Y
PENNSYLVANIA						
1 Brady	N	Y	N	Y	Y	Y
2 Fattah	N	Y	?	?	?	?
3 ***English***	Y	Y	Y	Y	Y	N
4 ***Hart***	Y	Y	N	Y	Y	N
5 ***Peterson***	Y	Y	Y	Y	Y	N
6 ***Gerlach***	N	Y	N	Y	Y	N
7 ***Weldon***	Y	Y	Y	Y	Y	N
8 ***Greenwood***	Y	Y	Y	Y	Y	N
9 ***Shuster, Bill***	Y	Y	N	Y	Y	N
10 ***Sherwood***	Y	Y	N	Y	Y	N
11 Kanjorski	N	Y	N	Y	Y	Y
12 Murtha	N	?	N	Y	Y	N
13 Hoeffel	N	Y	N	Y	Y	Y
14 Doyle	N	Y	N	Y	Y	Y
15 ***Toomey***	Y	Y	Y	Y	Y	N
16 ***Pitts***	Y	Y	Y	Y	Y	N
17 Holden	N	Y	N	Y	Y	Y
18 ***Murphy***	Y	Y	N	Y	+	N
19 ***Platts***	Y	Y	N	Y	Y	N
RHODE ISLAND						
1 Kennedy	N	Y	N	Y	Y	Y
2 Langevin	N	Y	N	Y	Y	Y
SOUTH CAROLINA						
1 ***Brown***	Y	Y	Y	Y	Y	N
2 ***Wilson***	Y	Y	Y	Y	Y	N
3 ***Barrett***	Y	Y	Y	N	Y	N
4 ***DeMint***	Y	Y	Y	Y	Y	N
5 Spratt	N	Y	N	Y	?	Y
6 Clyburn	N	Y	N	Y	Y	Y
SOUTH DAKOTA						
AL Vacant						

	198	199	200	201	202	203
TENNESSEE						
1 ***Jenkins***	Y	Y	N	N	Y	N
2 ***Duncan***	Y	Y	Y	N	Y	N
3 ***Wamp***	Y	Y	Y	N	Y	N
4 Davis	N	Y	N	Y	Y	Y
5 Cooper	N	Y	Y	N	Y	Y
6 Gordon	N	Y	Y	Y	Y	Y
7 ***Blackburn***	Y	Y	Y	N	Y	N
8 Tanner	N	Y	N	N	Y	Y
9 Ford	N	Y	N	Y	Y	Y
TEXAS						
1 Sandlin	N	Y	N	Y	Y	Y
2 Turner	N	Y	N	Y	Y	Y
3 ***Johnson, Sam***	Y	Y	?	?	?	?
4 ***Hall***	Y	Y	N	Y	Y	N
5 ***Hensarling***	Y	Y	Y	N	Y	N
6 ***Barton***	Y	Y	Y	N	Y	N
7 ***Culberson***	Y	Y	Y	Y	Y	N
8 ***Brady***	Y	Y	Y	N	Y	N
9 Lampson	N	Y	N	Y	Y	Y
10 Doggett	N	Y	Y	N	Y	Y
11 Edwards	N	Y	Y	Y	Y	N
12 ***Granger***	Y	Y	Y	N	Y	N
13 ***Thornberry***	Y	Y	Y	N	Y	N
14 ***Paul***	N	Y	N	N	Y	Y
15 Hinojosa	N	Y	N	Y	Y	Y
16 Reyes	N	Y	N	Y	Y	Y
17 Stenholm	N	Y	Y	N	Y	N
18 Jackson-Lee	N	Y	N	Y	Y	Y
19 ***Neugebauer***	Y	Y	Y	N	Y	N
20 Gonzalez	N	Y	N	Y	Y	Y
21 ***Smith***	Y	Y	Y	Y	Y	N
22 ***DeLay***	Y	Y	Y	N	Y	N
23 ***Bonilla***	Y	Y	N	N	Y	N
24 Frost	N	Y	N	Y	Y	Y
25 Bell	N	Y	N	Y	Y	Y
26 ***Burgess***	Y	Y	Y	N	Y	N
27 Ortiz	N	Y	N	Y	Y	Y
28 Rodriguez	N	Y	N	N	Y	Y
29 Green	N	Y	N	Y	Y	Y
30 Johnson, E.B.	N	Y	N	Y	Y	Y
31 ***Carter***	Y	Y	+	N	?	N
32 ***Sessions***	Y	Y	Y	N	Y	N
UTAH						
1 ***Bishop***	Y	Y	N	Y	Y	N
2 Matheson	N	Y	N	Y	Y	Y
3 ***Cannon***	Y	Y	N	N	Y	N
VERMONT						
AL *Sanders*	N	Y	N	Y	Y	Y
VIRGINIA						
1 ***Davis, Jo Ann***	Y	Y	N	Y	Y	N
2 ***Schrock***	Y	Y	Y	Y	Y	N
3 Scott	N	Y	N	Y	Y	Y
4 ***Forbes***	Y	Y	N	Y	Y	N
5 ***Goode***	N	Y	N	Y	Y	N
6 ***Goodlatte***	Y	Y	Y	N	Y	N
7 ***Cantor***	Y	Y	Y	Y	?	N
8 Moran	N	Y	Y	Y	Y	Y
9 Boucher	N	Y	N	Y	Y	Y
10 ***Wolf***	Y	Y	N	Y	Y	N
11 ***Davis, T.***	Y	Y	Y	Y	Y	N
WASHINGTON						
1 Inslee	N	Y	Y	Y	Y	Y
2 Larsen	N	Y	Y	Y	Y	Y
3 Baird	N	+	N	Y	Y	Y
4 ***Hastings***	Y	Y	Y	Y	Y	N
5 ***Nethercutt***	Y	Y	N	N	Y	N
6 Dicks	N	Y	Y	Y	Y	Y
7 McDermott	N	Y	Y	Y	Y	Y
8 ***Dunn***	Y	Y	Y	Y	Y	N
9 Smith	N	?	Y	Y	Y	Y
WEST VIRGINIA						
1 Mollohan	N	Y	N	Y	Y	Y
2 ***Capito***	Y	Y	Y	Y	Y	N
3 Rahall	N	Y	N	Y	Y	Y
WISCONSIN						
1 ***Ryan***	Y	Y	Y	Y	Y	N
2 Baldwin	N	Y	Y	Y	Y	Y
3 Kind	N	Y	N	Y	Y	Y
4 Kleczka	N	Y	N	Y	Y	Y
5 ***Sensenbrenner***	Y	Y	Y	N	Y	N
6 ***Petri***	Y	Y	Y	N	Y	Y
7 Obey	N	Y	Y	Y	Y	Y
8 ***Green***	Y	Y	Y	Y	Y	N
WYOMING						
AL ***Cubin***	Y	Y	Y	N	Y	N

Southern states - Ala., Ark., Fla., Ga., Ky., La., Miss., N.C., Okla., S.C., Tenn., Texas, Va.

Key

Y	Voted for (yea).
#	Paired for.
+	Announced for.
N	Voted against (nay).
X	Paired against.
–	Announced against.
P	Voted "present."
C	Voted "present" to avoid possible conflict of interest.
?	Did not vote or otherwise make a position known.

Democrats **Republicans** *Independents*

204. HR 4200. Fiscal 2005 Defense Authorization/Taiwan Officer Exchanges. Ryun, R-Kan., amendment that would require the Defense secretary to initiate officer training and exchange programs with the Taiwan military, which would focus on the defense of Taiwan against potential submarine and missile attacks. Adopted 290-132: R 206-14; D 83-118 (ND 60-86, SD 23-32); I 1-0. May 20, 2004.

205. HR 4200. Fiscal 2005 Defense Authorization/Recommit. Waxman, D-Calif., motion to recommit the bill to the House Armed Services Committee with instructions to add language that would express the sense of the House that a select committee should be established to investigate the treatment of detainees in the global war on terrorism, including allegations of abuse of Iraqi prisoners. Motion rejected 202-224: R 0-222; D 201-2 (ND 147-1, SD 54-1); I 1-0. May 20, 2004.

206. HR 4200. Fiscal 2005 Defense Authorization/Passage. Passage of the bill that would authorize $447.2 billion for defense programs, including $25 billion for operations in Iraq, for fiscal 2005. It would authorize up to $10.2 billion for missile defense, fund research for new nuclear, earth-penetrating weapons and delay the next scheduled round of base closures from 2005 to 2007. It also would require the Defense department to increase the number of active-duty Army service members by 30,000, boost Marine Corps active-duty levels by 9,000 and provide for a 3.5 percent pay hike for military personnel. Passed 391-34: R 221-1; D 169-33 (ND 116-31, SD 53-2); I 1-0. May 20, 2004.

207. H Con Res 432. Adjournment/Adoption. Adoption of the concurrent resolution that would provide for an adjournment of the House until 2 p.m., Tuesday, June 1. The resolution also would provide for an adjournment of the Senate until 12 p.m. on Tuesday, June 1. Adopted 222-193: R 214-1; D 8-191 (ND 7-137, SD 1-54); I 0-1. May 20, 2004.

208. HR 4359. Child Tax Credit/Democratic Substitute. Levin, D-Mich., substitute amendment that would extend through 2010 the $1,000 child tax credit. It would condition a permanent extension on passage of legislation that balances the budget by fiscal 2014 without using Social Security and Medicare trust funds. The cost of the substitute would be generally offset by applying an additional tax of 2.75 percent for 2005 through 2010 on individuals with incomes of more than $500,000 a year and married taxpayers with incomes of more than $1 million. Rejected 187-226: R 0-217; D 186-9 (ND 138-4, SD 48-5); I 1-0. May 20, 2004.

209. HR 4359. Child Tax Credit/Passage. Passage of the bill that would permanently extend the $1,000 per child tax credit that is scheduled to revert to $700 per child in 2005. It would increase the amount of income a taxpayer may earn before the credit begins to phase out from $75,000 to $125,000 for single individuals and from $110,000 to $250,000 for married couples. It also would allow military personnel to include combat pay in their gross earnings in order to calculate eligibility for the child tax credit. Passed 271-139: R 213-3; D 58-135 (ND 35-105, SD 23-30); I 0-1. May 20, 2004.

		204	205	206	207	208	209
ALABAMA							
1	*Bonner*	Y	N	Y	Y	N	Y
2	*Everett*	Y	N	Y	Y	N	N
3	*Rogers*	Y	N	Y	Y	N	Y
4	*Aderholt*	Y	N	Y	Y	N	Y
5	Cramer	Y	Y	Y	N	N	Y
6	*Bachus*	N	N	Y	Y	N	Y
7	Davis	N	Y	Y	N	Y	Y
ALASKA							
AL	*Young*	Y	N	Y	Y	N	Y
ARIZONA							
1	*Renzi*	N	N	Y	Y	N	Y
2	*Franks*	Y	N	Y	Y	N	Y
3	*Shadegg*	Y	N	Y	Y	N	Y
4	Pastor	N	Y	Y	N	Y	N
5	*Hayworth*	Y	N	Y	Y	N	Y
6	*Flake*	Y	N	Y	Y	N	Y
7	Grijalva	N	Y	N	N	Y	N
8	*Kolbe*	N	N	Y	Y	N	Y
ARKANSAS							
1	Berry	N	Y	Y	N	Y	N
2	Snyder	N	Y	Y	N	Y	N
3	*Boozman*	Y	N	Y	Y	N	Y
4	Ross	Y	Y	Y	N	Y	N
CALIFORNIA							
1	Thompson	Y	Y	Y	N	Y	N
2	*Herger*	Y	N	Y	Y	N	Y
3	*Ose*	Y	N	Y	Y	N	Y
4	*Doolittle*	Y	N	Y	Y	N	Y
5	Matsui	Y	Y	Y	N	Y	N
6	Woolsey	N	Y	N	N	Y	N
7	Miller, George	N	Y	N	N	Y	N
8	Pelosi	Y	Y	Y	N	Y	N
9	Lee	N	Y	N	N	Y	N
10	Tauscher	Y	Y	Y	N	Y	N
11	*Pombo*	Y	N	Y	Y	N	Y
12	Lantos	Y	Y	Y	N	Y	N
13	Stark	N	Y	N	N	Y	N
14	Eshoo	Y	Y	Y	N	Y	N
15	Honda	N	Y	N	N	Y	N
16	Lofgren	Y	Y	Y	N	?	?
17	Farr	N	Y	N	N	Y	N
18	Cardoza	N	Y	Y	N	Y	Y
19	*Radanovich*	Y	N	Y	Y	N	Y
20	Dooley	N	Y	Y	N	Y	N
21	*Nunes*	Y	N	Y	Y	N	Y
22	*Thomas*	Y	N	Y	Y	N	Y
23	Capps	N	Y	Y	N	Y	N
24	*Gallegly*	Y	N	Y	Y	?	?
25	*McKeon*	Y	N	Y	Y	N	Y
26	*Dreier*	Y	N	Y	Y	N	Y
27	Sherman	Y	Y	Y	N	Y	N
28	Berman	Y	Y	Y	N	Y	N
29	Schiff	Y	Y	Y	N	Y	N
30	Waxman	Y	Y	Y	N	Y	N
31	Becerra	?	Y	Y	N	Y	N
32	Solis	N	Y	N	N	Y	N
33	Watson	Y	Y	N	N	Y	N
34	Roybal-Allard	N	Y	N	N	Y	N
35	Waters	N	N	N	N	Y	N
36	Harman	Y	Y	Y	N	Y	N
37	Millender-McD.	Y	Y	Y	N	Y	N
38	Napolitano	N	Y	N	N	Y	N
39	Sánchez, Linda	Y	Y	Y	N	Y	N
40	*Royce*	Y	N	Y	Y	N	Y
41	*Lewis*	Y	N	Y	Y	N	Y
42	*Miller, Gary*	Y	N	Y	Y	?	?
43	Baca	N	Y	Y	N	Y	N
44	*Calvert*	Y	N	Y	Y	N	Y
45	*Bono*	Y	N	Y	Y	N	Y
46	*Rohrabacher*	Y	N	Y	Y	N	Y
47	Sanchez, Loretta	N	Y	Y	N	Y	N
48	*Cox*	Y	N	Y	Y	N	Y
49	*Issa*	Y	N	Y	Y	N	Y
50	*Cunningham*	Y	N	Y	Y	N	Y
51	Filner	N	Y	N	N	Y	Y
52	*Hunter*	Y	N	Y	Y	N	Y
53	Davis	Y	Y	Y	N	Y	N
COLORADO							
1	DeGette	N	Y	Y	N	Y	N
2	Udall	N	Y	Y	N	Y	Y
3	*McInnis*	Y	N	Y	Y	?	?
4	*Musgrave*	Y	N	Y	Y	N	Y
5	*Hefley*	Y	N	Y	Y	N	Y
6	*Tancredo*	Y	N	Y	?	N	Y
7	*Beauprez*	Y	N	Y	Y	N	Y
CONNECTICUT							
1	Larson	N	Y	Y	N	Y	N
2	*Simmons*	Y	N	Y	Y	N	Y
3	DeLauro	N	Y	N	N	Y	N
4	*Shays*	N	N	Y	Y	N	Y
5	*Johnson*	Y	N	Y	N	N	Y
DELAWARE							
AL	*Castle*	Y	N	Y	Y	N	Y
FLORIDA							
1	*Miller, J.*	Y	N	Y	Y	N	Y
2	Boyd	N	Y	Y	N	Y	N
3	Brown	Y	Y	Y	N	Y	Y
4	*Crenshaw*	Y	N	Y	Y	N	Y
5	*Brown-Waite*	Y	N	Y	Y	N	Y
6	*Stearns*	Y	N	Y	Y	N	Y
7	*Mica*	Y	N	Y	Y	N	Y
8	*Keller*	Y	N	Y	Y	N	Y
9	*Bilirakis*	Y	N	Y	Y	N	Y
10	*Young*	Y	N	Y	Y	N	Y
11	Davis	Y	Y	Y	N	Y	N
12	*Putnam*	Y	N	Y	Y	N	Y
13	*Harris*	Y	N	Y	Y	N	Y
14	*Goss*	N	N	Y	Y	N	Y
15	*Weldon*	Y	N	Y	Y	N	Y
16	*Foley*	Y	N	Y	Y	N	Y
17	Meek	N	Y	N	N	Y	N
18	*Ros-Lehtinen*	Y	N	Y	Y	N	Y
19	Wexler	Y	Y	Y	N	Y	N
20	Deutsch	?	?	?	?	?	?
21	*Diaz-Balart, L.*	Y	N	Y	Y	N	Y
22	*Shaw*	Y	N	Y	Y	N	Y
23	Hastings	Y	Y	Y	N	Y	N
24	*Feeney*	Y	N	Y	Y	N	Y
25	*Diaz-Balart, M.*	Y	N	Y	Y	N	Y
GEORGIA							
1	*Kingston*	Y	N	Y	Y	N	Y
2	Bishop	Y	Y	Y	N	Y	Y
3	Marshall	N	N	Y	N	?	Y
4	Majette	Y	Y	Y	N	Y	N
5	Lewis	N	Y	N	N	Y	N
6	*Isakson*	Y	N	Y	Y	N	Y
7	*Linder*	Y	N	Y	Y	N	Y
8	*Collins*	Y	N	Y	Y	N	Y
9	*Norwood*	?	?	?	?	?	?
10	*Deal*	Y	N	Y	Y	N	Y
11	*Gingrey*	Y	N	Y	Y	N	Y
12	*Burns*	Y	N	Y	Y	N	Y
13	Scott	Y	Y	Y	N	Y	N
HAWAII							
1	Abercrombie	N	Y	Y	N	Y	N
2	Case	Y	Y	Y	N	Y	N
IDAHO							
1	*Otter*	Y	N	Y	Y	N	Y
2	*Simpson*	Y	N	Y	Y	N	Y
ILLINOIS							
1	Rush	Y	Y	Y	N	?	?
2	Jackson	N	Y	N	N	Y	N
3	Lipinski	N	Y	Y	N	?	?
4	Gutierrez	N	Y	N	N	Y	?
5	Emanuel	N	Y	Y	N	Y	N
6	*Hyde*	Y	N	Y	Y	N	Y

ND Northern Democrats   SD Southern Democrats

	204	205	206	207	208	209
7 Davis	Y	Y	Y	N	Y	N
8 ***Crane***	Y	N	Y	Y	N	Y
9 Schakowsky	N	Y	N	N	Y	N
10 ***Kirk***	Y	N	Y	Y	N	Y
11 ***Weller***	Y	N	Y	Y	N	Y
12 Costello	Y	Y	Y	N	Y	Y
13 ***Biggert***	N	N	Y	Y	N	Y
14 ***Hastert***		N	Y	Y		
15 ***Johnson***	Y	N	Y	Y	N	Y
16 ***Manzullo***	N	N	Y	Y	N	Y
17 Evans	N	Y	Y	N	Y	N
18 ***LaHood***	N	N	Y	Y	N	Y
19 ***Shimkus***	Y	N	Y	Y	N	Y
INDIANA						
1 Visclosky	N	Y	Y	N	Y	N
2 ***Chocola***	Y	N	Y	Y	N	Y
3 ***Souder***	Y	N	Y	Y	N	Y
4 ***Buyer***	Y	N	Y	Y	N	Y
5 ***Burton***	Y	N	Y	Y	N	Y
6 ***Pence***	Y	N	Y	Y	N	Y
7 Carson	Y	Y	Y	N	Y	N
8 ***Hostettler***	Y	N	Y	Y	N	Y
9 Hill	N	Y	Y	N	Y	N
IOWA						
1 ***Nussle***	Y	N	Y	Y	N	Y
2 ***Leach***	?	?	?	?	?	?
3 Boswell	Y	Y	Y	N	Y	Y
4 ***Latham***	Y	N	Y	Y	N	Y
5 ***King***	Y	N	Y	Y	N	Y
KANSAS						
1 ***Moran***	Y	N	Y	Y	N	Y
2 ***Ryun***	Y	N	Y	Y	N	Y
3 Moore	N	Y	Y	N	Y	Y
4 ***Tiahrt***	Y	N	Y	Y	N	Y
KENTUCKY						
1 ***Whitfield***	Y	N	Y	Y	N	Y
2 ***Lewis***	Y	N	Y	Y	N	Y
3 ***Northup***	Y	N	Y	Y	N	Y
4 Lucas	Y	Y	Y	N	Y	Y
5 ***Rogers***	Y	N	Y	Y	N	Y
6 Chandler	Y	Y	Y	N	N	Y
LOUISIANA						
1 ***Vitter***	Y	N	Y	Y	N	Y
2 Jefferson	Y	Y	Y	N	Y	N
3 ***Tauzin***	?	?	?	?	?	?
4 ***McCrery***	Y	N	Y	Y	N	Y
5 Alexander	N	Y	Y	N	N	Y
6 ***Baker***	Y	N	Y	Y	N	Y
7 John	Y	Y	Y	N	Y	Y
MAINE						
1 Allen	N	Y	Y	N	Y	N
2 Michaud	Y	Y	Y	N	Y	Y
MARYLAND						
1 ***Gilchrest***	Y	N	Y	Y	N	Y
2 Ruppersberger	N	Y	Y	Y	Y	N
3 Cardin	N	Y	Y	N	Y	N
4 Wynn	N	Y	Y	Y	Y	Y
5 Hoyer	N	Y	Y	N	Y	N
6 ***Bartlett***	Y	N	Y	Y	N	Y
7 Cummings	Y	Y	Y	N	Y	N
8 Van Hollen	N	Y	Y	N	Y	N
MASSACHUSETTS						
1 Olver	N	Y	N	N	Y	N
2 Neal	Y	Y	Y	N	Y	N
3 McGovern	N	Y	Y	N	Y	N
4 Frank	Y	Y	N	N	Y	N
5 Meehan	N	Y	Y	N	Y	N
6 Tierney	N	Y	Y	N	Y	N
7 Markey	Y	Y	N	N	Y	N
8 Capuano	Y	Y	Y	N	Y	N
9 Lynch	Y	Y	Y	N	Y	Y
10 Delahunt	N	Y	Y	N	Y	N
MICHIGAN						
1 Stupak	Y	Y	Y	N	Y	Y
2 ***Hoekstra***	Y	N	Y	Y	N	Y
3 ***Ehlers***	Y	N	Y	Y	N	Y
4 ***Camp***	Y	N	Y	Y	N	Y
5 Kildee	Y	Y	Y	N	Y	N
6 ***Upton***	Y	N	Y	Y	N	Y
7 ***Smith***	Y	N	Y	Y	N	Y
8 ***Rogers***	Y	N	Y	Y	N	Y
9 ***Knollenberg***	Y	N	Y	Y	N	Y
10 ***Miller***	Y	N	Y	Y	N	Y
11 ***McCotter***	Y	N	Y	Y	N	Y
12 Levin	N	Y	Y	N	Y	N

	204	205	206	207	208	209
13 Kilpatrick	Y	Y	N	N	Y	N
14 Conyers	N	Y	?	N	Y	N
15 Dingell	Y	Y	Y	N	Y	N
MINNESOTA						
1 ***Gutknecht***	Y	N	Y	Y	N	Y
2 ***Kline***	Y	N	Y	Y	N	Y
3 ***Ramstad***	Y	N	Y	Y	N	Y
4 McCollum	N	Y	Y	N	Y	N
5 Sabo	N	Y	Y	Y	Y	N
6 ***Kennedy***	Y	N	Y	Y	N	Y
7 Peterson	Y	N	Y	N	N	Y
8 Oberstar	N	Y	N	N	Y	N
MISSISSIPPI						
1 ***Wicker***	Y	N	Y	Y	N	Y
2 Thompson	N	Y	Y	N	Y	Y
3 ***Pickering***	Y	N	Y	Y	N	Y
4 Taylor	N	Y	Y	N	Y	N
MISSOURI						
1 Clay	N	Y	Y	N	Y	N
2 ***Akin***	Y	N	Y	Y	N	Y
3 Gephardt	N	Y	Y	N	Y	Y
4 Skelton	N	Y	Y	N	Y	Y
5 McCarthy	N	Y	Y	N	Y	?
6 ***Graves***	Y	N	Y	Y	N	Y
7 ***Blunt***	Y	N	Y	Y	N	?
8 ***Emerson***	Y	N	Y	Y	N	Y
9 ***Hulshof***	Y	N	Y	Y	N	Y
MONTANA						
AL ***Rehberg***	Y	N	Y	Y	N	Y
NEBRASKA						
1 ***Bereuter***	N	N	Y	Y	N	Y
2 ***Terry***	Y	N	Y	Y	N	Y
3 ***Osborne***	Y	N	Y	Y	N	Y
NEVADA						
1 Berkley	Y	Y	Y	N	Y	Y
2 ***Gibbons***	Y	N	Y	Y	N	Y
3 ***Porter***	Y	N	Y	N	N	Y
NEW HAMPSHIRE						
1 ***Bradley***	Y	N	Y	Y	N	Y
2 ***Bass***	Y	N	Y	Y	N	Y
NEW JERSEY						
1 Andrews	Y	Y	Y	N	Y	N
2 ***LoBiondo***	Y	N	Y	Y	N	Y
3 ***Saxton***	Y	N	Y	Y	N	Y
4 ***Smith***	Y	N	Y	Y	N	Y
5 ***Garrett***	Y	N	Y	Y	N	Y
6 Pallone	Y	Y	Y	N	Y	N
7 ***Ferguson***	Y	N	Y	Y	N	?
8 Pascrell	N	Y	Y	N	Y	N
9 Rothman	N	Y	Y	N	Y	Y
10 Payne	N	Y	N	N	Y	N
11 ***Frelinghuysen***	Y	N	Y	Y	N	Y
12 Holt	N	Y	Y	N	Y	N
13 Menendez	Y	Y	Y	N	?	?
NEW MEXICO						
1 ***Wilson***	Y	N	Y	Y	N	N
2 ***Pearce***	Y	N	Y	Y	N	Y
3 Udall	Y	Y	Y	N	Y	N
NEW YORK						
1 Bishop	N	Y	Y	N	Y	Y
2 Israel	N	Y	Y	N	Y	Y
3 ***King***	Y	N	Y	Y	N	Y
4 McCarthy	N	Y	Y	N	Y	Y
5 Ackerman	Y	Y	Y	N	Y	N
6 Meeks	Y	Y	Y	N	Y	Y
7 Crowley	N	Y	Y	N	Y	Y
8 Nadler	N	Y	N	N	Y	N
9 Weiner	Y	Y	N	N	Y	Y
10 Towns	N	Y	N	N	Y	N
11 Owens	N	Y	N	?	?	?
12 Velázquez	N	Y	N	N	Y	N
13 ***Fossella***	Y	N	Y	Y	N	Y
14 Maloney	Y	Y	Y	?	Y	Y
15 Rangel	N	Y	N	N	Y	N
16 Serrano	N	Y	N	N	Y	N
17 Engel	Y	Y	Y	N	Y	Y
18 Lowey	Y	Y	Y	N	Y	Y
19 ***Kelly***	Y	N	Y	Y	N	Y
20 ***Sweeney***	Y	N	Y	Y	N	Y
21 McNulty	Y	Y	Y	N	Y	Y
22 Hinchey	N	Y	N	N	Y	N
23 ***McHugh***	Y	N	Y	Y	N	Y
24 ***Boehlert***	Y	N	Y	Y	N	Y
25 ***Walsh***	?	?	?	?	N	Y

	204	205	206	207	208	209
26 ***Reynolds***	Y	N	Y	Y	N	Y
27 ***Quinn***	?	N	Y	Y	N	Y
28 Slaughter	Y	Y	Y	N	Y	N
29 ***Houghton***	N	N	Y	Y	N	N
NORTH CAROLINA						
1 Ballance	?	?	?	?	?	?
2 Etheridge	Y	Y	Y	N	Y	Y
3 ***Jones***	Y	N	Y	Y	N	Y
4 Price	N	Y	Y	N	Y	Y
5 ***Burr***	?	?	?	?	?	?
6 ***Coble***	Y	N	Y	Y	N	Y
7 McIntyre	Y	Y	Y	N	?	?
8 ***Hayes***	Y	N	Y	Y	N	Y
9 ***Myrick***	Y	N	Y	Y	N	Y
10 ***Ballenger***	Y	N	Y	Y	N	Y
11 ***Taylor***	Y	N	Y	Y	N	Y
12 Watt	N	Y	N	N	Y	N
13 Miller	Y	Y	Y	N	Y	Y
NORTH DAKOTA						
AL Pomeroy	N	Y	Y	N	Y	Y
OHIO						
1 ***Chabot***	Y	N	Y	Y	N	Y
2 ***Portman***	Y	N	Y	Y	N	Y
3 ***Turner***	Y	N	Y	Y	N	Y
4 ***Oxley***	Y	N	Y	?	N	Y
5 ***Gillmor***	Y	N	Y	Y	N	Y
6 Strickland	N	Y	Y	N	Y	N
7 ***Hobson***	Y	N	Y	Y	N	Y
8 ***Boehner***	Y	N	Y	Y	N	Y
9 Kaptur	Y	Y	Y	?	Y	N
10 Kucinich	N	Y	N	N	Y	N
11 Jones	Y	Y	Y	?	Y	N
12 ***Tiberi***	Y	N	Y	Y	N	Y
13 Brown	Y	Y	Y	N	Y	N
14 ***LaTourette***	Y	N	Y	Y	?	Y
15 ***Pryce***	Y	N	Y	Y	N	Y
16 ***Regula***	Y	N	Y	Y	N	Y
17 Ryan	N	Y	Y	N	Y	Y
18 ***Ney***	Y	N	Y	Y	N	Y
OKLAHOMA						
1 ***Sullivan***	Y	N	Y	Y	N	Y
2 Carson	Y	Y	Y	N	N	Y
3 ***Lucas***	Y	N	Y	Y	N	Y
4 ***Cole***	Y	N	Y	Y	N	Y
5 ***Istook***	Y	N	Y	Y	N	Y
OREGON						
1 Wu	Y	Y	N	N	Y	Y
2 ***Walden***	Y	N	Y	Y	N	Y
3 Blumenauer	N	Y	N	N	Y	N
4 DeFazio	N	Y	Y	N	Y	Y
5 Hooley	Y	Y	Y	N	Y	Y
PENNSYLVANIA						
1 Brady	Y	Y	Y	N	Y	N
2 Fattah	?	Y	Y	N	Y	N
3 ***English***	Y	N	Y	?	N	Y
4 ***Hart***	Y	N	Y	Y	N	Y
5 ***Peterson***	Y	N	Y	Y	N	Y
6 ***Gerlach***	Y	N	Y	Y	N	Y
7 ***Weldon***	N	N	Y	?	N	Y
8 ***Greenwood***	Y	N	Y	?	N	Y
9 ***Shuster, Bill***	Y	N	Y	Y	N	Y
10 ***Sherwood***	Y	N	Y	Y	N	Y
11 Kanjorski	N	Y	Y	Y	N	N
12 Murtha	Y	Y	Y	Y	?	?
13 Hoeffel	Y	Y	Y	N	Y	N
14 Doyle	Y	Y	Y	N	Y	N
15 ***Toomey***	Y	N	Y	Y	N	Y
16 ***Pitts***	Y	N	Y	Y	N	Y
17 Holden	Y	Y	Y	N	Y	Y
18 ***Murphy***	Y	N	Y	Y	N	Y
19 ***Platts***	Y	N	Y	Y	N	Y
RHODE ISLAND						
1 Kennedy	Y	Y	Y	N	Y	N
2 Langevin	Y	Y	Y	N	Y	N
SOUTH CAROLINA						
1 ***Brown***	Y	N	Y	Y	N	Y
2 ***Wilson***	Y	N	Y	Y	N	Y
3 ***Barrett***	Y	N	Y	Y	N	Y
4 ***DeMint***	Y	N	Y	?	?	?
5 Spratt	N	Y	Y	N	Y	N
6 Clyburn	N	Y	Y	Y	Y	N
SOUTH DAKOTA						
AL Vacant						

	204	205	206	207	208	209
TENNESSEE						
1 ***Jenkins***	Y	N	Y	Y	N	Y
2 ***Duncan***	Y	N	Y	Y	N	Y
3 ***Wamp***	Y	N	Y	Y	N	Y
4 Davis	N	Y	Y	N	Y	Y
5 Cooper	N	Y	Y	N	Y	N
6 Gordon	N	Y	Y	N	Y	Y
7 ***Blackburn***	Y	N	Y	Y	N	Y
8 Tanner	N	Y	Y	N	Y	N
9 Ford	N	Y	Y	N	Y	Y
TEXAS						
1 Sandlin	N	Y	Y	N	N	Y
2 Turner	N	Y	Y	N	Y	?
3 ***Johnson, Sam***	?	?	?	?	?	?
4 ***Hall***	Y	N	Y	Y	N	Y
5 ***Hensarling***	Y	N	Y	Y	N	Y
6 ***Barton***	Y	N	Y	Y	N	Y
7 ***Culberson***	Y	N	Y	Y	N	Y
8 ***Brady***	Y	N	Y	Y	N	Y
9 Lampson	N	Y	Y	N	Y	Y
10 Doggett	N	Y	Y	N	Y	N
11 Edwards	Y	Y	Y	N	Y	N
12 ***Granger***	Y	N	Y	Y	N	Y
13 ***Thornberry***	N	N	Y	Y	N	Y
14 ***Paul***	N	N	N	Y	N	Y
15 Hinojosa	N	Y	Y	N	Y	N
16 Reyes	N	Y	Y	N	Y	N
17 Stenholm	Y	Y	Y	N	Y	N
18 Jackson-Lee	Y	Y	Y	N	Y	N
19 ***Neugebauer***	Y	N	Y	Y	N	Y
20 Gonzalez	N	Y	Y	N	Y	N
21 ***Smith***	Y	N	Y	Y	N	Y
22 ***DeLay***	Y	N	Y	Y	N	Y
23 ***Bonilla***	Y	N	Y	Y	N	Y
24 Frost	Y	Y	Y	N	Y	N
25 Bell	Y	Y	Y	N	Y	Y
26 ***Burgess***	Y	N	Y	Y	N	Y
27 Ortiz	N	Y	Y	N	Y	N
28 Rodriguez	N	Y	Y	N	Y	N
29 Green	N	Y	Y	N	Y	N
30 Johnson, E.B.	Y	Y	Y	N	Y	N
31 ***Carter***	Y	N	Y	Y	N	Y
32 ***Sessions***	Y	N	Y	Y	N	Y
UTAH						
1 ***Bishop***	Y	N	Y	Y	N	Y
2 Matheson	Y	Y	Y	N	N	Y
3 ***Cannon***	Y	N	Y	Y	N	Y
VERMONT						
AL *Sanders*	Y	Y	Y	N	Y	N
VIRGINIA						
1 ***Davis, Jo Ann***	Y	N	Y	Y	N	Y
2 ***Schrock***	Y	N	Y	Y	N	Y
3 Scott	N	Y	Y	N	Y	N
4 ***Forbes***	Y	N	Y	Y	N	Y
5 ***Goode***	Y	N	Y	Y	N	Y
6 ***Goodlatte***	Y	N	Y	Y	N	Y
7 ***Cantor***	Y	N	Y	Y	N	Y
8 Moran	N	Y	Y	N	Y	Y
9 Boucher	N	Y	Y	N	Y	Y
10 ***Wolf***	Y	N	Y	Y	N	Y
11 ***Davis, T.***	Y	N	Y	Y	N	Y
WASHINGTON						
1 Inslee	N	Y	Y	N	Y	N
2 Larsen	N	Y	Y	N	Y	N
3 Baird	N	Y	Y	N	Y	N
4 ***Hastings***	Y	N	Y	Y	N	Y
5 ***Nethercutt***	Y	N	Y	Y	N	Y
6 Dicks	N	Y	Y	Y	Y	N
7 McDermott	N	Y	N	N	Y	N
8 ***Dunn***	Y	N	Y	Y	N	Y
9 Smith	N	Y	Y	N	Y	N
WEST VIRGINIA						
1 Mollohan	Y	Y	Y	N	N	N
2 ***Capito***	Y	N	Y	?	N	Y
3 Rahall	N	Y	Y	N	Y	Y
WISCONSIN						
1 ***Ryan***	Y	N	Y	Y	N	Y
2 Baldwin	Y	Y	N	N	Y	N
3 Kind	N	Y	Y	N	Y	N
4 Kleczka	N	Y	Y	N	Y	N
5 ***Sensenbrenner***	Y	N	Y	Y	N	Y
6 ***Petri***	N	N	Y	Y	N	Y
7 Obey	N	Y	Y	N	Y	N
8 ***Green***	Y	N	Y	Y	N	Y
WYOMING						
AL ***Cubin***	Y	N	Y	Y	N	Y

Southern states - Ala., Ark., Fla., Ga., Ky., La., Miss., N.C., Okla., S.C., Tenn., Texas, Va.

210. H Con Res 295. Focus: HOPE Tribute/Adoption. Miller, R-Mich., motion to suspend the rules and adopt the concurrent resolution that would recognize Focus: HOPE, a Michigan-based civil and human rights group, for its commitment and contributions to human rights in Detroit and the United States. Motion agreed to 374-0: R 206-0; D 167-0 (ND 120-0, SD 47-0); I 1-0. A two-thirds majority of those present and voting (250 in this case) is required for adoption under suspension of the rules. June 1, 2004.

211. H Res 612. Richmond Firefighters Tribute/Adoption. Miller, R-Mich., motion to suspend the rules and adopt the resolution that would recognize and honor the firefighters, public servants and others who responded to a devastating fire in Richmond, Va., on March 26, 2004. Motion agreed to 377-0: R 206-0; D 170-0 (ND 122-0, SD 48-0); I 1-0. A two-thirds majority of those present and voting (252 in this case) is required for adoption under suspension of the rules. June 1, 2004.

212. H Con Res 417. Tuskegee Airmen Tribute/Adoption. Cole, R-Okla., motion to suspend the rules and adopt the concurrent resolution that would express the sense of Congress that the U.S. Air Force should continue to honor and learn from the Tuskegee Airmen, a group of African-American World War II fighter pilots. Motion agreed to 378-0: R 205-0; D 172-0 (ND 124-0, SD 48-0); I 1-0. A two-thirds majority of those present and voting (252 in this case) is required for adoption under suspension of the rules. June 1, 2004.

213. H J Res 83. Continuity of Congress Constitutional Amendment/ Previous Question. Hastings, R-Wash., motion to order the previous question (thus ending debate and possibility of amendment) on adoption of the rule (H Res 657) to provide for House floor consideration of a joint resolution to propose a constitutional amendment that would allow state governors to appoint new House members in the event many were killed or incapacitated. Motion agreed to 215-195: R 215-0; D 0-194 (ND 0-143, SD 0-51); I 0-1. June 2, 2004.

214. H J Res 83. Continuity of Congress Constitutional Amendment/ Rule. Adoption of the rule (H Res 657) to provide for House floor consideration of a joint resolution to propose a constitutional amendment that would allow state governors to appoint new House members in the event many were killed or incapacitated. Adopted 211-200: R 211-2; D 0-197 (ND 0-144, SD 0-53); I 0-1. June 2, 2004.

215. HR 444. Job Training and Worker Services/Previous Question. Pryce, R-Ohio, motion to order the previous question (thus ending debate and possibility of amendment) on a technical correction to the rule (H Res 656) to provide for House floor consideration of a bill that would authorize personal accounts and grants of up to $3,000 for unemployed individuals to use for job training or for services that might help in an employment search. Motion agreed to 214-196: R 214-0; D 0-195 (ND 0-143, SD 0-52); I 0-1. June 2, 2004.

216. HR 444. Job Training and Worker Services/Technical Correction. Pryce, R-Ohio, amendment that would make a technical correction to the rule (H Res 656) for House floor consideration of a bill that would authorize personal accounts and grants of up to $3,000 for unemployed individuals to use for job training or for services that might help in an employment search. Adopted 320-96: R 218-0; D 102-95 (ND 66-78, SD 36-17); I 0-1. June 2, 2004.

Key

Y	Voted for (yea).
#	Paired for.
+	Announced for.
N	Voted against (nay).
X	Paired against.
–	Announced against.
P	Voted "present."
C	Voted "present" to avoid possible conflict of interest.
?	Did not vote or otherwise make a position known.

Democrats **Republicans**
Independents

	210	211	212	213	214	215	216
ALABAMA							
1 *Bonner*	Y	Y	Y	Y	Y	Y	Y
2 *Everett*	Y	Y	Y	Y	Y	Y	Y
3 *Rogers*	Y	Y	Y	Y	Y	Y	Y
4 *Aderholt*	Y	Y	Y	Y	Y	Y	Y
5 Cramer	Y	Y	Y	N	N	N	Y
6 *Bachus*	+	+	+	+	+	+	+
7 Davis	?	?	?	N	N	N	N
ALASKA							
AL *Young*	Y	Y	Y	Y	Y	Y	Y
ARIZONA							
1 *Renzi*	Y	Y	Y	Y	Y	Y	Y
2 *Franks*	Y	Y	Y	Y	Y	Y	Y
3 *Shadegg*	Y	Y	Y	Y	Y	Y	Y
4 Pastor	Y	Y	Y	N	N	N	N
5 *Hayworth*	Y	Y	Y	Y	Y	Y	Y
6 *Flake*	Y	Y	Y	Y	Y	Y	Y
7 Grijalva	Y	Y	N	N	N	N	N
8 *Kolbe*	Y	Y	Y	Y	Y	Y	Y
ARKANSAS							
1 Berry	Y	Y	N	N	N	?	Y
2 Snyder	Y	Y	N	N	N	N	Y
3 *Boozman*	Y	Y	Y	Y	Y	Y	Y
4 Ross	Y	Y	N	N	N	N	Y
CALIFORNIA							
1 Thompson	Y	Y	N	N	N	N	Y
2 *Herger*	Y	Y	Y	Y	Y	Y	Y
3 *Ose*	Y	Y	Y	Y	Y	Y	Y
4 *Doolittle*	?	?	?	Y	Y	Y	Y
5 Matsui	Y	Y	N	N	N	N	Y
6 Woolsey	?	?	N	N	N	N	N
7 Miller, George	Y	Y	N	N	N	N	N
8 Pelosi	Y	Y	N	N	N	N	N
9 Lee	Y	Y	N	N	N	N	N
10 Tauscher	Y	Y	N	N	N	N	Y
11 *Pombo*	Y	Y	Y	Y	Y	Y	Y
12 Lantos	Y	Y	N	N	N	N	Y
13 Stark	Y	Y	N	N	N	N	N
14 Eshoo	Y	Y	N	N	N	N	N
15 Honda	Y	Y	N	N	N	N	N
16 Lofgren	Y	Y	N	N	N	N	N
17 Farr	Y	Y	N	N	N	N	N
18 Cardoza	Y	Y	N	N	N	N	Y
19 *Radanovich*	Y	Y	Y	Y	Y	Y	Y
20 Dooley	?	?	?	N	N	N	Y
21 *Nunes*	Y	Y	Y	Y	Y	Y	Y
22 *Thomas*	Y	Y	Y	Y	Y	Y	Y
23 Capps	Y	Y	N	N	N	N	Y
24 *Gallegly*	Y	Y	Y	Y	Y	Y	Y
25 *McKeon*	Y	Y	Y	Y	Y	Y	Y
26 *Dreier*	Y	Y	Y	Y	Y	Y	Y
27 Sherman	Y	Y	Y	N	N	N	Y
28 Berman	Y	Y	Y	N	N	N	Y
29 Schiff	Y	Y	Y	N	N	N	Y
30 Waxman	Y	Y	N	N	N	N	N
31 Becerra	?	?	?	N	N	N	Y
32 Solis	Y	Y	N	N	N	N	N
33 Watson	Y	Y	N	N	N	N	N
34 Roybal-Allard	Y	Y	N	N	N	N	N
35 Waters	?	?	N	N	N	N	N
36 Harman	Y	Y	N	N	N	N	Y

	210	211	212	213	214	215	216
37 Millender-McD.	Y	Y	Y	N	N	N	N
38 Napolitano	Y	Y	Y	N	N	N	N
39 Sánchez, Linda	Y	Y	Y	N	N	N	N
40 *Royce*	Y	Y	Y	Y	Y	Y	Y
41 *Lewis*	Y	Y	Y	Y	Y	?	Y
42 *Miller, Gary*	Y	Y	Y	Y	Y	Y	Y
43 Baca	Y	Y	N	N	N	N	N
44 *Calvert*	Y	Y	Y	Y	Y	Y	Y
45 *Bono*	Y	Y	Y	Y	Y	Y	Y
46 *Rohrabacher*	Y	Y	Y	P	Y	Y	Y
47 Sanchez, Loretta	Y	Y	N	N	N	N	N
48 *Cox*	Y	Y	Y	Y	Y	Y	Y
49 *Issa*	Y	Y	Y	Y	Y	Y	Y
50 *Cunningham*	Y	Y	Y	Y	Y	Y	Y
51 Filner	Y	Y	N	N	N	N	N
52 *Hunter*	Y	Y	Y	?	Y	Y	?
53 Davis	Y	Y	N	N	N	N	N
COLORADO							
1 DeGette	?	?	?	?	?	?	?
2 Udall	Y	Y	N	N	N	N	Y
3 *McInnis*	Y	Y	Y	Y	Y	Y	Y
4 *Musgrave*	Y	Y	Y	Y	Y	Y	Y
5 *Hefley*	?	?	Y	Y	Y	Y	Y
6 *Tancredo*	Y	Y	Y	?	?	?	Y
7 *Beauprez*	Y	Y	Y	Y	Y	Y	Y
CONNECTICUT							
1 Larson	Y	Y	N	N	N	N	Y
2 *Simmons*	Y	Y	Y	?	Y	Y	Y
3 DeLauro	Y	Y	N	N	N	N	N
4 *Shays*	Y	Y	Y	Y	Y	Y	Y
5 *Johnson*	Y	Y	Y	Y	Y	Y	Y
DELAWARE							
AL *Castle*	Y	Y	Y	Y	Y	Y	Y
FLORIDA							
1 *Miller, J.*	Y	Y	Y	Y	Y	Y	Y
2 Boyd	Y	Y	N	N	N	N	Y
3 Brown	Y	Y	N	N	N	N	Y
4 *Crenshaw*	Y	Y	Y	Y	Y	Y	Y
5 *Brown-Waite*	Y	Y	Y	Y	Y	Y	Y
6 *Stearns*	Y	Y	Y	Y	Y	Y	Y
7 *Mica*	Y	Y	?	Y	Y	?	Y
8 *Keller*	Y	Y	Y	Y	Y	Y	Y
9 *Bilirakis*	Y	Y	Y	Y	Y	Y	Y
10 *Young*	Y	Y	Y	Y	Y	Y	Y
11 Davis	?	?	?	?	?	?	?
12 *Putnam*	Y	Y	Y	Y	Y	Y	Y
13 *Harris*	Y	Y	Y	Y	Y	Y	Y
14 *Goss*	Y	Y	Y	Y	Y	Y	Y
15 *Weldon*	Y	Y	Y	Y	Y	Y	Y
16 *Foley*	Y	Y	Y	Y	Y	Y	Y
17 Meek	?	?	?	N	N	N	N
18 *Ros-Lehtinen*	Y	Y	Y	Y	Y	Y	Y
19 Wexler	Y	Y	N	N	N	Y	Y
20 Deutsch	?	?	?	?	?	?	?
21 *Diaz-Balart, L.*	Y	Y	Y	Y	Y	Y	Y
22 *Shaw*	Y	Y	?	Y	Y	Y	Y
23 Hastings	Y	Y	N	N	N	N	N
24 *Feeney*	Y	Y	Y	Y	Y	Y	Y
25 *Diaz-Balart, M.*	Y	Y	Y	Y	Y	Y	Y
GEORGIA							
1 *Kingston*	Y	Y	Y	Y	Y	Y	Y
2 Bishop	Y	Y	N	N	N	N	Y
3 Marshall	Y	Y	N	N	N	N	Y
4 Majette	Y	Y	N	N	N	N	Y
5 Lewis	Y	Y	N	N	N	N	N
6 *Isakson*	Y	Y	Y	Y	Y	Y	Y
7 *Linder*	Y	Y	Y	Y	Y	Y	Y
8 *Collins*	+	+	+	Y	Y	Y	Y
9 *Norwood*	Y	Y	Y	Y	Y	Y	Y
10 *Deal*	Y	Y	Y	Y	Y	Y	Y
11 *Gingrey*	Y	Y	Y	Y	Y	Y	Y
12 *Burns*	Y	Y	Y	Y	Y	Y	Y
13 Scott	Y	Y	N	N	N	N	Y
HAWAII							
1 Abercrombie	?	?	?	N	N	N	Y
2 Case	Y	Y	N	N	N	N	Y
IDAHO							
1 *Otter*	Y	Y	Y	Y	Y	Y	Y
2 *Simpson*	Y	Y	Y	Y	Y	Y	Y
ILLINOIS							
1 Rush	Y	Y	N	N	N	N	Y
2 Jackson	Y	Y	N	N	N	N	N
3 Lipinski	Y	Y	N	N	N	N	N
4 Gutierrez	?	?	?	N	N	N	N
5 Emanuel	+	+	+	N	N	N	N
6 *Hyde*	Y	Y	Y	Y	Y	Y	Y

ND Northern Democrats   SD Southern Democrats

	210	211	212	213	214	215	216
7 Davis	Y	Y	Y	N	N	N	N
8 ***Crane***	Y	Y	Y	Y	Y	Y	Y
9 Schakowsky	Y	Y	Y	N	N	N	N
10 ***Kirk***	Y	Y	Y	Y	Y	Y	Y
11 ***Weller***	Y	Y	Y	Y	Y	Y	Y
12 Costello	?	?	?	?	?	?	?
13 ***Biggert***	Y	Y	Y	Y	Y	Y	Y
14 ***Hastert***							
15 ***Johnson***	Y	Y	Y	Y	Y	Y	Y
16 ***Manzullo***	Y	Y	Y	Y	N	Y	Y
17 Evans	Y	Y	Y	N	N	N	N
18 ***LaHood***	Y	Y	Y	Y	N	Y	Y
19 ***Shimkus***	Y	Y	Y	Y	Y	Y	Y
INDIANA							
1 Visclosky	Y	Y	Y	N	N	N	N
2 ***Chocola***	Y	Y	Y	Y	Y	Y	Y
3 ***Souder***	?	?	?	Y	Y	Y	Y
4 ***Buyer***	Y	Y	Y	Y	Y	Y	Y
5 ***Burton***	Y	Y	Y	Y	Y	Y	Y
6 ***Pence***	Y	Y	Y	Y	Y	Y	Y
7 Carson	Y	Y	Y	N	N	N	Y
8 ***Hostettler***	Y	Y	Y	Y	Y	Y	Y
9 Hill	Y	Y	Y	N	N	N	Y
IOWA							
1 ***Nussle***	Y	Y	Y	Y	Y	Y	Y
2 ***Leach***	Y	Y	Y	Y	Y	Y	Y
3 Boswell	Y	Y	Y	N	N	N	Y
4 ***Latham***	Y	Y	Y	?	Y	Y	Y
5 ***King***	Y	Y	Y	Y	Y	Y	Y
KANSAS							
1 ***Moran***	Y	Y	Y	Y	Y	Y	Y
2 ***Ryun***	Y	Y	Y	Y	Y	Y	Y
3 Moore	Y	Y	Y	N	N	N	Y
4 ***Tiahrt***	Y	Y	Y	Y	Y	Y	Y
KENTUCKY							
1 ***Whitfield***	Y	Y	Y	Y	Y	Y	Y
2 ***Lewis***	Y	Y	Y	Y	Y	Y	Y
3 ***Northup***	Y	Y	Y	Y	+	Y	Y
4 Lucas	Y	Y	Y	N	N	N	N
5 ***Rogers***	?	?	?	Y	Y	Y	Y
6 Chandler	Y	Y	Y	N	N	N	N
LOUISIANA							
1 ***Vitter***	Y	Y	Y	Y	Y	Y	Y
2 Jefferson	Y	Y	Y	N	N	N	Y
3 ***Tauzin***	?	?	?	?	?	?	?
4 ***McCrery***	?	?	?	?	?	?	?
5 Alexander	Y	Y	Y	N	N	N	Y
6 ***Baker***	Y	Y	Y	Y	Y	Y	Y
7 John	?	?	?	N	N	N	Y
MAINE							
1 Allen	Y	Y	Y	N	N	N	Y
2 Michaud	?	?	?	N	N	N	Y
MARYLAND							
1 ***Gilchrest***	Y	Y	Y	Y	Y	Y	Y
2 Ruppersberger	Y	Y	Y	N	N	N	Y
3 Cardin	Y	Y	Y	N	N	N	Y
4 Wynn	Y	Y	Y	N	N	N	N
5 Hoyer	Y	Y	Y	N	N	N	N
6 ***Bartlett***	Y	Y	Y	Y	Y	Y	Y
7 Cummings	?	Y	Y	N	N	N	N
8 Van Hollen	Y	Y	Y	N	N	N	Y
MASSACHUSETTS							
1 Olver	Y	Y	Y	N	N	N	N
2 Neal	?	?	?	N	N	N	N
3 McGovern	Y	Y	Y	N	N	N	N
4 Frank	Y	Y	Y	N	N	N	N
5 Meehan	?	?	?	N	N	N	N
6 Tierney	Y	Y	Y	N	N	N	N
7 Markey	Y	Y	Y	N	N	N	N
8 Capuano	Y	Y	Y	N	N	N	N
9 Lynch	?	?	?	N	N	N	Y
10 Delahunt	Y	Y	Y	N	N	N	N
MICHIGAN							
1 Stupak	Y	Y	Y	N	N	N	Y
2 ***Hoekstra***	Y	Y	Y	Y	Y	Y	Y
3 ***Ehlers***	Y	Y	Y	Y	Y	Y	Y
4 ***Camp***	Y	Y	Y	Y	Y	Y	Y
5 Kildee	Y	Y	Y	N	N	N	N
6 ***Upton***	Y	Y	Y	Y	Y	Y	Y
7 ***Smith***	Y	Y	?	Y	Y	Y	Y
8 ***Rogers***	Y	Y	Y	Y	Y	Y	Y
9 ***Knollenberg***	Y	Y	Y	Y	Y	Y	Y
10 ***Miller***	Y	Y	Y	Y	Y	Y	Y
11 ***McCotter***	Y	Y	Y	Y	Y	Y	Y
12 Levin	Y	Y	Y	N	N	N	N

	210	211	212	213	214	215	216
13 Kilpatrick	Y	Y	Y	N	N	N	N
14 Conyers	?	?	?	N	N	N	N
15 Dingell	Y	Y	Y	?	N	N	N
MINNESOTA							
1 ***Gutknecht***	Y	Y	Y	Y	Y	Y	Y
2 ***Kline***	Y	Y	Y	Y	Y	Y	Y
3 ***Ramstad***	Y	Y	Y	Y	Y	Y	Y
4 McCollum	Y	Y	Y	N	N	N	Y
5 Sabo	Y	Y	Y	N	N	N	N
6 ***Kennedy***	Y	Y	Y	Y	Y	Y	Y
7 Peterson	Y	Y	Y	N	N	N	Y
8 Oberstar	Y	Y	Y	N	N	N	N
MISSISSIPPI							
1 ***Wicker***	Y	Y	Y	Y	Y	Y	Y
2 Thompson	Y	Y	Y	N	N	N	Y
3 ***Pickering***	Y	Y	Y	Y	Y	Y	Y
4 Taylor	Y	Y	Y	N	N	N	Y
MISSOURI							
1 Clay	Y	Y	Y	N	N	N	N
2 ***Akin***	Y	Y	Y	Y	Y	Y	Y
3 Gephardt	?	?	?	N	N	N	Y
4 Skelton	Y	Y	Y	N	N	N	N
5 McCarthy	Y	Y	Y	N	N	N	Y
6 ***Graves***	Y	Y	Y	Y	Y	Y	Y
7 ***Blunt***	Y	Y	Y	Y	Y	Y	Y
8 ***Emerson***	Y	Y	Y	?	?	?	?
9 ***Hulshof***	Y	Y	Y	Y	Y	Y	Y
MONTANA							
AL ***Rehberg***	Y	Y	Y	Y	Y	Y	Y
NEBRASKA							
1 ***Bereuter***	?	?	?	?	?	?	?
2 ***Terry***	Y	Y	Y	Y	Y	Y	Y
3 ***Osborne***	Y	Y	Y	Y	Y	Y	Y
NEVADA							
1 Berkley	?	?	?	?	?	?	?
2 ***Gibbons***	Y	Y	Y	Y	Y	Y	Y
3 ***Porter***	Y	Y	Y	Y	Y	Y	Y
NEW HAMPSHIRE							
1 ***Bradley***	Y	Y	Y	Y	Y	Y	Y
2 ***Bass***	?	?	?	Y	Y	Y	Y
NEW JERSEY							
1 Andrews	Y	Y	Y	N	N	N	N
2 ***LoBiondo***	Y	Y	Y	Y	Y	Y	Y
3 ***Saxton***	Y	Y	Y	Y	Y	Y	Y
4 ***Smith***	Y	Y	Y	Y	Y	Y	Y
5 ***Garrett***	Y	Y	Y	Y	Y	Y	Y
6 Pallone	Y	Y	Y	N	N	N	N
7 ***Ferguson***	Y	Y	Y	Y	Y	?	Y
8 Pascrell	Y	Y	Y	N	N	N	Y
9 Rothman	Y	Y	Y	N	N	N	N
10 Payne	?	?	?	N	N	N	N
11 ***Frelinghuysen***	Y	Y	Y	Y	Y	Y	Y
12 Holt	Y	Y	Y	N	N	N	Y
13 Menendez	Y	Y	Y	N	N	N	N
NEW MEXICO							
1 ***Wilson***	Y	Y	Y	?	?	?	?
2 ***Pearce***	Y	Y	Y	+	Y	Y	Y
3 Udall	Y	Y	Y	N	N	N	N
NEW YORK							
1 Bishop	Y	Y	Y	N	N	N	Y
2 Israel	Y	Y	Y	N	N	N	Y
3 ***King***	Y	Y	Y	Y	Y	Y	Y
4 McCarthy	Y	Y	Y	N	N	N	Y
5 Ackerman	Y	Y	Y	N	N	N	N
6 Meeks	Y	Y	Y	N	N	N	N
7 Crowley	Y	Y	Y	N	N	N	N
8 Nadler	Y	Y	Y	N	N	N	Y
9 Weiner	?	?	?	N	N	N	N
10 Towns	?	?	?	N	N	N	N
11 Owens	?	?	?	N	N	N	N
12 Velázquez	Y	Y	Y	N	N	N	N
13 ***Fossella***	Y	Y	Y	Y	Y	Y	Y
14 Maloney	?	?	?	N	N	N	Y
15 Rangel	?	?	?	N	N	N	N
16 Serrano	Y	Y	Y	N	N	N	N
17 Engel	Y	Y	Y	N	N	N	Y
18 Lowey	Y	Y	Y	N	N	N	Y
19 ***Kelly***	Y	Y	Y	Y	Y	Y	Y
20 ***Sweeney***	?	?	?	Y	Y	Y	Y
21 McNulty	Y	Y	Y	N	N	N	N
22 Hinchey	?	Y	Y	N	N	N	N
23 ***McHugh***	Y	Y	Y	Y	Y	Y	Y
24 ***Boehlert***	Y	Y	Y	Y	Y	Y	Y
25 ***Walsh***	Y	Y	Y	Y	Y	Y	Y

	210	211	212	213	214	215	216
26 ***Reynolds***	Y	Y	Y	Y	Y	Y	Y
27 ***Quinn***	Y	Y	Y	Y	Y	Y	Y
28 Slaughter	Y	Y	Y	N	N	N	N
29 ***Houghton***	Y	Y	Y	Y	Y	Y	Y
NORTH CAROLINA							
1 Ballance	?	?	?	?	?	?	?
2 Etheridge	Y	Y	Y	–	N	N	N
3 ***Jones***	Y	Y	Y	Y	Y	Y	Y
4 Price	Y	Y	Y	N	N	N	Y
5 ***Burr***	Y	Y	Y	Y	Y	Y	Y
6 ***Coble***	Y	Y	Y	Y	Y	Y	Y
7 McIntyre	Y	Y	Y	N	N	N	Y
8 ***Hayes***	Y	Y	Y	Y	?	Y	Y
9 ***Myrick***	Y	Y	Y	Y	Y	Y	Y
10 ***Ballenger***	Y	Y	Y	?	?	?	?
11 ***Taylor***	Y	Y	Y	Y	Y	Y	Y
12 Watt	Y	Y	Y	N	N	N	Y
13 Miller	Y	Y	Y	N	N	N	N
NORTH DAKOTA							
AL Pomeroy	Y	Y	Y	N	N	N	Y
OHIO							
1 ***Chabot***	?	?	?	Y	Y	Y	Y
2 ***Portman***	Y	Y	Y	Y	Y	Y	Y
3 ***Turner***	Y	Y	Y	Y	Y	Y	Y
4 ***Oxley***	+	+	+	Y	Y	Y	Y
5 ***Gillmor***	Y	Y	Y	Y	Y	Y	Y
6 Strickland	Y	Y	Y	N	N	?	Y
7 ***Hobson***	Y	Y	Y	Y	Y	Y	Y
8 ***Boehner***	?	?	?	Y	Y	Y	Y
9 Kaptur	Y	Y	Y	N	N	N	Y
10 Kucinich	Y	Y	Y	N	N	N	N
11 Jones	?	?	?	?	?	?	?
12 ***Tiberi***	Y	Y	Y	Y	Y	Y	Y
13 Brown	Y	Y	Y	N	N	N	N
14 ***LaTourette***	Y	Y	Y	Y	Y	Y	Y
15 ***Pryce***	Y	Y	Y	Y	Y	Y	Y
16 ***Regula***	Y	Y	Y	Y	Y	Y	Y
17 Ryan	Y	Y	Y	N	N	N	N
18 ***Ney***	Y	Y	Y	Y	Y	Y	Y
OKLAHOMA							
1 ***Sullivan***	?	?	?	Y	Y	Y	Y
2 Carson	?	?	?	?	?	?	?
3 ***Lucas***	Y	Y	Y	Y	Y	Y	Y
4 ***Cole***	Y	Y	Y	Y	Y	Y	Y
5 ***Istook***	?	?	?	Y	Y	Y	Y
OREGON							
1 Wu	Y	Y	Y	N	N	N	Y
2 ***Walden***	Y	Y	Y	Y	Y	Y	Y
3 Blumenauer	Y	Y	Y	N	N	N	N
4 DeFazio	Y	Y	Y	N	N	N	N
5 Hooley	Y	Y	Y	N	N	N	Y
PENNSYLVANIA							
1 Brady	?	?	?	N	N	N	N
2 Fattah	Y	Y	Y	N	N	N	Y
3 ***English***	?	?	Y	Y	Y	Y	Y
4 ***Hart***	Y	Y	Y	Y	Y	?	Y
5 ***Peterson***	Y	Y	Y	Y	?	Y	Y
6 ***Gerlach***	Y	Y	Y	Y	Y	Y	Y
7 ***Weldon***	Y	Y	Y	Y	Y	Y	Y
8 ***Greenwood***	Y	Y	Y	Y	Y	Y	Y
9 ***Shuster, Bill***	Y	Y	Y	Y	Y	Y	Y
10 ***Sherwood***	Y	Y	Y	Y	Y	Y	Y
11 Kanjorski	Y	Y	Y	N	N	N	Y
12 Murtha	Y	Y	Y	N	N	N	Y
13 Hoeffel	?	?	?	N	N	N	Y
14 Doyle	Y	Y	Y	N	N	N	Y
15 ***Toomey***	Y	Y	Y	Y	Y	Y	Y
16 ***Pitts***	Y	Y	Y	Y	Y	Y	Y
17 Holden	Y	Y	Y	N	N	N	Y
18 ***Murphy***	Y	Y	Y	Y	Y	Y	Y
19 ***Platts***	?	?	?	Y	Y	Y	Y
RHODE ISLAND							
1 Kennedy	Y	Y	Y	N	N	N	N
2 Langevin	Y	Y	Y	N	N	N	N
SOUTH CAROLINA							
1 ***Brown***	Y	Y	Y	Y	Y	Y	Y
2 ***Wilson***	Y	Y	Y	Y	Y	Y	Y
3 ***Barrett***	Y	Y	Y	Y	Y	Y	Y
4 ***DeMint***	?	?	?	?	?	?	?
5 Spratt	Y	Y	Y	N	N	N	Y
6 Clyburn	Y	Y	Y	N	N	N	Y
SOUTH DAKOTA							
AL Vacant							

	210	211	212	213	214	215	216
TENNESSEE							
1 ***Jenkins***	Y	Y	Y	Y	Y	Y	Y
2 ***Duncan***	?	?	?	Y	Y	Y	Y
3 ***Wamp***	?	?	?	Y	Y	Y	Y
4 Davis	Y	Y	Y	N	N	N	Y
5 Cooper	Y	Y	Y	N	N	N	Y
6 Gordon	Y	Y	Y	N	N	N	Y
7 ***Blackburn***	Y	Y	Y	Y	Y	Y	Y
8 Tanner	Y	Y	Y	N	N	N	Y
9 Ford	Y	Y	Y	N	N	N	N
TEXAS							
1 Sandlin	?	?	?	N	N	N	N
2 Turner	Y	Y	Y	N	N	N	Y
3 ***Johnson, Sam***	Y	Y	Y	Y	Y	Y	Y
4 ***Hall***	Y	Y	Y	Y	Y	Y	Y
5 ***Hensarling***	Y	Y	Y	Y	Y	Y	Y
6 ***Barton***	Y	Y	Y	Y	Y	Y	Y
7 ***Culberson***	Y	Y	Y	Y	Y	Y	Y
8 ***Brady***	Y	Y	Y	Y	Y	Y	Y
9 Lampson	Y	Y	Y	N	N	N	Y
10 Doggett	Y	Y	Y	N	N	N	Y
11 Edwards	?	Y	Y	?	N	N	N
12 ***Granger***	Y	Y	Y	Y	Y	Y	Y
13 ***Thornberry***	Y	Y	Y	Y	Y	Y	Y
14 ***Paul***	Y	Y	Y	Y	Y	Y	Y
15 Hinojosa	Y	Y	Y	N	N	N	N
16 Reyes	Y	Y	Y	N	N	N	Y
17 Stenholm	Y	Y	Y	N	N	N	Y
18 Jackson-Lee	?	?	Y	N	N	N	Y
19 ***Neugebauer***	Y	Y	Y	Y	Y	Y	Y
20 Gonzalez	Y	Y	Y	N	N	N	Y
21 ***Smith***	Y	Y	Y	Y	Y	Y	Y
22 ***DeLay***	Y	Y	Y	Y	Y	Y	Y
23 ***Bonilla***	Y	Y	Y	Y	Y	Y	Y
24 Frost	Y	Y	Y	N	N	N	N
25 Bell	Y	Y	Y	N	N	N	Y
26 ***Burgess***	Y	Y	Y	Y	Y	Y	Y
27 Ortiz	Y	Y	Y	N	N	N	N
28 Rodriguez	Y	Y	Y	N	N	N	Y
29 Green	Y	Y	Y	N	N	N	N
30 Johnson, E.B.	Y	Y	?	N	N	N	N
31 ***Carter***	Y	Y	Y	Y	Y	Y	Y
32 ***Sessions***	Y	Y	Y	Y	Y	Y	Y
UTAH							
1 ***Bishop***	Y	Y	Y	Y	Y	Y	Y
2 Matheson	Y	Y	Y	N	N	N	Y
3 ***Cannon***	Y	Y	Y	Y	Y	Y	Y
VERMONT							
AL *Sanders*	Y	Y	Y	N	N	N	N
VIRGINIA							
1 ***Davis, Jo Ann***	Y	Y	Y	Y	Y	Y	Y
2 ***Schrock***	Y	Y	Y	Y	Y	Y	Y
3 Scott	Y	Y	Y	N	N	N	Y
4 ***Forbes***	Y	Y	Y	Y	Y	Y	Y
5 ***Goode***	Y	Y	Y	Y	Y	Y	Y
6 ***Goodlatte***	Y	Y	Y	Y	Y	Y	Y
7 ***Cantor***	Y	Y	Y	Y	Y	Y	Y
8 Moran	Y	Y	Y	N	N	N	Y
9 Boucher	Y	Y	Y	N	N	N	Y
10 ***Wolf***	Y	Y	Y	Y	Y	Y	Y
11 ***Davis, T.***	Y	Y	Y	Y	Y	Y	Y
WASHINGTON							
1 Inslee	Y	Y	Y	N	N	N	N
2 Larsen	Y	Y	Y	N	N	N	N
3 Baird	Y	Y	Y	N	N	N	N
4 ***Hastings***	Y	Y	Y	Y	Y	Y	Y
5 ***Nethercutt***	Y	Y	Y	Y	Y	Y	Y
6 Dicks	?	?	?	N	N	N	Y
7 McDermott	Y	Y	Y	N	N	N	N
8 ***Dunn***	Y	Y	Y	Y	Y	Y	Y
9 Smith	Y	Y	Y	N	N	N	Y
WEST VIRGINIA							
1 Mollohan	Y	Y	Y	N	N	N	Y
2 ***Capito***	Y	Y	Y	Y	Y	Y	Y
3 Rahall	Y	Y	Y	N	N	N	Y
WISCONSIN							
1 ***Ryan***	Y	Y	Y	Y	Y	Y	Y
2 Baldwin	Y	Y	Y	N	N	N	Y
3 Kind	Y	Y	Y	N	N	N	Y
4 Kleczka	Y	Y	Y	N	N	N	N
5 ***Sensenbrenner***	Y	Y	Y	Y	Y	Y	Y
6 ***Petri***	Y	Y	Y	Y	Y	Y	Y
7 Obey	Y	Y	Y	N	N	N	N
8 ***Green***	Y	Y	Y	Y	Y	Y	Y
WYOMING							
AL ***Cubin***	Y	Y	Y	Y	Y	Y	Y

Southern states - Ala., Ark., Fla., Ga., Ky., La., Miss., N.C., Okla., S.C., Tenn., Texas, Va.

Key

Y	Voted for (yea).
#	Paired for.
+	Announced for.
N	Voted against (nay).
X	Paired against.
–	Announced against.
P	Voted "present."
C	Voted "present" to avoid possible conflict of interest.
?	Did not vote or otherwise make a position known.

Democrats   **Republicans**
Independents

217. HR 444. Job Training and Worker Services/Rule. Adoption of the rule (H Res 656) to provide for House floor consideration of a bill that would authorize personal accounts and grants of up to $3,000 for unemployed individuals to use for job training or for services that might help in an employment search. The rule, as amended, would provide for the addition of the texts of a bill (HR 4409) that would tighten standards for teacher training programs at colleges and universities, and a bill (HR 4411) that would authorize up to $120 million for post-secondary education programs. The rule specifies that if more than one of the bills pass the House, the text of those bills shall be combined into one measure. Adopted 220-196: R 219-0; D 1-195 (ND 1-142, SD 0-53); I 0-1. June 2, 2004.

218. H J Res 83. Continuity of Congress Constitutional Amendment/ Recommit. Lofgren, D-Calif., motion to recommit the bill to the House Judiciary Committee with instructions to hold hearings on a constitutional amendment addressing the continuity of Congress. Motion rejected 194-221: R 1-220; D 192-1 (ND 139-1, SD 53-0); I 1-0. June 2, 2004.

219. H J Res 83. Continuity of Congress Constitutional Amendment/ Passage. Passage of the joint resolution to propose a constitutional amendment that would allow state governors to appoint new House members in the event that many were killed or incapacitated. Each member would be allowed to choose at least two potential successors who could be appointed in the event of a catastrophe, until special elections could be held. Rejected 63-353: R 4-219; D 59-133 (ND 52-89, SD 7-44); I 0-1. A two-thirds majority vote of those present and voting (279 in this case) is required to pass a joint resolution proposing an amendment to the Constitution. June 2, 2004.

220. S J Res 28. 60th Anniversary of D-Day/Passage. Ryun, R-Kan., motion to suspend the rules and pass the joint resolution that would recognize the 60th anniversary of D-Day, the Allied landing at Normandy during World War II, and request that the president issue a proclamation calling on the American people to commemorate the day. Motion agreed to 419-0: R 223-0; D 195-0 (ND 142-0, SD 53-0); I 1-0. A two-thirds majority of those present and voting (280 in this case) is required for passage under suspension of the rules. June 2, 2004.

221. H Con Res 413. World War II Women Tribute/Adoption. McKeon, R-Calif., motion to suspend the rules and adopt the concurrent resolution that would honor women's contributions to the nation during World War II. Motion agreed to 417-0: R 223-0; D 193-0 (ND 141-0, SD 52-0); I 1-0. A two-thirds majority of those present and voting (278 in this case) is required for adoption under suspension of the rules. June 2, 2004.

222. HR 4109. Simplified Tax Form for Seniors/Passage. Foley, R-Fla., motion to suspend the rules and pass the bill that would permit taxpayers 65 years and older who do not itemize their deductions to file their taxes using a new, simplified "1040S" income tax return form, based on the 1040EZ tax form. Motion agreed to 418-0: R 222-0; D 195-0 (ND 143-0, SD 52-0); I 1-0. A two-thirds majority of those present and voting (279 in this case) is required for passage under suspension of the rules. June 2, 2004.

	217	218	219	220	221	222
ALABAMA						
1 *Bonner*	Y	N	N	Y	Y	Y
2 *Everett*	Y	N	N	Y	Y	Y
3 *Rogers*	Y	N	N	Y	Y	Y
4 *Aderholt*	Y	N	N	Y	Y	Y
5 Cramer	N	Y	N	Y	Y	Y
6 *Bachus*	+	N	N	Y	Y	Y
7 Davis	N	Y	N	Y	Y	Y
ALASKA						
AL *Young*	Y	N	N	Y	Y	Y
ARIZONA						
1 *Renzi*	Y	N	N	Y	Y	Y
2 *Franks*	Y	N	N	Y	Y	Y
3 *Shadegg*	Y	N	N	Y	Y	Y
4 Pastor	N	Y	N	Y	Y	Y
5 *Hayworth*	Y	N	N	Y	Y	Y
6 *Flake*	Y	N	N	Y	Y	Y
7 Grijalva	N	Y	N	Y	Y	Y
8 *Kolbe*	Y	N	N	Y	Y	Y
ARKANSAS						
1 Berry	N	Y	N	Y	Y	Y
2 Snyder	N	Y	N	Y	Y	Y
3 *Boozman*	Y	N	N	Y	Y	Y
4 Ross	N	Y	N	Y	Y	Y
CALIFORNIA						
1 Thompson	N	Y	N	Y	Y	Y
2 *Herger*	Y	N	N	Y	Y	Y
3 *Ose*	Y	N	N	Y	Y	Y
4 *Doolittle*	Y	N	N	Y	Y	Y
5 Matsui	N	Y	N	Y	Y	Y
6 Woolsey	N	Y	N	Y	Y	Y
7 Miller, George	N	Y	Y	Y	Y	Y
8 Pelosi	N	Y	N	Y	Y	Y
9 Lee	N	Y	N	Y	Y	Y
10 Tauscher	N	Y	Y	Y	Y	Y
11 *Pombo*	Y	N	N	Y	Y	Y
12 Lantos	N	Y	N	Y	Y	Y
13 Stark	N	?	?	?	?	?
14 Eshoo	N	Y	Y	Y	Y	Y
15 Honda	N	Y	Y	Y	Y	Y
16 Lofgren	N	Y	N	Y	Y	Y
17 Farr	N	Y	N	Y	Y	Y
18 Cardoza	N	Y	N	Y	Y	Y
19 *Radanovich*	Y	N	N	Y	Y	Y
20 Dooley	N	Y	Y	Y	Y	Y
21 *Nunes*	Y	N	N	Y	Y	Y
22 *Thomas*	Y	N	N	Y	Y	Y
23 Capps	N	Y	N	Y	Y	Y
24 *Gallegly*	Y	N	N	Y	Y	Y
25 *McKeon*	Y	N	N	Y	Y	Y
26 *Dreier*	Y	N	N	Y	Y	Y
27 Sherman	N	Y	Y	Y	Y	Y
28 Berman	N	Y	Y	Y	Y	Y
29 Schiff	N	Y	Y	Y	Y	Y
30 Waxman	N	Y	Y	Y	Y	Y
31 Becerra	N	Y	N	Y	Y	Y
32 Solis	N	Y	N	Y	Y	Y
33 Watson	N	Y	N	Y	Y	Y
34 Roybal-Allard	N	Y	N	Y	Y	Y
35 Waters	N	Y	N	Y	Y	Y
36 Harman	N	Y	N	Y	Y	Y

	217	218	219	220	221	222
37 Millender-McD.	N	Y	N	Y	Y	Y
38 Napolitano	N	+	+	Y	Y	Y
39 Sánchez, Linda	N	Y	Y	Y	Y	Y
40 *Royce*	Y	N	N	Y	Y	Y
41 *Lewis*	Y	N	N	Y	Y	Y
42 *Miller, Gary*	Y	N	N	Y	Y	Y
43 Baca	Y	N	N	Y	Y	Y
44 *Calvert*	Y	N	N	Y	Y	Y
45 *Bono*	Y	N	N	Y	Y	Y
46 *Rohrabacher*	Y	Y	N	Y	Y	Y
47 Sanchez, Loretta	N	Y	N	Y	Y	Y
48 *Cox*	Y	N	N	Y	Y	Y
49 *Issa*	Y	N	N	Y	Y	Y
50 *Cunningham*	Y	N	N	Y	Y	Y
51 Filner	Y	N	N	Y	Y	Y
52 *Hunter*	Y	N	N	Y	Y	Y
53 Davis	N	Y	N	Y	Y	Y
COLORADO						
1 DeGette	?	?	?	?	?	?
2 Udall	N	Y	N	Y	Y	Y
3 *McInnis*	Y	N	N	Y	Y	Y
4 *Musgrave*	Y	N	N	Y	Y	Y
5 *Hefley*	Y	N	N	Y	Y	Y
6 *Tancredo*	Y	N	N	Y	Y	Y
7 *Beauprez*	Y	N	N	Y	Y	Y
CONNECTICUT						
1 Larson	N	Y	Y	Y	Y	Y
2 *Simmons*	Y	N	Y	Y	Y	Y
3 DeLauro	N	Y	Y	Y	Y	Y
4 *Shays*	Y	N	Y	Y	Y	Y
5 *Johnson*	Y	N	Y	Y	Y	Y
DELAWARE						
AL *Castle*	Y	N	N	Y	Y	Y
FLORIDA						
1 *Miller, J.*	Y	N	N	Y	Y	Y
2 Boyd	N	Y	N	Y	Y	Y
3 Brown	N	Y	N	Y	Y	Y
4 *Crenshaw*	Y	N	N	Y	Y	Y
5 *Brown-Waite*	Y	N	N	Y	Y	Y
6 *Stearns*	Y	N	N	Y	Y	Y
7 *Mica*	Y	N	N	Y	Y	Y
8 *Keller*	Y	N	N	Y	Y	Y
9 *Bilirakis*	Y	N	N	Y	Y	Y
10 *Young*	Y	N	N	Y	Y	Y
11 Davis	?	?	?	?	?	?
12 *Putnam*	Y	N	N	Y	Y	Y
13 *Harris*	Y	N	N	Y	Y	Y
14 *Goss*	Y	N	N	Y	Y	Y
15 *Weldon*	Y	N	N	Y	Y	Y
16 *Foley*	Y	N	N	Y	Y	Y
17 Meek	N	Y	N	Y	Y	Y
18 *Ros-Lehtinen*	Y	N	N	Y	Y	Y
19 Wexler	N	Y	N	Y	Y	Y
20 Deutsch	?	?	?	?	?	?
21 *Diaz-Balart, L.*	Y	N	N	Y	Y	Y
22 *Shaw*	Y	N	N	Y	Y	Y
23 Hastings	N	Y	Y	Y	Y	Y
24 *Feeney*	Y	N	N	Y	Y	Y
25 *Diaz-Balart, M.*	Y	N	N	Y	Y	Y
GEORGIA						
1 *Kingston*	Y	N	N	Y	Y	Y
2 Bishop	N	Y	N	Y	Y	Y
3 Marshall	N	Y	N	Y	Y	Y
4 Majette	N	Y	N	Y	Y	Y
5 Lewis	N	Y	N	Y	Y	Y
6 *Isakson*	Y	N	N	Y	Y	Y
7 *Linder*	Y	N	N	Y	Y	Y
8 *Collins*	Y	N	N	Y	Y	Y
9 *Norwood*	Y	N	N	Y	Y	Y
10 *Deal*	Y	N	N	Y	Y	Y
11 *Gingrey*	Y	N	N	Y	Y	Y
12 *Burns*	Y	N	N	Y	Y	Y
13 Scott	N	Y	N	Y	Y	Y
HAWAII						
1 Abercrombie	N	Y	N	Y	Y	Y
2 Case	N	Y	Y	Y	Y	Y
IDAHO						
1 *Otter*	Y	N	N	Y	Y	Y
2 *Simpson*	Y	N	N	Y	Y	Y
ILLINOIS						
1 Rush	N	Y	N	Y	Y	Y
2 Jackson	N	Y	N	Y	Y	Y
3 Lipinski	N	Y	N	Y	Y	Y
4 Gutierrez	N	Y	Y	Y	?	Y
5 Emanuel	N	Y	N	Y	Y	Y
6 *Hyde*	Y	N	N	Y	Y	Y

ND Northern Democrats   SD Southern Democrats

	217	218	219	220	221	222
7 Davis	N	Y	N	Y	Y	Y
8 ***Crane***	Y	N	N	Y	Y	Y
9 Schakowsky	N	Y	Y	Y	Y	Y
10 ***Kirk***	Y	N	N	Y	Y	Y
11 ***Weller***	Y	N	N	Y	Y	Y
12 Costello	?	?	?	?	?	?
13 ***Biggert***	Y	N	N	Y	Y	Y
14 ***Hastert***						
15 ***Johnson***	Y	N	N	Y	Y	Y
16 ***Manzullo***	Y	N	N	Y	Y	Y
17 Evans	N	Y	Y	Y	Y	Y
18 ***LaHood***	Y	N	N	Y	Y	Y
19 ***Shimkus***	Y	N	N	Y	Y	Y
INDIANA						
1 Visclosky	N	Y	N	Y	Y	Y
2 ***Chocola***	Y	N	N	Y	Y	Y
3 ***Souder***	Y	N	Y	Y	Y	Y
4 ***Buyer***	Y	N	N	Y	Y	Y
5 ***Burton***	Y	N	N	Y	Y	Y
6 ***Pence***	Y	N	N	Y	Y	Y
7 Carson	N	Y	N	Y	Y	Y
8 ***Hostettler***	Y	N	N	Y	Y	Y
9 Hill	N	Y	N	Y	Y	Y
IOWA						
1 ***Nussle***	Y	N	N	Y	Y	Y
2 ***Leach***	Y	N	N	Y	Y	Y
3 Boswell	N	Y	N	Y	Y	Y
4 ***Latham***	Y	N	N	Y	Y	Y
5 ***King***	Y	N	N	Y	Y	Y
KANSAS						
1 ***Moran***	Y	N	N	Y	Y	Y
2 ***Ryun***	Y	N	N	Y	Y	Y
3 Moore	N	Y	N	Y	Y	Y
4 ***Tiahrt***	Y	N	N	Y	Y	Y
KENTUCKY						
1 ***Whitfield***	Y	N	N	Y	Y	Y
2 ***Lewis***	Y	N	N	Y	Y	Y
3 ***Northup***	Y	N	N	Y	Y	Y
4 Lucas	N	Y	Y	Y	Y	Y
5 ***Rogers***	Y	N	N	Y	Y	Y
6 Chandler	N	Y	Y	Y	Y	Y
LOUISIANA						
1 ***Vitter***	Y	N	Y	Y	Y	Y
2 Jefferson	N	Y	N	Y	Y	Y
3 ***Tauzin***	?	?	?	?	?	?
4 ***McCrery***	?	N	N	Y	Y	Y
5 Alexander	N	Y	N	Y	Y	Y
6 ***Baker***	Y	N	N	Y	Y	Y
7 John	N	Y	N	Y	Y	Y
MAINE						
1 Allen	N	Y	N	Y	Y	Y
2 Michaud	N	Y	N	Y	Y	Y
MARYLAND						
1 ***Gilchrest***	Y	N	N	Y	Y	Y
2 Ruppersberger	N	Y	Y	Y	Y	Y
3 Cardin	N	Y	N	Y	Y	Y
4 Wynn	N	Y	N	Y	Y	Y
5 Hoyer	N	Y	N	Y	Y	Y
6 ***Bartlett***	Y	N	N	Y	Y	Y
7 Cummings	N	?	N	Y	Y	Y
8 Van Hollen	N	Y	N	Y	Y	Y
MASSACHUSETTS						
1 Olver	N	Y	N	Y	Y	Y
2 Neal	N	Y	N	Y	Y	Y
3 McGovern	N	Y	N	Y	Y	Y
4 Frank	N	Y	N	Y	Y	Y
5 Meehan	N	Y	N	Y	Y	Y
6 Tierney	N	Y	N	Y	Y	Y
7 Markey	N	Y	N	Y	Y	Y
8 Capuano	N	Y	Y	Y	Y	Y
9 Lynch	N	Y	N	Y	Y	Y
10 Delahunt	N	Y	N	Y	Y	Y
MICHIGAN						
1 Stupak	N	Y	N	Y	Y	Y
2 ***Hoekstra***	Y	N	N	Y	Y	Y
3 ***Ehlers***	Y	N	N	Y	Y	Y
4 ***Camp***	Y	N	N	Y	Y	Y
5 Kildee	N	Y	N	Y	Y	Y
6 ***Upton***	Y	N	N	Y	Y	Y
7 ***Smith***	Y	N	N	Y	Y	Y
8 ***Rogers***	Y	N	N	Y	Y	Y
9 ***Knollenberg***	Y	N	N	Y	Y	Y
10 ***Miller***	Y	N	N	Y	Y	Y
11 ***McCotter***	Y	N	N	Y	Y	Y
12 Levin	N	Y	N	Y	Y	Y
13 Kilpatrick	N	Y	Y	Y	Y	Y
14 Conyers	N	?	?	?	?	Y
15 Dingell	N	Y	N	Y	Y	Y
MINNESOTA						
1 ***Gutknecht***	Y	N	N	Y	Y	Y
2 ***Kline***	Y	N	N	Y	Y	Y
3 ***Ramstad***	Y	N	N	Y	Y	Y
4 McCollum	N	Y	Y	Y	Y	Y
5 Sabo	N	Y	Y	Y	Y	Y
6 ***Kennedy***	Y	N	N	Y	Y	Y
7 Peterson	N	N	N	Y	Y	Y
8 Oberstar	N	Y	Y	Y	Y	Y
MISSISSIPPI						
1 ***Wicker***	Y	N	N	Y	Y	Y
2 Thompson	N	Y	N	Y	Y	Y
3 ***Pickering***	Y	?	N	Y	Y	Y
4 Taylor	N	Y	N	Y	Y	Y
MISSOURI						
1 Clay	N	Y	N	Y	Y	Y
2 ***Akin***	Y	N	N	Y	Y	Y
3 Gephardt	N	Y	Y	Y	Y	Y
4 Skelton	N	Y	N	Y	Y	Y
5 McCarthy	N	Y	N	Y	Y	Y
6 ***Graves***	Y	N	N	Y	Y	Y
7 ***Blunt***	Y	N	N	Y	Y	Y
8 ***Emerson***	?	?	?	?	?	?
9 ***Hulshof***	Y	N	N	Y	Y	Y
MONTANA						
AL ***Rehberg***	Y	N	N	Y	Y	Y
NEBRASKA						
1 ***Bereuter***	?	?	N	Y	Y	Y
2 ***Terry***	Y	N	N	Y	Y	Y
3 ***Osborne***	Y	N	N	Y	Y	Y
NEVADA						
1 Berkley	?	Y	Y	Y	Y	Y
2 ***Gibbons***	Y	N	N	Y	Y	Y
3 ***Porter***	Y	N	N	Y	Y	Y
NEW HAMPSHIRE						
1 ***Bradley***	Y	N	N	Y	Y	Y
2 ***Bass***	Y	N	N	Y	Y	Y
NEW JERSEY						
1 Andrews	N	Y	N	Y	Y	Y
2 ***LoBiondo***	Y	N	N	Y	Y	Y
3 ***Saxton***	Y	N	N	Y	Y	Y
4 ***Smith***	Y	N	N	Y	Y	Y
5 ***Garrett***	Y	N	N	Y	Y	Y
6 Pallone	N	Y	N	Y	Y	Y
7 ***Ferguson***	Y	N	N	Y	Y	Y
8 Pascrell	N	Y	N	Y	Y	Y
9 Rothman	N	Y	Y	Y	Y	Y
10 Payne	N	Y	Y	Y	Y	Y
11 ***Frelinghuysen***	Y	N	N	Y	Y	Y
12 Holt	N	Y	N	Y	Y	Y
13 Menendez	N	Y	N	Y	Y	Y
NEW MEXICO						
1 ***Wilson***	?	?	?	?	?	?
2 ***Pearce***	Y	N	N	Y	Y	Y
3 Udall	N	Y	N	Y	Y	Y
NEW YORK						
1 Bishop	N	Y	N	Y	Y	Y
2 Israel	N	Y	N	Y	Y	Y
3 ***King***	Y	N	N	Y	Y	Y
4 McCarthy	N	?	?	?	?	?
5 Ackerman	N	Y	N	Y	Y	Y
6 Meeks	N	Y	Y	Y	Y	Y
7 Crowley	N	Y	Y	Y	Y	Y
8 Nadler	N	?	?	?	?	?
9 Weiner	N	Y	Y	Y	Y	Y
10 Towns	?	Y	Y	Y	Y	Y
11 Owens	N	Y	N	Y	Y	Y
12 Velázquez	N	Y	N	Y	Y	Y
13 ***Fossella***	Y	N	N	Y	Y	Y
14 Maloney	N	Y	N	Y	Y	Y
15 Rangel	N	Y	Y	Y	Y	Y
16 Serrano	N	Y	N	Y	Y	Y
17 Engel	N	Y	Y	Y	Y	Y
18 Lowey	N	Y	Y	Y	Y	Y
19 ***Kelly***	Y	N	N	Y	Y	Y
20 ***Sweeney***	Y	N	N	Y	Y	Y
21 McNulty	N	Y	N	Y	Y	Y
22 Hinchey	N	Y	Y	Y	Y	Y
23 ***McHugh***	Y	N	N	Y	Y	Y
24 ***Boehlert***	Y	N	N	Y	Y	Y
25 ***Walsh***	Y	N	N	Y	Y	Y
26 ***Reynolds***	Y	N	N	Y	Y	Y
27 ***Quinn***	Y	N	N	Y	Y	Y
28 Slaughter	N	Y	Y	Y	Y	Y
29 ***Houghton***	Y	N	N	Y	Y	Y
NORTH CAROLINA						
1 Ballance	?	?	?	?	?	?
2 Etheridge	N	Y	N	Y	Y	Y
3 ***Jones***	Y	N	N	Y	Y	Y
4 Price	N	Y	N	Y	Y	Y
5 ***Burr***	Y	N	N	Y	Y	Y
6 ***Coble***	Y	N	N	Y	Y	Y
7 McIntyre	N	Y	N	Y	Y	Y
8 ***Hayes***	Y	N	N	Y	Y	Y
9 ***Myrick***	Y	N	N	Y	Y	Y
10 ***Ballenger***	?	N	N	Y	Y	Y
11 ***Taylor***	Y	N	N	Y	Y	Y
12 Watt	N	Y	P	Y	Y	Y
13 Miller	N	Y	Y	Y	Y	Y
NORTH DAKOTA						
AL Pomeroy	N	Y	N	Y	Y	Y
OHIO						
1 ***Chabot***	Y	N	N	Y	Y	Y
2 ***Portman***	Y	N	N	Y	Y	Y
3 ***Turner***	Y	N	N	Y	Y	Y
4 ***Oxley***	Y	N	N	Y	Y	Y
5 ***Gillmor***	Y	N	N	Y	Y	Y
6 Strickland	N	Y	Y	Y	Y	Y
7 ***Hobson***	Y	N	N	Y	Y	Y
8 ***Boehner***	Y	N	N	Y	Y	Y
9 Kaptur	N	Y	N	Y	Y	Y
10 Kucinich	N	Y	N	Y	Y	Y
11 Jones	?	Y	Y	Y	Y	Y
12 ***Tiberi***	Y	N	N	Y	Y	Y
13 Brown	N	Y	Y	Y	Y	Y
14 ***LaTourette***	Y	N	N	Y	Y	Y
15 ***Pryce***	Y	N	N	Y	Y	Y
16 ***Regula***	Y	N	N	Y	Y	Y
17 Ryan	N	Y	Y	Y	Y	Y
18 ***Ney***	Y	N	N	Y	Y	Y
OKLAHOMA						
1 ***Sullivan***	Y	N	N	Y	Y	Y
2 Carson	?	?	?	?	?	?
3 ***Lucas***	Y	N	N	Y	Y	Y
4 ***Cole***	Y	N	N	Y	Y	Y
5 ***Istook***	Y	N	N	Y	Y	Y
OREGON						
1 Wu	N	Y	N	Y	Y	Y
2 ***Walden***	Y	N	N	Y	Y	Y
3 Blumenauer	N	Y	Y	Y	Y	Y
4 DeFazio	N	Y	Y	Y	Y	Y
5 Hooley	N	Y	Y	Y	Y	Y
PENNSYLVANIA						
1 Brady	N	Y	N	Y	Y	Y
2 Fattah	N	Y	N	Y	Y	Y
3 ***English***	Y	N	N	Y	Y	Y
4 ***Hart***	Y	N	N	Y	Y	Y
5 ***Peterson***	Y	N	N	Y	Y	Y
6 ***Gerlach***	Y	N	N	Y	Y	Y
7 ***Weldon***	Y	N	N	Y	Y	Y
8 ***Greenwood***	Y	N	N	Y	Y	Y
9 ***Shuster, Bill***	Y	N	N	Y	Y	Y
10 ***Sherwood***	Y	N	N	Y	Y	?
11 Kanjorski	N	Y	N	Y	Y	Y
12 Murtha	N	Y	N	Y	Y	Y
13 Hoeffel	N	Y	N	Y	Y	Y
14 Doyle	N	Y	N	Y	Y	Y
15 ***Toomey***	Y	N	N	Y	Y	Y
16 ***Pitts***	Y	N	N	Y	Y	Y
17 Holden	N	Y	N	Y	Y	Y
18 ***Murphy***	Y	N	N	Y	Y	Y
19 ***Platts***	Y	N	N	Y	Y	Y
RHODE ISLAND						
1 Kennedy	N	Y	Y	Y	Y	Y
2 Langevin	N	Y	Y	Y	Y	Y
SOUTH CAROLINA						
1 ***Brown***	Y	N	N	Y	Y	Y
2 ***Wilson***	Y	N	N	Y	Y	Y
3 ***Barrett***	Y	N	N	Y	Y	Y
4 ***DeMint***	?	?	?	?	?	?
5 Spratt	N	Y	N	Y	Y	Y
6 Clyburn	N	Y	N	Y	Y	Y
SOUTH DAKOTA						
AL Vacant						
TENNESSEE						
1 ***Jenkins***	Y	N	N	Y	Y	Y
2 ***Duncan***	Y	N	N	Y	Y	Y
3 ***Wamp***	Y	N	N	Y	Y	Y
4 Davis	N	Y	Y	Y	Y	Y
5 Cooper	N	Y	N	Y	Y	Y
6 Gordon	N	Y	N	Y	?	?
7 ***Blackburn***	Y	N	N	Y	Y	Y
8 Tanner	N	Y	N	Y	Y	Y
9 Ford	N	Y	N	Y	Y	Y
TEXAS						
1 Sandlin	N	Y	N	Y	Y	Y
2 Turner	N	Y	N	Y	Y	Y
3 ***Johnson, Sam***	Y	N	N	Y	Y	Y
4 ***Hall***	Y	N	N	Y	Y	Y
5 ***Hensarling***	Y	N	N	Y	Y	Y
6 ***Barton***	Y	N	N	Y	Y	Y
7 ***Culberson***	Y	N	N	Y	Y	Y
8 ***Brady***	Y	N	N	Y	Y	Y
9 Lampson	N	Y	N	Y	Y	Y
10 Doggett	N	Y	N	Y	Y	Y
11 Edwards	N	Y	N	Y	Y	Y
12 ***Granger***	Y	N	N	Y	Y	Y
13 ***Thornberry***	Y	N	N	Y	Y	Y
14 ***Paul***	Y	N	N	Y	Y	Y
15 Hinojosa	N	Y	N	Y	Y	Y
16 Reyes	N	Y	N	Y	Y	Y
17 Stenholm	N	Y	N	Y	Y	Y
18 Jackson-Lee	N	Y	P	Y	Y	Y
19 ***Neugebauer***	Y	N	N	Y	Y	Y
20 Gonzalez	N	Y	N	Y	Y	Y
21 ***Smith***	Y	N	N	Y	Y	Y
22 ***DeLay***	Y	N	N	Y	Y	Y
23 ***Bonilla***	Y	N	N	Y	Y	Y
24 Frost	N	Y	Y	Y	Y	Y
25 Bell	N	Y	Y	Y	Y	Y
26 ***Burgess***	Y	N	N	Y	Y	Y
27 Ortiz	N	Y	N	Y	Y	Y
28 Rodriguez	N	Y	N	Y	Y	Y
29 Green	N	Y	N	Y	Y	Y
30 Johnson, E.B.	N	Y	N	Y	Y	Y
31 ***Carter***	Y	N	N	Y	Y	Y
32 ***Sessions***	Y	N	N	Y	Y	Y
UTAH						
1 ***Bishop***	Y	N	N	Y	Y	Y
2 Matheson	N	Y	Y	Y	Y	Y
3 ***Cannon***	Y	N	N	Y	Y	Y
VERMONT						
AL *Sanders*	N	Y	N	Y	Y	Y
VIRGINIA						
1 ***Davis, Jo Ann***	Y	N	N	Y	Y	Y
2 ***Schrock***	Y	N	N	Y	Y	Y
3 Scott	N	Y	N	Y	Y	Y
4 ***Forbes***	Y	N	N	Y	Y	Y
5 ***Goode***	Y	N	N	Y	Y	Y
6 ***Goodlatte***	Y	N	N	Y	Y	Y
7 ***Cantor***	Y	N	N	Y	Y	Y
8 Moran	N	Y	N	Y	Y	Y
9 Boucher	N	Y	N	Y	Y	Y
10 ***Wolf***	Y	N	N	Y	Y	Y
11 ***Davis, T.***	Y	N	N	Y	Y	Y
WASHINGTON						
1 Inslee	N	Y	Y	Y	Y	Y
2 Larsen	N	Y	Y	Y	Y	Y
3 Baird	N	Y	Y	Y	Y	Y
4 ***Hastings***	Y	N	N	Y	Y	Y
5 ***Nethercutt***	Y	N	N	Y	Y	Y
6 Dicks	N	Y	Y	Y	Y	Y
7 McDermott	N	Y	N	Y	Y	Y
8 ***Dunn***	Y	N	N	Y	Y	Y
9 Smith	Y	Y	Y	Y	Y	Y
WEST VIRGINIA						
1 Mollohan	N	Y	N	Y	Y	Y
2 ***Capito***	Y	N	N	Y	Y	Y
3 Rahall	N	Y	N	Y	Y	Y
WISCONSIN						
1 ***Ryan***	Y	N	N	Y	Y	Y
2 Baldwin	N	Y	N	Y	Y	Y
3 Kind	N	Y	N	Y	Y	Y
4 Kleczka	N	Y	N	Y	Y	Y
5 ***Sensenbrenner***	Y	N	N	Y	Y	Y
6 ***Petri***	Y	N	N	Y	Y	Y
7 Obey	N	Y	N	Y	Y	Y
8 ***Green***	Y	N	N	Y	Y	Y
WYOMING						
AL ***Cubin***	Y	N	N	Y	Y	Y

Southern states - Ala., Ark., Fla., Ga., Ky., La., Miss., N.C., Okla., S.C., Tenn., Texas, Va.

223. Procedural Motion/Journal. Approval of the House Journal of Wednesday, June 2, 2004. Approved 346-47: R 193-12; D 152-35 (ND 110-25, SD 42-10); I 1-0. June 3, 2004.

224. HR 444. Job Training and Worker Services/Recommit. Kildee, D-Mich., motion to recommit the bill to the House Education and the Workforce Committee with instructions to authorize an extension of the federal program to provide an additional 13 weeks of unemployment benefits for people who have exhausted their state jobless benefits. Motion rejected 199-216: R 2-216; D 196-0 (ND 143-0, SD 53-0); I 1-0. June 3, 2004.

225. HR 444. Job Training and Worker Services/Passage. Passage of the bill that would authorize personal accounts and grants of up to $3,000 for unemployed individuals to use for job training or for services that might help in an employment search. Workers who find a job before receiving 13 weeks of unemployment compensation could receive the balance remaining in their accounts as a cash re-employment bonus. Passed 213-203: R 213-4; D 0-198 (ND 0-144, SD 0-54); I 0-1. A "yea" was a vote in support of the president's position. June 3, 2004.

226. HR 3866. Steroid Control/Passage. Sensenbrenner, R-Wis., motion to suspend the rules and pass the bill that would broaden a ban on anabolic steroids to include products made with any of more than 50 performance-enhancing supplements. Motion agreed to 408-3: R 212-2; D 195-1 (ND 142-1, SD 53-0); I 1-0. A two-thirds majority of those present and voting (274 in this case) is required for passage under suspension of the rules. June 3, 2004.

227. HR 3550. Surface Transportation/Motion to Instruct. Oberstar, D-Minn., motion to instruct House conferees to insist on the "Safe Routes to School" provisions in the House-passed bill, which would provide $1 billion over six years for a grant program that encourages walking and biking by students. Motion agreed to 377-30: R 182-30; D 194-0 (ND 143-0, SD 51-0); I 1-0. June 3, 2004.

228. H Res 655. Tiananmen Square Protesters/Adoption. Smith, R-N.J., motion to suspend the rules and adopt the resolution that would express sympathy for the families of those killed, tortured and imprisoned for their participation in the 1989 Tiananmen Square protests, while condemning the ongoing human rights abuses by the Chinese government. Motion agreed to 400-1: R 206-1; D 193-0 (ND 142-0, SD 51-0); I 1-0. A two-thirds majority of those present and voting (268 in this case) is required for adoption under suspension of the rules. June 3, 2004.

* *Rep. Stephanie Herseth, D-S.D., was sworn in June 3, 2004, to fill the At Large seat vacated when Republican Bill Janklow resigned Jan. 20, 2003. The first vote for which Herseth was eligible was 224.*

Key

Y	Voted for (yea).
#	Paired for.
+	Announced for.
N	Voted against (nay).
X	Paired against.
–	Announced against.
P	Voted "present."
C	Voted "present" to avoid possible conflict of interest.
?	Did not vote or otherwise make a position known.

Democrats **Republicans**
Independents

	223	224	225	226	227	228
ALABAMA						
1 *Bonner*	Y	N	Y	Y	N	Y
2 *Everett*	Y	N	Y	Y	Y	Y
3 *Rogers*	Y	N	Y	Y	Y	Y
4 *Aderholt*	Y	N	Y	Y	Y	Y
5 Cramer	Y	Y	N	Y	Y	?
6 *Bachus*	Y	N	Y	Y	Y	Y
7 Davis	Y	Y	N	Y	Y	Y
ALASKA						
AL *Young*	?	N	Y	Y	Y	Y
ARIZONA						
1 *Renzi*	Y	N	Y	Y	Y	Y
2 *Franks*	Y	N	Y	Y	N	Y
3 *Shadegg*	Y	N	Y	Y	N	Y
4 Pastor	N	Y	N	Y	Y	Y
5 *Hayworth*	Y	N	Y	Y	N	Y
6 *Flake*	Y	N	Y	N	N	Y
7 Grijalva	?	Y	N	Y	Y	Y
8 *Kolbe*	Y	N	Y	Y	Y	Y
ARKANSAS						
1 Berry	Y	Y	N	Y	Y	Y
2 Snyder	Y	Y	N	Y	Y	Y
3 *Boozman*	Y	N	Y	Y	Y	Y
4 Ross	Y	Y	N	Y	Y	Y
CALIFORNIA						
1 Thompson	N	Y	N	Y	Y	Y
2 *Herger*	?	N	Y	Y	Y	Y
3 *Ose*	Y	N	Y	Y	Y	Y
4 *Doolittle*	Y	N	Y	Y	Y	Y
5 Matsui	Y	Y	N	Y	Y	Y
6 Woolsey	Y	Y	N	Y	Y	Y
7 Miller, George	N	Y	N	Y	Y	Y
8 Pelosi	Y	Y	N	Y	Y	Y
9 Lee	Y	Y	N	Y	Y	Y
10 Tauscher	Y	Y	N	Y	Y	Y
11 *Pombo*	Y	N	Y	Y	Y	Y
12 Lantos	Y	Y	N	Y	Y	Y
13 Stark	Y	Y	N	Y	Y	Y
14 Eshoo	Y	Y	N	Y	Y	Y
15 Honda	Y	Y	N	Y	Y	Y
16 Lofgren	Y	Y	N	Y	Y	Y
17 Farr	Y	Y	N	Y	Y	Y
18 Cardoza	Y	Y	N	Y	Y	Y
19 *Radanovich*	Y	N	Y	Y	Y	Y
20 Dooley	Y	Y	N	Y	Y	Y
21 *Nunes*	Y	N	Y	Y	Y	Y
22 *Thomas*	?	N	Y	Y	Y	Y
23 Capps	Y	Y	N	Y	Y	Y
24 *Gallegly*	Y	N	Y	Y	Y	Y
25 *McKeon*	Y	N	Y	Y	Y	Y
26 *Dreier*	Y	N	Y	Y	?	?
27 Sherman	Y	Y	N	Y	Y	Y
28 Berman	Y	Y	N	Y	Y	Y
29 Schiff	Y	Y	N	Y	Y	Y
30 Waxman	Y	Y	N	Y	Y	Y
31 Becerra	Y	Y	N	Y	Y	Y
32 Solis	Y	Y	N	Y	Y	Y
33 Watson	Y	–	?	Y	Y	Y
34 Roybal-Allard	Y	Y	N	Y	Y	Y
35 Waters	N	Y	N	Y	Y	Y
36 Harman	Y	Y	N	Y	Y	Y

	223	224	225	226	227	228
37 Millender-McD.	Y	Y	N	Y	Y	Y
38 Napolitano	Y	Y	N	Y	Y	Y
39 Sánchez, Linda	Y	Y	N	Y	Y	Y
40 *Royce*	Y	N	Y	Y	N	Y
41 *Lewis*	Y	N	Y	Y	Y	?
42 *Miller, Gary*	Y	N	Y	Y	Y	Y
43 Baca	Y	Y	N	Y	Y	Y
44 *Calvert*	Y	N	Y	Y	Y	Y
45 *Bono*	Y	N	Y	Y	Y	Y
46 *Rohrabacher*	?	N	Y	Y	Y	Y
47 Sanchez, Loretta	Y	N	Y	Y	Y	Y
48 *Cox*	Y	N	Y	Y	Y	Y
49 *Issa*	Y	N	Y	Y	Y	Y
50 *Cunningham*	Y	N	Y	Y	Y	Y
51 Filner	N	Y	N	Y	Y	Y
52 *Hunter*	?	N	Y	Y	Y	?
53 Davis	Y	Y	N	Y	Y	Y
COLORADO						
1 DeGette	?	?	?	?	?	?
2 Udall	N	Y	N	Y	Y	Y
3 *McInnis*	Y	N	Y	?	Y	?
4 *Musgrave*	Y	N	Y	Y	Y	Y
5 *Hefley*	N	N	Y	Y	Y	Y
6 *Tancredo*	P	N	N	Y	N	Y
7 *Beauprez*	Y	N	Y	Y	Y	Y
CONNECTICUT						
1 Larson	Y	Y	N	Y	Y	Y
2 *Simmons*	Y	N	Y	Y	Y	Y
3 DeLauro	Y	Y	N	Y	Y	Y
4 *Shays*	Y	Y	Y	Y	Y	Y
5 *Johnson*	Y	N	Y	Y	Y	Y
DELAWARE						
AL *Castle*	Y	N	Y	Y	Y	Y
FLORIDA						
1 *Miller, J.*	Y	N	N	Y	N	Y
2 Boyd	Y	Y	N	Y	Y	Y
3 Brown	Y	Y	N	Y	Y	Y
4 *Crenshaw*	Y	N	Y	Y	Y	Y
5 *Brown-Waite*	Y	N	Y	?	Y	Y
6 *Stearns*	Y	N	Y	Y	Y	Y
7 *Mica*	Y	N	Y	Y	Y	Y
8 *Keller*	Y	N	Y	Y	Y	Y
9 *Bilirakis*	Y	N	Y	Y	Y	Y
10 *Young*	Y	N	Y	Y	Y	Y
11 Davis	Y	Y	N	Y	Y	Y
12 *Putnam*	Y	N	Y	Y	Y	Y
13 *Harris*	Y	N	Y	Y	Y	Y
14 *Goss*	Y	N	Y	Y	Y	Y
15 *Weldon*	?	N	Y	Y	Y	Y
16 *Foley*	Y	N	Y	Y	Y	Y
17 Meek	Y	Y	N	Y	Y	Y
18 *Ros-Lehtinen*	Y	N	Y	Y	Y	Y
19 Wexler	?	Y	N	Y	Y	Y
20 Deutsch	?	?	?	?	?	?
21 *Diaz-Balart, L.*	Y	N	Y	Y	Y	Y
22 *Shaw*	Y	N	Y	Y	Y	Y
23 Hastings	N	Y	N	Y	Y	Y
24 *Feeney*	Y	N	?	?	Y	Y
25 *Diaz-Balart, M.*	Y	N	Y	Y	Y	Y
GEORGIA						
1 *Kingston*	?	N	Y	Y	N	Y
2 Bishop	Y	Y	N	Y	Y	Y
3 Marshall	Y	Y	N	Y	Y	?
4 Majette	Y	Y	N	Y	Y	Y
5 Lewis	Y	Y	N	Y	Y	Y
6 *Isakson*	Y	N	Y	Y	N	Y
7 *Linder*	Y	N	Y	Y	N	Y
8 *Collins*	Y	N	Y	Y	+	+
9 *Norwood*	Y	N	Y	Y	N	Y
10 *Deal*	Y	N	Y	Y	?	?
11 *Gingrey*	Y	N	Y	Y	Y	Y
12 *Burns*	Y	N	Y	Y	Y	Y
13 Scott	Y	Y	N	Y	Y	Y
HAWAII						
1 Abercrombie	Y	Y	N	Y	Y	Y
2 Case	Y	Y	N	Y	Y	Y
IDAHO						
1 *Otter*	N	N	Y	Y	Y	?
2 *Simpson*	Y	N	Y	Y	Y	Y
ILLINOIS						
1 Rush	Y	Y	N	Y	Y	Y
2 Jackson	Y	Y	N	Y	Y	Y
3 Lipinski	Y	Y	N	Y	Y	Y
4 Gutierrez	Y	Y	N	Y	Y	Y
5 Emanuel	Y	Y	N	Y	Y	Y
6 *Hyde*	Y	N	Y	Y	N	Y

ND Northern Democrats   SD Southern Democrats

	223	224	225	226	227	228
7 Davis	Y	Y	N	Y	Y	Y
8 ***Crane***	?	N	Y	Y	Y	Y
9 Schakowsky	N	Y	N	Y	Y	Y
10 ***Kirk***	Y	N	Y	Y	Y	Y
11 ***Weller***	N	N	Y	Y	Y	Y
12 Costello	N	Y	N	Y	Y	Y
13 ***Biggert***	Y	N	Y	Y	Y	Y
14 ***Hastert***						
15 ***Johnson***	Y	N	Y	Y	Y	Y
16 ***Manzullo***	Y	N	Y	Y	Y	Y
17 Evans	Y	Y	N	Y	Y	Y
18 ***LaHood***	Y	N	Y	Y	Y	Y
19 ***Shimkus***	Y	N	Y	Y	Y	Y
INDIANA						
1 Visclosky	N	Y	N	Y	Y	Y
2 ***Chocola***	Y	N	Y	Y	Y	Y
3 ***Souder***	Y	N	Y	Y	Y	Y
4 ***Buyer***	Y	N	Y	Y	Y	Y
5 ***Burton***	+	–	+	+	+	+
6 ***Pence***	Y	N	Y	Y	Y	Y
7 Carson	Y	Y	N	Y	Y	Y
8 ***Hostettler***	Y	N	N	Y	Y	Y
9 Hill	Y	Y	N	Y	Y	Y
IOWA						
1 ***Nussle***	Y	N	Y	Y	Y	Y
2 ***Leach***	Y	N	Y	Y	Y	Y
3 Boswell	Y	Y	N	Y	Y	Y
4 ***Latham***	Y	N	Y	Y	Y	Y
5 ***King***	Y	N	Y	Y	Y	Y
KANSAS						
1 ***Moran***	Y	N	Y	Y	Y	Y
2 ***Ryun***	Y	N	Y	Y	Y	Y
3 Moore	Y	Y	N	Y	Y	Y
4 ***Tiahrt***	Y	N	Y	Y	Y	Y
KENTUCKY						
1 ***Whitfield***	Y	N	Y	Y	Y	Y
2 ***Lewis***	Y	N	Y	Y	Y	Y
3 ***Northup***	Y	N	Y	Y	N	Y
4 Lucas	Y	Y	N	Y	Y	Y
5 ***Rogers***	Y	N	Y	Y	Y	Y
6 Chandler	Y	?	N	Y	Y	Y
LOUISIANA						
1 ***Vitter***	Y	N	Y	Y	Y	Y
2 Jefferson	?	Y	N	Y	?	Y
3 ***Tauzin***	?	?	?	?	?	?
4 ***McCrery***	Y	N	Y	Y	Y	Y
5 Alexander	Y	Y	N	Y	Y	Y
6 ***Baker***	Y	N	Y	Y	Y	Y
7 John	Y	Y	N	Y	?	?
MAINE						
1 Allen	Y	Y	N	Y	Y	Y
2 Michaud	Y	Y	N	Y	Y	Y
MARYLAND						
1 ***Gilchrest***	Y	N	Y	Y	Y	Y
2 Ruppersberger	Y	?	N	Y	Y	Y
3 Cardin	Y	Y	N	Y	Y	Y
4 Wynn	Y	Y	N	Y	Y	Y
5 Hoyer	Y	Y	N	Y	Y	Y
6 ***Bartlett***	?	N	Y	Y	Y	Y
7 Cummings	?	Y	N	Y	Y	Y
8 Van Hollen	Y	Y	N	Y	Y	Y
MASSACHUSETTS						
1 Olver	N	Y	N	Y	Y	?
2 Neal	Y	Y	N	Y	Y	Y
3 McGovern	Y	Y	N	Y	Y	Y
4 Frank	Y	Y	N	Y	Y	Y
5 Meehan	Y	Y	N	Y	Y	Y
6 Tierney	Y	Y	N	Y	Y	Y
7 Markey	Y	Y	N	Y	Y	Y
8 Capuano	?	?	?	?	?	?
9 Lynch	?	?	?	?	?	?
10 Delahunt	?	Y	N	Y	Y	Y
MICHIGAN						
1 Stupak	N	Y	N	Y	Y	Y
2 ***Hoekstra***	Y	N	Y	Y	N	Y
3 ***Ehlers***	Y	N	Y	Y	Y	Y
4 ***Camp***	Y	N	Y	Y	Y	Y
5 Kildee	Y	Y	N	Y	Y	Y
6 ***Upton***	Y	N	Y	Y	Y	Y
7 ***Smith***	?	?	?	?	?	?
8 ***Rogers***	Y	N	Y	Y	Y	Y
9 ***Knollenberg***	Y	N	Y	Y	Y	Y
10 ***Miller***	Y	N	Y	Y	Y	Y
11 ***McCotter***	Y	N	Y	Y	Y	Y
12 Levin	Y	Y	N	Y	Y	Y

	223	224	225	226	227	228
13 Kilpatrick	Y	Y	N	Y	Y	Y
14 Conyers	?	Y	N	Y	Y	Y
15 Dingell	Y	Y	N	Y	Y	Y
MINNESOTA						
1 ***Gutknecht***	N	N	Y	Y	Y	Y
2 ***Kline***	Y	N	Y	Y	Y	Y
3 ***Ramstad***	N	N	Y	Y	Y	Y
4 McCollum	Y	Y	N	Y	Y	Y
5 Sabo	N	Y	N	?	Y	Y
6 ***Kennedy***	N	N	Y	Y	Y	Y
7 Peterson	N	Y	N	Y	Y	Y
8 Oberstar	Y	Y	N	Y	Y	Y
MISSISSIPPI						
1 ***Wicker***	N	N	Y	Y	Y	Y
2 Thompson	N	Y	N	Y	Y	Y
3 ***Pickering***	Y	N	Y	Y	Y	Y
4 Taylor	N	Y	N	Y	Y	Y
MISSOURI						
1 Clay	Y	Y	N	Y	Y	Y
2 ***Akin***	Y	N	Y	Y	Y	Y
3 Gephardt	Y	Y	N	Y	Y	Y
4 Skelton	Y	Y	N	Y	Y	Y
5 McCarthy	Y	Y	N	Y	Y	Y
6 ***Graves***	N	N	Y	Y	Y	Y
7 ***Blunt***	Y	N	Y	Y	N	Y
8 ***Emerson***	?	?	?	?	?	?
9 ***Hulshof***	N	N	Y	Y	Y	Y
MONTANA						
AL ***Rehberg***	Y	N	Y	Y	Y	Y
NEBRASKA						
1 ***Bereuter***	Y	N	Y	Y	Y	Y
2 ***Terry***	Y	N	Y	Y	Y	Y
3 ***Osborne***	Y	N	Y	Y	Y	Y
NEVADA						
1 Berkley	Y	Y	N	Y	Y	Y
2 ***Gibbons***	Y	N	Y	Y	Y	Y
3 ***Porter***	Y	N	Y	Y	Y	Y
NEW HAMPSHIRE						
1 ***Bradley***	Y	N	Y	Y	Y	Y
2 ***Bass***	Y	N	Y	Y	Y	Y
NEW JERSEY						
1 Andrews	Y	Y	N	?	Y	Y
2 ***LoBiondo***	N	N	Y	Y	Y	Y
3 ***Saxton***	Y	N	Y	Y	Y	Y
4 ***Smith***	Y	N	Y	Y	Y	Y
5 ***Garrett***	Y	N	Y	Y	Y	Y
6 Pallone	Y	Y	N	Y	Y	Y
7 ***Ferguson***	Y	N	Y	Y	Y	Y
8 Pascrell	Y	Y	N	Y	Y	Y
9 Rothman	Y	Y	N	Y	Y	Y
10 Payne	Y	Y	N	Y	Y	Y
11 ***Frelinghuysen***	Y	N	Y	Y	Y	Y
12 Holt	Y	Y	N	Y	Y	Y
13 Menendez	Y	Y	N	Y	Y	Y
NEW MEXICO						
1 ***Wilson***	Y	N	Y	Y	Y	Y
2 ***Pearce***	Y	N	Y	Y	Y	Y
3 Udall	N	Y	N	Y	Y	Y
NEW YORK						
1 Bishop	Y	Y	N	Y	Y	Y
2 Israel	Y	Y	N	Y	Y	Y
3 ***King***	Y	N	Y	Y	Y	Y
4 McCarthy	Y	Y	N	Y	Y	Y
5 Ackerman	Y	Y	N	Y	Y	Y
6 Meeks	Y	Y	N	Y	Y	Y
7 Crowley	Y	Y	N	Y	Y	Y
8 Nadler	Y	Y	N	Y	Y	Y
9 Weiner	?	Y	N	Y	Y	Y
10 Towns	Y	Y	N	Y	Y	Y
11 Owens	Y	Y	N	Y	Y	Y
12 Velázquez	?	Y	N	Y	Y	Y
13 ***Fossella***	?	–	+	+	Y	Y
14 Maloney	Y	Y	N	Y	Y	Y
15 Rangel	Y	Y	N	Y	Y	Y
16 Serrano	Y	Y	N	Y	Y	Y
17 Engel	?	Y	N	Y	Y	Y
18 Lowey	Y	Y	N	Y	Y	Y
19 ***Kelly***	Y	N	Y	Y	Y	Y
20 ***Sweeney***	Y	N	Y	Y	Y	Y
21 McNulty	N	Y	N	Y	Y	Y
22 Hinchey	N	Y	N	Y	Y	Y
23 ***McHugh***	Y	N	Y	Y	Y	Y
24 ***Boehlert***	?	N	Y	Y	Y	Y
25 ***Walsh***	Y	N	Y	Y	Y	Y

	223	224	225	226	227	228
26 ***Reynolds***	Y	N	Y	Y	Y	Y
27 ***Quinn***	Y	?	?	?	?	?
28 Slaughter	?	Y	N	Y	+	+
29 ***Houghton***	Y	N	Y	Y	Y	?
NORTH CAROLINA						
1 Ballance	?	?	?	?	?	?
2 Etheridge	Y	Y	N	Y	Y	Y
3 ***Jones***	Y	N	Y	Y	Y	Y
4 Price	Y	Y	N	Y	Y	Y
5 ***Burr***	Y	N	Y	Y	Y	Y
6 ***Coble***	Y	N	Y	Y	Y	Y
7 McIntyre	Y	Y	N	Y	Y	Y
8 ***Hayes***	Y	N	Y	Y	Y	Y
9 ***Myrick***	Y	N	Y	Y	N	Y
10 ***Ballenger***	Y	N	Y	Y	Y	?
11 ***Taylor***	Y	N	Y	Y	Y	Y
12 Watt	Y	Y	N	Y	Y	Y
13 Miller	Y	Y	N	Y	Y	Y
NORTH DAKOTA						
AL Pomeroy	Y	Y	N	Y	Y	Y
OHIO						
1 ***Chabot***	Y	N	Y	Y	Y	Y
2 ***Portman***	Y	N	Y	Y	Y	Y
3 ***Turner***	Y	N	Y	Y	Y	Y
4 ***Oxley***	Y	N	Y	Y	Y	Y
5 ***Gillmor***	Y	N	Y	Y	Y	Y
6 Strickland	N	Y	N	Y	Y	Y
7 ***Hobson***	Y	N	Y	?	Y	Y
8 ***Boehner***	Y	N	Y	Y	Y	Y
9 Kaptur	Y	Y	N	Y	Y	Y
10 Kucinich	N	Y	N	N	Y	Y
11 Jones	Y	Y	N	Y	Y	Y
12 ***Tiberi***	Y	N	Y	Y	N	Y
13 Brown	Y	Y	N	Y	Y	Y
14 ***LaTourette***	Y	N	Y	Y	Y	Y
15 ***Pryce***	Y	N	Y	?	Y	Y
16 ***Regula***	Y	N	Y	Y	Y	Y
17 Ryan	Y	Y	N	Y	Y	Y
18 ***Ney***	Y	N	Y	Y	Y	Y
OKLAHOMA						
1 ***Sullivan***	Y	N	Y	Y	Y	Y
2 Carson	?	?	?	?	?	?
3 ***Lucas***	Y	N	Y	Y	Y	Y
4 ***Cole***	Y	N	Y	Y	Y	Y
5 ***Istook***	?	N	Y	Y	?	Y
OREGON						
1 Wu	N	Y	N	Y	Y	Y
2 ***Walden***	Y	N	Y	Y	Y	Y
3 Blumenauer	Y	Y	N	Y	Y	Y
4 DeFazio	N	Y	N	Y	Y	Y
5 Hooley	N	Y	N	Y	Y	Y
PENNSYLVANIA						
1 Brady	?	?	?	?	?	?
2 Fattah	Y	Y	N	Y	Y	Y
3 ***English***	N	N	Y	Y	Y	Y
4 ***Hart***	N	N	Y	Y	Y	Y
5 ***Peterson***	Y	N	Y	Y	Y	Y
6 ***Gerlach***	?	?	?	?	?	?
7 ***Weldon***	?	N	Y	Y	Y	Y
8 ***Greenwood***	Y	N	Y	Y	Y	Y
9 ***Shuster, Bill***	Y	N	Y	Y	Y	Y
10 ***Sherwood***	Y	N	Y	Y	Y	Y
11 Kanjorski	Y	Y	N	Y	Y	Y
12 Murtha	?	Y	N	Y	Y	Y
13 Hoeffel	Y	Y	N	Y	Y	Y
14 Doyle	Y	Y	N	Y	Y	Y
15 ***Toomey***	Y	N	Y	Y	N	Y
16 ***Pitts***	Y	N	Y	Y	Y	Y
17 Holden	Y	Y	N	Y	Y	Y
18 ***Murphy***	Y	N	Y	Y	Y	Y
19 ***Platts***	Y	N	Y	Y	Y	Y
RHODE ISLAND						
1 Kennedy	Y	Y	N	Y	Y	Y
2 Langevin	Y	Y	N	Y	Y	Y
SOUTH CAROLINA						
1 ***Brown***	Y	N	Y	Y	Y	Y
2 ***Wilson***	Y	N	Y	Y	N	?
3 ***Barrett***	Y	N	Y	Y	N	Y
4 ***DeMint***	?	?	?	?	?	?
5 Spratt	Y	Y	N	Y	Y	Y
6 Clyburn	Y	Y	N	?	Y	Y
SOUTH DAKOTA						
AL Herseth*		Y	N	Y	Y	Y

	223	224	225	226	227	228
TENNESSEE						
1 ***Jenkins***	Y	N	Y	Y	?	?
2 ***Duncan***	Y	N	Y	Y	Y	Y
3 ***Wamp***	Y	N	Y	Y	Y	Y
4 Davis	Y	Y	N	Y	Y	Y
5 Cooper	N	Y	N	Y	Y	Y
6 Gordon	Y	Y	N	Y	Y	Y
7 ***Blackburn***	Y	N	Y	Y	N	Y
8 Tanner	Y	Y	N	Y	Y	Y
9 Ford	N	Y	N	Y	Y	Y
TEXAS						
1 Sandlin	N	Y	N	Y	Y	Y
2 Turner	Y	Y	N	Y	Y	Y
3 ***Johnson, Sam***	?	?	?	?	?	?
4 ***Hall***	Y	N	Y	Y	Y	Y
5 ***Hensarling***	Y	N	Y	Y	Y	Y
6 ***Barton***	Y	N	Y	Y	Y	Y
7 ***Culberson***	Y	N	Y	Y	N	Y
8 ***Brady***	Y	N	Y	Y	Y	Y
9 Lampson	N	Y	N	Y	Y	Y
10 Doggett	Y	Y	N	Y	Y	Y
11 Edwards	Y	Y	N	Y	Y	Y
12 ***Granger***	Y	N	Y	Y	Y	Y
13 ***Thornberry***	?	N	Y	Y	N	Y
14 ***Paul***	Y	N	N	N	Y	N
15 Hinojosa	Y	Y	N	Y	Y	Y
16 Reyes	Y	Y	N	Y	Y	Y
17 Stenholm	Y	Y	N	Y	Y	Y
18 Jackson-Lee	Y	Y	N	Y	Y	Y
19 ***Neugebauer***	Y	N	Y	Y	Y	Y
20 Gonzalez	Y	Y	N	Y	Y	Y
21 ***Smith***	Y	N	Y	Y	Y	Y
22 ***DeLay***	Y	N	Y	Y	N	Y
23 ***Bonilla***	Y	N	Y	Y	N	Y
24 Frost	Y	Y	N	Y	Y	Y
25 Bell	N	Y	N	Y	Y	Y
26 ***Burgess***	Y	N	Y	Y	Y	Y
27 Ortiz	Y	Y	N	Y	Y	Y
28 Rodriguez	Y	Y	N	Y	Y	Y
29 Green	N	Y	N	Y	Y	Y
30 Johnson, E.B.	N	Y	N	Y	Y	Y
31 ***Carter***	Y	N	Y	Y	Y	Y
32 ***Sessions***	Y	N	Y	Y	Y	Y
UTAH						
1 ***Bishop***	Y	N	Y	Y	N	Y
2 Matheson	Y	Y	N	Y	Y	Y
3 ***Cannon***	Y	N	Y	Y	N	Y
VERMONT						
AL *Sanders*	Y	Y	N	Y	Y	Y
VIRGINIA						
1 ***Davis, Jo Ann***	Y	N	Y	Y	Y	Y
2 ***Schrock***	Y	N	Y	Y	N	Y
3 Scott	Y	Y	N	Y	?	Y
4 ***Forbes***	Y	N	Y	Y	Y	Y
5 ***Goode***	Y	Y	Y	Y	Y	Y
6 ***Goodlatte***	Y	N	Y	Y	Y	Y
7 ***Cantor***	Y	N	Y	Y	N	Y
8 Moran	Y	Y	N	Y	Y	Y
9 Boucher	Y	Y	N	Y	Y	Y
10 ***Wolf***	Y	N	Y	Y	Y	Y
11 ***Davis, T.***	Y	N	Y	Y	Y	Y
WASHINGTON						
1 Inslee	Y	Y	N	Y	Y	Y
2 Larsen	N	Y	N	Y	Y	Y
3 Baird	N	Y	N	Y	Y	Y
4 ***Hastings***	Y	N	Y	Y	Y	Y
5 ***Nethercutt***	Y	N	Y	Y	Y	Y
6 Dicks	Y	Y	N	Y	Y	Y
7 McDermott	N	Y	N	Y	Y	Y
8 ***Dunn***	Y	N	Y	Y	?	?
9 Smith	Y	Y	N	Y	Y	Y
WEST VIRGINIA						
1 Mollohan	Y	Y	N	Y	Y	Y
2 ***Capito***	Y	N	Y	Y	Y	Y
3 Rahall	Y	Y	N	Y	Y	Y
WISCONSIN						
1 ***Ryan***	Y	N	Y	Y	Y	Y
2 Baldwin	N	Y	N	Y	Y	Y
3 Kind	Y	Y	N	Y	Y	Y
4 Kleczka	Y	Y	N	Y	Y	Y
5 ***Sensenbrenner***	Y	N	Y	Y	Y	Y
6 ***Petri***	Y	N	Y	Y	Y	Y
7 Obey	Y	Y	N	Y	?	?
8 ***Green***	Y	N	Y	Y	Y	Y
WYOMING						
AL ***Cubin***	Y	N	Y	Y	Y	Y

Southern states - Ala., Ark., Fla., Ga., Ky., La., Miss., N.C., Okla., S.C., Tenn., Texas, Va.

Key

Y	Voted for (yea).
#	Paired for.
+	Announced for.
N	Voted against (nay).
X	Paired against.
–	Announced against.
P	Voted "present."
C	Voted "present" to avoid possible conflict of interest.
?	Did not vote or otherwise make a position known.

Democrats **Republicans**
Independents

229. H Res 663. Ronald Reagan Condolences/Adoption. Adoption of the resolution that would express profound regret and sorrow on the death of former President Ronald Reagan, who died June 5, 2004. Adopted 355-0: R 201-0; D 154-0 (ND 112-0, SD 42-0); I 0-0. June 8, 2004.

230. Procedural Motion/Journal. Approval of the House Journal of Friday, June 4, 2004. Approved 318-29: R 188-8; D 130-21 (ND 92-17, SD 38-4); I 0-0. June 8, 2004.

231. H Res 664. Ronald Reagan Tribute/Adoption. Adoption of the resolution that would express appreciation for former President Ronald Reagan's public service and condolences to the Reagan family. Reagan died June 5, 2004. Adopted 375-0: R 208-0; D 167-0 (ND 122-0, SD 45-0); I 0-0. June 9, 2004.

	229	230	231
ALABAMA			
1 *Bonner*	Y	Y	Y
2 *Everett*	Y	Y	Y
3 *Rogers*	Y	Y	Y
4 *Aderholt*	Y	Y	Y
5 Cramer	Y	Y	Y
6 *Bachus*	Y	Y	Y
7 Davis	Y	Y	Y
ALASKA			
AL *Young*	Y	Y	Y
ARIZONA			
1 *Renzi*	Y	Y	Y
2 *Franks*	Y	Y	Y
3 *Shadegg*	+	+	+
4 *Pastor*	Y	Y	Y
5 *Hayworth*	Y	Y	Y
6 *Flake*	Y	Y	Y
7 Grijalva	?	?	?
8 *Kolbe*	Y	Y	Y
ARKANSAS			
1 Berry	Y	Y	Y
2 Snyder	Y	Y	Y
3 *Boozman*	Y	Y	Y
4 Ross	Y	Y	Y
CALIFORNIA			
1 Thompson	Y	N	Y
2 *Herger*	Y	Y	Y
3 *Ose*	?	?	?
4 *Doolittle*	?	?	Y
5 Matsui	Y	Y	Y
6 Woolsey	?	?	?
7 Miller, George	Y	?	Y
8 Pelosi	Y	Y	Y
9 Lee	?	?	?
10 Tauscher	Y	Y	Y
11 *Pombo*	?	?	Y
12 Lantos	Y	Y	Y
13 Stark	?	?	?
14 Eshoo	Y	Y	Y
15 Honda	Y	Y	Y
16 Lofgren	?	?	?
17 Farr	Y	Y	Y
18 Cardoza	Y	Y	Y
19 *Radanovich*	Y	Y	Y
20 Dooley	?	?	Y
21 *Nunes*	Y	Y	Y
22 *Thomas*	Y	Y	Y
23 Capps	?	?	?
24 *Gallegly*	Y	Y	Y
25 *McKeon*	Y	Y	Y
26 *Dreier*	Y	Y	Y
27 Sherman	Y	Y	Y
28 Berman	Y	Y	Y
29 Schiff	Y	Y	Y
30 Waxman	Y	Y	Y
31 Becerra	?	?	Y
32 Solis	+	+	+
33 Watson	Y	Y	Y
34 Roybal-Allard	Y	Y	Y
35 Waters	Y	N	?
36 Harman	Y	Y	Y

	229	230	231
37 Millender-McD.	?	?	Y
38 Napolitano	Y	Y	Y
39 Sánchez, Linda	Y	Y	Y
40 *Royce*	?	?	Y
41 *Lewis*	Y	Y	Y
42 *Miller, Gary*	?	?	?
43 Baca	Y	Y	+
44 *Calvert*	Y	Y	Y
45 *Bono*	Y	Y	Y
46 *Rohrabacher*	Y	Y	Y
47 Sanchez, Loretta	Y	Y	Y
48 *Cox*	Y	Y	Y
49 *Issa*	Y	Y	Y
50 *Cunningham*	Y	Y	Y
51 Filner	Y	N	Y
52 *Hunter*	Y	Y	Y
53 Davis	Y	Y	Y
COLORADO			
1 DeGette	Y	Y	Y
2 Udall	Y	N	Y
3 *McInnis*	?	?	?
4 *Musgrave*	Y	Y	Y
5 *Hefley*	Y	Y	Y
6 *Tancredo*	Y	P	Y
7 *Beauprez*	Y	Y	Y
CONNECTICUT			
1 Larson	?	?	?
2 *Simmons*	Y	Y	Y
3 DeLauro	Y	Y	Y
4 *Shays*	Y	Y	Y
5 *Johnson*	Y	Y	Y
DELAWARE			
AL *Castle*	Y	Y	Y
FLORIDA			
1 *Miller, J.*	Y	Y	Y
2 Boyd	Y	Y	Y
3 Brown	Y	Y	Y
4 *Crenshaw*	Y	Y	Y
5 *Brown-Waite*	Y	Y	Y
6 *Stearns*	Y	Y	Y
7 *Mica*	Y	Y	Y
8 *Keller*	Y	Y	Y
9 *Bilirakis*	?	?	?
10 *Young*	Y	Y	Y
11 Davis	Y	Y	Y
12 *Putnam*	Y	Y	Y
13 *Harris*	Y	Y	Y
14 *Goss*	Y	Y	?
15 *Weldon*	Y	Y	Y
16 *Foley*	Y	Y	Y
17 Meek	Y	Y	Y
18 *Ros-Lehtinen*	?	?	?
19 Wexler	?	?	?
20 Deutsch	?	?	?
21 *Diaz-Balart, L.*	Y	Y	Y
22 *Shaw*	Y	Y	Y
23 Hastings	?	?	?
24 *Feeney*	Y	Y	Y
25 *Diaz-Balart, M.*	Y	Y	Y
GEORGIA			
1 *Kingston*	?	?	Y
2 Bishop	Y	Y	Y
3 Marshall	Y	Y	Y
4 Majette	?	?	?
5 Lewis	Y	Y	Y
6 *Isakson*	Y	Y	Y
7 *Linder*	Y	Y	Y
8 *Collins*	+	+	Y
9 *Norwood*	Y	Y	Y
10 *Deal*	Y	Y	Y
11 *Gingrey*	Y	Y	Y
12 *Burns*	?	?	Y
13 Scott	Y	Y	Y
HAWAII			
1 Abercrombie	Y	Y	Y
2 Case	?	?	?
IDAHO			
1 *Otter*	Y	N	Y
2 *Simpson*	Y	Y	Y
ILLINOIS			
1 Rush	?	?	?
2 Jackson	Y	Y	Y
3 Lipinski	Y	Y	Y
4 Gutierrez	?	?	?
5 Emanuel	Y	Y	Y
6 *Hyde*	Y	Y	Y

ND Northern Democrats   SD Southern Democrats

	229	230	231
7 Davis	Y	Y	Y
8 *Crane*	Y	?	Y
9 Schakowsky	Y	Y	Y
10 *Kirk*	Y	Y	Y
11 *Weller*	Y	N	Y
12 Costello	Y	N	Y
13 *Biggert*	Y	Y	Y
14 *Hastert*	Y		
15 *Johnson*	Y	Y	Y
16 *Manzullo*	Y	Y	Y
17 Evans	?	?	?
18 *LaHood*	Y	Y	Y
19 *Shimkus*	Y	Y	Y
INDIANA			
1 Visclosky	Y	N	Y
2 *Chocola*	Y	Y	Y
3 *Souder*	?	?	?
4 *Buyer*	Y	Y	Y
5 *Burton*	Y	Y	Y
6 *Pence*	Y	Y	Y
7 Carson	Y	Y	Y
8 *Hostettler*	Y	Y	Y
9 Hill	Y	Y	Y
IOWA			
1 *Nussle*	Y	Y	Y
2 *Leach*	Y	Y	?
3 Boswell	Y	Y	Y
4 *Latham*	Y	Y	Y
5 *King*	Y	Y	Y
KANSAS			
1 *Moran*	Y	N	Y
2 *Ryun*	Y	Y	Y
3 Moore	Y	Y	Y
4 *Tiahrt*	?	?	?
KENTUCKY			
1 *Whitfield*	Y	Y	Y
2 *Lewis*	Y	Y	Y
3 *Northup*	Y	Y	Y
4 Lucas	Y	Y	Y
5 *Rogers*	Y	Y	Y
6 Chandler	Y	Y	Y
LOUISIANA			
1 *Vitter*	Y	Y	Y
2 Jefferson	Y	?	Y
3 *Tauzin*	?	?	?
4 *McCrery*	?	Y	Y
5 Alexander	?	Y	Y
6 *Baker*	Y	Y	Y
7 John	Y	Y	Y
MAINE			
1 Allen	Y	Y	Y
2 Michaud	Y	Y	Y
MARYLAND			
1 *Gilchrest*	?	?	Y
2 Ruppersberger	Y	Y	Y
3 Cardin	Y	Y	Y
4 Wynn	Y	Y	Y
5 Hoyer	Y	Y	Y
6 *Bartlett*	Y	Y	Y
7 Cummings	Y	?	Y
8 Van Hollen	Y	Y	Y
MASSACHUSETTS			
1 Olver	Y	N	Y
2 Neal	Y	Y	Y
3 McGovern	Y	Y	Y
4 Frank	Y	Y	Y
5 Meehan	Y	Y	Y
6 Tierney	Y	Y	Y
7 Markey	Y	Y	Y
8 Capuano	Y	N	Y
9 Lynch	?	?	?
10 Delahunt	?	?	Y
MICHIGAN			
1 Stupak	?	?	Y
2 *Hoekstra*	Y	Y	Y
3 *Ehlers*	Y	Y	Y
4 *Camp*	Y	Y	Y
5 Kildee	Y	Y	Y
6 *Upton*	Y	Y	Y
7 *Smith*	Y	Y	Y
8 Rogers	Y	Y	Y
9 *Knollenberg*	Y	Y	Y
10 *Miller*	Y	Y	Y
11 *McCotter*	Y	Y	Y
12 Levin	Y	Y	Y

	229	230	231
13 Kilpatrick	+	+	Y
14 Conyers	?	?	?
15 Dingell	?	?	?
MINNESOTA			
1 *Gutknecht*	Y	?	Y
2 *Kline*	Y	Y	Y
3 *Ramstad*	Y	N	Y
4 McCollum	Y	Y	Y
5 Sabo	Y	N	Y
6 *Kennedy*	Y	N	Y
7 Peterson	Y	N	Y
8 Oberstar	Y	N	Y
MISSISSIPPI			
1 *Wicker*	Y	Y	Y
2 Thompson	Y	N	Y
3 *Pickering*	Y	Y	Y
4 Taylor	Y	N	Y
MISSOURI			
1 Clay	?	?	?
2 *Akin*	Y	Y	Y
3 Gephardt	?	?	?
4 Skelton	?	?	?
5 McCarthy	?	?	+
6 *Graves*	?	?	Y
7 *Blunt*	Y	Y	Y
8 *Emerson*	Y	Y	Y
9 *Hulshof*	Y	Y	Y
MONTANA			
AL *Rehberg*	Y	Y	Y
NEBRASKA			
1 *Bereuter*	Y	Y	Y
2 *Terry*	Y	Y	Y
3 *Osborne*	Y	?	Y
NEVADA			
1 Berkley	Y	Y	Y
2 *Gibbons*	Y	Y	Y
3 *Porter*	Y	Y	Y
NEW HAMPSHIRE			
1 *Bradley*	Y	Y	Y
2 *Bass*	Y	Y	Y
NEW JERSEY			
1 Andrews	Y	Y	Y
2 *LoBiondo*	Y	N	Y
3 *Saxton*	Y	Y	Y
4 *Smith*	Y	Y	Y
5 *Garrett*	Y	Y	Y
6 Pallone	Y	Y	Y
7 *Ferguson*	Y	Y	Y
8 Pascrell	Y	Y	Y
9 Rothman	?	?	?
10 Payne	?	?	?
11 *Frelinghuysen*	Y	Y	Y
12 Holt	Y	Y	Y
13 Menendez	?	?	Y
NEW MEXICO			
1 *Wilson*	Y	Y	Y
2 *Pearce*	Y	Y	Y
3 Udall	Y	N	Y
NEW YORK			
1 Bishop	Y	Y	Y
2 Israel	Y	Y	Y
3 *King*	?	?	?
4 McCarthy	Y	Y	Y
5 Ackerman	?	?	?
6 Meeks	Y	?	Y
7 Crowley	Y	Y	Y
8 Nadler	Y	Y	Y
9 Weiner	Y	Y	Y
10 Towns	Y	Y	?
11 Owens	Y	Y	Y
12 Velázquez	Y	Y	Y
13 *Fossella*	Y	Y	?
14 Maloney	Y	Y	Y
15 Rangel	?	?	?
16 Serrano	Y	Y	Y
17 Engel	Y	Y	Y
18 Lowey	Y	Y	Y
19 *Kelly*	Y	Y	Y
20 *Sweeney*	Y	Y	Y
21 McNulty	Y	Y	Y
22 Hinchey	Y	Y	Y
23 *McHugh*	Y	Y	Y
24 *Boehlert*	Y	Y	Y
25 *Walsh*	Y	Y	Y

	229	230	231
26 *Reynolds*	Y	Y	Y
27 *Quinn*	Y	Y	Y
28 Slaughter	Y	N	Y
29 Houghton	?	?	?
NORTH CAROLINA			
1 Ballance	?	?	?
2 Etheridge	Y	Y	Y
3 *Jones*	?	?	Y
4 Price	Y	Y	Y
5 *Burr*	Y	Y	Y
6 *Coble*	Y	Y	Y
7 McIntyre	Y	Y	Y
8 *Hayes*	Y	Y	Y
9 *Myrick*	Y	Y	Y
10 *Ballenger*	Y	Y	Y
11 *Taylor*	Y	Y	Y
12 Watt	Y	Y	Y
13 Miller	Y	Y	Y
NORTH DAKOTA			
AL Pomeroy	Y	Y	Y
OHIO			
1 *Chabot*	Y	Y	Y
2 *Portman*	Y	Y	Y
3 *Turner*	Y	Y	Y
4 *Oxley*	Y	Y	?
5 *Gillmor*	Y	N	Y
6 Strickland	Y	N	Y
7 *Hobson*	Y	Y	Y
8 *Boehner*	Y	Y	Y
9 Kaptur	?	?	?
10 Kucinich	?	?	?
11 Jones	Y	N	Y
12 *Tiberi*	Y	Y	Y
13 Brown	Y	Y	Y
14 *LaTourette*	Y	Y	Y
15 *Pryce*	Y	Y	Y
16 *Regula*	?	?	?
17 Ryan	Y	Y	Y
18 *Ney*	?	?	?
OKLAHOMA			
1 *Sullivan*	Y	Y	Y
2 Carson	?	?	?
3 *Lucas*	Y	Y	Y
4 *Cole*	Y	Y	Y
5 *Istook*	Y	Y	Y
OREGON			
1 Wu	Y	N	Y
2 *Walden*	Y	Y	Y
3 Blumenauer	Y	Y	Y
4 DeFazio	Y	Y	Y
5 Hooley	Y	Y	Y
PENNSYLVANIA			
1 Brady	?	?	?
2 Fattah	?	?	?
3 *English*	?	?	Y
4 *Hart*	Y	N	Y
5 *Peterson*	Y	Y	Y
6 *Gerlach*	Y	Y	Y
7 *Weldon*	Y	Y	Y
8 *Greenwood*	Y	Y	Y
9 *Shuster, Bill*	Y	Y	Y
10 *Sherwood*	Y	Y	Y
11 Kanjorski	Y	Y	Y
12 Murtha	?	?	Y
13 Hoeffel	Y	Y	Y
14 Doyle	Y	Y	Y
15 *Toomey*	Y	Y	Y
16 *Pitts*	Y	Y	Y
17 Holden	Y	Y	Y
18 *Murphy*	Y	Y	Y
19 *Platts*	Y	Y	Y
RHODE ISLAND			
1 Kennedy	Y	Y	Y
2 Langevin	Y	Y	Y
SOUTH CAROLINA			
1 *Brown*	Y	Y	Y
2 *Wilson*	Y	Y	Y
3 *Barrett*	Y	Y	Y
4 *DeMint*	?	?	?
5 Spratt	?	?	?
6 Clyburn	Y	Y	Y
SOUTH DAKOTA			
AL Herseth	Y	Y	Y

	229	230	231
TENNESSEE			
1 *Jenkins*	Y	Y	Y
2 *Duncan*	Y	Y	Y
3 *Wamp*	Y	Y	Y
4 Davis	Y	Y	Y
5 Cooper	Y	Y	Y
6 Gordon	Y	Y	Y
7 *Blackburn*	Y	Y	Y
8 Tanner	Y	Y	Y
9 Ford	Y	Y	Y
TEXAS			
1 Sandlin	Y	N	Y
2 Turner	?	?	?
3 *Johnson, Sam*	Y	Y	Y
4 *Hall*	Y	Y	Y
5 *Hensarling*	Y	Y	Y
6 *Barton*	Y	Y	Y
7 *Culberson*	Y	Y	Y
8 *Brady*	Y	Y	Y
9 Lampson	?	?	?
10 Doggett	Y	Y	Y
11 Edwards	Y	Y	Y
12 *Granger*	Y	Y	Y
13 *Thornberry*	Y	Y	Y
14 *Paul*	Y	Y	Y
15 Hinojosa	Y	Y	Y
16 Reyes	?	?	?
17 Stenholm	Y	Y	Y
18 Jackson-Lee	Y	Y	Y
19 *Neugebauer*	Y	Y	Y
20 Gonzalez	?	?	?
21 *Smith*	Y	Y	Y
22 *DeLay*	Y	Y	Y
23 *Bonilla*	?	?	Y
24 Frost	?	?	Y
25 Bell	Y	Y	Y
26 *Burgess*	Y	Y	Y
27 Ortiz	Y	Y	Y
28 Rodriguez	?	?	?
29 Green	Y	Y	Y
30 Johnson, E.B.	Y	N	Y
31 *Carter*	?	?	Y
32 *Sessions*	Y	Y	Y
UTAH			
1 *Bishop*	Y	Y	Y
2 Matheson	Y	Y	Y
3 *Cannon*	Y	Y	Y
VERMONT			
AL *Sanders*	?	?	?
VIRGINIA			
1 *Davis, Jo Ann*	Y	Y	Y
2 *Schrock*	Y	Y	Y
3 Scott	Y	Y	Y
4 *Forbes*	Y	Y	Y
5 *Goode*	Y	Y	Y
6 *Goodlatte*	Y	Y	Y
7 *Cantor*	Y	Y	Y
8 Moran	?	?	Y
9 Boucher	Y	Y	Y
10 *Wolf*	Y	Y	Y
11 *Davis, T.*	Y	Y	Y
WASHINGTON			
1 Inslee	Y	Y	Y
2 Larsen	Y	N	Y
3 Baird	Y	Y	Y
4 *Hastings*	Y	Y	Y
5 *Nethercutt*	Y	Y	Y
6 Dicks	Y	Y	Y
7 McDermott	?	?	Y
8 *Dunn*	?	?	?
9 Smith	Y	Y	Y
WEST VIRGINIA			
1 Mollohan	?	?	Y
2 *Capito*	Y	Y	Y
3 Rahall	?	?	?
WISCONSIN			
1 *Ryan*	Y	Y	Y
2 Baldwin	Y	Y	Y
3 Kind	Y	Y	Y
4 Kleczka	Y	Y	Y
5 *Sensenbrenner*	Y	Y	Y
6 *Petri*	Y	Y	Y
7 Obey	Y	Y	Y
8 *Green*	Y	Y	Y
WYOMING			
AL *Cubin*	?	?	Y

Southern states - Ala., Ark., Fla., Ga., Ky., La., Miss., N.C., Okla., S.C., Tenn., Texas, Va.

232. H J Res 97. Myanmar Sanctions/Passage. Thomas, R-Calif., motion to suspend the rules and pass the joint resolution that would extend for one year import restrictions on products from Myanmar, formerly known as Burma, until the president certifies that the Myanmar government has made significant progress toward practicing democracy and ending human rights violations. Motion agreed to 372-2: R 209-2; D 163-0 (ND 119-0, SD 44-0); I 0-0. A two-thirds majority of those present and voting (250 in this case) is required for passage under suspension of the rules. June 14, 2004.

233. H Res 669. Prostate Cancer Awareness/Adoption. Deal, R-Ga., motion to suspend the rules and adopt the resolution that would express the sense of the House commending health organizations for their efforts in supplying information about screening and treatment options for prostate cancer. It also would urge the government to ensure that providers supply prostate cancer patients with accurate information about various treatments. Motion agreed to 377-3: R 209-3; D 168-0 (ND 122-0, SD 46-0); I 0-0. A two-thirds majority of those present and voting (254 in this case) is required for adoption under suspension of the rules. June 14, 2004.

234. HR 4323. Emergency Defense Acquisitions/Passage. Hunter, R-Calif., motion to suspend the rules and pass the bill that would authorize the Defense secretary to waive certain acquisition regulations in order to obtain equipment needed by a military commander to prevent combat fatalities. Motion agreed to 285-97: R 211-2; D 74-94 (ND 43-79, SD 31-15); I 0-1. A two-thirds majority of those present and voting (255 in this case) is required for passage under suspension of the rules. June 14, 2004.

235. H Res 653. George Bush's 80th Birthday/Adoption. Carter, R-Texas, motion to suspend the rules and adopt the resolution that would congratulate former President George Bush on his 80th birthday. Motion agreed to 381-0: R 214-0; D 166-0 (ND 121-0, SD 45-0); I 1-0. A two-thirds majority of those present and voting (254 in this case) is required for adoption under suspension of the rules. June 14, 2004.

236. HR 4503, HR 4517. Energy Policy and Oil Facility Expansion/ Previous Question. Hastings, R-Wash., motion to order the previous question (thus ending debate and possibility of amendment) on adoption of the rule (H Res 671) to provide for House floor consideration of a bill that would implement a comprehensive national policy for energy conservation, research and development, and a bill that would make it easier to build and expand oil refineries. Motion agreed to 218-197: R 218-1; D 0-195 (ND 0-143, SD 0-52); I 0-1. June 15, 2004.

237. HR 4503, HR 4517. Energy Policy and Oil Facility Expansion/ Rule. Adoption of the rule (H Res 671) to provide for House floor consideration of a bill that would implement a comprehensive national policy for energy conservation, research and development, and a bill that would make it easier to build and expand oil refineries. Adopted 225-193: R 218-4; D 7-188 (ND 1-143, SD 6-45); I 0-1. June 15, 2004.

Rep. Frank W. Ballance, Jr., D-N.C., resigned effective June 11, 2004. The last vote for which he was eligible was 231.

Key

Y	Voted for (yea).
#	Paired for.
+	Announced for.
N	Voted against (nay).
X	Paired against.
–	Announced against.
P	Voted "present."
C	Voted "present" to avoid possible conflict of interest.
?	Did not vote or otherwise make a position known.

Democrats **Republicans**
Independents

	232	233	234	235	236	237
ALABAMA						
1 *Bonner*	Y	Y	Y	Y	Y	Y
2 *Everett*	Y	Y	Y	Y	Y	Y
3 *Rogers*	Y	Y	Y	Y	Y	Y
4 *Aderholt*	?	?	?	?	Y	Y
5 Cramer	Y	Y	Y	Y	N	N
6 *Bachus*	Y	Y	Y	Y	Y	Y
7 Davis	?	?	?	?	N	N
ALASKA						
AL *Young*	?	Y	Y	Y	Y	Y
ARIZONA						
1 *Renzi*	Y	Y	Y	Y	Y	Y
2 *Franks*	Y	Y	Y	Y	Y	Y
3 *Shadegg*	Y	N	Y	Y	Y	Y
4 Pastor	Y	Y	N	Y	N	N
5 *Hayworth*	Y	Y	Y	Y	Y	Y
6 *Flake*	N	N	Y	Y	Y	Y
7 Grijalva	Y	Y	N	Y	N	N
8 *Kolbe*	Y	Y	Y	Y	Y	Y
ARKANSAS						
1 Berry	Y	Y	N	Y	N	N
2 Snyder	Y	Y	Y	Y	N	N
3 *Boozman*	Y	Y	Y	Y	Y	Y
4 Ross	Y	Y	N	Y	N	N
CALIFORNIA						
1 Thompson	Y	Y	N	Y	N	N
2 *Herger*	Y	Y	Y	Y	Y	Y
3 *Ose*	Y	Y	Y	Y	Y	Y
4 *Doolittle*	Y	Y	Y	Y	Y	Y
5 Matsui	Y	Y	N	Y	N	N
6 Woolsey	?	?	?	?	N	N
7 *Miller, George*	?	?	?	?	N	N
8 Pelosi	?	?	?	?	N	N
9 Lee	Y	Y	N	Y	N	N
10 Tauscher	Y	Y	Y	Y	N	N
11 *Pombo*	Y	Y	Y	Y	Y	Y
12 Lantos	?	?	?	?	N	N
13 Stark	Y	Y	N	Y	N	N
14 Eshoo	Y	Y	N	Y	N	N
15 Honda	Y	Y	N	Y	N	N
16 Lofgren	Y	Y	N	Y	N	N
17 Farr	Y	Y	N	Y	N	N
18 Cardoza	Y	Y	N	Y	?	N
19 *Radanovich*	Y	Y	Y	Y	Y	Y
20 Dooley	?	?	?	?	N	N
21 *Nunes*	Y	Y	Y	Y	Y	Y
22 *Thomas*	Y	Y	Y	Y	Y	Y
23 Capps	Y	Y	N	Y	N	N
24 *Gallegly*	Y	Y	Y	Y	Y	Y
25 *McKeon*	Y	Y	Y	Y	Y	Y
26 *Dreier*	Y	Y	Y	Y	Y	Y
27 Sherman	Y	Y	N	Y	N	N
28 Berman	Y	Y	N	Y	N	N
29 Schiff	+	Y	Y	Y	N	N
30 Waxman	Y	Y	N	Y	N	N
31 Becerra	Y	Y	N	Y	N	N
32 Solis	Y	Y	N	Y	N	N
33 Watson	?	?	?	?	?	?
34 Roybal-Allard	Y	Y	N	Y	N	N
35 Waters	Y	Y	N	Y	N	?
36 Harman	Y	Y	N	Y	N	N

	232	233	234	235	236	237
37 Millender-McD.	?	?	?	?	?	?
38 Napolitano	Y	Y	N	Y	N	N
39 Sánchez, Linda	Y	Y	N	Y	N	N
40 *Royce*	Y	Y	Y	Y	Y	Y
41 *Lewis*	Y	Y	Y	Y	Y	Y
42 *Miller, Gary*	Y	Y	Y	Y	Y	Y
43 Baca	Y	Y	N	Y	N	N
44 *Calvert*	Y	Y	Y	Y	Y	Y
45 *Bono*	Y	Y	Y	Y	Y	Y
46 *Rohrabacher*	Y	Y	Y	Y	Y	Y
47 Sanchez, Loretta	Y	Y	Y	Y	N	N
48 *Cox*	Y	Y	Y	Y	Y	Y
49 *Issa*	Y	Y	Y	Y	Y	Y
50 *Cunningham*	Y	Y	Y	Y	Y	Y
51 Filner	Y	Y	N	Y	N	N
52 *Hunter*	Y	?	Y	Y	Y	Y
53 Davis	Y	Y	Y	Y	N	N
COLORADO						
1 DeGette	Y	Y	N	Y	N	N
2 Udall	Y	Y	N	Y	N	N
3 *McInnis*	Y	Y	Y	Y	Y	Y
4 *Musgrave*	Y	Y	Y	Y	Y	Y
5 *Hefley*	Y	Y	Y	Y	Y	Y
6 *Tancredo*	Y	Y	?	Y	Y	Y
7 *Beauprez*	Y	Y	Y	Y	Y	Y
CONNECTICUT						
1 Larson	Y	Y	Y	Y	N	N
2 *Simmons*	Y	Y	Y	Y	Y	Y
3 DeLauro	Y	Y	N	Y	N	N
4 *Shays*	?	?	?	?	N	N
5 *Johnson*	Y	Y	Y	Y	Y	Y
DELAWARE						
AL *Castle*	Y	Y	Y	Y	Y	N
FLORIDA						
1 *Miller, J.*	?	?	?	?	Y	Y
2 Boyd	Y	Y	N	Y	N	N
3 Brown	?	?	?	?	N	N
4 *Crenshaw*	Y	Y	Y	Y	Y	Y
5 *Brown-Waite*	Y	Y	Y	Y	?	?
6 *Stearns*	Y	Y	Y	Y	Y	Y
7 *Mica*	Y	Y	Y	Y	Y	Y
8 *Keller*	Y	Y	Y	Y	Y	Y
9 *Bilirakis*	?	?	?	?	Y	Y
10 *Young*	Y	Y	Y	Y	Y	Y
11 Davis	Y	Y	N	Y	N	N
12 *Putnam*	Y	Y	Y	Y	Y	Y
13 *Harris*	Y	Y	Y	Y	Y	Y
14 *Goss*	Y	Y	Y	Y	Y	Y
15 *Weldon*	Y	Y	Y	Y	Y	Y
16 *Foley*	Y	Y	Y	Y	Y	Y
17 Meek	Y	Y	N	Y	N	N
18 *Ros-Lehtinen*	Y	Y	Y	Y	Y	Y
19 Wexler	Y	Y	N	Y	N	N
20 Deutsch	?	?	?	?	–	–
21 *Diaz-Balart, L.*	Y	Y	Y	Y	Y	Y
22 *Shaw*	Y	Y	Y	Y	Y	Y
23 Hastings	Y	Y	N	Y	N	N
24 *Feeney*	Y	Y	Y	Y	Y	Y
25 *Diaz-Balart, M.*	Y	Y	Y	Y	?	Y
GEORGIA						
1 *Kingston*	Y	Y	Y	Y	Y	Y
2 Bishop	Y	Y	N	Y	N	N
3 Marshall	Y	Y	Y	Y	N	N
4 Majette	Y	Y	N	Y	N	N
5 Lewis	Y	Y	N	Y	N	N
6 *Isakson*	Y	Y	Y	Y	Y	Y
7 *Linder*	Y	Y	Y	Y	Y	Y
8 *Collins*	Y	Y	Y	+	+	
9 *Norwood*	Y	Y	Y	Y	Y	Y
10 *Deal*	Y	Y	Y	Y	Y	Y
11 *Gingrey*	Y	Y	Y	Y	Y	Y
12 *Burns*	Y	Y	Y	Y	Y	Y
13 Scott	Y	Y	Y	Y	N	N
HAWAII						
1 Abercrombie	Y	Y	N	Y	N	N
2 Case	Y	Y	Y	Y	N	N
IDAHO						
1 *Otter*	Y	Y	Y	Y	Y	Y
2 *Simpson*	Y	Y	Y	Y	Y	Y
ILLINOIS						
1 Rush	Y	Y	Y	Y	N	N
2 Jackson	Y	Y	Y	Y	N	N
3 Lipinski	?	?	?	?	N	N
4 Gutierrez	?	?	?	?	N	N
5 Emanuel	Y	Y	Y	Y	N	N
6 *Hyde*	Y	Y	Y	Y	Y	Y

ND Northern Democrats   SD Southern Democrats

	232	233	234	235	236	237
7 Davis	Y	Y	N	Y	N	N
8 ***Crane***	Y	Y	Y	Y	Y	Y
9 Schakowsky	Y	Y	N	Y	N	N
10 ***Kirk***	Y	Y	Y	Y	Y	Y
11 ***Weller***	Y	Y	Y	Y	Y	Y
12 Costello	Y	Y	Y	Y	N	N
13 ***Biggert***	Y	Y	Y	Y	Y	Y
14 ***Hastert***						
15 ***Johnson***	Y	Y	N	Y	Y	Y
16 ***Manzullo***	Y	Y	Y	Y	Y	Y
17 Evans	Y	Y	Y	Y	N	N
18 ***LaHood***	Y	Y	Y	Y	Y	Y
19 ***Shimkus***	Y	Y	Y	Y	Y	Y
INDIANA						
1 Visclosky	Y	Y	N	Y	N	N
2 ***Chocola***	Y	Y	Y	Y	Y	Y
3 ***Souder***	Y	Y	Y	Y	Y	Y
4 ***Buyer***	Y	Y	Y	Y	Y	Y
5 ***Burton***	+	+	+	+	+	+
6 ***Pence***	Y	Y	Y	Y	Y	Y
7 Carson	?	?	?	?	?	?
8 ***Hostettler***	Y	Y	Y	Y	Y	Y
9 Hill	Y	Y	Y	Y	N	N
IOWA						
1 ***Nussle***	?	?	Y	Y	Y	Y
2 ***Leach***	Y	Y	Y	Y	Y	N
3 Boswell	Y	Y	Y	Y	N	N
4 ***Latham***	Y	Y	Y	Y	Y	Y
5 ***King***	Y	Y	Y	Y	Y	Y
KANSAS						
1 ***Moran***	Y	Y	Y	Y	Y	Y
2 ***Ryun***	Y	Y	Y	Y	Y	Y
3 Moore	Y	Y	Y	Y	N	N
4 ***Tiahrt***	Y	Y	Y	Y	Y	Y
KENTUCKY						
1 ***Whitfield***	Y	Y	Y	Y	Y	Y
2 ***Lewis***	Y	Y	Y	Y	Y	Y
3 ***Northup***	Y	Y	Y	Y	Y	Y
4 Lucas	Y	Y	Y	Y	N	N
5 ***Rogers***	Y	Y	Y	Y	Y	Y
6 Chandler	Y	Y	N	Y	N	N
LOUISIANA						
1 ***Vitter***	Y	Y	Y	Y	Y	Y
2 Jefferson	Y	Y	N	Y	N	N
3 ***Tauzin***	Y	Y	Y	Y	Y	Y
4 ***McCrery***	Y	Y	Y	Y	Y	Y
5 Alexander	Y	Y	Y	Y	N	N
6 ***Baker***	Y	Y	Y	Y	Y	Y
7 John	?	?	?	?	?	?
MAINE						
1 Allen	Y	Y	N	Y	N	N
2 Michaud	Y	Y	Y	Y	N	N
MARYLAND						
1 ***Gilchrest***	Y	Y	Y	Y	Y	Y
2 Ruppersberger	?	?	?	?	N	N
3 Cardin	Y	Y	Y	Y	N	N
4 Wynn	Y	Y	N	Y	N	N
5 Hoyer	Y	Y	Y	Y	N	N
6 ***Bartlett***	Y	Y	N	Y	Y	Y
7 Cummings	Y	Y	N	Y	N	N
8 Van Hollen	Y	Y	Y	Y	N	N
MASSACHUSETTS						
1 Olver	Y	Y	N	Y	?	N
2 Neal	?	?	?	?	N	N
3 McGovern	Y	Y	N	Y	N	N
4 Frank	Y	Y	N	Y	N	N
5 Meehan	?	?	?	?	N	N
6 Tierney	Y	Y	N	Y	N	N
7 Markey	Y	Y	N	Y	N	N
8 Capuano	Y	Y	N	Y	N	N
9 Lynch	Y	Y	N	Y	N	N
10 Delahunt	Y	Y	N	Y	N	N
MICHIGAN						
1 Stupak	Y	Y	N	Y	N	N
2 ***Hoekstra***	Y	Y	Y	Y	Y	Y
3 ***Ehlers***	?	?	?	?	?	?
4 ***Camp***	Y	Y	Y	Y	Y	Y
5 Kildee	Y	Y	Y	Y	N	N
6 ***Upton***	Y	Y	Y	Y	Y	Y
7 ***Smith***	Y	Y	Y	Y	Y	Y
8 ***Rogers***	Y	Y	Y	Y	Y	Y
9 ***Knollenberg***	Y	Y	Y	Y	Y	Y
10 ***Miller***	Y	Y	Y	Y	Y	Y
11 ***McCotter***	Y	Y	Y	Y	Y	Y
12 Levin	Y	Y	N	Y	N	N

	232	233	234	235	236	237
13 Kilpatrick	+	+	+	+	N	N
14 Conyers	?	?	?	?	N	N
15 Dingell	Y	Y	N	Y	N	N
MINNESOTA						
1 ***Gutknecht***	Y	Y	Y	Y	Y	Y
2 ***Kline***	Y	Y	Y	Y	Y	Y
3 ***Ramstad***	Y	Y	Y	Y	Y	Y
4 McCollum	Y	Y	N	Y	N	N
5 Sabo	Y	Y	N	Y	N	N
6 ***Kennedy***	Y	Y	Y	Y	Y	Y
7 Peterson	Y	Y	N	Y	N	N
8 Oberstar	Y	Y	N	Y	N	N
MISSISSIPPI						
1 ***Wicker***	Y	Y	Y	Y	Y	Y
2 Thompson	Y	Y	Y	Y	N	N
3 ***Pickering***	Y	Y	Y	Y	Y	Y
4 Taylor	Y	Y	Y	Y	N	N
MISSOURI						
1 Clay	Y	Y	N	Y	N	N
2 ***Akin***	Y	Y	Y	Y	Y	Y
3 Gephardt	?	?	?	?	N	N
4 Skelton	Y	Y	Y	Y	N	N
5 McCarthy	Y	Y	Y	Y	N	N
6 ***Graves***	?	?	?	?	Y	Y
7 ***Blunt***	Y	Y	Y	Y	Y	Y
8 ***Emerson***	Y	Y	Y	Y	Y	Y
9 ***Hulshof***	Y	Y	Y	Y	Y	Y
MONTANA						
AL ***Rehberg***	Y	Y	Y	Y	Y	Y
NEBRASKA						
1 ***Bereuter***	Y	Y	Y	Y	Y	Y
2 ***Terry***	Y	Y	Y	Y	?	Y
3 ***Osborne***	Y	Y	Y	Y	Y	Y
NEVADA						
1 Berkley	Y	Y	N	Y	N	N
2 ***Gibbons***	Y	Y	Y	Y	Y	Y
3 ***Porter***	Y	Y	Y	Y	Y	Y
NEW HAMPSHIRE						
1 ***Bradley***	Y	Y	Y	Y	Y	Y
2 ***Bass***	Y	Y	Y	Y	Y	Y
NEW JERSEY						
1 Andrews	?	Y	Y	Y	N	N
2 ***LoBiondo***	Y	Y	Y	Y	Y	Y
3 ***Saxton***	Y	Y	Y	Y	Y	Y
4 ***Smith***	Y	Y	Y	Y	Y	Y
5 ***Garrett***	?	Y	Y	Y	Y	Y
6 Pallone	?	?	?	?	N	N
7 ***Ferguson***	Y	Y	Y	Y	Y	Y
8 Pascrell	?	?	?	?	?	?
9 Rothman	?	Y	Y	Y	N	N
10 Payne	?	?	?	?	N	N
11 ***Frelinghuysen***	Y	Y	Y	Y	Y	Y
12 Holt	Y	Y	N	Y	N	N
13 Menendez	Y	Y	Y	Y	N	N
NEW MEXICO						
1 ***Wilson***	Y	Y	Y	Y	Y	Y
2 ***Pearce***	Y	Y	Y	Y	Y	Y
3 Udall	Y	Y	N	Y	N	N
NEW YORK						
1 Bishop	Y	Y	Y	Y	N	N
2 Israel	Y	Y	Y	Y	N	N
3 ***King***	Y	Y	Y	Y	Y	Y
4 McCarthy	Y	Y	Y	Y	N	N
5 Ackerman	Y	Y	N	Y	N	N
6 Meeks	Y	Y	N	Y	N	N
7 Crowley	?	?	?	?	N	N
8 Nadler	?	?	?	?	N	N
9 Weiner	Y	Y	N	Y	N	N
10 Towns	Y	Y	Y	Y	N	N
11 Owens	Y	Y	N	Y	N	N
12 Velázquez	?	?	?	?	N	N
13 ***Fossella***	Y	Y	Y	Y	Y	Y
14 Maloney	Y	Y	N	?	N	N
15 Rangel	Y	Y	Y	Y	N	N
16 Serrano	?	?	?	?	N	N
17 Engel	Y	Y	Y	Y	N	N
18 Lowey	?	?	?	?	N	N
19 ***Kelly***	Y	Y	Y	Y	Y	Y
20 ***Sweeney***	Y	Y	Y	Y	Y	Y
21 McNulty	Y	Y	Y	Y	N	N
22 Hinchey	Y	Y	N	Y	N	N
23 ***McHugh***	Y	Y	Y	Y	Y	Y
24 ***Boehlert***	Y	Y	Y	Y	Y	Y
25 ***Walsh***	Y	Y	Y	Y	Y	Y

	232	233	234	235	236	237
26 ***Reynolds***	Y	Y	Y	Y	Y	Y
27 ***Quinn***	Y	Y	Y	Y	Y	Y
28 Slaughter	Y	Y	N	Y	N	N
29 ***Houghton***	Y	Y	Y	Y	Y	Y
NORTH CAROLINA						
1 Vacant*						
2 Etheridge	Y	Y	Y	Y	N	N
3 ***Jones***	Y	Y	Y	Y	Y	Y
4 Price	Y	Y	Y	Y	N	N
5 ***Burr***	?	?	?	?	Y	Y
6 ***Coble***	Y	Y	Y	Y	Y	Y
7 McIntyre	Y	Y	Y	Y	N	N
8 ***Hayes***	Y	Y	Y	Y	Y	Y
9 ***Myrick***	Y	Y	Y	Y	Y	Y
10 ***Ballenger***	Y	Y	Y	Y	Y	Y
11 ***Taylor***	?	?	?	?	Y	Y
12 Watt	Y	Y	N	Y	N	N
13 Miller	Y	Y	Y	Y	N	N
NORTH DAKOTA						
AL Pomeroy	Y	Y	Y	Y	N	N
OHIO						
1 ***Chabot***	Y	Y	Y	Y	Y	Y
2 ***Portman***	Y	Y	Y	Y	Y	Y
3 ***Turner***	Y	Y	Y	Y	Y	Y
4 ***Oxley***	Y	Y	Y	Y	Y	Y
5 ***Gillmor***	Y	Y	Y	Y	Y	Y
6 Strickland	Y	Y	N	Y	N	N
7 ***Hobson***	Y	Y	Y	Y	Y	Y
8 ***Boehner***	Y	Y	Y	Y	Y	Y
9 Kaptur	Y	Y	Y	Y	N	N
10 Kucinich	Y	Y	N	Y	N	N
11 Jones	Y	Y	N	Y	N	N
12 ***Tiberi***	Y	Y	Y	Y	Y	Y
13 Brown	Y	Y	N	Y	N	N
14 ***LaTourette***	Y	Y	Y	Y	Y	Y
15 ***Pryce***	Y	Y	Y	Y	Y	Y
16 ***Regula***	Y	Y	Y	Y	Y	Y
17 Ryan	Y	Y	N	Y	N	N
18 ***Ney***	Y	Y	Y	Y	Y	Y
OKLAHOMA						
1 ***Sullivan***	Y	Y	Y	Y	Y	Y
2 Carson	?	?	?	?	?	?
3 ***Lucas***	Y	Y	Y	Y	Y	Y
4 ***Cole***	Y	Y	Y	Y	Y	Y
5 ***Istook***	Y	Y	Y	Y	Y	Y
OREGON						
1 Wu	Y	Y	Y	Y	N	N
2 ***Walden***	Y	Y	Y	Y	Y	Y
3 Blumenauer	Y	Y	N	Y	N	N
4 DeFazio	Y	Y	N	Y	N	N
5 Hooley	Y	Y	N	Y	N	N
PENNSYLVANIA						
1 Brady	Y	Y	N	Y	N	N
2 Fattah	?	?	?	?	N	N
3 ***English***	Y	Y	Y	Y	Y	Y
4 ***Hart***	Y	Y	Y	Y	Y	Y
5 ***Peterson***	?	?	?	?	Y	N
6 ***Gerlach***	Y	Y	Y	Y	Y	Y
7 ***Weldon***	Y	Y	Y	Y	Y	Y
8 ***Greenwood***	Y	Y	Y	Y	Y	Y
9 ***Shuster, Bill***	Y	Y	Y	Y	Y	Y
10 ***Sherwood***	Y	Y	Y	Y	Y	Y
11 Kanjorski	Y	Y	N	Y	N	N
12 Murtha	Y	Y	N	Y	N	N
13 Hoeffel	?	?	?	?	N	N
14 Doyle	Y	Y	N	Y	N	N
15 ***Toomey***	?	?	?	?	Y	Y
16 ***Pitts***	Y	Y	Y	Y	Y	Y
17 Holden	Y	Y	Y	Y	N	N
18 ***Murphy***	Y	Y	Y	Y	Y	Y
19 ***Platts***	Y	Y	Y	Y	Y	Y
RHODE ISLAND						
1 Kennedy	Y	Y	N	Y	N	N
2 Langevin	Y	Y	N	Y	N	N
SOUTH CAROLINA						
1 ***Brown***	Y	Y	Y	Y	Y	Y
2 ***Wilson***	Y	Y	Y	Y	Y	Y
3 ***Barrett***	Y	Y	Y	Y	Y	Y
4 ***DeMint***	?	?	?	?	?	?
5 Spratt	Y	Y	Y	Y	N	N
6 Clyburn	Y	Y	Y	Y	N	N
SOUTH DAKOTA						
AL Herseth	Y	Y	Y	Y	N	N

	232	233	234	235	236	237
TENNESSEE						
1 ***Jenkins***	Y	Y	Y	Y	Y	Y
2 ***Duncan***	Y	Y	Y	Y	Y	Y
3 ***Wamp***	Y	Y	Y	Y	Y	Y
4 Davis	Y	Y	Y	Y	N	N
5 Cooper	Y	Y	Y	Y	N	N
6 Gordon	Y	Y	Y	Y	N	N
7 ***Blackburn***	Y	Y	Y	Y	Y	Y
8 Tanner	Y	Y	Y	Y	N	N
9 Ford	?	?	?	?	N	N
TEXAS						
1 Sandlin	Y	Y	Y	Y	N	Y
2 Turner	Y	Y	Y	?	N	?
3 ***Johnson, Sam***	Y	Y	Y	Y	Y	Y
4 ***Hall***	Y	Y	Y	Y	Y	Y
5 ***Hensarling***	Y	Y	Y	Y	Y	Y
6 ***Barton***	Y	Y	Y	Y	Y	Y
7 ***Culberson***	?	?	?	?	Y	Y
8 ***Brady***	Y	Y	Y	Y	Y	Y
9 Lampson	?	?	?	?	?	?
10 Doggett	Y	Y	N	Y	N	N
11 Edwards	?	Y	Y	Y	N	N
12 ***Granger***	Y	Y	Y	Y	Y	Y
13 ***Thornberry***	Y	Y	Y	Y	Y	Y
14 ***Paul***	N	N	Y	Y	Y	Y
15 Hinojosa	Y	Y	Y	Y	N	N
16 Reyes	?	?	?	?	N	Y
17 Stenholm	Y	Y	N	Y	N	N
18 Jackson-Lee	Y	Y	N	Y	N	N
19 ***Neugebauer***	Y	Y	Y	Y	Y	Y
20 Gonzalez	Y	Y	Y	Y	N	Y
21 ***Smith***	Y	Y	Y	Y	Y	Y
22 ***DeLay***	Y	Y	Y	Y	Y	Y
23 ***Bonilla***	Y	Y	Y	Y	Y	Y
24 Frost	?	?	?	?	N	N
25 Bell	?	?	?	?	N	N
26 ***Burgess***	Y	Y	Y	Y	Y	Y
27 Ortiz	Y	Y	Y	Y	N	Y
28 Rodriguez	Y	Y	Y	Y	N	Y
29 Green	Y	Y	Y	Y	N	Y
30 Johnson, E.B.	Y	Y	N	Y	N	N
31 ***Carter***	Y	Y	Y	Y	Y	Y
32 ***Sessions***	Y	Y	Y	Y	Y	Y
UTAH						
1 ***Bishop***	Y	Y	Y	Y	?	Y
2 Matheson	Y	Y	Y	Y	N	Y
3 ***Cannon***	Y	Y	Y	Y	Y	Y
VERMONT						
AL *Sanders*	?	?	N	Y	N	N
VIRGINIA						
1 ***Davis, Jo Ann***	Y	Y	Y	Y	Y	Y
2 ***Schrock***	Y	Y	Y	Y	Y	Y
3 Scott	?	Y	Y	Y	N	N
4 ***Forbes***	Y	Y	Y	Y	Y	Y
5 ***Goode***	Y	Y	Y	Y	Y	Y
6 ***Goodlatte***	Y	Y	Y	Y	Y	Y
7 ***Cantor***	Y	Y	Y	Y	Y	Y
8 Moran	Y	Y	Y	Y	N	N
9 Boucher	Y	Y	Y	Y	N	N
10 ***Wolf***	Y	Y	Y	Y	Y	Y
11 ***Davis, T.***	Y	Y	Y	Y	Y	Y
WASHINGTON						
1 Inslee	Y	Y	Y	Y	N	N
2 Larsen	Y	Y	Y	Y	N	N
3 Baird	Y	Y	Y	Y	N	N
4 ***Hastings***	Y	Y	Y	Y	Y	Y
5 ***Nethercutt***	Y	Y	Y	Y	Y	Y
6 Dicks	Y	Y	N	Y	N	N
7 McDermott	Y	Y	N	Y	N	N
8 ***Dunn***	Y	Y	Y	Y	Y	Y
9 Smith	Y	Y	Y	Y	N	N
WEST VIRGINIA						
1 Mollohan	?	?	?	?	N	N
2 ***Capito***	Y	Y	Y	Y	Y	Y
3 Rahall	Y	Y	N	Y	N	N
WISCONSIN						
1 ***Ryan***	Y	Y	Y	Y	Y	Y
2 Baldwin	Y	Y	N	Y	N	N
3 Kind	Y	Y	Y	Y	N	N
4 Kleczka	Y	Y	N	Y	N	N
5 ***Sensenbrenner***	Y	Y	Y	Y	Y	Y
6 ***Petri***	Y	Y	Y	Y	Y	Y
7 Obey	Y	Y	N	Y	N	N
8 ***Green***	Y	Y	Y	Y	Y	Y
WYOMING						
AL ***Cubin***	Y	Y	Y	Y	Y	Y

Southern states - Ala., Ark., Fla., Ga., Ky., La., Miss., N.C., Okla., S.C., Tenn., Texas, Va.

Key

Y Voted for (yea).
\# Paired for.
\+ Announced for.
N Voted against (nay).
X Paired against.
− Announced against.
P Voted "present."
C Voted "present" to avoid possible conflict of interest.
? Did not vote or otherwise make a position known.

•

Democrats **Republicans**
Independents

238. HR 4513, HR 4529. Alternative Energy Projects and ANWR Drilling/Previous Question. Reynolds, R-N.Y., motion to order the previous question (thus ending debate and possibility of amendment) on adoption of the rule (H Res 672) to provide for House floor consideration of a bill that would streamline licensing and siting for alternative energy projects on federal lands and a bill that would open a portion of Alaska's Arctic National Wildlife Refuge (ANWR) to oil and gas exploration. Motion agreed to 221-198: R 221-0; D 0-197 (ND 0-144, SD 0-53); I 0-1. June 15, 2004.

239. HR 4513, HR 4529. Alternative Energy Projects and ANWR Drilling/Rule. Adoption of the rule (H Res 672) to provide for House floor consideration of a bill that would streamline licensing and siting for alternative energy projects on federal lands and a bill that would open a portion of ANWR to oil and gas exploration. Adopted 226-193: R 218-2; D 8-190 (ND 0-145, SD 8-45); I 0-1. June 15, 2004.

240. HR 4503. Energy Policy/Recommit. Dingell, D-Mich., motion to recommit the bill to the Energy and Commerce Committee with instructions to strike the provisions and insert language aimed at reducing fraud and manipulation of energy markets and preventing future blackouts. It also would defer deliveries of crude oil to the Strategic Petroleum Reserve in an effort to control the costs of gasoline. Motion rejected 192-230: R 1-222; D 190-8 (ND 144-1, SD 46-7); I 1-0. June 15, 2004.

241. HR 4503. Energy Policy/Passage. Passage of the bill that would implement a comprehensive national policy for energy conservation, research and development. It would authorize $25.7 billion in tax breaks over 10 years and authorize $18 billion in loan guarantees for a natural gas pipeline from Alaska. It would require that gasoline sold in the United States contain an increased volume of ethanol. Makers of the gasoline additive MTBE would be protected from liability but would have to cease production of the additive by 2015. The bill would also impose reliability standards for electricity transmission networks and ease restrictions on utility ownership and mergers. Passed 244-178: R 198-25; D 46-152 (ND 20-125, SD 26-27); I 0-1. June 15, 2004.

242. HR 4513. Alternative Energy Projects/Passage. Passage of the bill that would streamline licensing and siting for alternative energy projects on federal lands. Federal agencies would not be required to identify alternate project locations, other than the proposed action and a "no action" alternative, when preparing an environmental assessment or impact statement for a renewable energy project. Passed 229-186: R 200-18; D 29-167 (ND 8-135, SD 21-32); I 0-1. June 15, 2004.

243. HR 4567. Fiscal 2005 Homeland Security Appropriations/Previous Question. L. Diaz-Balart, R-Fla., motion to order the previous question (thus ending debate and possibility of amendment) on adoption of the rule (H Res 675) to provide for House floor consideration of the bill that would appropriate $33.1 billion in fiscal 2005 for the Department of Homeland Security. Motion agreed to 224-205: R 224-0; D 0-204 (ND 0-149, SD 0-55); I 0-1. June 16, 2004.

	238	239	240	241	242	243
ALABAMA						
1 *Bonner*	Y	Y	N	Y	Y	Y
2 *Everett*	Y	Y	N	Y	Y	Y
3 *Rogers*	Y	Y	N	Y	Y	Y
4 *Aderholt*	Y	Y	N	Y	Y	Y
5 Cramer	N	N	Y	Y	Y	N
6 *Bachus*	Y	Y	N	Y	Y	Y
7 Davis	N	N	Y	Y	Y	N
ALASKA						
AL *Young*	Y	Y	N	Y	Y	Y
ARIZONA						
1 *Renzi*	Y	Y	N	Y	Y	Y
2 *Franks*	Y	Y	N	Y	Y	Y
3 *Shadegg*	Y	Y	N	Y	Y	Y
4 Pastor	N	N	Y	N	N	N
5 *Hayworth*	Y	Y	N	Y	Y	Y
6 *Flake*	Y	Y	N	Y	Y	Y
7 Grijalva	N	N	Y	N	N	N
8 *Kolbe*	Y	Y	N	Y	Y	Y
ARKANSAS						
1 Berry	N	N	Y	Y	Y	N
2 Snyder	N	N	Y	N	N	N
3 *Boozman*	Y	Y	N	Y	Y	Y
4 Ross	N	N	Y	Y	Y	N
CALIFORNIA						
1 Thompson	N	N	Y	N	N	N
2 *Herger*	Y	Y	N	Y	Y	Y
3 *Ose*	Y	Y	N	Y	Y	Y
4 *Doolittle*	Y	Y	N	Y	Y	Y
5 Matsui	N	N	Y	N	N	N
6 Woolsey	N	N	Y	N	N	N
7 Miller, George	N	N	Y	N	N	N
8 Pelosi	N	N	Y	N	N	N
9 Lee	N	N	Y	N	N	N
10 Tauscher	N	N	Y	N	N	N
11 *Pombo*	Y	Y	N	Y	Y	Y
12 Lantos	N	N	Y	N	N	N
13 Stark	N	N	Y	N	N	N
14 Eshoo	N	N	Y	N	N	N
15 Honda	N	N	Y	N	N	N
16 Lofgren	N	N	Y	N	N	N
17 Farr	N	N	Y	N	N	N
18 Cardoza	N	N	Y	N	N	N
19 *Radanovich*	Y	Y	N	Y	Y	Y
20 Dooley	N	N	Y	Y	N	N
21 *Nunes*	Y	Y	N	Y	Y	Y
22 *Thomas*	Y	Y	N	Y	Y	Y
23 Capps	N	N	Y	N	N	N
24 *Gallegly*	Y	Y	N	Y	Y	Y
25 *McKeon*	Y	Y	N	Y	Y	Y
26 *Dreier*	Y	Y	N	Y	Y	Y
27 Sherman	N	N	Y	N	N	N
28 Berman	N	N	Y	N	N	N
29 Schiff	N	N	Y	N	N	N
30 Waxman	N	N	Y	N	N	N
31 Becerra	N	N	Y	N	N	N
32 Solis	N	N	Y	N	N	N
33 Watson	?	?	?	?	?	N
34 Roybal-Allard	N	N	Y	N	N	N
35 Waters	N	N	Y	N	N	N
36 Harman	N	N	Y	N	N	N

	238	239	240	241	242	243
37 Millender-McD.	?	?	?	?	?	N
38 Napolitano	N	N	Y	N	N	N
39 Sánchez, Linda	N	N	Y	N	N	N
40 *Royce*	Y	Y	N	Y	Y	Y
41 *Lewis*	Y	Y	N	Y	Y	Y
42 *Miller, Gary*	Y	Y	N	Y	Y	Y
43 Baca	N	N	Y	N	Y	N
44 *Calvert*	Y	Y	N	Y	Y	Y
45 *Bono*	Y	Y	N	Y	Y	Y
46 *Rohrabacher*	Y	Y	N	Y	Y	Y
47 Sanchez, Loretta	N	N	Y	N	?	N
48 *Cox*	Y	Y	N	Y	Y	Y
49 *Issa*	Y	Y	N	Y	Y	Y
50 *Cunningham*	Y	Y	N	Y	Y	Y
51 Filner	N	N	Y	N	N	N
52 *Hunter*	Y	?	N	Y	Y	Y
53 Davis	N	N	Y	N	N	N
COLORADO						
1 DeGette	N	N	Y	N	N	N
2 Udall	N	N	Y	N	N	N
3 *McInnis*	Y	Y	N	Y	Y	Y
4 *Musgrave*	Y	Y	N	Y	Y	Y
5 *Hefley*	Y	Y	N	Y	Y	Y
6 *Tancredo*	Y	Y	N	Y	Y	Y
7 *Beauprez*	Y	Y	N	Y	Y	Y
CONNECTICUT						
1 Larson	N	N	Y	N	N	N
2 *Simmons*	Y	Y	N	Y	N	Y
3 DeLauro	N	N	Y	N	N	N
4 *Shays*	Y	Y	N	N	N	Y
5 *Johnson*	Y	Y	N	Y	N	Y
DELAWARE						
AL *Castle*	Y	N	N	N	N	Y
FLORIDA						
1 *Miller, J.*	Y	Y	N	Y	Y	Y
2 Boyd	N	N	Y	N	Y	N
3 Brown	N	N	Y	N	N	N
4 *Crenshaw*	Y	Y	N	Y	Y	Y
5 *Brown-Waite*	?	?	N	Y	Y	Y
6 *Stearns*	Y	Y	N	Y	Y	Y
7 *Mica*	Y	Y	N	Y	Y	Y
8 *Keller*	Y	Y	N	Y	Y	Y
9 *Bilirakis*	Y	Y	N	Y	Y	Y
10 *Young*	Y	Y	N	Y	Y	Y
11 Davis	N	N	Y	N	N	N
12 *Putnam*	Y	Y	N	Y	Y	Y
13 *Harris*	Y	Y	N	Y	Y	Y
14 *Goss*	Y	Y	N	Y	Y	Y
15 *Weldon*	Y	Y	N	Y	Y	Y
16 *Foley*	Y	Y	N	Y	Y	Y
17 Meek	N	N	Y	N	N	N
18 *Ros-Lehtinen*	Y	Y	N	Y	?	Y
19 Wexler	N	N	Y	N	N	N
20 Deutsch	−	−	−	+	?	N
21 *Diaz-Balart, L.*	Y	Y	?	?	?	Y
22 *Shaw*	Y	Y	N	Y	Y	Y
23 Hastings	N	N	Y	N	N	?
24 *Feeney*	Y	Y	N	Y	Y	Y
25 *Diaz-Balart, M.*	Y	Y	N	Y	Y	Y
GEORGIA						
1 *Kingston*	Y	Y	N	Y	Y	Y
2 Bishop	N	N	Y	Y	Y	N
3 Marshall	N	N	Y	N	Y	N
4 Majette	N	N	N	N	N	N
5 Lewis	N	N	Y	N	N	N
6 *Isakson*	Y	Y	N	Y	Y	Y
7 *Linder*	Y	Y	N	Y	Y	Y
8 *Collins*	+	+	N	−	+	Y
9 *Norwood*	Y	Y	N	Y	?	Y
10 *Deal*	Y	Y	N	Y	Y	Y
11 *Gingrey*	Y	Y	N	Y	Y	Y
12 *Burns*	Y	Y	N	Y	Y	Y
13 Scott	N	N	N	N	N	N
HAWAII						
1 Abercrombie	N	N	Y	N	Y	N
2 Case	N	N	Y	N	N	N
IDAHO						
1 *Otter*	Y	Y	N	Y	Y	Y
2 *Simpson*	Y	Y	N	Y	Y	Y
ILLINOIS						
1 Rush	N	N	Y	N	Y	N
2 Jackson	N	N	Y	N	N	N
3 Lipinski	N	N	Y	N	N	N
4 Gutierrez	N	N	Y	N	N	N
5 Emanuel	N	N	Y	N	N	N
6 *Hyde*	Y	Y	N	Y	Y	Y

ND Northern Democrats   SD Southern Democrats

	238	239	240	241	242	243
7 Davis	N	N	Y	N	N	N
8 ***Crane***	Y	Y	N	Y	Y	Y
9 Schakowsky	N	N	Y	N	N	N
10 ***Kirk***	Y	Y	N	N	N	Y
11 ***Weller***	Y	Y	N	Y	Y	Y
12 Costello	N	N	Y	Y	N	N
13 ***Biggert***	Y	Y	N	Y	Y	Y
14 ***Hastert***						
15 ***Johnson***	Y	Y	N	Y	N	Y
16 ***Manzullo***	Y	Y	N	Y	Y	Y
17 Evans	N	N	Y	Y	Y	N
18 ***LaHood***	Y	Y	N	Y	Y	Y
19 ***Shimkus***	Y	Y	N	Y	Y	Y
INDIANA						
1 Visclosky	N	N	Y	Y	N	N
2 ***Chocola***	Y	Y	N	Y	Y	Y
3 ***Souder***	Y	Y	N	Y	Y	Y
4 ***Buyer***	Y	Y	N	Y	Y	Y
5 ***Burton***	+	+	N	Y	Y	Y
6 ***Pence***	Y	Y	N	Y	Y	Y
7 Carson	?	?	?	?	?	N
8 ***Hostettler***	Y	Y	N	Y	Y	Y
9 Hill	N	N	Y	N	N	N
IOWA						
1 ***Nussle***	Y	Y	N	Y	Y	Y
2 ***Leach***	Y	Y	N	Y	Y	Y
3 Boswell	N	N	Y	Y	Y	N
4 ***Latham***	Y	Y	N	Y	Y	Y
5 ***King***	Y	Y	N	Y	Y	Y
KANSAS						
1 ***Moran***	Y	Y	N	Y	Y	Y
2 ***Ryun***	Y	Y	N	Y	Y	Y
3 Moore	N	N	Y	N	N	N
4 ***Tiahrt***	Y	Y	N	Y	?	Y
KENTUCKY						
1 ***Whitfield***	Y	Y	N	Y	Y	Y
2 ***Lewis***	Y	Y	N	Y	Y	Y
3 ***Northup***	Y	Y	N	Y	Y	Y
4 Lucas	N	N	Y	Y	Y	N
5 ***Rogers***	Y	Y	N	Y	Y	Y
6 Chandler	N	N	Y	N	N	N
LOUISIANA						
1 ***Vitter***	Y	Y	N	Y	Y	Y
2 Jefferson	N	N	Y	Y	N	N
3 ***Tauzin***	Y	Y	N	Y	?	Y
4 ***McCrery***	Y	Y	N	Y	Y	Y
5 Alexander	N	N	N	Y	Y	N
6 ***Baker***	Y	Y	N	Y	Y	Y
7 John	N	Y	N	Y	Y	N
MAINE						
1 Allen	N	N	Y	N	N	N
2 Michaud	N	N	Y	N	N	N
MARYLAND						
1 ***Gilchrest***	Y	Y	N	N	N	Y
2 Ruppersberger	N	N	Y	N	N	N
3 Cardin	N	N	Y	N	N	N
4 Wynn	N	N	Y	Y	Y	N
5 Hoyer	N	N	Y	N	N	N
6 ***Bartlett***	Y	Y	N	Y	Y	Y
7 Cummings	N	N	Y	N	?	N
8 Van Hollen	N	N	Y	N	N	N
MASSACHUSETTS						
1 Olver	N	N	Y	N	N	N
2 Neal	N	N	Y	N	N	N
3 McGovern	N	N	Y	N	N	N
4 Frank	N	N	Y	N	N	N
5 Meehan	N	N	Y	N	N	N
6 Tierney	N	N	Y	N	N	N
7 Markey	N	N	Y	N	N	N
8 Capuano	N	N	Y	N	N	N
9 Lynch	N	N	Y	N	N	N
10 Delahunt	N	N	Y	N	N	N
MICHIGAN						
1 Stupak	N	N	Y	N	N	N
2 ***Hoekstra***	Y	Y	N	Y	Y	Y
3 ***Ehlers***	?	?	?	?	?	Y
4 ***Camp***	Y	Y	N	Y	Y	Y
5 Kildee	N	N	Y	N	N	N
6 ***Upton***	Y	Y	N	Y	Y	Y
7 ***Smith***	Y	Y	N	Y	Y	Y
8 ***Rogers***	Y	Y	N	Y	Y	Y
9 ***Knollenberg***	Y	Y	N	Y	Y	Y
10 ***Miller***	Y	Y	N	Y	Y	Y
11 ***McCotter***	Y	Y	N	Y	Y	Y
12 Levin	N	N	Y	N	N	N

	238	239	240	241	242	243
13 Kilpatrick	N	N	Y	N	N	N
14 Conyers	N	N	Y	N	N	N
15 Dingell	N	N	Y	N	N	N
MINNESOTA						
1 ***Gutknecht***	Y	Y	N	Y	Y	Y
2 ***Kline***	Y	Y	N	Y	Y	Y
3 ***Ramstad***	Y	Y	N	Y	N	Y
4 McCollum	N	N	Y	N	N	N
5 Sabo	N	N	Y	N	N	N
6 ***Kennedy***	Y	Y	N	Y	Y	Y
7 Peterson	N	N	Y	Y	Y	N
8 Oberstar	N	N	Y	N	N	N
MISSISSIPPI						
1 ***Wicker***	Y	Y	N	Y	Y	Y
2 Thompson	N	N	Y	N	N	N
3 ***Pickering***	Y	?	N	Y	Y	Y
4 Taylor	N	N	Y	N	N	N
MISSOURI						
1 Clay	N	N	Y	N	N	N
2 ***Akin***	Y	Y	N	Y	Y	Y
3 Gephardt	N	N	Y	N	N	N
4 Skelton	N	N	Y	Y	N	N
5 McCarthy	N	N	Y	N	N	N
6 ***Graves***	Y	Y	N	Y	Y	Y
7 ***Blunt***	Y	Y	N	Y	Y	Y
8 ***Emerson***	Y	Y	N	Y	Y	Y
9 ***Hulshof***	Y	Y	N	Y	Y	Y
MONTANA						
AL ***Rehberg***	Y	Y	N	Y	Y	Y
NEBRASKA						
1 ***Bereuter***	Y	Y	N	Y	Y	Y
2 ***Terry***	Y	Y	N	Y	Y	Y
3 ***Osborne***	Y	Y	N	Y	Y	?
NEVADA						
1 Berkley	N	N	Y	N	N	N
2 ***Gibbons***	Y	Y	N	Y	Y	Y
3 ***Porter***	Y	Y	N	Y	Y	Y
NEW HAMPSHIRE						
1 ***Bradley***	Y	Y	N	N	Y	Y
2 ***Bass***	Y	Y	N	N	Y	Y
NEW JERSEY						
1 Andrews	N	N	Y	N	N	N
2 ***LoBiondo***	Y	Y	N	N	N	Y
3 ***Saxton***	Y	Y	N	N	N	Y
4 ***Smith***	Y	Y	N	N	N	Y
5 ***Garrett***	Y	Y	N	Y	Y	Y
6 Pallone	N	N	Y	N	N	N
7 ***Ferguson***	Y	Y	N	Y	N	Y
8 Pascrell	?	?	?	?	?	N
9 Rothman	N	N	Y	N	N	N
10 Payne	N	N	Y	N	N	N
11 ***Frelinghuysen***	Y	Y	N	Y	N	Y
12 Holt	N	N	Y	N	N	N
13 Menendez	N	N	Y	N	N	N
NEW MEXICO						
1 ***Wilson***	Y	Y	N	Y	Y	Y
2 ***Pearce***	Y	Y	N	Y	Y	Y
3 Udall	N	N	Y	N	N	N
NEW YORK						
1 Bishop	N	N	Y	N	N	N
2 Israel	N	N	Y	N	N	N
3 ***King***	Y	Y	N	N	Y	Y
4 McCarthy	N	N	Y	N	N	N
5 Ackerman	?	N	Y	N	N	N
6 Meeks	N	N	Y	N	N	N
7 Crowley	N	N	Y	N	N	N
8 Nadler	N	N	Y	N	N	N
9 Weiner	N	N	Y	N	N	N
10 Towns	N	N	Y	Y	Y	N
11 Owens	N	N	Y	N	N	N
12 Velázquez	N	N	Y	N	N	N
13 ***Fossella***	Y	Y	N	N	Y	Y
14 Maloney	N	N	Y	N	N	N
15 Rangel	N	N	Y	N	N	N
16 Serrano	N	N	Y	N	N	N
17 Engel	N	N	Y	N	N	N
18 Lowey	N	N	Y	N	N	N
19 ***Kelly***	Y	Y	N	N	N	Y
20 ***Sweeney***	Y	Y	N	N	Y	Y
21 McNulty	N	N	Y	N	N	N
22 Hinchey	N	N	Y	N	N	N
23 ***McHugh***	Y	N	N	Y	Y	Y
24 ***Boehlert***	Y	Y	N	N	N	Y
25 ***Walsh***	Y	Y	N	Y	Y	Y

	238	239	240	241	242	243
26 ***Reynolds***	Y	Y	N	Y	Y	Y
27 ***Quinn***	Y	Y	N	Y	Y	Y
28 Slaughter	N	N	Y	N	N	N
29 ***Houghton***	Y	Y	N	N	Y	Y
NORTH CAROLINA						
1 Vacant						
2 Etheridge	N	N	Y	N	N	N
3 ***Jones***	Y	Y	N	Y	Y	Y
4 Price	N	N	Y	N	N	N
5 ***Burr***	Y	Y	N	Y	Y	Y
6 ***Coble***	Y	Y	N	Y	Y	Y
7 McIntyre	N	N	Y	Y	N	N
8 ***Hayes***	Y	Y	N	Y	Y	Y
9 ***Myrick***	Y	Y	N	Y	Y	Y
10 ***Ballenger***	Y	Y	N	Y	Y	Y
11 ***Taylor***	Y	Y	N	Y	Y	Y
12 Watt	N	N	Y	N	N	N
13 Miller	N	N	Y	N	N	N
NORTH DAKOTA						
AL Pomeroy	N	N	Y	Y	N	N
OHIO						
1 ***Chabot***	Y	Y	N	Y	Y	Y
2 ***Portman***	Y	Y	N	Y	Y	Y
3 ***Turner***	Y	Y	N	Y	Y	Y
4 ***Oxley***	Y	Y	N	Y	Y	Y
5 ***Gillmor***	Y	Y	N	Y	Y	Y
6 Strickland	N	N	N	N	N	N
7 ***Hobson***	Y	Y	N	Y	Y	Y
8 ***Boehner***	Y	Y	N	Y	Y	Y
9 Kaptur	N	N	Y	N	N	N
10 Kucinich	N	N	Y	N	N	N
11 Jones	N	N	Y	N	N	N
12 ***Tiberi***	Y	Y	N	Y	Y	Y
13 Brown	N	N	Y	N	N	N
14 ***LaTourette***	Y	Y	N	Y	Y	Y
15 ***Pryce***	Y	Y	N	Y	Y	Y
16 ***Regula***	Y	Y	N	Y	Y	Y
17 Ryan	N	N	Y	N	N	N
18 ***Ney***	Y	Y	N	Y	Y	Y
OKLAHOMA						
1 ***Sullivan***	Y	Y	N	Y	Y	Y
2 Carson	?	?	?	?	?	N
3 ***Lucas***	Y	Y	N	Y	Y	Y
4 ***Cole***	Y	Y	N	Y	Y	Y
5 ***Istook***	Y	Y	N	Y	Y	Y
OREGON						
1 Wu	N	N	Y	N	N	N
2 ***Walden***	Y	Y	N	Y	Y	Y
3 Blumenauer	N	N	Y	N	N	N
4 DeFazio	N	N	Y	N	N	N
5 Hooley	N	N	Y	N	N	N
PENNSYLVANIA						
1 Brady	N	N	Y	N	N	N
2 Fattah	N	N	Y	N	N	N
3 ***English***	Y	Y	N	Y	Y	Y
4 ***Hart***	Y	Y	N	Y	Y	Y
5 ***Peterson***	Y	Y	N	Y	Y	Y
6 ***Gerlach***	Y	Y	N	Y	N	Y
7 ***Weldon***	Y	Y	N	Y	N	Y
8 ***Greenwood***	Y	Y	N	Y	Y	Y
9 ***Shuster, Bill***	Y	Y	N	Y	Y	Y
10 ***Sherwood***	Y	Y	N	Y	Y	Y
11 Kanjorski	N	N	Y	Y	N	N
12 Murtha	N	N	Y	Y	N	N
13 Hoeffel	N	N	Y	N	N	N
14 Doyle	N	N	Y	Y	N	N
15 ***Toomey***	Y	Y	N	Y	?	Y
16 ***Pitts***	Y	Y	N	Y	Y	Y
17 Holden	N	N	Y	Y	N	N
18 ***Murphy***	Y	Y	N	Y	Y	Y
19 ***Platts***	Y	Y	N	Y	Y	?
RHODE ISLAND						
1 Kennedy	N	N	Y	N	N	N
2 Langevin	N	N	Y	N	N	N
SOUTH CAROLINA						
1 ***Brown***	Y	Y	N	Y	Y	Y
2 ***Wilson***	Y	Y	N	Y	Y	Y
3 ***Barrett***	Y	Y	N	Y	Y	Y
4 ***DeMint***	?	?	?	?	?	?
5 Spratt	N	N	Y	N	N	N
6 Clyburn	N	N	Y	N	N	N
SOUTH DAKOTA						
AL Herseth	N	N	Y	Y	N	N

	238	239	240	241	242	243
TENNESSEE						
1 ***Jenkins***	Y	Y	N	Y	Y	Y
2 ***Duncan***	Y	Y	N	Y	Y	Y
3 ***Wamp***	Y	Y	N	Y	Y	Y
4 Davis	N	N	Y	Y	N	N
5 Cooper	N	N	Y	N	N	N
6 Gordon	N	N	Y	Y	N	N
7 ***Blackburn***	Y	Y	N	Y	Y	Y
8 Tanner	N	N	Y	N	N	N
9 Ford	N	N	Y	N	N	N
TEXAS						
1 Sandlin	N	Y	N	Y	Y	N
2 Turner	N	N	Y	Y	N	N
3 ***Johnson, Sam***	Y	Y	N	Y	Y	Y
4 ***Hall***	Y	Y	N	Y	Y	Y
5 ***Hensarling***	Y	Y	N	Y	Y	Y
6 ***Barton***	Y	Y	N	Y	Y	Y
7 ***Culberson***	Y	Y	N	Y	Y	Y
8 ***Brady***	Y	Y	N	Y	Y	Y
9 Lampson	?	?	Y	Y	Y	N
10 Doggett	N	N	Y	N	N	N
11 Edwards	N	Y	N	Y	Y	N
12 ***Granger***	Y	Y	N	Y	Y	Y
13 ***Thornberry***	Y	Y	N	Y	Y	Y
14 ***Paul***	Y	Y	N	N	Y	Y
15 Hinojosa	N	N	Y	Y	Y	N
16 Reyes	N	Y	Y	Y	Y	N
17 Stenholm	N	N	Y	Y	Y	N
18 Jackson-Lee	N	N	Y	Y	Y	N
19 ***Neugebauer***	Y	Y	N	Y	Y	Y
20 Gonzalez	N	Y	Y	Y	Y	N
21 ***Smith***	?	Y	N	Y	Y	Y
22 ***DeLay***	Y	Y	N	Y	Y	Y
23 ***Bonilla***	Y	Y	N	Y	Y	Y
24 Frost	N	N	Y	N	N	N
25 Bell	N	N	?	?	?	N
26 ***Burgess***	Y	Y	N	Y	Y	Y
27 Ortiz	N	Y	Y	Y	Y	N
28 Rodriguez	N	Y	Y	Y	Y	N
29 Green	N	Y	Y	Y	Y	N
30 Johnson, E.B.	N	N	Y	N	N	N
31 ***Carter***	Y	Y	N	Y	Y	Y
32 ***Sessions***	Y	Y	N	Y	Y	Y
UTAH						
1 ***Bishop***	Y	Y	N	Y	Y	Y
2 Matheson	N	N	N	Y	N	N
3 ***Cannon***	Y	Y	N	Y	Y	Y
VERMONT						
AL *Sanders*	N	N	Y	N	N	N
VIRGINIA						
1 ***Davis, Jo Ann***	Y	Y	N	Y	Y	Y
2 ***Schrock***	Y	Y	N	Y	Y	Y
3 Scott	N	N	Y	N	N	N
4 ***Forbes***	Y	Y	N	Y	Y	Y
5 ***Goode***	Y	Y	N	Y	Y	Y
6 ***Goodlatte***	Y	Y	N	Y	Y	Y
7 ***Cantor***	Y	Y	N	Y	Y	Y
8 Moran	N	N	Y	N	N	N
9 Boucher	N	N	Y	Y	N	N
10 ***Wolf***	Y	Y	N	N	N	Y
11 ***Davis, T.***	Y	Y	N	Y	Y	Y
WASHINGTON						
1 Inslee	N	N	Y	N	N	N
2 Larsen	N	N	Y	N	N	N
3 Baird	N	N	Y	N	N	N
4 ***Hastings***	Y	Y	N	Y	Y	Y
5 ***Nethercutt***	Y	Y	N	Y	Y	Y
6 Dicks	N	N	Y	N	N	N
7 McDermott	N	N	Y	N	N	N
8 ***Dunn***	Y	Y	N	Y	Y	Y
9 Smith	N	N	Y	N	N	N
WEST VIRGINIA						
1 Mollohan	N	N	Y	Y	N	N
2 ***Capito***	Y	Y	N	Y	Y	Y
3 Rahall	N	N	Y	N	N	N
WISCONSIN						
1 ***Ryan***	Y	Y	N	N	Y	Y
2 Baldwin	N	N	Y	N	N	N
3 Kind	N	N	Y	N	N	N
4 Kleczka	N	N	Y	N	N	N
5 ***Sensenbrenner***	Y	Y	N	N	Y	Y
6 ***Petri***	Y	Y	N	N	Y	Y
7 Obey	N	N	Y	N	N	N
8 ***Green***	Y	Y	N	N	Y	Y
WYOMING						
AL ***Cubin***	Y	Y	N	Y	Y	Y

Southern states - Ala., Ark., Fla., Ga., Ky., La., Miss., N.C., Okla., S.C., Tenn., Texas, Va.

Key

Y	Voted for (yea).
#	Paired for.
+	Announced for.
N	Voted against (nay).
X	Paired against.
−	Announced against.
P	Voted "present."
C	Voted "present" to avoid possible conflict of interest.
?	Did not vote or otherwise make a position known.

Democrats   ***Republicans***
Independents

---

244. HR 4567. Fiscal 2005 Homeland Security Appropriations/Rule. Adoption of the rule (H Res 675) to provide for House floor consideration of the bill that would appropriate $33.1 billion in fiscal 2005 for the Department of Homeland Security. Adopted 234-197: R 226-0; D 8-196 (ND 4-145, SD 4-51); I 0-1. June 16, 2004.

245. HR 4568. Fiscal 2005 Interior Appropriations/Rule. Adoption of the rule (H Res 674) to provide for House floor consideration of the bill that would appropriate $19.5 billion for the Interior Department, related agencies and programs in fiscal 2005. Adopted 428-1: R 226-0; D 201-1 (ND 147-1, SD 54-0); I 1-0. June 16, 2004.

246. HR 4517. Oil Refinery Expansion/Passage. Passage of the bill that would make it easier to build and expand oil refineries. It would designate the Department of Energy as the "lead agency" with authority over environmental reviews for refinery expansion and rebuilding, replacing the current system, which is spread over several agencies. Passed 239-192: R 206-20; D 33-171 (ND 11-138, SD 22-33); I 0-1. June 16, 2004.

247. HR 4545. Clean Air Act Waivers/Passage. Barton, R-Texas, motion to suspend the rules and pass the bill that would amend the Clean Air Act to allow the EPA to grant limited waivers from a state's fuel additive requirements during periods of fuel shortages. The bill would also impose a nationwide cap on the number of specialty fuel blends. Motion rejected 236-194: R 207-19; D 29-174 (ND 8-140, SD 21-34); I 0-1. A two-thirds majority of those present and voting (287 in this case) is required for passage under suspension of the rules. June 16, 2004.

248. HR 4568. Fiscal 2005 Interior Appropriations/Arts and Humanities Funding. Slaughter, D-N.Y., amendment that would provide an additional $10 million for the National Endowment for the Arts and an additional $3.5 million for the National Endowment for the Humanities. The amendment would be offset by cuts in administrative costs at the Interior Department. Adopted 241-185: R 48-178; D 192-7 (ND 143-1, SD 49-6); I 1-0. June 16, 2004.

249. HR 4568. Fiscal 2005 Interior Appropriations/Forest Service, Arts Funds. Tancredo, R-Colo., amendment that would provide an additional $23 million for the U.S. Forest Service and reduce funds for the National Endowment for the Arts by $60 million. Rejected 112-313: R 110-115; D 2-197 (ND 1-143, SD 1-54); I 0-1. June 16, 2004.

	244	245	246	247	248	249
ALABAMA						
1 *Bonner*	Y	Y	Y	Y	N	Y
2 *Everett*	Y	Y	Y	Y	N	Y
3 *Rogers*	Y	Y	Y	Y	N	Y
4 *Aderholt*	Y	Y	Y	Y	N	Y
5 Cramer	N	Y	Y	Y	Y	N
6 *Bachus*	Y	Y	Y	Y	N	Y
7 Davis	N	Y	N	Y	Y	N
ALASKA						
AL *Young*	Y	Y	Y	Y	N	N
ARIZONA						
1 *Renzi*	Y	Y	Y	Y	N	Y
2 *Franks*	Y	Y	Y	Y	N	Y
3 *Shadegg*	Y	Y	Y	Y	N	Y
4 Pastor	N	Y	N	N	Y	N
5 *Hayworth*	Y	Y	Y	Y	N	Y
6 *Flake*	Y	Y	Y	Y	N	Y
7 Grijalva	N	Y	N	N	Y	N
8 *Kolbe*	Y	Y	Y	Y	Y	N
ARKANSAS						
1 Berry	N	Y	Y	Y	Y	N
2 Snyder	N	Y	N	N	Y	N
3 *Boozman*	Y	Y	Y	Y	N	Y
4 Ross	N	Y	Y	Y	Y	N
CALIFORNIA						
1 Thompson	N	Y	N	N	Y	N
2 *Herger*	Y	Y	Y	Y	N	N
3 *Ose*	Y	Y	Y	Y	N	N
4 *Doolittle*	Y	Y	Y	Y	N	Y
5 Matsui	N	Y	N	N	Y	N
6 Woolsey	N	Y	N	N	Y	N
7 Miller, George	N	Y	N	N	Y	N
8 Pelosi	N	Y	N	N	Y	N
9 Lee	N	Y	N	N	Y	N
10 Tauscher	N	Y	N	N	Y	N
11 *Pombo*	Y	Y	Y	Y	N	Y
12 Lantos	N	Y	N	N	Y	N
13 Stark	N	Y	N	N	Y	N
14 Eshoo	N	Y	N	N	Y	N
15 Honda	N	Y	N	N	Y	N
16 Lofgren	N	Y	N	N	Y	N
17 Farr	N	Y	N	N	Y	N
18 Cardoza	N	Y	Y	N	Y	N
19 *Radanovich*	Y	Y	Y	Y	N	N
20 Dooley	N	Y	N	N	Y	N
21 *Nunes*	Y	Y	Y	Y	N	N
22 *Thomas*	Y	Y	Y	Y	N	N
23 Capps	N	Y	N	N	Y	N
24 *Gallegly*	Y	Y	Y	Y	N	Y
25 *McKeon*	Y	Y	Y	Y	N	N
26 *Dreier*	Y	Y	Y	Y	N	N
27 Sherman	N	Y	N	N	Y	N
28 Berman	N	Y	N	N	Y	N
29 Schiff	N	Y	N	N	Y	N
30 Waxman	N	Y	N	N	Y	N
31 Becerra	N	Y	N	N	Y	N
32 Solis	N	Y	N	N	Y	N
33 Watson	N	Y	N	N	Y	N
34 Roybal-Allard	N	Y	N	N	Y	N
35 Waters	N	Y	N	N	Y	N
36 Harman	N	Y	N	Y	Y	N
37 Millender-McD.	N	Y	Y	N	Y	N
38 Napolitano	N	Y	N	N	Y	N
39 Sánchez, Linda	N	Y	N	N	Y	N
40 *Royce*	Y	Y	Y	Y	N	Y
41 *Lewis*	Y	Y	Y	Y	N	N
42 *Miller, Gary*	Y	Y	Y	Y	N	N
43 Baca	N	Y	N	N	Y	N
44 *Calvert*	Y	Y	Y	Y	N	N
45 *Bono*	Y	Y	Y	Y	N	Y
46 *Rohrabacher*	Y	Y	Y	Y	N	Y
47 Sanchez, Loretta	N	Y	N	N	Y	N
48 *Cox*	Y	Y	Y	Y	N	Y
49 *Issa*	Y	Y	Y	Y	N	N
50 *Cunningham*	Y	Y	Y	Y	N	Y
51 Filner	N	Y	N	N	?	−
52 *Hunter*	Y	Y	Y	Y	N	Y
53 Davis	N	Y	N	N	Y	N
COLORADO						
1 DeGette	N	Y	N	N	Y	N
2 Udall	N	Y	N	N	Y	N
3 *McInnis*	Y	Y	Y	Y	N	Y
4 *Musgrave*	Y	Y	Y	Y	N	Y
5 *Hefley*	Y	Y	Y	Y	N	Y
6 *Tancredo*	Y	Y	Y	Y	N	Y
7 *Beauprez*	Y	Y	Y	Y	N	Y
CONNECTICUT						
1 Larson	N	Y	N	N	Y	N
2 *Simmons*	Y	Y	N	N	Y	N
3 DeLauro	N	Y	N	N	Y	N
4 *Shays*	Y	Y	N	N	Y	N
5 *Johnson*	Y	Y	N	N	Y	N
DELAWARE						
AL *Castle*	Y	Y	N	N	Y	N
FLORIDA						
1 *Miller, J.*	Y	Y	Y	Y	N	Y
2 Boyd	N	Y	Y	Y	N	Y
3 Brown	N	Y	N	N	Y	N
4 *Crenshaw*	Y	Y	Y	Y	N	Y
5 *Brown-Waite*	Y	Y	Y	Y	N	Y
6 *Stearns*	Y	Y	Y	Y	N	Y
7 *Mica*	Y	Y	Y	Y	N	Y
8 *Keller*	Y	Y	Y	Y	N	Y
9 *Bilirakis*	Y	Y	Y	Y	N	Y
10 *Young*	Y	Y	Y	Y	N	Y
11 Davis	N	?	N	N	Y	N
12 *Putnam*	Y	Y	Y	Y	N	Y
13 *Harris*	Y	Y	Y	Y	N	Y
14 *Goss*	Y	Y	Y	Y	N	Y
15 *Weldon*	Y	Y	Y	Y	N	Y
16 *Foley*	Y	Y	Y	Y	N	N
17 Meek	N	Y	N	N	Y	N
18 *Ros-Lehtinen*	Y	Y	Y	Y	N	N
19 Wexler	N	Y	N	N	Y	N
20 Deutsch	N	Y	N	N	Y	N
21 *Diaz-Balart, L.*	Y	Y	Y	Y	N	N
22 *Shaw*	Y	Y	Y	Y	N	N
23 Hastings	?	?	?	?	?	?
24 *Feeney*	Y	Y	Y	Y	N	Y
25 *Diaz-Balart, M.*	Y	Y	Y	Y	N	Y
GEORGIA						
1 *Kingston*	Y	Y	Y	Y	N	Y
2 Bishop	N	Y	Y	Y	Y	N
3 Marshall	N	Y	Y	Y	Y	N
4 Majette	Y	Y	N	N	Y	N
5 Lewis	N	Y	N	N	Y	N
6 *Isakson*	Y	Y	Y	Y	N	Y
7 *Linder*	Y	Y	Y	Y	N	Y
8 *Collins*	Y	Y	Y	Y	N	Y
9 *Norwood*	Y	Y	Y	Y	N	Y
10 *Deal*	Y	Y	Y	Y	N	Y
11 *Gingrey*	Y	Y	Y	Y	N	Y
12 *Burns*	Y	Y	Y	Y	N	Y
13 Scott	N	Y	N	Y	Y	N
HAWAII						
1 Abercrombie	N	Y	N	N	Y	N
2 Case	N	Y	N	N	Y	N
IDAHO						
1 *Otter*	Y	Y	Y	Y	N	Y
2 *Simpson*	Y	Y	Y	Y	N	Y
ILLINOIS						
1 Rush	Y	Y	N	N	Y	N
2 Jackson	N	Y	N	N	Y	N
3 Lipinski	Y	Y	Y	Y	N	N
4 Gutierrez	N	Y	N	N	Y	N
5 Emanuel	N	Y	N	N	Y	N
6 *Hyde*	Y	Y	Y	Y	N	Y

ND Northern Democrats   SD Southern Democrats

	244	245	246	247	248	249
7 Davis	N	Y	N	N	Y	N
8 ***Crane***	Y	Y	Y	Y	N	Y
9 Schakowsky	N	Y	N	N	Y	N
10 ***Kirk***	Y	Y	N	Y	Y	N
11 ***Weller***	Y	Y	Y	Y	N	N
12 Costello	N	Y	Y	Y	Y	N
13 ***Biggert***	Y	Y	Y	Y	Y	N
14 ***Hastert***						
15 ***Johnson***	Y	Y	N	Y	Y	N
16 ***Manzullo***	Y	Y	Y	Y	N	Y
17 Evans	N	Y	N	N	Y	N
18 ***LaHood***	Y	Y	Y	Y	Y	N
19 ***Shimkus***	Y	Y	Y	Y	N	Y
INDIANA						
1 Visclosky	N	Y	N	N	Y	N
2 ***Chocola***	Y	Y	Y	Y	N	N
3 ***Souder***	Y	Y	Y	Y	N	Y
4 ***Buyer***	Y	Y	Y	Y	N	Y
5 ***Burton***	Y	Y	Y	Y	N	Y
6 ***Pence***	Y	Y	Y	Y	N	Y
7 Carson	N	Y	N	N	Y	N
8 ***Hostettler***	Y	Y	Y	Y	N	Y
9 Hill	N	Y	N	N	Y	N
IOWA						
1 ***Nussle***	Y	Y	Y	Y	N	N
2 ***Leach***	Y	Y	N	N	Y	N
3 Boswell	N	Y	N	N	Y	N
4 ***Latham***	Y	Y	Y	Y	N	N
5 ***King***	Y	Y	Y	Y	N	Y
KANSAS						
1 ***Moran***	Y	Y	Y	Y	N	N
2 ***Ryun***	Y	Y	Y	Y	N	Y
3 Moore	N	Y	N	Y	Y	N
4 ***Tiahrt***	Y	Y	Y	Y	N	Y
KENTUCKY						
1 ***Whitfield***	Y	Y	Y	Y	N	N
2 ***Lewis***	Y	Y	Y	Y	N	Y
3 ***Northup***	Y	Y	Y	Y	N	N
4 Lucas	N	Y	Y	Y	N	N
5 ***Rogers***	Y	Y	Y	Y	N	N
6 Chandler	N	Y	N	N	Y	N
LOUISIANA						
1 ***Vitter***	Y	Y	Y	Y	N	Y
2 Jefferson	N	Y	N	N	Y	N
3 ***Tauzin***	Y	Y	Y	Y	N	Y
4 ***McCrery***	Y	Y	Y	Y	N	N
5 Alexander	Y	Y	Y	Y	Y	N
6 ***Baker***	Y	Y	Y	Y	N	N
7 John	N	Y	Y	Y	Y	N
MAINE						
1 Allen	N	Y	N	N	Y	N
2 Michaud	N	Y	N	N	Y	N
MARYLAND						
1 ***Gilchrest***	Y	Y	N	Y	Y	N
2 Ruppersberger	N	Y	N	N	Y	N
3 Cardin	N	Y	N	N	Y	N
4 Wynn	N	Y	N	N	Y	N
5 Hoyer	N	Y	N	N	Y	N
6 ***Bartlett***	Y	Y	Y	Y	N	Y
7 Cummings	N	Y	N	N	Y	N
8 Van Hollen	N	Y	N	N	Y	N
MASSACHUSETTS						
1 Olver	N	Y	N	N	Y	N
2 Neal	N	Y	N	N	Y	N
3 McGovern	N	Y	N	N	Y	N
4 Frank	N	Y	N	N	Y	N
5 Meehan	N	Y	N	N	Y	N
6 Tierney	N	Y	N	N	Y	N
7 Markey	N	Y	N	N	Y	N
8 Capuano	N	Y	N	N	Y	N
9 Lynch	N	Y	N	N	Y	N
10 Delahunt	N	?	N	N	Y	N
MICHIGAN						
1 Stupak	N	Y	N	N	Y	N
2 ***Hoekstra***	Y	Y	Y	Y	N	Y
3 ***Ehlers***	Y	Y	N	N	Y	N
4 ***Camp***	Y	Y	Y	Y	N	N
5 Kildee	N	Y	N	N	Y	N
6 ***Upton***	Y	Y	Y	Y	Y	N
7 ***Smith***	Y	Y	Y	Y	N	Y
8 ***Rogers***	Y	Y	Y	Y	N	N
9 ***Knollenberg***	Y	Y	Y	Y	N	N
10 ***Miller***	Y	Y	Y	Y	N	N
11 ***McCotter***	Y	Y	Y	Y	N	N
12 Levin	N	Y	N	N	Y	N
13 Kilpatrick	N	Y	N	N	Y	N
14 Conyers	N	Y	N	?	Y	N
15 Dingell	N	Y	N	N	Y	N
MINNESOTA						
1 ***Gutknecht***	Y	Y	Y	Y	N	Y
2 ***Kline***	Y	Y	Y	Y	N	Y
3 ***Ramstad***	Y	Y	N	Y	Y	N
4 McCollum	N	Y	N	N	Y	N
5 Sabo	N	Y	N	N	Y	N
6 ***Kennedy***	Y	Y	Y	Y	N	Y
7 Peterson	N	Y	Y	Y	Y	N
8 Oberstar	N	Y	N	N	Y	N
MISSISSIPPI						
1 ***Wicker***	Y	Y	Y	Y	N	Y
2 Thompson	N	Y	N	N	Y	N
3 ***Pickering***	Y	Y	Y	Y	N	Y
4 Taylor	N	Y	Y	N	N	Y
MISSOURI						
1 Clay	N	Y	N	N	Y	N
2 ***Akin***	Y	Y	Y	Y	N	Y
3 Gephardt	N	Y	N	N	?	?
4 Skelton	N	Y	Y	Y	N	N
5 McCarthy	N	Y	N	N	Y	N
6 ***Graves***	Y	Y	Y	Y	N	Y
7 ***Blunt***	Y	Y	Y	Y	N	Y
8 ***Emerson***	Y	Y	Y	Y	N	Y
9 ***Hulshof***	Y	Y	Y	Y	N	Y
MONTANA						
AL ***Rehberg***	Y	Y	Y	Y	N	N
NEBRASKA						
1 ***Bereuter***	Y	Y	Y	Y	Y	N
2 ***Terry***	Y	Y	Y	Y	N	N
3 ***Osborne***	Y	Y	Y	Y	N	N
NEVADA						
1 Berkley	N	Y	N	N	Y	N
2 ***Gibbons***	Y	Y	Y	Y	N	Y
3 ***Porter***	Y	Y	Y	Y	Y	N
NEW HAMPSHIRE						
1 ***Bradley***	Y	Y	Y	N	N	N
2 ***Bass***	Y	Y	Y	N	Y	N
NEW JERSEY						
1 Andrews	N	Y	N	N	Y	N
2 ***LoBiondo***	Y	Y	N	N	Y	N
3 ***Saxton***	Y	Y	N	N	Y	N
4 ***Smith***	Y	Y	N	N	N	N
5 ***Garrett***	Y	Y	Y	Y	N	Y
6 Pallone	N	Y	N	N	Y	N
7 ***Ferguson***	Y	Y	Y	Y	Y	N
8 Pascrell	N	Y	N	N	Y	N
9 Rothman	N	Y	N	N	Y	N
10 Payne	N	Y	N	N	Y	N
11 ***Frelinghuysen***	Y	Y	Y	Y	Y	N
12 Holt	N	Y	N	N	Y	N
13 Menendez	N	Y	N	N	Y	N
NEW MEXICO						
1 ***Wilson***	Y	Y	N	Y	N	N
2 ***Pearce***	Y	Y	Y	Y	N	N
3 Udall	N	Y	N	N	Y	N
NEW YORK						
1 Bishop	N	Y	N	N	Y	N
2 Israel	N	Y	N	N	Y	N
3 ***King***	Y	Y	Y	N	N	N
4 McCarthy	N	Y	N	N	Y	N
5 Ackerman	N	Y	N	N	Y	N
6 Meeks	N	Y	N	N	?	?
7 Crowley	N	Y	N	N	Y	N
8 Nadler	N	Y	N	N	Y	N
9 Weiner	N	Y	N	N	Y	N
10 Towns	N	Y	N	N	Y	N
11 Owens	N	Y	N	N	Y	N
12 Velázquez	N	Y	N	N	Y	N
13 ***Fossella***	Y	Y	N	N	Y	N
14 Maloney	N	Y	N	N	Y	N
15 Rangel	N	Y	Y	N	Y	N
16 Serrano	N	Y	N	N	Y	N
17 Engel	N	Y	N	N	Y	N
18 Lowey	N	Y	N	N	Y	N
19 ***Kelly***	Y	Y	N	N	Y	N
20 ***Sweeney***	Y	Y	Y	Y	Y	N
21 McNulty	N	Y	N	N	Y	N
22 Hinchey	N	Y	N	N	Y	N
23 ***McHugh***	Y	Y	Y	Y	Y	N
24 ***Boehlert***	Y	Y	N	N	Y	N
25 ***Walsh***	Y	Y	N	Y	Y	N
26 ***Reynolds***	Y	Y	Y	Y	N	N
27 ***Quinn***	Y	Y	Y	Y	Y	N
28 Slaughter	N	Y	N	N	Y	N
29 ***Houghton***	Y	Y	Y	Y	Y	N
NORTH CAROLINA						
1 Vacant						
2 Etheridge	N	Y	N	N	Y	N
3 ***Jones***	Y	Y	Y	Y	N	Y
4 Price	N	Y	N	N	Y	N
5 ***Burr***	Y	Y	Y	Y	N	N
6 ***Coble***	Y	Y	Y	Y	N	Y
7 McIntyre	N	Y	N	Y	N	N
8 ***Hayes***	Y	Y	Y	Y	N	Y
9 ***Myrick***	Y	Y	Y	Y	N	Y
10 ***Ballenger***	Y	Y	Y	Y	Y	N
11 ***Taylor***	Y	Y	Y	Y	N	Y
12 Watt	N	Y	N	N	Y	N
13 Miller	N	Y	N	N	Y	N
NORTH DAKOTA						
AL Pomeroy	N	Y	N	N	Y	N
OHIO						
1 ***Chabot***	Y	Y	Y	Y	N	Y
2 ***Portman***	Y	Y	Y	Y	Y	N
3 ***Turner***	Y	Y	Y	Y	Y	N
4 ***Oxley***	Y	Y	Y	Y	N	N
5 ***Gillmor***	Y	Y	Y	Y	N	N
6 Strickland	N	N	N	N	Y	N
7 ***Hobson***	Y	Y	Y	Y	N	N
8 ***Boehner***	Y	Y	Y	Y	N	Y
9 Kaptur	N	Y	N	N	Y	N
10 Kucinich	N	Y	N	N	Y	N
11 Jones	N	Y	N	N	Y	N
12 ***Tiberi***	Y	Y	Y	Y	N	N
13 Brown	N	Y	N	N	?	?
14 ***LaTourette***	Y	Y	Y	Y	Y	N
15 ***Pryce***	Y	Y	Y	Y	Y	N
16 ***Regula***	Y	Y	Y	Y	N	N
17 Ryan	N	Y	N	N	Y	N
18 ***Ney***	Y	Y	Y	Y	N	Y
OKLAHOMA						
1 ***Sullivan***	Y	Y	Y	Y	N	Y
2 Carson	Y	Y	Y	Y	Y	N
3 ***Lucas***	Y	Y	Y	Y	N	N
4 ***Cole***	Y	Y	Y	Y	N	N
5 ***Istook***	Y	Y	Y	Y	N	Y
OREGON						
1 Wu	N	Y	N	N	Y	N
2 ***Walden***	Y	Y	Y	Y	N	N
3 Blumenauer	N	Y	N	N	Y	N
4 DeFazio	N	Y	N	N	Y	Y
5 Hooley	N	Y	N	N	Y	N
PENNSYLVANIA						
1 Brady	N	Y	N	N	Y	N
2 Fattah	N	Y	N	N	Y	N
3 ***English***	Y	Y	Y	Y	Y	N
4 ***Hart***	Y	Y	Y	Y	Y	N
5 ***Peterson***	Y	Y	Y	Y	Y	N
6 ***Gerlach***	Y	Y	N	N	Y	N
7 ***Weldon***	Y	Y	Y	N	Y	N
8 ***Greenwood***	Y	Y	Y	Y	Y	N
9 ***Shuster, Bill***	Y	Y	Y	Y	N	N
10 ***Sherwood***	Y	Y	Y	Y	Y	N
11 Kanjorski	N	Y	N	N	Y	N
12 Murtha	N	Y	N	N	Y	N
13 Hoeffel	N	Y	N	N	Y	N
14 Doyle	N	Y	N	N	Y	N
15 ***Toomey***	Y	Y	Y	Y	N	Y
16 ***Pitts***	Y	Y	Y	Y	N	Y
17 Holden	N	Y	Y	Y	Y	N
18 ***Murphy***	Y	Y	Y	Y	N	Y
19 ***Platts***	Y	Y	Y	Y	Y	N
RHODE ISLAND						
1 Kennedy	N	Y	N	N	Y	N
2 Langevin	N	Y	N	N	Y	N
SOUTH CAROLINA						
1 ***Brown***	Y	Y	Y	Y	N	N
2 ***Wilson***	Y	Y	Y	Y	N	Y
3 ***Barrett***	Y	Y	Y	Y	N	Y
4 ***DeMint***	?	?	?	?	–	?
5 Spratt	N	Y	N	N	Y	N
6 Clyburn	N	Y	N	N	Y	N
SOUTH DAKOTA						
AL Herseth	Y	Y	Y	N	Y	N
TENNESSEE						
1 ***Jenkins***	Y	Y	Y	Y	N	N
2 ***Duncan***	Y	Y	Y	Y	Y	N
3 ***Wamp***	Y	Y	Y	Y	N	N
4 Davis	N	Y	Y	Y	Y	N
5 Cooper	Y	Y	N	N	Y	N
6 Gordon	N	Y	N	Y	Y	N
7 ***Blackburn***	Y	Y	Y	Y	N	Y
8 Tanner	N	Y	Y	N	N	N
9 Ford	N	Y	N	N	Y	N
TEXAS						
1 Sandlin	N	Y	Y	Y	Y	N
2 Turner	N	Y	Y	Y	N	N
3 ***Johnson, Sam***	Y	Y	Y	Y	N	Y
4 ***Hall***	Y	Y	Y	Y	N	Y
5 ***Hensarling***	Y	Y	Y	Y	N	Y
6 ***Barton***	Y	Y	Y	Y	N	N
7 ***Culberson***	Y	Y	Y	Y	N	Y
8 ***Brady***	Y	Y	Y	Y	N	Y
9 Lampson	N	Y	Y	N	Y	N
10 Doggett	N	Y	N	N	Y	N
11 Edwards	N	Y	Y	Y	Y	N
12 ***Granger***	Y	Y	Y	Y	N	N
13 ***Thornberry***	Y	Y	Y	Y	N	Y
14 ***Paul***	Y	Y	Y	Y	N	Y
15 Hinojosa	N	Y	Y	N	Y	N
16 Reyes	N	Y	Y	N	Y	N
17 Stenholm	N	Y	Y	Y	N	N
18 Jackson-Lee	N	Y	N	N	Y	N
19 ***Neugebauer***	Y	Y	Y	Y	N	Y
20 Gonzalez	N	Y	N	N	Y	N
21 ***Smith***	Y	Y	Y	Y	N	N
22 ***DeLay***	Y	Y	Y	Y	N	Y
23 ***Bonilla***	Y	Y	Y	Y	N	Y
24 Frost	N	Y	N	Y	Y	N
25 Bell	N	Y	N	N	Y	N
26 ***Burgess***	Y	Y	Y	Y	N	Y
27 Ortiz	N	Y	Y	Y	Y	N
28 Rodriguez	N	Y	Y	N	Y	N
29 Green	N	Y	N	N	Y	N
30 Johnson, E.B.	N	Y	N	N	Y	N
31 ***Carter***	Y	Y	Y	Y	N	Y
32 ***Sessions***	Y	Y	Y	Y	N	Y
UTAH						
1 ***Bishop***	Y	Y	Y	Y	N	?
2 Matheson	Y	Y	Y	Y	Y	N
3 ***Cannon***	Y	Y	Y	Y	N	Y
VERMONT						
AL *Sanders*	N	Y	N	N	Y	N
VIRGINIA						
1 ***Davis, Jo Ann***	Y	Y	Y	Y	N	Y
2 ***Schrock***	Y	Y	Y	Y	N	N
3 Scott	N	Y	N	N	Y	N
4 ***Forbes***	Y	Y	Y	Y	N	Y
5 ***Goode***	Y	Y	Y	Y	N	Y
6 ***Goodlatte***	Y	Y	Y	Y	N	Y
7 ***Cantor***	Y	Y	Y	Y	N	Y
8 Moran	N	Y	N	N	Y	N
9 Boucher	N	Y	N	N	Y	N
10 ***Wolf***	Y	Y	N	N	N	N
11 ***Davis, T.***	Y	Y	Y	Y	Y	N
WASHINGTON						
1 Inslee	N	Y	N	N	Y	N
2 Larsen	N	Y	N	N	Y	N
3 Baird	N	Y	N	N	Y	N
4 ***Hastings***	Y	Y	Y	Y	N	Y
5 ***Nethercutt***	Y	Y	Y	Y	N	N
6 Dicks	N	Y	N	N	Y	N
7 McDermott	N	Y	N	N	?	?
8 ***Dunn***	Y	Y	Y	Y	N	Y
9 Smith	N	Y	N	N	Y	N
WEST VIRGINIA						
1 Mollohan	N	Y	N	N	Y	N
2 ***Capito***	Y	Y	Y	Y	Y	N
3 Rahall	N	Y	N	N	Y	N
WISCONSIN						
1 ***Ryan***	Y	Y	Y	Y	N	Y
2 Baldwin	N	Y	N	N	Y	N
3 Kind	N	Y	N	Y	Y	N
4 Kleczka	N	Y	N	N	Y	N
5 ***Sensenbrenner***	Y	Y	Y	Y	N	Y
6 ***Petri***	Y	Y	Y	Y	N	Y
7 Obey	N	Y	N	N	Y	N
8 ***Green***	Y	Y	Y	Y	N	Y
WYOMING						
AL ***Cubin***	Y	Y	Y	Y	N	Y

Southern states - Ala., Ark., Fla., Ga., Ky., La., Miss., N.C., Okla., S.C., Tenn., Texas, Va.

Key

Y   Voted for (yea).
\#   Paired for.
\+   Announced for.
N   Voted against (nay).
X   Paired against.
−   Announced against.
P   Voted "present."
C   Voted "present" to avoid possible conflict of interest.
?   Did not vote or otherwise make a position known.

Democrats   ***Republicans***
Independents

---

250. HR 4568. Fiscal 2005 Interior Appropriations/Wildfire Fuel Reduction. Hooley, D-Ore., amendment that would increase funding for wildfire fuel-reduction programs by $6 million. It would be offset by decreasing appropriations to other programs covered under the bill. Rejected 186-241: R 23-203; D 162-38 (ND 131-14, SD 31-24); I 1-0. June 16, 2004.

251. HR 4568. Fiscal 2005 Interior Appropriations/Energy Smart Schools. Sanders, I-Vt., amendment that would provide $1 million for the Energy Smart Schools Program, which aims to improve the energy-efficiency of school buildings. Rejected 199-227: R 6-217; D 192-10 (ND 142-5, SD 50-5); I 1-0. June 16, 2004.

252. HR 4568. Fiscal 2005 Interior Appropriations/American Indian Sacred Sites. Rahall, D-W.Va., amendment that would prohibit funds from being used to adversely affect American Indian sacred sites on certain federal lands. Rejected 209-215: R 15-206; D 193-9 (ND 141-6, SD 52-3); I 1-0. June 16, 2004.

253. HR 4568. Fiscal 2005 Interior Appropriations/Tongass National Forest. Chabot, R-Ohio, amendment that would block the use of funds to plan or construct forest development roads in the Tongass National Forest in Alaska for the purposes of harvesting timber. Adopted 222-205: R 48-176; D 173-29 (ND 134-13, SD 39-16); I 1-0. June 16, 2004.

254. HR 4568. Fiscal 2005 Interior Appropriations/Forest Management Plans. Udall, D-N.M., amendment that would prohibit funds from being used to finalize or implement regulations that would change scientific and public input criteria related to developing forest management plans. Rejected 195-230: R 20-202; D 174-28 (ND 137-10, SD 37-18); I 1-0. A "nay" was a vote in support of the president's position. June 16, 2004.

255. HR 4568. Fiscal 2005 Interior Appropriations/Payments in Lieu of Taxes. Flake, R-Ariz., amendment that would increase the bill's appropriations by $15 million for payments in lieu of taxes, while reducing funding for the Smithsonian Institution by $13 million and the National Endowment for the Humanities by $2 million. Rejected 94-332: R 85-138; D 9-193 (ND 5-142, SD 4-51); I 0-1. June 16, 2004.

	250	251	252	253	254	255
ALABAMA						
1 *Bonner*	N	N	N	N	N	N
2 *Everett*	N	N	N	N	N	N
3 *Rogers*	N	N	N	N	N	N
4 *Aderholt*	N	N	N	N	N	N
5 Cramer	N	N	Y	Y	N	N
6 *Bachus*	N	N	N	N	N	Y
7 Davis	Y	Y	Y	Y	N	N
ALASKA						
AL *Young*	N	N	N	N	N	N
ARIZONA						
1 *Renzi*	Y	N	Y	N	N	Y
2 *Franks*	Y	N	N	N	N	Y
3 *Shadegg*	Y	N	N	N	N	Y
4 Pastor	Y	Y	Y	Y	Y	N
5 *Hayworth*	Y	N	N	N	N	Y
6 *Flake*	Y	N	N	N	N	Y
7 Grijalva	Y	Y	Y	Y	Y	N
8 *Kolbe*	N	N	N	N	N	N
ARKANSAS						
1 Berry	N	Y	Y	N	N	N
2 Snyder	Y	Y	Y	Y	Y	N
3 *Boozman*	N	N	N	N	N	Y
4 Ross	Y	Y	N	N	N	N
CALIFORNIA						
1 Thompson	Y	Y	Y	N	Y	N
2 *Herger*	N	N	N	N	N	Y
3 *Ose*	N	N	N	N	N	N
4 *Doolittle*	N	N	N	N	N	Y
5 Matsui	Y	Y	Y	Y	Y	N
6 Woolsey	Y	Y	Y	Y	Y	N
7 Miller, George	Y	Y	Y	Y	Y	N
8 Pelosi	Y	Y	Y	Y	Y	N
9 Lee	Y	Y	Y	Y	Y	N
10 Tauscher	N	Y	Y	Y	Y	N
11 *Pombo*	N	N	N	N	N	Y
12 Lantos	Y	Y	Y	Y	Y	N
13 Stark	Y	Y	Y	Y	Y	N
14 Eshoo	N	Y	Y	Y	Y	N
15 Honda	Y	Y	Y	Y	Y	N
16 Lofgren	Y	N	Y	Y	Y	N
17 Farr	Y	Y	Y	Y	Y	N
18 Cardoza	Y	Y	Y	Y	N	N
19 *Radanovich*	N	N	N	N	N	Y
20 Dooley	Y	Y	Y	Y	N	N
21 *Nunes*	N	N	N	N	N	N
22 *Thomas*	N	N	N	N	N	N
23 Capps	Y	Y	Y	Y	Y	N
24 *Gallegly*	N	N	N	N	N	N
25 *McKeon*	N	N	N	N	N	Y
26 *Dreier*	N	N	N	N	N	N
27 Sherman	Y	Y	Y	Y	Y	N
28 Berman	Y	Y	Y	Y	Y	N
29 Schiff	Y	Y	Y	Y	Y	N
30 Waxman	Y	Y	Y	Y	Y	N
31 Becerra	Y	Y	Y	Y	Y	N
32 Solis	Y	Y	Y	Y	Y	N
33 Watson	Y	Y	Y	Y	Y	N
34 Roybal-Allard	Y	Y	Y	Y	Y	N
35 Waters	Y	Y	Y	Y	Y	N
36 Harman	Y	Y	Y	Y	Y	N
37 Millender-McD.	Y	Y	Y	Y	Y	N
38 Napolitano	Y	Y	Y	Y	Y	N
39 Sánchez, Linda	Y	Y	Y	Y	Y	N
40 *Royce*	Y	N	N	Y	N	Y
41 *Lewis*	N	N	N	N	N	N
42 *Miller, Gary*	N	N	N	N	N	Y
43 Baca	Y	Y	Y	Y	N	N
44 *Calvert*	N	N	N	N	N	N
45 *Bono*	N	N	N	N	N	Y
46 *Rohrabacher*	Y	N	N	N	Y	N
47 Sanchez, Loretta	Y	N	N	N	N	Y
48 *Cox*	Y	N	N	N	N	Y
49 *Issa*	N	N	N	N	N	N
50 *Cunningham*	N	N	N	N	N	N
51 Filner	+	+	+	+	+	−
52 *Hunter*	N	N	N	N	N	N
53 Davis	Y	Y	Y	Y	Y	N
COLORADO						
1 DeGette	Y	Y	Y	Y	Y	N
2 Udall	Y	Y	Y	Y	Y	N
3 *McInnis*	Y	N	N	N	N	Y
4 *Musgrave*	N	N	N	N	N	Y
5 *Hefley*	Y	N	N	N	N	Y
6 *Tancredo*	Y	N	N	N	N	Y
7 *Beauprez*	Y	N	N	N	N	Y
CONNECTICUT						
1 Larson	Y	Y	Y	Y	Y	N
2 *Simmons*	N	Y	Y	Y	Y	N
3 DeLauro	Y	Y	Y	Y	Y	N
4 *Shays*	N	Y	Y	Y	Y	N
5 *Johnson*	N	Y	N	Y	Y	N
DELAWARE						
AL *Castle*	N	N	N	Y	N	N
FLORIDA						
1 *Miller, J.*	N	N	N	N	N	Y
2 Boyd	Y	Y	Y	N	N	Y
3 Brown	Y	Y	Y	Y	Y	N
4 *Crenshaw*	N	N	N	N	N	N
5 *Brown-Waite*	N	N	N	N	N	N
6 *Stearns*	N	N	N	N	N	N
7 *Mica*	N	N	N	N	N	N
8 *Keller*	N	N	N	N	N	N
9 *Bilirakis*	N	N	N	N	N	N
10 *Young*	N	N	N	N	N	N
11 Davis	Y	Y	Y	Y	Y	N
12 *Putnam*	N	N	N	N	N	N
13 *Harris*	N	N	N	N	N	N
14 *Goss*	N	N	N	N	N	N
15 *Weldon*	N	N	N	N	N	N
16 *Foley*	N	N	N	Y	N	N
17 Meek	Y	Y	Y	Y	Y	N
18 *Ros-Lehtinen*	N	N	N	N	N	N
19 Wexler	Y	Y	Y	Y	Y	N
20 Deutsch	Y	Y	Y	Y	Y	N
21 *Diaz-Balart, L.*	N	N	N	N	N	N
22 *Shaw*	N	N	N	N	N	N
23 Hastings	?	?	?	?	?	?
24 *Feeney*	N	N	N	N	N	N
25 *Diaz-Balart, M.*	N	N	N	N	N	N
GEORGIA						
1 *Kingston*	N	?	?	N	N	Y
2 Bishop	N	Y	Y	N	N	N
3 Marshall	N	Y	Y	N	N	N
4 Majette	N	Y	Y	Y	Y	N
5 Lewis	Y	Y	Y	Y	Y	N
6 *Isakson*	N	N	N	N	N	N
7 *Linder*	N	N	N	N	N	N
8 *Collins*	N	N	N	N	N	N
9 *Norwood*	N	N	N	N	N	Y
10 *Deal*	N	N	N	N	N	Y
11 *Gingrey*	N	N	N	N	N	Y
12 *Burns*	N	N	N	N	N	N
13 Scott	Y	Y	Y	Y	N	N
HAWAII						
1 Abercrombie	N	Y	N	Y	N	Y
2 Case	N	Y	Y	Y	Y	N
IDAHO						
1 *Otter*	Y	N	N	N	N	Y
2 *Simpson*	N	N	N	N	N	N
ILLINOIS						
1 Rush	Y	Y	Y	Y	Y	N
2 Jackson	Y	Y	Y	Y	Y	N
3 Lipinski	N	Y	Y	N	Y	N
4 Gutierrez	Y	Y	Y	Y	Y	N
5 Emanuel	Y	Y	Y	Y	Y	N
6 *Hyde*	N	N	Y	N	N	N

ND Northern Democrats   SD Southern Democrats

	250	251	252	253	254	255
7 Davis	Y	Y	Y	Y	Y	N
8 ***Crane***	N	N	N	N	N	N
9 Schakowsky	Y	Y	Y	Y	Y	N
10 ***Kirk***	N	N	N	Y	Y	N
11 ***Weller***	N	N	?	N	N	N
12 Costello	N	Y	Y	N	Y	N
13 ***Biggert***	N	N	N	Y	N	N
14 ***Hastert***						
15 ***Johnson***	N	N	N	Y	Y	N
16 ***Manzullo***	N	N	N	N	N	N
17 Evans	Y	Y	Y	Y	Y	N
18 ***LaHood***	N	N	N	N	N	N
19 ***Shimkus***	N	N	N	N	N	N
INDIANA						
1 Visclosky	Y	Y	Y	Y	Y	N
2 ***Chocola***	N	N	N	N	N	N
3 ***Souder***	N	N	N	N	N	Y
4 ***Buyer***	N	N	N	Y	N	N
5 ***Burton***	N	N	N	N	N	Y
6 ***Pence***	N	N	N	N	N	Y
7 Carson	Y	Y	Y	Y	Y	N
8 ***Hostettler***	N	N	N	N	N	Y
9 Hill	Y	N	Y	Y	Y	N
IOWA						
1 ***Nussle***	N	N	N	N	N	N
2 ***Leach***	N	Y	Y	Y	Y	N
3 Boswell	Y	Y	Y	N	N	N
4 ***Latham***	N	N	N	N	N	N
5 ***King***	N	N	N	N	N	Y
KANSAS						
1 ***Moran***	Y	N	N	N	N	Y
2 ***Ryun***	N	N	N	N	N	N
3 Moore	Y	Y	Y	Y	Y	N
4 ***Tiahrt***	N	N	N	N	N	N
KENTUCKY						
1 ***Whitfield***	N	N	N	Y	N	Y
2 ***Lewis***	N	N	N	N	N	Y
3 ***Northup***	N	N	N	N	N	N
4 Lucas	Y	Y	Y	N	N	N
5 ***Rogers***	N	N	N	N	N	Y
6 Chandler	Y	Y	Y	Y	Y	N
LOUISIANA						
1 ***Vitter***	N	N	N	N	N	Y
2 Jefferson	Y	Y	Y	Y	Y	N
3 ***Tauzin***	N	N	N	N	N	N
4 ***McCrery***	N	N	N	N	N	Y
5 Alexander	N	N	Y	N	N	N
6 ***Baker***	N	N	N	N	N	N
7 John	N	Y	Y	N	N	Y
MAINE						
1 Allen	Y	Y	Y	Y	Y	N
2 Michaud	Y	Y	Y	Y	Y	N
MARYLAND						
1 ***Gilchrest***	N	N	N	N	Y	N
2 Ruppersberger	Y	Y	Y	Y	Y	N
3 Cardin	Y	Y	Y	Y	Y	N
4 Wynn	Y	Y	Y	Y	Y	N
5 Hoyer	Y	Y	Y	Y	Y	N
6 ***Bartlett***	N	N	N	N	N	Y
7 Cummings	Y	Y	Y	Y	Y	N
8 Van Hollen	Y	Y	Y	Y	Y	N
MASSACHUSETTS						
1 Olver	Y	Y	Y	Y	Y	N
2 Neal	Y	Y	Y	Y	Y	N
3 McGovern	Y	Y	Y	Y	Y	N
4 Frank	Y	Y	Y	Y	Y	N
5 Meehan	Y	Y	Y	Y	Y	N
6 Tierney	Y	Y	Y	Y	Y	N
7 Markey	Y	Y	Y	Y	Y	N
8 Capuano	Y	Y	Y	N	Y	N
9 Lynch	Y	Y	Y	Y	Y	N
10 Delahunt	Y	Y	Y	Y	Y	N
MICHIGAN						
1 Stupak	Y	Y	Y	N	N	Y
2 ***Hoekstra***	N	N	N	N	N	N
3 ***Ehlers***	N	N	N	Y	Y	N
4 ***Camp***	N	N	Y	N	N	N
5 Kildee	Y	Y	Y	Y	Y	N
6 ***Upton***	N	N	Y	Y	N	N
7 ***Smith***	N	N	N	N	N	N
8 ***Rogers***	N	N	N	N	N	N
9 ***Knollenberg***	N	N	N	N	N	N
10 ***Miller***	N	N	N	N	N	N
11 ***McCotter***	N	N	N	N	N	N
12 Levin	Y	Y	Y	Y	Y	N
13 Kilpatrick	Y	Y	Y	Y	Y	N
14 Conyers	Y	Y	Y	Y	Y	N
15 Dingell	Y	Y	Y	Y	Y	N
MINNESOTA						
1 ***Gutknecht***	N	N	N	N	N	N
2 ***Kline***	N	N	N	N	N	N
3 ***Ramstad***	N	N	Y	Y	Y	N
4 McCollum	Y	Y	Y	Y	Y	N
5 Sabo	Y	Y	Y	Y	Y	N
6 ***Kennedy***	N	N	N	N	N	N
7 Peterson	Y	Y	Y	N	N	N
8 Oberstar	Y	Y	Y	N	N	N
MISSISSIPPI						
1 ***Wicker***	N	N	N	N	N	Y
2 Thompson	Y	Y	Y	N	Y	N
3 ***Pickering***	N	N	N	N	N	Y
4 Taylor	N	Y	Y	N	Y	N
MISSOURI						
1 Clay	Y	Y	Y	Y	Y	N
2 ***Akin***	N	N	N	N	N	N
3 Gephardt	?	?	?	?	?	?
4 Skelton	Y	Y	N	N	Y	N
5 McCarthy	Y	Y	Y	Y	Y	N
6 ***Graves***	N	N	N	N	N	Y
7 ***Blunt***	N	N	N	N	?	?
8 ***Emerson***	N	N	N	N	N	Y
9 ***Hulshof***	Y	N	N	N	N	Y
MONTANA						
AL ***Rehberg***	N	N	N	N	N	Y
NEBRASKA						
1 ***Bereuter***	N	N	N	N	N	N
2 ***Terry***	N	N	Y	N	–	N
3 ***Osborne***	N	N	N	N	N	N
NEVADA						
1 Berkley	Y	Y	Y	Y	Y	Y
2 ***Gibbons***	N	N	N	N	N	Y
3 ***Porter***	N	Y	N	N	N	Y
NEW HAMPSHIRE						
1 ***Bradley***	N	N	Y	Y	N	Y
2 ***Bass***	N	N	N	Y	N	Y
NEW JERSEY						
1 Andrews	Y	Y	Y	Y	Y	N
2 ***LoBiondo***	N	N	N	Y	Y	N
3 ***Saxton***	N	N	N	Y	Y	N
4 ***Smith***	N	N	N	Y	Y	N
5 ***Garrett***	N	N	N	Y	N	Y
6 Pallone	Y	Y	Y	Y	Y	N
7 ***Ferguson***	N	N	N	Y	Y	N
8 Pascrell	Y	Y	Y	Y	Y	N
9 Rothman	Y	Y	Y	Y	Y	N
10 Payne	Y	Y	Y	Y	Y	N
11 ***Frelinghuysen***	N	N	N	N	N	N
12 Holt	Y	Y	Y	Y	Y	N
13 Menendez	Y	Y	Y	Y	Y	N
NEW MEXICO						
1 ***Wilson***	Y	Y	Y	N	N	Y
2 ***Pearce***	N	N	N	N	N	Y
3 Udall	Y	Y	Y	Y	Y	N
NEW YORK						
1 Bishop	Y	Y	Y	Y	Y	N
2 Israel	Y	N	Y	Y	Y	N
3 ***King***	N	N	N	N	N	N
4 McCarthy	Y	Y	Y	Y	Y	N
5 Ackerman	Y	Y	Y	Y	Y	N
6 Meeks	?	Y	Y	Y	Y	N
7 Crowley	Y	Y	Y	Y	Y	N
8 Nadler	Y	Y	Y	Y	Y	N
9 Weiner	Y	Y	Y	Y	Y	N
10 Towns	Y	Y	Y	Y	Y	N
11 Owens	Y	Y	Y	Y	Y	N
12 Velázquez	Y	Y	Y	Y	Y	N
13 ***Fossella***	N	N	N	N	N	N
14 Maloney	Y	Y	Y	Y	Y	N
15 Rangel	Y	Y	Y	Y	Y	N
16 Serrano	Y	Y	Y	Y	Y	N
17 Engel	Y	Y	Y	Y	Y	N
18 Lowey	Y	Y	Y	Y	Y	N
19 ***Kelly***	N	N	N	Y	Y	Y
20 ***Sweeney***	N	N	N	N	N	N
21 McNulty	N	Y	Y	Y	Y	N
22 Hinchey	Y	Y	Y	Y	Y	N
23 ***McHugh***	N	N	N	N	N	N
24 ***Boehlert***	N	N	N	Y	Y	N
25 ***Walsh***	N	N	N	Y	N	N
26 ***Reynolds***	N	N	N	N	N	N
27 ***Quinn***	N	N	N	N	N	N
28 Slaughter	Y	Y	Y	Y	Y	N
29 ***Houghton***	N	N	Y	Y	Y	N
NORTH CAROLINA						
1 Vacant						
2 Etheridge	N	Y	Y	Y	N	N
3 ***Jones***	Y	N	N	Y	N	Y
4 Price	N	Y	Y	Y	Y	N
5 ***Burr***	N	N	N	N	N	N
6 ***Coble***	N	N	N	N	N	N
7 McIntyre	N	Y	Y	Y	N	N
8 ***Hayes***	N	N	N	N	N	Y
9 ***Myrick***	N	N	N	N	N	Y
10 ***Ballenger***	N	N	N	N	N	N
11 ***Taylor***	N	N	N	N	N	N
12 Watt	Y	Y	Y	Y	Y	N
13 Miller	N	Y	Y	Y	Y	N
NORTH DAKOTA						
AL Pomeroy	Y	Y	Y	Y	Y	Y
OHIO						
1 ***Chabot***	N	N	N	Y	N	Y
2 ***Portman***	N	N	N	Y	N	N
3 ***Turner***	N	N	N	N	N	N
4 ***Oxley***	N	N	?	N	N	N
5 ***Gillmor***	N	N	N	N	N	N
6 Strickland	Y	Y	Y	Y	Y	Y
7 ***Hobson***	N	N	N	N	N	N
8 ***Boehner***	N	N	N	N	N	N
9 Kaptur	Y	Y	Y	Y	Y	N
10 Kucinich	Y	Y	Y	Y	Y	N
11 Jones	Y	Y	Y	Y	Y	N
12 ***Tiberi***	N	N	N	Y	N	N
13 Brown	?	Y	Y	Y	Y	N
14 ***LaTourette***	N	?	?	?	?	?
15 ***Pryce***	N	N	N	Y	N	N
16 ***Regula***	N	N	N	N	N	N
17 Ryan	Y	Y	Y	Y	Y	N
18 ***Ney***	N	N	N	N	N	N
OKLAHOMA						
1 ***Sullivan***	N	N	N	N	N	N
2 Carson	Y	N	Y	N	N	N
3 ***Lucas***	N	N	N	N	N	N
4 ***Cole***	N	N	N	N	N	N
5 ***Istook***	N	N	N	N	N	N
OREGON						
1 Wu	Y	Y	Y	Y	Y	N
2 ***Walden***	Y	N	N	N	N	Y
3 Blumenauer	Y	Y	Y	Y	Y	N
4 DeFazio	Y	Y	Y	Y	Y	N
5 Hooley	Y	Y	Y	Y	Y	N
PENNSYLVANIA						
1 Brady	N	Y	Y	Y	Y	N
2 Fattah	Y	Y	Y	Y	Y	N
3 ***English***	N	N	N	Y	N	N
4 ***Hart***	N	N	N	Y	N	N
5 ***Peterson***	N	N	N	N	N	N
6 ***Gerlach***	N	N	N	Y	Y	N
7 ***Weldon***	N	N	N	Y	N	N
8 ***Greenwood***	N	N	N	Y	Y	N
9 ***Shuster, Bill***	N	N	N	N	N	N
10 ***Sherwood***	N	N	N	N	N	N
11 Kanjorski	Y	Y	Y	Y	N	N
12 Murtha	N	Y	N	Y	N	N
13 Hoeffel	N	Y	Y	Y	Y	N
14 Doyle	N	Y	Y	Y	Y	N
15 ***Toomey***	N	N	N	N	N	Y
16 ***Pitts***	N	N	N	Y	N	N
17 Holden	Y	Y	Y	Y	Y	N
18 ***Murphy***	N	N	N	Y	N	N
19 ***Platts***	N	N	N	Y	N	N
RHODE ISLAND						
1 Kennedy	Y	Y	Y	Y	Y	N
2 Langevin	Y	Y	Y	Y	Y	N
SOUTH CAROLINA						
1 ***Brown***	N	N	N	N	N	N
2 ***Wilson***	N	N	N	N	N	N
3 ***Barrett***	N	N	N	N	N	Y
4 ***DeMint***	?	?	?	?	?	?
5 Spratt	Y	Y	Y	Y	Y	N
6 Clyburn	Y	Y	Y	Y	Y	N
SOUTH DAKOTA						
AL Herseth	Y	Y	Y	Y	N	N
TENNESSEE						
1 ***Jenkins***	N	N	N	N	N	N
2 ***Duncan***	N	N	N	N	N	N
3 ***Wamp***	N	N	N	N	N	N
4 Davis	N	Y	Y	Y	N	N
5 Cooper	Y	Y	Y	Y	Y	N
6 Gordon	N	N	Y	Y	Y	N
7 ***Blackburn***	N	N	N	N	N	N
8 Tanner	N	Y	Y	N	Y	Y
9 Ford	Y	Y	Y	Y	Y	N
TEXAS						
1 Sandlin	N	Y	Y	Y	Y	N
2 Turner	N	Y	Y	N	N	Y
3 ***Johnson, Sam***	N	N	N	N	N	N
4 ***Hall***	N	N	N	N	N	N
5 ***Hensarling***	N	N	N	N	N	Y
6 ***Barton***	N	N	N	N	N	N
7 ***Culberson***	N	N	N	N	N	N
8 ***Brady***	N	N	N	N	N	Y
9 Lampson	N	Y	Y	Y	Y	N
10 Doggett	Y	Y	Y	Y	Y	N
11 Edwards	Y	Y	N	N	N	N
12 ***Granger***	N	?	?	?	?	?
13 ***Thornberry***	N	N	N	N	N	Y
14 ***Paul***	Y	N	Y	Y	N	Y
15 Hinojosa	N	Y	Y	Y	Y	N
16 Reyes	N	Y	Y	N	Y	N
17 Stenholm	N	N	N	N	N	N
18 Jackson-Lee	Y	Y	Y	Y	Y	N
19 ***Neugebauer***	N	N	N	N	N	N
20 Gonzalez	N	Y	Y	Y	Y	N
21 ***Smith***	N	N	N	N	N	N
22 ***DeLay***	N	N	N	N	N	N
23 ***Bonilla***	N	N	N	N	N	N
24 Frost	Y	Y	Y	Y	Y	N
25 Bell	Y	Y	Y	Y	Y	N
26 ***Burgess***	N	N	N	N	N	Y
27 Ortiz	N	Y	Y	N	Y	N
28 Rodriguez	Y	Y	Y	Y	Y	N
29 Green	N	Y	N	Y	Y	N
30 Johnson, E.B.	Y	Y	Y	Y	Y	N
31 ***Carter***	N	N	N	N	N	Y
32 ***Sessions***	N	N	N	N	N	Y
UTAH						
1 ***Bishop***	N	N	N	N	N	Y
2 Matheson	N	N	Y	Y	Y	Y
3 ***Cannon***	N	N	N	N	N	Y
VERMONT						
AL *Sanders*	Y	Y	Y	Y	Y	N
VIRGINIA						
1 ***Davis, Jo Ann***	N	N	Y	N	N	Y
2 ***Schrock***	N	N	N	N	N	N
3 Scott	Y	Y	Y	Y	Y	N
4 ***Forbes***	N	N	Y	N	N	N
5 ***Goode***	N	N	N	N	N	N
6 ***Goodlatte***	N	N	N	N	N	Y
7 ***Cantor***	N	N	N	N	N	Y
8 Moran	Y	Y	Y	Y	Y	N
9 Boucher	Y	Y	Y	Y	Y	N
10 ***Wolf***	N	N	N	N	N	N
11 ***Davis, T.***	N	N	N	N	Y	N
WASHINGTON						
1 Inslee	Y	Y	Y	Y	Y	N
2 Larsen	Y	Y	Y	N	Y	N
3 Baird	Y	Y	Y	Y	Y	N
4 ***Hastings***	Y	N	N	N	N	Y
5 ***Nethercutt***	N	N	N	N	N	Y
6 Dicks	Y	Y	N	N	Y	N
7 McDermott	Y	Y	Y	Y	Y	N
8 ***Dunn***	N	N	N	N	N	Y
9 Smith	Y	Y	N	Y	Y	N
WEST VIRGINIA						
1 Mollohan	N	N	Y	N	N	N
2 ***Capito***	N	N	N	Y	N	N
3 Rahall	Y	Y	Y	Y	Y	N
WISCONSIN						
1 ***Ryan***	Y	N	N	Y	N	Y
2 Baldwin	Y	Y	Y	Y	Y	N
3 Kind	Y	Y	Y	Y	Y	N
4 Kleczka	Y	Y	Y	Y	Y	N
5 ***Sensenbrenner***	N	N	N	Y	N	Y
6 ***Petri***	N	N	N	Y	N	Y
7 Obey	N	Y	Y	Y	Y	N
8 ***Green***	Y	N	N	Y	N	Y
WYOMING						
AL ***Cubin***	N	N	N	N	N	N

Southern states - Ala., Ark., Fla., Ga., Ky., La., Miss., N.C., Okla., S.C., Tenn., Texas, Va.

Key

Y	Voted for (yea).
#	Paired for.
+	Announced for.
N	Voted against (nay).
X	Paired against.
−	Announced against.
P	Voted "present."
C	Voted "present" to avoid possible conflict of interest.
?	Did not vote or otherwise make a position known.

Democrats **Republicans** *Independents*

256. HR 4520. Corporate Tax Overhaul/Previous Question. Reynolds, R-N.Y., motion to order the previous question (thus ending debate and possibility of amendment) on adoption of the rule (H Res 681) to provide for House floor consideration of the bill that would revoke an export tax break for U.S. manufacturers ruled an illegal trade subsidy by the World Trade Organization and provide for approximately $140 billion in new corporate tax cuts. Motion agreed to 233-193: R 225-0; D 8-192 (ND 0-145, SD 8-47); I 0-1. June 17, 2004.

257. HR 4520. Corporate Tax Overhaul/Rule. Adoption of the rule (H Res 681) to provide for House floor consideration of the bill that would revoke an export tax break for U.S. manufacturers ruled an illegal trade subsidy by the World Trade Organization and provide for approximately $140 billion in new corporate tax cuts. Adopted 230-195: R 219-6; D 11-188 (ND 2-142, SD 9-46); I 0-1. June 17, 2004.

258. HR 4520. Corporate Tax Overhaul/Recommit. Rangel, D-N.Y., motion to recommit the bill to the House Ways and Means Committee with instructions to strike the provisions of the bill and insert language that would revoke the export tax break for U.S. manufacturers. It also would allow taxpayers to deduct from their federal taxable income either state sales or state income tax payments. The cost would be offset by eliminating certain tax provisions, including denying some tax benefits to domestic corporations that reincorporate overseas to avoid U.S. income taxes. Motion rejected 193-235: R 0-225; D 192-10 (ND 145-2, SD 47-8); I 1-0. June 17, 2004.

259. HR 4520. Corporate Tax Overhaul/Passage. Passage of the bill that would revoke an export tax break for U.S. manufacturers ruled an illegal trade subsidy by the World Trade Organization, while providing for approximately $140 billion in new corporate tax cuts. Revenue raising offsets would reduce the cost of the bill to $34.4 billion over 11 years. It would include a buyout for tobacco farmers that could not exceed $9.6 billion. Passed 251-178: R 203-23; D 48-154 (ND 12-135, SD 36-19); I 0-1. June 17, 2004.

260. Procedural Motion/Journal. Approval of the House Journal of Wednesday, June 16, 2004. Approved 342-67: R 198-16; D 143-51 (ND 104-38, SD 39-13); I 1-0. June 17, 2004.

261. HR 4568. Fiscal 2005 Interior Appropriations/Bison in Yellowstone Park. Hinchey, D-N.Y., amendment that would bar funds from being used to kill, or assist in killing, bison in Yellowstone National Park. Rejected 202-215: R 34-184; D 167-31 (ND 131-13, SD 36-18); I 1-0. June 17, 2004.

	256	257	258	259	260	261
ALABAMA						
1 *Bonner*	Y	Y	N	Y	Y	N
2 *Everett*	Y	Y	N	Y	Y	N
3 *Rogers*	Y	Y	N	Y	Y	N
4 *Aderholt*	Y	Y	N	Y	Y	N
5 Cramer	N	N	Y	Y	Y	Y
6 *Bachus*	Y	Y	N	Y	Y	N
7 Davis	N	N	Y	Y	Y	Y
ALASKA						
AL *Young*	Y	Y	N	Y	Y	N
ARIZONA						
1 *Renzi*	Y	Y	N	Y	Y	N
2 *Franks*	Y	Y	N	Y	Y	N
3 *Shadegg*	Y	Y	N	Y	Y	N
4 Pastor	N	N	Y	N	N	Y
5 *Hayworth*	Y	Y	N	Y	Y	N
6 *Flake*	Y	Y	N	N	Y	N
7 Grijalva	N	N	Y	N	Y	Y
8 *Kolbe*	Y	Y	N	Y	Y	N
ARKANSAS						
1 Berry	N	N	Y	N	Y	N
2 Snyder	N	N	Y	Y	Y	Y
3 *Boozman*	Y	Y	N	Y	Y	N
4 Ross	N	N	Y	Y	?	N
CALIFORNIA						
1 Thompson	N	N	Y	Y	N	Y
2 *Herger*	Y	Y	N	Y	Y	N
3 *Ose*	Y	Y	N	Y	Y	N
4 *Doolittle*	Y	Y	N	Y	Y	N
5 Matsui	N	N	Y	N	N	Y
6 Woolsey	N	N	Y	N	N	Y
7 Miller, George	N	N	Y	N	N	Y
8 Pelosi	N	N	Y	N	N	Y
9 Lee	N	N	Y	N	N	Y
10 Tauscher	N	N	Y	N	N	Y
11 *Pombo*	Y	Y	N	Y	?	N
12 Lantos	N	N	Y	N	Y	Y
13 Stark	N	N	Y	N	N	Y
14 Eshoo	N	N	Y	N	N	Y
15 Honda	N	N	Y	N	Y	Y
16 Lofgren	N	N	Y	N	N	Y
17 Farr	N	N	Y	N	N	Y
18 Cardoza	N	N	Y	N	Y	N
19 *Radanovich*	Y	Y	N	Y	Y	N
20 Dooley	N	N	Y	Y	Y	N
21 *Nunes*	Y	Y	N	Y	Y	N
22 *Thomas*	Y	Y	N	Y	Y	N
23 Capps	N	N	Y	N	Y	Y
24 *Gallegly*	Y	Y	N	Y	Y	N
25 *McKeon*	Y	Y	N	Y	Y	N
26 *Dreier*	Y	Y	N	Y	Y	N
27 Sherman	N	N	Y	N	Y	Y
28 Berman	N	N	Y	N	Y	?
29 Schiff	N	N	Y	N	Y	Y
30 Waxman	N	?	Y	N	Y	Y
31 Becerra	N	N	Y	N	Y	Y
32 Solis	N	N	Y	N	Y	Y
33 Watson	N	N	Y	N	Y	Y
34 Roybal-Allard	N	N	Y	N	Y	Y
35 Waters	N	N	Y	N	N	Y
36 Harman	N	N	Y	N	Y	Y
37 Millender-McD.	N	N	Y	N	Y	Y
38 Napolitano	N	N	Y	N	Y	Y
39 Sánchez, Linda	N	N	Y	N	Y	Y
40 *Royce*	Y	Y	N	N	Y	N
41 *Lewis*	Y	Y	N	Y	?	N
42 *Miller, Gary*	Y	Y	N	Y	Y	N
43 Baca	N	N	Y	N	Y	N
44 *Calvert*	Y	Y	N	Y	Y	N
45 *Bono*	Y	Y	N	Y	Y	N
46 *Rohrabacher*	Y	Y	N	Y	Y	N
47 Sanchez, Loretta	N	N	Y	N	N	Y
48 *Cox*	Y	Y	N	Y	Y	?
49 *Issa*	Y	Y	N	Y	Y	N
50 *Cunningham*	Y	Y	N	Y	Y	N
51 Filner	N	N	Y	N	N	Y
52 *Hunter*	Y	Y	N	Y	Y	N
53 Davis	N	N	Y	N	Y	Y
COLORADO						
1 DeGette	N	N	Y	N	Y	Y
2 Udall	N	N	Y	N	N	Y
3 *McInnis*	Y	Y	N	Y	?	N
4 *Musgrave*	Y	Y	N	Y	Y	N
5 *Hefley*	Y	Y	N	N	N	N
6 *Tancredo*	Y	Y	N	N	P	N
7 *Beauprez*	Y	Y	N	Y	Y	N
CONNECTICUT						
1 Larson	N	N	Y	N	Y	Y
2 *Simmons*	Y	Y	N	Y	Y	Y
3 DeLauro	N	N	Y	N	Y	Y
4 *Shays*	Y	N	N	N	Y	Y
5 *Johnson*	Y	Y	N	Y	Y	Y
DELAWARE						
AL *Castle*	Y	N	N	N	Y	Y
FLORIDA						
1 *Miller, J.*	Y	Y	N	Y	Y	N
2 Boyd	N	N	Y	Y	Y	N
3 Brown	N	N	Y	N	Y	Y
4 *Crenshaw*	Y	Y	N	Y	Y	N
5 *Brown-Waite*	Y	Y	N	Y	Y	N
6 *Stearns*	Y	Y	N	Y	Y	N
7 *Mica*	Y	Y	N	Y	Y	N
8 *Keller*	Y	Y	N	Y	Y	N
9 *Bilirakis*	Y	Y	N	Y	Y	N
10 *Young*	Y	Y	N	Y	Y	N
11 Davis	N	N	Y	Y	Y	N
12 *Putnam*	Y	Y	N	Y	Y	N
13 *Harris*	Y	Y	N	Y	?	N
14 *Goss*	Y	Y	N	Y	Y	N
15 *Weldon*	Y	Y	N	Y	Y	N
16 *Foley*	Y	Y	N	Y	Y	N
17 Meek	N	N	Y	N	Y	Y
18 *Ros-Lehtinen*	N	Y	N	Y	Y	N
19 Wexler	N	N	Y	N	Y	Y
20 Deutsch	N	N	Y	N	Y	Y
21 *Diaz-Balart, L.*	Y	Y	N	Y	Y	N
22 *Shaw*	Y	Y	N	Y	Y	Y
23 Hastings	?	?	?	?	?	?
24 *Feeney*	Y	Y	N	Y	Y	N
25 *Diaz-Balart, M.*	Y	Y	N	Y	Y	N
GEORGIA						
1 *Kingston*	Y	Y	N	Y	Y	?
2 Bishop	Y	Y	N	Y	Y	N
3 Marshall	Y	Y	N	Y	N	N
4 Majette	N	N	Y	N	Y	N
5 Lewis	N	N	Y	N	N	Y
6 *Isakson*	Y	Y	N	Y	?	?
7 *Linder*	Y	Y	N	Y	Y	N
8 *Collins*	Y	Y	N	Y	Y	N
9 *Norwood*	Y	Y	N	Y	Y	N
10 *Deal*	Y	Y	N	Y	Y	N
11 *Gingrey*	Y	Y	N	Y	Y	N
12 *Burns*	Y	Y	N	Y	Y	N
13 Scott	N	N	Y	Y	Y	N
HAWAII						
1 Abercrombie	N	N	Y	Y	?	Y
2 Case	N	N	Y	N	Y	Y
IDAHO						
1 *Otter*	Y	Y	N	Y	N	N
2 *Simpson*	Y	Y	N	Y	Y	N
ILLINOIS						
1 Rush	N	N	Y	N	Y	Y
2 Jackson	N	N	Y	N	Y	Y
3 Lipinski	N	N	Y	N	?	?
4 Gutierrez	N	N	Y	N	Y	Y
5 Emanuel	N	N	Y	N	Y	Y
6 *Hyde*	Y	Y	N	Y	Y	N

ND Northern Democrats   SD Southern Democrats

	256	257	258	259	260	261
7 Davis	N	N	Y	Y	Y	Y
8 ***Crane***	Y	Y	N	Y	N	N
9 Schakowsky	N	N	Y	N	N	Y
10 ***Kirk***	Y	Y	N	N	Y	Y
11 ***Weller***	Y	Y	N	Y	N	N
12 Costello	N	N	Y	N	N	Y
13 ***Biggert***	Y	Y	N	Y	Y	Y
14 ***Hastert***				Y		
15 ***Johnson***	Y	N	N	N	Y	Y
16 ***Manzullo***	Y	Y	N	N	?	N
17 Evans	N	N	Y	N	N	Y
18 ***LaHood***	Y	Y	N	Y	Y	N
19 ***Shimkus***	Y	Y	N	Y	Y	N
INDIANA						
1 Visclosky	N	N	Y	N	N	Y
2 ***Chocola***	Y	Y	N	Y	Y	N
3 ***Souder***	Y	Y	N	Y	Y	N
4 ***Buyer***	Y	Y	N	Y	Y	N
5 ***Burton***	Y	Y	N	Y	Y	N
6 ***Pence***	Y	Y	N	Y	Y	N
7 Carson	N	N	Y	N	Y	Y
8 ***Hostettler***	Y	Y	N	Y	Y	N
9 Hill	N	N	Y	N	Y	Y
IOWA						
1 ***Nussle***	Y	Y	N	Y	Y	N
2 ***Leach***	Y	N	N	Y	Y	Y
3 Boswell	N	N	Y	Y	Y	N
4 ***Latham***	Y	Y	N	Y	Y	N
5 ***King***	Y	Y	N	Y	Y	N
KANSAS						
1 ***Moran***	Y	Y	N	Y	N	N
2 ***Ryun***	Y	Y	N	Y	Y	N
3 Moore	N	Y	Y	Y	Y	Y
4 ***Tiahrt***	Y	Y	N	Y	Y	N
KENTUCKY						
1 ***Whitfield***	Y	Y	N	Y	Y	Y
2 ***Lewis***	Y	Y	N	Y	Y	N
3 ***Northup***	Y	Y	N	N	Y	N
4 Lucas	Y	Y	N	Y	Y	Y
5 ***Rogers***	Y	Y	N	Y	Y	N
6 Chandler	Y	Y	N	Y	Y	Y
LOUISIANA						
1 ***Vitter***	Y	Y	N	Y	Y	N
2 Jefferson	N	N	Y	Y	N	Y
3 ***Tauzin***	Y	Y	N	Y	Y	N
4 ***McCrery***	Y	Y	N	Y	Y	N
5 Alexander	N	N	Y	Y	Y	N
6 ***Baker***	Y	Y	N	Y	Y	N
7 John	N	N	Y	Y	Y	N
MAINE						
1 Allen	N	N	Y	N	Y	Y
2 Michaud	N	N	Y	N	Y	Y
MARYLAND						
1 ***Gilchrest***	Y	Y	N	Y	Y	N
2 Ruppersberger	?	?	Y	Y	Y	Y
3 Cardin	N	N	Y	N	Y	Y
4 Wynn	N	N	Y	N	Y	Y
5 Hoyer	N	N	Y	N	Y	Y
6 ***Bartlett***	Y	Y	N	N	Y	N
7 Cummings	N	N	Y	N	Y	Y
8 Van Hollen	N	N	Y	N	Y	Y
MASSACHUSETTS						
1 Olver	N	N	Y	N	N	Y
2 Neal	N	N	Y	N	Y	Y
3 McGovern	N	N	Y	N	N	Y
4 Frank	N	N	Y	N	Y	Y
5 Meehan	N	N	Y	N	Y	Y
6 Tierney	N	N	Y	N	Y	Y
7 Markey	N	N	Y	N	Y	Y
8 Capuano	N	N	Y	N	N	Y
9 Lynch	N	N	Y	N	Y	Y
10 Delahunt	N	N	Y	N	Y	Y
MICHIGAN						
1 Stupak	N	N	Y	N	N	N
2 ***Hoekstra***	Y	Y	N	Y	Y	N
3 ***Ehlers***	Y	Y	N	Y	Y	Y
4 ***Camp***	Y	Y	N	Y	Y	N
5 Kildee	N	N	Y	N	Y	Y
6 ***Upton***	Y	Y	N	N	Y	Y
7 ***Smith***	Y	Y	N	Y	Y	?
8 ***Rogers***	Y	Y	N	Y	Y	N
9 ***Knollenberg***	Y	Y	N	Y	Y	?
10 ***Miller***	Y	Y	N	Y	Y	N
11 ***McCotter***	Y	Y	N	Y	Y	N
12 Levin	N	N	Y	N	N	Y
13 Kilpatrick	?	?	?	?	?	?
14 Conyers	?	?	?	?	?	?
15 Dingell	N	N	Y	N	Y	N
MINNESOTA						
1 ***Gutknecht***	Y	Y	N	Y	N	N
2 ***Kline***	Y	Y	N	Y	Y	N
3 ***Ramstad***	Y	Y	N	Y	N	Y
4 McCollum	N	N	Y	N	Y	Y
5 Sabo	N	N	Y	N	N	Y
6 ***Kennedy***	Y	Y	N	Y	N	N
7 Peterson	N	N	Y	Y	N	N
8 Oberstar	N	N	Y	N	N	N
MISSISSIPPI						
1 ***Wicker***	Y	Y	N	Y	N	N
2 Thompson	N	N	Y	Y	N	Y
3 ***Pickering***	Y	Y	N	Y	Y	N
4 Taylor	N	N	Y	N	N	Y
MISSOURI						
1 Clay	N	N	Y	N	Y	Y
2 ***Akin***	Y	Y	N	Y	Y	N
3 Gephardt	?	?	Y	N	?	Y
4 Skelton	N	N	Y	N	Y	Y
5 McCarthy	N	N	Y	N	Y	Y
6 ***Graves***	Y	Y	N	Y	N	N
7 ***Blunt***	Y	Y	N	Y	Y	N
8 ***Emerson***	Y	Y	N	Y	?	N
9 ***Hulshof***	Y	Y	N	Y	Y	N
MONTANA						
AL ***Rehberg***	Y	Y	N	Y	Y	N
NEBRASKA						
1 ***Bereuter***	Y	Y	N	Y	Y	?
2 ***Terry***	Y	Y	N	Y	Y	Y
3 ***Osborne***	Y	Y	N	Y	Y	N
NEVADA						
1 Berkley	N	N	Y	N	Y	Y
2 ***Gibbons***	Y	Y	N	Y	Y	N
3 ***Porter***	Y	Y	N	Y	N	N
NEW HAMPSHIRE						
1 ***Bradley***	Y	Y	N	N	Y	Y
2 ***Bass***	Y	Y	N	N	Y	Y
NEW JERSEY						
1 Andrews	N	N	Y	N	Y	Y
2 ***LoBiondo***	Y	Y	N	Y	N	Y
3 ***Saxton***	Y	Y	N	Y	?	Y
4 ***Smith***	Y	Y	N	Y	Y	Y
5 ***Garrett***	Y	Y	N	Y	Y	N
6 Pallone	N	N	Y	N	Y	Y
7 ***Ferguson***	Y	Y	N	Y	Y	Y
8 Pascrell	N	N	Y	N	Y	Y
9 Rothman	N	N	Y	N	Y	Y
10 Payne	N	N	Y	N	Y	Y
11 ***Frelinghuysen***	Y	Y	N	Y	Y	Y
12 Holt	N	N	Y	N	Y	Y
13 Menendez	N	N	Y	N	N	Y
NEW MEXICO						
1 ***Wilson***	Y	Y	N	N	Y	N
2 ***Pearce***	Y	Y	N	Y	Y	N
3 Udall	N	N	Y	N	N	Y
NEW YORK						
1 Bishop	N	N	Y	N	Y	Y
2 Israel	N	N	Y	N	Y	Y
3 ***King***	Y	Y	N	Y	Y	N
4 McCarthy	N	N	Y	N	Y	Y
5 Ackerman	N	N	Y	N	Y	Y
6 Meeks	N	N	Y	N	Y	Y
7 Crowley	N	N	Y	N	Y	Y
8 Nadler	N	N	Y	N	Y	Y
9 Weiner	N	N	Y	N	Y	Y
10 Towns	N	N	Y	N	N	Y
11 Owens	N	N	Y	N	Y	Y
12 Velázquez	N	N	Y	N	N	Y
13 ***Fossella***	Y	Y	N	Y	N	N
14 Maloney	N	N	Y	N	Y	Y
15 Rangel	N	N	Y	N	Y	Y
16 Serrano	N	N	Y	N	Y	Y
17 Engel	N	N	Y	N	Y	Y
18 Lowey	N	N	Y	N	Y	Y
19 ***Kelly***	Y	Y	N	Y	Y	Y
20 ***Sweeney***	Y	Y	N	Y	Y	N
21 McNulty	N	N	Y	N	N	Y
22 Hinchey	N	N	Y	N	N	Y
23 ***McHugh***	Y	Y	N	Y	Y	N
24 ***Boehlert***	Y	Y	N	Y	Y	N
25 ***Walsh***	Y	Y	N	Y	Y	N
26 ***Reynolds***	Y	Y	N	Y	Y	N
27 ***Quinn***	?	?	?	?	?	N
28 Slaughter	N	N	Y	N	?	Y
29 ***Houghton***	Y	Y	N	Y	Y	N
NORTH CAROLINA						
1 Vacant						
2 Etheridge	Y	Y	N	Y	Y	Y
3 ***Jones***	Y	Y	N	Y	Y	N
4 Price	N	N	Y	Y	Y	Y
5 ***Burr***	Y	Y	N	Y	Y	N
6 ***Coble***	Y	Y	N	Y	Y	N
7 McIntyre	Y	Y	N	Y	Y	N
8 ***Hayes***	Y	Y	N	Y	Y	N
9 ***Myrick***	Y	Y	N	Y	Y	N
10 ***Ballenger***	Y	Y	N	Y	Y	N
11 ***Taylor***	Y	Y	N	Y	Y	N
12 Watt	N	N	Y	Y	Y	Y
13 Miller	N	N	Y	Y	Y	Y
NORTH DAKOTA						
AL Pomeroy	N	N	N	N	Y	N
OHIO						
1 ***Chabot***	Y	Y	N	Y	Y	N
2 ***Portman***	Y	Y	N	Y	Y	N
3 ***Turner***	Y	Y	N	Y	Y	N
4 ***Oxley***	Y	Y	N	Y	Y	?
5 ***Gillmor***	Y	Y	N	Y	Y	N
6 Strickland	N	N	Y	N	N	Y
7 ***Hobson***	Y	Y	N	Y	Y	N
8 ***Boehner***	Y	Y	N	Y	Y	N
9 Kaptur	N	N	Y	N	Y	Y
10 Kucinich	N	N	Y	N	N	Y
11 Jones	N	N	Y	N	N	Y
12 ***Tiberi***	Y	Y	N	Y	N	Y
13 Brown	N	N	Y	N	Y	Y
14 ***LaTourette***	Y	Y	N	Y	Y	N
15 ***Pryce***	Y	Y	N	Y	Y	Y
16 ***Regula***	Y	Y	N	Y	Y	N
17 Ryan	N	N	Y	N	Y	Y
18 ***Ney***	Y	Y	N	Y	Y	N
OKLAHOMA						
1 ***Sullivan***	Y	Y	N	Y	Y	N
2 Carson	N	N	Y	Y	Y	N
3 ***Lucas***	Y	Y	N	Y	Y	N
4 ***Cole***	Y	Y	N	Y	Y	N
5 ***Istook***	Y	N	N	Y	Y	N
OREGON						
1 Wu	N	N	Y	Y	N	Y
2 ***Walden***	Y	Y	N	Y	Y	N
3 Blumenauer	N	N	Y	N	Y	Y
4 DeFazio	N	N	Y	N	N	Y
5 Hooley	N	N	Y	Y	Y	Y
PENNSYLVANIA						
1 Brady	N	N	Y	N	N	Y
2 Fattah	N	N	Y	N	Y	Y
3 ***English***	Y	Y	N	Y	N	Y
4 ***Hart***	Y	Y	N	Y	N	N
5 ***Peterson***	Y	Y	N	Y	Y	N
6 ***Gerlach***	Y	Y	N	Y	Y	Y
7 ***Weldon***	Y	Y	N	Y	Y	Y
8 ***Greenwood***	Y	Y	N	Y	Y	Y
9 ***Shuster, Bill***	Y	Y	N	Y	Y	N
10 ***Sherwood***	Y	Y	N	Y	Y	N
11 Kanjorski	N	N	Y	N	Y	Y
12 Murtha	N	N	Y	N	Y	Y
13 Hoeffel	N	N	Y	N	Y	Y
14 Doyle	N	N	Y	N	Y	Y
15 ***Toomey***	Y	Y	N	Y	Y	N
16 ***Pitts***	Y	Y	N	Y	Y	N
17 Holden	N	N	Y	N	Y	N
18 ***Murphy***	Y	Y	N	Y	Y	N
19 ***Platts***	Y	N	N	N	Y	Y
RHODE ISLAND						
1 Kennedy	N	N	Y	N	N	Y
2 Langevin	N	N	Y	N	Y	Y
SOUTH CAROLINA						
1 ***Brown***	Y	Y	N	Y	Y	N
2 ***Wilson***	Y	Y	N	Y	Y	N
3 ***Barrett***	Y	Y	N	Y	Y	N
4 ***DeMint***	?	?	?	?	?	?
5 Spratt	N	N	Y	Y	Y	Y
6 Clyburn	N	N	Y	Y	Y	Y
SOUTH DAKOTA						
AL Herseth	N	N	Y	Y	Y	N
TENNESSEE						
1 ***Jenkins***	Y	Y	N	Y	Y	N
2 ***Duncan***	Y	Y	N	Y	Y	N
3 ***Wamp***	Y	Y	N	Y	Y	Y
4 Davis	N	N	Y	Y	Y	Y
5 Cooper	N	N	Y	Y	N	N
6 Gordon	Y	Y	N	Y	Y	Y
7 ***Blackburn***	Y	Y	N	Y	Y	N
8 Tanner	N	N	Y	Y	N	N
9 Ford	N	N	Y	Y	N	Y
TEXAS						
1 Sandlin	N	N	Y	Y	N	N
2 Turner	N	N	Y	Y	Y	N
3 ***Johnson, Sam***	Y	Y	N	Y	Y	N
4 ***Hall***	Y	Y	N	Y	Y	N
5 ***Hensarling***	Y	Y	N	Y	Y	N
6 ***Barton***	Y	Y	N	Y	Y	N
7 ***Culberson***	Y	Y	N	Y	Y	N
8 ***Brady***	Y	Y	N	Y	Y	N
9 Lampson	N	N	Y	Y	Y	Y
10 Doggett	N	N	Y	N	?	Y
11 Edwards	N	N	Y	Y	Y	N
12 ***Granger***	Y	Y	N	Y	Y	N
13 ***Thornberry***	Y	Y	N	Y	Y	N
14 ***Paul***	Y	Y	N	Y	Y	N
15 Hinojosa	N	N	Y	N	Y	Y
16 Reyes	N	N	Y	N	Y	?
17 Stenholm	N	N	Y	Y	N	N
18 Jackson-Lee	N	N	Y	N	N	Y
19 ***Neugebauer***	Y	Y	N	Y	Y	N
20 Gonzalez	N	N	Y	N	Y	Y
21 ***Smith***	Y	Y	N	Y	Y	N
22 ***DeLay***	Y	Y	N	Y	?	N
23 ***Bonilla***	Y	Y	N	Y	Y	N
24 Frost	N	N	Y	Y	Y	N
25 Bell	N	N	Y	N	Y	Y
26 ***Burgess***	Y	Y	N	Y	Y	N
27 Ortiz	N	N	Y	N	Y	Y
28 Rodriguez	N	N	Y	N	Y	Y
29 Green	N	N	Y	N	N	Y
30 Johnson, E.B.	N	N	Y	N	N	N
31 ***Carter***	Y	Y	N	Y	Y	N
32 ***Sessions***	Y	Y	N	Y	Y	N
UTAH						
1 ***Bishop***	Y	Y	N	Y	Y	N
2 Matheson	N	Y	N	Y	Y	N
3 ***Cannon***	Y	Y	N	Y	Y	N
VERMONT						
AL *Sanders*	N	N	Y	N	Y	Y
VIRGINIA						
1 ***Davis, Jo Ann***	Y	Y	N	N	Y	N
2 ***Schrock***	Y	Y	N	Y	Y	N
3 Scott	N	N	Y	N	Y	Y
4 ***Forbes***	Y	Y	N	Y	Y	N
5 ***Goode***	Y	Y	N	Y	Y	Y
6 ***Goodlatte***	Y	Y	N	Y	Y	N
7 ***Cantor***	Y	Y	N	Y	Y	N
8 Moran	N	N	Y	N	Y	Y
9 Boucher	N	Y	Y	Y	?	Y
10 ***Wolf***	Y	Y	N	N	Y	N
11 ***Davis, T.***	Y	Y	N	N	Y	Y
WASHINGTON						
1 Inslee	N	N	Y	N	Y	Y
2 Larsen	N	N	Y	N	N	Y
3 Baird	N	N	Y	N	N	Y
4 ***Hastings***	Y	Y	N	Y	Y	N
5 ***Nethercutt***	Y	Y	N	Y	?	?
6 Dicks	N	N	Y	N	N	Y
7 McDermott	N	N	Y	N	N	Y
8 ***Dunn***	Y	Y	N	Y	Y	N
9 Smith	N	N	Y	N	?	?
WEST VIRGINIA						
1 Mollohan	N	N	Y	N	Y	Y
2 ***Capito***	Y	Y	N	N	Y	N
3 Rahall	N	N	Y	N	Y	Y
WISCONSIN						
1 ***Ryan***	Y	Y	N	Y	Y	N
2 Baldwin	N	N	Y	N	N	Y
3 Kind	N	N	Y	N	Y	Y
4 Kleczka	N	N	Y	N	Y	Y
5 ***Sensenbrenner***	Y	Y	N	N	Y	Y
6 ***Petri***	Y	Y	N	Y	Y	N
7 Obey	N	N	Y	N	Y	Y
8 ***Green***	Y	Y	N	Y	Y	Y
WYOMING						
AL ***Cubin***	Y	Y	N	Y	Y	N

Southern states - Ala., Ark., Fla., Ga., Ky., La., Miss., N.C., Okla., S.C., Tenn., Texas, Va.

Key

Y	Voted for (yea).
#	Paired for.
+	Announced for.
N	Voted against (nay).
X	Paired against.
–	Announced against.
P	Voted "present."
C	Voted "present" to avoid possible conflict of interest.
?	Did not vote or otherwise make a position known.

Democrats **Republicans**
Independents

262. HR 4568. Fiscal 2005 Interior Appropriations/Strategic Petroleum Reserve. Sanders, I-Vt., amendment that would prohibit the use of funds to maintain more than 647 million barrels of oil in the Strategic Petroleum Reserve, the level in the reserve as of mid-March 2004. Rejected 152-267: R 16-205; D 135-62 (ND 112-31, SD 23-31); I 1-0. June 17, 2004.

263. HR 4568. Fiscal 2005 Interior Appropriations/Snowmobiles in Yellowstone and Grand Teton Parks. Holt, D-N.J., amendment that would block funds from being used to do anything inconsistent with the phase-out of recreational snowmobile use in Yellowstone and Grand Teton National Parks. Rejected 198-224: R 28-195; D 170-28 (ND 128-16, SD 42-12); I 0-1. A "nay" was a vote in support of the president's position. June 17, 2004.

264. HR 4568. Fiscal 2005 Interior Appropriations/Passage. Passage of the bill that would appropriate $19.5 billion for the Interior Department, related agencies and programs in fiscal 2005. The bill would provide $3.6 billion for fighting wildfires, including $1 billion in supplemental funding $500 million in each of fiscal 2004 and 2005 that could be released for emergency fire conditions. It also would provide $3 billion for the Indian Health Service. The bill, as amended, would increase spending for the arts and humanities by $13.5 million and block the use of funds to plan or construct forest development roads in the Tongass National Forest in Alaska for harvesting timber. Passed 334-86: R 205-16; D 129-69 (ND 81-63, SD 48-6); I 0-1. June 17, 2004.

265. HR 4567. Fiscal 2005 Homeland Security Appropriations/Baggage Screener Cap. DeFazio, D-Ore., amendment that would strike language in the bill capping the number of full-time aviation screeners at 45,000. Rejected 180-228: R 4-213; D 175-15 (ND 128-8, SD 47-7); I 1-0. June 18, 2004 (in the session that began and the Congressional Record dated June 17, 2004).

266. HR 4567. Fiscal 2005 Homeland Security Appropriations/High-Threat Urban Areas. Sweeney, R-N.Y., amendment that would transfer $450 million from formula-based state and local homeland security programs to discretionary terrorism prevention programs for high-threat, high-density urban areas, such as New York City. Rejected 171-237: R 70-147; D 101-89 (ND 85-51, SD 16-38); I 0-1. June 18, 2004 (in the session that began and the Congressional Record dated June 17, 2004).

	262	263	264	265	266
ALABAMA					
1 *Bonner*	N	N	Y	N	N
2 *Everett*	N	N	Y	N	N
3 *Rogers*	N	N	Y	N	N
4 *Aderholt*	N	N	Y	N	N
5 Cramer	N	N	Y	N	N
6 *Bachus*	N	N	Y	N	N
7 Davis	Y	Y	Y	Y	N
ALASKA					
AL *Young*	N	N	Y	?	?
ARIZONA					
1 *Renzi*	N	N	Y	N	N
2 *Franks*	N	N	N	N	N
3 *Shadegg*	N	N	Y	N	Y
4 Pastor	Y	Y	Y	Y	N
5 *Hayworth*	N	N	Y	N	N
6 *Flake*	N	N	N	N	Y
7 Grijalva	Y	Y	N	Y	Y
8 *Kolbe*	N	N	Y	N	Y
ARKANSAS					
1 Berry	N	Y	N	N	N
2 Snyder	N	Y	Y	Y	N
3 *Boozman*	N	N	Y	N	N
4 Ross	Y	N	Y	Y	N
CALIFORNIA					
1 Thompson	Y	Y	Y	Y	Y
2 *Herger*	N	N	Y	N	N
3 *Ose*	N	N	Y	N	N
4 *Doolittle*	N	N	Y	N	N
5 Matsui	Y	Y	Y	Y	N
6 Woolsey	Y	Y	N	Y	Y
7 Miller, George	Y	Y	N	Y	Y
8 Pelosi	Y	Y	Y	Y	Y
9 Lee	Y	Y	N	Y	Y
10 Tauscher	Y	Y	Y	Y	Y
11 *Pombo*	N	N	Y	N	Y
12 Lantos	N	Y	Y	Y	Y
13 Stark	Y	Y	N	?	?
14 Eshoo	Y	Y	N	Y	Y
15 Honda	Y	Y	N	Y	Y
16 Lofgren	Y	Y	N	Y	Y
17 Farr	Y	Y	N	Y	Y
18 Cardoza	N	N	Y	Y	N
19 *Radanovich*	N	N	Y	N	Y
20 Dooley	N	Y	Y	?	?
21 *Nunes*	N	N	Y	N	N
22 *Thomas*	N	N	Y	N	N
23 Capps	Y	Y	N	Y	Y
24 *Gallegly*	N	N	Y	N	Y
25 *McKeon*	N	N	Y	N	N
26 *Dreier*	N	N	Y	N	Y
27 Sherman	N	Y	Y	Y	Y
28 Berman	?	?	?	?	?
29 Schiff	N	Y	N	Y	Y
30 Waxman	N	Y	N	?	?
31 Becerra	Y	Y	N	Y	Y
32 Solis	Y	Y	N	Y	Y
33 Watson	Y	Y	N	Y	Y
34 Roybal-Allard	Y	Y	Y	Y	Y
35 Waters	N	Y	N	Y	N
36 Harman	N	Y	Y	?	?

	262	263	264	265	266
37 Millender-McD.	Y	Y	Y	Y	Y
38 Napolitano	Y	Y	Y	Y	Y
39 Sánchez, Linda	Y	Y	N	Y	Y
40 *Royce*	Y	N	N	N	Y
41 *Lewis*	N	N	Y	N	N
42 *Miller, Gary*	N	N	Y	N	Y
43 Baca	Y	Y	Y	Y	Y
44 *Calvert*	N	N	Y	N	N
45 *Bono*	N	Y	N	N	N
46 *Rohrabacher*	Y	N	N	N	N
47 Sanchez, Loretta	Y	Y	Y	Y	Y
48 *Cox*	N	N	Y	N	Y
49 *Issa*	N	N	Y	N	N
50 *Cunningham*	N	N	Y	N	N
51 Filner	Y	N	Y	Y	Y
52 *Hunter*	N	N	Y	N	N
53 Davis	Y	Y	Y	Y	Y
COLORADO					
1 DeGette	N	N	Y	N	Y
2 Udall	N	N	Y	Y	Y
3 *McInnis*	N	N	Y	N	N
4 *Musgrave*	N	N	Y	N	Y
5 *Hefley*	N	N	Y	N	N
6 *Tancredo*	N	N	Y	N	Y
7 *Beauprez*	N	N	Y	N	N
CONNECTICUT					
1 Larson	Y	Y	N	Y	N
2 *Simmons*	Y	Y	Y	Y	N
3 DeLauro	Y	Y	N	Y	N
4 *Shays*	N	Y	N	N	Y
5 *Johnson*	Y	Y	Y	N	N
DELAWARE					
AL *Castle*	N	Y	N	Y	N
FLORIDA					
1 *Miller, J.*	N	N	N	N	N
2 Boyd	N	N	Y	N	N
3 Brown	Y	Y	Y	Y	Y
4 *Crenshaw*	N	N	Y	N	Y
5 *Brown-Waite*	N	N	N	N	N
6 *Stearns*	N	N	N	N	N
7 *Mica*	N	N	Y	N	N
8 *Keller*	N	N	Y	N	Y
9 *Bilirakis*	N	N	Y	N	N
10 *Young*	N	N	Y	N	N
11 Davis	Y	Y	Y	Y	Y
12 *Putnam*	N	N	Y	N	Y
13 *Harris*	N	N	Y	N	Y
14 *Goss*	N	Y	?	?	?
15 *Weldon*	N	N	Y	N	N
16 *Foley*	N	Y	Y	N	Y
17 Meek	Y	Y	Y	Y	Y
18 *Ros-Lehtinen*	N	N	Y	N	Y
19 Wexler	Y	Y	Y	Y	Y
20 Deutsch	?	?	?	?	?
21 *Diaz-Balart, L.*	N	N	Y	N	Y
22 *Shaw*	N	N	Y	N	N
23 Hastings	?	?	?	?	?
24 *Feeney*	N	N	Y	N	Y
25 *Diaz-Balart, M.*	N	N	Y	N	Y
GEORGIA					
1 *Kingston*	?	N	Y	N	N
2 Bishop	Y	N	Y	Y	N
3 Marshall	N	Y	Y	Y	N
4 Majette	Y	N	Y	N	Y
5 Lewis	Y	Y	N	Y	Y
6 *Isakson*	?	?	?	?	?
7 *Linder*	N	N	Y	N	N
8 *Collins*	N	N	N	N	N
9 *Norwood*	N	N	Y	N	N
10 *Deal*	N	N	Y	N	N
11 *Gingrey*	N	N	Y	N	N
12 *Burns*	N	N	Y	N	N
13 Scott	N	Y	Y	Y	Y
HAWAII					
1 Abercrombie	Y	Y	Y	Y	N
2 Case	N	Y	Y	Y	N
IDAHO					
1 *Otter*	N	N	Y	N	N
2 *Simpson*	N	N	Y	N	N
ILLINOIS					
1 Rush	Y	Y	Y	Y	Y
2 Jackson	Y	Y	N	Y	Y
3 Lipinski	?	?	?	?	?
4 Gutierrez	Y	Y	N	Y	Y
5 Emanuel	Y	Y	N	Y	Y
6 *Hyde*	N	N	Y	N	Y

ND Northern Democrats   SD Southern Democrats

	262	263	264	265	266
7 Davis	Y	Y	Y	Y	Y
8 ***Crane***	N	N	Y	N	N
9 Schakowsky	Y	Y	N	Y	Y
10 ***Kirk***	N	Y	Y	N	Y
11 ***Weller***	N	N	Y	N	N
12 Costello	N	Y	Y	Y	Y
13 ***Biggert***	N	Y	Y	N	N
14 ***Hastert***					
15 ***Johnson***	Y	Y	Y	N	N
16 ***Manzullo***	N	N	Y	N	N
17 Evans	Y	Y	N	Y	N
18 ***LaHood***	N	N	Y	N	N
19 ***Shimkus***	N	N	Y	N	N
INDIANA					
1 Visclosky	Y	Y	Y	N	N
2 ***Chocola***	N	N	Y	N	N
3 ***Souder***	N	Y	Y	N	N
4 ***Buyer***	N	N	Y	N	N
5 ***Burton***	N	N	Y	N	N
6 ***Pence***	N	N	Y	N	N
7 Carson	Y	Y	Y	N	N
8 ***Hostettler***	N	N	N	N	N
9 Hill	N	Y	Y	Y	N
IOWA					
1 ***Nussle***	N	N	Y	N	N
2 ***Leach***	N	Y	Y	N	N
3 Boswell	Y	N	N	Y	N
4 ***Latham***	N	N	Y	N	N
5 ***King***	N	N	N	N	N
KANSAS					
1 ***Moran***	Y	Y	Y	N	N
2 ***Ryun***	N	N	Y	N	N
3 Moore	N	Y	Y	Y	N
4 ***Tiahrt***	N	N	N	N	N
KENTUCKY					
1 ***Whitfield***	N	Y	Y	N	N
2 ***Lewis***	N	N	Y	N	N
3 ***Northup***	N	N	Y	N	N
4 Lucas	N	N	Y	Y	N
5 ***Rogers***	N	N	Y	N	N
6 Chandler	Y	Y	Y	Y	N
LOUISIANA					
1 ***Vitter***	N	N	Y	N	N
2 Jefferson	N	Y	Y	Y	Y
3 ***Tauzin***	N	N	Y	?	?
4 ***McCrery***	N	N	Y	N	N
5 Alexander	N	N	Y	Y	N
6 ***Baker***	N	N	Y	N	N
7 John	N	N	Y	N	N
MAINE					
1 Allen	N	N	N	Y	N
2 Michaud	Y	N	N	Y	N
MARYLAND					
1 ***Gilchrest***	N	Y	Y	N	N
2 Ruppersberger	Y	N	Y	Y	Y
3 Cardin	N	Y	Y	Y	Y
4 Wynn	N	Y	Y	Y	Y
5 Hoyer	N	Y	Y	Y	Y
6 ***Bartlett***	N	N	Y	N	N
7 Cummings	Y	Y	Y	Y	Y
8 Van Hollen	N	Y	N	Y	Y
MASSACHUSETTS					
1 Olver	Y	Y	Y	N	Y
2 Neal	Y	Y	Y	?	?
3 McGovern	Y	Y	N	Y	Y
4 Frank	Y	Y	N	Y	Y
5 Meehan	Y	Y	Y	Y	Y
6 Tierney	Y	Y	N	Y	Y
7 Markey	Y	Y	N	Y	Y
8 Capuano	Y	Y	N	Y	Y
9 Lynch	N	Y	N	Y	Y
10 Delahunt	Y	Y	N	Y	Y
MICHIGAN					
1 Stupak	Y	N	Y	Y	N
2 ***Hoekstra***	N	N	Y	N	N
3 ***Ehlers***	N	Y	Y	N	N
4 ***Camp***	N	N	Y	N	N
5 Kildee	Y	Y	Y	Y	N
6 ***Upton***	N	N	Y	N	N
7 ***Smith***	N	N	Y	N	N
8 ***Rogers***	N	N	Y	N	N
9 ***Knollenberg***	?	N	Y	N	N
10 ***Miller***	N	N	Y	N	N
11 ***McCotter***	N	N	Y	N	N
12 Levin	Y	Y	Y	Y	N

	262	263	264	265	266
13 Kilpatrick	?	?	?	N	Y
14 Conyers	?	?	?	Y	Y
15 Dingell	N	Y	N	Y	Y
MINNESOTA					
1 ***Gutknecht***	N	N	Y	N	N
2 ***Kline***	N	N	Y	N	Y
3 ***Ramstad***	N	N	Y	N	Y
4 McCollum	Y	Y	Y	N	N
5 Sabo	N	Y	Y	N	N
6 ***Kennedy***	N	N	Y	N	Y
7 Peterson	Y	N	Y	N	N
8 Oberstar	Y	N	Y	Y	N
MISSISSIPPI					
1 ***Wicker***	N	N	Y	N	N
2 Thompson	Y	Y	Y	Y	N
3 ***Pickering***	N	N	Y	?	?
4 Taylor	Y	N	Y	N	N
MISSOURI					
1 Clay	Y	Y	Y	?	?
2 ***Akin***	N	N	Y	N	Y
3 Gephardt	Y	Y	Y	?	?
4 Skelton	Y	Y	Y	Y	N
5 McCarthy	N	Y	N	Y	Y
6 ***Graves***	N	N	Y	N	N
7 ***Blunt***	N	N	Y	N	N
8 ***Emerson***	N	N	Y	N	N
9 ***Hulshof***	N	N	Y	N	N
MONTANA					
AL ***Rehberg***	N	N	Y	N	N
NEBRASKA					
1 ***Bereuter***	?	?	?	?	?
2 ***Terry***	Y	N	Y	N	N
3 ***Osborne***	N	N	Y	N	N
NEVADA					
1 Berkley	N	Y	Y	Y	Y
2 ***Gibbons***	N	N	Y	N	Y
3 ***Porter***	N	N	Y	Y	Y
NEW HAMPSHIRE					
1 ***Bradley***	N	N	Y	N	N
2 ***Bass***	N	N	Y	N	N
NEW JERSEY					
1 Andrews	Y	Y	N	Y	Y
2 ***LoBiondo***	N	Y	Y	N	Y
3 ***Saxton***	N	Y	Y	N	Y
4 ***Smith***	N	Y	Y	N	Y
5 ***Garrett***	N	Y	Y	N	Y
6 Pallone	Y	Y	N	Y	Y
7 ***Ferguson***	N	Y	Y	N	Y
8 Pascrell	Y	Y	N	Y	Y
9 Rothman	Y	Y	Y	Y	Y
10 Payne	Y	Y	N	Y	Y
11 ***Frelinghuysen***	N	N	Y	N	Y
12 Holt	Y	Y	N	Y	Y
13 Menendez	N	Y	N	Y	Y
NEW MEXICO					
1 ***Wilson***	N	N	Y	Y	N
2 ***Pearce***	N	N	Y	N	N
3 Udall	Y	Y	Y	Y	N
NEW YORK					
1 Bishop	Y	Y	N	Y	Y
2 Israel	N	Y	N	Y	Y
3 ***King***	N	N	Y	N	Y
4 McCarthy	Y	Y	Y	Y	Y
5 Ackerman	Y	Y	Y	Y	N
6 Meeks	Y	Y	Y	Y	Y
7 Crowley	Y	Y	Y	Y	Y
8 Nadler	Y	Y	N	Y	Y
9 Weiner	Y	Y	N	Y	Y
10 Towns	Y	Y	Y	Y	Y
11 Owens	Y	Y	N	Y	Y
12 Velázquez	Y	Y	N	Y	Y
13 ***Fossella***	N	N	Y	N	Y
14 Maloney	Y	Y	Y	Y	Y
15 Rangel	N	Y	Y	Y	Y
16 Serrano	?	Y	Y	Y	Y
17 Engel	Y	Y	Y	Y	Y
18 Lowey	Y	Y	Y	Y	Y
19 ***Kelly***	Y	Y	Y	Y	Y
20 ***Sweeney***	N	N	Y	N	Y
21 McNulty	Y	Y	Y	Y	Y
22 Hinchey	Y	Y	N	Y	Y
23 ***McHugh***	N	N	Y	N	Y
24 ***Boehlert***	N	N	Y	N	Y
25 ***Walsh***	N	Y	Y	N	Y

	262	263	264	265	266
26 ***Reynolds***	N	N	Y	N	Y
27 ***Quinn***	N	N	Y	N	Y
28 Slaughter	Y	Y	Y	?	?
29 ***Houghton***	N	N	Y	N	Y
NORTH CAROLINA					
1 Vacant					
2 Etheridge	N	Y	Y	Y	N
3 ***Jones***	Y	N	?	N	N
4 Price	N	Y	Y	N	N
5 ***Burr***	N	N	Y	N	N
6 ***Coble***	N	N	Y	N	N
7 McIntyre	Y	Y	Y	Y	N
8 ***Hayes***	N	N	Y	N	N
9 ***Myrick***	N	N	Y	N	Y
10 ***Ballenger***	N	N	Y	?	?
11 ***Taylor***	N	N	Y	N	N
12 Watt	Y	Y	Y	Y	N
13 Miller	Y	Y	Y	Y	N
NORTH DAKOTA					
AL Pomeroy	N	N	Y	Y	N
OHIO					
1 ***Chabot***	N	Y	Y	N	Y
2 ***Portman***	N	N	Y	N	Y
3 ***Turner***	N	N	Y	N	N
4 ***Oxley***	N	N	Y	N	N
5 ***Gillmor***	N	Y	Y	N	N
6 Strickland	Y	Y	N	Y	N
7 ***Hobson***	N	N	Y	N	N
8 ***Boehner***	N	N	Y	N	N
9 Kaptur	Y	Y	Y	Y	N
10 Kucinich	Y	Y	N	Y	N
11 Jones	Y	Y	Y	Y	Y
12 ***Tiberi***	N	N	Y	N	Y
13 Brown	Y	Y	N	Y	N
14 ***LaTourette***	N	N	Y	N	N
15 ***Pryce***	N	N	Y	N	Y
16 ***Regula***	N	N	Y	N	N
17 Ryan	Y	Y	Y	Y	N
18 ***Ney***	N	N	Y	N	N
OKLAHOMA					
1 ***Sullivan***	N	N	N	N	Y
2 Carson	N	Y	Y	Y	N
3 ***Lucas***	N	N	Y	N	N
4 ***Cole***	N	N	Y	N	N
5 ***Istook***	N	N	Y	N	N
OREGON					
1 Wu	Y	Y	N	Y	N
2 ***Walden***	N	N	Y	N	N
3 Blumenauer	Y	Y	N	Y	Y
4 DeFazio	Y	Y	Y	Y	N
5 Hooley	Y	Y	Y	Y	N
PENNSYLVANIA					
1 Brady	Y	Y	Y	Y	Y
2 Fattah	Y	Y	Y	Y	Y
3 ***English***	Y	Y	Y	N	N
4 ***Hart***	N	N	Y	N	N
5 ***Peterson***	N	N	Y	N	N
6 ***Gerlach***	N	N	Y	N	Y
7 ***Weldon***	N	N	Y	N	N
8 ***Greenwood***	Y	Y	Y	N	Y
9 ***Shuster, Bill***	N	N	Y	N	N
10 ***Sherwood***	N	N	Y	N	N
11 Kanjorski	Y	Y	Y	Y	N
12 Murtha	Y	N	Y	?	?
13 Hoeffel	Y	Y	N	Y	Y
14 Doyle	Y	Y	Y	Y	Y
15 ***Toomey***	N	N	N	N	N
16 ***Pitts***	N	N	Y	N	N
17 Holden	Y	Y	Y	Y	N
18 ***Murphy***	N	N	Y	N	Y
19 ***Platts***	N	N	Y	N	N
RHODE ISLAND					
1 Kennedy	Y	Y	Y	Y	Y
2 Langevin	Y	Y	Y	Y	N
SOUTH CAROLINA					
1 ***Brown***	N	N	Y	N	N
2 ***Wilson***	N	N	Y	N	N
3 ***Barrett***	N	N	Y	N	N
4 ***DeMint***	?	?	?	?	?
5 Spratt	N	Y	Y	Y	N
6 Clyburn	Y	Y	Y	Y	N
SOUTH DAKOTA					
AL Herseth	Y	N	Y	Y	N

	262	263	264	265	266
TENNESSEE					
1 ***Jenkins***	N	N	Y	N	N
2 ***Duncan***	N	N	Y	N	N
3 ***Wamp***	N	N	Y	N	N
4 Davis	N	Y	Y	Y	N
5 Cooper	N	Y	N	Y	Y
6 Gordon	N	Y	Y	?	?
7 ***Blackburn***	N	N	Y	N	N
8 Tanner	N	N	N	Y	N
9 Ford	N	Y	Y	Y	Y
TEXAS					
1 Sandlin	N	N	Y	Y	N
2 Turner	Y	Y	Y	Y	N
3 ***Johnson, Sam***	N	N	Y	?	?
4 ***Hall***	N	N	Y	N	N
5 ***Hensarling***	N	N	N	N	N
6 ***Barton***	N	N	Y	N	N
7 ***Culberson***	N	N	Y	N	Y
8 ***Brady***	N	N	Y	N	Y
9 Lampson	N	Y	Y	Y	Y
10 Doggett	Y	Y	Y	Y	N
11 Edwards	N	Y	Y	Y	N
12 ***Granger***	N	N	Y	N	Y
13 ***Thornberry***	N	N	Y	N	N
14 ***Paul***	Y	N	N	N	N
15 Hinojosa	Y	Y	Y	Y	N
16 Reyes	?	?	?	Y	N
17 Stenholm	N	N	Y	N	N
18 Jackson-Lee	Y	Y	N	Y	Y
19 ***Neugebauer***	N	N	Y	N	N
20 Gonzalez	N	Y	Y	Y	N
21 ***Smith***	N	N	Y	N	Y
22 ***DeLay***	N	N	Y	N	Y
23 ***Bonilla***	N	N	Y	N	Y
24 Frost	N	Y	Y	Y	N
25 Bell	N	Y	Y	Y	Y
26 ***Burgess***	N	N	Y	N	Y
27 Ortiz	N	N	Y	Y	N
28 Rodriguez	N	Y	Y	Y	N
29 Green	Y	Y	Y	Y	Y
30 Johnson, E.B.	Y	Y	Y	Y	N
31 ***Carter***	N	N	Y	N	Y
32 ***Sessions***	N	N	Y	N	Y
UTAH					
1 ***Bishop***	N	N	Y	N	N
2 Matheson	N	N	N	Y	N
3 ***Cannon***	N	N	Y	N	N
VERMONT					
AL *Sanders*	Y	N	N	Y	N
VIRGINIA					
1 ***Davis, Jo Ann***	Y	N	Y	N	N
2 ***Schrock***	N	N	?	N	N
3 Scott	Y	Y	Y	Y	Y
4 ***Forbes***	Y	N	Y	N	N
5 ***Goode***	Y	N	Y	N	N
6 ***Goodlatte***	Y	N	Y	N	N
7 ***Cantor***	N	N	Y	N	Y
8 Moran	Y	Y	Y	Y	Y
9 Boucher	Y	Y	Y	Y	N
10 ***Wolf***	N	N	Y	N	Y
11 ***Davis, T.***	N	N	Y	N	Y
WASHINGTON					
1 Inslee	Y	Y	Y	Y	N
2 Larsen	Y	Y	Y	Y	N
3 Baird	Y	Y	Y	Y	N
4 ***Hastings***	N	N	Y	N	N
5 ***Nethercutt***	?	?	?	?	?
6 Dicks	N	Y	Y	?	?
7 McDermott	Y	Y	Y	Y	N
8 ***Dunn***	N	N	Y	N	N
9 Smith	?	?	?	?	?
WEST VIRGINIA					
1 Mollohan	N	Y	Y	N	N
2 ***Capito***	N	Y	Y	N	N
3 Rahall	N	Y	N	Y	N
WISCONSIN					
1 ***Ryan***	N	N	Y	N	N
2 Baldwin	Y	Y	N	Y	N
3 Kind	Y	N	N	Y	N
4 Kleczka	Y	Y	N	Y	N
5 ***Sensenbrenner***	N	N	N	N	N
6 ***Petri***	N	N	N	N	N
7 Obey	Y	Y	N	Y	N
8 ***Green***	N	N	Y	N	N
WYOMING					
AL ***Cubin***	N	N	Y	N	N

Southern states - Ala., Ark., Fla., Ga., Ky., La., Miss., N.C., Okla., S.C., Tenn., Texas, Va.

Key

Y	Voted for (yea).
#	Paired for.
+	Announced for.
N	Voted against (nay).
X	Paired against.
−	Announced against.
P	Voted "present."
C	Voted "present" to avoid possible conflict of interest.
?	Did not vote or otherwise make a position known.

Democrats **Republicans** *Independents*

267. HR 4567. Fiscal 2005 Homeland Security Appropriations/ Research and Development. Jackson-Lee, D-Texas, amendment that would increase funding for research and development by $10 million while decreasing funding for management expenses by the same amount. Rejected 137-269: R 1-213; D 135-56 (ND 91-48, SD 44-8); I 1-0. June 18, 2004.

268. HR 4567. Fiscal 2005 Homeland Security Appropriations/ Offshore Contracts. DeLauro, D-Conn., amendment that would prevent the use of funds in the bill to carry out a contract with a U.S. company that incorporates offshore to avoid U.S. taxes. Rejected 182-221: R 18-194; D 163-27 (ND 126-12, SD 37-15); I 1-0. June 18, 2004.

269. HR 4567. Fiscal 2005 Homeland Security Appropriations/ Contract Immigration Services. Roybal-Allard, D-Calif., amendment that would prohibit the use of funds to privatize or contract out services provided by the Bureau of Citizenship and Immigration Services, which reviews citizenship applications, performs background checks, conducts interviews, and approves work authorizations and visa extensions. Adopted 242-163: R 49-163; D 192-0 (ND 139-0, SD 53-0); I 1-0. June 18, 2004.

270. HR 4567. Fiscal 2005 Homeland Security Appropriations/ Citizenship and Immigration Status. Tancredo, R-Colo., amendment that would prohibit the use of funds to assist state or local governments that have restrictions on exchanging information with the Bureau of Immigration and Customs Enforcement on an individual's citizenship or immigration status. Rejected 148-259: R 146-68; D 2-190 (ND 1-138, SD 1-52); I 0-1. June 18, 2004.

271. HR 4567. Fiscal 2005 Homeland Security Appropriations/ Urban Area Security. Maloney, D-N.Y., amendment that would limit to 80 the total number of grants available under the Urban Area Security Initiative, which provides discretionary funds to high-threat, high-density urban areas. Rejected 113-292: R 19-195; D 94-96 (ND 79-58, SD 15-38); I 0-1. June 18, 2004.

272. HR 4567. Fiscal 2005 Homeland Security Appropriations/ Privacy Study. Sabo, D-Minn., amendment that would authorize $2 million from the aviation security account for use by the Department of Homeland Security's privacy officer to conduct privacy impact assessments. Rejected 199-205: R 8-205; D 190-0 (ND 137-0, SD 53-0); I 1-0. June 18, 2004.

273. HR 4567. Fiscal 2005 Homeland Security Appropriations/ Unscreened Cargo. Markey, D-Mass., amendment that would bar the use of funds in the bill to approve, renew or implement any aviation cargo security plan that allows the transporting of unscreened or uninspected cargo on passenger planes. Rejected 191-211: R 43-169; D 147-42 (ND 111-25, SD 36-17); I 1-0. June 18, 2004.

	267	268	269	270	271	272	273
ALABAMA							
1 *Bonner*	N	N	N	Y	N	N	N
2 *Everett*	?	?	?	?	?	?	?
3 *Rogers*	N	N	Y	Y	N	N	N
4 *Aderholt*	N	N	N	Y	N	N	Y
5 Cramer	N	N	Y	N	N	Y	Y
6 *Bachus*	N	N	N	Y	N	N	N
7 Davis	Y	Y	Y	N	N	Y	Y
ALASKA							
AL *Young*	N	N	N	Y	N	N	N
ARIZONA							
1 *Renzi*	N	N	N	Y	N	N	N
2 *Franks*	N	N	N	Y	N	N	N
3 *Shadegg*	N	N	N	Y	N	N	N
4 Pastor	Y	Y	Y	N	Y	N	Y
5 *Hayworth*	N	N	N	Y	N	N	Y
6 *Flake*	N	N	N	Y	N	N	N
7 Grijalva	Y	Y	Y	N	Y	Y	Y
8 *Kolbe*	N	N	N	Y	N	N	N
ARKANSAS							
1 Berry	Y	Y	Y	N	N	Y	Y
2 Snyder	N	Y	Y	N	N	Y	Y
3 *Boozman*	N	N	N	Y	N	N	N
4 Ross	Y	Y	Y	N	N	Y	Y
CALIFORNIA							
1 Thompson	N	N	Y	N	Y	Y	Y
2 *Herger*	N	N	N	Y	N	N	N
3 *Ose*	N	N	N	Y	N	N	N
4 *Doolittle*	N	N	N	Y	N	N	N
5 Matsui	N	Y	Y	N	Y	Y	Y
6 Woolsey	Y	Y	Y	N	Y	Y	Y
7 Miller, George	N	Y	Y	N	Y	Y	Y
8 Pelosi	Y	Y	Y	N	Y	Y	Y
9 Lee	Y	Y	Y	N	Y	Y	Y
10 Tauscher	N	Y	Y	N	Y	Y	Y
11 *Pombo*	N	N	N	Y	N	N	N
12 Lantos	Y	Y	Y	N	Y	Y	Y
13 Stark	N	Y	Y	N	Y	Y	Y
14 Eshoo	N	Y	Y	N	Y	Y	Y
15 Honda	Y	Y	Y	N	Y	Y	Y
16 Lofgren	N	N	Y	N	Y	Y	Y
17 Farr	?	?	?	?	?	?	?
18 Cardoza	N	Y	Y	N	Y	Y	Y
19 *Radanovich*	N	N	N	Y	N	N	N
20 Dooley	N	N	Y	N	Y	N	N
21 *Nunes*	N	N	N	N	N	N	N
22 *Thomas*	N	N	?	?	?	?	?
23 Capps	Y	Y	Y	N	N	Y	N
24 *Gallegly*	N	N	N	Y	N	N	N
25 *McKeon*	N	N	N	Y	N	N	N
26 *Dreier*	N	N	N	Y	N	N	N
27 Sherman	N	Y	Y	N	Y	Y	Y
28 Berman	?	?	+	−	+	+	?
29 Schiff	N	Y	Y	N	Y	Y	Y
30 Waxman	?	?	?	?	?	?	?
31 Becerra	Y	Y	Y	N	Y	Y	Y
32 Solis	Y	Y	Y	N	Y	Y	Y
33 Watson	Y	Y	Y	N	Y	Y	Y
34 Roybal-Allard	Y	Y	Y	N	Y	Y	Y
35 Waters	Y	Y	Y	N	Y	N	N
36 Harman	N	Y	Y	N	Y	N	Y

	267	268	269	270	271	272	273
37 Millender-McD.	Y	Y	Y	N	Y	Y	Y
38 Napolitano	Y	Y	Y	N	Y	Y	Y
39 Sánchez, Linda	Y	Y	Y	N	Y	Y	Y
40 *Royce*	N	N	N	Y	N	N	N
41 *Lewis*	N	N	N	N	N	N	N
42 *Miller, Gary*	N	N	N	Y	N	N	N
43 Baca	Y	Y	Y	N	N	N	N
44 *Calvert*	N	N	N	N	N	N	N
45 *Bono*	N	N	N	N	N	N	N
46 *Rohrabacher*	N	N	N	Y	N	Y	N
47 Sanchez, Loretta	Y	Y	Y	N	Y	Y	Y
48 *Cox*	N	N	N	Y	N	N	N
49 *Issa*	N	N	N	Y	N	N	N
50 *Cunningham*	N	N	N	Y	N	N	N
51 Filner	Y	Y	Y	N	Y	Y	Y
52 *Hunter*	N	N	N	Y	N	N	N
53 Davis	Y	Y	Y	N	Y	Y	Y
COLORADO							
1 DeGette	Y	Y	Y	N	N	Y	Y
2 Udall	Y	N	Y	N	N	Y	Y
3 *McInnis*	N	N	N	Y	N	N	N
4 *Musgrave*	N	N	N	Y	N	N	N
5 *Hefley*	N	N	Y	Y	N	Y	N
6 *Tancredo*	N	N	Y	Y	Y	N	N
7 *Beauprez*	N	N	N	Y	N	N	N
CONNECTICUT							
1 Larson	Y	Y	Y	N	Y	Y	Y
2 *Simmons*	N	Y	Y	N	N	Y	Y
3 DeLauro	Y	Y	Y	N	Y	Y	Y
4 *Shays*	N	N	Y	Y	Y	Y	N
5 *Johnson*	N	Y	N	N	N	N	N
DELAWARE							
AL *Castle*	N	N	N	N	N	N	N
FLORIDA							
1 *Miller, J.*	N	N	N	Y	N	N	N
2 Boyd	N	Y	N	N	N	Y	Y
3 Brown	Y	Y	Y	Y	Y	Y	N
4 *Crenshaw*	N	N	N	Y	N	N	N
5 *Brown-Waite*	N	N	N	Y	N	N	Y
6 *Stearns*	N	N	N	Y	N	N	Y
7 *Mica*	N	N	N	Y	N	N	N
8 *Keller*	N	N	N	Y	N	N	N
9 *Bilirakis*	N	N	N	Y	N	N	N
10 *Young*	N	N	N	Y	N	N	N
11 Davis	Y	N	Y	N	N	Y	Y
12 *Putnam*	N	N	N	Y	N	N	N
13 *Harris*	N	N	N	Y	N	N	?
14 *Goss*	N	N	N	N	N	N	N
15 *Weldon*	N	N	?	Y	N	N	N
16 *Foley*	N	N	Y	N	Y	N	N
17 Meek	Y	Y	Y	N	Y	Y	Y
18 *Ros-Lehtinen*	N	N	N	Y	N	N	N
19 Wexler	Y	Y	Y	N	Y	Y	Y
20 Deutsch	?	?	?	?	?	?	?
21 *Diaz-Balart, L.*	N	N	N	Y	N	N	N
22 *Shaw*	N	N	N	Y	N	N	N
23 Hastings	?	?	?	?	?	?	?
24 *Feeney*	N	N	N	Y	N	N	N
25 *Diaz-Balart, M.*	N	N	N	Y	N	N	N
GEORGIA							
1 *Kingston*	N	N	N	Y	N	Y	N
2 Bishop	Y	Y	Y	N	N	Y	N
3 Marshall	Y	Y	Y	N	N	Y	Y
4 Majette	Y	Y	Y	N	N	Y	Y
5 Lewis	?	?	Y	N	N	Y	Y
6 *Isakson*	?	?	?	?	?	?	?
7 *Linder*	N	N	N	Y	N	N	N
8 *Collins*	−	−	−	+	−	−	−
9 *Norwood*	N	N	N	Y	N	N	N
10 *Deal*	N	N	N	Y	N	N	N
11 *Gingrey*	N	N	N	Y	N	N	N
12 *Burns*	N	N	N	Y	N	N	N
13 Scott	Y	Y	Y	N	Y	N	N
HAWAII							
1 Abercrombie	N	Y	Y	N	Y	Y	Y
2 Case	N	Y	Y	N	N	Y	Y
IDAHO							
1 *Otter*	N	N	N	Y	N	N	N
2 *Simpson*	N	N	N	Y	N	N	N
ILLINOIS							
1 Rush	Y	Y	Y	N	Y	Y	Y
2 Jackson	N	Y	Y	N	Y	Y	Y
3 Lipinski	?	?	?	?	?	?	?
4 Gutierrez	+	?	+	?	+	+	+
5 Emanuel	?	?	?	?	?	?	?
6 *Hyde*	N	N	Y	N	Y	N	N

ND Northern Democrats   SD Southern Democrats

	267	268	269	270	271	272	273
7 Davis	Y	Y	Y	N	Y	Y	N
8 ***Crane***	N	N	N	Y	N	N	N
9 Schakowsky	Y	Y	Y	N	?	?	?
10 ***Kirk***	N	N	N	N	N	N	Y
11 ***Weller***	N	N	N	N	N	N	N
12 Costello	Y	Y	Y	N	N	Y	N
13 ***Biggert***	N	N	N	N	N	N	N
14 ***Hastert***							
15 ***Johnson***	N	N	Y	N	N	N	Y
16 ***Manzullo***	N	N	N	Y	N	N	N
17 Evans	Y	Y	Y	N	N	Y	Y
18 ***LaHood***	N	N	Y	N	N	N	N
19 ***Shimkus***	N	N	Y	Y	Y	N	Y
INDIANA							
1 Visclosky	Y	Y	Y	N	N	Y	N
2 ***Chocola***	N	N	N	N	N	N	N
3 ***Souder***	N	N	N	Y	N	N	N
4 ***Buyer***	N	?	Y	Y	N	N	N
5 ***Burton***	N	N	N	Y	N	N	N
6 ***Pence***	N	?	N	Y	N	N	N
7 Carson	Y	Y	Y	N	Y	Y	Y
8 ***Hostettler***	N	N	Y	Y	N	N	N
9 Hill	N	Y	Y	N	N	Y	Y
IOWA							
1 ***Nussle***	N	N	N	N	N	N	N
2 ***Leach***	N	N	Y	N	N	Y	Y
3 Boswell	Y	N	Y	N	N	Y	N
4 ***Latham***	N	N	N	N	N	N	N
5 ***King***	N	N	N	Y	N	N	N
KANSAS							
1 ***Moran***	N	N	Y	Y	N	N	Y
2 ***Ryun***	N	N	N	Y	N	N	Y
3 Moore	Y	N	Y	N	N	Y	Y
4 ***Tiahrt***	N	N	N	Y	N	N	N
KENTUCKY							
1 ***Whitfield***	N	Y	N	Y	N	N	N
2 ***Lewis***	N	N	N	Y	N	N	N
3 ***Northup***	N	Y	N	N	N	N	N
4 Lucas	N	N	Y	N	N	Y	N
5 ***Rogers***	N	N	N	Y	N	N	N
6 Chandler	Y	Y	Y	N	N	Y	Y
LOUISIANA							
1 ***Vitter***	N	Y	N	Y	N	N	Y
2 Jefferson	Y	Y	Y	N	Y	Y	Y
3 ***Tauzin***	N	N	N	Y	N	N	N
4 ***McCrery***	N	N	N	Y	N	N	N
5 Alexander	Y	Y	Y	N	Y	Y	Y
6 ***Baker***	?	?	?	?	?	?	?
7 John	?	?	?	?	?	?	?
MAINE							
1 Allen	N	Y	Y	N	N	Y	N
2 Michaud	N	Y	Y	N	N	Y	N
MARYLAND							
1 ***Gilchrest***	N	N	N	Y	N	N	N
2 Ruppersberger	Y	Y	Y	N	Y	Y	N
3 Cardin	Y	Y	Y	N	Y	Y	Y
4 Wynn	Y	Y	Y	N	N	Y	N
5 Hoyer	Y	Y	Y	N	Y	Y	Y
6 ***Bartlett***	N	N	N	Y	N	N	N
7 Cummings	Y	Y	Y	N	N	Y	Y
8 Van Hollen	N	Y	Y	N	Y	Y	Y
MASSACHUSETTS							
1 Olver	Y	Y	Y	N	N	Y	Y
2 Neal	N	Y	Y	N	Y	Y	Y
3 McGovern	Y	Y	Y	N	Y	Y	Y
4 Frank	N	Y	Y	N	Y	Y	Y
5 Meehan	N	Y	Y	N	Y	Y	Y
6 Tierney	Y	Y	Y	N	?	?	?
7 Markey	N	Y	Y	N	Y	Y	Y
8 Capuano	Y	Y	Y	N	Y	Y	Y
9 Lynch	N	Y	Y	N	Y	Y	Y
10 Delahunt	Y	Y	Y	N	Y	Y	Y
MICHIGAN							
1 Stupak	N	Y	Y	N	N	Y	Y
2 ***Hoekstra***	N	N	N	Y	Y	N	N
3 ***Ehlers***	N	N	N	N	N	Y	N
4 ***Camp***	N	N	N	Y	N	N	N
5 Kildee	Y	Y	Y	N	N	Y	Y
6 ***Upton***	N	N	N	Y	N	N	Y
7 ***Smith***	N	N	N	Y	N	N	N
8 ***Rogers***	N	N	N	N	N	N	N
9 ***Knollenberg***	N	N	N	N	N	N	N
10 ***Miller***	N	N	N	Y	N	N	N
11 ***McCotter***	N	N	Y	Y	N	N	N
12 Levin	N	Y	Y	N	N	Y	Y
13 Kilpatrick	Y	Y	Y	N	N	Y	Y
14 Conyers	Y	Y	Y	N	Y	Y	Y
15 Dingell	N	Y	Y	N	N	Y	Y
MINNESOTA							
1 ***Gutknecht***	N	N	N	Y	N	N	N
2 ***Kline***	N	N	N	Y	N	N	N
3 ***Ramstad***	N	N	N	Y	N	N	Y
4 McCollum	N	Y	Y	N	N	Y	Y
5 Sabo	N	Y	Y	N	N	Y	Y
6 ***Kennedy***	N	N	N	N	Y	N	N
7 Peterson	N	Y	Y	Y	N	Y	N
8 Oberstar	N	Y	Y	N	N	Y	N
MISSISSIPPI							
1 ***Wicker***	N	N	N	Y	N	N	N
2 Thompson	Y	Y	Y	N	N	Y	N
3 ***Pickering***	N	N	N	Y	N	N	N
4 Taylor	N	Y	Y	Y	N	Y	Y
MISSOURI							
1 Clay	Y	Y	Y	N	Y	Y	N
2 ***Akin***	N	N	N	Y	N	N	N
3 Gephardt	Y	Y	Y	N	Y	Y	Y
4 Skelton	Y	Y	Y	N	N	Y	Y
5 McCarthy	Y	Y	Y	N	Y	Y	Y
6 ***Graves***	N	N	N	Y	N	N	N
7 ***Blunt***	N	N	N	N	N	N	N
8 ***Emerson***	N	Y	Y	Y	N	N	N
9 ***Hulshof***	N	N	N	Y	N	N	N
MONTANA							
AL ***Rehberg***	N	N	N	Y	N	N	N
NEBRASKA							
1 ***Bereuter***	?	?	?	?	?	?	?
2 ***Terry***	N	N	N	N	N	N	N
3 ***Osborne***	N	N	Y	N	N	N	N
NEVADA							
1 Berkley	Y	Y	Y	N	Y	Y	N
2 ***Gibbons***	?	?	?	?	?	?	?
3 ***Porter***	N	N	N	N	Y	N	Y
NEW HAMPSHIRE							
1 ***Bradley***	N	Y	N	Y	N	Y	Y
2 ***Bass***	N	Y	N	Y	N	N	Y
NEW JERSEY							
1 Andrews	Y	Y	Y	N	N	Y	Y
2 ***LoBiondo***	N	Y	Y	N	N	N	Y
3 ***Saxton***	N	N	Y	N	N	N	Y
4 ***Smith***	N	Y	Y	N	N	N	Y
5 ***Garrett***	N	N	N	Y	N	N	N
6 Pallone	Y	Y	Y	N	Y	Y	Y
7 ***Ferguson***	N	N	Y	N	Y	N	Y
8 Pascrell	N	Y	Y	N	Y	Y	Y
9 Rothman	Y	Y	Y	N	Y	Y	Y
10 Payne	Y	Y	Y	N	Y	Y	Y
11 ***Frelinghuysen***	N	N	N	N	Y	N	Y
12 Holt	Y	Y	Y	N	Y	Y	Y
13 Menendez	?	?	?	?	?	?	?
NEW MEXICO							
1 ***Wilson***	N	Y	N	N	N	N	N
2 ***Pearce***	N	N	N	N	N	N	N
3 Udall	Y	N	Y	N	N	Y	Y
NEW YORK							
1 Bishop	Y	Y	Y	N	Y	Y	Y
2 Israel	N	Y	Y	N	Y	Y	Y
3 ***King***	N	N	N	N	Y	N	Y
4 McCarthy	Y	Y	Y	N	Y	Y	Y
5 Ackerman	Y	Y	Y	N	Y	Y	Y
6 Meeks	Y	Y	Y	N	Y	Y	N
7 Crowley	Y	?	Y	N	Y	Y	N
8 Nadler	Y	Y	Y	N	Y	Y	Y
9 Weiner	Y	Y	Y	N	Y	Y	Y
10 Towns	Y	Y	Y	N	Y	Y	Y
11 Owens	Y	Y	Y	N	Y	Y	Y
12 Velázquez	Y	Y	Y	N	Y	Y	Y
13 ***Fossella***	N	N	N	N	Y	N	Y
14 Maloney	Y	Y	Y	N	Y	Y	Y
15 Rangel	Y	Y	Y	N	Y	Y	Y
16 Serrano	Y	Y	Y	N	Y	Y	Y
17 Engel	Y	Y	Y	N	Y	Y	N
18 Lowey	Y	Y	Y	N	Y	Y	Y
19 ***Kelly***	N	N	N	Y	Y	N	Y
20 ***Sweeney***	N	N	Y	Y	Y	N	N
21 McNulty	Y	Y	Y	N	Y	Y	Y
22 Hinchey	Y	Y	Y	N	Y	Y	Y
23 ***McHugh***	N	N	Y	Y	Y	N	N
24 ***Boehlert***	?	?	?	?	?	?	?
25 ***Walsh***	N	N	N	N	N	N	N
26 ***Reynolds***	N	N	N	N	Y	N	N
27 ***Quinn***	?	?	?	?	?	?	?
28 Slaughter	Y	Y	Y	N	Y	Y	Y
29 ***Houghton***	N	N	Y	N	Y	N	N
NORTH CAROLINA							
1 Vacant							
2 Etheridge	Y	N	Y	N	N	Y	Y
3 ***Jones***	N	N	Y	Y	N	N	Y
4 Price	Y	N	Y	N	N	Y	Y
5 ***Burr***	N	N	Y	N	N	N	N
6 ***Coble***	N	N	Y	Y	N	N	N
7 McIntyre	Y	Y	Y	N	N	Y	Y
8 ***Hayes***	N	Y	N	Y	N	N	N
9 ***Myrick***	N	N	N	Y	N	N	N
10 ***Ballenger***	?	?	?	?	?	?	?
11 ***Taylor***	N	N	Y	Y	N	N	N
12 Watt	Y	N	Y	N	N	Y	Y
13 Miller	Y	N	Y	N	N	Y	Y
NORTH DAKOTA							
AL Pomeroy	N	N	Y	N	N	Y	Y
OHIO							
1 ***Chabot***	N	N	N	Y	Y	Y	Y
2 ***Portman***	N	N	N	N	N	N	N
3 ***Turner***	N	N	Y	Y	N	N	Y
4 ***Oxley***	N	N	N	N	N	N	N
5 ***Gillmor***	N	N	N	Y	N	N	N
6 Strickland	N	Y	Y	N	N	Y	Y
7 ***Hobson***	N	N	N	N	N	?	N
8 ***Boehner***	?	?	?	?	?	?	?
9 Kaptur	Y	Y	Y	N	N	Y	?
10 Kucinich	Y	Y	Y	N	N	Y	Y
11 Jones	Y	Y	Y	N	Y	Y	N
12 ***Tiberi***	N	N	N	N	N	N	Y
13 Brown	Y	Y	Y	N	N	Y	N
14 ***LaTourette***	N	N	Y	N	N	N	N
15 ***Pryce***	N	N	?	N	N	N	N
16 ***Regula***	N	N	N	N	N	N	N
17 Ryan	Y	Y	Y	N	N	Y	N
18 ***Ney***	N	N	N	Y	N	N	Y
OKLAHOMA							
1 ***Sullivan***	N	N	N	N	N	N	N
2 Carson	Y	Y	Y	N	Y	Y	N
3 ***Lucas***	N	N	N	Y	N	N	N
4 ***Cole***	N	N	N	N	N	N	N
5 ***Istook***	N	N	N	Y	N	N	N
OREGON							
1 Wu	Y	Y	Y	N	N	Y	N
2 ***Walden***	N	N	N	Y	N	N	N
3 Blumenauer	Y	N	Y	N	Y	Y	Y
4 DeFazio	Y	Y	Y	N	N	Y	Y
5 Hooley	Y	N	Y	N	N	Y	Y
PENNSYLVANIA							
1 Brady	Y	Y	Y	N	Y	Y	Y
2 Fattah	Y	Y	Y	N	Y	Y	Y
3 ***English***	N	N	Y	N	N	N	N
4 ***Hart***	N	N	N	N	N	N	N
5 ***Peterson***	N	N	N	Y	N	N	N
6 ***Gerlach***	?	?	?	?	?	?	?
7 ***Weldon***	N	N	Y	Y	N	N	N
8 ***Greenwood***	?	N	N	Y	N	N	?
9 ***Shuster, Bill***	N	N	N	Y	N	N	N
10 ***Sherwood***	N	Y	N	N	N	N	N
11 Kanjorski	N	Y	Y	N	N	Y	Y
12 Murtha	N	Y	Y	N	N	Y	N
13 Hoeffel	?	?	?	?	?	?	?
14 Doyle	N	Y	Y	N	Y	Y	Y
15 ***Toomey***	N	N	N	Y	N	N	Y
16 ***Pitts***	N	N	N	Y	N	N	Y
17 Holden	N	Y	Y	N	N	Y	Y
18 ***Murphy***	N	N	N	N	N	N	N
19 ***Platts***	N	N	Y	Y	N	N	N
RHODE ISLAND							
1 Kennedy	Y	Y	Y	N	N	Y	Y
2 Langevin	N	Y	Y	N	N	Y	Y
SOUTH CAROLINA							
1 ***Brown***	N	N	N	Y	N	N	N
2 ***Wilson***	N	N	N	Y	N	N	N
3 ***Barrett***	N	N	N	Y	N	N	N
4 ***DeMint***	?	?	?	?	?	?	?
5 Spratt	Y	Y	Y	N	N	Y	Y
6 Clyburn	Y	Y	Y	N	N	Y	N
SOUTH DAKOTA							
AL Herseth	N	Y	Y	N	N	Y	Y
TENNESSEE							
1 ***Jenkins***	N	N	N	Y	N	N	N
2 ***Duncan***	N	Y	Y	Y	N	N	N
3 ***Wamp***	N	Y	N	Y	N	N	N
4 Davis	Y	Y	Y	N	N	Y	N
5 Cooper	Y	N	Y	N	Y	Y	Y
6 Gordon	Y	N	Y	N	N	Y	Y
7 ***Blackburn***	N	N	N	Y	N	N	N
8 Tanner	Y	N	Y	N	N	Y	Y
9 Ford	Y	N	Y	N	Y	Y	Y
TEXAS							
1 Sandlin	Y	Y	Y	N	Y	Y	N
2 Turner	Y	N	Y	N	N	Y	Y
3 ***Johnson, Sam***	N	N	N	Y	N	N	N
4 ***Hall***	N	N	N	N	N	N	N
5 ***Hensarling***	N	N	N	N	N	N	N
6 ***Barton***	N	N	Y	N	N	N	N
7 ***Culberson***	N	N	N	Y	N	N	N
8 ***Brady***	N	N	N	Y	N	N	N
9 Lampson	Y	Y	Y	N	N	Y	N
10 Doggett	Y	Y	Y	N	N	Y	Y
11 Edwards	Y	Y	Y	N	N	Y	N
12 ***Granger***	N	N	N	Y	N	N	N
13 ***Thornberry***	N	N	N	Y	N	N	N
14 ***Paul***	N	N	Y	Y	N	Y	N
15 Hinojosa	Y	Y	Y	N	N	Y	Y
16 Reyes	?	?	?	?	?	?	?
17 Stenholm	N	N	Y	N	N	Y	N
18 Jackson-Lee	Y	Y	Y	N	Y	Y	N
19 ***Neugebauer***	N	N	N	Y	N	N	N
20 Gonzalez	Y	Y	Y	N	Y	Y	N
21 ***Smith***	N	N	N	Y	N	N	N
22 ***DeLay***	N	N	N	Y	N	N	N
23 ***Bonilla***	N	N	N	Y	N	N	N
24 Frost	Y	Y	Y	N	N	Y	Y
25 Bell	Y	Y	Y	N	Y	Y	N
26 ***Burgess***	N	N	N	Y	N	N	N
27 Ortiz	Y	Y	Y	N	N	Y	Y
28 Rodriguez	Y	Y	Y	N	Y	Y	Y
29 Green	Y	Y	Y	N	Y	Y	N
30 Johnson, E.B.	Y	Y	Y	N	Y	Y	Y
31 ***Carter***	N	N	N	Y	N	N	N
32 ***Sessions***	N	N	N	Y	N	N	N
UTAH							
1 ***Bishop***	N	N	N	Y	N	N	N
2 Matheson	N	Y	Y	N	N	Y	N
3 ***Cannon***	N	N	N	N	N	N	N
VERMONT							
AL *Sanders*	Y	Y	Y	N	N	Y	Y
VIRGINIA							
1 ***Davis, Jo Ann***	N	Y	Y	Y	N	N	N
2 ***Schrock***	N	N	N	Y	N	N	N
3 Scott	Y	Y	Y	N	N	Y	Y
4 ***Forbes***	Y	N	Y	Y	N	N	N
5 ***Goode***	N	Y	Y	Y	N	N	N
6 ***Goodlatte***	N	–	N	Y	N	N	N
7 ***Cantor***	N	N	N	Y	N	N	N
8 Moran	N	N	Y	N	Y	Y	Y
9 Boucher	N	Y	Y	N	N	Y	Y
10 ***Wolf***	N	N	Y	N	N	N	N
11 ***Davis, T.***	N	N	Y	N	Y	N	N
WASHINGTON							
1 Inslee	Y	Y	Y	N	N	Y	Y
2 Larsen	N	Y	Y	N	N	Y	Y
3 Baird	?	?	?	?	?	?	?
4 ***Hastings***	N	N	N	N	N	N	N
5 ***Nethercutt***	N	Y	N	N	N	N	N
6 Dicks	N	N	Y	N	N	Y	Y
7 McDermott	Y	Y	Y	N	Y	Y	Y
8 ***Dunn***	N	N	N	N	N	N	N
9 Smith	?	?	?	?	?	?	?
WEST VIRGINIA							
1 Mollohan	N	Y	Y	N	N	Y	Y
2 ***Capito***	N	N	Y	N	N	N	Y
3 Rahall	Y	Y	Y	N	N	Y	N
WISCONSIN							
1 ***Ryan***	N	N	N	N	N	Y	Y
2 Baldwin	N	Y	Y	N	N	Y	Y
3 Kind	N	Y	Y	N	N	Y	Y
4 Kleczka	N	Y	Y	N	N	Y	Y
5 ***Sensenbrenner***	N	N	N	Y	N	N	N
6 ***Petri***	N	N	Y	N	N	N	N
7 Obey	N	Y	Y	N	N	Y	Y
8 ***Green***	N	N	Y	N	N	Y	Y
WYOMING							
AL ***Cubin***	N	N	N	Y	N	N	N

Southern states - Ala., Ark., Fla., Ga., Ky., La., Miss., N.C., Okla., S.C., Tenn., Texas, Va.

274. HR 4567. Fiscal 2005 Homeland Security Appropriations/Statewide Security Guard Contracts. Velázquez, D-N.Y., amendment that would prohibit the use of funds in the bill for the Federal Protective Service to terminate small business contracts and enter into statewide contracts for security guard services. Rejected 201-205: R 9-205; D 191-0 (ND 138-0, SD 53-0); I 1-0. June 18, 2004.

275. HR 4567. Fiscal 2005 Homeland Security Appropriations/Passage. Passage of the bill that would provide $33.1 billion in fiscal 2005 for the Department of Homeland Security, including $2.5 billion previously enacted for Project Bioshield. Passed 400-5: R 213-2; D 186-3 (ND 134-2, SD 52-1); I 1-0. June 18, 2004.

276. H Res 591. Community Bank Appreciation/Adoption. Renzi, R-Ariz., motion to suspend the rules and adopt the resolution that would support the designation of a "Community Banking Month" to raise public awareness and appreciation of community banking institutions. Motion agreed to 364-0: R 195-0; D 169-0 (ND 125-0, SD 44-0); I 0-0. A two-thirds majority of those present and voting (243 in this case) is required for adoption under suspension of the rules. June 21, 2004.

277. HR 4363. Homeownership Assistance/Passage. Green, R-Wis., motion to suspend the rules and pass the bill that would allow low- to moderate-income families who receive homes from nonprofit groups, such as Habitat for Humanity, to fulfill their obligation to contribute labor by helping the nonprofit to build homes other than their own. Motion agreed to 368-0: R 196-0; D 172-0 (ND 128-0, SD 44-0); I 0-0. A two-thirds majority of those present and voting (246 in this case) is required for passage under suspension of the rules. June 21, 2004.

278. H Res 660. Randy Johnson Tribute/Adoption. Miller, R-Mich., motion to suspend the rules and adopt the resolution that would congratulate professional baseball player Randy Johnson for pitching a perfect game May 18, 2004. Motion agreed to 367-0: R 195-0; D 172-0 (ND 129-0, SD 43-0); I 0-0. A two-thirds majority of those present and voting (245 in this case) is required for adoption under suspension of the rules. June 21, 2004.

279. HR 4613. Fiscal 2005 Defense Appropriations/Previous Question. Myrick, R-N.C., motion to order the previous question (thus ending debate and possibility of amendment) on adoption of the rule (H Res 683) to provide for House floor consideration of the bill that would appropriate $418 billion for defense programs for fiscal 2005. The rule also would allow a debt limit increase to be added to the bill in conference. Motion agreed to 220-196: R 220-0; D 0-195 (ND 0-142, SD 0-53); I 0-1. June 22, 2004.

280. HR 4613. Fiscal 2005 Defense Appropriations/Rule. Adoption of the rule (H Res 683) to provide for House floor consideration of the bill that would appropriate $418 billion for defense programs for fiscal 2005. The rule also would allow a debt limit increase to be added to the bill in conference. Adopted 221-197: R 220-1; D 1-195 (ND 1-143, SD 0-52); I 0-1. June 22, 2004.

Key

Y	Voted for (yea).
#	Paired for.
+	Announced for.
N	Voted against (nay).
X	Paired against.
−	Announced against.
P	Voted "present."
C	Voted "present" to avoid possible conflict of interest.
?	Did not vote or otherwise make a position known.

Democrats   *Republicans*   *Independents*

	274	275	276	277	278	279	280
ALABAMA							
1 *Bonner*	N	Y	Y	Y	Y	Y	Y
2 *Everett*	?	?	?	?	?	Y	Y
3 *Rogers*	N	Y	Y	Y	Y	Y	Y
4 *Aderholt*	N	Y	Y	Y	Y	Y	Y
5 Cramer	Y	Y	Y	Y	Y	N	N
6 *Bachus*	N	Y	Y	Y	Y	Y	Y
7 Davis	Y	Y	?	?	?	N	N
ALASKA							
AL *Young*	N	Y	Y	Y	Y	Y	Y
ARIZONA							
1 *Renzi*	N	Y	Y	Y	Y	Y	Y
2 *Franks*	N	Y	Y	Y	Y	Y	Y
3 *Shadegg*	N	Y	Y	Y	Y	Y	Y
4 Pastor	Y	Y	Y	Y	Y	N	N
5 *Hayworth*	N	Y	Y	Y	Y	Y	Y
6 *Flake*	N	N	Y	Y	Y	Y	Y
7 Grijalva	Y	Y	Y	Y	Y	N	N
8 *Kolbe*	N	Y	Y	Y	Y	Y	Y
ARKANSAS							
1 Berry	Y	N	Y	Y	Y	N	N
2 Snyder	Y	Y	Y	Y	Y	N	N
3 *Boozman*	N	Y	Y	Y	Y	N	N
4 Ross	Y	Y	Y	Y	Y	N	N
CALIFORNIA							
1 Thompson	Y	Y	Y	Y	Y	N	N
2 *Herger*	N	Y	Y	Y	Y	Y	Y
3 *Ose*	N	Y	Y	Y	Y	Y	Y
4 *Doolittle*	N	Y	Y	Y	Y	Y	Y
5 Matsui	Y	Y	?	?	?	N	N
6 Woolsey	Y	Y	Y	Y	Y	N	N
7 Miller, George	Y	Y	Y	Y	Y	?	N
8 Pelosi	Y	Y	?	?	?	N	N
9 Lee	Y	Y	Y	Y	Y	N	N
10 Tauscher	Y	Y	Y	Y	Y	N	N
11 *Pombo*	N	Y	Y	Y	Y	Y	Y
12 Lantos	Y	Y	Y	Y	Y	N	N
13 Stark	Y	Y	?	?	?	N	N
14 Eshoo	Y	Y	Y	Y	Y	N	N
15 Honda	Y	Y	Y	Y	Y	N	N
16 Lofgren	Y	Y	Y	Y	Y	N	N
17 Farr	?	?	Y	Y	Y	N	N
18 Cardoza	Y	Y	Y	Y	Y	N	N
19 *Radanovich*	N	Y	Y	Y	Y	Y	Y
20 Dooley	Y	Y	Y	Y	Y	N	N
21 *Nunes*	N	Y	Y	Y	Y	Y	Y
22 *Thomas*	?	?	Y	Y	Y	Y	Y
23 Capps	Y	Y	?	Y	Y	N	N
24 *Gallegly*	N	Y	?	?	?	Y	Y
25 *McKeon*	N	Y	Y	Y	Y	Y	Y
26 *Dreier*	N	Y	Y	Y	Y	?	Y
27 Sherman	Y	Y	Y	Y	Y	N	N
28 Berman	?	+	?	?	?	?	?
29 Schiff	Y	Y	Y	Y	Y	N	N
30 Waxman	?	?	?	?	?	N	N
31 Becerra	Y	Y	?	?	?	N	N
32 Solis	Y	Y	Y	Y	Y	N	N
33 Watson	Y	Y	Y	Y	Y	N	N
34 Roybal-Allard	Y	Y	Y	Y	Y	N	N
35 Waters	Y	Y	Y	Y	Y	N	N
36 Harman	Y	Y	Y	Y	Y	N	N
37 Millender-McD.	Y	Y	Y	Y	Y	N	N
38 Napolitano	Y	Y	Y	Y	Y	N	N
39 Sánchez, Linda	Y	N	Y	Y	Y	N	N
40 *Royce*	N	Y	?	?	?	Y	Y
41 *Lewis*	N	Y	Y	Y	Y	Y	Y
42 *Miller, Gary*	N	Y	Y	Y	Y	Y	Y
43 Baca	Y	Y	Y	Y	Y	N	N
44 *Calvert*	N	Y	Y	Y	Y	Y	Y
45 *Bono*	N	Y	Y	Y	Y	Y	Y
46 *Rohrabacher*	N	Y	Y	Y	Y	Y	Y
47 Sanchez, Loretta	Y	Y	Y	Y	Y	N	N
48 *Cox*	N	Y	Y	Y	Y	Y	Y
49 *Issa*	N	Y	Y	Y	Y	Y	Y
50 *Cunningham*	N	Y	Y	Y	Y	Y	Y
51 Filner	Y	Y	Y	Y	Y	N	N
52 *Hunter*	N	Y	Y	Y	Y	N	N
53 Davis	Y	Y	Y	Y	Y	N	N
COLORADO							
1 DeGette	Y	Y	Y	Y	Y	N	N
2 Udall	Y	Y	Y	Y	Y	N	N
3 *McInnis*	N	Y	?	?	?	?	?
4 *Musgrave*	N	Y	Y	Y	Y	Y	Y
5 *Hefley*	N	Y	Y	Y	Y	Y	Y
6 *Tancredo*	N	Y	Y	Y	Y	Y	Y
7 *Beauprez*	N	Y	Y	Y	Y	Y	Y
CONNECTICUT							
1 Larson	Y	Y	Y	Y	Y	N	N
2 *Simmons*	N	Y	Y	Y	Y	Y	Y
3 DeLauro	Y	Y	Y	Y	Y	N	N
4 *Shays*	N	Y	?	?	?	Y	Y
5 *Johnson*	N	Y	Y	Y	Y	Y	Y
DELAWARE							
AL *Castle*	N	Y	Y	Y	Y	Y	Y
FLORIDA							
1 *Miller, J.*	N	Y	?	?	?	Y	Y
2 Boyd	Y	Y	?	?	?	N	N
3 Brown	Y	Y	Y	Y	Y	N	N
4 *Crenshaw*	N	Y	Y	Y	Y	Y	Y
5 *Brown-Waite*	N	Y	Y	Y	Y	Y	Y
6 *Stearns*	N	Y	Y	Y	Y	Y	Y
7 *Mica*	N	Y	Y	Y	Y	Y	Y
8 *Keller*	N	Y	Y	Y	Y	Y	Y
9 *Bilirakis*	N	Y	Y	Y	Y	Y	Y
10 *Young*	N	Y	Y	Y	Y	Y	Y
11 Davis	Y	Y	Y	Y	Y	N	N
12 *Putnam*	N	Y	?	?	Y	Y	Y
13 *Harris*	N	Y	Y	Y	Y	Y	Y
14 *Goss*	N	Y	Y	Y	Y	Y	Y
15 *Weldon*	N	Y	Y	Y	Y	Y	Y
16 *Foley*	N	Y	Y	Y	Y	Y	Y
17 Meek	Y	Y	Y	Y	Y	N	N
18 *Ros-Lehtinen*	Y	Y	?	?	?	Y	Y
19 Wexler	Y	Y	?	?	?	N	N
20 Deutsch	Y	Y	?	?	?	?	?
21 *Diaz-Balart, L.*	N	Y	Y	Y	Y	Y	Y
22 *Shaw*	N	Y	Y	Y	Y	Y	Y
23 Hastings	?	?	?	?	?	?	?
24 *Feeney*	N	Y	Y	Y	Y	Y	Y
25 *Diaz-Balart, M.*	N	Y	Y	Y	Y	Y	Y
GEORGIA							
1 *Kingston*	N	Y	Y	Y	Y	Y	Y
2 Bishop	Y	Y	Y	Y	Y	N	N
3 Marshall	Y	Y	Y	Y	Y	N	N
4 Majette	Y	Y	?	?	Y	N	N
5 Lewis	Y	Y	Y	Y	Y	N	N
6 *Isakson*	?	?	?	?	?	Y	Y
7 *Linder*	N	Y	Y	Y	Y	Y	Y
8 *Collins*	−	+	+	+	+	+	+
9 *Norwood*	N	Y	Y	Y	Y	Y	Y
10 *Deal*	N	Y	Y	Y	Y	Y	Y
11 *Gingrey*	N	Y	Y	Y	Y	Y	Y
12 *Burns*	N	Y	Y	Y	Y	Y	Y
13 Scott	Y	Y	Y	Y	Y	N	N
HAWAII							
1 Abercrombie	Y	Y	Y	Y	Y	N	N
2 Case	Y	Y	Y	Y	Y	N	N
IDAHO							
1 *Otter*	N	Y	Y	Y	Y	Y	Y
2 *Simpson*	N	Y	Y	Y	Y	Y	Y
ILLINOIS							
1 Rush	Y	Y	?	?	?	N	N
2 Jackson	Y	Y	Y	Y	Y	N	N
3 Lipinski	?	?	?	?	Y	N	N
4 Gutierrez	+	+	?	?	?	N	N
5 Emanuel	?	?	?	?	Y	N	N
6 *Hyde*	N	Y	Y	Y	Y	Y	Y

ND Northern Democrats   SD Southern Democrats

	274	275	276	277	278	279	280
7 Davis	Y	Y	Y	Y	Y	N	N
8 ***Crane***	N	Y	Y	Y	Y	Y	Y
9 Schakowsky	?	?	?	Y	Y	N	N
10 ***Kirk***	N	Y	Y	Y	Y	Y	Y
11 ***Weller***	N	Y	+	Y	Y	Y	Y
12 Costello	Y	Y	Y	Y	Y	N	N
13 ***Biggert***	N	Y	Y	Y	Y	Y	Y
14 ***Hastert***		Y					
15 ***Johnson***	N	Y	Y	Y	Y	Y	Y
16 ***Manzullo***	Y	Y	Y	Y	Y	Y	Y
17 Evans	Y	Y	Y	Y	Y	N	N
18 ***LaHood***	Y	Y	Y	Y	Y	Y	Y
19 ***Shimkus***	N	Y	Y	Y	Y	Y	Y
INDIANA							
1 Visclosky	Y	Y	Y	Y	Y	N	N
2 ***Chocola***	N	Y	Y	Y	Y	Y	Y
3 ***Souder***	N	Y	Y	Y	Y	Y	Y
4 ***Buyer***	N	Y	Y	Y	Y	Y	Y
5 ***Burton***	N	Y	Y	Y	Y	Y	Y
6 ***Pence***	N	Y	Y	Y	Y	Y	Y
7 Carson	Y	Y	?	?	?	?	?
8 ***Hostettler***	N	Y	Y	Y	Y	Y	Y
9 Hill	Y	Y	Y	Y	Y	N	N
IOWA							
1 ***Nussle***	N	Y	Y	Y	Y	Y	Y
2 ***Leach***	N	Y	Y	Y	Y	Y	Y
3 Boswell	Y	Y	Y	Y	Y	N	N
4 ***Latham***	N	Y	Y	Y	Y	Y	Y
5 ***King***	N	Y	Y	Y	Y	Y	Y
KANSAS							
1 ***Moran***	N	Y	Y	Y	Y	Y	Y
2 ***Ryun***	N	Y	Y	Y	Y	Y	Y
3 Moore	Y	Y	Y	Y	Y	N	N
4 ***Tiahrt***	N	Y	Y	Y	Y	Y	Y
KENTUCKY							
1 ***Whitfield***	N	Y	Y	Y	Y	Y	Y
2 ***Lewis***	N	Y	Y	Y	Y	Y	Y
3 ***Northup***	N	Y	Y	Y	Y	Y	Y
4 Lucas	Y	Y	Y	Y	Y	N	N
5 ***Rogers***	N	Y	Y	Y	Y	Y	Y
6 Chandler	Y	Y	Y	Y	Y	N	N
LOUISIANA							
1 ***Vitter***	N	Y	?	?	?	Y	Y
2 Jefferson	Y	Y	Y	Y	Y	N	N
3 ***Tauzin***	N	Y	?	?	?	?	?
4 ***McCrery***	N	Y	Y	Y	Y	Y	Y
5 Alexander	Y	Y	Y	Y	Y	N	N
6 ***Baker***	?	?	?	?	?	Y	Y
7 John	?	?	?	?	?	N	N
MAINE							
1 Allen	Y	Y	Y	Y	Y	N	N
2 Michaud	Y	Y	Y	Y	Y	N	N
MARYLAND							
1 ***Gilchrest***	N	Y	Y	Y	Y	Y	Y
2 Ruppersberger	Y	Y	Y	Y	Y	N	N
3 Cardin	Y	Y	Y	Y	Y	N	N
4 Wynn	Y	Y	Y	Y	?	N	N
5 Hoyer	Y	Y	Y	Y	Y	N	N
6 ***Bartlett***	N	Y	Y	Y	Y	Y	N
7 Cummings	Y	Y	?	Y	Y	N	N
8 Van Hollen	Y	Y	Y	Y	Y	N	N
MASSACHUSETTS							
1 Olver	Y	Y	Y	Y	Y	N	N
2 Neal	Y	Y	Y	Y	Y	N	N
3 McGovern	Y	Y	?	?	?	N	N
4 Frank	Y	Y	Y	Y	Y	N	N
5 Meehan	Y	Y	?	?	?	N	N
6 Tierney	?	?	Y	Y	Y	N	N
7 Markey	Y	Y	Y	Y	Y	N	N
8 Capuano	Y	N	Y	Y	Y	N	N
9 Lynch	Y	Y	Y	Y	Y	N	N
10 Delahunt	Y	Y	Y	Y	Y	N	N
MICHIGAN							
1 Stupak	Y	Y	Y	Y	Y	N	N
2 ***Hoekstra***	Y	Y	?	?	?	Y	Y
3 ***Ehlers***	N	Y	Y	Y	Y	Y	Y
4 ***Camp***	N	Y	Y	Y	Y	Y	Y
5 Kildee	Y	Y	Y	Y	Y	N	N
6 ***Upton***	N	Y	Y	Y	Y	Y	Y
7 ***Smith***	N	Y	Y	Y	Y	Y	Y
8 ***Rogers***	N	Y	?	?	?	Y	Y
9 ***Knollenberg***	N	Y	Y	Y	Y	Y	Y
10 ***Miller***	N	Y	Y	Y	Y	Y	Y
11 ***McCotter***	Y	Y	Y	Y	Y	Y	Y
12 Levin	Y	Y	Y	Y	Y	N	N
13 Kilpatrick	Y	Y	Y	Y	Y	N	N
14 Conyers	Y	Y	Y	Y	Y	N	N
15 Dingell	Y	Y	Y	Y	Y	N	N
MINNESOTA							
1 ***Gutknecht***	N	Y	Y	Y	Y	Y	Y
2 ***Kline***	N	Y	Y	Y	Y	Y	Y
3 ***Ramstad***	N	Y	Y	Y	Y	Y	Y
4 McCollum	Y	Y	Y	Y	Y	N	N
5 Sabo	Y	Y	Y	Y	Y	N	N
6 ***Kennedy***	N	Y	Y	Y	Y	Y	Y
7 Peterson	Y	Y	Y	Y	Y	N	N
8 Oberstar	Y	Y	Y	Y	Y	N	N
MISSISSIPPI							
1 ***Wicker***	N	Y	Y	Y	Y	Y	Y
2 Thompson	Y	Y	Y	Y	Y	N	N
3 ***Pickering***	N	Y	Y	Y	Y	Y	Y
4 Taylor	Y	Y	Y	Y	Y	N	N
MISSOURI							
1 Clay	Y	Y	Y	Y	Y	N	N
2 ***Akin***	N	Y	Y	Y	Y	Y	Y
3 Gephardt	Y	?	?	?	?	?	?
4 Skelton	Y	Y	Y	Y	Y	N	N
5 McCarthy	Y	Y	Y	Y	Y	N	N
6 ***Graves***	N	Y	Y	Y	Y	Y	Y
7 ***Blunt***	N	Y	Y	Y	Y	Y	Y
8 ***Emerson***	N	Y	Y	Y	Y	Y	Y
9 ***Hulshof***	N	Y	?	?	?	Y	Y
MONTANA							
AL ***Rehberg***	N	Y	Y	Y	Y	Y	Y
NEBRASKA							
1 ***Bereuter***	?	?	?	?	?	?	?
2 ***Terry***	N	Y	Y	Y	Y	Y	Y
3 ***Osborne***	N	Y	Y	Y	Y	Y	Y
NEVADA							
1 Berkley	Y	Y	Y	Y	Y	N	N
2 ***Gibbons***	?	?	Y	Y	Y	Y	Y
3 ***Porter***	N	Y	?	?	?	Y	Y
NEW HAMPSHIRE							
1 ***Bradley***	N	Y	Y	Y	Y	Y	Y
2 ***Bass***	N	Y	Y	Y	Y	Y	Y
NEW JERSEY							
1 Andrews	Y	Y	Y	Y	Y	N	N
2 ***LoBiondo***	N	Y	Y	Y	Y	Y	Y
3 ***Saxton***	N	Y	Y	Y	Y	Y	Y
4 ***Smith***	N	Y	Y	Y	Y	Y	Y
5 ***Garrett***	N	Y	Y	Y	Y	Y	Y
6 Pallone	Y	Y	Y	Y	Y	N	N
7 ***Ferguson***	N	Y	Y	Y	Y	Y	Y
8 Pascrell	Y	Y	Y	Y	Y	N	N
9 Rothman	Y	Y	Y	Y	Y	N	N
10 Payne	Y	Y	Y	Y	Y	N	N
11 ***Frelinghuysen***	N	Y	Y	Y	Y	Y	Y
12 Holt	Y	Y	Y	Y	Y	N	N
13 Menendez	?	?	?	?	?	N	N
NEW MEXICO							
1 ***Wilson***	N	Y	Y	Y	Y	Y	Y
2 ***Pearce***	N	Y	Y	Y	Y	Y	Y
3 Udall	Y	Y	Y	Y	Y	N	N
NEW YORK							
1 Bishop	Y	Y	Y	Y	Y	N	N
2 Israel	Y	Y	Y	Y	Y	N	N
3 ***King***	Y	Y	Y	Y	Y	Y	Y
4 McCarthy	Y	Y	Y	Y	Y	N	N
5 Ackerman	Y	Y	Y	Y	Y	N	N
6 Meeks	Y	Y	?	?	?	N	N
7 Crowley	Y	Y	Y	Y	Y	N	N
8 Nadler	Y	Y	Y	Y	Y	N	N
9 Weiner	Y	Y	?	?	?	N	N
10 Towns	Y	Y	Y	Y	Y	N	N
11 Owens	Y	Y	?	?	?	N	N
12 Velázquez	Y	Y	Y	Y	Y	N	N
13 ***Fossella***	N	Y	Y	Y	Y	Y	Y
14 Maloney	Y	?	Y	Y	Y	N	N
15 Rangel	Y	Y	Y	Y	Y	?	?
16 Serrano	Y	Y	Y	Y	Y	N	N
17 Engel	Y	Y	?	?	?	N	N
18 Lowey	Y	Y	Y	Y	Y	N	N
19 ***Kelly***	N	Y	Y	Y	Y	Y	Y
20 ***Sweeney***	Y	Y	?	?	?	Y	Y
21 McNulty	Y	Y	Y	Y	Y	N	N
22 Hinchey	Y	Y	Y	Y	Y	N	N
23 ***McHugh***	Y	Y	Y	Y	Y	Y	Y
24 ***Boehlert***	?	?	Y	Y	Y	Y	Y
25 ***Walsh***	N	Y	Y	Y	Y	Y	Y
26 ***Reynolds***	N	Y	Y	Y	Y	Y	Y
27 ***Quinn***	?	?	Y	Y	Y	Y	Y
28 Slaughter	Y	Y	Y	Y	Y	N	N
29 ***Houghton***	N	Y	Y	Y	Y	Y	Y
NORTH CAROLINA							
1 Vacant							
2 Etheridge	Y	Y	Y	Y	Y	N	N
3 ***Jones***	N	Y	Y	Y	Y	Y	Y
4 Price	Y	Y	Y	Y	Y	N	N
5 ***Burr***	N	Y	?	?	?	Y	Y
6 ***Coble***	N	Y	Y	Y	Y	Y	Y
7 McIntyre	Y	Y	Y	Y	Y	N	N
8 ***Hayes***	N	Y	Y	Y	Y	Y	Y
9 ***Myrick***	N	Y	Y	Y	Y	Y	Y
10 ***Ballenger***	?	?	?	?	?	Y	Y
11 ***Taylor***	N	Y	?	?	?	Y	Y
12 Watt	Y	Y	Y	Y	Y	N	N
13 Miller	Y	Y	Y	Y	Y	N	N
NORTH DAKOTA							
AL Pomeroy	Y	Y	Y	Y	Y	N	N
OHIO							
1 ***Chabot***	N	Y	?	?	?	Y	Y
2 ***Portman***	N	Y	?	?	?	Y	Y
3 ***Turner***	N	Y	+	+	+	Y	Y
4 ***Oxley***	N	Y	Y	Y	Y	Y	Y
5 ***Gillmor***	N	Y	Y	Y	Y	Y	Y
6 Strickland	Y	Y	Y	Y	Y	N	N
7 ***Hobson***	N	Y	Y	Y	Y	Y	Y
8 ***Boehner***	?	?	Y	Y	Y	Y	Y
9 Kaptur	Y	Y	Y	Y	Y	N	N
10 Kucinich	Y	Y	Y	Y	Y	N	N
11 Jones	Y	Y	Y	Y	Y	?	N
12 ***Tiberi***	N	Y	Y	Y	Y	Y	Y
13 Brown	Y	Y	Y	Y	Y	N	N
14 ***LaTourette***	N	Y	Y	Y	Y	Y	Y
15 ***Pryce***	N	Y	Y	Y	Y	Y	Y
16 ***Regula***	N	Y	Y	Y	Y	Y	Y
17 Ryan	Y	Y	Y	Y	Y	N	N
18 ***Ney***	N	Y	Y	Y	Y	Y	Y
OKLAHOMA							
1 ***Sullivan***	N	Y	Y	Y	Y	Y	Y
2 Carson	Y	Y	?	?	?	N	N
3 ***Lucas***	N	Y	Y	Y	Y	Y	Y
4 ***Cole***	N	Y	Y	Y	Y	Y	Y
5 ***Istook***	N	Y	Y	Y	Y	Y	Y
OREGON							
1 Wu	Y	Y	Y	Y	Y	N	N
2 ***Walden***	N	Y	Y	Y	Y	Y	Y
3 Blumenauer	Y	Y	Y	Y	Y	N	N
4 DeFazio	Y	Y	Y	Y	Y	N	N
5 Hooley	Y	Y	Y	Y	Y	N	N
PENNSYLVANIA							
1 Brady	Y	Y	Y	Y	Y	N	N
2 Fattah	Y	Y	Y	Y	Y	N	N
3 ***English***	N	Y	Y	Y	Y	Y	Y
4 ***Hart***	N	Y	Y	Y	Y	Y	Y
5 ***Peterson***	N	Y	?	?	?	Y	Y
6 ***Gerlach***	?	?	Y	Y	Y	Y	Y
7 ***Weldon***	N	Y	Y	Y	Y	Y	Y
8 ***Greenwood***	N	Y	Y	Y	Y	Y	Y
9 ***Shuster, Bill***	N	Y	Y	Y	Y	Y	Y
10 ***Sherwood***	N	Y	Y	Y	Y	Y	Y
11 Kanjorski	Y	Y	Y	Y	Y	N	N
12 Murtha	Y	Y	?	?	?	N	Y
13 Hoeffel	Y	Y	Y	Y	Y	N	N
14 Doyle	Y	Y	Y	Y	Y	N	N
15 ***Toomey***	N	Y	?	?	?	Y	Y
16 ***Pitts***	N	Y	Y	Y	Y	Y	Y
17 Holden	Y	Y	Y	Y	Y	N	N
18 ***Murphy***	N	Y	Y	Y	Y	Y	Y
19 ***Platts***	N	Y	Y	Y	Y	Y	Y
RHODE ISLAND							
1 Kennedy	Y	Y	+	+	Y	N	N
2 Langevin	Y	Y	Y	Y	Y	N	N
SOUTH CAROLINA							
1 ***Brown***	N	Y	Y	Y	Y	Y	Y
2 ***Wilson***	N	Y	?	?	?	Y	Y
3 ***Barrett***	N	Y	Y	Y	Y	Y	Y
4 ***DeMint***	?	?	?	?	?	?	?
5 Spratt	Y	Y	Y	Y	Y	N	N
6 Clyburn	Y	Y	Y	Y	Y	N	N
SOUTH DAKOTA							
AL Herseth	Y	Y	Y	Y	Y	N	N
TENNESSEE							
1 ***Jenkins***	N	Y	?	?	?	Y	Y
2 ***Duncan***	N	Y	Y	Y	Y	Y	Y
3 ***Wamp***	N	Y	?	?	?	Y	Y
4 Davis	Y	Y	Y	Y	Y	N	N
5 Cooper	Y	Y	Y	Y	Y	N	N
6 Gordon	Y	Y	Y	Y	Y	N	N
7 ***Blackburn***	N	Y	Y	Y	Y	Y	Y
8 Tanner	Y	Y	Y	Y	Y	N	N
9 Ford	Y	Y	Y	Y	?	N	N
TEXAS							
1 Sandlin	Y	Y	Y	Y	Y	N	N
2 Turner	Y	Y	Y	Y	Y	N	N
3 ***Johnson, Sam***	N	Y	Y	Y	Y	Y	Y
4 ***Hall***	N	Y	Y	Y	Y	Y	Y
5 ***Hensarling***	N	Y	Y	Y	Y	Y	Y
6 ***Barton***	N	Y	Y	Y	Y	Y	Y
7 ***Culberson***	N	Y	Y	Y	Y	Y	Y
8 ***Brady***	N	Y	Y	Y	Y	Y	Y
9 Lampson	Y	Y	Y	Y	Y	N	N
10 Doggett	Y	Y	?	?	?	N	N
11 Edwards	Y	Y	Y	Y	Y	N	N
12 ***Granger***	N	Y	Y	Y	Y	Y	Y
13 ***Thornberry***	N	Y	Y	Y	Y	Y	Y
14 ***Paul***	N	N	Y	Y	Y	Y	Y
15 Hinojosa	Y	Y	?	?	?	N	N
16 Reyes	?	?	?	?	?	?	?
17 Stenholm	Y	Y	Y	Y	Y	N	N
18 Jackson-Lee	Y	Y	Y	Y	Y	N	N
19 ***Neugebauer***	N	Y	Y	Y	Y	Y	Y
20 Gonzalez	Y	Y	Y	Y	Y	N	N
21 ***Smith***	N	Y	Y	Y	Y	Y	Y
22 ***DeLay***	N	Y	Y	Y	Y	Y	Y
23 ***Bonilla***	N	Y	Y	Y	Y	Y	Y
24 Frost	Y	Y	?	?	?	N	N
25 Bell	Y	Y	Y	Y	Y	N	N
26 ***Burgess***	N	Y	Y	Y	Y	Y	Y
27 Ortiz	Y	Y	Y	Y	Y	N	N
28 Rodriguez	Y	Y	Y	Y	Y	N	N
29 Green	Y	Y	Y	Y	Y	N	?
30 Johnson, E.B.	Y	Y	Y	Y	Y	N	N
31 ***Carter***	N	Y	Y	Y	?	Y	Y
32 ***Sessions***	N	Y	Y	Y	Y	Y	Y
UTAH							
1 ***Bishop***	Y	Y	Y	Y	Y	Y	Y
2 Matheson	Y	Y	Y	Y	Y	N	N
3 ***Cannon***	N	Y	Y	Y	Y	Y	Y
VERMONT							
AL *Sanders*	Y	Y	?	?	?	N	N
VIRGINIA							
1 ***Davis, Jo Ann***	N	Y	Y	Y	Y	Y	Y
2 ***Schrock***	N	Y	Y	Y	Y	?	?
3 Scott	Y	Y	Y	Y	Y	N	N
4 ***Forbes***	N	Y	Y	Y	Y	Y	Y
5 ***Goode***	N	Y	Y	Y	Y	Y	Y
6 ***Goodlatte***	N	Y	Y	Y	Y	Y	Y
7 ***Cantor***	N	Y	Y	Y	Y	Y	Y
8 Moran	Y	Y	Y	Y	Y	N	N
9 Boucher	Y	Y	Y	Y	Y	N	N
10 ***Wolf***	N	Y	Y	Y	Y	Y	Y
11 ***Davis, T.***	N	Y	Y	Y	Y	Y	Y
WASHINGTON							
1 Inslee	Y	Y	Y	Y	Y	N	N
2 Larsen	Y	Y	Y	Y	Y	N	N
3 Baird	?	?	Y	Y	Y	N	N
4 ***Hastings***	N	Y	Y	Y	Y	Y	Y
5 ***Nethercutt***	N	Y	Y	Y	Y	Y	Y
6 Dicks	Y	Y	Y	Y	Y	N	N
7 McDermott	Y	Y	Y	Y	Y	N	N
8 ***Dunn***	N	Y	Y	Y	Y	Y	Y
9 Smith	?	?	Y	Y	Y	N	N
WEST VIRGINIA							
1 Mollohan	Y	Y	Y	Y	Y	?	?
2 ***Capito***	N	Y	Y	Y	Y	Y	Y
3 Rahall	Y	Y	Y	Y	Y	N	N
WISCONSIN							
1 ***Ryan***	N	Y	Y	Y	Y	Y	Y
2 Baldwin	Y	Y	Y	Y	Y	N	N
3 Kind	Y	Y	Y	Y	Y	N	N
4 Kleczka	Y	Y	Y	Y	Y	N	N
5 ***Sensenbrenner***	N	Y	Y	Y	Y	Y	Y
6 ***Petri***	N	Y	Y	Y	Y	Y	Y
7 Obey	Y	Y	Y	Y	Y	N	N
8 ***Green***	N	Y	Y	Y	Y	Y	Y
WYOMING							
AL ***Cubin***	N	Y	Y	Y	Y	Y	Y

Southern states - Ala., Ark., Fla., Ga., Ky., La., Miss., N.C., Okla., S.C., Tenn., Texas, Va.

Key

Y	Voted for (yea).
#	Paired for.
+	Announced for.
N	Voted against (nay).
X	Paired against.
–	Announced against.
P	Voted "present."
C	Voted "present" to avoid possible conflict of interest.
?	Did not vote or otherwise make a position known.

Democrats **Republicans**
Independents

---

281. H Con Res 449. Ray Charles Tribute/Adoption. Burns, R-Ga., motion to suspend the rules and adopt the concurrent resolution that would honor the life and accomplishments of musician Ray Charles, who died June 10, 2004. Motion agreed to 419-0: R 221-0; D 197-0 (ND 145-0, SD 52-0); I 1-0. A two-thirds majority of those present and voting (280 in this case) is required for adoption under suspension of the rules. June 22, 2004.

282. H Con Res 13. Blues Music Recognition/Adoption. Burns, R-Ga., motion to suspend the rules and adopt the concurrent resolution that would recognize the importance of blues music to the nation's cultural development and request that the president issue a proclamation to observe its importance. Motion agreed to 410-0: R 213-0; D 196-0 (ND 145-0, SD 51-0); I 1-0. A two-thirds majority of those present and voting (274 in this case) is required for adoption under suspension of the rules. June 22, 2004.

283. HR 4613. Fiscal 2005 Defense Appropriations/Civilian Worker Regulations. Inslee, D-Wash., amendment that would prohibit funds from being used to suspend or modify regulations that protect civilian Defense Department employees' collective bargaining and due process rights. Rejected 202-218: R 5-217; D 196-1 (ND 144-1, SD 52-0); I 1-0. June 22, 2004.

284. HR 4613. Fiscal 2005 Defense Appropriations/Passage. Passage of the bill that would appropriate $417 billion for defense programs for fiscal 2005, including $25 billion in emergency funding for operations in Iraq and Afghanistan. The total includes $120.6 billion for operations and maintenance, $77.4 billion for procurement and $9.7 billion for ballistic missile defense programs. It also would appropriate $104.2 billion for personnel, including $200 million to fund an additional 13,000 active duty Army and Marine Corps personnel. Passed 403-17: R 221-1; D 181-16 (ND 132-13, SD 49-3); I 1-0. June 22, 2004.

285. H Res 658. National Homeownership Month/Adoption. Miller, R-Calif., motion to suspend the rules and adopt the resolution that would recognize National Homeownership Month and the importance of homeownership in the United States. Motion agreed to 415-2: R 219-2; D 195-0 (ND 143-0, SD 52-0); I 1-0. A two-thirds majority of those present and voting (278 in this case) is required for adoption under suspension of the rules. June 22, 2004.

286. HR 4548. Fiscal 2005 Intelligence Authorization/Previous Question. Myrick, R-N.C., motion to order the previous question (thus ending debate and possibility of amendment) on adoption of the rule (H Res 686) to provide for House floor consideration of the bill that would authorize classified amounts in fiscal 2005 for U.S. intelligence activities and agencies. Motion agreed to 222-200: R 222-0; D 0-199 (ND 0-145, SD 0-54); I 0-1. June 23, 2004.

287. HR 4548. Fiscal 2005 Intelligence Authorization/Rule. Adoption of the rule (H Res 686) to provide for House floor consideration of the bill that would authorize classified amounts in fiscal 2005 for U.S. intelligence activities and agencies. Adopted 220-200: R 220-0; D 0-199 (ND 0-145, SD 0-54); I 0-1. June 23, 2004.

	281	282	283	284	285	286	287
ALABAMA							
1 *Bonner*	Y	Y	N	Y	Y	Y	Y
2 *Everett*	Y	Y	N	Y	Y	Y	Y
3 *Rogers*	Y	Y	N	Y	Y	Y	Y
4 *Aderholt*	Y	Y	N	Y	Y	Y	Y
5 Cramer	Y	Y	Y	Y	Y	N	N
6 *Bachus*	Y	Y	N	Y	Y	Y	Y
7 Davis	Y	Y	Y	Y	Y	N	N
ALASKA							
AL *Young*	Y	Y	N	Y	Y	Y	Y
ARIZONA							
1 *Renzi*	Y	Y	N	Y	Y	Y	Y
2 *Franks*	Y	Y	N	Y	Y	Y	Y
3 *Shadegg*	Y	Y	N	Y	Y	Y	Y
4 Pastor	Y	Y	Y	Y	Y	N	N
5 *Hayworth*	Y	Y	N	Y	Y	Y	Y
6 *Flake*	Y	Y	N	Y	N	Y	Y
7 Grijalva	Y	Y	Y	Y	Y	N	N
8 *Kolbe*	Y	Y	N	Y	Y	Y	Y
ARKANSAS							
1 Berry	Y	Y	Y	Y	Y	N	N
2 Snyder	Y	Y	Y	Y	Y	N	N
3 *Boozman*	Y	Y	N	Y	Y	Y	Y
4 Ross	Y	Y	Y	Y	Y	N	N
CALIFORNIA							
1 Thompson	Y	Y	Y	Y	Y	N	N
2 *Herger*	Y	Y	N	Y	Y	Y	Y
3 *Ose*	Y	Y	N	Y	Y	Y	Y
4 *Doolittle*	Y	Y	N	Y	Y	Y	Y
5 Matsui	Y	Y	Y	Y	Y	N	N
6 Woolsey	Y	Y	Y	N	Y	N	N
7 Miller, George	Y	Y	Y	Y	Y	N	N
8 Pelosi	Y	Y	Y	Y	Y	N	N
9 Lee	Y	Y	Y	N	Y	N	N
10 Tauscher	Y	Y	Y	Y	Y	N	N
11 *Pombo*	Y	Y	N	Y	Y	Y	Y
12 Lantos	Y	Y	Y	Y	?	N	N
13 Stark	Y	Y	Y	N	?	N	N
14 Eshoo	Y	Y	Y	Y	Y	N	N
15 Honda	Y	Y	Y	Y	Y	N	N
16 Lofgren	Y	Y	Y	Y	Y	N	N
17 Farr	Y	Y	Y	Y	Y	N	N
18 Cardoza	Y	Y	Y	Y	Y	N	N
19 *Radanovich*	Y	Y	N	Y	Y	Y	Y
20 Dooley	Y	Y	Y	Y	Y	N	N
21 *Nunes*	Y	Y	N	Y	Y	Y	Y
22 *Thomas*	Y	Y	N	Y	Y	Y	Y
23 Capps	Y	Y	Y	Y	Y	N	N
24 *Gallegly*	Y	Y	N	Y	Y	Y	Y
25 *McKeon*	Y	Y	N	Y	Y	Y	Y
26 *Dreier*	Y	Y	N	Y	Y	Y	Y
27 Sherman	Y	Y	Y	Y	Y	N	N
28 Berman	?	?	?	?	?	?	?
29 Schiff	Y	Y	Y	Y	Y	N	N
30 Waxman	Y	Y	Y	Y	Y	N	N
31 Becerra	Y	Y	Y	Y	Y	N	N
32 Solis	Y	Y	Y	Y	Y	N	N
33 Watson	Y	Y	Y	Y	Y	N	N
34 Roybal-Allard	Y	Y	Y	Y	Y	N	N
35 Waters	Y	Y	Y	N	Y	N	N
36 Harman	Y	Y	Y	Y	Y	N	N

	281	282	283	284	285	286	287
37 Millender-McD.	Y	Y	Y	Y	Y	N	N
38 Napolitano	Y	Y	Y	Y	Y	N	N
39 Sánchez, Linda	Y	Y	Y	Y	Y	N	N
40 *Royce*	Y	Y	N	Y	Y	Y	Y
41 *Lewis*	Y	Y	N	Y	Y	Y	Y
42 *Miller, Gary*	Y	Y	N	Y	Y	Y	Y
43 Baca	Y	Y	Y	Y	Y	N	N
44 *Calvert*	Y	Y	N	Y	Y	Y	Y
45 *Bono*	Y	Y	N	Y	Y	Y	Y
46 *Rohrabacher*	Y	Y	N	Y	Y	Y	Y
47 Sanchez, Loretta	Y	Y	Y	Y	Y	N	N
48 *Cox*	Y	Y	N	Y	Y	Y	?
49 *Issa*	Y	Y	N	Y	Y	Y	Y
50 *Cunningham*	Y	Y	N	Y	Y	Y	Y
51 Filner	Y	Y	Y	Y	Y	N	N
52 *Hunter*	Y	?	N	Y	Y	Y	Y
53 Davis	Y	Y	Y	Y	Y	N	N
COLORADO							
1 DeGette	Y	Y	Y	Y	Y	N	N
2 Udall	Y	Y	Y	Y	Y	N	N
3 *McInnis*	?	?	?	?	?	Y	Y
4 *Musgrave*	Y	Y	N	Y	Y	Y	Y
5 *Hefley*	Y	Y	N	Y	Y	Y	Y
6 *Tancredo*	Y	Y	N	Y	Y	Y	Y
7 *Beauprez*	Y	Y	N	Y	Y	Y	Y
CONNECTICUT							
1 Larson	Y	Y	Y	Y	Y	N	N
2 *Simmons*	Y	Y	Y	Y	Y	Y	Y
3 DeLauro	Y	Y	Y	Y	Y	N	N
4 *Shays*	Y	Y	N	Y	Y	Y	Y
5 *Johnson*	Y	Y	N	Y	Y	Y	Y
DELAWARE							
AL *Castle*	Y	Y	N	Y	Y	Y	Y
FLORIDA							
1 *Miller, J.*	Y	Y	N	Y	Y	Y	Y
2 Boyd	Y	Y	Y	Y	Y	N	N
3 Brown	Y	Y	Y	Y	Y	N	N
4 *Crenshaw*	Y	Y	N	Y	Y	Y	Y
5 *Brown-Waite*	Y	Y	N	Y	Y	Y	Y
6 *Stearns*	Y	Y	N	Y	Y	Y	Y
7 *Mica*	Y	Y	N	Y	Y	Y	Y
8 *Keller*	Y	Y	N	Y	Y	Y	Y
9 *Bilirakis*	Y	Y	N	Y	Y	Y	Y
10 *Young*	Y	Y	N	Y	Y	Y	Y
11 Davis	Y	Y	Y	Y	Y	N	N
12 *Putnam*	Y	Y	N	Y	Y	Y	Y
13 *Harris*	Y	Y	N	Y	Y	Y	Y
14 *Goss*	Y	Y	N	Y	Y	Y	Y
15 *Weldon*	Y	Y	N	Y	Y	Y	Y
16 *Foley*	Y	Y	N	Y	Y	Y	Y
17 Meek	Y	Y	Y	Y	Y	N	N
18 *Ros-Lehtinen*	Y	Y	N	Y	Y	Y	Y
19 Wexler	Y	Y	Y	Y	Y	N	N
20 Deutsch	?	?	?	+	+	?	?
21 *Diaz-Balart, L.*	Y	Y	N	Y	Y	Y	Y
22 *Shaw*	Y	Y	N	Y	Y	Y	Y
23 Hastings	?	?	?	?	?	?	?
24 *Feeney*	Y	Y	N	Y	Y	Y	Y
25 *Diaz-Balart, M.*	Y	Y	N	Y	Y	Y	Y
GEORGIA							
1 *Kingston*	Y	Y	N	Y	Y	Y	Y
2 Bishop	Y	Y	Y	Y	Y	N	N
3 Marshall	Y	Y	Y	Y	Y	N	N
4 Majette	Y	Y	Y	Y	Y	N	N
5 Lewis	Y	Y	Y	N	Y	N	N
6 *Isakson*	Y	Y	N	Y	Y	Y	Y
7 *Linder*	Y	Y	N	Y	Y	Y	Y
8 *Collins*	+	+	N	Y	Y	Y	Y
9 *Norwood*	Y	Y	N	Y	Y	Y	Y
10 *Deal*	Y	Y	N	Y	Y	Y	Y
11 *Gingrey*	Y	?	N	Y	Y	Y	Y
12 *Burns*	Y	Y	N	Y	Y	Y	Y
13 Scott	Y	Y	Y	Y	Y	N	N
HAWAII							
1 Abercrombie	Y	Y	Y	Y	Y	N	N
2 Case	Y	Y	Y	Y	Y	N	N
IDAHO							
1 *Otter*	Y	Y	N	Y	Y	Y	Y
2 *Simpson*	Y	Y	N	Y	Y	Y	Y
ILLINOIS							
1 Rush	Y	Y	Y	Y	Y	N	N
2 Jackson	Y	Y	Y	N	Y	N	N
3 Lipinski	Y	Y	Y	Y	Y	N	N
4 Gutierrez	Y	Y	Y	Y	Y	N	N
5 Emanuel	Y	Y	Y	Y	Y	N	N
6 *Hyde*	Y	Y	N	Y	Y	Y	Y

ND Northern Democrats   SD Southern Democrats

	281	282	283	284	285	286	287
7 Davis	Y	Y	Y	Y	Y	N	N
8 ***Crane***	Y	?	N	Y	Y	Y	Y
9 Schakowsky	Y	Y	Y	N	Y	N	N
10 ***Kirk***	Y	Y	N	Y	Y	Y	Y
11 ***Weller***	Y	Y	N	Y	Y	Y	Y
12 Costello	Y	Y	Y	Y	Y	N	N
13 ***Biggert***	Y	Y	N	Y	Y	Y	Y
14 ***Hastert***							
15 ***Johnson***	Y	Y	Y	Y	Y	Y	Y
16 ***Manzullo***	Y	Y	N	Y	Y	Y	Y
17 Evans	Y	Y	Y	Y	Y	N	N
18 ***LaHood***	Y	Y	N	Y	Y	Y	Y
19 ***Shimkus***	Y	Y	N	Y	Y	Y	Y
INDIANA							
1 Visclosky	Y	Y	Y	Y	Y	N	N
2 ***Chocola***	Y	Y	N	Y	Y	Y	Y
3 ***Souder***	Y	Y	N	Y	Y	Y	Y
4 ***Buyer***	Y	Y	N	Y	Y	Y	?
5 ***Burton***	Y	Y	N	Y	Y	Y	Y
6 ***Pence***	Y	Y	N	Y	Y	Y	Y
7 Carson	?	?	?	?	?	?	?
8 ***Hostettler***	Y	Y	N	Y	Y	Y	Y
9 Hill	Y	Y	Y	Y	Y	N	N
IOWA							
1 ***Nussle***	Y	Y	N	Y	Y	Y	Y
2 ***Leach***	Y	Y	N	Y	Y	Y	Y
3 Boswell	Y	Y	Y	Y	Y	N	N
4 ***Latham***	Y	Y	N	Y	Y	Y	Y
5 ***King***	Y	Y	N	Y	Y	Y	Y
KANSAS							
1 ***Moran***	Y	Y	N	Y	Y	Y	Y
2 ***Ryun***	Y	Y	N	Y	Y	Y	Y
3 Moore	Y	Y	Y	Y	Y	N	N
4 ***Tiahrt***	Y	Y	N	Y	Y	Y	Y
KENTUCKY							
1 ***Whitfield***	Y	Y	?	?	?	Y	Y
2 ***Lewis***	Y	Y	N	Y	Y	Y	Y
3 ***Northup***	Y	Y	N	Y	Y	Y	Y
4 Lucas	Y	Y	Y	Y	Y	N	N
5 ***Rogers***	Y	Y	N	Y	Y	Y	Y
6 Chandler	Y	Y	Y	Y	Y	N	N
LOUISIANA							
1 ***Vitter***	Y	Y	N	Y	Y	Y	Y
2 Jefferson	Y	Y	Y	Y	Y	N	N
3 ***Tauzin***	?	?	?	?	?	?	?
4 ***McCrery***	Y	Y	N	Y	Y	Y	Y
5 Alexander	Y	Y	Y	Y	Y	N	N
6 ***Baker***	Y	Y	N	Y	Y	Y	Y
7 John	Y	Y	Y	Y	Y	N	N
MAINE							
1 Allen	Y	Y	Y	Y	Y	N	N
2 Michaud	Y	Y	Y	Y	Y	N	N
MARYLAND							
1 ***Gilchrest***	Y	Y	N	Y	Y	Y	Y
2 Ruppersberger	Y	Y	Y	Y	Y	N	N
3 Cardin	Y	Y	Y	Y	Y	N	N
4 Wynn	Y	Y	Y	Y	Y	N	N
5 Hoyer	Y	Y	Y	Y	Y	N	N
6 ***Bartlett***	Y	Y	N	Y	Y	Y	Y
7 Cummings	Y	Y	Y	Y	Y	N	N
8 Van Hollen	Y	Y	Y	Y	Y	N	N
MASSACHUSETTS							
1 Olver	Y	Y	Y	Y	Y	N	N
2 Neal	Y	Y	Y	Y	Y	N	N
3 McGovern	Y	Y	Y	Y	Y	N	N
4 Frank	Y	Y	Y	Y	Y	N	N
5 Meehan	Y	Y	Y	Y	Y	N	N
6 Tierney	Y	Y	Y	Y	Y	N	N
7 Markey	Y	Y	Y	Y	Y	N	N
8 Capuano	Y	Y	Y	Y	Y	N	N
9 Lynch	Y	Y	Y	Y	Y	N	N
10 Delahunt	Y	Y	Y	Y	Y	N	N
MICHIGAN							
1 Stupak	Y	Y	Y	Y	Y	N	N
2 ***Hoekstra***	Y	Y	N	Y	Y	Y	Y
3 ***Ehlers***	Y	Y	N	Y	Y	Y	Y
4 ***Camp***	Y	Y	N	Y	Y	Y	Y
5 Kildee	Y	Y	Y	Y	Y	N	N
6 ***Upton***	Y	Y	N	Y	Y	Y	Y
7 ***Smith***	Y	Y	N	Y	Y	Y	Y
8 ***Rogers***	Y	Y	N	Y	Y	Y	Y
9 ***Knollenberg***	Y	Y	N	Y	Y	Y	Y
10 ***Miller***	Y	Y	N	Y	Y	Y	Y
11 ***McCotter***	Y	Y	N	Y	Y	Y	Y
12 Levin	Y	Y	Y	Y	Y	N	N
13 Kilpatrick	Y	Y	Y	Y	Y	N	N
14 Conyers	Y	Y	Y	N	Y	N	N
15 Dingell	Y	Y	Y	Y	Y	N	N
MINNESOTA							
1 ***Gutknecht***	Y	Y	N	Y	Y	Y	Y
2 ***Kline***	Y	Y	N	Y	Y	Y	Y
3 ***Ramstad***	Y	Y	N	Y	Y	Y	Y
4 McCollum	Y	Y	Y	Y	Y	N	N
5 Sabo	Y	Y	Y	Y	Y	N	N
6 ***Kennedy***	Y	Y	N	Y	Y	Y	Y
7 Peterson	Y	Y	Y	Y	Y	N	N
8 Oberstar	Y	Y	Y	Y	Y	N	N
MISSISSIPPI							
1 ***Wicker***	Y	Y	N	Y	Y	Y	Y
2 Thompson	Y	Y	Y	Y	Y	N	N
3 ***Pickering***	Y	?	N	Y	Y	Y	Y
4 Taylor	Y	Y	Y	Y	Y	N	N
MISSOURI							
1 Clay	Y	Y	Y	Y	Y	N	N
2 ***Akin***	Y	?	N	Y	Y	Y	Y
3 Gephardt	?	?	?	?	?	?	?
4 Skelton	Y	Y	Y	Y	Y	N	N
5 McCarthy	Y	Y	Y	Y	Y	N	N
6 ***Graves***	Y	Y	N	Y	Y	Y	Y
7 ***Blunt***	Y	?	N	Y	Y	Y	Y
8 ***Emerson***	Y	Y	N	Y	Y	Y	Y
9 ***Hulshof***	Y	Y	N	Y	Y	Y	Y
MONTANA							
AL ***Rehberg***	Y	Y	N	Y	Y	Y	Y
NEBRASKA							
1 ***Bereuter***	?	?	?	?	?	?	?
2 ***Terry***	Y	Y	N	Y	Y	Y	Y
3 ***Osborne***	Y	Y	N	Y	Y	Y	Y
NEVADA							
1 Berkley	Y	Y	Y	Y	Y	N	N
2 ***Gibbons***	Y	Y	N	Y	Y	Y	Y
3 ***Porter***	Y	Y	N	Y	Y	Y	Y
NEW HAMPSHIRE							
1 ***Bradley***	Y	Y	N	Y	Y	Y	Y
2 ***Bass***	Y	Y	N	Y	Y	Y	Y
NEW JERSEY							
1 Andrews	Y	Y	Y	Y	Y	N	N
2 ***LoBiondo***	Y	Y	N	Y	Y	Y	Y
3 ***Saxton***	Y	Y	N	Y	Y	Y	Y
4 ***Smith***	Y	Y	N	Y	Y	Y	Y
5 ***Garrett***	Y	Y	N	Y	Y	Y	Y
6 Pallone	Y	Y	Y	Y	Y	N	N
7 ***Ferguson***	Y	Y	N	Y	Y	Y	Y
8 Pascrell	Y	Y	Y	Y	Y	N	N
9 Rothman	Y	Y	Y	Y	Y	N	N
10 Payne	Y	Y	Y	N	Y	N	N
11 ***Frelinghuysen***	Y	Y	N	Y	Y	Y	Y
12 Holt	Y	Y	Y	Y	Y	N	N
13 Menendez	Y	Y	Y	Y	Y	N	N
NEW MEXICO							
1 ***Wilson***	Y	Y	N	Y	Y	Y	Y
2 ***Pearce***	Y	Y	N	Y	Y	Y	Y
3 Udall	Y	Y	Y	Y	Y	N	N
NEW YORK							
1 Bishop	Y	Y	Y	Y	Y	N	N
2 Israel	Y	Y	Y	Y	Y	?	?
3 ***King***	Y	Y	N	Y	Y	Y	Y
4 McCarthy	Y	Y	Y	Y	Y	N	N
5 Ackerman	Y	Y	Y	Y	Y	N	N
6 Meeks	Y	Y	Y	Y	Y	N	N
7 Crowley	Y	Y	Y	Y	Y	N	N
8 Nadler	Y	Y	Y	Y	Y	N	N
9 Weiner	Y	Y	Y	Y	Y	N	N
10 Towns	Y	Y	Y	Y	Y	N	N
11 Owens	Y	Y	Y	N	Y	N	N
12 Velázquez	Y	Y	Y	Y	Y	N	N
13 ***Fossella***	Y	Y	N	Y	Y	Y	Y
14 Maloney	Y	Y	Y	Y	Y	N	N
15 Rangel	Y	Y	Y	Y	Y	N	N
16 Serrano	Y	Y	Y	Y	Y	N	N
17 Engel	Y	Y	Y	Y	Y	N	N
18 Lowey	Y	Y	Y	Y	Y	N	N
19 ***Kelly***	Y	Y	N	Y	Y	Y	Y
20 ***Sweeney***	Y	Y	N	Y	Y	Y	Y
21 McNulty	Y	Y	Y	Y	Y	N	N
22 Hinchey	Y	Y	Y	Y	Y	N	N
23 ***McHugh***	Y	Y	N	Y	Y	Y	Y
24 ***Boehlert***	Y	Y	N	Y	Y	Y	Y
25 ***Walsh***	Y	Y	N	Y	Y	Y	Y
26 ***Reynolds***	Y	Y	N	Y	Y	Y	Y
27 ***Quinn***	Y	Y	N	Y	Y	Y	Y
28 Slaughter	Y	Y	Y	Y	Y	N	N
29 ***Houghton***	Y	Y	N	Y	Y	Y	Y
NORTH CAROLINA							
1 Vacant							
2 Etheridge	Y	Y	Y	Y	Y	N	N
3 ***Jones***	Y	Y	Y	Y	Y	Y	Y
4 Price	Y	Y	Y	Y	Y	N	N
5 ***Burr***	Y	Y	N	Y	Y	Y	Y
6 ***Coble***	Y	Y	N	Y	Y	Y	Y
7 McIntyre	Y	Y	Y	Y	Y	N	N
8 ***Hayes***	Y	Y	N	Y	Y	Y	Y
9 ***Myrick***	Y	Y	N	Y	?	Y	Y
10 ***Ballenger***	Y	Y	N	Y	Y	Y	Y
11 ***Taylor***	Y	Y	N	Y	Y	Y	Y
12 Watt	Y	Y	Y	N	Y	N	N
13 Miller	Y	Y	Y	Y	Y	N	N
NORTH DAKOTA							
AL Pomeroy	Y	Y	Y	Y	Y	N	N
OHIO							
1 ***Chabot***	Y	Y	N	Y	Y	Y	Y
2 ***Portman***	Y	Y	N	Y	Y	Y	Y
3 ***Turner***	Y	Y	N	Y	Y	Y	Y
4 ***Oxley***	Y	?	N	Y	Y	Y	Y
5 ***Gillmor***	Y	Y	N	Y	Y	Y	Y
6 Strickland	Y	Y	Y	Y	Y	N	N
7 ***Hobson***	Y	Y	N	Y	Y	Y	Y
8 ***Boehner***	Y	Y	N	Y	Y	Y	Y
9 Kaptur	Y	Y	Y	Y	Y	N	N
10 Kucinich	Y	Y	Y	N	Y	N	N
11 Jones	Y	Y	Y	Y	Y	N	N
12 ***Tiberi***	Y	Y	N	Y	Y	Y	Y
13 Brown	Y	Y	Y	Y	Y	N	N
14 ***LaTourette***	Y	Y	N	Y	Y	Y	Y
15 ***Pryce***	Y	Y	N	Y	Y	Y	Y
16 ***Regula***	Y	Y	N	Y	Y	Y	Y
17 Ryan	Y	Y	Y	Y	Y	N	N
18 ***Ney***	Y	Y	N	Y	Y	Y	Y
OKLAHOMA							
1 ***Sullivan***	Y	Y	N	Y	Y	Y	Y
2 Carson	Y	Y	Y	Y	Y	N	N
3 ***Lucas***	Y	Y	N	Y	Y	Y	Y
4 ***Cole***	Y	Y	N	Y	Y	Y	Y
5 ***Istook***	Y	Y	N	Y	Y	Y	Y
OREGON							
1 Wu	Y	Y	Y	Y	Y	N	N
2 ***Walden***	Y	Y	N	Y	Y	Y	Y
3 Blumenauer	Y	Y	Y	Y	Y	N	N
4 DeFazio	Y	Y	Y	Y	Y	N	N
5 Hooley	Y	Y	Y	Y	Y	N	N
PENNSYLVANIA							
1 Brady	Y	Y	Y	Y	Y	N	N
2 Fattah	Y	Y	Y	Y	Y	N	N
3 ***English***	Y	Y	N	Y	Y	Y	Y
4 ***Hart***	Y	Y	N	Y	Y	Y	Y
5 ***Peterson***	Y	Y	N	Y	Y	Y	Y
6 ***Gerlach***	Y	Y	N	Y	Y	Y	Y
7 ***Weldon***	Y	Y	N	Y	Y	?	?
8 ***Greenwood***	Y	Y	N	Y	Y	?	?
9 ***Shuster, Bill***	Y	Y	N	Y	Y	Y	Y
10 ***Sherwood***	Y	Y	N	Y	Y	Y	Y
11 Kanjorski	Y	Y	Y	Y	Y	N	N
12 Murtha	Y	Y	N	Y	Y	N	N
13 Hoeffel	Y	Y	Y	Y	Y	N	N
14 Doyle	Y	Y	Y	Y	Y	N	N
15 ***Toomey***	Y	Y	N	Y	Y	Y	Y
16 ***Pitts***	Y	Y	N	Y	Y	Y	Y
17 Holden	Y	Y	Y	Y	Y	N	N
18 ***Murphy***	Y	Y	N	Y	Y	Y	Y
19 ***Platts***	Y	Y	N	Y	Y	Y	Y
RHODE ISLAND							
1 Kennedy	Y	Y	Y	Y	Y	N	N
2 Langevin	Y	Y	Y	Y	Y	N	N
SOUTH CAROLINA							
1 ***Brown***	Y	Y	N	Y	Y	Y	Y
2 ***Wilson***	Y	Y	N	Y	Y	Y	Y
3 ***Barrett***	Y	Y	N	Y	Y	Y	Y
4 ***DeMint***	?	?	?	?	?	?	?
5 Spratt	Y	Y	Y	Y	Y	N	N
6 Clyburn	Y	Y	Y	Y	Y	N	N
SOUTH DAKOTA							
AL Herseth	Y	Y	Y	Y	Y	N	N
TENNESSEE							
1 ***Jenkins***	Y	Y	N	Y	Y	Y	Y
2 ***Duncan***	Y	Y	N	Y	Y	Y	Y
3 ***Wamp***	Y	Y	N	Y	Y	Y	Y
4 Davis	Y	Y	Y	Y	Y	N	N
5 Cooper	Y	Y	Y	Y	Y	N	N
6 Gordon	Y	Y	Y	Y	Y	N	N
7 ***Blackburn***	Y	Y	N	Y	Y	Y	Y
8 Tanner	Y	Y	Y	Y	Y	N	N
9 Ford	?	Y	Y	Y	Y	N	N
TEXAS							
1 Sandlin	Y	Y	Y	Y	Y	N	N
2 Turner	Y	?	Y	Y	Y	N	N
3 ***Johnson, Sam***	Y	Y	N	Y	Y	Y	Y
4 ***Hall***	Y	Y	N	Y	Y	Y	Y
5 ***Hensarling***	Y	Y	N	Y	Y	Y	Y
6 ***Barton***	Y	Y	N	Y	Y	Y	Y
7 ***Culberson***	Y	Y	N	Y	Y	Y	Y
8 ***Brady***	Y	Y	N	Y	Y	Y	Y
9 Lampson	Y	Y	Y	Y	Y	N	N
10 Doggett	Y	Y	Y	Y	Y	N	N
11 Edwards	Y	Y	Y	Y	Y	N	N
12 ***Granger***	Y	Y	N	Y	Y	Y	Y
13 ***Thornberry***	Y	Y	N	Y	Y	Y	Y
14 ***Paul***	Y	Y	N	N	N	Y	Y
15 Hinojosa	Y	?	+	+	+	N	N
16 Reyes	?	?	?	?	?	N	N
17 Stenholm	Y	Y	Y	Y	Y	N	N
18 Jackson-Lee	Y	Y	Y	N	Y	N	N
19 ***Neugebauer***	Y	Y	N	Y	Y	Y	Y
20 Gonzalez	Y	Y	Y	Y	Y	N	N
21 ***Smith***	Y	Y	N	Y	Y	Y	Y
22 ***DeLay***	Y	?	N	Y	Y	Y	Y
23 ***Bonilla***	Y	Y	N	Y	Y	Y	Y
24 Frost	Y	Y	Y	Y	Y	N	N
25 Bell	Y	Y	Y	Y	Y	N	N
26 ***Burgess***	Y	Y	N	Y	Y	Y	Y
27 Ortiz	Y	Y	Y	Y	Y	N	N
28 Rodriguez	Y	Y	Y	Y	Y	N	N
29 Green	Y	Y	Y	Y	Y	N	N
30 Johnson, E.B.	Y	Y	Y	Y	Y	N	N
31 ***Carter***	Y	Y	N	Y	Y	Y	Y
32 ***Sessions***	Y	Y	N	Y	Y	Y	Y
UTAH							
1 ***Bishop***	Y	Y	Y	Y	Y	Y	Y
2 Matheson	Y	Y	Y	Y	Y	N	N
3 ***Cannon***	Y	Y	N	Y	Y	Y	Y
VERMONT							
AL *Sanders*	Y	Y	Y	Y	Y	N	N
VIRGINIA							
1 ***Davis, Jo Ann***	Y	Y	N	Y	Y	Y	Y
2 ***Schrock***	?	?	N	Y	Y	Y	Y
3 Scott	Y	Y	Y	Y	Y	N	N
4 ***Forbes***	Y	Y	N	Y	Y	Y	Y
5 ***Goode***	Y	Y	N	Y	Y	Y	Y
6 ***Goodlatte***	Y	Y	N	Y	Y	Y	Y
7 ***Cantor***	Y	Y	N	Y	Y	Y	Y
8 Moran	Y	Y	Y	Y	Y	N	N
9 Boucher	Y	Y	Y	Y	Y	N	N
10 ***Wolf***	Y	Y	Y	Y	Y	Y	Y
11 ***Davis, T.***	Y	Y	N	Y	Y	Y	Y
WASHINGTON							
1 Inslee	Y	Y	Y	Y	Y	N	N
2 Larsen	Y	Y	Y	Y	Y	N	N
3 Baird	Y	Y	Y	Y	Y	N	N
4 ***Hastings***	Y	Y	N	Y	Y	Y	Y
5 ***Nethercutt***	Y	Y	N	Y	Y	Y	Y
6 Dicks	Y	Y	Y	Y	Y	N	N
7 McDermott	Y	Y	Y	N	Y	N	N
8 ***Dunn***	Y	Y	N	Y	Y	Y	Y
9 Smith	Y	Y	Y	Y	Y	N	N
WEST VIRGINIA							
1 Mollohan	?	?	?	?	?	N	N
2 ***Capito***	Y	Y	N	Y	Y	Y	Y
3 Rahall	Y	Y	Y	Y	Y	N	N
WISCONSIN							
1 ***Ryan***	Y	Y	N	Y	Y	Y	Y
2 Baldwin	Y	Y	Y	Y	Y	N	N
3 Kind	Y	Y	Y	Y	Y	N	N
4 Kleczka	Y	Y	Y	Y	Y	N	N
5 ***Sensenbrenner***	Y	Y	N	Y	Y	Y	Y
6 ***Petri***	Y	Y	N	Y	Y	Y	Y
7 Obey	Y	Y	Y	Y	Y	N	N
8 ***Green***	Y	Y	N	Y	Y	Y	Y
WYOMING							
AL ***Cubin***	Y	Y	N	Y	Y	Y	Y

Southern states - Ala., Ark., Fla., Ga., Ky., La., Miss., N.C., Okla., S.C., Tenn., Texas, Va.

Key

Y Voted for (yea).
\# Paired for.
+ Announced for.
N Voted against (nay).
X Paired against.
− Announced against.
P Voted "present."
C Voted "present" to avoid possible conflict of interest.
? Did not vote or otherwise make a position known.

•

Democrats   **Republicans**
Independents

288. HR 4635. Surface Transportation Extension/Passage. Young, R-Alaska, motion to suspend the rules and pass the bill that would extend funding for highway, transit and transportation safety programs for an additional month, through July 31, 2004. The bill includes $27 billion in contract authority for federal-aid highway programs. Motion agreed to 418-0: R 220-0; D 197-0 (ND 144-0, SD 53-0); I 1-0. A two-thirds majority of those present and voting (279 in this case) is required for passage under suspension of the rules. June 23, 2004.

289. HR 4053. Caucus of Democratic Countries/Passage. Ros-Lehtinen, R-Fla., motion to suspend the rules and pass the bill that would call on the State Department to establish a caucus of democratic countries at the United Nations and other international organizations to promote common positions on issues. Motion agreed to 365-56: R 166-56; D 198-0 (ND 145-0, SD 53-0); I 1-0. A two-thirds majority of those present and voting (281 in this case) is required for passage under suspension of the rules. June 23, 2004.

290. H Con Res 460. U.S. Approval of Israeli Plan/Adoption. Ros-Lehtinen, R-Fla., motion to suspend the rules and adopt the concurrent resolution that would endorse President Bush's approval of Israeli plans to unilaterally withdraw from Gaza, maintain some Israeli settlements in the West Bank and effectively reject Palestinian refugees' "right of return" to what is now Israel. Motion agreed to 407-9: R 220-1; D 186-8 (ND 135-8, SD 51-0); I 1-0. A two-thirds majority of those present and voting (280 in this case) is required for adoption under suspension of the rules. June 23, 2004.

291. HR 4548. Fiscal 2005 Intelligence Authorization/Libyan Disarmament. Boehlert, R-N.Y., amendment that would express the sense of Congress that the world has been made safer with the removal of Libya's weapons of mass destruction and acknowledge that the disarmament would not have been possible without U.S. resolve in the war on terror. Adopted 335-83: R 222-1; D 113-81 (ND 66-75, SD 47-6); I 0-1. June 23, 2004.

292. HR 4548. Fiscal 2005 Intelligence Authorization/Terrorist Detention. Johnson, R-Texas, amendment that would express the sense of Congress that the apprehension, detention and interrogation of terrorists are fundamental to the successful prosecution of the war on terror. Adopted 366-51: R 222-0; D 143-51 (ND 96-45, SD 47-6); I 1-0. June 23, 2004.

293. HR 4548. Fiscal 2005 Intelligence Authorization/Intelligence Community Support. Rogers, R-Mich., amendment that would express the sense of Congress in support of the efforts of the intelligence community. Adopted 222-195: R 222-0; D 0-194 (ND 0-141, SD 0-53); I 0-1. June 23, 2004.

294. HR 4548. Fiscal 2005 Intelligence Authorization/Iraq Oil-for-Food Program. Shays, R-Conn., amendment that would express the sense of Congress that the heads of each intelligence agency should make information about the U.N. Iraq Oil-for-Food Program available to congressional committees. Adopted 419-0: R 223-0; D 195-0 (ND 141-0, SD 54-0); I 1-0. June 23, 2004.

	288	289	290	291	292	293	294
ALABAMA							
1 *Bonner*	Y	N	Y	Y	Y	Y	Y
2 *Everett*	Y	N	Y	Y	Y	Y	Y
3 *Rogers*	Y	Y	Y	Y	Y	Y	Y
4 *Aderholt*	Y	N	Y	Y	Y	Y	Y
5 Cramer	Y	Y	Y	Y	Y	N	Y
6 *Bachus*	Y	Y	Y	Y	Y	Y	Y
7 Davis	Y	Y	Y	Y	Y	N	Y
ALASKA							
AL *Young*	Y	Y	Y	Y	Y	Y	Y
ARIZONA							
1 *Renzi*	Y	N	Y	Y	Y	Y	Y
2 *Franks*	Y	N	Y	Y	Y	Y	Y
3 *Shadegg*	Y	N	Y	Y	Y	Y	Y
4 Pastor	Y	Y	N	N	N	N	Y
5 *Hayworth*	Y	N	Y	Y	Y	Y	Y
6 *Flake*	Y	N	Y	Y	Y	Y	Y
7 Grijalva	Y	Y	N	N	N	N	Y
8 *Kolbe*	Y	Y	Y	Y	Y	?	Y
ARKANSAS							
1 Berry	Y	Y	Y	Y	Y	N	Y
2 Snyder	Y	Y	Y	Y	Y	N	Y
3 *Boozman*	Y	Y	Y	Y	Y	Y	Y
4 Ross	Y	Y	Y	Y	Y	N	Y
CALIFORNIA							
1 Thompson	Y	Y	N	N	N	N	Y
2 *Herger*	Y	N	Y	Y	Y	Y	Y
3 *Ose*	Y	Y	Y	Y	Y	Y	Y
4 *Doolittle*	Y	Y	Y	Y	Y	Y	Y
5 Matsui	Y	Y	Y	Y	Y	N	Y
6 Woolsey	Y	Y	N	N	N	N	Y
7 Miller, George	Y	Y	N	N	N	N	Y
8 Pelosi	Y	Y	Y	Y	N	N	Y
9 Lee	Y	Y	N	N	N	N	Y
10 Tauscher	Y	Y	Y	Y	Y	N	Y
11 *Pombo*	Y	Y	Y	Y	Y	Y	Y
12 Lantos	Y	Y	Y	Y	Y	N	Y
13 Stark	Y	N	N	N	N	N	Y
14 Eshoo	Y	Y	Y	Y	Y	N	Y
15 Honda	Y	Y	Y	N	Y	N	Y
16 Lofgren	Y	Y	Y	Y	Y	N	Y
17 Farr	Y	Y	N	N	N	N	Y
18 Cardoza	Y	Y	Y	Y	Y	N	Y
19 *Radanovich*	Y	Y	Y	Y	Y	Y	Y
20 Dooley	Y	Y	Y	Y	Y	N	Y
21 *Nunes*	Y	Y	Y	Y	Y	Y	Y
22 *Thomas*	Y	Y	Y	Y	Y	Y	Y
23 Capps	Y	Y	Y	N	Y	N	Y
24 *Gallegly*	Y	Y	Y	Y	Y	Y	Y
25 *McKeon*	Y	Y	Y	Y	Y	Y	Y
26 *Dreier*	Y	Y	Y	Y	Y	Y	Y
27 Sherman	Y	Y	Y	N	Y	N	Y
28 Berman	?	?	?	?	?	?	?
29 Schiff	Y	Y	Y	Y	Y	N	Y
30 Waxman	Y	Y	N	Y	Y	N	Y
31 Becerra	Y	Y	N	Y	N	N	Y
32 Solis	Y	Y	N	Y	N	N	Y
33 Watson	Y	Y	P	N	Y	N	Y
34 Roybal-Allard	Y	Y	N	Y	N	N	Y
35 Waters	Y	Y	N	N	N	N	Y
36 Harman	Y	Y	Y	Y	Y	N	Y

	288	289	290	291	292	293	294
37 Millender-McD.	Y	Y	Y	N	N	N	Y
38 Napolitano	Y	Y	Y	N	Y	N	Y
39 Sánchez, Linda	Y	Y	Y	Y	Y	N	Y
40 *Royce*	Y	Y	Y	Y	Y	Y	Y
41 *Lewis*	Y	Y	Y	Y	Y	Y	Y
42 *Miller, Gary*	Y	Y	Y	Y	Y	Y	Y
43 Baca	Y	Y	Y	Y	Y	N	Y
44 *Calvert*	Y	Y	Y	Y	Y	Y	Y
45 *Bono*	Y	Y	Y	Y	Y	Y	Y
46 *Rohrabacher*	Y	Y	Y	Y	Y	Y	Y
47 Sanchez, Loretta	Y	Y	Y	Y	Y	N	Y
48 *Cox*	Y	Y	Y	Y	Y	Y	Y
49 *Issa*	Y	Y	Y	Y	Y	Y	Y
50 *Cunningham*	Y	Y	Y	Y	Y	Y	Y
51 Filner	Y	Y	N	N	N	N	Y
52 *Hunter*	?	Y	Y	Y	Y	Y	Y
53 Davis	Y	Y	Y	Y	Y	N	Y
COLORADO							
1 DeGette	Y	Y	Y	Y	Y	N	Y
2 Udall	Y	Y	Y	Y	Y	N	Y
3 *McInnis*	Y	Y	Y	Y	Y	Y	Y
4 *Musgrave*	Y	N	Y	Y	Y	Y	Y
5 *Hefley*	Y	Y	Y	Y	Y	Y	Y
6 *Tancredo*	Y	N	Y	Y	Y	Y	Y
7 *Beauprez*	Y	Y	Y	Y	Y	Y	Y
CONNECTICUT							
1 Larson	Y	Y	N	N	N	N	Y
2 *Simmons*	Y	Y	Y	Y	Y	Y	Y
3 DeLauro	Y	Y	Y	N	N	N	Y
4 *Shays*	Y	Y	Y	Y	Y	Y	Y
5 *Johnson*	Y	Y	Y	Y	Y	Y	Y
DELAWARE							
AL *Castle*	Y	Y	Y	Y	Y	Y	Y
FLORIDA							
1 *Miller, J.*	Y	N	Y	Y	Y	Y	Y
2 Boyd	Y	Y	Y	Y	Y	N	Y
3 Brown	Y	Y	Y	Y	Y	N	Y
4 *Crenshaw*	Y	Y	Y	Y	Y	Y	Y
5 *Brown-Waite*	Y	Y	Y	Y	Y	Y	Y
6 *Stearns*	Y	Y	Y	Y	Y	Y	Y
7 *Mica*	Y	Y	Y	Y	Y	Y	Y
8 *Keller*	Y	Y	Y	Y	Y	Y	Y
9 *Bilirakis*	Y	Y	Y	Y	Y	Y	Y
10 *Young*	Y	Y	Y	Y	Y	Y	Y
11 Davis	Y	Y	Y	Y	Y	N	Y
12 *Putnam*	Y	Y	Y	Y	Y	Y	Y
13 *Harris*	Y	N	Y	Y	Y	Y	Y
14 *Goss*	Y	Y	Y	Y	Y	Y	Y
15 *Weldon*	Y	N	?	Y	Y	Y	Y
16 *Foley*	Y	Y	Y	Y	Y	Y	Y
17 Meek	?	?	?	Y	Y	N	Y
18 *Ros-Lehtinen*	Y	Y	Y	Y	Y	Y	Y
19 Wexler	Y	Y	Y	Y	Y	N	Y
20 Deutsch	?	?	?	?	?	?	?
21 *Diaz-Balart, L.*	Y	Y	Y	Y	Y	Y	Y
22 *Shaw*	Y	Y	Y	Y	Y	Y	Y
23 Hastings	?	?	?	?	?	?	?
24 *Feeney*	Y	N	Y	Y	Y	Y	Y
25 *Diaz-Balart, M.*	Y	Y	Y	Y	Y	Y	Y
GEORGIA							
1 *Kingston*	Y	Y	Y	Y	Y	Y	Y
2 Bishop	Y	Y	Y	Y	Y	N	Y
3 Marshall	Y	Y	Y	Y	Y	N	Y
4 Majette	Y	Y	Y	Y	Y	N	Y
5 Lewis	Y	Y	N	N	N	N	Y
6 *Isakson*	Y	N	Y	Y	Y	Y	Y
7 *Linder*	Y	Y	Y	Y	?	Y	Y
8 *Collins*	Y	N	Y	Y	Y	Y	Y
9 *Norwood*	Y	N	Y	Y	Y	Y	Y
10 *Deal*	Y	N	Y	Y	Y	Y	Y
11 *Gingrey*	Y	Y	Y	Y	Y	Y	Y
12 *Burns*	Y	Y	Y	Y	Y	Y	Y
13 Scott	Y	Y	Y	Y	Y	N	Y
HAWAII							
1 Abercrombie	Y	Y	Y	N	N	N	Y
2 Case	Y	Y	Y	Y	Y	N	Y
IDAHO							
1 *Otter*	Y	N	Y	Y	Y	Y	Y
2 *Simpson*	Y	Y	Y	Y	Y	Y	Y
ILLINOIS							
1 Rush	Y	Y	Y	N	N	N	Y
2 Jackson	Y	Y	Y	N	N	N	Y
3 Lipinski	Y	Y	Y	Y	Y	N	Y
4 Gutierrez	Y	Y	Y	N	N	N	Y
5 Emanuel	Y	Y	Y	N	Y	N	Y
6 *Hyde*	Y	Y	Y	Y	Y	Y	Y

ND Northern Democrats   SD Southern Democrats

	288	289	290	291	292	293	294
7 Davis	Y	Y	Y	N	Y	N	Y
8 ***Crane***	Y	Y	Y	Y	Y	Y	Y
9 Schakowsky	Y	Y	Y	N	N	N	Y
10 ***Kirk***	Y	Y	+	Y	Y	Y	Y
11 ***Weller***	Y	Y	Y	Y	Y	Y	Y
12 Costello	Y	Y	Y	N	Y	N	Y
13 ***Biggert***	Y	Y	Y	Y	Y	Y	Y
14 ***Hastert***							
15 ***Johnson***	Y	Y	Y	Y	Y	Y	Y
16 ***Manzullo***	Y	N	Y	Y	Y	Y	Y
17 Evans	Y	Y	Y	Y	Y	N	Y
18 ***LaHood***	Y	Y	Y	Y	Y	Y	Y
19 ***Shimkus***	Y	Y	Y	Y	Y	Y	Y
INDIANA							
1 Visclosky	Y	Y	Y	N	Y	N	Y
2 ***Chocola***	Y	N	Y	Y	Y	Y	Y
3 ***Souder***	Y	?	Y	Y	Y	Y	Y
4 ***Buyer***	Y	Y	Y	?	?	?	?
5 ***Burton***	Y	Y	Y	Y	Y	Y	Y
6 ***Pence***	Y	N	Y	Y	Y	Y	Y
7 Carson	?	?	?	?	?	?	?
8 ***Hostettler***	Y	N	Y	Y	Y	Y	Y
9 Hill	Y	Y	Y	Y	Y	N	Y
IOWA							
1 ***Nussle***	Y	Y	Y	Y	Y	Y	Y
2 ***Leach***	Y	Y	Y	Y	Y	Y	Y
3 Boswell	Y	Y	Y	Y	Y	N	Y
4 ***Latham***	Y	Y	Y	Y	Y	Y	Y
5 ***King***	Y	N	Y	Y	Y	Y	Y
KANSAS							
1 ***Moran***	Y	N	Y	Y	Y	Y	Y
2 ***Ryun***	Y	Y	Y	Y	Y	Y	Y
3 Moore	Y	Y	Y	Y	Y	N	Y
4 ***Tiahrt***	Y	N	Y	Y	Y	Y	Y
KENTUCKY							
1 ***Whitfield***	Y	Y	Y	Y	Y	Y	Y
2 ***Lewis***	Y	Y	Y	Y	Y	Y	Y
3 ***Northup***	Y	Y	Y	Y	Y	Y	Y
4 Lucas	Y	Y	Y	Y	Y	N	Y
5 ***Rogers***	Y	Y	Y	Y	Y	Y	Y
6 Chandler	Y	Y	Y	Y	Y	N	Y
LOUISIANA							
1 ***Vitter***	Y	Y	Y	Y	Y	Y	Y
2 Jefferson	Y	Y	Y	Y	Y	N	Y
3 ***Tauzin***	?	?	?	?	?	?	?
4 ***McCrery***	Y	Y	Y	Y	Y	Y	Y
5 Alexander	Y	Y	Y	Y	Y	N	Y
6 ***Baker***	Y	Y	Y	Y	Y	Y	Y
7 John	Y	Y	Y	Y	Y	N	Y
MAINE							
1 Allen	Y	Y	Y	N	Y	N	Y
2 Michaud	Y	Y	Y	N	Y	N	Y
MARYLAND							
1 ***Gilchrest***	Y	Y	Y	Y	Y	Y	Y
2 Ruppersberger	Y	Y	Y	Y	Y	N	Y
3 Cardin	Y	Y	Y	Y	Y	N	Y
4 Wynn	Y	Y	Y	Y	Y	N	Y
5 Hoyer	Y	Y	Y	Y	Y	N	Y
6 ***Bartlett***	Y	N	Y	Y	Y	Y	Y
7 Cummings	Y	Y	Y	N	N	N	Y
8 Van Hollen	Y	Y	Y	N	Y	N	Y
MASSACHUSETTS							
1 Olver	Y	Y	Y	N	Y	N	Y
2 Neal	Y	Y	Y	N	Y	N	Y
3 McGovern	Y	Y	Y	N	Y	N	Y
4 Frank	Y	Y	Y	N	N	N	Y
5 Meehan	Y	Y	Y	N	Y	N	Y
6 Tierney	Y	Y	Y	N	N	N	Y
7 Markey	Y	Y	Y	N	N	N	Y
8 Capuano	Y	Y	Y	N	N	N	Y
9 Lynch	Y	Y	Y	N	Y	N	Y
10 Delahunt	Y	Y	Y	N	N	N	Y
MICHIGAN							
1 Stupak	Y	Y	Y	Y	N	N	Y
2 ***Hoekstra***	Y	N	Y	Y	Y	Y	Y
3 ***Ehlers***	Y	Y	Y	Y	Y	Y	Y
4 ***Camp***	Y	Y	Y	Y	Y	Y	Y
5 Kildee	Y	Y	Y	Y	Y	N	Y
6 ***Upton***	Y	Y	Y	Y	Y	Y	Y
7 ***Smith***	Y	N	Y	Y	Y	Y	Y
8 ***Rogers***	Y	Y	Y	Y	Y	Y	Y
9 ***Knollenberg***	Y	Y	Y	Y	Y	Y	Y
10 ***Miller***	Y	Y	Y	Y	Y	Y	Y
11 ***McCotter***	Y	Y	Y	Y	Y	Y	Y
12 Levin	Y	Y	Y	N	N	N	Y

	288	289	290	291	292	293	294
13 Kilpatrick	Y	Y	N	N	N	N	Y
14 Conyers	Y	Y	N	N	N	N	Y
15 Dingell	Y	Y	N	Y	Y	N	Y
MINNESOTA							
1 ***Gutknecht***	Y	Y	Y	Y	Y	Y	Y
2 ***Kline***	Y	Y	Y	Y	Y	Y	Y
3 ***Ramstad***	Y	Y	Y	Y	Y	Y	Y
4 McCollum	Y	Y	Y	N	N	N	Y
5 Sabo	Y	Y	Y	N	Y	N	Y
6 ***Kennedy***	Y	Y	Y	Y	Y	Y	Y
7 Peterson	Y	Y	Y	Y	Y	N	Y
8 Oberstar	Y	Y	Y	N	Y	N	Y
MISSISSIPPI							
1 ***Wicker***	Y	Y	Y	Y	Y	Y	Y
2 Thompson	Y	Y	Y	N	Y	N	Y
3 ***Pickering***	Y	Y	Y	Y	Y	Y	Y
4 Taylor	Y	Y	Y	Y	Y	N	Y
MISSOURI							
1 Clay	Y	Y	Y	?	?	?	?
2 ***Akin***	Y	N	Y	Y	Y	Y	Y
3 Gephardt	?	?	?	?	?	?	?
4 Skelton	Y	Y	Y	Y	Y	N	Y
5 McCarthy	Y	Y	Y	Y	Y	N	Y
6 ***Graves***	Y	Y	Y	Y	Y	Y	Y
7 ***Blunt***	Y	Y	Y	Y	Y	Y	Y
8 ***Emerson***	Y	N	Y	Y	Y	Y	Y
9 ***Hulshof***	Y	Y	Y	Y	Y	Y	Y
MONTANA							
AL ***Rehberg***	Y	Y	Y	Y	Y	Y	Y
NEBRASKA							
1 ***Bereuter***	?	?	?	?	?	?	?
2 ***Terry***	Y	Y	Y	Y	Y	Y	Y
3 ***Osborne***	Y	Y	Y	Y	Y	Y	Y
NEVADA							
1 Berkley	Y	Y	Y	N	Y	N	Y
2 ***Gibbons***	Y	Y	Y	Y	Y	Y	Y
3 ***Porter***	Y	Y	Y	Y	Y	Y	Y
NEW HAMPSHIRE							
1 ***Bradley***	Y	Y	Y	Y	Y	Y	Y
2 ***Bass***	Y	Y	Y	Y	Y	Y	Y
NEW JERSEY							
1 Andrews	Y	Y	Y	Y	Y	N	Y
2 ***LoBiondo***	Y	Y	Y	Y	Y	Y	Y
3 ***Saxton***	Y	Y	Y	Y	Y	Y	Y
4 ***Smith***	Y	Y	Y	Y	Y	Y	Y
5 ***Garrett***	Y	N	Y	Y	Y	Y	Y
6 Pallone	Y	Y	Y	Y	Y	N	Y
7 ***Ferguson***	Y	Y	Y	Y	Y	Y	Y
8 Pascrell	Y	Y	Y	N	Y	N	Y
9 Rothman	Y	Y	Y	Y	Y	N	Y
10 Payne	Y	Y	P	N	N	N	Y
11 ***Frelinghuysen***	Y	Y	Y	Y	Y	Y	Y
12 Holt	Y	Y	Y	Y	Y	N	Y
13 Menendez	Y	Y	Y	Y	Y	N	Y
NEW MEXICO							
1 ***Wilson***	Y	Y	Y	Y	Y	Y	Y
2 ***Pearce***	Y	Y	Y	Y	Y	Y	Y
3 Udall	Y	Y	Y	N	Y	N	Y
NEW YORK							
1 Bishop	Y	Y	Y	Y	Y	N	Y
2 Israel	?	?	?	?	?	?	?
3 ***King***	Y	Y	Y	Y	Y	Y	Y
4 McCarthy	Y	Y	Y	Y	Y	N	Y
5 Ackerman	Y	Y	Y	Y	Y	N	Y
6 Meeks	Y	Y	Y	N	Y	N	Y
7 Crowley	Y	Y	Y	Y	Y	N	Y
8 Nadler	Y	Y	Y	N	N	N	Y
9 Weiner	Y	Y	Y	?	?	?	?
10 Towns	Y	Y	Y	N	Y	N	Y
11 Owens	Y	Y	Y	N	N	N	Y
12 Velázquez	Y	Y	Y	N	N	N	Y
13 ***Fossella***	Y	Y	Y	Y	Y	Y	Y
14 Maloney	Y	Y	Y	N	N	N	Y
15 Rangel	Y	Y	Y	?	?	?	?
16 Serrano	Y	Y	Y	N	N	N	Y
17 Engel	Y	Y	Y	Y	Y	N	Y
18 Lowey	Y	Y	Y	Y	Y	N	Y
19 ***Kelly***	Y	Y	Y	Y	Y	Y	Y
20 ***Sweeney***	Y	Y	Y	Y	Y	Y	Y
21 McNulty	Y	Y	Y	Y	Y	N	Y
22 Hinchey	Y	Y	Y	N	Y	N	Y
23 ***McHugh***	Y	Y	Y	Y	Y	Y	Y
24 ***Boehlert***	Y	Y	Y	Y	Y	Y	Y
25 ***Walsh***	Y	Y	Y	Y	Y	Y	Y

	288	289	290	291	292	293	294
26 ***Reynolds***	Y	Y	Y	Y	Y	Y	Y
27 ***Quinn***	Y	Y	Y	Y	Y	Y	Y
28 Slaughter	Y	Y	Y	N	N	N	Y
29 ***Houghton***	Y	Y	Y	Y	Y	Y	Y
NORTH CAROLINA							
1 Vacant							
2 Etheridge	Y	Y	Y	Y	Y	N	Y
3 ***Jones***	Y	N	Y	Y	Y	Y	Y
4 Price	Y	Y	Y	Y	Y	N	Y
5 ***Burr***	Y	Y	Y	Y	Y	Y	Y
6 ***Coble***	Y	N	Y	Y	Y	Y	Y
7 McIntyre	Y	Y	Y	Y	Y	N	Y
8 ***Hayes***	Y	N	Y	Y	Y	Y	Y
9 ***Myrick***	Y	N	Y	Y	Y	Y	Y
10 ***Ballenger***	Y	Y	Y	Y	Y	Y	Y
11 ***Taylor***	?	Y	Y	Y	Y	Y	Y
12 Watt	Y	Y	P	N	N	N	Y
13 Miller	Y	Y	Y	Y	Y	N	Y
NORTH DAKOTA							
AL Pomeroy	Y	Y	Y	Y	Y	N	Y
OHIO							
1 ***Chabot***	Y	Y	Y	Y	Y	Y	Y
2 ***Portman***	Y	Y	Y	Y	Y	Y	Y
3 ***Turner***	Y	Y	Y	Y	Y	Y	Y
4 ***Oxley***	Y	Y	Y	Y	Y	Y	Y
5 ***Gillmor***	Y	Y	Y	Y	Y	Y	Y
6 Strickland	Y	Y	Y	N	Y	N	Y
7 ***Hobson***	Y	Y	Y	Y	Y	Y	Y
8 ***Boehner***	Y	Y	Y	Y	Y	Y	Y
9 Kaptur	Y	Y	Y	Y	Y	N	Y
10 Kucinich	Y	Y	N	N	N	N	Y
11 Jones	?	Y	Y	N	N	N	Y
12 ***Tiberi***	Y	Y	Y	Y	Y	Y	Y
13 Brown	Y	Y	Y	N	Y	N	Y
14 ***LaTourette***	Y	Y	Y	Y	Y	Y	Y
15 ***Pryce***	Y	Y	Y	Y	Y	Y	Y
16 ***Regula***	Y	Y	Y	Y	Y	Y	Y
17 Ryan	Y	Y	Y	Y	Y	N	Y
18 ***Ney***	Y	Y	Y	Y	Y	Y	Y
OKLAHOMA							
1 ***Sullivan***	Y	Y	Y	Y	Y	Y	Y
2 Carson	Y	Y	Y	Y	Y	N	Y
3 ***Lucas***	Y	Y	Y	Y	Y	Y	Y
4 ***Cole***	Y	Y	Y	Y	Y	Y	Y
5 ***Istook***	Y	Y	Y	Y	Y	Y	Y
OREGON							
1 Wu	Y	Y	Y	Y	Y	N	Y
2 ***Walden***	Y	Y	Y	Y	Y	Y	Y
3 Blumenauer	Y	Y	Y	N	N	N	Y
4 DeFazio	Y	Y	Y	Y	Y	N	Y
5 Hooley	Y	Y	Y	Y	Y	N	Y
PENNSYLVANIA							
1 Brady	Y	Y	Y	Y	Y	N	Y
2 Fattah	Y	Y	Y	Y	Y	N	Y
3 ***English***	Y	Y	Y	Y	Y	Y	Y
4 ***Hart***	Y	Y	Y	Y	Y	Y	Y
5 ***Peterson***	Y	Y	Y	Y	Y	Y	Y
6 ***Gerlach***	Y	Y	Y	Y	Y	Y	Y
7 ***Weldon***	?	?	Y	Y	Y	Y	Y
8 ***Greenwood***	?	Y	Y	Y	Y	Y	Y
9 ***Shuster, Bill***	Y	Y	Y	Y	Y	Y	Y
10 ***Sherwood***	Y	Y	Y	Y	Y	Y	Y
11 Kanjorski	Y	Y	Y	N	N	N	Y
12 Murtha	Y	Y	Y	Y	Y	N	Y
13 Hoeffel	Y	Y	Y	Y	Y	N	Y
14 Doyle	Y	Y	Y	Y	Y	N	Y
15 ***Toomey***	Y	N	Y	Y	Y	Y	Y
16 ***Pitts***	Y	Y	Y	Y	Y	Y	Y
17 Holden	Y	Y	Y	Y	Y	N	Y
18 ***Murphy***	Y	Y	Y	Y	Y	Y	Y
19 ***Platts***	Y	Y	Y	Y	Y	Y	Y
RHODE ISLAND							
1 Kennedy	Y	Y	Y	Y	Y	N	Y
2 Langevin	Y	Y	Y	Y	Y	N	Y
SOUTH CAROLINA							
1 ***Brown***	Y	Y	Y	Y	Y	Y	Y
2 ***Wilson***	Y	Y	Y	Y	Y	Y	Y
3 ***Barrett***	Y	N	Y	Y	Y	Y	Y
4 ***DeMint***	?	?	?	?	?	?	?
5 Spratt	Y	Y	Y	Y	Y	N	Y
6 Clyburn	Y	Y	Y	Y	Y	N	Y
SOUTH DAKOTA							
AL Herseth	Y	Y	Y	Y	Y	N	Y

	288	289	290	291	292	293	294
TENNESSEE							
1 ***Jenkins***	Y	Y	Y	Y	Y	Y	Y
2 ***Duncan***	Y	N	Y	Y	Y	Y	Y
3 ***Wamp***	Y	N	Y	Y	Y	Y	Y
4 Davis	Y	Y	Y	Y	Y	N	Y
5 Cooper	Y	Y	Y	Y	Y	N	Y
6 Gordon	Y	Y	Y	Y	Y	N	Y
7 ***Blackburn***	Y	Y	Y	Y	Y	Y	Y
8 Tanner	Y	Y	Y	Y	Y	N	Y
9 Ford	Y	Y	Y	Y	Y	N	Y
TEXAS							
1 Sandlin	Y	Y	Y	Y	Y	N	Y
2 Turner	Y	Y	Y	Y	Y	N	Y
3 ***Johnson, Sam***	Y	N	Y	Y	Y	Y	Y
4 ***Hall***	Y	Y	Y	Y	Y	Y	Y
5 ***Hensarling***	Y	N	Y	Y	Y	Y	Y
6 ***Barton***	Y	Y	Y	Y	Y	Y	Y
7 ***Culberson***	Y	N	Y	Y	Y	Y	Y
8 ***Brady***	Y	Y	Y	Y	Y	Y	Y
9 Lampson	Y	Y	Y	Y	Y	N	Y
10 Doggett	Y	Y	Y	N	N	N	Y
11 Edwards	Y	Y	Y	Y	Y	N	Y
12 ***Granger***	Y	Y	Y	Y	Y	Y	Y
13 ***Thornberry***	Y	Y	Y	Y	Y	Y	Y
14 ***Paul***	Y	N	N	N	Y	Y	Y
15 Hinojosa	Y	Y	Y	Y	Y	N	Y
16 Reyes	Y	Y	Y	Y	Y	N	Y
17 Stenholm	Y	Y	Y	Y	Y	N	Y
18 Jackson-Lee	Y	Y	Y	N	N	N	Y
19 ***Neugebauer***	Y	N	?	Y	Y	Y	Y
20 Gonzalez	Y	Y	Y	Y	Y	N	Y
21 ***Smith***	Y	Y	Y	Y	Y	Y	Y
22 ***DeLay***	Y	Y	Y	Y	Y	Y	Y
23 ***Bonilla***	Y	Y	Y	Y	Y	Y	Y
24 Frost	Y	Y	Y	Y	Y	N	Y
25 Bell	Y	Y	Y	Y	Y	N	Y
26 ***Burgess***	Y	N	Y	Y	Y	Y	Y
27 Ortiz	Y	Y	Y	Y	Y	N	Y
28 Rodriguez	Y	Y	Y	Y	Y	N	Y
29 Green	Y	Y	Y	Y	Y	N	Y
30 Johnson, E.B.	Y	Y	Y	Y	N	N	Y
31 ***Carter***	Y	N	Y	Y	Y	Y	Y
32 ***Sessions***	Y	Y	Y	Y	Y	Y	Y
UTAH							
1 ***Bishop***	Y	N	Y	Y	Y	Y	Y
2 Matheson	Y	Y	Y	Y	Y	N	Y
3 ***Cannon***	Y	N	Y	Y	Y	Y	Y
VERMONT							
AL *Sanders*	Y	Y	Y	N	Y	N	Y
VIRGINIA							
1 ***Davis, Jo Ann***	Y	N	Y	Y	Y	Y	Y
2 ***Schrock***	Y	N	Y	Y	Y	Y	Y
3 Scott	Y	Y	Y	N	N	N	Y
4 ***Forbes***	Y	N	Y	Y	Y	Y	Y
5 ***Goode***	Y	N	Y	Y	Y	Y	Y
6 ***Goodlatte***	Y	N	Y	Y	Y	Y	Y
7 ***Cantor***	Y	Y	Y	Y	Y	Y	Y
8 Moran	Y	Y	Y	?	?	–	Y
9 Boucher	Y	Y	?	Y	Y	N	Y
10 ***Wolf***	Y	Y	Y	Y	Y	Y	Y
11 ***Davis, T.***	Y	Y	Y	Y	Y	Y	Y
WASHINGTON							
1 Inslee	Y	Y	Y	N	Y	N	Y
2 Larsen	Y	Y	Y	Y	Y	N	Y
3 Baird	Y	Y	Y	Y	Y	N	Y
4 ***Hastings***	Y	Y	Y	Y	Y	Y	Y
5 ***Nethercutt***	Y	Y	Y	Y	Y	Y	Y
6 Dicks	Y	Y	Y	Y	N	N	Y
7 McDermott	Y	Y	Y	?	?	?	?
8 ***Dunn***	Y	Y	Y	Y	Y	Y	Y
9 Smith	Y	Y	Y	Y	Y	N	Y
WEST VIRGINIA							
1 Mollohan	Y	Y	Y	Y	Y	N	Y
2 ***Capito***	Y	Y	Y	Y	Y	Y	Y
3 Rahall	Y	Y	Y	N	Y	N	Y
WISCONSIN							
1 ***Ryan***	Y	Y	Y	Y	Y	Y	Y
2 Baldwin	Y	Y	Y	N	N	N	Y
3 Kind	Y	Y	Y	Y	Y	N	Y
4 Kleczka	Y	Y	Y	N	N	N	Y
5 ***Sensenbrenner***	Y	Y	Y	Y	Y	Y	Y
6 ***Petri***	Y	Y	Y	Y	Y	Y	Y
7 Obey	Y	Y	Y	N	Y	N	Y
8 ***Green***	Y	Y	Y	Y	Y	Y	Y
WYOMING							
AL ***Cubin***	Y	N	Y	Y	Y	Y	Y

Southern states - Ala., Ark., Fla., Ga., Ky., La., Miss., N.C., Okla., S.C., Tenn., Texas, Va.

Key

Y	Voted for (yea).
#	Paired for.
+	Announced for.
N	Voted against (nay).
X	Paired against.
–	Announced against.
P	Voted "present."
C	Voted "present" to avoid possible conflict of interest.
?	Did not vote or otherwise make a position known.

Democrats **Republicans** *Independents*

295. HR 4548. Fiscal 2005 Intelligence Authorization/Iraq-al Qaeda Connections. Kucinich, D-Ohio, amendment that would direct the CIA's inspector general to audit the evidence of the pre-Sept. 11, 2001, relationship between Saddam Hussein's regime and al Qaeda. Adopted 343-76: R 148-75; D 194-1 (ND 140-1, SD 54-0); I 1-0. June 23, 2004.

296. HR 4548. Fiscal 2005 Intelligence Authorization/Open-Source Intelligence. Simmons, R-Conn., amendment that would direct the CIA director to report to Congress on the progress the intelligence community is making in utilizing open-source intelligence. Adopted 417-1: R 222-0; D 194-1 (ND 140-1, SD 54-0); I 1-0. June 23, 2004.

297. HR 4548. Fiscal 2005 Intelligence Authorization/Treatment of Prisoners. Reyes, D-Texas, amendment that would withhold 25 percent of the funds available to intelligence agencies, including the CIA, until the appropriate congressional committees receive all documents related to the handling and treatment of detainees in Iraq; Afghanistan; Guantánamo Bay, Cuba; and elsewhere. Rejected 149-270: R 3-220; D 145-50 (ND 113-28, SD 32-22); I 1-0. June 23, 2004.

298. HR 4548. Fiscal 2005 Intelligence Authorization/Terrorist Detention. Johnson, R-Texas, amendment that would express the sense of Congress that the apprehension, detention and interrogation of terrorists are fundamental to the successful prosecution of the war on terror. Adopted 304-116: R 223-0; D 81-115 (ND 43-99, SD 38-16); I 0-1. (Previously, in vote 292, the House adopted the Johnson amendment in the Committee of the Whole.) June 23, 2004.

299. HR 4548. Fiscal 2005 Intelligence Authorization/Recommit. Peterson, D-Minn., motion to recommit the bill to the House Intelligence Committee with instructions to fully fund authorizations for counter-terrorism programs. Motion rejected 197-224: R 0-224; D 196-0 (ND 142-0, SD 54-0); I 1-0. June 23, 2004.

300. HR 4548. Fiscal 2005 Intelligence Authorization/Passage. Passage of the bill that would authorize classified amounts in fiscal 2005 for U.S. intelligence activities and agencies including the CIA, the National Security Agency, the National Geospatial-Intelligence Agency and the Defense Intelligence Agency. The bill, as amended, would direct the CIA's inspector general to audit the evidence of the pre-Sept. 11, 2001, relationship between Saddam Hussein's regime and al Qaeda. Passed 360-61: R 221-3; D 138-58 (ND 89-53, SD 49-5); I 1-0. June 23, 2004.

301. H Res 685. Fiscal 2005 Budget Resolution Revision/Adoption. Adoption of the resolution that would revise the conference report on the fiscal 2005 budget resolution (S Con Res 95) to provide $14.2 billion in additional funds for education, homeland security, veterans, health and other programs. The increased spending would be offset by reducing or eliminating $18.9 billion in tax cuts for couples with incomes of more than $1 million. The remaining $4.7 billion would be used for deficit reduction. Rejected 184-230: R 2-217; D 181-13 (ND 137-4, SD 44-9); I 1-0. June 24, 2004.

	295	296	297	298	299	300	301
ALABAMA							
1 *Bonner*	N	Y	N	Y	N	Y	N
2 *Everett*	N	Y	N	Y	N	Y	N
3 *Rogers*	N	Y	N	Y	N	Y	N
4 *Aderholt*	N	Y	N	Y	N	Y	N
5 Cramer	Y	Y	Y	Y	Y	Y	Y
6 *Bachus*	Y	Y	N	Y	N	Y	N
7 Davis	Y	Y	N	Y	Y	Y	Y
ALASKA							
AL *Young*	Y	Y	N	Y	N	Y	N
ARIZONA							
1 *Renzi*	Y	Y	N	Y	N	Y	N
2 *Franks*	N	Y	N	Y	N	Y	N
3 *Shadegg*	N	Y	N	Y	N	Y	N
4 Pastor	Y	Y	Y	N	Y	N	Y
5 *Hayworth*	Y	Y	N	Y	N	Y	N
6 *Flake*	N	Y	N	Y	N	Y	N
7 Grijalva	Y	Y	Y	N	Y	N	Y
8 *Kolbe*	Y	Y	N	Y	N	Y	N
ARKANSAS							
1 Berry	Y	Y	Y	Y	Y	Y	Y
2 Snyder	Y	Y	N	Y	Y	Y	Y
3 *Boozman*	N	Y	N	Y	N	Y	N
4 Ross	Y	Y	Y	Y	Y	Y	Y
CALIFORNIA							
1 Thompson	Y	Y	Y	N	Y	N	Y
2 *Herger*	N	Y	N	Y	N	Y	N
3 *Ose*	Y	Y	N	Y	N	Y	N
4 *Doolittle*	N	Y	N	Y	N	Y	N
5 Matsui	Y	Y	Y	N	Y	N	Y
6 Woolsey	Y	Y	Y	N	Y	N	Y
7 Miller, George	Y	Y	Y	N	Y	N	Y
8 Pelosi	Y	Y	Y	N	Y	N	Y
9 Lee	Y	Y	Y	N	Y	N	Y
10 Tauscher	Y	Y	Y	N	Y	N	Y
11 *Pombo*	Y	Y	N	Y	N	Y	N
12 Lantos	Y	Y	Y	Y	Y	Y	Y
13 Stark	Y	Y	Y	N	Y	N	Y
14 Eshoo	Y	Y	Y	N	Y	N	Y
15 Honda	Y	Y	Y	N	Y	N	Y
16 Lofgren	Y	Y	Y	N	Y	N	Y
17 Farr	Y	Y	Y	N	Y	N	Y
18 Cardoza	Y	Y	Y	Y	Y	Y	Y
19 *Radanovich*	N	Y	N	Y	N	Y	N
20 Dooley	Y	Y	Y	Y	Y	Y	Y
21 *Nunes*	Y	Y	N	Y	N	Y	N
22 *Thomas*	Y	Y	N	Y	N	Y	N
23 Capps	Y	Y	Y	N	Y	N	Y
24 *Gallegly*	Y	Y	N	Y	N	Y	N
25 *McKeon*	N	Y	N	Y	N	Y	N
26 *Dreier*	Y	Y	N	Y	N	Y	N
27 Sherman	Y	Y	Y	Y	Y	Y	Y
28 Berman	?	?	?	?	?	?	?
29 Schiff	Y	Y	Y	Y	Y	Y	Y
30 Waxman	Y	Y	Y	N	Y	N	Y
31 Becerra	Y	Y	Y	N	Y	N	Y
32 Solis	Y	Y	Y	N	Y	N	Y
33 Watson	Y	Y	Y	N	Y	N	Y
34 Roybal-Allard	Y	Y	Y	N	Y	N	Y
35 Waters	Y	Y	Y	N	Y	N	Y
36 Harman	Y	Y	Y	N	Y	Y	Y

	295	296	297	298	299	300	301
37 Millender-McD.	Y	Y	Y	N	Y	Y	Y
38 Napolitano	Y	Y	Y	N	Y	N	Y
39 Sánchez, Linda	Y	Y	Y	N	Y	N	Y
40 *Royce*	Y	Y	N	Y	N	Y	N
41 *Lewis*	Y	Y	N	Y	N	Y	N
42 *Miller, Gary*	Y	Y	N	Y	N	Y	N
43 Baca	Y	Y	Y	Y	Y	N	Y
44 *Calvert*	Y	Y	N	Y	N	Y	N
45 *Bono*	Y	Y	N	Y	N	Y	N
46 *Rohrabacher*	Y	Y	N	Y	N	Y	N
47 Sanchez, Loretta	Y	Y	Y	Y	Y	Y	Y
48 *Cox*	Y	Y	N	Y	N	Y	N
49 *Issa*	Y	Y	N	Y	N	Y	N
50 *Cunningham*	Y	Y	N	Y	N	Y	N
51 Filner	Y	Y	Y	N	Y	N	Y
52 *Hunter*	N	Y	N	Y	N	Y	N
53 Davis	Y	Y	N	Y	Y	Y	Y
COLORADO							
1 DeGette	Y	Y	Y	N	Y	Y	Y
2 Udall	Y	Y	Y	N	Y	Y	Y
3 *McInnis*	Y	Y	N	Y	N	Y	N
4 *Musgrave*	N	Y	N	Y	N	Y	N
5 *Hefley*	N	Y	N	Y	N	Y	N
6 *Tancredo*	N	Y	N	Y	N	Y	N
7 *Beauprez*	Y	Y	N	Y	N	Y	N
CONNECTICUT							
1 Larson	Y	Y	Y	N	Y	N	Y
2 *Simmons*	Y	Y	Y	N	Y	N	Y
3 DeLauro	Y	Y	Y	N	Y	N	Y
4 *Shays*	Y	Y	N	Y	N	Y	N
5 *Johnson*	Y	Y	N	Y	N	Y	N
DELAWARE							
AL *Castle*	Y	Y	N	Y	N	Y	N
FLORIDA							
1 *Miller, J.*	Y	Y	N	Y	N	Y	N
2 Boyd	Y	Y	Y	Y	Y	Y	Y
3 Brown	Y	Y	Y	N	Y	Y	Y
4 *Crenshaw*	Y	Y	N	Y	N	Y	N
5 *Brown-Waite*	Y	Y	N	Y	N	Y	N
6 *Stearns*	Y	Y	N	Y	N	Y	N
7 *Mica*	N	Y	N	Y	N	Y	N
8 *Keller*	Y	Y	N	Y	N	Y	N
9 *Bilirakis*	N	Y	N	Y	N	Y	N
10 *Young*	Y	Y	N	Y	N	Y	N
11 Davis	Y	Y	Y	Y	Y	Y	Y
12 *Putnam*	N	Y	N	Y	N	Y	N
13 *Harris*	Y	Y	N	Y	N	Y	N
14 *Goss*	Y	Y	N	Y	N	Y	N
15 *Weldon*	N	Y	N	Y	N	Y	N
16 *Foley*	Y	Y	N	Y	N	Y	N
17 Meek	Y	Y	Y	N	Y	Y	Y
18 *Ros-Lehtinen*	Y	Y	N	Y	N	Y	N
19 Wexler	Y	Y	Y	Y	Y	Y	Y
20 Deutsch	?	?	?	?	?	?	?
21 *Diaz-Balart, L.*	N	Y	N	Y	N	Y	N
22 *Shaw*	N	Y	N	Y	N	Y	N
23 Hastings	?	?	?	?	?	?	?
24 *Feeney*	N	Y	N	Y	N	Y	N
25 *Diaz-Balart, M.*	N	Y	N	Y	N	Y	N
GEORGIA							
1 *Kingston*	N	Y	N	Y	N	Y	N
2 Bishop	Y	Y	Y	Y	Y	Y	Y
3 Marshall	Y	Y	Y	Y	Y	Y	Y
4 Majette	Y	Y	Y	N	Y	N	Y
5 Lewis	Y	Y	Y	N	Y	N	Y
6 *Isakson*	Y	Y	N	Y	N	Y	N
7 *Linder*	Y	Y	N	Y	N	Y	?
8 *Collins*	N	Y	N	Y	N	Y	N
9 *Norwood*	Y	Y	N	Y	N	Y	N
10 *Deal*	Y	Y	N	Y	N	Y	N
11 *Gingrey*	Y	Y	N	Y	N	Y	N
12 *Burns*	Y	Y	N	Y	N	Y	N
13 Scott	Y	Y	Y	Y	Y	Y	Y
HAWAII							
1 Abercrombie	Y	N	Y	N	Y	N	Y
2 Case	Y	Y	N	Y	Y	Y	Y
IDAHO							
1 *Otter*	Y	Y	Y	Y	N	N	N
2 *Simpson*	Y	Y	N	Y	N	Y	N
ILLINOIS							
1 Rush	Y	Y	Y	N	Y	N	Y
2 Jackson	Y	Y	Y	N	Y	N	Y
3 Lipinski	Y	Y	N	Y	N	Y	Y
4 Gutierrez	Y	Y	Y	N	Y	Y	Y
5 Emanuel	Y	Y	Y	N	Y	N	Y
6 *Hyde*	N	Y	N	Y	N	Y	N

ND Northern Democrats   SD Southern Democrats

	295	296	297	298	299	300	301
7 Davis	Y	Y	Y	N	Y	N	Y
8 ***Crane***	Y	Y	N	Y	N	Y	N
9 Schakowsky	Y	Y	Y	N	Y	N	Y
10 ***Kirk***	Y	Y	N	Y	N	Y	N
11 ***Weller***	Y	Y	N	Y	N	Y	N
12 Costello	Y	Y	N	N	Y	Y	Y
13 ***Biggert***	Y	Y	N	Y	N	Y	N
14 ***Hastert***				Y	N	Y	
15 ***Johnson***	Y	Y	N	Y	N	Y	N
16 ***Manzullo***	Y	Y	N	Y	N	Y	N
17 Evans	Y	Y	Y	N	Y	N	Y
18 ***LaHood***	Y	Y	N	Y	N	Y	Y
19 ***Shimkus***	Y	Y	N	Y	N	Y	N
INDIANA							
1 Visclosky	Y	Y	Y	N	Y	N	Y
2 ***Chocola***	Y	Y	N	Y	N	Y	N
3 ***Souder***	N	Y	N	Y	N	Y	N
4 ***Buyer***	?	?	?	?	?	?	N
5 ***Burton***	Y	Y	N	Y	N	Y	N
6 ***Pence***	Y	Y	N	Y	N	Y	N
7 Carson	?	?	?	?	?	?	?
8 ***Hostettler***	N	Y	N	Y	N	Y	N
9 Hill	Y	Y	N	Y	Y	Y	N
IOWA							
1 ***Nussle***	Y	Y	N	Y	N	Y	N
2 ***Leach***	Y	Y	N	Y	N	Y	N
3 Boswell	Y	Y	N	Y	Y	Y	Y
4 ***Latham***	Y	Y	N	Y	N	Y	N
5 ***King***	Y	Y	N	Y	N	Y	N
KANSAS							
1 ***Moran***	Y	Y	N	Y	N	Y	N
2 ***Ryun***	N	Y	N	Y	N	Y	N
3 Moore	Y	Y	N	Y	Y	Y	N
4 ***Tiahrt***	Y	Y	N	Y	N	Y	N
KENTUCKY							
1 ***Whitfield***	N	Y	N	Y	N	Y	N
2 ***Lewis***	N	Y	N	Y	N	Y	N
3 ***Northup***	Y	Y	N	Y	N	Y	N
4 Lucas	Y	Y	Y	Y	Y	Y	Y
5 ***Rogers***	Y	Y	N	Y	N	Y	N
6 Chandler	Y	Y	N	Y	Y	Y	Y
LOUISIANA							
1 ***Vitter***	Y	Y	N	Y	N	Y	N
2 Jefferson	Y	Y	Y	N	Y	Y	Y
3 ***Tauzin***	?	?	?	?	?	?	?
4 ***McCrery***	N	Y	N	Y	N	Y	N
5 Alexander	Y	Y	N	Y	Y	Y	N
6 ***Baker***	N	Y	N	Y	N	Y	N
7 John	Y	Y	N	Y	Y	Y	Y
MAINE							
1 Allen	Y	Y	Y	N	Y	Y	Y
2 Michaud	Y	Y	N	Y	Y	Y	Y
MARYLAND							
1 ***Gilchrest***	Y	Y	N	Y	N	Y	N
2 Ruppersberger	Y	Y	Y	Y	Y	Y	Y
3 Cardin	Y	Y	Y	Y	Y	Y	Y
4 Wynn	Y	Y	Y	N	Y	Y	Y
5 Hoyer	Y	Y	Y	N	Y	Y	Y
6 ***Bartlett***	Y	Y	N	Y	N	Y	N
7 Cummings	Y	Y	Y	N	Y	Y	Y
8 Van Hollen	Y	Y	Y	Y	Y	Y	Y
MASSACHUSETTS							
1 Olver	Y	Y	Y	N	Y	N	Y
2 Neal	Y	Y	Y	N	Y	Y	Y
3 McGovern	Y	Y	Y	N	Y	Y	Y
4 Frank	Y	Y	Y	N	Y	Y	Y
5 Meehan	Y	Y	Y	N	Y	Y	Y
6 Tierney	Y	Y	Y	N	Y	Y	Y
7 Markey	Y	Y	Y	N	Y	N	Y
8 Capuano	Y	Y	Y	N	Y	N	Y
9 Lynch	Y	Y	Y	Y	Y	Y	Y
10 Delahunt	Y	Y	Y	N	Y	Y	Y
MICHIGAN							
1 Stupak	Y	Y	Y	N	Y	Y	Y
2 ***Hoekstra***	Y	Y	N	Y	N	Y	N
3 ***Ehlers***	Y	Y	N	Y	N	Y	N
4 ***Camp***	Y	Y	N	Y	N	Y	N
5 Kildee	Y	Y	N	Y	Y	Y	Y
6 ***Upton***	Y	Y	N	Y	N	Y	N
7 ***Smith***	Y	Y	N	Y	N	Y	N
8 ***Rogers***	Y	Y	N	Y	N	Y	N
9 ***Knollenberg***	N	Y	N	Y	N	Y	N
10 ***Miller***	N	Y	N	Y	N	Y	N
11 ***McCotter***	Y	Y	N	Y	N	Y	N
12 Levin	Y	Y	N	N	Y	Y	Y
13 Kilpatrick	Y	Y	Y	N	Y	N	Y
14 Conyers	Y	Y	Y	N	Y	N	Y
15 Dingell	Y	Y	Y	N	Y	Y	Y
MINNESOTA							
1 ***Gutknecht***	Y	Y	N	Y	N	Y	N
2 ***Kline***	Y	Y	N	Y	N	Y	N
3 ***Ramstad***	Y	Y	N	Y	N	Y	N
4 McCollum	Y	Y	Y	N	Y	Y	Y
5 Sabo	Y	Y	Y	N	Y	Y	Y
6 ***Kennedy***	Y	Y	N	Y	N	Y	N
7 Peterson	Y	Y	Y	Y	Y	Y	N
8 Oberstar	Y	Y	Y	N	Y	N	Y
MISSISSIPPI							
1 ***Wicker***	Y	Y	N	Y	N	Y	N
2 Thompson	Y	Y	Y	N	Y	Y	Y
3 ***Pickering***	Y	Y	N	Y	N	Y	N
4 Taylor	Y	Y	N	Y	Y	Y	N
MISSOURI							
1 Clay	?	?	?	?	?	?	Y
2 ***Akin***	N	Y	N	Y	N	Y	N
3 Gephardt	?	?	?	?	?	?	?
4 Skelton	Y	Y	Y	Y	Y	Y	Y
5 McCarthy	Y	Y	Y	N	Y	Y	Y
6 ***Graves***	Y	Y	N	Y	N	Y	N
7 ***Blunt***	N	Y	N	Y	N	Y	N
8 ***Emerson***	Y	Y	N	Y	N	Y	N
9 ***Hulshof***	Y	Y	N	Y	N	Y	N
MONTANA							
AL ***Rehberg***	Y	Y	N	Y	N	Y	N
NEBRASKA							
1 ***Bereuter***	?	?	?	?	?	?	?
2 ***Terry***	Y	?	N	Y	N	Y	N
3 ***Osborne***	Y	Y	N	Y	N	Y	N
NEVADA							
1 Berkley	Y	Y	N	N	Y	Y	Y
2 ***Gibbons***	Y	Y	N	Y	N	Y	N
3 ***Porter***	Y	Y	N	Y	N	Y	N
NEW HAMPSHIRE							
1 ***Bradley***	Y	Y	N	Y	N	Y	N
2 ***Bass***	Y	Y	N	Y	N	Y	N
NEW JERSEY							
1 Andrews	Y	Y	Y	Y	Y	Y	Y
2 ***LoBiondo***	Y	Y	N	Y	N	Y	N
3 ***Saxton***	Y	Y	N	Y	N	Y	N
4 ***Smith***	Y	Y	N	Y	N	Y	N
5 ***Garrett***	N	Y	N	Y	N	Y	N
6 Pallone	Y	Y	Y	Y	Y	N	Y
7 ***Ferguson***	Y	Y	N	Y	N	Y	N
8 Pascrell	Y	Y	Y	Y	Y	Y	Y
9 Rothman	Y	Y	Y	Y	Y	Y	Y
10 Payne	Y	Y	Y	N	Y	N	Y
11 ***Frelinghuysen***	Y	Y	N	Y	N	Y	N
12 Holt	Y	Y	Y	Y	Y	N	Y
13 Menendez	Y	Y	Y	N	Y	Y	Y
NEW MEXICO							
1 ***Wilson***	Y	Y	Y	Y	N	Y	Y
2 ***Pearce***	Y	Y	N	Y	N	Y	N
3 Udall	Y	Y	Y	N	Y	Y	Y
NEW YORK							
1 Bishop	Y	Y	N	Y	Y	Y	Y
2 Israel	?	?	?	?	?	?	Y
3 ***King***	N	Y	N	Y	N	Y	N
4 McCarthy	Y	Y	N	Y	Y	Y	Y
5 Ackerman	Y	Y	Y	N	Y	Y	Y
6 Meeks	Y	Y	Y	N	Y	Y	?
7 Crowley	Y	Y	Y	Y	Y	Y	Y
8 Nadler	Y	Y	Y	N	Y	Y	Y
9 Weiner	?	?	?	N	Y	N	Y
10 Towns	Y	Y	Y	N	Y	Y	Y
11 Owens	Y	Y	Y	N	Y	Y	Y
12 Velázquez	Y	Y	Y	N	Y	N	Y
13 ***Fossella***	N	Y	N	?	N	Y	N
14 Maloney	Y	Y	Y	N	Y	Y	Y
15 Rangel	?	?	?	?	?	?	Y
16 Serrano	Y	Y	Y	N	Y	N	Y
17 Engel	Y	Y	Y	Y	Y	Y	Y
18 Lowey	Y	Y	Y	Y	Y	Y	Y
19 ***Kelly***	N	Y	N	Y	N	Y	N
20 ***Sweeney***	Y	Y	N	Y	N	Y	N
21 McNulty	Y	Y	N	Y	Y	Y	Y
22 Hinchey	Y	Y	N	N	Y	Y	Y
23 ***McHugh***	Y	Y	N	Y	N	Y	N
24 ***Boehlert***	Y	Y	N	Y	N	Y	N
25 ***Walsh***	Y	Y	N	Y	N	Y	N
26 ***Reynolds***	Y	Y	N	Y	N	Y	N
27 ***Quinn***	Y	Y	N	Y	N	Y	?
28 Slaughter	Y	Y	Y	N	Y	N	Y
29 ***Houghton***	N	Y	N	Y	N	Y	N
NORTH CAROLINA							
1 Vacant							
2 Etheridge	Y	Y	N	Y	Y	Y	Y
3 ***Jones***	Y	Y	N	Y	N	Y	N
4 Price	Y	Y	N	Y	Y	Y	Y
5 ***Burr***	Y	Y	N	Y	N	Y	N
6 ***Coble***	Y	Y	N	Y	N	Y	N
7 McIntyre	Y	Y	Y	Y	Y	Y	Y
8 ***Hayes***	Y	Y	N	Y	N	Y	N
9 ***Myrick***	Y	Y	N	Y	N	Y	N
10 ***Ballenger***	N	Y	N	Y	N	Y	N
11 ***Taylor***	N	Y	N	Y	N	Y	N
12 Watt	Y	Y	Y	N	Y	N	Y
13 Miller	Y	Y	N	Y	Y	Y	Y
NORTH DAKOTA							
AL Pomeroy	Y	Y	N	Y	Y	Y	Y
OHIO							
1 ***Chabot***	Y	Y	N	Y	N	Y	N
2 ***Portman***	Y	Y	N	Y	N	Y	N
3 ***Turner***	Y	Y	N	Y	N	Y	N
4 ***Oxley***	N	Y	N	Y	N	Y	N
5 ***Gillmor***	Y	Y	N	Y	N	Y	N
6 Strickland	Y	Y	N	N	Y	Y	Y
7 ***Hobson***	Y	Y	N	Y	N	Y	N
8 ***Boehner***	N	Y	N	Y	N	Y	N
9 Kaptur	Y	Y	Y	N	Y	Y	Y
10 Kucinich	Y	Y	Y	N	Y	N	Y
11 Jones	Y	Y	Y	N	Y	N	?
12 ***Tiberi***	Y	Y	N	Y	N	Y	N
13 Brown	Y	Y	N	N	Y	Y	?
14 ***LaTourette***	Y	Y	N	Y	N	Y	N
15 ***Pryce***	Y	Y	N	Y	N	Y	N
16 ***Regula***	Y	Y	N	Y	N	Y	N
17 Ryan	Y	Y	N	N	Y	N	Y
18 ***Ney***	Y	Y	N	Y	N	Y	N
OKLAHOMA							
1 ***Sullivan***	Y	Y	N	Y	N	Y	N
2 Carson	Y	Y	N	Y	Y	Y	N
3 ***Lucas***	N	Y	N	Y	N	Y	N
4 ***Cole***	Y	Y	N	Y	N	Y	N
5 ***Istook***	Y	Y	N	Y	N	Y	N
OREGON							
1 Wu	Y	Y	Y	Y	Y	Y	Y
2 ***Walden***	Y	Y	N	Y	N	Y	N
3 Blumenauer	Y	Y	Y	N	Y	N	Y
4 DeFazio	Y	Y	Y	Y	Y	Y	Y
5 Hooley	Y	Y	Y	Y	Y	Y	Y
PENNSYLVANIA							
1 Brady	Y	Y	Y	N	Y	Y	Y
2 Fattah	Y	Y	Y	N	Y	N	Y
3 ***English***	Y	Y	N	Y	N	Y	N
4 ***Hart***	N	Y	N	Y	N	Y	N
5 ***Peterson***	Y	Y	N	Y	N	Y	N
6 ***Gerlach***	Y	Y	N	Y	N	Y	N
7 ***Weldon***	Y	Y	N	Y	N	Y	N
8 ***Greenwood***	Y	Y	N	Y	N	Y	N
9 ***Shuster, Bill***	Y	Y	N	Y	N	Y	N
10 ***Sherwood***	N	Y	N	Y	N	Y	N
11 Kanjorski	Y	Y	N	N	Y	Y	Y
12 Murtha	Y	Y	N	N	Y	Y	Y
13 Hoeffel	Y	Y	Y	N	Y	Y	Y
14 Doyle	Y	Y	Y	N	Y	Y	?
15 ***Toomey***	Y	Y	N	Y	N	Y	N
16 ***Pitts***	Y	Y	N	Y	N	Y	N
17 Holden	Y	Y	N	Y	Y	Y	Y
18 ***Murphy***	N	Y	N	Y	N	Y	N
19 ***Platts***	Y	Y	N	Y	N	Y	N
RHODE ISLAND							
1 Kennedy	Y	Y	N	Y	Y	Y	Y
2 Langevin	Y	Y	Y	N	Y	Y	Y
SOUTH CAROLINA							
1 ***Brown***	Y	Y	N	Y	N	Y	N
2 ***Wilson***	N	Y	N	Y	N	Y	N
3 ***Barrett***	N	Y	N	Y	N	Y	N
4 ***DeMint***	?	?	?	?	?	?	?
5 Spratt	Y	Y	N	Y	Y	Y	Y
6 Clyburn	Y	Y	Y	N	Y	Y	Y
SOUTH DAKOTA							
AL Herseth	Y	Y	N	Y	Y	Y	Y
TENNESSEE							
1 ***Jenkins***	N	Y	N	Y	N	Y	N
2 ***Duncan***	Y	Y	N	Y	N	N	N
3 ***Wamp***	N	Y	N	Y	N	Y	N
4 Davis	Y	Y	N	Y	Y	Y	N
5 Cooper	Y	Y	N	Y	Y	Y	Y
6 Gordon	Y	Y	N	Y	Y	Y	Y
7 ***Blackburn***	N	Y	N	Y	N	Y	N
8 Tanner	Y	Y	N	Y	Y	Y	N
9 Ford	Y	Y	N	Y	Y	Y	Y
TEXAS							
1 Sandlin	Y	Y	Y	Y	Y	Y	N
2 Turner	Y	Y	Y	Y	Y	Y	Y
3 ***Johnson, Sam***	N	Y	N	Y	N	Y	N
4 ***Hall***	Y	Y	N	Y	N	Y	N
5 ***Hensarling***	N	Y	N	Y	N	Y	N
6 ***Barton***	N	Y	N	Y	N	Y	?
7 ***Culberson***	N	Y	N	Y	N	Y	N
8 ***Brady***	N	Y	N	Y	N	Y	N
9 Lampson	Y	Y	Y	Y	Y	Y	Y
10 Doggett	Y	Y	Y	N	Y	Y	Y
11 Edwards	Y	Y	N	Y	Y	Y	Y
12 ***Granger***	N	Y	N	Y	N	Y	?
13 ***Thornberry***	N	Y	N	Y	N	Y	N
14 ***Paul***	Y	Y	Y	Y	N	N	N
15 Hinojosa	Y	Y	Y	N	Y	Y	Y
16 Reyes	Y	Y	Y	Y	Y	N	?
17 Stenholm	Y	Y	N	Y	Y	Y	N
18 Jackson-Lee	Y	Y	Y	N	Y	N	Y
19 ***Neugebauer***	N	Y	N	Y	N	Y	N
20 Gonzalez	Y	Y	Y	Y	Y	Y	Y
21 ***Smith***	Y	Y	N	Y	N	Y	?
22 ***DeLay***	N	Y	N	Y	N	Y	N
23 ***Bonilla***	N	Y	N	Y	N	Y	N
24 Frost	Y	Y	N	Y	Y	Y	Y
25 Bell	Y	Y	Y	Y	Y	Y	Y
26 ***Burgess***	N	Y	N	Y	N	Y	N
27 Ortiz	Y	Y	Y	Y	Y	Y	Y
28 Rodriguez	Y	Y	Y	N	Y	Y	Y
29 Green	Y	Y	Y	Y	Y	N	Y
30 Johnson, E.B.	Y	Y	Y	N	Y	Y	Y
31 ***Carter***	N	Y	N	Y	N	Y	N
32 ***Sessions***	Y	Y	N	Y	N	Y	N
UTAH							
1 ***Bishop***	N	Y	N	Y	N	Y	N
2 Matheson	Y	Y	N	Y	Y	Y	N
3 ***Cannon***	N	Y	N	Y	N	Y	N
VERMONT							
AL *Sanders*	Y	Y	Y	N	Y	Y	Y
VIRGINIA							
1 ***Davis, Jo Ann***	Y	Y	N	Y	N	Y	N
2 ***Schrock***	N	Y	N	Y	N	Y	N
3 Scott	Y	Y	Y	N	Y	Y	Y
4 ***Forbes***	Y	Y	N	Y	N	Y	N
5 ***Goode***	Y	Y	N	Y	N	Y	N
6 ***Goodlatte***	Y	Y	N	Y	N	Y	N
7 ***Cantor***	N	Y	N	Y	N	Y	N
8 Moran	Y	Y	Y	N	Y	Y	Y
9 Boucher	Y	Y	N	Y	Y	Y	Y
10 ***Wolf***	Y	Y	N	Y	N	Y	N
11 ***Davis, T.***	Y	Y	N	Y	N	Y	N
WASHINGTON							
1 Inslee	Y	Y	N	N	Y	Y	Y
2 Larsen	Y	Y	Y	Y	Y	Y	Y
3 Baird	N	Y	N	Y	Y	Y	Y
4 ***Hastings***	N	Y	N	Y	N	Y	N
5 ***Nethercutt***	Y	Y	N	Y	N	Y	N
6 Dicks	Y	Y	Y	N	Y	Y	Y
7 McDermott	?	?	?	?	?	?	?
8 ***Dunn***	Y	Y	N	Y	N	Y	N
9 Smith	Y	Y	Y	Y	Y	Y	Y
WEST VIRGINIA							
1 Mollohan	Y	Y	Y	N	Y	N	Y
2 ***Capito***	Y	Y	N	Y	N	Y	N
3 Rahall	Y	Y	Y	N	Y	Y	Y
WISCONSIN							
1 ***Ryan***	N	Y	N	Y	N	Y	N
2 Baldwin	Y	Y	Y	N	Y	N	Y
3 Kind	Y	Y	N	Y	Y	Y	Y
4 Kleczka	Y	Y	Y	N	Y	N	Y
5 ***Sensenbrenner***	N	Y	N	Y	N	Y	N
6 ***Petri***	N	Y	N	Y	N	Y	N
7 Obey	Y	Y	Y	N	Y	N	Y
8 ***Green***	Y	Y	N	Y	N	Y	N
WYOMING							
AL ***Cubin***	Y	Y	N	Y	N	Y	N

Southern states - Ala., Ark., Fla., Ga., Ky., La., Miss., N.C., Okla., S.C., Tenn., Texas, Va.

Key

302. HR 4663. Budget Enforcement/Previous Question. Hastings, R-Wash., motion to order the previous question (thus ending debate and possibility of amendment) on adoption of the rule (H Res 692) to provide for House floor consideration of the bill that would set statutory caps on discretionary spending for fiscal years 2005 and 2006, and institute pay-as-you-go rules requiring any mandatory spending increases to be offset by reductions in spending. Motion agreed to 217-197: R 217-0; D 0-196 (ND 0-142, SD 0-54); I 0-1. June 24, 2004.

303. HR 4663. Budget Enforcement/Rule. Adoption of the rule (H Res 692) to provide for House floor consideration of the bill that would set statutory caps on discretionary spending for fiscal years 2005 and 2006, and institute pay-as-you-go rules requiring any mandatory spending increases to be offset by reductions in spending. Adopted 217-197: R 217-0; D 0-196 (ND 0-142, SD 0-54); I 0-1. June 24, 2004.

304. H Res 676. Civil Rights Act 40th Anniversary/Adoption. Sensenbrenner, R-Wis., motion to suspend the rules and adopt the resolution that would honor the 40th anniversary of the passage of the Civil Rights Act of 1964. Motion agreed to 414-1: R 217-1; D 196-0 (ND 142-0, SD 54-0); I 1-0. A two-thirds majority of those present and voting (277 in this case) is required for adoption under suspension of the rules. June 24, 2004.

305. HR 4663. Budget Enforcement/Federal Sunset Commission. Brady, R-Texas, amendment that would establish a 12-member Federal Sunset Commission to review all federal agencies for their efficiency, effectiveness, redundancy and need. Adopted 272-140: R 208-11; D 64-128 (ND 32-108, SD 32-20); I 0-1. June 24, 2004.

306. HR 4663. Budget Enforcement/Budget Categories. Chocola, R-Ind., amendment that would replace the current 20 budget functions in budget resolutions with the following five categories: mandatory spending; defense discretionary spending; non-defense discretionary spending, emergency spending and interest on the debt. Rejected 126-290: R 120-100; D 6-189 (ND 5-136, SD 1-53); I 0-1. June 24, 2004.

307. HR 4663. Budget Enforcement/Budget Committee Discretion. Castle, R-Del., amendment that would eliminate the requirement to provide budget authority and outlays for the 20 separate functions in the budget resolution. It would grant the House and Senate Budget committees the discretion to include any functional categories they deem appropriate in the budget resolution. Rejected 185-230: R 172-48; D 13-181 (ND 7-133, SD 6-48); I 0-1. June 24, 2004.

308. HR 4663. Budget Enforcement/Entitlement Caps. Hensarling, R-Texas, amendment that would limit annual spending increases for entitlement programs other than Social Security to the growth in inflation plus the increase in the number of eligible beneficiaries. Rejected 96-317: R 96-120; D 0-196 (ND 0-142, SD 0-54); I 0-1. June 24, 2004.

	302	303	304	305	306	307	308
ALABAMA							
1 *Bonner*	Y	Y	Y	N	Y	N	N
2 *Everett*	Y	Y	Y	N	N	N	N
3 *Rogers*	Y	Y	Y	Y	Y	Y	N
4 *Aderholt*	Y	Y	Y	Y	N	N	N
5 Cramer	N	N	Y	N	N	N	N
6 *Bachus*	Y	Y	Y	Y	Y	Y	N
7 Davis	N	N	Y	N	N	N	N
ALASKA							
AL *Young*	Y	Y	Y	N	N	N	N
ARIZONA							
1 *Renzi*	Y	Y	Y	N	N	N	N
2 *Franks*	Y	Y	Y	Y	Y	Y	Y
3 *Shadegg*	Y	Y	Y	Y	Y	Y	Y
4 Pastor	N	N	Y	N	N	N	N
5 *Hayworth*	Y	Y	Y	Y	Y	Y	Y
6 *Flake*	Y	Y	Y	Y	Y	Y	Y
7 Grijalva	N	N	Y	N	N	N	N
8 *Kolbe*	Y	Y	Y	N	N	Y	N
ARKANSAS							
1 Berry	N	N	Y	N	N	N	N
2 Snyder	N	N	Y	Y	N	N	N
3 *Boozman*	Y	Y	Y	Y	Y	Y	N
4 Ross	N	N	Y	N	N	N	N
CALIFORNIA							
1 Thompson	N	N	Y	N	N	N	N
2 *Herger*	Y	Y	Y	Y	Y	Y	?
3 *Ose*	Y	Y	Y	N	N	Y	Y
4 *Doolittle*	Y	Y	?	Y	N	Y	Y
5 Matsui	N	N	Y	N	N	N	N
6 Woolsey	N	N	Y	N	N	N	N
7 Miller, George	N	N	Y	N	N	N	N
8 Pelosi	N	N	Y	N	N	N	N
9 Lee	N	N	Y	N	N	N	N
10 Tauscher	N	N	Y	N	N	N	N
11 *Pombo*	Y	Y	Y	N	N	N	Y
12 Lantos	N	N	Y	N	N	N	N
13 Stark	N	N	Y	N	N	N	N
14 Eshoo	N	N	Y	N	N	N	N
15 Honda	N	N	Y	N	N	N	N
16 Lofgren	N	N	Y	N	N	N	N
17 Farr	N	N	Y	N	N	N	N
18 Cardoza	N	N	Y	N	N	N	N
19 *Radanovich*	Y	Y	Y	Y	N	Y	N
20 Dooley	N	N	Y	N	N	N	N
21 *Nunes*	Y	Y	Y	N	N	N	N
22 *Thomas*	Y	Y	Y	N	Y	Y	N
23 Capps	N	N	Y	N	N	N	N
24 *Gallegly*	Y	Y	Y	N	Y	Y	N
25 *McKeon*	Y	Y	Y	Y	Y	Y	Y
26 *Dreier*	Y	Y	Y	N	Y	N	N
27 Sherman	N	N	Y	N	N	N	N
28 Berman	?	?	?	?	?	?	?
29 Schiff	N	N	Y	N	N	N	N
30 Waxman	N	N	Y	N	N	N	N
31 Becerra	N	N	Y	N	N	N	N
32 Solis	N	N	Y	N	N	N	N
33 Watson	N	N	Y	N	N	N	N
34 Roybal-Allard	N	N	Y	?	N	N	N
35 Waters	N	N	Y	N	N	N	N
36 Harman	N	N	Y	N	N	Y	N

	302	303	304	305	306	307	308
37 Millender-McD.	N	N	Y	N	N	N	N
38 Napolitano	N	N	Y	N	N	N	N
39 Sánchez, Linda	N	N	Y	N	N	N	N
40 *Royce*	Y	Y	Y	Y	Y	Y	Y
41 *Lewis*	Y	Y	Y	Y	N	Y	N
42 *Miller, Gary*	Y	Y	Y	Y	Y	Y	Y
43 Baca	N	N	Y	N	N	N	N
44 *Calvert*	Y	Y	Y	Y	N	Y	N
45 *Bono*	Y	Y	Y	Y	Y	Y	N
46 *Rohrabacher*	Y	Y	Y	Y	Y	Y	Y
47 Sanchez, Loretta	N	N	Y	N	N	N	N
48 *Cox*	Y	Y	Y	Y	Y	Y	Y
49 *Issa*	Y	Y	Y	N	N	Y	?
50 *Cunningham*	Y	Y	Y	Y	N	N	N
51 Filner	N	N	Y	N	N	N	N
52 *Hunter*	Y	Y	Y	N	N	N	N
53 Davis	N	N	Y	N	N	N	N
COLORADO							
1 DeGette	N	N	Y	N	N	N	N
2 Udall	N	N	Y	N	N	N	N
3 *McInnis*	Y	Y	Y	Y	Y	Y	N
4 *Musgrave*	Y	Y	Y	Y	Y	Y	Y
5 *Hefley*	Y	Y	Y	N	Y	N	N
6 *Tancredo*	Y	Y	Y	Y	Y	Y	N
7 *Beauprez*	Y	Y	Y	Y	Y	Y	Y
CONNECTICUT							
1 Larson	N	N	Y	N	N	N	N
2 *Simmons*	Y	Y	Y	Y	N	Y	N
3 DeLauro	N	N	Y	N	N	N	N
4 *Shays*	Y	Y	Y	Y	N	Y	N
5 *Johnson*	Y	Y	Y	Y	N	Y	N
DELAWARE							
AL *Castle*	Y	Y	Y	Y	N	Y	N
FLORIDA							
1 *Miller, J.*	Y	Y	Y	Y	Y	Y	Y
2 Boyd	N	N	Y	N	N	N	N
3 Brown	N	N	Y	N	N	N	N
4 *Crenshaw*	Y	Y	Y	Y	N	Y	N
5 *Brown-Waite*	Y	Y	Y	N	N	N	N
6 *Stearns*	Y	Y	Y	N	N	N	N
7 *Mica*	Y	Y	Y	N	N	Y	N
8 *Keller*	Y	Y	Y	Y	Y	Y	Y
9 *Bilirakis*	Y	Y	Y	Y	N	N	N
10 *Young*	Y	Y	Y	N	N	N	N
11 Davis	N	N	Y	N	N	N	N
12 *Putnam*	Y	Y	Y	N	N	Y	N
13 *Harris*	Y	Y	?	Y	Y	Y	Y
14 *Goss*	Y	Y	Y	N	N	N	N
15 *Weldon*	Y	Y	Y	Y	N	Y	N
16 *Foley*	Y	Y	Y	N	N	Y	N
17 Meek	N	N	Y	N	N	N	N
18 *Ros-Lehtinen*	Y	Y	Y	Y	Y	Y	?
19 Wexler	N	N	Y	N	N	N	N
20 Deutsch	?	?	?	?	?	?	?
21 *Diaz-Balart, L.*	Y	Y	Y	Y	Y	Y	N
22 *Shaw*	Y	Y	Y	Y	N	Y	N
23 Hastings	?	?	?	?	?	?	?
24 *Feeney*	Y	Y	Y	Y	Y	Y	Y
25 *Diaz-Balart, M.*	Y	Y	Y	Y	Y	Y	Y
GEORGIA							
1 *Kingston*	Y	Y	Y	N	Y	Y	Y
2 Bishop	N	N	Y	N	N	N	N
3 Marshall	N	N	Y	N	N	N	N
4 Majette	N	N	Y	N	N	N	N
5 Lewis	N	N	Y	N	N	N	N
6 *Isakson*	Y	Y	Y	Y	N	Y	N
7 *Linder*	?	?	?	Y	N	Y	N
8 *Collins*	Y	Y	Y	?	?	?	?
9 *Norwood*	Y	Y	Y	Y	Y	Y	Y
10 *Deal*	Y	Y	Y	Y	Y	Y	Y
11 *Gingrey*	Y	Y	Y	Y	Y	Y	Y
12 *Burns*	Y	Y	Y	Y	Y	Y	Y
13 Scott	N	N	Y	N	N	N	N
HAWAII							
1 Abercrombie	N	N	Y	N	N	N	N
2 Case	N	N	Y	Y	N	?	N
IDAHO							
1 *Otter*	Y	Y	Y	Y	Y	N	Y
2 *Simpson*	Y	Y	Y	N	N	N	N
ILLINOIS							
1 Rush	N	N	Y	N	N	N	N
2 Jackson	N	N	Y	N	N	N	N
3 Lipinski	N	N	Y	N	N	N	N
4 Gutierrez	N	N	Y	N	N	N	N
5 Emanuel	N	N	Y	N	N	N	N
6 *Hyde*	Y	Y	Y	N	N	N	N

ND Northern Democrats   SD Southern Democrats

	302	303	304	305	306	307	308
7 Davis	N	N	Y	N	N	N	N
8 ***Crane***	Y	Y	Y	Y	Y	Y	Y
9 Schakowsky	N	N	Y	N	N	N	N
10 ***Kirk***	Y	+	Y	Y	Y	Y	N
11 ***Weller***	Y	Y	Y	Y	Y	N	N
12 Costello	N	N	Y	Y	N	N	N
13 ***Biggert***	Y	Y	Y	Y	Y	Y	N
14 ***Hastert***							
15 ***Johnson***	Y	Y	Y	Y	N	N	N
16 ***Manzullo***	Y	Y	Y	Y	Y	Y	Y
17 Evans	N	N	Y	N	N	N	N
18 ***LaHood***	Y	Y	Y	N	N	N	N
19 ***Shimkus***	Y	Y	Y	Y	Y	Y	Y
INDIANA							
1 Visclosky	N	N	Y	N	N	N	N
2 ***Chocola***	Y	Y	Y	Y	Y	Y	Y
3 ***Souder***	Y	Y	Y	Y	Y	Y	Y
4 ***Buyer***	Y	Y	Y	Y	N	Y	N
5 ***Burton***	Y	Y	Y	Y	Y	Y	N
6 ***Pence***	Y	Y	Y	Y	Y	Y	Y
7 Carson	?	?	?	?	?	?	?
8 ***Hostettler***	Y	Y	Y	Y	Y	Y	Y
9 Hill	N	N	Y	N	N	N	N
IOWA							
1 ***Nussle***	Y	Y	Y	Y	N	Y	N
2 ***Leach***	Y	Y	Y	Y	Y	Y	N
3 Boswell	N	N	Y	Y	Y	Y	N
4 ***Latham***	Y	Y	Y	Y	N	Y	N
5 ***King***	Y	Y	Y	Y	Y	Y	Y
KANSAS							
1 ***Moran***	Y	Y	Y	Y	Y	Y	Y
2 ***Ryun***	Y	Y	Y	Y	Y	Y	Y
3 Moore	N	N	Y	Y	Y	N	N
4 ***Tiahrt***	Y	Y	Y	Y	N	Y	Y
KENTUCKY							
1 ***Whitfield***	Y	Y	Y	Y	N	Y	N
2 ***Lewis***	Y	Y	Y	Y	N	Y	N
3 ***Northup***	Y	Y	Y	Y	N	Y	N
4 Lucas	N	N	Y	Y	N	Y	N
5 ***Rogers***	Y	Y	Y	Y	N	Y	N
6 Chandler	N	N	Y	N	N	N	N
LOUISIANA							
1 ***Vitter***	Y	Y	Y	Y	Y	Y	Y
2 Jefferson	N	N	Y	?	N	N	N
3 ***Tauzin***	?	?	?	?	?	?	?
4 ***McCrery***	Y	Y	Y	Y	Y	Y	N
5 Alexander	N	N	Y	Y	N	N	N
6 ***Baker***	Y	Y	Y	N	N	Y	N
7 John	N	N	Y	Y	N	N	N
MAINE							
1 Allen	N	N	Y	N	N	N	N
2 Michaud	N	N	Y	N	N	N	N
MARYLAND							
1 ***Gilchrest***	Y	Y	Y	Y	N	Y	N
2 Ruppersberger	N	N	Y	Y	N	N	N
3 Cardin	N	N	Y	N	N	N	N
4 Wynn	N	N	Y	N	N	N	N
5 Hoyer	N	N	Y	N	N	N	N
6 ***Bartlett***	Y	Y	Y	Y	Y	Y	Y
7 Cummings	N	N	Y	N	N	N	N
8 Van Hollen	N	N	Y	N	N	N	N
MASSACHUSETTS							
1 Olver	N	N	Y	N	N	N	N
2 Neal	N	N	Y	N	N	N	N
3 McGovern	N	N	Y	N	N	N	N
4 Frank	N	N	Y	N	N	N	N
5 Meehan	N	N	Y	Y	N	N	N
6 Tierney	N	N	Y	N	N	N	N
7 Markey	N	N	Y	N	N	N	N
8 Capuano	N	N	Y	N	N	N	N
9 Lynch	N	N	Y	N	N	N	N
10 Delahunt	N	N	Y	N	N	N	N
MICHIGAN							
1 Stupak	N	N	Y	N	N	N	N
2 ***Hoekstra***	Y	Y	Y	Y	Y	Y	Y
3 ***Ehlers***	Y	Y	Y	Y	Y	Y	N
4 ***Camp***	Y	Y	Y	Y	Y	Y	N
5 Kildee	N	N	Y	N	N	N	N
6 ***Upton***	Y	Y	Y	Y	Y	Y	N
7 ***Smith***	Y	Y	Y	Y	Y	Y	Y
8 ***Rogers***	Y	Y	Y	Y	Y	Y	N
9 ***Knollenberg***	Y	Y	Y	Y	N	Y	N
10 ***Miller***	Y	Y	Y	N	N	N	N
11 ***McCotter***	Y	Y	Y	Y	N	N	N
12 Levin	N	N	Y	N	N	N	N

	302	303	304	305	306	307	308
13 Kilpatrick	N	N	Y	N	N	N	N
14 Conyers	N	N	Y	N	N	?	N
15 Dingell	N	N	Y	N	N	N	N
MINNESOTA							
1 ***Gutknecht***	Y	?	Y	Y	Y	Y	Y
2 ***Kline***	Y	Y	Y	Y	Y	Y	Y
3 ***Ramstad***	Y	Y	Y	Y	Y	Y	N
4 McCollum	N	N	Y	N	N	N	N
5 Sabo	N	N	Y	N	N	N	N
6 ***Kennedy***	Y	Y	Y	Y	Y	Y	Y
7 Peterson	N	N	Y	Y	N	N	N
8 Oberstar	N	N	Y	N	N	N	N
MISSISSIPPI							
1 ***Wicker***	Y	Y	Y	Y	N	Y	N
2 Thompson	N	N	Y	N	N	N	N
3 ***Pickering***	Y	Y	Y	Y	N	Y	N
4 Taylor	N	N	Y	Y	N	Y	N
MISSOURI							
1 Clay	N	N	Y	N	N	N	N
2 ***Akin***	Y	Y	Y	Y	Y	Y	Y
3 Gephardt	?	?	?	?	?	?	?
4 Skelton	N	N	Y	Y	N	Y	N
5 McCarthy	N	N	Y	N	N	N	N
6 ***Graves***	Y	Y	Y	Y	N	N	N
7 ***Blunt***	Y	Y	Y	Y	Y	Y	Y
8 ***Emerson***	Y	Y	Y	Y	N	Y	N
9 ***Hulshof***	Y	Y	Y	Y	Y	Y	N
MONTANA							
AL ***Rehberg***	Y	Y	Y	Y	N	Y	N
NEBRASKA							
1 ***Bereuter***	?	?	?	?	?	?	?
2 ***Terry***	Y	Y	Y	Y	N	Y	N
3 ***Osborne***	Y	Y	Y	Y	N	Y	N
NEVADA							
1 Berkley	N	N	Y	N	N	N	N
2 ***Gibbons***	Y	Y	Y	Y	N	Y	Y
3 ***Porter***	Y	Y	Y	Y	N	N	N
NEW HAMPSHIRE							
1 ***Bradley***	Y	Y	Y	Y	N	Y	N
2 ***Bass***	Y	Y	Y	Y	Y	Y	Y
NEW JERSEY							
1 Andrews	N	N	Y	N	N	N	N
2 ***LoBiondo***	Y	Y	Y	Y	N	Y	N
3 ***Saxton***	Y	Y	Y	Y	N	N	N
4 ***Smith***	Y	Y	Y	Y	N	N	N
5 ***Garrett***	Y	Y	Y	Y	Y	Y	Y
6 Pallone	N	N	Y	N	N	N	N
7 ***Ferguson***	Y	Y	Y	Y	N	Y	N
8 Pascrell	N	N	Y	N	N	N	N
9 Rothman	N	N	Y	?	?	?	?
10 Payne	N	N	Y	N	N	N	N
11 ***Frelinghuysen***	Y	Y	Y	N	N	Y	N
12 Holt	N	N	Y	N	N	N	N
13 Menendez	N	N	Y	N	N	N	N
NEW MEXICO							
1 ***Wilson***	Y	Y	Y	N	Y	N	N
2 ***Pearce***	Y	Y	Y	Y	Y	Y	Y
3 Udall	N	N	Y	Y	N	N	N
NEW YORK							
1 Bishop	N	N	Y	N	N	N	N
2 Israel	N	N	Y	Y	N	N	N
3 ***King***	Y	Y	Y	Y	N	N	N
4 McCarthy	N	N	Y	N	N	N	N
5 Ackerman	N	N	Y	N	N	N	N
6 Meeks	?	?	?	?	N	N	N
7 Crowley	N	N	Y	N	N	N	N
8 Nadler	N	N	Y	N	N	N	N
9 Weiner	N	N	Y	N	N	N	N
10 Towns	N	N	Y	N	N	N	N
11 Owens	N	N	Y	N	N	N	N
12 Velázquez	N	N	Y	?	N	N	N
13 ***Fossella***	Y	Y	Y	Y	Y	Y	N
14 Maloney	N	N	Y	N	N	N	N
15 Rangel	N	N	Y	N	N	N	N
16 Serrano	N	N	Y	N	N	N	N
17 Engel	N	N	Y	N	N	N	N
18 Lowey	N	N	Y	N	N	N	N
19 ***Kelly***	Y	Y	Y	Y	N	Y	N
20 ***Sweeney***	Y	Y	Y	Y	N	Y	N
21 McNulty	N	N	Y	Y	N	N	N
22 Hinchey	N	N	Y	N	N	N	N
23 ***McHugh***	Y	Y	Y	Y	N	Y	N
24 ***Boehlert***	Y	Y	Y	Y	N	Y	N
25 ***Walsh***	Y	Y	Y	Y	N	N	N

	302	303	304	305	306	307	308
26 ***Reynolds***	Y	Y	Y	Y	Y	Y	N
27 ***Quinn***	?	?	?	Y	N	N	N
28 Slaughter	N	N	Y	N	N	N	N
29 ***Houghton***	Y	Y	Y	Y	Y	N	N
NORTH CAROLINA							
1 Vacant							
2 Etheridge	N	N	Y	N	N	N	N
3 ***Jones***	Y	Y	Y	Y	Y	Y	N
4 Price	N	N	Y	N	N	N	N
5 ***Burr***	Y	Y	Y	Y	N	Y	N
6 ***Coble***	Y	Y	Y	Y	Y	N	Y
7 McIntyre	N	N	Y	Y	N	N	N
8 ***Hayes***	Y	Y	Y	Y	N	N	N
9 ***Myrick***	Y	Y	Y	Y	Y	Y	Y
10 ***Ballenger***	Y	Y	Y	Y	Y	Y	Y
11 ***Taylor***	Y	Y	Y	Y	N	Y	Y
12 Watt	N	N	Y	N	N	N	N
13 Miller	N	N	Y	N	N	N	N
NORTH DAKOTA							
AL Pomeroy	N	N	Y	N	N	N	N
OHIO							
1 ***Chabot***	Y	Y	Y	Y	Y	Y	Y
2 ***Portman***	Y	Y	Y	Y	N	Y	N
3 ***Turner***	Y	Y	Y	Y	N	N	N
4 ***Oxley***	Y	Y	Y	Y	N	N	N
5 ***Gillmor***	Y	Y	Y	Y	N	Y	N
6 Strickland	N	N	Y	N	N	N	N
7 ***Hobson***	Y	Y	Y	Y	N	N	N
8 ***Boehner***	Y	Y	Y	Y	Y	Y	Y
9 Kaptur	N	N	Y	N	N	N	N
10 Kucinich	N	N	Y	N	N	N	N
11 Jones	?	?	?	?	?	?	?
12 ***Tiberi***	?	Y	Y	Y	Y	Y	N
13 Brown	?	?	?	N	N	N	N
14 ***LaTourette***	Y	Y	Y	Y	N	N	N
15 ***Pryce***	Y	Y	Y	Y	Y	Y	N
16 ***Regula***	Y	Y	Y	Y	N	Y	N
17 Ryan	N	N	Y	N	N	N	N
18 ***Ney***	Y	Y	Y	Y	Y	Y	N
OKLAHOMA							
1 ***Sullivan***	Y	Y	Y	Y	Y	Y	Y
2 Carson	N	N	Y	Y	N	N	N
3 ***Lucas***	Y	Y	Y	Y	N	N	N
4 ***Cole***	?	Y	Y	Y	Y	Y	Y
5 ***Istook***	Y	Y	Y	Y	N	Y	Y
OREGON							
1 Wu	N	N	Y	Y	N	N	N
2 ***Walden***	Y	Y	Y	Y	N	Y	N
3 Blumenauer	N	N	Y	N	?	N	N
4 DeFazio	N	N	Y	Y	N	N	N
5 Hooley	N	N	Y	Y	N	N	N
PENNSYLVANIA							
1 Brady	N	N	Y	N	N	N	N
2 Fattah	N	N	Y	N	N	N	N
3 ***English***	Y	Y	Y	Y	N	Y	N
4 ***Hart***	Y	Y	Y	Y	Y	Y	?
5 ***Peterson***	Y	Y	Y	Y	N	N	N
6 ***Gerlach***	Y	Y	Y	Y	Y	Y	N
7 ***Weldon***	Y	Y	Y	Y	N	Y	N
8 ***Greenwood***	Y	Y	Y	N	Y	Y	N
9 ***Shuster, Bill***	Y	Y	Y	Y	Y	Y	N
10 ***Sherwood***	Y	Y	Y	Y	N	N	N
11 Kanjorski	N	N	Y	Y	N	N	N
12 Murtha	N	N	Y	N	Y	Y	N
13 Hoeffel	N	N	Y	Y	N	N	N
14 Doyle	N	N	Y	N	N	N	N
15 ***Toomey***	Y	Y	Y	Y	Y	Y	Y
16 ***Pitts***	Y	Y	Y	Y	Y	Y	Y
17 Holden	N	N	Y	Y	Y	Y	N
18 ***Murphy***	Y	Y	Y	Y	N	N	Y
19 ***Platts***	Y	Y	Y	Y	Y	Y	N
RHODE ISLAND							
1 Kennedy	N	N	Y	N	N	N	N
2 Langevin	N	N	Y	N	N	N	N
SOUTH CAROLINA							
1 ***Brown***	Y	Y	Y	Y	N	Y	N
2 ***Wilson***	Y	Y	Y	Y	Y	Y	Y
3 ***Barrett***	Y	Y	Y	Y	Y	Y	Y
4 ***DeMint***	?	?	?	Y	Y	N	Y
5 Spratt	N	N	Y	N	N	N	N
6 Clyburn	N	N	Y	N	N	N	N
SOUTH DAKOTA							
AL Herseth	N	N	Y	Y	N	Y	N

	302	303	304	305	306	307	308
TENNESSEE							
1 ***Jenkins***	Y	Y	Y	Y	N	Y	N
2 ***Duncan***	Y	Y	Y	Y	Y	Y	Y
3 ***Wamp***	Y	Y	Y	Y	N	Y	N
4 Davis	N	N	Y	Y	N	Y	N
5 Cooper	N	N	Y	Y	N	N	N
6 Gordon	N	N	Y	Y	N	N	N
7 ***Blackburn***	Y	Y	Y	Y	Y	Y	Y
8 Tanner	N	N	Y	Y	N	Y	N
9 Ford	N	N	Y	N	N	N	N
TEXAS							
1 Sandlin	N	N	Y	Y	N	N	N
2 Turner	N	N	Y	Y	N	N	N
3 ***Johnson, Sam***	Y	Y	Y	Y	Y	Y	Y
4 ***Hall***	Y	Y	Y	Y	N	Y	Y
5 ***Hensarling***	Y	Y	Y	Y	Y	Y	Y
6 ***Barton***	?	?	?	?	?	?	?
7 ***Culberson***	Y	Y	Y	Y	N	Y	Y
8 ***Brady***	Y	Y	Y	Y	Y	Y	Y
9 Lampson	N	N	Y	Y	N	N	N
10 Doggett	N	N	Y	Y	N	N	N
11 Edwards	N	N	Y	Y	N	N	N
12 ***Granger***	?	?	?	?	?	?	?
13 ***Thornberry***	Y	Y	Y	Y	Y	Y	Y
14 ***Paul***	Y	Y	N	Y	N	Y	Y
15 Hinojosa	N	N	Y	Y	N	N	N
16 Reyes	N	N	Y	Y	N	N	N
17 Stenholm	N	N	Y	Y	N	Y	N
18 Jackson-Lee	N	N	Y	N	N	N	N
19 ***Neugebauer***	Y	Y	Y	Y	Y	Y	Y
20 Gonzalez	N	N	Y	Y	N	N	N
21 ***Smith***	?	?	?	Y	N	Y	N
22 ***DeLay***	Y	Y	Y	Y	Y	Y	Y
23 ***Bonilla***	Y	Y	Y	Y	N	Y	N
24 Frost	N	N	Y	Y	N	N	N
25 Bell	N	N	Y	Y	N	N	N
26 ***Burgess***	Y	Y	Y	Y	Y	Y	Y
27 Ortiz	N	N	Y	Y	N	N	N
28 Rodriguez	N	N	Y	Y	N	N	N
29 Green	N	N	Y	Y	Y	Y	N
30 Johnson, E.B.	N	N	Y	Y	N	N	N
31 ***Carter***	Y	Y	Y	Y	Y	Y	Y
32 ***Sessions***	Y	Y	Y	Y	Y	Y	Y
UTAH							
1 ***Bishop***	Y	Y	Y	Y	Y	Y	Y
2 Matheson	N	N	Y	Y	N	N	N
3 ***Cannon***	Y	Y	Y	Y	Y	Y	Y
VERMONT							
AL *Sanders*	N	N	Y	N	N	N	N
VIRGINIA							
1 ***Davis, Jo Ann***	Y	Y	Y	Y	Y	Y	N
2 ***Schrock***	Y	Y	Y	Y	Y	Y	Y
3 Scott	N	N	Y	N	N	N	N
4 ***Forbes***	Y	Y	Y	Y	Y	Y	Y
5 ***Goode***	Y	Y	Y	Y	Y	N	Y
6 ***Goodlatte***	Y	Y	Y	Y	Y	N	Y
7 ***Cantor***	Y	Y	Y	Y	Y	Y	N
8 Moran	N	N	Y	N	N	N	N
9 Boucher	N	N	Y	Y	N	N	N
10 ***Wolf***	Y	Y	Y	Y	N	N	N
11 ***Davis, T.***	Y	Y	Y	?	?	?	?
WASHINGTON							
1 Inslee	N	N	Y	N	N	N	N
2 Larsen	N	N	Y	N	N	N	N
3 Baird	N	N	Y	Y	N	N	N
4 ***Hastings***	Y	Y	Y	?	?	?	?
5 ***Nethercutt***	Y	Y	Y	Y	N	Y	N
6 Dicks	N	N	Y	N	N	N	N
7 McDermott	?	?	?	?	?	?	?
8 ***Dunn***	Y	Y	Y	Y	Y	Y	Y
9 Smith	N	N	Y	Y	Y	Y	N
WEST VIRGINIA							
1 Mollohan	N	N	Y	?	?	?	?
2 ***Capito***	Y	Y	Y	Y	N	N	N
3 Rahall	N	N	Y	N	N	N	N
WISCONSIN							
1 ***Ryan***	Y	Y	Y	Y	Y	Y	Y
2 Baldwin	N	N	Y	N	N	N	N
3 Kind	N	N	Y	Y	N	N	N
4 Kleczka	N	N	Y	Y	N	N	N
5 ***Sensenbrenner***	Y	Y	Y	Y	Y	Y	Y
6 ***Petri***	Y	Y	Y	Y	Y	Y	N
7 Obey	N	N	Y	N	N	N	N
8 ***Green***	Y	Y	Y	Y	Y	Y	Y
WYOMING							
AL ***Cubin***	Y	Y	Y	Y	Y	N	Y

Southern states - Ala., Ark., Fla., Ga., Ky., La., Miss., N.C., Okla., S.C., Tenn., Texas, Va.

WWW.CQ.COM

2004 CQ ALMANAC — H-103

Key

Y	Voted for (yea).
#	Paired for.
+	Announced for.
N	Voted against (nay).
X	Paired against.
–	Announced against.
P	Voted "present."
C	Voted "present" to avoid possible conflict of interest.
?	Did not vote or otherwise make a position known.

Democrats   **Republicans**
Independents

309. HR 4663. Budget Enforcement/Automatic Continuing Resolution. Hensarling, R-Texas, amendment that would provide for an automatic continuing resolution if appropriations bills are not passed by the beginning of the fiscal year. It would set funding levels at or below the prior year's level. Rejected 111-304: R 111-109; D 0-194 (ND 0-140, SD 0-54); I 0-1. June 24, 2004.

310. HR 4663. Budget Enforcement/Budget Analysis. Kirk, R-Ill., amendment that would require the Congressional Budget Office to prepare an annual analysis comparing budgeted entitlement spending to actual entitlement spending, with an account-by-account breakdown to show spending trends. Adopted 289-121: R 199-19; D 90-101 (ND 58-80, SD 32-21); I 0-1. June 24, 2004.

311. HR 4663. Budget Enforcement/Joint Budget Resolution. Ryan, R-Wis., amendment that would change the current non-binding budget resolution from a concurrent resolution to a joint resolution that requires the president's signature and, if signed, has the force of law. Rejected 97-312: R 87-130; D 10-181 (ND 6-132, SD 4-49); I 0-1. June 24, 2004.

312. HR 4663. Budget Enforcement/Budget Protection Accounts. Ryan, R-Wis., amendment that would establish Budget Protection Accounts for mandatory and discretionary spending which would allow Congress to place budget savings in a "lockbox" to be used for deficit reduction at the end of the fiscal year. Rejected 137-272: R 118-98; D 19-173 (ND 9-130, SD 10-43); I 0-1. June 24, 2004.

313. HR 4663. Budget Enforcement/Expedited Rescissions. Ryan, R-Wis., amendment that would provide for expedited congressional consideration of presidential proposals to eliminate specific spending items in appropriations bills. Rejected 174-237: R 129-89; D 45-147 (ND 21-118, SD 24-29); I 0-1. June 24, 2004.

	309	310	311	312	313
ALABAMA					
1 *Bonner*	N	Y	N	N	Y
2 *Everett*	N	N	N	N	N
3 *Rogers*	N	Y	N	N	N
4 *Aderholt*	N	N	N	N	N
5 Cramer	N	Y	N	N	N
6 *Bachus*	N	Y	N	N	N
7 Davis	N	N	N	N	N
ALASKA					
AL *Young*	N	N	N	N	N
ARIZONA					
1 *Renzi*	N	Y	N	Y	N
2 *Franks*	Y	Y	Y	Y	Y
3 *Shadegg*	Y	Y	Y	Y	Y
4 Pastor	N	Y	N	N	N
5 *Hayworth*	Y	Y	Y	Y	Y
6 *Flake*	Y	Y	Y	Y	Y
7 Grijalva	N	N	N	N	N
8 *Kolbe*	N	Y	N	N	N
ARKANSAS					
1 Berry	N	Y	N	N	N
2 Snyder	N	Y	N	N	Y
3 *Boozman*	N	Y	N	N	Y
4 Ross	N	Y	N	N	N
CALIFORNIA					
1 Thompson	N	Y	N	N	N
2 *Herger*	Y	Y	Y	Y	Y
3 *Ose*	Y	Y	N	Y	Y
4 *Doolittle*	N	Y	N	N	N
5 Matsui	N	N	N	N	N
6 Woolsey	N	N	N	N	N
7 Miller, George	N	Y	N	N	N
8 Pelosi	N	N	N	N	N
9 Lee	N	N	N	N	N
10 Tauscher	N	Y	N	N	N
11 *Pombo*	Y	Y	N	Y	Y
12 Lantos	N	Y	N	N	N
13 Stark	N	N	N	N	N
14 Eshoo	N	Y	N	N	N
15 Honda	N	N	N	N	N
16 Lofgren	N	Y	N	N	Y
17 Farr	N	N	N	N	N
18 Cardoza	N	Y	N	N	Y
19 *Radanovich*	Y	N	N	Y	Y
20 Dooley	N	Y	N	N	Y
21 *Nunes*	Y	Y	N	Y	Y
22 *Thomas*	Y	Y	N	N	Y
23 Capps	N	Y	N	N	N
24 *Gallegly*	N	Y	N	Y	Y
25 *McKeon*	Y	Y	N	Y	Y
26 *Dreier*	N	Y	N	N	N
27 Sherman	N	Y	N	N	N
28 Berman	?	?	?	?	?
29 Schiff	N	Y	N	N	?
30 Waxman	N	N	N	N	N
31 Becerra	N	N	N	N	N
32 Solis	N	N	N	N	N
33 Watson	N	N	N	N	N
34 Roybal-Allard	N	N	N	N	N
35 Waters	?	N	N	N	N
36 Harman	N	Y	N	Y	Y

	309	310	311	312	313
37 Millender-McD.	N	N	N	N	N
38 Napolitano	N	Y	N	N	N
39 Sánchez, Linda	N	N	N	N	N
40 *Royce*	Y	Y	Y	Y	Y
41 *Lewis*	N	N	N	?	N
42 *Miller, Gary*	N	Y	N	Y	Y
43 Baca	N	N	N	N	N
44 *Calvert*	N	Y	N	N	N
45 *Bono*	N	Y	N	N	N
46 *Rohrabacher*	Y	Y	Y	Y	Y
47 Sanchez, Loretta	N	Y	N	N	N
48 *Cox*	Y	Y	?	?	Y
49 *Issa*	Y	Y	N	N	Y
50 *Cunningham*	N	Y	N	N	N
51 Filner	N	N	N	N	N
52 *Hunter*	N	Y	N	N	N
53 Davis	N	Y	N	N	N
COLORADO					
1 DeGette	N	N	N	N	N
2 Udall	N	Y	N	N	Y
3 *McInnis*	Y	Y	Y	Y	Y
4 *Musgrave*	Y	Y	Y	Y	Y
5 *Hefley*	Y	Y	Y	Y	Y
6 *Tancredo*	Y	Y	Y	Y	Y
7 *Beauprez*	Y	Y	Y	Y	Y
CONNECTICUT					
1 Larson	N	N	N	N	N
2 *Simmons*	N	Y	N	N	N
3 DeLauro	N	N	N	N	N
4 *Shays*	Y	Y	Y	Y	Y
5 *Johnson*	N	Y	N	N	Y
DELAWARE					
AL *Castle*	N	Y	Y	Y	Y
FLORIDA					
1 *Miller, J.*	Y	Y	Y	Y	Y
2 Boyd	N	Y	N	N	Y
3 Brown	N	N	N	N	N
4 *Crenshaw*	N	Y	N	N	N
5 *Brown-Waite*	Y	Y	Y	Y	Y
6 *Stearns*	Y	Y	Y	Y	Y
7 *Mica*	Y	Y	N	N	N
8 *Keller*	Y	Y	Y	Y	Y
9 *Bilirakis*	Y	Y	N	Y	N
10 *Young*	N	N	N	N	N
11 Davis	N	Y	Y	Y	Y
12 *Putnam*	N	Y	N	Y	Y
13 *Harris*	Y	Y	Y	Y	Y
14 *Goss*	N	?	?	?	?
15 *Weldon*	N	Y	N	N	N
16 *Foley*	Y	Y	N	Y	Y
17 Meek	N	Y	N	N	N
18 *Ros-Lehtinen*	N	Y	N	Y	Y
19 Wexler	N	N	N	N	N
20 Deutsch	?	?	?	?	?
21 *Diaz-Balart, L.*	N	Y	N	N	N
22 *Shaw*	N	Y	N	N	N
23 Hastings	?	?	?	?	?
24 *Feeney*	Y	Y	Y	Y	Y
25 *Diaz-Balart, M.*	Y	Y	Y	Y	Y
GEORGIA					
1 *Kingston*	N	Y	N	N	N
2 Bishop	N	N	N	N	N
3 Marshall	N	Y	N	N	Y
4 Majette	N	Y	N	N	Y
5 Lewis	N	N	N	N	N
6 *Isakson*	Y	Y	Y	Y	Y
7 *Linder*	Y	Y	Y	Y	Y
8 *Collins*	?	?	?	?	?
9 *Norwood*	Y	Y	N	Y	Y
10 *Deal*	Y	Y	N	Y	Y
11 *Gingrey*	Y	Y	Y	Y	Y
12 *Burns*	N	Y	Y	Y	Y
13 Scott	N	Y	N	N	N
HAWAII					
1 Abercrombie	N	N	N	N	N
2 Case	N	Y	Y	Y	Y
IDAHO					
1 *Otter*	Y	Y	Y	Y	Y
2 *Simpson*	N	N	N	N	N
ILLINOIS					
1 Rush	N	N	N	N	N
2 Jackson	N	N	N	N	N
3 Lipinski	N	Y	N	N	N
4 Gutierrez	N	N	N	N	N
5 Emanuel	N	N	N	N	N
6 *Hyde*	N	Y	N	N	N

ND Northern Democrats   SD Southern Democrats

	309	310	311	312	313
7 Davis	N	N	N	N	N
8 *Crane*	Y	Y	Y	Y	Y
9 Schakowsky	N	N	?	N	N
10 *Kirk*	N	Y	Y	N	Y
11 *Weller*	N	Y	N	N	N
12 Costello	N	Y	N	N	N
13 *Biggert*	N	Y	Y	Y	Y
14 *Hastert*					
15 *Johnson*	N	Y	N	Y	N
16 *Manzullo*	Y	Y	Y	Y	Y
17 Evans	?	N	N	N	N
18 *LaHood*	N	N	N	N	N
19 *Shimkus*	Y	Y	Y	Y	Y
INDIANA					
1 Visclosky	N	N	N	N	N
2 *Chocola*	Y	Y	Y	Y	Y
3 *Souder*	Y	Y	Y	Y	N
4 *Buyer*	N	Y	N	N	N
5 *Burton*	N	Y	N	N	N
6 *Pence*	Y	Y	Y	Y	Y
7 Carson	?	?	?	?	?
8 *Hostettler*	Y	Y	Y	Y	Y
9 Hill	N	Y	N	Y	N
IOWA					
1 *Nussle*	Y	Y	Y	N	Y
2 *Leach*	N	Y	N	N	N
3 Boswell	N	Y	N	Y	Y
4 *Latham*	N	Y	N	N	N
5 *King*	Y	Y	Y	Y	Y
KANSAS					
1 *Moran*	Y	Y	N	Y	Y
2 *Ryun*	Y	Y	Y	Y	Y
3 Moore	N	Y	Y	N	N
4 *Tiahrt*	N	Y	N	N	N
KENTUCKY					
1 *Whitfield*	N	N	N	N	N
2 *Lewis*	N	Y	N	N	N
3 *Northup*	N	Y	N	N	N
4 Lucas	N	Y	Y	Y	Y
5 *Rogers*	N	N	N	N	N
6 Chandler	N	Y	N	N	N
LOUISIANA					
1 *Vitter*	Y	Y	Y	Y	Y
2 Jefferson	N	N	N	N	N
3 *Tauzin*	?	?	?	?	?
4 *McCrery*	Y	Y	N	Y	Y
5 Alexander	N	Y	N	N	Y
6 *Baker*	Y	N	Y	N	N
7 John	N	Y	N	Y	Y
MAINE					
1 Allen	N	N	N	N	N
2 Michaud	N	Y	N	N	N
MARYLAND					
1 *Gilchrest*	N	Y	N	N	Y
2 Ruppersberger	N	N	N	N	Y
3 Cardin	N	N	Y	N	Y
4 Wynn	N	N	N	N	N
5 Hoyer	N	N	N	N	Y
6 *Bartlett*	Y	Y	Y	Y	Y
7 Cummings	N	N	N	N	N
8 Van Hollen	N	Y	N	N	N
MASSACHUSETTS					
1 Olver	N	N	N	N	N
2 Neal	N	Y	N	N	N
3 McGovern	N	N	N	N	N
4 Frank	N	N	N	N	N
5 Meehan	N	Y	N	N	N
6 Tierney	N	Y	N	N	N
7 Markey	N	N	N	N	N
8 Capuano	N	Y	N	N	N
9 Lynch	N	Y	N	N	N
10 Delahunt	N	Y	N	N	N
MICHIGAN					
1 Stupak	N	Y	N	N	N
2 *Hoekstra*	Y	Y	Y	Y	Y
3 *Ehlers*	N	Y	N	N	Y
4 *Camp*	N	Y	Y	Y	Y
5 Kildee	N	N	N	N	N
6 *Upton*	Y	Y	Y	Y	Y
7 *Smith*	Y	Y	N	Y	Y
8 *Rogers*	N	Y	N	N	N
9 *Knollenberg*	N	Y	N	N	N
10 *Miller*	N	Y	N	N	N
11 *McCotter*	N	Y	N	N	N
12 Levin	N	Y	N	N	N

	309	310	311	312	313
13 Kilpatrick	N	N	N	N	N
14 Conyers	N	N	N	N	N
15 Dingell	N	N	N	N	N
MINNESOTA					
1 *Gutknecht*	Y	Y	Y	Y	Y
2 *Kline*	Y	Y	Y	Y	Y
3 *Ramstad*	Y	Y	Y	Y	Y
4 McCollum	N	N	N	N	N
5 Sabo	N	N	N	N	N
6 *Kennedy*	Y	Y	Y	Y	Y
7 Peterson	N	Y	Y	Y	Y
8 Oberstar	N	N	N	N	N
MISSISSIPPI					
1 *Wicker*	N	Y	N	N	N
2 Thompson	N	N	N	N	N
3 *Pickering*	N	Y	N	N	N
4 Taylor	N	Y	N	N	Y
MISSOURI					
1 Clay	N	N	N	N	N
2 *Akin*	Y	Y	Y	Y	Y
3 Gephardt	?	?	?	?	?
4 Skelton	N	Y	N	N	N
5 McCarthy	N	N	N	N	N
6 *Graves*	N	Y	N	N	N
7 *Blunt*	N	Y	N	N	Y
8 *Emerson*	N	Y	N	N	N
9 *Hulshof*	Y	Y	Y	Y	Y
MONTANA					
AL *Rehberg*	N	Y	N	N	Y
NEBRASKA					
1 *Bereuter*	?	?	?	?	?
2 *Terry*	Y	Y	Y	Y	Y
3 *Osborne*	N	Y	N	N	Y
NEVADA					
1 Berkley	N	N	N	N	N
2 *Gibbons*	Y	Y	Y	Y	Y
3 *Porter*	N	N	N	N	Y
NEW HAMPSHIRE					
1 *Bradley*	N	Y	N	Y	Y
2 *Bass*	Y	Y	N	Y	Y
NEW JERSEY					
1 Andrews	N	N	N	N	Y
2 *LoBiondo*	N	Y	N	Y	Y
3 *Saxton*	N	N	N	N	N
4 *Smith*	N	Y	N	N	N
5 *Garrett*	Y	Y	Y	Y	Y
6 Pallone	N	N	N	N	N
7 *Ferguson*	N	Y	N	Y	Y
8 Pascrell	N	Y	N	N	N
9 Rothman	?	?	?	?	?
10 Payne	N	N	N	N	N
11 *Frelinghuysen*	N	Y	N	N	N
12 Holt	N	N	N	N	N
13 Menendez	N	N	N	N	N
NEW MEXICO					
1 *Wilson*	Y	Y	N	Y	Y
2 *Pearce*	N	Y	N	N	N
3 Udall	N	Y	N	N	Y
NEW YORK					
1 Bishop	N	N	N	N	N
2 Israel	N	Y	N	N	N
3 *King*	N	Y	N	N	N
4 McCarthy	N	Y	N	N	N
5 Ackerman	N	N	N	N	N
6 Meeks	N	?	N	N	N
7 Crowley	N	N	N	N	N
8 Nadler	N	N	N	N	N
9 Weiner	N	N	N	N	N
10 Towns	N	N	N	N	N
11 Owens	N	N	N	N	N
12 Velázquez	N	N	N	N	N
13 *Fossella*	Y	?	?	?	?
14 Maloney	N	N	N	N	N
15 Rangel	N	N	N	N	?
16 Serrano	N	N	N	N	N
17 Engel	N	N	N	N	N
18 Lowey	N	N	N	N	N
19 *Kelly*	N	Y	N	Y	Y
20 *Sweeney*	N	Y	N	N	N
21 McNulty	N	Y	N	N	N
22 Hinchey	N	N	N	N	N
23 *McHugh*	N	N	N	N	N
24 *Boehlert*	N	Y	Y	Y	Y
25 *Walsh*	N	Y	N	N	N

	309	310	311	312	313
26 *Reynolds*	Y	Y	N	Y	N
27 *Quinn*	N	N	N	N	N
28 Slaughter	N	N	N	N	N
29 *Houghton*	N	Y	N	N	N
NORTH CAROLINA					
1 Vacant					
2 Etheridge	N	N	N	N	Y
3 *Jones*	N	Y	Y	Y	N
4 Price	N	Y	N	N	Y
5 *Burr*	Y	Y	N	Y	Y
6 *Coble*	Y	Y	Y	Y	Y
7 McIntyre	N	Y	N	Y	Y
8 *Hayes*	N	Y	N	N	N
9 *Myrick*	Y	Y	Y	Y	Y
10 *Ballenger*	Y	Y	Y	Y	Y
11 *Taylor*	N	Y	N	N	N
12 Watt	N	?	?	?	?
13 Miller	N	Y	N	N	N
NORTH DAKOTA					
AL Pomeroy	N	Y	N	N	N
OHIO					
1 *Chabot*	Y	Y	Y	Y	Y
2 *Portman*	N	Y	Y	N	Y
3 *Turner*	N	Y	N	N	Y
4 *Oxley*	N	Y	N	Y	N
5 *Gillmor*	Y	Y	Y	Y	Y
6 Strickland	N	N	N	N	N
7 *Hobson*	N	Y	N	N	N
8 *Boehner*	Y	N	Y	Y	Y
9 Kaptur	N	N	N	N	N
10 Kucinich	N	N	N	N	N
11 Jones	?	?	?	?	?
12 *Tiberi*	Y	Y	N	N	N
13 Brown	N	N	N	N	N
14 *LaTourette*	N	N	N	N	N
15 *Pryce*	N	Y	N	N	Y
16 *Regula*	N	Y	N	N	N
17 Ryan	N	Y	N	N	N
18 *Ney*	N	Y	N	N	N
OKLAHOMA					
1 *Sullivan*	Y	Y	N	N	N
2 Carson	N	Y	N	Y	N
3 *Lucas*	N	Y	N	N	N
4 *Cole*	Y	Y	Y	Y	Y
5 *Istook*	N	Y	N	N	N
OREGON					
1 Wu	N	Y	N	N	N
2 *Walden*	Y	Y	Y	Y	Y
3 Blumenauer	N	Y	N	N	N
4 DeFazio	N	Y	N	N	Y
5 Hooley	N	Y	N	N	Y
PENNSYLVANIA					
1 Brady	N	N	N	N	N
2 Fattah	N	N	N	N	N
3 *English*	Y	Y	Y	N	Y
4 *Hart*	Y	Y	Y	Y	Y
5 *Peterson*	N	Y	N	N	N
6 *Gerlach*	N	Y	N	N	N
7 *Weldon*	N	Y	N	N	N
8 *Greenwood*	Y	Y	Y	Y	Y
9 *Shuster, Bill*	Y	Y	N	N	N
10 *Sherwood*	N	Y	N	N	N
11 Kanjorski	N	?	?	?	N
12 Murtha	N	N	N	N	N
13 Hoeffel	N	Y	N	N	Y
14 Doyle	N	?	?	?	N
15 *Toomey*	Y	Y	Y	Y	Y
16 *Pitts*	Y	Y	N	Y	Y
17 Holden	N	Y	N	N	N
18 *Murphy*	N	Y	N	Y	Y
19 *Platts*	N	Y	N	N	Y
RHODE ISLAND					
1 Kennedy	N	Y	N	N	N
2 Langevin	N	Y	Y	Y	Y
SOUTH CAROLINA					
1 *Brown*	N	Y	N	N	N
2 *Wilson*	Y	Y	Y	Y	Y
3 *Barrett*	Y	Y	Y	Y	Y
4 *DeMint*	Y	Y	Y	Y	Y
5 Spratt	N	Y	N	N	Y
6 Clyburn	N	N	N	N	N
SOUTH DAKOTA					
AL Herseth	N	Y	N	Y	Y

	309	310	311	312	313
TENNESSEE					
1 *Jenkins*	N	Y	N	N	N
2 *Duncan*	Y	Y	Y	Y	Y
3 *Wamp*	N	Y	N	N	N
4 Davis	N	Y	N	Y	Y
5 Cooper	N	Y	N	N	Y
6 Gordon	N	Y	N	N	Y
7 *Blackburn*	Y	Y	Y	Y	Y
8 Tanner	N	Y	N	Y	Y
9 Ford	N	Y	N	N	N
TEXAS					
1 Sandlin	N	Y	N	N	Y
2 Turner	N	Y	N	Y	Y
3 *Johnson, Sam*	Y	Y	Y	Y	N
4 *Hall*	N	Y	N	Y	N
5 *Hensarling*	Y	Y	Y	Y	Y
6 *Barton*	?	?	?	?	?
7 *Culberson*	N	Y	N	N	N
8 *Brady*	Y	Y	Y	Y	Y
9 Lampson	N	Y	N	N	Y
10 Doggett	N	N	Y	Y	Y
11 Edwards	N	N	N	N	N
12 *Granger*	?	?	?	?	?
13 *Thornberry*	N	Y	Y	Y	Y
14 *Paul*	Y	Y	Y	Y	N
15 Hinojosa	N	N	N	N	N
16 Reyes	N	N	N	N	N
17 Stenholm	N	Y	Y	Y	Y
18 Jackson-Lee	N	N	N	N	N
19 *Neugebauer*	Y	Y	Y	Y	Y
20 Gonzalez	N	N	N	N	N
21 *Smith*	Y	Y	N	Y	Y
22 *DeLay*	N	Y	N	N	N
23 *Bonilla*	N	N	N	N	N
24 Frost	N	Y	N	N	Y
25 Bell	N	N	N	N	N
26 *Burgess*	N	Y	Y	Y	N
27 Ortiz	N	N	N	N	N
28 Rodriguez	N	N	N	N	N
29 Green	N	Y	N	N	N
30 Johnson, E.B.	N	N	N	N	Y
31 *Carter*	N	Y	Y	Y	N
32 *Sessions*	Y	Y	Y	Y	Y
UTAH					
1 *Bishop*	Y	Y	N	Y	Y
2 Matheson	N	Y	Y	Y	Y
3 *Cannon*	Y	Y	N	Y	Y
VERMONT					
AL *Sanders*	N	N	N	N	N
VIRGINIA					
1 *Davis, Jo Ann*	Y	Y	N	N	N
2 *Schrock*	Y	Y	Y	Y	Y
3 Scott	N	Y	N	N	N
4 *Forbes*	Y	Y	N	Y	Y
5 *Goode*	Y	Y	N	Y	Y
6 *Goodlatte*	Y	Y	N	Y	Y
7 *Cantor*	Y	Y	N	Y	Y
8 Moran	N	N	N	N	N
9 Boucher	N	N	N	N	N
10 *Wolf*	N	N	N	N	N
11 *Davis, T.*	?	?	?	?	?
WASHINGTON					
1 Inslee	N	Y	N	N	N
2 Larsen	N	Y	N	N	N
3 Baird	N	Y	N	N	N
4 *Hastings*	?	?	?	?	?
5 *Nethercutt*	N	Y	N	N	N
6 Dicks	N	N	N	N	N
7 McDermott	?	?	?	?	?
8 *Dunn*	Y	Y	N	Y	Y
9 Smith	N	Y	N	Y	Y
WEST VIRGINIA					
1 Mollohan	?	?	?	?	?
2 *Capito*	N	Y	N	Y	Y
3 Rahall	N	N	N	N	N
WISCONSIN					
1 *Ryan*	Y	Y	Y	Y	Y
2 Baldwin	N	N	N	N	N
3 Kind	N	Y	N	N	Y
4 Kleczka	N	?	?	?	?
5 *Sensenbrenner*	Y	Y	Y	Y	Y
6 *Petri*	N	Y	N	N	Y
7 Obey	N	N	N	N	N
8 *Green*	Y	Y	Y	Y	Y
WYOMING					
AL *Cubin*	Y	Y	Y	Y	Y

Southern states - Ala., Ark., Fla., Ga., Ky., La., Miss., N.C., Okla., S.C., Tenn., Texas, Va.

Key

Y	Voted for (yea).
#	Paired for.
+	Announced for.
N	Voted against (nay).
X	Paired against.
–	Announced against.
P	Voted "present."
C	Voted "present" to avoid possible conflict of interest.
?	Did not vote or otherwise make a position known.

Democrats **Republicans**
Independents

314. HR 4663. Budget Enforcement/Democratic Substitute. Spratt, D-S.C., substitute amendment that would restore pay-as-you-go rules for new tax cuts and mandatory spending increases through Sept. 30, 2009. It also would set discretionary spending caps of $832.5 billion in fiscal 2005 and $856.9 billion in fiscal 2006. Rejected 179-233: R 3-214; D 175-19 (ND 133-8, SD 42-11); I 1-0. June 24, 2004.

315. HR 4663. Budget Enforcement/Hensarling Substitute. Hensarling, R-Texas, substitute amendment that would make several major changes to the current budget process including turning the non-binding concurrent budget resolution into a joint resolution that would have the force of law, and requiring a two-thirds supermajority vote in both houses for spending that exceeds the budget. Rejected 88-326: R 88-130; D 0-195 (ND 0-142, SD 0-53); I 0-1. June 24, 2004.

316. HR 4663. Budget Enforcement/Kirk Substitute. Kirk, R-Ill., substitute amendment that would make several changes to the current budget process including restoring pay-as-you-go offset requirements for mandatory spending increases for fiscal 2005, 2006 and 2007. It also would place a cap on entitlement spending, with the exception of Social Security and Medicare, and require automatic cuts in entitlement spending in any year in which spending exceeds the cap. Rejected 120-296: R 120-100; D 0-195 (ND 0-142, SD 0-53); I 0-1. June 24, 2004.

317. HR 4663. Budget Enforcement/Recommit. Stenholm, D-Texas, motion to recommit the bill to the House Budget Committee with instructions to restore pay-as-you-go rules for both tax cuts and mandatory spending. Motion rejected 196-218: R 0-218; D 195-0 (ND 142-0, SD 53-0); I 1-0. June 25, 2004 (in the session that began and the Congressional Record dated June 24, 2004).

318. HR 4663. Budget Enforcement/Passage. Passage of the bill that would set statutory caps on discretionary spending for fiscal years 2005 and 2006, and institute pay-as-you-go rules that require any mandatory spending increases to be offset. The bill, as amended, would require the Congressional Budget Office to prepare an annual analysis comparing budgeted entitlement spending to actual entitlement spending, with an account-by-account breakdown to show spending trends. Rejected 146-268: R 146-72; D 0-195 (ND 0-142, SD 0-53); I 0-1. A "yea" was a vote in support of the president's position. June 25, 2004 (in the session that began and the Congressional Record dated June 24, 2004).

319. H Res 691. Iraqi Sovereignty/Adoption. Adoption of the resolution that would congratulate the interim government of Iraq on its pending assumption of sovereign authority and express the sense of Congress that U.S. armed forces operating in Iraq after June 30, 2004, will remain under the full authority of U.S. commanders. Adopted 352-57: R 213-1; D 138-56 (ND 89-52, SD 49-4); I 1-0. June 25, 2004 (in the session that began and the Congressional Record dated June 24, 2004).

	314	315	316	317	318	319
ALABAMA						
1 *Bonner*	N	Y	Y	N	N	Y
2 *Everett*	N	N	N	N	N	Y
3 *Rogers*	N	N	N	N	N	Y
4 *Aderholt*	N	N	N	N	N	Y
5 Cramer	N	N	Y	N	N	Y
6 *Bachus*	N	N	N	Y	N	Y
7 Davis	Y	N	N	Y	N	Y
ALASKA						
AL *Young*	N	N	N	N	Y	Y
ARIZONA						
1 *Renzi*	N	N	N	N	N	Y
2 *Franks*	N	Y	Y	N	Y	Y
3 *Shadegg*	N	Y	Y	N	Y	Y
4 Pastor	Y	N	N	Y	N	N
5 *Hayworth*	N	Y	Y	N	Y	Y
6 *Flake*	N	Y	Y	N	Y	Y
7 Grijalva	Y	N	N	Y	N	N
8 *Kolbe*	N	N	N	N	Y	Y
ARKANSAS						
1 Berry	N	N	N	Y	N	Y
2 Snyder	Y	N	N	Y	N	Y
3 *Boozman*	N	N	N	Y	N	Y
4 Ross	Y	N	N	Y	N	Y
CALIFORNIA						
1 Thompson	N	N	N	Y	N	Y
2 *Herger*	N	Y	Y	N	Y	Y
3 *Ose*	N	N	N	N	Y	Y
4 *Doolittle*	N	N	N	N	Y	Y
5 Matsui	Y	N	N	Y	N	Y
6 Woolsey	Y	N	N	Y	N	N
7 Miller, George	Y	N	N	Y	N	N
8 Pelosi	Y	N	N	Y	N	N
9 Lee	Y	N	N	Y	N	N
10 Tauscher	Y	N	N	Y	N	Y
11 *Pombo*	N	N	N	N	Y	Y
12 Lantos	Y	N	N	Y	N	Y
13 Stark	Y	N	N	Y	N	N
14 Eshoo	Y	N	N	Y	N	N
15 Honda	Y	N	N	Y	N	N
16 Lofgren	Y	N	N	Y	N	Y
17 Farr	Y	N	N	Y	N	N
18 Cardoza	Y	N	N	Y	N	Y
19 *Radanovich*	N	Y	Y	N	Y	Y
20 Dooley	Y	N	N	Y	N	Y
21 *Nunes*	N	N	Y	N	Y	Y
22 *Thomas*	N	N	N	N	Y	Y
23 Capps	Y	N	N	Y	N	Y
24 *Gallegly*	N	N	N	N	Y	Y
25 *McKeon*	N	Y	Y	N	N	Y
26 *Dreier*	N	N	N	N	Y	Y
27 Sherman	Y	N	N	Y	N	Y
28 Berman	?	?	?	?	?	?
29 Schiff	Y	N	N	Y	N	Y
30 Waxman	Y	N	N	Y	N	Y
31 Becerra	Y	N	N	Y	N	Y
32 Solis	Y	N	N	Y	N	N
33 Watson	Y	N	N	Y	N	N
34 Roybal-Allard	Y	N	N	Y	N	Y
35 Waters	Y	N	N	Y	N	N
36 Harman	Y	N	N	Y	N	Y

	314	315	316	317	318	319
37 Millender-McD.	Y	N	N	Y	N	Y
38 Napolitano	Y	N	N	Y	N	Y
39 Sánchez, Linda	Y	N	N	Y	N	Y
40 *Royce*	N	Y	Y	N	Y	Y
41 *Lewis*	N	N	N	N	N	Y
42 *Miller, Gary*	N	Y	Y	N	N	Y
43 Baca	N	N	N	Y	N	Y
44 *Calvert*	N	N	N	N	N	Y
45 *Bono*	N	N	N	N	N	Y
46 *Rohrabacher*	N	Y	N	N	N	Y
47 Sanchez, Loretta	Y	N	N	Y	N	Y
48 *Cox*	N	Y	Y	N	Y	Y
49 *Issa*	N	N	N	N	Y	Y
50 *Cunningham*	N	N	N	N	N	Y
51 Filner	Y	N	N	Y	N	N
52 *Hunter*	N	N	N	N	N	Y
53 Davis	Y	N	N	Y	N	Y
COLORADO						
1 DeGette	Y	N	N	Y	N	N
2 Udall	Y	N	N	Y	N	Y
3 *McInnis*	N	N	Y	N	Y	Y
4 *Musgrave*	N	Y	Y	N	N	Y
5 *Hefley*	N	Y	Y	N	Y	?
6 *Tancredo*	N	Y	Y	N	Y	Y
7 *Beauprez*	N	Y	Y	N	Y	Y
CONNECTICUT						
1 Larson	Y	N	N	Y	N	N
2 *Simmons*	N	N	N	N	N	Y
3 DeLauro	Y	N	N	Y	N	Y
4 *Shays*	N	N	Y	N	Y	Y
5 *Johnson*	N	N	Y	N	Y	Y
DELAWARE						
AL *Castle*	N	N	Y	N	Y	Y
FLORIDA						
1 *Miller, J.*	N	Y	Y	N	Y	Y
2 Boyd	N	N	N	Y	N	Y
3 Brown	Y	N	N	Y	N	Y
4 *Crenshaw*	N	N	N	N	N	Y
5 *Brown-Waite*	N	N	Y	N	Y	Y
6 *Stearns*	N	Y	Y	N	Y	Y
7 *Mica*	N	N	N	N	N	Y
8 *Keller*	N	N	N	N	Y	Y
9 *Bilirakis*	N	Y	N	N	N	Y
10 *Young*	N	N	N	N	N	Y
11 Davis	N	N	N	Y	N	Y
12 *Putnam*	N	Y	Y	N	Y	Y
13 *Harris*	N	Y	Y	N	Y	Y
14 *Goss*	N	N	N	N	N	Y
15 *Weldon*	N	N	N	N	N	Y
16 *Foley*	N	N	N	N	Y	Y
17 Meek	Y	N	N	Y	N	Y
18 *Ros-Lehtinen*	N	N	N	N	Y	Y
19 Wexler	Y	N	N	Y	N	N
20 Deutsch	?	?	?	?	?	?
21 *Diaz-Balart, L.*	N	N	N	N	Y	Y
22 *Shaw*	N	N	N	N	N	Y
23 Hastings	?	?	?	?	?	?
24 *Feeney*	N	Y	Y	N	Y	Y
25 *Diaz-Balart, M.*	N	Y	N	Y	N	Y
GEORGIA						
1 *Kingston*	N	N	N	N	N	Y
2 Bishop	Y	N	N	Y	N	Y
3 Marshall	N	N	N	Y	N	Y
4 Majette	Y	N	N	Y	N	Y
5 Lewis	Y	N	N	Y	N	N
6 *Isakson*	N	Y	Y	N	Y	Y
7 *Linder*	N	N	Y	N	Y	Y
8 *Collins*	?	?	?	?	?	?
9 *Norwood*	N	Y	Y	N	Y	Y
10 *Deal*	N	Y	Y	N	Y	Y
11 *Gingrey*	N	Y	Y	N	Y	Y
12 *Burns*	N	N	N	N	Y	Y
13 Scott	Y	N	N	Y	N	Y
HAWAII						
1 Abercrombie	Y	N	N	Y	N	Y
2 Case	Y	N	N	Y	N	Y
IDAHO						
1 *Otter*	N	Y	Y	N	Y	Y
2 *Simpson*	N	N	N	N	N	Y
ILLINOIS						
1 Rush	Y	N	N	Y	N	N
2 Jackson	Y	N	N	Y	N	N
3 Lipinski	N	N	N	Y	N	Y
4 Gutierrez	Y	N	N	Y	N	N
5 Emanuel	Y	N	N	Y	N	Y
6 *Hyde*	N	N	Y	N	Y	Y

ND Northern Democrats   SD Southern Democrats

	314	315	316	317	318	319
7 Davis	Y	N	N	Y	N	Y
8 ***Crane***	N	Y	Y	N	Y	Y
9 Schakowsky	Y	N	N	Y	N	N
10 ***Kirk***	N	N	Y	N	Y	Y
11 ***Weller***	N	N	Y	N	N	Y
12 Costello	Y	N	N	Y	N	Y
13 ***Biggert***	N	N	Y	N	Y	Y
14 ***Hastert***						
15 ***Johnson***	N	N	N	N	Y	Y
16 ***Manzullo***	N	Y	Y	N	Y	Y
17 Evans	Y	N	N	Y	N	Y
18 ***LaHood***	N	N	N	N	N	Y
19 ***Shimkus***	N	Y	Y	N	Y	Y
INDIANA						
1 Visclosky	Y	N	N	Y	N	Y
2 ***Chocola***	N	Y	Y	N	Y	Y
3 ***Souder***	N	N	N	N	N	Y
4 ***Buyer***	N	N	N	N	Y	Y
5 ***Burton***	N	N	Y	N	Y	Y
6 ***Pence***	N	Y	Y	N	Y	Y
7 Carson	?	?	?	?	?	?
8 ***Hostettler***	N	Y	Y	N	Y	Y
9 Hill	N	N	N	Y	N	Y
IOWA						
1 ***Nussle***	N	N	N	N	Y	Y
2 ***Leach***	Y	N	N	N	N	Y
3 Boswell	Y	N	N	Y	N	Y
4 ***Latham***	N	N	N	N	N	Y
5 ***King***	N	Y	Y	N	Y	Y
KANSAS						
1 ***Moran***	N	Y	N	N	Y	Y
2 ***Ryun***	N	Y	Y	N	Y	Y
3 Moore	Y	N	N	Y	N	Y
4 ***Tiahrt***	N	N	Y	N	N	Y
KENTUCKY						
1 ***Whitfield***	N	N	N	N	N	Y
2 ***Lewis***	N	N	N	N	N	Y
3 ***Northup***	N	N	N	N	N	Y
4 Lucas	N	N	N	Y	N	Y
5 ***Rogers***	N	N	N	N	N	Y
6 Chandler	Y	N	N	Y	N	Y
LOUISIANA						
1 ***Vitter***	N	Y	Y	N	Y	Y
2 Jefferson	Y	N	N	Y	N	Y
3 ***Tauzin***	?	?	?	?	?	?
4 ***McCrery***	N	Y	Y	N	Y	Y
5 Alexander	N	N	N	Y	N	Y
6 ***Baker***	N	?	N	N	Y	Y
7 John	N	N	N	Y	N	Y
MAINE						
1 Allen	Y	N	N	Y	N	Y
2 Michaud	Y	N	N	Y	N	Y
MARYLAND						
1 ***Gilchrest***	N	N	Y	N	Y	Y
2 Ruppersberger	Y	N	N	Y	N	Y
3 Cardin	Y	N	N	Y	N	Y
4 Wynn	Y	N	N	Y	N	Y
5 Hoyer	Y	N	N	Y	N	Y
6 ***Bartlett***	N	Y	Y	N	Y	Y
7 Cummings	Y	N	N	Y	N	N
8 Van Hollen	Y	N	N	Y	N	Y
MASSACHUSETTS						
1 Olver	Y	N	N	Y	N	N
2 Neal	Y	N	N	Y	N	N
3 McGovern	Y	N	N	Y	N	N
4 Frank	Y	N	N	Y	N	N
5 Meehan	Y	N	N	Y	N	N
6 Tierney	Y	N	N	Y	N	N
7 Markey	Y	N	N	Y	N	N
8 Capuano	Y	N	N	Y	N	Y
9 Lynch	Y	N	N	Y	N	Y
10 Delahunt	Y	N	N	Y	N	N
MICHIGAN						
1 Stupak	Y	N	N	Y	N	Y
2 ***Hoekstra***	N	Y	Y	N	Y	Y
3 ***Ehlers***	N	N	Y	N	Y	Y
4 ***Camp***	N	N	N	N	Y	Y
5 Kildee	Y	N	N	Y	N	Y
6 ***Upton***	N	N	Y	N	Y	Y
7 ***Smith***	N	N	Y	?	?	?
8 ***Rogers***	N	N	Y	N	Y	Y
9 ***Knollenberg***	N	N	N	N	N	Y
10 ***Miller***	N	N	N	N	N	Y
11 ***McCotter***	N	N	N	N	Y	Y
12 Levin	Y	N	N	Y	N	Y

	314	315	316	317	318	319
13 Kilpatrick	Y	N	N	Y	N	N
14 Conyers	Y	N	N	Y	N	N
15 Dingell	Y	N	N	Y	N	Y
MINNESOTA						
1 ***Gutknecht***	N	Y	Y	N	Y	Y
2 ***Kline***	N	Y	Y	N	Y	Y
3 ***Ramstad***	N	N	N	N	Y	Y
4 McCollum	Y	N	N	Y	N	N
5 Sabo	Y	N	N	Y	N	N
6 ***Kennedy***	N	Y	Y	N	Y	Y
7 Peterson	N	N	N	Y	N	Y
8 Oberstar	Y	N	N	Y	N	N
MISSISSIPPI						
1 ***Wicker***	N	N	N	N	N	Y
2 Thompson	Y	N	N	Y	N	Y
3 ***Pickering***	N	N	N	N	Y	Y
4 Taylor	N	N	N	Y	N	Y
MISSOURI						
1 Clay	Y	N	N	Y	N	N
2 ***Akin***	N	Y	Y	N	Y	Y
3 Gephardt	?	?	?	?	?	?
4 Skelton	Y	N	N	Y	N	Y
5 McCarthy	Y	N	N	Y	N	N
6 ***Graves***	N	N	N	N	Y	Y
7 ***Blunt***	N	Y	Y	N	Y	Y
8 ***Emerson***	N	N	N	N	N	Y
9 ***Hulshof***	N	N	Y	N	Y	Y
MONTANA						
AL ***Rehberg***	N	N	Y	N	Y	Y
NEBRASKA						
1 ***Bereuter***	?	?	?	?	?	?
2 ***Terry***	N	Y	Y	N	Y	Y
3 ***Osborne***	N	N	N	N	N	Y
NEVADA						
1 Berkley	Y	N	N	Y	N	Y
2 ***Gibbons***	N	Y	Y	N	Y	Y
3 ***Porter***	N	N	N	N	N	Y
NEW HAMPSHIRE						
1 ***Bradley***	N	N	N	N	Y	Y
2 ***Bass***	N	N	Y	N	Y	Y
NEW JERSEY						
1 Andrews	Y	N	N	Y	N	Y
2 ***LoBiondo***	N	N	N	N	N	Y
3 ***Saxton***	N	N	N	N	N	Y
4 ***Smith***	N	N	N	N	N	Y
5 ***Garrett***	N	Y	Y	N	Y	Y
6 Pallone	Y	N	N	Y	N	N
7 ***Ferguson***	N	N	N	N	N	Y
8 Pascrell	Y	N	N	Y	N	Y
9 Rothman	?	?	?	?	?	?
10 Payne	Y	N	N	Y	N	N
11 ***Frelinghuysen***	N	N	N	N	N	Y
12 Holt	Y	N	N	Y	N	N
13 Menendez	Y	N	N	Y	N	Y
NEW MEXICO						
1 ***Wilson***	Y	N	N	N	N	Y
2 ***Pearce***	N	N	N	N	Y	Y
3 Udall	Y	N	N	Y	N	Y
NEW YORK						
1 Bishop	Y	N	N	Y	N	Y
2 Israel	Y	N	N	Y	N	Y
3 ***King***	N	N	N	N	N	Y
4 McCarthy	Y	N	N	Y	N	Y
5 Ackerman	Y	N	N	Y	N	Y
6 Meeks	Y	N	N	Y	N	Y
7 Crowley	Y	N	N	Y	N	Y
8 Nadler	Y	N	N	Y	N	N
9 Weiner	Y	N	N	Y	N	Y
10 Towns	Y	N	N	Y	N	N
11 Owens	Y	N	N	Y	N	N
12 Velázquez	Y	N	N	Y	N	N
13 ***Fossella***	?	N	Y	N	Y	Y
14 Maloney	Y	N	N	Y	N	N
15 Rangel	Y	N	N	Y	N	N
16 Serrano	Y	N	N	Y	N	N
17 Engel	Y	N	N	Y	N	Y
18 Lowey	Y	N	N	Y	N	Y
19 ***Kelly***	N	N	N	N	Y	Y
20 ***Sweeney***	N	N	N	N	N	Y
21 McNulty	Y	N	N	Y	N	Y
22 Hinchey	Y	N	N	Y	N	N
23 ***McHugh***	N	N	N	N	N	Y
24 ***Boehlert***	N	N	Y	N	Y	Y
25 ***Walsh***	N	N	N	N	N	Y

	314	315	316	317	318	319
26 ***Reynolds***	N	N	Y	N	Y	Y
27 ***Quinn***	N	N	N	N	N	Y
28 Slaughter	Y	N	N	Y	N	Y
29 ***Houghton***	N	?	?	?	?	?
NORTH CAROLINA						
1 Vacant						
2 Etheridge	Y	N	N	Y	N	Y
3 ***Jones***	Y	Y	N	N	Y	Y
4 Price	Y	N	N	Y	N	Y
5 ***Burr***	N	N	N	N	Y	Y
6 ***Coble***	N	Y	Y	N	N	Y
7 McIntyre	Y	N	N	Y	N	Y
8 ***Hayes***	N	N	N	N	N	Y
9 ***Myrick***	N	Y	Y	N	Y	Y
10 ***Ballenger***	N	Y	Y	?	?	?
11 ***Taylor***	N	N	N	N	N	Y
12 Watt	?	N	N	Y	N	N
13 Miller	Y	N	N	Y	N	Y
NORTH DAKOTA						
AL Pomeroy	Y	N	N	Y	N	Y
OHIO						
1 ***Chabot***	N	Y	Y	N	Y	Y
2 ***Portman***	N	N	Y	N	Y	Y
3 ***Turner***	N	Y	Y	N	Y	Y
4 ***Oxley***	N	N	N	N	Y	Y
5 ***Gillmor***	N	N	Y	N	Y	Y
6 Strickland	Y	N	N	Y	N	Y
7 ***Hobson***	N	N	N	N	N	?
8 ***Boehner***	N	Y	N	N	Y	Y
9 Kaptur	Y	N	N	Y	N	N
10 Kucinich	Y	N	N	Y	N	N
11 Jones	?	?	?	?	?	?
12 ***Tiberi***	N	N	Y	N	Y	Y
13 Brown	Y	N	N	Y	N	N
14 ***LaTourette***	N	N	N	N	N	Y
15 ***Pryce***	N	N	Y	N	Y	Y
16 ***Regula***	N	N	N	N	N	Y
17 Ryan	Y	N	N	Y	N	Y
18 ***Ney***	N	N	N	N	Y	Y
OKLAHOMA						
1 ***Sullivan***	?	Y	Y	N	Y	Y
2 Carson	N	N	N	Y	N	Y
3 ***Lucas***	N	N	N	N	Y	Y
4 ***Cole***	N	Y	Y	N	Y	Y
5 ***Istook***	N	?	N	N	N	Y
OREGON						
1 Wu	Y	N	N	Y	N	Y
2 ***Walden***	N	N	N	N	N	Y
3 Blumenauer	Y	N	N	Y	N	N
4 DeFazio	Y	N	N	Y	N	Y
5 Hooley	Y	N	N	Y	N	Y
PENNSYLVANIA						
1 Brady	Y	N	N	Y	N	Y
2 Fattah	Y	N	N	Y	N	Y
3 ***English***	N	Y	Y	N	N	Y
4 ***Hart***	N	Y	Y	N	Y	Y
5 ***Peterson***	N	N	N	N	N	Y
6 ***Gerlach***	N	N	N	N	N	Y
7 ***Weldon***	N	N	N	N	Y	Y
8 ***Greenwood***	N	N	Y	N	Y	Y
9 ***Shuster, Bill***	N	Y	N	N	Y	Y
10 ***Sherwood***	N	N	N	N	N	Y
11 Kanjorski	Y	N	N	Y	N	Y
12 Murtha	N	N	N	Y	N	?
13 Hoeffel	Y	N	N	Y	N	Y
14 Doyle	Y	N	N	Y	N	Y
15 ***Toomey***	N	Y	Y	N	Y	Y
16 ***Pitts***	N	Y	Y	N	Y	Y
17 Holden	Y	N	N	Y	N	Y
18 ***Murphy***	N	N	Y	N	Y	Y
19 ***Platts***	N	N	N	N	Y	Y
RHODE ISLAND						
1 Kennedy	Y	N	N	Y	N	Y
2 Langevin	Y	N	N	Y	N	Y
SOUTH CAROLINA						
1 ***Brown***	N	N	Y	N	Y	Y
2 ***Wilson***	N	Y	Y	N	Y	Y
3 ***Barrett***	N	Y	Y	N	Y	Y
4 ***DeMint***	N	Y	Y	N	Y	Y
5 Spratt	Y	N	N	Y	N	Y
6 Clyburn	Y	N	N	Y	N	Y
SOUTH DAKOTA						
AL Herseth	Y	N	N	Y	N	Y

	314	315	316	317	318	319
TENNESSEE						
1 ***Jenkins***	N	Y	Y	N	Y	Y
2 ***Duncan***	N	Y	Y	N	Y	Y
3 ***Wamp***	N	N	N	N	N	Y
4 Davis	Y	N	N	Y	N	Y
5 Cooper	Y	N	N	Y	N	Y
6 Gordon	Y	?	?	?	?	?
7 ***Blackburn***	N	Y	Y	N	Y	Y
8 Tanner	N	N	N	Y	N	Y
9 Ford	Y	N	N	Y	N	Y
TEXAS						
1 Sandlin	Y	N	N	Y	N	Y
2 Turner	Y	N	N	Y	N	Y
3 ***Johnson, Sam***	N	Y	Y	N	Y	Y
4 ***Hall***	N	N	N	N	N	Y
5 ***Hensarling***	N	Y	Y	N	Y	Y
6 ***Barton***	?	?	?	?	?	?
7 ***Culberson***	N	N	N	N	N	Y
8 ***Brady***	N	Y	Y	N	Y	Y
9 Lampson	Y	N	N	Y	N	Y
10 Doggett	Y	N	N	Y	N	Y
11 Edwards	Y	N	N	Y	N	Y
12 ***Granger***	?	?	?	?	?	?
13 ***Thornberry***	N	Y	Y	N	Y	Y
14 ***Paul***	N	Y	Y	N	Y	N
15 Hinojosa	Y	N	N	Y	N	Y
16 Reyes	Y	N	N	Y	N	Y
17 Stenholm	N	N	N	Y	N	Y
18 Jackson-Lee	Y	N	N	Y	N	Y
19 ***Neugebauer***	N	Y	Y	N	Y	Y
20 Gonzalez	Y	N	N	Y	N	Y
21 ***Smith***	N	N	N	N	N	Y
22 ***DeLay***	N	N	Y	N	Y	Y
23 ***Bonilla***	N	N	N	N	N	Y
24 Frost	Y	N	N	Y	N	Y
25 Bell	Y	N	N	Y	N	Y
26 ***Burgess***	N	Y	Y	N	Y	Y
27 Ortiz	Y	N	N	Y	N	Y
28 Rodriguez	Y	N	N	Y	N	Y
29 Green	Y	N	N	Y	N	Y
30 Johnson, E.B.	Y	N	N	Y	N	Y
31 ***Carter***	N	Y	Y	N	Y	Y
32 ***Sessions***	N	Y	Y	N	Y	?
UTAH						
1 ***Bishop***	N	Y	Y	N	Y	Y
2 Matheson	N	N	N	Y	N	Y
3 ***Cannon***	?	Y	Y	N	Y	Y
VERMONT						
AL *Sanders*	Y	N	N	Y	N	Y
VIRGINIA						
1 ***Davis, Jo Ann***	N	N	N	N	N	Y
2 ***Schrock***	N	Y	Y	N	Y	?
3 Scott	Y	N	N	Y	N	N
4 ***Forbes***	N	N	Y	N	Y	Y
5 ***Goode***	N	Y	Y	N	Y	Y
6 ***Goodlatte***	N	N	Y	N	Y	Y
7 ***Cantor***	N	Y	Y	N	Y	Y
8 Moran	Y	N	N	Y	N	Y
9 Boucher	Y	N	N	Y	N	Y
10 ***Wolf***	N	N	N	N	N	Y
11 ***Davis, T.***	?	N	N	N	N	Y
WASHINGTON						
1 Inslee	Y	N	N	Y	N	Y
2 Larsen	Y	N	N	Y	N	Y
3 Baird	Y	N	N	Y	N	Y
4 ***Hastings***	?	?	?	?	?	?
5 ***Nethercutt***	N	N	N	N	N	Y
6 Dicks	Y	N	N	Y	N	Y
7 McDermott	?	?	?	?	?	?
8 ***Dunn***	N	Y	Y	N	Y	Y
9 Smith	Y	N	N	Y	N	Y
WEST VIRGINIA						
1 Mollohan	?	?	?	?	?	?
2 ***Capito***	N	N	N	N	Y	Y
3 Rahall	N	N	N	Y	N	Y
WISCONSIN						
1 ***Ryan***	N	Y	Y	N	Y	Y
2 Baldwin	Y	N	N	Y	N	N
3 Kind	Y	N	N	Y	N	Y
4 Kleczka	?	N	N	Y	N	N
5 ***Sensenbrenner***	N	Y	Y	N	Y	Y
6 ***Petri***	N	N	N	N	Y	Y
7 Obey	N	N	N	Y	N	Y
8 ***Green***	N	Y	Y	N	Y	Y
WYOMING						
AL ***Cubin***	N	Y	Y	N	Y	Y

Southern states - Ala., Ark., Fla., Ga., Ky., La., Miss., N.C., Okla., S.C., Tenn., Texas, Va.

Key

Y	Voted for (yea).
#	Paired for.
+	Announced for.
N	Voted against (nay).
X	Paired against.
–	Announced against.
P	Voted "present."
C	Voted "present" to avoid possible conflict of interest.
?	Did not vote or otherwise make a position known.

Democrats **Republicans**
Independents

320. HR 4614. Fiscal 2005 Energy and Water Appropriations/Previous Question. Sessions, R-Texas, motion to order the previous question (thus ending debate and possibility of amendment) on adoption of the rule (H Res 694) to provide for House floor consideration of the bill that would provide $28.5 billion in fiscal 2005 spending for energy and water development projects. Motion agreed to 209-182: R 209-1; D 0-180 (ND 0-132, SD 0-48); I 0-1. June 25, 2004.

321. HR 4614. Fiscal 2005 Energy and Water Appropriations/Renewable Energy Programs. Sanders, I-Vt., amendment that would increase funding for renewable energy sources by $30 million, to be offset by a decrease in the Advanced Simulation and Computing program in the weapons activities budget. Rejected 150-241: R 17-188; D 132-53 (ND 108-27, SD 24-26); I 1-0. June 25, 2004.

322. HR 4614. Fiscal 2005 Energy and Water Appropriations/Defense Non-Proliferation Programs. Wilson, R-N.M., amendment that would increase funding for defense-related nuclear non-proliferation programs by $5 million, to be offset by cuts in administrative funds. Rejected 163-224: R 54-149; D 108-75 (ND 84-49, SD 24-26); I 1-0. June 25, 2004.

323. HR 4614. Fiscal 2005 Energy and Water Appropriations/Global Threat Reduction. Meehan, D-Mass., amendment that would increase funding for the Global Threat Reduction initiative by $30 million, while decreasing funding for nuclear weapons programs by the same amount. Rejected 151-235: R 7-195; D 143-40 (ND 115-18, SD 28-22); I 1-0. June 25, 2004.

324. HR 4614. Fiscal 2005 Energy and Water Appropriations/Across-the-Board Cut. Hefley, R-Colo., amendment that would reduce total discretionary funding in the bill by 1 percent. Rejected 68-319: R 65-138; D 3-180 (ND 1-132, SD 2-48); I 0-1. June 25, 2004.

325. HR 4614. Fiscal 2005 Energy and Water Appropriations/Passage. Passage of the bill that would provide $28.5 billion in fiscal 2005 spending for energy and water development projects. Passed 370-16: R 189-13; D 180-3 (ND 130-3, SD 50-0); I 1-0. June 25, 2004.

	320	321	322	323	324	325
ALABAMA						
1 *Bonner*	Y	N	N	N	N	Y
2 *Everett*	Y	N	N	N	N	Y
3 *Rogers*	Y	N	N	N	N	Y
4 *Aderholt*	Y	N	N	N	N	Y
5 Cramer	N	N	N	N	N	Y
6 *Bachus*	Y	N	N	N	Y	Y
7 Davis	N	Y	Y	Y	N	Y
ALASKA						
AL *Young*	?	?	?	?	?	?
ARIZONA						
1 *Renzi*	Y	N	Y	N	N	Y
2 *Franks*	Y	N	Y	N	Y	N
3 *Shadegg*	Y	N	Y	N	Y	N
4 Pastor	N	N	N	N	N	Y
5 *Hayworth*	Y	N	Y	N	Y	Y
6 *Flake*	Y	N	Y	N	Y	N
7 Grijalva	N	Y	Y	Y	N	Y
8 *Kolbe*	Y	N	N	N	N	Y
ARKANSAS						
1 Berry	N	N	N	N	N	Y
2 Snyder	N	N	Y	Y	N	Y
3 *Boozman*	Y	N	N	N	N	Y
4 Ross	N	N	N	N	N	Y
CALIFORNIA						
1 Thompson	N	N	N	Y	N	Y
2 *Herger*	Y	N	N	N	N	Y
3 *Ose*	Y	N	N	N	N	Y
4 *Doolittle*	N	N	?	Y	N	Y
5 Matsui	N	N	?	Y	N	Y
6 Woolsey	N	N	N	Y	N	Y
7 Miller, George	N	N	N	Y	N	Y
8 Pelosi	N	N	N	Y	N	Y
9 Lee	N	Y	Y	Y	N	Y
10 Tauscher	N	N	N	N	N	Y
11 *Pombo*	Y	N	N	N	N	Y
12 Lantos	N	N	Y	Y	N	Y
13 Stark	?	Y	Y	Y	N	Y
14 Eshoo	N	N	N	N	N	Y
15 Honda	N	N	N	N	N	Y
16 Lofgren	N	N	N	N	N	Y
17 Farr	N	Y	Y	N	N	Y
18 Cardoza	N	N	N	N	N	Y
19 *Radanovich*	Y	N	N	N	N	Y
20 Dooley	N	?	?	?	?	?
21 *Nunes*	Y	N	N	N	N	Y
22 *Thomas*	Y	?	?	?	?	?
23 Capps	N	Y	N	Y	N	Y
24 *Gallegly*	Y	N	N	N	N	Y
25 *McKeon*	Y	N	N	N	N	Y
26 *Dreier*	Y	N	N	N	N	Y
27 Sherman	N	Y	Y	Y	N	Y
28 Berman	?	?	?	?	?	?
29 Schiff	N	N	Y	Y	N	Y
30 Waxman	?	Y	Y	Y	N	Y
31 Becerra	N	Y	Y	Y	N	Y
32 Solis	N	Y	Y	Y	N	Y
33 Watson	N	Y	Y	Y	N	Y
34 Roybal-Allard	N	Y	N	N	N	Y
35 Waters	N	Y	N	Y	N	Y
36 Harman	N	?	?	?	?	?

	320	321	322	323	324	325
37 Millender-McD.	N	Y	Y	Y	N	Y
38 Napolitano	N	Y	Y	Y	N	Y
39 Sánchez, Linda	N	Y	Y	Y	N	Y
40 *Royce*	Y	N	Y	N	Y	N
41 *Lewis*	Y	N	N	N	N	Y
42 *Miller, Gary*	Y	N	N	N	N	Y
43 Baca	N	Y	Y	Y	N	Y
44 *Calvert*	Y	N	N	N	N	Y
45 *Bono*	Y	N	N	N	N	Y
46 *Rohrabacher*	Y	N	N	N	Y	Y
47 Sanchez, Loretta	N	N	Y	Y	N	Y
48 *Cox*	?	N	Y	N	N	Y
49 *Issa*	+	N	N	N	N	Y
50 *Cunningham*	Y	?	?	?	?	?
51 Filner	N	Y	Y	Y	N	Y
52 *Hunter*	Y	N	?	?	N	Y
53 Davis	N	N	Y	N	N	Y
COLORADO						
1 DeGette	N	Y	Y	Y	N	Y
2 Udall	N	Y	Y	Y	N	Y
3 *McInnis*	Y	N	N	N	N	Y
4 *Musgrave*	Y	N	N	N	Y	Y
5 *Hefley*	Y	N	Y	N	Y	Y
6 *Tancredo*	Y	N	N	N	Y	Y
7 *Beauprez*	Y	N	N	N	Y	Y
CONNECTICUT						
1 Larson	N	N	N	N	N	Y
2 *Simmons*	Y	Y	Y	Y	N	Y
3 DeLauro	N	N	Y	Y	N	Y
4 *Shays*	Y	Y	N	Y	N	Y
5 *Johnson*	Y	N	Y	N	N	Y
DELAWARE						
AL *Castle*	Y	N	N	N	N	Y
FLORIDA						
1 *Miller, J.*	Y	N	N	N	Y	Y
2 Boyd	N	?	?	?	?	?
3 Brown	N	Y	N	Y	N	Y
4 *Crenshaw*	Y	N	N	N	N	Y
5 *Brown-Waite*	Y	N	N	N	N	Y
6 *Stearns*	Y	N	N	N	N	N
7 *Mica*	Y	N	N	N	N	Y
8 *Keller*	Y	N	N	N	Y	Y
9 *Bilirakis*	Y	N	N	N	N	Y
10 *Young*	Y	N	N	N	N	Y
11 Davis	N	Y	N	Y	N	Y
12 *Putnam*	Y	N	N	N	N	Y
13 *Harris*	Y	N	N	N	N	Y
14 *Goss*	Y	N	N	N	N	Y
15 *Weldon*	?	N	N	N	N	Y
16 *Foley*	Y	N	N	N	N	Y
17 Meek	N	Y	N	N	N	Y
18 *Ros-Lehtinen*	N	Y	N	N	N	Y
19 Wexler	?	Y	Y	Y	N	Y
20 Deutsch	?	?	?	?	?	?
21 *Diaz-Balart, L.*	Y	N	N	N	N	Y
22 *Shaw*	Y	N	N	N	N	Y
23 Hastings	?	?	?	?	?	?
24 *Feeney*	Y	N	N	N	Y	Y
25 *Diaz-Balart, M.*	Y	N	N	Y	N	Y
GEORGIA						
1 *Kingston*	Y	N	N	N	N	Y
2 Bishop	N	Y	N	N	N	Y
3 Marshall	N	N	Y	N	N	Y
4 Majette	N	Y	Y	Y	N	Y
5 Lewis	N	?	?	?	?	?
6 *Isakson*	Y	?	?	?	?	?
7 *Linder*	Y	N	N	N	Y	Y
8 *Collins*	?	?	?	?	?	?
9 *Norwood*	?	N	Y	N	Y	Y
10 *Deal*	Y	?	?	?	?	?
11 *Gingrey*	Y	N	N	N	Y	Y
12 *Burns*	Y	N	N	N	N	Y
13 Scott	N	N	N	N	N	Y
HAWAII						
1 Abercrombie	N	Y	Y	Y	N	Y
2 Case	N	Y	Y	Y	N	Y
IDAHO						
1 *Otter*	Y	N	Y	N	Y	Y
2 *Simpson*	Y	N	N	N	N	Y
ILLINOIS						
1 Rush	N	Y	Y	Y	N	Y
2 Jackson	N	Y	Y	Y	N	Y
3 Lipinski	?	?	?	?	?	?
4 Gutierrez	N	Y	Y	Y	N	Y
5 Emanuel	N	Y	N	Y	N	Y
6 *Hyde*	Y	N	N	N	N	Y

ND Northern Democrats   SD Southern Democrats

	320	321	322	323	324	325
7 Davis	N	Y	Y	Y	N	Y
8 ***Crane***	Y	N	N	N	Y	Y
9 Schakowsky	N	Y	Y	Y	N	Y
10 ***Kirk***	Y	N	N	N	N	Y
11 ***Weller***	Y	N	Y	N	N	?
12 Costello	N	Y	N	N	N	Y
13 ***Biggert***	Y	N	N	N	N	Y
14 ***Hastert***						
15 ***Johnson***	Y	Y	N	N	N	Y
16 ***Manzullo***	Y	N	Y	N	Y	Y
17 Evans	N	Y	Y	Y	N	Y
18 ***LaHood***	Y	N	N	N	N	Y
19 ***Shimkus***	Y	N	Y	N	Y	Y
INDIANA						
1 Visclosky	N	N	N	N	N	Y
2 ***Chocola***	Y	N	N	N	Y	Y
3 ***Souder***	Y	N	N	N	N	Y
4 ***Buyer***	Y	N	N	N	Y	Y
5 ***Burton***	Y	N	N	N	Y	Y
6 ***Pence***	Y	N	N	N	Y	Y
7 Carson	?	?	?	?	?	?
8 ***Hostettler***	Y	N	N	N	Y	N
9 Hill	N	N	N	N	N	Y
IOWA						
1 ***Nussle***	Y	Y	N	N	N	Y
2 ***Leach***	Y	Y	Y	Y	N	Y
3 Boswell	N	Y	Y	Y	N	Y
4 ***Latham***	Y	Y	N	N	N	Y
5 ***King***	Y	N	N	N	Y	Y
KANSAS						
1 ***Moran***	Y	Y	Y	N	Y	Y
2 ***Ryun***	Y	?	?	?	?	?
3 Moore	N	Y	Y	Y	N	Y
4 ***Tiahrt***	Y	N	N	N	N	Y
KENTUCKY						
1 ***Whitfield***	Y	N	N	N	N	Y
2 ***Lewis***	Y	N	N	N	Y	Y
3 ***Northup***	Y	N	N	N	N	Y
4 Lucas	N	N	N	N	N	Y
5 ***Rogers***	Y	N	N	N	N	Y
6 Chandler	N	N	Y	Y	N	Y
LOUISIANA						
1 ***Vitter***	?	?	?	?	?	?
2 Jefferson	N	Y	Y	Y	N	Y
3 ***Tauzin***	?	?	?	?	?	?
4 ***McCrery***	Y	N	N	N	N	Y
5 Alexander	N	Y	N	N	N	Y
6 ***Baker***	Y	N	N	N	N	Y
7 John	?	?	?	?	?	?
MAINE						
1 Allen	N	Y	Y	Y	N	Y
2 Michaud	N	Y	Y	Y	N	Y
MARYLAND						
1 ***Gilchrest***	Y	N	Y	N	N	Y
2 Ruppersberger	N	Y	Y	Y	N	Y
3 Cardin	N	Y	Y	Y	N	Y
4 Wynn	N	N	N	Y	N	Y
5 Hoyer	N	Y	N	N	N	Y
6 ***Bartlett***	Y	Y	N	N	Y	Y
7 Cummings	?	Y	N	Y	N	Y
8 Van Hollen	N	Y	Y	Y	N	Y
MASSACHUSETTS						
1 Olver	N	Y	N	Y	N	Y
2 Neal	N	Y	N	Y	N	Y
3 McGovern	N	Y	N	Y	N	Y
4 Frank	N	Y	Y	Y	N	Y
5 Meehan	N	Y	Y	Y	N	Y
6 Tierney	N	Y	Y	Y	N	Y
7 Markey	N	Y	Y	Y	N	Y
8 Capuano	N	Y	N	Y	N	Y
9 Lynch	N	N	N	Y	N	Y
10 Delahunt	N	?	?	?	?	?
MICHIGAN						
1 Stupak	N	Y	N	Y	N	Y
2 ***Hoekstra***	Y	N	N	N	N	Y
3 ***Ehlers***	Y	Y	Y	N	N	Y
4 ***Camp***	Y	N	N	N	N	Y
5 Kildee	N	Y	Y	Y	N	Y
6 ***Upton***	Y	N	N	N	N	Y
7 ***Smith***	Y	?	?	?	?	?
8 ***Rogers***	Y	N	N	N	Y	Y
9 ***Knollenberg***	Y	N	N	N	N	Y
10 ***Miller***	Y	N	N	N	N	Y
11 ***McCotter***	Y	N	N	N	Y	Y
12 Levin	N	Y	N	Y	N	Y

	320	321	322	323	324	325
13 Kilpatrick	N	+	−	+	−	+
14 Conyers	N	Y	Y	Y	N	Y
15 Dingell	N	Y	Y	Y	N	Y
MINNESOTA						
1 ***Gutknecht***	Y	N	N	N	Y	Y
2 ***Kline***	Y	N	N	N	N	Y
3 ***Ramstad***	Y	Y	N	N	Y	Y
4 McCollum	N	Y	Y	Y	N	Y
5 Sabo	N	Y	N	?	?	?
6 ***Kennedy***	Y	N	N	N	N	Y
7 Peterson	N	Y	N	Y	N	Y
8 Oberstar	?	Y	N	Y	N	Y
MISSISSIPPI						
1 ***Wicker***	Y	N	N	N	N	Y
2 Thompson	N	Y	N	Y	N	Y
3 ***Pickering***	Y	N	N	N	N	Y
4 Taylor	N	N	Y	Y	Y	Y
MISSOURI						
1 Clay	?	Y	N	Y	N	Y
2 ***Akin***	Y	N	N	N	N	Y
3 Gephardt	?	?	?	?	?	?
4 Skelton	N	N	Y	Y	N	Y
5 McCarthy	N	+	+	+	−	+
6 ***Graves***	Y	N	Y	N	Y	Y
7 ***Blunt***	Y	N	N	N	N	Y
8 ***Emerson***	Y	N	N	N	N	Y
9 ***Hulshof***	Y	N	Y	N	N	Y
MONTANA						
AL ***Rehberg***	Y	N	N	N	N	Y
NEBRASKA						
1 ***Bereuter***	?	N	Y	N	N	Y
2 ***Terry***	Y	Y	N	N	N	N
3 ***Osborne***	Y	N	N	N	N	Y
NEVADA						
1 Berkley	N	Y	Y	Y	N	N
2 ***Gibbons***	Y	N	Y	N	Y	N
3 ***Porter***	Y	N	Y	N	Y	N
NEW HAMPSHIRE						
1 ***Bradley***	Y	N	Y	N	Y	Y
2 ***Bass***	Y	N	Y	N	Y	Y
NEW JERSEY						
1 Andrews	N	Y	Y	Y	N	N
2 ***LoBiondo***	Y	N	N	N	N	Y
3 ***Saxton***	Y	N	N	N	N	Y
4 ***Smith***	Y	Y	Y	Y	N	Y
5 ***Garrett***	Y	N	N	N	Y	Y
6 Pallone	N	Y	N	Y	N	Y
7 ***Ferguson***	Y	N	N	N	N	Y
8 Pascrell	N	Y	N	Y	N	Y
9 Rothman	?	?	?	?	?	?
10 Payne	N	Y	Y	Y	N	Y
11 ***Frelinghuysen***	Y	N	N	N	N	Y
12 Holt	N	Y	Y	Y	N	Y
13 Menendez	N	Y	N	Y	N	Y
NEW MEXICO						
1 ***Wilson***	Y	N	Y	N	N	Y
2 ***Pearce***	Y	N	Y	N	N	Y
3 Udall	N	Y	Y	Y	N	Y
NEW YORK						
1 Bishop	N	Y	N	Y	N	Y
2 Israel	N	Y	N	N	N	Y
3 ***King***	Y	N	?	?	?	?
4 McCarthy	N	Y	Y	Y	N	Y
5 Ackerman	?	?	?	?	?	?
6 Meeks	N	Y	N	Y	N	Y
7 Crowley	N	Y	Y	Y	N	Y
8 Nadler	N	Y	Y	Y	N	Y
9 Weiner	?	Y	Y	Y	N	Y
10 Towns	N	Y	N	Y	N	Y
11 Owens	N	Y	Y	Y	N	Y
12 Velázquez	N	Y	N	Y	N	Y
13 ***Fossella***	Y	N	N	N	N	Y
14 Maloney	N	Y	Y	Y	N	Y
15 Rangel	N	Y	Y	Y	N	Y
16 Serrano	N	Y	N	Y	N	Y
17 Engel	?	Y	Y	Y	N	Y
18 Lowey	N	Y	?	?	?	?
19 ***Kelly***	Y	Y	Y	N	N	Y
20 ***Sweeney***	Y	N	N	N	N	Y
21 McNulty	N	Y	Y	Y	N	Y
22 Hinchey	N	Y	Y	Y	N	Y
23 ***McHugh***	Y	N	N	N	N	Y
24 ***Boehlert***	Y	Y	N	N	N	Y
25 ***Walsh***	Y	N	N	N	N	Y

	320	321	322	323	324	325
26 ***Reynolds***	Y	?	?	?	?	?
27 ***Quinn***	Y	N	N	N	N	Y
28 Slaughter	−	+	+	+	−	+
29 ***Houghton***	Y	?	?	?	?	?
NORTH CAROLINA						
1 Vacant						
2 Etheridge	N	N	Y	Y	N	Y
3 ***Jones***	Y	?	?	?	?	?
4 Price	N	Y	Y	Y	N	Y
5 ***Burr***	Y	N	N	N	N	Y
6 ***Coble***	Y	?	?	?	?	?
7 McIntyre	N	N	Y	Y	N	Y
8 ***Hayes***	Y	N	N	N	N	Y
9 ***Myrick***	Y	N	N	N	Y	Y
10 ***Ballenger***	Y	N	N	?	?	?
11 ***Taylor***	Y	N	N	N	Y	Y
12 Watt	N	Y	N	Y	N	Y
13 Miller	N	Y	Y	Y	N	Y
NORTH DAKOTA						
AL Pomeroy	N	Y	Y	Y	N	Y
OHIO						
1 ***Chabot***	Y	N	Y	N	Y	Y
2 ***Portman***	Y	N	N	N	N	Y
3 ***Turner***	Y	N	N	N	N	Y
4 ***Oxley***	Y	N	N	N	N	Y
5 ***Gillmor***	Y	N	Y	N	N	Y
6 Strickland	N	Y	Y	Y	N	Y
7 ***Hobson***	Y	N	N	N	N	Y
8 ***Boehner***	Y	N	N	N	Y	Y
9 Kaptur	?	Y	Y	Y	N	Y
10 Kucinich	N	Y	Y	Y	N	N
11 Jones	?	Y	Y	N	N	Y
12 ***Tiberi***	Y	N	N	N	N	Y
13 Brown	N	Y	Y	Y	N	Y
14 ***LaTourette***	Y	N	N	N	N	Y
15 ***Pryce***	Y	?	?	?	?	?
16 ***Regula***	Y	N	N	N	N	Y
17 Ryan	N	Y	Y	Y	N	Y
18 ***Ney***	Y	N	N	N	N	Y
OKLAHOMA						
1 ***Sullivan***	Y	N	Y	N	Y	Y
2 Carson	N	N	Y	N	N	Y
3 ***Lucas***	Y	N	Y	N	N	Y
4 ***Cole***	Y	N	N	N	N	Y
5 ***Istook***	Y	N	N	N	N	Y
OREGON						
1 Wu	N	Y	Y	Y	N	Y
2 ***Walden***	Y	N	Y	N	N	Y
3 Blumenauer	N	Y	Y	Y	N	Y
4 DeFazio	N	Y	Y	Y	N	Y
5 Hooley	N	Y	Y	Y	N	Y
PENNSYLVANIA						
1 Brady	N	N	N	N	N	Y
2 Fattah	N	Y	N	Y	N	Y
3 ***English***	Y	N	Y	N	N	Y
4 ***Hart***	Y	N	N	N	N	Y
5 ***Peterson***	?	?	?	?	?	?
6 ***Gerlach***	Y	N	N	N	N	Y
7 ***Weldon***	Y	N	N	N	N	Y
8 ***Greenwood***	Y	N	Y	N	N	Y
9 ***Shuster, Bill***	Y	N	N	N	N	Y
10 ***Sherwood***	Y	N	N	N	N	Y
11 Kanjorski	N	N	N	N	N	Y
12 Murtha	N	N	N	N	N	Y
13 Hoeffel	N	Y	Y	Y	N	Y
14 Doyle	N	Y	N	N	N	Y
15 ***Toomey***	Y	N	N	N	Y	N
16 ***Pitts***	Y	N	Y	N	Y	Y
17 Holden	N	N	N	N	N	Y
18 ***Murphy***	Y	N	N	N	N	Y
19 ***Platts***	?	N	N	N	N	Y
RHODE ISLAND						
1 Kennedy	N	Y	Y	Y	N	Y
2 Langevin	N	Y	Y	Y	N	Y
SOUTH CAROLINA						
1 ***Brown***	Y	N	N	N	N	Y
2 ***Wilson***	Y	N	N	N	Y	Y
3 ***Barrett***	Y	N	N	N	Y	Y
4 ***DeMint***	Y	N	N	N	Y	Y
5 Spratt	N	N	Y	Y	N	Y
6 Clyburn	N	Y	N	Y	N	Y
SOUTH DAKOTA						
AL Herseth	N	Y	Y	Y	N	Y

	320	321	322	323	324	325
TENNESSEE						
1 ***Jenkins***	Y	N	N	N	N	Y
2 ***Duncan***	Y	N	N	N	Y	Y
3 ***Wamp***	Y	N	N	N	N	Y
4 Davis	N	N	N	N	N	Y
5 Cooper	N	Y	Y	Y	N	Y
6 Gordon	N	N	Y	Y	N	Y
7 ***Blackburn***	Y	N	N	N	Y	Y
8 Tanner	N	Y	N	N	Y	Y
9 Ford	?	Y	N	Y	N	Y
TEXAS						
1 Sandlin	N	N	Y	N	N	Y
2 Turner	N	N	Y	N	Y	Y
3 ***Johnson, Sam***	?	N	N	N	Y	Y
4 ***Hall***	Y	N	N	N	N	Y
5 ***Hensarling***	Y	N	Y	N	Y	N
6 ***Barton***	?	?	?	?	?	?
7 ***Culberson***	Y	N	N	N	N	Y
8 ***Brady***	Y	N	Y	N	Y	Y
9 Lampson	N	Y	N	N	N	Y
10 Doggett	N	Y	Y	Y	N	Y
11 Edwards	N	N	N	N	N	Y
12 ***Granger***	Y	N	N	N	N	Y
13 ***Thornberry***	Y	N	Y	N	N	Y
14 ***Paul***	Y	?	?	?	?	?
15 Hinojosa	−	Y	Y	N	N	Y
16 Reyes	?	N	N	N	N	Y
17 Stenholm	N	N	N	N	N	Y
18 Jackson-Lee	N	Y	Y	Y	N	Y
19 ***Neugebauer***	Y	N	N	N	Y	Y
20 Gonzalez	N	N	Y	Y	N	Y
21 ***Smith***	Y	N	N	N	N	Y
22 ***DeLay***	Y	N	N	N	N	Y
23 ***Bonilla***	Y	N	N	N	N	Y
24 Frost	N	N	N	N	N	Y
25 Bell	N	N	N	Y	N	Y
26 ***Burgess***	Y	?	?	?	?	?
27 Ortiz	N	N	N	N	N	Y
28 Rodriguez	?	?	?	?	?	?
29 Green	N	Y	N	N	N	Y
30 Johnson, E.B.	N	N	N	Y	N	Y
31 ***Carter***	Y	N	N	N	N	Y
32 ***Sessions***	Y	N	N	N	Y	Y
UTAH						
1 ***Bishop***	Y	N	N	N	Y	Y
2 Matheson	N	N	Y	Y	N	Y
3 ***Cannon***	Y	N	N	N	Y	Y
VERMONT						
AL *Sanders*	N	Y	Y	Y	N	Y
VIRGINIA						
1 ***Davis, Jo Ann***	Y	N	N	N	Y	Y
2 ***Schrock***	Y	N	N	N	N	Y
3 Scott	N	Y	Y	Y	N	Y
4 ***Forbes***	Y	N	N	N	N	Y
5 ***Goode***	?	N	N	N	N	Y
6 ***Goodlatte***	Y	N	N	N	N	Y
7 ***Cantor***	Y	N	N	N	N	Y
8 Moran	N	Y	N	Y	N	Y
9 Boucher	N	N	Y	N	N	Y
10 ***Wolf***	Y	N	N	N	N	Y
11 ***Davis, T.***	Y	N	Y	N	N	Y
WASHINGTON						
1 Inslee	N	Y	Y	Y	N	Y
2 Larsen	N	Y	Y	Y	N	Y
3 Baird	N	Y	N	Y	N	Y
4 ***Hastings***	?	?	?	?	?	?
5 ***Nethercutt***	N	N	N	N	N	Y
6 Dicks	N	?	?	?	?	?
7 McDermott	N	Y	Y	Y	N	Y
8 ***Dunn***	?	?	?	?	?	?
9 Smith	N	N	Y	Y	Y	Y
WEST VIRGINIA						
1 Mollohan	?	?	?	?	?	?
2 ***Capito***	Y	N	N	N	N	Y
3 Rahall	N	Y	N	Y	N	Y
WISCONSIN						
1 ***Ryan***	Y	Y	Y	N	Y	Y
2 Baldwin	N	Y	Y	Y	N	Y
3 Kind	N	Y	Y	Y	N	Y
4 Kleczka	N	Y	Y	Y	N	Y
5 ***Sensenbrenner***	Y	Y	Y	Y	Y	N
6 ***Petri***	Y	N	N	Y	Y	Y
7 Obey	N	Y	Y	Y	N	Y
8 ***Green***	Y	Y	Y	Y	Y	Y
WYOMING						
AL ***Cubin***	?	?	?	?	?	?

Southern states - Ala., Ark., Fla., Ga., Ky., La., Miss., N.C., Okla., S.C., Tenn., Texas, Va.

326. H Con Res 410. Marshall Islands Constitution Anniversary/Adoption. Flake, R-Ariz., motion to suspend the rules and adopt the concurrent resolution that would recognize the 25th anniversary of the adoption of the constitution of the Republic of the Marshall Islands and recognize the nation as an important ally of the United States. Motion agreed to 379-0: R 210-0; D 168-0 (ND 123-0, SD 45-0); I 1-0. A two-thirds majority of those present and voting (253 in this case) is required for adoption under suspension of the rules. July 6, 2004.

327. H Con Res 257. Posthumous Medal of Freedom/Adoption. Miller, R-Mich., motion to suspend the rules and adopt the concurrent resolution that would express the sense of the Congress that the late Harry W. Colmery, a previous national commander of the American Legion, should be posthumously awarded the Presidential Medal of Freedom for his legal and military contributions to the nation. Motion agreed to 381-1: R 208-1; D 172-0 (ND 125-0, SD 47-0); I 1-0. A two-thirds majority of those present and voting (255 in this case) is required for adoption under suspension of the rules. July 6, 2004.

328. HR 4754. Fiscal 2005 Commerce, Justice, State Appropriations/Small Business Administration Funding. Manzullo, R-Ill., amendment that would increase funding for the Small Business Administration's 7(a) loan program by $79 million and offset the increase with cuts in other programs. Adopted 281-137: R 87-135; D 193-2 (ND 141-1, SD 52-1); I 1-0. July 7, 2004.

329. HR 4754. Fiscal 2005 Commerce, Justice, State Appropriations/Cuba Gift and Travel Restrictions. Flake, R-Ariz., amendment that would prohibit the use of funds in the bill to implement the Commerce Department's new restrictions on gift parcels shipped to Cuba and the amount of personal baggage allowed for travelers to Cuba. Adopted 221-194: R 46-176; D 174-18 (ND 127-13, SD 47-5); I 1-0. A "nay" was a vote in support of the president's position. July 7, 2004.

330. HR 4754. Fiscal 2005 Commerce, Justice, State Appropriations/Law Enforcement Funding. Weiner, D-N.Y., amendment that would increase funding by $107 million for law enforcement grants under the Community Oriented Policing Services program, offset by funding cuts for the Census Bureau. Rejected 206-212: R 74-148; D 131-64 (ND 99-43, SD 32-21); I 1-0. July 7, 2004.

331. HR 4754. Fiscal 2005 Commerce, Justice, State Appropriations/Short-Form Census. Hefley, R-Colo., amendment that would eliminate funding for the early design and planning process for the 2010 Short-Form Only census. Rejected 71-342: R 67-152; D 4-189 (ND 2-139, SD 2-50); I 0-1. July 7, 2004.

332. HR 4754. Fiscal 2005 Commerce, Justice, State Appropriations/Commerce Department Funding. Kucinich, D-Ohio, amendment that would reduce funding by $50,000 for Commerce Department management expenses and increase it by the same amount. (The purpose of the amendment was to generate debate on the makeup of the President's Manufacturing Council.) Adopted 232-186: R 37-185; D 194-1 (ND 142-0, SD 52-1); I 1-0. July 7, 2004.

333. HR 4754. Fiscal 2005 Commerce, Justice, State Appropriations/UNESCO Funds. Paul, R-Texas, amendment that would prohibit the use of funds in the bill to pay for any U.S. contribution to the United National Educational, Scientific, and Cultural Organization (UNESCO). Rejected 135-283: R 132-90; D 3-192 (ND 1-141, SD 2-51); I 0-1. July 7, 2004.

Key

Y	Voted for (yea).
#	Paired for.
+	Announced for.
N	Voted against (nay).
X	Paired against.
−	Announced against.
P	Voted "present."
C	Voted "present" to avoid possible conflict of interest.
?	Did not vote or otherwise make a position known.

Democrats   *Republicans*
Independents

	326	327	328	329	330	331	332	333
ALABAMA								
1 Bonner	Y	Y	N	N	N	N	N	Y
2 Everett	Y	Y	N	Y	N	Y	N	Y
3 Rogers	Y	Y	N	N	Y	N	N	N
4 Aderholt	?	?	N	Y	N	?	Y	Y
5 Cramer	Y	Y	Y	Y	N	Y	N	N
6 Bachus	?	Y	N	N	N	N	N	Y
7 Davis	Y	Y	Y	N	N	N	Y	N
ALASKA								
AL *Young*	Y	Y	N	?	?	?	?	?
ARIZONA								
1 Renzi	Y	Y	N	Y	N	N	N	Y
2 Franks	Y	Y	N	N	Y	N	N	Y
3 Shadegg	Y	N	N	N	Y	N	Y	Y
4 Pastor	Y	Y	Y	N	Y	N	Y	N
5 Hayworth	Y	N	N	N	N	N	N	Y
6 Flake	Y	N	Y	N	Y	N	Y	Y
7 Grijalva	Y	Y	Y	N	Y	N	Y	N
8 Kolbe	Y	Y	N	N	N	N	N	N
ARKANSAS								
1 Berry	Y	Y	Y	Y	N	Y	N	N
2 Snyder	Y	Y	Y	Y	Y	N	Y	N
3 Boozman	Y	Y	Y	N	Y	N	Y	Y
4 Ross	Y	Y	Y	Y	Y	N	Y	N
CALIFORNIA								
1 Thompson	Y	Y	Y	Y	Y	N	Y	N
2 Herger	Y	Y	N	N	N	Y	N	Y
3 Ose	Y	Y	N	Y	N	N	N	N
4 Doolittle	Y	Y	?	?	?	?	?	?
5 Matsui	Y	Y	Y	Y	Y	N	Y	N
6 Woolsey	Y	Y	Y	Y	Y	N	Y	N
7 Miller, George	Y	Y	Y	Y	Y	N	Y	N
8 Pelosi	?	?	Y	Y	Y	N	Y	N
9 Lee	Y	Y	Y	Y	Y	N	Y	N
10 Tauscher	Y	Y	Y	Y	Y	N	Y	N
11 Pombo	?	?	Y	N	N	N	N	Y
12 Lantos	Y	Y	Y	Y	Y	N	Y	N
13 Stark	Y	Y	Y	Y	Y	N	Y	N
14 Eshoo	Y	Y	Y	Y	Y	N	Y	N
15 Honda	?	?	?	?	?	?	?	?
16 Lofgren	Y	Y	Y	Y	Y	N	Y	N
17 Farr	Y	Y	Y	Y	Y	N	Y	N
18 Cardoza	Y	Y	Y	?	Y	N	Y	N
19 *Radanovich*	Y	Y	Y	N	N	N	N	Y
20 Dooley	Y	Y	Y	Y	N	N	Y	N
21 *Nunes*	Y	N	N	N	N	N	N	N
22 *Thomas*	Y	N	N	N	?	N	N
23 Capps	Y	Y	Y	Y	Y	N	Y	N
24 *Gallegly*	Y	Y	N	N	N	N	N	N
25 *McKeon*	Y	Y	N	N	N	N	N	N
26 *Dreier*	Y	N	N	N	N	N	N	N
27 Sherman	Y	Y	Y	Y	Y	N	Y	N
28 Berman	Y	N	Y	N	Y	N	Y	N
29 Schiff	Y	Y	Y	Y	Y	N	Y	N
30 Waxman	Y	Y	Y	Y	Y	N	Y	N
31 Becerra	?	?	Y	Y	Y	N	Y	N
32 Solis	?	?	Y	Y	Y	N	Y	N
33 Watson	Y	Y	Y	Y	Y	N	Y	N
34 Roybal-Allard	Y	Y	Y	Y	Y	N	Y	N
35 Waters	Y	Y	Y	Y	Y	N	Y	N
36 Harman	?	?	Y	Y	Y	N	Y	N

	326	327	328	329	330	331	332	333
37 Millender-McD.	Y	Y	Y	Y	N	N	Y	N
38 Napolitano	Y	Y	Y	Y	N	N	Y	N
39 Sánchez, Linda	Y	Y	Y	Y	N	N	Y	N
40 *Royce*	Y	Y	N	N	Y	N	Y	N
41 *Lewis*	Y	N	N	N	N	N	N	N
42 *Miller, Gary*	Y	N	N	N	Y	N	N	N
43 Baca	Y	Y	Y	Y	N	N	Y	N
44 *Calvert*	Y	N	N	N	N	N	N	N
45 *Bono*	Y	N	N	N	N	N	N	N
46 *Rohrabacher*	Y	N	N	N	Y	N	N	Y
47 Sanchez, Loretta	Y	Y	Y	Y	Y	N	Y	N
48 *Cox*	Y	Y	N	N	N	N	N	N
49 *Issa*	Y	N	N	N	Y	N	N	N
50 *Cunningham*	Y	N	N	N	N	N	N	N
51 Filner	?	?	Y	Y	Y	N	Y	N
52 *Hunter*	Y	?	Y	N	Y	Y	Y	Y
53 Davis	Y	Y	Y	Y	N	N	Y	N
COLORADO								
1 DeGette	Y	Y	Y	Y	Y	N	Y	N
2 Udall	?	?	Y	Y	Y	N	Y	N
3 *McInnis*	?	?	?	N	N	N	Y	N
4 *Musgrave*	Y	Y	N	N	N	N	Y	Y
5 *Hefley*	Y	N	N	N	Y	Y	N	Y
6 *Tancredo*	?	?	Y	N	N	Y	N	Y
7 *Beauprez*	Y	Y	N	N	N	N	N	N
CONNECTICUT								
1 Larson	Y	Y	Y	Y	Y	N	Y	N
2 *Simmons*	Y	N	N	N	Y	N	Y	N
3 DeLauro	Y	Y	Y	Y	Y	N	Y	N
4 *Shays*	Y	N	Y	N	N	N	Y	N
5 *Johnson*	Y	N	Y	N	N	N	N	N
DELAWARE								
AL *Castle*	Y	Y	Y	Y	N	N	N	N
FLORIDA								
1 *Miller, J.*	Y	N	N	N	N	Y	N	Y
2 Boyd	Y	Y	Y	N	N	N	Y	N
3 Brown	Y	Y	Y	N	N	N	Y	N
4 *Crenshaw*	Y	N	N	N	N	N	N	Y
5 *Brown-Waite*	Y	Y	N	Y	N	Y	N	Y
6 *Stearns*	Y	Y	N	N	N	N	N	Y
7 *Mica*	Y	Y	N	N	N	N	N	N
8 *Keller*	Y	N	N	N	Y	N	N	Y
9 *Bilirakis*	Y	Y	N	N	N	N	N	Y
10 *Young*	?	?	N	?	?	?	?	?
11 Davis	Y	Y	Y	N	N	N	Y	N
12 *Putnam*	Y	Y	N	N	N	N	N	N
13 *Harris*	Y	Y	N	N	N	N	N	N
14 *Goss*	?	?	N	N	N	N	N	N
15 *Weldon*	Y	N	N	N	N	N	N	N
16 *Foley*	Y	N	N	N	Y	N	N	N
17 Meek	Y	Y	Y	?	?	?	Y	N
18 *Ros-Lehtinen*	Y	N	N	N	N	N	N	N
19 Wexler	Y	Y	Y	Y	N	N	Y	N
20 Deutsch	?	?	?	?	?	?	?	?
21 *Diaz-Balart, L.*	Y	N	N	N	N	N	N	N
22 *Shaw*	Y	N	N	N	N	N	N	N
23 Hastings	?	?	?	?	?	?	?	?
24 *Feeney*	Y	N	N	N	Y	N	Y	Y
25 *Diaz-Balart, M.*	Y	N	N	N	N	N	N	N
GEORGIA								
1 *Kingston*	Y	N	N	N	N	Y	N	Y
2 Bishop	Y	Y	Y	Y	N	Y	N	Y
3 Marshall	Y	Y	Y	Y	Y	Y	Y	N
4 Majette	?	?	Y	Y	N	N	Y	N
5 Lewis	Y	Y	Y	Y	N	N	Y	N
6 *Isakson*	Y	N	N	N	N	N	N	Y
7 *Linder*	Y	N	N	N	N	N	N	N
8 *Collins*	?	?	?	?	?	?	?	?
9 *Norwood*	Y	N	N	N	N	Y	N	Y
10 *Deal*	Y	N	N	N	N	Y	N	Y
11 *Gingrey*	Y	N	N	N	Y	N	N	Y
12 *Burns*	Y	Y	Y	N	N	N	N	N
13 Scott	Y	Y	Y	Y	N	N	Y	N
HAWAII								
1 Abercrombie	Y	Y	Y	Y	Y	N	Y	N
2 Case	Y	Y	Y	Y	N	N	Y	N
IDAHO								
1 *Otter*	Y	Y	Y	Y	Y	N	Y	N
2 *Simpson*	Y	N	N	N	N	N	N	Y
ILLINOIS								
1 Rush	Y	Y	Y	Y	Y	N	Y	N
2 Jackson	Y	Y	Y	Y	Y	N	Y	N
3 Lipinski	Y	Y	Y	Y	Y	N	Y	N
4 Gutierrez	?	?	Y	N	Y	?	Y	N
5 Emanuel	Y	Y	Y	Y	N	Y	Y	N
6 *Hyde*	Y	N	N	N	N	N	Y	Y

ND Northern Democrats   SD Southern Democrats

	326	327	328	329	330	331	332	333
7 Davis	Y	Y	Y	Y	N	N	Y	N
8 ***Crane***	Y	Y	N	N	N	N	N	Y
9 Schakowsky	Y	Y	Y	Y	N	N	Y	N
10 ***Kirk***	Y	Y	N	N	N	N	N	N
11 ***Weller***	?	?	N	N	N	N	N	N
12 Costello	Y	Y	Y	Y	Y	N	Y	N
13 ***Biggert***	Y	Y	N	Y	N	N	N	N
14 ***Hastert***								
15 ***Johnson***	Y	Y	Y	Y	Y	N	N	N
16 ***Manzullo***	Y	Y	Y	N	Y	Y	Y	Y
17 Evans	Y	Y	Y	Y	Y	N	Y	N
18 ***LaHood***	Y	Y	?	?	?	?	?	?
19 ***Shimkus***	Y	Y	N	Y	Y	N	Y	Y
INDIANA								
1 Visclosky	Y	Y	Y	Y	N	N	Y	N
2 ***Chocola***	Y	Y	N	N	Y	Y	N	Y
3 ***Souder***	Y	Y	N	N	Y	N	N	Y
4 ***Buyer***	Y	Y	N	N	N	Y	N	Y
5 ***Burton***	Y	Y	N	N	N	Y	N	Y
6 ***Pence***	Y	Y	Y	N	N	Y	N	Y
7 Carson	?	?	?	?	?	?	?	?
8 ***Hostettler***	Y	Y	N	Y	N	Y	N	Y
9 Hill	Y	Y	Y	Y	N	N	Y	N
IOWA								
1 ***Nussle***	Y	Y	N	N	N	N	Y	N
2 ***Leach***	Y	Y	Y	Y	Y	N	Y	N
3 Boswell	Y	Y	Y	Y	Y	N	Y	N
4 ***Latham***	Y	Y	N	N	N	N	N	N
5 ***King***	Y	Y	Y	N	N	Y	N	Y
KANSAS								
1 ***Moran***	Y	Y	Y	Y	Y	Y	N	Y
2 ***Ryun***	Y	Y	Y	N	N	Y	N	Y
3 Moore	Y	Y	Y	Y	N	N	Y	N
4 ***Tiahrt***	Y	Y	Y	N	N	N	N	Y
KENTUCKY								
1 ***Whitfield***	Y	Y	N	N	N	N	N	N
2 ***Lewis***	Y	Y	N	N	N	N	N	Y
3 ***Northup***	Y	Y	N	N	N	N	N	N
4 Lucas	Y	Y	Y	Y	Y	N	Y	N
5 ***Rogers***	Y	Y	N	N	N	N	N	N
6 Chandler	Y	Y	Y	?	Y	N	Y	N
LOUISIANA								
1 ***Vitter***	Y	Y	N	N	Y	Y	N	Y
2 Jefferson	Y	Y	Y	Y	Y	N	Y	N
3 ***Tauzin***	?	?	?	?	?	?	?	?
4 ***McCrery***	Y	Y	N	N	N	N	N	Y
5 Alexander	Y	Y	Y	Y	Y	N	Y	N
6 ***Baker***	Y	Y	N	N	Y	N	N	N
7 John	?	?	?	N	Y	N	Y	N
MAINE								
1 Allen	Y	Y	Y	Y	Y	N	Y	N
2 Michaud	Y	Y	Y	Y	Y	N	Y	N
MARYLAND								
1 ***Gilchrest***	Y	Y	N	Y	N	N	N	N
2 Ruppersberger	Y	Y	Y	Y	Y	N	Y	N
3 Cardin	?	?	?	?	?	?	?	?
4 Wynn	Y	Y	Y	Y	Y	N	Y	N
5 Hoyer	?	?	Y	Y	N	N	Y	N
6 ***Bartlett***	Y	Y	Y	Y	Y	Y	N	Y
7 Cummings	?	?	Y	Y	N	N	Y	N
8 Van Hollen	Y	Y	Y	Y	N	N	Y	N
MASSACHUSETTS								
1 Olver	Y	Y	Y	Y	N	N	Y	N
2 Neal	Y	Y	Y	Y	Y	N	Y	N
3 McGovern	Y	Y	Y	Y	Y	N	Y	N
4 Frank	Y	Y	Y	Y	Y	N	Y	N
5 Meehan	Y	Y	Y	Y	Y	N	Y	N
6 Tierney	Y	Y	Y	Y	Y	N	Y	N
7 Markey	Y	Y	Y	Y	Y	N	Y	N
8 Capuano	Y	Y	Y	Y	Y	N	Y	N
9 Lynch	Y	Y	Y	Y	Y	N	Y	N
10 Delahunt	?	?	Y	Y	Y	N	Y	N
MICHIGAN								
1 Stupak	Y	Y	Y	Y	Y	N	Y	N
2 ***Hoekstra***	?	?	Y	N	N	N	Y	Y
3 ***Ehlers***	Y	Y	N	Y	N	N	N	N
4 ***Camp***	Y	Y	N	Y	Y	N	N	N
5 Kildee	Y	Y	Y	Y	Y	N	Y	N
6 ***Upton***	Y	Y	N	Y	N	Y	N	N
7 ***Smith***	Y	Y	N	Y	N	Y	N	Y
8 ***Rogers***	Y	Y	N	N	N	N	N	Y
9 ***Knollenberg***	Y	Y	N	N	N	N	N	N
10 ***Miller***	Y	Y	N	N	N	N	N	N
11 ***McCotter***	Y	Y	Y	N	Y	N	Y	Y
12 Levin	Y	Y	Y	Y	Y	N	Y	N
13 Kilpatrick	Y	Y	Y	Y	N	N	Y	N
14 Conyers	?	Y	Y	?	N	N	Y	N
15 Dingell	Y	Y	Y	Y	N	N	Y	N
MINNESOTA								
1 ***Gutknecht***	Y	Y	Y	Y	N	Y	N	Y
2 ***Kline***	Y	Y	Y	N	N	N	N	Y
3 ***Ramstad***	Y	Y	Y	Y	Y	Y	N	N
4 McCollum	Y	Y	Y	Y	Y	N	Y	N
5 Sabo	Y	Y	Y	Y	N	N	Y	N
6 ***Kennedy***	Y	Y	Y	N	N	N	N	N
7 Peterson	?	?	Y	Y	Y	N	Y	Y
8 Oberstar	Y	Y	Y	Y	N	N	Y	N
MISSISSIPPI								
1 ***Wicker***	Y	Y	N	N	N	N	N	N
2 Thompson	?	?	Y	Y	N	N	Y	N
3 ***Pickering***	Y	Y	Y	N	Y	N	N	Y
4 Taylor	Y	Y	Y	Y	Y	Y	Y	Y
MISSOURI								
1 Clay	Y	Y	Y	Y	N	N	Y	N
2 ***Akin***	Y	Y	N	N	N	?	N	Y
3 Gephardt	?	?	?	N	N	N	Y	N
4 Skelton	Y	Y	Y	N	Y	Y	Y	N
5 McCarthy	Y	Y	Y	Y	Y	N	Y	N
6 ***Graves***	Y	Y	Y	Y	Y	Y	N	Y
7 ***Blunt***	Y	Y	N	N	N	N	N	N
8 ***Emerson***	Y	Y	N	Y	N	N	N	Y
9 ***Hulshof***	Y	Y	Y	N	Y	N	N	Y
MONTANA								
AL ***Rehberg***	Y	Y	Y	Y	Y	N	N	Y
NEBRASKA								
1 ***Bereuter***	Y	Y	N	Y	Y	N	N	N
2 ***Terry***	Y	Y	Y	N	Y	Y	N	Y
3 ***Osborne***	Y	Y	N	Y	Y	N	N	N
NEVADA								
1 Berkley	Y	Y	Y	N	Y	N	Y	N
2 ***Gibbons***	Y	Y	N	N	Y	N	Y	Y
3 ***Porter***	Y	Y	Y	N	Y	N	Y	N
NEW HAMPSHIRE								
1 ***Bradley***	Y	Y	Y	N	Y	Y	Y	N
2 ***Bass***	Y	Y	N	Y	N	N	N	N
NEW JERSEY								
1 Andrews	Y	Y	Y	N	Y	N	Y	N
2 ***LoBiondo***	Y	Y	Y	N	Y	N	Y	N
3 ***Saxton***	Y	Y	N	N	Y	N	Y	N
4 ***Smith***	?	?	N	N	Y	N	Y	N
5 ***Garrett***	Y	Y	N	N	N	N	N	Y
6 Pallone	Y	Y	Y	N	N	N	Y	N
7 ***Ferguson***	Y	Y	Y	N	Y	N	Y	N
8 Pascrell	?	?	Y	N	Y	N	Y	N
9 Rothman	Y	Y	Y	N	Y	N	Y	N
10 Payne	?	?	Y	Y	N	N	Y	N
11 ***Frelinghuysen***	Y	Y	Y	N	N	N	N	N
12 Holt	Y	Y	Y	Y	Y	N	Y	N
13 Menendez	Y	Y	Y	N	N	N	Y	N
NEW MEXICO								
1 ***Wilson***	Y	Y	Y	N	Y	N	N	N
2 ***Pearce***	Y	Y	N	N	N	N	N	Y
3 Udall	Y	Y	Y	Y	Y	N	Y	N
NEW YORK								
1 Bishop	Y	Y	Y	Y	Y	N	Y	N
2 Israel	Y	Y	Y	Y	N	N	Y	N
3 ***King***	Y	Y	N	N	Y	N	Y	Y
4 McCarthy	?	?	Y	Y	Y	N	Y	N
5 Ackerman	Y	Y	Y	N	Y	N	Y	N
6 Meeks	Y	Y	Y	Y	Y	N	Y	N
7 Crowley	Y	Y	Y	Y	N	N	Y	N
8 Nadler	Y	Y	Y	Y	N	N	Y	N
9 Weiner	Y	Y	Y	Y	N	N	Y	N
10 Towns	Y	Y	Y	Y	N	N	Y	N
11 Owens	Y	Y	Y	Y	Y	N	Y	N
12 Velázquez	Y	Y	Y	Y	N	N	Y	N
13 ***Fossella***	Y	Y	N	N	Y	Y	Y	Y
14 Maloney	Y	Y	Y	Y	N	N	Y	N
15 Rangel	Y	Y	Y	Y	Y	N	Y	N
16 Serrano	Y	Y	Y	Y	N	N	Y	N
17 Engel	?	?	Y	Y	N	N	Y	N
18 Lowey	?	Y	Y	Y	Y	N	Y	N
19 ***Kelly***	Y	Y	Y	N	N	N	N	N
20 ***Sweeney***	?	?	N	N	N	N	N	N
21 McNulty	Y	Y	Y	Y	Y	N	Y	N
22 Hinchey	?	?	?	?	?	?	?	?
23 ***McHugh***	Y	Y	Y	Y	Y	N	Y	N
24 ***Boehlert***	Y	Y	Y	Y	Y	N	Y	N
25 ***Walsh***	Y	Y	N	N	N	N	N	N
26 ***Reynolds***	Y	Y	N	N	Y	Y	N	Y
27 ***Quinn***	Y	Y	N	N	Y	N	Y	Y
28 Slaughter	?	?	Y	Y	Y	N	Y	N
29 ***Houghton***	Y	Y	N	Y	N	Y	N	N
NORTH CAROLINA								
1 Vacant								
2 Etheridge	Y	Y	Y	Y	Y	N	Y	N
3 ***Jones***	Y	Y	N	N	Y	N	Y	Y
4 Price	?	Y	Y	Y	Y	N	Y	N
5 ***Burr***	Y	Y	Y	N	Y	N	N	Y
6 ***Coble***	Y	Y	Y	Y	Y	Y	N	Y
7 McIntyre	?	?	Y	N	Y	N	Y	Y
8 ***Hayes***	Y	Y	Y	N	N	N	N	Y
9 ***Myrick***	Y	Y	N	N	N	Y	N	Y
10 ***Ballenger***	Y	Y	N	N	N	N	N	N
11 ***Taylor***	Y	N	N	N	N	N	N	N
12 Watt	Y	Y	Y	Y	Y	N	Y	N
13 Miller	?	Y	Y	Y	Y	N	Y	N
NORTH DAKOTA								
AL Pomeroy	Y	Y	Y	Y	Y	N	Y	N
OHIO								
1 ***Chabot***	Y	Y	Y	N	Y	Y	N	Y
2 ***Portman***	Y	Y	N	N	N	N	N	N
3 ***Turner***	Y	Y	N	Y	N	N	N	N
4 ***Oxley***	Y	Y	Y	N	N	N	N	N
5 ***Gillmor***	Y	Y	Y	N	N	Y	N	N
6 Strickland	Y	Y	Y	Y	Y	N	Y	N
7 ***Hobson***	Y	Y	N	N	N	N	N	N
8 ***Boehner***	Y	Y	N	N	N	N	N	Y
9 Kaptur	Y	Y	Y	Y	Y	N	Y	N
10 Kucinich	Y	Y	Y	Y	Y	N	Y	N
11 Jones	?	?	?	?	?	?	?	?
12 ***Tiberi***	Y	Y	Y	Y	N	N	N	Y
13 Brown	?	?	?	Y	Y	N	Y	N
14 ***LaTourette***	Y	Y	Y	N	N	N	Y	N
15 ***Pryce***	Y	Y	Y	N	N	N	N	N
16 ***Regula***	Y	Y	N	N	N	N	N	N
17 Ryan	Y	Y	Y	Y	Y	N	Y	N
18 ***Ney***	Y	Y	Y	Y	N	N	Y	Y
OKLAHOMA								
1 ***Sullivan***	Y	?	Y	N	N	Y	N	Y
2 Carson	?	?	Y	Y	Y	N	Y	N
3 ***Lucas***	Y	Y	Y	N	N	N	N	Y
4 ***Cole***	Y	Y	N	N	N	N	N	N
5 ***Istook***	Y	Y	?	N	N	N	N	Y
OREGON								
1 Wu	Y	Y	Y	N	Y	N	Y	N
2 ***Walden***	Y	Y	Y	N	Y	N	N	N
3 Blumenauer	Y	Y	Y	?	?	?	?	?
4 DeFazio	Y	Y	Y	Y	Y	N	Y	N
5 Hooley	Y	Y	Y	Y	Y	N	Y	N
PENNSYLVANIA								
1 Brady	Y	Y	Y	Y	Y	N	Y	N
2 Fattah	Y	Y	Y	Y	Y	N	Y	N
3 ***English***	Y	Y	N	Y	N	N	Y	N
4 ***Hart***	Y	Y	Y	N	N	N	Y	Y
5 ***Peterson***	?	?	N	Y	N	N	N	Y
6 ***Gerlach***	Y	Y	Y	N	Y	N	Y	N
7 ***Weldon***	Y	Y	Y	N	Y	N	Y	N
8 ***Greenwood***	Y	Y	N	Y	Y	N	N	N
9 ***Shuster, Bill***	Y	Y	Y	N	N	N	N	Y
10 ***Sherwood***	Y	Y	N	Y	N	N	N	N
11 Kanjorski	Y	Y	Y	Y	Y	N	Y	N
12 Murtha	Y	Y	Y	Y	N	N	Y	N
13 Hoeffel	Y	Y	Y	Y	Y	N	Y	N
14 Doyle	Y	Y	Y	Y	Y	N	Y	N
15 ***Toomey***	Y	Y	N	N	N	N	N	Y
16 ***Pitts***	?	?	N	N	N	N	N	Y
17 Holden	Y	Y	Y	Y	Y	N	Y	N
18 ***Murphy***	Y	Y	Y	N	Y	N	Y	Y
19 ***Platts***	Y	Y	Y	N	N	N	Y	Y
RHODE ISLAND								
1 Kennedy	Y	Y	Y	Y	Y	N	Y	N
2 Langevin	Y	Y	Y	Y	Y	N	Y	N
SOUTH CAROLINA								
1 ***Brown***	Y	Y	N	N	N	N	N	Y
2 ***Wilson***	Y	Y	N	N	N	Y	N	N
3 ***Barrett***	Y	Y	N	N	N	N	N	Y
4 ***DeMint***	Y	Y	Y	Y	N	Y	N	Y
5 Spratt	Y	Y	Y	Y	N	N	Y	N
6 Clyburn	?	?	Y	Y	N	N	Y	N
SOUTH DAKOTA								
AL Herseth	Y	Y	Y	Y	Y	N	Y	N
TENNESSEE								
1 ***Jenkins***	?	?	N	N	N	N	N	Y
2 ***Duncan***	Y	Y	Y	N	N	Y	N	Y
3 ***Wamp***	Y	Y	N	N	N	N	N	Y
4 Davis	Y	Y	Y	Y	Y	N	Y	N
5 Cooper	Y	Y	Y	Y	N	N	Y	N
6 Gordon	Y	Y	Y	Y	N	N	Y	N
7 ***Blackburn***	Y	Y	Y	N	N	N	N	Y
8 Tanner	Y	Y	Y	Y	N	N	Y	N
9 Ford	Y	Y	Y	Y	Y	N	Y	N
TEXAS								
1 Sandlin	Y	Y	Y	Y	N	N	Y	N
2 Turner	Y	Y	Y	Y	N	N	Y	N
3 ***Johnson, Sam***	Y	Y	Y	N	N	Y	N	Y
4 ***Hall***	Y	Y	Y	N	N	N	N	N
5 ***Hensarling***	Y	Y	N	N	N	Y	N	Y
6 ***Barton***	Y	Y	N	N	N	N	N	N
7 ***Culberson***	Y	Y	N	N	N	N	N	Y
8 ***Brady***	Y	Y	N	N	N	N	N	Y
9 Lampson	Y	Y	Y	Y	Y	N	Y	N
10 Doggett	Y	Y	Y	Y	Y	N	Y	N
11 Edwards	Y	Y	Y	Y	Y	N	Y	N
12 ***Granger***	Y	Y	N	N	N	N	N	N
13 ***Thornberry***	Y	Y	N	N	N	Y	N	Y
14 ***Paul***	Y	Y	Y	Y	Y	Y	N	Y
15 Hinojosa	Y	Y	Y	Y	N	N	Y	N
16 Reyes	Y	Y	Y	Y	Y	N	Y	N
17 Stenholm	?	?	Y	Y	Y	N	Y	N
18 Jackson-Lee	Y	Y	Y	Y	Y	N	Y	N
19 ***Neugebauer***	Y	Y	Y	N	Y	Y	N	Y
20 Gonzalez	Y	Y	Y	Y	N	N	Y	N
21 ***Smith***	Y	Y	N	N	N	N	N	N
22 ***DeLay***	?	?	N	N	N	N	N	Y
23 ***Bonilla***	Y	Y	N	N	N	N	N	Y
24 Frost	Y	Y	Y	Y	Y	N	Y	N
25 Bell	Y	Y	Y	Y	Y	N	Y	N
26 ***Burgess***	Y	Y	Y	N	N	N	N	Y
27 Ortiz	Y	Y	Y	Y	Y	N	Y	N
28 Rodriguez	Y	Y	Y	Y	Y	N	Y	N
29 Green	Y	Y	Y	Y	Y	N	Y	N
30 Johnson, E.B.	Y	Y	Y	Y	N	N	Y	N
31 ***Carter***	Y	Y	N	N	N	N	N	N
32 ***Sessions***	Y	Y	N	N	Y	Y	N	Y
UTAH								
1 ***Bishop***	Y	Y	Y	N	Y	N	N	Y
2 Matheson	Y	Y	Y	Y	Y	N	Y	N
3 ***Cannon***	Y	Y	N	N	N	N	N	Y
VERMONT								
AL *Sanders*	Y	Y	Y	Y	Y	N	Y	N
VIRGINIA								
1 ***Davis, Jo Ann***	Y	Y	Y	N	N	Y	Y	Y
2 ***Schrock***	Y	Y	Y	N	N	N	N	Y
3 Scott	Y	Y	Y	Y	Y	?	Y	N
4 ***Forbes***	Y	Y	Y	N	N	N	N	Y
5 ***Goode***	Y	Y	Y	N	N	N	N	Y
6 ***Goodlatte***	Y	Y	N	N	N	N	N	Y
7 ***Cantor***	Y	Y	N	N	N	N	N	Y
8 Moran	Y	Y	N	Y	N	N	Y	N
9 Boucher	Y	Y	Y	Y	Y	N	Y	N
10 ***Wolf***	Y	Y	N	N	N	N	N	N
11 ***Davis, T.***	Y	Y	Y	N	N	N	N	N
WASHINGTON								
1 Inslee	Y	Y	Y	Y	Y	N	Y	N
2 Larsen	Y	Y	Y	Y	Y	N	Y	N
3 Baird	Y	Y	Y	Y	Y	Y	Y	N
4 ***Hastings***	Y	Y	N	N	N	N	N	Y
5 ***Nethercutt***	Y	Y	Y	Y	Y	N	N	N
6 Dicks	Y	Y	Y	Y	Y	N	Y	N
7 McDermott	Y	Y	Y	Y	Y	N	Y	N
8 ***Dunn***	Y	Y	N	N	Y	N	N	N
9 Smith	Y	Y	Y	Y	Y	N	Y	N
WEST VIRGINIA								
1 Mollohan	Y	Y	Y	Y	N	N	Y	N
2 ***Capito***	Y	Y	Y	N	N	N	Y	N
3 Rahall	Y	Y	Y	Y	Y	N	Y	N
WISCONSIN								
1 ***Ryan***	Y	Y	N	Y	N	Y	N	Y
2 Baldwin	Y	Y	Y	Y	Y	N	Y	N
3 Kind	Y	Y	Y	Y	Y	N	Y	N
4 Kleczka	?	?	Y	Y	Y	N	Y	N
5 ***Sensenbrenner***	Y	Y	N	Y	N	Y	N	Y
6 ***Petri***	Y	Y	N	Y	N	Y	N	Y
7 Obey	Y	Y	Y	Y	Y	N	Y	N
8 ***Green***	Y	Y	Y	N	Y	Y	N	Y
WYOMING								
AL ***Cubin***	Y	Y	Y	Y	N	Y	N	Y

Southern states - Ala., Ark., Fla., Ga., Ky., La., Miss., N.C., Okla., S.C., Tenn., Texas, Va.

334. HR 4754. Fiscal 2005 Commerce, Justice, State Appropriations/ Medical Marijuana. Farr, D-Calif., amendment that would prohibit the use of funds to prevent the implementation of state laws authorizing the use of marijuana for medical reasons in Alaska, California, Colorado, Hawaii, Maine, Maryland, Nevada, Oregon, Vermont or Washington state. Rejected 148-268: R 19-202; D 128-66 (ND 111-31, SD 17-35); I 1-0. July 7, 2004.

335. HR 4754. Fiscal 2005 Commerce, Justice, State Appropriations/ United Nations Funding. Paul, R-Texas, amendment that would prohibit the use of funds in the bill to pay any U.S. contribution to the United Nations or any affiliated agency of the United Nations. Rejected 83-335: R 80-142; D 3-192 (ND 2-140, SD 1-52); I 0-1. July 7, 2004.

336. HR 4755. Fiscal 2005 Legislative Branch Appropriations/Rule. Adoption of the rule (H Res 707) to provide for House floor consideration of the bill that would appropriate $2.75 billion in fiscal 2005 for legislative branch operations. Adopted 223-194: R 221-0; D 2-193 (ND 2-141, SD 0-52); I 0-1. July 8, 2004.

337. HR 3598. Manufacturing Technology/Rule. Adoption of the rule (H Res 706) to provide for House floor consideration of the bill that would authorize $470 million in fiscal 2005 through 2008 for the Manufacturing Extension Partnership Program, which provides technical assistance to small- and medium-sized manufacturers. Adopted 217-196: R 217-0; D 0-195 (ND 0-143, SD 0-52); I 0-1. July 8, 2004.

338. HR 3980. Windstorm Impact Program/Passage. Neugebauer, R-Texas, motion to suspend the rules and pass the bill that would establish the National Windstorm Impact Reduction Program, which would coordinate federal efforts and consult with academic and private-sector entities to reduce the loss of life and property from windstorms. Motion agreed to 387-26: R 194-25; D 192-1 (ND 140-1, SD 52-0); I 1-0. A two-thirds majority of those present and voting (276 in this case) is required for passage under suspension of the rules. July 8, 2004.

339. HR 4754. Fiscal 2005 Commerce, Justice, State Appropriations/ Surveillance of Library Records. Sanders, I-Vt., amendment that would prohibit funds from being used to make an application under the Foreign Intelligence Surveillance Act to acquire library circulation records, library patron lists, library Internet records, bookseller sales records or bookseller customer lists. Rejected 210-210: R 18-206; D 191-4 (ND 142-2, SD 49-2); I 1-0. A "nay" was a vote in support of the president's position. July 8, 2004.

340. HR 4754. Fiscal 2005 Commerce, Justice, State Appropriations/ HIV/AIDS Funding. Akin, R-Mo., amendment that would prohibit funds from being used for HIV/AIDS programs that do not explicitly oppose legalizing sex trafficking and prostitution. Adopted 306-113: R 220-3; D 86-110 (ND 55-90, SD 31-20); I 0-0. July 8, 2004.

341. HR 4754. Fiscal 2005 Commerce, Justice, State Appropriations/Immigration and Citizenship Information. King, R-Iowa, amendment that would provide $1 million to enforce an existing law that prohibits localities from refusing to allow their officers to provide information to the federal government on the citizenship or immigration status of an individual. The spending would be offset by reducing Justice Department salaries and expenses by $1 million. Rejected 139-278: R 134-87; D 5-190 (ND 1-143, SD 4-47); I 0-1. July 8, 2004.

Key

Y	Voted for (yea).
#	Paired for.
+	Announced for.
N	Voted against (nay).
X	Paired against.
−	Announced against.
P	Voted "present."
C	Voted "present" to avoid possible conflict of interest.
?	Did not vote or otherwise make a position known.

Democrats **Republicans**
Independents

	334	335	336	337	338	339	340	341
ALABAMA								
1 *Bonner*	N	Y	Y	Y	Y	N	Y	Y
2 *Everett*	N	Y	Y	Y	Y	N	Y	Y
3 *Rogers*	N	Y	Y	Y	Y	N	Y	Y
4 *Aderholt*	N	N	Y	Y	Y	N	Y	Y
5 Cramer	N	N	N	Y	Y	Y	Y	N
6 *Bachus*	N	Y	Y	?	N	Y	N	Y
7 Davis	N	N	N	N	Y	Y	N	N
ALASKA								
AL *Young*	?	?	Y	Y	Y	Y	Y	?
ARIZONA								
1 *Renzi*	N	Y	Y	Y	Y	Y	Y	Y
2 *Franks*	N	Y	Y	Y	Y	N	Y	Y
3 *Shadegg*	N	N	Y	Y	N	Y	N	Y
4 Pastor	Y	N	N	N	Y	Y	N	N
5 *Hayworth*	N	Y	Y	Y	Y	N	Y	Y
6 *Flake*	Y	Y	Y	Y	N	Y	N	Y
7 Grijalva	Y	N	N	N	Y	Y	N	N
8 *Kolbe*	N	Y	Y	Y	N	N	N	N
ARKANSAS								
1 Berry	N	N	?	?	?	?	?	?
2 Snyder	N	N	N	N	Y	Y	N	N
3 *Boozman*	N	Y	Y	Y	Y	N	Y	Y
4 Ross	N	N	N	N	Y	Y	N	N
CALIFORNIA								
1 Thompson	Y	N	N	N	Y	Y	N	N
2 *Herger*	N	Y	Y	Y	Y	N	Y	Y
3 *Ose*	N	N	Y	Y	Y	N	Y	N
4 *Doolittle*	N	Y	Y	Y	Y	N	Y	Y
5 Matsui	?	?	N	N	Y	N	N	N
6 Woolsey	Y	N	N	N	Y	Y	N	N
7 Miller, George	Y	N	N	N	Y	Y	N	N
8 Pelosi	Y	N	N	N	Y	Y	N	N
9 Lee	Y	N	N	N	Y	Y	N	N
10 Tauscher	Y	N	N	N	Y	Y	N	N
11 *Pombo*	N	Y	Y	Y	N	Y	N	Y
12 Lantos	Y	N	N	N	Y	Y	N	N
13 Stark	Y	N	N	N	Y	Y	N	N
14 Eshoo	Y	N	N	N	Y	Y	N	N
15 Honda	?	?	N	?	?	Y	N	N
16 Lofgren	Y	N	N	N	Y	P	N	N
17 Farr	Y	N	N	N	Y	Y	N	N
18 Cardoza	N	N	N	N	Y	Y	N	N
19 *Radanovich*	N	Y	Y	Y	Y	N	Y	N
20 Dooley	Y	N	N	N	Y	Y	N	N
21 *Nunes*	N	Y	Y	Y	Y	N	Y	N
22 *Thomas*	N	N	Y	Y	Y	N	Y	N
23 Capps	Y	N	N	N	Y	Y	N	N
24 *Gallegly*	N	N	Y	Y	Y	N	Y	Y
25 *McKeon*	N	N	Y	Y	Y	N	Y	N
26 *Dreier*	N	N	Y	Y	Y	N	Y	N
27 Sherman	Y	N	N	?	Y	Y	N	N
28 Berman	Y	N	N	N	Y	Y	N	N
29 Schiff	Y	N	N	N	Y	Y	N	N
30 Waxman	Y	N	N	N	Y	Y	N	N
31 Becerra	Y	N	N	N	Y	Y	N	N
32 Solis	Y	N	N	N	Y	Y	N	N
33 Watson	Y	N	N	N	Y	Y	N	N
34 Roybal-Allard	Y	N	N	N	Y	Y	N	N
35 Waters	Y	N	N	?	Y	Y	N	N
36 Harman	Y	N	N	N	Y	Y	N	N

	334	335	336	337	338	339	340	341
37 Millender-McD.	Y	N	N	Y	Y	Y	N	N
38 Napolitano	Y	N	N	N	Y	Y	N	?
39 Sánchez, Linda	Y	N	N	Y	Y	Y	N	N
40 *Royce*	N	N	Y	Y	N	Y	N	Y
41 *Lewis*	N	N	Y	Y	Y	N	Y	N
42 *Miller, Gary*	N	N	Y	Y	Y	N	Y	Y
43 Baca	N	N	N	N	Y	Y	N	N
44 *Calvert*	N	N	Y	Y	Y	N	Y	N
45 *Bono*	N	N	Y	Y	Y	N	Y	Y
46 *Rohrabacher*	Y	Y	Y	Y	N	Y	N	Y
47 Sanchez, Loretta	N	N	N	Y	Y	Y	N	N
48 *Cox*	N	N	Y	Y	Y	N	Y	Y
49 *Issa*	N	N	Y	Y	N	Y	N	N
50 *Cunningham*	N	N	Y	Y	Y	N	Y	N
51 Filner	Y	N	N	N	Y	Y	N	N
52 *Hunter*	N	Y	Y	Y	Y	N	Y	N
53 Davis	Y	N	N	N	Y	Y	N	N
COLORADO								
1 DeGette	Y	N	N	N	Y	Y	N	N
2 Udall	Y	N	N	Y	Y	Y	N	N
3 *McInnis*	N	Y	Y	Y	N	Y	N	Y
4 *Musgrave*	N	N	Y	Y	Y	N	Y	Y
5 *Hefley*	Y	Y	Y	N	N	Y	N	Y
6 *Tancredo*	Y	Y	Y	Y	Y	Y	Y	Y
7 *Beauprez*	Y	N	Y	Y	Y	N	Y	Y
CONNECTICUT								
1 Larson	Y	N	N	Y	Y	Y	N	N
2 *Simmons*	Y	N	Y	Y	Y	Y	N	N
3 DeLauro	Y	N	N	N	Y	Y	N	N
4 *Shays*	N	N	Y	Y	N	Y	N	Y
5 *Johnson*	Y	N	Y	Y	Y	N	N	N
DELAWARE								
AL *Castle*	N	N	Y	Y	Y	Y	Y	Y
FLORIDA								
1 *Miller, J.*	N	Y	Y	Y	N	N	Y	Y
2 Boyd	N	N	N	N	Y	Y	N	N
3 Brown	N	N	N	N	Y	Y	N	N
4 *Crenshaw*	N	N	Y	Y	Y	N	Y	N
5 *Brown-Waite*	N	Y	Y	Y	Y	N	Y	N
6 *Stearns*	N	Y	Y	Y	N	N	Y	Y
7 *Mica*	N	Y	?	Y	Y	N	Y	N
8 *Keller*	N	Y	Y	Y	Y	N	Y	N
9 *Bilirakis*	N	N	Y	Y	Y	N	Y	N
10 *Young*	?	?	Y	Y	?	N	Y	N
11 Davis	Y	N	N	Y	Y	Y	N	N
12 *Putnam*	N	Y	Y	Y	N	N	Y	N
13 *Harris*	N	Y	Y	Y	Y	N	Y	Y
14 *Goss*	N	N	Y	Y	N	Y	N	Y
15 *Weldon*	N	Y	Y	Y	N	N	Y	Y
16 *Foley*	N	Y	Y	Y	Y	N	Y	Y
17 Meek	?	?	?	?	?	Y	N	N
18 *Ros-Lehtinen*	N	N	Y	Y	N	N	Y	Y
19 Wexler	Y	N	N	Y	Y	N	N	N
20 Deutsch	?	?	?	?	?	?	?	?
21 *Diaz-Balart, L.*	N	N	Y	Y	Y	N	Y	N
22 *Shaw*	N	N	Y	Y	Y	Y	Y	Y
23 Hastings	?	?	?	?	?	?	?	?
24 *Feeney*	N	Y	Y	Y	Y	N	Y	Y
25 *Diaz-Balart, M.*	N	N	Y	Y	Y	N	Y	N
GEORGIA								
1 *Kingston*	N	Y	Y	Y	N	N	Y	Y
2 Bishop	Y	N	N	Y	?	?	?	
3 Marshall	N	N	N	Y	Y	Y	N	N
4 Majette	Y	N	N	Y	Y	Y	N	N
5 Lewis	Y	N	N	N	Y	Y	N	N
6 *Isakson*	N	N	Y	Y	Y	N	Y	N
7 *Linder*	N	Y	Y	Y	N	N	Y	N
8 *Collins*	?	?	?	?	?	?	?	?
9 *Norwood*	N	Y	Y	Y	N	Y	N	Y
10 *Deal*	N	Y	Y	Y	N	Y	N	Y
11 *Gingrey*	N	Y	Y	Y	Y	N	Y	Y
12 *Burns*	N	N	Y	Y	N	N	Y	Y
13 Scott	Y	N	N	N	Y	Y	N	N
HAWAII								
1 Abercrombie	Y	N	N	Y	Y	Y	N	N
2 Case	Y	N	N	N	Y	Y	N	N
IDAHO								
1 *Otter*	Y	Y	Y	Y	N	Y	Y	Y
2 *Simpson*	Y	Y	Y	Y	N	Y	Y	Y
ILLINOIS								
1 Rush	Y	N	N	N	?	Y	N	N
2 Jackson	Y	N	N	N	Y	Y	N	N
3 Lipinski	Y	N	N	N	Y	Y	N	N
4 Gutierrez	Y	N	N	N	Y	Y	N	N
5 Emanuel	N	N	N	N	Y	Y	N	N
6 *Hyde*	N	N	Y	Y	Y	N	Y	N

ND Northern Democrats   SD Southern Democrats

	334	335	336	337	338	339	340	341
7 Davis	Y	N	N	N	Y	Y	N	N
8 ***Crane***	N	N	Y	Y	Y	N	Y	Y
9 Schakowsky	Y	N	N	N	Y	Y	N	N
10 ***Kirk***	N	N	Y	Y	Y	Y	Y	N
11 ***Weller***	N	N	Y	Y	Y	N	Y	N
12 Costello	N	N	N	N	Y	Y	Y	N
13 ***Biggert***	N	N	Y	Y	Y	N	Y	N
14 ***Hastert***						N		
15 ***Johnson***	Y	N	Y	Y	Y	Y	Y	N
16 ***Manzullo***	N	Y	Y	Y	Y	N	Y	Y
17 Evans	Y	N	N	N	Y	Y	N	N
18 ***LaHood***	?	?	?	?	?	?	?	?
19 ***Shimkus***	N	N	Y	Y	Y	N	Y	Y
INDIANA								
1 Visclosky	N	N	N	N	Y	Y	Y	N
2 ***Chocola***	N	N	Y	Y	Y	N	Y	Y
3 ***Souder***	N	N	Y	Y	Y	N	Y	Y
4 ***Buyer***	N	N	Y	Y	Y	N	Y	Y
5 ***Burton***	N	Y	Y	Y	N	N	Y	N
6 ***Pence***	N	N	Y	Y	Y	N	Y	Y
7 Carson	?	?	?	?	?	?	?	?
8 ***Hostettler***	N	Y	Y	Y	N	N	Y	Y
9 Hill	N	N	N	N	Y	Y	Y	N
IOWA								
1 ***Nussle***	N	N	Y	Y	Y	N	Y	Y
2 ***Leach***	Y	N	Y	Y	Y	Y	Y	N
3 Boswell	N	N	N	N	Y	Y	Y	N
4 ***Latham***	N	N	Y	Y	Y	N	Y	Y
5 ***King***	N	N	Y	Y	Y	N	Y	Y
KANSAS								
1 ***Moran***	N	Y	Y	Y	Y	Y	Y	Y
2 ***Ryun***	N	Y	Y	Y	Y	N	Y	Y
3 Moore	N	N	N	N	Y	Y	Y	N
4 ***Tiahrt***	N	N	Y	Y	Y	N	Y	N
KENTUCKY								
1 ***Whitfield***	N	N	Y	Y	Y	N	Y	N
2 ***Lewis***	N	Y	Y	Y	Y	N	Y	Y
3 ***Northup***	N	N	Y	Y	Y	N	Y	N
4 Lucas	N	N	N	N	Y	Y	Y	N
5 ***Rogers***	N	N	Y	Y	Y	N	Y	N
6 Chandler	N	N	N	N	Y	Y	Y	Y
LOUISIANA								
1 ***Vitter***	N	N	Y	Y	Y	N	Y	Y
2 Jefferson	Y	N	N	N	Y	Y	N	N
3 ***Tauzin***	?	?	?	?	?	?	?	?
4 ***McCrery***	N	N	Y	Y	Y	N	Y	Y
5 Alexander	N	N	N	N	Y	Y	Y	N
6 ***Baker***	N	N	Y	Y	Y	N	Y	Y
7 John	N	N	N	N	Y	Y	Y	N
MAINE								
1 Allen	Y	N	N	N	Y	Y	Y	N
2 Michaud	Y	N	N	N	Y	Y	Y	N
MARYLAND								
1 ***Gilchrest***	Y	N	Y	Y	Y	N	Y	N
2 Ruppersberger	Y	N	N	N	Y	Y	Y	N
3 Cardin	?	?	N	N	Y	Y	Y	N
4 Wynn	Y	N	N	N	?	Y	Y	N
5 Hoyer	Y	N	N	N	Y	Y	N	N
6 ***Bartlett***	Y	Y	Y	Y	Y	Y	Y	Y
7 Cummings	N	N	N	N	Y	Y	N	N
8 Van Hollen	Y	N	N	N	Y	Y	N	N
MASSACHUSETTS								
1 Olver	Y	N	N	N	Y	Y	N	N
2 Neal	Y	N	N	N	Y	Y	N	N
3 McGovern	Y	N	N	N	Y	Y	N	N
4 Frank	Y	N	N	N	Y	Y	N	N
5 Meehan	Y	N	?	N	Y	Y	N	N
6 Tierney	Y	N	N	N	Y	Y	N	N
7 Markey	Y	N	N	N	Y	Y	N	N
8 Capuano	Y	N	N	N	Y	Y	N	N
9 Lynch	N	N	N	N	Y	Y	Y	N
10 Delahunt	Y	N	N	N	Y	Y	Y	N
MICHIGAN								
1 Stupak	N	N	N	N	Y	Y	Y	N
2 ***Hoekstra***	N	N	Y	Y	Y	N	Y	Y
3 ***Ehlers***	N	N	Y	Y	Y	Y	Y	N
4 ***Camp***	N	N	Y	Y	Y	N	Y	Y
5 Kildee	N	N	N	N	Y	Y	Y	N
6 ***Upton***	N	N	Y	Y	Y	N	Y	Y
7 ***Smith***	N	N	Y	Y	Y	N	Y	Y
8 ***Rogers***	N	N	Y	Y	Y	N	Y	N
9 ***Knollenberg***	N	N	Y	?	Y	N	Y	N
10 ***Miller***	N	N	Y	Y	Y	N	Y	Y
11 ***McCotter***	N	Y	Y	Y	Y	N	Y	Y
12 Levin	N	N	N	N	Y	Y	N	N

	334	335	336	337	338	339	340	341
13 Kilpatrick	Y	N	N	N	Y	Y	N	N
14 Conyers	Y	N	N	N	Y	Y	N	N
15 Dingell	Y	N	N	N	Y	Y	N	N
MINNESOTA								
1 ***Gutknecht***	N	N	Y	Y	Y	N	Y	Y
2 ***Kline***	N	N	Y	Y	Y	N	Y	Y
3 ***Ramstad***	N	N	Y	Y	Y	N	Y	Y
4 McCollum	Y	N	N	N	Y	Y	Y	N
5 Sabo	Y	Y	N	N	Y	Y	N	N
6 ***Kennedy***	N	N	Y	Y	Y	N	Y	Y
7 Peterson	N	Y	N	N	Y	Y	Y	N
8 Oberstar	Y	N	N	N	Y	Y	Y	N
MISSISSIPPI								
1 ***Wicker***	N	N	Y	Y	?	N	Y	N
2 Thompson	N	N	N	N	Y	Y	N	N
3 ***Pickering***	N	N	Y	Y	Y	N	Y	Y
4 Taylor	N	Y	N	Y	Y	Y	Y	Y
MISSOURI								
1 Clay	Y	N	N	N	Y	Y	N	N
2 ***Akin***	N	Y	Y	Y	Y	N	Y	Y
3 Gephardt	Y	N	?	?	?	?	?	?
4 Skelton	N	N	N	N	Y	Y	Y	N
5 McCarthy	Y	N	N	N	Y	Y	N	N
6 ***Graves***	Y	N	Y	Y	Y	N	Y	Y
7 ***Blunt***	N	N	Y	Y	Y	N	Y	Y
8 ***Emerson***	N	N	Y	Y	Y	N	Y	Y
9 ***Hulshof***	N	Y	Y	Y	Y	N	Y	Y
MONTANA								
AL ***Rehberg***	N	Y	Y	Y	Y	N	Y	Y
NEBRASKA								
1 ***Bereuter***	N	N	Y	Y	Y	N	Y	N
2 ***Terry***	N	N	Y	Y	Y	N	Y	N
3 ***Osborne***	N	N	Y	Y	Y	N	Y	N
NEVADA								
1 Berkley	Y	N	N	N	Y	Y	N	N
2 ***Gibbons***	N	Y	Y	Y	Y	N	Y	Y
3 ***Porter***	Y	N	Y	Y	Y	Y	Y	N
NEW HAMPSHIRE								
1 ***Bradley***	N	N	Y	Y	Y	N	Y	Y
2 ***Bass***	N	N	Y	Y	Y	N	Y	N
NEW JERSEY								
1 Andrews	Y	N	N	N	Y	Y	N	N
2 ***LoBiondo***	N	N	Y	Y	Y	N	Y	N
3 ***Saxton***	N	N	Y	Y	Y	N	Y	N
4 ***Smith***	N	N	Y	Y	Y	N	Y	N
5 ***Garrett***	Y	Y	Y	Y	Y	N	Y	Y
6 Pallone	N	N	N	N	Y	Y	N	N
7 ***Ferguson***	N	N	Y	Y	Y	N	Y	N
8 Pascrell	Y	N	N	N	Y	Y	N	N
9 Rothman	N	N	N	N	Y	Y	Y	N
10 Payne	Y	N	N	N	Y	Y	N	N
11 ***Frelinghuysen***	N	N	Y	Y	Y	N	Y	N
12 Holt	Y	N	N	N	Y	Y	N	N
13 Menendez	N	N	N	N	Y	Y	N	N
NEW MEXICO								
1 ***Wilson***	N	N	Y	Y	Y	N	Y	N
2 ***Pearce***	N	N	Y	Y	Y	N	Y	Y
3 Udall	Y	N	N	N	Y	Y	Y	N
NEW YORK								
1 Bishop	Y	N	N	N	Y	Y	Y	N
2 Israel	Y	N	N	N	Y	Y	Y	N
3 ***King***	N	N	Y	Y	Y	N	Y	N
4 McCarthy	Y	N	N	N	Y	Y	Y	N
5 Ackerman	Y	N	N	N	Y	Y	N	N
6 Meeks	N	N	N	N	Y	Y	N	N
7 Crowley	Y	N	N	N	Y	Y	N	N
8 Nadler	Y	N	N	N	Y	Y	N	N
9 Weiner	Y	N	N	N	Y	Y	N	N
10 Towns	Y	N	N	N	Y	Y	N	N
11 Owens	Y	N	N	N	Y	Y	Y	N
12 Velázquez	Y	N	N	N	Y	Y	N	N
13 ***Fossella***	N	N	Y	Y	Y	N	Y	N
14 Maloney	Y	N	N	N	Y	Y	N	N
15 Rangel	Y	N	N	N	Y	Y	Y	N
16 Serrano	Y	N	N	N	Y	Y	N	N
17 Engel	Y	N	N	N	Y	Y	N	N
18 Lowey	Y	N	N	N	Y	Y	N	N
19 ***Kelly***	N	N	Y	Y	Y	N	Y	Y
20 ***Sweeney***	N	N	Y	Y	Y	N	Y	N
21 McNulty	N	N	N	N	Y	Y	Y	N
22 Hinchey	?	?	?	?	?	?	?	?
23 ***McHugh***	N	N	Y	Y	Y	N	Y	Y
24 ***Boehlert***	Y	N	Y	Y	Y	Y	Y	N
25 ***Walsh***	N	N	Y	Y	Y	N	Y	N

	334	335	336	337	338	339	340	341
26 ***Reynolds***	N	N	Y	Y	Y	N	Y	N
27 ***Quinn***	N	N	?	?	?	?	?	?
28 Slaughter	Y	N	N	N	Y	Y	Y	N
29 ***Houghton***	N	N	Y	Y	Y	N	Y	N
NORTH CAROLINA								
1 Vacant								
2 Etheridge	N	N	N	N	Y	Y	Y	N
3 ***Jones***	N	Y	Y	Y	N	N	Y	Y
4 Price	Y	N	N	N	Y	Y	N	N
5 ***Burr***	N	N	Y	Y	Y	N	Y	N
6 ***Coble***	N	Y	Y	Y	N	N	Y	Y
7 McIntyre	N	N	N	N	Y	Y	Y	N
8 ***Hayes***	N	Y	Y	Y	Y	N	Y	Y
9 ***Myrick***	N	Y	Y	Y	N	N	Y	Y
10 ***Ballenger***	N	N	Y	Y	Y	N	Y	N
11 ***Taylor***	N	N	Y	Y	Y	N	Y	N
12 Watt	Y	N	N	N	Y	Y	N	N
13 Miller	N	N	N	N	Y	Y	Y	N
NORTH DAKOTA								
AL Pomeroy	N	N	N	N	Y	Y	Y	N
OHIO								
1 ***Chabot***	N	N	Y	Y	Y	N	Y	Y
2 ***Portman***	N	N	Y	Y	Y	N	Y	Y
3 ***Turner***	N	N	Y	Y	Y	N	Y	N
4 ***Oxley***	N	N	?	?	?	N	Y	N
5 ***Gillmor***	N	N	Y	Y	Y	N	Y	N
6 Strickland	Y	N	N	N	Y	Y	Y	N
7 ***Hobson***	N	N	Y	Y	Y	N	Y	N
8 ***Boehner***	N	N	Y	Y	Y	N	Y	N
9 Kaptur	Y	N	N	N	Y	Y	Y	N
10 Kucinich	Y	N	N	N	Y	Y	N	N
11 Jones	?	?	N	N	Y	Y	N	N
12 ***Tiberi***	N	Y	Y	Y	Y	N	Y	N
13 Brown	Y	N	N	N	Y	Y	N	N
14 ***LaTourette***	Y	N	Y	Y	Y	N	Y	N
15 ***Pryce***	N	N	Y	Y	Y	N	Y	N
16 ***Regula***	N	N	Y	Y	Y	N	Y	N
17 Ryan	Y	N	N	N	Y	Y	Y	N
18 ***Ney***	N	Y	Y	Y	Y	Y	Y	Y
OKLAHOMA								
1 ***Sullivan***	N	Y	Y	Y	Y	N	Y	Y
2 Carson	N	N	N	N	Y	Y	Y	N
3 ***Lucas***	N	Y	Y	Y	Y	N	Y	Y
4 ***Cole***	N	N	Y	Y	Y	N	Y	Y
5 ***Istook***	N	Y	Y	Y	Y	N	Y	Y
OREGON								
1 Wu	N	N	N	N	Y	Y	Y	N
2 ***Walden***	N	N	Y	Y	Y	N	Y	N
3 Blumenauer	?	?	?	?	?	?	?	?
4 DeFazio	Y	N	N	N	Y	Y	Y	N
5 Hooley	Y	N	N	N	Y	Y	Y	N
PENNSYLVANIA								
1 Brady	Y	N	N	N	Y	Y	N	N
2 Fattah	Y	N	N	N	N	Y	N	N
3 ***English***	N	N	Y	Y	Y	N	Y	N
4 ***Hart***	N	N	Y	Y	Y	N	Y	N
5 ***Peterson***	N	N	Y	Y	Y	N	Y	?
6 ***Gerlach***	N	N	Y	Y	Y	N	Y	N
7 ***Weldon***	N	N	Y	Y	Y	N	Y	N
8 ***Greenwood***	N	N	Y	Y	Y	N	Y	Y
9 ***Shuster, Bill***	N	Y	Y	Y	Y	N	Y	Y
10 ***Sherwood***	N	N	Y	Y	Y	N	Y	N
11 Kanjorski	Y	N	N	N	Y	Y	Y	N
12 Murtha	N	N	N	N	Y	Y	N	N
13 Hoeffel	N	N	N	N	Y	Y	Y	N
14 Doyle	Y	N	N	N	Y	Y	N	N
15 ***Toomey***	N	N	Y	Y	N	N	Y	Y
16 ***Pitts***	N	N	Y	Y	Y	N	Y	Y
17 Holden	N	N	N	N	Y	Y	Y	N
18 ***Murphy***	N	N	Y	Y	Y	N	Y	N
19 ***Platts***	N	Y	?	?	?	N	Y	Y
RHODE ISLAND								
1 Kennedy	Y	N	N	N	Y	Y	Y	N
2 Langevin	N	N	N	N	Y	Y	Y	N
SOUTH CAROLINA								
1 ***Brown***	N	N	Y	Y	Y	N	Y	N
2 ***Wilson***	N	N	Y	Y	Y	N	Y	Y
3 ***Barrett***	N	Y	Y	Y	Y	N	Y	Y
4 ***DeMint***	N	N	Y	Y	Y	N	Y	Y
5 Spratt	N	N	N	N	Y	Y	Y	N
6 Clyburn	N	N	N	N	Y	Y	N	N
SOUTH DAKOTA								
AL Herseth	N	N	N	N	Y	Y	Y	N

	334	335	336	337	338	339	340	341
TENNESSEE								
1 ***Jenkins***	N	N	Y	Y	Y	N	Y	Y
2 ***Duncan***	N	Y	Y	Y	N	Y	Y	Y
3 ***Wamp***	N	Y	Y	Y	Y	N	Y	Y
4 Davis	N	N	N	N	Y	Y	Y	N
5 Cooper	N	N	N	N	Y	Y	Y	N
6 Gordon	N	N	N	N	Y	Y	Y	N
7 ***Blackburn***	N	Y	Y	Y	N	N	Y	Y
8 Tanner	N	N	N	N	Y	Y	Y	Y
9 Ford	N	N	N	N	Y	Y	N	N
TEXAS								
1 Sandlin	N	N	N	N	Y	Y	Y	N
2 Turner	N	N	N	N	Y	Y	Y	N
3 ***Johnson, Sam***	N	Y	Y	Y	N	N	Y	Y
4 ***Hall***	?	N	Y	Y	Y	N	Y	N
5 ***Hensarling***	N	N	Y	Y	Y	N	Y	Y
6 ***Barton***	N	N	Y	Y	Y	N	Y	N
7 ***Culberson***	N	Y	Y	Y	N	N	Y	Y
8 ***Brady***	N	N	Y	Y	Y	N	Y	Y
9 Lampson	N	N	N	N	Y	Y	Y	N
10 Doggett	Y	N	N	N	Y	Y	N	N
11 Edwards	N	N	N	N	Y	N	Y	N
12 ***Granger***	N	N	Y	Y	Y	N	Y	N
13 ***Thornberry***	N	N	Y	Y	Y	N	Y	Y
14 ***Paul***	Y	Y	Y	Y	N	Y	Y	Y
15 Hinojosa	N	N	N	N	Y	Y	Y	N
16 Reyes	N	N	N	N	Y	Y	Y	N
17 Stenholm	N	N	N	N	Y	N	Y	N
18 Jackson-Lee	Y	N	N	N	Y	Y	N	N
19 ***Neugebauer***	N	Y	Y	Y	Y	N	Y	Y
20 Gonzalez	Y	N	N	N	Y	Y	N	N
21 ***Smith***	N	N	Y	Y	Y	N	Y	Y
22 ***DeLay***	N	Y	Y	Y	Y	N	Y	Y
23 ***Bonilla***	N	N	Y	Y	Y	N	Y	N
24 Frost	N	N	N	N	Y	Y	Y	N
25 Bell	Y	N	N	N	Y	?	?	?
26 ***Burgess***	N	Y	Y	Y	Y	N	Y	Y
27 Ortiz	N	N	N	N	Y	Y	Y	N
28 Rodriguez	Y	N	N	N	Y	Y	N	N
29 Green	N	N	N	N	Y	Y	Y	N
30 Johnson, E.B.	Y	N	N	N	Y	Y	N	N
31 ***Carter***	N	N	Y	Y	Y	N	Y	Y
32 ***Sessions***	N	Y	Y	Y	N	N	Y	Y
UTAH								
1 ***Bishop***	N	Y	Y	Y	Y	N	Y	Y
2 Matheson	N	N	N	N	Y	Y	Y	Y
3 ***Cannon***	N	Y	Y	Y	N	N	Y	N
VERMONT								
AL *Sanders*	Y	N	N	N	Y	Y	?	N
VIRGINIA								
1 ***Davis, Jo Ann***	N	Y	Y	Y	Y	N	Y	Y
2 ***Schrock***	N	N	Y	Y	Y	N	Y	Y
3 Scott	Y	N	N	N	Y	Y	N	N
4 ***Forbes***	N	Y	Y	Y	Y	N	Y	Y
5 ***Goode***	N	Y	Y	Y	N	N	Y	Y
6 ***Goodlatte***	N	N	Y	Y	Y	N	Y	Y
7 ***Cantor***	N	Y	Y	Y	Y	N	Y	Y
8 Moran	Y	N	N	N	Y	Y	N	N
9 Boucher	?	N	N	N	Y	Y	Y	N
10 ***Wolf***	N	N	Y	Y	Y	N	Y	N
11 ***Davis, T.***	N	N	Y	Y	Y	N	Y	N
WASHINGTON								
1 Inslee	Y	N	N	N	Y	Y	Y	N
2 Larsen	Y	N	N	N	Y	Y	N	N
3 Baird	Y	N	N	N	Y	Y	Y	N
4 ***Hastings***	N	Y	Y	Y	Y	N	Y	N
5 ***Nethercutt***	N	N	Y	Y	Y	N	Y	N
6 Dicks	Y	N	N	N	Y	Y	Y	N
7 McDermott	Y	N	N	N	Y	Y	N	N
8 ***Dunn***	N	N	Y	Y	Y	N	Y	N
9 Smith	Y	N	N	N	Y	Y	Y	N
WEST VIRGINIA								
1 Mollohan	N	N	N	N	Y	Y	N	N
2 ***Capito***	N	N	Y	Y	Y	N	Y	N
3 Rahall	N	N	N	N	Y	Y	Y	N
WISCONSIN								
1 ***Ryan***	N	N	Y	Y	Y	N	Y	Y
2 Baldwin	Y	N	N	N	Y	Y	N	N
3 Kind	Y	N	N	N	Y	Y	Y	N
4 Kleczka	Y	N	N	N	Y	Y	Y	N
5 ***Sensenbrenner***	N	Y	Y	Y	N	N	Y	Y
6 ***Petri***	N	N	Y	Y	Y	Y	Y	Y
7 Obey	Y	N	N	N	Y	Y	N	N
8 ***Green***	N	N	Y	Y	Y	N	Y	Y
WYOMING								
AL ***Cubin***	N	Y	Y	Y	Y	N	Y	Y

Southern states - Ala., Ark., Fla., Ga., Ky., La., Miss., N.C., Okla., S.C., Tenn., Texas, Va.

Key

Y	Voted for (yea).
#	Paired for.
+	Announced for.
N	Voted against (nay).
X	Paired against.
–	Announced against.
P	Voted "present."
C	Voted "present" to avoid possible conflict of interest.
?	Did not vote or otherwise make a position known.

Democrats **Republicans**
Independents

342. HR 4754. Fiscal 2005 Commerce, Justice, State Appropriations/ Contributions to International Organizations. Smith, R-Mich., amendment that would reduce funding for U.S. contributions to international organizations, such as the United Nations, by $20 million. Rejected 129-291: R 122-101; D 7-189 (ND 2-143, SD 5-46); I 0-1. July 8, 2004.

343. HR 4754. Fiscal 2005 Commerce, Justice, State Appropriations/ Federal Claims Court. Hefley, R-Colo., amendment that would limit funding for the U.S. Court of Federal Claims to $7.5 million. Rejected 67-347: R 65-154; D 2-192 (ND 2-141, SD 0-51); I 0-1. July 8, 2004.

344. HR 4754. Fiscal 2005 Commerce, Justice, State Appropriation/ Across-the-Board Cut. Hefley, R-Colo., amendment that would reduce overall spending in the bill by 1 percent. Rejected 81-327: R 76-142; D 5-184 (ND 2-138, SD 3-46); I 0-1. July 8, 2004.

345. HR 4754. Fiscal 2005 Commerce, Justice, State Appropriations/ Recommit. Hoyer, D-Md., motion to recommit the bill to the House Appropriations Committee with instructions to add language that would prohibit funds from being used to make an application under the Foreign Intelligence Surveillance Act to acquire library circulation records, library patron lists, library Internet records, bookseller sales records or bookseller customer lists. Motion rejected 194-223: R 2-220; D 191-3 (ND 143-1, SD 48-2); I 1-0. July 8, 2004.

346. HR 4754. Fiscal 2005 Commerce, Justice, State Appropriations/ Passage. Passage of the bill that would provide $43.5 billion for the departments of Commerce, Justice and State and the federal judiciary and related agencies in fiscal 2005. It would provide $20.8 billion for the Justice Department, $5.7 billion for the Commerce Department and $9 billion for the State Department and international broadcasting agencies. Passed 397-18: R 204-16; D 192-2 (ND 143-1, SD 49-1); I 1-0. July 8, 2004.

347. Procedural Motion/Adjourn. Nadler, D-N.Y., motion to adjourn. Motion rejected 64-324: R 1-211; D 63-113 (ND 53-73, SD 10-40); I 0-0. July 8, 2004.

	342	343	344	345	346	347
ALABAMA						
1 *Bonner*	Y	N	N	N	Y	N
2 *Everett*	Y	Y	Y	N	Y	N
3 *Rogers*	Y	N	N	N	Y	N
4 *Aderholt*	N	N	N	N	Y	N
5 Cramer	Y	N	N	Y	Y	N
6 *Bachus*	N	N	N	N	Y	N
7 Davis	N	N	N	Y	Y	N
ALASKA						
AL *Young*	Y	Y	N	N	Y	N
ARIZONA						
1 *Renzi*	Y	N	N	N	Y	N
2 *Franks*	Y	Y	Y	N	N	N
3 *Shadegg*	Y	Y	Y	N	N	N
4 Pastor	N	N	N	Y	Y	Y
5 *Hayworth*	Y	N	Y	N	Y	N
6 *Flake*	Y	Y	Y	N	N	N
7 Grijalva	N	N	N	Y	Y	Y
8 *Kolbe*	N	N	N	N	Y	N
ARKANSAS						
1 Berry	?	?	?	?	Y	Y
2 Snyder	N	N	N	Y	Y	Y
3 *Boozman*	Y	N	N	N	Y	N
4 Ross	N	N	N	Y	Y	N
CALIFORNIA						
1 Thompson	N	N	N	Y	Y	N
2 *Herger*	Y	Y	Y	N	Y	N
3 *Ose*	N	N	N	N	Y	N
4 *Doolittle*	N	N	N	N	Y	N
5 Matsui	N	N	N	Y	Y	Y
6 Woolsey	N	N	N	Y	Y	N
7 Miller, George	N	N	N	Y	Y	N
8 Pelosi	N	N	N	Y	Y	Y
9 Lee	N	N	N	Y	Y	N
10 Tauscher	N	N	N	Y	Y	N
11 *Pombo*	Y	N	N	N	Y	N
12 Lantos	N	N	N	Y	Y	Y
13 Stark	N	N	N	Y	Y	?
14 Eshoo	N	N	?	Y	Y	?
15 Honda	N	N	N	Y	Y	N
16 Lofgren	N	N	N	P	Y	N
17 Farr	N	N	N	Y	Y	Y
18 Cardoza	N	N	N	Y	Y	N
19 *Radanovich*	N	N	N	N	Y	N
20 Dooley	N	N	N	Y	Y	?
21 *Nunes*	N	N	N	N	Y	N
22 *Thomas*	N	N	N	N	Y	N
23 Capps	N	N	N	Y	Y	Y
24 *Gallegly*	Y	N	N	N	Y	N
25 *McKeon*	Y	N	N	N	Y	N
26 *Dreier*	N	N	N	N	Y	N
27 Sherman	N	N	N	Y	Y	N
28 Berman	N	N	N	Y	Y	N
29 Schiff	N	N	N	Y	Y	N
30 Waxman	N	N	N	Y	?	?
31 Becerra	N	N	N	Y	Y	N
32 Solis	N	N	N	Y	Y	Y
33 Watson	N	N	N	Y	Y	Y
34 Roybal-Allard	N	N	N	Y	Y	Y
35 Waters	N	N	N	Y	Y	Y
36 Harman	N	N	N	Y	Y	N
37 Millender-McD.	N	N	N	Y	Y	N
38 Napolitano	N	N	N	Y	Y	N
39 Sánchez, Linda	N	N	N	Y	Y	?
40 *Royce*	Y	Y	Y	N	Y	N
41 *Lewis*	N	N	N	N	Y	N
42 *Miller, Gary*	Y	Y	Y	N	Y	N
43 Baca	N	N	N	Y	Y	?
44 *Calvert*	N	N	N	N	Y	N
45 *Bono*	N	N	N	N	Y	N
46 *Rohrabacher*	Y	Y	Y	N	Y	N
47 Sanchez, Loretta	N	N	N	Y	Y	N
48 *Cox*	N	N	Y	N	?	N
49 *Issa*	N	N	Y	N	Y	N
50 *Cunningham*	Y	N	N	N	Y	N
51 Filner	N	N	N	Y	Y	N
52 *Hunter*	Y	Y	N	N	Y	?
53 Davis	N	N	N	Y	Y	N
COLORADO						
1 DeGette	N	N	N	Y	Y	N
2 Udall	N	N	Y	N	Y	N
3 *McInnis*	Y	Y	N	N	Y	N
4 *Musgrave*	Y	Y	Y	N	Y	N
5 *Hefley*	Y	Y	Y	N	N	N
6 *Tancredo*	Y	Y	Y	N	Y	N
7 *Beauprez*	N	Y	Y	N	Y	N
CONNECTICUT						
1 Larson	N	N	N	Y	Y	Y
2 *Simmons*	N	N	N	N	Y	N
3 DeLauro	N	N	N	Y	Y	Y
4 *Shays*	N	N	N	N	Y	N
5 *Johnson*	N	N	N	N	Y	N
DELAWARE						
AL *Castle*	N	N	N	Y	Y	N
FLORIDA						
1 *Miller, J.*	Y	Y	Y	N	N	N
2 Boyd	N	N	N	Y	Y	Y
3 Brown	N	N	N	Y	Y	N
4 *Crenshaw*	N	N	N	N	Y	N
5 *Brown-Waite*	Y	N	N	N	Y	N
6 *Stearns*	Y	Y	Y	N	Y	N
7 *Mica*	Y	Y	Y	N	Y	N
8 *Keller*	Y	Y	Y	N	Y	N
9 *Bilirakis*	N	N	N	N	Y	N
10 *Young*	N	N	N	Y	Y	?
11 Davis	N	N	?	Y	Y	N
12 *Putnam*	N	N	N	N	Y	N
13 *Harris*	N	N	N	N	Y	N
14 *Goss*	N	N	N	N	?	?
15 *Weldon*	N	N	N	N	Y	N
16 *Foley*	N	N	?	N	Y	N
17 Meek	N	N	N	Y	Y	N
18 *Ros-Lehtinen*	N	N	N	N	Y	N
19 Wexler	N	N	N	Y	Y	N
20 Deutsch	?	?	?	?	?	?
21 *Diaz-Balart, L.*	N	N	?	N	Y	N
22 *Shaw*	N	N	N	N	Y	N
23 Hastings	?	?	?	?	?	?
24 *Feeney*	N	Y	Y	N	Y	N
25 *Diaz-Balart, M.*	N	N	Y	N	Y	N
GEORGIA						
1 *Kingston*	Y	Y	N	N	Y	N
2 Bishop	?	?	?	?	?	?
3 Marshall	N	N	N	Y	Y	N
4 Majette	N	N	N	Y	Y	N
5 Lewis	N	N	N	Y	Y	N
6 *Isakson*	Y	Y	?	?	?	?
7 *Linder*	Y	N	N	Y	N	N
8 *Collins*	?	?	?	?	?	?
9 *Norwood*	Y	Y	Y	N	N	?
10 *Deal*	Y	N	N	N	Y	N
11 *Gingrey*	Y	N	N	N	Y	N
12 *Burns*	N	N	N	N	Y	N
13 Scott	N	N	N	Y	Y	N
HAWAII						
1 Abercrombie	N	N	N	Y	Y	Y
2 Case	N	N	N	Y	Y	N
IDAHO						
1 *Otter*	Y	Y	Y	N	N	N
2 *Simpson*	Y	N	N	N	Y	N
ILLINOIS						
1 Rush	N	N	Y	Y	Y	N
2 Jackson	N	N	N	Y	Y	N
3 Lipinski	N	N	?	Y	Y	Y
4 Gutierrez	N	N	N	Y	Y	Y
5 Emanuel	N	N	N	Y	Y	N
6 *Hyde*	N	N	N	N	Y	N

ND Northern Democrats   SD Southern Democrats

	342	343	344	345	346	347
7 Davis	N	N	N	Y	Y	Y
8 ***Crane***	Y	N	Y	N	Y	N
9 Schakowsky	N	N	N	Y	Y	Y
10 ***Kirk***	N	?	N	N	Y	N
11 ***Weller***	N	?	N	N	Y	?
12 Costello	Y	N	N	Y	Y	N
13 ***Biggert***	N	N	N	N	Y	N
14 ***Hastert***				N		N
15 ***Johnson***	N	N	N	N	Y	N
16 ***Manzullo***	Y	Y	N	N	Y	N
17 Evans	N	N	N	Y	Y	Y
18 ***LaHood***	?	?	?	?	?	?
19 ***Shimkus***	Y	N	Y	N	Y	N
INDIANA						
1 Visclosky	N	Y	N	Y	Y	N
2 ***Chocola***	Y	N	Y	N	Y	N
3 ***Souder***	Y	N	N	N	Y	N
4 ***Buyer***	Y	N	N	N	Y	N
5 ***Burton***	Y	N	Y	N	Y	N
6 ***Pence***	Y	Y	Y	N	Y	N
7 Carson	?	?	?	?	?	?
8 ***Hostettler***	Y	N	Y	N	Y	N
9 Hill	N	N	N	Y	Y	N
IOWA						
1 ***Nussle***	N	N	N	N	Y	N
2 ***Leach***	N	N	N	Y	Y	N
3 Boswell	N	N	N	Y	Y	N
4 ***Latham***	N	N	N	N	Y	N
5 ***King***	Y	N	Y	N	Y	N
KANSAS						
1 ***Moran***	Y	N	N	N	Y	N
2 ***Ryun***	Y	Y	Y	N	Y	N
3 Moore	N	N	N	Y	Y	N
4 ***Tiahrt***	Y	N	N	N	Y	N
KENTUCKY						
1 ***Whitfield***	Y	N	N	N	Y	N
2 ***Lewis***	Y	Y	Y	N	Y	N
3 ***Northup***	N	N	N	N	Y	N
4 Lucas	N	N	N	Y	Y	N
5 ***Rogers***	N	N	N	N	Y	N
6 Chandler	N	N	N	Y	Y	N
LOUISIANA						
1 ***Vitter***	Y	Y	Y	N	Y	N
2 Jefferson	N	N	N	Y	Y	N
3 ***Tauzin***	?	?	?	?	?	?
4 ***McCrery***	Y	N	N	N	Y	N
5 Alexander	N	N	N	Y	Y	N
6 ***Baker***	Y	N	Y	N	Y	N
7 John	N	N	N	Y	Y	N
MAINE						
1 Allen	N	N	N	Y	Y	Y
2 Michaud	N	N	N	Y	Y	N
MARYLAND						
1 ***Gilchrest***	N	N	N	N	Y	N
2 Ruppersberger	N	N	N	Y	Y	N
3 Cardin	N	N	N	Y	Y	N
4 Wynn	N	N	N	Y	Y	Y
5 Hoyer	N	N	N	Y	Y	N
6 ***Bartlett***	Y	Y	Y	N	Y	N
7 Cummings	N	N	N	Y	Y	N
8 Van Hollen	N	N	N	Y	Y	N
MASSACHUSETTS						
1 Olver	N	N	N	Y	Y	Y
2 Neal	N	N	N	Y	Y	Y
3 McGovern	N	N	N	Y	Y	Y
4 Frank	N	N	N	Y	Y	Y
5 Meehan	N	N	N	Y	Y	Y
6 Tierney	N	N	N	Y	Y	Y
7 Markey	N	N	N	Y	Y	Y
8 Capuano	N	N	Y	Y	N	Y
9 Lynch	N	N	N	Y	Y	Y
10 Delahunt	N	N	N	Y	Y	?
MICHIGAN						
1 Stupak	N	N	?	Y	Y	?
2 ***Hoekstra***	Y	N	Y	N	Y	N
3 ***Ehlers***	N	N	N	N	Y	N
4 ***Camp***	Y	N	N	N	Y	N
5 Kildee	N	N	N	Y	Y	N
6 ***Upton***	N	N	N	N	Y	N
7 ***Smith***	Y	Y	N	N	Y	?
8 ***Rogers***	N	N	Y	N	Y	N
9 ***Knollenberg***	N	N	N	N	Y	N
10 ***Miller***	N	N	N	N	Y	N
11 ***McCotter***	Y	N	N	N	Y	N
12 Levin	N	N	N	Y	Y	Y

	342	343	344	345	346	347
13 Kilpatrick	N	N	N	Y	Y	Y
14 Conyers	N	N	N	Y	Y	N
15 Dingell	N	N	N	Y	Y	N
MINNESOTA						
1 ***Gutknecht***	Y	Y	Y	N	N	N
2 ***Kline***	Y	Y	N	N	Y	N
3 ***Ramstad***	Y	Y	Y	N	Y	N
4 McCollum	N	N	N	Y	Y	N
5 Sabo	N	N	N	Y	Y	?
6 ***Kennedy***	Y	N	N	N	Y	N
7 Peterson	Y	N	N	Y	Y	Y
8 Oberstar	N	N	N	Y	Y	Y
MISSISSIPPI						
1 ***Wicker***	N	N	N	N	Y	N
2 Thompson	N	N	N	Y	Y	N
3 ***Pickering***	N	N	N	N	Y	N
4 Taylor	Y	N	Y	Y	N	Y
MISSOURI						
1 Clay	N	N	N	Y	Y	N
2 ***Akin***	Y	N	Y	N	Y	N
3 Gephardt	?	?	?	?	?	?
4 Skelton	N	N	N	Y	Y	Y
5 McCarthy	N	N	N	Y	Y	Y
6 ***Graves***	Y	Y	Y	N	Y	N
7 ***Blunt***	N	N	N	N	Y	N
8 ***Emerson***	N	N	N	N	Y	N
9 ***Hulshof***	Y	N	N	N	Y	N
MONTANA						
AL ***Rehberg***	Y	Y	N	N	Y	N
NEBRASKA						
1 ***Bereuter***	N	N	N	N	Y	N
2 ***Terry***	N	Y	Y	N	Y	N
3 ***Osborne***	Y	N	N	N	Y	N
NEVADA						
1 Berkley	N	N	N	Y	Y	N
2 ***Gibbons***	Y	N	Y	N	Y	N
3 ***Porter***	N	N	N	N	Y	N
NEW HAMPSHIRE						
1 ***Bradley***	Y	Y	N	N	Y	N
2 ***Bass***	Y	N	Y	N	Y	N
NEW JERSEY						
1 Andrews	N	N	N	Y	Y	Y
2 ***LoBiondo***	N	N	N	N	Y	N
3 ***Saxton***	N	N	N	N	Y	N
4 ***Smith***	N	N	N	N	Y	N
5 ***Garrett***	Y	Y	Y	N	Y	N
6 Pallone	N	N	N	Y	Y	Y
7 ***Ferguson***	N	N	N	N	Y	N
8 Pascrell	N	N	N	Y	Y	?
9 Rothman	N	N	N	Y	Y	N
10 Payne	N	N	N	Y	Y	N
11 ***Frelinghuysen***	N	N	N	N	Y	N
12 Holt	N	N	N	Y	Y	N
13 Menendez	N	N	N	Y	Y	N
NEW MEXICO						
1 ***Wilson***	N	N	N	N	Y	N
2 ***Pearce***	N	N	N	N	Y	N
3 Udall	N	N	N	Y	Y	N
NEW YORK						
1 Bishop	N	N	N	Y	Y	N
2 Israel	N	N	N	Y	Y	N
3 ***King***	N	N	N	N	Y	N
4 McCarthy	N	N	N	Y	Y	N
5 Ackerman	N	N	N	Y	Y	?
6 Meeks	N	N	N	Y	Y	?
7 Crowley	N	N	N	Y	Y	N
8 Nadler	N	N	N	Y	Y	Y
9 Weiner	N	N	N	Y	Y	N
10 Towns	N	N	N	Y	Y	Y
11 Owens	N	N	N	Y	Y	Y
12 Velázquez	N	N	N	Y	Y	Y
13 ***Fossella***	Y	N	Y	N	Y	N
14 Maloney	N	N	N	Y	Y	Y
15 Rangel	N	N	N	Y	Y	?
16 Serrano	N	N	N	Y	Y	N
17 Engel	N	N	N	Y	Y	N
18 Lowey	N	N	N	Y	Y	N
19 ***Kelly***	N	N	N	N	Y	N
20 ***Sweeney***	N	N	N	N	Y	N
21 McNulty	N	N	N	Y	Y	N
22 Hinchey	?	?	?	?	?	?
23 ***McHugh***	N	N	N	N	Y	N
24 ***Boehlert***	N	N	?	N	Y	N
25 ***Walsh***	N	N	N	N	Y	N

	342	343	344	345	346	347
26 ***Reynolds***	N	?	N	N	Y	N
27 ***Quinn***	?	?	?	?	?	?
28 Slaughter	N	N	N	Y	Y	N
29 ***Houghton***	N	N	N	N	Y	N
NORTH CAROLINA						
1 Vacant						
2 Etheridge	N	N	N	Y	Y	N
3 ***Jones***	Y	Y	Y	N	N	N
4 Price	N	N	N	Y	Y	N
5 ***Burr***	N	N	N	N	Y	N
6 ***Coble***	Y	Y	Y	N	Y	N
7 McIntyre	Y	N	N	Y	Y	N
8 ***Hayes***	Y	N	N	N	Y	N
9 ***Myrick***	Y	Y	N	N	Y	N
10 ***Ballenger***	N	N	N	N	Y	N
11 ***Taylor***	N	N	N	N	Y	N
12 Watt	N	N	N	Y	Y	?
13 Miller	N	N	N	Y	Y	Y
NORTH DAKOTA						
AL Pomeroy	N	N	N	Y	Y	N
OHIO						
1 ***Chabot***	Y	Y	Y	N	Y	N
2 ***Portman***	N	N	N	N	Y	N
3 ***Turner***	N	N	N	N	Y	?
4 ***Oxley***	N	N	N	N	Y	?
5 ***Gillmor***	Y	N	N	N	Y	N
6 Strickland	N	N	N	Y	Y	Y
7 ***Hobson***	N	N	N	N	Y	N
8 ***Boehner***	N	N	N	N	Y	N
9 Kaptur	N	N	?	Y	Y	Y
10 Kucinich	N	?	N	Y	Y	Y
11 Jones	N	?	N	Y	Y	Y
12 ***Tiberi***	N	N	N	N	Y	N
13 Brown	N	N	N	Y	Y	N
14 ***LaTourette***	N	N	N	N	Y	N
15 ***Pryce***	N	N	N	N	Y	N
16 ***Regula***	N	N	N	N	Y	N
17 Ryan	N	N	?	Y	Y	Y
18 ***Ney***	Y	N	N	N	Y	N
OKLAHOMA						
1 ***Sullivan***	Y	N	N	N	Y	N
2 Carson	N	N	N	Y	Y	N
3 ***Lucas***	N	N	N	N	Y	N
4 ***Cole***	N	N	N	N	Y	N
5 ***Istook***	Y	N	N	N	Y	N
OREGON						
1 Wu	N	N	N	Y	Y	N
2 ***Walden***	Y	N	N	N	Y	N
3 Blumenauer	?	?	?	?	?	?
4 DeFazio	N	N	N	Y	Y	Y
5 Hooley	N	N	N	Y	Y	N
PENNSYLVANIA						
1 Brady	N	N	N	Y	Y	Y
2 Fattah	N	N	N	Y	Y	N
3 ***English***	N	N	N	N	Y	N
4 ***Hart***	Y	N	N	N	Y	N
5 ***Peterson***	Y	N	N	N	Y	N
6 ***Gerlach***	N	N	N	N	Y	N
7 ***Weldon***	N	N	N	N	Y	N
8 ***Greenwood***	N	N	?	N	Y	N
9 ***Shuster, Bill***	Y	N	N	N	Y	N
10 ***Sherwood***	N	N	N	N	Y	N
11 Kanjorski	N	N	N	Y	Y	N
12 Murtha	N	N	N	Y	Y	?
13 Hoeffel	N	N	N	Y	Y	N
14 Doyle	N	N	N	Y	Y	?
15 ***Toomey***	Y	Y	Y	N	N	N
16 ***Pitts***	N	Y	Y	N	Y	?
17 Holden	N	N	N	Y	Y	?
18 ***Murphy***	Y	N	N	N	Y	N
19 ***Platts***	Y	N	N	N	Y	N
RHODE ISLAND						
1 Kennedy	N	N	N	Y	Y	N
2 Langevin	N	N	N	Y	Y	N
SOUTH CAROLINA						
1 ***Brown***	N	N	N	N	Y	N
2 ***Wilson***	Y	N	Y	N	Y	N
3 ***Barrett***	Y	N	Y	N	Y	N
4 ***DeMint***	Y	Y	Y	N	Y	N
5 Spratt	N	N	N	Y	Y	N
6 Clyburn	N	N	N	Y	Y	?
SOUTH DAKOTA						
AL Herseth	N	N	N	Y	Y	N

	342	343	344	345	346	347
TENNESSEE						
1 ***Jenkins***	Y	N	Y	N	Y	N
2 ***Duncan***	Y	Y	Y	N	N	N
3 ***Wamp***	Y	N	N	N	Y	?
4 Davis	N	N	N	Y	Y	N
5 Cooper	N	N	N	Y	Y	N
6 Gordon	Y	N	N	Y	Y	N
7 ***Blackburn***	Y	Y	Y	N	Y	N
8 Tanner	N	N	Y	Y	Y	N
9 Ford	N	N	?	Y	Y	Y
TEXAS						
1 Sandlin	N	N	N	Y	Y	N
2 Turner	N	N	N	?	?	N
3 ***Johnson, Sam***	Y	Y	Y	N	Y	N
4 ***Hall***	Y	N	Y	N	Y	N
5 ***Hensarling***	Y	Y	Y	N	N	N
6 ***Barton***	Y	N	Y	N	Y	N
7 ***Culberson***	Y	N	?	N	Y	N
8 ***Brady***	N	?	Y	N	Y	Y
9 Lampson	N	N	N	Y	Y	N
10 Doggett	N	N	Y	Y	Y	Y
11 Edwards	N	N	N	N	Y	N
12 ***Granger***	N	N	N	N	Y	N
13 ***Thornberry***	Y	N	Y	N	Y	N
14 ***Paul***	Y	Y	Y	Y	N	N
15 Hinojosa	N	N	N	Y	Y	N
16 Reyes	N	N	N	Y	Y	N
17 Stenholm	Y	N	N	N	Y	Y
18 Jackson-Lee	N	N	N	Y	Y	Y
19 ***Neugebauer***	Y	Y	Y	N	Y	N
20 Gonzalez	N	N	N	Y	Y	N
21 ***Smith***	N	N	N	N	Y	N
22 ***DeLay***	Y	N	N	N	Y	N
23 ***Bonilla***	N	N	N	N	Y	N
24 Frost	N	N	N	Y	Y	N
25 Bell	?	?	?	?	?	?
26 ***Burgess***	Y	N	Y	N	Y	N
27 Ortiz	N	N	N	Y	Y	N
28 Rodriguez	N	N	N	Y	Y	N
29 Green	N	N	N	Y	Y	N
30 Johnson, E.B.	N	N	N	Y	?	Y
31 ***Carter***	Y	N	N	N	Y	N
32 ***Sessions***	Y	Y	Y	N	Y	N
UTAH						
1 ***Bishop***	Y	Y	Y	N	Y	N
2 Matheson	N	N	N	Y	Y	N
3 ***Cannon***	Y	N	N	N	Y	N
VERMONT						
AL *Sanders*	N	N	N	Y	Y	?
VIRGINIA						
1 ***Davis, Jo Ann***	Y	Y	N	N	Y	N
2 ***Schrock***	N	N	N	N	Y	N
3 Scott	N	N	N	Y	Y	N
4 ***Forbes***	Y	N	N	N	Y	N
5 ***Goode***	Y	Y	N	N	Y	?
6 ***Goodlatte***	Y	Y	N	N	Y	N
7 ***Cantor***	Y	N	N	N	Y	N
8 Moran	N	N	N	Y	Y	N
9 Boucher	N	N	N	Y	Y	N
10 ***Wolf***	N	N	N	N	Y	N
11 ***Davis, T.***	N	N	N	N	Y	N
WASHINGTON						
1 Inslee	N	N	N	Y	Y	N
2 Larsen	N	N	N	Y	Y	?
3 Baird	N	N	N	Y	Y	?
4 ***Hastings***	Y	Y	N	N	Y	N
5 ***Nethercutt***	N	N	N	N	Y	N
6 Dicks	N	N	N	Y	Y	N
7 McDermott	N	N	N	Y	Y	Y
8 ***Dunn***	N	N	N	N	Y	N
9 Smith	N	N	N	N	Y	?
WEST VIRGINIA						
1 Mollohan	N	N	N	Y	Y	N
2 ***Capito***	N	N	N	N	Y	N
3 Rahall	N	N	N	Y	Y	N
WISCONSIN						
1 ***Ryan***	Y	Y	Y	N	Y	N
2 Baldwin	N	N	N	Y	Y	Y
3 Kind	N	N	N	Y	Y	N
4 Kleczka	N	N	N	Y	Y	N
5 ***Sensenbrenner***	Y	Y	Y	N	Y	N
6 ***Petri***	Y	Y	Y	N	N	N
7 Obey	N	N	N	Y	Y	Y
8 ***Green***	Y	Y	N	N	Y	N
WYOMING						
AL ***Cubin***	N	Y	Y	N	N	N

Southern states - Ala., Ark., Fla., Ga., Ky., La., Miss., N.C., Okla., S.C., Tenn., Texas, Va.

Key

Y	Voted for (yea).
#	Paired for.
+	Announced for.
N	Voted against (nay).
X	Paired against.
–	Announced against.
P	Voted "present."
C	Voted "present" to avoid possible conflict of interest.
?	Did not vote or otherwise make a position known.

Democrats   ***Republicans***
Independents

348. HR 2828. CalFed Water Program/Appeal Ruling of the Chair. Hastings, R-Wash., motion to table (kill) the Frank, D-Mass., appeal of the ruling of the chair that certain words spoken by Frank violated Rule XVII of the House, which requires that a member's remarks in debate shall be confined to a question under debate. Motion agreed to 197-165: R 194-0; D 3-164 (ND 0-124, SD 3-40); I 0-1. July 9, 2004.

349. Procedural Motion/Adjourn. McGovern, D-Mass., motion to adjourn. Motion rejected 54-334: R 1-210; D 52-124 (ND 40-91, SD 12-33); I 1-0. July 9, 2004.

350. HR 2828. CalFed Water Program/Previous Question. Hastings, R-Wash., motion to order the previous question (thus ending debate and possibility of amendment) on adoption of the rule (H Res 711) to provide for House floor consideration of the bill that would authorize $389 million for fiscal 2005 through fiscal 2008 for six federal agencies to conduct various water projects in California. Motion agreed to 216-180: R 214-0; D 2-179 (ND 2-132, SD 0-47); I 0-1. July 9, 2004.

351. HR 2828. CalFed Water Program/Rule. Adoption of the rule (H Res 711) to provide for House floor consideration of the bill that would authorize $389 million for fiscal 2005 through fiscal 2008 for six federal agencies to conduct various water projects in California. Adopted 237-158: R 213-0; D 24-157 (ND 17-118, SD 7-39); I 0-1. July 9, 2004.

352. HR 2828. CalFed Water Program/Rule Reconsideration. Hastings, R-Wash., motion to table (kill) the Wicker, R-Miss., motion to reconsider the vote on adoption of the rule (H Res 711) to provide for House floor consideration of the bill that would authorize $389 million for fiscal 2005 through fiscal 2008 for six federal agencies to conduct various water projects in California. Motion agreed to 210-181: R 208-0; D 2-180 (ND 2-131, SD 0-49); I 0-1. July 9, 2004.

353. Procedural Motion/Adjourn. McGovern, D-Mass., motion to adjourn. Motion rejected 41-353: R 1-207; D 39-146 (ND 31-105, SD 8-41); I 1-0. July 9, 2004.

354. HR 2828. CalFed Water Program/Recommit. Miller, D-Calif., motion to recommit the bill to the House Resources Committee with instructions to strike a provision in the bill that would require the Interior secretary to determine a proposed water project's feasibility and notify Congress if it was feasible. Congress would then have 120 days to disapprove the project or it would be automatically authorized. Motion rejected 139-255: R 0-212; D 138-43 (ND 112-21, SD 26-22); I 1-0. (Subsequently, the bill was passed by voice vote.) July 9, 2004.

	348	349	350	351	352	353	354
ALABAMA							
1 *Bonner*	Y	N	Y	Y	Y	N	N
2 *Everett*	Y	N	Y	Y	Y	N	N
3 *Rogers*	Y	N	Y	Y	Y	N	N
4 *Aderholt*	Y	N	Y	Y	Y	N	N
5 Cramer	N	N	N	N	N	N	N
6 *Bachus*	Y	N	Y	Y	Y	?	N
7 Davis	N	N	N	N	N	N	N
ALASKA							
AL *Young*	?	?	Y	Y	Y	N	N
ARIZONA							
1 *Renzi*	Y	N	Y	Y	Y	N	N
2 *Franks*	Y	N	Y	Y	Y	N	N
3 *Shadegg*	Y	N	Y	Y	Y	N	N
4 Pastor	N	N	N	Y	N	Y	Y
5 *Hayworth*	Y	N	Y	Y	Y	N	N
6 *Flake*	?	N	Y	Y	Y	N	N
7 Grijalva	N	Y	N	N	N	Y	Y
8 *Kolbe*	N	N	Y	Y	Y	N	N
ARKANSAS							
1 Berry	N	N	N	N	N	N	N
2 Snyder	N	Y	N	N	N	N	Y
3 *Boozman*	Y	N	Y	Y	?	N	N
4 Ross	N	N	N	N	N	N	Y
CALIFORNIA							
1 Thompson	N	N	N	N	N	N	Y
2 *Herger*	?	N	Y	Y	Y	N	N
3 *Ose*	Y	N	Y	Y	Y	N	N
4 *Doolittle*	Y	N	Y	Y	Y	N	N
5 Matsui	N	Y	N	N	N	Y	Y
6 Woolsey	N	Y	N	N	N	Y	Y
7 Miller, George	?	N	N	N	N	N	Y
8 Pelosi	N	Y	N	N	N	N	Y
9 Lee	?	?	?	?	?	?	?
10 Tauscher	N	N	N	N	N	N	Y
11 *Pombo*	Y	N	Y	Y	Y	N	N
12 Lantos	N	Y	N	N	N	Y	Y
13 Stark	N	Y	N	N	N	Y	Y
14 Eshoo	N	N	N	N	N	N	Y
15 Honda	N	Y	N	N	N	N	Y
16 Lofgren	N	Y	N	N	?	Y	Y
17 Farr	N	Y	N	N	N	N	Y
18 Cardoza	N	N	?	Y	P	N	Y
19 *Radanovich*	Y	N	Y	Y	Y	N	N
20 Dooley	?	N	N	N	N	N	Y
21 *Nunes*	Y	N	Y	Y	Y	N	N
22 *Thomas*	Y	N	Y	Y	Y	N	N
23 Capps	N	N	N	N	N	N	Y
24 *Gallegly*	Y	N	Y	Y	Y	N	N
25 *McKeon*	?	N	Y	Y	Y	N	N
26 *Dreier*	Y	N	Y	Y	Y	N	N
27 Sherman	N	N	N	N	N	N	Y
28 Berman	N	Y	N	N	N	N	Y
29 Schiff	N	N	N	N	N	N	Y
30 Waxman	?	?	?	?	?	?	?
31 Becerra	N	N	N	N	N	N	Y
32 Solis	N	Y	N	N	N	N	Y
33 Watson	?	Y	N	N	N	N	Y
34 Roybal-Allard	N	N	N	N	N	N	Y
35 Waters	?	?	N	N	N	Y	Y
36 Harman	N	N	N	N	N	N	Y

	348	349	350	351	352	353	354
37 Millender-McD.	N	Y	N	Y	N	N	N
38 Napolitano	N	N	N	Y	Y	N	N
39 Sánchez, Linda	N	Y	N	N	N	N	Y
40 *Royce*	Y	N	Y	Y	Y	N	N
41 *Lewis*	Y	N	Y	Y	Y	N	N
42 *Miller, Gary*	Y	N	Y	Y	Y	N	N
43 Baca	N	Y	N	Y	N	N	N
44 *Calvert*	Y	N	Y	Y	Y	N	N
45 *Bono*	?	N	Y	Y	Y	N	N
46 *Rohrabacher*	?	N	Y	Y	Y	N	N
47 Sanchez, Loretta	N	N	N	Y	N	N	N
48 *Cox*	?	?	Y	Y	Y	N	N
49 *Issa*	Y	N	Y	Y	Y	N	N
50 *Cunningham*	Y	N	Y	Y	Y	N	N
51 Filner	N	Y	N	N	N	Y	Y
52 *Hunter*	Y	N	Y	Y	?	N	N
53 Davis	N	N	N	N	N	N	Y
COLORADO							
1 DeGette	N	N	N	N	N	N	Y
2 Udall	N	Y	N	N	N	N	Y
3 *McInnis*	Y	N	Y	Y	Y	N	N
4 *Musgrave*	Y	N	Y	Y	Y	N	N
5 *Hefley*	Y	N	Y	Y	Y	N	N
6 *Tancredo*	Y	N	Y	Y	Y	N	N
7 *Beauprez*	Y	N	Y	Y	Y	N	N
CONNECTICUT							
1 Larson	N	Y	N	N	N	Y	Y
2 *Simmons*	Y	N	Y	?	Y	N	N
3 DeLauro	N	N	N	N	N	Y	Y
4 *Shays*	Y	N	Y	Y	Y	N	N
5 *Johnson*	Y	N	Y	Y	Y	?	N
DELAWARE							
AL *Castle*	Y	N	Y	Y	Y	N	N
FLORIDA							
1 *Miller, J.*	Y	N	Y	Y	Y	N	N
2 Boyd	N	?	N	N	N	N	N
3 Brown	?	?	?	?	N	N	N
4 *Crenshaw*	Y	N	Y	Y	Y	N	N
5 *Brown-Waite*	Y	N	Y	Y	Y	N	N
6 *Stearns*	Y	N	Y	Y	Y	N	N
7 *Mica*	Y	N	Y	Y	Y	N	N
8 *Keller*	Y	N	Y	Y	Y	N	N
9 *Bilirakis*	Y	N	Y	Y	Y	N	N
10 *Young*	Y	N	Y	Y	Y	N	N
11 Davis	N	Y	N	N	N	N	Y
12 *Putnam*	Y	N	Y	Y	Y	N	N
13 *Harris*	Y	N	Y	Y	Y	N	N
14 *Goss*	Y	N	Y	Y	Y	N	N
15 *Weldon*	Y	N	Y	Y	Y	N	N
16 *Foley*	Y	N	Y	Y	Y	N	N
17 Meek	N	N	N	N	N	N	Y
18 *Ros-Lehtinen*	?	N	Y	Y	Y	N	N
19 Wexler	?	?	?	?	?	?	?
20 Deutsch	N	N	N	N	N	N	Y
21 *Diaz-Balart, L.*	?	N	Y	Y	Y	?	N
22 *Shaw*	Y	N	Y	Y	Y	N	N
23 Hastings	?	?	?	?	?	?	?
24 *Feeney*	Y	N	Y	Y	Y	N	N
25 *Diaz-Balart, M.*	Y	N	Y	Y	Y	N	N
GEORGIA							
1 *Kingston*	Y	N	Y	Y	Y	N	N
2 Bishop	N	N	N	Y	N	Y	N
3 Marshall	N	N	N	?	N	N	N
4 *Majette*	?	?	?	?	?	?	?
5 Lewis	N	Y	N	N	N	Y	Y
6 *Isakson*	?	?	?	?	?	?	?
7 *Linder*	?	N	Y	Y	N	N	N
8 *Collins*	?	?	?	?	?	?	?
9 *Norwood*	?	?	?	?	?	?	?
10 *Deal*	?	?	?	?	?	?	?
11 *Gingrey*	Y	N	Y	Y	Y	N	N
12 *Burns*	Y	N	Y	Y	Y	N	N
13 Scott	N	N	N	N	N	N	Y
HAWAII							
1 Abercrombie	N	N	N	N	N	Y	Y
2 Case	?	N	N	N	N	N	N
IDAHO							
1 *Otter*	?	N	Y	Y	Y	N	N
2 *Simpson*	Y	N	Y	Y	Y	N	N
ILLINOIS							
1 Rush	N	N	N	N	N	N	Y
2 Jackson	N	N	N	N	N	N	Y
3 Lipinski	?	?	?	?	?	?	?
4 Gutierrez	N	Y	N	N	N	N	Y
5 Emanuel	N	Y	N	N	N	N	Y
6 *Hyde*	Y	N	Y	Y	Y	N	N

ND Northern Democrats   SD Southern Democrats

	348	349	350	351	352	353	354
7 Davis	N	Y	N	N	N	N	Y
8 ***Crane***	Y	N	Y	Y	Y	N	N
9 Schakowsky	N	Y	N	N	N	Y	Y
10 ***Kirk***	Y	N	Y	Y	Y	N	–
11 ***Weller***	Y	N	Y	Y	Y	N	N
12 Costello	N	N	N	Y	N	N	N
13 ***Biggert***	Y	N	Y	Y	Y	N	N
14 ***Hastert***		N	Y				N
15 ***Johnson***	Y	N	Y	Y	Y	N	N
16 ***Manzullo***	Y	N	Y	Y	Y	N	N
17 Evans	N	Y	N	N	N	N	N
18 ***LaHood***	?	?	?	?	?	?	?
19 ***Shimkus***	Y	Y	Y	Y	Y	Y	N
INDIANA							
1 Visclosky	N	N	N	N	N	N	Y
2 ***Chocola***	Y	N	Y	Y	Y	N	N
3 ***Souder***	Y	N	Y	Y	?	N	N
4 ***Buyer***	Y	N	Y	Y	Y	N	N
5 ***Burton***	?	N	Y	Y	Y	N	N
6 ***Pence***	Y	N	Y	Y	Y	N	N
7 Carson	?	?	?	?	?	?	?
8 ***Hostettler***	Y	N	Y	Y	Y	N	N
9 Hill	N	N	N	N	N	N	Y
IOWA							
1 ***Nussle***	Y	?	Y	Y	Y	N	N
2 ***Leach***	Y	N	Y	Y	Y	N	N
3 Boswell	N	N	N	N	N	N	N
4 ***Latham***	Y	N	Y	Y	Y	N	N
5 ***King***	Y	N	Y	Y	Y	N	N
KANSAS							
1 ***Moran***	Y	N	Y	Y	Y	N	N
2 ***Ryun***	Y	N	Y	Y	Y	N	N
3 Moore	N	N	N	N	N	N	N
4 ***Tiahrt***	Y	N	Y	Y	Y	N	N
KENTUCKY							
1 ***Whitfield***	Y	N	Y	Y	Y	N	N
2 ***Lewis***	Y	N	Y	Y	Y	N	N
3 ***Northup***	Y	N	Y	Y	Y	N	N
4 Lucas	N	N	N	N	N	N	N
5 ***Rogers***	Y	N	Y	Y	Y	N	N
6 Chandler	N	N	N	N	N	N	Y
LOUISIANA							
1 ***Vitter***	Y	N	Y	Y	Y	N	N
2 Jefferson	?	Y	N	N	N	Y	Y
3 ***Tauzin***	?	?	?	?	?	?	?
4 ***McCrery***	Y	N	Y	Y	Y	?	N
5 Alexander	Y	Y	N	Y	N	N	Y
6 ***Baker***	Y	N	Y	Y	Y	N	N
7 John	?	?	?	?	?	?	?
MAINE							
1 Allen	N	Y	N	N	N	Y	Y
2 Michaud	N	N	N	N	N	N	Y
MARYLAND							
1 ***Gilchrest***	Y	N	Y	Y	Y	N	N
2 Ruppersberger	N	N	N	N	N	N	Y
3 Cardin	N	N	N	N	N	N	Y
4 Wynn	N	N	N	N	N	N	Y
5 Hoyer	N	N	N	N	N	N	Y
6 ***Bartlett***	Y	N	Y	Y	Y	N	N
7 Cummings	?	?	N	N	N	N	Y
8 Van Hollen	N	N	N	N	N	N	Y
MASSACHUSETTS							
1 Olver	N	N	N	N	N	N	Y
2 Neal	N	Y	N	N	N	Y	Y
3 McGovern	N	Y	N	N	N	Y	Y
4 Frank	N	Y	N	N	N	N	Y
5 Meehan	N	N	N	N	N	N	Y
6 Tierney	N	Y	N	N	N	Y	Y
7 Markey	N	N	N	N	N	N	Y
8 Capuano	N	Y	N	N	N	Y	Y
9 Lynch	N	N	N	Y	N	N	Y
10 Delahunt	?	?	?	?	?	?	?
MICHIGAN							
1 Stupak	N	Y	N	N	N	Y	Y
2 ***Hoekstra***	Y	N	Y	Y	Y	N	N
3 ***Ehlers***	Y	N	Y	Y	Y	N	N
4 ***Camp***	Y	N	Y	Y	Y	?	N
5 Kildee	N	N	N	Y	N	N	Y
6 ***Upton***	Y	N	Y	Y	Y	N	N
7 ***Smith***	Y	N	Y	Y	Y	N	N
8 ***Rogers***	Y	N	Y	Y	Y	N	N
9 ***Knollenberg***	Y	N	Y	Y	Y	N	N
10 ***Miller***	Y	N	Y	Y	Y	N	N
11 ***McCotter***	Y	N	Y	Y	Y	N	N
12 Levin	N	N	N	N	N	N	Y
13 Kilpatrick	N	N	N	N	N	Y	Y
14 Conyers	N	Y	N	N	N	Y	Y
15 Dingell	N	Y	N	N	N	Y	Y
MINNESOTA							
1 ***Gutknecht***	Y	N	Y	Y	?	?	?
2 ***Kline***	Y	N	Y	Y	Y	N	N
3 ***Ramstad***	Y	N	Y	Y	Y	N	N
4 McCollum	N	N	N	N	N	N	N
5 Sabo	N	N	Y	N	N	N	N
6 ***Kennedy***	Y	N	Y	Y	Y	N	N
7 Peterson	N	N	N	Y	N	N	N
8 Oberstar	?	N	Y	N	N	N	N
MISSISSIPPI							
1 ***Wicker***	Y	N	Y	Y	Y	N	N
2 Thompson	N	N	N	N	N	N	Y
3 ***Pickering***	Y	N	Y	Y	Y	N	N
4 Taylor	Y	N	N	N	N	N	Y
MISSOURI							
1 Clay	?	?	?	?	?	Y	Y
2 ***Akin***	Y	N	Y	Y	Y	N	N
3 Gephardt	?	?	?	?	?	?	?
4 Skelton	N	N	N	N	N	N	N
5 McCarthy	N	Y	N	N	N	Y	Y
6 ***Graves***	Y	N	Y	Y	Y	N	N
7 ***Blunt***	Y	N	Y	Y	Y	N	N
8 ***Emerson***	Y	N	Y	Y	Y	N	N
9 ***Hulshof***	Y	N	Y	Y	Y	N	N
MONTANA							
AL ***Rehberg***	Y	N	Y	Y	Y	N	N
NEBRASKA							
1 ***Bereuter***	Y	N	Y	Y	Y	N	N
2 ***Terry***	Y	N	Y	Y	Y	N	N
3 ***Osborne***	Y	N	Y	Y	Y	N	N
NEVADA							
1 Berkley	N	N	N	N	N	N	Y
2 ***Gibbons***	Y	N	Y	Y	Y	N	N
3 ***Porter***	Y	N	Y	Y	Y	N	N
NEW HAMPSHIRE							
1 ***Bradley***	Y	N	Y	Y	Y	N	N
2 ***Bass***	Y	N	Y	Y	Y	N	N
NEW JERSEY							
1 Andrews	N	N	N	N	N	N	Y
2 ***LoBiondo***	Y	N	Y	Y	Y	N	N
3 ***Saxton***	Y	N	Y	Y	Y	N	N
4 ***Smith***	Y	N	Y	Y	Y	N	N
5 ***Garrett***	Y	N	Y	Y	Y	N	N
6 Pallone	N	N	N	N	N	N	Y
7 ***Ferguson***	Y	N	Y	Y	Y	N	N
8 Pascrell	N	N	N	N	N	N	Y
9 Rothman	N	Y	N	N	N	N	Y
10 Payne	N	N	N	N	N	Y	Y
11 ***Frelinghuysen***	Y	N	Y	Y	Y	N	N
12 Holt	N	N	N	N	N	N	Y
13 Menendez	N	N	N	Y	N	N	Y
NEW MEXICO							
1 ***Wilson***	Y	N	Y	Y	Y	N	N
2 ***Pearce***	Y	N	Y	Y	Y	N	N
3 Udall	N	N	N	N	N	N	Y
NEW YORK							
1 Bishop	?	?	?	?	?	?	?
2 Israel	N	N	N	N	N	N	Y
3 ***King***	Y	N	Y	Y	Y	N	?
4 McCarthy	N	Y	N	N	N	N	Y
5 Ackerman	?	?	?	?	?	?	?
6 Meeks	?	?	?	?	?	?	?
7 Crowley	N	Y	N	N	N	Y	Y
8 Nadler	N	N	N	N	N	N	Y
9 Weiner	N	N	N	N	N	N	Y
10 Towns	N	Y	N	N	N	Y	Y
11 Owens	?	Y	N	N	N	Y	Y
12 Velázquez	N	Y	N	N	N	Y	Y
13 ***Fossella***	Y	–	+	Y	Y	N	N
14 Maloney	N	N	N	N	N	N	Y
15 Rangel	N	N	N	N	N	N	?
16 Serrano	N	N	N	N	N	N	Y
17 Engel	?	?	N	N	N	N	Y
18 Lowey	N	N	N	N	N	N	Y
19 ***Kelly***	Y	N	Y	Y	Y	N	N
20 ***Sweeney***	?	?	?	?	?	?	N
21 McNulty	N	N	N	N	N	N	Y
22 Hinchey	?	?	?	?	?	?	?
23 ***McHugh***	Y	N	Y	Y	Y	N	N
24 ***Boehlert***	Y	N	Y	Y	Y	N	N
25 ***Walsh***	Y	N	Y	Y	Y	N	N
26 ***Reynolds***	?	N	Y	Y	Y	N	N
27 ***Quinn***	?	?	?	?	?	?	?
28 Slaughter	N	N	N	N	N	N	Y
29 ***Houghton***	Y	N	Y	Y	Y	N	N
NORTH CAROLINA							
1 Vacant							
2 Etheridge	N	N	N	N	N	N	Y
3 ***Jones***	Y	N	Y	Y	Y	N	N
4 Price	N	N	N	N	N	N	Y
5 ***Burr***	Y	N	Y	Y	Y	N	N
6 ***Coble***	Y	N	Y	Y	Y	N	N
7 McIntyre	?	N	N	N	N	N	Y
8 ***Hayes***	Y	N	Y	Y	Y	N	N
9 ***Myrick***	Y	N	Y	Y	Y	N	N
10 ***Ballenger***	Y	N	Y	Y	Y	N	N
11 ***Taylor***	Y	N	Y	Y	Y	N	N
12 Watt	N	N	N	N	N	N	Y
13 Miller	N	Y	N	N	N	Y	Y
NORTH DAKOTA							
AL Pomeroy	N	Y	N	N	N	N	Y
OHIO							
1 ***Chabot***	Y	N	Y	Y	Y	N	N
2 ***Portman***	Y	N	Y	Y	Y	N	N
3 ***Turner***	Y	N	Y	Y	Y	N	N
4 ***Oxley***	Y	N	Y	Y	Y	N	N
5 ***Gillmor***	?	N	Y	Y	Y	N	N
6 Strickland	N	N	N	N	N	N	Y
7 ***Hobson***	Y	N	Y	Y	Y	N	N
8 ***Boehner***	Y	N	Y	Y	Y	N	N
9 Kaptur	N	N	N	N	N	N	Y
10 Kucinich	N	N	N	N	N	N	Y
11 Jones	?	?	?	?	?	?	?
12 ***Tiberi***	Y	N	Y	Y	Y	N	N
13 Brown	N	N	N	N	N	N	Y
14 ***LaTourette***	Y	N	Y	Y	Y	N	N
15 ***Pryce***	Y	N	Y	Y	Y	N	N
16 ***Regula***	Y	N	Y	Y	Y	N	N
17 Ryan	N	N	N	N	N	N	Y
18 ***Ney***	Y	N	Y	Y	Y	N	N
OKLAHOMA							
1 ***Sullivan***	?	N	Y	Y	Y	N	N
2 Carson	N	N	N	N	N	N	N
3 ***Lucas***	Y	N	Y	Y	Y	N	N
4 ***Cole***	Y	N	Y	Y	Y	N	N
5 ***Istook***	Y	N	Y	Y	Y	N	N
OREGON							
1 Wu	N	N	N	N	N	N	Y
2 ***Walden***	Y	N	Y	Y	Y	N	N
3 Blumenauer	?	?	?	?	?	?	?
4 DeFazio	N	N	N	N	N	N	Y
5 Hooley	N	N	N	N	N	N	Y
PENNSYLVANIA							
1 Brady	N	N	N	N	N	N	Y
2 Fattah	?	?	?	?	?	?	?
3 ***English***	?	N	Y	Y	Y	N	N
4 ***Hart***	Y	N	Y	Y	?	N	N
5 ***Peterson***	Y	N	Y	Y	Y	N	N
6 ***Gerlach***	?	?	?	?	?	?	?
7 ***Weldon***	Y	N	Y	Y	Y	N	N
8 ***Greenwood***	Y	N	Y	Y	Y	N	N
9 ***Shuster, Bill***	Y	N	Y	Y	Y	N	N
10 ***Sherwood***	Y	N	Y	Y	Y	N	N
11 Kanjorski	N	N	N	N	N	N	Y
12 Murtha	N	N	N	Y	N	N	Y
13 Hoeffel	N	N	N	N	N	N	Y
14 Doyle	N	N	N	N	N	N	Y
15 ***Toomey***	Y	N	Y	Y	Y	N	N
16 ***Pitts***	?	?	?	?	?	?	?
17 Holden	N	N	N	N	N	N	Y
18 ***Murphy***	Y	N	Y	Y	Y	N	N
19 ***Platts***	?	?	?	?	?	?	?
RHODE ISLAND							
1 Kennedy	N	N	N	N	N	N	N
2 Langevin	N	N	N	N	N	N	Y
SOUTH CAROLINA							
1 ***Brown***	Y	N	Y	Y	Y	N	N
2 ***Wilson***	Y	N	Y	Y	Y	N	N
3 ***Barrett***	Y	N	Y	Y	Y	N	N
4 ***DeMint***	Y	N	Y	Y	Y	N	N
5 Spratt	N	Y	N	N	N	N	Y
6 Clyburn	N	Y	N	N	N	N	Y
SOUTH DAKOTA							
AL Herseth	N	N	N	N	N	N	N
TENNESSEE							
1 ***Jenkins***	Y	N	Y	Y	?	N	N
2 ***Duncan***	Y	N	Y	Y	Y	N	N
3 ***Wamp***	Y	N	Y	Y	Y	N	N
4 Davis	N	N	N	N	N	N	N
5 Cooper	N	N	N	N	N	N	Y
6 Gordon	N	N	N	N	N	N	N
7 ***Blackburn***	Y	N	Y	Y	Y	N	N
8 Tanner	?	?	?	?	N	N	?
9 Ford	N	Y	N	N	N	Y	N
TEXAS							
1 Sandlin	N	N	N	N	N	N	N
2 Turner	?	?	N	N	N	N	Y
3 ***Johnson, Sam***	?	N	Y	Y	Y	N	N
4 ***Hall***	Y	N	Y	Y	Y	N	N
5 ***Hensarling***	Y	N	Y	Y	Y	N	N
6 ***Barton***	?	N	Y	Y	Y	N	N
7 ***Culberson***	?	?	?	?	?	?	?
8 ***Brady***	Y	N	Y	Y	Y	N	?
9 Lampson	N	N	N	N	N	N	N
10 Doggett	N	Y	N	N	N	N	Y
11 Edwards	N	N	N	N	N	N	N
12 ***Granger***	Y	N	Y	Y	Y	N	N
13 ***Thornberry***	Y	N	Y	Y	Y	N	N
14 ***Paul***	?	?	?	?	?	?	?
15 Hinojosa	?	N	N	Y	N	N	N
16 Reyes	?	?	?	?	?	?	?
17 Stenholm	N	N	N	N	N	N	N
18 Jackson-Lee	N	Y	N	Y	N	Y	Y
19 ***Neugebauer***	Y	N	Y	Y	Y	N	N
20 Gonzalez	N	N	N	Y	N	N	N
21 ***Smith***	Y	N	Y	Y	Y	N	N
22 ***DeLay***	Y	N	Y	Y	Y	N	N
23 ***Bonilla***	Y	N	Y	Y	Y	N	N
24 Frost	N	N	N	N	N	N	N
25 Bell	?	?	?	?	?	?	?
26 ***Burgess***	Y	N	Y	Y	Y	N	N
27 Ortiz	N	N	N	Y	N	N	N
28 Rodriguez	N	N	N	Y	N	Y	N
29 Green	?	?	?	?	?	?	?
30 Johnson, E.B.	N	Y	N	N	N	Y	Y
31 ***Carter***	Y	N	Y	Y	Y	N	N
32 ***Sessions***	Y	N	Y	Y	Y	N	N
UTAH							
1 ***Bishop***	Y	N	Y	Y	Y	N	N
2 Matheson	N	N	N	Y	N	N	N
3 ***Cannon***	Y	N	Y	Y	Y	N	N
VERMONT							
AL *Sanders*	N	Y	N	N	N	Y	Y
VIRGINIA							
1 ***Davis, Jo Ann***	Y	N	Y	Y	Y	N	N
2 ***Schrock***	Y	N	Y	Y	Y	N	N
3 Scott	N	N	N	N	N	N	Y
4 ***Forbes***	Y	N	Y	Y	Y	N	N
5 ***Goode***	?	N	Y	Y	Y	N	N
6 ***Goodlatte***	Y	N	Y	Y	Y	N	N
7 ***Cantor***	Y	N	Y	Y	Y	N	N
8 Moran	N	N	N	N	N	N	N
9 Boucher	Y	N	N	N	N	N	Y
10 ***Wolf***	Y	N	Y	Y	Y	N	N
11 ***Davis, T.***	Y	N	Y	Y	Y	N	N
WASHINGTON							
1 Inslee	N	N	N	N	N	N	Y
2 Larsen	?	N	N	N	N	N	Y
3 Baird	N	?	N	N	N	N	Y
4 ***Hastings***	Y	N	Y	Y	Y	N	N
5 ***Nethercutt***	Y	N	Y	Y	Y	N	N
6 Dicks	N	N	N	N	N	N	?
7 McDermott	N	N	N	N	Y	N	Y
8 ***Dunn***	?	N	Y	Y	Y	N	N
9 Smith	N	N	N	N	N	N	Y
WEST VIRGINIA							
1 Mollohan	N	N	N	Y	N	N	Y
2 ***Capito***	Y	N	Y	Y	Y	N	N
3 Rahall	N	N	N	Y	N	N	Y
WISCONSIN							
1 ***Ryan***	Y	N	Y	Y	Y	N	N
2 Baldwin	N	Y	N	N	N	Y	Y
3 Kind	N	N	N	Y	N	N	Y
4 Kleczka	?	N	N	N	N	N	Y
5 ***Sensenbrenner***	Y	N	Y	Y	Y	N	N
6 ***Petri***	Y	N	Y	Y	Y	N	N
7 Obey	N	N	N	N	N	N	Y
8 ***Green***	Y	N	Y	Y	Y	N	N
WYOMING							
AL ***Cubin***	Y	N	Y	Y	Y	N	N

Southern states - Ala., Ark., Fla., Ga., Ky., La., Miss., N.C., Okla., S.C., Tenn., Texas, Va

Key

Y	Voted for (yea).
#	Paired for.
+	Announced for.
N	Voted against (nay).
X	Paired against.
–	Announced against.
P	Voted "present."
C	Voted "present" to avoid possible conflict of interest.
?	Did not vote or otherwise make a position known.

Democrats **Republicans**
Independents

355. HR 3598. Manufacturing Technology/Increased Authorization. Gordon, D-Tenn., amendment that would increase authorization for the Manufacturing Extension Partnership program to $120.6 million in fiscal 2005, $132.4 million in fiscal 2006, $145.3 million in fiscal 2007 and $159.5 million in fiscal 2008. Rejected 170-192: R 4-192; D 165-0 (ND 122-0, SD 43-0); I 1-0. July 9, 2004.

356. HR 3598. Manufacturing Technology/Re-Competition for Funds. Jackson-Lee, D-Texas, amendment that would prohibit the use of funds to require centers participating in the Manufacturing Extension Partnership program to re-compete for funds that already have been approved. Rejected 166-197: R 2-194; D 163-3 (ND 120-1, SD 43-2); I 1-0. July 9, 2004.

357. HR 3598. Manufacturing Technology/Manufacturing and Technology Administration. Larson, D-Conn., amendment that would establish a Manufacturing and Technology Administration within the Commerce Department. It would direct the president to appoint an undersecretary of Commerce for manufacturing and technology to supervise the new office. Rejected 170-189: R 5-188; D 164-1 (ND 119-1, SD 45-0); I 1-0. July 9, 2004.

358. HR 3598. Manufacturing Technology/Recommit. Costello, D-Ill., motion to recommit the bill to the House Science Committee with instructions to include language that would require the Commerce Department to complete an independent study on the outsourcing of U.S. jobs and provide policy recommendations based on these findings. Motion rejected 171-193: R 3-193; D 167-0 (ND 122-0, SD 45-0); I 1-0. (Subsequently, the bill was passed by voice vote.) July 9, 2004.

359. HR 4755. Fiscal 2005 Legislative Branch Appropriations/GAO Funding. Holt, D-N.J., amendment that would increase funding for the Government Accountability Office by $30 million, offset by cuts to the Architect of the Capitol's administration account and the Government Printing Office. Rejected 115-252: R 5-196; D 110-56 (ND 83-36, SD 27-20); I 0-0. July 12, 2004.

360. HR 4755. Fiscal 2005 Legislative Branch Appropriations/Across-the-Board Cut. Hefley, R-Colo., amendment that would reduce all discretionary spending in the bill by 1 percent. Rejected 87-278: R 74-124; D 13-154 (ND 3-117, SD 10-37); I 0-0. July 12, 2004.

	355	356	357	358	359	360
ALABAMA						
1 *Bonner*	N	N	N	N	N	N
2 *Everett*	N	N	?	N	N	Y
3 *Rogers*	N	N	N	N	N	N
4 *Aderholt*	N	N	N	N	N	N
5 Cramer	Y	Y	Y	Y	N	N
6 *Bachus*	N	N	N	N	?	?
7 Davis	Y	Y	Y	Y	Y	N
ALASKA						
AL *Young*	N	N	N	N	N	N
ARIZONA						
1 *Renzi*	N	N	N	N	N	N
2 *Franks*	?	N	N	N	N	Y
3 *Shadegg*	N	N	N	N	N	Y
4 Pastor	+	Y	Y	Y	N	N
5 *Hayworth*	N	N	N	N	N	Y
6 *Flake*	N	N	N	N	N	Y
7 Grijalva	Y	Y	Y	Y	Y	N
8 *Kolbe*	N	N	N	N	N	N
ARKANSAS						
1 Berry	Y	Y	Y	Y	N	N
2 Snyder	Y	Y	Y	Y	Y	N
3 *Boozman*	N	N	N	N	N	N
4 Ross	Y	Y	Y	Y	N	N
CALIFORNIA						
1 Thompson	Y	Y	Y	Y	N	N
2 *Herger*	N	N	N	N	N	Y
3 *Ose*	N	N	N	N	N	N
4 *Doolittle*	N	N	N	N	N	N
5 Matsui	Y	Y	Y	Y	N	N
6 Woolsey	Y	Y	Y	Y	N	N
7 Miller, George	Y	Y	Y	?	?	?
8 Pelosi	?	?	?	?	Y	N
9 Lee	?	?	?	?	?	?
10 Tauscher	Y	Y	Y	Y	Y	N
11 *Pombo*	N	N	N	N	N	N
12 Lantos	Y	Y	Y	Y	N	N
13 Stark	Y	Y	Y	Y	?	?
14 Eshoo	Y	Y	Y	Y	N	N
15 Honda	Y	Y	Y	Y	Y	N
16 Lofgren	?	?	?	?	Y	N
17 Farr	Y	Y	Y	Y	N	N
18 Cardoza	Y	Y	?	Y	N	N
19 *Radanovich*	N	N	N	N	N	N
20 Dooley	Y	Y	Y	Y	?	?
21 *Nunes*	N	N	N	N	N	N
22 *Thomas*	N	N	N	N	N	N
23 Capps	Y	Y	Y	Y	N	N
24 *Gallegly*	N	N	?	N	N	N
25 *McKeon*	N	N	N	N	N	N
26 *Dreier*	N	N	N	N	N	N
27 Sherman	Y	Y	Y	Y	Y	N
28 Berman	Y	?	Y	Y	N	N
29 Schiff	Y	Y	Y	Y	N	N
30 Waxman	?	?	?	?	?	?
31 Becerra	?	?	?	Y	Y	N
32 Solis	Y	Y	Y	Y	N	N
33 Watson	Y	Y	Y	Y	N	N
34 Roybal-Allard	Y	Y	Y	Y	Y	N
35 Waters	Y	Y	Y	Y	N	N
36 Harman	Y	Y	Y	Y	N	N

	355	356	357	358	359	360
37 Millender-McD.	Y	Y	Y	N	N	N
38 Napolitano	Y	Y	Y	Y	Y	N
39 Sánchez, Linda	Y	Y	Y	Y	N	N
40 *Royce*	N	N	N	N	N	Y
41 *Lewis*	N	N	N	N	N	N
42 *Miller, Gary*	N	N	N	N	N	N
43 Baca	?	?	?	Y	N	N
44 *Calvert*	?	?	?	N	N	N
45 *Bono*	N	N	N	N	N	N
46 *Rohrabacher*	N	N	N	N	N	Y
47 Sanchez, Loretta	Y	Y	Y	Y	Y	N
48 *Cox*	N	N	N	N	N	N
49 *Issa*	N	N	N	N	N	N
50 *Cunningham*	N	N	N	N	N	N
51 Filner	Y	Y	Y	Y	Y	N
52 *Hunter*	?	?	?	N	N	N
53 Davis	Y	Y	Y	Y	Y	N
COLORADO						
1 DeGette	Y	Y	Y	Y	Y	N
2 Udall	Y	Y	Y	Y	N	N
3 *McInnis*	N	N	N	N	N	N
4 *Musgrave*	N	N	N	N	N	Y
5 *Hefley*	N	N	N	N	N	Y
6 *Tancredo*	–	–	–	–	N	Y
7 *Beauprez*	N	N	N	N	N	N
CONNECTICUT						
1 Larson	Y	Y	Y	Y	N	N
2 *Simmons*	N	N	Y	N	N	N
3 DeLauro	Y	Y	Y	Y	+	–
4 *Shays*	N	N	Y	N	?	?
5 *Johnson*	?	?	?	?	Y	N
DELAWARE						
AL *Castle*	N	N	N	N	N	N
FLORIDA						
1 *Miller, J.*	N	N	N	N	N	Y
2 Boyd	?	?	?	Y	N	N
3 Brown	Y	Y	Y	Y	?	?
4 *Crenshaw*	N	N	N	N	N	N
5 *Brown-Waite*	N	N	N	N	Y	N
6 *Stearns*	N	N	N	N	Y	Y
7 *Mica*	?	?	?	?	N	Y
8 *Keller*	N	N	N	N	?	?
9 *Bilirakis*	N	N	N	N	N	N
10 *Young*	N	N	N	N	N	N
11 Davis	Y	Y	Y	Y	Y	N
12 *Putnam*	N	N	N	N	N	N
13 *Harris*	N	N	N	N	N	N
14 *Goss*	?	?	?	?	?	?
15 *Weldon*	N	N	N	N	N	N
16 *Foley*	N	N	N	N	N	N
17 Meek	Y	Y	Y	Y	N	N
18 *Ros-Lehtinen*	N	N	N	N	N	N
19 Wexler	?	?	?	?	?	?
20 Deutsch	?	?	?	?	?	?
21 *Diaz-Balart, L.*	N	N	N	N	N	N
22 *Shaw*	?	?	?	?	N	N
23 Hastings	?	?	?	Y	Y	N
24 *Feeney*	N	N	N	N	?	?
25 *Diaz-Balart, M.*	N	N	N	N	N	Y
GEORGIA						
1 *Kingston*	N	N	N	N	N	N
2 Bishop	Y	Y	Y	Y	N	N
3 Marshall	Y	N	Y	Y	Y	Y
4 *Majette*	?	?	?	?	?	?
5 Lewis	Y	Y	Y	Y	N	N
6 *Isakson*	?	?	?	?	?	?
7 *Linder*	?	?	?	N	N	N
8 *Collins*	?	?	?	–	–	+
9 *Norwood*	?	?	?	?	N	Y
10 *Deal*	?	?	?	N	N	Y
11 *Gingrey*	N	N	N	N	N	N
12 *Burns*	N	N	N	N	N	N
13 Scott	Y	Y	Y	Y	N	N
HAWAII						
1 Abercrombie	Y	Y	Y	Y	N	N
2 Case	?	?	?	?	Y	N
IDAHO						
1 *Otter*	N	N	N	N	N	Y
2 *Simpson*	N	N	N	N	N	N
ILLINOIS						
1 Rush	Y	Y	Y	Y	Y	N
2 Jackson	Y	Y	Y	Y	Y	N
3 Lipinski	?	?	?	?	?	?
4 Gutierrez	Y	Y	?	Y	?	?
5 Emanuel	+	+	+	+	Y	N
6 *Hyde*	N	N	N	N	N	N

ND Northern Democrats   SD Southern Democrats

	355	356	357	358	359	360
7 Davis	Y	Y	Y	Y	Y	N
8 ***Crane***	N	N	N	N	N	Y
9 Schakowsky	Y	Y	Y	Y	Y	N
10 ***Kirk***	N	N	N	N	N	N
11 ***Weller***	N	N	N	N	N	N
12 Costello	Y	Y	Y	Y	N	N
13 ***Biggert***	N	N	N	N	N	N
14 ***Hastert***						
15 ***Johnson***	N	N	N	N	N	N
16 ***Manzullo***	N	N	N	N	N	N
17 Evans	Y	Y	Y	Y	Y	N
18 ***LaHood***	?	?	?	?	N	N
19 ***Shimkus***	N	N	N	Y	N	Y
INDIANA						
1 Visclosky	Y	Y	Y	Y	N	N
2 ***Chocola***	N	N	N	N	N	Y
3 ***Souder***	N	N	N	N	N	Y
4 ***Buyer***	N	N	N	N	N	Y
5 ***Burton***	N	N	N	N	–	+
6 ***Pence***	N	N	N	N	N	Y
7 Carson	?	?	?	?	?	?
8 ***Hostettler***	N	N	N	N	?	?
9 Hill	Y	Y	Y	Y	Y	N
IOWA						
1 ***Nussle***	N	N	N	N	N	N
2 ***Leach***	?	?	?	N	Y	N
3 Boswell	Y	Y	Y	Y	Y	N
4 ***Latham***	N	N	N	N	N	N
5 ***King***	N	N	–	N	N	Y
KANSAS						
1 ***Moran***	N	N	N	N	N	Y
2 ***Ryun***	N	N	N	N	N	Y
3 Moore	Y	Y	Y	Y	?	?
4 ***Tiahrt***	N	N	N	N	–	–
KENTUCKY						
1 ***Whitfield***	N	N	N	N	?	?
2 ***Lewis***	N	N	N	N	N	Y
3 ***Northup***	N	N	N	N	N	N
4 Lucas	Y	Y	Y	Y	N	N
5 ***Rogers***	N	N	N	N	N	N
6 Chandler	Y	Y	Y	Y	Y	N
LOUISIANA						
1 ***Vitter***	N	N	N	N	?	?
2 Jefferson	?	Y	Y	Y	Y	N
3 ***Tauzin***	?	?	?	?	N	N
4 ***McCrery***	N	N	N	N	N	N
5 Alexander	Y	Y	Y	Y	N	N
6 ***Baker***	N	N	N	N	?	?
7 John	?	?	?	?	N	N
MAINE						
1 Allen	Y	Y	Y	Y	Y	N
2 Michaud	Y	Y	Y	Y	Y	N
MARYLAND						
1 ***Gilchrest***	N	N	N	N	N	N
2 Ruppersberger	Y	Y	Y	Y	Y	N
3 Cardin	Y	Y	Y	Y	Y	N
4 Wynn	Y	Y	Y	?	N	N
5 Hoyer	Y	Y	Y	Y	N	N
6 ***Bartlett***	N	N	N	N	N	Y
7 Cummings	Y	Y	Y	Y	N	N
8 Van Hollen	Y	Y	Y	Y	N	N
MASSACHUSETTS						
1 Olver	Y	Y	Y	Y	Y	N
2 Neal	Y	Y	Y	Y	Y	N
3 McGovern	+	+	+	+	Y	N
4 Frank	Y	Y	Y	Y	?	?
5 Meehan	Y	Y	Y	Y	?	?
6 Tierney	Y	Y	Y	Y	?	?
7 Markey	Y	Y	Y	Y	?	?
8 Capuano	Y	Y	Y	Y	?	?
9 Lynch	Y	Y	Y	Y	Y	N
10 Delahunt	?	?	?	?	?	?
MICHIGAN						
1 Stupak	Y	Y	Y	Y	Y	N
2 ***Hoekstra***	N	N	N	N	N	N
3 ***Ehlers***	N	N	N	N	N	N
4 ***Camp***	?	?	?	?	N	N
5 Kildee	Y	Y	Y	Y	N	N
6 ***Upton***	N	N	N	N	N	N
7 ***Smith***	N	N	N	N	N	Y
8 ***Rogers***	N	N	?	N	N	N
9 ***Knollenberg***	N	N	N	N	N	N
10 ***Miller***	N	N	N	N	N	N
11 ***McCotter***	N	N	N	N	N	Y
12 Levin	Y	Y	Y	Y	N	N

	355	356	357	358	359	360
13 Kilpatrick	+	+	+	+	N	N
14 Conyers	Y	Y	Y	Y	?	?
15 Dingell	Y	Y	Y	Y	Y	N
MINNESOTA						
1 ***Gutknecht***	?	?	?	?	?	?
2 ***Kline***	N	N	N	N	N	N
3 ***Ramstad***	N	N	N	N	N	Y
4 McCollum	Y	Y	Y	Y	Y	N
5 Sabo	Y	Y	Y	Y	?	?
6 ***Kennedy***	N	N	N	N	N	Y
7 Peterson	Y	N	N	Y	N	N
8 Oberstar	Y	Y	Y	Y	N	N
MISSISSIPPI						
1 ***Wicker***	N	N	N	N	N	N
2 Thompson	Y	Y	Y	Y	Y	N
3 ***Pickering***	N	N	N	N	N	N
4 Taylor	Y	Y	Y	Y	N	Y
MISSOURI						
1 Clay	Y	Y	Y	Y	Y	N
2 ***Akin***	N	N	N	N	N	Y
3 Gephardt	?	?	?	?	?	?
4 Skelton	Y	?	Y	Y	?	N
5 McCarthy	Y	Y	Y	Y	Y	N
6 ***Graves***	N	N	N	N	N	Y
7 ***Blunt***	N	N	N	N	N	N
8 ***Emerson***	N	N	N	Y	N	N
9 ***Hulshof***	N	N	N	N	N	Y
MONTANA						
AL ***Rehberg***	N	N	N	N	N	N
NEBRASKA						
1 ***Bereuter***	N	N	N	N	Y	N
2 ***Terry***	N	N	N	N	N	N
3 ***Osborne***	N	N	N	N	N	N
NEVADA						
1 Berkley	?	?	?	?	Y	N
2 ***Gibbons***	N	N	N	N	N	Y
3 ***Porter***	Y	Y	N	N	N	N
NEW HAMPSHIRE						
1 ***Bradley***	N	N	N	N	N	Y
2 ***Bass***	N	N	N	N	–	+
NEW JERSEY						
1 Andrews	Y	Y	Y	Y	?	?
2 ***LoBiondo***	N	N	N	N	N	Y
3 ***Saxton***	N	N	N	N	N	N
4 ***Smith***	N	N	N	N	N	N
5 ***Garrett***	N	N	N	N	?	?
6 Pallone	Y	Y	Y	Y	Y	N
7 ***Ferguson***	N	N	N	N	N	N
8 Pascrell	Y	Y	Y	Y	?	?
9 Rothman	Y	Y	?	Y	Y	N
10 Payne	?	?	?	?	Y	N
11 ***Frelinghuysen***	N	N	N	N	N	N
12 Holt	Y	Y	Y	Y	Y	N
13 Menendez	Y	Y	Y	Y	?	?
NEW MEXICO						
1 ***Wilson***	N	N	N	N	N	N
2 ***Pearce***	N	N	N	N	N	N
3 Udall	Y	Y	Y	Y	Y	N
NEW YORK						
1 Bishop	?	?	?	?	Y	N
2 Israel	Y	Y	Y	Y	Y	N
3 ***King***	N	N	N	N	N	?
4 McCarthy	Y	Y	Y	Y	Y	N
5 Ackerman	?	?	?	?	Y	N
6 Meeks	?	?	?	?	N	N
7 Crowley	Y	Y	Y	Y	Y	N
8 Nadler	Y	Y	Y	Y	Y	N
9 Weiner	Y	Y	Y	Y	Y	N
10 Towns	Y	Y	Y	Y	N	N
11 Owens	Y	Y	Y	Y	+	–
12 Velázquez	Y	Y	Y	Y	Y	N
13 ***Fossella***	N	N	N	N	?	?
14 Maloney	Y	Y	Y	Y	?	?
15 Rangel	Y	Y	Y	Y	Y	N
16 Serrano	Y	Y	Y	Y	N	N
17 Engel	Y	Y	Y	Y	?	?
18 Lowey	Y	Y	Y	Y	N	N
19 ***Kelly***	N	N	N	N	Y	N
20 ***Sweeney***	N	N	N	N	N	N
21 McNulty	?	?	?	?	Y	N
22 Hinchey	?	?	?	?	?	?
23 ***McHugh***	N	N	N	N	N	N
24 ***Boehlert***	N	N	N	N	N	N
25 ***Walsh***	N	N	N	N	N	N

	355	356	357	358	359	360
26 ***Reynolds***	N	N	N	N	N	N
27 ***Quinn***	?	?	?	?	?	?
28 Slaughter	Y	Y	Y	Y	Y	N
29 ***Houghton***	?	?	?	?	?	?
NORTH CAROLINA						
1 Vacant						
2 Etheridge	Y	Y	Y	Y	Y	N
3 ***Jones***	N	N	N	N	N	Y
4 Price	Y	Y	Y	Y	Y	N
5 ***Burr***	Y	N	N	N	?	?
6 ***Coble***	?	?	?	?	N	Y
7 McIntyre	Y	Y	Y	Y	Y	N
8 ***Hayes***	N	N	N	N	N	Y
9 ***Myrick***	N	N	N	N	N	Y
10 ***Ballenger***	N	N	N	N	N	N
11 ***Taylor***	N	N	N	N	N	N
12 Watt	Y	Y	Y	Y	Y	N
13 Miller	Y	Y	Y	Y	Y	N
NORTH DAKOTA						
AL Pomeroy	Y	Y	Y	Y	N	N
OHIO						
1 ***Chabot***	N	N	N	N	N	Y
2 ***Portman***	N	N	N	N	N	N
3 ***Turner***	N	N	N	N	N	N
4 ***Oxley***	N	N	N	N	N	–
5 ***Gillmor***	?	?	?	?	N	N
6 Strickland	Y	Y	Y	Y	Y	N
7 ***Hobson***	N	N	N	N	N	N
8 ***Boehner***	N	N	N	N	N	N
9 Kaptur	Y	Y	Y	Y	Y	N
10 Kucinich	Y	Y	Y	Y	Y	N
11 Jones	?	?	?	?	Y	N
12 ***Tiberi***	N	N	N	N	N	N
13 Brown	Y	Y	Y	Y	Y	N
14 ***LaTourette***	?	?	?	?	N	N
15 ***Pryce***	N	N	N	N	N	N
16 ***Regula***	N	N	N	N	N	N
17 Ryan	Y	Y	Y	Y	Y	N
18 ***Ney***	N	N	Y	N	N	N
OKLAHOMA						
1 ***Sullivan***	N	N	N	N	N	N
2 Carson	Y	Y	Y	Y	?	?
3 ***Lucas***	N	N	N	N	N	N
4 ***Cole***	N	N	N	N	N	N
5 ***Istook***	N	N	N	N	N	N
OREGON						
1 Wu	Y	Y	Y	Y	Y	N
2 ***Walden***	N	N	N	N	N	N
3 Blumenauer	?	?	?	?	N	N
4 DeFazio	Y	Y	Y	Y	Y	Y
5 Hooley	Y	Y	Y	Y	Y	Y
PENNSYLVANIA						
1 Brady	Y	Y	Y	Y	N	N
2 Fattah	?	?	?	?	?	?
3 ***English***	N	N	N	N	N	N
4 ***Hart***	N	N	N	N	N	N
5 ***Peterson***	N	N	N	N	?	?
6 ***Gerlach***	?	?	?	?	N	N
7 ***Weldon***	N	N	N	N	N	N
8 ***Greenwood***	N	N	N	?	Y	N
9 ***Shuster, Bill***	N	N	N	N	?	?
10 ***Sherwood***	N	N	N	N	N	N
11 Kanjorski	Y	Y	Y	Y	Y	N
12 Murtha	Y	Y	Y	Y	N	N
13 Hoeffel	?	?	?	?	?	?
14 Doyle	Y	Y	Y	Y	Y	N
15 ***Toomey***	N	N	N	N	?	?
16 ***Pitts***	?	?	?	?	N	Y
17 Holden	Y	Y	Y	Y	N	N
18 ***Murphy***	N	N	N	N	N	N
19 ***Platts***	?	?	?	?	N	N
RHODE ISLAND						
1 Kennedy	Y	Y	Y	Y	N	N
2 Langevin	Y	Y	Y	Y	N	N
SOUTH CAROLINA						
1 ***Brown***	N	N	N	N	N	N
2 ***Wilson***	N	N	N	N	?	?
3 ***Barrett***	N	N	N	N	N	Y
4 ***DeMint***	?	?	?	?	?	?
5 Spratt	Y	Y	Y	Y	Y	N
6 Clyburn	Y	Y	Y	Y	Y	N
SOUTH DAKOTA						
AL Herseth	Y	Y	Y	Y	N	N

	355	356	357	358	359	360
TENNESSEE						
1 ***Jenkins***	N	N	N	N	N	Y
2 ***Duncan***	N	N	N	N	Y	Y
3 ***Wamp***	?	?	?	?	N	Y
4 Davis	Y	Y	Y	Y	N	Y
5 Cooper	Y	Y	Y	Y	Y	Y
6 Gordon	Y	Y	Y	Y	Y	N
7 ***Blackburn***	N	?	N	N	N	Y
8 Tanner	Y	Y	Y	Y	N	Y
9 Ford	Y	Y	Y	Y	N	N
TEXAS						
1 Sandlin	?	Y	Y	Y	Y	N
2 Turner	?	Y	Y	Y	N	N
3 ***Johnson, Sam***	N	N	N	N	N	N
4 ***Hall***	N	Y	N	N	N	Y
5 ***Hensarling***	N	N	N	N	N	Y
6 ***Barton***	N	N	N	N	N	Y
7 ***Culberson***	?	?	?	?	N	N
8 ***Brady***	N	N	N	N	N	Y
9 Lampson	Y	Y	Y	Y	Y	Y
10 Doggett	Y	Y	?	Y	Y	Y
11 Edwards	Y	Y	Y	Y	Y	Y
12 ***Granger***	N	N	N	N	N	N
13 ***Thornberry***	N	N	N	N	N	N
14 ***Paul***	?	?	?	?	N	Y
15 Hinojosa	Y	Y	Y	Y	?	?
16 Reyes	?	?	?	?	N	N
17 Stenholm	Y	N	Y	Y	N	Y
18 Jackson-Lee	Y	Y	Y	Y	Y	N
19 ***Neugebauer***	N	N	N	N	N	Y
20 Gonzalez	Y	Y	Y	Y	Y	N
21 ***Smith***	N	N	N	N	N	N
22 ***DeLay***	N	N	N	N	N	N
23 ***Bonilla***	N	N	N	N	N	N
24 Frost	Y	Y	Y	Y	N	N
25 Bell	?	?	?	?	?	?
26 ***Burgess***	N	N	N	N	N	Y
27 Ortiz	?	?	?	?	N	N
28 Rodriguez	Y	Y	Y	Y	Y	N
29 Green	?	?	?	?	Y	Y
30 Johnson, E.B.	Y	Y	Y	+	+	–
31 ***Carter***	N	N	N	N	N	N
32 ***Sessions***	N	N	N	N	N	Y
UTAH						
1 ***Bishop***	N	N	N	N	?	?
2 Matheson	Y	Y	Y	Y	Y	N
3 ***Cannon***	N	N	N	N	N	Y
VERMONT						
AL *Sanders*	Y	Y	Y	Y	?	?
VIRGINIA						
1 ***Davis, Jo Ann***	N	N	N	N	N	Y
2 ***Schrock***	N	N	N	N	N	Y
3 Scott	Y	Y	Y	Y	?	?
4 ***Forbes***	N	N	N	N	N	Y
5 ***Goode***	Y	N	N	N	N	Y
6 ***Goodlatte***	N	N	N	N	N	Y
7 ***Cantor***	N	N	N	N	N	N
8 Moran	Y	Y	Y	Y	N	N
9 Boucher	Y	Y	Y	Y	Y	N
10 ***Wolf***	N	N	N	N	N	N
11 ***Davis, T.***	?	?	?	?	N	?
WASHINGTON						
1 Inslee	Y	Y	Y	Y	Y	N
2 Larsen	Y	Y	Y	Y	Y	N
3 Baird	Y	Y	Y	Y	N	N
4 ***Hastings***	N	N	N	N	N	N
5 ***Nethercutt***	N	N	N	N	N	N
6 Dicks	?	?	?	?	?	?
7 McDermott	Y	Y	Y	Y	Y	N
8 ***Dunn***	N	N	N	N	N	N
9 Smith	Y	Y	Y	Y	Y	Y
WEST VIRGINIA						
1 Mollohan	Y	Y	Y	Y	Y	N
2 ***Capito***	N	N	N	N	N	N
3 Rahall	?	?	?	?	N	N
WISCONSIN						
1 ***Ryan***	N	N	N	N	N	Y
2 Baldwin	Y	Y	Y	Y	Y	N
3 Kind	Y	Y	Y	Y	Y	N
4 Kleczka	Y	Y	Y	Y	Y	N
5 ***Sensenbrenner***	N	N	N	N	N	Y
6 ***Petri***	N	N	N	N	N	Y
7 Obey	Y	Y	Y	Y	Y	N
8 ***Green***	Y	N	N	N	N	Y
WYOMING						
AL ***Cubin***	N	N	N	N	N	Y

Southern states - Ala., Ark., Fla., Ga., Ky., La., Miss., N.C., Okla., S.C., Tenn., Texas, Va.

Key

Y	Voted for (yea).
#	Paired for.
+	Announced for.
N	Voted against (nay).
X	Paired against.
–	Announced against.
P	Voted "present."
C	Voted "present" to avoid possible conflict of interest.
?	Did not vote or otherwise make a position known.

Democrats **Republicans**
Independents

361. HR 4755. Fiscal 2005 Legislative Branch Appropriations/ Recommit. Sherman, D-Calif., motion to recommit the bill to the House Appropriations Committee with instructions to insert language that would prohibit committee mailing expenses from exceeding an aggregate amount of $25,000. Motion rejected 163-205: R 3-197; D 160-8 (ND 114-7, SD 46-1); I 0-0. July 12, 2004.

362. HR 4755. Fiscal 2005 Legislative Branch Appropriations/Passage. Passage of the bill that would appropriate $2.75 billion in fiscal 2005 for legislative branch operations, excluding funds for Senate operations. Passed 327-43: R 173-27; D 154-16 (ND 110-12, SD 44-4); I 0-0. July 12, 2004.

363. HR 4766. Fiscal 2005 Agriculture Appropriations/Sudden Oak Death. Hooley, D-Ore., amendment that would increase funding by $5 million for the prevention of sudden oak death, a disease that is killing oaks and other plant species mainly in the western United States. It would be offset by cuts in the Agriculture Buildings and Facilities and Rental Payments account. Adopted 260-160: R 63-158; D 196-2 (ND 144-1, SD 52-1); I 1-0. July 13, 2004.

364. HR 4766. Fiscal 2005 Agriculture Appropriations/Animal and Plant Health Inspection Service. Weiner, D-N.Y., amendment that would increase funding by $18 million for the Animal and Plant Health Inspection Service, to be offset by cuts in Agriculture Department building and facility accounts. Adopted 223-197: R 26-195; D 196-2 (ND 145-0, SD 51-2); I 1-0. July 13, 2004.

365. HR 4613. Fiscal 2005 Defense Appropriations/Motion to Close Conference. Lewis, R-Calif., motion to close portions of the conference on the bill that would appropriate funding for defense programs for fiscal 2005. Motion agreed to 411-6: R 221-0; D 189-6 (ND 138-6, SD 51-0); I 1-0. July 13, 2004.

366. HR 4766. Fiscal 2005 Agriculture Appropriations/Civil Rights and Education Funding Increases. Baca, D-Calif., amendment that would increase funding by $250,000 for the Office of the Secretary for Civil Rights and $1.5 million for research and education activities, to be offset by cuts in rural development. Rejected 205-209: R 11-207; D 193-2 (ND 142-0, SD 51-2); I 1-0. July 13, 2004.

	361	362	363	364	365	366
ALABAMA						
1 *Bonner*	N	Y	N	N	Y	N
2 *Everett*	N	Y	N	N	Y	N
3 *Rogers*	N	Y	N	N	Y	Y
4 *Aderholt*	N	Y	N	N	Y	N
5 Cramer	Y	Y	Y	Y	Y	Y
6 *Bachus*	?	?	N	N	Y	N
7 Davis	Y	Y	Y	Y	Y	Y
ALASKA						
AL *Young*	N	Y	N	N	Y	N
ARIZONA						
1 *Renzi*	N	Y	N	N	Y	N
2 *Franks*	N	N	N	N	Y	N
3 *Shadegg*	N	Y	N	N	Y	N
4 Pastor	Y	Y	Y	Y	Y	Y
5 *Hayworth*	N	N	N	N	Y	N
6 *Flake*	N	N	N	N	Y	N
7 Grijalva	Y	Y	Y	Y	Y	Y
8 *Kolbe*	N	Y	N	N	Y	N
ARKANSAS						
1 Berry	Y	N	Y	Y	Y	Y
2 Snyder	Y	Y	Y	Y	Y	Y
3 *Boozman*	N	Y	N	N	Y	N
4 Ross	Y	Y	Y	Y	Y	Y
CALIFORNIA						
1 Thompson	Y	Y	Y	Y	Y	Y
2 *Herger*	N	Y	N	N	Y	N
3 *Ose*	N	Y	Y	Y	Y	Y
4 *Doolittle*	N	N	N	N	Y	N
5 Matsui	Y	Y	Y	Y	Y	Y
6 Woolsey	Y	Y	Y	Y	Y	?
7 Miller, George	?	?	Y	Y	Y	Y
8 Pelosi	Y	Y	Y	Y	Y	Y
9 Lee	?	?	?	?	?	?
10 Tauscher	Y	Y	Y	Y	Y	Y
11 *Pombo*	N	Y	Y	N	Y	N
12 Lantos	Y	Y	Y	Y	Y	Y
13 Stark	?	?	Y	Y	N	?
14 Eshoo	Y	Y	Y	Y	Y	Y
15 Honda	Y	Y	Y	Y	Y	Y
16 Lofgren	Y	N	Y	Y	Y	Y
17 Farr	Y	Y	Y	Y	Y	Y
18 Cardoza	N	Y	Y	Y	?	Y
19 *Radanovich*	N	Y	N	Y	N	N
20 Dooley	?	?	?	Y	Y	Y
21 *Nunes*	N	N	N	N	Y	N
22 *Thomas*	N	Y	N	Y	N	N
23 Capps	Y	Y	Y	Y	Y	Y
24 *Gallegly*	N	Y	Y	N	Y	N
25 *McKeon*	N	Y	N	Y	N	N
26 *Dreier*	N	Y	N	N	Y	N
27 Sherman	Y	N	Y	Y	N	Y
28 Berman	Y	Y	Y	Y	Y	Y
29 Schiff	Y	Y	Y	Y	Y	Y
30 Waxman	?	?	Y	Y	Y	Y
31 Becerra	Y	Y	Y	Y	Y	Y
32 Solis	Y	Y	Y	Y	Y	Y
33 Watson	Y	Y	Y	Y	Y	Y
34 Roybal-Allard	Y	Y	Y	Y	Y	Y
35 Waters	Y	Y	Y	Y	Y	Y
36 Harman	?	Y	Y	Y	Y	Y

	361	362	363	364	365	366
37 Millender-McD.	Y	Y	Y	Y	Y	Y
38 Napolitano	Y	Y	Y	Y	Y	Y
39 Sánchez, Linda	Y	Y	Y	Y	Y	Y
40 *Royce*	N	N	Y	N	Y	N
41 *Lewis*	N	?	N	N	Y	N
42 *Miller, Gary*	N	Y	N	Y	N	N
43 Baca	N	Y	Y	Y	Y	Y
44 *Calvert*	N	Y	N	N	Y	N
45 *Bono*	N	Y	N	Y	N	N
46 *Rohrabacher*	N	N	N	N	Y	N
47 Sanchez, Loretta	Y	Y	Y	Y	Y	Y
48 *Cox*	N	N	N	N	Y	N
49 *Issa*	N	Y	N	Y	N	N
50 *Cunningham*	N	Y	N	N	Y	N
51 Filner	Y	Y	Y	Y	Y	Y
52 *Hunter*	N	N	N	N	Y	N
53 Davis	Y	Y	Y	Y	Y	Y
COLORADO						
1 DeGette	Y	Y	Y	Y	Y	Y
2 Udall	Y	Y	Y	Y	Y	Y
3 *McInnis*	N	N	N	N	Y	N
4 *Musgrave*	N	Y	N	N	Y	N
5 *Hefley*	N	N	N	N	Y	N
6 *Tancredo*	N	Y	N	N	Y	N
7 *Beauprez*	N	Y	N	N	Y	N
CONNECTICUT						
1 Larson	Y	Y	Y	Y	Y	Y
2 *Simmons*	N	Y	Y	Y	Y	Y
3 DeLauro	+	+	Y	Y	Y	Y
4 *Shays*	?	?	Y	Y	Y	Y
5 *Johnson*	N	Y	Y	N	Y	N
DELAWARE						
AL *Castle*	N	Y	N	N	Y	N
FLORIDA						
1 *Miller, J.*	N	N	N	N	Y	N
2 Boyd	Y	Y	Y	Y	Y	Y
3 Brown	?	?	Y	Y	Y	Y
4 *Crenshaw*	N	Y	N	N	Y	N
5 *Brown-Waite*	N	Y	N	N	Y	N
6 *Stearns*	N	N	Y	N	Y	N
7 *Mica*	N	Y	N	N	Y	N
8 *Keller*	N	Y	N	N	Y	N
9 *Bilirakis*	N	Y	N	N	Y	N
10 *Young*	?	N	N	N	Y	N
11 Davis	Y	Y	Y	Y	?	Y
12 *Putnam*	N	Y	N	N	Y	N
13 *Harris*	N	Y	N	N	Y	N
14 *Goss*	?	?	N	N	Y	N
15 *Weldon*	N	Y	N	N	Y	N
16 *Foley*	N	Y	N	N	Y	N
17 Meek	Y	Y	Y	Y	Y	Y
18 *Ros-Lehtinen*	N	N	N	N	Y	N
19 Wexler	?	?	Y	Y	Y	Y
20 Deutsch	?	?	?	?	?	?
21 *Diaz-Balart, L.*	N	Y	N	N	Y	N
22 *Shaw*	N	Y	N	N	Y	N
23 Hastings	Y	Y	Y	Y	Y	Y
24 *Feeney*	N	Y	N	N	Y	N
25 *Diaz-Balart, M.*	N	Y	N	N	Y	N
GEORGIA						
1 *Kingston*	N	Y	N	N	Y	N
2 Bishop	Y	Y	Y	Y	Y	Y
3 Marshall	Y	Y	Y	Y	Y	Y
4 Majette	?	?	?	?	?	?
5 Lewis	Y	Y	Y	Y	Y	Y
6 *Isakson*	?	?	?	?	?	?
7 *Linder*	N	Y	N	N	Y	N
8 *Collins*	–	+	+	–	+	–
9 *Norwood*	N	Y	N	N	Y	N
10 *Deal*	N	Y	N	N	Y	N
11 *Gingrey*	N	Y	N	N	Y	N
12 *Burns*	N	Y	N	Y	N	Y
13 Scott	Y	Y	Y	Y	Y	Y
HAWAII						
1 Abercrombie	N	Y	Y	Y	Y	Y
2 Case	N	Y	Y	Y	Y	Y
IDAHO						
1 *Otter*	N	N	Y	N	Y	N
2 *Simpson*	N	Y	N	N	Y	N
ILLINOIS						
1 Rush	Y	Y	N	Y	Y	Y
2 Jackson	Y	Y	Y	Y	Y	Y
3 Lipinski	Y	Y	Y	Y	Y	Y
4 Gutierrez	?	?	Y	Y	Y	Y
5 Emanuel	Y	Y	Y	Y	Y	Y
6 *Hyde*	N	Y	N	Y	Y	N

ND Northern Democrats   SD Southern Democrats

	361	362	363	364	365	366
7 Davis	Y	Y	Y	Y	Y	Y
8 ***Crane***	N	Y	N	N	Y	N
9 Schakowsky	Y	Y	Y	Y	Y	Y
10 ***Kirk***	N	Y	N	N	Y	N
11 ***Weller***	N	Y	N	Y	Y	Y
12 Costello	Y	N	Y	Y	Y	Y
13 ***Biggert***	N	Y	N	Y	Y	N
14 ***Hastert***						
15 ***Johnson***	N	Y	N	N	Y	N
16 ***Manzullo***	N	Y	Y	N	Y	N
17 Evans	Y	Y	Y	Y	Y	Y
18 ***LaHood***	N	Y	Y	N	Y	N
19 ***Shimkus***	N	Y	Y	N	Y	N
INDIANA						
1 Visclosky	Y	Y	Y	Y	Y	Y
2 ***Chocola***	N	Y	N	N	Y	N
3 ***Souder***	N	N	Y	Y	Y	N
4 ***Buyer***	N	Y	N	N	Y	N
5 ***Burton***	–	+	N	N	Y	N
6 ***Pence***	N	Y	N	N	Y	N
7 Carson	?	?	?	?	?	?
8 ***Hostettler***	?	?	N	N	Y	N
9 Hill	Y	Y	Y	Y	Y	Y
IOWA						
1 ***Nussle***	N	Y	N	N	Y	N
2 ***Leach***	N	Y	Y	N	Y	Y
3 Boswell	Y	Y	Y	Y	Y	Y
4 ***Latham***	N	Y	N	N	Y	N
5 ***King***	N	Y	N	N	Y	N
KANSAS						
1 ***Moran***	N	Y	N	N	Y	N
2 ***Ryun***	N	Y	N	N	Y	N
3 Moore	Y	N	Y	Y	Y	Y
4 ***Tiahrt***	–	+	N	N	Y	N
KENTUCKY						
1 ***Whitfield***	?	?	Y	N	Y	N
2 ***Lewis***	N	Y	N	N	Y	N
3 ***Northup***	N	Y	N	N	Y	N
4 Lucas	Y	Y	Y	Y	Y	Y
5 ***Rogers***	N	Y	N	N	Y	N
6 Chandler	Y	Y	Y	Y	Y	Y
LOUISIANA						
1 ***Vitter***	?	?	?	?	?	?
2 Jefferson	Y	Y	Y	Y	?	Y
3 ***Tauzin***	N	Y	N	N	Y	N
4 ***McCrery***	N	Y	N	N	Y	N
5 Alexander	Y	Y	Y	Y	Y	Y
6 ***Baker***	?	?	N	N	Y	N
7 John	Y	Y	Y	Y	Y	Y
MAINE						
1 Allen	Y	Y	Y	Y	Y	Y
2 Michaud	Y	Y	Y	Y	Y	Y
MARYLAND						
1 ***Gilchrest***	N	Y	N	N	Y	N
2 Ruppersberger	Y	Y	Y	Y	Y	Y
3 Cardin	Y	Y	Y	Y	Y	Y
4 Wynn	Y	Y	Y	Y	Y	Y
5 Hoyer	Y	Y	Y	Y	Y	Y
6 ***Bartlett***	N	N	Y	N	Y	N
7 Cummings	Y	Y	Y	Y	Y	Y
8 Van Hollen	Y	Y	Y	Y	Y	Y
MASSACHUSETTS						
1 Olver	Y	Y	Y	Y	Y	Y
2 Neal	Y	Y	Y	Y	Y	Y
3 McGovern	Y	Y	Y	Y	Y	Y
4 Frank	?	?	Y	Y	Y	Y
5 Meehan	?	?	Y	Y	Y	Y
6 Tierney	?	?	Y	Y	Y	Y
7 Markey	?	?	Y	Y	Y	Y
8 Capuano	?	?	Y	Y	Y	Y
9 Lynch	Y	Y	Y	Y	Y	Y
10 Delahunt	?	?	Y	Y	Y	Y
MICHIGAN						
1 Stupak	Y	N	Y	Y	Y	Y
2 ***Hoekstra***	N	Y	N	N	Y	N
3 ***Ehlers***	N	Y	Y	Y	Y	Y
4 ***Camp***	N	Y	N	N	Y	N
5 Kildee	Y	N	Y	Y	Y	Y
6 ***Upton***	N	Y	Y	Y	Y	N
7 ***Smith***	N	N	N	N	Y	N
8 ***Rogers***	N	Y	Y	N	Y	N
9 ***Knollenberg***	N	Y	N	N	Y	N
10 ***Miller***	N	Y	N	N	Y	N
11 ***McCotter***	N	Y	N	Y	Y	N
12 Levin	Y	Y	Y	Y	Y	Y
13 Kilpatrick	Y	Y	Y	Y	Y	Y
14 Conyers	?	?	Y	Y	Y	Y
15 Dingell	N	Y	Y	Y	Y	Y
MINNESOTA						
1 ***Gutknecht***	?	?	?	?	?	?
2 ***Kline***	N	Y	N	N	Y	N
3 ***Ramstad***	N	Y	Y	N	Y	N
4 McCollum	Y	N	Y	Y	Y	Y
5 Sabo	?	?	Y	Y	Y	Y
6 ***Kennedy***	N	N	N	N	Y	N
7 Peterson	Y	Y	Y	Y	Y	Y
8 Oberstar	Y	Y	Y	Y	Y	Y
MISSISSIPPI						
1 ***Wicker***	N	Y	N	N	Y	N
2 Thompson	Y	Y	Y	Y	Y	Y
3 ***Pickering***	N	Y	N	N	Y	N
4 Taylor	Y	N	Y	Y	Y	N
MISSOURI						
1 Clay	Y	Y	Y	Y	Y	Y
2 ***Akin***	N	Y	N	N	Y	N
3 Gephardt	?	?	?	?	?	Y
4 Skelton	Y	Y	Y	Y	Y	Y
5 McCarthy	Y	Y	Y	Y	Y	Y
6 ***Graves***	N	N	N	N	Y	N
7 ***Blunt***	N	Y	N	N	Y	N
8 ***Emerson***	N	Y	N	N	Y	N
9 ***Hulshof***	N	N	N	N	Y	N
MONTANA						
AL ***Rehberg***	N	Y	N	N	Y	N
NEBRASKA						
1 ***Bereuter***	N	Y	Y	Y	Y	?
2 ***Terry***	N	Y	N	N	Y	N
3 ***Osborne***	N	Y	N	N	Y	N
NEVADA						
1 Berkley	Y	Y	Y	Y	Y	Y
2 ***Gibbons***	N	Y	N	N	Y	N
3 ***Porter***	N	Y	N	N	Y	Y
NEW HAMPSHIRE						
1 ***Bradley***	N	Y	Y	N	Y	Y
2 ***Bass***	N	Y	Y	N	Y	Y
NEW JERSEY						
1 Andrews	?	?	Y	Y	Y	Y
2 ***LoBiondo***	N	N	Y	Y	Y	N
3 ***Saxton***	N	Y	?	?	?	?
4 ***Smith***	N	Y	Y	Y	Y	N
5 ***Garrett***	?	?	N	N	Y	N
6 Pallone	Y	Y	Y	Y	Y	Y
7 ***Ferguson***	N	Y	N	Y	Y	N
8 Pascrell	?	?	Y	Y	Y	Y
9 Rothman	Y	Y	Y	Y	Y	Y
10 Payne	Y	Y	Y	Y	Y	Y
11 ***Frelinghuysen***	N	Y	N	N	Y	N
12 Holt	Y	Y	Y	Y	Y	Y
13 Menendez	?	?	Y	Y	Y	Y
NEW MEXICO						
1 ***Wilson***	N	Y	N	N	Y	Y
2 ***Pearce***	N	Y	N	N	Y	N
3 Udall	Y	Y	Y	Y	N	Y
NEW YORK						
1 Bishop	Y	Y	Y	Y	Y	Y
2 Israel	Y	Y	Y	Y	Y	Y
3 ***King***	?	?	Y	Y	Y	N
4 McCarthy	Y	Y	Y	Y	Y	Y
5 Ackerman	Y	Y	Y	Y	Y	Y
6 Meeks	Y	Y	Y	Y	Y	Y
7 Crowley	Y	Y	Y	Y	Y	Y
8 Nadler	Y	Y	Y	Y	Y	Y
9 Weiner	Y	Y	Y	Y	Y	Y
10 Towns	Y	Y	Y	Y	Y	Y
11 Owens	+	?	Y	Y	Y	Y
12 Velázquez	Y	Y	Y	Y	Y	Y
13 ***Fossella***	?	?	Y	Y	Y	N
14 Maloney	?	?	Y	Y	Y	Y
15 Rangel	Y	Y	Y	Y	Y	Y
16 Serrano	Y	Y	Y	Y	Y	Y
17 Engel	?	?	Y	Y	Y	Y
18 Lowey	Y	Y	Y	Y	Y	Y
19 ***Kelly***	N	Y	Y	Y	Y	N
20 ***Sweeney***	N	Y	Y	Y	Y	N
21 McNulty	Y	Y	Y	Y	Y	Y
22 Hinchey	?	?	Y	Y	N	Y
23 ***McHugh***	N	Y	Y	Y	Y	N
24 ***Boehlert***	N	Y	Y	Y	Y	N
25 ***Walsh***	N	Y	N	N	Y	N
26 ***Reynolds***	N	Y	N	N	Y	N
27 ***Quinn***	?	?	Y	N	Y	N
28 Slaughter	Y	N	Y	Y	Y	Y
29 ***Houghton***	?	?	N	N	Y	?
NORTH CAROLINA						
1 Vacant						
2 Etheridge	Y	Y	Y	Y	Y	Y
3 ***Jones***	N	N	N	N	Y	N
4 Price	Y	Y	Y	Y	Y	Y
5 ***Burr***	?	?	N	N	Y	N
6 ***Coble***	Y	N	N	N	Y	N
7 McIntyre	Y	Y	Y	Y	Y	Y
8 ***Hayes***	N	Y	N	N	Y	N
9 ***Myrick***	N	Y	N	N	Y	N
10 ***Ballenger***	N	Y	N	N	Y	N
11 ***Taylor***	N	Y	N	Y	Y	N
12 Watt	Y	Y	Y	Y	Y	Y
13 Miller	Y	Y	Y	Y	Y	Y
NORTH DAKOTA						
AL Pomeroy	Y	Y	Y	Y	Y	Y
OHIO						
1 ***Chabot***	N	Y	N	N	Y	N
2 ***Portman***	N	Y	N	N	Y	N
3 ***Turner***	N	Y	Y	N	Y	N
4 ***Oxley***	–	+	N	N	Y	N
5 ***Gillmor***	N	Y	N	N	Y	N
6 Strickland	Y	Y	Y	Y	Y	Y
7 ***Hobson***	N	Y	N	N	Y	N
8 ***Boehner***	N	Y	N	N	Y	N
9 Kaptur	Y	Y	Y	Y	Y	Y
10 Kucinich	Y	Y	Y	Y	N	Y
11 Jones	Y	Y	Y	Y	Y	?
12 ***Tiberi***	N	Y	N	N	Y	N
13 Brown	Y	Y	Y	Y	Y	Y
14 ***LaTourette***	N	Y	Y	Y	Y	N
15 ***Pryce***	N	Y	N	N	Y	N
16 ***Regula***	N	Y	N	N	Y	N
17 Ryan	Y	Y	Y	Y	Y	Y
18 ***Ney***	N	Y	N	N	Y	N
OKLAHOMA						
1 ***Sullivan***	N	Y	Y	N	Y	N
2 Carson	?	?	N	Y	Y	Y
3 ***Lucas***	N	Y	N	N	Y	N
4 ***Cole***	N	Y	N	N	Y	?
5 ***Istook***	N	Y	?	?	?	?
OREGON						
1 Wu	Y	N	Y	Y	Y	Y
2 ***Walden***	N	Y	Y	N	Y	N
3 Blumenauer	Y	Y	Y	Y	Y	Y
4 DeFazio	Y	Y	Y	Y	N	Y
5 Hooley	Y	Y	Y	Y	Y	Y
PENNSYLVANIA						
1 Brady	Y	Y	Y	Y	Y	Y
2 Fattah	?	?	Y	Y	Y	Y
3 ***English***	N	Y	N	N	Y	N
4 ***Hart***	N	Y	N	N	Y	N
5 ***Peterson***	?	?	N	N	Y	N
6 ***Gerlach***	N	Y	Y	N	Y	N
7 ***Weldon***	N	Y	Y	N	Y	N
8 ***Greenwood***	N	Y	N	N	Y	N
9 ***Shuster, Bill***	?	?	Y	N	Y	N
10 ***Sherwood***	N	Y	N	N	Y	N
11 Kanjorski	Y	Y	Y	Y	Y	Y
12 Murtha	Y	Y	Y	Y	Y	Y
13 Hoeffel	?	?	Y	Y	Y	Y
14 Doyle	Y	Y	Y	Y	Y	Y
15 ***Toomey***	?	?	N	N	Y	N
16 ***Pitts***	N	Y	N	N	Y	N
17 Holden	Y	Y	Y	Y	Y	Y
18 ***Murphy***	N	Y	N	N	Y	N
19 ***Platts***	N	Y	Y	N	Y	N
RHODE ISLAND						
1 Kennedy	Y	Y	Y	Y	Y	Y
2 Langevin	Y	Y	Y	Y	Y	Y
SOUTH CAROLINA						
1 ***Brown***	N	Y	N	N	Y	N
2 ***Wilson***	?	?	N	N	Y	N
3 ***Barrett***	N	Y	N	N	Y	N
4 ***DeMint***	?	?	N	N	Y	N
5 Spratt	Y	Y	Y	Y	Y	Y
6 Clyburn	Y	Y	Y	Y	Y	Y
SOUTH DAKOTA						
AL Herseth	Y	Y	Y	Y	Y	Y
TENNESSEE						
1 ***Jenkins***	N	Y	N	N	Y	N
2 ***Duncan***	N	N	N	N	Y	N
3 ***Wamp***	N	Y	Y	N	Y	N
4 Davis	Y	Y	Y	Y	Y	Y
5 Cooper	Y	Y	Y	N	Y	Y
6 Gordon	Y	Y	Y	Y	Y	Y
7 ***Blackburn***	N	Y	Y	N	Y	N
8 Tanner	Y	Y	Y	Y	Y	Y
9 Ford	Y	Y	Y	Y	Y	Y
TEXAS						
1 Sandlin	Y	Y	Y	Y	Y	Y
2 Turner	Y	Y	Y	Y	Y	Y
3 ***Johnson, Sam***	N	Y	N	N	Y	N
4 ***Hall***	N	Y	N	N	Y	N
5 ***Hensarling***	N	N	N	N	Y	N
6 ***Barton***	N	Y	N	N	Y	N
7 ***Culberson***	N	Y	N	N	Y	N
8 ***Brady***	N	Y	N	N	Y	N
9 Lampson	Y	Y	Y	Y	Y	Y
10 Doggett	Y	N	Y	Y	Y	Y
11 Edwards	Y	Y	Y	Y	Y	Y
12 ***Granger***	N	Y	N	N	Y	N
13 ***Thornberry***	N	Y	N	N	Y	N
14 ***Paul***	Y	N	N	Y	Y	N
15 Hinojosa	?	?	Y	Y	Y	Y
16 Reyes	Y	Y	Y	Y	Y	Y
17 Stenholm	Y	Y	Y	Y	Y	Y
18 Jackson-Lee	Y	Y	+	+	?	+
19 ***Neugebauer***	N	N	N	N	Y	N
20 Gonzalez	Y	Y	Y	Y	Y	Y
21 ***Smith***	N	Y	N	N	Y	N
22 ***DeLay***	N	Y	N	N	Y	N
23 ***Bonilla***	N	Y	N	N	Y	N
24 Frost	Y	Y	Y	Y	Y	Y
25 Bell	?	?	Y	Y	Y	Y
26 ***Burgess***	N	Y	N	N	Y	N
27 Ortiz	N	Y	Y	Y	Y	Y
28 Rodriguez	Y	Y	Y	Y	Y	Y
29 Green	Y	N	Y	N	Y	Y
30 Johnson, E.B.	+	+	Y	Y	Y	Y
31 ***Carter***	N	Y	N	N	Y	N
32 ***Sessions***	N	Y	N	N	Y	N
UTAH						
1 ***Bishop***	?	?	N	N	Y	N
2 Matheson	Y	N	Y	Y	Y	Y
3 ***Cannon***	N	Y	N	N	Y	N
VERMONT						
AL *Sanders*	?	?	Y	Y	Y	Y
VIRGINIA						
1 ***Davis, Jo Ann***	N	N	N	N	Y	N
2 ***Schrock***	N	Y	N	N	Y	N
3 Scott	?	Y	Y	Y	Y	Y
4 ***Forbes***	N	N	N	N	Y	Y
5 ***Goode***	N	N	N	N	Y	N
6 ***Goodlatte***	N	Y	N	N	Y	N
7 ***Cantor***	N	Y	N	N	Y	N
8 Moran	Y	Y	Y	Y	Y	Y
9 Boucher	Y	Y	Y	Y	Y	N
10 ***Wolf***	N	Y	N	N	Y	N
11 ***Davis, T.***	?	?	N	Y	Y	N
WASHINGTON						
1 Inslee	Y	Y	Y	Y	Y	Y
2 Larsen	Y	Y	Y	?	?	?
3 Baird	Y	Y	Y	Y	Y	Y
4 ***Hastings***	N	Y	Y	N	Y	N
5 ***Nethercutt***	N	Y	Y	N	Y	N
6 Dicks	?	?	Y	Y	Y	Y
7 McDermott	Y	Y	Y	Y	N	Y
8 ***Dunn***	N	Y	N	N	Y	N
9 Smith	Y	Y	Y	Y	Y	Y
WEST VIRGINIA						
1 Mollohan	Y	Y	Y	Y	Y	Y
2 ***Capito***	N	Y	N	N	Y	N
3 Rahall	N	Y	Y	Y	Y	Y
WISCONSIN						
1 ***Ryan***	N	Y	N	N	Y	N
2 Baldwin	Y	Y	Y	Y	Y	Y
3 Kind	Y	N	Y	Y	Y	Y
4 Kleczka	Y	Y	Y	Y	Y	?
5 ***Sensenbrenner***	N	N	Y	N	Y	N
6 ***Petri***	N	N	N	N	Y	N
7 Obey	Y	N	Y	Y	Y	Y
8 ***Green***	N	N	Y	Y	Y	N
WYOMING						
AL ***Cubin***	N	Y	N	N	Y	N

Southern states - Ala., Ark., Fla., Ga., Ky., La., Miss., N.C., Okla., S.C., Tenn., Texas, Va.

Key

Y	Voted for (yea).
#	Paired for.
+	Announced for.
N	Voted against (nay).
X	Paired against.
–	Announced against.
P	Voted "present."
C	Voted "present" to avoid possible conflict of interest.
?	Did not vote or otherwise make a position known.

• Democrats **Republicans** *Independents*

367. HR 4766. Fiscal 2005 Agriculture Appropriations/Food Stamps. Tancredo, R-Colo., amendment that would prohibit funds under the food stamp program from being used to contravene existing immigration law requiring that food stamp applicants have an affidavit of support by a sponsor. Rejected 156-262: R 148-71; D 8-190 (ND 3-142, SD 5-48); I 0-1. July 13, 2004.

368. HR 4766. Fiscal 2005 Agriculture Appropriations/Market Access Program. Chabot, R-Ohio, amendment that would prohibit the use of funds in the bill to carry out the activities of the Market Access Program, which funds the advertising and marketing of agricultural projects overseas. Rejected 72-347: R 60-159; D 12-187 (ND 11-136, SD 1-51); I 0-1. July 13, 2004.

369. HR 4766. Fiscal 2005 Agriculture Appropriations/Farmers Market Programs. Kaptur, D-Ohio, amendment that would increase funding by $6 million for the farmers market promotion program to be offset by reductions in the Office of the Chief Information Officer account. Rejected 206-213: R 8-211; D 197-2 (ND 146-0, SD 51-2); I 1-0. July 13, 2004.

370. HR 4766. Fiscal 2005 Agriculture Appropriations/Passage. Passage of the bill that would appropriate $83.7 billion for agriculture, rural development and nutrition programs in fiscal 2005, including $33.6 billion for the food stamp program, $16.5 billion for the Commodity Credit Corporation, $11.4 billion for child nutrition programs, $2.4 billion for rural development programs and $1.5 billion for the Food and Drug Administration. Passed 389-31: R 204-16; D 184-15 (ND 135-11, SD 49-4); I 1-0. July 13, 2004.

371. HR 4759. U.S.-Australia Trade/Rule. Adoption of the rule (H Res 712) to provide for House floor consideration of the bill that would implement a trade agreement reducing tariffs and trade barriers between the United States and Australia. Adopted 337-89: R 225-0; D 112-88 (ND 72-73, SD 40-15); I 0-1. July 14, 2004.

372. H Res 705. World Trade Organization Tax Rules/Adoption. English, R-Pa., motion to suspend the rules and adopt the resolution that would urge the president to report to Congress next year on efforts to resolve the World Trade Organization's disparate treatment of direct and indirect taxes, which allows indirect taxes on exports to be rebated. Motion agreed to 423-1: R 223-1; D 199-0 (ND 144-0, SD 55-0); I 1-0. A two-thirds majority of those present and voting (283 in this case) is required for adoption under suspension of the rules. July 14, 2004.

	367	368	369	370	371	372
ALABAMA						
1 *Bonner*	N	N	N	Y	Y	Y
2 *Everett*	Y	N	N	Y	Y	Y
3 *Rogers*	Y	N	N	Y	Y	Y
4 *Aderholt*	Y	N	N	Y	Y	Y
5 Cramer	Y	N	Y	Y	Y	Y
6 *Bachus*	Y	Y	N	Y	Y	Y
7 Davis	N	N	Y	Y	Y	Y
ALASKA						
AL *Young*	N	N	N	Y	Y	Y
ARIZONA						
1 *Renzi*	Y	N	N	Y	Y	Y
2 *Franks*	Y	Y	N	Y	Y	Y
3 *Shadegg*	Y	Y	N	Y	Y	Y
4 Pastor	N	N	Y	Y	Y	Y
5 *Hayworth*	Y	Y	N	Y	Y	Y
6 *Flake*	Y	Y	N	N	Y	Y
7 Grijalva	N	N	Y	Y	N	Y
8 *Kolbe*	Y	N	N	Y	Y	Y
ARKANSAS						
1 Berry	N	N	N	Y	N	Y
2 Snyder	N	N	Y	Y	Y	Y
3 *Boozman*	Y	N	N	Y	Y	Y
4 Ross	Y	N	Y	Y	Y	Y
CALIFORNIA						
1 Thompson	N	N	N	Y	Y	Y
2 *Herger*	Y	N	N	Y	Y	Y
3 *Ose*	Y	N	N	Y	Y	Y
4 *Doolittle*	Y	N	Y	Y	Y	Y
5 Matsui	N	N	Y	Y	Y	Y
6 Woolsey	N	N	Y	Y	Y	Y
7 Miller, George	N	N	Y	Y	N	Y
8 Pelosi	N	N	Y	Y	Y	Y
9 Lee	?	?	?	?	N	Y
10 Tauscher	N	N	Y	Y	Y	Y
11 *Pombo*	Y	N	N	Y	Y	Y
12 Lantos	N	N	Y	Y	N	Y
13 Stark	N	N	N	N	N	Y
14 Eshoo	N	N	Y	Y	Y	Y
15 Honda	N	N	Y	Y	Y	Y
16 Lofgren	N	N	Y	Y	Y	Y
17 Farr	N	N	Y	Y	N	Y
18 Cardoza	N	N	Y	Y	N	Y
19 *Radanovich*	N	N	N	Y	Y	Y
20 Dooley	N	N	N	Y	Y	Y
21 *Nunes*	N	N	N	Y	Y	Y
22 *Thomas*	N	N	N	Y	Y	Y
23 Capps	N	N	Y	Y	Y	Y
24 *Gallegly*	Y	N	N	Y	Y	Y
25 *McKeon*	Y	N	N	Y	Y	Y
26 *Dreier*	N	N	N	Y	Y	Y
27 Sherman	N	N	Y	Y	Y	Y
28 Berman	N	N	Y	Y	Y	Y
29 Schiff	N	N	Y	Y	Y	Y
30 Waxman	N	Y	Y	Y	Y	Y
31 Becerra	N	N	Y	Y	N	Y
32 Solis	N	N	Y	Y	N	Y
33 Watson	N	N	Y	Y	N	Y
34 Roybal-Allard	N	N	Y	Y	Y	Y
35 Waters	N	N	Y	Y	Y	Y
36 Harman	N	N	Y	Y	Y	Y

	367	368	369	370	371	372
37 Millender-McD.	N	N	Y	Y	N	Y
38 Napolitano	N	Y	Y	Y	Y	Y
39 Sánchez, Linda	N	N	Y	Y	N	Y
40 *Royce*	Y	Y	N	N	Y	Y
41 *Lewis*	N	N	N	Y	Y	Y
42 *Miller, Gary*	Y	Y	N	Y	Y	Y
43 Baca	N	N	N	Y	N	Y
44 *Calvert*	N	N	N	Y	Y	Y
45 *Bono*	N	N	N	Y	Y	Y
46 *Rohrabacher*	Y	Y	N	N	Y	Y
47 Sanchez, Loretta	N	N	Y	Y	Y	Y
48 *Cox*	N	N	N	Y	Y	Y
49 *Issa*	N	N	N	Y	Y	Y
50 *Cunningham*	Y	N	N	Y	Y	Y
51 Filner	N	N	Y	Y	N	Y
52 *Hunter*	Y	N	N	Y	Y	Y
53 Davis	N	Y	Y	Y	Y	Y
COLORADO						
1 DeGette	N	N	Y	Y	Y	Y
2 Udall	N	Y	Y	Y	Y	Y
3 *McInnis*	Y	Y	N	Y	Y	Y
4 *Musgrave*	Y	N	Y	Y	Y	Y
5 *Hefley*	Y	Y	N	Y	Y	Y
6 *Tancredo*	Y	Y	N	N	Y	Y
7 *Beauprez*	Y	N	N	Y	Y	Y
CONNECTICUT						
1 Larson	N	N	Y	Y	N	Y
2 *Simmons*	N	N	Y	Y	Y	Y
3 DeLauro	N	N	Y	Y	N	Y
4 *Shays*	Y	Y	N	N	Y	Y
5 *Johnson*	Y	N	N	N	Y	Y
DELAWARE						
AL *Castle*	N	Y	N	Y	Y	Y
FLORIDA						
1 *Miller, J.*	Y	Y	N	Y	Y	Y
2 Boyd	Y	Y	Y	Y	Y	Y
3 Brown	N	N	Y	Y	Y	Y
4 *Crenshaw*	Y	N	N	Y	Y	Y
5 *Brown-Waite*	Y	N	Y	Y	Y	Y
6 *Stearns*	Y	N	N	Y	Y	Y
7 *Mica*	Y	N	N	Y	Y	Y
8 *Keller*	Y	N	N	Y	Y	Y
9 *Bilirakis*	Y	N	N	Y	Y	Y
10 *Young*	N	N	N	Y	Y	Y
11 Davis	N	Y	Y	Y	Y	Y
12 *Putnam*	Y	N	N	Y	Y	Y
13 *Harris*	Y	N	N	Y	Y	Y
14 *Goss*	Y	N	N	Y	Y	Y
15 *Weldon*	Y	N	N	Y	Y	Y
16 *Foley*	Y	N	N	Y	Y	Y
17 Meek	N	N	Y	Y	N	Y
18 *Ros-Lehtinen*	N	N	Y	Y	N	Y
19 Wexler	N	N	Y	Y	N	Y
20 Deutsch	?	?	?	?	N	Y
21 *Diaz-Balart, L.*	N	N	Y	Y	Y	Y
22 *Shaw*	N	N	N	Y	Y	Y
23 Hastings	N	N	Y	Y	N	Y
24 *Feeney*	Y	N	N	Y	Y	Y
25 *Diaz-Balart, M.*	N	N	Y	Y	Y	Y
GEORGIA						
1 *Kingston*	Y	N	N	Y	Y	Y
2 Bishop	N	N	Y	Y	N	Y
3 Marshall	N	N	Y	Y	N	Y
4 Majette	?	?	?	?	?	?
5 Lewis	N	N	Y	Y	Y	Y
6 *Isakson*	?	?	?	?	?	?
7 *Linder*	Y	Y	N	Y	Y	Y
8 *Collins*	+	–	–	Y	Y	Y
9 *Norwood*	Y	N	N	Y	Y	Y
10 *Deal*	Y	N	Y	Y	Y	Y
11 *Gingrey*	Y	N	N	Y	Y	Y
12 *Burns*	Y	N	N	Y	Y	Y
13 Scott	N	N	Y	Y	Y	Y
HAWAII						
1 Abercrombie	N	N	Y	Y	N	Y
2 Case	N	N	Y	Y	Y	Y
IDAHO						
1 *Otter*	Y	N	N	Y	Y	Y
2 *Simpson*	Y	N	N	Y	Y	Y
ILLINOIS						
1 Rush	N	N	Y	Y	N	Y
2 Jackson	N	N	Y	Y	Y	Y
3 Lipinski	N	N	Y	Y	Y	Y
4 Gutierrez	N	N	Y	Y	Y	Y
5 Emanuel	N	N	Y	Y	Y	Y
6 *Hyde*	N	Y	N	Y	Y	Y

ND Northern Democrats   SD Southern Democrats

	367	368	369	370	371	372
7 Davis	N	N	Y	Y	N	Y
8 ***Crane***	Y	N	N	N	Y	Y
9 Schakowsky	N	Y	Y	Y	N	Y
10 ***Kirk***	N	Y	N	Y	Y	Y
11 ***Weller***	N	N	N	Y	Y	Y
12 Costello	N	N	Y	Y	N	Y
13 ***Biggert***	N	N	N	Y	Y	Y
14 ***Hastert***						
15 ***Johnson***	N	N	N	Y	Y	Y
16 ***Manzullo***	Y	Y	N	Y	Y	Y
17 Evans	N	N	Y	Y	Y	Y
18 ***LaHood***	N	N	N	Y	Y	Y
19 ***Shimkus***	Y	N	N	Y	Y	Y
INDIANA						
1 Visclosky	N	N	Y	Y	Y	Y
2 ***Chocola***	Y	N	N	Y	Y	Y
3 ***Souder***	Y	N	N	Y	Y	Y
4 ***Buyer***	Y	N	N	N	Y	Y
5 ***Burton***	Y	Y	N	Y	Y	?
6 ***Pence***	Y	Y	N	Y	Y	Y
7 Carson	?	N	?	?	?	?
8 ***Hostettler***	Y	Y	N	Y	Y	Y
9 Hill	N	N	Y	Y	Y	Y
IOWA						
1 ***Nussle***	N	N	N	Y	Y	Y
2 ***Leach***	N	N	Y	Y	Y	Y
3 Boswell	N	N	Y	Y	N	Y
4 ***Latham***	N	N	N	Y	Y	Y
5 ***King***	Y	Y	N	Y	Y	Y
KANSAS						
1 ***Moran***	Y	N	N	Y	Y	Y
2 ***Ryun***	Y	N	N	Y	Y	Y
3 Moore	N	N	Y	Y	Y	?
4 ***Tiahrt***	N	N	N	Y	Y	Y
KENTUCKY						
1 ***Whitfield***	N	N	N	Y	Y	Y
2 ***Lewis***	Y	N	N	N	Y	Y
3 ***Northup***	Y	N	N	Y	Y	Y
4 Lucas	N	N	Y	Y	Y	Y
5 ***Rogers***	Y	N	N	Y	Y	Y
6 Chandler	N	N	Y	Y	Y	Y
LOUISIANA						
1 ***Vitter***	?	?	?	+	Y	Y
2 Jefferson	N	N	Y	Y	Y	Y
3 ***Tauzin***	N	N	N	Y	Y	Y
4 ***McCrery***	Y	N	N	Y	Y	Y
5 Alexander	N	N	Y	Y	N	Y
6 ***Baker***	Y	N	N	Y	Y	Y
7 John	N	N	N	Y	Y	Y
MAINE						
1 Allen	N	N	Y	Y	Y	Y
2 Michaud	N	N	Y	Y	N	Y
MARYLAND						
1 ***Gilchrest***	N	N	N	Y	Y	Y
2 Ruppersberger	N	N	Y	Y	Y	Y
3 Cardin	N	N	Y	Y	Y	Y
4 Wynn	N	N	Y	Y	Y	Y
5 Hoyer	N	N	Y	Y	Y	Y
6 ***Bartlett***	Y	Y	N	Y	Y	Y
7 Cummings	N	N	Y	Y	Y	Y
8 Van Hollen	N	Y	Y	Y	Y	Y
MASSACHUSETTS						
1 Olver	N	N	Y	Y	Y	Y
2 Neal	N	N	Y	Y	N	Y
3 McGovern	N	N	Y	Y	N	Y
4 Frank	N	N	Y	N	N	Y
5 Meehan	N	N	Y	N	N	Y
6 Tierney	N	N	Y	Y	N	Y
7 Markey	N	N	Y	N	N	Y
8 Capuano	N	N	Y	N	N	Y
9 Lynch	N	N	Y	Y	Y	Y
10 Delahunt	N	N	Y	Y	N	Y
MICHIGAN						
1 Stupak	N	N	Y	N	N	Y
2 ***Hoekstra***	Y	Y	N	Y	Y	Y
3 ***Ehlers***	N	Y	N	Y	Y	Y
4 ***Camp***	Y	N	N	Y	Y	Y
5 Kildee	N	N	Y	Y	N	Y
6 ***Upton***	Y	N	N	Y	Y	Y
7 ***Smith***	Y	Y	N	Y	Y	Y
8 ***Rogers***	Y	N	N	Y	Y	Y
9 ***Knollenberg***	N	N	N	Y	Y	Y
10 ***Miller***	Y	N	N	Y	Y	Y
11 ***McCotter***	Y	N	N	Y	Y	Y
12 Levin	N	N	Y	Y	Y	Y

	367	368	369	370	371	372
13 Kilpatrick	N	N	Y	Y	N	Y
14 Conyers	N	N	Y	N	Y	Y
15 Dingell	N	N	Y	Y	Y	Y
MINNESOTA						
1 ***Gutknecht***	?	?	?	?	Y	Y
2 ***Kline***	Y	N	N	Y	Y	Y
3 ***Ramstad***	Y	Y	N	Y	Y	Y
4 McCollum	N	Y	Y	Y	N	Y
5 Sabo	N	N	Y	Y	N	Y
6 ***Kennedy***	Y	N	N	Y	Y	Y
7 Peterson	N	N	Y	Y	N	Y
8 Oberstar	N	N	Y	Y	N	Y
MISSISSIPPI						
1 ***Wicker***	Y	N	N	Y	Y	Y
2 Thompson	N	N	Y	Y	N	Y
3 ***Pickering***	Y	N	N	Y	Y	Y
4 Taylor	Y	N	Y	Y	N	Y
MISSOURI						
1 Clay	N	N	Y	Y	Y	Y
2 ***Akin***	Y	N	N	Y	Y	Y
3 Gephardt	N	N	Y	Y	Y	Y
4 Skelton	N	N	Y	Y	Y	Y
5 McCarthy	N	N	Y	Y	Y	Y
6 ***Graves***	Y	N	N	Y	Y	Y
7 ***Blunt***	N	N	N	Y	Y	Y
8 ***Emerson***	N	N	N	Y	Y	Y
9 ***Hulshof***	N	N	Y	Y	Y	Y
MONTANA						
AL ***Rehberg***	Y	N	N	Y	Y	Y
NEBRASKA						
1 ***Bereuter***	?	?	?	?	Y	Y
2 ***Terry***	Y	N	N	Y	Y	Y
3 ***Osborne***	N	N	N	Y	Y	Y
NEVADA						
1 Berkley	N	Y	Y	Y	Y	Y
2 ***Gibbons***	Y	Y	N	Y	Y	Y
3 ***Porter***	N	N	N	Y	Y	Y
NEW HAMPSHIRE						
1 ***Bradley***	Y	Y	N	Y	Y	Y
2 ***Bass***	Y	Y	N	Y	Y	Y
NEW JERSEY						
1 Andrews	N	Y	Y	Y	N	Y
2 ***LoBiondo***	N	Y	N	Y	Y	Y
3 ***Saxton***	?	?	?	?	Y	Y
4 ***Smith***	N	Y	N	Y	Y	Y
5 ***Garrett***	Y	Y	N	Y	Y	Y
6 Pallone	N	N	Y	Y	N	Y
7 ***Ferguson***	N	Y	N	Y	Y	Y
8 Pascrell	N	Y	Y	N	N	Y
9 Rothman	N	N	Y	Y	N	Y
10 Payne	N	N	Y	Y	N	Y
11 ***Frelinghuysen***	N	Y	N	Y	Y	Y
12 Holt	N	N	Y	Y	N	Y
13 Menendez	N	N	Y	Y	Y	Y
NEW MEXICO						
1 ***Wilson***	N	N	N	Y	Y	Y
2 ***Pearce***	N	N	N	Y	Y	Y
3 Udall	N	N	Y	Y	Y	Y
NEW YORK						
1 Bishop	N	N	Y	Y	Y	Y
2 Israel	N	N	Y	Y	Y	Y
3 ***King***	N	N	N	Y	Y	Y
4 McCarthy	N	N	Y	Y	Y	Y
5 Ackerman	N	N	Y	Y	N	Y
6 Meeks	N	N	Y	Y	Y	Y
7 Crowley	N	N	Y	Y	Y	Y
8 Nadler	N	N	Y	Y	N	Y
9 Weiner	N	N	Y	Y	N	Y
10 Towns	N	N	Y	Y	Y	Y
11 Owens	N	N	Y	Y	N	Y
12 Velázquez	N	N	Y	Y	N	Y
13 ***Fossella***	Y	Y	N	Y	Y	Y
14 Maloney	N	N	Y	Y	Y	Y
15 Rangel	N	N	Y	Y	?	?
16 Serrano	N	N	Y	Y	Y	Y
17 Engel	N	N	Y	Y	Y	Y
18 Lowey	N	N	Y	Y	Y	Y
19 ***Kelly***	Y	N	Y	Y	Y	Y
20 ***Sweeney***	Y	N	N	Y	Y	Y
21 McNulty	N	N	Y	Y	N	Y
22 Hinchey	N	N	Y	Y	N	Y
23 ***McHugh***	Y	N	N	Y	Y	Y
24 ***Boehlert***	N	N	N	Y	Y	Y
25 ***Walsh***	N	N	N	Y	Y	Y

	367	368	369	370	371	372
26 ***Reynolds***	N	N	N	Y	Y	Y
27 ***Quinn***	Y	N	N	Y	Y	Y
28 Slaughter	N	N	Y	Y	N	Y
29 ***Houghton***	?	?	?	?	Y	Y
NORTH CAROLINA						
1 Vacant						
2 Etheridge	N	N	Y	Y	N	Y
3 ***Jones***	Y	N	N	Y	Y	Y
4 Price	N	N	Y	Y	Y	Y
5 ***Burr***	N	N	N	N	Y	Y
6 ***Coble***	Y	N	N	N	Y	Y
7 McIntyre	N	N	Y	Y	N	Y
8 ***Hayes***	Y	N	N	Y	Y	Y
9 ***Myrick***	Y	Y	N	Y	Y	Y
10 ***Ballenger***	N	N	N	Y	Y	Y
11 ***Taylor***	Y	N	N	Y	Y	Y
12 Watt	N	N	Y	Y	Y	Y
13 Miller	N	N	Y	Y	Y	Y
NORTH DAKOTA						
AL Pomeroy	N	N	Y	Y	N	Y
OHIO						
1 ***Chabot***	Y	Y	N	Y	Y	Y
2 ***Portman***	N	Y	N	Y	Y	Y
3 ***Turner***	N	N	N	Y	Y	Y
4 ***Oxley***	N	N	N	Y	Y	Y
5 ***Gillmor***	Y	N	N	Y	Y	Y
6 Strickland	N	N	Y	Y	N	Y
7 ***Hobson***	N	N	N	Y	Y	Y
8 ***Boehner***	N	N	N	Y	Y	Y
9 Kaptur	N	N	Y	Y	N	Y
10 Kucinich	N	N	Y	N	N	Y
11 Jones	?	N	Y	Y	N	Y
12 ***Tiberi***	Y	Y	N	Y	Y	Y
13 Brown	N	Y	Y	Y	N	Y
14 ***LaTourette***	N	N	N	Y	Y	Y
15 ***Pryce***	N	N	N	Y	Y	Y
16 ***Regula***	N	N	N	Y	Y	Y
17 Ryan	N	N	Y	Y	N	Y
18 ***Ney***	N	N	N	Y	Y	Y
OKLAHOMA						
1 ***Sullivan***	Y	N	N	Y	Y	Y
2 Carson	Y	?	Y	Y	N	Y
3 ***Lucas***	Y	N	N	Y	Y	Y
4 ***Cole***	N	N	N	Y	Y	Y
5 ***Istook***	?	?	?	?	?	?
OREGON						
1 Wu	N	N	Y	Y	Y	Y
2 ***Walden***	Y	N	N	Y	Y	Y
3 Blumenauer	N	N	Y	Y	Y	Y
4 DeFazio	Y	N	Y	Y	N	Y
5 Hooley	Y	N	Y	Y	Y	Y
PENNSYLVANIA						
1 Brady	N	N	Y	Y	N	Y
2 Fattah	N	N	Y	Y	Y	Y
3 ***English***	Y	N	N	Y	Y	Y
4 ***Hart***	Y	N	N	Y	Y	Y
5 ***Peterson***	Y	N	N	Y	Y	Y
6 ***Gerlach***	N	N	N	Y	Y	Y
7 ***Weldon***	N	N	N	Y	Y	Y
8 ***Greenwood***	Y	N	Y	Y	Y	Y
9 ***Shuster, Bill***	Y	Y	N	Y	Y	Y
10 ***Sherwood***	N	N	N	Y	Y	Y
11 Kanjorski	N	N	Y	Y	Y	Y
12 Murtha	N	N	Y	Y	Y	Y
13 Hoeffel	N	N	Y	Y	?	?
14 Doyle	N	N	Y	Y	Y	Y
15 ***Toomey***	Y	Y	N	Y	Y	Y
16 ***Pitts***	Y	Y	N	Y	Y	Y
17 Holden	N	N	Y	Y	Y	Y
18 ***Murphy***	Y	N	N	Y	Y	Y
19 ***Platts***	Y	N	Y	Y	Y	Y
RHODE ISLAND						
1 Kennedy	N	N	Y	Y	N	Y
2 Langevin	N	N	Y	Y	Y	Y
SOUTH CAROLINA						
1 ***Brown***	Y	N	N	Y	Y	Y
2 ***Wilson***	Y	Y	N	Y	Y	Y
3 ***Barrett***	Y	Y	N	Y	Y	Y
4 ***DeMint***	Y	Y	N	Y	Y	Y
5 Spratt	N	N	Y	Y	Y	Y
6 Clyburn	N	N	Y	Y	N	Y
SOUTH DAKOTA						
AL Herseth	N	N	Y	Y	N	Y

	367	368	369	370	371	372
TENNESSEE						
1 ***Jenkins***	N	N	N	Y	Y	Y
2 ***Duncan***	Y	Y	N	Y	Y	Y
3 ***Wamp***	Y	Y	N	Y	Y	Y
4 Davis	N	N	Y	Y	Y	Y
5 Cooper	N	N	Y	Y	Y	Y
6 Gordon	Y	N	Y	N	Y	Y
7 ***Blackburn***	Y	N	N	Y	Y	Y
8 Tanner	N	N	Y	Y	Y	Y
9 Ford	N	N	Y	Y	Y	Y
TEXAS						
1 Sandlin	N	N	Y	Y	Y	Y
2 Turner	N	N	Y	Y	Y	Y
3 ***Johnson, Sam***	Y	N	N	Y	Y	Y
4 ***Hall***	N	N	N	Y	Y	Y
5 ***Hensarling***	Y	Y	N	Y	Y	Y
6 ***Barton***	N	N	N	Y	Y	Y
7 ***Culberson***	Y	Y	N	Y	Y	Y
8 ***Brady***	Y	N	N	Y	Y	Y
9 Lampson	N	N	Y	Y	Y	Y
10 Doggett	N	Y	Y	Y	Y	Y
11 Edwards	N	N	Y	Y	Y	Y
12 ***Granger***	N	N	N	Y	Y	Y
13 ***Thornberry***	N	N	N	Y	Y	Y
14 ***Paul***	Y	Y	N	N	Y	N
15 Hinojosa	N	N	Y	Y	Y	Y
16 Reyes	N	N	Y	Y	Y	Y
17 Stenholm	N	N	Y	Y	Y	Y
18 Jackson-Lee	+	–	+	+	Y	Y
19 ***Neugebauer***	Y	N	N	Y	Y	Y
20 Gonzalez	N	N	Y	Y	Y	Y
21 ***Smith***	Y	N	N	Y	Y	Y
22 ***DeLay***	Y	Y	N	Y	Y	Y
23 ***Bonilla***	N	N	N	Y	Y	Y
24 Frost	N	N	Y	Y	Y	Y
25 Bell	N	N	Y	Y	Y	Y
26 ***Burgess***	Y	Y	N	Y	Y	Y
27 Ortiz	N	N	Y	Y	Y	Y
28 Rodriguez	N	N	Y	Y	Y	Y
29 Green	N	N	Y	Y	N	Y
30 Johnson, E.B.	N	N	Y	Y	Y	Y
31 ***Carter***	Y	Y	N	Y	Y	Y
32 ***Sessions***	Y	N	N	Y	Y	Y
UTAH						
1 ***Bishop***	N	N	N	Y	Y	Y
2 Matheson	Y	N	Y	Y	Y	Y
3 ***Cannon***	N	N	N	Y	Y	Y
VERMONT						
AL *Sanders*	N	N	Y	Y	N	Y
VIRGINIA						
1 ***Davis, Jo Ann***	Y	Y	N	Y	Y	Y
2 ***Schrock***	Y	N	N	Y	Y	Y
3 Scott	N	N	Y	Y	Y	Y
4 ***Forbes***	Y	N	N	Y	Y	Y
5 ***Goode***	Y	N	N	N	Y	Y
6 ***Goodlatte***	Y	N	N	Y	Y	Y
7 ***Cantor***	Y	N	N	Y	Y	Y
8 Moran	N	N	Y	N	Y	Y
9 Boucher	N	N	Y	N	Y	Y
10 ***Wolf***	N	N	N	Y	Y	Y
11 ***Davis, T.***	N	N	N	Y	Y	Y
WASHINGTON						
1 Inslee	N	N	Y	Y	Y	Y
2 Larsen	?	?	?	?	Y	Y
3 Baird	N	N	Y	Y	N	Y
4 ***Hastings***	Y	N	Y	Y	Y	Y
5 ***Nethercutt***	Y	N	N	Y	Y	Y
6 Dicks	N	N	Y	Y	Y	Y
7 McDermott	N	N	Y	N	N	Y
8 ***Dunn***	Y	N	N	Y	Y	Y
9 Smith	N	N	Y	N	Y	Y
WEST VIRGINIA						
1 Mollohan	N	N	Y	Y	N	Y
2 ***Capito***	Y	N	N	Y	Y	Y
3 Rahall	N	N	Y	Y	N	Y
WISCONSIN						
1 ***Ryan***	Y	N	N	Y	Y	Y
2 Baldwin	N	N	Y	Y	N	Y
3 Kind	N	N	Y	Y	?	?
4 Kleczka	N	N	Y	Y	N	Y
5 ***Sensenbrenner***	Y	Y	N	N	Y	Y
6 ***Petri***	Y	Y	Y	Y	Y	Y
7 Obey	N	N	Y	Y	N	Y
8 ***Green***	Y	N	Y	Y	Y	Y
WYOMING						
AL ***Cubin***	Y	N	N	Y	Y	Y

Southern states - Ala., Ark., Fla., Ga., Ky., La., Miss., N.C., Okla., S.C., Tenn., Texas, Va.

Key

Y   Voted for (yea).
\#   Paired for.
\+   Announced for.
N   Voted against (nay).
X   Paired against.
–   Announced against.
P   Voted "present."
C   Voted "present" to avoid possible conflict of interest.
?   Did not vote or otherwise make a position known.

Democrats   **Republicans**
Independents

373. HR 4418. Customs, Immigration and Trade Agencies Authorization/Passage. Thomas, R-Calif., motion to suspend the rules and pass the bill that would authorize $21 billion in fiscal 2005-06 for the U.S. Customs and Border Protection bureau and the U.S. Immigration and Customs Enforcement bureau. It also would authorize $83 million for the Office of the U.S. Trade Representative and $127 million for the U.S. International Trade Commission in fiscal 2005 and 2006. Motion agreed to 341-85: R 222-3; D 119-81 (ND 82-63, SD 37-18); I 0-1. A two-thirds majority of those present and voting (284 in this case) is required for passage under suspension of the rules. July 14, 2004.

374. H Res 576. Intellectual Property Rights in China/Adoption. Ballenger, R-N.C., motion to suspend the rules and adopt the resolution that would urge the Chinese government to coordinate a nationwide intellectual property rights enforcement campaign and to vigorously pursue counterfeiting and piracy cases. Motion agreed to 416-3: R 219-3; D 196-0 (ND 143-0, SD 53-0); I 1-0. A two-thirds majority of those present and voting (280 in this case) is required for adoption under suspension of the rules. July 14, 2004.

375. HR 4759. U.S.-Australia Trade/Passage. Passage of the bill that would implement a trade agreement reducing tariffs and trade barriers between the United States and Australia. It would give all U.S. agricultural exports to Australia immediate duty-free access, phase out U.S. duties on Australian beef and lamb exports, and slightly increase the current U.S. quota for Australian dairy exports. Passed 314-109: R 198-24; D 116-84 (ND 75-70, SD 41-14); I 0-1. A "yea" was a vote in support of the president's position. July 14, 2004.

376. S 15. Project Bioshield/Passage. Passage of the bill that would authorize $5.6 billion over 10 years for the Health and Human Services Department (HHS) to carry out Project Bioshield, an administration initiative to develop and stockpile vaccines, medications and other countermeasures to combat a bioterrorism attack. Passed (thus cleared for the president) 414-2: R 222-2; D 191-0 (ND 138-0, SD 53-0); I 1-0. A "yea" was a vote in support of the president's position. July 14, 2004.

377. H Res 615. Israel and the United Nations/Adoption. Ros-Lehtinen, R-Fla., motion to suspend the rules and adopt the resolution that would express the sense of the House in support of giving Israel full membership in the Western European and Others Group of the United Nations. Motion agreed to 418-0: R 222-0; D 195-0 (ND 143-0, SD 52-0); I 1-0. A two-thirds majority of those present and voting (280 in this case) is required for adoption under suspension of the rules. July 15, 2004.

378. H Res 713. International Court of Justice/Adoption. Pence, R-Ind., motion to suspend the rules and adopt the resolution that would deplore the misuse of the International Court of Justice by a majority of members of the U.N. General Assembly for narrow political purposes including interference in the Palestinian-Israeli conflict. Motion agreed to 361-45: R 214-4; D 147-40 (ND 100-36, SD 47-4); I 0-1. A two-thirds majority of those present and voting (273 in this case) is required for adoption under suspension of the rules. July 15, 2004.

	373	374	375	376	377	378
ALABAMA						
1 *Bonner*	Y	Y	Y	Y	Y	Y
2 *Everett*	Y	Y	Y	Y	Y	Y
3 *Rogers*	Y	Y	Y	Y	Y	Y
4 *Aderholt*	Y	Y	Y	Y	Y	Y
5 Cramer	Y	Y	Y	Y	Y	Y
6 *Bachus*	Y	Y	Y	Y	Y	Y
7 Davis	N	Y	Y	Y	Y	Y
ALASKA						
AL *Young*	Y	Y	Y	Y	Y	Y
ARIZONA						
1 *Renzi*	Y	Y	Y	Y	Y	Y
2 *Franks*	Y	Y	Y	Y	+	+
3 *Shadegg*	Y	Y	Y	Y	Y	Y
4 Pastor	Y	N	Y	N	Y	N
5 *Hayworth*	Y	Y	Y	Y	Y	Y
6 *Flake*	Y	Y	Y	N	Y	Y
7 Grijalva	Y	N	Y	N	Y	N
8 *Kolbe*	Y	Y	Y	Y	Y	Y
ARKANSAS						
1 Berry	Y	Y	N	Y	Y	Y
2 Snyder	Y	Y	Y	Y	Y	Y
3 *Boozman*	Y	Y	Y	Y	Y	Y
4 Ross	Y	Y	Y	Y	Y	Y
CALIFORNIA						
1 Thompson	Y	Y	Y	Y	Y	Y
2 *Herger*	Y	?	Y	Y	Y	Y
3 *Ose*	Y	Y	Y	Y	Y	Y
4 *Doolittle*	Y	Y	Y	Y	Y	Y
5 Matsui	Y	Y	Y	Y	Y	Y
6 Woolsey	N	Y	N	Y	Y	Y
7 Miller, George	N	Y	N	Y	N	N
8 Pelosi	N	Y	Y	Y	Y	Y
9 Lee	N	Y	N	Y	N	N
10 Tauscher	Y	Y	Y	Y	Y	Y
11 *Pombo*	Y	Y	N	Y	Y	Y
12 Lantos	Y	Y	N	Y	Y	Y
13 Stark	N	N	N	Y	N	N
14 Eshoo	Y	Y	Y	Y	Y	Y
15 Honda	Y	Y	Y	Y	Y	Y
16 Lofgren	Y	Y	Y	Y	Y	N
17 Farr	N	?	Y	Y	Y	N
18 Cardoza	Y	Y	N	Y	Y	Y
19 *Radanovich*	Y	Y	Y	Y	Y	Y
20 Dooley	Y	Y	Y	?	Y	Y
21 *Nunes*	Y	Y	P	Y	Y	Y
22 *Thomas*	Y	Y	Y	Y	Y	Y
23 Capps	Y	Y	Y	Y	Y	N
24 *Gallegly*	Y	Y	Y	Y	Y	Y
25 *McKeon*	Y	Y	Y	Y	Y	Y
26 *Dreier*	Y	Y	Y	Y	Y	Y
27 Sherman	N	Y	Y	Y	Y	Y
28 Berman	Y	Y	Y	Y	Y	Y
29 Schiff	Y	Y	Y	Y	Y	Y
30 Waxman	N	Y	N	Y	Y	Y
31 Becerra	N	Y	Y	Y	P	N
32 Solis	Y	Y	N	Y	Y	N
33 Watson	N	Y	Y	Y	Y	?
34 Roybal-Allard	Y	Y	Y	Y	Y	Y
35 Waters	N	Y	N	Y	Y	N
36 Harman	Y	Y	Y	Y	Y	Y
37 Millender-McD.	Y	Y	N	Y	Y	Y
38 Napolitano	Y	Y	Y	Y	Y	Y
39 Sánchez, Linda	N	Y	N	Y	Y	Y
40 *Royce*	Y	Y	Y	Y	Y	Y
41 *Lewis*	Y	Y	Y	Y	Y	Y
42 *Miller, Gary*	Y	Y	Y	Y	Y	Y
43 Baca	Y	Y	N	Y	Y	Y
44 *Calvert*	Y	Y	Y	Y	Y	Y
45 *Bono*	Y	Y	Y	Y	Y	Y
46 *Rohrabacher*	Y	Y	Y	Y	Y	N
47 Sanchez, Loretta	N	Y	N	Y	Y	Y
48 *Cox*	Y	Y	Y	Y	Y	Y
49 *Issa*	Y	Y	Y	Y	Y	N
50 *Cunningham*	Y	Y	Y	Y	Y	P
51 Filner	N	Y	N	Y	N	Y
52 *Hunter*	Y	Y	Y	Y	Y	Y
53 Davis	Y	Y	Y	Y	Y	Y
COLORADO						
1 DeGette	Y	Y	Y	Y	Y	N
2 Udall	N	Y	N	Y	Y	Y
3 *McInnis*	Y	Y	Y	Y	Y	Y
4 *Musgrave*	Y	Y	Y	Y	Y	Y
5 *Hefley*	Y	Y	Y	Y	Y	Y
6 *Tancredo*	Y	Y	Y	Y	Y	Y
7 *Beauprez*	Y	Y	Y	Y	Y	Y
CONNECTICUT						
1 Larson	N	Y	N	Y	Y	Y
2 *Simmons*	Y	Y	Y	Y	Y	Y
3 DeLauro	Y	Y	N	Y	Y	Y
4 *Shays*	Y	Y	Y	Y	Y	Y
5 *Johnson*	Y	Y	Y	Y	Y	Y
DELAWARE						
AL *Castle*	Y	Y	Y	Y	Y	Y
FLORIDA						
1 *Miller, J.*	Y	Y	Y	Y	Y	Y
2 Boyd	Y	Y	Y	Y	Y	Y
3 Brown	N	Y	N	Y	Y	Y
4 *Crenshaw*	Y	Y	Y	Y	Y	Y
5 *Brown-Waite*	Y	Y	Y	Y	Y	Y
6 *Stearns*	Y	Y	Y	Y	Y	Y
7 *Mica*	Y	Y	Y	Y	Y	Y
8 *Keller*	Y	Y	Y	Y	Y	Y
9 *Bilirakis*	Y	Y	Y	Y	Y	Y
10 *Young*	Y	Y	Y	Y	?	?
11 Davis	Y	Y	Y	Y	Y	Y
12 *Putnam*	Y	Y	Y	Y	Y	Y
13 *Harris*	Y	Y	Y	Y	Y	Y
14 *Goss*	Y	Y	Y	Y	Y	Y
15 *Weldon*	Y	Y	Y	Y	Y	Y
16 *Foley*	Y	Y	Y	Y	Y	Y
17 Meek	N	Y	Y	Y	Y	Y
18 *Ros-Lehtinen*	Y	N	?	Y	Y	Y
19 Wexler	Y	Y	Y	Y	Y	Y
20 Deutsch	Y	Y	N	?	?	?
21 *Diaz-Balart, L.*	Y	N	Y	Y	Y	Y
22 *Shaw*	Y	Y	Y	Y	Y	Y
23 Hastings	N	Y	N	Y	Y	Y
24 *Feeney*	Y	Y	Y	Y	Y	Y
25 *Diaz-Balart, M.*	Y	N	Y	Y	Y	Y
GEORGIA						
1 *Kingston*	Y	Y	Y	Y	Y	Y
2 Bishop	N	Y	Y	Y	Y	Y
3 Marshall	Y	Y	N	Y	Y	Y
4 Majette	?	?	?	?	?	?
5 Lewis	N	Y	Y	Y	Y	N
6 *Isakson*	?	?	?	?	?	?
7 *Linder*	Y	Y	Y	Y	Y	Y
8 *Collins*	Y	Y	?	?	?	?
9 *Norwood*	Y	Y	Y	Y	Y	Y
10 *Deal*	Y	Y	Y	Y	Y	Y
11 *Gingrey*	Y	Y	Y	Y	Y	Y
12 *Burns*	Y	Y	Y	Y	Y	Y
13 Scott	Y	Y	Y	Y	Y	Y
HAWAII						
1 Abercrombie	Y	Y	N	Y	Y	N
2 Case	Y	Y	N	Y	Y	P
IDAHO						
1 *Otter*	Y	Y	N	Y	Y	Y
2 *Simpson*	Y	Y	N	Y	Y	Y
ILLINOIS						
1 Rush	N	Y	N	Y	Y	N
2 Jackson	N	Y	N	Y	Y	N
3 Lipinski	Y	Y	N	Y	Y	Y
4 Gutierrez	N	Y	N	Y	Y	Y
5 Emanuel	Y	Y	N	Y	Y	Y
6 *Hyde*	Y	Y	Y	Y	Y	Y

ND Northern Democrats   SD Southern Democrats

	373	374	375	376	377	378
7 Davis	Y	Y	N	Y	Y	N
8 ***Crane***	Y	Y	Y	Y	Y	Y
9 Schakowsky	N	Y	N	Y	Y	Y
10 ***Kirk***	Y	Y	Y	Y	Y	Y
11 ***Weller***	Y	Y	Y	Y	Y	Y
12 Costello	Y	Y	N	Y	Y	Y
13 ***Biggert***	Y	Y	Y	Y	Y	Y
14 ***Hastert***						
15 ***Johnson***	Y	Y	Y	Y	Y	Y
16 ***Manzullo***	Y	?	Y	Y	Y	Y
17 Evans	Y	Y	N	Y	Y	Y
18 ***LaHood***	Y	Y	Y	Y	Y	N
19 ***Shimkus***	Y	Y	Y	Y	Y	Y
INDIANA						
1 Visclosky	Y	Y	Y	Y	Y	Y
2 ***Chocola***	Y	Y	Y	Y	Y	Y
3 ***Souder***	Y	Y	Y	Y	Y	Y
4 ***Buyer***	Y	Y	Y	Y	Y	Y
5 ***Burton***	Y	Y	N	Y	Y	Y
6 ***Pence***	Y	Y	Y	Y	Y	Y
7 Carson	?	?	?	?	?	?
8 ***Hostettler***	Y	Y	N	Y	Y	Y
9 Hill	Y	Y	Y	Y	Y	Y
IOWA						
1 ***Nussle***	Y	Y	Y	Y	Y	Y
2 ***Leach***	Y	Y	Y	Y	Y	P
3 Boswell	Y	Y	Y	Y	Y	Y
4 ***Latham***	Y	Y	Y	Y	Y	Y
5 ***King***	Y	Y	Y	Y	Y	Y
KANSAS						
1 ***Moran***	Y	Y	N	Y	Y	Y
2 ***Ryun***	Y	Y	Y	Y	Y	Y
3 Moore	Y	Y	Y	Y	Y	Y
4 ***Tiahrt***	Y	Y	Y	Y	Y	Y
KENTUCKY						
1 ***Whitfield***	Y	Y	Y	Y	Y	Y
2 ***Lewis***	Y	Y	Y	Y	Y	Y
3 ***Northup***	Y	Y	Y	Y	Y	Y
4 Lucas	Y	Y	Y	Y	Y	Y
5 ***Rogers***	Y	Y	Y	Y	Y	Y
6 Chandler	Y	Y	Y	Y	Y	Y
LOUISIANA						
1 ***Vitter***	Y	Y	Y	Y	Y	Y
2 Jefferson	N	Y	Y	Y	Y	P
3 ***Tauzin***	Y	Y	Y	Y	Y	Y
4 ***McCrery***	Y	Y	Y	Y	Y	Y
5 Alexander	Y	Y	N	Y	Y	Y
6 ***Baker***	Y	Y	Y	Y	Y	Y
7 John	Y	Y	Y	Y	Y	Y
MAINE						
1 Allen	Y	Y	Y	Y	Y	Y
2 Michaud	Y	Y	N	Y	Y	Y
MARYLAND						
1 ***Gilchrest***	Y	Y	Y	Y	Y	Y
2 Ruppersberger	Y	Y	Y	Y	Y	Y
3 Cardin	Y	Y	Y	?	Y	Y
4 Wynn	N	Y	Y	Y	Y	N
5 Hoyer	N	Y	Y	Y	Y	Y
6 ***Bartlett***	Y	Y	Y	Y	Y	Y
7 Cummings	N	Y	N	Y	Y	Y
8 Van Hollen	Y	Y	Y	Y	Y	Y
MASSACHUSETTS						
1 Olver	N	Y	Y	Y	Y	Y
2 Neal	N	?	Y	Y	Y	Y
3 McGovern	N	Y	Y	Y	Y	Y
4 Frank	N	Y	N	?	Y	Y
5 Meehan	Y	Y	Y	Y	Y	Y
6 Tierney	N	Y	N	Y	Y	Y
7 Markey	N	Y	N	Y	Y	Y
8 Capuano	N	Y	Y	Y	Y	P
9 Lynch	N	Y	Y	Y	Y	Y
10 Delahunt	Y	Y	N	Y	Y	?
MICHIGAN						
1 Stupak	N	Y	N	Y	Y	Y
2 ***Hoekstra***	Y	Y	N	Y	Y	Y
3 ***Ehlers***	Y	Y	Y	Y	Y	Y
4 ***Camp***	Y	Y	Y	Y	Y	Y
5 Kildee	Y	Y	N	Y	Y	Y
6 ***Upton***	Y	Y	Y	Y	Y	Y
7 ***Smith***	Y	Y	N	Y	Y	Y
8 ***Rogers***	Y	Y	Y	Y	Y	Y
9 ***Knollenberg***	Y	Y	Y	Y	Y	Y
10 ***Miller***	Y	Y	Y	Y	Y	Y
11 ***McCotter***	Y	Y	Y	Y	Y	Y
12 Levin	Y	Y	Y	Y	Y	Y

	373	374	375	376	377	378
13 Kilpatrick	N	Y	Y	Y	?	N
14 Conyers	N	Y	N	?	?	N
15 Dingell	Y	Y	Y	?	Y	N
MINNESOTA						
1 ***Gutknecht***	Y	Y	N	Y	Y	Y
2 ***Kline***	Y	Y	Y	Y	Y	Y
3 ***Ramstad***	Y	Y	Y	Y	Y	Y
4 McCollum	N	Y	N	Y	Y	Y
5 Sabo	Y	Y	N	Y	Y	P
6 ***Kennedy***	Y	Y	Y	Y	Y	Y
7 Peterson	Y	Y	N	Y	Y	Y
8 Oberstar	N	Y	N	Y	Y	Y
MISSISSIPPI						
1 ***Wicker***	Y	Y	Y	Y	Y	Y
2 Thompson	N	Y	N	Y	?	?
3 ***Pickering***	Y	Y	Y	Y	Y	Y
4 Taylor	N	Y	N	Y	Y	Y
MISSOURI						
1 Clay	N	Y	Y	Y	Y	N
2 ***Akin***	Y	Y	Y	Y	Y	Y
3 Gephardt	Y	Y	Y	?	Y	Y
4 Skelton	Y	Y	Y	Y	Y	Y
5 McCarthy	N	Y	Y	Y	Y	Y
6 ***Graves***	Y	Y	Y	Y	Y	Y
7 ***Blunt***	Y	Y	Y	Y	Y	Y
8 ***Emerson***	Y	Y	N	Y	Y	Y
9 ***Hulshof***	Y	Y	Y	Y	Y	Y
MONTANA						
AL ***Rehberg***	Y	Y	N	Y	Y	Y
NEBRASKA						
1 ***Bereuter***	Y	Y	Y	Y	Y	P
2 ***Terry***	Y	Y	Y	Y	Y	Y
3 ***Osborne***	Y	Y	N	Y	Y	Y
NEVADA						
1 Berkley	Y	Y	Y	Y	Y	Y
2 ***Gibbons***	Y	Y	Y	Y	Y	Y
3 ***Porter***	Y	Y	Y	Y	Y	Y
NEW HAMPSHIRE						
1 ***Bradley***	Y	Y	Y	Y	Y	Y
2 ***Bass***	Y	Y	N	Y	Y	Y
NEW JERSEY						
1 Andrews	N	Y	N	Y	Y	Y
2 ***LoBiondo***	Y	Y	Y	Y	Y	Y
3 ***Saxton***	Y	Y	Y	Y	Y	Y
4 ***Smith***	Y	Y	Y	Y	Y	Y
5 ***Garrett***	Y	Y	Y	Y	Y	Y
6 Pallone	N	Y	N	Y	Y	Y
7 ***Ferguson***	Y	Y	Y	Y	Y	Y
8 Pascrell	N	Y	N	Y	Y	Y
9 Rothman	N	Y	N	Y	Y	Y
10 Payne	N	Y	N	Y	Y	N
11 ***Frelinghuysen***	Y	Y	Y	Y	Y	Y
12 Holt	Y	Y	Y	Y	Y	P
13 Menendez	Y	Y	Y	Y	Y	Y
NEW MEXICO						
1 ***Wilson***	Y	Y	Y	Y	Y	Y
2 ***Pearce***	Y	Y	N	Y	Y	Y
3 Udall	N	Y	N	Y	Y	Y
NEW YORK						
1 Bishop	N	Y	Y	Y	Y	Y
2 Israel	Y	Y	Y	Y	Y	Y
3 ***King***	Y	Y	Y	Y	Y	Y
4 McCarthy	Y	Y	Y	Y	Y	Y
5 Ackerman	Y	Y	Y	Y	Y	Y
6 Meeks	N	Y	Y	Y	Y	Y
7 Crowley	Y	Y	Y	Y	Y	Y
8 Nadler	Y	Y	N	Y	Y	Y
9 Weiner	Y	Y	Y	Y	Y	Y
10 Towns	N	Y	Y	Y	Y	Y
11 Owens	N	Y	N	Y	Y	Y
12 Velázquez	N	Y	N	Y	Y	P
13 ***Fossella***	Y	Y	Y	Y	Y	Y
14 Maloney	Y	Y	Y	Y	Y	Y
15 Rangel	?	?	?	?	Y	Y
16 Serrano	Y	Y	N	Y	Y	Y
17 Engel	Y	Y	Y	Y	Y	Y
18 Lowey	Y	Y	Y	Y	Y	Y
19 ***Kelly***	Y	Y	Y	Y	Y	Y
20 ***Sweeney***	Y	Y	Y	Y	Y	Y
21 McNulty	Y	Y	N	Y	Y	Y
22 Hinchey	N	Y	N	Y	Y	N
23 ***McHugh***	Y	Y	Y	Y	Y	Y
24 ***Boehlert***	Y	Y	Y	Y	Y	Y
25 ***Walsh***	Y	Y	Y	Y	Y	Y

	373	374	375	376	377	378
26 ***Reynolds***	Y	Y	Y	Y	Y	Y
27 ***Quinn***	Y	Y	N	Y	Y	Y
28 Slaughter	Y	Y	N	Y	Y	Y
29 ***Houghton***	Y	Y	Y	?	Y	Y
NORTH CAROLINA						
1 Vacant						
2 Etheridge	Y	Y	Y	Y	Y	Y
3 ***Jones***	N	Y	N	Y	Y	Y
4 Price	Y	Y	Y	Y	Y	N
5 ***Burr***	Y	Y	Y	Y	Y	Y
6 ***Coble***	Y	Y	Y	Y	Y	Y
7 McIntyre	Y	Y	N	Y	Y	Y
8 ***Hayes***	N	Y	N	Y	Y	Y
9 ***Myrick***	Y	Y	Y	Y	Y	Y
10 ***Ballenger***	Y	Y	Y	Y	Y	Y
11 ***Taylor***	Y	Y	N	Y	Y	Y
12 Watt	N	Y	Y	Y	Y	N
13 Miller	Y	Y	Y	Y	Y	Y
NORTH DAKOTA						
AL Pomeroy	Y	Y	N	Y	Y	?
OHIO						
1 ***Chabot***	Y	Y	Y	Y	Y	Y
2 ***Portman***	Y	Y	Y	Y	Y	Y
3 ***Turner***	Y	Y	Y	Y	Y	Y
4 ***Oxley***	Y	Y	Y	Y	Y	Y
5 ***Gillmor***	Y	Y	Y	Y	Y	Y
6 Strickland	Y	Y	N	Y	Y	Y
7 ***Hobson***	Y	Y	Y	Y	Y	Y
8 ***Boehner***	Y	Y	Y	Y	Y	Y
9 Kaptur	Y	Y	N	Y	Y	N
10 Kucinich	N	Y	N	Y	Y	N
11 Jones	N	Y	Y	Y	Y	Y
12 ***Tiberi***	Y	Y	Y	Y	Y	Y
13 Brown	Y	Y	N	Y	Y	Y
14 ***LaTourette***	Y	Y	Y	Y	Y	Y
15 ***Pryce***	Y	Y	Y	Y	Y	Y
16 ***Regula***	Y	Y	Y	Y	Y	Y
17 Ryan	N	Y	N	Y	Y	N
18 ***Ney***	Y	Y	Y	Y	Y	Y
OKLAHOMA						
1 ***Sullivan***	Y	Y	Y	Y	Y	Y
2 Carson	Y	?	N	Y	Y	Y
3 ***Lucas***	Y	Y	N	Y	Y	Y
4 ***Cole***	Y	Y	Y	Y	Y	Y
5 ***Istook***	?	?	?	Y	Y	Y
OREGON						
1 Wu	Y	Y	Y	Y	Y	Y
2 ***Walden***	Y	Y	Y	Y	Y	Y
3 Blumenauer	N	Y	Y	Y	Y	P
4 DeFazio	Y	Y	N	Y	Y	P
5 Hooley	Y	Y	Y	Y	Y	Y
PENNSYLVANIA						
1 Brady	N	Y	N	Y	Y	Y
2 Fattah	N	Y	N	Y	Y	N
3 ***English***	Y	Y	Y	Y	Y	Y
4 ***Hart***	Y	Y	Y	Y	Y	Y
5 ***Peterson***	Y	Y	Y	Y	Y	Y
6 ***Gerlach***	Y	Y	Y	Y	Y	Y
7 ***Weldon***	Y	Y	Y	Y	Y	Y
8 ***Greenwood***	Y	Y	Y	Y	?	?
9 ***Shuster, Bill***	Y	Y	Y	Y	Y	Y
10 ***Sherwood***	Y	Y	Y	Y	Y	Y
11 Kanjorski	Y	Y	N	Y	Y	N
12 Murtha	Y	Y	Y	Y	Y	Y
13 Hoeffel	?	?	?	?	?	?
14 Doyle	N	Y	Y	Y	Y	Y
15 ***Toomey***	Y	Y	Y	Y	Y	Y
16 ***Pitts***	Y	Y	Y	Y	Y	Y
17 Holden	Y	Y	Y	Y	+	+
18 ***Murphy***	Y	Y	Y	Y	Y	Y
19 ***Platts***	Y	Y	Y	Y	Y	Y
RHODE ISLAND						
1 Kennedy	N	Y	Y	Y	Y	Y
2 Langevin	N	Y	Y	Y	Y	Y
SOUTH CAROLINA						
1 ***Brown***	Y	Y	Y	Y	Y	Y
2 ***Wilson***	Y	Y	Y	Y	Y	Y
3 ***Barrett***	Y	Y	Y	Y	Y	Y
4 ***DeMint***	Y	Y	Y	Y	Y	Y
5 Spratt	Y	?	N	Y	Y	Y
6 Clyburn	N	Y	N	Y	Y	Y
SOUTH DAKOTA						
AL Herseth	Y	Y	N	Y	Y	Y

	373	374	375	376	377	378
TENNESSEE						
1 ***Jenkins***	Y	Y	Y	Y	Y	Y
2 ***Duncan***	Y	Y	Y	Y	Y	Y
3 ***Wamp***	Y	Y	Y	Y	Y	Y
4 Davis	Y	Y	Y	Y	Y	Y
5 Cooper	Y	Y	Y	Y	Y	Y
6 Gordon	Y	Y	Y	Y	Y	Y
7 ***Blackburn***	Y	Y	Y	Y	Y	Y
8 Tanner	Y	Y	Y	Y	Y	Y
9 Ford	N	Y	Y	?	Y	Y
TEXAS						
1 Sandlin	Y	Y	Y	Y	Y	Y
2 Turner	N	Y	Y	Y	Y	Y
3 ***Johnson, Sam***	Y	Y	Y	Y	Y	Y
4 ***Hall***	Y	Y	Y	Y	Y	Y
5 ***Hensarling***	Y	Y	Y	Y	Y	Y
6 ***Barton***	Y	Y	Y	Y	Y	Y
7 ***Culberson***	Y	Y	Y	Y	Y	Y
8 ***Brady***	Y	Y	Y	Y	Y	Y
9 Lampson	Y	Y	Y	Y	Y	Y
10 Doggett	N	Y	Y	Y	Y	P
11 Edwards	Y	Y	Y	Y	Y	Y
12 ***Granger***	Y	Y	Y	Y	Y	Y
13 ***Thornberry***	Y	Y	Y	Y	Y	Y
14 ***Paul***	N	Y	N	N	Y	N
15 Hinojosa	Y	Y	Y	Y	Y	Y
16 Reyes	N	Y	Y	Y	?	Y
17 Stenholm	Y	Y	Y	Y	Y	Y
18 Jackson-Lee	N	Y	Y	Y	Y	Y
19 ***Neugebauer***	Y	Y	Y	Y	Y	Y
20 Gonzalez	Y	Y	Y	Y	Y	Y
21 ***Smith***	Y	Y	Y	Y	Y	Y
22 ***DeLay***	Y	Y	Y	Y	Y	Y
23 ***Bonilla***	Y	Y	Y	Y	Y	Y
24 Frost	Y	Y	Y	Y	Y	Y
25 Bell	N	Y	Y	Y	Y	Y
26 ***Burgess***	Y	Y	Y	Y	Y	Y
27 Ortiz	Y	Y	Y	Y	Y	Y
28 Rodriguez	Y	Y	Y	Y	Y	Y
29 Green	Y	Y	Y	Y	Y	Y
30 Johnson, E.B.	Y	Y	Y	Y	Y	Y
31 ***Carter***	Y	Y	Y	Y	Y	Y
32 ***Sessions***	Y	Y	Y	Y	Y	Y
UTAH						
1 ***Bishop***	Y	Y	N	Y	Y	Y
2 Matheson	Y	Y	Y	Y	Y	Y
3 ***Cannon***	Y	Y	Y	Y	Y	Y
VERMONT						
AL *Sanders*	N	Y	N	Y	Y	N
VIRGINIA						
1 ***Davis, Jo Ann***	Y	Y	Y	Y	Y	Y
2 ***Schrock***	Y	Y	Y	Y	Y	Y
3 Scott	Y	Y	N	Y	Y	Y
4 ***Forbes***	Y	Y	Y	Y	Y	Y
5 ***Goode***	Y	?	N	Y	Y	Y
6 ***Goodlatte***	Y	Y	Y	Y	Y	Y
7 ***Cantor***	Y	Y	Y	Y	Y	Y
8 Moran	Y	Y	Y	Y	Y	N
9 Boucher	Y	Y	N	Y	Y	Y
10 ***Wolf***	Y	Y	Y	Y	Y	Y
11 ***Davis, T.***	Y	Y	Y	Y	Y	Y
WASHINGTON						
1 Inslee	N	Y	Y	Y	Y	N
2 Larsen	Y	Y	Y	Y	Y	Y
3 Baird	Y	Y	Y	Y	Y	N
4 ***Hastings***	Y	Y	Y	Y	Y	Y
5 ***Nethercutt***	Y	Y	Y	Y	Y	Y
6 Dicks	Y	Y	Y	Y	Y	Y
7 McDermott	N	Y	Y	Y	Y	N
8 ***Dunn***	Y	Y	Y	Y	Y	Y
9 Smith	Y	Y	Y	Y	Y	Y
WEST VIRGINIA						
1 Mollohan	Y	Y	N	Y	Y	N
2 ***Capito***	Y	Y	Y	Y	Y	Y
3 Rahall	Y	Y	N	Y	Y	N
WISCONSIN						
1 ***Ryan***	Y	Y	Y	Y	Y	Y
2 Baldwin	N	Y	N	Y	Y	Y
3 Kind	?	?	?	?	Y	Y
4 Kleczka	Y	Y	N	?	Y	N
5 ***Sensenbrenner***	Y	Y	N	Y	Y	Y
6 ***Petri***	Y	Y	Y	Y	Y	P
7 Obey	N	Y	N	Y	Y	N
8 ***Green***	Y	Y	N	Y	Y	Y
WYOMING						
AL ***Cubin***	Y	Y	Y	Y	Y	Y

Southern states - Ala., Ark., Fla., Ga., Ky., La., Miss., N.C., Okla., S.C., Tenn., Texas, Va.

Key

Y	Voted for (yea).
#	Paired for.
+	Announced for.
N	Voted against (nay).
X	Paired against.
–	Announced against.
P	Voted "present."
C	Voted "present" to avoid possible conflict of interest.
?	Did not vote or otherwise make a position known.

Democrats **Republicans**
Independents

379. H Con Res 462. Reaffirming U.S.-Taiwan Relations/Adoption. Smith, R-N.J., motion to suspend the rules and adopt the concurrent resolution that would reaffirm Congress' commitment to the Taiwan Relations Act and call on the president and Congress to determine whether China's military modernization and weapons procurement program requires that the United States make additional weapons available to Taiwan. Motion agreed to 400-18: R 220-2; D 179-16 (ND 129-14, SD 50-2); I 1-0. A two-thirds majority of those present and voting (279 in this case) is required for adoption under suspension of the rules. July 15, 2004.

380. HR 4818. Fiscal 2005 Foreign Operations Appropriations/World Bank Funding. Sherman, D-Calif., amendment that would cut $359 million in funding for the World Bank while increasing funding for the child survival account by $290 million. Rejected 111-312: R 59-164; D 52-147 (ND 41-105, SD 11-42); I 0-1. July 15, 2004.

381. HR 4818. Fiscal 2005 Foreign Operations Appropriations/Aid to Egypt. Lantos, D-Calif., amendment that would increase funding for economic aid to Egypt by $570 million, to be offset by a reduction in military aid to Egypt. Rejected 131-287: R 63-156; D 68-130 (ND 56-90, SD 12-40); I 0-1. A "nay" was a vote in support of the president's position. July 15, 2004.

382. HR 4818. Fiscal 2005 Foreign Operations Appropriations/Millennium Challenge Account. Kennedy, R-Minn., amendment that would add $250 million for the Millennium Challenge Corporation and $90 million for the president's Global HIV/AIDS initiative. It would cut $425 million from the U.S. contribution to the World Bank's International Development Association. Rejected 133-288: R 90-132; D 42-156 (ND 35-111, SD 7-45); I 1-0. July 15, 2004.

383. HR 4818. Fiscal 2005 Foreign Operations Appropriations/Millennium Challenge Account. Paul, R-Texas, amendment that would eliminate funding for the Millennium Challenge Account. Rejected 41-379: R 37-184; D 4-194 (ND 3-143, SD 1-51); I 0-1. July 15, 2004.

384. Procedural Motion/Appeal Ruling of the Chair. Buyer, R-Ind., motion to table (kill) the Brown, D-Fla., appeal of the ruling of the chair that certain words spoken by Brown, that were taken down and read at the Clerk's desk, violate rules or precedents of the House. Motion agreed to 219-187: R 219-0; D 0-186 (ND 0-139, SD 0-47); I 0-1. July 15, 2004.

	379	380	381	382	383	384
ALABAMA						
1 *Bonner*	Y	N	N	N	N	Y
2 *Everett*	Y	N	Y	N	Y	Y
3 *Rogers*	Y	N	N	N	N	Y
4 *Aderholt*	Y	N	N	N	N	Y
5 Cramer	Y	N	N	N	N	N
6 *Bachus*	Y	Y	Y	Y	N	Y
7 Davis	Y	N	N	N	N	N
ALASKA						
AL *Young*	Y	N	N	N	N	Y
ARIZONA						
1 *Renzi*	Y	N	Y	N	N	Y
2 *Franks*	Y	Y	N	Y	Y	Y
3 *Shadegg*	Y	N	N	Y	N	Y
4 Pastor	Y	N	N	N	N	N
5 *Hayworth*	Y	N	N	Y	N	Y
6 *Flake*	Y	Y	Y	Y	Y	Y
7 Grijalva	N	N	N	N	N	N
8 *Kolbe*	Y	N	N	N	N	Y
ARKANSAS						
1 Berry	Y	N	N	Y	N	N
2 Snyder	Y	N	N	Y	N	N
3 *Boozman*	Y	N	N	N	N	Y
4 Ross	Y	N	Y	N	N	N
CALIFORNIA						
1 Thompson	Y	N	N	N	N	N
2 *Herger*	Y	N	N	N	N	Y
3 *Ose*	Y	N	N	N	N	Y
4 *Doolittle*	Y	N	N	N	N	Y
5 Matsui	Y	N	N	N	N	N
6 Woolsey	Y	Y	Y	Y	N	N
7 Miller, George	N	N	N	N	N	N
8 Pelosi	N	N	N	N	N	N
9 Lee	N	N	N	N	N	N
10 Tauscher	Y	N	N	N	N	N
11 *Pombo*	Y	N	N	Y	Y	Y
12 Lantos	Y	Y	Y	N	?	N
13 Stark	N	N	N	N	N	N
14 Eshoo	Y	N	N	N	N	N
15 Honda	Y	N	Y	N	N	N
16 Lofgren	N	Y	N	N	N	N
17 Farr	Y	N	Y	N	N	N
18 Cardoza	Y	Y	Y	Y	N	N
19 *Radanovich*	Y	N	N	N	N	Y
20 Dooley	Y	N	N	N	N	?
21 *Nunes*	Y	N	N	N	N	Y
22 *Thomas*	Y	N	N	N	N	Y
23 Capps	Y	N	N	N	N	N
24 *Gallegly*	Y	N	Y	N	N	Y
25 *McKeon*	Y	N	N	N	N	Y
26 *Dreier*	Y	N	N	N	N	Y
27 Sherman	Y	Y	Y	Y	N	N
28 Berman	Y	N	N	N	N	N
29 Schiff	Y	N	N	N	N	N
30 Waxman	Y	Y	Y	N	N	?
31 Becerra	P	N	Y	Y	N	N
32 Solis	Y	N	N	N	N	N
33 Watson	Y	N	N	N	N	N
34 Roybal-Allard	Y	N	N	N	N	?
35 Waters	N	Y	Y	?	N	N
36 Harman	Y	N	N	N	N	N

	379	380	381	382	383	384
37 Millender-McD.	Y	N	N	N	N	N
38 Napolitano	Y	Y	Y	N	N	N
39 Sánchez, Linda	Y	Y	Y	N	N	N
40 *Royce*	Y	Y	Y	Y	Y	Y
41 *Lewis*	Y	N	N	N	N	Y
42 *Miller, Gary*	Y	N	N	N	Y	Y
43 Baca	Y	N	N	N	N	N
44 *Calvert*	Y	N	N	N	N	Y
45 *Bono*	Y	N	N	N	N	Y
46 *Rohrabacher*	Y	Y	N	Y	N	Y
47 Sanchez, Loretta	Y	N	N	N	N	N
48 *Cox*	Y	Y	N	Y	Y	Y
49 *Issa*	Y	N	N	N	N	Y
50 *Cunningham*	Y	N	N	N	N	Y
51 Filner	N	Y	Y	N	N	N
52 *Hunter*	Y	N	N	N	N	Y
53 Davis	Y	N	N	N	N	N
COLORADO						
1 DeGette	Y	N	N	N	N	N
2 Udall	Y	N	N	N	N	N
3 *McInnis*	Y	N	N	Y	Y	?
4 *Musgrave*	Y	N	Y	N	N	Y
5 *Hefley*	Y	Y	N	Y	N	Y
6 *Tancredo*	Y	N	N	Y	Y	Y
7 *Beauprez*	Y	N	Y	N	N	Y
CONNECTICUT						
1 Larson	Y	N	Y	N	N	N
2 *Simmons*	Y	N	Y	N	Y	N
3 DeLauro	Y	N	N	N	N	N
4 *Shays*	Y	N	N	N	N	Y
5 *Johnson*	Y	N	N	N	N	Y
DELAWARE						
AL *Castle*	Y	N	N	N	N	Y
FLORIDA						
1 *Miller, J.*	Y	N	N	N	Y	Y
2 Boyd	Y	N	N	N	N	N
3 Brown	Y	N	N	N	N	N
4 *Crenshaw*	Y	N	N	N	N	Y
5 *Brown-Waite*	Y	N	N	N	N	Y
6 *Stearns*	Y	Y	Y	Y	N	Y
7 *Mica*	Y	N	N	Y	N	Y
8 *Keller*	Y	N	?	N	Y	Y
9 *Bilirakis*	Y	Y	N	Y	N	Y
10 *Young*	?	N	N	N	N	Y
11 Davis	Y	N	N	N	N	N
12 *Putnam*	Y	N	N	N	N	Y
13 *Harris*	Y	N	N	Y	N	Y
14 *Goss*	Y	N	N	N	N	Y
15 *Weldon*	Y	N	Y	N	N	Y
16 *Foley*	Y	N	N	N	N	Y
17 Meek	Y	N	N	N	N	N
18 *Ros-Lehtinen*	Y	Y	Y	N	Y	Y
19 Wexler	Y	Y	N	N	N	N
20 Deutsch	?	?	?	?	?	?
21 *Diaz-Balart, L.*	Y	Y	N	N	N	Y
22 *Shaw*	Y	N	N	N	N	Y
23 Hastings	Y	Y	Y	N	N	N
24 *Feeney*	Y	Y	Y	Y	Y	Y
25 *Diaz-Balart, M.*	Y	Y	Y	N	N	Y
GEORGIA						
1 *Kingston*	Y	N	N	Y	Y	Y
2 Bishop	Y	N	N	N	N	N
3 Marshall	Y	N	N	N	N	N
4 Majette	?	?	?	?	?	?
5 Lewis	Y	N	N	N	N	N
6 *Isakson*	?	?	?	?	?	?
7 *Linder*	Y	N	N	N	N	Y
8 *Collins*	?	?	?	?	?	?
9 *Norwood*	Y	Y	Y	N	N	Y
10 *Deal*	Y	Y	Y	Y	N	Y
11 *Gingrey*	Y	Y	Y	N	N	Y
12 *Burns*	Y	N	Y	Y	N	Y
13 Scott	Y	N	N	N	N	N
HAWAII						
1 Abercrombie	N	N	Y	Y	N	N
2 Case	Y	N	N	N	N	N
IDAHO						
1 *Otter*	N	N	Y	N	Y	Y
2 *Simpson*	Y	N	Y	Y	N	Y
ILLINOIS						
1 Rush	Y	Y	N	Y	N	N
2 Jackson	Y	N	N	N	N	N
3 Lipinski	Y	N	N	N	N	N
4 Gutierrez	Y	N	Y	N	N	N
5 Emanuel	Y	N	Y	N	N	N
6 *Hyde*	Y	N	Y	N	N	Y

ND Northern Democrats   SD Southern Democrats

	379	380	381	382	383	384
7 Davis	Y	N	N	N	N	N
8 ***Crane***	Y	N	Y	Y	N	Y
9 Schakowsky	Y	N	N	N	N	N
10 ***Kirk***	Y	N	N	N	N	Y
11 ***Weller***	Y	N	Y	Y	N	Y
12 Costello	Y	Y	N	N	N	N
13 ***Biggert***	Y	N	N	N	N	Y
14 ***Hastert***						Y
15 ***Johnson***	Y	N	N	N	N	Y
16 ***Manzullo***	Y	Y	N	Y	N	Y
17 Evans	Y	N	Y	N	N	N
18 ***LaHood***	Y	N	N	N	N	Y
19 ***Shimkus***	Y	Y	N	Y	N	Y
INDIANA						
1 Visclosky	Y	N	N	N	N	N
2 ***Chocola***	Y	N	Y	Y	N	Y
3 ***Souder***	Y	Y	Y	Y	N	Y
4 ***Buyer***	Y	N	?	N	N	Y
5 ***Burton***	Y	Y	Y	Y	N	Y
6 ***Pence***	Y	Y	Y	Y	N	Y
7 Carson	?	?	?	?	?	?
8 ***Hostettler***	Y	Y	N	Y	Y	Y
9 Hill	Y	N	N	N	N	N
IOWA						
1 ***Nussle***	Y	N	N	N	N	Y
2 ***Leach***	Y	N	Y	Y	N	Y
3 Boswell	Y	Y	Y	N	N	N
4 ***Latham***	Y	N	N	N	N	Y
5 ***King***	Y	N	Y	N	Y	Y
KANSAS						
1 ***Moran***	Y	Y	Y	N	Y	Y
2 ***Ryun***	Y	N	N	N	N	Y
3 Moore	Y	N	N	Y	N	N
4 ***Tiahrt***	Y	N	Y	N	N	Y
KENTUCKY						
1 ***Whitfield***	Y	N	N	N	N	Y
2 ***Lewis***	Y	Y	N	N	N	Y
3 ***Northup***	Y	N	Y	Y	N	Y
4 Lucas	Y	N	N	N	N	N
5 ***Rogers***	Y	N	N	N	N	Y
6 Chandler	Y	Y	Y	Y	N	N
LOUISIANA						
1 ***Vitter***	Y	Y	N	N	N	Y
2 Jefferson	Y	N	N	N	N	N
3 ***Tauzin***	Y	Y	N	Y	N	Y
4 ***McCrery***	Y	N	N	N	N	Y
5 Alexander	Y	N	N	N	N	?
6 ***Baker***	Y	N	N	N	N	Y
7 John	Y	N	N	N	N	N
MAINE						
1 Allen	Y	N	N	N	N	N
2 Michaud	Y	N	N	N	N	N
MARYLAND						
1 ***Gilchrest***	Y	N	N	N	N	Y
2 Ruppersberger	Y	N	N	N	N	N
3 Cardin	Y	N	Y	N	N	N
4 Wynn	Y	N	N	N	N	N
5 Hoyer	Y	N	N	N	N	N
6 ***Bartlett***	Y	Y	N	Y	Y	Y
7 Cummings	Y	?	N	Y	N	N
8 Van Hollen	Y	N	N	N	N	N
MASSACHUSETTS						
1 Olver	Y	N	N	N	N	N
2 Neal	Y	N	Y	N	N	N
3 McGovern	Y	N	N	N	N	N
4 Frank	Y	N	Y	N	N	N
5 Meehan	Y	Y	Y	N	N	N
6 Tierney	Y	N	Y	N	N	N
7 Markey	Y	Y	Y	N	N	N
8 Capuano	Y	N	N	N	N	N
9 Lynch	Y	N	Y	N	N	N
10 Delahunt	Y	N	Y	Y	N	N
MICHIGAN						
1 Stupak	Y	N	Y	N	N	N
2 ***Hoekstra***	Y	N	N	N	N	Y
3 ***Ehlers***	Y	N	N	N	N	Y
4 ***Camp***	Y	N	Y	N	N	Y
5 Kildee	Y	N	Y	N	N	N
6 ***Upton***	Y	N	N	N	N	Y
7 ***Smith***	Y	Y	Y	N	Y	Y
8 ***Rogers***	Y	N	N	Y	N	Y
9 ***Knollenberg***	Y	N	N	N	N	Y
10 ***Miller***	Y	N	N	N	N	Y
11 ***McCotter***	Y	N	N	Y	N	Y
12 Levin	Y	N	N	N	N	N

	379	380	381	382	383	384
13 Kilpatrick	Y	N	N	N	N	N
14 Conyers	Y	N	?	N	N	N
15 Dingell	Y	N	N	N	N	N
MINNESOTA						
1 ***Gutknecht***	Y	Y	N	Y	N	Y
2 ***Kline***	Y	N	N	Y	N	Y
3 ***Ramstad***	Y	Y	Y	Y	N	Y
4 McCollum	N	N	Y	N	N	N
5 Sabo	P	N	N	N	N	N
6 ***Kennedy***	Y	Y	N	Y	N	Y
7 Peterson	Y	Y	Y	N	Y	?
8 Oberstar	N	Y	Y	N	N	N
MISSISSIPPI						
1 ***Wicker***	Y	N	N	N	N	Y
2 Thompson	?	N	N	N	N	N
3 ***Pickering***	Y	N	Y	Y	N	Y
4 Taylor	Y	Y	N	N	Y	N
MISSOURI						
1 Clay	Y	N	N	Y	N	N
2 ***Akin***	Y	N	N	Y	N	Y
3 Gephardt	Y	N	N	N	N	?
4 Skelton	Y	N	N	N	N	N
5 McCarthy	Y	N	Y	N	N	–
6 ***Graves***	Y	Y	N	N	Y	Y
7 ***Blunt***	Y	N	N	N	N	Y
8 ***Emerson***	Y	N	N	Y	N	Y
9 ***Hulshof***	Y	N	N	Y	N	Y
MONTANA						
AL ***Rehberg***	Y	N	N	N	N	Y
NEBRASKA						
1 ***Bereuter***	Y	N	N	N	N	Y
2 ***Terry***	Y	N	N	Y	N	Y
3 ***Osborne***	Y	N	N	N	N	Y
NEVADA						
1 Berkley	Y	Y	Y	Y	N	N
2 ***Gibbons***	Y	N	N	Y	Y	Y
3 ***Porter***	Y	Y	Y	Y	N	Y
NEW HAMPSHIRE						
1 ***Bradley***	Y	N	N	Y	N	Y
2 ***Bass***	Y	Y	N	Y	N	Y
NEW JERSEY						
1 Andrews	Y	Y	N	Y	N	N
2 ***LoBiondo***	Y	Y	Y	Y	N	Y
3 ***Saxton***	Y	N	Y	N	N	Y
4 ***Smith***	Y	Y	Y	N	N	Y
5 ***Garrett***	Y	N	N	Y	Y	Y
6 Pallone	Y	Y	Y	Y	N	N
7 ***Ferguson***	Y	Y	Y	Y	N	Y
8 Pascrell	Y	N	N	Y	N	N
9 Rothman	Y	Y	N	Y	N	N
10 Payne	Y	Y	Y	N	N	N
11 ***Frelinghuysen***	Y	N	N	N	N	Y
12 Holt	Y	N	N	N	N	N
13 Menendez	Y	N	N	N	N	N
NEW MEXICO						
1 ***Wilson***	Y	N	N	N	N	Y
2 ***Pearce***	Y	N	N	N	N	Y
3 Udall	Y	N	Y	Y	N	N
NEW YORK						
1 Bishop	Y	Y	Y	Y	N	N
2 Israel	P	Y	Y	Y	N	N
3 ***King***	Y	Y	Y	Y	N	Y
4 McCarthy	Y	N	Y	Y	N	N
5 Ackerman	Y	Y	Y	Y	N	N
6 Meeks	Y	N	N	N	N	?
7 Crowley	Y	Y	Y	N	N	N
8 Nadler	Y	Y	Y	Y	N	N
9 Weiner	Y	Y	Y	Y	N	N
10 Towns	Y	N	Y	N	N	N
11 Owens	Y	Y	N	N	N	N
12 Velázquez	Y	N	N	N	N	N
13 ***Fossella***	Y	Y	Y	Y	N	Y
14 Maloney	Y	N	N	N	N	N
15 Rangel	Y	N	N	N	N	N
16 Serrano	Y	N	N	N	N	N
17 Engel	Y	Y	Y	Y	N	N
18 Lowey	Y	N	N	N	N	N
19 ***Kelly***	Y	N	N	N	N	Y
20 ***Sweeney***	Y	Y	Y	N	N	Y
21 McNulty	Y	Y	Y	Y	N	N
22 Hinchey	Y	N	N	N	N	N
23 ***McHugh***	Y	N	N	N	N	Y
24 ***Boehlert***	Y	N	N	N	N	Y
25 ***Walsh***	Y	N	N	N	N	Y

	379	380	381	382	383	384
26 ***Reynolds***	Y	N	Y	N	N	Y
27 ***Quinn***	Y	?	?	?	?	?
28 Slaughter	Y	N	N	N	N	N
29 ***Houghton***	Y	N	N	N	N	?
NORTH CAROLINA						
1 Vacant						
2 Etheridge	Y	N	N	N	N	N
3 ***Jones***	?	Y	?	N	Y	Y
4 Price	Y	N	N	N	N	N
5 ***Burr***	Y	N	Y	Y	N	Y
6 ***Coble***	Y	Y	Y	Y	Y	Y
7 McIntyre	Y	Y	N	Y	N	N
8 ***Hayes***	Y	Y	Y	N	Y	?
9 ***Myrick***	Y	N	N	Y	N	Y
10 ***Ballenger***	Y	N	N	N	N	Y
11 ***Taylor***	Y	N	N	N	N	Y
12 Watt	P	N	N	Y	N	N
13 Miller	Y	N	N	N	N	N
NORTH DAKOTA						
AL Pomeroy	Y	N	N	N	N	N
OHIO						
1 ***Chabot***	Y	Y	Y	Y	Y	Y
2 ***Portman***	Y	N	N	N	N	Y
3 ***Turner***	Y	N	N	N	N	Y
4 ***Oxley***	Y	N	N	N	N	Y
5 ***Gillmor***	Y	N	N	N	N	Y
6 Strickland	Y	Y	N	Y	N	N
7 ***Hobson***	Y	N	N	N	N	Y
8 ***Boehner***	Y	N	N	Y	N	Y
9 Kaptur	Y	N	N	N	N	N
10 Kucinich	N	Y	N	Y	Y	N
11 Jones	Y	N	N	N	N	N
12 ***Tiberi***	Y	N	Y	N	N	Y
13 Brown	Y	Y	Y	N	N	?
14 ***LaTourette***	Y	N	N	Y	N	Y
15 ***Pryce***	Y	N	Y	N	N	Y
16 ***Regula***	Y	N	N	N	N	Y
17 Ryan	Y	Y	N	Y	N	N
18 ***Ney***	Y	N	N	N	N	Y
OKLAHOMA						
1 ***Sullivan***	Y	N	Y	Y	N	Y
2 Carson	Y	N	N	N	N	N
3 ***Lucas***	Y	N	N	N	N	Y
4 ***Cole***	Y	N	N	N	N	Y
5 ***Istook***	Y	N	N	N	?	Y
OREGON						
1 Wu	Y	Y	Y	Y	N	N
2 ***Walden***	Y	N	N	Y	N	Y
3 Blumenauer	Y	N	Y	N	N	N
4 DeFazio	Y	Y	Y	Y	N	N
5 Hooley	Y	Y	Y	N	N	N
PENNSYLVANIA						
1 Brady	Y	N	N	N	N	N
2 Fattah	Y	N	N	N	N	N
3 ***English***	Y	Y	N	Y	N	Y
4 ***Hart***	Y	N	N	Y	N	Y
5 ***Peterson***	Y	N	?	?	?	Y
6 ***Gerlach***	Y	N	N	N	N	Y
7 ***Weldon***	Y	N	N	N	N	Y
8 ***Greenwood***	?	?	?	?	?	?
9 ***Shuster, Bill***	Y	N	Y	Y	Y	Y
10 ***Sherwood***	Y	N	N	N	N	Y
11 Kanjorski	Y	N	N	N	N	N
12 Murtha	Y	N	N	N	N	N
13 Hoeffel	?	N	Y	N	N	N
14 Doyle	Y	N	N	N	N	N
15 ***Toomey***	Y	Y	N	Y	Y	Y
16 ***Pitts***	Y	Y	N	Y	N	Y
17 Holden	+	–	–	–	–	N
18 ***Murphy***	Y	N	N	N	N	Y
19 ***Platts***	Y	Y	N	Y	N	Y
RHODE ISLAND						
1 Kennedy	Y	N	Y	N	N	N
2 Langevin	Y	N	Y	N	N	N
SOUTH CAROLINA						
1 ***Brown***	Y	N	N	N	N	Y
2 ***Wilson***	Y	N	N	N	N	Y
3 ***Barrett***	Y	Y	Y	N	N	Y
4 ***DeMint***	Y	Y	N	Y	N	?
5 Spratt	Y	N	N	N	N	N
6 Clyburn	Y	Y	N	N	N	N
SOUTH DAKOTA						
AL Herseth	Y	N	N	N	N	N

	379	380	381	382	383	384
TENNESSEE						
1 ***Jenkins***	Y	N	N	N	N	Y
2 ***Duncan***	Y	Y	N	N	Y	Y
3 ***Wamp***	Y	Y	N	N	Y	Y
4 Davis	Y	N	Y	N	N	?
5 Cooper	Y	N	Y	N	N	N
6 Gordon	Y	Y	Y	N	N	N
7 ***Blackburn***	Y	N	N	N	N	Y
8 Tanner	Y	Y	N	N	N	N
9 Ford	Y	N	N	N	N	?
TEXAS						
1 Sandlin	Y	N	N	N	N	N
2 Turner	N	N	N	Y	N	N
3 ***Johnson, Sam***	Y	N	N	N	N	Y
4 ***Hall***	Y	Y	Y	N	N	Y
5 ***Hensarling***	Y	N	N	Y	N	Y
6 ***Barton***	Y	N	N	N	N	Y
7 ***Culberson***	Y	N	N	N	N	Y
8 ***Brady***	Y	N	N	N	N	Y
9 Lampson	Y	N	N	N	N	N
10 Doggett	Y	?	?	?	?	?
11 Edwards	Y	Y	Y	N	N	N
12 ***Granger***	Y	N	N	N	N	Y
13 ***Thornberry***	Y	N	N	Y	N	Y
14 ***Paul***	N	Y	N	Y	Y	?
15 Hinojosa	Y	N	N	N	N	N
16 Reyes	Y	N	N	N	N	N
17 Stenholm	Y	Y	?	?	?	?
18 Jackson-Lee	Y	N	Y	N	N	N
19 ***Neugebauer***	Y	N	N	Y	N	Y
20 Gonzalez	Y	N	N	N	N	N
21 ***Smith***	Y	N	N	N	N	Y
22 ***DeLay***	Y	N	Y	N	N	Y
23 ***Bonilla***	Y	N	N	N	N	Y
24 Frost	Y	N	Y	N	N	N
25 Bell	Y	N	N	N	N	?
26 ***Burgess***	Y	N	N	N	Y	Y
27 Ortiz	Y	N	N	N	N	N
28 Rodriguez	Y	Y	N	N	N	N
29 Green	Y	N	Y	Y	N	N
30 Johnson, E.B.	Y	N	N	N	N	N
31 ***Carter***	Y	N	N	N	N	Y
32 ***Sessions***	Y	N	N	Y	N	Y
UTAH						
1 ***Bishop***	Y	N	N	N	N	Y
2 Matheson	Y	Y	Y	N	N	N
3 ***Cannon***	Y	N	Y	N	N	Y
VERMONT						
AL *Sanders*	Y	N	N	Y	N	N
VIRGINIA						
1 ***Davis, Jo Ann***	Y	Y	N	N	Y	Y
2 ***Schrock***	Y	N	Y	Y	N	Y
3 Scott	Y	N	Y	N	N	N
4 ***Forbes***	Y	Y	N	N	N	Y
5 ***Goode***	Y	N	Y	Y	Y	Y
6 ***Goodlatte***	Y	Y	N	Y	Y	Y
7 ***Cantor***	Y	N	Y	Y	N	Y
8 Moran	N	N	N	N	N	N
9 Boucher	Y	N	N	N	N	?
10 ***Wolf***	Y	N	N	N	N	Y
11 ***Davis, T.***	Y	N	N	N	N	Y
WASHINGTON						
1 Inslee	Y	N	N	Y	N	N
2 Larsen	Y	N	N	N	N	N
3 Baird	Y	N	N	N	N	N
4 ***Hastings***	Y	N	N	N	N	Y
5 ***Nethercutt***	Y	N	N	Y	N	Y
6 Dicks	Y	N	N	N	N	N
7 McDermott	N	N	N	N	N	N
8 ***Dunn***	Y	N	N	N	N	Y
9 Smith	Y	N	N	N	N	N
WEST VIRGINIA						
1 Mollohan	Y	N	N	N	N	N
2 ***Capito***	Y	N	N	Y	N	Y
3 Rahall	N	Y	N	N	Y	N
WISCONSIN						
1 ***Ryan***	Y	N	Y	Y	N	Y
2 Baldwin	Y	N	N	N	N	N
3 Kind	Y	N	Y	Y	N	?
4 Kleczka	Y	N	N	N	N	N
5 ***Sensenbrenner***	Y	Y	Y	Y	N	Y
6 ***Petri***	Y	N	N	N	N	Y
7 Obey	N	N	N	N	N	N
8 ***Green***	Y	N	N	Y	N	Y
WYOMING						
AL ***Cubin***	Y	N	N	Y	N	Y

Southern states - Ala., Ark., Fla., Ga., Ky., La., Miss., N.C., Okla., S.C., Tenn., Texas, Va.

Key

Y	Voted for (yea).
#	Paired for.
+	Announced for.
N	Voted against (nay).
X	Paired against.
–	Announced against.
P	Voted "present."
C	Voted "present" to avoid possible conflict of interest.
?	Did not vote or otherwise make a position known.

Democrats   **Republicans**
Independents

385. HR 4818. Fiscal 2005 Foreign Operations Appropriations/U.N. Inspection of U.S. Elections. Buyer, R-Ind., amendment that would add language that would prohibit use of funds in the bill to request the United Nations to assess the validity of elections in the United States. Adopted 243-161: R 210-0; D 33-160 (ND 16-128, SD 17-32); I 0-1. July 15, 2004.

386. HR 4818. Fiscal 2005 Foreign Operations Appropriations/Export-Import Bank Funding. Sanders, I-Vt., amendment that would prohibit the Export-Import Bank from approving direct loans or loan guarantees to companies incorporated in Bermuda, Barbados, the Cayman Islands, Antigua or Panama. Adopted 270-132: R 82-129; D 187-3 (ND 138-3, SD 49-0); I 1-0. July 15, 2004.

387. HR 4818. Fiscal 2005 Foreign Operations Appropriations/International Criminal Court. Nethercutt, R-Wash., amendment that would prohibit Economic Support Fund assistance to the government of any country that is a party to the International Criminal Court (ICC) and has yet to pledge that it would not surrender U.S. nationals to the ICC. Adopted 241-166: R 201-11; D 40-154 (ND 22-122, SD 18-32); I 0-1. July 15, 2004.

388. HR 4818. Fiscal 2005 Foreign Operations Appropriations/Sub-Saharan Africa Aid. Jackson-Lee, D-Texas, amendment that would require at least $5 million in agricultural development funds for sub-Saharan Africa be made available for small-scale irrigation, water and drainage, post-harvest storage, crop intensification, crop and livestock diversification and rural infrastructure. Rejected 164-243: R 3-209; D 160-34 (ND 114-29, SD 46-5); I 1-0. July 15, 2004.

389. HR 4818. Fiscal 2005 Foreign Operations Appropriations/Aid for Saudi Arabia. Weiner, D-N.Y., amendment that would prohibit any funds in the bill from being used for assistance to Saudi Arabia. Adopted 217-191: R 60-152; D 156-39 (ND 120-24, SD 36-15); I 1-0. A "nay" was a vote in support of the president's position. July 15, 2004.

390. HR 4818. Fiscal 2005 Foreign Operations Appropriations/Passage. Passage of the bill that would appropriate $19.4 billion in fiscal 2005 for foreign operations. Passed 365-41: R 177-34; D 187-7 (ND 139-4, SD 48-3); I 1-0. July 15, 2004.

	385	386	387	388	389	390
ALABAMA						
1 *Bonner*	?	?	?	?	?	?
2 *Everett*	Y	N	Y	N	Y	Y
3 *Rogers*	Y	N	Y	N	Y	Y
4 *Aderholt*	?	N	Y	N	N	Y
5 Cramer	?	?	?	?	?	?
6 *Bachus*	Y	Y	Y	N	N	Y
7 Davis	N	Y	N	Y	Y	Y
ALASKA						
AL *Young*	Y	Y	Y	N	N	Y
ARIZONA						
1 *Renzi*	Y	Y	Y	N	Y	Y
2 *Franks*	Y	N	Y	N	Y	N
3 *Shadegg*	Y	N	Y	N	N	Y
4 Pastor	N	Y	N	Y	N	Y
5 *Hayworth*	Y	Y	Y	N	Y	Y
6 *Flake*	Y	N	Y	N	Y	N
7 Grijalva	N	Y	N	Y	N	Y
8 *Kolbe*	Y	N	N	N	N	Y
ARKANSAS						
1 Berry	N	Y	N	N	Y	N
2 Snyder	N	Y	N	Y	N	Y
3 *Boozman*	Y	N	Y	N	N	Y
4 Ross	N	Y	Y	Y	Y	Y
CALIFORNIA						
1 Thompson	N	Y	N	N	Y	Y
2 *Herger*	Y	N	Y	N	N	N
3 *Ose*	Y	Y	Y	N	Y	Y
4 *Doolittle*	Y	N	Y	N	N	Y
5 Matsui	N	Y	Y	Y	Y	Y
6 Woolsey	N	Y	N	N	N	Y
7 Miller, George	N	Y	N	Y	Y	?
8 Pelosi	N	Y	N	Y	Y	Y
9 Lee	N	Y	N	Y	Y	Y
10 Tauscher	N	Y	N	Y	Y	Y
11 *Pombo*	Y	N	Y	N	N	N
12 Lantos	N	Y	N	Y	Y	Y
13 Stark	N	Y	N	Y	Y	Y
14 Eshoo	N	Y	N	N	Y	Y
15 Honda	N	Y	N	Y	Y	Y
16 Lofgren	N	Y	N	Y	Y	Y
17 Farr	N	Y	N	Y	Y	Y
18 Cardoza	N	Y	N	Y	Y	Y
19 *Radanovich*	?	?	?	?	?	?
20 Dooley	?	?	?	?	?	?
21 *Nunes*	Y	N	Y	N	N	Y
22 *Thomas*	Y	N	Y	N	N	Y
23 Capps	N	+	N	Y	Y	Y
24 *Gallegly*	Y	Y	Y	N	N	Y
25 *McKeon*	Y	N	Y	N	N	Y
26 *Dreier*	Y	N	Y	N	N	Y
27 Sherman	N	Y	N	Y	Y	Y
28 Berman	N	Y	N	Y	Y	Y
29 Schiff	N	Y	N	Y	Y	Y
30 Waxman	N	Y	N	Y	Y	Y
31 Becerra	N	Y	N	Y	Y	Y
32 Solis	N	Y	N	Y	Y	Y
33 Watson	N	?	N	Y	Y	Y
34 Roybal-Allard	?	?	?	?	?	?
35 Waters	N	Y	N	N	Y	Y
36 Harman	N	Y	N	Y	Y	Y

	385	386	387	388	389	390
37 Millender-McD.	N	Y	N	Y	Y	Y
38 Napolitano	N	Y	N	Y	Y	Y
39 Sánchez, Linda	N	Y	N	Y	Y	Y
40 *Royce*	Y	Y	Y	N	Y	N
41 *Lewis*	Y	N	Y	N	N	Y
42 *Miller, Gary*	Y	N	Y	N	N	Y
43 Baca	N	Y	N	Y	Y	Y
44 *Calvert*	Y	N	Y	N	N	Y
45 *Bono*	Y	N	Y	N	N	Y
46 *Rohrabacher*	Y	Y	Y	N	Y	N
47 Sanchez, Loretta	N	Y	N	Y	Y	Y
48 *Cox*	Y	Y	Y	N	N	Y
49 *Issa*	Y	Y	Y	N	N	Y
50 *Cunningham*	Y	Y	Y	N	N	Y
51 Filner	N	Y	N	Y	Y	Y
52 *Hunter*	Y	Y	Y	N	N	Y
53 Davis	N	Y	N	Y	Y	Y
COLORADO						
1 DeGette	N	Y	N	Y	Y	Y
2 Udall	N	Y	N	Y	Y	Y
3 *McInnis*	?	?	?	?	?	?
4 *Musgrave*	Y	N	Y	N	Y	Y
5 *Hefley*	Y	N	N	N	N	N
6 *Tancredo*	Y	Y	Y	Y	Y	N
7 *Beauprez*	Y	N	Y	N	N	Y
CONNECTICUT						
1 Larson	N	Y	N	Y	Y	Y
2 *Simmons*	Y	Y	Y	N	Y	Y
3 DeLauro	N	Y	N	Y	Y	Y
4 *Shays*	Y	Y	Y	N	N	Y
5 *Johnson*	Y	Y	Y	N	N	Y
DELAWARE						
AL *Castle*	Y	N	Y	N	N	Y
FLORIDA						
1 *Miller, J.*	Y	N	Y	N	N	N
2 Boyd	Y	Y	Y	N	Y	N
3 Brown	N	Y	N	Y	Y	Y
4 *Crenshaw*	?	N	Y	N	N	Y
5 *Brown-Waite*	Y	Y	Y	N	N	Y
6 *Stearns*	Y	Y	Y	N	Y	N
7 *Mica*	Y	Y	Y	N	N	Y
8 *Keller*	Y	Y	Y	N	N	Y
9 *Bilirakis*	Y	Y	Y	N	Y	Y
10 *Young*	?	?	?	?	?	?
11 Davis	N	Y	N	Y	Y	Y
12 *Putnam*	Y	N	Y	N	N	Y
13 *Harris*	Y	N	Y	N	N	Y
14 *Goss*	Y	N	N	N	N	Y
15 *Weldon*	Y	N	Y	N	N	Y
16 *Foley*	Y	N	Y	N	N	Y
17 Meek	N	Y	N	Y	Y	Y
18 *Ros-Lehtinen*	Y	Y	Y	N	Y	Y
19 Wexler	N	Y	N	Y	Y	Y
20 Deutsch	?	?	?	?	?	?
21 *Diaz-Balart, L.*	?	?	?	?	?	?
22 *Shaw*	Y	N	Y	N	N	Y
23 Hastings	N	Y	N	Y	Y	Y
24 *Feeney*	Y	N	Y	N	N	?
25 *Diaz-Balart, M.*	Y	N	Y	N	N	Y
GEORGIA						
1 *Kingston*	Y	N	Y	N	N	Y
2 Bishop	N	Y	N	Y	Y	Y
3 Marshall	Y	Y	Y	Y	Y	Y
4 Majette	?	?	?	?	?	?
5 Lewis	N	Y	N	N	Y	Y
6 *Isakson*	?	?	?	?	?	?
7 *Linder*	Y	N	Y	N	Y	Y
8 *Collins*	?	?	?	?	?	?
9 *Norwood*	Y	Y	Y	N	Y	N
10 *Deal*	?	?	?	?	?	?
11 *Gingrey*	Y	Y	Y	N	N	Y
12 *Burns*	Y	Y	Y	N	N	Y
13 Scott	N	Y	N	Y	Y	Y
HAWAII						
1 Abercrombie	N	Y	N	Y	Y	Y
2 Case	N	Y	N	N	Y	Y
IDAHO						
1 *Otter*	Y	N	Y	N	Y	N
2 *Simpson*	Y	N	Y	N	N	Y
ILLINOIS						
1 Rush	N	Y	N	Y	Y	Y
2 Jackson	N	Y	N	Y	Y	Y
3 Lipinski	Y	Y	N	Y	Y	Y
4 Gutierrez	N	Y	N	?	Y	Y
5 Emanuel	N	Y	N	Y	Y	Y
6 *Hyde*	Y	Y	Y	N	N	Y

ND Northern Democrats   SD Southern Democrats

	385	386	387	388	389	390
7 Davis	N	Y	N	Y	Y	Y
8 ***Crane***	Y	N	Y	N	N	Y
9 Schakowsky	N	Y	N	Y	Y	Y
10 ***Kirk***	Y	N	N	N	Y	Y
11 ***Weller***	Y	N	Y	N	N	Y
12 Costello	Y	Y	Y	Y	Y	Y
13 ***Biggert***	Y	N	N	N	N	Y
14 ***Hastert***						
15 ***Johnson***	Y	N	Y	N	Y	Y
16 ***Manzullo***	Y	Y	Y	N	Y	Y
17 Evans	N	Y	N	Y	Y	Y
18 ***LaHood***	Y	N	Y	N	N	Y
19 ***Shimkus***	Y	N	Y	N	N	Y
INDIANA						
1 Visclosky	N	Y	N	N	N	Y
2 ***Chocola***	Y	N	Y	N	N	Y
3 ***Souder***	Y	N	Y	N	Y	Y
4 ***Buyer***	Y	N	Y	N	N	Y
5 ***Burton***	Y	Y	Y	N	Y	Y
6 ***Pence***	Y	N	Y	N	N	Y
7 Carson	?	?	?	?	?	?
8 ***Hostettler***	Y	Y	Y	Y	Y	N
9 Hill	N	Y	N	N	Y	Y
IOWA						
1 ***Nussle***	Y	N	Y	N	N	Y
2 ***Leach***	Y	N	Y	N	Y	Y
3 Boswell	N	Y	Y	Y	Y	Y
4 ***Latham***	Y	N	N	N	N	Y
5 ***King***	Y	N	Y	N	N	Y
KANSAS						
1 ***Moran***	Y	N	Y	N	N	N
2 ***Ryun***	?	?	?	?	?	?
3 Moore	N	Y	Y	Y	Y	Y
4 ***Tiahrt***	Y	N	Y	N	N	Y
KENTUCKY						
1 ***Whitfield***	Y	Y	Y	N	N	N
2 ***Lewis***	Y	N	Y	N	N	Y
3 ***Northup***	Y	Y	Y	N	N	Y
4 Lucas	N	Y	N	Y	N	Y
5 ***Rogers***	Y	Y	Y	N	N	Y
6 Chandler	Y	Y	Y	Y	Y	Y
LOUISIANA						
1 ***Vitter***	Y	N	Y	N	N	Y
2 Jefferson	?	?	?	Y	Y	Y
3 ***Tauzin***	Y	N	Y	N	N	Y
4 ***McCrery***	Y	N	Y	N	N	Y
5 Alexander	Y	Y	Y	Y	Y	Y
6 ***Baker***	Y	N	Y	N	Y	Y
7 John	N	Y	Y	N	Y	Y
MAINE						
1 Allen	N	Y	N	Y	N	Y
2 Michaud	N	Y	N	Y	Y	Y
MARYLAND						
1 ***Gilchrest***	Y	N	Y	N	N	Y
2 Ruppersberger	N	Y	N	N	N	Y
3 Cardin	N	Y	N	N	Y	Y
4 Wynn	N	Y	N	Y	Y	Y
5 Hoyer	N	Y	N	Y	Y	Y
6 ***Bartlett***	Y	N	Y	N	Y	N
7 Cummings	N	Y	N	Y	Y	Y
8 Van Hollen	N	Y	N	Y	Y	Y
MASSACHUSETTS						
1 Olver	N	Y	N	Y	Y	Y
2 Neal	N	Y	N	Y	Y	Y
3 McGovern	N	Y	N	Y	Y	Y
4 Frank	N	Y	N	N	Y	Y
5 Meehan	N	Y	N	Y	Y	Y
6 Tierney	N	Y	N	Y	Y	Y
7 Markey	N	Y	N	Y	Y	Y
8 Capuano	N	Y	N	Y	Y	Y
9 Lynch	N	Y	Y	Y	Y	Y
10 Delahunt	N	Y	N	Y	Y	Y
MICHIGAN						
1 Stupak	N	Y	N	N	Y	N
2 ***Hoekstra***	Y	N	Y	N	N	Y
3 ***Ehlers***	Y	N	N	N	N	Y
4 ***Camp***	Y	Y	Y	N	N	Y
5 Kildee	N	Y	N	Y	N	Y
6 ***Upton***	Y	Y	Y	N	N	Y
7 ***Smith***	Y	N	Y	N	N	N
8 ***Rogers***	Y	Y	Y	N	N	Y
9 ***Knollenberg***	Y	N	N	N	N	Y
10 ***Miller***	Y	Y	Y	N	N	Y
11 ***McCotter***	Y	Y	Y	N	Y	Y
12 Levin	N	Y	N	Y	Y	Y
13 Kilpatrick	N	Y	N	Y	N	Y
14 Conyers	N	Y	N	Y	N	Y
15 Dingell	N	Y	N	Y	N	Y
MINNESOTA						
1 ***Gutknecht***	Y	Y	Y	N	N	N
2 ***Kline***	Y	N	Y	N	N	Y
3 ***Ramstad***	Y	Y	Y	N	Y	Y
4 McCollum	N	Y	N	Y	Y	Y
5 Sabo	N	Y	N	N	Y	Y
6 ***Kennedy***	Y	?	Y	N	N	Y
7 Peterson	Y	Y	Y	N	N	Y
8 Oberstar	N	Y	N	Y	Y	Y
MISSISSIPPI						
1 ***Wicker***	Y	N	Y	N	N	Y
2 Thompson	N	Y	N	Y	N	Y
3 ***Pickering***	Y	Y	Y	N	N	Y
4 Taylor	Y	Y	Y	Y	N	N
MISSOURI						
1 Clay	N	Y	N	Y	Y	Y
2 ***Akin***	Y	N	Y	N	N	N
3 Gephardt	N	Y	N	Y	Y	Y
4 Skelton	Y	Y	Y	Y	N	Y
5 McCarthy	−	+	−	+	+	+
6 ***Graves***	Y	N	Y	N	Y	N
7 ***Blunt***	Y	N	Y	N	N	Y
8 ***Emerson***	Y	Y	Y	N	Y	Y
9 ***Hulshof***	Y	N	Y	N	N	N
MONTANA						
AL ***Rehberg***	Y	N	Y	N	N	Y
NEBRASKA						
1 ***Bereuter***	Y	N	N	N	N	Y
2 ***Terry***	Y	N	Y	N	Y	Y
3 ***Osborne***	Y	N	Y	N	N	Y
NEVADA						
1 Berkley	N	Y	N	Y	Y	Y
2 ***Gibbons***	Y	N	Y	N	N	N
3 ***Porter***	Y	Y	Y	N	Y	Y
NEW HAMPSHIRE						
1 ***Bradley***	Y	Y	Y	N	N	Y
2 ***Bass***	Y	Y	Y	N	N	Y
NEW JERSEY						
1 Andrews	Y	Y	N	N	Y	Y
2 ***LoBiondo***	Y	Y	Y	N	Y	Y
3 ***Saxton***	Y	Y	Y	N	N	Y
4 ***Smith***	Y	Y	Y	N	Y	Y
5 ***Garrett***	Y	N	Y	N	Y	Y
6 Pallone	N	Y	N	Y	Y	Y
7 ***Ferguson***	Y	Y	Y	N	Y	Y
8 Pascrell	N	Y	Y	Y	Y	Y
9 Rothman	N	Y	N	N	Y	Y
10 Payne	N	Y	N	Y	Y	Y
11 ***Frelinghuysen***	?	?	?	?	?	?
12 Holt	N	Y	N	Y	Y	Y
13 Menendez	N	Y	N	N	Y	Y
NEW MEXICO						
1 ***Wilson***	Y	Y	Y	N	N	Y
2 ***Pearce***	Y	N	Y	N	N	Y
3 Udall	N	Y	Y	Y	Y	Y
NEW YORK						
1 Bishop	N	Y	N	N	Y	Y
2 Israel	N	Y	Y	Y	Y	Y
3 ***King***	Y	Y	Y	N	N	Y
4 McCarthy	N	Y	Y	Y	Y	Y
5 Ackerman	N	Y	N	Y	Y	Y
6 Meeks	N	?	N	Y	Y	Y
7 Crowley	N	N	N	Y	Y	Y
8 Nadler	N	Y	N	Y	Y	Y
9 Weiner	N	Y	N	Y	Y	Y
10 Towns	N	Y	N	Y	Y	Y
11 Owens	N	Y	N	Y	Y	Y
12 Velázquez	N	Y	N	Y	Y	Y
13 ***Fossella***	Y	N	Y	N	N	Y
14 Maloney	N	Y	N	Y	Y	Y
15 Rangel	N	Y	N	Y	Y	Y
16 Serrano	N	Y	N	N	Y	Y
17 Engel	N	Y	N	Y	Y	Y
18 Lowey	N	Y	N	N	Y	Y
19 ***Kelly***	Y	N	Y	N	Y	Y
20 ***Sweeney***	Y	N	Y	N	N	Y
21 McNulty	Y	Y	Y	Y	Y	Y
22 Hinchey	N	Y	N	Y	Y	Y
23 ***McHugh***	Y	Y	Y	N	N	Y
24 ***Boehlert***	Y	Y	Y	N	N	Y
25 ***Walsh***	Y	N	N	N	N	Y
26 ***Reynolds***	Y	N	Y	N	N	Y
27 ***Quinn***	?	?	?	?	?	?
28 Slaughter	N	Y	N	Y	Y	Y
29 ***Houghton***	?	?	?	?	?	?
NORTH CAROLINA						
1 Vacant						
2 Etheridge	N	Y	N	Y	N	Y
3 ***Jones***	Y	Y	Y	Y	Y	N
4 Price	N	Y	N	Y	N	Y
5 ***Burr***	Y	N	Y	N	N	Y
6 ***Coble***	Y	Y	Y	N	Y	Y
7 McIntyre	Y	Y	Y	Y	Y	Y
8 ***Hayes***	?	?	?	?	?	?
9 ***Myrick***	Y	N	Y	N	N	Y
10 ***Ballenger***	Y	N	Y	N	N	Y
11 ***Taylor***	Y	Y	N	N	N	Y
12 Watt	N	Y	N	Y	N	Y
13 Miller	N	Y	N	Y	Y	Y
NORTH DAKOTA						
AL Pomeroy	Y	N	Y	N	N	Y
OHIO						
1 ***Chabot***	Y	Y	Y	N	Y	Y
2 ***Portman***	Y	N	Y	N	N	Y
3 ***Turner***	Y	N	Y	N	N	Y
4 ***Oxley***	Y	N	Y	N	N	Y
5 ***Gillmor***	Y	Y	Y	N	N	Y
6 Strickland	N	Y	N	Y	Y	Y
7 ***Hobson***	Y	N	Y	N	N	Y
8 ***Boehner***	Y	N	Y	N	N	Y
9 Kaptur	?	?	?	?	?	?
10 Kucinich	N	Y	N	Y	N	N
11 Jones	N	Y	N	Y	Y	Y
12 ***Tiberi***	Y	Y	Y	N	N	Y
13 Brown	N	Y	N	Y	Y	Y
14 ***LaTourette***	Y	Y	Y	N	N	Y
15 ***Pryce***	Y	Y	Y	N	N	Y
16 ***Regula***	Y	Y	Y	N	N	Y
17 Ryan	N	Y	N	Y	Y	Y
18 ***Ney***	Y	Y	Y	N	N	Y
OKLAHOMA						
1 ***Sullivan***	Y	N	Y	N	N	Y
2 Carson	Y	Y	Y	Y	Y	Y
3 ***Lucas***	Y	N	Y	N	N	N
4 ***Cole***	Y	N	Y	N	N	Y
5 ***Istook***	Y	N	Y	N	N	Y
OREGON						
1 Wu	N	Y	Y	Y	Y	Y
2 ***Walden***	Y	N	Y	N	Y	Y
3 Blumenauer	N	N	N	N	Y	Y
4 DeFazio	Y	Y	Y	Y	Y	N
5 Hooley	N	Y	Y	Y	Y	Y
PENNSYLVANIA						
1 Brady	N	Y	N	Y	N	Y
2 Fattah	N	Y	N	Y	N	Y
3 ***English***	Y	Y	Y	N	N	Y
4 ***Hart***	Y	N	Y	N	N	Y
5 ***Peterson***	Y	Y	Y	N	N	Y
6 ***Gerlach***	Y	Y	Y	N	N	Y
7 ***Weldon***	Y	Y	Y	N	N	Y
8 ***Greenwood***	?	?	?	?	?	?
9 ***Shuster, Bill***	Y	Y	Y	N	Y	Y
10 ***Sherwood***	Y	Y	Y	N	N	Y
11 Kanjorski	N	Y	Y	N	N	Y
12 Murtha	N	Y	Y	N	N	Y
13 Hoeffel	N	Y	N	Y	Y	Y
14 Doyle	N	Y	N	Y	N	Y
15 ***Toomey***	Y	N	Y	N	Y	N
16 ***Pitts***	Y	N	Y	N	N	Y
17 Holden	Y	Y	Y	N	Y	Y
18 ***Murphy***	Y	Y	Y	N	N	Y
19 ***Platts***	Y	Y	Y	N	Y	Y
RHODE ISLAND						
1 Kennedy	N	Y	N	Y	Y	Y
2 Langevin	N	Y	Y	Y	Y	Y
SOUTH CAROLINA						
1 ***Brown***	Y	N	Y	N	N	Y
2 ***Wilson***	Y	N	Y	N	N	Y
3 ***Barrett***	Y	N	Y	N	N	Y
4 ***DeMint***	Y	N	Y	N	N	Y
5 Spratt	Y	Y	N	Y	N	Y
6 Clyburn	N	Y	N	Y	N	Y
SOUTH DAKOTA						
AL Herseth	Y	Y	Y	Y	Y	Y
TENNESSEE						
1 ***Jenkins***	?	?	?	?	?	?
2 ***Duncan***	Y	Y	Y	N	Y	N
3 ***Wamp***	Y	Y	Y	N	Y	Y
4 Davis	Y	Y	Y	Y	Y	Y
5 Cooper	Y	Y	N	Y	Y	Y
6 Gordon	Y	Y	N	N	Y	Y
7 ***Blackburn***	Y	N	Y	N	N	Y
8 Tanner	Y	Y	Y	Y	Y	N
9 Ford	?	?	N	Y	Y	Y
TEXAS						
1 Sandlin	Y	Y	Y	Y	N	Y
2 Turner	Y	Y	Y	Y	N	Y
3 ***Johnson, Sam***	Y	N	Y	N	N	Y
4 ***Hall***	Y	N	Y	N	N	Y
5 ***Hensarling***	Y	N	Y	N	N	Y
6 ***Barton***	Y	N	Y	N	N	Y
7 ***Culberson***	Y	N	Y	N	N	Y
8 ***Brady***	Y	N	Y	N	N	Y
9 Lampson	N	Y	N	Y	Y	Y
10 Doggett	?	?	?	?	?	?
11 Edwards	Y	Y	Y	Y	Y	Y
12 ***Granger***	Y	N	Y	N	N	Y
13 ***Thornberry***	Y	N	Y	N	N	Y
14 ***Paul***	Y	Y	Y	N	Y	N
15 Hinojosa	N	Y	N	Y	Y	Y
16 Reyes	N	Y	Y	Y	Y	Y
17 Stenholm	?	?	?	?	?	?
18 Jackson-Lee	N	Y	N	Y	Y	Y
19 ***Neugebauer***	Y	N	Y	N	Y	Y
20 Gonzalez	N	Y	N	Y	Y	Y
21 ***Smith***	Y	N	Y	N	N	Y
22 ***DeLay***	Y	N	Y	N	N	Y
23 ***Bonilla***	Y	N	Y	N	N	Y
24 Frost	Y	Y	Y	Y	N	Y
25 Bell	N	Y	N	Y	Y	Y
26 ***Burgess***	Y	N	Y	N	N	Y
27 Ortiz	N	Y	Y	Y	Y	Y
28 Rodriguez	N	Y	N	Y	Y	Y
29 Green	Y	Y	Y	Y	Y	Y
30 Johnson, E.B.	N	Y	N	Y	N	Y
31 ***Carter***	Y	N	Y	N	N	Y
32 ***Sessions***	Y	N	Y	N	N	Y
UTAH						
1 ***Bishop***	Y	N	Y	N	N	Y
2 Matheson	Y	Y	Y	Y	Y	Y
3 ***Cannon***	Y	N	Y	N	N	Y
VERMONT						
AL *Sanders*	N	Y	N	Y	Y	Y
VIRGINIA						
1 ***Davis, Jo Ann***	Y	Y	Y	N	Y	N
2 ***Schrock***	Y	N	Y	N	N	Y
3 Scott	N	Y	N	Y	Y	Y
4 ***Forbes***	Y	N	Y	N	Y	Y
5 ***Goode***	Y	Y	Y	N	Y	N
6 ***Goodlatte***	Y	N	Y	N	Y	N
7 ***Cantor***	Y	N	Y	N	N	Y
8 Moran	N	Y	N	Y	Y	Y
9 Boucher	N	Y	N	Y	N	Y
10 ***Wolf***	Y	Y	Y	N	N	Y
11 ***Davis, T.***	Y	N	Y	N	N	Y
WASHINGTON						
1 Inslee	N	Y	N	Y	Y	Y
2 Larsen	Y	Y	N	Y	Y	Y
3 Baird	Y	Y	N	N	Y	Y
4 ***Hastings***	Y	N	Y	N	N	Y
5 ***Nethercutt***	Y	Y	Y	N	N	Y
6 Dicks	Y	Y	N	Y	Y	Y
7 McDermott	N	Y	N	Y	Y	Y
8 ***Dunn***	Y	N	Y	N	N	Y
9 Smith	Y	Y	N	Y	Y	Y
WEST VIRGINIA						
1 Mollohan	N	Y	N	Y	N	Y
2 ***Capito***	Y	Y	Y	N	N	Y
3 Rahall	N	Y	N	Y	N	N
WISCONSIN						
1 ***Ryan***	Y	N	Y	N	Y	Y
2 Baldwin	N	Y	N	Y	N	Y
3 Kind	Y	Y	N	Y	N	Y
4 Kleczka	N	Y	N	Y	N	Y
5 ***Sensenbrenner***	Y	Y	Y	N	Y	N
6 ***Petri***	Y	Y	Y	N	N	Y
7 Obey	N	Y	N	N	N	Y
8 ***Green***	Y	Y	Y	N	N	Y
WYOMING						
AL ***Cubin***	Y	N	Y	N	Y	N

Southern states - Ala., Ark., Fla., Ga., Ky., La., Miss., N.C., Okla., S.C., Tenn., Texas, Va.

Key

Y	Voted for (yea).
#	Paired for.
+	Announced for.
N	Voted against (nay).
X	Paired against.
–	Announced against.
P	Voted "present."
C	Voted "present" to avoid possible conflict of interest.
?	Did not vote or otherwise make a position known.

Democrats **Republicans** *Independents*

---

391. HR 1587. Vietnam Human Rights/Passage. Smith, R-N.J., motion to suspend the rules and pass the bill that would freeze annual non-humanitarian assistance to Vietnam at fiscal 2004 levels unless the president submits a report showing that Vietnam has made progress in respecting religious freedom, property rights and human rights. Motion agreed to 323-45: R 172-23; D 151-22 (ND 111-18, SD 40-4); I 0-0. A two-thirds majority of those present and voting (246 in this case) is required for passage under suspension of the rules. July 19, 2004.

392. S Con Res 114. Child Hunger/Adoption. Smith, R-N.J., motion to suspend the rules and adopt the concurrent resolution that would express Congress' grave concern about the continuing problem of hunger and the need to feed hungry and malnourished children around the world. Motion agreed to 367-4: R 194-4; D 173-0 (ND 129-0, SD 44-0); I 0-0. A two-thirds majority of those present and voting (248 in this case) is required for adoption under suspension of the rules. July 19, 2004.

393. S 2264. Ugandan Crisis/Passage. Royce, R-Calif., motion to suspend the rules and pass the bill that would express the sense of Congress that the U.S. government should work to support a peaceful resolution of the conflict in northern and eastern Uganda, and require the State Department to submit a report to Congress on the Ugandan conflict. Motion agreed to 371-1: R 197-1; D 173-0 (ND 129-0, SD 44-0); I 1-0. A two-thirds majority of those present and voting (248 in this case) is required for passage under suspension of the rules. July 19, 2004.

394. HR 3574. Stock Options Overhaul/Option Pricing Models. Sherman, D-Calif., amendment that would strike language in the bill that would require companies to use a pricing model, known as "zero volatility," that assumes there will be no change in the value of an underlying stock, when calculating the value of the stock options provided to a company's top five executives. Rejected 126-296: R 17-204; D 108-92 (ND 89-57, SD 19-35); I 1-0. July 20, 2004.

395. HR 3574. Stock Options Overhaul/SEC Authority. Maloney, D-N.Y., amendment that would add language stating that nothing in the bill can be construed to impair or limit the authority of the Securities and Exchange Commission to establish accounting standards or principles. Rejected 114-308: R 12-208; D 101-100 (ND 87-60, SD 14-40); I 1-0. July 20, 2004.

396. HR 3574. Stock Options Overhaul/Substitute. Kanjorski, D-Pa., substitute amendment that would require the Securities and Exchange Commission to oversee an inclusive process in setting accounting standards for equity-based compensation. It also would express the sense of Congress that preserving the integrity of the accounting standard-setting process and the independence of the Financial Accounting Standards Board is crucial to financial accounting and markets. Rejected 127-293: R 23-195; D 103-98 (ND 86-61, SD 17-37); I 1-0. July 20, 2004.

397. HR 3574. Stock Options Overhaul/Passage. Passage of the bill that would block a Financial Accounting Standards Board rule set to take effect in December that would require stock options to be accounted for as an expense. The bill would require the deduction of only stock options provided to the five highest-paid executives, and would mandate a study of the economic impact of expensing all stock options. Passed 312-111: R 198-22; D 114-88 (ND 73-75, SD 41-13); I 0-1. July 20, 2004.

398. HR 4850. Fiscal 2005 District of Columbia Appropriations/Across-the-Board Cut. Hefley, R-Colo., amendment that would reduce all discretionary appropriations in the bill by 1 percent. Rejected 113-309: R 106-115; D 7-193 (ND 2-145, SD 5-48); I 0-1. July 20, 2004.

	391	392	393	394	395	396	397	398
ALABAMA								
1 *Bonner*	?	?	?	N	N	N	Y	N
2 *Everett*	?	Y	Y	N	N	N	Y	Y
3 *Rogers*	Y	Y	Y	N	N	N	Y	N
4 *Aderholt*	Y	Y	Y	N	N	N	Y	N
5 Cramer	?	?	?	N	N	N	Y	N
6 *Bachus*	Y	Y	Y	N	N	N	Y	N
7 Davis	Y	Y	Y	N	N	N	Y	N
ALASKA								
AL *Young*	Y	Y	Y	N	N	N	Y	N
ARIZONA								
1 *Renzi*	+	+	+	N	N	N	Y	N
2 *Franks*	Y	Y	Y	N	N	N	Y	Y
3 *Shadegg*	Y	Y	Y	N	N	N	Y	Y
4 Pastor	Y	Y	Y	Y	Y	Y	N	N
5 *Hayworth*	Y	Y	Y	N	N	N	Y	N
6 *Flake*	N	N	Y	N	N	N	Y	Y
7 Grijalva	Y	Y	Y	Y	Y	Y	N	N
8 *Kolbe*	N	Y	Y	N	N	N	Y	N
ARKANSAS								
1 Berry	Y	Y	Y	Y	Y	Y	N	N
2 Snyder	Y	Y	Y	N	N	N	Y	N
3 *Boozman*	Y	Y	Y	N	N	N	Y	Y
4 Ross	Y	Y	Y	N	N	N	Y	N
CALIFORNIA								
1 Thompson	Y	Y	Y	N	N	N	N	N
2 *Herger*	N	Y	Y	N	N	N	Y	Y
3 *Ose*	N	Y	Y	N	N	N	Y	N
4 *Doolittle*	Y	Y	Y	N	N	N	Y	N
5 Matsui	Y	Y	Y	Y	Y	Y	N	N
6 Woolsey	Y	Y	Y	N	N	N	Y	N
7 Miller, George	N	Y	Y	Y	Y	Y	N	N
8 Pelosi	?	?	?	N	N	N	Y	N
9 Lee	?	?	?	Y	Y	Y	N	N
10 Tauscher	Y	Y	Y	N	N	N	Y	N
11 *Pombo*	Y	Y	Y	N	N	N	Y	N
12 Lantos	Y	Y	Y	N	N	N	Y	N
13 Stark	Y	Y	Y	Y	Y	Y	N	N
14 Eshoo	N	Y	Y	N	N	N	Y	N
15 Honda	Y	Y	Y	N	N	N	Y	N
16 Lofgren	Y	Y	Y	N	N	N	Y	N
17 Farr	Y	Y	Y	N	N	N	Y	N
18 Cardoza	Y	Y	Y	N	N	N	Y	N
19 *Radanovich*	Y	Y	Y	N	N	N	Y	N
20 Dooley	N	Y	Y	N	N	N	Y	N
21 *Nunes*	Y	Y	Y	N	N	N	Y	N
22 *Thomas*	N	Y	Y	N	N	?	N	Y
23 Capps	Y	Y	Y	Y	Y	Y	N	N
24 *Gallegly*	Y	Y	Y	N	N	N	Y	N
25 *McKeon*	?	?	?	N	N	N	Y	N
26 *Dreier*	N	Y	Y	N	N	N	Y	N
27 Sherman	Y	Y	Y	Y	Y	Y	N	N
28 Berman	Y	Y	Y	Y	Y	Y	N	N
29 Schiff	Y	Y	Y	N	N	N	Y	N
30 Waxman	Y	Y	Y	Y	Y	Y	N	N
31 Becerra	Y	Y	Y	Y	Y	Y	N	N
32 Solis	Y	Y	Y	Y	Y	Y	N	N
33 Watson	Y	Y	Y	Y	Y	Y	N	N
34 Roybal-Allard	Y	Y	Y	Y	Y	Y	N	N
35 Waters	Y	Y	Y	Y	Y	Y	N	N
36 Harman	Y	Y	Y	N	N	N	Y	N

	391	392	393	394	395	396	397	398
37 Millender-McD.	Y	Y	Y	N	N	N	Y	N
38 Napolitano	Y	Y	Y	Y	Y	Y	N	N
39 Sánchez, Linda	Y	Y	Y	Y	Y	Y	N	N
40 *Royce*	Y	Y	Y	N	N	N	Y	N
41 *Lewis*	Y	Y	Y	N	N	N	Y	N
42 *Miller, Gary*	Y	Y	Y	N	N	N	Y	N
43 Baca	Y	Y	Y	N	N	N	Y	N
44 *Calvert*	Y	Y	Y	N	N	N	Y	N
45 *Bono*	Y	Y	Y	N	N	N	Y	N
46 *Rohrabacher*	Y	Y	Y	N	N	N	Y	Y
47 Sanchez, Loretta	Y	Y	Y	N	N	N	Y	N
48 *Cox*	Y	Y	N	N	N	N	Y	N
49 *Issa*	Y	Y	Y	N	N	N	Y	N
50 *Cunningham*	Y	Y	Y	N	N	N	Y	N
51 Filner	Y	Y	Y	Y	Y	Y	N	N
52 *Hunter*	?	?	N	N	N	N	Y	N
53 Davis	Y	Y	Y	Y	Y	Y	N	N
COLORADO								
1 DeGette	Y	Y	Y	N	N	N	Y	N
2 Udall	Y	Y	Y	N	N	N	Y	N
3 *McInnis*	N	Y	Y	N	N	Y	Y	Y
4 *Musgrave*	Y	Y	Y	N	N	N	Y	Y
5 *Hefley*	Y	Y	Y	N	N	N	Y	Y
6 *Tancredo*	Y	Y	Y	N	N	Y	Y	Y
7 *Beauprez*	Y	Y	Y	N	N	N	Y	Y
CONNECTICUT								
1 Larson	Y	Y	Y	N	N	N	Y	N
2 *Simmons*	N	Y	Y	N	N	N	Y	N
3 DeLauro	Y	Y	Y	Y	Y	Y	N	N
4 *Shays*	N	Y	Y	Y	Y	Y	N	N
5 *Johnson*	Y	Y	Y	N	N	?	Y	N
DELAWARE								
AL *Castle*	Y	Y	Y	Y	Y	Y	N	N
FLORIDA								
1 *Miller, J.*	Y	N	N	N	N	N	Y	Y
2 Boyd	Y	Y	Y	N	N	N	Y	N
3 Brown	Y	Y	Y	Y	N	Y	N	N
4 *Crenshaw*	Y	Y	Y	N	N	N	Y	N
5 *Brown-Waite*	Y	Y	Y	N	N	N	Y	Y
6 *Stearns*	Y	Y	Y	N	N	N	Y	N
7 *Mica*	Y	Y	Y	N	N	N	Y	N
8 *Keller*	Y	Y	Y	N	N	N	Y	N
9 *Bilirakis*	Y	Y	Y	N	N	N	Y	N
10 *Young*	?	?	N	N	N	N	Y	N
11 Davis	Y	Y	Y	Y	Y	Y	N	N
12 *Putnam*	Y	Y	Y	N	N	N	Y	N
13 *Harris*	Y	Y	Y	N	N	N	Y	–
14 *Goss*	N	Y	Y	N	N	N	Y	Y
15 *Weldon*	Y	Y	Y	N	N	N	Y	Y
16 *Foley*	Y	Y	Y	N	N	N	Y	N
17 Meek	Y	Y	Y	Y	N	N	Y	N
18 *Ros-Lehtinen*	?	?	N	N	N	N	Y	N
19 Wexler	?	?	Y	Y	Y	Y	N	N
20 Deutsch	?	?	Y	Y	Y	Y	N	N
21 *Diaz-Balart, L.*	Y	Y	Y	N	N	N	Y	N
22 *Shaw*	Y	Y	Y	N	N	N	Y	N
23 Hastings	N	Y	Y	Y	Y	Y	N	N
24 *Feeney*	Y	Y	Y	N	N	N	Y	Y
25 *Diaz-Balart, M.*	Y	Y	Y	N	N	N	Y	Y
GEORGIA								
1 *Kingston*	?	?	?	N	N	N	Y	N
2 Bishop	N	Y	Y	N	N	N	Y	N
3 Marshall	Y	Y	Y	Y	Y	Y	N	?
4 *Majette*	?	?	?	?	?	?	?	?
5 Lewis	Y	Y	Y	N	N	N	N	N
6 *Isakson*	?	?	?	?	?	?	?	?
7 *Linder*	Y	Y	Y	N	N	N	Y	Y
8 *Collins*	?	?	?	?	?	?	?	?
9 *Norwood*	Y	Y	Y	N	N	N	Y	Y
10 *Deal*	Y	Y	Y	N	N	N	Y	N
11 *Gingrey*	Y	Y	Y	N	N	N	+	Y
12 *Burns*	Y	Y	Y	N	N	N	Y	Y
13 Scott	Y	Y	Y	N	N	N	Y	N
HAWAII								
1 Abercrombie	?	?	?	Y	Y	Y	N	N
2 Case	Y	Y	Y	N	N	N	Y	N
IDAHO								
1 *Otter*	Y	Y	Y	N	N	N	Y	Y
2 *Simpson*	Y	Y	Y	N	N	N	Y	Y
ILLINOIS								
1 Rush	?	?	?	Y	Y	Y	N	N
2 Jackson	N	Y	Y	Y	Y	Y	N	N
3 Lipinski	?	?	?	Y	Y	Y	N	N
4 Gutierrez	?	?	?	Y	Y	Y	N	N
5 Emanuel	Y	Y	Y	Y	Y	Y	N	N
6 *Hyde*	Y	Y	Y	N	N	N	Y	N

ND Northern Democrats   SD Southern Democrats

	391	392	393	394	395	396	397	398
7 Davis	?	?	?	Y	Y	Y	Y	N
8 ***Crane***	N	Y	Y	N	N	N	Y	Y
9 Schakowsky	Y	Y	Y	Y	Y	Y	N	N
10 ***Kirk***	Y	Y	Y	N	N	N	Y	N
11 ***Weller***	N	Y	Y	N	N	N	Y	N
12 Costello	N	Y	Y	Y	Y	Y	N	N
13 ***Biggert***	N	Y	Y	N	N	N	Y	N
14 ***Hastert***								
15 ***Johnson***	Y	Y	Y	N	Y	Y	Y	N
16 ***Manzullo***	Y	Y	Y	N	N	N	Y	Y
17 Evans	N	Y	Y	Y	N	Y	N	N
18 ***LaHood***	Y	Y	Y	N	N	N	N	N
19 ***Shimkus***	N	Y	Y	N	N	Y	N	Y
INDIANA								
1 Visclosky	Y	Y	Y	Y	Y	Y	N	N
2 ***Chocola***	?	?	?	N	N	N	Y	Y
3 ***Souder***	Y	Y	Y	N	N	N	Y	N
4 ***Buyer***	Y	Y	Y	N	N	N	Y	?
5 ***Burton***	Y	Y	Y	N	N	N	Y	Y
6 ***Pence***	Y	Y	Y	N	N	N	Y	Y
7 Carson	?	?	?	?	?	?	?	?
8 ***Hostettler***	Y	Y	Y	N	N	N	Y	Y
9 Hill	Y	Y	Y	N	N	N	Y	N
IOWA								
1 ***Nussle***	Y	Y	Y	N	N	N	Y	N
2 ***Leach***	Y	Y	Y	Y	Y	Y	N	N
3 Boswell	Y	Y	Y	N	N	N	Y	N
4 ***Latham***	Y	Y	Y	N	N	N	Y	N
5 ***King***	Y	Y	Y	N	N	N	Y	Y
KANSAS								
1 ***Moran***	Y	Y	Y	N	N	N	Y	Y
2 ***Ryun***	?	?	?	N	N	N	Y	N
3 Moore	Y	Y	Y	N	N	N	Y	N
4 ***Tiahrt***	Y	Y	Y	N	N	N	Y	N
KENTUCKY								
1 ***Whitfield***	Y	Y	Y	N	N	N	Y	N
2 ***Lewis***	Y	Y	Y	N	N	N	Y	Y
3 ***Northup***	Y	Y	Y	N	N	N	Y	N
4 Lucas	Y	Y	Y	N	N	N	Y	N
5 ***Rogers***	Y	Y	Y	N	N	N	Y	N
6 Chandler	Y	Y	Y	N	N	N	Y	N
LOUISIANA								
1 ***Vitter***	?	?	?	N	N	N	Y	Y
2 Jefferson	Y	Y	Y	N	N	N	Y	N
3 ***Tauzin***	Y	Y	Y	N	N	N	Y	N
4 ***McCrery***	?	?	?	?	?	?	?	N
5 Alexander	Y	Y	Y	Y	Y	Y	N	N
6 ***Baker***	?	Y	Y	N	N	N	Y	Y
7 John	?	?	?	N	N	N	Y	N
MAINE								
1 Allen	Y	Y	Y	N	N	N	Y	N
2 Michaud	Y	Y	Y	Y	N	N	Y	N
MARYLAND								
1 ***Gilchrest***	Y	Y	Y	Y	Y	Y	N	N
2 Ruppersberger	N	Y	Y	N	N	N	Y	N
3 Cardin	Y	Y	Y	Y	Y	Y	N	N
4 Wynn	Y	Y	Y	N	Y	N	Y	N
5 Hoyer	Y	Y	Y	Y	Y	Y	N	N
6 ***Bartlett***	Y	Y	Y	N	N	N	Y	Y
7 Cummings	Y	Y	Y	N	Y	Y	N	N
8 Van Hollen	Y	Y	Y	N	Y	Y	N	N
MASSACHUSETTS								
1 Olver	N	Y	Y	Y	Y	Y	N	N
2 Neal	Y	Y	Y	Y	Y	Y	N	N
3 McGovern	Y	Y	Y	N	N	N	Y	N
4 Frank	Y	Y	Y	Y	Y	Y	N	N
5 Meehan	Y	Y	Y	N	N	N	Y	N
6 Tierney	Y	Y	Y	Y	Y	Y	N	N
7 Markey	Y	Y	Y	Y	Y	Y	N	N
8 Capuano	Y	Y	Y	N	N	N	Y	N
9 Lynch	Y	Y	Y	N	N	N	Y	N
10 Delahunt	?	?	?	Y	Y	Y	Y	N
MICHIGAN								
1 Stupak	Y	Y	Y	Y	Y	Y	N	N
2 ***Hoekstra***	Y	Y	Y	N	N	N	Y	Y
3 ***Ehlers***	Y	Y	Y	Y	N	N	Y	N
4 ***Camp***	Y	Y	Y	N	N	N	Y	N
5 Kildee	Y	Y	Y	N	N	Y	N	N
6 ***Upton***	Y	Y	Y	N	N	N	Y	Y
7 ***Smith***	N	Y	Y	Y	?	Y	N	N
8 ***Rogers***	Y	Y	Y	N	N	N	Y	Y
9 ***Knollenberg***	Y	Y	Y	N	N	N	Y	N
10 ***Miller***	?	?	?	N	N	N	Y	N
11 ***McCotter***	Y	Y	Y	N	N	N	Y	Y
12 Levin	Y	Y	Y	Y	Y	Y	N	N
13 Kilpatrick	+	+	+	N	N	N	N	N
14 Conyers	N	Y	Y	Y	Y	Y	N	N
15 Dingell	Y	Y	Y	Y	Y	Y	N	N
MINNESOTA								
1 ***Gutknecht***	Y	Y	Y	N	N	N	Y	Y
2 ***Kline***	Y	Y	Y	N	N	N	Y	N
3 ***Ramstad***	Y	Y	Y	N	N	N	Y	Y
4 McCollum	Y	Y	Y	Y	Y	Y	Y	N
5 Sabo	N	Y	Y	Y	Y	Y	N	N
6 ***Kennedy***	Y	Y	Y	N	N	N	Y	Y
7 Peterson	Y	Y	Y	Y	Y	Y	N	N
8 Oberstar	N	Y	Y	Y	Y	Y	N	N
MISSISSIPPI								
1 ***Wicker***	Y	Y	Y	N	N	N	Y	N
2 Thompson	Y	Y	Y	Y	Y	Y	N	N
3 ***Pickering***	Y	Y	Y	N	N	N	Y	Y
4 Taylor	Y	Y	Y	Y	Y	Y	N	Y
MISSOURI								
1 Clay	?	?	?	Y	Y	Y	Y	N
2 ***Akin***	Y	Y	Y	N	N	N	Y	Y
3 Gephardt	?	?	?	N	N	N	Y	N
4 Skelton	Y	Y	Y	Y	N	N	Y	N
5 McCarthy	Y	Y	Y	N	N	N	Y	N
6 ***Graves***	Y	Y	Y	N	N	N	Y	Y
7 ***Blunt***	Y	Y	Y	N	N	N	Y	N
8 ***Emerson***	N	Y	Y	N	N	N	N	N
9 ***Hulshof***	?	?	?	N	N	N	Y	Y
MONTANA								
AL ***Rehberg***	Y	Y	Y	N	N	N	Y	Y
NEBRASKA								
1 ***Bereuter***	Y	Y	Y	Y	Y	Y	N	N
2 ***Terry***	Y	Y	Y	N	N	N	N	Y
3 ***Osborne***	Y	Y	Y	N	N	Y	N	N
NEVADA								
1 Berkley	Y	Y	Y	N	N	?	Y	N
2 ***Gibbons***	Y	Y	Y	N	N	N	Y	Y
3 ***Porter***	Y	Y	Y	N	N	N	Y	N
NEW HAMPSHIRE								
1 ***Bradley***	Y	Y	Y	N	N	N	Y	Y
2 ***Bass***	Y	Y	Y	Y	N	Y	N	Y
NEW JERSEY								
1 Andrews	Y	Y	Y	Y	Y	Y	Y	N
2 ***LoBiondo***	Y	Y	Y	N	N	N	Y	N
3 ***Saxton***	Y	Y	Y	N	N	N	Y	N
4 ***Smith***	Y	Y	Y	N	N	N	Y	N
5 ***Garrett***	Y	Y	Y	N	N	N	Y	Y
6 Pallone	Y	Y	Y	Y	N	N	Y	N
7 ***Ferguson***	?	?	?	?	?	?	?	?
8 Pascrell	Y	Y	Y	Y	Y	Y	N	N
9 Rothman	Y	Y	Y	Y	Y	Y	N	N
10 Payne	?	?	?	Y	Y	Y	N	N
11 ***Frelinghuysen***	?	?	?	N	N	N	Y	N
12 Holt	Y	Y	Y	Y	Y	N	Y	N
13 Menendez	?	?	?	N	N	N	Y	N
NEW MEXICO								
1 ***Wilson***	Y	Y	Y	N	N	N	Y	N
2 ***Pearce***	Y	Y	Y	N	N	N	Y	N
3 Udall	Y	Y	Y	N	N	N	Y	N
NEW YORK								
1 Bishop	Y	Y	Y	Y	Y	Y	N	N
2 Israel	Y	Y	Y	N	N	N	Y	N
3 ***King***	Y	Y	Y	N	N	N	Y	N
4 McCarthy	Y	Y	Y	N	N	N	Y	N
5 Ackerman	Y	Y	Y	Y	Y	Y	Y	N
6 Meeks	Y	Y	Y	N	N	N	Y	N
7 Crowley	Y	Y	Y	N	N	N	Y	N
8 Nadler	N	Y	Y	Y	Y	Y	N	N
9 Weiner	Y	Y	Y	Y	Y	Y	N	N
10 Towns	?	?	?	N	Y	Y	N	N
11 Owens	Y	Y	Y	Y	Y	Y	Y	N
12 Velázquez	Y	Y	Y	N	N	N	Y	N
13 ***Fossella***	Y	Y	Y	Y	Y	Y	N	Y
14 Maloney	Y	Y	Y	Y	Y	Y	N	N
15 Rangel	Y	Y	Y	Y	Y	Y	Y	N
16 Serrano	Y	Y	Y	Y	Y	Y	N	N
17 Engel	Y	Y	Y	?	Y	Y	Y	N
18 Lowey	Y	Y	Y	Y	Y	Y	N	N
19 ***Kelly***	Y	Y	Y	N	N	N	Y	N
20 ***Sweeney***	?	?	?	N	N	N	Y	N
21 McNulty	Y	Y	Y	Y	Y	Y	N	N
22 Hinchey	Y	Y	Y	Y	Y	Y	N	N
23 ***McHugh***	Y	Y	Y	N	N	N	Y	Y
24 ***Boehlert***	Y	Y	Y	N	N	N	Y	Y
25 ***Walsh***	Y	Y	Y	N	N	N	Y	N
26 ***Reynolds***	Y	Y	Y	N	N	N	Y	N
27 ***Quinn***	?	?	?	?	?	?	?	?
28 Slaughter	Y	Y	Y	Y	Y	Y	N	N
29 ***Houghton***	?	?	?	N	N	N	Y	N
NORTH CAROLINA								
1 Vacant								
2 Etheridge	Y	Y	Y	N	N	N	Y	N
3 ***Jones***	N	Y	Y	N	Y	N	Y	Y
4 Price	Y	Y	Y	N	N	N	Y	N
5 ***Burr***	Y	Y	Y	N	N	N	Y	N
6 ***Coble***	N	Y	Y	N	N	N	Y	Y
7 McIntyre	?	?	?	N	N	N	Y	N
8 ***Hayes***	?	?	?	N	N	N	Y	Y
9 ***Myrick***	Y	Y	Y	N	N	N	Y	Y
10 ***Ballenger***	?	?	?	?	?	?	?	N
11 ***Taylor***	N	Y	Y	N	N	N	Y	Y
12 Watt	?	?	?	Y	Y	Y	N	N
13 Miller	Y	Y	Y	N	Y	N	Y	N
NORTH DAKOTA								
AL Pomeroy	Y	Y	Y	Y	Y	Y	N	N
OHIO								
1 ***Chabot***	Y	Y	Y	N	N	N	Y	Y
2 ***Portman***	Y	Y	Y	N	N	N	Y	N
3 ***Turner***	Y	Y	Y	N	N	N	Y	N
4 ***Oxley***	Y	Y	Y	N	N	N	Y	Y
5 ***Gillmor***	Y	Y	Y	Y	Y	Y	N	N
6 Strickland	Y	Y	Y	Y	Y	Y	N	Y
7 ***Hobson***	Y	Y	Y	N	N	N	Y	N
8 ***Boehner***	Y	Y	Y	N	N	N	Y	N
9 Kaptur	Y	Y	Y	Y	Y	Y	N	N
10 Kucinich	N	Y	Y	Y	Y	Y	N	N
11 Jones	?	?	?	Y	N	Y	N	N
12 ***Tiberi***	Y	Y	Y	N	N	N	Y	N
13 Brown	Y	Y	Y	Y	Y	Y	N	N
14 ***LaTourette***	Y	Y	Y	N	N	N	Y	N
15 ***Pryce***	N	Y	Y	N	N	N	Y	N
16 ***Regula***	Y	Y	Y	N	N	N	Y	N
17 Ryan	Y	Y	Y	Y	Y	Y	N	N
18 ***Ney***	Y	Y	Y	N	N	N	Y	N
OKLAHOMA								
1 ***Sullivan***	Y	Y	Y	N	N	N	Y	Y
2 Carson	?	?	?	N	N	N	Y	N
3 ***Lucas***	Y	Y	Y	N	N	N	Y	N
4 ***Cole***	Y	Y	Y	N	N	N	N	N
5 ***Istook***	Y	Y	Y	N	N	N	Y	N
OREGON								
1 Wu	Y	Y	Y	N	Y	N	Y	N
2 ***Walden***	Y	Y	Y	N	N	N	Y	N
3 Blumenauer	Y	Y	Y	N	N	N	Y	N
4 DeFazio	Y	Y	Y	Y	Y	Y	N	N
5 Hooley	Y	Y	Y	N	N	N	Y	N
PENNSYLVANIA								
1 Brady	Y	Y	Y	Y	Y	Y	N	N
2 Fattah	?	?	?	Y	Y	Y	N	N
3 ***English***	Y	Y	Y	N	N	N	Y	N
4 ***Hart***	Y	Y	Y	N	N	N	Y	N
5 ***Peterson***	?	?	?	N	N	N	Y	N
6 ***Gerlach***	Y	Y	Y	N	N	N	Y	N
7 ***Weldon***	Y	Y	Y	Y	N	N	Y	N
8 ***Greenwood***	?	?	?	N	N	?	Y	N
9 ***Shuster, Bill***	Y	Y	Y	N	N	N	Y	Y
10 ***Sherwood***	Y	Y	Y	N	N	N	Y	N
11 Kanjorski	Y	Y	Y	Y	Y	Y	N	N
12 Murtha	Y	Y	Y	Y	Y	Y	N	N
13 Hoeffel	Y	Y	Y	?	?	Y	N	N
14 Doyle	Y	Y	Y	Y	Y	Y	N	N
15 ***Toomey***	?	?	?	N	N	N	Y	Y
16 ***Pitts***	?	?	?	N	N	N	Y	Y
17 Holden	Y	Y	Y	N	N	N	Y	N
18 ***Murphy***	Y	Y	Y	N	N	N	Y	N
19 ***Platts***	Y	Y	Y	Y	N	Y	N	Y
RHODE ISLAND								
1 Kennedy	?	?	?	N	N	N	Y	N
2 Langevin	Y	Y	Y	N	N	N	Y	N
SOUTH CAROLINA								
1 ***Brown***	Y	Y	Y	N	N	N	Y	N
2 ***Wilson***	Y	Y	Y	N	N	N	Y	Y
3 ***Barrett***	Y	Y	Y	N	N	N	Y	Y
4 ***DeMint***	?	?	?	N	N	N	Y	Y
5 Spratt	?	?	?	Y	Y	Y	N	N
6 Clyburn	Y	Y	Y	Y	Y	Y	N	N
SOUTH DAKOTA								
AL Herseth	Y	Y	Y	N	N	N	Y	N
TENNESSEE								
1 ***Jenkins***	Y	Y	Y	N	N	N	Y	Y
2 ***Duncan***	Y	Y	Y	Y	N	N	Y	Y
3 ***Wamp***	Y	Y	Y	N	N	N	Y	Y
4 Davis	Y	Y	Y	N	N	N	Y	Y
5 Cooper	N	Y	Y	?	?	?	?	?
6 Gordon	Y	Y	Y	N	N	N	Y	N
7 ***Blackburn***	Y	Y	Y	N	N	N	Y	Y
8 Tanner	N	Y	Y	N	N	N	Y	Y
9 Ford	Y	Y	Y	N	N	Y	Y	N
TEXAS								
1 Sandlin	Y	Y	Y	N	N	N	Y	N
2 Turner	Y	Y	Y	N	N	N	Y	N
3 ***Johnson, Sam***	Y	N	Y	N	N	N	Y	N
4 ***Hall***	Y	Y	Y	N	N	Y	Y	N
5 ***Hensarling***	Y	Y	Y	N	N	N	Y	Y
6 ***Barton***	Y	Y	Y	N	N	N	Y	Y
7 ***Culberson***	?	?	?	N	N	N	Y	N
8 ***Brady***	Y	Y	Y	N	N	N	Y	Y
9 Lampson	Y	Y	Y	N	N	N	Y	N
10 Doggett	Y	Y	Y	Y	N	N	Y	Y
11 Edwards	Y	Y	Y	N	N	N	Y	N
12 ***Granger***	?	?	?	N	N	N	Y	N
13 ***Thornberry***	Y	Y	Y	N	N	N	Y	Y
14 ***Paul***	N	N	N	N	N	N	Y	Y
15 Hinojosa	?	?	?	N	N	N	Y	N
16 Reyes	Y	Y	Y	N	N	N	Y	N
17 Stenholm	Y	Y	Y	N	N	N	Y	Y
18 Jackson-Lee	Y	Y	Y	Y	Y	Y	N	N
19 ***Neugebauer***	+	Y	Y	N	N	N	Y	Y
20 Gonzalez	Y	Y	Y	N	N	N	Y	N
21 ***Smith***	Y	Y	Y	N	N	N	Y	N
22 ***DeLay***	Y	Y	Y	N	N	N	Y	N
23 ***Bonilla***	Y	Y	Y	N	N	N	Y	N
24 Frost	?	?	?	N	N	N	Y	N
25 Bell	?	?	?	Y	N	Y	Y	N
26 ***Burgess***	Y	Y	Y	N	N	N	Y	Y
27 Ortiz	Y	Y	Y	N	N	N	Y	N
28 Rodriguez	Y	Y	Y	Y	N	N	Y	N
29 Green	Y	Y	Y	N	N	N	Y	N
30 Johnson, E.B.	Y	Y	Y	N	N	N	Y	N
31 ***Carter***	Y	Y	Y	N	N	N	Y	Y
32 ***Sessions***	Y	Y	Y	N	N	N	Y	Y
UTAH								
1 ***Bishop***	Y	Y	Y	N	N	N	Y	Y
2 Matheson	Y	Y	Y	N	N	N	Y	?
3 ***Cannon***	Y	Y	Y	N	N	N	Y	Y
VERMONT								
AL *Sanders*	?	?	Y	Y	Y	Y	N	N
VIRGINIA								
1 ***Davis, Jo Ann***	Y	Y	Y	N	N	N	Y	Y
2 ***Schrock***	Y	Y	Y	N	N	N	Y	Y
3 Scott	Y	Y	Y	N	N	Y	N	N
4 ***Forbes***	Y	Y	Y	N	N	N	Y	Y
5 ***Goode***	Y	Y	Y	N	N	Y	N	Y
6 ***Goodlatte***	Y	Y	Y	N	N	N	Y	Y
7 ***Cantor***	N	Y	Y	N	N	N	Y	N
8 Moran	Y	Y	Y	N	N	N	Y	N
9 Boucher	Y	Y	Y	N	N	N	Y	N
10 ***Wolf***	Y	Y	Y	N	N	N	Y	N
11 ***Davis, T.***	Y	Y	Y	N	N	N	Y	N
WASHINGTON								
1 Inslee	?	?	?	N	N	N	Y	N
2 Larsen	N	Y	Y	N	N	N	Y	N
3 Baird	Y	Y	Y	N	N	N	Y	N
4 ***Hastings***	Y	Y	Y	N	N	N	Y	N
5 ***Nethercutt***	Y	Y	Y	N	N	N	Y	N
6 Dicks	N	Y	Y	N	N	N	Y	N
7 McDermott	N	Y	Y	Y	Y	Y	N	N
8 ***Dunn***	Y	Y	Y	N	N	N	Y	N
9 Smith	Y	Y	Y	N	N	N	Y	Y
WEST VIRGINIA								
1 Mollohan	Y	Y	Y	N	N	N	Y	N
2 ***Capito***	Y	Y	Y	N	N	N	Y	N
3 Rahall	Y	Y	Y	Y	Y	Y	N	N
WISCONSIN								
1 ***Ryan***	Y	Y	Y	N	N	N	Y	Y
2 Baldwin	N	Y	Y	Y	Y	Y	N	N
3 Kind	Y	Y	Y	N	N	N	Y	N
4 Kleczka	?	?	?	Y	Y	Y	N	N
5 ***Sensenbrenner***	Y	Y	Y	N	N	N	Y	Y
6 ***Petri***	Y	Y	Y	Y	Y	Y	N	Y
7 Obey	N	Y	Y	Y	Y	Y	N	N
8 ***Green***	Y	Y	Y	N	N	N	Y	Y
WYOMING								
AL ***Cubin***	Y	Y	Y	N	N	N	Y	Y

Southern states - Ala., Ark., Fla., Ga., Ky., La., Miss., N.C., Okla., S.C., Tenn., Texas, Va.

399. HR 4850. Fiscal 2005 District of Columbia Appropriations/ Passage. Passage of the bill that would appropriate $560 million in fiscal 2005 spending and allow the use of $8.2 billion in local funds for government operations and services in the District of Columbia. Passed 371-54: R 182-40; D 188-14 (ND 139-8, SD 49-6); I 1-0. July 20, 2004.

400. HR 4837. Fiscal 2005 Military Construction Appropriations/ Previous Question. Myrick, R-N.C., motion to order the previous question (thus ending debate and possibility of amendment) on adoption of the rule (H Res 732) to provide for House floor consideration of the bill that would provide $10 billion in fiscal 2005 for military construction projects, including family housing and barrack construction and modernization. Motion agreed to 217-197: R 217-1; D 0-195 (ND 0-144, SD 0-51); I 0-1. July 21, 2004.

401. HR 4837. Fiscal 2005 Military Construction Appropriations/ Rule. Adoption of the rule (H Res 732) to provide for House floor consideration of the bill that would provide $10 billion in fiscal 2005 for military construction projects, including family housing and barrack construction and modernization. Adopted 212-211: R 212-9; D 0-201 (ND 0-147, SD 0-54); I 0-1. July 21, 2004.

402. H Res 723. Apollo 11 Anniversary/Adoption. Hall, R-Texas, motion to suspend the rules and adopt the resolution that would recognize the 35th anniversary of the Apollo 11 lunar landing, commend the astronauts and other NASA employees who worked on the mission and support continued U.S. leadership in space exploration. Motion agreed to 416-0: R 218-0; D 197-0 (ND 143-0, SD 54-0); I 1-0. A two-thirds majority of those present and voting (278 in this case) is required for adoption under suspension of the rules. July 21, 2004.

403. HR 4608. Bob Michel VA Outpatient Clinic/Passage. Smith, R-N.J., motion to suspend the rules and pass the bill that would name a veterans outpatient clinic in Peoria, Ill., as the "Bob Michel Department of Veterans Affairs Outpatient Clinic," after former Rep. Robert H. Michel, R-Ill. (1957-95), who served as minority leader from 1981 to 1995. Motion agreed to 407-0: R 212-0; D 194-0 (ND 141-0, SD 53-0); I 1-0. A two-thirds majority of those present and voting (272 in this case) is required for passage under suspension of the rules. July 21, 2004.

404. HR 2443. Coast Guard Reauthorization/Conference Report. Adoption of the conference report on the bill that would authorize $8.2 billion in fiscal 2005 for Coast Guard programs and activities, including $5.4 billion for operating expenses. Adopted (thus sent to the Senate) 425-1: R 223-1; D 201-0 (ND 147-0, SD 54-0); I 1-0. July 21, 2004.

405. HR 4840. Small Business Taxes/Passage. Portman, R-Ohio, motion to suspend the rules and pass the bill that would extend through 2007 provisions included in current tax law increasing expensing and cost limits on qualifying business property. Motion agreed to 424-0: R 222-0; D 201-0 (ND 147-0, SD 54-0); I 1-0. A two-thirds majority of those present and voting (283 in this case) is required for passage under suspension of the rules. July 21, 2004.

406. HR 4879. Military Housing Spending Cap/Passage. Hunter, R-Calif., motion to suspend the rules and pass the bill that would increase the spending cap on the Pentagon's Military Housing Privatization Program from $850 million to $1.35 billion. Motion agreed to 423-0: R 221-0; D 201-0 (ND 146-0, SD 55-0); I 1-0. A two-thirds majority of those present and voting (282 in this case) is required for passage under suspension of the rules. July 21, 2004.

* Rep. G.K. Butterfield, D-N.C., was sworn in July 21, 2004 to replace Democrat Rep. Frank W. Ballance Jr., who resigned effective June 11, 2004. The first vote for which Butterfield was eligible was vote 405.

Key

Y	Voted for (yea).
#	Paired for.
+	Announced for.
N	Voted against (nay).
X	Paired against.
−	Announced against.
P	Voted "present."
C	Voted "present" to avoid possible conflict of interest.
?	Did not vote or otherwise make a position known.

Democrats **Republicans** *Independents*

	399	400	401	402	403	404	405	406
ALABAMA								
1 *Bonner*	Y	Y	Y	Y	Y	Y	Y	Y
2 *Everett*	N	Y	Y	Y	Y	Y	Y	Y
3 *Rogers*	Y	Y	Y	Y	Y	Y	Y	Y
4 *Aderholt*	Y	Y	Y	Y	Y	Y	Y	Y
5 Cramer	Y	N	N	Y	Y	Y	Y	Y
6 *Bachus*	Y	Y	Y	Y	Y	Y	Y	Y
7 Davis	Y	N	N	Y	Y	Y	Y	Y
ALASKA								
AL *Young*	Y	Y	Y	Y	Y	Y	Y	Y
ARIZONA								
1 *Renzi*	Y	Y	Y	Y	Y	Y	Y	Y
2 *Franks*	N	Y	Y	Y	Y	Y	Y	Y
3 *Shadegg*	Y	Y	Y	Y	Y	Y	Y	Y
4 Pastor	Y	N	N	Y	Y	Y	Y	Y
5 *Hayworth*	N	Y	Y	Y	Y	Y	Y	Y
6 *Flake*	N	Y	N	Y	Y	Y	Y	Y
7 Grijalva	Y	N	N	Y	Y	Y	Y	Y
8 *Kolbe*	Y	Y	Y	Y	Y	Y	Y	Y
ARKANSAS								
1 Berry	N	N	N	Y	Y	Y	Y	Y
2 Snyder	Y	N	N	Y	Y	Y	Y	Y
3 *Boozman*	Y	Y	Y	Y	Y	Y	Y	Y
4 Ross	N	N	N	Y	Y	Y	Y	Y
CALIFORNIA								
1 Thompson	Y	N	N	Y	Y	Y	Y	Y
2 *Herger*	N	Y	Y	Y	Y	Y	Y	Y
3 *Ose*	Y	Y	Y	Y	Y	Y	Y	Y
4 *Doolittle*	Y	Y	Y	Y	Y	Y	Y	Y
5 Matsui	Y	N	N	Y	Y	Y	Y	Y
6 Woolsey	Y	N	N	Y	Y	Y	Y	Y
7 Miller, George	N	N	N	Y	Y	Y	Y	Y
8 Pelosi	Y	N	N	Y	Y	Y	Y	Y
9 Lee	Y	N	N	Y	Y	Y	Y	Y
10 Tauscher	Y	N	N	Y	Y	Y	Y	Y
11 *Pombo*	Y	Y	Y	Y	Y	Y	Y	Y
12 Lantos	Y	N	N	Y	Y	Y	Y	Y
13 Stark	Y	N	N	Y	Y	Y	Y	Y
14 Eshoo	Y	N	N	Y	Y	Y	Y	Y
15 Honda	Y	N	N	Y	Y	Y	Y	Y
16 Lofgren	Y	N	N	Y	Y	Y	Y	Y
17 Farr	Y	N	N	Y	Y	Y	Y	Y
18 Cardoza	Y	N	N	Y	Y	Y	Y	Y
19 *Radanovich*	Y	Y	Y	Y	Y	Y	Y	Y
20 Dooley	Y	N	N	Y	Y	Y	Y	Y
21 *Nunes*	Y	Y	Y	Y	Y	Y	Y	Y
22 *Thomas*	Y	Y	Y	Y	Y	Y	Y	Y
23 Capps	Y	N	N	Y	Y	Y	Y	Y
24 *Gallegly*	Y	Y	Y	Y	Y	Y	Y	Y
25 *McKeon*	Y	Y	Y	Y	Y	Y	Y	Y
26 *Dreier*	Y	Y	Y	Y	Y	Y	Y	Y
27 Sherman	Y	N	N	Y	Y	Y	Y	Y
28 Berman	Y	N	N	Y	Y	Y	Y	Y
29 Schiff	Y	N	N	Y	Y	Y	Y	Y
30 Waxman	Y	N	N	?	?	Y	Y	Y
31 Becerra	Y	N	N	Y	Y	Y	Y	Y
32 Solis	Y	N	N	Y	Y	Y	Y	Y
33 Watson	Y	N	N	Y	Y	Y	Y	Y
34 Roybal-Allard	Y	N	N	Y	Y	Y	Y	Y
35 Waters	Y	N	N	Y	Y	Y	Y	Y
36 Harman	Y	N	N	Y	Y	Y	Y	Y

	399	400	401	402	403	404	405	406
37 Millender-McD.	Y	N	N	Y	Y	Y	Y	Y
38 Napolitano	Y	N	N	?	Y	Y	Y	Y
39 Sánchez, Linda	Y	N	N	Y	Y	Y	Y	Y
40 *Royce*	N	Y	Y	Y	Y	Y	Y	Y
41 *Lewis*	Y	Y	Y	Y	Y	Y	Y	Y
42 *Miller, Gary*	Y	Y	Y	Y	Y	Y	Y	Y
43 Baca	Y	N	N	Y	Y	Y	Y	Y
44 *Calvert*	Y	Y	Y	Y	Y	Y	Y	Y
45 *Bono*	Y	Y	Y	Y	Y	Y	Y	Y
46 *Rohrabacher*	Y	Y	Y	Y	Y	Y	Y	Y
47 Sanchez, Loretta	Y	N	N	Y	Y	Y	Y	Y
48 *Cox*	Y	Y	Y	Y	Y	Y	Y	Y
49 *Issa*	Y	Y	Y	Y	Y	Y	Y	Y
50 *Cunningham*	Y	Y	Y	Y	Y	Y	Y	Y
51 Filner	Y	N	N	Y	Y	Y	Y	Y
52 *Hunter*	Y	Y	Y	Y	Y	Y	Y	Y
53 Davis	Y	N	N	Y	Y	Y	Y	Y
COLORADO								
1 DeGette	Y	N	N	Y	Y	Y	Y	Y
2 Udall	Y	N	N	Y	Y	Y	Y	Y
3 *McInnis*	Y	Y	Y	Y	Y	Y	Y	Y
4 *Musgrave*	Y	Y	Y	Y	Y	Y	Y	Y
5 *Hefley*	N	Y	Y	Y	Y	Y	Y	Y
6 *Tancredo*	Y	Y	Y	Y	Y	Y	Y	Y
7 *Beauprez*	Y	Y	Y	Y	Y	Y	Y	Y
CONNECTICUT								
1 Larson	Y	N	N	Y	Y	Y	Y	Y
2 *Simmons*	N	Y	Y	Y	Y	Y	Y	Y
3 DeLauro	Y	N	N	?	Y	Y	Y	Y
4 *Shays*	Y	Y	Y	Y	Y	Y	Y	Y
5 *Johnson*	Y	Y	Y	Y	Y	Y	Y	Y
DELAWARE								
AL *Castle*	Y	Y	Y	Y	Y	Y	Y	Y
FLORIDA								
1 *Miller, J.*	N	Y	Y	Y	Y	Y	Y	Y
2 Boyd	Y	N	N	Y	Y	Y	Y	Y
3 Brown	Y	N	N	Y	Y	Y	Y	Y
4 *Crenshaw*	Y	Y	Y	Y	Y	Y	Y	Y
5 *Brown-Waite*	Y	Y	Y	Y	Y	Y	Y	Y
6 *Stearns*	N	Y	Y	Y	Y	Y	Y	Y
7 *Mica*	Y	Y	Y	Y	Y	Y	Y	Y
8 *Keller*	Y	Y	Y	Y	Y	Y	Y	Y
9 *Bilirakis*	Y	Y	Y	Y	Y	Y	Y	Y
10 *Young*	Y	Y	Y	Y	Y	Y	Y	Y
11 Davis	Y	N	N	Y	Y	Y	Y	Y
12 *Putnam*	Y	Y	Y	Y	Y	Y	Y	Y
13 *Harris*	Y	Y	Y	Y	Y	Y	Y	Y
14 *Goss*	N	Y	Y	Y	Y	Y	Y	Y
15 *Weldon*	Y	Y	Y	Y	Y	Y	Y	Y
16 *Foley*	Y	Y	Y	Y	Y	Y	Y	Y
17 Meek	Y	N	N	Y	Y	Y	Y	Y
18 *Ros-Lehtinen*	Y	Y	?	?	Y	Y	Y	Y
19 Wexler	N	N	N	Y	Y	Y	Y	Y
20 Deutsch	N	?	?	?	?	?	?	?
21 *Diaz-Balart, L.*	Y	Y	Y	Y	Y	Y	Y	Y
22 *Shaw*	Y	Y	Y	Y	Y	Y	Y	Y
23 Hastings	Y	N	N	Y	Y	Y	Y	Y
24 *Feeney*	Y	Y	Y	Y	Y	Y	Y	Y
25 *Diaz-Balart, M.*	Y	Y	Y	Y	Y	Y	Y	Y
GEORGIA								
1 *Kingston*	Y	Y	Y	Y	Y	Y	Y	Y
2 Bishop	Y	N	N	Y	Y	Y	Y	Y
3 Marshall	Y	N	N	Y	Y	Y	Y	Y
4 Majette	?	?	?	?	?	?	?	?
5 Lewis	Y	N	N	Y	Y	Y	?	Y
6 *Isakson*	?	?	?	?	?	Y	Y	Y
7 *Linder*	Y	Y	Y	Y	Y	Y	Y	Y
8 *Collins*	?	?	?	?	?	?	?	?
9 *Norwood*	N	Y	Y	Y	Y	Y	Y	Y
10 *Deal*	N	Y	Y	Y	Y	Y	Y	Y
11 *Gingrey*	Y	Y	Y	Y	Y	Y	Y	Y
12 *Burns*	Y	Y	Y	Y	Y	Y	Y	Y
13 Scott	Y	N	N	Y	Y	Y	Y	Y
HAWAII								
1 Abercrombie	Y	N	N	Y	Y	Y	Y	Y
2 Case	Y	N	N	Y	Y	Y	Y	Y
IDAHO								
1 *Otter*	N	Y	Y	Y	Y	Y	Y	Y
2 *Simpson*	Y	Y	Y	Y	Y	Y	Y	Y
ILLINOIS								
1 Rush	Y	N	N	Y	Y	Y	Y	Y
2 Jackson	Y	N	N	Y	Y	Y	Y	Y
3 Lipinski	Y	N	N	Y	Y	Y	Y	Y
4 Gutierrez	Y	N	N	Y	Y	Y	Y	Y
5 Emanuel	Y	N	N	Y	Y	Y	Y	Y
6 *Hyde*	Y	Y	Y	Y	Y	Y	Y	Y

ND Northern Democrats   SD Southern Democrats

	399	400	401	402	403	404	405	406
7 Davis	Y	N	N	Y	Y	Y	Y	Y
8 ***Crane***	Y	Y	Y	Y	Y	Y	Y	Y
9 Schakowsky	Y	N	N	Y	Y	Y	Y	Y
10 ***Kirk***	Y	Y	Y	Y	Y	Y	Y	Y
11 ***Weller***	Y	Y	Y	Y	Y	Y	Y	Y
12 Costello	Y	N	N	Y	Y	Y	Y	Y
13 ***Biggert***	N	Y	Y	Y	Y	Y	Y	Y
14 ***Hastert***		Y	Y					
15 ***Johnson***	Y	Y	Y	Y	Y	Y	Y	Y
16 ***Manzullo***	N	Y	Y	Y	Y	Y	Y	Y
17 Evans	N	N	N	Y	Y	Y	Y	Y
18 ***LaHood***	Y	Y	Y	Y	Y	Y	Y	Y
19 ***Shimkus***	Y	Y	Y	Y	Y	Y	Y	Y
INDIANA								
1 Visclosky	Y	N	N	Y	Y	Y	Y	Y
2 ***Chocola***	Y	Y	Y	Y	Y	Y	Y	Y
3 ***Souder***	Y	?	Y	Y	Y	Y	Y	Y
4 ***Buyer***	Y	Y	Y	Y	Y	Y	Y	Y
5 ***Burton***	Y	Y	Y	Y	Y	Y	Y	Y
6 ***Pence***	Y	Y	Y	Y	Y	Y	Y	Y
7 Carson	?	?	?	?	?	?	?	?
8 ***Hostettler***	N	Y	Y	Y	Y	Y	Y	Y
9 Hill	Y	N	N	Y	Y	Y	Y	Y
IOWA								
1 ***Nussle***	Y	Y	N	Y	Y	Y	Y	Y
2 ***Leach***	Y	Y	Y	Y	Y	Y	Y	Y
3 Boswell	N	N	N	Y	Y	Y	Y	Y
4 ***Latham***	Y	Y	Y	Y	Y	Y	Y	Y
5 ***King***	N	Y	N	Y	Y	Y	Y	Y
KANSAS								
1 ***Moran***	Y	Y	Y	Y	Y	Y	Y	Y
2 ***Ryun***	Y	Y	Y	Y	Y	Y	Y	Y
3 Moore	Y	N	N	Y	Y	Y	Y	Y
4 ***Tiahrt***	Y	Y	Y	Y	Y	Y	Y	Y
KENTUCKY								
1 ***Whitfield***	Y	Y	Y	Y	Y	Y	Y	Y
2 ***Lewis***	Y	Y	Y	Y	Y	Y	Y	Y
3 ***Northup***	Y	Y	Y	Y	Y	Y	Y	Y
4 Lucas	Y	N	N	Y	Y	Y	Y	Y
5 ***Rogers***	Y	Y	Y	Y	Y	Y	Y	Y
6 Chandler	Y	N	N	Y	Y	Y	Y	Y
LOUISIANA								
1 ***Vitter***	Y	Y	Y	Y	Y	Y	Y	Y
2 Jefferson	Y	N	N	Y	Y	Y	Y	Y
3 ***Tauzin***	Y	Y	Y	Y	?	Y	Y	?
4 ***McCrery***	Y	Y	Y	Y	Y	Y	Y	Y
5 Alexander	Y	N	N	Y	Y	Y	Y	Y
6 ***Baker***	Y	Y	Y	Y	Y	Y	Y	Y
7 John	Y	N	N	Y	Y	Y	Y	Y
MAINE								
1 Allen	Y	N	N	Y	Y	Y	Y	Y
2 Michaud	N	N	N	Y	Y	Y	Y	Y
MARYLAND								
1 ***Gilchrest***	Y	Y	Y	Y	?	Y	Y	Y
2 Ruppersberger	Y	N	N	Y	Y	Y	Y	Y
3 Cardin	Y	N	N	Y	Y	Y	Y	Y
4 Wynn	Y	N	N	Y	Y	Y	Y	Y
5 Hoyer	Y	N	N	Y	Y	Y	Y	Y
6 ***Bartlett***	N	Y	Y	Y	Y	Y	Y	Y
7 Cummings	Y	N	N	Y	Y	Y	Y	Y
8 Van Hollen	Y	N	N	Y	Y	Y	Y	Y
MASSACHUSETTS								
1 Olver	Y	N	N	Y	Y	Y	Y	Y
2 Neal	Y	N	N	Y	Y	Y	Y	Y
3 McGovern	Y	N	N	Y	Y	Y	Y	Y
4 Frank	Y	?	N	Y	Y	Y	Y	Y
5 Meehan	Y	N	N	Y	Y	Y	Y	Y
6 Tierney	N	N	N	Y	Y	Y	Y	Y
7 Markey	Y	N	N	Y	Y	Y	Y	Y
8 Capuano	Y	N	N	Y	Y	Y	Y	Y
9 Lynch	Y	?	N	Y	Y	Y	Y	Y
10 Delahunt	Y	N	N	Y	Y	Y	Y	Y
MICHIGAN								
1 Stupak	Y	N	N	Y	Y	Y	Y	Y
2 ***Hoekstra***	Y	Y	Y	Y	Y	Y	Y	Y
3 ***Ehlers***	Y	Y	Y	Y	Y	Y	Y	Y
4 ***Camp***	Y	Y	Y	Y	Y	Y	Y	Y
5 Kildee	Y	N	N	Y	Y	Y	Y	Y
6 ***Upton***	Y	Y	Y	Y	Y	Y	Y	Y
7 ***Smith***	N	Y	Y	Y	Y	Y	Y	Y
8 ***Rogers***	Y	Y	Y	Y	Y	Y	Y	Y
9 ***Knollenberg***	Y	Y	Y	Y	Y	Y	Y	Y
10 ***Miller***	Y	Y	Y	Y	Y	Y	Y	Y
11 ***McCotter***	Y	Y	Y	Y	Y	Y	Y	Y
12 Levin	Y	N	N	Y	Y	Y	Y	Y

	399	400	401	402	403	404	405	406
13 Kilpatrick	Y	N	N	Y	Y	Y	Y	Y
14 Conyers	Y	N	N	Y	Y	Y	Y	Y
15 Dingell	Y	N	N	?	Y	Y	Y	Y
MINNESOTA								
1 ***Gutknecht***	N	Y	N	Y	Y	Y	Y	Y
2 ***Kline***	Y	Y	Y	Y	Y	Y	Y	Y
3 ***Ramstad***	N	Y	Y	Y	Y	Y	Y	Y
4 McCollum	Y	N	N	Y	Y	Y	Y	Y
5 Sabo	Y	N	N	Y	Y	Y	Y	Y
6 ***Kennedy***	Y	Y	Y	Y	Y	Y	Y	Y
7 Peterson	N	N	N	Y	Y	Y	Y	Y
8 Oberstar	Y	N	N	Y	Y	Y	Y	Y
MISSISSIPPI								
1 ***Wicker***	Y	Y	Y	Y	Y	Y	Y	Y
2 Thompson	Y	N	N	Y	Y	Y	Y	Y
3 ***Pickering***	Y	Y	Y	Y	?	Y	Y	Y
4 Taylor	N	N	N	Y	Y	Y	Y	Y
MISSOURI								
1 Clay	Y	N	N	Y	Y	Y	Y	Y
2 ***Akin***	Y	Y	Y	Y	Y	Y	Y	Y
3 Gephardt	Y	N	N	Y	Y	Y	Y	Y
4 Skelton	Y	N	N	Y	Y	Y	Y	Y
5 McCarthy	Y	N	N	Y	Y	Y	Y	Y
6 ***Graves***	N	Y	Y	Y	Y	Y	Y	Y
7 ***Blunt***	Y	Y	Y	Y	Y	Y	Y	Y
8 ***Emerson***	Y	Y	Y	Y	Y	Y	Y	Y
9 ***Hulshof***	Y	Y	Y	Y	Y	Y	Y	Y
MONTANA								
AL ***Rehberg***	Y	Y	Y	Y	Y	Y	Y	Y
NEBRASKA								
1 ***Bereuter***	Y	Y	Y	Y	Y	Y	Y	Y
2 ***Terry***	Y	Y	Y	Y	Y	Y	Y	Y
3 ***Osborne***	Y	Y	Y	Y	Y	Y	Y	Y
NEVADA								
1 Berkley	Y	N	N	Y	Y	Y	Y	Y
2 ***Gibbons***	Y	Y	Y	Y	Y	Y	Y	Y
3 ***Porter***	Y	Y	N	Y	Y	Y	Y	Y
NEW HAMPSHIRE								
1 ***Bradley***	Y	Y	Y	Y	Y	Y	Y	Y
2 ***Bass***	Y	Y	Y	Y	Y	Y	Y	Y
NEW JERSEY								
1 Andrews	Y	N	N	Y	Y	Y	Y	Y
2 ***LoBiondo***	Y	Y	Y	Y	Y	Y	Y	Y
3 ***Saxton***	Y	+	+	+	+	Y	Y	Y
4 ***Smith***	Y	Y	Y	Y	Y	Y	Y	Y
5 ***Garrett***	Y	Y	N	Y	Y	Y	Y	Y
6 Pallone	Y	N	N	Y	Y	Y	Y	Y
7 ***Ferguson***	?	?	?	?	?	?	?	?
8 Pascrell	Y	N	N	Y	Y	Y	Y	Y
9 Rothman	Y	N	N	Y	Y	Y	Y	Y
10 Payne	Y	N	N	Y	Y	Y	Y	Y
11 ***Frelinghuysen***	Y	Y	Y	Y	Y	Y	Y	Y
12 Holt	Y	N	N	Y	Y	Y	Y	Y
13 Menendez	Y	N	N	Y	Y	Y	Y	Y
NEW MEXICO								
1 ***Wilson***	Y	N	N	Y	Y	Y	Y	Y
2 ***Pearce***	Y	Y	Y	Y	Y	Y	Y	Y
3 Udall	Y	N	N	Y	Y	Y	Y	Y
NEW YORK								
1 Bishop	Y	N	N	Y	Y	Y	Y	Y
2 Israel	Y	N	N	Y	Y	Y	Y	Y
3 ***King***	Y	?	?	?	?	?	Y	Y
4 McCarthy	Y	N	N	Y	Y	Y	Y	Y
5 Ackerman	Y	N	N	Y	Y	Y	Y	Y
6 Meeks	Y	N	N	?	?	Y	Y	Y
7 Crowley	Y	N	N	Y	Y	Y	Y	Y
8 Nadler	Y	N	N	Y	Y	Y	Y	Y
9 Weiner	Y	N	N	Y	Y	Y	Y	Y
10 Towns	Y	N	N	Y	Y	Y	Y	Y
11 Owens	Y	N	N	Y	Y	Y	Y	Y
12 Velázquez	Y	N	N	Y	Y	Y	Y	Y
13 ***Fossella***	N	Y	Y	Y	Y	Y	Y	Y
14 Maloney	Y	N	N	Y	Y	Y	Y	Y
15 Rangel	Y	N	N	?	?	Y	Y	Y
16 Serrano	Y	N	N	Y	Y	Y	Y	Y
17 Engel	Y	N	N	Y	Y	Y	Y	Y
18 Lowey	Y	N	N	Y	Y	Y	Y	Y
19 ***Kelly***	Y	Y	Y	Y	Y	Y	Y	Y
20 ***Sweeney***	Y	Y	Y	Y	Y	Y	Y	Y
21 McNulty	Y	N	N	Y	Y	Y	Y	Y
22 Hinchey	Y	N	N	Y	Y	Y	Y	Y
23 ***McHugh***	N	Y	Y	Y	?	Y	Y	Y
24 ***Boehlert***	N	Y	Y	Y	Y	Y	Y	Y
25 ***Walsh***	Y	Y	Y	Y	Y	Y	Y	Y

	399	400	401	402	403	404	405	406
26 ***Reynolds***	Y	Y	Y	Y	Y	Y	?	?
27 ***Quinn***	?	?	?	?	?	?	?	?
28 Slaughter	Y	N	N	Y	Y	Y	Y	Y
29 ***Houghton***	Y	Y	Y	Y	Y	Y	Y	Y
NORTH CAROLINA								
1 Butterfield*							Y	Y
2 Etheridge	N	N	N	Y	Y	Y	Y	Y
3 ***Jones***	N	Y	Y	?	?	Y	Y	Y
4 Price	Y	?	N	Y	Y	Y	Y	Y
5 ***Burr***	Y	Y	Y	Y	Y	Y	Y	Y
6 ***Coble***	N	Y	Y	Y	Y	Y	Y	Y
7 McIntyre	Y	N	N	Y	Y	Y	Y	Y
8 ***Hayes***	Y	Y	Y	Y	Y	Y	Y	Y
9 ***Myrick***	Y	Y	Y	Y	Y	Y	Y	Y
10 ***Ballenger***	Y	Y	Y	Y	Y	Y	Y	Y
11 ***Taylor***	N	Y	Y	Y	Y	Y	Y	Y
12 Watt	Y	N	N	Y	Y	Y	Y	Y
13 Miller	Y	N	N	Y	Y	Y	Y	Y
NORTH DAKOTA								
AL Pomeroy	Y	N	N	Y	Y	Y	Y	Y
OHIO								
1 ***Chabot***	Y	Y	Y	Y	Y	Y	Y	Y
2 ***Portman***	Y	Y	Y	Y	Y	Y	Y	Y
3 ***Turner***	Y	Y	Y	Y	Y	Y	Y	Y
4 ***Oxley***	Y	?	Y	Y	Y	Y	Y	Y
5 ***Gillmor***	Y	Y	Y	Y	Y	Y	Y	Y
6 Strickland	Y	?	?	?	?	Y	Y	Y
7 ***Hobson***	Y	Y	Y	Y	Y	Y	Y	Y
8 ***Boehner***	Y	Y	Y	Y	Y	Y	Y	Y
9 Kaptur	Y	N	N	Y	Y	Y	Y	Y
10 Kucinich	Y	N	N	Y	Y	Y	Y	Y
11 Jones	Y	N	N	Y	Y	Y	Y	Y
12 ***Tiberi***	Y	Y	Y	Y	Y	Y	Y	Y
13 Brown	Y	N	N	Y	Y	?	?	?
14 ***LaTourette***	Y	Y	Y	Y	Y	Y	Y	Y
15 ***Pryce***	Y	Y	Y	Y	Y	Y	Y	Y
16 ***Regula***	Y	Y	Y	Y	Y	Y	Y	Y
17 Ryan	Y	N	N	Y	Y	Y	Y	Y
18 ***Ney***	Y	Y	Y	Y	Y	Y	+	+
OKLAHOMA								
1 ***Sullivan***	Y	Y	Y	Y	Y	Y	Y	Y
2 Carson	Y	N	N	Y	Y	Y	Y	Y
3 ***Lucas***	Y	Y	Y	Y	Y	Y	Y	Y
4 ***Cole***	Y	Y	Y	Y	?	Y	Y	Y
5 ***Istook***	Y	?	?	?	?	Y	Y	Y
OREGON								
1 Wu	Y	N	N	Y	Y	Y	Y	Y
2 ***Walden***	Y	Y	Y	Y	Y	Y	Y	Y
3 Blumenauer	Y	N	N	Y	Y	Y	Y	Y
4 DeFazio	Y	N	N	Y	Y	Y	Y	Y
5 Hooley	Y	N	N	Y	Y	Y	Y	Y
PENNSYLVANIA								
1 Brady	Y	N	N	Y	Y	Y	Y	Y
2 Fattah	Y	N	N	Y	Y	Y	Y	Y
3 ***English***	Y	Y	Y	Y	Y	Y	Y	Y
4 ***Hart***	Y	Y	Y	Y	Y	Y	Y	Y
5 ***Peterson***	Y	Y	Y	Y	Y	Y	Y	Y
6 ***Gerlach***	Y	Y	Y	Y	Y	Y	Y	Y
7 ***Weldon***	Y	Y	Y	Y	Y	Y	Y	Y
8 ***Greenwood***	Y	Y	Y	Y	Y	Y	Y	Y
9 ***Shuster, Bill***	Y	Y	Y	Y	Y	Y	Y	Y
10 ***Sherwood***	Y	Y	Y	Y	Y	Y	Y	Y
11 Kanjorski	Y	N	N	Y	Y	Y	Y	Y
12 Murtha	Y	N	N	Y	Y	Y	Y	Y
13 Hoeffel	Y	N	N	Y	Y	Y	Y	Y
14 Doyle	Y	N	N	Y	Y	Y	Y	Y
15 ***Toomey***	N	Y	Y	Y	Y	Y	Y	Y
16 ***Pitts***	Y	?	Y	Y	Y	Y	Y	Y
17 Holden	Y	N	N	Y	Y	Y	Y	Y
18 ***Murphy***	Y	Y	Y	Y	Y	Y	Y	Y
19 ***Platts***	Y	Y	Y	Y	Y	Y	Y	Y
RHODE ISLAND								
1 Kennedy	Y	N	N	Y	Y	Y	Y	?
2 Langevin	Y	N	N	Y	Y	Y	Y	Y
SOUTH CAROLINA								
1 ***Brown***	Y	Y	Y	Y	Y	Y	Y	Y
2 ***Wilson***	Y	Y	Y	Y	Y	Y	Y	Y
3 ***Barrett***	Y	Y	Y	Y	Y	Y	Y	Y
4 ***DeMint***	Y	Y	Y	Y	Y	Y	Y	Y
5 Spratt	Y	N	N	Y	Y	Y	Y	Y
6 Clyburn	Y	N	N	Y	?	Y	Y	Y
SOUTH DAKOTA								
AL Herseth	Y	N	N	Y	Y	Y	Y	Y

	399	400	401	402	403	404	405	406
TENNESSEE								
1 ***Jenkins***	Y	Y	Y	Y	Y	Y	Y	Y
2 ***Duncan***	N	Y	Y	Y	Y	Y	Y	Y
3 ***Wamp***	Y	Y	Y	Y	Y	Y	Y	Y
4 Davis	Y	N	N	Y	Y	Y	Y	Y
5 Cooper	Y	N	N	Y	Y	Y	Y	Y
6 Gordon	Y	?	N	Y	Y	Y	Y	Y
7 ***Blackburn***	Y	Y	Y	Y	Y	Y	Y	Y
8 Tanner	Y	N	N	Y	Y	Y	Y	Y
9 Ford	Y	N	N	Y	Y	Y	Y	Y
TEXAS								
1 Sandlin	Y	N	N	Y	Y	Y	Y	Y
2 Turner	Y	N	N	Y	Y	Y	Y	Y
3 ***Johnson, Sam***	Y	Y	Y	Y	Y	Y	Y	Y
4 ***Hall***	Y	Y	Y	Y	Y	Y	Y	Y
5 ***Hensarling***	N	Y	N	Y	Y	Y	Y	Y
6 ***Barton***	Y	Y	Y	Y	Y	Y	Y	Y
7 ***Culberson***	Y	Y	Y	Y	?	Y	Y	Y
8 ***Brady***	Y	Y	Y	Y	Y	Y	Y	Y
9 Lampson	Y	N	N	Y	Y	Y	Y	Y
10 Doggett	Y	N	N	Y	Y	Y	Y	Y
11 Edwards	Y	N	N	Y	Y	Y	Y	Y
12 ***Granger***	Y	Y	Y	Y	Y	Y	Y	Y
13 ***Thornberry***	Y	Y	Y	Y	Y	Y	Y	Y
14 ***Paul***	N	Y	Y	Y	Y	N	Y	Y
15 Hinojosa	Y	N	N	Y	Y	Y	Y	Y
16 Reyes	Y	N	N	Y	Y	Y	Y	Y
17 Stenholm	N	N	N	Y	Y	Y	Y	Y
18 Jackson-Lee	Y	N	N	Y	Y	Y	Y	Y
19 ***Neugebauer***	N	Y	Y	Y	Y	Y	Y	Y
20 Gonzalez	Y	N	N	Y	Y	Y	Y	Y
21 ***Smith***	Y	Y	Y	Y	Y	Y	Y	Y
22 ***DeLay***	Y	Y	Y	Y	Y	Y	Y	Y
23 ***Bonilla***	Y	Y	Y	Y	Y	Y	Y	Y
24 Frost	Y	N	N	Y	Y	Y	Y	Y
25 Bell	Y	?	N	Y	Y	Y	Y	Y
26 ***Burgess***	Y	Y	Y	Y	Y	Y	Y	Y
27 Ortiz	Y	N	N	Y	Y	Y	Y	Y
28 Rodriguez	Y	N	N	Y	Y	Y	Y	Y
29 Green	Y	N	N	Y	Y	Y	Y	Y
30 Johnson, E.B.	Y	N	N	Y	Y	Y	Y	Y
31 ***Carter***	Y	Y	Y	Y	Y	Y	Y	Y
32 ***Sessions***	Y	Y	Y	Y	Y	Y	Y	Y
UTAH								
1 ***Bishop***	Y	Y	Y	Y	Y	Y	Y	Y
2 Matheson	?	N	N	Y	Y	Y	Y	Y
3 ***Cannon***	Y	Y	Y	Y	Y	Y	Y	Y
VERMONT								
AL *Sanders*	Y	N	N	Y	Y	Y	Y	Y
VIRGINIA								
1 ***Davis, Jo Ann***	N	Y	Y	Y	Y	Y	Y	Y
2 ***Schrock***	Y	Y	Y	Y	Y	Y	Y	Y
3 Scott	Y	N	N	Y	Y	Y	Y	Y
4 ***Forbes***	Y	Y	Y	Y	Y	Y	Y	Y
5 ***Goode***	N	Y	Y	Y	Y	Y	Y	Y
6 ***Goodlatte***	N	Y	Y	Y	Y	Y	Y	Y
7 ***Cantor***	Y	Y	Y	Y	Y	Y	Y	Y
8 Moran	Y	N	N	Y	Y	Y	Y	Y
9 Boucher	Y	N	N	Y	Y	Y	Y	Y
10 ***Wolf***	Y	Y	Y	Y	Y	Y	Y	Y
11 ***Davis, T.***	Y	Y	Y	Y	Y	Y	Y	Y
WASHINGTON								
1 Inslee	Y	N	N	Y	Y	Y	Y	Y
2 Larsen	Y	N	N	Y	Y	Y	Y	Y
3 Baird	Y	N	N	Y	Y	Y	Y	Y
4 ***Hastings***	Y	Y	Y	Y	Y	Y	Y	Y
5 ***Nethercutt***	Y	Y	Y	Y	Y	Y	Y	Y
6 Dicks	Y	N	N	Y	Y	Y	Y	Y
7 McDermott	N	N	N	Y	Y	Y	Y	Y
8 ***Dunn***	?	Y	Y	Y	Y	Y	Y	Y
9 Smith	Y	N	N	Y	Y	Y	Y	Y
WEST VIRGINIA								
1 Mollohan	Y	?	N	Y	Y	Y	Y	Y
2 ***Capito***	Y	Y	Y	Y	Y	Y	Y	Y
3 Rahall	N	N	N	Y	Y	Y	Y	Y
WISCONSIN								
1 ***Ryan***	Y	Y	Y	Y	Y	Y	Y	Y
2 Baldwin	Y	N	N	Y	Y	Y	Y	Y
3 Kind	Y	N	N	Y	Y	Y	Y	Y
4 Kleczka	Y	N	N	Y	Y	Y	Y	Y
5 ***Sensenbrenner***	N	Y	Y	Y	Y	Y	Y	Y
6 ***Petri***	N	Y	Y	Y	Y	Y	Y	Y
7 Obey	Y	N	N	Y	Y	Y	Y	Y
8 ***Green***	Y	Y	Y	Y	Y	Y	Y	Y
WYOMING								
AL ***Cubin***	N	Y	Y	Y	Y	Y	Y	Y

Southern states - Ala., Ark., Fla., Ga., Ky., La., Miss., N.C., Okla., S.C., Tenn., Texas, Va.

407. HR 4842. U.S.-Morocco Trade/Rule. Adoption of the rule (H Res 738) to provide for House floor consideration of the bill that would implement a trade agreement that would reduce tariffs and trade barriers between the United States and Morocco. Adopted 345-76: R 219-0; D 126-75 (ND 82-63, SD 44-12); I 0-1. July 22, 2004.

408. HR 4175. Veterans' Compensation Adjustment/Passage. Smith, R-N.J., motion to suspend the rules and pass the bill that would increase the amounts paid to veterans for disability compensation and to their survivors for dependency and indemnity compensation by the same cost-of-living adjustment payable to Social Security recipients. Motion agreed to 421-0: R 221-0; D 199-0 (ND 144-0, SD 55-0); I 1-0. A two-thirds majority of those present and voting (281 in this case) is required for passage under suspension of the rules. July 22, 2004.

409. H Res 728. Terrorists and Elections/Adoption. Ney, R-Ohio, motion to suspend the rules and adopt the resolution that would express the sense of the House that terrorists will never cause the postponement of a presidential election and that no individual or agency should be able to postpone the date of a presidential election. Motion agreed to 419-2: R 218-1; D 200-1 (ND 143-1, SD 57-0); I 1-0. A two-thirds majority of those present and voting (281 in this case) is required for adoption under suspension of the rules. July 22, 2004.

410. HR 3313. Court Review of Defense of Marriage Act/Passage. Passage of the bill that would a remove a provision in the 1996 "Defense of Marriage Act" from the jurisdiction of federal courts. That provision allows states to refuse to recognize same-sex marriage licenses issued in other states or jurisdictions. Passed 233-194: R 206-17; D 27-176 (ND 7-139, SD 20-37); I 0-1. A "yea" was a vote in support of the president's position. July 22, 2004.

411. HR 4056. Commercial Aviation Missile-Defense/Passage. Mica, R-Fla., motion to suspend the rules and pass the bill that would require the Federal Aviation Administration to establish a process for certifying missile defense systems to protect airports and airplanes from shoulder-fired weapons. Motion agreed to 423-0: R 220-0; D 202-0 (ND 145-0, SD 57-0); I 1-0. A two-thirds majority of those present and voting (282 in this case) is required for passage under suspension of the rules. July 22, 2004.

412. H Res 652. Belarus Elections/Adoption. Leach, R-Iowa, motion to suspend the rules and adopt the resolution that would express support for the establishment of a full democracy in Belarus and urge Belarusian authorities to ensure full transparency, access and representation for the 2004 parliamentary elections. Motion agreed to 421-0: R 219-0; D 201-0 (ND 144-0, SD 57-0); I 1-0. A two-thirds majority of those present and voting (281 in this case) is required for adoption under suspension of the rules. July 22, 2004.

413. HR 4842. U.S.-Morocco Trade/Passage. Passage of the bill that would implement a trade agreement that would reduce tariffs and trade barriers between the United States and Morocco. It would make more than 95 percent of bilateral trade in consumer and industrial products duty-free immediately, with all remaining tariffs eliminated within nine years. It also would reduce some agricultural tariffs. Passed 323-99: R 203-18; D 120-80 (ND 77-66, SD 43-14); I 0-1. A "yea" was a vote in support of the president's position. July 22, 2004.

414. H Con Res 436. Democracy in South Africa/Adoption. Leach, R-Iowa, motion to suspend the rules and adopt the concurrent resolution that would applaud South Africa for its transition to a democracy and the progress achieved during 10 years of majority rule. Motion agreed to 422-0: R 222-0; D 199-0 (ND 143-0, SD 56-0); I 1-0. A two-thirds majority of those present and voting (282 in this case) is required for adoption under suspension of the rules. July 22, 2004.

Key

Y	Voted for (yea).
#	Paired for.
+	Announced for.
N	Voted against (nay).
X	Paired against.
−	Announced against.
P	Voted "present."
C	Voted "present" to avoid possible conflict of interest.
?	Did not vote or otherwise make a position known.

Democrats **Republicans** *Independents*

	407	408	409	410	411	412	413	414
ALABAMA								
1 *Bonner*	Y	Y	Y	Y	Y	Y	Y	Y
2 *Everett*	Y	Y	Y	Y	Y	Y	Y	Y
3 *Rogers*	Y	Y	Y	Y	Y	Y	N	Y
4 *Aderholt*	Y	Y	Y	Y	Y	Y	N	Y
5 Cramer	N	Y	Y	Y	Y	Y	Y	Y
6 *Bachus*	Y	Y	?	Y	Y	Y	Y	Y
7 Davis	Y	Y	N	Y	Y	Y	Y	Y
ALASKA								
AL *Young*	Y	Y	Y	Y	Y	Y	Y	Y
ARIZONA								
1 *Renzi*	Y	Y	Y	Y	Y	Y	Y	Y
2 *Franks*	Y	Y	Y	Y	Y	Y	Y	Y
3 *Shadegg*	Y	Y	Y	Y	Y	Y	Y	Y
4 Pastor	N	Y	N	Y	N	Y	N	Y
5 *Hayworth*	Y	Y	Y	Y	Y	Y	Y	Y
6 *Flake*	Y	Y	Y	Y	Y	Y	Y	Y
7 Grijalva	N	Y	N	Y	N	Y	N	Y
8 *Kolbe*	Y	Y	Y	N	Y	Y	Y	Y
ARKANSAS								
1 Berry	N	Y	Y	Y	Y	Y	N	Y
2 Snyder	Y	Y	Y	N	Y	Y	Y	Y
3 *Boozman*	Y	Y	Y	Y	Y	Y	Y	Y
4 Ross	Y	Y	Y	Y	Y	Y	Y	Y
CALIFORNIA								
1 Thompson	Y	Y	Y	N	Y	Y	Y	Y
2 *Herger*	Y	Y	Y	Y	Y	Y	Y	Y
3 *Ose*	Y	Y	Y	N	Y	Y	Y	Y
4 *Doolittle*	Y	Y	Y	Y	Y	Y	Y	Y
5 Matsui	Y	Y	Y	N	Y	Y	Y	Y
6 Woolsey	N	Y	N	Y	N	Y	N	Y
7 Miller, George	Y	Y	N	Y	N	Y	N	Y
8 Pelosi	Y	Y	N	Y	Y	Y	Y	Y
9 Lee	N	Y	N	Y	N	Y	N	Y
10 Tauscher	Y	Y	Y	N	Y	Y	Y	Y
11 *Pombo*	Y	Y	Y	Y	Y	Y	Y	Y
12 Lantos	Y	Y	Y	N	Y	Y	N	Y
13 Stark	N	Y	N	Y	N	Y	N	Y
14 Eshoo	Y	Y	Y	N	Y	Y	Y	Y
15 Honda	Y	Y	Y	N	Y	Y	N	Y
16 Lofgren	N	Y	?	N	Y	Y	N	Y
17 Farr	Y	Y	Y	N	Y	Y	N	Y
18 Cardoza	Y	Y	Y	N	Y	Y	Y	Y
19 *Radanovich*	Y	Y	Y	Y	Y	Y	Y	Y
20 Dooley	Y	Y	Y	N	Y	Y	Y	Y
21 *Nunes*	Y	Y	Y	Y	Y	Y	Y	Y
22 *Thomas*	Y	Y	Y	Y	Y	Y	Y	Y
23 Capps	Y	Y	Y	N	Y	Y	Y	Y
24 *Gallegly*	Y	Y	Y	Y	Y	Y	Y	Y
25 *McKeon*	Y	Y	Y	Y	Y	Y	Y	Y
26 *Dreier*	Y	Y	Y	Y	Y	Y	Y	Y
27 Sherman	N	Y	Y	N	Y	Y	N	Y
28 Berman	Y	?	Y	N	Y	Y	N	Y
29 Schiff	Y	Y	Y	N	Y	Y	Y	Y
30 Waxman	Y	Y	Y	N	Y	Y	N	Y
31 Becerra	N	Y	Y	N	Y	Y	N	Y
32 Solis	N	Y	Y	N	Y	Y	N	Y
33 Watson	N	Y	Y	N	Y	Y	N	Y
34 Roybal-Allard	Y	Y	Y	N	Y	Y	N	Y
35 Waters	N	Y	Y	N	Y	Y	N	Y
36 Harman	Y	Y	Y	N	Y	Y	Y	Y

	407	408	409	410	411	412	413	414
37 Millender-McD.	Y	Y	Y	N	Y	Y	Y	Y
38 Napolitano	N	Y	Y	N	Y	Y	N	Y
39 *Sánchez, Linda*	N	Y	Y	N	Y	Y	N	Y
40 *Royce*	Y	Y	Y	Y	Y	Y	Y	Y
41 *Lewis*	Y	Y	Y	Y	Y	Y	Y	Y
42 *Miller, Gary*	Y	Y	Y	Y	Y	Y	Y	Y
43 Baca	N	Y	Y	N	Y	Y	N	Y
44 *Calvert*	Y	Y	Y	Y	Y	Y	Y	Y
45 *Bono*	Y	Y	Y	N	Y	Y	Y	Y
46 *Rohrabacher*	Y	Y	Y	Y	Y	Y	Y	Y
47 Sanchez, Loretta	Y	Y	Y	N	Y	Y	Y	Y
48 *Cox*	Y	Y	Y	Y	Y	Y	Y	Y
49 *Issa*	Y	Y	Y	Y	Y	Y	Y	Y
50 *Cunningham*	Y	Y	Y	Y	Y	Y	Y	Y
51 Filner	N	Y	N	Y	N	Y	N	Y
52 *Hunter*	Y	Y	Y	Y	Y	Y	N	Y
53 Davis	Y	Y	Y	N	Y	Y	Y	Y
COLORADO								
1 DeGette	Y	Y	Y	N	Y	Y	Y	Y
2 Udall	N	Y	Y	N	Y	Y	Y	Y
3 *McInnis*	Y	Y	N	Y	Y	Y	Y	Y
4 *Musgrave*	Y	Y	Y	Y	Y	Y	Y	Y
5 *Hefley*	Y	Y	Y	Y	Y	Y	Y	Y
6 *Tancredo*	Y	Y	Y	Y	Y	Y	Y	Y
7 *Beauprez*	Y	Y	Y	Y	Y	Y	Y	Y
CONNECTICUT								
1 Larson	N	Y	Y	N	Y	Y	N	Y
2 *Simmons*	?	Y	Y	N	Y	Y	Y	Y
3 DeLauro	N	Y	Y	N	Y	Y	N	Y
4 *Shays*	Y	Y	Y	N	Y	Y	Y	Y
5 *Johnson*	Y	Y	Y	N	Y	Y	Y	Y
DELAWARE								
AL *Castle*	Y	Y	Y	N	Y	Y	Y	Y
FLORIDA								
1 *Miller, J.*	Y	Y	Y	Y	Y	Y	Y	Y
2 Boyd	Y	Y	Y	N	Y	Y	Y	Y
3 Brown	Y	Y	Y	N	Y	Y	N	Y
4 *Crenshaw*	Y	Y	Y	Y	Y	Y	Y	Y
5 *Brown-Waite*	Y	Y	Y	Y	Y	Y	Y	Y
6 *Stearns*	Y	Y	Y	Y	Y	Y	Y	Y
7 *Mica*	Y	Y	Y	Y	Y	Y	Y	Y
8 *Keller*	Y	Y	Y	Y	Y	Y	Y	Y
9 *Bilirakis*	Y	Y	Y	Y	Y	Y	Y	Y
10 *Young*	Y	Y	?	Y	Y	Y	Y	Y
11 Davis	Y	Y	Y	N	Y	Y	Y	Y
12 *Putnam*	Y	Y	Y	Y	Y	Y	Y	Y
13 *Harris*	Y	Y	Y	Y	Y	Y	Y	Y
14 *Goss*	Y	Y	Y	Y	Y	Y	Y	Y
15 *Weldon*	Y	Y	Y	Y	Y	Y	Y	Y
16 *Foley*	Y	Y	Y	N	Y	Y	Y	Y
17 Meek	Y	Y	Y	N	Y	Y	Y	Y
18 *Ros-Lehtinen*	Y	Y	Y	Y	Y	Y	Y	Y
19 Wexler	Y	Y	Y	N	Y	Y	Y	Y
20 Deutsch	Y	Y	Y	N	Y	Y	Y	Y
21 *Diaz-Balart, L.*	Y	Y	Y	Y	Y	?	Y	Y
22 *Shaw*	Y	Y	Y	Y	Y	Y	Y	Y
23 Hastings	N	Y	Y	N	Y	Y	N	Y
24 *Feeney*	Y	Y	Y	Y	Y	Y	Y	Y
25 *Diaz-Balart, M.*	Y	Y	Y	Y	Y	?	Y	Y
GEORGIA								
1 *Kingston*	Y	Y	Y	Y	Y	Y	Y	Y
2 Bishop	Y	Y	Y	N	Y	Y	Y	Y
3 Marshall	N	Y	Y	Y	N	Y	N	Y
4 Majette	?	?	Y	N	Y	Y	N	Y
5 Lewis	Y	Y	Y	N	Y	Y	Y	Y
6 *Isakson*	Y	Y	Y	Y	Y	Y	Y	Y
7 *Linder*	Y	Y	Y	Y	Y	Y	Y	Y
8 *Collins*	?	?	?	?	?	?	?	?
9 *Norwood*	Y	Y	Y	Y	Y	Y	Y	Y
10 *Deal*	Y	Y	Y	Y	Y	Y	Y	Y
11 *Gingrey*	Y	Y	Y	Y	Y	Y	Y	Y
12 *Burns*	Y	Y	Y	Y	Y	Y	N	Y
13 Scott	Y	Y	Y	N	Y	Y	Y	Y
HAWAII								
1 Abercrombie	Y	Y	Y	N	Y	Y	Y	Y
2 Case	Y	Y	Y	N	Y	Y	Y	Y
IDAHO								
1 *Otter*	Y	Y	Y	Y	Y	Y	Y	Y
2 *Simpson*	Y	Y	Y	Y	Y	Y	Y	Y
ILLINOIS								
1 Rush	Y	Y	Y	N	Y	Y	N	Y
2 Jackson	N	Y	Y	N	Y	Y	N	Y
3 Lipinski	N	Y	Y	N	Y	Y	N	Y
4 Gutierrez	Y	Y	Y	N	Y	Y	N	Y
5 Emanuel	Y	Y	Y	N	Y	Y	Y	Y
6 *Hyde*	Y	Y	Y	N	Y	Y	Y	Y

ND Northern Democrats   SD Southern Democrats

	407	408	409	410	411	412	413	414
7 Davis	Y	Y	Y	N	Y	Y	N	Y
8 ***Crane***	Y	Y	Y	Y	Y	Y	Y	Y
9 Schakowsky	N	Y	Y	N	Y	Y	N	Y
10 ***Kirk***	?	?	?	?	?	?	?	?
11 ***Weller***	Y	Y	Y	Y	Y	Y	Y	Y
12 Costello	N	Y	Y	Y	Y	Y	N	Y
13 ***Biggert***	Y	Y	Y	N	Y	Y	Y	Y
14 ***Hastert***				Y				
15 ***Johnson***	Y	Y	Y	Y	Y	Y	Y	Y
16 ***Manzullo***	Y	Y	Y	Y	Y	Y	Y	Y
17 Evans	N	Y	Y	N	Y	Y	N	Y
18 ***LaHood***	Y	Y	Y	Y	Y	Y	Y	Y
19 ***Shimkus***	Y	Y	Y	Y	Y	Y	Y	Y
INDIANA								
1 Visclosky	N	Y	Y	N	Y	Y	N	Y
2 ***Chocola***	Y	Y	Y	Y	Y	Y	Y	Y
3 ***Souder***	Y	Y	Y	Y	Y	Y	Y	Y
4 ***Buyer***	Y	Y	Y	Y	Y	Y	Y	Y
5 ***Burton***	Y	Y	Y	Y	Y	Y	N	Y
6 ***Pence***	Y	Y	Y	Y	Y	Y	Y	Y
7 Carson	?	?	?	?	?	?	?	?
8 ***Hostettler***	Y	Y	Y	Y	Y	Y	N	Y
9 Hill	Y	Y	Y	N	Y	Y	Y	Y
IOWA								
1 ***Nussle***	Y	Y	Y	Y	Y	Y	Y	Y
2 ***Leach***	Y	Y	Y	N	Y	Y	Y	Y
3 Boswell	Y	Y	Y	N	Y	Y	Y	Y
4 ***Latham***	Y	Y	Y	Y	Y	Y	Y	Y
5 ***King***	Y	Y	Y	Y	Y	Y	Y	Y
KANSAS								
1 ***Moran***	Y	Y	Y	Y	Y	Y	Y	Y
2 ***Ryun***	Y	Y	Y	Y	Y	Y	Y	Y
3 Moore	Y	Y	Y	N	Y	Y	Y	Y
4 ***Tiahrt***	Y	Y	Y	Y	Y	Y	Y	Y
KENTUCKY								
1 ***Whitfield***	Y	Y	Y	Y	Y	Y	Y	Y
2 ***Lewis***	Y	Y	Y	Y	Y	Y	Y	Y
3 ***Northup***	Y	Y	Y	Y	Y	Y	Y	Y
4 Lucas	Y	Y	Y	Y	Y	Y	Y	Y
5 ***Rogers***	Y	Y	Y	Y	Y	Y	Y	Y
6 Chandler	Y	Y	Y	Y	Y	Y	Y	Y
LOUISIANA								
1 ***Vitter***	Y	Y	Y	Y	Y	Y	Y	Y
2 Jefferson	Y	Y	Y	N	Y	Y	Y	Y
3 ***Tauzin***	Y	Y	Y	Y	Y	Y	Y	Y
4 ***McCrery***	Y	Y	Y	Y	Y	Y	Y	Y
5 Alexander	N	Y	Y	Y	Y	Y	N	Y
6 ***Baker***	Y	Y	Y	Y	Y	Y	Y	Y
7 John	Y	Y	Y	Y	Y	Y	Y	Y
MAINE								
1 Allen	Y	Y	Y	N	Y	Y	Y	Y
2 Michaud	N	Y	Y	N	Y	Y	N	Y
MARYLAND								
1 ***Gilchrest***	Y	Y	Y	N	Y	Y	Y	Y
2 Ruppersberger	Y	Y	Y	N	Y	Y	Y	Y
3 Cardin	Y	Y	Y	N	Y	Y	Y	Y
4 Wynn	Y	Y	Y	N	Y	Y	Y	Y
5 Hoyer	Y	Y	Y	N	Y	Y	Y	Y
6 ***Bartlett***	Y	Y	Y	Y	Y	Y	Y	Y
7 Cummings	N	Y	Y	N	Y	Y	Y	Y
8 Van Hollen	Y	Y	Y	N	Y	Y	Y	Y
MASSACHUSETTS								
1 Olver	N	Y	Y	N	Y	Y	N	Y
2 Neal	Y	Y	Y	N	Y	Y	Y	Y
3 McGovern	N	Y	Y	N	Y	Y	N	Y
4 Frank	Y	Y	Y	N	Y	Y	N	Y
5 Meehan	Y	Y	Y	N	Y	Y	?	?
6 Tierney	N	Y	Y	N	Y	Y	N	Y
7 Markey	N	Y	Y	N	Y	Y	N	Y
8 Capuano	N	Y	Y	N	Y	?	N	Y
9 Lynch	Y	Y	Y	N	Y	Y	Y	Y
10 Delahunt	N	Y	Y	N	Y	Y	N	Y
MICHIGAN								
1 Stupak	N	Y	Y	N	Y	Y	Y	Y
2 ***Hoekstra***	Y	Y	Y	Y	Y	Y	Y	Y
3 ***Ehlers***	Y	Y	Y	Y	Y	Y	Y	Y
4 ***Camp***	Y	Y	Y	Y	Y	Y	Y	Y
5 Kildee	N	Y	Y	N	Y	Y	N	Y
6 ***Upton***	Y	Y	Y	Y	Y	Y	Y	Y
7 ***Smith***	Y	Y	Y	Y	Y	Y	Y	Y
8 ***Rogers***	Y	Y	Y	Y	Y	Y	Y	Y
9 ***Knollenberg***	Y	Y	Y	Y	Y	Y	Y	Y
10 ***Miller***	Y	Y	Y	Y	Y	Y	Y	Y
11 ***McCotter***	Y	Y	Y	Y	Y	Y	Y	Y
12 Levin	Y	Y	Y	N	Y	Y	Y	Y
13 Kilpatrick	Y	Y	Y	N	Y	Y	Y	Y
14 Conyers	N	Y	Y	N	Y	Y	N	Y
15 Dingell	Y	Y	Y	N	Y	Y	Y	Y
MINNESOTA								
1 ***Gutknecht***	Y	Y	Y	Y	Y	Y	Y	Y
2 ***Kline***	Y	Y	Y	Y	Y	Y	Y	Y
3 ***Ramstad***	Y	Y	Y	Y	Y	Y	Y	Y
4 McCollum	Y	Y	Y	N	Y	Y	Y	Y
5 Sabo	N	Y	Y	N	Y	Y	N	Y
6 ***Kennedy***	Y	Y	Y	Y	Y	Y	Y	Y
7 Peterson	N	Y	Y	Y	Y	Y	N	Y
8 Oberstar	N	Y	Y	N	Y	Y	N	Y
MISSISSIPPI								
1 ***Wicker***	Y	Y	Y	Y	Y	Y	Y	Y
2 Thompson	Y	Y	Y	N	Y	Y	N	Y
3 ***Pickering***	Y	Y	Y	Y	Y	Y	Y	Y
4 Taylor	N	Y	Y	Y	Y	Y	N	Y
MISSOURI								
1 Clay	Y	Y	Y	N	Y	Y	Y	Y
2 ***Akin***	Y	Y	Y	Y	Y	Y	Y	Y
3 Gephardt	?	?	?	N	?	?	?	?
4 Skelton	Y	Y	Y	Y	Y	Y	Y	Y
5 McCarthy	Y	Y	Y	N	Y	Y	Y	Y
6 ***Graves***	Y	Y	Y	Y	Y	Y	Y	Y
7 ***Blunt***	Y	Y	Y	Y	Y	Y	Y	Y
8 ***Emerson***	Y	Y	Y	Y	Y	Y	N	Y
9 ***Hulshof***	Y	Y	Y	Y	Y	Y	Y	Y
MONTANA								
AL ***Rehberg***	Y	Y	Y	Y	Y	Y	Y	Y
NEBRASKA								
1 ***Bereuter***	Y	Y	Y	N	Y	Y	Y	Y
2 ***Terry***	Y	Y	Y	Y	Y	Y	Y	Y
3 ***Osborne***	Y	Y	Y	Y	Y	Y	Y	Y
NEVADA								
1 Berkley	Y	Y	Y	N	Y	Y	Y	Y
2 ***Gibbons***	Y	Y	Y	Y	Y	Y	Y	Y
3 ***Porter***	Y	Y	Y	Y	Y	Y	Y	Y
NEW HAMPSHIRE								
1 ***Bradley***	Y	Y	Y	Y	Y	Y	Y	Y
2 ***Bass***	?	?	Y	N	Y	Y	Y	Y
NEW JERSEY								
1 Andrews	Y	Y	Y	N	Y	Y	N	Y
2 ***LoBiondo***	Y	Y	Y	Y	Y	Y	Y	Y
3 ***Saxton***	Y	Y	Y	Y	Y	Y	Y	Y
4 ***Smith***	Y	Y	Y	Y	Y	Y	Y	Y
5 ***Garrett***	Y	Y	Y	Y	Y	Y	Y	Y
6 Pallone	N	Y	Y	N	Y	Y	N	Y
7 ***Ferguson***	Y	Y	Y	Y	Y	Y	Y	Y
8 Pascrell	N	Y	Y	N	Y	Y	N	Y
9 Rothman	N	Y	Y	N	Y	Y	Y	Y
10 Payne	N	Y	Y	N	Y	Y	N	Y
11 ***Frelinghuysen***	Y	Y	Y	Y	Y	Y	Y	Y
12 Holt	Y	Y	Y	N	Y	Y	N	Y
13 Menendez	Y	Y	Y	N	Y	Y	Y	Y
NEW MEXICO								
1 ***Wilson***	Y	Y	Y	Y	Y	Y	Y	Y
2 ***Pearce***	Y	Y	Y	Y	Y	Y	Y	Y
3 Udall	N	Y	Y	N	Y	Y	Y	Y
NEW YORK								
1 Bishop	Y	Y	Y	N	Y	Y	Y	Y
2 Israel	Y	Y	Y	N	Y	Y	Y	Y
3 ***King***	Y	Y	Y	Y	Y	Y	Y	Y
4 McCarthy	Y	Y	Y	N	Y	Y	Y	Y
5 Ackerman	Y	Y	Y	N	Y	Y	Y	?
6 Meeks	Y	Y	Y	N	Y	Y	Y	Y
7 Crowley	Y	Y	Y	N	Y	Y	Y	Y
8 Nadler	N	Y	Y	N	Y	Y	N	Y
9 Weiner	Y	Y	Y	N	Y	Y	Y	Y
10 Towns	Y	Y	Y	N	Y	Y	Y	Y
11 Owens	N	Y	Y	N	Y	Y	N	Y
12 Velázquez	N	Y	Y	N	Y	Y	N	Y
13 ***Fossella***	Y	Y	Y	Y	Y	Y	Y	Y
14 Maloney	Y	Y	Y	N	Y	Y	Y	Y
15 Rangel	Y	Y	Y	N	Y	Y	Y	Y
16 Serrano	Y	Y	Y	N	Y	Y	N	Y
17 Engel	Y	Y	Y	N	Y	Y	Y	Y
18 Lowey	?	?	?	?	?	?	?	?
19 ***Kelly***	Y	Y	Y	Y	Y	Y	Y	Y
20 ***Sweeney***	Y	Y	Y	Y	Y	Y	Y	Y
21 McNulty	N	Y	Y	N	Y	Y	N	Y
22 Hinchey	N	Y	Y	N	Y	Y	N	Y
23 ***McHugh***	Y	Y	Y	Y	Y	Y	Y	Y
24 ***Boehlert***	Y	Y	Y	Y	Y	Y	Y	Y
25 ***Walsh***	Y	Y	Y	Y	Y	Y	Y	Y
26 ***Reynolds***	Y	Y	Y	Y	Y	Y	Y	Y
27 ***Quinn***	?	?	?	?	?	?	?	?
28 Slaughter	N	Y	Y	N	Y	Y	N	Y
29 ***Houghton***	Y	Y	Y	N	Y	Y	Y	Y
NORTH CAROLINA								
1 Butterfield	Y	Y	Y	N	Y	Y	N	Y
2 Etheridge	Y	Y	Y	N	Y	Y	Y	Y
3 ***Jones***	Y	Y	Y	Y	Y	Y	N	Y
4 Price	Y	Y	Y	N	Y	Y	Y	Y
5 ***Burr***	Y	Y	Y	Y	Y	Y	N	Y
6 ***Coble***	Y	Y	Y	Y	Y	Y	N	Y
7 McIntyre	N	Y	Y	Y	Y	Y	N	Y
8 ***Hayes***	Y	Y	Y	Y	Y	Y	N	Y
9 ***Myrick***	Y	Y	Y	Y	Y	Y	N	Y
10 ***Ballenger***	Y	Y	Y	Y	Y	Y	Y	Y
11 ***Taylor***	Y	Y	Y	Y	Y	Y	N	Y
12 Watt	N	?	Y	N	Y	Y	Y	Y
13 Miller	N	Y	Y	N	Y	Y	N	Y
NORTH DAKOTA								
AL Pomeroy	Y	Y	Y	N	Y	Y	Y	Y
OHIO								
1 ***Chabot***	Y	Y	Y	Y	Y	Y	Y	Y
2 ***Portman***	Y	Y	Y	Y	?	?	Y	Y
3 ***Turner***	Y	Y	Y	Y	Y	Y	Y	Y
4 ***Oxley***	Y	Y	Y	Y	Y	Y	Y	Y
5 ***Gillmor***	Y	Y	?	Y	Y	Y	Y	Y
6 Strickland	N	Y	Y	N	Y	Y	N	Y
7 ***Hobson***	Y	Y	Y	Y	Y	Y	Y	Y
8 ***Boehner***	Y	Y	Y	Y	Y	Y	Y	Y
9 Kaptur	Y	Y	Y	N	Y	Y	N	Y
10 Kucinich	?	?	?	?	?	?	?	?
11 Jones	Y	Y	Y	N	Y	Y	Y	Y
12 ***Tiberi***	Y	Y	Y	Y	Y	Y	Y	Y
13 Brown	N	Y	Y	N	Y	Y	N	Y
14 ***LaTourette***	Y	Y	Y	Y	Y	Y	Y	Y
15 ***Pryce***	Y	Y	Y	Y	Y	Y	Y	Y
16 ***Regula***	Y	Y	Y	Y	Y	Y	Y	Y
17 Ryan	N	Y	Y	N	Y	Y	N	Y
18 ***Ney***	Y	Y	Y	Y	Y	Y	Y	Y
OKLAHOMA								
1 ***Sullivan***	?	Y	Y	Y	Y	Y	Y	Y
2 Carson	Y	Y	Y	Y	Y	Y	Y	Y
3 ***Lucas***	Y	Y	Y	Y	Y	Y	Y	Y
4 ***Cole***	Y	Y	Y	Y	Y	Y	Y	Y
5 ***Istook***	Y	Y	Y	Y	?	Y	Y	Y
OREGON								
1 Wu	N	Y	Y	N	Y	Y	N	Y
2 ***Walden***	Y	Y	Y	Y	Y	Y	Y	Y
3 Blumenauer	Y	Y	Y	N	Y	Y	Y	Y
4 DeFazio	N	Y	Y	N	Y	Y	N	Y
5 Hooley	Y	Y	Y	N	Y	Y	Y	Y
PENNSYLVANIA								
1 Brady	N	Y	Y	N	Y	Y	N	Y
2 Fattah	Y	Y	Y	N	Y	Y	Y	Y
3 ***English***	Y	Y	Y	N	Y	Y	Y	Y
4 ***Hart***	Y	Y	Y	Y	Y	Y	Y	Y
5 ***Peterson***	Y	Y	Y	Y	Y	Y	Y	Y
6 ***Gerlach***	Y	Y	Y	N	Y	Y	Y	Y
7 ***Weldon***	Y	Y	Y	Y	Y	Y	Y	Y
8 ***Greenwood***	?	?	?	?	?	?	?	?
9 ***Shuster, Bill***	Y	Y	Y	Y	Y	Y	Y	Y
10 ***Sherwood***	Y	Y	Y	Y	Y	Y	Y	Y
11 Kanjorski	N	Y	Y	N	Y	Y	N	Y
12 Murtha	N	Y	Y	N	Y	Y	N	Y
13 Hoeffel	Y	Y	Y	N	Y	Y	Y	Y
14 Doyle	N	Y	Y	N	Y	Y	N	Y
15 ***Toomey***	Y	Y	Y	Y	Y	Y	Y	Y
16 ***Pitts***	Y	Y	Y	Y	Y	Y	Y	Y
17 Holden	N	Y	Y	Y	Y	Y	N	Y
18 ***Murphy***	Y	Y	Y	Y	Y	Y	Y	Y
19 ***Platts***	Y	Y	Y	Y	Y	Y	Y	Y
RHODE ISLAND								
1 Kennedy	Y	Y	Y	N	Y	Y	Y	Y
2 Langevin	Y	Y	Y	N	Y	Y	Y	Y
SOUTH CAROLINA								
1 ***Brown***	Y	Y	Y	Y	Y	Y	Y	Y
2 ***Wilson***	Y	Y	Y	Y	Y	Y	N	Y
3 ***Barrett***	Y	Y	Y	Y	Y	Y	N	Y
4 ***DeMint***	Y	Y	Y	Y	Y	Y	Y	Y
5 Spratt	N	Y	Y	N	Y	Y	N	Y
6 Clyburn	Y	Y	Y	N	Y	Y	Y	Y
SOUTH DAKOTA								
AL Herseth	Y	Y	Y	Y	Y	Y	Y	Y
TENNESSEE								
1 ***Jenkins***	Y	Y	Y	Y	Y	Y	Y	Y
2 ***Duncan***	Y	Y	Y	Y	Y	Y	Y	Y
3 ***Wamp***	Y	Y	Y	Y	Y	Y	N	Y
4 Davis	Y	Y	Y	Y	Y	Y	Y	Y
5 Cooper	Y	Y	Y	N	Y	Y	Y	Y
6 Gordon	Y	Y	Y	Y	Y	Y	Y	Y
7 ***Blackburn***	Y	Y	Y	Y	Y	Y	Y	Y
8 Tanner	Y	Y	Y	Y	Y	Y	Y	Y
9 Ford	Y	Y	Y	N	Y	Y	Y	?
TEXAS								
1 Sandlin	Y	Y	Y	Y	Y	Y	Y	Y
2 Turner	Y	Y	Y	Y	Y	Y	Y	Y
3 ***Johnson, Sam***	Y	Y	Y	Y	Y	Y	Y	Y
4 ***Hall***	Y	Y	Y	Y	Y	Y	Y	Y
5 ***Hensarling***	Y	Y	Y	Y	Y	Y	Y	Y
6 ***Barton***	Y	Y	Y	Y	Y	Y	Y	Y
7 ***Culberson***	Y	Y	Y	Y	Y	Y	Y	Y
8 ***Brady***	Y	Y	Y	Y	Y	Y	Y	Y
9 Lampson	Y	Y	Y	N	Y	Y	Y	Y
10 Doggett	Y	Y	Y	N	Y	Y	N	Y
11 Edwards	Y	Y	Y	Y	Y	Y	Y	Y
12 ***Granger***	Y	Y	Y	Y	Y	Y	Y	Y
13 ***Thornberry***	Y	Y	Y	Y	Y	Y	Y	Y
14 ***Paul***	?	?	?	?	?	?	?	?
15 Hinojosa	Y	Y	Y	N	Y	Y	Y	Y
16 Reyes	Y	Y	Y	N	Y	Y	Y	Y
17 Stenholm	Y	Y	Y	Y	Y	Y	Y	Y
18 Jackson-Lee	Y	Y	Y	N	Y	Y	Y	Y
19 ***Neugebauer***	Y	Y	Y	Y	Y	Y	Y	Y
20 Gonzalez	Y	Y	Y	N	Y	Y	Y	Y
21 ***Smith***	Y	Y	Y	Y	Y	Y	Y	Y
22 ***DeLay***	Y	Y	Y	Y	Y	Y	Y	Y
23 ***Bonilla***	Y	Y	Y	Y	Y	Y	Y	Y
24 Frost	Y	Y	Y	N	Y	Y	Y	Y
25 Bell	Y	Y	Y	N	Y	Y	Y	Y
26 ***Burgess***	Y	Y	Y	Y	Y	Y	Y	Y
27 Ortiz	Y	Y	Y	N	Y	Y	Y	Y
28 Rodriguez	Y	Y	Y	N	Y	Y	Y	Y
29 Green	N	Y	Y	N	Y	Y	N	Y
30 Johnson, E.B.	Y	Y	Y	N	Y	Y	Y	Y
31 ***Carter***	Y	Y	Y	Y	Y	Y	Y	Y
32 ***Sessions***	Y	Y	Y	Y	Y	Y	Y	Y
UTAH								
1 ***Bishop***	Y	Y	Y	Y	Y	Y	Y	Y
2 Matheson	Y	Y	Y	Y	Y	Y	Y	Y
3 ***Cannon***	Y	Y	Y	Y	Y	Y	?	Y
VERMONT								
AL *Sanders*	N	Y	Y	N	Y	Y	N	Y
VIRGINIA								
1 ***Davis, Jo Ann***	Y	Y	Y	Y	Y	Y	Y	Y
2 ***Schrock***	Y	Y	Y	Y	Y	Y	Y	Y
3 Scott	Y	Y	Y	N	Y	Y	Y	Y
4 ***Forbes***	Y	Y	Y	Y	Y	Y	Y	Y
5 ***Goode***	Y	Y	Y	Y	Y	Y	N	Y
6 ***Goodlatte***	Y	Y	Y	Y	Y	Y	Y	Y
7 ***Cantor***	Y	Y	Y	Y	Y	Y	Y	Y
8 Moran	Y	Y	Y	N	Y	Y	Y	Y
9 Boucher	N	Y	Y	Y	Y	Y	N	Y
10 ***Wolf***	Y	Y	Y	Y	Y	Y	Y	Y
11 ***Davis, T.***	Y	Y	Y	Y	Y	Y	Y	Y
WASHINGTON								
1 Inslee	Y	Y	Y	N	Y	Y	Y	Y
2 Larsen	Y	Y	Y	N	Y	Y	Y	Y
3 Baird	Y	Y	N	N	Y	Y	Y	Y
4 ***Hastings***	Y	Y	Y	Y	Y	Y	Y	Y
5 ***Nethercutt***	Y	Y	Y	Y	Y	Y	Y	Y
6 Dicks	Y	Y	Y	N	Y	Y	Y	Y
7 McDermott	Y	Y	Y	N	Y	Y	Y	Y
8 ***Dunn***	Y	Y	Y	Y	Y	Y	Y	Y
9 Smith	Y	Y	Y	N	Y	Y	Y	Y
WEST VIRGINIA								
1 Mollohan	N	Y	Y	N	Y	Y	N	Y
2 ***Capito***	Y	Y	Y	Y	Y	Y	Y	Y
3 Rahall	N	Y	Y	Y	Y	Y	Y	Y
WISCONSIN								
1 ***Ryan***	Y	Y	Y	Y	Y	Y	Y	Y
2 Baldwin	N	Y	Y	N	Y	Y	N	Y
3 Kind	Y	Y	Y	N	Y	Y	Y	Y
4 Kleczka	N	Y	Y	N	Y	Y	?	Y
5 ***Sensenbrenner***	Y	Y	Y	Y	Y	Y	Y	Y
6 ***Petri***	Y	Y	Y	Y	Y	Y	Y	Y
7 Obey	N	Y	Y	N	Y	Y	Y	Y
8 ***Green***	Y	Y	Y	Y	Y	Y	Y	Y
WYOMING								
AL ***Cubin***	Y	Y	Y	Y	Y	Y	Y	Y

Southern states - Ala., Ark., Fla., Ga., Ky., La., Miss., N.C., Okla., S.C., Tenn., Texas, Va.

Key

Y	Voted for (yea).
#	Paired for.
+	Announced for.
N	Voted against (nay).
X	Paired against.
−	Announced against.
P	Voted "present."
C	Voted "present" to avoid possible conflict of interest.
?	Did not vote or otherwise make a position known.

Democrats **Republicans** *Independents*

---

415. H Con Res 418. U.S.-Japan Relations/Adoption. Leach, R-Iowa, motion to suspend the rules and adopt the concurrent resolution that would recognize the historical importance of the 150th anniversary of diplomatic relations between the United States and Japan. Motion agreed to 416-0: R 220-0; D 195-0 (ND 139-0, SD 56-0); I 1-0. A two-thirds majority of those present and voting (278 in this case) is required for adoption under suspension of the rules. July 22, 2004.

416. HR 4837. Fiscal 2005 Military Construction Appropriations/ Recommit. Obey, D-Wis., motion to recommit the bill to the House Appropriations Committee with instructions to add language that would increase the spending cap on the Military Housing Privatization Program from $850 million to $1.3 billion. Motion rejected 201-217: R 2-217; D 198-0 (ND 141-0, SD 57-0); I 1-0. July 22, 2004.

417. HR 4837. Fiscal 2005 Military Construction Appropriations/ Passage. Passage of the bill that would provide $10 billion in fiscal 2005 for military construction projects, including $5.3 billion for military construction, $4.2 billion for family housing, and $246 million for base realignment and closure projects. Passed 420-1: R 221-0; D 198-1 (ND 141-1, SD 57-0); I 1-0. July 22, 2004.

418. HR 4613. Fiscal 2005 Defense Appropriations/Conference Report. Adoption of the conference report on the bill that would appropriate $417.5 billion for the Defense Department and related agencies, including $391.2 billion for the Pentagon and $25 billion in emergency spending for military operations in Iraq and Afghanistan. Adopted (thus sent to the Senate) 410-12: R 221-0; D 188-12 (ND 133-10, SD 55-2); I 1-0. July 22, 2004.

419. H Con Res 469. Attack on Jewish Center in Argentina/Adoption. Leach, R-Iowa, motion to suspend the rules and adopt the concurrent resolution that would reiterate Congress' condemnation of the 1994 attack on the AMIA Jewish Community Center in Buenos Aires, Argentina, and honor the victims of the attack. Motion agreed to 422-0: R 221-0; D 200-0 (ND 143-0, SD 57-0); I 1-0. A two-thirds majority of those present and voting (282 in this case) is required for adoption under suspension of the rules. July 22, 2004.

420. H Con Res 467. Genocide in Sudan/Adoption. Tancredo, R-Colo., motion to suspend the rules and adopt the concurrent resolution that would declare that the violence in the Darfur region of Sudan constitutes genocide and would urge the president to make the same declaration and lead an effort to prevent genocide in the region. Motion agreed to 422-0: R 221-0; D 200-0 (ND 143-0, SD 57-0); I 1-0. A two-thirds majority of those present and voting (282 in this case) is required for adoption under suspension of the rules. July 22, 2004.

421. HR 1308. Child Tax Credit/Motion to Instruct. Stenholm, D-Texas, motion to instruct House conferees to insist on a conference agreement that would extend expiring tax provisions without increasing the federal budget deficit. Motion rejected 198-222: R 2-218; D 195-4 (ND 139-4, SD 56-0); I 1-0. July 22, 2004.

	415	416	417	418	419	420	421
ALABAMA							
1 *Bonner*	Y	N	Y	Y	Y	Y	N
2 *Everett*	Y	N	Y	Y	Y	Y	N
3 *Rogers*	Y	N	Y	Y	Y	Y	N
4 *Aderholt*	Y	N	Y	Y	Y	Y	N
5 Cramer	Y	Y	Y	Y	Y	Y	Y
6 *Bachus*	Y	N	Y	Y	Y	Y	N
7 Davis	Y	Y	Y	Y	Y	Y	Y
ALASKA							
AL *Young*	Y	N	Y	Y	Y	Y	N
ARIZONA							
1 *Renzi*	Y	N	Y	Y	Y	Y	N
2 *Franks*	Y	N	Y	Y	Y	Y	N
3 *Shadegg*	Y	N	Y	Y	Y	Y	N
4 Pastor	Y	Y	Y	Y	Y	Y	Y
5 *Hayworth*	Y	N	Y	Y	Y	Y	N
6 *Flake*	Y	Y	Y	Y	Y	Y	Y
7 Grijalva	Y	Y	Y	N	Y	Y	Y
8 *Kolbe*	Y	N	Y	Y	Y	Y	N
ARKANSAS							
1 Berry	Y	Y	Y	Y	Y	Y	Y
2 Snyder	Y	Y	Y	Y	Y	Y	Y
3 *Boozman*	Y	Y	Y	Y	Y	Y	Y
4 Ross	Y	Y	Y	Y	Y	Y	Y
CALIFORNIA							
1 Thompson	Y	Y	Y	Y	Y	Y	Y
2 *Herger*	Y	N	Y	Y	Y	Y	N
3 *Ose*	Y	N	Y	Y	Y	Y	N
4 *Doolittle*	Y	N	Y	Y	Y	Y	N
5 Matsui	Y	Y	Y	Y	Y	Y	Y
6 Woolsey	Y	Y	Y	N	Y	Y	Y
7 Miller, George	Y	Y	Y	Y	Y	Y	Y
8 Pelosi	Y	Y	Y	Y	Y	Y	Y
9 Lee	Y	Y	Y	N	Y	Y	Y
10 Tauscher	Y	Y	Y	Y	Y	Y	Y
11 *Pombo*	Y	N	Y	Y	Y	Y	N
12 Lantos	Y	Y	Y	Y	Y	Y	Y
13 Stark	Y	Y	Y	N	Y	Y	Y
14 Eshoo	Y	Y	Y	Y	Y	Y	Y
15 Honda	Y	Y	Y	Y	Y	Y	Y
16 Lofgren	Y	Y	Y	Y	Y	Y	Y
17 Farr	Y	Y	Y	Y	Y	Y	Y
18 Cardoza	Y	Y	Y	Y	Y	Y	Y
19 *Radanovich*	Y	N	Y	Y	Y	Y	N
20 Dooley	Y	Y	Y	Y	Y	Y	Y
21 *Nunes*	Y	N	Y	Y	Y	Y	N
22 *Thomas*	Y	N	Y	Y	Y	Y	N
23 Capps	Y	Y	Y	Y	Y	Y	Y
24 *Gallegly*	Y	N	Y	Y	Y	Y	N
25 *McKeon*	Y	N	Y	Y	Y	Y	N
26 *Dreier*	Y	N	Y	Y	Y	Y	N
27 Sherman	Y	Y	Y	Y	Y	Y	Y
28 Berman	Y	Y	Y	Y	Y	Y	Y
29 Schiff	?	Y	Y	Y	Y	Y	Y
30 Waxman	Y	Y	Y	Y	Y	Y	Y
31 Becerra	Y	Y	Y	Y	Y	Y	Y
32 Solis	Y	Y	Y	Y	Y	Y	Y
33 Watson	Y	Y	Y	Y	Y	Y	Y
34 Roybal-Allard	Y	Y	Y	Y	Y	Y	Y
35 Waters	?	Y	Y	Y	Y	Y	Y
36 Harman	Y	Y	Y	Y	Y	Y	Y

	415	416	417	418	419	420	421
37 Millender-McD.	Y	Y	Y	Y	Y	Y	Y
38 Napolitano	Y	Y	Y	Y	Y	Y	Y
39 Sánchez, Linda	Y	Y	Y	Y	Y	Y	Y
40 *Royce*	Y	N	Y	Y	Y	Y	N
41 *Lewis*	Y	N	Y	Y	Y	Y	N
42 *Miller, Gary*	Y	N	Y	Y	Y	Y	N
43 Baca	Y	Y	Y	Y	Y	Y	Y
44 *Calvert*	?	N	Y	Y	Y	Y	N
45 *Bono*	Y	N	Y	Y	Y	Y	N
46 *Rohrabacher*	Y	?	?	Y	Y	Y	N
47 Sanchez, Loretta	Y	Y	Y	Y	Y	Y	Y
48 *Cox*	Y	N	Y	Y	Y	Y	N
49 *Issa*	Y	N	Y	Y	Y	Y	N
50 *Cunningham*	Y	N	Y	Y	Y	Y	N
51 Filner	Y	Y	Y	Y	Y	Y	Y
52 *Hunter*	Y	N	Y	Y	Y	Y	N
53 Davis	Y	Y	Y	Y	Y	Y	Y
COLORADO							
1 DeGette	Y	Y	Y	Y	Y	Y	Y
2 Udall	Y	Y	Y	Y	Y	Y	Y
3 *McInnis*	Y	N	Y	Y	Y	Y	N
4 *Musgrave*	Y	N	Y	Y	Y	Y	N
5 *Hefley*	Y	N	Y	Y	Y	Y	N
6 *Tancredo*	Y	N	Y	Y	Y	Y	N
7 *Beauprez*	Y	N	Y	Y	Y	Y	N
CONNECTICUT							
1 Larson	Y	Y	Y	Y	Y	Y	Y
2 *Simmons*	Y	N	Y	Y	Y	Y	N
3 DeLauro	Y	Y	Y	Y	Y	Y	Y
4 *Shays*	Y	Y	Y	Y	Y	Y	N
5 *Johnson*	Y	N	Y	Y	Y	Y	N
DELAWARE							
AL *Castle*	Y	N	Y	Y	Y	Y	N
FLORIDA							
1 *Miller, J.*	Y	N	Y	Y	Y	Y	N
2 Boyd	Y	Y	Y	Y	Y	Y	Y
3 Brown	Y	Y	Y	Y	Y	Y	Y
4 *Crenshaw*	Y	N	Y	Y	Y	Y	N
5 *Brown-Waite*	Y	N	Y	Y	Y	Y	N
6 *Stearns*	Y	N	Y	Y	Y	Y	N
7 *Mica*	Y	N	Y	Y	Y	Y	N
8 *Keller*	Y	N	Y	Y	Y	Y	N
9 *Bilirakis*	Y	N	Y	Y	Y	Y	N
10 *Young*	Y	N	Y	Y	Y	Y	N
11 Davis	Y	Y	Y	Y	Y	Y	Y
12 *Putnam*	Y	N	Y	Y	Y	Y	N
13 *Harris*	Y	N	Y	Y	Y	Y	N
14 *Goss*	Y	N	Y	Y	Y	Y	N
15 *Weldon*	Y	N	Y	Y	Y	Y	N
16 *Foley*	Y	N	Y	Y	Y	Y	N
17 Meek	Y	Y	Y	Y	Y	Y	Y
18 *Ros-Lehtinen*	Y	N	Y	Y	Y	Y	N
19 Wexler	Y	Y	Y	Y	Y	Y	Y
20 Deutsch	Y	Y	Y	Y	Y	Y	Y
21 *Diaz-Balart, L.*	Y	N	Y	Y	Y	Y	N
22 *Shaw*	Y	N	Y	Y	Y	Y	N
23 Hastings	Y	Y	Y	Y	Y	Y	Y
24 *Feeney*	Y	N	Y	Y	Y	Y	N
25 *Diaz-Balart, M.*	Y	N	Y	Y	Y	Y	N
GEORGIA							
1 *Kingston*	Y	N	Y	Y	Y	Y	N
2 Bishop	Y	Y	Y	Y	Y	Y	Y
3 Marshall	Y	Y	Y	Y	Y	Y	Y
4 Majette	Y	Y	Y	Y	Y	Y	Y
5 Lewis	Y	Y	Y	N	Y	Y	Y
6 *Isakson*	Y	N	Y	Y	Y	Y	N
7 *Linder*	Y	N	Y	Y	Y	Y	N
8 *Collins*	?	?	?	?	?	?	?
9 *Norwood*	Y	N	Y	Y	Y	Y	N
10 *Deal*	Y	N	Y	Y	Y	Y	N
11 *Gingrey*	Y	N	Y	Y	Y	Y	N
12 *Burns*	Y	N	Y	Y	Y	Y	N
13 Scott	Y	Y	Y	Y	Y	Y	Y
HAWAII							
1 Abercrombie	Y	Y	Y	Y	Y	Y	Y
2 Case	Y	Y	Y	Y	Y	Y	Y
IDAHO							
1 *Otter*	Y	N	Y	Y	Y	Y	N
2 *Simpson*	Y	N	Y	Y	Y	Y	N
ILLINOIS							
1 Rush	Y	Y	Y	Y	Y	Y	Y
2 Jackson	Y	Y	Y	Y	Y	Y	Y
3 Lipinski	Y	Y	Y	Y	Y	Y	Y
4 Gutierrez	Y	Y	Y	Y	Y	Y	Y
5 Emanuel	Y	Y	Y	Y	Y	Y	Y
6 *Hyde*	Y	N	Y	Y	Y	Y	N

ND Northern Democrats   SD Southern Democrats

	415	416	417	418	419	420	421
7 Davis	Y	Y	Y	Y	Y	Y	Y
8 ***Crane***	Y	N	Y	Y	Y	Y	N
9 Schakowsky	Y	Y	Y	N	Y	Y	Y
10 ***Kirk***	?	?	?	?	?	?	?
11 ***Weller***	Y	N	Y	Y	Y	Y	N
12 Costello	Y	Y	Y	Y	Y	Y	Y
13 ***Biggert***	Y	N	Y	Y	Y	Y	N
14 ***Hastert***							
15 ***Johnson***	Y	N	Y	Y	Y	Y	N
16 ***Manzullo***	Y	N	Y	Y	Y	Y	N
17 Evans	Y	Y	Y	Y	Y	Y	Y
18 ***LaHood***	Y	N	Y	Y	Y	Y	N
19 ***Shimkus***	Y	N	Y	Y	Y	Y	N
INDIANA							
1 Visclosky	Y	Y	Y	Y	Y	Y	Y
2 ***Chocola***	Y	N	Y	Y	Y	Y	N
3 ***Souder***	Y	N	Y	Y	Y	Y	N
4 ***Buyer***	Y	N	Y	Y	Y	Y	N
5 ***Burton***	Y	N	Y	Y	Y	Y	N
6 ***Pence***	Y	N	Y	Y	Y	Y	N
7 Carson	?	?	?	?	?	?	?
8 ***Hostettler***	Y	N	Y	Y	Y	Y	N
9 Hill	Y	Y	Y	Y	Y	Y	Y
IOWA							
1 ***Nussle***	Y	N	Y	Y	Y	Y	N
2 ***Leach***	Y	N	Y	Y	Y	Y	N
3 Boswell	Y	Y	Y	Y	Y	Y	Y
4 ***Latham***	Y	N	Y	Y	Y	Y	N
5 ***King***	Y	N	Y	Y	Y	Y	N
KANSAS							
1 ***Moran***	Y	N	Y	Y	Y	Y	N
2 ***Ryun***	Y	N	Y	Y	Y	Y	N
3 Moore	Y	Y	Y	Y	Y	Y	Y
4 ***Tiahrt***	Y	N	Y	Y	Y	Y	N
KENTUCKY							
1 ***Whitfield***	Y	N	Y	Y	Y	Y	N
2 ***Lewis***	Y	N	Y	Y	Y	Y	N
3 ***Northup***	Y	N	Y	Y	Y	Y	N
4 Lucas	Y	Y	Y	Y	Y	Y	Y
5 ***Rogers***	Y	N	Y	Y	Y	Y	N
6 Chandler	Y	Y	Y	Y	Y	Y	Y
LOUISIANA							
1 ***Vitter***	Y	N	Y	Y	Y	Y	N
2 Jefferson	Y	Y	Y	Y	Y	Y	Y
3 ***Tauzin***	Y	N	Y	Y	Y	Y	N
4 ***McCrery***	Y	N	Y	Y	Y	Y	N
5 Alexander	Y	Y	Y	Y	Y	Y	Y
6 ***Baker***	Y	N	Y	Y	Y	Y	N
7 John	Y	Y	Y	Y	Y	Y	Y
MAINE							
1 Allen	Y	Y	Y	Y	Y	Y	Y
2 Michaud	Y	Y	Y	Y	Y	Y	Y
MARYLAND							
1 ***Gilchrest***	Y	N	Y	Y	Y	Y	N
2 Ruppersberger	Y	Y	Y	Y	Y	Y	Y
3 Cardin	Y	Y	Y	Y	Y	Y	Y
4 Wynn	Y	Y	Y	Y	Y	Y	Y
5 Hoyer	Y	Y	Y	Y	Y	Y	Y
6 ***Bartlett***	Y	N	Y	Y	Y	Y	N
7 Cummings	Y	Y	Y	Y	Y	Y	Y
8 Van Hollen	Y	Y	Y	Y	Y	Y	Y
MASSACHUSETTS							
1 Olver	Y	Y	Y	Y	Y	Y	Y
2 Neal	Y	Y	Y	Y	Y	Y	Y
3 McGovern	Y	Y	Y	Y	Y	Y	Y
4 Frank	Y	Y	Y	Y	Y	Y	Y
5 Meehan	?	?	?	?	?	?	?
6 Tierney	Y	Y	Y	Y	Y	Y	Y
7 Markey	Y	Y	Y	Y	Y	Y	Y
8 Capuano	Y	Y	Y	Y	Y	Y	Y
9 Lynch	Y	Y	Y	Y	Y	Y	Y
10 Delahunt	Y	Y	Y	Y	Y	Y	Y
MICHIGAN							
1 Stupak	Y	Y	Y	Y	Y	Y	Y
2 ***Hoekstra***	Y	N	Y	Y	Y	Y	N
3 ***Ehlers***	Y	N	Y	Y	Y	Y	N
4 ***Camp***	Y	N	Y	Y	Y	Y	N
5 Kildee	Y	Y	Y	Y	Y	Y	Y
6 ***Upton***	Y	N	Y	Y	Y	Y	N
7 ***Smith***	Y	N	Y	Y	Y	Y	Y
8 ***Rogers***	Y	N	Y	Y	Y	Y	N
9 ***Knollenberg***	Y	N	Y	Y	Y	Y	N
10 ***Miller***	Y	N	Y	Y	Y	Y	N
11 ***McCotter***	Y	N	Y	Y	Y	Y	N
12 Levin	Y	Y	Y	Y	Y	Y	Y
13 Kilpatrick	Y	Y	Y	Y	Y	Y	Y
14 Conyers	?	Y	?	N	Y	Y	Y
15 Dingell	Y	Y	Y	Y	Y	Y	Y
MINNESOTA							
1 ***Gutknecht***	Y	N	Y	Y	Y	Y	N
2 ***Kline***	Y	N	Y	Y	Y	Y	N
3 ***Ramstad***	Y	N	Y	Y	Y	Y	N
4 McCollum	Y	Y	Y	Y	Y	Y	Y
5 Sabo	?	Y	Y	Y	Y	Y	Y
6 ***Kennedy***	Y	N	Y	Y	Y	Y	N
7 Peterson	Y	Y	Y	Y	Y	Y	Y
8 Oberstar	Y	Y	Y	Y	Y	Y	Y
MISSISSIPPI							
1 ***Wicker***	Y	N	Y	Y	Y	Y	N
2 Thompson	Y	Y	Y	Y	Y	Y	Y
3 ***Pickering***	Y	N	Y	Y	Y	Y	N
4 Taylor	Y	Y	Y	Y	Y	Y	Y
MISSOURI							
1 Clay	Y	?	?	?	?	?	?
2 ***Akin***	Y	N	Y	Y	Y	Y	N
3 Gephardt	?	?	?	?	?	?	?
4 Skelton	Y	Y	Y	Y	Y	Y	Y
5 McCarthy	Y	Y	Y	Y	Y	Y	Y
6 ***Graves***	Y	N	Y	Y	Y	Y	N
7 ***Blunt***	Y	N	Y	Y	Y	Y	N
8 ***Emerson***	Y	N	Y	Y	Y	Y	N
9 ***Hulshof***	Y	N	Y	Y	Y	Y	N
MONTANA							
AL ***Rehberg***	Y	N	Y	Y	Y	Y	N
NEBRASKA							
1 ***Bereuter***	Y	N	Y	Y	Y	Y	N
2 ***Terry***	Y	N	Y	Y	Y	Y	N
3 ***Osborne***	Y	N	Y	Y	Y	Y	N
NEVADA							
1 Berkley	Y	Y	Y	Y	Y	Y	Y
2 ***Gibbons***	Y	N	Y	Y	Y	Y	N
3 ***Porter***	Y	N	Y	Y	Y	Y	N
NEW HAMPSHIRE							
1 ***Bradley***	Y	N	Y	Y	Y	Y	N
2 ***Bass***	Y	N	Y	Y	Y	Y	N
NEW JERSEY							
1 Andrews	Y	Y	Y	Y	Y	Y	Y
2 ***LoBiondo***	Y	N	Y	Y	Y	Y	N
3 ***Saxton***	Y	N	Y	Y	Y	Y	N
4 ***Smith***	Y	N	Y	Y	Y	Y	N
5 ***Garrett***	Y	N	Y	Y	Y	Y	N
6 Pallone	Y	Y	Y	Y	Y	Y	Y
7 ***Ferguson***	Y	N	Y	?	?	?	?
8 Pascrell	Y	Y	Y	Y	Y	Y	Y
9 Rothman	Y	Y	Y	Y	Y	Y	Y
10 Payne	Y	Y	Y	N	Y	Y	Y
11 ***Frelinghuysen***	Y	N	Y	Y	Y	Y	N
12 Holt	Y	Y	Y	Y	Y	Y	Y
13 Menendez	Y	Y	Y	Y	Y	Y	Y
NEW MEXICO							
1 ***Wilson***	Y	Y	Y	Y	Y	Y	N
2 ***Pearce***	Y	N	Y	Y	Y	Y	N
3 Udall	Y	Y	Y	Y	Y	Y	Y
NEW YORK							
1 Bishop	Y	Y	Y	Y	Y	Y	Y
2 Israel	Y	Y	Y	Y	Y	Y	Y
3 ***King***	Y	N	Y	Y	Y	Y	N
4 McCarthy	Y	Y	Y	Y	Y	Y	Y
5 Ackerman	?	?	?	?	?	?	?
6 Meeks	Y	?	Y	Y	Y	Y	Y
7 Crowley	Y	Y	Y	Y	Y	Y	Y
8 Nadler	Y	Y	Y	Y	Y	Y	Y
9 Weiner	Y	Y	Y	Y	Y	Y	Y
10 Towns	Y	Y	Y	Y	Y	Y	Y
11 Owens	Y	Y	Y	N	Y	Y	Y
12 Velázquez	Y	Y	Y	Y	Y	Y	Y
13 ***Fossella***	Y	N	Y	Y	Y	Y	N
14 Maloney	Y	Y	Y	Y	Y	Y	Y
15 Rangel	Y	Y	Y	Y	Y	Y	Y
16 Serrano	Y	Y	Y	Y	Y	Y	Y
17 Engel	Y	Y	Y	Y	Y	Y	Y
18 Lowey	?	?	?	?	?	?	?
19 ***Kelly***	Y	N	Y	Y	Y	Y	N
20 ***Sweeney***	Y	N	Y	Y	Y	Y	N
21 McNulty	Y	Y	Y	Y	Y	Y	Y
22 Hinchey	Y	Y	Y	Y	Y	Y	Y
23 ***McHugh***	Y	N	Y	Y	Y	Y	N
24 ***Boehlert***	Y	N	Y	Y	Y	Y	N
25 ***Walsh***	Y	N	Y	Y	Y	Y	N
26 ***Reynolds***	Y	N	Y	Y	Y	Y	N
27 ***Quinn***	?	?	?	?	?	?	?
28 Slaughter	Y	Y	Y	Y	Y	Y	Y
29 ***Houghton***	Y	N	Y	Y	Y	Y	N
NORTH CAROLINA							
1 Butterfield	Y	Y	Y	Y	Y	Y	Y
2 Etheridge	Y	Y	Y	Y	Y	Y	Y
3 ***Jones***	Y	Y	Y	Y	Y	Y	Y
4 Price	Y	Y	Y	Y	Y	Y	Y
5 ***Burr***	Y	N	Y	Y	Y	Y	N
6 ***Coble***	Y	N	Y	Y	Y	Y	N
7 McIntyre	Y	Y	Y	Y	Y	Y	Y
8 ***Hayes***	Y	N	Y	Y	Y	Y	N
9 ***Myrick***	Y	N	Y	Y	Y	Y	N
10 ***Ballenger***	Y	N	Y	Y	Y	Y	N
11 ***Taylor***	Y	N	Y	Y	Y	Y	N
12 Watt	Y	Y	Y	N	Y	Y	Y
13 Miller	Y	Y	Y	Y	Y	Y	Y
NORTH DAKOTA							
AL Pomeroy	Y	Y	Y	Y	Y	Y	Y
OHIO							
1 ***Chabot***	Y	N	Y	Y	Y	Y	N
2 ***Portman***	Y	N	Y	Y	Y	Y	N
3 ***Turner***	Y	N	Y	Y	Y	Y	N
4 ***Oxley***	Y	N	Y	Y	Y	Y	N
5 ***Gillmor***	Y	N	Y	Y	Y	Y	N
6 Strickland	Y	Y	Y	Y	Y	Y	Y
7 ***Hobson***	?	N	Y	Y	Y	Y	N
8 ***Boehner***	Y	N	Y	Y	Y	Y	N
9 Kaptur	Y	Y	Y	Y	Y	Y	Y
10 Kucinich	?	?	Y	N	Y	Y	Y
11 Jones	Y	Y	Y	Y	Y	Y	Y
12 ***Tiberi***	Y	N	Y	Y	Y	Y	N
13 Brown	Y	Y	Y	Y	Y	Y	Y
14 ***LaTourette***	Y	N	Y	Y	Y	Y	N
15 ***Pryce***	Y	N	Y	Y	Y	Y	N
16 ***Regula***	Y	N	Y	Y	Y	Y	N
17 Ryan	Y	Y	Y	Y	Y	Y	Y
18 ***Ney***	Y	N	Y	Y	Y	Y	N
OKLAHOMA							
1 ***Sullivan***	Y	N	Y	Y	Y	Y	N
2 Carson	Y	Y	Y	Y	Y	Y	Y
3 ***Lucas***	Y	N	Y	Y	Y	Y	N
4 ***Cole***	Y	N	Y	Y	Y	Y	N
5 ***Istook***	Y	N	Y	Y	Y	Y	N
OREGON							
1 Wu	Y	Y	Y	Y	Y	Y	Y
2 ***Walden***	Y	N	Y	Y	Y	Y	N
3 Blumenauer	Y	Y	Y	Y	Y	Y	Y
4 DeFazio	Y	Y	Y	Y	Y	Y	Y
5 Hooley	Y	Y	Y	Y	Y	Y	Y
PENNSYLVANIA							
1 Brady	Y	Y	Y	Y	Y	Y	N
2 Fattah	Y	Y	Y	Y	Y	Y	Y
3 ***English***	Y	N	Y	Y	Y	Y	N
4 ***Hart***	Y	?	Y	Y	Y	Y	N
5 ***Peterson***	Y	N	Y	Y	Y	Y	N
6 ***Gerlach***	Y	N	Y	Y	Y	Y	N
7 ***Weldon***	Y	N	Y	Y	Y	Y	N
8 ***Greenwood***	?	?	?	?	?	?	?
9 ***Shuster, Bill***	Y	N	Y	Y	Y	Y	N
10 ***Sherwood***	Y	N	Y	Y	Y	Y	N
11 Kanjorski	Y	Y	Y	Y	Y	Y	N
12 Murtha	Y	Y	Y	Y	Y	Y	N
13 Hoeffel	Y	Y	Y	Y	Y	Y	Y
14 Doyle	Y	Y	Y	Y	Y	Y	Y
15 ***Toomey***	Y	N	Y	Y	Y	Y	N
16 ***Pitts***	Y	N	Y	Y	Y	Y	N
17 Holden	Y	Y	Y	Y	Y	Y	Y
18 ***Murphy***	Y	N	Y	Y	Y	Y	N
19 ***Platts***	Y	N	Y	Y	Y	Y	N
RHODE ISLAND							
1 Kennedy	Y	Y	Y	Y	Y	Y	Y
2 Langevin	Y	Y	Y	Y	Y	Y	Y
SOUTH CAROLINA							
1 ***Brown***	Y	N	Y	Y	Y	Y	N
2 ***Wilson***	Y	N	Y	Y	Y	Y	N
3 ***Barrett***	Y	N	Y	Y	Y	Y	N
4 ***DeMint***	Y	N	Y	Y	Y	Y	N
5 Spratt	Y	Y	Y	Y	Y	Y	Y
6 Clyburn	Y	Y	Y	Y	Y	Y	Y
SOUTH DAKOTA							
AL Herseth	Y	Y	Y	Y	Y	Y	Y
TENNESSEE							
1 ***Jenkins***	Y	N	Y	Y	Y	Y	N
2 ***Duncan***	Y	N	Y	Y	Y	Y	N
3 ***Wamp***	Y	N	Y	Y	Y	Y	N
4 Davis	Y	Y	Y	Y	Y	Y	Y
5 Cooper	Y	Y	Y	Y	Y	Y	Y
6 Gordon	Y	Y	Y	Y	Y	Y	Y
7 ***Blackburn***	Y	N	Y	Y	Y	Y	N
8 Tanner	Y	Y	Y	Y	Y	Y	Y
9 Ford	?	Y	Y	Y	Y	Y	Y
TEXAS							
1 Sandlin	Y	Y	Y	Y	Y	Y	Y
2 Turner	Y	Y	Y	Y	Y	Y	Y
3 ***Johnson, Sam***	Y	N	Y	Y	Y	Y	N
4 ***Hall***	Y	N	Y	Y	Y	Y	N
5 ***Hensarling***	Y	N	Y	Y	Y	Y	N
6 ***Barton***	Y	N	Y	Y	Y	Y	N
7 ***Culberson***	Y	?	Y	Y	Y	Y	N
8 ***Brady***	Y	N	Y	Y	Y	Y	N
9 Lampson	Y	Y	Y	Y	Y	Y	Y
10 Doggett	Y	Y	Y	Y	Y	Y	Y
11 Edwards	Y	Y	Y	Y	Y	Y	Y
12 ***Granger***	Y	N	Y	Y	Y	Y	N
13 ***Thornberry***	Y	N	Y	Y	Y	Y	N
14 ***Paul***	?	?	?	?	?	?	?
15 Hinojosa	Y	Y	Y	Y	Y	Y	Y
16 Reyes	Y	Y	Y	Y	Y	Y	Y
17 Stenholm	Y	Y	Y	Y	Y	Y	Y
18 Jackson-Lee	Y	Y	Y	Y	Y	Y	Y
19 ***Neugebauer***	Y	N	Y	Y	Y	Y	N
20 Gonzalez	Y	Y	Y	Y	Y	Y	Y
21 ***Smith***	Y	N	Y	Y	Y	Y	N
22 ***DeLay***	Y	N	Y	Y	Y	Y	N
23 ***Bonilla***	Y	N	Y	Y	Y	Y	N
24 Frost	Y	Y	Y	Y	Y	Y	Y
25 Bell	Y	Y	Y	Y	Y	Y	Y
26 ***Burgess***	Y	N	Y	Y	Y	Y	N
27 Ortiz	Y	Y	Y	Y	Y	Y	Y
28 Rodriguez	Y	Y	Y	Y	Y	Y	Y
29 Green	Y	Y	Y	Y	Y	Y	Y
30 Johnson, E.B.	Y	Y	Y	Y	Y	Y	Y
31 ***Carter***	Y	N	Y	Y	Y	Y	N
32 ***Sessions***	Y	N	Y	Y	Y	Y	N
UTAH							
1 ***Bishop***	Y	N	Y	Y	Y	Y	N
2 Matheson	Y	Y	Y	Y	Y	Y	Y
3 ***Cannon***	Y	N	Y	Y	Y	Y	N
VERMONT							
AL *Sanders*	Y	Y	Y	Y	Y	Y	Y
VIRGINIA							
1 ***Davis, Jo Ann***	Y	N	Y	Y	Y	Y	N
2 ***Schrock***	Y	N	Y	Y	Y	Y	N
3 Scott	Y	Y	Y	Y	Y	Y	Y
4 ***Forbes***	Y	N	Y	Y	Y	Y	N
5 ***Goode***	Y	N	Y	Y	Y	Y	N
6 ***Goodlatte***	Y	N	Y	Y	Y	Y	N
7 ***Cantor***	Y	N	Y	Y	Y	Y	N
8 Moran	Y	Y	Y	Y	Y	Y	?
9 Boucher	Y	Y	Y	Y	Y	Y	Y
10 ***Wolf***	Y	N	Y	Y	Y	Y	N
11 ***Davis, T.***	Y	N	Y	Y	Y	Y	N
WASHINGTON							
1 Inslee	Y	Y	Y	Y	Y	Y	Y
2 Larsen	Y	Y	Y	Y	Y	Y	Y
3 Baird	Y	Y	Y	Y	Y	Y	Y
4 ***Hastings***	Y	N	Y	Y	Y	Y	N
5 ***Nethercutt***	Y	N	Y	Y	Y	Y	N
6 Dicks	Y	Y	Y	Y	Y	Y	Y
7 McDermott	Y	Y	Y	N	Y	Y	Y
8 ***Dunn***	Y	N	Y	Y	Y	Y	N
9 Smith	Y	Y	Y	Y	Y	Y	Y
WEST VIRGINIA							
1 Mollohan	Y	Y	Y	Y	Y	Y	N
2 ***Capito***	Y	N	Y	Y	Y	Y	N
3 Rahall	Y	Y	Y	Y	Y	Y	Y
WISCONSIN							
1 ***Ryan***	Y	N	Y	Y	Y	Y	N
2 Baldwin	Y	Y	Y	Y	Y	Y	Y
3 Kind	Y	Y	Y	Y	Y	Y	Y
4 Kleczka	Y	Y	Y	Y	Y	Y	Y
5 ***Sensenbrenner***	Y	N	Y	Y	Y	Y	N
6 ***Petri***	Y	N	Y	Y	Y	Y	?
7 Obey	Y	Y	N	Y	Y	Y	Y
8 ***Green***	Y	N	Y	Y	Y	Y	N
WYOMING							
AL ***Cubin***	Y	N	Y	Y	Y	Y	N

Southern states - Ala., Ark., Fla., Ga., Ky., La., Miss., N.C., Okla., S.C., Tenn., Texas, Va.

Key

Y	Voted for (yea).
#	Paired for.
+	Announced for.
N	Voted against (nay).
X	Paired against.
–	Announced against.
P	Voted "present."
C	Voted "present" to avoid possible conflict of interest.
?	Did not vote or otherwise make a position known.

Democrats   **Republicans**
Independents

422. HR 4381. Harvey and Bernice Jones Post Office/Passage. Miller, R-Mich., motion to suspend the rules and pass the bill that would designate a post office in Springdale, Ark., after local philanthropists Harvey and Bernice Jones. Motion agreed to 382-0: R 202-0; D 179-0 (ND 131-0, SD 47-0); I 1-0. A two-thirds majority of those present and voting (256 in this case) is required for passage under suspension of the rules. Sept. 7, 2004.

423. HR 4556. William Carey Lee Post Office Building/Passage. Miller, R-Mich., motion to suspend the rules and pass the bill that would designate a post office in Dunn, N.C., after Gen. William Carey Lee, the first commanding general of the 101st Airborne parachute troops during World Wars I and II. Motion agreed to 380-0: R 202-0; D 177-0 (ND 131-0, SD 46-0); I 1-0. A two-thirds majority of those present and voting (254 in this case) is required for passage under suspension of the rules. Sept. 7, 2004.

424. HR 5006. Fiscal 2005 Labor-HHS-Education Appropriations/ Previous Question. Pryce, R-Ohio, motion to order the previous question (thus ending debate and possibility of amendment) on adoption of the rule (H Res 754) to provide for House floor consideration of the bill that would appropriate $496.6 billion for the Labor, Health and Human Services, and Education departments and related agencies. Motion agreed to 209-190: R 209-0; D 0-189 (ND 0-136, SD 0-53); I 0-1. (Subsequently, the rule was adopted by voice vote.) Sept. 8, 2004.

425. HR 5006. Fiscal 2005 Labor-HHS-Education Appropriations/ Health Statistics. Jackson-Lee, D-Texas, amendment that would increase funding for National Center for Health Statistics surveys by $2.5 million and the National Center on Minority Health and Health Disparities by $1.5 million. It would be offset by a $4 million decrease in funding for competitive abstinence education grants. Rejected 112-305: R 0-219; D 111-86 (ND 86-55, SD 25-31); I 1-0. Sept. 8, 2004.

426. HR 5006. Fiscal 2005 Labor-HHS-Education Appropriations/ Hepatitis C Research. Jackson-Lee, D-Texas, amendment that would provide $1 million to the Centers for Disease Control and Prevention for Hepatitis C research. The spending would be offset by decreasing funding for abstinence education by $1 million. Rejected 156-261: R 3-215; D 152-46 (ND 117-25, SD 35-21); I 1-0. Sept. 8, 2004.

427. HR 5006. Fiscal 2005 Labor-HHS-Education Appropriations/ LIHEAP. Sanders, I-Vt., amendment that would increase funding by $22 million for the Low-Income Home Energy Assistance Program (LIHEAP) and the weatherization assistance program. The spending would be offset by a $26 million cut in funding for Health and Human Services departmental management. Adopted 305-114: R 107-112; D 197-2 (ND 142-1, SD 55-1); I 1-0. Sept. 8, 2004.

428. HR 5006. Fiscal 2005 Labor-HHS-Education Appropriations/ Discretionary Spending Reduction. Hefley, R-Colo., amendment that would reduce the discretionary spending in the bill by $1.4 billion. Rejected 79-333: R 75-139; D 4-193 (ND 1-141, SD 3-52); I 0-1. Sept. 8, 2004.

[1] *Rep. Rodney Alexander of Louisiana switched parties from Democrat to Republican, effective Sept. 7, 2004.*

[2] *Rep. Doug Bereuter, R-Neb., resigned effective August 31, 2004 The last vote for which he was eligible was vote 421.*

	422	423	424	425	426	427	428
ALABAMA							
1 *Bonner*	Y	Y	Y	N	N	N	N
2 *Everett*	Y	Y	Y	N	N	N	N
3 *Rogers*	Y	Y	Y	N	N	N	N
4 *Aderholt*	Y	Y	Y	N	N	N	N
5 Cramer	Y	Y	N	N	N	Y	N
6 *Bachus*	Y	Y	Y	N	N	N	N
7 Davis	Y	Y	N	Y	Y	Y	N
ALASKA							
AL *Young*	?	?	?	?	?	?	?
ARIZONA							
1 *Renzi*	+	+	Y	N	N	Y	N
2 *Franks*	?	?	Y	N	N	N	Y
3 *Shadegg*	Y	Y	Y	N	N	N	Y
4 Pastor	Y	Y	N	Y	Y	Y	N
5 *Hayworth*	Y	Y	Y	N	N	Y	Y
6 *Flake*	+	+	+	–	–	–	Y
7 Grijalva	+	+	–	+	+	+	N
8 *Kolbe*	?	?	Y	N	N	N	N
ARKANSAS							
1 Berry	Y	Y	N	N	N	Y	N
2 Snyder	Y	Y	N	N	N	Y	N
3 *Boozman*	Y	Y	Y	N	N	N	N
4 Ross	Y	Y	N	N	N	Y	N
CALIFORNIA							
1 Thompson	Y	Y	N	N	N	Y	N
2 *Herger*	Y	Y	Y	N	N	N	Y
3 *Ose*	Y	Y	N	N	N	N	N
4 *Doolittle*	Y	Y	Y	N	N	N	N
5 Matsui	Y	Y	N	Y	N	Y	N
6 Woolsey	Y	Y	N	Y	Y	Y	N
7 Miller, George	Y	Y	N	Y	Y	Y	N
8 Pelosi	Y	Y	N	Y	Y	Y	N
9 Lee	Y	Y	N	Y	Y	Y	N
10 Tauscher	Y	Y	N	N	N	Y	N
11 *Pombo*	Y	Y	Y	N	N	N	N
12 Lantos	Y	Y	N	Y	N	Y	N
13 Stark	?	?	N	Y	Y	Y	N
14 Eshoo	Y	Y	N	N	N	Y	N
15 Honda	Y	Y	N	Y	N	Y	N
16 Lofgren	Y	Y	N	N	N	Y	N
17 Farr	Y	Y	N	Y	Y	Y	N
18 Cardoza	Y	Y	N	N	N	Y	N
19 *Radanovich*	Y	Y	N	N	N	N	N
20 Dooley	Y	Y	N	?	N	?	N
21 *Nunes*	?	?	Y	N	N	N	N
22 *Thomas*	Y	Y	N	N	N	N	N
23 Capps	Y	Y	N	Y	Y	Y	N
24 *Gallegly*	+	+	Y	N	N	N	N
25 *McKeon*	Y	Y	N	N	N	N	N
26 *Dreier*	Y	Y	N	N	N	N	N
27 Sherman	Y	Y	N	Y	Y	Y	N
28 Berman	Y	Y	N	Y	Y	Y	N
29 Schiff	Y	Y	N	N	N	Y	N
30 Waxman	Y	Y	N	Y	Y	Y	N
31 Becerra	Y	Y	N	Y	Y	Y	N
32 Solis	Y	Y	N	Y	Y	Y	N
33 Watson	Y	Y	N	Y	Y	Y	?
34 Roybal-Allard	Y	Y	N	N	N	Y	N
35 Waters	Y	Y	N	Y	Y	Y	N
36 Harman	Y	Y	N	Y	Y	Y	N

	422	423	424	425	426	427	428
37 Millender-McD.	Y	Y	N	Y	Y	Y	–
38 Napolitano	Y	Y	N	Y	Y	Y	N
39 Sánchez, Linda	Y	Y	N	Y	Y	Y	N
40 *Royce*	Y	Y	N	N	N	N	N
41 *Lewis*	Y	Y	?	N	N	Y	N
42 *Miller, Gary*	Y	Y	N	N	N	N	N
43 Baca	Y	Y	N	N	N	Y	N
44 *Calvert*	Y	Y	Y	N	N	N	N
45 *Bono*	Y	Y	N	N	N	Y	?
46 *Rohrabacher*	Y	Y	N	N	N	N	N
47 Sanchez, Loretta	Y	Y	N	Y	Y	Y	N
48 *Cox*	Y	Y	N	N	N	N	N
49 *Issa*	Y	Y	N	N	N	N	N
50 *Cunningham*	Y	Y	N	N	N	N	N
51 Filner	Y	Y	N	Y	Y	Y	N
52 *Hunter*	Y	Y	Y	N	N	Y	N
53 Davis	Y	Y	N	N	N	Y	N
COLORADO							
1 DeGette	Y	Y	N	Y	Y	Y	N
2 Udall	Y	Y	?	Y	Y	Y	N
3 *McInnis*	?	?	?	N	N	N	Y
4 *Musgrave*	Y	Y	N	N	N	N	N
5 *Hefley*	Y	Y	N	N	N	N	Y
6 *Tancredo*	Y	Y	N	N	N	N	Y
7 *Beauprez*	Y	Y	Y	N	N	Y	N
CONNECTICUT							
1 Larson	Y	Y	N	Y	Y	Y	N
2 *Simmons*	Y	Y	?	N	N	Y	N
3 DeLauro	Y	Y	N	Y	Y	Y	N
4 *Shays*	Y	Y	Y	N	N	Y	N
5 *Johnson*	Y	Y	N	N	N	Y	N
DELAWARE							
AL *Castle*	Y	Y	Y	N	N	Y	N
FLORIDA							
1 *Miller, J.*	Y	Y	N	N	N	Y	N
2 Boyd	Y	Y	N	N	N	Y	N
3 Brown	Y	Y	N	Y	Y	Y	N
4 *Crenshaw*	Y	Y	Y	N	N	N	N
5 *Brown-Waite*	Y	Y	N	N	N	Y	N
6 *Stearns*	Y	Y	Y	N	N	N	Y
7 *Mica*	Y	Y	N	N	N	N	N
8 *Keller*	Y	Y	N	N	N	N	N
9 *Bilirakis*	?	?	?	N	N	?	Y
10 *Young*	Y	Y	N	N	N	N	N
11 Davis	?	?	N	N	N	Y	N
12 *Putnam*	?	?	?	N	N	N	N
13 *Harris*	Y	Y	N	N	N	N	N
14 *Goss*	?	?	Y	N	N	N	?
15 *Weldon*	Y	Y	N	N	N	N	N
16 *Foley*	Y	Y	Y	N	N	Y	N
17 Meek	Y	Y	N	Y	Y	Y	N
18 *Ros-Lehtinen*	Y	Y	N	N	N	Y	N
19 Wexler	?	?	N	Y	Y	Y	N
20 Deutsch	Y	Y	N	Y	Y	Y	N
21 *Diaz-Balart, L.*	Y	Y	N	N	N	N	N
22 *Shaw*	Y	Y	N	N	N	N	N
23 Hastings	Y	Y	N	Y	Y	Y	N
24 *Feeney*	Y	Y	N	N	N	N	Y
25 *Diaz-Balart, M.*	Y	Y	Y	N	N	N	Y
GEORGIA							
1 *Kingston*	Y	Y	Y	N	N	N	Y
2 Bishop	Y	Y	N	N	N	Y	N
3 Marshall	Y	Y	N	N	N	Y	N
4 *Majette*	?	?	N	Y	Y	Y	N
5 Lewis	Y	Y	N	Y	Y	Y	N
6 *Isakson*	Y	Y	N	N	N	N	N
7 *Linder*	Y	Y	Y	N	N	N	Y
8 *Collins*	Y	Y	N	N	N	N	N
9 *Norwood*	Y	Y	?	N	N	N	Y
10 *Deal*	Y	Y	N	N	N	Y	N
11 *Gingrey*	Y	Y	N	N	N	N	N
12 *Burns*	Y	Y	Y	N	N	Y	N
13 Scott	Y	Y	N	Y	N	Y	N
HAWAII							
1 Abercrombie	Y	Y	N	Y	Y	Y	N
2 Case	Y	Y	N	Y	Y	Y	N
IDAHO							
1 *Otter*	Y	Y	Y	N	N	N	Y
2 *Simpson*	?	?	Y	N	N	N	N
ILLINOIS							
1 Rush	?	?	N	Y	Y	Y	N
2 Jackson	Y	Y	N	Y	Y	Y	N
3 Lipinski	?	?	N	N	P	N	Y
4 Gutierrez	+	+	N	Y	Y	Y	N
5 Emanuel	Y	Y	N	Y	Y	Y	N
6 *Hyde*	Y	Y	Y	N	N	Y	N

ND Northern Democrats   SD Southern Democrats

	422	423	424	425	426	427	428
7 Davis	Y	Y	N	Y	Y	Y	N
8 ***Crane***	Y	Y	Y	N	N	Y	?
9 Schakowsky	Y	Y	N	N	Y	Y	N
10 ***Kirk***	Y	Y	Y	N	N	Y	N
11 ***Weller***	Y	Y	Y	N	N	Y	N
12 Costello	Y	Y	N	N	N	Y	N
13 ***Biggert***	Y	Y	Y	N	N	Y	N
14 ***Hastert***							
15 ***Johnson***	Y	Y	Y	N	N	Y	N
16 ***Manzullo***	Y	Y	Y	N	N	N	N
17 Evans	Y	Y	N	Y	N	Y	N
18 ***LaHood***	Y	Y	Y	N	N	Y	N
19 ***Shimkus***	Y	Y	Y	N	N	Y	Y
INDIANA							
1 Visclosky	Y	Y	N	N	Y	Y	N
2 ***Chocola***	Y	Y	Y	N	N	Y	Y
3 ***Souder***	Y	Y	Y	N	N	Y	N
4 ***Buyer***	Y	Y	Y	N	N	N	Y
5 ***Burton***	Y	Y	Y	N	N	N	Y
6 ***Pence***	Y	Y	Y	N	N	N	Y
7 Carson	?	?	N	Y	Y	Y	N
8 ***Hostettler***	Y	Y	Y	N	N	Y	Y
9 Hill	Y	Y	N	N	N	Y	N
IOWA							
1 ***Nussle***	Y	Y	Y	N	N	Y	N
2 ***Leach***	Y	Y	Y	N	N	Y	N
3 Boswell	Y	Y	N	N	N	Y	N
4 ***Latham***	?	?	Y	N	N	Y	N
5 ***King***	Y	Y	Y	N	N	Y	Y
KANSAS							
1 ***Moran***	Y	Y	Y	N	N	Y	N
2 ***Ryun***	Y	Y	Y	N	N	Y	N
3 Moore	Y	Y	N	N	N	Y	N
4 ***Tiahrt***	Y	Y	Y	N	N	Y	N
KENTUCKY							
1 ***Whitfield***	Y	Y	Y	N	N	N	Y
2 ***Lewis***	Y	Y	Y	N	N	Y	Y
3 ***Northup***	Y	Y	Y	N	N	N	N
4 Lucas	Y	Y	N	N	N	Y	N
5 ***Rogers***	Y	Y	Y	N	N	N	N
6 Chandler	Y	Y	?	N	N	Y	N
LOUISIANA							
1 ***Vitter***	Y	Y	Y	N	N	Y	Y
2 Jefferson	Y	Y	N	Y	Y	Y	N
3 ***Tauzin***	?	?	?	?	?	?	?
4 ***McCrery***	Y	Y	Y	N	N	Y	N
5 ***Alexander*** [1]	Y	Y	Y	N	N	Y	N
6 ***Baker***	?	?	Y	N	N	Y	N
7 John	?	?	?	N	N	Y	N
MAINE							
1 Allen	Y	Y	N	Y	Y	Y	N
2 Michaud	Y	Y	N	N	N	Y	N
MARYLAND							
1 ***Gilchrest***	Y	Y	Y	N	N	Y	N
2 Ruppersberger	Y	Y	N	Y	Y	Y	N
3 Cardin	Y	Y	N	N	Y	Y	N
4 Wynn	Y	Y	N	Y	Y	Y	N
5 Hoyer	Y	Y	N	N	Y	Y	N
6 ***Bartlett***	Y	Y	Y	N	N	Y	Y
7 Cummings	Y	Y	N	Y	Y	Y	?
8 Van Hollen	Y	Y	N	Y	Y	Y	N
MASSACHUSETTS							
1 Olver	Y	Y	N	N	Y	Y	N
2 Neal	Y	Y	N	Y	Y	Y	N
3 McGovern	Y	Y	N	Y	Y	Y	N
4 Frank	Y	Y	N	Y	Y	Y	N
5 Meehan	Y	Y	N	Y	Y	Y	N
6 Tierney	Y	Y	N	Y	Y	Y	N
7 Markey	Y	Y	N	Y	Y	Y	N
8 Capuano	Y	Y	N	Y	Y	Y	N
9 Lynch	Y	Y	N	Y	Y	Y	N
10 Delahunt	Y	Y	N	N	Y	Y	N
MICHIGAN							
1 Stupak	Y	Y	N	N	Y	Y	N
2 ***Hoekstra***	Y	Y	Y	N	N	Y	N
3 ***Ehlers***	Y	Y	Y	N	N	Y	N
4 ***Camp***	Y	Y	Y	N	N	Y	N
5 Kildee	Y	Y	N	Y	Y	Y	N
6 ***Upton***	Y	Y	Y	N	N	Y	N
7 ***Smith***	Y	Y	Y	N	N	N	?
8 ***Rogers***	Y	Y	Y	N	N	Y	N
9 ***Knollenberg***	Y	Y	Y	N	N	N	N
10 ***Miller***	Y	Y	Y	N	N	Y	N
11 ***McCotter***	Y	Y	Y	N	N	Y	Y
12 Levin	Y	Y	N	N	Y	Y	N
13 Kilpatrick	Y	Y	N	N	Y	Y	N
14 Conyers	Y	Y	?	Y	Y	Y	N
15 Dingell	Y	Y	N	Y	Y	Y	N
MINNESOTA							
1 ***Gutknecht***	Y	Y	Y	N	N	Y	Y
2 ***Kline***	Y	Y	Y	N	N	Y	N
3 ***Ramstad***	Y	Y	Y	N	N	Y	N
4 McCollum	P	P	N	N	Y	Y	N
5 Sabo	Y	Y	N	N	Y	Y	N
6 ***Kennedy***	Y	Y	Y	N	N	Y	N
7 Peterson	Y	Y	N	N	N	Y	N
8 Oberstar	?	?	N	N	Y	Y	N
MISSISSIPPI							
1 ***Wicker***	Y	Y	Y	N	N	N	N
2 Thompson	Y	Y	N	Y	Y	Y	N
3 ***Pickering***	Y	Y	Y	N	N	Y	N
4 Taylor	Y	Y	N	N	N	Y	Y
MISSOURI							
1 Clay	Y	Y	?	Y	Y	Y	N
2 ***Akin***	Y	Y	Y	N	?	N	Y
3 Gephardt	?	?	N	Y	Y	Y	?
4 Skelton	Y	Y	N	N	N	Y	N
5 McCarthy	Y	Y	N	Y	Y	Y	N
6 ***Graves***	Y	Y	Y	N	N	Y	Y
7 ***Blunt***	Y	Y	Y	N	N	N	N
8 ***Emerson***	Y	Y	Y	N	N	Y	N
9 ***Hulshof***	?	?	Y	N	N	Y	N
MONTANA							
AL ***Rehberg***	Y	Y	Y	N	N	Y	N
NEBRASKA							
1 Vacant [2]							
2 ***Terry***	Y	Y	Y	N	N	N	Y
3 ***Osborne***	Y	Y	Y	N	N	Y	N
NEVADA							
1 Berkley	Y	Y	N	Y	Y	Y	N
2 ***Gibbons***	Y	Y	Y	N	N	Y	Y
3 ***Porter***	Y	Y	Y	N	N	Y	N
NEW HAMPSHIRE							
1 ***Bradley***	Y	Y	Y	N	N	Y	N
2 ***Bass***	Y	Y	Y	N	N	Y	Y
NEW JERSEY							
1 Andrews	Y	Y	?	Y	Y	Y	N
2 ***LoBiondo***	Y	Y	Y	N	N	Y	N
3 ***Saxton***	Y	Y	Y	N	N	Y	N
4 ***Smith***	Y	Y	Y	N	N	Y	N
5 ***Garrett***	Y	Y	Y	N	N	N	Y
6 Pallone	Y	Y	N	Y	Y	Y	N
7 ***Ferguson***	Y	Y	Y	N	N	Y	N
8 Pascrell	Y	Y	N	N	Y	Y	N
9 Rothman	Y	Y	N	Y	Y	Y	N
10 Payne	Y	Y	?	Y	Y	Y	N
11 ***Frelinghuysen***	Y	Y	Y	N	N	Y	N
12 Holt	Y	Y	N	Y	Y	Y	N
13 Menendez	Y	Y	N	Y	Y	Y	N
NEW MEXICO							
1 ***Wilson***	Y	Y	Y	N	Y	Y	N
2 ***Pearce***	Y	Y	Y	N	N	N	N
3 Udall	Y	Y	N	Y	Y	Y	N
NEW YORK							
1 Bishop	Y	Y	N	Y	Y	Y	N
2 Israel	Y	Y	N	Y	Y	Y	N
3 ***King***	Y	Y	Y	N	N	Y	N
4 McCarthy	Y	Y	?	Y	Y	Y	N
5 Ackerman	Y	Y	N	Y	Y	Y	N
6 Meeks	Y	Y	N	Y	Y	Y	N
7 Crowley	Y	Y	N	Y	Y	Y	N
8 Nadler	Y	Y	N	Y	Y	Y	N
9 Weiner	Y	Y	N	Y	Y	Y	N
10 Towns	?	?	N	Y	Y	Y	N
11 Owens	+	+	?	Y	Y	Y	N
12 Velázquez	Y	Y	N	Y	Y	Y	N
13 ***Fossella***	Y	Y	Y	N	N	Y	Y
14 Maloney	Y	Y	N	Y	Y	Y	N
15 Rangel	Y	?	N	Y	Y	Y	N
16 Serrano	Y	Y	N	Y	Y	Y	N
17 Engel	?	?	?	?	?	?	?
18 Lowey	Y	Y	N	N	N	Y	N
19 ***Kelly***	Y	Y	Y	N	N	Y	N
20 ***Sweeney***	Y	Y	Y	N	N	Y	N
21 McNulty	Y	Y	N	Y	Y	Y	N
22 Hinchey	Y	Y	N	Y	Y	Y	N
23 ***McHugh***	Y	Y	Y	N	N	Y	N
24 ***Boehlert***	Y	Y	?	N	N	Y	N
25 ***Walsh***	Y	Y	Y	N	N	Y	N
26 ***Reynolds***	Y	Y	Y	N	N	Y	N
27 ***Quinn***	Y	Y	Y	N	N	Y	N
28 Slaughter	Y	Y	N	Y	Y	Y	N
29 ***Houghton***	Y	Y	Y	N	N	Y	N
NORTH CAROLINA							
1 Butterfield	Y	Y	N	Y	Y	Y	N
2 Etheridge	Y	Y	N	N	Y	Y	N
3 ***Jones***	Y	Y	Y	N	N	Y	Y
4 Price	Y	Y	N	N	Y	Y	N
5 ***Burr***	?	?	Y	N	N	Y	N
6 ***Coble***	Y	Y	Y	N	N	Y	Y
7 McIntyre	Y	Y	N	N	N	Y	N
8 ***Hayes***	Y	Y	Y	N	N	N	Y
9 ***Myrick***	Y	Y	Y	N	N	N	Y
10 ***Ballenger***	?	?	?	?	?	?	?
11 ***Taylor***	Y	Y	Y	N	N	N	N
12 Watt	?	?	N	Y	Y	Y	N
13 Miller	Y	Y	N	N	Y	Y	N
NORTH DAKOTA							
AL Pomeroy	Y	Y	N	N	N	Y	N
OHIO							
1 ***Chabot***	Y	Y	Y	N	N	Y	Y
2 ***Portman***	Y	Y	Y	N	N	Y	–
3 ***Turner***	Y	Y	Y	N	N	N	N
4 ***Oxley***	Y	Y	Y	N	N	N	N
5 ***Gillmor***	Y	Y	Y	N	N	Y	N
6 Strickland	Y	Y	N	N	N	Y	N
7 ***Hobson***	Y	Y	?	N	N	N	N
8 ***Boehner***	Y	Y	Y	N	N	N	N
9 Kaptur	Y	Y	N	Y	Y	Y	N
10 Kucinich	Y	Y	N	N	N	Y	N
11 Jones	+	+	?	?	Y	Y	N
12 ***Tiberi***	Y	Y	Y	N	N	N	N
13 Brown	Y	Y	N	Y	Y	Y	N
14 ***LaTourette***	Y	Y	Y	N	N	Y	N
15 ***Pryce***	Y	Y	Y	N	N	N	N
16 ***Regula***	?	?	Y	N	N	N	N
17 Ryan	?	?	?	?	?	?	?
18 ***Ney***	Y	Y	Y	N	N	Y	?
OKLAHOMA							
1 ***Sullivan***	Y	Y	Y	N	N	N	Y
2 Carson	?	?	N	N	N	Y	N
3 ***Lucas***	?	?	Y	N	N	N	N
4 ***Cole***	Y	Y	Y	N	N	N	N
5 ***Istook***	Y	Y	Y	N	N	N	?
OREGON							
1 Wu	Y	Y	N	Y	Y	Y	N
2 ***Walden***	Y	Y	Y	N	N	N	N
3 Blumenauer	Y	Y	N	N	Y	Y	N
4 DeFazio	Y	Y	N	Y	Y	Y	N
5 Hooley	Y	Y	N	N	N	Y	Y
PENNSYLVANIA							
1 Brady	Y	Y	N	Y	Y	Y	N
2 Fattah	Y	Y	N	Y	Y	Y	N
3 ***English***	Y	Y	Y	N	N	Y	N
4 ***Hart***	Y	Y	Y	N	N	Y	N
5 ***Peterson***	Y	Y	Y	N	N	Y	N
6 ***Gerlach***	Y	Y	Y	N	N	Y	N
7 ***Weldon***	Y	Y	Y	N	N	Y	N
8 ***Greenwood***	Y	Y	Y	N	Y	N	N
9 ***Shuster, Bill***	Y	Y	Y	N	N	Y	Y
10 ***Sherwood***	Y	Y	Y	N	N	N	N
11 Kanjorski	Y	Y	N	N	N	Y	N
12 Murtha	?	?	N	N	N	Y	N
13 Hoeffel	?	?	N	Y	Y	Y	N
14 Doyle	Y	Y	N	N	N	Y	N
15 ***Toomey***	Y	Y	Y	N	N	N	Y
16 ***Pitts***	Y	Y	Y	N	N	N	Y
17 Holden	Y	Y	N	N	N	Y	N
18 ***Murphy***	Y	Y	Y	N	N	Y	N
19 ***Platts***	Y	Y	Y	N	N	Y	N
RHODE ISLAND							
1 Kennedy	Y	Y	N	Y	Y	Y	N
2 Langevin	Y	Y	N	N	Y	Y	N
SOUTH CAROLINA							
1 ***Brown***	Y	Y	Y	N	N	N	N
2 ***Wilson***	Y	Y	Y	N	N	N	Y
3 ***Barrett***	Y	Y	Y	N	N	N	Y
4 ***DeMint***	Y	Y	Y	N	N	N	Y
5 Spratt	Y	Y	N	N	Y	Y	N
6 Clyburn	Y	?	N	N	Y	Y	N
SOUTH DAKOTA							
AL Herseth	Y	Y	N	N	N	Y	N
TENNESSEE							
1 ***Jenkins***	Y	Y	Y	N	N	N	Y
2 ***Duncan***	Y	Y	Y	N	N	N	Y
3 ***Wamp***	Y	Y	Y	N	N	N	N
4 Davis	Y	Y	N	N	N	Y	Y
5 Cooper	Y	Y	N	Y	Y	Y	N
6 Gordon	Y	Y	N	N	N	Y	N
7 ***Blackburn***	Y	Y	Y	N	N	N	Y
8 Tanner	Y	Y	N	Y	Y	Y	Y
9 Ford	Y	Y	N	Y	Y	Y	N
TEXAS							
1 Sandlin	Y	Y	N	Y	Y	Y	N
2 Turner	Y	Y	N	N	N	Y	N
3 ***Johnson, Sam***	Y	Y	Y	N	N	N	N
4 ***Hall***	Y	Y	Y	N	N	Y	N
5 ***Hensarling***	Y	Y	Y	N	N	N	Y
6 ***Barton***	Y	Y	Y	N	N	N	Y
7 ***Culberson***	Y	Y	?	N	N	N	N
8 ***Brady***	?	?	?	N	N	N	Y
9 Lampson	?	?	?	N	N	Y	N
10 Doggett	Y	Y	N	Y	Y	Y	N
11 Edwards	?	Y	N	N	N	Y	N
12 ***Granger***	Y	Y	Y	N	N	N	N
13 ***Thornberry***	Y	Y	Y	N	N	N	Y
14 ***Paul***	Y	Y	Y	N	N	Y	Y
15 Hinojosa	Y	Y	N	Y	Y	Y	N
16 Reyes	Y	Y	N	N	Y	Y	N
17 Stenholm	Y	Y	N	N	N	Y	N
18 Jackson-Lee	Y	Y	N	Y	Y	Y	N
19 ***Neugebauer***	Y	Y	Y	N	N	Y	Y
20 Gonzalez	Y	Y	N	N	Y	Y	N
21 ***Smith***	Y	Y	Y	N	N	N	N
22 ***DeLay***	Y	Y	Y	N	N	N	N
23 ***Bonilla***	Y	Y	Y	N	N	N	N
24 Frost	?	?	N	N	Y	Y	N
25 Bell	Y	Y	N	Y	Y	Y	N
26 ***Burgess***	Y	Y	Y	N	N	Y	Y
27 Ortiz	Y	Y	N	N	N	Y	N
28 Rodriguez	Y	Y	N	Y	Y	Y	N
29 Green	Y	Y	N	Y	Y	Y	N
30 Johnson, E.B.	Y	Y	N	Y	Y	Y	N
31 ***Carter***	Y	Y	Y	N	N	N	N
32 ***Sessions***	?	?	Y	N	N	N	Y
UTAH							
1 ***Bishop***	Y	Y	Y	N	N	N	Y
2 Matheson	Y	Y	N	N	N	Y	N
3 ***Cannon***	?	?	?	?	?	?	?
VERMONT							
AL *Sanders*	Y	Y	N	Y	Y	Y	N
VIRGINIA							
1 ***Davis, Jo Ann***	Y	Y	Y	N	N	Y	Y
2 ***Schrock***	?	?	?	?	?	?	?
3 Scott	Y	Y	N	N	Y	Y	N
4 ***Forbes***	Y	Y	Y	N	N	N	N
5 ***Goode***	Y	Y	Y	N	N	N	N
6 ***Goodlatte***	Y	Y	Y	N	N	N	N
7 ***Cantor***	Y	Y	Y	N	N	N	N
8 Moran	Y	?	N	Y	Y	N	?
9 Boucher	Y	Y	N	N	N	Y	N
10 ***Wolf***	Y	Y	Y	N	N	Y	N
11 ***Davis, T.***	Y	Y	Y	N	Y	N	N
WASHINGTON							
1 Inslee	Y	Y	N	Y	Y	Y	N
2 Larsen	Y	Y	N	Y	Y	Y	N
3 Baird	Y	Y	N	Y	Y	Y	N
4 ***Hastings***	Y	Y	Y	N	N	N	N
5 ***Nethercutt***	+	+	+	–	–	+	–
6 Dicks	Y	Y	N	?	?	?	N
7 McDermott	Y	Y	N	Y	Y	Y	N
8 ***Dunn***	Y	Y	Y	?	?	N	N
9 Smith	Y	Y	N	?	Y	Y	N
WEST VIRGINIA							
1 Mollohan	?	?	?	?	?	?	?
2 ***Capito***	Y	Y	Y	N	N	Y	N
3 Rahall	Y	Y	N	N	N	Y	N
WISCONSIN							
1 ***Ryan***	Y	Y	Y	N	N	Y	Y
2 Baldwin	Y	Y	N	Y	Y	Y	N
3 Kind	Y	Y	N	N	Y	Y	N
4 Kleczka	Y	Y	?	N	Y	Y	N
5 ***Sensenbrenner***	Y	Y	Y	N	N	Y	Y
6 ***Petri***	Y	Y	Y	N	N	Y	N
7 Obey	Y	Y	N	N	Y	Y	N
8 ***Green***	Y	Y	Y	N	N	Y	N
WYOMING							
AL ***Cubin***	Y	Y	Y	N	N	N	N

Southern states - Ala., Ark., Fla., Ga., Ky., La., Miss., N.C., Okla., S.C., Tenn., Texas, Va.

Key

Y	Voted for (yea).
#	Paired for.
+	Announced for.
N	Voted against (nay).
X	Paired against.
–	Announced against.
P	Voted "present."
C	Voted "present" to avoid possible conflict of interest.
?	Did not vote or otherwise make a position known.

Democrats **Republicans** *Independents*

429. HR 5006. Fiscal 2005 Labor-HHS-Education Appropriations/ Pension Benefit Guaranty Corporation. Miller, D-Calif., amendment that would require the Pension Benefit Guaranty Corporation to make the financial status of company pension plans available to workers who participate in the plans. Adopted 268-148: R 67-148; D 200-0 (ND 145-0, SD 55-0); I 1-0. Sept. 8, 2004.

430. HR 5006. Fiscal 2005 Labor-HHS-Education Appropriations/ Motion to Rise. Regula, R-Ohio, motion to rise from the Committee of the Whole. Motion agreed to 216-195: R 215-0; D 1-194 (ND 1-141, SD 0-53); I 0-1. Sept. 8, 2004.

431. H Res 757. Sept. 11 Remembrance/Adoption. Adoption of the resolution that would express the sense of the House on the anniversary of the Sept. 11, 2001, terrorist attacks. The resolution would extend the deepest sympathies of the House to the victims of the attacks and thank foreign leaders and citizens of all nations who have assisted the United States in its fight against terrorism. Adopted 406-16: R 218-1; D 187-15 (ND 133-14, SD 54-1); I 1-0. Sept. 9, 2004.

432. HR 1308. Child Tax Credit and Military Tax Breaks/Motion to Instruct. Hill, D-Ind., motion to instruct conferees to insist on a conference report that would extend expiring tax relief provisions without increasing the federal budget deficit. Motion rejected 203-216: R 2-216; D 200-0 (ND 146-0, SD 54-0); I 1-0. Sept. 9, 2004.

433. S 2634. Youth Suicide Prevention/Passage. Barton, R-Texas, motion to suspend the rules and pass the bill that would authorize $82 million over three years for grants to universities and states for youth suicide intervention and prevention programs and for creation of a technical assistance center. The bill would require parental consent for certain school-sponsored programs. Motion agreed to 352-64: R 153-64; D 198-0 (ND 145-0, SD 53-0); I 1-0. A two-thirds majority of those present and voting (280 in this case) is required for passage under suspension of the rules. Sept. 9, 2004.

434. HR 5006. Fiscal 2005 Labor-HHS-Education Appropriations/ Overtime Pay Regulations. Obey, D-Wis., amendment that would prohibit funds in the bill from being used to administer or implement any regulation that would take away eligibility for overtime for workers. It would allow the enforcement of regulations that extend overtime protection to certain low-income workers. Adopted 223-193: R 22-193; D 200-0 (ND 146-0, SD 54-0); I 1-0. A "nay" was a vote in support of the president's position. Sept. 9, 2004.

	429	430	431	432	433	434
ALABAMA						
1 *Bonner*	N	Y	Y	N	N	N
2 *Everett*	N	Y	Y	N	N	N
3 *Rogers*	N	Y	Y	N	Y	N
4 *Aderholt*	Y	Y	Y	N	N	N
5 Cramer	Y	N	Y	Y	Y	Y
6 *Bachus*	N	Y	Y	N	Y	N
7 Davis	Y	N	Y	Y	Y	Y
ALASKA						
AL *Young*	?	?	?	?	?	?
ARIZONA						
1 *Renzi*	Y	Y	Y	N	Y	N
2 *Franks*	N	Y	Y	N	N	N
3 *Shadegg*	N	Y	Y	N	N	N
4 Pastor	Y	N	Y	Y	Y	Y
5 *Hayworth*	N	Y	Y	N	N	N
6 *Flake*	N	Y	Y	N	N	N
7 Grijalva	Y	N	Y	Y	Y	Y
8 *Kolbe*	N	Y	Y	N	Y	N
ARKANSAS						
1 Berry	Y	N	Y	Y	Y	Y
2 Snyder	Y	N	Y	Y	Y	Y
3 *Boozman*	N	Y	Y	N	Y	N
4 Ross	Y	N	Y	Y	Y	Y
CALIFORNIA						
1 Thompson	Y	N	Y	Y	Y	Y
2 *Herger*	N	Y	Y	N	N	N
3 *Ose*	N	Y	Y	N	N	N
4 *Doolittle*	N	Y	Y	N	N	N
5 Matsui	Y	N	Y	Y	Y	Y
6 Woolsey	Y	N	N	Y	Y	Y
7 Miller, George	Y	N	Y	Y	Y	Y
8 Pelosi	Y	N	Y	Y	Y	Y
9 Lee	Y	N	N	Y	Y	Y
10 Tauscher	Y	N	Y	Y	Y	Y
11 *Pombo*	N	Y	Y	N	N	N
12 Lantos	Y	N	Y	Y	Y	Y
13 Stark	Y	N	N	Y	Y	Y
14 Eshoo	Y	N	Y	Y	Y	Y
15 Honda	Y	N	N	Y	Y	Y
16 Lofgren	Y	N	Y	Y	Y	Y
17 Farr	Y	N	Y	Y	Y	Y
18 Cardoza	Y	N	Y	Y	Y	Y
19 *Radanovich*	N	Y	Y	N	N	N
20 Dooley	Y	N	Y	Y	Y	Y
21 *Nunes*	N	Y	Y	N	N	N
22 *Thomas*	N	Y	Y	N	Y	N
23 Capps	Y	N	Y	Y	Y	Y
24 *Gallegly*	Y	Y	Y	N	Y	N
25 *McKeon*	N	Y	Y	N	Y	N
26 *Dreier*	N	Y	Y	N	N	N
27 Sherman	Y	N	Y	Y	Y	Y
28 Berman	Y	N	Y	Y	Y	Y
29 Schiff	Y	N	Y	Y	Y	Y
30 Waxman	Y	N	Y	Y	Y	Y
31 Becerra	Y	N	Y	Y	Y	Y
32 Solis	Y	N	Y	Y	Y	Y
33 Watson	Y	N	Y	Y	Y	Y
34 Roybal-Allard	Y	N	Y	Y	Y	Y
35 Waters	Y	N	N	Y	Y	?
36 Harman	Y	N	Y	Y	Y	Y

	429	430	431	432	433	434
37 Millender-McD.	Y	N	Y	Y	Y	Y
38 Napolitano	Y	N	Y	Y	Y	Y
39 Sánchez, Linda	Y	N	Y	Y	Y	Y
40 *Royce*	N	Y	Y	N	N	N
41 *Lewis*	N	Y	Y	N	Y	N
42 *Miller, Gary*	N	Y	Y	N	Y	N
43 Baca	Y	N	Y	Y	Y	Y
44 *Calvert*	N	Y	Y	N	Y	N
45 *Bono*	?	?	Y	N	Y	N
46 *Rohrabacher*	Y	Y	Y	N	Y	N
47 Sanchez, Loretta	Y	N	Y	Y	Y	Y
48 *Cox*	N	Y	Y	N	Y	N
49 *Issa*	N	Y	Y	N	Y	N
50 *Cunningham*	Y	Y	Y	N	Y	N
51 Filner	Y	N	Y	Y	Y	Y
52 *Hunter*	?	Y	Y	N	Y	N
53 Davis	Y	N	Y	Y	Y	Y
COLORADO						
1 DeGette	Y	N	Y	Y	Y	Y
2 Udall	Y	N	Y	Y	Y	Y
3 *McInnis*	N	Y	Y	N	Y	N
4 *Musgrave*	N	Y	Y	N	N	N
5 *Hefley*	Y	Y	Y	N	N	N
6 *Tancredo*	N	Y	Y	N	N	N
7 *Beauprez*	N	Y	Y	N	Y	N
CONNECTICUT						
1 Larson	Y	N	Y	Y	Y	Y
2 *Simmons*	Y	Y	Y	Y	Y	Y
3 DeLauro	Y	N	Y	Y	Y	Y
4 *Shays*	Y	Y	Y	Y	Y	Y
5 *Johnson*	Y	Y	Y	N	Y	N
DELAWARE						
AL *Castle*	Y	Y	Y	Y	Y	N
FLORIDA						
1 *Miller, J.*	N	Y	Y	N	N	N
2 Boyd	Y	N	Y	Y	Y	Y
3 Brown	Y	N	Y	Y	Y	Y
4 *Crenshaw*	N	Y	Y	N	Y	N
5 *Brown-Waite*	Y	Y	Y	N	Y	N
6 *Stearns*	N	Y	Y	N	N	N
7 *Mica*	N	Y	Y	N	Y	N
8 *Keller*	N	Y	Y	N	N	N
9 *Bilirakis*	Y	Y	Y	N	Y	N
10 *Young*	N	Y	Y	N	Y	N
11 Davis	Y	N	Y	Y	Y	Y
12 *Putnam*	N	Y	Y	N	Y	N
13 *Harris*	N	Y	Y	N	Y	N
14 *Goss*	?	?	?	?	?	?
15 *Weldon*	N	Y	Y	N	Y	N
16 *Foley*	N	Y	Y	N	Y	N
17 Meek	Y	N	Y	Y	?	Y
18 *Ros-Lehtinen*	N	Y	Y	N	Y	N
19 Wexler	Y	N	?	?	?	Y
20 Deutsch	Y	N	Y	Y	Y	Y
21 *Diaz-Balart, L.*	N	Y	Y	N	Y	N
22 *Shaw*	N	Y	Y	N	Y	N
23 Hastings	Y	N	Y	Y	Y	Y
24 *Feeney*	N	Y	Y	N	N	N
25 *Diaz-Balart, M.*	N	Y	Y	N	Y	N
GEORGIA						
1 *Kingston*	N	Y	Y	N	N	N
2 Bishop	Y	N	Y	Y	Y	Y
3 Marshall	Y	N	Y	Y	Y	Y
4 *Majette*	Y	N	Y	?	?	+
5 Lewis	Y	N	Y	Y	Y	Y
6 *Isakson*	N	Y	Y	N	Y	N
7 *Linder*	Y	Y	Y	N	Y	N
8 *Collins*	Y	Y	Y	N	Y	N
9 *Norwood*	N	?	Y	N	Y	N
10 *Deal*	N	Y	Y	N	N	N
11 *Gingrey*	N	Y	Y	N	N	N
12 *Burns*	N	Y	Y	N	Y	N
13 Scott	Y	N	Y	Y	Y	Y
HAWAII						
1 Abercrombie	Y	N	Y	Y	Y	Y
2 Case	Y	N	Y	Y	Y	Y
IDAHO						
1 *Otter*	N	Y	Y	N	N	N
2 *Simpson*	N	Y	Y	N	Y	N
ILLINOIS						
1 Rush	Y	N	Y	Y	Y	Y
2 Jackson	Y	N	N	Y	Y	Y
3 Lipinski	Y	N	Y	Y	Y	Y
4 Gutierrez	Y	N	Y	Y	Y	Y
5 Emanuel	Y	N	Y	Y	Y	Y
6 *Hyde*	Y	Y	Y	N	N	N

ND Northern Democrats   SD Southern Democrats

	429	430	431	432	433	434
7 Davis	Y	N	Y	Y	Y	Y
8 ***Crane***	?	?	Y	N	N	N
9 Schakowsky	Y	N	N	Y	Y	Y
10 ***Kirk***	Y	Y	Y	N	Y	N
11 ***Weller***	Y	Y	Y	N	Y	N
12 Costello	Y	N	Y	Y	Y	Y
13 ***Biggert***	N	Y	Y	N	Y	N
14 ***Hastert***		Y	Y			N
15 ***Johnson***	Y	Y	Y	N	Y	Y
16 ***Manzullo***	Y	Y	Y	N	N	N
17 Evans	Y	N	Y	Y	Y	Y
18 ***LaHood***	N	Y	Y	N	Y	Y
19 ***Shimkus***	Y	Y	Y	N	Y	N
INDIANA						
1 Visclosky	Y	N	Y	Y	Y	Y
2 ***Chocola***	N	Y	Y	N	Y	N
3 ***Souder***	N	Y	Y	N	Y	N
4 ***Buyer***	N	Y	Y	N	Y	N
5 ***Burton***	N	Y	Y	N	N	N
6 ***Pence***	N	Y	Y	N	N	N
7 Carson	Y	N	Y	Y	Y	Y
8 ***Hostettler***	N	Y	Y	N	N	N
9 Hill	Y	N	Y	Y	Y	Y
IOWA						
1 ***Nussle***	?	?	Y	N	Y	Y
2 ***Leach***	Y	Y	Y	N	Y	Y
3 Boswell	Y	N	Y	Y	Y	Y
4 ***Latham***	N	Y	Y	N	Y	N
5 ***King***	N	Y	Y	N	N	N
KANSAS						
1 ***Moran***	Y	Y	Y	N	Y	N
2 ***Ryun***	N	Y	Y	N	Y	N
3 Moore	Y	N	Y	Y	Y	Y
4 ***Tiahrt***	N	Y	Y	N	Y	N
KENTUCKY						
1 ***Whitfield***	Y	Y	Y	N	Y	N
2 ***Lewis***	N	Y	Y	N	N	N
3 ***Northup***	N	Y	Y	N	Y	N
4 Lucas	Y	N	Y	Y	Y	Y
5 ***Rogers***	N	Y	Y	N	Y	N
6 Chandler	Y	N	Y	Y	Y	Y
LOUISIANA						
1 ***Vitter***	N	Y	Y	N	Y	N
2 Jefferson	Y	N	Y	Y	Y	Y
3 ***Tauzin***	?	?	?	?	?	?
4 ***McCrery***	N	Y	Y	N	Y	N
5 ***Alexander***	N	Y	Y	N	Y	N
6 ***Baker***	N	Y	Y	N	Y	N
7 John	Y	N	Y	Y	Y	Y
MAINE						
1 Allen	Y	N	Y	Y	Y	Y
2 Michaud	Y	N	Y	Y	Y	Y
MARYLAND						
1 ***Gilchrest***	Y	Y	Y	N	Y	N
2 Ruppersberger	Y	N	Y	Y	Y	Y
3 Cardin	Y	N	Y	Y	Y	Y
4 Wynn	Y	N	Y	Y	Y	Y
5 Hoyer	Y	N	Y	Y	Y	Y
6 ***Bartlett***	N	Y	Y	N	N	N
7 Cummings	Y	N	Y	Y	?	Y
8 Van Hollen	Y	N	Y	Y	Y	Y
MASSACHUSETTS						
1 Olver	Y	N	Y	Y	Y	Y
2 Neal	Y	N	Y	Y	Y	Y
3 McGovern	Y	?	Y	Y	Y	Y
4 Frank	Y	N	N	Y	Y	Y
5 Meehan	Y	N	Y	Y	Y	Y
6 Tierney	Y	N	Y	Y	Y	Y
7 Markey	Y	N	N	Y	Y	Y
8 Capuano	Y	N	Y	Y	Y	Y
9 Lynch	Y	N	Y	Y	Y	Y
10 Delahunt	Y	N	Y	Y	Y	Y
MICHIGAN						
1 Stupak	Y	N	Y	Y	Y	Y
2 ***Hoekstra***	N	Y	Y	N	Y	N
3 ***Ehlers***	Y	Y	Y	N	Y	N
4 ***Camp***	Y	Y	Y	N	Y	N
5 Kildee	Y	N	Y	Y	Y	Y
6 ***Upton***	Y	Y	Y	N	Y	Y
7 ***Smith***	N	Y	Y	N	N	N
8 ***Rogers***	Y	Y	Y	N	Y	N
9 ***Knollenberg***	N	Y	Y	N	Y	N
10 ***Miller***	Y	Y	Y	N	Y	N
11 ***McCotter***	Y	Y	Y	N	Y	Y
12 Levin	Y	N	Y	Y	Y	Y
13 Kilpatrick	Y	N	Y	Y	Y	Y
14 Conyers	Y	N	N	Y	Y	Y
15 Dingell	Y	N	Y	Y	Y	Y
MINNESOTA						
1 ***Gutknecht***	N	Y	Y	N	N	N
2 ***Kline***	N	Y	Y	N	N	N
3 ***Ramstad***	Y	Y	Y	N	Y	N
4 McCollum	Y	N	Y	Y	Y	Y
5 Sabo	Y	N	Y	Y	Y	Y
6 ***Kennedy***	Y	Y	Y	N	Y	N
7 Peterson	Y	N	Y	Y	Y	Y
8 Oberstar	Y	N	Y	Y	Y	Y
MISSISSIPPI						
1 ***Wicker***	N	Y	Y	N	Y	N
2 Thompson	Y	N	Y	Y	Y	Y
3 ***Pickering***	N	Y	Y	N	Y	N
4 Taylor	Y	N	Y	Y	Y	Y
MISSOURI						
1 Clay	Y	N	Y	Y	Y	Y
2 ***Akin***	N	Y	Y	N	N	N
3 Gephardt	?	?	Y	Y	Y	Y
4 Skelton	Y	N	Y	Y	Y	Y
5 McCarthy	Y	N	Y	Y	Y	Y
6 ***Graves***	N	Y	Y	N	Y	N
7 ***Blunt***	N	Y	Y	N	Y	N
8 ***Emerson***	Y	Y	Y	N	Y	Y
9 ***Hulshof***	N	Y	Y	N	Y	N
MONTANA						
AL ***Rehberg***	N	Y	Y	N	Y	N
NEBRASKA						
1 Vacant						
2 ***Terry***	N	Y	Y	N	Y	N
3 ***Osborne***	N	Y	Y	N	Y	N
NEVADA						
1 Berkley	Y	N	Y	Y	Y	Y
2 ***Gibbons***	Y	Y	Y	N	Y	N
3 ***Porter***	Y	Y	Y	N	Y	N
NEW HAMPSHIRE						
1 ***Bradley***	Y	Y	Y	N	Y	N
2 ***Bass***	Y	Y	Y	N	Y	N
NEW JERSEY						
1 Andrews	Y	N	Y	Y	Y	Y
2 ***LoBiondo***	Y	Y	Y	N	Y	Y
3 ***Saxton***	N	Y	Y	N	Y	Y
4 ***Smith***	Y	Y	Y	N	Y	Y
5 ***Garrett***	N	Y	Y	N	N	N
6 Pallone	Y	N	Y	Y	Y	Y
7 ***Ferguson***	Y	Y	Y	N	Y	Y
8 Pascrell	Y	N	Y	Y	Y	Y
9 Rothman	Y	N	Y	Y	Y	Y
10 Payne	Y	N	Y	Y	?	Y
11 ***Frelinghuysen***	N	Y	Y	N	Y	N
12 Holt	Y	N	Y	Y	Y	Y
13 Menendez	Y	N	Y	Y	Y	Y
NEW MEXICO						
1 ***Wilson***	Y	Y	Y	N	Y	N
2 ***Pearce***	N	Y	Y	N	Y	N
3 Udall	Y	N	Y	Y	Y	Y
NEW YORK						
1 Bishop	Y	N	Y	Y	Y	Y
2 Israel	Y	N	Y	Y	Y	Y
3 ***King***	Y	Y	Y	N	Y	Y
4 McCarthy	Y	N	Y	Y	Y	Y
5 Ackerman	Y	N	Y	Y	Y	Y
6 Meeks	Y	N	Y	Y	Y	Y
7 Crowley	Y	N	Y	Y	Y	Y
8 Nadler	Y	N	Y	Y	Y	Y
9 Weiner	Y	N	Y	Y	Y	Y
10 Towns	Y	N	Y	Y	Y	Y
11 Owens	Y	N	Y	Y	Y	Y
12 Velázquez	Y	N	Y	Y	Y	Y
13 ***Fossella***	Y	Y	Y	N	Y	N
14 Maloney	Y	N	Y	Y	Y	Y
15 Rangel	Y	N	Y	Y	Y	Y
16 Serrano	Y	N	Y	Y	Y	Y
17 Engel	?	?	Y	Y	Y	Y
18 Lowey	Y	N	Y	Y	Y	Y
19 ***Kelly***	Y	Y	Y	N	Y	Y
20 ***Sweeney***	Y	Y	Y	N	Y	Y
21 McNulty	Y	N	Y	Y	Y	Y
22 Hinchey	Y	N	N	Y	Y	Y
23 ***McHugh***	Y	Y	Y	N	Y	Y
24 ***Boehlert***	Y	Y	Y	N	Y	Y
25 ***Walsh***	Y	Y	Y	N	Y	N
26 ***Reynolds***	N	Y	Y	N	Y	N
27 ***Quinn***	Y	Y	Y	N	Y	?
28 Slaughter	Y	N	Y	?	Y	Y
29 ***Houghton***	Y	Y	Y	N	Y	N
NORTH CAROLINA						
1 Butterfield	Y	N	Y	Y	Y	Y
2 Etheridge	Y	N	Y	Y	Y	Y
3 ***Jones***	Y	Y	Y	N	N	Y
4 Price	Y	N	Y	Y	Y	Y
5 ***Burr***	Y	Y	Y	N	?	N
6 ***Coble***	Y	Y	Y	N	N	N
7 McIntyre	Y	N	Y	Y	Y	Y
8 ***Hayes***	N	Y	Y	N	Y	N
9 ***Myrick***	N	Y	Y	N	N	N
10 ***Ballenger***	?	?	?	?	?	?
11 ***Taylor***	Y	Y	Y	N	Y	N
12 Watt	Y	N	Y	Y	Y	Y
13 Miller	Y	N	Y	Y	Y	Y
NORTH DAKOTA						
AL Pomeroy	Y	N	Y	Y	Y	Y
OHIO						
1 ***Chabot***	Y	Y	Y	N	Y	N
2 ***Portman***	N	Y	Y	N	Y	N
3 ***Turner***	N	Y	Y	N	Y	N
4 ***Oxley***	N	Y	Y	N	Y	N
5 ***Gillmor***	N	Y	Y	N	Y	N
6 Strickland	Y	?	Y	Y	Y	Y
7 ***Hobson***	N	Y	Y	N	Y	N
8 ***Boehner***	N	Y	Y	N	Y	N
9 Kaptur	Y	N	Y	Y	Y	Y
10 Kucinich	Y	N	N	Y	Y	Y
11 Jones	Y	N	Y	Y	Y	Y
12 ***Tiberi***	N	Y	Y	N	Y	N
13 Brown	Y	N	Y	Y	Y	Y
14 ***LaTourette***	Y	Y	Y	N	Y	Y
15 ***Pryce***	N	Y	Y	N	Y	N
16 ***Regula***	N	Y	Y	N	Y	N
17 Ryan	?	?	?	?	?	?
18 ***Ney***	?	?	Y	N	Y	N
OKLAHOMA						
1 ***Sullivan***	N	Y	Y	N	N	N
2 Carson	Y	N	Y	Y	Y	Y
3 ***Lucas***	N	Y	Y	N	N	?
4 ***Cole***	N	Y	Y	N	Y	N
5 ***Istook***	N	Y	Y	N	N	N
OREGON						
1 Wu	Y	N	Y	Y	Y	Y
2 ***Walden***	N	Y	Y	N	Y	N
3 Blumenauer	Y	N	Y	Y	Y	Y
4 DeFazio	Y	N	Y	Y	Y	Y
5 Hooley	Y	N	Y	Y	Y	Y
PENNSYLVANIA						
1 Brady	Y	N	Y	Y	Y	Y
2 Fattah	Y	N	Y	Y	Y	Y
3 ***English***	Y	Y	Y	N	Y	Y
4 ***Hart***	Y	Y	Y	N	Y	N
5 ***Peterson***	N	Y	Y	N	N	N
6 ***Gerlach***	Y	Y	Y	N	Y	N
7 ***Weldon***	Y	Y	Y	N	Y	N
8 ***Greenwood***	N	Y	?	?	?	?
9 ***Shuster, Bill***	Y	Y	Y	N	Y	?
10 ***Sherwood***	N	Y	Y	N	N	N
11 Kanjorski	Y	N	Y	Y	Y	?
12 Murtha	Y	N	Y	Y	Y	Y
13 Hoeffel	Y	N	Y	Y	Y	Y
14 Doyle	Y	N	Y	Y	Y	Y
15 ***Toomey***	N	Y	?	?	?	?
16 ***Pitts***	N	Y	Y	N	Y	N
17 Holden	Y	N	Y	Y	Y	Y
18 ***Murphy***	Y	Y	Y	N	Y	Y
19 ***Platts***	Y	Y	Y	N	Y	N
RHODE ISLAND						
1 Kennedy	Y	N	Y	Y	Y	Y
2 Langevin	Y	N	Y	Y	Y	Y
SOUTH CAROLINA						
1 ***Brown***	N	Y	Y	N	Y	N
2 ***Wilson***	N	Y	Y	N	Y	N
3 ***Barrett***	N	Y	Y	N	N	N
4 ***DeMint***	N	Y	Y	N	Y	N
5 Spratt	Y	N	Y	Y	Y	Y
6 Clyburn	Y	?	Y	Y	Y	?
SOUTH DAKOTA						
AL Herseth	Y	N	Y	Y	Y	Y
TENNESSEE						
1 ***Jenkins***	Y	Y	Y	N	Y	N
2 ***Duncan***	Y	Y	Y	N	Y	N
3 ***Wamp***	Y	Y	Y	N	Y	N
4 Davis	Y	N	Y	Y	Y	Y
5 Cooper	Y	N	Y	Y	Y	Y
6 Gordon	Y	N	Y	Y	Y	Y
7 ***Blackburn***	N	Y	Y	N	Y	N
8 Tanner	Y	N	Y	Y	Y	Y
9 Ford	Y	N	Y	Y	Y	Y
TEXAS						
1 Sandlin	Y	N	Y	Y	Y	Y
2 Turner	Y	N	Y	Y	Y	Y
3 ***Johnson, Sam***	N	Y	Y	N	N	?
4 ***Hall***	N	Y	Y	N	Y	N
5 ***Hensarling***	N	Y	Y	N	N	N
6 ***Barton***	N	Y	Y	N	Y	N
7 ***Culberson***	N	Y	Y	N	N	N
8 ***Brady***	N	Y	Y	N	Y	N
9 Lampson	Y	N	Y	Y	Y	Y
10 Doggett	Y	N	Y	Y	Y	Y
11 Edwards	Y	N	Y	Y	Y	Y
12 ***Granger***	N	Y	Y	N	Y	N
13 ***Thornberry***	N	Y	Y	N	N	N
14 ***Paul***	N	?	N	N	N	N
15 Hinojosa	Y	?	Y	Y	Y	Y
16 Reyes	Y	N	Y	Y	Y	Y
17 Stenholm	Y	N	Y	Y	Y	Y
18 Jackson-Lee	Y	N	Y	Y	Y	Y
19 ***Neugebauer***	N	Y	Y	N	N	N
20 Gonzalez	Y	N	Y	Y	Y	Y
21 ***Smith***	N	Y	Y	N	Y	N
22 ***DeLay***	N	Y	Y	N	Y	N
23 ***Bonilla***	N	Y	Y	N	N	N
24 Frost	Y	N	Y	Y	Y	Y
25 Bell	Y	N	Y	Y	Y	Y
26 ***Burgess***	N	Y	Y	N	Y	N
27 Ortiz	Y	N	Y	Y	Y	Y
28 Rodriguez	Y	N	Y	Y	Y	Y
29 Green	Y	N	Y	Y	Y	Y
30 Johnson, E.B.	Y	N	Y	Y	Y	Y
31 ***Carter***	N	Y	Y	N	N	N
32 ***Sessions***	N	Y	Y	N	Y	N
UTAH						
1 ***Bishop***	N	Y	Y	N	N	N
2 Matheson	Y	N	Y	Y	Y	Y
3 ***Cannon***	?	?	?	?	?	?
VERMONT						
AL *Sanders*	Y	N	Y	Y	Y	Y
VIRGINIA						
1 ***Davis, Jo Ann***	N	Y	Y	N	Y	N
2 ***Schrock***	?	?	?	?	?	?
3 Scott	Y	N	Y	Y	Y	Y
4 ***Forbes***	N	Y	Y	N	Y	N
5 ***Goode***	N	Y	Y	N	Y	N
6 ***Goodlatte***	N	Y	Y	N	Y	N
7 ***Cantor***	N	Y	Y	N	N	N
8 Moran	?	?	Y	Y	Y	Y
9 Boucher	Y	N	Y	Y	Y	Y
10 ***Wolf***	Y	Y	Y	N	Y	N
11 ***Davis, T.***	N	Y	Y	N	Y	N
WASHINGTON						
1 Inslee	Y	N	Y	Y	Y	Y
2 Larsen	Y	N	Y	Y	Y	Y
3 Baird	Y	N	Y	Y	Y	Y
4 ***Hastings***	N	Y	Y	N	Y	N
5 ***Nethercutt***	+	+	+	−	+	?
6 Dicks	Y	N	Y	Y	Y	Y
7 McDermott	Y	N	N	Y	Y	Y
8 ***Dunn***	N	Y	Y	N	Y	N
9 Smith	Y	Y	Y	Y	Y	Y
WEST VIRGINIA						
1 Mollohan	?	?	?	?	?	Y
2 ***Capito***	Y	Y	Y	N	Y	Y
3 Rahall	Y	N	Y	Y	Y	Y
WISCONSIN						
1 ***Ryan***	N	Y	Y	N	N	N
2 Baldwin	Y	N	Y	Y	Y	Y
3 Kind	Y	N	Y	Y	Y	Y
4 Kleczka	Y	?	Y	Y	Y	Y
5 ***Sensenbrenner***	N	Y	Y	N	N	N
6 ***Petri***	N	Y	Y	N	N	N
7 Obey	Y	N	Y	Y	Y	Y
8 ***Green***	N	Y	Y	N	Y	N
WYOMING						
AL ***Cubin***	N	Y	Y	N	N	N

Southern states - Ala., Ark., Fla., Ga., Ky., La., Miss., N.C., Okla., S.C., Tenn., Texas, Va.

Key

Y	Voted for (yea).
#	Paired for.
+	Announced for.
N	Voted against (nay).
X	Paired against.
–	Announced against.
P	Voted "present."
C	Voted "present" to avoid possible conflict of interest.
?	Did not vote or otherwise make a position known.

Democrats **Republicans**
Independents

---

435. HR 5006. Fiscal 2005 Labor-HHS-Education Appropriations/ American Indian Tribes. Hayworth, R-Ariz., amendment that would prohibit the use of funds by the National Labor Relations Board to exercise its jurisdiction over American Indian tribes. Rejected 185-227: R 172-39; D 13-187 (ND 6-138, SD 7-49); I 0-1. Sept. 9, 2004.

436. HR 5006. Fiscal 2005 Labor-HHS-Education Appropriations/ Student Loans. Kildee, D-Mich., amendment that would prohibit funding for companies that receive a special 9.5 percent interest return on federally subsidized student loans. Adopted 413-3: R 211-3; D 201-0 (ND 145-0, SD 56-0); I 1-0. Sept. 9, 2004.

437. HR 5006. Fiscal 2005 Labor-HHS-Education Appropriations/ HHS Departmental Management Funding. Stark, D-Calif., amendment that would cut funding for general departmental management in the Department of Health and Human Services by $84,500. Rejected 195-216: R 4-210; D 190-6 (ND 141-2, SD 49-4); I 1-0. Sept. 9, 2004.

438. HR 5006. Fiscal 2005 Labor-HHS-Education Appropriations/ Mental Health Programs. Paul, R-Texas, amendment that would ban the use of funds in the bill to create or implement any new or universal mental health screening program. Rejected 95-315: R 94-118; D 1-196 (ND 0-142, SD 1-54); I 0-1. Sept. 9, 2004.

439. HR 5006. Fiscal 2005 Labor-HHS-Education Appropriations/ Social Security Benefits. Hayworth, R-Ariz., amendment that would prohibit the use of funds to pay salaries of Social Security Administration employees to administer Social Security benefit payments under a totalization agreement with Mexico. Rejected 178-225: R 149-61; D 28-164 (ND 13-126, SD 15-38); I 1-0. Sept. 9, 2004.

440. HR 5006. Fiscal 2005 Labor-HHS-Education Appropriations/ Passage. Passage of the bill that would appropriate $496.6 billion, including $142.5 billion in discretionary spending, for the Labor, Health and Human Services, and Education departments and related agencies in fiscal 2005. It would provide $57.7 billion for the Education Department, including $12.2 billion for special education; $14.9 billion for the Labor Department; and $374.3 billion for Health and Human Services, including $28.4 billion for the National Institutes of Health. Passed 388-13: R 195-13; D 192-0 (ND 139-0, SD 53-0); I 1-0. Sept. 9, 2004.

	435	436	437	438	439	440
ALABAMA						
1 *Bonner*	Y	Y	N	Y	Y	Y
2 *Everett*	Y	Y	N	Y	Y	?
3 *Rogers*	Y	Y	N	N	Y	Y
4 *Aderholt*	Y	Y	N	Y	Y	Y
5 Cramer	Y	Y	Y	N	Y	Y
6 *Bachus*	Y	Y	N	Y	N	Y
7 Davis	Y	Y	Y	N	N	Y
ALASKA						
AL *Young*	?	?	?	?	?	?
ARIZONA						
1 *Renzi*	Y	Y	N	N	Y	Y
2 *Franks*	Y	Y	N	Y	Y	N
3 *Shadegg*	Y	Y	N	Y	Y	Y
4 Pastor	N	Y	Y	N	N	Y
5 *Hayworth*	Y	Y	N	N	Y	Y
6 *Flake*	Y	Y	N	Y	Y	N
7 Grijalva	N	Y	Y	N	N	Y
8 *Kolbe*	Y	Y	N	Y	Y	Y
ARKANSAS						
1 Berry	N	Y	Y	N	N	Y
2 Snyder	N	Y	N	N	N	Y
3 *Boozman*	Y	Y	N	Y	Y	Y
4 Ross	N	Y	Y	N	N	Y
CALIFORNIA						
1 Thompson	N	Y	Y	N	N	Y
2 *Herger*	Y	Y	N	Y	Y	Y
3 *Ose*	Y	Y	N	Y	N	Y
4 *Doolittle*	Y	Y	N	Y	Y	Y
5 Matsui	N	Y	Y	N	N	Y
6 Woolsey	N	Y	Y	N	N	Y
7 Miller, George	N	Y	Y	N	N	Y
8 Pelosi	N	Y	Y	N	N	Y
9 Lee	N	Y	Y	N	N	Y
10 Tauscher	N	Y	Y	N	N	Y
11 *Pombo*	N	Y	N	Y	Y	Y
12 Lantos	N	Y	Y	N	N	Y
13 Stark	N	Y	Y	N	N	Y
14 Eshoo	N	Y	Y	N	N	Y
15 Honda	N	Y	Y	N	N	Y
16 Lofgren	N	Y	Y	N	N	Y
17 Farr	N	Y	Y	N	N	Y
18 Cardoza	N	Y	Y	N	?	?
19 *Radanovich*	Y	Y	N	N	?	?
20 Dooley	N	Y	Y	N	N	Y
21 *Nunes*	Y	Y	N	N	Y	Y
22 *Thomas*	N	Y	N	N	N	Y
23 Capps	N	Y	Y	N	N	Y
24 *Gallegly*	Y	Y	N	N	Y	Y
25 *McKeon*	Y	Y	N	N	N	Y
26 *Dreier*	Y	Y	N	N	N	Y
27 Sherman	N	Y	Y	N	N	Y
28 Berman	N	Y	Y	N	N	Y
29 Schiff	N	Y	Y	N	N	Y
30 Waxman	N	Y	Y	N	N	Y
31 Becerra	N	Y	Y	N	N	Y
32 Solis	N	Y	Y	N	N	Y
33 Watson	N	Y	Y	N	N	Y
34 Roybal-Allard	N	Y	Y	N	N	Y
35 Waters	N	Y	Y	N	N	Y
36 Harman	N	Y	N	N	N	Y

	435	436	437	438	439	440
37 Millender-McD.	N	Y	N	N	N	Y
38 Napolitano	N	Y	Y	N	N	Y
39 Sánchez, Linda	N	Y	Y	N	N	Y
40 *Royce*	Y	Y	N	Y	Y	N
41 *Lewis*	Y	Y	N	N	N	Y
42 *Miller, Gary*	Y	Y	N	Y	Y	Y
43 Baca	N	Y	Y	N	N	Y
44 *Calvert*	Y	Y	N	N	Y	Y
45 *Bono*	Y	Y	N	N	Y	Y
46 *Rohrabacher*	Y	Y	N	Y	Y	N
47 Sanchez, Loretta	N	Y	Y	N	N	Y
48 *Cox*	Y	Y	N	Y	Y	?
49 *Issa*	Y	Y	N	N	N	Y
50 *Cunningham*	Y	Y	N	N	Y	Y
51 Filner	N	Y	Y	N	N	Y
52 *Hunter*	Y	Y	N	Y	Y	Y
53 Davis	N	Y	Y	N	N	Y
COLORADO						
1 DeGette	N	Y	Y	N	N	Y
2 Udall	N	Y	Y	N	N	Y
3 *McInnis*	Y	Y	N	?	?	?
4 *Musgrave*	Y	Y	N	Y	Y	Y
5 *Hefley*	Y	Y	N	Y	N	Y
6 *Tancredo*	Y	Y	N	Y	Y	N
7 *Beauprez*	Y	Y	N	N	N	Y
CONNECTICUT						
1 Larson	N	Y	Y	N	N	Y
2 *Simmons*	N	Y	N	N	N	Y
3 DeLauro	N	Y	Y	N	N	Y
4 *Shays*	N	Y	N	N	Y	Y
5 *Johnson*	N	Y	N	N	N	Y
DELAWARE						
AL *Castle*	Y	Y	N	N	N	Y
FLORIDA						
1 *Miller, J.*	Y	Y	N	Y	N	N
2 Boyd	Y	Y	N	Y	N	Y
3 Brown	N	Y	Y	N	N	Y
4 *Crenshaw*	Y	Y	N	N	N	Y
5 *Brown-Waite*	Y	Y	N	Y	Y	Y
6 *Stearns*	N	Y	N	Y	N	Y
7 *Mica*	Y	Y	N	N	N	Y
8 *Keller*	Y	Y	N	Y	N	Y
9 *Bilirakis*	Y	Y	N	Y	N	Y
10 *Young*	Y	Y	N	N	N	Y
11 Davis	N	Y	N	N	N	Y
12 *Putnam*	Y	Y	N	Y	N	Y
13 *Harris*	Y	Y	N	N	N	Y
14 *Goss*	?	?	?	?	?	Y
15 *Weldon*	Y	Y	N	N	N	Y
16 *Foley*	Y	Y	N	Y	N	Y
17 Meek	N	Y	N	N	N	Y
18 *Ros-Lehtinen*	?	Y	N	N	?	?
19 Wexler	N	Y	Y	N	N	Y
20 Deutsch	N	Y	Y	N	N	Y
21 *Diaz-Balart, L.*	Y	Y	N	N	N	?
22 *Shaw*	Y	Y	N	N	N	Y
23 Hastings	N	Y	Y	N	N	Y
24 *Feeney*	Y	Y	N	Y	Y	Y
25 *Diaz-Balart, M.*	Y	Y	N	N	Y	Y
GEORGIA						
1 *Kingston*	Y	N	N	Y	Y	Y
2 Bishop	N	Y	Y	N	N	Y
3 Marshall	N	Y	N	Y	N	Y
4 Majette	N	Y	Y	N	N	Y
5 Lewis	N	Y	Y	N	N	Y
6 *Isakson*	Y	Y	N	N	Y	Y
7 *Linder*	Y	Y	N	Y	Y	Y
8 *Collins*	Y	Y	N	Y	Y	Y
9 *Norwood*	Y	Y	N	Y	Y	Y
10 *Deal*	Y	Y	N	Y	Y	Y
11 *Gingrey*	Y	Y	N	Y	Y	Y
12 *Burns*	Y	Y	N	Y	Y	Y
13 Scott	N	Y	Y	N	N	Y
HAWAII						
1 Abercrombie	N	Y	Y	N	N	Y
2 Case	N	Y	Y	N	N	Y
IDAHO						
1 *Otter*	Y	Y	N	Y	Y	Y
2 *Simpson*	Y	Y	N	Y	Y	Y
ILLINOIS						
1 Rush	N	Y	Y	?	Y	Y
2 Jackson	N	Y	N	N	N	Y
3 Lipinski	N	Y	Y	N	?	?
4 Gutierrez	N	Y	?	N	N	Y
5 Emanuel	N	Y	N	N	N	Y
6 *Hyde*	Y	Y	N	N	N	Y

ND Northern Democrats   SD Southern Democrats

	435	436	437	438	439	440
7 Davis	N	Y	Y	N	N	Y
8 ***Crane***	Y	Y	N	Y	N	Y
9 Schakowsky	N	Y	Y	N	N	Y
10 ***Kirk***	N	Y	N	N	Y	Y
11 ***Weller***	Y	Y	N	N	N	Y
12 Costello	N	Y	Y	N	Y	Y
13 ***Biggert***	Y	Y	N	Y	N	Y
14 ***Hastert***						
15 ***Johnson***	N	Y	N	Y	Y	Y
16 ***Manzullo***	Y	Y	N	Y	Y	Y
17 Evans	N	Y	Y	N	N	Y
18 ***LaHood***	Y	Y	N	N	Y	Y
19 ***Shimkus***	N	Y	N	N	Y	Y
INDIANA						
1 Visclosky	N	Y	Y	N	N	Y
2 ***Chocola***	Y	Y	N	Y	Y	Y
3 ***Souder***	Y	Y	N	Y	N	Y
4 ***Buyer***	Y	Y	N	N	Y	Y
5 ***Burton***	N	Y	N	Y	Y	Y
6 ***Pence***	Y	Y	N	Y	Y	Y
7 Carson	N	Y	Y	N	N	Y
8 ***Hostettler***	Y	Y	N	Y	Y	N
9 Hill	N	Y	Y	N	Y	Y
IOWA						
1 ***Nussle***	Y	Y	N	N	N	Y
2 ***Leach***	Y	Y	N	N	N	Y
3 Boswell	N	Y	Y	N	Y	Y
4 ***Latham***	Y	Y	N	N	N	Y
5 ***King***	Y	Y	N	Y	Y	Y
KANSAS						
1 ***Moran***	?	?	?	?	?	?
2 ***Ryun***	Y	Y	N	Y	Y	Y
3 Moore	N	Y	?	N	Y	Y
4 ***Tiahrt***	Y	Y	N	Y	N	Y
KENTUCKY						
1 ***Whitfield***	Y	Y	N	Y	Y	Y
2 ***Lewis***	Y	Y	N	N	Y	Y
3 ***Northup***	Y	Y	N	N	N	Y
4 Lucas	N	Y	Y	N	N	Y
5 ***Rogers***	Y	Y	N	N	Y	Y
6 Chandler	N	Y	Y	N	Y	Y
LOUISIANA						
1 ***Vitter***	Y	Y	N	Y	Y	Y
2 Jefferson	N	Y	Y	N	N	Y
3 ***Tauzin***	?	?	?	?	?	?
4 ***McCrery***	Y	Y	N	N	N	Y
5 ***Alexander***	Y	Y	N	N	Y	Y
6 ***Baker***	Y	Y	N	N	Y	Y
7 John	Y	Y	?	N	Y	Y
MAINE						
1 Allen	N	Y	Y	N	N	Y
2 Michaud	N	Y	Y	N	N	Y
MARYLAND						
1 ***Gilchrest***	Y	Y	N	N	N	Y
2 Ruppersberger	N	Y	Y	N	N	Y
3 Cardin	N	Y	Y	N	N	Y
4 Wynn	N	Y	Y	N	N	Y
5 Hoyer	N	Y	Y	N	N	Y
6 ***Bartlett***	Y	Y	N	Y	Y	N
7 Cummings	N	Y	Y	N	N	Y
8 Van Hollen	N	Y	Y	N	N	Y
MASSACHUSETTS						
1 Olver	N	Y	Y	N	N	Y
2 Neal	N	Y	Y	N	N	Y
3 McGovern	N	Y	Y	N	N	Y
4 Frank	N	Y	Y	N	N	Y
5 Meehan	N	Y	Y	N	?	?
6 Tierney	N	Y	Y	N	N	Y
7 Markey	N	Y	Y	N	N	Y
8 Capuano	N	Y	Y	N	N	Y
9 Lynch	N	Y	Y	N	N	Y
10 Delahunt	?	?	?	?	?	?
MICHIGAN						
1 Stupak	Y	Y	Y	N	N	Y
2 ***Hoekstra***	N	Y	N	Y	Y	Y
3 ***Ehlers***	N	Y	N	N	N	Y
4 ***Camp***	Y	Y	N	Y	Y	Y
5 Kildee	N	Y	Y	N	N	Y
6 ***Upton***	N	Y	N	Y	Y	Y
7 ***Smith***	Y	Y	N	Y	Y	Y
8 ***Rogers***	Y	Y	N	Y	Y	Y
9 ***Knollenberg***	Y	Y	N	N	N	Y
10 ***Miller***	Y	Y	N	Y	Y	Y
11 ***McCotter***	Y	Y	N	Y	Y	Y
12 Levin	N	Y	Y	N	N	Y
13 Kilpatrick	N	Y	Y	N	N	Y
14 Conyers	N	Y	Y	N	N	Y
15 Dingell	N	Y	Y	N	N	Y
MINNESOTA						
1 ***Gutknecht***	Y	Y	Y	Y	Y	Y
2 ***Kline***	Y	Y	N	N	Y	Y
3 ***Ramstad***	Y	Y	N	Y	Y	Y
4 McCollum	N	Y	Y	N	N	Y
5 Sabo	N	Y	Y	N	N	Y
6 ***Kennedy***	Y	Y	N	Y	Y	Y
7 Peterson	Y	Y	Y	N	Y	Y
8 Oberstar	Y	Y	Y	N	N	Y
MISSISSIPPI						
1 ***Wicker***	Y	Y	N	N	N	Y
2 Thompson	N	Y	Y	N	N	Y
3 ***Pickering***	Y	Y	N	N	N	Y
4 Taylor	Y	Y	Y	Y	Y	Y
MISSOURI						
1 Clay	N	Y	Y	N	N	Y
2 ***Akin***	Y	Y	N	Y	Y	Y
3 Gephardt	?	?	?	?	?	?
4 Skelton	N	Y	Y	N	Y	Y
5 McCarthy	N	Y	Y	N	N	Y
6 ***Graves***	Y	Y	N	Y	Y	Y
7 ***Blunt***	Y	N	N	N	N	Y
8 ***Emerson***	Y	Y	N	N	Y	Y
9 ***Hulshof***	Y	Y	N	N	Y	Y
MONTANA						
AL ***Rehberg***	Y	Y	N	N	Y	Y
NEBRASKA						
1 Vacant						
2 ***Terry***	?	Y	N	Y	Y	Y
3 ***Osborne***	Y	Y	N	N	N	Y
NEVADA						
1 Berkley	N	Y	Y	N	N	Y
2 ***Gibbons***	N	Y	N	N	Y	Y
3 ***Porter***	N	Y	N	N	N	Y
NEW HAMPSHIRE						
1 ***Bradley***	Y	Y	Y	N	Y	Y
2 ***Bass***	Y	Y	N	N	Y	Y
NEW JERSEY						
1 Andrews	N	Y	Y	N	N	Y
2 ***LoBiondo***	N	Y	N	N	Y	Y
3 ***Saxton***	N	Y	N	N	Y	Y
4 ***Smith***	N	Y	N	N	N	Y
5 ***Garrett***	Y	Y	N	Y	Y	Y
6 Pallone	N	Y	Y	N	N	Y
7 ***Ferguson***	N	Y	N	N	N	Y
8 Pascrell	N	Y	Y	N	N	Y
9 Rothman	N	Y	Y	N	N	Y
10 Payne	N	Y	Y	N	N	Y
11 ***Frelinghuysen***	Y	Y	N	N	N	Y
12 Holt	N	Y	Y	N	N	Y
13 Menendez	N	Y	Y	N	N	Y
NEW MEXICO						
1 ***Wilson***	Y	Y	N	N	N	N
2 ***Pearce***	Y	Y	N	N	N	Y
3 Udall	N	Y	Y	N	N	Y
NEW YORK						
1 Bishop	N	Y	Y	N	N	Y
2 Israel	N	Y	Y	N	Y	Y
3 ***King***	N	Y	N	N	N	Y
4 McCarthy	N	Y	Y	N	N	Y
5 Ackerman	N	Y	Y	N	N	Y
6 Meeks	N	Y	Y	N	N	Y
7 Crowley	N	Y	Y	N	N	Y
8 Nadler	N	Y	Y	N	N	Y
9 Weiner	N	Y	Y	N	N	Y
10 Towns	N	Y	Y	N	?	?
11 Owens	N	Y	Y	N	N	Y
12 Velázquez	N	Y	Y	N	N	Y
13 ***Fossella***	N	Y	N	N	Y	Y
14 Maloney	N	Y	Y	N	N	Y
15 Rangel	N	Y	Y	N	?	Y
16 Serrano	N	Y	Y	N	N	Y
17 Engel	N	Y	Y	N	N	Y
18 Lowey	N	Y	Y	N	N	Y
19 ***Kelly***	Y	Y	N	N	Y	Y
20 ***Sweeney***	N	Y	N	N	Y	Y
21 McNulty	N	Y	Y	?	N	Y
22 Hinchey	N	Y	Y	N	N	Y
23 ***McHugh***	N	Y	N	N	Y	Y
24 ***Boehlert***	N	Y	N	N	Y	Y
25 ***Walsh***	N	Y	N	N	N	Y
26 ***Reynolds***	Y	Y	N	N	Y	Y
27 ***Quinn***	?	?	?	?	?	?
28 Slaughter	N	Y	Y	N	N	Y
29 ***Houghton***	N	Y	N	N	N	Y
NORTH CAROLINA						
1 Butterfield	N	Y	Y	N	N	Y
2 Etheridge	N	Y	Y	N	N	Y
3 ***Jones***	Y	Y	Y	Y	Y	N
4 Price	N	Y	Y	N	N	Y
5 ***Burr***	Y	Y	N	N	Y	Y
6 ***Coble***	Y	Y	N	Y	Y	Y
7 McIntyre	N	Y	Y	N	Y	Y
8 ***Hayes***	Y	Y	N	Y	Y	Y
9 ***Myrick***	Y	Y	N	Y	Y	Y
10 ***Ballenger***	?	?	?	?	?	?
11 ***Taylor***	Y	Y	N	N	Y	Y
12 Watt	N	Y	Y	N	N	Y
13 Miller	N	Y	Y	N	N	Y
NORTH DAKOTA						
AL Pomeroy	Y	Y	Y	N	N	Y
OHIO						
1 ***Chabot***	Y	Y	N	Y	Y	Y
2 ***Portman***	Y	Y	N	N	N	Y
3 ***Turner***	N	Y	N	N	N	Y
4 ***Oxley***	Y	Y	N	N	N	Y
5 ***Gillmor***	Y	Y	N	N	Y	Y
6 Strickland	N	Y	Y	N	N	Y
7 ***Hobson***	Y	Y	N	N	N	Y
8 ***Boehner***	Y	Y	N	N	N	Y
9 Kaptur	N	Y	Y	N	N	Y
10 Kucinich	N	Y	Y	N	N	Y
11 Jones	N	Y	Y	N	N	Y
12 ***Tiberi***	Y	Y	N	N	N	Y
13 Brown	N	Y	Y	N	N	?
14 ***LaTourette***	Y	Y	N	N	Y	Y
15 ***Pryce***	Y	Y	N	N	N	Y
16 ***Regula***	Y	Y	N	N	N	Y
17 Ryan	?	?	?	?	?	?
18 ***Ney***	Y	Y	N	N	Y	Y
OKLAHOMA						
1 ***Sullivan***	Y	Y	N	Y	Y	Y
2 Carson	Y	Y	Y	N	Y	Y
3 ***Lucas***	?	?	?	?	?	?
4 ***Cole***	Y	Y	N	Y	Y	Y
5 ***Istook***	?	N	N	?	Y	Y
OREGON						
1 Wu	N	Y	Y	N	Y	Y
2 ***Walden***	Y	Y	N	N	Y	Y
3 Blumenauer	N	Y	Y	N	N	Y
4 DeFazio	N	Y	Y	N	Y	Y
5 Hooley	N	Y	Y	N	Y	Y
PENNSYLVANIA						
1 Brady	N	Y	Y	N	N	Y
2 Fattah	N	Y	Y	N	N	Y
3 ***English***	Y	Y	N	N	N	Y
4 ***Hart***	Y	Y	N	Y	Y	Y
5 ***Peterson***	N	Y	N	N	?	?
6 ***Gerlach***	Y	Y	N	N	N	Y
7 ***Weldon***	N	Y	N	N	Y	Y
8 ***Greenwood***	?	?	?	?	?	?
9 ***Shuster, Bill***	?	?	?	?	?	?
10 ***Sherwood***	Y	Y	N	N	N	Y
11 Kanjorski	?	?	?	?	?	?
12 Murtha	N	Y	Y	N	N	Y
13 Hoeffel	N	Y	Y	N	N	Y
14 Doyle	N	Y	Y	N	N	Y
15 ***Toomey***	?	?	?	?	?	?
16 ***Pitts***	N	Y	N	Y	Y	Y
17 Holden	N	Y	Y	N	N	Y
18 ***Murphy***	N	Y	N	N	N	Y
19 ***Platts***	N	Y	N	N	Y	Y
RHODE ISLAND						
1 Kennedy	N	Y	Y	N	N	Y
2 Langevin	N	Y	Y	?	?	?
SOUTH CAROLINA						
1 ***Brown***	Y	Y	N	N	Y	Y
2 ***Wilson***	Y	Y	N	N	N	Y
3 ***Barrett***	Y	Y	N	Y	Y	Y
4 ***DeMint***	Y	Y	N	Y	Y	Y
5 Spratt	N	Y	Y	N	N	Y
6 Clyburn	N	Y	Y	N	N	Y
SOUTH DAKOTA						
AL Herseth	Y	Y	Y	N	Y	Y
TENNESSEE						
1 ***Jenkins***	Y	Y	N	N	Y	Y
2 ***Duncan***	Y	Y	N	Y	Y	Y
3 ***Wamp***	Y	Y	N	N	Y	Y
4 Davis	N	Y	Y	N	Y	Y
5 Cooper	N	Y	Y	N	N	Y
6 Gordon	N	Y	Y	N	Y	Y
7 ***Blackburn***	Y	Y	N	Y	Y	Y
8 Tanner	Y	Y	?	?	?	?
9 Ford	N	Y	?	N	N	Y
TEXAS						
1 Sandlin	N	Y	N	N	Y	Y
2 Turner	N	Y	Y	N	?	?
3 ***Johnson, Sam***	Y	Y	N	N	Y	Y
4 ***Hall***	Y	Y	N	N	N	Y
5 ***Hensarling***	Y	Y	N	Y	Y	N
6 ***Barton***	Y	Y	N	N	Y	Y
7 ***Culberson***	Y	Y	N	Y	Y	Y
8 ***Brady***	Y	Y	N	Y	Y	Y
9 Lampson	N	Y	Y	N	Y	Y
10 Doggett	N	Y	Y	N	N	Y
11 Edwards	N	Y	Y	N	Y	Y
12 ***Granger***	Y	Y	N	N	Y	Y
13 ***Thornberry***	Y	Y	N	Y	Y	Y
14 ***Paul***	Y	Y	Y	Y	Y	N
15 Hinojosa	N	Y	Y	N	N	Y
16 Reyes	N	Y	Y	N	?	?
17 Stenholm	N	Y	Y	N	Y	Y
18 Jackson-Lee	N	Y	Y	N	N	Y
19 ***Neugebauer***	Y	Y	N	Y	Y	Y
20 Gonzalez	N	Y	Y	N	N	Y
21 ***Smith***	Y	Y	N	N	Y	Y
22 ***DeLay***	Y	Y	N	Y	Y	Y
23 ***Bonilla***	Y	Y	N	N	N	Y
24 Frost	N	Y	Y	N	Y	Y
25 Bell	N	Y	Y	N	N	Y
26 ***Burgess***	Y	Y	N	Y	Y	Y
27 Ortiz	N	Y	Y	N	N	Y
28 Rodriguez	N	Y	Y	N	N	Y
29 Green	N	Y	Y	N	N	Y
30 Johnson, E.B.	N	Y	Y	N	N	Y
31 ***Carter***	Y	Y	N	N	Y	Y
32 ***Sessions***	Y	Y	N	Y	Y	Y
UTAH						
1 ***Bishop***	Y	Y	N	Y	Y	Y
2 Matheson	Y	Y	Y	N	Y	Y
3 ***Cannon***	?	?	?	?	?	?
VERMONT						
AL *Sanders*	N	Y	Y	N	Y	Y
VIRGINIA						
1 ***Davis, Jo Ann***	Y	Y	N	Y	Y	Y
2 ***Schrock***	?	?	?	?	?	?
3 Scott	N	Y	Y	N	N	Y
4 ***Forbes***	Y	Y	N	Y	Y	Y
5 ***Goode***	Y	Y	N	Y	Y	Y
6 ***Goodlatte***	Y	Y	N	Y	Y	Y
7 ***Cantor***	Y	Y	N	Y	N	Y
8 Moran	N	Y	Y	N	N	Y
9 Boucher	N	Y	Y	N	N	Y
10 ***Wolf***	N	Y	N	N	Y	Y
11 ***Davis, T.***	Y	Y	N	N	Y	Y
WASHINGTON						
1 Inslee	N	Y	Y	N	N	Y
2 Larsen	N	Y	Y	N	N	Y
3 Baird	N	Y	Y	N	N	Y
4 ***Hastings***	Y	Y	N	N	N	Y
5 ***Nethercutt***	+	+	–	–	–	+
6 Dicks	N	Y	Y	N	N	Y
7 McDermott	N	Y	Y	N	N	Y
8 ***Dunn***	Y	Y	N	N	N	Y
9 Smith	N	Y	Y	N	N	Y
WEST VIRGINIA						
1 Mollohan	N	Y	Y	N	N	Y
2 ***Capito***	Y	Y	N	N	Y	Y
3 Rahall	N	Y	Y	N	N	Y
WISCONSIN						
1 ***Ryan***	N	Y	N	Y	Y	Y
2 Baldwin	N	Y	Y	N	N	Y
3 Kind	N	Y	Y	N	N	Y
4 Kleczka	?	Y	Y	N	N	Y
5 ***Sensenbrenner***	N	Y	N	Y	Y	Y
6 ***Petri***	N	Y	N	Y	Y	Y
7 Obey	N	Y	Y	N	N	Y
8 ***Green***	N	Y	N	Y	Y	Y
WYOMING						
AL ***Cubin***	Y	Y	N	Y	Y	Y

Southern states - Ala., Ark., Fla., Ga., Ky., La., Miss., N.C., Okla., S.C., Tenn., Texas, Va.

Key

Y	Voted for (yea).
#	Paired for.
+	Announced for.
N	Voted against (nay).
X	Paired against.
−	Announced against.
P	Voted "present."
C	Voted "present" to avoid possible conflict of interest.
?	Did not vote or otherwise make a position known.

Democrats ***Republicans***
Independents

441. H Con Res 363. Human Rights in Syria/Adoption. Ros-Lehtinen, R-Fla., motion to suspend the rules and adopt the concurrent resolution that would condemn human rights violations by the Syrian government and call for a U.N. resolution condemning the abuses. Motion agreed to 342-0: R 187-0; D 155-0 (ND 109-0, SD 46-0); I 0-0. A two-thirds majority of those present and voting (228 in this case) is required for adoption under suspension of the rules. Sept. 13, 2004.

442. H Res 667. Democracy in Hong Kong/Adoption. Ros-Lehtinen, R-Fla., motion to suspend the rules and adopt the resolution that would express the House's position that the people of Hong Kong should determine the pace and scope of constitutional changes. Motion agreed to 345-0: R 189-0; D 155-0 (ND 110-0, SD 45-0); I 1-0. A two-thirds majority of those present and voting (230 in this case) is required for adoption under suspension of the rules. Sept. 13, 2004.

443. H Res 760. Terrorist Attacks in Russia/Adoption. Royce, R-Calif., motion to suspend the rules and adopt the resolution that would condemn the terrorist attacks against the Russian Federation in August and September 2004. Motion agreed to 347-0: R 191-0; D 155-0 (ND 109-0, SD 46-0); I 1-0. A two-thirds majority of those present and voting (232 in this case) is required for adoption under suspension of the rules. Sept. 13, 2004.

444. HR 4571. Frivolous Lawsuits/Rule. Adoption of the rule (H Res 766) to provide for House floor consideration of the bill that would increase federal sanctions on lawyers who file meritless civil lawsuits. Adopted 228-165: R 207-0; D 21-164 (ND 11-122, SD 10-42); I 0-1. Sept. 14, 2004.

445. HR 3369. Legal Protection for Nonprofit Athletic Groups/ Passage. Sensenbrenner, R-Wis., motion to suspend the rules and pass the bill that would provide immunity for properly licensed, certified or authorized nonprofit athletic organizations in lawsuits that claim negligence resulting from rules enforced during an approved sports practice or competition. Motion rejected 217-176: R 201-5; D 16-170 (ND 5-127, SD 11-43); I 0-1. A two-thirds majority of those present and voting (262 in this case) is required for passage under suspension of the rules. Sept. 14, 2004.

446. HR 1787. Firefighting Equipment Liability Protection/Passage. Sensenbrenner, R-Wis., motion to suspend the rules and pass the bill that would prohibit lawsuits against those who donate surplus fire-control or fire-rescue equipment, such as hoses or protective clothing, to volunteer fire departments. Motion agreed to 397-3: R 210-1; D 186-2 (ND 133-1, SD 53-1); I 1-0. A two-thirds majority of those present and voting (267 in this case) is required for passage under suspension of the rules. Sept. 14, 2004.

	441	442	443	444	445	446
ALABAMA						
1 *Bonner*	Y	Y	Y	?	?	?
2 *Everett*	?	?	?	Y	Y	Y
3 *Rogers*	Y	Y	Y	Y	Y	Y
4 *Aderholt*	Y	Y	Y	Y	Y	Y
5 Cramer	Y	Y	Y	Y	Y	Y
6 *Bachus*	Y	Y	Y	Y	Y	Y
7 Davis	Y	Y	Y	N	N	Y
ALASKA						
AL *Young*	Y	Y	Y	Y	Y	Y
ARIZONA						
1 *Renzi*	Y	Y	Y	Y	Y	Y
2 *Franks*	Y	Y	Y	Y	Y	Y
3 *Shadegg*	Y	Y	Y	Y	Y	Y
4 Pastor	Y	Y	Y	N	N	Y
5 *Hayworth*	Y	Y	Y	Y	Y	Y
6 *Flake*	Y	Y	Y	Y	N	Y
7 Grijalva	?	?	?	N	N	Y
8 *Kolbe*	Y	Y	Y	Y	Y	Y
ARKANSAS						
1 Berry	Y	Y	Y	N	N	Y
2 Snyder	Y	Y	Y	N	N	Y
3 *Boozman*	?	?	?	Y	Y	Y
4 Ross	Y	Y	Y	N	N	Y
CALIFORNIA						
1 Thompson	Y	Y	Y	N	N	Y
2 *Herger*	?	?	?	Y	Y	Y
3 *Ose*	Y	Y	Y	Y	Y	Y
4 *Doolittle*	Y	Y	Y	Y	Y	Y
5 Matsui	?	?	?	N	N	Y
6 Woolsey	Y	Y	?	N	N	Y
7 Miller, George	Y	Y	?	N	N	Y
8 Pelosi	Y	Y	Y	N	N	Y
9 Lee	Y	Y	Y	N	N	Y
10 Tauscher	Y	Y	Y	N	N	Y
11 *Pombo*	Y	Y	Y	Y	Y	Y
12 Lantos	Y	Y	Y	N	N	Y
13 Stark	?	?	?	N	N	Y
14 Eshoo	Y	Y	Y	N	N	Y
15 Honda	Y	Y	Y	N	N	Y
16 Lofgren	Y	Y	Y	N	N	Y
17 Farr	Y	Y	Y	N	N	Y
18 Cardoza	Y	Y	Y	N	N	Y
19 *Radanovich*	Y	Y	Y	Y	Y	Y
20 Dooley	Y	Y	Y	N	N	Y
21 *Nunes*	Y	Y	Y	Y	Y	Y
22 *Thomas*	Y	Y	Y	Y	Y	Y
23 Capps	Y	Y	Y	N	N	Y
24 *Gallegly*	Y	Y	Y	Y	Y	Y
25 *McKeon*	?	Y	Y	Y	Y	Y
26 *Dreier*	Y	Y	Y	Y	Y	Y
27 Sherman	Y	Y	Y	N	N	Y
28 Berman	Y	Y	Y	N	N	Y
29 Schiff	Y	Y	Y	N	N	Y
30 Waxman	?	?	?	N	N	Y
31 Becerra	Y	Y	Y	N	N	Y
32 Solis	Y	Y	Y	N	N	Y
33 Watson	Y	Y	Y	N	N	Y
34 Roybal-Allard	Y	Y	Y	N	N	Y
35 Waters	P	P	Y	N	N	Y
36 Harman	Y	Y	Y	N	N	Y

	441	442	443	444	445	446
37 Millender-McD.	Y	Y	Y	N	N	Y
38 Napolitano	Y	Y	Y	N	N	Y
39 Sánchez, Linda	Y	Y	Y	N	N	Y
40 *Royce*	Y	Y	Y	Y	Y	Y
41 *Lewis*	Y	Y	Y	Y	Y	Y
42 *Miller, Gary*	Y	Y	Y	Y	Y	Y
43 Baca	Y	Y	Y	N	N	Y
44 *Calvert*	Y	Y	Y	Y	Y	Y
45 *Bono*	Y	Y	Y	Y	Y	Y
46 *Rohrabacher*	Y	Y	Y	?	?	Y
47 Sanchez, Loretta	Y	Y	Y	N	N	Y
48 *Cox*	Y	Y	Y	Y	Y	Y
49 *Issa*	Y	Y	Y	Y	+	Y
50 *Cunningham*	Y	Y	Y	Y	Y	Y
51 Filner	Y	Y	Y	N	N	Y
52 *Hunter*	Y	Y	Y	?	?	?
53 Davis	Y	Y	Y	N	N	Y
COLORADO						
1 DeGette	Y	Y	Y	N	N	Y
2 Udall	Y	Y	Y	N	N	Y
3 *McInnis*	?	?	?	?	?	?
4 *Musgrave*	Y	Y	Y	Y	Y	Y
5 *Hefley*	Y	Y	Y	Y	Y	Y
6 *Tancredo*	Y	Y	Y	Y	Y	Y
7 *Beauprez*	?	?	?	?	?	?
CONNECTICUT						
1 Larson	Y	Y	Y	N	N	Y
2 *Simmons*	Y	Y	Y	Y	Y	Y
3 DeLauro	Y	Y	Y	N	N	Y
4 *Shays*	Y	Y	Y	Y	Y	Y
5 *Johnson*	Y	Y	Y	Y	Y	Y
DELAWARE						
AL *Castle*	Y	Y	Y	Y	Y	Y
FLORIDA						
1 *Miller, J.*	Y	Y	Y	Y	Y	Y
2 Boyd	Y	Y	Y	Y	Y	Y
3 Brown	Y	Y	Y	N	N	Y
4 *Crenshaw*	Y	Y	Y	Y	Y	Y
5 *Brown-Waite*	Y	Y	Y	Y	Y	Y
6 *Stearns*	Y	Y	Y	Y	Y	Y
7 *Mica*	Y	Y	Y	Y	Y	Y
8 *Keller*	Y	Y	Y	Y	Y	Y
9 *Bilirakis*	Y	Y	Y	Y	Y	Y
10 *Young*	Y	Y	Y	Y	Y	Y
11 Davis	Y	Y	Y	N	N	Y
12 *Putnam*	Y	Y	Y	Y	Y	Y
13 *Harris*	Y	Y	Y	Y	Y	?
14 *Goss*	?	?	?	?	?	?
15 *Weldon*	Y	Y	Y	Y	Y	Y
16 *Foley*	Y	Y	Y	Y	Y	Y
17 Meek	Y	Y	Y	N	N	Y
18 *Ros-Lehtinen*	Y	Y	Y	Y	Y	Y
19 Wexler	Y	Y	Y	N	N	Y
20 Deutsch	Y	Y	Y	N	N	Y
21 *Diaz-Balart, L.*	Y	Y	Y	Y	Y	Y
22 *Shaw*	Y	Y	Y	Y	Y	Y
23 Hastings	?	?	?	?	?	?
24 *Feeney*	Y	Y	Y	Y	Y	Y
25 *Diaz-Balart, M.*	Y	Y	Y	Y	Y	Y
GEORGIA						
1 *Kingston*	Y	Y	Y	Y	Y	Y
2 Bishop	Y	Y	Y	N	N	Y
3 Marshall	Y	Y	Y	N	N	Y
4 *Majette*	?	?	?	N	N	Y
5 Lewis	Y	Y	Y	N	N	Y
6 *Isakson*	?	?	?	Y	Y	Y
7 *Linder*	Y	Y	Y	Y	Y	Y
8 *Collins*	Y	Y	Y	Y	Y	Y
9 *Norwood*	Y	Y	Y	Y	Y	Y
10 *Deal*	Y	Y	Y	Y	Y	Y
11 *Gingrey*	Y	Y	Y	Y	Y	Y
12 *Burns*	Y	Y	Y	Y	Y	Y
13 Scott	Y	Y	Y	N	Y	Y
HAWAII						
1 Abercrombie	Y	Y	Y	N	N	Y
2 Case	Y	Y	Y	N	Y	Y
IDAHO						
1 *Otter*	Y	Y	Y	Y	N	Y
2 *Simpson*	?	Y	Y	Y	Y	Y
ILLINOIS						
1 Rush	Y	Y	Y	N	N	Y
2 Jackson	Y	Y	Y	N	N	Y
3 Lipinski	?	?	?	N	N	Y
4 Gutierrez	?	?	?	N	N	Y
5 Emanuel	Y	Y	Y	N	N	Y
6 *Hyde*	Y	Y	Y	Y	Y	Y

ND Northern Democrats   SD Southern Democrats

	441	442	443	444	445	446
7 Davis	Y	Y	Y	N	N	Y
8 ***Crane***	Y	Y	Y	Y	Y	Y
9 Schakowsky	?	?	?	N	N	Y
10 ***Kirk***	Y	Y	Y	Y	Y	Y
11 ***Weller***	Y	Y	Y	Y	Y	Y
12 Costello	Y	Y	Y	N	N	Y
13 ***Biggert***	+	+	+	Y	Y	Y
14 ***Hastert***						
15 ***Johnson***	Y	Y	Y	Y	Y	Y
16 ***Manzullo***	Y	Y	Y	Y	N	Y
17 Evans	?	?	?	N	N	Y
18 ***LaHood***	Y	Y	Y	Y	Y	Y
19 ***Shimkus***	Y	Y	Y	Y	Y	Y
INDIANA						
1 Visclosky	Y	Y	Y	N	N	Y
2 ***Chocola***	Y	Y	Y	Y	Y	Y
3 ***Souder***	Y	Y	Y	Y	Y	Y
4 ***Buyer***	Y	Y	Y	Y	Y	Y
5 ***Burton***	Y	Y	Y	Y	Y	Y
6 ***Pence***	Y	Y	Y	Y	Y	Y
7 Carson	Y	Y	Y	N	N	Y
8 ***Hostettler***	Y	Y	Y	Y	Y	Y
9 Hill	Y	Y	Y	N	N	Y
IOWA						
1 ***Nussle***	Y	Y	Y	Y	Y	Y
2 ***Leach***	Y	Y	Y	Y	Y	Y
3 Boswell	Y	Y	Y	N	N	Y
4 ***Latham***	Y	Y	Y	Y	Y	Y
5 ***King***	Y	Y	Y	Y	Y	Y
KANSAS						
1 ***Moran***	Y	Y	Y	Y	Y	Y
2 ***Ryun***	Y	Y	Y	Y	Y	Y
3 Moore	Y	Y	Y	Y	N	Y
4 ***Tiahrt***	Y	Y	Y	Y	Y	Y
KENTUCKY						
1 ***Whitfield***	Y	Y	Y	?	?	?
2 ***Lewis***	Y	Y	Y	Y	Y	Y
3 ***Northup***	Y	Y	Y	Y	Y	Y
4 Lucas	?	?	?	?	Y	Y
5 ***Rogers***	?	?	?	?	?	?
6 Chandler	Y	Y	Y	N	Y	Y
LOUISIANA						
1 ***Vitter***	?	?	?	Y	Y	Y
2 Jefferson	Y	Y	Y	N	N	Y
3 ***Tauzin***	?	?	?	?	?	?
4 ***McCrery***	Y	Y	Y	Y	Y	Y
5 ***Alexander***	Y	Y	Y	Y	Y	Y
6 ***Baker***	?	?	?	?	Y	Y
7 John	Y	Y	Y	N	N	Y
MAINE						
1 Allen	Y	Y	Y	N	N	Y
2 Michaud	Y	Y	Y	N	N	Y
MARYLAND						
1 ***Gilchrest***	Y	Y	Y	Y	Y	Y
2 Ruppersberger	Y	Y	Y	N	+	Y
3 Cardin	Y	Y	Y	N	N	Y
4 Wynn	Y	Y	Y	N	Y	Y
5 Hoyer	Y	Y	Y	N	N	Y
6 ***Bartlett***	Y	Y	Y	Y	Y	Y
7 Cummings	Y	Y	Y	N	N	Y
8 Van Hollen	Y	Y	Y	N	N	Y
MASSACHUSETTS						
1 Olver	Y	Y	Y	N	N	Y
2 Neal	?	?	?	N	N	Y
3 McGovern	?	?	?	N	N	Y
4 Frank	Y	Y	Y	N	N	Y
5 Meehan	Y	Y	Y	N	N	Y
6 Tierney	Y	Y	Y	N	N	Y
7 Markey	?	?	?	N	N	Y
8 Capuano	–	+	+	N	N	Y
9 Lynch	?	?	?	N	N	Y
10 Delahunt	Y	Y	Y	N	N	Y
MICHIGAN						
1 Stupak	Y	Y	Y	N	N	Y
2 ***Hoekstra***	?	?	?	Y	Y	Y
3 ***Ehlers***	Y	Y	Y	Y	Y	Y
4 ***Camp***	Y	Y	Y	Y	Y	Y
5 Kildee	Y	Y	Y	Y	N	Y
6 ***Upton***	Y	Y	Y	Y	Y	Y
7 ***Smith***	?	?	?	?	Y	Y
8 ***Rogers***	+	+	+	Y	Y	Y
9 ***Knollenberg***	Y	Y	Y	Y	Y	Y
10 ***Miller***	Y	Y	Y	Y	Y	Y
11 ***McCotter***	Y	Y	Y	Y	Y	Y
12 Levin	Y	Y	Y	N	N	Y

	441	442	443	444	445	446
13 Kilpatrick	Y	Y	Y	N	N	Y
14 Conyers	?	?	?	?	?	?
15 Dingell	Y	Y	Y	N	N	Y
MINNESOTA						
1 ***Gutknecht***	Y	Y	Y	Y	Y	Y
2 ***Kline***	Y	Y	Y	Y	Y	Y
3 ***Ramstad***	Y	Y	Y	Y	Y	Y
4 McCollum	Y	Y	Y	N	N	Y
5 Sabo	?	?	?	N	N	Y
6 ***Kennedy***	Y	Y	Y	Y	Y	Y
7 Peterson	Y	Y	Y	Y	N	Y
8 Oberstar	Y	Y	Y	N	N	Y
MISSISSIPPI						
1 ***Wicker***	Y	Y	Y	Y	Y	Y
2 Thompson	?	?	?	N	N	Y
3 ***Pickering***	Y	Y	Y	Y	Y	Y
4 Taylor	+	+	+	Y	Y	Y
MISSOURI						
1 Clay	?	?	?	?	?	?
2 ***Akin***	Y	Y	Y	Y	Y	Y
3 Gephardt	?	?	?	?	?	?
4 Skelton	Y	Y	Y	N	N	Y
5 McCarthy	Y	Y	Y	N	N	Y
6 ***Graves***	Y	Y	Y	Y	Y	Y
7 ***Blunt***	Y	Y	Y	Y	Y	Y
8 ***Emerson***	?	?	?	?	Y	Y
9 ***Hulshof***	Y	Y	Y	Y	Y	Y
MONTANA						
AL ***Rehberg***	Y	Y	Y	Y	Y	Y
NEBRASKA						
1 Vacant						
2 ***Terry***	Y	Y	Y	Y	N	Y
3 ***Osborne***	Y	Y	Y	Y	Y	Y
NEVADA						
1 Berkley	Y	Y	Y	N	N	Y
2 ***Gibbons***	Y	Y	Y	Y	Y	Y
3 ***Porter***	Y	Y	Y	Y	Y	Y
NEW HAMPSHIRE						
1 ***Bradley***	Y	Y	Y	Y	Y	Y
2 ***Bass***	Y	Y	Y	Y	Y	Y
NEW JERSEY						
1 Andrews	Y	Y	Y	N	N	Y
2 ***LoBiondo***	Y	Y	Y	Y	Y	Y
3 ***Saxton***	?	?	?	Y	Y	Y
4 ***Smith***	Y	Y	Y	Y	Y	Y
5 ***Garrett***	Y	Y	Y	Y	Y	Y
6 Pallone	Y	Y	Y	N	N	Y
7 ***Ferguson***	Y	Y	Y	Y	Y	Y
8 Pascrell	?	?	?	?	N	Y
9 Rothman	Y	Y	Y	N	N	Y
10 Payne	Y	Y	Y	N	N	Y
11 ***Frelinghuysen***	Y	Y	Y	Y	Y	Y
12 Holt	Y	Y	Y	N	N	Y
13 Menendez	Y	Y	Y	N	N	Y
NEW MEXICO						
1 ***Wilson***	Y	?	Y	Y	Y	Y
2 ***Pearce***	Y	Y	Y	Y	Y	Y
3 Udall	?	?	?	N	N	Y
NEW YORK						
1 Bishop	Y	Y	Y	N	N	Y
2 Israel	Y	Y	Y	Y	N	Y
3 ***King***	Y	Y	Y	Y	Y	Y
4 McCarthy	Y	Y	Y	N	N	Y
5 Ackerman	?	?	?	?	?	?
6 Meeks	Y	Y	Y	N	N	Y
7 Crowley	?	?	?	?	?	?
8 Nadler	Y	Y	Y	N	N	N
9 Weiner	?	?	?	N	N	Y
10 Towns	?	?	?	?	?	?
11 Owens	?	?	?	?	?	?
12 Velázquez	Y	Y	Y	?	?	?
13 ***Fossella***	Y	Y	Y	Y	Y	Y
14 Maloney	Y	Y	Y	N	N	Y
15 Rangel	?	Y	Y	N	N	Y
16 Serrano	?	?	?	?	?	?
17 Engel	?	?	?	?	?	?
18 Lowey	Y	Y	Y	N	N	Y
19 ***Kelly***	Y	Y	Y	Y	Y	Y
20 ***Sweeney***	?	?	?	?	Y	Y
21 McNulty	Y	Y	Y	Y	N	Y
22 Hinchey	?	?	?	N	N	Y
23 ***McHugh***	Y	Y	Y	Y	Y	Y
24 ***Boehlert***	?	?	?	?	?	?
25 ***Walsh***	Y	Y	Y	Y	Y	Y

	441	442	443	444	445	446
26 ***Reynolds***	Y	Y	Y	Y	Y	Y
27 ***Quinn***	?	?	?	?	Y	Y
28 Slaughter	+	+	+	–	–	+
29 ***Houghton***	?	?	?	?	?	?
NORTH CAROLINA						
1 Butterfield	Y	Y	Y	N	N	Y
2 Etheridge	Y	Y	Y	N	N	Y
3 ***Jones***	Y	Y	Y	Y	Y	Y
4 Price	Y	Y	Y	N	N	Y
5 ***Burr***	?	?	?	Y	Y	Y
6 ***Coble***	Y	Y	Y	Y	Y	Y
7 McIntyre	Y	Y	Y	N	N	Y
8 ***Hayes***	Y	Y	Y	Y	Y	Y
9 ***Myrick***	Y	Y	Y	Y	Y	Y
10 ***Ballenger***	?	?	?	?	?	?
11 ***Taylor***	?	?	?	Y	Y	Y
12 Watt	Y	Y	Y	N	N	Y
13 Miller	Y	Y	Y	N	N	Y
NORTH DAKOTA						
AL Pomeroy	Y	Y	Y	N	N	Y
OHIO						
1 ***Chabot***	Y	Y	Y	Y	Y	Y
2 ***Portman***	Y	Y	Y	Y	Y	Y
3 ***Turner***	Y	Y	Y	Y	Y	Y
4 ***Oxley***	Y	Y	Y	?	Y	Y
5 ***Gillmor***	Y	Y	Y	Y	Y	Y
6 Strickland	Y	Y	Y	N	N	Y
7 ***Hobson***	Y	Y	Y	Y	Y	Y
8 ***Boehner***	Y	Y	Y	Y	Y	Y
9 Kaptur	?	?	?	?	N	Y
10 Kucinich	?	?	?	N	N	Y
11 Jones	Y	Y	Y	N	N	Y
12 ***Tiberi***	Y	Y	Y	Y	Y	Y
13 Brown	+	+	+	N	N	Y
14 ***LaTourette***	?	?	?	?	Y	Y
15 ***Pryce***	?	?	?	?	?	Y
16 ***Regula***	?	Y	Y	Y	Y	Y
17 Ryan	Y	Y	Y	N	N	Y
18 ***Ney***	Y	Y	Y	Y	Y	Y
OKLAHOMA						
1 ***Sullivan***	Y	Y	Y	Y	Y	Y
2 Carson	?	?	?	N	Y	Y
3 ***Lucas***	Y	Y	Y	Y	Y	Y
4 ***Cole***	Y	Y	Y	Y	Y	Y
5 ***Istook***	Y	Y	Y	?	?	Y
OREGON						
1 Wu	Y	Y	Y	N	N	Y
2 ***Walden***	Y	Y	Y	Y	Y	Y
3 Blumenauer	Y	Y	Y	N	N	Y
4 DeFazio	Y	Y	Y	N	N	Y
5 Hooley	Y	Y	Y	N	N	Y
PENNSYLVANIA						
1 Brady	Y	Y	Y	N	N	Y
2 Fattah	Y	Y	Y	N	N	Y
3 ***English***	?	?	?	Y	Y	Y
4 ***Hart***	Y	Y	Y	Y	Y	Y
5 ***Peterson***	?	?	?	Y	Y	Y
6 ***Gerlach***	?	?	?	Y	Y	Y
7 ***Weldon***	Y	Y	Y	Y	Y	Y
8 ***Greenwood***	Y	Y	Y	?	?	?
9 ***Shuster, Bill***	Y	Y	Y	Y	Y	Y
10 ***Sherwood***	Y	Y	Y	Y	Y	Y
11 Kanjorski	Y	Y	Y	N	N	Y
12 Murtha	?	?	?	N	N	Y
13 Hoeffel	?	?	?	?	?	?
14 Doyle	Y	Y	Y	N	N	Y
15 ***Toomey***	?	?	?	Y	Y	Y
16 ***Pitts***	Y	Y	Y	Y	Y	Y
17 Holden	Y	Y	Y	Y	Y	Y
18 ***Murphy***	Y	Y	Y	Y	Y	Y
19 ***Platts***	Y	Y	Y	Y	Y	Y
RHODE ISLAND						
1 Kennedy	+	+	+	–	–	+
2 Langevin	?	?	?	?	?	?
SOUTH CAROLINA						
1 ***Brown***	Y	Y	Y	Y	Y	Y
2 ***Wilson***	Y	Y	Y	Y	Y	Y
3 ***Barrett***	Y	Y	Y	Y	Y	Y
4 ***DeMint***	?	?	?	?	Y	Y
5 Spratt	Y	Y	Y	N	N	Y
6 Clyburn	Y	Y	Y	?	N	Y
SOUTH DAKOTA						
AL Herseth	Y	Y	Y	N	Y	Y

	441	442	443	444	445	446
TENNESSEE						
1 ***Jenkins***	Y	Y	Y	Y	Y	Y
2 ***Duncan***	Y	Y	Y	Y	Y	Y
3 ***Wamp***	Y	Y	Y	Y	Y	Y
4 Davis	Y	Y	Y	Y	Y	Y
5 Cooper	Y	Y	Y	Y	N	Y
6 Gordon	Y	Y	Y	N	N	Y
7 ***Blackburn***	Y	Y	Y	?	?	?
8 Tanner	Y	Y	Y	N	N	Y
9 Ford	Y	Y	Y	N	N	Y
TEXAS						
1 Sandlin	?	?	?	N	Y	Y
2 Turner	?	?	?	N	N	Y
3 ***Johnson, Sam***	Y	Y	Y	Y	Y	Y
4 ***Hall***	Y	Y	Y	Y	Y	Y
5 ***Hensarling***	Y	Y	Y	Y	Y	Y
6 ***Barton***	Y	Y	Y	Y	Y	Y
7 ***Culberson***	Y	Y	Y	Y	Y	Y
8 ***Brady***	Y	Y	Y	Y	Y	Y
9 Lampson	Y	Y	Y	N	N	Y
10 Doggett	Y	Y	Y	N	N	Y
11 Edwards	Y	Y	Y	N	Y	Y
12 ***Granger***	Y	Y	Y	Y	Y	Y
13 ***Thornberry***	Y	Y	Y	Y	Y	Y
14 ***Paul***	?	?	?	Y	N	N
15 Hinojosa	Y	Y	Y	–	N	Y
16 Reyes	Y	Y	Y	N	N	Y
17 Stenholm	Y	Y	Y	Y	Y	Y
18 Jackson-Lee	Y	Y	Y	N	N	Y
19 ***Neugebauer***	Y	Y	Y	Y	Y	Y
20 Gonzalez	Y	Y	Y	N	N	Y
21 ***Smith***	Y	Y	Y	Y	Y	Y
22 ***DeLay***	Y	Y	Y	Y	Y	Y
23 ***Bonilla***	Y	Y	Y	Y	Y	Y
24 Frost	?	?	?	N	N	Y
25 Bell	Y	Y	Y	N	N	Y
26 ***Burgess***	Y	Y	Y	Y	Y	Y
27 Ortiz	Y	Y	Y	N	N	Y
28 Rodriguez	Y	Y	Y	N	N	Y
29 Green	Y	?	Y	N	N	Y
30 Johnson, E.B.	+	+	+	?	?	?
31 ***Carter***	+	+	+	Y	Y	Y
32 ***Sessions***	Y	Y	Y	Y	Y	Y
UTAH						
1 ***Bishop***	?	?	?	Y	Y	Y
2 Matheson	Y	Y	Y	Y	Y	Y
3 ***Cannon***	?	?	?	?	?	?
VERMONT						
AL *Sanders*	?	Y	Y	N	N	Y
VIRGINIA						
1 ***Davis, Jo Ann***	Y	Y	Y	Y	Y	Y
2 ***Schrock***	?	?	?	?	?	?
3 Scott	Y	Y	Y	N	N	N
4 ***Forbes***	Y	Y	Y	Y	Y	Y
5 ***Goode***	Y	Y	Y	Y	Y	Y
6 ***Goodlatte***	Y	Y	Y	Y	Y	Y
7 ***Cantor***	Y	Y	Y	Y	Y	Y
8 Moran	Y	Y	Y	Y	N	Y
9 Boucher	Y	Y	Y	N	N	Y
10 ***Wolf***	Y	Y	Y	Y	Y	Y
11 ***Davis, T.***	Y	Y	Y	Y	Y	Y
WASHINGTON						
1 Inslee	?	?	?	N	N	Y
2 Larsen	Y	Y	Y	N	N	Y
3 Baird	Y	Y	Y	N	N	Y
4 ***Hastings***	Y	Y	Y	Y	Y	Y
5 ***Nethercutt***	+	+	+	Y	Y	Y
6 Dicks	Y	Y	Y	N	?	Y
7 McDermott	Y	Y	Y	N	N	Y
8 ***Dunn***	Y	Y	Y	Y	?	Y
9 Smith	?	?	?	Y	N	Y
WEST VIRGINIA						
1 Mollohan	Y	Y	Y	N	N	Y
2 ***Capito***	Y	Y	Y	Y	Y	Y
3 Rahall	Y	Y	Y	N	N	Y
WISCONSIN						
1 ***Ryan***	Y	Y	Y	Y	Y	Y
2 Baldwin	Y	Y	Y	N	N	Y
3 Kind	Y	Y	Y	N	N	Y
4 Kleczka	?	?	?	?	?	?
5 ***Sensenbrenner***	Y	Y	Y	Y	Y	Y
6 ***Petri***	Y	Y	Y	Y	Y	Y
7 Obey	Y	Y	Y	Y	N	Y
8 ***Green***	Y	Y	Y	Y	Y	Y
WYOMING						
AL ***Cubin***	Y	Y	Y	Y	Y	Y

Southern states - Ala., Ark., Fla., Ga., Ky., La., Miss., N.C., Okla., S.C., Tenn., Texas, Va.

Key

Y	Voted for (yea).
#	Paired for.
+	Announced for.
N	Voted against (nay).
X	Paired against.
–	Announced against.
P	Voted "present."
C	Voted "present" to avoid possible conflict of interest.
?	Did not vote or otherwise make a position known.

Democrats **Republicans**
Independents

447. HR 1084. Legal Protection for Volunteer Pilots/Passage. Sensenbrenner, R-Wis., motion to suspend the rules and pass the bill that would provide liability protection to nonprofit volunteer pilots, referral agencies and volunteer pilot organizations on public benefit missions for harm caused to passengers during flights. It would apply only to pilots who are licensed and insured. Motion agreed to 385-12: R 205-3; D 179-9 (ND 126-8, SD 53-1); I 1-0. A two-thirds majority of those present and voting (265 in this case) is required for passage under suspension of the rules. Sept. 14, 2004.

448. HR 4571. Frivolous Lawsuits/Democratic Substitute. Turner, D-Texas, substitute amendment that would increase federal sanctions on lawyers who file meritless civil lawsuits. It would require mandatory sanctions against those filing such lawsuits, including required payment of costs and attorney fees. It also would prevent a court from sealing or otherwise restricting access to a court record unless the court finds that such a restriction is justified. Rejected 177-226: R 2-211; D 174-15 (ND 128-8, SD 46-7); I 1-0. Sept. 14, 2004.

449. HR 4571. Frivolous Lawsuits/Recommit. DeLauro, D-Conn., motion to recommit the bill to the House Judiciary Committee with instructions to add language stating that the provisions of the bill are not applicable to foreign corporations that acquire a domestic corporation in a corporation repatriation transaction. Motion rejected 196-211: R 6-211; D 189-0 (ND 136-0, SD 53-0); I 1-0. Sept. 14, 2004.

450. HR 4571. Frivolous Lawsuits/Passage. Passage of the bill that would increase federal sanctions on lawyers who file meritless civil lawsuits. It would restore mandatory sanctions against those filing such lawsuits instead of giving judges the discretion to implement sanctions. The bill would strike the "safe harbor" provision of Rule 11 of the Federal Rules of Civil Procedure that allows lawyers to avoid sanctions by withdrawing or correcting questionable claims. Passed 229-174: R 213-3; D 16-171 (ND 5-131, SD 11-40); I 0-0. Sept. 14, 2004.

451. HR 5025. Fiscal 2005 Transportation-Treasury Appropriations/Previous Question. Reynolds, R-N.Y., motion to order the previous question (thus ending debate and possibility of amendment) on adoption of the rule (H Res 770) to provide for House floor consideration of the bill that would appropriate $89.8 billion in fiscal 2005 for the departments of Treasury and Transportation and related agencies. Motion agreed to 235-170: R 121-91; D 114-78 (ND 88-50, SD 26-28); I 0-1. (Subsequently, the rule was adopted by voice vote.) Sept. 14, 2004.

	447	448	449	450	451
ALABAMA					
1 *Bonner*	?	?	?	?	?
2 *Everett*	Y	N	N	Y	Y
3 *Rogers*	Y	N	N	Y	N
4 *Aderholt*	Y	N	N	Y	N
5 Cramer	Y	N	Y	Y	Y
6 *Bachus*	?	N	N	Y	Y
7 Davis	Y	Y	Y	N	Y
ALASKA					
AL *Young*	Y	N	N	Y	Y
ARIZONA					
1 *Renzi*	Y	N	N	Y	N
2 *Franks*	Y	N	N	Y	Y
3 *Shadegg*	Y	N	N	Y	Y
4 Pastor	Y	Y	Y	N	Y
5 *Hayworth*	Y	N	N	Y	N
6 *Flake*	Y	N	N	Y	Y
7 Grijalva	Y	Y	Y	N	Y
8 *Kolbe*	Y	N	N	Y	Y
ARKANSAS					
1 Berry	Y	Y	Y	N	N
2 Snyder	Y	N	Y	N	N
3 *Boozman*	Y	N	N	Y	N
4 Ross	Y	Y	Y	N	N
CALIFORNIA					
1 Thompson	Y	Y	Y	N	Y
2 *Herger*	Y	N	N	Y	Y
3 *Ose*	Y	N	N	Y	N
4 *Doolittle*	Y	N	N	N	Y
5 Matsui	Y	Y	Y	N	Y
6 Woolsey	Y	Y	Y	N	Y
7 Miller, George	Y	Y	Y	N	Y
8 Pelosi	Y	Y	Y	N	Y
9 Lee	Y	Y	Y	N	Y
10 Tauscher	Y	Y	Y	N	Y
11 *Pombo*	Y	N	N	Y	Y
12 Lantos	Y	Y	Y	N	Y
13 Stark	N	Y	Y	N	Y
14 Eshoo	Y	Y	Y	N	Y
15 Honda	Y	Y	Y	N	Y
16 Lofgren	N	N	Y	N	N
17 Farr	Y	Y	Y	N	Y
18 Cardoza	Y	Y	Y	Y	N
19 *Radanovich*	Y	?	N	Y	Y
20 Dooley	Y	Y	Y	N	Y
21 *Nunes*	Y	N	N	Y	Y
22 *Thomas*	Y	N	N	Y	Y
23 Capps	Y	Y	Y	N	N
24 *Gallegly*	Y	N	N	Y	Y
25 *McKeon*	Y	N	N	Y	Y
26 *Dreier*	Y	N	N	Y	Y
27 Sherman	Y	Y	Y	N	Y
28 Berman	Y	N	Y	N	Y
29 Schiff	Y	Y	Y	N	Y
30 Waxman	Y	Y	Y	N	Y
31 Becerra	Y	Y	Y	N	N
32 Solis	Y	Y	Y	N	Y
33 Watson	Y	Y	Y	N	Y
34 Roybal-Allard	Y	Y	Y	N	Y
35 Waters	N	Y	Y	N	Y
36 Harman	Y	Y	Y	N	Y

	447	448	449	450	451
37 Millender-McD.	Y	Y	Y	N	Y
38 Napolitano	Y	Y	Y	N	N
39 Sánchez, Linda	Y	Y	Y	N	N
40 *Royce*	Y	N	N	Y	N
41 *Lewis*	Y	N	N	Y	Y
42 *Miller, Gary*	Y	N	N	Y	Y
43 Baca	Y	Y	Y	N	Y
44 *Calvert*	Y	N	N	Y	Y
45 *Bono*	Y	N	N	Y	Y
46 *Rohrabacher*	Y	N	N	Y	Y
47 Sanchez, Loretta	Y	Y	Y	N	N
48 *Cox*	Y	N	N	Y	Y
49 *Issa*	+	N	N	Y	Y
50 *Cunningham*	Y	N	N	Y	Y
51 Filner	Y	Y	Y	N	N
52 *Hunter*	?	N	N	Y	Y
53 Davis	Y	Y	Y	N	N
COLORADO					
1 DeGette	Y	Y	Y	N	N
2 Udall	Y	Y	Y	N	N
3 *McInnis*	?	?	?	?	?
4 *Musgrave*	Y	N	N	Y	N
5 *Hefley*	Y	N	N	Y	Y
6 *Tancredo*	Y	N	N	Y	N
7 *Beauprez*	?	N	N	Y	N
CONNECTICUT					
1 Larson	Y	Y	Y	N	Y
2 *Simmons*	Y	N	N	Y	N
3 DeLauro	Y	Y	Y	N	Y
4 *Shays*	Y	N	N	Y	N
5 *Johnson*	Y	N	N	Y	N
DELAWARE					
AL *Castle*	Y	N	N	Y	N
FLORIDA					
1 *Miller, J.*	Y	?	?	?	?
2 Boyd	Y	Y	Y	N	N
3 Brown	Y	Y	Y	N	Y
4 *Crenshaw*	Y	N	N	Y	Y
5 *Brown-Waite*	Y	N	Y	N	Y
6 *Stearns*	Y	N	N	Y	N
7 *Mica*	Y	N	N	Y	Y
8 *Keller*	Y	N	N	Y	N
9 *Bilirakis*	Y	N	N	Y	Y
10 *Young*	Y	N	N	Y	Y
11 Davis	Y	Y	Y	N	Y
12 *Putnam*	Y	N	N	Y	Y
13 *Harris*	Y	N	N	Y	N
14 *Goss*	?	?	N	Y	Y
15 *Weldon*	Y	N	N	Y	Y
16 *Foley*	Y	N	N	Y	Y
17 Meek	Y	Y	Y	N	Y
18 *Ros-Lehtinen*	?	N	N	Y	Y
19 Wexler	N	Y	Y	N	Y
20 Deutsch	Y	Y	Y	N	N
21 *Diaz-Balart, L.*	Y	N	N	Y	Y
22 *Shaw*	Y	N	N	Y	Y
23 Hastings	?	?	?	?	?
24 *Feeney*	Y	N	N	Y	Y
25 *Diaz-Balart, M.*	?	N	N	Y	Y
GEORGIA					
1 *Kingston*	Y	N	N	Y	Y
2 Bishop	Y	Y	Y	N	Y
3 Marshall	Y	?	?	?	N
4 Majette	Y	Y	Y	N	N
5 Lewis	Y	Y	Y	N	Y
6 *Isakson*	Y	N	N	Y	N
7 *Linder*	Y	N	N	Y	Y
8 *Collins*	Y	N	N	Y	Y
9 *Norwood*	Y	N	N	Y	Y
10 *Deal*	Y	N	Y	N	Y
11 *Gingrey*	Y	N	N	Y	Y
12 *Burns*	Y	N	N	Y	N
13 Scott	Y	Y	Y	Y	Y
HAWAII					
1 Abercrombie	?	Y	Y	N	Y
2 Case	Y	Y	Y	N	Y
IDAHO					
1 *Otter*	Y	N	N	Y	Y
2 *Simpson*	Y	N	N	Y	Y
ILLINOIS					
1 Rush	Y	Y	Y	N	Y
2 Jackson	Y	Y	Y	N	Y
3 Lipinski	Y	Y	Y	N	Y
4 Gutierrez	Y	Y	Y	N	Y
5 Emanuel	Y	Y	Y	N	Y
6 *Hyde*	Y	N	N	Y	Y

ND Northern Democrats SD Southern Democrats

	447	448	449	450	451
7 Davis	Y	Y	Y	N	Y
8 *Crane*	Y	Y	N	N	Y
9 Schakowsky	Y	Y	Y	N	Y
10 *Kirk*	Y	Y	N	Y	N
11 *Weller*	Y	N	Y	Y	N
12 Costello	Y	Y	N	N	N
13 *Biggert*	Y	N	Y	Y	Y
14 Hastert					
15 Johnson	Y	Y	Y	Y	Y
16 *Manzullo*	N	N	N	Y	N
17 Evans	Y	Y	Y	N	N
18 *LaHood*	Y	Y	Y	Y	Y
19 *Shimkus*	Y	N	N	Y	N
INDIANA					
1 Visclosky	Y	Y	Y	N	Y
2 *Chocola*	Y	N	Y	Y	N
3 *Souder*	Y	N	Y	Y	N
4 *Buyer*	Y	N	Y	Y	Y
5 *Burton*	Y	N	Y	Y	?
6 *Pence*	Y	N	Y	Y	N
7 Carson	Y	Y	Y	N	N
8 *Hostettler*	Y	N	Y	Y	N
9 Hill	Y	Y	Y	N	N
IOWA					
1 *Nussle*	Y	N	N	Y	N
2 *Leach*	Y	N	N	Y	Y
3 Boswell	Y	Y	Y	N	N
4 *Latham*	Y	N	N	Y	N
5 *King*	Y	N	N	Y	Y
KANSAS					
1 *Moran*	Y	N	N	Y	N
2 *Ryun*	Y	N	N	Y	N
3 Moore	Y	Y	Y	N	N
4 *Tiahrt*	Y	N	N	Y	N
KENTUCKY					
1 *Whitfield*	?	?	?	?	?
2 *Lewis*	Y	N	N	Y	N
3 *Northup*	Y	N	Y	Y	N
4 Lucas	Y	N	Y	N	N
5 *Rogers*	?	N	N	Y	Y
6 Chandler	Y	Y	Y	N	N
LOUISIANA					
1 *Vitter*	Y	N	N	Y	N
2 Jefferson	Y	Y	Y	N	Y
3 *Tauzin*	?	?	?	?	?
4 *McCrery*	Y	N	N	Y	N
5 *Alexander*	Y	N	N	Y	N
6 *Baker*	Y	N	N	Y	?
7 John	Y	Y	Y	?	N
MAINE					
1 Allen	Y	N	Y	N	N
2 Michaud	Y	Y	Y	N	N
MARYLAND					
1 *Gilchrest*	Y	N	N	Y	Y
2 Ruppersberger	Y	Y	Y	N	Y
3 Cardin	Y	Y	Y	N	Y
4 Wynn	Y	Y	Y	N	Y
5 Hoyer	Y	Y	Y	N	Y
6 *Bartlett*	Y	N	N	Y	N
7 Cummings	Y	Y	Y	N	Y
8 Van Hollen	Y	Y	Y	N	Y
MASSACHUSETTS					
1 Olver	Y	Y	Y	N	Y
2 Neal	Y	Y	Y	N	Y
3 McGovern	Y	Y	Y	N	Y
4 Frank	Y	Y	Y	N	Y
5 Meehan	Y	Y	Y	N	Y
6 Tierney	Y	Y	Y	N	Y
7 Markey	N	N	Y	N	Y
8 Capuano	Y	Y	Y	N	Y
9 Lynch	Y	Y	Y	N	N
10 Delahunt	Y	Y	Y	N	Y
MICHIGAN					
1 Stupak	Y	Y	Y	N	N
2 *Hoekstra*	Y	N	N	Y	N
3 *Ehlers*	Y	N	N	Y	N
4 *Camp*	Y	N	N	Y	Y
5 Kildee	Y	Y	Y	N	N
6 *Upton*	Y	N	N	Y	Y
7 *Smith*	Y	N	N	Y	N
8 *Rogers*	Y	N	N	Y	N
9 *Knollenberg*	Y	N	N	Y	N
10 *Miller*	Y	N	N	Y	N
11 *McCotter*	Y	N	N	Y	N
12 Levin	Y	Y	Y	N	Y

	447	448	449	450	451
13 Kilpatrick	Y	Y	Y	N	Y
14 Conyers	?	?	?	?	?
15 Dingell	Y	Y	Y	N	Y
MINNESOTA					
1 *Gutknecht*	Y	N	N	Y	Y
2 *Kline*	Y	N	N	Y	Y
3 *Ramstad*	Y	N	N	Y	N
4 McCollum	Y	Y	Y	N	Y
5 Sabo	Y	Y	Y	N	Y
6 *Kennedy*	Y	N	N	Y	N
7 Peterson	N	Y	Y	N	Y
8 Oberstar	Y	Y	Y	N	Y
MISSISSIPPI					
1 *Wicker*	Y	N	N	Y	Y
2 Thompson	Y	Y	Y	N	Y
3 *Pickering*	Y	N	N	Y	Y
4 Taylor	Y	N	Y	Y	N
MISSOURI					
1 Clay	?	Y	Y	N	Y
2 *Akin*	Y	N	N	Y	Y
3 Gephardt	?	?	?	?	?
4 Skelton	Y	Y	Y	N	Y
5 McCarthy	Y	Y	Y	N	Y
6 *Graves*	Y	N	N	Y	N
7 *Blunt*	Y	N	N	Y	N
8 *Emerson*	Y	N	N	Y	N
9 *Hulshof*	Y	N	N	Y	N
MONTANA					
AL *Rehberg*	Y	N	N	Y	Y
NEBRASKA					
1 Vacant					
2 *Terry*	N	N	N	Y	N
3 *Osborne*	Y	N	N	Y	Y
NEVADA					
1 Berkley	Y	Y	Y	N	N
2 *Gibbons*	Y	N	N	Y	N
3 *Porter*	Y	N	Y	Y	N
NEW HAMPSHIRE					
1 *Bradley*	Y	N	N	Y	N
2 *Bass*	Y	N	N	Y	Y
NEW JERSEY					
1 Andrews	Y	N	Y	N	Y
2 *LoBiondo*	Y	N	N	Y	N
3 *Saxton*	Y	N	N	Y	Y
4 *Smith*	Y	N	N	Y	Y
5 *Garrett*	Y	N	N	Y	Y
6 Pallone	Y	Y	Y	N	Y
7 *Ferguson*	Y	N	Y	N	Y
8 Pascrell	Y	Y	Y	N	Y
9 Rothman	Y	Y	Y	N	Y
10 Payne	Y	Y	Y	N	Y
11 *Frelinghuysen*	Y	N	N	?	Y
12 Holt	Y	Y	Y	N	N
13 Menendez	Y	Y	Y	N	Y
NEW MEXICO					
1 *Wilson*	Y	N	N	Y	N
2 *Pearce*	Y	N	N	Y	N
3 Udall	Y	Y	Y	N	N
NEW YORK					
1 Bishop	Y	Y	Y	N	N
2 Israel	Y	Y	Y	N	Y
3 *King*	Y	N	N	Y	N
4 McCarthy	Y	Y	Y	N	Y
5 Ackerman	Y	?	?	?	?
6 Meeks	Y	Y	Y	N	Y
7 Crowley	?	?	?	?	?
8 Nadler	N	Y	Y	N	Y
9 Weiner	Y	Y	Y	N	Y
10 Towns	?	?	?	?	?
11 Owens	?	?	?	?	?
12 Velázquez	?	?	?	?	Y
13 *Fossella*	Y	N	N	Y	N
14 Maloney	Y	Y	Y	N	Y
15 Rangel	Y	Y	Y	N	Y
16 Serrano	?	?	?	?	?
17 Engel	?	?	?	?	?
18 Lowey	Y	Y	Y	N	Y
19 *Kelly*	Y	N	N	Y	N
20 *Sweeney*	Y	N	N	Y	N
21 McNulty	Y	Y	Y	N	Y
22 Hinchey	N	Y	Y	N	Y
23 *McHugh*	Y	N	N	Y	N
24 *Boehlert*	?	?	?	?	?
25 Walsh	Y	N	N	Y	N

	447	448	449	450	451
26 *Reynolds*	Y	N	N	Y	Y
27 *Quinn*	Y	N	N	Y	Y
28 Slaughter	+	+	+	-	-
29 Houghton	?	N	N	Y	Y
NORTH CAROLINA					
1 Butterfield	Y	Y	Y	N	Y
2 Etheridge	Y	Y	Y	N	N
3 *Jones*	Y	N	N	Y	N
4 Price	Y	Y	Y	N	N
5 *Burr*	Y	N	N	Y	N
6 *Coble*	Y	N	N	Y	N
7 McIntyre	Y	N	N	Y	N
8 *Hayes*	Y	N	N	Y	N
9 *Myrick*	Y	N	N	Y	N
10 *Ballenger*	?	?	?	?	?
11 *Taylor*	Y	Y	N	Y	N
12 Watt	Y	Y	Y	N	Y
13 Miller	Y	Y	Y	N	N
NORTH DAKOTA					
AL Pomeroy	Y	Y	Y	N	N
OHIO					
1 *Chabot*	Y	N	N	Y	N
2 *Portman*	Y	N	N	Y	Y
3 *Turner*	Y	N	N	Y	Y
4 *Oxley*	Y	N	N	Y	Y
5 *Gillmor*	Y	N	N	Y	Y
6 Strickland	Y	Y	Y	N	N
7 *Hobson*	Y	N	N	Y	Y
8 *Boehner*	Y	N	N	Y	Y
9 Kaptur	Y	Y	Y	N	N
10 Kucinich	Y	Y	Y	N	N
11 Jones	Y	Y	Y	N	N
12 *Tiberi*	Y	N	N	Y	Y
13 Brown	Y	Y	Y	N	N
14 *LaTourette*	Y	N	N	Y	Y
15 *Pryce*	Y	N	N	Y	Y
16 *Regula*	Y	N	N	Y	Y
17 Ryan	N	Y	Y	N	N
18 *Ney*	Y	N	N	Y	Y
OKLAHOMA					
1 *Sullivan*	Y	N	N	Y	N
2 Carson	Y	Y	Y	N	N
3 *Lucas*	Y	N	N	Y	Y
4 *Cole*	Y	N	N	Y	Y
5 *Istook*	Y	?	N	Y	Y
OREGON					
1 Wu	Y	Y	Y	N	N
2 *Walden*	Y	N	N	Y	N
3 Blumenauer	Y	Y	Y	N	Y
4 DeFazio	Y	Y	Y	N	N
5 Hooley	Y	Y	Y	N	N
PENNSYLVANIA					
1 Brady	Y	Y	Y	N	Y
2 Fattah	Y	Y	Y	N	Y
3 *English*	Y	N	N	Y	N
4 *Hart*	Y	N	N	Y	N
5 *Peterson*	Y	N	N	Y	N
6 *Gerlach*	Y	N	N	Y	N
7 *Weldon*	Y	N	N	Y	N
8 *Greenwood*	?	?	N	Y	N
9 *Shuster, Bill*	Y	N	N	Y	N
10 *Sherwood*	Y	N	N	Y	?
11 Kanjorski	Y	Y	Y	N	Y
12 Murtha	Y	Y	Y	N	Y
13 Hoeffel	?	?	N	Y	Y
14 Doyle	Y	Y	Y	N	Y
15 *Toomey*	Y	N	N	Y	N
16 *Pitts*	Y	N	N	Y	N
17 Holden	Y	Y	Y	N	N
18 *Murphy*	Y	N	N	Y	N
19 *Platts*	Y	N	N	Y	N
RHODE ISLAND					
1 Kennedy	+	+	+	-	Y
2 Langevin	?	?	?	?	?
SOUTH CAROLINA					
1 *Brown*	Y	N	N	Y	Y
2 *Wilson*	Y	N	N	Y	Y
3 *Barrett*	Y	N	N	Y	N
4 *DeMint*	Y	N	N	Y	N
5 Spratt	Y	Y	Y	N	Y
6 Clyburn	Y	Y	Y	N	Y
SOUTH DAKOTA					
AL Herseth	Y	Y	Y	N	N

	447	448	449	450	451
TENNESSEE					
1 *Jenkins*	Y	N	N	Y	N
2 *Duncan*	Y	N	N	Y	N
3 *Wamp*	Y	N	N	Y	N
4 *Davis*	Y	N	Y	Y	N
5 Cooper	Y	Y	Y	N	N
6 Gordon	Y	Y	Y	N	N
7 *Blackburn*	?	?	?	?	?
8 Tanner	Y	N	N	Y	N
9 Ford	Y	Y	Y	N	N
TEXAS					
1 Sandlin	Y	Y	Y	N	N
2 Turner	Y	N	Y	Y	N
3 *Johnson, Sam*	Y	N	N	Y	N
4 *Hall*	Y	N	N	Y	N
5 *Hensarling*	Y	N	N	Y	N
6 *Barton*	Y	N	N	Y	N
7 *Culberson*	Y	N	N	Y	N
8 *Brady*	Y	N	N	Y	N
9 Lampson	Y	Y	Y	N	N
10 Doggett	Y	Y	Y	N	N
11 Edwards	Y	Y	Y	N	N
12 *Granger*	Y	N	N	Y	N
13 *Thornberry*	N	N	N	Y	N
14 *Paul*	N	N	N	Y	N
15 Hinojosa	Y	Y	Y	N	N
16 Reyes	Y	Y	Y	N	N
17 Stenholm	Y	N	N	Y	Y
18 Jackson-Lee	Y	N	Y	N	Y
19 *Neugebauer*	Y	N	N	Y	N
20 Gonzalez	Y	Y	Y	N	N
21 *Smith*	Y	N	N	Y	N
22 *DeLay*	Y	N	N	Y	N
23 *Bonilla*	Y	N	N	Y	N
24 Frost	Y	Y	Y	N	N
25 Bell	Y	Y	Y	N	N
26 *Burgess*	Y	N	N	Y	N
27 Ortiz	Y	Y	Y	N	N
28 Rodriguez	Y	Y	Y	N	N
29 Green	Y	Y	Y	N	N
30 Johnson, E.B.	?	?	?	?	?
31 *Carter*	Y	N	N	Y	N
32 *Sessions*	Y	N	N	Y	N
UTAH					
1 *Bishop*	Y	N	N	Y	N
2 Matheson	Y	N	Y	Y	N
3 *Cannon*	?	?	?	?	?
VERMONT					
AL *Sanders*	Y	Y	Y	?	N
VIRGINIA					
1 *Davis, Jo Ann*	Y	N	N	Y	N
2 *Schrock*	?	?	?	?	?
3 Scott	Y	N	N	Y	Y
4 *Forbes*	Y	N	N	Y	N
5 *Goode*	Y	N	Y	N	N
6 *Goodlatte*	Y	N	N	Y	N
7 *Cantor*	Y	N	N	Y	N
8 Moran	Y	Y	Y	N	Y
9 Boucher	Y	Y	Y	N	N
10 *Wolf*	Y	N	N	Y	Y
11 *Davis, T.*	Y	N	N	Y	N
WASHINGTON					
1 Inslee	Y	Y	Y	N	N
2 Larsen	Y	Y	Y	N	N
3 Baird	Y	Y	Y	N	N
4 *Hastings*	Y	N	N	Y	N
5 *Nethercutt*	Y	N	N	Y	?
6 Dicks	Y	Y	Y	N	N
7 McDermott	Y	Y	Y	N	Y
8 *Dunn*	Y	N	N	Y	N
9 Smith	Y	Y	Y	N	N
WEST VIRGINIA					
1 Mollohan	Y	N	N	Y	N
2 *Capito*	Y	N	N	Y	N
3 Rahall	Y	Y	Y	N	N
WISCONSIN					
1 *Ryan*	Y	N	N	Y	N
2 Baldwin	Y	Y	Y	N	Y
3 Kind	Y	Y	Y	N	N
4 Kleczka	?	?	?	?	?
5 *Sensenbrenner*	Y	N	N	Y	N
6 *Petri*	Y	N	N	Y	N
7 Obey	Y	Y	Y	N	N
8 *Green*	Y	N	N	Y	N
WYOMING					
AL *Cubin*	Y	N	N	Y	Y

Southern states - Ala., Ark., Fla., Ga., Ky., La., Miss., N.C., Okla., S.C., Tenn., Texas, Va.

452. HR 5025. Fiscal 2005 Transportation-Treasury Appropriations/ Mexican Identification Cards. Oxley, R-Ohio, amendment that would strike language that would prohibit the Treasury Department from using funds in the bill to implement regulations allowing financial institutions to accept Mexican "matricula consular" identification documents. Adopted 222-177: R 49-161; D 172-16 (ND 128-7, SD 44-9); I 1-0. A "yea" was a vote in support of the president's position. Sept. 14, 2004.

453. HR 5025. Fiscal 2005 Transportation-Treasury Appropriations/ Federal Contracts for Caribbean Companies. DeLauro, D-Conn., amendment that would add a section prohibiting the use of the funds in the bill to enter into contracts with companies located in Bermuda, Barbados, the Cayman Islands, Antigua or Panama, parts of the Caribbean commonly used as tax havens. Rejected 189-211: R 15-196; D 173-15 (ND 129-6, SD 44-9); I 1-0. Sept. 14, 2004.

454. HR 5025. Fiscal 2005 Transportation-Treasury Appropriations/ Financial Crimes Enforcement Network. Kelly, R-N.Y., amendment that would increase funding for salaries and expenses in the Financial Crimes Enforcement Network by $25.5 million, to be offset by reductions in General Services Administrations accounts for space rentals and building operations. Adopted 360-37: R 180-29; D 179-8 (ND 127-7, SD 52-1); I 1-0. Sept. 14, 2004.

455. HR 5025. Fiscal 2005 Transportation-Treasury Appropriations/ Discretionary Spending Reduction. Hefley, R-Colo., amendment that would reduce the discretionary spending in the bill by 1 percent. Rejected 69-333: R 66-142; D 3-190 (ND 1-139, SD 2-51); I 0-1. Sept. 15, 2004.

456. HR 5025. Fiscal 2005 Transportation-Treasury Appropriations/ Health Accounts. Moran, D-Va., amendment that would prohibit the use of funds in the bill to implement or establish health savings or reimbursement accounts under the Federal Employees Health Benefits Program. Rejected 181-223: R 7-204; D 173-19 (ND 128-11, SD 45-8); I 1-0. Sept. 15, 2004.

Key

Y	Voted for (yea).
#	Paired for.
+	Announced for.
N	Voted against (nay).
X	Paired against.
–	Announced against.
P	Voted "present."
C	Voted "present" to avoid possible conflict of interest.
?	Did not vote or otherwise make a position known.

Democrats · **Republicans** · *Independents*

	452	453	454	455	456
ALABAMA					
1 *Bonner*	?	?	?	?	?
2 *Everett*	?	?	?	?	?
3 *Rogers*	N	N	Y	N	N
4 *Aderholt*	N	N	N	N	N
5 Cramer	N	N	Y	N	N
6 *Bachus*	Y	N	Y	?	N
7 Davis	Y	Y	Y	N	Y
ALASKA					
AL *Young*	?	?	?	N	N
ARIZONA					
1 *Renzi*	N	N	Y	N	N
2 *Franks*	N	N	Y	Y	N
3 *Shadegg*	N	N	Y	Y	N
4 Pastor	Y	Y	N	N	Y
5 *Hayworth*	N	N	Y	N	Y
6 *Flake*	Y	N	Y	Y	N
7 Grijalva	Y	Y	Y	N	Y
8 *Kolbe*	Y	N	Y	N	N
ARKANSAS					
1 Berry	Y	Y	Y	N	Y
2 Snyder	Y	Y	Y	N	Y
3 *Boozman*	N	N	Y	N	N
4 Ross	Y	Y	Y	N	Y
CALIFORNIA					
1 Thompson	Y	Y	Y	N	Y
2 *Herger*	N	N	Y	Y	N
3 *Ose*	Y	N	Y	N	N
4 *Doolittle*	N	N	Y	N	N
5 Matsui	Y	Y	?	N	Y
6 Woolsey	Y	Y	Y	N	Y
7 Miller, George	Y	Y	Y	N	Y
8 Pelosi	Y	Y	Y	N	Y
9 Lee	Y	Y	Y	N	Y
10 Tauscher	Y	Y	Y	N	Y
11 *Pombo*	N	N	Y	N	N
12 Lantos	Y	Y	Y	N	Y
13 Stark	Y	Y	Y	N	Y
14 Eshoo	Y	Y	Y	N	Y
15 Honda	Y	Y	Y	N	Y
16 Lofgren	Y	Y	Y	N	Y
17 Farr	Y	Y	Y	N	Y
18 Cardoza	Y	Y	Y	N	N
19 *Radanovich*	N	N	Y	N	N
20 Dooley	Y	N	Y	N	N
21 *Nunes*	N	N	Y	?	N
22 *Thomas*	N	N	Y	N	N
23 Capps	Y	Y	Y	N	Y
24 *Gallegly*	N	N	Y	?	?
25 *McKeon*	N	N	Y	N	N
26 *Dreier*	N	N	Y	N	N
27 Sherman	Y	Y	Y	N	Y
28 Berman	Y	Y	Y	N	Y
29 Schiff	Y	Y	Y	N	Y
30 Waxman	Y	Y	Y	N	Y
31 Becerra	Y	Y	Y	N	Y
32 Solis	Y	Y	Y	N	Y
33 Watson	Y	Y	Y	N	Y
34 Roybal-Allard	Y	Y	Y	N	Y
35 Waters	Y	N	N	N	Y
36 Harman	Y	Y	Y	N	Y

	452	453	454	455	456
37 Millender-McD.	Y	Y	Y	N	Y
38 Napolitano	Y	Y	Y	N	Y
39 Sánchez, Linda	Y	Y	Y	N	Y
40 *Royce*	N	Y	Y	Y	N
41 *Lewis*	N	N	N	N	N
42 *Miller, Gary*	N	N	Y	N	N
43 Baca	Y	Y	Y	N	Y
44 *Calvert*	N	N	Y	N	N
45 *Bono*	N	N	Y	N	N
46 *Rohrabacher*	N	N	Y	Y	N
47 Sanchez, Loretta	Y	Y	Y	N	Y
48 *Cox*	N	N	Y	Y	N
49 *Issa*	N	N	Y	N	N
50 *Cunningham*	N	N	N	N	N
51 Filner	Y	Y	Y	N	Y
52 *Hunter*	N	Y	Y	N	N
53 Davis	Y	Y	Y	N	Y
COLORADO					
1 DeGette	Y	Y	Y	N	Y
2 Udall	Y	Y	Y	N	Y
3 *McInnis*	?	?	?	?	?
4 *Musgrave*	N	N	Y	N	N
5 *Hefley*	N	N	Y	N	N
6 *Tancredo*	N	N	Y	N	N
7 *Beauprez*	Y	N	Y	N	Y
CONNECTICUT					
1 Larson	Y	Y	Y	N	Y
2 *Simmons*	Y	Y	Y	N	Y
3 DeLauro	Y	Y	Y	N	Y
4 *Shays*	N	N	Y	N	N
5 *Johnson*	N	N	Y	N	N
DELAWARE					
AL *Castle*	Y	N	Y	N	N
FLORIDA					
1 *Miller, J.*	?	?	?	?	?
2 Boyd	N	N	Y	N	N
3 Brown	Y	Y	Y	N	Y
4 *Crenshaw*	N	N	Y	N	N
5 *Brown-Waite*	N	N	Y	N	N
6 *Stearns*	N	Y	Y	Y	N
7 *Mica*	N	N	Y	N	N
8 *Keller*	N	N	Y	N	N
9 *Bilirakis*	N	N	Y	N	N
10 *Young*	N	N	Y	N	N
11 Davis	Y	Y	Y	N	Y
12 *Putnam*	N	N	Y	N	N
13 *Harris*	N	N	Y	N	N
14 *Goss*	?	?	?	N	N
15 *Weldon*	N	N	Y	N	N
16 *Foley*	N	N	Y	N	N
17 Meek	Y	Y	Y	N	Y
18 *Ros-Lehtinen*	Y	N	Y	N	N
19 Wexler	Y	Y	Y	N	Y
20 Deutsch	Y	Y	Y	N	Y
21 *Diaz-Balart, L.*	Y	N	Y	N	N
22 *Shaw*	N	N	Y	N	N
23 Hastings	Y	Y	Y	N	Y
24 *Feeney*	N	N	Y	N	N
25 *Diaz-Balart, M.*	Y	N	Y	Y	N
GEORGIA					
1 *Kingston*	N	N	N	N	N
2 Bishop	Y	Y	Y	N	N
3 Marshall	N	Y	Y	N	N
4 Majette	Y	Y	Y	N	Y
5 Lewis	Y	Y	Y	N	Y
6 *Isakson*	N	N	Y	N	N
7 *Linder*	N	N	Y	N	N
8 *Collins*	N	N	N	N	N
9 *Norwood*	N	N	N	Y	N
10 *Deal*	N	N	N	Y	?
11 *Gingrey*	N	N	Y	N	N
12 *Burns*	N	N	Y	N	N
13 Scott	Y	Y	Y	N	Y
HAWAII					
1 Abercrombie	Y	Y	Y	N	Y
2 Case	N	N	Y	N	N
IDAHO					
1 *Otter*	N	N	Y	N	Y
2 *Simpson*	N	N	Y	N	N
ILLINOIS					
1 Rush	Y	Y	Y	N	Y
2 Jackson	Y	Y	Y	N	Y
3 Lipinski	N	N	Y	N	N
4 Gutierrez	Y	Y	Y	N	Y
5 Emanuel	Y	Y	Y	N	Y
6 *Hyde*	N	N	Y	N	N

ND Northern Democrats   SD Southern Democrats

	452	453	454	455	456
7 Davis	Y	Y	Y	N	Y
8 *Crane*	N	N	Y	N	N
9 Schakowsky	Y	Y	Y	N	Y
10 *Kirk*	N	N	Y	N	N
11 *Weller*	Y	N	Y	N	N
12 Costello	Y	N	Y	N	N
13 *Biggert*	Y	N	Y	N	N
14 *Hastert*					
15 *Johnson*	N	N	N	N	N
16 *Manzullo*	N	N	Y	N	N
17 Evans	Y	N	Y	N	Y
18 *LaHood*	N	N	Y	N	N
19 *Shimkus*	N	N	Y	N	N
INDIANA					
1 Visclosky	N	Y	N	N	Y
2 *Chocola*	N	N	Y	N	N
3 *Souder*	N	N	Y	N	N
4 *Buyer*	N	N	Y	N	N
5 *Burton*	N	N	N	N	N
6 *Pence*	N	N	Y	N	N
7 Carson	Y	Y	Y	N	Y
8 *Hostettler*	N	N	N	N	N
9 Hill	Y	Y	Y	N	Y
IOWA					
1 *Nussle*	Y	N	Y	N	N
2 *Leach*	Y	N	Y	N	N
3 Boswell	Y	Y	Y	N	Y
4 *Latham*	Y	N	Y	N	N
5 King	N	N	N	N	N
KANSAS					
1 *Moran*	N	N	Y	N	N
2 *Ryun*	N	N	Y	N	N
3 Moore	Y	Y	Y	N	Y
4 *Tiahrt*	N	N	Y	N	N
KENTUCKY					
1 *Whitfield*	N	N	Y	N	N
2 *Lewis*	N	N	Y	N	N
3 *Northup*	N	N	Y	N	N
4 Lucas	Y	Y	Y	N	N
5 *Rogers*	N	N	Y	N	N
6 Chandler	N	Y	Y	N	Y
LOUISIANA					
1 *Vitter*	N	N	Y	N	N
2 Jefferson	Y	Y	Y	N	Y
3 *Tauzin*	?	?	?	?	?
4 *McCrery*	Y	N	Y	N	N
5 *Alexander*	N	N	Y	?	?
6 *Baker*	?	?	?	?	?
7 John	?	?	?	?	?
MAINE					
1 Allen	Y	Y	Y	N	Y
2 Michaud	Y	Y	Y	N	Y
MARYLAND					
1 *Gilchrest*	Y	N	Y	N	N
2 Ruppersberger	Y	Y	Y	N	Y
3 Cardin	Y	Y	Y	N	Y
4 Wynn	Y	Y	Y	N	Y
5 Hoyer	Y	Y	Y	N	Y
6 *Bartlett*	N	N	Y	N	Y
7 Cummings	Y	Y	Y	N	Y
8 Van Hollen	Y	Y	Y	N	Y
MASSACHUSETTS					
1 Olver	Y	Y	N	N	Y
2 Neal	Y	Y	Y	N	Y
3 McGovern	Y	Y	Y	N	Y
4 Frank	Y	Y	Y	N	Y
5 Meehan	Y	Y	Y	N	Y
6 Tierney	Y	Y	Y	N	Y
7 Markey	Y	Y	Y	N	Y
8 Capuano	Y	Y	Y	N	Y
9 Lynch	Y	Y	Y	N	Y
10 Delahunt	Y	Y	Y	N	Y
MICHIGAN					
1 Stupak	Y	Y	Y	N	Y
2 *Hoekstra*	N	N	Y	Y	N
3 *Ehlers*	Y	N	Y	N	N
4 *Camp*	N	N	Y	N	N
5 Kildee	Y	Y	Y	N	Y
6 *Upton*	N	N	Y	N	N
7 *Smith*	N	N	N	Y	N
8 *Rogers*	?	N	Y	Y	N
9 *Knollenberg*	N	N	N	N	N
10 *Miller*	N	N	Y	N	N
11 *McCotter*	N	N	Y	N	N
12 Levin	Y	Y	Y	N	Y

	452	453	454	455	456
13 Kilpatrick	Y	Y	Y	N	Y
14 Conyers	?	?	?	?	?
15 Dingell	Y	Y	Y	N	Y
MINNESOTA					
1 *Gutknecht*	N	N	Y	Y	N
2 *Kline*	N	N	Y	N	N
3 *Ramstad*	N	N	Y	N	N
4 McCollum	Y	Y	Y	N	Y
5 Sabo	Y	Y	Y	N	Y
6 *Kennedy*	Y	N	Y	N	N
7 Peterson	N	Y	Y	N	N
8 Oberstar	Y	Y	Y	N	Y
MISSISSIPPI					
1 *Wicker*	N	N	N	N	N
2 Thompson	Y	Y	Y	N	Y
3 *Pickering*	Y	N	N	N	N
4 Taylor	?	?	?	?	?
MISSOURI					
1 Clay	?	?	?	N	Y
2 *Akin*	N	N	Y	N	N
3 Gephardt	?	?	?	N	Y
4 Skelton	Y	N	Y	N	Y
5 McCarthy	Y	Y	Y	N	Y
6 *Graves*	N	N	Y	N	N
7 *Blunt*	Y	N	Y	N	N
8 *Emerson*	N	N	Y	N	N
9 *Hulshof*	Y	N	Y	N	N
MONTANA					
AL *Rehberg*	N	N	Y	N	N
NEBRASKA					
1 Vacant					
2 *Terry*	Y	N	N	Y	N
3 *Osborne*	Y	N	Y	N	N
NEVADA					
1 Berkley	Y	Y	Y	?	?
2 *Gibbons*	N	N	Y	N	N
3 *Porter*	Y	N	Y	N	N
NEW HAMPSHIRE					
1 *Bradley*	N	Y	Y	N	N
2 *Bass*	N	Y	Y	Y	N
NEW JERSEY					
1 Andrews	Y	Y	Y	N	Y
2 *LoBiondo*	N	Y	Y	N	Y
3 *Saxton*	N	Y	Y	N	N
4 *Smith*	N	Y	Y	N	N
5 *Garrett*	N	N	Y	?	N
6 Pallone	Y	Y	Y	N	Y
7 *Ferguson*	N	N	Y	N	N
8 Pascrell	Y	Y	Y	N	Y
9 Rothman	Y	Y	Y	N	Y
10 Payne	Y	Y	Y	N	Y
11 *Frelinghuysen*	N	N	Y	N	N
12 Holt	Y	Y	Y	N	Y
13 Menendez	Y	Y	Y	N	Y
NEW MEXICO					
1 *Wilson*	Y	N	Y	–	N
2 *Pearce*	Y	N	Y	N	N
3 Udall	Y	Y	Y	N	Y
NEW YORK					
1 Bishop	Y	Y	Y	N	Y
2 Israel	Y	Y	Y	N	Y
3 *King*	Y	Y	Y	N	Y
4 McCarthy	Y	Y	Y	N	Y
5 Ackerman	?	?	?	?	?
6 Meeks	Y	Y	Y	N	Y
7 Crowley	?	?	?	?	?
8 Nadler	Y	Y	Y	N	Y
9 Weiner	?	?	?	N	Y
10 Towns	?	?	?	N	Y
11 Owens	?	?	?	N	Y
12 Velázquez	Y	Y	Y	N	Y
13 *Fossella*	N	N	Y	N	Y
14 Maloney	Y	Y	Y	N	Y
15 Rangel	Y	Y	Y	N	Y
16 Serrano	?	?	?	?	?
17 Engel	?	?	?	?	?
18 Lowey	Y	Y	Y	N	Y
19 *Kelly*	Y	Y	Y	N	N
20 *Sweeney*	N	N	Y	N	N
21 McNulty	Y	Y	Y	N	Y
22 Hinchey	Y	Y	Y	N	Y
23 *McHugh*	N	N	Y	N	Y
24 *Boehlert*	?	?	?	?	?
25 *Walsh*	Y	Y	Y	N	N

	452	453	454	455	456
26 *Reynolds*	N	N	Y	Y	N
27 *Quinn*	Y	N	Y	N	N
28 Slaughter	+	+	+	–	+
29 Houghton	?	?	?	N	N
NORTH CAROLINA					
1 Butterfield	Y	Y	Y	N	Y
2 Etheridge	Y	N	Y	N	Y
3 *Jones*	N	Y	N	Y	Y
4 Price	Y	N	Y	N	Y
5 *Burr*	N	N	Y	N	N
6 *Coble*	N	N	Y	N	N
7 McIntyre	N	N	Y	N	Y
8 *Hayes*	N	N	Y	N	N
9 *Myrick*	N	N	N	Y	N
10 *Ballenger*	?	?	?	?	?
11 *Taylor*	Y	Y	Y	N	N
12 Watt	Y	Y	Y	N	Y
13 Miller	Y	N	Y	N	Y
NORTH DAKOTA					
AL Pomeroy	Y	N	Y	N	N
OHIO					
1 *Chabot*	N	N	Y	N	N
2 *Portman*	N	N	Y	N	N
3 *Turner*	N	N	Y	N	N
4 *Oxley*	Y	N	Y	N	N
5 *Gillmor*	Y	N	Y	N	N
6 Strickland	Y	Y	Y	N	Y
7 *Hobson*	N	N	Y	N	N
8 *Boehner*	Y	N	Y	N	N
9 Kaptur	Y	Y	Y	Y	Y
10 Kucinich	Y	Y	Y	N	Y
11 Jones	Y	Y	Y	N	Y
12 *Tiberi*	N	N	Y	N	N
13 Brown	Y	Y	Y	N	N
14 *LaTourette*	Y	N	Y	N	N
15 *Pryce*	Y	N	Y	N	N
16 *Regula*	N	N	Y	N	N
17 Ryan	N	Y	Y	N	Y
18 *Ney*	Y	N	Y	N	N
OKLAHOMA					
1 *Sullivan*	N	N	Y	N	N
2 Carson	N	N	Y	N	Y
3 *Lucas*	Y	N	Y	N	N
4 *Cole*	N	N	Y	N	N
5 *Istook*	N	N	N	N	N
OREGON					
1 Wu	Y	Y	Y	N	Y
2 *Walden*	N	N	Y	N	N
3 Blumenauer	Y	N	Y	N	Y
4 DeFazio	N	Y	Y	N	Y
5 Hooley	Y	Y	Y	N	Y
PENNSYLVANIA					
1 Brady	Y	Y	Y	N	Y
2 Fattah	Y	Y	Y	N	Y
3 *English*	Y	N	?	N	N
4 *Hart*	Y	N	Y	N	N
5 *Peterson*	N	N	Y	N	N
6 *Gerlach*	Y	N	Y	N	N
7 *Weldon*	N	N	Y	N	N
8 *Greenwood*	N	N	Y	N	N
9 *Shuster, Bill*	N	N	Y	N	N
10 *Sherwood*	?	?	?	N	N
11 Kanjorski	Y	N	Y	N	Y
12 Murtha	?	?	?	N	Y
13 Hoeffel	Y	Y	Y	N	Y
14 Doyle	Y	Y	Y	N	Y
15 *Toomey*	Y	N	Y	N	N
16 *Pitts*	N	N	Y	N	N
17 Holden	N	N	Y	N	Y
18 *Murphy*	N	N	Y	N	N
19 *Platts*	N	N	Y	N	N
RHODE ISLAND					
1 Kennedy	Y	Y	Y	N	?
2 Langevin	?	?	?	?	?
SOUTH CAROLINA					
1 *Brown*	N	N	Y	N	N
2 *Wilson*	Y	N	Y	N	N
3 *Barrett*	N	N	Y	N	N
4 *DeMint*	N	N	Y	N	N
5 Spratt	Y	N	Y	N	Y
6 Clyburn	Y	Y	Y	N	Y
SOUTH DAKOTA					
AL Herseth	Y	Y	Y	N	Y

	452	453	454	455	456
TENNESSEE					
1 *Jenkins*	N	N	Y	Y	N
2 *Duncan*	N	N	Y	?	N
3 *Wamp*	N	N	Y	N	N
4 Davis	Y	Y	Y	Y	Y
5 Cooper	Y	N	Y	N	Y
6 Gordon	Y	N	Y	N	Y
7 *Blackburn*	N	N	Y	N	N
8 Tanner	N	N	Y	N	Y
9 Ford	Y	Y	Y	N	Y
TEXAS					
1 Sandlin	Y	Y	Y	N	Y
2 Turner	Y	Y	Y	N	Y
3 *Johnson, Sam*	N	N	N	N	N
4 *Hall*	N	N	Y	N	N
5 *Hensarling*	Y	N	Y	?	?
6 *Barton*	N	N	Y	N	N
7 *Culberson*	N	N	Y	N	N
8 *Brady*	N	N	Y	N	N
9 Lampson	Y	Y	Y	N	Y
10 Doggett	Y	Y	Y	N	Y
11 Edwards	Y	Y	Y	N	Y
12 *Granger*	N	N	Y	N	N
13 *Thornberry*	N	N	N	N	N
14 *Paul*	N	N	N	N	N
15 Hinojosa	Y	Y	Y	N	Y
16 Reyes	Y	Y	Y	N	Y
17 Stenholm	N	Y	Y	N	Y
18 Jackson-Lee	Y	Y	Y	N	Y
19 *Neugebauer*	N	N	Y	N	N
20 Gonzalez	Y	Y	Y	N	Y
21 *Smith*	N	N	Y	N	N
22 *DeLay*	N	N	Y	N	N
23 *Bonilla*	N	N	?	N	N
24 Frost	Y	Y	Y	N	Y
25 Bell	Y	Y	Y	N	Y
26 *Burgess*	N	N	Y	N	N
27 Ortiz	Y	Y	Y	N	Y
28 Rodriguez	Y	Y	Y	N	Y
29 Green	Y	Y	Y	N	Y
30 Johnson, E.B.	?	?	?	–	+
31 *Carter*	N	N	Y	N	N
32 *Sessions*	N	N	Y	N	N
UTAH					
1 *Bishop*	N	N	Y	N	N
2 Matheson	Y	Y	Y	N	N
3 *Cannon*	?	?	?	?	?
VERMONT					
AL *Sanders*	Y	Y	Y	N	Y
VIRGINIA					
1 *Davis, Jo Ann*	N	N	Y	Y	N
2 *Schrock*	?	?	?	?	?
3 Scott	Y	Y	Y	N	Y
4 *Forbes*	N	N	Y	N	N
5 *Goode*	N	Y	N	N	Y
6 *Goodlatte*	N	N	Y	N	N
7 *Cantor*	N	N	Y	N	N
8 Moran	Y	N	N	N	Y
9 Boucher	N	Y	Y	N	Y
10 *Wolf*	N	N	Y	N	Y
11 *Davis, T.*	Y	N	N	N	N
WASHINGTON					
1 Inslee	Y	Y	Y	N	Y
2 Larsen	Y	Y	Y	N	Y
3 Baird	Y	Y	Y	N	Y
4 *Hastings*	Y	N	Y	N	N
5 *Nethercutt*	?	+	+	–	–
6 Dicks	Y	Y	Y	N	Y
7 McDermott	Y	Y	Y	N	Y
8 *Dunn*	?	?	?	N	?
9 Smith	Y	Y	Y	N	Y
WEST VIRGINIA					
1 Mollohan	Y	Y	N	N	Y
2 *Capito*	N	N	Y	N	N
3 Rahall	Y	Y	Y	N	Y
WISCONSIN					
1 *Ryan*	N	N	Y	N	N
2 Baldwin	Y	Y	Y	N	Y
3 Kind	Y	Y	Y	N	Y
4 Kleczka	?	?	?	N	Y
5 *Sensenbrenner*	N	N	Y	N	N
6 *Petri*	N	N	Y	N	N
7 Obey	Y	Y	Y	?	?
8 *Green*	N	N	Y	N	N
WYOMING					
AL *Cubin*	N	N	Y	N	N

Southern states - Ala., Ark., Fla., Ga., Ky., La., Miss., N.C., Okla., S.C., Tenn., Texas, Va.

457. HR 5025. Fiscal 2005 Transportation-Treasury Appropriations/ Federal Job Outsourcing. Van Hollen, D-Md., amendment that would prohibit any funds in the bill from being used to implement a May 29, 2003, Office of Management and Budget rule streamlining the outsourcing of work by federal agencies. Adopted 210-187: R 24-184; D 185-3 (ND 139-1, SD 46-2); I 1-0. A "nay" was a vote in support of the president's position. Sept. 21, 2004.

458. HR 5025. Fiscal 2005 Transportation-Treasury Appropriations/ Pension Plan Conversion. Sanders, I-Vt., amendment that would prohibit any funds in the bill from being used to help overturn a July 31, 2003, district court ruling that determined that IBM Corp.'s conversion of its pension plan to a cash-balance plan violated the pension age-discrimination provisions of the Employee Retirement Income Security Act of 1974. Adopted 237-162: R 52-157; D 184-5 (ND 137-3, SD 47-2); I 1-0. Sept. 21, 2004.

459. HR 5025. Fiscal 2005 Transportation-Treasury Appropriations/ Health Plans. Norton, D-D.C., amendment that would prohibit any funds in the bill from being used to enter into or renew any contract for a high-deductible health plan under the Federal Employees Health Benefits Program that does not require enrollees to remain enrolled for at least three consecutive years from the date of initial enrollment. Rejected 175-224: R 7-203; D 167-21 (ND 130-9, SD 37-12); I 1-0. Sept. 21, 2004.

460. HR 5025. Fiscal 2005 Transportation-Treasury Appropriations/ Cuban Travel Restrictions. Davis, D-Fla., amendment that would prohibit the use of funds in the bill to implement, administer or enforce new administration restrictions on travel to Cuba that allow individuals to visit immediate relatives there once every three years for a maximum of two consecutive weeks. Adopted 225-174: R 39-170; D 185-4 (ND 139-1, SD 46-3); I 1-0. A "nay" was a vote in support of the president's position. Sept. 21, 2004.

461. HR 5025. Fiscal 2005 Transportation-Treasury Appropriations/ Economic Embargo on Cuba. Rangel, D-N.Y., amendment that would add a section prohibiting the use of funds to implement, administer or enforce the economic embargo on Cuba. Rejected 188-225: R 25-188; D 162-37 (ND 125-20, SD 37-17); I 1-0. A "nay" was a vote in support of the president's position. Sept. 22, 2004.

462. HR 5025. Fiscal 2005 Transportation-Treasury Appropriations/ Federal Safety Standards for Foreign Trucks. Olver, D-Mass., amendment that would prohibit the Transportation Department from using funds in the bill to implement or enforce a proposed regulation that would provide foreign-operated and foreign-built trucks operating in the United States with a 24-month exemption to comply with federal safety standards before the final rule's effective date. Adopted 339-70: R 141-69; D 197-1 (ND 143-1, SD 54-0); I 1-0. A "nay" was a vote in support of the president's position. Sept. 22, 2004.

463. HR 5025. Fiscal 2005 Transportation-Treasury Appropriations/ Federal Trust Funds. Stenholm, D-Texas, amendment that would prohibit the use of funds in the bill to pay the salaries of Treasury Department employees who take any actions that would take money from or suspend investment into various federal trust funds, including the Social Security Trust Funds, the Military Retirement Trust Fund and the Unemployment Trust Fund, in order to circumvent the federal debt limit. Adopted 404-8: R 205-7; D 198-1 (ND 145-0, SD 53-1); I 1-0. Sept. 22, 2004.

464. HR 5025. Fiscal 2005 Transportation-Treasury Appropriations/ Recommit. Obey, D-Wis., motion to recommit the bill to the House Appropriations Committee with instructions to restore funding for several programs and agencies, including the Federal Highway Administration, the National Highway Traffic Safety Administration, the Federal Railroad Administration, the Federal Transit Administration and the Surface Transportation Board. Motion rejected 201-210: R 1-210; D 199-0 (ND 145-0, SD 54-0); I 1-0. Sept. 22, 2004.

Key

Y	Voted for (yea).
#	Paired for.
+	Announced for.
N	Voted against (nay).
X	Paired against.
–	Announced against.
P	Voted "present."
C	Voted "present" to avoid possible conflict of interest.
?	Did not vote or otherwise make a position known.

Democrats **Republicans**
Independents

	457	458	459	460	461	462	463	464
ALABAMA								
1 *Bonner*	?	?	?	?	?	?	?	?
2 *Everett*	N	N	N	N	N	Y	N	N
3 *Rogers*	N	N	N	N	N	Y	N	N
4 *Aderholt*	N	N	N	N	N	Y	N	N
5 Cramer	Y	Y	N	Y	Y	Y	Y	Y
6 *Bachus*	N	N	N	N	N	Y	N	N
7 Davis	Y	Y	Y	N	Y	Y	Y	Y
ALASKA								
AL *Young*	N	N	N	N	N	Y	N	N
ARIZONA								
1 *Renzi*	N	Y	N	N	N	N	Y	N
2 *Franks*	N	N	N	N	N	N	Y	N
3 *Shadegg*	N	N	N	N	N	N	N	N
4 Pastor	Y	Y	N	Y	Y	Y	Y	Y
5 *Hayworth*	N	N	N	N	N	Y	N	N
6 *Flake*	N	N	Y	N	N	Y	N	N
7 Grijalva	Y	Y	Y	Y	Y	Y	Y	Y
8 *Kolbe*	N	N	N	N	N	N	N	N
ARKANSAS								
1 Berry	Y	Y	Y	Y	Y	Y	Y	Y
2 Snyder	Y	Y	Y	Y	Y	Y	Y	Y
3 *Boozman*	N	N	N	N	Y	Y	Y	N
4 Ross	Y	Y	Y	Y	Y	Y	Y	Y
CALIFORNIA								
1 Thompson	Y	Y	Y	Y	Y	Y	Y	Y
2 *Herger*	N	N	N	Y	Y	N	Y	N
3 *Ose*	N	N	N	N	N	N	N	N
4 *Doolittle*	N	N	N	N	N	Y	N	N
5 Matsui	?	?	?	N	Y	Y	Y	?
6 Woolsey	Y	Y	Y	Y	Y	Y	Y	Y
7 Miller, George	Y	Y	Y	Y	Y	Y	Y	Y
8 Pelosi	Y	Y	Y	Y	Y	Y	Y	Y
9 Lee	Y	Y	Y	Y	Y	Y	Y	Y
10 Tauscher	Y	Y	Y	Y	Y	Y	Y	Y
11 *Pombo*	N	N	N	N	N	Y	Y	N
12 Lantos	Y	Y	Y	Y	Y	Y	?	Y
13 Stark	Y	Y	Y	Y	Y	Y	Y	Y
14 Eshoo	Y	Y	Y	Y	Y	Y	Y	Y
15 Honda	+	+	+	Y	Y	Y	Y	Y
16 Lofgren	Y	Y	Y	Y	Y	Y	Y	Y
17 Farr	Y	Y	Y	Y	Y	Y	Y	Y
18 Cardoza	Y	Y	N	Y	Y	Y	Y	Y
19 *Radanovich*	N	N	N	N	N	N	Y	N
20 Dooley	Y	Y	N	Y	N	Y	Y	Y
21 *Nunes*	N	N	N	N	N	Y	Y	N
22 *Thomas*	N	N	N	N	N	N	N	N
23 Capps	Y	Y	Y	Y	Y	Y	Y	Y
24 *Gallegly*	N	N	N	N	N	Y	Y	N
25 *McKeon*	N	N	N	N	N	N	Y	N
26 *Dreier*	N	N	N	N	N	Y	N	N
27 Sherman	Y	Y	Y	Y	N	Y	Y	Y
28 Berman	Y	Y	Y	Y	Y	Y	Y	Y
29 Schiff	Y	Y	N	Y	N	Y	Y	Y
30 Waxman	Y	Y	Y	Y	Y	Y	Y	Y
31 Becerra	Y	Y	Y	Y	Y	+	Y	Y
32 Solis	Y	Y	Y	Y	Y	Y	Y	Y
33 Watson	Y	Y	Y	Y	Y	Y	Y	Y
34 Roybal-Allard	Y	Y	Y	Y	Y	Y	Y	Y
35 Waters	Y	Y	Y	Y	Y	Y	Y	Y
36 Harman	Y	N	Y	N	Y	Y	Y	Y

	457	458	459	460	461	462	463	464
37 Millender-McD.	?	?	?	?	?	?	?	?
38 Napolitano	Y	Y	Y	Y	Y	Y	Y	Y
39 Sánchez, Linda	Y	Y	Y	Y	Y	Y	Y	Y
40 *Royce*	N	Y	N	N	N	N	Y	N
41 *Lewis*	N	N	N	N	N	N	N	N
42 *Miller, Gary*	N	N	N	N	N	N	Y	N
43 Baca	Y	Y	Y	Y	Y	Y	Y	Y
44 *Calvert*	N	N	N	N	N	N	Y	N
45 *Bono*	N	N	Y	N	N	Y	Y	N
46 *Rohrabacher*	?	N	N	N	N	Y	N	N
47 Sanchez, Loretta	Y	Y	Y	Y	Y	Y	Y	Y
48 *Cox*	N	N	N	N	N	?	Y	N
49 *Issa*	N	N	N	N	N	N	Y	N
50 *Cunningham*	N	N	N	N	N	Y	Y	N
51 Filner	Y	Y	Y	Y	Y	Y	Y	Y
52 *Hunter*	N	N	N	N	N	Y	Y	N
53 Davis	Y	Y	Y	Y	Y	Y	Y	Y
COLORADO								
1 DeGette	Y	Y	Y	Y	Y	Y	Y	Y
2 Udall	Y	Y	Y	Y	Y	Y	Y	Y
3 *McInnis*	?	?	?	?	?	?	?	?
4 *Musgrave*	N	Y	N	N	N	N	Y	N
5 *Hefley*	N	N	N	N	N	N	Y	N
6 *Tancredo*	–	–	–	–	N	Y	Y	N
7 *Beauprez*	N	N	N	N	N	Y	Y	N
CONNECTICUT								
1 Larson	Y	Y	Y	Y	Y	Y	Y	Y
2 *Simmons*	Y	Y	Y	N	N	Y	Y	Y
3 DeLauro	Y	Y	Y	Y	Y	Y	Y	Y
4 *Shays*	N	N	N	Y	Y	Y	Y	N
5 *Johnson*	N	N	N	Y	Y	Y	Y	N
DELAWARE								
AL *Castle*	N	N	N	Y	N	Y	Y	N
FLORIDA								
1 *Miller, J.*	?	?	?	?	?	?	?	?
2 Boyd	Y	Y	N	N	Y	Y	Y	Y
3 Brown	?	?	?	N	Y	Y	Y	Y
4 *Crenshaw*	N	N	N	N	N	Y	Y	N
5 *Brown-Waite*	N	Y	N	N	N	Y	Y	N
6 *Stearns*	N	N	N	N	N	N	Y	N
7 *Mica*	N	N	N	N	N	Y	N	?
8 *Keller*	N	N	N	N	N	N	Y	N
9 *Bilirakis*	N	Y	N	N	N	Y	Y	N
10 *Young*	N	N	N	N	N	Y	Y	N
11 Davis	Y	Y	Y	Y	N	Y	Y	Y
12 *Putnam*	N	N	N	N	N	Y	N	N
13 *Harris*	N	N	N	N	N	Y	N	N
14 *Goss*	?	?	?	?	?	?	?	N
15 *Weldon*	N	N	N	N	N	N	N	N
16 *Foley*	N	N	N	N	N	Y	Y	?
17 Meek	?	Y	Y	Y	Y	Y	Y	Y
18 *Ros-Lehtinen*	N	N	N	N	N	Y	Y	N
19 Wexler	Y	Y	Y	?	?	?	?	Y
20 Deutsch	Y	Y	Y	Y	Y	Y	Y	Y
21 *Diaz-Balart, L.*	N	N	N	N	N	Y	Y	N
22 *Shaw*	N	N	N	N	N	Y	Y	?
23 Hastings	Y	Y	Y	Y	Y	Y	Y	Y
24 *Feeney*	N	N	N	N	N	N	Y	N
25 *Diaz-Balart, M.*	N	N	N	N	N	N	Y	N
GEORGIA								
1 *Kingston*	N	N	N	N	N	Y	N	N
2 Bishop	?	?	?	?	?	?	?	?
3 Marshall	Y	Y	Y	Y	Y	Y	Y	Y
4 Majette	?	?	?	?	N	Y	Y	?
5 Lewis	Y	Y	Y	Y	Y	Y	Y	Y
6 *Isakson*	?	?	?	?	N	Y	N	N
7 *Linder*	N	N	N	N	N	N	N	N
8 *Collins*	N	N	N	N	N	N	N	N
9 *Norwood*	N	N	N	N	N	N	Y	N
10 *Deal*	N	N	N	N	N	Y	N	N
11 *Gingrey*	N	N	N	N	N	N	Y	N
12 *Burns*	N	N	N	N	N	N	Y	N
13 Scott	Y	Y	Y	Y	Y	Y	Y	Y
HAWAII								
1 Abercrombie	Y	Y	Y	Y	Y	Y	Y	Y
2 Case	Y	Y	N	Y	N	Y	Y	Y
IDAHO								
1 *Otter*	N	N	N	Y	N	Y	N	N
2 *Simpson*	N	N	N	N	Y	N	Y	N
ILLINOIS								
1 Rush	Y	Y	Y	Y	Y	Y	Y	Y
2 Jackson	Y	Y	Y	Y	Y	Y	Y	Y
3 Lipinski	Y	Y	Y	Y	Y	Y	Y	Y
4 Gutierrez	?	?	?	?	N	Y	Y	Y
5 Emanuel	Y	Y	Y	Y	Y	Y	Y	Y
6 *Hyde*	Y	Y	N	N	N	Y	Y	N

ND Northern Democrats   SD Southern Democrats

	457	458	459	460	461	462	463	464
7 Davis	Y	Y	Y	Y	Y	Y	Y	Y
8 ***Crane***	N	N	N	N	N	N	Y	N
9 Schakowsky	Y	Y	Y	Y	Y	Y	Y	Y
10 ***Kirk***	N	Y	N	N	–	+	+	–
11 ***Weller***	N	N	N	N	N	Y	Y	N
12 Costello	Y	Y	Y	Y	Y	Y	Y	Y
13 ***Biggert***	N	N	N	Y	Y	N	Y	N
14 ***Hastert***								
15 ***Johnson***	Y	N	N	Y	Y	Y	Y	N
16 ***Manzullo***	N	Y	N	N	?	?	?	?
17 Evans	Y	Y	Y	Y	Y	Y	Y	Y
18 ***LaHood***	Y	Y	N	Y	N	Y	Y	N
19 ***Shimkus***	Y	Y	N	Y	Y	Y	Y	N
INDIANA								
1 Visclosky	?	?	?	?	Y	Y	Y	Y
2 ***Chocola***	N	N	N	N	N	N	Y	N
3 ***Souder***	N	N	N	N	N	Y	Y	N
4 ***Buyer***	N	N	N	N	N	Y	Y	N
5 ***Burton***	N	Y	N	N	N	Y	Y	N
6 ***Pence***	N	N	N	N	N	N	Y	N
7 Carson	Y	Y	Y	Y	Y	Y	Y	Y
8 ***Hostettler***	Y	N	N	Y	N	Y	Y	N
9 Hill	Y	Y	N	Y	Y	Y	Y	Y
IOWA								
1 ***Nussle***	N	Y	N	N	Y	Y	Y	N
2 ***Leach***	N	Y	N	Y	Y	Y	Y	N
3 Boswell	Y	Y	Y	Y	Y	Y	Y	Y
4 ***Latham***	N	Y	N	N	Y	Y	Y	N
5 ***King***	N	N	N	N	N	Y	Y	N
KANSAS								
1 ***Moran***	N	N	N	Y	Y	Y	Y	N
2 ***Ryun***	N	N	N	N	N	Y	Y	N
3 Moore	Y	Y	Y	Y	Y	Y	Y	Y
4 ***Tiahrt***	N	N	N	N	N	N	Y	N
KENTUCKY								
1 ***Whitfield***	N	Y	N	N	N	Y	Y	N
2 ***Lewis***	Y	N	N	N	N	Y	Y	N
3 ***Northup***	N	Y	N	N	N	Y	Y	N
4 Lucas	Y	N	N	Y	Y	Y	Y	Y
5 ***Rogers***	N	N	N	N	N	Y	Y	N
6 Chandler	Y	Y	Y	Y	N	Y	Y	Y
LOUISIANA								
1 ***Vitter***	N	N	N	N	N	N	Y	N
2 Jefferson	Y	Y	Y	Y	Y	Y	Y	Y
3 ***Tauzin***	?	?	?	?	?	?	?	?
4 ***McCrery***	N	N	N	N	N	N	Y	N
5 ***Alexander***	Y	N	N	N	N	Y	Y	N
6 ***Baker***	N	N	N	N	N	N	Y	N
7 John	?	?	?	?	Y	Y	Y	Y
MAINE								
1 Allen	Y	Y	Y	Y	Y	Y	Y	Y
2 Michaud	Y	Y	Y	Y	Y	Y	Y	Y
MARYLAND								
1 ***Gilchrest***	N	Y	N	Y	N	Y	Y	N
2 Ruppersberger	Y	Y	Y	Y	Y	Y	Y	Y
3 Cardin	Y	Y	Y	Y	N	Y	Y	Y
4 Wynn	Y	Y	Y	Y	Y	Y	Y	Y
5 Hoyer	Y	Y	Y	Y	Y	Y	Y	Y
6 ***Bartlett***	N	N	N	Y	N	N	Y	N
7 Cummings	Y	Y	Y	Y	Y	Y	Y	Y
8 Van Hollen	Y	Y	Y	Y	Y	Y	Y	Y
MASSACHUSETTS								
1 Olver	Y	Y	Y	Y	Y	Y	Y	Y
2 Neal	Y	Y	Y	Y	Y	Y	Y	Y
3 McGovern	Y	Y	Y	Y	Y	Y	Y	Y
4 Frank	Y	Y	Y	Y	Y	Y	Y	Y
5 Meehan	Y	Y	Y	Y	Y	Y	Y	Y
6 Tierney	Y	Y	Y	Y	Y	Y	Y	Y
7 Markey	Y	Y	Y	Y	Y	Y	Y	Y
8 Capuano	Y	Y	Y	Y	Y	Y	Y	Y
9 Lynch	Y	Y	Y	Y	Y	Y	Y	Y
10 Delahunt	Y	Y	Y	Y	Y	Y	Y	Y
MICHIGAN								
1 Stupak	Y	Y	Y	Y	Y	Y	Y	Y
2 ***Hoekstra***	?	?	?	?	?	?	?	?
3 ***Ehlers***	N	N	N	Y	N	Y	Y	N
4 ***Camp***	N	Y	N	N	N	Y	Y	N
5 Kildee	Y	Y	Y	Y	Y	Y	Y	Y
6 ***Upton***	N	Y	N	N	Y	Y	Y	N
7 ***Smith***	N	N	N	Y	N	Y	Y	N
8 ***Rogers***	N	N	N	N	N	Y	Y	N
9 ***Knollenberg***	N	N	N	N	N	N	Y	N
10 ***Miller***	N	Y	N	N	N	Y	Y	N
11 ***McCotter***	N	Y	N	N	N	Y	Y	N
12 Levin	Y	Y	Y	Y	Y	Y	Y	Y
13 Kilpatrick	Y	Y	Y	Y	Y	Y	Y	Y
14 Conyers	Y	Y	Y	Y	Y	Y	Y	Y
15 Dingell	Y	Y	Y	Y	Y	Y	Y	Y
MINNESOTA								
1 ***Gutknecht***	Y	Y	N	N	N	Y	Y	N
2 ***Kline***	N	N	N	N	N	Y	Y	N
3 ***Ramstad***	N	N	N	Y	Y	N	Y	N
4 McCollum	Y	Y	Y	Y	Y	Y	Y	Y
5 Sabo	Y	Y	Y	Y	Y	Y	Y	Y
6 ***Kennedy***	N	N	N	N	N	N	Y	N
7 Peterson	Y	Y	Y	Y	Y	Y	Y	Y
8 Oberstar	Y	Y	Y	Y	Y	Y	Y	Y
MISSISSIPPI								
1 ***Wicker***	?	?	?	?	?	?	?	?
2 Thompson	Y	Y	Y	Y	Y	Y	Y	Y
3 ***Pickering***	N	N	N	Y	N	Y	Y	N
4 Taylor	Y	Y	N	Y	Y	Y	Y	Y
MISSOURI								
1 Clay	Y	Y	Y	Y	Y	Y	Y	Y
2 ***Akin***	N	N	N	N	N	Y	Y	N
3 Gephardt	Y	Y	Y	Y	?	?	?	?
4 Skelton	Y	Y	Y	N	N	Y	Y	Y
5 McCarthy	Y	Y	Y	Y	Y	Y	Y	Y
6 ***Graves***	N	N	N	Y	Y	Y	Y	N
7 ***Blunt***	N	N	N	N	N	N	Y	N
8 ***Emerson***	Y	Y	N	Y	Y	Y	Y	N
9 ***Hulshof***	N	N	N	N	N	Y	Y	N
MONTANA								
AL ***Rehberg***	N	N	N	Y	N	Y	Y	N
NEBRASKA								
1 Vacant								
2 ***Terry***	N	N	N	N	N	Y	Y	N
3 ***Osborne***	N	N	N	Y	Y	N	Y	N
NEVADA								
1 Berkley	Y	Y	?	Y	N	Y	Y	Y
2 ***Gibbons***	N	N	N	N	N	Y	Y	N
3 ***Porter***	N	N	N	N	N	Y	Y	N
NEW HAMPSHIRE								
1 ***Bradley***	N	N	N	N	N	Y	Y	N
2 ***Bass***	N	N	N	Y	N	Y	Y	N
NEW JERSEY								
1 Andrews	Y	Y	Y	Y	N	Y	Y	Y
2 ***LoBiondo***	Y	Y	N	N	N	Y	Y	N
3 ***Saxton***	N	Y	N	N	N	Y	Y	N
4 ***Smith***	Y	Y	N	N	N	Y	Y	N
5 ***Garrett***	N	N	N	N	N	N	Y	N
6 Pallone	Y	Y	Y	Y	N	Y	Y	Y
7 ***Ferguson***	N	Y	N	N	N	Y	Y	N
8 Pascrell	Y	Y	Y	Y	N	Y	Y	Y
9 Rothman	Y	Y	Y	Y	N	Y	Y	Y
10 Payne	Y	Y	Y	Y	Y	Y	Y	Y
11 ***Frelinghuysen***	N	Y	N	N	N	Y	Y	N
12 Holt	Y	Y	Y	Y	N	Y	Y	Y
13 Menendez	Y	Y	Y	Y	N	Y	Y	Y
NEW MEXICO								
1 ***Wilson***	N	Y	N	N	N	Y	Y	N
2 ***Pearce***	N	N	N	N	N	N	Y	N
3 Udall	Y	Y	Y	Y	Y	Y	Y	Y
NEW YORK								
1 Bishop	Y	Y	Y	Y	Y	Y	Y	Y
2 Israel	Y	Y	Y	Y	Y	Y	Y	Y
3 ***King***	?	?	?	?	N	Y	Y	N
4 McCarthy	Y	Y	Y	Y	Y	Y	Y	Y
5 Ackerman	Y	Y	Y	Y	N	Y	Y	Y
6 Meeks	Y	N	Y	Y	?	?	Y	Y
7 Crowley	Y	N	Y	Y	Y	Y	Y	Y
8 Nadler	Y	Y	Y	Y	Y	Y	Y	Y
9 Weiner	Y	Y	Y	Y	Y	Y	Y	Y
10 Towns	Y	Y	Y	Y	Y	Y	Y	Y
11 Owens	Y	Y	Y	Y	Y	Y	Y	Y
12 Velázquez	Y	Y	Y	Y	Y	Y	Y	Y
13 ***Fossella***	N	Y	N	N	N	Y	Y	N
14 Maloney	Y	Y	Y	Y	Y	Y	Y	Y
15 Rangel	Y	Y	Y	Y	Y	Y	Y	Y
16 Serrano	Y	Y	Y	Y	Y	Y	Y	Y
17 Engel	Y	Y	Y	Y	N	Y	Y	Y
18 Lowey	Y	Y	Y	Y	Y	Y	Y	Y
19 ***Kelly***	Y	Y	N	N	N	Y	Y	N
20 ***Sweeney***	Y	Y	N	N	N	Y	Y	N
21 McNulty	Y	Y	Y	Y	Y	Y	Y	Y
22 Hinchey	?	?	?	?	Y	Y	Y	Y
23 ***McHugh***	Y	Y	Y	N	N	Y	Y	N
24 ***Boehlert***	Y	Y	N	Y	N	Y	Y	N
25 ***Walsh***	Y	Y	N	N	N	Y	Y	N
26 ***Reynolds***	N	N	N	N	N	Y	Y	N
27 ***Quinn***	Y	Y	N	N	N	Y	Y	N
28 Slaughter	Y	Y	Y	Y	Y	Y	Y	Y
29 ***Houghton***	N	N	N	Y	Y	Y	Y	N
NORTH CAROLINA								
1 Butterfield	Y	Y	Y	Y	Y	Y	Y	Y
2 Etheridge	Y	Y	Y	Y	N	Y	Y	Y
3 ***Jones***	Y	Y	N	N	N	?	Y	N
4 Price	Y	Y	Y	Y	Y	Y	Y	Y
5 ***Burr***	Y	N	Y	N	N	Y	Y	N
6 ***Coble***	N	Y	N	N	N	Y	Y	N
7 McIntyre	Y	Y	Y	N	N	Y	Y	Y
8 ***Hayes***	N	N	N	N	N	Y	Y	N
9 ***Myrick***	N	N	N	N	N	N	Y	N
10 ***Ballenger***	N	N	N	N	N	N	Y	N
11 ***Taylor***	N	Y	N	N	N	N	Y	N
12 Watt	Y	Y	Y	Y	Y	Y	Y	Y
13 Miller	Y	Y	Y	Y	N	Y	Y	Y
NORTH DAKOTA								
AL Pomeroy	Y	Y	Y	Y	Y	Y	Y	Y
OHIO								
1 ***Chabot***	N	N	N	N	N	Y	Y	N
2 ***Portman***	N	N	N	N	N	Y	N	N
3 ***Turner***	N	Y	N	N	N	Y	Y	N
4 ***Oxley***	N	N	N	N	N	N	Y	N
5 ***Gillmor***	N	N	N	N	N	Y	Y	N
6 Strickland	Y	Y	Y	?	Y	Y	Y	Y
7 ***Hobson***	N	N	N	N	N	Y	Y	N
8 ***Boehner***	N	N	N	N	N	N	Y	N
9 Kaptur	Y	Y	Y	Y	Y	Y	Y	Y
10 Kucinich	Y	Y	Y	Y	Y	Y	Y	Y
11 Jones	Y	Y	Y	Y	Y	Y	Y	Y
12 ***Tiberi***	N	N	N	Y	Y	N	Y	N
13 Brown	Y	Y	Y	Y	Y	Y	Y	Y
14 ***LaTourette***	Y	Y	N	N	N	Y	Y	N
15 ***Pryce***	N	N	N	N	N	N	Y	N
16 ***Regula***	N	N	N	N	N	Y	Y	N
17 Ryan	Y	Y	Y	Y	Y	Y	Y	Y
18 ***Ney***	N	Y	N	Y	N	Y	Y	N
OKLAHOMA								
1 ***Sullivan***	N	N	N	N	N	Y	Y	N
2 Carson	?	?	?	?	Y	Y	Y	Y
3 ***Lucas***	N	N	N	N	N	Y	Y	N
4 ***Cole***	N	N	Y	N	N	Y	Y	N
5 ***Istook***	N	N	N	N	N	N	Y	N
OREGON								
1 Wu	Y	Y	N	Y	N	Y	Y	Y
2 ***Walden***	N	N	N	N	N	Y	Y	N
3 Blumenauer	?	?	?	?	Y	Y	Y	Y
4 DeFazio	Y	Y	Y	Y	Y	Y	Y	Y
5 Hooley	Y	Y	N	Y	Y	Y	Y	Y
PENNSYLVANIA								
1 Brady	Y	Y	Y	Y	Y	Y	Y	Y
2 Fattah	Y	Y	Y	Y	Y	Y	Y	Y
3 ***English***	Y	N	N	N	N	Y	Y	N
4 ***Hart***	N	N	N	N	?	?	?	?
5 ***Peterson***	N	N	N	Y	Y	Y	Y	N
6 ***Gerlach***	N	Y	N	N	N	Y	Y	N
7 ***Weldon***	N	Y	N	Y	N	Y	Y	N
8 ***Greenwood***	?	?	?	?	?	?	?	?
9 ***Shuster, Bill***	N	N	N	N	N	Y	Y	N
10 ***Sherwood***	N	N	N	N	N	Y	Y	N
11 Kanjorski	Y	Y	Y	Y	Y	Y	Y	Y
12 Murtha	Y	Y	Y	Y	N	Y	Y	Y
13 Hoeffel	Y	Y	Y	Y	Y	Y	Y	Y
14 Doyle	Y	Y	Y	Y	Y	Y	Y	Y
15 ***Toomey***	N	N	N	Y	N	N	Y	N
16 ***Pitts***	N	N	N	N	N	N	Y	N
17 Holden	Y	Y	Y	Y	N	Y	Y	Y
18 ***Murphy***	N	N	N	N	?	?	?	?
19 ***Platts***	N	Y	N	N	N	Y	Y	N
RHODE ISLAND								
1 Kennedy	Y	Y	Y	Y	N	Y	Y	Y
2 Langevin	Y	Y	Y	Y	Y	Y	Y	Y
SOUTH CAROLINA								
1 ***Brown***	N	N	N	N	N	Y	Y	N
2 ***Wilson***	N	N	N	N	N	Y	Y	N
3 ***Barrett***	N	N	N	N	N	N	Y	N
4 ***DeMint***	?	?	?	?	N	N	?	N
5 Spratt	Y	Y	Y	Y	N	Y	Y	Y
6 Clyburn	Y	Y	Y	Y	Y	Y	Y	Y
SOUTH DAKOTA								
AL Herseth	Y	Y	Y	Y	Y	Y	Y	Y
TENNESSEE								
1 ***Jenkins***	?	?	?	?	N	Y	Y	N
2 ***Duncan***	N	N	N	N	N	Y	Y	N
3 ***Wamp***	N	N	N	N	N	Y	Y	N
4 Davis	Y	Y	N	Y	Y	Y	Y	Y
5 Cooper	Y	N	N	Y	Y	Y	Y	Y
6 Gordon	Y	Y	Y	Y	Y	Y	Y	Y
7 ***Blackburn***	N	N	N	N	N	N	Y	N
8 Tanner	Y	Y	N	Y	Y	Y	Y	Y
9 Ford	Y	Y	Y	Y	Y	Y	Y	Y
TEXAS								
1 Sandlin	?	?	?	?	Y	Y	Y	Y
2 Turner	N	Y	N	Y	Y	Y	Y	Y
3 ***Johnson, Sam***	N	N	N	N	N	N	N	N
4 ***Hall***	N	N	N	N	N	Y	Y	N
5 ***Hensarling***	?	?	?	?	?	?	?	?
6 ***Barton***	N	N	N	N	N	N	Y	N
7 ***Culberson***	?	?	N	N	N	N	Y	N
8 ***Brady***	N	N	N	Y	N	N	Y	N
9 Lampson	Y	Y	N	Y	Y	Y	Y	Y
10 Doggett	Y	Y	Y	Y	Y	Y	Y	Y
11 Edwards	Y	Y	Y	Y	Y	Y	Y	Y
12 ***Granger***	N	N	N	N	N	N	Y	N
13 ***Thornberry***	N	N	N	N	N	N	Y	N
14 ***Paul***	N	N	N	Y	Y	Y	Y	N
15 Hinojosa	Y	Y	Y	Y	Y	Y	Y	Y
16 Reyes	Y	Y	Y	Y	Y	Y	Y	Y
17 Stenholm	N	Y	N	Y	Y	Y	Y	Y
18 Jackson-Lee	Y	Y	Y	Y	Y	Y	Y	Y
19 ***Neugebauer***	N	N	N	N	N	Y	Y	N
20 Gonzalez	Y	Y	N	Y	Y	Y	Y	Y
21 ***Smith***	N	N	N	N	N	N	Y	N
22 ***DeLay***	N	N	N	N	N	N	Y	N
23 ***Bonilla***	N	N	N	N	N	N	Y	N
24 Frost	?	?	?	?	N	Y	Y	Y
25 Bell	Y	Y	Y	Y	Y	Y	Y	Y
26 ***Burgess***	N	Y	N	N	N	Y	Y	N
27 Ortiz	Y	Y	Y	Y	N	Y	Y	Y
28 Rodriguez	Y	Y	Y	Y	N	Y	Y	Y
29 Green	Y	Y	N	Y	N	Y	Y	Y
30 Johnson, E.B.	Y	Y	Y	Y	Y	Y	Y	Y
31 ***Carter***	N	N	N	N	N	N	Y	N
32 ***Sessions***	N	N	N	N	N	N	Y	N
UTAH								
1 ***Bishop***	N	N	N	N	N	?	Y	N
2 Matheson	Y	Y	Y	Y	Y	Y	Y	Y
3 ***Cannon***	?	?	?	?	?	?	?	?
VERMONT								
AL *Sanders*	Y	Y	Y	Y	Y	Y	Y	Y
VIRGINIA								
1 ***Davis, Jo Ann***	Y	N	N	N	N	Y	Y	N
2 ***Schrock***	?	?	?	?	N	N	N	N
3 Scott	Y	Y	Y	Y	Y	Y	N	Y
4 ***Forbes***	N	N	N	N	N	Y	Y	N
5 ***Goode***	N	Y	Y	N	N	Y	Y	N
6 ***Goodlatte***	N	N	N	N	N	Y	Y	N
7 ***Cantor***	N	N	N	N	N	N	Y	N
8 Moran	Y	Y	Y	Y	Y	Y	Y	Y
9 Boucher	Y	Y	Y	Y	Y	Y	Y	Y
10 ***Wolf***	N	N	Y	N	N	Y	Y	N
11 ***Davis, T.***	N	N	Y	?	N	N	N	N
WASHINGTON								
1 Inslee	Y	Y	Y	Y	Y	Y	Y	Y
2 Larsen	Y	Y	Y	Y	Y	Y	Y	Y
3 Baird	?	?	?	?	?	?	?	?
4 ***Hastings***	N	N	N	N	N	N	Y	N
5 ***Nethercutt***	N	N	N	Y	Y	N	Y	N
6 Dicks	Y	Y	Y	Y	Y	Y	Y	Y
7 McDermott	Y	Y	Y	Y	Y	Y	Y	Y
8 ***Dunn***	?	?	?	?	N	N	Y	N
9 Smith	N	Y	Y	Y	Y	Y	Y	Y
WEST VIRGINIA								
1 Mollohan	?	?	?	?	Y	Y	Y	Y
2 ***Capito***	Y	Y	N	N	N	Y	Y	N
3 Rahall	Y	Y	Y	Y	Y	Y	Y	Y
WISCONSIN								
1 ***Ryan***	N	N	N	Y	Y	Y	Y	N
2 Baldwin	Y	Y	Y	Y	Y	Y	Y	Y
3 Kind	Y	Y	Y	Y	Y	Y	Y	Y
4 Kleczka	Y	Y	Y	Y	Y	Y	Y	Y
5 ***Sensenbrenner***	N	N	N	N	N	Y	Y	N
6 ***Petri***	N	Y	N	N	N	Y	Y	N
7 Obey	Y	Y	Y	Y	Y	Y	Y	Y
8 ***Green***	N	N	N	N	N	Y	Y	N
WYOMING								
AL ***Cubin***	N	N	N	Y	N	N	Y	N

Southern states - Ala., Ark., Fla., Ga., Ky., La., Miss., N.C., Okla., S.C., Tenn., Texas, Va.

465. HR 5025. Fiscal 2005 Transportation-Treasury Appropriations. Passage of the fiscal 2005 spending bill for the departments of Transportation and Treasury. Nearly 50 percent of the $89.8 billion approved in committee was cut during floor debate, including more than 80 percent of transportation funds. Passed 397-12: R 199-10; D 197-2 (ND 143-2, SD 54-0); I 1-0. Sept. 22, 2004.

466. HR 2028. Pledge of Allegiance/Supreme Court Jurisdiction. Watt, D-N.C., amendment that would strike language in the bill that would prohibit the Supreme Court from hearing any cases relating to the constitutionality of the Pledge of Allegiance. Rejected 202-217: R 25-193; D 176-24 (ND 139-8, SD 37-16); I 1-0. Sept. 23, 2004.

467. HR 2028. Pledge of Allegiance/Passage. Passage of the bill that would prohibit federal district and appellate courts and the Supreme Court from hearing cases challenging the constitutionality of the Pledge of Allegiance. It would allow the Superior Court of the District of Columbia and the District of Columbia Court of Appeals to continue considering such cases. Passed 247-173: R 213-6; D 34-166 (ND 12-135, SD 22-31); I 0-1. Sept. 23, 2004.

468. HR 1057. Adoption Tax Credit/Passage. Camp, R-Mich., motion to suspend the rules and pass the bill that would permanently extend a provision enacted in the 2001 tax law that increased the adoption tax credit from $5,000 ($6,000 for children with special needs) to $10,000. Motion agreed to 414-0: R 214-0; D 199-0 (ND 146-0, SD 53-0); I 1-0. A two-thirds majority of those present and voting (276 in this case) is required for passage under suspension of the rules. Sept. 23, 2004.

469. HR 1308. Family and Corporate Tax Breaks/Previous Question. Reynolds, R-N.Y., motion to order the previous question (thus ending debate and possibility of amendment) on adoption of the rule (H Res 785) that would waive the two-thirds majority vote requirement for same-day consideration of the rule on the conference report. Motion agreed to 211-196: R 211-0; D 0-195 (ND 0-142, SD 0-53); I 0-1. Sept. 23, 2004.

470. HR 1308. Family and Corporate Tax Breaks/Previous Question. Motion to order the previous question (thus ending debate and possibility of amendment) on adoption of the rule (H Res 794) to provide for House floor consideration of the conference report on the bill that would extend several tax breaks for individuals and businesses. Motion agreed to 212-193: R 212-0; D 0-192 (ND 0-141, SD 0-51); I 0-1. (Subsequently, the rule was adopted by voice vote.) Sept. 23, 2004.

471. HR 1308. Family and Corporate Tax Breaks/Rule. Adoption of the rule (H Res 794) to provide for House floor consideration of the conference report on the bill that would extend several tax breaks for individuals and businesses. Adopted 235-167: R 212-0; D 23-166 (ND 11-128, SD 12-38); I 0-1. Sept. 23, 2004.

472. HR 1308. Family and Corporate Tax Breaks/Conference Report. Adoption of the conference report on the bill that would extend the $1,000 per child tax credit through 2009, the upper limit for the current 10 percent bracket through 2010 and tax breaks for married couples through 2008. It also would provide a one-year extension of current income exemptions from the alternative minimum tax and extend the expiring research and development tax credit through 2005. Adopted (thus sent to the Senate) 339-65: R 213-0; D 125-65 (ND 83-57, SD 42-8); I 1-0. A "yea" was a vote in support of the president's position. Sept. 23, 2004.

Key

Y	Voted for (yea).
#	Paired for.
+	Announced for.
N	Voted against (nay).
X	Paired against.
–	Announced against.
P	Voted "present."
C	Voted "present" to avoid possible conflict of interest.
?	Did not vote or otherwise make a position known.

Democrats **Republicans**
Independents

	465	466	467	468	469	470	471	472
ALABAMA								
1 *Bonner*	?	?	?	?	?	?	?	?
2 *Everett*	Y	N	Y	Y	Y	Y	Y	Y
3 *Rogers*	Y	N	Y	Y	Y	Y	Y	Y
4 *Aderholt*	Y	N	Y	Y	Y	Y	Y	Y
5 Cramer	Y	N	Y	N	N	N	Y	Y
6 *Bachus*	Y	N	Y	Y	Y	Y	Y	Y
7 Davis	Y	Y	N	Y	N	N	N	Y
ALASKA								
AL *Young*	Y	N	Y	Y	Y	Y	Y	Y
ARIZONA								
1 *Renzi*	Y	N	Y	Y	Y	Y	Y	Y
2 *Franks*	N	N	Y	Y	Y	Y	Y	Y
3 *Shadegg*	Y	N	Y	Y	Y	Y	Y	Y
4 Pastor	Y	Y	N	Y	N	N	N	Y
5 *Hayworth*	Y	N	Y	Y	Y	Y	Y	Y
6 *Flake*	N	N	Y	Y	Y	Y	Y	Y
7 Grijalva	Y	Y	N	Y	N	N	N	Y
8 *Kolbe*	Y	Y	N	Y	Y	Y	Y	Y
ARKANSAS								
1 Berry	Y	N	Y	Y	N	N	N	N
2 Snyder	Y	Y	N	Y	N	N	N	Y
3 *Boozman*	Y	N	Y	Y	Y	Y	Y	Y
4 Ross	Y	N	Y	N	N	N	N	N
CALIFORNIA								
1 Thompson	Y	Y	N	Y	N	N	N	N
2 *Herger*	Y	N	Y	Y	Y	Y	Y	Y
3 *Ose*	Y	Y	N	Y	Y	Y	Y	Y
4 *Doolittle*	Y	N	Y	Y	Y	Y	Y	Y
5 Matsui	Y	N	Y	N	N	N	N	Y
6 Woolsey	Y	Y	N	Y	N	N	N	N
7 Miller, George	Y	Y	N	Y	N	N	N	N
8 Pelosi	Y	Y	N	Y	N	N	N	N
9 Lee	Y	Y	N	Y	N	N	N	N
10 Tauscher	Y	Y	N	Y	N	N	N	Y
11 *Pombo*	Y	N	Y	Y	Y	Y	Y	Y
12 Lantos	Y	Y	N	Y	N	N	N	Y
13 Stark	Y	Y	N	?	N	N	N	N
14 Eshoo	Y	Y	N	Y	N	N	N	Y
15 Honda	Y	Y	N	Y	N	N	N	N
16 Lofgren	Y	Y	N	Y	N	N	N	Y
17 Farr	Y	Y	N	Y	N	N	N	N
18 Cardoza	Y	Y	N	Y	N	N	N	Y
19 *Radanovich*	Y	N	Y	Y	Y	Y	Y	Y
20 Dooley	Y	Y	N	Y	N	N	N	Y
21 *Nunes*	Y	N	Y	Y	?	?	?	Y
22 *Thomas*	Y	N	Y	Y	Y	Y	Y	Y
23 Capps	Y	Y	N	Y	N	N	?	N
24 *Gallegly*	Y	N	Y	Y	Y	Y	Y	Y
25 *McKeon*	Y	N	Y	Y	Y	Y	Y	Y
26 *Dreier*	Y	N	Y	Y	Y	Y	Y	Y
27 Sherman	Y	Y	N	Y	N	N	N	Y
28 Berman	Y	N	N	Y	N	N	N	Y
29 Schiff	Y	Y	N	Y	N	N	N	Y
30 Waxman	Y	Y	N	Y	N	N	N	N
31 Becerra	Y	Y	N	Y	N	N	N	N
32 Solis	Y	Y	N	Y	N	N	N	N
33 Watson	Y	Y	N	Y	N	N	N	N
34 Roybal-Allard	Y	Y	N	Y	N	N	N	N
35 Waters	Y	Y	N	Y	N	N	N	N
36 Harman	Y	Y	N	Y	N	N	N	N

	465	466	467	468	469	470	471	472
37 Millender-McD.	?	Y	N	Y	N	N	N	N
38 Napolitano	Y	Y	N	Y	N	N	N	Y
39 Sánchez, Linda	Y	Y	N	Y	N	N	N	Y
40 *Royce*	N	N	Y	Y	Y	Y	Y	Y
41 *Lewis*	Y	N	Y	Y	Y	Y	Y	Y
42 *Miller, Gary*	Y	N	Y	Y	Y	Y	Y	Y
43 Baca	Y	Y	N	Y	N	N	N	Y
44 *Calvert*	Y	N	Y	Y	Y	Y	Y	Y
45 *Bono*	Y	N	Y	Y	Y	Y	Y	Y
46 *Rohrabacher*	Y	N	Y	Y	Y	Y	Y	Y
47 Sanchez, Loretta	Y	Y	N	Y	N	N	N	Y
48 *Cox*	?	N	Y	Y	Y	Y	Y	Y
49 *Issa*	Y	N	Y	Y	Y	Y	Y	Y
50 *Cunningham*	Y	N	Y	Y	Y	Y	Y	Y
51 Filner	Y	Y	N	Y	N	N	N	N
52 *Hunter*	Y	N	Y	Y	N	N	N	Y
53 Davis	Y	Y	N	Y	N	N	Y	Y
COLORADO								
1 DeGette	Y	Y	N	Y	N	N	N	N
2 Udall	Y	N	Y	?	?	?	?	?
3 *McInnis*	?	N	Y	Y	Y	Y	Y	Y
4 *Musgrave*	Y	N	Y	Y	Y	Y	Y	Y
5 *Hefley*	N	N	Y	Y	Y	Y	Y	Y
6 *Tancredo*	Y	N	Y	Y	?	Y	Y	Y
7 *Beauprez*	Y	N	Y	Y	Y	Y	Y	Y
CONNECTICUT								
1 Larson	Y	Y	N	Y	N	N	N	N
2 *Simmons*	Y	Y	Y	Y	Y	Y	Y	Y
3 DeLauro	Y	Y	N	Y	N	N	N	N
4 *Shays*	Y	Y	N	Y	Y	Y	Y	Y
5 *Johnson*	Y	Y	Y	Y	Y	Y	Y	Y
DELAWARE								
AL *Castle*	N	Y	Y	Y	Y	Y	Y	Y
FLORIDA								
1 *Miller, J.*	?	?	?	?	?	?	?	?
2 Boyd	Y	N	Y	N	N	N	N	Y
3 Brown	Y	Y	N	Y	N	N	N	Y
4 *Crenshaw*	Y	N	Y	N	N	N	N	Y
5 *Brown-Waite*	Y	N	Y	Y	Y	Y	Y	Y
6 *Stearns*	Y	N	Y	Y	Y	Y	Y	Y
7 *Mica*	Y	N	Y	Y	Y	Y	Y	Y
8 *Keller*	Y	N	Y	Y	Y	Y	Y	Y
9 *Bilirakis*	Y	N	Y	Y	Y	Y	Y	Y
10 *Young*	Y	N	Y	Y	Y	Y	Y	Y
11 Davis	Y	N	Y	N	N	N	N	Y
12 *Putnam*	Y	N	Y	Y	Y	Y	Y	Y
13 *Harris*	Y	N	Y	Y	Y	Y	Y	Y
14 *Goss*	Y	?	?	Y	Y	Y	Y	?
15 *Weldon*	Y	N	Y	Y	Y	Y	Y	Y
16 *Foley*	?	Y	Y	Y	Y	Y	Y	Y
17 Meek	Y	Y	N	Y	N	N	N	N
18 *Ros-Lehtinen*	Y	N	Y	Y	Y	Y	Y	Y
19 Wexler	?	Y	N	Y	N	N	N	N
20 Deutsch	Y	N	Y	N	N	N	N	Y
21 *Diaz-Balart, L.*	Y	N	Y	Y	Y	Y	Y	Y
22 *Shaw*	Y	N	Y	Y	Y	Y	Y	Y
23 Hastings	Y	Y	N	Y	N	N	N	N
24 *Feeney*	Y	N	Y	Y	Y	Y	Y	Y
25 *Diaz-Balart, M.*	Y	N	Y	Y	Y	Y	Y	Y
GEORGIA								
1 *Kingston*	Y	N	Y	Y	Y	Y	Y	Y
2 Bishop	?	?	?	?	?	?	?	?
3 Marshall	Y	N	Y	N	N	N	N	Y
4 *Majette*	Y	Y	N	Y	N	?	N	Y
5 Lewis	Y	Y	N	Y	N	N	N	N
6 *Isakson*	Y	N	Y	Y	Y	Y	Y	Y
7 *Linder*	Y	N	Y	Y	Y	Y	Y	Y
8 *Collins*	Y	N	Y	Y	Y	?	?	?
9 *Norwood*	Y	N	Y	Y	Y	Y	Y	Y
10 *Deal*	Y	N	Y	?	?	?	?	?
11 *Gingrey*	Y	N	Y	Y	Y	Y	Y	Y
12 *Burns*	Y	N	Y	Y	Y	Y	Y	Y
13 Scott	Y	Y	N	Y	N	N	N	Y
HAWAII								
1 Abercrombie	Y	Y	N	Y	N	N	Y	Y
2 Case	Y	N	N	Y	N	N	Y	Y
IDAHO								
1 *Otter*	N	Y	Y	Y	Y	Y	Y	Y
2 *Simpson*	Y	Y	Y	Y	Y	Y	Y	Y
ILLINOIS								
1 Rush	Y	Y	N	Y	N	N	N	N
2 Jackson	Y	Y	N	Y	N	N	N	N
3 Lipinski	Y	Y	Y	Y	N	?	?	?
4 Gutierrez	Y	Y	N	Y	N	N	N	N
5 Emanuel	Y	N	N	Y	N	N	N	Y
6 *Hyde*	Y	N	Y	Y	Y	Y	Y	Y

ND Northern Democrats   SD Southern Democrats

	465	466	467	468	469	470	471	472
7 Davis	Y	Y	N	Y	N	N	N	N
8 ***Crane***	Y	N	Y	Y	Y	Y	Y	Y
9 Schakowsky	Y	Y	N	Y	N	N	N	N
10 ***Kirk***	+	Y	Y	Y	Y	Y	Y	Y
11 ***Weller***	Y	N	Y	Y	Y	Y	Y	Y
12 Costello	Y	N	Y	Y	N	N	N	Y
13 ***Biggert***	Y	Y	N	Y	Y	Y	Y	Y
14 ***Hastert***								Y
15 ***Johnson***	Y	N	Y	Y	Y	Y	Y	Y
16 ***Manzullo***	?	N	Y	Y	?	Y	Y	Y
17 Evans	Y	Y	N	Y	N	N	N	Y
18 ***LaHood***	Y	N	Y	Y	Y	Y	Y	Y
19 ***Shimkus***	N	N	Y	Y	Y	Y	Y	Y
INDIANA								
1 Visclosky	Y	Y	N	Y	N	N	N	N
2 ***Chocola***	Y	N	Y	Y	Y	Y	Y	Y
3 ***Souder***	Y	N	Y	Y	Y	Y	Y	Y
4 ***Buyer***	Y	N	Y	Y	Y	Y	Y	Y
5 ***Burton***	Y	N	Y	Y	Y	Y	Y	Y
6 ***Pence***	Y	N	Y	Y	Y	Y	Y	Y
7 Carson	Y	Y	N	Y	N	N	N	Y
8 ***Hostettler***	Y	N	Y	Y	Y	Y	Y	Y
9 Hill	Y	Y	N	Y	N	N	N	N
IOWA								
1 ***Nussle***	Y	N	Y	Y	Y	Y	Y	Y
2 ***Leach***	Y	Y	Y	Y	Y	Y	Y	Y
3 Boswell	Y	Y	Y	Y	N	N	N	Y
4 ***Latham***	Y	N	Y	Y	Y	Y	Y	Y
5 ***King***	Y	N	Y	Y	Y	Y	Y	Y
KANSAS								
1 ***Moran***	Y	N	Y	Y	Y	Y	Y	Y
2 ***Ryun***	Y	N	Y	Y	Y	Y	Y	Y
3 Moore	Y	Y	N	Y	N	N	Y	Y
4 ***Tiahrt***	Y	N	Y	+	Y	Y	Y	Y
KENTUCKY								
1 ***Whitfield***	Y	N	Y	Y	Y	Y	Y	Y
2 ***Lewis***	Y	N	Y	Y	Y	Y	Y	Y
3 ***Northup***	Y	N	Y	Y	Y	Y	Y	Y
4 Lucas	Y	?	?	?	?	?	?	?
5 ***Rogers***	Y	N	Y	Y	Y	Y	Y	Y
6 Chandler	Y	N	Y	Y	N	N	Y	Y
LOUISIANA								
1 ***Vitter***	Y	?	?	?	?	?	?	?
2 Jefferson	Y	Y	N	Y	N	N	N	Y
3 ***Tauzin***	?	?	?	?	?	?	?	?
4 ***McCrery***	Y	N	Y	Y	Y	Y	Y	Y
5 ***Alexander***	Y	N	Y	Y	Y	Y	Y	Y
6 ***Baker***	Y	N	Y	Y	Y	Y	Y	Y
7 John	Y	N	Y	Y	N	N	N	Y
MAINE								
1 Allen	Y	Y	N	Y	N	N	N	Y
2 Michaud	Y	Y	N	Y	N	N	N	Y
MARYLAND								
1 ***Gilchrest***	Y	Y	N	Y	Y	Y	Y	Y
2 Ruppersberger	Y	Y	N	Y	N	N	N	Y
3 Cardin	Y	Y	N	Y	N	N	N	Y
4 Wynn	Y	Y	Y	Y	N	N	N	Y
5 Hoyer	Y	Y	N	Y	N	N	N	N
6 ***Bartlett***	Y	N	Y	Y	Y	Y	Y	Y
7 Cummings	Y	Y	N	Y	N	N	N	Y
8 Van Hollen	Y	Y	N	Y	N	N	N	Y
MASSACHUSETTS								
1 Olver	Y	Y	N	Y	N	N	N	N
2 Neal	Y	Y	N	Y	N	N	N	N
3 McGovern	Y	Y	N	Y	N	N	N	Y
4 Frank	Y	Y	N	Y	N	N	N	N
5 Meehan	?	Y	N	Y	N	N	N	N
6 Tierney	Y	Y	N	Y	N	N	N	N
7 Markey	Y	Y	N	Y	N	N	N	N
8 Capuano	Y	Y	N	Y	N	N	N	N
9 Lynch	Y	Y	N	Y	N	N	N	Y
10 Delahunt	Y	Y	N	Y	N	?	?	?
MICHIGAN								
1 Stupak	Y	Y	N	Y	N	N	N	Y
2 ***Hoekstra***	?	N	Y	Y	Y	Y	Y	Y
3 ***Ehlers***	Y	N	Y	Y	Y	Y	Y	Y
4 ***Camp***	Y	N	Y	Y	Y	Y	Y	Y
5 Kildee	Y	Y	N	Y	N	N	N	Y
6 ***Upton***	Y	Y	Y	Y	Y	Y	Y	Y
7 ***Smith***	Y	N	Y	Y	Y	Y	Y	Y
8 ***Rogers***	Y	N	Y	?	Y	Y	Y	Y
9 ***Knollenberg***	Y	N	Y	Y	Y	Y	Y	Y
10 ***Miller***	Y	N	Y	Y	Y	Y	Y	Y
11 ***McCotter***	Y	N	Y	Y	Y	Y	Y	Y
12 Levin	Y	Y	N	Y	N	N	N	Y
13 Kilpatrick	Y	Y	N	Y	N	N	N	N
14 Conyers	Y	Y	N	Y	N	N	N	N
15 Dingell	Y	Y	N	Y	N	N	N	Y
MINNESOTA								
1 ***Gutknecht***	Y	N	Y	Y	Y	Y	Y	Y
2 ***Kline***	Y	N	Y	Y	Y	Y	Y	Y
3 ***Ramstad***	Y	N	Y	Y	Y	Y	Y	Y
4 McCollum	Y	Y	N	Y	N	N	N	N
5 Sabo	Y	Y	N	Y	N	N	N	N
6 ***Kennedy***	Y	N	Y	Y	Y	Y	Y	Y
7 Peterson	Y	N	Y	Y	N	N	N	Y
8 Oberstar	Y	Y	N	Y	N	N	N	N
MISSISSIPPI								
1 ***Wicker***	?	N	Y	Y	Y	Y	Y	Y
2 Thompson	Y	?	?	?	?	?	?	?
3 ***Pickering***	Y	N	Y	Y	Y	Y	Y	Y
4 Taylor	Y	N	Y	Y	N	N	N	N
MISSOURI								
1 Clay	Y	Y	N	Y	N	N	N	N
2 ***Akin***	Y	N	Y	Y	Y	Y	Y	Y
3 Gephardt	?	Y	N	?	?	?	?	Y
4 Skelton	Y	N	Y	Y	N	N	Y	Y
5 McCarthy	Y	Y	N	Y	N	–	?	+
6 ***Graves***	Y	?	?	?	?	?	?	?
7 ***Blunt***	Y	N	Y	Y	Y	Y	Y	Y
8 ***Emerson***	Y	N	Y	Y	Y	Y	Y	Y
9 ***Hulshof***	Y	N	Y	Y	Y	Y	Y	Y
MONTANA								
AL ***Rehberg***	Y	N	Y	Y	Y	Y	Y	Y
NEBRASKA								
1 Vacant								
2 ***Terry***	Y	N	Y	Y	Y	Y	Y	Y
3 ***Osborne***	Y	N	Y	Y	?	?	?	?
NEVADA								
1 Berkley	Y	Y	N	Y	N	N	Y	Y
2 ***Gibbons***	Y	N	Y	Y	Y	Y	Y	Y
3 ***Porter***	Y	N	Y	Y	Y	Y	Y	Y
NEW HAMPSHIRE								
1 ***Bradley***	Y	N	Y	Y	Y	Y	Y	Y
2 ***Bass***	Y	Y	Y	Y	Y	Y	Y	Y
NEW JERSEY								
1 Andrews	Y	Y	N	Y	N	N	N	N
2 ***LoBiondo***	Y	N	Y	Y	Y	Y	Y	Y
3 ***Saxton***	Y	N	Y	Y	Y	Y	Y	Y
4 ***Smith***	Y	N	Y	Y	Y	Y	Y	Y
5 ***Garrett***	Y	N	Y	Y	?	?	?	?
6 Pallone	Y	Y	N	Y	N	N	N	N
7 ***Ferguson***	Y	N	Y	Y	Y	Y	Y	Y
8 Pascrell	Y	Y	N	Y	N	N	N	Y
9 Rothman	Y	Y	N	Y	N	N	N	Y
10 Payne	Y	Y	N	Y	N	N	N	N
11 ***Frelinghuysen***	Y	N	Y	Y	Y	Y	Y	Y
12 Holt	Y	Y	N	Y	N	N	N	N
13 Menendez	Y	Y	N	Y	N	N	N	N
NEW MEXICO								
1 ***Wilson***	Y	N	Y	Y	Y	Y	Y	Y
2 ***Pearce***	Y	N	Y	Y	Y	Y	Y	Y
3 Udall	Y	Y	N	Y	N	N	N	Y
NEW YORK								
1 Bishop	Y	Y	N	Y	N	N	N	Y
2 Israel	Y	Y	N	Y	N	N	N	Y
3 ***King***	Y	N	Y	Y	Y	Y	Y	Y
4 McCarthy	Y	Y	N	Y	N	N	N	Y
5 Ackerman	Y	Y	N	Y	N	N	N	Y
6 Meeks	Y	Y	N	Y	N	N	N	Y
7 Crowley	Y	Y	N	Y	N	N	Y	Y
8 Nadler	Y	Y	N	Y	N	N	N	Y
9 Weiner	Y	Y	N	Y	N	N	N	Y
10 Towns	Y	Y	N	Y	N	N	N	N
11 Owens	Y	Y	N	Y	N	N	N	N
12 Velázquez	Y	Y	N	Y	N	N	N	Y
13 ***Fossella***	Y	Y	Y	Y	Y	Y	Y	Y
14 Maloney	Y	Y	N	Y	N	N	Y	+
15 Rangel	Y	Y	N	Y	N	N	N	Y
16 Serrano	Y	Y	N	Y	N	N	N	Y
17 Engel	Y	Y	N	Y	N	N	N	Y
18 Lowey	Y	Y	N	Y	N	N	Y	Y
19 ***Kelly***	Y	N	Y	Y	Y	Y	Y	Y
20 ***Sweeney***	Y	N	Y	Y	Y	Y	Y	Y
21 McNulty	Y	Y	N	Y	N	N	N	Y
22 Hinchey	Y	Y	N	Y	N	N	N	Y
23 ***McHugh***	Y	N	Y	Y	Y	Y	Y	Y
24 ***Boehlert***	Y	Y	Y	Y	Y	Y	Y	Y
25 ***Walsh***	Y	N	Y	Y	Y	Y	Y	Y
26 ***Reynolds***	?	N	Y	Y	Y	Y	Y	Y
27 ***Quinn***	Y	?	?	?	?	?	?	?
28 Slaughter	Y	Y	N	Y	N	N	N	Y
29 ***Houghton***	Y	Y	Y	Y	Y	Y	Y	Y
NORTH CAROLINA								
1 Butterfield	Y	Y	N	Y	N	N	Y	Y
2 Etheridge	Y	Y	Y	Y	N	N	N	Y
3 ***Jones***	N	N	Y	Y	Y	Y	Y	Y
4 Price	Y	Y	N	Y	N	N	N	Y
5 ***Burr***	Y	N	Y	Y	Y	Y	Y	Y
6 ***Coble***	Y	N	Y	Y	Y	Y	Y	Y
7 McIntyre	Y	N	Y	Y	N	N	Y	Y
8 ***Hayes***	Y	N	Y	Y	Y	Y	Y	Y
9 ***Myrick***	Y	N	Y	Y	?	?	?	?
10 ***Ballenger***	Y	N	Y	Y	Y	Y	Y	Y
11 ***Taylor***	Y	N	Y	Y	Y	Y	Y	Y
12 Watt	Y	Y	N	Y	N	N	N	Y
13 Miller	Y	Y	N	Y	N	N	N	Y
NORTH DAKOTA								
AL Pomeroy	Y	Y	N	Y	N	N	N	Y
OHIO								
1 ***Chabot***	Y	N	Y	Y	Y	Y	Y	Y
2 ***Portman***	Y	N	Y	Y	Y	Y	Y	Y
3 ***Turner***	Y	N	Y	Y	+	Y	Y	Y
4 ***Oxley***	Y	N	Y	Y	Y	Y	Y	Y
5 ***Gillmor***	?	N	Y	Y	Y	Y	Y	Y
6 Strickland	Y	Y	N	Y	N	N	N	Y
7 ***Hobson***	Y	N	Y	Y	Y	Y	Y	Y
8 ***Boehner***	Y	N	Y	Y	Y	Y	Y	Y
9 Kaptur	Y	Y	N	Y	N	N	N	Y
10 Kucinich	N	Y	N	Y	N	N	N	Y
11 Jones	Y	Y	N	Y	N	N	N	Y
12 ***Tiberi***	Y	N	Y	Y	Y	Y	Y	Y
13 Brown	Y	Y	N	Y	N	N	N	Y
14 ***LaTourette***	Y	N	Y	Y	Y	Y	Y	Y
15 ***Pryce***	Y	Y	Y	Y	Y	Y	Y	Y
16 ***Regula***	Y	N	Y	Y	Y	Y	Y	Y
17 Ryan	Y	Y	Y	Y	N	N	N	Y
18 ***Ney***	Y	N	Y	Y	Y	Y	Y	Y
OKLAHOMA								
1 ***Sullivan***	Y	N	Y	Y	Y	Y	Y	Y
2 Carson	Y	N	Y	Y	N	N	N	Y
3 ***Lucas***	Y	N	Y	Y	Y	Y	Y	Y
4 ***Cole***	Y	N	Y	Y	Y	Y	Y	Y
5 ***Istook***	Y	N	Y	Y	?	?	?	+
OREGON								
1 Wu	Y	Y	N	Y	N	N	Y	Y
2 ***Walden***	Y	N	Y	Y	Y	Y	Y	Y
3 Blumenauer	Y	Y	N	Y	N	N	N	N
4 DeFazio	Y	Y	N	Y	N	N	?	Y
5 Hooley	Y	Y	N	Y	N	N	N	Y
PENNSYLVANIA								
1 Brady	Y	Y	N	Y	N	N	N	N
2 Fattah	Y	Y	N	Y	?	N	N	?
3 ***English***	Y	Y	Y	?	Y	Y	Y	Y
4 ***Hart***	?	N	Y	Y	Y	Y	Y	Y
5 ***Peterson***	Y	N	Y	Y	Y	Y	Y	Y
6 ***Gerlach***	Y	N	Y	Y	Y	Y	Y	Y
7 ***Weldon***	Y	N	Y	?	Y	Y	Y	Y
8 ***Greenwood***	?	Y	Y	Y	Y	Y	Y	Y
9 ***Shuster, Bill***	Y	N	Y	Y	Y	Y	Y	Y
10 ***Sherwood***	Y	N	Y	Y	Y	Y	Y	Y
11 Kanjorski	Y	Y	N	Y	N	N	N	N
12 Murtha	Y	Y	N	Y	N	N	N	N
13 Hoeffel	Y	Y	N	Y	N	N	N	Y
14 Doyle	Y	Y	N	Y	N	N	N	N
15 ***Toomey***	Y	N	Y	Y	Y	Y	Y	Y
16 ***Pitts***	Y	N	Y	Y	Y	Y	Y	Y
17 Holden	Y	N	Y	Y	N	N	N	Y
18 ***Murphy***	?	N	Y	Y	Y	Y	Y	Y
19 ***Platts***	Y	N	Y	Y	Y	Y	Y	Y
RHODE ISLAND								
1 Kennedy	Y	Y	N	Y	N	N	N	Y
2 Langevin	Y	Y	N	Y	N	N	N	Y
SOUTH CAROLINA								
1 ***Brown***	Y	N	Y	Y	Y	Y	Y	Y
2 ***Wilson***	Y	N	Y	Y	Y	Y	Y	Y
3 ***Barrett***	Y	N	Y	Y	Y	Y	Y	Y
4 ***DeMint***	Y	N	Y	Y	Y	Y	Y	Y
5 Spratt	Y	Y	N	Y	N	N	N	Y
6 Clyburn	Y	Y	Y	Y	N	N	N	Y
SOUTH DAKOTA								
AL Herseth	Y	N	Y	Y	?	?	?	?
TENNESSEE								
1 ***Jenkins***	Y	N	Y	Y	Y	Y	Y	Y
2 ***Duncan***	Y	N	Y	Y	Y	Y	Y	Y
3 ***Wamp***	Y	N	Y	Y	Y	Y	Y	Y
4 Davis	Y	N	Y	Y	N	N	Y	Y
5 Cooper	Y	Y	N	Y	N	N	N	N
6 Gordon	Y	N	Y	Y	N	N	?	Y
7 ***Blackburn***	Y	N	Y	Y	Y	Y	Y	Y
8 Tanner	Y	Y	Y	Y	N	N	N	N
9 Ford	Y	Y	Y	Y	N	N	N	Y
TEXAS								
1 Sandlin	Y	N	Y	Y	N	N	Y	Y
2 Turner	Y	N	Y	Y	N	N	N	Y
3 ***Johnson, Sam***	Y	N	Y	Y	Y	Y	Y	Y
4 ***Hall***	Y	N	Y	Y	Y	Y	Y	Y
5 ***Hensarling***	?	N	Y	Y	Y	Y	Y	Y
6 ***Barton***	Y	N	Y	Y	Y	Y	Y	Y
7 ***Culberson***	Y	N	Y	Y	Y	Y	Y	Y
8 ***Brady***	Y	N	Y	Y	Y	Y	Y	Y
9 Lampson	Y	Y	Y	Y	N	N	N	Y
10 Doggett	Y	Y	N	Y	N	N	?	?
11 Edwards	Y	N	Y	Y	N	N	N	Y
12 ***Granger***	Y	N	Y	Y	Y	Y	Y	Y
13 ***Thornberry***	Y	N	Y	Y	Y	Y	Y	Y
14 ***Paul***	N	N	Y	Y	Y	Y	?	Y
15 Hinojosa	Y	Y	N	Y	N	N	Y	Y
16 Reyes	Y	Y	N	Y	N	N	Y	Y
17 Stenholm	Y	N	Y	Y	N	N	N	Y
18 Jackson-Lee	Y	Y	N	Y	N	N	N	Y
19 ***Neugebauer***	Y	N	Y	Y	Y	Y	Y	Y
20 Gonzalez	Y	Y	N	Y	N	N	N	Y
21 ***Smith***	Y	N	Y	Y	Y	Y	Y	Y
22 ***DeLay***	Y	N	Y	Y	Y	Y	Y	Y
23 ***Bonilla***	Y	N	Y	Y	Y	Y	Y	Y
24 Frost	Y	Y	N	Y	N	N	Y	Y
25 Bell	Y	Y	N	Y	N	N	N	Y
26 ***Burgess***	Y	N	Y	Y	Y	Y	Y	Y
27 Ortiz	Y	Y	N	Y	N	N	Y	Y
28 Rodriguez	Y	Y	N	Y	N	N	N	?
29 Green	Y	Y	N	Y	N	?	?	?
30 Johnson, E.B.	Y	Y	N	Y	N	N	N	Y
31 ***Carter***	Y	N	Y	Y	Y	Y	Y	Y
32 ***Sessions***	Y	N	Y	Y	Y	Y	Y	Y
UTAH								
1 ***Bishop***	Y	N	Y	Y	Y	Y	Y	Y
2 Matheson	Y	N	Y	Y	N	N	Y	Y
3 ***Cannon***	?	?	?	?	?	?	?	?
VERMONT								
AL *Sanders*	Y	Y	N	Y	N	N	N	Y
VIRGINIA								
1 ***Davis, Jo Ann***	Y	N	Y	Y	Y	Y	Y	Y
2 ***Schrock***	Y	N	Y	Y	Y	Y	Y	Y
3 Scott	Y	Y	N	Y	N	N	N	N
4 ***Forbes***	Y	N	Y	Y	Y	Y	Y	Y
5 ***Goode***	Y	N	Y	Y	Y	Y	Y	Y
6 ***Goodlatte***	Y	N	Y	Y	Y	Y	Y	Y
7 ***Cantor***	Y	N	Y	Y	Y	Y	Y	Y
8 Moran	Y	Y	N	Y	N	N	N	Y
9 Boucher	Y	Y	Y	Y	N	N	Y	Y
10 ***Wolf***	Y	N	Y	Y	Y	Y	Y	Y
11 ***Davis, T.***	Y	Y	Y	Y	Y	Y	Y	Y
WASHINGTON								
1 Inslee	Y	Y	N	Y	N	N	N	N
2 Larsen	Y	Y	N	Y	N	N	N	N
3 Baird	?	Y	N	Y	N	N	N	Y
4 ***Hastings***	Y	N	Y	Y	Y	Y	Y	Y
5 ***Nethercutt***	Y	?	Y	Y	Y	Y	Y	Y
6 Dicks	Y	Y	N	Y	N	N	N	N
7 McDermott	Y	Y	N	Y	N	N	N	N
8 ***Dunn***	?	N	Y	Y	Y	Y	Y	Y
9 Smith	Y	?	?	?	?	?	?	?
WEST VIRGINIA								
1 Mollohan	Y	N	Y	Y	N	N	N	N
2 ***Capito***	Y	N	Y	Y	Y	Y	Y	Y
3 Rahall	Y	N	Y	Y	N	N	N	Y
WISCONSIN								
1 ***Ryan***	Y	N	Y	Y	Y	Y	Y	Y
2 Baldwin	Y	Y	N	Y	N	N	N	Y
3 Kind	Y	Y	N	Y	N	N	N	Y
4 Kleczka	Y	?	?	?	?	?	?	?
5 ***Sensenbrenner***	N	N	Y	Y	Y	Y	Y	Y
6 ***Petri***	Y	N	Y	Y	Y	Y	Y	Y
7 Obey	N	Y	N	Y	N	N	N	N
8 ***Green***	Y	N	Y	Y	Y	Y	Y	Y
WYOMING								
AL ***Cubin***	Y	N	Y	Y	Y	Y	Y	Y

Southern states - Ala., Ark., Fla., Ga., Ky., La., Miss., N.C., Okla., S.C., Tenn., Texas, Va.

473. HR 4200. Fiscal 2005 Defense Authorization/Motion to Instruct. Pelosi, D-Calif., motion to instruct House conferees to accept provisions in the Senate bill that would broaden the categories covered by hate crimes to include crimes motivated by the victim's gender, sexual orientation or disability. Motion agreed to 213-186: R 31-177; D 182-9 (ND 138-0, SD 44-9); I 0-0. Sept. 28, 2004.

474. HR 4200. Fiscal 2005 Defense Authorization/Motion to Close Conference. Saxton, R-N.J., motion to close portions of the conference on the bill that would authorize funding for defense programs for fiscal 2005. Motion agreed to 396-0: R 207-0; D 189-0 (ND 136-0, SD 53-0); I 0-0. Sept. 28, 2004.

475. S 2363. Boys and Girls Clubs/Passage. Sensenbrenner, R-Wis., motion to suspend the rules and pass the bill that would authorize $450 million in grants for the Boys and Girls Clubs of America over five years and increase the number of chapters nationwide to 5,000 by 2011. Motion agreed to 374-19: R 185-19; D 189-0 (ND 136-0, SD 53-0); I 0-0. A two-thirds majority of those present and voting (262 in this case) is required for passage under suspension of the rules. Sept. 28, 2004.

476. HR 4520. Corporate Tax Overhaul/Motion to Instruct. Neal, D-Mass., motion to instruct House conferees to insist on a conference agreement that would not increase the federal deficit, and accept provisions in the Senate bill that would close tax shelters and end certain tax practices regarded as abusive. Motion rejected 205-215: R 4-214; D 200-1 (ND 147-0, SD 53-1); I 1-0. Sept. 29, 2004.

477. HR 3193. District of Columbia Gun Laws/Passage. Passage of the bill that would repeal the District of Columbia's laws that prohibit the sale and possession of handguns, handgun ammunition and semiautomatic weapons not banned by federal law. It would eliminate the District's firearm registration program and supersede the portion of city code that requires weapons to be kept unloaded and disassembled, or with the trigger locked. It would limit the possession of weapons to residents' homes and property, and prohibit any firearm from being carried on District streets. Passed 250-171: R 198-22; D 52-148 (ND 24-122, SD 28-26); I 0-1. Sept. 29, 2004.

478. H J Res 107. Fiscal 2005 Continuing Resolution/Recommit. Obey, D-Wis., motion to recommit the joint resolution to the Appropriations Committee with instructions to increase funding for the Veterans Health Administration, lift the cap on private military housing, implement the State Children's Health Insurance Program for 750,000 children, eliminate $1 billion in special student loan subsidies and provide additional funding for FBI counterterrorism and counterintelligence programs, education and health programs. Motion rejected 200-221: R 1-219; D 198-2 (ND 146-1, SD 52-1); I 1-0. Sept. 29, 2004.

479. H J Res 107. Fiscal 2005 Continuing Resolution/Passage. Passage of the joint resolution that would provide continuing appropriations through Nov. 20 for all federal departments and agencies whose fiscal 2005 appropriations bills have not been enacted. Passed 389-32: R 188-31; D 200-1 (ND 147-0, SD 53-1); I 1-0. Sept. 29, 2004.

480. HR 5183. Surface Transportation Extension/Recommit. DeFazio, D-Ore., motion to recommit the bill to the Transportation and Infrastructure Committee with instructions to increase each number in the bill by 12.85 percent. Motion rejected 199-218: R 0-217; D 198-1 (ND 146-0, SD 52-1); I 1-0. Sept. 30, 2004.

* Rep. Porter J. Goss, R-Fla., resigned effective Sept. 23, 2004. The last vote for which he was eligible was vote 472.

Key

Y	Voted for (yea).
#	Paired for.
+	Announced for.
N	Voted against (nay).
X	Paired against.
–	Announced against.
P	Voted "present."
C	Voted "present" to avoid possible conflict of interest.
?	Did not vote or otherwise make a position known.

Democrats **Republicans**
Independents

	473	474	475	476	477	478	479	480
ALABAMA								
1 Bonner	N	Y	Y	N	Y	N	Y	N
2 Everett	N	Y	Y	N	Y	N	Y	N
3 Rogers	N	Y	Y	N	Y	N	Y	N
4 Aderholt	N	Y	Y	N	Y	N	Y	N
5 Cramer	Y	Y	Y	Y	Y	Y	Y	Y
6 Bachus	N	Y	Y	N	Y	N	Y	N
7 Davis	Y	Y	Y	Y	Y	Y	Y	Y
ALASKA								
AL Young	N	Y	Y	N	Y	N	Y	N
ARIZONA								
1 Renzi	N	Y	Y	N	Y	N	Y	N
2 Franks	N	Y	N	N	Y	N	N	N
3 Shadegg	N	Y	N	N	Y	N	N	N
4 Pastor	Y	Y	Y	N	Y	Y	Y	Y
5 Hayworth	N	Y	Y	N	Y	N	Y	N
6 Flake	N	Y	N	N	Y	N	N	N
7 Grijalva	Y	Y	Y	Y	N	Y	Y	Y
8 Kolbe	N	Y	Y	N	Y	N	Y	N
ARKANSAS								
1 Berry	N	Y	Y	Y	Y	Y	Y	Y
2 Snyder	Y	Y	Y	Y	N	Y	Y	Y
3 Boozman	N	Y	N	Y	N	Y	N	Y
4 Ross	Y	Y	Y	Y	Y	Y	Y	Y
CALIFORNIA								
1 Thompson	Y	Y	Y	Y	N	Y	Y	Y
2 Herger	N	Y	Y	N	Y	N	Y	N
3 Ose	N	Y	?	N	Y	N	Y	N
4 Doolittle	N	Y	Y	N	Y	N	Y	N
5 Matsui	Y	Y	Y	Y	N	Y	Y	Y
6 Woolsey	Y	Y	Y	Y	N	Y	Y	Y
7 Miller, George	Y	Y	Y	Y	N	Y	Y	Y
8 Pelosi	Y	?	?	Y	N	Y	Y	Y
9 Lee	Y	Y	Y	Y	N	Y	Y	Y
10 Tauscher	Y	Y	Y	Y	N	Y	Y	Y
11 Pombo	N	Y	N	N	Y	N	Y	N
12 Lantos	Y	Y	Y	Y	N	Y	Y	Y
13 Stark	Y	?	?	Y	N	Y	Y	Y
14 Eshoo	Y	Y	Y	Y	N	Y	Y	Y
15 Honda	+	+	+	Y	N	Y	Y	Y
16 Lofgren	Y	Y	Y	Y	N	Y	Y	Y
17 Farr	Y	Y	Y	Y	N	Y	Y	Y
18 Cardoza	Y	Y	Y	Y	N	Y	Y	Y
19 Radanovich	N	Y	N	Y	N	Y	N	Y
20 Dooley	?	?	?	Y	N	Y	Y	Y
21 Nunes	N	Y	Y	N	Y	N	Y	N
22 Thomas	N	Y	Y	N	Y	N	Y	N
23 Capps	Y	Y	Y	Y	N	Y	Y	Y
24 Gallegly	N	Y	Y	N	Y	N	Y	N
25 McKeon	N	Y	Y	N	Y	N	Y	N
26 Dreier	N	Y	Y	N	Y	N	Y	N
27 Sherman	Y	Y	Y	Y	N	Y	Y	Y
28 Berman	Y	Y	Y	Y	N	Y	Y	Y
29 Schiff	Y	Y	Y	Y	N	Y	Y	Y
30 Waxman	Y	Y	Y	Y	N	Y	Y	Y
31 Becerra	Y	Y	Y	Y	N	Y	Y	Y
32 Solis	Y	Y	Y	Y	N	Y	Y	Y
33 Watson	Y	Y	Y	Y	N	Y	Y	Y
34 Roybal-Allard	Y	Y	Y	Y	N	Y	Y	Y
35 Waters	Y	Y	Y	Y	N	Y	Y	Y
36 Harman	Y	Y	Y	Y	N	Y	Y	Y

	473	474	475	476	477	478	479	480
37 Millender-McD.	Y	Y	Y	N	Y	Y	Y	Y
38 Napolitano	Y	Y	Y	Y	N	Y	Y	Y
39 Sánchez, Linda	+	+	+	Y	N	Y	Y	Y
40 Royce	N	Y	Y	N	Y	N	N	N
41 Lewis	N	Y	Y	N	Y	N	Y	N
42 Miller, Gary	N	Y	Y	N	Y	N	Y	N
43 Baca	Y	Y	Y	Y	N	Y	Y	Y
44 Calvert	N	Y	Y	N	Y	N	Y	N
45 Bono	N	Y	Y	N	Y	N	N	N
46 Rohrabacher	N	Y	Y	N	Y	N	Y	N
47 Sanchez, Loretta	Y	Y	Y	Y	N	Y	Y	Y
48 Cox	N	Y	Y	N	Y	N	Y	N
49 Issa	N	Y	Y	N	Y	N	Y	N
50 Cunningham	N	Y	Y	N	Y	N	Y	N
51 Filner	Y	Y	Y	Y	N	Y	Y	Y
52 Hunter	?	?	?	N	Y	N	Y	N
53 Davis	Y	Y	Y	N	Y	Y	Y	Y
COLORADO								
1 DeGette	Y	Y	Y	Y	N	Y	Y	Y
2 Udall	Y	Y	Y	Y	N	Y	Y	Y
3 McInnis	N	Y	N	Y	N	Y	N	Y
4 Musgrave	N	Y	Y	N	Y	N	Y	N
5 Hefley	N	Y	N	Y	N	Y	N	Y
6 Tancredo	N	Y	Y	N	Y	N	Y	N
7 Beauprez	N	Y	Y	N	Y	N	N	N
CONNECTICUT								
1 Larson	Y	Y	Y	Y	N	Y	Y	Y
2 Simmons	Y	Y	Y	Y	N	Y	N	Y
3 DeLauro	Y	Y	Y	Y	N	Y	Y	Y
4 Shays	?	?	?	N	N	N	Y	N
5 Johnson	Y	Y	Y	N	N	Y	N	Y
DELAWARE								
AL Castle	Y	?	Y	N	N	N	Y	N
FLORIDA								
1 Miller, J.	N	Y	N	N	Y	N	N	N
2 Boyd	N	Y	Y	Y	Y	Y	Y	Y
3 Brown	Y	Y	Y	Y	N	Y	Y	?
4 Crenshaw	N	Y	N	Y	N	Y	N	N
5 Brown-Waite	N	Y	Y	N	Y	N	?	N
6 Stearns	N	Y	N	Y	N	Y	N	N
7 Mica	N	Y	Y	N	Y	N	Y	N
8 Keller	N	Y	Y	N	Y	N	Y	N
9 Bilirakis	N	Y	Y	N	Y	N	Y	N
10 Young	N	Y	Y	N	N	Y	N	N
11 Davis	Y	Y	Y	Y	N	Y	Y	Y
12 Putnam	?	?	?	?	?	?	?	N
13 Harris	N	Y	Y	N	Y	N	Y	?
14 Vacant*								
15 Weldon	?	?	?	?	?	?	?	N
16 Foley	Y	Y	Y	N	Y	N	Y	N
17 Meek	Y	Y	Y	?	?	?	?	?
18 Ros-Lehtinen	Y	Y	Y	N	Y	N	Y	Y
19 Wexler	Y	Y	Y	Y	N	Y	Y	Y
20 Deutsch	Y	Y	Y	Y	N	Y	Y	Y
21 Diaz-Balart, L.	Y	?	?	N	Y	N	Y	Y
22 Shaw	Y	Y	Y	N	Y	N	Y	Y
23 Hastings	?	?	?	?	?	?	?	?
24 Feeney	N	Y	?	N	Y	N	N	N
25 Diaz-Balart, M.	Y	Y	Y	N	Y	N	Y	?
GEORGIA								
1 Kingston	?	?	?	N	Y	N	Y	N
2 Bishop	Y	Y	Y	Y	Y	Y	Y	Y
3 Marshall	Y	Y	Y	Y	Y	Y	Y	Y
4 Majette	?	?	?	Y	Y	Y	Y	Y
5 Lewis	Y	Y	Y	Y	N	?	Y	Y
6 Isakson	?	?	?	N	Y	N	Y	N
7 Linder	N	Y	Y	N	Y	N	Y	N
8 Collins	N	Y	?	N	Y	N	Y	N
9 Norwood	N	Y	Y	N	Y	N	Y	N
10 Deal	N	Y	N	N	Y	N	Y	N
11 Gingrey	N	Y	Y	N	Y	N	Y	N
12 Burns	Y	Y	Y	N	Y	N	Y	N
13 Scott	Y	Y	Y	N	Y	N	Y	Y
HAWAII								
1 Abercrombie	Y	Y	Y	Y	N	Y	Y	Y
2 Case	Y	Y	Y	Y	N	Y	Y	Y
IDAHO								
1 Otter	N	Y	N	N	Y	N	Y	N
2 Simpson	N	Y	N	Y	N	Y	N	Y
ILLINOIS								
1 Rush	Y	Y	Y	Y	N	Y	Y	Y
2 Jackson	Y	Y	Y	Y	N	Y	Y	Y
3 Lipinski	Y	Y	Y	Y	N	Y	Y	Y
4 Gutierrez	+	+	+	Y	N	Y	Y	Y
5 Emanuel	Y	Y	Y	Y	N	Y	Y	Y
6 Hyde	N	Y	Y	N	N	Y	N	N

ND Northern Democrats   SD Southern Democrats

	473	474	475	476	477	478	479	480
7 Davis	Y	Y	Y	Y	N	Y	Y	?
8 ***Crane***	N	Y	Y	N	Y	N	Y	N
9 Schakowsky	Y	Y	Y	Y	N	Y	Y	Y
10 ***Kirk***	Y	Y	Y	N	N	N	Y	N
11 ***Weller***	Y	Y	Y	N	Y	N	Y	N
12 Costello	Y	Y	Y	Y	Y	Y	Y	Y
13 ***Biggert***	Y	Y	Y	N	Y	N	Y	N
14 ***Hastert***								
15 ***Johnson***	N	Y	Y	N	Y	N	Y	N
16 ***Manzullo***	N	Y	N	N	Y	N	N	N
17 Evans	Y	Y	Y	N	Y	Y	Y	Y
18 ***LaHood***	Y	Y	Y	N	Y	N	Y	N
19 ***Shimkus***	Y	Y	Y	N	Y	N	Y	N
INDIANA								
1 Visclosky	Y	Y	Y	Y	N	Y	Y	Y
2 ***Chocola***	N	Y	Y	N	Y	N	Y	N
3 ***Souder***	N	Y	Y	N	Y	N	Y	N
4 ***Buyer***	N	Y	Y	N	Y	N	Y	N
5 ***Burton***	N	Y	Y	N	Y	N	Y	N
6 ***Pence***	N	Y	N	N	Y	N	N	N
7 Carson	Y	Y	Y	Y	N	Y	Y	Y
8 ***Hostettler***	N	Y	Y	N	Y	N	N	N
9 Hill	Y	Y	Y	Y	Y	Y	Y	Y
IOWA								
1 ***Nussle***	N	Y	Y	N	Y	N	Y	N
2 ***Leach***	Y	Y	Y	Y	N	Y	Y	N
3 Boswell	Y	Y	Y	Y	Y	Y	Y	Y
4 ***Latham***	N	Y	Y	N	Y	N	Y	N
5 ***King***	N	Y	N	N	Y	N	N	N
KANSAS								
1 ***Moran***	N	Y	Y	N	Y	N	Y	N
2 ***Ryun***	N	Y	Y	N	Y	N	Y	N
3 Moore	Y	Y	Y	Y	N	Y	Y	Y
4 ***Tiahrt***	?	Y	Y	N	Y	N	Y	N
KENTUCKY								
1 ***Whitfield***	N	Y	Y	N	Y	N	Y	N
2 ***Lewis***	N	Y	Y	N	Y	N	Y	N
3 ***Northup***	N	Y	Y	N	Y	N	Y	N
4 Lucas	N	Y	Y	Y	Y	Y	Y	Y
5 ***Rogers***	?	?	?	N	Y	N	Y	N
6 Chandler	Y	Y	Y	Y	Y	Y	Y	Y
LOUISIANA								
1 ***Vitter***	N	Y	Y	N	Y	N	Y	N
2 Jefferson	Y	Y	Y	Y	N	Y	Y	Y
3 ***Tauzin***	?	?	?	?	?	?	?	?
4 ***McCrery***	N	Y	Y	N	Y	N	Y	N
5 ***Alexander***	N	Y	Y	N	Y	N	Y	N
6 ***Baker***	N	Y	Y	N	Y	N	Y	N
7 John	?	?	?	Y	Y	Y	Y	Y
MAINE								
1 Allen	Y	Y	Y	Y	N	Y	Y	Y
2 Michaud	Y	Y	Y	Y	Y	Y	Y	Y
MARYLAND								
1 ***Gilchrest***	Y	Y	Y	N	N	N	Y	N
2 Ruppersberger	Y	Y	Y	Y	N	Y	Y	Y
3 Cardin	Y	Y	Y	Y	N	Y	Y	Y
4 Wynn	Y	Y	Y	Y	N	Y	Y	Y
5 Hoyer	Y	Y	Y	Y	N	Y	Y	Y
6 ***Bartlett***	N	Y	Y	N	Y	N	N	N
7 Cummings	Y	Y	Y	Y	N	Y	Y	Y
8 Van Hollen	Y	Y	Y	Y	N	Y	Y	Y
MASSACHUSETTS								
1 Olver	Y	Y	Y	Y	N	Y	Y	Y
2 Neal	Y	Y	Y	Y	N	Y	Y	Y
3 McGovern	Y	Y	Y	Y	N	Y	Y	Y
4 Frank	Y	Y	Y	Y	N	Y	Y	Y
5 Meehan	Y	Y	Y	Y	N	Y	Y	Y
6 Tierney	Y	Y	Y	Y	N	Y	Y	Y
7 Markey	Y	Y	Y	Y	N	Y	Y	Y
8 Capuano	Y	Y	Y	Y	N	Y	Y	Y
9 Lynch	Y	Y	Y	Y	N	Y	Y	Y
10 Delahunt	Y	Y	Y	Y	N	Y	Y	Y
MICHIGAN								
1 Stupak	Y	Y	Y	Y	Y	Y	Y	Y
2 ***Hoekstra***	N	Y	Y	N	Y	N	Y	N
3 ***Ehlers***	N	Y	Y	N	Y	N	Y	N
4 ***Camp***	N	Y	Y	N	Y	N	Y	N
5 Kildee	Y	Y	Y	Y	N	Y	Y	Y
6 ***Upton***	N	Y	Y	N	Y	N	Y	N
7 ***Smith***	N	Y	Y	N	Y	N	N	N
8 ***Rogers***	N	Y	Y	N	Y	N	Y	N
9 ***Knollenberg***	N	Y	Y	N	Y	N	Y	N
10 ***Miller***	N	Y	Y	N	Y	N	Y	N
11 ***McCotter***	N	Y	Y	N	Y	N	Y	N
12 Levin	Y	Y	Y	Y	N	Y	Y	Y
13 Kilpatrick	Y	Y	Y	Y	N	Y	Y	Y
14 Conyers	Y	Y	Y	Y	N	Y	Y	Y
15 Dingell	Y	Y	Y	Y	Y	Y	Y	Y
MINNESOTA								
1 ***Gutknecht***	N	Y	Y	N	Y	N	N	N
2 ***Kline***	N	Y	Y	N	Y	N	Y	N
3 ***Ramstad***	N	Y	Y	N	N	N	Y	N
4 McCollum	Y	Y	Y	Y	N	Y	Y	Y
5 Sabo	Y	Y	Y	Y	N	Y	Y	Y
6 ***Kennedy***	N	Y	Y	N	Y	N	Y	N
7 Peterson	Y	Y	Y	Y	Y	N	Y	Y
8 Oberstar	Y	Y	Y	Y	Y	Y	Y	Y
MISSISSIPPI								
1 ***Wicker***	N	Y	Y	N	Y	N	Y	N
2 Thompson	Y	Y	Y	Y	N	Y	Y	Y
3 ***Pickering***	N	Y	Y	N	Y	N	Y	N
4 Taylor	N	Y	Y	Y	Y	N	Y	Y
MISSOURI								
1 Clay	Y	Y	Y	Y	N	Y	Y	Y
2 ***Akin***	N	Y	N	N	Y	N	N	N
3 Gephardt	?	?	?	?	?	?	?	Y
4 Skelton	Y	Y	Y	Y	Y	Y	Y	Y
5 McCarthy	Y	Y	Y	Y	N	Y	Y	Y
6 ***Graves***	N	Y	Y	N	Y	N	Y	N
7 ***Blunt***	N	Y	Y	?	Y	N	Y	N
8 ***Emerson***	N	Y	Y	N	Y	N	Y	N
9 ***Hulshof***	N	Y	Y	N	Y	N	Y	N
MONTANA								
AL ***Rehberg***	N	Y	Y	N	Y	N	Y	N
NEBRASKA								
1 Vacant								
2 ***Terry***	N	Y	Y	N	Y	N	Y	N
3 ***Osborne***	N	Y	Y	N	Y	N	Y	N
NEVADA								
1 Berkley	Y	Y	Y	Y	N	Y	Y	Y
2 ***Gibbons***	N	Y	Y	N	Y	N	Y	N
3 ***Porter***	Y	Y	Y	N	Y	N	Y	N
NEW HAMPSHIRE								
1 ***Bradley***	N	Y	Y	Y	Y	N	Y	N
2 ***Bass***	Y	Y	Y	N	Y	N	Y	N
NEW JERSEY								
1 Andrews	Y	Y	Y	Y	N	Y	Y	Y
2 ***LoBiondo***	Y	Y	Y	N	Y	N	Y	N
3 ***Saxton***	Y	Y	Y	N	N	N	Y	N
4 ***Smith***	Y	Y	Y	N	N	N	Y	N
5 ***Garrett***	N	Y	N	N	Y	N	N	N
6 Pallone	Y	Y	Y	Y	N	Y	Y	Y
7 ***Ferguson***	Y	Y	Y	N	N	N	Y	N
8 Pascrell	Y	Y	Y	Y	N	Y	Y	Y
9 Rothman	Y	Y	Y	Y	N	Y	Y	Y
10 Payne	?	?	?	Y	N	Y	Y	Y
11 ***Frelinghuysen***	Y	Y	Y	N	N	N	Y	N
12 Holt	Y	Y	Y	Y	N	Y	Y	Y
13 Menendez	Y	Y	Y	Y	N	Y	Y	Y
NEW MEXICO								
1 ***Wilson***	N	Y	Y	Y	Y	N	Y	N
2 ***Pearce***	N	Y	Y	N	Y	N	Y	N
3 Udall	Y	Y	Y	Y	N	Y	Y	Y
NEW YORK								
1 Bishop	Y	Y	Y	Y	N	Y	Y	Y
2 Israel	Y	Y	Y	Y	N	Y	Y	Y
3 ***King***	N	Y	Y	N	N	N	Y	N
4 McCarthy	Y	Y	Y	Y	N	Y	Y	Y
5 Ackerman	Y	Y	Y	Y	N	Y	Y	Y
6 Meeks	?	?	?	Y	N	Y	Y	?
7 Crowley	Y	Y	Y	Y	N	Y	Y	Y
8 Nadler	Y	Y	Y	Y	N	Y	Y	Y
9 Weiner	Y	Y	Y	Y	N	Y	Y	Y
10 Towns	Y	Y	Y	Y	N	Y	Y	Y
11 Owens	Y	Y	Y	Y	N	Y	Y	Y
12 Velázquez	Y	Y	Y	Y	N	Y	Y	Y
13 ***Fossella***	N	Y	Y	N	Y	N	Y	N
14 Maloney	Y	Y	Y	Y	N	Y	Y	Y
15 Rangel	Y	Y	Y	Y	N	Y	Y	Y
16 Serrano	Y	Y	Y	Y	N	Y	Y	Y
17 Engel	Y	Y	Y	Y	N	Y	Y	Y
18 Lowey	Y	Y	Y	Y	N	Y	Y	Y
19 ***Kelly***	Y	Y	Y	N	Y	N	Y	N
20 ***Sweeney***	N	Y	Y	N	Y	N	Y	N
21 McNulty	Y	Y	Y	Y	N	Y	Y	Y
22 Hinchey	Y	Y	Y	Y	N	Y	Y	Y
23 ***McHugh***	N	Y	Y	N	Y	N	Y	N
24 ***Boehlert***	?	?	?	?	?	?	?	?
25 ***Walsh***	N	Y	Y	N	N	N	Y	N
26 ***Reynolds***	N	Y	Y	N	Y	N	Y	N
27 ***Quinn***	N	Y	Y	N	N	N	Y	N
28 Slaughter	Y	Y	Y	Y	N	Y	Y	Y
29 ***Houghton***	N	Y	?	N	N	N	Y	N
NORTH CAROLINA								
1 Butterfield	Y	Y	Y	Y	N	Y	Y	Y
2 Etheridge	Y	Y	Y	Y	N	Y	Y	Y
3 ***Jones***	N	Y	N	N	Y	N	N	N
4 Price	Y	Y	Y	Y	N	Y	Y	Y
5 ***Burr***	?	?	?	N	Y	N	Y	N
6 ***Coble***	N	Y	Y	N	Y	N	Y	N
7 McIntyre	N	Y	Y	Y	Y	Y	Y	Y
8 ***Hayes***	N	Y	Y	N	Y	N	Y	N
9 ***Myrick***	N	Y	Y	N	Y	N	N	N
10 ***Ballenger***	?	?	?	N	Y	N	Y	N
11 ***Taylor***	N	Y	Y	N	Y	N	Y	N
12 Watt	Y	Y	Y	Y	N	Y	Y	Y
13 Miller	Y	Y	Y	Y	N	Y	Y	Y
NORTH DAKOTA								
AL Pomeroy	Y	Y	Y	Y	Y	Y	Y	Y
OHIO								
1 ***Chabot***	N	Y	Y	N	Y	N	N	N
2 ***Portman***	N	Y	Y	N	Y	N	Y	N
3 ***Turner***	N	Y	Y	N	Y	N	Y	N
4 ***Oxley***	N	Y	Y	N	Y	N	Y	N
5 ***Gillmor***	N	Y	Y	N	Y	N	Y	N
6 Strickland	Y	Y	Y	Y	Y	Y	Y	Y
7 ***Hobson***	N	Y	Y	N	Y	N	Y	N
8 ***Boehner***	N	Y	Y	N	Y	N	Y	N
9 Kaptur	Y	Y	Y	Y	N	Y	Y	Y
10 Kucinich	Y	Y	Y	Y	N	Y	Y	Y
11 Jones	?	?	?	Y	N	Y	Y	Y
12 ***Tiberi***	N	Y	Y	N	Y	N	Y	N
13 Brown	Y	Y	Y	Y	N	Y	Y	Y
14 ***LaTourette***	N	Y	Y	N	Y	N	Y	N
15 ***Pryce***	N	Y	Y	N	Y	N	Y	N
16 ***Regula***	N	Y	Y	N	Y	N	Y	N
17 Ryan	Y	Y	Y	Y	Y	Y	Y	Y
18 ***Ney***	N	Y	Y	N	Y	N	Y	N
OKLAHOMA								
1 ***Sullivan***	N	Y	Y	N	Y	N	Y	N
2 Carson	N	Y	Y	Y	Y	Y	Y	Y
3 ***Lucas***	N	Y	Y	N	Y	N	Y	N
4 ***Cole***	N	Y	Y	N	Y	N	Y	N
5 ***Istook***	N	Y	N	N	Y	N	Y	N
OREGON								
1 Wu	Y	Y	Y	Y	N	Y	Y	Y
2 ***Walden***	Y	Y	Y	N	Y	N	Y	N
3 Blumenauer	Y	Y	Y	Y	N	Y	Y	Y
4 DeFazio	Y	Y	Y	Y	Y	Y	Y	Y
5 Hooley	Y	Y	Y	Y	N	Y	Y	Y
PENNSYLVANIA								
1 Brady	Y	Y	Y	Y	N	Y	Y	Y
2 Fattah	?	?	?	Y	N	Y	Y	Y
3 ***English***	Y	Y	Y	N	Y	N	Y	N
4 ***Hart***	N	Y	Y	N	Y	N	Y	N
5 ***Peterson***	N	Y	Y	N	Y	N	Y	N
6 ***Gerlach***	Y	Y	Y	N	Y	N	Y	N
7 ***Weldon***	?	?	?	N	Y	N	Y	?
8 ***Greenwood***	Y	Y	Y	N	N	N	Y	N
9 ***Shuster, Bill***	N	Y	Y	N	Y	N	Y	N
10 ***Sherwood***	N	Y	Y	N	Y	N	Y	N
11 Kanjorski	Y	Y	Y	Y	Y	Y	Y	Y
12 Murtha	?	?	?	Y	Y	Y	Y	Y
13 Hoeffel	?	?	?	?	?	?	?	Y
14 Doyle	Y	Y	Y	Y	N	Y	Y	Y
15 ***Toomey***	N	Y	N	N	Y	N	N	N
16 ***Pitts***	N	Y	Y	N	Y	N	N	N
17 Holden	Y	Y	Y	Y	Y	Y	Y	Y
18 ***Murphy***	N	Y	Y	N	Y	N	Y	N
19 ***Platts***	Y	Y	Y	N	Y	N	Y	N
RHODE ISLAND								
1 Kennedy	Y	Y	Y	Y	N	Y	Y	Y
2 Langevin	Y	Y	Y	Y	N	Y	Y	Y
SOUTH CAROLINA								
1 ***Brown***	N	Y	Y	N	Y	N	Y	N
2 ***Wilson***	N	Y	Y	N	Y	N	Y	N
3 ***Barrett***	?	?	?	N	Y	N	N	N
4 ***DeMint***	?	?	?	N	Y	N	Y	N
5 Spratt	Y	Y	Y	Y	N	Y	Y	Y
6 Clyburn	Y	Y	Y	Y	N	Y	Y	Y
SOUTH DAKOTA								
AL Herseth	Y	Y	Y	Y	Y	Y	Y	Y
TENNESSEE								
1 ***Jenkins***	N	Y	Y	N	Y	N	Y	N
2 ***Duncan***	N	Y	Y	N	Y	N	N	N
3 ***Wamp***	N	Y	Y	N	Y	N	Y	N
4 Davis	N	Y	Y	Y	Y	Y	Y	Y
5 Cooper	Y	Y	Y	Y	Y	Y	N	Y
6 Gordon	Y	Y	Y	Y	Y	Y	Y	Y
7 ***Blackburn***	N	Y	Y	N	Y	N	Y	N
8 Tanner	N	Y	Y	Y	Y	Y	Y	Y
9 Ford	Y	Y	Y	Y	Y	Y	Y	Y
TEXAS								
1 Sandlin	Y	Y	Y	Y	Y	Y	Y	Y
2 Turner	Y	Y	Y	Y	Y	Y	Y	Y
3 ***Johnson, Sam***	N	Y	N	N	Y	N	Y	N
4 ***Hall***	N	Y	Y	N	Y	N	Y	N
5 ***Hensarling***	N	Y	N	N	Y	N	N	N
6 ***Barton***	N	Y	Y	N	Y	N	Y	N
7 ***Culberson***	N	Y	N	N	Y	N	Y	N
8 ***Brady***	N	Y	Y	N	Y	N	Y	N
9 Lampson	Y	Y	Y	Y	Y	Y	Y	Y
10 Doggett	Y	Y	Y	Y	N	Y	Y	Y
11 Edwards	Y	Y	Y	Y	Y	Y	Y	Y
12 ***Granger***	N	Y	Y	N	Y	N	Y	N
13 ***Thornberry***	N	Y	Y	N	Y	N	Y	N
14 ***Paul***	N	Y	N	N	Y	N	N	N
15 Hinojosa	Y	Y	Y	Y	Y	Y	Y	Y
16 Reyes	Y	Y	Y	Y	Y	Y	Y	Y
17 Stenholm	N	Y	Y	Y	Y	Y	Y	N
18 Jackson-Lee	Y	Y	Y	Y	N	Y	Y	Y
19 ***Neugebauer***	N	Y	Y	N	Y	N	Y	N
20 Gonzalez	Y	Y	Y	Y	N	Y	Y	Y
21 ***Smith***	N	Y	Y	N	Y	N	Y	N
22 ***DeLay***	N	Y	Y	N	Y	N	Y	N
23 ***Bonilla***	N	Y	Y	?	Y	N	Y	N
24 Frost	Y	Y	Y	Y	N	Y	Y	Y
25 Bell	Y	Y	Y	Y	N	Y	Y	Y
26 ***Burgess***	N	Y	Y	N	Y	N	Y	N
27 Ortiz	Y	Y	Y	Y	Y	Y	Y	Y
28 Rodriguez	Y	Y	Y	Y	N	Y	Y	Y
29 Green	Y	Y	Y	Y	Y	Y	Y	Y
30 Johnson, E.B.	Y	Y	Y	Y	N	Y	Y	Y
31 ***Carter***	N	Y	Y	N	Y	N	Y	N
32 ***Sessions***	N	Y	Y	N	Y	N	Y	N
UTAH								
1 ***Bishop***	N	Y	Y	N	Y	N	Y	N
2 Matheson	Y	Y	Y	Y	Y	Y	Y	Y
3 ***Cannon***	?	?	?	?	?	?	?	?
VERMONT								
AL *Sanders*	?	?	?	Y	N	Y	Y	Y
VIRGINIA								
1 ***Davis, Jo Ann***	N	Y	Y	N	Y	N	Y	N
2 ***Schrock***	N	Y	Y	N	Y	N	Y	N
3 Scott	Y	Y	Y	Y	N	Y	Y	Y
4 ***Forbes***	N	Y	Y	N	Y	N	Y	N
5 ***Goode***	N	Y	Y	N	Y	N	Y	N
6 ***Goodlatte***	N	Y	Y	N	Y	N	Y	N
7 ***Cantor***	N	Y	Y	N	Y	N	Y	N
8 Moran	Y	Y	Y	Y	N	Y	Y	Y
9 Boucher	Y	Y	Y	Y	Y	Y	Y	Y
10 ***Wolf***	N	Y	Y	N	N	N	Y	N
11 ***Davis, T.***	N	Y	Y	N	N	N	Y	N
WASHINGTON								
1 Inslee	Y	Y	Y	Y	N	Y	Y	Y
2 Larsen	Y	Y	Y	Y	N	Y	Y	Y
3 Baird	Y	Y	Y	Y	Y	Y	Y	Y
4 ***Hastings***	N	Y	Y	N	Y	N	Y	N
5 ***Nethercutt***	?	?	?	?	?	?	?	?
6 Dicks	Y	Y	Y	Y	Y	Y	Y	Y
7 McDermott	Y	Y	Y	Y	N	Y	Y	Y
8 ***Dunn***	N	Y	Y	N	Y	N	Y	N
9 Smith	Y	Y	Y	Y	N	Y	Y	Y
WEST VIRGINIA								
1 Mollohan	Y	Y	Y	Y	Y	Y	Y	Y
2 ***Capito***	N	Y	Y	Y	Y	Y	Y	N
3 Rahall	Y	Y	Y	Y	Y	Y	Y	Y
WISCONSIN								
1 ***Ryan***	N	Y	Y	N	Y	N	N	N
2 Baldwin	Y	Y	Y	Y	N	Y	Y	Y
3 Kind	Y	Y	Y	Y	Y	Y	Y	Y
4 Kleczka	Y	Y	Y	Y	N	Y	Y	Y
5 ***Sensenbrenner***	N	Y	Y	N	Y	N	N	N
6 ***Petri***	N	Y	Y	N	Y	N	N	N
7 Obey	Y	Y	Y	Y	P	Y	Y	Y
8 ***Green***	N	Y	Y	N	Y	N	N	N
WYOMING								
AL ***Cubin***	?	?	?	N	Y	N	N	N

Southern states - Ala., Ark., Fla., Ga., Ky., La., Miss., N.C., Okla., S.C., Tenn., Texas, Va.

Key

Y	Voted for (yea).
#	Paired for.
+	Announced for.
N	Voted against (nay).
X	Paired against.
–	Announced against.
P	Voted "present."
C	Voted "present" to avoid possible conflict of interest.
?	Did not vote or otherwise make a position known.

Democrats **Republicans** *Independents*

481. HR 5183. Surface Transportation Extension/Passage. Passage of the bill that would extend funding for highway, transit and transportation safety programs for an additional eight months, through May 31, 2005. The bill also would reauthorize the 18.4-cents-per-gallon gasoline tax. Passed 409-8: R 209-8; D 199-0 (ND 146-0, SD 53-0); I 1-0. Sept. 30, 2004.

482. HR 5149. Temporary Welfare Reauthorization/Passage. Herger, R-Calif., motion to suspend the rules and pass the bill that would extend, through March 31, 2005, the Temporary Assistance for Needy Families block grant program. Motion agreed to 416-0: R 217-0; D 198-0 (ND 145-0, SD 53-0); I 1-0. A two-thirds majority of those present and voting (278 in this case) is required for passage under suspension of the rules. Sept. 30, 2004.

483. HR 4231. Department of Veterans Affairs Nurse Recruitment/Passage. Smith, R-N.J., motion to suspend the rules and pass the bill that would authorize the department to establish a pilot program to study the use of outside recruitment, advertising and communications agencies, and the use of interactive and online technologies to improve its nurse recruitment program. Motion agreed to 411-1: R 216-1; D 194-0 (ND 142-0, SD 52-0); I 1-0. A two-thirds majority of those present and voting (275 in this case) is required for passage under suspension of the rules. Sept. 30, 2004.

484. H J Res 106. Same-Sex Marriage Ban Constitutional Amendment/Passage. Passage of the joint resolution to propose a constitutional amendment to define marriage as consisting only of the union of a man and a woman. The U.S. Constitution or any state's constitution could not be construed to require that marriage or any other constructs of marriage be conferred to any other union. Rejected 227-186: R 191-27; D 36-158 (ND 7-135, SD 29-23); I 0-1. A two-thirds majority vote of those present and voting (276 in this case) is required to pass a joint resolution proposing an amendment to the Constitution. A "yea" was a vote in support of the president's position. Sept. 30, 2004.

485. H Con Res 501. Duke Ellington Tribute/Adoption. Burns, R-Ga., motion to suspend the rules and adopt the concurrent resolution that would honor the life and work of Duke Ellington, recognize the 30th anniversary of the Duke Ellington School of the Arts and support the annual Duke Ellington Jazz Festival to be held in Washington, D.C. Motion agreed to 391-0: R 205-0; D 185-0 (ND 134-0, SD 51-0); I 1-0. A two-thirds majority of those present and voting (261 in this case) is required for adoption under suspension of the rules. Sept. 30, 2004.

486. H Res 792. United Negro College Fund Anniversary/Adoption. Burns, R-Ga., motion to suspend the rules and adopt the resolution that would honor the United Negro College Fund on its 60th anniversary. Motion agreed to 386-0: R 201-0; D 184-0 (ND 133-0, SD 51-0); I 1-0. A two-thirds majority of those present and voting (258 in this case) is required for adoption under suspension of the rules. Sept. 30, 2004.

	481	482	483	484	485	486
ALABAMA						
1 Bonner	Y	Y	Y	Y	Y	Y
2 Everett	Y	Y	Y	Y	Y	Y
3 Rogers	Y	Y	Y	Y	Y	Y
4 Aderholt	Y	Y	Y	Y	Y	Y
5 Cramer	Y	Y	Y	Y	Y	Y
6 Bachus	Y	Y	Y	Y	?	Y
7 Davis	Y	Y	Y	Y	Y	Y
ALASKA						
AL *Young*	Y	Y	Y	Y	Y	Y
ARIZONA						
1 *Renzi*	Y	Y	Y	Y	Y	Y
2 *Franks*	N	Y	Y	Y	Y	Y
3 *Shadegg*	Y	Y	Y	Y	Y	Y
4 Pastor	Y	Y	Y	N	Y	Y
5 *Hayworth*	Y	Y	Y	Y	Y	Y
6 *Flake*	N	Y	Y	Y	Y	Y
7 Grijalva	Y	Y	Y	N	Y	Y
8 *Kolbe*	Y	Y	Y	N	Y	Y
ARKANSAS						
1 Berry	Y	Y	Y	Y	Y	Y
2 Snyder	Y	Y	Y	N	Y	Y
3 *Boozman*	Y	Y	Y	Y	Y	Y
4 Ross	Y	Y	Y	Y	Y	Y
CALIFORNIA						
1 Thompson	Y	Y	Y	N	Y	Y
2 *Herger*	Y	Y	Y	N	Y	Y
3 *Ose*	Y	Y	Y	N	Y	Y
4 *Doolittle*	Y	Y	Y	N	Y	Y
5 Matsui	Y	Y	Y	N	Y	Y
6 Woolsey	Y	Y	Y	N	Y	Y
7 Miller, George	Y	Y	Y	N	Y	Y
8 Pelosi	Y	Y	Y	N	Y	Y
9 Lee	Y	Y	Y	N	Y	Y
10 Tauscher	Y	Y	Y	N	Y	Y
11 *Pombo*	Y	Y	Y	Y	Y	Y
12 Lantos	Y	Y	Y	N	Y	Y
13 Stark	Y	Y	Y	N	?	?
14 Eshoo	Y	Y	?	N	Y	Y
15 Honda	Y	Y	Y	N	Y	Y
16 Lofgren	Y	Y	Y	N	Y	Y
17 Farr	Y	Y	Y	N	Y	Y
18 Cardoza	Y	Y	Y	N	Y	Y
19 *Radanovich*	Y	Y	Y	Y	Y	Y
20 Dooley	Y	Y	Y	N	Y	Y
21 *Nunes*	Y	Y	Y	Y	Y	Y
22 *Thomas*	Y	Y	Y	Y	Y	Y
23 Capps	Y	Y	Y	N	Y	?
24 *Gallegly*	Y	Y	Y	Y	Y	Y
25 *McKeon*	Y	Y	Y	Y	Y	Y
26 *Dreier*	Y	Y	Y	N	Y	Y
27 Sherman	Y	Y	Y	N	Y	Y
28 Berman	Y	Y	Y	N	Y	Y
29 Schiff	Y	Y	Y	N	Y	Y
30 Waxman	Y	Y	Y	N	Y	Y
31 Becerra	Y	Y	Y	N	Y	Y
32 Solis	Y	Y	Y	N	Y	Y
33 Watson	Y	Y	Y	N	Y	Y
34 Roybal-Allard	Y	Y	Y	N	Y	Y
35 Waters	Y	Y	Y	N	Y	Y
36 Harman	?	?	?	?	?	?

	481	482	483	484	485	486
37 Millender-McD.	Y	Y	Y	N	Y	Y
38 Napolitano	Y	Y	Y	N	Y	Y
39 Sánchez, Linda	Y	Y	Y	N	Y	Y
40 *Royce*	Y	Y	Y	Y	Y	Y
41 *Lewis*	Y	Y	Y	Y	Y	Y
42 *Miller, Gary*	Y	Y	Y	Y	?	?
43 Baca	Y	Y	Y	N	Y	Y
44 *Calvert*	Y	Y	Y	Y	Y	Y
45 *Bono*	Y	Y	Y	N	Y	Y
46 *Rohrabacher*	Y	Y	Y	Y	Y	Y
47 Sanchez, Loretta	Y	Y	Y	N	Y	Y
48 *Cox*	Y	Y	Y	N	Y	Y
49 *Issa*	Y	Y	Y	Y	Y	Y
50 *Cunningham*	Y	Y	Y	Y	Y	Y
51 Filner	Y	Y	Y	N	Y	Y
52 *Hunter*	Y	Y	Y	?	?	?
53 Davis	Y	Y	Y	N	Y	Y
COLORADO						
1 DeGette	Y	Y	Y	N	Y	Y
2 Udall	Y	Y	Y	N	Y	Y
3 *McInnis*	Y	Y	Y	N	Y	Y
4 *Musgrave*	Y	Y	Y	Y	Y	Y
5 *Hefley*	Y	Y	Y	Y	Y	?
6 *Tancredo*	Y	Y	Y	Y	Y	Y
7 *Beauprez*	Y	Y	Y	Y	Y	Y
CONNECTICUT						
1 Larson	Y	Y	Y	N	Y	Y
2 *Simmons*	Y	Y	Y	N	Y	Y
3 DeLauro	Y	Y	Y	N	Y	Y
4 *Shays*	Y	Y	Y	N	Y	Y
5 *Johnson*	Y	Y	Y	N	?	?
DELAWARE						
AL *Castle*	Y	Y	Y	N	Y	Y
FLORIDA						
1 *Miller, J.*	Y	Y	Y	Y	Y	Y
2 Boyd	Y	Y	Y	N	Y	Y
3 Brown	?	?	?	?	?	?
4 *Crenshaw*	Y	Y	Y	Y	Y	Y
5 *Brown-Waite*	Y	Y	Y	Y	Y	Y
6 *Stearns*	N	Y	Y	Y	Y	Y
7 *Mica*	Y	Y	Y	Y	Y	Y
8 *Keller*	Y	Y	Y	Y	Y	Y
9 *Bilirakis*	Y	Y	Y	Y	Y	Y
10 *Young*	Y	Y	Y	Y	Y	Y
11 Davis	Y	Y	Y	N	Y	Y
12 *Putnam*	Y	Y	Y	Y	Y	Y
13 *Harris*	?	?	?	Y	Y	Y
14 Vacant						
15 *Weldon*	Y	Y	Y	Y	Y	Y
16 *Foley*	Y	Y	Y	N	Y	?
17 Meek	?	?	?	?	?	?
18 *Ros-Lehtinen*	?	?	?	?	?	?
19 Wexler	Y	Y	Y	N	Y	Y
20 Deutsch	Y	Y	Y	N	Y	Y
21 *Diaz-Balart, L.*	?	?	?	?	?	?
22 *Shaw*	Y	Y	Y	N	Y	Y
23 Hastings	?	?	?	?	?	?
24 *Feeney*	Y	Y	Y	Y	Y	Y
25 *Diaz-Balart, M.*	?	?	?	?	?	?
GEORGIA						
1 *Kingston*	Y	Y	Y	Y	Y	Y
2 Bishop	Y	Y	Y	Y	Y	Y
3 Marshall	Y	Y	Y	Y	Y	Y
4 Majette	Y	Y	Y	N	Y	Y
5 Lewis	Y	Y	Y	N	Y	Y
6 *Isakson*	Y	Y	Y	Y	Y	Y
7 *Linder*	Y	Y	Y	Y	Y	Y
8 *Collins*	Y	Y	Y	Y	Y	Y
9 *Norwood*	Y	Y	Y	Y	Y	Y
10 *Deal*	Y	Y	Y	Y	?	?
11 *Gingrey*	Y	Y	Y	Y	Y	Y
12 *Burns*	Y	Y	Y	Y	Y	Y
13 Scott	Y	Y	Y	Y	Y	Y
HAWAII						
1 Abercrombie	Y	Y	Y	N	Y	Y
2 Case	Y	Y	Y	N	Y	Y
IDAHO						
1 *Otter*	Y	Y	Y	Y	Y	Y
2 *Simpson*	Y	Y	Y	Y	Y	Y
ILLINOIS						
1 Rush	Y	Y	Y	N	Y	Y
2 Jackson	Y	Y	Y	N	Y	Y
3 Lipinski	Y	Y	Y	N	Y	Y
4 Gutierrez	Y	Y	Y	N	Y	Y
5 Emanuel	Y	Y	Y	N	?	?
6 *Hyde*	Y	Y	Y	Y	Y	Y

ND Northern Democrats   SD Southern Democrats

	481	482	483	484	485	486
7 Davis	?	?	?	?	?	?
8 ***Crane***	Y	Y	Y	Y	Y	Y
9 Schakowsky	Y	Y	Y	N	Y	Y
10 ***Kirk***	Y	Y	Y	N	Y	Y
11 ***Weller***	Y	Y	Y	Y	Y	Y
12 Costello	Y	Y	Y	Y	Y	Y
13 ***Biggert***	Y	Y	Y	N	Y	Y
14 ***Hastert***				Y	Y	
15 ***Johnson***	Y	Y	Y	Y	Y	Y
16 ***Manzullo***	Y	Y	Y	Y	Y	Y
17 Evans	Y	Y	Y	N	Y	Y
18 ***LaHood***	Y	Y	Y	Y	Y	Y
19 ***Shimkus***	Y	Y	Y	Y	?	?
INDIANA						
1 Visclosky	Y	Y	Y	N	Y	Y
2 ***Chocola***	Y	Y	Y	Y	Y	Y
3 ***Souder***	Y	Y	Y	Y	Y	Y
4 ***Buyer***	Y	Y	Y	Y	Y	Y
5 ***Burton***	Y	Y	Y	Y	Y	Y
6 ***Pence***	Y	Y	?	Y	Y	Y
7 Carson	Y	Y	Y	N	Y	Y
8 ***Hostettler***	Y	Y	Y	N	Y	Y
9 Hill	Y	Y	Y	N	Y	Y
IOWA						
1 ***Nussle***	Y	Y	Y	Y	Y	Y
2 ***Leach***	Y	Y	Y	N	Y	Y
3 Boswell	Y	Y	Y	N	?	?
4 ***Latham***	Y	Y	Y	Y	Y	Y
5 ***King***	Y	Y	Y	Y	Y	Y
KANSAS						
1 ***Moran***	Y	Y	Y	Y	Y	Y
2 ***Ryun***	Y	Y	Y	Y	Y	Y
3 Moore	Y	Y	?	N	Y	Y
4 ***Tiahrt***	Y	Y	Y	Y	Y	Y
KENTUCKY						
1 ***Whitfield***	Y	Y	Y	Y	Y	Y
2 ***Lewis***	Y	Y	Y	Y	Y	Y
3 ***Northup***	Y	Y	Y	Y	Y	Y
4 Lucas	Y	Y	Y	Y	?	?
5 ***Rogers***	Y	Y	Y	Y	Y	Y
6 Chandler	Y	Y	Y	Y	Y	Y
LOUISIANA						
1 ***Vitter***	Y	Y	Y	Y	Y	Y
2 Jefferson	Y	Y	Y	Y	Y	Y
3 ***Tauzin***	?	?	?	?	?	?
4 ***McCrery***	Y	Y	Y	Y	Y	Y
5 ***Alexander***	Y	Y	Y	Y	Y	Y
6 ***Baker***	Y	Y	Y	Y	Y	Y
7 John	Y	Y	Y	Y	Y	Y
MAINE						
1 Allen	Y	Y	?	N	Y	Y
2 Michaud	Y	Y	Y	N	Y	Y
MARYLAND						
1 ***Gilchrest***	Y	Y	Y	N	Y	Y
2 Ruppersberger	Y	Y	Y	N	Y	Y
3 Cardin	Y	Y	Y	N	Y	Y
4 Wynn	Y	Y	Y	N	Y	Y
5 Hoyer	Y	Y	Y	N	Y	Y
6 ***Bartlett***	Y	Y	Y	Y	Y	Y
7 Cummings	Y	Y	Y	N	Y	Y
8 Van Hollen	Y	Y	Y	N	Y	Y
MASSACHUSETTS						
1 Olver	Y	Y	Y	N	?	?
2 Neal	Y	Y	Y	N	Y	Y
3 McGovern	Y	Y	Y	N	Y	Y
4 Frank	Y	Y	Y	N	Y	Y
5 Meehan	Y	Y	Y	N	Y	Y
6 Tierney	Y	Y	Y	N	Y	Y
7 Markey	Y	Y	Y	N	Y	Y
8 Capuano	Y	Y	Y	N	Y	Y
9 Lynch	Y	Y	Y	N	Y	Y
10 Delahunt	Y	Y	Y	N	Y	Y
MICHIGAN						
1 Stupak	Y	Y	Y	N	Y	Y
2 ***Hoekstra***	Y	Y	Y	Y	Y	Y
3 ***Ehlers***	Y	Y	Y	Y	Y	Y
4 ***Camp***	Y	Y	Y	Y	Y	Y
5 Kildee	Y	Y	Y	N	Y	Y
6 ***Upton***	Y	Y	Y	Y	Y	Y
7 ***Smith***	Y	Y	N	Y	Y	Y
8 ***Rogers***	Y	Y	Y	Y	Y	?
9 ***Knollenberg***	Y	Y	Y	N	Y	Y
10 ***Miller***	Y	Y	Y	Y	Y	Y
11 ***McCotter***	Y	Y	Y	Y	Y	Y
12 Levin	Y	Y	Y	N	Y	Y
13 Kilpatrick	Y	Y	Y	N	?	?
14 Conyers	Y	Y	Y	N	Y	Y
15 Dingell	Y	Y	Y	N	Y	Y
MINNESOTA						
1 ***Gutknecht***	Y	Y	Y	Y	?	?
2 ***Kline***	Y	Y	Y	Y	Y	Y
3 ***Ramstad***	Y	Y	Y	Y	Y	Y
4 McCollum	Y	Y	Y	N	?	?
5 Sabo	Y	Y	Y	N	Y	Y
6 ***Kennedy***	Y	Y	Y	Y	Y	Y
7 Peterson	Y	Y	Y	Y	Y	Y
8 Oberstar	Y	Y	Y	?	?	?
MISSISSIPPI						
1 ***Wicker***	Y	Y	Y	Y	Y	Y
2 Thompson	Y	Y	Y	Y	Y	Y
3 ***Pickering***	Y	Y	Y	Y	Y	Y
4 Taylor	Y	Y	Y	Y	Y	Y
MISSOURI						
1 Clay	Y	Y	Y	N	Y	Y
2 ***Akin***	Y	Y	Y	Y	Y	Y
3 Gephardt	Y	?	?	N	Y	Y
4 Skelton	Y	Y	Y	Y	Y	Y
5 McCarthy	Y	Y	Y	N	Y	Y
6 ***Graves***	Y	Y	Y	Y	Y	Y
7 ***Blunt***	Y	Y	Y	Y	Y	Y
8 ***Emerson***	Y	Y	Y	Y	Y	Y
9 ***Hulshof***	Y	Y	Y	Y	Y	Y
MONTANA						
AL ***Rehberg***	Y	Y	Y	Y	Y	Y
NEBRASKA						
1 Vacant						
2 ***Terry***	Y	Y	Y	Y	Y	Y
3 ***Osborne***	Y	Y	Y	Y	Y	Y
NEVADA						
1 Berkley	Y	Y	Y	N	Y	Y
2 ***Gibbons***	Y	Y	Y	N	Y	Y
3 ***Porter***	Y	Y	Y	Y	Y	Y
NEW HAMPSHIRE						
1 ***Bradley***	Y	Y	Y	Y	Y	Y
2 ***Bass***	Y	Y	Y	N	Y	Y
NEW JERSEY						
1 Andrews	Y	Y	Y	N	Y	Y
2 ***LoBiondo***	Y	Y	Y	Y	Y	Y
3 ***Saxton***	?	Y	Y	Y	Y	Y
4 ***Smith***	Y	Y	Y	Y	Y	Y
5 ***Garrett***	Y	Y	Y	Y	Y	Y
6 Pallone	Y	Y	Y	N	Y	Y
7 ***Ferguson***	Y	Y	Y	Y	Y	Y
8 Pascrell	Y	Y	Y	N	Y	Y
9 Rothman	Y	Y	Y	N	Y	Y
10 Payne	Y	Y	Y	N	Y	Y
11 ***Frelinghuysen***	Y	Y	Y	N	Y	Y
12 Holt	Y	Y	Y	N	Y	Y
13 Menendez	Y	Y	Y	?	?	?
NEW MEXICO						
1 ***Wilson***	Y	Y	Y	Y	Y	Y
2 ***Pearce***	Y	Y	Y	Y	Y	Y
3 Udall	Y	Y	Y	N	Y	Y
NEW YORK						
1 Bishop	Y	Y	Y	N	Y	Y
2 Israel	Y	Y	Y	N	Y	Y
3 ***King***	Y	Y	Y	Y	?	?
4 McCarthy	Y	Y	Y	N	Y	Y
5 Ackerman	Y	Y	Y	N	?	?
6 Meeks	?	?	?	?	?	?
7 Crowley	Y	Y	Y	N	Y	Y
8 Nadler	Y	Y	Y	N	Y	Y
9 Weiner	Y	Y	Y	N	Y	Y
10 Towns	Y	Y	Y	N	Y	Y
11 Owens	Y	Y	Y	N	Y	Y
12 Velázquez	Y	Y	Y	N	Y	Y
13 ***Fossella***	Y	Y	Y	Y	Y	Y
14 Maloney	Y	Y	Y	N	Y	Y
15 Rangel	Y	Y	Y	?	?	?
16 Serrano	Y	Y	Y	N	Y	Y
17 Engel	Y	Y	Y	N	Y	Y
18 Lowey	Y	Y	Y	N	Y	Y
19 ***Kelly***	Y	Y	Y	Y	Y	Y
20 ***Sweeney***	Y	Y	Y	N	Y	Y
21 McNulty	Y	Y	Y	N	Y	Y
22 Hinchey	Y	Y	Y	N	Y	Y
23 ***McHugh***	Y	Y	Y	Y	Y	Y
24 ***Boehlert***	?	?	?	?	?	?
25 ***Walsh***	Y	Y	Y	Y	Y	Y
26 ***Reynolds***	Y	Y	Y	Y	Y	Y
27 ***Quinn***	Y	Y	Y	Y	Y	Y
28 Slaughter	Y	Y	Y	N	Y	Y
29 ***Houghton***	Y	Y	Y	N	Y	Y
NORTH CAROLINA						
1 Butterfield	Y	Y	Y	N	Y	Y
2 Etheridge	Y	Y	Y	Y	Y	Y
3 ***Jones***	N	Y	Y	Y	Y	Y
4 Price	Y	Y	Y	N	Y	Y
5 ***Burr***	Y	Y	Y	Y	Y	Y
6 ***Coble***	Y	Y	Y	Y	Y	Y
7 McIntyre	Y	Y	Y	Y	Y	Y
8 ***Hayes***	Y	Y	Y	Y	?	?
9 ***Myrick***	Y	Y	Y	Y	?	Y
10 ***Ballenger***	Y	Y	Y	Y	Y	?
11 ***Taylor***	Y	Y	Y	Y	Y	Y
12 Watt	Y	Y	Y	N	Y	Y
13 Miller	Y	Y	Y	N	Y	Y
NORTH DAKOTA						
AL Pomeroy	Y	Y	Y	N	Y	Y
OHIO						
1 ***Chabot***	Y	Y	Y	Y	Y	Y
2 ***Portman***	Y	Y	Y	Y	Y	Y
3 ***Turner***	Y	Y	Y	Y	Y	Y
4 ***Oxley***	N	Y	Y	Y	Y	Y
5 ***Gillmor***	Y	Y	Y	Y	Y	Y
6 Strickland	Y	Y	Y	N	Y	Y
7 ***Hobson***	Y	Y	Y	N	Y	Y
8 ***Boehner***	Y	Y	Y	Y	Y	Y
9 Kaptur	Y	Y	Y	N	Y	Y
10 Kucinich	Y	Y	Y	N	Y	Y
11 Jones	Y	Y	Y	N	Y	Y
12 ***Tiberi***	Y	Y	Y	Y	Y	Y
13 Brown	Y	Y	Y	N	Y	Y
14 ***LaTourette***	Y	Y	Y	Y	Y	Y
15 ***Pryce***	Y	Y	Y	N	Y	Y
16 ***Regula***	Y	Y	Y	Y	Y	Y
17 Ryan	Y	Y	Y	N	Y	Y
18 ***Ney***	Y	Y	Y	Y	Y	Y
OKLAHOMA						
1 ***Sullivan***	Y	Y	Y	Y	Y	?
2 Carson	Y	Y	Y	Y	Y	Y
3 ***Lucas***	Y	Y	Y	Y	Y	Y
4 ***Cole***	Y	Y	Y	Y	Y	Y
5 ***Istook***	Y	Y	Y	Y	?	Y
OREGON						
1 Wu	Y	Y	Y	N	Y	Y
2 ***Walden***	Y	Y	Y	Y	Y	Y
3 Blumenauer	Y	Y	Y	N	Y	Y
4 DeFazio	Y	Y	Y	N	Y	Y
5 Hooley	Y	Y	Y	N	Y	Y
PENNSYLVANIA						
1 Brady	Y	Y	Y	N	Y	Y
2 Fattah	Y	Y	Y	N	Y	Y
3 ***English***	Y	Y	Y	Y	Y	Y
4 ***Hart***	Y	Y	Y	Y	Y	Y
5 ***Peterson***	Y	Y	Y	Y	Y	?
6 ***Gerlach***	Y	Y	Y	N	Y	Y
7 ***Weldon***	Y	Y	Y	Y	Y	Y
8 ***Greenwood***	Y	Y	Y	N	?	?
9 ***Shuster, Bill***	Y	Y	Y	Y	Y	Y
10 ***Sherwood***	Y	Y	Y	Y	Y	Y
11 Kanjorski	Y	Y	Y	N	Y	Y
12 Murtha	Y	Y	Y	?	?	?
13 Hoeffel	Y	Y	Y	N	Y	Y
14 Doyle	Y	Y	Y	N	Y	Y
15 ***Toomey***	N	Y	Y	Y	Y	Y
16 ***Pitts***	Y	Y	Y	Y	Y	Y
17 Holden	Y	Y	Y	Y	Y	Y
18 ***Murphy***	Y	Y	Y	Y	Y	Y
19 ***Platts***	Y	Y	Y	Y	Y	Y
RHODE ISLAND						
1 Kennedy	Y	Y	Y	N	Y	Y
2 Langevin	Y	Y	Y	N	Y	Y
SOUTH CAROLINA						
1 ***Brown***	Y	Y	Y	Y	Y	Y
2 ***Wilson***	Y	Y	Y	Y	Y	Y
3 ***Barrett***	Y	Y	Y	Y	Y	Y
4 ***DeMint***	Y	Y	Y	Y	Y	Y
5 Spratt	Y	Y	Y	Y	Y	Y
6 Clyburn	Y	Y	Y	N	Y	Y
SOUTH DAKOTA						
AL Herseth	Y	Y	Y	Y	Y	Y
TENNESSEE						
1 ***Jenkins***	Y	Y	Y	Y	Y	Y
2 ***Duncan***	Y	Y	Y	Y	Y	Y
3 ***Wamp***	Y	Y	Y	Y	Y	Y
4 Davis	Y	Y	Y	Y	Y	Y
5 Cooper	Y	Y	Y	Y	Y	Y
6 Gordon	Y	Y	Y	Y	Y	Y
7 ***Blackburn***	Y	Y	Y	Y	Y	Y
8 Tanner	Y	Y	Y	Y	Y	Y
9 Ford	Y	Y	Y	Y	Y	Y
TEXAS						
1 Sandlin	Y	Y	Y	Y	Y	Y
2 Turner	Y	Y	?	N	Y	Y
3 ***Johnson, Sam***	Y	Y	Y	Y	Y	Y
4 ***Hall***	Y	Y	Y	Y	Y	Y
5 ***Hensarling***	N	Y	Y	Y	Y	Y
6 ***Barton***	Y	Y	Y	Y	Y	Y
7 ***Culberson***	Y	Y	Y	Y	Y	Y
8 ***Brady***	Y	?	Y	Y	?	?
9 Lampson	Y	Y	Y	Y	Y	Y
10 Doggett	Y	Y	Y	N	Y	Y
11 Edwards	Y	Y	Y	Y	Y	Y
12 ***Granger***	Y	Y	Y	Y	Y	Y
13 ***Thornberry***	Y	Y	Y	Y	Y	Y
14 ***Paul***	N	Y	Y	N	Y	Y
15 Hinojosa	Y	Y	Y	N	Y	Y
16 Reyes	Y	Y	Y	?	?	?
17 Stenholm	Y	Y	Y	Y	Y	Y
18 Jackson-Lee	Y	Y	Y	N	Y	Y
19 ***Neugebauer***	Y	Y	Y	Y	Y	Y
20 Gonzalez	Y	Y	Y	N	Y	Y
21 ***Smith***	Y	Y	Y	Y	Y	Y
22 ***DeLay***	Y	Y	Y	Y	Y	Y
23 ***Bonilla***	Y	Y	Y	Y	Y	Y
24 Frost	Y	Y	Y	N	Y	Y
25 Bell	Y	Y	Y	N	Y	Y
26 ***Burgess***	Y	Y	Y	Y	Y	Y
27 Ortiz	Y	Y	Y	Y	Y	Y
28 Rodriguez	Y	Y	Y	N	Y	Y
29 Green	Y	Y	Y	N	Y	Y
30 Johnson, E.B.	Y	Y	Y	N	Y	Y
31 ***Carter***	Y	Y	Y	Y	Y	Y
32 ***Sessions***	Y	Y	Y	Y	Y	Y
UTAH						
1 ***Bishop***	Y	Y	Y	Y	Y	Y
2 Matheson	Y	Y	Y	Y	Y	Y
3 ***Cannon***	?	?	?	?	?	?
VERMONT						
AL *Sanders*	Y	Y	Y	N	Y	Y
VIRGINIA						
1 ***Davis, Jo Ann***	Y	Y	Y	Y	Y	Y
2 ***Schrock***	Y	Y	Y	Y	Y	Y
3 Scott	Y	Y	Y	N	Y	Y
4 ***Forbes***	Y	Y	Y	Y	Y	Y
5 ***Goode***	Y	Y	Y	Y	Y	Y
6 ***Goodlatte***	Y	Y	Y	Y	Y	Y
7 ***Cantor***	Y	Y	Y	Y	Y	Y
8 Moran	Y	Y	Y	N	Y	Y
9 Boucher	Y	Y	Y	Y	Y	Y
10 ***Wolf***	Y	Y	Y	Y	Y	Y
11 ***Davis, T.***	Y	Y	Y	Y	?	?
WASHINGTON						
1 Inslee	Y	Y	Y	N	Y	Y
2 Larsen	Y	Y	Y	N	Y	Y
3 Baird	Y	Y	Y	N	Y	Y
4 ***Hastings***	Y	Y	Y	Y	Y	Y
5 ***Nethercutt***	?	?	?	?	?	?
6 Dicks	Y	Y	Y	N	Y	Y
7 McDermott	Y	Y	Y	N	Y	Y
8 ***Dunn***	Y	Y	Y	?	?	?
9 Smith	Y	Y	Y	N	Y	Y
WEST VIRGINIA						
1 Mollohan	Y	Y	Y	N	Y	Y
2 ***Capito***	Y	Y	Y	Y	Y	Y
3 Rahall	Y	Y	Y	Y	Y	Y
WISCONSIN						
1 ***Ryan***	Y	Y	Y	Y	Y	Y
2 Baldwin	Y	Y	Y	N	Y	Y
3 Kind	Y	Y	Y	N	Y	Y
4 Kleczka	Y	Y	Y	N	Y	Y
5 ***Sensenbrenner***	Y	Y	Y	Y	Y	Y
6 ***Petri***	Y	Y	Y	Y	Y	Y
7 Obey	Y	Y	Y	N	Y	Y
8 ***Green***	Y	Y	Y	Y	Y	Y
WYOMING						
AL ***Cubin***	Y	Y	Y	Y	Y	Y

Southern states - Ala., Ark., Fla., Ga., Ky., La., Miss., N.C., Okla., S.C., Tenn., Texas, Va.

Key

Y	Voted for (yea).
#	Paired for.
+	Announced for.
N	Voted against (nay).
X	Paired against.
–	Announced against.
P	Voted "present."
C	Voted "present" to avoid possible conflict of interest.
?	Did not vote or otherwise make a position known.

Democrats ***Republicans***
Independents

487. S Con Res 76. Holocaust Survivors Tribute/Adoption. Gibbons, R-Nev., motion to suspend the rules and adopt the concurrent resolution that would recognize Nov. 2, 2003, as "A Tribute to Survivors" at the U.S. Holocaust Memorial Museum. Motion agreed to 331-0: R 183-0; D 147-0 (ND 110-0, SD 37-0); I 1-0. A two-thirds majority of those present and voting (221 in this case) is required for adoption under suspension of the rules. Oct. 4, 2004.

488. S 1814. Federal Land Transfer/Passage. Gibbons, R-Nev., motion to suspend the rules and pass the bill that would transfer ownership of the Mingo Job Corps Civilian Conservation Center in Puxico, Mo., from the Interior Department's U.S. Fish and Wildlife Service to the Agriculture Department's Forest Service. Motion agreed to 333-0: R 184-0; D 148-0 (ND 111-0, SD 37-0); I 1-0. A two-thirds majority of those present and voting (222 in this case) is required for passage under suspension of the rules. Oct. 4, 2004.

489. H Res 567. Dental Care for Children/Adoption. Bilirakis, R-Fla., motion to suspend the rules and adopt the resolution that would congratulate the American Dental Association for establishing and sponsoring the "Give Kids a Smile" program. Motion agreed to 338-0: R 187-0; D 150-0 (ND 112-0, SD 38-0); I 1-0. A two-thirds majority of those present and voting (226 in this case) is required for adoption under suspension of the rules. Oct. 4, 2004.

490. S 878. Additional Federal Judgeships/Previous Question. Sessions, R-Texas, motion to order the previous question (thus ending debate and possibility of amendment) on adoption of the rule (H Res 814) to provide for House floor consideration of the bill that would create new district and circuit court judgeships. Motion agreed to 198-171: R 198-0; D 0-170 (ND 0-124, SD 0-46); I 0-1. Oct. 5, 2004.

491. S 878. Additional Federal Judgeships/Rule. Adoption of the rule (H Res 814) to provide for House floor consideration of the bill that would create new district and circuit court judgeships. Adopted 206-173: R 203-0; D 3-172 (ND 1-128, SD 2-44); I 0-1. Oct. 5, 2004.

492. S 878. Additional Federal Judgeships/9th Circuit Court of Appeals Division. Simpson, R-Idaho, amendment that would split the current U.S. Court of Appeals for the 9th Circuit into three circuits. It would reorganize the 9th Circuit to include California, Hawaii, Guam and the Northern Mariana Islands. It also would create a new 12th Circuit made up of Arizona, Idaho, Montana and Nevada and a new 13th Circuit made up of Alaska, Oregon and Washington. Adopted 205-194: R 200-11; D 5-182 (ND 2-135, SD 3-47); I 0-1. Oct. 5, 2004.

493. S 878. Additional Federal Judgeships/Recommit. Berman, D-Calif., motion to recommit the bill to the Judiciary Committee with instructions to add a section that would allow for an appeal of a judge's decision to not recuse himself from a particular case. Motion rejected 190-216: R 0-213; D 189-3 (ND 139-2, SD 50-1); I 1-0. (Subsequently, the bill was passed by voice vote.) Oct. 5, 2004.

	487	488	489	490	491	492	493
ALABAMA							
1 Bonner	Y	Y	Y	Y	Y	Y	N
2 Everett	Y	Y	Y	Y	Y	Y	N
3 Rogers	Y	Y	Y	Y	Y	Y	N
4 Aderholt	Y	Y	Y	Y	Y	Y	N
5 Cramer	Y	Y	Y	N	N	N	Y
6 Bachus	Y	Y	Y	Y	Y	Y	N
7 Davis	Y	Y	Y	N	N	N	Y
ALASKA							
AL Young	?	?	?	Y	Y	Y	N
ARIZONA							
1 Renzi	Y	Y	Y	Y	Y	Y	N
2 Franks	Y	Y	Y	Y	Y	Y	N
3 Shadegg	?	?	?	Y	Y	Y	N
4 Pastor	Y	Y	Y	N	N	N	Y
5 Hayworth	Y	Y	Y	Y	Y	Y	N
6 Flake	Y	Y	Y	Y	Y	Y	N
7 Grijalva	?	?	?	N	N	N	Y
8 Kolbe	Y	Y	Y	Y	Y	Y	N
ARKANSAS							
1 Berry	Y	Y	Y	N	N	N	Y
2 Snyder	Y	Y	Y	N	N	N	Y
3 Boozman	Y	Y	Y	Y	Y	Y	N
4 Ross	Y	Y	Y	N	N	N	Y
CALIFORNIA							
1 Thompson	Y	Y	Y	N	N	N	Y
2 Herger	?	Y	Y	Y	Y	Y	N
3 Ose	Y	Y	Y	Y	Y	Y	N
4 Doolittle	Y	Y	Y	Y	Y	Y	N
5 Matsui	?	?	?	N	N	N	?
6 Woolsey	Y	Y	Y	N	N	N	Y
7 Miller, George	Y	Y	Y	N	N	N	Y
8 Pelosi	?	?	?	N	N	N	Y
9 Lee	Y	Y	Y	N	N	N	Y
10 Tauscher	Y	Y	Y	N	N	N	Y
11 Pombo	Y	Y	Y	Y	Y	Y	N
12 Lantos	?	?	?	?	?	N	Y
13 Stark	Y	Y	Y	N	N	N	Y
14 Eshoo	Y	Y	Y	N	N	N	Y
15 Honda	Y	Y	Y	N	N	N	Y
16 Lofgren	Y	Y	Y	N	N	N	Y
17 Farr	Y	Y	Y	N	N	N	Y
18 Cardoza	Y	Y	Y	N	N	N	Y
19 Radanovich	Y	Y	Y	Y	Y	Y	N
20 Dooley	Y	Y	Y	N	N	N	Y
21 Nunes	?	?	?	Y	Y	Y	N
22 Thomas	Y	Y	Y	Y	Y	Y	N
23 Capps	Y	Y	Y	N	N	N	Y
24 Gallegly	?	?	?	Y	Y	Y	N
25 McKeon	Y	Y	Y	Y	Y	Y	N
26 Dreier	Y	Y	Y	Y	Y	Y	N
27 Sherman	Y	Y	Y	N	N	N	Y
28 Berman	Y	?	?	N	N	N	Y
29 Schiff	Y	Y	Y	N	N	N	Y
30 Waxman	Y	Y	Y	N	N	N	Y
31 Becerra	?	?	?	N	N	N	Y
32 Solis	Y	Y	Y	N	N	N	Y
33 Watson	?	?	?	N	N	N	Y
34 Roybal-Allard	Y	Y	Y	N	N	N	Y
35 Waters	Y	Y	Y	?	?	N	Y
36 Harman	Y	Y	Y	N	N	N	Y

	487	488	489	490	491	492	493
37 Millender-McD.	?	?	?	?	?	?	?
38 Napolitano	Y	Y	Y	?	?	N	Y
39 Sánchez, Linda	Y	Y	Y	N	N	N	Y
40 Royce	?	Y	Y	Y	Y	Y	N
41 Lewis	Y	Y	Y	Y	Y	Y	N
42 Miller, Gary	Y	Y	Y	Y	Y	Y	N
43 Baca	Y	Y	Y	N	N	N	Y
44 Calvert	Y	Y	Y	Y	Y	Y	N
45 Bono	Y	Y	Y	Y	Y	Y	N
46 Rohrabacher	Y	Y	Y	Y	Y	Y	N
47 Sanchez, Loretta	Y	Y	Y	N	N	N	Y
48 Cox	Y	Y	Y	Y	Y	Y	N
49 Issa	Y	Y	Y	Y	Y	Y	N
50 Cunningham	Y	Y	Y	Y	Y	Y	N
51 Filner	Y	Y	Y	N	N	N	Y
52 Hunter	Y	Y	Y	Y	Y	Y	N
53 Davis	Y	Y	Y	N	N	N	Y
COLORADO							
1 DeGette	Y	Y	Y	N	N	N	Y
2 Udall	Y	Y	Y	N	N	N	Y
3 McInnis	Y	Y	Y	Y	Y	Y	N
4 Musgrave	Y	Y	Y	Y	Y	Y	N
5 Hefley	Y	Y	Y	Y	Y	Y	N
6 Tancredo	Y	?	Y	Y	Y	Y	N
7 Beauprez	Y	Y	Y	Y	Y	Y	N
CONNECTICUT							
1 Larson	Y	Y	Y	?	N	N	Y
2 Simmons	Y	Y	Y	Y	Y	N	N
3 DeLauro	Y	Y	Y	N	N	N	Y
4 Shays	?	?	?	Y	Y	N	N
5 Johnson	Y	Y	Y	Y	Y	Y	N
DELAWARE							
AL Castle	Y	Y	Y	Y	Y	N	N
FLORIDA							
1 Miller, J.	Y	Y	Y	Y	Y	Y	N
2 Boyd	Y	Y	Y	N	N	N	Y
3 Brown	?	?	?	?	?	?	?
4 Crenshaw	Y	Y	Y	Y	Y	Y	N
5 Brown-Waite	?	?	?	Y	Y	Y	N
6 Stearns	Y	Y	Y	Y	Y	Y	N
7 Mica	Y	Y	Y	Y	Y	Y	N
8 Keller	Y	Y	Y	Y	Y	Y	N
9 Bilirakis	Y	Y	Y	Y	Y	Y	N
10 Young	Y	Y	Y	Y	Y	Y	N
11 Davis	Y	Y	Y	N	Y	N	Y
12 Putnam	Y	Y	Y	Y	Y	Y	N
13 Harris	Y	Y	Y	?	?	Y	N
14 Vacant							
15 Weldon	Y	Y	Y	Y	Y	Y	N
16 Foley	Y	Y	Y	Y	Y	Y	N
17 Meek	?	?	?	N	N	N	Y
18 Ros-Lehtinen	Y	Y	Y	Y	Y	Y	N
19 Wexler	Y	Y	Y	?	?	N	Y
20 Deutsch	Y	Y	Y	N	N	N	Y
21 Diaz-Balart, L.	Y	Y	Y	Y	Y	Y	N
22 Shaw	?	?	?	Y	Y	Y	N
23 Hastings	?	?	?	?	?	?	?
24 Feeney	Y	Y	Y	Y	Y	Y	N
25 Diaz-Balart, M.	Y	Y	Y	Y	Y	Y	N
GEORGIA							
1 Kingston	Y	Y	Y	Y	Y	Y	N
2 Bishop	?	Y	Y	N	N	N	Y
3 Marshall	Y	Y	Y	N	N	N	Y
4 Majette	?	?	?	?	?	?	?
5 Lewis	Y	Y	Y	?	?	N	Y
6 Isakson	?	?	?	?	?	?	?
7 Linder	Y	Y	Y	Y	Y	Y	N
8 Collins	Y	Y	Y	Y	Y	Y	N
9 Norwood	Y	Y	Y	?	?	?	?
10 Deal	Y	Y	Y	Y	Y	Y	N
11 Gingrey	Y	Y	Y	Y	Y	Y	N
12 Burns	Y	Y	Y	Y	Y	Y	N
13 Scott	?	?	?	N	N	N	Y
HAWAII							
1 Abercrombie	Y	Y	Y	–	–	–	+
2 Case	Y	Y	Y	N	N	N	Y
IDAHO							
1 Otter	Y	Y	Y	?	Y	Y	N
2 Simpson	Y	Y	Y	Y	Y	Y	N
ILLINOIS							
1 Rush	?	?	?	N	N	N	Y
2 Jackson	Y	Y	Y	N	N	N	Y
3 Lipinski	?	?	?	?	N	N	Y
4 Gutierrez	+	+	+	N	N	N	Y
5 Emanuel	Y	Y	Y	N	N	N	Y
6 Hyde							

ND Northern Democrats   SD Southern Democrats

	487	488	489	490	491	492	493
7 Davis	Y	Y	Y	N	N	N	Y
8 ***Crane***	Y	Y	Y	Y	Y	Y	N
9 Schakowsky	Y	Y	Y	N	N	N	Y
10 ***Kirk***	Y	Y	Y	?	?	Y	N
11 ***Weller***	Y	Y	Y	Y	Y	Y	N
12 Costello	Y	Y	Y	N	N	N	Y
13 ***Biggert***	Y	Y	Y	Y	Y	Y	N
14 ***Hastert***							N
15 ***Johnson***	Y	Y	Y	Y	Y	N	N
16 ***Manzullo***	Y	Y	Y	Y	Y	Y	N
17 Evans	Y	Y	Y	N	N	N	Y
18 ***LaHood***	Y	Y	Y	Y	Y	Y	N
19 ***Shimkus***	?	?	?	Y	Y	Y	N
INDIANA							
1 Visclosky	Y	Y	Y	N	N	N	Y
2 ***Chocola***	Y	Y	Y	Y	Y	Y	N
3 ***Souder***	Y	Y	Y	?	?	Y	N
4 ***Buyer***	?	?	?	?	?	?	N
5 ***Burton***	+	+	+	Y	Y	Y	N
6 ***Pence***	Y	Y	Y	Y	Y	Y	N
7 Carson	Y	Y	Y	N	N	N	Y
8 ***Hostettler***	Y	Y	Y	?	Y	Y	N
9 Hill	?	?	?	N	N	N	Y
IOWA							
1 ***Nussle***	Y	Y	Y	Y	Y	Y	N
2 ***Leach***	Y	Y	Y	Y	Y	Y	N
3 Boswell	Y	Y	Y	N	N	N	Y
4 ***Latham***	Y	Y	Y	Y	Y	Y	N
5 ***King***	Y	Y	Y	Y	Y	Y	N
KANSAS							
1 ***Moran***	Y	Y	Y	Y	Y	Y	N
2 ***Ryun***	Y	Y	Y	Y	Y	Y	N
3 Moore	Y	Y	Y	N	N	N	Y
4 ***Tiahrt***	Y	Y	Y	Y	Y	Y	N
KENTUCKY							
1 ***Whitfield***	Y	Y	Y	Y	Y	Y	N
2 ***Lewis***	Y	Y	Y	Y	Y	Y	N
3 ***Northup***	Y	Y	Y	Y	Y	Y	N
4 Lucas	Y	Y	Y	N	N	N	Y
5 ***Rogers***	Y	Y	Y	Y	Y	Y	N
6 Chandler	Y	Y	Y	N	N	N	Y
LOUISIANA							
1 ***Vitter***	?	?	?	Y	Y	Y	N
2 Jefferson	Y	Y	Y	N	N	N	Y
3 ***Tauzin***	?	?	?	?	?	?	?
4 ***McCrery***	Y	Y	Y	Y	Y	Y	N
5 ***Alexander***	?	?	?	?	?	Y	N
6 ***Baker***	Y	Y	Y	Y	Y	Y	N
7 John	?	?	?	?	?	?	?
MAINE							
1 Allen	Y	Y	Y	N	N	N	Y
2 Michaud	Y	Y	Y	N	N	N	Y
MARYLAND							
1 ***Gilchrest***	?	?	?	Y	Y	N	N
2 Ruppersberger	?	?	?	N	N	N	Y
3 Cardin	Y	Y	Y	N	N	N	Y
4 Wynn	Y	Y	Y	?	?	N	Y
5 Hoyer	Y	Y	Y	N	N	N	Y
6 ***Bartlett***	Y	?	?	Y	Y	Y	N
7 Cummings	?	?	?	N	N	N	Y
8 Van Hollen	Y	Y	Y	N	N	N	Y
MASSACHUSETTS							
1 Olver	Y	Y	Y	N	N	N	Y
2 Neal	?	?	?	N	N	N	Y
3 McGovern	?	?	?	?	?	N	Y
4 Frank	Y	Y	Y	N	N	N	Y
5 Meehan	Y	Y	Y	N	N	N	Y
6 Tierney	Y	Y	Y	N	N	N	Y
7 Markey	Y	Y	Y	N	N	N	Y
8 Capuano	?	?	?	N	N	N	Y
9 Lynch	?	?	?	N	N	N	Y
10 Delahunt	Y	Y	Y	N	N	?	Y
MICHIGAN							
1 Stupak	Y	Y	Y	N	N	N	Y
2 ***Hoekstra***	Y	Y	Y	Y	Y	Y	N
3 ***Ehlers***	Y	Y	Y	Y	Y	Y	N
4 ***Camp***	Y	Y	Y	Y	Y	Y	N
5 Kildee	Y	Y	Y	N	N	N	Y
6 ***Upton***	Y	Y	Y	Y	Y	Y	N
7 ***Smith***	?	?	?	Y	Y	Y	N
8 ***Rogers***	Y	Y	Y	Y	Y	Y	N
9 ***Knollenberg***	Y	Y	Y	Y	Y	Y	N
10 ***Miller***	Y	Y	Y	Y	Y	Y	N
11 ***McCotter***	Y	Y	Y	Y	Y	Y	N
12 Levin	Y	Y	Y	N	N	N	Y

	487	488	489	490	491	492	493
13 Kilpatrick	?	?	?	N	N	N	Y
14 Conyers	?	Y	Y	N	N	N	Y
15 Dingell	Y	Y	Y	N	N	?	Y
MINNESOTA							
1 ***Gutknecht***	Y	Y	Y	Y	Y	Y	N
2 ***Kline***	Y	Y	Y	Y	Y	Y	N
3 ***Ramstad***	Y	Y	Y	Y	Y	Y	N
4 McCollum	Y	Y	Y	N	N	N	Y
5 Sabo	Y	Y	Y	N	N	N	Y
6 ***Kennedy***	Y	Y	Y	Y	Y	Y	N
7 Peterson	Y	Y	Y	N	Y	Y	N
8 Oberstar	Y	Y	Y	?	?	N	Y
MISSISSIPPI							
1 ***Wicker***	Y	Y	Y	?	Y	Y	N
2 Thompson	Y	Y	Y	N	N	N	Y
3 ***Pickering***	?	?	?	Y	Y	Y	N
4 Taylor	Y	Y	Y	N	N	Y	Y
MISSOURI							
1 Clay	Y	Y	Y	?	?	?	Y
2 ***Akin***	Y	Y	Y	Y	Y	Y	N
3 Gephardt	?	?	?	?	?	?	?
4 Skelton	Y	Y	Y	N	N	N	Y
5 McCarthy	Y	Y	Y	N	N	N	Y
6 ***Graves***	Y	Y	Y	Y	Y	Y	N
7 ***Blunt***	Y	Y	Y	Y	Y	Y	N
8 ***Emerson***	Y	Y	Y	Y	Y	Y	N
9 ***Hulshof***	Y	Y	Y	Y	Y	Y	N
MONTANA							
AL ***Rehberg***	Y	Y	Y	Y	Y	Y	N
NEBRASKA							
1 Vacant							
2 ***Terry***	?	?	?	?	?	?	?
3 ***Osborne***	Y	Y	Y	Y	Y	Y	N
NEVADA							
1 Berkley	Y	Y	Y	N	N	N	Y
2 ***Gibbons***	Y	Y	Y	Y	Y	Y	N
3 ***Porter***	Y	Y	Y	Y	Y	Y	N
NEW HAMPSHIRE							
1 ***Bradley***	Y	Y	Y	Y	Y	Y	N
2 ***Bass***	Y	Y	Y	Y	Y	Y	N
NEW JERSEY							
1 Andrews	Y	Y	Y	N	N	N	Y
2 ***LoBiondo***	Y	Y	Y	Y	Y	Y	N
3 ***Saxton***	Y	?	Y	Y	Y	Y	N
4 ***Smith***	Y	Y	Y	Y	Y	Y	N
5 ***Garrett***	Y	Y	Y	Y	Y	Y	N
6 Pallone	?	?	?	N	N	N	Y
7 ***Ferguson***	Y	Y	Y	Y	Y	Y	N
8 Pascrell	Y	Y	Y	N	N	N	Y
9 Rothman	Y	Y	Y	?	N	N	Y
10 Payne	?	?	?	?	?	?	?
11 ***Frelinghuysen***	Y	Y	Y	Y	Y	Y	N
12 Holt	Y	Y	Y	N	N	N	Y
13 Menendez	?	?	Y	N	N	N	Y
NEW MEXICO							
1 ***Wilson***	Y	Y	Y	Y	Y	N	N
2 ***Pearce***	Y	Y	Y	Y	Y	Y	N
3 Udall	Y	Y	Y	N	N	N	Y
NEW YORK							
1 Bishop	Y	Y	Y	N	N	N	Y
2 Israel	Y	Y	Y	N	N	N	Y
3 ***King***	Y	Y	Y	Y	Y	Y	N
4 McCarthy	?	?	?	N	N	N	Y
5 Ackerman	?	?	?	N	N	?	Y
6 Meeks	Y	Y	Y	?	?	?	?
7 Crowley	Y	Y	Y	N	N	N	Y
8 Nadler	?	?	?	N	N	N	Y
9 Weiner	Y	Y	Y	?	N	N	Y
10 Towns	?	?	?	?	?	?	Y
11 Owens	?	?	?	N	N	N	Y
12 Velázquez	Y	Y	Y	N	N	N	Y
13 ***Fossella***	Y	Y	Y	?	Y	Y	N
14 Maloney	Y	Y	Y	N	N	N	Y
15 Rangel	?	Y	Y	N	N	N	Y
16 Serrano	Y	Y	Y	N	N	N	Y
17 Engel	Y	Y	Y	?	?	N	Y
18 Lowey	Y	Y	Y	N	N	N	Y
19 ***Kelly***	Y	Y	Y	Y	Y	Y	N
20 ***Sweeney***	?	?	?	?	?	Y	N
21 McNulty	Y	Y	Y	N	N	N	Y
22 Hinchey	Y	Y	Y	?	?	N	Y
23 ***McHugh***	Y	Y	Y	Y	Y	Y	N
24 ***Boehlert***	?	?	?	?	?	?	?
25 ***Walsh***	Y	Y	Y	Y	Y	Y	N

	487	488	489	490	491	492	493
26 ***Reynolds***	Y	Y	Y	Y	Y	Y	N
27 ***Quinn***	Y	Y	Y	?	?	Y	N
28 Slaughter	Y	Y	Y	N	N	N	Y
29 ***Houghton***	?	?	?	Y	Y	Y	N
NORTH CAROLINA							
1 Butterfield	Y	Y	Y	N	N	N	Y
2 Etheridge	Y	Y	Y	N	N	N	Y
3 ***Jones***	Y	Y	Y	Y	Y	Y	N
4 Price	Y	Y	Y	N	N	N	Y
5 ***Burr***	Y	Y	Y	Y	Y	Y	N
6 ***Coble***	Y	Y	Y	Y	Y	Y	N
7 McIntyre	Y	Y	Y	N	N	Y	Y
8 ***Hayes***	Y	Y	Y	Y	Y	Y	S
9 ***Myrick***	?	?	?	?	?	Y	N
10 ***Ballenger***	Y	Y	Y	Y	Y	Y	N
11 ***Taylor***	?	?	?	Y	Y	Y	N
12 Watt	?	?	?	N	N	N	Y
13 Miller	Y	Y	Y	N	N	N	N
NORTH DAKOTA							
AL Pomeroy	Y	Y	Y	N	N	Y	Y
OHIO							
1 ***Chabot***	Y	Y	Y	Y	Y	Y	N
2 ***Portman***	?	?	?	?	?	?	?
3 ***Turner***	?	?	?	Y	Y	Y	N
4 ***Oxley***	Y	Y	Y	Y	Y	Y	N
5 ***Gillmor***	Y	Y	Y	Y	Y	Y	N
6 Strickland	Y	Y	Y	N	N	N	Y
7 ***Hobson***	?	?	?	Y	Y	Y	N
8 ***Boehner***	Y	Y	Y	Y	Y	Y	N
9 Kaptur	Y	Y	Y	N	N	N	Y
10 Kucinich	Y	Y	Y	?	?	?	?
11 Jones	?	?	?	?	?	N	Y
12 ***Tiberi***	Y	Y	Y	Y	Y	Y	N
13 Brown	?	?	?	N	N	N	Y
14 ***LaTourette***	Y	Y	Y	Y	Y	Y	N
15 ***Pryce***	Y	Y	Y	Y	Y	Y	N
16 ***Regula***	Y	Y	Y	Y	Y	Y	N
17 Ryan	Y	Y	Y	N	N	N	Y
18 ***Ney***	Y	Y	Y	Y	Y	Y	N
OKLAHOMA							
1 ***Sullivan***	?	Y	Y	Y	Y	?	N
2 Carson	?	?	?	N	N	N	Y
3 ***Lucas***	Y	Y	Y	Y	Y	Y	N
4 ***Cole***	Y	Y	Y	Y	Y	Y	N
5 ***Istook***	Y	Y	Y	Y	Y	Y	N
OREGON							
1 Wu	Y	Y	Y	N	N	N	Y
2 ***Walden***	Y	Y	Y	Y	Y	Y	N
3 Blumenauer	Y	Y	Y	N	N	N	Y
4 DeFazio	Y	Y	Y	N	N	N	Y
5 Hooley	Y	Y	Y	N	N	N	Y
PENNSYLVANIA							
1 Brady	?	?	?	N	N	N	Y
2 Fattah	?	?	?	N	N	N	Y
3 ***English***	Y	Y	Y	Y	Y	Y	N
4 ***Hart***	Y	Y	Y	Y	Y	Y	N
5 ***Peterson***	?	?	?	Y	Y	Y	N
6 ***Gerlach***	?	?	?	Y	Y	Y	N
7 ***Weldon***	?	?	?	?	?	?	?
8 ***Greenwood***	?	?	?	?	?	?	?
9 ***Shuster, Bill***	Y	Y	Y	Y	Y	Y	N
10 ***Sherwood***	Y	Y	Y	Y	Y	Y	N
11 Kanjorski	Y	Y	Y	N	N	N	Y
12 Murtha	?	?	?	N	N	N	Y
13 Hoeffel	?	?	?	?	?	?	?
14 Doyle	Y	Y	Y	N	N	N	Y
15 ***Toomey***	?	?	?	?	?	Y	N
16 ***Pitts***	Y	Y	Y	Y	Y	Y	N
17 Holden	Y	Y	Y	N	N	N	Y
18 ***Murphy***	Y	Y	Y	Y	Y	Y	N
19 ***Platts***	Y	Y	Y	Y	Y	Y	N
RHODE ISLAND							
1 Kennedy	?	?	?	N	N	N	Y
2 Langevin	Y	Y	Y	N	N	N	Y
SOUTH CAROLINA							
1 ***Brown***	Y	Y	Y	Y	Y	Y	N
2 ***Wilson***	Y	Y	Y	Y	Y	Y	N
3 ***Barrett***	Y	Y	Y	Y	Y	Y	N
4 ***DeMint***	?	?	?	?	?	?	?
5 Spratt	Y	Y	Y	N	N	N	Y
6 Clyburn	Y	Y	Y	N	N	N	Y
SOUTH DAKOTA							
AL Herseth	Y	Y	Y	N	N	N	Y

	487	488	489	490	491	492	493
TENNESSEE							
1 ***Jenkins***	Y	Y	Y	Y	Y	Y	N
2 ***Duncan***	?	Y	Y	Y	Y	Y	N
3 ***Wamp***	?	?	?	Y	Y	Y	N
4 Davis	Y	Y	Y	N	N	N	Y
5 Cooper	?	?	?	N	N	N	Y
6 Gordon	Y	Y	Y	N	N	N	Y
7 ***Blackburn***	Y	Y	Y	Y	Y	Y	N
8 Tanner	Y	Y	Y	N	N	N	Y
9 Ford	Y	Y	Y	N	N	N	Y
TEXAS							
1 Sandlin	?	?	?	N	Y	N	Y
2 Turner	Y	Y	Y	?	?	N	Y
3 ***Johnson, Sam***	Y	Y	Y	Y	Y	Y	N
4 ***Hall***	Y	Y	Y	?	?	Y	N
5 ***Hensarling***	Y	Y	Y	Y	Y	Y	N
6 ***Barton***	Y	Y	Y	Y	Y	Y	N
7 ***Culberson***	Y	Y	Y	Y	Y	Y	N
8 ***Brady***	Y	Y	Y	Y	Y	Y	N
9 Lampson	?	?	?	?	?	?	?
10 Doggett	?	?	?	?	?	?	Y
11 Edwards	Y	Y	Y	N	N	N	Y
12 ***Granger***	Y	Y	Y	Y	Y	Y	N
13 ***Thornberry***	Y	Y	Y	Y	Y	Y	N
14 ***Paul***	Y	Y	Y	Y	Y	Y	N
15 Hinojosa	+	Y	Y	N	N	N	Y
16 Reyes	?	?	?	N	N	N	Y
17 Stenholm	Y	Y	Y	?	?	Y	Y
18 Jackson-Lee	?	?	?	N	N	N	Y
19 ***Neugebauer***	Y	Y	Y	Y	Y	Y	N
20 Gonzalez	Y	Y	Y	N	N	N	Y
21 ***Smith***	Y	Y	Y	Y	Y	Y	N
22 ***DeLay***	Y	Y	Y	Y	Y	Y	N
23 ***Bonilla***	Y	Y	Y	Y	Y	Y	N
24 Frost	?	?	?	N	N	N	Y
25 Bell	Y	Y	Y	N	N	N	Y
26 ***Burgess***	Y	Y	Y	Y	Y	Y	N
27 Ortiz	?	?	?	N	N	N	Y
28 Rodriguez	?	?	?	N	N	N	Y
29 Green	Y	?	Y	N	N	N	Y
30 Johnson, E.B.	Y	Y	Y	N	N	N	Y
31 ***Carter***	Y	Y	Y	Y	Y	Y	N
32 ***Sessions***	Y	Y	Y	Y	Y	Y	N
UTAH							
1 ***Bishop***	?	?	?	Y	Y	Y	N
2 Matheson	Y	Y	Y	N	N	N	Y
3 ***Cannon***	?	?	?	?	?	?	?
VERMONT							
AL *Sanders*	Y	Y	Y	N	N	N	Y
VIRGINIA							
1 ***Davis, Jo Ann***	Y	Y	Y	Y	Y	Y	N
2 ***Schrock***	Y	Y	Y	Y	Y	Y	N
3 Scott	Y	Y	Y	N	N	N	Y
4 ***Forbes***	?	?	?	?	?	?	?
5 ***Goode***	?	?	?	?	?	?	?
6 ***Goodlatte***	Y	Y	Y	Y	Y	Y	N
7 ***Cantor***	Y	Y	Y	Y	Y	Y	N
8 Moran	Y	?	?	N	N	N	Y
9 Boucher	Y	Y	Y	N	N	N	Y
10 ***Wolf***	Y	Y	Y	Y	Y	Y	N
11 ***Davis, T.***	Y	Y	Y	Y	Y	Y	N
WASHINGTON							
1 Inslee	Y	Y	Y	N	N	N	Y
2 Larsen	?	?	?	?	N	N	Y
3 Baird	Y	Y	Y	?	?	N	Y
4 ***Hastings***	Y	Y	Y	Y	Y	Y	N
5 ***Nethercutt***	?	?	?	?	?	?	?
6 Dicks	?	?	?	N	N	N	Y
7 McDermott	Y	Y	Y	N	N	N	Y
8 ***Dunn***	Y	?	Y	Y	Y	Y	N
9 Smith	Y	Y	Y	N	N	N	Y
WEST VIRGINIA							
1 Mollohan	?	?	?	?	?	N	Y
2 ***Capito***	Y	Y	Y	Y	Y	Y	N
3 Rahall	Y	Y	Y	N	N	N	Y
WISCONSIN							
1 ***Ryan***	Y	Y	Y	Y	Y	Y	N
2 Baldwin	Y	Y	Y	N	N	N	Y
3 Kind	Y	Y	Y	N	N	N	Y
4 Kleczka	Y	Y	Y	N	N	N	Y
5 ***Sensenbrenner***	Y	Y	Y	Y	Y	Y	N
6 ***Petri***	Y	Y	Y	Y	Y	Y	N
7 Obey	Y	Y	Y	N	N	N	Y
8 ***Green***	Y	Y	Y	Y	Y	Y	N
WYOMING							
AL ***Cubin***	Y	Y	Y	?	Y	Y	N

Southern states - Ala., Ark., Fla., Ga., Ky., La., Miss., N.C., Okla., S.C., Tenn., Texas, Va.

494. HR 163. Reinstatement of the Draft/Passage. McHugh, R-N.Y., motion to suspend the rules and pass the bill that would require all citizens age 18 to 26 to perform two years of service in the military, the commissioned corps of the National Oceanic and Atmospheric Administration or the Public Health Service. Individuals with disabilities or those with conscientious objections could participate in designated civilian activities promoting national security or homeland defense. Motion rejected 2-402: R 0-215; D 2-186 (ND 2-136, SD 0-50); I 0-1. A two-thirds majority of those present and voting (270 in this case) is required for passage under suspension of the rules. Oct. 5, 2004.

495. HR 2929. Spyware Programs/Passage. Barton, R-Texas, motion to suspend the rules and pass the bill that would require software companies to obtain permission from computer users before installing programs that can collect personal information and distribute it to third parties. It also would allow the Federal Trade Commission to levy a fine of up to $3 million against companies that download such software onto users' computers without permission. Motion agreed to 399-1: R 211-1; D 187-0 (ND 138-0, SD 49-0); I 1-0. A two-thirds majority of those present and voting (267 in this case) is required for passage under suspension of the rules. Oct. 5, 2004.

496. HR 5011. Sale of Financial Policies on Military Bases/Passage. Baker, R-La., motion to suspend the rules and pass the bill that would ban the sale of contractual plan mutual funds on military bases and grant state insurance commissioners the authority to regulate most insurance sales to military personnel. Motion agreed to 396-2: R 212-2; D 183-0 (ND 134-0, SD 49-0); I 1-0. A two-thirds majority of those present and voting (266 in this case) is required for passage under suspension of the rules. Oct. 5, 2004.

497. HR 5107. DNA Testing/Passage. Passage of the bill that would authorize grants to help states eliminate the backlog in the testing of DNA samples, promote use of forensic technology to identify missing persons and train first-responders in the handling of biological crime evidence. It would establish new procedures to allow inmates to obtain post-conviction DNA testing and authorize $755 million over five years to speed the processing of unanalyzed biological crime evidence. The bill also would create a new set of statutory victims' rights. Passed 393-14: R 198-14; D 194-0 (ND 141-0, SD 53-0); I 1-0. Oct. 6, 2004.

498. HR 4850. Fiscal 2005 District of Columbia Appropriations/ Conference Report. Adoption of the conference report on the bill that would appropriate $560 million in fiscal 2005 for the District of Columbia and approve the city's own $8.3 billion budget. Adopted (thus sent to the Senate) 377-36: R 184-29; D 192-7 (ND 141-3, SD 51-4); I 1-0. Oct. 6, 2004.

499. HR 5212. Fiscal 2005 Supplemental Appropriations/Previous Question. Putnam, R-Fla., motion to order the previous question (thus ending debate and possibility of amendment) on adoption of the rule (H Res 819) to provide for House floor consideration of the bill that would appropriate $11 billion in emergency supplemental funding for hurricane victims in Florida and other states. Motion agreed to 216-186: R 216-0; D 0-185 (ND 0-135, SD 0-50); I 0-1. (Subsequently, the rule as amended was adopted by voice vote.) Oct. 6, 2004.

Key

Y	Voted for (yea).
#	Paired for.
+	Announced for.
N	Voted against (nay).
X	Paired against.
–	Announced against.
P	Voted "present."
C	Voted "present" to avoid possible conflict of interest.
?	Did not vote or otherwise make a position known.

Democrats **Republicans**
Independents

	494	495	496	497	498	499
ALABAMA						
1 *Bonner*	N	Y	Y	Y	Y	Y
2 *Everett*	N	Y	Y	Y	Y	Y
3 *Rogers*	N	Y	Y	Y	Y	Y
4 *Aderholt*	N	Y	Y	Y	Y	Y
5 Cramer	N	Y	Y	Y	Y	N
6 *Bachus*	N	Y	Y	Y	Y	Y
7 Davis	N	Y	Y	Y	Y	N
ALASKA						
AL *Young*	N	Y	Y	Y	Y	Y
ARIZONA						
1 *Renzi*	N	Y	?	Y	Y	Y
2 *Franks*	N	Y	Y	Y	N	Y
3 *Shadegg*	N	Y	Y	N	N	Y
4 Pastor	N	Y	Y	Y	Y	N
5 *Hayworth*	N	Y	Y	Y	N	Y
6 *Flake*	N	Y	N	N	N	Y
7 Grijalva	N	Y	Y	Y	Y	N
8 *Kolbe*	N	Y	Y	Y	Y	Y
ARKANSAS						
1 Berry	N	Y	Y	Y	N	N
2 Snyder	N	Y	Y	Y	Y	N
3 *Boozman*	N	Y	Y	Y	Y	Y
4 Ross	N	Y	Y	Y	Y	N
CALIFORNIA						
1 Thompson	N	Y	Y	Y	Y	N
2 *Herger*	N	Y	Y	Y	Y	Y
3 *Ose*	N	Y	Y	Y	Y	Y
4 *Doolittle*	N	Y	Y	Y	Y	Y
5 Matsui	N	Y	Y	Y	Y	N
6 Woolsey	N	Y	?	Y	N	N
7 Miller, George	N	Y	Y	Y	Y	N
8 Pelosi	N	Y	Y	Y	Y	?
9 Lee	N	Y	Y	Y	Y	N
10 Tauscher	N	Y	Y	Y	Y	N
11 *Pombo*	N	Y	Y	Y	Y	Y
12 Lantos	N	Y	Y	Y	Y	N
13 Stark	N	Y	Y	Y	Y	N
14 Eshoo	N	Y	Y	Y	Y	N
15 Honda	N	Y	Y	Y	Y	N
16 Lofgren	N	Y	Y	Y	Y	N
17 Farr	N	Y	Y	Y	Y	N
18 Cardoza	N	Y	Y	Y	Y	N
19 *Radanovich*	N	Y	Y	Y	Y	Y
20 Dooley	?	?	?	Y	Y	N
21 *Nunes*	N	Y	Y	Y	Y	Y
22 *Thomas*	N	Y	Y	Y	Y	N
23 Capps	N	Y	Y	Y	Y	N
24 *Gallegly*	N	Y	Y	Y	Y	Y
25 *McKeon*	N	Y	Y	Y	Y	Y
26 *Dreier*	N	Y	Y	Y	Y	Y
27 Sherman	N	Y	?	Y	Y	N
28 Berman	N	Y	Y	Y	Y	N
29 Schiff	N	Y	Y	Y	Y	N
30 Waxman	N	Y	Y	Y	Y	?
31 Becerra	N	Y	Y	?	Y	N
32 Solis	N	Y	Y	Y	Y	N
33 Watson	N	Y	Y	Y	Y	N
34 Roybal-Allard	N	Y	Y	Y	Y	N
35 Waters	N	Y	Y	Y	Y	N
36 Harman	N	Y	Y	Y	Y	?

	494	495	496	497	498	499
37 Millender-McD.	?	?	?	?	?	?
38 Napolitano	N	Y	?	Y	Y	N
39 Sánchez, Linda	N	Y	Y	Y	Y	?
40 *Royce*	N	Y	Y	Y	N	Y
41 *Lewis*	N	Y	Y	Y	Y	Y
42 *Miller, Gary*	N	Y	Y	Y	Y	Y
43 Baca	N	Y	Y	Y	Y	N
44 *Calvert*	N	Y	Y	Y	Y	Y
45 *Bono*	N	Y	Y	Y	Y	Y
46 *Rohrabacher*	N	Y	Y	Y	Y	Y
47 Sanchez, Loretta	N	Y	Y	Y	Y	N
48 *Cox*	?	?	?	Y	Y	?
49 *Issa*	N	Y	Y	Y	Y	Y
50 *Cunningham*	N	Y	Y	Y	Y	Y
51 Filner	N	Y	Y	Y	Y	N
52 *Hunter*	N	Y	Y	Y	Y	Y
53 Davis	N	Y	Y	Y	Y	N
COLORADO						
1 DeGette	N	Y	Y	Y	Y	N
2 Udall	N	Y	Y	Y	Y	N
3 *McInnis*	N	Y	Y	Y	Y	Y
4 *Musgrave*	N	Y	Y	Y	Y	Y
5 *Hefley*	N	?	Y	N	Y	Y
6 *Tancredo*	N	Y	Y	Y	?	Y
7 *Beauprez*	N	Y	Y	Y	Y	Y
CONNECTICUT						
1 Larson	N	Y	Y	Y	Y	N
2 *Simmons*	N	?	Y	Y	Y	Y
3 DeLauro	N	Y	Y	Y	Y	N
4 *Shays*	N	Y	Y	Y	Y	Y
5 *Johnson*	N	Y	Y	Y	Y	Y
DELAWARE						
AL *Castle*	N	Y	Y	Y	Y	Y
FLORIDA						
1 *Miller, J.*	N	Y	Y	N	N	Y
2 Boyd	N	Y	Y	Y	Y	N
3 Brown	?	?	?	Y	Y	N
4 *Crenshaw*	N	Y	Y	Y	Y	Y
5 *Brown-Waite*	N	Y	Y	N	N	Y
6 *Stearns*	N	Y	Y	Y	Y	Y
7 *Mica*	N	Y	Y	Y	Y	Y
8 *Keller*	N	Y	Y	Y	Y	Y
9 *Bilirakis*	N	Y	Y	Y	Y	Y
10 *Young*	N	Y	Y	Y	Y	Y
11 Davis	N	Y	Y	Y	Y	N
12 *Putnam*	N	Y	Y	Y	Y	Y
13 *Harris*	N	Y	Y	Y	Y	Y
14 Vacant						
15 *Weldon*	N	Y	Y	Y	Y	Y
16 *Foley*	N	Y	Y	Y	Y	Y
17 Meek	N	Y	Y	Y	Y	N
18 *Ros-Lehtinen*	N	Y	Y	Y	Y	Y
19 Wexler	N	Y	Y	?	Y	N
20 Deutsch	N	Y	Y	Y	Y	N
21 *Diaz-Balart, L.*	N	Y	Y	Y	Y	Y
22 *Shaw*	N	Y	Y	Y	Y	Y
23 Hastings	N	Y	Y	Y	Y	N
24 *Feeney*	N	Y	Y	Y	Y	Y
25 *Diaz-Balart, M.*	N	Y	Y	Y	Y	Y
GEORGIA						
1 *Kingston*	N	Y	Y	?	?	?
2 Bishop	N	Y	Y	Y	Y	N
3 Marshall	N	Y	Y	Y	Y	N
4 *Majette*	?	?	?	?	?	?
5 Lewis	N	Y	Y	Y	Y	N
6 *Isakson*	N	Y	Y	Y	Y	Y
7 *Linder*	N	Y	Y	Y	Y	Y
8 *Collins*	N	Y	Y	Y	Y	Y
9 *Norwood*	?	?	?	?	?	?
10 *Deal*	N	Y	Y	Y	Y	Y
11 *Gingrey*	N	Y	Y	Y	Y	Y
12 *Burns*	N	Y	Y	Y	Y	Y
13 Scott	N	Y	Y	Y	Y	N
HAWAII						
1 Abercrombie	N	Y	Y	Y	Y	N
2 Case	N	Y	Y	Y	Y	N
IDAHO						
1 *Otter*	N	Y	Y	Y	N	Y
2 *Simpson*	N	Y	Y	Y	Y	?
ILLINOIS						
1 Rush	N	Y	Y	Y	Y	N
2 Jackson	N	Y	Y	Y	Y	N
3 Lipinski	N	Y	Y	Y	Y	N
4 Gutierrez	N	Y	Y	Y	Y	N
5 Emanuel	N	Y	Y	Y	Y	N
6 *Hyde*	N	Y	Y	?	?	Y

ND Northern Democrats   SD Southern Democrats

	494	495	496	497	498	499
7 Davis	N	Y	Y	Y	Y	N
8 ***Crane***	N	Y	Y	Y	Y	Y
9 Schakowsky	N	Y	Y	Y	Y	N
10 ***Kirk***	N	Y	Y	Y	Y	Y
11 ***Weller***	N	Y	Y	Y	Y	Y
12 Costello	N	Y	Y	Y	Y	N
13 ***Biggert***	N	Y	Y	Y	Y	Y
14 ***Hastert***	N					
15 ***Johnson***	N	Y	Y	Y	Y	Y
16 ***Manzullo***	N	Y	Y	Y	N	Y
17 Evans	N	Y	Y	Y	Y	N
18 ***LaHood***	N	Y	Y	Y	Y	Y
19 ***Shimkus***	N	Y	Y	Y	Y	Y
INDIANA						
1 Visclosky	N	Y	Y	Y	Y	N
2 ***Chocola***	N	Y	Y	Y	Y	Y
3 ***Souder***	N	Y	Y	Y	Y	Y
4 ***Buyer***	N	Y	Y	Y	Y	Y
5 ***Burton***	N	Y	Y	Y	Y	Y
6 ***Pence***	N	Y	Y	N	Y	Y
7 Carson	N	Y	Y	Y	Y	N
8 ***Hostettler***	N	Y	Y	Y	Y	Y
9 Hill	N	Y	Y	Y	Y	N
IOWA						
1 ***Nussle***	N	Y	Y	Y	Y	Y
2 ***Leach***	N	Y	Y	Y	Y	Y
3 Boswell	N	Y	Y	Y	N	N
4 ***Latham***	N	Y	Y	Y	Y	Y
5 ***King***	N	Y	Y	Y	Y	Y
KANSAS						
1 ***Moran***	N	Y	Y	Y	Y	Y
2 ***Ryun***	N	Y	Y	Y	N	Y
3 Moore	N	Y	Y	Y	N	N
4 ***Tiahrt***	N	Y	Y	Y	Y	Y
KENTUCKY						
1 ***Whitfield***	N	Y	Y	Y	Y	Y
2 ***Lewis***	N	Y	Y	Y	Y	Y
3 ***Northup***	N	Y	Y	Y	Y	Y
4 Lucas	N	Y	Y	Y	Y	N
5 ***Rogers***	N	Y	Y	Y	Y	Y
6 Chandler	N	Y	Y	?	Y	N
LOUISIANA						
1 ***Vitter***	N	Y	Y	Y	Y	Y
2 Jefferson	N	Y	Y	Y	Y	?
3 ***Tauzin***	?	?	?	?	?	?
4 ***McCrery***	N	Y	Y	Y	Y	Y
5 ***Alexander***	N	Y	Y	Y	Y	Y
6 ***Baker***	N	Y	Y	Y	Y	Y
7 John	?	?	?	Y	Y	?
MAINE						
1 Allen	N	Y	Y	Y	Y	N
2 Michaud	N	Y	Y	Y	Y	N
MARYLAND						
1 ***Gilchrest***	N	Y	Y	Y	Y	Y
2 Ruppersberger	N	Y	Y	Y	Y	?
3 Cardin	N	Y	Y	Y	Y	N
4 Wynn	N	Y	Y	Y	Y	N
5 Hoyer	N	Y	Y	Y	Y	N
6 ***Bartlett***	N	Y	Y	Y	N	Y
7 Cummings	N	Y	Y	Y	Y	N
8 Van Hollen	N	Y	Y	Y	Y	N
MASSACHUSETTS						
1 Olver	N	Y	Y	Y	Y	N
2 Neal	N	Y	Y	Y	Y	?
3 McGovern	N	Y	Y	Y	Y	N
4 Frank	N	Y	Y	Y	Y	N
5 Meehan	N	Y	Y	Y	Y	N
6 Tierney	N	Y	Y	Y	N	N
7 Markey	N	Y	Y	Y	Y	N
8 Capuano	N	Y	Y	Y	Y	N
9 Lynch	N	Y	Y	Y	Y	N
10 Delahunt	N	Y	Y	Y	Y	N
MICHIGAN						
1 Stupak	N	Y	Y	Y	Y	N
2 ***Hoekstra***	N	Y	Y	Y	Y	Y
3 ***Ehlers***	N	Y	Y	Y	Y	Y
4 ***Camp***	N	Y	Y	Y	Y	Y
5 Kildee	N	Y	Y	Y	Y	N
6 ***Upton***	N	Y	Y	Y	Y	Y
7 ***Smith***	N	Y	Y	Y	N	Y
8 ***Rogers***	N	Y	Y	Y	Y	Y
9 ***Knollenberg***	N	Y	Y	Y	Y	Y
10 ***Miller***	N	Y	Y	Y	Y	Y
11 ***McCotter***	N	Y	Y	Y	Y	Y
12 Levin	N	Y	Y	Y	Y	N
13 Kilpatrick	N	Y	Y	Y	Y	N
14 Conyers	N	Y	Y	Y	Y	N
15 Dingell	N	Y	Y	Y	Y	N
MINNESOTA						
1 ***Gutknecht***	N	Y	Y	Y	Y	Y
2 ***Kline***	N	Y	Y	Y	Y	Y
3 ***Ramstad***	N	Y	Y	Y	Y	Y
4 McCollum	N	Y	Y	Y	Y	N
5 Sabo	N	Y	Y	Y	Y	N
6 ***Kennedy***	N	Y	Y	Y	Y	Y
7 Peterson	N	Y	Y	Y	Y	N
8 Oberstar	N	Y	Y	Y	Y	N
MISSISSIPPI						
1 ***Wicker***	N	Y	Y	Y	Y	Y
2 Thompson	N	Y	Y	Y	Y	N
3 ***Pickering***	N	Y	Y	Y	Y	Y
4 Taylor	N	Y	Y	Y	N	N
MISSOURI						
1 Clay	N	Y	Y	Y	Y	?
2 ***Akin***	N	Y	Y	Y	N	Y
3 Gephardt	?	?	?	?	?	?
4 Skelton	N	Y	Y	Y	Y	N
5 McCarthy	N	Y	Y	Y	Y	N
6 ***Graves***	N	Y	Y	Y	N	Y
7 ***Blunt***	N	Y	Y	Y	Y	Y
8 ***Emerson***	N	Y	Y	Y	Y	Y
9 ***Hulshof***	N	Y	Y	Y	Y	Y
MONTANA						
AL ***Rehberg***	N	Y	Y	Y	Y	Y
NEBRASKA						
1 Vacant						
2 ***Terry***	–	Y	Y	Y	Y	Y
3 ***Osborne***	N	Y	Y	Y	Y	Y
NEVADA						
1 Berkley	N	Y	Y	Y	Y	N
2 ***Gibbons***	N	Y	Y	Y	Y	Y
3 ***Porter***	N	Y	Y	Y	Y	Y
NEW HAMPSHIRE						
1 ***Bradley***	N	Y	Y	Y	Y	Y
2 ***Bass***	N	Y	Y	?	?	Y
NEW JERSEY						
1 Andrews	N	Y	Y	Y	Y	N
2 ***LoBiondo***	N	Y	Y	Y	Y	Y
3 ***Saxton***	N	Y	Y	Y	Y	Y
4 ***Smith***	N	Y	Y	Y	Y	Y
5 ***Garrett***	N	Y	Y	N	Y	Y
6 Pallone	N	Y	Y	Y	Y	N
7 ***Ferguson***	N	Y	Y	Y	Y	Y
8 Pascrell	N	Y	Y	Y	Y	N
9 Rothman	N	Y	Y	Y	Y	N
10 Payne	N	Y	Y	Y	Y	N
11 ***Frelinghuysen***	N	Y	Y	Y	Y	Y
12 Holt	N	Y	Y	Y	Y	N
13 Menendez	N	Y	Y	Y	Y	N
NEW MEXICO						
1 ***Wilson***	N	Y	Y	Y	Y	Y
2 ***Pearce***	N	Y	Y	Y	Y	Y
3 Udall	N	Y	Y	Y	Y	N
NEW YORK						
1 Bishop	N	Y	Y	Y	Y	N
2 Israel	N	Y	Y	Y	Y	N
3 ***King***	N	Y	Y	Y	?	Y
4 McCarthy	N	Y	Y	Y	Y	N
5 Ackerman	N	Y	Y	Y	Y	N
6 Meeks	?	?	?	Y	Y	N
7 Crowley	N	Y	Y	Y	Y	N
8 Nadler	N	Y	Y	Y	Y	N
9 Weiner	N	Y	Y	Y	Y	N
10 Towns	N	Y	Y	?	?	?
11 Owens	N	Y	Y	Y	Y	N
12 Velázquez	N	Y	Y	Y	Y	N
13 ***Fossella***	N	Y	Y	Y	N	Y
14 Maloney	N	Y	Y	Y	Y	N
15 Rangel	N	Y	?	Y	Y	N
16 Serrano	N	Y	Y	Y	Y	N
17 Engel	N	Y	Y	Y	Y	N
18 Lowey	N	Y	Y	Y	Y	N
19 ***Kelly***	N	Y	Y	Y	Y	Y
20 ***Sweeney***	N	Y	Y	Y	Y	Y
21 McNulty	N	Y	Y	Y	Y	N
22 Hinchey	N	Y	Y	Y	Y	N
23 ***McHugh***	N	Y	Y	Y	N	Y
24 ***Boehlert***	?	?	?	?	?	?
25 ***Walsh***	N	Y	Y	Y	Y	Y
26 ***Reynolds***	N	Y	Y	Y	Y	Y
27 ***Quinn***	N	Y	Y	Y	Y	Y
28 Slaughter	?	?	?	?	?	?
29 ***Houghton***	N	Y	Y	?	?	?
NORTH CAROLINA						
1 Butterfield	N	Y	Y	Y	Y	N
2 Etheridge	N	Y	Y	Y	Y	N
3 ***Jones***	N	Y	Y	N	N	Y
4 Price	N	Y	Y	Y	Y	N
5 ***Burr***	N	Y	Y	Y	Y	Y
6 ***Coble***	N	Y	Y	Y	N	Y
7 McIntyre	?	?	?	Y	N	N
8 ***Hayes***	N	Y	Y	Y	Y	Y
9 ***Myrick***	N	Y	Y	Y	Y	Y
10 ***Ballenger***	N	Y	Y	Y	Y	Y
11 ***Taylor***	N	Y	Y	Y	Y	Y
12 Watt	N	Y	Y	Y	Y	?
13 Miller	N	Y	Y	Y	Y	N
NORTH DAKOTA						
AL Pomeroy	N	Y	Y	Y	Y	N
OHIO						
1 ***Chabot***	N	Y	Y	Y	Y	Y
2 ***Portman***	?	?	?	Y	Y	Y
3 ***Turner***	N	Y	Y	Y	Y	Y
4 ***Oxley***	N	Y	Y	Y	Y	Y
5 ***Gillmor***	N	Y	Y	Y	Y	Y
6 Strickland	N	Y	Y	Y	Y	N
7 ***Hobson***	N	Y	Y	Y	Y	Y
8 ***Boehner***	N	Y	Y	Y	Y	Y
9 Kaptur	?	?	?	?	Y	N
10 Kucinich	?	?	?	Y	Y	N
11 Jones	?	?	?	Y	Y	?
12 ***Tiberi***	N	Y	Y	Y	Y	Y
13 Brown	?	?	?	Y	Y	N
14 ***LaTourette***	N	?	Y	Y	Y	Y
15 ***Pryce***	?	?	?	Y	Y	Y
16 ***Regula***	N	Y	Y	Y	Y	Y
17 Ryan	N	Y	Y	Y	Y	N
18 ***Ney***	N	Y	Y	Y	Y	Y
OKLAHOMA						
1 ***Sullivan***	N	Y	Y	Y	Y	Y
2 Carson	N	Y	Y	Y	Y	?
3 ***Lucas***	N	Y	Y	Y	Y	Y
4 ***Cole***	N	Y	Y	Y	Y	Y
5 ***Istook***	N	Y	Y	?	Y	Y
OREGON						
1 Wu	N	Y	Y	Y	Y	N
2 ***Walden***	N	Y	Y	Y	Y	Y
3 Blumenauer	N	Y	Y	Y	Y	N
4 DeFazio	N	Y	Y	Y	Y	N
5 Hooley	N	Y	Y	Y	Y	N
PENNSYLVANIA						
1 Brady	N	Y	Y	Y	Y	N
2 Fattah	N	Y	Y	Y	Y	N
3 ***English***	N	Y	Y	Y	Y	Y
4 ***Hart***	N	Y	Y	Y	Y	Y
5 ***Peterson***	N	Y	Y	Y	Y	Y
6 ***Gerlach***	N	Y	Y	Y	Y	Y
7 ***Weldon***	N	Y	Y	Y	Y	Y
8 ***Greenwood***	?	?	?	Y	Y	Y
9 ***Shuster, Bill***	N	Y	Y	Y	Y	Y
10 ***Sherwood***	N	Y	Y	?	?	Y
11 Kanjorski	N	Y	Y	Y	Y	N
12 Murtha	Y	Y	?	Y	Y	N
13 Hoeffel	?	?	?	Y	Y	?
14 Doyle	N	Y	Y	Y	Y	N
15 ***Toomey***	N	Y	Y	Y	N	Y
16 ***Pitts***	N	Y	Y	Y	Y	Y
17 Holden	N	Y	Y	Y	Y	N
18 ***Murphy***	N	Y	Y	Y	Y	Y
19 ***Platts***	N	Y	Y	Y	N	Y
RHODE ISLAND						
1 Kennedy	N	Y	Y	Y	Y	N
2 Langevin	N	Y	Y	Y	Y	N
SOUTH CAROLINA						
1 ***Brown***	N	Y	Y	Y	Y	Y
2 ***Wilson***	N	Y	Y	Y	Y	Y
3 ***Barrett***	N	Y	Y	N	Y	Y
4 ***DeMint***	?	?	?	?	?	?
5 Spratt	N	Y	Y	Y	Y	N
6 Clyburn	N	Y	Y	Y	Y	N
SOUTH DAKOTA						
AL Herseth	N	Y	Y	Y	Y	N
TENNESSEE						
1 ***Jenkins***	N	Y	Y	Y	Y	Y
2 ***Duncan***	N	Y	Y	N	N	Y
3 ***Wamp***	N	Y	Y	Y	Y	Y
4 Davis	N	Y	Y	Y	Y	N
5 Cooper	N	Y	Y	Y	Y	N
6 Gordon	N	Y	Y	Y	Y	N
7 ***Blackburn***	N	Y	Y	Y	Y	Y
8 Tanner	N	Y	Y	Y	Y	N
9 Ford	N	Y	Y	Y	Y	N
TEXAS						
1 Sandlin	?	?	?	Y	Y	N
2 Turner	N	Y	Y	Y	Y	N
3 ***Johnson, Sam***	N	Y	Y	N	Y	Y
4 ***Hall***	N	Y	Y	?	Y	Y
5 ***Hensarling***	N	Y	Y	N	N	Y
6 ***Barton***	N	Y	Y	Y	Y	Y
7 ***Culberson***	N	Y	Y	N	Y	Y
8 ***Brady***	N	Y	Y	Y	Y	Y
9 Lampson	?	?	?	Y	Y	N
10 Doggett	N	Y	Y	Y	Y	N
11 Edwards	N	Y	Y	Y	Y	N
12 ***Granger***	N	Y	Y	N	Y	Y
13 ***Thornberry***	N	Y	Y	Y	Y	Y
14 ***Paul***	N	N	N	?	?	?
15 Hinojosa	N	Y	Y	Y	Y	?
16 Reyes	N	Y	Y	Y	Y	N
17 Stenholm	N	Y	Y	Y	Y	N
18 Jackson-Lee	N	Y	Y	Y	Y	N
19 ***Neugebauer***	N	Y	Y	Y	Y	Y
20 Gonzalez	N	Y	Y	Y	Y	N
21 ***Smith***	N	Y	Y	Y	Y	Y
22 ***DeLay***	N	Y	Y	Y	Y	Y
23 ***Bonilla***	N	Y	Y	Y	Y	Y
24 Frost	N	Y	Y	Y	Y	N
25 Bell	N	Y	Y	Y	Y	N
26 ***Burgess***	N	Y	Y	N	Y	Y
27 Ortiz	N	Y	Y	Y	Y	N
28 Rodriguez	N	Y	Y	Y	Y	N
29 Green	N	Y	Y	Y	N	N
30 Johnson, E.B.	N	Y	Y	Y	Y	N
31 ***Carter***	N	Y	Y	N	Y	Y
32 ***Sessions***	N	Y	Y	Y	Y	Y
UTAH						
1 ***Bishop***	N	Y	Y	Y	Y	Y
2 Matheson	N	Y	Y	Y	Y	N
3 ***Cannon***	?	?	?	Y	Y	Y
VERMONT						
AL *Sanders*	N	Y	Y	Y	Y	N
VIRGINIA						
1 ***Davis, Jo Ann***	N	Y	Y	Y	Y	Y
2 ***Schrock***	N	Y	Y	Y	Y	Y
3 Scott	N	Y	Y	Y	Y	N
4 ***Forbes***	?	?	?	Y	Y	Y
5 ***Goode***	N	Y	Y	Y	N	Y
6 ***Goodlatte***	N	Y	Y	Y	N	Y
7 ***Cantor***	N	Y	Y	Y	Y	Y
8 Moran	N	+	+	Y	Y	N
9 Boucher	N	Y	Y	Y	Y	N
10 ***Wolf***	N	Y	Y	Y	Y	Y
11 ***Davis, T.***	N	Y	Y	Y	Y	Y
WASHINGTON						
1 Inslee	N	Y	Y	Y	Y	N
2 Larsen	N	Y	Y	Y	Y	N
3 Baird	N	Y	Y	Y	Y	N
4 ***Hastings***	N	Y	Y	Y	Y	Y
5 ***Nethercutt***	?	?	?	?	?	?
6 Dicks	N	Y	Y	Y	Y	N
7 McDermott	N	Y	Y	Y	Y	N
8 ***Dunn***	N	Y	Y	Y	Y	Y
9 Smith	N	Y	Y	Y	Y	N
WEST VIRGINIA						
1 Mollohan	N	Y	Y	Y	Y	N
2 ***Capito***	N	Y	Y	Y	Y	Y
3 Rahall	N	Y	Y	Y	Y	N
WISCONSIN						
1 ***Ryan***	N	Y	Y	Y	Y	Y
2 Baldwin	N	Y	Y	Y	Y	N
3 Kind	N	Y	Y	Y	Y	N
4 Kleczka	?	?	?	?	?	?
5 ***Sensenbrenner***	N	Y	Y	Y	N	Y
6 ***Petri***	N	Y	Y	Y	N	Y
7 Obey	N	Y	Y	Y	Y	N
8 ***Green***	N	Y	Y	Y	Y	Y
WYOMING						
AL ***Cubin***	N	Y	Y	Y	N	Y

Southern states - Ala., Ark., Fla., Ga., Ky., La., Miss., N.C., Okla., S.C., Tenn., Texas, Va.

Key

Y	Voted for (yea).
#	Paired for.
+	Announced for.
N	Voted against (nay).
X	Paired against.
–	Announced against.
P	Voted "present."
C	Voted "present" to avoid possible conflict of interest.
?	Did not vote or otherwise make a position known.

Democrats **Republicans**
Independents

500. HR 5212. Fiscal 2005 Supplemental Appropriations/Discretionary Funding Cut. Hensarling, R-Texas, amendment that would offset the $11 billion cost of the emergency supplemental with a proportional reduction of fiscal 2005 discretionary funding. It would exempt the Departments of Defense, Homeland Security and Veterans Affairs from the funding cut. Rejected 89-321: R 88-127; D 1-193 (ND 0-139, SD 1-54); I 0-1. Oct. 6, 2004.

501. HR 5212. Fiscal 2005 Supplemental Appropriations/Passage. Passage of the bill that would provide $11 billion in emergency supplemental appropriations for fiscal 2005 for hurricane victims in Florida and other states. It also would provide $2.9 billion in emergency assistance for agricultural producers affected by drought conditions. Passed 412-0: R 218-0; D 193-0 (ND 138-0, SD 55-0); I 1-0. Oct. 6, 2004.

502. HR 4567. Fiscal 2005 Homeland Security Appropriations/Motion to Instruct. Sabo, D-Minn., motion to instruct House conferees to insist on a conference report that includes the highest possible funding levels for homeland security first-responders, domestic preparedness, emergency management performance grants, fire grants, flood maps and disaster mitigation programs. Motion agreed to 395-16: R 199-16; D 195-0 (ND 140-0, SD 55-0); I 1-0. Oct. 7, 2004.

503 HR 4661. Spyware Programs/Passage. Goodlatte, R-Va., motion to suspend the rules and pass the bill that would establish criminal penalties, including imprisonment for up to two years, for anyone who intentionally gains unauthorized access to a computer in order to steal information or damage the machine. Anyone who intentionally gained access in furtherance of a federal crime could serve up to five years in prison. The bill would authorize a total of $40 million over four years to fund federal prosecutions in order to discourage spyware use. Motion agreed to 415-0: R 219-0; D 195-0 (ND 141-0, SD 54-0); I 1-0. A two-thirds majority of those present and voting (277 in this case) is required for passage under suspension of the rules. Oct. 7, 2004.

504. HR 5213. Research Review Reports/Passage. Bilirakis, R-Fla., motion to suspend the rules and pass the bill that would require reports to Congress from the National Institutes of Health on spinal cord injury and paralysis research, and the Centers for Disease Control and Prevention on inflammatory bowel disease epidemiological studies. The Government Accountability Office would be required to conduct studies on Medicare and Medicaid coverage standards for patients with inflammatory bowel disease and on the problems patients encounter when applying for disability insurance benefits. Motion agreed to 418-0: R 221-0; D 196-0 (ND 141-0, SD 55-0); I 1-0. A two-thirds majority of those present and voting (279 in this case) is required for passage under suspension of the rules. Oct. 7, 2004.

505. HR 5186. Student Loan Guarantees and Forgiveness/Passage. Boehner, R-Ohio, motion to suspend the rules and pass the bill that would eliminate for one year loan guarantees that allow some lenders to receive a 9.5 percent rate of return on certain student loans compared with the current market rate of about 3.5 percent paid by most students. It also would increase, from $5,000 to $17,500, the amount of loan forgiveness for math, science and special-education teachers who agree to teach for five or more years in elementary and secondary schools in high-poverty areas. Motion agreed to 414-0: R 218-0; D 195-0 (ND 140-0, SD 55-0); I 1-0. A two-thirds majority of those present and voting (276 in this case) is required for passage under suspension of the rules. Oct. 7, 2004.

	500	501	502	503	504	505
ALABAMA						
1 *Bonner*	N	Y	Y	Y	Y	Y
2 *Everett*	N	Y	Y	Y	Y	Y
3 *Rogers*	N	Y	Y	Y	Y	Y
4 *Aderholt*	N	Y	Y	Y	Y	Y
5 Cramer	N	Y	Y	Y	Y	Y
6 *Bachus*	?	Y	N	Y	Y	Y
7 Davis	N	Y	Y	Y	Y	Y
ALASKA						
AL *Young*	?	?	Y	Y	Y	Y
ARIZONA						
1 *Renzi*	N	Y	Y	Y	Y	Y
2 *Franks*	Y	Y	Y	Y	Y	Y
3 *Shadegg*	Y	Y	N	Y	Y	Y
4 Pastor	N	Y	Y	Y	Y	Y
5 *Hayworth*	Y	Y	Y	Y	Y	Y
6 *Flake*	Y	Y	N	Y	Y	Y
7 Grijalva	N	Y	Y	Y	Y	Y
8 Kolbe	N	Y	N	Y	Y	Y
ARKANSAS						
1 Berry	N	Y	Y	Y	Y	Y
2 Snyder	N	Y	Y	Y	Y	Y
3 *Boozman*	Y	Y	Y	Y	Y	Y
4 Ross	N	Y	Y	Y	Y	Y
CALIFORNIA						
1 Thompson	N	Y	Y	Y	Y	Y
2 *Herger*	Y	Y	Y	Y	Y	Y
3 *Ose*	N	Y	Y	Y	Y	Y
4 *Doolittle*	N	Y	Y	Y	Y	Y
5 Matsui	N	Y	Y	Y	Y	Y
6 Woolsey	N	Y	Y	Y	Y	Y
7 Miller, George	N	Y	Y	Y	Y	Y
8 Pelosi	?	?	Y	Y	Y	Y
9 Lee	N	Y	Y	Y	Y	Y
10 Tauscher	N	Y	Y	Y	Y	Y
11 *Pombo*	N	Y	Y	Y	Y	Y
12 Lantos	N	Y	Y	Y	Y	Y
13 Stark	?	?	Y	Y	Y	Y
14 Eshoo	N	Y	Y	Y	Y	Y
15 Honda	N	Y	Y	Y	Y	Y
16 Lofgren	N	Y	Y	Y	Y	Y
17 Farr	N	Y	Y	Y	Y	Y
18 Cardoza	N	Y	Y	Y	Y	Y
19 *Radanovich*	Y	Y	?	Y	Y	Y
20 Dooley	?	?	Y	Y	Y	Y
21 *Nunes*	N	Y	Y	Y	Y	Y
22 *Thomas*	N	Y	Y	Y	Y	Y
23 Capps	N	Y	Y	Y	Y	Y
24 *Gallegly*	N	Y	Y	Y	Y	Y
25 *McKeon*	N	Y	Y	Y	Y	Y
26 *Dreier*	N	Y	Y	Y	Y	Y
27 Sherman	N	Y	Y	Y	Y	Y
28 Berman	N	Y	Y	Y	Y	Y
29 Schiff	N	Y	Y	Y	Y	Y
30 Waxman	N	Y	Y	Y	Y	Y
31 Becerra	N	Y	Y	Y	Y	Y
32 Solis	N	Y	Y	Y	Y	Y
33 Watson	N	Y	Y	Y	Y	Y
34 Roybal-Allard	N	Y	Y	Y	Y	Y
35 Waters	N	Y	Y	Y	Y	Y
36 Harman	N	Y	Y	Y	Y	Y

	500	501	502	503	504	505
37 Millender-McD.	?	?	?	?	?	?
38 Napolitano	N	Y	Y	Y	Y	Y
39 Sánchez, Linda	N	Y	Y	Y	Y	Y
40 *Royce*	Y	Y	Y	Y	Y	Y
41 *Lewis*	N	Y	Y	Y	Y	Y
42 *Miller, Gary*	Y	Y	Y	Y	Y	Y
43 Baca	N	Y	Y	Y	Y	Y
44 *Calvert*	N	Y	Y	Y	Y	Y
45 *Bono*	N	Y	Y	Y	Y	Y
46 *Rohrabacher*	Y	Y	Y	Y	Y	Y
47 Sanchez, Loretta	N	Y	Y	Y	Y	Y
48 *Cox*	Y	Y	Y	?	Y	Y
49 *Issa*	N	Y	Y	Y	Y	Y
50 *Cunningham*	N	Y	Y	Y	Y	Y
51 Filner	N	Y	?	?	?	Y
52 *Hunter*	N	Y	Y	Y	Y	?
53 Davis	N	Y	Y	Y	Y	Y
COLORADO						
1 DeGette	N	Y	Y	Y	Y	Y
2 Udall	N	Y	Y	Y	Y	Y
3 *McInnis*	Y	Y	Y	Y	Y	Y
4 *Musgrave*	Y	Y	N	Y	Y	Y
5 *Hefley*	Y	Y	Y	Y	Y	Y
6 *Tancredo*	Y	Y	Y	Y	Y	Y
7 *Beauprez*	Y	Y	Y	Y	Y	Y
CONNECTICUT						
1 Larson	N	Y	Y	Y	Y	Y
2 *Simmons*	N	Y	Y	Y	Y	Y
3 DeLauro	N	Y	Y	Y	Y	Y
4 *Shays*	N	Y	Y	Y	Y	Y
5 *Johnson*	N	Y	?	Y	Y	Y
DELAWARE						
AL *Castle*	N	Y	Y	Y	Y	Y
FLORIDA						
1 *Miller, J.*	Y	Y	Y	Y	Y	Y
2 Boyd	N	Y	Y	Y	Y	Y
3 Brown	N	Y	Y	Y	Y	Y
4 *Crenshaw*	N	Y	Y	Y	Y	Y
5 *Brown-Waite*	Y	Y	Y	Y	Y	?
6 *Stearns*	N	Y	Y	Y	Y	Y
7 *Mica*	N	Y	Y	Y	Y	Y
8 *Keller*	Y	Y	Y	Y	Y	Y
9 *Bilirakis*	N	Y	Y	Y	Y	Y
10 *Young*	N	Y	Y	?	Y	Y
11 Davis	N	Y	Y	Y	Y	Y
12 *Putnam*	N	Y	Y	Y	Y	Y
13 *Harris*	Y	Y	Y	Y	Y	Y
14 Vacant						
15 *Weldon*	N	Y	Y	Y	Y	Y
16 *Foley*	N	Y	Y	Y	Y	Y
17 Meek	N	Y	Y	Y	Y	Y
18 *Ros-Lehtinen*	N	Y	Y	Y	Y	Y
19 Wexler	N	Y	Y	Y	Y	Y
20 Deutsch	N	Y	Y	Y	Y	Y
21 *Diaz-Balart, L.*	N	Y	Y	Y	Y	Y
22 *Shaw*	N	Y	Y	Y	Y	Y
23 Hastings	N	Y	Y	Y	Y	Y
24 *Feeney*	Y	Y	N	Y	Y	Y
25 *Diaz-Balart, M.*	N	Y	Y	Y	Y	Y
GEORGIA						
1 *Kingston*	?	?	N	Y	Y	Y
2 Bishop	N	Y	Y	Y	Y	Y
3 Marshall	N	Y	Y	Y	Y	Y
4 *Majette*	N	Y	?	?	?	?
5 Lewis	N	Y	Y	Y	Y	Y
6 *Isakson*	N	Y	Y	Y	Y	Y
7 *Linder*	N	Y	N	Y	Y	Y
8 *Collins*	Y	Y	Y	Y	Y	Y
9 *Norwood*	?	?	?	?	?	?
10 *Deal*	Y	Y	Y	Y	Y	Y
11 *Gingrey*	Y	Y	Y	Y	Y	Y
12 *Burns*	N	Y	Y	Y	Y	Y
13 Scott	N	Y	Y	?	Y	Y
HAWAII						
1 Abercrombie	N	Y	Y	Y	Y	Y
2 Case	N	Y	Y	Y	Y	Y
IDAHO						
1 *Otter*	Y	Y	Y	Y	Y	Y
2 *Simpson*	N	Y	Y	Y	Y	Y
ILLINOIS						
1 Rush	N	Y	Y	Y	Y	Y
2 Jackson	N	Y	Y	Y	Y	Y
3 Lipinski	N	Y	Y	Y	Y	Y
4 Gutierrez	N	Y	Y	Y	Y	Y
5 Emanuel	N	Y	Y	Y	Y	Y
6 *Hyde*	N	Y	Y	Y	Y	Y

ND Northern Democrats   SD Southern Democrats

	500	501	502	503	504	505
7 Davis	N	Y	Y	Y	Y	Y
8 ***Crane***	Y	Y	Y	Y	Y	Y
9 Schakowsky	N	Y	Y	Y	Y	Y
10 ***Kirk***	N	Y	Y	Y	Y	Y
11 ***Weller***	N	Y	Y	Y	Y	Y
12 Costello	N	Y	Y	Y	Y	Y
13 ***Biggert***	N	Y	Y	Y	Y	Y
14 ***Hastert***						
15 ***Johnson***	N	Y	Y	Y	Y	Y
16 ***Manzullo***	Y	Y	Y	Y	Y	Y
17 Evans	N	Y	Y	Y	Y	Y
18 ***LaHood***	N	Y	Y	Y	Y	Y
19 ***Shimkus***	N	Y	Y	Y	Y	Y
INDIANA						
1 Visclosky	N	Y	Y	Y	Y	Y
2 ***Chocola***	Y	Y	Y	Y	Y	Y
3 ***Souder***	N	Y	Y	Y	Y	Y
4 ***Buyer***	N	Y	Y	Y	Y	Y
5 ***Burton***	Y	Y	Y	Y	Y	Y
6 ***Pence***	Y	Y	Y	Y	Y	Y
7 Carson	N	Y	Y	Y	Y	Y
8 ***Hostettler***	Y	Y	Y	Y	Y	Y
9 Hill	N	Y	Y	Y	Y	Y
IOWA						
1 ***Nussle***	Y	Y	Y	Y	Y	Y
2 ***Leach***	N	Y	Y	Y	Y	Y
3 Boswell	N	Y	Y	Y	Y	Y
4 ***Latham***	N	Y	Y	Y	Y	Y
5 ***King***	Y	Y	Y	Y	Y	Y
KANSAS						
1 ***Moran***	Y	Y	Y	Y	Y	Y
2 ***Ryun***	N	Y	Y	Y	Y	Y
3 Moore	N	Y	Y	Y	Y	Y
4 ***Tiahrt***	Y	Y	Y	Y	Y	Y
KENTUCKY						
1 ***Whitfield***	Y	Y	Y	Y	Y	Y
2 ***Lewis***	Y	Y	Y	Y	Y	Y
3 ***Northup***	N	Y	Y	Y	Y	Y
4 Lucas	N	Y	Y	Y	Y	Y
5 ***Rogers***	N	Y	Y	Y	Y	Y
6 Chandler	N	Y	Y	Y	Y	Y
LOUISIANA						
1 ***Vitter***	N	Y	?	Y	Y	Y
2 Jefferson	N	Y	Y	Y	Y	Y
3 ***Tauzin***	?	?	?	?	?	?
4 ***McCrery***	N	Y	Y	Y	Y	Y
5 ***Alexander***	N	Y	Y	Y	Y	Y
6 ***Baker***	N	Y	Y	Y	Y	Y
7 John	N	Y	Y	Y	Y	Y
MAINE						
1 Allen	N	Y	Y	Y	Y	Y
2 Michaud	N	Y	Y	Y	Y	Y
MARYLAND						
1 ***Gilchrest***	N	Y	Y	Y	Y	Y
2 Ruppersberger	N	Y	Y	Y	Y	Y
3 Cardin	N	Y	Y	Y	Y	Y
4 Wynn	N	Y	Y	Y	Y	Y
5 Hoyer	N	Y	Y	Y	Y	Y
6 ***Bartlett***	Y	Y	Y	Y	Y	Y
7 Cummings	N	Y	Y	Y	Y	Y
8 Van Hollen	N	Y	Y	Y	Y	Y
MASSACHUSETTS						
1 Olver	N	Y	Y	Y	Y	Y
2 Neal	?	?	?	?	?	?
3 McGovern	N	Y	Y	Y	Y	Y
4 Frank	N	Y	Y	Y	Y	Y
5 Meehan	N	Y	Y	Y	Y	Y
6 Tierney	N	Y	Y	Y	Y	Y
7 Markey	N	Y	Y	Y	Y	Y
8 Capuano	N	Y	Y	Y	Y	Y
9 Lynch	N	Y	Y	Y	Y	Y
10 Delahunt	N	Y	Y	Y	Y	Y
MICHIGAN						
1 Stupak	N	Y	Y	Y	Y	Y
2 ***Hoekstra***	Y	Y	Y	Y	Y	Y
3 ***Ehlers***	N	Y	N	Y	Y	Y
4 ***Camp***	N	Y	Y	Y	Y	Y
5 Kildee	N	Y	Y	Y	Y	Y
6 ***Upton***	N	Y	Y	Y	Y	Y
7 ***Smith***	Y	Y	Y	Y	Y	Y
8 ***Rogers***	N	Y	Y	Y	Y	Y
9 ***Knollenberg***	N	Y	Y	Y	Y	Y
10 ***Miller***	N	Y	Y	Y	Y	Y
11 ***McCotter***	N	Y	Y	Y	Y	Y
12 Levin	N	Y	Y	Y	Y	Y
13 Kilpatrick	N	Y	?	?	?	?
14 Conyers	N	Y	Y	Y	Y	Y
15 Dingell	N	Y	Y	Y	Y	Y
MINNESOTA						
1 ***Gutknecht***	Y	Y	Y	Y	Y	Y
2 ***Kline***	Y	Y	Y	Y	Y	Y
3 ***Ramstad***	Y	Y	Y	Y	Y	Y
4 McCollum	N	Y	Y	Y	Y	Y
5 Sabo	N	Y	Y	Y	Y	Y
6 ***Kennedy***	N	Y	Y	Y	Y	Y
7 Peterson	N	Y	Y	Y	Y	Y
8 Oberstar	N	Y	Y	Y	Y	Y
MISSISSIPPI						
1 ***Wicker***	N	Y	Y	Y	Y	Y
2 Thompson	N	Y	Y	Y	Y	Y
3 ***Pickering***	N	Y	Y	Y	Y	Y
4 Taylor	Y	Y	Y	Y	Y	Y
MISSOURI						
1 Clay	N	Y	Y	Y	Y	Y
2 ***Akin***	Y	Y	Y	Y	Y	Y
3 Gephardt	?	?	?	?	?	?
4 Skelton	N	Y	Y	Y	Y	Y
5 McCarthy	N	Y	Y	Y	Y	Y
6 ***Graves***	Y	Y	Y	Y	Y	Y
7 ***Blunt***	Y	Y	Y	Y	Y	Y
8 ***Emerson***	N	Y	Y	Y	Y	Y
9 ***Hulshof***	N	Y	?	Y	Y	Y
MONTANA						
AL ***Rehberg***	Y	Y	Y	Y	Y	Y
NEBRASKA						
1 Vacant						
2 ***Terry***	N	Y	Y	Y	Y	Y
3 ***Osborne***	N	Y	Y	Y	Y	Y
NEVADA						
1 Berkley	N	Y	Y	Y	Y	Y
2 ***Gibbons***	Y	Y	Y	Y	Y	Y
3 ***Porter***	N	Y	Y	Y	Y	Y
NEW HAMPSHIRE						
1 ***Bradley***	N	Y	Y	Y	Y	Y
2 ***Bass***	N	Y	Y	Y	Y	Y
NEW JERSEY						
1 Andrews	N	Y	Y	Y	Y	Y
2 ***LoBiondo***	N	Y	Y	Y	Y	Y
3 ***Saxton***	N	Y	Y	Y	Y	Y
4 ***Smith***	N	Y	Y	Y	Y	Y
5 ***Garrett***	Y	Y	N	Y	Y	Y
6 Pallone	N	Y	Y	Y	Y	Y
7 ***Ferguson***	N	Y	Y	Y	Y	Y
8 Pascrell	N	Y	Y	Y	Y	Y
9 Rothman	N	Y	Y	Y	Y	Y
10 Payne	N	Y	Y	Y	Y	Y
11 ***Frelinghuysen***	N	Y	Y	Y	Y	Y
12 Holt	N	Y	Y	Y	Y	Y
13 Menendez	N	Y	Y	Y	Y	Y
NEW MEXICO						
1 ***Wilson***	N	Y	Y	Y	Y	Y
2 ***Pearce***	N	Y	N	Y	Y	Y
3 Udall	N	Y	Y	Y	Y	Y
NEW YORK						
1 Bishop	N	Y	Y	Y	Y	Y
2 Israel	N	Y	?	Y	Y	Y
3 ***King***	N	Y	Y	Y	Y	Y
4 McCarthy	N	Y	Y	Y	Y	Y
5 Ackerman	N	Y	Y	Y	Y	Y
6 Meeks	N	Y	Y	Y	Y	Y
7 Crowley	N	Y	Y	Y	Y	Y
8 Nadler	N	Y	Y	Y	Y	Y
9 Weiner	N	Y	Y	Y	Y	Y
10 Towns	?	?	?	?	?	?
11 Owens	N	Y	Y	Y	Y	Y
12 Velázquez	N	Y	Y	Y	Y	Y
13 ***Fossella***	Y	Y	Y	Y	Y	Y
14 Maloney	N	Y	Y	Y	Y	Y
15 Rangel	N	?	Y	Y	Y	Y
16 Serrano	N	Y	Y	Y	Y	Y
17 Engel	N	Y	Y	Y	Y	Y
18 Lowey	N	Y	Y	Y	Y	Y
19 ***Kelly***	N	Y	Y	Y	Y	Y
20 ***Sweeney***	N	Y	Y	Y	Y	Y
21 McNulty	N	Y	Y	Y	Y	Y
22 Hinchey	N	Y	Y	Y	Y	Y
23 ***McHugh***	N	Y	Y	Y	Y	Y
24 ***Boehlert***	?	?	?	?	?	?
25 ***Walsh***	N	Y	Y	Y	Y	Y
26 ***Reynolds***	N	Y	Y	Y	Y	Y
27 ***Quinn***	N	Y	Y	Y	Y	Y
28 Slaughter	?	?	?	?	?	?
29 ***Houghton***	?	?	Y	Y	Y	Y
NORTH CAROLINA						
1 Butterfield	N	Y	Y	Y	Y	Y
2 Etheridge	N	Y	Y	Y	Y	Y
3 ***Jones***	Y	Y	N	Y	Y	Y
4 Price	N	Y	Y	Y	Y	Y
5 ***Burr***	N	Y	Y	Y	Y	Y
6 ***Coble***	Y	Y	Y	Y	Y	Y
7 McIntyre	N	Y	Y	Y	Y	Y
8 ***Hayes***	N	Y	Y	Y	Y	Y
9 ***Myrick***	Y	Y	Y	Y	Y	Y
10 ***Ballenger***	Y	Y	Y	Y	Y	Y
11 ***Taylor***	N	Y	Y	Y	Y	?
12 Watt	?	?	Y	Y	Y	Y
13 Miller	N	Y	Y	Y	Y	Y
NORTH DAKOTA						
AL Pomeroy	N	Y	Y	Y	Y	Y
OHIO						
1 ***Chabot***	Y	Y	Y	Y	Y	Y
2 ***Portman***	Y	Y	Y	Y	Y	Y
3 ***Turner***	Y	Y	Y	Y	Y	Y
4 ***Oxley***	N	Y	Y	Y	Y	Y
5 ***Gillmor***	N	Y	Y	Y	Y	Y
6 Strickland	N	Y	Y	Y	Y	Y
7 ***Hobson***	N	Y	Y	Y	Y	Y
8 ***Boehner***	Y	Y	Y	Y	Y	Y
9 Kaptur	N	Y	Y	Y	Y	Y
10 Kucinich	N	Y	Y	Y	Y	Y
11 Jones	?	?	Y	Y	Y	Y
12 ***Tiberi***	N	Y	N	Y	Y	Y
13 Brown	N	Y	Y	Y	Y	Y
14 ***LaTourette***	N	Y	Y	Y	Y	Y
15 ***Pryce***	N	Y	Y	Y	Y	Y
16 ***Regula***	N	Y	Y	Y	Y	Y
17 Ryan	N	Y	Y	Y	Y	Y
18 ***Ney***	N	Y	Y	Y	Y	Y
OKLAHOMA						
1 ***Sullivan***	Y	Y	?	Y	Y	Y
2 Carson	N	Y	Y	Y	Y	Y
3 ***Lucas***	N	Y	Y	Y	Y	Y
4 ***Cole***	Y	Y	Y	Y	Y	Y
5 ***Istook***	?	Y	Y	Y	Y	Y
OREGON						
1 Wu	N	Y	Y	Y	Y	Y
2 ***Walden***	N	Y	Y	Y	Y	Y
3 Blumenauer	N	Y	Y	Y	Y	Y
4 DeFazio	N	Y	Y	Y	Y	Y
5 Hooley	N	Y	Y	Y	Y	Y
PENNSYLVANIA						
1 Brady	N	Y	Y	Y	Y	Y
2 Fattah	N	Y	Y	Y	Y	?
3 ***English***	N	Y	Y	Y	Y	Y
4 ***Hart***	Y	Y	Y	Y	Y	Y
5 ***Peterson***	N	Y	Y	Y	Y	Y
6 ***Gerlach***	N	Y	Y	Y	Y	Y
7 ***Weldon***	N	Y	?	Y	Y	Y
8 ***Greenwood***	N	Y	Y	?	?	?
9 ***Shuster, Bill***	N	Y	Y	Y	Y	Y
10 ***Sherwood***	N	Y	Y	Y	Y	Y
11 Kanjorski	N	Y	Y	Y	Y	Y
12 Murtha	N	Y	Y	Y	Y	Y
13 Hoeffel	N	Y	Y	Y	Y	Y
14 Doyle	N	Y	Y	Y	Y	Y
15 ***Toomey***	Y	Y	N	Y	Y	Y
16 ***Pitts***	Y	Y	Y	Y	Y	Y
17 Holden	N	Y	Y	Y	Y	Y
18 ***Murphy***	N	Y	Y	Y	Y	Y
19 ***Platts***	N	Y	Y	Y	Y	Y
RHODE ISLAND						
1 Kennedy	N	Y	Y	Y	Y	Y
2 Langevin	N	Y	Y	Y	Y	Y
SOUTH CAROLINA						
1 ***Brown***	N	Y	Y	Y	Y	Y
2 ***Wilson***	Y	Y	Y	Y	Y	Y
3 ***Barrett***	Y	Y	Y	Y	Y	Y
4 ***DeMint***	?	Y	Y	Y	Y	Y
5 Spratt	N	Y	Y	Y	Y	Y
6 Clyburn	N	Y	Y	Y	Y	Y
SOUTH DAKOTA						
AL Herseth	N	Y	Y	Y	Y	Y
TENNESSEE						
1 ***Jenkins***	Y	Y	Y	Y	Y	Y
2 ***Duncan***	Y	Y	N	Y	Y	Y
3 ***Wamp***	N	Y	Y	Y	Y	Y
4 Davis	N	Y	Y	Y	Y	Y
5 Cooper	N	Y	Y	Y	Y	Y
6 Gordon	N	Y	Y	Y	Y	Y
7 ***Blackburn***	Y	Y	Y	Y	Y	Y
8 Tanner	N	Y	Y	Y	Y	Y
9 Ford	N	Y	Y	Y	Y	Y
TEXAS						
1 Sandlin	N	Y	Y	Y	Y	Y
2 Turner	N	Y	Y	Y	Y	Y
3 ***Johnson, Sam***	Y	Y	Y	Y	Y	Y
4 ***Hall***	N	Y	Y	Y	Y	Y
5 ***Hensarling***	Y	Y	Y	Y	Y	Y
6 ***Barton***	Y	Y	Y	Y	Y	Y
7 ***Culberson***	N	Y	?	Y	Y	Y
8 ***Brady***	Y	Y	Y	Y	Y	Y
9 Lampson	N	Y	Y	Y	Y	Y
10 Doggett	N	Y	Y	Y	Y	Y
11 Edwards	N	Y	Y	Y	Y	Y
12 ***Granger***	N	Y	Y	Y	Y	Y
13 ***Thornberry***	Y	Y	Y	Y	Y	Y
14 ***Paul***	?	?	?	?	?	?
15 Hinojosa	N	Y	Y	Y	Y	Y
16 Reyes	N	Y	Y	Y	Y	Y
17 Stenholm	N	Y	Y	Y	Y	Y
18 Jackson-Lee	N	Y	Y	Y	Y	Y
19 ***Neugebauer***	N	Y	Y	Y	Y	Y
20 Gonzalez	N	Y	Y	Y	Y	Y
21 ***Smith***	N	Y	Y	Y	Y	Y
22 ***DeLay***	N	Y	Y	Y	Y	Y
23 ***Bonilla***	N	Y	Y	Y	Y	Y
24 Frost	N	Y	Y	Y	Y	Y
25 Bell	N	Y	Y	Y	Y	Y
26 ***Burgess***	Y	Y	Y	Y	Y	Y
27 Ortiz	N	Y	Y	Y	Y	Y
28 Rodriguez	N	Y	Y	Y	Y	Y
29 Green	N	Y	Y	Y	Y	Y
30 Johnson, E.B.	N	Y	Y	Y	Y	Y
31 ***Carter***	Y	Y	Y	Y	Y	Y
32 ***Sessions***	N	Y	Y	Y	Y	Y
UTAH						
1 ***Bishop***	Y	Y	Y	Y	Y	Y
2 Matheson	N	Y	Y	Y	Y	Y
3 ***Cannon***	Y	Y	Y	Y	Y	Y
VERMONT						
AL *Sanders*	N	Y	Y	Y	Y	Y
VIRGINIA						
1 ***Davis, Jo Ann***	Y	Y	Y	Y	Y	Y
2 ***Schrock***	Y	Y	Y	Y	Y	Y
3 Scott	N	Y	Y	Y	Y	Y
4 ***Forbes***	Y	Y	Y	Y	Y	Y
5 ***Goode***	Y	Y	Y	Y	Y	Y
6 ***Goodlatte***	Y	Y	Y	Y	Y	Y
7 ***Cantor***	N	Y	Y	Y	Y	Y
8 Moran	N	Y	Y	Y	Y	Y
9 Boucher	N	Y	Y	Y	Y	Y
10 ***Wolf***	N	Y	Y	Y	Y	Y
11 ***Davis, T.***	Y	Y	Y	Y	Y	Y
WASHINGTON						
1 Inslee	N	Y	Y	Y	Y	Y
2 Larsen	N	Y	Y	Y	Y	Y
3 Baird	N	Y	Y	Y	Y	Y
4 ***Hastings***	N	Y	Y	Y	Y	Y
5 ***Nethercutt***	?	?	Y	Y	Y	Y
6 Dicks	N	Y	Y	Y	Y	Y
7 McDermott	N	Y	Y	Y	Y	Y
8 ***Dunn***	N	Y	N	Y	Y	Y
9 Smith	N	Y	Y	Y	Y	Y
WEST VIRGINIA						
1 Mollohan	N	Y	Y	Y	Y	Y
2 ***Capito***	N	Y	Y	Y	Y	Y
3 Rahall	N	Y	Y	Y	Y	Y
WISCONSIN						
1 ***Ryan***	Y	Y	Y	Y	Y	Y
2 Baldwin	N	Y	Y	Y	Y	Y
3 Kind	N	Y	Y	Y	Y	Y
4 Kleczka	?	?	?	?	?	?
5 ***Sensenbrenner***	Y	Y	Y	Y	Y	Y
6 ***Petri***	Y	Y	Y	Y	Y	Y
7 Obey	N	Y	Y	Y	Y	Y
8 ***Green***	Y	Y	Y	Y	Y	Y
WYOMING						
AL ***Cubin***	Y	Y	Y	Y	Y	Y

Southern states - Ala., Ark., Fla., Ga., Ky., La., Miss., N.C., Okla., S.C., Tenn., Texas, Va.

Key

Y	Voted for (yea).
#	Paired for.
+	Announced for.
N	Voted against (nay).
X	Paired against.
−	Announced against.
P	Voted "present."
C	Voted "present" to avoid possible conflict of interest.
?	Did not vote or otherwise make a position known.

Democrats **Republicans** *Independents*

506. HR 4520. Corporate Tax Overhaul/Consideration of Rule. Adoption of the resolution (H Res 828) that would waive the two-thirds vote requirement for same day consideration of the rule (H Res 830) to provide for House floor consideration of the conference report on the bill that would revoke an export tax break for U.S. manufacturers ruled an illegal trade subsidy by the World Trade Organization and provide for $137 billion in new tax cuts. Adopted 222-195: R 219-0; D 3-194 (ND 0-142, SD 3-52); I 0-1. Oct. 7, 2004.

507. S 1134. Economic Development Administration/Passage. LaTourette, R-Ohio, motion to suspend the rules and pass the bill that would reauthorize the Commerce Department's Economic Development Administration through 2008. Motion agreed to 388-31: R 190-30; D 197-1 (ND 143-0, SD 54-1); I 1-0. A two-thirds majority of those present and voting (280 in this case) is required for passage under suspension of the rules. Oct. 7, 2004.

508. HR 5061. Assistance for Sudan/Passage. Tancredo, R-Colo., motion to suspend the rules and pass the bill that would authorize $450 million over three years for humanitarian assistance in Sudan's Darfur region and eastern Chad and for reconstruction efforts in areas of southern Sudan. Motion agreed to 412-3: R 215-3; D 196-0 (ND 141-0, SD 55-0); I 1-0. A two-thirds majority of those present and voting (277 in this case) is required for passage under suspension of the rules. Oct. 7, 2004.

509. HR 4520. Corporate Tax Overhaul/Conference Report. Adoption of the conference report on the bill that would repeal an export provision in the U.S. tax code that has been ruled an unfair subsidy by the World Trade Organization, and would provide $137 billion in new tax cuts for corporations over 10 years. It also includes a $10 billion buyout of tobacco farmers. The cost of the tax breaks would be offset by curbs on tax-avoidance practices. Adopted (thus sent to the Senate) 280-141: R 207-16; D 73-124 (ND 25-118, SD 48-6); I 0-1. Oct. 7, 2004.

510. HR 10. Intelligence Overhaul/Substitute. Menendez, D-N.J., substitute amendment that would reorganize 15 U.S. intelligence agencies and create a national intelligence director with authority over all intelligence agency budgets and personnel. It also would modify laws relating to intelligence community management, authorize new diplomatic and foreign aid programs to combat terrorism, provide an integrated screening system, improve counterterrorist travel intelligence and establish a Privacy and Civil Liberties Oversight Board. Rejected 203-213: R 8-212; D 194-1 (ND 141-0, SD 53-1); I 1-0. Oct. 8, 2004 (in the session that began and the Congressional Record dated Oct. 7, 2004).

511. HR 10. Intelligence Overhaul/Information Access. Souder, R-Ind., amendment that would direct the Homeland Security secretary to ensure that all security screening personnel have access to law enforcement and intelligence information maintained by the Department of Homeland Security. The secretary would be required to provide Congress with an overview of all department agencies, databases, and other capabilities relating to terrorism, drug trafficking, illegal immigration, screening, investigations, and inspection of goods or individuals entering the United States. The secretary also would be required to submit a plan to Congress within 180 days on actions taken and plans to improve access and the flow of information. Adopted 410-0: R 215-0; D 194-0 (ND 140-0, SD 54-0); I 1-0. Oct. 8, 2004 (in the session that began and the Congressional Record dated Oct. 7, 2004).

	506	507	508	509	510	511
ALABAMA						
1 Bonner	Y	Y	Y	Y	N	Y
2 Everett	Y	Y	Y	Y	N	Y
3 Rogers	Y	Y	Y	Y	N	Y
4 Aderholt	Y	Y	Y	Y	N	Y
5 Cramer	N	Y	Y	Y	Y	Y
6 Bachus	Y	Y	Y	Y	N	Y
7 Davis	N	Y	Y	Y	Y	Y
ALASKA						
AL Young	Y	Y	Y	Y	N	Y
ARIZONA						
1 Renzi	Y	Y	Y	Y	N	Y
2 Franks	Y	N	Y	Y	N	Y
3 Shadegg	Y	N	Y	Y	N	Y
4 Pastor	N	Y	Y	N	Y	Y
5 Hayworth	Y	Y	Y	Y	N	Y
6 Flake	Y	N	N	Y	N	Y
7 Grijalva	N	Y	Y	N	Y	Y
8 Kolbe	Y	Y	Y	Y	N	Y
ARKANSAS						
1 Berry	N	Y	Y	Y	Y	Y
2 Snyder	N	Y	Y	Y	Y	Y
3 Boozman	Y	Y	Y	Y	N	Y
4 Ross	N	Y	Y	Y	Y	Y
CALIFORNIA						
1 Thompson	N	Y	Y	Y	Y	Y
2 Herger	Y	Y	Y	Y	N	Y
3 Ose	Y	Y	Y	N	N	Y
4 Doolittle	Y	Y	Y	Y	N	Y
5 Matsui	N	Y	Y	N	Y	Y
6 Woolsey	N	Y	N	Y	Y	Y
7 Miller, George	N	Y	Y	N	Y	Y
8 Pelosi	N	Y	Y	N	Y	Y
9 Lee	N	Y	N	Y	Y	Y
10 Tauscher	N	Y	Y	N	Y	Y
11 Pombo	Y	Y	Y	Y	N	Y
12 Lantos	N	Y	Y	N	Y	Y
13 Stark	N	Y	Y	N	?	?
14 Eshoo	N	Y	Y	N	Y	Y
15 Honda	N	Y	Y	N	Y	Y
16 Lofgren	N	Y	N	Y	Y	Y
17 Farr	N	Y	Y	N	Y	Y
18 Cardoza	N	Y	Y	N	Y	Y
19 Radanovich	?	Y	Y	Y	N	Y
20 Dooley	N	Y	Y	Y	Y	Y
21 Nunes	Y	Y	Y	Y	N	Y
22 Thomas	Y	Y	Y	Y	N	Y
23 Capps	N	Y	Y	N	Y	Y
24 Gallegly	Y	Y	Y	Y	N	Y
25 McKeon	Y	Y	Y	Y	N	Y
26 Dreier	Y	Y	Y	Y	N	Y
27 Sherman	N	Y	Y	N	Y	Y
28 Berman	N	Y	Y	N	Y	Y
29 Schiff	N	Y	Y	N	Y	Y
30 Waxman	N	Y	Y	N	Y	Y
31 Becerra	N	Y	Y	N	Y	Y
32 Solis	N	Y	Y	N	Y	Y
33 Watson	N	Y	Y	N	Y	Y
34 Roybal-Allard	N	Y	Y	N	Y	Y
35 Waters	N	Y	Y	N	Y	Y
36 Harman	N	Y	Y	N	Y	Y
37 Millender-McD.	?	?	?	?	?	?
38 Napolitano	N	Y	Y	N	Y	Y
39 Sánchez, Linda	N	Y	Y	N	Y	Y
40 Royce	Y	N	Y	Y	N	Y
41 Lewis	Y	Y	Y	Y	N	Y
42 Miller, Gary	Y	N	N	Y	N	Y
43 Baca	N	Y	Y	N	Y	Y
44 Calvert	Y	Y	Y	Y	N	Y
45 Bono	Y	Y	Y	Y	N	Y
46 Rohrabacher	Y	N	Y	Y	N	Y
47 Sanchez, Loretta	N	Y	Y	N	Y	Y
48 Cox	Y	N	Y	Y	N	Y
49 Issa	Y	Y	Y	Y	N	Y
50 Cunningham	Y	Y	Y	Y	N	Y
51 Filner	?	?	?	?	?	?
52 Hunter	Y	N	Y	Y	N	Y
53 Davis	N	Y	Y	N	Y	Y
COLORADO						
1 DeGette	N	Y	Y	N	Y	Y
2 Udall	N	Y	Y	Y	Y	Y
3 McInnis	Y	Y	Y	Y	N	Y
4 Musgrave	Y	Y	Y	Y	N	Y
5 Hefley	Y	N	N	Y	N	Y
6 Tancredo	Y	Y	Y	Y	N	Y
7 Beauprez	Y	Y	Y	Y	N	Y
CONNECTICUT						
1 Larson	N	Y	Y	N	Y	Y
2 Simmons	Y	Y	Y	Y	Y	Y
3 DeLauro	N	Y	Y	N	Y	Y
4 Shays	Y	Y	Y	Y	Y	Y
5 Johnson	Y	Y	Y	Y	N	Y
DELAWARE						
AL Castle	Y	Y	Y	N	Y	Y
FLORIDA						
1 Miller, J.	Y	N	Y	N	Y	Y
2 Boyd	N	Y	Y	Y	Y	Y
3 Brown	N	Y	Y	N	Y	Y
4 Crenshaw	Y	Y	Y	Y	N	Y
5 Brown-Waite	Y	Y	Y	Y	N	Y
6 Stearns	Y	N	Y	Y	N	Y
7 Mica	Y	Y	Y	Y	N	Y
8 Keller	Y	Y	Y	Y	N	Y
9 Bilirakis	Y	Y	Y	Y	N	Y
10 Young	Y	Y	Y	Y	N	Y
11 Davis	N	Y	Y	Y	Y	Y
12 Putnam	Y	Y	Y	Y	N	Y
13 Harris	Y	Y	Y	Y	N	Y
14 Vacant						
15 Weldon	Y	Y	Y	Y	N	Y
16 Foley	Y	Y	Y	Y	N	Y
17 Meek	N	Y	Y	N	Y	Y
18 Ros-Lehtinen	Y	Y	Y	N	?	?
19 Wexler	N	Y	Y	N	Y	Y
20 Deutsch	N	Y	Y	Y	Y	Y
21 Diaz-Balart, L.	Y	Y	Y	N	N	Y
22 Shaw	Y	Y	Y	Y	N	Y
23 Hastings	N	Y	Y	N	Y	Y
24 Feeney	Y	Y	Y	Y	N	Y
25 Diaz-Balart, M.	Y	Y	Y	N	N	Y
GEORGIA						
1 Kingston	Y	Y	Y	Y	N	Y
2 Bishop	Y	Y	Y	Y	Y	Y
3 Marshall	N	Y	Y	N	Y	Y
4 Majette	?	?	?	?	?	?
5 Lewis	N	Y	Y	N	Y	Y
6 Isakson	Y	Y	Y	Y	N	Y
7 Linder	Y	Y	Y	Y	N	Y
8 Collins	Y	Y	Y	Y	N	Y
9 Norwood	?	?	?	?	?	?
10 Deal	Y	Y	Y	Y	N	Y
11 Gingrey	Y	Y	Y	Y	N	Y
12 Burns	Y	Y	Y	Y	N	Y
13 Scott	Y	Y	Y	Y	Y	Y
HAWAII						
1 Abercrombie	N	Y	Y	N	Y	Y
2 Case	N	Y	Y	N	Y	Y
IDAHO						
1 Otter	Y	N	Y	Y	N	Y
2 Simpson	Y	Y	Y	Y	N	Y
ILLINOIS						
1 Rush	N	Y	?	N	Y	Y
2 Jackson	N	Y	Y	N	Y	Y
3 Lipinski	N	Y	Y	?	?	?
4 Gutierrez	N	Y	Y	N	Y	Y
5 Emanuel	N	Y	Y	N	Y	Y
6 Hyde	Y	Y	Y	Y	N	Y

ND Northern Democrats   SD Southern Democrats

	506	507	508	509	510	511
7 Davis	N	Y	Y	Y	Y	Y
8 ***Crane***	Y	Y	Y	Y	N	Y
9 Schakowsky	N	Y	Y	N	Y	Y
10 ***Kirk***	Y	Y	Y	N	N	Y
11 ***Weller***	Y	Y	?	Y	N	Y
12 Costello	N	Y	Y	N	Y	Y
13 ***Biggert***	Y	Y	Y	Y	N	Y
14 ***Hastert***				Y	N	
15 ***Johnson***	Y	Y	Y	Y	Y	Y
16 ***Manzullo***	Y	Y	Y	Y	N	Y
17 Evans	N	Y	Y	N	Y	Y
18 ***LaHood***	Y	Y	Y	N	N	Y
19 ***Shimkus***	Y	Y	Y	Y	N	Y
INDIANA						
1 Visclosky	N	Y	Y	N	Y	Y
2 ***Chocola***	Y	N	Y	Y	N	Y
3 ***Souder***	Y	N	Y	Y	N	Y
4 ***Buyer***	Y	Y	?	Y	N	Y
5 ***Burton***	Y	Y	Y	Y	N	Y
6 ***Pence***	Y	N	Y	Y	N	Y
7 Carson	N	Y	Y	N	Y	Y
8 ***Hostettler***	Y	N	Y	Y	N	Y
9 Hill	N	Y	Y	Y	Y	Y
IOWA						
1 ***Nussle***	Y	Y	Y	Y	N	Y
2 ***Leach***	Y	Y	Y	Y	Y	Y
3 Boswell	N	Y	Y	Y	Y	Y
4 ***Latham***	Y	Y	Y	Y	N	Y
5 ***King***	Y	N	Y	Y	N	Y
KANSAS						
1 ***Moran***	Y	Y	Y	Y	N	Y
2 ***Ryun***	?	?	Y	Y	N	Y
3 Moore	N	Y	Y	Y	Y	Y
4 ***Tiahrt***	Y	Y	Y	Y	N	Y
KENTUCKY						
1 ***Whitfield***	Y	Y	Y	Y	N	Y
2 ***Lewis***	Y	Y	Y	Y	N	Y
3 ***Northup***	Y	Y	Y	Y	N	Y
4 Lucas	N	Y	Y	Y	Y	Y
5 ***Rogers***	Y	Y	Y	Y	N	Y
6 Chandler	N	Y	Y	Y	Y	Y
LOUISIANA						
1 ***Vitter***	Y	Y	Y	Y	N	Y
2 Jefferson	N	Y	Y	Y	Y	Y
3 ***Tauzin***	?	?	?	?	?	?
4 ***McCrery***	Y	Y	Y	Y	N	Y
5 ***Alexander***	Y	Y	Y	Y	N	Y
6 ***Baker***	Y	Y	Y	Y	?	?
7 John	N	Y	Y	Y	Y	Y
MAINE						
1 Allen	N	Y	Y	N	Y	Y
2 Michaud	N	Y	Y	N	Y	Y
MARYLAND						
1 ***Gilchrest***	Y	Y	Y	Y	N	Y
2 Ruppersberger	N	Y	Y	Y	Y	Y
3 Cardin	N	Y	Y	N	Y	Y
4 Wynn	N	Y	Y	Y	Y	Y
5 Hoyer	N	Y	Y	N	Y	Y
6 ***Bartlett***	Y	Y	Y	Y	N	Y
7 Cummings	N	Y	Y	N	Y	Y
8 Van Hollen	N	Y	Y	N	Y	Y
MASSACHUSETTS						
1 Olver	N	Y	Y	N	Y	Y
2 Neal	N	Y	Y	N	Y	Y
3 McGovern	N	Y	Y	N	Y	Y
4 Frank	N	Y	Y	N	Y	Y
5 Meehan	N	Y	Y	N	Y	Y
6 Tierney	N	Y	Y	N	Y	Y
7 Markey	N	Y	Y	N	Y	Y
8 Capuano	N	Y	Y	N	Y	Y
9 Lynch	N	Y	Y	N	Y	Y
10 Delahunt	N	Y	Y	N	Y	Y
MICHIGAN						
1 Stupak	N	Y	Y	N	Y	Y
2 ***Hoekstra***	Y	Y	Y	Y	N	Y
3 ***Ehlers***	Y	Y	Y	Y	N	Y
4 ***Camp***	Y	Y	Y	Y	N	Y
5 Kildee	N	Y	Y	N	Y	Y
6 ***Upton***	Y	Y	Y	N	Y	Y
7 ***Smith***	Y	N	Y	Y	N	?
8 ***Rogers***	Y	Y	Y	Y	N	Y
9 ***Knollenberg***	Y	Y	Y	Y	N	Y
10 ***Miller***	Y	Y	Y	Y	N	Y
11 ***McCotter***	Y	Y	Y	Y	N	Y
12 Levin	N	Y	Y	N	Y	Y
13 Kilpatrick	?	?	?	N	Y	Y
14 Conyers	N	Y	Y	N	Y	Y
15 Dingell	N	Y	Y	N	Y	Y
MINNESOTA						
1 ***Gutknecht***	Y	Y	Y	Y	N	Y
2 ***Kline***	Y	Y	Y	Y	N	Y
3 ***Ramstad***	Y	Y	Y	Y	N	Y
4 McCollum	N	Y	Y	N	Y	Y
5 Sabo	N	Y	Y	N	Y	Y
6 ***Kennedy***	Y	Y	Y	Y	N	Y
7 Peterson	N	Y	Y	Y	Y	Y
8 Oberstar	N	Y	Y	N	Y	Y
MISSISSIPPI						
1 ***Wicker***	Y	Y	Y	Y	N	Y
2 Thompson	N	Y	Y	Y	Y	Y
3 ***Pickering***	Y	Y	Y	Y	N	Y
4 Taylor	N	N	Y	Y	Y	Y
MISSOURI						
1 Clay	N	Y	Y	N	Y	Y
2 ***Akin***	Y	Y	Y	Y	N	Y
3 Gephardt	?	?	?	?	?	?
4 Skelton	N	Y	Y	Y	Y	Y
5 McCarthy	N	Y	Y	N	Y	Y
6 ***Graves***	Y	Y	Y	Y	N	Y
7 ***Blunt***	Y	Y	Y	Y	N	Y
8 ***Emerson***	Y	Y	Y	Y	N	Y
9 ***Hulshof***	Y	Y	Y	Y	N	Y
MONTANA						
AL ***Rehberg***	Y	Y	Y	Y	N	Y
NEBRASKA						
1 Vacant						
2 ***Terry***	Y	Y	Y	Y	N	Y
3 ***Osborne***	Y	Y	?	Y	N	Y
NEVADA						
1 Berkley	N	Y	Y	Y	Y	Y
2 ***Gibbons***	Y	Y	Y	Y	N	Y
3 ***Porter***	Y	Y	Y	Y	N	Y
NEW HAMPSHIRE						
1 ***Bradley***	Y	Y	Y	N	N	Y
2 ***Bass***	Y	Y	Y	N	N	Y
NEW JERSEY						
1 Andrews	N	Y	Y	N	Y	Y
2 ***LoBiondo***	Y	Y	Y	Y	N	Y
3 ***Saxton***	Y	Y	Y	Y	N	Y
4 ***Smith***	Y	Y	Y	Y	N	Y
5 ***Garrett***	Y	N	Y	Y	N	Y
6 Pallone	N	Y	Y	N	Y	Y
7 ***Ferguson***	Y	Y	Y	Y	Y	Y
8 Pascrell	N	Y	Y	N	Y	Y
9 Rothman	N	Y	Y	N	Y	Y
10 Payne	N	Y	Y	N	Y	Y
11 ***Frelinghuysen***	Y	Y	Y	Y	N	Y
12 Holt	N	Y	Y	N	Y	Y
13 Menendez	N	Y	Y	N	Y	Y
NEW MEXICO						
1 ***Wilson***	Y	Y	Y	N	N	Y
2 ***Pearce***	Y	Y	Y	Y	N	Y
3 Udall	N	Y	Y	N	Y	Y
NEW YORK						
1 Bishop	N	Y	Y	N	Y	Y
2 Israel	N	Y	Y	N	Y	Y
3 ***King***	Y	Y	Y	Y	N	Y
4 McCarthy	N	Y	Y	N	Y	Y
5 Ackerman	N	Y	Y	N	Y	Y
6 Meeks	N	Y	Y	Y	Y	Y
7 Crowley	N	Y	Y	Y	Y	Y
8 Nadler	N	Y	Y	N	Y	Y
9 Weiner	N	Y	Y	N	Y	Y
10 Towns	N	Y	Y	?	?	?
11 Owens	N	Y	Y	N	Y	Y
12 Velázquez	N	Y	Y	N	Y	Y
13 ***Fossella***	Y	Y	Y	Y	Y	Y
14 Maloney	N	Y	Y	N	Y	Y
15 Rangel	N	Y	Y	N	Y	Y
16 Serrano	N	Y	Y	N	Y	Y
17 Engel	N	Y	Y	N	Y	Y
18 Lowey	N	Y	Y	N	Y	Y
19 ***Kelly***	Y	Y	Y	Y	N	Y
20 ***Sweeney***	Y	Y	Y	Y	N	Y
21 McNulty	N	Y	Y	N	Y	Y
22 Hinchey	?	?	?	N	Y	Y
23 ***McHugh***	Y	Y	Y	Y	N	Y
24 ***Boehlert***	?	?	?	?	?	?
25 ***Walsh***	Y	Y	Y	Y	N	Y
26 ***Reynolds***	Y	Y	Y	Y	N	Y
27 ***Quinn***	?	?	?	Y	Y	Y
28 Slaughter	?	?	?	?	?	?
29 ***Houghton***	Y	Y	Y	Y	?	?
NORTH CAROLINA						
1 Butterfield	N	Y	Y	Y	Y	Y
2 Etheridge	N	Y	Y	Y	Y	Y
3 ***Jones***	Y	N	Y	Y	N	Y
4 Price	N	Y	Y	Y	Y	Y
5 ***Burr***	Y	Y	Y	Y	N	Y
6 ***Coble***	Y	Y	Y	Y	N	Y
7 McIntyre	N	Y	Y	Y	Y	Y
8 ***Hayes***	Y	Y	Y	Y	N	Y
9 ***Myrick***	Y	N	Y	Y	N	Y
10 ***Ballenger***	Y	Y	Y	Y	N	?
11 ***Taylor***	Y	Y	Y	Y	N	Y
12 Watt	N	Y	Y	Y	Y	Y
13 Miller	N	Y	Y	Y	Y	Y
NORTH DAKOTA						
AL Pomeroy	N	Y	Y	Y	Y	Y
OHIO						
1 ***Chabot***	Y	N	Y	Y	N	Y
2 ***Portman***	Y	Y	Y	Y	N	Y
3 ***Turner***	Y	Y	Y	Y	N	Y
4 ***Oxley***	Y	Y	Y	Y	N	Y
5 ***Gillmor***	Y	Y	Y	Y	N	Y
6 Strickland	N	Y	Y	N	Y	Y
7 ***Hobson***	Y	Y	Y	Y	N	Y
8 ***Boehner***	Y	Y	Y	Y	N	Y
9 Kaptur	N	Y	Y	Y	Y	Y
10 Kucinich	N	Y	Y	N	Y	Y
11 Jones	?	Y	?	N	Y	Y
12 ***Tiberi***	Y	Y	Y	Y	N	Y
13 Brown	N	Y	Y	N	Y	Y
14 ***LaTourette***	Y	Y	Y	Y	N	Y
15 ***Pryce***	Y	Y	Y	Y	N	Y
16 ***Regula***	Y	Y	Y	Y	N	Y
17 Ryan	N	Y	Y	N	Y	Y
18 ***Ney***	Y	Y	Y	Y	N	Y
OKLAHOMA						
1 ***Sullivan***	Y	Y	Y	Y	N	Y
2 Carson	Y	Y	Y	Y	Y	Y
3 ***Lucas***	Y	Y	Y	Y	N	Y
4 ***Cole***	Y	Y	Y	Y	N	Y
5 ***Istook***	Y	Y	Y	Y	N	Y
OREGON						
1 Wu	N	Y	Y	Y	Y	Y
2 ***Walden***	Y	Y	Y	Y	N	Y
3 Blumenauer	N	Y	Y	N	Y	Y
4 DeFazio	N	Y	Y	N	Y	Y
5 Hooley	N	Y	Y	Y	Y	Y
PENNSYLVANIA						
1 Brady	N	Y	Y	N	Y	Y
2 Fattah	N	Y	Y	N	Y	Y
3 ***English***	Y	Y	Y	Y	N	Y
4 ***Hart***	Y	Y	Y	Y	N	Y
5 ***Peterson***	Y	Y	Y	Y	N	Y
6 ***Gerlach***	Y	Y	Y	Y	N	Y
7 ***Weldon***	Y	Y	Y	Y	N	Y
8 ***Greenwood***	Y	Y	Y	Y	N	Y
9 ***Shuster, Bill***	Y	Y	Y	Y	N	Y
10 ***Sherwood***	Y	Y	Y	Y	N	Y
11 Kanjorski	N	Y	Y	N	Y	Y
12 Murtha	N	Y	Y	N	?	?
13 Hoeffel	N	Y	Y	N	Y	Y
14 Doyle	N	Y	Y	N	Y	Y
15 ***Toomey***	Y	N	Y	Y	N	Y
16 ***Pitts***	Y	Y	Y	Y	N	Y
17 Holden	N	Y	Y	N	Y	Y
18 ***Murphy***	Y	Y	Y	Y	N	Y
19 ***Platts***	Y	N	Y	N	N	Y
RHODE ISLAND						
1 Kennedy	N	Y	Y	N	Y	Y
2 Langevin	N	Y	Y	N	Y	Y
SOUTH CAROLINA						
1 ***Brown***	Y	Y	Y	Y	N	Y
2 ***Wilson***	Y	Y	Y	Y	N	Y
3 ***Barrett***	Y	N	Y	Y	N	Y
4 ***DeMint***	Y	Y	Y	Y	N	Y
5 Spratt	N	Y	Y	Y	Y	Y
6 Clyburn	N	Y	Y	Y	Y	Y
SOUTH DAKOTA						
AL Herseth	N	Y	Y	Y	Y	Y
TENNESSEE						
1 ***Jenkins***	Y	Y	Y	Y	N	Y
2 ***Duncan***	Y	Y	Y	Y	N	Y
3 ***Wamp***	Y	Y	Y	Y	N	Y
4 Davis	N	Y	Y	Y	Y	Y
5 Cooper	N	Y	Y	Y	Y	Y
6 Gordon	N	Y	Y	Y	Y	Y
7 ***Blackburn***	Y	Y	Y	Y	N	Y
8 Tanner	N	Y	Y	Y	Y	Y
9 Ford	N	Y	Y	Y	Y	Y
TEXAS						
1 Sandlin	N	Y	Y	Y	Y	Y
2 Turner	N	Y	Y	Y	Y	Y
3 ***Johnson, Sam***	Y	N	Y	Y	N	Y
4 ***Hall***	Y	Y	Y	Y	N	Y
5 ***Hensarling***	Y	N	Y	Y	N	Y
6 ***Barton***	Y	Y	Y	Y	N	Y
7 ***Culberson***	Y	N	Y	Y	N	Y
8 ***Brady***	Y	Y	Y	Y	N	Y
9 Lampson	N	Y	Y	Y	Y	Y
10 Doggett	N	Y	Y	N	Y	Y
11 Edwards	N	Y	Y	Y	Y	Y
12 ***Granger***	Y	Y	Y	Y	N	Y
13 ***Thornberry***	Y	Y	Y	Y	N	Y
14 ***Paul***	?	?	?	?	?	?
15 Hinojosa	N	Y	Y	Y	Y	Y
16 Reyes	N	Y	Y	Y	Y	Y
17 Stenholm	N	Y	Y	Y	Y	Y
18 Jackson-Lee	N	Y	Y	Y	Y	Y
19 ***Neugebauer***	Y	Y	Y	Y	N	Y
20 Gonzalez	N	Y	Y	Y	Y	Y
21 ***Smith***	Y	Y	Y	Y	N	Y
22 ***DeLay***	Y	Y	Y	Y	N	Y
23 ***Bonilla***	Y	Y	Y	Y	N	Y
24 Frost	N	Y	Y	Y	Y	Y
25 Bell	N	Y	Y	Y	Y	Y
26 ***Burgess***	Y	Y	Y	Y	N	Y
27 Ortiz	N	Y	Y	?	?	?
28 Rodriguez	N	Y	Y	Y	Y	Y
29 Green	N	Y	Y	Y	Y	Y
30 Johnson, E.B.	N	Y	Y	Y	Y	Y
31 ***Carter***	Y	Y	Y	Y	N	Y
32 ***Sessions***	Y	Y	Y	Y	N	Y
UTAH						
1 ***Bishop***	Y	Y	Y	Y	N	Y
2 Matheson	N	Y	Y	Y	Y	Y
3 ***Cannon***	Y	Y	Y	Y	N	Y
VERMONT						
AL *Sanders*	N	Y	Y	N	Y	Y
VIRGINIA						
1 ***Davis, Jo Ann***	Y	Y	Y	Y	N	Y
2 ***Schrock***	Y	Y	Y	Y	N	?
3 Scott	N	Y	Y	N	Y	Y
4 ***Forbes***	Y	Y	Y	Y	N	Y
5 ***Goode***	Y	Y	Y	Y	N	Y
6 ***Goodlatte***	Y	Y	Y	Y	N	Y
7 ***Cantor***	Y	Y	Y	Y	N	Y
8 Moran	N	Y	Y	N	Y	Y
9 Boucher	N	Y	Y	Y	Y	Y
10 ***Wolf***	Y	Y	Y	N	N	Y
11 ***Davis, T.***	Y	Y	Y	Y	N	Y
WASHINGTON						
1 Inslee	N	Y	Y	Y	Y	Y
2 Larsen	N	Y	Y	Y	Y	Y
3 Baird	N	Y	Y	Y	Y	Y
4 ***Hastings***	Y	Y	Y	Y	N	Y
5 ***Nethercutt***	Y	Y	Y	Y	N	Y
6 Dicks	N	Y	Y	Y	Y	Y
7 McDermott	N	Y	Y	N	Y	Y
8 ***Dunn***	Y	Y	Y	Y	N	Y
9 Smith	N	Y	Y	Y	Y	Y
WEST VIRGINIA						
1 Mollohan	N	Y	Y	N	Y	Y
2 ***Capito***	Y	Y	Y	Y	N	Y
3 Rahall	N	Y	Y	N	Y	Y
WISCONSIN						
1 ***Ryan***	Y	Y	Y	Y	N	Y
2 Baldwin	N	Y	Y	N	Y	Y
3 Kind	N	Y	Y	N	Y	Y
4 Kleczka	N	Y	Y	N	Y	?
5 ***Sensenbrenner***	Y	N	Y	N	N	Y
6 ***Petri***	Y	N	Y	Y	N	Y
7 Obey	N	Y	Y	N	Y	Y
8 ***Green***	Y	Y	Y	Y	N	Y
WYOMING						
AL ***Cubin***	Y	N	Y	Y	N	Y

Southern states - Ala., Ark., Fla., Ga., Ky., La., Miss., N.C., Okla., S.C., Tenn., Texas, Va.

Key

Y	Voted for (yea).
#	Paired for.
+	Announced for.
N	Voted against (nay).
X	Paired against.
–	Announced against.
P	Voted "present."
C	Voted "present" to avoid possible conflict of interest.
?	Did not vote or otherwise make a position known.

Democrats   ***Republicans***
Independents

512. HR 10. Intelligence Overhaul/Drug Enforcement Administration. Kirk, R-Ill., amendment that would require the president to submit a report to the House and Senate Select Intelligence and Judiciary committees within 180 days of enactment of the bill detailing the practicality of incorporating the Drug Enforcement Administration into the intelligence community. Adopted 414-0: R 221-0; D 192-0 (ND 140-0, SD 52-0); I 1-0. Oct. 8, 2004.

513. HR 10. Intelligence Overhaul/Possession of Terrorist Weapons. Sessions, R-Texas, amendment that would make the unauthorized possession of shoulder-fired guided missiles, atomic weapons, "dirty" bombs and smallpox virus a federal crime punishable by mandatory penalties of up to $2 million in fines plus 30 years in prison, life imprisonment or death if the violation results in a person's death. Adopted 385-30: R 220-0; D 164-30 (ND 116-26, SD 48-4); I 1-0. Oct. 8, 2004.

514. HR 10. Intelligence Overhaul/Punishment for Terrorist Acts. Carter, R-Texas, amendment that would change the federal criminal code to apply the death penalty or life imprisonment for a terrorist offense that results in a person's death. Adopted 344-72: R 218-3; D 126-68 (ND 80-62, SD 46-6); I 0-1. Oct. 8, 2004.

515. HR 10. Intelligence Overhaul/Pretrial Detention of Terrorist Suspects. Goodlatte, R-Va., amendment that would create a rebuttable presumption of pretrial detention of a defendant charged with a terrorist offense if there is probable cause that he or she committed a terrorist attack. It also would give judges the discretion to impose lifetime supervision of defendants who have been convicted of terrorist offenses. Adopted 333-84: R 219-2; D 114-81 (ND 68-75, SD 46-6); I 0-1. Oct. 8, 2004.

516. HR 10. Intelligence Overhaul/Deportation Requirements. Green, R-Wis., amendment that would provide that all terrorist-related grounds of inadmissibility would also be grounds for deportation. It also would make it an inadmissible and deportable offense to attend a terrorist training camp, and it would strengthen the grounds of inadmissibility and deportability regarding monetary or material support to terrorist organizations. Adopted 283-132: R 219-1; D 64-130 (ND 28-115, SD 36-15); I 0-1. Oct. 8, 2004.

517. HR 10. Intelligence Overhaul/Expedited Deportation of Aliens. Smith, R-N.J., amendment that would remove the section of the bill that would require expedited removal of aliens that have been in the country for fewer than five years without a hearing or future review. Adopted 212-203: R 32-189; D 179-14 (ND 137-4, SD 42-10); I 1-0. Oct. 8, 2004.

518. HR 10. Intelligence Overhaul/Asylum Rights and Refugee Protections. Smith, R-N.J., amendment that would remove the section of the bill that would restrict asylum rights and refugee protections. Rejected 197-219: R 21-200; D 175-19 (ND 135-7, SD 40-12); I 1-0. Oct. 8, 2004.

	512	513	514	515	516	517	518
ALABAMA							
1 *Bonner*	Y	Y	Y	Y	Y	N	N
2 *Everett*	Y	Y	Y	Y	Y	N	N
3 *Rogers*	Y	Y	Y	Y	Y	N	N
4 *Aderholt*	Y	Y	Y	Y	Y	N	N
5 Cramer	Y	Y	Y	Y	Y	N	N
6 *Bachus*	Y	Y	Y	Y	Y	N	N
7 Davis	Y	Y	Y	Y	Y	Y	Y
ALASKA							
AL *Young*	Y	Y	Y	Y	Y	N	N
ARIZONA							
1 *Renzi*	Y	Y	Y	Y	Y	N	N
2 *Franks*	Y	Y	Y	Y	Y	N	N
3 *Shadegg*	Y	Y	Y	Y	Y	N	N
4 Pastor	Y	Y	Y	N	N	Y	Y
5 *Hayworth*	Y	Y	Y	Y	Y	N	N
6 *Flake*	Y	Y	Y	Y	Y	N	N
7 Grijalva	N	N	N	N	N	Y	Y
8 *Kolbe*	Y	Y	Y	Y	Y	Y	Y
ARKANSAS							
1 Berry	Y	Y	Y	Y	Y	Y	Y
2 Snyder	Y	Y	Y	Y	Y	Y	Y
3 *Boozman*	Y	Y	Y	Y	Y	N	N
4 Ross	Y	Y	Y	Y	Y	N	N
CALIFORNIA							
1 Thompson	Y	Y	Y	N	N	Y	Y
2 *Herger*	Y	Y	Y	Y	Y	N	N
3 *Ose*	Y	Y	Y	Y	Y	N	N
4 *Doolittle*	Y	Y	Y	Y	Y	N	N
5 Matsui	?	?	?	?	?	?	?
6 Woolsey	Y	N	N	N	N	Y	Y
7 Miller, George	Y	N	N	N	N	Y	Y
8 Pelosi	Y	N	N	N	N	Y	Y
9 Lee	Y	N	N	N	N	Y	Y
10 Tauscher	Y	Y	Y	N	N	Y	Y
11 *Pombo*	Y	Y	Y	Y	Y	N	N
12 Lantos	Y	Y	Y	N	N	Y	Y
13 Stark	Y	N	N	N	N	Y	Y
14 Eshoo	Y	Y	Y	N	N	Y	Y
15 Honda	Y	N	N	N	N	Y	Y
16 Lofgren	Y	Y	Y	N	N	Y	Y
17 Farr	Y	N	N	N	N	Y	Y
18 Cardoza	Y	Y	Y	Y	Y	Y	Y
19 *Radanovich*	Y	Y	Y	Y	Y	N	N
20 Dooley	Y	Y	Y	Y	N	Y	Y
21 *Nunes*	Y	Y	Y	Y	Y	N	N
22 *Thomas*	Y	Y	Y	Y	Y	N	N
23 Capps	Y	Y	Y	N	N	Y	Y
24 *Gallegly*	Y	Y	Y	Y	Y	N	N
25 *McKeon*	Y	Y	Y	Y	Y	N	N
26 *Dreier*	Y	Y	Y	Y	Y	N	N
27 Sherman	Y	Y	N	N	N	Y	Y
28 Berman	Y	Y	N	N	N	Y	Y
29 Schiff	Y	Y	Y	N	N	Y	Y
30 Waxman	Y	N	N	N	N	Y	Y
31 Becerra	Y	N	N	N	N	Y	Y
32 Solis	Y	N	N	N	N	Y	Y
33 Watson	Y	N	N	N	N	Y	Y
34 Roybal-Allard	Y	N	N	N	N	Y	Y
35 Waters	Y	N	N	N	N	Y	Y
36 Harman	Y	Y	Y	Y	N	Y	Y

	512	513	514	515	516	517	518
37 Millender-McD.	Y	Y	N	N	N	Y	Y
38 Napolitano	Y	Y	N	Y	N	Y	Y
39 Sánchez, Linda	Y	Y	N	N	N	Y	Y
40 *Royce*	Y	Y	Y	Y	Y	N	N
41 *Lewis*	Y	Y	Y	Y	Y	N	N
42 *Miller, Gary*	Y	Y	Y	Y	N	Y	N
43 Baca	Y	Y	Y	Y	N	Y	Y
44 *Calvert*	Y	Y	Y	Y	Y	N	N
45 *Bono*	Y	Y	Y	Y	Y	N	N
46 *Rohrabacher*	Y	Y	Y	Y	Y	N	N
47 Sanchez, Loretta	Y	Y	N	N	Y	Y	Y
48 *Cox*	Y	?	Y	Y	Y	N	N
49 *Issa*	Y	Y	Y	Y	Y	N	N
50 *Cunningham*	Y	Y	Y	Y	Y	N	N
51 Filner	+	+	+	+	–	+	+
52 *Hunter*	Y	Y	Y	Y	Y	N	N
53 Davis	Y	Y	Y	Y	N	Y	Y
COLORADO							
1 DeGette	Y	Y	N	N	N	Y	Y
2 Udall	Y	Y	Y	N	Y	N	Y
3 *McInnis*	Y	Y	Y	Y	Y	N	N
4 *Musgrave*	Y	Y	Y	Y	Y	N	N
5 *Hefley*	Y	Y	Y	Y	Y	N	N
6 *Tancredo*	Y	Y	Y	Y	Y	N	N
7 *Beauprez*	Y	Y	Y	Y	Y	N	N
CONNECTICUT							
1 Larson	Y	Y	Y	N	N	Y	Y
2 *Simmons*	Y	Y	Y	Y	Y	Y	Y
3 DeLauro	Y	Y	Y	N	Y	Y	Y
4 *Shays*	Y	Y	Y	Y	Y	Y	Y
5 *Johnson*	Y	Y	Y	Y	Y	Y	Y
DELAWARE							
AL *Castle*	Y	Y	Y	Y	N	Y	N
FLORIDA							
1 *Miller, J.*	Y	Y	Y	Y	Y	N	N
2 Boyd	Y	Y	Y	Y	Y	N	N
3 Brown	Y	Y	Y	N	Y	Y	Y
4 *Crenshaw*	Y	Y	Y	Y	Y	N	N
5 *Brown-Waite*	Y	Y	Y	Y	Y	N	N
6 *Stearns*	Y	Y	Y	Y	Y	N	N
7 *Mica*	Y	Y	Y	Y	Y	N	N
8 *Keller*	Y	Y	Y	Y	Y	N	N
9 *Bilirakis*	Y	Y	Y	Y	Y	N	N
10 *Young*	Y	Y	Y	Y	Y	N	N
11 Davis	Y	Y	Y	Y	N	Y	Y
12 *Putnam*	Y	Y	Y	Y	Y	N	N
13 *Harris*	Y	Y	Y	Y	Y	N	N
15 *Weldon*	Y	Y	Y	Y	Y	N	N
14 Vacant							
16 *Foley*	Y	Y	Y	Y	Y	N	Y
17 Meek	?	?	?	?	?	?	?
18 *Ros-Lehtinen*	Y	Y	Y	Y	Y	N	Y
19 Wexler	Y	Y	Y	N	Y	Y	Y
20 Deutsch	Y	Y	Y	Y	Y	Y	Y
21 *Diaz-Balart, L.*	Y	Y	Y	Y	N	Y	Y
22 *Shaw*	Y	Y	Y	Y	Y	N	N
23 Hastings	Y	N	N	N	N	Y	Y
24 *Feeney*	Y	Y	Y	Y	Y	N	N
25 *Diaz-Balart, M.*	Y	Y	Y	Y	Y	Y	Y
GEORGIA							
1 *Kingston*	Y	Y	Y	Y	Y	N	N
2 Bishop	Y	Y	Y	Y	Y	Y	Y
3 Marshall	Y	Y	Y	Y	Y	N	N
4 Majette	?	?	?	?	?	?	?
5 Lewis	Y	N	N	N	N	Y	Y
6 *Isakson*	Y	Y	Y	Y	Y	N	N
7 *Linder*	Y	Y	Y	Y	Y	N	N
8 *Collins*	Y	Y	Y	Y	Y	N	N
9 *Norwood*	?	?	?	?	?	?	?
10 *Deal*	Y	Y	Y	Y	Y	N	N
11 *Gingrey*	Y	Y	Y	Y	Y	N	N
12 *Burns*	Y	Y	Y	Y	Y	N	N
13 Scott	Y	Y	Y	Y	Y	Y	Y
HAWAII							
1 Abercrombie	Y	Y	N	N	N	Y	Y
2 Case	Y	Y	Y	Y	Y	N	N
IDAHO							
1 *Otter*	Y	Y	Y	N	Y	N	N
2 *Simpson*	Y	Y	Y	Y	Y	N	N
ILLINOIS							
1 Rush	Y	N	N	N	N	Y	Y
2 Jackson	Y	N	N	N	N	Y	Y
3 Lipinski	?	?	?	?	?	?	?
4 Gutierrez	Y	N	N	N	N	Y	Y
5 Emanuel	Y	Y	Y	N	N	Y	Y
6 *Hyde*	Y	Y	Y	Y	Y	N	N

ND Northern Democrats   SD Southern Democrats

	512	513	514	515	516	517	518
7 Davis	Y	Y	N	N	N	Y	Y
8 ***Crane***	Y	Y	Y	Y	Y	N	N
9 Schakowsky	Y	Y	N	N	N	Y	Y
10 ***Kirk***	Y	Y	Y	Y	Y	Y	N
11 ***Weller***	Y	Y	Y	Y	Y	N	N
12 Costello	Y	Y	Y	Y	Y	Y	Y
13 ***Biggert***	Y	Y	Y	Y	Y	Y	N
14 ***Hastert***							
15 ***Johnson***	Y	Y	Y	N	Y	Y	Y
16 ***Manzullo***	Y	Y	Y	Y	Y	N	N
17 Evans	Y	Y	Y	Y	N	Y	Y
18 ***LaHood***	Y	Y	Y	Y	Y	N	N
19 ***Shimkus***	Y	Y	Y	Y	Y	N	N
INDIANA							
1 Visclosky	Y	Y	Y	N	Y	Y	Y
2 ***Chocola***	Y	Y	Y	Y	Y	N	N
3 ***Souder***	Y	Y	Y	Y	Y	Y	N
4 ***Buyer***	Y	Y	Y	Y	Y	N	N
5 ***Burton***	Y	Y	Y	Y	Y	N	N
6 ***Pence***	Y	Y	Y	Y	Y	N	N
7 Carson	Y	N	N	N	N	Y	Y
8 ***Hostettler***	Y	Y	Y	Y	Y	N	N
9 Hill	Y	Y	Y	Y	Y	Y	N
IOWA							
1 ***Nussle***	Y	Y	Y	Y	Y	N	N
2 ***Leach***	Y	Y	Y	Y	Y	Y	N
3 Boswell	Y	Y	Y	Y	Y	Y	Y
4 ***Latham***	Y	Y	Y	Y	Y	N	N
5 ***King***	Y	Y	Y	Y	Y	N	N
KANSAS							
1 ***Moran***	Y	Y	Y	Y	Y	N	N
2 ***Ryun***	Y	Y	Y	Y	Y	N	N
3 Moore	Y	Y	Y	Y	Y	Y	N
4 ***Tiahrt***	Y	Y	Y	Y	Y	N	N
KENTUCKY							
1 ***Whitfield***	Y	Y	Y	Y	Y	N	N
2 ***Lewis***	Y	Y	Y	Y	Y	N	N
3 ***Northup***	Y	Y	Y	Y	Y	Y	N
4 Lucas	Y	Y	Y	Y	Y	Y	N
5 ***Rogers***	Y	Y	Y	Y	Y	N	N
6 Chandler	Y	Y	Y	Y	Y	N	N
LOUISIANA							
1 ***Vitter***	Y	Y	Y	Y	Y	N	N
2 Jefferson	Y	Y	Y	Y	Y	Y	Y
3 ***Tauzin***	?	?	?	?	?	?	?
4 ***McCrery***	Y	Y	Y	Y	Y	N	N
5 ***Alexander***	Y	Y	Y	Y	Y	N	N
6 ***Baker***	Y	Y	Y	Y	Y	N	N
7 John	Y	Y	Y	Y	Y	N	N
MAINE							
1 Allen	Y	Y	Y	N	N	Y	Y
2 Michaud	Y	Y	Y	N	N	Y	Y
MARYLAND							
1 ***Gilchrest***	Y	Y	Y	Y	Y	Y	N
2 Ruppersberger	Y	?	Y	Y	Y	Y	N
3 Cardin	Y	Y	Y	Y	N	Y	Y
4 Wynn	Y	Y	Y	Y	N	Y	Y
5 Hoyer	Y	Y	Y	Y	N	Y	Y
6 ***Bartlett***	Y	Y	Y	Y	Y	Y	N
7 Cummings	Y	Y	Y	Y	N	Y	Y
8 Van Hollen	Y	Y	N	Y	N	Y	Y
MASSACHUSETTS							
1 Olver	Y	N	N	N	N	Y	Y
2 Neal	Y	Y	Y	N	N	Y	Y
3 McGovern	Y	Y	N	N	N	Y	Y
4 Frank	Y	Y	N	N	N	Y	Y
5 Meehan	Y	Y	Y	N	N	Y	Y
6 Tierney	Y	Y	N	N	N	Y	Y
7 Markey	Y	N	N	N	N	Y	Y
8 Capuano	Y	Y	N	N	N	Y	Y
9 Lynch	Y	Y	Y	Y	N	Y	Y
10 Delahunt	Y	Y	N	N	N	Y	Y
MICHIGAN							
1 Stupak	Y	Y	Y	Y	N	Y	Y
2 ***Hoekstra***	Y	Y	N	Y	Y	N	N
3 ***Ehlers***	Y	Y	N	Y	Y	N	Y
4 ***Camp***	Y	Y	Y	Y	Y	N	N
5 Kildee	Y	N	N	Y	N	Y	Y
6 ***Upton***	Y	Y	Y	Y	Y	N	N
7 ***Smith***	Y	Y	Y	Y	Y	N	N
8 ***Rogers***	Y	Y	Y	Y	Y	N	N
9 ***Knollenberg***	Y	Y	Y	Y	Y	N	N
10 ***Miller***	Y	Y	Y	Y	Y	N	N
11 ***McCotter***	Y	Y	Y	Y	Y	N	N
12 Levin	Y	Y	N	Y	N	Y	Y

	512	513	514	515	516	517	518
13 Kilpatrick	Y	Y	N	N	N	Y	Y
14 Conyers	?	Y	N	N	N	Y	Y
15 Dingell	Y	Y	Y	N	Y	Y	Y
MINNESOTA							
1 ***Gutknecht***	Y	Y	Y	Y	Y	N	N
2 ***Kline***	Y	Y	Y	Y	Y	N	N
3 ***Ramstad***	Y	Y	Y	Y	Y	N	N
4 McCollum	Y	N	N	Y	N	Y	Y
5 Sabo	Y	N	N	Y	N	Y	Y
6 ***Kennedy***	Y	Y	Y	Y	Y	N	N
7 Peterson	Y	Y	Y	Y	Y	Y	N
8 Oberstar	Y	N	N	N	N	Y	Y
MISSISSIPPI							
1 ***Wicker***	Y	Y	Y	Y	Y	N	N
2 Thompson	Y	Y	Y	Y	Y	Y	Y
3 ***Pickering***	Y	Y	Y	Y	Y	N	N
4 Taylor	Y	Y	Y	Y	Y	N	N
MISSOURI							
1 Clay	?	Y	N	N	N	Y	Y
2 ***Akin***	Y	Y	Y	Y	Y	N	N
3 Gephardt	?	?	?	?	?	?	?
4 Skelton	Y	Y	Y	Y	Y	Y	Y
5 McCarthy	+	N	N	N	N	Y	Y
6 ***Graves***	Y	Y	Y	Y	Y	N	N
7 ***Blunt***	Y	Y	Y	Y	Y	N	N
8 ***Emerson***	Y	Y	Y	Y	Y	N	N
9 ***Hulshof***	Y	Y	Y	Y	Y	N	N
MONTANA							
AL ***Rehberg***	Y	Y	Y	Y	Y	N	N
NEBRASKA							
1 Vacant							
2 ***Terry***	Y	Y	Y	Y	Y	Y	Y
3 ***Osborne***	Y	Y	Y	Y	Y	N	N
NEVADA							
1 Berkley	Y	Y	Y	Y	N	Y	Y
2 ***Gibbons***	Y	Y	Y	Y	Y	N	N
3 ***Porter***	Y	Y	Y	Y	Y	Y	Y
NEW HAMPSHIRE							
1 ***Bradley***	Y	Y	Y	Y	Y	N	N
2 ***Bass***	Y	Y	Y	Y	Y	N	N
NEW JERSEY							
1 Andrews	Y	Y	Y	Y	N	Y	Y
2 ***LoBiondo***	Y	Y	Y	Y	Y	N	N
3 ***Saxton***	Y	Y	Y	Y	Y	N	N
4 ***Smith***	Y	Y	N	Y	Y	Y	Y
5 ***Garrett***	Y	Y	Y	Y	Y	N	N
6 Pallone	Y	Y	Y	N	N	Y	Y
7 ***Ferguson***	Y	Y	Y	Y	Y	N	N
8 Pascrell	Y	Y	Y	Y	Y	Y	Y
9 Rothman	Y	Y	Y	N	N	Y	Y
10 Payne	Y	N	N	N	N	Y	Y
11 ***Frelinghuysen***	Y	Y	Y	Y	Y	N	N
12 Holt	Y	N	N	N	N	Y	Y
13 Menendez	Y	Y	Y	Y	N	Y	Y
NEW MEXICO							
1 ***Wilson***	Y	Y	Y	Y	N	Y	Y
2 ***Pearce***	Y	Y	Y	Y	Y	N	N
3 Udall	Y	Y	Y	N	Y	Y	Y
NEW YORK							
1 Bishop	Y	Y	Y	Y	Y	Y	Y
2 Israel	Y	Y	Y	Y	N	Y	Y
3 ***King***	Y	Y	Y	Y	Y	Y	Y
4 McCarthy	Y	Y	Y	Y	N	Y	Y
5 Ackerman	Y	Y	Y	N	N	Y	Y
6 Meeks	Y	Y	N	N	N	Y	Y
7 Crowley	Y	Y	Y	Y	N	Y	Y
8 Nadler	Y	Y	N	N	N	Y	Y
9 Weiner	Y	Y	Y	N	N	Y	Y
10 Towns	?	?	?	?	?	?	?
11 Owens	Y	Y	N	N	N	Y	Y
12 Velázquez	Y	N	N	N	N	Y	Y
13 ***Fossella***	Y	Y	Y	Y	Y	Y	N
14 Maloney	Y	Y	Y	N	N	Y	Y
15 Rangel	Y	N	N	N	N	Y	Y
16 Serrano	Y	Y	N	N	N	Y	Y
17 Engel	Y	Y	Y	Y	N	?	Y
18 Lowey	Y	Y	Y	Y	N	Y	Y
19 ***Kelly***	Y	Y	Y	Y	Y	N	N
20 ***Sweeney***	Y	Y	Y	Y	Y	N	N
21 McNulty	Y	Y	Y	Y	Y	Y	Y
22 Hinchey	Y	Y	N	N	N	Y	Y
23 ***McHugh***	Y	Y	Y	Y	Y	N	N
24 ***Boehlert***	?	?	?	?	?	?	?
25 ***Walsh***	Y	Y	Y	Y	Y	Y	Y

	512	513	514	515	516	517	518
26 ***Reynolds***	Y	Y	Y	Y	Y	N	N
27 ***Quinn***	Y	Y	Y	Y	Y	N	N
28 Slaughter	?	?	?	?	?	?	?
29 ***Houghton***	Y	Y	Y	Y	Y	Y	Y
NORTH CAROLINA							
1 Butterfield	Y	Y	Y	Y	Y	Y	Y
2 Etheridge	Y	Y	Y	Y	Y	Y	Y
3 ***Jones***	Y	Y	Y	Y	Y	N	N
4 Price	Y	Y	Y	Y	N	Y	Y
5 ***Burr***	Y	Y	Y	Y	Y	N	Y
6 ***Coble***	Y	Y	Y	Y	Y	N	N
7 McIntyre	Y	Y	Y	Y	Y	Y	N
8 ***Hayes***	Y	Y	Y	Y	Y	N	N
9 ***Myrick***	Y	Y	Y	Y	Y	N	N
10 ***Ballenger***	Y	Y	Y	Y	Y	?	?
11 ***Taylor***	Y	Y	Y	Y	Y	N	N
12 Watt	Y	N	N	N	N	Y	Y
13 Miller	Y	Y	Y	Y	Y	Y	Y
NORTH DAKOTA							
AL Pomeroy	Y	Y	Y	Y	Y	Y	Y
OHIO							
1 ***Chabot***	Y	Y	Y	Y	Y	N	N
2 ***Portman***	Y	Y	Y	Y	Y	N	N
3 ***Turner***	Y	Y	Y	Y	Y	N	N
4 ***Oxley***	Y	Y	Y	Y	Y	N	N
5 ***Gillmor***	Y	Y	Y	Y	Y	N	N
6 Strickland	Y	Y	Y	N	N	Y	Y
7 ***Hobson***	Y	Y	Y	Y	Y	N	N
8 ***Boehner***	Y	Y	Y	Y	Y	N	N
9 Kaptur	Y	Y	Y	Y	Y	?	?
10 Kucinich	Y	N	N	N	N	Y	Y
11 Jones	Y	Y	N	N	N	Y	Y
12 ***Tiberi***	Y	Y	Y	Y	Y	N	N
13 Brown	Y	Y	Y	N	N	Y	Y
14 ***LaTourette***	Y	Y	Y	Y	Y	Y	N
15 ***Pryce***	Y	Y	Y	Y	Y	N	N
16 ***Regula***	Y	Y	Y	Y	Y	N	N
17 Ryan	Y	Y	Y	N	Y	Y	Y
18 ***Ney***	Y	Y	Y	Y	Y	N	N
OKLAHOMA							
1 ***Sullivan***	Y	Y	Y	Y	?	N	N
2 Carson	Y	Y	Y	Y	Y	N	N
3 ***Lucas***	Y	Y	Y	Y	Y	N	N
4 ***Cole***	Y	Y	Y	Y	Y	N	N
5 ***Istook***	Y	Y	Y	Y	Y	N	N
OREGON							
1 Wu	Y	Y	Y	Y	Y	Y	Y
2 ***Walden***	Y	Y	Y	Y	Y	N	N
3 Blumenauer	Y	N	N	N	N	Y	Y
4 DeFazio	Y	Y	Y	Y	Y	N	Y
5 Hooley	Y	Y	Y	Y	Y	Y	Y
PENNSYLVANIA							
1 Brady	Y	Y	Y	Y	N	Y	Y
2 Fattah	Y	Y	N	N	N	Y	Y
3 ***English***	Y	Y	Y	Y	Y	N	N
4 ***Hart***	Y	Y	Y	Y	Y	N	N
5 ***Peterson***	Y	Y	Y	Y	Y	N	N
6 ***Gerlach***	Y	Y	Y	Y	Y	Y	Y
7 ***Weldon***	Y	Y	Y	Y	Y	Y	Y
8 ***Greenwood***	Y	Y	Y	Y	Y	Y	N
9 ***Shuster, Bill***	Y	Y	Y	Y	Y	N	N
10 ***Sherwood***	Y	Y	Y	Y	Y	N	N
11 Kanjorski	Y	Y	Y	Y	N	Y	Y
12 Murtha	Y	Y	Y	Y	N	Y	Y
13 Hoeffel	Y	Y	Y	Y	N	Y	Y
14 Doyle	Y	Y	Y	Y	Y	Y	Y
15 ***Toomey***	Y	Y	Y	Y	Y	N	N
16 ***Pitts***	Y	Y	Y	Y	Y	N	N
17 Holden	Y	Y	Y	Y	Y	N	N
18 ***Murphy***	Y	Y	Y	Y	Y	N	N
19 ***Platts***	Y	Y	Y	Y	Y	N	N
RHODE ISLAND							
1 Kennedy	Y	Y	Y	Y	N	Y	Y
2 Langevin	Y	Y	Y	Y	Y	Y	Y
SOUTH CAROLINA							
1 ***Brown***	Y	Y	Y	Y	Y	N	N
2 ***Wilson***	Y	Y	Y	Y	Y	N	N
3 ***Barrett***	Y	Y	Y	Y	Y	N	N
4 ***DeMint***	Y	Y	Y	Y	Y	N	N
5 Spratt	Y	Y	Y	Y	Y	Y	Y
6 Clyburn	Y	Y	Y	Y	Y	Y	Y
SOUTH DAKOTA							
AL Herseth	Y	Y	Y	Y	Y	Y	Y

	512	513	514	515	516	517	518
TENNESSEE							
1 ***Jenkins***	Y	Y	Y	Y	Y	N	N
2 ***Duncan***	Y	Y	Y	Y	Y	N	N
3 ***Wamp***	Y	Y	Y	Y	Y	N	N
4 Davis	Y	Y	Y	Y	Y	N	N
5 Cooper	Y	Y	Y	Y	Y	Y	Y
6 Gordon	Y	Y	Y	Y	Y	Y	Y
7 ***Blackburn***	Y	Y	Y	Y	Y	N	N
8 Tanner	Y	Y	Y	Y	Y	Y	Y
9 Ford	Y	Y	Y	Y	Y	Y	Y
TEXAS							
1 Sandlin	Y	Y	Y	Y	Y	Y	Y
2 Turner	Y	Y	Y	Y	Y	Y	Y
3 ***Johnson, Sam***	Y	Y	Y	Y	Y	N	N
4 ***Hall***	Y	Y	Y	Y	Y	N	N
5 ***Hensarling***	Y	Y	Y	Y	Y	N	N
6 ***Barton***	Y	Y	Y	Y	Y	N	N
7 ***Culberson***	?	?	?	?	?	N	N
8 ***Brady***	Y	Y	Y	Y	Y	N	N
9 Lampson	Y	Y	Y	Y	Y	Y	Y
10 Doggett	Y	Y	Y	N	N	Y	Y
11 Edwards	Y	Y	Y	Y	Y	N	N
12 ***Granger***	Y	Y	Y	Y	Y	N	N
13 ***Thornberry***	Y	Y	Y	Y	Y	N	N
14 ***Paul***	?	?	?	?	?	?	?
15 Hinojosa	+	+	+	+	−	+	+
16 Reyes	Y	Y	Y	Y	N	Y	Y
17 Stenholm	Y	Y	Y	Y	Y	N	N
18 Jackson-Lee	Y	Y	N	N	N	Y	Y
19 ***Neugebauer***	Y	Y	Y	Y	Y	N	N
20 Gonzalez	Y	Y	Y	Y	N	Y	Y
21 ***Smith***	Y	Y	Y	Y	Y	N	N
22 ***DeLay***	Y	Y	Y	Y	Y	N	N
23 ***Bonilla***	Y	Y	Y	Y	Y	N	N
24 Frost	Y	Y	Y	Y	Y	Y	Y
25 Bell	Y	Y	Y	Y	N	Y	Y
26 ***Burgess***	Y	Y	Y	Y	Y	N	N
27 Ortiz	?	?	?	?	?	?	?
28 Rodriguez	Y	Y	Y	Y	N	Y	Y
29 Green	Y	Y	Y	Y	Y	Y	Y
30 Johnson, E.B.	Y	Y	N	Y	?	Y	Y
31 ***Carter***	Y	Y	Y	Y	Y	N	N
32 ***Sessions***	Y	Y	Y	Y	Y	N	N
UTAH							
1 ***Bishop***	Y	Y	Y	Y	Y	N	N
2 Matheson	Y	Y	Y	Y	Y	N	N
3 ***Cannon***	Y	Y	Y	Y	Y	N	N
VERMONT							
AL *Sanders*	Y	Y	N	N	N	Y	Y
VIRGINIA							
1 ***Davis, Jo Ann***	Y	Y	Y	Y	Y	N	N
2 ***Schrock***	Y	Y	Y	Y	Y	N	N
3 Scott	Y	N	N	N	N	Y	Y
4 ***Forbes***	Y	Y	Y	Y	Y	N	N
5 ***Goode***	Y	Y	Y	Y	Y	N	N
6 ***Goodlatte***	Y	Y	Y	Y	Y	N	N
7 ***Cantor***	Y	Y	Y	Y	Y	N	N
8 Moran	Y	Y	Y	Y	N	Y	Y
9 Boucher	Y	Y	Y	Y	Y	Y	Y
10 ***Wolf***	Y	Y	Y	Y	Y	Y	N
11 ***Davis, T.***	Y	Y	Y	Y	Y	Y	Y
WASHINGTON							
1 Inslee	Y	Y	Y	N	N	Y	Y
2 Larsen	Y	Y	Y	N	N	Y	Y
3 Baird	Y	Y	Y	Y	N	Y	Y
4 ***Hastings***	Y	Y	Y	Y	Y	N	N
5 ***Nethercutt***	Y	Y	Y	Y	Y	N	N
6 Dicks	Y	Y	Y	N	N	Y	Y
7 McDermott	Y	N	N	N	N	Y	Y
8 ***Dunn***	Y	Y	Y	Y	Y	N	N
9 Smith	Y	Y	Y	N	N	Y	Y
WEST VIRGINIA							
1 Mollohan	Y	N	N	N	N	Y	Y
2 ***Capito***	Y	Y	Y	Y	Y	N	N
3 Rahall	Y	Y	Y	Y	Y	Y	Y
WISCONSIN							
1 ***Ryan***	Y	Y	Y	Y	Y	N	N
2 Baldwin	Y	Y	N	N	N	Y	Y
3 Kind	Y	Y	Y	Y	N	Y	Y
4 Kleczka	Y	Y	N	Y	N	Y	Y
5 ***Sensenbrenner***	Y	Y	Y	Y	Y	N	N
6 ***Petri***	Y	Y	Y	Y	Y	Y	N
7 Obey	Y	Y	?	Y	N	Y	Y
8 ***Green***	Y	Y	Y	Y	Y	N	N
WYOMING							
AL ***Cubin***	Y	Y	Y	Y	Y	N	N

Southern states - Ala., Ark., Fla., Ga., Ky., La., Miss., N.C., Okla., S.C., Tenn., Texas, Va.

Key

Y	Voted for (yea).
#	Paired for.
+	Announced for.
N	Voted against (nay).
X	Paired against.
–	Announced against.
P	Voted "present."
C	Voted "present" to avoid possible conflict of interest.
?	Did not vote or otherwise make a position known.

Democrats **Republicans**
Independents

519. HR 10. Intelligence Overhaul/Border Construction. Ose, R-Calif., amendment that would expedite construction to fill two gaps in the 14-mile barrier along the U.S.-Mexico border in San Diego, Calif. Adopted 256-160: R 215-6; D 41-153 (ND 14-128, SD 27-25); I 0-1. Oct. 8, 2004.

520. HR 10. Intelligence Overhaul/Mutual Aid Agreements. Weldon, R-Pa., amendment that would require the Department of Homeland Security to establish a program to identify and catalog existing mutual aid agreements between local jurisdictions to provide emergency assistance, disseminate examples of the best practices used in developing such agreements, and inventory terrorist attack or emergency federal response capabilities. Adopted 415-0: R 220-0; D 194-0 (ND 142-0, SD 52-0); I 1-0. Oct. 8, 2004.

521. HR 10. Intelligence Overhaul/Expedited Deportation of Aliens. Separate vote at the request of Sensenbrenner, R-Wis., on the Smith, R-N.J., amendment that would remove the section of the bill that would require expedited removal of aliens who have been in the country for fewer than five years without a hearing or future review. Rejected 203-210: R 25-193; D 177-17 (ND 136-6, SD 41-11); I 1-0. Oct. 8, 2004.

522. HR 10. Intelligence Overhaul/Recommit. Maloney, D-N.Y., motion to recommit the bill to the Select Intelligence Committee with instructions to substitute the text of the Senate-passed bill (S 2845). Motion rejected 193-223: R 2-219; D 190-4 (ND 139-3, SD 51-1); I 1-0. Oct. 8, 2004.

523. HR 10. Intelligence Overhaul/Passage. Passage of the bill that would reorganize 15 U.S. intelligence agencies and create a national intelligence director, who would give guidance on budgets. It also would create a national intelligence center and allow aliens to be deported without judicial review. The number of border-patrol agents would increase from 10,000 to 20,000 over the next five years. The bill, as amended, would make attending a terrorist training camp a deportable offense and toughen penalties for those charged with financially aiding terrorist groups. Passed 282-134: R 213-8; D 69-125 (ND 33-109, SD 36-16); I 0-1. Oct. 8, 2004.

524. HR 4200. Fiscal 2005 Defense Authorization/Previous Question. Myrick, R-N.C., motion to order the previous question (thus ending debate and possibility of amendment) on adoption of the rule (H Res 843) to provide for House floor consideration of the conference report on the bill that would authorize $445.6 billion for the Defense Department and the Energy Department's national security programs. Motion agreed to 225-175: R 206-5; D 19-169 (ND 10-127, SD 9-42); I 0-1. (Subsequently, the rule was adopted by voice vote.) Oct. 8, 2004.

	519	520	521	522	523	524
ALABAMA						
1 *Bonner*	Y	Y	N	Y	Y	Y
2 *Everett*	Y	Y	N	Y	Y	Y
3 *Rogers*	Y	Y	N	Y	Y	Y
4 *Aderholt*	Y	Y	N	Y	Y	Y
5 Cramer	Y	Y	N	Y	Y	Y
6 *Bachus*	Y	Y	N	Y	Y	Y
7 Davis	N	Y	Y	Y	Y	N
ALASKA						
AL *Young*	Y	Y	N	N	N	Y
ARIZONA						
1 *Renzi*	Y	Y	N	N	Y	Y
2 *Franks*	Y	Y	?	N	Y	Y
3 *Shadegg*	Y	Y	N	N	Y	Y
4 Pastor	N	Y	Y	Y	N	N
5 *Hayworth*	Y	Y	N	N	Y	Y
6 *Flake*	Y	Y	N	N	Y	Y
7 Grijalva	N	Y	Y	Y	N	N
8 *Kolbe*	Y	Y	Y	N	Y	Y
ARKANSAS						
1 Berry	Y	Y	Y	Y	Y	N
2 Snyder	N	Y	Y	Y	Y	Y
3 *Boozman*	Y	Y	N	N	Y	Y
4 Ross	N	Y	Y	Y	Y	N
CALIFORNIA						
1 Thompson	N	Y	Y	Y	N	N
2 *Herger*	Y	Y	N	N	Y	Y
3 *Ose*	Y	Y	N	N	Y	Y
4 *Doolittle*	Y	Y	N	N	Y	Y
5 Matsui	?	?	?	?	?	?
6 Woolsey	N	Y	Y	Y	N	N
7 Miller, George	N	Y	Y	Y	N	N
8 Pelosi	N	Y	Y	Y	N	N
9 Lee	N	Y	Y	Y	N	N
10 Tauscher	N	Y	Y	Y	N	N
11 *Pombo*	Y	?	N	N	Y	Y
12 Lantos	N	Y	Y	Y	N	N
13 Stark	N	Y	Y	Y	N	N
14 Eshoo	N	Y	Y	Y	N	N
15 Honda	N	Y	Y	Y	N	N
16 Lofgren	N	Y	Y	Y	N	N
17 Farr	N	Y	Y	Y	N	N
18 Cardoza	Y	Y	Y	Y	Y	N
19 *Radanovich*	Y	Y	N	N	Y	?
20 Dooley	N	Y	Y	Y	Y	N
21 *Nunes*	Y	Y	N	N	Y	Y
22 *Thomas*	Y	Y	N	N	Y	Y
23 Capps	N	Y	Y	Y	N	N
24 *Gallegly*	Y	Y	N	N	Y	?
25 *McKeon*	Y	Y	N	N	Y	Y
26 *Dreier*	Y	Y	N	N	Y	Y
27 Sherman	N	Y	Y	Y	N	N
28 Berman	N	Y	Y	Y	N	N
29 Schiff	N	Y	Y	Y	N	N
30 Waxman	N	Y	Y	Y	N	N
31 Becerra	N	Y	Y	Y	N	N
32 Solis	N	Y	Y	Y	N	N
33 Watson	N	Y	Y	Y	N	N
34 Roybal-Allard	N	Y	Y	Y	N	N
35 Waters	N	Y	Y	Y	N	N
36 Harman	N	Y	Y	Y	Y	N

	519	520	521	522	523	524
37 Millender-McD.	N	Y	Y	Y	N	N
38 Napolitano	N	Y	Y	Y	N	N
39 Sánchez, Linda	N	Y	Y	Y	N	Y
40 *Royce*	Y	Y	N	N	Y	Y
41 *Lewis*	Y	Y	N	N	Y	Y
42 *Miller, Gary*	Y	Y	N	N	Y	?
43 Baca	N	Y	Y	Y	N	N
44 *Calvert*	Y	Y	N	N	Y	Y
45 *Bono*	Y	Y	N	N	Y	Y
46 *Rohrabacher*	Y	Y	N	N	Y	Y
47 Sanchez, Loretta	N	Y	Y	N	Y	Y
48 *Cox*	Y	Y	N	N	Y	Y
49 *Issa*	Y	Y	N	N	Y	?
50 *Cunningham*	Y	Y	?	N	Y	Y
51 Filner	–	+	+	+	–	–
52 *Hunter*	Y	Y	N	N	Y	Y
53 Davis	N	Y	Y	Y	N	N
COLORADO						
1 DeGette	N	Y	Y	Y	N	N
2 Udall	N	Y	Y	Y	N	N
3 *McInnis*	Y	Y	N	N	Y	Y
4 *Musgrave*	Y	Y	N	N	Y	Y
5 *Hefley*	Y	Y	N	N	Y	Y
6 *Tancredo*	Y	Y	N	N	Y	Y
7 *Beauprez*	Y	Y	N	N	Y	Y
CONNECTICUT						
1 Larson	N	Y	Y	Y	N	N
2 *Simmons*	Y	Y	Y	N	Y	Y
3 DeLauro	N	Y	Y	Y	N	N
4 *Shays*	N	Y	Y	N	Y	Y
5 *Johnson*	Y	Y	Y	N	Y	Y
DELAWARE						
AL *Castle*	Y	Y	N	Y	Y	Y
FLORIDA						
1 *Miller, J.*	Y	Y	N	N	Y	Y
2 Boyd	N	Y	Y	Y	N	Y
3 Brown	N	Y	Y	Y	Y	N
4 *Crenshaw*	Y	Y	N	N	Y	Y
5 *Brown-Waite*	Y	Y	N	Y	Y	Y
6 *Stearns*	Y	Y	N	N	Y	Y
7 *Mica*	Y	Y	N	N	Y	Y
8 *Keller*	Y	Y	N	N	Y	Y
9 *Bilirakis*	Y	Y	N	N	Y	Y
10 *Young*	Y	Y	N	N	Y	Y
11 Davis	N	Y	Y	Y	Y	N
12 *Putnam*	Y	Y	N	N	Y	Y
13 *Harris*	Y	Y	N	N	Y	Y
14 Vacant						
15 *Weldon*	Y	Y	N	N	Y	Y
16 *Foley*	Y	Y	N	N	Y	Y
17 *Meek*	?	?	?	?	?	?
18 *Ros-Lehtinen*	Y	Y	N	N	Y	Y
19 Wexler	N	Y	Y	Y	N	N
20 Deutsch	N	Y	Y	Y	N	N
21 *Diaz-Balart, L.*	Y	Y	N	N	Y	Y
22 *Shaw*	Y	Y	N	N	Y	Y
23 Hastings	N	Y	Y	Y	N	N
24 *Feeney*	Y	Y	N	N	Y	Y
25 *Diaz-Balart, M.*	N	Y	Y	N	N	Y
GEORGIA						
1 *Kingston*	Y	Y	N	N	Y	Y
2 Bishop	Y	Y	Y	Y	Y	N
3 Marshall	Y	Y	N	N	Y	N
4 Majette	?	?	?	?	?	?
5 Lewis	N	Y	Y	Y	N	N
6 *Isakson*	Y	Y	N	N	Y	Y
7 *Linder*	Y	Y	N	N	Y	Y
8 *Collins*	Y	Y	N	N	Y	?
9 *Norwood*	?	?	?	?	?	?
10 *Deal*	Y	Y	N	N	Y	Y
11 *Gingrey*	Y	Y	N	N	Y	Y
12 *Burns*	Y	Y	N	N	Y	Y
13 Scott	Y	Y	Y	Y	Y	N
HAWAII						
1 Abercrombie	N	Y	Y	Y	N	N
2 Case	N	Y	N	Y	Y	Y
IDAHO						
1 *Otter*	Y	Y	N	N	Y	Y
2 *Simpson*	Y	Y	N	N	Y	Y
ILLINOIS						
1 Rush	N	Y	Y	Y	N	N
2 Jackson	N	Y	Y	Y	N	N
3 Lipinski	?	?	?	?	?	?
4 Gutierrez	N	Y	Y	Y	N	N
5 Emanuel	N	Y	Y	Y	N	N
6 *Hyde*	Y	Y	N	N	Y	Y

ND Northern Democrats   SD Southern Democrats

	519	520	521	522	523	524
7 Davis	N	Y	Y	Y	N	N
8 ***Crane***	Y	Y	N	N	Y	Y
9 Schakowsky	N	Y	Y	Y	N	N
10 ***Kirk***	Y	Y	Y	N	Y	Y
11 ***Weller***	Y	Y	N	N	Y	Y
12 Costello	N	Y	Y	Y	N	N
13 ***Biggert***	Y	Y	N	N	Y	Y
14 ***Hastert***				N	Y	
15 ***Johnson***	Y	Y	Y	N	Y	Y
16 ***Manzullo***	Y	Y	N	N	Y	Y
17 Evans	N	Y	Y	Y	N	N
18 ***LaHood***	Y	Y	N	N	N	Y
19 ***Shimkus***	Y	Y	N	N	Y	N
INDIANA						
1 Visclosky	N	Y	Y	Y	N	N
2 ***Chocola***	Y	Y	N	N	Y	Y
3 ***Souder***	Y	Y	Y	N	Y	Y
4 ***Buyer***	Y	Y	N	N	Y	Y
5 ***Burton***	Y	Y	N	N	Y	?
6 ***Pence***	Y	Y	N	N	Y	Y
7 Carson	N	Y	Y	Y	N	N
8 ***Hostettler***	Y	Y	N	N	Y	N
9 Hill	Y	Y	Y	Y	Y	N
IOWA						
1 ***Nussle***	Y	Y	N	N	Y	Y
2 ***Leach***	Y	Y	Y	Y	Y	?
3 Boswell	N	Y	Y	Y	Y	N
4 ***Latham***	Y	Y	N	N	Y	Y
5 ***King***	Y	Y	N	N	Y	Y
KANSAS						
1 ***Moran***	Y	Y	N	N	Y	Y
2 ***Ryun***	Y	Y	N	N	Y	Y
3 Moore	Y	Y	N	Y	Y	N
4 ***Tiahrt***	Y	Y	N	N	Y	Y
KENTUCKY						
1 ***Whitfield***	Y	Y	N	N	Y	Y
2 ***Lewis***	Y	Y	N	N	Y	Y
3 ***Northup***	Y	Y	N	N	Y	Y
4 Lucas	Y	Y	Y	Y	Y	N
5 ***Rogers***	Y	Y	N	N	Y	Y
6 Chandler	Y	Y	N	Y	Y	Y
LOUISIANA						
1 ***Vitter***	Y	Y	N	N	Y	Y
2 Jefferson	N	Y	Y	Y	N	N
3 ***Tauzin***	?	?	?	?	?	?
4 ***McCrery***	Y	Y	N	N	Y	Y
5 ***Alexander***	Y	Y	N	N	Y	Y
6 ***Baker***	Y	Y	N	N	Y	Y
7 John	Y	Y	N	Y	Y	N
MAINE						
1 Allen	N	Y	Y	Y	N	N
2 Michaud	Y	Y	Y	Y	Y	N
MARYLAND						
1 ***Gilchrest***	Y	Y	N	N	Y	Y
2 Ruppersberger	N	Y	Y	Y	Y	N
3 Cardin	N	Y	Y	Y	Y	Y
4 Wynn	N	Y	Y	Y	N	N
5 Hoyer	N	Y	Y	Y	Y	N
6 ***Bartlett***	Y	Y	Y	N	Y	Y
7 Cummings	N	Y	Y	Y	N	N
8 Van Hollen	N	Y	Y	Y	N	N
MASSACHUSETTS						
1 Olver	N	Y	Y	Y	N	N
2 Neal	N	Y	Y	Y	N	N
3 McGovern	N	Y	Y	Y	N	N
4 Frank	N	Y	Y	Y	N	?
5 Meehan	N	Y	Y	Y	N	N
6 Tierney	N	Y	Y	Y	N	N
7 Markey	N	Y	Y	Y	N	?
8 Capuano	N	Y	Y	Y	N	N
9 Lynch	Y	Y	Y	Y	N	N
10 Delahunt	N	Y	Y	Y	N	N
MICHIGAN						
1 Stupak	N	Y	Y	Y	N	N
2 ***Hoekstra***	Y	Y	N	N	Y	Y
3 ***Ehlers***	Y	Y	N	N	Y	Y
4 ***Camp***	Y	Y	N	N	Y	Y
5 Kildee	N	Y	Y	Y	N	N
6 ***Upton***	Y	Y	N	N	Y	Y
7 ***Smith***	Y	Y	N	N	Y	Y
8 ***Rogers***	Y	Y	N	N	Y	Y
9 ***Knollenberg***	Y	Y	N	N	Y	Y
10 ***Miller***	Y	Y	N	N	Y	Y
11 ***McCotter***	Y	Y	N	N	Y	Y
12 Levin	N	Y	Y	Y	N	N
13 Kilpatrick	N	Y	Y	Y	N	N
14 Conyers	N	Y	Y	Y	N	N
15 Dingell	N	Y	Y	Y	N	N
MINNESOTA						
1 ***Gutknecht***	Y	Y	N	N	Y	Y
2 ***Kline***	Y	Y	N	N	Y	Y
3 ***Ramstad***	Y	Y	N	N	Y	Y
4 McCollum	N	Y	Y	Y	N	N
5 Sabo	N	Y	Y	N	N	N
6 ***Kennedy***	Y	Y	N	N	Y	Y
7 Peterson	Y	Y	N	Y	Y	N
8 Oberstar	N	Y	Y	Y	N	N
MISSISSIPPI						
1 ***Wicker***	Y	Y	N	N	Y	Y
2 Thompson	N	Y	Y	Y	Y	N
3 ***Pickering***	Y	Y	N	N	Y	Y
4 Taylor	Y	Y	N	Y	Y	N
MISSOURI						
1 Clay	N	Y	Y	Y	Y	?
2 ***Akin***	Y	Y	N	N	Y	Y
3 Gephardt	?	?	?	?	?	?
4 Skelton	Y	Y	Y	Y	Y	N
5 McCarthy	N	Y	Y	Y	Y	N
6 ***Graves***	Y	Y	N	N	Y	Y
7 ***Blunt***	Y	Y	N	N	Y	Y
8 ***Emerson***	Y	Y	N	N	Y	Y
9 ***Hulshof***	Y	Y	N	N	Y	Y
MONTANA						
AL ***Rehberg***	Y	Y	N	N	Y	Y
NEBRASKA						
1 Vacant						
2 ***Terry***	Y	Y	N	N	Y	Y
3 ***Osborne***	Y	Y	N	N	Y	Y
NEVADA						
1 Berkley	N	Y	Y	Y	N	N
2 ***Gibbons***	Y	Y	N	N	Y	Y
3 ***Porter***	Y	Y	Y	N	Y	Y
NEW HAMPSHIRE						
1 ***Bradley***	Y	Y	N	N	Y	N
2 ***Bass***	Y	Y	N	N	Y	–
NEW JERSEY						
1 Andrews	N	Y	Y	Y	Y	Y
2 ***LoBiondo***	Y	Y	N	N	Y	Y
3 ***Saxton***	Y	Y	N	N	Y	Y
4 ***Smith***	Y	Y	Y	N	Y	Y
5 ***Garrett***	Y	Y	N	N	Y	Y
6 Pallone	N	Y	Y	Y	N	N
7 ***Ferguson***	Y	Y	N	N	Y	Y
8 Pascrell	N	Y	Y	Y	N	N
9 Rothman	N	Y	Y	Y	Y	N
10 Payne	N	Y	Y	Y	N	N
11 ***Frelinghuysen***	Y	Y	N	N	Y	Y
12 Holt	N	Y	Y	Y	N	N
13 Menendez	N	Y	Y	Y	N	N
NEW MEXICO						
1 ***Wilson***	N	Y	Y	N	N	N
2 ***Pearce***	Y	Y	N	N	Y	Y
3 Udall	N	Y	Y	Y	N	N
NEW YORK						
1 Bishop	Y	Y	Y	Y	Y	N
2 Israel	Y	Y	Y	Y	Y	N
3 ***King***	Y	Y	Y	N	Y	Y
4 McCarthy	N	Y	Y	Y	Y	N
5 Ackerman	N	Y	Y	Y	N	N
6 Meeks	N	Y	Y	Y	N	?
7 Crowley	N	Y	Y	Y	N	N
8 Nadler	N	Y	Y	Y	N	N
9 Weiner	N	Y	Y	Y	N	N
10 Towns	?	?	?	?	?	?
11 Owens	N	Y	Y	Y	N	N
12 Velázquez	N	Y	Y	Y	N	N
13 ***Fossella***	Y	Y	N	N	Y	Y
14 Maloney	N	Y	Y	Y	N	N
15 Rangel	N	Y	Y	Y	N	N
16 Serrano	N	Y	Y	Y	N	N
17 Engel	N	Y	Y	Y	N	N
18 Lowey	N	Y	Y	Y	Y	N
19 ***Kelly***	Y	Y	N	N	Y	Y
20 ***Sweeney***	Y	Y	N	N	Y	Y
21 McNulty	N	Y	Y	Y	N	N
22 Hinchey	N	Y	Y	Y	N	N
23 ***McHugh***	Y	Y	N	N	Y	Y
24 ***Boehlert***	?	?	?	?	?	?
25 ***Walsh***	Y	Y	Y	N	Y	Y
26 ***Reynolds***	Y	Y	N	N	Y	Y
27 ***Quinn***	Y	Y	N	N	Y	Y
28 Slaughter	?	?	?	?	?	?
29 ***Houghton***	Y	Y	Y	N	Y	Y
NORTH CAROLINA						
1 Butterfield	Y	Y	Y	Y	Y	N
2 Etheridge	Y	Y	Y	Y	Y	N
3 ***Jones***	Y	Y	?	?	?	?
4 Price	N	Y	Y	Y	Y	N
5 ***Burr***	Y	Y	N	N	Y	Y
6 ***Coble***	Y	Y	N	N	Y	Y
7 McIntyre	Y	Y	N	Y	Y	N
8 ***Hayes***	Y	Y	N	N	Y	Y
9 ***Myrick***	Y	Y	N	N	Y	Y
10 ***Ballenger***	?	?	?	?	?	?
11 ***Taylor***	Y	Y	N	N	Y	Y
12 Watt	N	Y	Y	Y	N	N
13 Miller	N	Y	Y	Y	Y	N
NORTH DAKOTA						
AL Pomeroy	N	Y	Y	Y	Y	N
OHIO						
1 ***Chabot***	Y	Y	N	N	Y	Y
2 ***Portman***	Y	Y	N	N	Y	Y
3 ***Turner***	Y	Y	N	N	Y	Y
4 ***Oxley***	Y	Y	N	N	Y	Y
5 ***Gillmor***	N	Y	N	N	Y	Y
6 Strickland	N	Y	Y	Y	N	N
7 ***Hobson***	Y	Y	N	N	Y	Y
8 ***Boehner***	Y	Y	N	N	Y	Y
9 Kaptur	?	?	?	?	?	?
10 Kucinich	N	Y	Y	Y	N	N
11 Jones	N	Y	Y	Y	N	N
12 ***Tiberi***	Y	Y	N	N	Y	Y
13 Brown	N	Y	Y	Y	N	N
14 ***LaTourette***	Y	Y	Y	N	Y	Y
15 ***Pryce***	Y	Y	N	N	Y	Y
16 ***Regula***	Y	Y	N	N	Y	Y
17 Ryan	N	Y	Y	Y	N	N
18 ***Ney***	Y	Y	N	N	Y	Y
OKLAHOMA						
1 ***Sullivan***	Y	Y	N	N	Y	Y
2 Carson	Y	Y	N	Y	Y	N
3 ***Lucas***	Y	Y	N	N	Y	Y
4 ***Cole***	Y	Y	N	N	Y	Y
5 ***Istook***	Y	Y	N	N	Y	Y
OREGON						
1 Wu	N	Y	Y	Y	Y	N
2 ***Walden***	Y	Y	N	N	Y	Y
3 Blumenauer	N	Y	Y	Y	N	Y
4 DeFazio	N	Y	N	Y	Y	N
5 Hooley	N	Y	Y	Y	Y	N
PENNSYLVANIA						
1 Brady	N	Y	Y	Y	N	N
2 Fattah	N	Y	Y	Y	N	N
3 ***English***	Y	Y	N	N	Y	Y
4 ***Hart***	Y	Y	N	N	Y	Y
5 ***Peterson***	Y	Y	N	N	Y	Y
6 ***Gerlach***	Y	Y	Y	N	Y	Y
7 ***Weldon***	Y	Y	Y	N	Y	Y
8 ***Greenwood***	Y	Y	Y	N	Y	?
9 ***Shuster, Bill***	Y	Y	N	N	Y	Y
10 ***Sherwood***	Y	Y	N	N	Y	Y
11 Kanjorski	Y	Y	Y	Y	N	N
12 Murtha	Y	Y	Y	N	N	?
13 Hoeffel	N	Y	Y	Y	Y	N
14 Doyle	N	Y	Y	Y	N	N
15 ***Toomey***	Y	Y	N	N	Y	Y
16 ***Pitts***	Y	Y	N	N	Y	Y
17 Holden	Y	Y	N	Y	Y	N
18 ***Murphy***	Y	Y	N	N	Y	Y
19 ***Platts***	Y	Y	N	N	Y	Y
RHODE ISLAND						
1 Kennedy	N	Y	Y	Y	Y	N
2 Langevin	N	Y	Y	Y	Y	N
SOUTH CAROLINA						
1 ***Brown***	Y	Y	N	N	Y	Y
2 ***Wilson***	Y	Y	N	N	Y	Y
3 ***Barrett***	Y	Y	N	N	Y	Y
4 ***DeMint***	Y	Y	N	N	Y	Y
5 Spratt	Y	Y	Y	Y	Y	Y
6 Clyburn	N	Y	Y	Y	Y	N
SOUTH DAKOTA						
AL Herseth	N	Y	Y	Y	Y	N
TENNESSEE						
1 ***Jenkins***	Y	Y	N	N	Y	Y
2 ***Duncan***	Y	Y	N	N	N	Y
3 ***Wamp***	Y	Y	N	N	N	Y
4 Davis	Y	Y	N	Y	Y	N
5 Cooper	Y	Y	Y	Y	N	Y
6 Gordon	Y	Y	Y	Y	Y	Y
7 ***Blackburn***	Y	Y	N	N	Y	Y
8 Tanner	Y	Y	Y	Y	N	N
9 Ford	Y	Y	Y	Y	N	?
TEXAS						
1 Sandlin	Y	Y	Y	Y	Y	N
2 Turner	Y	Y	Y	Y	Y	N
3 ***Johnson, Sam***	Y	Y	N	N	Y	Y
4 ***Hall***	Y	Y	N	N	Y	Y
5 ***Hensarling***	Y	Y	N	N	Y	Y
6 ***Barton***	Y	Y	N	N	Y	Y
7 ***Culberson***	Y	Y	N	N	Y	Y
8 ***Brady***	Y	Y	N	N	Y	Y
9 Lampson	Y	Y	Y	Y	Y	N
10 Doggett	N	Y	Y	Y	N	Y
11 Edwards	Y	Y	N	Y	Y	N
12 ***Granger***	Y	Y	N	N	Y	Y
13 ***Thornberry***	Y	Y	N	N	Y	Y
14 ***Paul***	?	?	?	?	?	?
15 Hinojosa	–	+	+	+	+	–
16 Reyes	Y	Y	Y	Y	N	N
17 Stenholm	Y	Y	N	Y	Y	Y
18 Jackson-Lee	N	Y	Y	Y	N	N
19 ***Neugebauer***	Y	Y	N	N	Y	Y
20 Gonzalez	N	Y	Y	Y	N	N
21 ***Smith***	Y	Y	N	N	Y	Y
22 ***DeLay***	Y	Y	N	N	Y	Y
23 ***Bonilla***	Y	Y	N	N	Y	Y
24 Frost	Y	Y	Y	Y	Y	N
25 Bell	N	Y	Y	Y	Y	N
26 ***Burgess***	Y	Y	N	N	Y	Y
27 Ortiz	?	?	?	?	?	?
28 Rodriguez	N	Y	Y	Y	N	N
29 Green	N	Y	Y	Y	N	N
30 Johnson, E.B.	N	Y	Y	Y	N	N
31 ***Carter***	Y	Y	N	N	Y	Y
32 ***Sessions***	Y	Y	N	N	Y	Y
UTAH						
1 ***Bishop***	Y	Y	N	N	Y	Y
2 Matheson	Y	Y	N	Y	Y	N
3 ***Cannon***	Y	Y	N	N	Y	Y
VERMONT						
AL *Sanders*	N	Y	Y	Y	N	N
VIRGINIA						
1 ***Davis, Jo Ann***	Y	Y	N	N	Y	N
2 ***Schrock***	Y	Y	N	N	Y	Y
3 Scott	N	Y	Y	Y	N	N
4 ***Forbes***	Y	Y	N	N	Y	Y
5 ***Goode***	Y	Y	N	N	Y	Y
6 ***Goodlatte***	Y	Y	N	N	Y	Y
7 ***Cantor***	Y	Y	N	N	Y	Y
8 Moran	N	Y	Y	Y	N	Y
9 Boucher	Y	Y	Y	Y	Y	N
10 ***Wolf***	Y	Y	Y	N	Y	Y
11 ***Davis, T.***	Y	Y	Y	N	Y	Y
WASHINGTON						
1 Inslee	N	Y	Y	Y	N	Y
2 Larsen	N	Y	Y	Y	N	Y
3 Baird	N	Y	Y	Y	N	N
4 ***Hastings***	Y	Y	N	N	Y	Y
5 ***Nethercutt***	Y	Y	N	N	Y	Y
6 Dicks	N	Y	Y	Y	N	Y
7 McDermott	N	Y	Y	Y	N	N
8 ***Dunn***	Y	Y	N	N	Y	Y
9 Smith	Y	Y	Y	Y	N	Y
WEST VIRGINIA						
1 Mollohan	N	Y	Y	Y	N	N
2 ***Capito***	Y	Y	N	N	Y	Y
3 Rahall	N	Y	Y	Y	N	N
WISCONSIN						
1 ***Ryan***	Y	Y	N	N	Y	Y
2 Baldwin	N	Y	Y	Y	N	N
3 Kind	N	Y	Y	Y	Y	N
4 Kleczka	N	Y	Y	Y	N	N
5 ***Sensenbrenner***	Y	Y	N	N	Y	Y
6 ***Petri***	Y	Y	Y	N	Y	Y
7 Obey	N	Y	Y	N	N	N
8 ***Green***	Y	Y	N	N	Y	Y
WYOMING						
AL ***Cubin***	Y	Y	N	N	Y	Y

Southern states - Ala., Ark., Fla., Ga., Ky., La., Miss., N.C., Okla., S.C., Tenn., Texas, Va.

Key

Y	Voted for (yea).
#	Paired for.
+	Announced for.
N	Voted against (nay).
X	Paired against.
−	Announced against.
P	Voted "present."
C	Voted "present" to avoid possible conflict of interest.
?	Did not vote or otherwise make a position known.

Democrats   **Republicans**
Independents

525. S 2845. Intelligence Overhaul/Motion to Instruct. Gutierrez, D-Ill., motion to instruct House conferees to reject certain immigration provisions in the bill, including language that would allow the expedited removal of undocumented individuals and those who restrict asylum rights and refugee protections. Motion rejected 169-229: R 3-207; D 165-22 (ND 130-6, SD 35-16); I 1-0. Oct. 8, 2004.

526. H Res 845. DeLay Investigation of Conduct/Motion to Table. Blunt, R-Mo., motion to table (kill) the Pelosi, D-Calif., resolution that would authorize and direct the Committee on Standards of Official Conduct to establish an investigative subcommittee to determine whether there is substantial reason to believe that Majority Leader Tom DeLay, R-Texas, has violated the House's Code of Official Conduct or other relevant laws, rules or regulations. It also would allow the committee to retain a special counsel to assist in its investigation. Motion agreed to 210-182: R 210-0; D 0-181 (ND 0-131, SD 0-50); I 0-1. Oct. 8, 2004.

527. H Con Res 518. Adjournment/Adoption. Adoption of the concurrent resolution that would provide for an adjournment of the House until 2 p.m., Tuesday, Nov. 16. The resolution also would provide for an adjournment of the Senate until 12 p.m. on Nov. 15 or until 12 p.m. on Nov. 16, or until such time as may be specified by congressional leaders. Adopted 204-169: R 198-1; D 6-167 (ND 6-118, SD 0-49); I 0-1. Oct. 9, 2004.

528. HR 4200. Fiscal 2005 Defense Authorization/Conference Report. Adoption of the conference report on the bill that would authorize $445.6 billion for the Defense Department and the Energy Department's national security programs. It would authorize $25 billion in additional funds for operations in Iraq and provide more than $2 billion for increased protection of U.S. troops there. It would maintain the 2005 schedule for military base closings and require the Army and Marine Corps to increase their numbers by 20,000 and 3,000, respectively, in fiscal 2005. It also would direct the Air Force to purchase up to 100 refueling tanker planes under competitive bidding and provide for a 3.5 percent pay increase for military personnel. Adopted (thus sent to the Senate) 359-14: R 198-0; D 160-14 (ND 112-13, SD 48-1); I 1-0. Oct. 9, 2004.

529. HR 4837. Fiscal 2005 Military Construction Appropriations/Conference Report. Adoption of the conference report on the bill that would provide $10 billion for military construction, and family and troop housing. It would provide $5.5 billion for military construction projects, $4.1 billion for military and family housing and $246 million for base realignment and closure activities. It also includes $14.5 billion in supplement appropriations: $11.6 billion for aid to hurricane victims and $2.9 billion to assist farmers hurt by droughts and hurricanes. Adopted (thus sent to the Senate) 374-0: R 198-0; D 175-0 (ND 125-0, SD 50-0); I 1-0. Oct. 9, 2004.

530. HR 4567. Fiscal 2005 Homeland Security Appropriations/Conference Report. Adoption of the conference report on the bill that would appropriate $33.1 billion in fiscal 2005 for the Department of Homeland Security and related agencies. The bill includes $6.3 billion for customs and border protection, $5.2 billion for the Transportation Security Administration, $7.4 billion for the Coast Guard, $1.2 billion for the Secret Service and $5.5 billion for emergency preparedness and response. Adopted (thus sent to the Senate) 368-0: R 193-0; D 174-0 (ND 124-0, SD 50-0); I 1-0. Oct. 9, 2004.

	525	526	527	528	529	530
ALABAMA						
1 *Bonner*	N	Y	Y	Y	Y	Y
2 *Everett*	N	Y	Y	Y	Y	?
3 *Rogers*	N	Y	Y	Y	Y	Y
4 *Aderholt*	N	Y	Y	Y	Y	Y
5 Cramer	N	N	N	Y	Y	Y
6 *Bachus*	N	Y	Y	Y	Y	?
7 Davis	Y	N	N	Y	Y	Y
ALASKA						
AL *Young*	N	Y	Y	Y	Y	Y
ARIZONA						
1 *Renzi*	N	Y	Y	Y	Y	Y
2 *Franks*	N	Y	Y	Y	Y	Y
3 *Shadegg*	N	Y	Y	Y	Y	Y
4 Pastor	Y	N	Y	Y	Y	Y
5 *Hayworth*	N	Y	Y	Y	Y	Y
6 *Flake*	N	Y	Y	Y	Y	Y
7 Grijalva	Y	N	N	Y	Y	Y
8 *Kolbe*	Y	Y	Y	Y	Y	Y
ARKANSAS						
1 Berry	Y	N	N	Y	Y	Y
2 Snyder	Y	N	N	Y	Y	Y
3 *Boozman*	N	Y	Y	Y	Y	Y
4 Ross	Y	N	N	Y	Y	Y
CALIFORNIA						
1 Thompson	Y	N	N	Y	Y	Y
2 *Herger*	N	Y	Y	Y	Y	Y
3 *Ose*	N	Y	Y	Y	Y	Y
4 *Doolittle*	N	Y	Y	Y	Y	Y
5 Matsui	?	?	−	+	+	+
6 Woolsey	Y	N	N	N	Y	Y
7 Miller, George	Y	N	?	?	?	?
8 Pelosi	Y	N	N	Y	Y	Y
9 Lee	Y	N	N	N	Y	Y
10 Tauscher	Y	N	N	Y	Y	Y
11 *Pombo*	N	Y	Y	Y	Y	Y
12 Lantos	Y	N	N	Y	Y	Y
13 Stark	Y	N	N	N	Y	Y
14 Eshoo	Y	N	?	?	?	?
15 Honda	Y	N	N	N	Y	Y
16 Lofgren	Y	N	N	Y	Y	Y
17 Farr	Y	N	N	Y	Y	Y
18 Cardoza	Y	N	N	Y	Y	Y
19 *Radanovich*	?	?	Y	Y	Y	Y
20 Dooley	Y	?	N	Y	Y	Y
21 *Nunes*	N	Y	Y	Y	Y	Y
22 *Thomas*	N	Y	Y	Y	Y	Y
23 Capps	Y	N	N	Y	Y	Y
24 *Gallegly*	?	?	?	?	?	?
25 *McKeon*	N	Y	Y	Y	Y	Y
26 *Dreier*	N	Y	Y	Y	Y	Y
27 Sherman	Y	N	N	Y	Y	Y
28 Berman	Y	N	N	Y	Y	Y
29 Schiff	Y	N	N	Y	Y	Y
30 Waxman	Y	N	Y	Y	Y	Y
31 Becerra	Y	N	N	Y	Y	Y
32 Solis	Y	N	N	Y	Y	Y
33 Watson	Y	N	N	Y	Y	Y
34 Roybal-Allard	Y	P	N	Y	Y	Y
35 Waters	?	N	?	?	?	?
36 Harman	Y	N	N	Y	Y	Y

	525	526	527	528	529	530
37 Millender-McD.	Y	N	N	Y	Y	Y
38 Napolitano	Y	N	N	Y	Y	Y
39 Sánchez, Linda	Y	N	N	Y	Y	Y
40 *Royce*	N	Y	Y	Y	Y	Y
41 *Lewis*	N	?	Y	Y	Y	Y
42 *Miller, Gary*	?	?	?	?	?	?
43 Baca	Y	N	N	Y	Y	Y
44 *Calvert*	N	Y	Y	Y	Y	Y
45 *Bono*	N	Y	Y	Y	Y	Y
46 *Rohrabacher*	N	Y	Y	Y	Y	Y
47 Sanchez, Loretta	Y	N	N	Y	Y	Y
48 *Cox*	N	Y	Y	Y	Y	Y
49 *Issa*	?	?	?	?	?	?
50 *Cunningham*	N	Y	Y	Y	Y	Y
51 Filner	+	−	+	+	+	+
52 *Hunter*	N	Y	Y	Y	Y	Y
53 Davis	Y	N	N	Y	Y	Y
COLORADO						
1 DeGette	Y	N	N	Y	Y	Y
2 Udall	Y	N	N	Y	Y	Y
3 *McInnis*	N	Y	Y	Y	Y	Y
4 *Musgrave*	N	Y	Y	Y	Y	Y
5 *Hefley*	N	Y	Y	Y	Y	Y
6 *Tancredo*	N	Y	Y	Y	Y	Y
7 *Beauprez*	N	Y	Y	Y	Y	Y
CONNECTICUT						
1 Larson	Y	N	N	Y	Y	Y
2 *Simmons*	N	Y	Y	Y	Y	Y
3 DeLauro	Y	N	N	Y	Y	Y
4 *Shays*	N	Y	Y	Y	Y	Y
5 *Johnson*	N	Y	Y	Y	?	?
DELAWARE						
AL *Castle*	N	Y	Y	Y	Y	Y
FLORIDA						
1 *Miller, J.*	N	Y	Y	Y	Y	Y
2 Boyd	N	N	N	Y	Y	Y
3 Brown	Y	N	N	Y	Y	Y
4 *Crenshaw*	N	Y	Y	Y	Y	Y
5 *Brown-Waite*	N	Y	Y	Y	Y	Y
6 *Stearns*	N	Y	Y	Y	Y	Y
7 *Mica*	N	?	?	?	?	?
8 *Keller*	N	Y	Y	Y	Y	Y
9 *Bilirakis*	N	Y	Y	Y	Y	Y
10 *Young*	N	Y	Y	Y	Y	Y
11 Davis	Y	N	N	Y	Y	Y
12 *Putnam*	N	Y	Y	Y	Y	Y
13 *Harris*	N	Y	Y	Y	Y	Y
14 Vacant						
15 *Weldon*	N	Y	Y	Y	Y	Y
16 *Foley*	N	Y	+	?	+	+
17 Meek	?	?	?	?	?	?
18 *Ros-Lehtinen*	N	Y	?	?	?	?
19 Wexler	Y	N	N	Y	Y	Y
20 Deutsch	Y	N	N	Y	Y	Y
21 *Diaz-Balart, L.*	?	?	Y	Y	Y	Y
22 *Shaw*	N	Y	Y	Y	Y	Y
23 Hastings	Y	N	N	Y	Y	Y
24 *Feeney*	N	Y	Y	Y	Y	Y
25 *Diaz-Balart, M.*	N	Y	Y	Y	Y	Y
GEORGIA						
1 *Kingston*	N	Y	Y	Y	Y	Y
2 Bishop	Y	N	N	Y	Y	Y
3 Marshall	N	N	N	Y	Y	Y
4 *Majette*	?	?	?	?	?	?
5 Lewis	Y	N	N	N	Y	Y
6 *Isakson*	N	Y	?	?	?	?
7 *Linder*	N	Y	Y	Y	Y	Y
8 *Collins*	?	Y	Y	Y	Y	Y
9 *Norwood*	?	?	?	?	?	?
10 *Deal*	N	Y	Y	Y	Y	Y
11 *Gingrey*	N	Y	Y	Y	Y	Y
12 *Burns*	N	Y	Y	Y	Y	Y
13 Scott	Y	N	N	Y	Y	Y
HAWAII						
1 Abercrombie	Y	N	N	Y	Y	Y
2 Case	N	N	N	Y	Y	Y
IDAHO						
1 *Otter*	N	Y	Y	Y	Y	Y
2 *Simpson*	N	Y	Y	Y	Y	Y
ILLINOIS						
1 Rush	Y	N	N	Y	Y	Y
2 Jackson	Y	N	N	N	Y	Y
3 Lipinski	?	?	?	?	?	?
4 Gutierrez	Y	N	N	Y	Y	Y
5 Emanuel	Y	N	N	Y	Y	Y
6 *Hyde*	N	Y	Y	Y	Y	Y

ND Northern Democrats   SD Southern Democrats

	525	526	527	528	529	530
7 Davis	Y	N	N	Y	Y	Y
8 **Crane**	N	Y	Y	Y	Y	Y
9 Schakowsky	Y	N	N	N	Y	Y
10 **Kirk**	N	Y	Y	Y	Y	Y
11 **Weller**	N	Y	Y	Y	Y	Y
12 Costello	N	N	N	Y	Y	Y
13 **Biggert**	N	Y	Y	Y	Y	Y
14 **Hastert**		Y	Y			
15 **Johnson**	N	Y	?	Y	Y	Y
16 **Manzullo**	N	Y	Y	Y	Y	Y
17 Evans	Y	N	N	Y	Y	Y
18 **LaHood**	?	?	?	?	?	?
19 **Shimkus**	N	Y	Y	Y	Y	Y
INDIANA						
1 Visclosky	Y	N	?	?	?	?
2 **Chocola**	N	Y	Y	Y	Y	Y
3 **Souder**	N	Y	Y	Y	Y	Y
4 **Buyer**	N	Y	Y	Y	Y	Y
5 **Burton**	?	?	?	?	?	?
6 **Pence**	N	Y	Y	Y	Y	Y
7 Carson	Y	N	N	Y	Y	Y
8 **Hostettler**	N	Y	Y	Y	Y	Y
9 Hill	N	N	N	Y	Y	Y
IOWA						
1 **Nussle**	N	Y	Y	?	?	?
2 **Leach**	Y	Y	Y	Y	Y	Y
3 Boswell	Y	N	N	Y	Y	Y
4 **Latham**	N	Y	Y	Y	Y	Y
5 **King**	N	Y	Y	Y	Y	?
KANSAS						
1 **Moran**	N	Y	Y	Y	Y	Y
2 **Ryun**	N	Y	Y	Y	Y	Y
3 Moore	N	N	N	Y	Y	Y
4 **Tiahrt**	N	Y	Y	?	Y	Y
KENTUCKY						
1 **Whitfield**	N	Y	Y	Y	Y	Y
2 **Lewis**	N	Y	Y	Y	Y	Y
3 **Northup**	N	Y	Y	Y	Y	Y
4 Lucas	N	N	N	Y	Y	Y
5 **Rogers**	N	Y	Y	Y	Y	Y
6 Chandler	N	N	N	Y	Y	Y
LOUISIANA						
1 **Vitter**	N	Y	Y	Y	Y	Y
2 Jefferson	Y	N	N	Y	Y	Y
3 **Tauzin**	?	?	?	?	?	?
4 **McCrery**	N	Y	Y	Y	Y	Y
5 **Alexander**	N	Y	Y	Y	Y	Y
6 **Baker**	N	Y	Y	Y	Y	Y
7 John	N	N	N	Y	Y	Y
MAINE						
1 Allen	Y	N	N	Y	Y	Y
2 Michaud	Y	N	N	Y	Y	Y
MARYLAND						
1 **Gilchrest**	N	Y	Y	Y	Y	Y
2 Ruppersberger	Y	N	N	Y	Y	Y
3 Cardin	Y	N	N	Y	Y	Y
4 Wynn	Y	N	N	Y	Y	Y
5 Hoyer	Y	N	N	Y	Y	Y
6 **Bartlett**	N	Y	Y	Y	Y	Y
7 Cummings	Y	N	N	Y	Y	Y
8 Van Hollen	Y	N	N	Y	Y	Y
MASSACHUSETTS						
1 Olver	Y	N	N	Y	Y	Y
2 Neal	Y	N	N	Y	Y	Y
3 McGovern	Y	N	N	Y	Y	Y
4 Frank	?	?	N	Y	Y	Y
5 Meehan	Y	N	?	?	?	?
6 Tierney	Y	N	N	Y	Y	Y
7 Markey	?	?	?	N	Y	Y
8 Capuano	Y	N	N	Y	Y	Y
9 Lynch	Y	N	N	Y	Y	Y
10 Delahunt	Y	P	N	Y	Y	Y
MICHIGAN						
1 Stupak	Y	N	?	?	?	?
2 **Hoekstra**	N	Y	Y	Y	Y	Y
3 **Ehlers**	N	Y	Y	Y	Y	Y
4 **Camp**	N	Y	Y	Y	Y	Y
5 Kildee	Y	N	N	Y	Y	Y
6 **Upton**	N	Y	Y	Y	Y	Y
7 **Smith**	N	Y	Y	Y	Y	Y
8 **Rogers**	N	Y	Y	Y	Y	Y
9 **Knollenberg**	N	Y	Y	Y	Y	Y
10 **Miller**	N	Y	Y	Y	Y	Y
11 **McCotter**	N	Y	Y	Y	Y	Y
12 Levin	Y	N	N	Y	Y	Y
13 Kilpatrick	Y	N	?	?	?	?
14 Conyers	Y	N	Y	N	Y	Y
15 Dingell	Y	N	N	Y	Y	Y
MINNESOTA						
1 **Gutknecht**	N	Y	Y	Y	Y	Y
2 **Kline**	N	Y	Y	Y	Y	Y
3 **Ramstad**	N	Y	Y	Y	Y	Y
4 McCollum	Y	N	N	Y	Y	Y
5 Sabo	Y	N	N	Y	Y	Y
6 **Kennedy**	N	Y	Y	Y	Y	Y
7 Peterson	N	N	N	Y	Y	Y
8 Oberstar	Y	N	?	?	?	?
MISSISSIPPI						
1 **Wicker**	N	Y	Y	Y	Y	Y
2 Thompson	Y	N	N	Y	Y	Y
3 **Pickering**	N	Y	Y	Y	Y	Y
4 Taylor	N	N	N	Y	Y	Y
MISSOURI						
1 Clay	?	?	?	?	?	?
2 **Akin**	N	Y	Y	Y	Y	Y
3 Gephardt	?	?	?	?	?	?
4 Skelton	Y	N	N	Y	Y	Y
5 McCarthy	Y	N	N	Y	Y	Y
6 **Graves**	N	Y	Y	Y	Y	Y
7 **Blunt**	N	Y	Y	Y	Y	Y
8 **Emerson**	N	Y	Y	Y	Y	Y
9 **Hulshof**	N	Y	Y	Y	Y	Y
MONTANA						
AL **Rehberg**	N	Y	Y	Y	Y	Y
NEBRASKA						
1 Vacant						
2 **Terry**	N	Y	Y	Y	Y	Y
3 **Osborne**	N	Y	Y	Y	Y	Y
NEVADA						
1 Berkley	Y	N	N	Y	Y	Y
2 **Gibbons**	N	Y	Y	Y	Y	Y
3 **Porter**	N	Y	Y	Y	Y	Y
NEW HAMPSHIRE						
1 **Bradley**	N	Y	Y	Y	Y	Y
2 **Bass**	–	+	Y	Y	Y	Y
NEW JERSEY						
1 Andrews	Y	N	N	Y	Y	Y
2 **LoBiondo**	N	Y	Y	Y	Y	Y
3 **Saxton**	N	Y	Y	Y	Y	Y
4 **Smith**	N	Y	Y	Y	Y	Y
5 **Garrett**	N	Y	Y	Y	Y	Y
6 Pallone	Y	N	N	Y	Y	Y
7 **Ferguson**	N	Y	Y	Y	Y	Y
8 Pascrell	Y	N	N	Y	Y	Y
9 Rothman	Y	N	N	Y	Y	Y
10 Payne	Y	N	N	N	Y	Y
11 **Frelinghuysen**	N	Y	Y	Y	Y	Y
12 Holt	Y	N	N	Y	Y	Y
13 Menendez	Y	N	N	Y	Y	Y
NEW MEXICO						
1 **Wilson**	Y	Y	Y	Y	Y	Y
2 **Pearce**	N	Y	Y	Y	Y	Y
3 Udall	Y	N	N	Y	Y	Y
NEW YORK						
1 Bishop	Y	N	N	Y	Y	Y
2 Israel	Y	N	N	Y	Y	Y
3 **King**	N	?	?	?	?	?
4 McCarthy	Y	N	N	Y	Y	Y
5 Ackerman	Y	N	N	Y	Y	Y
6 Meeks	?	?	?	?	?	?
7 Crowley	Y	N	N	Y	Y	Y
8 Nadler	Y	N	N	Y	Y	Y
9 Weiner	Y	N	N	Y	Y	Y
10 Towns	?	?	?	?	?	?
11 Owens	Y	N	N	Y	Y	Y
12 Velázquez	Y	N	N	N	Y	Y
13 **Fossella**	N	Y	Y	Y	Y	Y
14 Maloney	Y	N	N	Y	Y	Y
15 Rangel	Y	N	N	Y	Y	Y
16 Serrano	Y	N	N	N	Y	Y
17 Engel	Y	N	N	Y	Y	Y
18 Lowey	Y	N	N	Y	Y	Y
19 **Kelly**	N	Y	Y	Y	Y	Y
20 **Sweeney**	N	Y	Y	Y	Y	Y
21 McNulty	Y	N	N	Y	Y	Y
22 Hinchey	Y	N	N	Y	Y	Y
23 **McHugh**	N	Y	Y	Y	Y	Y
24 **Boehlert**	?	?	?	?	?	?
25 **Walsh**	N	Y	Y	Y	Y	?
26 **Reynolds**	N	Y	Y	Y	Y	Y
27 **Quinn**	N	?	?	?	?	?
28 Slaughter	?	?	?	?	?	?
29 **Houghton**	N	Y	Y	Y	Y	Y
NORTH CAROLINA						
1 Butterfield	Y	N	N	Y	Y	Y
2 Etheridge	Y	N	N	Y	Y	Y
3 **Jones**	?	?	?	?	?	?
4 Price	Y	N	N	Y	Y	Y
5 **Burr**	N	Y	Y	Y	Y	Y
6 **Coble**	N	Y	Y	Y	Y	Y
7 McIntyre	N	N	N	Y	Y	Y
8 **Hayes**	N	Y	Y	Y	Y	Y
9 **Myrick**	N	Y	Y	Y	Y	Y
10 **Ballenger**	?	?	?	?	?	?
11 **Taylor**	N	Y	Y	Y	Y	?
12 Watt	Y	N	N	Y	Y	Y
13 Miller	Y	N	N	Y	Y	Y
NORTH DAKOTA						
AL Pomeroy	Y	N	N	Y	Y	Y
OHIO						
1 **Chabot**	N	Y	Y	Y	Y	Y
2 **Portman**	N	Y	Y	Y	Y	Y
3 **Turner**	N	Y	Y	Y	Y	Y
4 **Oxley**	N	Y	?	?	?	?
5 **Gillmor**	N	Y	Y	Y	Y	Y
6 Strickland	Y	N	N	Y	Y	Y
7 **Hobson**	N	Y	?	?	?	?
8 **Boehner**	N	Y	Y	Y	Y	Y
9 Kaptur	?	?	?	?	?	?
10 Kucinich	Y	N	N	N	Y	Y
11 Jones	Y	P	?	?	?	?
12 **Tiberi**	N	Y	?	?	?	?
13 Brown	Y	N	?	?	?	?
14 **LaTourette**	N	Y	Y	Y	Y	Y
15 **Pryce**	N	Y	Y	Y	Y	Y
16 **Regula**	N	Y	Y	Y	Y	Y
17 Ryan	Y	N	N	Y	Y	Y
18 **Ney**	N	Y	?	?	?	?
OKLAHOMA						
1 **Sullivan**	N	Y	Y	Y	Y	Y
2 Carson	N	N	N	Y	Y	Y
3 **Lucas**	N	Y	Y	Y	Y	Y
4 **Cole**	N	Y	Y	Y	Y	Y
5 **Istook**	N	Y	?	?	?	?
OREGON						
1 Wu	Y	N	N	Y	Y	Y
2 **Walden**	N	Y	Y	Y	Y	Y
3 Blumenauer	Y	N	N	Y	Y	Y
4 DeFazio	?	N	N	Y	Y	Y
5 Hooley	Y	N	N	Y	Y	Y
PENNSYLVANIA						
1 Brady	Y	N	N	Y	Y	Y
2 Fattah	Y	N	?	?	?	?
3 **English**	N	Y	Y	Y	Y	Y
4 **Hart**	N	Y	Y	Y	Y	Y
5 **Peterson**	N	Y	?	?	?	?
6 **Gerlach**	N	Y	Y	Y	Y	Y
7 **Weldon**	N	Y	Y	Y	Y	Y
8 **Greenwood**	?	?	?	?	?	?
9 **Shuster, Bill**	N	Y	Y	Y	Y	Y
10 **Sherwood**	N	Y	Y	Y	Y	Y
11 Kanjorski	Y	N	N	Y	Y	Y
12 Murtha	Y	N	Y	Y	Y	?
13 Hoeffel	Y	N	?	?	?	?
14 Doyle	Y	P	?	?	?	?
15 **Toomey**	N	Y	Y	Y	Y	Y
16 **Pitts**	N	Y	Y	Y	Y	Y
17 Holden	Y	N	N	Y	Y	Y
18 **Murphy**	N	Y	Y	Y	Y	Y
19 **Platts**	N	Y	Y	Y	Y	Y
RHODE ISLAND						
1 Kennedy	Y	N	N	Y	Y	Y
2 Langevin	Y	N	N	Y	Y	Y
SOUTH CAROLINA						
1 **Brown**	N	Y	Y	Y	Y	Y
2 **Wilson**	N	Y	Y	Y	Y	Y
3 **Barrett**	N	Y	Y	Y	Y	Y
4 **DeMint**	N	Y	Y	Y	Y	Y
5 Spratt	Y	N	N	Y	Y	Y
6 Clyburn	Y	N	N	Y	Y	Y
SOUTH DAKOTA						
AL Herseth	Y	N	N	Y	Y	Y
TENNESSEE						
1 **Jenkins**	N	Y	Y	Y	Y	Y
2 **Duncan**	N	Y	?	?	?	?
3 **Wamp**	N	Y	Y	Y	Y	Y
4 Davis	N	N	N	Y	Y	Y
5 Cooper	Y	N	N	Y	Y	Y
6 Gordon	N	N	N	Y	Y	Y
7 **Blackburn**	N	Y	Y	Y	Y	Y
8 Tanner	N	N	N	Y	Y	Y
9 Ford	?	?	N	?	Y	Y
TEXAS						
1 Sandlin	Y	N	N	Y	Y	Y
2 Turner	N	N	N	Y	Y	Y
3 **Johnson, Sam**	N	Y	Y	Y	Y	Y
4 **Hall**	N	Y	Y	Y	Y	Y
5 **Hensarling**	N	Y	Y	Y	Y	Y
6 **Barton**	N	Y	Y	Y	Y	Y
7 **Culberson**	N	Y	Y	Y	Y	Y
8 **Brady**	N	Y	?	Y	Y	Y
9 Lampson	Y	N	N	Y	Y	Y
10 Doggett	Y	N	?	?	?	?
11 Edwards	N	N	N	Y	Y	Y
12 **Granger**	N	Y	Y	Y	Y	Y
13 **Thornberry**	N	Y	Y	Y	Y	Y
14 **Paul**	?	?	?	?	?	?
15 Hinojosa	+	–	?	?	?	?
16 Reyes	Y	N	N	Y	Y	Y
17 Stenholm	N	N	N	Y	Y	Y
18 Jackson-Lee	Y	N	N	Y	Y	Y
19 **Neugebauer**	N	Y	Y	Y	Y	Y
20 Gonzalez	Y	N	N	Y	Y	Y
21 **Smith**	N	Y	Y	Y	Y	Y
22 **DeLay**	N	Y	Y	Y	Y	Y
23 **Bonilla**	N	Y	Y	Y	Y	Y
24 Frost	Y	N	N	Y	Y	Y
25 Bell	Y	N	N	Y	Y	Y
26 **Burgess**	N	Y	Y	Y	Y	Y
27 Ortiz	?	?	?	?	?	?
28 Rodriguez	Y	N	N	Y	Y	Y
29 Green	Y	N	?	?	?	?
30 Johnson, E.B.	Y	?	N	Y	Y	Y
31 **Carter**	N	Y	Y	Y	Y	Y
32 **Sessions**	N	Y	Y	Y	Y	Y
UTAH						
1 **Bishop**	N	Y	Y	Y	Y	Y
2 Matheson	N	N	N	Y	Y	Y
3 **Cannon**	N	Y	Y	Y	Y	Y
VERMONT						
AL *Sanders*	Y	N	N	Y	Y	Y
VIRGINIA						
1 **Davis, Jo Ann**	N	Y	Y	Y	Y	Y
2 **Schrock**	N	Y	Y	Y	Y	Y
3 Scott	Y	N	N	Y	Y	Y
4 **Forbes**	N	Y	Y	Y	Y	Y
5 **Goode**	N	Y	Y	Y	Y	Y
6 **Goodlatte**	N	Y	Y	Y	Y	Y
7 **Cantor**	N	Y	Y	Y	Y	Y
8 Moran	Y	N	?	Y	Y	Y
9 Boucher	N	N	N	Y	Y	Y
10 **Wolf**	N	Y	Y	Y	Y	Y
11 **Davis, T.**	N	Y	Y	Y	Y	Y
WASHINGTON						
1 Inslee	Y	N	N	Y	Y	Y
2 Larsen	Y	N	?	?	?	?
3 Baird	Y	N	N	Y	Y	Y
4 **Hastings**	N	Y	Y	Y	Y	Y
5 **Nethercutt**	N	Y	Y	Y	Y	Y
6 Dicks	Y	N	N	Y	Y	Y
7 McDermott	Y	N	N	N	Y	Y
8 **Dunn**	N	Y	?	?	?	?
9 Smith	Y	N	N	Y	Y	Y
WEST VIRGINIA						
1 Mollohan	Y	P	Y	Y	Y	Y
2 **Capito**	N	Y	Y	Y	Y	Y
3 Rahall	Y	N	N	Y	Y	Y
WISCONSIN						
1 **Ryan**	N	Y	Y	Y	Y	Y
2 Baldwin	Y	N	N	Y	Y	Y
3 Kind	Y	N	N	Y	Y	Y
4 Kleczka	Y	?	?	?	?	?
5 **Sensenbrenner**	N	Y	Y	Y	Y	Y
6 **Petri**	N	Y	Y	Y	Y	Y
7 Obey	Y	N	N	Y	Y	Y
8 **Green**	N	Y	N	Y	Y	Y
WYOMING						
AL **Cubin**	N	Y	Y	Y	Y	Y

Southern states - Ala., Ark., Fla., Ga., Ky., La., Miss., N.C., Okla., S.C., Tenn., Texas, Va.

Key

Y	Voted for (yea).
#	Paired for.
+	Announced for.
N	Voted against (nay).
X	Paired against.
−	Announced against.
P	Voted "present."
C	Voted "present" to avoid possible conflict of interest.
?	Did not vote or otherwise make a position known.

Democrats **Republicans**
Independents

---

531. H J Res 110. Battle of the Bulge 60th Anniversary/Passage. King, R-N.Y., motion to suspend the rules and pass the joint resolution that would recognize the 60th anniversary of the Battle of the Bulge in World War II. It would honor veterans and those killed in the battle, and would reaffirm the bonds of friendship between the United States, Belgium and Luxembourg. Motion agreed to 392-0: R 212-0; D 179-0 (ND 127-0, SD 52-0); I 1-0. A two-thirds majority of those present and voting (262 in this case) is required for passage under suspension of the rules. Nov. 16, 2004.

532. HR 1417. Copyright Royalty Regulation/Concur with Senate Amendment. Sensenbrenner, R-Wis., motion to suspend the rules and concur with a Senate amendment to the bill that would establish three new judgeships, called copyright royalty judges, to determine copyright royalty rates and the distribution of royalties. The U.S. Copyright Office would review their rulings for legal errors. Motion agreed to (thus cleared for the president) 407-0: R 216-0; D 190-0 (ND 138-0, SD 52-0); I 1-0. A two-thirds majority of those present and voting (272 in this case) is required for passage under suspension of the rules. Nov. 17, 2004.

533. S 2302. Doctor Visas/Passage. Sensenbrenner, R-Wis., motion to suspend the rules and pass the bill that would provide a two-year extension, retroactive to May 2006, of a visa program waiver that allows foreign nationals who complete medical school in the United States to stay in the country if they agree to work for three years as physicians in specified rural and urban areas. Motion agreed to 407-4: R 213-4; D 193-0 (ND 139-0, SD 54-0); I 1-0. A two-thirds majority of those present and voting (274 in this case) is required for passage under suspension of the rules. Nov. 17, 2004.

534. S 2986. Debt Limit Increase/Previous Question. Reynolds, R-N.Y., motion to order the previous question (thus ending debate and possibility of amendment) on adoption of the rule (H Res 856) to provide for House floor consideration of the bill that would increase the federal debt limit to $8.18 trillion. Motion agreed to 205-191: R 205-0; D 0-190 (ND 0-136, SD 0-54); I 0-1. (Subsequently, the rule was adopted by voice vote.) Nov. 18, 2004.

535. S 2986. Debt Limit Increase/Motion to Commit. Stenholm, D-Texas, motion to commit the bill to the Ways and Means Committee with instructions that the provisions of the bill not apply after April 15, 2005. Motion rejected 194-218: R 0-218; D 193-0 (ND 138-0, SD 55-0); I 1-0. Nov. 18, 2004.

536. S 2986. Debt Limit Increase/Passage. Passage of the bill that would increase the federal debt limit to $8.18 trillion, an $800 billion increase. Passed (thus cleared for the president) 208-204: R 208-10; D 0-193 (ND 0-138, SD 0-55); I 0-1. Nov. 18, 2004.

	531	532	533	534	535	536
ALABAMA						
1 *Bonner*	Y	Y	Y	Y	N	Y
2 *Everett*	Y	Y	Y	Y	N	Y
3 *Rogers*	Y	Y	Y	Y	N	Y
4 *Aderholt*	Y	Y	Y	Y	N	Y
5 Cramer	Y	Y	Y	N	Y	N
6 *Bachus*	Y	Y	Y	Y	N	Y
7 Davis	Y	Y	Y	N	Y	N
ALASKA						
AL *Young*	Y	Y	Y	Y	N	Y
ARIZONA						
1 *Renzi*	Y	Y	Y	Y	N	Y
2 *Franks*	Y	Y	Y	Y	N	Y
3 *Shadegg*	Y	Y	Y	Y	N	Y
4 Pastor	Y	Y	Y	N	Y	N
5 *Hayworth*	Y	Y	Y	Y	N	Y
6 *Flake*	Y	Y	Y	N	Y	N
7 Grijalva	Y	Y	Y	N	Y	N
8 *Kolbe*	Y	Y	Y	Y	N	Y
ARKANSAS						
1 Berry	Y	Y	Y	N	Y	N
2 Snyder	Y	Y	Y	N	Y	N
3 *Boozman*	Y	Y	Y	Y	N	Y
4 Ross	Y	Y	Y	N	Y	N
CALIFORNIA						
1 Thompson	Y	Y	Y	N	Y	N
2 *Herger*	Y	Y	Y	Y	N	Y
3 *Ose*	Y	Y	Y	Y	N	N
4 *Doolittle*	Y	Y	Y	Y	N	Y
5 Matsui	Y	Y	Y	?	?	?
6 Woolsey	Y	Y	Y	N	Y	N
7 Miller, George	Y	Y	Y	N	Y	N
8 Pelosi	Y	Y	Y	N	Y	N
9 Lee	Y	Y	Y	N	Y	N
10 Tauscher	Y	Y	Y	N	Y	N
11 *Pombo*	Y	Y	Y	Y	N	Y
12 Lantos	Y	Y	N	Y	N	Y
13 Stark	?	?	?	?	?	?
14 Eshoo	Y	Y	Y	N	Y	N
15 Honda	Y	Y	Y	N	Y	N
16 Lofgren	Y	Y	Y	N	Y	N
17 Farr	Y	Y	Y	N	Y	N
18 Cardoza	Y	Y	Y	N	Y	N
19 *Radanovich*	Y	Y	Y	?	N	Y
20 Dooley	?	?	?	?	?	?
21 *Nunes*	Y	Y	Y	Y	N	Y
22 *Thomas*	Y	Y	Y	Y	N	Y
23 Capps	?	Y	Y	N	Y	N
24 *Gallegly*	Y	Y	Y	Y	N	Y
25 *McKeon*	Y	Y	Y	Y	N	Y
26 *Dreier*	Y	Y	Y	Y	N	Y
27 Sherman	Y	Y	Y	N	Y	N
28 Berman	Y	Y	Y	N	Y	N
29 Schiff	Y	Y	Y	N	Y	N
30 Waxman	?	Y	Y	N	Y	N
31 Becerra	Y	Y	Y	N	Y	N
32 Solis	Y	Y	Y	N	Y	N
33 Watson	?	Y	Y	N	Y	N
34 Roybal-Allard	?	Y	Y	N	Y	N
35 Waters	?	Y	Y	N	Y	N
36 Harman	Y	Y	Y	N	Y	N

	531	532	533	534	535	536
37 Millender-McD.	?	?	?	?	?	?
38 Napolitano	Y	Y	Y	N	Y	N
39 Sánchez, Linda	Y	Y	Y	N	Y	N
40 *Royce*	Y	Y	Y	Y	N	Y
41 *Lewis*	Y	Y	Y	Y	N	Y
42 *Miller, Gary*	Y	Y	Y	?	N	Y
43 Baca	Y	Y	Y	N	Y	N
44 *Calvert*	Y	Y	Y	Y	N	Y
45 *Bono*	Y	Y	Y	Y	N	Y
46 *Rohrabacher*	Y	Y	N	Y	N	Y
47 Sanchez, Loretta	Y	Y	Y	N	Y	N
48 *Cox*	?	Y	Y	Y	N	Y
49 *Issa*	Y	Y	Y	Y	N	Y
50 *Cunningham*	Y	Y	Y	Y	N	Y
51 Filner	Y	Y	Y	N	Y	N
52 *Hunter*	?	Y	Y	Y	N	Y
53 Davis	Y	Y	Y	N	Y	N
COLORADO						
1 DeGette	Y	Y	Y	N	Y	N
2 Udall	Y	Y	Y	N	Y	N
3 *McInnis*	?	Y	Y	Y	N	Y
4 *Musgrave*	Y	?	?	?	?	?
5 *Hefley*	Y	Y	Y	Y	N	Y
6 *Tancredo*	Y	Y	Y	?	?	?
7 *Beauprez*	Y	Y	Y	Y	N	Y
CONNECTICUT						
1 Larson	Y	Y	Y	N	Y	N
2 *Simmons*	Y	Y	Y	?	N	Y
3 DeLauro	Y	Y	Y	N	Y	N
4 *Shays*	Y	Y	Y	Y	N	Y
5 *Johnson*	Y	Y	Y	Y	N	Y
DELAWARE						
AL *Castle*	Y	Y	Y	Y	N	Y
FLORIDA						
1 *Miller, J.*	Y	Y	Y	Y	N	Y
2 Boyd	Y	Y	Y	N	Y	N
3 Brown	?	Y	N	Y	N	N
4 *Crenshaw*	Y	Y	Y	Y	N	Y
5 *Brown-Waite*	Y	Y	Y	Y	N	Y
6 *Stearns*	Y	Y	Y	?	N	Y
7 *Mica*	Y	Y	Y	Y	N	Y
8 *Keller*	Y	Y	Y	Y	N	Y
9 *Bilirakis*	Y	Y	Y	Y	N	Y
10 *Young*	Y	Y	Y	Y	N	Y
11 Davis	?	Y	N	Y	N	N
12 *Putnam*	Y	Y	Y	Y	N	Y
14 Vacant						
13 *Harris*	Y	Y	Y	Y	N	Y
15 *Weldon*	Y	Y	Y	Y	N	Y
16 *Foley*	Y	Y	Y	Y	N	Y
17 Meek	Y	Y	Y	N	Y	N
18 *Ros-Lehtinen*	Y	Y	Y	Y	N	Y
19 Wexler	Y	Y	Y	N	Y	N
20 Deutsch	Y	Y	Y	N	Y	N
21 *Diaz-Balart, L.*	Y	Y	Y	Y	N	Y
22 *Shaw*	Y	Y	Y	Y	N	Y
23 Hastings	?	Y	Y	N	Y	N
24 *Feeney*	Y	?	Y	?	?	?
25 *Diaz-Balart, M.*	Y	Y	Y	Y	N	Y
GEORGIA						
1 *Kingston*	Y	Y	Y	N	Y	Y
2 Bishop	Y	Y	Y	N	Y	N
3 Marshall	Y	Y	Y	N	Y	N
4 Majette	Y	Y	Y	N	Y	N
5 Lewis	Y	Y	Y	N	Y	N
6 *Isakson*	?	Y	Y	Y	N	Y
7 *Linder*	?	Y	Y	Y	N	Y
8 *Collins*	Y	Y	Y	Y	N	Y
9 *Norwood*	?	?	?	?	?	?
10 *Deal*	Y	Y	Y	Y	N	Y
11 *Gingrey*	Y	Y	Y	Y	N	Y
12 *Burns*	Y	Y	Y	Y	N	Y
13 Scott	Y	Y	Y	N	Y	N
HAWAII						
1 Abercrombie	Y	Y	Y	N	Y	N
2 Case	Y	Y	Y	N	Y	N
IDAHO						
1 *Otter*	Y	Y	Y	Y	N	Y
2 *Simpson*	Y	Y	Y	Y	N	Y
ILLINOIS						
1 Rush	Y	Y	Y	N	Y	N
2 Jackson	Y	Y	Y	N	Y	N
3 Lipinski	?	Y	Y	?	?	?
4 Gutierrez	?	Y	Y	N	Y	N
5 Emanuel	Y	Y	Y	N	Y	N
6 *Hyde*	Y	Y	Y	Y	N	Y

ND Northern Democrats   SD Southern Democrats

	531	532	533	534	535	536
7 Davis	Y	Y	Y	N	Y	N
8 ***Crane***	Y	Y	Y	?	N	Y
9 Schakowsky	Y	Y	Y	N	Y	N
10 ***Kirk***	Y	Y	Y	Y	N	Y
11 ***Weller***	Y	Y	Y	?	?	?
12 Costello	Y	Y	Y	N	Y	N
13 ***Biggert***	Y	Y	Y	Y	N	Y
14 ***Hastert***					N	Y
15 ***Johnson***	Y	Y	Y	Y	N	Y
16 ***Manzullo***	Y	Y	Y	Y	N	Y
17 Evans	Y	Y	Y	N	Y	N
18 ***LaHood***	Y	Y	Y	Y	N	Y
19 ***Shimkus***	Y	Y	Y	Y	N	Y
INDIANA						
1 Visclosky	Y	Y	Y	N	Y	N
2 ***Chocola***	Y	Y	Y	Y	N	Y
3 ***Souder***	Y	Y	Y	Y	N	Y
4 ***Buyer***	Y	Y	Y	Y	N	Y
5 ***Burton***	Y	Y	Y	Y	N	Y
6 ***Pence***	Y	Y	Y	Y	N	Y
7 Carson	Y	Y	Y	N	Y	N
8 ***Hostettler***	Y	Y	Y	Y	N	Y
9 Hill	Y	?	Y	N	Y	N
IOWA						
1 ***Nussle***	Y	Y	Y	Y	N	Y
2 ***Leach***	Y	Y	Y	Y	N	Y
3 Boswell	Y	Y	Y	N	Y	N
4 ***Latham***	Y	Y	Y	Y	N	Y
5 ***King***	Y	Y	Y	Y	N	Y
KANSAS						
1 ***Moran***	Y	Y	Y	Y	N	Y
2 ***Ryun***	Y	Y	Y	Y	N	Y
3 Moore	Y	Y	Y	N	Y	N
4 ***Tiahrt***	Y	Y	Y	Y	N	Y
KENTUCKY						
1 ***Whitfield***	Y	Y	Y	Y	N	Y
2 ***Lewis***	Y	Y	Y	Y	N	Y
3 ***Northup***	Y	Y	Y	Y	N	Y
4 Lucas	Y	Y	Y	N	Y	N
5 ***Rogers***	Y	Y	Y	Y	N	Y
6 Chandler	Y	Y	Y	N	Y	N
LOUISIANA						
1 ***Vitter***	Y	Y	Y	Y	N	Y
2 Jefferson	Y	Y	Y	N	Y	N
3 ***Tauzin***	Y	Y	Y	Y	N	Y
4 ***McCrery***	Y	Y	Y	Y	N	Y
5 ***Alexander***	Y	Y	Y	Y	N	Y
6 ***Baker***	Y	Y	Y	Y	N	Y
7 John	Y	?	?	?	Y	N
MAINE						
1 Allen	Y	Y	Y	N	Y	N
2 Michaud	Y	Y	Y	N	Y	N
MARYLAND						
1 ***Gilchrest***	Y	Y	Y	Y	N	Y
2 Ruppersberger	Y	Y	Y	N	Y	N
3 Cardin	Y	Y	Y	N	Y	N
4 Wynn	Y	Y	Y	N	Y	N
5 Hoyer	Y	Y	Y	N	Y	N
6 ***Bartlett***	Y	Y	Y	Y	N	N
7 Cummings	Y	Y	Y	N	Y	N
8 Van Hollen	Y	Y	Y	N	Y	N
MASSACHUSETTS						
1 Olver	Y	Y	Y	N	Y	N
2 Neal	?	Y	Y	N	Y	N
3 McGovern	Y	Y	Y	N	Y	N
4 Frank	Y	Y	Y	N	Y	N
5 Meehan	Y	Y	Y	N	Y	N
6 Tierney	Y	Y	Y	N	Y	N
7 Markey	Y	Y	Y	N	Y	N
8 Capuano	Y	Y	Y	N	Y	N
9 Lynch	?	Y	Y	N	Y	N
10 Delahunt	?	Y	Y	N	Y	N
MICHIGAN						
1 Stupak	Y	Y	Y	N	Y	N
2 ***Hoekstra***	Y	Y	Y	Y	N	Y
3 ***Ehlers***	Y	Y	Y	Y	N	Y
4 ***Camp***	Y	Y	Y	Y	N	Y
5 Kildee	Y	Y	Y	N	Y	N
6 ***Upton***	Y	Y	Y	Y	N	Y
7 ***Smith***	Y	Y	Y	Y	N	N
8 ***Rogers***	Y	Y	Y	Y	N	Y
9 ***Knollenberg***	Y	Y	Y	Y	N	Y
10 ***Miller***	Y	Y	Y	Y	N	Y
11 ***McCotter***	Y	Y	Y	Y	N	Y
12 Levin	Y	Y	Y	N	Y	N
13 Kilpatrick	Y	+	+	N	Y	N
14 Conyers	Y	Y	Y	N	Y	N
15 Dingell	Y	Y	Y	N	Y	N
MINNESOTA						
1 ***Gutknecht***	Y	Y	Y	Y	N	Y
2 ***Kline***	Y	Y	Y	Y	N	Y
3 ***Ramstad***	Y	Y	Y	Y	N	Y
4 McCollum	Y	Y	Y	N	Y	N
5 Sabo	Y	Y	Y	N	Y	N
6 ***Kennedy***	Y	Y	Y	Y	N	Y
7 Peterson	Y	Y	Y	N	Y	N
8 Oberstar	Y	Y	Y	N	Y	N
MISSISSIPPI						
1 ***Wicker***	Y	Y	Y	Y	N	Y
2 Thompson	Y	Y	Y	N	Y	N
3 ***Pickering***	Y	Y	Y	Y	N	Y
4 Taylor	Y	Y	Y	N	Y	N
MISSOURI						
1 Clay	?	Y	Y	N	Y	N
2 ***Akin***	Y	Y	Y	Y	N	Y
3 Gephardt	?	?	?	?	?	?
4 Skelton	Y	Y	Y	N	Y	N
5 McCarthy	Y	Y	Y	N	Y	N
6 ***Graves***	Y	?	?	Y	N	Y
7 ***Blunt***	Y	Y	Y	Y	N	Y
8 ***Emerson***	Y	Y	Y	Y	N	Y
9 ***Hulshof***	Y	Y	Y	Y	N	Y
MONTANA						
AL ***Rehberg***	Y	Y	Y	Y	N	Y
NEBRASKA						
1 Vacant						
2 ***Terry***	Y	Y	Y	Y	N	Y
3 ***Osborne***	Y	Y	Y	Y	N	Y
NEVADA						
1 Berkley	Y	Y	Y	N	Y	N
2 ***Gibbons***	Y	Y	Y	Y	N	N
3 ***Porter***	Y	Y	Y	Y	N	Y
NEW HAMPSHIRE						
1 ***Bradley***	Y	Y	Y	Y	N	Y
2 ***Bass***	Y	Y	Y	Y	N	Y
NEW JERSEY						
1 Andrews	Y	Y	Y	N	Y	N
2 ***LoBiondo***	Y	Y	Y	Y	N	Y
3 ***Saxton***	Y	Y	Y	Y	N	Y
4 ***Smith***	Y	Y	Y	Y	N	Y
5 ***Garrett***	Y	Y	Y	Y	N	Y
6 Pallone	Y	Y	Y	N	Y	N
7 ***Ferguson***	Y	Y	Y	Y	N	Y
8 Pascrell	Y	Y	Y	N	Y	N
9 Rothman	Y	Y	?	N	Y	N
10 Payne	Y	Y	Y	N	Y	N
11 ***Frelinghuysen***	Y	Y	Y	Y	N	Y
12 Holt	Y	Y	Y	N	Y	N
13 Menendez	Y	Y	Y	N	Y	N
NEW MEXICO						
1 ***Wilson***	Y	Y	Y	Y	N	Y
2 ***Pearce***	Y	Y	Y	Y	N	Y
3 Udall	Y	Y	Y	N	Y	N
NEW YORK						
1 Bishop	Y	Y	Y	N	Y	N
2 Israel	Y	Y	Y	N	Y	N
3 ***King***	Y	Y	Y	Y	N	Y
4 McCarthy	?	?	?	?	?	?
5 Ackerman	Y	Y	Y	?	?	?
6 Meeks	Y	Y	Y	N	Y	N
7 Crowley	Y	Y	Y	N	Y	N
8 Nadler	Y	Y	Y	N	Y	N
9 Weiner	Y	Y	Y	N	Y	N
10 Towns	Y	Y	Y	N	Y	N
11 Owens	Y	Y	Y	N	Y	N
12 Velázquez	Y	Y	Y	N	Y	N
13 ***Fossella***	Y	Y	Y	Y	N	Y
14 Maloney	Y	Y	Y	N	Y	N
15 Rangel	Y	Y	Y	?	Y	N
16 Serrano	Y	Y	Y	N	Y	N
17 Engel	Y	?	Y	N	Y	N
18 Lowey	?	Y	Y	N	Y	N
19 ***Kelly***	Y	Y	Y	Y	N	Y
20 ***Sweeney***	Y	Y	Y	Y	N	Y
21 McNulty	Y	Y	Y	N	Y	N
22 Hinchey	Y	Y	Y	N	Y	N
23 ***McHugh***	Y	Y	Y	Y	N	Y
24 ***Boehlert***	Y	Y	Y	Y	N	Y
25 ***Walsh***	Y	Y	Y	Y	N	Y
26 ***Reynolds***	Y	Y	Y	Y	N	Y
27 ***Quinn***	Y	Y	Y	?	?	?
28 Slaughter	Y	Y	Y	N	Y	N
29 ***Houghton***	?	Y	Y	?	N	Y
NORTH CAROLINA						
1 Butterfield	Y	Y	Y	N	Y	N
2 Etheridge	Y	Y	Y	N	Y	N
3 ***Jones***	Y	Y	N	Y	N	N
4 Price	Y	Y	Y	N	Y	N
5 ***Burr***	?	?	?	?	N	Y
6 ***Coble***	Y	Y	Y	Y	N	Y
7 McIntyre	Y	Y	Y	N	Y	N
8 ***Hayes***	Y	Y	Y	Y	N	Y
9 ***Myrick***	Y	Y	Y	Y	N	Y
10 ***Ballenger***	Y	Y	Y	Y	N	Y
11 ***Taylor***	?	Y	Y	Y	N	Y
12 Watt	Y	Y	Y	N	Y	N
13 Miller	Y	Y	Y	N	Y	N
NORTH DAKOTA						
AL Pomeroy	Y	Y	Y	N	Y	N
OHIO						
1 ***Chabot***	Y	Y	Y	Y	N	Y
2 ***Portman***	Y	Y	Y	Y	N	Y
3 ***Turner***	Y	Y	Y	Y	N	Y
4 ***Oxley***	Y	Y	Y	?	N	Y
5 ***Gillmor***	Y	Y	Y	Y	N	Y
6 Strickland	Y	Y	Y	N	Y	N
7 ***Hobson***	Y	Y	Y	Y	N	Y
8 ***Boehner***	Y	Y	Y	?	N	Y
9 Kaptur	Y	Y	Y	N	Y	N
10 Kucinich	Y	Y	Y	N	Y	N
11 Jones	?	Y	Y	N	Y	N
12 ***Tiberi***	Y	Y	Y	Y	N	Y
13 Brown	Y	Y	Y	N	Y	N
14 ***LaTourette***	Y	Y	Y	Y	N	Y
15 ***Pryce***	Y	Y	Y	Y	N	Y
16 ***Regula***	Y	Y	Y	Y	N	Y
17 Ryan	Y	Y	Y	N	Y	N
18 ***Ney***	Y	Y	Y	Y	N	Y
OKLAHOMA						
1 ***Sullivan***	Y	Y	Y	Y	N	?
2 Carson	Y	Y	Y	?	?	?
3 ***Lucas***	Y	Y	Y	Y	N	Y
4 ***Cole***	Y	Y	Y	Y	N	Y
5 ***Istook***	Y	Y	Y	Y	N	Y
OREGON						
1 Wu	Y	Y	Y	N	Y	N
2 ***Walden***	Y	Y	Y	Y	N	Y
3 Blumenauer	Y	Y	Y	N	Y	N
4 DeFazio	Y	Y	Y	N	Y	N
5 Hooley	Y	Y	Y	N	Y	N
PENNSYLVANIA						
1 Brady	Y	Y	Y	N	Y	N
2 Fattah	Y	Y	Y	N	Y	N
3 ***English***	Y	Y	Y	?	N	Y
4 ***Hart***	Y	Y	Y	Y	N	Y
5 ***Peterson***	Y	Y	Y	Y	N	Y
6 ***Gerlach***	Y	Y	Y	Y	N	Y
7 ***Weldon***	Y	Y	Y	Y	N	Y
8 ***Greenwood***	Y	Y	Y	?	N	Y
9 ***Shuster, Bill***	Y	Y	Y	Y	N	Y
10 ***Sherwood***	Y	Y	Y	Y	N	Y
11 Kanjorski	Y	Y	Y	N	Y	N
12 Murtha	?	?	?	N	Y	N
13 Hoeffel	?	Y	Y	?	?	?
14 Doyle	Y	Y	Y	N	Y	N
15 ***Toomey***	?	?	?	?	?	?
16 ***Pitts***	Y	Y	Y	Y	N	Y
17 Holden	Y	Y	Y	N	Y	N
18 ***Murphy***	Y	Y	Y	Y	N	Y
19 ***Platts***	Y	Y	Y	Y	N	Y
RHODE ISLAND						
1 Kennedy	Y	Y	Y	N	Y	N
2 Langevin	?	Y	Y	N	Y	N
SOUTH CAROLINA						
1 ***Brown***	Y	Y	Y	Y	N	Y
2 ***Wilson***	Y	Y	Y	Y	N	Y
3 ***Barrett***	Y	Y	Y	Y	N	Y
4 ***DeMint***	?	Y	Y	Y	N	Y
5 Spratt	Y	Y	Y	N	Y	N
6 Clyburn	Y	Y	Y	N	Y	N
SOUTH DAKOTA						
AL Herseth	Y	Y	Y	N	Y	N
TENNESSEE						
1 ***Jenkins***	Y	Y	Y	Y	N	Y
2 ***Duncan***	Y	Y	N	Y	N	N
3 ***Wamp***	Y	Y	Y	Y	N	Y
4 Davis	Y	Y	Y	N	Y	N
5 Cooper	Y	Y	Y	N	Y	N
6 Gordon	Y	Y	Y	N	Y	N
7 ***Blackburn***	Y	Y	Y	Y	N	Y
8 Tanner	Y	?	Y	N	Y	N
9 Ford	Y	Y	Y	N	Y	N
TEXAS						
1 Sandlin	Y	Y	Y	N	Y	N
2 Turner	Y	Y	Y	N	Y	N
3 ***Johnson, Sam***	Y	Y	Y	Y	N	Y
4 ***Hall***	Y	Y	Y	Y	N	Y
5 ***Hensarling***	Y	Y	Y	Y	N	Y
6 ***Barton***	Y	Y	Y	Y	N	Y
7 ***Culberson***	Y	Y	Y	Y	N	Y
8 ***Brady***	Y	Y	Y	Y	N	Y
9 Lampson	Y	Y	Y	N	Y	N
10 Doggett	Y	Y	Y	N	Y	N
11 Edwards	Y	Y	Y	N	Y	N
12 ***Granger***	Y	Y	Y	Y	N	Y
13 ***Thornberry***	Y	Y	Y	Y	N	Y
14 ***Paul***	Y	Y	Y	Y	N	N
15 Hinojosa	Y	Y	Y	N	Y	N
16 Reyes	Y	Y	Y	N	Y	N
17 Stenholm	Y	?	Y	N	Y	N
18 Jackson-Lee	?	Y	Y	N	Y	N
19 ***Neugebauer***	Y	Y	Y	Y	N	Y
20 Gonzalez	Y	Y	Y	N	Y	N
21 ***Smith***	Y	Y	Y	Y	N	Y
22 ***DeLay***	Y	Y	Y	Y	N	Y
23 ***Bonilla***	Y	Y	Y	Y	N	Y
24 Frost	Y	Y	Y	N	Y	N
25 Bell	Y	Y	Y	N	Y	N
26 ***Burgess***	Y	?	?	Y	N	Y
27 Ortiz	Y	?	?	N	Y	N
28 Rodriguez	Y	Y	Y	N	Y	N
29 Green	Y	Y	Y	N	Y	N
30 Johnson, E.B.	Y	Y	Y	N	Y	N
31 ***Carter***	Y	Y	Y	Y	N	Y
32 ***Sessions***	Y	Y	Y	Y	N	Y
UTAH						
1 ***Bishop***	Y	Y	Y	Y	N	Y
2 Matheson	Y	Y	Y	N	Y	N
3 ***Cannon***	?	?	?	?	?	?
VERMONT						
AL *Sanders*	Y	Y	Y	N	Y	N
VIRGINIA						
1 ***Davis, Jo Ann***	Y	Y	Y	Y	N	N
2 ***Schrock***	?	Y	Y	?	N	Y
3 Scott	Y	Y	Y	N	Y	N
4 ***Forbes***	Y	Y	Y	Y	N	Y
5 ***Goode***	Y	Y	N	Y	N	N
6 ***Goodlatte***	Y	Y	Y	Y	N	Y
7 ***Cantor***	Y	Y	Y	Y	N	Y
8 Moran	Y	Y	Y	N	Y	N
9 Boucher	Y	Y	Y	N	Y	N
10 ***Wolf***	Y	Y	Y	Y	N	Y
11 ***Davis, T.***	Y	Y	Y	Y	N	Y
WASHINGTON						
1 Inslee	Y	Y	Y	N	Y	N
2 Larsen	Y	Y	Y	N	Y	N
3 Baird	Y	Y	Y	N	Y	N
4 ***Hastings***	Y	Y	Y	Y	N	Y
5 ***Nethercutt***	?	Y	Y	?	N	Y
6 Dicks	Y	Y	Y	N	Y	N
7 McDermott	?	?	?	?	?	?
8 ***Dunn***	Y	?	?	?	?	?
9 Smith	Y	Y	Y	N	Y	N
WEST VIRGINIA						
1 Mollohan	Y	Y	Y	N	Y	N
2 ***Capito***	Y	Y	Y	Y	N	Y
3 Rahall	Y	Y	Y	N	Y	N
WISCONSIN						
1 ***Ryan***	Y	Y	Y	Y	N	Y
2 Baldwin	Y	Y	Y	N	Y	N
3 Kind	Y	Y	Y	N	Y	N
4 Kleczka	Y	?	?	?	?	?
5 ***Sensenbrenner***	Y	Y	Y	Y	N	Y
6 ***Petri***	Y	Y	Y	Y	N	Y
7 Obey	Y	Y	Y	N	Y	N
8 ***Green***	Y	Y	Y	Y	N	Y
WYOMING						
AL ***Cubin***	Y	?	?	Y	N	Y

Southern states - Ala., Ark., Fla., Ga., Ky., La., Miss., N.C., Okla., S.C., Tenn., Texas, Va.

Key

Y	Voted for (yea).
#	Paired for.
+	Announced for.
N	Voted against (nay).
X	Paired against.
−	Announced against.
P	Voted "present."
C	Voted "present" to avoid possible conflict of interest.
?	Did not vote or otherwise make a position known.

Democrats **Republicans**
Independents

---

537. HR 1350. IDEA Reauthorization/Conference Report. Adoption of the conference report on the bill that would reauthorize and amend the Individuals with Disabilities Act (IDEA) through 2011 to provide public education for children with disabilities. It would authorize $12.4 billion for states and school districts in fiscal 2005, increasing by $2.3 billion per year through 2011. It would authorize such sums as necessary after that. It also would maintain some student discipline rules under current law, reduce paperwork burdens for teachers, and change several procedures for handling complaints under IDEA. Adopted (thus sent to the Senate) 397-3: R 209-3; D 188-0 (ND 134-0, SD 54-0); I 0-0. Nov. 19, 2004.

538. HR 4818, H J Res 114. Fiscal 2005 Appropriations Bills/Same-Day Consideration. Adoption of the rule (H Res 846) that would waive the two-thirds majority vote requirement for same-day consideration of the rule on the conference report for the omnibus appropriations bill (HR 4818) and the continuing resolution (H J Res 114) for fiscal 2005. Adopted 234-159: R 209-0; D 25-158 (ND 15-115, SD 10-43); I 0-1. Nov. 20, 2004.

539. H Res 853. Boy Scouts Recognition/Adoption. Sensenbrenner, R-Wis., motion to suspend the rules and adopt the resolution that would recognize the public service efforts of the Boys Scouts of America. Motion agreed to 391-3: R 210-0; D 180-3 (ND 127-3, SD 53-0); I 1-0. A two-thirds majority of those present and voting (263 in this case) is required for adoption under suspension of the rules. Nov. 20, 2004.

540. HR 4818, H J Res 114. Fiscal 2005 Appropriations Bills/Rule. Adoption of the rule (H Res 866), as amended, to provide for House floor consideration of the conference report on the bill that would provide fiscal 2005 omnibus appropriations for all federal departments and agencies whose regular fiscal 2005 spending bills have not been enacted, and a continuing resolution, through Dec. 3, 2004, for fiscal 2005. Adopted 233-158: R 212-0; D 21-157 (ND 14-113, SD 7-44); I 0-1. Nov. 20, 2004.

541. HR 5382. Space Tourism/Passage. Rohrabacher, R-Calif., motion to suspend the rules and pass the bill that would authorize the Federal Aviation Administration to regulate the commercial human space flight industry. For the first eight years, the FAA could only prohibit technologies already proven to cause serious or near-fatal injuries. Motion agreed to 269-120: R 206-2; D 63-117 (ND 37-91, SD 26-26); I 0-1. A two-thirds majority of those present and voting (260 in this case) is required for passage under suspension of the rules. Nov. 20, 2004.

542. HR 4818. Fiscal 2005 Omnibus Appropriations/Conference Report. Adoption of the conference report on the bill that would provide $388.4 billion in discretionary spending in fiscal 2005 for all federal departments and agencies whose fiscal 2005 spending bills have not been enacted. The measure incorporates nine previously separate appropriations bills: Agriculture; Commerce-Justice-State; Energy and Water; Foreign Operations; Interior; Labor-HHS-Education; Transportation and Treasury; Legislative Branch and VA-HUD. The total does not includes a 0.8 percent across-the-board cut in all discretionary accounts in the omnibus. Adopted (thus sent to the Senate) 344-51: R 183-27; D 160-24 (ND 113-18, SD 47-6); I 1-0. Nov. 20, 2004.

	537	538	539	540	541	542
ALABAMA						
1 *Bonner*	Y	Y	Y	Y	Y	Y
2 *Everett*	Y	Y	Y	Y	Y	Y
3 *Rogers*	Y	Y	Y	Y	Y	Y
4 *Aderholt*	Y	Y	Y	Y	Y	Y
5 Cramer	Y	Y	Y	Y	Y	Y
6 *Bachus*	Y	?	?	?	?	?
7 Davis	Y	N	Y	N	Y	Y
ALASKA						
AL *Young*	?	?	Y	Y	N	Y
ARIZONA						
1 *Renzi*	Y	Y	Y	Y	Y	Y
2 *Franks*	Y	Y	Y	Y	Y	N
3 *Shadegg*	Y	Y	Y	Y	Y	N
4 Pastor	Y	N	Y	N	Y	Y
5 *Hayworth*	Y	Y	Y	Y	Y	Y
6 *Flake*	N	Y	Y	Y	N	N
7 Grijalva	Y	N	Y	N	N	N
8 *Kolbe*	Y	Y	Y	Y	Y	Y
ARKANSAS						
1 Berry	?	N	Y	N	N	Y
2 Snyder	Y	Y	Y	Y	Y	Y
3 *Boozman*	Y	Y	Y	Y	Y	Y
4 Ross	Y	N	Y	N	Y	Y
CALIFORNIA						
1 Thompson	Y	N	Y	N	N	Y
2 *Herger*	Y	Y	Y	Y	Y	Y
3 *Ose*	Y	Y	Y	Y	Y	Y
4 *Doolittle*	Y	Y	Y	Y	Y	Y
5 Matsui	?	N	Y	N	Y	Y
6 Woolsey	Y	N	N	N	N	N
7 Miller, George	Y	N	Y	N	N	Y
8 Pelosi	Y	N	Y	N	N	Y
9 Lee	Y	N	Y	N	N	N
10 Tauscher	Y	N	Y	N	N	N
11 *Pombo*	Y	Y	Y	Y	Y	Y
12 Lantos	Y	N	Y	N	Y	Y
13 Stark	Y	?	?	N	N	N
14 Eshoo	Y	N	Y	N	Y	Y
15 Honda	Y	N	Y	N	N	Y
16 Lofgren	Y	N	Y	N	Y	N
17 Farr	Y	N	Y	N	Y	Y
18 Cardoza	Y	N	Y	N	Y	Y
19 *Radanovich*	Y	Y	Y	Y	Y	Y
20 Dooley	Y	N	Y	Y	Y	Y
21 *Nunes*	Y	Y	Y	Y	Y	Y
22 *Thomas*	Y	N	Y	N	Y	N
23 Capps	Y	N	Y	N	N	Y
24 *Gallegly*	Y	Y	Y	Y	Y	Y
25 *McKeon*	Y	Y	Y	Y	Y	Y
26 *Dreier*	Y	Y	Y	Y	Y	Y
27 Sherman	Y	N	Y	N	N	Y
28 Berman	Y	N	Y	N	N	Y
29 Schiff	Y	N	Y	N	N	Y
30 Waxman	Y	N	Y	N	N	Y
31 Becerra	Y	N	Y	N	N	Y
32 Solis	Y	N	Y	N	N	Y
33 Watson	Y	N	Y	N	N	Y
34 Roybal-Allard	Y	N	Y	N	N	Y
35 Waters	Y	?	?	?	?	?
36 Harman	Y	N	Y	N	Y	Y

	537	538	539	540	541	542
37 Millender-McD.	?	?	?	?	?	?
38 Napolitano	Y	N	Y	N	N	Y
39 Sánchez, Linda	Y	N	Y	N	N	Y
40 *Royce*	Y	Y	Y	Y	Y	N
41 *Lewis*	Y	Y	Y	Y	Y	Y
42 *Miller, Gary*	Y	Y	Y	Y	Y	Y
43 Baca	Y	N	Y	N	N	Y
44 *Calvert*	Y	Y	Y	Y	Y	Y
45 *Bono*	Y	Y	Y	Y	Y	Y
46 *Rohrabacher*	Y	Y	Y	Y	Y	N
47 Sanchez, Loretta	Y	N	Y	N	Y	Y
48 *Cox*	Y	Y	Y	Y	Y	N
49 *Issa*	Y	Y	Y	Y	Y	Y
50 *Cunningham*	+	Y	Y	?	Y	Y
51 Filner	Y	N	N	N	N	N
52 *Hunter*	Y	Y	Y	Y	Y	Y
53 Davis	Y	N	Y	N	Y	Y
COLORADO						
1 DeGette	Y	N	Y	N	N	N
2 Udall	Y	N	Y	N	Y	Y
3 *McInnis*	Y	Y	Y	Y	Y	Y
4 *Musgrave*	?	?	?	?	?	?
5 *Hefley*	Y	Y	Y	Y	Y	N
6 *Tancredo*	Y	Y	Y	Y	Y	N
7 *Beauprez*	Y	Y	Y	Y	Y	Y
CONNECTICUT						
1 Larson	Y	N	Y	N	?	Y
2 *Simmons*	Y	Y	Y	Y	Y	Y
3 DeLauro	Y	N	Y	N	N	Y
4 *Shays*	Y	Y	Y	Y	Y	Y
5 *Johnson*	Y	Y	Y	Y	Y	Y
DELAWARE						
AL *Castle*	Y	Y	Y	Y	Y	Y
FLORIDA						
1 *Miller, J.*	Y	Y	Y	Y	Y	Y
2 Boyd	Y	N	Y	N	Y	Y
3 Brown	Y	N	Y	N	Y	Y
4 *Crenshaw*	Y	Y	Y	Y	Y	Y
5 *Brown-Waite*	Y	Y	Y	Y	Y	Y
6 *Stearns*	Y	Y	Y	Y	Y	Y
7 *Mica*	Y	Y	Y	Y	Y	Y
8 *Keller*	Y	Y	Y	Y	Y	Y
9 *Bilirakis*	Y	Y	Y	Y	Y	Y
10 *Young*	Y	Y	Y	Y	Y	Y
11 Davis	Y	N	Y	N	N	Y
12 *Putnam*	Y	Y	Y	Y	?	Y
13 *Harris*	Y	Y	Y	Y	Y	Y
14 Vacant						
15 *Weldon*	Y	Y	Y	Y	Y	Y
16 *Foley*	Y	Y	Y	Y	Y	Y
17 Meek	Y	N	Y	N	N	Y
18 *Ros-Lehtinen*	Y	Y	Y	Y	Y	Y
19 Wexler	Y	N	Y	?	Y	Y
20 Deutsch	Y	?	?	?	?	?
21 *Diaz-Balart, L.*	Y	Y	Y	Y	Y	Y
22 *Shaw*	Y	Y	Y	Y	Y	Y
23 Hastings	Y	N	Y	N	N	Y
24 *Feeney*	Y	?	?	?	?	?
25 *Diaz-Balart, M.*	Y	Y	Y	Y	Y	Y
GEORGIA						
1 *Kingston*	Y	Y	Y	Y	Y	Y
2 Bishop	Y	Y	Y	Y	Y	Y
3 Marshall	Y	N	Y	N	Y	Y
4 *Majette*	Y	Y	Y	N	N	N
5 Lewis	Y	N	Y	N	N	Y
6 *Isakson*	Y	Y	Y	Y	Y	Y
7 *Linder*	Y	Y	Y	Y	Y	Y
8 *Collins*	+	+	+	+	+	+
9 *Norwood*	?	?	?	?	?	?
10 *Deal*	Y	Y	Y	Y	Y	N
11 *Gingrey*	Y	Y	Y	Y	Y	Y
12 *Burns*	Y	Y	Y	Y	Y	Y
13 Scott	Y	N	Y	Y	Y	Y
HAWAII						
1 Abercrombie	Y	N	Y	N	Y	Y
2 Case	Y	?	?	?	?	?
IDAHO						
1 *Otter*	Y	Y	Y	Y	Y	Y
2 *Simpson*	Y	Y	Y	Y	Y	Y
ILLINOIS						
1 Rush	Y	N	Y	N	N	Y
2 Jackson	Y	N	Y	N	N	N
3 Lipinski	?	?	?	?	?	?
4 Gutierrez	Y	N	Y	N	N	Y
5 Emanuel	Y	N	Y	N	N	Y
6 *Hyde*	Y	Y	Y	Y	Y	Y

ND Northern Democrats   SD Southern Democrats

	537	538	539	540	541	542
7 Davis	Y	N	Y	N	N	Y
8 ***Crane***	Y	Y	Y	Y	Y	Y
9 Schakowsky	Y	N	Y	N	N	N
10 ***Kirk***	Y	Y	Y	Y	?	Y
11 ***Weller***	?	?	?	?	?	?
12 Costello	Y	N	Y	N	N	N
13 ***Biggert***	Y	Y	Y	Y	Y	Y
14 ***Hastert***				Y		Y
15 ***Johnson***	Y	Y	Y	Y	Y	Y
16 ***Manzullo***	Y	Y	Y	Y	Y	Y
17 Evans	Y	N	Y	N	N	Y
18 ***LaHood***	Y	Y	Y	Y	Y	Y
19 ***Shimkus***	Y	Y	Y	Y	Y	Y
INDIANA						
1 Visclosky	Y	N	Y	N	Y	Y
2 ***Chocola***	Y	Y	Y	Y	Y	Y
3 ***Souder***	Y	Y	Y	Y	Y	Y
4 ***Buyer***	Y	Y	Y	Y	Y	Y
5 ***Burton***	Y	Y	Y	Y	Y	Y
6 ***Pence***	Y	Y	Y	Y	Y	Y
7 Carson	Y	N	Y	N	N	Y
8 ***Hostettler***	Y	Y	Y	Y	Y	N
9 Hill	Y	N	Y	?	?	Y
IOWA						
1 ***Nussle***	Y	Y	Y	Y	Y	Y
2 ***Leach***	Y	Y	Y	Y	Y	Y
3 Boswell	Y	N	Y	?	?	?
4 ***Latham***	Y	Y	Y	Y	Y	Y
5 ***King***	Y	Y	Y	Y	Y	Y
KANSAS						
1 ***Moran***	Y	Y	Y	Y	Y	Y
2 ***Ryun***	Y	Y	Y	Y	Y	Y
3 Moore	Y	Y	Y	Y	N	Y
4 ***Tiahrt***	Y	Y	Y	Y	Y	Y
KENTUCKY						
1 ***Whitfield***	Y	Y	Y	Y	Y	Y
2 ***Lewis***	Y	Y	Y	Y	Y	Y
3 ***Northup***	Y	Y	Y	Y	Y	Y
4 Lucas	Y	Y	Y	N	N	Y
5 ***Rogers***	Y	Y	Y	Y	Y	Y
6 Chandler	Y	Y	Y	N	N	Y
LOUISIANA						
1 ***Vitter***	Y	Y	Y	Y	Y	Y
2 Jefferson	Y	N	Y	N	N	N
3 ***Tauzin***	Y	Y	Y	Y	Y	Y
4 ***McCrery***	Y	Y	Y	Y	Y	Y
5 ***Alexander***	Y	Y	Y	Y	Y	Y
6 ***Baker***	Y	Y	Y	Y	Y	Y
7 John	Y	?	?	?	?	?
MAINE						
1 Allen	Y	N	Y	N	N	Y
2 Michaud	Y	Y	Y	Y	N	Y
MARYLAND						
1 ***Gilchrest***	Y	Y	Y	Y	Y	Y
2 Ruppersberger	Y	Y	Y	?	Y	Y
3 Cardin	Y	N	Y	N	N	Y
4 Wynn	Y	Y	Y	Y	Y	Y
5 Hoyer	Y	N	Y	N	N	Y
6 ***Bartlett***	Y	Y	Y	Y	Y	N
7 Cummings	Y	N	Y	N	N	Y
8 Van Hollen	Y	N	Y	N	Y	Y
MASSACHUSETTS						
1 Olver	Y	N	Y	N	N	Y
2 Neal	Y	N	Y	N	N	Y
3 McGovern	Y	N	Y	?	N	Y
4 Frank	Y	N	N	N	N	Y
5 Meehan	?	?	?	?	?	?
6 Tierney	Y	N	Y	N	N	Y
7 Markey	Y	N	Y	N	N	N
8 Capuano	Y	N	Y	N	N	Y
9 Lynch	Y	N	Y	N	?	Y
10 Delahunt	Y	?	?	?	?	?
MICHIGAN						
1 Stupak	Y	N	Y	Y	N	Y
2 ***Hoekstra***	Y	Y	Y	Y	Y	Y
3 ***Ehlers***	Y	Y	Y	Y	Y	Y
4 ***Camp***	Y	Y	Y	Y	Y	Y
5 Kildee	Y	N	Y	N	N	Y
6 ***Upton***	Y	?	?	?	?	?
7 ***Smith***	Y	Y	Y	Y	Y	?
8 ***Rogers***	Y	Y	Y	Y	Y	Y
9 ***Knollenberg***	Y	Y	Y	Y	Y	Y
10 ***Miller***	Y	Y	Y	Y	Y	Y
11 ***McCotter***	Y	Y	Y	Y	Y	Y
12 Levin	Y	N	Y	N	N	Y
13 Kilpatrick	Y	N	Y	N	N	Y
14 Conyers	?	N	Y	?	N	N
15 Dingell	Y	N	N	N	N	N
MINNESOTA						
1 ***Gutknecht***	Y	Y	Y	Y	Y	Y
2 ***Kline***	Y	Y	Y	Y	Y	Y
3 ***Ramstad***	Y	Y	Y	Y	Y	Y
4 McCollum	Y	Y	Y	N	N	Y
5 Sabo	Y	Y	Y	N	N	Y
6 ***Kennedy***	Y	Y	Y	Y	Y	Y
7 Peterson	Y	N	Y	N	Y	Y
8 Oberstar	Y	N	Y	N	N	Y
MISSISSIPPI						
1 ***Wicker***	Y	Y	Y	Y	Y	Y
2 Thompson	Y	N	Y	N	Y	Y
3 ***Pickering***	Y	Y	Y	Y	Y	Y
4 Taylor	Y	N	Y	N	N	N
MISSOURI						
1 Clay	Y	N	Y	N	Y	Y
2 ***Akin***	Y	Y	Y	Y	Y	N
3 Gephardt	?	?	?	?	?	?
4 Skelton	Y	N	Y	?	?	?
5 McCarthy	Y	N	Y	N	N	Y
6 ***Graves***	Y	Y	Y	Y	?	?
7 ***Blunt***	Y	Y	Y	Y	Y	Y
8 ***Emerson***	Y	Y	Y	Y	Y	Y
9 ***Hulshof***	Y	Y	Y	Y	Y	Y
MONTANA						
AL ***Rehberg***	Y	Y	Y	Y	Y	Y
NEBRASKA						
1 Vacant						
2 ***Terry***	Y	Y	Y	Y	Y	N
3 ***Osborne***	Y	Y	Y	Y	Y	Y
NEVADA						
1 Berkley	Y	N	Y	N	N	Y
2 ***Gibbons***	Y	Y	Y	Y	Y	N
3 ***Porter***	Y	Y	Y	Y	Y	Y
NEW HAMPSHIRE						
1 ***Bradley***	Y	Y	Y	Y	Y	Y
2 ***Bass***	Y	Y	Y	Y	N	Y
NEW JERSEY						
1 Andrews	Y	N	Y	N	N	Y
2 ***LoBiondo***	Y	Y	Y	Y	Y	Y
3 ***Saxton***	+	Y	Y	Y	Y	Y
4 ***Smith***	Y	Y	Y	Y	Y	Y
5 ***Garrett***	N	Y	Y	Y	Y	N
6 Pallone	Y	Y	Y	N	N	Y
7 ***Ferguson***	Y	Y	Y	Y	Y	Y
8 Pascrell	Y	Y	Y	N	N	Y
9 Rothman	?	?	?	?	?	+
10 Payne	Y	N	Y	N	N	N
11 ***Frelinghuysen***	Y	Y	Y	Y	Y	Y
12 Holt	Y	N	Y	N	Y	Y
13 Menendez	Y	N	Y	N	N	Y
NEW MEXICO						
1 ***Wilson***	Y	Y	Y	Y	Y	Y
2 ***Pearce***	Y	Y	Y	Y	Y	Y
3 Udall	Y	N	Y	N	N	Y
NEW YORK						
1 Bishop	Y	N	Y	N	N	Y
2 Israel	Y	N	Y	N	N	Y
3 ***King***	Y	Y	Y	Y	Y	Y
4 McCarthy	+	?	?	?	?	?
5 Ackerman	Y	?	?	?	?	?
6 Meeks	Y	N	Y	N	Y	Y
7 Crowley	Y	N	Y	N	N	Y
8 Nadler	Y	N	Y	N	N	Y
9 Weiner	Y	N	Y	N	N	Y
10 Towns	Y	?	?	?	?	?
11 Owens	Y	?	?	N	Y	Y
12 Velázquez	?	N	Y	N	N	Y
13 ***Fossella***	Y	Y	Y	Y	Y	N
14 Maloney	Y	N	Y	N	Y	Y
15 Rangel	Y	N	Y	Y	N	Y
16 Serrano	Y	N	Y	N	N	Y
17 Engel	Y	N	Y	Y	N	Y
18 Lowey	Y	N	Y	N	N	Y
19 ***Kelly***	Y	Y	Y	Y	Y	Y
20 ***Sweeney***	Y	Y	Y	Y	Y	Y
21 McNulty	Y	N	Y	N	Y	Y
22 Hinchey	Y	N	Y	N	N	Y
23 ***McHugh***	Y	Y	Y	Y	Y	Y
24 ***Boehlert***	Y	Y	Y	Y	Y	Y
25 ***Walsh***	Y	Y	Y	Y	Y	Y
26 ***Reynolds***	Y	Y	Y	Y	Y	Y
27 ***Quinn***	?	?	?	?	?	?
28 Slaughter	Y	N	Y	N	N	Y
29 ***Houghton***	Y	Y	Y	Y	Y	Y
NORTH CAROLINA						
1 Butterfield	Y	Y	Y	Y	Y	Y
2 Etheridge	Y	N	Y	N	N	Y
3 ***Jones***	Y	Y	Y	Y	Y	N
4 Price	Y	N	Y	N	Y	Y
5 ***Burr***	Y	?	?	?	?	?
6 ***Coble***	Y	Y	Y	Y	Y	Y
7 McIntyre	Y	N	Y	N	N	Y
8 ***Hayes***	Y	Y	Y	Y	Y	Y
9 ***Myrick***	Y	Y	Y	Y	Y	Y
10 ***Ballenger***	Y	Y	Y	Y	Y	?
11 ***Taylor***	Y	Y	Y	Y	Y	Y
12 Watt	Y	N	Y	N	Y	Y
13 Miller	Y	Y	Y	N	Y	Y
NORTH DAKOTA						
AL Pomeroy	Y	N	Y	N	Y	Y
OHIO						
1 ***Chabot***	Y	Y	Y	Y	Y	N
2 ***Portman***	Y	Y	Y	Y	Y	Y
3 ***Turner***	Y	Y	Y	Y	Y	Y
4 ***Oxley***	Y	Y	Y	Y	Y	Y
5 ***Gillmor***	Y	?	?	?	?	?
6 Strickland	Y	N	Y	N	Y	Y
7 ***Hobson***	Y	?	?	?	?	?
8 ***Boehner***	Y	Y	Y	Y	Y	Y
9 Kaptur	?	N	Y	N	N	Y
10 Kucinich	Y	N	Y	N	N	N
11 Jones	Y	N	Y	N	N	Y
12 ***Tiberi***	Y	Y	Y	Y	Y	Y
13 Brown	Y	N	Y	N	N	Y
14 ***LaTourette***	Y	Y	Y	Y	Y	Y
15 ***Pryce***	Y	Y	Y	Y	Y	Y
16 ***Regula***	Y	Y	Y	Y	Y	Y
17 Ryan	Y	N	Y	N	N	Y
18 ***Ney***	Y	Y	Y	Y	Y	Y
OKLAHOMA						
1 ***Sullivan***	Y	Y	Y	Y	Y	Y
2 Carson	Y	N	Y	N	Y	Y
3 ***Lucas***	Y	Y	Y	Y	Y	Y
4 ***Cole***	Y	Y	Y	Y	Y	Y
5 ***Istook***	Y	Y	Y	Y	Y	Y
OREGON						
1 Wu	Y	N	Y	N	N	Y
2 ***Walden***	Y	Y	Y	Y	Y	Y
3 Blumenauer	Y	?	?	?	?	?
4 DeFazio	Y	N	Y	N	N	Y
5 Hooley	Y	N	Y	N	N	Y
PENNSYLVANIA						
1 Brady	Y	?	?	Y	N	Y
2 Fattah	Y	?	?	?	?	?
3 ***English***	Y	Y	Y	Y	Y	Y
4 ***Hart***	Y	Y	Y	Y	?	Y
5 ***Peterson***	Y	Y	Y	Y	Y	Y
6 ***Gerlach***	Y	Y	Y	Y	Y	Y
7 ***Weldon***	?	Y	Y	Y	Y	Y
8 ***Greenwood***	Y	Y	Y	Y	Y	Y
9 ***Shuster, Bill***	Y	Y	Y	Y	Y	Y
10 ***Sherwood***	Y	Y	Y	Y	Y	Y
11 Kanjorski	Y	Y	Y	Y	Y	Y
12 Murtha	?	Y	Y	Y	Y	Y
13 Hoeffel	?	N	Y	N	N	N
14 Doyle	Y	Y	Y	Y	Y	Y
15 ***Toomey***	?	?	?	?	?	?
16 ***Pitts***	Y	Y	Y	Y	Y	N
17 Holden	Y	N	Y	Y	N	Y
18 ***Murphy***	Y	Y	Y	Y	Y	Y
19 ***Platts***	Y	Y	Y	Y	Y	Y
RHODE ISLAND						
1 Kennedy	Y	N	Y	N	N	Y
2 Langevin	Y	N	Y	N	N	Y
SOUTH CAROLINA						
1 ***Brown***	Y	Y	Y	Y	Y	Y
2 ***Wilson***	Y	Y	Y	Y	Y	Y
3 ***Barrett***	Y	Y	Y	Y	Y	Y
4 ***DeMint***	Y	Y	Y	Y	Y	N
5 Spratt	Y	N	Y	N	N	Y
6 Clyburn	Y	N	Y	N	Y	Y
SOUTH DAKOTA						
AL Herseth	Y	N	Y	N	N	Y
TENNESSEE						
1 ***Jenkins***	Y	Y	Y	Y	Y	Y
2 ***Duncan***	Y	Y	Y	Y	Y	N
3 ***Wamp***	Y	Y	Y	Y	Y	Y
4 Davis	Y	N	Y	N	N	Y
5 Cooper	Y	N	Y	N	N	Y
6 Gordon	Y	?	?	Y	Y	Y
7 ***Blackburn***	Y	Y	Y	Y	Y	Y
8 Tanner	Y	N	Y	N	N	N
9 Ford	Y	N	Y	N	N	N
TEXAS						
1 Sandlin	Y	N	Y	N	N	Y
2 Turner	Y	N	Y	?	?	?
3 ***Johnson, Sam***	?	Y	?	Y	Y	Y
4 ***Hall***	Y	Y	Y	Y	Y	Y
5 ***Hensarling***	Y	Y	Y	Y	Y	N
6 ***Barton***	Y	Y	Y	Y	Y	Y
7 ***Culberson***	Y	?	Y	Y	Y	Y
8 ***Brady***	Y	Y	Y	Y	Y	Y
9 Lampson	Y	N	Y	N	Y	Y
10 Doggett	Y	N	Y	N	N	Y
11 Edwards	Y	N	Y	N	N	Y
12 ***Granger***	Y	Y	Y	Y	Y	Y
13 ***Thornberry***	Y	Y	Y	Y	Y	Y
14 ***Paul***	N	Y	Y	Y	Y	N
15 Hinojosa	Y	N	Y	N	Y	Y
16 Reyes	Y	N	Y	N	Y	Y
17 Stenholm	Y	N	Y	N	N	N
18 Jackson-Lee	Y	N	Y	N	Y	Y
19 ***Neugebauer***	Y	Y	Y	Y	Y	Y
20 Gonzalez	Y	N	Y	N	N	Y
21 ***Smith***	Y	Y	Y	Y	Y	Y
22 ***DeLay***	Y	Y	Y	Y	Y	Y
23 ***Bonilla***	Y	Y	Y	Y	Y	Y
24 Frost	?	Y	Y	Y	N	Y
25 Bell	Y	Y	Y	N	Y	Y
26 ***Burgess***	Y	Y	Y	Y	Y	Y
27 Ortiz	Y	N	Y	N	Y	Y
28 Rodriguez	Y	N	Y	N	Y	Y
29 Green	Y	N	Y	N	N	Y
30 Johnson, E.B.	Y	N	Y	N	N	Y
31 ***Carter***	Y	Y	Y	Y	Y	Y
32 ***Sessions***	Y	Y	Y	Y	Y	Y
UTAH						
1 ***Bishop***	Y	Y	Y	Y	Y	Y
2 Matheson	Y	Y	Y	N	N	Y
3 ***Cannon***	?	?	?	?	?	?
VERMONT						
AL *Sanders*	?	N	Y	N	N	Y
VIRGINIA						
1 ***Davis, Jo Ann***	Y	Y	Y	Y	Y	N
2 ***Schrock***	Y	Y	Y	Y	Y	Y
3 Scott	Y	N	Y	N	N	Y
4 ***Forbes***	Y	Y	Y	Y	Y	Y
5 ***Goode***	Y	Y	Y	Y	Y	Y
6 ***Goodlatte***	Y	Y	Y	Y	Y	Y
7 ***Cantor***	Y	Y	Y	Y	Y	Y
8 Moran	Y	N	Y	?	N	Y
9 Boucher	Y	N	Y	N	Y	Y
10 ***Wolf***	Y	Y	Y	Y	Y	Y
11 ***Davis, T.***	Y	?	?	Y	Y	Y
WASHINGTON						
1 Inslee	Y	N	Y	N	N	N
2 Larsen	Y	N	Y	N	N	Y
3 Baird	Y	N	Y	N	N	P
4 ***Hastings***	Y	Y	Y	Y	Y	Y
5 ***Nethercutt***	Y	Y	Y	Y	Y	Y
6 Dicks	Y	Y	Y	Y	N	Y
7 McDermott	+	–	?	–	–	–
8 ***Dunn***	?	?	?	?	?	?
9 Smith	Y	Y	Y	N	Y	Y
WEST VIRGINIA						
1 Mollohan	Y	Y	Y	Y	Y	Y
2 ***Capito***	Y	Y	Y	Y	Y	Y
3 Rahall	?	N	Y	N	N	Y
WISCONSIN						
1 ***Ryan***	Y	Y	Y	Y	Y	N
2 Baldwin	Y	N	Y	N	N	Y
3 Kind	Y	?	?	?	?	?
4 Kleczka	?	?	?	?	?	Y
5 ***Sensenbrenner***	Y	Y	Y	Y	Y	Y
6 ***Petri***	Y	Y	Y	Y	Y	Y
7 Obey	Y	N	Y	N	N	Y
8 ***Green***	Y	Y	Y	Y	Y	N
WYOMING						
AL ***Cubin***	Y	Y	Y	Y	Y	Y

Southern states - Ala., Ark., Fla., Ga., Ky., La., Miss., N.C., Okla., S.C., Tenn., Texas, Va.

Key

Y	Voted for (yea).
#	Paired for.
+	Announced for.
N	Voted against (nay).
X	Paired against.
–	Announced against.
P	Voted "present."
C	Voted "present" to avoid possible conflict of interest.
?	Did not vote or otherwise make a position known.

Democrats   **Republicans**
Independents

543. HR 4818. Fiscal 2005 Omnibus Appropriations Technical Corrections/Adoption. Young, R-Fla., motion to suspend the rules and adopt the concurrent resolution (H Con Res 528) that would make several changes to the conference report on the bill that would provide $388.4 billion in discretionary spending in fiscal 2005 for all federal departments and agencies whose fiscal 2005 spending bills have not been enacted. The resolution would delete a provision that would allow appropriators and their staff to view income tax returns as part of their oversight of IRS operations. Motion agreed to 381-0: R 206-0; D 174-0 (ND 126-0, SD 48-0); I 1-0. A two-thirds majority of those present and voting (254 in this case) is required for adoption under suspension of the rules. Dec. 6, 2004.

544. S 2845. Intelligence Overhaul/Conference Report. Adoption of the conference report on the bill that would reorganize 15 U.S. intelligence agencies and create a new director of national intelligence to oversee all U.S. intelligence activities and determine the intelligence budget. The director would be allowed to move no more than 5 percent of an agency's budget. The National Counterterrorism Center would serve as the primary organization for analyzing and integrating all U.S. intelligence pertaining to terrorism and counterterrorism. The measure would authorize approximately 10,000 additional border patrol agents over five years, and new programs and pilot projects to upgrade airport and airplane security. The FBI would be allowed to conduct surveillance and wiretaps on suspected terrorists who have no ties to any foreign country or entity. Adopted (thus sent to the Senate) 336-75: R 152-67; D 183-8 (ND 133-7, SD 50-1); I 1-0. A "yea" was a vote in support of the president's position. Dec. 7, 2004.

	543	544
ALABAMA		
1 *Bonner*	Y	Y
2 *Everett*	Y	N
3 *Rogers*	Y	Y
4 *Aderholt*	Y	N
5 Cramer	Y	Y
6 *Bachus*	Y	N
7 Davis	?	?
ALASKA		
AL *Young*	?	?
ARIZONA		
1 *Renzi*	Y	Y
2 *Franks*	Y	Y
3 *Shadegg*	Y	Y
4 Pastor	Y	Y
5 *Hayworth*	Y	N
6 *Flake*	Y	N
7 Grijalva	Y	Y
8 *Kolbe*	Y	Y
ARKANSAS		
1 Berry	Y	Y
2 Snyder	Y	Y
3 *Boozman*	Y	N
4 Ross	Y	Y
CALIFORNIA		
1 Thompson	Y	Y
2 *Herger*	Y	Y
3 *Ose*	Y	N
4 *Doolittle*	Y	Y
5 Matsui	Y	Y
6 Woolsey	Y	Y
7 Miller, George	Y	Y
8 Pelosi	Y	Y
9 Lee	Y	Y
10 Tauscher	Y	Y
11 *Pombo*	Y	N
12 Lantos	Y	Y
13 Stark	Y	Y
14 Eshoo	Y	Y
15 Honda	Y	Y
16 Lofgren	Y	Y
17 Farr	Y	Y
18 Cardoza	Y	Y
19 *Radanovich*	Y	N
20 Dooley	?	?
21 *Nunes*	Y	Y
22 *Thomas*	Y	Y
23 Capps	Y	Y
24 *Gallegly*	Y	N
25 *McKeon*	?	Y
26 *Dreier*	Y	Y
27 Sherman	Y	Y
28 Berman	Y	Y
29 Schiff	Y	Y
30 Waxman	Y	Y
31 Becerra	Y	Y
32 Solis	Y	Y
33 Watson	Y	Y
34 Roybal-Allard	Y	Y
35 Waters	Y	Y
36 Harman	Y	Y

	543	544
37 Millender-McD.	Y	Y
38 Napolitano	Y	Y
39 Sánchez, Linda	Y	Y
40 *Royce*	Y	N
41 *Lewis*	Y	Y
42 *Miller, Gary*	Y	N
43 Baca	?	Y
44 *Calvert*	Y	N
45 *Bono*	Y	Y
46 *Rohrabacher*	Y	N
47 Sanchez, Loretta	Y	Y
48 *Cox*	Y	Y
49 *Issa*	Y	N
50 *Cunningham*	Y	Y
51 Filner	Y	Y
52 *Hunter*	Y	Y
53 Davis	Y	Y
COLORADO		
1 DeGette	Y	Y
2 Udall	Y	Y
3 *McInnis*	?	N
4 *Musgrave*	Y	Y
5 *Hefley*	Y	N
6 *Tancredo*	Y	N
7 *Beauprez*	Y	Y
CONNECTICUT		
1 Larson	Y	Y
2 *Simmons*	Y	Y
3 DeLauro	+	Y
4 *Shays*	Y	Y
5 *Johnson*	Y	Y
DELAWARE		
AL *Castle*	Y	Y
FLORIDA		
1 *Miller, J.*	Y	Y
2 Boyd	Y	Y
3 Brown	Y	Y
4 *Crenshaw*	Y	Y
5 *Brown-Waite*	Y	N
6 *Stearns*	Y	Y
7 *Mica*	Y	Y
8 *Keller*	Y	Y
9 *Bilirakis*	Y	Y
10 *Young*	Y	Y
11 Davis	?	?
12 *Putnam*	Y	Y
13 *Harris*	Y	Y
14 Vacant		
15 *Weldon*	Y	N
16 *Foley*	Y	Y
17 Meek	Y	Y
18 *Ros-Lehtinen*	Y	Y
19 Wexler	Y	Y
20 Deutsch	Y	Y
21 *Diaz-Balart, L.*	Y	Y
22 *Shaw*	Y	Y
23 Hastings	?	?
24 *Feeney*	Y	Y
25 *Diaz-Balart, M.*	Y	Y
GEORGIA		
1 *Kingston*	Y	N
2 Bishop	Y	Y
3 Marshall	Y	Y
4 Majette	Y	Y
5 Lewis	Y	Y
6 *Isakson*	Y	Y
7 *Linder*	Y	Y
8 *Collins*	?	N
9 *Norwood*	?	?
10 *Deal*	Y	N
11 *Gingrey*	Y	N
12 *Burns*	Y	Y
13 Scott	Y	Y
HAWAII		
1 Abercrombie	?	?
2 Case	?	?
IDAHO		
1 *Otter*	Y	N
2 *Simpson*	Y	N
ILLINOIS		
1 Rush	?	Y
2 Jackson	Y	Y
3 Lipinski	?	?
4 Gutierrez	+	Y
5 Emanuel	Y	Y
6 *Hyde*	?	Y

ND Northern Democrats   SD Southern Democrats

		543	544
7	Davis	Y	Y
8	*Crane*	Y	N
9	Schakowsky	Y	Y
10	*Kirk*	Y	Y
11	*Weller*	Y	Y
12	Costello	Y	Y
13	*Biggert*	Y	Y
14	*Hastert*	Y	Y
15	*Johnson*	Y	Y
16	*Manzullo*	Y	N
17	Evans	Y	Y
18	*LaHood*	Y	N
19	*Shimkus*	Y	Y

INDIANA

		543	544
1	Visclosky	Y	Y
2	*Chocola*	Y	Y
3	*Souder*	Y	Y
4	*Buyer*	Y	Y
5	*Burton*	Y	Y
6	*Pence*	Y	Y
7	Carson	Y	Y
8	*Hostettler*	Y	N
9	Hill	Y	Y

IOWA

		543	544
1	*Nussle*	?	Y
2	*Leach*	Y	Y
3	Boswell	?	?
4	*Latham*	Y	Y
5	*King*	Y	N

KANSAS

		543	544
1	*Moran*	Y	Y
2	*Ryun*	Y	Y
3	Moore	Y	Y
4	*Tiahrt*	Y	Y

KENTUCKY

		543	544
1	*Whitfield*	Y	Y
2	*Lewis*	Y	N
3	*Northup*	Y	Y
4	*Lucas*	Y	?
5	*Rogers*	Y	Y
6	Chandler	Y	Y

LOUISIANA

		543	544
1	*Vitter*	?	Y
2	Jefferson	?	Y
3	*Tauzin*	Y	Y
4	*McCrery*	Y	Y
5	*Alexander*	Y	Y
6	*Baker*	Y	Y
7	John	Y	Y

MAINE

		543	544
1	Allen	Y	Y
2	Michaud	Y	Y

MARYLAND

		543	544
1	*Gilchrest*	Y	Y
2	Ruppersberger	Y	Y
3	Cardin	Y	Y
4	Wynn	Y	Y
5	Hoyer	Y	Y
6	*Bartlett*	Y	N
7	Cummings	?	Y
8	Van Hollen	Y	Y

MASSACHUSETTS

		543	544
1	Olver	Y	Y
2	Neal	?	Y
3	McGovern	Y	Y
4	Frank	Y	Y
5	Meehan	Y	Y
6	Tierney	Y	Y
7	Markey	Y	Y
8	Capuano	Y	Y
9	Lynch	Y	Y
10	Delahunt	?	Y

MICHIGAN

		543	544
1	Stupak	Y	Y
2	*Hoekstra*	Y	Y
3	*Ehlers*	Y	Y
4	*Camp*	Y	N
5	Kildee	Y	Y
6	*Upton*	Y	Y
7	*Smith*	Y	?
8	*Rogers*	Y	Y
9	*Knollenberg*	Y	Y
10	*Miller*	Y	Y
11	*McCotter*	Y	Y
12	Levin	Y	Y

		543	544
13	Kilpatrick	Y	Y
14	Conyers	Y	Y
15	Dingell	Y	Y

MINNESOTA

		543	544
1	*Gutknecht*	Y	N
2	*Kline*	Y	Y
3	*Ramstad*	Y	Y
4	McCollum	Y	Y
5	Sabo	Y	N
6	*Kennedy*	Y	Y
7	Peterson	Y	Y
8	Oberstar	Y	N

MISSISSIPPI

		543	544
1	*Wicker*	Y	Y
2	Thompson	Y	Y
3	*Pickering*	Y	Y
4	Taylor	Y	Y

MISSOURI

		543	544
1	Clay	Y	Y
2	*Akin*	Y	Y
3	Gephardt	Y	Y
4	Skelton	Y	Y
5	McCarthy	Y	Y
6	*Graves*	Y	Y
7	*Blunt*	Y	Y
8	*Emerson*	Y	Y
9	*Hulshof*	Y	Y

MONTANA

		543	544
AL	*Rehberg*	Y	N

NEBRASKA

		543	544
1	Vacant		
2	*Terry*	Y	Y
3	*Osborne*	Y	Y

NEVADA

		543	544
1	Berkley	Y	Y
2	*Gibbons*	Y	Y
3	*Porter*	Y	Y

NEW HAMPSHIRE

		543	544
1	*Bradley*	Y	Y
2	*Bass*	Y	Y

NEW JERSEY

		543	544
1	Andrews	Y	Y
2	*LoBiondo*	Y	Y
3	*Saxton*	Y	Y
4	*Smith*	Y	Y
5	*Garrett*	Y	Y
6	Pallone	?	Y
7	*Ferguson*	Y	Y
8	Pascrell	Y	Y
9	Rothman	Y	Y
10	Payne	Y	+
11	*Frelinghuysen*	Y	Y
12	Holt	Y	Y
13	Menendez	Y	Y

NEW MEXICO

		543	544
1	*Wilson*	?	Y
2	*Pearce*	Y	Y
3	Udall	Y	Y

NEW YORK

		543	544
1	Bishop	Y	Y
2	Israel	Y	Y
3	*King*	Y	Y
4	McCarthy	Y	Y
5	Ackerman	Y	Y
6	Meeks	Y	Y
7	Crowley	Y	Y
8	Nadler	Y	Y
9	Weiner	?	Y
10	Towns	?	Y
11	Owens	Y	Y
12	Velázquez	Y	Y
13	*Fossella*	Y	Y
14	Maloney	Y	Y
15	Rangel	Y	Y
16	Serrano	Y	Y
17	Engel	Y	Y
18	Lowey	Y	Y
19	*Kelly*	Y	Y
20	*Sweeney*	?	N
21	McNulty	Y	Y
22	Hinchey	Y	Y
23	*McHugh*	Y	Y
24	*Boehlert*	?	?
25	*Walsh*	Y	Y

		543	544
26	*Reynolds*	Y	Y
27	*Quinn*	Y	Y
28	Slaughter	Y	Y
29	*Houghton*	?	?

NORTH CAROLINA

		543	544
1	Butterfield	Y	Y
2	Etheridge	Y	Y
3	*Jones*	?	N
4	Price	Y	Y
5	*Burr*	Y	?
6	*Coble*	Y	N
7	McIntyre	Y	Y
8	*Hayes*	Y	Y
9	*Myrick*	Y	Y
10	*Ballenger*	?	?
11	*Taylor*	Y	N
12	Watt	Y	Y
13	Miller	Y	Y

NORTH DAKOTA

		543	544
AL	Pomeroy	Y	Y

OHIO

		543	544
1	*Chabot*	Y	N
2	*Portman*	Y	Y
3	*Turner*	Y	Y
4	*Oxley*	Y	Y
5	*Gillmor*	Y	Y
6	Strickland	Y	Y
7	*Hobson*	Y	Y
8	*Boehner*	Y	Y
9	Kaptur	Y	Y
10	Kucinich	Y	N
11	Jones	?	?
12	*Tiberi*	Y	Y
13	Brown	Y	Y
14	*LaTourette*	Y	Y
15	*Pryce*	Y	Y
16	*Regula*	Y	Y
17	Ryan	Y	Y
18	*Ney*	Y	Y

OKLAHOMA

		543	544
1	*Sullivan*	Y	N
2	Carson	?	Y
3	*Lucas*	Y	N
4	*Cole*	Y	Y
5	*Istook*	Y	N

OREGON

		543	544
1	Wu	Y	Y
2	*Walden*	Y	Y
3	Blumenauer	Y	Y
4	DeFazio	Y	Y
5	Hooley	Y	Y

PENNSYLVANIA

		543	544
1	Brady	Y	Y
2	Fattah	?	?
3	*English*	Y	Y
4	*Hart*	Y	Y
5	*Peterson*	Y	Y
6	*Gerlach*	Y	Y
7	*Weldon*	Y	Y
8	*Greenwood*	Y	Y
9	*Shuster, Bill*	Y	Y
10	*Sherwood*	Y	Y
11	Kanjorski	Y	Y
12	Murtha	?	N
13	Hoeffel	Y	Y
14	Doyle	Y	Y
15	*Toomey*	Y	Y
16	*Pitts*	Y	N
17	Holden	Y	Y
18	*Murphy*	Y	Y
19	*Platts*	Y	Y

RHODE ISLAND

		543	544
1	Kennedy	Y	Y
2	Langevin	Y	Y

SOUTH CAROLINA

		543	544
1	*Brown*	Y	Y
2	*Wilson*	Y	Y
3	*Barrett*	Y	N
4	*DeMint*	Y	Y
5	Spratt	Y	Y
6	Clyburn	Y	Y

SOUTH DAKOTA

		543	544
AL	Herseth	Y	Y

TENNESSEE

		543	544
1	*Jenkins*	Y	N
2	*Duncan*	Y	N
3	*Wamp*	Y	N
4	Davis	Y	Y
5	Cooper	Y	Y
6	Gordon	?	N
7	*Blackburn*	Y	N
8	Tanner	Y	Y
9	Ford	Y	Y

TEXAS

		543	544
1	Sandlin	Y	Y
2	Turner	Y	Y
3	*Johnson, Sam*	Y	N
4	*Hall*	Y	Y
5	*Hensarling*	Y	Y
6	*Barton*	Y	N
7	*Culberson*	Y	N
8	*Brady*	Y	Y
9	Lampson	Y	Y
10	Doggett	Y	Y
11	Edwards	Y	Y
12	*Granger*	?	Y
13	*Thornberry*	Y	Y
14	*Paul*	Y	N
15	Hinojosa	Y	Y
16	Reyes	?	Y
17	Stenholm	Y	Y
18	Jackson-Lee	Y	Y
19	*Neugebauer*	Y	N
20	Gonzalez	Y	Y
21	*Smith*	Y	N
22	*DeLay*	Y	Y
23	*Bonilla*	Y	Y
24	Frost	Y	Y
25	Bell	?	?
26	*Burgess*	Y	N
27	Ortiz	Y	Y
28	Rodriguez	Y	Y
29	Green	Y	Y
30	Johnson, E.B.	Y	Y
31	*Carter*	Y	Y
32	*Sessions*	Y	Y

UTAH

		543	544
1	*Bishop*	Y	N
2	Matheson	Y	Y
3	*Cannon*	?	?

VERMONT

		543	544
AL	*Sanders*	Y	Y

VIRGINIA

		543	544
1	*Davis, Jo Ann*	Y	N
2	*Schrock*	?	Y
3	Scott	Y	Y
4	*Forbes*	Y	N
5	*Goode*	Y	N
6	*Goodlatte*	Y	Y
7	*Cantor*	Y	Y
8	Moran	Y	Y
9	Boucher	Y	Y
10	*Wolf*	+	Y
11	*Davis, T.*	Y	Y

WASHINGTON

		543	544
1	Inslee	Y	Y
2	Larsen	?	Y
3	Baird	Y	Y
4	*Hastings*	?	Y
5	*Nethercutt*	?	Y
6	Dicks	?	Y
7	McDermott	Y	N
8	*Dunn*	Y	Y
9	Smith	Y	Y

WEST VIRGINIA

		543	544
1	Mollohan	Y	N
2	*Capito*	Y	Y
3	Rahall	?	?

WISCONSIN

		543	544
1	*Ryan*	Y	Y
2	Baldwin	Y	Y
3	Kind	?	Y
4	Kleczka	?	Y
5	*Sensenbrenner*	Y	Y
6	*Petri*	Y	Y
7	Obey	Y	N
8	*Green*	Y	N

WYOMING

		543	544
AL		Y	N

Southern states - Ala., Ark., Fla., Ga., Ky., La., Miss., N.C., Okla., S.C., Tenn., Texas, Va.

House Roll Call Votes
By Subject

House Votes

Appendix S

SENATE ROLL CALL VOTES

Senate Roll Call Votes By Bill Number

Senate Bills

S 15, S-23

S 150, S-19

S 1072, S-7

S 1248, S-22

S 1350, S-22

S 1637, S-10, S-15, S-17, S-20, S-21, S-22

S 1805, S-8, S-9, S-10

S 2061, S-8

S 2062, S-33

S 2207, S-17

S 2290, S-18

S 2329, S-18

S 2400, S-23, S-24, S-25, S-27, S-28, S-29, S-30, S-31, S-32

S 2677, S-35

S 2845, S-41, S-42, S-47

S 2986, S-45

S Con Res 95, S-11, S-12, S-13, S-14

S J Res 40, S-34

S Res 319, S-12

S Res 356, S-21

S Res 373, S-26

S Res 393, S-32

S Res 445, S-43, S-44

S Res 454, S-44

House Bills

H J Res 97, S-32

HR 4, S-16

HR 1047, S-46

HR 1308, S-40

HR 1997, S-15

HR 2673, S-4

HR 3104, S-23

HR 3108, S-5, S-6, S-17

HR 4520, S-34, S-44

HR 4567, S-36, S-37, S-38, S-39

HR 4613, S-32, S-35

HR 4755, S-40

HR 4759, S-34

HR 4818, S-46

HR 4837, S-40

	1	2	3
ALABAMA			
Shelby	Y	Y	Y
Sessions	Y	Y	Y
ALASKA			
Stevens	Y	Y	Y
Murkowski, L.	Y	Y	Y
ARIZONA			
McCain	N	N	N
Kyl	Y	Y	Y
ARKANSAS			
Lincoln	N	N	Y
Pryor	N	N	Y
CALIFORNIA			
Feinstein	N	Y	Y
Boxer	N	N	N
COLORADO			
Campbell	N	Y	Y
Allard	Y	Y	N
CONNECTICUT			
Dodd	N	N	Y
Lieberman	?	?	?
DELAWARE			
Biden	N	N	N
Carper	N	Y	Y
FLORIDA			
Graham	N	N	N
Nelson	N	N	Y
GEORGIA			
Miller	Y	Y	Y
Chambliss	?	?	?
HAWAII			
Inouye	?	Y	Y
Akaka	N	N	Y
IDAHO			
Craig	Y	Y	Y
Crapo	Y	Y	Y
ILLINOIS			
Fitzgerald	Y	Y	Y
Durbin	N	N	Y
INDIANA			
Lugar	Y	Y	Y
Bayh	N	N	N

	1	2	3
IOWA			
Grassley	Y	Y	Y
Harkin	N	Y	Y
KANSAS			
Brownback	Y	Y	Y
Roberts	Y	Y	Y
KENTUCKY			
McConnell	Y	Y	Y
Bunning	Y	Y	Y
LOUISIANA			
Breaux	N	Y	Y
Landrieu	N	Y	Y
MAINE			
Snowe	N	N	N
Collins	Y	Y	Y
MARYLAND			
Sarbanes	N	N	N
Mikulski	N	Y	Y
MASSACHUSETTS			
Kennedy	N	N	N
Kerry	-	-	-
MICHIGAN			
Levin	N	N	N
Stabenow	N	N	N
MINNESOTA			
Dayton	?	Y	N
Coleman	Y	Y	Y
MISSISSIPPI			
Cochran	Y	Y	Y
Lott	Y	Y	Y
MISSOURI			
Bond	Y	Y	Y
Talent	Y	Y	Y
MONTANA			
Burns	Y	Y	Y
Baucus	?	?	?
NEBRASKA			
Hagel	Y	?	?
Nelson	N	Y	Y
NEVADA			
Reid	N	Y	Y
Ensign	N	N	N

	1	2	3
NEW HAMPSHIRE			
Gregg	Y	Y	Y
Sununu	Y	Y	Y
NEW JERSEY			
Lautenberg	N	N	N
Corzine	N	N	N
NEW MEXICO			
Domenici	Y	?	+
Bingaman	N	Y	Y
NEW YORK			
Schumer	N	Y	Y
Clinton	N	N	N
NORTH CAROLINA			
Edwards	?	?	?
Dole	Y	Y	Y
NORTH DAKOTA			
Conrad	N	N	N
Dorgan	N	N	N
OHIO			
DeWine	Y	Y	Y
Voinovich	Y	Y	Y
OKLAHOMA			
Nickles	Y	Y	Y
Inhofe	Y	Y	Y
OREGON			
Wyden	N	N	N
Smith	Y	Y	Y
PENNSYLVANIA			
Specter	Y	Y	Y
Santorum	Y	Y	Y
RHODE ISLAND			
Reed	N	N	N
Chafee	Y	Y	Y
SOUTH CAROLINA			
Hollings	Y	Y	Y
Graham	Y	Y	Y
SOUTH DAKOTA			
Daschle	N	N	N
Johnson	N	N	N
TENNESSEE			
Frist	N	Y	Y
Alexander	Y	Y	Y

	1	2	3
TEXAS			
Hutchison	Y	Y	Y
Cornyn	Y	Y	Y
UTAH			
Hatch	Y	Y	Y
Bennett	Y	Y	Y
VERMONT			
Leahy	N	Y	N
Jeffords	N	N	N
VIRGINIA			
Warner	Y	Y	Y
Allen	Y	Y	Y
WASHINGTON			
Murray	Y	Y	Y
Cantwell	N	N	Y
WEST VIRGINIA			
Byrd	N	N	N
Rockefeller	N	N	N
WISCONSIN			
Kohl	N	N	N
Feingold	N	N	N
WYOMING			
Thomas	Y	Y	Y
Enzi	Y	Y	Y

Key

Y	Voted for (yea).
#	Paired for.
+	Announced for.
N	Voted against (nay).
X	Paired against.
–	Announced against.
P	Voted "present."
C	Voted "present" to avoid possible conflict of interest.
?	Did not vote or otherwise make a position known.

Democrats **Republicans**
Independents

ND Northern Democrats   SD Southern Democrats

Southern states - Ala., Ark., Fla., Ga., Ky., La., Miss., N.C., Okla., S.C., Tenn., Texas, Va.

1. HR 2673. Fiscal 2004 Omnibus Appropriations/Cloture. Motion to invoke cloture (thus limiting debate) on the conference report on the bill that would provide a total of $820 billion in fiscal 2004 spending, including $328.1 billion in discretionary spending, for all federal departments and agencies whose regular fiscal 2004 spending bills have not been enacted. Motion rejected 48-45: R 45-5; D 3-39 (ND 1-33, SD 2-6); I 0-1. Three-fifths of the total Senate (60) is required to invoke cloture. Jan. 20, 2004.

2. HR 2673. Fiscal 2004 Omnibus Appropriations/Cloture. Motion to invoke cloture (thus limiting debate) on the conference report on the bill that would provide a total of $820 billion in fiscal 2004 spending, including $328.1 billion in discretionary spending, for all federal departments and agencies whose regular fiscal 2004 spending bills have not been enacted. Motion agreed to 61-32: R 45-3; D 16-28 (ND 12-24, SD 4-4); I 0-1. Three-fifths of the total Senate (60) is required to invoke cloture. Jan. 22, 2004.

3. HR 2673. Fiscal 2004 Omnibus Appropriations/Conference Report. Adoption of the conference report on the bill that would provide a total of $820 billion in fiscal 2004, including $328.1 billion in discretionary spending, for all federal departments and agencies whose regular fiscal 2004 spending bills have not been enacted. Discretionary spending totals include $16.9 billion for the Agriculture Department, Food and Drug Administration, Commodity Futures Trading Commission and related agencies; $37.7 billion for the Commerce, Justice and State departments and judicial agencies; $545 million for the District of Columbia; $17.3 billion for foreign aid and export assistance; $139.8 billion for the Labor, Health and Human Services, and Education departments; $27.5 billion for the Transportation and Treasury departments and related independent agencies; and $91 billion for the Veterans Affairs, and Housing and Urban Development departments. Adopted (thus cleared for the president) 65-28: R 44-4; D 21-23 (ND 14-22, SD 7-1); I 0-1. Jan. 22, 2004.

	4	5	6
ALABAMA			
Shelby	Y	Y	Y
Sessions	N	N	Y
ALASKA			
Stevens	Y	Y	Y
Murkowski, L.	N	Y	Y
ARIZONA			
McCain	N	N	Y
Kyl	N	N	Y
ARKANSAS			
Lincoln	Y	Y	Y
Pryor	Y	Y	Y
CALIFORNIA			
Feinstein	Y	Y	Y
Boxer	Y	Y	Y
COLORADO			
Campbell	N	Y	Y
Allard	N	Y	Y
CONNECTICUT			
Dodd	Y	Y	Y
Lieberman	?	?	?
DELAWARE			
Biden	?	Y	Y
Carper	Y	Y	Y
FLORIDA			
Graham	Y	Y	Y
Nelson	Y	Y	Y
GEORGIA			
Miller	Y	Y	Y
Chambliss	?	?	?
HAWAII			
Inouye	Y	Y	Y
Akaka	Y	Y	Y
IDAHO			
Craig	N	Y	Y
Crapo	N	Y	Y
ILLINOIS			
Fitzgerald	N	N	Y
Durbin	Y	Y	Y
INDIANA			
Lugar	Y	Y	Y
Bayh	Y	Y	Y

	4	5	6
IOWA			
Grassley	Y	Y	Y
Harkin	Y	Y	Y
KANSAS			
Brownback	Y	Y	Y
Roberts	Y	Y	Y
KENTUCKY			
McConnell	Y	Y	Y
Bunning	N	Y	Y
LOUISIANA			
Breaux	Y	Y	Y
Landrieu	Y	Y	Y
MAINE			
Snowe	N	Y	Y
Collins	Y	Y	Y
MARYLAND			
Sarbanes	Y	Y	Y
Mikulski	?	Y	Y
MASSACHUSETTS			
Kennedy	Y	Y	Y
Kerry	+	+	+
MICHIGAN			
Levin	Y	Y	Y
Stabenow	Y	Y	Y
MINNESOTA			
Dayton	Y	Y	Y
Coleman	Y	Y	Y
MISSISSIPPI			
Cochran	Y	Y	Y
Lott	N	Y	Y
MISSOURI			
Bond	Y	Y	Y
Talent	Y	Y	Y
MONTANA			
Burns	N	Y	Y
Baucus	+	?	?
NEBRASKA			
Hagel	N	Y	Y
Nelson	Y	Y	Y
NEVADA			
Reid	N	Y	Y
Ensign	N	N	Y

	4	5	6
NEW HAMPSHIRE			
Gregg	Y	Y	Y
Sununu	N	Y	Y
NEW JERSEY			
Lautenberg	Y	Y	Y
Corzine	Y	Y	Y
NEW MEXICO			
Domenici	Y	Y	Y
Bingaman	Y	Y	Y
NEW YORK			
Schumer	Y	Y	Y
Clinton	Y	Y	Y
NORTH CAROLINA			
Edwards	?	?	?
Dole	N	Y	Y
NORTH DAKOTA			
Conrad	Y	Y	Y
Dorgan	Y	Y	Y
OHIO			
DeWine	Y	Y	Y
Voinovich	Y	Y	Y
OKLAHOMA			
Nickles	N	N	Y
Inhofe	–	N	Y
OREGON			
Wyden	Y	Y	Y
Smith	Y	Y	Y
PENNSYLVANIA			
Specter	Y	Y	Y
Santorum	N	Y	Y
RHODE ISLAND			
Reed	Y	Y	Y
Chafee	N	N	Y
SOUTH CAROLINA			
Hollings	Y	Y	Y
Graham	N	Y	Y
SOUTH DAKOTA			
Daschle	Y	Y	Y
Johnson	Y	Y	Y
TENNESSEE			
Frist	Y	Y	Y
Alexander	Y	Y	Y

Key

Y	Voted for (yea).
#	Paired for.
+	Announced for.
N	Voted against (nay).
X	Paired against.
–	Announced against.
P	Voted "present."
C	Voted "present" to avoid possible conflict of interest.
?	Did not vote or otherwise make a position known.

Democrats **Republicans** *Independents*

	4	5	6
TEXAS			
Hutchison	N	Y	Y
Cornyn	N	Y	Y
UTAH			
Hatch	Y	Y	Y
Bennett	Y	Y	Y
VERMONT			
Leahy	Y	Y	Y
Jeffords	Y	Y	Y
VIRGINIA			
Warner	Y	Y	Y
Allen	Y	Y	Y
WASHINGTON			
Murray	Y	Y	Y
Cantwell	Y	Y	Y
WEST VIRGINIA			
Byrd	Y	Y	Y
Rockefeller	Y	Y	Y
WISCONSIN			
Kohl	Y	Y	Y
Feingold	Y	Y	Y
WYOMING			
Thomas	N	N	Y
Enzi	Y	Y	Y

ND Northern Democrats   SD Southern Democrats

Southern states - Ala., Ark., Fla., Ga., Ky., La., Miss., N.C., Okla., S.C., Tenn., Texas, Va.

4. HR 3108. Pension Funding/PBGC Liability Limit. Rockefeller, D-W.Va., motion to table (kill) the Kyl, R-Ariz., amendment to the Grassley, R-Iowa, substitute amendment. The Kyl amendment would release the Pension Benefit Guaranty Corporation (PBGC) from obligations for any pension benefits accrued by workers at a company that terminates its pension plan while operating under a waiver from deficit reduction contribution requirements. If a plan fails more than two years after the relief period ends, the PBGC would insure the plan's full obligations. The Grassley substitute would temporarily replace the 30-year Treasury rate with a rate based on long-term corporate bonds for certain pension plan funding requirements. Motion agreed to 67-25: R 25-24; D 41-1 (ND 33-1, SD 8-0); I 1-0. Jan. 27, 2004.

5. HR 3108. Pension Funding/Passage. Passage of the bill that would temporarily replace the 30-year Treasury rate with a rate based on long-term corporate bonds for certain pension plan funding requirements. The bill also would relieve airlines and steelmakers of billions in "catch-up" contributions required of companies with chronically underfunded pensions. Companies in other industries also could apply for the relief. It also would allow Greyhound Lines Inc. to skip its deficit-reduction contribution for two years. Multi-employer plans would be allowed to delay accounting for two years of losses in their pension funds. Passed 86-9: R 41-9; D 44-0 (ND 36-0, SD 8-0); I 1-0. (Before passage, the Senate adopted the Grassley, R-Iowa., substitute amendment, as amended, by voice vote.) Jan. 28, 2004.

6. Sharpe Nomination/Confirmation. Confirmation of President Bush's nomination of Gary L. Sharpe of New York to be a judge for the U.S. District Court for the Northern District of New York. Confirmed 95-0: R 50-0; D 44-0 (ND 36-0, SD 8-0); I 1-0. A "yea" was a vote in support of the president's position. Jan. 28, 2004.

	7	8
ALABAMA		
Shelby	Y	Y
Sessions	Y	Y
ALASKA		
Stevens	?	Y
Murkowski, L.	?	Y
ARIZONA		
McCain	N	Y
Kyl	N	Y
ARKANSAS		
Lincoln	Y	Y
Pryor	Y	Y
CALIFORNIA		
Feinstein	Y	Y
Boxer	Y	Y
COLORADO		
Campbell	Y	Y
Allard	Y	Y
CONNECTICUT		
Dodd	N	Y
Lieberman	?	?
DELAWARE		
Biden	?	Y
Carper	Y	Y
FLORIDA		
Graham	N	Y
Nelson	Y	Y
GEORGIA		
Miller	Y	Y
Chambliss	Y	Y
HAWAII		
Inouye	Y	Y
Akaka	N	Y
IDAHO		
Craig	Y	Y
Crapo	Y	Y
ILLINOIS		
Fitzgerald	Y	Y
Durbin	+	Y
INDIANA		
Lugar	Y	Y
Bayh	Y	Y

	7	8
IOWA		
Grassley	Y	Y
Harkin	+	Y
KANSAS		
Brownback	Y	Y
Roberts	Y	Y
KENTUCKY		
McConnell	Y	Y
Bunning	Y	Y
LOUISIANA		
Breaux	Y	Y
Landrieu	Y	Y
MAINE		
Snowe	Y	Y
Collins	Y	Y
MARYLAND		
Sarbanes	Y	Y
Mikulski	Y	Y
MASSACHUSETTS		
Kennedy	Y	Y
Kerry	+	+
MICHIGAN		
Levin	Y	Y
Stabenow	Y	Y
MINNESOTA		
Dayton	Y	Y
Coleman	?	Y
MISSISSIPPI		
Cochran	Y	Y
Lott	Y	Y
MISSOURI		
Bond	Y	Y
Talent	Y	Y
MONTANA		
Burns	?	Y
Baucus	Y	Y
NEBRASKA		
Hagel	Y	Y
Nelson	Y	Y
NEVADA		
Reid	Y	Y
Ensign	?	Y

	7	8
NEW HAMPSHIRE		
Gregg	N	Y
Sununu	N	Y
NEW JERSEY		
Lautenberg	Y	Y
Corzine	Y	Y
NEW MEXICO		
Domenici	Y	Y
Bingaman	Y	Y
NEW YORK		
Schumer	Y	Y
Clinton	Y	Y
NORTH CAROLINA		
Edwards	?	?
Dole	Y	Y
NORTH DAKOTA		
Conrad	Y	Y
Dorgan	Y	Y
OHIO		
DeWine	Y	Y
Voinovich	Y	Y
OKLAHOMA		
Nickles	Y	Y
Inhofe	Y	Y
OREGON		
Wyden	Y	Y
Smith	Y	Y
PENNSYLVANIA		
Specter	N	Y
Santorum	Y	Y
RHODE ISLAND		
Reed	?	Y
Chafee	Y	Y
SOUTH CAROLINA		
Hollings	?	?
Graham	Y	Y
SOUTH DAKOTA		
Daschle	Y	Y
Johnson	Y	Y
TENNESSEE		
Frist	Y	Y
Alexander	Y	Y

	7	8
TEXAS		
Hutchison	N	Y
Cornyn	Y	Y
UTAH		
Hatch	Y	Y
Bennett	?	Y
VERMONT		
Leahy	Y	Y
Jeffords	Y	Y
VIRGINIA		
Warner	Y	Y
Allen	Y	Y
WASHINGTON		
Murray	Y	Y
Cantwell	Y	Y
WEST VIRGINIA		
Byrd	Y	Y
Rockefeller	Y	Y
WISCONSIN		
Kohl	N	Y
Feingold	N	Y
WYOMING		
Thomas	Y	Y
Enzi	Y	Y

Key

Y	Voted for (yea).
#	Paired for.
+	Announced for.
N	Voted against (nay).
X	Paired against.
–	Announced against.
P	Voted "present."
C	Voted "present" to avoid possible conflict of interest.
?	Did not vote or otherwise make a position known.

Democrats   **Republicans**
Independents

ND Northern Democrats   SD Southern Democrats

Southern states - Ala., Ark., Fla., Ga., Ky., La., Miss., N.C., Okla., S.C., Tenn., Texas, Va.

7. S 1072. Highway Funding/Cloture. Motion to invoke cloture (thus limiting debate) on the motion to proceed to consideration of the bill that would authorize $318 billion in federal aid for highways, highway safety programs and transit programs over six years. Motion agreed to 75-11: R 39-6; D 35-5 (ND 29-4, SD 6-1); I 1-0. Three-fifths of the total Senate (60) is required to invoke cloture. Feb. 2, 2004.

8. Filip Nomination/Confirmation. Confirmation of President Bush's nomination of Mark R. Filip of Illinois to be a judge for the U.S. District Court for the Northern District of Illinois. Confirmed 96-0: R 51-0; D 44-0 (ND 37-0, SD 7-0); I 1-0. A "yea" was a vote in support of the president's position. Feb. 4, 2004.

ALABAMA	9	10	11	12	13	14
Shelby	N	Y	N	Y	N	Y
Sessions	N	Y	N	N	N	N
ALASKA						
Stevens	Y	Y	N	Y	N	Y
Murkowski, L.	Y	Y	N	Y	N	Y
ARIZONA						
McCain	N	N	Y	N	Y	N
Kyl	Y	N	Y	N	Y	N
ARKANSAS						
Lincoln	N	Y	N	Y	N	Y
Pryor	N	Y	N	Y	N	Y
CALIFORNIA						
Feinstein	N	Y	Y	Y	N	Y
Boxer	N	Y	Y	Y	N	Y
COLORADO						
Campbell	Y	Y	Y	N	Y	N
Allard	Y	Y	N	N	Y	Y
CONNECTICUT						
Dodd	N	Y	N	Y	N	Y
Lieberman	N	Y	N	Y	N	Y
DELAWARE						
Biden	N	Y	N	Y	N	Y
Carper	N	Y	N	Y	N	Y
FLORIDA						
Graham	Y	?	?	?	N	N
Nelson	N	Y	Y	Y	N	Y
GEORGIA						
Miller	Y	Y	N	N	Y	N
Chambliss	Y	Y	N	N	Y	N
HAWAII						
Inouye	N	Y	N	Y	N	Y
Akaka	N	Y	N	Y	N	Y
IDAHO						
Craig	Y	Y	N	Y	N	Y
Crapo	Y	Y	N	Y	N	Y
ILLINOIS						
Fitzgerald	N	Y	N	N	N	Y
Durbin	N	Y	Y	Y	N	Y
INDIANA						
Lugar	Y	Y	Y	N	N	Y
Bayh	N	Y	N	Y	N	Y

IOWA	9	10	11	12	13	14
Grassley	Y	Y	N	Y	N	Y
Harkin	Y	Y	N	Y	N	Y
KANSAS						
Brownback	Y	Y	N	N	Y	N
Roberts	Y	Y	N	Y	N	Y
KENTUCKY						
McConnell	Y	Y	N	Y	N	N
Bunning	Y	Y	N	Y	N	Y
LOUISIANA						
Breaux	N	Y	N	Y	N	Y
Landrieu	N	Y	N	Y	N	Y
MAINE						
Snowe	Y	Y	N	Y	N	Y
Collins	Y	Y	N	Y	N	Y
MARYLAND						
Sarbanes	N	Y	N	Y	N	Y
Mikulski	N	Y	Y	Y	N	Y
MASSACHUSETTS						
Kennedy	N	Y	N	Y	N	Y
Kerry	−	+	−	+	−	+
MICHIGAN						
Levin	N	Y	N	Y	N	Y
Stabenow	N	Y	Y	Y	N	Y
MINNESOTA						
Dayton	N	Y	N	Y	N	Y
Coleman	Y	Y	N	Y	N	Y
MISSISSIPPI						
Cochran	Y	Y	N	Y	N	Y
Lott	Y	Y	N	Y	N	Y
MISSOURI						
Bond	Y	Y	N	Y	N	Y
Talent	Y	Y	N	Y	N	Y
MONTANA						
Burns	Y	Y	N	N	N	Y
Baucus	Y	Y	N	Y	N	Y
NEBRASKA						
Hagel	Y	Y	N	N	N	Y
Nelson	Y	Y	N	Y	N	+
NEVADA						
Reid	Y	Y	N	Y	N	Y
Ensign	Y	N	N	N	Y	N

NEW HAMPSHIRE	9	10	11	12	13	14
Gregg	Y	N	N	N	Y	N
Sununu	Y	N	Y	N	Y	N
NEW JERSEY						
Lautenberg	N	Y	N	Y	N	Y
Corzine	N	Y	N	Y	N	Y
NEW MEXICO						
Domenici	Y	Y	N	Y	N	Y
Bingaman	N	Y	N	Y	N	Y
NEW YORK						
Schumer	N	Y	N	Y	N	Y
Clinton	N	Y	N	Y	N	Y
NORTH CAROLINA						
Edwards	?	?	?	?	?	?
Dole	N	Y	N	Y	N	Y
NORTH DAKOTA						
Conrad	Y	Y	N	Y	N	Y
Dorgan	Y	Y	N	Y	N	Y
OHIO						
DeWine	N	Y	N	Y	N	Y
Voinovich	Y	Y	N	Y	N	Y
OKLAHOMA						
Nickles	Y	Y	N	N	Y	N
Inhofe	Y	Y	N	Y	N	Y
OREGON						
Wyden	N	Y	N	Y	N	Y
Smith	N	Y	N	Y	N	Y
PENNSYLVANIA						
Specter	Y	N	?	?	Y	N
Santorum	Y	N	?	N	Y	N
RHODE ISLAND						
Reed	N	Y	N	Y	N	Y
Chafee	N	Y	N	Y	N	Y
SOUTH CAROLINA						
Graham	Y	Y	N	Y	N	Y
Hollings	N	N	N	Y	N	Y
SOUTH DAKOTA						
Johnson	Y	Y	N	Y	N	Y
Daschle	Y	Y	N	Y	N	Y
TENNESSEE						
Frist	N	Y	N	Y	N	Y
Alexander	Y	Y	N	N	Y	N

TEXAS	9	10	11	12	13	14
Hutchison	Y	N	Y	N	Y	N
Cornyn	Y	Y	Y	Y	N	Y
UTAH						
Hatch	Y	Y	N	Y	Y	Y
Bennett	Y	Y	N	Y	Y	Y
VERMONT						
Leahy	Y	Y	N	Y	N	Y
Jeffords	Y	Y	N	Y	N	Y
VIRGINIA						
Warner	N	Y	N	Y	N	Y
Allen	Y	Y	N	Y	N	Y
WASHINGTON						
Murray	N	Y	N	Y	N	Y
Cantwell	N	Y	N	Y	N	Y
WEST VIRGINIA						
Byrd	Y	Y	N	Y	N	Y
Rockefeller	Y	Y	N	Y	N	Y
WISCONSIN						
Kohl	Y	N	Y	N	N	N
Feingold	Y	N	Y	N	Y	N
WYOMING						
Thomas	Y	Y	N	Y	N	Y
Enzi	Y	Y	N	N	Y	Y

ND Northern Democrats   SD Southern Democrats

Southern states - Ala., Ark., Fla., Ga., Ky., La., Miss., N.C., Okla., S.C., Tenn., Texas, Va.

9. S 1072. Highway Funding/Seat Belt Use. Inhofe, R-Okla., motion to table (kill) the Warner, R-Va., amendment to the Inhofe substitute amendment. The Warner amendment would require states to prove a 90 percent seat belt use rate or enact primary seat belt laws by fiscal 2006. Failure would affect the availability of a state's highway construction funds. The substitute would authorize $318 billion in federal aid for highways, highway safety programs and transit programs over six years. Motion agreed to 57-41: R 41-10; D 15-31 (ND 13-25, SD 2-6); I 1-0. Feb. 11, 2004.

10. S 1072. Highway Funding/Cloture. Motion to invoke cloture (thus limiting debate) on the Inhofe, R-Okla., substitute amendment. The substitute would authorize $318 billion in federal aid for highways, highway safety programs and transit programs over six years. Motion agreed to 86-11: R 43-8; D 42-3 (ND 36-2, SD 6-1); I 1-0. Three-fifths of the total Senate (60) is required to invoke cloture. Feb. 12, 2004.

11. S 1072. Highway Funding/Formula Funding. Hutchison, R-Texas, amendment to the Inhofe, R-Okla., substitute amendment. The Hutchison amendment would allocate $9.25 billion for the Infrastructure Performance and Maintenance Program to increase formula highway funding for all states that have a funding floor of a 90.5 percent rate-of-return in fiscal 2004. The amendment would provide that the rate-of-return would increase incrementally until it reached 95 percent in fiscal 2009. Rejected 17-78: R 7-42; D 10-35 (ND 9-29, SD 1-6); I 0-1. Feb. 12, 2004.

12. S 1072. Highway Funding/Budgetary Points of Order. Bond, R-Mo., motion to waive the Budget Act with respect to all points of order against the Inhofe, R-Okla., substitute amendment that would authorize $318 billion in federal aid for highways, highway safety programs and transit programs over six years. Motion agreed to 72-24: R 30-20; D 41-4 (ND 35-3, SD 6-1); I 1-0. A three-fifths majority vote (60) of the total Senate is required to waive the Budget Act. Feb. 12, 2004.

13. S 1072. Highway Funding/Total Cost Reduction. Kyl, R-Ariz., amendment to the Inhofe, R-Okla., substitute amendment. The Kyl amendment would reduce the total cost of the surface transportation measure from $318 billion to $256 billion, to match the president's fiscal 2005 budget request. Rejected 20-78: R 18-33; D 2-44 (ND 1-37, SD 1-7); I 0-1. A "yea" was a vote in support of the president's position. Feb. 12, 2004.

14. S 1072. Highway Funding/Passage. Passage of the bill that would authorize $318.9 billion in federal aid for highways, highway safety programs and transit programs over six years. The total would include $255 billion for highways, $56.5 billion for transit and $6 billion for safety programs. The bill would ensure that states receive a 95 percent return on their Highway Trust Fund contributions by 2009. Passed 76-21: R 34-17; D 41-4 (ND 35-2, SD 6-2); I 1-0. (Before passage, the Senate adopted the Inhofe, R-Okla., substitute amendment, as amended, by voice vote.) A "nay" was a vote in support of the president's position. Feb. 12, 2004.

ALABAMA	15	16	17	18	19	20	21	22
Shelby	N	Y	N	N	Y	N	Y	N
Sessions	Y	Y	N	N	Y	N	Y	N
ALASKA								
Stevens	Y	Y	Y	N	Y	N	Y	N
Murkowski, L.	Y	Y	Y	Y	?	?	?	?
ARIZONA								
McCain	Y	Y	Y	Y	Y	N	Y	N
Kyl	Y	Y	N	N	Y	N	Y	N
ARKANSAS								
Lincoln	N	Y	Y	Y	Y	N	Y	N
Pryor	N	Y	Y	Y	Y	N	Y	N
CALIFORNIA								
Feinstein	N	N	Y	Y	N	Y	N	Y
Boxer	?	N	Y	Y	N	Y	N	Y
COLORADO								
Campbell	Y	Y	?	?	?	?	?	?
Allard	Y	Y	N	N	Y	N	Y	N
CONNECTICUT								
Dodd	N	N	Y	Y	N	Y	N	Y
Lieberman	N	Y	Y	Y	N	Y	N	Y
DELAWARE								
Biden	N	N	Y	Y	N	Y	N	Y
Carper	N	Y	Y	Y	N	Y	N	Y
FLORIDA								
Graham	N	N	Y	Y	N	Y	N	Y
Nelson	N	Y	Y	Y	N	Y	N	Y
GEORGIA								
Miller	?	?	N	N	Y	N	Y	N
Chambliss	Y	Y	N	N	Y	N	Y	N
HAWAII								
Inouye	N	N	Y	Y	N	Y	N	Y
Akaka	N	N	Y	Y	N	Y	N	Y
IDAHO								
Craig	Y	Y	N	N	Y	N	Y	N
Crapo	N	Y	N	N	Y	N	Y	N
ILLINOIS								
Fitzgerald	Y	Y	Y	N	N	N	N	N
Durbin	N	N	Y	Y	N	Y	N	Y
INDIANA								
Lugar	Y	Y	Y	N	Y	N	Y	N
Bayh	N	Y	Y	Y	Y	Y	Y	Y

IOWA	15	16	17	18	19	20	21	22
Grassley	Y	Y	Y	N	Y	N	Y	N
Harkin	N	N	Y	Y	N	Y	N	Y
KANSAS								
Brownback	Y	Y	Y	N	Y	N	Y	N
Roberts	Y	Y	Y	N	Y	N	Y	N
KENTUCKY								
McConnell	Y	Y	Y	N	Y	N	Y	N
Bunning	Y	Y	N	N	Y	N	Y	N
LOUISIANA								
Breaux	N	Y	Y	Y	Y	N	Y	N
Landrieu	N	Y	Y	Y	Y	N	Y	N
MAINE								
Snowe	Y	Y	Y	Y	Y	N	Y	N
Collins	Y	Y	Y	Y	Y	N	Y	N
MARYLAND								
Sarbanes	N	N	Y	Y	N	Y	N	Y
Mikulski	N	N	Y	Y	N	Y	N	Y
MASSACHUSETTS								
Kennedy	N	N	Y	Y	N	Y	?	?
Kerry	−	−	+	+	−	+	−	+
MICHIGAN								
Levin	N	N	Y	Y	N	Y	N	Y
Stabenow	N	Y	Y	Y	N	Y	N	Y
MINNESOTA								
Dayton	N	Y	Y	Y	N	Y	Y	Y
Coleman	Y	Y	Y	N	Y	N	Y	N
MISSISSIPPI								
Cochran	Y	Y	N	N	Y	N	Y	N
Lott	Y	Y	N	N	Y	N	Y	N
MISSOURI								
Bond	Y	Y	N	N	Y	N	Y	N
Talent	Y	Y	N	N	Y	N	Y	N
MONTANA								
Burns	Y	Y	N	N	Y	N	Y	N
Baucus	N	Y	Y	Y	Y	N	Y	N
NEBRASKA								
Hagel	Y	Y	Y	N	Y	N	Y	N
Nelson	N	Y	Y	Y	N	Y	N	Y
NEVADA								
Reid	N	Y	Y	Y	N	Y	N	Y
Ensign	Y	Y	N	N	Y	N	Y	N

NEW HAMPSHIRE	15	16	17	18	19	20	21	22
Gregg	Y	Y	Y	N	Y	N	Y	N
Sununu	Y	Y	N	N	Y	N	Y	N
NEW JERSEY								
Lautenberg	N	N	Y	Y	N	Y	N	Y
Corzine	?	N	Y	Y	N	Y	N	Y
NEW MEXICO								
Domenici	Y	Y	Y	Y	N	Y	?	?
Bingaman	N	Y	Y	Y	N	Y	N	Y
NEW YORK								
Schumer	N	N	Y	Y	N	Y	N	Y
Clinton	N	N	Y	Y	N	Y	N	Y
NORTH CAROLINA								
Edwards	?	?	?	?	?	?	?	?
Dole	Y	Y	N	N	Y	N	Y	N
NORTH DAKOTA								
Conrad	N	Y	Y	Y	N	Y	Y	Y
Dorgan	N	Y	Y	Y	Y	Y	N	Y
OHIO								
DeWine	Y	Y	Y	N	Y	N	Y	N
Voinovich	Y	Y	Y	Y	Y	N	Y	N
OKLAHOMA								
Nickles	Y	Y	N	N	Y	N	Y	N
Inhofe	Y	Y	N	N	Y	N	Y	N
OREGON								
Wyden	N	N	Y	Y	N	Y	N	Y
Smith	Y	Y	Y	N	Y	N	Y	N
PENNSYLVANIA								
Specter	Y	Y	N	Y	N	Y	N	Y
Santorum	Y	Y	Y	N	Y	N	Y	N
RHODE ISLAND								
Reed	N	N	Y	Y	N	Y	N	Y
Chafee	Y	Y	Y	Y	N	Y	N	Y
SOUTH CAROLINA								
Hollings	N	N	Y	Y	N	Y	N	Y
Graham	N	Y	N	N	Y	N	Y	N
SOUTH DAKOTA								
Daschle	N	Y	Y	Y	Y	Y	Y	Y
Johnson	−	Y	N	Y	N	Y	N	Y
TENNESSEE								
Frist	Y	Y	Y	N	Y	N	Y	N
Alexander	Y	Y	N	Y	N	Y	N	Y

Key

Y	Voted for (yea).
#	Paired for.
+	Announced for.
N	Voted against (nay).
X	Paired against.
−	Announced against.
P	Voted "present."
C	Voted "present" to avoid possible conflict of interest.
?	Did not vote or otherwise make a position known.

Democrats   ***Republicans***
Independents

TEXAS	15	16	17	18	19	20	21	22
Hutchison	Y	Y	Y	N	Y	N	Y	N
Cornyn	Y	Y	N	N	Y	N	Y	N
UTAH								
Hatch	Y	Y	N	N	Y	N	Y	N
Bennett	?	Y	Y	N	Y	N	Y	N
VERMONT								
Leahy	N	Y	Y	Y	N	Y	N	Y
Jeffords	N	Y	Y	Y	N	Y	N	Y
VIRGINIA								
Warner	Y	Y	N	Y	N	Y	N	Y
Allen	Y	Y	N	N	Y	N	Y	N
WASHINGTON								
Murray	N	N	Y	Y	N	Y	N	Y
Cantwell	N	N	Y	Y	N	Y	N	Y
WEST VIRGINIA								
Byrd	Y	Y	Y	Y	N	Y	N	Y
Rockefeller	N	Y	Y	Y	Y	Y	Y	N
WISCONSIN								
Kohl	N	Y	Y	Y	N	Y	N	Y
Feingold	N	Y	Y	Y	N	Y	N	Y
WYOMING								
Thomas	Y	Y	N	N	Y	N	Y	N
Enzi	Y	Y	N	N	Y	N	Y	N

ND Northern Democrats   SD Southern Democrats

Southern states - Ala., Ark., Fla., Ga., Ky., La., Miss., N.C., Okla., S.C., Tenn., Texas, Va.

15. S 2061. Medical Malpractice/Cloture. Motion to invoke cloture (thus limiting debate) on the motion to proceed to consideration of the bill that would place caps on damage awards in medical malpractice lawsuits against obstetricians and gynecologists. Motion rejected 48-45: R 47-3; D 1-41 (ND 1-34, SD 0-7); I 0-1. Three-fifths of the total Senate (60) is required to invoke cloture. A "yea" was a vote in support of the president's position. Feb. 24, 2004.

16. S 1805. Gun Liability/Cloture. Motion to invoke cloture (thus limiting debate) on the motion to proceed to consideration of the bill that would bar certain civil lawsuits against manufacturers, distributors, dealers and importers of firearms and ammunition, principally those lawsuits aimed at making them liable for gun violence. Motion agreed to 75-22: R 50-1; D 24-21 (ND 19-19, SD 5-2); I 1-0. Three-fifths of the total Senate (60) is required to invoke cloture. Feb. 25, 2004.

17. S 1805. Gun Liability/Gun Safety Devices. Boxer, D-Calif., amendment, as amended, to prohibit the sale or transfer of handguns by a licensed manufacturer, importer or dealer unless a secure gun storage or safety device is provided for each handgun. It would exempt gun transfers to U.S. or state government agencies and law enforcement officials. It would impose penalties of up to $2,500 and license suspension or revocation for manufacturers, dealers or importers who sell a handgun without such a device. Adopted 70-27: R 25-25; D 44-2 (ND 37-1, SD 7-1); I 1-0. Feb. 26, 2004.

18. S 1805. Gun Liability/Temporary Unemployment Compensation. Cantwell, D-Wash., motion to waive the Budget Act with respect to the Nickles, R-Okla., point of order against the Cantwell amendment that would extend for six months, from Dec. 31, 2003, to June 30, 2004, the federal program to provide an additional 13 weeks of unemployment benefits for people who have exhausted their state jobless benefits. Motion rejected 58-39: R 12-38; D 45-1 (ND 38-0, SD 7-1); I 1-0. A three-fifths majority vote (60) of the total Senate is required to waive the Budget Act. Feb. 26, 2004.

19. S 1805. Gun Liability/Sniper Victim Lawsuits. Frist, R-Tenn., amendment that would allow lawsuits involving a shooting victim of John Allen Muhammad or Lee Boyd Malvo to proceed as long as the lawsuit qualifies for an exemption under the provisions of the underlying bill. Adopted 59-37: R 45-4; D 14-32 (ND 8-30, SD 6-2); I 0-1. Feb. 26, 2004.

20. S 1805. Gun Liability/Sniper Victim Lawsuits. Mikulski, D-Md., amendment that would create a specific exemption in the underlying bill to permit lawsuits involving a shooting victim of John Allen Muhammad or Lee Boyd Malvo. Rejected 40-56: R 3-46; D 36-10 (ND 33-5, SD 3-5); I 1-0. Feb. 26, 2004.

21. S 1805. Gun Liability/Law Enforcement Lawsuits. Frist, R-Tenn., amendment that would clarify that an officer or employee of any federal, state or local law enforcement agency could recover damages authorized under federal or state law in a civil action as long as the lawsuit qualifies for an exemption under the provisions of the underlying bill. Adopted 60-34: R 44-4; D 16-29 (ND 10-27, SD 6-2); I 0-1. Feb. 26, 2004.

22. S 1805. Gun Liability/Law Enforcement Lawsuits. Corzine, D-N.J., amendment that would clarify that none of the bill's provisions would prohibit an officer or employee of any federal, state or local law enforcement agency from recovering damages authorized under federal or state law in a civil action. Rejected 38-56: R 3-45; D 34-11 (ND 31-6, SD 3-5); I 1-0. Feb. 26, 2004.

	23	24	25	26	27
ALABAMA					
Shelby	N	N	N	Y	Y
Sessions	N	N	N	Y	Y
ALASKA					
Stevens	N	N	N	Y	Y
Murkowski, L.	?	N	N	Y	Y
ARIZONA					
McCain	?	N	Y	Y	Y
Kyl	N	N	N	Y	Y
ARKANSAS					
Lincoln	N	Y	Y	Y	Y
Pryor	N	Y	Y	Y	Y
CALIFORNIA					
Feinstein	Y	Y	Y	Y	Y
Boxer	?	Y	Y	Y	Y
COLORADO					
Campbell	N	N	N	Y	Y
Allard	N	N	N	Y	Y
CONNECTICUT					
Dodd	Y	Y	Y	N	Y
Lieberman	Y	Y	Y	Y	Y
DELAWARE					
Biden	+	Y	Y	Y	Y
Carper	Y	Y	Y	Y	N
FLORIDA					
Graham	?	Y	Y	Y	Y
Nelson	Y	Y	Y	Y	Y
GEORGIA					
Miller	N	N	N	Y	Y
Chambliss	N	N	N	Y	Y
HAWAII					
Inouye	Y	Y	Y	N	Y
Akaka	?	Y	Y	N	N
IDAHO					
Craig	N	N	N	Y	Y
Crapo	N	N	N	Y	Y
ILLINOIS					
Fitzgerald	Y	Y	Y	N	Y
Durbin	Y	Y	Y	N	Y
INDIANA					
Lugar	N	Y	Y	Y	Y
Bayh	N	Y	Y	Y	Y

	23	24	25	26	27
IOWA					
Grassley	N	N	N	Y	Y
Harkin	Y	Y	Y	Y	Y
KANSAS					
Brownback	N	N	N	Y	Y
Roberts	N	N	N	Y	Y
KENTUCKY					
McConnell	N	N	N	Y	Y
Bunning	N	N	N	Y	Y
LOUISIANA					
Breaux	N	Y	Y	Y	Y
Landrieu	N	N	Y	Y	Y
MAINE					
Snowe	N	Y	N	Y	Y
Collins	N	Y	N	Y	Y
MARYLAND					
Sarbanes	Y	Y	Y	N	N
Mikulski	Y	Y	Y	Y	Y
MASSACHUSETTS					
Kennedy	?	Y	Y	N	N
Kerry	+	Y	Y	Y	Y
MICHIGAN					
Levin	Y	Y	Y	Y	N
Stabenow	Y	Y	Y	Y	Y
MINNESOTA					
Dayton	N	Y	Y	Y	Y
Coleman	N	N	N	Y	Y
MISSISSIPPI					
Cochran	N	N	N	Y	Y
Lott	N	N	N	Y	Y
MISSOURI					
Bond	N	N	N	Y	Y
Talent	N	N	N	Y	Y
MONTANA					
Burns	N	N	N	Y	Y
Baucus	N	N	N	Y	Y
NEBRASKA					
Hagel	N	N	Y	Y	Y
Nelson	N	N	N	Y	Y
NEVADA					
Reid	N	N	Y	Y	Y
Ensign	N	N	N	Y	Y

	23	24	25	26	27
NEW HAMPSHIRE					
Gregg	N	Y	N	Y	Y
Sununu	N	N	N	Y	Y
NEW JERSEY					
Lautenberg	?	Y	Y	N	N
Corzine	?	Y	Y	Y	N
NEW MEXICO					
Domenici	N	N	N	Y	?
Bingaman	Y	Y	Y	Y	Y
NEW YORK					
Schumer	Y	Y	Y	Y	Y
Clinton	Y	Y	Y	Y	Y
NORTH CAROLINA					
Edwards	?	Y	Y	Y	?
Dole	N	N	N	Y	Y
NORTH DAKOTA					
Conrad	N	Y	Y	Y	Y
Dorgan	N	Y	Y	Y	Y
OHIO					
DeWine	Y	Y	Y	Y	Y
Voinovich	?	Y	Y	Y	Y
OKLAHOMA					
Nickles	N	N	N	Y	Y
Inhofe	N	N	N	Y	Y
OREGON					
Wyden	Y	Y	Y	Y	N
Smith	N	Y	N	Y	Y
PENNSYLVANIA					
Specter	N	N	N	Y	Y
Santorum	N	N	N	Y	Y
RHODE ISLAND					
Reed	Y	Y	Y	Y	Y
Chafee	Y	Y	Y	Y	Y
SOUTH CAROLINA					
Hollings	Y	Y	Y	Y	N
Graham	?	N	N	Y	Y
SOUTH DAKOTA					
Daschle	N	Y	Y	Y	Y
Johnson	N	?	?	?	?
TENNESSEE					
Frist	N	N	N	Y	Y
Alexander	N	N	N	Y	Y

	23	24	25	26	27
TEXAS					
Hutchison	N	N	N	Y	Y
Cornyn	N	N	N	Y	Y
UTAH					
Hatch	N	N	N	Y	Y
Bennett	N	N	N	Y	Y
VERMONT					
Leahy	Y	Y	Y	Y	Y
Jeffords	N	Y	Y	Y	Y
VIRGINIA					
Warner	Y	Y	Y	Y	Y
Allen	N	N	N	Y	Y
WASHINGTON					
Murray	Y	Y	Y	Y	Y
Cantwell	Y	Y	Y	Y	N
WEST VIRGINIA					
Byrd	Y	Y	Y	Y	Y
Rockefeller	N	Y	Y	Y	Y
WISCONSIN					
Kohl	Y	Y	Y	Y	Y
Feingold	Y	N	Y	N	Y
WYOMING					
Thomas	N	N	N	Y	Y
Enzi	N	N	N	Y	Y

ND Northern Democrats   SD Southern Democrats

Southern states - Ala., Ark., Fla., Ga., Ky., La., Miss., N.C., Okla., S.C., Tenn., Texas, Va.

23. S 1805. Gun Liability/Foreseeable Injury Liability. Bingaman, D-N.M., amendment that would clarify that a manufacturer or seller of a firearm would be liable for foreseeable injuries to consumers who purchase a firearm. It would modify the definition of reasonably foreseeable in the bill to mean "the reasonable anticipation that harm or injury is likely to result." Rejected 28-59: R 4-43; D 24-15 (ND 22-10, SD 2-5); I 0-1. March 1, 2004.

24. S 1805. Gun Liability/Assault Weapons Ban. Feinstein, D-Calif., amendment that would provide a 10-year reauthorization of the assault weapons ban set to expire in September 2004. Adopted 52-47: R 10-41; D 41-6 (ND 34-4, SD 7-2); I 1-0. March 2, 2004.

25. S 1805. Gun Liability/Gun Show Checks. McCain, R-Ariz., amendment that would require criminal background checks on all firearm transactions at gun shows where at least 75 guns are sold. Exemptions would be provided for dealers selling guns from their homes as well as members-only gun swaps and meets conducted by nonprofit hunting clubs. Adopted 53-46: R 8-43; D 44-3 (ND 36-2, SD 8-1); I 1-0. March 2, 2004.

26. S 1805. Gun Liability/Concealed Handguns. Campbell, R-Colo., amendment that would exempt off-duty and retired law enforcement officers from state laws that prohibit the carrying of concealed handguns. Adopted 91-8: R 50-1; D 40-7 (ND 31-7, SD 9-0); I 1-0. March 2, 2004.

27. S 1805. Gun Liability/Armor-Piercing Ammunition. Frist, R-Tenn., amendment that would require the attorney general to commission a study to determine if a uniform standard for the testing of projectiles against body armor is feasible. It also would increase the penalties for violent or drug trafficking crimes in which the perpetrator uses or possesses armor-piercing ammunition. If death resulted from the use of such ammunition, a person could be imprisoned up to life or face the death penalty. Adopted 85-12: R 50-0; D 34-12 (ND 27-11, SD 7-1); I 1-0. March 2, 2004.

	28	29	30	31	32
ALABAMA					
Shelby	N	Y	N	Y	Y
Sessions	N	Y	N	Y	Y
ALASKA					
Stevens	N	Y	N	Y	N
Murkowski, L.	N	Y	N	Y	Y
ARIZONA					
McCain	N	Y	Y	Y	N
Kyl	N	Y	N	Y	N
ARKANSAS					
Lincoln	N	Y	Y	Y	Y
Pryor	N	Y	Y	Y	Y
CALIFORNIA					
Feinstein	Y	N	N	Y	Y
Boxer	Y	N	N	Y	Y
COLORADO					
Campbell	N	Y	N	Y	N
Allard	N	Y	N	Y	N
CONNECTICUT					
Dodd	Y	N	N	Y	Y
Lieberman	Y	N	Y	Y	Y
DELAWARE					
Biden	Y	N	N	?	Y
Carper	Y	N	N	Y	Y
FLORIDA					
Graham	Y	N	N	?	Y
Nelson	Y	N	N	?	Y
GEORGIA					
Miller	N	Y	N	Y	Y
Chambliss	N	Y	N	Y	N
HAWAII					
Inouye	Y	N	N	Y	Y
Akaka	Y	N	N	Y	Y
IDAHO					
Craig	N	Y	N	Y	N
Crapo	N	Y	N	Y	N
ILLINOIS					
Fitzgerald	N	N	N	Y	N
Durbin	Y	N	N	Y	Y
INDIANA					
Lugar	N	N	Y	Y	N
Bayh	Y	N	N	Y	Y

	28	29	30	31	32
IOWA					
Grassley	N	Y	N	Y	Y
Harkin	Y	N	N	Y	Y
KANSAS					
Brownback	N	Y	N	Y	N
Roberts	N	Y	N	Y	N
KENTUCKY					
McConnell	N	Y	N	Y	Y
Bunning	N	Y	N	Y	Y
LOUISIANA					
Breaux	N	Y	Y	?	?
Landrieu	N	Y	N	Y	Y
MAINE					
Snowe	N	Y	N	Y	Y
Collins	N	Y	N	Y	Y
MARYLAND					
Sarbanes	Y	N	N	Y	Y
Mikulski	Y	N	N	Y	Y
MASSACHUSETTS					
Kennedy	Y	N	N	Y	Y
Kerry	Y	N	N	+	+
MICHIGAN					
Levin	Y	N	N	Y	Y
Stabenow	Y	N	N	Y	Y
MINNESOTA					
Dayton	Y	N	N	Y	Y
Coleman	N	Y	N	Y	Y
MISSISSIPPI					
Cochran	N	Y	N	Y	N
Lott	N	Y	N	Y	N
MISSOURI					
Bond	N	Y	N	Y	Y
Talent	N	Y	N	Y	Y
MONTANA					
Burns	N	Y	N	Y	N
Baucus	N	Y	N	Y	Y
NEBRASKA					
Hagel	N	Y	N	Y	N
Nelson	N	Y	N	Y	Y
NEVADA					
Reid	N	Y	N	Y	Y
Ensign	N	Y	N	Y	Y

	28	29	30	31	32
NEW HAMPSHIRE					
Gregg	N	Y	N	Y	N
Sununu	N	Y	N	Y	N
NEW JERSEY					
Lautenberg	Y	N	N	Y	Y
Corzine	Y	N	N	Y	Y
NEW MEXICO					
Domenici	?	?	N	Y	Y
Bingaman	N	N	N	Y	Y
NEW YORK					
Schumer	Y	N	N	Y	Y
Clinton	Y	N	N	Y	Y
NORTH CAROLINA					
Edwards	?	?	?	?	?
Dole	N	Y	N	Y	Y
NORTH DAKOTA					
Conrad	N	N	N	Y	Y
Dorgan	N	Y	N	Y	Y
OHIO					
DeWine	N	N	N	Y	Y
Voinovich	N	Y	Y	Y	Y
OKLAHOMA					
Nickles	N	Y	N	Y	N
Inhofe	N	Y	N	Y	Y
OREGON					
Wyden	Y	N	N	Y	Y
Smith	N	Y	N	Y	Y
PENNSYLVANIA					
Specter	N	Y	N	Y	Y
Santorum	N	Y	N	Y	Y
RHODE ISLAND					
Reed	Y	N	N	Y	Y
Chafee	Y	N	N	Y	Y
SOUTH CAROLINA					
Hollings	Y	N	N	Y	Y
Graham	N	Y	N	Y	Y
SOUTH DAKOTA					
Daschle	N	Y	Y	Y	Y
Johnson	?	?	?	+	?
TENNESSEE					
Alexander	N	Y	N	Y	N
Frist	N	Y	N	Y	Y

	28	29	30	31	32
TEXAS					
Hutchison	N	Y	N	Y	Y
Cornyn	N	Y	N	Y	N
UTAH					
Hatch	N	Y	N	Y	N
Bennett	N	Y	N	Y	N
VERMONT					
Leahy	N	N	N	Y	Y
Jeffords	N	N	N	Y	Y
VIRGINIA					
Warner	N	N	N	Y	N
Allen	N	Y	N	Y	Y
WASHINGTON					
Murray	Y	N	N	Y	Y
Cantwell	Y	N	N	Y	Y
WEST VIRGINIA					
Byrd	Y	N	N	Y	Y
Rockefeller	Y	Y	N	Y	Y
WISCONSIN					
Kohl	Y	N	N	Y	Y
Feingold	Y	N	N	Y	Y
WYOMING					
Thomas	N	Y	N	Y	N
Enzi	N	Y	N	Y	N

Key

Y   Voted for (yea).
\#   Paired for.
\+   Announced for.
N   Voted against (nay).
X   Paired against.
–   Announced against.
P   Voted "present."
C   Voted "present" to avoid possible conflict of interest.
?   Did not vote or otherwise make a position known.

Democrats   ***Republicans***
Independents

ND Northern Democrats   SD Southern Democrats

Southern states - Ala., Ark., Fla., Ga., Ky., La., Miss., N.C., Okla., S.C., Tenn., Texas, Va.

28. S 1805. Gun Liability/Armor-Piercing Ammunition. Kennedy, D-Mass., amendment that would expand the definition of armor-piercing ammunition to include a projectile that could be used in a handgun and could penetrate body armor worn by law enforcement officers. The new definition also would include a projectile for a centerfire rifle, designed or marketed with the ability to pierce body armor. It would require the attorney general to promulgate standards for the uniform testing of projectiles against body armor. Rejected 34-63: R 1-49; D 33-13 (ND 30-8, SD 3-5); I 0-1. March 2, 2004.

29. S 1805. Gun Liability/Expanded Negligence Exemption. Craig, R-Idaho, motion to table (kill) the Levin, D-Mich., amendment that would exempt from the provisions of the bill civil lawsuits in which gross negligence or reckless conduct of a defendant led to the death or injury of another person. Motion agreed to 56-41: R 45-5; D 11-35 (ND 6-32, SD 5-3); I 0-1. March 2, 2004.

30. S 1805. Gun Liability/Passage. Passage of the bill that would bar certain civil lawsuits against manufacturers, distributors, dealers and importers of firearms and ammunition, principally those lawsuits aimed at making them liable for gun violence. Trade groups also would be protected. The bill would require the dismissal of pending lawsuits against the gun industry, except for those involving a defect in a weapon or ammunition. The bill, as amended, includes the provisions on background checks at gun shows, 10-year reauthorization of the assault weapons ban and increased penalties for certain crimes involving armor-piercing ammunition. Rejected 8-90: R 3-48; D 5-41 (ND 2-36, SD 3-5); I 0-1. March 2, 2004.

31. S 1637. Corporate Tax Overhaul/Research and Development Credit Extension. Hatch, R-Utah amendment that would provide for an 18-month extension of the research and development tax credit. Adopted 93-0: R 51-0; D 41-0 (ND 36-0, SD 5-0); I 1-0. (Before adoption, the Senate adopted by voice vote a Bingaman, D-N.M., amendment to the Hatch amendment.) March 3, 2004.

32. S 1637. Corporate Tax Overhaul/Outsourcing. Dodd, D-Conn., amendment that would prohibit a federal government contract, including state contracts with any federal funding, from being performed outside the United States. The measure, as amended, would require that within 90 days of the bill's enactment the Commerce secretary make an initial certification that the provisions in the amendment would not result in the loss of more jobs than they would protect and would not harm the U.S. economy. The certification would need to be renewed on or before Jan. 1 of each year for the amendment provisions to take effect for that coming year. National security agencies, including the Defense and Homeland Security departments, intelligence services and programs and certain Energy Department programs, would be exempt from the provisions barring offshore contracts. Adopted 70-26: R 25-26; D 44-0 (ND 37-0, SD 7-0); I 1-0. (Before adoption, the Senate adopted by voice vote a McConnell, R-Ky., amendment and a McCain, R-Ariz., amendment to the Dodd amendment.) March 4, 2004.

	33	34	35	36	37	38
ALABAMA						
Shelby	N	N	N	N	Y	N
Sessions	N	N	N	N	Y	N
ALASKA						
Stevens	N	N	N	N	Y	N
Murkowski, L.	N	N	N	N	Y	N
ARIZONA						
McCain	N	Y	N	N	Y	Y
Kyl	N	N	N	N	Y	N
ARKANSAS						
Lincoln	Y	Y	Y	Y	Y	Y
Pryor	Y	Y	Y	Y	Y	Y
CALIFORNIA						
Feinstein	Y	Y	Y	Y	Y	Y
Boxer	Y	Y	Y	Y	Y	Y
COLORADO						
Campbell	N	N	N	N	Y	N
Allard	N	N	N	N	Y	N
CONNECTICUT						
Dodd	Y	Y	Y	Y	Y	Y
Lieberman	Y	Y	Y	Y	Y	Y
DELAWARE						
Biden	Y	Y	Y	Y	N	Y
Carper	Y	?	Y	Y	N	Y
FLORIDA						
Graham	Y	Y	Y	Y	Y	Y
Nelson	Y	Y	Y	Y	Y	Y
GEORGIA						
Miller	N	N	N	N	Y	N
Chambliss	N	N	N	N	Y	N
HAWAII						
Inouye	Y	Y	Y	Y	Y	Y
Akaka	Y	Y	Y	Y	Y	Y
IDAHO						
Craig	N	N	N	N	Y	N
Crapo	N	N	N	N	Y	N
ILLINOIS						
Fitzgerald	N	N	N	N	Y	N
Durbin	Y	Y	Y	Y	Y	Y
INDIANA						
Lugar	N	N	N	N	Y	N
Bayh	Y	Y	Y	Y	Y	Y

	33	34	35	36	37	38
IOWA						
Grassley	N	N	N	N	Y	N
Harkin	Y	Y	Y	Y	Y	Y
KANSAS						
Brownback	N	N	N	N	Y	N
Roberts	N	N	N	N	Y	N
KENTUCKY						
McConnell	N	N	N	N	Y	N
Bunning	N	N	N	N	Y	N
LOUISIANA						
Breaux	Y	Y	Y	Y	Y	Y
Landrieu	Y	Y	Y	Y	Y	Y
MAINE						
Snowe	N	N	N	N	Y	Y
Collins	N	N	N	N	Y	Y
MARYLAND						
Sarbanes	Y	Y	Y	Y	Y	Y
Mikulski	Y	Y	Y	Y	Y	Y
MASSACHUSETTS						
Kennedy	Y	Y	Y	Y	Y	Y
Kerry	?	?	?	Y	Y	Y
MICHIGAN						
Levin	Y	Y	Y	Y	Y	Y
Stabenow	Y	Y	Y	Y	Y	Y
MINNESOTA						
Dayton	Y	Y	Y	Y	Y	Y
Coleman	N	N	N	N	Y	N
MISSISSIPPI						
Cochran	N	N	N	N	Y	N
Lott	N	N	N	N	Y	N
MISSOURI						
Bond	N	N	N	N	Y	N
Talent	N	N	N	N	Y	N
MONTANA						
Burns	N	N	N	N	Y	N
Baucus	Y	N	Y	Y	Y	Y
NEBRASKA						
Hagel	N	N	N	N	Y	N
Nelson	Y	N	Y	N	Y	N
NEVADA						
Reid	Y	Y	Y	Y	Y	Y
Ensign	N	N	N	N	Y	N

	33	34	35	36	37	38
NEW HAMPSHIRE						
Gregg	N	N	N	N	N	N
Sununu	N	N	N	N	Y	N
NEW JERSEY						
Lautenberg	Y	Y	Y	Y	Y	Y
Corzine	Y	Y	Y	Y	Y	Y
NEW MEXICO						
Domenici	N	N	N	N	Y	N
Bingaman	Y	Y	Y	Y	Y	Y
NEW YORK						
Schumer	Y	Y	Y	Y	Y	Y
Clinton	Y	Y	Y	Y	Y	Y
NORTH CAROLINA						
Edwards	?	Y	Y	Y	Y	Y
Dole	N	N	N	N	Y	N
NORTH DAKOTA						
Conrad	Y	Y	Y	Y	Y	Y
Dorgan	Y	Y	Y	Y	Y	Y
OHIO						
DeWine	N	N	N	N	Y	N
Voinovich	N	N	N	N	Y	N
OKLAHOMA						
Nickles	N	N	N	N	Y	N
Inhofe	N	N	N	N	Y	N
OREGON						
Wyden	Y	Y	Y	Y	Y	Y
Smith	N	N	N	N	Y	N
PENNSYLVANIA						
Specter	N	N	N	N	Y	N
Santorum	N	N	N	N	Y	N
RHODE ISLAND						
Reed	Y	Y	Y	Y	Y	Y
Chafee	Y	N	N	Y	Y	Y
SOUTH CAROLINA						
Hollings	Y	Y	Y	Y	Y	Y
Graham	N	N	N	N	Y	N
SOUTH DAKOTA						
Daschle	Y	Y	Y	Y	Y	Y
Johnson	?	?	?	?	?	?
TENNESSEE						
Frist	N	N	N	N	Y	N
Alexander	N	N	N	N	Y	N

Key

Y	Voted for (yea).
#	Paired for.
+	Announced for.
N	Voted against (nay).
X	Paired against.
−	Announced against.
P	Voted "present."
C	Voted "present" to avoid possible conflict of interest.
?	Did not vote or otherwise make a position known.

Democrats **Republicans**
Independents

	33	34	35	36	37	38
TEXAS						
Hutchison	N	N	N	N	Y	N
Cornyn	N	N	N	N	Y	N
UTAH						
Hatch	N	N	N	N	Y	N
Bennett	N	N	N	N	Y	N
VERMONT						
Leahy	Y	Y	Y	Y	Y	Y
Jeffords	Y	Y	Y	Y	N	Y
VIRGINIA						
Warner	N	N	N	N	Y	N
Allen	N	N	N	N	Y	N
WASHINGTON						
Murray	Y	Y	Y	Y	Y	Y
Cantwell	Y	Y	Y	Y	Y	Y
WEST VIRGINIA						
Byrd	Y	Y	Y	Y	Y	N
Rockefeller	Y	Y	Y	Y	Y	Y
WISCONSIN						
Kohl	Y	Y	Y	Y	Y	Y
Feingold	Y	Y	Y	Y	Y	Y
WYOMING						
Thomas	N	N	N	N	Y	N
Enzi	N	N	N	N	Y	N

ND Northern Democrats   SD Southern Democrats

Southern states - Ala., Ark., Fla., Ga., Ky., La., Miss., N.C., Okla., S.C., Tenn., Texas, Va.

33. S Con Res 95. Fiscal 2005 Budget Resolution/Budgetary Point of Order. Conrad, D-N.D., amendment that would create a 60-vote point of order against any direct spending or revenue legislation that would increase the on-budget deficit in any fiscal year until the budget is balanced without using money from the Social Security surplus. Rejected 46-51: R 1-50; D 44-1 (ND 37-0, SD 7-1); I 1-0. March 9, 2004.

34. S Con Res 95. Fiscal 2005 Budget Resolution/Veterans' Health Care. Daschle, D-S.D., amendment that would create a reserve fund that would allow up to $2.7 billion in additional spending for veterans' medical programs. It also would increase the amount dedicated to deficit reduction by $2.7 billion. The spending would be offset by reducing tax breaks for taxpayers with incomes of more than $1 million per year. Rejected 44-53: R 1-50; D 42-3 (ND 34-2, SD 8-1); I 1-0. March 9, 2004.

35. S Con Res 95. Fiscal 2005 Budget Resolution/Education Funding. Murray, D-Wash., amendment that would create a reserve fund that would allow an increase of up to $8.6 billion in education programs. It also would increase the amount dedicated for deficit reduction by $8.6 billion. The spending would be offset by revenue increases. Rejected 46-52: R 0-51; D 45-1 (ND 37-0, SD 8-1); I 1-0. March 10, 2004.

36. S Con Res 95. Fiscal 2005 Budget Resolution/Reconciliation Instructions. Byrd, D-W.Va., amendment that would strike reconciliation instructions from the resolution. The instructions would direct the Finance Committee to report legislation that would reduce revenues by $80.6 billion for fiscal 2005 through 2009. The instructions would accommodate an extension of the expiring $1,000 child tax credit, continue the 10 percent income tax bracket at present income levels and extend relief of the so-called marriage penalty. Rejected 47-52: R 1-50; D 45-2 (ND 37-1, SD 8-1); I 1-0. March 10, 2004.

37. S Con Res 95. Fiscal 2005 Budget Resolution/Defense Spending. Warner, R-Va., amendment that would increase the recommended level of defense spending in the underlying resolution by $6.9 billion. The amendment contains no offsets. Adopted 95-4: R 50-1; D 45-2 (ND 36-2, SD 9-0); I 0-1. March 10, 2004.

38. S Con Res 95. Fiscal 2005 Budget Resolution/PAYGO Rules. Feingold, D-Wis., amendment that would restore pay-as-you-go (PAYGO) rules, which would create a 60-vote point of order against any direct spending or revenue legislation that would increase the on-budget deficit or cause an on-budget deficit. Tax cuts and new entitlement spending would have to be offset with revenue increases or spending cuts. Adopted 51-48: R 4-47; D 46-1 (ND 38-0, SD 8-1); I 1-0. March 10, 2004.

ALABAMA	39	40	41	42	43	44	45
Shelby	N	N	N	N	Y	N	N
Sessions	N	N	N	N	Y	N	N
ALASKA							
Stevens	N	N	N	N	Y	N	N
Murkowski, L.	N	N	N	N	Y	N	N
ARIZONA							
McCain	N	N	N	N	Y	N	Y
Kyl	N	N	N	N	Y	N	N
ARKANSAS							
Lincoln	Y	Y	Y	Y	Y	Y	N
Pryor	Y	Y	Y	Y	Y	Y	N
CALIFORNIA							
Feinstein	Y	Y	Y	Y	Y	Y	Y
Boxer	Y	Y	Y	Y	Y	Y	Y
COLORADO							
Campbell	N	N	N	N	Y	N	N
Allard	N	N	N	N	Y	N	N
CONNECTICUT							
Dodd	Y	Y	Y	Y	Y	Y	Y
Lieberman	Y	Y	Y	Y	Y	Y	Y
DELAWARE							
Biden	Y	Y	Y	Y	Y	Y	Y
Carper	Y	Y	Y	Y	Y	Y	Y
FLORIDA							
Graham	Y	Y	Y	Y	Y	Y	Y
Nelson	Y	Y	Y	Y	Y	Y	Y
GEORGIA							
Miller	N	N	N	N	Y	N	N
Chambliss	N	N	N	N	Y	N	N
HAWAII							
Inouye	Y	Y	Y	Y	Y	Y	Y
Akaka	Y	Y	Y	Y	Y	Y	Y
IDAHO							
Craig	N	N	N	N	Y	N	N
Crapo	N	N	N	N	Y	N	N
ILLINOIS							
Fitzgerald	N	N	N	N	Y	N	N
Durbin	Y	Y	Y	Y	Y	Y	Y
INDIANA							
Lugar	N	N	N	N	Y	N	N
Bayh	Y	Y	Y	Y	Y	Y	Y

IOWA	39	40	41	42	43	44	45
Grassley	N	N	N	N	Y	N	N
Harkin	Y	Y	Y	Y	Y	Y	Y
KANSAS							
Brownback	N	N	N	N	Y	N	N
Roberts	N	N	N	N	Y	N	N
KENTUCKY							
McConnell	N	N	N	N	Y	N	N
Bunning	N	N	N	N	Y	N	N
LOUISIANA							
Breaux	Y	Y	N	Y	Y	Y	N
Landrieu	Y	Y	Y	Y	Y	Y	N
MAINE							
Snowe	Y	N	N	N	Y	N	Y
Collins	Y	N	N	N	Y	N	Y
MARYLAND							
Sarbanes	Y	Y	Y	Y	Y	Y	Y
Mikulski	Y	Y	Y	Y	Y	Y	Y
MASSACHUSETTS							
Kennedy	Y	Y	Y	Y	Y	Y	Y
Kerry	Y	Y	?	?	?	?	?
MICHIGAN							
Levin	Y	Y	Y	Y	Y	Y	Y
Stabenow	Y	Y	Y	Y	Y	Y	Y
MINNESOTA							
Dayton	Y	Y	Y	Y	Y	Y	Y
Coleman	Y	N	N	N	Y	N	N
MISSISSIPPI							
Cochran	N	N	N	N	Y	N	N
Lott	N	N	N	N	Y	N	N
MISSOURI							
Bond	Y	N	N	N	Y	N	N
Talent	N	N	N	N	Y	N	N
MONTANA							
Burns	N	N	?	N	Y	N	N
Baucus	Y	Y	N	N	Y	N	Y
NEBRASKA							
Hagel	N	N	N	N	Y	N	N
Nelson	Y	Y	N	N	Y	N	Y
NEVADA							
Reid	Y	Y	?	?	?	?	?
Ensign	N	N	?	N	Y	N	N

NEW HAMPSHIRE	39	40	41	42	43	44	45
Gregg	N	N	N	N	Y	N	N
Sununu	N	N	N	N	Y	N	N
NEW JERSEY							
Lautenberg	?	Y	Y	Y	Y	Y	Y
Corzine	Y	Y	Y	Y	Y	Y	Y
NEW MEXICO							
Domenici	?	?	N	N	Y	N	N
Bingaman	Y	Y	Y	Y	Y	Y	Y
NEW YORK							
Schumer	Y	Y	Y	Y	Y	Y	Y
Clinton	Y	Y	Y	Y	Y	Y	Y
NORTH CAROLINA							
Edwards	Y	Y	?	?	?	?	?
Dole	N	N	N	N	Y	N	N
NORTH DAKOTA							
Conrad	Y	Y	Y	Y	Y	Y	Y
Dorgan	Y	Y	Y	Y	Y	Y	Y
OHIO							
DeWine	Y	N	N	N	Y	N	N
Voinovich	N	N	N	N	Y	N	N
OKLAHOMA							
Nickles	N	N	N	N	Y	N	N
Inhofe	N	N	N	N	Y	N	N
OREGON							
Wyden	Y	Y	Y	Y	Y	Y	Y
Smith	Y	N	N	N	Y	N	N
PENNSYLVANIA							
Specter	Y	N	N	N	Y	N	N
Santorum	N	N	N	N	Y	N	N
RHODE ISLAND							
Reed	Y	Y	Y	Y	Y	Y	Y
Chafee	Y	N	N	N	Y	N	Y
SOUTH CAROLINA							
Hollings	Y	Y	Y	Y	Y	Y	Y
Graham	N	N	N	N	Y	N	N
SOUTH DAKOTA							
Daschle	Y	Y	Y	Y	Y	Y	Y
Johnson	?	?	?	?	?	?	?
TENNESSEE							
Frist	N	N	N	N	Y	N	N
Alexander	N	N	N	N	Y	N	N

Key

Y	Voted for (yea).
#	Paired for.
+	Announced for.
N	Voted against (nay).
X	Paired against.
–	Announced against.
P	Voted "present."
C	Voted "present" to avoid possible conflict of interest.
?	Did not vote or otherwise make a position known.

Democrats **Republicans**
Independents

TEXAS	39	40	41	42	43	44	45
Hutchison	N	N	N	N	Y	N	N
Cornyn	N	N	N	N	Y	N	N
UTAH							
Hatch	N	N	N	N	Y	N	N
Bennett	N	N	N	N	Y	N	N
VERMONT							
Leahy	Y	Y	Y	Y	Y	Y	Y
Jeffords	Y	Y	Y	Y	Y	Y	Y
VIRGINIA							
Warner	N	N	N	N	Y	N	N
Allen	N	N	N	N	Y	N	N
WASHINGTON							
Murray	Y	Y	Y	Y	Y	Y	Y
Cantwell	Y	Y	Y	Y	Y	Y	Y
WEST VIRGINIA							
Byrd	?	?	Y	Y	Y	Y	Y
Rockefeller	Y	Y	Y	Y	Y	Y	Y
WISCONSIN							
Kohl	Y	Y	Y	Y	Y	Y	Y
Feingold	Y	Y	Y	Y	Y	Y	Y
WYOMING							
Thomas	N	N	N	N	Y	N	N
Enzi	N	N	N	N	Y	N	N

ND Northern Democrats   SD Southern Democrats

Southern states - Ala., Ark., Fla., Ga., Ky., La., Miss., N.C., Okla., S.C., Tenn., Texas, Va.

39. S Con Res 95. Fiscal 2005 Budget Resolution/Reconciliation Instructions. Baucus, R-Mont., amendment that would strike reconciliation instructions that direct the Finance Committee to achieve $14 billion in mandatory spending reductions through cuts in Medicaid and the earned income tax credit. Adopted 53-43: R 8-42; D 44-1 (ND 36-0, SD 8-1); I 1-0. March 10, 2004.

40. S Con Res 95. Fiscal 2005 Budget Resolution/Veterans' Health Care. Nelson, D-Fla., amendment that would create a reserve fund that would allow up to $1.8 billion in additional spending for veterans' medical programs. The spending would be offset by revenue increases. Rejected 46-51: R 0-50; D 45-1 (ND 37-0, SD 8-1); I 1-0. March 10, 2004.

41. S Con Res 95. Fiscal 2005 Budget Resolution/Job Creation Initiatives and Tax Credits. Boxer, D-Calif., amendment that would create a reserve fund that would allow increases of up to $24 billion for fiscal 2005 through 2009 for employment initiatives including tax credits for companies that create new U.S.-based manufacturing jobs and small businesses that provide health care coverage. It also would prohibit the use of tax dollars to outsource non-defense and non-homeland security government contracts abroad. Employers would be required to provide advanced notice to workers whose jobs may be moved abroad. The spending would be offset by reducing tax breaks for taxpayers with incomes of more than $1 million per year. Rejected 41-53: R 0-49; D 40-4 (ND 34-2, SD 6-2); I 1-0. March 11, 2004.

42. S Con Res 95. Fiscal 2005 Budget Resolution/Firefighter Funding. Sarbanes, D-Md., amendment that would create a reserve fund that would al- low up to $1.4 billion in additional funds in fiscal 2005 for firefighter grant and assistance programs. The spending would be offset with revenue increases. Rejected 41-55: R 0-51; D 40-4 (ND 34-2, SD 6-2); I 1-0. March 11, 2004.

43. S Res 319. Madrid Bombings/Adoption. Adoption of the resolution that would express the sense of the Senate that Americans are outraged and shocked by the train bombings in Madrid, Spain, and express condolences and support to the people of Spain. It would urge the United States to offer immediate assistance to the Spanish government to bring those responsible for the acts to justice. Adopted 96-0: R 51-0; D 44-0 (ND 36-0, SD 8-0); I 1-0. March 11, 2004.

44. S Con Res 95. Fiscal 2005 Budget Resolution/Law Enforcement Funding. Dorgan, D-N.D., amendment that would create a reserve fund that would allow up to $1.1 billion in additional funding for law enforcement programs. It also would increase the amount dedicated to deficit reduction by $1.1 billion. The spending would be offset by reducing tax breaks for taxpayers with incomes of more than $1 million per year. Rejected 41-55: R 0-51; D 40-4 (ND 34-2, SD 6-2); I 1-0. March 11, 2004.

45. S Con Res 95. Fiscal 2005 Budget Resolution/Superfund Program. Lautenberg, D-N.J., amendment that would increase spending by $8.3 billion for the superfund program for fiscal 2005 through 2009. It would provide for reinstating polluter fees to fund the cleanup of superfund sites. It also would increase the amount dedicated to deficit reduction by $8.3 billion. Rejected 44-52: R 4-47; D 39-5 (ND 36-0, SD 3-5); I 1-0. March 11, 2004.

	46	47	48	49	50	51	52
ALABAMA							
Shelby	N	N	N	N	N	N	N
Sessions	N	N	N	N	N	N	N
ALASKA							
Stevens	N	N	N	N	N	N	N
Murkowski, L.	N	N	N	N	N	N	N
ARIZONA							
McCain	N	N	N	N	N	N	N
Kyl	N	N	N	N	N	N	N
ARKANSAS							
Lincoln	N	Y	Y	Y	Y	Y	Y
Pryor	Y	Y	Y	Y	Y	Y	Y
CALIFORNIA							
Feinstein	Y	Y	Y	Y	Y	Y	Y
Boxer	Y	Y	Y	Y	Y	Y	Y
COLORADO							
Campbell	N	N	N	N	N	N	N
Allard	N	N	N	N	N	N	N
CONNECTICUT							
Dodd	Y	Y	Y	Y	Y	Y	Y
Lieberman	Y	Y	Y	Y	Y	Y	Y
DELAWARE							
Biden	Y	Y	Y	Y	Y	Y	Y
Carper	Y	Y	Y	Y	Y	Y	N
FLORIDA							
Graham	N	Y	Y	Y	Y	Y	Y
Nelson	Y	Y	Y	Y	Y	Y	Y
GEORGIA							
Miller	N	N	N	N	N	N	N
Chambliss	N	N	N	N	N	N	N
HAWAII							
Inouye	Y	Y	Y	Y	Y	Y	Y
Akaka	Y	Y	Y	Y	Y	Y	Y
IDAHO							
Craig	N	N	N	N	N	N	N
Crapo	N	N	?	N	N	N	N
ILLINOIS							
Fitzgerald	N	N	N	N	N	N	N
Durbin	Y	Y	Y	Y	Y	Y	Y
INDIANA							
Lugar	N	N	N	N	N	N	N
Bayh	N	Y	Y	Y	Y	Y	Y

	46	47	48	49	50	51	52
IOWA							
Grassley	N	N	N	N	N	N	N
Harkin	Y	Y	Y	Y	Y	Y	Y
KANSAS							
Brownback	N	N	N	N	N	N	N
Roberts	N	N	N	N	N	N	N
KENTUCKY							
McConnell	N	N	N	N	N	N	N
Bunning	N	N	N	N	N	N	N
LOUISIANA							
Breaux	N	Y	Y	N	N	Y	Y
Landrieu	N	Y	Y	Y	Y	Y	Y
MAINE							
Snowe	N	N	N	N	N	N	N
Collins	N	N	N	N	N	N	N
MARYLAND							
Sarbanes	Y	Y	Y	Y	Y	Y	Y
Mikulski	Y	Y	Y	Y	Y	Y	Y
MASSACHUSETTS							
Kennedy	Y	Y	Y	Y	Y	Y	Y
Kerry	?	?	?	?	?	?	?
MICHIGAN							
Levin	Y	Y	Y	Y	Y	Y	Y
Stabenow	N	Y	Y	Y	Y	Y	Y
MINNESOTA							
Dayton	N	Y	Y	Y	Y	Y	Y
Coleman	N	N	N	N	N	N	N
MISSISSIPPI							
Cochran	N	N	N	N	N	N	N
Lott	N	N	N	N	N	N	N
MISSOURI							
Bond	N	N	N	N	N	N	N
Talent	N	N	N	N	N	N	N
MONTANA							
Burns	N	N	N	N	N	N	N
Baucus	N	Y	N	Y	N	N	N
NEBRASKA							
Hagel	N	N	N	N	N	N	N
Nelson	N	N	N	N	N	N	Y
NEVADA							
Reid	?	?	?	?	?	?	?
Ensign	N	N	N	N	N	N	N

	46	47	48	49	50	51	52
NEW HAMPSHIRE							
Gregg	N	N	N	N	N	N	N
Sununu	N	N	N	N	N	N	N
NEW JERSEY							
Lautenberg	Y	Y	Y	Y	Y	Y	Y
Corzine	Y	Y	Y	Y	Y	Y	Y
NEW MEXICO							
Domenici	N	N	N	N	N	N	N
Bingaman	Y	Y	Y	Y	N	Y	Y
NEW YORK							
Schumer	N	Y	Y	Y	Y	Y	Y
Clinton	Y	Y	Y	Y	Y	Y	Y
NORTH CAROLINA							
Edwards	?	?	Y	Y	Y	Y	?
Dole	N	N	N	N	N	N	N
NORTH DAKOTA							
Conrad	N	Y	Y	Y	N	Y	Y
Dorgan	N	Y	Y	Y	Y	Y	Y
OHIO							
DeWine	Y	N	N	N	N	N	N
Voinovich	N	N	N	?	N	N	N
OKLAHOMA							
Nickles	N	N	N	N	N	N	N
Inhofe	N	N	N	N	N	N	N
OREGON							
Wyden	Y	Y	Y	Y	Y	Y	Y
Smith	N	N	N	N	N	N	N
PENNSYLVANIA							
Specter	N	N	N	N	N	N	N
Santorum	N	N	N	N	N	N	N
RHODE ISLAND							
Reed	Y	Y	Y	Y	Y	Y	Y
Chafee	Y	N	N	N	N	Y	N
SOUTH CAROLINA							
Hollings	N	Y	Y	Y	Y	Y	Y
Graham	N	N	N	N	N	N	N
SOUTH DAKOTA							
Daschle	N	Y	Y	Y	Y	Y	Y
Johnson	?	?	?	?	?	?	?
TENNESSEE							
Frist	N	N	N	N	N	N	N
Alexander	N	N	N	N	N	N	N

Key

Y	Voted for (yea).
#	Paired for.
+	Announced for.
N	Voted against (nay).
X	Paired against.
−	Announced against.
P	Voted "present."
C	Voted "present" to avoid possible conflict of interest.
?	Did not vote or otherwise make a position known.

Democrats **Republicans**
Independents

	46	47	48	49	50	51	52
TEXAS							
Hutchison	N	N	N	N	N	N	N
Cornyn	N	N	N	N	N	N	N
UTAH							
Hatch	N	N	N	N	N	N	N
Bennett	N	N	N	N	N	N	N
VERMONT							
Leahy	Y	Y	Y	Y	Y	Y	Y
Jeffords	Y	Y	Y	Y	Y	Y	Y
VIRGINIA							
Warner	N	N	N	N	N	N	N
Allen	N	N	N	N	N	N	N
WASHINGTON							
Murray	Y	Y	Y	Y	Y	Y	Y
Cantwell	Y	Y	Y	Y	Y	Y	Y
WEST VIRGINIA							
Byrd	Y	Y	Y	Y	Y	Y	Y
Rockefeller	Y	Y	Y	Y	Y	Y	Y
WISCONSIN							
Kohl	Y	Y	Y	Y	Y	Y	Y
Feingold	Y	Y	Y	Y	Y	Y	Y
WYOMING							
Thomas	N	N	N	N	N	N	N
Enzi	N	N	N	N	N	N	N

ND Northern Democrats   SD Southern Democrats

Southern states - Ala., Ark., Fla., Ga., Ky., La., Miss., N.C., Okla., S.C., Tenn., Texas, Va.

46. S Con Res 95. Fiscal 2005 Budget Resolution/Health Programs Funding. Harkin, D-Iowa, amendment that would create a reserve fund that would allow up to $30.5 billon in additional spending in fiscal 2005 through 2009 for medical research and for health services, such as tobacco cessation programs, mental health and substance abuse programs. It also would increase the amount dedicated to deficit reduction by $2 billion. The spending would be offset by increasing the cigarette tax by 61 cents per pack. Rejected 32-64: R 2-49; D 29-15 (ND 27-9, SD 2-6); I 1-0. March 11, 2004.

47. S Con Res 95. Fiscal 2005 Budget Resolution/Health Insurance Coverage. Lincoln, D-Ark., amendment that would increase spending by $60 billion from fiscal 2005 through 2009 to provide health insurance coverage to people without insurance. The spending would be offset by revenue increases. Rejected 43-53: R 0-51; D 42-2 (ND 35-1, SD 7-1); I 1-0. March 11, 2004.

48. S Con Res 95. Fiscal 2005 Budget Resolution/Discretionary Spending Increase. Byrd, D-W.Va., amendment that would create a reserve fund that would allow up to $11.2 billion in additional spending in fiscal 2005 for law enforcement and first-responder grants, education, veterans' medical care, global HIV/AIDS, surface transportation, medical research and Homeland Security Department programs. The spending would be offset by revenue increases. Rejected 43-53: R 0-50; D 42-3 (ND 34-2, SD 8-1); I 1-0. March 11, 2004.

49. S Con Res 95. Fiscal 2005 Budget Resolution/Budgetary Point of Order. Bingaman, D-N.M., motion to waive the Budget Act with respect to the Nickles, R-Okla., point of order against the Bingaman amendment that would create a 60-vote point of order against legislation that increases the number of

taxpayers affected by the alternative minimum tax, except for measures to extend expiring provisions related to the $1,000 child tax credit, the 10 percent income tax bracket, and the so-called marriage penalty. Motion rejected 43-53: R 0-50; D 42-3 (ND 35-1, SD 7-2); I 1-0. A three-fifths majority vote (60) of the total Senate is required to waive the Budget Act. March 11, 2004.

50. S Con Res 95. Fiscal 2005 Budget Resolution/Homeland Security Funding. Lieberman, D-Conn., amendment that would create a reserve fund that would allow up to $6.8 billion in additional spending for homeland security programs. The spending would be offset by reducing tax breaks for taxpayers with incomes of more than $1 million per year. Rejected 40-57: R 0-51; D 39-6 (ND 33-3, SD 6-3); I 1-0. March 11, 2004.

51. S Con Res 95. Fiscal 2005 Budget Resolution/Pell Grant Funding. Kennedy, D-Mass., amendment that would create a reserve fund that would allow up to $4.9 billion in additional spending in fiscal 2005 for Pell Grants. It also would increase the amount dedicated to deficit reduction by $4.9 billion. The spending would be offset by revenue increases. Rejected 44-53: R 1-50; D 42-3 (ND 34-2, SD 8-1); I 1-0. March 11, 2004.

52. S Con Res 95. Fiscal 2005 Budget Resolution/Indian Health Service Funding. Daschle, D-S.D., amendment that would create a reserve fund that would allow up to $3.4 billion in additional spending in fiscal 2005 for Indian Health Service clinical services. The spending would be offset by a reduction in tax cuts for individuals with incomes in excess of $1 million or by other revenue increases. Rejected 42-54: R 0-51; D 41-3 (ND 34-2, SD 7-1); I 1-0. March 11, 2004.

	53	54	55	56	57	58	59
ALABAMA							
Shelby	N	N	Y	Y	N	Y	Y
Sessions	N	N	Y	N	N	Y	Y
ALASKA							
Stevens	N	N	Y	Y	N	Y	Y
Murkowski, L.	N	N	Y	Y	N	Y	Y
ARIZONA							
McCain	N	Y	Y	N	N	Y	Y
Kyl	N	N	Y	N	N	Y	Y
ARKANSAS							
Lincoln	Y	Y	N	Y	Y	N	Y
Pryor	Y	Y	N	Y	Y	N	Y
CALIFORNIA							
Feinstein	Y	Y	N	Y	Y	N	Y
Boxer	Y	Y	N	Y	Y	N	Y
COLORADO							
Campbell	N	N	Y	N	N	Y	?
Allard	N	N	Y	N	N	Y	Y
CONNECTICUT							
Dodd	Y	N	N	Y	N	Y	N
Lieberman	Y	Y	N	Y	Y	N	?
DELAWARE							
Biden	Y	Y	N	Y	Y	N	Y
Carper	N	Y	N	Y	Y	N	Y
FLORIDA							
Graham	Y	Y	N	Y	Y	N	Y
Nelson	Y	Y	N	Y	Y	N	Y
GEORGIA							
Miller	N	N	Y	Y	N	Y	Y
Chambliss	N	N	Y	Y	N	Y	Y
HAWAII							
Inouye	Y	Y	N	Y	Y	N	Y
Akaka	Y	Y	N	Y	Y	N	Y
IDAHO							
Craig	N	N	Y	N	N	Y	Y
Crapo	N	N	Y	N	N	Y	Y
ILLINOIS							
Fitzgerald	N	Y	Y	N	N	Y	Y
Durbin	Y	Y	N	Y	Y	N	Y
INDIANA							
Lugar	N	N	Y	N	N	Y	Y
Bayh	Y	N	Y	Y	N	Y	Y

	53	54	55	56	57	58	59
IOWA							
Grassley	N	N	Y	Y	N	Y	Y
Harkin	Y	Y	N	Y	Y	N	Y
KANSAS							
Brownback	N	N	Y	N	N	Y	Y
Roberts	N	N	Y	Y	N	Y	Y
KENTUCKY							
McConnell	N	N	Y	Y	N	Y	Y
Bunning	N	N	Y	N	N	Y	Y
LOUISIANA							
Breaux	N	N	N	N	N	N	Y
Landrieu	Y	Y	N	Y	Y	N	Y
MAINE							
Snowe	N	N	Y	N	Y	Y	Y
Collins	N	Y	Y	N	Y	Y	Y
MARYLAND							
Sarbanes	Y	Y	N	Y	Y	N	Y
Mikulski	Y	Y	N	Y	Y	N	Y
MASSACHUSETTS							
Kennedy	Y	N	N	Y	Y	N	Y
Kerry	?	?	?	?	?	?	?
MICHIGAN							
Levin	Y	Y	N	Y	Y	N	Y
Stabenow	Y	Y	N	Y	Y	N	Y
MINNESOTA							
Dayton	Y	Y	N	Y	Y	N	Y
Coleman	N	Y	Y	Y	N	Y	Y
MISSISSIPPI							
Cochran	N	N	Y	Y	N	Y	Y
Lott	N	Y	Y	Y	N	N	Y
MISSOURI							
Bond	N	N	Y	N	N	Y	Y
Talent	N	Y	Y	Y	N	Y	Y
MONTANA							
Burns	N	N	Y	N	N	Y	Y
Baucus	Y	Y	N	Y	Y	N	Y
NEBRASKA							
Hagel	N	N	Y	N	N	Y	Y
Nelson	Y	Y	N	Y	N	N	Y
NEVADA							
Reid	?	?	?	?	?	?	?
Ensign	N	N	Y	Y	N	Y	Y

	53	54	55	56	57	58	59
NEW HAMPSHIRE							
Gregg	N	N	Y	Y	N	Y	Y
Sununu	N	Y	Y	N	N	Y	Y
NEW JERSEY							
Lautenberg	Y	Y	N	Y	Y	N	Y
Corzine	Y	Y	N	Y	Y	N	Y
NEW MEXICO							
Domenici	N	N	Y	N	N	Y	?
Bingaman	Y	Y	N	Y	Y	N	Y
NEW YORK							
Schumer	Y	Y	N	Y	Y	N	Y
Clinton	Y	Y	N	Y	Y	N	Y
NORTH CAROLINA							
Edwards	?	?	?	?	?	?	?
Dole	N	N	Y	Y	N	Y	Y
NORTH DAKOTA							
Conrad	Y	Y	N	Y	Y	N	Y
Dorgan	Y	Y	N	Y	Y	N	Y
OHIO							
DeWine	N	Y	Y	Y	N	Y	Y
Voinovich	N	Y	Y	N	N	Y	Y
OKLAHOMA							
Nickles	N	N	Y	N	N	Y	Y
Inhofe	N	N	Y	N	N	Y	Y
OREGON							
Wyden	Y	Y	N	Y	Y	N	Y
Smith	N	N	Y	Y	N	Y	Y
PENNSYLVANIA							
Specter	N	Y	Y	Y	N	Y	Y
Santorum	N	N	Y	Y	N	Y	Y
RHODE ISLAND							
Reed	Y	Y	N	Y	Y	N	Y
Chafee	N	N	N	Y	N	Y	Y
SOUTH CAROLINA							
Hollings	Y	Y	N	Y	Y	N	Y
Graham	N	Y	Y	N	N	Y	Y
SOUTH DAKOTA							
Daschle	Y	Y	N	Y	Y	N	Y
Johnson	?	?	?	?	?	?	?
TENNESSEE							
Frist	N	N	Y	N	N	Y	Y
Alexander	N	N	Y	N	N	Y	Y

	53	54	55	56	57	58	59
TEXAS							
Hutchison	N	N	Y	Y	N	Y	Y
Cornyn	N	N	Y	Y	N	Y	Y
UTAH							
Hatch	N	N	Y	Y	N	Y	Y
Bennett	N	N	Y	Y	N	Y	Y
VERMONT							
Leahy	Y	Y	N	Y	Y	N	Y
Jeffords	Y	Y	N	Y	Y	N	?
VIRGINIA							
Warner	N	?	Y	Y	N	Y	Y
Allen	N	Y	Y	N	N	Y	Y
WASHINGTON							
Murray	Y	N	N	Y	N	Y	Y
Cantwell	Y	N	N	Y	N	Y	Y
WEST VIRGINIA							
Byrd	Y	Y	N	Y	Y	N	Y
Rockefeller	Y	Y	N	Y	Y	N	Y
WISCONSIN							
Kohl	Y	Y	N	Y	Y	N	Y
Feingold	Y	Y	N	Y	Y	N	Y
WYOMING							
Thomas	N	N	Y	N	N	Y	Y
Enzi	N	N	Y	N	N	Y	Y

Key

Y	Voted for (yea).
#	Paired for.
+	Announced for.
N	Voted against (nay).
X	Paired against.
–	Announced against.
P	Voted "present."
C	Voted "present" to avoid possible conflict of interest.
?	Did not vote or otherwise make a position known.

Democrats   ***Republicans***
Independents

ND Northern Democrats   SD Southern Democrats

Southern states - Ala., Ark., Fla., Ga., Ky., La., Miss., N.C., Okla., S.C., Tenn., Texas, Va.

53. S Con Res 95. Fiscal 2005 Budget Resolution/After-School Program Funding. Dodd, D-Conn., amendment that would create a reserve fund that would allow up to $1 billion in additional spending for the 21st Century Community Learning Centers program. It also would increase the amount dedicated for deficit reduction by $4.9 billion. The spending would be offset by revenue increases. Rejected 42-54: R 0-51; D 41-3 (ND 35-1, SD 6-2); I 1-0. March 11, 2004.

54. S Con Res 95. Fiscal 2005 Budget Resolution/Homeland Security Funding. Levin, D-Mich., amendment that would increase funding by $1.7 billion for Homeland Security grants and assistance for first-responders and firefighters and for port security measures. It assumes the funding would be offset by the cancellation of planned future deliveries of oil to the Strategic Petroleum Reserve. Adopted 52-43: R 14-36; D 37-7 (ND 31-5, SD 6-2); I 1-0. March 11, 2004.

55. S Con Res 95. Fiscal 2005 Budget Resolution/Budgetary Point of Order. McConnell, R-Ky., motion to waive the Budget Act with respect to the Baucus, D-Mont., point of order against the McConnell amendment that would create a 60-vote point of order against legislation that seeks to increase taxes on the top income tax bracket without an exemption for small businesses. Motion rejected 51-45: R 50-1; D 1-43 (ND 0-36, SD 1-7); I 0-1. A three-fifths majority (60) of the entire Senate is required to waive the Budget Act. March 11, 2004.

56. S Con Res 95. Fiscal 2005 Budget Resolution/NIH Funding. Specter, R-Pa., amendment that would increase funding for the National Institutes of Health by $2 billion. The spending would be offset by using unspecified funds contained in the measure. Adopted 72-24: R 28-23; D 43-1 (ND 36-0, SD 7-1); I 1-0. March 11, 2004.

57. S Con Res 95. Fiscal 2005 Budget Resolution/Debt Limit. Lautenberg, D-N.J., amendment that would strike reconciliation instructions from the resolution for the Finance Committee to report legislation that would increase the statutory debt limit. Rejected 42-54: R 0-51; D 41-3 (ND 35-1, SD 6-2); I 1-0. March 11, 2004.

58. S Con Res 95. Fiscal 2005 Budget Resolution/Adoption. Adoption of the concurrent resolution to adopt a five-year budget plan that would limit fiscal 2005 discretionary spending to $821 billion. It would allow an $80.6 billion five-year tax cut package to be protected by reconciliation rules. Under pay-as-you-go rules (PAYGO), any tax cuts or new entitlement spending would have to be offset with revenue increases or entitlement cuts. The resolution would set aside $30 billion for additional fiscal 2005 spending to support military operations in Iraq and Afghanistan. Adopted 51-45: R 50-1; D 1-43 (ND 0-36, SD 1-7); I 0-1. March 12, 2004 (in the session that began and the Congressional Record dated March 11, 2004).

59. Guirola Nomination/Confirmation. Confirmation of President Bush's nomination of Louis Guirola Jr., of Mississippi to be a judge for the U.S. District Court for the Southern District of Mississippi. Confirmed 92-0: R 49-0; D 43-0 (ND 35-0, SD 8-0); I 0-0. A "yea" was a vote in support of the president's position. March 12, 2004 (in the session that began and the Congressional Record dated March 11, 2004).

	60	61	62	63
ALABAMA				
Shelby	Y	N	N	Y
Sessions	Y	N	N	Y
ALASKA				
Stevens	Y	N	N	Y
Murkowski, L.	Y	N	N	Y
ARIZONA				
McCain	Y	N	N	Y
Kyl	Y	N	N	Y
ARKANSAS				
Lincoln	N	Y	Y	N
Pryor	N	Y	Y	Y
CALIFORNIA				
Feinstein	N	Y	Y	N
Boxer	N	Y	Y	N
COLORADO				
Campbell	Y	N	N	Y
Allard	Y	N	N	Y
CONNECTICUT				
Dodd	N	Y	Y	N
Lieberman	N	Y	Y	N
DELAWARE				
Biden	N	?	Y	N
Carper	N	Y	Y	Y
FLORIDA				
Graham	N	Y	Y	N
Nelson	N	Y	Y	N
GEORGIA				
Miller	Y	N	N	Y
Chambliss	Y	N	N	Y
HAWAII				
Inouye	N	Y	Y	N
Akaka	N	Y	Y	N
IDAHO				
Craig	Y	N	N	Y
Crapo	Y	N	N	Y
ILLINOIS				
Fitzgerald	Y	N	N	Y
Durbin	N	Y	Y	N
INDIANA				
Lugar	Y	N	N	Y
Bayh	N	Y	Y	N

	60	61	62	63
IOWA				
Grassley	Y	N	N	Y
Harkin	N	Y	Y	N
KANSAS				
Brownback	Y	N	N	Y
Roberts	Y	N	N	Y
KENTUCKY				
McConnell	Y	N	N	Y
Bunning	Y	N	N	Y
LOUISIANA				
Breaux	N	N	Y	Y
Landrieu	N	Y	Y	Y
MAINE				
Snowe	Y	Y	N	N
Collins	Y	Y	N	N
MARYLAND				
Sarbanes	N	Y	Y	N
Mikulski	N	Y	Y	N
MASSACHUSETTS				
Kennedy	N	Y	Y	N
Kerry	–	Y	+	N
MICHIGAN				
Levin	N	Y	Y	N
Stabenow	N	Y	Y	N
MINNESOTA				
Dayton	N	Y	Y	Y
Coleman	Y	N	N	Y
MISSISSIPPI				
Cochran	Y	N	N	Y
Lott	Y	N	N	Y
MISSOURI				
Bond	Y	N	N	Y
Talent	Y	N	N	Y
MONTANA				
Burns	Y	N	N	Y
Baucus	N	Y	Y	N
NEBRASKA				
Hagel	Y	N	N	Y
Nelson	N	N	N	Y
NEVADA				
Reid	N	Y	Y	Y
Ensign	Y	N	N	Y

	60	61	62	63
NEW HAMPSHIRE				
Gregg	Y	N	N	?
Sununu	Y	N	N	Y
NEW JERSEY				
Lautenberg	N	Y	Y	N
Corzine	N	Y	Y	N
NEW MEXICO				
Domenici	Y	N	N	Y
Bingaman	N	Y	Y	Y
NEW YORK				
Schumer	N	Y	Y	N
Clinton	N	Y	Y	N
NORTH CAROLINA				
Edwards	?	Y	Y	N
Dole	Y	N	N	Y
NORTH DAKOTA				
Conrad	N	Y	Y	N
Dorgan	N	Y	Y	Y
OHIO				
DeWine	Y	N	N	Y
Voinovich	Y	N	N	Y
OKLAHOMA				
Nickles	Y	N	N	Y
Inhofe	Y	N	N	Y
OREGON				
Wyden	N	Y	Y	N
Smith	Y	N	N	Y
PENNSYLVANIA				
Specter	Y	Y	N	Y
Santorum	Y	N	N	Y
RHODE ISLAND				
Reed	N	Y	Y	N
Chafee	Y	Y	N	N
SOUTH CAROLINA				
Hollings	N	Y	Y	N
Graham	Y	N	N	Y
SOUTH DAKOTA				
Daschle	N	Y	Y	Y
Johnson	N	Y	Y	N
TENNESSEE				
Frist	N	N	N	Y
Alexander	Y	N	N	Y

	60	61	62	63
TEXAS				
Hutchison	Y	N	Y	Y
Cornyn	Y	N	N	Y
UTAH				
Hatch	Y	N	N	Y
Bennett	Y	N	N	Y
VERMONT				
Leahy	N	Y	Y	N
Jeffords	N	Y	Y	N
VIRGINIA				
Warner	Y	N	N	Y
Allen	Y	N	N	Y
WASHINGTON				
Murray	N	Y	Y	N
Cantwell	N	Y	Y	N
WEST VIRGINIA				
Byrd	N	Y	Y	N
Rockefeller	N	Y	Y	Y
WISCONSIN				
Kohl	N	Y	Y	N
Feingold	N	Y	N	N
WYOMING				
Thomas	Y	N	N	Y
Enzi	Y	N	N	Y

Key

Y	Voted for (yea).
#	Paired for.
+	Announced for.
N	Voted against (nay).
X	Paired against.
–	Announced against.
P	Voted "present."
C	Voted "present" to avoid possible conflict of interest.
?	Did not vote or otherwise make a position known.

Democrats **Republicans**
Independents

ND Northern Democrats   SD Southern Democrats

Southern states - Ala., Ark., Fla., Ga., Ky., La., Miss., N.C., Okla., S.C., Tenn., Texas, Va.

60. S 1637. Corporate Tax Overhaul/Cloture. Motion to invoke cloture (thus limiting debate) on the Frist, R-Tenn., motion to recommit the bill to the Finance Committee with instructions that it report the bill back to the Senate with language that includes all amendments previously adopted to the bill and additional provisions that would extend so-called Liberty Zone private activity bonds for New York City for five years to help businesses recovering from the Sept. 11, 2001, terrorist attacks; permit a tax deduction for private mortgage insurance payments in addition to interest payments on the mortgage itself; and provide a 50 percent tax credit to employers for wages the employer continues to pay to reservists and National Guard members called to active duty, with a maximum credit of $7,500 per employee. Motion rejected 51-47: R 50-1; D 1-45 (ND 0-38, SD 1-7); I 0-1. Three-fifths of the total Senate (60) is required to invoke cloture. March 24, 2004.

61. HR 1997. Fetal Protection/Democratic Substitute. Feinstein, D-Calif., substitute amendment that would make it a criminal offense to interrupt the normal course of or terminate a pregnancy during the commission of a violent crime against a pregnant woman. It would establish criminal penalties, equal to those that would apply if the pregnant woman were injured or killed, for those who affect the pregnancy. The death penalty could not be imposed for such crimes. The provisions would not apply to consensual abortion or to a woman's actions with respect to her pregnancy. The amendment does not include a provision that specifically defines an "unborn child." Rejected 49-50:

R 4-47; D 44-3 (ND 37-1, SD 7-2); I 1-0. A "nay" was a vote in support of the president's position. March 25, 2004.

62. HR 1997. Fetal Protection/Domestic Violence Leave Extension. Murray, D-Wash., motion to waive the Budget Act with respect to the Nickles, R-Okla., point of order against the Murray amendment that would expand the Family and Medical Leave Act to allow victims of domestic violence and sexual assault to take leave from work for up to 30 days. It also would allow victims of domestic violence, stalking or sexual assault to receive unemployment insurance if they have lost their job as a result. Motion rejected 46-53: R 1-50; D 44-3 (ND 36-2, SD 8-1); I 1-0. A three-fifths majority (60) of the entire Senate is required to waive the Budget Act. March 25, 2004.

63. HR 1997. Fetal Protection/Passage. Passage of the bill that would make it a criminal offense to injure or kill a fetus during the commission of a violent crime. The measure would establish criminal penalties, equal to those that would apply if the pregnant woman were injured or killed, for those who harm a fetus, regardless of the perpetrator's knowledge of the pregnancy or intent to harm the fetus. The bill states that its provisions should not be interpreted to apply to consensual abortion or to a woman's actions with respect to her pregnancy. The death penalty could not be imposed under this bill. Passed (thus cleared for the president) 61-38: R 48-2; D 13-35 (ND 9-30, SD 4-5); I 0-1. A "yea" was a vote in support of the president's position. March 25, 2004.

	64	65
ALABAMA		
Shelby	Y	Y
Sessions	N	Y
ALASKA		
Stevens	Y	Y
Murkowski, L.	Y	?
ARIZONA		
McCain	Y	Y
Kyl	N	Y
ARKANSAS		
Lincoln	Y	N
Pryor	Y	N
CALIFORNIA		
Feinstein	Y	N
Boxer	Y	N
COLORADO		
Campbell	Y	Y
Allard	N	Y
CONNECTICUT		
Dodd	Y	N
Lieberman	Y	N
DELAWARE		
Biden	Y	N
Carper	Y	N
FLORIDA		
Graham	Y	N
Nelson	Y	N
GEORGIA		
Miller	N	N
Chambliss	N	Y
HAWAII		
Inouye	Y	N
Akaka	Y	N
IDAHO		
Craig	N	Y
Crapo	N	Y
ILLINOIS		
Fitzgerald	Y	Y
Durbin	Y	N
INDIANA		
Lugar	Y	Y
Bayh	Y	N

	64	65
IOWA		
Grassley	Y	Y
Harkin	Y	N
KANSAS		
Brownback	Y	Y
Roberts	Y	Y
KENTUCKY		
McConnell	N	Y
Bunning	Y	Y
LOUISIANA		
Breaux	Y	N
Landrieu	Y	N
MAINE		
Snowe	Y	Y
Collins	Y	Y
MARYLAND		
Sarbanes	Y	N
Mikulski	Y	N
MASSACHUSETTS		
Kennedy	Y	N
Kerry	+	–
MICHIGAN		
Levin	Y	N
Stabenow	Y	N
MINNESOTA		
Dayton	Y	N
Coleman	Y	Y
MISSISSIPPI		
Cochran	Y	Y
Lott	N	Y
MISSOURI		
Bond	Y	Y
Talent	Y	Y
MONTANA		
Burns	N	Y
Baucus	Y	N
NEBRASKA		
Hagel	Y	Y
Nelson	Y	N
NEVADA		
Reid	Y	N
Ensign	N	Y

	64	65
NEW HAMPSHIRE		
Gregg	N	Y
Sununu	N	Y
NEW JERSEY		
Lautenberg	Y	N
Corzine	Y	N
NEW MEXICO		
Domenici	?	Y
Bingaman	Y	N
NEW YORK		
Schumer	Y	N
Clinton	Y	N
NORTH CAROLINA		
Edwards	Y	N
Dole	Y	Y
NORTH DAKOTA		
Conrad	Y	N
Dorgan	Y	N
OHIO		
DeWine	Y	Y
Voinovich	Y	Y
OKLAHOMA		
Nickles	N	Y
Inhofe	N	Y
OREGON		
Wyden	Y	N
Smith	Y	Y
PENNSYLVANIA		
Specter	Y	Y
Santorum	N	Y
RHODE ISLAND		
Reed	Y	N
Chafee	Y	Y
SOUTH CAROLINA		
Hollings	Y	N
Graham	Y	Y
SOUTH DAKOTA		
Daschle	Y	N
Johnson	Y	N
TENNESSEE		
Frist	Y	Y
Alexander	Y	Y

Key

Y	Voted for (yea).
#	Paired for.
+	Announced for.
N	Voted against (nay).
X	Paired against.
–	Announced against.
P	Voted "present."
C	Voted "present" to avoid possible conflict of interest.
?	Did not vote or otherwise make a position known.

Democrats **Republicans**
Independents

	64	65
TEXAS		
Hutchison	Y	Y
Cornyn	N	Y
UTAH		
Hatch	Y	Y
Bennett	Y	Y
VERMONT		
Leahy	Y	N
Jeffords	Y	N
VIRGINIA		
Warner	Y	Y
Allen	N	Y
WASHINGTON		
Murray	Y	N
Cantwell	Y	N
WEST VIRGINIA		
Byrd	Y	N
Rockefeller	Y	N
WISCONSIN		
Kohl	Y	N
Feingold	Y	N
WYOMING		
Thomas	N	Y
Enzi	N	Y

ND Northern Democrats   SD Southern Democrats

Southern states - Ala., Ark., Fla., Ga., Ky., La., Miss., N.C., Okla., S.C., Tenn., Texas, Va.

64. HR 4. Welfare Reauthorization/Child Care Funding. Snowe, R-Maine, amendment that would increase mandatory child care funding by $6 billion over the next five years. The spending would be offset by extending expiring Customs user fees. Adopted 78-20: R 31-19; D 46-1 (ND 38-0, SD 8-1); I 1-0. A "nay" was a vote in support of the president's position. March 30, 2004.

65. HR 4. Welfare Reauthorization/Cloture. Motion to invoke cloture (thus limiting debate) on the committee substitute amendment that would reauthorize the Temporary Assistance for Needy Families block grant program through fiscal 2008. It would increase the number of hours welfare recipients would be required to work each week and authorize $200 million a year to fund programs to promote marriage. It would increase mandatory child care funding by $7 billion over the next five years. Motion rejected 51-47: R 50-0; D 1-46 (ND 0-38, SD 1-8); I 0-1. Three-fifths of the total Senate (60) is required to invoke cloture. April 1, 2004.

Senate Votes 66, 67, 68

	66	67	68
ALABAMA			
Shelby	N	Y	Y
Sessions	Y	Y	N
ALASKA			
Stevens	Y	Y	Y
Murkowski, L.	Y	Y	Y
ARIZONA			
McCain	Y	N	N
Kyl	Y	N	N
ARKANSAS			
Lincoln	N	N	Y
Pryor	N	N	Y
CALIFORNIA			
Feinstein	N	N	Y
Boxer	N	N	Y
COLORADO			
Campbell	Y	Y	Y
Allard	Y	Y	Y
CONNECTICUT			
Dodd	N	N	N
Lieberman	?	?	Y
DELAWARE			
Biden	N	N	Y
Carper	N	N	Y
FLORIDA			
Graham	N	N	Y
Nelson	N	N	Y
GEORGIA			
Miller	Y	Y	Y
Chambliss	Y	Y	Y
HAWAII			
Inouye	N	N	Y
Akaka	N	N	?
IDAHO			
Craig	Y	Y	Y
Crapo	N	Y	Y
ILLINOIS			
Fitzgerald	Y	Y	N
Durbin	N	N	Y
INDIANA			
Lugar	Y	Y	Y
Bayh	N	N	Y

	66	67	68
IOWA			
Grassley	Y	Y	Y
Harkin	N	N	Y
KANSAS			
Brownback	Y	Y	Y
Roberts	Y	Y	Y
KENTUCKY			
McConnell	Y	Y	Y
Bunning	Y	Y	Y
LOUISIANA			
Breaux	N	Y	Y
Landrieu	N	N	Y
MAINE			
Snowe	Y	Y	Y
Collins	Y	Y	Y
MARYLAND			
Sarbanes	N	N	N
Mikulski	N	N	N
MASSACHUSETTS			
Kennedy	N	N	N
Kerry	–	–	?
MICHIGAN			
Levin	N	N	Y
Stabenow	N	N	Y
MINNESOTA			
Dayton	N	N	Y
Coleman	Y	Y	Y
MISSISSIPPI			
Cochran	Y	Y	Y
Lott	Y	Y	Y
MISSOURI			
Bond	Y	Y	Y
Talent	Y	Y	Y
MONTANA			
Burns	Y	Y	Y
Baucus	N	N	Y
NEBRASKA			
Hagel	Y	Y	Y
Nelson	N	Y	Y
NEVADA			
Reid	N	N	N
Ensign	Y	Y	N

	66	67	68
NEW HAMPSHIRE			
Gregg	Y	N	Y
Sununu	Y	N	Y
NEW JERSEY			
Lautenberg	N	N	N
Corzine	N	N	N
NEW MEXICO			
Domenici	Y	Y	Y
Bingaman	N	N	Y
NEW YORK			
Schumer	N	N	Y
Clinton	N	N	Y
NORTH CAROLINA			
Edwards	N	N	?
Dole	Y	Y	Y
NORTH DAKOTA			
Conrad	N	N	Y
Dorgan	N	N	Y
OHIO			
DeWine	Y	Y	Y
Voinovich	Y	Y	Y
OKLAHOMA			
Nickles	Y	Y	N
Inhofe	Y	Y	Y
OREGON			
Wyden	N	N	Y
Smith	Y	Y	Y
PENNSYLVANIA			
Specter	Y	Y	Y
Santorum	Y	Y	Y
RHODE ISLAND			
Reed	N	N	N
Chafee	Y	Y	N
SOUTH CAROLINA			
Hollings	N	N	Y
Graham	N	Y	Y
SOUTH DAKOTA			
Daschle	N	N	N
Johnson	N	N	Y
TENNESSEE			
Frist	Y	Y	Y
Alexander	Y	Y	Y

	66	67	68
TEXAS			
Hutchison	Y	Y	Y
Cornyn	Y	Y	Y
UTAH			
Hatch	Y	Y	Y
Bennett	Y	Y	Y
VERMONT			
Leahy	N	N	N
Jeffords	N	N	Y
VIRGINIA			
Warner	Y	Y	Y
Allen	Y	Y	Y
WASHINGTON			
Murray	?	?	Y
Cantwell	N	N	Y
WEST VIRGINIA			
Byrd	N	N	N
Rockefeller	N	N	Y
WISCONSIN			
Kohl	N	N	Y
Feingold	N	N	N
WYOMING			
Thomas	Y	Y	Y
Enzi	Y	Y	Y

Key

Y Voted for (yea).
\# Paired for.
+ Announced for.
N Voted against (nay).
X Paired against.
– Announced against.
P Voted "present."
C Voted "present" to avoid possible conflict of interest.
? Did not vote or otherwise make a position known.

Democrats **Republicans**
Independents

ND Northern Democrats SD Southern Democrats

Southern states - Ala., Ark., Fla., Ga., Ky., La., Miss., N.C., Okla., S.C., Tenn., Texas, Va.

66. S 2207. Medical Malpractice/Cloture. Motion to invoke cloture (thus limiting debate) on the motion to proceed to consideration of the bill that would seek to curb damages against emergency and trauma center personnel, as well as obstetricians and gynecologists. The bill would cap punitive damages at $250,000, or double the amount of economic compensation awarded, whichever amount is greater. Motion rejected 49-48: R 48-3; D 1-44 (ND 0-36, SD 1-8); I 0-1. Three-fifths of the total Senate (60) is required to invoke cloture. A "yea" was a vote in support of the president's position. April 7, 2004.

67. S 1637. Corporate Tax Overhaul/Cloture. Motion to invoke cloture (thus limiting debate) on the Frist, R-Tenn., motion to recommit the bill to the Finance Committee with instructions that it report the bill back to the Senate with language that includes all amendments previously adopted to the bill and additional provisions that would extend so-called Liberty Zone private activity bonds for New York City for five years to help businesses recovering from the Sept. 11, 2001, terrorist attacks; permit a tax deduction for private mortgage in-

surance payments in addition to interest payments on the mortgage itself; and provide a 50 percent tax credit to employers for wages the employer continues to pay to reservists and National Guard members called to active duty, with a maximum credit of $7,500 per employee. Additional provisions would also include $13 billion in energy tax cuts and a welfare-to-work tax credit. Motion rejected 50-47: R 47-4; D 3-42 (ND 1-35, SD 2-7); I 0-1. Three-fifths of the total Senate (60) is required to invoke cloture. April 7, 2004.

68. HR 3108. Pension Funding/Conference Report. Adoption of the conference report on the bill that would allow companies to reduce contributions to their pension plans by temporarily altering the formula used to calculate whether those contributions are enough to cover liabilities. The new formula would use a rate based on yields on a corporate bond index. The bill also would ease funding rules for about 4 percent of multi-employer pension plans, giving them a grace period to account for losses. Adopted (thus cleared for the president) 78-19: R 44-7; D 33-12 (ND 25-12, SD 8-0); I 1-0. A "yea" was a vote in support of the president's position. April 8, 2004.

	69	70
ALABAMA		
Shelby	Y	Y
Sessions	Y	Y
ALASKA		
Stevens	Y	Y
Murkowski, L.	Y	Y
ARIZONA		
McCain	Y	Y
Kyl	Y	Y
ARKANSAS		
Lincoln	N	Y
Pryor	N	Y
CALIFORNIA		
Feinstein	N	Y
Boxer	N	Y
COLORADO		
Campbell	?	?
Allard	Y	Y
CONNECTICUT		
Dodd	N	Y
Lieberman	N	Y
DELAWARE		
Biden	N	Y
Carper	N	Y
FLORIDA		
Graham	N	Y
Nelson	N	Y
GEORGIA		
Miller	Y	Y
Chambliss	Y	Y
HAWAII		
Inouye	N	Y
Akaka	N	Y
IDAHO		
Craig	Y	Y
Crapo	Y	Y
ILLINOIS		
Fitzgerald	Y	Y
Durbin	N	Y
INDIANA		
Lugar	Y	Y
Bayh	N	Y

	69	70
IOWA		
Grassley	Y	Y
Harkin	N	Y
KANSAS		
Brownback	Y	Y
Roberts	Y	Y
KENTUCKY		
McConnell	Y	Y
Bunning	Y	Y
LOUISIANA		
Breaux	N	Y
Landrieu	N	Y
MAINE		
Snowe	Y	Y
Collins	Y	Y
MARYLAND		
Sarbanes	N	Y
Mikulski	N	Y
MASSACHUSETTS		
Kennedy	N	Y
Kerry	?	?
MICHIGAN		
Levin	N	Y
Stabenow	N	Y
MINNESOTA		
Dayton	N	Y
Coleman	Y	Y
MISSISSIPPI		
Cochran	Y	Y
Lott	Y	Y
MISSOURI		
Bond	Y	Y
Talent	Y	Y
MONTANA		
Burns	Y	Y
Baucus	N	Y
NEBRASKA		
Hagel	Y	Y
Nelson	N	Y
NEVADA		
Reid	N	Y
Ensign	Y	Y

	69	70
NEW HAMPSHIRE		
Gregg	Y	Y
Sununu	Y	Y
NEW JERSEY		
Lautenberg	N	Y
Corzine	N	Y
NEW MEXICO		
Domenici	Y	Y
Bingaman	N	Y
NEW YORK		
Schumer	N	Y
Clinton	N	Y
NORTH CAROLINA		
Edwards	N	Y
Dole	Y	Y
NORTH DAKOTA		
Conrad	N	Y
Dorgan	N	Y
OHIO		
DeWine	Y	Y
Voinovich	Y	Y
OKLAHOMA		
Nickles	Y	Y
Inhofe	Y	Y
OREGON		
Wyden	N	Y
Smith	Y	Y
PENNSYLVANIA		
Specter	?	?
Santorum	Y	Y
RHODE ISLAND		
Reed	N	Y
Chafee	Y	Y
SOUTH CAROLINA		
Hollings	N	N
Graham	Y	Y
SOUTH DAKOTA		
Daschle	N	Y
Johnson	N	Y
TENNESSEE		
Frist	Y	Y
Alexander	Y	Y

	69	70
TEXAS		
Hutchison	Y	Y
Cornyn	Y	Y
UTAH		
Hatch	Y	Y
Bennett	Y	Y
VERMONT		
Leahy	N	Y
Jeffords	N	Y
VIRGINIA		
Warner	Y	Y
Allen	Y	Y
WASHINGTON		
Murray	N	Y
Cantwell	N	Y
WEST VIRGINIA		
Byrd	N	Y
Rockefeller	N	Y
WISCONSIN		
Kohl	N	Y
Feingold	N	Y
WYOMING		
Thomas	Y	Y
Enzi	Y	Y

Key

Y	Voted for (yea).
#	Paired for.
+	Announced for.
N	Voted against (nay).
X	Paired against.
–	Announced against.
P	Voted "present."
C	Voted "present" to avoid possible conflict of interest.
?	Did not vote or otherwise make a position known.

Democrats   ***Republicans***
Independents

ND Northern Democrats   SD Southern Democrats

Southern states - Ala., Ark., Fla., Ga., Ky., La., Miss., N.C., Okla., S.C., Tenn., Texas, Va.

69. S 2290. Asbestos Claims Fund/Cloture. Motion to invoke cloture (thus limiting debate) on the motion to proceed to the bill that would establish a fund to pay thousands of asbestos-exposure claims outside the court system via a no-fault fund of as much as $124 billion. The fund would be financed through contributions from defendant corporations and insurers, which would be shielded in return from most future lawsuits related to asbestos exposure. Motion rejected 50-47: R 49-0; D 1-46 (ND 0-38, SD 1-8); I 0-1. Three-fifths of the total Senate (60) is required to invoke cloture. April 22, 2004.

70. S 2329. Victims' Rights/Passage. Passage of the bill that would provide victims of crime or their representatives the right to be heard at public proceedings and would require judicial officials to take victims' safety into account when deciding the fate of defendants. It would provide victims the right to reasonable, accurate and timely notice of any public proceeding involving the crime or of any release or escape of the accused. It also would authorize $122.3 million from fiscal 2005 through 2009 for grants administered by the Justice Department to encourage states to establish and maintain programs to carry out the provisions related to crime victims' rights and for the development of a notification system of dates and criminal proceedings for crime victims. Passed 96-1: R 49-0; D 46-1 (ND 38-0, SD 8-1); I 1-0. April 22, 2004.

	71	72	73	74	75	76	77
ALABAMA							
Shelby	Y	Y	N	Y	Y	Y	Y
Sessions	Y	Y	N	Y	Y	Y	Y
ALASKA							
Stevens	Y	Y	N	Y	Y	Y	N
Murkowski, L.	Y	Y	N	Y	Y	Y	Y
ARIZONA							
McCain	Y	Y	N	N	Y	Y	Y
Kyl	Y	Y	N	Y	Y	Y	Y
ARKANSAS							
Lincoln	Y	Y	Y	Y	Y	N	Y
Pryor	Y	Y	Y	Y	N	N	Y
CALIFORNIA							
Feinstein	N	N	N	N	N	N	Y
Boxer	Y	Y	N	Y	Y	N	Y
COLORADO							
Campbell	Y	Y	Y	Y	Y	Y	Y
Allard	Y	Y	N	Y	Y	Y	Y
CONNECTICUT							
Dodd	Y	N	Y	N	N	Y	N
Lieberman	Y	Y	N	N	N	Y	N
DELAWARE							
Biden	?	N	Y	N	N	N	Y
Carper	N	N	Y	Y	N	N	Y
FLORIDA							
Graham	N	?	Y	N	N	N	N
Nelson	Y	N	Y	N	N	N	Y
GEORGIA							
Miller	?	Y	N	Y	Y	Y	Y
Chambliss	Y	Y	N	Y	Y	Y	Y
HAWAII							
Inouye	?	N	Y	N	Y	N	Y
Akaka	N	N	Y	N	N	N	Y
IDAHO							
Craig	Y	Y	N	Y	Y	Y	Y
Crapo	Y	Y	N	Y	Y	Y	Y
ILLINOIS							
Fitzgerald	?	Y	N	Y	Y	Y	Y
Durbin	N	N	Y	Y	N	N	Y
INDIANA							
Lugar	Y	Y	Y	Y	Y	N	Y
Bayh	Y	Y	Y	N	Y	N	Y
IOWA							
Grassley	Y	Y	N	Y	Y	Y	Y
Harkin	Y	Y	Y	Y	N	N	Y
KANSAS							
Brownback	Y	Y	N	N	Y	Y	Y
Roberts	Y	Y	N	Y	Y	Y	Y
KENTUCKY							
McConnell	Y	Y	N	Y	Y	Y	Y
Bunning	Y	Y	N	Y	Y	+	+
LOUISIANA							
Breaux	Y	N	Y	Y	N	?	?
Landrieu	?	N	Y	Y	Y	Y	Y
MAINE							
Snowe	Y	Y	N	N	Y	Y	Y
Collins	Y	Y	N	N	Y	Y	Y
MARYLAND							
Sarbanes	?	N	Y	N	N	N	Y
Mikulski	?	Y	Y	N	Y	N	Y
MASSACHUSETTS							
Kennedy	Y	N	Y	N	N	N	Y
Kerry	?	?	?	?	?	?	?
MICHIGAN							
Levin	Y	N	Y	N	N	N	Y
Stabenow	Y	Y	Y	N	Y	N	Y
MINNESOTA							
Dayton	Y	Y	Y	Y	Y	Y	Y
Coleman	Y	Y	N	Y	Y	Y	Y
MISSISSIPPI							
Cochran	Y	Y	N	Y	N	Y	Y
Lott	Y	Y	N	N	Y	Y	Y
MISSOURI							
Bond	Y	Y	N	Y	Y	Y	Y
Talent	Y	Y	N	Y	Y	Y	Y
MONTANA							
Burns	Y	Y	N	Y	Y	Y	Y
Baucus	Y	Y	Y	N	Y	Y	Y
NEBRASKA							
Hagel	?	Y	Y	Y	Y	Y	Y
Nelson	Y	Y	Y	Y	Y	Y	Y
NEVADA							
Reid	Y	Y	Y	Y	N	N	Y
Ensign	Y	Y	N	N	Y	Y	Y
NEW HAMPSHIRE							
Gregg	Y	Y	N	N	Y	Y	Y
Sununu	Y	Y	N	N	Y	Y	Y
NEW JERSEY							
Lautenberg	?	N	N	N	N	N	N
Corzine	Y	N	N	N	Y	Y	Y
NEW MEXICO							
Domenici	Y	N	N	Y	Y	Y	Y
Bingaman	Y	N	Y	N	N	N	N
NEW YORK							
Schumer	Y	N	N	N	Y	Y	Y
Clinton	N	N	N	N	N	N	Y
NORTH CAROLINA							
Edwards	?	N	Y	?	?	N	Y
Dole	Y	Y	N	Y	Y	Y	Y
NORTH DAKOTA							
Conrad	Y	Y	Y	Y	N	N	Y
Dorgan	Y	Y	Y	Y	N	N	Y
OHIO							
DeWine	Y	Y	N	Y	N	N	Y
Voinovich	N	N	N	Y	N	N	Y
OKLAHOMA							
Nickles	Y	Y	N	Y	Y	Y	Y
Inhofe	Y	Y	N	Y	Y	Y	Y
OREGON							
Wyden	Y	Y	N	Y	Y	Y	Y
Smith	Y	Y	N	Y	Y	Y	Y
PENNSYLVANIA							
Specter	?	?	N	Y	Y	Y	Y
Santorum	Y	Y	N	Y	Y	Y	Y
RHODE ISLAND							
Reed	Y	Y	N	N	N	N	Y
Chafee	?	N	N	N	Y	N	Y
SOUTH CAROLINA							
Hollings	N	N	Y	N	Y	N	Y
Graham	Y	?	N	N	Y	Y	Y
SOUTH DAKOTA							
Daschle	Y	Y	Y	Y	N	N	Y
Johnson	Y	Y	Y	Y	N	N	Y
TENNESSEE							
Frist	Y	Y	N	Y	Y	Y	Y
Alexander	N	N	N	Y	N	N	Y
TEXAS							
Hutchison	Y	N	N	N	N	Y	Y
Cornyn	Y	N	N	N	Y	Y	Y
UTAH							
Hatch	Y	Y	N	Y	Y	Y	Y
Bennett	Y	Y	N	Y	Y	?	?
VERMONT							
Leahy	Y	Y	N	N	Y	Y	Y
Jeffords	N	N	Y	N	Y	Y	Y
VIRGINIA							
Warner	Y	Y	N	Y	Y	Y	Y
Allen	Y	Y	N	Y	Y	Y	Y
WASHINGTON							
Murray	Y	Y	Y	N	Y	Y	Y
Cantwell	Y	Y	Y	N	Y	Y	Y
WEST VIRGINIA							
Byrd	Y	N	Y	N	Y	N	Y
Rockefeller	N	Y	Y	N	N	N	Y
WISCONSIN							
Kohl	?	Y	Y	N	N	Y	Y
Feingold	Y	N	Y	N	N	N	Y
WYOMING							
Thomas	Y	N	N	Y	Y	Y	Y
Enzi	?	N	N	Y	N	N	Y

ND Northern Democrats   SD Southern Democrats

Southern states - Ala., Ark., Fla., Ga., Ky., La., Miss., N.C., Okla., S.C., Tenn., Texas, Va.

Key

Y   Voted for (yea).
Paired for.
+   Announced for.
N   Voted against (nay).
X   Paired against.
−   Announced against.
P   Voted "present."
C   Voted "present" to avoid possible conflict of interest.
?   Did not vote or otherwise make a position known.

Democrats   **Republicans**
Independents

---

71. S 150. Internet Tax Moratorium/Cloture. Motion to invoke cloture (thus limiting debate) on the motion to proceed to the bill that would permanently ban states from imposing taxes on Internet access. Motion agreed to 74-11: R 44-2; D 30-8 (ND 26-6, SD 4-2); I 0-1. Three-fifths of the total Senate (60) is required to invoke cloture. April 26, 2004.

72. S 150. Internet Tax Moratorium/Internet Access Definition. McCain, R-Ariz., motion to table (kill) the Hutchison, R-Texas, amendment to the McCain substitute amendment. The Hutchison amendment would specify that the definition of Internet access service would not include a tax levied on or measured by net income, capital stock, net worth or property value. It also would not apply to any payment made for the use of a public right-of-way or in lieu of a fee for the use of a public right-of-way, including an access line fee, franchise fee, license fee or gross receipt fee. The substitute would extend the Internet tax moratorium for four years. Motion agreed to 64-32: R 41-8; D 23-23 (ND 20-18, SD 3-5); I 0-1. April 27, 2004.

73. S 150. Internet Tax Moratorium/Cloture. Motion to invoke cloture (thus limiting debate) on the Daschle, D-S.D., amendment that would require that gasoline sold in or introduced into the United States contain renewable fuel in specific amounts, beginning with 3.1 billion gallons in 2005 and increasing each year to 5 billion gallons in 2012. Motion rejected 40-59: R 2-49; D 37-10 (ND 29-9, SD 8-1); I 1-0. Three-fifths of the total Senate (60) is required to invoke cloture. April 29, 2004.

74. S 150. Internet Tax Moratorium/Cloture. Motion to invoke cloture (thus limiting debate) on the Domenici, R-N.M., amendment to the Daschle, D-S.D., amendment. The Domenici amendment would overhaul the nation's energy policies, authorize mandatory electricity reliability standards, and include provisions on wind, nuclear, hydrogen and solar energy. Motion rejected 55-43: R 39-12; D 16-30 (ND 10-28, SD 6-2); I 0-1. Three-fifths of the total Senate (60) is required to invoke cloture. April 29, 2004.

75. S 150. Internet Tax Moratorium/Cloture. Motion to invoke cloture (thus limiting debate) on the McCain, R-Ariz., substitute amendment that would extend the Internet tax moratorium for four years. It also would prohibit two or more states from taxing the same online purchase and would bar taxes that specifically target Internet commerce. Motion agreed to 64-34: R 46-5; D 18-28 (ND 15-23, SD 3-5); I 0-1. Three-fifths of the total Senate (60) is required to invoke cloture. April 29, 2004.

76. S 150. Internet Tax Moratorium/DSL Tax Moratorium Extension. McCain, R-Ariz., motion to table (kill) the Feinstein, D-Calif., amendment to the McCain substitute amendment. The Feinstein amendment would extend the exemption from the bill's provisions to four years for states and localities that already tax consumer digital subscriber line (DSL) services. Motion agreed to 59-37: R 43-6; D 16-30 (ND 13-25, SD 3-5); I 0-1. April 29, 2004.

77. S 150. Internet Tax Moratorium/Passage. Passage of the bill, as amended, that would extend the Internet tax moratorium for four years. It also would prohibit two or more states from taxing the same online purchase and would bar taxes that specifically target Internet commerce. It would allow states and localities to tax Voice Over Internet Protocol service. It also would require a General Accounting Office study of the tax moratorium's impact on state and local economies. Passed 93-3: R 49-0; D 43-3 (ND 36-2, SD 7-1); I 1-0. April 29, 2004.

	78	79	80	81	82	83	84	85
ALABAMA								
Shelby	Y	N	N	N	N	Y	N	Y
Sessions	Y	N	N	N	N	Y	N	Y
ALASKA								
Stevens	Y	N	N	N	N	Y	Y	Y
Murkowski, L.	Y	N	N	N	N	Y	Y	Y
ARIZONA								
McCain	Y	N	N	N	N	Y	N	Y
Kyl	Y	N	N	N	N	Y	N	Y
ARKANSAS								
Lincoln	Y	Y	Y	N	N	N	Y	Y
Pryor	Y	Y	Y	N	N	N	Y	Y
CALIFORNIA								
Feinstein	Y	Y	Y	Y	N	N	Y	Y
Boxer	Y	Y	Y	N	N	N	Y	Y
COLORADO								
Campbell	Y	N	N	N	N	Y	Y	Y
Allard	Y	N	N	N	N	Y	N	Y
CONNECTICUT								
Dodd	Y	Y	Y	Y	N	Y	N	Y
Lieberman	Y	Y	Y	Y	N	Y	Y	Y
DELAWARE								
Biden	Y	Y	Y	N	N	N	Y	Y
Carper	Y	Y	Y	Y	N	N	Y	Y
FLORIDA								
Graham	Y	Y	Y	Y	Y	N	Y	Y
Nelson	Y	Y	Y	Y	N	N	Y	Y
GEORGIA								
Miller	Y	N	N	N	N	Y	Y	Y
Chambliss	Y	N	N	N	N	Y	Y	Y
HAWAII								
Inouye	Y	Y	Y	Y	N	Y	N	Y
Akaka	Y	Y	Y	Y	N	Y	N	Y
IDAHO								
Craig	Y	N	N	N	N	Y	Y	Y
Crapo	Y	N	N	N	N	Y	Y	Y
ILLINOIS								
Fitzgerald	Y	N	N	N	N	Y	N	Y
Durbin	Y	Y	Y	Y	Y	N	Y	N
INDIANA								
Lugar	Y	N	N	N	N	Y	Y	Y
Bayh	Y	Y	Y	Y	N	N	N	Y

	78	79	80	81	82	83	84	85
IOWA								
Grassley	Y	N	N	N	N	Y	N	Y
Harkin	Y	Y	Y	Y	Y	N	N	N
KANSAS								
Brownback	Y	N	N	N	N	Y	Y	Y
Roberts	Y	N	N	N	N	Y	Y	Y
KENTUCKY								
McConnell	Y	N	N	N	N	Y	Y	Y
Bunning	Y	N	N	N	N	Y	Y	Y
LOUISIANA								
Breaux	Y	Y	Y	Y	N	Y	Y	Y
Landrieu	Y	Y	Y	Y	Y	N	Y	Y
MAINE								
Snowe	Y	Y	Y	N	N	Y	N	Y
Collins	Y	N	Y	N	N	Y	N	Y
MARYLAND								
Sarbanes	Y	Y	Y	Y	Y	N	Y	Y
Mikulski	Y	Y	Y	Y	Y	N	Y	Y
MASSACHUSETTS								
Kennedy	Y	Y	Y	Y	N	Y	N	Y
Kerry	?	?	?	?	?	?	?	?
MICHIGAN								
Levin	Y	Y	Y	Y	N	Y	N	Y
Stabenow	Y	Y	Y	Y	N	N	Y	Y
MINNESOTA								
Dayton	Y	Y	Y	Y	Y	N	Y	N
Coleman	Y	N	Y	N	N	Y	Y	Y
MISSISSIPPI								
Cochran	Y	N	N	N	N	Y	Y	Y
Lott	Y	N	N	N	N	Y	N	Y
MISSOURI								
Bond	Y	N	N	N	N	Y	Y	Y
Talent	Y	N	N	N	N	Y	Y	Y
MONTANA								
Burns	Y	N	N	N	N	Y	N	Y
Baucus	Y	Y	Y	N	N	Y	Y	Y
NEBRASKA								
Hagel	Y	N	N	N	N	Y	N	Y
Nelson	Y	Y	Y	N	N	Y	Y	Y
NEVADA								
Reid	Y	Y	Y	N	Y	N	Y	Y
Ensign	Y	N	N	N	N	Y	N	Y

	78	79	80	81	82	83	84	85
NEW HAMPSHIRE								
Gregg	Y	N	N	N	N	Y	N	Y
Sununu	Y	N	N	N	N	Y	N	Y
NEW JERSEY								
Lautenberg	Y	Y	Y	N	Y	N	Y	Y
Corzine	Y	Y	Y	N	N	N	Y	Y
NEW MEXICO								
Domenici	Y	N	N	N	N	Y	Y	Y
Bingaman	Y	Y	Y	Y	N	N	Y	Y
NEW YORK								
Schumer	Y	Y	Y	Y	N	N	Y	Y
Clinton	Y	Y	Y	Y	N	N	Y	Y
NORTH CAROLINA								
Edwards	Y	Y	Y	Y	N	Y	N	Y
Dole	Y	N	N	N	N	Y	N	Y
NORTH DAKOTA								
Conrad	Y	Y	Y	Y	N	N	Y	Y
Dorgan	Y	Y	Y	Y	N	N	N	Y
OHIO								
DeWine	Y	N	N	N	N	Y	Y	Y
Voinovich	Y	N	N	N	N	Y	Y	Y
OKLAHOMA								
Nickles	Y	N	N	N	N	Y	N	Y
Inhofe	Y	N	N	N	N	Y	N	Y
OREGON								
Wyden	Y	Y	Y	Y	N	N	Y	Y
Smith	Y	N	Y	N	N	Y	Y	Y
PENNSYLVANIA								
Specter	Y	Y	Y	N	N	Y	Y	Y
Santorum	Y	N	N	N	N	Y	Y	Y
RHODE ISLAND								
Reed	Y	Y	Y	Y	N	N	Y	Y
Chafee	Y	Y	N	N	N	Y	Y	Y
SOUTH CAROLINA								
Hollings	Y	Y	Y	Y	N	N	Y	Y
Graham	Y	N	Y	N	N	Y	Y	Y
SOUTH DAKOTA								
Daschle	Y	Y	Y	Y	N	N	Y	Y
Johnson	Y	Y	Y	Y	N	N	Y	Y
TENNESSEE								
Frist	Y	N	N	N	N	Y	Y	Y
Alexander	Y	N	N	N	N	Y	Y	Y

	78	79	80	81	82	83	84	85
TEXAS								
Hutchison	Y	N	N	N	N	Y	Y	Y
Cornyn	Y	N	N	N	N	Y	Y	Y
UTAH								
Hatch	Y	N	N	N	N	Y	Y	Y
Bennett	Y	N	N	N	N	Y	Y	Y
VERMONT								
Leahy	Y	Y	Y	N	N	Y	N	Y
Jeffords	Y	Y	Y	N	N	Y	N	Y
VIRGINIA								
Warner	Y	N	N	N	N	Y	Y	Y
Allen	Y	N	N	N	N	Y	Y	Y
WASHINGTON								
Murray	Y	Y	Y	N	N	Y	N	Y
Cantwell	Y	Y	Y	N	N	Y	N	Y
WEST VIRGINIA								
Byrd	Y	Y	Y	Y	Y	N	Y	Y
Rockefeller	Y	Y	Y	Y	Y	N	Y	Y
WISCONSIN								
Kohl	Y	Y	Y	Y	N	N	Y	Y
Feingold	Y	Y	Y	Y	N	N	Y	Y
WYOMING								
Thomas	Y	N	N	N	N	Y	N	?
Enzi	Y	N	N	N	N	Y	Y	Y

ND Northern Democrats SD Southern Democrats

Southern states - Ala., Ark., Fla., Ga., Ky., La., Miss., N.C., Okla., S.C., Tenn., Texas, Va.

78. S 1637. Corporate Tax Overhaul/Overtime Pay Rules Exemption. Gregg, R-N.H., amendment that would exempt certain professions from new Labor Department rules that overhaul eligibility standards for overtime pay. The list of exemptions would include 55 different groups, such as registered nurses; oil and gas pipeline, field and platform workers; steel workers; teachers; firefighters; police officers; funeral directors; and longshoremen. Adopted 99-0: R 51-0; D 47-0 (ND 38-0, SD 9-0); I 1-0. May 4, 2004.

79. S 1637. Corporate Tax Overhaul/Overtime Pay Rules. Harkin, D-Iowa, amendment that would block implementation of language in a new Labor Department rule that would cause some workers to lose their eligibility for overtime pay. Adopted 52-47: R 5-46; D 46-1 (ND 38-0, SD 8-1); I 1-0. A "nay" was a vote in support of the president's position. May 4, 2004.

80. S 1637. Corporate Tax Overhaul/Trade Adjustment Assistance. Wyden, D-Ore., motion to waive the Budget Act with respect to the Nickles, R-Okla., point of order against the Wyden amendment that would extend eligibility for trade adjustment assistance (TAA) to service workers, including government workers who have lost their jobs because of foreign trade since Nov. 4, 2002. It would lower the age of eligibility for the wage insurance program from 50 to 40, and it would expand TAA by covering home mortgage loans and by increasing the health care tax credit from 65 percent to 75 percent. Motion rejected 54-45: R 8-43; D 45-2 (ND 37-1, SD 8-1); I 1-0. A three-fifths majority (60) of the entire Senate is required to waive the Budget Act. May 4, 2004.

81. S 1637. Corporate Tax Overhaul/Corporate Profits Repatriation. Breaux, D-La., amendment that would require companies to spend offshore profits on job creation, research and development, capital investment or funding pension plans in order to be eligible for a reduced tax rate of 5.25 percent. Rejected 31-68: R 1-50; D 30-17 (ND 25-13, SD 5-4); I 0-1. May 5, 2004.

82. S 1637. Corporate Tax Overhaul/Manufacturing Jobs Tax Credit. Graham, D-Fla., amendment that would strike from the underlying bill all international tax provisions and the tax deduction provisions related to income attributable to U.S. production activities. It would replace them with a new tax credit equal to 1.66 percent of the wages an employer paid to each employee in manufacturing up to $35,000 per employee. Rejected 22-77: R 0-51; D 22-25 (ND 17-21, SD 5-4); I 0-1. May 5, 2004.

83. S 1637. Corporate Tax Overhaul/Corporate Reimportation Tax. Grassley, R-Iowa, motion to table (kill) the Dorgan, D-N.D., amendment that would partially repeal a tax deferral regulation for U.S. multinational companies by requiring those companies to pay federal income taxes on foreign factories when goods are reimported back into the United States. Employers also would be required to notify employees and the Labor Department when jobs will be moved offshore, including the number of jobs affected, the relocation destination of those jobs and the reason for the relocation. Motion agreed to 60-39: R 51-0; D 8-39 (ND 5-33, SD 3-6); I 1-0. May 5, 2004.

84. S 1637. Corporate Tax Overhaul/Brownfields Demonstration Program. Allard, R-Colo., amendment that would authorize $2 billion for a new type of tax-exempt bond, called "green bonds," for a brownfields demonstration program for projects that use renewable energy and environmentally friendly construction techniques. Adopted 76-23: R 34-17; D 42-5 (ND 33-5, SD 9-0); I 0-1. May 5, 2004.

85. Negroponte Nomination/Confirmation. Confirmation of President Bush's nomination of John D. Negroponte of New York to be ambassador to Iraq. Confirmed 95-3: R 50-0; D 44-3 (ND 35-3, SD 9-0); I 1-0. A "yea" was a vote in support of the president's position. May 6, 2004.

Senate Votes 86, 87, 88, 89, 90

	86	87	88	89	90
ALABAMA					
Shelby	Y	Y	N	N	N
Sessions	Y	Y	N	N	N
ALASKA					
Stevens	Y	Y	N	N	N
Murkowski, L.	?	Y	Y	N	N
ARIZONA					
McCain	?	N	Y	Y	?
Kyl	Y	Y	N	Y	N
ARKANSAS					
Lincoln	Y	Y	Y	N	N
Pryor	Y	Y	Y	N	N
CALIFORNIA					
Feinstein	Y	Y	Y	N	N
Boxer	Y	Y	Y	Y	N
COLORADO					
Campbell	Y	Y	N	N	N
Allard	Y	Y	N	N	N
CONNECTICUT					
Dodd	Y	Y	Y	Y	Y
Lieberman	Y	Y	Y	N	N
DELAWARE					
Biden	Y	Y	Y	Y	N
Carper	Y	Y	Y	N	N
FLORIDA					
Graham	Y	N	Y	Y	Y
Nelson	Y	Y	Y	N	N
GEORGIA					
Miller	Y	Y	N	N	N
Chambliss	Y	Y	N	N	N
HAWAII					
Inouye	Y	Y	Y	N	Y
Akaka	Y	Y	Y	N	Y
IDAHO					
Craig	Y	Y	N	N	N
Crapo	Y	Y	N	N	N
ILLINOIS					
Fitzgerald	Y	Y	N	N	N
Durbin	Y	Y	Y	N	Y
INDIANA					
Lugar	Y	Y	N	N	N
Bayh	Y	?	Y	N	N
IOWA					
Grassley	Y	Y	N	N	N
Harkin	Y	Y	Y	N	Y
KANSAS					
Brownback	Y	Y	N	N	N
Roberts	Y	Y	N	N	N
KENTUCKY					
McConnell	Y	Y	N	N	N
Bunning	Y	Y	N	N	N
LOUISIANA					
Breaux	Y	Y	Y	N	N
Landrieu	Y	Y	Y	N	N
MAINE					
Snowe	Y	Y	Y	N	N
Collins	Y	Y	Y	N	N
MARYLAND					
Sarbanes	Y	Y	Y	N	Y
Mikulski	Y	Y	Y	N	Y
MASSACHUSETTS					
Kennedy	Y	Y	Y	Y	Y
Kerry	?	?	?	?	?
MICHIGAN					
Levin	Y	Y	Y	N	Y
Stabenow	Y	Y	Y	N	N
MINNESOTA					
Dayton	Y	Y	Y	N	Y
Coleman	?	Y	N	N	N
MISSISSIPPI					
Cochran	Y	Y	N	N	N
Lott	Y	Y	N	N	N
MISSOURI					
Bond	Y	Y	N	N	N
Talent	Y	Y	Y	N	N
MONTANA					
Burns	Y	Y	N	N	N
Baucus	Y	Y	Y	N	N
NEBRASKA					
Hagel	Y	Y	N	N	N
Nelson	Y	Y	Y	N	N
NEVADA					
Reid	Y	Y	Y	N	Y
Ensign	Y	Y	N	N	N

	86	87	88	89	90
NEW HAMPSHIRE					
Gregg	Y	N	N	Y	N
Sununu	Y	N	N	Y	N
NEW JERSEY					
Lautenberg	+	N	Y	Y	N
Corzine	Y	N	Y	Y	N
NEW MEXICO					
Domenici	Y	Y	N	N	N
Bingaman	Y	Y	Y	N	N
NEW YORK					
Schumer	Y	Y	Y	N	N
Clinton	Y	Y	Y	N	Y
NORTH CAROLINA					
Edwards	?	Y	Y	?	?
Dole	Y	Y	Y	N	N
NORTH DAKOTA					
Conrad	Y	Y	Y	N	Y
Dorgan	Y	Y	Y	N	Y
OHIO					
DeWine	Y	Y	Y	N	N
Voinovich	Y	Y	Y	N	N
OKLAHOMA					
Nickles	Y	Y	N	N	N
Inhofe	Y	Y	N	N	N
OREGON					
Wyden	Y	Y	Y	N	N
Smith	Y	Y	Y	N	N
PENNSYLVANIA					
Specter	?	Y	N	N	N
Santorum	Y	Y	N	N	N
RHODE ISLAND					
Reed	Y	Y	Y	N	Y
Chafee	Y	Y	Y	N	N
SOUTH CAROLINA					
Hollings	?	N	Y	Y	Y
Graham	Y	Y	N	N	N
SOUTH DAKOTA					
Daschle	Y	Y	Y	N	N
Johnson	Y	Y	Y	N	N
TENNESSEE					
Frist	Y	Y	N	N	N
Alexander	Y	Y	N	N	N

	86	87	88	89	90
TEXAS					
Hutchison	Y	Y	N	N	N
Cornyn	Y	Y	N	N	N
UTAH					
Hatch	Y	Y	N	N	N
Bennett	Y	Y	N	N	N
VERMONT					
Leahy	Y	Y	Y	N	Y
Jeffords	Y	Y	Y	N	Y
VIRGINIA					
Warner	Y	Y	N	N	N
Allen	Y	Y	N	N	N
WASHINGTON					
Murray	Y	Y	Y	N	N
Cantwell	Y	Y	Y	N	N
WEST VIRGINIA					
Byrd	Y	Y	Y	N	Y
Rockefeller	Y	Y	Y	N	Y
WISCONSIN					
Kohl	Y	Y	Y	N	Y
Feingold	Y	N	Y	Y	Y
WYOMING					
Thomas	Y	Y	N	N	N
Enzi	Y	Y	N	N	N

Key

Y	Voted for (yea).
#	Paired for.
+	Announced for.
N	Voted against (nay).
X	Paired against.
−	Announced against.
P	Voted "present."
C	Voted "present" to avoid possible conflict of interest.
?	Did not vote or otherwise make a position known.

Democrats **Republicans**
Independents

ND Northern Democrats   SD Southern Democrats

Southern states - Ala., Ark., Fla., Ga., Ky., La., Miss., N.C., Okla., S.C., Tenn., Texas, Va.

86. S Res 356. Treatment of Iraqi Prisoners/Adoption. Adoption of the resolution that would condemn the abuse of Iraqi prisoners at Abu Ghraib prison and join with the president in expressing apology for the humiliations suffered by the prisoners in Iraq and their families. It would call for an investigation by members of the Senate and the president into the alleged abuses and urge that all individuals responsible for such acts be held accountable. It also would express support for Americans who are serving nobly abroad to improve the lives of Iraqis. Adopted 92-0: R 47-0; D 44-0 (ND 37-0, SD 7-0); I 1-0. May 10, 2004.

87. S 1637. Corporate Tax Overhaul/Cloture. Motion to invoke cloture (thus limiting debate) on the bill that would revoke an export tax break for U.S. manufacturers ruled an illegal trade subsidy by the World Trade Organization. The legislation would replace the export tax break with more than $170 billion in new corporate tax breaks over 10 years. The cost would be offset through the repeal of the export subsidy and through other revenue-raising provisions. Motion agreed to 90-8: R 48-3; D 41-5 (ND 34-3, SD 7-2); I 1-0. Three-fifths of the total Senate (60) is required to invoke cloture. May 11, 2004.

88. S 1637. Corporate Tax Overhaul/Unemployment Insurance. Cantwell, D-Wash., motion to waive the Budget Act with respect to the Nickles, R-Okla., point of order against the Cantwell amendment that would extend to Nov. 30, 2004, the federal program to provide an additional 13 weeks of unemployment benefits for people who have exhausted their state jobless benefits. Motion rejected 59-40: R 12-39; D 46-1 (ND 38-0, SD 8-1); I 1-0. A three-fifths majority (60) of the total Senate is required to waive the Budget Act. May 11, 2004.

89. S 1637. Corporate Tax Overhaul/Energy Tax Provisions. McCain, R-Ariz., amendment that would strike provisions in the bill that would provide $18 billion in energy tax breaks. Rejected 13-85: R 4-47; D 9-37 (ND 7-31, SD 2-6); I 0-1. May 11, 2004.

90. S 1637. Corporate Tax Overhaul/Manufacturing Tax Deduction. Hollings, D-S.C., amendment that would strike $39 billion in tax breaks on overseas income from the bill. The amendment would provide for an immediate 9 percent tax deduction for domestic manufacturers. Rejected 23-74: R 0-50; D 22-24 (ND 20-18, SD 2-6); I 1-0. May 11, 2004.

	91	92	93	94
ALABAMA				
Shelby	Y	Y	N	Y
Sessions	Y	Y	N	Y
ALASKA				
Stevens	Y	Y	N	Y
Murkowski, L.	Y	Y	Y	Y
ARIZONA				
McCain	?	Y	Y	Y
Kyl	N	Y	N	Y
ARKANSAS				
Lincoln	Y	Y	Y	Y
Pryor	Y	Y	Y	Y
CALIFORNIA				
Feinstein	Y	Y	Y	Y
Boxer	Y	Y	Y	Y
COLORADO				
Campbell	Y	Y	N	Y
Allard	Y	Y	N	Y
CONNECTICUT				
Dodd	Y	Y	Y	Y
Lieberman	Y	Y	Y	Y
DELAWARE				
Biden	Y	Y	Y	Y
Carper	Y	Y	Y	Y
FLORIDA				
Graham	N	Y	Y	Y
Nelson	Y	Y	Y	Y
GEORGIA				
Miller	Y	Y	N	Y
Chambliss	Y	Y	N	Y
HAWAII				
Inouye	Y	Y	Y	Y
Akaka	Y	Y	Y	Y
IDAHO				
Craig	Y	Y	N	Y
Crapo	Y	Y	N	Y
ILLINOIS				
Fitzgerald	Y	Y	N	Y
Durbin	Y	Y	Y	Y
INDIANA				
Lugar	Y	Y	N	Y
Bayh	Y	Y	Y	Y

	91	92	93	94
IOWA				
Grassley	Y	Y	N	Y
Harkin	Y	Y	Y	Y
KANSAS				
Brownback	Y	Y	N	Y
Roberts	Y	Y	Y	Y
KENTUCKY				
McConnell	Y	Y	N	Y
Bunning	Y	Y	N	Y
LOUISIANA				
Breaux	Y	Y	Y	Y
Landrieu	Y	Y	Y	Y
MAINE				
Snowe	Y	Y	Y	Y
Collins	Y	Y	Y	Y
MARYLAND				
Sarbanes	Y	Y	Y	Y
Mikulski	Y	Y	Y	Y
MASSACHUSETTS				
Kennedy	Y	Y	Y	Y
Kerry	?	?	?	?
MICHIGAN				
Levin	Y	Y	Y	Y
Stabenow	Y	Y	Y	N
MINNESOTA				
Dayton	Y	Y	Y	Y
Coleman	Y	Y	Y	?
MISSISSIPPI				
Cochran	Y	Y	N	Y
Lott	Y	Y	N	Y
MISSOURI				
Bond	Y	Y	N	Y
Talent	Y	Y	N	Y
MONTANA				
Burns	Y	Y	N	Y
Baucus	Y	Y	Y	Y
NEBRASKA				
Hagel	Y	Y	Y	Y
Nelson	Y	Y	Y	Y
NEVADA				
Reid	Y	Y	Y	Y
Ensign	Y	Y	N	Y

	91	92	93	94
NEW HAMPSHIRE				
Gregg	N	Y	N	Y
Sununu	N	Y	N	Y
NEW JERSEY				
Lautenberg	Y	Y	Y	Y
Corzine	Y	Y	Y	Y
NEW MEXICO				
Domenici	Y	Y	N	Y
Bingaman	Y	Y	Y	Y
NEW YORK				
Schumer	Y	Y	Y	Y
Clinton	Y	Y	Y	Y
NORTH CAROLINA				
Edwards	?	Y	Y	Y
Dole	Y	Y	N	Y
NORTH DAKOTA				
Conrad	Y	Y	Y	Y
Dorgan	Y	Y	Y	Y
OHIO				
DeWine	Y	Y	N	Y
Voinovich	Y	Y	N	Y
OKLAHOMA				
Nickles	Y	N	N	Y
Inhofe	Y	Y	N	Y
OREGON				
Wyden	Y	Y	Y	Y
Smith	Y	Y	N	Y
PENNSYLVANIA				
Specter	Y	Y	Y	Y
Santorum	Y	?	?	Y
RHODE ISLAND				
Reed	Y	Y	Y	Y
Chafee	Y	Y	Y	Y
SOUTH CAROLINA				
Hollings	N	?	?	Y
Graham	Y	Y	N	Y
SOUTH DAKOTA				
Daschle	Y	Y	Y	Y
Johnson	Y	Y	Y	Y
TENNESSEE				
Frist	Y	Y	N	Y
Alexander	Y	Y	N	Y

Key

Y	Voted for (yea).
#	Paired for.
+	Announced for.
N	Voted against (nay).
X	Paired against.
–	Announced against.
P	Voted "present."
C	Voted "present" to avoid possible conflict of interest.
?	Did not vote or otherwise make a position known.

Democrats **Republicans**
Independents

	91	92	93	94
TEXAS				
Hutchison	Y	Y	N	Y
Cornyn	Y	Y	N	Y
UTAH				
Hatch	Y	Y	N	Y
Bennett	Y	Y	N	Y
VERMONT				
Leahy	Y	Y	Y	N
Jeffords	Y	Y	Y	N
VIRGINIA				
Warner	Y	Y	Y	Y
Allen	Y	Y	N	Y
WASHINGTON				
Murray	Y	Y	Y	Y
Cantwell	Y	Y	Y	Y
WEST VIRGINIA				
Byrd	Y	Y	Y	Y
Rockefeller	Y	Y	Y	Y
WISCONSIN				
Kohl	Y	Y	Y	Y
Feingold	Y	Y	Y	Y
WYOMING				
Thomas	Y	Y	N	Y
Enzi	Y	Y	N	Y

ND Northern Democrats   SD Southern Democrats

Southern states - Ala., Ark., Fla., Ga., Ky., La., Miss., N.C., Okla., S.C., Tenn., Texas, Va.

91. S 1637. Corporate Tax Overhaul/Passage. Passage of the bill that would revoke an export tax break for U.S. manufacturers ruled an illegal trade subsidy by the World Trade Organization. It would replace the export tax break with more than $170 billion in new corporate tax breaks over 10 years. The cost would be offset through the repeal of the export subsidy and through other revenue-raising provisions. The bill also includes $18 billion in energy-related tax breaks. The bill, as amended, would block the Labor Department from implementing new rules overhauling eligibility standards for overtime pay. Passed 92-5: R 47-3; D 44-2 (ND 38-0, SD 6-2); I 1-0. May 11, 2004.

92. S 1248. IDEA Reauthorization/IDEA Funding. Gregg, R-N.H., amendment that would authorize discretionary spending increases of $2.3 billion per year to provide for full federal funding by 2011 of 40 percent of the average per pupil expenditures for certain programs under the Individuals with Disabilities Education Act. Adopted 96-1: R 49-1; D 46-0 (ND 38-0, SD 8-0); I 1-0. May 12, 2004.

93. S 1248. IDEA Reauthorization/IDEA Funding. Harkin, D-Iowa, motion to waive the Budget Act with respect to the Gregg, R-N.H., point of order against the Harkin amendment that would increase funding by $2.2 billion annually over the next six years to provide for full federal funding by 2010 of 40 percent of the average per pupil expenditures for certain programs under IDEA. The entire increase would be mandatory spending. Motion rejected 56-41: R 10-40; D 45-1 (ND 38-0, SD 7-1); I 1-0. A three-fifths majority (60) of the total Senate is required to waive the Budget Act. A "nay" was a vote in support of the president's position. May 12, 2004.

94. HR 1350. IDEA Reauthorization/Passage. Passage of the bill that would reauthorize the Individuals with Disabilities Education Act (IDEA). It would authorize discretionary spending increases of $2.3 billion per year to provide for full federal funding by 2011 of 40 percent of the average per pupil expenditures for certain programs under the IDEA. It would streamline student discipline measures, adding serious bodily injury to the offenses that could give rise to suspension. Parents who dispute a discipline decision would be granted an expedited hearing within 20 days of a request. Passed 95-3: R 50-0; D 45-2 (ND 36-2, SD 9-0); I 0-1. (Before passage, the Senate struck all after the enacting clause and inserted the text of S 1248, as amended.) May 13, 2004.

	95	96	97	98	99
ALABAMA					
Shelby	Y	Y	Y	N	Y
Sessions	Y	Y	Y	N	Y
ALASKA					
Stevens	Y	Y	Y	Y	Y
Murkowski, L.	?	Y	Y	Y	Y
ARIZONA					
McCain	Y	Y	Y	N	Y
Kyl	Y	Y	Y	N	Y
ARKANSAS					
Lincoln	Y	Y	Y	N	Y
Pryor	Y	Y	Y	Y	Y
CALIFORNIA					
Feinstein	Y	Y	Y	Y	Y
Boxer	+	Y	Y	Y	Y
COLORADO					
Campbell	Y	Y	Y	N	Y
Allard	Y	Y	Y	N	Y
CONNECTICUT					
Dodd	Y	Y	Y	Y	Y
Lieberman	Y	Y	Y	N	Y
DELAWARE					
Biden	+	Y	Y	N	Y
Carper	Y	Y	Y	N	Y
FLORIDA					
Graham	Y	Y	Y	N	Y
Nelson	Y	Y	Y	Y	Y
GEORGIA					
Miller	?	Y	Y	N	Y
Chambliss	?	Y	Y	N	Y
HAWAII					
Inouye	?	?	?	?	Y
Akaka	Y	Y	Y	N	Y
IDAHO					
Craig	Y	Y	Y	Y	Y
Crapo	Y	Y	Y	Y	Y
ILLINOIS					
Fitzgerald	Y	Y	Y	Y	Y
Durbin	Y	Y	Y	Y	Y
INDIANA					
Lugar	Y	Y	Y	N	Y
Bayh	Y	Y	Y	Y	Y

	95	96	97	98	99
IOWA					
Grassley	Y	Y	Y	N	Y
Harkin	Y	Y	Y	N	Y
KANSAS					
Brownback	+	Y	Y	N	Y
Roberts	+	Y	Y	N	Y
KENTUCKY					
McConnell	Y	Y	Y	N	Y
Bunning	Y	Y	+	+	Y
LOUISIANA					
Breaux	Y	Y	Y	Y	Y
Landrieu	Y	Y	Y	Y	Y
MAINE					
Snowe	Y	Y	Y	Y	Y
Collins	Y	Y	Y	Y	Y
MARYLAND					
Sarbanes	Y	Y	Y	Y	Y
Mikulski	Y	Y	Y	Y	Y
MASSACHUSETTS					
Kennedy	Y	Y	Y	N	Y
Kerry	?	?	?	?	?
MICHIGAN					
Levin	Y	Y	Y	N	Y
Stabenow	+	Y	Y	Y	Y
MINNESOTA					
Dayton	Y	Y	Y	Y	Y
Coleman	Y	Y	Y	N	Y
MISSISSIPPI					
Cochran	Y	Y	Y	Y	Y
Lott	Y	Y	Y	Y	Y
MISSOURI					
Bond	Y	Y	Y	N	Y
Talent	Y	Y	Y	N	Y
MONTANA					
Burns	Y	Y	Y	N	Y
Baucus	Y	Y	Y	Y	Y
NEBRASKA					
Hagel	Y	Y	Y	N	Y
Nelson	Y	Y	Y	Y	Y
NEVADA					
Reid	?	Y	Y	N	Y
Ensign	?	Y	Y	N	Y

	95	96	97	98	99
NEW HAMPSHIRE					
Gregg	Y	Y	Y	Y	Y
Sununu	Y	Y	Y	Y	Y
NEW JERSEY					
Lautenberg	Y	Y	?	?	Y
Corzine	?	Y	Y	Y	Y
NEW MEXICO					
Domenici	Y	Y	Y	Y	Y
Bingaman	?	Y	Y	Y	Y
NEW YORK					
Schumer	Y	Y	Y	Y	Y
Clinton	Y	Y	Y	Y	Y
NORTH CAROLINA					
Edwards	Y	Y	Y	Y	Y
Dole	Y	Y	Y	N	Y
NORTH DAKOTA					
Conrad	Y	Y	Y	Y	Y
Dorgan	Y	Y	Y	Y	Y
OHIO					
DeWine	Y	Y	Y	N	Y
Voinovich	Y	Y	Y	N	Y
OKLAHOMA					
Nickles	Y	Y	Y	N	Y
Inhofe	+	Y	Y	Y	Y
OREGON					
Wyden	Y	Y	Y	N	Y
Smith	Y	Y	Y	N	Y
PENNSYLVANIA					
Specter	Y	Y	Y	Y	Y
Santorum	Y	Y	Y	N	Y
RHODE ISLAND					
Reed	Y	Y	Y	N	Y
Chafee	Y	Y	Y	Y	Y
SOUTH CAROLINA					
Hollings	Y	Y	Y	Y	Y
Graham	Y	Y	Y	N	Y
SOUTH DAKOTA					
Daschle	+	Y	Y	Y	Y
Johnson	Y	Y	Y	Y	Y
TENNESSEE					
Frist	?	Y	Y	Y	Y
Alexander	Y	Y	Y	N	Y

Key

Y	Voted for (yea).
#	Paired for.
+	Announced for.
N	Voted against (nay).
X	Paired against.
−	Announced against.
P	Voted "present."
C	Voted "present" to avoid possible conflict of interest.
?	Did not vote or otherwise make a position known.

Democrats **Republicans**
Independents

	95	96	97	98	99
TEXAS					
Hutchison	Y	Y	Y	Y	Y
Cornyn	Y	Y	Y	N	Y
UTAH					
Hatch	Y	Y	Y	Y	Y
Bennett	Y	Y	Y	Y	Y
VERMONT					
Leahy	Y	Y	Y	N	Y
Jeffords	?	Y	Y	N	Y
VIRGINIA					
Warner	Y	Y	Y	N	Y
Allen	Y	Y	Y	N	Y
WASHINGTON					
Murray	Y	Y	Y	Y	Y
Cantwell	Y	Y	Y	N	Y
WEST VIRGINIA					
Byrd	Y	Y	Y	N	Y
Rockefeller	Y	Y	Y	N	Y
WISCONSIN					
Kohl	Y	Y	Y	N	Y
Feingold	Y	Y	Y	N	Y
WYOMING					
Thomas	Y	Y	Y	N	Y
Enzi	Y	Y	Y	N	Y

ND Northern Democrats   SD Southern Democrats

Southern states - Ala., Ark., Fla., Ga., Ky., La., Miss., N.C., Okla., S.C., Tenn., Texas, Va.

95. S 2400. Fiscal 2005 Defense Authorization/Health Care and Disability Benefits. Hutchison, R-Texas, amendment that would authorize medical and dental care for service academy cadets and midshipmen, and Reserve Officer Training Corps participants who incur injury or aggravate an illness or disease in the line of duty. Adopted 82-0: R 44-0; D 38-0 (ND 30-0, SD 8-0); I 0-0. May 17, 2004.

96. HR 3104. Military Medals/Passage. Passage of the bill that would provide for the establishment of separate campaign medals to be awarded to members of the military who participate in operations in Iraq or Afghanistan. Passed 98-0: R 51-0; D 46-0 (ND 37-0, SD 9-0); I 1-0. May 18, 2004.

97. Cooke Nomination/Confirmation. Confirmation of President Bush's nomination of Marcia G. Cooke of Florida to be a judge for the U.S. District Court for the Southern District of Florida. Confirmed 96-0: R 50-0; D 45-0 (ND 36-0, SD 9-0); I 1-0. A "yea" was a vote in support of the president's position. May 18, 2004.

98. S 2400. Fiscal 2005 Defense Authorization/Overseas Base Closures. Lott, R-Miss., amendment that would require the 2005 base realignment and closure round to apply only to U.S. military installations located overseas, delaying new U.S. domestic base closings until 2007. It also would require the Defense secretary to submit a detailed plan for reducing overseas bases. Rejected 47-49: R 21-29; D 26-19 (ND 20-16, SD 6-3); I 0-1. A "nay" was a vote in support of the president's position. May 18, 2004.

99. S 15. Project Bioshield/Passage. Passage of the bill that would authorize $5.6 billion over 10 years for the Department of Health and Human Services (HHS) to carry out Project Bioshield, an administration initiative to develop and stockpile vaccines, medications and other countermeasures to combat a bioterrorism attack. It would transfer overall responsibility for the Strategic National Stockpile to HHS and allow the department to contract the purchase of drugs and other stockpile items. It also would give the government authority to promote additional research and development of measures to counter biological, chemical, nuclear and radiological agents, including allowing an expedited award process for grants and projects. In the event of a national emergency, the bill would allow the distribution of treatments not yet approved by the Food and Drug Administration, along with those originally approved for other uses. Passed 99-0: R 51-0; D 47-0 (ND 38-0, SD 9-0); I 1-0. (Before passage, the Senate adopted by voice vote a Gregg, R-N.H., substitute amendment.) A "yea" was a vote in support of the president's position. May 19, 2004.

	100	101	102	103
ALABAMA				
Shelby	N	N	Y	Y
Sessions	Y	N	Y	?
ALASKA				
Stevens	Y	N	Y	Y
Murkowski, L.	Y	N	Y	Y
ARIZONA				
McCain	Y	N	Y	Y
Kyl	Y	N	Y	Y
ARKANSAS				
Lincoln	N	Y	Y	Y
Pryor	N	Y	Y	Y
CALIFORNIA				
Feinstein	N	Y	Y	Y
Boxer	N	Y	Y	Y
COLORADO				
Campbell	Y	N	Y	Y
Allard	Y	N	Y	Y
CONNECTICUT				
Dodd	N	Y	Y	Y
Lieberman	N	Y	Y	Y
DELAWARE				
Biden	N	Y	Y	Y
Carper	N	Y	Y	Y
FLORIDA				
Graham	N	Y	Y	Y
Nelson	N	Y	Y	Y
GEORGIA				
Miller	Y	N	Y	?
Chambliss	N	N	Y	Y
HAWAII				
Inouye	N	Y	Y	Y
Akaka	N	Y	Y	Y
IDAHO				
Craig	Y	N	Y	Y
Crapo	N	N	Y	Y
ILLINOIS				
Fitzgerald	Y	N	Y	Y
Durbin	N	Y	Y	Y
INDIANA				
Lugar	Y	N	Y	Y
Bayh	N	Y	Y	Y

	100	101	102	103
IOWA				
Grassley	Y	N	Y	Y
Harkin	N	Y	Y	N
KANSAS				
Brownback	Y	N	Y	Y
Roberts	Y	N	Y	Y
KENTUCKY				
McConnell	Y	N	Y	Y
Bunning	Y	N	Y	Y
LOUISIANA				
Breaux	N	Y	Y	Y
Landrieu	N	Y	Y	Y
MAINE				
Snowe	Y	Y	Y	Y
Collins	N	Y	Y	Y
MARYLAND				
Sarbanes	N	Y	Y	Y
Mikulski	N	Y	Y	Y
MASSACHUSETTS				
Kennedy	N	Y	Y	Y
Kerry	?	?	?	?
MICHIGAN				
Levin	N	Y	Y	Y
Stabenow	N	Y	Y	Y
MINNESOTA				
Dayton	N	Y	Y	Y
Coleman	N	N	Y	Y
MISSISSIPPI				
Cochran	Y	N	Y	Y
Lott	N	N	Y	Y
MISSOURI				
Bond	Y	N	Y	Y
Talent	Y	N	Y	Y
MONTANA				
Burns	Y	N	Y	Y
Baucus	N	N	Y	Y
NEBRASKA				
Hagel	Y	N	Y	Y
Nelson	N	Y	Y	Y
NEVADA				
Reid	N	Y	Y	Y
Ensign	Y	N	Y	Y

	100	101	102	103
NEW HAMPSHIRE				
Gregg	Y	N	Y	Y
Sununu	Y	N	Y	Y
NEW JERSEY				
Lautenberg	N	Y	Y	Y
Corzine	N	Y	Y	Y
NEW MEXICO				
Domenici	Y	N	Y	Y
Bingaman	N	Y	Y	Y
NEW YORK				
Schumer	N	Y	Y	Y
Clinton	N	Y	Y	Y
NORTH CAROLINA				
Edwards	N	Y	Y	Y
Dole	Y	N	Y	Y
NORTH DAKOTA				
Conrad	N	Y	Y	Y
Dorgan	N	Y	Y	Y
OHIO				
DeWine	N	N	Y	Y
Voinovich	N	N	Y	Y
OKLAHOMA				
Nickles	Y	N	Y	Y
Inhofe	Y	N	Y	Y
OREGON				
Wyden	N	Y	Y	Y
Smith	N	N	Y	Y
PENNSYLVANIA				
Specter	N	Y	Y	Y
Santorum	Y	N	Y	Y
RHODE ISLAND				
Reed	N	Y	Y	Y
Chafee	N	N	Y	Y
SOUTH CAROLINA				
Hollings	N	Y	Y	Y
Graham	N	N	Y	Y
SOUTH DAKOTA				
Daschle	N	Y	Y	Y
Johnson	N	Y	Y	Y
TENNESSEE				
Frist	Y	N	Y	Y
Alexander	Y	N	Y	Y

Key

Y	Voted for (yea).
#	Paired for.
+	Announced for.
N	Voted against (nay).
X	Paired against.
–	Announced against.
P	Voted "present."
C	Voted "present" to avoid possible conflict of interest.
?	Did not vote or otherwise make a position known.

Democrats **Republicans**
Independents

	100	101	102	103
TEXAS				
Hutchison	Y	N	Y	?
Cornyn	Y	N	Y	Y
UTAH				
Hatch	N	N	Y	Y
Bennett	N	N	Y	Y
VERMONT				
Leahy	N	Y	Y	Y
Jeffords	N	Y	Y	Y
VIRGINIA				
Warner	Y	N	?	Y
Allen	N	N	Y	Y
WASHINGTON				
Murray	N	Y	Y	Y
Cantwell	N	Y	Y	Y
WEST VIRGINIA				
Byrd	N	Y	Y	Y
Rockefeller	N	Y	Y	Y
WISCONSIN				
Kohl	N	Y	Y	Y
Feingold	N	Y	Y	Y
WYOMING				
Thomas	Y	N	Y	Y
Enzi	Y	N	Y	Y

ND Northern Democrats   SD Southern Democrats

Southern states - Ala., Ark., Fla., Ga., Ky., La., Miss., N.C., Okla., S.C., Tenn., Texas, Va.

100. S 2400. Fiscal 2005 Defense Authorization/Tobacco Attorney Fees. Kyl, R-Ariz., amendment that would express the sense of the Senate that legislation should be enacted that would impose an excise tax on a plaintiff's attorney in tobacco litigation cases equal to 5 percent of the excess fee transaction that exceeds $20,000 per hour. The revenue would be used to pay for military equipment, including heavily armored Humvees, body armor, unmanned aerial vehicles and ammunition. Rejected 37-62: R 36-15; D 1-46 (ND 0-38, SD 1-8); I 0-1. May 19, 2004.

101. S 2400. Fiscal 2005 Defense Authorization/U.S. Foreign Subsidiaries. Lautenberg, D-N.J. amendment that would require that any restrictions on transactions of U.S. companies that do business with countries determined to be state sponsors of terrorism also apply to their foreign subsidiaries, where there is at least 50 percent ownership by the U.S. company. Rejected 49-50: R 3-48; D 45-2 (ND 37-1, SD 8-1); I 1-0. May 19, 2004.

102. Gruender Nomination/Confirmation. Confirmation of President Bush's nomination of Raymond W. Gruender of Missouri to be a judge for the U.S. Court of Appeals for the 8th Circuit. Confirmed 97-1: R 50-0; D 46-1 (ND 37-1, SD 9-0); I 1-0. A "yea" was a vote in support of the president's position. May 20, 2004.

103. Van Antwerpen Nomination/Confirmation. Confirmation of President Bush's nomination of Franklin S. Van Antwerpen of Pennsylvania to be a judge for the U.S. Court of Appeals for the 3rd Circuit. Confirmed 96-0: R 49-0; D 46-0 (ND 38-0, SD 8-0); I 1-0. A "yea" was a vote in support of the president's position. May 20, 2004.

	104	105	106	107	108	109	110
ALABAMA							
Shelby	Y	Y	Y	N	Y	Y	Y
Sessions	Y	N	Y	N	Y	Y	Y
ALASKA							
Stevens	Y	N	Y	N	Y	Y	Y
Murkowski, L.	?	Y	Y	N	Y	Y	Y
ARIZONA							
McCain	Y	Y	Y	Y	Y	Y	Y
Kyl	Y	N	Y	N	Y	Y	Y
ARKANSAS							
Lincoln	Y	Y	Y	Y	Y	Y	Y
Pryor	Y	Y	Y	Y	Y	Y	Y
CALIFORNIA							
Feinstein	Y	Y	Y	Y	Y	Y	Y
Boxer	Y	Y	Y	Y	Y	Y	Y
COLORADO							
Campbell	?	?	?	?	?	?	?
Allard	Y	N	Y	N	Y	Y	Y
CONNECTICUT							
Dodd	Y	Y	Y	Y	Y	Y	Y
Lieberman	Y	Y	Y	Y	Y	Y	Y
DELAWARE							
Biden	Y	Y	Y	Y	Y	Y	?
Carper	Y	Y	Y	Y	Y	Y	Y
FLORIDA							
Graham	?	Y	Y	Y	Y	Y	Y
Nelson	Y	Y	Y	Y	Y	Y	Y
GEORGIA							
Miller	Y	N	Y	N	?	?	?
Chambliss	Y	Y	Y	N	Y	Y	Y
HAWAII							
Inouye	Y	Y	Y	Y	Y	Y	Y
Akaka	Y	Y	Y	Y	Y	Y	Y
IDAHO							
Craig	Y	Y	Y	N	Y	Y	Y
Crapo	Y	Y	Y	N	Y	Y	Y
ILLINOIS							
Fitzgerald	Y	Y	?	N	Y	Y	Y
Durbin	Y	Y	Y	Y	Y	Y	Y
INDIANA							
Lugar	Y	Y	Y	N	Y	Y	Y
Bayh	Y	Y	Y	Y	Y	Y	Y

	104	105	106	107	108	109	110
IOWA							
Grassley	Y	N	Y	N	Y	Y	Y
Harkin	+	Y	Y	Y	Y	Y	Y
KANSAS							
Brownback	Y	N	Y	N	Y	Y	Y
Roberts	Y	N	Y	N	Y	Y	Y
KENTUCKY							
McConnell	Y	N	Y	N	Y	Y	Y
Bunning	+	N	Y	N	Y	Y	Y
LOUISIANA							
Breaux	Y	Y	Y	Y	Y	Y	Y
Landrieu	Y	Y	Y	Y	Y	Y	Y
MAINE							
Snowe	Y	N	Y	N	Y	Y	Y
Collins	Y	Y	Y	N	Y	Y	Y
MARYLAND							
Sarbanes	?	Y	Y	Y	Y	Y	Y
Mikulski	Y	Y	Y	Y	Y	Y	Y
MASSACHUSETTS							
Kennedy	Y	Y	Y	Y	Y	Y	Y
Kerry	?	?	?	?	?	?	?
MICHIGAN							
Levin	Y	Y	Y	Y	Y	Y	Y
Stabenow	Y	Y	Y	Y	Y	Y	Y
MINNESOTA							
Dayton	Y	Y	Y	Y	Y	Y	Y
Coleman	Y	Y	Y	Y	Y	Y	Y
MISSISSIPPI							
Cochran	Y	N	Y	N	Y	Y	Y
Lott	Y	N	Y	N	Y	Y	Y
MISSOURI							
Bond	Y	N	Y	N	Y	Y	Y
Talent	Y	Y	Y	N	Y	Y	Y
MONTANA							
Burns	Y	N	Y	N	Y	Y	Y
Baucus	?	?	?	?	?	?	?
NEBRASKA							
Hagel	Y	Y	Y	N	Y	Y	Y
Nelson	Y	Y	Y	Y	Y	Y	Y
NEVADA							
Reid	Y	Y	Y	Y	Y	Y	Y
Ensign	Y	Y	Y	N	Y	Y	Y

	104	105	106	107	108	109	110
NEW HAMPSHIRE							
Gregg	Y	Y	Y	N	Y	Y	Y
Sununu	Y	N	Y	N	Y	Y	Y
NEW JERSEY							
Lautenberg	?	Y	Y	Y	Y	Y	Y
Corzine	?	Y	Y	Y	Y	Y	?
NEW MEXICO							
Domenici	Y	?	Y	N	Y	Y	Y
Bingaman	Y	Y	Y	Y	Y	Y	Y
NEW YORK							
Schumer	Y	Y	Y	Y	Y	Y	Y
Clinton	Y	Y	Y	Y	Y	Y	Y
NORTH CAROLINA							
Edwards	?	?	?	?	?	?	?
Dole	Y	N	Y	N	Y	Y	Y
NORTH DAKOTA							
Conrad	Y	Y	Y	Y	Y	Y	Y
Dorgan	Y	Y	Y	Y	Y	Y	Y
OHIO							
DeWine	Y	Y	Y	N	Y	Y	Y
Voinovich	Y	Y	Y	N	Y	Y	Y
OKLAHOMA							
Nickles	Y	N	Y	N	Y	Y	Y
Inhofe	Y	N	Y	N	Y	Y	Y
OREGON							
Wyden	Y	Y	Y	Y	Y	Y	Y
Smith	Y	Y	Y	Y	Y	Y	Y
PENNSYLVANIA							
Specter	Y	Y	Y	N	Y	Y	Y
Santorum	Y	N	Y	N	Y	Y	Y
RHODE ISLAND							
Reed	Y	Y	Y	Y	Y	Y	Y
Chafee	Y	Y	Y	N	Y	Y	Y
SOUTH CAROLINA							
Hollings	Y	Y	Y	N	Y	Y	Y
Graham	Y	Y	Y	N	Y	Y	Y
SOUTH DAKOTA							
Daschle	Y	Y	Y	Y	Y	Y	Y
Johnson	Y	Y	Y	Y	Y	Y	Y
TENNESSEE							
Frist	Y	N	Y	N	Y	Y	Y
Alexander	Y	Y	Y	N	Y	Y	Y

Key

Y	Voted for (yea).
#	Paired for.
+	Announced for.
N	Voted against (nay).
X	Paired against.
–	Announced against.
P	Voted "present."
C	Voted "present" to avoid possible conflict of interest.
?	Did not vote or otherwise make a position known.

Democrats   **Republicans**
Independents

	104	105	106	107	108	109	110
TEXAS							
Hutchison	Y	Y	Y	N	Y	Y	Y
Cornyn	Y	N	Y	N	Y	Y	Y
UTAH							
Hatch	Y	Y	Y	N	Y	Y	Y
Bennett	Y	Y	Y	N	Y	Y	Y
VERMONT							
Leahy	Y	Y	Y	Y	Y	Y	Y
Jeffords	Y	Y	Y	Y	Y	Y	Y
VIRGINIA							
Warner	Y	N	Y	N	Y	Y	Y
Allen	Y	Y	Y	N	Y	Y	Y
WASHINGTON							
Murray	Y	Y	Y	Y	Y	Y	Y
Cantwell	Y	Y	Y	Y	Y	Y	Y
WEST VIRGINIA							
Byrd	Y	Y	Y	Y	Y	Y	Y
Rockefeller	Y	Y	Y	Y	Y	Y	Y
WISCONSIN							
Kohl	Y	Y	Y	Y	Y	Y	Y
Feingold	Y	Y	Y	Y	Y	Y	Y
WYOMING							
Thomas	Y	N	Y	N	Y	Y	Y
Enzi	Y	N	Y	N	Y	Y	Y

ND Northern Democrats   SD Southern Democrats

Southern states - Ala., Ark., Fla., Ga., Ky., La., Miss., N.C., Okla., S.C., Tenn., Texas, Va.

104. Saylor Nomination/Confirmation. Confirmation of President Bush's nomination of F. Dennis Saylor IV, of Massachusetts to be a judge for the U.S. District Court for the District of Massachusetts. Confirmed 89-0: R 48-0; D 40-0 (ND 33-0, SD 7-0); I 1-0. A "yea" was a vote in support of the president's position. June 1, 2004.

105. S 2400. Fiscal 2005 Defense Authorization/TRICARE Expansion. Daschle, D-S.D., and Graham, R-S.C., amendment that would expand eligibility for the military's TRICARE health program to National Guard and Army Reserve forces and their families while they are on inactive status. It would enable reservists to pay premiums to receive health care benefits beyond the limited ones to which they are currently entitled. Reservists would be responsible for paying a portion of the premiums to receive health care benefits with the remainder covered by the federal government. Adopted 70-25: R 25-24; D 44-1 (ND 37-0, SD 7-1); I 1-0. June 2, 2004.

106. S 2400. Fiscal 2005 Defense Authorization/Supplemental Military Funding. Warner, R-Va., amendment that would authorize an additional $25 billion for military operations in Iraq and Afghanistan. The total authorized funding would include $14.5 billion for the Army, $1 billion for the Navy, $2 billion for the Marine Corps and $1 billion for the Air Force. Up to $2.5 billion of the authorized funding could be transferred among specific categories outlined in the amendment, contingent on prior congressional notification. Adopted 95-0: R 49-0; D 45-0 (ND 37-0, SD 8-0); I 1-0. June 2, 2004.

107. S 2400. Fiscal 2005 Defense Authorization/Nuclear Waste Cleanup. Cantwell, D-Wash., amendment that would strike language in the underlying bill that pertains to the Energy Department's classification of high-level nuclear waste at a South Carolina site. It would insert provisions that would require the department to continue activities related to the storage, retrieval, treatment and separation of tank waste from the reprocessing of spent nuclear fuel currently managed as high-level radioactive waste in accordance with state-approved treatment and closure plans. It would authorize $350 million for the cleanup of such sites in Idaho, South Carolina and Washington. Rejected 48-48: R 3-47; D 44-1 (ND 37-0, SD 7-1); I 1-0. June 3, 2004.

108. Townes Nomination/Confirmation. Confirmation of President Bush's nomination of Sandra L. Townes of New York to be a judge for the U.S. District Court for the Eastern District of New York. Confirmed 95-0: R 50-0; D 44-0 (ND 37-0, SD 7-0); I 1-0. A "yea" was a vote in support of the president's position. June 3, 2004.

109. Karas Nomination/Confirmation. Confirmation of President Bush's nomination of Kenneth M. Karas of New York to be a judge for the U.S. District Court for the Southern District of New York. Confirmed 95-0: R 50-0; D 44-0 (ND 37-0, SD 7-0); I 1-0. A "yea" was a vote in support of the president's position. June 3, 2004.

110. Herrera Nomination/Confirmation. Confirmation of President Bush's nomination of Judith C. Herrera of New Mexico to be a judge for the U.S. District Court for the District of New Mexico. Confirmed 93-0: R 50-0; D 42-0 (ND 35-0, SD 7-0); I 1-0. A "yea" was a vote in support of the president's position. June 3, 2004.

	111
ALABAMA	
Shelby	Y
Sessions	Y
ALASKA	
Stevens	Y
Murkowski, L.	Y
ARIZONA	
McCain	Y
Kyl	Y
ARKANSAS	
Lincoln	Y
Pryor	Y
CALIFORNIA	
Feinstein	Y
Boxer	Y
COLORADO	
Campbell	Y
Allard	Y
CONNECTICUT	
Dodd	Y
Lieberman	Y
DELAWARE	
Biden	Y
Carper	Y
FLORIDA	
Graham	Y
Nelson	Y
GEORGIA	
Miller	Y
Chambliss	Y
HAWAII	
Inouye	Y
Akaka	Y
IDAHO	
Craig	Y
Crapo	Y
ILLINOIS	
Fitzgerald	Y
Durbin	Y
INDIANA	
Lugar	Y
Bayh	Y

	111
IOWA	
Grassley	Y
Harkin	Y
KANSAS	
Brownback	Y
Roberts	Y
KENTUCKY	
McConnell	Y
Bunning	Y
LOUISIANA	
Breaux	Y
Landrieu	Y
MAINE	
Snowe	Y
Collins	Y
MARYLAND	
Sarbanes	Y
Mikulski	Y
MASSACHUSETTS	
Kennedy	Y
Kerry	?
MICHIGAN	
Levin	Y
Stabenow	Y
MINNESOTA	
Dayton	Y
Coleman	Y
MISSISSIPPI	
Cochran	Y
Lott	Y
MISSOURI	
Bond	Y
Talent	Y
MONTANA	
Burns	Y
Baucus	?
NEBRASKA	
Hagel	Y
Nelson	Y
NEVADA	
Reid	Y
Ensign	Y

	111
NEW HAMPSHIRE	
Gregg	Y
Sununu	Y
NEW JERSEY	
Lautenberg	Y
Corzine	Y
NEW MEXICO	
Domenici	Y
Bingaman	Y
NEW YORK	
Schumer	Y
Clinton	Y
NORTH CAROLINA	
Edwards	Y
Dole	Y
NORTH DAKOTA	
Conrad	Y
Dorgan	Y
OHIO	
DeWine	Y
Voinovich	Y
OKLAHOMA	
Nickles	Y
Inhofe	Y
OREGON	
Wyden	Y
Smith	Y
PENNSYLVANIA	
Specter	Y
Santorum	Y
RHODE ISLAND	
Reed	Y
Chafee	Y
SOUTH CAROLINA	
Hollings	Y
Graham	Y
SOUTH DAKOTA	
Daschle	Y
Johnson	Y
TENNESSEE	
Frist	Y
Alexander	Y

Key

Y	Voted for (yea).
#	Paired for.
+	Announced for.
N	Voted against (nay).
X	Paired against.
–	Announced against.
P	Voted "present."
C	Voted "present" to avoid possible conflict of interest.
?	Did not vote or otherwise make a position known.

Democrats **Republicans**
Independents

	111
TEXAS	
Hutchison	Y
Cornyn	Y
UTAH	
Hatch	Y
Bennett	Y
VERMONT	
Leahy	Y
Jeffords	Y
VIRGINIA	
Warner	Y
Allen	Y
WASHINGTON	
Murray	Y
Cantwell	Y
WEST VIRGINIA	
Byrd	Y
Rockefeller	Y
WISCONSIN	
Kohl	Y
Feingold	Y
WYOMING	
Thomas	Y
Enzi	Y

ND Northern Democrats   SD Southern Democrats

Southern states - Ala., Ark., Fla., Ga., Ky., La., Miss., N.C., Okla., S.C., Tenn., Texas, Va.

111. S Res 373. Ronald Reagan Condolences/Adoption. Adoption of the resolution that would express profound sorrow and deep regret over the death of former President Ronald Reagan, who died June 5, 2004. It also would commemorate his life and service. Adopted 98-0: R 51-0; D 46-0 (ND 37-0, SD 9-0); I 1-0. June 9, 2004.

	112	113	114	115	116	117	118
ALABAMA							
Shelby	Y	N	N	Y	Y	Y	Y
Sessions	Y	N	N	Y	Y	Y	Y
ALASKA							
Stevens	Y	N	Y	Y	Y	Y	Y
Murkowski, L.	Y	N	Y	Y	Y	Y	Y
ARIZONA							
McCain	Y	N	N	Y	Y	Y	Y
Kyl	Y	N	N	Y	Y	Y	Y
ARKANSAS							
Lincoln	Y	Y	Y	Y	Y	Y	N
Pryor	Y	Y	Y	Y	Y	Y	N
CALIFORNIA							
Feinstein	Y	Y	Y	Y	Y	Y	N
Boxer	Y	Y	Y	Y	Y	Y	N
COLORADO							
Campbell	Y	N	Y	Y	Y	Y	Y
Allard	Y	N	N	Y	Y	Y	Y
CONNECTICUT							
Dodd	Y	Y	Y	Y	Y	Y	N
Lieberman	Y	Y	Y	Y	Y	Y	N
DELAWARE							
Biden	?	Y	Y	Y	Y	Y	N
Carper	?	Y	Y	Y	Y	Y	N
FLORIDA							
Graham	Y	Y	Y	Y	Y	Y	N
Nelson	Y	N	Y	Y	Y	Y	Y
GEORGIA							
Miller	Y	N	Y	Y	Y	Y	Y
Chambliss	Y	N	N	Y	Y	Y	Y
HAWAII							
Inouye	Y	Y	Y	Y	Y	Y	N
Akaka	Y	Y	Y	Y	Y	Y	N
IDAHO							
Craig	Y	N	N	Y	Y	Y	Y
Crapo	Y	N	N	Y	Y	Y	Y
ILLINOIS							
Fitzgerald	Y	N	N	Y	Y	Y	Y
Durbin	Y	Y	Y	Y	Y	Y	N
INDIANA							
Lugar	Y	N	Y	Y	Y	Y	Y
Bayh	Y	N	Y	Y	Y	Y	N

	112	113	114	115	116	117	118
IOWA							
Grassley	Y	N	N	Y	Y	Y	Y
Harkin	Y	Y	Y	Y	Y	Y	N
KANSAS							
Brownback	Y	N	N	Y	Y	Y	Y
Roberts	Y	N	N	Y	Y	Y	Y
KENTUCKY							
McConnell	Y	N	N	Y	Y	Y	Y
Bunning	Y	N	N	Y	Y	Y	Y
LOUISIANA							
Breaux	Y	Y	Y	Y	Y	Y	N
Landrieu	Y	Y	Y	Y	Y	Y	N
MAINE							
Snowe	Y	N	Y	Y	Y	Y	Y
Collins	Y	N	Y	Y	Y	Y	Y
MARYLAND							
Sarbanes	Y	Y	Y	Y	Y	Y	N
Mikulski	Y	Y	Y	Y	Y	Y	N
MASSACHUSETTS							
Kennedy	Y	Y	Y	Y	Y	Y	N
Kerry	?	?	?	?	?	?	?
MICHIGAN							
Levin	Y	Y	Y	Y	Y	Y	N
Stabenow	Y	Y	Y	Y	Y	Y	N
MINNESOTA							
Dayton	Y	Y	Y	Y	Y	Y	N
Coleman	Y	N	Y	Y	Y	Y	Y
MISSISSIPPI							
Cochran	Y	N	Y	Y	Y	Y	Y
Lott	Y	N	N	Y	Y	Y	Y
MISSOURI							
Bond	Y	N	Y	Y	Y	Y	Y
Talent	Y	N	N	Y	Y	Y	Y
MONTANA							
Burns	Y	N	N	Y	Y	Y	Y
Baucus	Y	Y	Y	Y	Y	Y	N
NEBRASKA							
Hagel	Y	N	N	Y	Y	Y	Y
Nelson	Y	N	Y	Y	Y	Y	N
NEVADA							
Reid	Y	Y	Y	Y	Y	Y	N
Ensign	Y	N	Y	Y	Y	Y	Y

	112	113	114	115	116	117	118
NEW HAMPSHIRE							
Gregg	Y	N	Y	Y	Y	Y	Y
Sununu	Y	N	N	Y	Y	Y	Y
NEW JERSEY							
Lautenberg	Y	Y	Y	Y	Y	Y	N
Corzine	?	Y	Y	Y	Y	Y	N
NEW MEXICO							
Domenici	Y	N	N	Y	Y	Y	Y
Bingaman	Y	Y	Y	Y	Y	Y	?
NEW YORK							
Schumer	Y	Y	Y	Y	Y	Y	N
Clinton	Y	Y	Y	Y	Y	Y	N
NORTH CAROLINA							
Edwards	?	Y	Y	Y	Y	Y	?
Dole	Y	N	N	Y	Y	Y	Y
NORTH DAKOTA							
Conrad	Y	Y	Y	Y	Y	Y	N
Dorgan	Y	Y	Y	Y	Y	Y	N
OHIO							
DeWine	Y	N	Y	Y	Y	Y	Y
Voinovich	Y	N	Y	Y	Y	Y	Y
OKLAHOMA							
Nickles	Y	N	N	Y	Y	Y	Y
Inhofe	Y	N	N	Y	Y	Y	Y
OREGON							
Wyden	Y	Y	Y	Y	Y	Y	N
Smith	Y	N	Y	Y	Y	Y	Y
PENNSYLVANIA							
Specter	Y	N	N	Y	Y	Y	Y
Santorum	Y	N	N	Y	Y	Y	Y
RHODE ISLAND							
Reed	Y	Y	Y	Y	Y	Y	N
Chafee	Y	Y	Y	Y	Y	Y	Y
SOUTH CAROLINA							
Hollings	Y	N	Y	Y	Y	Y	N
Graham	Y	N	N	Y	Y	Y	Y
SOUTH DAKOTA							
Daschle	Y	Y	Y	Y	Y	Y	N
Johnson	Y	Y	Y	Y	Y	Y	N
TENNESSEE							
Frist	Y	N	N	Y	Y	Y	Y
Alexander	Y	N	Y	Y	Y	Y	Y

	112	113	114	115	116	117	118
TEXAS							
Hutchison	Y	N	N	Y	Y	Y	Y
Cornyn	Y	N	N	Y	Y	Y	Y
UTAH							
Hatch	?	N	N	Y	Y	Y	Y
Bennett	Y	N	Y	Y	Y	Y	Y
VERMONT							
Leahy	+	+	Y	Y	Y	Y	N
Jeffords	?	?	?	?	?	?	N
VIRGINIA							
Warner	Y	N	N	Y	Y	Y	Y
Allen	Y	N	Y	Y	Y	Y	Y
WASHINGTON							
Murray	Y	Y	Y	Y	Y	Y	N
Cantwell	Y	Y	Y	Y	Y	Y	N
WEST VIRGINIA							
Byrd	Y	Y	Y	Y	Y	Y	N
Rockefeller	Y	Y	Y	Y	Y	Y	Y
WISCONSIN							
Kohl	?	Y	Y	Y	Y	Y	N
Feingold	Y	Y	Y	Y	Y	Y	N
WYOMING							
Thomas	Y	N	N	Y	Y	Y	Y
Enzi	Y	N	N	Y	Y	Y	Y

Key

Y	Voted for (yea).
#	Paired for.
+	Announced for.
N	Voted against (nay).
X	Paired against.
–	Announced against.
P	Voted "present."
C	Voted "present" to avoid possible conflict of interest.
?	Did not vote or otherwise make a position known.

Democrats **Republicans**
Independents

ND Northern Democrats   SD Southern Democrats

Southern states - Ala., Ark., Fla., Ga., Ky., La., Miss., N.C., Okla., S.C., Tenn., Texas, Va.

112. S 2400. Fiscal 2005 Defense Authorization/Equipment Reimbursement. Dodd, D-Conn., amendment that would require the Defense secretary to reimburse members of the armed forces deployed in operations in Iraq or Afghanistan for the cost of any protective, safety or health equipment purchased by or on behalf of such members by their families, nonprofit organizations or community groups for use in connection with the operations. Adopted 91-0: R 50-0; D 41-0 (ND 33-0, SD 8-0); I 0-0. June 14, 2004.

113. S 2400. Fiscal 2005 Defense Authorization/Nuclear Weapons. Kennedy, D-Mass., amendment that would prohibit the use of $36.6 million authorized in the underlying bill for two Energy Department programs: a study of Robust Nuclear Earth Penetrator "bunker buster" weapons and a Stockpile Services Advanced Concepts Initiative, which includes research into a "low yield" nuclear weapon. Rejected 42-55: R 1-50; D 41-5 (ND 35-2, SD 6-3); I 0-0. June 15, 2004.

114. S 2400. Fiscal 2005 Defense Authorization/Hate Crimes. Smith, R-Ore., amendment that would broaden the categories covered by hate crimes to include crimes motivated by the victim's gender, sexual orientation or disability. Such crimes may be prosecuted in federal court. The amendment would require the Justice Department to certify that bias was a motivating factor in the crime and that state or local law enforcement officials have been consulted and the state does not object to the federal government assuming jurisdiction. It would authorize $5 million per year for fiscal 2005 and 2006 for the Justice Department to assist states and local authorities in investigating and prosecuting hate crimes. Adopted 65-33: R 18-33; D 47-0 (ND 38-0,SD 9-0); I 0-0. June 15, 2004.

115. Hopkins Nomination/Confirmation. Confirmation of President Bush's nomination of Virginia E. Hopkins of Alabama to be a judge for the U.S. District Court for the Northern District of Alabama. Confirmed 98-0: R 51-0; D 47-0 (ND 38-0, SD 9-0); I 0-0. A "yea" was a vote in support of the president's position. June 15, 2004.

116. Martinez Nomination/Confirmation. Confirmation of President Bush's nomination of Ricardo S. Martinez of Washington to be a judge for the U.S. District Court for the Western District of Washington. Confirmed 98-0: R 51-0; D 47-0 (ND 38-0, SD 9-0); I 0-0. A "yea" was a vote in support of the president's position. June 15, 2004.

117. Pratter Nomination/Confirmation. Confirmation of President Bush's nomination of Gene E.K. Pratter of Pennsylvania to be a judge for the U.S. District Court for the Eastern District of Pennsylvania. Confirmed 98-0: R 51-0; D 47-0 (ND 38-0, SD 9-0); I 0-0. A "yea" was a vote in support of the president's position. June 15, 2004.

118. S 2400. Fiscal 2005 Defense Authorization/Military Interrogations. Warner, R-Va., motion to table (kill) the Dodd, D-Conn., amendment that would prohibit the use of private contractors to conduct prisoner interrogations at U.S. military facilities. Motion agreed to 54-43: R 51-0; D 3-42 (ND 1-36, SD 2-6); I 0-1. June 16, 2004.

	119	120	121	122	123	124
ALABAMA						
Shelby	Y	N	Y	Y	Y	N
Sessions	Y	N	Y	Y	Y	N
ALASKA						
Stevens	Y	N	Y	Y	Y	N
Murkowski, L.	Y	N	Y	Y	Y	N
ARIZONA						
McCain	Y	N	Y	Y	Y	N
Kyl	Y	N	Y	Y	Y	N
ARKANSAS						
Lincoln	Y	Y	Y	Y	Y	Y
Pryor	Y	Y	Y	Y	Y	N
CALIFORNIA						
Feinstein	Y	Y	Y	Y	Y	Y
Boxer	Y	Y	Y	Y	Y	Y
COLORADO						
Campbell	Y	N	Y	Y	Y	N
Allard	Y	N	Y	Y	Y	N
CONNECTICUT						
Dodd	Y	Y	Y	Y	Y	Y
Lieberman	Y	Y	Y	Y	Y	N
DELAWARE						
Biden	Y	Y	Y	Y	Y	Y
Carper	Y	Y	Y	Y	Y	Y
FLORIDA						
Graham	?	Y	Y	Y	Y	Y
Nelson	Y	Y	Y	Y	Y	N
GEORGIA						
Miller	Y	N	Y	Y	Y	N
Chambliss	Y	N	Y	Y	Y	N
HAWAII						
Inouye	Y	Y	Y	Y	Y	Y
Akaka	Y	Y	Y	Y	Y	Y
IDAHO						
Craig	Y	N	Y	Y	Y	N
Crapo	Y	N	Y	Y	Y	N
ILLINOIS						
Fitzgerald	Y	N	Y	Y	Y	N
Durbin	Y	Y	Y	Y	Y	Y
INDIANA						
Lugar	Y	N	?	?	?	N
Bayh	Y	Y	Y	Y	Y	N
IOWA						
Grassley	Y	N	Y	Y	Y	N
Harkin	Y	Y	Y	Y	Y	Y
KANSAS						
Brownback	Y	N	Y	Y	Y	N
Roberts	Y	N	Y	Y	Y	N
KENTUCKY						
McConnell	Y	N	Y	Y	Y	N
Bunning	Y	N	Y	Y	Y	N
LOUISIANA						
Breaux	Y	Y	Y	Y	Y	Y
Landrieu	Y	Y	Y	Y	Y	Y
MAINE						
Snowe	Y	N	Y	Y	Y	N
Collins	Y	N	Y	Y	Y	N
MARYLAND						
Sarbanes	Y	Y	Y	Y	Y	Y
Mikulski	Y	Y	Y	Y	Y	Y
MASSACHUSETTS						
Kennedy	Y	Y	Y	Y	Y	Y
Kerry	?	?	?	?	?	?
MICHIGAN						
Levin	Y	Y	Y	Y	Y	Y
Stabenow	Y	Y	Y	Y	Y	Y
MINNESOTA						
Dayton	Y	Y	Y	Y	Y	Y
Coleman	Y	N	Y	Y	Y	N
MISSISSIPPI						
Cochran	Y	N	Y	Y	Y	N
Lott	Y	N	Y	Y	Y	N
MISSOURI						
Bond	Y	N	Y	Y	Y	N
Talent	Y	N	Y	Y	Y	N
MONTANA						
Burns	Y	N	Y	Y	Y	N
Baucus	Y	Y	Y	Y	Y	Y
NEBRASKA						
Hagel	Y	N	Y	Y	Y	N
Nelson	Y	Y	Y	Y	Y	N
NEVADA						
Reid	Y	Y	Y	Y	Y	Y
Ensign	Y	N	Y	Y	Y	N
NEW HAMPSHIRE						
Gregg	Y	N	Y	Y	Y	N
Sununu	Y	N	Y	Y	Y	N
NEW JERSEY						
Lautenberg	Y	Y	Y	Y	Y	Y
Corzine	Y	Y	Y	Y	Y	Y
NEW MEXICO						
Domenici	Y	N	Y	Y	Y	N
Bingaman	Y	Y	Y	Y	Y	Y
NEW YORK						
Schumer	Y	Y	Y	Y	Y	Y
Clinton	Y	Y	Y	Y	Y	N
NORTH CAROLINA						
Edwards	?	?	?	?	?	Y
Dole	Y	N	Y	Y	Y	N
NORTH DAKOTA						
Conrad	Y	Y	Y	Y	Y	Y
Dorgan	Y	Y	Y	Y	Y	Y
OHIO						
DeWine	Y	N	Y	Y	Y	N
Voinovich	Y	N	Y	Y	Y	N
OKLAHOMA						
Nickles	Y	N	Y	Y	Y	N
Inhofe	Y	N	Y	Y	Y	N
OREGON						
Wyden	Y	Y	Y	Y	Y	Y
Smith	Y	N	Y	Y	Y	N
PENNSYLVANIA						
Specter	Y	N	Y	Y	Y	N
Santorum	Y	N	Y	Y	Y	N
RHODE ISLAND						
Reed	Y	Y	Y	Y	Y	Y
Chafee	Y	N	Y	Y	Y	N
SOUTH CAROLINA						
Hollings	Y	Y	Y	Y	Y	Y
Graham	Y	N	Y	Y	Y	N
SOUTH DAKOTA						
Daschle	Y	Y	Y	Y	Y	Y
Johnson	Y	Y	Y	Y	Y	Y
TENNESSEE						
Frist	Y	N	Y	Y	Y	N
Alexander	Y	N	Y	Y	Y	N
TEXAS						
Hutchison	Y	N	Y	Y	Y	N
Cornyn	Y	N	Y	Y	Y	N
UTAH						
Hatch	Y	N	Y	Y	Y	N
Bennett	Y	N	Y	Y	Y	N
VERMONT						
Leahy	Y	Y	Y	Y	Y	Y
Jeffords	Y	Y	Y	Y	Y	Y
VIRGINIA						
Warner	Y	N	Y	Y	Y	N
Allen	Y	N	Y	Y	Y	N
WASHINGTON						
Murray	Y	Y	Y	Y	Y	Y
Cantwell	Y	Y	Y	Y	Y	Y
WEST VIRGINIA						
Byrd	Y	Y	Y	Y	Y	Y
Rockefeller	Y	Y	Y	Y	Y	Y
WISCONSIN						
Kohl	Y	Y	Y	Y	Y	Y
Feingold	Y	Y	Y	Y	Y	Y
WYOMING						
Thomas	Y	N	Y	Y	Y	N
Enzi	Y	N	Y	Y	Y	N

Key

Y	Voted for (yea).
#	Paired for.
+	Announced for.
N	Voted against (nay).
X	Paired against.
−	Announced against.
P	Voted "present."
C	Voted "present" to avoid possible conflict of interest.
?	Did not vote or otherwise make a position known.

Democrats   **Republicans**
Independents

ND Northern Democrats   SD Southern Democrats

Southern states - Ala., Ark., Fla., Ga., Ky., La., Miss., N.C., Okla., S.C., Tenn., Texas, Va.

119. S 2400. Fiscal 2005 Defense Authorization/Wartime Profiteering. Warner, R-Va., amendment that would extend federal jurisdiction to include fraudulent offenses committed overseas by contractors who make false claims or statements in connection with military or rebuilding activities. Adopted 97-0: R 51-0; D 45-0 (ND 38-0, SD 7-0); I 1-0. June 16, 2004.

120. S 2400. Fiscal 2005 Defense Authorization/Wartime Profiteering. Leahy, D-Vt., amendment that would make profiteering on contracts in connection with military or rebuilding activities in Iraq, Afghanistan or other countries punishable by up to 20 years in federal prison and $1 million in fines. Rejected 46-52: R 0-51; D 45-1 (ND 38-0, SD 7-1); I 1-0. June 16, 2004.

121. Duffey Nomination/Confirmation. Confirmation of President Bush's nomination of William S. Duffey Jr. of Georgia to be a judge for the U.S. District Court for the Northern District of Georgia. Confirmed 97-0: R 50-0; D 46-0 (ND 38-0, SD 8-0); I 1-0. A "yea" was a vote in support of the president's position. June 16, 2004.

122. Stengel Nomination/Confirmation. Confirmation of President Bush's nomination of Lawrence F. Stengel of Pennsylvania to be a judge for the U.S. District Court for the Eastern District of Pennsylvania. Confirmed 97-0: R 50-0; D 46-0 (ND 38-0, SD 8-0); I 1-0. A "yea" was a vote in support of the president's position. June 16, 2004.

123. Diamond Nomination/Confirmation. Confirmation of President Bush's nomination of Paul S. Diamond of Pennsylvania to be a judge for the U.S. District Court for the Eastern District of Pennsylvania. Confirmed 97-0: R 50-0; D 46-0 (ND 38-0, SD 8-0); I 1-0. A "yea" was a vote in support of the president's position. June 16, 2004.

124. S 2400. Fiscal 2005 Defense Authorization/Missile Defense. Boxer, D-Calif., amendment that would provide that the ground-based midcourse defense element of the national ballistic missile defense system cannot be deployed for initial defensive operations until the Defense secretary certifies that the capabilities of the system to perform its defense mission have been confirmed by operationally realistic testing of the system. Rejected 42-57: R 1-50; D 40-7 (ND 34-4, SD 6-3); I 1-0. June 17, 2004.

	125	126	127	128	129	130
ALABAMA						
Shelby	Y	Y	Y	Y	Y	N
Sessions	Y	Y	Y	Y	Y	N
ALASKA						
Stevens	Y	Y	Y	Y	Y	N
Murkowski, L.	Y	Y	Y	Y	Y	N
ARIZONA						
McCain	Y	Y	Y	Y	Y	N
Kyl	Y	Y	Y	Y	Y	N
ARKANSAS						
Lincoln	N	Y	Y	Y	Y	Y
Pryor	N	Y	Y	Y	Y	N
CALIFORNIA						
Feinstein	N	Y	Y	Y	Y	Y
Boxer	N	Y	Y	Y	Y	Y
COLORADO						
Campbell	Y	Y	Y	Y	Y	N
Allard	Y	Y	Y	Y	Y	N
CONNECTICUT						
Dodd	N	Y	Y	Y	Y	Y
Lieberman	N	Y	Y	Y	Y	Y
DELAWARE						
Biden	N	Y	Y	Y	Y	Y
Carper	N	Y	Y	Y	Y	Y
FLORIDA						
Graham	N	Y	Y	Y	Y	Y
Nelson	N	Y	Y	Y	Y	Y
GEORGIA						
Miller	Y	Y	Y	Y	Y	N
Chambliss	Y	Y	Y	Y	Y	N
HAWAII						
Inouye	N	Y	Y	Y	Y	Y
Akaka	N	Y	Y	Y	Y	Y
IDAHO						
Craig	Y	Y	Y	Y	N	N
Crapo	Y	Y	Y	Y	Y	N
ILLINOIS						
Fitzgerald	Y	Y	Y	Y	Y	N
Durbin	N	Y	N	Y	Y	Y
INDIANA						
Lugar	Y	Y	Y	Y	Y	N
Bayh	Y	Y	Y	Y	Y	N

	125	126	127	128	129	130
IOWA						
Grassley	Y	Y	Y	Y	Y	N
Harkin	N	Y	Y	Y	Y	Y
KANSAS						
Brownback	Y	Y	Y	Y	Y	N
Roberts	Y	Y	Y	Y	Y	N
KENTUCKY						
McConnell	Y	Y	Y	Y	Y	N
Bunning	Y	Y	Y	Y	Y	N
LOUISIANA						
Breaux	N	Y	Y	Y	Y	Y
Landrieu	Y	Y	Y	Y	Y	Y
MAINE						
Snowe	Y	Y	Y	Y	Y	N
Collins	Y	Y	Y	Y	Y	N
MARYLAND						
Sarbanes	N	Y	Y	Y	Y	Y
Mikulski	N	Y	Y	Y	Y	Y
MASSACHUSETTS						
Kennedy	N	Y	Y	Y	Y	Y
Kerry	?	?	?	?	?	?
MICHIGAN						
Levin	N	Y	Y	Y	Y	Y
Stabenow	N	Y	Y	Y	Y	Y
MINNESOTA						
Dayton	N	Y	Y	Y	Y	Y
Coleman	Y	Y	Y	Y	Y	N
MISSISSIPPI						
Cochran	Y	Y	Y	Y	Y	N
Lott	Y	Y	Y	Y	Y	N
MISSOURI						
Bond	Y	Y	Y	Y	Y	N
Talent	Y	Y	Y	Y	Y	N
MONTANA						
Burns	Y	Y	Y	Y	Y	N
Baucus	N	Y	Y	Y	Y	N
NEBRASKA						
Hagel	Y	Y	Y	Y	Y	N
Nelson	Y	Y	Y	Y	Y	N
NEVADA						
Reid	N	Y	Y	Y	Y	Y
Ensign	Y	Y	Y	Y	Y	N

	125	126	127	128	129	130
NEW HAMPSHIRE						
Gregg	Y	Y	Y	Y	Y	N
Sununu	Y	Y	Y	Y	Y	N
NEW JERSEY						
Lautenberg	N	Y	Y	Y	Y	Y
Corzine	N	Y	Y	Y	Y	Y
NEW MEXICO						
Domenici	Y	Y	Y	Y	Y	N
Bingaman	N	Y	Y	Y	Y	Y
NEW YORK						
Schumer	N	Y	Y	Y	Y	Y
Clinton	N	Y	Y	Y	Y	Y
NORTH CAROLINA						
Edwards	N	Y	Y	Y	Y	Y
Dole	Y	Y	Y	Y	Y	N
NORTH DAKOTA						
Conrad	N	Y	Y	Y	Y	Y
Dorgan	N	Y	Y	Y	Y	Y
OHIO						
DeWine	Y	Y	Y	Y	Y	N
Voinovich	Y	Y	Y	Y	Y	N
OKLAHOMA						
Nickles	Y	Y	Y	Y	Y	N
Inhofe	Y	Y	Y	Y	?	?
OREGON						
Wyden	N	Y	Y	Y	Y	Y
Smith	Y	Y	Y	Y	N	N
PENNSYLVANIA						
Specter	Y	Y	Y	Y	Y	N
Santorum	Y	Y	Y	Y	N	N
RHODE ISLAND						
Reed	N	Y	Y	Y	Y	Y
Chafee	Y	Y	Y	Y	Y	Y
SOUTH CAROLINA						
Hollings	N	Y	Y	Y	Y	Y
Graham	Y	Y	Y	Y	Y	N
SOUTH DAKOTA						
Daschle	N	Y	Y	Y	Y	Y
Johnson	N	Y	Y	Y	Y	Y
TENNESSEE						
Frist	Y	Y	Y	Y	Y	N
Alexander	Y	Y	Y	Y	Y	N

Key

Y	Voted for (yea).
#	Paired for.
+	Announced for.
N	Voted against (nay).
X	Paired against.
−	Announced against.
P	Voted "present."
C	Voted "present" to avoid possible conflict of interest.
?	Did not vote or otherwise make a position known.

Democrats **Republicans**
Independents

	125	126	127	128	129	130
TEXAS						
Hutchison	Y	Y	Y	Y	Y	N
Cornyn	Y	Y	Y	Y	Y	N
UTAH						
Hatch	Y	Y	Y	Y	Y	N
Bennett	Y	Y	Y	Y	?	?
VERMONT						
Leahy	N	Y	Y	Y	Y	Y
Jeffords	N	Y	Y	Y	Y	Y
VIRGINIA						
Warner	Y	Y	Y	Y	Y	N
Allen	Y	Y	Y	Y	Y	N
WASHINGTON						
Murray	N	Y	Y	Y	Y	Y
Cantwell	N	Y	Y	Y	Y	Y
WEST VIRGINIA						
Byrd	N	Y	Y	Y	Y	Y
Rockefeller	N	Y	Y	Y	Y	Y
WISCONSIN						
Kohl	N	Y	Y	Y	Y	Y
Feingold	N	Y	Y	Y	Y	Y
WYOMING						
Thomas	Y	Y	Y	Y	N	N
Enzi	Y	Y	Y	Y	Y	N

ND Northern Democrats   SD Southern Democrats

Southern states - Ala., Ark., Fla., Ga., Ky., La., Miss., N.C., Okla., S.C., Tenn., Texas, Va.

125. S 2400. Fiscal 2005 Defense Authorization/Missile Defense. Warner, R-Va., amendment to the Reed, D-R.I., amendment. The Warner amendment would require that no later than Feb. 1, 2005, the Defense secretary, in consultation with the director of the Operational Test and Evaluation office, establish criteria for operationally realistic testing of field prototypes developed under the ballistic missile defense program. The Defense secretary would be responsible for ensuring no later than Oct. 1, 2005, that a test of the ballistic missile defense system is conducted consistent with the criteria established. The Reed amendment would require the Defense Department to conduct, on an independent basis, operationally realistic testing of the prototypes developed under the ballistic missile defense program. The director of the Operational Test and Evaluation office would be responsible for approving and evaluating the tests. Adopted 55-44: R 51-0; D 4-43 (ND 2-36, SD 2-7); I 0-1. (Subsequently, the Reed amendment, as amended, was adopted by voice vote.) June 17, 2004.

126. Robart Nomination/Confirmation. Confirmation of President Bush's nomination of James L. Robart of Washington to be a judge for the U.S. District Court for the Western District of Washington. Confirmed 99-0: R 51-0; D 47-0 (ND 38-0, SD 9-0); I 1-0. A "yea" was a vote in support of the president's position. June 17, 2004.

127. Benitez Nomination/Confirmation. Confirmation of President Bush's nomination of Roger T. Benitez of California to be a judge for the U.S. District Court for the Southern District of California. Confirmed 98-1: R 51-0; D 46-1 (ND 37-1, SD 9-0); I 1-0. A "yea" was a vote in support of the president's position. June 17, 2004.

128. Boyle Nomination/Confirmation. Confirmation of President Bush's nomination of Jane J. Boyle of Texas to be a judge for the U.S. District Court for the Northern District of Texas. Confirmed 99-0: R 51-0; D 47-0 (ND 38-0, SD 9-0); I 1-0. A "yea" was a vote in support of the president's position. June 17, 2004.

129. S 2400. Fiscal 2005 Defense Authorization/Troop Increase. Reed, D-R.I., amendment that would increase the authorized end strength for active-duty Army personnel by 20,000 soldiers in fiscal 2005. As amended, it would require the additional troops to be covered by the $25 billion authorized for operations in Iraq and Afghanistan or from another future supplemental appropriation. Adopted 93-4: R 45-4; D 47-0 (ND 38-0, SD 9-0); I 1-0. June 17, 2004.

130. S 2400. Fiscal 2005 Defense Authorization/Tax Rate Increase. Biden, D-Del., amendment that would provide that the top income tax rate be increased from 35 percent to 36 percent starting in 2005 until 2010. It would provide that the funds made available by the increase be used to pay for security and stabilization operations in Iraq. Rejected 44-53: R 1-48; D 42-5 (ND 35-3, SD 7-2); I 1-0. June 17, 2004.

	131	132	133	134	135	136	137
ALABAMA							
Shelby	Y	N	N	Y	Y	N	Y
Sessions	Y	N	N	Y	Y	N	Y
ALASKA							
Stevens	Y	N	N	Y	Y	N	Y
Murkowski, L.	Y	N	N	Y	Y	N	Y
ARIZONA							
McCain	Y	Y	N	Y	N	Y	Y
Kyl	Y	N	N	Y	Y	N	Y
ARKANSAS							
Lincoln	Y	N	Y	Y	N	Y	Y
Pryor	Y	N	Y	Y	N	Y	N
CALIFORNIA							
Feinstein	N	Y	Y	Y	N	Y	Y
Boxer	N	Y	Y	Y	N	Y	Y
COLORADO							
Campbell	Y	N	N	Y	Y	N	Y
Allard	Y	N	N	Y	Y	N	Y
CONNECTICUT							
Dodd	?	?	Y	Y	N	Y	N
Lieberman	N	Y	N	Y	Y	Y	Y
DELAWARE							
Biden	N	N	Y	N	Y	N	Y
Carper	N	N	Y	Y	N	Y	Y
FLORIDA							
Graham	N	Y	Y	Y	N	Y	Y
Nelson	N	Y	N	Y	N	Y	Y
GEORGIA							
Miller	?	N	N	Y	Y	N	Y
Chambliss	Y	N	N	Y	Y	N	Y
HAWAII							
Inouye	N	Y	Y	Y	N	Y	N
Akaka	N	Y	Y	Y	N	Y	N
IDAHO							
Craig	Y	N	N	Y	Y	N	Y
Crapo	Y	N	N	Y	Y	N	Y
ILLINOIS							
Fitzgerald	?	Y	Y	Y	Y	Y	N
Durbin	N	Y	Y	Y	Y	Y	N
INDIANA							
Lugar	Y	N	N	Y	Y	N	Y
Bayh	Y	N	N	Y	N	Y	Y

	131	132	133	134	135	136	137
IOWA							
Grassley	Y	N	N	Y	Y	N	Y
Harkin	N	Y	Y	Y	N	Y	N
KANSAS							
Brownback	Y	N	N	Y	Y	–	+
Roberts	Y	N	N	Y	Y	N	Y
KENTUCKY							
McConnell	Y	N	N	Y	Y	N	Y
Bunning	Y	N	N	Y	Y	N	Y
LOUISIANA							
Breaux	Y	N	Y	N	N	Y	N
Landrieu	Y	N	Y	Y	N	Y	N
MAINE							
Snowe	Y	Y	N	Y	N	Y	Y
Collins	Y	N	N	Y	Y	Y	Y
MARYLAND							
Sarbanes	N	Y	Y	Y	N	Y	N
Mikulski	N	Y	Y	Y	N	Y	Y
MASSACHUSETTS							
Kennedy	N	Y	Y	Y	N	Y	N
Kerry	?	?	Y	Y	N	?	?
MICHIGAN							
Levin	Y	N	Y	Y	N	Y	Y
Stabenow	N	Y	Y	Y	N	Y	Y
MINNESOTA							
Dayton	N	Y	Y	Y	N	Y	Y
Coleman	Y	N	N	Y	Y	N	Y
MISSISSIPPI							
Cochran	Y	N	N	Y	Y	N	Y
Lott	Y	N	N	Y	Y	N	Y
MISSOURI							
Bond	Y	N	N	Y	Y	N	Y
Talent	Y	N	N	Y	Y	N	Y
MONTANA							
Burns	?	N	N	Y	Y	N	Y
Baucus	N	Y	Y	Y	N	Y	N
NEBRASKA							
Hagel	Y	N	N	Y	Y	N	Y
Nelson	Y	N	N	Y	N	Y	Y
NEVADA							
Reid	N	Y	Y	Y	N	Y	N
Ensign	Y	N	N	Y	Y	N	Y

	131	132	133	134	135	136	137
NEW HAMPSHIRE							
Gregg	Y	N	N	Y	Y	N	Y
Sununu	Y	N	N	Y	Y	N	Y
NEW JERSEY							
Lautenberg	N	Y	Y	Y	N	Y	N
Corzine	N	Y	Y	Y	N	Y	N
NEW MEXICO							
Domenici	Y	N	N	Y	Y	N	Y
Bingaman	Y	Y	Y	Y	Y	Y	N
NEW YORK							
Schumer	N	Y	Y	Y	N	Y	Y
Clinton	?	?	Y	Y	N	Y	Y
NORTH CAROLINA							
Edwards	N	Y	Y	Y	N	Y	Y
Dole	Y	N	N	Y	Y	N	Y
NORTH DAKOTA							
Conrad	N	Y	Y	Y	N	N	Y
Dorgan	N	Y	Y	Y	N	Y	Y
OHIO							
DeWine	Y	N	N	Y	Y	N	Y
Voinovich	Y	N	N	Y	N	N	Y
OKLAHOMA							
Nickles	Y	N	N	Y	Y	N	Y
Inhofe	+	?	N	Y	Y	N	Y
OREGON							
Wyden	N	Y	Y	Y	N	Y	Y
Smith	N	N	N	Y	Y	N	Y
PENNSYLVANIA							
Specter	Y	N	N	Y	Y	N	Y
Santorum	Y	N	N	Y	Y	N	Y
RHODE ISLAND							
Reed	N	Y	Y	Y	N	Y	N
Chafee	Y	N	N	Y	Y	N	Y
SOUTH CAROLINA							
Hollings	N	Y	Y	Y	N	Y	N
Graham	Y	N	N	Y	Y	N	Y
SOUTH DAKOTA							
Daschle	N	Y	Y	Y	N	Y	N
Johnson	N	Y	Y	Y	N	Y	N
TENNESSEE							
Frist	Y	N	N	Y	Y	N	Y
Alexander	+	–	N	Y	Y	N	Y

	131	132	133	134	135	136	137
TEXAS							
Hutchison	Y	N	N	Y	Y	N	Y
Cornyn	Y	N	N	Y	Y	N	Y
UTAH							
Hatch	Y	N	N	Y	Y	N	Y
Bennett	?	?	N	Y	Y	N	Y
VERMONT							
Leahy	N	Y	Y	Y	N	Y	N
Jeffords	N	Y	Y	Y	Y	Y	N
VIRGINIA							
Warner	Y	N	N	Y	Y	N	Y
Allen	Y	N	N	Y	Y	N	Y
WASHINGTON							
Murray	N	Y	Y	Y	N	Y	Y
Cantwell	N	Y	Y	Y	N	Y	Y
WEST VIRGINIA							
Byrd	N	Y	Y	Y	N	Y	Y
Rockefeller	N	Y	Y	Y	N	Y	Y
WISCONSIN							
Kohl	N	Y	Y	Y	N	Y	Y
Feingold	N	Y	Y	Y	N	Y	N
WYOMING							
Thomas	?	?	N	Y	Y	N	Y
Enzi	Y	N	N	Y	Y	N	Y

ND Northern Democrats   SD Southern Democrats

Southern states - Ala., Ark., Fla., Ga., Ky., La., Miss., N.C., Okla., S.C., Tenn., Texas, Va.

131. S 2400. Fiscal 2005 Defense Authorization/Media Coverage. Warner, R-Va., amendment that would express the sense of Congress that the Defense Department policy prohibiting media coverage of the return to the United States of the remains of armed forces members who died overseas appropriately protects the privacy of their families and friends, and is consistent with the Constitution's guarantees of freedom of speech and press. Adopted 52-38: R 44-1; D 8-36 (ND 4-32, SD 4-4); I 0-1. June 21, 2004.

132. S 2400. Fiscal 2005 Defense Authorization/Media Coverage. Lautenberg, D-N.J., amendment that would require that no later than 60 days after enactment of the bill, the Defense secretary develop a protocol that permits media coverage of the return to the United States of coffins containing the remains of members of the armed forces who died overseas. The protocol would be required to ensure the preservation of the dignity of the occasion of the return and the confidentiality of the members' identity. Rejected 39-54: R 3-44; D 35-10 (ND 31-5, SD 4-5); I 1-0. June 21, 2004.

133. S 2400. Fiscal 2005 Defense Authorization/Missile Defense. Levin, D-Mich., amendment that would shift $515.5 million in the bill from the Missile Defense Agency's ground-based midcourse interceptors to nuclear nonproliferation programs and other homeland security and anti-terrorism activities. Rejected 44-56: R 0-51; D 43-5 (ND 36-3, SD 7-2); I 1-0. June 22, 2004.

134. S 2400. Fiscal 2005 Defense Authorization/Broadcast Indecency. Brownback, R-Kan., amendment to the Brownback amendment. The second-degree amendment would provide that television or radio broadcasters could be penalized up to $275,000 per violation or day of violations for airing obscene, indecent or profane programming. It would provide that a broadcaster could be fined no more than $3 million for multiple violations. The underlying amendment includes identical language. Adopted 99-1: R 51-0; D 47-1 (ND 38-0, SD 9-1); I 1-0. (Subsequently, the underlying Brownback amendment was adopted by voice vote.) June 22, 2004.

135. S 2400. Fiscal 2004 Defense Authorization/"Buy America" Provisions. McCain, R-Ariz., substitute amendment to the Dayton, D-Minn., amendment. The McCain amendment would allow the Defense secretary to waive the application of any domestic source requirements with respect to items that are grown, reprocessed, reused, produced or manufactured in seven foreign countries that have a "declaration of principles" with the United States. The Dayton amendment would strike language in the underlying bill that would allow the Defense secretary to waive the requirements with regard to 21 countries that have a "memorandum of understanding" with the United States. Adopted 54-46: R 48-3; D 5-43 (ND 4-35, SD 1-8); I 1-0. June 22, 2004.

136. S 2400. Fiscal 2005 Defense Authorization/Reserves Retirement. Corzine, D-N.J., motion to waive the Budget Act with respect to the Warner, R-Va., point of order against the Corzine amendment that would reduce from 60 to 55 the age at which certain members of the National Guard and Army Reserves could receive retirement benefits. Motion rejected 49-49: R 3-47; D 45-2 (ND 37-1, SD 8-1); I 1-0. A three-fifths majority (60) of the total Senate is required to waive the Budget Act. (Subsequently, the chair upheld the point of order, and the amendment fell.) June 23, 2004.

137. S 2400. Fiscal 2005 Defense Authorization/Iraq Reports. McConnell, R-Ky., amendment that would require that no later than 120 days after the bill's enactment the president submit an unclassified report to Congress on the strategy of U.S. and coalition forces in Iraq regarding stabilization and rebuilding. Adopted 71-27: R 50-0; D 21-26 (ND 17-21, SD 4-5); I 0-1. June 23, 2004.

	138	139	140	141	142	143	144	145
ALABAMA								
Shelby	N	N	N	Y	Y	Y	N	N
Sessions	N	N	N	Y	Y	Y	N	N
ALASKA								
Stevens	N	N	N	Y	Y	Y	N	N
Murkowski, L.	N	N	N	Y	Y	Y	N	N
ARIZONA								
McCain	Y	N	N	Y	Y	N	N	N
Kyl	N	N	N	Y	Y	Y	N	N
ARKANSAS								
Lincoln	Y	Y	Y	Y	Y	N	Y	Y
Pryor	Y	Y	Y	Y	Y	N	Y	Y
CALIFORNIA								
Feinstein	Y	N	Y	N	Y	N	Y	N
Boxer	Y	Y	Y	Y	Y	N	Y	Y
COLORADO								
Campbell	N	N	N	Y	Y	Y	N	N
Allard	N	N	N	Y	Y	Y	N	N
CONNECTICUT								
Dodd	Y	Y	N	Y	Y	N	Y	Y
Lieberman	N	N	N	Y	Y	N	Y	Y
DELAWARE								
Biden	Y	Y	Y	Y	Y	N	Y	Y
Carper	Y	Y	Y	Y	Y	N	Y	Y
FLORIDA								
Graham	Y	Y	N	Y	Y	N	Y	Y
Nelson	Y	Y	Y	Y	Y	N	Y	Y
GEORGIA								
Miller	N	N	N	Y	Y	Y	N	N
Chambliss	N	N	N	Y	Y	Y	N	N
HAWAII								
Inouye	Y	Y	Y	Y	Y	N	Y	Y
Akaka	Y	Y	Y	Y	Y	N	Y	Y
IDAHO								
Craig	N	N	N	Y	Y	Y	N	N
Crapo	N	N	N	Y	?	Y	N	N
ILLINOIS								
Fitzgerald	N	Y	N	Y	Y	N	Y	N
Durbin	Y	Y	Y	Y	Y	N	Y	Y
INDIANA								
Lugar	N	N	N	Y	Y	Y	N	N
Bayh	Y	N	N	Y	Y	N	Y	Y

	138	139	140	141	142	143	144	145
IOWA								
Grassley	N	N	N	Y	Y	Y	N	N
Harkin	Y	Y	Y	Y	Y	N	Y	Y
KANSAS								
Brownback	–	–	–	+	+	+	–	–
Roberts	N	N	N	Y	Y	Y	N	N
KENTUCKY								
McConnell	N	N	N	Y	Y	Y	N	N
Bunning	N	N	N	Y	Y	Y	N	N
LOUISIANA								
Breaux	Y	Y	Y	Y	Y	N	Y	Y
Landrieu	Y	Y	Y	Y	Y	N	Y	Y
MAINE								
Snowe	N	N	N	Y	Y	Y	N	Y
Collins	N	N	N	Y	Y	Y	N	Y
MARYLAND								
Sarbanes	Y	Y	Y	Y	Y	N	Y	Y
Mikulski	Y	Y	Y	Y	Y	N	Y	Y
MASSACHUSETTS								
Kennedy	Y	Y	Y	Y	Y	N	Y	Y
Kerry	?	?	?	?	?	?	?	?
MICHIGAN								
Levin	Y	Y	Y	Y	Y	N	Y	Y
Stabenow	Y	Y	Y	Y	Y	N	Y	Y
MINNESOTA								
Dayton	Y	Y	Y	Y	Y	N	Y	Y
Coleman	N	N	N	Y	Y	Y	N	N
MISSISSIPPI								
Cochran	N	N	N	Y	Y	Y	N	N
Lott	N	N	N	Y	Y	Y	N	N
MISSOURI								
Bond	N	N	N	Y	Y	Y	N	N
Talent	N	N	N	Y	Y	Y	N	N
MONTANA								
Burns	N	N	N	Y	Y	Y	N	N
Baucus	Y	Y	Y	Y	Y	N	Y	Y
NEBRASKA								
Hagel	Y	N	N	Y	Y	N	N	N
Nelson	Y	Y	N	Y	Y	N	Y	Y
NEVADA								
Reid	Y	Y	Y	Y	Y	N	Y	Y
Ensign	N	N	N	Y	Y	Y	N	N

	138	139	140	141	142	143	144	145
NEW HAMPSHIRE								
Gregg	N	N	N	Y	Y	Y	N	N
Sununu	N	N	N	Y	Y	?	?	?
NEW JERSEY								
Lautenberg	Y	Y	Y	Y	Y	N	Y	Y
Corzine	Y	Y	Y	Y	Y	N	Y	Y
NEW MEXICO								
Domenici	N	N	N	Y	Y	Y	N	N
Bingaman	Y	Y	Y	Y	Y	?	?	?
NEW YORK								
Schumer	Y	Y	Y	Y	Y	N	Y	Y
Clinton	Y	Y	N	Y	Y	N	Y	Y
NORTH CAROLINA								
Edwards	Y	Y	Y	Y	Y	N	Y	Y
Dole	N	N	N	Y	Y	Y	N	N
NORTH DAKOTA								
Conrad	Y	Y	Y	Y	Y	N	Y	Y
Dorgan	Y	Y	Y	Y	Y	N	Y	Y
OHIO								
DeWine	N	N	N	Y	Y	Y	N	N
Voinovich	N	N	N	Y	Y	Y	N	N
OKLAHOMA								
Nickles	N	N	N	Y	Y	Y	N	N
Inhofe	N	N	N	Y	Y	Y	N	N
OREGON								
Wyden	Y	Y	Y	Y	Y	N	Y	Y
Smith	N	N	N	Y	?	Y	N	N
PENNSYLVANIA								
Specter	N	N	N	Y	Y	N	N	Y
Santorum	N	N	N	Y	Y	Y	N	N
RHODE ISLAND								
Reed	Y	Y	Y	Y	Y	N	Y	Y
Chafee	N	N	N	Y	Y	Y	N	N
SOUTH CAROLINA								
Hollings	Y	Y	Y	Y	Y	?	Y	Y
Graham	N	N	N	Y	Y	N	N	N
SOUTH DAKOTA								
Daschle	Y	Y	Y	Y	Y	N	Y	Y
Johnson	Y	Y	Y	Y	Y	N	Y	Y
TENNESSEE								
Frist	N	N	N	Y	Y	Y	N	N
Alexander	N	N	N	Y	Y	Y	N	N

	138	139	140	141	142	143	144	145
TEXAS								
Hutchison	N	N	N	Y	Y	Y	N	N
Cornyn	N	N	N	Y	Y	Y	N	N
UTAH								
Hatch	N	N	N	Y	?	Y	N	N
Bennett	N	N	N	Y	?	Y	N	N
VERMONT								
Leahy	Y	Y	Y	Y	Y	N	Y	Y
Jeffords	Y	Y	Y	Y	Y	N	Y	Y
VIRGINIA								
Warner	N	N	N	Y	Y	Y	N	N
Allen	N	N	N	Y	Y	Y	N	N
WASHINGTON								
Murray	Y	Y	Y	Y	Y	N	Y	Y
Cantwell	Y	Y	Y	Y	Y	N	Y	Y
WEST VIRGINIA								
Byrd	Y	Y	Y	Y	Y	N	Y	Y
Rockefeller	Y	Y	Y	Y	Y	N	Y	Y
WISCONSIN								
Kohl	Y	Y	Y	Y	Y	N	Y	Y
Feingold	Y	Y	Y	Y	Y	N	Y	Y
WYOMING								
Thomas	N	N	N	Y	Y	Y	N	N
Enzi	N	N	N	Y	Y	Y	N	N

Key

Y	Voted for (yea).
#	Paired for.
+	Announced for.
N	Voted against (nay).
X	Paired against.
–	Announced against.
P	Voted "present."
C	Voted "present" to avoid possible conflict of interest.
?	Did not vote or otherwise make a position known.

Democrats **Republicans**
Independents

ND Northern Democrats   SD Southern Democrats

Southern states - Ala., Ark., Fla., Ga., Ky., La., Miss., N.C., Okla., S.C., Tenn., Texas, Va.

138. S 2400. Fiscal 2005 Defense Authorization/Iraq Reports. Kennedy, D-Mass., amendment that would require that no later than 30 days after the bill's enactment the president submit an unclassified report to Congress on the strategy of the United States regarding stabilization and rebuilding in Iraq, an estimate on the number of U.S. troops that will be serving in Iraq as of Dec. 31, 2005, and the percentage of such forces that will be members of the National Guard and Army Reserves. Rejected 48-50: R 2-48; D 45-2 (ND 37-1, SD 8-1); I 1-0. June 23, 2004.

139. S 2400. Fiscal 2005 Defense Authorization/Missile Defense. Reed, D-R.I., amendment that would condition $550.5 million of the Missile Defense Agency's request for ground-based midcourse interceptors on certification by the Operational Test and Evaluation office that the system is effective and suitable for combat. Rejected 45-53: R 0-50; D 44-3 (ND 36-2, SD 8-1); I 1-0. June 23, 2004.

140. S 2400. Fiscal 2005 Defense Authorization/Troop Limit. Byrd, D-W.Va., amendment that would cap the number of military troops and civilian contractors in Colombia at 500 each. Rejected 40-58: R 1-49; D 38-9 (ND 32-6, SD 6-3); I 1-0. June 23, 2004.

141. Sanchez Nomination/Confirmation. Confirmation of President Bush's nomination of Juan R. Sanchez of Pennsylvania to be a judge for the U.S. District Court for the Eastern District of Pennsylvania. Confirmed 98-0: R 50-0; D 47-0 (ND 38-0, SD 9-0); I 1-0. A "yea" was a vote in support of the president's position. June 23, 2004.

142. Kelley Nomination/Confirmation. Confirmation of President Bush's nomination of Walter D. Kelley Jr. of Virginia to be a judge for the U.S. District Court for the Eastern District of Virginia. Confirmed 94-0: R 46-0;

D 47-0 (ND 38-0, SD 9-0); I 1-0. A "yea" was a vote in support of the president's position. June 23, 2004.

143. S 2400. Fiscal 2005 Defense Authorization/Prisoner Reports. Hatch, R-Utah, motion to table (kill) the Leahy, D-Vt., amendment that would require the Defense Department to provide Congress with a number of reports pertaining to detainees at U.S. military prisons worldwide, including a report on all prisoner interrogations techniques approved by U.S. officials. It also would require the department to submit all International Committee of the Red Cross reports regarding treatment of prisoners in U.S. custody in Iraq, Afghanistan and Guantánamo Bay, Cuba. Motion rejected 45-50: R 44-5; D 1-44 (ND 0-37, SD 1-7); I 0-1. June 23, 2004.

144. S 2400. Fiscal 2005 Defense Authorization/Prisoner Reports. Leahy, D-Vt., amendment to the Leahy amendment. The amendment would direct the attorney general to submit to the Judiciary Committee all documents in the possession of the Justice Department produced since Jan. 20, 2001, regarding the treatment and interrogation of detainees held in U.S. custody. Rejected 46-50: R 0-49; D 45-1 (ND 37-0, SD 8-1); I 1-0. (Subsequently, the underlying Leahy amendment was adopted by voice vote.) June 23, 2004.

145. S 2400. Fiscal 2005 Defense Authorization/Veterans' Health Benefits. Daschle, D-S.D., motion to waive the Budget Act with respect to the Nickles, R-Okla., point of order against the Daschle amendment that would authorize an increase in health benefits for veterans by keeping discretionary spending at fiscal 2004 levels and providing mandatory funds adjusted by a formula specified in the amendment. Motion rejected 49-48: R 3-46; D 45-2 (ND 37-1, SD 8-1); I 1-0. A three-fifths majority (60) of the total Senate is required to waive the Budget Act. (Subsequently, the chair upheld the point of order, and the amendment fell.) June 23, 2004.

Senate Votes 146, 147, 148, 149, 150, 151, 152

	146	147	148	149	150	151	152
ALABAMA							
Shelby	Y	Y	Y	Y	Y	Y	Y
Sessions	Y	N	Y	Y	Y	Y	Y
ALASKA							
Stevens	Y	Y	Y	Y	Y	Y	Y
Murkowski, L.	Y	Y	Y	Y	Y	Y	Y
ARIZONA							
McCain	Y	Y	Y	Y	Y	Y	Y
Kyl	Y	N	Y	Y	Y	Y	Y
ARKANSAS							
Lincoln	Y	Y	N	Y	Y	Y	Y
Pryor	Y	Y	N	Y	Y	Y	Y
CALIFORNIA							
Feinstein	Y	Y	N	Y	Y	Y	N
Boxer	Y	Y	N	Y	Y	Y	N
COLORADO							
Campbell	Y	Y	Y	Y	Y	Y	Y
Allard	Y	Y	Y	Y	Y	Y	Y
CONNECTICUT							
Dodd	Y	Y	N	Y	Y	Y	Y
Lieberman	Y	Y	N	Y	Y	Y	Y
DELAWARE							
Biden	Y	Y	N	Y	Y	Y	Y
Carper	Y	Y	N	Y	Y	Y	Y
FLORIDA							
Graham	Y	Y	N	Y	Y	Y	Y
Nelson	Y	Y	N	Y	Y	N	Y
GEORGIA							
Miller	Y	Y	Y	Y	Y	Y	Y
Chambliss	Y	Y	Y	Y	Y	Y	Y
HAWAII							
Inouye	Y	Y	Y	Y	Y	Y	N
Akaka	Y	Y	N	Y	Y	Y	N
IDAHO							
Craig	Y	Y	Y	Y	Y	Y	Y
Crapo	Y	Y	Y	Y	Y	Y	Y
ILLINOIS							
Fitzgerald	Y	Y	Y	Y	Y	Y	Y
Durbin	Y	Y	N	Y	Y	Y	Y
INDIANA							
Lugar	Y	?	?	?	?	?	?
Bayh	Y	Y	N	Y	Y	Y	Y

	146	147	148	149	150	151	152
IOWA							
Grassley	Y	Y	Y	Y	Y	Y	Y
Harkin	Y	Y	N	Y	Y	Y	N
KANSAS							
Brownback	+	Y	Y	Y	Y	Y	Y
Roberts	Y	Y	Y	Y	?	Y	Y
KENTUCKY							
McConnell	Y	Y	Y	Y	Y	Y	Y
Bunning	Y	N	Y	Y	Y	Y	Y
LOUISIANA							
Breaux	Y	Y	N	Y	Y	Y	Y
Landrieu	Y	Y	N	Y	Y	Y	Y
MAINE							
Snowe	Y	Y	Y	Y	Y	Y	Y
Collins	Y	Y	Y	Y	Y	Y	Y
MARYLAND							
Sarbanes	Y	Y	N	Y	Y	Y	N
Mikulski	Y	Y	N	Y	Y	Y	N
MASSACHUSETTS							
Kennedy	Y	Y	N	Y	Y	Y	N
Kerry	?	?	?	?	?	?	?
MICHIGAN							
Levin	Y	Y	N	Y	Y	Y	N
Stabenow	Y	Y	N	Y	Y	Y	N
MINNESOTA							
Dayton	Y	Y	N	Y	Y	Y	N
Coleman	Y	Y	Y	Y	Y	Y	Y
MISSISSIPPI							
Cochran	Y	Y	Y	Y	Y	Y	Y
Lott	Y	Y	Y	Y	Y	Y	Y
MISSOURI							
Bond	Y	Y	Y	Y	Y	Y	Y
Talent	Y	Y	Y	Y	Y	Y	Y
MONTANA							
Burns	Y	Y	Y	Y	Y	Y	Y
Baucus	Y	Y	Y	Y	Y	Y	N
NEBRASKA							
Hagel	Y	Y	Y	Y	Y	Y	Y
Nelson	Y	Y	N	Y	Y	Y	Y
NEVADA							
Reid	Y	Y	N	Y	Y	Y	N
Ensign	Y	Y	Y	Y	Y	Y	Y

	146	147	148	149	150	151	152
NEW HAMPSHIRE							
Gregg	Y	Y	Y	Y	Y	Y	Y
Sununu	?	Y	Y	Y	Y	N	Y
NEW JERSEY							
Lautenberg	Y	Y	N	Y	Y	Y	N
Corzine	Y	Y	N	Y	Y	Y	N
NEW MEXICO							
Domenici	Y	Y	N	Y	Y	Y	Y
Bingaman	Y	Y	N	Y	Y	Y	Y
NEW YORK							
Schumer	Y	Y	N	Y	Y	Y	Y
Clinton	Y	Y	N	Y	Y	Y	N
NORTH CAROLINA							
Edwards	Y	Y	N	Y	Y	Y	N
Dole	Y	N	Y	Y	Y	Y	Y
NORTH DAKOTA							
Conrad	Y	Y	N	Y	Y	Y	Y
Dorgan	Y	Y	N	Y	Y	Y	Y
OHIO							
DeWine	Y	Y	N	Y	Y	Y	Y
Voinovich	Y	Y	Y	Y	Y	Y	Y
OKLAHOMA							
Nickles	Y	Y	Y	Y	Y	Y	?
Inhofe	Y	N	Y	Y	Y	Y	Y
OREGON							
Wyden	Y	Y	N	Y	Y	Y	N
Smith	Y	Y	N	Y	Y	Y	N
PENNSYLVANIA							
Specter	Y	Y	N	Y	Y	Y	Y
Santorum	Y	N	Y	Y	Y	Y	Y
RHODE ISLAND							
Reed	Y	Y	N	Y	Y	Y	N
Chafee	Y	Y	Y	Y	Y	Y	Y
SOUTH CAROLINA							
Hollings	Y	Y	Y	Y	Y	Y	Y
Graham	Y	Y	Y	Y	Y	Y	Y
SOUTH DAKOTA							
Daschle	Y	Y	N	Y	Y	Y	N
Johnson	Y	Y	N	Y	Y	Y	N
TENNESSEE							
Frist	Y	Y	Y	Y	Y	Y	Y
Alexander	Y	Y	Y	Y	Y	Y	Y

	146	147	148	149	150	151	152
TEXAS							
Hutchison	Y	Y	Y	Y	Y	Y	Y
Cornyn	Y	N	Y	Y	Y	Y	Y
UTAH							
Hatch	Y	Y	Y	Y	Y	Y	Y
Bennett	Y	Y	Y	Y	Y	Y	Y
VERMONT							
Leahy	Y	Y	N	Y	Y	Y	N
Jeffords	Y	Y	N	Y	Y	N	N
VIRGINIA							
Warner	Y	Y	Y	Y	Y	Y	Y
Allen	Y	Y	Y	Y	Y	Y	Y
WASHINGTON							
Murray	Y	Y	N	Y	Y	Y	N
Cantwell	Y	Y	N	Y	Y	Y	Y
WEST VIRGINIA							
Byrd	Y	Y	Y	Y	Y	N	Y
Rockefeller	Y	Y	N	Y	Y	Y	Y
WISCONSIN							
Kohl	Y	Y	N	Y	Y	Y	Y
Feingold	Y	Y	N	Y	Y	Y	Y
WYOMING							
Thomas	Y	N	Y	Y	Y	Y	Y
Enzi	Y	N	Y	Y	N	Y	Y

Key

Y	Voted for (yea).
#	Paired for.
+	Announced for.
N	Voted against (nay).
X	Paired against.
–	Announced against.
P	Voted "present."
C	Voted "present" to avoid possible conflict of interest.
?	Did not vote or otherwise make a position known.

Democrats **Republicans**
Independents

ND Northern Democrats   SD Southern Democrats

Southern states - Ala., Ark., Fla., Ga., Ky., La., Miss., N.C., Okla., S.C., Tenn., Texas, Va.

146. S 2400. Fiscal 2005 Defense Authorization/Passage. Passage of the bill that would authorize $447.2 billion for the Defense Department and for the Energy Department's national security programs, including $25 billion in emergency funding for military operations in Iraq and Afghanistan. It also would increase the authorized end strength for active-duty Army personnel by 20,000 soldiers in fiscal 2005 and authorize $10.2 billion in missile defense funding. The bill includes an across-the-board military pay raise of 3.5 percent and would give members of the National Guard and Reserve access to the military's Tricare health system even when they are on inactive status. Passed 97-0: R 49-0; D 47-0 (ND 38-0, SD 9-0); I 1-0. June 23, 2004.

147. HR 4613. Fiscal 2005 Defense Appropriations/Overseas Military Funding. Byrd, D-W.Va., amendment that would express the sense of the Senate that any funds for ongoing military operations overseas, including those in Iraq and Afghanistan, should be included in the president's annual budget request and that such funds, when allocated in appropriations bills, should be placed in specific accounts. Adopted 89-9: R 41-9; D 47-0 (ND 38-0, SD 9-0); I 1-0. June 24, 2004.

148. HR 4613. Fiscal 2005 Defense Appropriations/Disaster Assistance. Stevens, R-Alaska, motion to table (kill) the Biden, D-Del., amendment that would add $118 million in emergency funding for disaster and famine assistance efforts in response to the humanitarian crisis in the Darfur region of Sudan and Chad. Motion agreed to 53-45: R 48-2; D 5-42 (ND 3-35, SD 2-7); I 0-1. June 24, 2004.

149. HR 4613. Fiscal 2005 Defense Appropriations/Passage. Passage of the bill that would appropriate $416.2 billion in fiscal 2005 for the Defense Department and related agencies, including $25 billion in emergency funding for operations in Iraq and Afghanistan. It would provide $104 billion for military personnel, including a 3.5 percent pay raise for military personnel. As amended, it also would appropriate an additional $95 million in emergency funding for disaster and famine assistance efforts in the Darfur region of Sudan and Chad. Passed 98-0: R 50-0; D 47-0 (ND 38-0, SD 9-0); I 1-0. June 24, 2004.

150. H J Res 97. Myanmar Sanctions/Passage. Passage of the joint resolution that would extend for one year import restrictions on products from Myanmar, formerly known as Burma, until the president certifies that the Myanmar government has made significant progress toward practicing democracy and ending human rights violations. Passed (thus cleared for the president) 96-1: R 48-1; D 47-0 (ND 38-0, SD 9-0); I 1-0. June 24, 2004.

151. S Res 393. Middle East Peace Process/Adoption. Adoption of the resolution that would express the sense of the Senate in support of U.S. policy in the Middle East peace process. Adopted 95-3: R 49-1; D 46-1 (ND 37-1, SD 9-0); I 0-1. June 24, 2004.

152. Sykes Nomination/Confirmation. Confirmation of President Bush's nomination of Diane S. Sykes of Wisconsin to be a judge for the U.S. Court of Appeals for the 7th Circuit. Confirmed 70-27: R 49-0; D 21-26 (ND 14-24, SD 7-2); I 0-1. A "yea" was a vote in support of the president's position. June 24, 2004.

	153	154
ALABAMA		
Shelby	Y	N
Sessions	Y	Y
ALASKA		
Stevens	Y	Y
Murkowski, L.	?	Y
ARIZONA		
McCain	Y	N
Kyl	Y	Y
ARKANSAS		
Lincoln	Y	N
Pryor	Y	N
CALIFORNIA		
Feinstein	N	N
Boxer	N	?
COLORADO		
Campbell	Y	?
Allard	Y	Y
CONNECTICUT		
Dodd	N	N
Lieberman	N	N
DELAWARE		
Biden	N	?
Carper	N	N
FLORIDA		
Graham	N	N
Nelson	N	N
GEORGIA		
Miller	Y	Y
Chambliss	Y	Y
HAWAII		
Inouye	N	N
Akaka	N	N
IDAHO		
Craig	Y	N
Crapo	Y	Y
ILLINOIS		
Fitzgerald	Y	?
Durbin	N	N
INDIANA		
Lugar	Y	Y
Bayh	N	N

	153	154
IOWA		
Grassley	Y	Y
Harkin	N	N
KANSAS		
Brownback	Y	Y
Roberts	Y	Y
KENTUCKY		
McConnell	Y	Y
Bunning	Y	Y
LOUISIANA		
Breaux	Y	N
Landrieu	Y	N
MAINE		
Snowe	N	Y
Collins	N	Y
MARYLAND		
Sarbanes	N	N
Mikulski	N	?
MASSACHUSETTS		
Kennedy	N	N
Kerry	?	?
MICHIGAN		
Levin	N	N
Stabenow	N	N
MINNESOTA		
Dayton	N	N
Coleman	Y	Y
MISSISSIPPI		
Cochran	Y	Y
Lott	Y	Y
MISSOURI		
Bond	Y	Y
Talent	Y	Y
MONTANA		
Burns	Y	Y
Baucus	N	N
NEBRASKA		
Hagel	Y	?
Nelson	Y	Y
NEVADA		
Reid	N	N
Ensign	Y	?

	153	154
NEW HAMPSHIRE		
Gregg	Y	Y
Sununu	Y	Y
NEW JERSEY		
Lautenberg	N	N
Corzine	N	N
NEW MEXICO		
Domenici	Y	Y
Bingaman	N	N
NEW YORK		
Schumer	N	N
Clinton	N	?
NORTH CAROLINA		
Edwards	?	?
Dole	Y	Y
NORTH DAKOTA		
Conrad	N	N
Dorgan	N	N
OHIO		
DeWine	Y	Y
Voinovich	Y	Y
OKLAHOMA		
Nickles	Y	Y
Inhofe	Y	Y
OREGON		
Wyden	N	N
Smith	Y	Y
PENNSYLVANIA		
Specter	Y	Y
Santorum	Y	?
RHODE ISLAND		
Reed	N	N
Chafee	N	Y
SOUTH CAROLINA		
Hollings	N	N
Graham	Y	Y
SOUTH DAKOTA		
Daschle	N	N
Johnson	N	N
TENNESSEE		
Frist	Y	Y
Alexander	Y	Y

Key

	153	154
TEXAS		
Hutchison	N	Y
Cornyn	Y	Y
UTAH		
Hatch	Y	Y
Bennett	Y	Y
VERMONT		
Leahy	N	N
Jeffords	N	N
VIRGINIA		
Warner	N	Y
Allen	Y	Y
WASHINGTON		
Murray	N	N
Cantwell	N	N
WEST VIRGINIA		
Byrd	N	?
Rockefeller	N	N
WISCONSIN		
Kohl	N	N
Feingold	N	N
WYOMING		
Thomas	Y	Y
Enzi	Y	?

ND Northern Democrats   SD Southern Democrats

Southern states - Ala., Ark., Fla., Ga., Ky., La., Miss., N.C., Okla., S.C., Tenn., Texas, Va.

153. Holmes Nomination/Confirmation. Confirmation of President Bush's nomination of J. Leon Holmes of Arkansas to be a judge for the U.S. District Court for the Eastern District of Arkansas. Confirmed 51-46: R 45-5; D 6-40 (ND 1-37, SD 5-3); I 0-1. A "yea" was a vote in support of the president's position. July 6, 2004.

154. S 2062. Class Action Lawsuits/Cloture. Motion to invoke cloture (thus limiting debate) on the bill that would allow class action cases involving at least 100 plaintiffs to be sent to federal court if at least $5 million is at stake and fewer than two-thirds of the plaintiffs live in the same state as the defendant. Motion rejected 44-43: R 42-3; D 2-39 (ND 1-32, SD 1-7); I 0-1. Three-fifths of the total Senate (60) is required to invoke cloture. A "yea" was a vote in support of the president's position. July 8, 2004.

	155	156	157
ALABAMA			
Shelby	Y	Y	N
Sessions	Y	Y	N
ALASKA			
Stevens	Y	Y	Y
Murkowski, L.	Y	Y	Y
ARIZONA			
McCain	N	Y	Y
Kyl	Y	Y	N
ARKANSAS			
Lincoln	N	Y	Y
Pryor	N	Y	Y
CALIFORNIA			
Feinstein	N	Y	Y
Boxer	N	Y	Y
COLORADO			
Campbell	N	Y	Y
Allard	Y	Y	N
CONNECTICUT			
Dodd	N	Y	Y
Lieberman	N	Y	Y
DELAWARE			
Biden	N	Y	Y
Carper	N	Y	P
FLORIDA			
Graham	N	Y	Y
Nelson	N	Y	?
GEORGIA			
Miller	Y	Y	Y
Chambliss	Y	Y	Y
HAWAII			
Inouye	N	N	Y
Akaka	N	N	Y
IDAHO			
Craig	Y	Y	Y
Crapo	Y	Y	Y
ILLINOIS			
Fitzgerald	Y	Y	N
Durbin	N	Y	Y
INDIANA			
Lugar	Y	Y	Y
Bayh	N	Y	Y

	155	156	157
IOWA			
Grassley	Y	Y	Y
Harkin	N	Y	Y
KANSAS			
Brownback	Y	Y	Y
Roberts	Y	Y	N
KENTUCKY			
McConnell	Y	Y	Y
Bunning	Y	Y	Y
LOUISIANA			
Breaux	N	Y	Y
Landrieu	N	Y	Y
MAINE			
Snowe	N	N	Y
Collins	N	Y	Y
MARYLAND			
Sarbanes	N	Y	Y
Mikulski	N	Y	Y
MASSACHUSETTS			
Kennedy	N	Y	Y
Kerry	?	?	?
MICHIGAN			
Levin	N	Y	Y
Stabenow	N	Y	Y
MINNESOTA			
Dayton	N	N	Y
Coleman	Y	Y	Y
MISSISSIPPI			
Cochran	Y	Y	Y
Lott	Y	Y	N
MISSOURI			
Bond	Y	Y	Y
Talent	Y	Y	Y
MONTANA			
Burns	Y	Y	N
Baucus	N	?	?
NEBRASKA			
Hagel	Y	Y	Y
Nelson	Y	Y	Y
NEVADA			
Reid	N	N	Y
Ensign	Y	Y	Y

	155	156	157
NEW HAMPSHIRE			
Gregg	Y	Y	N
Sununu	N	Y	N
NEW JERSEY			
Lautenberg	N	Y	Y
Corzine	N	Y	Y
NEW MEXICO			
Domenici	Y	?	?
Bingaman	N	Y	Y
NEW YORK			
Schumer	N	N	Y
Clinton	N	Y	Y
NORTH CAROLINA			
Edwards	?	?	?
Dole	Y	Y	Y
NORTH DAKOTA			
Conrad	N	N	Y
Dorgan	N	N	Y
OHIO			
DeWine	Y	Y	Y
Voinovich	Y	N	Y
OKLAHOMA			
Nickles	Y	Y	N
Inhofe	Y	Y	?
OREGON			
Wyden	N	Y	Y
Smith	Y	Y	Y
PENNSYLVANIA			
Specter	Y	Y	Y
Santorum	Y	Y	N
RHODE ISLAND			
Reed	N	Y	Y
Chafee	N	Y	Y
SOUTH CAROLINA			
Hollings	N	Y	Y
Graham	Y	Y	Y
SOUTH DAKOTA			
Daschle	N	N	Y
Johnson	N	N	Y
TENNESSEE			
Frist	Y	Y	Y
Alexander	Y	Y	Y

Key

Y	Voted for (yea).
#	Paired for.
+	Announced for.
N	Voted against (nay).
X	Paired against.
−	Announced against.
P	Voted "present."
C	Voted "present" to avoid possible conflict of interest.
?	Did not vote or otherwise make a position known.

Democrats   **Republicans**
Independents

	155	156	157
TEXAS			
Hutchison	Y	Y	Y
Cornyn	Y	Y	Y
UTAH			
Hatch	Y	Y	Y
Bennett	Y	Y	Y
VERMONT			
Leahy	N	N	Y
Jeffords	N	Y	N
VIRGINIA			
Warner	Y	Y	Y
Allen	Y	Y	Y
WASHINGTON			
Murray	N	Y	Y
Cantwell	N	Y	Y
WEST VIRGINIA			
Byrd	Y	N	Y
Rockefeller	N	N	Y
WISCONSIN			
Kohl	N	N	Y
Feingold	N	N	Y
WYOMING			
Thomas	Y	Y	N
Enzi	Y	Y	N

ND Northern Democrats   SD Southern Democrats

Southern states - Ala., Ark., Fla., Ga., Ky., La., Miss., N.C., Okla., S.C., Tenn., Texas, Va.

155. S J Res 40. Same-Sex Marriage Ban Constitutional Amendment/ Cloture. Motion to invoke cloture (thus limiting debate) on the motion to proceed to the joint resolution to propose a constitutional amendment that would define marriage as consisting only of the union of a man and a woman. It would provide that the U.S. Constitution or any state's constitution could not be construed to require that marriage or any other constructs of marriage be conferred to any other union. Motion rejected 48-50: R 45-6; D 3-43 (ND 2-36, SD 1-7); I 0-1. Three-fifths of the total Senate (60) is required to invoke cloture. A "yea" was a vote in support of the president's position. July 14, 2004.

156. HR 4759. U.S.-Australia Trade/Passage. Passage of the bill that would implement a trade agreement that would reduce tariffs and trade barriers between the United States and Australia. It would give all U.S. agricultural exports to Australia immediate duty-free access, phase out U.S. duties on Australian beef and lamb exports, and slightly increase the current U.S. quota for Australian dairy exports. Passed (thus cleared for the president) 80-16: R 48-2; D 31-14 (ND 23-14, SD 8-0); I 1-0. A "yea" was a vote in support of the president's position. July 15, 2004.

157. HR 4520. Corporate Tax Overhaul/Tobacco Buyout and FDA Regulation. DeWine, R-Ohio, amendment to the McConnell, R-Ky. (for Grassley, R-Iowa), substitute amendment. The DeWine amendment would give the Food and Drug Administration (FDA) authority to regulate the manufacture and sale of tobacco products. It would also eliminate the federal quota and price support programs for certain tobacco farmers, authorize $12 billion over 10 years for the transition from the current quota program, and fund the buyout through assessments on tobacco companies. The substitute amendment would insert the text of S 1637 as passed by the Senate. Adopted 78-15: R 35-14; D 43-0 (ND 36-0, SD 7-0); I 0-1. (Subsequently, the substitute was adopted by voice vote and the bill, as amended, was passed by voice vote.) July 15, 2004.

	158	159	160	161	162	163
ALABAMA						
Shelby	Y	N	Y	Y	Y	Y
Sessions	Y	N	Y	Y	Y	Y
ALASKA						
Stevens	Y	Y	Y	Y	Y	Y
Murkowski, L.	Y	Y	Y	Y	Y	Y
ARIZONA						
McCain	Y	Y	Y	Y	Y	Y
Kyl	Y	Y	Y	Y	Y	Y
ARKANSAS						
Lincoln	N	Y	N	Y	Y	Y
Pryor	N	Y	N	N	N	Y
CALIFORNIA						
Feinstein	N	Y	N	N	N	Y
Boxer	N	Y	N	N	N	Y
COLORADO						
Campbell	Y	Y	Y	Y	Y	Y
Allard	Y	Y	Y	Y	Y	Y
CONNECTICUT						
Dodd	N	Y	N	N	N	Y
Lieberman	N	Y	N	N	N	Y
DELAWARE						
Biden	Y	Y	N	N	N	Y
Carper	N	Y	N	N	N	Y
FLORIDA						
Graham	N	Y	N	N	N	?
Nelson	N	Y	N	N	N	Y
GEORGIA						
Miller	?	Y	Y	Y	Y	Y
Chambliss	Y	Y	Y	Y	Y	Y
HAWAII						
Inouye	N	Y	N	N	N	Y
Akaka	N	N	N	N	N	Y
IDAHO						
Craig	Y	Y	Y	Y	Y	Y
Crapo	Y	Y	Y	Y	Y	Y
ILLINOIS						
Fitzgerald	Y	Y	Y	Y	Y	Y
Durbin	N	Y	N	N	N	Y
INDIANA						
Lugar	Y	Y	Y	Y	Y	Y
Bayh	N	Y	N	N	N	Y

	158	159	160	161	162	163
IOWA						
Grassley	Y	Y	Y	Y	Y	Y
Harkin	N	N	N	N	N	?
KANSAS						
Brownback	Y	Y	Y	Y	Y	Y
Roberts	Y	Y	Y	Y	Y	Y
KENTUCKY						
McConnell	Y	Y	Y	Y	Y	Y
Bunning	Y	Y	Y	Y	Y	Y
LOUISIANA						
Breaux	N	Y	N	N	N	Y
Landrieu	N	Y	N	N	N	Y
MAINE						
Snowe	Y	Y	Y	Y	Y	Y
Collins	Y	Y	Y	Y	Y	Y
MARYLAND						
Sarbanes	N	Y	N	N	N	Y
Mikulski	N	Y	N	N	N	Y
MASSACHUSETTS						
Kennedy	N	Y	N	N	N	Y
Kerry	?	?	?	?	?	?
MICHIGAN						
Levin	N	Y	N	N	N	Y
Stabenow	N	Y	N	N	N	Y
MINNESOTA						
Dayton	N	Y	N	N	N	Y
Coleman	Y	Y	Y	Y	Y	Y
MISSISSIPPI						
Cochran	Y	Y	Y	Y	Y	Y
Lott	Y	Y	Y	Y	Y	Y
MISSOURI						
Bond	Y	Y	Y	Y	Y	Y
Talent	Y	Y	Y	Y	Y	Y
MONTANA						
Burns	Y	Y	Y	Y	Y	Y
Baucus	N	Y	N	N	N	Y
NEBRASKA						
Hagel	Y	Y	Y	Y	Y	Y
Nelson	Y	Y	N	Y	Y	Y
NEVADA						
Reid	N	N	N	N	N	Y
Ensign	Y	Y	Y	Y	Y	Y

	158	159	160	161	162	163
NEW HAMPSHIRE						
Gregg	Y	Y	Y	Y	?	Y
Sununu	Y	Y	Y	Y	Y	Y
NEW JERSEY						
Lautenberg	N	Y	N	N	N	Y
Corzine	N	Y	N	N	N	Y
NEW MEXICO						
Domenici	Y	Y	Y	Y	Y	Y
Bingaman	N	Y	N	N	N	Y
NEW YORK						
Schumer	N	Y	N	N	N	Y
Clinton	N	Y	N	N	N	Y
NORTH CAROLINA						
Edwards	?	?	?	?	?	?
Dole	Y	N	Y	Y	Y	Y
NORTH DAKOTA						
Conrad	N	Y	N	N	N	Y
Dorgan	N	N	N	N	N	Y
OHIO						
DeWine	Y	Y	Y	Y	Y	Y
Voinovich	Y	N	Y	Y	Y	Y
OKLAHOMA						
Nickles	Y	Y	Y	Y	Y	Y
Inhofe	Y	Y	Y	Y	Y	Y
OREGON						
Wyden	N	Y	N	N	N	Y
Smith	Y	Y	Y	Y	Y	Y
PENNSYLVANIA						
Specter	Y	Y	Y	Y	Y	Y
Santorum	Y	Y	Y	Y	Y	Y
RHODE ISLAND						
Reed	N	Y	N	N	N	Y
Chafee	Y	Y	Y	Y	Y	Y
SOUTH CAROLINA						
Hollings	N	N	N	N	N	Y
Graham	Y	N	Y	Y	Y	Y
SOUTH DAKOTA						
Daschle	N	Y	N	N	N	Y
Johnson	N	Y	N	N	N	Y
TENNESSEE						
Frist	Y	Y	Y	Y	Y	Y
Alexander	Y	Y	Y	Y	Y	Y

Key

Y	Voted for (yea).
#	Paired for.
+	Announced for.
N	Voted against (nay).
X	Paired against.
–	Announced against.
P	Voted "present."
C	Voted "present" to avoid possible conflict of interest.
?	Did not vote or otherwise make a position known.

Democrats **Republicans**
Independents

	158	159	160	161	162	163
TEXAS						
Hutchison	Y	Y	Y	Y	Y	Y
Cornyn	Y	Y	Y	Y	Y	Y
UTAH						
Hatch	Y	Y	Y	Y	Y	Y
Bennett	Y	Y	Y	Y	Y	Y
VERMONT						
Leahy	N	N	N	N	N	Y
Jeffords	N	Y	N	N	N	Y
VIRGINIA						
Warner	Y	Y	Y	Y	Y	Y
Allen	Y	Y	Y	Y	Y	Y
WASHINGTON						
Murray	N	Y	N	N	N	Y
Cantwell	N	Y	N	N	N	Y
WEST VIRGINIA						
Byrd	N	N	N	N	N	Y
Rockefeller	N	Y	N	N	N	Y
WISCONSIN						
Kohl	N	Y	N	N	N	Y
Feingold	N	N	N	N	N	Y
WYOMING						
Thomas	Y	Y	Y	Y	Y	Y
Enzi	Y	Y	Y	Y	Y	Y

ND Northern Democrats   SD Southern Democrats

Southern states - Ala., Ark., Fla., Ga., Ky., La., Miss., N.C., Okla., S.C., Tenn., Texas, Va.

158. Myers Nomination/Cloture. Motion to invoke cloture (thus limiting debate) on President Bush's nomination of William G. Myers III of Idaho to be a judge for the U.S. Court of Appeals for the 9th Circuit. Motion rejected 53-44: R 51-0; D 2-43 (ND 2-36, SD 0-7); I 0-1. Three-fifths of the total Senate (60) is required to invoke cloture. A "yea" was a vote in support of the president's position. July 20, 2004.

159. S 2677. U.S.-Morocco Trade/Passage. Passage of the bill that would implement a trade agreement that would reduce tariffs and trade barriers between the United States and Morocco. It would make more than 95 percent of bilateral trade in consumer and industrial products duty-free immediately, with all remaining tariffs eliminated within nine years. It also would reduce some agricultural tariffs. Passed 85-13: R 46-5; D 38-8 (ND 31-7, SD 7-1); I 1-0. A "yea" was a vote in support of the president's position. July 21, 2004.

160. Saad Nomination/Cloture. Motion to invoke cloture (thus limiting debate) on President Bush's nomination of Henry W. Saad of Michigan to be a judge for the U.S. Court of Appeals for the 6th Circuit. Motion rejected 52-46: R 51-0; D 1-45 (ND 0-38, SD 1-7); I 0-1. Three-fifths of the total Senate (60) is required to invoke cloture. A "yea" was a vote in support of the president's position. July 22, 2004.

161. Griffin Nomination/Cloture. Motion to invoke cloture (thus limiting debate) on President Bush's nomination of Richard A. Griffin of Michigan to be a judge for the U.S. Court of Appeals for the 6th Circuit. Motion rejected 54-44: R 51-0; D 3-43 (ND 1-37, SD 2-6); I 0-1. Three-fifths of the total Senate (60) is required to invoke cloture. A "yea" was a vote in support of the president's position. July 22, 2004.

162. McKeague Nomination/Cloture. Motion to invoke cloture (thus limiting debate) on President Bush's nomination of David W. McKeague of Michigan to be a judge for the U.S. Court of Appeals for the 6th Circuit. Motion rejected 53-44: R 50-0; D 3-43 (ND 1-37, SD 2-6); I 0-1. Three-fifths of the total Senate (60) is required to invoke cloture. A "yea" was a vote in support of the president's position. July 22, 2004.

163. HR 4613. Fiscal 2005 Defense Appropriations/Conference Report. Adoption of the conference report on the bill that would appropriate $417.5 billion for the Defense Department and related agencies, including $391.2 billion for the Pentagon and $25 billion in emergency spending for military operations in Iraq and Afghanistan. Adopted (thus cleared for the president) 96-0: R 51-0; D 44-0 (ND 37-0, SD 7-0); I 1-0. July 22, 2004.

	164	165	166	167	168
ALABAMA					
Shelby	Y	Y	N	Y	N
Sessions	Y	Y	N	Y	N
ALASKA					
Stevens	Y	Y	N	Y	N
Murkowski, L.	?	?	N	Y	N
ARIZONA					
McCain	Y	Y	N	Y	N
Kyl	Y	Y	N	Y	N
ARKANSAS					
Lincoln	Y	Y	Y	N	Y
Pryor	Y	Y	Y	N	Y
CALIFORNIA					
Feinstein	Y	Y	Y	N	Y
Boxer	Y	Y	Y	N	Y
COLORADO					
Campbell	Y	Y	N	Y	N
Allard	Y	Y	N	Y	N
CONNECTICUT					
Dodd	Y	Y	Y	N	Y
Lieberman	Y	Y	Y	N	Y
DELAWARE					
Biden	Y	Y	Y	N	Y
Carper	Y	Y	Y	N	Y
FLORIDA					
Graham	?	?	Y	N	Y
Nelson	Y	Y	Y	N	Y
GEORGIA					
Miller	Y	Y	N	Y	N
Chambliss	Y	Y	N	Y	N
HAWAII					
Inouye	Y	Y	Y	N	Y
Akaka	?	?	?	?	?
IDAHO					
Craig	Y	Y	N	Y	N
Crapo	Y	Y	N	Y	N
ILLINOIS					
Fitzgerald	Y	Y	Y	N	Y
Durbin	Y	Y	Y	N	Y
INDIANA					
Lugar	Y	Y	N	Y	N
Bayh	Y	Y	Y	N	Y

	164	165	166	167	168
IOWA					
Grassley	Y	Y	N	Y	N
Harkin	Y	N	Y	N	Y
KANSAS					
Brownback	Y	Y	N	Y	N
Roberts	Y	Y	N	Y	N
KENTUCKY					
McConnell	Y	Y	N	Y	N
Bunning	Y	Y	N	Y	N
LOUISIANA					
Breaux	Y	Y	Y	N	Y
Landrieu	Y	Y	Y	N	Y
MAINE					
Snowe	Y	Y	N	N	Y
Collins	Y	Y	N	Y	Y
MARYLAND					
Sarbanes	Y	Y	Y	N	Y
Mikulski	Y	Y	Y	N	Y
MASSACHUSETTS					
Kennedy	Y	Y	Y	N	Y
Kerry	?	?	?	?	?
MICHIGAN					
Levin	Y	Y	Y	N	Y
Stabenow	Y	Y	Y	N	Y
MINNESOTA					
Dayton	Y	Y	Y	N	Y
Coleman	Y	Y	N	Y	N
MISSISSIPPI					
Cochran	Y	Y	N	Y	N
Lott	Y	Y	N	Y	N
MISSOURI					
Bond	Y	Y	N	Y	Y
Talent	?	Y	N	Y	N
MONTANA					
Burns	Y	Y	N	Y	N
Baucus	Y	Y	Y	N	Y
NEBRASKA					
Hagel	Y	Y	N	Y	N
Nelson	Y	Y	Y	N	Y
NEVADA					
Reid	Y	Y	Y	N	Y
Ensign	Y	Y	N	Y	N

	164	165	166	167	168
NEW HAMPSHIRE					
Gregg	Y	Y	N	Y	N
Sununu	Y	Y	N	Y	N
NEW JERSEY					
Lautenberg	Y	Y	Y	N	Y
Corzine	Y	Y	Y	N	Y
NEW MEXICO					
Domenici	Y	Y	N	Y	N
Bingaman	Y	Y	Y	N	Y
NEW YORK					
Schumer	Y	Y	Y	N	Y
Clinton	?	?	?	?	?
NORTH CAROLINA					
Edwards	?	?	?	?	?
Dole	Y	Y	N	Y	N
NORTH DAKOTA					
Conrad	Y	Y	Y	N	Y
Dorgan	Y	Y	Y	N	Y
OHIO					
DeWine	Y	Y	Y	N	Y
Voinovich	Y	Y	N	Y	N
OKLAHOMA					
Nickles	Y	Y	N	Y	N
Inhofe	Y	Y	N	Y	N
OREGON					
Wyden	Y	Y	N	Y	N
Smith	Y	Y	N	Y	N
PENNSYLVANIA					
Specter	Y	Y	Y	N	Y
Santorum	?	?	N	Y	N
RHODE ISLAND					
Reed	Y	Y	Y	N	Y
Chafee	Y	Y	N	N	Y
SOUTH CAROLINA					
Hollings	Y	Y	Y	N	Y
Graham	?	Y	N	Y	N
SOUTH DAKOTA					
Daschle	Y	Y	Y	N	Y
Johnson	Y	Y	Y	N	Y
TENNESSEE					
Frist	Y	Y	N	Y	N
Alexander	Y	Y	N	Y	N

	164	165	166	167	168
TEXAS					
Hutchison	Y	Y	Y	Y	N
Cornyn	Y	Y	N	Y	N
UTAH					
Hatch	Y	Y	N	Y	N
Bennett	Y	Y	N	Y	N
VERMONT					
Leahy	Y	Y	Y	N	Y
Jeffords	Y	Y	Y	N	Y
VIRGINIA					
Warner	Y	Y	Y	N	Y
Allen	Y	Y	Y	Y	Y
WASHINGTON					
Murray	Y	Y	Y	N	Y
Cantwell	Y	Y	Y	N	Y
WEST VIRGINIA					
Byrd	Y	Y	Y	N	Y
Rockefeller	Y	Y	Y	N	Y
WISCONSIN					
Kohl	Y	Y	Y	N	Y
Feingold	Y	Y	Y	N	Y
WYOMING					
Thomas	Y	Y	N	Y	N
Enzi	Y	Y	N	Y	N

ND Northern Democrats   SD Southern Democrats

Southern states - Ala., Ark., Fla., Ga., Ky., La., Miss., N.C., Okla., S.C., Tenn., Texas, Va.

164. Covington Nomination/Confirmation. Confirmation of President Bush's nomination of Virginia Maria Hernandez Covington of Florida to be a judge for the U.S. District Court for the Middle District of Florida. Confirmed 91-0: R 47-0; D 43-0 (ND 36-0, SD 7-0); I 1-0. A "yea" was a vote in support of the president's position. Sept. 7, 2004.

165. Schneider Nomination/Confirmation. Confirmation of President Bush's nomination of Michael H. Schneider Sr. of Texas to be a judge for the U.S. District Court for the Eastern District of Texas. Confirmed 92-1: R 49-0; D 42-1 (ND 35-1, SD 7-0); I 1-0. A "yea" was a vote in support of the president's position. Sept. 7, 2004.

166. HR 4567. Fiscal 2005 Homeland Security Appropriations/ Port Security. Schumer, D-N.Y., motion to waive the Budget Act with respect to the Cochran, R-Miss., point of order against the Schumer amendment. The Schumer amendment would provide an additional $150 million for port security research and development grants in high-threat, high-density urban areas. Motion rejected 50-46: R 6-45; D 43-1 (ND 36-0, SD 7-1); I 1-0. A three-fifths majority (60) of the total Senate is required to waive the Budget Act. (Subsequently, the chair upheld the point of order, and the amendment fell.) Sept. 8, 2004.

167. HR 4567. Fiscal 2005 Homeland Security Appropriations/ Contract Immigration Services. Thomas, R-Wyo., amendment to the Leahy, D-Vt., amendment. The Thomas amendment would prohibit the use of funds to privatize or contract out services provided by the Bureau of Citizenship and Immigration Services, unless the Homeland Security secretary submits a report to Congress within 60 days of the contract award that includes a strategy for mitigating potential adverse effects on federal employees. The Leahy amendment would prohibit the use of funds to privatize or contract out services provided by the Bureau of Citizenship and Immigration Services. Adopted 49-47: R 48-3; D 1-43 (ND 0-36, SD 1-7); I 0-1. Sept. 8, 2004.

168. HR 4567. Fiscal 2005 Homeland Security Appropriations/ Contract Immigration Services. Leahy, D-Vt., amendment to the Leahy amendment. The perfecting amendment would revert the base amendment to its original text, which would prohibit the use of funds to privatize or contract out services provided by the Bureau of Citizenship and Immigration Services. Adopted 49-47: R 5-46; D 43-1 (ND 36-0, SD 7-1); I 1-0. (Subsequently, the underlying Leahy amendment was adopted by voice vote.) A "nay" was a vote in support of the president's position. Sept. 8, 2004.

	169	170	171	172
ALABAMA				
Shelby	N	N	N	Y
Sessions	N	N	N	Y
ALASKA				
Stevens	N	N	N	Y
Murkowski, L.	N	Y	N	Y
ARIZONA				
McCain	N	N	N	N
Kyl	N	N	N	Y
ARKANSAS				
Lincoln	Y	Y	Y	N
Pryor	Y	Y	Y	N
CALIFORNIA				
Feinstein	Y	Y	Y	N
Boxer	Y	Y	Y	N
COLORADO				
Campbell	N	N	N	?
Allard	N	N	N	Y
CONNECTICUT				
Dodd	Y	Y	Y	N
Lieberman	Y	Y	Y	N
DELAWARE				
Biden	Y	Y	Y	N
Carper	Y	Y	Y	N
FLORIDA				
Graham	Y	Y	Y	N
Nelson	Y	Y	Y	N
GEORGIA				
Miller	N	N	N	Y
Chambliss	N	N	N	Y
HAWAII				
Inouye	Y	Y	Y	N
Akaka	?	?	?	?
IDAHO				
Craig	N	N	N	Y
Crapo	N	N	N	Y
ILLINOIS				
Fitzgerald	N	N	N	Y
Durbin	Y	Y	Y	N
INDIANA				
Lugar	N	N	N	Y
Bayh	Y	N	Y	N

	169	170	171	172
IOWA				
Grassley	N	N	N	Y
Harkin	Y	Y	Y	N
KANSAS				
Brownback	N	N	N	N
Roberts	N	N	N	Y
KENTUCKY				
McConnell	N	N	N	Y
Bunning	N	N	N	Y
LOUISIANA				
Breaux	Y	Y	Y	N
Landrieu	Y	Y	Y	N
MAINE				
Snowe	N	N	N	Y
Collins	N	N	N	Y
MARYLAND				
Sarbanes	Y	Y	Y	N
Mikulski	Y	Y	Y	N
MASSACHUSETTS				
Kennedy	Y	Y	Y	N
Kerry	?	?	?	?
MICHIGAN				
Levin	Y	Y	Y	N
Stabenow	Y	Y	Y	N
MINNESOTA				
Dayton	Y	Y	Y	N
Coleman	N	N	N	Y
MISSISSIPPI				
Cochran	N	N	N	Y
Lott	N	N	N	Y
MISSOURI				
Bond	N	N	N	Y
Talent	N	N	N	Y
MONTANA				
Burns	N	N	N	Y
Baucus	Y	N	Y	N
NEBRASKA				
Hagel	N	N	N	Y
Nelson	Y	N	Y	N
NEVADA				
Reid	Y	Y	Y	N
Ensign	N	N	N	Y

	169	170	171	172
NEW HAMPSHIRE				
Gregg	N	N	N	Y
Sununu	N	N	N	Y
NEW JERSEY				
Lautenberg	Y	Y	Y	N
Corzine	Y	Y	Y	?
NEW MEXICO				
Domenici	N	N	N	Y
Bingaman	Y	Y	Y	N
NEW YORK				
Schumer	Y	Y	Y	N
Clinton	?	?	?	?
NORTH CAROLINA				
Edwards	?	?	?	?
Dole	?	?	?	?
NORTH DAKOTA				
Conrad	N	N	N	N
Dorgan	Y	Y	Y	N
OHIO				
DeWine	N	N	Y	N
Voinovich	N	N	N	Y
OKLAHOMA				
Nickles	N	N	N	?
Inhofe	N	N	N	Y
OREGON				
Wyden	Y	Y	Y	N
Smith	N	N	N	?
PENNSYLVANIA				
Specter	?	?	?	Y
Santorum	N	N	N	Y
RHODE ISLAND				
Reed	Y	Y	Y	N
Chafee	N	N	N	Y
SOUTH CAROLINA				
Hollings	Y	Y	Y	N
Graham	N	N	N	Y
SOUTH DAKOTA				
Daschle	Y	Y	Y	N
Johnson	Y	Y	Y	N
TENNESSEE				
Frist	N	N	N	Y
Alexander	N	N	N	Y

Key

Y	Voted for (yea).
#	Paired for.
+	Announced for.
N	Voted against (nay).
X	Paired against.
–	Announced against.
P	Voted "present."
C	Voted "present" to avoid possible conflict of interest.
?	Did not vote or otherwise make a position known.

Democrats **Republicans**
Independents

	169	170	171	172
TEXAS				
Hutchison	N	N	Y	Y
Cornyn	N	N	N	Y
UTAH				
Hatch	N	N	N	Y
Bennett	N	N	N	Y
VERMONT				
Leahy	Y	Y	Y	N
Jeffords	Y	Y	Y	N
VIRGINIA				
Warner	N	N	N	Y
Allen	N	N	N	Y
WASHINGTON				
Murray	Y	Y	Y	N
Cantwell	Y	Y	Y	N
WEST VIRGINIA				
Byrd	Y	Y	Y	N
Rockefeller	Y	Y	Y	N
WISCONSIN				
Kohl	Y	Y	Y	N
Feingold	Y	Y	Y	N
WYOMING				
Thomas	N	N	N	Y
Enzi	N	N	N	Y

ND Northern Democrats   SD Southern Democrats

Southern states - Ala., Ark., Fla., Ga., Ky., La., Miss., N.C., Okla., S.C., Tenn., Texas, Va.

169. HR 4567. Fiscal 2005 Homeland Security Appropriations/Spending Increase. Byrd, D-W.Va., motion to waive the Budget Act with respect to the Cochran, R-Miss., point of order against the Byrd amendment. The Byrd amendment would increase overall homeland security spending in the bill by $2 billion, including $440 million for grants to high-threat, high-security urban areas, $350 million for rail and mass transit security, $324 million for the Coast Guard, $236 million for port and border security, $150 million for aviation security and $100 million for additional fire personnel. Motion rejected 43-51: R 0-49; D 42-2 (ND 35-1, SD 7-1); I 1-0. A three-fifths majority vote (60) of the total Senate is required to waive the Budget Act. (Subsequently, the chair upheld the point of order, and the amendment fell.) Sept. 9, 2004.

170. HR 4567. Fiscal 2005 Homeland Security Appropriations/First-Responder Funding. Reid, D-Nev., motion to waive the Budget Act with respect to the Cochran, R-Miss., point of order against the Dodd, D-Conn., amendment. The Dodd amendment would increase funding for police, firefighters and other state and local emergency personnel by $15.8 billion, to be offset by reducing tax breaks enacted in the 2001 tax law for individuals making more than $1 million. Motion rejected 41-53: R 1-48; D 39-5 (ND 33-3,

SD 6-2); I 1-0. A three-fifths majority (60) of the total Senate is required to waive the Budget Act. (Subsequently, the chair upheld the point of order, and the amendment fell.) Sept. 9, 2004.

171. HR 4567. Fiscal 2005 Homeland Security Appropriations/Port Security Grants. Murray, D-Wash., motion to waive the Budget Act with respect to the Cochran, R-Miss., point of order against the Murray amendment, which would increase funding for port security grants by $300 million. Motion rejected 45-49: R 2-47; D 42-2 (ND 35-1, SD 7-1); I 1-0. A three-fifths majority (60) of the total Senate is required to waive the Budget Act. (Subsequently, the chair upheld the point of order, and the amendment fell.) Sept. 9, 2004.

172. HR 4567. Fiscal 2005 Homeland Security Appropriations/Communication Interoperability. Cochran, R-Miss., motion to table (kill) the Boxer, D-Calif., amendment that would increase funding by $70 million to improve the interoperability of state and local communication systems, to be offset by a reduction in the human resources account. Motion agreed to 46-45: R 45-2; D 1-42 (ND 0-35, SD 1-7); I 0-1. Sept. 9, 2004.

	173	174	175	176	177	178	179
ALABAMA							
Shelby	Y	N	N	Y	Y	N	N
Sessions	Y	N	N	Y	?	N	?
ALASKA							
Stevens	Y	N	N	Y	Y	N	N
Murkowski, L.	Y	N	Y	Y	Y	N	N
ARIZONA							
McCain	Y	N	N	Y	Y	N	N
Kyl	?	?	N	Y	Y	N	N
ARKANSAS							
Lincoln	Y	Y	Y	N	N	Y	Y
Pryor	Y	Y	Y	N	N	Y	Y
CALIFORNIA							
Feinstein	N	Y	Y	N	N	Y	Y
Boxer	N	Y	Y	N	N	Y	Y
COLORADO							
Campbell	?	?	?	?	?	?	?
Allard	Y	N	N	Y	Y	N	N
CONNECTICUT							
Dodd	N	Y	Y	N	N	Y	Y
Lieberman	N	Y	Y	N	N	Y	Y
DELAWARE							
Biden	N	Y	Y	N	N	Y	Y
Carper	Y	N	Y	N	N	N	Y
FLORIDA							
Graham	N	Y	Y	N	N	Y	Y
Nelson	N	Y	Y	N	?	?	Y
GEORGIA							
Miller	Y	N	N	Y	Y	N	N
Chambliss	Y	N	N	Y	Y	N	N
HAWAII							
Inouye	N	Y	Y	N	N	Y	Y
Akaka	?	?	?	?	?	?	?
IDAHO							
Craig	Y	N	N	Y	Y	N	N
Crapo	Y	N	N	Y	Y	N	N
ILLINOIS							
Fitzgerald	Y	N	N	Y	Y	N	N
Durbin	N	Y	Y	N	N	Y	Y
INDIANA							
Lugar	Y	N	N	Y	Y	N	N
Bayh	Y	N	Y	N	N	Y	N

	173	174	175	176	177	178	179
IOWA							
Grassley	Y	N	N	Y	Y	N	N
Harkin	Y	Y	Y	N	N	Y	Y
KANSAS							
Brownback	+	?	N	Y	Y	N	N
Roberts	Y	N	N	Y	Y	N	N
KENTUCKY							
McConnell	Y	N	N	Y	Y	N	N
Bunning	Y	N	?	?	?	?	N
LOUISIANA							
Breaux	Y	Y	Y	N	N	Y	Y
Landrieu	N	Y	Y	N	N	Y	Y
MAINE							
Snowe	N	N	N	Y	Y	N	Y
Collins	Y	Y	Y	Y	Y	N	Y
MARYLAND							
Sarbanes	N	Y	Y	N	N	Y	Y
Mikulski	N	Y	Y	N	N	Y	Y
MASSACHUSETTS							
Kennedy	N	Y	Y	N	N	Y	Y
Kerry	?	?	?	?	?	?	?
MICHIGAN							
Levin	N	Y	Y	N	N	Y	Y
Stabenow	N	Y	Y	N	N	Y	Y
MINNESOTA							
Dayton	N	Y	Y	N	N	Y	Y
Coleman	Y	N	N	Y	Y	N	N
MISSISSIPPI							
Cochran	Y	N	N	Y	Y	N	N
Lott	Y	N	N	Y	Y	N	N
MISSOURI							
Bond	Y	N	Y	Y	Y	N	N
Talent	Y	N	Y	Y	Y	N	N
MONTANA							
Burns	Y	?	N	Y	Y	N	N
Baucus	Y	Y	Y	N	N	Y	Y
NEBRASKA							
Hagel	Y	N	N	Y	Y	N	N
Nelson	Y	N	Y	N	N	Y	Y
NEVADA							
Reid	N	Y	Y	N	N	Y	Y
Ensign	N	N	N	Y	Y	N	N

	173	174	175	176	177	178	179
NEW HAMPSHIRE							
Gregg	?	?	N	Y	Y	N	N
Sununu	Y	N	N	Y	Y	N	N
NEW JERSEY							
Lautenberg	N	Y	Y	N	N	Y	Y
Corzine	?	?	Y	N	N	Y	Y
NEW MEXICO							
Domenici	Y	N	N	Y	Y	N	N
Bingaman	N	N	Y	N	N	Y	Y
NEW YORK							
Schumer	N	Y	Y	N	N	Y	Y
Clinton	N	Y	Y	N	N	Y	Y
NORTH CAROLINA							
Edwards	?	?	?	?	?	?	?
Dole	Y	N	N	Y	Y	N	N
NORTH DAKOTA							
Conrad	Y	N	Y	N	N	Y	Y
Dorgan	Y	N	Y	N	N	Y	Y
OHIO							
DeWine	Y	N	N	Y	Y	N	N
Voinovich	?	?	N	Y	Y	N	N
OKLAHOMA							
Nickles	Y	N	N	Y	Y	N	N
Inhofe	Y	N	N	Y	Y	N	N
OREGON							
Wyden	N	Y	Y	N	N	Y	Y
Smith	Y	N	N	Y	Y	N	N
PENNSYLVANIA							
Specter	N	N	Y	N	Y	Y	Y
Santorum	Y	N	N	Y	Y	N	N
RHODE ISLAND							
Reed	?	?	Y	N	N	Y	Y
Chafee	?	?	N	Y	Y	N	N
SOUTH CAROLINA							
Hollings	N	Y	Y	N	N	Y	Y
Graham	Y	N	N	Y	Y	N	N
SOUTH DAKOTA							
Daschle	Y	Y	Y	N	N	Y	Y
Johnson	N	Y	Y	N	N	Y	Y
TENNESSEE							
Frist	Y	N	N	Y	Y	N	N
Alexander	Y	N	N	Y	Y	N	N

	173	174	175	176	177	178	179
TEXAS							
Hutchison	Y	N	N	N	Y	Y	N
Cornyn	Y	N	N	Y	Y	N	N
UTAH							
Hatch	Y	N	N	Y	Y	N	N
Bennett	Y	N	N	Y	Y	N	N
VERMONT							
Leahy	N	Y	Y	N	N	Y	Y
Jeffords	Y	Y	Y	N	N	Y	Y
VIRGINIA							
Warner	Y	N	N	Y	Y	N	N
Allen	Y	N	N	Y	Y	N	Y
WASHINGTON							
Murray	N	Y	Y	N	N	Y	Y
Cantwell	N	Y	Y	N	N	Y	Y
WEST VIRGINIA							
Byrd	N	Y	Y	N	N	Y	Y
Rockefeller	N	Y	Y	N	N	Y	Y
WISCONSIN							
Kohl	N	Y	Y	N	N	Y	Y
Feingold	N	Y	Y	N	N	Y	Y
WYOMING							
Thomas	Y	N	N	Y	Y	N	N
Enzi	Y	N	N	Y	Y	N	N

ND Northern Democrats   SD Southern Democrats

Southern states - Ala., Ark., Fla., Ga., Ky., La., Miss., N.C., Okla., S.C., Tenn., Texas, Va.

173. HR 4567. Fiscal 2005 Homeland Security Appropriations/ Hazmat Trucks. Cochran, R-Miss., motion to table (kill) the Schumer, D-N.Y., amendment that would provide $70 million for a tracking system for hazardous materials trucks and background checks for commercial driver's licenses, to be offset by a reduction in the human resources account. Motion agreed to 55-34: R 42-3; D 12-31 (ND 8-27, SD 4-4); I 1-0. Sept. 13, 2004.

174. HR 4567. Fiscal 2005 Homeland Security Appropriations/Coast Guard Funding. Lautenberg, D-N.J., motion to waive the Budget Act with respect to the Cochran, R-Miss., point of order against the Lautenberg amendment. The Lautenberg amendment would increase funding by $100 million for Coast Guard non-homeland security activities such as fishing enforcement and search and rescue operations. Motion rejected 38-50: R 1-43; D 36-7 (ND 29-6, SD 7-1); I 1-0. A three-fifths majority (60) of the total Senate is required to waive the Budget Act. (Subsequently, the chair upheld the point of order, and the amendment fell.) Sept. 13, 2004.

175. HR 4567. Fiscal 2005 Homeland Security Appropriations/ Firefighter Grants. Mikulski, D-Md., motion to waive the Budget Act with respect to the Cochran, R-Miss., point of order against the Mikulski amendment. The Mikulski amendment would increase funding for firefighter assistance grants by $150 million. Motion rejected 50-45: R 5-44; D 44-1 (ND 37-0, SD 7-1); I 1-0. A three-fifths majority (60) of the total Senate is required to waive the Budget Act. (Subsequently, the chair upheld the point of order, and the amendment fell.) Sept. 14, 2004.

176. HR 4567. Fiscal 2005 Homeland Security Appropriations/ Chemical Facility Security. Cochran, R-Miss., motion to table (kill) the Corzine, D-N.J., amendment that would increase funding by $70 million for enhancing security around chemical facilities, to be offset by a reduction in the

human resources account. Motion agreed to 48-47: R 47-2; D 1-44 (ND 0-37, SD 1-7); I 0-1. Sept. 14, 2004.

177. HR 4567. Fiscal 2005 Homeland Security Appropriations/ Contract Employee Benefits. Cochran, R-Miss., motion to table (kill) the Dayton, D-Minn., amendment that would prohibit funds from being used for the protection of federally owned buildings unless the Department of Homeland Security implements procedures to ensure that private security firms contracted by the agency are required to get approval from their employees before changing employee benefits. Motion agreed to 49-45: R 48-0; D 1-44 (ND 0-37, SD 1-7); I 0-1. Sept. 14, 2004.

178. HR 4567. Fiscal 2005 Homeland Security Appropriations/ High-Threat Area Funding. Clinton, D-N.Y., motion to waive the Budget Act with respect to the Cochran, R-Miss., point of order against the Clinton amendment. The Clinton amendment would increase funding for high-threat urban areas by $625 million. Motion rejected 44-50: R 2-47; D 41-3 (ND 35-2, SD 6-1); I 1-0. A three-fifths majority (60) of the total Senate is required to waive the Budget Act. (Subsequently, the chair upheld the point of order, and the amendment fell.) Sept. 14, 2004.

179. HR 4567. Fiscal 2005 Homeland Security Appropriations/ Spending Increase. Byrd, D-W.Va., motion to waive the Budget Act with respect to the Cochran, R-Miss., point of order against the Byrd amendment. The Byrd amendment would increase funding for homeland security programs by $470 million, including $225 million for state and local programs and $70 million for baggage screening. It also would bar funds from being used to purchase petroleum for the Strategic Petroleum Reserve in fiscal 2005. Motion rejected 48-47: R 5-44; D 42-3 (ND 35-2, SD 7-1); I 1-0. A three-fifths majority (60) of the total Senate is required to waive the Budget Act. (Subsequently, the chair upheld the point of order, and the amendment fell.) Sept. 14, 2004.

	180	181	182	183	184
ALABAMA					
Shelby	Y	N	N	Y	Y
Sessions	?	?	?	?	?
ALASKA					
Stevens	Y	N	N	Y	Y
Murkowski, L.	Y	N	N	Y	Y
ARIZONA					
McCain	Y	N	N	N	Y
Kyl	Y	N	N	Y	Y
ARKANSAS					
Lincoln	N	Y	Y	Y	Y
Pryor	N	Y	Y	Y	Y
CALIFORNIA					
Feinstein	N	Y	Y	N	Y
Boxer	N	Y	Y	N	Y
COLORADO					
Campbell	?	?	?	?	?
Allard	Y	N	N	Y	Y
CONNECTICUT					
Dodd	N	Y	Y	N	Y
Lieberman	N	Y	Y	N	Y
DELAWARE					
Biden	N	Y	Y	N	Y
Carper	N	Y	N	Y	Y
FLORIDA					
Graham	N	Y	Y	N	Y
Nelson	N	Y	Y	N	Y
GEORGIA					
Miller	Y	N	N	Y	Y
Chambliss	Y	N	N	Y	Y
HAWAII					
Inouye	N	Y	Y	N	Y
Akaka	?	?	?	?	?
IDAHO					
Craig	Y	N	N	Y	Y
Crapo	Y	N	N	Y	Y
ILLINOIS					
Fitzgerald	Y	N	N	Y	Y
Durbin	N	Y	N	Y	Y
INDIANA					
Lugar	Y	N	N	Y	Y
Bayh	N	Y	Y	Y	Y
IOWA					
Grassley	Y	N	N	Y	Y
Harkin	N	Y	Y	Y	Y
KANSAS					
Brownback	Y	N	N	Y	Y
Roberts	Y	N	N	Y	Y
KENTUCKY					
McConnell	Y	N	N	Y	Y
Bunning	Y	N	N	Y	Y
LOUISIANA					
Breaux	N	Y	Y	N	Y
Landrieu	N	Y	Y	N	Y
MAINE					
Snowe	Y	N	N	Y	Y
Collins	Y	N	N	Y	Y
MARYLAND					
Sarbanes	N	Y	Y	N	Y
Mikulski	N	Y	Y	N	Y
MASSACHUSETTS					
Kennedy	N	Y	Y	N	Y
Kerry	?	?	?	?	?
MICHIGAN					
Levin	N	Y	Y	N	Y
Stabenow	N	Y	Y	N	Y
MINNESOTA					
Dayton	N	Y	Y	Y	Y
Coleman	Y	N	N	Y	Y
MISSISSIPPI					
Cochran	Y	N	N	Y	Y
Lott	?	?	?	?	?
MISSOURI					
Bond	Y	N	N	Y	Y
Talent	Y	N	N	Y	Y
MONTANA					
Burns	Y	N	N	Y	Y
Baucus	N	Y	Y	Y	Y
NEBRASKA					
Hagel	Y	N	Y	Y	Y
Nelson	N	Y	Y	Y	Y
NEVADA					
Reid	N	Y	Y	N	Y
Ensign	Y	N	N	N	Y
NEW HAMPSHIRE					
Gregg	Y	N	N	Y	Y
Sununu	Y	N	N	Y	Y
NEW JERSEY					
Lautenberg	N	Y	Y	N	Y
Corzine	N	Y	Y	N	Y
NEW MEXICO					
Domenici	Y	N	?	?	?
Bingaman	N	N	N	N	Y
NEW YORK					
Schumer	N	Y	Y	N	Y
Clinton	N	Y	Y	N	Y
NORTH CAROLINA					
Edwards	?	?	?	?	?
Dole	Y	N	N	Y	Y
NORTH DAKOTA					
Conrad	N	N	N	Y	Y
Dorgan	N	N	N	Y	Y
OHIO					
DeWine	Y	N	N	N	Y
Voinovich	Y	N	N	Y	Y
OKLAHOMA					
Nickles	Y	N	N	Y	Y
Inhofe	Y	N	N	Y	Y
OREGON					
Wyden	N	Y	Y	Y	Y
Smith	Y	N	N	Y	Y
PENNSYLVANIA					
Specter	Y	Y	Y	N	Y
Santorum	Y	N	N	Y	Y
RHODE ISLAND					
Reed	N	Y	Y	N	Y
Chafee	Y	N	N	Y	Y
SOUTH CAROLINA					
Hollings	N	Y	Y	N	Y
Graham	Y	N	N	Y	Y
SOUTH DAKOTA					
Daschle	N	Y	Y	Y	Y
Johnson	N	Y	Y	Y	Y
TENNESSEE					
Frist	Y	N	N	Y	Y
Alexander	Y	N	N	Y	Y
TEXAS					
Hutchison	Y	N	Y	N	Y
Cornyn	Y	N	N	N	Y
UTAH					
Hatch	Y	N	N	Y	Y
Bennett	Y	N	N	Y	Y
VERMONT					
Leahy	N	Y	Y	N	Y
Jeffords	N	Y	Y	N	Y
VIRGINIA					
Warner	Y	N	N	N	Y
Allen	Y	N	N	N	Y
WASHINGTON					
Murray	N	Y	Y	N	Y
Cantwell	N	Y	Y	N	Y
WEST VIRGINIA					
Byrd	N	Y	Y	N	Y
Rockefeller	N	Y	Y	Y	Y
WISCONSIN					
Kohl	N	Y	Y	Y	Y
Feingold	N	Y	Y	Y	Y
WYOMING					
Thomas	Y	N	N	Y	Y
Enzi	Y	N	N	Y	Y

Key

Y	Voted for (yea).
#	Paired for.
+	Announced for.
N	Voted against (nay).
X	Paired against.
−	Announced against.
P	Voted "present."
C	Voted "present" to avoid possible conflict of interest.
?	Did not vote or otherwise make a position known.

Democrats **Republicans**
Independents

ND Northern Democrats   SD Southern Democrats

Southern states - Ala., Ark., Fla., Ga., Ky., La., Miss., N.C., Okla., S.C., Tenn., Texas, Va.

180. HR 4567. Fiscal 2005 Homeland Security Appropriations/Scowcroft Commission Report. Cochran, R-Miss., motion to table (kill) the Kennedy, D-Mass., amendment that would require the Bush administration to declassify a 2002 report by a commission led by former national security adviser Brent Scowcroft that recommended a stronger director of central intelligence. Motion agreed to 49-45: R 48-0; D 1-44 (ND 0-37, SD 1-7); I 0-1. Sept. 14, 2004.

181. HR 4567. Fiscal 2005 Homeland Security Appropriations/Rail Security Funds. Schumer, D-N.Y., motion to waive the Budget Act with respect to the Cochran, R-Miss., point of order against the Schumer amendment. The Schumer amendment would increase funding for rail and transit security by $350 million. Motion rejected 43-51: R 1-47; D 41-4 (ND 34-3, SD 7-1); I 1-0. A three-fifths majority (60) of the total Senate is required to waive the Budget Act. (Subsequently, the chair upheld the point of order, and the amendment fell.) Sept. 14, 2004.

182. HR 4567. Fiscal 2005 Homeland Security Appropriations/Immigration Security. Schumer, D-N.Y., motion to waive the Budget Act with respect to the Cochran, R-Miss., point of order against the Schumer amendment. The Schumer amendment would increase funding for immigration security measures by $350 million, including $200 million for biometric technologies. Motion rejected 44-49: R 3-44; D 40-5 (ND 33-4, SD 7-1); I 1-0. A three-fifths majority (60) of the total Senate is required to waive the Budget Act. (Subsequently, the chair upheld the point of order, and the amendment fell.) Sept. 14, 2004.

183. HR 4567. Fiscal 2005 Homeland Security Appropriations/ Threat-Based Allocations. Cochran, R-Miss., motion to table (kill) the Clinton, D-N.Y., amendment that would require the secretary of Homeland Security to distribute formula-based grants to states and localities based on threat and vulnerability assessments. Motion agreed to 54-39: R 37-10; D 17-28 (ND 14-23, SD 3-5); I 0-1. Sept. 14, 2004.

184. HR 4567. Fiscal 2005 Homeland Security Appropriations/ Passage. Passage of the bill that would provide $33.8 billion in fiscal 2005 for the Department of Homeland Security and related agencies, 5 percent more than the administration's request. The bill, as amended, would also provide an estimated $2.9 billion in emergency aid to agricultural producers affected by natural disasters. Passed 93-0: R 47-0; D 45-0 (ND 37-0, SD 8-0); I 1-0. Sept. 14, 2004.

	185	186	187	188
ALABAMA				
Shelby	Y	Y	Y	Y
Sessions	Y	Y	Y	Y
ALASKA				
Stevens	Y	Y	Y	Y
Murkowski, L.	Y	Y	Y	Y
ARIZONA				
McCain	Y	Y	Y	Y
Kyl	Y	Y	Y	Y
ARKANSAS				
Lincoln	Y	Y	Y	Y
Pryor	Y	Y	Y	Y
CALIFORNIA				
Feinstein	Y	Y	Y	Y
Boxer	Y	Y	Y	Y
COLORADO				
Campbell	Y	Y	Y	Y
Allard	Y	Y	Y	Y
CONNECTICUT				
Dodd	Y	Y	N	Y
Lieberman	Y	Y	Y	Y
DELAWARE				
Biden	Y	Y	N	Y
Carper	Y	Y	Y	Y
FLORIDA				
Graham	?	Y	Y	Y
Nelson	Y	Y	Y	Y
GEORGIA				
Miller	Y	Y	Y	Y
Chambliss	Y	Y	Y	Y
HAWAII				
Inouye	?	Y	Y	?
Akaka	?	?	?	?
IDAHO				
Craig	Y	Y	Y	Y
Crapo	Y	Y	Y	Y
ILLINOIS				
Fitzgerald	Y	Y	Y	Y
Durbin	Y	Y	N	Y
INDIANA				
Lugar	Y	Y	Y	Y
Bayh	Y	Y	Y	Y

	185	186	187	188
IOWA				
Grassley	Y	Y	Y	Y
Harkin	Y	Y	N	Y
KANSAS				
Brownback	Y	Y	Y	Y
Roberts	Y	Y	Y	Y
KENTUCKY				
McConnell	+	Y	Y	Y
Bunning	Y	Y	Y	Y
LOUISIANA				
Breaux	Y	Y	Y	Y
Landrieu	Y	Y	Y	Y
MAINE				
Snowe	Y	Y	Y	N
Collins	Y	Y	Y	Y
MARYLAND				
Sarbanes	Y	Y	N	Y
Mikulski	Y	Y	Y	Y
MASSACHUSETTS				
Kennedy	Y	Y	N	?
Kerry	?	?	?	?
MICHIGAN				
Levin	Y	Y	N	Y
Stabenow	Y	Y	N	Y
MINNESOTA				
Dayton	Y	Y	Y	Y
Coleman	+	Y	Y	Y
MISSISSIPPI				
Cochran	Y	Y	Y	Y
Lott	Y	Y	Y	Y
MISSOURI				
Bond	Y	Y	Y	Y
Talent	Y	Y	Y	Y
MONTANA				
Burns	Y	Y	Y	Y
Baucus	Y	Y	Y	Y
NEBRASKA				
Hagel	Y	Y	Y	Y
Nelson	Y	Y	Y	Y
NEVADA				
Reid	Y	Y	Y	Y
Ensign	Y	N	Y	Y

	185	186	187	188
NEW HAMPSHIRE				
Gregg	Y	Y	Y	Y
Sununu	Y	?	Y	Y
NEW JERSEY				
Lautenberg	Y	Y	N	Y
Corzine	Y	Y	N	Y
NEW MEXICO				
Domenici	Y	Y	Y	Y
Bingaman	Y	Y	N	Y
NEW YORK				
Schumer	Y	Y	Y	Y
Clinton	Y	Y	N	Y
NORTH CAROLINA				
Edwards	?	?	?	?
Dole	Y	Y	Y	Y
NORTH DAKOTA				
Conrad	Y	N	N	Y
Dorgan	Y	Y	Y	Y
OHIO				
DeWine	Y	Y	Y	Y
Voinovich	Y	Y	Y	Y
OKLAHOMA				
Nickles	Y	Y	Y	Y
Inhofe	?	Y	Y	Y
OREGON				
Wyden	Y	Y	N	Y
Smith	Y	Y	Y	Y
PENNSYLVANIA				
Specter	Y	Y	?	Y
Santorum	Y	Y	?	Y
RHODE ISLAND				
Reed	Y	Y	N	Y
Chafee	Y	Y	Y	N
SOUTH CAROLINA				
Hollings	Y	Y	Y	N
Graham	Y	Y	Y	Y
SOUTH DAKOTA				
Daschle	Y	Y	Y	Y
Johnson	Y	Y	Y	Y
TENNESSEE				
Frist	Y	Y	Y	Y
Alexander	+	Y	Y	Y

	185	186	187	188
TEXAS				
Hutchison	Y	Y	Y	Y
Cornyn	Y	Y	Y	Y
UTAH				
Hatch	Y	Y	Y	Y
Bennett	Y	Y	Y	Y
VERMONT				
Leahy	Y	Y	N	Y
Jeffords	Y	Y	?	Y
VIRGINIA				
Warner	Y	Y	Y	Y
Allen	Y	Y	Y	Y
WASHINGTON				
Murray	Y	Y	Y	Y
Cantwell	Y	Y	Y	Y
WEST VIRGINIA				
Byrd	Y	Y	N	Y
Rockefeller	Y	Y	N	Y
WISCONSIN				
Kohl	Y	Y	Y	Y
Feingold	Y	Y	Y	Y
WYOMING				
Thomas	Y	Y	Y	Y
Enzi	Y	Y	Y	Y

ND Northern Democrats   SD Southern Democrats

Southern states - Ala., Ark., Fla., Ga., Ky., La., Miss., N.C., Okla., S.C., Tenn., Texas, Va.

Key

Y	Voted for (yea).
#	Paired for.
+	Announced for.
N	Voted against (nay).
X	Paired against.
–	Announced against.
P	Voted "present."
C	Voted "present" to avoid possible conflict of interest.
?	Did not vote or otherwise make a position known.

Democrats   **Republicans**
Independents

185. HR 4837. Fiscal 2005 Military Construction Appropriations/ Passage. Passage of the bill that would appropriate $10 billion for military construction, family housing, and base realignment and closure projects in fiscal 2005. It would provide $4.2 billion for family housing, $5.3 billion for military construction projects and $246 million for base realignment and closure programs. Passed 91-0: R 47-0; D 43-0 (ND 36-0, SD 7-0); I 1-0. Sept. 21, 2004.

186. HR 4755. Fiscal 2005 Legislative Branch Appropriations/Passage. Passage of the bill that would appropriate $3.6 billion in fiscal 2005 for legislative branch operations, including $725 million for Senate operations. Passed 94-2: R 49-1; D 44-1 (ND 36-1, SD 8-0); I 1-0. (Before passage, the Senate incorporated the text of S 2666 into the bill.) Sept. 21, 2004.

187. Goss Nomination/Confirmation. Confirmation of President Bush's nomination of Porter J. Goss of Florida to be director of central intelligence. Confirmed 77-17: R 49-0; D 28-17 (ND 20-17, SD 8-0); I 0-0. A "yea" was a vote in support of the president's position. Sept. 22, 2004.

188. HR 1308. Family and Corporate Tax Breaks/Conference Report. Adoption of the conference report on the bill that would extend the $1,000 per child tax credit through 2009, the upper limit for the current 10 percent bracket through 2010 and tax breaks for married couples through 2008. It also would provide a one-year extension of current income exemptions from the alternative minimum tax and extend the expiring research and development tax credit through 2005. Adopted (thus cleared for the president) 92-3: R 49-2; D 42-1 (ND 35-0, SD 7-1); I 1-0. A "yea" was a vote in support of the president's position. Sept. 23, 2004.

	189	190	191	192	193	194
ALABAMA						
Shelby	Y	Y	Y	N	Y	Y
Sessions	Y	Y	Y	Y	N	Y
ALASKA						
Stevens	Y	Y	Y	Y	N	Y
Murkowski, L.	Y	Y	Y	N	Y	Y
ARIZONA						
McCain	Y	Y	Y	Y	?	?
Kyl	Y	Y	Y	Y	?	?
ARKANSAS						
Lincoln	Y	Y	Y	Y	Y	N
Pryor	Y	Y	Y	Y	Y	N
CALIFORNIA						
Feinstein	Y	Y	N	Y	Y	N
Boxer	Y	Y	Y	Y	?	?
COLORADO						
Campbell	Y	Y	Y	Y	Y	Y
Allard	Y	Y	Y	Y	Y	Y
CONNECTICUT						
Dodd	Y	Y	Y	Y	Y	N
Lieberman	Y	Y	Y	Y	Y	Y
DELAWARE						
Biden	Y	Y	Y	Y	?	?
Carper	Y	Y	Y	Y	Y	N
FLORIDA						
Graham	Y	Y	Y	Y	?	?
Nelson	Y	Y	Y	Y	?	?
GEORGIA						
Miller	Y	Y	Y	Y	?	Y
Chambliss	Y	Y	Y	Y	Y	Y
HAWAII						
Inouye	Y	Y	Y	Y	N	N
Akaka	?	?	?	?	?	?
IDAHO						
Craig	Y	Y	Y	N	Y	Y
Crapo	Y	Y	Y	N	Y	Y
ILLINOIS						
Fitzgerald	Y	Y	Y	Y	Y	Y
Durbin	Y	Y	Y	Y	Y	?
INDIANA						
Lugar	Y	Y	Y	Y	Y	Y
Bayh	Y	Y	Y	N	Y	N

	189	190	191	192	193	194
IOWA						
Grassley	Y	Y	Y	Y	Y	Y
Harkin	Y	Y	Y	N	Y	N
KANSAS						
Brownback	Y	Y	Y	N	Y	+
Roberts	Y	Y	Y	N	Y	Y
KENTUCKY						
McConnell	Y	Y	Y	Y	Y	Y
Bunning	Y	Y	Y	Y	Y	Y
LOUISIANA						
Breaux	Y	Y	Y	Y	Y	N
Landrieu	Y	Y	Y	Y	Y	N
MAINE						
Snowe	Y	Y	Y	N	Y	N
Collins	Y	Y	Y	Y	Y	Y
MARYLAND						
Sarbanes	Y	Y	Y	Y	Y	N
Mikulski	Y	Y	Y	Y	Y	N
MASSACHUSETTS						
Kennedy	Y	Y	Y	Y	Y	N
Kerry	?	?	?	?	?	?
MICHIGAN						
Levin	Y	Y	Y	Y	Y	N
Stabenow	Y	Y	N	Y	Y	N
MINNESOTA						
Dayton	Y	Y	Y	Y	Y	N
Coleman	Y	Y	Y	Y	Y	Y
MISSISSIPPI						
Cochran	Y	Y	Y	Y	N	Y
Lott	Y	Y	Y	N	Y	Y
MISSOURI						
Bond	Y	Y	Y	N	Y	Y
Talent	Y	Y	Y	Y	Y	Y
MONTANA						
Burns	Y	Y	Y	Y	N	Y
Baucus	Y	Y	Y	Y	Y	N
NEBRASKA						
Hagel	Y	Y	Y	Y	Y	Y
Nelson	Y	Y	Y	Y	Y	N
NEVADA						
Reid	Y	Y	Y	Y	Y	N
Ensign	Y	Y	Y	Y	Y	Y

	189	190	191	192	193	194
NEW HAMPSHIRE						
Gregg	Y	Y	Y	Y	Y	Y
Sununu	Y	Y	Y	Y	Y	Y
NEW JERSEY						
Lautenberg	Y	Y	Y	Y	Y	N
Corzine	Y	?	Y	Y	Y	N
NEW MEXICO						
Domenici	Y	Y	Y	Y	?	?
Bingaman	Y	Y	Y	Y	Y	N
NEW YORK						
Schumer	Y	Y	Y	Y	Y	N
Clinton	Y	Y	Y	Y	Y	N
NORTH CAROLINA						
Edwards	?	?	?	?	?	?
Dole	Y	Y	Y	Y	Y	Y
NORTH DAKOTA						
Conrad	Y	Y	Y	N	Y	N
Dorgan	Y	Y	Y	Y	Y	N
OHIO						
DeWine	Y	Y	Y	N	Y	Y
Voinovich	Y	Y	Y	Y	Y	Y
OKLAHOMA						
Nickles	Y	Y	Y	Y	Y	Y
Inhofe	Y	Y	Y	Y	Y	Y
OREGON						
Wyden	Y	Y	Y	N	Y	N
Smith	Y	Y	Y	Y	Y	Y
PENNSYLVANIA						
Specter	Y	Y	N	N	Y	N
Santorum	Y	Y	Y	N	Y	Y
RHODE ISLAND						
Reed	Y	Y	Y	Y	Y	N
Chafee	Y	Y	Y	Y	Y	Y
SOUTH CAROLINA						
Hollings	Y	Y	Y	Y	N	N
Graham	Y	Y	Y	Y	Y	Y
SOUTH DAKOTA						
Daschle	Y	Y	Y	Y	Y	N
Johnson	Y	Y	Y	Y	Y	N
TENNESSEE						
Frist	Y	Y	Y	Y	Y	Y
Alexander	Y	Y	Y	N	Y	Y

	189	190	191	192	193	194
TEXAS						
Hutchison	Y	Y	Y	Y	Y	Y
Cornyn	Y	Y	Y	Y	Y	Y
UTAH						
Hatch	Y	Y	Y	N	Y	Y
Bennett	Y	Y	Y	N	Y	Y
VERMONT						
Leahy	Y	Y	Y	Y	Y	N
Jeffords	Y	Y	Y	Y	Y	N
VIRGINIA						
Warner	Y	Y	Y	Y	Y	Y
Allen	Y	Y	Y	Y	Y	Y
WASHINGTON						
Murray	Y	Y	Y	Y	Y	Y
Cantwell	Y	Y	Y	Y	Y	N
WEST VIRGINIA						
Byrd	Y	Y	N	Y	N	N
Rockefeller	Y	Y	Y	Y	Y	N
WISCONSIN						
Kohl	Y	Y	Y	Y	Y	N
Feingold	Y	Y	Y	Y	Y	N
WYOMING						
Thomas	Y	Y	Y	Y	Y	Y
Enzi	Y	Y	Y	Y	Y	Y

Key

Y	Voted for (yea).
#	Paired for.
+	Announced for.
N	Voted against (nay).
X	Paired against.
−	Announced against.
P	Voted "present."
C	Voted "present" to avoid possible conflict of interest.
?	Did not vote or otherwise make a position known.

Democrats   **Republicans**
Independents

ND Northern Democrats   SD Southern Democrats

Southern states - Ala., Ark., Fla., Ga., Ky., La., Miss., N.C., Okla., S.C., Tenn., Texas, Va.

189. S 2845. Intelligence Overhaul/Transportation Security. McCain, R-Ariz., amendment that would require the Homeland Security secretary to develop and implement a comprehensive national transportation security plan, integrate and consolidate airline "no fly" lists and improve explosive detection capabilities at aircraft passenger checkpoints. Adopted 97-0: R 51-0; D 45-0 (ND 37-0, SD 8-0); I 1-0. Sept. 28, 2004.

190. S 2845. Intelligence Overhaul/Air Cargo Security. Hutchison, R-Texas, amendment that would require the Homeland Security secretary to implement a program that would screen all aircraft cargo. Adopted 96-0: R 51-0; D 44-0 (ND 36-0, SD 8-0); I 1-0. Sept. 28, 2004.

191. S 2845. Intelligence Overhaul/NID Term of Office. Collins, R-Maine, motion to table (kill) the Specter, R-Pa., amendment that would specify a fixed 10-year term for the national intelligence director. Motion agreed to 93-4: R 50-1; D 42-3 (ND 34-3, SD 8-0); I 1-0. Sept. 28, 2004.

192. S 2845. Intelligence Overhaul/Increased NID Authority. Collins, R-Maine, motion to table (kill) the Specter, R-Pa., amendment that would increase the authority of the national intelligence director to include direct operational control over several intelligence agencies, including the CIA, National Security Agency and certain military intelligence agencies. Motion agreed to 78-19: R 36-15; D 41-4 (ND 33-4, SD 8-0); I 1-0. Sept. 28, 2004.

193. S 2845. Intelligence Overhaul/National Intelligence Coordinator. Collins, R-Maine, motion to table (kill) the Hollings, D-S.C., substitute amendment that would strike the text of the bill and insert language that would create a national intelligence coordinator as a member of the National Security Council. The new position would coordinate the performance of all U.S. intelligence and intelligence-related activities and assume the staff and resources currently assigned to the director of central intelligence. Motion agreed to 82-7: R 43-5; D 38-2 (ND 34-1, SD 4-1); I 1-0. Sept. 30, 2004.

194. S 2845. Intelligence Overhaul/Foreign Subsidiaries. Collins, R-Maine, motion to table (kill) the Lautenberg, D-N.J., amendment that would bar foreign subsidiaries of U.S. companies from doing business with countries considered sponsors of terrorism. Motion agreed to 47-41: R 45-2; D 2-38 (ND 1-33, SD 1-5); I 0-1. Sept. 30, 2004.

ALABAMA	195	196	197	198	199
Shelby	Y	N	Y	Y	Y
Sessions	Y	N	N	Y	Y
ALASKA					
Stevens	N	N	N	Y	Y
Murkowski, L.	N	N	Y	Y	Y
ARIZONA					
McCain	Y	Y	Y	Y	Y
Kyl	N	N	Y	Y	Y
ARKANSAS					
Lincoln	Y	Y	Y	Y	Y
Pryor	Y	Y	Y	Y	Y
CALIFORNIA					
Feinstein	Y	Y	Y	Y	Y
Boxer	Y	Y	Y	Y	Y
COLORADO					
Campbell	Y	N	Y	Y	Y
Allard	Y	N	Y	Y	Y
CONNECTICUT					
Dodd	N	Y	Y	Y	Y
Lieberman	Y	Y	Y	Y	Y
DELAWARE					
Biden	N	Y	?	Y	Y
Carper	Y	Y	Y	Y	Y
FLORIDA					
Graham	?	?	Y	Y	Y
Nelson	Y	Y	Y	Y	Y
GEORGIA					
Miller	Y	N	Y	Y	Y
Chambliss	Y	N	Y	Y	Y
HAWAII					
Inouye	N	N	N	Y	Y
Akaka	?	?	?	Y	Y
IDAHO					
Craig	Y	N	Y	Y	Y
Crapo	Y	N	Y	Y	Y
ILLINOIS					
Fitzgerald	Y	N	Y	Y	Y
Durbin	Y	Y	Y	Y	Y
INDIANA					
Lugar	Y	N	Y	Y	Y
Bayh	Y	Y	Y	Y	Y

IOWA	195	196	197	198	199
Grassley	Y	Y	Y	Y	Y
Harkin	N	Y	Y	Y	Y
KANSAS					
Brownback	Y	N	Y	Y	Y
Roberts	Y	N	Y	Y	Y
KENTUCKY					
McConnell	Y	N	Y	Y	Y
Bunning	Y	N	Y	Y	Y
LOUISIANA					
Breaux	Y	Y	Y	Y	Y
Landrieu	Y	Y	Y	Y	Y
MAINE					
Snowe	Y	Y	Y	Y	Y
Collins	Y	Y	Y	Y	Y
MARYLAND					
Sarbanes	N	Y	Y	Y	Y
Mikulski	Y	Y	Y	Y	Y
MASSACHUSETTS					
Kennedy	?	?	Y	Y	Y
Kerry	?	?	?	?	?
MICHIGAN					
Levin	Y	Y	N	Y	Y
Stabenow	N	Y	Y	Y	Y
MINNESOTA					
Dayton	N	Y	Y	Y	Y
Coleman	Y	Y	Y	Y	Y
MISSISSIPPI					
Cochran	N	N	N	Y	Y
Lott	Y	Y	Y	Y	Y
MISSOURI					
Bond	Y	N	Y	Y	Y
Talent	Y	N	Y	Y	Y
MONTANA					
Burns	N	N	N	Y	Y
Baucus	N	Y	Y	Y	Y
NEBRASKA					
Hagel	N	Y	Y	Y	Y
Nelson	Y	N	Y	Y	Y
NEVADA					
Reid	N	Y	Y	Y	Y
Ensign	Y	Y	N	Y	Y

NEW HAMPSHIRE	195	196	197	198	199
Gregg	N	Y	Y	Y	Y
Sununu	Y	Y	Y	Y	Y
NEW JERSEY					
Lautenberg	N	Y	Y	Y	Y
Corzine	?	?	?	Y	Y
NEW MEXICO					
Domenici	N	N	Y	Y	Y
Bingaman	Y	Y	Y	Y	Y
NEW YORK					
Schumer	Y	Y	Y	Y	Y
Clinton	Y	Y	Y	Y	Y
NORTH CAROLINA					
Edwards	?	?	?	?	?
Dole	Y	N	Y	Y	Y
NORTH DAKOTA					
Conrad	Y	N	N	Y	Y
Dorgan	N	Y	Y	Y	Y
OHIO					
DeWine	Y	Y	Y	Y	Y
Voinovich	Y	Y	Y	Y	Y
OKLAHOMA					
Nickles	Y	N	Y	Y	Y
Inhofe	?	?	Y	Y	Y
OREGON					
Wyden	Y	Y	Y	Y	Y
Smith	Y	N	Y	Y	Y
PENNSYLVANIA					
Specter	Y	Y	Y	Y	Y
Santorum	Y	Y	Y	Y	Y
RHODE ISLAND					
Reed	N	Y	Y	Y	Y
Chafee	N	Y	Y	Y	Y
SOUTH CAROLINA					
Hollings	?	?	Y	Y	N
Graham	Y	Y	Y	Y	Y
SOUTH DAKOTA					
Daschle	Y	Y	Y	Y	Y
Johnson	N	Y	Y	Y	Y
TENNESSEE					
Frist	Y	N	Y	Y	Y
Alexander	Y	Y	Y	Y	Y

Key

Y	Voted for (yea).
#	Paired for.
+	Announced for.
N	Voted against (nay).
X	Paired against.
–	Announced against.
P	Voted "present."
C	Voted "present" to avoid possible conflict of interest.
?	Did not vote or otherwise make a position known.

Democrats **Republicans**
Independents

TEXAS	195	196	197	198	199
Hutchison	Y	N	Y	Y	Y
Cornyn	?	Y	N	Y	Y
UTAH					
Hatch	Y	N	Y	Y	Y
Bennett	N	N	Y	Y	Y
VERMONT					
Leahy	N	Y	Y	Y	Y
Jeffords	N	Y	Y	Y	Y
VIRGINIA					
Warner	N	N	Y	Y	Y
Allen	Y	N	Y	Y	Y
WASHINGTON					
Murray	Y	Y	Y	Y	Y
Cantwell	Y	Y	Y	Y	Y
WEST VIRGINIA					
Byrd	N	N	N	Y	N
Rockefeller	Y	Y	Y	Y	Y
WISCONSIN					
Kohl	N	Y	Y	Y	Y
Feingold	Y	Y	Y	Y	Y
WYOMING					
Thomas	N	N	Y	Y	Y
Enzi	Y	N	Y	Y	Y

ND Northern Democrats   SD Southern Democrats

Southern states - Ala., Ark., Fla., Ga., Ky., La., Miss., N.C., Okla., S.C., Tenn., Texas, Va.

195. S 2845. Intelligence Overhaul/Reduced NID Budget Authority. Collins, R-Maine, motion to table (kill) the Byrd, D-W.Va., amendment that would strike language in the bill that would establish new budget accounts for use by the national intelligence director. It also would place restrictions on the new director's authority to transfer funds including requiring approval from the Office of Management and Budget director and Congress, capping the total transfer to $100 million per fiscal year and requiring it to be less than 5 percent of an agency's total budget. Motion agreed to 62-29: R 37-12; D 25-16 (ND 19-16, SD 6-0); I 0-1. Oct. 4, 2004.

196. S 2845. Intelligence Overhaul/Disclosure of Funding Amounts. Lieberman, D-Conn., motion to table (kill) the Stevens, R-Alaska, amendment that would strike the section of the bill that would require the public disclosure of the aggregate top-line amount of intelligence funding. Motion agreed to 55-37: R 18-32; D 36-5 (ND 31-4, SD 5-1); I 1-0. Oct. 4, 2004.

197. S 2845. Intelligence Overhaul/Cloture. Motion to invoke cloture (thus limiting debate) on the bill that would create a national intelligence director with budget authority and a national counterterrorism center, based on

recommendations of the Sept. 11 commission. Motion agreed to 85-10: R 45-6; D 39-4 (ND 31-4, SD 8-0); I 1-0. Three-fifths of the total Senate (60) is required to invoke cloture. Oct. 5, 2004.

198. S 2845. Intelligence Overhaul/Intelligence Funding Authorization. Roberts, R-Kan., amendment that would clarify that funds appropriated for intelligence activities must be specifically authorized in accordance with the National Security Act of 1947. Adopted 98-0: R 51-0; D 46-0 (ND 38-0, SD 8-0); I 1-0. Oct. 6, 2004.

199. S 2845. Intelligence Overhaul/Passage. Passage of the bill that would reorganize 15 U.S. intelligence agencies and create a national intelligence director with the power to freely transfer money among the CIA, National Security Agency and other defense and civilian agencies. It also would create a counterterrorism center with operational planning capabilities and a Privacy and Civil Liberties Oversight Board to investigate use of intelligence powers and act as a watchdog on civil liberties concerns. Passed 96-2: R 51-0; D 44-2 (ND 37-1, SD 7-1); I 1-0. Oct. 6, 2004.

	200	201	202	203
ALABAMA				
Shelby	N	N	Y	N
Sessions	Y	N	Y	N
ALASKA				
Stevens	N	N	Y	N
Murkowski, L.	N	N	Y	N
ARIZONA				
McCain	Y	Y	N	N
Kyl	Y	Y	Y	N
ARKANSAS				
Lincoln	N	Y	N	Y
Pryor	N	Y	N	Y
CALIFORNIA				
Feinstein	N	Y	Y	Y
Boxer	N	N	Y	Y
COLORADO				
Campbell	N	N	Y	?
Allard	N	N	Y	N
CONNECTICUT				
Dodd	N	N	Y	Y
Lieberman	Y	Y	N	?
DELAWARE				
Carper	N	Y	N	Y
Biden	Y	Y	Y	Y
FLORIDA				
Graham	N	Y	N	?
Nelson	N	N	N	Y
GEORGIA				
Miller	N	N	Y	N
Chambliss	?	?	?	?
HAWAII				
Inouye	N	N	Y	Y
Akaka	N	N	N	Y
IDAHO				
Craig	N	N	Y	N
Crapo	Y	Y	Y	N
ILLINOIS				
Fitzgerald	Y	Y	N	N
Durbin	N	N	Y	Y
INDIANA				
Lugar	Y	Y	N	Y
Bayh	Y	Y	N	N

	200	201	202	203
IOWA				
Grassley	N	N	Y	N
Harkin	N	N	Y	Y
KANSAS				
Brownback	N	N	Y	N
Roberts	Y	N	Y	N
KENTUCKY				
McConnell	N	N	N	N
Bunning	N	N	Y	N
LOUISIANA				
Breaux	N	N	N	Y
Landrieu	N	N	N	Y
MAINE				
Snowe	Y	N	N	N
Collins	Y	Y	N	N
MARYLAND				
Sarbanes	N	N	Y	Y
Mikulski	N	N	Y	Y
MASSACHUSETTS				
Kennedy	N	N	Y	Y
Kerry	?	?	?	?
MICHIGAN				
Levin	N	Y	N	N
Stabenow	N	N	Y	Y
MINNESOTA				
Dayton	N	N	N	N
Coleman	N	Y	N	Y
MISSISSIPPI				
Cochran	N	N	Y	N
Lott	Y	Y	Y	?
MISSOURI				
Bond	N	N	N	N
Talent	N	Y	N	N
MONTANA				
Burns	N	N	N	N
Baucus	N	N	Y	N
NEBRASKA				
Hagel	N	Y	Y	Y
Nelson	N	N	N	Y
NEVADA				
Reid	N	N	N	N
Ensign	Y	N	N	N

	200	201	202	203
NEW HAMPSHIRE				
Gregg	N	N	?	?
Sununu	Y	Y	N	N
NEW JERSEY				
Lautenberg	N	N	N	N
Corzine	N	N	Y	Y
NEW MEXICO				
Domenici	N	?	?	?
Bingaman	N	Y	Y	Y
NEW YORK				
Schumer	N	N	Y	N
Clinton	N	N	Y	Y
NORTH CAROLINA				
Edwards	?	?	?	?
Dole	N	N	N	N
NORTH DAKOTA				
Conrad	N	N	Y	Y
Dorgan	N	N	Y	Y
OHIO				
DeWine	Y	N	Y	N
Voinovich	Y	Y	N	N
OKLAHOMA				
Nickles	Y	Y	N	N
Inhofe	N	Y	N	N
OREGON				
Wyden	N	N	Y	N
Smith	N	N	Y	N
PENNSYLVANIA				
Specter	N	Y	Y	N
Santorum	Y	Y	N	N
RHODE ISLAND				
Reed	N	N	Y	Y
Chafee	N	Y	N	Y
SOUTH CAROLINA				
Hollings	N	N	N	?
Graham	Y	Y	N	N
SOUTH DAKOTA				
Daschle	N	N	N	Y
Johnson	N	N	Y	Y
TENNESSEE				
Frist	N	N	N	N
Alexander	Y	Y	N	N

Key

Y	Voted for (yea).
#	Paired for.
+	Announced for.
N	Voted against (nay).
X	Paired against.
–	Announced against.
P	Voted "present."
C	Voted "present" to avoid possible conflict of interest.
?	Did not vote or otherwise make a position known.

Democrats **Republicans**
Independents

	200	201	202	203
TEXAS				
Hutchison	N	N	Y	N
Cornyn	N	Y	Y	N
UTAH				
Hatch	N	N	Y	N
Bennett	N	N	Y	N
VERMONT				
Leahy	N	N	Y	Y
Jeffords	N	Y	Y	Y
VIRGINIA				
Warner	N	N	Y	N
Allen	N	N	Y	N
WASHINGTON				
Murray	N	N	N	N
Cantwell	Y	N	Y	Y
WEST VIRGINIA				
Byrd	N	N	Y	N
Rockefeller	N	N	N	N
WISCONSIN				
Kohl	N	N	Y	Y
Feingold	Y	Y	Y	Y
WYOMING				
Thomas	N	N	Y	N
Enzi	N	Y	N	N

ND Northern Democrats   SD Southern Democrats

Southern states - Ala., Ark., Fla., Ga., Ky., La., Miss., N.C., Okla., S.C., Tenn., Texas, Va.

200. S Res 445. Senate Intelligence Oversight/Authorization and Appropriation Authority. McCain, R-Ariz., amendment to the McConnell, R-Ky., substitute amendment. The McCain amendment would give an Intelligence Appropriations Subcommittee both authorization and appropriation authority. The substitute would transform the Governmental Affairs Committee into the Homeland Security and Governmental Affairs Committee, with jurisdiction over much of the Homeland Security Department. It also would create an Intelligence Appropriations Subcommittee, merge the Military Construction and Defense Appropriations subcommittees, eliminate term limits for members of the Intelligence Committee and shrink its size by two slots. Rejected 23-74: R 18-32; D 5-41 (ND 5-33, SD 0-8); I 0-1. Oct. 7, 2004.

201. S Res 445. Senate Intelligence Oversight/Transportation Security Administration. McCain, R-Ariz., amendment to the McConnell, R-Ky., substitute amendment. The McCain amendment would place the Transportation Security Administration under the jurisdiction of the proposed Homeland Se-

curity and Governmental Affairs Committee. Rejected 33-63: R 21-28; D 11-35 (ND 8-30, SD 3-5); I 1-0. Oct. 7, 2004.

202. S Res 445. Senate Intelligence Oversight/Secret Service Jurisdiction. Hatch, R-Utah, amendment to the McConnell, R-Ky., substitute amendment. The Hatch amendment would exempt the Secret Service from the jurisdiction of the proposed Homeland Security and Governmental Affairs Committee. Adopted 54-41: R 26-22; D 27-19 (ND 26-12, SD 1-7); I 1-0. Oct. 7, 2004.

203. S Res 445. Senate Intelligence Oversight/Ex-Officio Members. Biden, D-Del., amendment to the McConnell, R-Ky., substitute amendment. The Biden amendment would make the chairman and ranking member of the Foreign Relations Committee ex-officio members of the Intelligence Committee, without voting rights or the ability to help establish a quorum. Rejected 36-54: R 5-41; D 30-13 (ND 25-12, SD 5-1); I 1-0. Oct. 7, 2004.

	204	205	206	207	208	209	210	211
ALABAMA								
Shelby	Y	Y	Y	Y	Y	Y	Y	Y
Sessions	Y	Y	Y	Y	Y	N	N	Y
ALASKA								
Stevens	Y	Y	N	Y	Y	Y	Y	Y
Murkowski, L.	Y	Y	N	Y	Y	N	Y	Y
ARIZONA								
McCain	N	Y	N	Y	N	N	N	?
Kyl	Y	Y	Y	Y	Y	N	Y	Y
ARKANSAS								
Lincoln	Y	Y	Y	N	Y	Y	Y	Y
Pryor	Y	Y	N	N	Y	Y	Y	Y
CALIFORNIA								
Feinstein	Y	Y	Y	N	Y	Y	Y	N
Boxer	Y	?	?	?	?	?	?	N
COLORADO								
Campbell	?	?	?	?	?	?	?	?
Allard	Y	Y	Y	Y	Y	Y	Y	Y
CONNECTICUT								
Dodd	Y	Y	Y	N	Y	Y	N	N
Lieberman	?	?	N	N	N	Y	Y	Y
DELAWARE								
Biden	Y	Y	Y	N	Y	Y	?	N
Carper	Y	Y	N	N	Y	Y	N	N
FLORIDA								
Graham	?	?	Y	N	Y	N	Y	?
Nelson	Y	Y	Y	N	Y	Y	Y	Y
GEORGIA								
Miller	Y	Y	?	?	?	?	Y	?
Chambliss	?	?	?	?	?	?	?	?
HAWAII								
Inouye	Y	N	Y	N	Y	Y	Y	Y
Akaka	Y	Y	N	N	Y	N	N	N
IDAHO								
Craig	Y	Y	?	?	?	?	Y	Y
Crapo	Y	Y	Y	Y	Y	Y	Y	Y
ILLINOIS								
Fitzgerald	Y	Y	N	Y	N	Y	Y	Y
Durbin	Y	Y	N	N	Y	Y	?	N
INDIANA								
Lugar	Y	Y	N	Y	Y	Y	Y	Y
Bayh	Y	Y	?	?	?	?	?	Y

	204	205	206	207	208	209	210	211
IOWA								
Grassley	Y	Y	Y	Y	Y	Y	Y	Y
Harkin	Y	Y	Y	N	Y	Y	Y	N
KANSAS								
Brownback	Y	Y	N	Y	Y	Y	Y	Y
Roberts	Y	Y	N	Y	Y	Y	Y	Y
KENTUCKY								
McConnell	Y	Y	Y	Y	Y	Y	Y	Y
Bunning	Y	Y	Y	Y	Y	Y	Y	Y
LOUISIANA								
Breaux	Y	N	?	?	?	?	Y	Y
Landrieu	Y	Y	Y	N	Y	Y	N	Y
MAINE								
Snowe	Y	Y	N	Y	Y	Y	Y	Y
Collins	N	Y	N	Y	N	Y	Y	N
MARYLAND								
Sarbanes	Y	Y	?	?	?	?	?	N
Mikulski	Y	Y	Y	N	Y	Y	Y	Y
MASSACHUSETTS								
Kennedy	Y	Y	Y	N	Y	Y	N	N
Kerry	?	?	?	?	?	?	?	?
MICHIGAN								
Levin	Y	Y	N	N	Y	Y	N	N
Stabenow	Y	Y	N	Y	Y	Y	Y	Y
MINNESOTA								
Dayton	Y	Y	Y	N	Y	Y	Y	Y
Coleman	Y	Y	N	Y	N	Y	Y	Y
MISSISSIPPI								
Cochran	Y	Y	N	Y	Y	Y	Y	Y
Lott	Y	Y	N	Y	Y	N	Y	Y
MISSOURI								
Bond	Y	Y	Y	N	Y	Y	Y	Y
Talent	Y	Y	N	Y	Y	Y	Y	Y
MONTANA								
Burns	Y	Y	Y	Y	Y	Y	Y	Y
Baucus	Y	Y	Y	N	Y	Y	Y	Y
NEBRASKA								
Hagel	Y	Y	N	Y	Y	Y	Y	Y
Nelson	Y	Y	Y	N	Y	Y	Y	Y
NEVADA								
Reid	Y	Y	Y	N	Y	Y	Y	Y
Ensign	Y	Y	Y	Y	Y	N	Y	Y

	204	205	206	207	208	209	210	211
NEW HAMPSHIRE								
Gregg	Y	Y	Y	Y	Y	N	?	N
Sununu	?	?	?	?	?	?	?	?
NEW JERSEY								
Lautenberg	Y	Y	N	N	Y	Y	?	?
Corzine	Y	Y	Y	N	Y	Y	?	N
NEW MEXICO								
Domenici	Y	Y	Y	Y	Y	Y	Y	Y
Bingaman	Y	Y	Y	N	Y	Y	Y	Y
NEW YORK								
Schumer	Y	Y	Y	N	Y	Y	?	Y
Clinton	Y	Y	Y	N	Y	Y	?	Y
NORTH CAROLINA								
Edwards	?	?	?	?	?	?	?	?
Dole	Y	Y	Y	Y	Y	Y	Y	Y
NORTH DAKOTA								
Conrad	Y	Y	Y	N	Y	Y	N	Y
Dorgan	Y	Y	Y	N	Y	Y	Y	?
OHIO								
DeWine	Y	Y	N	Y	Y	N	N	N
Voinovich	N	Y	N	Y	N	N	Y	Y
OKLAHOMA								
Nickles	Y	Y	Y	N	Y	Y	Y	Y
Inhofe	Y	Y	N	Y	N	Y	Y	Y
OREGON								
Wyden	Y	Y	Y	N	Y	Y	Y	Y
Smith	Y	Y	Y	Y	Y	Y	Y	Y
PENNSYLVANIA								
Specter	Y	Y	?	?	?	?	?	?
Santorum	Y	Y	Y	Y	Y	N	Y	Y
RHODE ISLAND								
Reed	Y	Y	Y	N	Y	Y	N	N
Chafee	Y	Y	Y	Y	Y	N	Y	N
SOUTH CAROLINA								
Hollings	?	?	?	?	?	?	?	?
Graham	Y	?	?	?	?	?	Y	Y
SOUTH DAKOTA								
Daschle	Y	Y	Y	N	Y	Y	Y	Y
Johnson	Y	Y	Y	N	Y	Y	Y	Y
TENNESSEE								
Frist	Y	Y	N	Y	Y	Y	Y	Y
Alexander	Y	N	Y	Y	Y	Y	Y	Y

Key

Y	Voted for (yea).
#	Paired for.
+	Announced for.
N	Voted against (nay).
X	Paired against.
–	Announced against.
P	Voted "present."
C	Voted "present" to avoid possible conflict of interest.
?	Did not vote or otherwise make a position known.

Democrats **Republicans**
Independents

	204	205	206	207	208	209	210	211
TEXAS								
Hutchison	Y	Y	N	Y	Y	N	?	Y
Cornyn	Y	Y	?	?	?	?	?	Y
UTAH								
Hatch	Y	Y	N	Y	Y	Y	Y	Y
Bennett	Y	N	N	Y	Y	Y	Y	Y
VERMONT								
Leahy	?	?	Y	N	Y	Y	?	?
Jeffords	Y	Y	N	N	Y	Y	Y	Y
VIRGINIA								
Warner	Y	Y	N	Y	Y	Y	Y	Y
Allen	Y	N	N	Y	Y	Y	Y	Y
WASHINGTON								
Murray	Y	Y	Y	N	Y	Y	Y	Y
Cantwell	Y	Y	Y	N	Y	Y	Y	Y
WEST VIRGINIA								
Byrd	Y	Y	N	N	Y	Y	N	N
Rockefeller	Y	Y	N	N	Y	Y	Y	N
WISCONSIN								
Kohl	Y	Y	Y	N	Y	Y	P	P
Feingold	Y	Y	Y	N	Y	Y	Y	Y
WYOMING								
Thomas	Y	Y	Y	Y	Y	Y	Y	Y
Enzi	Y	Y	Y	Y	Y	N	Y	Y

ND Northern Democrats SD Southern Democrats

Southern states - Ala., Ark., Fla., Ga., Ky., La., Miss., N.C., Okla., S.C., Tenn., Texas, Va.

204. S Res 445. Senate Intelligence Oversight/Cloture. Motion to invoke cloture (thus limiting debate) on the McConnell, R-Ky., substitute amendment that would transform the Governmental Affairs Committee into the Homeland Security and Governmental Affairs Committee. It also would create an Intelligence Appropriations Subcommittee. Motion agreed to 88-3: R 45-3; D 42-0 (ND 36-0, SD 6-0); I 1-0. Three-fifths of the total Senate (60) is required to invoke cloture. Oct. 8, 2004.

205. Procedural Motion/Require Attendance. Frist, R-Tenn., motion to instruct the sergeant at arms to request the attendance of absent senators. Motion agreed to 85-4: R 45-2; D 39-2 (ND 34-1, SD 5-1); I 1-0. Oct. 8, 2004.

206. S Res 445. Senate Intelligence Oversight/Budget Process Authority. Nickles, R-Okla., amendment to the Nickles amendment to the McConnell, R-Ky., substitute amendment. The Nickles amendment would grant sole jurisdiction over the congressional budget process to the Budget Committee and specify that it would share jurisdiction with the Governmental Affairs Committee over the nomination of the Office of Management and Budget (OMB) director. The underlying Nickles amendment includes similar language but would not grant joint jurisdiction over the OMB director nomination. Adopted 50-35: R 19-25; D 31-9 (ND 27-8, SD 4-1); I 0-1. (Subsequently, the underlying Nickles amendment, as amended, was adopted by voice vote.) Oct. 9, 2004.

207. S Res 445. Senate Intelligence Oversight/Subcommittee Consolidation. Hutchison, R-Texas, amendment to the McConnell, R-Ky., substitute amendment. The Hutchison amendment would strike language merging the Military Construction and Defense Appropriations subcommittees. Adopted 44-41: R 44-0; D 0-40 (ND 0-35, SD 0-5); I 0-1. (Subsequently, the substitute amendment was adopted by voice vote.) Oct. 9, 2004.

208. S Res 445. Senate Intelligence Oversight/Adoption. Adoption of the resolution, as amended, that would transform the Governmental Affairs Committee into the Homeland Security and Governmental Affairs Committee, with jurisdiction over much of the Homeland Security Department. It also would create an Intelligence Appropriations Subcommittee, eliminate term limits for members of the Select Intelligence Committee and shrink its size by two slots. The resolution, as amended, would retain Judiciary Committee jurisdiction over the Secret Service. Adopted 79-6: R 39-5; D 39-1 (ND 34-1, SD 5-0); I 1-0. Oct. 9, 2004.

209. S Res 454. Disaster Assistance/Adoption. Adoption of the resolution that would express the sense of the Senate that Congress should provide emergency spending for disaster assistance to eligible agricultural producers that is not offset by subsequent cuts to the farm bill. Adopted 71-14: R 30-14; D 40-0 (ND 35-0, SD 5-0); I 1-0. Oct. 9, 2004.

210. HR 4520. Corporate Tax Overhaul/Cloture. Motion to invoke cloture (thus limiting debate) on the conference report on the bill that would repeal an export provision in the U.S. tax code that has been ruled an unfair subsidy by the World Trade Organization and provide for $137 billion in new tax cuts. Motion agreed to 66-14: R 41-3; D 24-11 (ND 19-9, SD 5-2); I 1-0. Three-fifths of the total Senate (60) is required to invoke cloture. Oct. 10, 2004.

211. HR 4520. Corporate Tax Overhaul/Conference Report. Adoption of the conference report on the bill that would repeal an export provision in the U.S. tax code that has been ruled an unfair subsidy by the World Trade Organization and provide for $137 billion in new tax cuts for corporations over 10 years. It also includes a $10 billion buyout of tobacco farmers. The cost of the tax breaks would be offset by curbs on tax-avoidance practices. Adopted (thus cleared for the president) 69-17: R 43-3; D 25-14 (ND 20-14, SD 5-0); I 1-0. Oct. 11, 2004.

	212	213
ALABAMA		
Shelby	Y	Y
Sessions	Y	Y
ALASKA		
Stevens	Y	Y
Murkowski, L.	Y	Y
ARIZONA		
McCain	Y	Y
Kyl	Y	Y
ARKANSAS		
Lincoln	Y	N
Pryor	Y	N
CALIFORNIA		
Feinstein	Y	N
Boxer	Y	N
COLORADO		
Campbell	Y	Y
Allard	Y	Y
CONNECTICUT		
Dodd	N	N
Lieberman	Y	N
DELAWARE		
Biden	?	–
Carper	N	N
FLORIDA		
Graham	Y	N
Nelson	Y	N
GEORGIA		
Miller	Y	Y
Chambliss	Y	Y
HAWAII		
Inouye	Y	N
Akaka	N	N
IDAHO		
Craig	Y	Y
Crapo	Y	Y
ILLINOIS		
Fitzgerald	Y	Y
Durbin	N	N
INDIANA		
Lugar	Y	Y
Bayh	Y	N

	212	213
IOWA		
Grassley	Y	Y
Harkin	Y	N
KANSAS		
Brownback	Y	Y
Roberts	Y	Y
KENTUCKY		
McConnell	Y	Y
Bunning	Y	Y
LOUISIANA		
Breaux	?	Y
Landrieu	Y	N
MAINE		
Snowe	Y	Y
Collins	Y	Y
MARYLAND		
Sarbanes	Y	N
Mikulski	N	N
MASSACHUSETTS		
Kennedy	N	N
Kerry	Y	N
MICHIGAN		
Levin	N	N
Stabenow	N	N
MINNESOTA		
Dayton	Y	N
Coleman	Y	Y
MISSISSIPPI		
Cochran	Y	Y
Lott	Y	Y
MISSOURI		
Bond	Y	Y
Talent	Y	Y
MONTANA		
Burns	Y	Y
Baucus	Y	N
NEBRASKA		
Hagel	Y	Y
Nelson	Y	N
NEVADA		
Reid	Y	#
Ensign	Y	N

	212	213
NEW HAMPSHIRE		
Gregg	Y	Y
Sununu	Y	Y
NEW JERSEY		
Lautenberg	N	N
Corzine	N	N
NEW MEXICO		
Domenici	Y	Y
Bingaman	Y	N
NEW YORK		
Schumer	Y	N
Clinton	Y	X
NORTH CAROLINA		
Edwards	Y	N
Dole	Y	Y
NORTH DAKOTA		
Conrad	Y	N
Dorgan	Y	N
OHIO		
DeWine	Y	Y
Voinovich	Y	Y
OKLAHOMA		
Nickles	Y	Y
Inhofe	Y	Y
OREGON		
Wyden	Y	N
Smith	Y	Y
PENNSYLVANIA		
Specter	Y	Y
Santorum	?	Y
RHODE ISLAND		
Reed	N	N
Chafee	Y	Y
SOUTH CAROLINA		
Hollings	Y	N
Graham	Y	Y
SOUTH DAKOTA		
Daschle	N	N
Johnson	Y	N
TENNESSEE		
Frist	Y	Y
Alexander	Y	Y

	212	213
TEXAS		
Hutchison	Y	Y
Cornyn	Y	Y
UTAH		
Hatch	Y	Y
Bennett	Y	Y
VERMONT		
Leahy	Y	–
Jeffords	Y	N
VIRGINIA		
Warner	Y	Y
Allen	Y	Y
WASHINGTON		
Murray	Y	N
Cantwell	Y	N
WEST VIRGINIA		
Byrd	Y	N
Rockefeller	Y	N
WISCONSIN		
Kohl	Y	N
Feingold	Y	N
WYOMING		
Thomas	Y	Y
Enzi	Y	Y

Key

Y	Voted for (yea).
#	Paired for.
+	Announced for.
N	Voted against (nay).
X	Paired against.
–	Announced against.
P	Voted "present."
C	Voted "present" to avoid possible conflict of interest.
?	Did not vote or otherwise make a position known.

Democrats   **Republicans**
Independents

ND Northern Democrats   SD Southern Democrats

Southern states - Ala., Ark., Fla., Ga., Ky., La., Miss., N.C., Okla., S.C., Tenn., Texas, Va.

212. Harvey Nomination/Confirmation. Confirmation of President Bush's nomination of Francis J. Harvey of California to be secretary of the Army. Confirmed 85-12: R 50-0; D 34-12 (ND 26-12, SD 8-0); I 1-0. A "yea" was a vote in support of the president's position. Nov. 16, 2004.

213. S 2986. Debt Limit Increase/Passage. Passage of the bill that would increase the federal debt limit to $8.18 trillion, an $800 billion increase. Passed 52-44: R 50-1; D 2-42 (ND 0-35, SD 2-7); I 0-1. Nov. 17, 2004.

	214	215
ALABAMA		
Shelby	Y	Y
Sessions	Y	N
ALASKA		
Stevens	Y	Y
Murkowski, L.	Y	Y
ARIZONA		
McCain	Y	N
Kyl	Y	N
ARKANSAS		
Lincoln	Y	Y
Pryor	Y	Y
CALIFORNIA		
Feinstein	Y	Y
Boxer	Y	N
COLORADO		
Campbell	Y	?
Allard	Y	Y
CONNECTICUT		
Dodd	Y	N
Lieberman	Y	Y
DELAWARE		
Biden	Y	?
Carper	Y	N
FLORIDA		
Graham	?	N
Nelson	Y	Y
GEORGIA		
Miller	Y	Y
Chambliss	Y	Y
HAWAII		
Inouye	Y	Y
Akaka	Y	N
IDAHO		
Craig	Y	Y
Crapo	Y	Y
ILLINOIS		
Fitzgerald	Y	Y
Durbin	Y	N
INDIANA		
Lugar	?	?
Bayh	Y	N

	214	215
IOWA		
Grassley	Y	Y
Harkin	Y	Y
KANSAS		
Brownback	Y	Y
Roberts	Y	Y
KENTUCKY		
McConnell	Y	Y
Bunning	Y	Y
LOUISIANA		
Breaux	Y	Y
Landrieu	Y	Y
MAINE		
Snowe	Y	Y
Collins	Y	Y
MARYLAND		
Sarbanes	Y	N
Mikulski	Y	Y
MASSACHUSETTS		
Kennedy	Y	N
Kerry	Y	N
MICHIGAN		
Levin	Y	N
Stabenow	Y	N
MINNESOTA		
Dayton	N	Y
Coleman	N	Y
MISSISSIPPI		
Cochran	Y	Y
Lott	Y	Y
MISSOURI		
Bond	Y	Y
Talent	Y	Y
MONTANA		
Burns	Y	Y
Baucus	Y	Y
NEBRASKA		
Hagel	Y	N
Nelson	Y	N
NEVADA		
Reid	Y	Y
Ensign	Y	N

	214	215
NEW HAMPSHIRE		
Gregg	Y	?
Sununu	Y	Y
NEW JERSEY		
Lautenberg	Y	N
Corzine	Y	N
NEW MEXICO		
Domenici	Y	Y
Bingaman	Y	Y
NEW YORK		
Schumer	Y	Y
Clinton	?	Y
NORTH CAROLINA		
Edwards	Y	N
Dole	Y	Y
NORTH DAKOTA		
Conrad	Y	N
Dorgan	Y	Y
OHIO		
DeWine	Y	Y
Voinovich	Y	Y
OKLAHOMA		
Nickles	Y	Y
Inhofe	Y	N
OREGON		
Wyden	Y	Y
Smith	Y	Y
PENNSYLVANIA		
Specter	Y	Y
Santorum	Y	Y
RHODE ISLAND		
Reed	Y	N
Chafee	Y	Y
SOUTH CAROLINA		
Hollings	Y	?
Graham	Y	Y
SOUTH DAKOTA		
Daschle	Y	Y
Johnson	Y	Y
TENNESSEE		
Frist	Y	Y
Alexander	Y	Y

Key

Y	Voted for (yea).
#	Paired for.
+	Announced for.
N	Voted against (nay).
X	Paired against.
–	Announced against.
P	Voted "present."
C	Voted "present" to avoid possible conflict of interest.
?	Did not vote or otherwise make a position known.

Democrats **Republicans**
Independents

	214	215
TEXAS		
Hutchison	?	Y
Cornyn	Y	Y
UTAH		
Hatch	Y	Y
Bennett	Y	Y
VERMONT		
Leahy	?	N
Jeffords	?	N
VIRGINIA		
Warner	Y	Y
Allen	Y	Y
WASHINGTON		
Murray	Y	Y
Cantwell	Y	Y
WEST VIRGINIA		
Byrd	N	N
Rockefeller	Y	N
WISCONSIN		
Kohl	N	N
Feingold	N	N
WYOMING		
Thomas	Y	Y
Enzi	?	Y

ND Northern Democrats   SD Southern Democrats

Southern states - Ala., Ark., Fla., Ga., Ky., La., Miss., N.C., Okla., S.C., Tenn., Texas, Va.

214. HR 1047. Miscellaneous Tariffs and Trade/Cloture. Motion to invoke cloture (thus limiting debate) on the conference report on the bill that would suspend duties on hundreds of specific imported goods, authorize reimbursement for duties on certain previously imported goods and make several technical corrections to trade laws. Motion agreed to 88-5: R 47-1; D 41-4 (ND 33-4, SD 8-0); I 0-0. Three-fifths of the total Senate (60) is required to invoke cloture. (Subsequently, the conference report was adopted by voice vote.) Nov. 19, 2004.

215. HR 4818. Fiscal 2005 Omnibus Appropriations/Conference Report. Adoption of the conference report on the bill that would provide $388.4 billion in discretionary spending in fiscal 2005 for all federal departments and agencies whose fiscal 2005 spending bills have not been enacted. The measure incorporates nine previously separate appropriations bills: Agriculture; Commerce-Justice-State; Energy and Water; Foreign Operations; Interior; Labor-HHS-Education; Transportation and Treasury; Legislative Branch and VA-HUD. The total does not include a 0.8 percent across-the-board cut in all discretionary accounts in the omnibus. Adopted (thus cleared for the president) 65-30: R 42-6; D 23-23 (ND 17-21, SD 6-2); I 0-1. Nov. 20, 2004.

Senate Vote 216

State / Senator	216
ALABAMA	
Shelby	Y
Sessions	Y
ALASKA	
Stevens	Y
Murkowski, L.	Y
ARIZONA	
McCain	Y
Kyl	Y
ARKANSAS	
Lincoln	Y
Pryor	Y
CALIFORNIA	
Feinstein	Y
Boxer	Y
COLORADO	
Campbell	?
Allard	Y
CONNECTICUT	
Dodd	Y
Lieberman	Y
DELAWARE	
Biden	Y
Carper	Y
FLORIDA	
Graham	Y
Nelson	Y
GEORGIA	
Miller	Y
Chambliss	Y
HAWAII	
Inouye	?
Akaka	Y
IDAHO	
Craig	Y
Crapo	Y
ILLINOIS	
Fitzgerald	Y
Durbin	Y
INDIANA	
Lugar	Y
Bayh	Y

State / Senator	216
IOWA	
Grassley	Y
Harkin	+
KANSAS	
Brownback	Y
Roberts	Y
KENTUCKY	
McConnell	Y
Bunning	Y
LOUISIANA	
Breaux	Y
Landrieu	Y
MAINE	
Snowe	Y
Collins	Y
MARYLAND	
Sarbanes	Y
Mikulski	Y
MASSACHUSETTS	
Kennedy	Y
Kerry	Y
MICHIGAN	
Levin	Y
Stabenow	Y
MINNESOTA	
Dayton	Y
Coleman	Y
MISSISSIPPI	
Cochran	Y
Lott	?
MISSOURI	
Bond	?
Talent	Y
MONTANA	
Burns	Y
Baucus	Y
NEBRASKA	
Hagel	Y
Nelson	Y
NEVADA	
Reid	Y
Ensign	Y

State / Senator	216
NEW HAMPSHIRE	
Gregg	Y
Sununu	Y
NEW JERSEY	
Lautenberg	Y
Corzine	Y
NEW MEXICO	
Domenici	Y
Bingaman	Y
NEW YORK	
Schumer	Y
Clinton	Y
NORTH CAROLINA	
Edwards	Y
Dole	Y
NORTH DAKOTA	
Conrad	Y
Dorgan	Y
OHIO	
DeWine	Y
Voinovich	Y
OKLAHOMA	
Nickles	?
Inhofe	N
OREGON	
Wyden	Y
Smith	?
PENNSYLVANIA	
Specter	Y
Santorum	Y
RHODE ISLAND	
Reed	Y
Chafee	Y
SOUTH CAROLINA	
Hollings	?
Graham	Y
SOUTH DAKOTA	
Daschle	Y
Johnson	Y
TENNESSEE	
Frist	Y
Alexander	Y

State / Senator	216
TEXAS	
Hutchison	Y
Cornyn	Y
UTAH	
Hatch	+
Bennett	Y
VERMONT	
Leahy	Y
Jeffords	Y
VIRGINIA	
Warner	Y
Allen	Y
WASHINGTON	
Murray	Y
Cantwell	Y
WEST VIRGINIA	
Byrd	N
Rockefeller	Y
WISCONSIN	
Kohl	Y
Feingold	Y
WYOMING	
Thomas	Y
Enzi	Y

ND Northern Democrats   SD Southern Democrats

Southern states - Ala., Ark., Fla., Ga., Ky., La., Miss., N.C., Okla., S.C., Tenn., Texas, Va.

216. S 2845. Intelligence Overhaul/Conference Report. Adoption of the conference report on the bill that would reorganize 15 U.S. intelligence agencies and create a new director of national intelligence to oversee all U.S. intelligence activities and determine the intelligence budget. The director would be allowed to move no more than 5 percent of an agency's budget. The National Counterterrorism Center would serve as the primary organization for analyzing and integrating all U.S. intelligence pertaining to terrorism and counterterrorism. The measure would authorize approximately 10,000 additional border patrol agents over five years, and new programs and pilot projects to upgrade airport and airplane security. The FBI would be allowed to conduct surveillance and wiretaps on suspected terrorists who have no ties to any foreign country or entity. Adopted (thus cleared for the president) 89-2: R 44-1; D 44-1 (ND 36-1, SD 8-0); I 1-0. A "yea" was a vote in support of the president's position. Dec. 8, 2004.

Senate Roll Call Votes
By Subject

Appendix I

GENERAL INDEX

General Index